LEAVING CERTIFI

LESS STRESS MORE SUCCESS

Physics Revision

Brendan Casserly
and
Bernard Horgan

Gill & Macmillan

Gill & Macmillan
Hume Avenue
Park West
Dublin 12
www.gillmacmillan.ie

© Brendan Casserly and Bernard Horgan 2011

978 0 7171 4706 9

Design by Liz White Designs
Print origination and artwork by MPS Limited, a Macmillan Company

The paper used in this book is made from the wood pulp of managed forests.
For every tree felled, at least one tree is planted, thereby renewing natural resources.

CONTENTS

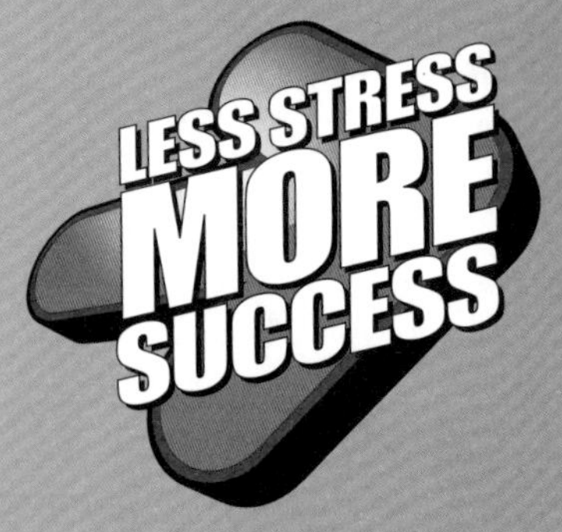

Introduction

 To learn:
- How to revise most effectively
- Being prepared on the day of the exam
- The layout of the exam paper
- How the questions are marked
- Mandatory experiments

 Note: Material that is to be studied only by those taking Higher level is indicated in the text.

Every student has a textbook. The aim of this revision book is to help you get as high a mark as possible in your Leaving Certificate so it is modelled not just on the syllabus, but **on the examination paper! In other words, it is exam focused!** Both options, Option 1 and Option 2, are covered. This revision book can be used in conjunction with any textbook.

If you want to do well in your Leaving Certificate, then two things are essential:
- Revise effectively.
- Be prepared on the day of the examination.

How to revise most effectively

- It is important to study somewhere you feel reasonably comfortable. Turn off the TV and computer. Now turn off your mobile phone! Believe it or not, the world can get along fine without you for a few hours. Besides, if somebody texts, you can catch up on it later.
- **Make out a study plan.** Don't just keep it in your head. Put it down on paper and post it above your desk.
- Be realistic. Plan to study for two hours at a time broken up into 25- to 30-minute sessions.
- If you have covered a topic in school, revise it briefly that night while it is still fresh in your mind. Don't say, *I'll wait until the end of the week and then revise it all.*

Remember, it is easier to learn in small pieces.
- Occasionally go back over chapters you studied a month ago.
- Study definitions not just so that you will be able to repeat them but so that you will be better able to understand the topic.

Don't get hung up on more difficult material. First, master key material such as mandatory experiments, definitions and formulae, which are straightforward and yield easier marks.

- From time to time attempt a question from a past paper. Try to do it within the appropriate time, then check your answer. **This is the ultimate test of how effective your revision is**.
- Draw a **simple** diagram, and see if you can label all the parts properly.
- Finally, take advantage of the weekend to get in some extra study, **but leave time for recreation as well**.

How to be prepared on the day of the exam

- Pack everything you need the night before.
- Arrive early. Ever had the experience of starting late and being all hot and bothered trying to catch up? Not a good idea.
- Be familiar with the layout of the paper. Revision and the mock exam will help here.

    Section A: 4 questions – do 3, 40 marks each.

    Section B: 8 questions – do 5, 56 marks each.
- Start with your best question. Then your next best and so on. This way, if you are short of time, at least your best questions will be done.

Time yourself as follows

- Reading the paper and selecting questions: 10 minutes.
- Section A: 3 questions, 17 minutes each, 51 minutes.
- Section B: 5 questions, 22 minutes each, 110 minutes.
- Reviewing your answers: 9 minutes.
- Stick fairly closely to the above, with perhaps a little extra time for Section B questions, which carry 56 marks each.

Read the paper right through, underlining key words as you go, before deciding what questions to do.

Remember, generally one point of information earns 3 marks so if part of a question is assigned 12 marks the examiner is looking for four points.

Things not to do

- Do not stay up late studying the night before. A tired student is a poor student. In fact, it might be a better idea to relax and watch a DVD before going to bed early.
- Do not get up very early so as to spend time revising the whole course! Have a quick look over a few points but no more.

The layout of the exam paper

The paper consists of two sections. Section A contains 4 questions, based on the mandatory experiments, of which you must answer 3 questions. Section B consists of 8 questions, of which you must do 5.

How the questions are marked

Generally speaking, the paper is marked in units of 3 marks. Another way of looking at this is that if 12 marks are allocated to part of a question, then the examiner is looking for four pieces of information worth 3 marks each. However, in question 5 each part is worth 7 marks so you get 3 marks for the first piece of information and 4 marks for the second.

Mandatory experiments

It is important to realise which experiments are mandatory and which are not, though several non-mandatory experiments also appear on examination papers.

The mandatory experiments are:

1. **HL** To investigate the relationship between period and length for a simple pendulum
2. To measure g by free fall
3. To show that acceleration is proportional to force
4. To verify the principle of conservation of momentum
5. To measure the velocity of a body
6. To measure the acceleration of a body
7. To investigate the laws of equilibrium for a set of coplanar forces
8. To find the focal length of a concave mirror
9. To verify Snell's law
10. To find the refractive index of a rectangular glass block
11. To find the refractive index of a liquid
12. To find the focal length of a converging lens
13. To measure the wavelength of monochromatic light using a diffraction grating
14. To measure the velocity of sound using a resonance tube
15. To investigate the variation of the fundamental frequency of a string with length
16. **HL** To investigate the variation of the fundamental frequency of a string with tension
17. To draw the calibration curve of a thermometer using a mercury thermometer as a standard
18. To verify Boyle's law
19. To find the specific heat capacity of a metal

20 • To find the specific heat capacity of a liquid
21 • To find the specific latent heat of fusion of ice
22 • To find the specific latent heat of vaporisation of water
23 • To investigate how the current flowing through various conductors varies with potential difference applied
24 • To measure the resistivity of the material of a wire
25 • To investigate how the resistance of a metallic conductor varies with temperature
26 • To investigate how the resistance of a thermistor varies with temperature
27 • To verify Joule's law

Tables of mandatory experiment topics that have come up in Section A in the past

Higher Level

2010	$F \propto a$	Latent heat of vaporisation of water	Snell's law	Variation of resistance of thermistor with temperature
2009	g by free fall	Focal length of a converging lens	$f \propto T$	Resistivity
2008	Pendulum	Latent heat of fusion of ice	Wavelength of light	Variation of R with temperature for a metallic conductor
2007	Equilibrium	SHC of water	Focal length of a concave mirror	Variation of I with V for a diode
2006	Pendulum	Wavelength of light	Speed of sound	Joule's law
2005	Momentum	Latent heat of vaporisation of water	Snell's law	Variation of I with V for a bulb

Ordinary Level

2010	$F \propto a$	S.H.C. of substance	Focal length of concave mirror	Resistivity
2009	g by free fall	Latent heat of fusion of ice	$f \propto \ell$	R of thermistor
2008	a for a moving trolley	Speed of sound	Refractive index	Variation of I with V for a diode
2007	Equilibrium	Wavelength of light	Calibration curve of thermometer	Joule's law
2006	Momentum	Snell's law	$f \propto \ell$	Variation of R with temperature for a metallic conductor
2005	$a \propto F$	Latent heat of vaporisation of water	Focal length of a converging lens	Resistivity

SECTION A

Mandatory Experiments

Mechanics Experiments
Exam paper question 1

 To learn:

- How to describe the mandatory mechanics experiments in points
- How to gain maximum marks from the short **FAQs** that appear towards the end of many mechanics questions in Section A
- How to decide what to **graph** against what

exam focus

- There are no extra marks for heavy, overwritten descriptions of an experiment.
- There is no need to list the equipment. This will be clear from the labelled diagram.
- Pay attention to the FAQs, as many marks are lost here.

key point

Be aware of the importance of percentage error. If you are measuring something 10 cm long and you make an error of 1 cm, the percentage error is 10%, but if you are measuring something 100 cm long the percentage error would be only 1%.

key point

If a question involves a formula, ignore the constants and you will see what to graph. For example, the following experiment involves the formula $g = \frac{4\pi^2 l}{T^2}$, so eliminate $4\pi^2$ and graph l (Y axis) against T^2 (X axis).

Mandatory experiment

 Aim: To investigate the relationship between period and length for a simple pendulum (and hence to calculate g)

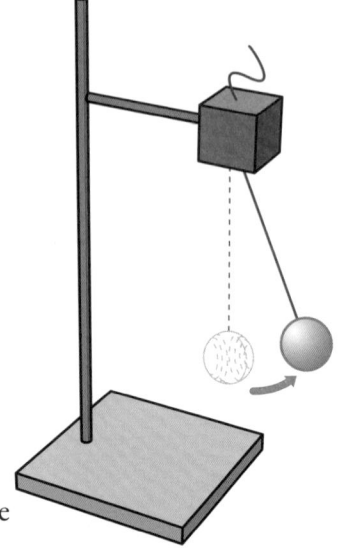

Method:

1. Attach the pendulum bob to one end of a light thread and clamp the other end of the thread between two pieces of cork.
2. Set the pendulum swinging through a small angle and take the time for 50 oscillations.

3. Find the periodic time T for one oscillation.

4. Carefully measure l, the distance from the cork to the centre of the pendulum bob.

5. Repeat for different values of l.

6. Plot a graph of l against T^2. A straight line through the origin implies that $l \propto T^2$.

The slope of this graph gives the value of $\dfrac{l}{T^2}$.

7. g can now be calculated from the formula $g = \dfrac{4\pi^2 l}{T^2}$

FAQs

Why is a light thread used?
So that practically all the mass is concentrated in the bob.

Why must the angle be kept small?
The pendulum formula is only valid for small angles.

Why is the time for one oscillation not measured directly?
It might be too small to register on the timer and there could be a large percentage error.

Why could the number of oscillations be reduced if the length of the pendulum were increased?
Because the time for each oscillation would be increased so the overall time would be about the same.

How would you ensure that the length of the pendulum remained constant?
Use inextensible string.

Mandatory experiment

Aim: To measure *g* by free fall

Method:

1. With the switch K in position 1, the ball bearing is attached to the electromagnet with a small piece of paper between them.

2. When the switch is thrown to position 2, the ball bearing is released and the timer T starts.

3. When the ball bearing hits the trapdoor, the timer stops. The time for the free fall is now known.

4. Repeat a number of times and take the **minimum** time, *t*.

5. Measure *s* carefully. $s = ut + \dfrac{1}{2}at^2$.

In this case $u = 0$ so that $s = \dfrac{1}{2}gt^2 \Rightarrow g = \dfrac{2s}{t^2}$.

'*g*' can now be calculated.

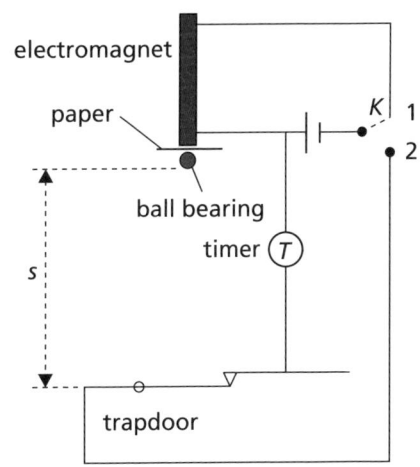

Note: *s* should be at least 1 m.

FAQs

In an experiment to measure g *by free fall, give two precautions that should be taken to ensure a more accurate result.*

Measure from the bottom of the ball bearing. Use large values of *s* (smaller percentage error). Set the trapdoor as sensitively as possible. Take the shortest time not the average time.

What is the piece of paper for?

To make sure that the ball bearing does not become magnetised.

Give two ways of minimising the effect of air resistance in the experiment.

Make sure the object is small, spherical, dense, smooth and that there are no draughts.

Using a tickertape timer

A tickertape timer puts a dot on a tape every 0.02 of a second. If the tape is moving with uniform velocity, the dots are equally spaced. However, if the tape is accelerating, the distance between the dots is increasing. In this case the acceleration can be calculated as follows.

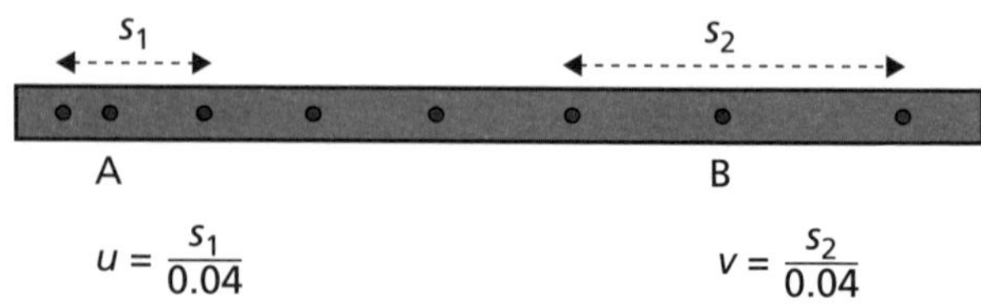

$$u = \frac{s_1}{0.04}$$

$$v = \frac{s_2}{0.04}$$

1. Measure s_1, the distance over two spaces at the start of the tape. (Taking two spaces also reduces percentage error.) Now calculate u as above.
2. Measure s_2, the distance over two spaces towards the end of the tape.
3. Calculate v as above.

   The time t is the time taken to go from A to B.

   $$a = \frac{(v - u)}{t}$$

Mandatory experiment

Aim: To show that acceleration is proportional to force

Method:

1. Set up the apparatus as shown in the diagram.
2. Raise one end of the plank until, with a slight push, the trolley moves with constant speed.
3. Place a weight in the pan and let the trolley accelerate down the slope. Note the force F and calculate the acceleration from the tickertape.

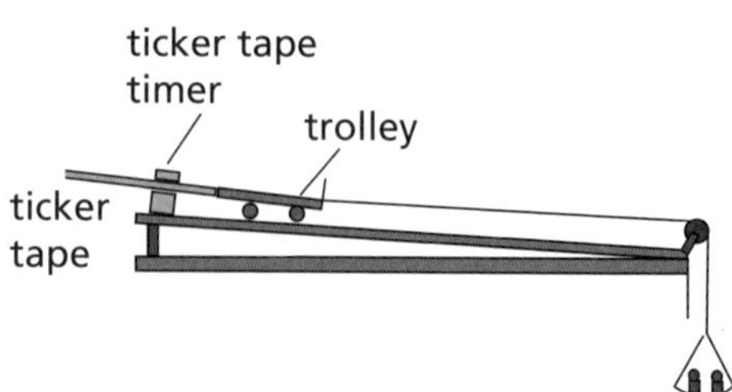

4. Remove one disc from the pan and place it on the trolley.
5. The experiment is repeated a number of times, varying the accelerating force *F* in each case by varying the mass in the scale pan.

A graph of *F* against *a* gives a straight line through the origin showing that *a* α *F*.

FAQ

When you remove a disc from the scale pan why place it on the trolley?
So that the total mass moving, scale pan plus trolley, remains constant. **You cannot proceed with more than two variables.**

> **key point**
>
> You cannot proceed with more than two variables. This is a **general rule**. If you want to show that a α F, then mass must remain constant.

Mandatory experiment

Aim: To verify the principle of conservation of momentum

Method:
1. Level the air track.
2. Find the mass of each complete rider.
3. Set up the apparatus as shown in the diagram.
4. Give the first rider a slight push to set it in motion. As it passes the first light gate, the beam of light is interrupted and the transit time measured.

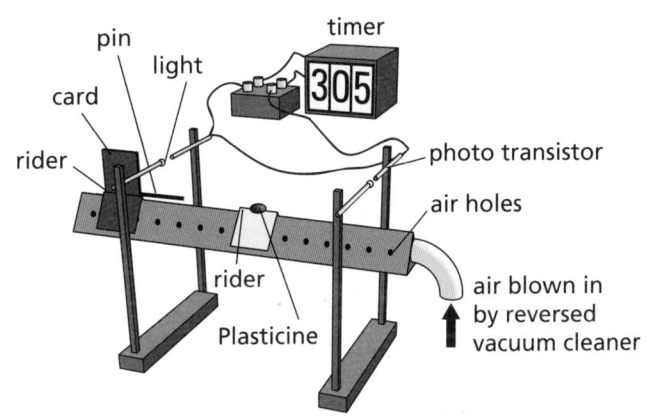

5. On impact the pin penetrates the Plasticine and the two riders move along together. The new transit time is recorded as the card interrupts the beam of light at the second light gate.
6. You should find that:
   mass of the first rider × velocity before impact
   = combined mass of riders × velocity after impact.
The air track with a single rider can be used to measure velocity.

FAQ

In an experiment to verify the principle of conservation of momentum, how was the effect of friction minimised?
By using an air cushion between the surfaces of the track and the rider.

Mandatory experiment

Aim: To measure the velocity of a body

Method:

1. Give the rider a slight push in order to set it moving.
2. The transit time for the card gives the time it takes the rider to travel 0.1 m.
3. $\dfrac{\text{Distance}}{\text{Time}}$ gives the velocity.

Mandatory experiment

Aim: To measure the acceleration of a body

Method:

1. Place the photo transistors 1 m apart for convenience.
2. Give the first rider a push in order to set it moving.
3. Note the transit time as it passes through the first light gate. This is the time it takes to travel 0.1 m.

   $\dfrac{\text{Distance}}{\text{Time}}$ gives the initial velocity u.

4. Repeat for the second light gate to get the final velocity v.
5. The distance s is 1 m.
6. Calculate the acceleration from the formula $v^2 = u^2 + 2as$.

Mandatory experiment

Aim: To investigate the laws of equilibrium for a set of coplanar forces

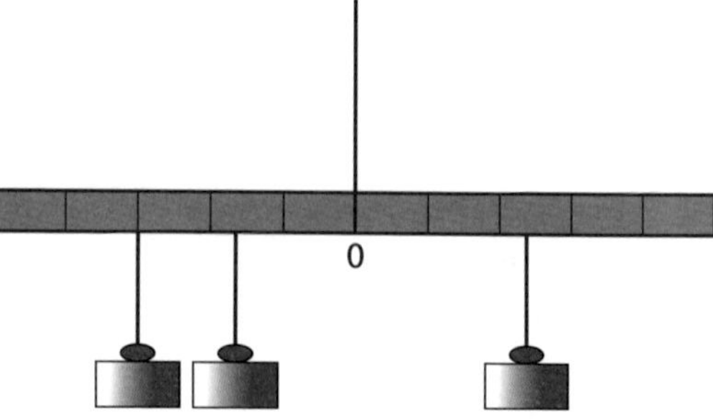

Method:

1. Find the mass of a metre stick and hang it from a stand.
2. Adjust the thread until the metre stick is balanced horizontally. The thread is now at the centre of gravity of the metre stick.
3. Hang a number of masses on the metre stick and adjust their positions until the metre stick balances.
4. Calculate the moments about O.

Result: The sum of the clockwise moments equals the sum of the anticlockwise moments.

5. Leaving the masses as they are, hang the metre stick from a suitable spring balance.
Result: The reading on the spring balance equals the sum of all the weights including the weight of the metre stick (remember weight = mass × *g*).
Conclusion: The two laws of equilibrium have been obeyed.

FAQ

In an experiment to investigate the laws of equilibrium why is it important to have the metre stick horizontal (or, if you use spring balances, to have them vertical)?
So that the distances measured along the metre stick are perpendicular distances.

If you are asked to draw a **suitable** graph, this means that the given table of data must be modified before the graph is drawn. If there is a formula involved, write it down, ignore the constants and you will see what you need to graph and therefore how the data needs to be modified. (See exam question below.)

Exam question

Q: The following results were obtained by a student in an experiment to measure *g*, the acceleration due to gravity, using a simple pendulum.

Length/*m*	0.2	0.4	0.6	0.8	1	1.2	1.4	1.6
Time for 30 oscillations/*s*	27	37.8	46.5	53.7	60.6	66.0	70.8	76.4

Draw a **suitable** graph and hence determine the value of *g*.

A: This question involves a formula since $g = \dfrac{4\pi^2 l}{T^2}$. **In a case like this ignore the constants** $(4\pi^2)$ **and you will see what to graph.** You must plot a graph of *l* against T^2.

To do this you must divide the bottom line of the table by 30 to get the time for **one oscillation** and then square it, resulting in the following table.

l/m		0.2	0.4	0.6	0.8	1	1.2	1.4	1.6
T^2/sec^2		0.8	1.6	2.4	3.2	4.1	4.8	5.6	6.5

Now draw your graph and use the slope to get $\dfrac{l}{T^2}$.

- The slope is $\dfrac{1.6}{6.5} = 0.246$.

- Multiplying this by $4\pi^2$ gives $g = 9.72$ cm s^{-2}.

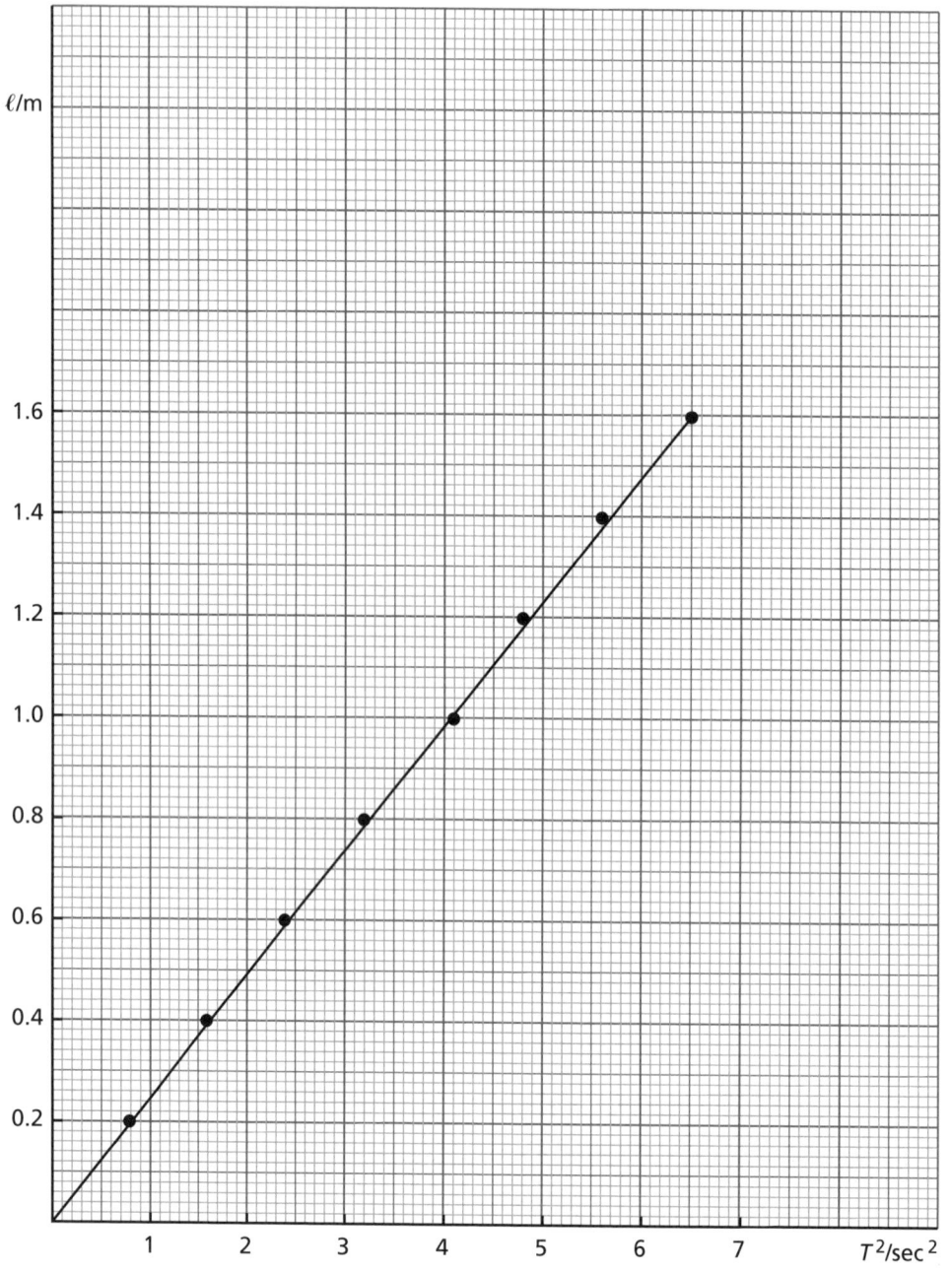

2 Light and Sound Experiments

Exam paper questions 2/3

 aims To learn:
- How to describe mandatory light and sound experiments in points
- How to calculate the velocity of sound in air from given data

Mandatory experiment

Aim: To find the focal length of a concave mirror

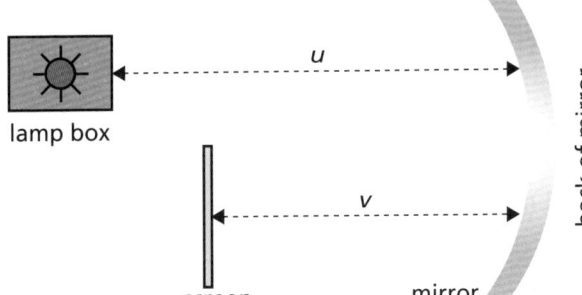

lamp box

screen   mirror

u

v

back of mirror

Method:

1. Set up the apparatus as shown in the diagram.
2. Adjust the position of the screen until a sharp image of the slit is formed on it.
3. Measure u and v.
4. Calculate the focal length from the formula
$$\frac{1}{f} = \frac{1}{u} + \frac{1}{v}$$
5. Repeat for different positions of the lamp box and find the average value of f.

FAQs

How would an approximate value of the focal length be found?
By focusing the image of a distant object on a screen. Distance from mirror to screen gives an approximate value of f.

What would be the advantage of getting an approximate value?
To avoid placing the object near or inside f.

What are the main sources of error?
Not measuring from the pole of the mirror, not getting a sharp enough image, not checking for zero error on metre stick.

Remember, if you are given a table of data for the previous experiment (see Question 3 2007 Higher Level) and asked to calculate f by drawing a suitable graph, there is no need to graph $\frac{1}{v}$ against $\frac{1}{u}$. Simply:

Graph v against u.

Find the point on the curve where $v = u$

Now $\dfrac{1}{u} + \dfrac{1}{u} = \dfrac{1}{f} \Rightarrow \dfrac{2}{u} = \dfrac{1}{f} \Rightarrow 2f = u$

$$f = \frac{1}{2}u.$$

Mandatory experiment

Aim: To verify Snell's law

Method:

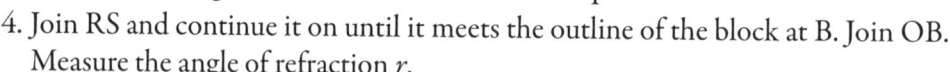

1. Draw the outline of a glass block on a sheet of paper. Remove the block.
2. Draw a normal NO to the side of the block and a line making an angle of incidence of 20° with NO. Replace the block. Stick two pins P and Q on the line.
3. Stick two pins R and S in line with the images of P and Q as seen through the block. Remove block and pins.
4. Join RS and continue it on until it meets the outline of the block at B. Join OB. Measure the angle of refraction r.
5. Repeat this procedure for angles of incidence of 30°, 40°, etc. and plot a graph of **sin i** against **sin r**.

Result: The result should be a straight line through the origin, which verifies Snell's law.

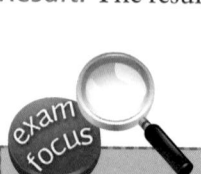

Remember, this experiment can also be used to find the refractive index of a rectangular glass block as the slope of the graph $\left(\dfrac{\sin i}{\sin r}\right)$ gives the refractive index or you can do it as shown in the next experiment.

Mandatory experiment

Aim: To find the refractive index of a rectangular glass block

Method:

1. Draw a straight line on a sheet of paper.
2. Stand a glass block on its end over the line.
3. Move the search pin up and down until it coincides, without parallax, with the image of the line as seen in the block.
4. Fix the search pin to the side of the block and measure the apparent depth.
5. Now measure the real depth of the block.
6. The refractive index =
$$\frac{\text{real depth}}{\text{apparent depth}}.$$

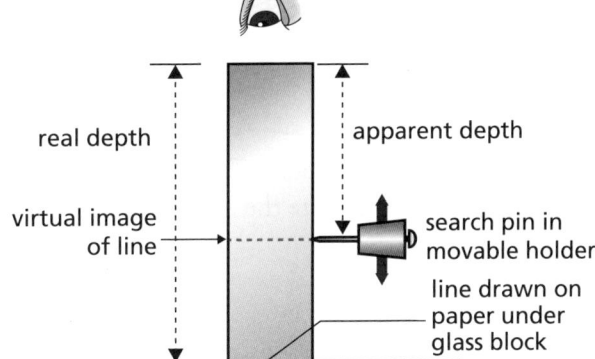

real depth | apparent depth

virtual image of line

search pin in movable holder

line drawn on paper under glass block

Mandatory experiment

Aim: To find the refractive index of a liquid

Method:

1. Set up the apparatus as shown in the diagram.
2. Move the search pin up and down until it coincides, without parallax, with the image of the line as seen in the liquid.
3. Fix the search pin to the side of the beaker and measure the apparent depth.
4. Measure the real depth of the beaker.
5. Refractive index $= \dfrac{\text{real depth}}{\text{apparent depth}}.$

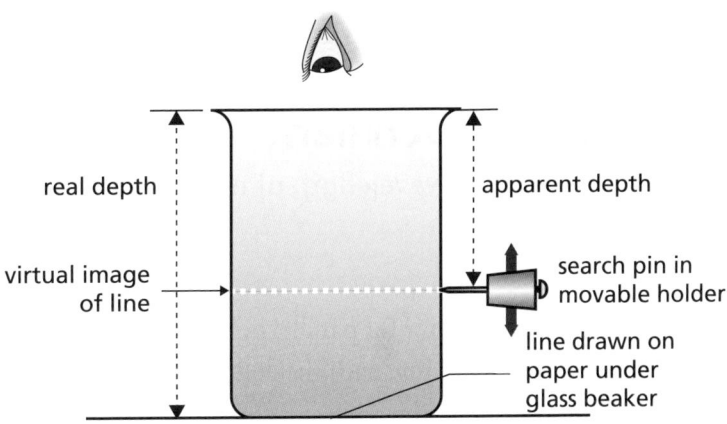

real depth | apparent depth

virtual image of line

search pin in movable holder

line drawn on paper under glass beaker

Mandatory experiment

Aim: To find the focal length of a converging lens

Method:

1. Set up the apparatus as shown in the diagram.
2. Adjust the position of the lens until a sharp image of the slit in the lamp box is formed on the screen.
3. Measure u and v.
4. Calculate f from the formula $\dfrac{1}{f} = \dfrac{1}{u} + \dfrac{1}{v}$
5. Repeat for different positions of the lamp box and calculate the average value of f.

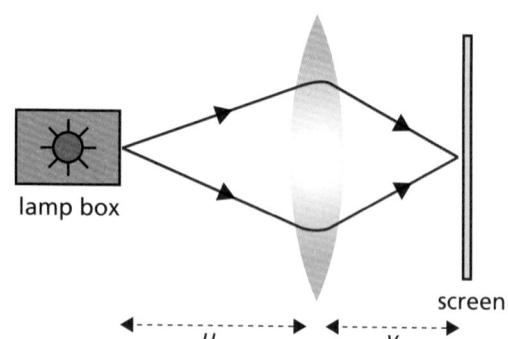

lamp box

screen

u v

FAQs

In an experiment to find the focal length of a converging lens:

(a) How was the image distance measured?

Get a sharp image, then measure the distance from the **centre** of the lens to the screen.

(b) Give two precautions when measuring the image distance.

Measure from centre of lens, measure perpendicular distance, check for zero error on metre stick.

(c) What difficulty would arise if the student placed the object 10 cm from the lens?

If the object was inside the focus, it would result in a virtual image that could not be caught on the screen.

Mandatory experiment

Aim: To measure the wavelength of monochromatic light using a diffraction grating

Method:

1. Adjust the spectrometer for parallel light.
2. Place the telescope in line with the collimator.
3. Clamp the grating on the table at right angles to the collimator.
4. Rotate the telescope to the left until the cross wires are on the first order image. Note the angle.
5. Repeat for the first order image on the right. The difference between the two readings gives 2θ.

The grating element d is indicated on the grating.

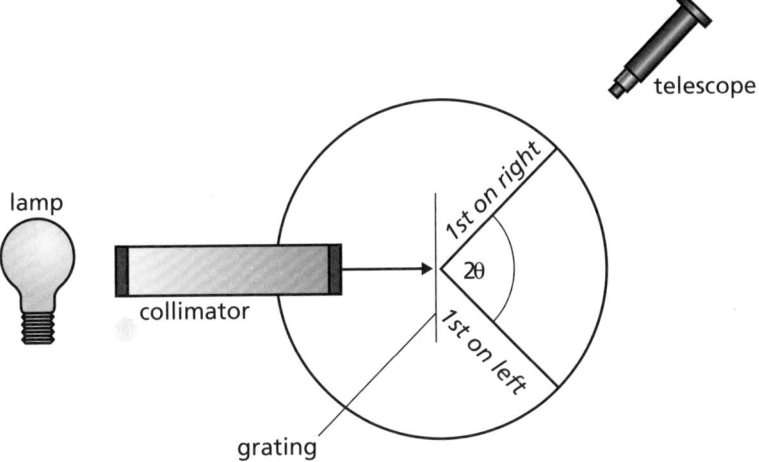

Result: λ can now be calculated from the formula $n\lambda = d \sin \theta$.

FAQs

If you were carrying out an experiment to measure the wavelength of monochromatic light using a spectrometer what step(s) would you take in each of the following cases:

(a) If the images seen in the telescope were very faint

Widen the collimator slit.

(b) If the cross wires were unclear

Focus the telescope.

(c) If the images on one side were above the centre of the eyepiece

Level the spectrometer table.

Mandatory experiment

Aim: To measure the velocity of sound using a resonance tube

Method:

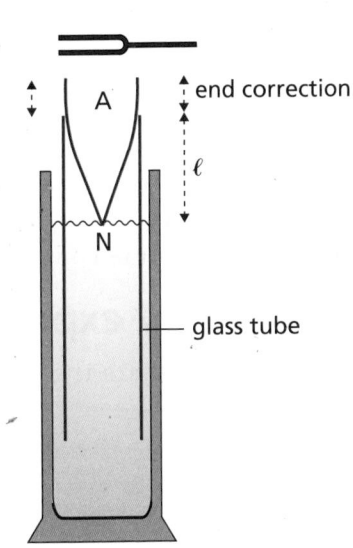

1. Strike a tuning fork of known frequency and hold it over the air column in the tube.

2. Slowly raise the tube until the sound reaches a maximum. This is called the first position of resonance. (The antinode is not exactly at the top of the tube but a small distance c, known as the end correction, above it.) Measure the distance l.

3. Take the end correction c as being 0.3 times the diameter of the tube.

4. $\dfrac{\lambda}{4} = l + 0.3d \implies \lambda = 4(l + 0.3d)$.

5. The velocity c can now be calculated from the formula $c = f\lambda$ where f is the frequency of the fork.

The velocity of sound in air is approximately 330 m s^{-1}.

Mandatory experiment

Aim: To investigate the variation of the fundamental frequency of a string with length

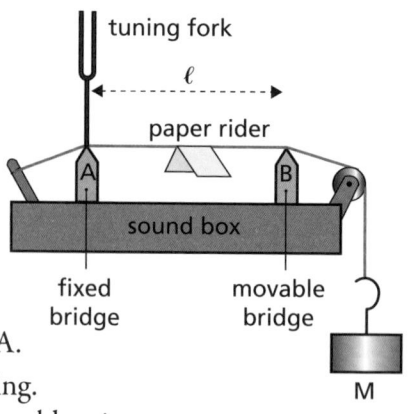

Method:

1. Set the tension of the string at a convenient value and leave it fixed.
2. Strike a tuning fork of known frequency on a block of wood and place it in contact with bridge A.
3. Adjust B until the paper rider is thrown off the string. The string is now in resonance with the fork and would emit a note of the same frequency. Measure *l*.
4. Repeat this procedure with forks of different frequencies.
5. If you have been able to get 5 or more readings, draw a graph of *f* against $\frac{1}{l}$. You should get a straight line through the origin.

Conclusion: $f \propto \frac{1}{l}$.

The frequency of a stretched string is inversely proportional to its length.

FAQs

In an experiment to investigate the variation of the fundamental frequency of a string with length:

(a) How was the tension measured?

The weight of pan and contents or reading on a Newton balance.

(b) How did the student know that resonance occurred?

The paper rider jumped.

(c) Why was it necessary to keep the tension constant?

Because you cannot proceed with more than two variables. THIS IS A GENERAL RULE. If you are investigating frequency against length, then tension must be constant.

All FAQ questions in this book are typical of what has appeared on Leaving Certificate papers in the past or is likely to in the future. Also note that in the exam question on p. 15, Question 3 Higher Level 2006, 25 out of 40 marks go for FAQs!

HL Mandatory experiment

Aim: To investigate the variation of the fundamental frequency of a string with tension

Method:

1. Set the length of the string at a convenient value and leave it fixed.

2. Strike a tuning fork of known frequency on a block of wood and hold it in contact with the bridge A.

3. Adjust the tension until the paper is thrown off the string. Note the tension.

4. Repeat this procedure with a number of forks of different frequency. Plot a graph of f against $\sqrt{T}$.

Result: A straight line through the origin.

Conclusion: $f \propto \sqrt{T}$.

The frequency of a stretched string is directly proportional to the square root of the tension.

Exam question

2006 Higher level question 3

Q: A cylindrical column of air closed at one end and three different tuning forks were used in an experiment to measure the speed of sound in air. A tuning fork of frequency f was set vibrating and held over the column of air.

The length of the column of air was adjusted until it was vibrating at its first harmonic and its length l was then measured. This procedure was repeated for each tuning fork. Finally, the diameter of the column of air was measured. The following data was recorded.

f/Hz	512	480	426
l/cm	16.0	17.2	19.4

Diameter of column of air = 2.05 cm.

Explain:

(i) How the length of the column of air was adjusted

A: By raising or lowering the open pipe in the water.

(ii) How the frequency of the column of air was measured

A: When resonance occurs f of air column = f of fork.

(iii) How the diameter of the column of air was measured

A: Using a Vernier callipers to measure the internal diameter of the pipe.

(iv) How it was known that the air column was vibrating at its first harmonic

A: A loud sound, indicating resonance, was heard.

(v) Using all the data, calculate the speed of sound in air.

A: $\lambda_1 = 4(l_1 + 0.3d) = 4(0.16 + 0.3 \times 0.0205) = 4(0.16615) = 0.6646$

$v_1 = f\lambda_1 = 512 \times 0.6646 = 340.3$ m s^{-1}

Similarly $v_2 = 342$ m s^{-1} $v_3 = 341.1$ m s^{-1}

Average $v = 341.13$ m s^{-1}

aims To learn:
- How to describe the mandatory heat experiments in points
- How to answer FAQs on heat experiments
- How to calculate the specific latent heat of fusion of ice from given data

Mandatory experiment

Aim: To draw the calibration curve of a thermometer using a mercury thermometer as standard

Method:

1. Set up the apparatus as shown in the diagram. Read the temperature and the voltage.
2. Raise the temperature of the water by 10° C. Read the temperature and the voltage.
3. Repeat the procedure until you have at least 5 readings. Plot a graph of temperature against voltage.

Boyle's law

At constant temperature the pressure of a fixed mass of gas is inversely proportional to its volume. (pV is constant.)

Mandatory experiment

Aim: To verify Boyle's law

Method:

1. Set up the apparatus as shown in the diagram.
2. Open the tap and pump up the oil as far as possible or until the gauge reaches its maximum reading. Close the tap.

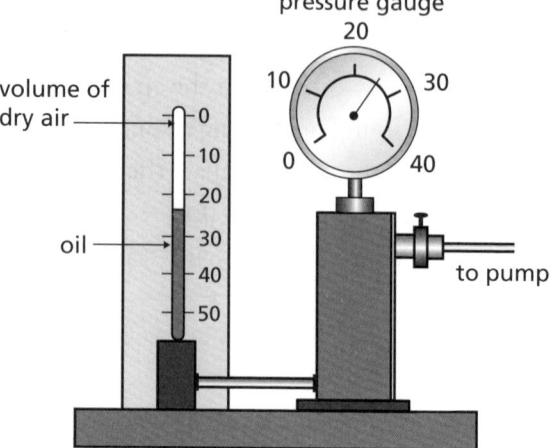

3. Wait a few minutes before reading the pressure and the volume.

4. Open the tap slightly until the pressure falls to a convenient reading. Close the tap, wait a few minutes and read the new pressure and volume.

5. Repeat this about seven times and plot a graph of p against $\frac{1}{V}$

The result should be a straight line through the origin showing

$$p \propto \frac{1}{V} \Rightarrow pV \text{ is constant.}$$

FAQs

In an experiment to verify Boyle's law how would you make sure that the temperature remains constant?
Allow time between readings for the temperature to settle.

If the pump is disconnected and the tap is open, will there be any reading on the gauge?
The gauge will read atmospheric pressure.

Mandatory experiment

Aim: To find the specific heat capacity of a metal

Method:

1. Find the mass of the block of metal.

2. Set up the apparatus as shown in the diagram.

3. Read the initial temperature on the thermometer and zero the joulemeter.

4. Allow current to flow until a temperature rise of at least 5° C has been achieved.

5. Wait a few minutes for the heat to spread throughout the metal block before taking the final temperature.

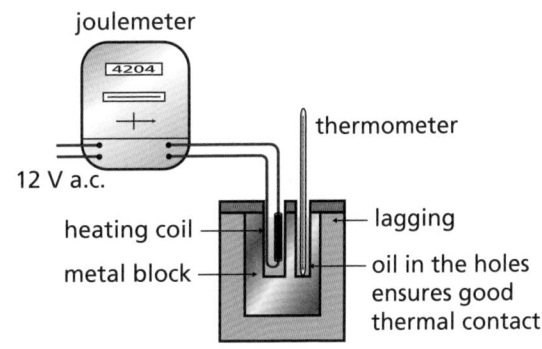

Formula: $\Delta E = mc\Delta\theta$.

In words, energy = mass × SHC × change in temperature.

Reading on joulemeter = mass × SHC × rise in temperature of block. SHC is the only unknown.

Mandatory experiment

Aim: To find the specific heat capacity of a liquid

Method:

1. Find the mass of the calorimeter.
2. Find the mass of the calorimeter plus the liquid.
3. Set up the apparatus as shown in the diagram.
4. Note the initial temperature of the liquid.
5. Zero the joulemeter and allow current to flow until a temperature rise of at least 5° C has been achieved.
6. Note the final temperature and the final joulemeter reading.
7. The specific heat capacity can be calculated from the following equation:

   Heat supplied = heat gained by calorimeter + heat gained by liquid.

SHC of liquid is the only unknown.

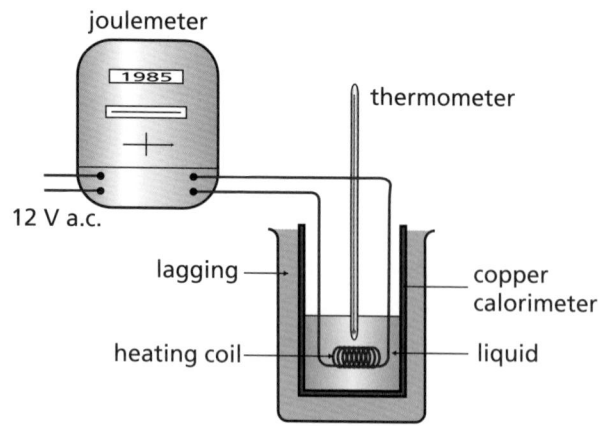

Mandatory experiment

Aim: To find the specific latent heat of fusion of ice

Method:

1. Place some small lumps of ice in water and keep taking the temperature until it reaches 0° C.
2. In the meantime find the mass of a calorimeter.
3. Add some slightly warmed water to the calorimeter and find the mass of the calorimeter plus water.
4. Lag the calorimeter as shown in the diagram and take the initial temperature.
5. Dry the lumps of ice on blotting paper and add them, one at a time, to the water.

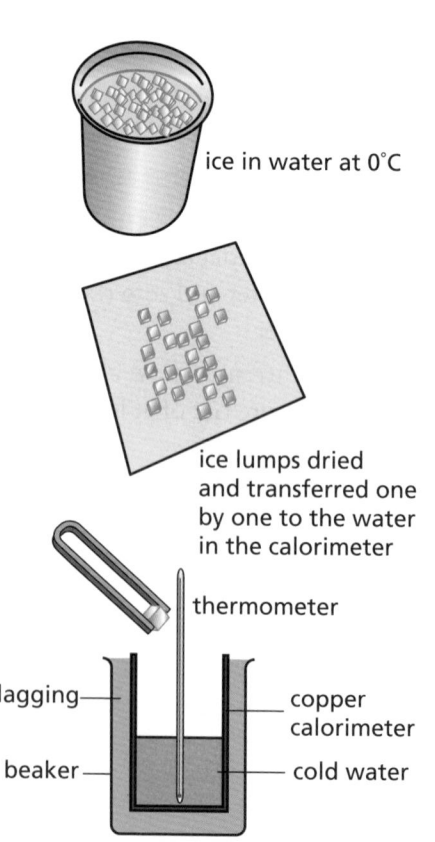

6. When all the ice has been added, stir until it dissolves and take the final temperature.

7. Find the mass of calorimeter + water + melted ice.

8. The specific latent heat of fusion of ice can be calculated from the following equation:

Heat needed to melt ice + heat needed to raise the temperature of resulting water = heat lost by calorimeter + heat lost by water.

Formula for heat energy needed to melt the ice:
$E = ml$ where l is the latent heat of fusion of ice.
(See worked example on p. 21.)

FAQs

In an experiment to measure the specific latent heat of fusion of ice:

(a) What would be the advantage of having the room temperature approximately halfway between the initial and final temperature of the water?

The heat lost to the surroundings by the warm water at the beginning would be approximately equal to the heat gained from the surroundings by the cold water at the end.

(b) Why is the ice dried before adding it to the water?

The aim is to add ice, not melted ice (water), which has already taken in its latent heat of fusion.

(c) Why should you use warm water in the calorimeter?

To melt the ice more quickly.

(d) Why should you use melting ice?

Because melting ice is at 0° C.

(e) How would you find the mass of the ice added?

Subtract the mass of calorimeter plus water from the final mass of calorimeter plus contents.

Mandatory experiment

Aim: To find the specific latent heat of vaporisation of water

Method:

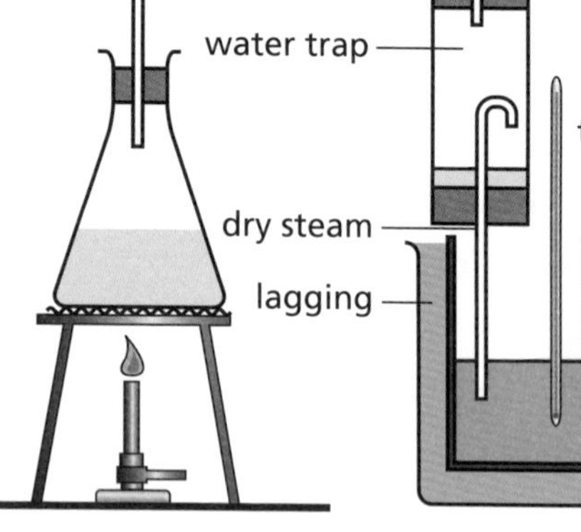

1. Weigh the calorimeter. Weigh the calorimeter and water. Take the temperature of the water.
2. Set up the apparatus as shown in the diagram.
3. Allow steam to pass into the water in the calorimeter until the temperature has risen by about 20° C to 25° C.
4. Finally, re-weigh the calorimeter and contents to find the mass of steam condensed.

wet steam
water trap
thermometer
dry steam
lagging
copper calorimeter

5. The latent heat of vaporisation of water can be calculated from the equation:

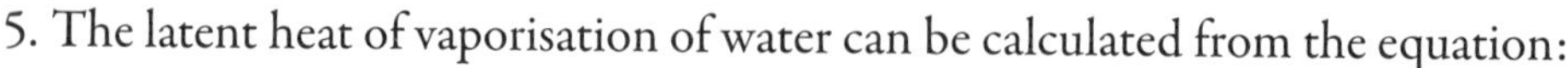

Heat lost by steam + heat lost by resulting water = heat gained by calorimeter + heat gained by water

FAQs

In an experiment to measure the specific latent heat of vaporisation of water:

(a) Why was dry steam used?
To make sure that only dry steam, and not condensed steam (water), is added to the calorimeter.

(b) How was the steam dried?
By using a water trap to trap the condensed steam. It also helps to insulate the delivery tube and have it sloping backwards towards the steam generator.

exam focus

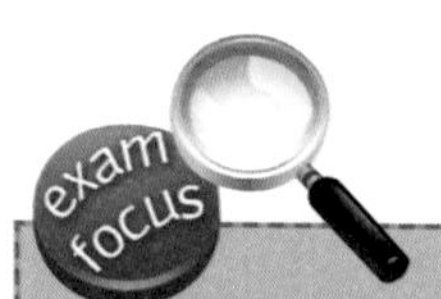

Remember, most people believe that if you are familiar with one method of doing an experiment that is sufficient. This is generally true but not always! For example, most people would use the electrical method given above to find the specific heat capacity of water but take a look at Question 2, 2007 Higher Level where it is found by adding hot copper to water in a copper calorimeter.

(c) Why is the rise in temperature often the least accurate value?
Standard thermometers only read to 1°.

(d) Give two ways of improving the accuracy of this value.
Use a thermometer that reads to 0.1 degrees. Reduce percentage error by using more steam and less water. Increase insulation.

(e) Why would a thermometer with low heat capacity increase accuracy?
It would absorb less heat from the water in the calorimeter.

(f) Why should the calorimeter be polished?
To reduce heat loss by radiation.

(g) How would you find the mass of the steam added?
Subtract mass of calorimeter plus water from the final mass of calorimeter plus water plus condensed steam.

Exam questions

Q 1: The specific heat capacity of water was found by adding hot copper to water in a copper calorimeter.

(a) Describe how the copper was heated and how its temperature was measured.

A: The copper was heated as shown in the diagram and the temperature was read from the thermometer.

(b) Give two precautions which were taken to minimise heat loss to the surroundings.

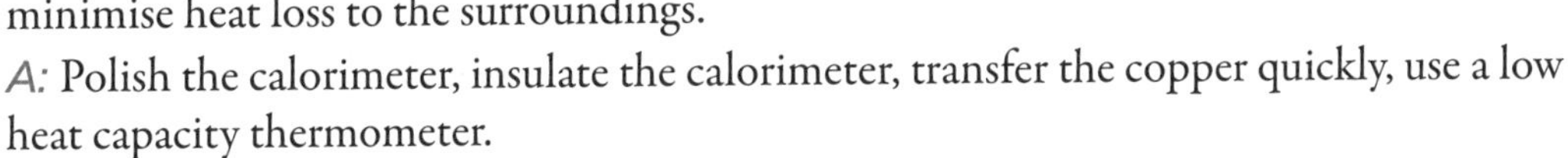

A: Polish the calorimeter, insulate the calorimeter, transfer the copper quickly, use a low heat capacity thermometer.

Q 2: In an experiment to find the specific latent heat of fusion of ice the following readings were obtained.

mass of copper calorimeter	= 50 g
mass of calorimeter + water	= 145 g
initial temperature of water	= 25° C
final temperature	= 5° C
mass of calorimeter + water + melted ice	= 170 g

Find the specific latent heat of fusion of ice.

A: Specific heat capacity of water = 4,200 J kg^{-1}K^{-1}
Specific heat capacity of copper = 400 J Kg^{-1}K^{-1}

Heat gained by ice in melting	Heat to raise resulting water by 5° C	Heat lost by calorimeter	Heat lost by warm water
0.025 × l	(0.025 × 4,200 × 5)	(0.05 × 400 × 20)	(0.095 × 4,200 × 20)

$0.025l + 525 = 400 + 7,980$
$0.025l = 8,380 - 525 = 7,855$
$l = \dfrac{7,855}{0.025} = 314,200 \, J = 314.2 \, kJ \, kg^{-1}$

4 ⟩ Electrical Experiments
Exam paper question 4

 aims To learn:
- How to describe mandatory electrical experiments in points
- How to answer FAQs on the above
- How to get maximum marks from graphs

Mandatory experiment

Aim: To investigate how the current flowing through various conductors varies with potential difference applied

Method:

1. Set up the apparatus as shown in the diagram.
2. Set the variable resistor to give a small potential difference (voltage). Note the voltage and the current.
3. Adjust the variable resistor to give a slightly larger voltage. Note voltage and current again.
4. Repeat 4 or 5 more times.
5. Draw a graph of voltage (Y axis) against current (X axis).

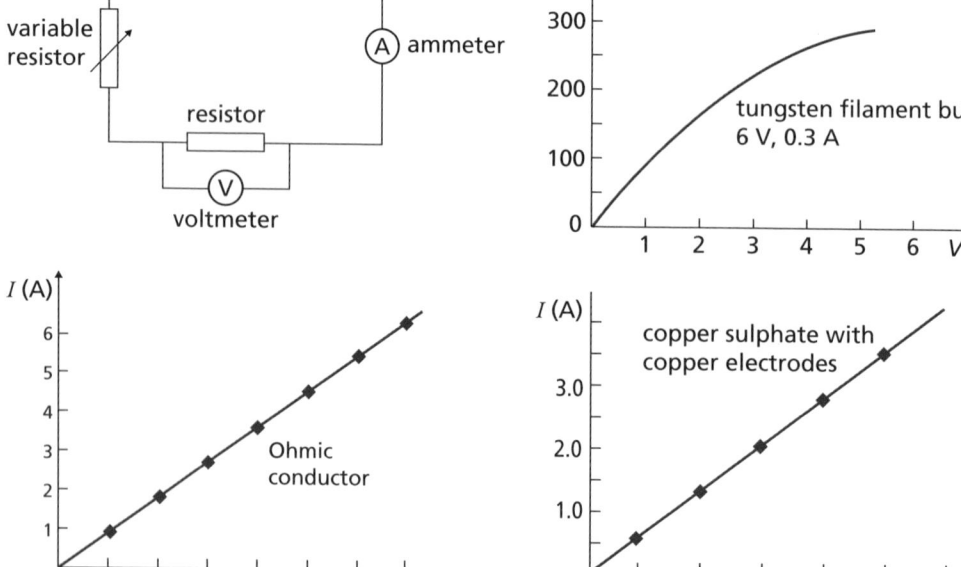

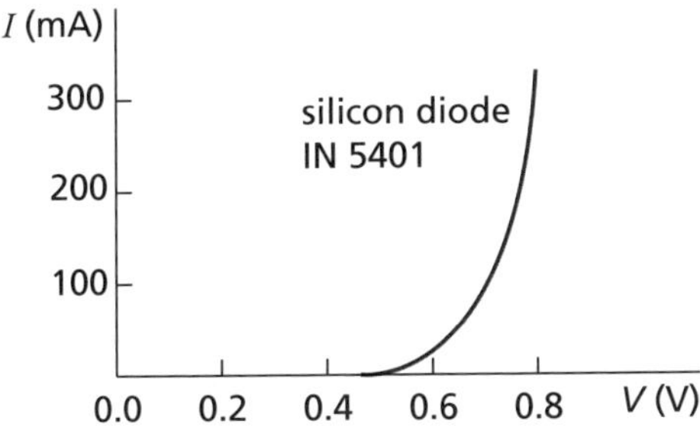

At constant temperature the current flowing through a metallic conductor is directly proportional to the potential difference across it.

This is Ohm's law.

Not all conductors are Ohmic (obey Ohm's law).

FAQs

On a graph showing the relationship between current and voltage for a metal at constant temperature, how would the graph change if the temperature was increasing?

At constant temperature the graph would be linear (Ohm's law) but as the temperature increased the resistance would increase and the slope of the graph would decrease to give a curved graph.

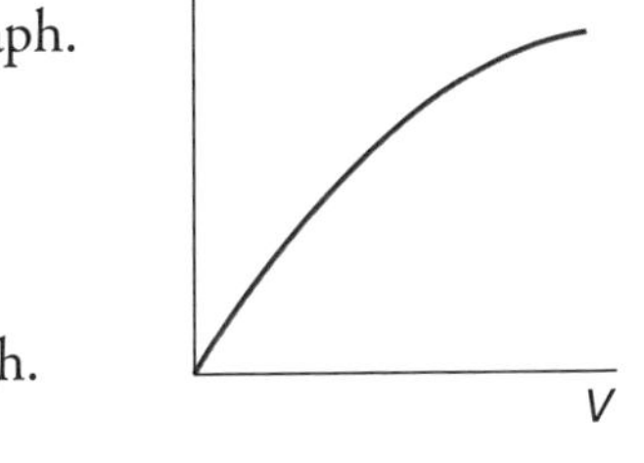

In the case of a similar experiment using a filament bulb, why would the resistance of the bulb change during the experiment?

As the current increases, the temperature of the filament increases making it more difficult for electrons to pass through.

How would the graph for an ionic solution be altered if the concentration of the solution was reduced?

Reducing the concentration would mean fewer ions, fewer charge carriers, greater resistance leading to a reduction in the slope of the graph.

*In an experiment to investigate the variation of current with potential difference for a copper sulphate solution, draw a sketch of the graph that would be obtained if **inactive** electrodes were used.*

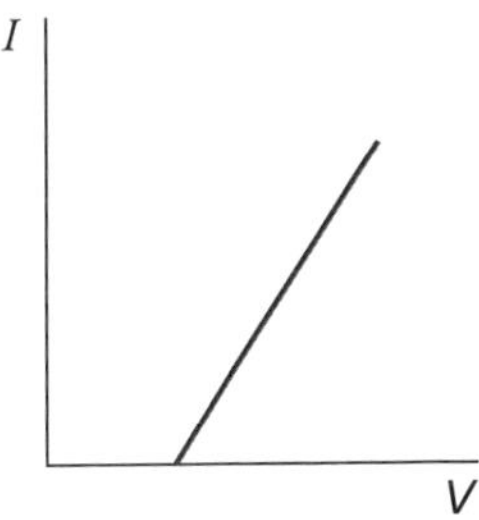

In an experiment to investigate the variation of current with potential difference for a semiconductor diode, if the student changed the diode to reverse bias what changes should be made to the original circuit?

Replace the milliammeter with a microammeter and make sure the voltmeter is in parallel with a series combination of the diode and microammeter.

Mandatory experiment

Aim: To measure the resistivity of the material of a wire

Method:

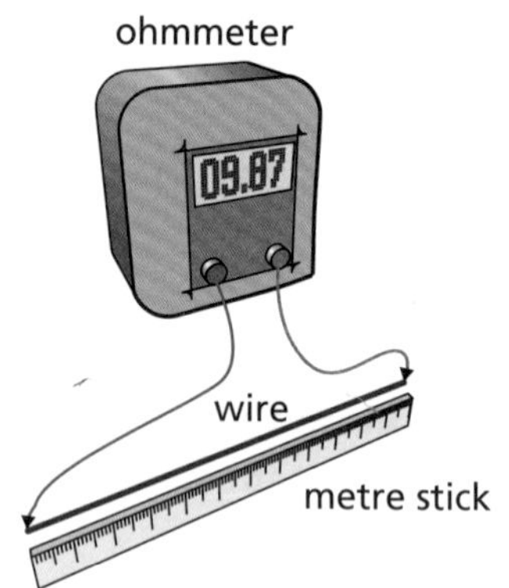

ohmmeter

wire

metre stick

1. Connect the wire to a digital ohmmeter and measure the exact length of nichrome wire between the leads.
2. Measure the resistance of the wire with the ohmmeter.
3. Check the micrometer for zero error.
4. Measure the diameter of the wire at a number of places with a micrometer screw gauge and take the average of these as the diameter.
5. Calculate the cross sectional area of the wire assuming it is perfectly circular.
   $(A = \pi r^2)$
6. Calculate the resistivity of the material from the formula $\rho = \dfrac{RA}{l}$.

FAQs

In an experiment to measure the resistivity of the material of a wire:

(a) Name an instrument used to measure the diameter of the wire and explain how it is used.

Micrometer screw gauge. Place the wire between the two jaws and tighten them. Do not over tighten. Read the two scales to get a more accurate answer.

(b) Why is the diameter of the wire measured at several points?
To find the average diameter as the wire may not be uniform.

(c) Give two precautions that should be taken when measuring the length of the wire.
Make sure the wire is taut and there are no kinks in it. Measure only the length of the resistance wire, not the leads.

Mandatory experiment

Aim: To investigate how the resistance of a metallic conductor varies with temperature

Method:

1. Set up the apparatus as shown in the diagram.
2. Heat the water slowly to raise the temperature to about 90° C. Note temperature and resistance.

3. Remove the burner and note the temperature and resistance at intervals of 10° C as the temperature falls.

4. Plot a graph of R against θ. It should look like the graph in the diagram.

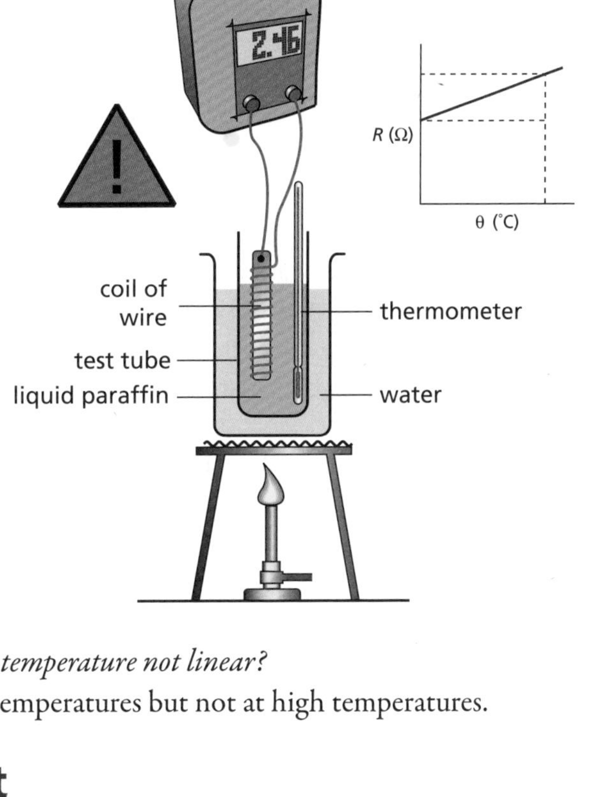

FAQs

In an experiment to investigate the variation in the resistance of a metallic conductor with temperature, why is glycerol or paraffin used?

Because it is a poor conductor of electricity so there can be no short circuit between the turns of the coil of wire.

Why is the relationship between the resistance of a metallic conductor and its temperature not linear?

It is linear over a very narrow range of temperatures but not at high temperatures.

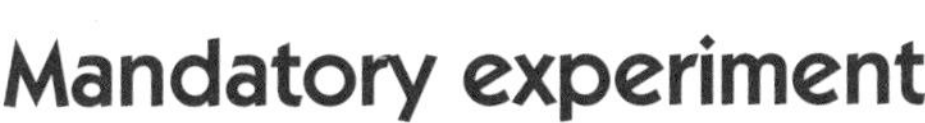

Mandatory experiment

Aim: To investigate how the resistance of a thermistor varies with temperature

Method:

1. Set up the apparatus as shown in the diagram.

2. Heat the water slowly to about 90° C. Note resistance and temperature.

3. Note the resistance and temperature at intervals of 10° C as the temperature falls.

4. Plot a graph of R against θ. It should be similar to the graph in the diagram.

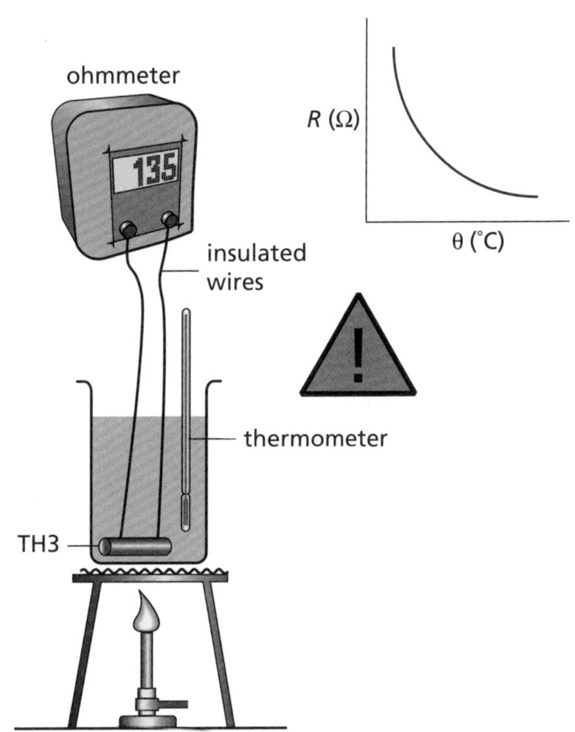

Mandatory experiment

Aim: To verify Joule's law

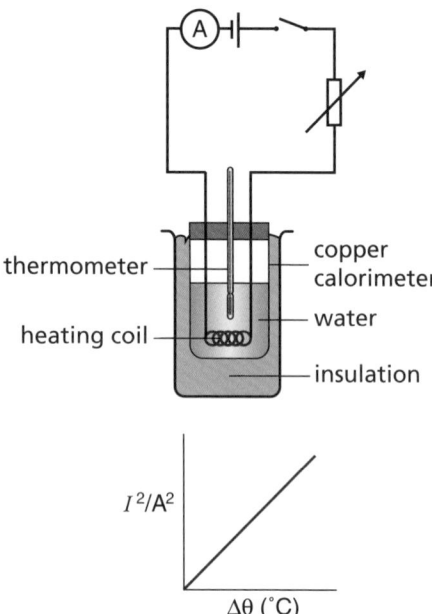

Method:

1. Set up the apparatus as shown in the diagram.
2. Add enough water to cover the heating element in the calorimeter. Note the temperature of the water.
3. Pass a current of 0.5 A through the coil for 5 minutes keeping the current constant by adjusting the variable resistor. Note the rise in temperature.
4. Repeat for currents of 1 A, 1.5 A, 2 A, etc. noting current and temperature rise in each case.
5. Draw a graph of temperature rise $\Delta\theta$ against I^2.

The result is a straight line through the origin, which proves Joule's law.

FAQ

In an experiment to verify Joule's law, why was the current allowed to flow for the same fixed length of time in each case?

Once again we cannot proceed with more than two variables.

Many experiments involve graphs. To get maximum marks:
- Label axes clearly (V/volts, I/amps).
- Choose a scale to make the graph as big as possible. (Lower percentage error.)
- Plot 6 or 7 points carefully.
- Draw the line of best fit. (In effect using only the best readings.)
- In finding the slope, take two points as far apart as possible. This lessens percentage error.

Exam question

2004 Higher level question 4

Q: In an experiment to measure the resistivity of nichrome wire, the resistance and length of the nichrome wire were found. The diameter of the wire was then measured at several points along its length. The following data was recorded.

Resistance of wire $= 32.1\ \Omega$

Length of wire $= 90.1$ cm

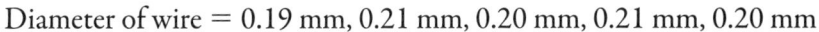

The most common mistake here is not converting measurements to standard units.

Diameter of wire $= 0.19$ mm, 0.21 mm, 0.20 mm, 0.21 mm, 0.20 mm

Use this data to calculate a value for the resistivity of nichrome.

A: Average diameter of wire $= 0.202$ mm $\Rightarrow$ radius $= 0.101$ mm $= 0.101 \times 10^{-3}$ m.

$A = \pi r^2 = 3.14 \times (0.101 \times 10^{-3})^2 = 3.2 \times 10^{-8}\ \text{m}^2$

$\rho = \dfrac{RA}{l} = (32.1)\left(\dfrac{3.2 \times 10^{-8}}{0.901}\right) = 1.1 \times 10^{-6}\ \Omega\ \text{m}$

SECTION B

Theory

5 Mechanics

aims To learn:

- Mechanics definitions and formulae
- How to answer FAQs on mechanics
- How to solve longer problems on mechanics

exam focus

The State Examinations Commission booklet of Formulae and Tables **does not contain definitions and laws** so, for revision purposes, it is most convenient to have relevant laws, formulae and definitions together as they are in this and all following chapters. You should check the SEC formula and tables book if you are not sure of a formula or unit.

Vectors and scalars

- Any quantity which has both magnitude and direction is a vector.
- Any quantity which has magnitude only is a scalar.
- **(HL)** Parallelogram law: If two vectors are represented by two adjacent sides *ab* and *ad* of a parallelogram *abcd* then the diagonal *ac* represents their resultant.
- A vector has no components at right angles to itself.

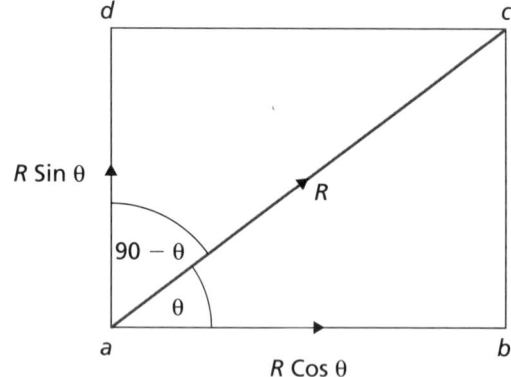

Linear motion

- Displacement is the distance of a body, in a given direction, from a fixed point.
- Velocity is speed in a given direction.
- Acceleration is the rate of change of velocity.
- **(HL)** Equations of motion: $V = u + at$, $s = ut + \frac{1}{2}at^2$, $v^2 = u^2 + 2as$

- A body has acceleration if either its speed or direction is changing.
- Ignoring air resistance, the acceleration due to gravity is the same for all bodies at the same place.
- g always acts downwards towards the centre of the earth.
- A body at its highest point has zero velocity but not zero acceleration. (Acceleration due to gravity still operates.)

Forces

- A force is anything which changes, or tends to change, the motion of a body in magnitude or direction.
- An unbalanced force causes motion.
- The force with which the earth attracts a body is called the weight of the body.
- The mass of a body is the amount of matter in it.
- Momentum is the product of the mass and velocity of a body.
- **Newton's laws of motion:**
  1. A body remains at rest or moving with uniform velocity unless an unbalanced force acts on it.
  2. The rate of change of momentum is proportional to the force causing it and takes place in the direction of that force.
  3. To every action there is an equal and opposite reaction. Action and reaction never act on the same body.
- Force = mass × acceleration
- Weight = mass × g
- A newton is the force which gives an acceleration of 1 ms^{-2} to a mass of 1 kg.
- Principle of conservation of momentum: If no external force acts on a system of colliding bodies the total momentum of the bodies remains constant.
- Impulse = force × time = change in momentum
  Mathematically $Ft = mv - mu$.

Moments

- The point at which the whole weight of a body appears to act is called its centre of gravity.
- The principle of stable design is to have a low centre of gravity and a wide base.
- A lever is a rigid body that is free to rotate about a fixed point called the fulcrum.
- The moment of a force about a point is force × the perpendicular distance from the point to the line of action of the force.

- The principle of moments states that when a body is in equilibrium the sum of the clockwise moments **about any point** is equal to the sum of the anticlockwise moments about that point.

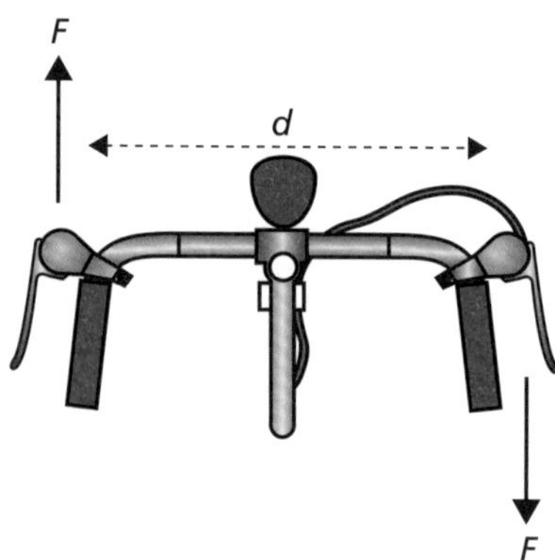

- The conditions for equilibrium are:
  1. The principle of moments must apply.
  2. The vector sum of the forces in any direction is zero.
- The moment of a **couple** is the product of one force × the perpendicular distance between them.

Work, energy and power

- Work = force by distance moved in the direction of the force
- A joule is the work done when a force of 1 newton moves its point of application 1 m.
- Potential energy is energy due to position or mechanical condition. $E_p = mgh$
- Kinetic energy is energy due to motion. $E_k = \frac{1}{2}mv^2$
- The law of conservation of energy states that energy can neither be created nor destroyed; it simply changes from one form to another.
- Power is the amount of work done per second.
- 1 watt = 1 joule s^{-1}
- Friction is a force which opposes relative motion between two bodies in contact.
- Lubricants reduce friction.
- Viscosity is resistance to flow in fluids.
- A sphere falling through a fluid has three forces acting on it:
  1. Its weight W acting downwards
  2. An upthrust U due to displaced fluid
  3. A frictional force F acting upwards

  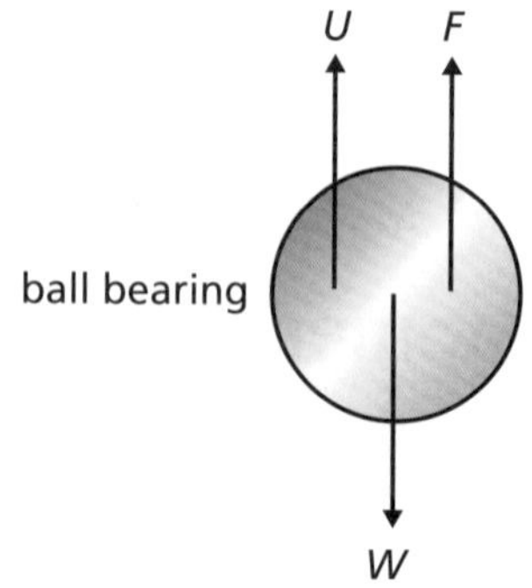

  ball bearing

  W and U are constant. As the sphere begins to fall, it accelerates but, as its velocity increases, F also increases until $U + F = W$ and the net force on the sphere is zero. It now continues to fall with uniform velocity known as terminal velocity.

Density and pressure

- The mass of unit volume of a substance is called its density.
- Pressure is force per unit area.
- The unit of pressure is the pascal. $1\ \text{Pa} = 1\ \text{N}\,\text{m}^{-2}$
- Pressure in a fluid depends on depth, density and acceleration due to gravity. $P = \rho g h$
- Archimedes' Principle: A body partly or wholly immersed in a fluid experiences an upthrust equal to the weight of the fluid displaced.
- Law of flotation: A floating body displaces its own weight of fluid.

Circular motion

HL

- The angle in radians $= \dfrac{\text{arc}}{\text{radius}} \Rightarrow \theta = \dfrac{s}{r}$.

- The angular velocity is the rate of change of angle in radians per second. $\omega = \dfrac{\theta}{t}$

- The periodic time $T = \dfrac{2\pi}{\omega}$

- Linear velocity $= \dfrac{\text{arc}}{t} = \dfrac{r\theta}{t} = r\omega$

  $v = r\omega$

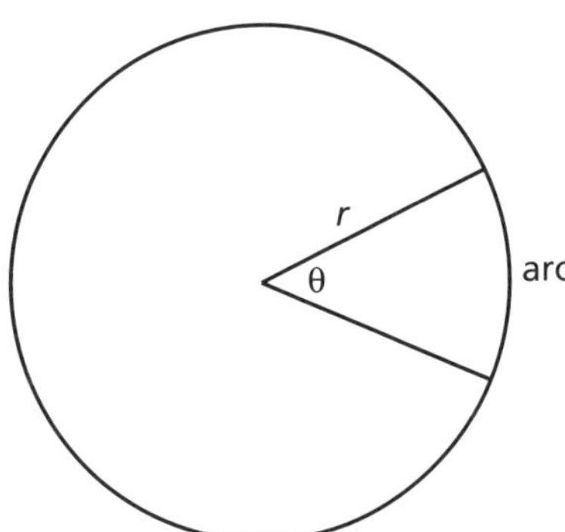

- Acceleration towards the centre of a circle

  $a = r\omega^2$ or $a = \dfrac{v^2}{r}$

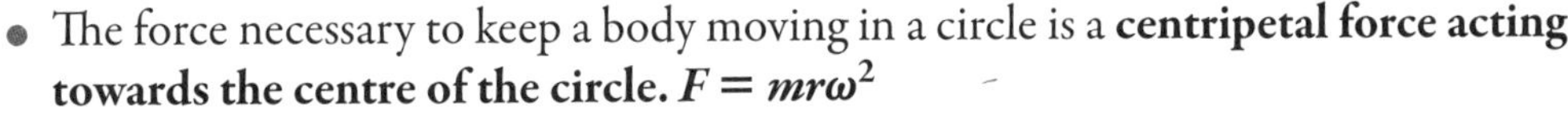

- The force necessary to keep a body moving in a circle is a **centripetal force acting towards the centre of the circle.** $F = mr\omega^2$

  or $F = \dfrac{mv^2}{r}$

- Law of gravitation: The force of attraction between any two bodies is proportional to the product of their masses and inversely proportional to the square of the distance between them.

  $F \propto \dfrac{(M_1 M_2)}{d^2} \Rightarrow F = \dfrac{(G M_1 M_2)}{d^2}$

  $mg = \dfrac{GmM}{d^2} \Rightarrow \dfrac{g}{G} = \dfrac{M}{d^2}$ or $g = \dfrac{GM}{d^2}$

exam focus

Instead of giving a definition or stating a law you may simply give a formula, if there is one, **provided you say what each symbol in the formula represents!**

HL Kepler's laws of planetary motion

1. The planets move in elliptical orbits round the sun as one focus.
2. The line joining the sun and the planet sweeps out equal areas in equal time intervals.
3. The square of the periodic time of a planet is proportional to the cube of its mean distance from the sun.

$$\frac{GmM}{r^2} = mr\omega^2 = mr\left(\frac{4\pi^2}{T^2}\right) \Rightarrow T^2 = \frac{4\pi^2 r^3}{GM}$$

Mathematically this is Kepler's third law.

Question 6 2005 Higher Level: A satellite is in circular orbit round the planet Saturn. Derive the relationship between the period of the satellite, the mass of Saturn and the radius of the orbit. **The relationship between period, mass and radius is in fact Kepler's third law so simply derive it as above.**

HL Satellites in orbit

For a signal to be transmitted from earth to a satellite and from there to somewhere else on earth, the satellite must always be directly above the same point on earth. In other words, the period of the satellite must be the same as the period of rotation of the earth, i.e. 24 hours. The satellite is now said to be in a **geostationary** or **parking** orbit.

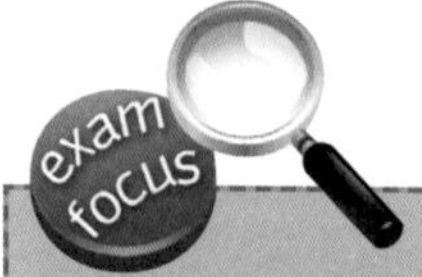

The two most popular questions in Section B are Question 5 and Question 12. Answer all 10 parts in Question 5 but only 2 parts in Question 12.

HL Simple harmonic motion

- Hooke's law: Provided a spring is not extended beyond its elastic limit the extension is proportional to the load.
- The motion of a body is simple harmonic motion if its acceleration towards a particular point is directly proportional to its displacement from that point.
- $a = -\omega^2 s$ **is a mathematical definition of simple harmonic motion.**

  The minus indicates that the body begins to retard as it passes through 0, the centre of its motion.
- When a particle is undergoing simple harmonic motion its acceleration is maximum when its displacement is maximum.

FAQs

Give an example where a body has acceleration but zero velocity.
A body that has been thrown vertically upwards and is at its greatest height.

When does a body travelling at constant speed have an acceleration?
When it is changing direction.

Why is it easier to turn a nut using a longer spanner rather than a shorter one?
The distance from the effort to the fulcrum is greater, giving a greater turning effect.

State the law of flotation.
A floating body displaces its own weight of fluid.

A container contains 5 kg of water. If the area of the base of the container is 0.5 m^2, what is the pressure on the base?
$$P = \frac{F}{A} = \frac{(5 \times 9.8)}{0.5} = 98 \text{ Pa.}$$

What is the relationship between the acceleration due to gravity g and the distance from the centre of the earth?
$$g \propto \frac{1}{d^2}$$

A particle travels at constant speed of 10 ms^{-1} in a circle of radius 2 m. What is its angular velocity?
$$v = r\omega \Rightarrow \omega = \frac{v}{r} = \frac{10}{2} = 5 \text{ radians per second.}$$

The moon orbits the earth. What is the relationship between the period of the moon and the radius of its orbit?
$T^2 \propto R^3$. (Kepler's third law)

Exam questions

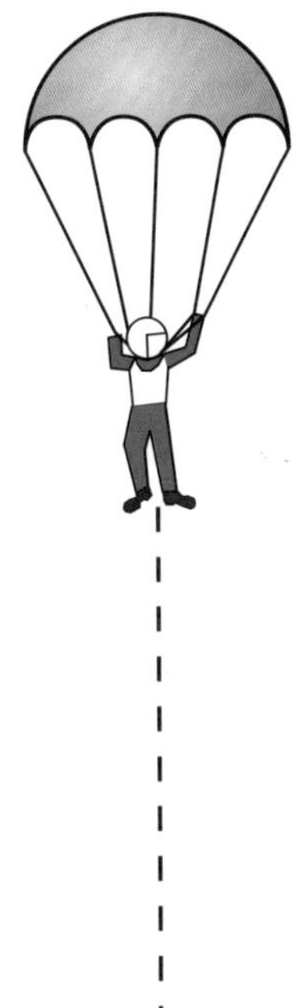

Q 1: A parachutist is falling with a vertical velocity of 15 m s^{-1} when he is blown by the wind, which has a horizontal velocity of 8 m s^{-1}. Calculate the resultant velocity of the parachutist. At a certain instant during the descent he is directly over a point X on the ground. He lands 10 seconds later at a point Y. What is the distance XY?

A: $R^2 = 15^2 + 8^2 = 289$
$\Rightarrow R = 17$ m s^{-1}.

Y   X

$\text{Tan}^{-1}\dfrac{8}{15} = \tan^{-1} 0.5333 = 28°$ to the vertical.

$v = 17 \text{ m s}^{-1}$ at 28° to the vertical

Distance in any direction = velocity in that direction × time.

XY = 8 × 10 = 80 m.

Q 2: A body leaves a point A and moves in a straight line with uniform velocity of 36 m s^{-1}. Seven seconds later another body of mass 2 kg at rest at A is acted on by a constant force of 4 newtons and moves in the same direction as the first body. How long will it take the second body to catch up on the first body?

A: For the second body $F = ma \Rightarrow 4 = 2a \Rightarrow a = 2 \text{ m s}^{-2}$

$S_1 = ut + \frac{1}{2}at^2$ but since $u = 0$ $s_1 = \frac{1}{2}at^2 = \frac{1}{2}(2)t^2 = t^2$

For the first body distance = velocity × time

$S_2 = 36(t + 7) = 36t + 252$

When they meet $s_1 = s_2 \Rightarrow t^2 =$

$36t + 252$

$\Rightarrow t^2 - 36t - 252 = 0$

$\Rightarrow (t - 42)(t + 6) = 0$

$\Rightarrow t = 42$ seconds.

Note: Cannot be −6 seconds.

Q 3: Given that the mass of the earth is 6×10^{24} kg and that the radius of the earth is 6.4×10^6 m calculate the height above the earth's surface of a satellite which is in geostationary orbit.

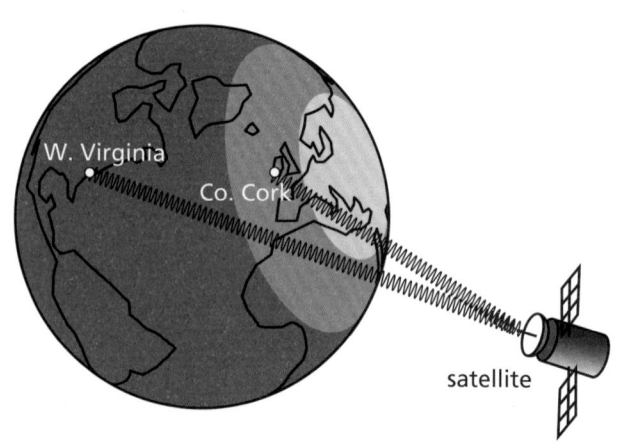

satellite

A: $\dfrac{4\pi^2 r^3}{GM} = T^2 \Rightarrow r^3 = \dfrac{GMT^2}{4\pi^2} = \dfrac{6.67 \times 10^{-11} \times 6 \times 10^{24} \times (24 \times 3,600)^2}{4 \times 3.14^2}$

$\qquad = 7.575 \times 10^{22} \text{ m} \Rightarrow r = 4.231 \times 10^7 \text{ m}$

The height above the earth's surface is the radius of the satellite's orbit minus the radius of the earth.

$h = 4.231 \times 10^7 - 6.4 \times 10^6 = 3.591 \times 10^7 \text{ m}.$

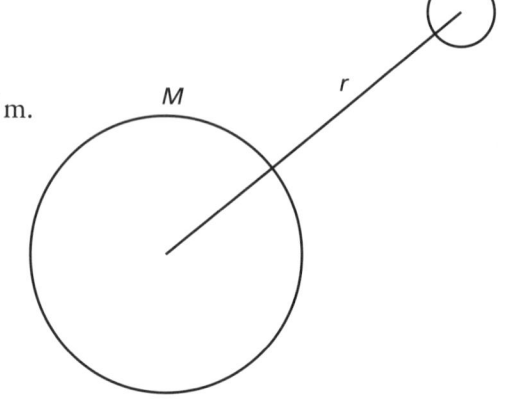

6 Light and Sound

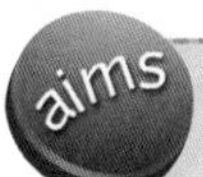 **aims**

To learn:
- All light and sound formulae
- All light and sound definitions
- Wave definitions
- How to get maximum marks for FAQs in light and sound
- Applications of light and sound

Light and reflection

- Light is a form of energy.
- The laws of reflection are:
  1. The angle of reflection (r) equals the angle of incidence (i).
  2. The incident ray, the normal and the reflected ray are all in the same plane.
- A real image is formed by the actual intersection of light rays. It can be formed on a screen and is always inverted.
- A virtual image is formed by the apparent intersection of rays. It cannot be formed on a screen and is always erect.
- A concave mirror forms a virtual image when the object is inside the focus.
- $\dfrac{1}{f} = \dfrac{1}{v} + \dfrac{1}{u}$ where f is the focal length, v is the image distance and u is the object distance.
- $m = \dfrac{v}{u}$ where m is the magnification.
  (These formulae are also used for lenses.)
- Concave mirrors are used as reflectors in headlamps, as makeup mirrors and by dentists.
- Convex mirrors give a wide field of view and are used as rearview mirrors in cars, in buses, in shops and at dangerous junctions.

Refraction of light

- Refraction: Light bends when it passes from one medium to another medium of different density.
- Laws of refraction:
  1. $\dfrac{\sin i}{\sin r}$ is constant for two given media (Snell's law).

  $\dfrac{\sin i}{\sin r}$ is known as the refractive index n.

2. The incident ray, refracted ray and normal are all in the same plane.

- $n = \dfrac{\sin i}{\sin r} = \dfrac{\text{real depth}}{\text{apparent depth}}$

  $= \dfrac{\text{velocity of light in medium 1}}{\text{velocity of light in medium 2}}$

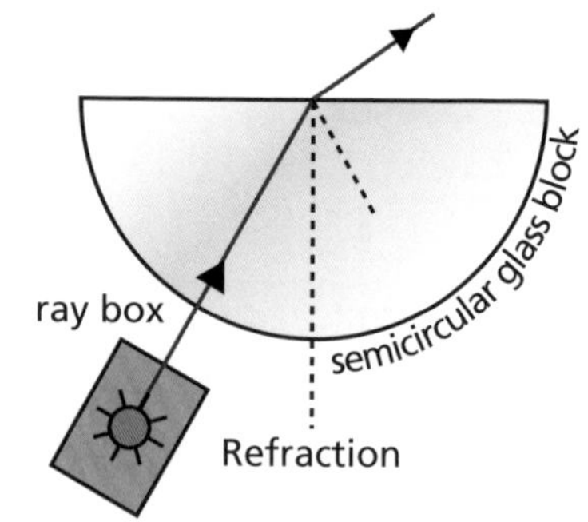

ray box

semicircular glass block

Refraction

- The critical angle is the angle of incidence in the denser medium corresponding to an angle of refraction of 90° in the less dense medium.

- $n = \dfrac{1}{\sin C}$

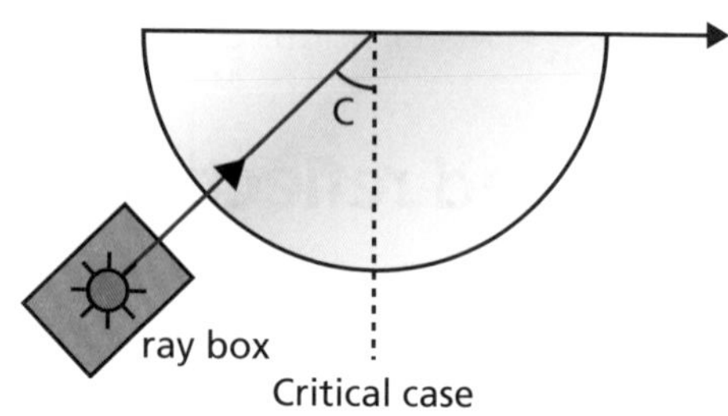

ray box

Critical case

- Total internal reflection occurs when the angle of incidence in the denser medium is greater than the critical angle.

- Total internal reflection is used in periscopes, prism binoculars, reflectors, fibre optics (communication and endoscopes).

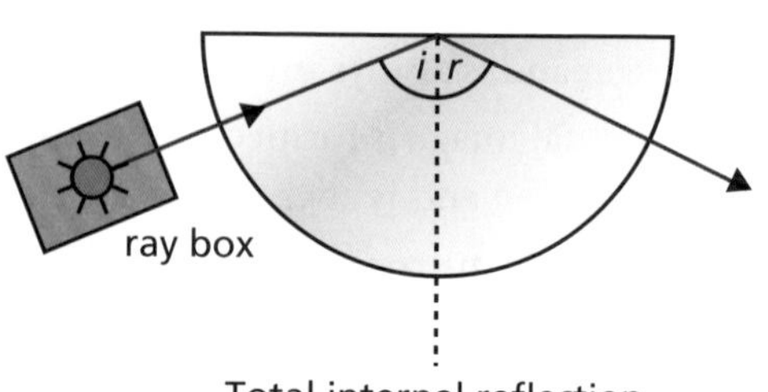

ray box

Total internal reflection

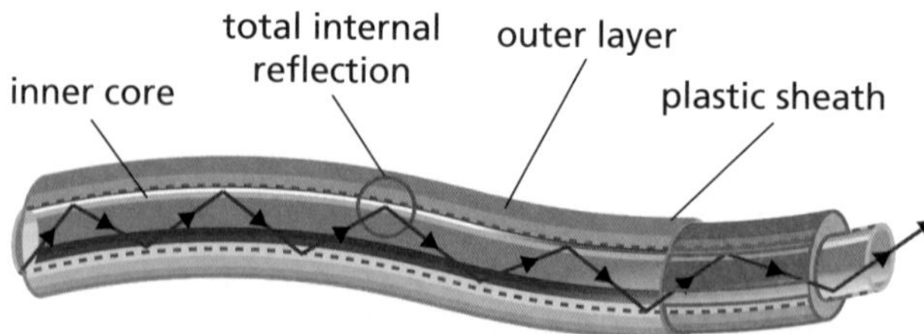

total internal reflection   outer layer

inner core   plastic sheath

A fibre optic cable: The cable is made of inner and outer layers of glass in which light travels at different speeds. Total internal reflection occurs at the boundary between these layers. Scratches on the plastic covering will not cause a loss of light, because the light does not reach this part of the fibre.

Lenses

- A converging lens forms a virtual image only when the object is inside the focus.
- A diverging lens **always** forms a virtual, erect, diminished image.
- For a converging lens, f is positive.

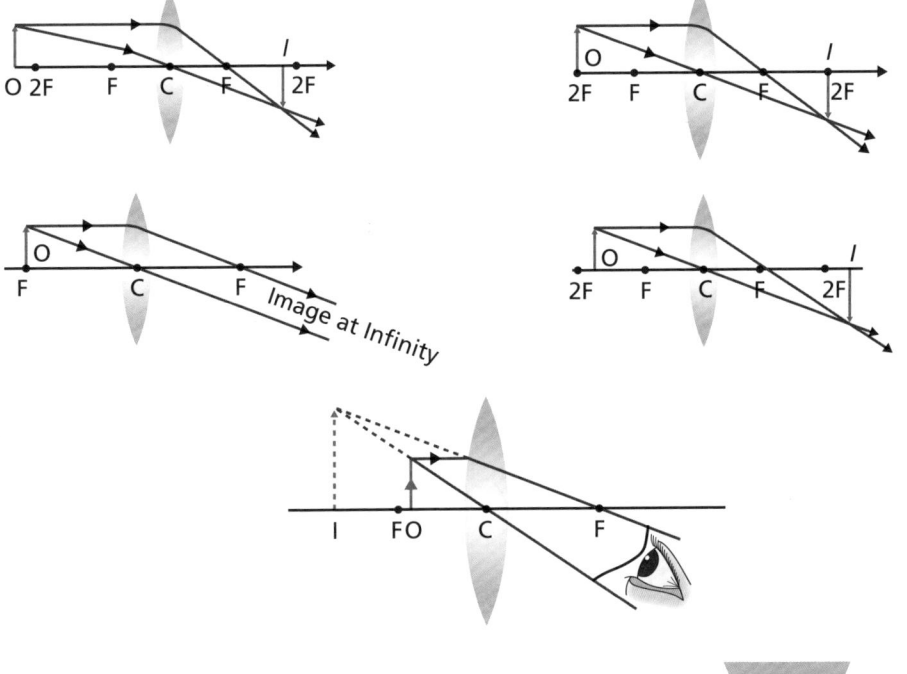

- For a diverging lens, f is negative.
- The power of a lens: $P = \dfrac{1}{f}$
- For two lenses in contact:
  $P = P_1 + P_2$

diverging lens

The eye

- Accommodation means that the eye focuses objects at different distances from it onto the retina by changing the shape, and consequently the focal length, of the lens.
- Short sight (myopia) and long sight can be corrected by the use of the appropriate lenses.

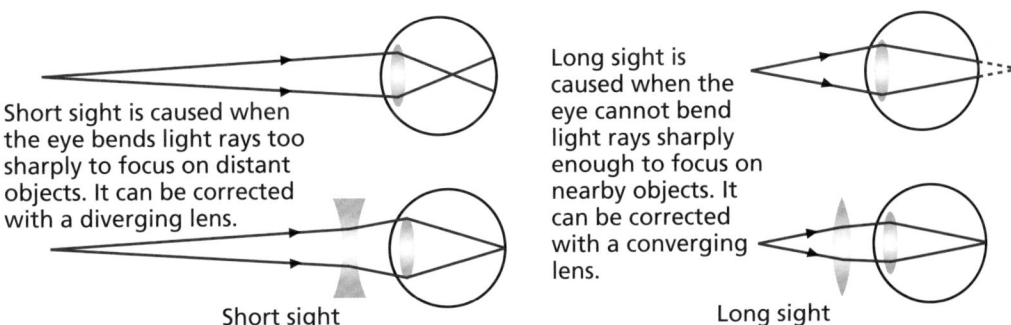

Short sight is caused when the eye bends light rays too sharply to focus on distant objects. It can be corrected with a diverging lens.

Long sight is caused when the eye cannot bend light rays sharply enough to focus on nearby objects. It can be corrected with a converging lens.

Short sight

Long sight

Waves

- Transverse waves are waves which travel perpendicular to the direction of vibration of the particles.
- Longitudinal waves travel parallel to the direction of vibration of the particles.
- Velocity = frequency × wavelength. ($c = f \times \lambda$)
- Interference means that when two or more waves meet, the resultant displacement equals the algebraic sum of the individual displacements.
- Constructive interference occurs when two waves combine to give a wave of larger amplitude.
- Destructive interference occurs when two waves meet to give a wave of smaller amplitude.

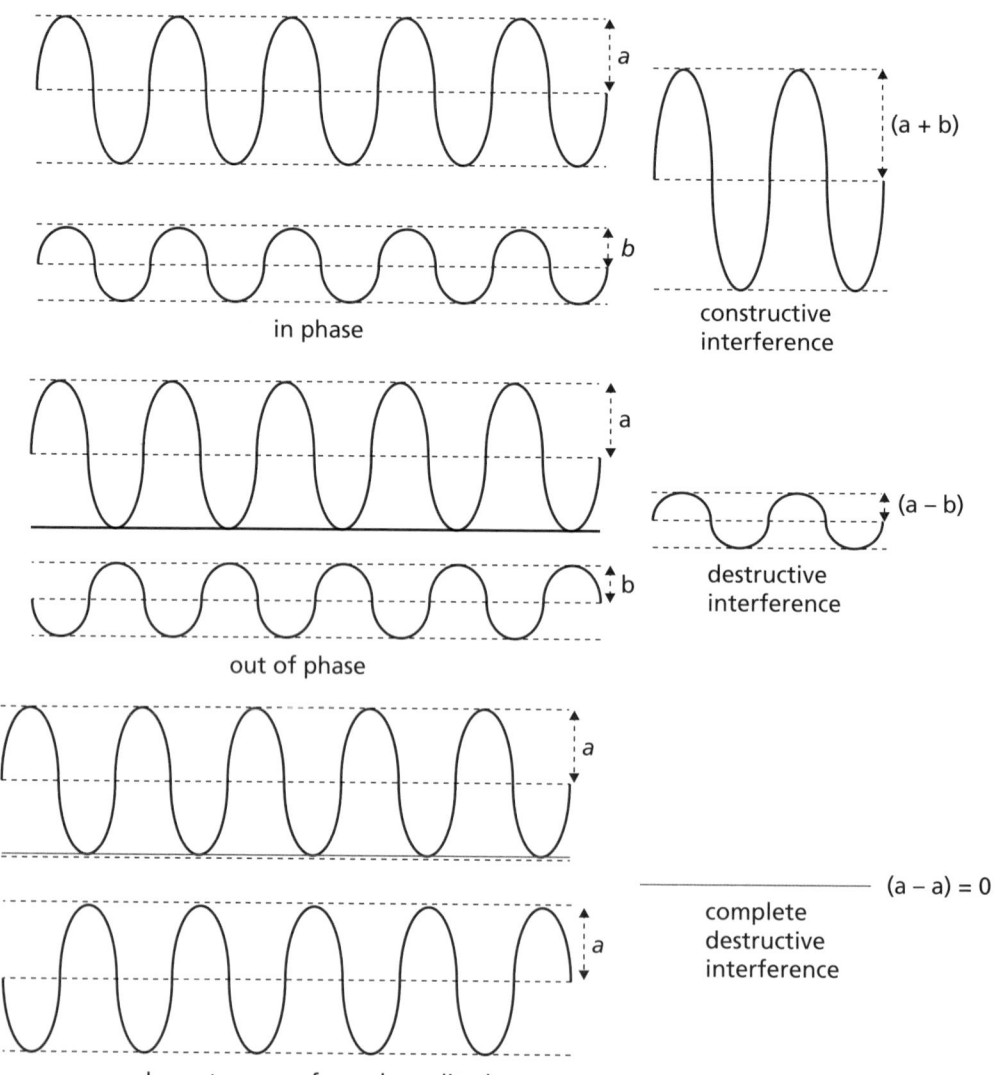

in phase

constructive interference

out of phase

destructive interference

coherent waves of equal amplitude
half a wavelength out of phase

complete destructive interference

- Coherent sources are sources that have the same frequency and are in phase.
- The spreading of waves into the geometric shadow of an obstacle is called **diffraction.**
- The longer the wavelength, the greater the diffraction.

Derivation of diffraction grating formula

Consider two rays emerging in a direction making an angle θ with the grating. If, when these rays are brought together by a converging lens, their path differences is a whole number of wavelengths **nλ**, the result will be constructive interference and a bright image.

From the diagram $\dfrac{n\lambda}{d} = \sin \theta \Rightarrow \mathbf{n\lambda = d \sin \theta}$.

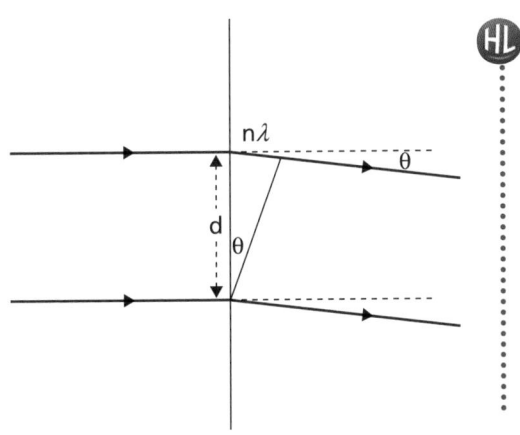

Diffraction grating

Polarisation

Light waves are transverse, which means that they vibrate at right angles to the direction in which they are travelling. The vibrations radiate out like a disc from the centre of the wave path.

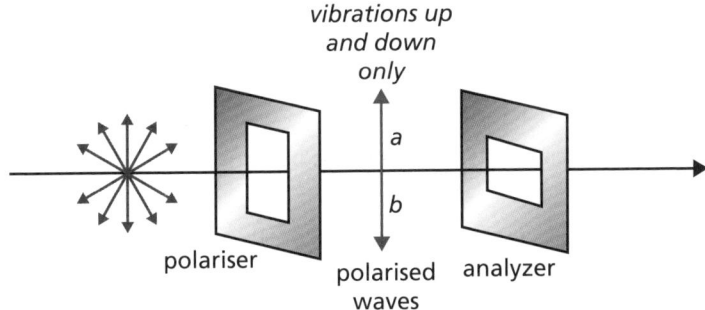

Polaroid material

When they meet a polariser, only vibrations in one direction, *ab*, will pass through. The light has now been polarised. An analyser can be used to confirm that polarisation has taken place.

- Polarisation means that wave vibrations are confined to one plane.
- Only transverse waves can be polarised.
- The fact that light can be polarised shows that light waves are transverse.

The electromagnetic spectrum

- The electromagnetic spectrum consists of waves which are based on vibrating electric and magnetic fields.
- The spectrum goes from gamma rays and X-rays to microwaves and radio waves.
- **Dispersion** is the splitting up of white light into its constituent colours.
- The primary colours of light are red, green and blue.
- Complementary colours are a primary colour and a secondary colour, which together give white.
- Dispersion by refraction: Long wavelengths refracted least.
- Dispersion by diffraction: Long wavelengths diffracted most.

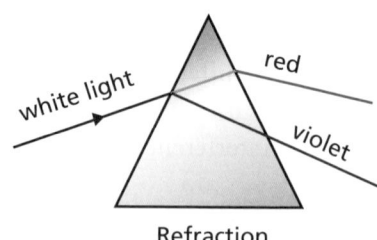

Refraction

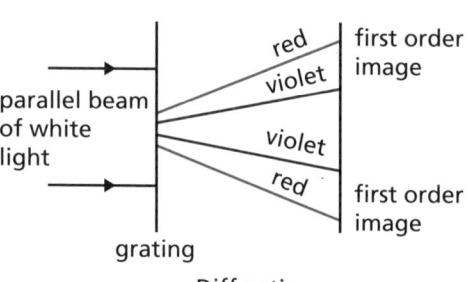

Diffraction

- An emission spectrum is a spectrum given out by a substance whose atoms are in an excited state.
- An absorption spectrum is a spectrum that is continuous except for certain missing wavelengths.
- Fraunhofer lines are dark lines in the spectrum of the sun due to absorption.

exam focus

You can lose marks by putting in the wrong units, or no units at all, with your answer. The State Examinations Commission booklet of Formulae and Tables contains symbols and units on pages 65 to 71.

Sound

- The pitch of a note depends on the frequency.
- The loudness depends on amplitude (and frequency).
- Harmonics are frequencies which are multiples of the fundamental frequency.
- The quality of a note depends on the harmonics present.
- **Resonance** is the transfer of energy between two bodies of the same natural frequency.
- A pendulum has a natural frequency of vibration that depends on its length so it can be used **to demonstrate resonance**.

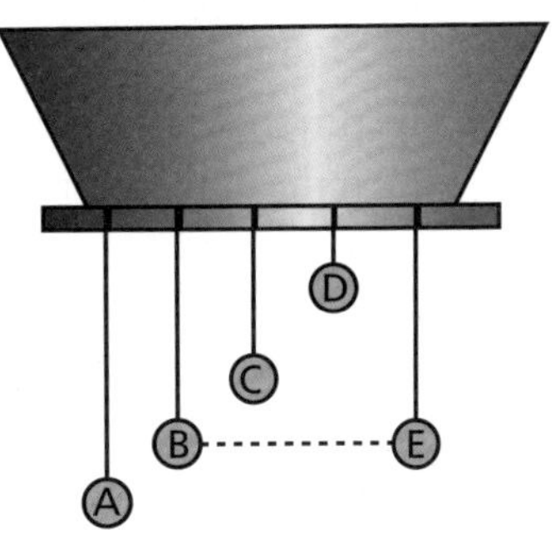

The heavy pendulum E is set in motion. This causes the others to vibrate but B vibrates most. This is because B and E are the same length and have the same natural frequency of vibration.

- A stationary wave is produced when two waves of the same frequency and amplitude meet when moving in opposite directions.
- The distance between successive nodes is half a wavelength.
- The distance between a node and an antinode is quarter of a wavelength.

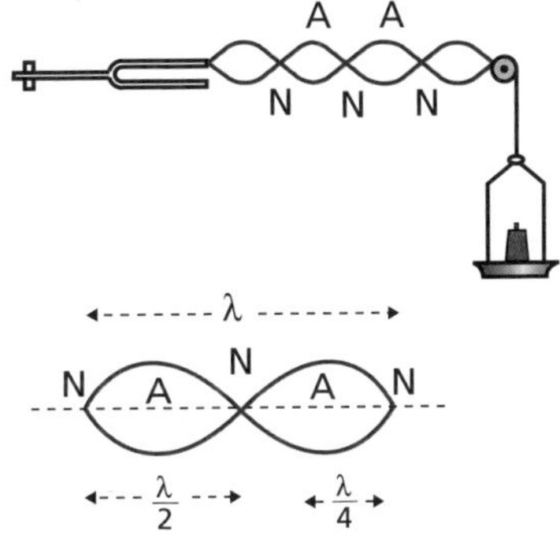

- The frequency of a stretched string depends on the length, the tension and the mass of unit length.

$$f = \frac{1}{2l}\sqrt{\frac{T}{\mu}}$$

- The **Doppler** effect is the change in the frequency of waves due to relative motion between the source and the observer.

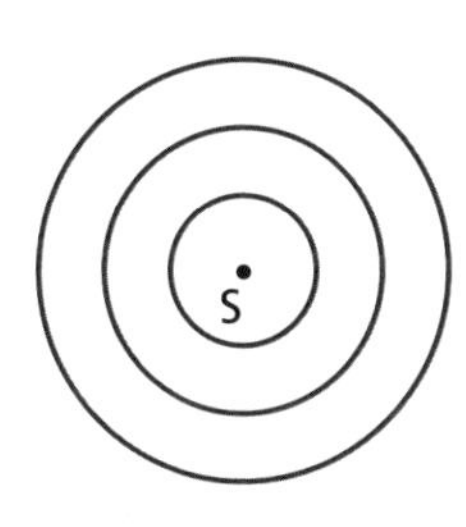
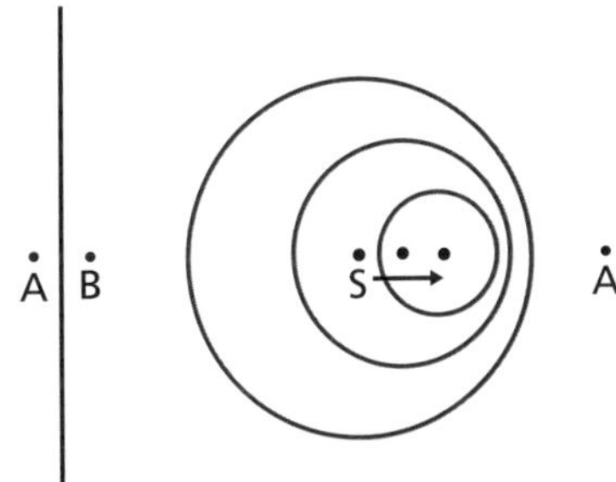

- The Doppler formula is $f' = \dfrac{fc}{(c \pm u)}$

- Sound intensity is the energy per second passing through 1 square metre held at right angles to the direction in which the sound is travelling.

- The threshold of hearing is the lowest intensity to which the human ear can respond when the frequency is 1 kHz. (**Sound intensity** $10^{-12} \, \text{W m}^{-2}$)

key point

- The unit of sound intensity is the watt per metre squared (W m^{-2}) not the Bel or decibel.
- Sound intensity level is measured in decibels (dB).

- The bel (B) is the relative change in intensity between two sounds if the intensity of one is 10 times the intensity of the other.

- **Number of bels** $= \log_{10} \dfrac{I_2}{I_1}$

- **Sound intensity level** $= \log_{10}\left(\dfrac{I}{10^{-12}}\right)$ B or $10 \log_{10}\left(\dfrac{I}{10^{-12}}\right)$ dB

To demonstrate that sound is a wave motion

As you walk slowly from A to B the sound level rises and falls due to constructive and destructive interference. This shows the wave nature of sound.

source

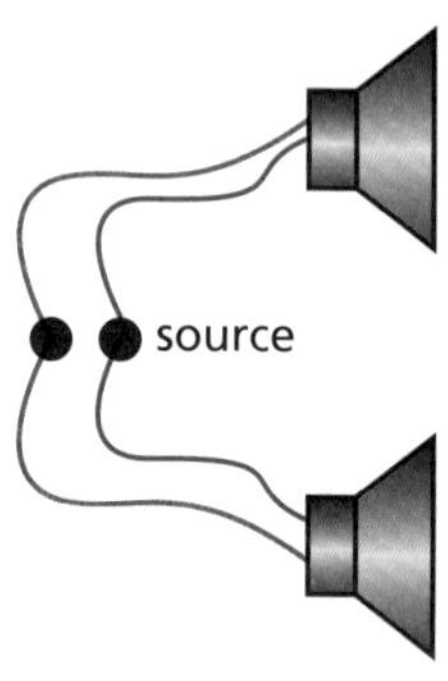

FAQs

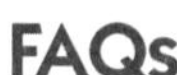

Why do dentists use concave mirrors?
Because they can produce an erect magnified image.

A diverging lens cannot be used as a magnifying glass. Explain why.
It always forms a diminished image.

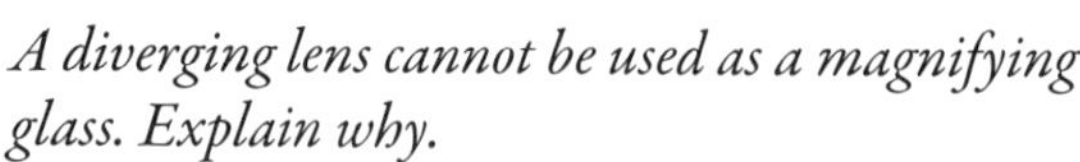

Why is a filament light bulb not an efficient source of light?
Only a small percentage of the output is light energy.

Why is a fluorescent tube an efficient source of light?
A high percentage of the electrical energy is converted to light.

Describe an experiment to show that light waves are transverse waves.
Observe a light source through two pieces of Polaroid material. Rotate one piece slowly until the light dims to zero. Polarisation of light has occurred and only transverse waves can be polarised.

The refractive index of a liquid is 1.35. What is the critical angle for this liquid?

$$n = \frac{1}{\sin C} \Rightarrow \sin C = \frac{1}{n} = \frac{1}{1.35} = 0.74. \ C = 47.8° = 47° \ 48'.$$

In fibre optics why is each fibre coated with glass of lower refractive index?
Because total internal reflection can occur only when light tries to pass from a denser to a less dense medium.

Give two reasons why the telecommunications industry uses optical fibres instead of copper conductors to transmit signals.
Take up less space, carry more information, more flexible, less interference, need to be boosted less often.

What two phenomena occur when light passes through a pair of narrow slits?
Diffraction and interference.

Why does diffraction not occur when light passes through a window?
The window is too wide relative to the wavelength of light.

How is infra-red radiation detected?
By its heating effect (on a blackened thermometer bulb).

What does the loudness of a musical note depend on?
The amplitude and the frequency.

What does the quality of a musical note depend on?
The overtones or harmonics.

As a person approaches a loudspeaker the sound intensity doubles. What is the increase in sound intensity level?

$$\text{Log}\left(\frac{I_2}{I_1}\right) = \log 2 = 0.3 \text{ Bels} = 3\text{dB}.$$

Sound intensity level can be measured in dB or dB(A). What is the difference between the two scales?
The dB(A) scale is a weighted scale adapted to the frequency response of the human ear.

Give two applications of the Doppler effect.
Speed traps, studying the movement of stars (red shift), weather forecasting, tracking satellites.

How does resonance occur in an acoustic guitar?
Energy is transferred to the air inside the sound box, which then vibrates at the same frequency as the string.

What is the relationship between tension and frequency for a stretched string?
$f \propto \sqrt{T}$

HL Exam question

2007 Higher level question 7

Q: (a) What is the Doppler effect?
Explain, with the aid of a labelled diagram, how this phenomenon occurs.
A: See Doppler effect diagram on p. 43. As the source s moves towards A and away from B the observer at A receives waves of reduced wavelength and **increased frequency** while the observer at B receives waves of increased wavelength and **reduced frequency**.
(b) An emission line spectrum of a star was analysed using the Doppler effect. Describe how an emission line spectrum is produced.
A: A monatomic gas is given energy and the electrons move up to a higher energy level. However, the atoms are now in an excited state so electrons drop down again, emitting their excess energy as electromagnetic radiation as they do so. E = hf so that different energy drops give different discrete frequencies or wavelengths of light.
(c) The red line emitted by a hydrogen discharge tube in the laboratory has a wavelength of 656 nm. The same red line in the hydrogen spectrum of a moving star has a wavelength of 720 nm. Is the star approaching the earth? Justify your answer.
A: No. The wavelength has increased so the frequency has decreased which, according to the Doppler effect, means the source (star) is moving away from the earth.
Q: Calculate:
(i) The frequency of the red line in the star's spectrum

A: $c = f'\lambda \Rightarrow f' = \dfrac{c}{\lambda} = \dfrac{(3 \times 10^8)}{(720 \times 10^{-9})} = 4.17 \times 10^{14}\,\text{Hz}$

(ii) The speed of the moving star (Speed of light $= 3.00 \times 10^8\,\text{m s}^{-1}$)

A: $f = \dfrac{(3 \times 10^8)}{(656 \times 10^{-9})} = 4.57 \times 10^{14}\,\text{Hz}$

$f' = \dfrac{fc}{(c+u)} \Rightarrow 4.17 \times 10^{14} = \dfrac{(4.57 \times 10^{14})(3 \times 10^8)}{(3 \times 10^8 + u)}$

$\Rightarrow (3 \times 10^8 + u) = \dfrac{(4.57 \times 10^{14})(3 \times 10^8)}{(4.17 \times 10^{14})}$

$\Rightarrow 3 \times 10^8 + u = 1.096 \times 3 \times 10^8 = 3.288 \times 10^8$

$\Rightarrow u = 0.288 \times 10^8 = 2.88 \times 10^7\,\text{m s}^{-1}.$

7 Heat

Heat, temperature and thermometers

- Heat is a form of energy.
- Temperature is a measure of how hot a body is.
- Temperature indicates the level of heat, or degree of hotness, in a body not the amount of heat.
- A **thermometric property** is a property that changes measurably as the temperature changes.
- As well as a thermometric property, a good thermometer should have accuracy, a wide range, sensitivity, low heat capacity and be quick to reach thermal equilibrium.
- Boyle's law: At constant temperature the pressure of a fixed mass of gas is inversely proportional to the volume. $\left(P \propto \dfrac{1}{V} \right)$

- An ideal gas is a gas that obeys Boyle's law exactly. Many gases approach the ideal at lower pressures.
- $-273.15°$ C is known as absolute zero.

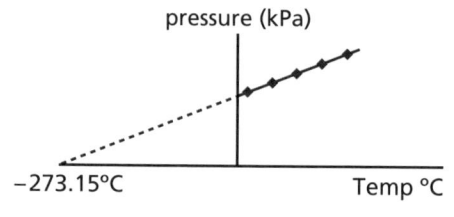

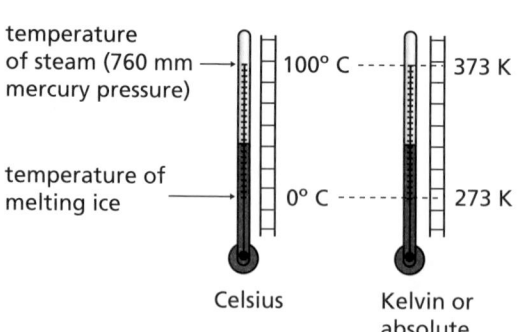

Transmission of heat

- Conduction is the way heat travels through a substance from one particle to the next. (The particles themselves do not travel.)
- Convection is the way heat travels through a fluid by the movement of heated particles.
- Heat radiation is the transfer of heat energy by electromagnetic waves.
- Dark surfaces are better than bright surfaces at absorbing and radiating heat.
- The solar constant is the average energy per second falling normally on 1 m² of the earth's atmosphere. (Unit $W\,m^{-2}$)
- The U-value is a measure of the heat lost per second through each square metre for every 1 K difference in temperature between the inside and the outside. ($W\,m^{-2}K^{-1}$)
- Insulation reduces the U-value.

Heat capacity and latent heat

- The heat capacity of a body is the heat required to raise its temperature by 1 K.
- The specific heat capacity of a substance is the amount of heat required to raise the temperature of 1 kg of that substance by 1 K.
- The amount of heat energy gained or lost = mass $\times$ SHC $\times$ change in temperature. ($\Delta E = m.c.\Delta\theta$)
- There is no change of temperature during a change of state.
- Latent heat is the heat involved when a substance changes state without changing temperature.

- The specific latent heat of fusion of ice is the amount of heat needed to change 1 kg of ice to water without change of temperature. $(\Delta E = ml)$
- The specific latent heat of vaporisation of water is the amount of heat needed to change 1 kg of water to steam without change of temperature. $(\Delta E = ml)$
- A heat pump transfers heat from one area to another, e.g. a refrigerator.

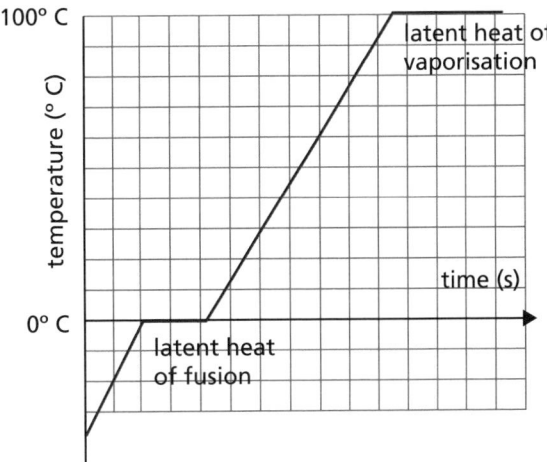

FAQs

Why is it necessary to have a standard thermometer?
Because thermometers based on different thermometric properties give different readings at the same temperature.

What is the thermometric property of a thermocouple?
The emf (voltage) generated.

Name a thermometric property other than emf.
Length, volume, pressure, resistance, colour.

The solar constant is 1.35 kW m^{-2}. What is the average amount of energy falling normally on each square metre of the earth's atmosphere in one year?
Solar constant × time $= (1.35 \times 10^3)(3.1536 \times 10^7)$
$$= 4.26 \times 10^{10} \text{ J.}$$

The average value for the solar constant in Ireland is 1.2 × 10^2 W m^{-2}. What is the average energy falling normally on an area of 5 m^2 in Ireland in 1 minute?
$(1.2 \times 10^2)(5)(60) = 3.6 \times 10^4$ J.

Storage heaters have a large heat capacity. Explain why.
Because they contain materials of high **specific** heat capacity.

Why does the temperature of an athlete reduce when she perspires?
Because as she perspires the water takes (latent) heat energy from the body to evaporate the water.

ⒽⓁ Exam questions

2009 Higher level question 11

Q: Read the following passage and answer the accompanying questions.

The sun is a major source of 'green' energy. In Ireland solar heating systems and geothermal systems are used to get energy from the sun. There are two main types of solar heating systems, flat-plate collectors and vacuum-tube collectors.

- A flat-plate collector is usually an aluminium box with a glass cover on top and a blackened plate on the bottom. A copper pipe is laid on the bottom of the box, like a hose on the ground; water is passed through the pipe and transfers the absorbed heat to a domestic hot water system.

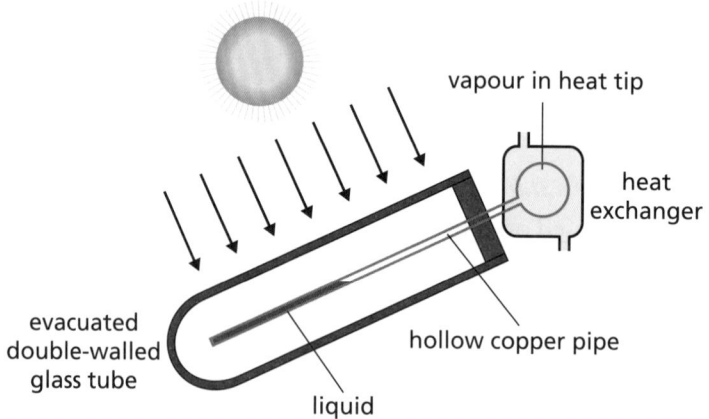

- In a vacuum-tube collector each tube consists of an evacuated double-walled silvered glass tube in which there is a hollow copper pipe containing a liquid. The liquid inside the copper pipe is vaporised and expands into the heat tip. There the vapour liquefies and the latent heat released is transferred, using a heat exchanger, to the domestic hot water system. The condensed liquid returns to the copper pipe and the cycle is repeated.

In a geothermal heating system a heat pump is used to extract solar energy stored in the ground and transfer it to the domestic hot water system.

(a) What is the maximum energy that can fall on an area of 8 m² in one hour if the solar constant is 1.35 W m⁻²?

A: $1{,}350 \times 8 \times 3{,}600 = 3.888 \times 10^7 \, \text{J}$

(b) Why is the bottom of a flat-plate collector blackened?

A: Because black surfaces are better absorbers of radiated heat.

(c) How much energy is required to raise the temperature of 500 litres of water from 20° C to 50° C?

A: $\Delta E = mc\Delta\theta = 500 \times 4{,}200 \times 30 = 6.3 \times 10^7 \, \text{J}$

(d) The liquid in a vacuum-tube solar collector has a large specific latent heat of vaporisation. Why?

A: So that more latent heat will be released during the change of state when the vapour liquefies.

(e) Name the three ways in which heat could be lost from a vacuum-tube solar collector.

A: Conduction, convection, radiation.

(f) How is the sun's energy trapped in a vacuum-tube solar collector?

A: Evacuated walls prevent conduction and convection and silvered walls prevent radiation. (Just as in a vacuum flask.)

(g) Describe, in terms of heat transfer, the operation of a heat pump.

A: Energy is taken from one body, making it colder, to another body, making it hotter.

(h) Give an advantage of a geothermal heating system over a solar heating system.

A: Geothermal systems function all the time, solar systems function only during daylight hours.

2006 Higher level question 12 (c)

Q: Define (i) power (ii) specific heat capacity.

A: Power is the amount of work done per second *or* the rate at which energy is changed from one form to another.

Specific heat capacity of a substance is the amount of heat required to raise the temperature of 1 kg of that substance by 1 K.

Q: 400 g of water at a temperature of $15°C$ is placed in an electric kettle. The power rating of the kettle is 3.0 kW.

(Specific heat capacity of water $= 4,200 \text{ J kg}^{-1} \text{K}^{-1}$)

Calculate:

(i) The energy required to raise the temperature of the water to $100°C$

A: $0.4 \times 4,200 \times 85 = 142,800 = 1.428 \times 10^5 \text{ J}$

(ii) The energy supplied by the kettle per second

A: $3.0 \text{ kW} = 3 \text{ kilojoules} = 3,000 = 3 \times 10^3 \text{ Js}^{-1}$

(iii) The least amount of time it would take to heat the water to $100°C$

A: Time $\dfrac{142,800}{3,000} = 47.6$ seconds

Q: In reality the time taken to heat the water will be greater. Explain why.

A: Inevitably, heat will be lost to the surroundings by conduction, convection and radiation.

8 Electricity – Static, Electric Fields and Capacitance

aims To learn:
- Definitions and formulae
- How to answer FAQs on static electricity, electric fields and capacitance
- How to solve problems on electric fields and capacitance

exam focus

- Check formulae and units in the SEC Formulae and Tables book.
- Illustrate your answer with clear simple labelled diagrams where possible.
- Always give the correct unit in your final answer to a numerical question.
- Where the quantity is a vector you must give the direction.

Static electricity

- All atoms are made up of three sub-atomic particles: protons, neutrons and electrons.

	Proton	Neutron	Electron
Mass	1 a.m.u.	1 a.m.u.	$\frac{1}{1,840}$ a.m.u.
Charge	+1	0	−1
Location	nucleus	nucleus	orbits around nucleus

- Static electric charges are produced by friction between two different materials.
- There are two types of charge – positive and negative.
- Like charges repel each other, unlike charges attract each other.
- A body becomes positively charged when it loses electrons.
- A body becomes negatively charged when it gains electrons.

- Conductors are substances through which electric charges can pass freely.
- Insulators are substances through which electric charges cannot pass.

Conductor	Current carriers	Examples
Solid	Electrons	Copper, aluminium
Liquid	Positive and negative ions	Salt water, copper sulphate solution
Gas	Electrons and ions	Fluorescent and neon gas tubes

Electric charge

- Electric charge (q) is measured in coulombs.
- A coulomb is the quantity of electric charge that passes when a current of one ampere flows for one second.
- $q = It$ (charge = current by time)
- The gold leaf electroscope is used to:
  - (a) Detect electric charge
  - (b) Identify the charge – positive or negative
  - (c) Compare the size of charges
  - (d) Distinguish between a conductor and an insulator

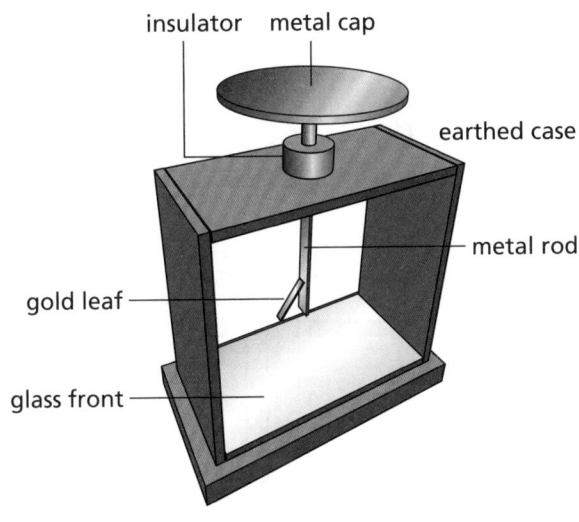

insulator   metal cap

earthed case

metal rod

gold leaf

glass front

How an electroscope is charged by induction

- Bring charged insulator close to electroscope.
- Earth the electroscope.
- Remove charged insulator.

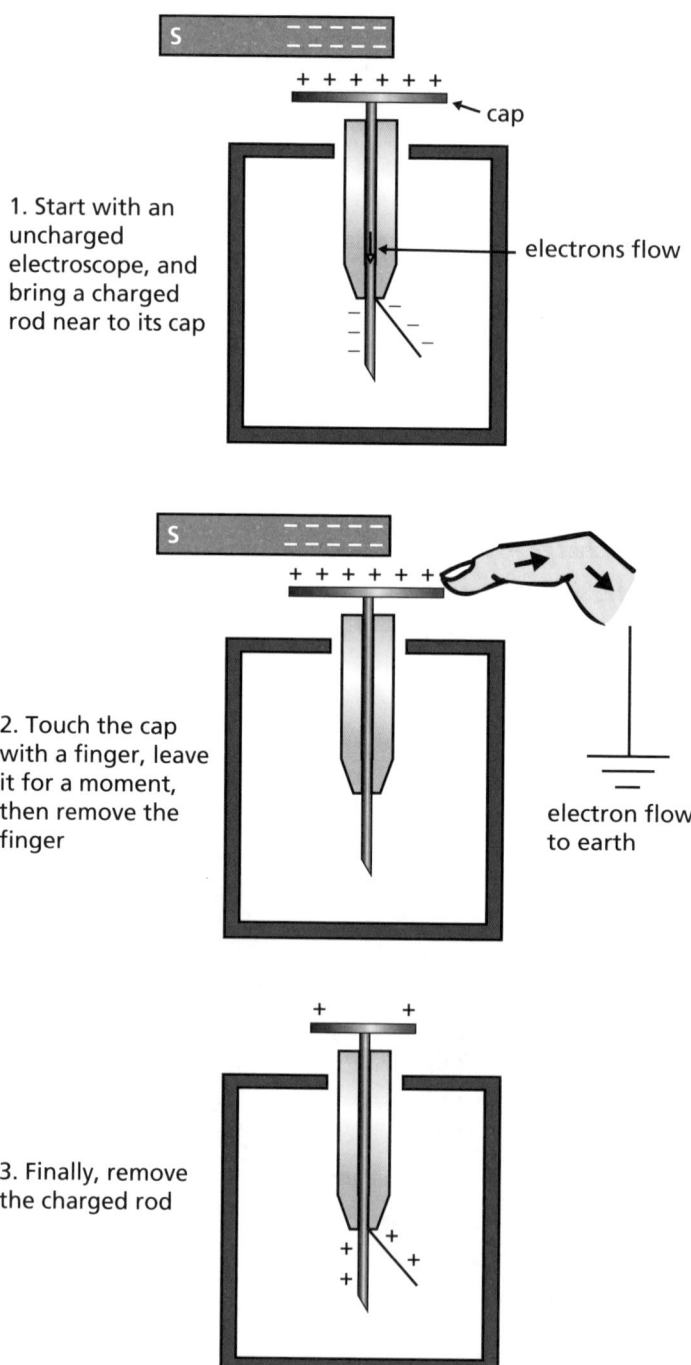

1. Start with an uncharged electroscope, and bring a charged rod near to its cap

cap

electrons flow

2. Touch the cap with a finger, leave it for a moment, then remove the finger

electron flow to earth

3. Finally, remove the charged rod

The induced charge is opposite to the inducing charge.

- Charge on a sphere is uniformly distributed.
- Charge on a pear-shaped conductor is concentrated near the pointed end.
- Charge is found only on the outside of a charged conductor.
- The greater the curvature of a conductor (the more pointed it is), the greater the charge density.
- Point discharge is where the high charge density at a point ionises the air nearby. Some of these ions are discharged at the point and reduce the charge on the conductor.
- A lightning conductor uses point discharge to reduce the effects of electrical storms.

proof plane

spherical conductor

pear-shaped conductor

insulating stands

Effects of static electricity

Static charge built up when you rub your shoes on a carpet can reach a potential of 20,000 volts. You get a shock when you are earthed by touching a metal.

Technicians earth themselves by touching a conductor to prevent static charges damaging electronic equipment.

Fabric conditioners contain chemicals that reduce static electricity in clothes.

The aircraft and pumps are first connected together and earthed to discharge any static charges when refuelling.

Computers have an earthed metal cage around the vulnerable parts to screen them from static discharge.

Electric fields

- Coulomb's law: The force between two point charges is directly proportional to the product of the charges and inversely proportional to the square of the distance between them.
- $F = \left(\dfrac{1}{4\pi\varepsilon} \right) \dfrac{q_1 q_2}{d^2}$

  ε is the permittivity of the material between the charges.
  Permittivity is a property that affects the force between the charges.
- Coulomb's law is an example of an inverse square law.
- An electric field is the space around a charge in which the charge has an effect.
- An electric field line is the line along which a positive charge will move when placed in the electric field.

HL

- Electric field strength at a point is the force per unit positive charge at that point.
- Electric field strength: $E = \dfrac{F}{q}$
- Electric field strength is a vector quantity.

Describe how an electric field pattern may be demonstrated in the laboratory.

1. Switch on power.
2. Semolina particles line up to show field pattern.

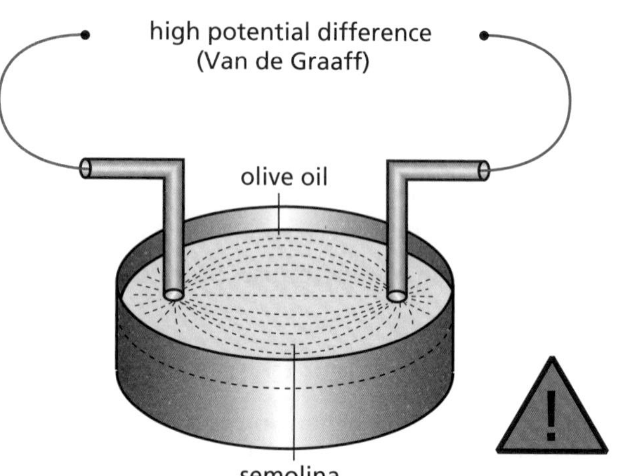

Electric potential

- The potential difference between two points is the work done in moving a charge of one coulomb from one point to the other.
- Potential difference is measured in volts.
- A potential difference of one volt exists between two points where one joule of work is done in moving one coulomb between these points.
- $V = \dfrac{W}{q}$

high potential difference (Van de Graaff)

olive oil

semolina

- Equipotentials are points at the same potential.
- Charge will move only when there is a potential difference between two points and always moves toward the point at lower potential.

Capacitors and capacitance

- A capacitor is a device for storing a small quantity of electric charge.
- When a capacitor is connected to a battery, the current flows to the capacitor for a very short time.
- Once the capacitor is charged to the same voltage as the battery, there is no difference in potential between them – no more current flows.
- Capacitance is the ratio of the charge on a capacitor to the potential difference applied across it.
- $C = \dfrac{q}{V}$

   Note: Capacitance is inversely proportional to voltage.
- Capacitance is measured in farads (F).
- Farad (F): A capacitor has a capacitance of one farad when the ratio of charge to potential difference on it is one coulomb per volt.

Parallel plate capacitor

The simplest form of capacitor consists of a pair of metal plates separated by a thin sheet of insulating material. The insulating material is known as the dielectric.

$$C = \frac{\varepsilon A}{d}$$

How would you demonstrate that the capacitance of a parallel plate capacitor depends on the distance between its plates?

1. Earth one plate and place a charge on the other plate.
2. Slowly separate plates.
3. Leaves diverge, indicating voltage increasing so the capacitance is lowered.

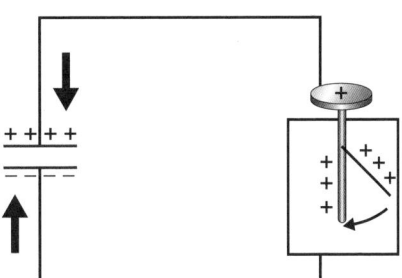

1. Connect digital multimeter, with scale set to capacitance setting, to the plates.
2. Switch on meter and slowly separate the plates.
   Capacitance reading is lowered.

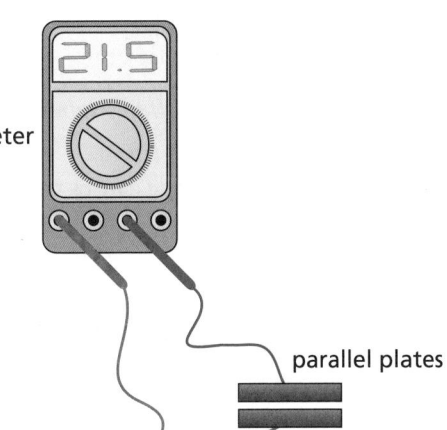

multimeter

parallel plates

Energy stored in a capacitor

- The energy stored in the capacitor is the energy supplied by the battery to charge the capacitor.
- $W = \frac{1}{2}CV^2$

Capacitors in circuits

When you connect a capacitor to a battery (direct current – d.c.), the current flows to the capacitor for a very short time. Once the capacitor is charged to the same voltage as the battery, there is no difference in potential between them and no more current flows.

- There is no continuous flow of current in a capacitor circuit with d.c.
- Capacitors do not conduct in a d.c. circuit.
- Current flows in a capacitor circuit with a.c.
- The larger the capacitance, the greater the current flow with a.c.
- The greater the frequency, the greater the current flow with a.c.

Uses of capacitors

Capacitors are used in a camera flash unit, to store electric charge, in back-up power supplies for computers, to filter high-frequency a.c from low frequency a.c. in hi-fi sound systems, to tune radios and to smooth rectified a.c.

FAQs

Why do the leaves of a gold leaf electroscope diverge when a positively charged rod is brought close to the metal cap?
Electrons are attracted up towards the rod, leaving a shortage of electrons (+ charge) on both leaves, which then diverge.

Why does the gold leaf collapse when a positively charged rod is held close to the electroscope and the metal cap is then earthed?
Earthing the electroscope causes the charge to flow to ground.

How is the cap of the electroscope earthed?
Touch it with your finger.

Name two hazards caused by static electricity.
Electric shock, explosions when fuelling aircraft, electric storms.

Explain why all the charge resides on the surface of a Van de Graff generator's dome.
Like charges repel and charges are a maximum distance apart on the outside surface of the dome.

Name two ways in which a lightning conductor prevents a building from being damaged.
It neutralises charged clouds and conducts charge to earth.

Give a use for a capacitor.
Storing charge, radio tuning, filtering, smoothing, storing energy, camera flash.

Why is Coulomb's law an example of the inverse square law?
The force is inversely proportional to the distance squared.

List the factors that affect the capacitance of a parallel plate capacitor.
Common area of plates, distance apart and permittivity medium between plates.

What is the net charge on a capacitor?
Zero.

Calculate the energy stored in a 5 μF capacitor when a potential difference of 20 V is applied to it.

$$W = \frac{1}{2}CV^2 = \frac{1}{2}(5 \times 10^{-6})(20)^2 = 1.0 \times 10^{-3}\,\mathrm{J}$$

Give two differences between the gravitational force and the electrostatic force between two electrons.
Gravitational force is much smaller than the electrostatic force.
Gravitational force is attractive only; electrostatic force between two electrons is repulsive.

Exam questions

2009 Higher level question 9 (part)

HL

Q: The ability of a capacitor to store energy is the basis of a defibrillator. During a heart attack the chambers of the heart fail to pump blood because their muscle fibres contract and relax randomly. To save the victim, the heart muscle must be shocked to re-establish its normal rhythm. A defibrillator is used to shock the heart muscle.
A 64 μF capacitor in a defibrillator is charged to a potential difference of 2,500 V. The capacitor is discharged through electrodes attached to the chest of a heart attack victim.

Calculate:

(i) The charge stored on each plate of the capacitor

A: $q = CV = (64 \times 10^{-6})(2{,}500)$

$\quad q = 0.16\,\mathrm{C}$

(ii) The energy stored in the capacitor

A: $E = \frac{1}{2}CV^2$

$\quad E = \frac{1}{2}(64 \times 10^{-6})(2{,}500)^2$

$\quad E = 200\,\mathrm{J}$

(iii) The average current that flows through the victim when the capacitor discharges in a time of 10 ms

A: $I = \dfrac{q}{t} = \dfrac{0.16}{10 \times 10^{-3}}$

$\quad I = 16\,\mathrm{A}$

(iv) The average power generated as the capacitor discharges

A: $P = \dfrac{W}{t} = \dfrac{E}{t} = \dfrac{200}{10 \times 10^{-3}}$

$P = 20{,}000 \text{ W}$

2007 Higher level question 8

Q: The dome of a Van de Graff generator is charged. The dome has a diameter of 30 cm and its charge is 4 C.

A 5 μC point charge is placed 7 cm from the surface of the dome.

Calculate:

(i) The electric field strength at a point 7 cm from the dome

A: $E = \dfrac{q_1 q_2}{4\pi \varepsilon d^2}$

Electric field strength is force per unit charge so take a charge of 1 coulomb at the given point

$E = \dfrac{(1)(4)}{4\pi(8.9 \times 10^{-12})(0.22)^2}$

Note: The charge on the dome is taken as being at the centre so the distance between the charges is the radius of the dome plus 7 cm $(0.15 + 0.07 = 0.22 \text{ m})$

$E = 7.39 \times 10^{11} \text{ N C}^{-1}$

(ii) The electrostatic force exerted on the 5 μC point charge

A: $F = E q$

$F = (7.39 \times 10^{11})(5 \times 10^{-6})$

$F = 3.69 \times 10^{6} \text{ N}$

2006 Higher level question 12 (b)

Q: The plates of an air-filled parallel plate capacitor have a common area of 40 cm^2 and are 1 cm apart. The capacitor is connected to a 12 V d.c. supply.

Calculate:

(i) The capacitance of the capacitor

A: $C = \dfrac{\varepsilon A}{d}$

$C = \dfrac{(8.85 \times 10^{-12})(40 \times 10^{-4})}{(0.01)}$

$C = 3.54 \times 10^{-12} \text{ F}$

(ii) The magnitude of the charge on each plate.

A: $Q = C V$

$Q = (3.54 \times 10^{-12})(12)$

$= 4.25 \times 10^{-11} \text{ C}$

9 Simple Electric Circuits

aims To learn:
- Definitions and formulae for electric circuits
- How to answer FAQs on electric circuits
- How to solve problems involving voltage, current, resistance and resistivity

Electric circuits

- Electricity will flow only if there is a complete circuit and a potential difference across the circuit.
- An electric current is a flow of electric charge.
- Electric current is measured in amperes.
- A potential difference of one volt exists between any two points when one joule of energy is expended in moving one coulomb between them.
- $V = \dfrac{W}{q}$
- Potential difference is measured in volts.
- Electromotive force is the total work done (energy) in moving one coulomb of electric charge round a complete circuit loop.
- $\text{emf} = \dfrac{\text{energy}}{\text{coulomb}} = \dfrac{\text{joules}}{\text{coulomb}}$
- Batteries (or cells), generators and other sources of electrical energy have emfs.

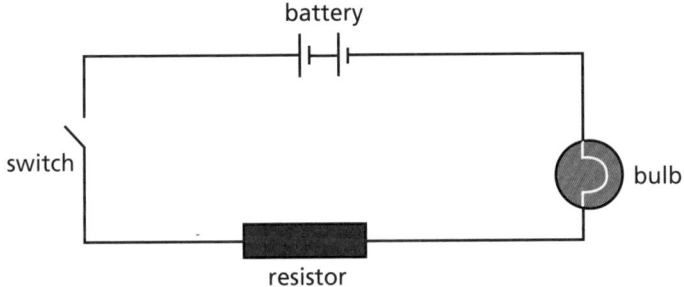

The simple cell

- Any combination of two different electrodes in an electrolyte is a simple cell.
- The simple cell converts chemical energy into electrical energy.
- Dry cells are primary cells and convert chemical energy into electrical energy in a non-reversible way.

- Rechargeable cells are secondary cells, which means they can be recharged many times.

Resistance

- An object has a resistance if energy is used in passing electricity through it.
- Ohm's law: At constant temperature, the current passing through a metallic conductor is directly proportional to the potential difference across it.
- Resistance is the ratio of the potential difference across a conductor to the current flowing through it.

- $R = \dfrac{V}{I}$

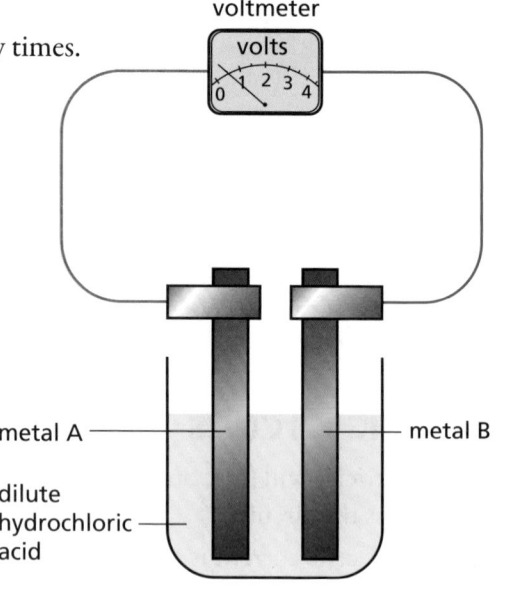

- Unit of resistance is the ohm (Ω).
- The ohm is the resistance of a conductor when a potential difference of 1 volt across it produces a current flow of 1 amp through it.
- All conductors are NOT ohmic (i.e. obey Ohm's law). Semiconductor diodes, thermistors, gases and certain electrolytes are not ohmic.
- A rheostat is a variable resistance that controls the current flowing through a circuit.

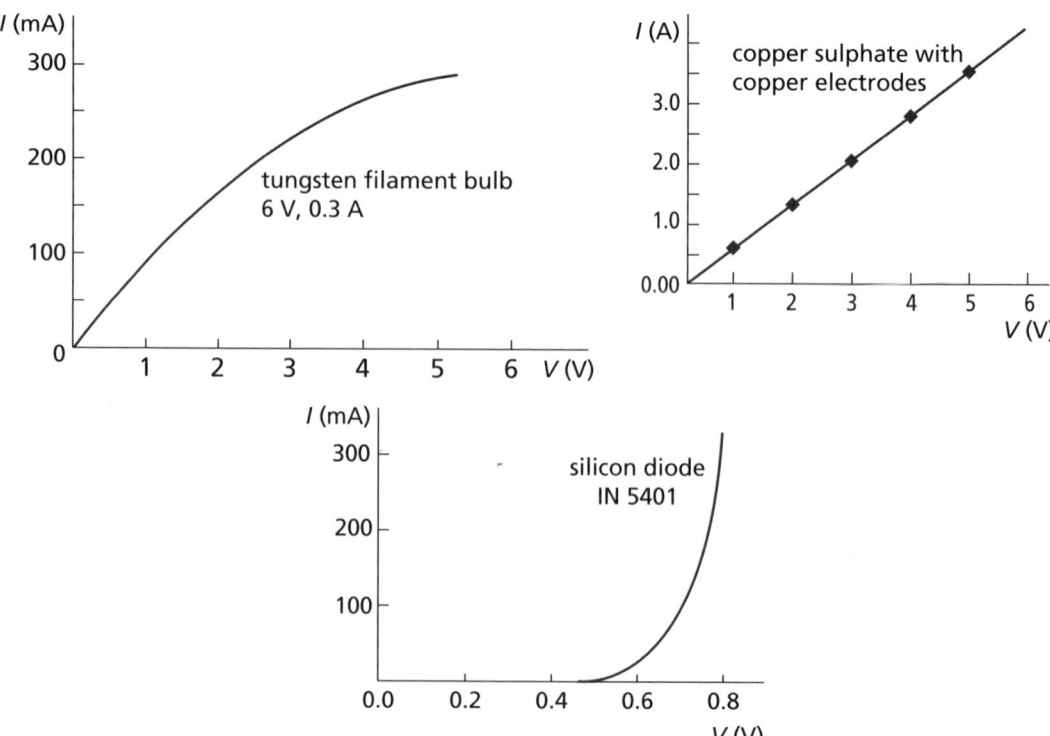

Rules for currents and potential differences in circuits

1. The sum of the currents entering a point in a circuit equals the sum of the currents leaving it.

$$I = I_1 + I_2 + I_3$$

2. The emf of the circuit equals the sum of all the potential differences in the circuit.

$$E = V_1 + V_2 + V_3$$

Resistances in series

The two resistors are connected in a line, so the same current I flows through both.

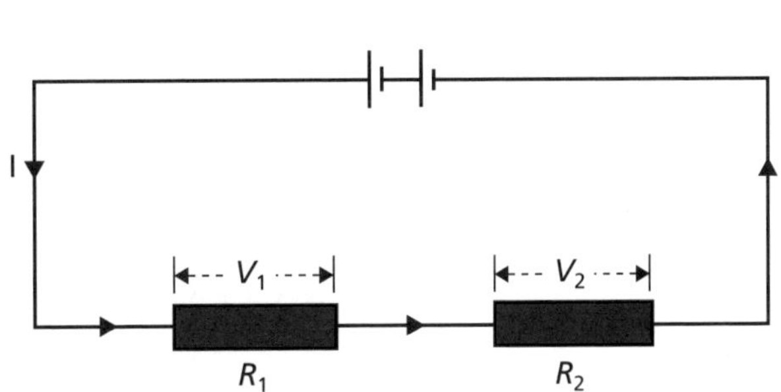

$V = V_1 + V_2$

but $V = IR$ (Ohm's law)

$IR = IR_1 + IR_2$ dividing by I we get

$R = R_1 + R_2$

Resistances in parallel

The potential difference between two points is the same regardless of the path followed. The potential difference across each of the resistances, from A to B, is V.

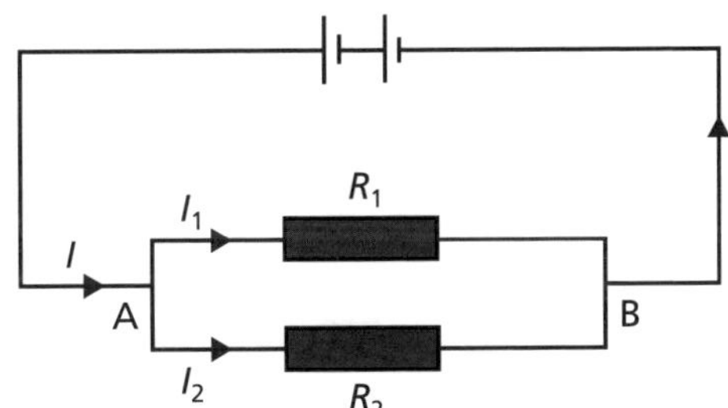

$I = I_1 + I_2$

From Ohm's law:

$$I = \frac{V}{R}$$

$$\frac{V}{R} = \frac{V}{R_1} + \frac{V}{R_2}$$

dividing by V we get:

$$\frac{1}{R} = \frac{1}{R_1} + \frac{1}{R_2}$$

Electricity in the home

- In a ring main circuit the live and neutral wires each form a ring or loop. This gives two independent paths for the current to any point and reduces the thickness of wire needed. A third loop is formed by the earth wire.
- The live wire is always connected through the switch.
- A fuse is a piece of wire that melts and breaks the circuit if a circuit becomes overloaded – too big a current.

- In an electric plug the fuse is always on the live wire.

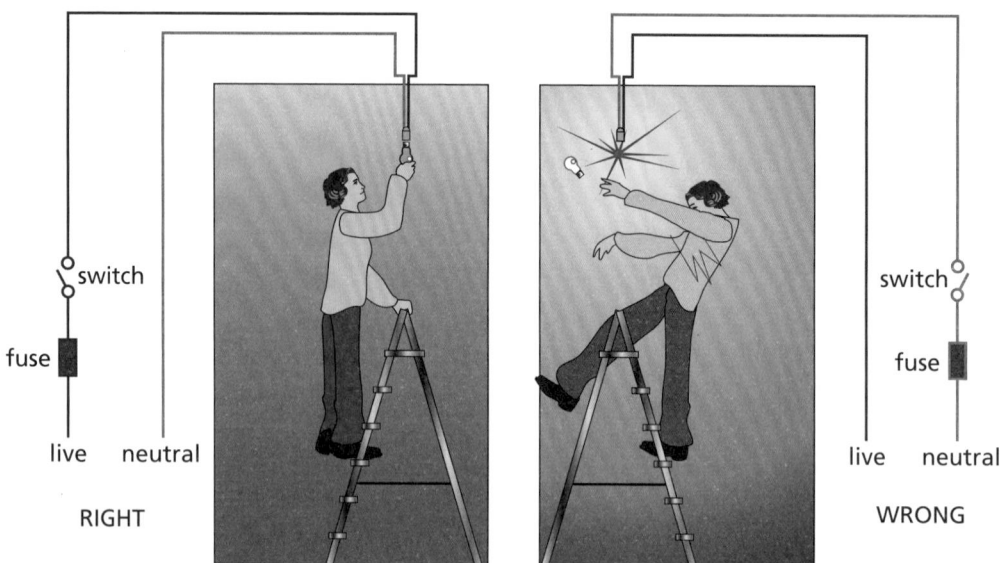

- A miniature circuit breaker (MCB) or trip switch is a mechanical device that cuts off the current when the current exceeds a particular value.

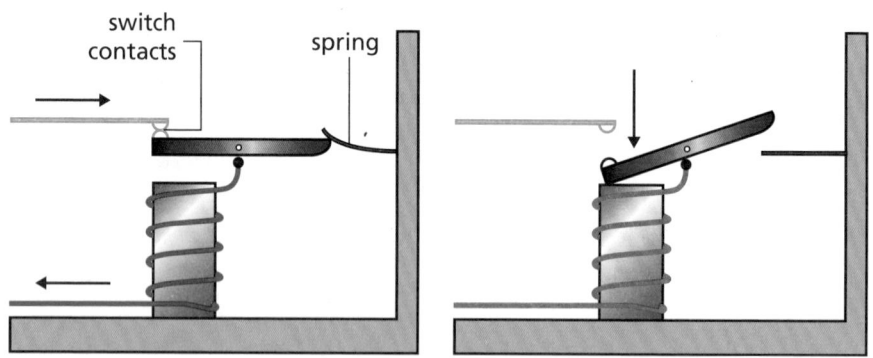

Circuit breaker. If the current in the coil is too big, the solenoid pulls the contacts open.

- Earthing a circuit gives a low resistance path to earth.
- Bonding ensures that there is always an unbroken low resistance path for the current to flow to earth by connecting all the metal objects in a bathroom – pipes, metal parts of shower and bath – to a good earth.
- Double-insulated appliances have all live connections insulated and all metal parts are also insulated.
- The RCD (or ELCB) is a trip switch that cuts off the current very quickly when a fault in an appliance causes a small current to flow to earth.

Measuring resistances

- An ohmmeter uses Ohm's law to measure resistance.

ohmmeter

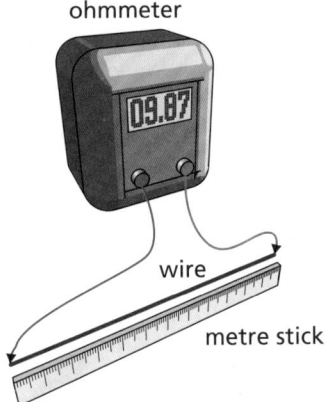

wire

metre stick

From Ohm's law: $R = VI$

The emf of the cell is taken as V: by measuring I we get a value for R.

Resistance of a metallic conductor

- R is proportional to the length of the wire – l.
- R is inversely proportional to the cross-sectional area of the wire A.
- $R = \dfrac{kl}{A}$
- The constant k depends on the material of the wire called the resistivity (ρ) of the metal.
- $R = \dfrac{\rho l}{A}$
- $\rho = \dfrac{RA}{l}$
- Unit of resistivity is the ohm metre = Ωm.

Resistance varies with temperature

- The resistance of a material varies with temperature.
- The resistance of most metals increases with temperature. The resistance of semiconductors such as silicon and germanium decreases with temperature.
- The resistance of alloys such as magnanin does not vary appreciably with temperature.

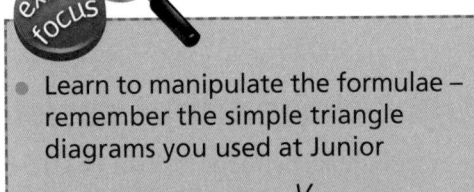

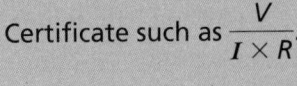

- Learn to manipulate the formulae – remember the simple triangle diagrams you used at Junior Certificate such as $\dfrac{V}{I \times R}$.

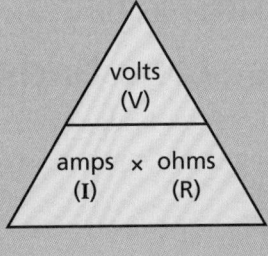

volts
(V)

amps × ohms
(I)   (R)

watts

amps × volts

- Remember the three Cs in answering questions: Clear, Concise and Correct.

- Read the terms used in the question – 'explain' is quite different from 'define'.

- A thermistor is a semiconductor device whose resistance changes greatly with temperature.
- The resistance of a thermistor falls sharply with increasing temperature typically from 500 Ω at 25° C to 10 Ω at 200° C.

Light-dependent resistor (LDR)

- A light-dependent resistor (LDR) is a semiconductor whose resistance changes with the amount of light falling on it.
- The resistance of the cadmium sulphide (CdS) light-dependent resistor is about 10 MΩ in the dark and falls to about 1 kΩ in normal daylight.

Wheatstone bridge

The Wheatstone bridge circuit measures resistance by comparing an unknown resistance with a known standard resistance.

$$\frac{R_1}{R_2} = \frac{R_3}{R_4}$$

The ratio of resistances R_1 and R_2 is usually a power of 10 (10, 100, etc.). R_3 is a variable resistance that can be set to known values. R_4 is the resistance being measured.

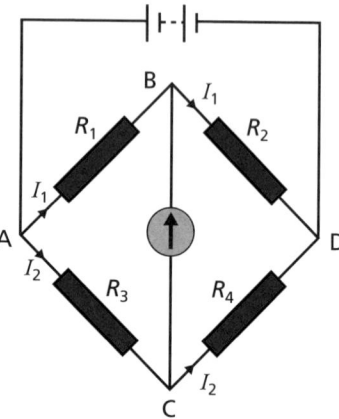

Wheatstone bridge

Uses of the Wheatstone bridge

- Strain gauges: Strain increases the length of the wire and so increases its resistance.
- Fire alarm: A fire affects the resistance of a thermistor nearer the fire far more than the other resistors. This unbalances the Wheatstone bridge and sets off the alarm.
- The Wheatstone bridge circuit can also be used as a thermostat to maintain a steady temperature in an oven.
- Flame failure device: If the pilot flame goes out, the thermistor goes cold, its resistance increases and the bridge is now unbalanced. The p.d. across the bridge operates a solenoid and shuts off the fuel.

Potential divider (potentiometer)

A single voltage supply can give a variety of different voltages by using a potential divider.

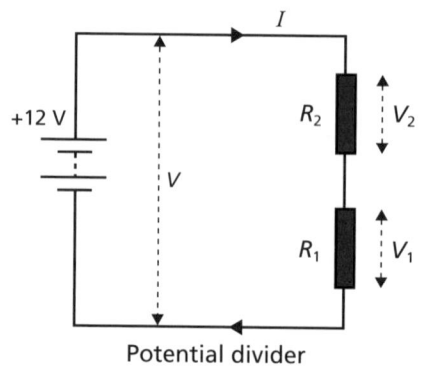

Potential divider

Clearly the supply voltage was divided between the two resistors in proportion to their resistances.

The rheostat and potential divider look alike – and frequently the same device can be connected to one circuit as a rheostat and to another circuit as a potential divider. It is important to realise that the principle of operation is not the same.

FAQs

State Ohm's law.

At constant temperature, the current passing through a metallic conductor is directly proportional to the potential difference across it.

$$\frac{V}{I} = R$$

What happens to the resistance of a thermistor when heated?

The resistance decreases.

Give a use for a thermistor.

Thermometer, heat sensor, temperature control.

What will happen when a current of 20 A flows through a fuse marked 13 A?

The fuse blows and current stops.

What is the colour of the earth wire in an electric cable?

Green and yellow.

Name a common material used to conduct electricity in electric cables.

Copper or aluminium.

Why is the coating on electric cables made from plastic?

For safety, as plastic is an insulator.

Why are some appliances not earthed?

They are double insulated.

What is the advantage of connecting lights in parallel?

If one goes, the others still work/lights are brighter.

What is the colour of the wire that should be connected to the fuse in a plug?

Brown: The live wire always goes through the fuse.

What is the function of a fuse?

It is a safety device that prevents too high a current flowing. It prevents overheating in a circuit.

Explain how a fuse works.

The fuse wire heats up and breaks the circuit if the current is too high.

Name a device with the same function as a fuse.

Circuit breaker, trip switch, RCD/MCB.

Explain how a residual current device (RCD) operates.
When an electrical device is operated correctly, no current flows to earth so the current in the live is the same as the current in the neutral. If a fault develops, the currents are not the same. The RCD detects this and trips a switch to cut off the current.

What is the purpose of a miniature circuit breaker (MCB)?
It breaks the circuit when too large a current flows. Its advantage over a fuse is that it can be reset. If a fuse blows, it has to be replaced.

Give one advantage of a residual current device (RCD) over a miniature circuit breaker (MCB).
RCD responds very quickly and responds to tiny currents.

When will an RCD (residual current device) disconnect a circuit?
When the current flowing in differs from the current flowing out (when current leaks to earth).

An RCD is rated 30 mA. What is the significance of this current?
If the current flowing to earth exceeds 30 mA, the RCD trips and breaks the circuit.

If an electrical device has exposed metal parts, how is the risk of electrocution minimised?
By earthing the metal parts or using double insulation.

HL Exam questions

2007 Higher level question 9

Q: Define:
(i) Resistance
A: Voltage divided by current $\dfrac{V}{I}$

(ii) Resistivity
A: $\rho = \dfrac{RA}{l}$

where R is resistance, A is cross-sectional area and l is length.

Q: A metre bridge was used to measure the resistance of a sample of nichrome wire. The diagram indicates the readings taken when the metre bridge was balanced. The nichrome wire has a length of 220 mm and a radius of 0.11 mm.

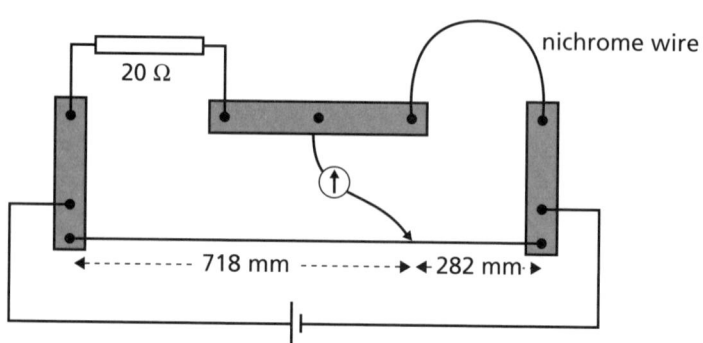

Calculate:

(i) The resistance of the nichrome wire

A: The metre bridge is a Wheatstone bridge circuit.

$$\frac{R_1}{R_2} = \frac{l_1}{l_2} = \frac{R_3}{R_4}$$

Substituting: $\dfrac{R}{20} = \dfrac{282}{718}$

$R = 7.86\,\Omega$

(ii) The resistivity of nichrome

A: $\rho = \dfrac{RA}{l}$

$A = \pi r^2 = (3.14)(0.11 \times 10^{-3})^2 = 3.801 \times 10^{-8}\,\text{m}^2$

$\rho = \dfrac{(7.86)(3.801 \times 10^{-8})}{0.22}$

$= 1.36 \times 10^{-6}\,\Omega\,\text{m}$

Q: Sketch a graph to show the relationship between the temperature and the resistance of the nichrome wire as its temperature is increased.

What happens to the resistance of the wire:

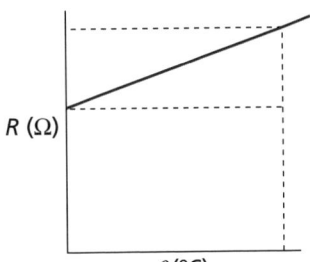

(i) As its temperature falls below $0°\text{C}$?

A: The *resistance* decreases.

(ii) As its length is increased?

A: The *resistance* increases.

(iii) If its diameter is increased?

A: The *resistance* decreases.

Q: Name another device, apart from a metre bridge, that can be used to measure resistance.

A: Ohmmeter (or multimeter) or Wheatstone bridge.

Q: Give one advantage and one disadvantage of using this device instead of a metre bridge.

A: Ohmmeter/multimeter:

Advantage: Very compact, portable, faster method, etc.

Disadvantage: Less accurate, difficult to calibrate.

Wheatstone bridge:

Advantage: Compact, portable, more accurate.

Disadvantage: More difficult to understand, expensive.

2005 Higher level question 9 (part)

Q: In the circuit diagram, the resistance of the thermistor at room temperature is 500 Ω.
At room temperature, calculate:

(i) The total resistance of the circuit

A: $\dfrac{1}{R} = \dfrac{1}{500} + \dfrac{1}{750}$

$R = 300\ \Omega$

$R_T = 300 + 300 = 600\ \Omega$

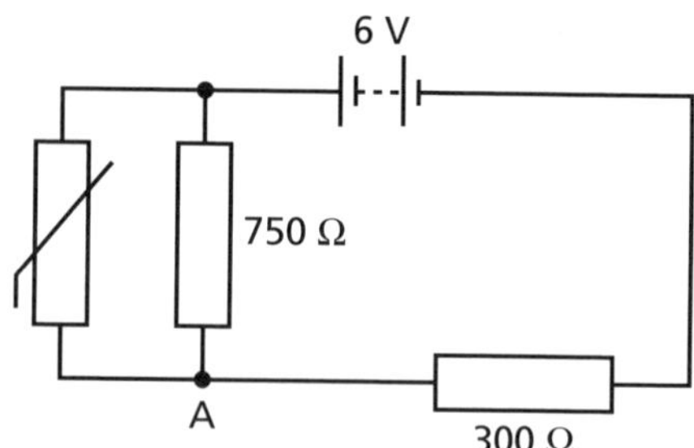

(ii) The current flowing through the 750 Ω
  resistor

A: The current flowing through the circuit is:

$I = \left(\dfrac{V}{R}\right) = \dfrac{6}{600} = 0.01\ \text{A}$

The voltage across the parallel branch is:

$V = (0.01)(300) = 3\ V$

The current flowing through the 750 Ω resistor is:

$I = \dfrac{V}{R} = \dfrac{3}{750}$

$= 4 \times 10^{-3}\ \text{A or 4 mA}$

Q: As the temperature of the room increases, explain why:

(iii) The resistance of the thermistor decreases

A: • Temperature increases so more energy is added to the thermistor.
  • More electrons released.
  • More electrons available for conduction.

(iv) The potential at A increases

A: Resistance of thermistor decreases so resistance of thermistor and 750 Ω branch
decreases.

The potential drop across thermistor and 750 Ω combination decreases.

So potential at A increases.

10 Effects of Electric Current

aims To learn:

- Definitions and formulae for the effects of electric current
- How to answer FAQs on the effects of electric current
- How to solve problems involving heating, voltage, current, resistance and resistivity

Magnets

- A magnet is a piece of iron, cobalt or nickel (or alloys of these) that can attract other pieces of the same metals.
- When a magnet is free to swing, it settles in a north–south direction.
- A compass contains a magnetic needle.
- Like magnetic poles repel.
- Unlike magnetic poles attract.

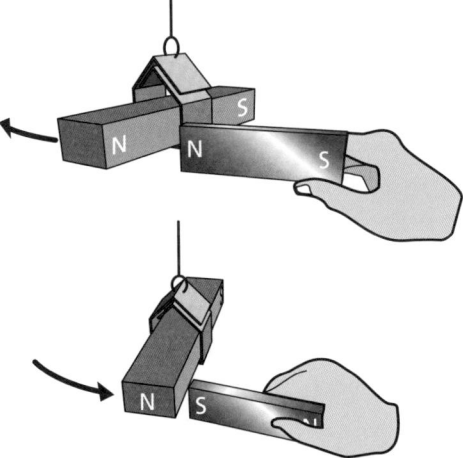

Magnetic fields

- A magnetic field is the space within which a magnetic force has an effect.
- The magnetic field line is the path along which a north pole would move if it were free to do so.

Describe how you would show the magnetic field around a bar magnet.

1. Put a bar magnet on a sheet of paper and mark the outline of the magnet.
2. Put the plotting compass close to the north pole of the magnet. Mark the tip and tail of the compass needle.
3. Repeat to produce the magnetic field pattern.

The direction of the compass gives the direction of the magnetic field lines.

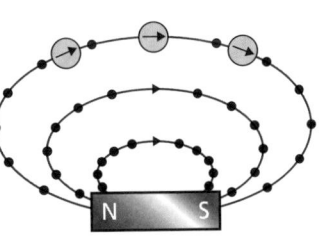

Magnetic effect of an electric current

- A conductor carrying an electric current has a magnetic effect.

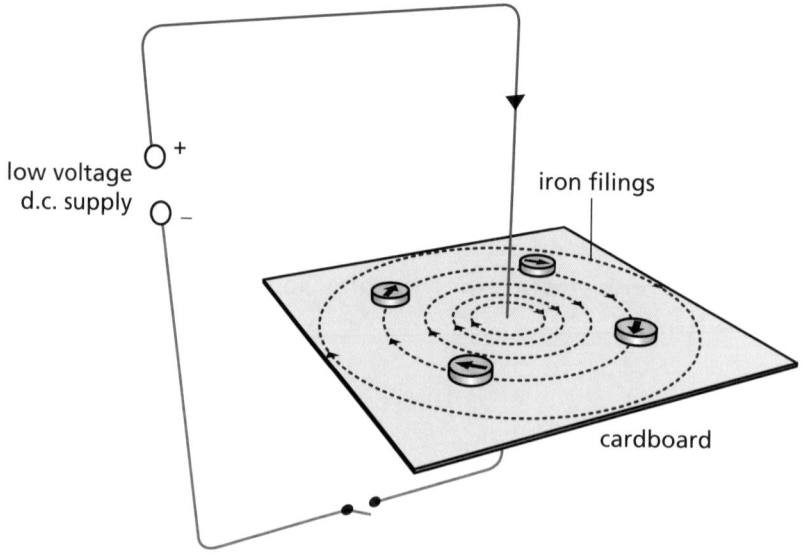

- An electromagnet is based on this principle.
- An electromagnet is produced when an electric current flows through a coil of wire wrapped around an iron core.

Describe an experiment to show the magnetic field due to a current in a solenoid.

1. Switch on the current.
2. The direction of the compass changes. Mark the tip and tail of the compass needle.
3. Repeat to produce the magnetic field pattern.

Conclusion: The direction of the compass gives the direction of the magnetic field lines.

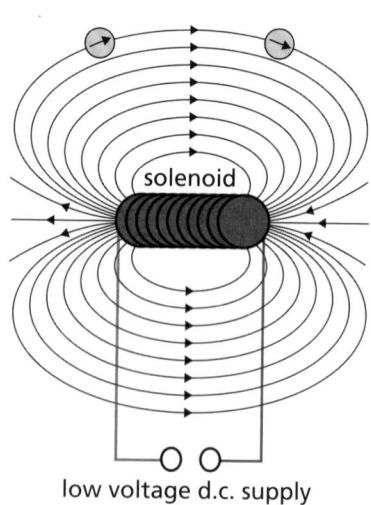

Magnetic flux

- The total magnetic flux depends on the strength of the magnet that produces the flux.
- Magnetic flux (Φ) is measured in webers (Wb).
- Magnetic flux density (B) is the magnetic flux per unit area at right angles to the direction of the magnetic field lines.

- $B = \dfrac{\Phi}{A}$

- The unit of magnetic flux density is the tesla (T).
- Magnetic flux density is a vector.
- The direction of the magnetic flux density is the direction of the field lines through the area.

Uses of magnets

- Magnets are used as catches on cupboard doors.
- Magnetic seals are used on fridge doors.
- Magnets are also used in electric motors, loudspeakers and dynamos.
- Electromagnets are used on cranes in scrap yards, in relays and in electric doorbells.

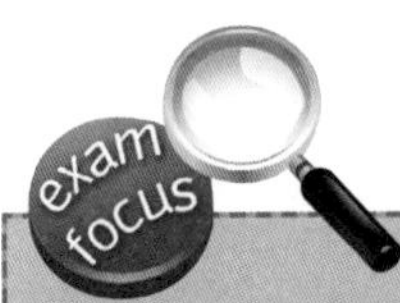

Questions on the effects of electric currents usually involve the heating effect, which often involves formulae from the heat section. Revise the formulae from the heat section. Ask yourself what the question is asking. A question on the heating effect of current – 'Explain, in terms of movement of electrons, why light is emitted when a metal is heated' (Q7/2008) – is about the red light not the heat.

Heating effect

- Joule's law: The heat produced in a fixed time for a given resistance is proportional to the current squared. $H \propto I^2$
- The heating effect is also proportional to the resistance and the time:
  $H = I^2Rt$

Power

- The power is the energy produced or consumed per second.
- The unit of power is the watt (W).

$$power = \frac{energy}{seconds}$$

$$P = \frac{J}{t} = \frac{I^2Rt}{t} = I^2R = V.I$$

watts = volts × amps

- $P = V.I$

Electricity supply

The ESB transfers energy at a high voltage.

Heat loss due to current flowing through the cables, by Joule's law, depends on the current squared and the resistance. The resistance is constant, so the heat loss depends on the square of the current. To minimise heat loss it makes sense to keep the current low. This can be done only by transmission at high voltage.

The kilowatt hour

- A 1-kilowatt appliance left on for one hour uses 1 kilowatt hour of electrical energy.
- kilowatt hours = kilowatts $\times$ hours

Chemical effect: Electrolysis

- Electric current is carried through the solution by the movement of ions.

An electrolyte is a substance that, molten or in solution, conducts electricity by the movement of ions.

Electrolysis is the process of causing chemical changes by passing an electric current through an electrolyte.

Commercial uses of electrolysis

- Electrolytic refining of metals
- Electroplating

Electrolytes and Ohm's law

- Electrolytes obey Ohm's law when precautions are taken to exclude any 'back' emfs.

$CuSO_4$ with copper electrodes: This obeys Ohm's law as the copper ions discharged at the cathode are immediately replaced by copper atoms entering the solution as ions at the anode.

$CuSO_4$ with inert (platinum) electrodes: This does not follow Ohm's law as oxygen is produced at the anode. The oxygen and the platinum electrode produce a 'back' emf that must be overcome before current will flow. (See graph for copper sulphate, bottom diagram, p. 23.)

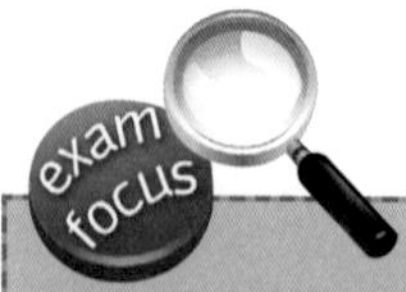

STS (Science, Technology and Society) questions on the everyday applications of science are usually reasonably easy. See 2008 Question 7 on the next page.

FAQs

Why does a magnet that is free to rotate point towards the north?
Any reference to (earth's) magnetic field/like poles repel/unlike poles attract.

Give one use of the earth's magnetic field.
Compass, navigation, protective layer around the earth.

Define magnetic flux.
Magnetic flux = magnetic flux density × area

What is a magnetic field?
A magnetic field is the space within which a magnetic force has an effect.

Draw a sketch of the magnetic field around a bar magnet.

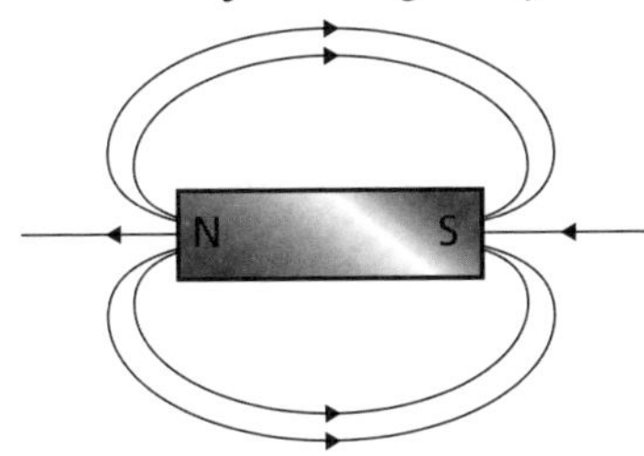

Give one use of an electromagnet.
Electric bell, solenoid, scrap yard crane.

State one advantage of an electromagnet over an ordinary magnet.
You can switch the electromagnet off. You can vary the strength of the electromagnet by varying the current.

Explain why higher voltages are used in the transmission of electrical energy.
Higher voltage implies smaller current and therefore less energy lost as heat.

How would you reduce the energy lost in cables?
Use thicker wire, materials of lower resistivity, higher voltage (EHT).

What are the charge carriers when an electric current passes through an electrolyte?
Ions.

Exam questions

2008 Higher level question 7 (part)

Q: A toaster has a power rating of 1,050 W when it is connected to the mains supply. Its heating coil is made of nichrome and it has a resistance of 12 Ω. The coil is 40 m long and it has a circular cross-section of diameter 2.2 mm.

Calculate:
(i) The resistivity of nichrome

A: $\rho = \dfrac{RA}{l}$

$A = \pi r^2 = (3.14)(1.1 \times 10^{-3})^2 = 3.801 \times 10^{-6}\,\text{m}^2$

$\rho = (12)\left(\dfrac{3.801 \times 10^{-8}}{40}\right)$

$= 1.14 \times 10^{-6}\,\Omega\text{m}$

(ii) The heat generated by the toaster in 2 minutes if it has an efficiency of 96%.

A: Heat generated = power × time

$$H = 1{,}050 \times 120 = 1.26 \times 10^5$$

96% of $1.26 \times 10^5 = 1.21 \times 10^5\,\text{J}$

Q: The toaster has exposed metal parts. How is the risk of electrocution minimised?

A: The metal parts of the toaster are earthed. If you make contact with live metal, the RCD would trip as a small current would flow to earth.

Q: When the toaster is on, the coil emits red light. Explain, in terms of movement of electrons, why light is emitted when a metal is heated.

A: The electrons gain energy and jump to a higher energy state. They quickly drop back to their more stable ground state and release the energy in red and infra-red light.

2009 Ordinary level question 8 (part)

Q: A coffee maker has a power rating of 800 W. What is the most suitable fuse for the plug of the coffee maker?

A: $P = VI$

$800 = 230 \times I$

$I = \dfrac{800}{230} = 3.4\,\text{A}$

So the most suitable fuse is a 5 A fuse.

Q: If the coffee maker is used for 150 minutes, calculate:

The number of units of electricity used by the coffee maker

A: Units of electricity = Kilowatts × time in hours

$= 0.8 \times 2.5$

$= 2\,\text{Kw hrs or 2. units}$

Q: The cost of the electricity used if each unit of electricity costs 15 cent

A: Cost = 2 units @ 15 cent = 30 cent

2006 Higher level question 9 (part)

HL

Q: What is the resistance of the filament of a light bulb, rated 40 W, when it is connected to the mains?

A: $P = \dfrac{V^2}{R}$

$40 = \dfrac{(230)^2}{R}$

$R = \dfrac{52,900}{40}$

$R = 1,322.5 \ \Omega$

Q: Explain why the resistance of the bulb is different when it is not connected to the mains.

A: Because the cold filament has a lower resistance than the hot filament of the bulb when switched on.

You should now review the Exam Question from 2006 Higher Level paper (Question 12 (c)) in Chapter 7, page 51.

11 The Force on a Current-carrying Conductor in a Magnetic Field

 To learn:

- Definitions and formulae for the effects of a force on a current-carrying conductor in a magnetic field
- How to answer FAQs on the effects of a force on a current-carrying conductor in a magnetic field
- How to solve problems involving the effects of a force on a current-carrying conductor in a magnetic field

The force on a current-carrying conductor in a magnetic field

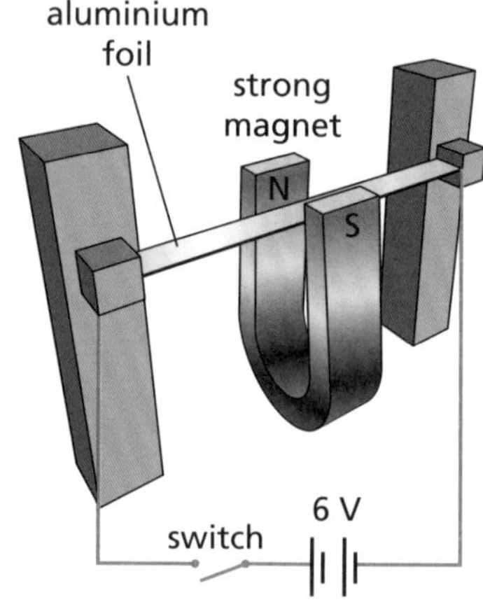

A current-carrying conductor in a magnetic field experiences a force.

Describe an experiment to show that there is a force on a current-carrying conductor in a magnetic field.

1. Switch on the currrent.
2. The aluminium foil moves.

Conclusion: A current-carrying conductor in a magnetic field experiences a force.

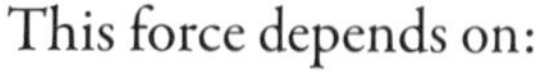

This force depends on:

1. The current
2. The length of the conductor in the magnetic field
3. The magnetic flux density through the conductor **at right angles**

$$F = IlB$$

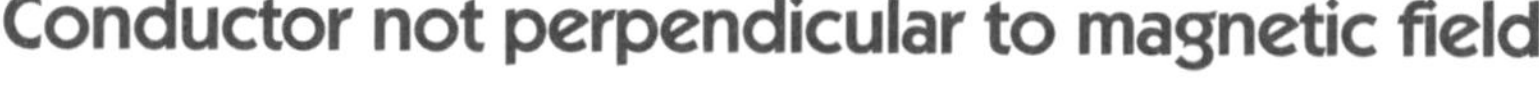

Conductor not perpendicular to magnetic field

It is only the component of the magnetic field perpendicular to the current that produces a force on the conductor. This component is $B \sin \theta$, where θ is the angle between the conductor and the magnetic field lines.

Left-hand motor rule

Set your forefinger along the direction of the magnetic field. Set your centre finger along the direction of the current. Now your thumb gives you the direction of the force or movement.

The left-hand motor rule gives the direction of the force.

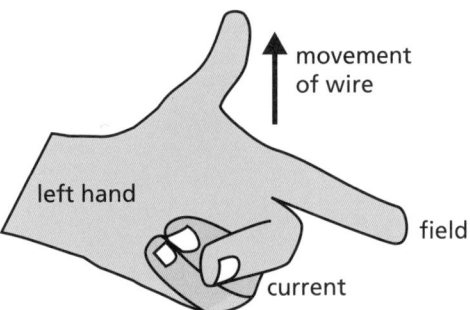

movement
of wire

left hand

field

current

key point

- The basic physical principle of moving-coil loudspeakers, electric motors and moving-coil meters is that there is a force on a current-carrying conductor in a magnetic field.
- The energy conversion involved in these effects is electrical to kinetic.

Magnetic flux density

The force on a current-carrying conductor in a magnetic field can be used to measure the strength of the magnetic field: the magnetic flux density.

- $B = \dfrac{F}{Il}$

- The magnetic flux density (B) is one tesla when a current of one ampere flowing through a conductor of 1 metre length in a magnetic field produces a force of 1 newton.

exam focus

The definition, in words, of magnetic flux density is rather awkward. In an exam simply put down the formula above *but say what each symbol stands for.*

The force on a charged particle in a magnetic field

$F = qvB$

Where the charged particle has a charge of q coulombs and is moving with a velocity of $v \text{ ms}^{-1}$.

Forces between currents

- There is a force between two conductors carrying a current.
- Each conductor produces a magnetic field when current flows through it. The other conductor is then a current-carrying conductor in a magnetic field and experiences a force.
- When current flows in the same direction, the conductors are attracted toward each other.
- When current flows in opposite directions, the conductors repel each other.
- The unit of electric current, the ampere, is defined in terms of the force between currents.

- The ampere is that constant current which, if maintained in two infinitely long conductors of negligible cross-section 1 metre apart in a vacuum, would produce between the conductors a force of 2×10^{-7} newtons per metre length.

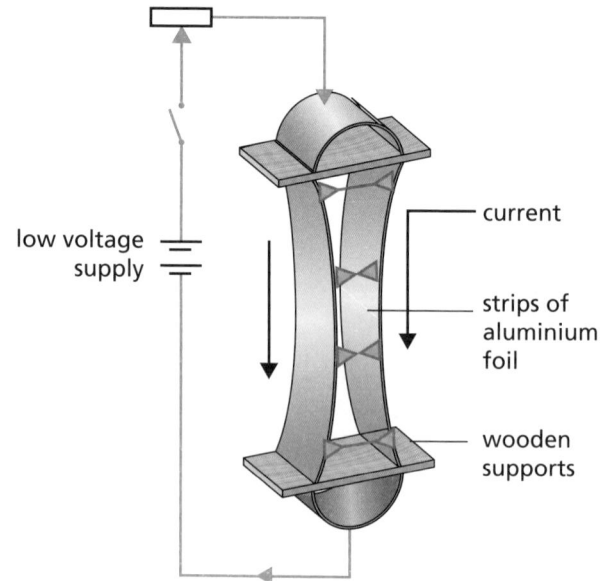

low voltage supply

current

strips of aluminium foil

wooden supports

Currents in the *same* direction *attract* each other

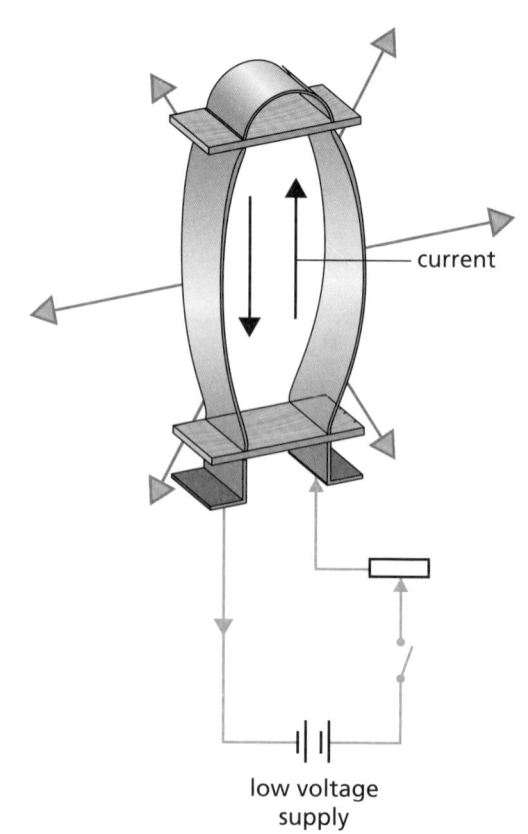

current

low voltage supply

Currents in *opposite* directions *repel* each other

FAQs

State the principle on which the definition of the ampere is based.

Force between two conductors carrying current./A current-carrying conductor experiences a force in a magnetic field.

What is the force exerted on an electron when it is in an electric field of strength 5 N C^{-1}?

$F = E q$

$F = 5(1.6 \times 10^{-19})$

$F = 8.0 \times 10^{-19}\,\text{N}$

Name two devices that are based on the fact that there is a force on a current-carrying conductor in a magnetic field.

Electric motor, loudspeaker, ammeter, etc.

Exam questions

2005 Ordinary level question 9

Q: Describe an experiment to show that a current-carrying conductor in a magnetic field experiences a force.

A: 1. Switch on the current.

    2. Conductor moves.

Conclusion: A current-carrying conductor in a magnetic field experiences a force.

Q: State two factors on which the size of this force depends.

A: The current *I*.

The strength of magnetic field *B*.

The length of conductor.

The angle between the conductor and the magnetic field lines *θ*.

Q: An electron, charge 1.6×10^{-19} C, is travelling at a velocity of 5×10^5 m s^{-1} at right angles to a magnetic field of flux density 3 T. What is the force on the electron?

A: $F = qvB$

$= (1.6 \times 10^{-19})(5 \times 10^5)(3)$

$= 24 \times 10^{-14}$

$= 2.4 \times 10^{-13}\,\text{N}$

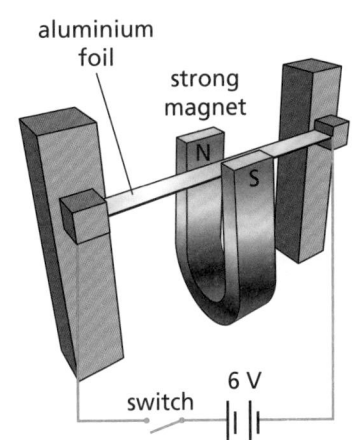

aluminium foil

strong magnet

N

S

6 V

switch

2006 Ordinary level question 10

Q: When the switch is closed, the aluminium foil experiences an upward force. Name a device based on this effect.

A: Loudspeaker, ammeter or electric motor.

Q: Describe what happens if:

(i) The current flows in the opposite direction

A: The foil moves in the opposite direction because the force is now downwards.

(ii) A larger current flows through the aluminium foil

A: There is a greater force on the foil and a greater movement.

(iii) The aluminium foil is placed parallel to the magnetic field

A: Nothing happens as there is no force on the foil.

Q: Calculate the force on the aluminium foil of length 10 cm if a current of 1.5 A flows through it when it is placed in a magnetic field of flux density 3.0 T.

A: $F = IlB$

$F = (1.5)(0.1)(3)$

$ = 0.45\text{ N}$

2009 Ordinary level question 9

Q: The diagram shows a compass placed near a wire connected to a battery and a switch.

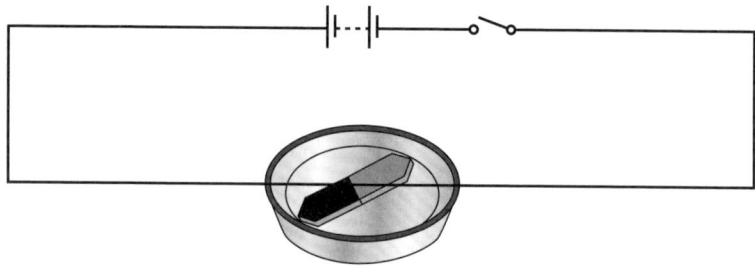

What happens to the compass when the switch is closed?

A: The compass needle moves.

Q: What does this tell you about an electric current?

A: An electric current produces a magnetic field that deflects the compass needle.

Q: What happens to the compass when the switch is opened?

A: The compass needle returns to its original position.

Q: The wire is then placed between the poles of a U-shaped magnet as shown in the diagram.

Describe what happens to the wire when a current flows through it.

A: The wire moves.

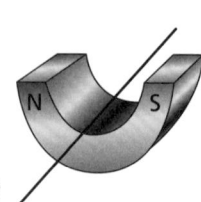

Q: What would happen if the current flowed in the opposite direction?

A: The wire would move in the opposite direction.

2006 Higher level question 9

HL

Q: What is an electric current?

A: A flow of electric *charge*.

Q: Define the ampere, the SI unit of current.

A: The ampere is that constant current which, if maintained in two infinitely long conductors of negligible cross-section one metre apart in a vacuum, would produce between the conductors a force of 2×10^{-7} newtons per metre length.

Q: Describe an experiment to demonstrate the principle on which the definition of the ampere is based.

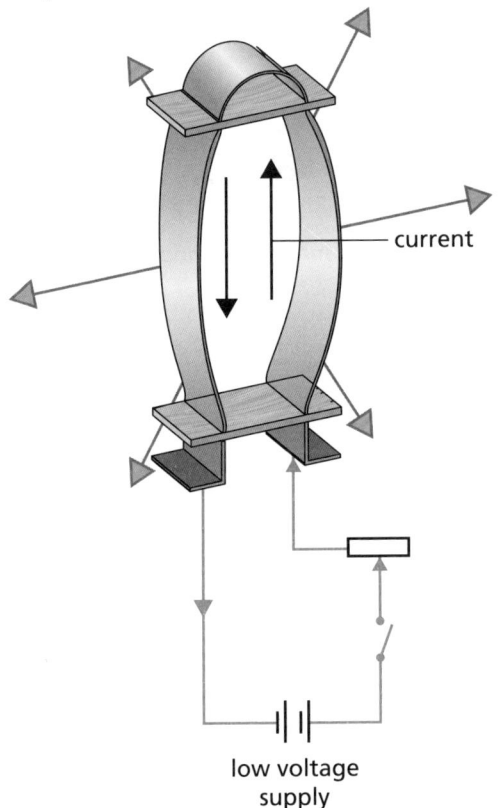

current

low voltage
supply

A: 1. Switch on the current.

    2. The aluminium strips move.

Conclusion: There is a force between two conductors carrying a current.

12 Electromagnetic Induction

aims To learn:

- Definitions and formulae for electromagnetic induction
- How to answer FAQs on electromagnetic induction
- How to solve problems involving electromagnetic induction

Electromagnetic induction

- Relative movement between a magnet and a coil causes an electric current to flow in the coil.
- Electromagnetic induction means that an emf is induced whenever the magnetic flux cutting a conductor changes.
- Faraday's law: Whenever there is a change in the magnetic flux cutting a circuit, an emf is induced, the strength of which is proportional to the rate of change of flux cutting the circuit.

- $$E = -\frac{d\phi}{dt}$$

  where E is the emf induced, $\frac{d\phi}{dt}$ is the instantaneous rate of change of magnetic flux with time and the negative sign is due to Lenz's law.

- $$E = -N\frac{d\phi}{dt}$$

  where N is the number of turns of wire in the conductor.

- Lenz's law: The direction of the induced emf is always such as to oppose the change causing it.

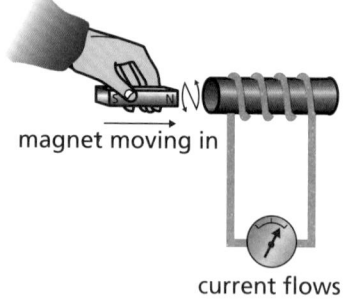

magnet moving in

current flows

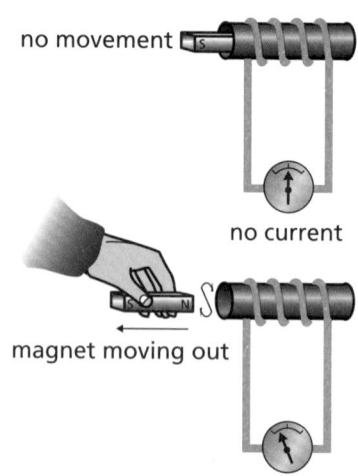

no movement

no current

magnet moving out

current flows opposite way

exam focus

Don't confuse force on a current-carrying conductor in a magnetic field (electrical energy to kinetic) with electromagnetic induction (kinetic energy to electrical).

key point

Relative movement happens when the magnet (magnetic field) and the coil move at different speeds. Neither needs to be stationary.

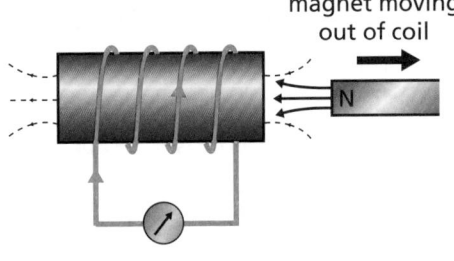

magnet moving into coil

field set up by induced current

Magnet repelled by field of coil

magnet moving out of coil

field set up by induced current

Magnet attracted by field of coil

- The emf generated by a rotating coil is an alternating emf with a sine wave pattern as seen on the oscilloscope.
- Electromagnetic induction is conversion of mechanical energy into electrical energy.
- The unit of magnetic flux is the weber.
- The weber (Wb): The magnetic flux which, in a circuit of one turn, produces an emf of one volt as the flux is reduced to zero at a uniform rate in one second.
- $\Phi = BA$; the weber (Wb) is the magnetic flux passing through an area of 1 m^2 in a magnetic field of flux density one tesla.

Peak values

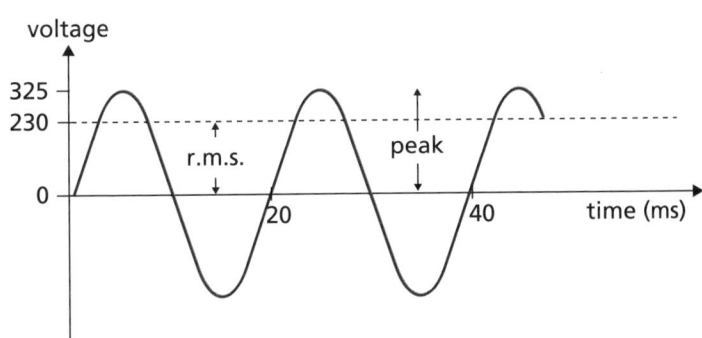

- The maximum value shown on the oscilloscope is called the peak value.
- Root mean square value: The average value used to represent an alternating voltage is called the root mean square (rms) value.
- The peak value of the voltage V_0 is $\sqrt{2}$ times the root mean square value:

$$V_{rms} = \frac{V_0}{\sqrt{2}}$$

- As the current is directly related to the voltage:

$$I_{rms} = \frac{I_0}{\sqrt{2}}$$

Transformers change a.c. voltages

- A transformer is used to change the voltage of the a.c. supply.
- A transformer consists of separate primary and secondary coils of insulated wire on a laminated soft iron frame. The resistance of the coils is kept low to prevent power losses.

  When an alternating voltage is applied across the primary coil it produces an alternating magnetic flux through the primary and soft iron core. This flux cuts through the secondary coil and induces an emf in it.

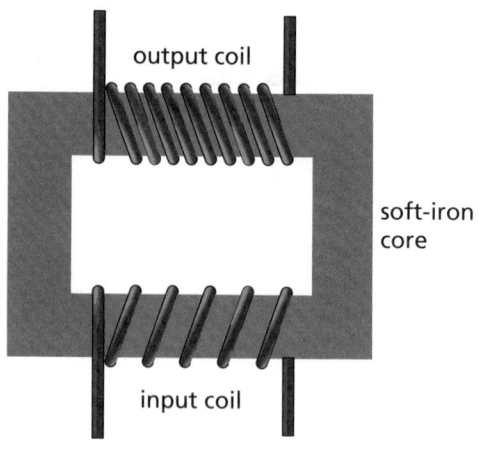

- $$\frac{V_i}{V_o} = \frac{N_P}{N_S}$$

  The ratio of secondary turns to primary turns determines whether the transformer is a 'step-up' or 'step-down' transformer.

  Step-up transformer – voltage increased
  Step-down transformer – voltage decreased

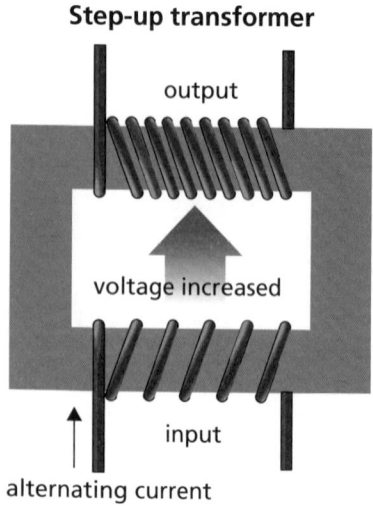

Step-up transformer

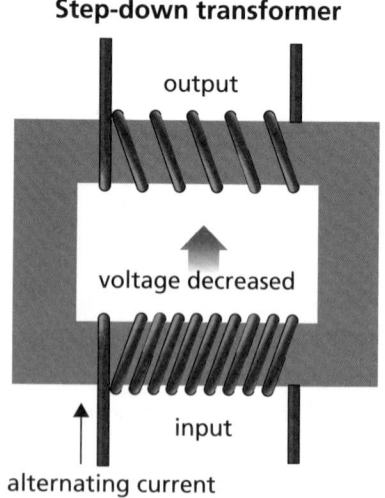

Step-down transformer

Uses of transformers

The ESB uses transformers to 'step up' voltage for transmission of energy and then 'step down' the voltage to supply electrical energy to homes, offices and factories.

Transformers are used to step down voltage for electronic circuits. In fact, we use transformers whenever an appliance needs a voltage different from the mains voltage.

Use simple labelled diagrams to complement your explanations of electromagnetic induction and its applications such as transformers.

Mutual induction

When an emf is generated in the secondary coil by a change in the magnetic field produced by the primary coil, this is mutual induction.

Self-induction

An emf is generated in a coil by a change in the magnetic field of the same coil. This is self-induction.

Inductors and a.c.

An emf is generated in any coil when the current is changing. These coils have an inductance and are called inductors.

The greater the inductance of the coil, the smaller the current passed by an inductor when connected to a.c.

FAQs

What is electromagnetic induction?
An emf is induced whenever the magnetic flux cutting a conductor changes

or

Relative movement between a magnet and a coil causes an electric current to flow in the coil.

What is the energy change that takes place in electromagnetic induction?
Mechanical energy changes into electrical energy.

Give one application of electromagnetic induction.
Bicycle dynamo, generator, induction motor, induction cooker.

State Faraday's law of electromagnetic induction.
Whenever there is a change in the magnetic flux cutting a circuit, an emf is induced, the strength of which is proportional to the rate of change of flux cutting the circuit.

State Lenz's law of electromagnetic induction.
The direction of the induced emf is always such as to oppose the change causing it.

What is a transformer used for?
A transformer is used to change the voltage of the a.c. supply.

What is meant by a.c.?
Alternating current.

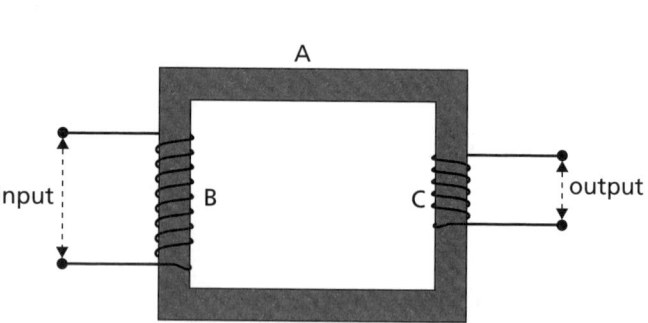

magnet moving in

How would you demonstrate that a magnet and a coil can be used to produce electricity?

1. Move the magnet relative to the coil.
2. The needle on the galvanometer moves.

current flows

Conclusion: emf is produced.

The diagram shows a transformer. Name the parts labelled A and B.
A = Laminated soft iron
B = Primary or input coil

Name a device that uses a transformer.
Mobile phone charger, television, power supply.

The input voltage of a transformer is 230 V. The primary has 4,600 turns and the secondary has 120 turns. Calculate the output voltage.

$$\frac{V_i}{V_o} = \frac{Np}{Ns}$$

$$\frac{230}{V_o} = \frac{4{,}600}{120}$$

$$V_o = \frac{203 \times 120}{4{,}600} = 6 \text{ V}$$

Exam questions

Q: The ESB voltage is 230 V (rms value). What is the peak value of the ESB voltage to your house?

A: Peak value $= \sqrt{2}\,(200) = 325 \text{ V}$

2009 Higher level question 5 (part)

Q: What is the average emf induced in a coil of 20 turns when the magnetic flux cutting it decreases from 2.3 Wb to 1.4 Wb in 0.4 s?

A: $E = -N \dfrac{d\phi}{dt}$

$= -20 \left(\dfrac{0.9}{0.4} \right)$

$= 45 \text{ V}$

2008 Higher level question 8 (part)

Q: A bar magnet is attached to a string and allowed to swing as shown in the diagram. A copper sheet is then placed underneath the magnet. Explain why the amplitude of the swings decreases rapidly.

A: • The swinging magnetic field moves through the conductor copper sheet.

• This induces an emf in the copper sheet.

• Current flows in the copper sheet, which produces a magnetic field.

• The direction by Lenz's law opposes the change causing it, i.e. the swinging magnet.

• This causes the magnet to slow down.

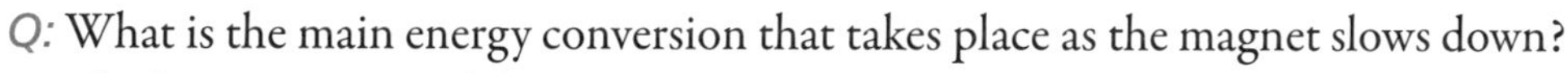

Q: What is the main energy conversion that takes place as the magnet slows down?

A: The kinetic energy of the magnet is converted to electrical energy and heat.

Q: A metal loop of wire in the shape of a square of side 5 cm enters a magnetic field of flux density 8 T. The loop is perpendicular to the field and is travelling at a speed of 5 m s^{-1}.

(i) How long does it take the loop to completely enter the field?

A: $t = \dfrac{5 \times 10^{-2}}{5}$ s

$= 1 \times 10^{-2}$ s

(ii) What is the magnetic flux cutting the loop when it is completely in the magnetic field?

A: $\Phi = B A$

$= 8 \, (5 \times 10^{-2})^2$

$= 2 \times 10^{-2}$ Wb

(iii) What is the average emf induced in the loop as it enters the magnetic field?

A: Average emf $= -\dfrac{\Delta \phi}{\Delta t} = \dfrac{2 \times 10^{-2} \text{ Wb}}{1 \times 10^{-2} \text{ s}} = 2 \text{ V}$

2007 Higher level question 12 (c) (part)

Q: Describe an experiment to demonstrate Faraday's law.

A: 1. Move the magnet towards coil.
Observation: The needle of the galvanometer deflects, indicating that current is flowing.
The faster the magnet moves, the greater the deflection of the galvanometer.

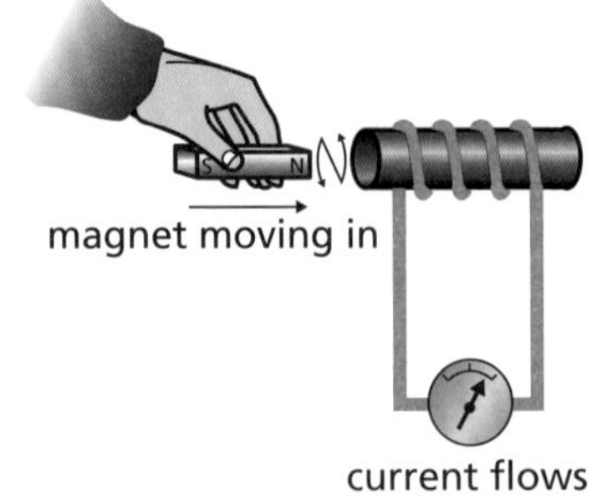

magnet moving in

current flows

Q: A resistor is connected in series with an ammeter and an a.c. power supply. A current flows in the circuit. The resistor is then replaced with a coil. The resistance of the circuit does not change.

What is the effect on the current flowing in the circuit?

A: The current is reduced.

Q: Justify your answer.

A: The coil has a self-inductance that induces an emf in the coil. This is a back emf (Lenz's law).

2005 Higher level question 12 (b) (part)

Q: A square coil of side 5 cm lies perpendicular to a magnetic field of flux density 4.0 T. The coil consists of 200 turns of wire.

What is the magnetic flux cutting the coil?

A: $A = (0.05)^2 = 0.0025$

$\varphi = BA = (4)(0.0025)$

$\varphi = 0.01$ Wb

Q: The coil is rotated through an angle of 90° in 0.2 seconds. Calculate the magnitude of the average emf induced in the coil while it is being rotated.

A: $E = -N\left(\dfrac{\Delta\varphi}{\Delta t}\right)$

$\dfrac{\Delta\varphi}{\Delta t} = \dfrac{(0.01 - 0)}{0.2} = 0.05$

As the coil rotates through 90° the magnetic flux cutting the coil goes from 0.01 Wb to zero.

$E = -200(0.05)$

$E = 10$ V

13 Semiconductors

 To learn:
- Definitions for semiconductors
- How to answer FAQs on semiconductors
- How to solve problems involving semiconductors

Semiconductors

- Conductors have loosely bound electrons in their outer electron orbits that are free to move.
- Insulators have very tightly bound electrons.
- Semiconductors are substances with outer electrons that are not free to move but which require little energy to free them for conduction.
- Silicon and germanium are semiconductors.
- Intrinsic conduction is the movement of charges through a pure semiconductor.
- The intrinsic current is very small and depends on the temperature of the semiconductor.
- Extrinsic conduction is the movement of charges through a doped semiconductor.
- Doping is the process of adding a small amount of another element to a pure semiconductor to increase its conductivity.
- An n-type semiconductor is a semiconductor in which electrons are the majority carriers.
- A p-type semiconductor is a semiconductor in which 'holes' are the majority carriers.

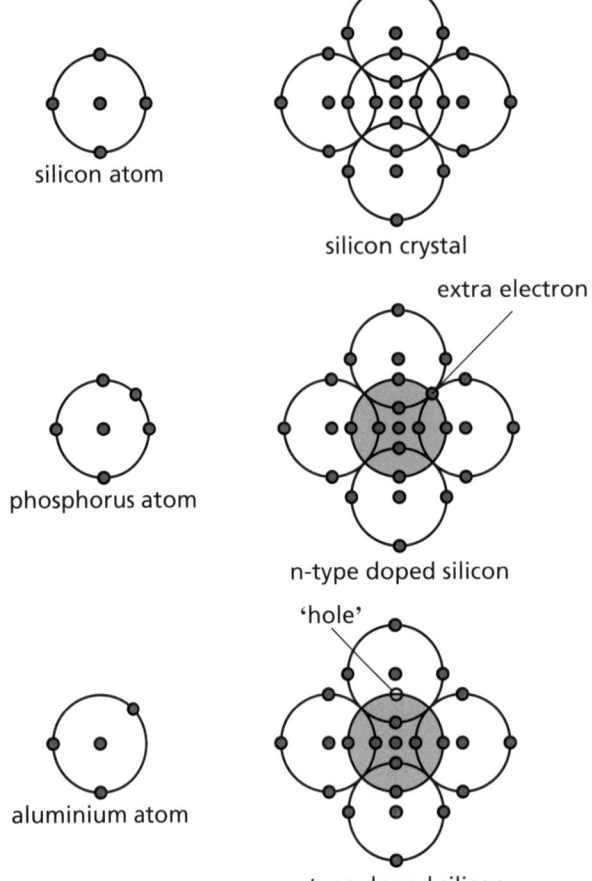

silicon atom

silicon crystal

extra electron

phosphorus atom

n-type doped silicon

'hole'

aluminium atom

p-type doped silicon

Movement of holes

The movement of 'positive charge' or 'holes'
in p-type semiconductors is caused by the
movement of electrons in the opposite direction.

	Majority carriers	Minority carriers
n-type	electrons	holes
p-type	holes	electrons

exam focus
- Semiconductors is a short section in the core physics course.
- Questions are on explaining the basic ideas behind the diode and its applications.

The diode is a p-n junction

- The diode is formed from a single piece of silicon crystal that is doped by a p-type element on one side and an n-type element on the other.

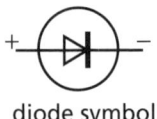

diode symbol

Unbiased junction

An unbiased p-n junction has a junction area (depletion layer) that has few charges available for conduction as the electrons migrate from the n-type to the p-type. This acts as a barrier to the movement of charges.

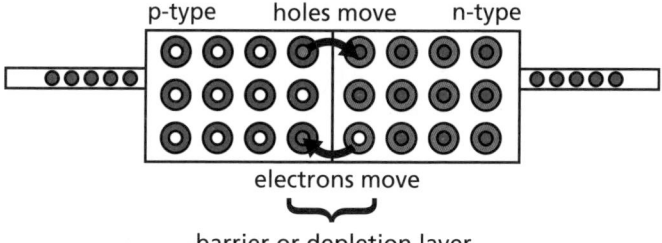

barrier or depletion layer

Forward-biased junction

This is a p-n junction with the positive terminal of the battery connected to the p-type side and the negative terminal connected to the n-type side. A small voltage (0·6 V for a silicon diode and 0·1 V for a germanium diode) must be applied before any current will flow in a forward-biased junction.

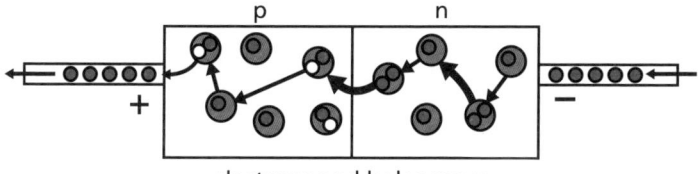

electrons and holes move

Reverse-biased junction

This has the positive terminal of the battery connected to the n-type material and the negative terminal connected to the p-type material. A reverse-biased p-n junction does not conduct any significant current.

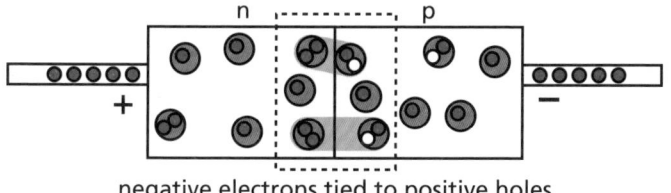

negative electrons tied to positive holes
when n-type is positive ~no current flows

key point

When dealing with conduction through a diode the charge carriers are electrons and 'holes'.

The diode is a half-wave rectifier

Current flows through a diode only when it is forward-biased so that only half of every wave of the a.c. cycle produces a flow of current. The output flows in one direction only and is direct current.

LEDs and photodiodes

- The LED (light-emitting diode) gives off light when electricity passes through the p-n junction.
- The photodiode is a reverse-biased p-n junction that conducts more electricity when light falls it.

FAQs

Give two ways in which a photodiode differs from an LED.
Photodiodes need to take in light; LEDs give out light.
A photodiode operates in reverse bias; an LED operates in forward bias.

Name one use for a photodiode.
A photodiode is used in light meters, burglar alarms, automatic doors, for reading bar codes, as a flame sensor in oil burners.

What are the charge carriers when an electric current passes through a semiconductor?
Electrons and positive holes.

Why is silicon a semiconductor?
It has a resistance between that of a conductor and an insulator.

Sketch a graph to show the variation of current with potential difference for a semiconductor diode in forward bias.

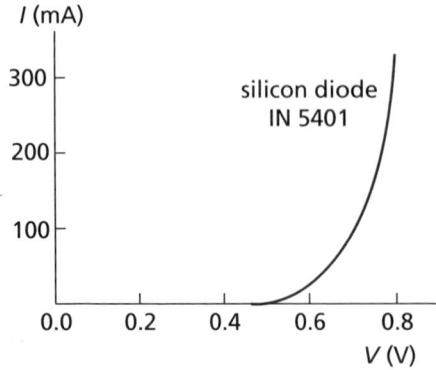

Give a use of a semiconductor diode.
A rectifier.

Name a material used as a semiconductor.
Silicon, germanium.

Exam questions

2009 Higher level question 12 (b)

Q: A semiconductor diode is formed when small quantities of phosphorus and boron are added to adjacent layers of a crystal of silicon to increase its conduction.

Explain how the presence of phosphorus and boron makes the silicon a better conductor.

A: Adding phosphorus increases the number of electrons available for conduction. Adding boron increases the number of 'holes' available for conduction.

Q: What happens at the boundary of the two adjacent layers?

A: An unbiased p-n junction has a junction area (depletion layer) that has few charges available for conduction as the electrons migrate from the n-type to the p-type. This acts as a barrier to the movement of charges.

Q: Describe what happens at the boundary when the semiconductor diode is:

Forward biased

A: The diode conducts. The applied voltage reduces the size of the depletion layer.

Reverse biased

A: The diode does not conduct. The applied voltage increases the size of the depletion layer.

2009 Ordinary level question 12 (c)

Q: A p-n junction (diode) is formed by <u>doping</u> adjacent layers of a <u>semiconductor</u>, and a depletion layer is formed at the junction. Explain the underlined terms.

A: Doping: The process of adding a small amount of another element to a pure semiconductor to increase its conductivity.

Semiconductor: A semiconductor has a resistance between that of a conductor and an insulator.

Q: How does the depletion layer form?
A: Holes and electrons combine at the p-n junction, leaving an area without charge carriers.

Q: The diagram shows two diodes connected to two bulbs A and B, a 6 V d.c. supply and a switch. What is observed when the switch is closed?
A: Bulb A lights and bulb B does not light.

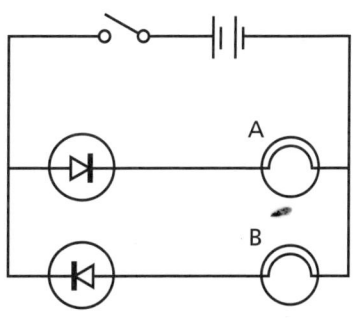

Q: Explain why this happens.
A: Diode near bulb A is forward biased and conducts electricity, which lights the bulb.
Diode near bulb B is reverse biased and does not conduct electricity – the bulb does not light.

14

Electrons, Photoelectric Effect and X-rays

aims To learn:
- Definitions and formulae for photoelectric effect and X-rays
- How to answer FAQs on photoelectric effect and X-rays
- How to solve problems involving photoelectric effect and X-rays

Thermionic emission

- Thermionic emission is the emission of electrons from a hot metal surface.
- Work function is the minimum amount of energy necessary to release an electron from the surface of a metal.
- Electrons are emitted from the surface of a hot metal.
- The higher the temperature of the metal, the more electrons are emitted.
- Electrons are accelerated across the vacuum only when the anode is at a positive potential.
- The greater the positive potential of the anode, the greater the current up to a limit – the saturation current.

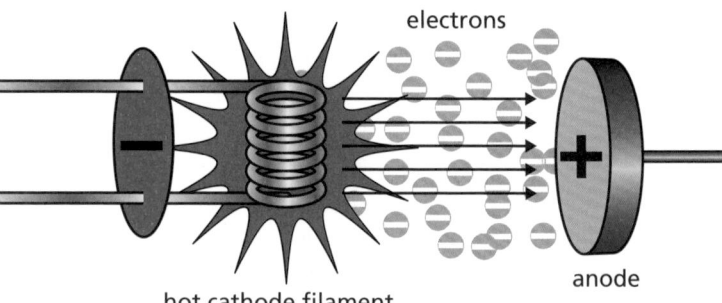

electrons

hot cathode filament

anode

Cathode ray tube

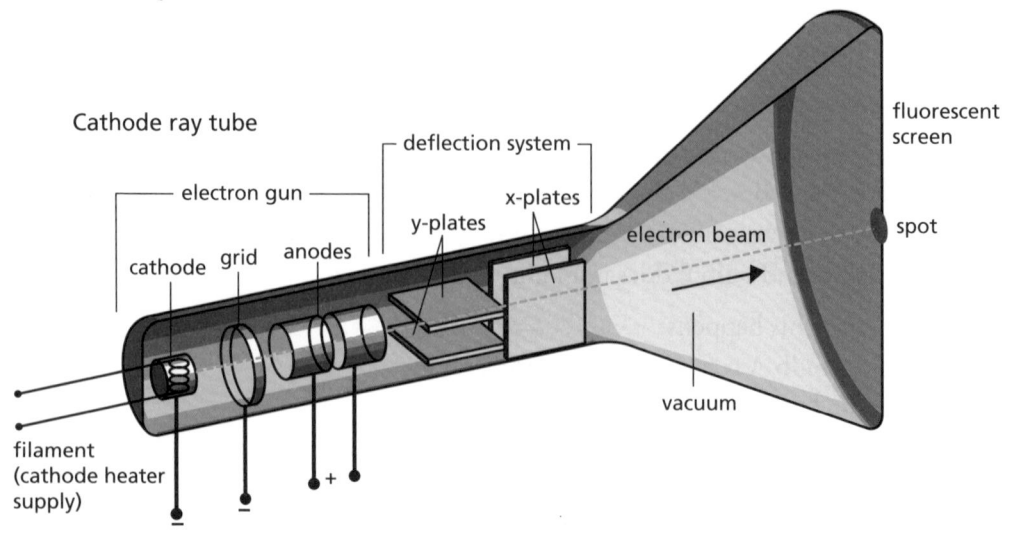

Cathode ray tube

electron gun

deflection system

fluorescent screen

cathode grid anodes

y-plates

x-plates

electron beam

spot

filament (cathode heater supply)

vacuum

Uses of thermionic emission

Oscilloscope: An oscilloscope is a cathode ray tube used to measure a.c. frequencies and voltages. Vertical and horizontal plates deflect the electron beam. A voltage across the Y-plates produces a deflection of the beam proportional to the voltage. A voltage is applied to the X-plates that deflects the beam steadily across the screen and then jumps back rapidly. This is the time-base circuit and can be varied from microseconds to about 10 seconds. A combination of the two deflections produces the oscilloscope trace.

A cathode ray oscilloscope is used to display the signal trace in an electrocardiograph that monitors the electrical activity of the heart.

Television: The first television sets were cathode ray tubes.

Cathode ray tubes have been replaced by Plasma, LCD and LED based screens in both television and oscilloscopes.

Cathode rays are electrons

In 1895 J.B. Perrin showed that cathode rays have a negative electric charge. Cathode rays are electrons.

Electrons have a negative charge.

In 1897 J.J. Thomson showed that electrons are deflected by a magnetic field in a way that shows they are a beam of negative charge.

He also deflected electrons with an electric field.

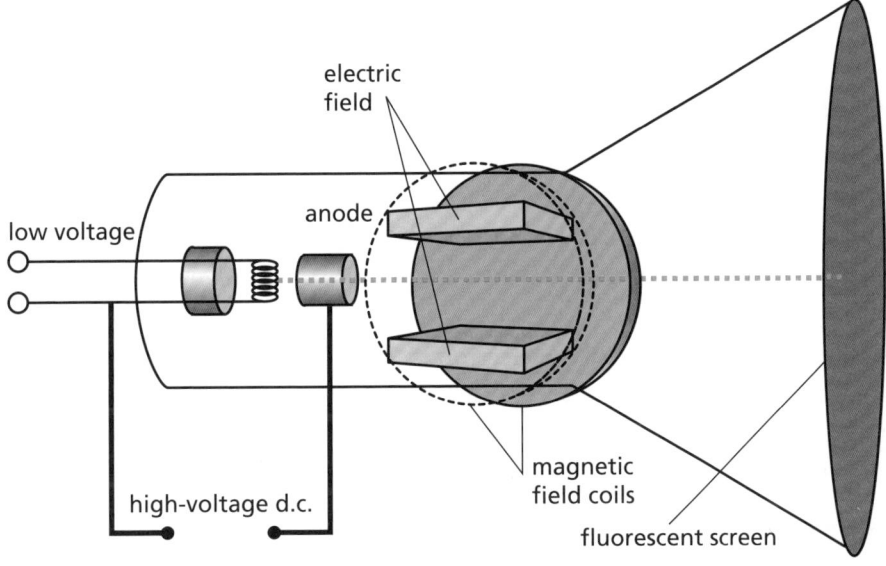

Properties of electrons

Electrons have the following properties:

- Cause fluorescence when they strike certain substances
- Affect photographic plates
- Travel in straight lines
- Are deflected by magnetic and electric fields in a direction, which shows them to be negative
- Cause a heating effect when they strike a small target
- Can pass through a thin metal foil
- Produce X-rays when they strike a heavy metal target
- Have a nature that is independent of the metal used in the cathode

The idea that there was a natural unit of electricity in each atom was suggested by George Johnstone Stoney of Galway. Stoney named this unit an electron.

Energy of an electron

- **The kinetic energy gained by an electron accelerated across a potential difference of V volts is $E_k = qV$ where q is the charge on the electron.**
- An electron accelerated across a potential difference of 1 volt has an energy of one electron-volt or 1 eV.
- $1\ eV = 1.6 \times 10^{-19}\ J$
- When the voltage is 1,000 V the energy is 1 keV.
- A MeV is 10^6 eV and a GeV is 10^9 eV.

The charge of the electron

Thomson measured the ratio of the electric charge of the electron to the mass of the electron in 1897.

He found that the specific charge (charge to mass ratio) of the electron did not vary.

An electron is a particle found in all matter that carries the fundamental unit of negative charge.

Millikan measured the charge of the electron in 1909. The smallest charge measured by Millikan was 1.6×10^{-19} C and every other charge was a whole number multiple of this charge. He concluded from this and from other evidence that the charge of the electron is 1.6×10^{-19} C.

The mass of the electron

The value of $\dfrac{e}{m}$ is 1.76×10^{11} C kg^{-1} (from Thomson's experiment). The charge of the electron is 1.6×10^{-19} C (from Millikan). We can calculate the mass of the electron from these values.

$$\frac{e}{m} = 1.76 \times 10^{11}$$
$$e = 1.6 \times 10^{-19}$$
$$\Rightarrow m = 9.09 \times 10^{-31} \text{ kg}$$

The mass of the hydrogen atom is about 2,000 times the mass of the electron.

Photoelectric emission

Photoelectric emission is the emission of electrons from the surface of a metal when electromagnetic radiation of suitable frequency falls on it.

Experiments on the photoelectric effect showed that:

- Electrons are emitted when light of suitable frequency falls on a metal surface.
- Below a certain frequency of light (the threshold frequency) no electrons are emitted regardless of the intensity of the light.
- The number of electrons emitted depends on the intensity of the light.
- The energy of the electrons emitted depends on the frequency of the light.
- The threshold frequency is the minimum frequency of light necessary to cause photoelectric emission.

Photoelectric emission could not be explained by the wave theory of light.

To demonstrate photoelectric emission

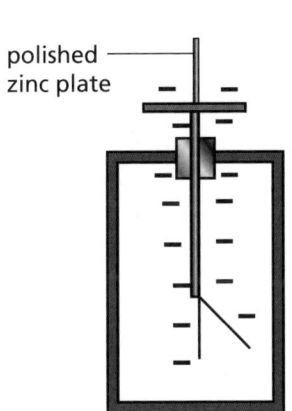

polished zinc plate

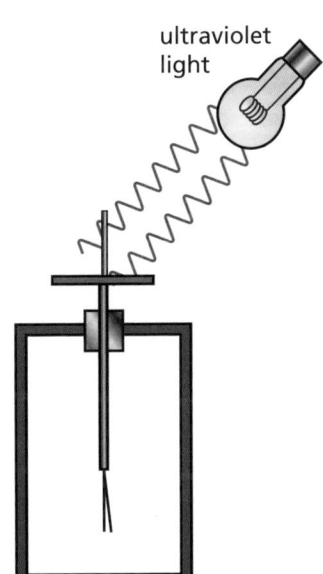

ultraviolet light

1. Clean the surface of a zinc plate with fine emery paper. Attach the plate to the cap of an electroscope.
2. Charge the electroscope with a negative charge.
3. Shine an ultraviolet (UV) lamp onto the zinc plate.
4. The leaf slowly falls, indicating that the zinc plate and the electroscope have lost their charge.

What would happen if you charged the electroscope with a positive charge?

When the plate is positively charged it attracts back the negative charge and so no charge is lost.

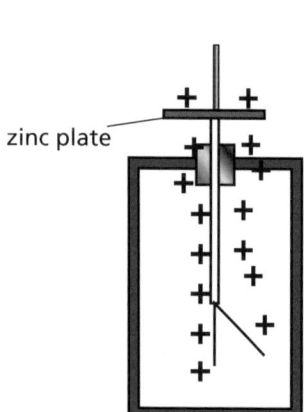

zinc plate

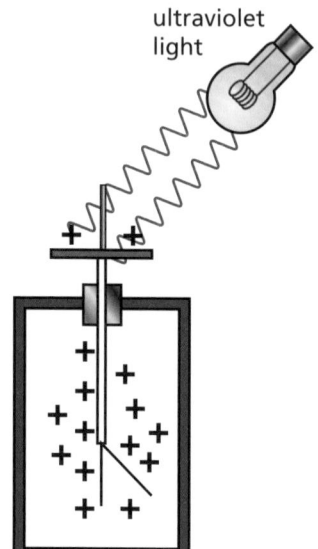

ultraviolet light

Planck's quantum theory

- Max Planck said that light (and other electromagnetic energy) is emitted and absorbed in a small 'packet' or quantum. Each quantum contains a definite amount of energy that depends only on the frequency of the light.

- The quantum of energy is given by the equation:

$$E = hf$$

where h is Planck's constant.

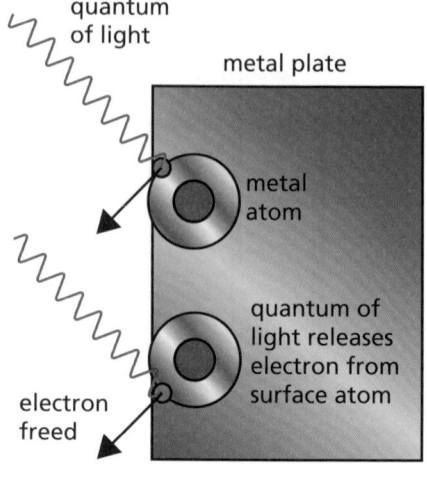

quantum of light

metal plate

metal atom

quantum of light releases electron from surface atom

electron freed

Einstein's photoelectric law

HL

- Each quantum of light travels closely concentrated in space. A quantum of light energy is called a photon.
- In photoelectric emission a photon gives up all its energy to one electron.
- The energy of the photon must be greater than the work function of metal for photoelectric emission.
- A photon is a quantum of light energy whose energy is given by Planck's equation $E = hf$.
- The work function is the minimum amount of energy necessary to release an electron from the surface of a metal.
- When a photon has an energy hf, greater than the work function ϕ, the remainder of the photon energy $(hf - \phi)$ is the maximum amount of kinetic energy the electron can have.
- Einstein's photoelectric law: $hf = \phi + \frac{1}{2} mv_{max}^2$
- A photon has wave properties in that its energy depends on the frequency and also particle properties by being closely confined in space and by interacting with matter as a single unit.
- The threshold frequency (f_0) is the minimum frequency of light necessary to cause photoelectric emission.

Photocell

A photocell is a vacuum tube with a concave cathode made from a material that emits photoelectrons easily. Photoelectrons are emitted when light above the threshold frequency falls on it.

The photoelectric current is directly related to the intensity of light falling on the photocell.

Uses of photocells

Photocells are used in burglar alarms, smoke alarms, automatic doors, safety switches on cutting machinery, laboratory light meters, optical soundtrack in film and control sensors in central heating boilers.

Solid state photodiodes, photoresistors, light-dependent resistors (LDRs) and phototransistors have replaced the photocell in many of these uses.

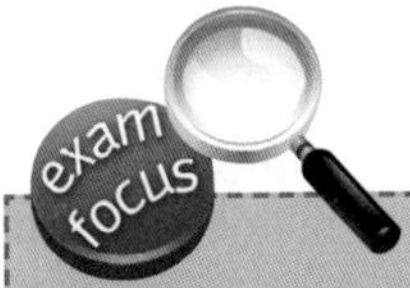

exam focus

You must answer the specific question asked. **Properties** of X-rays are not the same as **uses** of X-rays.

X-rays

Wilhelm Roentgen discovered X-rays in 1895. X-rays were found to have the following properties:

- X-rays are produced when fast electrons strike a solid body.
- X-rays produce fluorescence.
- X-rays blacken photographic emulsions. Roentgen took the first radiograph of his wife's hand.
- X-rays cannot be deflected by electric and magnetic fields.
- X-rays travel in straight lines and cannot be reflected or refracted easily.
- X-rays cause ionisation of the air.
- X-rays are diffracted by thin crystals.
- X-rays penetrate most substances.
- X-rays are absorbed by materials depending on the thickness and the density of the substance.
- X-rays are electromagnetic radiation of extremely short wavelength. X-rays have wavelengths from 10^{-9} to 10^{-15} m.

Hot-cathode X-ray tube

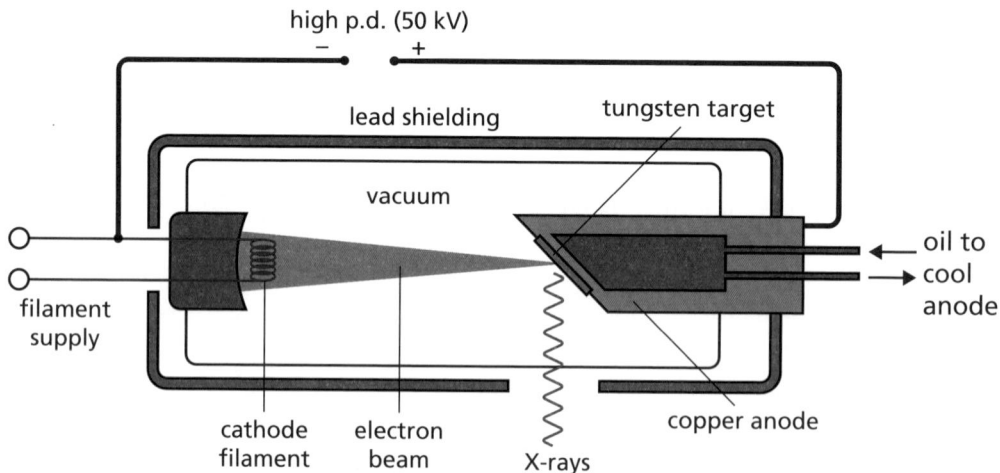

- The hot-cathode X-ray tube has a hot cathode that produces electrons by thermionic emission.
- A vacuum ensures that nothing slows the electrons.
- A tungsten target is set into the anode.
- The high voltage (>50 kV) across the tube accelerates the electrons.
- The high-energy electrons hit the tungsten target in the anode and produce X-rays.

- Only 1% of the electrons produce X-rays.
- About 99% of the electrons produce heat in the anode. The heat produced is dissipated by cooling fins or cooling liquids circulated through the anode.
- A lead shield with a small window ensures that X-rays are emitted in one direction.
- X-ray intensity depends on the temperature of the cathode.
- X-ray penetrating power depends on voltage across the tube.

key point

X-rays are emitted when an electron falls from an outer electron orbit (high energy level) to an inner orbit (lower energy). This happens when a fast electron knocks an electron out of an inner orbit. An electron from an outer orbit falls into this vacant place. The energy given off is an X-ray.

- X-ray production is the inverse process of photoelectric emission.
- In photoelectric emission photon energy frees an electron.
- In X-ray emission the electron energy frees an X-ray photon.

Detection of X-rays

X-rays are detected by fluorescence in some materials and by a blackening of photographic film.

Uses of X-rays

X-rays are used to diagnose and locate breaks in bones. CAT scans form images from a number of X-ray 'slices' through the body. Very penetrating X-rays are used in X-ray therapy to destroy cancer cells.

X-rays are used to check welds in pressure vessels and in aircraft bodies as well as detecting cracks in machinery under stress.

X-rays are used in security checks of baggage in airports. Research scientists use X-ray diffraction to discover the structure of crystals and large molecules.

Harmful effects of X-rays

X-rays have the same harmful effects as other ionising radiation (radioactive substances). Radiographers wear lead-lined aprons and stand behind lead glass screens to prevent radiation damage.

FAQs

How are electrons accelerated in a cathode ray tube?
By a very large voltage (EHT) across the tube.

What is the force exerted on an electron when it is in an electric field of strength $5 \, N \, C^{-1}$?
$F = Eq = 5(1.6 \times 10^{-19}) = 8 \times 10^{-19} \, N.$

Give two properties of the electron.
An electron has a small mass (9.1×10^{-31} kg), a negative charge (1.6×10^{-19} C) and orbits the nucleus.

Give two ways of deflecting a beam of electrons.
An electric field and a magnetic field.

If an electron is accelerated through a potential difference V, what equation relates the velocity to the potential difference?
$eV = \frac{1}{2}mv^2$

What is the photoelectric effect?
The emission of electrons from the surface of a metal when electromagnetic radiation of suitable frequency falls on it.

Give one application of the photoelectric effect.
Burglar alarms, automatic doors, control of burners in central heating, soundtrack in films.

In photoelectric emission what does the velocity of the emitted electrons depend on?
The work function of the metal and the energy of the photons.

What are X-rays?
X-rays are electromagnetic radiation of extremely short wavelength.

How are X-rays produced?
By accelerating electrons across a tube to strike a heavy metal anode.

How are electrons produced in an X-ray tube?
Electrons are produced by thermionic emission at the hot cathode.

State two properties of X-rays.
Electromagnetic waves, have short wavelength, cause ionisation, penetrate materials, no mass, no charge, affect photographic film, etc.

Who discovered X-rays?
Roentgen.

HL Exam questions

2008 Higher level question 11 (part)

Q: High-energy radiation of frequency 3.3×10^{14} Hz is used in medicine. What is the energy of a photon of this radiation?

A: $E = hf$

$E = (6.6 \times 10^{-34}) \cdot (3.3 \times 10^{14})$

$\quad = 2.18 \times 10^{-19}$ J

2005 Higher level question 12 (d) (part)

Q: Write down an expression for Einstein's photoelectric law.

A: $hf = \phi + \frac{1}{2} mv_{max}^2$

Q: Summarise Einstein's explanation of the photoelectric effect.

A: 1. Each quantum of light travels closely concentrated in space. A quantum of light energy is called a photon.
   2. In photoelectric emission a photon gives up all its energy to one electron.
   3. The energy of the photon must be greater than the work function of metal for photoelectric emission.

2006 Higher level question 12 (part)

Q: Calculate the kinetic energy gained by an electron when it is accelerated through a potential difference of 50 kV in an X-ray tube.

A: $E = qV$
$$= (1.6 \times 10^{-19})(50 \times 10^3)$$
$$= 8.0 \times 10^{-15} J$$

Q: Calculate the minimum wavelength of an X-ray emitted from the anode.

A: $E = hf = \dfrac{hc}{\lambda}$

$$\lambda = (6.6 \times 10^{-34})) \times \frac{(3.0 \times 10^8)}{(8.0 \times 10^{-15})}$$

$$= 2.475 \times 10^{-11} \, m$$

(Planck constant $= 6.6 \times 10^{-34} J$ s; speed of light $= 3.0 \times 10^8 \, m \, s^{-1}$; charge on electron $= 1.6 \times 10^{-19} C$)

2009 Higher level question 8

Q: What is a photon?

A: A photon is a quantum of light energy whose energy is given by Planck's equation
$E = hf$.

Q: An investigation was carried out to establish the relationship between the current flowing in a photocell and the frequency of the light incident on it. The graph illustrates the relationship.

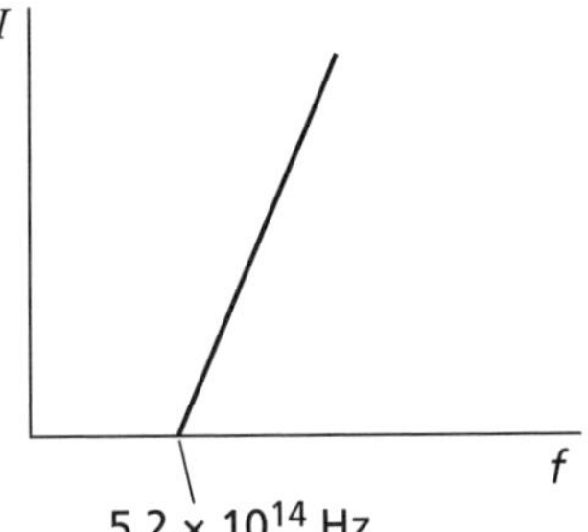

5.2×10^{14} Hz

Draw a labelled diagram of the structure of a photocell.

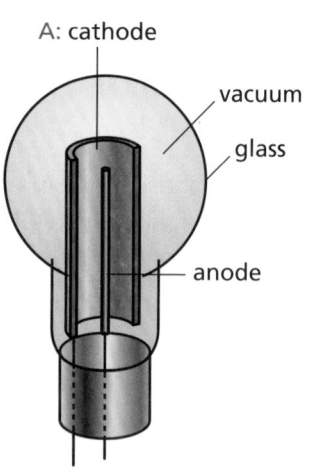

A: cathode

vacuum

glass

anode

Q: Using the graph on the previous page, calculate the work function of the metal.

A: The threshold frequency f_0 from the graph is 5.2×10^{14} Hz

$\phi = hf_0$

$\quad = (6.6 \times 10^{-34})(5.2 \times 10^{14})$

$\quad = 3.432 \times 10^{-19}$ J

Q: What is the maximum speed of an emitted electron when light of wavelength 550 nm is incident on the photocell?

A: $hf = \phi + \frac{1}{2} mv^2_{max}$

$\frac{1}{2} mv^2_{max} = hf - \phi$

$\frac{1}{2} mv^2_{max} = \dfrac{hc}{\lambda} - \phi$

Substituting:

$\frac{1}{2} mv^2_{max} = \dfrac{(6.6 \times 10^{-34})(3.0 \times 10^8)}{(550 \times 10^{-9})} - (3.432 \times 10^{-19})$

$\quad = 3.6 \times 10^{-19} - 3.432 \times 10^{-19}$

$\quad = 1.68 \times 10^{-20}$

$v^2 = \dfrac{2(1.68 \times 10^{-20})}{m}$

$\quad = \dfrac{2(1.68 \times 10^{-20})}{(9.1 \times 10^{-31})}$

$\quad = 3.516 \times 10^{10}$

$v = 1.922 \times 10^5$ ms^{-1}

Q: Explain why a current does not flow in the photocell when the frequency of the light is less than 5.2×10^{14} Hz.

A: Light with a frequency less than threshold frequency does not release electrons so current does not flow.

Q: The relationship between the current flowing in a photocell and the intensity of the light incident on the photocell was then investigated. Readings were taken and a graph was drawn to show the relationship.

Draw a sketch of the graph obtained.

A: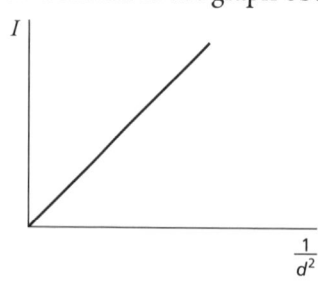

I

$\dfrac{1}{d^2}$

Q: How was the intensity of the light varied?

A: By varying the distance from light source to photocell.

Q: What conclusion about the nature of light can be drawn from these investigations?

A: Light is made up of photons.

2009 Ordinary level question 12 (d)

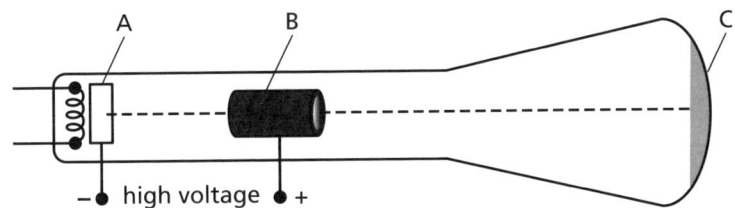

Q: The diagram shows a simple cathode ray tube. Thermionic emission occurs at plate A.

(i) What is thermionic emission?

A: Thermionic emission is the emission of electrons from a hot metal surface.

(ii) What are cathode rays?

A: Cathode rays are a beam of high-speed electrons.

(iii) Why is there a high voltage between A and B?

A: To accelerate the beam of electrons across the tube.

(iv) What happens to the cathode rays when they hit the screen C?

A: They produce a bright spot on the screen.

(v) Give a use for a cathode ray tube.

A: Oscilloscope, television.

2008 Ordinary level question 12 (c)

Q: What is the photoelectric effect?

A: The emission of electrons from the surface of a metal when electromagnetic radiation of suitable frequency falls on it.

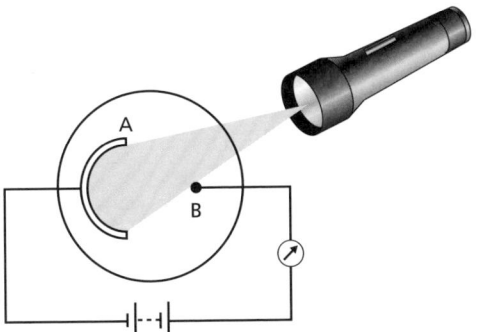

Q: A photocell is connected to a sensitive galvanometer as shown in the diagram. When light from the torch falls on the photocell, a current is detected by the galvanometer.

(i) Name the parts of the photocell labelled A and B.

A: A = Photocathode

   B = Photoanode

(ii) How can you vary the brightness of the light falling on the photocell?

A: Move it away from the photocell.

(iii) How does the brightness of the light affect the current?

A: The brighter the light, the greater the current.

(iv) Give a use for a photocell.

A: Burglar alarms, automatic door, control burners in heating systems, safety switches, light meters, solar cells, soundtrack in film.

2007 Ordinary level question 10

Q: What are X-rays?

A: X-rays are electromagnetic radiation of extremely short wavelength.

Q: Give one use for X-rays.

A: To photograph bones, to treat cancer, to detect flaws in materials.

Q: The diagram shows a simple X-ray tube.

Name the parts labelled A, B and C.

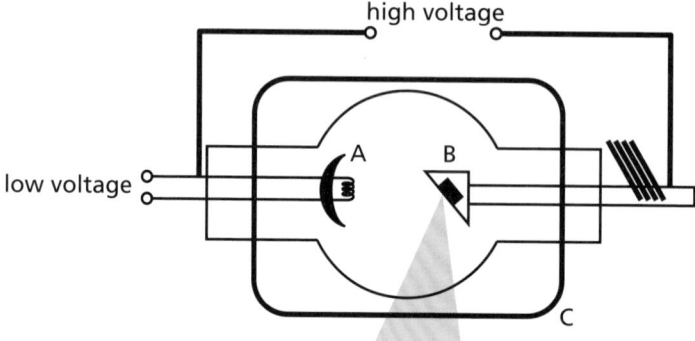

Q: A = Cathode/(heating coil)

   B = Anode or target

   C = Lead shield

(i) Explain how the electrons are emitted from A.

A: By thermionic emission.

(ii) What is the purpose of the high voltage supply?

A: To accelerate electrons across the tube.

(iii) What happens when the electrons hit part B?

A: X-rays are emitted.

(iv) Name a suitable material to use for part B.

A: Tungsten.

(v) Give one safety precaution when using X-rays.

A: Use a lead apron to shield your body from the X-rays.

15 Radioactivity and Nuclear Energy

Alpha, beta and gamma radiation

Henri Becquerel discovered that uranium salts produced a type of penetrating radiation. The Curies chemically separated substances that produce penetrating radiation naturally. Polonium, Thorium and Radium are some radioactive elements.

- Natural radioactivity is the spontaneous disintegration of the nucleus with the emission of alpha (α), beta (β) or gamma (γ) radiation.
- Penetrating power increases:

$$\alpha < \beta < \gamma$$

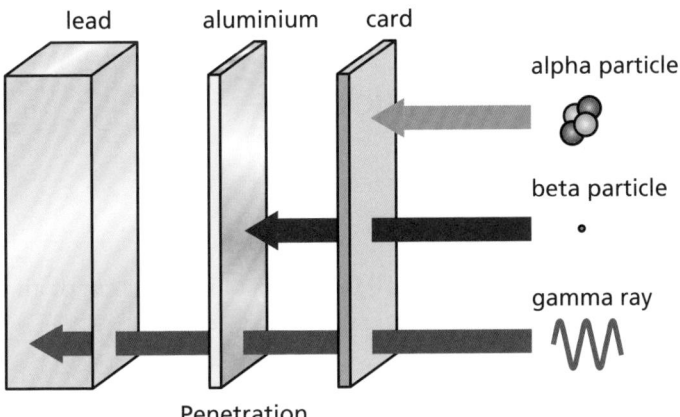

Penetration

- Ionising power increases:

$$\gamma < \beta < \alpha$$

- The greater the ionising effect, the lesser the penetration as ionising the substances takes energy from the radiation.

How would you demonstrate the penetration of α, β and γ radiation?

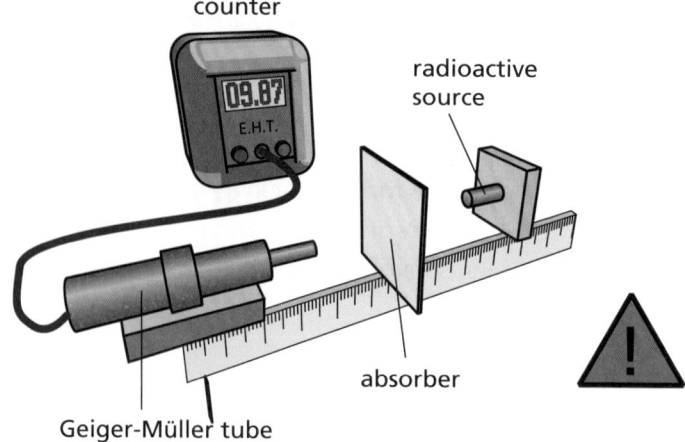

α radiation

1. Take a reading of the 'background radiation'.
2. Place the alpha source in front of the G-M tube. Take a reading.
3. Slowly move the alpha source away from the G-M tube. Where the reading is the same as the background's count, the alpha radiation is not reaching the G-M tube. This is the range of alpha-particles in air.
4. With the alpha source in front of the tube add sheets of suitable absorbers until the alpha-particles are stopped. Repeat for β and γ.

Alpha-particles are helium nuclei

Properties of alpha-particles:

- Cause fluorescence
- Blacken photographic plates
- Are strongly ionising – producing 10,000 pairs of ions per cm of air travelled
- Have weak penetration – are stopped by paper or 5 cm of air
- Have an electric charge of +2 (or $+3.2 \times 10^{-19}$ C)
- Have an atomic mass of 4 a.m.u.
- Have velocities ranging from 0.5% to 1% of the speed of light
- Are identical to doubly ionised helium atoms

An α particle is a combination of two protons and two neutrons ejected from the nucleus. The emission of an α particle from the nucleus takes two protons and two neutrons from the nucleus. This leaves a nucleus with an atomic number two less and an atomic mass four less.

$$^{228}_{90}\text{Th} \rightarrow \,^{224}_{88}\text{Ra} + \,^{4}_{2}\text{He}$$

Beta particles are high-speed electrons

Properties of beta particles:

- Cause fluorescence
- Blacken photographic plates
- Are moderately ionising – producing about 100 pairs of ions per cm of air travelled
- Are moderately penetrating – are stopped by about 500 cm of air
- Have a negative electric charge (-1.6×10^{-19} C)
- Have the same mass (when at rest) as the electron
- Have velocities ranging from 30% to 70% of the speed of light
- Are high-speed electrons originating in the nucleus

A β particle is a high-speed electron ejected by the decay in the nucleus of a neutron into a proton.

$$^{212}_{82}\text{Pb} \rightarrow {}^{212}_{83}\text{Bi} + \beta$$

As the sum of the atomic numbers and of the mass numbers on each side must be equal, the β particle is written as $_{-1}^{0}e$

$$^{212}_{82}\text{Pb} \rightarrow {}^{212}_{83}\text{Bi} + {}_{-1}^{0}e$$

Gamma rays are electromagnetic radiation of extremely short wavelength

Properties of gamma rays:

- Cause slight fluorescence
- Blacken photographic plates
- Are only weakly ionising
- Are very penetrating – passing through a considerable thickness of material
- Have no electric charge, are not deflected by electric or magnetic fields
- Have zero mass
- Have the same velocity as light
- Can be diffracted
- Produce a photoelectric effect
- Are shown by measurements to have shorter wavelengths than X-rays

When a nucleus emits a γ ray photon, the structure of the nucleus does not change.

How to detect radiation

Geiger-Müller tube

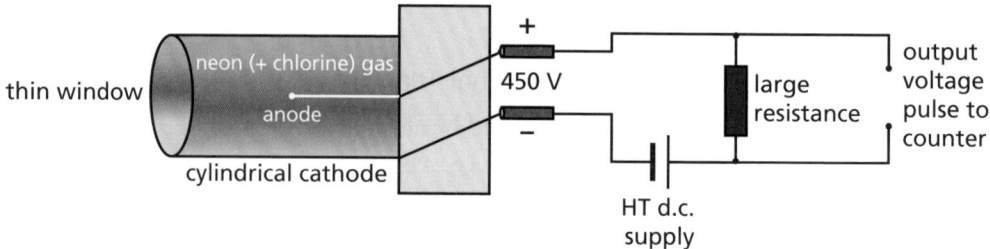

- The principle of the Geiger-Müller (G-M) tube is that radiation ionises the gas in the tube and produces an electric current. The G-M tube consists of a central thin wire anode and a cylindrical cathode maintained at a potential difference of 500 V.
- The tube contains a monatomic gas (neon) at low pressure.
- A Geiger-Müller tube and electronic counter is called a Geiger counter.

Solid-state detector

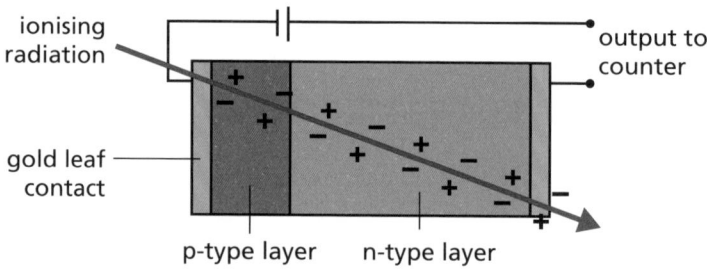

Solid state detector (p-n junction in reverse bias)

- A solid-state detector consists of a diode – a 'p-n' in 'reverse bias'.
- When radiation passes through the diode it 'knocks out' electrons, produces more charge carriers and a pulse of electricity flows.
- The solid-state detector can detect very low energy particles and can distinguish between different types of radiation.

The structure of the atom

Rutherford's gold foil experiment

Rutherford put forward a model of the atom that has all the positive charge concentrated in a very small volume – the nucleus.

The nucleus has a radius of the order of 10^{-15} m. The size of the atom – the space occupied by the electrons – is much greater. The radius of the atom is of the order of 10^{-10} m.

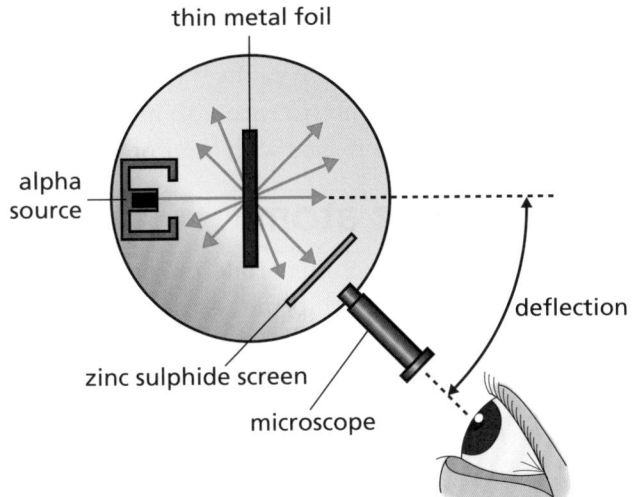

thin metal foil

alpha source

deflection

zinc sulphide screen

microscope

Rutherford discovered the proton in 1919

Rutherford proved that when an alpha-particle bombards a nitrogen nucleus it is changed (transmuted) to oxygen and that a proton was given off in the nuclear reaction.

$$^{4}_{2}\text{He} + ^{14}_{7}\text{N} \rightarrow ^{17}_{8}\text{O} + ^{1}_{1}\text{H}$$

Chadwick discovered the neutron in 1932

Chadwick showed that the radiation emitted when an alpha-particle strikes a beryllium nucleus was due to a particle with a mass close to that of the proton but with no electric charge – the neutron.

$$^{9}_{4}\text{Be} + ^{4}_{2}\text{He} \rightarrow ^{12}_{6}\text{C} + ^{1}_{0}\text{n}$$

The nucleus is composed of protons and neutrons.

- **Atomic number of an element (Z):** The number of protons in the nucleus of the atom of the element.

  It is also the number of electrons around the nucleus of a neutral atom of the element.

- **Isotopes:** Atoms of the same atomic number (of the same element – same number of protons) but with a different atomic mass (different number of neutrons).

  The most common isotope of carbon is used as the standard to compare the masses of different isotopes. An atom of this isotope of carbon is taken as having a mass of 12 atomic mass units.

- **Relative atomic mass:** The mass of an atom in atomic mass units, where the mass of the carbon-12 isotope is taken as having a mass of 12 units.

- **Mass number (A):** This is the whole number nearest to the relative atomic mass of an atom. It gives the number of protons and neutrons in the nucleus.

Lasers

A laser tube produces a beam of light in which all the waves are of the same frequency and in phase. As a result of constructive interference a beam of high energy light is produced. This narrow beam can be controlled with great precision.

The Bohr model of the atom

- Electrons can exist only in certain definite orbits, or energy levels, around the nucleus. As long as they are in these orbits they do not lose energy.
- When an electron drops from one energy level to a lower level it emits the excess energy in a photon.
- Planck's equation gives the wavelength:

$E_2 - E_1 = hf$

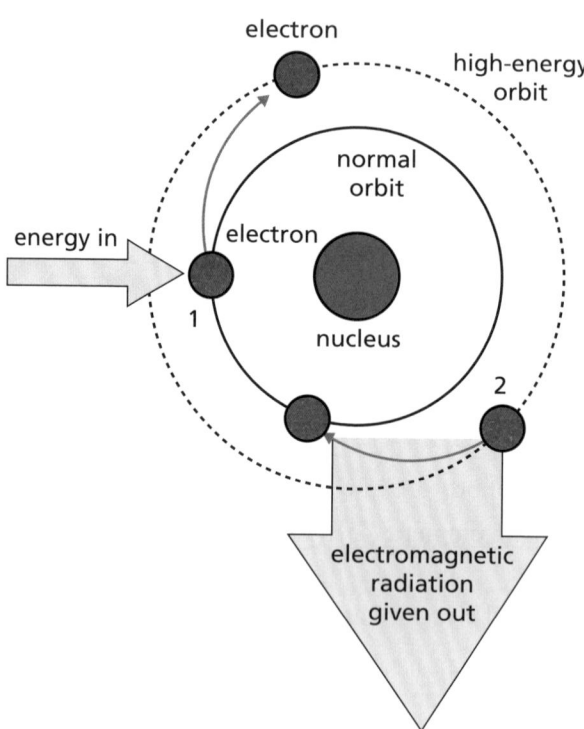

- An emission spectrum is a spectrum given out by a substance when its atoms are excited.

  Line spectra are explained by the Bohr model as the wavelengths emitted when an electron jumps from one energy level to another.

Radioactive decay

The rate at which radiation is emitted from a given substance depends only on the amount of the substance present (the number of atoms of the radioactive substance).

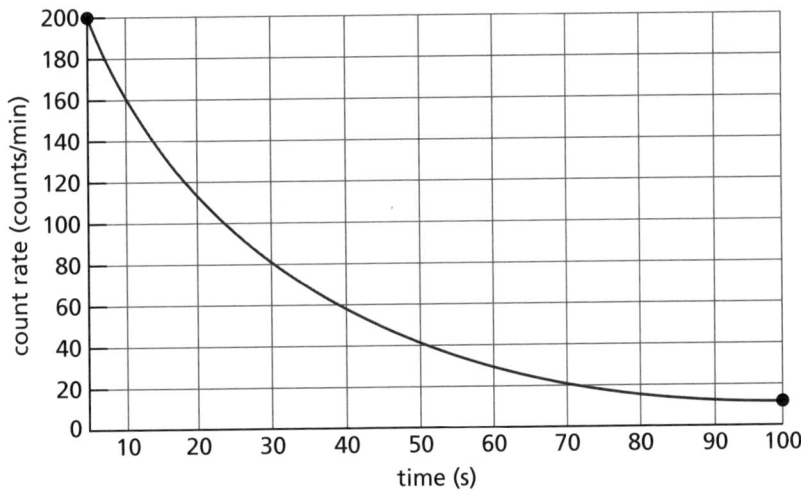

- Law of radioactive decay: The rate of radioactive decay depends only on number of atoms of radioactive substance present.
- Rate of decay $= -\lambda N$

  Where λ is the decay constant (the negative sign indicates that it is a 'decay' process) and N is the number of atoms in the sample.
- The rate of decay is the number of nuclear disintegrations occurring per second.
- The becquerel (Bq) is a rate of decay of one disintegration per second.
- The half-life ($T_{\frac{1}{2}}$) is the time taken for half the number of atoms of a radioactive substance to decay.

Half-life and decay constant

- A substance with a short half-life decays very fast and has a big decay constant.
- A substance with a long half-life decays very slowly and has a small decay constant.
- Decay constant and half-life are inversely related.

$$T_{\frac{1}{2}} = \frac{\ln 2}{\lambda}$$

$$= \frac{0.693}{\lambda}$$

Nuclear reactions

- Conservation of electric charge: This requires that the sum of the atomic numbers of the initial nuclei must equal the sum of the atomic numbers of the resultant nuclei.
- Conservation of mass-energy: Energy is conserved in any individual reaction, provided that mass is taken as a form of energy according to the equation $E = mc^2$.

- Conservation of momentum: The momentum before the reaction equals the momentum after.
- The total number of nucleons also remains unchanged.

Uses of radioisotopes and radiation hazards

Natural radioactivity is radioactivity produced by substances found in nature – substances like uranium, radium and thorium.

Artificial radioactivity is radioactivity produced by bombarding non-radioactive isotopes with charged particles or neutrons.

Radioactive isotopes have many uses in medicine, agriculture, research and industry.

Medical uses of radioisotopes

Radioisotopes are used:

1. Like X-rays to produce photographic images of the inside of the body
2. To kill cancerous cells
3. To sterilise prepacked syringes, scalpels, bandages and dressings as well as heat-sensitive medicines. Exposing substances to γ radiation does not make them radioactive.

Injections of salt containing the radioisotope sodium-24 into the bloodstream enable doctors to chart the flow of blood through the body.

Plutonium-238 radioisotope is used to generate electricity to power heart pacemakers.

Industrial uses of radioisotopes

Smoke detectors.

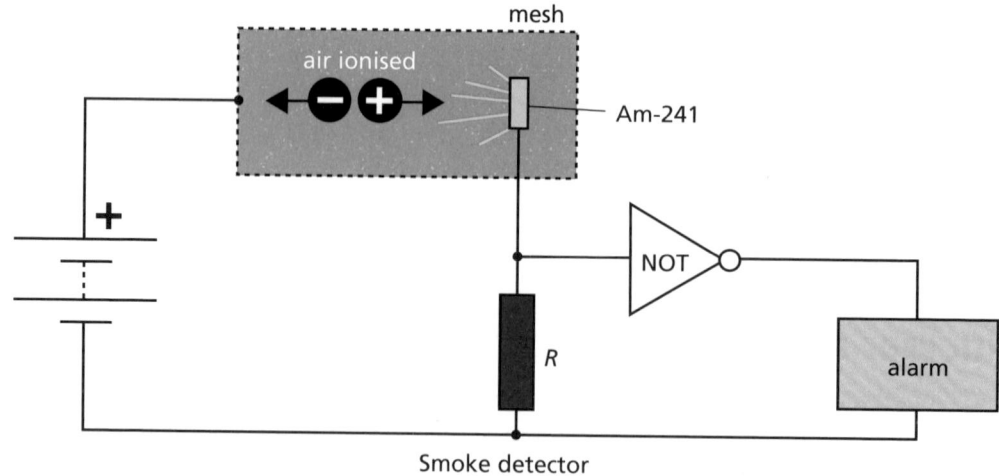

Smoke detector

Radioisotope generators power satellites and warning beacons at sea.

Gamma-ray photography is used to check jet engines, aircraft frames and pipelines.

Gamma rays are used to check the thickness of materials.

Radioisotope tracers are used to check pipes for leaks.

Agricultural uses of radioisotopes

Very high levels of γ radiation are used to sterilise foods.

The radioisotope phosphorus-32 (in a phosphate fertiliser) is used in agricultural research to monitor the intake of phosphates by plants.

Another use is in treating male insect pests with γ radiation – this makes them sterile.

Research uses of radioisotopes

Radioactive isotopes decay at a known rate and so can be used to determine the age of things.

Carbon dating uses the relative amounts of radioactive carbon-14 to carbon-12 to give a measure of the age of a dead plant or animal sample.

Uranium-238 dating uses the relative amounts of uranium-238 and lead-206 to date the age of the rock.

Radioactivation analysis

When a tiny sample of a substance is bombarded with neutrons it turns into radioactive isotopes of the same elements. The half-lives of these isotopes and the wavelengths of the gamma rays emitted enable scientists to identify the substances.

Effects of ionising radiation on your health

High levels of radiation kill cells. Long-term exposure to low-level radiation can lead to an increased incidence of cancer.

Alpha-particle radiation

Alpha radiation is stopped by the layer of dead cells above the live skin tissue. Alpha radiation is very dangerous if alpha emitters are taken into live tissue in a skin cut or breathed into the lungs in dust, liquid or gas. This is because it is a strongly ionising radiation and this causes great damage to cells.

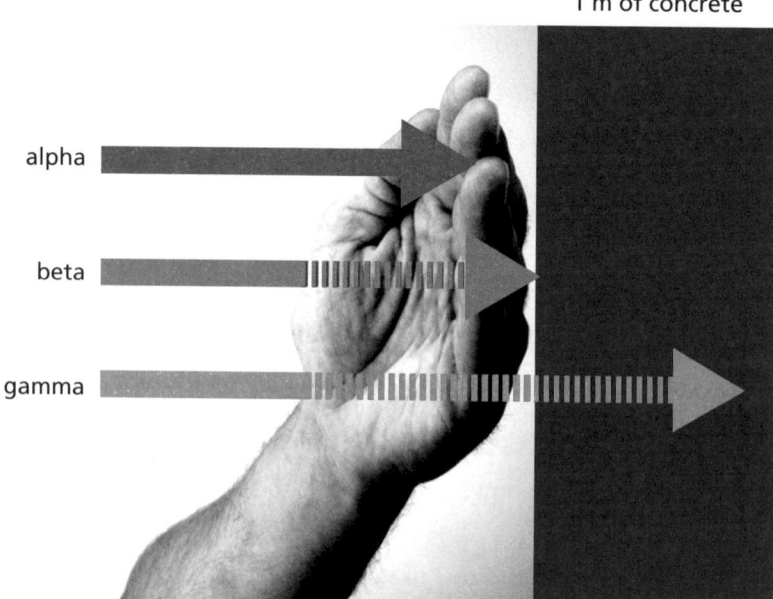

1 m of concrete

alpha

beta

gamma

Beta particle radiation

Beta particles can penetrate about 1 cm of body tissue. Beta emitters endanger skin tissue but do not affect the deeper organs of the body unless taken in through dust, liquids or gas.

Gamma radiation and X-rays

Both of these radiations can penetrate right through the body and so endanger all parts of the body. Gamma emitters are potentially more dangerous than X-rays because gamma emitters can be taken inside the body.

Radiation risks

The risk from medical X-rays is extremely small. Modern radiography has reduced the exposure to very low levels. Doctors have replaced X-rays with safer imaging techniques like MRI scans, ultrasound scans and optical fibre scopes.

Radon is a particular danger.

Radon gas is an alpha-particle emitter. Long-term exposure to radon gas can cause lung cancer.

Radiation protection

1. Assume that there is no safe dose.
2. Keep all unavoidable doses as small as possible.

3. Any deliberate exposure – such as using radioisotopes to diagnose illness – should have some benefit that outweighs the danger.

Nuclear energy

Einstein showed that mass and energy are related by the equation $E = mc^2$ where m is the mass of the body and c is the speed of light.

- Einstein's mass-energy equation $(E = mc^2)$: When a small amount of matter seems to disappear, a large amount of energy is released in its place.

Conservation of mass and conservation of energy taken separately do not work with nuclear reactions. Only conservation of mass-energy combined works with nuclear reactions. Mass-energy conservation was confirmed experimentally by Cockcroft and Walton:

$$^1_1H + ^7_3Li \rightarrow ^4_2He + ^4_2He$$

Cockcroft and Walton's experiment was the first direct confirmation of Einstein's prediction of the equivalence of mass and energy.

Fission

A single atom of uranium 235 undergoing fission

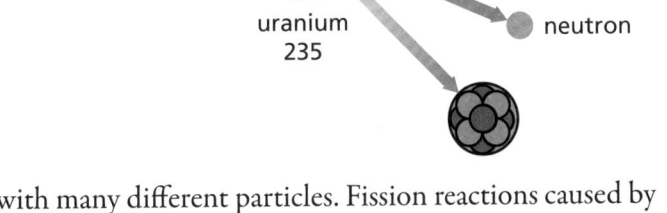

- **Fission is the splitting of the nucleus of a heavy element into two or more smaller nuclei with the emission of neutrons and a large amount of energy.**
- Great amounts of energy are released in nuclear fission. Fission reactions can be caused by bombarding the nucleus with many different particles. Fission reactions caused by neutrons are the most important.

Why does fission happen with large atoms?

In large atoms the nucleons are relatively far apart from each other. The nuclear forces are not strong enough at these distances so that the repulsive forces between the protons tend to split the nucleus when a neutron hits it.

Uranium fission

U-238 undergoes radiative capture and very little fission.

Fission: $^{238}_{92}U + ^1_0n \rightarrow$ 2 fragments + neutrons

Radiative capture: $^{238}_{92}U + ^1_0n \rightarrow ^{238}_{92}U + ^1_0n$ + gamma

U-235 undergoes fission and little radiative capture.

Fission: $^{235}_{92}U + ^{1}_{0}n \rightarrow 2$ fragments + neutrons

Radiative capture: $^{235}_{92}U + ^{1}_{0}n \rightarrow ^{235}_{92}U + ^{1}_{0}n$ + gamma

U-238 is the more abundant isotope (99.2%) mainly radiative capture and undergoes fission only with fast neutrons

U-235 (0.7%) mainly fission with fast and slow neutrons

Chain reaction

- Chain reaction: A reaction where each fission event produces at least one further fission.

A chain reaction is achieved by using uranium enriched with more pure uranium, U-235. Uncontrolled fission chain reactions use U-235 or plutonium 239 (Pu-239).

Nuclear reactors

A nuclear reactor produces energy by fission in uranium fuel rods. The energy is used to boil water and drive a steam turbine generator set.

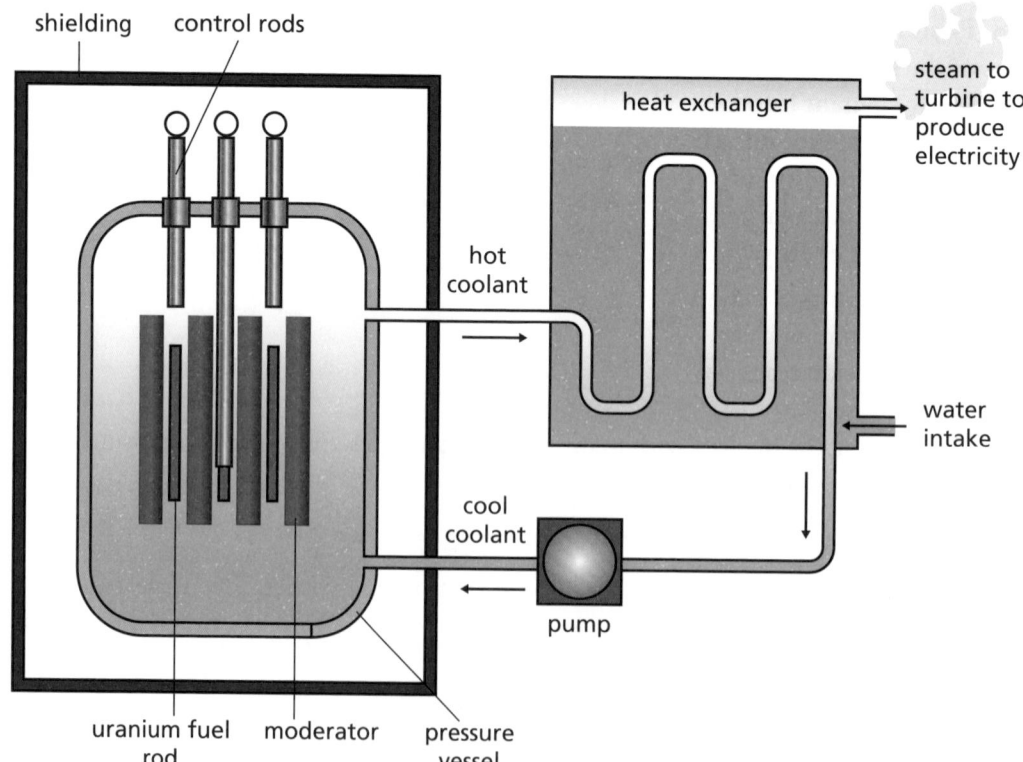

- **Fuel rods:** The fuel rods are made from natural uranium, enriched in U-235.
- **Moderator:** The moderator rapidly slows down neutrons to the energy that allows fission to happen. The moderator is a material like graphite or heavy water that slows down the neutrons without undergoing nuclear reactions.

- **Control rods:** Control rods are made from a neutron absorber like cadmium or boron steel. The rods are adjusted by raising or lowering them into the reactor core so that just one fission-producing neutron results from each fission. This controls the rate of fission.
- **Shielding:** The reactor core is contained in a sealed vessel to prevent radiation from escaping.
- **Heat exchanger:** A nuclear reactor heats the boiler indirectly through a heat exchanger.

Dangers of fission reactors

1. Even though many reactors have a good safety record, the potential for large-scale disaster is always present.
2. Disposal of nuclear waste, including highly radioactive old nuclear reactors.
3. Reprocessing of used (spent) fuel rods from reactor cores.

Fusion

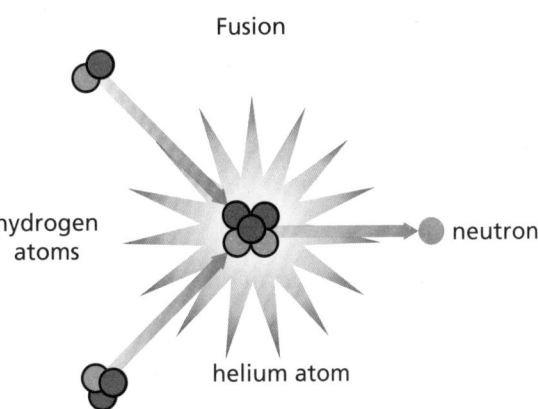

Fusion

- **Fusion is the union of light nuclei to form a heavier nucleus with the emission of large amounts of energy.**
- $^2_1H + ^2_1H \rightarrow ^3_2He + ^1_0n + energy$

hydrogen atoms

neutron

helium atom

Experimental fusion reactors

Experimental fusion reactors are attempting to produce sustained fusion of a plasma of hydrogen isotopes – a high-temperature mixture of deuterium and tritium. At temperatures of many hundred million degrees, all atoms are ionised and electrically charged. This plasma is kept in place in a doughnut-shaped tube called a tokamak with a powerful magnetic field.

Lithium metal is used as a heat exchanger because it is a good conductor of heat.

Lithium also 'breeds' tritium when struck by neutrons. The tritium can later be extracted for use as fuel for further fusion.

exam focus

- Do not confuse fission and fusion. Fission is the splitting of a nucleus; fusion is joining nuclei together.
- Moderators and control rods in a nuclear reactor are not the same: a moderator slows neutrons; control rods absorb neutrons.

Controlled fusion is attractive as an energy source

1. Low fuel cost: 700 grams of deuterium could power a 200 MW station for one day.
2. Fuel is readily available from water. There is sufficient deuterium on earth to last for 2×10^4 million years at current energy consumption rates.
3. No radioactive wastes of long half-life to dispose of.
4. Fusion is not a chain reaction – it cannot get out of control.

FAQs

In a nuclear fission reactor neutrons are slowed down after being emitted. Why?
Only slow neutrons cause fission.

What is the purpose of a moderator in a nuclear reactor?
To slow down the neutrons.

What is the source of the sun's energy?
Fusion of hydrogen gas.

Why does the amount of carbon-12 in dead tissue remain unchanged?
It is not radioactive, it is stable.

Name a material used as shielding in a nuclear reactor.
Lead or concrete.

The half-life of a radioactive element is three days. What fraction of a sample of the radioactive element will remain after nine days?
$\dfrac{1}{8}$

What is nuclear fusion?
Fusion is the union of light nuclei to form a heavier nucleus with the emission of large amounts of energy.

What are isotopes?
Isotopes are atoms of the same element with different mass number.

What is meant by radioactivity?
Radioactivity is the spontaneous disintegration of the nucleus with the emission of alpha (α), beta (β) or gamma (γ) radiation.

Name a detector of radioactivity.
Geiger-Muller tube, Geiger counter, solid-state detector, photographic film.

Explain the term 'half-life'.
Half-life is the time taken for half the number of atoms of a radioactive substance to decay.

Give one use of a radioactive isotope.
To detect disease, to cure cancers, to sterilise instruments, in smoke detectors, to detect leaks, in carbon dating.

Exam questions

2006 Ordinary level question 9

The diagram shows a simple nuclear fission reactor.

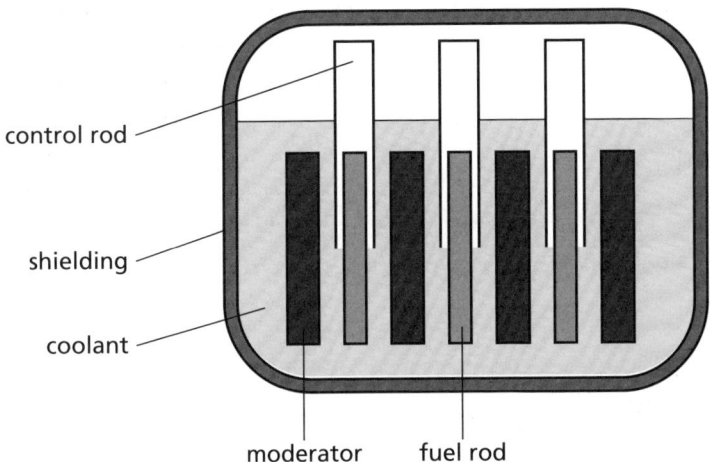

Q: Energy is released in a fission reactor when a chain reaction occurs in the fuel rods.

(i) What is meant by fission?

A: Fission is the splitting of the nucleus of a heavy element into two or more smaller nuclei with the emission of neutrons and a large amount of energy.

Q: Name a material in which fission occurs.

A: Uranium, Plutonium.

(ii) Describe how a chain reaction occurs in the fuel rods.

A: Chain reaction: a reaction where each fission event produces at least one further fission.

Q: Explain how the chain reaction is controlled.

A: Using control rods made from a neutron absorber like cadmium or boron steel. The rods are adjusted by raising or lowering them into the reactor core so that just one fission-producing neutron results from each fission. This controls the rate of fission.

(iii) What is the purpose of the shielding?

A: To prevent radiation escaping into the environment.

(iv) Describe what happens to the coolant when the reactor is working.

A: The coolant gets hot.

(v) Give one effect of a nuclear fission reactor on the environment.

A: It creates nuclear waste.

(vi) Give one precaution that should be taken when storing radioactive materials.

A: Store in lead, use a tongs when handling, store in a locked room, use appropriate warning signs.

2008 Ordinary level question 10

Q: Give two properties of an electron.

A: Negatively charged, deflected by electric and magnetic fields, small mass, outside nucleus.

Q: The diagram shows the arrangement used by Rutherford to investigate the structure of the atom. During the investigation he fired alpha-particles at a thin sheet of gold foil in a vacuum.

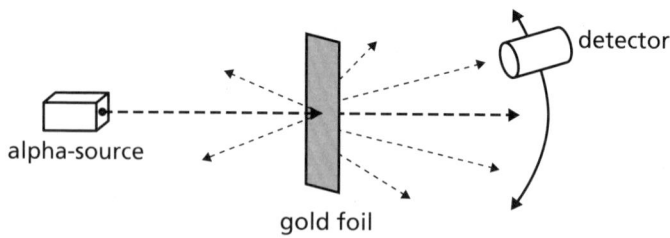

(i) What are alpha-particles?

A: A combination of two protons and two neutrons ejected from the nucleus – a helium (nucleus).

(ii) Describe what happened to the alpha-particles during the experiment.

A: Most went straight through. Some were deflected by various degrees. Some were bounced back.

(iii) What conclusion did Rutherford make about the structure of the atom?

A: The atom is mainly empty space with a dense nucleus, which is positively charged.

(iv) How are the electrons arranged in the atom?

A: They orbit the nucleus.

(v) Name a device used to detect alpha-particles.

A: Geiger-Müller tube, solid-state detector.

(vi) Why was it necessary to carry out this experiment in a vacuum?

A: Because alpha-particles would be stopped by a few centimetres of air.

HL 2009 Higher level question 12 (d)

Q: Smoke detectors use a very small quantity of the element americium-241. This element does not exist in nature and was discovered during the Manhattan Project in 1944. Alpha-particles are produced by the americium-241 in a smoke detector.

(i) Give the structure of an alpha-particle.

A: $^4_2$He or helium nucleus containing 2 protons and 2 neutrons.

(ii) How are the alpha-particles produced?

A: Americium-241 is radioactive and undergoes α-decay.

(iii) Why do these alpha-particles not pose a health risk?

A: Alpha-particles are good ionisers and have a very short range.

Q: Americium-241 has a decay constant of $5.1 \times 10^{-11}\,s^{-1}$.
Calculate its half-life in years.

A: $T_{\frac{1}{2}} = \dfrac{ln2}{\lambda}$

$= \dfrac{0.693}{5.1 \times 10^{-11}}$

$= 1.359 \times 10^{10}\,s$

$= 1.51 \times 10^{5}\,days$

$= 413.7\,years$

Q: Explain why americium-241 does not exist naturally.

A: Americium-241 is radioactive and has a relatively short half-life compared to the age of the universe. Any Am-241 that may have existed has undergone radioactive decay.

2005 Higher level question 8 (part)

Q: Cobalt-60 is a radioactive isotope with a half-life of 5.26 years and emits beta particles.

(i) Write an equation to represent the decay of cobalt-60.

A: $^{60}_{27}Co \rightarrow\, ^{60}_{28}Ni +\, ^{0}_{-1}e$

(ii) Calculate the decay constant of cobalt-60.

A: $\lambda = \dfrac{\ln 2}{T_{1/2}}$

$= \dfrac{0.693}{1.66} \times 10^{8}\,s$

$= 4.18 \times 10^{-9}\,s^{-1}$

(iii) Calculate the rate of decay of a sample of cobalt-60 when it has 2.5×10^{21} atoms.

A: Rate of Decay:

$\dfrac{dN}{dt} = (-)\lambda N$

$= 4.18 \times 10^{-9} \times 2.5 \times 10^{21}$

$= 1.045 \times 10^{13}\,s^{-1}\,or\,Bq$

2006 Higher level question 8

Q: Distinguish between fission and fusion.

A: Fission is the splitting of the nucleus of a heavy element into two or more smaller nuclei with the emission of neutrons and a large amount of energy.

Fusion is the union of light nuclei to form a heavier nucleus with the emission of large amounts of energy.

Q: The core of our sun is extremely hot and acts as a fusion reactor.

Why are large temperatures required for fusion to occur?

A: Because the nuclei are positively charged and the force of repulsion must be overcome to join them together.

Q: In the sun a series of different fusion reactions take place.
In one of the reactions, 2 isotopes of helium, each with a mass number of 3, combine to form another isotope of helium with the release of 2 protons.
Write an equation for this nuclear reaction.

A: $_2^3\text{He} + _2^3\text{He} \rightarrow _2^4\text{He} + 2\,_1^1\text{H}$

Q: Controlled nuclear fusion has been achieved on earth using the following reaction.
$_1^2\text{H} + _1^3\text{H} \rightarrow _2^4\text{He} + _0^1\text{n}$
What condition is necessary for this reaction to take place on earth?

A: Very high temperature.

Q: Calculate the energy released during this reaction.

A: mass of reactants $= 8.346 \times 10^{-27}\,\text{kg}$

mass of products $= 8.318 \times 10^{-27}\,\text{kg}$

loss in mass (mass defect) $= 2.8 \times 10^{-29}\,\text{kg}$

$$E = mc^2$$
$$E = (2.8 \times 10^{-29})(2.998 \times 10^8)^2$$
$$= 2.5166 \times 10^{-12}\,\text{J}$$
$$= 2.52 \times 10^{-12}\,\text{J}$$

Q: Give one benefit of a terrestrial fusion reactor under each of the following headings:
(i) Fuel

A: Easily available, plentiful and cheap.

(ii) Energy

A: Vast amounts of energy are released from a small mass of fuel.

(iii) Pollution

A: Little or no radioactive waste produced.

speed of light $= 2.998 \times 10^{-8}\,\text{m s}^{-1}$

mass of hydrogen-2 nucleus $= 3.342 \times 10^{-27}\,\text{kg}$

mass of hydrogen-3 nucleus $= 5.004 \times 10^{-27}\,\text{kg}$

mass of helium nucleus $= 6.644 \times 10^{-27}\,\text{kg}$

mass of neutron $= 1.674 \times 10^{-27}\,\text{kg}$

aims To learn:
- Definitions and formulae for particle physics
- How to answer FAQs on particle physics
- How to solve problems involving particle physics

Definitions and formulae

Rutherford's nuclear model of the atom

The discovery of the electron, proton and neutron and Rutherford's nuclear model of the atom changed the picture of an atom to a nucleus of protons and neutrons surrounded by orbiting electrons.

Conservation of momentum in nuclear reactions

When a nucleus emits an α particle the nucleus recoils in the same way as a gun when a shot is fired.

Conservation of momentum: momentum before = momentum after

The neutrino

When β particles are emitted by radioactive decay the process seemed to contradict conservation of energy and conservation of momentum. This led Pauli to suggest that another particle – a neutrino – was emitted in the decay. When the neutrino is taken into account, energy and momentum are conserved.

$$_0^1n \rightarrow {}_1^1p + {}_{-1}^{0}e + {}_0^0\nu$$

Neutrinos are also emitted in other nuclear reactions involving electrons.

The neutrino ($_0^0\nu$) has zero charge and mass like the photon but has momentum and energy.

Conservation of mass-energy

- Einstein's mass-energy equation: $E = mc^2$

  where m is the mass of the body and c is the speed of light.
- When a small amount of matter seems to disappear, a large amount of energy is released in its place.

Cockcroft and Walton split the nucleus

Mass-energy conservation was confirmed when a lithium target was bombarded by protons.

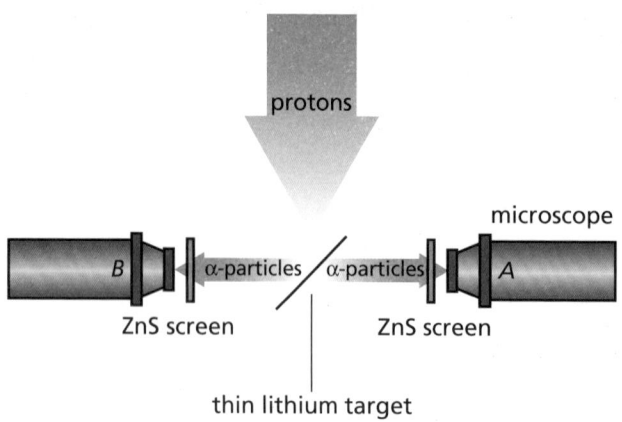

Cockcroft and Walton's experiment was the first direct confirmation of Einstein's prediction of the equivalence of mass and energy.

Machines to smash the nucleus

Linear accelerators

Cockcroft and Walton accelerated protons in a straight line – a linear accelerator.

Circular accelerators

A more compact way of accelerating particles was developed in 1930 by Lawrence. The cyclotron he invented was about the size of a dinner plate and had the following characteristics.

- The particles are charged and can be accelerated by an electric field. A magnetic field at right angles to the direction of the particles forces them into a circular path.
- Each time they come to the gap between the two semicircles the electric field accelerates them across the gap.
- The frequency of the electric field ensures that this happens at the correct moment.

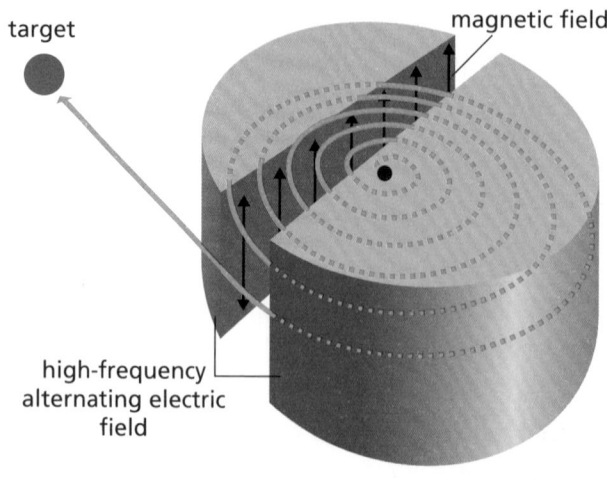

The synchrocyclotron adjusts the frequency to compensate for relativity effects and allow particles to accelerate to very high velocities.

The synchrotron adjusts the strength of the magnetic field to keep the particles moving in phase to adjust for relativity effects.

The Large Hadron Collider is a circular accelerator, 27 km in circumference, built by CERN on the Swiss-French border near Geneva to accelerate particles up to energies of 7 TeV.

- Linear accelerators accelerated charged particles in a straight line.
- Circular accelerators (cyclotrons, synchrocyclotrons and synchrotrons) accelerate charged particles in circular paths.

Mass-energy conversions

Antiparticles

The first antiparticle was discovered by Anderson in cosmic rays in 1932. He found a particle with the same mass as the electron but with a positive electric charge. This positive electron is the positron.

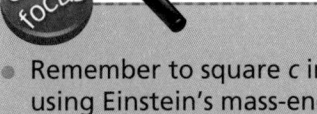

exam focus

- Remember to square c in using Einstein's mass-energy equation $E = mc^2$
- Remember to convert energy measured in eV values into joules.
- Don't confuse mass-energy with kinetic energy.

Converting energy into mass: pair production

Electron-positron pairs are produced when high-energy photons pass close to a nucleus – this is another example of mass-energy equivalence. The photon disappears and is replaced by two particles of equal mass and charge moving in opposite directions.

$$\gamma \rightarrow e^- + e^+$$

This process is called pair production.

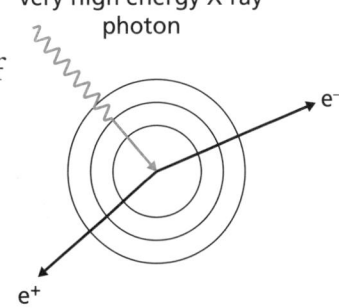

very high energy X-ray photon

Pair production

Annihilation

When an electron and a positron meet they annihilate each other and are replaced by two photons moving in opposite directions.

$$e^- + e^+ \rightarrow \gamma + \gamma$$

We have already calculated the mass-energy of the electron-positron pair to be 1.02 MeV. As this produces 2 γ ray photons the energy of each photon must be 0.51 Mev.

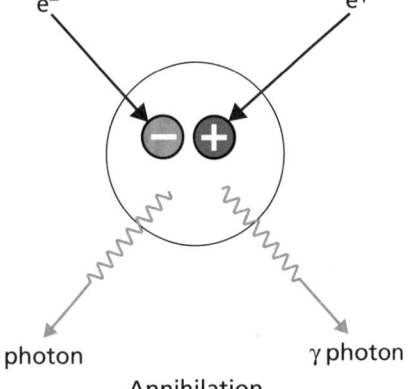

γ photon   γ photon

Annihilation

Antiprotons

It takes considerably more energy to produce a proton-antiproton pair because the mass of a proton is nearly 2,000 times that of an electron.

When a proton meets an antiproton they produce strange particles that in turn decay into other particles.

Proton + antiproton → pion and antipion

$$p^+ + p^- \rightarrow \pi^+ + \pi^-$$

High-energy collisions

High-energy cosmic rays colliding with particles in the earth's atmosphere produce many strange particles such as the 'pion'.

Pions are formed when high-energy protons in the cosmic rays collide. The pion is a very short-lived particle and decays into another strange particle (a muon μ) and a neutrino in about 10^{-8} of a second.

Proton-proton collisions

Scientists artificially produced many strange particles with high-energy electron or proton collisions in accelerators. These particles are identical to the particles produced in cosmic rays.

Einstein's mass-energy equation works both ways – mass changes into energy but energy can also change into mass. When high-energy protons collide, some of the enormous energy changes into mass.

> **key point**
> - Pair production is the conversion of energy into mass.
> - Pair annihilation is the conversion of mass into energy.

Many other strange particles (with lifetimes of 10^{-6} to 10^{-20} seconds) are produced in high-energy proton collisions.

$p^+ + p^+ \rightarrow p^+ + p^+ + (p^+ + p^-)$:	proton-antiproton pair produced
$p^+ + p^+ \rightarrow p^+ + p^+ + \pi^0$:	neutral pion produced
$p^+ + p^+ \rightarrow d^+ + \pi^+$:	deuteron (proton-neutron combination) and pion produced
$p^+ + p^+ \rightarrow p^+ + \Sigma^+ + K^0$:	proton, sigma baryon and kaon (K meson) produced

Fundamental forces of nature

There are four fundamental forces in nature:

- The strong nuclear force
- The weak nuclear force
- The electromagnetic force
- The gravitational force

Electromagnetic and gravitational forces are easy to observe and have been known for a long time. They have an effect at a great distance and cause many of the forces we see in everyday life.

Strong and weak nuclear forces were not discovered until the twentieth century. These forces act on subatomic particles and only work at very short-range subatomic distances.

Force	Relative Strength	Range	Purpose
Strong nuclear force	1 Very strong	Very short distances	Holds proton and neutrons together in nucleus
Electromagnetic force	10^{-2} 100 times weaker than strong nuclear force	Extends over great distances; obeys inverse square law	Holds atoms and molecules together
Weak nuclear force	10^{-13} Weaker than electromagnetic	Very short distances	Involved in beta particle decay
Gravitational force	10^{-40} Weakest of fundamental forces	Extends over enormous distances; obeys inverse square law	Holds universe together

The ultimate structure of matter?

Matter seems to be built from two groups of particles – hadrons (nuclear particles) and leptons (non-nuclear particles).

Leptons are indivisible and are fundamental particles. Hadrons are divided into baryons ('heavy' particles) and mesons (intermediate particles).

- Baryons are a combination of three quarks.
- Mesons are a combination of a quark and an antiquark.
- The best-known baryons are protons and neutrons, and the best-known mesons are pions and kaons.

Quarks

Murray Gell-Mann and George Zweig proposed a model that reduced all the heavy particles to combinations of three fundamental particles – Gell-Mann named the particles 'quarks'.

The three-quark model was soon found to be inadequate and was rapidly extended to six quarks (and six antiquarks). The quarks are named Up, Down, Strange, Charmed, Bottom and Top.

Quarks have a fractional electric charge – some have $\frac{1}{3}$ electron charge, other have $\frac{2}{3}$ electron charge.

Quark	Charge	Antiquark	Charge
Up (u)	$+\frac{2}{3}$	Up ($\bar{u}$)	$-\frac{2}{3}$
Down (d)	$-\frac{1}{3}$	Down ($\bar{d}$)	$+\frac{1}{3}$
Strange (s)	$-\frac{1}{3}$	Strange ($\bar{s}$)	$+\frac{1}{3}$
Charmed (c)	$+\frac{2}{3}$	Charmed ($\bar{c}$)	$-\frac{2}{3}$
Bottom (b)	$-\frac{1}{3}$	Bottom ($\bar{b}$)	$+\frac{1}{3}$
Top (t)	$+\frac{2}{3}$	Top ($\bar{t}$)	$-\frac{2}{3}$

All heavy particles are combinations of quarks.

Baryons are combinations of three quarks. Mesons are a quark-antiquark pair.

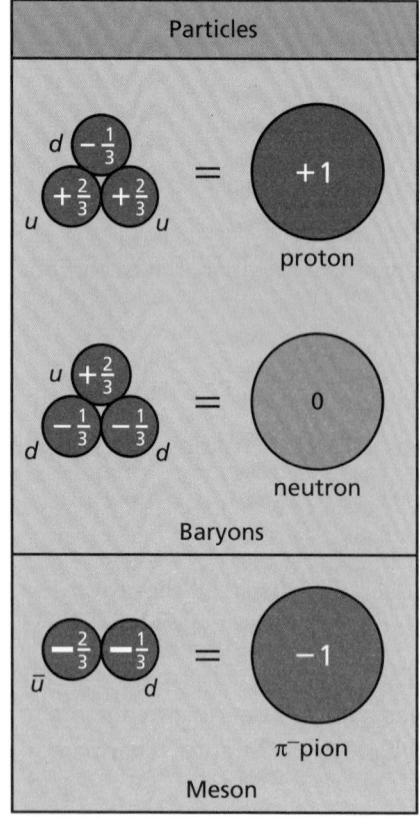

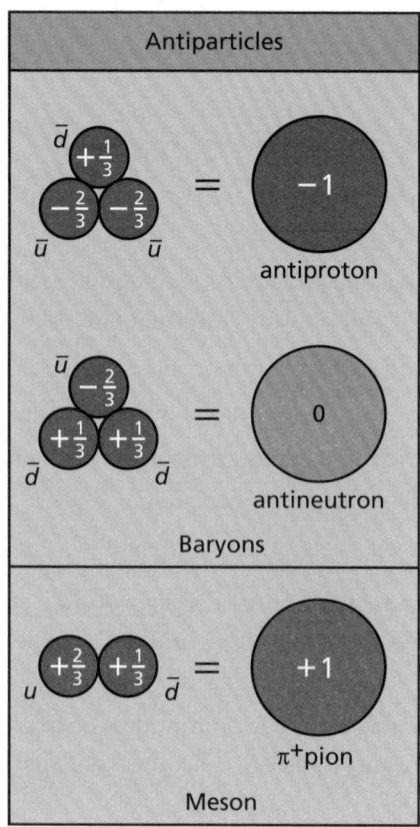

Matter is now seen as made up of leptons and baryons. Leptons are fundamental particles and are not subject to the strong nuclear force.

Baryons and mesons are all composed of quarks. The fundamental particles are six quarks and also six leptons.

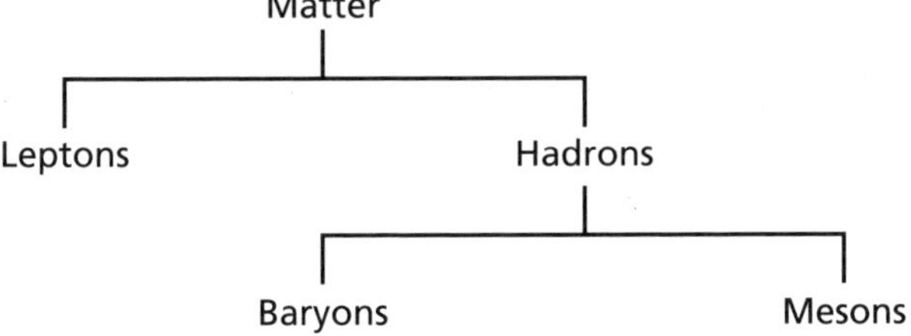

FAQs

Compare the properties of an electron with those of a positron.
Their masses are equal and their charges are equal but opposite in sign.

What happens when an electron meets a positron?
Annihilation with the emission of energy in the form of gamma rays.

Give one advantage of circular particle accelerators over linear accelerators.
Circular accelerators are more compact and the energy of the particles is progressively increased.

Name the three positively charged quarks.
Up, Top, Charmed.

Give the quark composition of a proton.
Up, Up, Down.

Give the quark composition of a neutron.
Up, Down, Down.

A kaon consists of a Strange quark and an Up antiquark. What type of hadron is a kaon?
A meson.

What is the difference in the quark composition of a baryon and a meson?
A baryon is composed of three quarks, a meson of one quark and one antiquark.

Arrange the fundamental forces of nature in increasing order of strength.
Gravitational, weak nuclear, electromagnetic, strong nuclear.

Give the range of each of the fundamental forces of nature.
Strong nuclear – short range (10^{-15}m), weak nuclear – short range (10^{-18}m), gravitational – infinite, electromagnetic – infinite.

Name the fundamental force of nature that holds the nucleus together.
Strong nuclear.

Name the three negatively charged leptons.

Electron (e), muon (μ) and tau (τ).

The existence of the neutrino was proposed in 1930 but it was not detected until 1956. Give two reasons why it is difficult to detect a neutrino.

The neutrino is uncharged, has very small (almost zero) mass and interacts weakly with matter.

Explain why high voltages can be used to accelerate alpha-particles and protons but not neutrons.

Alpha-particles and protons are charged but neutrons are not charged.

In an accelerator, two high-speed protons collide and a series of new particles is produced, in addition to the two original protons. Explain why new particles are produced.

The kinetic energy of the protons is converted into the mass of the new particles.

In beta decay it appeared that momentum was not conserved. How did Fermi's theory of radioactive decay resolve this?

By suggesting the emission of a neutrino that had the missing energy and momentum. The neutrino was theorised by Pauli in 1930 but was not discovered until 1956.

Exam questions

2009 Higher level question 10 (a)

In 1932 Cockcroft and Walton succeeded in splitting lithium nuclei by bombarding them with artificially accelerated protons using a linear accelerator. Each time a lithium nucleus was split a pair of alpha-particles was produced.

Q: How were the protons accelerated?
A: By a high voltage.

Q: How were the alpha-particles detected?
A: By observing flashes of light (scintillations) on a zinc sulphide screen.

Q: Write a nuclear equation to represent the splitting of a lithium nucleus by a proton.
A: $^{7}_{3}\text{Li} + ^{1}_{1}\text{H} \rightarrow ^{4}_{2}\text{He} + ^{4}_{2}\text{He}$

Q: Calculate the energy released in this reaction.
A: Loss in mass:
(mass of Li nucleus + mass of proton) − (mass of two alpha-particles)
$(1.33186 \times 10^{-26}) - (1.32894 \times 10^{-26})$
2.92×10^{-29} kg
Energy released: $E = mc^2$
$E = (2.92 \times 10^{-29})(2.9979 \times 10^{8})^2$
2.6×10^{-12} J

Q: Most of the accelerated protons did not split a lithium nucleus. Explain why.
A: Many of the protons did not collide with the lithium nucleus as the atom is mostly empty space.

Cockcroft and Walton's apparatus is now displayed at CERN in Switzerland, where very high energy protons are used in the Large Hadron Collider. In the Large Hadron Collider, two beams of protons are accelerated to high energies in a circular accelerator. The two beams of protons then collide, producing new particles. Each proton in the beams has a kinetic energy of 2.0 GeV.

Q: Explain why new particles are formed.
A: The kinetic energy of the protons is changed into mass.

Q: What is the maximum net mass of the new particles created per collision?
A: Total energy of the proton-proton collision is the energy of the two protons:
$2 \times 2 \text{ GeV} = 4 \text{ GeV}$
Maximum mass created is the mass equivalent of 4GeV

$$m = \frac{E}{c^2}$$

$$m = \frac{(4 \times 10^9)(1.6 \times 10^{-19})}{(2.9979 \times 10^8)^2}$$

$$= \frac{6.4 \times 10^{-10}}{8.9874 \times 10^{16}}$$

$$= 7.121 \times 10^{-27} \text{ kg}$$

Q: What is the advantage of using circular particle accelerators in particle physics?
A: Circular accelerators are more compact, the energy of the particles is progressively increased and greater particle speeds can be achieved.
(mass of alpha-particle $= 6.6447 \times 10^{-27}$ kg; mass of proton $= 1.6726 \times 10^{-27}$ kg; mass of lithium nucleus $= 1.1646 \times 10^{-26}$ kg; speed of light $= 2.9979 \times 10^8$ m s^{-1}; charge on electron $= 1.6022 \times 10^{-19}$ C)

2008 Higher level question 10 (a) (part)

In a circular accelerator, two protons, each with a kinetic energy of 1 GeV, travelling in opposite directions, collide.
After the collision two protons and three pions are emitted.
Q: What is the net charge of the three pions?
A: Zero.

Q: Justify your answer.
A: Electric charge is conserved in reactions.

Q: Calculate:

(i) The combined kinetic energy of the particles after the collision

A: Using conservation of mass-energy:

Mass-energy before collision equals mass-energy after collision

Mass-energy before collision: $2 p_+ + 2\text{GeV}$

Mass-energy after collision: $2p_+ + 3$ pions + K.E.

$$2\,\text{GeV} = 3 \text{ pions} + \text{K.E.}$$

energy equivalent of mass of one pion:

$$E = m\,c^2$$
$$= (2.4842 \times 10^{-28})(2.9979 \times 10^8)^2$$
$$= 2.2327 \times 10^{-11}\,\text{J}$$

For three pions:

$$E = 6.6980 \times 10^{-11}\,\text{J}$$

$$2\,\text{GeV} = (2 \times 10^9) \times (1.6022 \times 10^{-19})\,\text{J}$$

$$\text{K.E.} = 2\,\text{GeV} - 3 \text{ pions}$$
$$= 3.2044 \times 10^{-10} - 6.6980 \times 10^{-11}$$
$$= 2.535 \times 10^{-10}\,\text{J}$$

(ii) The maximum number of pions that could have been created during the collision

A: If all the K.E. was converted into mass:

Number of pions equivalent to K.E.

$$= \frac{2.535 \times 10^{-10}}{2.2327 \times 10^{-11}}$$
$$= 11.35$$

Maximum number of pions from K.E. = 11 pions

Maximum number of pions = $11 + 3 = 14$

(charge on electron = 1.6022×10^{-19} C; mass of proton = 1.6726×10^{-27} kg; mass of pion = 2.4842×10^{-28} kg; speed of light = 2.9979×108 m s^{-1})

2006 Higher level question 10 (a) (part)

Q: A neutral pion is unstable with a decay constant of 2.5×10^{12} s^{-1}. What is the half-life of a neutral pion?

A: $\lambda T_{\frac{1}{2}} = \ln 2 = 0.693$

$$T_{\frac{1}{2}} = \frac{0.693}{2.5 \times 10^{12}}$$
$$T_{\frac{1}{2}} = 2.772 \times 10^{-13}\,\text{s}$$

2007 Higher level question 10 (a) (part)

Q: (i) Draw a labelled diagram to show how Cockcroft and Walton accelerated the protons.

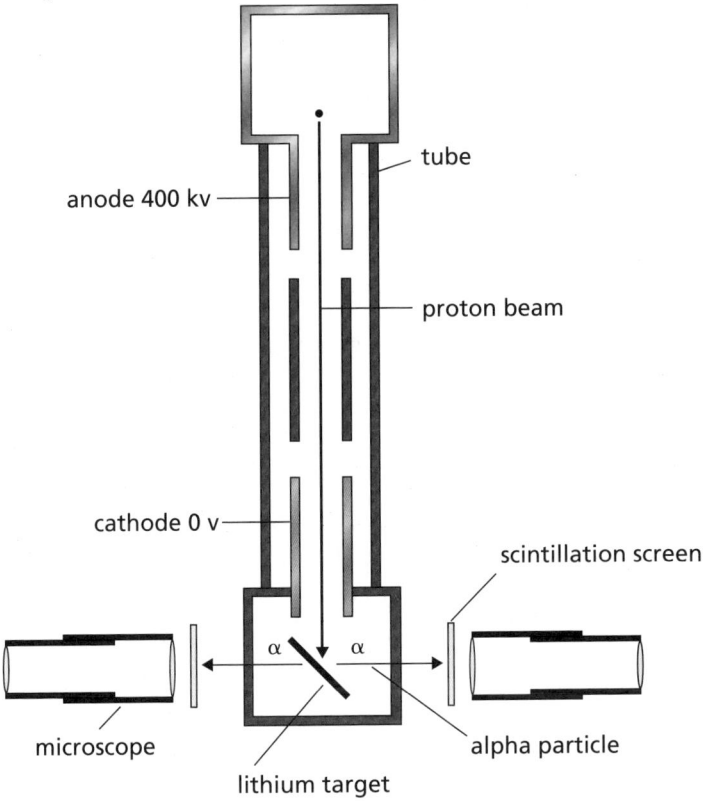

A: Labels: anode, cathode, lithium target, two alpha particles (helium nuclei).

Q: What is the velocity of a proton when it is accelerated from rest through a potential difference of 700 kV?

A: $W = qV$

$$= (1.6022 \times 10^{-19})(7.00 \times 10^5)$$

$$W = \frac{1}{2}mv^2$$

$$v^2 = \frac{2W}{m}$$

$$= \frac{2(1.6022 \times 10^{-19})(7.00 \times 10^5)}{1.6726 \times 10^{-27}}$$

$$= 1.341 \times 10^{14}$$

$$v = 1.16 \times 10^7 \text{ m s}^{-1}$$

(charge on electron = 1.6022×10^{-19} C; mass of proton = 1.6726×10^{-27} kg)

17 Option 2 – Applied Electricity

Note: Chapter 17 is for Higher Level students only.

 To learn:
- Definitions and formulae for applied electricity
- How to answer FAQs on applied electricity
- How to solve problems involving applied electricity

Definitions and formulae

Electromagnetic relay

- An electromagnetic relay is a device that enables a small current in one circuit to switch on (or off) a large current in an adjoining circuit.
- Lights and heated windows in a car are all switched on using electromagnetic relays.

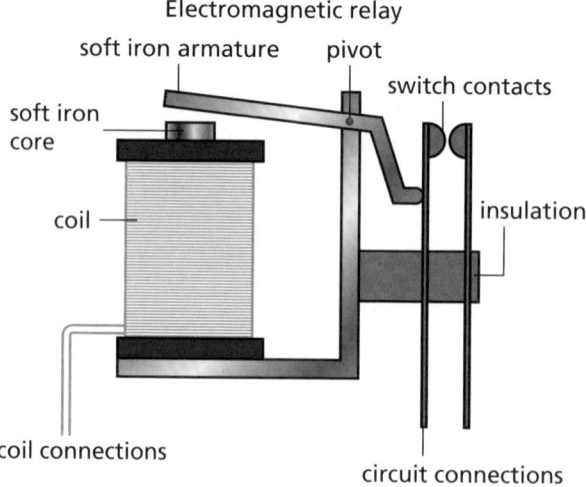

Electromagnetic relay

soft iron armature   pivot

switch contacts

soft iron core

coil

insulation

coil connections

circuit connections

 key point

The basic principle of the D.C. Motor, the Moving Coil Loudspeaker and the Moving Coil Meter is that a current-carrying conductor in a magnetic field experiences a force.

Simple d.c. motor

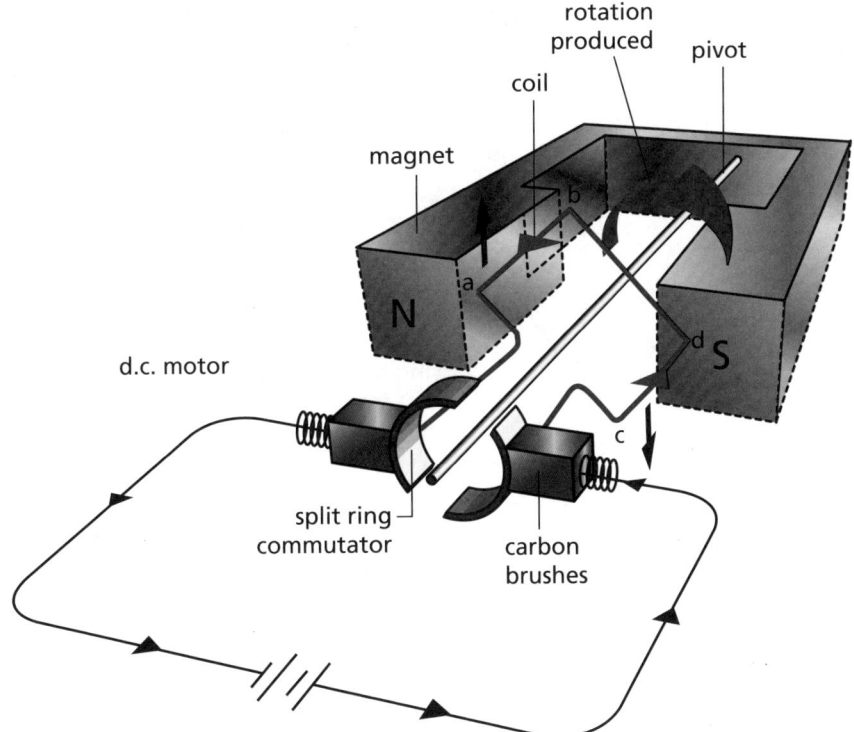

When a current flows through the coil, one side experiences an upward force, the other a downward force that causes the coil to rotate.

- The coil is wound on a frame of laminated soft iron between concave magnetic poles, which gives a concentrated radial magnetic field.
- The brushes enable current to enter the coil while still allowing the coil to rotate.
- The commutator causes the current in the coil to change direction every half turn so that the torque is always in the same direction.
- As the coil rotates the magnetic flux cutting it changes, producing a back emf (Lenz's law), which slows down the motor to a steady speed.
- Simple d.c. motors are used in tape recorders, video recorders, automatic cameras and starter motors in cars.

Loudspeakers

When current flows the coil experiences a force that causes the cone to move at the frequency of the current.

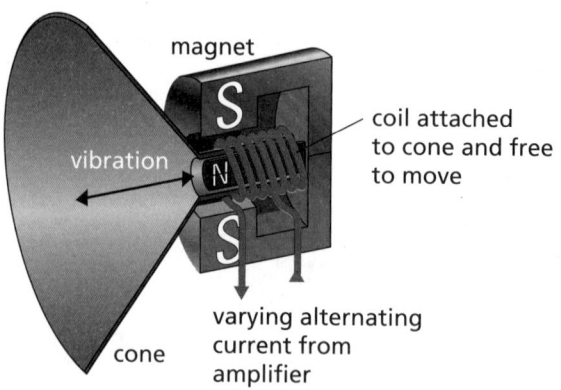

Moving coil meters

The current to and from the coil goes through hairsprings causing a couple, which turns the coil.

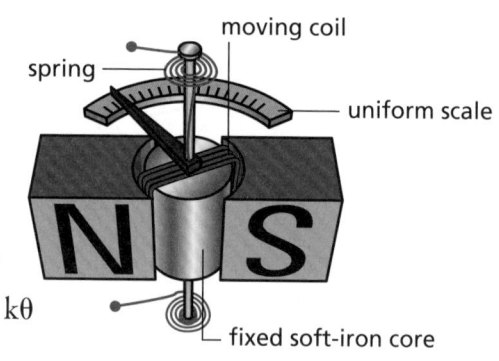

- The spring produces an opposing couple, which depends on the spring constant k and the angle θ through which it turns.
- The couple produced by the coil $= nIAB$
  The opposing couple due to the spring $= k\theta$
  When the pointer is at rest $nIAB = k\theta$
  As n, B, A and k are constants $I \propto \theta$

A sensitive galvanometer that produces a large angular deflection (θ) for a small current is made by using:

- A strong magnet, B is large
- A coil of many turns, n is big
- A coil of large area, a is large
- A weak spring, k is small

Damping

The coil of the galvanometer is wound on an aluminium frame. The frame produces a 'back' emf when it cuts through the magnetic field and slows down the coil.

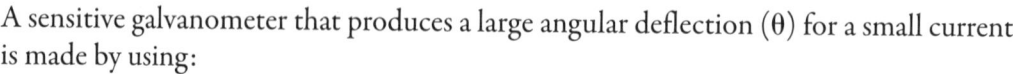

Ammeter

A galvanometer is converted to an ammeter by connecting a small resistance in parallel with it.

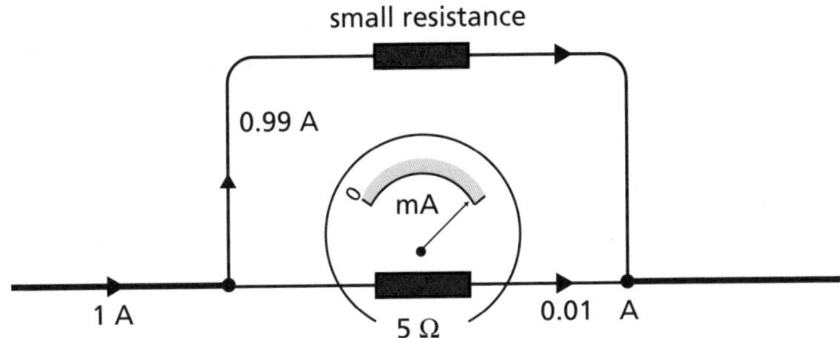

The parallel resistor is called a 'shunt' resistance. In theory, the resistance of the ammeter should be zero. In practice the resistance of the ammeter is as small as possible.

Voltmeter

A galvanometer is converted to a voltmeter by connecting a large resistance in series. In theory, the resistance of the voltmeter should be infinitely large and so allow no current through the voltmeter. In practice it is as large as possible.

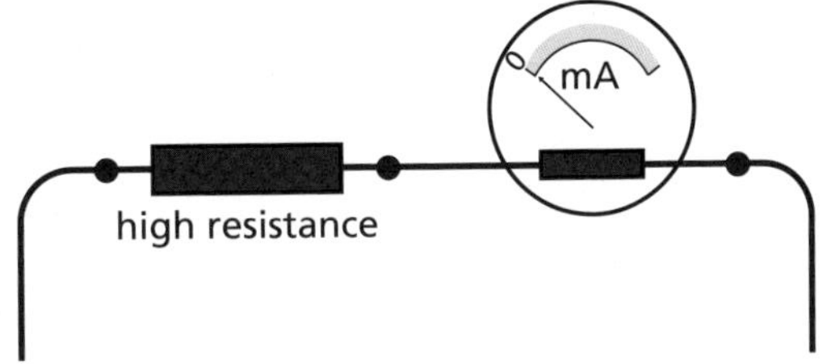

To convert a galvanometer to a voltmeter

Limitations of moving coil meters

- The moving coil galvanometer cannot measure alternating current (a.c.).
- Only small currents can be measured directly because of the fine wire in the coil.

Ohmmeter

A galvanometer is converted to an ohmmeter by connecting a dry cell (1.5 V) in series with resistor R_s. The series resistor is necessary to ensure that a big current does not flow through the galvanometer.

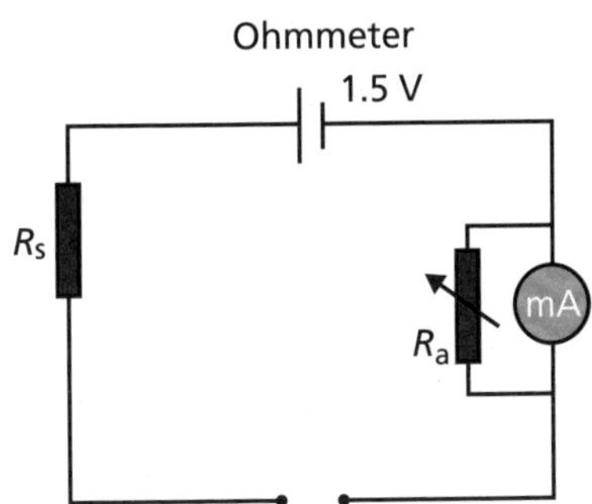

There is also an adjusting resistor R_a that allows you to compensate for changes in the emf of the battery as it ages.

The ohmmeter scale is not linear and it is not an accurate instrument, often having an error of 10%.

Ohmmeters are used:

- To test a circuit for continuity – to ensure that there are no breaks in a circuit
- To get approximate values of resistances

The induction coil

An induction coil is a device that steps up low voltage **d.c.** to high voltage **d.c.**
The induction coil was invented at Maynooth in 1836 by Nicholas Callan.

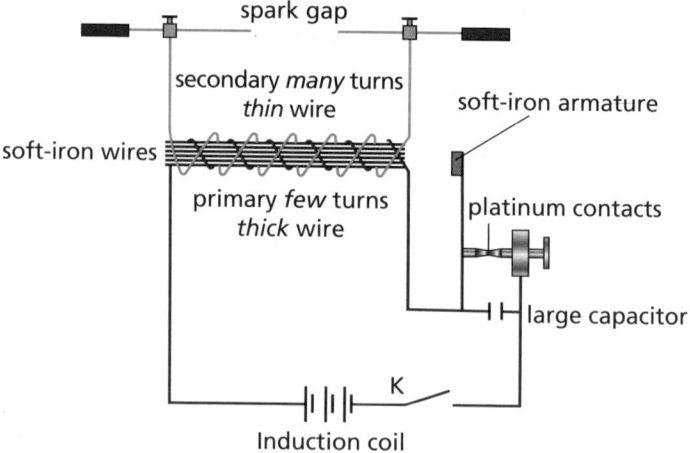

Induction coil

How the induction coil works

- When the switch is closed current flows through the primary coil. This causes a magnetic field, which cuts the secondary coil.
- It also magnetises the core, which attracts the armature breaking the circuit and causing the magnetic field to collapse.
- This rapid change in the field cutting the secondary coil induces a large emf in the secondary coil, which can cause sparks several centimetres long across the gap.

What does the capacitor do?

The 'back' emf in the primary coil charges the capacitor. This takes the energy from the circuit so sparking at the contacts is stopped.

Uses of induction coil

An induction coil is used in the ignition system of a car and in an electric fence.

The a.c. generator

As the coil is rotated the magnetic flux cutting the coil is continually changing and an emf is induced. The emf from a generator is increased by:

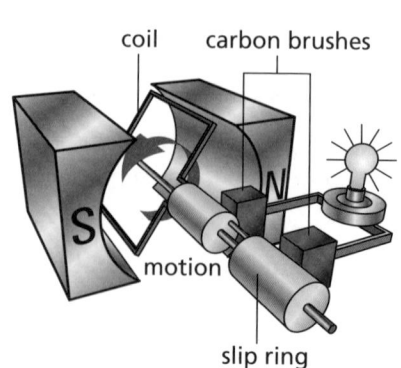

- Using a strong magnet (or electromagnet)
- Using a laminated soft iron core to produce a large magnetic flux density
- Using a large number of turns of wire in the armature
- Increasing the speed of rotation

key point

- In a generator or a motor the current in the coil is always alternating.
- For d.c. in the outside circuit a split ring commutator is used.
- For a.c. in the outside circuit slip rings are used.

Induction effects in metals

When a motor or dynamo moves, the soft iron core of the armature cuts through the magnetic flux. This induces an emf in the core and causes currents (called eddy currents) to flow. If the core is made of one piece, the induced currents flow through the resistance of the core material and produce much heat ($H = I^2Rt$). This effect is prevented by making the core of sheets, or laminations, of soft iron that are electrically insulated from each other. The current induced in each sheet is small and so the heat loss due to eddy currents is small.

Efficiency of transformers

If the transformer is 100% efficient:

Power of primary circuit = power of secondary coil

$V_i . I_i = V_o . I_o$

An efficient transformer has:

- Low resistance coils to reduce heating losses
- Closely wound primary and secondary coils to ensure that all the magnetic flux links the coils
- Laminated core to (a) produce total linkage of magnetic flux and (b) reduce eddy current losses
- Core of soft magnetic material to ensure small energy losses in bringing about the constant changes in the magnetic field.

Most transformers have efficiencies in excess of 99%.

Some practical uses of induction effects

The induction furnace, damping in moving coil meters and balances.

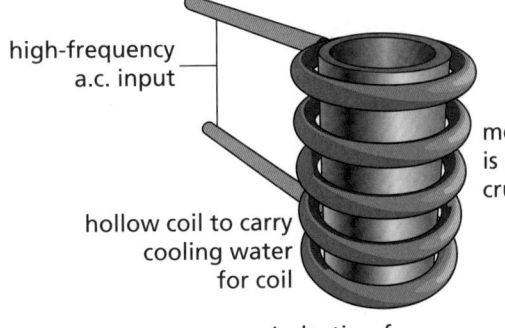

high-frequency a.c. input

metal to be melted is placed inside this crucible

hollow coil to carry cooling water for coil

Induction furnace

Principle of the induction motor

The rotating magnet induces a current in the copper disc. The disc begins to rotate in the same direction as the magnet and so reduces the relative motion between disc and magnet (the induced current opposes the change causing it). This principle is used in a car speedometer.

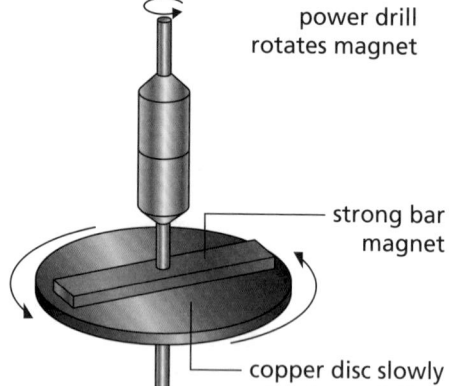

Principle of induction motor

power drill rotates magnet

strong bar magnet

copper disc slowly accelerates to follow the magnet

pivot

The simple induction motor

The simple induction motor consists of a rotor that moves and a fixed stator. This is mounted on a free-moving axle. The rotor consists of a cylinder of copper with a core of iron. This is mounted on a shaft and is free to rotate. Around this is fitted a stator. The stator consists of two electromagnets set at right angles to each other and around the rotor. The magnetic field produced by the two electromagnets appears to rotate around the rotor for each complete cycle of the a.c. – in effect, a rotating magnetic flux sweeping round the stator. The rotor attempts to eliminate the relative motion between itself and the rotating magnetic flux by rotating in the same direction. This induces the rotor to spin at the same rate.

key point

- The basic principle of motors, loudspeakers and meters is that a current-carrying conductor in a magnetic field experiences a force.
- The basic principle of generators, transformers and induction coils is that an emf is induced whenever the magnetic flux cutting a conductor changes.

Semiconductors

Applications of the diode: rectification

When a.c. is connected to a diode, the diode is forward-biased when the a.c. voltage is positive and current flows through the diode. When the a.c. voltage is negative the diode is reverse-biased and current does not flow. This is half-wave rectification. The output flows in one direction only and so is direct current. A rectifier changes a.c. to d.c.

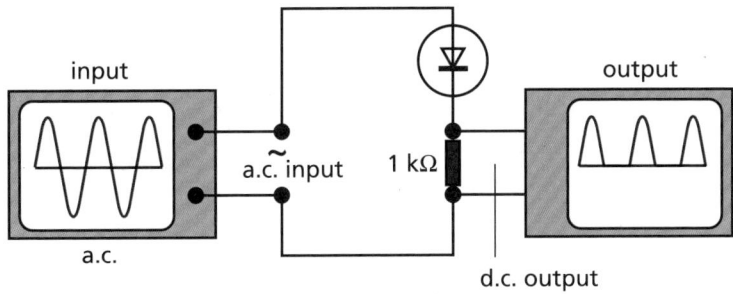

Half-wave rectifier

Bridge rectifier: full-wave rectification

A bridge rectifier, or full-wave rectifier, is an arrangement of four diodes. This allows a flow of current for the complete a.c. cycle. The addition of a smoothing circuit of an inductor and a capacitor converts the varying d.c. output to smooth d.c.

Light-emitting diode (LED)

- The LED gives off light when electricity passes through the p-n junction.
- The maximum current an LED can safely pass is very small (about 50 mA) and the forward voltage is about 2.0 V. A series resistor is required to keep the current below the maximum value.

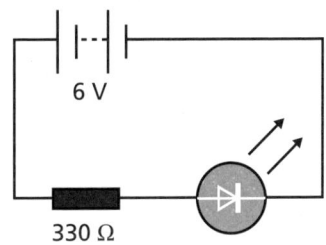

Uses of LEDs

LEDs are used as a light source, as current on/off indicators, as the numerical display in some calculators and as part of an optical switch. The LED is better than filament bulbs because of:

- Their small size
- The very small current required to operate them
- Their long life
- The fast speed at which they operate

Photodiode

The photodiode is a reverse bias diode that conducts only when light falls on the p-n junction.

It consists of a p-n junction with a 'window' that exposes the junction to light.

The photodiode is operated in reverse bias. When light energy falls on the junction, electrons and 'holes' are produced in the semiconductor. This increases the current in proportion to the intensity of the light falling on it.

Optical switch

This consists of an LED and a photodiode. When current flows through the LED it emits light. The light falls on the photodiode. Current flows through the photodiode and completes the circuit.

Optical switches have many applications. They are used as safety guards in machines, end-of-tape indicators in tape recorders, out-of-paper controls in printers and as smoke alarms.

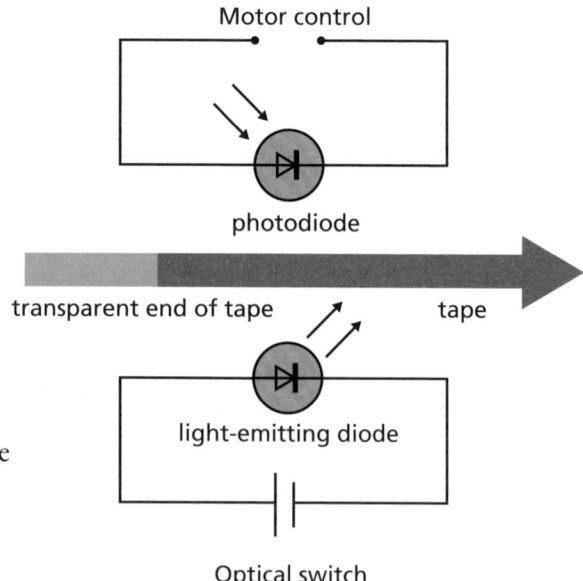

Motor control

photodiode

transparent end of tape   tape

light-emitting diode

Optical switch

Transistors

Bipolar transistor

There are two p-n junctions in the transistor.

npn transistor

symbol	currents	
collector +	collector current	c ┬ +
base current		
base		b ⎯⎯ p-type base
		n
		n
− emitter	emitter current	e ┃ −
		n-type emitter sends electrons through the base to the collector

The transistor operates with:

- The emitter-base junction forward-biased
- The base-collector junction reverse-biased

How the transistor works

Once the voltage across the forward-biased emitter-base junction is greater than 0.6 V, electrons flow from the emitter into the base. Since the base is very thin the electrons do not have to go very far to be attracted by the positive voltage on the collector. In this way most of the electrons flowing from the emitter reach the collector (even though the base-collector junction is negatively-biased). About 99% of the electrons flowing from the emitter to the base reach the collector. Once the emitter-base voltage falls below 0.6 V the current is cut off.

- The transistor can be switched on and off by the base voltage.
- The base voltage controls the base current, which in turn controls the collector current.
- The amplification factor or 'gain' of the transistor is k: $I_c = k I_b$.
- $I_e = I_c + I_b$

Transistor as a switch

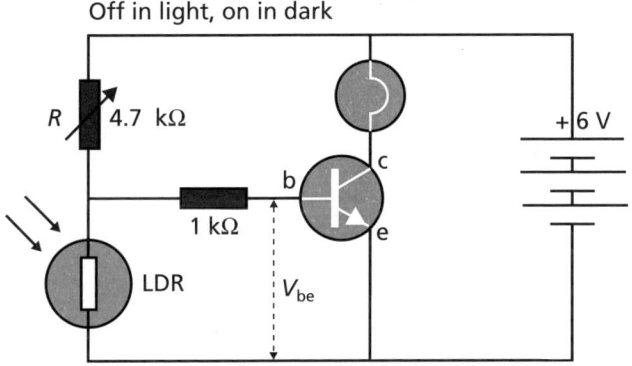

Off in light, on in dark

Load resistor

The load resistor R_L converts large changes in the collector current to large changes in the voltage across R_L.

Bias resistor

The bias resistor is a large series resistor that limits the base current I_b to a safe value. It sets a suitable base voltage and keeps the base-emitter junction forward-biased.

- If the output voltage is taken across R_L, the transistor acts as a **voltage amplifier.**

- If the output is taken across the transistor, as in the following diagram, the transistor acts as a **voltage inverter** so the voltage is both **amplified and inverted.**

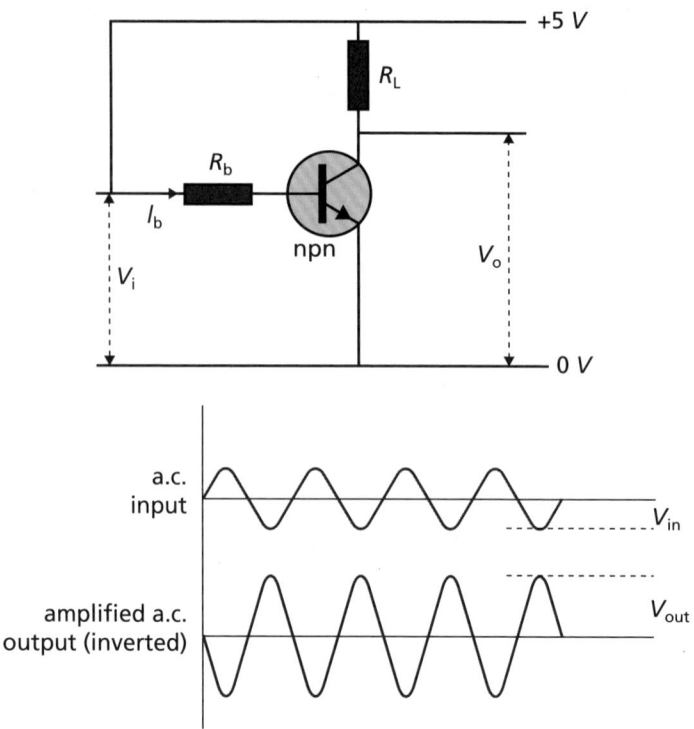

Logic gates

- Logic gate: A device that gives an output signal only when certain conditions are met in the input signal.
- AND gate: A circuit where there is an output only when BOTH inputs are ON.

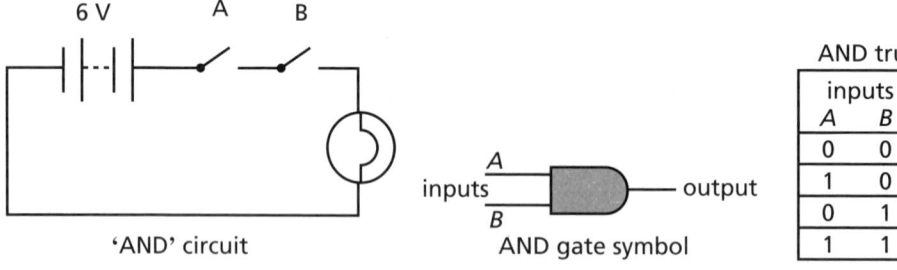

'AND' circuit

AND gate symbol

AND truth table

inputs		output
A	B	
0	0	0
1	0	0
0	1	0
1	1	1

- OR gate: A circuit where there is an output when EITHER input is ON.

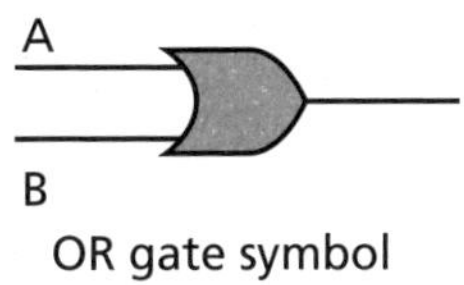

OR gate symbol

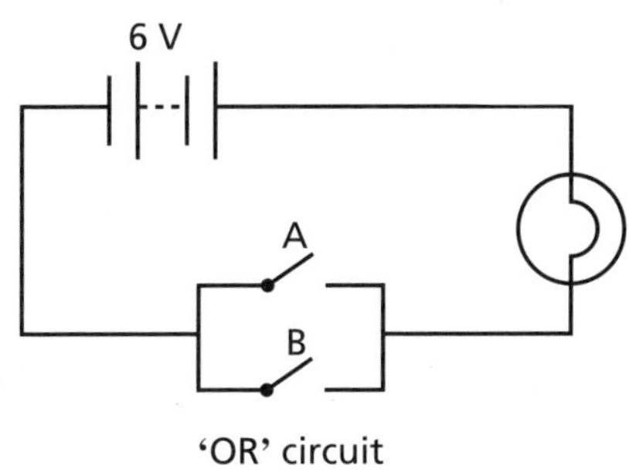

'OR' circuit

OR truth table

inputs		output
A	B	
0	0	0
1	0	1
0	1	1
1	1	1

- NOT gate: A circuit where there is an output only when the input is OFF.
- The voltage inverter acts as a NOT gate. When the input is high, the output is low and when the input is low, the output is high.
- All the sorting, processing, control and other functions in digital computers are carried out by semiconductor logic gates built into the integrated circuits.

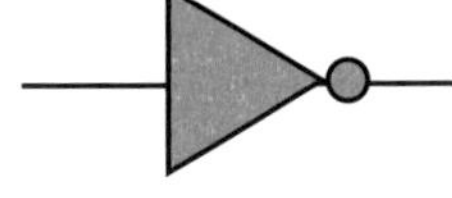

NOT gate symbol

NOT truth table

inputs	output
0	1
1	0

AND, OR and NOT gates are in practice made as integrated circuits (ICs) with connections for inputs, power supply and output.

FAQs

What is the function of a commutator in a d.c. motor?
To let the current in the coil change direction every half turn so that the torque is always in the same direction.

What is the function of the brushes in an electric motor?
To enable current to enter the coil while still allowing the coil to rotate.

What is the function of the magnet in an electric motor?
To provide a magnetic field so that the current-carrying conductor experiences a force that moves the coil.

What is the main energy conversion that takes place in an electric motor?
Electrical energy to kinetic energy.

Why does the motor turn when current flows through the coil?
Because a current-carrying conductor in a magnetic field experiences a force.

What is the function of a moving coil galvanometer?
A galvanometer measures very small currents. It can also show the direction of the current.

Why does the magnet in a moving coil galvanometer have curved pole faces?
To give a radial magnetic field and a uniform scale.

How can a galvanometer be converted into a voltmeter?
By connecting a large resistance in series.

Draw a diagram to show how a galvanometer can be converted into an ammeter.

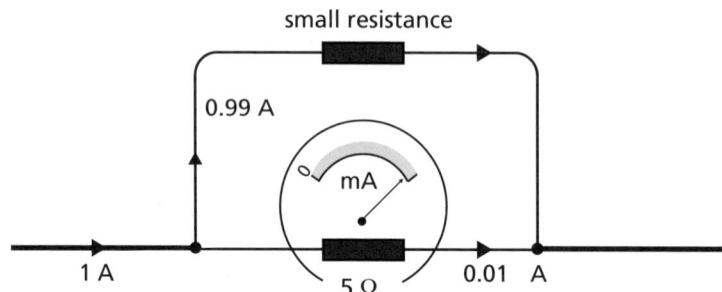

How would you convert a galvanometer to an ohmmeter?
Connect it in series with a battery and a rheostat.

How are the slip rings connected to an external circuit in an a.c. generator?
By means of metal or carbon brushes.

What is the function of an induction coil?
To change low voltage d.c. to high voltage d.c.

Why are both coils wrapped on the same soft iron core?
To maximise flux linkage for greater efficiency.

Name the three currents flowing in a transistor and give the relationship between them.

The emitter, base and collector currents. $I_e = I_c + I_b$.

Draw the basic structure of a bipolar transistor.

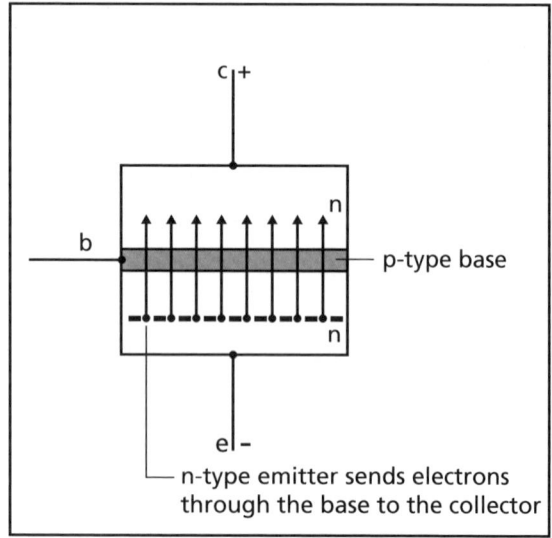

What is the significance of the work of George Boole in modern-day electronics?
He developed Boolean algebra, which is the basis of the logic used in logic gates.

Draw the truth table for the AND gate.

Name the Irish physicist who invented the induction coil.
Nicholas Callan.

AND truth table

inputs		output
A	B	
0	0	0
1	0	0
0	1	0
1	1	1

Exam questions

2005 Higher level question 11 (b) (part)

Q: (i) List three factors that affect the force on a current-carrying conductor placed near a magnet.
A: Magnetic flux density (B), current (I), length (l), sin θ.
(iv) Draw a sketch of the output voltage from an a.c. generator.
A: voltage

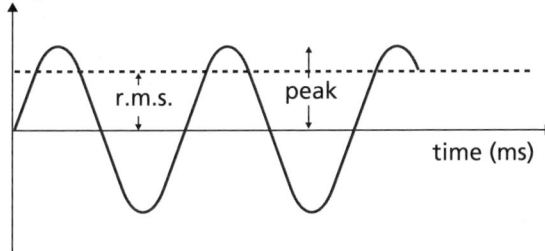

(vi) A transformer and an induction coil can both be used to change a small voltage into a larger voltage. What is the basic difference in the operation of these two devices?
A: **Transformer:** A transformer operates on a.c. The input and output voltages are a.c. Current flows through the output coil.
Induction coil: An induction coil operates on d.c. The input and output voltages are d.c. High voltage sparks jump across the gap in the secondary coil.
Q: Give two factors that affect the efficiency of a transformer.
A: Heat losses (I^2R) in coils due to eddy currents in the core, poor flux linkage, resistance of the coil.

2008 Higher level question 10 (b) (part)

Q: The transistor was one of the most important inventions of the twentieth century.
The diagram shows the circuit of a voltage amplifier.

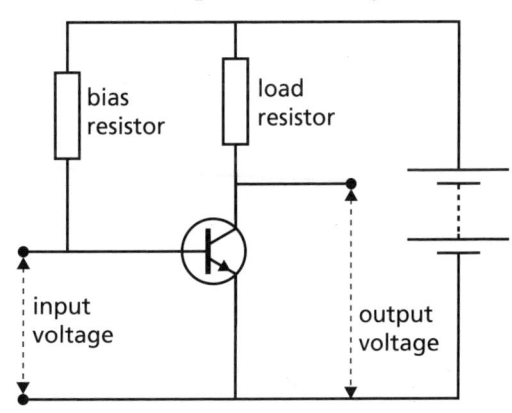

What is the purpose of:

(i) The bias resistor

A: The bias resistor is a large series resistor that sets the base voltage V_b, which limits the base current I_b to a safe value. It ensures that the base-emitter junction is forward-biased.

(ii) The load resistor

A: It converts large changes in the collector current (I_c) to large changes in the voltage across it.

$$[V = I_c R]$$

Q: A varying voltage is applied to the amplifier. Draw a sketch of the input and output voltages, using the same axes and scales.

A:

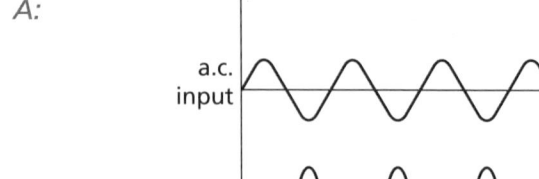

a.c. input ... V_{in}

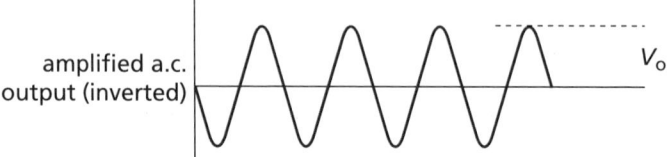

amplified a.c. output (inverted) ... V_{out}

Q: A NOT gate is a voltage inverter. Draw a circuit diagram to show how a transistor can be used as a voltage inverter.

A:

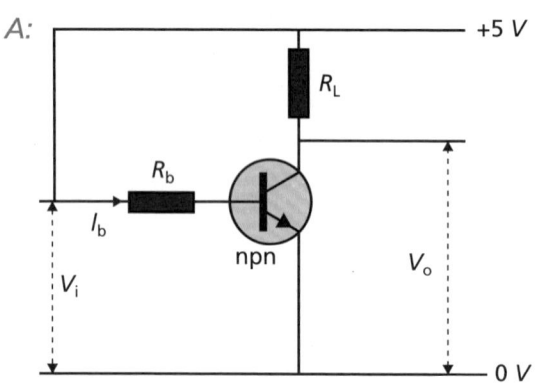

Q: Give the truth table of a NOT gate.

A: NOT truth table

inputs	output
0	1
1	0

2007 Higher level question 10 (b) (part)

Principle of induction motor

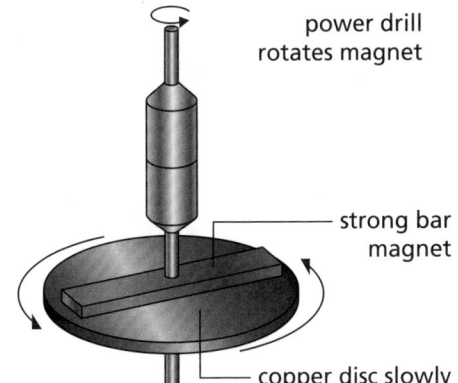

Q: The induction motor was invented by Nicholas Tesla. Give an advantage of an induction motor over a d.c. motor.

A: There are no brushes so there is no sparking and less friction.

A constant rate of rotation.

Q: Describe an experiment to demonstrate the principle on which the induction motor operates.

A: 1. Place the copper disc on the pivot.

2. Rotate magnet over disc.

3. The disc rotates in same direction as magnet.

2006 Higher level question 10 (b)

Q: What is a transistor?

A: A transistor is a semiconductor device that acts as a switch or an amplifier.

Q: Describe the structure of a bipolar transistor.

A: 3 layers npn – emitter, base, collector.

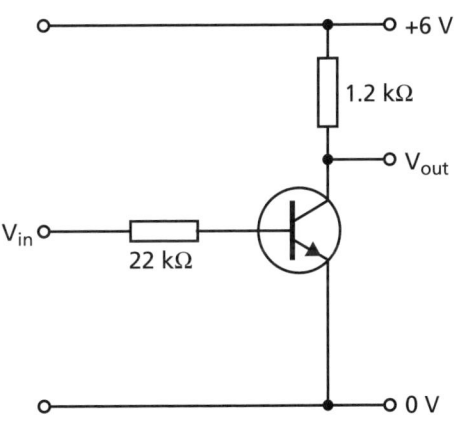

Q: The circuit diagram represents a voltage inverter.

What is the function of each resistor in the circuit?

A: The 1.2 kΩ resistor is a load resistor. It converts large changes in the collector current (I_c) to large changes in the voltage across it.

The 22 kΩ resistor is a protective resistor (bias) that limits current to base.

Q: Explain why the output voltage is almost 0 V when the input voltage is 6 V.

A: When the input voltage is 6 V the base current is large and the transistor switches on. The collector current I_c flows through the transistor and 1.2 kΩ resistor. The transistor resistance is low so the output voltage across it almost 0 V.

Q: Calculate the collector current when the input voltage is 6 V. (Assume that the output voltage is 0 V.)

A: $I = \dfrac{V}{R}$

$I = \dfrac{6}{1,200}$

$I = 0.005$ A

2004 Higher level question 10 (b) (part)

Q: A moving coil galvanometer has a resistance of 100 Ω and a full-scale deflection of 5.00 mA. Calculate the size of the resistor required to convert it into an ammeter with a full-scale deflection of 1.00 A. What is the effective resistance of the ammeter?

A: current through galvanometer = 0.005 A

current through resistor = 0.995 A

But: $V_R = V_G$

$(0.995)\,R = (0.005)(100)$

$R = 0.503\ \Omega$

$$\frac{1}{R_t} = \frac{1}{R_1} + \frac{1}{R_2}$$

$$= \frac{1}{0.503} + \frac{1}{100}$$

$R_t = 0.500\ \Omega$

Philips'

INTERNATIONAL

ATLAS

GEORGE PHILIP

Maps and Index

Edited by:
Bill Willett, B.A., Cartographic Editor, David Gaylard and
Raymond Smith, B.Sc., George Philip and Son Ltd

Maps prepared by George Philip Cartographic Services Ltd
under the direction of Alan Poynter, M.A., Director of Cartography

Exploring the Universe

This section has been produced for George Philip & Son
by Antler Books Ltd, 11 Rathbone Place, London W1P 1DE.
Artwork and diagrams: Steven Begg and Peter Bull
Picture Sources: Aspect Picture Library; British Tourist
Authority; Daily Telegraph; Federation of Astronomical
Societies; Hale Observatories; Malcolm Johnson/Chris Walker;
Kim Lindley; Paul Money; Geoff Pearce; Picturepoint; Royal
Astronomical Society; Royal Observatory, Edinburgh; Colin
Taylor.
Editorial: Brian Jones
Editorial Assistants: Sue Bilton and Lesley Spencer
Design: Slapstick Design
Colour Separations: BBE Colour Ltd

First Edition 1986

British Library Cataloguing in Publication Data

Philips' international atlas
  1. Atlases, British
  912   G1021

ISBN 0-540-05514-X

© 1986 George Philip & Son Ltd

Printed in Great Britain by George Philip Printers Ltd.

Preface

'To some kind of men it is an extraordinary delight to study, to looke upon a geographicall
map and to behold, as it were, all the remote Provinces, Towns, Citties of the world...'
(Robert Burton *The Anatomy of Melancholy* 1621)

These days, coffee tables rather than book shelves seem to be the repository of many large-format books. One of the objectives of the International Atlas is to present to the reader all the maps, at adequate scales, that are reasonably needed for everyday reference, and, moreover, in a page size that is comfortable to handle and refer to. The size is convenient for the book shelf, or even the coffee table.

The title of Philips' International Atlas is apt in a number of senses; the outlook of the maps that have been selected for the atlas is international, the policy with regard to name forms is international and there is a section of statistics giving the important facts for the principal nations of the world. Furthermore, the atlas is more than international in that there is a part of the volume devoted to placing our planet within the context of the universe.

The first set of maps in the atlas are of the world, one physical, the other political, and then the form of the atlas is to take each continent in turn, beginning with a physical map and a political map and then going to a larger scale for each part of the continent. (Large scale means the representative fraction, quoted in the scale, gets smaller and the map shows more detail; 1:2 million is larger than 1:5 million.)

Within each continent there are regional maps usually at a scale of between 1:5 and 1:15 million. At these scales there are usually a large number of countries shown on each map, and so these maps have been coloured politically to quickly show the reader the political make-up of the region. For example, there is a politically-coloured map of central Europe at 1:5 million and one of the complete United States at 1:12 million. Following such maps as these, the more densely populated areas are covered on larger scales, and so the reader has maps of the British Isles at 1:2 million, and, to give a few more examples, maps of France, Chicago and California at 1:2.5 million and the more densely populated parts of Russia at 1:5 million.

The International Atlas is the first time that George Philip has combined a full world atlas with a complete introduction to astronomy. Exploring the Universe covers all aspects of this fascinating subject, from the formation of the Solar System and the composition of the sun to the mysteries of deep space – black holes, quasars and the possibility of life elsewhere. This section is essential reading for the amateur astronomer and for anyone who would like to know more about what lies beyond Earth.

The statistical section lists the major countries of the world and gives information that describes such features as their demography, economy, production and trade. More is said about the aims and content of this section in its introduction.

The index, at the end of the book, together with the contents list and maps and the list of selected references, which follow this page, help the user find both larger features such as countries and regions, or smaller features such as towns and villages.

International boundaries have been drawn to show the *de facto* situation where there are rival claims to territory.

Finally, a word about the name forms that appear on the maps and in the index. The main form of the names is always given in the local form, which is the spelling used by the people of that particular country. Where necessary, the English conventional name form is given in brackets on the maps and cross-referenced in the index. Thus the city of Munich, Germany, is rendered as München, but the English form, Munich, is given in brackets, and cross-referenced to the main form in the index. For countries that do not use a Roman script, place names have been transcribed according to the standard systems adopted by the British and U.S. Geographic Name authorities. For Chinese place names, the modern Pinyin system has been used, with some of the more well known forms in brackets; Beijing (Peking) is an example, and both of these spellings will be in the index.

B M Willett

Contents

Exploring the Universe

The World

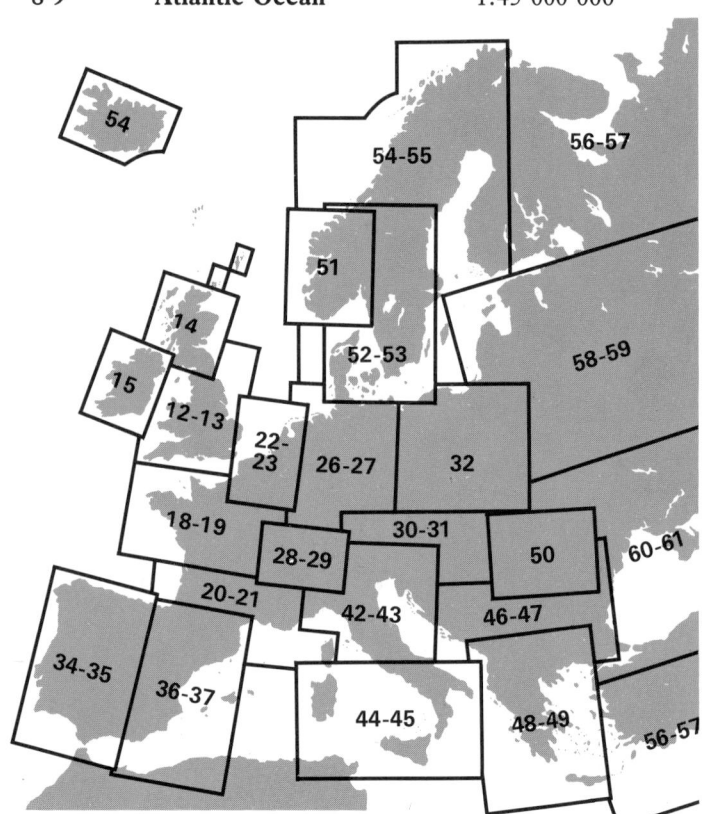

Europe

Asia

Contents

Australia and New Zealand

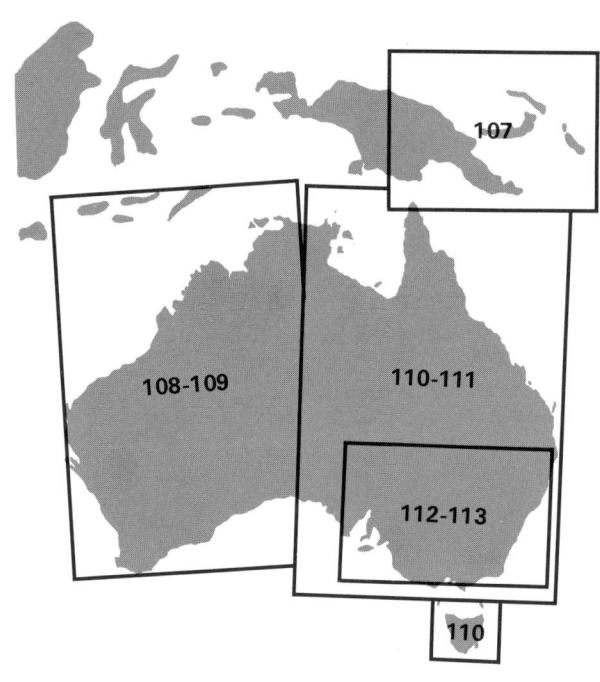
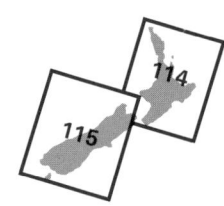

Africa

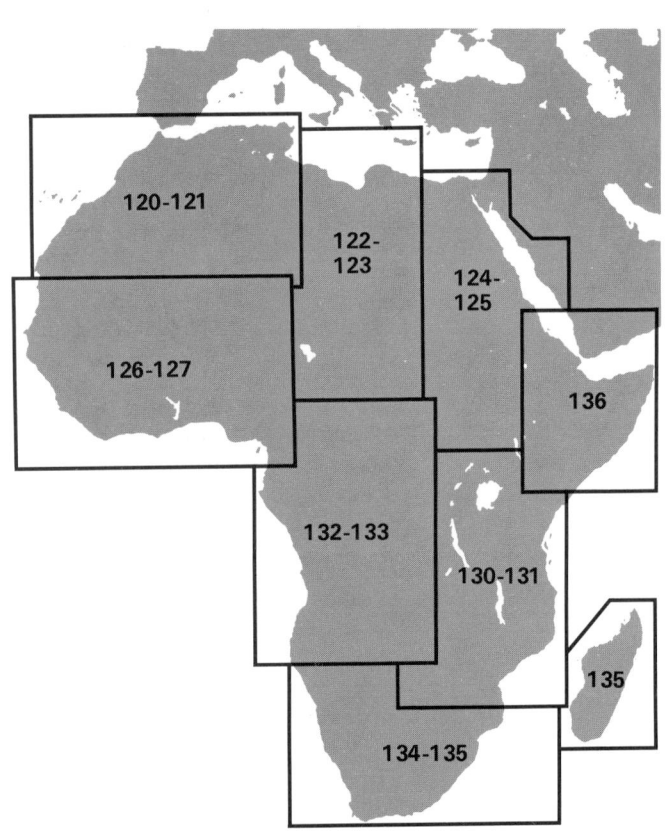

North America

South America

Economic Statistics

Index

Selected References

These selected references are additional to the contents list on the previous page and are included to take the reader directly to the page required for certain well known and used names. The list includes country names and names of large geographical features, mountains and seas, for example. The page quoted will be the one where the feature appears as a whole and at the largest scale.

Economic Statistics

Introduction

It is the aim of these statistics to present for the largest countries a picture of their character and position in the world in such a way that comparisons between countries may be made and a wide variety of basic questions answered.

The chosen items of information are the most important within the general categories of area and demography, natural resources, industrial production and trade. The arrangement of columns corresponds to these categories, the first column being general and the rest refer to the four categories.

In case some of the terms are unfamiliar, explanations are given below in the appropriate part of the Notes.

Table Arrangement

Country
1. Form of Government.
2 Language.
3. Currency.
4. Exchange rates (Spring 1986).

Area and population
1. Area (thousand sq. km.)
2. Population (thousands) and density (Estimates, June 1984).
3. Birth and Death rates per thousand population Annual Increase (percentage, 1980-84).
4. Urban population (thousands) Percentage of total population.
5. Capital and population (thousands).

Production
1. GDP (million $) 1982/84 and average annual growth rate, 1975-81;
   GDP per capita 1982/84 and annual growth rate, 1975-81.
   Industrial origin of GDP, percentage distribution.
2. Agricultural production, thousand tonnes.
3. Livestock, thousand head.
4. Fish caught, thousand tonnes, 1983.
5. Roundwood 1983, thousand cubic m.
6. Minerals mined, thousand tonnes.
   Gas in terajoules
   Coal — million tonnes
   Gold — tonnes
   Silver — tonnes
   Diamonds — thousand carats
   Uranium — tonnes
   Iron ore — million tonnes
   Lignite — million tonnes
   Crude petroleum — million tonnes.

Manufactures
1. Production/Consumption of all energy, million tonnes of coal equivalent 1983.
   Electricity production, million kWh (percentage hydro-electricity, nuclear, geothermal).
2. Manufactures, (thousand tonnes)
   (a) Agricultural 1983/84
   (b) Industrial 1982/84
   Sawnwood, thousand cubic m.
3. Communications: telephones and cars in use (thousands) 1981/82.
   Railway, passenger-km and tonne-km (millions) 1983/84
   Airlines, passenger-km and tonne-km (thousands) 1983/84.
   Sea cargo, loaded and unloaded (thousand tonnes).

Trade
Export and Import totals, million $.
List of major items.
Main trading partners in order of importance.
Invisible trade balance, million $, 1983-84.
Revenue from tourism, million $, 1982.
Aid given or received, million $
(Annual average 1979-81)

General Notes

As far as possible the figures refer to 1983/84. When they are for different years or periods, for example, for the Exchange Rate or the GDP growth figures, the appropriate date is mentioned in the table description above. For the urban and capital populations the most recent estimates or figures from the latest censuses are given; these may be 5–10 years old.

Column One
The exchange rates for the £ and U.S. $ are shown.
The C.F.A. franc is the unit of currency used throughout the African countries associated with France. (C.F.A. = Communauté Financière Africaine.)

Column Two
The area figure is for the total area of the country, including inland water bodies.
The birth and death rates are the latest figures that are available. The annual rate of change in the population is expressed as an average for the years 1980–84. The figure includes the natural net balance of births and deaths and also migration.

Column Three
The GDP in line 1 is the Gross Domestic Product. In Communist countries the best similar measure is the NMP, the Net Material Product.
The Gross Domestic Product is a measure of a country's total production of goods and services. The figures are expressed in 'purchaser's values' which means the cost in the market of goods and services on delivery to the purchaser; that is the cost of materials, production, trade and transport charges. Imported goods and services are excluded.
The Net Material Product is not wholly comparable to the GDP; it is the total net value of goods and production services, including taxes, in one year. Excluded are public administration, defence, personal and professional services. The figure should be used with caution and treated as a general indicator.
A second figure is given for the GDP expressed per capita, and an annual average rate of change is added after both.
The Industrial Origin of the GDP comes in the next line and is divided into three categories, Agriculture, Industry and Other. The percentage figures show which part of the GDP is contributed by each category.
Roundwood refers to the forest output of wood in its natural state as felled.

Column Four
The production and consumption of various types of energy has been converted to one measure – the heat energy obtained from burning one tonne of coal, – the 'coal equivalent'. The production figure is based on the home production of coal, lignite, crude petroleum, natural gas and hydro- and nuclear electricity. Imported energy sources are included in the consumption figure.
Sawnwood is timber in its first state of processing.
Energy Petroleum Products include particular products obtained from crude petroleum or shale oil. These products are motor and aviation gasolenes, jet fuels and kerosene, gas, diesel and residual oils and liquefied petroleum gas.

Column Five
Exports are f.o.b. and imports c.i.f.
Trade partners are listed in order of importance.
f.o.b. (free on board) A valuation of the cost of goods, plus insurance and freight to the border of the exporting country.
c.i.f. (cost, insurance, freight) A valuation of the cost of goods, plus insurance and freight to the border of the importing country.
The invisible trade balance is the net balance of earnings from, and expenditure on the exchange of non-physical ('invisible') goods. The most important activities are international banking, investment, insurance, shipping and tourism.
The revenue from tourism is the total income, not a net balance.
Aid is a general term for all planned assistance to the developing countries. Aid comes from governments and from private organisations.
A second distinction can be made between bilateral and multilateral aid. Bilateral aid is arranged between two governments according to their own arrangements; this method accounts for just over 80% of all aid. Multilateral aid is given through institutions such as the World Bank, the E.E.C., regional institutions like the Colombo plan and other U.N. agencies.

Abbreviations

. . .	data not available	c	carats (thousand)	m²	square metres	hydr	hydro-electric
t	tonnes, – the metric tonne	grt	gross registered tons (thousand)	m³	cubic metres	geo	geothermal
kg	kilogrammes	hl	hectolitres (thousand)	kWh	kilowatt-hour	M	million
km	kilometres	m	metres	nucl	nuclear	T	thousand

AFGHANISTAN

1. Republic
2. Pashto, Persian
3. Afghani
4. $1 = 65.50
   £1 = 99.00

1. 648 th. sq. km.
2. 17 672; 28 per sq. km.
3. BR 48; DR 22; AI 0.04%
4. Urb. pop.: 2 376 (16%)
5. Kabul 1 127

1. GDP $1 858 (. . .); $111 (. . .)
   Agric. 69%, Indust. 14%, Others 17%
2. Wheat 2 850   Maize 800
   Cottonseed 44   Cotton lint 22
3. Sheep 20 000   Cattle 3 750
   Goats 3 000
5. Roundwood 6 681
6. Coal 0.1   Natural gas 99.5
   Salt 30

1. 3.6/0.9; 1 025 kWh (80% hydr.)
2a. Sugar 6   Sawnwood 400
    Meat 252
b. Cement 87   Cotton woven 23Mm
3. Telephones 32; Cars 37
   Air: 231 pass.-km.; 39 ton-km.

Exports: $708   Imports: $695
Cotton   Food
Natural gas   Textiles
Dried fruit   Petroleum products
Fresh fruit   Machinery
Exports to: U.S.S.R., U.K., Pakistan
Imports from: U.S.S.R., Japan, Iran
Aid received (net): $44.2

ALBANIA

1. Republic
2. Albanian
3. Lek
4. $1 = 6.75
   £1 = 10.20

1. 29 th. sq. km.
2. 2 901; 100 per sq. km.
3. BR 26; DR 6; AI 2.2%
4. Urb. pop.: 961 (34%)
5. Tirana 202

1. NMP . . . (9.2%); . . . (6.2%)
2. Wheat 600   Maize 400
   Cottonseed 10   Cotton lint 6
3. Sheep 1 200   Goats 700
5. Roundwood 2 330
6. Lignite 1 020   Crude petroleum 3.5
   Chrome 900   Copper 14.0
   Nickel 9.0

1. 6.8/3.6; 2 885 kWh (68% hydr.)
2a. Sugar 40   Sawnwood 200
b. Cement 1 088   Copper 10
   Cotton woven . . . Wool woven . . .

Exports: . . .   Imports: . . .
Fuels and Minerals   Machinery
Exports to: India, Czechoslovakia, Poland, E. Germany
Imports from: India, Czechoslovakia, Poland, E. Germany

ALGERIA

1. Republic
2. Arabic, French
3. Algerian Dinar
4. $1 = 4.80
   £1 = 7.25

1. 2 382 th. sq. km.
2. 21 272; 9 per sq. km.
3. BR 47; DR 13; AI 3.3%
4. Urb. pop.: 9 785 (46%)
5. Algiers 1 740

1. GDP $44 926 (8.7%); $2 262 (5.3%)
   Agric. 6%, Indust. 40%, Other 54%
2. Wheat 1 200   Barley 588
   Grapes 360   Oranges 228
3. Sheep 14 700   Goats 3 000
4. Fish 70
5. Roundwood 1 685
6. Crude petroleum 30.3 Natural gas 516
   Iron ore 2.0   Phosphates 893
   Lead 5

1. 85.1/12.8; 8 520 kWh (4% hydr.)
2a. Wine 215   Meat 192
    Sawnwood 13
b. Cotton yarn 19.9   Cement 4 500
   Petroleum products 28.8
3. Telephones 607; Cars 574
   Rail: 1 506 pass.-km.; 2 016 ton-km.
   Air: 2 610 pass.-km.; 253 ton-km.
   Sea: 44 824 loaded; 13 299 unloaded

Exports: $11 861   Imports: $10 286
Crude petroleum   Machinery
Wine   Iron and steel
Natural gas   Food
Exports to: France, W. Germany, U.S.A., Italy
Imports from: France, W. Germany, Italy, U.S.A.
Revenue from tourism: $167
Aid received (net): $187.9

ANGOLA

1. Republic
2. Portuguese
3. Kwanza
4. $1 = 28.98
   £1 = 43.80

1. 1 247 th. sq. km.
2. 8 540; 7 per sq. km.
3. BR 24; DR 24; AI 1.3%
4. Urb. pop.: 1 964 (23%)
5. Luanda 700

1. GDP $2 701 (. . .); $432 (. . .)
2. Coffee 27   Sugar cane 360
   Maize 500   Palm oil 40
3. Cattle 3 350   Goats 955
4. Fish 112
5. Roundwood 9 003
6. Crude petroleum 10.3 Diamonds 920c

1. 12.4/1.0; 1 740 kWh (74% hydr.)
2a. Sugar 34   Sawnwood 160
b. Cement 3 600   Cotton yarn 3
3. Telephones 28; Cars 40
   Rail: 858 pass.-km.; 96 ton-km.
   Sea: 5 590 loaded; 1 608 unloaded

Exports: $2 029   Imports: $636
Coffee   Machinery
Diamonds   Metals
Crude petroleum
Exports to: U.S.A., Portugal, Canada, Japan
Imports from: Portugal, W. Germany, South Africa, U.S.A.
Aid received (net): $53.4

ARGENTINA

1. Republic
2. Spanish
3. Austral
4. $1 = 0.83
   £1 = 1.25

1. 2 767 th. sq. km.
2. 30 097; 11 per sq. km.
3. BR 24; DR 8; AI 1.3%
4. Urb. pop.: 27 398 (83%)
5. Buenos Aires 9 927

1. GDP $122 195 (1.3%); $4 124 (1.0%)
   Agric. 13%, Indust. 35%, Others 52%
2. Wheat 13 000   Maize 9 500
   Linseed 703   Oranges 580
   Wool 155   Grapes 2 759
3. Cattle 53 500   Sheep 30 000
4. Fish 416
5. Roundwood 10 520
6. Coal 0.5   Zinc 35
   Crude petroleum 23.2 Lead 29
   Natural gas 427   Silver 62

1. 56.8/50.9; 42 998 kWh (43% hydr., 8% nucl.)
2a. Meat 3 482   Wine 2 000
    Sugar 1 450   Sawnwood 1 163
b. Cotton yarn 91.2   Steel 2 508
   Petroleum products 21.9 Vehicles:
   Cement 5 220   pass. 144, comm. 30
   Iron 2 600
3. Telephones 2 767; Cars 2 368
   Rail: 10 524 pass.-km.; 11 244 ton-km.
   Air: 6 252 pass.-km.; 722 ton-km.
   Sea: 35 184 loaded; 5 568 unloaded

Exports: $8 107   Imports: $4 583
Meat   Machinery
Cereals   Iron and steel
Wool   Non-ferrous metals
Exports to: Italy, Netherlands, Brazil, U.S.A.
Imports from: U.S.A., W. Germany, Brazil, Japan
Invisible trade balance: –$6 479
Revenue from tourism: $516
Aid received (net): $149.1

AUSTRALIA

1. Commonwealth
2. English
3. Australian Dollar
4. $1 = 1.38
   £1 = 2.08

1. 7 687 th. sq. km.
2. 15 544; 2 per sq. km.
3. BR 15; DR 7; AI 1.2%
4. Urb. pop.: 13 368 (86%)
5. Canberra 256

1. GDP $166 691 (2.6%); $10 981 (1.3%)
   Agric. 6%, Indust. 27%, Others 67%
2. Wheat 18 580   Barley 5 470
   Oats 1 470   Wool 729
   Oranges 380   Other fruits 3 000
3. Sheep 139 242   Cattle 22 161
4. Fish 169
5. Roundwood 16 015
6. Coal 124.5   Lead 440
   Crude petroleum 23.9 Zinc 657
   Natural gas 463   Manganese 1 033
   Gold 39   Iron ore 57.6
   Nickel 76.9   Bauxite 32 182
   Copper 240   Silver 1 063
   Diamonds 5 700c   Uranium 3 211t

1. 135.4/92.0; 106 287 kWh (12% hydr.)
2a. Meat 2 304   Sugar 3 550
    Sawnwood 2 794   Butter & cheese 279
b. Wool yarn 20   Cement 5 100
   Steel 6 168   Radios 143
   Petroleum products 26.3 Vehicles:
                       pass. 371, comm. 29
3. Telephones 7 153; Cars 6 819
   Rail: . . .; 39 444 ton-km.
   Air: 26 124 pass.-km.; 2 953 ton-km.
   Sea: 209 832 loaded; 22 572 unloaded

Exports: $23 998   Imports: $23 424
Wool   Machinery
Cereals   Vehicles
Metals   Textiles
Meat   Crude petroleum
Exports to: Japan, U.S.A., New Zealand
Imports from: U.S.A., Japan, U.K., W. Germany
Invisible trade balance: –$6 740
Revenue from tourism: $1 097
Aid given (net): $812

AUSTRIA

1. Federal Republic
2. German
3. Austrian Schilling
4. $1 = 15.53
   £1 = 23.48

1. 84 th. sq. km.
2. 7 552; 90 per sq. km.
3. BR 12; DR 12; AI 0.0%
4. Urb. pop.: 3 927 (52%)
5. Vienna 1 531

1. GDP $58 490 (3.0%); $7 747 (3.0%)
   Agric. 4%, Indust. 28%, Others 68%
2. Wheat 1 501   Barley 1 517
   Potatoes 1 138   Rye 380
   Maize 1 542   Pears 151
3. Pigs 3 881   Cattle 2 633
5. Roundwood 13 670
6. Lignite 219   Iron ore 1.1
   Crude petroleum 1.3 Magnesite 1 006
   Natural gas 49   Antimony 0.5
   Salt 501   Lead 4
   Zinc 21

1. 8.6/26.7; 42 625 kWh (72% hydr.)
2a. Wine 252   Sugar 457
    Sawnwood 6 308   Meat 763
b. Cotton yarn 16.8   Wool yarn 5.1
   Steel 5 316   Aluminium 94
   Petroleum products 6.8
3. Telephones 3 178; Cars 2 361
   Rail: 7 217 pass.-km.; 11 244 ton-km.
   Air: 1 404 pass.-km.; 135 ton-km.

Exports: $15 741   Imports: $19 631
Machinery   Machinery
Iron and steel   Food
Textiles   Textiles
Sawnwood   Vehicles
                       Chemical products
Exports to: W. Germany, Italy, Switzerland, U.K.
Imports from: W. Germany, Switzerland, Italy, France
Invisible trade balance: +$2 865
Revenue from tourism: $5 649
Aid given (net): $285

BANGLADESH

1. Republic
2. Bengali
3. Taka
4. $1 = 29.87
   £1 = 45.15

1. 144 th. sq. km.
2. 96 730; 722 per sq. km.
3. BR 47; DR 19; AI 2.4%
4. Urb. pop.: 9 673 (10%)
5. Dacca 3 459

1. GDP $15 298 (. . .); $158 (. . .)
   Agric. 48%, Indust. 9%, Others 43%
2. Rice 21 500   Bananas 680
   Tea 46   Jute 733
3. Cattle 36 300   Goats 12 050
4. Fish 729
5. Roundwood 32 051
6. Natural gas 79.0

1. 2.8/4.6; 3 758 kWh (18% hydr.)
2a. Sugar 165   Sawnwood 196
b. Cotton yarn 46.8   Cement 326
3. Telephones 122; Cars 44
   Rail: 5 366 pass.-km.; 831 ton-km.
   Air: 1 430 pass.-km.; 149 ton-km.
   Sea: 1 056 loaded; 6 948 unloaded

Exports: $934   Imports: $2 042
Exports to: U.S.A., Pakistan, U.S.S.R., U.K.
Imports from: Japan, U.S.A., U.K.
Revenue from tourism: $10
Aid received (net): $1 142.7

For detailed table headings and notes see first page of this section

2

Country	Area and Population	Production	Manufactures	Trade

BELGIUM
1. Kingdom
2. French, Flemish, German
3. Belgian Franc
4. $1 = 45.48
   £1 = 68.75
	1. 33 th. sq. km.
	2. 9 877; 300 per sq. km.
	3. BR 12; DR 11; AI 0.1%
	4. Urb. pop.: 8 790 (89%)
	5. Brussels 989
		1. GDP $75 306 (2.3%); $7 638 (2.2%)
		   Agric. 2%, Indust. 25%, Others 73%
		2. Wheat 1 330 Barley 935
		   Potatoes 1 650 Apples 260
		3. Pigs 5 300 Cattle 3 171
		4. Fish 49
		5. Roundwood 3 041
		6. Coal 6.3
			1. 10.0/48.9; 52 706 kWh (2% hydr., 46% nucl.)
			2a. Sugar 900 Sawnwood 695
			b. Cotton yarn 46.8 Wool yarn 92
			   Steel 11 304 Copper 418
			   Coke oven coke 5 106 Plastics 2 000
			   Petroleum products 19.3 Vehicles:
			   Iron 8 964 pass. 890, comm. 39
			3. Telephones 3 819; Cars 3 231
			   Rail: 6 456 pass.-km.; 7 884 ton-km.
			   Air: 5 652 pass.-km.; 967 ton-km.
			   Sea: 47 052 loaded; 72 096 unloaded
				Exports: $51 699 Imports: $55 247
				(incl. Luxembourg) (incl. Luxembourg)
				Iron and steel Machinery
				Vehicles Vehicles
				Machinery Non-ferrous metals
				Non-ferrous metals Diamonds
				Textiles Petrol
				Trade is principally with: W. Germany, France,
				Netherlands, U.K.
				Invisible trade balance (incl. Luxembourg): +$2 281
				Revenue from tourism: $1 578
				Aid given (net): $2 274

BENIN
1. Republic
2. French
3. C.F.A. Franc
4. $1 = 352.13
   £1 = 532.25
	1. 113 th. sq. km.
	2. 3 825; 35 per sq. km.
	3. BR 51; DR 25; AI 3.5%
	4. Urb. pop.: 1 314 (39%)
	5. Porto-Novo 208
		1. GDP $1 035 (−4.3%); $303 (−6.3%)
		   Agric. 44%, Indust. 6%, Others 50%
		2. Cassava 639 Palm oil 40
		   Maize 379 Cottonseed 34
		   Groundnuts 58
		3. Goats 1 000 Cattle 875
		4. Fish 21
		5. Roundwood 4 210
			1. . . ./0.2; 5 kWh
			2a. Sawnwood 9
			3. Telephones 9; Cars 17
			   Rail: 83 pass.-km.; 94 ton-km.
			   Air: 212 pass.-km.; 41 ton-km.
			   Sea: 110 loaded; 749 unloaded
				Exports: $43 Imports: $476
				Palm oil Manufactured
				Oilseeds products
				Cotton, Cocoa Machinery
				Exports to: France, Netherlands, U.K.
				Imports from: France, W. Germany, Netherlands, U.K.
				Aid received (net): $87.1

BOLIVIA
1. Republic
2. Spanish
3. Bolivian Peso
4. $1 = 1.9 mill.
   £1 = 2.88 mill.
	1. 1 099 th. sq. km.
	2. 6 253; 6 per sq. km.
	3. BR 47; DR 18; AI 2.7%
	4. Urb. pop.: 2 822 (46%)
	5. La Paz 881, Sucre 64
		1. GDP $6 238 (3.2%); $1 054 (0.4%)
		   Agric. 22%, Indust. 23%, Others 55%
		2. Maize 489 Barley 40
		   Potatoes 650 Oranges 95
		3. Sheep 9 200 Cattle 4 300
		5. Roundwood 1 272
		6. Antimony 9.3 Crude petroleum 1.6
		   Tin 19.9 Silver 142t
		   Tungsten 3 997t Zinc 38
		   Natural gas 88.5 Copper 2
		   Lead 7
			1. 4.9/2.1; 1 698 kWh (72% hydr.)
			2a. Sugar 198 Sawnwood 97
			b. Cement 325 Tin 14
			3. Telephones 49; Cars 50
			   Rail: 529 pass.-km.; 646 ton-km.
			   Air: 876 pass.-km.; 95 ton-km.
				Exports: $773 Imports: $631
				Tin ore Cars
				Crude petroleum Flour
				Exports to: U.K., Argentina, U.S.A.
				Imports from: U.S.A., Japan, Argentina, Brazil
				Invisible trade balance: −$436
				Aid received (net): $211.3

BRAZIL
1. Federal Republic
2. Portuguese
3. Cruzado
4. $1 = 13.79
   £1 = 20.84
	1. 8 512 th. sq. km.
	2. 132 580; 16 per sq. km.
	3. BR 32; DR 9; AI 2.2%
	4. Urb. pop.: 86 611 (68%)
	5. Brasilia 1 306
		1. GDP $283 076 (6.5%); $2 232 (3.9%)
		   Agric. 10%, Indust. 25%, Others 65%
		2. Maize 21 174 Rice 9 023
		   Cassava 21 275 Soya beans 15 537
		   Bananas 6 968 Oranges 13 372
		   Cottonseed 1 179 Tobacco 415
		3. Cattle 132 801 Pigs 33 000
		4. Fish 845
		5. Roundwood 220 248
		6. Coal 7.5 Crude petroleum 12.8
		   Iron ore 66.0 Natural gas 64.8
		   Manganese 941 Asbestos 159
		   Gold 55.1 Tin 20.0
		   Bauxite 6 271 Zinc 79
		   Copper 26 Silver 69
			1. 50.3/85.7; 161 970 kWh (94% hydr.)
			2a. Meat 4 847 Sugar 9 100
			   Sawnwood 15 852
			b. Cotton fabric 1 207Mm Iron 17 904
			   Steel 18 384 Aluminium 400
			   Cement 19 488 Petroleum products 43.2
			   Vehicles:
			   pass. 536, comm. 384
			3. Telephones 8 536; Cars 9 922
			   Rail: 13 133 pass.-km.; 79 269 ton-km.
			   Air: 17 229 pass.-km.; 2 229 ton-km.
			   Sea: 141 732 loaded; 53 856 unloaded
				Exports: $27 005 Imports: $15 210
				Coffee Machinery
				Cotton Crude petroleum
				Iron ore Cereals
				Machinery Non-ferrous metals
				Exports to: U.S.A., W. Germany, Netherlands, Japan
				Imports from: U.S.A., W. Germany, Japan,
				Saudi Arabia, Iraq
				Invisible trade balance: −$13 414
				Revenue from tourism: $1 608
				Aid received (net): $556.4

BULGARIA
1. Republic
2. Bulgar
3. Lev
4. $1 = 0.91
   £1 = 1.37
	1. 111 th. sq. km.
	2. 8 961; 81 per sq. km.
	3. BR 14; DR 11; AI 0.4%
	4. Urb. pop.: 5 775 (68%)
	5. Sofia 1 094
		1. NMP $34 000 (6.0%); $3 800 (5.8%)
		   Agric. 18%, Indust. 57%, Others 25%
		2. Wheat 3 600 Maize 3 000
		   Tobacco 125 Grapes 1 000
		3. Sheep 10 978 Pigs 3 769
		4. Fish 121
		5. Roundwood 4 756
		6. Coal 0.2 Crude petroleum 0.6
		   Lignite 32.1 Zinc 65
		   Iron ore 0.6 Lead 95
		   Silver 26 Copper 73
			1. 18.8/50.2; 42 534 kWh (8% hydr., 29% nucl.)
			2a. Meat 722 Sawnwood 1 345
			   Wine 510 Sugar 145
			b. Cotton yarn 82.8 Iron 1 584
			   Steel 2 868 Cement 5 712
			   Petroleum products 11.4
			3. Telephones 1 513; Cars 480
			   Rail: 7 536 pass.-km.; 18 132 ton-km.
			   Air: 980 pass.-km.; 99 ton-km.
			   Sea: 4 488 loaded; 24 750 unloaded
				Exports: $12 829 Imports: $12 668
				Cigarettes Machinery
				Alcoholic drinks Ferrous metals
				Clothing Petroleum products
				The principal trade is with U.S.S.R. and E. Germany
				Revenue from tourism: $265

BURKINA FASO
1. Republic
2. French
3. C.F.A. Franc
4. $1 = 352.13
   £1 = 532.25
	1. 274 th. sq. km.
	2. 6 582; 24 per sq. km.
	3. BR 48; DR 24; AI 2.3%
	4. Urb. pop.: 362 (6%)
	5. Ouagadougou 286
		1. GDP $1 079 (6.6%); $163 (4.7%)
		   Agric. 37%, Indust. 11%, Others 52%
		2. Millet/sorghum 1 150 Maize 60
		   Rice 40 Groundnuts 77
		3. Cattle 2 800 Goats 2 600
		5. Roundwood 7 281
		6. Gold . . .
			1. . . ./0.2; 115 kWh
			2a. Meat 60
			3. Telephones 6; Cars 12
			   Air: 215 pass.-km.; 41 ton-km.
				Exports: $57 Imports: $288
				Livestock Manufactured goods
				Cotton Foods
				Exports to: Ivory Coast, France, China
				Imports from: France, U.S.A., Ivory Coast
				Aid received (net): $208.7

BURMA
1. Republic
2. Burmese
3. Kyat
4. $1 = 7.28
   £1 = 11
	1. 677 th. sq. km.
	2. 37 614; 58 per sq. km.
	3. BR 39; DR 14; AI 2.5%
	4. Urb. pop.: 8 455 (24%)
	5. Rangoon 2 459
		1. GDP $6 176 (6.3%); $165 (3.5%)
		   Agric. 50%, Indust. 11%, Others 39%
		2. Rice 14 500 Groundnuts 601
		   Tobacco 62 Jute 55
		3. Cattle 9 550 Buffaloes 2 100
		4. Fish 586
		5. Roundwood 19 254
		6. Crude petroleum 1.5 Zinc 4
		   Lead 8 Silver 18
		   Tin 1.9
			1. 3.0/2.5; 1 872 kWh (60% hydr.)
			2a. Sugar 56 Sawnwood 415
			b. Lead 8 Cotton yarn 8.4
			3. Telephones 37; Cars 48
			   Rail: 4 008 pass.-km.; 648 ton-km.
			   Air: 239 pass.-km.; 23 ton-km.
			   Sea: 1 248 loaded; 528 unloaded
				Exports: $310 Imports: $239
				Sawnwood Machinery
				Rice Textiles
				Exports to: Japan, Indonesia, Vietnam
				Imports from: Japan, China, W. Germany, U.K.,
				Singapore
				Invisible trade balance: −$73.2
				Aid received (net): $318.9

CAMBODIA
1. Republic
2. French, Cambodian
3. Riel
4. $1 = ?
   £1 = ?
	1. 181 th. sq. km.
	2. 7 149; 40 per sq. km.
	3. BR 30; DR 40; AI 2.9%
	4. Urb. pop.: 714 (10%)
	5. Phnom Penh 500
		1. GDP $592 (. . .); $83 (. . .)
		   Agric. 41%, Indust. 17%, Others 42%
		2. Rice 1 300 Maize 75
		   Rubber 14 Bananas 84
		3. Cattle 1 466 Pigs 1 008
		4. Fish 64
		5. Roundwood 5 229
			1. . . ./0.02; 140 kWh (41% hydr.)
			2a. Sawnwood 43
			3. Telephones 71; Cars 25
				Exports: . . . Imports: . . .
				Rubber Machinery
				Rice Textiles
				Cattle Iron and steel
				Exports to: Vietnam, Hong Kong, Singapore
				Imports from: France, Japan, China, Thailand, U.S.A.
				Aid received (net): $172.8

For detailed table headings and notes see first page of this section

Country	Area and Population	Production	Manufactures	Trade
CAMEROON 1. Republic 2. French, English 3. C.F.A. Franc 4. $1 = 352.13 £1 = 532.25	1. 475 th. sq. km. 2. 9 467; 21 per sq. km. 3. BR 43; DR 19; AI 2.5% 4. Urb. pop.: 1 984 (28%) 5. Yaoundé 485	1. GDP $7 786 (3.7%); $871 (1.8%) Agric. 23%, Indust. 26%, Others 51% 2. Coffee 127　Groundnuts 80 Cocoa 115　Palm oil 81 3. Goats 2 000　Cattle 3 730 4. Fish 84 5. Roundwood 9 904	1. 8.4/4.1; 1 804 kWh (95% hydr.) 2a. Sawnwood 426 b. Aluminium 77 3. Telephones 22; Cars 55 Rail: 492 pass.-km.; 864 ton-km. Air: 581 pass.-km.; 99 ton-km. Sea: 996 loaded; 3 000 unloaded	Exports: $883　Imports: $1 107 Cocoa　Manufactured goods Coffee Exports to: France, Netherlands, W. Germany Imports from: France, W. Germany, U.S.A. Aid received (net): $263.5
CANADA 1. Commonwealth 2. English, French 3. Canadian Dollar 4. $1 = 1.39 £1 = 2.10	1. 9 976 th. sq. km. 2. 25 150; 3 per sq. km. 3. BR 15; DR 7; AI 1.2% 4. Urb. pop.: 18 435 (76%) 5. Ottawa 738	1. GDP $327 555 (3.1%); $13 034 (2.0%) Agric. 3%, Indust. 23%, Others 74% 2. Wheat 21 199　Barley 10 252 Oats 2 670　Maize 7 024 3. Cattle 12 284　Pigs 10 760 4. Fish 1 337 5. Roundwood 141 502 6. Iron ore 22.6　Crude petroleum 71.2 Coal 32.1　Natural gas 2 740 Copper 712　Zinc 1 207 Nickel 174.2　Asbestos 829 Gold 81.3　Salt 7 542 Lead 307　Silver 1 171 Lignite 25.3　Uranium 6 758	1. 281.0/238.6; 408 443 kWh (65% hydr., 12% nucl.) 2a. Sawnwood 48 469　Wood pulp 19 295 Paper 13 353　Sugar 14 b. Iron 9 840　Steel 14 700 Aluminium 1 091　Copper 465 Televisions 450　Petroleum products 75.3 Vehicles:　Cement 8 856 pass. 1 033, comm. 809 3. Telephones 16 944; Cars 10 199 Rail: 2 088 pass.-km.; 244 668 ton-km. Air: 32 140 pass.-km.; 3 813 ton-km. Sea: 125 000 loaded; 49 000 unloaded	Exports: $86 817　Imports: $73 999 Vehicles　Machinery Machinery　Vehicles Paper and cardboard　Iron and steel Non-ferrous metals　Textiles Wood pulp　Crude petroleum Sawnwood　Fruit and vegetables Crude petroleum Wheat Trade is principally with: U.S.A., U.K., Japan Invisible trade balance: −$15 414 Revenue from tourism: $2 447 Aid given (net): $2 721
CENTRAL AFRICAN REPUBLIC 1. Republic 2. French 3. C.F.A. Franc 4. $1 = 352.13 £1 = 532.25	1. 623 th. sq. km. 2. 2 508; 4 per sq. km. 3. BR 44; DR 23; AI 2.2% 4. Urb. pop.: 834 (35%) 5. Bangui 387	1. GDP $796 (6.2%); $342 (3.2%) Agric. 32%, Indust. 15%, Others 53% 2. Maize 43　Cassava 900 Bananas 147　Coffee 15 Groundnuts 130　Cottonseed 20 3. Goats 960　Cattle 1 500 5. Roundwood 3 049 6. Diamonds 300	1. . . ./0.1; 68 kWh (96% hydr.) 2a. Meat 42　Sawnwood 63 3. Telephones 5; Cars 14 Air: 220 pass.-km.; 42 ton-km.	Exports: $109　Imports: $127 Diamonds　Machinery Cotton, Coffee　Vehicles Exports to: France, Belgium, Luxembourg Imports from: France, W. Germany, Japan Aid received (net): $97.6
CHAD 1. Republic 2. French 3. C.F.A. Franc 4. $1 = 352.13 £1 = 532.25	1. 1 284 th. sq. km. 2. 4 901; 4 per sq. km. 3. BR 44; DR 24; AI 2.3% 4. Urb. pop.: 882 (18%) 5. N'Djamena 303	1. GDP $665 (−4.5%); $165 (−6.6%) Agric. 41%, Indust. 17%, Others 42% 2. Millet 320　Groundnuts 80 Cottonseed 72　Cotton 40 3. Cattle 3 400　Goats 2 000 4. Fish 110 5. Roundwood 8 112	1. . . ./0.1; 65 kWh 2a. Meat 46 3. Telephones 6; Cars 10 Air: 229 pass.-km.; 43 ton-km.	Exports: $58　Imports: $109 Cotton　Petroleum products Meat　Machinery Exports to: France, Nigeria, Cameroon Imports from: France, Nigeria, Netherlands Aid received (net): $58.2
CHILE 1. Republic 2. Spanish 3. Chilean Peso 4. $1 = 186.83 £1 = 282.48	1. 757 th. sq. km. 2. 11 878; 16 per sq. km. 3. BR 21; DR 6; AI 1.6% 4. Urb. pop.: 9 653 (83%) 5. Santiago 4 132	1. GDP $17 796 (7.6%); $1 524 (5.8%) Agric. 6%, Indust. 31%, Others 63% 2. Wheat 988　Grapes 1 050 Wool 21　Tobacco 8 3. Sheep 6 300　Cattle 3 870 4. Fish 3 978 5. Roundwood 12 849 6. Coal 1.2　Iron ore 3.4 Crude petroleum 1.8　Copper 1 290 Natural gas 36.7　Molybdenum 15.3 Gold 18.0　Nickel 12.7 Silver 487　Lead 1	1. 6.5/10.6; 12 624 kWh (70% hydr.) 2a. Meat 361　Sawnwood 1 610 Sugar 332　Wood pulp 796 Wine 520 b. Iron 600　Steel 684 Copper 833　Fertilizers 139 Cement 1 296 3. Telephones 595; Cars 562 Rail: 1 428 pass.-km.; 2 304 ton-km. Air: 1 824 pass.-km.; 315 ton-km. Sea: 11 832 loaded; 5 268 unloaded	Exports: $3 657　Imports: $3 191 Copper, Iron ore,　Machinery Fishmeal, Saltpetre　Food Manufactured products Chemical products Exports to: Japan, W. Germany, U.K., Argentina, U.S.A., Brazil Invisible trade balance: −$2 452 Revenue from tourism: $123 Aid received (net): $22.5
CHINA 1. Republic 2. Chinese and others 3. Renminbi Yuan 4. $1 = 3.32 £1 = 4.88	1. 9 597 th. sq. km. 2. 1 049 705; 109 per sq. km. 3. BR 22; DR 8; AI 1.2% 4. Urb. pop.: 252 360 (24%) 5. Peking 9 330	1. GDP $224 263 (. . .); $218 (. . .) Agric. 45%, Indust. 42%, Others 13% 2. Rice 181 028　Wheat 87 682 Maize 72 690　Soya beans 9 710 Groundnuts 4 900　Oranges 1 495 Tobacco 1 526　Sorghum 8 532 Tea 505　Cotton lint 6 077 Rye 1 500　Cottonseed 12 162 Jute 1 489 3. Pigs 304 424　Sheep 98 916 4. Fish 5 213 5. Roundwood 231 650 6. Coal 736.2　Manganese 480 Crude petroleum 112.5　Natural gas 475 Tungsten 12.5　Iron ore 37.0 Tin 17.5　Salt 15 875 Lead 165　Bauxite 2 000 Copper 180　Zinc 190 Gold 65.0　Nickel 175 Silver 90	1. 682.6/629.1; 351 440 kWh (25% hydr.) 2a. Meat 18 335　Sawnwood 244.10 Sugar 5 119 b. Iron 41 160　Steel 43 320 Aluminium 425　Cement 121 000 Cotton yarn 3 226　Petroleum products 75.4 3. Telephones 4 425; Cars 283 Rail: 203 604 pass.-km.; 722 316 ton-km. Air: 5 750 pass.-km.; 603 ton-km. Sea: 47 268 loaded; 57 192 unloaded	Exports: $24 278　Imports: $25 495 Agricultural products　Grain Textiles　Cotton products Minerals　Machinery Crude petroleum　Primary materials Petrol Exports to: Hong Kong, U.S.S.R., Japan, Singapore Imports from: Japan, Australia, U.S.S.R., Canada Revenue from tourism: $843
COLOMBIA 1. Republic 2. Spanish 3. Columbian Peso 4. $1 = 183.99 £1 = 278.10	1. 1 139 th. sq. km. 2. 28 217; 282 per sq. km. 3. BR 32; DR 8; AI 2.2% 4. Urb. pop.: 18 632 (66%) 5. Bogotá 4 486	1. GDP $32 414 (5.7%); $1 149 (2.8%) Agric. 18%, Indust. 24%, Others 58% 2. Maize 874　Rice 1 696 Palm oil 121　Cassava 2 000 Bananas 3 500　Coffee 780 Cottonseed 200　Tobacco 37 Cotton lint 107 3. Cattle 23 860　Pigs 2 386 4. Fish 56 5. Roundwood 16 553 6. Coal 5.6　Silver 3t Natural gas 181　Gold 21.3 Crude petroleum 8.2　Iron ore 0.2	1. 26.3/25.0; 27 100 kWh (72% hydr.) 2a. Meat 878　Paper 366 Sugar 1 176　Sawnwood 721 b. Iron 246　Steel 276 Petroleum products 8.5　Cement 5 280 3. Telephones 1 842; Cars 599 Rail: 192 pass.-km.; 720 ton-km. Air: 550 pass.-km.; 714 ton-km. Sea: 7 128 loaded; 6 636 unloaded	Exports: $3 462　Imports: $4 052 Coffee　Machinery Crude petroleum　Vehicles Cotton　Iron and steel Bananas　Organic chemicals Sugar and honey Exports to: U.S.A., W. Germany, Venezuela Imports from: U.S.A., W. Germany, Venezuela Invisible trade balance: −$1 754 Revenue from tourism: $624 Aid received (net): $265.6
CONGO 1. Popular Republic 2. French 3. C.F.A. Franc 4. $1 = 352.13 £1 = 532.25	1. 342 th. sq. km. 2. 1 695; 5 per sq. km. 3. BR 45; DR 19; AI 2.6% 4. Urb. pop.: 932 (55%) 5. Brazzaville 422	1. GDP $1 918 (. . .); $1 128 (. . .) Agric. 8%, Indust. 48%, Others 44% 2. Cassava 600　Palm oil 15 3. Goats 182　Cattle 68 4. Fish 32 5. Roundwood 2 238 6. Diamonds. . .　Crude petroleum 5.9	1. 7.8/0.2; 185 kWh (92% hydr.) 2a. Sugar 21　Sawnwood 66 3. Telephones 17; Cars 27 Rail: 408 pass.-km.; 480 ton-km. Air: 247 pass.-km.; 45 ton-km. Sea: 3 084 loaded; 600 unloaded	Exports: $1 066　Imports: $806 Timber　Machinery Manufactured products Exports to: France, Italy, U.S.A., Brazil, Spain Imports from: France, U.S.A., Gabon, W. Germany Aid received (net): $75.1

For detailed table headings and notes see first page of this section

Country	Area and Population	Production	Manufactures	Trade

CUBA

Area and Population
1. Republic
2. Spanish
3. Cuban Peso
4. $1 = 0.68
   £1 = 1.29

1. 111 th. sq. km.
2. 9 992; 90 per sq. km.
3. BR 17; DR 6; AI 0.6%
4. Urb. pop.: 6 861 (70%)
5. Havana 1 951

Production
1. NMP $15 244 (. . .); $1 526 (. . .)
   Agric. 10%, Indust. 35%, Others 55%
2. Rice 555 — Cassava 340
   Coffee 21 — Oranges 374
   Sugar cane 75 000 — Tobacco 45
3. Cattle 6 400 — Pigs 2 300
4. Fish 198
5. Roundwood 3 193
6. Chrome 34 — Nickel 38.0
   Copper 3 — Crude petroleum 0.7

Manufactures
1. 1.1/1.3; 11 551 kWh (0.5% hydr.)
2a. Meat 343 — Sawnwood 108
   Sugar 8 331
b. Petroleum products 6.0 — Cotton, woven 138Mm²
   Cement 3 348
3. Telephones 406; Cars 182
   Rail: 2 352 pass.-km.; 2 808 ton-km.
   Air: 1 100 pass.-km.; 112 ton-km.
   Sea: 2 208 loaded; 2 712 unloaded

Trade
Exports: $6 172 — Imports: $8 144
Sugar — Machinery
Minerals — Cereals
Tobacco — Fertilizers
— Petroleum products
Exports to: U.S.S.R., Japan, Spain
Imports from: U.S.S.R., Japan
Aid received (net): $28.1

CYPRUS

Area and Population
1. Republic (split between Greek and Turkish parts)
2. Greek, Turkish and English
3. Cypriot Pound
4. $1 = 0.51
   £1 = 0.77

1. 9 th. sq. km.
2. 657; 73 per sq. km.
3. BR 20; DR 9; AI 1.2%
4. Urb. pop.: 276 (42%)
5. Nicosia 161

Production
1. GDP $2 009 (9.3%); $3 043 (8.7%)
   Agric. 9%, Indust. 17%, Others 74%
2. Barley 90 — Potatoes 180
   Grapes 205 — Oranges 147
3. Sheep 500 — Goats 360
5. Roundwood 5.74
6. Copper 1.1 — Asbestos 17.3
   Chrome 17

Manufactures
1. . . ./1.2; 1 221 kWh
2a. Wine 56 — Sawnwood 55
b. Cement 852
3. Telephones 128; Cars 106
   Air: 851 pass.-km.; 18 ton-km.
   Sea: 1 812 loaded; 3 168 unloaded

Trade
Exports: $575 — Imports: $1 364
Vegetables — Machinery
Citrus fruits — Textiles
Copper — Vehicles
Exports to: U.K., Saudi Arabia, Iraq
Imports from: U.K., W. Germany, Italy, Iraq, Greece
Revenue from tourism: $292

CZECHOSLOVAKIA

Area and Population
1. Socialist Republic
2. Czech, Slovak
3. Koruna
4. $1 = 10.08
   £1 = 15.23

1. 128 th. sq. km.
2. 15 459; 124 per sq. km.
3. BR 19; DR 12; AI 0.4%
4. Urb. pop.: 10 357 (67%)
5. Prague 1 190

Production
1. GDP $44 112 (3.2%); $2 853 (2.6%)
   Agric. 8%, Indust. 59%, Others 33%
2. Barley 3 677 — Wheat 6 170
   Oats 479 — Potatoes 3 978
   Apples 378 — Tomatoes 79
3. Pigs 7 070 — Cattle 5 190
5. Roundwood 19 206
6. Coal 26.4 — Silver 32t
   Lignite 104.7 — Crude petroleum 0.5
   Iron ore 0.5 — Antimony 1
   Natural gas 0.8 — Lead 3
   Tin 0.2

Manufactures
1. 67.7/96.9; 76 275 kWh (5% hydr., 8% nucl.)
2a. Meat 1 460 — Sawnwood 5 143
   Sugar 815 — Butter and cheese 344
   Beer 24.9 Mhl
b. Iron 9 624 — Steel 14 832
   Aluminium 32 — Plastics 1 034
   Wool yarn 57 — Petroleum products 13.5
   Cotton yarn 140
3. Telephones 3 226; Cars 2 442
   Rail: 19 320 pass.-km.; 73 992 ton-km.
   Air: 1 592 pass.-km.; 164 ton-km.

Trade
Exports: $17 196 — Imports: $17 080
Machinery — Machinery
Manufactured goods — Petroleum
Iron and steel — Non-ferrous metals
Vehicles — Iron and steel
Main trade is with: U.S.S.R., E. Germany, Poland, Hungary
Revenue from tourism: $243

DENMARK

Area and Population
1. Kingdom
2. Danish
3. Danish Krone
4. $1 = 8.15
   £1 = 12.33

1. 43 th. sq. km.
2. 5 112; 12.2 per sq. km.
3. BR 10; DR 11; AI 0.1%
4. Urb. pop.: 4 243 (83%)
5. Copenhagen 1 366

Production
1. GDP $50 252 (2.1%); $9 834 (1.8%)
   Agric. 5%, Indust. 18%, Others 77%
2. Barley 6 072 — Oats 150
   Rye 608 — Wheat 2 446
   Potatoes 1 121 — Apples 116
   Rape seed 517
3. Pigs 9 000 — Cattle 2 900
4. Fish 1 862
5. Roundwood 2 953
6. Crude petroleum 2.1

Manufactures
1. 3.1/22.2; 22 186 kWh
2a. Pork 1 041 — Beef 248
   Butter and cheese 400 — Sugar 595
b. Cotton yarn 2.0 — Steel 528
   Petroleum products 6.5 — Ships (grt.) 376
3. Telephones 3 453; Cars 1 367
   Rail: 48 036 pass.-km.; 18 888 ton-km.
   Air: 3 193 pass.-km.; 412 ton-km.
   Sea: 11 784 loaded; 31 020 unloaded

Trade
Exports: $16 349 — Imports: $16 973
Machinery — Machinery
Pork — Manufactured products
Other meat — Iron and steel
Fish — Textiles
Exports to: Sweden, U.K., W. Germany
Imports from: W. Germany, Sweden, U.K.
Invisible trade balance: −$1 499
Revenue from tourism: $1 305
Aid given (net): $774

ECUADOR

Area and Population
1. Republic
2. Spanish
3. Sucre
4. $1 = 125.25
   £1 = 189.49

1. 284 th. sq. km.
2. 9 115; 33 per sq. km.
3. BR 38; DR 10; AI 3.1%
4. Urb. pop.: 3 978 (45%)
5. Quito 1 110

Production
1. GDP $11 684 (6.0%); $1 283 (2.5%)
   Agric. 14%, Indust. 36%, Others 50%
2. Maize 300 — Rice 470
   Bananas/Plantains 2 600 — Oranges 350
   Cocoa 80 — Coffee 90
3. Cattle 3 300 — Sheep 2 311
4. Fish 307
5. Roundwood 7 795
6. Crude petroleum 12.6 — Gold 5.4
   Nickel 16.5

Manufactures
1. 17.8/5.8; 4 289 kWh (40% hydr.)
2a. Meat 238 — Sawnwood 980
   Sugar 328
b. Petroleum products 3.6
3. Telephones 290; Cars 70
   Rail: 230 pass.-km.; 625 ton-km.
   Air: 862 pass.-km.; 117 ton-km.
   Sea: 5 319 loaded; 2 451 unloaded

Trade
Exports: $2 581 — Imports: $1 716
Bananas — Machinery
Coffee — Vehicles
Cocoa — Chemical products
Exports to: U.S.A., Panama, Colombia, Chile
Imports from: U.S.A., W. Germany, Japan
Invisible trade balance: −$1 085
Revenue from tourism: $131
Aid received (net): $126.8

EGYPT

Area and Population
1. Republic
2. Arabic
3. Egyptian Pound
4. $1 = 0.83
   £1 = 2.06

1. 1 001 th. sq. km.
2. 45 817; 46 per sq. km.
3. BR 38; DR 10; AI 2.5%
4. Urb. pop.: 19 255 (44%)
5. Cairo 6 818

Production
1. GDP $31 750 (8.7%); $711 (6.0%)
   Agric. 19%, Indust. 29%, Others 52%
2. Maize 3 600 — Wheat 1 815
   Rice 2 236 — Tomatoes 2 600
   Oranges 1 450 — Dates 450
   Cotton lint 390 — Cottonseed 677
3. Cattle 1 825 — Buffaloes 2 410
4. Fish 140
5. Roundwood 1 935
6. Iron ore 1.1 — Salt 853
   Crude petroleum 39.3 — Phosphates 647

Manufactures
1. 56.5/25.9; 23 520 kWh (50% hydr.)
2a. Meat 543 — Sugar 780
b. Cotton yarn 244 — Iron 700
   Wool yarn 14.3 — Steel 1 000
   Fertilizers 600 — Cement 4 595
   Petroleum products 16.9
3. Telephones 522; Cars 461
   Rail: 10 995 pass.-km.; 2 472 ton-km.
   Air: 3 643 pass.-km.; 395 ton-km.
   Sea: 10 944 loaded; 33 084 unloaded

Trade
Exports: $3 215 — Imports: $10 274
Cotton — Machinery
Rice — Manufactured products
Cotton lint — Wheat
Fruit and vegetables — Vehicles
Exports to: U.S.S.R., Italy, Netherlands
Imports from: U.S.A., France, Italy, U.K., W. Germany
Invisible trade balance: −$277
Revenue from tourism: $386
Aid received (net): $1 477.5

ETHIOPIA

Area and Population
1. Republic
2. Amharic
3. Ethiopian Birr
4. $1 = 2.09
   £1 = 3.16

1. 1 222 th. sq. km.
2. 42 441; 35 per sq. km.
3. BR 49; DR 23; AI 2.6%
4. Urb. pop.: 4 719 (14%)
5. Addis-Ababa 1 478

Production
1. GDP $4 429 (. . .); $135 (. . .)
   Agric. 45%, Indust. 10%, Others 45%
2. Barley 848 — Millet 145
   Coffee 240 — Maize 1 275
3. Cattle 26 000 — Sheep 23 450
5. Roundwood 29 764
6. Gold 400kg — Salt 124

Manufactures
1. 0.07/0.84; 753 kWh (75% hydr.)
2a. Sugar 198 — Sawnwood 45
b. Cotton yarn 9.2 — Cement 159
3. Telephones 86; Cars 43
   Rail: 310 pass.-km.; 131 ton-km.
   Air: 762 pass.-km.; 97 ton-km.
   Sea: 547 loaded; 1 753 unloaded

Trade
Exports: $416 — Imports: $942
Coffee — Machinery
Hides — Manufactured products
Exports to: U.S.A., Djibouti, Saudi Arabia
Imports from: Japan, W. Germany, Kuwait, Italy, Saudi Arabia
Aid received (net): $201.8

FINLAND

Area and Population
1. Republic
2. Finnish, Swedish
3. Markka
4. $1 = 4.99
   £1 = 7.54

1. 337 th. sq. km.
2. 4 882; 16 per sq. km.
3. BR 13; DR 9; AI 0.3%
4. Urb. pop.: 2 873 (60%)
5. Helsinki 932

Production
1. GDP $47 148 (3.4%); $9 661 (3.1%)
   Agric. 7%, Indust. 24%, Others 69%
2. Wheat 478 — Barley 1 715
   Oats 1 321 — Potatoes 745
3. Cattle 1 620 — Pigs 1 383
4. Fish 157
5. Roundwood 38 439
6. Iron ore 0.7 — Chrome 170
   Titanium 164 — Copper 31
   Zinc 60 — Gold 784kg
   Silver 27t

Manufactures
1. 4.1/21.6; 40 236 kWh (33% hydr., 42% nucl.)
2a. Meat 320 — Butter and cheese 152
   Sawnwood 8 023 — Wood pulp 7 200
b. Paper 6 400 — Newsprint 1 556
   Iron 2 028 — Steel 2 628
   Cotton yarn 7.2 — Ships (grt.) 315
   Petroleum products 9.2
3. Telephones 2 511; Cars 1 352
   Rail: 3 276 pass.-km.; 7 980 ton-km.
   Air: 2 589 pass.-km.; 297 ton-km.
   Sea: 20 724 loaded; 30 260 unloaded

Trade
Exports: $13 505 — Imports: $12 443
Paper and cardboard — Machinery
Wood pulp — Crude petroleum
Sawnwood — Petroleum products
Machinery — Iron and steel
Ships and boats — Textiles
Clothing — Vehicles
Exports to: U.K., Sweden, U.S.S.R, W. Germany
Imports from: Sweden, W. Germany, U.S.S.R., U.K.
Invisible trade balance: −$1 323
Revenue from tourism: $579
Aid given (net): $150

For detailed table headings and notes see first page of this section

5

Country	Area and Population	Production	Manufactures	Trade
FRANCE 1. Republic 2. French 3. French Franc 4. $1 = 7.04 £1 = 10.65	1. 547 th. sq. km. 2. 54 947; 101 per sq. km. 3. BR 14; DR 10; AI 0.3% 4. Urb. pop.: 43 958 (80%) 5. Paris 8 510	1. GDP $445 913 (2.8%); $8 115 (2.4%) Agric. 4%, Indust. 26%, Others 70% 2. Wheat 32 884 / Barley 11 543 Oats 1 875 / Maize 10 321 Potatoes 6 200 / Sugarbeet 27 790 Apples 2 935 / Grapes 9 400 Tomatoes 790 / Pears 485 Tobacco 37 / Wool 23 Rape seed 1 354 3. Cattle 23 570 / Pigs 11 400 Sheep 12 260 / Goats 1 200 Horses 310 4. Fish 784 5. Roundwood 39 839 6. Coal 16.6 / Iron ore 4.5 Crude petroleum 1 680 / Lead 2 Natural gas 231 / Zinc 36 Salt 6 579 / Potash 1 651 Bauxite 1 530 / Nickel 6.9 Silver 24 / Uranium 3 299	1. 57.0/208.2; 283 400 kWh (25% hydr., 48% nucl.) 2a. Meat 5 585 / Butter and cheese 1 855 Wine 6 447 / Beer 22.4 Mhl Sugar 4 340 / Sawnwood 9 367 b. Iron 15 420 / Steel 19 020 Aluminium 510 / Cement 22 716 Plastics 2 694 / Paper 5 300 Synthetic fibres 38 / Petroleum products 68.2 Cotton yarn 193 / Wool yarn 107 Ships (grt.) 221 / Radios 2 733 Vehicles: pass. 2 910, comm. 424 3. Telephones 26 940; Cars 19 300 Rail: 60 276 pass.-km.; 60 120 ton-km. Air: 37 916 pass.-km.; 5 670 ton-km. Sea: 52 284 loaded; 172 332 unloaded	Exports: $93 276 / Imports: $103 807 Machinery / Machinery Vehicles / Petrol Iron and steel / Iron and steel Textiles / Non-ferrous metals Wheat / Vehicles Organic chemical products / Textile fibres Non-ferrous metals / Meat Petroleum products / Fruits Petrol Wine Exports to: W. Germany, Belgium-Luxembourg, Italy, U.K. Imports from: W. Germany, Italy, Belgium-Luxembourg, U.S.A. Invisible trade balance: +$5 190 Revenue from tourism: $6 991 Aid given (net): $9 418
FRENCH GUIANA 1. French Overseas Dept. 2. French 3. Franc 4. $1 = 7.04 £1 = 10.65	1. 91 th. sq. km. 2. 72; 0.8 per sq. km. 3. BR 30; DR 7; AI 3.4% 4. Urb. pop.: 48 (67%) 5. Cayenne 38	2. Cassava 8 / Bananas 1 3. Pigs 10 / Cattle 14 5. Roundwood 254 6. Gold 160kg	1. . . ./0.19; 150 kWh 2a. Sugar. . . / Sawnwood 19 3. Telephones 18; Cars 10 Sea: 25 loaded; 219 unloaded	Exports: $37 / Imports: $249 Timber / Machinery Exports to: France, U.S.A., Japan Imports from: France, Trinidad and Tobago Aid received (net): $95.4
GABON 1. Republic 2. French, Bantu 3. C.F.A. Franc 4. $1 = 352.13 £1 = 532.25	1. 268 th. sq. km. 2. 1 131; 4 per sq. km. 3. BR 33; DR 19; AI 1.6% 4. Urb. pop.: 367 (32%) 5. Libreville 350	1. GDP $3 603 (. .); $3 246 (. .) Agric. 5%, Indust. 49%, Others 46% 2. Cassava 265 / Bananas 178 Cocoa 2 3. Goats 60 / Sheep 80 4. Fish 52 5. Roundwood 2 608 6. Crude petroleum 7.5 / Gold 20kg Manganese 928 / Uranium 1 007	1. 11.8/1.1; 535 kWh (48% hydr.) 2a. Sawnwood 108 / Beer 0.6Mhl b. Petroleum products 1.3 3. Telephones 7; Cars 22 Air: 430 pass.-km.; 67 ton-km. Sea: 8 040 loaded; 631 unloaded	Exports: $1 975 / Imports: $853 Petrol / Manufactured products Sawnwood / Machinery Manganese ores / Vehicles Exports to: France, U.S.A., Argentina Imports from: France, U.S.A., Japan Aid received (net): $47.8
GERMANY (EAST) 1. Republic 2. German 3. Ostmark 4. $1 = 2.21 £1 = 3.34	1. 108 th. sq. km. (including E. Berlin) 2. 16 671; 157 per sq. km. 3. BR 14; DR 13; AI –0.1% 4. Urb. pop.: 12 784 (77%) 5. Berlin (East) 1 173	1. GDP $72 820 (3.3%); $4 368 (3.4%) Agric. 9%, Indust. 74%, Others 17% 2. Barley 4 400 / Rye 2 300 Wheat 4 100 / Potatoes 8 000 Apples 500 / Rape seed 303 3. Pigs 13 058 / Cattle 5 908 Sheep 2 359 4. Fish 240 5. Roundwood 10 908 6. Lignite 296.3 / Natural gas 145 Copper 12 / Potash 3 431 Salt 3 126 / Tin 2.5 Coal 1.0 / Silver 40	1. 91.7/121.8; 104 928 kWh (12% hydr., 1.6% nucl.) 2a. Meat 1 812 / Butter 297 Sugar 690 / Beer 25.4Mhl Sawnwood 2 446 b. Cotton yarn 134 / Wool yarn 37 Iron 2 352 / Steel 7 572 Ships (grt.) 350 / Petroleum products 19.4 Vehicles: pass. 202, comm. 41 3. Telephones 3 252; Cars 3 000 Rail: 22 920 pass.-km.; 56 652 ton-km. Air: . . . pass.-km.; . . . ton-km. Sea: 4 000 loaded; 15 500 unloaded	Exports: $24 836 / Imports: $22 940 Machinery / Machinery Vehicles / Crude petroleum Consumer goods / Iron ore Coal Fuels The principal trade is with: U.S.S.R., Czechoslovakia, W. Germany, Poland
GERMANY (WEST) 1. Federal Republic 2. German 3. Deutschmark 4. $1 = 2.21 £1 = 3.34	1. 249 th. sq. km. (including W. Berlin) 2. 61 181; 251 per sq. km. 3. BR 10; DR 11; AI –0.2% 4. Urb. pop.: 52 616 (86%) 5. Bonn 293	1. GDP $554 511 (3.5%); $9 064 (3.6%) Agric. 2%, Indust. 31%, Others 67% 2. Barley 10 284 / Wheat 10 223 Rye 1 930 / Potatoes 7 753 Apples 1 752 / Grapes 1 066 3. Pigs 23 449 / Cattle 15 552 4. Fish 306 5. Roundwood 29 485 6. Coal 84.0 / Zinc 113 Lignite 127.3 / Natural gas 635 Iron ore 0.3 / Crude petroleum 0.3 Salt 11 266 / Potash 2 419 Silver 38 / Lead 27	1. 157.8/339.7; 373 813 kWh (5% hydr., 18% nucl.) 2a. Meat 5 239 / Butter and cheese 1 444 Sugar 3 150 / Sawnwood 9 500 Wine 810 / Beer 91.2Mhl b. Cotton yarn 194 / Wool yarn 48 Iron 30 360 / Steel 39 384 Aluminium 1 219 / Radios 2 864 Vehicles: / Petroleum products 76.6 pass. 3 788, comm. 264 / Ships (grt.) 489 Synthetic fibres 143 3. Telephones 30 122; Cars 25 036 Rail: 38 616 pass.-km.; 59 844 ton-km. Air: 21 625 pass.-km.; 3 746 ton-km. Sea: 43 632 loaded; 84 984 unloaded	Exports: $169 784 / Imports: $151 246 Machinery / Machinery Vehicles / Non-ferrous metals Iron and steel / Crude petroleum Textiles / Iron and steel Organic chemicals / Textiles / Food Exports to: France, Netherlands, U.S.A., Belgium-Luxembourg, Italy Imports from: Netherlands, France, Belgium-Luxembourg, Italy, U.S.A. Invisible trade balance: –$5 200 Revenue from tourism: $5 614 Aid given (net): $7 467
GHANA 1. Republic 2. English 3. Cedi 4. $1 = 90.39 £1 = 136.62	1. 239 th. sq. km. 2. 13 151; 55 per sq. km. 3. BR 47; DR 16; AI 3.3% 4. Urb. pop.: 4 044 (31%) 5. Accra 965	1. GDP $8 182 (2.3%); $668 (–1.2%) Agric. 51%, Indust. 6%, Others 43% 2. Cassava 1 900 / Cocoa 188 Groundnuts 90 / Maize 534 3. Sheep 2 000 / Goats 2 000 4. Fish 228 5. Roundwood 9 803 6. Bauxite 64 / Manganese 76.2 Gold 11.6 / Diamonds 350	1. 0.4/1.2; 2 589 kWh (98% hydr.) 2a. Sawnwood 381 / Beer 0.3Mhl 3. Telephones 70; Cars 108 Rail: 314 pass.-km.; 92 ton-km. Air: 291 pass.-km.; 31 ton-km. Sea: 1 471 loaded; 2 493 unloaded	Exports: $57 / Imports: $247 Cocoa / Manufactured goods Aluminium / Machinery Exports to: U.K., U.S.A., W. Germany, U.S.S.R., Netherlands Imports from: U.S.A., U.K., W. Germany, Nigeria Invisible trade balance: –$219 Aid received (net): $175.2
GREECE 1. Republic 2. Greek 3. Drachma 4. $1 = 140.1 £1 = 211.76	1. 132 th. sq. km. 2. 9 896; 76 per sq. km. 3. BR 13; DR 9; AI 0.6% 4. Urb. pop.: 6 432 (65%) 5. Athens 3 027	1. GDP $29 361 (3.7%); $2 966 (2.5%) Agric. 15%, Indust. 19%, Others 66% 2. Wheat 2 646 / Potatoes 980 Olives 1 400 / Tomatoes 2 250 Grapes 1 565 / Tobacco 137 3. Sheep 8 500 / Goats 4 650 4. Fish 100 5. Roundwood 2 624 6. Bauxite 2 386 / Lignite 32.4 Chrome 35 / Magnesite 891 Zinc 23 / Lead 22 Nickel 13.6	1. 7.9/21.4; 22 262 kWh (10% hydr.) 2a. Olive oil 285 / Wine 540 Butter and cheese 262 / Sawnwood 390 b. Cotton yarn 119 / Steel 900 Cement 13 320 / Aluminium 136 Petroleum products 12.8 3. Telephones 2 957; Cars 999 Rail: 1 536 pass.-km.; 768 ton-km. Air: 4 924 pass.-km.; 507 ton-km. Sea: 20 328 loaded; 28 224 unloaded	Exports: $4 811 / Imports: $9 434 Tobacco / Machinery Iron and steel / Ships and boats Raisins / Vehicles Aluminium / Iron and steel: Crude petroleum Cotton Exports to: W. Germany, Italy, France, Saudi Arabia Imports from: W. Germany, Italy, Japan Invisible trade balance: +$466 Revenue from tourism: $1 527

For detailed table headings and notes see first page of this section

Country	Area and Population	Production		Manufactures		Trade	

GUINEA

1. Republic
2. French
3. Guinean Franc
4. $1 = 339.89
   £1 = 513.74

1. 246 th. sq. km.
2. 5 931; 24 per sq. km.
3. BR 47; DR 25; AI 2.3%
4. Urb. pop.: 1 378 (26%)
5. Conakry 763

1. GDP $1 910 (. . .); $369 (. . .)
2. Cassava 650
   Coffee 15
   Sweet potatoes 73
3. Sheep 455
4. Roundwood 3 644
5. Roundwood 3 644
6. Bauxite 14 738

Rice 400
Bananas 350
Palm oil 45
Cattle 1 850

Diamonds 40

1. 0.01/0.42; 500 kWh (16% hydr.)
2a. Sawnwood 90
3. Telephones 10; Cars 10
   Air: 144 pass.-km.; 14 ton-km.
   Sea: 10 000 loaded; 545 unloaded

Exports: $70
  Bauxite and
  aluminium
  Iron ore
  Coffee
Main trade is with: Portugal, Sweden
Aid received (net): $82.3

Imports: $100
  Machinery
  Manufactured goods
  Foods

HAITI

1. Republic
2. French, Creole
3. Gourde
4. $1 = 5.00
   £1 = 7.56

1. 28 th. sq. km.
2. 5 185; 85 per sq. km.
3. BR 42; DR 16; AI 2.5%
4. Urb. pop.: 1 452 (28%)
5. Port-au-Prince 888

1. GDP $1 029 (4.1%); $199 (2.3%)
   Agric. 32%, Indust. 17%, Others 51%
2. Bananas 550
   Cocoa 3
3. Pigs 500
4. Roundwood 5 624
5. Roundwood 5 624
6. Bauxite 377

Sisal 11
Coffee 38
Goats 1 100

1. 0.03/0.3; 373 kWh (70% hydr.)
2a. Meat 64
3. Telephones 18; Cars 17
   Sea: 723 loaded; 561 unloaded.

Sugar 35

Exports: $187
  Coffee
  Bauxite
  Sugar
  Sisal
Exports to: U.S.A. France, Belgium-Luxembourg
Imports from: U.S.A., Neth. Antilles, Japan, Canada,
Aid received (net): $101.5

Imports: $314
  Foods
  Textiles
  Machinery
  Mineral oils

HONG KONG

1. British colony
2. English, Chinese
3. Hong Kong Dollar
4. $1 = 7.77
   £1 = 11.74

1. 1.04 th. sq. km.
2. 5 364; 5 157 per sq. km.
3. BR 14; DR 5; AI 2.1%
4. Urb. pop.: 4 573 (92%)
5. Hong Kong 1 184

1. GDP $26 786 (12.0%); $4 997 (8.8%)
   Agric. 1%, Indust. 21%, Others 78%
2. Rice 1
3. Pigs 500
4. Fish 189
5. Roundwood 180
6. Iron ore . . .

Cattle 5

1. . . ./102; 16 482 kWh
2a. Cotton yarn 137
   Sawnwood 262
3. Telephones 1 823; Cars 228
   Rail: 1 476 pass.-km.; 96 ton-km.
   Sea: 13 980 loaded; 33 504 unloaded

Wool yarn 6

Exports: $28 317
  Clothing
  Textiles
  Toys and games
  Radios
Exports to: U.S.A., U.K., Japan, W. Germany
Imports from: Japan, China, U.S.A., U.K., Singapore
Revenue from tourism: $1 457
Aid received (net): $19.8

Imports: $28 567
  Textiles
  Machines
  Diamonds
  Cotton

HUNGARY

1. Republic
2. Hungarian
3. Forint
4. $1 = 45.84
   £1 = 69.29

1. 93 th. sq. km.
2. 10 665; 116 per sq. km.
3. BR 12; DR 14; AI 0.7%
4. Urb. pop.: 5 810 (54%)
5. Budapest 2 064

1. NMP $15 705 (3.4%); $1 473 (3.1%)
   Agric. 13%, Indust. 38%, Others 49%
2. Maize 6 700
   Potatoes 1 300
   Apples 1 144
3. Pigs 9 844
4. Fish 44
5. Roundwood 6 396
6. Coal 2.6
   Lignite 22.5
   Natural gas 249

Wheat 7 300
Tobacco 17
Grapes 850
Sheep 2 977

Bauxite 2 994
Manganese 17.6
Crude petroleum 27.0

1. 22.4/39.8; 25 775 kWh (0.6% hydr., 10% nucl.)
2a. Sugar 533
   Wine 535
b. Iron 2 100
   Aluminium 74
   Wool yarn 11
3. Telephones 1 297; Cars 1 182
   Rail: 10 512 pass.-km.; 22 308 ton-km.
   Air: 1 208 pass.-km.; 130 ton-km.

Sawnwood 1 180
Beer 7.9 Mhl
Steel 3 744
Cotton yarn 56.4
Petroleum products 7.4

Exports: $8 563
  Machinery
  Vehicles
  Fruit and vegetables
  Iron and steel
  Medicinal products
Main trade is with: U.S.S.R., W. Germany, E.Germany,
Czechoslovakia
Invisible trade balance: –$609
Revenue from tourism: $394

Imports: $8 109
  Machinery
  Vehicles
  Iron and steel
  Crude petroleum
  Petroleum products
  Chemical products

ICELAND

1. Republic
2. Icelandic
3. Icelandic Krona
4. $1 = 41.25
   £1 = 62.35

1. 103 th. sq. km.
2. 240; 2 per sq. km.
3. BR 18; DR 7; AI 1.1%
4. Urb. pop.: 207 (89%)
5. Reykjavik 124

1. GDP $2 636 (4.1%); $10 983 (3.1%)
2. Potatoes 13
3. Sheep 770
4. Fish 839

Whaling 352

1. 0.5/1.1; 3 781 kWh (95% hydr., 4.8% geo.)
2a. Meat 25
b. Aluminium 82
3. Telephones 111; Cars 95
   Air: 1 405 pass.-km.; 151 ton-km.
   Sea: 502 loaded; 1 358 unloaded

Exports: $728
  Fish, frozen and fresh
  Fish, salted and
  smoked
  Fish meal
  Aluminium
  Cod liver oil
Exports to: U.S.A., U.K., W. Germany
Imports from: W. Germany, U.K., U.S.S.R., Denmark,
Sweden

Imports: $820
  Machinery
  Petroleum products
  Textiles
  Iron and steel
  Paper and cardboard

INDIA

1. Federal Republic
2. Hindi, English
3. Indian Rupee
4. $1 = 12.29
   £1 = 18.57

1. 3 288 th. sq. km.
2. 745 012; 227 per sq. km.
3. BR 34; DR 12; AI 2.0%
4. Urb. pop.: 159 727 (23%)
5. Delhi 5 729

1. GDP $173 883 (3.7%); $233 (1.7%)
   Agric. 29%, Indust. 17%, Others 54%
2. Wheat 45 148
   Rice 91 000
   Coffee 103
   Sorghum 1 180
   Jute 1 404
   Cottonseed 2 500
3. Cattle 182 160
4. Fish 2 520
5. Roundwood 232 537
6. Coal 144.7
   Iron ore 25.8
   Bauxite 2 306
   Copper 47
   Zinc 44
   Gold 2.0

Millet 11 800
Tea 645
Tobacco 497
Rubber 185
Cotton lint 1 250

Goats 80 800

Manganese 442
Chrome 390
Crude petroleum 25.8
Lead 19
Diamonds 14
Silver 25

1. 159.8/169.3; 147 952 kWh (35% hydr., 1.4% nucl.)
2a. Sugar 6 420
   Sawnwood 10 976
b. Iron 9 588
   Aluminium 268
   Cement 29 028
   Radios 1 563
3. Telephones 2 982; Cars 1 068
   Rail: 220 464 pass.-km.; 172 536 ton-km.
   Air: 13 259 pass.-km.; 1 625 ton-km.
   Sea: 38 900 loaded; 40 380 unloaded

Butter 740

Steel 10 344
Zinc 55
Cotton yarn 1 093
Petroleum products 26.7

Exports: $8 474
  Jute products
  Tea
  Iron ore
  Iron and steel
  Cotton goods
Exports to: U.S.A., Japan, U.S.S.R., UK
Imports from: U.S.A., U.K., Japan, W. Germany
Invisible trade balance: –$621
Revenue from tourism: $800
Aid received (net): $1 933.4

Imports: $13 501
  Machinery
  Wheat
  Petrol
  Cotton
  Iron and steel

INDONESIA

1. Republic
2. Bahasa Indonesia
3. Rupiah
4. $1 = 1 123.63
   £1 = 1 698.36

1. 1 905 th. sq. km.
2. 159 895; 88 per sq. km.
3. BR 36; DR 15; AI 1.8%
4. Urb. pop.: 32 845 (22%)
5. Jakarta 6 503

1. GDP $79 994 (7.9%); $500 (6.0%)
   Agric. 25%, Indust. 30%, Others 45%
2. Cassava 14 000
   Rice 37 500
   Coffee 329
   Palm oil 1 000
   Rubber 1 150
3. Cattle 6 800
4. Fish 2 112
5. Roundwood 122 249
6. Coal 1.1
   Bauxite 1 003
   Nickel 47.8
   Diamonds 2.7
   Silver 35

Groundnuts 820
Copra 800
Tea 115
Tobacco 118

Goats 7 910

Tin 23.2
Natural gas 690
Crude petroleum 66.3
Copper 86

1. 120.1/38.3; 15 280 kWh (10% hydr.)
2a. Meat 537
   Sugar 1 675
b. Cement 6 612
   Petroleum products 20.8
3. Telephones 584; Cars 791
   Rail: 6 384 pass.-km.; 1 176 ton-km.
   Air: 8 044 pass.-km.; 875 ton-km.
   Sea: 107 124 loaded; 24 876 unloaded

Sawnwood 6 314

Tin 23

Exports: $21 858
  Crude petroleum
  Petroleum products
  Rubber
  Coffee
  Tin
  Spices
Exports to: Japan, Singapore, U.S.A.,
Trinidad and Tobago
Imports from: U.S.A., W. Germany, Japan, Singapore
Aid received (net): $1 176.4

Imports: $13 882
  Machinery
  Textiles
  Iron and steel
  Vehicles
  Rice

IRAN

1. Islamic Republic
2. Persian
3. Rial
4. $1 = 78.56
   £1 = 118.75

1. 1 648 th. sq. km.
2. 43 414; 27 per sq. km.
3. BR 43; DR 12; AI 3%
4. Urb. pop.: 20 774 (50%)
5. Teheran 4 589

1. GDP $128 921 (–4.7%); $3 161 (–7.0%)
   Agric. 18%, Indust. 26%, Others 56%
2. Wheat 5 500
   Rice 1 230
   Dates 330
   Raisins 52
3. Sheep 34 000
4. Roundwood 5 721
6. Natural gas 264
   Chrome 40
   Lead 20
   Silver 30

Cottonseed 180
Cotton lint 95
Tea 45
Tobacco 25
Goats 13 600

Crude petroleum 107.9
Zinc 30
Salt 750

1. 190.8/47.3; 29 900 kWh (22% hydr.)
2a. Sugar 725
b. Cotton yarn 88
   Cement 10 270
3. Telephones 1 049; Cars 933
   Rail: 2 526 pass.-km.; 3 861 ton-km.
   Air: 1 852 pass.-km.; 215 ton-km.
   Sea: 80 000 loaded; 6 000 unloaded

Sawnwood 163
Wool yarn 19
Petroleum products 25.5

Exports: $19 414
  Crude petroleum
  Petroleum products
  Carpets
Exports to: U.S.S.R., W. Germany, U.S.A., Italy,
Saudi Arabia
Imports from: W. Germany, U.S.A., Japan, U.K.
Invisible trade balance: –$3 442

Imports: $11 539
  Machinery
  Iron and steel
  Vehicles
  Textiles

For detailed table headings and notes see first page of this section

Country	Area and Population	Production	Manufactures	Trade
IRAQ 1. Republic 2. Arabic 3. Iraq Dinar 4. $1 = 0.31 £1 = 0.47	1. 435 th. sq. km. 2. 15 356; 35 per sq. km. 3. BR 47; DR 13; AI 3.5% 4. Urb. pop.: 8 683 (68%) 5. Bagdad 2 969	1. GDP $48 879 (. . .); $3 700 (. . .) Agric. 7%, Indust. 60%, Others 33% 2. Barley 300 / Rice 95 Wheat 300 / Dates 115 Cottonseed 6 3. Sheep 8 300 / Goats 2 300 5. Roundwood 113 6. Natural gas 17 / Crude petroleum 60.7	1. 69.1/9.2; 13 700 kWh (4% hydr.) 2b. Petroleum products 7.7 3. Telephones 185; Cars 170 Rail: 797 pass.-km.; 2 254 ton-km. Air: 1 470 pass.-km.; 187 ton-km. Sea: 95 750 loaded; 4 004 unloaded	Exports: $10 530 / Imports: $7 903 Crude petroleum / Manufactured goods Dates / Machinery / Food Exports to: India, China, Kuwait Imports from: U.K., W. Germany, Japan Revenue from tourism: $170 Aid received (net): $12.4
IRELAND 1. Republic 2. Irish, English 3. Irish pound 4. $1 = 0.73 £1 = 1.10	1. 70 th. sq. km. 2. 3 535; 51 per sq. km. 3. BR 19; DR 9; AI 2.0% 4. Urb. pop.: 1 914 (56%) 5. Dublin 915	1. GDP $16 613 (3.7%); $4 733 (2.5%) Agric. 11%, Indust. 24%, Others 65% 2. Barley 1 600 / Wheat 660 Potatoes 1 000 / Wool 10 Tomatoes 19 3. Cattle 6 759 / Sheep 3 754 4. Fish 203 5. Roundwood 1 026 6. Lead 37 / Zinc 206 Coal 0.06 / Natural gas 83	1. 4.3/11.2; 11 178 kWh (11% hydr.) 2a. Meat 638 / Sawnwood 247 Butter and cheese 216 b. Wool yarn 5.2 / Petroleum products 0.7 Cotton yarn 20 3. Telephones 720; Cars 714 Rail: 816 pass.-km.; 552 ton-km. Air: 2 343 pass.-km.; 285 ton-km. Sea: 5 000 loaded; 14 500 unloaded	Exports: $9 629 / Imports: $9 663 Cattle / Machinery Beef / Textiles Dairy products / Vehicles Non-ferrous metals / Iron and steel Machinery / Crude petroleum Main trade is with U.K. Exports to: U.S.A., France, W. Germany, Netherlands, Belgium-Lux Imports from: U.S.A., W. Germany, France, Italy, Japan Invisible trade balance: –$1 589 Revenue from tourism: $477
ISRAEL 1. Republic 2. Hebrew, Arabic 3. Shekel 4. $1 = 1.49 £1 = 2.25	1. 21 th. sq. km. 2. 4 194; 210 per sq. km. 3. BR 24; DR 7; AI 2.1% 4. Urb. pop.: 3 525 (87%) 5. Jerusalem 429	1. GDP $24 483 (3.1%); $6 075 (0.8%) Agric. 4%, Indust. 23%, Others 73% 2. Wheat 130 / Cottonseed 187 Oranges 921 / Cotton lint 94 Grapefruits 409 / Tomatoes 359 3. Cattle 330 / Sheep 240 4. Fish 22 5. Roundwood 118 6. Phosphates 1 966 / Potash 1 000 Salt 145 / Crude petroleum 0.02	1. 0.1/10.2; 14 578 kWh 2a. Meat 234 / Butter and cheese 66 Wine 33 b. Cotton yarn 16.8 / Wool yarn 5.6 Cement 1 884 3. Telephones 1 230; Cars 519 Rail: 221 pass.-km.; 827 ton-km. Air: 4 648 pass.-km.; 720 ton-km. Sea: 7 080 loaded; 9 576 unloaded	Exports: $5 804 / Imports: $8 411 Diamonds / Machinery Fruit / Diamonds Clothing / Iron and steel Exports to: U.S.A., W. Germany, U.K., Hong Kong Imports from: U.S.A., W. Germany, U.K., Netherlands, Switzerland Invisible trade balance: –$2 213 Revenue from tourism: $900 Aid received (net): $957.3
ITALY 1. Republic 2. Italian 3. Italian Lira 4. $1 = 1 512.40 £1 = 2 286.00	1. 301 th. sq. km. 2. 56 983; 194 per sq. km. 3. BR 10; DR 9; AI 0.3% 4. Urb. pop.: 40 453 (71%) 5. Rome 2 831	1. GDP $316 190 (3.6%); $5 549 (3.2%) Agric. 5%, Indust. 27%, Others 68% 2. Wheat 10 005 / Maize 6 781 Tomatoes 6 143 / Grapes 11 200 Olives 2 050 / Tobacco 153 Oranges 1 700 / Apples 2 050 Pears 1 070 / Lemons 690 3. Cattle 9 113 / Sheep 9 228 4. Fish 478 5. Roundwood 5 658 6. Lignite 1 950 / Natural gas 501 Zinc 43 / Crude petroleum 2.2 Asbestos 139 / Bauxite 13 Lead 24	1. 27.6/172.6; 182 880 kWh (24% hydr., 3.1% nucl., 1.4% geo.) 2a. Meat 3 732 / Butter and cheese 731 Sugar 1 370 / Wine 7 000 Olives 430 / Sawnwood 2 264 b. Iron 11 892 / Steel 23 076 Aluminium 513 / Woven silk 20 Cotton yarn 150 / Wool yarn 319 Televisions 1 719 / Ships (grt.) 233 Petroleum products 71.4 / Vehicles: Synthetic fibres 595 / pass. 1 439, comm. 160 3. Telephones 20 453; Cars 18 603 Rail: 37 128 pass.-km.; 17 868 ton-km. Air: 15 143 pass.-km.; 1 953 ton-km. Sea: 34 512 loaded; 187 584 unloaded	Exports: $73 303 / Imports: $84 215 Machinery / Machinery Vehicles / Petroleum Textiles / Non-ferrous metals Clothing / Iron and steel Petroleum products / Textile fibres Shoes / Cereals Iron and steel / Vehicles Fruit / Meat Exports to: France, W. Germany, U.S.A., U.K. Imports from: W. Germany, France, U.S.A. Invisible trade balance: +$2 026 Revenue from tourism: $8 234 Aid given (net): $3 676
IVORY COAST 1. Republic 2. French 3. C.F.A. Franc 4. $1 = 352.13 £1 = 532.25	1. 322 th. sq. km. 2. 9 464; 30 per sq. km. 3. BR 46; DR 20; AI 3.4% 4. Urb. pop.: 4 169 (44%) 5. Abidjan 1 850	1. GDP $7 586 (7.1%); $856 (2.9%) Agric. 27%, Indust. 11%, Others 62% 2. Rice 490 / Coffee 285 Cassava 800 / Cocoa 411 3. Sheep 1 400 / Goats 1 400 4. Fish 94 5. Roundwood 11 839 6. Diamonds 70	1. 1.9/1.8; 1 932 kWh (90% hydr.) 2a. Sawnwood 805 / Petroleum products 2.7 3. Telephones 88; Cars 167 Rail: 852 pass.-km.; 576 ton-km. Air: 316 pass.-km.; 51 ton-km. Sea: 4 536 loaded; 4 848 unloaded	Exports: $2 067 / Imports: $1 340 Cocoa / Machinery Coffee / Vehicles Exports to: France, U.S.A., Italy, Netherlands Imports from: France, W. Germany, U.S.A Invisible trade balance: –$1 172 Aid received (net): $224.4
JAMAICA 1. Commonwealth 2. English 3. Jamaica Dollar 4. $1 = 5.83 £1 = 8.82	1. 11 th. sq. km. 2. 2 301; 209 per sq. km. 3. BR 23; DR 5; AI 1.4% 4. Urb. pop.: 1 191 (52%) 5. Kingston 671	1. GDP $3 185 (–2.5%); $1 428 (–3.6%) Agric. 7%, Indust. 22%, Others 71% 2. Bananas 185 / Copra 7 Oranges 32 / Sugar cane 2 655 3. Goats 420 / Cattle 318 4. Fish 9 5. Roundwood 39 6. Bauxite 8 735	1. 0.02/3.0; 2 350 kWh (6% hydr.) 2a. Meat 50 / Sugar 193 b. Petroleum products 1.2 3. Telephones 60; Cars 124 Rail: 83 pass.-km.; 186 ton-km. Air: 1 230 pass.-km.; 129 ton-km. Sea: 8 335 loaded; 4 018 unloaded	Exports: $781 / Imports: $1 178 Bauxite and / Machinery aluminium / Textiles Sugar / Petroleum Bananas Exports to: U.S.A., U.K., Canada, Norway Imports from: U.S.A., Venezuela, U.K. Revenue from tourism: $338 Aid received (net): $166.2
JAPAN 1. Constitutional Monarchy 2. Japanese 3. Japanese Yen 4. $1 = 172.01 £1 = 260.00	1. 372 th. sq. km. (incl. Ryukyu Arch.) 2. 120 018; 323 per sq. km. 3. BR 13; DR 6; AI 0.6% 4. Urb. pop.: 89 187 (74%) 5. Tokyo 11 676	1. GDP $1 183 975 (5.0%); $9 928 (4.1%) Agric. 3%, Indust. 31%, Others 66% 2. Rice 14 848 / Potatoes 3 584 Tomatoes 791 / Apples 986 Pears 480 Tea 102 / Oranges/mandarines 2 552 Tobacco 137 3. Pigs 10 423 / Cattle 4 682 4. Fish 11 250 5. Roundwood 32 813 6. Coal 16.6 / Lead 49 Natural gas 90 / Manganese 27 Crude petroleum 0.2 / Zinc 253 Iron ore 0.3 / Gold 3.0 Copper 43 / Silver 324	1. 43.8/403.9; 602 357 kWh (14% hydr., 18% nucl.) 2a. Meat 3 344 / Sugar 905 Beer 48.4 Mhl / Sawnwood 29 670 b. Iron 81 816 / Steel 105 588 Aluminium 1 106 / Plastics 5 701 Cotton yarn 436 / Wool yarn 122 Silk 10 500 / Newsprint 2 715 Synthetic fibres 425 / Petroleum Vehicles: / products 153.8 pass. 7 073, comm. 4 037 / Radios 14 318 TV receivers 12 796 / Ships (grt.) 9 395 3. Telephones 56 284; Cars 25 539 Rail: 325 008 pass.-km.; 23 184 ton-km. Air: 55 731 pass.-km.; 6 986 ton-km. Sea: 94 320 loaded; 602 664 unloaded	Exports: $170 132 / Imports: $136 492 Iron and steel / Crude petroleum Electrical machinery / Machinery Textiles / Sawnwood Other machinery / Iron ore Vehicles / Textile fibres Ships and boats / Non-ferrous metals / Cereals Exports to: U.S.A., S. Korea, W. Germany Imports from: U.S.A., Australia, Saudi Arabia, Indonesia Invisible trade balance: –$7 750 Revenue from tourism: $763 Aid given (net): $8 593
KENYA 1. Republic 2. Bantu, English 3. Kenyan Shilling 4. $1 = 15.85 £1 = 23.95	1. 583 th. sq. km. 2. 19 563; 34 per sq. km. 3. BR 56; DR 14; AI 4.1% 4. Urb. pop.: 2 382 (15%) 5. Nairobi 1 200	1. GDP $5 442 (5.4%); $279 (1.2%) Agric. 27%, Indust. 11%, Others 62% 2. Maize 1 275 / Cottonseed 17 Coffee 95 / Tea 116 3. Cattle 12 000 / Goats 8 300 Sheep 6 700 4. Fish 97 5. Roundwood 29 330 6. Salt 83 / Soda ash 153	1. 0.2/1.8; 2 166 kWh (68% hydr.) 2a. Sugar 391 / Sawnwood 181 b. Cement 1 140 / Petroleum products 2.8 3. Telephones 217; Cars 115 Rail: 8 665 pass.-km.; 3 536 ton-km. (incl. Tanzania and Uganda) Air: 942 pass.-km.; 110 ton-km. Sea: 1 512 loaded; 3 792 unloaded	Exports: $1 084 / Imports: $1 501 Coffee / Machinery Tea / Vehicles Petroleum products / Petroleum Pyrethrum / Iron and steel Exports to: U.K., W. Germany, Uganda Imports from: U.K., Japan, W. Germany, U.S.A., Iran Revenue from tourism: $185 Aid received (net): $445.6

For detailed table headings and notes see first page of this section

Country	Area and Population	Production	Manufactures	Trade

KOREA (NORTH)

1. Republic
2. Korean
3. Won
4. $1 = 0.94
   £1 = 1.42

1. 121 th. sq. km.
2. 19 891; 164 per sq. km.
3. BR 33; DR 8; AI 2.3%
4. Urb. pop.: 12 171 (62%)
5. Pyongyang 1 500

2. Rice 5 400   Maize 2 580
   Potatoes 1 700   Tobacco 52
3. Pigs 2 700   Cattle 1 025*
4. Fish 1 600
5. Roundwood 6 200
6. Coal 37.1   Zinc 150
   Lead 110   Tungsten 500t
   Iron ore 4.8   Copper 10
   Gold 5.0   Silver 50

1. 47.8/52.3; 41 000 kWh (64% hydr.)
2a. Sawnwood 280
  b. Cotton . . .   Lead 95
     Steel 6 500   Zinc 115
     Iron 3 000   Fertilizers 860
     Petroleum products 2.9
3. Sea: 1 300 loaded; 2 000 unloaded

Exports: . . .   Imports: . . .
Minerals   Machinery
Metal products
Main trade is with U.S.S.R.

KOREA (SOUTH)

1. Republic
2. Korean
3. Won
4. $1 = 888.82
   £1 = 1 343.45

1. 98 th. sq. km.
2. 40 578; 414 per sq. km.
3. BR 23; DR 6; AI 1.4%
4. Urb. pop.: 21 434 (53%)
5. Seoul 8 367

1. GDP $81 129 (7.2%); $1 999 (5.6%)
   Agric. 14%, Indust. 30%, Others 56%
2. Rice 7 970   Barley 804
   Potatoes 436   Cottonseed 2
3. Pigs 3 649   Cattle 2 215
4. Fish 2 400
5. Roundwood 10 189
6. Coal 20.6   Gold 2.2
   Iron ore 0.7   Tungsten 2.5
   Zinc 54   Silver 70

1. 13.9/57.8; 53 047 kWh (5% hydr., 17% nucl.)
2a. Meat 679   Sawnwood 3 518
  b. Cotton yarn 275   Steel 5 016
     Radios 5 500   Iron 8 904
     Petroleum products 22.7   Cars 167
3. Telephones 2 898; Cars 360
   Rail: 21 227 pass.-km.; 10 625 ton-km.
   Air: 12 101 pass.-km.; 2 180 ton-km.
   Sea: 26 292 loaded; 79 020 unloaded

Exports: $29 245   Imports: $30 631
Clothing   Machinery
Plywood   Rice
Textiles   Petrol
Exports to: U.S.A., Japan, Saudi Arabia
Imports from: Japan, U.S.A., Saudi Arabia
Invisible trade balance: −$876
Revenue from tourism: $502
Aid received (net): $531.8

LAOS

1. Democratic Republic
2. Laotian, French
3. Kip
4. $1 = 34.99
   £1 = 52.89

1. 237 th. sq. km.
2. 4 019; 17 per sq. km.
3. BR 43; DR 17; AI 2.5%
4. Urb. pop.: 647 (15%)
5. Vientiane 120

1. GDP $300 (. . .); $87 (. . .)
2. Rice 1 322   Coffee 4
   Cottonseed 14   Tobacco 4
3. Pigs 1 350   Buffaloes 915
5. Roundwood 3 920
6. Tin 0.6

1. 0.1/0.3; 1 250 kWh (95% hydr.)
2a. Sawnwood 41
  b. Woven silk. . .
3. Telephones 6; Cars 15
   Air: 10 pass.-km.; 2 ton-km.

Exports: $33   Imports: $125
Sawnwood   Agricultural products
Tin   Petroleum products
  Vehicles
Exports to: Thailand, Malaysia, Hong Kong
Imports from: Thailand, Japan, France, W. Germany
Aid received (net): $43.3

LEBANON

1. Republic
2. Arabic, French
3. Lebanese pound
4. $1 = 24.69
   £1 = 37.32

1. 10 th. sq. km.
2. 2 644; 264 per sq. km.
3. BR 30; DR 9; AI −0.01%
4. Urb. pop.: 2 062 (78%)
5. Beirut 702

1. GDP $3 438 (. . .); $1 273 (. . .)
   Agric. 8%, Indust. 13%, Others 79%
2. Wheat 18   Oranges 200
   Apples 128   Grapes 160
   Tomatoes 125   Tobacco 4
3. Goats 440   Sheep 130
5. Roundwood 252
6. Salt 5

1. 0.1/2.0; 1 220 kWh (46% hydr.)
2a. Sugar 12   Sawnwood 33
  b. Cotton yarn. . .   Petroleum products 0.7
3. Telephones 192; Cars 315
   Rail: 2 pass.-km.; 42 ton-km.
   Air: 968 pass.-km.; 555 ton-km.
   Sea: 2 000 loaded; 2 500 unloaded

Exports: $886   Imports: $3 615
Fruit   Machinery
Machinery   Textiles
Vegetables   Vehicles
Eggs   Petroleum products
Exports to: Saudi Arabia, Syria, Libya, Kuwait
Imports from: U.S.A., W. Germany, France, Italy, U.K.
Aid received (net): $77.2

LIBYA

1. People's Republic
2. Arabic
3. Libyan Dinar
4. $1 = 0.30
   £1 = 0.45

1. 1 760 th. sq. km.
2. 3 624; 2.1 per sq. km.
3. BR 38; DR 13; AI 3.9%
4. Urb. pop.: 2 211 (61%)
5. Tripoli 980

1. GDP $29 885 (7.7%); $8 974 (3.5%)
   Agric. 2%, Indust. 52%, Others 46%
2. Barley 70   Tomatoes 245
   Dates 98   Olives 110
   Tobacco 1   Groundnuts 14
3. Sheep 4 800   Goats 1 500
5. Roundwood 631
6. Crude petroleum 54.3   Natural gas 384

1. 91.9/19.1; 7 150 kWh
2a. Olive oil 16
  b. Petroleum products 4.9
3. Telephones 41; Cars 400
   Air: 1 473 pass.-km.; 121 ton-km.
   Sea: 53 530 loaded; 12 680 unloaded

Exports: $11 136   Imports: $7 175
Crude petroleum   Machinery
  Vehicles
Exports to: W. Germany, Italy, U.S.A, France, Spain
Imports from: Italy, U.K., W. Germany, France, Japan
Aid received (net): $13.7

LUXEMBOURG

1. Grand Duchy
2. Luxembourgeois, French, German
3. Luxembourg Franc
4. $1 = 45.05
   £1 = 68.10

1. 2.6 th. sq. km.
2. 363; 140 per sq. km.
3. BR 12; DR 11; AI −0.1%
4. Urb. pop.: 283 (78%)
5. Luxembourg 79

1. GDP $3 344 (2.7%); $9 289 (2.7%)
   Agric. 3%, Indust. 29%, Others 68%
2. Oats 33
6. Iron ore 0.3

1. 0.1/3.8; 797 kWh (55% hydr.)
2a. Wine 16   Beer 0.7 Mhl
    Sawnwood 917
  b. Iron 2 772   Steel 3 948
3. Telephones 228; Cars 138
   Rail: 288 pass.-km.; 588 ton-km.
   Air: 92 pass.-km.; 9 ton-km.

Exports: (See Belgium)   Imports: (See Belgium)

MADAGASCAR

1. Republic
2. Malagasy, French
3. Malagasy Franc
4. $1 = 571.31
   £1 = 863.53

1. 587 th. sq. km.
2. 9 731; 17 per sq. km.
3. BR 45; DR 18; AI 2.8%
4. Urb. pop.: 1 239 (16%)
5. Antananarivo 400

1. GDP $2 991 (1.8%); $325 (−0.8%)
   Agric. 33%, Indust. 19%, Others 48%
2. Rice 2 132   Cassava 2 047
   Bananas 224   Sisal 20
   Coffee 81   Groundnuts 32
3. Cattle 10 400   Goats 1 800
4. Fish 55
5. Roundwood 6 262
6. Graphite 13   Gold 3kg
   Chrome 45

1. 0.03/0.6; 450 kWh (55% hydr.)
2a. Sugar 99   Sawnwood 234
  b. Cotton yarn. . .   Cement 36
3. Telephones 38; Cars 61
   Rail: 275 pass.-km.; 216 ton-km.
   Air: 506 pass.-km.; 75 ton-km.
   Sea: 312 loaded; 756 unloaded

Exports: $296   Imports: $387
Coffee   Manufactured goods
Spices   Machinery
Exports to: France, U.S.A., Indonesia
Imports from: France, W. Germany, China
Invisible trade balance: −$97
Aid received (net): $159.6

MALAWI

1. Republic
2. Bantu, English
3. Kwacha
4. $1 = 1.78
   £1 = 2.69

1. 118 th. sq. km.
2. 6 839; 73 per sq. km.
3. BR 49; DR 25; AI 3.2%
4. Urb. pop.: 752 (11%)
5. Lilongwe 99

1. GDP $1 334 (5.7%); $208 (3.0%)
   Agric. 37%, Indust. 13%, Others 50%
2. Maize 1 400   Groundnuts 180
   Tea 34   Tobacco 70
   Cottonseed 18   Cotton lint 7
3. Goats 770   Cattle 910
4. Fish 58
5. Roundwood 6 458

1. 0.06/0.3; 486 kWh (94% hydr.)
2a. Sawnwood 43   Beer 0.6Mhl
3. Telephones 29; Cars 14
   Rail: 108 pass.-km.; 120 ton-km.
   Air: 96 pass.-km.; 10 ton-km.

Exports: $292   Imports: $279
Tobacco   Machinery
Tea   Textiles
Groundnuts   Vehicles
Exports to: U.K., U.S.A., W. Germany, Netherlands
Imports from: U.K., Japan, South Africa
Invisible trade balance: −$128
Aid received (net): $162.6

MALAYSIA

1. Federation
2. Malay, Chinese, English and others
3. Ringgit
4. $1 = 2.54
   £1 = 3.84

1. 330 th. sq. km.
2. 15 193; 46 per sq. km.
3. BR 31; DR 7; AI 2.3%
4. Urb. pop.: 4 713 (31%)
5. Kuala Lumpur 938

1. GDP $23 796 (8.2%); $1 566 (4.8%)
   Agric. 20%, Indust. 31%, Others 49%
2. Rice 1 755   Palm oil 3 717
   Copra 212   Bananas 450
   Pineapples 181   Rubber 1 497
3. Pigs 2 050   Cattle 575
4. Fish 741
5. Roundwood 41 877
6. Iron ore 0.1   Tin 41.3
   Crude petroleum 23.0   Tungsten 49
   Gold 185kg   Copper 28

1. 28.2/13.3; 12 135 kWh (11% hydr.)
2a. Meat 245   Sawnwood 6 050
  b. Cement 3 468   Petroleum products 8.4
     Tin 47
3. Telephones 717; Cars 900
   Rail: 1 500 pass.-km.; 1 056 ton-km. (incl. Singapore)
   Air: 5 418 pass.-km.; 658 ton-km.
   Sea: 30 108 loaded; 22 140 unloaded

Exports: $13 917   Imports: $13 987
Rubber   Machinery
Tin   Crude petroleum
Sawnwood   Vehicles
Fish   Textiles
Palm oil   Rice
  Iron and steel
  Foods
Exports to: Singapore, Japan, U.S.A., U.K., Netherlands
Imports from: Japan, U.K., Singapore, Australia, W. Germany
Aid received (net): $218.4

For detailed table headings and notes see first page of this section

Country	Area and Population	Production	Manufactures	Trade

MALI

1. Republic
2. French, Arabic
3. Mali Franc
4. $1 = 352.13
   £1 = 532.25

1. 1 240 th. sq. km.
2. 7 973; 6.4 per sq. km.
3. BR 43; DR 18; AI 2.7%
4. Urb. pop.: 1 331 (18%)
5. Bamako 419

1. GDP $2 179 (. . .); $297 (. . .)
2. Millet 800
   Groundnuts 100   Rice 142
   3. Sheep 6 300   Cottonseed 96
   4. Fish 33   Cattle 6 000
   5. Roundwood 4 583

1. 0.01/0.20; 110 kWh (46% hydr.)
2a. Sugar 10   Meat 118
3. Telephones 5; Cars 20
   Rail: 156 pass.-km.; 132 ton-km.
   Air: 110 pass.-km.; 11 ton-km.

Exports: $167   Imports: $344
Cattle   Manufactured goods
Fish   Machinery
Cotton   Vehicles
Exports to: France, Ivory Coast, China, U.K.
Imports from: France, Ivory Coast, China, Senegal
Aid received (net): $214.6

MALTA

1. Commonwealth
2. Maltese, English
3. Maltese Pound
4. $1 = 0.40
   £1 = 0.60

1. 0.32 th. sq. km.
2. 380; 1 188 per sq. km.
3. BR 15; DR 8; AI 0.7%
4. Urb. pop.: 357 (94%)
5. Valetta 14

1. GDP $937 (10.2%); $2 466 (8.0%)
   Agric. 4%, Indust. 31%, Others 65%
2. Potatoes 13   Wheat 5
   Tomatoes 15   Grapes 3
   3. Pigs 54   Goats 5

1. . . ./0.5; 675 kWh
2a. Wine 2
3. Telephones 91; Cars 75
   Air: 644 pass.-km.; 60 ton-km.
   Sea: 168 loaded; 1 404 unloaded

Exports: $394   Imports: $717
Clothing   Foods
Textiles   Manufactured goods
Exports to: U.K., Libya, W. Germany
Imports from: U.K., Italy, W. Germany, U.S.A
Revenue from tourism: $185

MAURITANIA

1. Republic
2. Arabic, French
3. Ouguiya
4. $1 = 76.98
   £1 = 116.35

1. 1 031 th. sq. km.
2. 1 832; 1.8 per sq. km.
3. BR 50; DR 23; AI 2.9%
4. Urb. pop.: 421 (23%)
5. Nouakchott 135

1. GDP $811 (0.7%); $483 (−2.1%)
   Agric. 22%, Indust. 19%, Others 59%
2. Millet 15   Dates 10
   4. Sheep 5 000   Cattle 1 300
   5. Roundwood 54
   6. Iron ore 5.9

1. . . ./0.29; 102 kWh
3. Telephones . . .; Cars 8
   Air: 251 pass.-km.; 45 ton-km.
   Sea: 7 022 loaded; 294 unloaded

Exports: $294   Imports: $194
Iron ore   Machinery
Fish   Foods
Exports to: France, U.K., W. Germany, Spain, Italy, Belgium
Imports from: France, U.S.A., U.K., Senegal
Aid received (net): $113.3

MEXICO

1. Federal Republic
2. Spanish
3. Mexican Peso
4. $1 = 503.14
   £1 = 760.75

1. 1 973 th. sq. km.
2. 76 792; 39 per sq. km.
3. BR 38; DR 6; AI 2.6%
4. Urb. pop.: 50 683 (66%)
5. Mexico 14 750

1. GDP $171 267 (7.1%); $2 284 (4.0%)
   Agric. 7%, Indust. 31%, Others 62%
2. Maize 14 050   Copra 120
   Bananas 1 500   Sorghum 6 729
   Wheat 4 262   Tomatoes 1 320
   Oranges 1 600   Coffee 262
   Pineapples 400   Cottonseed 395
   Tobacco 62
   3. Cattle 37 500   Pigs 18 370
   4. Fish 1 070
   5. Roundwood 19 805
   6. Crude petroleum 136.6
   Natural gas 1 048   Lead 183
   Coal 5.8   Zinc 290
   Iron ore 5.3   Silver 1 987
   Copper 189   Gold 6.9
   Tin 0.5   Mercury 275t

1. 259.8/130.4; 82 343 kWh (25% hydr., 1.6% geo.)
2a. Meat 1 871   Sugar 3 260
   Sawnwood 1 539
   b. Iron 5 544   Steel 7 284
   Aluminium 64   Radios 663
   Cotton yarn . . .   Cement 18 384
   Petroleum products 63.8   Vehicles:
      pass. 246, comm. 62
3. Telephones 5 511; Cars 5 221
   Rail: 5 808 pass.-km.; 44 640 ton-km.
   Air: 13 465 pass.-km.; 1 330 ton-km.
   Sea: 72 108 loaded; 10 932 unloaded

Exports: $11 207   Imports: $23 462
Cotton   Machinery
Sugar   Vehicles
Tomatoes   Organic chemical
Coffee   products
Cattle   Iron and steel
Machinery   Paper and cardboard
   Petroleum products
Exports to: U.S.A., Spain, Japan, W. Germany, Brazil
Imports from: U.S.A., W. Germany, Japan, France
Invisible trade balance: −$9 654
Revenue from tourism: $1 406
Aid received (net): $542.5

MONGOLIA

1. People's Republic
2. Mongol
3. Tugrik
4. $1 = 3.35
   £1 = 5.07

1. 1 565 th. sq. km.
2. 1 820; 1.2 per sq. km.
3. BR 37; DR 8; AI 2.7%
4. Urb. pop.: 928 (51%)
5. Ulan-Bator 419

2. Wheat 459   Potatoes 123
3. Sheep 14 400   Goats 4 549
5. Roundwood 2 390
6. Coal 0.4   Lignite 4.1
   Tin 1.0   Copper 128
   Molybdenum 700t

1. 1.8/2.8; 1 975 kWh
2a. Wool . . .   Meat 229
   Sawnwood 470
   b. Cement 106
3. Telephones 31; Cars . . .
   Rail: 297 pass.-km.; 3 449 ton-km.

Exports: $436   Imports: $655
Livestock   Consumer goods
Wool   Machinery
Meat   Raw materials

MOROCCO

1. Kingdom
2. Arabic, French, Spanish
3. Dirham
4. $1 = 9.06
   £1 = 13.70

1. 447 th. sq. km.
2. 21 408; 48 per sq. km.
3. BR 45; DR 14; AI 3.3%
4. Urb. pop.: 8 444 (42%)
5. Rabat 842

1. GDP $14 697 (4.3%); $687 (1.2%)
   Agric. 14%, Indust. 23%, Others 63%
2. Barley 1 405   Wheat 1 989
   Oranges 746   Grapes 230
   Dates 40   Olives 250
   3. Sheep 12 000   Goats 4 500
   4. Fish 440
   5. Roundwood 1 695
   6. Coal 0.4   Cobalt 773t
   Iron ore 0.1   Lead 101
   Antimony 1.0   Phosphates 20 106
   Copper 22   Silver 127

1. 1.0/6.6; 6 010 kWh (9% hydr.)
2a. Meat 300   Wine 45
   Olive oil 34   Sawnwood 149
   Sugar 451
   b. Petroleum products 4.0   Wool yarn . . .
   Cement 3 336
3. Telephones 241; Cars 447
   Rail: 1 608 pass.-km.; 4 572 ton-km.
   Air: 1 827 pass.-km.; 203 ton-km.
   Sea: 19 428 loaded; 11 244 unloaded

Exports: $2 095   Imports: $3 861
Phosphates   Machinery
Oranges   Manufactured goods
Vegetables
Exports to: France, W. Germany, Italy, Spain
Imports from: France, U.S.A., W. Germany, Italy, Spain
Revenue from tourism: $425
Aid received (net): $350.8

MOZAMBIQUE

1. People's Republic
2. Portuguese, Bantu
3. Metica
4. $1 = 40.38
   £1 = 61.03

1. 802 th. sq. km.
2. 13 602; 17 per sq. km.
3. BR 45; DR 17; AI 3.1%
4. Urb. pop.: 1 539 (13%)
5. Maputo 384

1. GDP $3 272 (. . .); $322 (. . .)
2. Cassava 3 150   Maize 330
   Copra 65   Groundnuts 70
   Cottonseed 35   Sisal 4
   3. Cattle 1 320   Goats 355
   5. Roundwood 14 585
   6. Coal 0.5

1. 1.1/1.3; 6 426 kWh (94% hydr.)
2a. Sugar 95   Sawnwood 33
   Beer 0.5Mhl
   b. Petroleum products 0.7
3. Telephones 56; Cars 110
   Rail: 570 pass.-km.; 1 509 ton-km.
   Air: 614 pass.-km.; 67 ton-km.
   Sea: 2 613 loaded; 1 260 unloaded

Exports: $86   Imports: $487
Cotton   Machinery
Cashew nuts   Vehicles
Sugar   Iron and steel
Tea   Petroleum
Exports to: Portugal, S. Africa, U.K., U.S.A
Imports from: Portugal, S.Africa, W. Germany, U.K.
Aid received (net): $148.5

NAMIBIA

1. Mandated Territory
2. English, African dialects
3. Rand
4. $1 = 1.99
   £1 = 3.01

1. 824 th. sq. km.
2. 1 507; 1.8 per sq. km.
3. BR 45; DR 19; AI 2.8%
4. Urb. pop.: 407 (27%)
5. Windhoek 61

1. (incl. with South Africa)
2. Maize 40   Millet 20
   3. Sheep 6 000   Cattle 2 000
   4. Fish 341
   5. Roundwood . . .
   6. Copper 50   Zinc 31
   Lead 43   Diamonds 930
   Vanadium . . .   Tin 0.8
   Silver 106   Uranium 3 713

2a. Meat 68
b. Copper . . .   Lead 29
3. Telephones 57; Cars . . .
   Rail: see South Africa

Exports: . . . (Trade included with South Africa)   Imports: . . .

NEPAL

1. Kingdom
2. Nepalese, Hindu
3. Nepalese Rupee
4. $1 = 20.50
   £1 = 30.98

1. 141 th. sq. km.
2. 16 107; 118 per sq. km.
3. BR 44; DR 21; AI 2.3%
4. Urb. pop.: 956 (51%)
5. Katmandu 235

1. GDP $2 212 (2.6%); $141 (−0.4%)
   Agric. 53%, Indust. 4%, Others 43%
2. Rice 2 760   Maize 751
   Wheat 634   Jute 25
   3. Cattle 7 000   Goats 2 600
   5. Roundwood 14 684

1. 0.02/0.2; 257 kWh (80% hydr.)
2a. Sugar 23   Sawnwood 220
3. Telephones 11; Cars . . .
   Air: 250 pass.-km.; 24 ton-km.

Exports: $97   Imports: $163
Food grains   Textiles
Livestock   Petroleum products
Jute   Iron and steel
Timber   Machinery
   Tea
Main trade is with India
Aid received (net): $153.4

For detailed table headings and notes see first page of this section

Country	Area and Population	Production	Manufactures	Trade

NETHERLANDS

Area and Population
1. Kingdom
2. Dutch
3. Gilder
4. $1 = 2.49
   £1 = 3.77

1. 37 th. sq. km.
2. 14 420; 424 per sq. km.
3. BR 12; DR 8; AI 0.4%
4. Urb. pop.: 12 591 (88%)
5. Amsterdam 994, The Hague 672

Production
1. GDP $111 259 (2.5%); $7 716 (1.8%)
   Agric. 4%, Indust. 26%, Others 70%
2. Barley 192 / Wheat 1 133
   Tomatoes 491 / Apples 400
   Pears 96 / Potatoes 6 673
3. Pigs 11 000 / Cattle 5 500
4. Fish 503
5. Roundwood 905
6. Crude petroleum 2.5 / Natural gas 2 691
   Salt 3 124 / Coal 4.3

Manufactures
1. 109.7/91.9; 59 639 kWh (6% nucl.)
2a. Meat 2 264 (Pork 1 100) / Sugar 1 000
    Sawnwood 312 / Butter and cheese 772
b. Iron 4 920 / Steel 3 736
   Wool yarn 6.5 / Cotton yarn 7.2
   Petroleum products 47.1 / Vehicles:
   Plastics 2 500 / pass. 108, comm. 19
   Ships (grt.) 151
3. Telephones 7 697; Cars 4 650
   Rail: 8 940 pass.-km.; 3 120 ton-km.
   Air: 16 282 pass.-km.; 2 589 ton-km.
   Sea: 80 676 loaded; 244 056 unloaded

Trade
Exports: $65 881 / Imports: $62 136
Machinery / Machinery
Textiles / Crude petroleum
Chemical products / Textiles
Petroleum / Vehicles
Meat / Iron and steel
Iron and steel / Clothing
Vegetables / Non-ferrous metals
Exports to: W. Germany, Belgium-Luxembourg, France, U.K., Italy, U.S.A
Imports from: W. Germany, Belgium-Luxembourg, U.S.A., France, U.K., Italy
Invisible trade balance: +$394
Revenue from tourism: $520
Aid given (net): $1 818

NEW ZEALAND

Area and Population
1. Commonwealth
2. English
3. New Zealand Dollar
4. $1 = 1.75
   £1 = 2.64

1. 269 th. sq. km.
2. 3 233; 12 per sq. km.
3. BR 16; DR 8; AI 0.8%
4. Urb. pop.: 2 683 (83%)
5. Wellington 343

Production
1. GDP $21 554 (. . .); $6 736 (. . .)
   Agric. 10%, Indust. 25%, Others 65%
2. Barley 589 / Pears 15
   Apples 200 / Wheat 294
   Tomatoes 60 / Wool 363
3. Sheep 70 344 / Cattle 7 910
4. Fish 142
5. Roundwood 10 021
6. Coal 1.8 / Lignite 0.2
   Natural gas 85 / Gold 0.3
   Crude petroleum 0.7 / Silver 7

Manufactures
1. 8.4/11.7; 25 527 kWh (77% hydr., 4% geo.)
2a. Meat 1 212 / Butter and cheese 410
    Sawnwood 2 154 / Wood pulp 1 043
    Wine 58
b. Petroleum products 2.3 / Vehicles:
   Cement 828 / pass. 79, comm. 25
   Wool yarn 19
3. Telephones 1 730; Cars 1 337
   Rail: 396 pass.-km.; 3 168 ton-km.
   Air: 5 900 pass.-km.; 784 ton-km.
   Sea: 9 012 loaded; 7 464 unloaded

Trade
Exports: $5 358 / Imports: $6 010
Meat / Machinery
Wool / Textiles
Butter / Vehicles
Cheese / Iron and steel
/ Petroleum products
Exports to: U.K., Japan, Australia
Imports from: U.K., W. Germany, U.S.A., Japan
Invisible trade balance: –$1 416
Revenue from tourism: $226
Aid given (net): $87

NICARAGUA

Area and Population
1. Republic
2. Spanish
3. Cordoba
4. $1 = 27.95
   £1 = 42.24

1. 130 th. sq. km.
2. 3 162; 24 per sq. km.
3. BR 46; DR 12; AI 3.3%
4. Urb. pop.: 1 459 (46%)
5. Managua 615

Production
1. GDP $2 955 (1.7%); $998 (–1.9%)
   Agric. 25%, Indust. 21%, Others 54%
2. Maize 219 / Rice 162
   Bananas 213 / Coffee 46
   Cottonseed 126 / Cotton lint 85
3. Cattle 2 000 / Pigs 540
5. Roundwood 3 370
6. Gold 1.5

Manufactures
1. 0.07/0.9; 1 080 kWh (49% hydr., 2.7% geo.)
2a. Sugar 258 / Meat 87
    Sawnwood 222
b. Cement 100
3. Telephones 43; Cars 38
   Rail: 21 pass.-km.; 19 ton-km.
   Air: 120 pass.-km.; 12 ton-km.
   Sea: 366 loaded; 1 000 unloaded

Trade
Exports: $385 / Imports: $826
Cotton / Machinery
Meat / Textiles
Coffee / Iron and steel
Exports to: U.S.A., Japan, Costa Rica, W. Germany
Imports from: U.S.A., Guatemala, Costa Rica, W. Germany, Japan, Venezuela
Aid received (net): $171.4

NIGER

Area and Population
1. Republic
2. Arabic, French
3. C.F.A. Franc
4. $1 = 352.13
   £1 = 532.25

1. 1 267 th. sq. km.
2. 5 940; 4.7 per sq. km.
3. BR 51; DR 25; AI 2.8%
4. Urb. pop.: 832 (14%)
5. Niamey 225

Production
1. GDP $2 513 (. . .); $473 (. . .)
   Agric. 43%, Indust. 16%, Others 41%
2. Groundnuts 74 / Millet 900
3. Goats 7 500 / Cattle 3 500
5. Roundwood 3 731
6. Tin 50t / Uranium 2 906

Manufactures
1. 0.04/0.3; 252 kWh
2a. Meat 108
3. Telephones 10; Cars 13
   Air: 225 pass.-km.; 42 ton-km.

Trade
Exports: $333 / Imports: $442
Groundnuts / Manufactured goods
Exports to: France, Italy, Nigeria
Imports from: France, Ivory Coast, W. Germany
Aid received (net): $189.0

NIGERIA

Area and Population
1. Federal Republic
2. English, W. African
3. Naira
4. $1 = 1.00
   £1 = 1.52

1. 924 th. sq. km.
2. 92 037; 101 per sq. km.
3. BR 51; DR 25; AI 3.3%
4. Urb. pop.: 20 248 (22%)
5. Lagos 1 477

Production
1. GDP $64 956 (1.7%); $730 (–1.5%)
   Agric. 25%, Indust. 25%, Others 50%
2. Cassava 11 800 / Millet 3 000
   Rubber 55 / Cocoa 160
   Groundnuts 550 / Cottonseed 32
   Sorghum 3 000
3. Goats 26 000 / Cattle 11 800
4. Fish 515
5. Roundwood 85 760
6. Coal 0.2 / Natural gas 220
   Tin 1.3 / Crude petroleum 70.4

Manufactures
1. 96.8/17.0; 8 500 kWh (29% hydr.)
2a. Meat 810 / Sugar 58
    Sawnwood 2 703
b. Petroleum products 6.9 / Cement 3 600
3. Telephones 128; Cars 115
   Rail: 784 pass.-km.; 970 ton-km.
   Air: 2 252 pass.-km.; 230 ton-km.
   Sea: 58 088 loaded; 15 497 unloaded

Trade
Exports: $11 317 / Imports: $13 440
Petroleum / Machinery
Cocoa / Textiles
Groundnuts / Vehicles
Tin / Iron and steel
Exports to: Bermuda, U.S.A., Netherlands
Imports from: U.K., W. Germany, U.S.A., Japan
Invisible trade balance: –$2 146
Aid received (net): $76.8

NORWAY

Area and Population
1. Kingdom
2. Norwegian
3. Norwegian Krone
4. $1 = 7.04
   £1 = 10.64

1. 324 th. sq. km.
2. 4 140; 13 per sq. km.
3. BR 12; DR 10; AI 0.3%
4. Urb. pop.: 2 893 (71%)
5. Oslo 643

Production
1. GDP $49 149 (4.2%); $11 872 (3.8%)
   Agric. 3%, Indust. 32%, Others 65%
2. Barley 700 / Apples 48
   Oats 527 / Potatoes 470
3. Sheep 2 351 / Cattle 976
4. Fish 2 822
5. Roundwood 9 553
6. Coal 0.5 / Molybdenum 303
   Iron ore 2.5 / Vanadium 100
   Copper 22 / Zinc 29
   Titanium 544 / Natural gas 1 032
   Crude petroleum 34.2 / Lead 4
   Silver 7

Manufactures
1. 93.3/23.8; 106 243 kWh (99.4% hydr.)
2a. Butter and cheese 94 / Sawnwood 2 362
    Canned fish 32 / Wood pulp 1 641
b. Iron 1 368 / Steel 888
   Magnesium 48 / Aluminium 768
   Paper 1 400 / Wool yarn 3.2
   Ships (grt.) 99 / Petroleum products 7.0
3. Telephones 1 992; Cars 1 405
   Rail: 2 184 pass.-km.; 2 652 ton-km.
   Air: 4 118 pass.-km.; 498 ton-km.
   Sea: 47 088 loaded; 17 616 unloaded

Trade
Exports: $18 892 / Imports: $13 889
Non-ferrous metals / Machinery
(mainly aluminium) / Ships and boats
Ships and boats / Vehicles
Machinery / Iron and steel
Paper and cardboard / Textiles
Fish / Non-ferrous metals
Iron and steel / Petroleum products
Exports to: U.K., Sweden, W. Germany, Denmark, U.S.A.
Imports from: Sweden, W. Germany, U.K., U.S.A., Denmark
Invisible trade balance: –$1 381
Aid given (net): $702

PAKISTAN

Area and Population
1. Republic
2. Urdu, English
3. Pakistan Rupee
4. $1 = 16.14
   £1 = 24.40

1. 804 th. sq. km.
2. 93 286; 120 per sq. km.
3. BR 42; DR 10; AI 3.1%
4. Urb. pop.: 26 082 (29%)
5. Islamabad 201

Production
1. GDP $31 138 (6.4%); $334 (3.6%)
   Agric. 22%, Indust. 19%, Others 59%
2. Rice 5 009 / Wheat 11 053
   Dates 225 / Maize 1 100
   Tobacco 75 / Rape seed 251
   Cotton lint 990 / Cottonseed 1 980
3. Cattle 16 352 / Sheep 24 272
4. Fish 343
5. Roundwood 19 095
6. Coal 1.2 / Salt 796
   Natural gas 319 / Crude petroleum 0.7
   Chrome 7

Manufactures
1. 14.3/21.7; 19 636 kWh (53% hydr., 1% nucl.)
2a. Meat 973 / Sugar 1 258
    Sawnwood 55 / Jute 1
b. Petroleum products 4.1 / Cotton yarn 414
   Cement 4 500
3. Telephones 358; Cars 301
   Rail: 18 288 pass.-km.; 7 368 ton-km.
   Air: 6 425 pass.-km.; 820 ton-km.
   Sea: 2 352 loaded; 12 408 unloaded

Trade
Exports: $2 592 / Imports: $5 873
Textiles / Machinery
Cotton / Iron and steel
Leather / Fertilizer
Rice / Crude petroleum
/ Vehicles
Exports to: China, Japan, Iran, U.K.
Imports from: U.S.A., U.K., Japan, W. Germany
Invisible trade balance: –$635
Aid received (net): $730.8

PANAMA

Area and Population
1. Republic
2. Spanish
3. Balboa
4. $1 = 1.0
   £1 = 1.51

1. 77 th. sq. km.
2. 2 134; 28 per sq. km.
3. BR 26; DR 6; AI 2.2%
4. Urb. pop.: 899 (49%)
5. Panama 655

Production
1. GDP $4 541 (6.1%); $2 132 (3.6%)
   Agric. 9%, Indust. 9%, Others 82%
2. Rice 175 / Bananas 1 183
   Coffee 9 / Oranges 66
3. Cattle 1 470 / Pigs 200
4. Fish 166
5. Roundwood 2 047

Manufactures
1. 0.1/1.5; 2 239 kWh (39% hydr.)
2a. Meat 73 / Sugar 180
    Sawnwood 53
b. Petroleum products 2.4
3. Telephones 185; Cars 104
   Air: 400 pass.-km.; 51 ton-km.
   Sea: 79 512 loaded; 63 204 unloaded

Trade
Exports: $256 / Imports: $1 423
Bananas / Manufactured goods
Petroleum products / Petroleum
/ Machinery
Exports to: U.S.A., W. Germany
Imports from: U.S.A., Ecuador, Venezuela, Saudi Arabia
Invisible trade balance: +$631
Aid received (net): $68.1

For detailed table headings and notes see first page of this section

Country	Area and Population	Production	Manufactures	Trade

PERU

Area and Population
1. Republic
2. Spanish
3. Intl (1 000 Sol)
4. $1 = 13.92
   £1 = 21.05

1. 1 285 th. sq. km.
2. 19 198; 15 per sq. km.
3. BR 38; DR 12; AI 2.6%
4. Urb. pop.: 11 108 (64%)
5. Lima 5 258

Production
1. GDP $11 428 (2.1%); $595 (−0.7%)
   Agric. 8%, Indust. 36%, Others 56%
2. Maize 576 | Rice 1 134
   Oranges 155 | Coffee 92
   Cottonseed 165 | Potatoes 1 515
3. Sheep 14 500 | Cattle 2 825
4. Fish 1 487
5. Roundwood 7 775
6. Iron ore 2.5 | Gold 5.4t
   Antimony 0.5 | Silver 1 773
   Copper 364 | Zinc 568
   Lead 198 | Tungsten 720
   Molybdenum 2 563 | Crude petroleum 10.0
   Tin 3.0

Manufactures
1. 14.7/11.8; 9 328 kWh (78% hydr.)
2a. Meat 423 | Fish meal
   Sugar 532 | Sawnwood 577
   b. Cotton yarn. . . | Copper 219
3. Telephones 475; Cars 300
   Rail: 651 pass.-km.; 612 ton-km.
   Air: 1 685 pass.-km.; 246 ton-km.
   Sea: 8 298 loaded; 3 199 unloaded

Trade
Exports: $3 131 | Imports: $1 870
Copper | Machinery
Fish meal | Chemical products
Iron ore | Wheat
Cotton | Iron and steel
Exports to: U.S.A., Japan, Italy
Imports from: U.S.A., Ecuador, Venezuela
Invisible trade balance: −$1 417
Revenue from tourism: $465
Aid received (net): $329.4

PHILIPPINES

Area and Population
1. Republic
2. Tagalog, English
3. Philippine Peso
4. $1 = 20.08
   £1 = 30.35

1. 300 th. sq. km.
2. 53 351; 179 per sq. km.
3. BR 34; DR 8; AI 2.5%
4. Urb. pop.: 17 943 (37%)
5. Manila 1 630

Production
1. GDP $27 750 (6.0%); $520 (3.2%)
   Agric. 25%, Indust. 27%, Others 48%
2. Maize 3 400 | Rice 8 280
   Bananas 4 380 | Pineapples 1 200
   Coffee 145 | Copra 1 400
   Tobacco 55
3. Pigs 7 779 | Buffaloes 2 900
4. Fish 1 837
5. Roundwood 35 787
6. Coal 0.4 | Copper 233
   Iron ore 2.6 | Gold 34.1
   Chrome 360 | Silver 50
   Nickel 15.6

Manufactures
1. 2.6/16.3; 20 761 kWh (20% hydr., 14% geo.)
2a. Meat 761 | Sawnwood 1 222
   Salted fish 48 | Sugar 2 400
   b. Plastics . . . | Cotton yarn 39
   Petroleum products 7.8 | Cement 3 660
   Copper 99
3. Telephones 731; Cars 561
   Rail: 228 pass.-km.; 12 ton-km.
   Air: 7 369 pass.-km.; 881 ton-km.
   Sea: 12 672 loaded; 18 972 unloaded

Trade
Exports: $5 005 | Imports: $7 980
Wood | Machinery
Sugar | Petroleum
Copra | Vehicles
Copper | Iron and steel
Exports to: U.S.A., Japan, Netherlands
Imports from: Japan, U.S.A., Saudi Arabia
Invisible trade balance: −$958
Revenue from tourism: $450
Aid received (net): $648.2

POLAND

Area and Population
1. People's Republic
2. Polish
3. Złoty
4. $1 = 166.46
   £1 = 251.60

1. 313 th. sq. km.
2. 36 914; 121 per sq. km.
3. BR 19; DR 9; AI 0.9%
4. Urb. pop.: 21 493 (59%)
5. Warsaw 1 649

Production
1. NMP $58 867 (−0.8%); $1 595 (−1.6%)
   Agric. 17%, Indust. 50%, Others 33%
2. Barley 3 555 | Wheat 6 010
   Rye 9 540 | Oats 2 604
   Potatoes 37 437 | Apples 1 566
   Tobacco 100 | Rape seed 911
3. Pigs 16 657 | Cattle 11 197
4. Fish 735
5. Roundwood 24 681
6. Coal 191.6 | Nickel 2
   Lignite 50.4 | Zinc 191
   Copper 431 | Natural gas 166
   Lead 53 | Salt 4 326
   Silver 744

Manufactures
1. 170.9/161.4; 125 821 kWh (2.6% hydr.)
2a. Meat 2 299 | Sawnwood 6 764
   Butter and cheese 721 | Sugar 1 891
   Salted fish 18
   b. Iron 9 624 | Steel 16 536
   Aluminium 46 | Plastics 671
   Cotton yarn 179 | Wool yarn 79.2
   Petroleum products 9.9 | Vehicles:
   Ships (grt.) 317 | pass. 280, comm. 55
3. Telephones 3 506; Cars 2 871
   Rail: 53 184 pass.-km.; 123 504 ton-km.
   Air: 778 pass.-km.; 72 ton-km.
   Sea: 22 406 loaded; 15 844 unloaded

Trade
Exports: $11 687 | Imports: $10 633
Coal | Dairy products
Ships and boats | Iron ore
Meat | Crude petroleum
Dairy products | Cotton
Machinery | Wheat
Clothing | Iron and steel
| Petroleum products
| Machinery
Main trade is with: U.S.S.R., W. Germany,
Czechoslovakia, E. Germany
Revenue from tourism: $65

PORTUGAL

Area and Population
1. Republic
2. Portuguese
3. Escudo
4. $1 = 144.23
   £1 = 218.0

1. 92 th. sq. km.
2. 10 164; 110 per sq. km.
3. BR 14; DR 10; AI 0.7%
4. Urb. pop.: 2 905 (30%)
5. Lisbon 1 612

Production
1. GDP $23 811 (4.9%); $2 344 (4.1%)
   Agric. 8%, Indust. 30%, Others 62%
2. Wheat 475 | Maize 530
   Grapes 1 020 | Olives 300
   Tomatoes 881 | Wool 9
3. Sheep 5 000 | Pigs 3 450
4. Fish 246
5. Roundwood 8 278
6. Coal 0.2 | Tin 0.3
   Iron ore 22.7 | Tungsten 1 187
   Copper 2.6 | Gold 2t

Manufactures
1. 1.2/13.2; 18 161 kWh (45% hydr.)
2a. Meat 448 | Sawnwood 2 360
   Canned fish 47 | Salted fish 15
   Wine 730 | Olive oil 50
   b. Iron 468 | Steel 400
   Petroleum products 7.2 | Vehicles:
   Cotton yarn 107 | pass. 55, comm. 35
   Wool yarn 3.5
3. Telephones 1 456; Cars 1 346
   Rail: 5 448 pass.-km.; 1 236 ton-km.
   Air: 4 174 pass.-km.; 483 ton-km.
   Sea: 4 100 loaded; 19 000 unloaded

Trade
Exports: $5 184 | Imports: $7 797
Textiles | Machinery
Clothing | Vehicles
Wine | Iron and steel
Diamonds | Cotton
Machinery | Diamonds
Fish | Cereals
Cork | Crude petroleum
Exports to: U.K., France, W. Germany
Imports from: W. Germany, U.K., U.S.A., France
Invisible trade balance: −$665
Revenue from tourism: $878

ROMANIA

Area and Population
1. Socialist Republic
2. Romanian
3. Leu
4. $1 = 12.55
   £1 = 18.98

1. 238 th. sq. km.
2. 22 897; 100 per sq. km.
3. BR 18; DR 10; AI 0.8%
4. Urb. pop.: 10 905 (49%)
5. Bucharest 1 979

Production
1. NMP $17 915 (7.2%); $843 (6.3%)
   Agric. 15%, Indust. 58%, Others 27%
2. Maize 13 000 | Wheat 7 900
   Grapes 1 600 | Tomatoes 1 800
   Tobacco 32 | Sunflower seed 890
3. Sheep 18 451 | Pigs 14 347
4. Fish 243
5. Roundwood 22 953
6. Coal 7.8 | Lead 20
   Lignite 36.0 | Manganese 18
   Iron ore 0.5 | Natural gas 1 570
   Bauxite 460 | Crude petroleum 12.5
   Zinc 39 | Copper 30
   Silver 23

Manufactures
1. 92.4/101.4; 70 260 kWh (14% hydr.)
2a. Meat 1 744 | Sawnwood 4 948
   Sugar 610 | Butter and cheese 155
   b. Iron 8 184 | Steel 13 800
   Petroleum products 21.6 | Cotton yarn 172
   Silk 120 | Wool yarn 74
   Fertilizers 2 600 | Aluminium 215
3. Telephones 1 196; Cars 235
   Rail: 25 578 pass.-km.; 71 110 ton-km.
   Air: 1 145 pass.-km.; 102 ton-km.
   Sea: 10 000 loaded; 22 000 unloaded

Trade
Exports: $13 241 | Imports: $9 959
Machinery | Machinery
Consumer goods | Iron ore
Petroleum products | Coke
Cereals | Vehicles
| Iron goods
Exports to: U.S.S.R., E. Germany, W. Germany
Imports from: U.S.S.R., E. Germany, W. Germany
Revenue from tourism: $280

SAUDI ARABIA

Area and Population
1. Kingdom
2. Arabic
3. Rial
4. $1 = 3.64
   £1 = 5.51

1. 2 150 th. sq. km.
2. 11 093; 5 per sq. km.
3. BR 46; DR 14; AI 3.9%
4. Urb. pop.: 7 685 (71%)
5. Ar Riyād 667

Production
1. GDP $120 937 (8.7%); $12 094 (4.1%)
   Agric. 2%, Indust. 53%, Others 45%
2. Wheat 1 300 | Millet/Sorghum 112
   Dates 450 | Tomatoes 350
3. Sheep 3 600 | Goats 2 350
6. Crude petroleum 226.3 | Natural gas 50

Manufactures
1. 385.3/37.4; 32 000 kWh
2b. Petroleum products 40.4 | Cement 5 263
3. Telephones 789; Cars 153
   Rail: 105 pass.-km.; 393 ton-km.
   Air: 12 277 pass.-km.; 1 478 ton-km.
   Sea: 299 257 loaded; 30 000 unloaded

Trade
Exports: $36 834 | Imports: $33 696
Crude petroleum | Machinery
Petroleum products | Vehicles
| Food
Exports to: Japan, Italy, France, U.S.A.
Imports from: U.S.A., Japan, W. Germany
Invisible trade balance: −$25 123

SENEGAL

Area and Population
1. Republic
2. French, West African
3. C.F.A. Franc
4. $1 = 352.13
   £1 = 532.25

1. 196 th. sq. km.
2. 6 397; 33 per sq. km.
3. BR 55; DR 23; AI 2.7%
4. Urb. pop.: 1 713 (34%)
5. Dakar 799

Production
1. GDP $2 117 (1.1%); $331 (−1.5%)
2. Millet 471 | Rice 120
   Bananas 2 | Groundnuts 682
3. Cattle 2 200 | Goats 1 000
4. Fish 213
5. Roundwood 3 894
6. Phosphates 1 254 | Salt 170
   Titanium. . . | Zirconium. . .

Manufactures
1. . . ./1.0; 631 kWh
2a. Sawnwood 11
   b. Petroleum products 1.0 | Cement 375
3. Telephones 40; Cars 65
   Rail: 426 pass.-km.; 158 ton-km.
   Air: 229 pass.-km.; 42 ton-km.
   Sea: 2 448 loaded; 2 880 unloaded

Trade
Exports: $416 | Imports: $1 039
Groundnut oil | Food
Groundnuts | Manufactured goods
| Machinery
Main trade is with France
Aid received (net): $323.7

For detailed table headings and notes see first page of this section

Country	Area and Population	Production	Manufactures	Trade

SINGAPORE

1. Republic	1. 0.58 th. sq. km.
2. English, Chinese, Malay, Tamil	2. 2 529; 4 360 per sq. km.
3. Singapore Dollar	3. BR 16; DR 5; AI 1.2%
4. $1 = 2.18	4. Urb. pop.: 2 529 (100%)
£1 = 3.29	5. Singapore 2 517

Production
1. GDP $17 848 (9.0%); $7 083 (7.6%)
   Agric. 1%, Indust. 25%, Others 74%
3. Pigs 1 310 — Cattle 1
4. Fish 20

Manufactures
1. . . ./13.4; 8 626 kWh
2a. Meat 105 — Sawnwood 418
b. Petroleum products 29.2
3. Telephones 775; Cars 195
   Rail: see Malaysia
   Air: 18 161 pass.-km.; 2 466 ton-km.
   Sea: 35 665 loaded; 59 995 unloaded

Trade
Exports: $24 108 — Imports: $28 712
Rubber — Machinery
Petroleum products — Textiles
Machinery — Rubber
Exports to: Malaysia, U.S.A., Japan
Imports from: Japan, Malaysia, U.S.A., Saudi Arabia
Invisible trade balance: +$3 594
Revenue from tourism: $1 916
Aid received (net): $11.4

SOUTH AFRICA

1. Republic	1. 1 221 th. sq. km.
2. English, Afrikaans	2. 31 586; 26 per sq. km.
3. Rand	3. BR 38; DR 15; AI 2.5%
4. $1 = 1.99	4. Urb. pop.: 17 372 (55%)
£1 = 3.01	5. Pretoria 739; Cape Town 1 491

Production
1. GDP $73 556 (3.5%); $2 448 (0.7%)
   Agric. 5%, Indust. 38%, Others 57%
2. Maize 4 440 — Wheat 2 150
   Oranges 495 — Pineapples 153
   Grapes 1 700 — Cottonseed 58
   Tobacco 37 — Wool 109
3. Sheep 31 650 — Cattle 12 895
4. Fish 600
5. Roundwood 20 524
6. Coal 158 — Manganese 3 181
   Iron 15.6 — Asbestos 221
   Copper 212 — Antimony 7.5
   Chrome 2 870 — Nickel 22.5
   Gold 683.3 — Diamonds 9 800
   Tin 2.3 — Zinc 103
   Lead 95 — Silver 218
   Uranium 6 045

Manufactures
1. 105.9/99.9; 109 185 kWh (0.7% hydr.)
2a. Meat 1 206 — Sugar 2 500
   Wine 896 — Beer 9.2Mhl
   Sawnwood 1 550
b. Iron 8 580 — Steel 7 824
   Copper 148 — Cotton yarn 38
   Wool yarn 20 — Petroleum products 14.3
   Vehicles: — Cement 8 112
   pass. 273, comm. 114
3. Telephones 2 933; Cars 2 499
   Rail: . . . pass.-km.; 82 052 ton-km.
   Air: 9 287 pass.-km.; 1 175 ton-km.
   Sea: 69 276 loaded; 26 758 unloaded

Trade
Exports: $9 334 — Imports: $14 956
Diamonds — Machinery
Fruit — Vehicles
Wool — Textiles
Gold — Crude petroleum
Copper — Petroleum products
Iron and steel — Chemical products
Cereals
Exports to: U.K., Japan, U.S.A., W. Germany
Imports from: U.K., U.S.A., W. Germany, Japan
Invisible trade balance: −$3 297

SPAIN

1. Monarchy	1. 505 th. sq. km.
2. Spanish	2. 38 333; 76 per sq. km.
3. Spanish Peseta	3. BR 13; DR 7; AI 0.8%
4. $1 = 140.59	4. Urb. pop.: 34 500 (91%)
£1 = 212.50	5. Madrid 3 188

Production
1. GDP $149 193 (1.6%); $3 853 (0.7%)
   Agric. 6%, Indust. 27%, Others 67%
2. Barley 10 695 — Wheat 6 044
   Tomatoes 2 553 — Oranges 1 310
   Grapes 5 569 — Olives 3 418
   Cottonseed 87 — Cotton lint 55
   Tobacco 44 — Wool 23
3. Sheep 16 600 — Pigs 12 400
4. Fish 1 240
5. Roundwood 14 823
6. Coal 15.1 — Lead 96
   Lignite 24.4 — Tungsten 550t
   Iron ore 3.7 — Mercury 1 416t
   Copper 64 — Zinc 228
   Crude petroleum 3.2 — Tin 0.4
   Silver 221

Manufactures
1. 27.7/81.8; 115 450 kWh (24% hydr., 8% nucl.)
2a. Meat 2 635 — Sugar 1 328
   Olive oil 727 — Wine 3 554
   Sawnwood 2 720
b. Cotton yarn 69 — Wool yarn 30
   Silk 13 — Copper 156
   Iron 5 364 — Steel 13 572
   Aluminium 421 — Ships (grt.) 141
   Petroleum products 39.8 — Vehicles:
   Cement 25 500 — pass. 1 174, comm. 32
3. Telephones 12 386; Cars 8 354
   Rail: 15 576 pass.-km.; 11 820 ton-km.
   Air: 16 457 pass.-km.; 1 960 ton-km.
   Sea: 44 652 loaded; 88 752 unloaded

Trade
Exports: $23 544 — Imports: $28 812
Machinery — Machinery
Fruits — Crude petroleum
Vegetables — Iron and steel
Footwear — Organic chemicals
Petroleum products — Maize
Textiles — Soya
Ships and boats — Sawnwood
Olive oil — Copper
Exports to: U.S.A., W. Germany, France, U.K
Imports from: U.S.A., W. Germany, France, Saudi Arabia
Invisible trade balance: +$5 217
Revenue from tourism: $7 126

SRI LANKA

1. Republic	1. 66 th. sq. km.
2. Sinhalese, English, Tamil	2. 15 606; 240 per sq. km.
3. Sri Lanka Rupee	3. BR 26; DR 6; AI 2.0%
4. $1 = 27.72	4. Urb. pop.: 3 194 (20%)
£1 = 41.90	5. Colombo 1 412

Production
1. GDP $4 768 (5.6%); $309 (3.8%)
   Agric. 26%, Indust. 16%, Others 58%
2. Rice 2 270 — Cassava 650
   Tea 230 — Copra 100
   Rubber 145 — Tobacco 17
3. Cattle 1 738 — Buffaloes 951
4. Fish 222
5. Roundwood 8 363
6. Graphite 8 — Salt 129
   Titanium 90

Manufactures
1. 0.2/2.1; 2 114 kWh (58% hydr.)
2a. Meat 35 — Sawnwood 418
b. Cotton yarn 7.2 — Petroleum products 1.2
3. Telephones 110; Cars 132
   Rail: 2 256 pass.-km.; 240 ton-km.
   Air: 1 947 pass.-km.; 210 ton-km.
   Sea: 1 932 loaded; 3 588 unloaded

Trade
Exports: $1 454 — Imports: $1 845
Tea — Machinery
Rubber — Rice
Copra — Sugar
Coconuts — Flour
Coconut fibre — Textiles
— Petroleum products
Exports to: U.K., Pakistan, China, U.S.A.
Imports from: Saudi Arabia, Iran, U.S.A.
Revenue from tourism: $147
Aid received (net): $355.4

SUDAN

1. Republic	1. 2 506 th. sq. km.
2. Arabic, Hamitic, English	2. 20 945; 8.8 per sq. km.
3. Sudanese Pound	3. BR 47; DR 19; AI 2.9%
4. $1 = 2.50	4. Urb. pop.: 4 153 (20%)
£1 = 3.78	5. Khartoum 476

Production
1. GDP $6 634 (. . .); $345 (. . .)
   Agric. 36%, Indust. 10%, Others 54%
2. Millet 2 340 — Wheat 162
   Dates 115 — Groundnuts 420
   Sorghum 1 450 — Cottonseed 416
   Cotton lint 219
3. Cattle 19 600 — Sheep 20 000
5. Roundwood 38 157
6. Chrome 20 — Salt 150

Manufactures
1. 0.06/1.6; 1 010 kWh (50% hydr.)
2a. Meat 469 — Sugar 462
b. Cement 211 — Petroleum products 1.5
   Cotton fabrics . . .
3. Telephones 68; Cars 55
   Rail: . . . pass.-km.; 2 285 ton-km.
   Air: 657 pass.-km.; 70 ton-km.
   Sea: 916 loaded; 2 642 unloaded

Trade
Exports: $624 — Imports: $1 354
Cotton — Machinery
Gum arabic — Cotton fabrics
Sesame — Petroleum products
Groundnuts
Exports to: Saudi Arabia, China, Japan, Italy
Imports from: U.K., W. Germany, Japan, India
Aid received (net): $434.9

SWEDEN

1. Kingdom	1. 450 th. sq. km.
2. Swedish	2. 8 337; 20 per sq. km.
3. Krona	3. BR 11; DR 11; AI 0.01%
4. $1 = 7.11	4. Urb. pop.: 6 920 (83%)
£1 = 10.75	5. Stockholm 1 420

Production
1. GDP $88 048 (1.2%); $10 570 (1.0%)
   Agric. 3%, Indust. 21%, Others 76%
2. Oats 1 904 — Barley 2 733
   Wheat 1 776 — Apples 121
   Potatoes 1 307 — Rape seed 382
3. Pigs 2 670 — Cattle 1 875
4. Fish 265
5. Roundwood 53 294
6. Iron ore 11.8 — Lead 81
   Copper 86 — Zinc 207
   Gold 3.4 — Silver 180

Manufactures
1. 13.0/38.3; 109 635 kWh (59% hydr., 37% nucl.)
2a. Meat 562 — Butter and cheese 194
   Sugar 411 — Sawnwood 11 762
   Wood pulp 8 600
b. Iron 2 208 — Steel 4 704
   Aluminium 114 — Copper 64
   Paper 6 300 — Ships (grt.) 178
   Petroleum products 13.1 — Vehicles:
   — pass. 314, comm. 36
3. Telephones 6 888; Cars 2 936
   Rail: 6 480 pass.-km.; 16 944 ton-km.
   Air: 5 573 pass.-km.; 683 ton-km.
   Sea: 42 876 loaded; 48 780 unloaded

Trade
Exports: $29 781 — Imports: $26 572
Machinery — Machinery
Iron and steel — Petroleum products
Paper and cardboard — Vehicles
Wood pulp — Textiles
Vehicles — Iron and steel
Sawnwood — Non-ferrous metals
Ships and boats — Clothing
Iron ore — Crude petroleum
Exports to: U.K., W. Germany, Denmark, Norway
Imports from: W. Germany, U.K., U.S.A., Denmark
Invisible trade balance: −$2 530
Aid given (net): $1 397

SWITZERLAND

1. Federal Republic	1. 41 th. sq. km.
2. German, French, Italian	2. 6 442; 161 per sq. km.
3. Swiss Franc	3. BR 12; DR 9; AI −0.3%
4. $1 = 1.85	4. Urb. pop.: 3 801 (59%)
£1 = 2.79	5. Bern 301

Production
1. GDP $97 120 (1.9%); $15 081 (1.9%)
   Agric. 2%, Indust. 21%, Others 77%
2. Potatoes 944 — Apples 360
   Wheat 577 — Pears 135
3. Cattle 1 943 — Pigs 2 004
5. Roundwood 4 295
6. Salt 272

Manufactures
1. 6.3/23.6; 51 819 kWh (70% hydr., 28% nucl.)
2a. Meat 480 — Butter and cheese 169
   Wine 118 — Beer 4.2 Mhl
   Sawnwood 1 760
b. Iron 10 — Steel 900
   Aluminium 102 — Cotton yarn 49
   Petroleum products 4.2
3. Telephones 4 802; Cars 2 473
   Rail: 8 964 pass.-km.; 6 888 ton-km.
   Air: 11 773 pass.-km.; 1 550 ton-km.

Trade
Exports: $25 863 — Imports: $29 469
Machinery — Machinery
Watches — Vehicles
Textiles — Iron and steel
Medicines — Textiles
Organic chemical products — Petroleum products
Exports to: W. Germany, France, U.S.A., Italy, U.K.
Imports from: W. Germany, France, Italy, U.S.A., U.K.
Invisible trade balance: +$7 505
Revenue from tourism: $3 015
Aid given (net): $2 268

For detailed table headings and notes see first page of this section

Country	Area and Population	Production	Manufactures	Trade

SYRIA

1. Republic
2. Arabic
3. Syrian Pound
4. $1 = 5.95
   £1 = 9.00

1. 185 th. sq. km.
2. 9 934; 54 per sq. km.
3. BR 45; DR 9; AI 3.7%
4. Urb. pop.: 4 370 (47%)
5. Damascus 1 112

1. GDP $19 140 (5.9%); $1 927 (2.0%)
   Agric. 20%, Indust. 17%, Others 63%
2. Barley 302   Wheat 1 051
   Grapes 440   Olives 370
   Tomatoes 740   Tobacco 15
   Cottonseed 300
3. Sheep 14 000   Goats 1 000
4. Roundwood 44
6. Crude petroleum 8.0 Salt 88
   Phosphates 1 231

1. 14.1/9.1; 4 428 kWh (70% hydr.)
2a. Meat 201   Sugar 85
    Olive oil 85
b. Cement 4 284   Cotton, woven 35
   Petroleum products 8.0
3. Telephones 429; Cars 45
   Rail: 756 pass.-km.; 960 ton-km.
   Air: 947 pass.-km.; 98 ton-km.
   Sea: 7 656 loaded; 11 124 unloaded

Exports: $1 853   Imports: $4 116
Cotton   Machinery
Livestock   Iron and steel
Crude petroleum   Vehicles
Vegetables   Textiles
Wheat   Crude petroleum
Exports to: France, Italy, Greece, U.S.A.
Imports from: W. Germany, Italy, France, Iraq, Romania
Aid received (net): $162.7

TAIWAN

1. Republic
2. Chinese
3. New Dollar
4. $1 = 38.60
   £1 = 58.34

1. 36 th. sq. km.
2. 19 012; 528 per sq. km.
3. BR 20; DR 5; AI 2.1%
4. Urb. pop.: 11 407 (60%)
5. Tai-pei 2 271

1. GDP $58 000 (. . .); $3 146 (. . .)
   Agric. 6%, Indust. 36%, Others 58%
2. Rice 2 244   Bananas 203
   Groundnuts 86   Citrus fruits 354
   Pineapples 245   Tea 24
   Soya beans 9.5
3. Pigs 6 569   Cattle 130
4. Fish 1 003
5. Roundwood 700
6. Coal 4.2   Gold 1.6t

1. 6 029/48 527; 49 286 kWh (3% hydr., 18% nucl.)
2a. Sugar 619   Sawnwood 563
    Meat . . .
b. Steel 5 627   Aluminium 38
   Cotton yarn . . .   Televisions 5 165
   Petroleum products 20
3. Telephones 4 855; Cars 688
   Rail: 7 321 pass.-km.; 2 685 ton-km.
   Air: 866 pass.-km.; 3.2 ton-km.
   Sea: 36 887 loaded; 62 440 unloaded

Exports: $30 456   Imports: $21 959
Textiles   Machinery
Electrical goods   Crude petroleum
Timber products   Iron and steel
Plastics   Chemicals
Exports to: U.S.A., Japan, Saudi Arabia
Imports from: Japan, U.S.A., Kuwait

TANZANIA

1. Federal Republic
2. Swahili
3. Tanzanian Shilling
4. $1 = 18.72
   £1 = 28.30

1. 945 th. sq. km.
2. 21 062; 24 per sq. km.
3. BR 51; DR 17; AI 3.5%
4. Urb. pop.: 2 412 (14%)
5. Dar-es-Salaam 757

1. GDP $5 127 (2.7%); $299 (–0.4%)
   Agric. 46%, Indust. 9%, Others 45%
2. Maize 1 131   Cassava 5 600
   Bananas 2 000   Coffee 50
   Cottonseed 91   Cotton lint 47
   Tobacco 10   Sisal 40
3. Cattle 14 500   Goats 6 100
4. Fish 272
5. Roundwood 39 770
6. Gold 0.2   Diamonds 360

1. 0.06/0.9; 705 kWh (77% hydr.)
2a. Meat 220   Sawnwood 34
    Sugar 143   Beer 0.6Mhl
3. Telephones 66; Cars 44
   Rail: see Kenya
   Air: 210 pass.-km.; 20 ton-km.
   Sea: 1 080 loaded; 3 180 unloaded

Exports: $366   Imports: $822
Coffee   Machinery
Cotton   Vehicles
Diamonds   Textiles
Sisal   Petroleum products
Cashew nuts   Iron and steel
Exports to: U.K., W. Germany, U.S.A., Italy
Imports from: U.K., Japan, Netherlands, W. Germany
Aid received (net): $651.5

THAILAND

1. Kingdom
2. Thai
3. Baht
4. $1 = 26.17
   £1 = 39.56

1. 514 th. sq. km.
2. 50 396; 98 per sq. km.
3. BR 31; DR 8; AI 2.1%
4. Urb. pop.: 7 632 (17%)
5. Bangkok 5 468

1. GDP $36 529 (7.4%); $725 (5.0%)
   Agric. 20%, Indust. 21%, Others 59%
2. Maize 4 150   Rice 19 200
   Bananas 2 045   Pineapples 1 650
   Jute 199   Rubber 580
   Cottonseed 82   Tobacco 90
   Cassava 19 985   Palm oil 81
3. Buffaloes 6 150   Cattle 4 620
4. Fish 2 250
5. Roundwood 40 415
6. Lignite 2.3   Natural gas 57
   Tungsten 562   Iron ore 1.9
   Tin 21.6   Antimony 2.9
   Manganese 3.0   Lead 20

1. 3.5/17.4; 18 875 kWh (22% hydr.)
2a. Meat 783   Sawnwood 930
    Sugar 2 350
b. Cotton yarn 101   Petroleum products 7.8
   Cement 8 244   Tin 20
   Vehicles:
   pass. 36, comm. 75
3. Telephones 529; Cars 451
   Rail: 9 231 pass.-km.; 2 421 ton-km.
   Air: 8 611 pass.-km.; 1 095 ton-km.
   Sea: 17 760 loaded; 17 484 unloaded

Exports: $7 413   Imports: $10 398
Rice   Machinery
Maize   Vehicles
Rubber   Iron and steel
Fruit and vegetables Crude petroleum
Tin
Exports to: Japan, U.S.A., Singapore, Netherlands, Indonesia
Imports from: Japan, U.S.A., W. Germany, Saudi Arabia
Invisible trade balance: –$1 226
Revenue from tourism: $972
Aid received (net): $624.4

TOGO

1. Republic
2. Bantu, Hamitic, French
3. C.F.A. Franc
4. $1 = 352.13
   £1 = 532.25

1. 57 th. sq. km.
2. 2 872; 50 per sq. km.
3. BR 46; DR 17; AI 2.9%
4. Urb. pop.: 624 (22%)
5. Lomé 283

1. GDP $815 (2.7%); $296 (0.2%)
   Agric. 27%, Indust. 15%, Others 58%
2. Cassava 345   Cocoa 15
   Coffee 6   Groundnuts 20
   Palm oil 14
3. Goats 740   Sheep 840
5. Roundwood 745
6. Phosphates 2 081

1. . . ./0.6; 173 kWh (16% hydr.)
2a. Food industries
3. Telephones 10; Cars 2
   Rail: 104 pass.-km.; 13 ton-km.
   Air: 153 pass.-km.; 14 ton-km.
   Sea: 704 loaded; 995 unloaded

Exports: $162   Imports: $284
Cocoa   Cotton fabric
Phosphates   Machinery
Coffee   Food
                 Vehicles
Exports to: France, W. Germany, Netherlands
Imports from: France, W. Germany, U.K, U.S.A.
Aid received (net): $107

TRINIDAD & TOBAGO

1. Commonwealth
2. English
3. Trinidad and Tobago Dollars
4. $1 = 3.60
   £1 = 5.44

1. 5 th. sq. km.
2. 1 166; 233 per sq. km.
3. BR 25; DR 7; AI 0.9%
4. Urb. pop.: 243 (22%)
5. Port of Spain 60

1. GDP $8 115 (6.2%); $7 056 (4.6%)
   Agric. 2%, Indust. 29%, Others 69%
2. Rice 18   Bananas 8
   Oranges 7   Grapefruits 7
   Cocoa 2   Coffee 2
   Copra 6
3. Cattle 76   Pigs 62
5. Roundwood 67
6. Natural gas 119   Crude petroleum 8.4

1. 16.1/6.4; 2 300 kWh
2a. Sugar 71   Beer 0.3 Mhl
b. Petroleum products 4.2
3. Telephones 67; Cars 132
   Air: 1 540 pass.-km.; 149 ton-km.
   Sea: 12 798 loaded; 11 094 unloaded

Exports: $2 194   Imports: $2 101
Petroleum products Crude petroleum
Petroleum   Manufactured goods
Exports to: U.S.A., Netherlands, Surinam
Imports from: U.S.A., U.K., Saudi Arabia, Indonesia
Revenue from tourism: $163
Aid received (net): $5

TUNISIA

1. Republic
2. Arabic, French
3. Dinar
4. $1 = 0.72
   £1 = 1.09

1. 164 th. sq. km.
2. 937; 42 per sq. km.
3. BR 33; DR 11; AI 2.5%
4. Urb. pop.: 2 779 (50%)
5. Tunis 774

1. GDP $8 132 (6.4%); $1 208 (3.8%)
   Agric. 13%, Indust. 23%, Others 64%
2. Wheat 711   Tomatoes 430
   Oranges 130   Olives 400
   Grapes 112   Dates 50
3. Sheep 5 230   Cattle 600
4. Fish 67
5. Roundwood 2 673
6. Lead 6   Crude petroleum 5.7
   Iron ore 0.2   Phosphates 5 796
   Natural gas 17.6

1. 8.7/4.3; 3 531 kWh (1% hydr.)
2a. Sugar 7   Wine 70
    Meat 107   Olive oil 90
b. Petroleum products 1.8
3. Telephones 200; Cars 102
   Rail: 744 pass.-km.; 1 692 ton-km.
   Air: 1 531 pass.-km.; 154 ton-km.
   Sea: 2 856 loaded; 6 744 unloaded

Exports: $1 618   Imports: $2 420
Petroleum   Machinery
Olive oil   Wheat
Phosphates   Textiles
Fertilizer   Iron and steel
Exports to: France, Italy, Greece, W. Germany
Imports from: France, W. Germany, Italy
Revenue from tourism: $555
Aid received (net): $257.3

TURKEY

1. Republic
2. Turkish
3. Lira
4. $1 = 656.62
   £1 = 992.48

1. 780 th. sq. km.
2. 48 265; 63 per sq. km.
3. BR 35; DR 10; AI 2.3%
4. Urb. pop.: 20 673 (43%)
5. Ankara 2 276

1. GDP $40 551 (3.4%); $858 (1.3%)
   Agric. 18%, Indust. 28%, Others 54%
2. Barley 6 500   Wheat 17 235
   Apples 1 900   Oranges 744
   Rye 360   Grapes 3 300
   Tomatoes 4 000   Cottonseed 938
   Cotton lint 586   Wool 63
   Tobacco 210
3. Sheep 48 630   Goats 16 732
4. Fish 567
5. Roundwood 19 193
6. Coal 7.1   Zinc 51
   Lignite 24.3   Crude petroleum 2.0
   Iron ore 1.9   Antimony 0.2
   Chrome 520   Mercury 161t
   Bauxite 128   Copper 27

1. 15.5/35.5; 27 321 kWh (42% hydr.)
2a. Meat 900   Sawnwood 4 117
    Sugar 1 630   Wine 37
    Olive oil 143
b. Iron 228   Steel 2 748
   Cotton yarn 54   Wool yarn 5.3
   Petroleum products 14.2 Copper 39
   Cement 15 744
3. Telephones 2 104; Cars 472
   Rail: 6 624 pass.-km.; 7 680 ton-km.
   Air: 1 177 pass.-km.; 126 ton-km.
   Sea: 45 144 loaded; 36 312 unloaded

Exports: $7 086   Imports: $10 822
Cotton   Machinery
Nuts   Vehicles
Tobacco   Fertilizer
Raisins   Crude petroleum
                   Iron and steel
Exports to: W. Germany, U.S.A., Italy, France
Imports from: W. Germany, U.S.A., Iran, Italy, France
Revenue from tourism: $370

For detailed table headings and notes see first page of this section

Country	Area and Population	Production	Manufactures	Trade

UGANDA

1. Republic
2. English, Bantu
3. Ugandan Shilling
4. $1 = 1 422.00
  £1 = 2 149.00

1. 236 th. sq. km.
2. 14 961; 63 per sq. km.
3. BR 50; DR 16; AI 5.5%
4. Urb. pop.: 1 061 (7%)
5. Kampala 332

Production
1. GDP $3 360 (−0.4%); $238 (−3.7%)
  Agric. 73%, Indust. 6%, Others 21%
2. Cassava 1 650 Millet/Sorghum 980
  Coffee 204 Tea 3
  Cottonseed 42 Groundnuts 100
3. Cattle 5 200 Goats 2 500
4. Fish 172
5. Roundwood 26 255
6. Tin 0.1 Tungsten 20t
  Lead 8

Manufactures
1. 0.08/0.3; 650 kWh (99% hydr.)
2a. Meat 156 Sugar 6
  Sawnwood 24
3. Telephones 43; Cars 35
  Rail: see Kenya
  Air: 125 pass.-km.; 41 ton-km.

Trade
Exports: $399 Imports: $293
Coffee Manufactured goods
Cotton Machinery
Copper Vehicles
Exports to: U.K., U.S.A., Spain, France
Imports from: U.K., W. Germany, Kenya, Brazil
Aid received (net): $99.7

UNITED KINGDOM

1. Kingdom
2. English
3. English Pound
4. $1 = 0.66

1. 245 th. sq. km.
2. 56 488; 231 per sq. km.
3. BR 13; DR 12; AI −0.0%
4. Urb. pop.: 50 618 (91%)
5. London 6 767

Production
1. GDP $367 983 (0.8%); $6 514 (0.8%)
  Agric. 2%, Indust. 29%, Others 69%
2. Barley 10 958 Wheat 14 960
  Oats 550 Potatoes 7 398
  Apples 344 Wool 51
3. Sheep 34 802 Cattle 13 213
4. Fish 847
5. Roundwood 3 950
6. Coal 51.3 Natural gas 1 628
  Iron ore 0.1 Crude petroleum 122.1
  Tin 5.0 Salt 6 311
  Lead 4

Manufactures
1. 328.7/260.2; 276 227 kWh (2% hydr., 18% nucl.)
2a. Meat 3 199 Sawnwood 1 691
  Butter and cheese 450 Sugar 1 400
  Beer 59.8 Mhl
b. Iron 9 672 Steel 15 120
  Aluminium 462 Lead 338
  Copper 137 Plastics 2 051
  Cotton yarn 89 Wool yarn 126
  Synthetic fibres 175 Paper 3 200
  Radios 407 Petroleum products 69.9
  Vehicles: Ships (grt.) 204
  pass. 910, comm. 224 Cement 13 488
3. Telephones 27 784; Cars 15 910
  Rail: 30 084 pass.-km.; 12 456 ton-km.
  Air: 53 645 pass.-km.; 6 606 ton-km.
  Sea: 136 140 loaded; 136 128 unloaded

Trade
Exports: $101 332 Imports: $109 270
Machinery Machinery
Vehicles Crude petroleum
Textiles Non-ferrous metals
Diamonds Fruit and vegetables
Non-ferrous metals Diamonds
Iron and steel Minerals
Alcoholic drinks Cereals
Aircraft Butter
  Meat
  Textiles
Exports to: U.S.A., W. Germany, France, Ireland, Belgium-Luxembourg, Netherlands
Imports from: U.S.A., W. Germany, France, Netherlands
Invisible trade balance: + $9 690
Revenue from tourism: $5 144
Aid given (net): $11 615

UNITED STATES

1. Federal Republic
2. English
3. U.S. Dollar
4. £1 = 1.51

1. 9 373 th. sq. km.
2. 236 681; 25 per sq. km.
3. BR 16; DR 9; AI 0.8%
4. Urb. pop.: 167 050 (71%)
5. Washington 3 061

Production
1. GDP $3 276 000 (3.1%); $13 968 (2.1%)
  Agric. 2%, Indust. 24%, Others 66%
2. Barley 12 988 Potatoes 16 404
  Maize 194 475 Wheat 70 638
  Sorghum 21 994 Rye 823
  Oranges 6 566 Grapefruit 1 945
  Wine 1 620 Soya beans 50 643
  Cottonseed 4 811 Tobacco 791
  Rice 6 216 Cotton 2 894
3. Cattle 114 040 Pigs 55 819
4. Fish 4 143
5. Roundwood 437 762
6. Coal 750.3 Nickel 8.7
  Iron ore 32.8 Tungsten 980t
  Bauxite 856 Vanadium 1 969t
  Copper 1 091 Natural gas 15 879
  Gold 71.5 Crude petroleum 435.8
  Lead 333 Potash 1 429
  Molybdenum 15 Phosphates 42 573
  Zinc 278 Silver 1 382
  Lignite 57.3 Uranium 8 138

Manufactures
1. 1 904.6/2 174.8; 2 367 634 kWh (14% hydr., 12% nucl, 0.2% geo.)
2a. Meat 25 627 Butter and cheese 2 910
  Sugar 5 394 Wine 1 620
  Sawnwood 78 110 Wood pulp 47 700
b. Cotton yarn 1 064 Wool yarn 58
  Synthetic fibres 286 Silk fabric 83 863 M ft^2
  Paper 58 800 Copper 1 500
  Magnesium 144 Iron 47 088
  Steel 82 716 Aluminium 5 759
  Plastics 12 418 Petroleum products 604
  Vehicles: Radios 7 661
  pass. 7 622, comm. 3 076 Ships (grt.) 118
3. Telephones 181 892; Cars 123 461
  Rail: 17 695 pass.-km.; 1 341 717 ton-km.
  Air: 408 997 pass.-km.; 47 144 ton-km.
  Sea: 327 768 loaded; 332 424 unloaded

Trade
Exports: $217 888 Imports: $341 177
Machinery Vehicles
Vehicles Machinery
Aircraft Iron and steel
Cereals Non-ferrous metals
Chemical products Crude petroleum
Iron and steel Petroleum products
Non-ferrous metals Clothing
Soya Paper and cardboard
Metals Textiles
Coal Metals
Textiles
Exports to: Canada, Japan, U.K., W. Germany, Mexico
Imports from: Canada, Japan, W. Germany, U.K., Mexico
Invisible trade balance: + $18 750
Revenue from tourism: $11 293
Aid given (net): $17 870

URUGUAY

1. Republic
2. Spanish
3. Uruguayan Peso
4. $1 = 139.69
  £1 = 211.14

1. 176 th. sq. km.
2. 2 990; 17 per sq. km.
3. BR 18; DR 9; AI 0.7%
4. Urb. pop.: 2 502 (84%)
5. Montevideo 1 362

Production
1. GDP $3 980 (3.9%); $1 331 (3.4%)
  Agric. 12%, Indust. 22%, Others 66%
2. Maize 120 Wheat 450
  Grapes 117 Oranges 50
  Linseed 8 Wool 91
3. Sheep 23 337 Cattle 9 491
4. Fish 144
5. Roundwood 2 975

Manufactures
1. 0.9/2.1; 7 343 kWh (98% hydr.)
2a. Meat 438 Sawnwood 16
  Sugar 91
b. Petroleum products 2.2
3. Telephones 294; Cars 281
  Rail: 339 pass.-km.; 205 ton-km.
  Air: 293 pass.-km.; 28 ton-km.
  Sea: 570 loaded; 454 unloaded

Trade
Exports: $925 Imports: $736
Beef Machinery
Wool Vehicles
Hides and skins Crude petroleum
Exports to: W. Germany, Brazil, U.S.A.
Imports from: Argentina, Brazil, U.S.A., Iraq
Aid received (net): $17.1

U.S.S.R.

1. Socialist Republic
2. Russian and others
3. Rouble
4. $1 = 0.71
  £1 = 1.07

1. 22 402 th. sq. km.
2. 275 000; 12 per sq. km.
3. BR 20; DR 11; AI 0.9%
4. Urb. pop.: 173 185 (64%)
5. Moscow 8 537

Production
1. NMP $711 818 (4.1%); $2 588 (3.2%)
  Agric. 20%, Indust. 46%, Others 34%
2. Barley 42 000 Wheat 76 000
  Maize 13 000 Potatoes 85 300
  Grapes 7 500 Rye 10 500
  Flax 480 Cotton 2 400
  Tomatoes 7 500 Cottonseed 5 350
  Tobacco 350
3. Sheep 145 265 Cattle 119 558
4. Fish 9 757
5. Roundwood 355 900
6. Coal 483.3 Tungsten 9 100t
  Iron ore 148.2 Zinc 980
  Bauxite 6 200 Natural gas 18 638
  Chrome 2 500 Crude petroleum 613.0
  Copper 1 020 Phosphates 27 700
  Lead 570 Potash 9 294
  Manganese 3 457 Salt 16 200
  Molybdenum 11 Asbestos 2 250
  Nickel 175 Diamonds 12 000
  Gold 270.0 Tin 10.0
  Lignite 153.0 Silver 1 600

Manufactures
1. 2 065.5/1 611.5; 1 408 100 kWh (13% hydr., 6% nucl.)
2a. Meat 16 839 Sawnwood 109 200
  Butter and cheese 3 269 Sugar 8 350
  Wine 3 800
b. Iron 110 496 Steel 153 996
  Aluminium 2 300 Copper 1 380
  Magnesium 80 Paper 8 900
  Cotton yarn 1 658 Wool yarn 457
  Synthetic fibres 645 Radios 8 906
  Petroleum products 420 Vehicles:
  pass. 1 296, comm. 866
3. Telephones 25 069; Cars 9 631
  Rail: 347 852 pass.-km.; 3 464 480 ton-km.
  Air: 172 206 pass.-km.; 18 517 ton-km.
  Sea: 162 000 loaded; 63 000 unloaded

Trade
Exports: $91 649 Imports: $80 624
Machinery Machinery
Iron and steel Clothing
Crude petroleum Ships
Non-ferrous metals Iron and steel
Petroleum products Minerals
Sawnwood Railway rolling stock
Cotton Shoes
Vehicles
Main trade is with: E.Germany, Poland, Czechoslovakia, Bulgaria, Hungary

VENEZUELA

1. Republic
2. Spanish
3. Bolivar
4. $1 = 19.33
  £1 = 29.21

1. 912 th. sq. km.
2. 16 851; 19 per sq. km.
3. BR 37; DR 6; AI 3.3%
4. Urb. pop.: 10 936 (65%)
5. Caracas 2 944

Production
1. GDP $46 461 (2.8%); $2 757 (−0.2%)
  Agric. 7%, Indust. 40%, Others 53%
2. Maize 547 Bananas 1 403
  Oranges 362 Tomatoes 127
  Cocoa 12 Coffee 61
  Cottonseed 25 Sesame 38
3. Cattle 12 283 Pigs 2 584
4. Fish 227
5. Roundwood 1 300
6. Iron ore 8.1 Natural gas 645
  Gold 863kg Crude petroleum 85.9
  Diamonds 300 Coal 0.04

Manufactures
1. 165.9/50.1; 41 700 kWh (41% hydr.)
2a. Meat 778 Sawnwood 210
  Sugar 423
b. Iron 2 400 Steel 2 772
  Cotton yarn . . . Synthetic fibres 17
  Cement 6 000 Vehicles:
  Petroleum products 40.4 pass. 235, comm. 66
3. Telephones 789; Cars 1 643
  Rail: 19 pass.-km.; 29 ton-km.
  Air: 5 031 pass.-km.; 563 ton-km.
  Sea: 60 821 loaded; 12 093 unloaded

Trade
Exports: $7 792 Imports: $6 676
Crude petroleum Machinery
Petroleum products Vehicles
Iron ore Iron and steel
Coffee Cereals
  Manufactured goods
Exports to: U.S.A., Neth. Antilles, Canada
Imports from: U.S.A., W. Germany, Japan
Invisible trade balance: −$3 524

For detailed table headings and notes see first page of this section

15

Country	Area and Population	Production	Manufactures	Trade

VIETNAM
1. Democratic Republic
2. Vietnamese
3. Dông
4. $1 = 12.46
  £1 = 18.83
	1. 330 th. sq. km.
	2. 58 307; 179 per sq. km.
	3. BR 39; DR 12; AI 2.0%
	4. Urb. pop.: 11 661 (20%)
	5. Hanoi 2 571
		1. GDP $4 682 (. . .); $98 (. . .)
		  Agric. 29%, Indust. 7%, Others 64%
		2. Rice 15 416 Cassava 2 900
		  Groundnuts 87 Tea 29
		  Maize 475 Tobacco 27
		3. Cattle 2 010 Pigs 11 202
		4. Fish 710
		5. Roundwood 23 676
		6. Coal 5.3 Phosphates 220
		  Salt 900 Tin 0.5
			1. 6.2/7.2; 4 200 kWh (38% hydr.)
			2a. Sawnwood 520
			  b. Cotton yarn 36 Cement 798
			3. Telephones 47; Cars 66
			  Rail: 4 043 pass.-km.; 980 ton-km.
			  Air: 389 pass.-km.; 5 ton-km.
			  Sea: 680 loaded; 5 000 unloaded
				Exports: $440 Imports: $1 210
				Main trade is with:
				U.S.S.R. and other Communist countries, Japan,
				France, Singapore, Hong Kong
				Aid received (net): $266

YEMEN, NORTH
1. Republic
2. Arabic
3. Riyal
4. $1 = 7.02
  £1 = 10.61
	1. 195 th. sq. km.
	2. 6 660; 34 per sq. km.
	3. BR 49; DR 24; AI 2.3%
	4. Urb. pop.: 1 149 (18%)
	5. Sana 278
		1. GDP $1 122 (5.4%); $212 (3.4%)
		  Agric. 61%, Indust. 3%, Others 36%
		2. Wheat 50 Coffee 3
		  Cottonseed 3
		3. Sheep 1 823 Cattle 950
			1. . . ./1.2; 285 kWh
			3. Telephones 4; Cars. . .
			  Air: 490 pass.-km.; 49 ton-km.
			  Sea: 40 loaded; 2 000 unloaded
				Exports: $39 Imports: $1 521
				Exports to: China, S. Yemen, Italy, Saudi Arabia
				Imports from: Saudi Arabia, Japan, India
				Aid received (net): $137.5

YEMEN, SOUTH
1. People's Republic
2. Arabic
3. South Yemen Dinar
4. $1 = 0.34
  £1 = 0.52
	1. 333 th. sq. km.
	2. 2 225; 7 per sq. km.
	3. BR 48; DR 23; AI 1.9%
	4. Urb. pop.: 823 (37%)
	5. Aden 264
		1. GDP $290 (. . .); $176 (. . .)
		  Agric. 19%, Indust. 17%, Others 64%
		2. Millet 80 Wheat 15
		  Dates 11 Cottonseed 10
		3. Goats 1 380 Sheep 1 000
		4. Fish 74
		5. Roundwood 270
			1. . . ./1.7; 180 kWh
			2b. Petroleum products 3.1
			3. Telephones 9; Cars 11
			  Sea: 1 426 loaded; 2 204 unloaded
				Exports: $430 Imports: $673
				  Petroleum products Petroleum
				  Cotton Cotton fabic
				       Cereals
				Exports to: U.K., Yemen, South Africa
				Imports from: Iran, Kuwait, Japan
				Aid received (net): $51.0

YUGOSLAVIA
1. Federal Republic
2. Croatian, Serbian
3. Yugoslavian Dinar
4. $1 = 337.47
  £1 = 510.08
	1. 256 th. sq. km.
	2. 22 963; 90 per sq. km.
	3. BR 16; DR 9; AI 0.8%
	4. Urb. pop.: 10 333 (45%)
	5. Belgrade 1 407
		1. NMP $49 736 (5.4%); $2 196 (4.5%)
		  Agric. 14%, Indust. 42%, Others 44%
		2. Maize 11 265 Wheat 5 596
		  Grapes 1 560 Wool 10
		  Tobacco 75
		3. Sheep 7 458 Pigs 9 337
		4. Fish 80
		5. Roundwood 15 381
		6. Coal 0.3 Gold 4.2
		  Lignite 54.5 Lead 114
		  Iron ore 1.8 Silver 128
		  Antimony 0.9 Zinc 86
		  Bauxite 3 347 Copper 138
		  Crude petroleum 4.0 Natural gas 105
			1. 33.5/52.9; 71 571 kWh (30% hydr., 5% nucl., 9% geo)
			2a. Meat 1 629 Sawnwood 4 413
			  Sugar 985 Wine 750
			  b. Iron 3 264 Steel 1 956
			  Copper 128 Lead 120
			  Cotton yarn 119 Wool yarn 50
			  Synthetic fibres 58 Ships (grt.) 199
			  Petroleum products 12.3
			3. Telephones 2 303; Cars 2 568
			  Rail: 11 508 pass.-km.; 28 476 ton-km.
			  Air: 2 870 pass.-km.; 318 ton-km.
			  Sea: 6 312 loaded; 22 080 unloaded
				Exports: $9 811 Imports: $11 538
				  Machinery Machinery
				  Non-ferrous metals Iron and steel
				  Ships and boats Vehicles
				  Clothing Textile fibres
				  Meat Textiles
				  Textiles Non-ferrous metals
				  Iron and steel Chemical products
				  Shoes Crude petroleum
				Exports to: Italy, U.S.S.R., W. Germany
				Imports from: W. Germany, Italy, U.S.S.R
				Invisible trade balance: +$2 144
				Revenue from tourism: $844

ZAÏRE
1. Democratic Republic
2. Kiswahili, etc
3. Zaïre
4. $1 = 54.52
  £1 = 82.42
	1. 2 345 th. sq. km.
	2. 29 671; 13 per sq. km.
	3. BR 46; DR 17; AI 2.9%
	4. Urb. pop.: 9 010 (34%)
	5. Kinshasa 2 444
		1. GDP $5 443 (−3.7%); $180 (−6.7%)
		  Agric. 26%, Indust. 16%, Others 58%
		2. Cassava 14 800 Maize 680
		  Coffee 80 Groundnuts 380
		  Palm oil 140 Rubber 24
		  Bananas 1 805 Cottonseed 50
		3. Goats 2 910 Cattle 1 300
		4. Fish 102
		5. Roundwood 31 265
		6. Cobalt 11 Tin 2.4
		  Copper 501 Zinc 75
		  Manganese . . . Diamonds 18 500
		  Gold 6.0 Tungsten 85t
		  Crude petroleum 1.3 Silver 25
			1. 2.3/2.1; 4 213 kWh (99% hydr.)
			2a. Sugar 45 Beer 5.0Mhl
			  Sawnwood 121
			  b. Copper 225 Zinc 66
			  Petroleum products 0.6 Cement 400
			3. Telephones 27; Cars 40
			  Rail: 467 pass.-km.; 2 203 ton-km.
			  Air: 683 pass.-km.; 93 ton-km.
			  Sea: 845 loaded; 1 513 unloaded
				Exports: $1 004 Imports: $682
				  Copper Machinery
				  Diamonds Vehicles
				  Cobalt Petroleum products
				  Coffee Cotton fabric
				  Palm oil Cereals
				Exports to: Belgium-Luxembourg, U.K., U.S.A.
				Imports from: Belgium-Luxembourg, U.S.A., France,
				W. Germany
				Aid received (net): $410.9

ZAMBIA
1. Republic
2. English
3. Kwacha
4. $1 = 7.09
  £1 = 10.72
	1. 753 th. sq. km.
	2. 6 445; 8.6 per sq. km.
	3. BR 48; DR 17; AI 3.3%
	4. Urb. pop.: 3 029 (47%)
	5. Lusaka 538
		1. GDP $2 767 (−1.6%); $443 (−4.5%)
		  Agric. 14%, Indust. 35%, Others 51%
		2. Maize 857 Tobacco 3
		  Millet/sorghum 27 Groundnuts 19
		3. Cattle 2 400 Goats 355
		4. Fish 67
		5. Roundwood 9 171
		6. Coal 0.5 Tin . . .
		  Cobalt 2.4t Gold 0.3
		  Copper 565 Silver 28
		  Lead 19 Zinc 41
			1. 1.6/2.2; 10 071 kWh (99% hydr.)
			2a. Meat 88 Sugar 141
			  Sawnwood 42
			  b. Copper 523 Zinc 29
			  Lead 9 Cement 252
			3. Telephones 61; Cars 68
			  Air: 557 pass.-km.; 74 ton-km.
				Exports: $648 Imports: $566
				  Copper Machinery
				  Zinc Vehicles
				  Lead Textiles
				  Cobalt Iron and steel
				  Tobacco Petroleum products
				Exports to: Japan, U.K., W. Germany, U.S.A.
				Imports from: U.K., Saudi Arabia, U.S.A.
				Aid received (net): $290.1

ZIMBABWE
1. Republic
2. English
3. Zimbabwe Dollar
4. $1 = 1.60
  £1 = 2.42
	1. 391 th. sq. km.
	2. 7 980; 20 per sq. km.
	3. BR 47; DR 14; AI 3.5%
	4. Urb. pop.: 1 823 (24%)
	5. Harare 681
		1. GDP $6 612 (3.2%); $876 (0%)
		  Agric. 13%, Indust. 27%, Others 60%
		2. Maize 1 501 Millet/sorghum 132
		  Groundnuts 70 Tobacco 118
		3. Cattle 5 500 Goats 1 100
		5. Roundwood 6 696
		6. Coal 3.1 Gold 14.5t
		  Iron ore 0.5 Nickel 11.1
		  Chrome 420 Tin 1.2
		  Copper 21 Asbestos 153
		  Silver 38
			1. 2.9/3.8; 4 426 kWh (84% hydr.)
			2a. Meat 116 Sugar 457
			  Sawnwood 131
			  b. Iron 420 Steel 528
			  Copper 23 Cement 648
			3. Telephones 224; Cars 176
			  Rail: . . . pass.-km.; 6 259 ton-km.
			  Air: 541 pass.-km.; 58 ton-km.
				Exports: $1 008 Imports: $959
				  Tobacco Machinery
				  Asbestos Textiles
				  Copper Vehicles
				  Gold Mineral fuels
				Main trade is with: U.K., W. Germany, U.S.A.
				Aid received (net): $136.1

For detailed table headings and notes see first page of this section

Exploring the Universe

Introduction by Heather Couper,
President, British Astronomical Association

In just a generation, we have learned more about the universe than throughout the whole history of mankind. There has been nothing short of a revolution in astronomy.

Much of this new knowledge derives directly from our forays into space. Probes have now visited all the planets except Neptune and Pluto, turning them from once-mysterious points of light in the night sky to real, solid worlds in their own right. Satellites in orbit keep watch on the further reaches of the universe, telling of dramas whose alarm calls can never penetrate to the Earth's surface. Meanwhile, down on the ground, the revolution has been fuelled by 'space spin-offs' : electronics and computers. Astronomers can now take any incoming signal and wring it dry of nearly every scrap of information.

Out of all this has grown the 'new astronomy' : a universe of quasars, pulsars, black holes, the Big Bang. But despite all this new knowledge — in some ways, because of it — we are really no nearer to comprehending the universe. There is still so much we don't know. Did the universe really begin in a Big Bang? Will it last forever? Is there life beyond that on our own planet? And, even closer to home, there are still questions begging answers — for instance, where *did* the Moon come from?

In *Exploring the Universe*, Brian Jones takes stock of the universe as we know it at the end of the twentieth century. It is a fascinating blend of the familiar and the unfamiliar; the explained and the unexplained. And, in the end, we find that the universe is not solely the preserve of the scientist. In these days of increasing specialization and sophistication, the ever-watchful amateur astronomer's contributions have become even more essential. In the universe, all of us have a part to play.

History of Astronomy

Stonehenge, built in prehistoric times on Salisbury Plain, England.

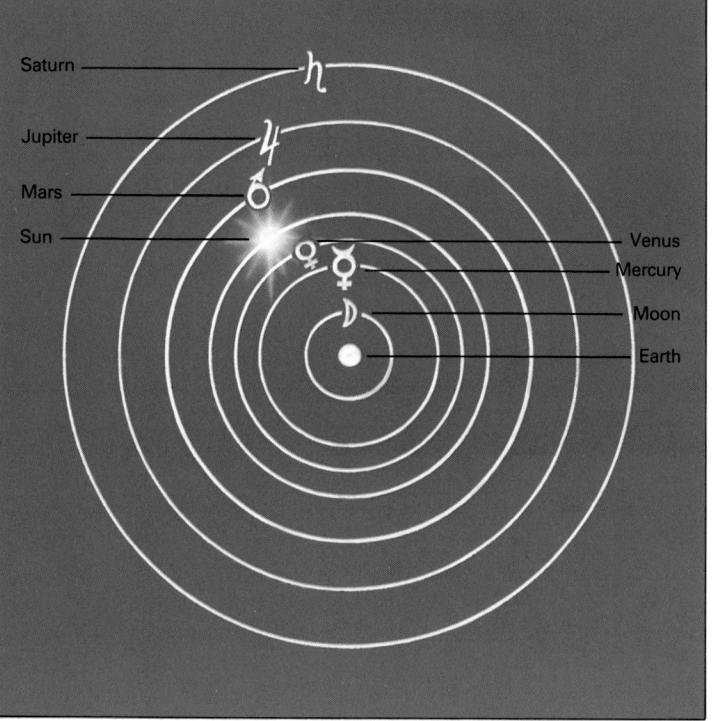

Man has always been fascinated by the stars. Although at first he had no real understanding as to what the stars might be, as time passed he eventually began to study them in a more scientific way. He linked the progression of the various star groups to the seasons on Earth, and eventually began to grasp an idea of time and how its rate of passing was indicated in the heavens. The Egyptians introduced the 365-day calendar in about 3000 BC. They also divided the stars into constellations and made accurate measurements of stellar positions. Astronomy flourished in China three millennia ago, where observers kept records of many celestial events including comets and eclipses, a great number of which have come down to us.

Observatories were built to help the early star watchers mark the positions of the rising and setting of the Sun and Moon at certain times of the year. It may be that some prehistoric monuments, such as Stonehenge on Salisbury Plain in England, were built by prehistoric man to mark the rising and setting of the Sun and Moon at certain times of the year.

The Greeks

The next great period of interest in astronomy came with the Greek era, during the centuries between the birth of Thales of Miletus in 624 BC and the death of Ptolemy in AD 180. The early Greek astronomers drew their knowledge from the Egyptians. Thales himself, in true Egyptian tradition, regarded the Earth as being a flat body situated at the centre of the universe. Aristarchus (310–250 BC) suggested that the Earth circled the Sun, but his ideas were not generally accepted.

One of the greatest of the Greek astronomers was Aristotle. It was through his reasoning that the old idea of a flat Earth was finally discounted. He noticed that the height above the horizon of the bright star Canopus changed according to the latitude of the observer. From Alexandria it was easily seen although from Athens, further to the north, the star disappeared below the southern horizon. This effect could only be explained by assuming the Earth to be a globe.

No account of the history of astronomy would be complete without mention of Ptolemy. His book *The Almagest*, summing up the work of philosophers before him, contained an account of what has become known as the Ptolemaic Theory. This put forward the idea that the Earth was situated at the centre of the universe with the Sun, Moon and planets revolving around it at different distances. Well beyond Saturn, then the outermost known planet, lay the sphere of fixed stars. The Ptolemaic Theory remained for centuries the most popular and widely believed idea as to the construction of the heavens.

The death of Ptolemy marked the end of the Greek era and centuries were to pass before any further significant progress was made. Astronomy owed its revival, some 800 years later, to astrology. The Arabs drew up improved star catalogues and tables which allowed the positions and movements of the planets to be plotted as well as being of great benefit to navigation. They also gave names to some of the brighter stars, many of which are still in use today including Betelgeuse in Orion and Deneb in Cygnus.

Interest in astronomy spread to Europe. The need for accurate measurements of stellar positions increased as navigation by the stars became more and more common. However, the general progress of astronomy was slow because the old ideas of Aristotle and his Earth-centred system held firm. Yet under the Ptolemaic Theory the motions of the planets through the sky could not be fully explained, and astronomers were becoming more and more convinced that something was wrong.

Renaissance Discoveries

The first major threat to the old system came in 1543 with the publication of *De Revolutionibus Orbium Coelestium* (Concerning the Revolutions of the Celestial Spheres) by Nicolas Copernicus. Born in Torun, Poland, in 1473, Copernicus had long thought that the Ptolemaic Theory was both clumsy and impractical. After years of studying both his own observations and those of other astronomers he came to the conclusion that the Earth was just one of a number of planets following circular orbits around the Sun. Such ideas were regarded as heresy by the Church authorities and Copernicus knew he was treading dangerous ground. For this reason he waited until he was on his deathbed before publishing his ideas.

After the work of Copernicus astronomers became increasingly convinced that the Sun was indeed at the centre of the universe. The Copernican System had its dissenters, however, one of which was the astronomer Tycho Brahe. Born in Denmark in 1546, Tycho's reputation as a brilliant observer was second to none. Although he had a lifelong interest in astronomy, his career really started in 1572 when he noticed a bright 'new star' in the constellation of Cassiopeia. We now know that this was a super-

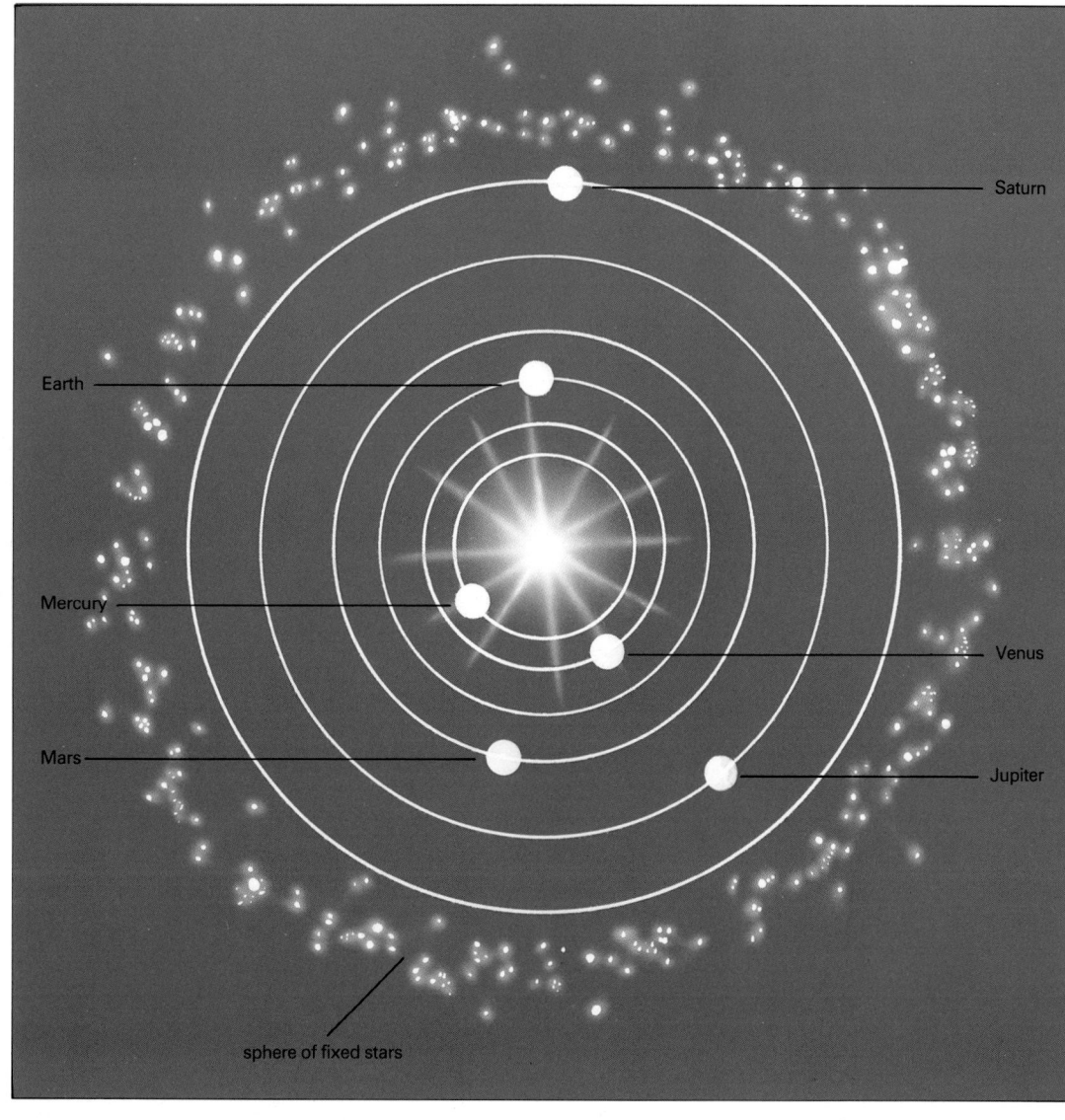

Saturn

Earth

Mercury

Mars

Venus

Jupiter

sphere of fixed stars

young mathematician called Johann Kepler. When Tycho died in 1601 he was succeeded by Kepler, who also inherited all his observations. Unlike Tycho, Kepler supported the Copernican System, although he noticed that the circular planetary orbits Copernicus had suggested did not fully explain the planets' actual observed motions through the sky.

Kepler examined Tycho's observations and attempted to explain the movements of the planets with different orbital shapes. Eventually he found that the planets orbited the Sun in elliptical paths with the Sun at one focus of the ellipse. After this discovery it did not take long to realize that the orbital speed of a planet varied according to its distance from the Sun. This explained the discrepancies between the Copernican System and the actual observed paths of the planets. At last, correct order had been established in the Solar System. Johann Kepler had laid the foundations for the astronomers of the future to study the heavens and to expand on their rapidly growing knowledge of the universe in which they lived.

nova, an event which signals the end of a massive star. Tycho's Star, as the object came to be known, was actually first seen by Wolfgang Schuler some five days before Tycho, but it was Tycho who made a series of observations and measurements of the star, eventually

publishing his results in a small book. News of his work spread and eventually reached King Frederick II of Denmark, who offered to build Tycho an observatory on the island of Hveen, some 3 miles (5 km) out from the Swedish coast. The observatory was erected in 1576 and,

over the next two decades, Tycho carried out detailed observations of the stars and planets, resulting in a star catalogue that surpassed anything then available.

In 1599, Tycho left Denmark and established an observatory in Prague. He took on an assistant, a

Two types of ellipse.

Left: An eccentric ellipse where the two foci are relatively far apart. Many comets have orbits like this where they are close to the Sun for only a very short fraction of their total orbital period.

Right: An ellipse which is fairly close to being a circle and which resembles a typical planetary orbit.

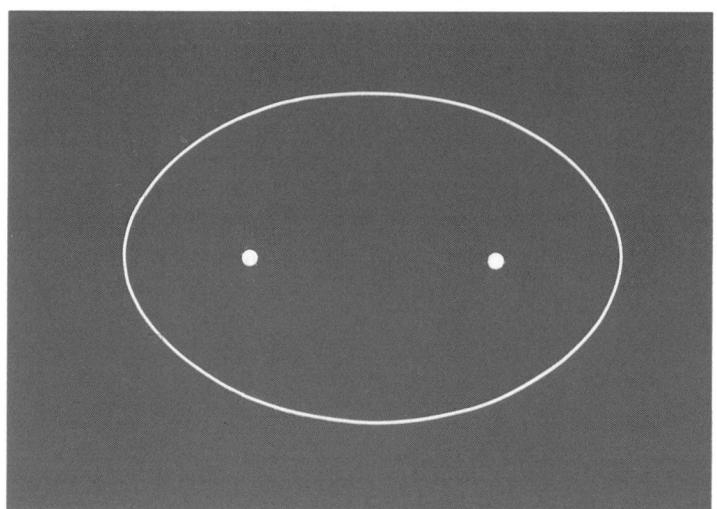

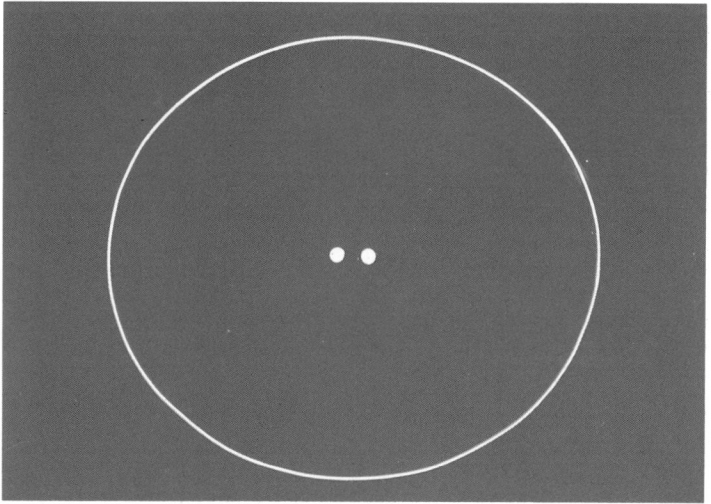

Formation of the Solar System

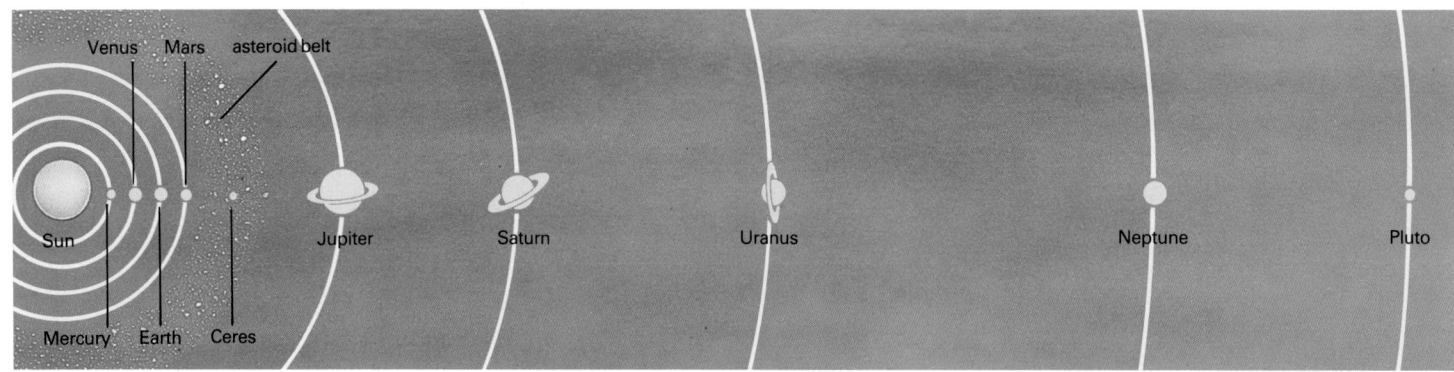

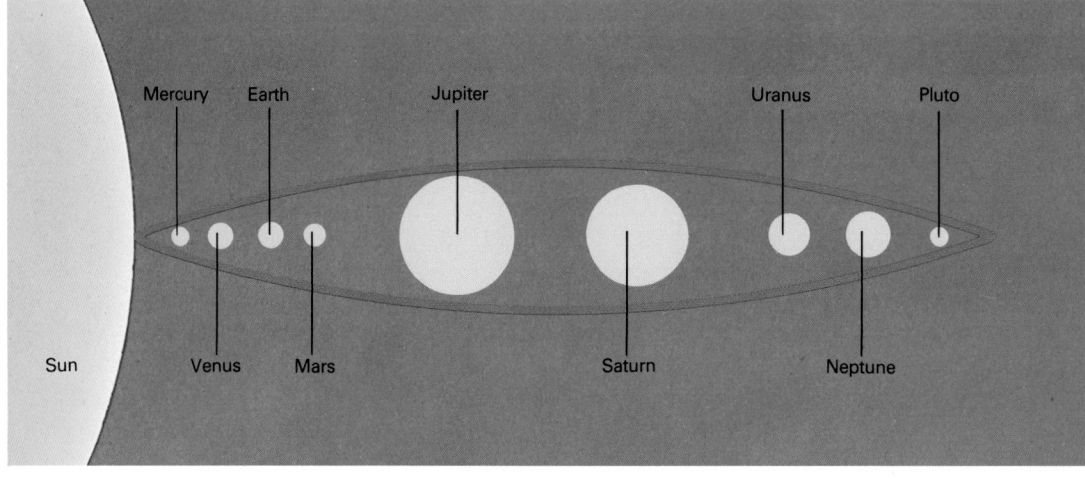

Above: A map of the Solar System showing the relative distances of the planets from the Sun. The position of the main asteroid belt is also shown, together with Ceres, the largest of the asteroids. The size of the Sun is not shown to scale.

Right: Passing star theory. According to a now discredited theory developed by Sir James Jeans, a cigar-shaped filament was dragged from the Sun by a passing star. The larger planets formed from the central region whilst the small planets condensed from the material at each end.

Our Earth is a member of the Solar System, a collection of planets, planetary satellites, asteroids, comets, meteoroids and dust orbiting the Sun. The Sun is an average star, just one of countless thousands known to exist in our Galaxy. Although we can pride ourselves on our current knowledge of the Sun and planets, we are still uncertain about the formation of the Solar System.

Astronomers agree on some points, one of which is that the Solar System is approximately 4.5 billion years old. This conclusion has been reached by calculating the age of meteorites, most of which are believed to have remained unchanged since they were formed from interstellar dust at the same time as the planets themselves took shape.

There is less agreement on the process of formation, although the composition and arrangement of the Solar System give us various clues. For example, all the planets, with the exception of Pluto, orbit the Sun in roughly the same plane. The planets are also split into two distinct groups. The four inner planets – Mercury, Venus, Earth and Mars – are all rocky and comparatively small, whilst the next four – Jupiter, Saturn, Uranus and Neptune – are large, gaseous worlds with no solid surface, made up of such materials as hydrogen, helium and methane. Pluto seems to be a small, rocky world, similar in composition to the four inner planets.

The most popular theory is that the Solar System condensed from a spinning dust and gas cloud. This cloud gradually became disc-shaped with most of the material being concentrated in the central region. As time went on this region condensed through gravity, gradually becoming hotter and hotter until the heat pressure eventually triggered off the nuclear reactions which cause the Sun and stars to give off their light.

In the meantime things were happening in the disc surrounding the protostar we know as the Sun. The heavier elements in the cloud were gravitationally attracted towards the inner regions and it is from these that the terrestrial planets were formed. The four gaseous planets came into being from the lighter elements, present as ice particles in the freezing temperatures of space, collecting together to form the gas giants we see today. Any traces of gaseous material left after the formation of the planets were quickly pushed out into space by the constant emission of gas from the young Sun acting as a cosmic broom, sweeping the interplanetary regions clear. Even now we can still detect a much reduced but perpetual wave of gas escaping from our parent star.

Although this theory does much to explain the formation of the Sun and planets, many other ideas have been proposed. In 1796 the French astronomer Pierre Simon de Laplace introduced his Nebular Hypothesis. This stated that the original gas cloud contracted and shrank, and while doing so threw off rings of matter. These rings condensed into planets with the outermost members of the Solar System being formed first. Laplace's idea was popular for a long time, although it has not stood up to the rigours of mathematical examination. For one thing it has been shown that rings of matter would not form planets as Laplace had stated. Also, if this idea were correct, then the planets would orbit the Sun in the plane of the solar equator, which is not the case.

Passing star theories were fashionable for a time, the first of which was proposed by Chamberlain and Moulton in 1900. They suggested that a star, wandering through space, passed close to the Sun and dragged material away from it, the resulting cloud eventually condensing to form the present Solar System. Sir James Jeans advanced a similar idea but suggested that a cigar-shaped filament was drawn out from the Sun with the larger planets forming from the central region of the cloud and the smaller ones from the ends. Although none of these theories was proved to be correct, they did pave the way for the modern day concept of the origins of the Solar System.

The Search for Planets Elsewhere

As all the stars are thought to have been born within gas clouds, the formation of the Solar System round our Sun suggests that planetary systems may well have formed round other stars. However, it is one thing to speculate on the existence of other planetary systems, but it is a very different proposition to detect them. The light from such an object would be so faint that it would be totally swamped in the glare from the parent star.

It is theoretically possible to detect the presence of extra-solar planets by carrying out detailed observations of the proper motions of stars. If a sufficiently large planet were in orbit around a star then gravitational interaction between the two bodies would produce a 'wobble' in the observed motion of the star. Peter van de Kamp carried out observations of nearby Barnard's Star and reported such a wobble. He concluded that there must be two Jupiter-sized planets in orbit around Barnard's Star. However, van de Kamp's results were questioned by astronomers and eventually dismissed as being due to instrumental error. In order to detect planets in this way it is clear that extremely accurate measurements are required. Subsequent observations of Barnard's Star have shown no irregularities in its proper motion, although the possibility of smaller, Earth-sized objects orbiting the star cannot yet be ruled out.

In 1983 the Infra Red Astronomy Satellite (IRAS) discovered a ring of particles surrounding Vega. This material could be a planetary system and may well resemble our own Solar System, with objects ranging in size from tiny meteorites upwards. IRAS also discovered similar rings around Fomalhaut and more than 40 other stars.

As yet we have no conclusive proof that other planetary systems exist, but the search will go on. Although it seems that Earth-based telescopes cannot hope to detect such objects visually, orbital telescopes, such as IRAS, together with purely optical instruments, may have more success.

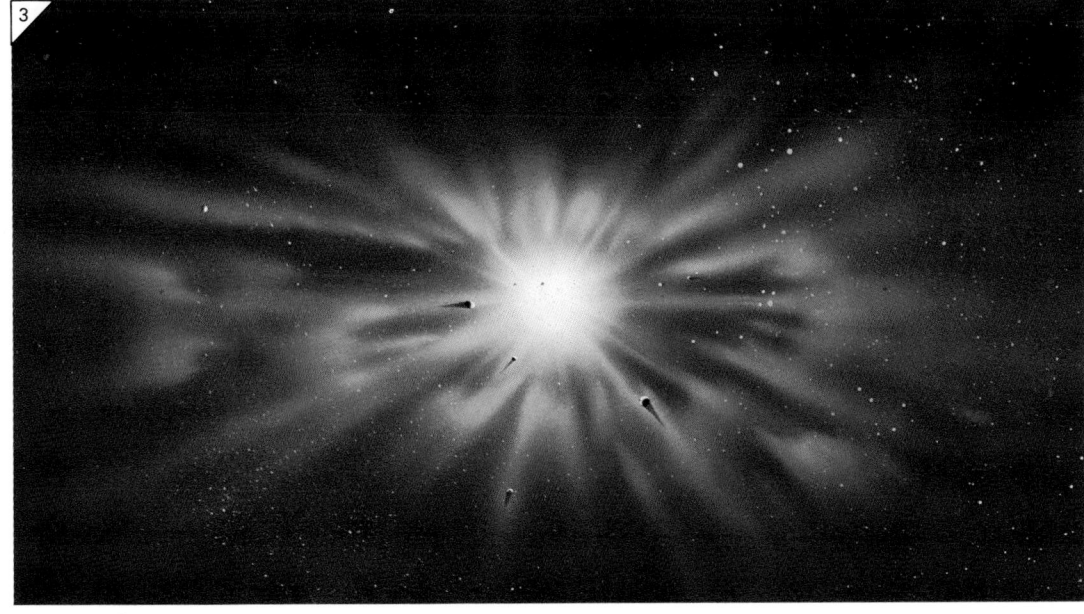

These pictures illustrate the evolution of the Solar System:
1. A spinning dust and gas cloud draws together under the force of gravity.
2. The gas cloud contracts, planets are formed and the central region of the cloud compresses and heats up.
3. The Sun eventually ignites and surplus dust and gas is driven from the region between the planets.

Interplanetary Debris

Comets

There are few sights more awe-inspiring than that of a giant comet hanging in the sky, yet appearances can be deceptive. Awesome as they are, comets are made up of very tenuous material and actually contain very little mass. They are thought to originate from a vast cloud of matter which completely surrounds the Solar System and stretches out from just beyond the orbit of Pluto to a distance of almost two light years. Known as Oort's Cloud, its existence was first proposed by the Dutch astronomer Jan Oort in 1950. It is thought that the gravitational influence of passing stars releases clumps of matter from the cloud, setting them off on paths towards the inner reaches of the Solar System in the form of comets.

While a comet is well away from the warming influence of the Sun it resembles nothing more than a dirty snowball consisting of ice and dust particles frozen together. It is only when the orbit of the comet brings it nearer to the Sun that light and heat from our parent star act on it, causing the ice in the nucleus to vaporize. The material released forms a cloud around the nucleus known as the coma. As the comet gets closer, solar energy pushes particles in the coma out to form one or more tails, thereby giving the comet its characteristic appearance. Because comet tails are formed in this way they always point away from the Sun and when the comet retreats into space the tail precedes it. As the distance between the comet and the Sun increases the tail and coma gradually disappear, leaving the cold, icy nucleus.

At each close approach to the Sun, a comet loses some of its mass to surrounding space through interaction with the solar wind – the constant stream of energized particles emitted by the Sun. As a result, those comets with short orbital periods tend to be small and faint with sometimes very little of their original mass. Encke's Comet, for example, orbits the Sun once every 3.3 years and can be seen only with optical aid. On the other hand, those comets with long periods can be quite spectacular. Halley's Comet, with a period of approximately 76 years, can be quite an impressive object. Other notable comets have been Comet Bennett of 1970 and Comet West of 1976, both of which have

extremely long orbits which take them out towards the very edge of the Solar System. Perhaps the most interesting thing about these ethereal members of the Sun's family is their unpredictability. Bright comets can appear at any time and anywhere in the sky. When they do, they seldom fail to impress.

Right: The structure of a comet.

Below: The orbits of Halley's Comet and Encke's Comet. The latter has the shortest known period for a comet (3.3 years) and is classed as a short-period comet. On the other hand, medium-period Halley's Comet takes about 76 years to travel round the Sun.

Bottom: Halley's Comet seen from an Earth orbiter with, inset, a photograph of the comet taken in 1910 by the Transvaal Observatory.

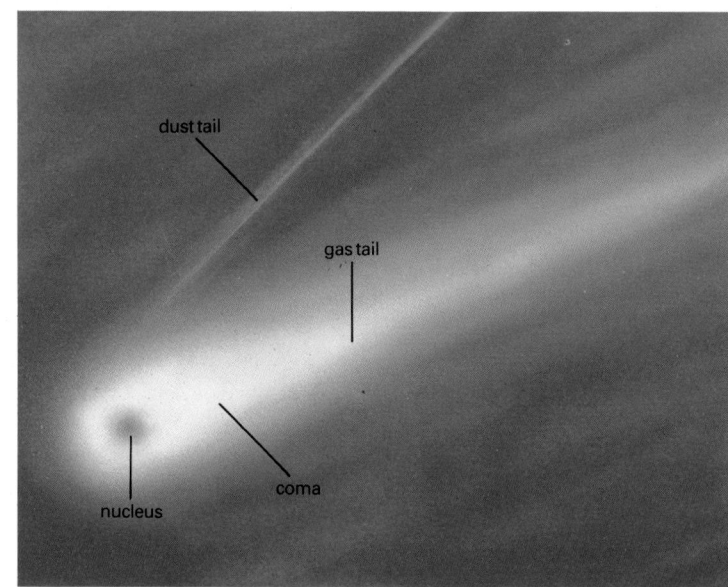

dust tail
gas tail
coma
nucleus

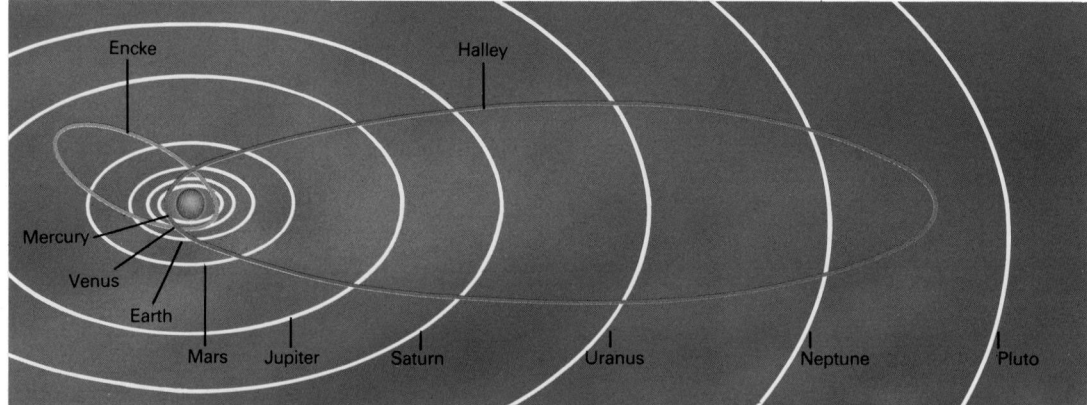

Encke
Halley
Mercury
Venus
Earth
Mars
Jupiter
Saturn
Uranus
Neptune
Pluto

Meteors and Meteorites

As a comet is gradually pulled apart through constant interaction with the Sun, particles become scattered all along its orbit. Should any of these particles wander close to the Earth they may be pulled down through the atmosphere by the Earth's gravity. The result is a sometimes brilliant streak of light moving quickly against the stellar background as the particle is destroyed by atmospheric friction. It is this effect that has led to meteors being commonly referred to as shooting stars.

At certain predictable times of the year the Earth passes through the orbital paths of various comets, resulting in relatively concentrated bombardments of shooting stars known as meteor showers. These meteor showers occur at well defined times of the year. It is easy to tell whether a meteor is a member of a shower. Because all the meteors in any particular shower come from the same cometary orbit, they all seem to radiate from the same point in space, known as the radiant. Each meteor travels in a path parallel to the others in the same shower, but they all originate from the same apparent point. A good analogy is that of a straight road. If you stand in the road, its edges seem to converge in the distance, although this is only an optical effect. If you look up into a clear, dark sky for any length of time you will be unlucky not to see a meteor or two, but when a shower is active the number of observed meteors can rise dramatically, sometimes reaching an hourly rate of a hundred or more. Lone meteors may be related to cometary debris in the same way as showers.

Whilst the vast majority of meteors disintegrate completely in the atmosphere, some are of sufficient size to survive the passage to Earth, at least partially. These are known as meteorites. It has been found that certain meteorites and a number of asteroids have similar characteristics, indicating that some meteorites may have their origin within the asteroid belt. The Earth's surface carries the scars of past meteoritic impacts, perhaps the best known being the large meteorite crater in Arizona, caused by an impact which occurred many thousands of years ago. It is disturbing to imagine what would happen if a large meteorite landed on one of the Earth's major cities, but the probability of such an occurrence is only once every 300 million years or so. A little less likely, perhaps, than the efforts of various film producers would have us believe.

Glows in the Zodiac

Looking towards the west where the Sun has set, if the sky is really dark and pollution free, a faint glow may sometimes be seen extending up from the horizon. Depending on the sky conditions, this glow may be followed along the zodiac, cutting through the plane of the ecliptic. This is the zodiacal light, and it arises from the reflection of sunlight by countless billions of tiny particles lying in a flat ring surrounding the Sun. A concentration of the light may be visible at a point in the sky opposite that of the Sun. This is the Gegenschein (German for counterglow).

The particles that form this disc originate mainly from comets, in particular the material lost by the comet as it passes the Sun, although some are the result of collisions between asteroids long ago in the history of the Solar System. Their numbers are vast, yet they are very thinly spread, a typical cubic mile of space containing only about twelve individual particles.

The eventual fate of this interplanetary dust is varied. Some may spiral in towards the Sun adding an insignificant contribution to the solar mass. Some may be pulled down toward the surfaces of passing planets, whilst the lightest particles are propelled out of the Solar System by the relentless pressure of light from our star.

In today's world the zodiacal light and the Gegenschein are difficult to observe, their faint glows being devoured by the pollution within our atmosphere. Yet their presence in the night sky bears testament to cometary passages of eons past and proves that the residue of comets long dead can still put on a brave show.

Arizona meteorite crater, USA.

The Inner Planets

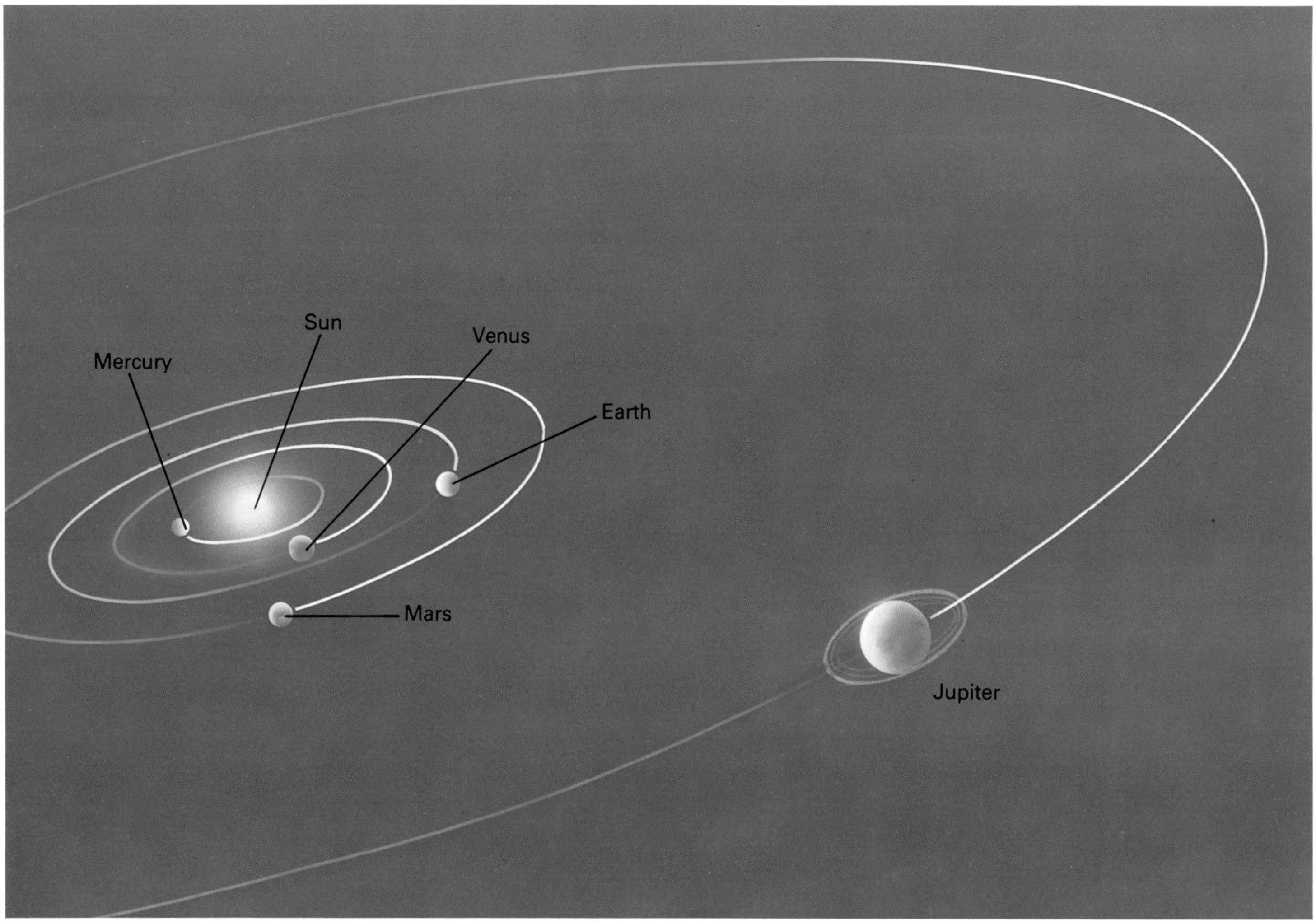

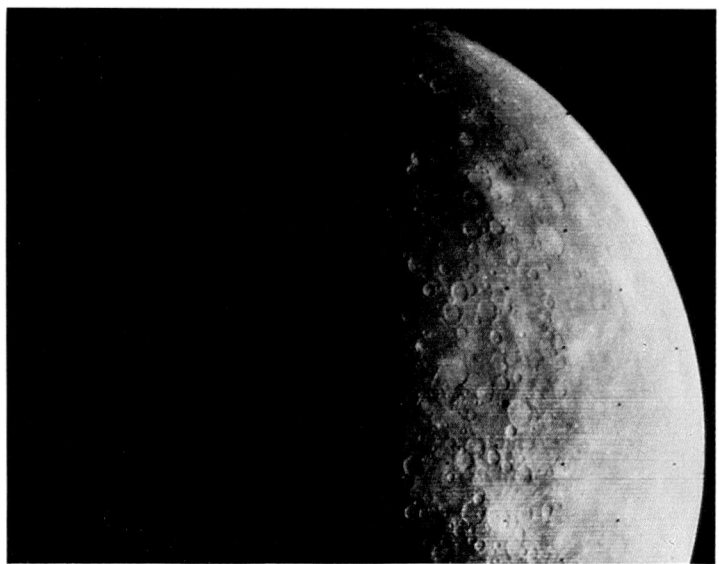

Mercury
Sun
Venus
Earth
Mars
Jupiter

The Terrestrial Planets

The four inner members of the Solar System are known as the terrestrial planets. Mercury, Venus, Earth and Mars are all rocky bodies, with surfaces that clearly display the marks of vulcanism, meteoritic bombardment, and, in the case of Mars and the Earth, atmospheric and other erosion.

Mercury is the innermost member of our Solar System, orbiting the Sun once every 88 days at an average distance of 36 million miles (57.9 million km). Because Mercury is so close to the Sun, it is never really conspicuous and is visible only for a short time in the west after sunset or in the east before sunrise. As a result, early observers had great difficulty in seeing any surface detail. Our knowledge was dramatically increased in 1974, when the American spacecraft Mariner 10 sent back

the first detailed photographs. They showed Mercury to be a heavily-cratered world with mountainous regions and a small number of smoother, mare-type areas similar to those found on the Moon.

In contrast, Venus is one of the brightest objects in the sky, this brilliance being due to the reflection of sunlight from dense clouds which completely enshroud the planet, hiding its surface from view. Again, we have obtained detailed knowledge of Venus only very recently. Radar-mapping from spacecraft has revealed a largely flat terrain but with a number of conspicuous highland regions. These include Ishtar Terra and Aphrodite Terra, both of which are many miles higher than the surrounding surface.

Almost three quarters of the Earth is covered by water, and the land area is characterized by much geological activity. Although vol-

Above: The inner planets and Jupiter, closest of the outer planets. All orbit the Sun in the same direction.

Below: Mercury photographed from Mariner 10 at a distance of 310,000 miles.

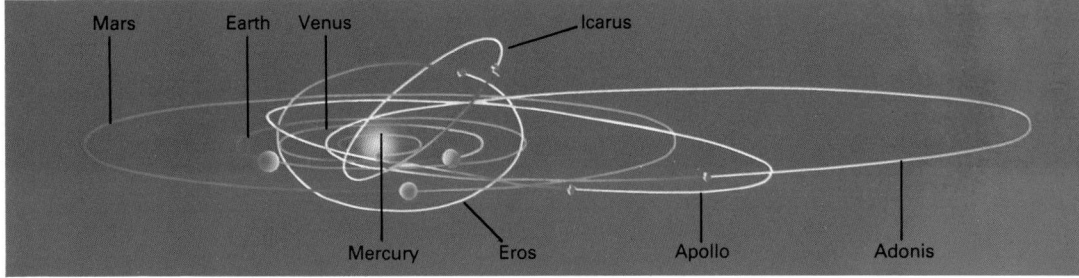

Right: The inner planets and some of the asteroids, all of which orbit the Sun in the same direction. Some asteroids, however, such as Eros, appear to move in reverse, having been pulled into a highly inclined orbit, possibly as a result of being perturbed by another body.

Below: Venus viewed from Mariner 10.

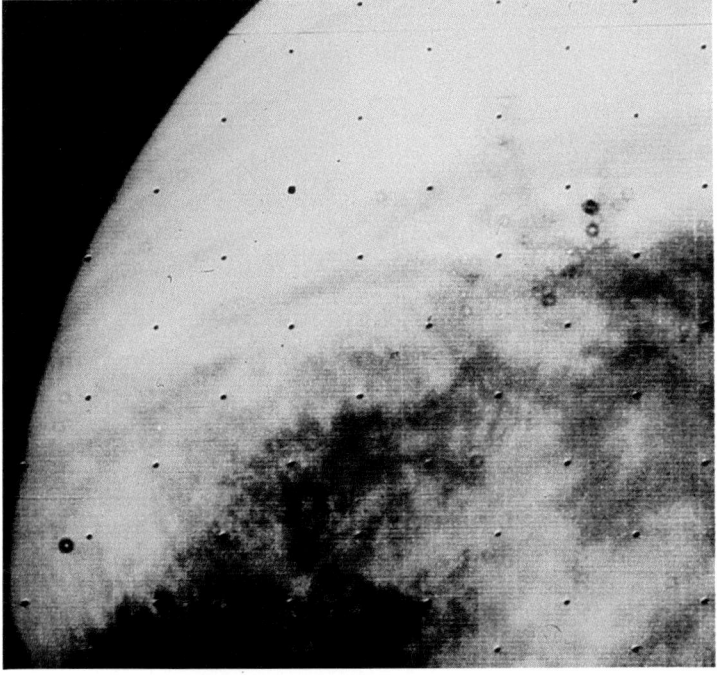

canoes, mountains and valleys are prominent features to us, the Earth's destructive, erosive forces ensure that many of these are short-lived on the geological time scale. Our planet also has a rich atmosphere which supports a wide diversity of life forms, another factor which helps to make the Earth unique.

Mars has a very thin atmosphere, composed mainly of carbon dioxide but containing traces of water vapour that produce cloud formations high above the Martian surface. The planet can boast features so large that they dwarf those found elsewhere in the Solar System. Olympus Mons is the largest volcano known with a height of around 15 miles (24 km) and a caldera (summit crater) some 40 miles (64 km) across. The Vallis Marineris is a huge canyon 2500 miles (4000 km) long and 45 miles (72 km) across at its widest point. Mars has two moons – Phobos and Deimos – discovered in 1877 by Asaph Hall. They are both tiny, irregular chunks of rock and probably represent captured asteroids.

The Asteroids

In 1772 Johann Bode drew attention to an interesting numerical relationship which made sense of the fact that the gaps between planets increase rapidly with distance from the Sun. Known as the

Titius-Bode law, it had first been proposed by Johann Titius in 1766, and it suggested that a hitherto-undiscovered planet was orbiting the Sun between Mars and Jupiter because the sequence of known planets did not quite fit what the law predicted. A look at any scale diagram of the Solar System will reveal that the family of major planets is indeed split into two groups by a gap at this point. The first discovery of a minor planet in this area was made quite accidentally by Giuseppe Piazzi on 1 January 1801 from his observatory at Palermo, Sicily. It was given the name Ceres, and further discoveries soon followed – those of Pallas in 1802, Juno in 1804 and Vesta in 1807. No more discoveries were made until 1845 when the Prussian astronomer Karl Hencke came across tiny Astrea. Since then not a year has passed without further minor planets coming to light.

We now know that many thousands of these tiny worlds orbit the Sun. Most of them keep to the region between Mars and Jupiter, but a few have very eccentric orbits. One notable example is Icarus which can come to within 13 million miles (21 million km) of the Sun, whilst at the other extreme the orbit of Hidalgo carries it out almost as far as Saturn. Chiron, discovered in 1977 by Charles Kowal, spends most of its orbit out between the paths of Saturn and Uranus.

The origin of the asteroids is not certain. They may represent the debris left over from the formation of the Solar System, or they could be the remains of a planet which broke up long ago. Earth-based telescopes can tell us little about these miniature worlds, but it is possible that some meteorites originated within the asteroid belt and if this is the case they could be important sources of information in our efforts to unlock the early secrets of our Solar System.

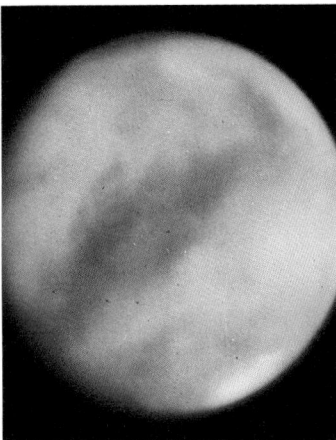

Above: Telescopic view of Mars.

Left: The surface of Mars as seen from the American Viking 1 space craft which landed on the planet in 1976.

The Outer Planets

The Gas Giants

Jupiter is the largest planet in the Solar System with a diameter of 89,250 miles (142,800 km) and is composed mainly of hydrogen with smaller amounts of methane and ammonia. Even a small telescope will show cloud belts on the surface of Jupiter representing the upper layers of the Jovian atmosphere. Jupiter also has a large number of satellites, the four largest of which – Io, Europa, Ganymede and Callisto – can be seen through binoculars. The Voyager spacecraft sent back a wealth of information about these tiny bodies including photographs of the restless, volcanic surface of Io and a gigantic crater on Callisto, echoing a massive meteoritic impact long ago.

Like Jupiter, Saturn is composed mainly of hydrogen, but with traces of helium and methane. Its diameter of 75,000 miles (120,000 km) makes it the second largest planet in the Solar System. Saturn also has a large satellite family, the brightest of which – Titan – can easily be seen through only moderate optical aid. Saturn is perhaps the most beautiful of all the planets, with a ring system that is a glorious sight. As seen from Earth the rings are split into three main parts – the outer A-ring, the central B-ring and the faint inner C-ring, or crêpe ring. The Voyager missions revealed that each of the main rings is actually split up into many smaller ringlets, rather like a gigantic gramophone record.

Uranus is the seventh planet out from the Sun, which it orbits over a period of 84 years at a mean distance of around 1783 million miles (2870 million km). In 1977 Uranus was found to have a system of five rings. Subsequent observation, coupled with the results of the Voyager fly-by in early 1986, increased the number to eleven. Closer examination has revealed that there is in fact a single ring system comprised mainly of tenuous material in which there are brighter portions corresponding to the observed ringlets. The Voyager mission has also increased the number of known Uranian satellites from five to at least fifteen, although none of the latest discoveries is bright enough to be seen by Earth-based astronomers.

The outermost of the gaseous planets, Neptune, lies over a billion miles beyond Uranus. It was discovered in 1846 by Johann Galle and

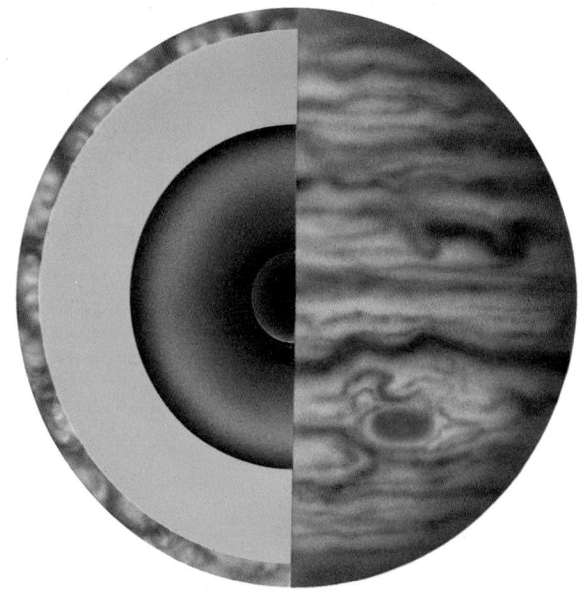

Above: Jupiter with red spot, satellite Io and its shadow.

Left: Cross section of Jupiter. Although thought to be mainly comprised of gases and liquids, it is generally believed that Jupiter has a rocky core surrounded by regions of liquid hydrogen in highly compressed states (the level of compression decreasing with increasing distance from the core). The outer, visible layer of atmosphere consists of hydrogen and helium.

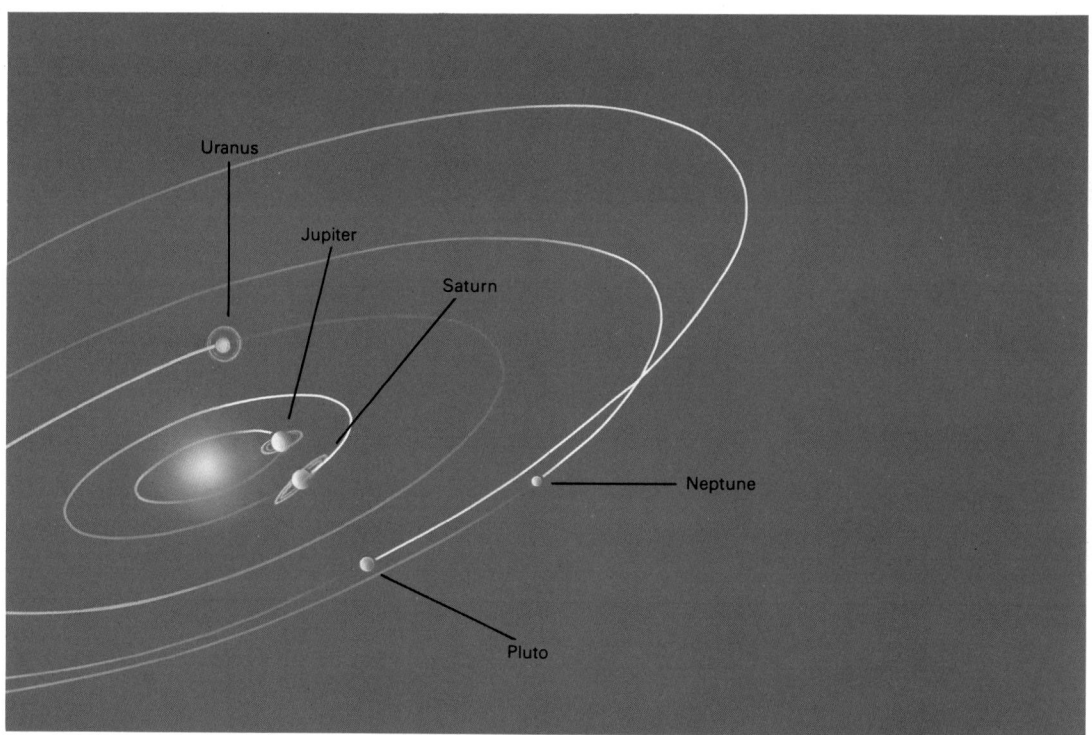

Orbits of the outer planets. Note that Pluto sometimes comes within the orbital path of Neptune.

Heinrich d'Arrest from the Berlin Observatory. Neptune was found to orbit the Sun at a mean distance of 2811 million miles (4497 million km), taking almost 165 years to complete one orbit. There are two satellites in orbit around the planet – Triton and Nereid – although the Voyager spacecraft, due to pass Neptune in August 1989, may reveal more.

TABLE OF PLANETARY DATA

	MEAN DISTANCE FROM THE SUN (miles)	ORBITAL PERIOD	AXIAL ROTATION (Equatorial)	EQUATORIAL DIAMETER (miles)	NUMBER OF SATELLITES
MERCURY	36,193,750	88 days	58.65 days	3049	0
VENUS	67,625,000	224.7 days	243 days	7565	0
EARTH	93,498,687	365.256 days	23.935 hours	7972	1
MARS	142,437,500	687 days	24.62 hours	4246	2
JUPITER	486,475,000	11.86 years	9 hrs 50 mins	89,250	16
SATURN	891,875,000	29.46 years	10 hrs 15 mins	75,000	21
URANUS	1,783,000,000	84.01 years	17 hrs 14 mins	32,375	15
NEPTUNE	2,811,000,000	164.8 years	15.8 hours	30,937	2
PLUTO	3,666,000,000	248 years	6.3 days	1500	1

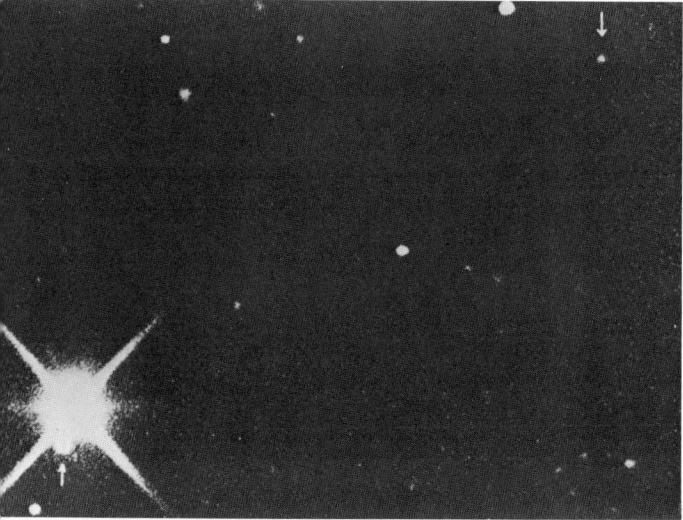

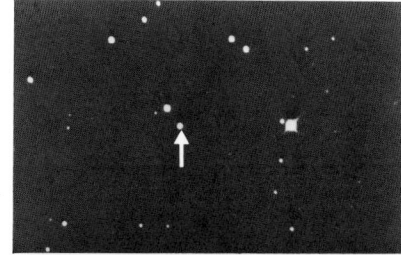

In 1978 Pluto was found to have a satellite. A photograph of the planet taken by James W. Christy showed an elongated image, suggesting the presence of a moon. Similar effects were noticed on earlier exposures and the discovery was confirmed later on in the year. This satellite, Charon, moves round Pluto in an elongated orbit over a period of 6.39 days. Its diameter is estimated at around 750 miles (1200 km), about half that of Pluto itself. This means that the Pluto-Charon system resembles a double planet rather than a planet and satellite.

It may be that Pluto was formed in a different part of the Solar System and was put into its present orbit by the gravitational effect created as a body passed through our region of space long ago. This would explain why Pluto's composition is rocky, not gaseous.

Because Pluto is so far away we will probably have to wait until spacecraft make the long journey out to the furthest reaches of the Solar System before we learn much more about Clyde Tombaugh's dim little world.

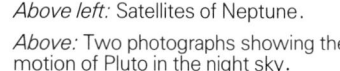

Above left: Satellites of Neptune.

Above: Two photographs showing the motion of Pluto in the night sky.

Left: Saturn and its rings.

Pluto

The outermost planet in the Solar System was discovered by Clyde Tombaugh in 1930. It was found to orbit the Sun once every 248 years at a mean distance of 3666 million miles (5865 million km). Named rather appropriately after the Guardian of the Underworld, Pluto is so far away that even the world's largest telescopes barely show a disc, and it is difficult to glean any information from Earth-based observations.

As a result of the Voyager 2 fly-by in early 1986, Uranus is now known to have fifteen satellites and a system of eleven rings.

The Sun

The Sun is just one of well over 100 billion other stars in our Galaxy. Yet to us it is the most important star in the sky, giving out the light and heat so essential to life on our planet. The Sun also constantly releases a stream of invisible energized particles, known as the solar wind, from which we are protected by the Earth's atmosphere. The Sun is the only star close enough to study in detail and astronomers are constantly monitoring the activity of the Sun and the effects that it has on our region of space.

The Structure of the Sun

There are three regions of the Sun visible to us; the photosphere, the chromosphere and the corona. The photosphere is the thin, visible inner layer of the Sun's atmosphere and it is from here that practically all the Sun's light is emitted. Turbulent energy currents inside the Sun give the photosphere a granular formation which is apparent if the Sun is examined closely. This is also the region where sunspots appear, marking relatively cool areas of the solar surface. The dark central umbra of a typical sunspot has a temperature in the region of 4000 deg K*, a sharp contrast with the rest of the photosphere where

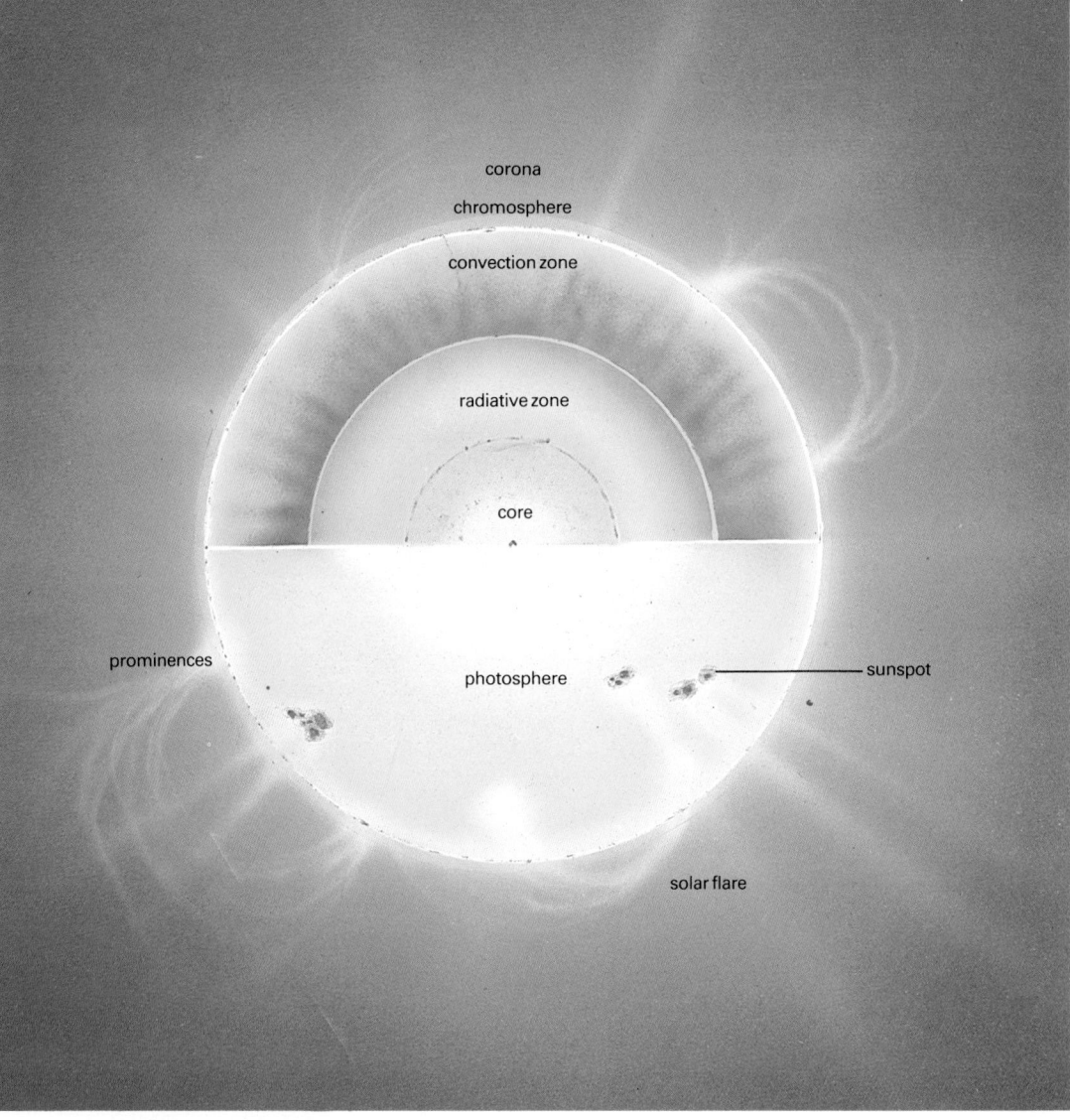

Right: Cross section of the Sun. Faculae (not shown on this diagram) can also be observed on the Sun. They are luminous clouds comprised mainly of hydrogen which are found above the solar surface, usually appearing in the regions where sunspots are about to form.

temperatures of 6000 deg K are normal. Luminous clouds of hydrogen, known as faculae, are sometimes associated with sunspots and can be seen at the edge of the Sun's disc in regions where sunspots are to appear. Sunspots also give rise to flares. Seen as bright filaments of light escaping from sunspot regions, they were discovered in 1859 by Richard Carrington.

Energy released by the Sun passes from the photosphere through the almost transparent chromosphere, a region of tenuous gas some 1200 miles (2000 km) thick.

The temperature of the material in the chromosphere increases from 4500 deg K near the photosphere to more than 10,000 deg K in its outer reaches. Features known as spicules can sometimes be seen escaping from the base of the

* The lowest theoretically possible temperature is absolute zero, where it is believed that all atomic and molecular motion ceases. It is equal to −273.15 deg C, but usually expressed as zero degrees Kelvin (0 deg K). The Kelvin scale is commonly used to express stellar temperatures, although when such high temperatures are being described, the difference between similar values on the Kelvin and Centigrade scales is negligible.

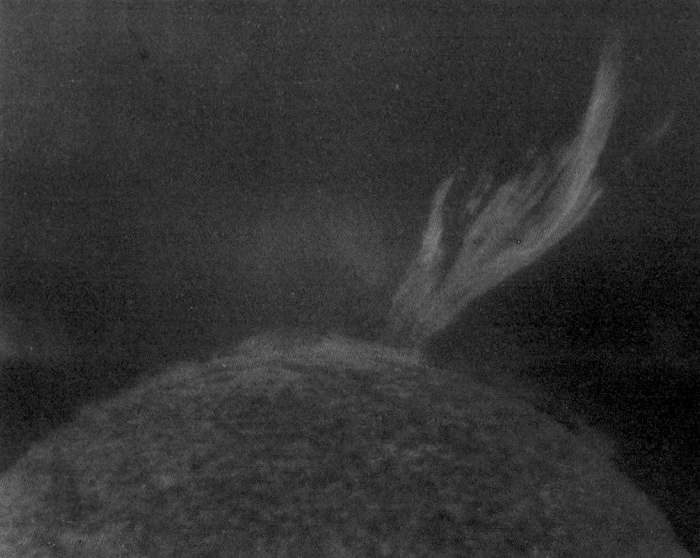

Left: A solar flare.

chromosphere at speeds approaching 15 miles (25 km) per second. They can reach heights of 7000 miles (10,000 km) or more, eventually melting into the corona.

Above the chromosphere is a thin transition zone through which energy passes to the corona. Like the chromosphere, the corona is made up of very tenuous material. Unless special equipment is used both the chromosphere and the corona only become visible during a total solar eclipse when the bright solar disc is hidden by the Moon. Inside the transition zone the temperature of the material changes abruptly from around 20,000 to 500,000 deg K, eventually reaching a maximum of between 1 and 2 million degrees in the inner corona. This levels out to 1 million degrees in the outer corona.* The corona itself has no well defined limits and simply thins out with increasing distance from the Sun, eventually dissipating into interplanetary space. Although the temperature of the corona material is very high, this zone cannot be described as 'hot' in the generally accepted sense of the word. The particles making up the corona have high temperatures, but are so thinly spread that their overall mass is extremely low and any sensation of heat is lost.

Like other regions of the solar atmosphere, the corona is marked by a number of individual features. Eruptive prominences can rise from the base of the corona at tremendous speeds, sometimes reaching heights of 1.25 million miles or more. In contrast are quiescent prominences, which are much more stable and generally last much longer.

The corona is also marked by what are known as coronal holes. These are best described as 'quiet'

It is not known with certainty why the temperature increases through the chromosphere and corona. A theory exists, however, which attempts to explain the chromospheric increase. Mechanical energy is transported through the photosphere in the form of pressure waves, at speeds of roughly 560 miles (1100 km) per hour. As these waves pass through the less dense regions of the chromosphere their amplitude increases. Shock waves are set up; the energy from which is released as heat, thereby raising the temperature of the chromosphere with increasing altitude. This does not explain the tremendous increases in the corona, although prolonged study may yet provide an answer.

Above: The full disc of the Sun.

Below: A view of the Aurora Borealis.

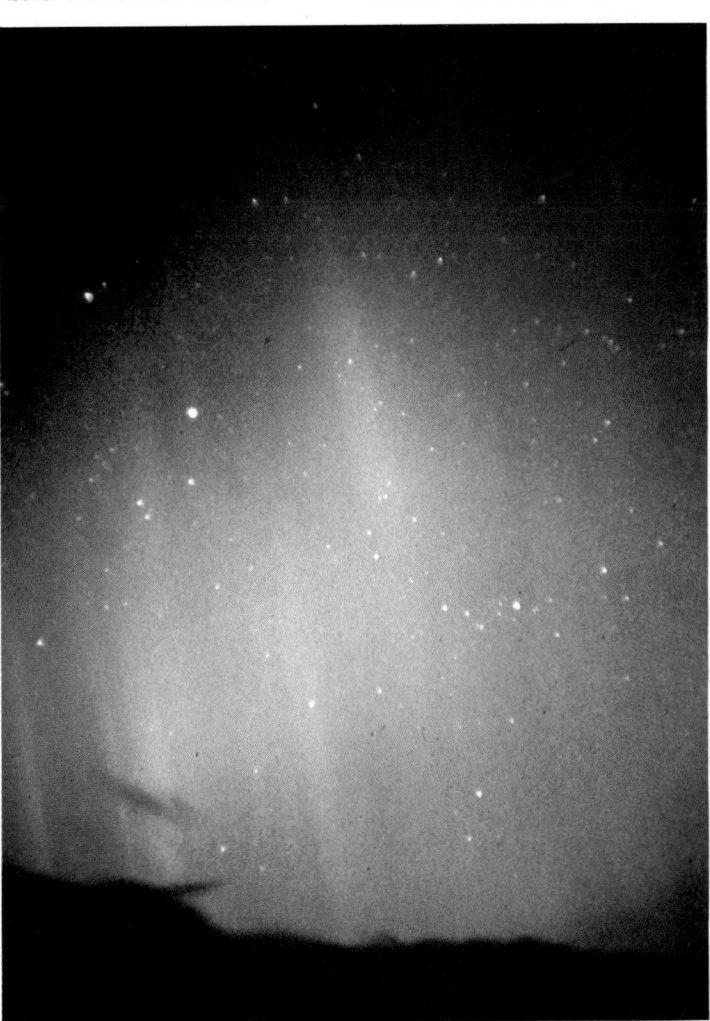

areas of the corona and where they appear there is a sharp increase in the number of energized particles escaping from the Sun. When one of these denser particle streams reaches the Earth, charged particles enter the Earth's upper

atmosphere in greater numbers and are responsible for an increase in the spectacular visual displays known as aurorae, caused by interaction between the particles and gas molecules in the atmosphere.

Production of the Sun's Light and Energy

The Sun's energy is produced as a result of nuclear reactions at its core. The temperature in this region is around 15 million deg K which, together with the tremendous pressure equal to 100 million times the atmospheric pressure at the Earth's surface, brings about a nuclear fusion reaction in which hydrogen is converted into helium. As this process takes place four hydrogen nuclei are fused together to form one nucleus of helium. During the reaction some mass is lost and is released in the form of energy. This released energy is carried away from the core by convection, eventually reaching the surface where it escapes as light and heat. Well over half a billion tons of hydrogen are converted into helium every second, resulting in a mass loss of some 4 million tons. Although this may seem high, it makes very little difference to the overall mass of the Sun. Our star has been producing energy this way for the best part of 4.5 billion years and we fully expect a similar time to pass before the solar hydrogen supply runs out.

Neutrinos

The reactions that produce the Sun's energy also give rise to neutrinos. These tiny particles have neither mass nor electrical charge and are projected from the Sun at the speed of light. Neutrinos are extremely difficult to detect. They are entirely unaffected by solid bodies such as the Earth or other planets and simply pass straight through any such object they meet. Until recently astronomers were unable to measure the rate of neutrino flow, but a way of detecting them has now been devised. Neutrinos have occasionally been found to react with chlorine atoms, converting them into atoms of argon-37 and detection of argon-37 atoms is made relatively easy by the fact that they are radioactive. The Homestake Mine, a gold mine at Lead in South Dakota, is now the site of an experiment designed to capture neutrinos. A giant tank containing over 100,000 gallons of chlorine solution has been placed nearly a mile underground and is intended to trap any neutrinos that pass through the overlying rock. The rate of capture is measured by the number of argon-37 atoms produced. This rate, although lower than expected, has at least been constant, and through this experiment we may find out more about the inner regions of the star we call the Sun.

The Moon

The Moon is our closest celestial neighbour and centuries of observation coupled with over two decades of study by both manned and unmanned spacecraft have taught us a great deal about our companion. It is one of the largest satellites in proportion to its primary planet in the Solar System, its diameter being over a quarter of the Earth's and its mass being equal to 1/81 of that of our planet. The most noticeable feature of the Moon from the Earth is that it always keeps the same face towards us, a consequence of the fact that it revolves on its axis once in the time it takes to orbit the Earth. However, because the Moon's orbit is elliptical the orbital speed varies as the Moon is alternately nearer and further from us. Consequently, the axial rotation and orbital periods become slightly out-of-sequence and the Moon appears to 'wobble' slightly from side to side. These lunar 'librations', discovered by Galileo in the early part of the 17th century, enable us to see up to 59% of the total lunar surface. The rest is hidden from Earth-based observers and can only be seen with the help of space probes. The first of these was the Russian Luna 3, which flew behind the Moon in 1959 and sent back the first photographs of this region.

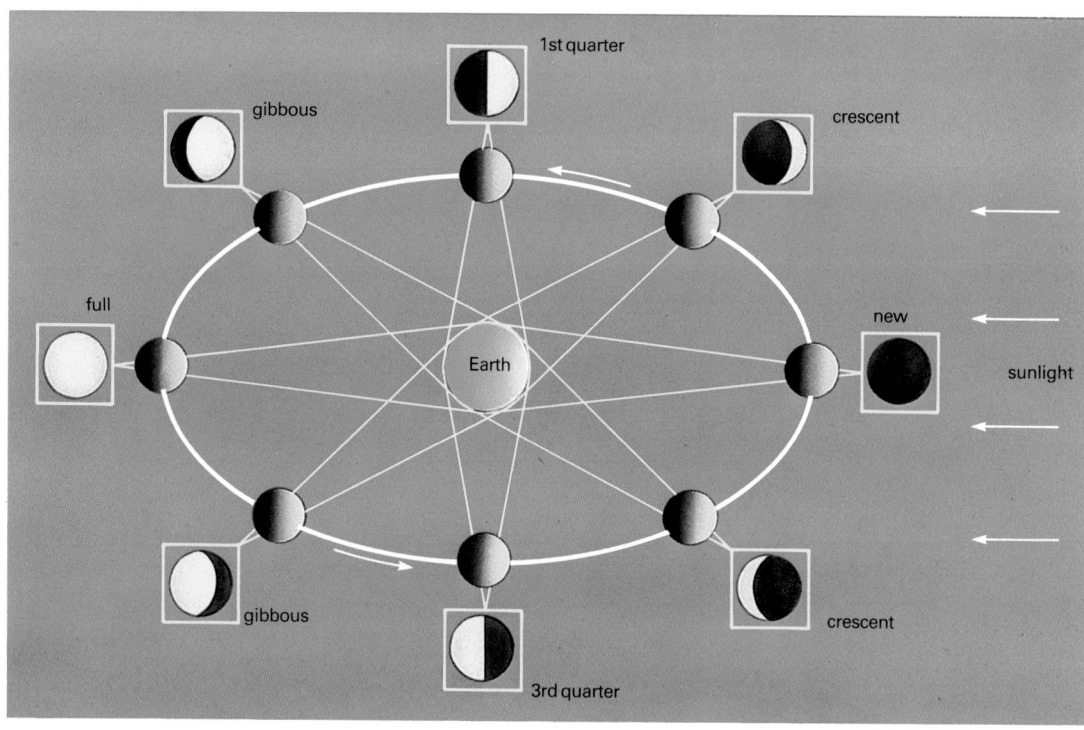

Above: The phases of the Moon showing (inside the boxes) how each phase looks from the Earth.

Below: The full lunar disc viewed from lunar orbit.

The Origin of the Moon

In spite of many years of observation, the origin of the Moon remains a mystery. The principal theories fall into three main categories; that the Moon was once part of the Earth, that it condensed from material surrounding our planet or that it was captured by the Earth's gravity.

The fission hypothesis states that a lump of matter was ejected from the young, rapidly-spinning Earth. A variation on this idea proposes that a number of particles were released which eventually collected together to form the Moon. However, both of these ideas have been discounted. Although we know that the original axial rotation period of the Earth was much shorter that it is today, it would have had to be as little as three hours in order that material would be thrown off. Also, if either of these hypotheses were correct then both the Earth and the Moon would have similar compositions, which is not the case. Other theories are that either the Moon condensed from a cloud of particles which once surrounded the Earth, or that the Moon formed separately and that its orbit carried it close enough to the Earth to allow it to be captured by the gravity of our planet. Both theories account for the different make-up of the Earth and the Moon, and although neither has been totally accepted, they may at least hint at the truth behind the origin of our satellite.

Lunar Highlands and Lowlands

The lunar surface is divided into two distinct types of terrain – the cratered highland regions and the darker, smoother maria. Most of the lunar surface – around 75% – is of the highland type. Astronomers believe that, as the Moon cooled down early on in its history, solidifying matter formed a crust on its surface. This crust was then bombarded by meteorites leaving a cratered terrain much like that we see today. Volcanic activity followed, creating large, smooth areas of lava in basins left by the cosmic bombardment. These smooth areas, or maria, were then subjected to further, less severe meteoritic bombardment which created the lunar surface that exists now. As time went on, much of the original meteoritic debris found throughout the Solar System was 'swept up' by the planets as they travelled through space.

Right: Mare Tranquillitatis (the Sea of Tranquillity), the site of the first manned lunar landing, that of Apollo 11 in July 1969.

Structure of the Moon

Seismometers left on the Moon by the Apollo astronauts have helped scientists to put together a picture of the lunar interior. The seismic waves from both natural and artificial tremors (moonquakes and, for example, tremors caused by a lunar landing vehicle) were examined, their rates of travel through the lunar interior being found to vary according to the density of material through which they passed. The crust has been found to have a depth of around 40 miles (60 km) with a top layer of bedrock created by the bombardment of meteorites. Beneath the crust is the upper mantle, or lithosphere, made up of denser material and stretching down to a depth of 650 miles (1000 km). It is at the base of the lithosphere that moonquakes originate. Just below the lithosphere is the partly molten asthenosphere, or outer core, which is believed to surround a small, possibly metallic core with a diameter which is considered to be no more than 370 miles (600 km).

Variations in the orbital speed of the American Orbiter 5 spacecraft in 1968 led to the discovery of localized areas of the lunar surface where the gravitational pull of the Moon is stronger. Cracks in the lithosphere seem to have allowed lava from the outer core to seep up towards the surface. This matter appears to have cooled down and solidified just beneath the lunar surface, creating areas of relatively high density. The presence of these areas of mass-concentration, or 'mascons', has been verified by the careful study of the orbital paths of other lunar satellites.

Lunar Features

Of the many different features visible on the lunar surface by far the most prominent are the craters. The small, simple craters, with diameters of up to around 6 miles (10 km), are bowl-shaped formations with outer walls in the form of a ring of debris thrown up from the original meteoritic impact. The larger, complex craters, such as Gassendi, have diameters ranging in size up to 125 miles (200 km). They have flat floors with a central peak and the slippage of material inside the crater rim has led to stepped or terraced formations inside the walls. Largest of all are the basins with diameters of over 125 miles. They are similar to the complex craters except that they possess a central ring rather than a peak. A notable example is the 550-mile (900-km) diameter Mare Orientale (Eastern Sea), which has multiple ring systems created by the material (ejecta) thrown out by a large meteoritic impact.

A number of craters have prominent ray systems extending from them and it has recently been discovered that these rays are caused by the scattering of fine ejecta after the original meteoritic impact.

Older craters can be seen to have suffered erosion from subsequent impacts and the floors and walls of many craters are peppered with smaller craterlets. Maria have had a similar history. After volcanic activity filled the low lying areas of the Moon's surface with lava, meteorites bombarded the newly formed landscape forming many craters of different sizes. Rilles are other lava-related features. As the lava solidified, flows still occurred in channels under the surface, but once the source of lava dried up, the channels emptied and collapsed in on themselves. As a result, long, snake-like depressions on the floor of the maria were created, such as those found traversing Oceanus Procellarum (Ocean of Storms).

The Tides

The tides are produced as a direct result of the Moon's gravitational influence on the Earth. Every particle on the Earth is affected by this force, although its strength varies according to distance from the Moon. This variation is known as differential acceleration, the movements produced being centred on the Earth's core. The Moon's gravitational influence is greatest on the hemisphere that faces it, and the effect is to produce tidal bulge. The hemisphere facing away from the Moon is subject to a weaker pull and is accelerated in the opposite direction, thereby producing another tidal bulge. As the Earth rotates these tidal bulges sweep in a westward direction producing a twice daily rise and fall in the level of the oceans at any particular point on the Earth's surface.

The Sun also exerts a gravitational effect on the Earth, although this is much less than that produced by the Moon. However, when the Sun, Moon and Earth are in line with each other, as at New Moon and Full Moon, there is an increased tidal effect caused by the joint action of solar and lunar gravity. The comparatively high tides thus produced are known as spring tides. When the Sun and Moon are at right angles to each other, as at first and last quarter, the two effects tend to cancel each other out, producing the smaller neap tides.

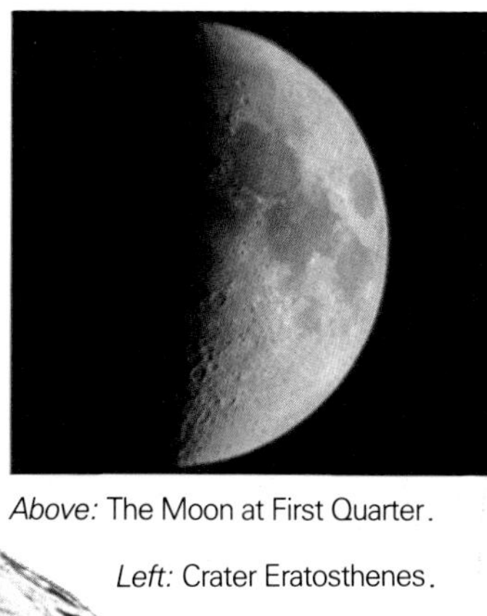

Above: The Moon at First Quarter.

Left: Crater Eratosthenes.

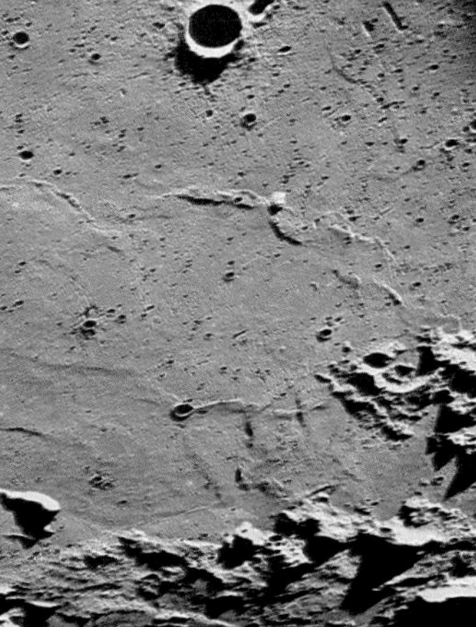

Celestial Hide and Seek

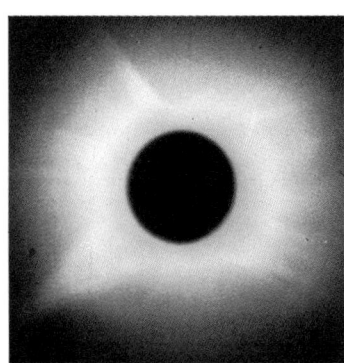

Above: Total eclipse of the Sun.

Right: A lunar eclipse.

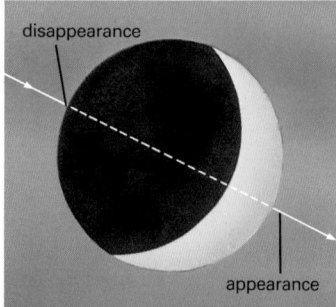

Above: Path of an occulted star or planet as it disappears behind the Moon as seen from Earth.

Solar Eclipses

Although the Sun is a great deal bigger than the Moon, it is much further away. Because of their relative positions, both bodies appear to have roughly the same apparent diameter and when the Moon passes between the Sun and Earth it can completely cover the solar disc. This event is known as a solar eclipse, which may be *total, annular* or *partial*. An eclipse is *total* when the apparent diameter of the Moon is equal to or greater than that of the Sun. However, because the Moon's orbit is elliptical its apparent diameter varies, appearing larger when the Moon is at its closest point. The Earth's orbit around the Sun is also elliptical resulting in a variation of the Sun's apparent diameter. Should an eclipse occur when the lunar disc is not large enough to cover the Sun, we see what is called an *annular* eclipse, with the Sun visible as a ring around the edge of the Moon.

The dark, central region of the shadow cast by the Moon is called the umbra. As the Earth turns on its axis and the Moon travels along its orbit, this umbral shadow passes across the surface of our planet, its path tracing those parts of the world from which a total eclipse will be seen. On either side is the region of the penumbra, from which a *partial* eclipse will be seen with only part of the solar disc obscured. Partial eclipses can also occur with no related total eclipse when the line up of Sun, Moon and Earth is not exact.

Lunar Eclipses

Less spectacular, though still quite interesting, are lunar eclipses, which occur when the Earth passes between the Sun and Moon. When the Moon is in the Earth's

shadow on these occasions there is a considerable darkening of the lunar disc. The Moon does not disappear completely, however, because sunlight is refracted through the Earth's atmosphere onto the lunar surface and during eclipse the Moon takes on a deep coppery-red hue.

There are three types of lunar eclipse – *total, partial* and *penumbral.* A *total* eclipse occurs when the entire Moon passes through the umbra of the Earth's shadow, although there is a partial phase both before and after totality as the Moon passes through the penumbra. During a *partial* eclipse the Moon does not completely enter the umbra, whilst during a *penumbral* eclipse it passes through the penumbra only.

There can only be a maximum of five solar eclipses in any one year and for lunar eclipses the

Left: Theory of a solar eclipse.

Below: Theory of a lunar eclipse.

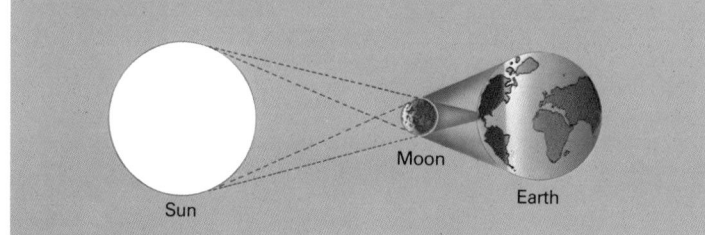

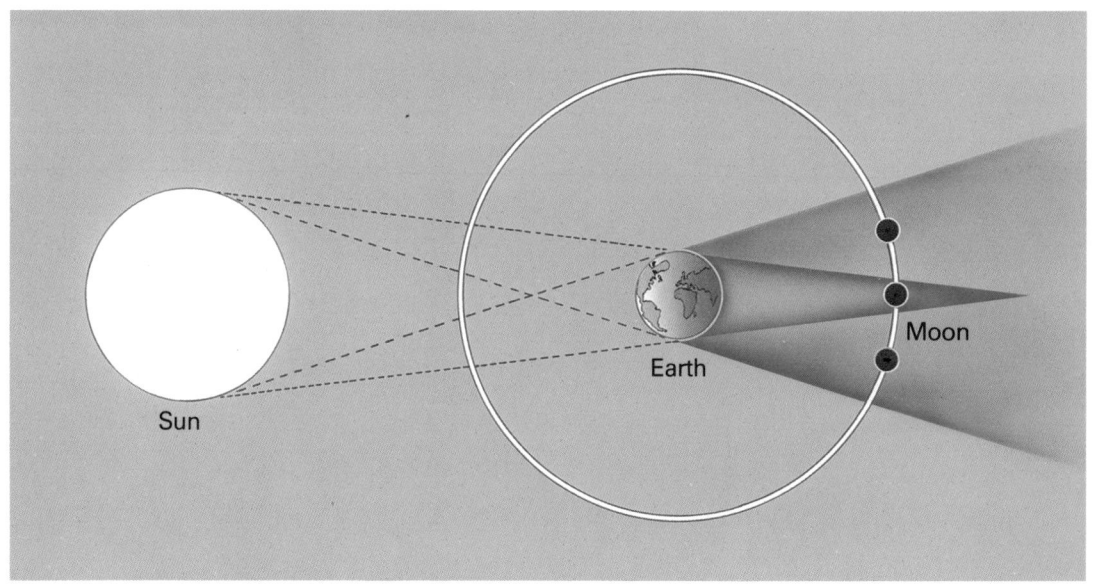

maximum is three. However, over a period of time more lunar eclipses will be seen from any one place as they are visible over the entire hemisphere facing the Moon. Solar eclipses can be seen only from areas on and around the path of totality.

Solar eclipses can only occur at New Moon, when the Sun and Moon are at the same point in the sky. Similarly, lunar eclipses take place when the Moon is full and at a point in the sky directly opposite to that of the Sun. However, eclipses do not happen every month. Although the Moon's orbit is centred on the Earth, its plane is tilted with respect to the ecliptic, or plane of the Earth's orbit around the

Sun. Therefore the Moon normally appears to pass either above or below the Sun. An eclipse of either type is only possible when the Moon is crossing the ecliptic, resulting in a lining up of the three bodies. Eclipses of the same type repeat after an interval of just over 18 years, known as the Saros period. After this time the Sun, Moon and Earth return to almost the same relative positions.

Occultations

Occultations occur when one celestial body passes in front of another and hides it from view. As the Moon moves along its orbit it occults a great number of stars together with an occasional planet,

whilst the planets themselves can occult either stars or their own satellites. The observation of occultations is important, particularly in the case of the Moon. Stellar positions are known with great accuracy, but, paradoxically, the precise path of the Moon around the Earth is not. Because the Moon has no atmosphere the light from an occulted star appears to 'snap out' suddenly as it disappears behind the lunar disc. This makes it easy to determine the exact position of the Moon against the background of stars at that time.

Although lunar occultations of stars are fairly common, the brighter planets rarely cross the Moon's path. Venus, Mars, Jupiter and Saturn can all be occulted but the opportunities to see these events are few and far between. Even rarer are occultations of stars by planets. Because of their comparatively small apparent diameters, planets occult very few stars. However, an important discovery was made during such an occultation when Uranus passed in front of a faint star on 10 March 1977. As the star approached the planet its light was seen to 'wink' five times. This was repeated after occultation, each wink being symmetrical with the first series. Astronomers deduced that there must be a ring system around Uranus, a fact which has since been verified.

Oppositions and Conjunctions

The opposition of a planet occurs when it is opposite to the Sun in the sky. When opposition takes place the Sun, Earth and planet are all exactly in line with the Earth in the middle. The planet can be seen

for most of the night and is actually due south at midnight. The inner planets, Mercury and Venus, cannot come to opposition; only the outer planets can, and when they do they are at their closest to the Earth and most favourably placed for observation.

Conjunctions occur when two objects, for example a planet and a star, appear to be very close to each other as seen from Earth. The term is, however, most commonly used in relation to the Sun. The two inner planets are at inferior conjunction when positioned between the Sun and the Earth, whilst any planet is said to be at superior conjunction when situated at the other side of the Sun as seen from Earth. When a planet is at conjunction it is above the horizon at the same time as the Sun and is practically unobservable at that time.

During inferior conjunction, if the lining up is exact, a transit occurs and the planet can be seen as a tiny black speck crossing the solar disc. Although transits are fairly uncommon, those of Venus are particularly so, and the next Venusian transit will not take place until 2004.

Retrograde Motion

Any object that orbits the Sun in a direction opposite to that of the earth is said to have retrograde motion. None of the planets or asteroids has been found to have retrograde motion, yet there are many comets which have, the most notable example being Halley's Comet. Planetary satellites can also have retrograde motion. For instance, Phoebe, one of the moons of Saturn, orbits the planet in the opposite direction from the rest.

Although none of the planets orbit the Sun in retrograde orbits, they can occasionally appear to move backwards against the backdrop of stars. This apparent motion takes place when the Earth, because of its faster orbital speed, 'overtakes' the planet. The observed retrograde motion is therefore due to nothing more than a line of sight effect.

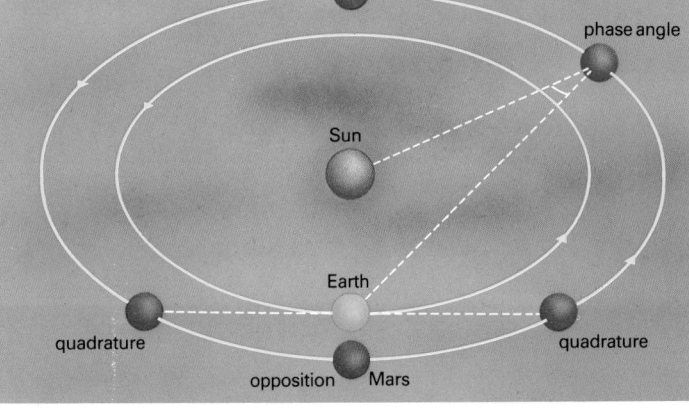

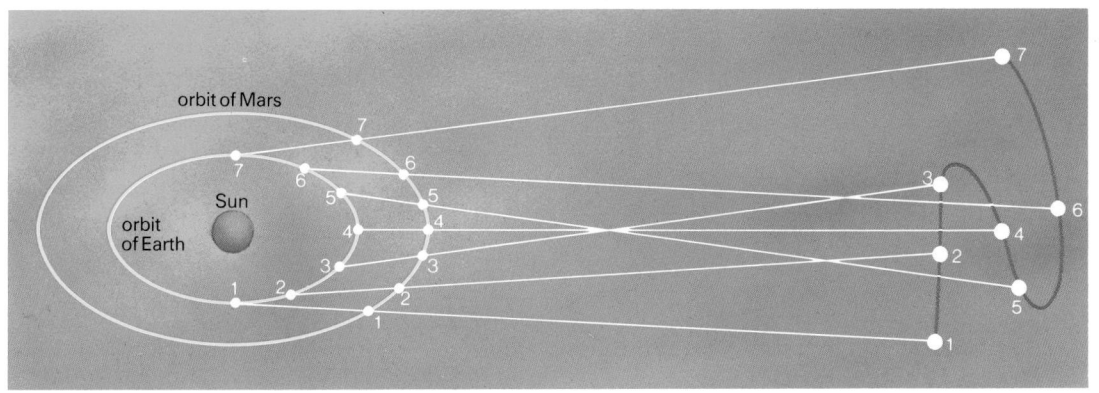

Above: Opposition and conjunction of a typical outer planet. It can be seen that Mars is in line with the Sun in each case. The planet is due south at midnight when at opposition and unobservable when at conjunction.

Left: The conjunction of Venus. Conjunction occurs when the inner planet — in this case Venus — is in line with the Earth and Sun.

Left: Because the Earth has a greater orbital velocity than any of the outer planets, it can overtake them, resulting in apparent retrograde motion between positions 3 and 5. This means that the planet will 'move' from east to west rather than the usual west to east against the stellar background.

The Stars

Looking up at a clear, dark sky, you will see many tiny points of light. The vast majority will be stars, but a few will be planets (or even passing aeroplanes), and if you look at the sky over a period of time differences between bodies will become apparent. Stars will appear to be stationary in the night sky whereas planets can be seen moving slowly across the stellar background from night to night as they orbit the Sun. Stars are also distinguished by the fact that they shine by creating their own light, like our Sun, rather than by reflecting light from another body, as planets do.

Stellar Distances

The stars are all very remote, and it would be impractical to try and express their distances in miles. Instead, astronomers use another unit – the light year. Light travels at just over 186,000 miles (300,000 km) per second; the distance it travels in a year (around 6 million, million miles) is the standard unit of cosmic distance. On this scale the Moon is 1.5 light seconds away, the Sun just over 8 light minutes and the nearest star, Proxima Centauri, 4.3 light years.

Various methods are used to measure the actual distances to the stars. The nearest ones have their distances determined by

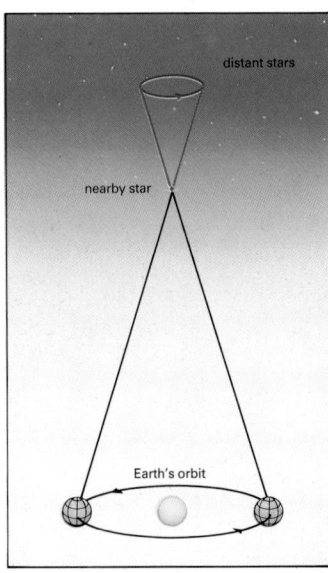

Below: Stellar parallax is used to measure the distance to the stars which are relatively close to Earth. Once the angle of shift of the star is determined this can be used with the known shift in position of the Earth to work out the distance to the star.

trigonometrical parallax; the apparent angular shift of the star against the background of more distant stars when viewed from two different positions. Two observations are made of the star, when the Earth is at opposite points in its orbit around the Sun. Using the diameter of the Earth's orbit as a base line, and knowing the angular shift, it is a straightforward task to work out the distance to the star. The first star to have its distance measured by parallax was 61 Cygni, by Friedrich Bessel in 1838, and it was found to lie at a distance of around 11 light years. The further away a star is, however, the smaller will be the angle of parallax, and the distance of a star more than 70 light years or so away can be more satisfactorily estimated by the method of comparison. A remote star is compared with one of a similar type which lies at a known distance. Assuming that similar types of star have identical brightnesses, an estimate is made of the star's distance by comparing its apparent and actual luminosities. In other words, astronomers can tell how far away a star is by measuring its brightness, providing they can classify its type.

Magnitudes

The stars all appear to have different brightnesses, with prominent objects such as Vega and Betelgeuse contrasting with faint stars on the edge of naked eye visibility. To express the brightness of stars, or other celestial bodies, astronomers class them according to

their magnitude, fainter stars having higher magnitude numbers than their brighter counterparts. This system was first introduced by Hipparchus in 150 BC. He gave the faintest stars a magnitude of 6 and the brightest a value of 1. The system used today is essentially the same, although accurate methods of measurement enable magnitudes to be assessed to within 0.01 and the scale has had to be extended to include minus values in order to incorporate very bright stars. The magnitude of Sirius, the brightest star in the sky, is −1.4.

The above system only classes the stars according to their apparent brightnesses and some stars, although appearing fainter, may have actual, or intrinsic, luminosities far exceeding those of apparently brighter objects. To grade a star according to its actual luminosity, astronomers use the apparent magnitude that the star would have if it were at a distance of 32.6 light years. At this distance, Sirius would shine with a magnitude of 1.3 whilst Rigel, normally appearing fainter than Sirius, would appear as an intensely bright star of magnitude −7. In reality, Rigel is over 100 times as far away as Sirius. This standard value of brightness is known as the absolute magnitude and is a far better indication of a star's actual luminosity.

Colours

Stars vary not only in brightness but also in colour. Our own Sun is yellow as is the bright star Capella

Above: The surface of a hypothetical planet orbiting a binary star system.

in Auriga. Sirius in Canis Major is white whilst Rigel is a brilliant blue-white star in Orion. Also in Orion is the conspicuous red star Betelgeuse. The brightest star in Taurus is the orange-red Aldebaran which is similar in colour to Antares, the principal star in the constellation Scorpius. The colour of a star is a good indication of its temperature. Hottest of all are the blue stars, contrasting sharply with the much cooler red stars which have surface temperatures in the order of only a few thousand deg K.

Spectral Classes

Although the stars are remote we are able to tell a great deal about their temperature and make-up by studying their spectra. When the light from a star is passed through a prism it is split up into its constituent colours, ranging from long wavelength red through to shorter wavelength violet. A high density gas, such as that found inside a star, produces a continuous spectrum with an unbroken sequence of colours. However, the light being examined must pass through the low-density gas which surrounds the star. Low-density gas produces an emission spectrum with isolated bright lines, each one a result of a particular element within the gas. A star's spectrum, therefore, takes the form of a continuous band of colours with an emission

spectrum superimposed upon it. The lines of this emission spectrum show up as dark bands in contrast to the brighter spectrum underneath, and are indicative of elements present within the atmosphere of the star.

Stars can be classified according to their spectra. This classification is denoted by a letter from the sequence – O, B, A, F, G, K, M, R, N and S. The hot blue stars are of type O and have surface temperatures in the order of 30,000 degrees or more, whilst the coolest stars are classed as M, R, N or S and have temperatures of only 3000 deg K or less. Each of the above classes can be further divided according to temperature by the addition of a number after the letter. The hottest stars in a particular class are designated 0 whilst 9 denotes the coolest. For example, the hottest B-type stars are B0, the next B1 and so on through to B9. The Sun, with a surface temperature in the region of 6000 deg K, is classed as a G2 type star.

Sizes of Stars

As well as varying considerably in temperature, stars can differ greatly in diameter. Supergiant stars can be many hundreds of times larger than the Sun. For example, Arcturus in Bootes has a diameter of around 11 million miles (18 million km), whilst even this is dwarfed by Antares which is around 280 million miles (450 million km) across. The Sun is a fairly average star with a diameter of 865,000 miles (1.4 million km). The smallest classes of star include white dwarfs which are typically only a few thousand miles across, and the tiny neutron stars with average diameters of only a few miles.

Double and Multiple Star Systems

There are two basic forms of double star – optical doubles and binary systems. Optical doubles are made up of two stars which are not actually related to each other and only appear to be close to each other because they happen to lie in the same line of sight as seen from the Earth. Binary systems, on the other hand, are comprised of two stars which are gravitationally bound and orbit each other around their common centre of gravity.

The stars in many binary systems are so close together that even the world's largest telescopes are unable to resolve them. These are known as *Spectroscopic Binaries* and astronomers are only able to detect the individual stars within the system by examining

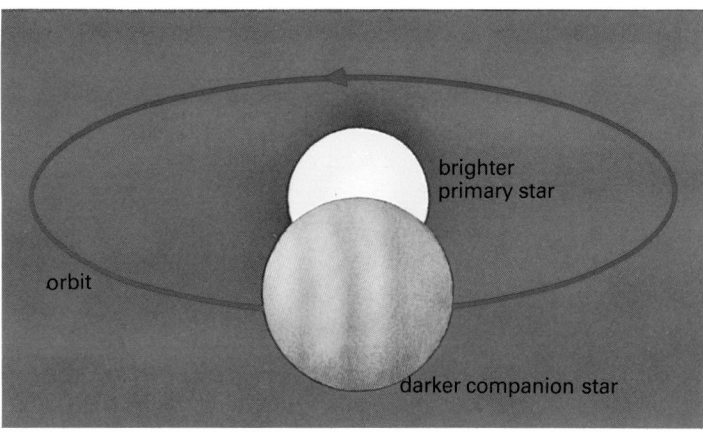
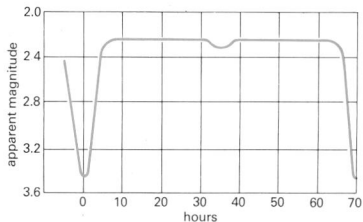

Above: The light curve of an eclipsing binary, or indeed of any variable star, shows the changing brightness of the star. The one shown here is typical of an eclipsing binary system.

Left: Diagram of an eclipsing binary system. As the darker star eclipses the brighter component, the overall brightness of the system is reduced. There is another slight reduction as the fainter star passes behind the brighter one.

their combined spectrum. In 1842 the German mathematician Christian Doppler suggested that the wavelength of light emitted by a moving light source, such as a star, would be shortened if the star was approaching us and lengthened if it was receding, in comparison to what we would see if the star were stationary. This idea was expanded on a few years later by the French physicist Hippolyte Fizeau who proposed that the emission lines in the spectrum of a star would behave in the same way. In other words, the lines would be shifted towards the red or long-wavelength end of the spectrum in the case of a receding star and towards the blue or short-wavelength end if the star were approaching.

Most of the stars within our Galaxy are members of multiple star systems. The many examples include Alcor and Mizar in the handle of the Plough and Epsilon Lyrae, found close to the prominent star Vega in the constellation of Lyra. Alcor and Mizar are two white stars which form a conspicuous naked-eye double and moderate optical aid will show that Mizar is itself a double, the fainter component having been discovered by the Italian astronomer Giovanni Riccioli in 1651. It has since been found that these two stars, Mizar A and Mizar B, are actually binary systems in their own right. Epsilon Lyrae is another conspicuous double visible to the unaided eye, and a telescope will show that each of these two stars, Epsilon 1 and Epsilon 2, is double again. The two components of Epsilon 1 orbit each other once every 1166 years whilst those of Epsilon 2 take 585 years to complete one orbit.

Variable Stars

A variable star is one whose brightness varies on either a regular or irregular basis. There are basically two types of variable star. *Intrinsic Variables* are those which vary

because of changes taking place within the star itself, whilst *Extrinsic Variables* are those whose brightness varies as a result of the action of some other object, either another star or clouds of material. There are also the spectacular *Novae*, whose brightness may change dramatically.

There are many different types of intrinsic variable, including *Periodic Variables*, where the luminosity varies in a regular way; *Irregular Variables* where the changes in light output show no sign of regularity and *Semi-regular Variables* whose variations show a certain amount of regularity, although this is by no means constant.

Perhaps the most interesting group are the *Cepheid Variables*. The first star of this group to be recognized was Delta Cephei, discovered by the English astronomer John Goodricke in 1784. Cepheid variables are quite numerous and around 700 are known within our Galaxy alone. Their changes in light output are regular and can last anything from 1 to 50 days. Delta Cephei varies between magnitudes 3.6 and 4.3 over a period of 5.4 days, these variations being due, as with all the Cepheids, to changes in the temperature and size of the star. Cepheids are especially important because there is a distinct relationship between their periods and their actual luminosities. This relationship was discovered by the American astronomer Henrietta Leavitt in 1912, and has proved to be extremely important in the estimation of distances to other galaxies. The existence of this period-luminosity relationship means that the intrinsic brightness of the star can be deduced by assessing the period of a Cepheid variable. By comparing this value to the apparent magnitude as seen from Earth, it is a straightforward task to calculate the distance of the star.

Extrinsic variables include two groups – *Eclipsing Binaries* and

T Tauri stars. Eclipsing binaries are double star systems in which the two stars orbit around each other. The orbital plane is in line with the Earth resulting in alternate eclipses of each star by the other. A typical eclipsing binary is Algol in the constellation of Perseus, the variability of which was first noticed by Montanari as long ago as 1667. In the Algol system a fainter red star orbits a hot blue star, and as the fainter star passes in front of its brighter companion the magnitude of the system drops from 2.1 to 3.3 and back again over a period of 2.87 days. There is a further but very slight drop in luminosity as the fainter star is eclipsed by the brighter one. T Tauri stars are young stars which are surrounded by dust. This dust can pass in front of the star obscuring its light, causing the irregular fluctuations in luminosity associated with this type of star.

Novae are stars which suddenly brighten to perhaps tens of thousands of times their original luminosity over a period of only a few hours, after which they decrease in magnitude to somewhere near their original brightness. One of the brightest novae of recent years was discovered in Cygnus in August, 1975. It reached a magnitude of 1.8, making it around a million times more luminous than the Sun. Novae are known for their unpredictability and many are discovered by amateur astronomers who regularly search the sky for such events. *Supernovae* are the explosions of stars following violent gravitational collapse.

Stellar Evolution

Our Galaxy contains over a hundred billion stars of which there are many different types. For example, observation shows that temperatures and diameters vary considerably. Our own Sun is an average member of the Galaxy with properties typical of many other stars, so that by studying it astronomers can piece together a great deal of information on stellar evolution and behaviour. Yet a full picture can be obtained only by observing the many different types of star, and from such work we are getting closer to a full understanding of how stars are born, how they live and how they eventually die.

Stars are born inside vast interstellar clouds which are composed mainly of hydrogen. The process starts with the contraction of the cloud, brought about when its mass becomes great enough to induce a gravitational compression which overcomes the cloud's outward thermal pressure. The cloud collapses into individual clumps, with each clump giving rise to a star. This localized break up of the cloud is known as fragmentation and as the compression continues the internal temperature of each clump rises. The heat is unable to escape because of the increased density of the outer layers and eventually reaches such a level as to create further thermal pressure. This in turn halts the gravitational collapse. The result is a relatively dense object which we call a protostar.

How the protostar develops from here depends on its mass. For those stars with a mass similar to that of the Sun the gravitational collapse results in a hot, central region, or nucleus, which grows hotter as the outer layers of the star

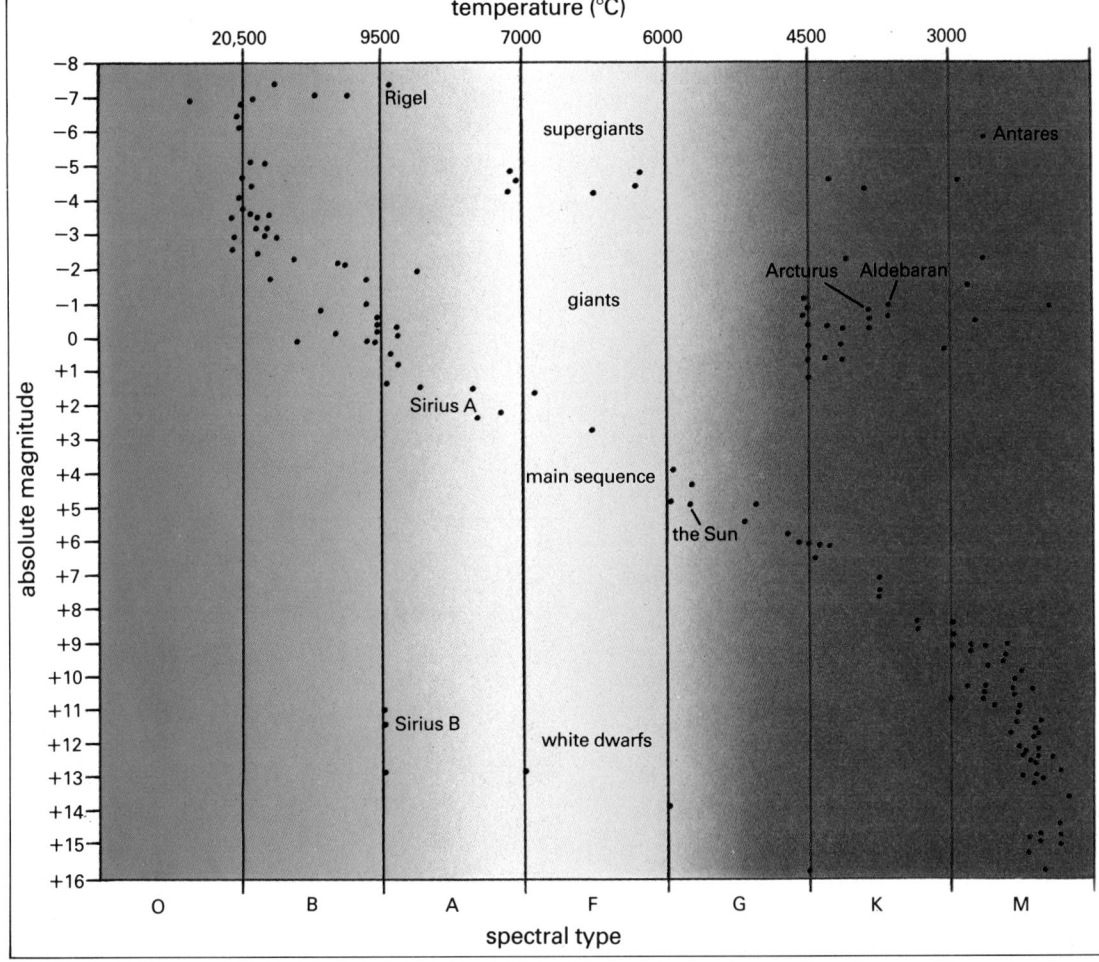

are pulled in. Eventually the temperature at the nucleus reaches 10 million deg K and thermonuclear reactions start in which the hydrogen present in the core is converted to helium. The outward pressure induced by this radiation stabilizes the star, ensuring a lifetime of around 10 billion years

before the hydrogen fuel is used up.

Whereas solar mass stars are fairly long-lived, stars with greater masses have relatively short lives and produce energy through the hydrogen-helium conversion for perhaps only a few million years. The greater the mass of the star,

Above: The Hertzsprung-Russell diagram plots the absolute magnitude (luminosity) of a star against its spectral class and temperature. It reveals an interesting pattern for most stars (the main sequence), notable exceptions being supergiants, giants and white dwarfs.

Left: Evolution of stars. (1) Fragmentation of interstellar gas and dust clouds takes place, thus forming protostars (2). The central region of each star collapses and internal temperatures rise, creating nuclear reactions, the energy from which halts the collapse. The star joins the main sequence (3). Single solar mass stars continue to belong to the main sequence until their hydrogen supply runs out (4a). The outer layers expand and the star becomes a giant (5) and sometimes a supergiant (6). The core contracts, the outer layers collapse, and the star becomes a white dwarf (7). Gravitational energy is converted into heat as the collapse takes place. This heat slowly radiates into space and a black dwarf (8) results. Very massive stars (4b) develop unstable cores (9). Their outer layers are thrown out in a supernova explosion (10) and the core collapses to form a neutron star (11), a pulsar (12) or a black hole (13).

the higher its rate of fuel consumption, and a star of around 10 solar masses may use up its hydrogen supply in only a million years or so.

Whatever the mass of the star, the supply of hydrogen eventually diminishes and the reactions which produce helium gradually cease. The result is an overall contraction of the star coupled with a reduction in its energy output. The helium-rich core also collapses although the envelope of hydrogen surrounding it continues to convert into helium. As well as adding to the mass of the core, this continued reaction halts the contraction of the outer layers of the star. However, the core continues to collapse until its internal temperature reaches 100 million deg K. There is also tremendous pressure within the core, and these two factors instigate further reactions in which the helium is converted into carbon. The radiation produced pushes away the outer layers of the star causing it to expand to many times its original size. The star has now turned into a red giant.

White Dwarfs
There comes a time in the life of every red giant when all the hydrogen is used up. Then there is nothing to stop the gravitational collapse of the star. A star with a core of up to 1.4 solar masses will contract to form a white dwarf, made up of material so tightly packed that it will have a density of around a million times that of water. More massive stars may also end up as white dwarfs, although for this to happen the star would have to lose some of its mass to bring it to within the 1.4 solar mass limit. White dwarfs are appropriately named. Although these stars contain almost as much material as the Sun, they have diameters of no more than a few thousand miles. Energy is no longer being created, and although the surface temperature of a white dwarf will be reasonably high, its luminosity will be low. Eventually all the remaining light and heat will leak away into space and a black dwarf will result – the final demise of a solar mass star.

Neutron Stars
For stars with cores of between 1.5 and 3 solar masses the collapse generally advances past the white dwarf stage. Under the tremendous force of gravity the protons and electrons within the star are forced together to form neutrons. The result is a neutron star. This packing together of the material within the star leads to incredible densities, and it is believed that a single cubic centimetre of neutron star would

weigh millions of tonnes. Although a typical neutron star would have a mass several times that of the Sun, its diameter would only be in the region of 20 miles (30 km).

Pulsars
In AD 1054, Chinese astronomers witnessed the appearance of a new and extremely bright star in the constellation of Taurus. What they actually saw was a supernova, a colossal explosion signalling the death of a massive star. The final gravitational collapse of these stars is so forceful that the internal temperature soars rapidly. Violent nuclear reactions take place, the star explodes and for a while it can become up to a billion times more luminous than the Sun. The star's outer layers are thrown off into surrounding space (see *Nebulae and Star Clusters* for further explanation) whilst the core collapses to form a neutron star. The scattered remains of the 1054 supernova are represented by the gaseous filaments of the Crab Nebula. Observation has shown that the neutron star at the heart of the Crab Nebula spins on its axis 30 times a second, and that it emits radio pulses synchronous with this rotation. This regular 'pulsing' has led to the use of the term 'pulsars'. Since the first pulsar was discovered in 1967 many more have come to light, and the current total stands at over 300. Their rotation periods have been found to range from 1/30 second, in the case of the Crab Pulsar, to over 4 seconds. The Crab Pulsar is unusual, however, in that it flashes optically in time with the radio

Below: Vela supernova remnant.

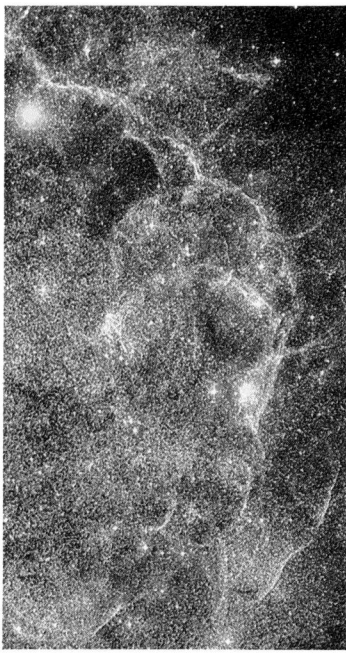

emissions. Only one other pulsar, the Vela supernova remnant, has been found to do the same.

The rapidly-spinning, superdense neutron stars are, indeed, incredible objects and seem to defy the imagination. Yet with the gravitational collapse of the most massive stars, those of 8 solar masses or more, even the fantastic properties of pulsars can be surpassed....

Black Holes
An object's gravitational force is related to both its mass and its diameter. If the Earth had the same diameter, but was made up of much more tightly-packed material, the pull of gravity at its surface would increase. Another way of looking at this relationship is in terms of escape velocity. In order to break free of the Earth's gravitational pull a rocket would have to travel at a velocity of at least 7 miles (11 km) per second. But a white dwarf is so dense that its escape velocity lies somewhere in the region of 2000 miles (3200 km) per second, equivalent to 1/90 the speed of light. And a typical neutron star has an escape velocity of around 125,000 miles (200,000 km) per second, or some 7/10 the speed of light...

Stars with cores of around 8 solar masses or more contain so much material that the final gravitational collapse goes past the white dwarf and neutron star stages. Nothing can stop the tremendous pull that the collapsing core exerts upon itself and it is crushed to ever increasing densities. The diameter of the star decreases whilst the pull of gravity at the surface increases rapidly, eventually producing an escape velocity which exceeds the speed of light. As this point is passed, light ceases to escape from the star, and, to any outside observer, it seems to wink out of sight. The intense gravitational pull of the totally collapsed star diminishes with increasing distance from the star until a point is reached where light can escape. This is the 'event horizon' and the region of space it encloses – known as a black hole – is forever hidden from view.

Black holes represent the theoretical final state of very massive stars. As their name suggests, we cannot see them, but it has been possible to detect them through the study of binary stars. A binary star system is composed of two stars in orbit around each other, and it is possible to calculate the mass of each star as well as their orbital periods. There are many binary systems known that contain either a white dwarf or a neutron star, and in these systems the gravi-

tational attraction of the denser companion pulls gas from the larger star into orbit around it. The ring of gas, known as an 'accretion disc', gets hotter as it is carried around the dwarf star, eventually emitting X-rays. Many of the X-ray sources that are known to exist in our Galaxy are of this nature, most of them being associated with neutron stars. However, during the early 1970s an X-ray source was discovered which didn't quite fit the standard pattern. This source was named Cygnus X-1. The brighter component of this binary system, HDE 226868, was found to be a supergiant blue star which orbited an unseen companion once every 5½ days or so. Analysis showed that this companion had a mass some 5 times that of our Sun. Astronomers believe that this object is a black hole and that X-rays are thrown out as gas in the accretion disc is sucked through the event horizon. A number of these exotic binary systems are suspected, although only prolonged research will help to confirm their existence. In the meantime, the mysteries of black holes are explored as much through imaginative postulation as through scientific observation.

Footnote:
Although many stars have proper names, only the twenty or so brightest have names which are commonly used. Star names have a wide variety of origins, Arabic, Greek and Latin being the three principal sources for those in use today. In the early 17th century the German astronomer Johann Bayer introduced a system whereby the stars within a constellation were designated by a Greek letter followed by the genitive form of the constellation name. The brightest star in a particular group was referred to as Alpha, the second Beta, and so on. Many of the fainter stars are often known by either a catalogue number, such as GC 6636 in Auriga (from the Boss General Catalogue) or after the name of their discoverer, such as the faint Barnard's Star, discovered by E.E. Barnard in 1916.

Nebulae and Star Clusters

Above: Rosette Nebula in Monoceros.

Left: The Trifid Nebula consists mainly of glowing hydrogen gas. 'Dark lanes' of silhouetted dust can be seen crossing the disc making the nebula resemble a pansy.

Below: Pleiades cluster. This is a cluster of young blue-white stars surrounded by reflection nebulosity, traces of the original gas cloud from which the stars were formed.

Nebulae

Faint, diffuse patches of light can be seen at various points in the sky. Closer examination will reveal that these objects are actually vast interstellar clouds of gas and dust known as nebulae, a name originating from the Latin word 'nebula' meaning cloud. Although a few are visible to the naked eye, many more can be seen with the help of moderate optical equipment, taking the form of either luminous or dark patches seen against the starry background.

These vast clouds are divided into three basic forms: emission, reflection and dark nebulae, and there are also what are known as planetary nebulae. Emission nebulae glow as a result of the stars within them exciting the surrounding gas. The stars are very hot and give out ultraviolet radiation, which becomes absorbed by the gas and causes it to give out visible light. A typical example is the Rosette Nebula in Monoceros, which is situated at a distance of around 3000 light years and has an apparent diameter roughly twice that of a full Moon. Deep within this nebula can be seen a cluster of hot blue-white stars which cause the gas to glow, and it also contains what are thought to be protostars. These are clumps of contracting material in which the internal temperatures and pressures increase to the point where a nuclear reaction is sparked off and a new star is born. Another emission nebula is the Orion Nebula, seen just below the three stars which form the Belt of Orion, and this nebula too is thought to be the birthplace of stars.

Reflection nebulae shine as a result of starlight being reflected from dust particles in the cloud. For example, the stars in the Pleiades cluster are surrounded by reflection nebulosity, the remnants of the material from which the stars were originally formed. Although these stars are not hot enough to cause the gas within the nebula to shine, the dust acts as an efficient reflector of starlight. The Horsehead Nebula in Orion is a fine example of a dark nebula, a cloud of material which contains no stars and which obscures the light from stars and other objects behind it. The Horsehead can be seen silhouetted against the bright background radiation of the emission nebula IC 434. First detected in 1889, the Horsehead Nebula was initially thought to be nothing more than a gap in this bright cloud of gas. However, we now know the true nature of this and other similar nebulae.

Planetary nebulae are the luminous shells of gas surrounding the hot stars known as white dwarfs. As a star collapses and the surface layers are ejected into surrounding space, the hot, inner regions of the star are exposed, resulting in an increased surface temperature of around 50,000 deg K. The energy released from the star excites the surrounding gas shell, causing it to shine. Planetary nebulae are seen to be expanding at speeds of around 9 to 12½ miles (15 to 20 km) per second, although this rate decreases with increasing distance from the star. Perhaps the most famous planetary nebula is the Ring Nebula in the constellation of Lyra. The blue central star is very hot, and on the point of the collapse which will turn it into a white dwarf.

Below: Horsehead Nebula in Orion south of Zeta Orionis.

Supernovae

As a very massive star undergoes final gravitational collapse, the temperature of its interior soars rapidly. This can produce a violent explosion, known as a supernova, which throws the star's outer layers into surrounding space. The scattered remnants of stars which have suffered such outbursts can be seen at various locations in the sky, one of the most famous examples being the Vela supernova remnant, a cloud of material which was ejected during a supernova explosion around 10,000 years ago. However, to describe such nebulae as 'supernova remnants' is somewhat misleading, as much of the gas visible does not actually originate from within the star itself but from surrounding space. The shock wave from the supernova sweeps through the interstellar regions, picking up gas and heating it to very high temperatures. This heating causes the gas to give off radiation at many wavelengths, including that of visible light.

Star Clusters

There are two distinct types of star cluster – *Open* and *Globular*. Open clusters (also known as *Galactic Clusters*) are quite common and over a thousand are known to exist within our Galaxy alone. The vast majority are found to lie on the galactic plane within the spiral arms of the Galaxy, and follow more or less circular orbits around the galactic nucleus. There are many open clusters which will be revealed with moderate optical aid and quite a few can be seen with the naked eye. A notable example is the Sword Handle Double Cluster in Perseus. Lying at a distance of around 7000 light years, this beautiful double cluster appears to be only a few million years old, and it is thought that both components were born within the same interstellar gas cloud. The total mass of the Sword Handle is around 7000 times that of the Sun and most of the stars within it are blue-white, although a few red stars can be seen.

Generally speaking, an open cluster contains several hundred stars, and in some cases interstellar gas and dust, left over from the original formation of the cluster. Most of the stars are similar in composition to the Sun and consist mainly of hydrogen together with some helium and small traces of other, heavier elements.

The stars within open clusters have their own individual motions and there is only a weak gravitational attraction between them. Consequently stars can break away from their companions and it is estimated that in a typical galactic cluster the escape rate is roughly one star every 100,000 years. The open clusters we see today must all therefore be fairly young on the cosmic time scale and it is also very likely that many of the individual stars in the Galaxy were originally members of such stellar gatherings.

Globular clusters are quite different in both nature and distribution. These objects are found outside the Galaxy and move around the galactic nucleus in highly elongated orbits, many of which are greatly inclined to the galactic plane. As with the open clusters, many globulars are visible to the naked eye, appearing as small, diffuse patches of light. However, telescopes reveal that these clusters are vast, spherical formations containing anything between one hundred thousand and a million stars, but no interstellar gas. Whereas open clusters are rarely more than 30 light years across, globular clusters are much larger with diameters ranging from 25 to 350 light years. Around 200 globulars are known. The stars within them are fairly tightly packed and the distances between them are measured in terms of light months rather than light years. As a result, the stars in globular clusters are strongly attracted to each other, and unlike their galactic counterparts they tend to stay together longer. However, observation has suggested that when individual stars pass close to each other, they may set up gravitational perturbations that could result in their ejection into surrounding space. On the other hand, this reaction may also work in reverse, with stars being pushed towards the centre of the cluster. This leads to an even denser gathering of stars in these regions which may result in the formation of both binary systems and black holes. Many globular clusters have been found to emit violent bursts of X-rays and it is believed that these originate from black holes situated at their centres.

The best known example is the Great Globular in Hercules. Lying at a distance of around 25,000 light years, this cluster has a diameter of about 170 light years. As with other objects of this type, the stars within the Great Globular are mainly red giants – much cooler and older than the stars found within galactic clusters.

As well as those in orbit around our Galaxy, globular clusters have been detected around other galaxies. These include the nearby Andromeda Spiral and the more distant elliptical galaxy Messier 87 in Virgo. Situated at a distance of around 40 million light years, Messier 87 has been found to have up to 15,000 globular clusters in orbit around it.

Below: Omega Centauri, the largest of the globular star clusters in the Milky Way and probably also the oldest.

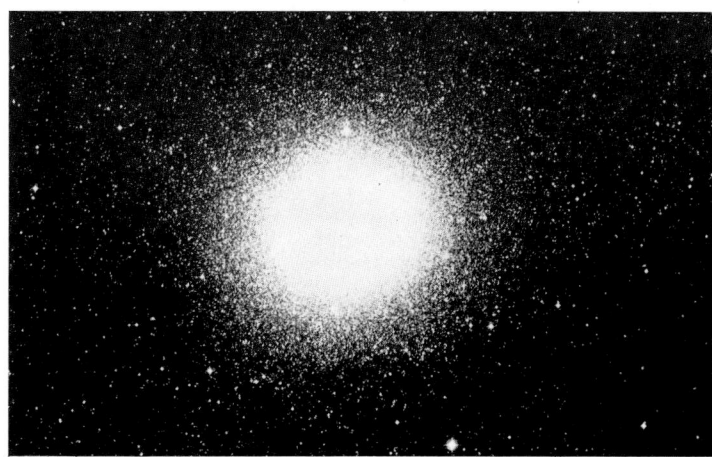

Below: Globular clusters around the Galaxy.

The Milky Way and Beyond

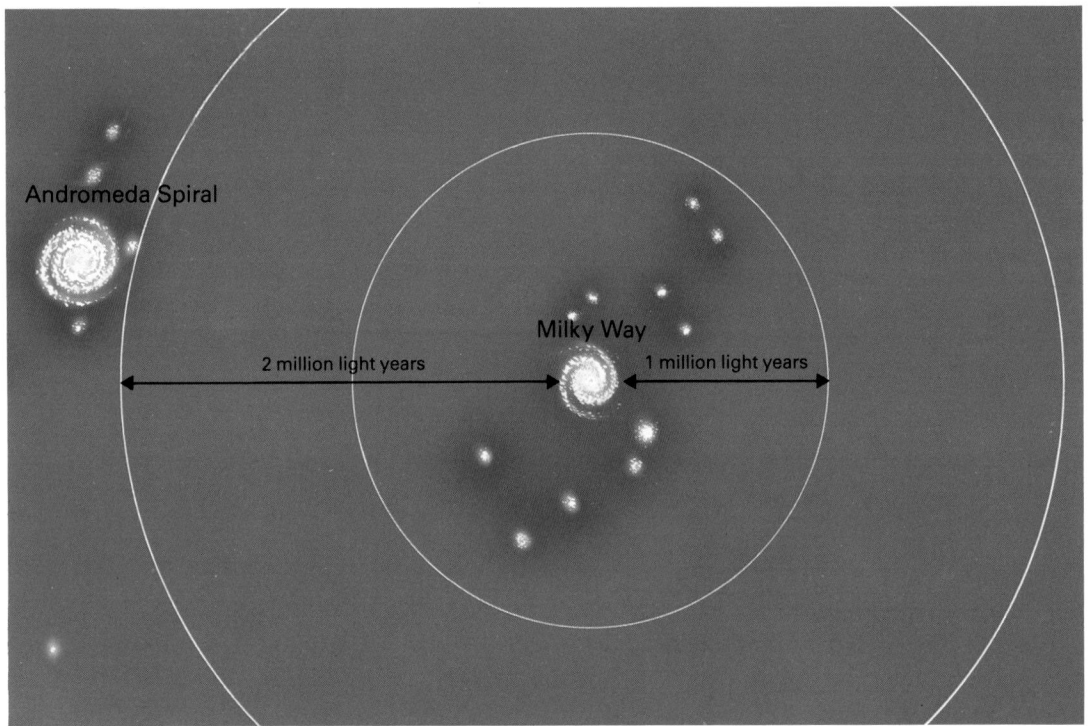

Andromeda Spiral

2 million light years

Milky Way

1 million light years

Left: The galaxies within the Local Group appear to be concentrated around the two dominant members of the system – our own Milky Way and the Andromeda Spiral. Although many small, faint galaxies are known to exist within the Local Group, it is likely that there are many more which are yet to be discovered.

Virtually all the celestial objects visible to the unaided eye are members of the Milky Way Galaxy, a gigantic spiral-shaped system containing over 100 billion stars, including our Sun, and many star clusters, nebulae and other deep-sky objects. Of the other galaxies that can be seen without optical aid, the largest is the Andromeda Spiral which, together with the Milky Way and around two dozen other star systems, makes up a collection of galaxies known as the Local Group. Beyond this region a great number of other galaxies can be observed, some isolated, some

in small groups and others in clusters which sometimes contain many thousands of galaxies. When compared with these vast clusters our own Local Group is relatively tiny. In all, around 100 million galaxies are known, spreading out towards the very edge of the observable universe.

Classification of Galaxies

Galaxies exist in many different shapes and sizes and are normally classified into two principal types according to a system proposed by the American astronomer Edwin

Hubble in 1925. *Elliptical Galaxies* are uniform in appearance and can vary in shape from almost spherical to flattened discs. In contrast, *Spiral Galaxies* are made up of a central, almost spherical bulge containing the nucleus surrounded by a disc in which spiral arms can be seen. The ratio between the size of the nucleus and the area of the spiral arms can vary, with some galaxies having large nuclei and closely packed spiral arms, while others possess small nuclei and arms which are much less tightly packed. The stars in spiral galaxies orbit around the galactic centre,

those in the arms trailing behind those close to the nucleus. *Barred Spiral Galaxies* have a central bar crossing the nucleus with spiral arms trailing from the ends of the bar. In addition to elliptical and spiral galaxies there are also two other types: *Lenticular Galaxies* have a central bulge and a surrounding disc, but they show no evidence of spiral arms; *Irregular Galaxies*, as their name suggests, have no well-defined shape or structure.

The total mass of a galaxy is normally given in terms of solar masses. For example, the Andromeda Spiral has a mass of around 300 billion times that of the Sun, or 300 billion solar masses. However, this mass is not entirely composed of stars and a significant percentage may be in the form of interstellar gas and dust, found particularly within the discs of spiral galaxies and also throughout irregular galaxies where it may represent up to 25 percent of the total galactic mass. In contrast, elliptical galaxies contain little or no such interstellar material.

Galaxies vary considerably in size. One of the smallest known galaxies is Leo I which lies at a distance of around 750,000 light years. Leo I is classed as a dwarf spheroidal galaxy and has a diameter of just over 2000 light years. The Andromeda Spiral, on the other hand, is one of the largest galaxies known with a diameter of over 160,000 light years.

The Milky Way

On a clear, dark night a faint misty band may be seen crossing the sky. This band is the Milky Way and has been observed for centuries. However, Galileo was the first to reveal its true nature in the early 17th cen-

Sa   Sb   Sc

Elliptical galaxies

Spiral galaxies

SO

Barred spiral galaxies

E0   E3   E7

SBa   SBb   SBc

Left: Galaxies are normally classified according to their shape as indicated in the Hubble system. The three main types of galaxy are elliptical, spiral and barred spiral. In addition, SO type galaxies fall between the elliptical and spiral types, as they have a central bulge although the surrounding disc contains no spiral arms.

tury. He found that the Milky Way was made up of countless numbers of faint stars. Although these are not bright enough to be seen separately with the unaided eye, collectively they produce the misty band of starlight that we see spanning the sky.

The Milky Way effect is a result of the fact that the Solar System is situated on the edge of a spiral arm some 30,000 light years from the galactic centre. As we look along the plane of the Galaxy, either towards or away from the nucleus, we see a large number of stars. In contrast, if we observe in a direction perpendicular to the galactic plane the number of stars we see is considerably reduced. We cannot see the centre of our Galaxy, which lies in the direction of the constellation Sagittarius, because it is hidden from us by vast clouds of interstellar dust lying in our line of sight.

The Galaxy is a typical spiral galaxy and, like other spirals, it has three main regions; the disc, a central bulge and a halo. The disc is the region containing the spiral arms and is very thin in comparison to its overall diameter with a thickness of less than 1000 light years. Our Galaxy has a total of four spiral arms, known as (from the centre) the Norma Arm, the Sagittarius Arm, the Orion Arm and the Perseus Arm. The Solar System lies between the Orion and Perseus Arms. As with other spirals, the arms contain a great many relatively young, hot stars, classed as Population I, which formed up to 5 billion years ago. There are also large amounts of interstellar gas and dust. This material constitutes between 5 and 10 percent of the mass of the Galaxy. The central bulge has a much lower proportion of this interstellar material and a higher concentration of stars. These stars are of Population II and are much older than their counterparts in the galactic disc, having formed in the region of 10 billion years ago or more, not long after the Galaxy itself. The central bulge is roughly 3000 light years thick and some 18,000 light years in diameter. The halo is a spherical region surrounding the galactic centre. It contains very old stars of Population II which are thought to have formed up to 15 billion years ago. Because these stars are concentrated into globular clusters which orbit the galactic centre, studying their paths can help us determine the position of the centre of the Galaxy.

Clusters of Galaxies

Clusters of galaxies exist throughout the universe. Some are small and contain only a few galaxies

Above: This is how our Milky Way would appear to an exterior observer. The central bulge is surrounded by the galactic disc containing the spiral arms. The Sun is located roughly two thirds of the way out from the centre of the Galaxy.

Left: Situated some 10 million light years away is a cluster of galaxies centred on the spiral galaxy M81. Known as the Ursa Major-Camelopardalis Group, it is one of the nearest to our own Local Group and contains a mixture of spiral and irregular galaxies.

Below: Quasar 3c273.

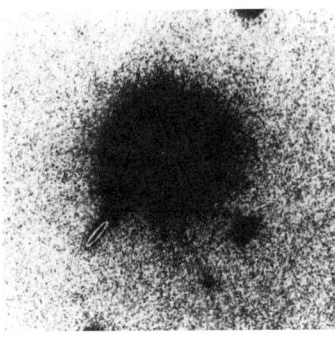

whilst others are enormous in comparison and may contain several thousand members. It is also known that clusters are grouped into superclusters – clusters of clusters. The Local Group, to which the Milky Way Galaxy belongs, has over twenty members, the largest two being our own Galaxy and the Andromeda Spiral. The rest of the Local Group are a mixture of elliptical, spiral and irregular galaxies, many of which are concentrated around the two dominant members. The total mass of the Local Group is some 650 billion solar masses, with around 70 percent of this mass being attributable to the Milky Way Galaxy and the Andromeda Spiral. The Local Group is a member of the Local Supercluster which itself is centred on the Virgo cluster of galaxies.

There are many other clusters of galaxies in the neighbourhood of the Local Group, the largest of which are the clusters in Eridanus, Pavo-Indus, Virgo and Canes Venatici. One of the closest is that associated with the two bright galaxies Messier 81 and Messier 82 in Ursa Major. M81 is a large spiral galaxy, whilst M82, appearing at first sight to be irregular, may actually be a spiral seen edge-on which has been deformed through gravitational interaction with nearby M81. M81 is the dominant member of the cluster which lies at a distance of almost 10 million light years.

Throughout the universe galaxies can be seen receding from each other, a phenomenon that is thought to derive from the birth of the universe. However, in each cluster the galaxies are not moving apart, although an individual galaxy can move around within its own cluster. Astronomers have calculated the mass that is required for a cluster to produce the gravitational

attraction that will keep the galaxies in the cluster together, but these theoretical calculations of the total mass required for stability do not always match up with the observed mass. This so-called missing mass problem is still to be satisfactorily explained, but the answer may lie in intergalactic dust and gas between the galaxies, which has not yet been detected.

Peculiar Galaxies

There are many types of galaxy which do not fit in with the Hubble classification, including radio galaxies and Seyfert galaxies. Although many galaxies emit radio waves, those known as *Radio Galaxies* are very strong emitters at these wavelengths. Two of the first to be identified were Centaurus A and Virgo A in 1949 and in each case it has been shown that most of the radio emission comes from two extended lobes situated at either side of the galaxy, thought to have been ejected from the galaxies in violent explosions. *Seyfert Galaxies* have small but very bright nuclei and emit large amounts of infra-red radiation.

Quasars

It was while astronomers were carrying out research into radio galaxies that they discovered a class of object which, although star-like in appearance, radiated vast amounts of energy. These objects were called quasi-stellar objects, or quasars, and were found to lie at vast distances. Quasars are very compact and, because they are visible at such great distances, must be highly luminous. For many years their true nature was unknown although we now know that many quasars are actually highly active galactic nuclei. Over 200 have been found to lie within galaxies, including the nearest, 3c273. The nebulosity around 3c273 resembles a gigantic elliptical galaxy.

One of the most distant quasars is PKS 2000–330 which lies some 15 billion light years away. Because it is so remote, the light from PKS 2000–330 was just over halfway towards us at the time of the birth of the Solar System, around 4.5 billion years ago. Quasars are the most remote and active class of object known to astronomers, and their study may help us to unlock some of the long-held secrets of the universe.

The Mysteries of the Universe

The Evolving Universe

The universe, by definition, contains everything we know to exist, and throughout the universe matter can be seen to obey the laws of physics. With the unaided eye we can see thousands of stars together with a small number of nebulae and star clusters, all of which are contained within the confines of our own Galaxy. Telescopes reveal much more, including millions of other galaxies far beyond our own. Telescopes have probed almost to the edge of the universe and objects have been detected which lie at colossal distances. The quasar PKS 2000–330, discovered with the 64-metre radio telescope at Parkes, Australia, in the early 1970s, has been found to lie some 15 billion light years away, a distance which is thought to place it towards the edge of the observable universe. The initial discovery by the Parkes telescope was made at radio wavelengths, the object being identified optically some years later by astronomers using the 3.9-metre Anglo-Australian Telescope at Siding Spring Observatory, Australia.

As we have seen, our own Galaxy is just one of around two dozen which make up a cluster of galaxies known as the Local Group. Throughout space other clusters can be detected, many of which are far larger than our own. Until quite recently it was thought that galaxies and clusters of galaxies were uniformly distributed through space, but it has now been shown that this might not be the case. Recent observations have revealed large voids in space, rather like gigantic bubbles. Galaxies seem to be gathered in long chain-like structures, concentrated in the regions where the bubbles intersect. The gigantic voids enclosed by the bubbles are thought to have originated shortly after the birth of the universe. Initially, massive stars were formed which eventually exploded, producing localized increases in temperature and causing shock waves to sweep clear of matter vast spherical areas of space (the bubble-like voids), thereby creating the shells of gas from which galaxies came into being.

The Birth of the Universe

Astronomers believe that the universe came into being some 15 billion years ago in a gigantic explosion known as the Big Bang. Before this event took place, all the matter we now see spread through the universe was packed into an incredibly dense formation commonly referred to as the 'cosmic egg', an idea first proposed by the Belgian astronomer Georges Lemaitre in 1927. Much of the observational evidence we have supports the Big Bang theory. It has been found that the universe is expanding with clusters of galaxies spreading out from each other at a uniform rate. The rate at which any pair of clusters moves apart is directly related to the distance between them. If two such clusters are 400 million light years apart they will be receding from each other at half the rate of two that are 800 million light years apart. This rate of expansion, as well as the expansion itself, can be traced back to a time when all the matter in the universe, including every galaxy, was compressed into the same region of space. This collection of matter was the cosmic egg that was to be ripped asunder in the Big Bang.

Immediately after the Big Bang the matter which emerged was incredibly hot, with a temperature in excess of a billion deg K, and it was not until about 3 minutes after the event that the temperature had dropped sufficiently to permit the formation of helium. About a million years later the temperature had fallen to around 3000 deg K, thus allowing the formation of hydrogen, currently the most abundant element in the universe. The final significant milestone in the early history of the universe came some billion years after the Big Bang with the formation of the galaxies. As

Below: Hot gas flows from the surface of a giant star to form an accretion disc around a nearby black hole. As the gas is sucked into the black hole it is heated to colossal temperatures reaching millions of degrees Kelvin. This causes the gas to emit X-rays which we can detect from satellites in orbit around the Earth.

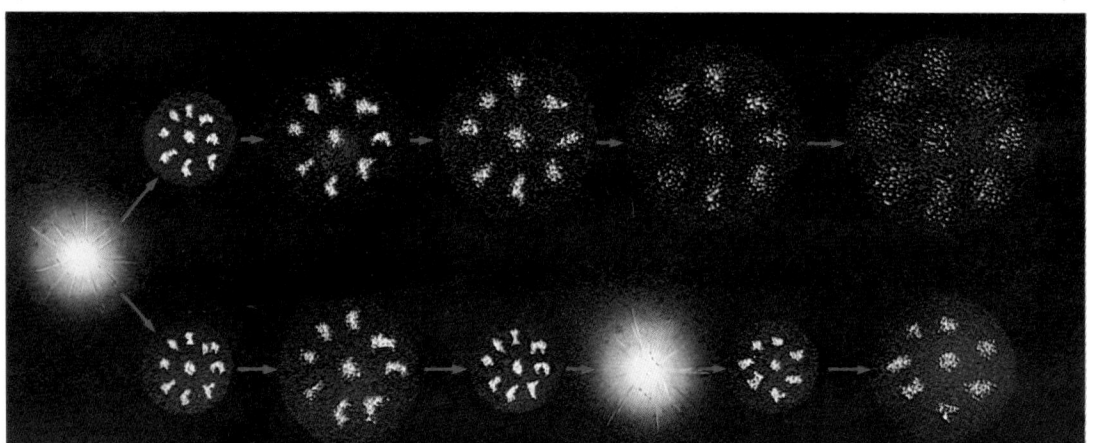

Left: There are two main theories as to the eventual fate of the universe. According to the continuously-expanding theory, the universe will expand forever and the galaxies will become less and less active as they move apart and the stars within them die. Alternatively, according to the pulsating universe theory, there is sufficient matter within the universe eventually to halt the expansion and bring about a collapse. This collapse could result in a single, extremely dense mass which may then undergo a further 'Big Bang' explosion, thereby creating another universe from the remnants of the old.

we have seen, the gas which was expanding was not uniformly spread and there were regions which contained larger and denser amounts of material. It was in these regions that galaxies developed as a result of the gas particles collecting together through mutual gravitational attraction. Once formed, the galaxies gathered to form clusters and superclusters. About 3 billion years later stars began to form within the galaxies. Star formation is continuing to take place and can be observed within the vast interstellar clouds of gas and dust which exist throughout our own and other galaxies.

The Fate of the Universe

Opinions are divided as to the eventual fate of the universe, alternative theories depending upon the amount of material present throughout it. According to the pulsating universe theory, first put forward by the American cosmologist Allan Sandage, the expansion that we see taking place today will eventually stop and the universe will then collapse back on itself. As the galaxies approach each other they will merge, individual stars will collide and eventually all the matter in the universe will come together to form an incredibly hot, superdense mass. Another Big Bang will then occur causing the universe to expand again. The main drawback to this theory is that the observed density of material throughout the universe is not enough to create the gravitational influence necessary to halt the expansion. Although there may be undiscovered material around, perhaps in the form of intergalactic dust, it seems unlikely that this will be sufficient to stop the expansion and to bring about a collapse.

Far more popular among astronomers is the expanding universe theory, which states that the universe will expand forever, gradually becoming less and less active as the galaxies move apart and the stars within them die, creating vast cosmic graveyards. Cold white dwarfs and black holes would be left in place of the beautiful stars that are predominant today. These black holes may then spiral in towards the denser inner regions of their own galaxies, devouring all around them. So, each of the countless galaxies we now see in the sky may be destined to end their lives as gigantic black holes.

The Evolution of the Earth

The Solar System was formed about 4.5 billion years ago from a spinning cloud of interstellar gas and dust. The central region of this cloud condensed to form the Sun, whilst the planets took shape from the disc of material surrounding it. The heavier elements present in the disc were concentrated near the inner regions and from these the four rocky, terrestrial planets were formed. At the same time the four gaseous planets took shape from the lighter elements in the outer regions of the disc. The origins of Pluto remain something of a mystery. It is believed to be a rocky, terrestrial-type planet, so it does not fit the theory.

As the Earth cooled a surface crust formed. Composed of basalt silicate rocks, its depth varies from up to 5 miles (8 km) thick under the oceans to around 40 miles (65 km) under the continents. The crust, together with the upper part of the mantle upon which it lies, forms the lithosphere which reaches to a depth of 60 miles (100 km). The lithosphere is divided into a number of plates which move around on top of the asthenosphere, a further region of mantle which extends to a depth of 450 miles (700 km). It is this movement, known as continental drift, which has resulted in the disposi-

tion of land and sea that we see today.

Geologists believe that the continental land masses reached their present positions after an original 'super-continent' broke up about 600 million years ago. By the time of the Cretaceous Period, between 65 and 140 million years ago, the process of continental drift had begun to create the land masses we recognize on modern maps. When plates come together a great deal of geological activity can occur, including the formation of mountain ranges. The lofty peaks of the Himalayas, for example, mark the boundary between the land mass we know as India and the Asian continent, which joined together about 50 million years ago.

The Origin of Life

The origin of life on our planet has been the subject of much controversy. It is generally believed that life arose around 3500 million years ago, an assumption based on the evidence for life found in rocks formed at this time. There are many theories which attempt to explain how life originated, one of which has been put forward by Fred Hoyle and Chandra Wickramasinghe and suggests that life was brought to Earth by comets from interstellar clouds. Living cells which formed inside these clouds are, according to the theory, de-

posited on the surfaces of planets by passing comets. If this is true then life similar to our own may be common throughout the Galaxy. Hoyle and Wickramasinghe's idea is based on a similar theory put forward early this century by the Swedish chemist Svante Arrhenius. He suggested that simple organisms were seeded on the Earth by either comets or meteorites from regions outside the Solar System.

The generally accepted idea is that life arose in the early atmosphere of Earth. It is thought that volcanic activity introduced such gases as carbon dioxide, water vapour, nitrogen and carbon monoxide into the environment as well as creating the oceans which now cover a large percentage of the surface area of our planet. Provided that traces of methane and ammonia were present in the atmosphere, the formation of amino acids could have been triggered off by the input of energy from, for example, bolts of lightning, heat from volcanic activity or even sunlight. Amino acids are recognized as the building blocks of protein, which plays an essential rôle in all biological functions. The composition of the atmosphere has changed since those early times, largely through the photosynthetic action of plants. Fuelled by the energy of sunlight, these create oxygen from the intake of carbon dioxide and water.

Whichever way life originated on our planet, the event which triggered it off was a matter of chance and, improbable as it may have been, something similar may have happened elsewhere. It is possible that the universe is teeming with other civilizations, all of which evolved through a chemical accident similar to that which led to the complexity of life on Earth we know today.

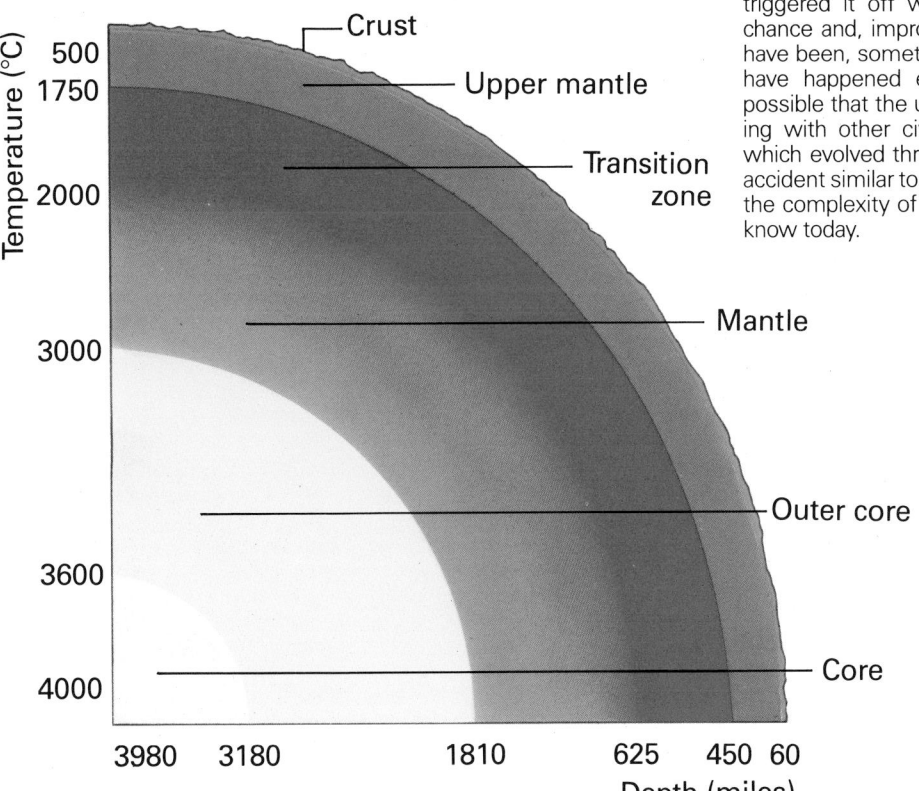

Right: Internal structure of the Earth.

Space Exploration and the Search for Life Elsewhere

Although the existence of extra-terrestrial life has yet to be proved, it would be foolish to assume that our Earth is unique in harbouring life. Our Galaxy alone contains well over a hundred billion stars and is just one of around a hundred million other galaxies spread across the entire observable universe. Yet up to now attempts to locate life elsewhere have failed. In the meantime man himself has started on the long, arduous journey which will eventually take him to the stars. Although our home is here on Earth, our future lies in space, and the first tiny but significant steps towards that goal have already been taken.

The Dawning of the Space Age

The space age began on 4 October 1957 with the launch of the Russian satellite Sputnik 1 which orbited the Earth for 96 days. Signals from the radio transmitter on Sputnik 1 were received for three weeks as they heralded man's latest frontier. The Russians launched Sputnik 2 in early November and it was only in January of the following year that the American space programme finally got under way with the launch of Explorer 1.

On 12 April 1961, the Russians initiated the first manned mission. Yuri Alekseyevich Gagarin was launched into space in Vostok 1, a 91-inch (2.3-metre) diameter sphere, from a site at Tyuratam in central Russia. Shortly afterwards the US President John Kennedy announced to the world the ultimate goal of the American space programme; to put a man on the Moon and return him safely to Earth before the decade was out. The space race had begun. Manned exploration of space now advanced rapidly. The early single-astronaut American Mercury capsules were succeeded by the twin-piloted Gemini craft, which provided experience in a number of different areas that would be essential to any proposed lunar landing mission. These included oribital docking procedure and relatively prolonged space journeys. In spite of the increased momentum of the American space effort, the Russians scored a number of 'firsts'.

Valentina Tereshkova was the first woman in space in June 1963, the first launch with a multiple crew was that of Voskhod 1 in October 1964 and the first spacewalk was by Alexei Leonov in March 1965. However, the initiation of the American Apollo programme, and in particular the first manned spaceflight around the Moon by Apollo 8 in December 1968, put paid to any further Russian interest in the race to the Moon. The Apollo series culminated in a number of moon landings, the first of which was the historic Apollo 11 mission in July 1969. On that mission Neil Armstrong became the first man to set foot on the lunar surface, capturing the attention of the world as the American dream promised by President Kennedy became a reality.

The Space Shuttle

Man had proved that he could live and work in the hostile environment of space and the subsequent American Skylab and Russian Salyut space stations were to provide working quarters for long-term manned missions. At the same time research was being directed towards reducing the cost of space exploration, in particular the use of non-recoverable launch vehicles. The introduction of the American Space Shuttle was a big step forward in this respect, as this was the first re-usable spacecraft which could be employed on a large number of separate launches. Extremely versatile, the shuttle can

be used to launch and retrieve satellites and to carry astronauts to and from Earth orbit. With the shuttle, it is now also possible for specialists, such as scientists, doctors and engineers, to be taken into the weightless conditions of space to carry out experiments which may prove beneficial to mankind. The Space Shuttle heralds the first positive step by man in his efforts to colonize space. Yet as we attempt to gain independence from our planet, the question of whether life already exists elsewhere in our Galaxy remains unanswered.

The Search for Extra-Terrestrial Life

Although we can only speculate about the existence of life elsewhere in the Galaxy, our immediate planetary neighbours are more accessible for investigation. For many years it was believed that Mars might be home to intelligent life. Towards the end of the 19th century the Italian astronomer Giovanni Schiaparelli saw what he thought were linear features on the Martian surface. He named them 'canali' which, correctly translated, means 'channels'. However, the American astronomer Percival Lowell, amongst others, mis-translated 'canali' as 'canals', a word which suggested that they might be artificial waterways. Lowell thought that a highly-advanced civilization might have built a gigantic system of canals to

An artist's impression of organisms that could theoretically develop within the gaseous atmosphere of a planet like Jupiter.

irrigate the desert-like surface of Mars with water from the polar ice caps. It was eventually shown that the lines seen by Schiaparelli were actually made up of many small, unconnected features and, sadly perhaps, the idea of an advanced Martian civilization disappeared. However, the possibility of simpler life forms on the planet was not ruled out and in 1976 two American spacecraft made successful soft landings on the Martian surface. These were the Viking missions and amongst their experiments were some that were designed to test the Martian soil for indications of life. Although these experiments failed to produce any conclusive evidence, the possibility of simple life forms on Mars cannot be discounted. Primitive organisms may also exist elsewhere in the Solar System. For example, Carl Sagan and E.E. Salpeter of Cornell University have suggested that life may have evolved within the cloud layers of Jupiter which are rich in such materials as hydrogen, methane and water. They have proposed a number of different organisms which, in theory, could exist in such an environment.

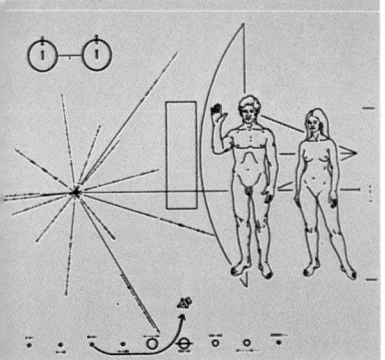

Above: The plaque carried by the Pioneer 10 and Pioneer 11 space probes portraying their human builders, and diagrams indicating the positions of Earth and the Solar System.

Below: The Arecibo Radio Message. A binary counting convention is established in the top row. The atomic number of the elements from which we are made is specified in the second row. The vertical white block represents the number of nucleotides in the genes of the red creature (man). Our planetary system is shown in yellow, the third planet having particular significance. The radio telescope transmitting the message is in violet.

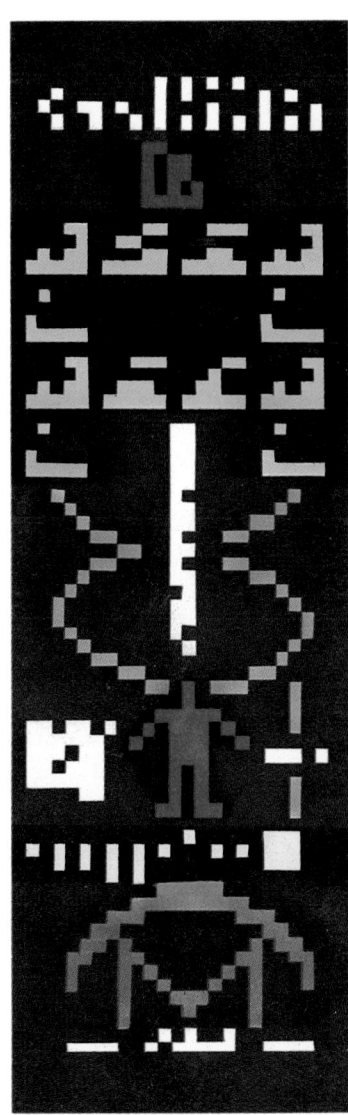

Messages to the Stars

In the early 1970s two American space probes, Pioneer 10 and Pioneer 11, were launched on missions to explore Jupiter and Saturn. Once their work was completed, their trajectories took them out of the Solar System towards interstellar space. Each craft carries a small plaque containing a pictorial message from the planet Earth. Should any alien civilization find one of the probes, they will be able to piece together an idea of what human beings look like and where they are located in the Galaxy.

A more sophisticated form of message is carried by each of the Voyager probes. Voyager 1 and Voyager 2 each carry a record storing pictorial information about the Earth and the people who live on it. Pictures of famous buildings, aeroplanes, railways, telescopes, rockets and other examples of technology have been combined with verbal greetings in a number of languages. Samples of music from many different cultures form a large part of the message. The records are accompanied by instructions on how to play them and by a suitable cartridge and stylus. Although the records themselves will far outlive their creators, they will bear testament to our efforts to contact our cosmic neighbours.

Interstellar distances are vast and the chances of any of these messages being found are certainly minimal, even if the Galaxy were teeming with life. A number of astronomers have tried to assess the probability of life-supporting planetary systems round other stars. In 1961, the American astronomer Frank Drake advanced a formula which attempted to calculate the number of advanced civilizations within our Galaxy. This formula is based on a calculation of the number of stars in the Galaxy, on an assessment of how many have planetary systems, on an estimate of the number of planetary systems which could support life, and then finally on an assessment of the factors which permit the development of a technologically advanced civilization. The final, and from our viewpoint the most worrying, factor is whether any civilization, having reached our stage of development, will go on to destroy itself. This is the one ingredient of the Drake formula which can be said to lie in the hands of each and every civilization that reaches the stage of advanced technology, and those who progress beyond it can be said, perhaps, to be truly intelligent!

Apart from assessing the probability of life elsewhere, attempts have been made to establish contact with alien beings by intercepting signals from space. For example, in the Russian CETI project (Communication with Extra-Terrestrial Intelligence), a total of 600 nearby stars have been examined on a 21-centimetre (8¼-inch) wavelength. This particular frequency was chosen because it corresponds to the emission frequency of hydrogen, the most common element in the universe, and it was assumed that the same logic would be used by other civilizations who would also transmit at this particular wavelength. So far the results have proved negative, although experiments such as this will, no doubt, be continued.

Signals have also been transmitted into space, most notably a message from the Arecibo Radio Telescope in 1974. This message was directed at the Great Globular Cluster in Hercules, which lies at a distance of around 25,000 light years. Even if the message were to be picked up and a reply sent back, we could not expect to receive it for 50,000 years. Certainly, communication on a cosmic scale is a lengthy operation! What action we would take if such a signal were received is uncertain. However, if we overcome the problems of our seemingly natural inclinations towards self-destruction, perhaps we may be ready to establish a rapport with our distant neighbours and to join the galactic community.

The giant 1000-foot (305-metre) radio telescope at Arecibo, Puerto Rico, the largest dish-type radio telescope in the world. The Arecibo telescope has been used in the search for signals from extraterrestrial civilizations as well as to beam signals from Earth for possible interception by other intelligences.

Telescopes and Observatories

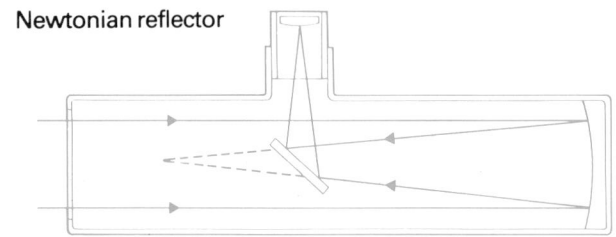

Newtonian reflector

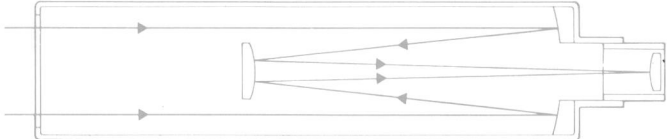

Cassegrain reflector

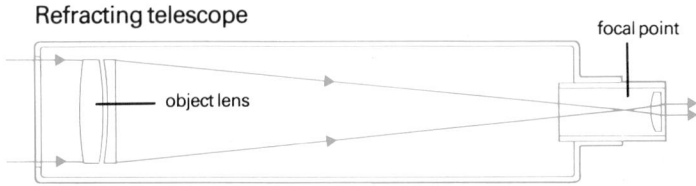

Refracting telescope

focal point

object lens

Top: The Newtonian reflector which uses a primary mirror to reflect the light, via a secondary mirror, to an eyepiece in the side of the tube.

Centre: The Cassegrain reflector also uses a mirror to reflect the light up the tube although the secondary mirror is convex and throws the light back through a hole in the centre of the primary where the eyepiece is situated.

Bottom: The refractor telescope uses a lens to collect the light and bring it into focus.

Above: The 40-inch refractor at Yerkes Observatory, USA, the world's largest refracting telescope.

Below: The Hale 200-inch reflector inside its dome at Palomar Observatory, California, USA.

The modern astronomer has many fine telescopes at his disposal. The United States, Australia, Hawaii and others all play host to giant observatories. Yet it must be borne in mind that these optical master-pieces are the descendants of the small, crudely constructed and sometimes unwieldy instruments used by the pioneers in observ-ational astronomy. The work of Galileo, Herschel and others paved the way for our modern day view of the universe.

Most of the large telescopes in current use are of the reflecting type; they use a specially shaped mirror (primary) to gather the light from the star and reflect it to the eyepiece where the image that is produced is magnified. The most popular type of reflector is the Newtonian, a system devised by the English scientist Isaac Newton in 1668. Newton's first telescope had a primary mirror only 1-inch (25mm) in diameter, making it virtually useless for observing. However, it demonstrated the Newtonian optical system which eventually proved to be so popular that this type of telescope is used more than any other by today's amateur astronomer. Other reflect-ing systems include the Maksutov, which incorporates both mirrors and lenses, and the Cassegrain. In the Cassegrain the secondary mir-ror reflects the light from the object being viewed, through a hole in the centre of the primary; it is a more compact telescope.

One of the largest optical tele-scopes currently in use is the 5-metre (200-inch) Hale reflector at Palomar Observatory, California, USA Completed in 1948, this giant instrument has helped astronomers to make many pioneering discoveries. Larger still is the 6-metre (236.2-inch) reflector at Zelenchukskaya Observatory in the USSR. One of the world's best equipped observation centres is the Kitt Peak National Observa-tory near Tucson, Arizona. Among its array of telescopes can be found the McMath solar telescope and

the 4-metre (158-inch) Mayall Tele-scope.

Before mirrors were used to gather sunlight, the only type of telescope available was the refractor, using a lens instead of a mirror. The first refractors, such as those used by Galileo, were extremely crude. The lens (objective) had a single component which resulted in chromatic aberration. Light is a mixture of different wavelengths ranging from red through to violet and the lens will focus the wavelengths at the long (red) end of the spectrum at a point further away from the lens than those at the short (violet) end. Wavelengths other than red and violet are brought to focus at points between these two, resulting in a series of images and false colour. Modern refractors use objectives made up of several components, each of a different type of glass, which helps to eliminate chromatic aberration. These achromatic object glasses, as they are known, are designed to bring two of the different wavelengths to a common focus with only a slight deviation for the rest. However, chromatic aberration cannot be completely eliminated. The largest refractor in the world is situated at the Yerkes Observatory in America. Completed in 1897, it has an objective with a diameter of 40-inches (1-metre).

There is quite a problem in providing a satisfactory mount for a telescope. For small instruments the alt-azimuth mount, which allows movement both vertically (altitude) and horizontally (azimuth), is usually suitable. The drawback with the alt-azimuth mount is that the telescope has to be moved in two axes in order to keep the star in the field of view. This problem is overcome with an equatorial mount which has both polar and declination axes. The telescope is set up with the polar axis parallel to that of the Earth. Once the star is brought into view it is kept there by clamping down the declination axis and moving the telescope around the polar axis only, in the opposite direction to the rotation of the Earth.

Contrary to popular belief, large telescopes and expensive optical equipment are not essential to enjoy astronomy. Although certain branches of research do require larger instruments, there is plenty of opportunity for those with limited means to enjoy the night sky. The wide field of view and bright images produced by binoculars make them the ideal instrument for both the beginner and the more advanced observer who wish to spend a few hours wandering about the heavens. Binoculars are

Altitude-azimuth mounting with axes that move vertically and horizontally.

Altitude-azimuth mount

The equatorial mount is aligned with the celestial pole, the polar axis being set parallel to the Earth's axis. The actual angle depends on the latitude of the observer. Once aligned correctly, the telescope can be made to follow the path of a star through the sky by movement in one axis only.

Polar axis

Equatorial (or declination) axis

Equatorial mount

classed A x B, where A is the magnification and B the diameter of the main lenses. The ideal size for astronomical work is 7 x 50. These have a wide field of view coupled with large objectives which can gather plenty of light.

Invisible Astronomy
It has recently been discovered that, as well as emitting visible light, many of the objects we see in the sky throw out radiation at different wavelengths to which our eyes are not sensitive. Instruments have been designed to pick up these various signals and gamma, X-ray, ultra-violet, infra-red and radio emissions can now all be detected. However, apart from visible light and radio waves, the Earth's atmosphere absorbs almost all forms of radiation. X-rays and gamma rays are absorbed in the upper atmosphere — X-rays by individual atoms and gamma rays by atomic nuclei — whilst ultra-violet radiation is absorbed by

molecules in the ozone layer. Infra-red emissions are absorbed by water vapour, although this problem can be overcome reasonably well by siting infra-red telescopes at altitudes high enough to escape the water vapour in our atmosphere. One example is the 150-inch (3.8-metre) United Kingdom Infra-Red Telescope (UKIRT) at Mauna Kea, Hawaii, which has been housed at a height of around 14,000 feet (4500 metres). Satellites now play a major role in astronomy, enabling us to send instruments designed to pick up X-rays, gamma rays and ultra-violet radiation above the atmosphere.

Because radio waves have no difficulty passing through the atmosphere, the radio astronomer carries out his work from ground-based instruments, and there are many radio telescopes around the world. The largest fully-steerable radio telescope is the giant 330-foot (100-metre) dish at Bonn, Germany, although the most famous is the 250-foot (76-metre) instrument at Jodrell Bank, England. There is a non-steerable radio telescope to dwarf both these at Arecibo, Puerto Rico. This 1000-foot (305-metre) instrument is so large that it had to be built into a natural valley in the hills.

Astro-photography
To photograph the night sky the only equipment needed is a camera with a suitable lens and film. The camera should be of the single lens reflex (SLR) type with a shutter that can be held open indefinitely. A sturdy tripod is also essential as the camera should be held steady throughout each exposure. Star fields, meteors and artificial satellites can be photographed quite easily, exposure varying between a few seconds to around 30 minutes or more. An exposure longer than 30 seconds will produce star trails because of the rotation of the Earth. If pinpoint images are required, or for detailed photographs of the Moon and planets, some sort of drive is needed. The camera can be attached to an equatorially mounted telescope equipped with an automatic drive system. Lunar details can be photographed with a telephoto lens, although in many cases the telescope itself can be used as a lens. This will enable close-up views to be obtained of the planets, star clusters and other deep sky objects.

GLOSSARY OF TERMS

Asteroid: One of a vast number of small, rocky bodies which orbit the Sun, generally between the orbits of Mars and Jupiter. Otherwise known as Minor Planets.

Asthenosphere: A region of the Earth's mantle which is semi-fluid and upon which the crust moves during the process of continental drift (plate tectonics). Also denotes the semi-molten outer core of the Moon. (See *Lithosphere*).

Aurora: Diffuse patches of light seen at high northern latitudes (Aurora Borealis) and high southern latitudes (Aurora Australis), caused by the effects of charged particles entering the upper atmosphere.

Big Bang: Currently the most popular theory as to the origin of the universe which states that all the matter in the universe emerged from a super-dense primordial mass when it exploded some 15 billion years ago (see *Cosmic Egg*).

Billion: A figure equal to 1000 million (1,000,000,000).

Binary Star System: A system of two stars which orbit each other around their common centre of gravity.

Black Hole: The region of space surrounding the totally collapsed remnant of a very massive star. In this region the gravitational field of the collapsed star is so powerful that not even light can escape.

Coma: The cloud of tenuous gas and dust surrounding the nucleus of a comet.

Comet: An object made up of dust, gas and icy material which orbits the Sun. Many comets have highly eccentric orbits.

Conjunction: The apparent close alignment of two bodies as seen from Earth. Inferior Conjunction occurs when one of the inner planets is directly between the Sun and Earth. Superior Conjunction occurs when a planet is exactly at the opposite side of the Sun as seen from Earth (and so is invisible).

Continental Drift: The theory that modern day continents were formed through the drifting of land masses.

Copernican System: The system proposed by the Polish astronomer Nicolas Copernicus which placed the Sun at the centre of the universe with the planets moving round it in circular orbits.

Cosmic Egg: The name given to the primordial mass which exploded in the Big Bang.

Crater: Walled depressions, roughly circular in shape, which range in diameter from tiny dents to features hundreds of miles across. Although craters are found on many planets and satellites, they are most prominent on the Moon.

Crust: The Earth's outermost layer which ranges in thickness from about 5 miles (8 km) under the oceans up to 40 miles (65 km) under the continental land masses. The term also refers to the Moon's outermost layer which is about 40 miles (65 km) deep (see *Mantle*).

Galaxy: A large star system which may contain up to a thousand billion stars together with interstellar material in the form of gas and dust.

Gegenschein: A very faint glow seen opposite the Sun in the sky, possibly caused by the reflection of sunlight from thinly spread interplanetary material.

Hertzsprung-Russell Diagram: A diagram which relates the temperature of a star to its brightness (see *Main Sequence*).

Kelvin Temperature Scale: The scale of temperature which starts at absolute zero — minus 273 deg C — which is the lowest possible temperature. At this point all atomic and molecular action stops.

Light Year: The distance light travels in a year — almost 6 million million miles.

Lithosphere: The crust and upper mantle of the Earth or Moon. In the case of the

The future of astronomy probably lies in observatories constructed in space or on the Moon, as in this artist's impression.

Earth the lithosphere is divided into a number of plates which move around on top of the asthenosphere.

Local Group: The cluster of galaxies of which our Milky Way Galaxy is a member.

Lunar Eclipse: An eclipse of the Moon occurs when the Moon passes into the shadow cast by the Earth.

Magnitude: The scale by which the brightness of a star or other celestial object is expressed. Apparent magnitude is the apparent brightness as seen from Earth; absolute magnitude is the apparent brightness that the object would have if viewed from a distance of 32.6 light years. Absolute magnitude is a better guide to the actual brightness of an object.

Main Sequence: The classification on the Hertzsprung-Russell diagram into which stars fall for most of their existence.

Mantle: The region of the Earth or Moon lying above the core and below the crust (see *Asthenosphere and Lithosphere*).

Maria: Dark, flat plains, a predominant feature of the lunar surface.

Mascon: (MASS-CONcentration). A region of the Moon which has a stronger than average gravitational field. This is thought to be due to relatively dense material situated below the surface.

Meteor: A particle in space, seen as a visible streak of light when it enters the Earth's atmosphere at high speed and burns up through atmospheric friction.

Meteor Radiant: The point in the sky from which shower meteors appear to originate.

Meteor Shower: The higher than normal concentration of meteors that results when Earth passes through the orbital path of a comet and intercepts relatively large amounts of cometary dust particles. Because all meteors within a particular shower follow parallel paths they all seem to radiate from one particular point — the meteor radiant.

Meteorite: A particle which is large enough to survive the fall through the atmosphere and reach the Earth's surface.

Meteoroid: General name applied to meteoritic particles in space.

Milky Way: The faint, luminous band of light seen to cross a dark sky, made up of the combined light of vast numbers of stars too faint to be seen individually. These stars lie along the plane of the Galaxy in the direction of the galactic centre.

Nebula: A cloud of gas and dust in space. Reflection nebulae shine because they reflect the light from nearby stars; emission nebulae shine because the gas is excited by energy from stars embedded within them;

dark nebulae contain no stars and appear as dark, non-luminous patches against a relatively bright background.

Nebular Hypothesis: The theory which states that the Sun and planets formed from a spinning dust and gas cloud.

Neutrino: Particles which apppear to have neither mass nor electrical charge and which are discharged from certain types of nuclear reactions such as those inside the Sun.

Neutron Star: An extremely dense object in which the protons and electrons have been forced together to form neutrons. Neutron stars are a result of the gravitational collapse of stars with masses between 1.5 and 3 times that of the Sun.

Occultation: The passage of one celestial body in front of another as seen from Earth, when the more distant object is temporarily hidden from view.

Oort's Cloud: A vast cloud of cometary material thought to surround the Solar System beyond the orbit of Pluto and from which comets are believed to originate. Its existence was first proposed in 1950 by the astronomer Jan Oort.

Opposition: The position occupied by a celestial object when it is directly opposite the Sun in the sky, and therefore due south at midnight. Usually used to refer to one of the planets with orbits greater than the Earth's.

Passing Star Theory: The theory suggesting that the planets were formed from the material dragged from the Sun by the gravitational influence of a passing star.

Planets: The major members of the Sun's family consisting of five, rocky, terrestrial objects — Mercury, Venus, Earth, Mars and Pluto — and four gaseous bodies — Jupiter, Saturn, Uranus and Neptune.

Protostar: The stage in a star's evolution before the start of nuclear reactions.

Ptolemaic Theory: The system popularized by the Greek astronomer Ptolemy which placed the Earth at the centre of the universe with the Sun, Moon and planets in orbit around it.

Pulsar: A rapidly-spinning neutron star which emits bursts of radio energy at very short, regular intervals.

Quasars: Extremely distant, highly luminous objects, now thought to be active galactic nuclei.

Retrograde Motion: 1. This term is most commonly applied to the apparent motion of an outer planet as seen from Earth. Because the Earth has a faster orbital speed it 'overtakes' the outer planet, which thus appears to move backwards in the sky.

2. Objects which orbit the Sun in a different direction to the Earth (i.e. east to west instead of west to east), or satellites which orbit their planets in a similar fashion, are also said to have retrograde motion.

Rilles: Long, snake-like features, caused by the collapse of underground channels, particularly prominent on the lunar surface.

Saros Period: A similar pattern of lunar and solar eclipses recurs after an interval of just over 18 years, known as the Saros Period.

Satellite: An object which orbits a planet, e.g., the Moon is classed as a satellite of the Earth, Titan as a satellite of Saturn, etc. The Earth also has many artificial satellites in the form of spacecraft and other objects.

Solar Eclipse: An eclipse of the Sun occurs when the Moon passes directly between the Sun and the Earth.

Solar Mass: A mass equivalent to that of the Sun.

Solar System: The Sun and the objects in its sphere of influence — planets, planetary satellites, asteroids, comets, meteoroids and interplanetary dust.

Solar Wind: The stream of energized particles emitted by the Sun which passes through the interplanetary region.

Star Cluster: A cluster of stars. Open clusters are loose collections of stars; globular clusters are vast, spherical formations of stars.

The Sun: The star closest to the Earth and the dominant member of the Solar System.

Supernova: An explosion which marks the end of a massive star and in which most of the stellar material is blown away into surrounding space.

Supernova Remnant: The gaseous remnant of a star which has undergone a supernova explosion, seen as a shell of gas expanding from the remains of the original star.

White Dwarf: The dense, collapsed remnant of a star with a mass of up to 1.4 times that of the Sun.

Zodiac: The band of sky through which the Sun and planets seem to move.

Zodiacal Light: A faint glow extending upwards from the point on the horizon at which the Sun has set, caused by the reflection of sunlight from tiny particles.

WORLD ATLAS

Map Symbols

Settlements

◌ PARIS   ■ Berne   ◉ Livorno   ◉ Brugge   ◎ Algeciras   ○ Fréjus   ○ Oberammergau   ○ Thira

Settlement symbols and type styles vary according to the scale of each map and indicate the importance of towns on the map rather than specific population figures

Ruins or Archæological Sites   ∴   Wells in Desert   ᵕ

Administration

International Boundaries   ‒‒‒‒‒

International Boundaries (Undefined)   ⸺ ⸺ ⸺

Internal Boundaries   ⸺⸺⸺

National Parks

Country Names

NICARAGUA

Administrative Area Names

KENT

CALABRIA

International boundaries show the *de facto* situation where there are rival claims to territory

Communications

Principal Roads   ⸺⸺

Other Roads   ⌒⌒

Trails and Seasonal Roads   ∼⸺∼∼⸺

Passes   ⋈

Airfields   ✧

Principal Shipping Routes   ⸻ 3386 ⸻

Principal Railways   ∼⸺

Other Railways   ⸺∼

Railways Under Construction   ∼∼⸻∼

Railways Tunnels   ⊐---⊏

Principal Canals   ⸽⸽⸽⸽⸽⸽⸽

Principal Oil Pipelines   ⸺⸺∼

Physical Features

Perennial Streams   ∽

Intermittent Streams   ------

Perennial Lakes   ⬭

Intermittent Lakes   ⬭

Swamps and Marshes

Permanent Ice and Glaciers

Elevations in metres   ▲ 8848

Sea Depths in metres   ▾ 8050

Height of Lake Surface
Above Sea Level in metres   *1134*

Elevation and Depth Tints

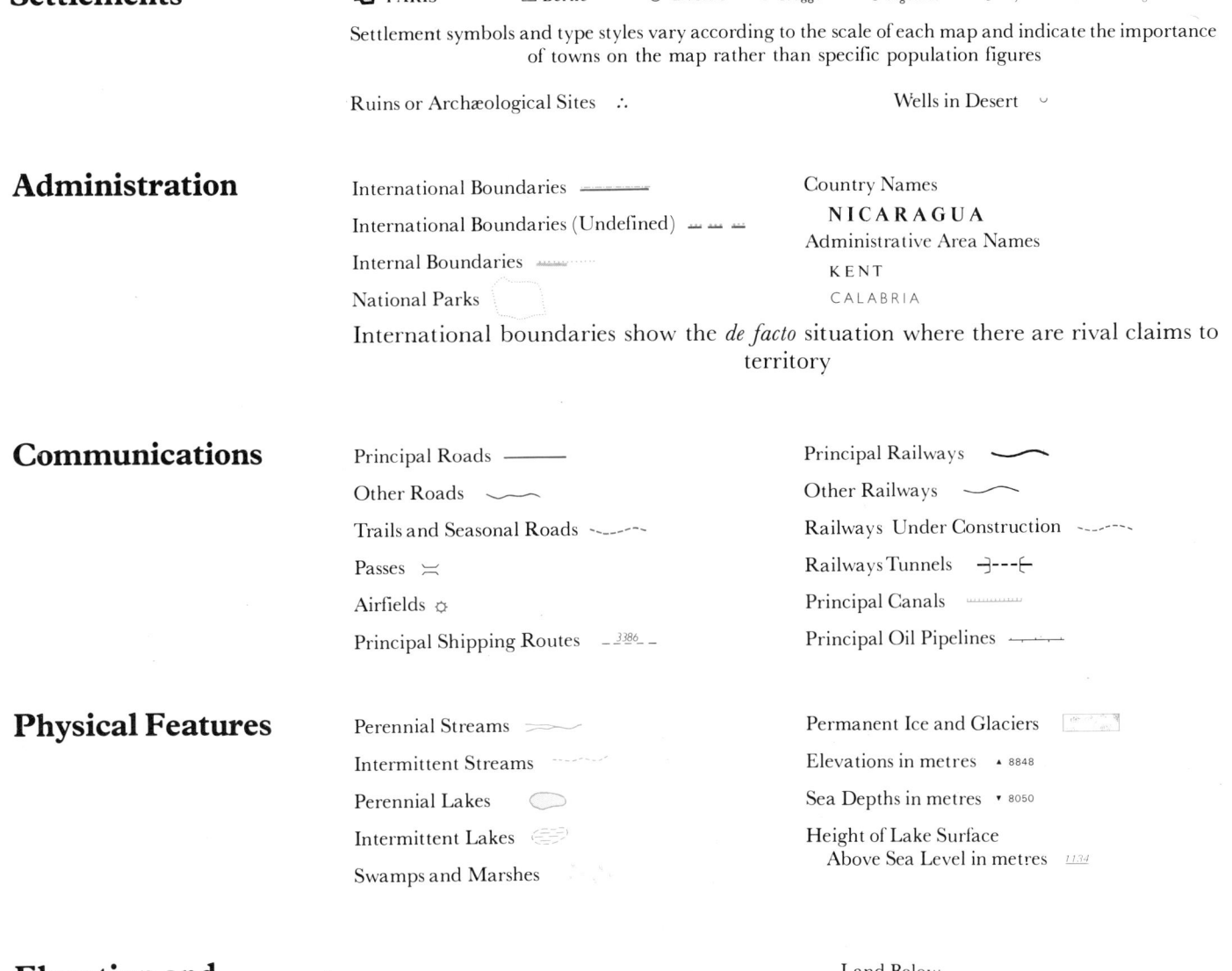

Some of the maps have different contours to highlight and clarify the principal relief features

Projection: Hammer Equal Area

ARCTIC OCEAN

Zemlya Frantsa Iosifa   Novaya Zemlya
Barents Sea   Kara   Severnaya   Laptev Sea   New Siberian Is.   East Siberian Sea
Nord Kapp   Sea   Zemlya   Tiksi   Nizhne-Kolymsk   Arctic Circle   Anadyr
Murmansk   Salekhard   Ust Port   Verkhoyansk   Bering Sea

NORWAY   Arkhangelsk   Ob   Yenisey   Lena   Vilyuysk   Kamchatka
Narvik   Oslo   SWEDEN   FINLAND   Helsinki   UNION   OF   SOVIET   SOCIALIST   REPUBLICS   Petropavlovsk-Kamchatskiy
Stockholm   Leningrad   RUSSIAN   SOVIET   FEDERATIVE   SOCIALIST   SOCIALIST   REPUBLIC   Okhotsk   Sea of   Okhotsk
DENMARK   Yaroslavl   EST.   Perm   Sverdlovsk   Tomsk   Krasnoyarsk   L.Baykal   Komsomolsk   C.Lopatka
Hamburg   WHITE   Moskva   Kazan   Novosibirsk   Novokuznetsk   Irkutsk   Ulan Ude   Khabarovsk   Sakhalin   Kuril Is.
POLAND   Warszawa   Kuybyshev   Ufa   Chelyabinsk   Omsk   Barnaul   Ulaanbaatar   Amur   Vladivostok   Sapporo
GERM   Berlin   Minsk   RUSSIA   Voronezh   Saratov   Orenburg   Irtysh   MONGOLIA   Harbin   Changchun   Hakodate
Praha   CZECH   Lvov   Kharkov   Volga   Volgograd   KAZAKHSTAN   Karaganda   Shenyang   N.KOREA   Pyŏngyang   JAPAN
Wien   AUSTRIA   Budapest   UKRAINE   Rostov   Astrakhan   Aral   L.Balkhash   Alma Ata   Beijing   Tianjin   Sŏul   Sea of   Japan   Tōkyō
Milano   ITALY   ROMANIA   Bucuresti   Odessa   Groznyy   Caspian   Sea   UZBEKISTAN   KIRGIZIA   Tashkent   Taiyuan   Dalian   S.KOREA   Kyoto   Yokohama
Roma   YUGOSLAVIA   Beograd   BULGARIA   Black   Sea   Tbilisi   Samarkand   CHINA   Jinan   Qingdao   Pusan   Kōbe   Nagoya
Barcelona   Napoli   Sardinia   Sofiya   Istanbul   Yerevan   Baku   TURKMENISTAN   Dushanbe   Lanzhou   Xi'an   Huang   Ho   Kitakyūshū   Ōsaka
Tunis   Sicily   Athinai   GREECE   TURKEY   Ankara   Tabriz   Ashkhabad   AFGHANISTAN   Kabul   Srinagar   XIZANG   (TIBET)   Lhasa   Chengdu   Wuhan   Nanjing   Shanghai
MALTA   Crete   CYPRUS   Halab   SYRIA   Dimashq   Baghdād   Tehrān   Mashhad   Rawalpindi   Lahore   Chongqing   Chang Jiang   Changsha   East China   Sea
Tarābulus   Banghāzī   El Iskandariya   Bayrūt   Amman   IRAQ   IRAN   (PERSIA)   Esfahan   PAKISTAN   Delhi   NEPAL   Kanpur   Lucknow   Fuzhou   PACIFIC
Mediterranean Sea   El Tel Aviv-Yafo   JORDAN   Abādān   Shiraz   Agra   Ganga   Chang   Guangzhou   TAIWAN   (FORMOSA)   Taibei   OCEAN
LIBYA   El Qāhira   EGYPT   Nile   KUWAIT   The Gulf   Karachi   INDIA   Kunming   Hong Kong   Tropic of Cancer
Aswān   Ar Riyād   QATAR   BAHRAIN   U.A.E.   Ahmadabad   Nagpur   Dhaka   BURMA   Mandalay   Hanoi   Hainan   South China   Sea
Red   SAUDI   OMAN   Arabian   Bombay   Pune   Bay of   Bengal   Rangoon   VIET   NAM   Manila
NIGER   CHAD   Omdurmân   El Khartûm   Sea   YEMEN   ARABIA   Sea   Hyderabad   Madras   Andaman Is.   THAILAND   Bangkok   PHILIPPINES
Kano   SUDAN   SOUTH   YEMEN   Aden   Gulf of Aden   Socotra   (S.Yemen)   Bangalore   (India)   Nicobar Is.   CAMBODIA   Cebu
NIGERIA   L.Chad   Ndjamena   Asmera   DJIBOUTI   Lakshadweep Is.   (India)   Phanh Bho   Ho Chi Minh   Phnom Penh   Yap   Marshall Is.
Abidjan   CAMEROON   CENTRAL   AFRICAN   REPUBLIC   Addis Abeba   ETHIOPIA   SRI LANKA   (CEYLON)   MALAYSIA   Belau   Guam   Wake I.   (U.S)
EQUAT. GUINEA   Douala   Bangui   ZAIRE   SOMALI REP.   Colombo   Dondra Hd.   Medan   Kuala Lumpur   BRUNEI   SABAH   Northern   Marianas   (U.S)
Libreville   Yaoundé   (CONGO)   Kisangani   KENYA   L.Turkana   MALDIVES   PEN. MALAYSIA   Kuching   Caroline Is.   Truk   Ponape   TRUST TERRITORY OF
SAO TOME   CONGO   Kasai   UGANDA   Kampala   Victoria   Nairobi   INDIAN   SINGAPORE   Borneo   THE PACIFIC ISLANDS   (U.S)   KIRIBATI
PRINCIPE   GABON   Brazzaville   Kinshasa   Equator   Sumatera   Sulawesi   Maluku   NAURU
CABINDA   Luanda   TANZANIA   Mombasa   Zanzibar   Dar es Salaam   Amirante   Is.   Chagos Arch.   (Br.)   Palembang   INDONESIA   Irian   PAPUA   New Ireland
ANGOLA   Benguela   Lubumbashi   L.   Tanganyika   SEYCHELLES   OCEAN   Aldabra   Jakarta   Ujung Pandang   Jawa   Surabaya   Banjarmasin   Jaya   NEW   Rabaul   New   SOLOMON IS.   TUVALU
ZAMBIA   Lusaka   Malawi   COMORO   Diego Garcia   (Br.)   Bandung   Java   Sunda Islands   Timor   GUINEA   Port   Moresby   Britain   Louisiade   Arch.   Santa Cruz Is.
Lusaka   MALAWI   Zomba   MADAGASCAR   Christmas I.   (Australia)   Arafura Sea   C.York   VANUATU   Vanua Levu
NAMIBIA   ZIMBABWE   Bulawayo   Harare   MOZAMBIQUE   Antananarivo   Rodriguez   Cocos   (Keeling Is.)   (Australia)   Timor Sea   Darwin   New   Caledonia   FIJI   Viti Levu   Suva
Windhoek   BOTSWANA   Mozambique Chan.   MAURITIUS   Réunion   (Fr.)   NORTHERN   TERRITORY   Townsville   Cairns   Norfolk I.   (Australia)
WEST   Gaborone   Pretoria   Maputo   SWAZ   Tropic of Capricorn   North West C.   WESTERN   QUEENSLAND   Alice Springs   Rockhampton
SOUTH   AFRICA   Johannesburg   LES.   Durban   AUSTRALIA   AUSTRALIA   SOUTH   AUSTRALIA   Brisbane
Cape Town   C.of Good Hope   Port Elizabeth   Amsterdam   (Fr.)   St.Paul   (Fr.)   Perth   Kalgoorlie-Boulder   NEW SOUTH   WALES   Lord Howe   (Australia)
Pr.Edward Is.   (South Africa)   Crozet Is.   (Fr.)   Kerguelen   (Fr.)   Fremantle   C.Leeuwin   Great   Australian   Bight   Adelaide   VICTORIA   Sydney   Canberra   Newcastle   North C.   Auckland   North I.
SOUTHERN   OCEAN   McDonald I.   (Australia)   Heard I.   (Australia)   TASMANIA   Melbourne   Tasman   Sea   NEW   ZEALAND   Wellington   C.Farewell   Christchurch
Bouvet I.   (Nor.)   Hobart   Stewart I.   Bounty Is.   (N.Z)   South I.   Dunedin
Enderby Land   Antarctic Circle   Antipodes Is.   (N.Z)   Auckland I.   (N.Z)
d Land   DEPENDENCY   Wilkes Land   Macquarie I.   (Australia)   Campbell I.   (N.Z)
East from Greenwich   AUSTRALIAN DEPENDENCY   TERRE ADELIE   Balleny Is.   Ross Sea

80 180 160 140 120 100 80 60 40 20

Queen Elizabeth Is.   Ellesmere I.

North Magnetic Pole   **Greenland**

Bering Str.   Yukon   Victoria I.   **Baffin**   Davis Str.

60   Mt. McKinley   Gt. Bear L.   **Island**   Arctic O.

Bering   Sea   Gt. Slave L.   Hudson Str.   C. Farewell   **Iceland**

Aleutian Is.   Hudson   Bay   Labrador   **British Isles**

Vancouver I.   L. Winnipeg   Great Lakes   **Newfoundland**

40   St. Lawrence   C. Race   **Ib**

Mt. Whitney   Arkansas   Ohio   Appalachian Mts.   **Azores**   Str. of Gibraltar

4418   Missouri   Mississippi   C. Hatteras

Lower California   Rio Grande   **Bermuda**   **Canary Is.**   **Atlas**

Hawaiian Is.   Gulf of Mexico   Florida Str.   **Bahama Islands**   **A T L A N T I C**   Tropic of C

20   Mauna Kea   Popocatepetl   **Cuba**   Hispaniola   **S**

4202   5452   Yucatan   **Greater Antilles**   C.Verde Is.   C. Verde

Citlaltepetl   Jamaica   **Lesser Antilles**

5700   **Caribbean Sea**

P A C I F I C   Isthmus of Panama   Orinoco   **Guiana Highlands**   **O C E A N**   C. Palmas   **G**

Palmyra Is.   Llanos   Roraima 2772

Tabuaeran   Galapagos Is.   Chimborazo   Negro

Kiritimati   6267   **Selvas**   Amazon   C. de São Roque   Equator

0

Madeira   Tocantins   **Ascension**

Phoenix Is.   Marquesas Is.   **Mato Grosso**   St. Helena

Tokelau Is.   **O C E A N**   Society Is.   Tuamotu Archipelago   Paraguay   **Brazilian Highlands**

Samoa Is.   Tahiti   L. Titicaca   Gran Chaco   C. Frio

Cook Is.   Paraná

20   Tonga Is.   Tubuai Is.   Atacama Desert   **Pampas**   R. de la Plata   Tropic of Capr

Pitcairn I.   Ojos del Salado   **A n d e s**

Easter I.   6863   Paraná   Tristan da C

Kermadec Is.   Aconcagua   Negro

6960   **Patagonia**

Chatham Is.   40   Falkland Is.   S. Georgia

Tierra del Fuego

Magellan's Str.   C. Horn   **Drake Passage**

60   **Antarctic Peninsula**   **Weddell Sea**

Graham Land   Palmer Land   Caird Coast

Ross Sea   Byrd Land   Ellsworth Land   **Coats Land**   20

80   180   160   140   120   100   80   60   40   West from Gree

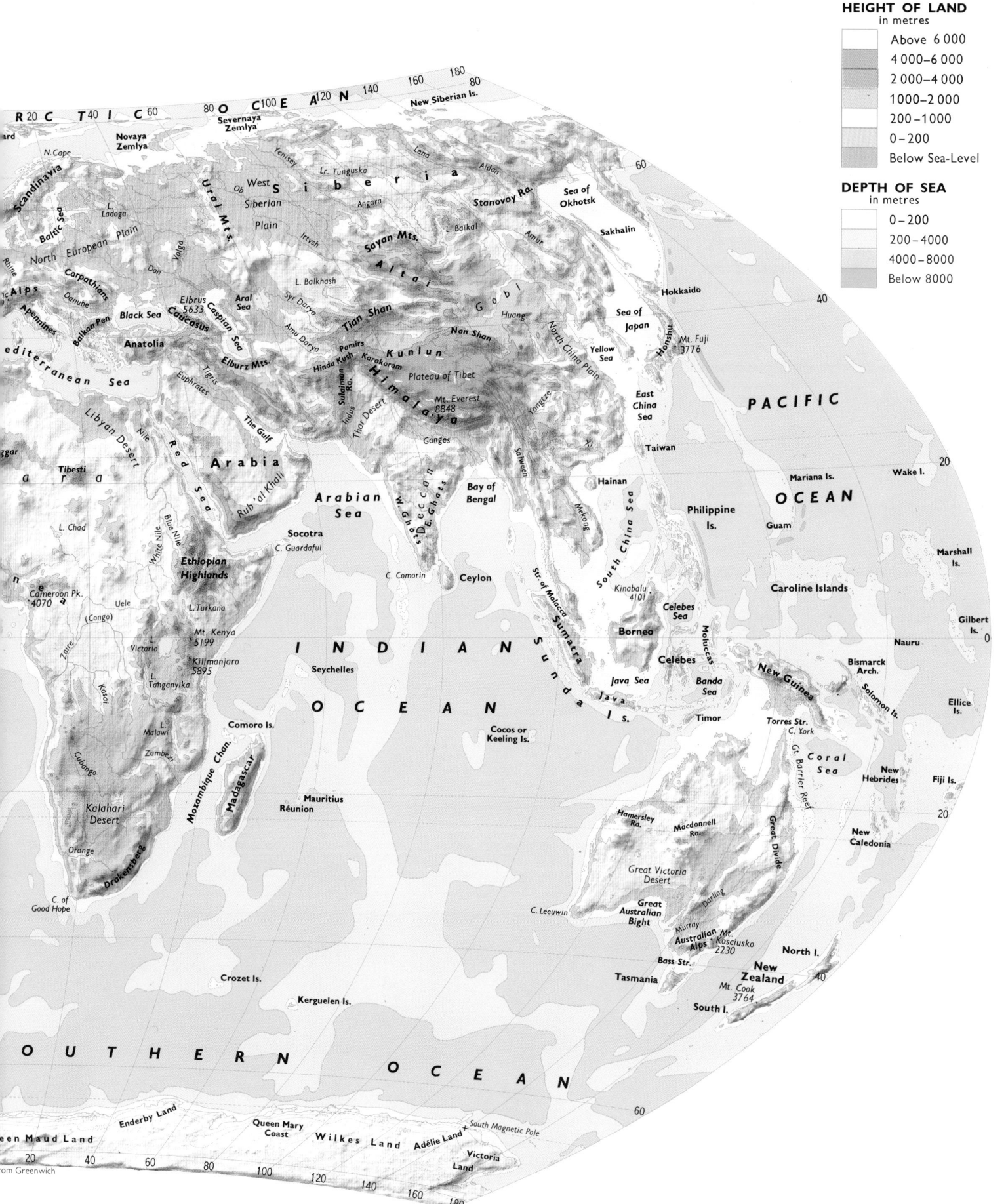

HEIGHT OF LAND
in metres
Above 6 000
4 000–6 000
2 000–4 000
1000–2 000
200–1000
0–200
Below Sea-Level

DEPTH OF SEA
in metres
0–200
200–4000
4000–8000
Below 8000

R 20 C T 40 I C 60   O   C 80 100 E 120 A 140 N 160   180 80
New Siberian Is.

N. Cape
Novaya
Zemlya
Severnaya
Zemlya
Scandinavia
L.
Ladoga
Baltic
Sea
Ob
West
Siberian
Plain
S i b e r i a
Yenisey
Lr. Tunguska
Lena
Aldan
Angora
Stanovoy Ra.
Sea of
Okhotsk
60
North European Plain
Ural Mts.
Irtysh
Sayan Mts.
L. Baikal
Amur
Sakhalin
Rhine
Volga
Don
L. Balkhash
A l t a i
Hokkaido
Carpathians
Alps
Apennines
Danube
Aral
Sea
Elbrus
5633
Caspian Sea
Tian Shan
G o b i
Huang
Sea of
Japan
40
Black Sea
Caucasus
Syr Darya
Nan Shan
North China Plain
Honshu
Mt. Fuji
3776
Balkan Pen.
Anatolia
Amu Darya
Pamirs
Kunlun
Yellow
Sea
editerranean   Sea
Elburz Mts.
Hindu Kush
Karakoram
Plateau of Tibet
East
China
Sea
PACIFIC
Tigris
Euphrates
Suleiman Ra.
H i m a l a y a
Mt. Everest
8848
Yangtze
Nile
Libyan Desert
The Gulf
Thar Desert
Ganges
Salween
Xi
Taiwan
20
zgar
a
r
a
Tibesti
Red Sea
Arabia
Rub' al Khali
W. Ghats
Deccan
E. Ghats
Bay of
Bengal
Mekong
Hainan
South China Sea
OCEAN
Mariana Is.
Wake I.
L. Chad
Arabian
Sea
Socotra
C. Guardafui
C. Comorin
Ceylon
Str. of Malacca
Philippine
Is.
Guam
Cameroon Pk.
4070
(Congo)
Uele
Ethiopian
Highlands
L. Turkana
Seychelles
I N D I A N
S u m a t r a
S u n d a   I s.
Kinabalu
4101
Caroline Islands
Marshall
Is.
Zaire
L.
Victoria
Mt. Kenya
5199
Borneo
Celebes
Sea
Gilbert
Is.
0
Kasai
Kilimanjaro
5895
O C E A N
Java Sea
Celebes
Moluccas
New Guinea
Nauru
L.
Tanganyika
Comoro Is.
Cocos or
Keeling Is.
Java
Banda
Sea
Timor
Bismarck
Arch.
Ellice
Is.
Cubango
Mozambique Chan.
Madagascar
Mauritius
Réunion
Torres Str.
C. York
Coral
Sea
New
Hebrides
Fiji Is.
Kalahari
Desert
L.
Malawi
Zambezi
Hamersley
Ra.
Macdonnell
Ra.
Gt. Barrier Reef
Great Divide
20
Orange
Drakensberg
Great Victoria
Desert
New
Caledonia
C. of
Good Hope
C. Leeuwin
Great
Australian
Bight
Murray
Darling
Australian
Alps
Mt.
Kosciusko
2230
North I.
Crozet Is.
Bass Str.
New
Zealand
Kerguelen Is.
Tasmania
Mt. Cook
3764
South I.
40
OUTHERN   O C E A N
60
Enderby Land
Queen Mary
Coast
Wilkes Land
Adélie Land
South Magnetic Pole
een Maud Land
20
40
60
80
100
120
140
160
180
Victoria
Land
rom Greenwich

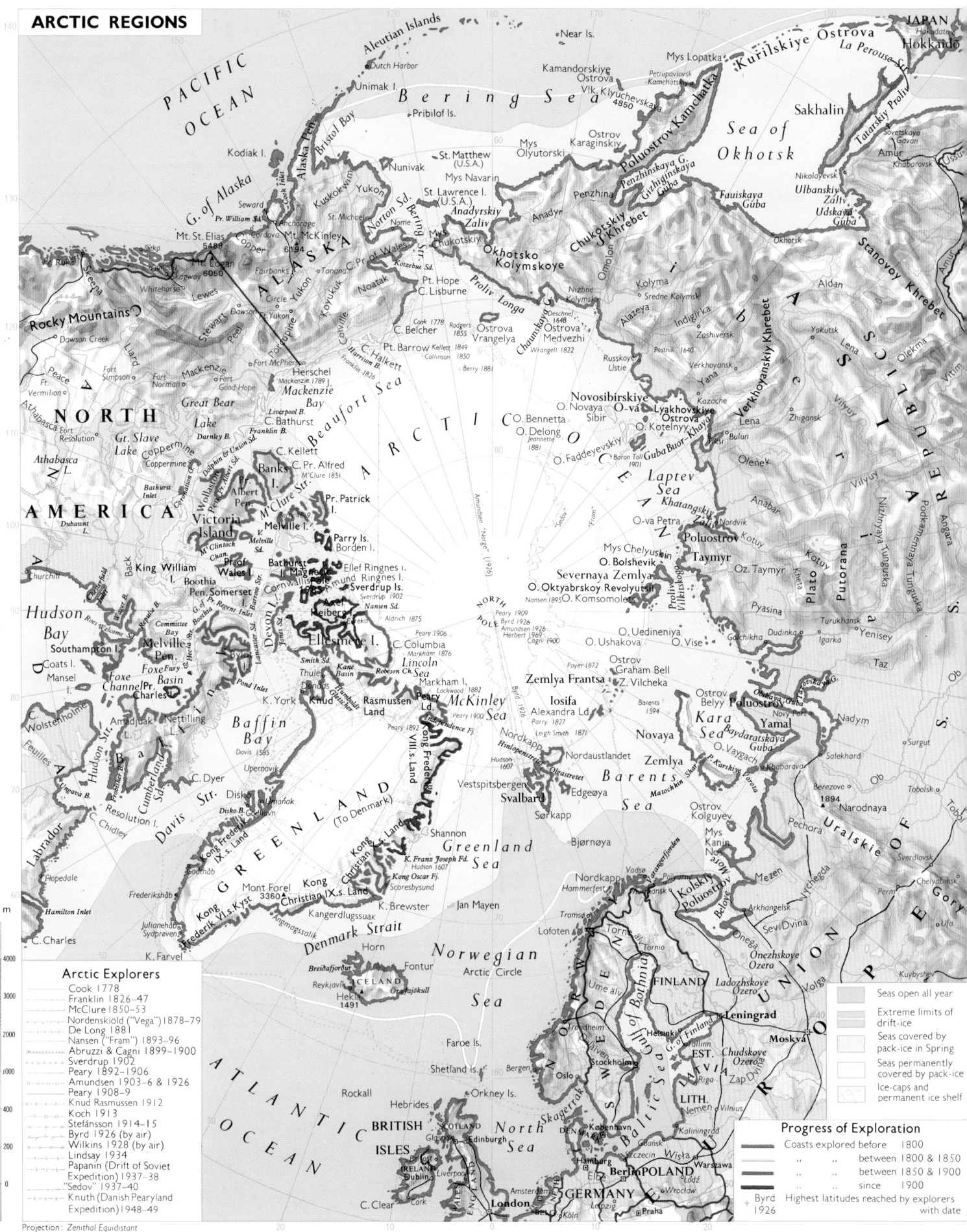

ARCTIC REGIONS

PACIFIC OCEAN

Aleutian Islands
Near Is.
Dutch Harbor
Unimak I.
Bering Sea
JAPAN
Hokkaido
La Perouse Str.
Kurilskiye Ostrova
Mys Lopatka
Kamandorskiye Ostrova
Petropavlovsk-Kamchatskiy
Vlk. Klyuchevskaya 4850
Poluostrov Kamchatka
Sakhalin
Sea of Okhotsk
Tatarskiy Proliv
Sovetskaya Gavan
Amur
Khabarovsk
Pribilof Is.
St. Matthew (U.S.A.)
Mys Olyutorski
Ostrov Karaginskiy
Penzhinskaya G.
Gizhiginskaya Guba
Nikolayevsk
Ulbanskiy Zaliv
Udskaya Guba
Stanovoy Khrebet
Ussuri
Kodiak I.
G. of Alaska
Seward
Pr. William Sd.
Anchorage
Cordova
Cook Inlet
Kenai Pen.
Alaska Pen.
Bristol Bay
Kuskokwim
Nunivak
Yukon
Norton Sd.
Bering Str.
Nome
St. Michael
St Lawrence I. (U.S.A.)
Mys Navarin
Anadyrskiy Zaliv
Anadyr
Penzhina
Okhotsko Kolymskoye
Chukotskiy Khrebet
Okhotsk
Fauiskaya Guba
ALASKA
Mt. St. Elias 5488
Mt. McKinley 6194
Copper
Mt. Logan 6050
Fairbanks
Tanana
C. Pr. of Wales
Kotzebue Sd.
Mys Chukotskiy
Proliv Longa
Omolon
Kolyma
Sredne Kolymsk
Nizhne Kolymsk
Aldan
Whitehorse
Lewes
Skagway
Circle
Yukon
Koyukuk
Noatak
Pt. Hope
C. Lisburne
Cook 1778
Rodgers 1855
Ostrova Vrangelya
Ostrova Medvezhi
Wrangell 1822
Alazeya
Indigirka
Zashiversk
Postmin 1640
Yakutsk
Lena
Vilyuy
Zhigansk
Bulun
Olekma
ROCKY MOUNTAINS
Dawson Creek
Stewart
Peel
Porcupine
Fort Yukon
Dawson
C. Belcher
Pt. Barrow
C. Halkett
Kellett 1849
Collinson 1850
Berry 1881
Deshnet 1648
Russkoye Ustie
Verkhoyansk
Yana
Kazache
Verkhoyanskiy Khrebet
Vitim
Peace
Ft. Vermilion
Liard
Fort Simpson
Fort Norman
Fort Good Hope
Fort McPherson
Herschel I.
Mackenzie 1789
Mackenzie Bay
Liverpool B.
C. Bathurst
Darnley B.
Franklin I.
Beaufort Sea
Franklin 1826
Harrison 1826
A R C T I C   O C E A N
O. Novaya Sibir
O-va Lyakhovskiye
O. Kotelnyy
Novosibirskiye Ostrova
Kazache
Lena
Nordvik
Olenek
Yakutsk
ATHABASCA L.
Fort Resolution
Great Bear Lake
Gt. Slave Lake
Coppermine
Dolphin & Union Str.
N O R T H
Dubawnt L.
Bathurst Inlet
Coronation Gulf
Wollaston Pen.
Banks I.
C. Pr. Alfred
McClure 1851
Prince Patrick I.
O. Bennetta
O. Delong
Jeannette 1881
O. Faddeyevskiy
Baron Toll 1901
Guba Buor-Khaya
A M E R I C A
Victoria Island
McClintock Chan.
Prince of Wales I.
V. Melville Sd.
Melville I.
M'Clure Str.
Parry Is.
Borden I.
Ellef Ringnes I.
Amund Ringnes I.
Sverdrup Is.
Sverdrup 1902
Nansen Sd.
Lincoln Sea
Aldrich 1875
Laptev Sea
Khatangskiy Zaliv
O-va Petra
Mys Chelyuskin
O. Bolshevik
Severnaya Zemlya
O. Oktyabrskoy Revolyutsii
O. Komsomolets
Nansen 1895
Poluostrov Taymyr
Oz. Taymyr
Kheta
Kotuy
Plato Putorana
Pyasina
Anabar
King William I.
Boothia Pen.
Somerset I.
Cornwallis I.
Bathurst I.
Magnetic Pole
G. of Pr. Regent Inlet
Devon I.
Axel Heiberg
Ellesmere I.
C. Columbia
Markham 1876
NORTH POLE
Amundsen "Norge" (1926)
Peary 1909
Byrd 1926
Amundsen 1926
Herbert 1969
Cagni 1900
O. Uedineniya
O. Vise
O. Ushakova
Turukhansk
Dudinka
Igarka
Yenisey
Taz
Ob
HUDSON BAY
Churchill
Southampton I.
Coats I.
Mansel
Melville Pen.
Foxe Channel
Pr. Charles I.
Foxe Basin
Committee Bay
Repulse B.
Boothia
Fury & Hecla Str.
Lancaster Sd.
Jones Sd.
Smith Sd.
Kane Basin
Robeson Ch. Sea
Markham I.
Lockwood 1882
Peary Ld.
Rasmussen Land
Knud
K. York
Thule
Independence Fj.
McKinley Sea
Peary 1906
Peary 1900
Peary 1892
Payer 1872
Zemlya Frantsa Iosifa
Alexandra Ld
Parry 1827
Leigh Smith 1871
Ostrov Graham Bell
Z. Vilcheka
Barents 1594
Ostrov Belyy
Poluostrov Yamal
Baydaratskaya Guba
Oskara Guba
Novy Port
Nadym
Salekhard
Surgut
Ob
Coppermine
Back
Dubawnt L.
Coats I.
Mansel
Nettilling L.
Amadjuak L.
Wolstenholme
Baffin Bay
Davis 1585
Upernavik
Pond Inlet
Disko B.
Godhavn
Umanak
K. Frederik VIII.s Land
Danmarkshavn
Kong Frederik VIII.s Land
V. Frantsa
Novaya Zemlya
Kara Sea
Matochkin Shar
Malyye Karmakuly
P. Karskiye Vorota
Ostrov Vaygach
Ostrov Kolguyev
Narodnaya 1894
Pechora
Uralskie Gory
U N I O N   O F
Labrador
Hopedale
Ungava B.
C. Chidley
Resolution I.
Cumberland Sd.
Davis Str.
C. Dyer
Disko
Holsteinsborg
Sukkertoppen
GREENLAND
(To Denmark)
Shannon
K. Franz Joseph Fd.
Hudson 1607
Kong Oscar Fj.
Scoresbysund
Greenland Sea
Nordaustlandet
Vestspitsbergen
Svalbard
Sørkapp
Edgeøya
Ostrov Kolguyev
Barents Sea
Mys Kanin Nos
Mezen
Narodnaya 1894
Berezovo
Tobolsk
Tobol
Hamilton Inlet
C. Charles
Julianehåb
Sydproven
K. Farvel
Kong Frederik VI.s Kyst
Mont Forel 3360
Kong Christian IX.s Land
Angmagssalik
Kangerdlugssuak
K. Brewster
Jan Mayen
Bjørnøya
Nordkapp
Hammerfest
Vadsø
Varangerfjorden
Kolskiy Poluostrov
Beloye More
Arkhangelsk
Sev. Dvina
Onega
Onezhskoye Ozero
Chudskoye Ozero
Perm
Chelyabinsk
Sverdlovsk
Ufa
Frederikshåb
Godthåb
Mont Forel 3360
Christian IX.s Land
Denmark Strait
Horn
Breidafjörður
Reykjavík
ICELAND
Hekla 1491
Öræfajökull
Norwegian Sea
Fontur
Arctic Circle
Tromsø
Lofoten
Narvik
Bodø
Torne
Tornio
Ume älv
FINLAND
Helsinki
Leningrad
Moskvá
Ladozhskoye Ozero
Onezhskoye Ozero
Volga
Kuybyshev
Faroe Is.
Shetland Is.
N O R W A Y
S W E D E N
Trondheim
Bergen
Oslo
Stockholm
Gulf of Bothnia
Gulf of Finland
Tallinn
EST.
Chudskoye Ozero
LATVIA
Riga
Zap. Dvina
LITH.
Vilnius
Nemen
ATLANTIC OCEAN
Rockall
Hebrides
Orkney Is.
North Sea
Skagerrak
København
DENMARK
Kattegat
Gdańsk
Kaliningrad
Szczecin
BRITISH ISLES
SCOTLAND
Glasgow
Edinburgh
ENGLAND
IRELAND
Dublin
Liverpool
London
C. Clear
Cork
Hamburg
Berlin
POLAND
Warszawa
Wisła
Łódź
Wrocław
GERMANY
Amsterdam
BEL.
Köln
Elbe
Leipzig
Praha

U N I O N   O F   S O V I E T   S O C I A L I S T   R E P U B L I C S

E U R O P E

Arctic Explorers
.... Cook 1778
—·—·— Franklin 1826–47
·········· McClure 1850–53
·-·-·-·- Nordenskiöld ("Vega")1878–79
·········· De Long 1881
—·—·— Nansen ("Fram") 1893–96
++++++ Abruzzi & Cagni 1899–1900
········· Sverdrup 1902
·-·-·-· Peary 1892–1906
·········· Amundsen 1903–6 & 1926
········· Peary 1908–9
·········· Knud Rasmussen 1912
—·—·— Koch 1913
++++++ Stefánsson 1914–15
·-·-·-· Byrd 1926 (by air)
········· Wilkins 1928 (by air)
·········· Lindsay 1934
·-·-·-· Papanin (Drift of Soviet
          Expedition) 1937–38
········· "Sedov" 1937–40
—·—·— Knuth (Danish Pearyland
          Expedition) 1948–49

Seas open all year
Extreme limits of drift-ice
Seas covered by pack-ice in Spring
Seas permanently covered by pack-ice
Ice-caps and permanent ice shelf

Progress of Exploration
——— Coasts explored before 1800
———   ,,   ,,   between 1800 & 1850
———   ,,   ,,   between 1850 & 1900
———   ,,   ,,   since 1900
+ Byrd 1926   Highest latitudes reached by explorers with date

Projection: Zenithal Equidistant

ft   m
12,000 4000
9000 3000
6000 2000
3000 1000
      400
      200
0   0

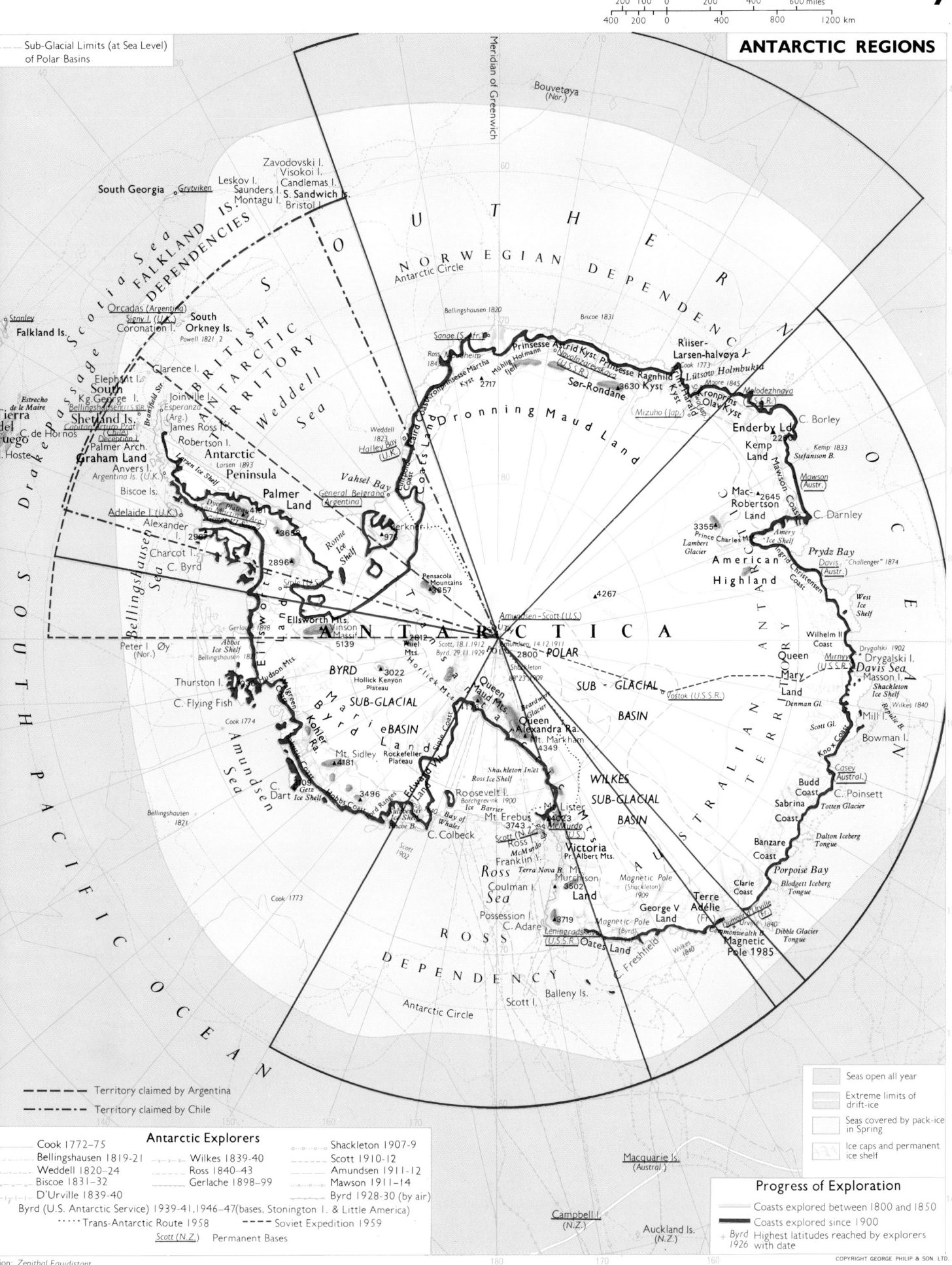

1:35 000 000

200 100 0 200 400 600 miles

400 200 0 400 800 1200 km

Sub-Glacial Limits (at Sea Level) of Polar Basins

Meridian of Greenwich

Bouvetøya (Nor.)

SOUTHERN

Zavodovski I.
Visokoi I.
Leskov I.
Candlemas I.
Saunders I.
Montagu I.
Bristol I.
S. Sandwich Is.

South Georgia _Grytviken_

Scotia Sea

NORWEGIAN DEPENDENCY

Antarctic Circle

Bellingshausen 1820

Biscoe 1831

FALKLAND IS.
DEPENDENCIES

Orcadas (Argentina)
Signy I. (U.K.) **South
Coronation I. Orkney Is.**
Powell 1821-2

Sange (S. Afr.) Ls.

Prinsesse Astrid Kyst Prinsesse Ragnhild
Cook 1773 Kyst
Mühlig Holmann Novolazarevskaya
(U.S.S.R.)

Riiser-
Larsen-halvøya
Lützow Holmbukta

D E P E N D E N C Y

Stanley
Falkland Is.

Estrecho
de la Maire

Tierra
del
Fuego

Clarence I.

**South
Kg George I.
Shetland Is.**
Bellingshausen (U.S.S.R.)
Deception I.
Capitan Arturo Prat (Chile)

Elephant I.

Joinville I.
Esperanza
(Arg.)
James Ross I.
Robertson I.

BRITISH
ANTARCTIC
TERRITORY

Weddell
Sea

Coats Land

Coats Land

Ross Mühlheim
1842

Prinsesse Martha
Kyst 2717

Dronning Maud Land

Sør-Rondane 3630 Kyst

Møre 1845

Kronprins
Olav Kyst

Mizuho (Jap.)

Malodezhnaya
(U.S.S.R.)

Enderby Ld
C. Borley
22
Kemp Kemp 1833
Land Stefansson I.
Mawson
(Austr.)

Anvers I.
Argentina Is. (U.K.)
Biscoe Is.

**Graham
Land**

Palmer Arch.

Antarctic
Peninsula

Larsen 1893

Palmer
Land

Weddell
1823
Halley Bay
(U.K.)

Vahsel Bay

General Belgrano
(Argentina)

INDIAN

Mac-
Robertson
Land

C. Darnley

Prince Charles Mts.
3355 Amery
Lambert Ice Shelf
Glacier

Prydz Bay

Davis "Challenger" 1874
(Austr.)

Adelaide I. (U.K.)
**Alexander
I.** 290

Charcot I.
C. Byrd

2896

Ronne Ice
Shelf

970

Pensacola
Mountains
3657

American
Highland

West
Ice
Shelf

OCEAN

Bellingshausen
Sea

Peter I. Øy
(Nor.)

Abbot
Ice Shelf
Bellingshausen 1821

Ellsworth Mts.
Vinson
Massif
5139

Thiel
Mts.

4267

Amundsen-Scott (U.S.)

Scott, 18.1.1912
Byrd, 29.11.1929
2800 Amundsen 14.12.1911 POLAR
SOUTH POLE
Shackleton

Wilhelm II
Coast

Queen
Mary
Land

Murnyy
(U.S.S.R.)

Drygalski 1902
Davis Sea
Masson I.
Shackleton
Ice Shelf

ANTARCTICA

SOUTH PACIFIC

Thurston I.

C. Flying Fish

Cook 1774

Gerlache 1898

BYRD
Hollick Kenyon
Plateau
3022

Horlick Mts.

SUB-GLACIAL
BASIN

Vostok (U.S.S.R.)

Denman Gl.

Scott Gl.

Mill I.
Knox Coast
Bowman I.

Amundsen
Sea

Mt. Sidley
4181

SUB-GLACIAL
eBASIN

Marie
Byrd
Land

Rockefeller
Plateau

Kohler
Ra.

Queen
Maud Mts.

Beardmore
Glacier

Queen
Alexandra Ra.
Mt. Markham
4349

WILKES
SUB-GLACIAL
BASIN

Casey
(Austr.)

Budd
Coast

Sabrina
Coast

C. Poinsett

Totten Glacier

OCEAN

Bellingshausen
1821

C. Dart
Getz
Ice Shelf

3496

Ross Ice Shelf

Shackleton Inlet

Roosevelt I.
Ross
Ice Barrier

Borchgrevink 1900

Bay of
Whales

Cook 1773

Cook 1773

C. Colbeck

Scott (N.Z.)
Scott
1902

McMurdo

Mt. Erebus
3743
Ross I.
McMurdo
(U.S.)

Mt. Lister
4023

Victoria

Pr. Albert Mts.

Franklin I.
Terra Nova B.

AUSTRALIAN ANTARCTIC TERRITORY

Banzare
Coast

Dalton Iceberg
Tongue

Porpoise Bay

Blodgett Iceberg
Tongue

Clarie
Coast

**Terre
Adélie**
(Fr.)

Dumont d'Urville 1840

ROSS

Ross
Sea

Coulman I.

Possession I.

C. Adare

DEPENDENCY

Balleny Is.

Scott I.

Antarctic Circle

Murchison
Land 3502

Magnetic Pole
(Shackleton)
1909

3719

Magnetic Pole
(Byrd)

Leningradskaya
(U.S.S.R.) Oates Land

George V
Land

C. Freshfield

Commonwealth B.

Wilkes
1840

Dibble Glacier
Tongue

**Magnetic
Pole 1985**

Territory claimed by Argentina

Territory claimed by Chile

Macquarie Is.
(Austral.)

Seas open all year

Extreme limits of
drift-ice

Seas covered by pack-ice
in Spring

Ice caps and permanent
ice shelf

Antarctic Explorers

Cook 1772–75
Bellingshausen 1819–21
Weddell 1820–24
Biscoe 1831–32
D'Urville 1839–40

Wilkes 1839–40
Ross 1840–43
Gerlache 1898–99

Shackleton 1907-9
Scott 1910-12
Amundsen 1911-12
Mawson 1911–14
Byrd 1928-30 (by air)

Byrd (U.S. Antarctic Service) 1939-41,1946–47(bases, Stonington I. & Little America)

Trans-Antarctic Route 1958   Soviet Expedition 1959

Scott (N.Z.)   Permanent Bases

Progress of Exploration

Coasts explored between 1800 and 1850

Coasts explored since 1900

+ Byrd
1926 Highest latitudes reached by explorers
with date

ection: Zenithal Equidistant

COPYRIGHT GEORGE PHILIP & SON LTD

ARCTIC OCEAN
Svalbard
Greenland Sea
Norwegian Sea
Barents Sea
Kara Sea
Novaya Zemlya
Severnaya Zemlya
Zemlya Frantsa Iosifa
Jan Mayen
ICELAND
Reykjavik
GREENLAND
Denmark Strait
Baffin Bay
Davis Strait
Baffin Island
Ellesmere Island
Queen Elizabeth Islands
Hudson Bay
James Bay
Labrador
Labrador Basin
Newfoundland
Grand Banks
Nova Scotia
Beaufort Sea
CANADA
UNITED STATES
Montreal
Toronto
Ottawa
Boston
New York
Philadelphia
Baltimore
Washington
Chicago
Detroit
Winnipeg
St. Louis
New Orleans
Houston
Dallas
Denver
Miami
Gulf of Mexico
Florida
Bermuda
Sargasso Sea
West Indies
BAHAMAS
CUBA
La Habana
Caribbean Sea
Hispaniola
MEXICO
Mexico
HONDURAS
NICARAGUA
COLOMBIA
Bogotá
VENEZUELA
Caracas
North American Basin
NORTH ATLANTIC OCEAN
Mid-Atlantic Ridge
Azores
Canary Basin
Cape Verde Basin
Tropic of Cancer
Madeira
Islas Canarias
C. VERDE IS.
Dakar
SENEGAL
MAURITANIA
WESTERN SAHARA
MOROCCO
Casablanca
ALGERIA
Alger
TUNISIA
LIBYA
NIGER
CHAD
NIGERIA
Lagos
GHANA
Accra
BENIN
TOGO
BURKINA FASO
CAMEROON
Gulf of Guinea
Sahara
Mediterranean Sea
PORTUGAL
Lisboa
SPAIN
Madrid
Barcelona
FRANCE
Paris
Bay of Biscay
UNITED KINGDOM
London
Glasgow
Dublin
North Sea
Amsterdam
Hamburg
Berlin
POLAND
Warszawa
SWEDEN
Stockholm
Oslo
FINLAND
Helsinki
Leningrad
U.S.S.R.
Moskva
Roma
Napoli
GREECE
ROMANIA
BULGARIA
YUGOSLAVIA
HUNGARY
AUSTRIA
CZECHOSLOVAKIA
Sicilia
Sardegna
Corse

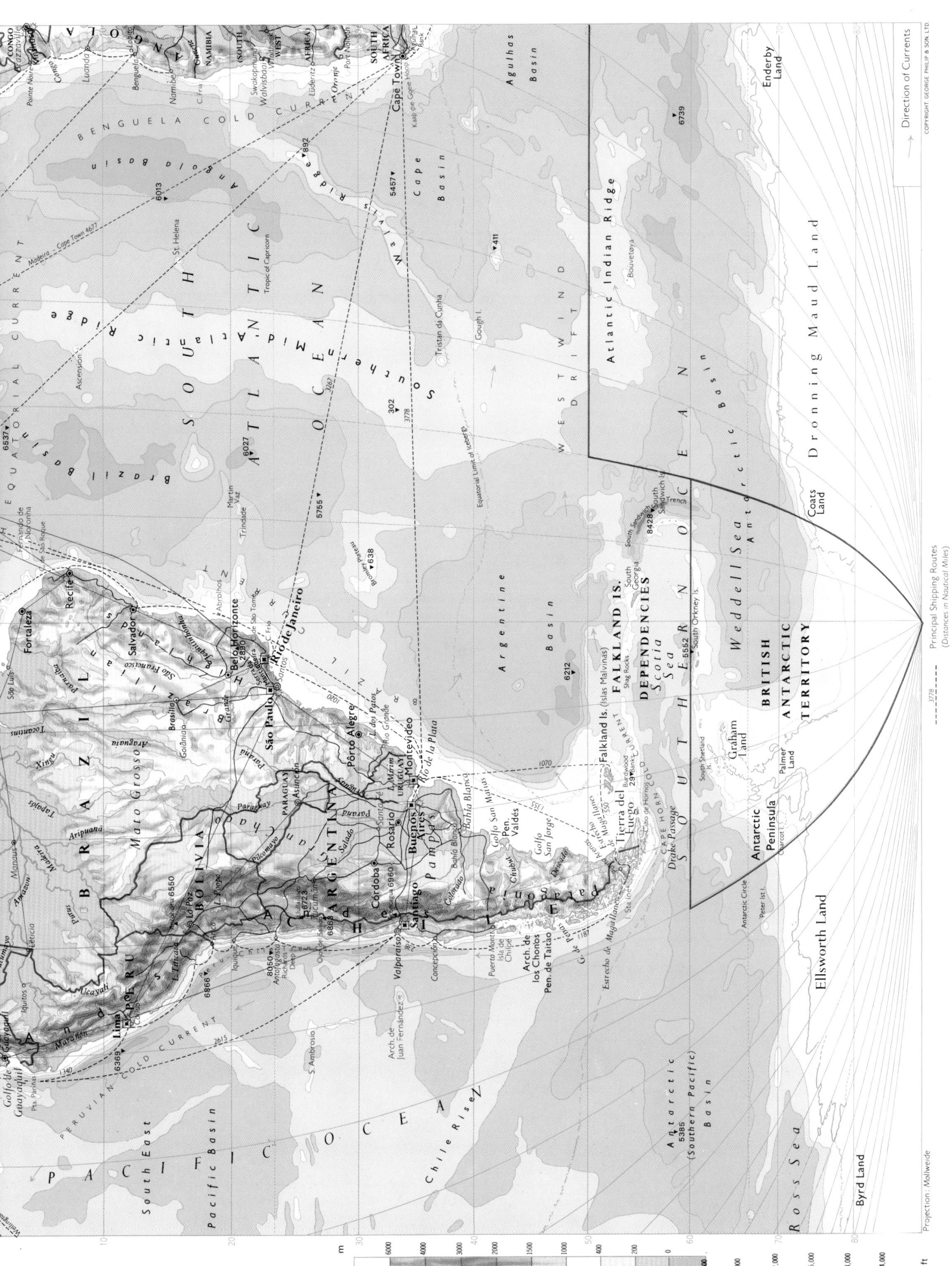

1:45 000 000

9

--- Direction of Currents

COPYRIGHT GEORGE PHILIP & SON, LTD.

CONGO
Brazzaville
Pointe Noire
Cabinda
Congo
Luanda
Benguela
Namibe
C. Fria
ANGOLA
NAMIBIA
(SOUTH
WEST
AFRICA)
Swakopmund
Walvisbaai
Lüderitz
SOUTH
AFRICA
Orange
Port Nolloth
Cape Town
Kaap die Goeie Hoop

BENGUELA COLD CURRENT

Angola Basin

6013

Madeira - Cape Town 4677

St. Helena

Ascension

Fernando de Noronha
Pta. de São Roque

Recife
Fortaleza
São Luís

B R A Z I L

Manaus
Amazon
Madeira
Tapajós
Xingu
Araguaia
Mato Grosso
Tocantins
Goiânia
Brasília
Belo Horizonte

Iquitos
Ucayali
Marañón
PERU
Lima
Callao
Pta. Parinas
Golfo de Guayaquil
Guayaquil

BOLIVIA
La Paz
Lago de 6550
Titicaca
Sea 6550

6866

8050
Antofagasta
Iquique

6369
1340

2015

PERUVIAN COLD CURRENT

Arica
Atacama
Deep

Arch. de
Juan Fernández
S. Ambrosio

Valparaíso
Santiago
Concepción

CHILE
ARGENTINA

6960
6728
Córdoba

Mendoza

Río de la Plata
Buenos Aires
Montevideo
URUGUAY
Rosario
Paraná
Santa Fé

PARAGUAY
Asunción
Paraguay
Pilcomayo
Salado

Pampas

Bahía Blanca
Colorado
Negro
Bahía Blanca

Pôrto Alegre
L. dos Patos
Rio Grande
L. Mirim

São Paulo
Santos
Rio de Janeiro
C. Frio
São Francisco
Salvador
R. Doce
Vitória
Cabo de São Tomé

Trindade
Martin Vaz

5755

638
Bromley Plateau

302
3778

5457

Cape
Basin

Walvis Ridge

Cape
Basin

411

Tristan da Cunha
Gough I.

Agulhas
Basin

6739

Tropic of Capricorn

S O U T H

A T L A N T I C

O C E A N

Brazil Basin

Mid-Atlantic Ridge

Southern

S O U T H   E Q U A T O R I A L   C U R R E N T

6537

6027

892

1000

Puerto Montt
Isla de
Chiloé
Arch. de
los Chonos
Pen. de Taitao

Golfo
Corcovado

1187

Estrecho de Magallanes

BRAZIL CURRENT

Argentine

Basin

6212

1070

Golfo San Matías
Pen.
Valdés
Golfo
San Jorge
Sta. Inés

Río Gallegos
Río Grande
Tierra del
Fuego
CAPE HORN
Cabo de Hornos
Drake Passage

Estados
750
Burdwood
Bank
29
Shag Rocks

FALKLAND IS.
Falkland Is. (Islas Malvinas)
5552

FALKLAND
DEPENDENCIES
South
Georgia
South Orkney Is.
South
Sandwich Is.
South Sandwich
Trench 8428

Scotia
Sea

South Shetland Is.

Graham Land

Antarctic
Peninsula
Palmer
Land
Dézolat I.

BRITISH
ANTARCTIC
TERRITORY

Peter I st I.

Antarctic Circle

Ellsworth Land

Byrd Land

Ross Sea

Antarctic
5385
(Southern Pacific)
Basin

Chile Rise

S O U T H

P A C I F I C   O C E A N

South Pacific Basin

South East
Pacific Basin

S O U T H E R N   O C E A N

Weddell Sea

Coats
Land

Enderby
Land

Dronning Maud Land

Atlantic Indian Ridge

Bouvetøya

W E S T   W I N D   D R I F T

Antarctic Basin

Equatorial Limit of Icebergs

Antarctic

3778

------- Principal Shipping Routes
(Distances in Nautical Miles)
——— Principal Air Routes

Projection: Mollweide

m
6000
4000
3000
2000
1500
1000
400
200
0

ft
18,000
12,000
9000
6000
4500
3000
1200
600
0
-200 -600

m
2000
4000
5000
6000
8000

ft
6000
12,000
15,000
18,000
24,000

1:20 000 000

| 100 | | 100 | 200 | 300 | 400 | 500 miles |

| 100 | 0 | 200 | 400 | 600 | 800 km |

Ob

Ural Mountains

Pechora

Kama

Obshchiri Syrt

Ural

CASPIAN SEA
-28

Volga

Terek

Kuma

Caucasus
5633 Elbrus
5196

Araks

L. Van

L. Urmia

Euphrates

Tundra

Volga Uplands

Mezen

N. Dvina

Onega

L. Onega

Don

Rybinsk Res.

Volga

Oka

Tsimlyansk Res.

Manych

Don

Uzd

Sea of Azov

Str. of Kerch

Rion

Kizil-Irmak

L. Tuz

3710

Anatolia

Taurus

Cyprus 1951

Kanin Peninsula

White Sea

Kola Peninsula

Central Russian Uplands

Ukraine

Dniepr (Dnieper)

Crimea

BLACK SEA
2211

Bosporus

S. of Marmara

1786

Ida

North Cape

Nordkinn

Lihari

Lapland

Finland

L. Ladoga

Neva

L. Chudskoye

Plain

Dvina (W. Dvina)

Niemen

Pripyat

Pripyat Marshes

Bug

Danube

Prut

Carpathians

Transylvanian Alps

Wallachia

Balkans

Rhodope

Balkan Peninsula

Pindus

Aegean Sea

Crete

L. Inari

Muonio

Torne

2123

Finland

G. of Finland

G. of Riga

Gotland

Wisla (Vistula)

Tisza

Maros

2655

Tatra

Danube

Plain of Hungary

Drave

Sava

Dinaric Alps

5121
C. Matapan

Morea

Ionian Is.

Ionian Sea

North Cape

Vesterålen

Lofoten

Kjolen Mts.

Scandinavia

2469

2468 Sulitjelma

Ume

Indals

Vänern

Vättern

Mälaren

Kattegat

Skagerrak

Jutland

Odra (Oder)

Sudetes

Erz Geb.

Bohemian For.

Elbe

Danube

Carpathians

Bakony For.

Morava

Moldau

Drave

Dinaric Alps

ALPS

Gran Sasso
2914

ADRIATIC SEA

Str. of Otranto

Apennines

Vesuvius
1277

Etna
3263

Sicily

Str. of Messina

Calabria

Valencia I.

BALTIC SEA

NORTH SEA

Weser

Harz
1142

Black For.

Weser

Rhine

Helgoland

Heligoland

Netherlands

Meuse

Ardennes

Vosges

Jura

4807

Mont Blanc

Ligurian Sea

Corsica

Str. of Bonifacio

Sardinia

C. Blanco

Tyrrhenian Sea

Malta

C. Bon

MEDITERRANEAN SEA

3734

NORWEGIAN SEA

Shetland Is.

Orkney Is.

Faroe Is.

Fisher Bank

Dogger Bank

NORTH SEA

Lindesnes

Rhine

Rhône

Geneva

G. of Lyons

Central Massif

Mt. Dore
1886

Cévennes

Maritime Alps

Plateau of the Shotts

Arctic Circle

Iceland

Hekla
1491

Oræfa Jökull
2119

ATLANTIC

Rockall

Hebrides

British Isles

Ben Nevis
1343

Great Britain

Snowdon
1085

Pennines

Irish Sea

Ireland

Thames

English Channel

Land's End

C. Clear

Brittany

Seine

Loire

Gironde

Garonne

Bay of Biscay

4861

Pyrenees

Pico de Aneto
3404

Cantabrian Mts.

Old Castile

New Castile

Iberian Peninsula

Douro

Sa. de Guadarrama

Sa. de Estrela

Sierra Morena

Guadalquivir

Andalusia

Sa. Nevada
3478

Str. of Gibraltar

C. Trafalgar

C. Spartel

Tagus

Ebro

Balearic Is.

OCEAN

C. Finisterre

C. da Roca (Lisbon)

C. St. Vincent

West from Greenwich   East from Greenwich

ft	m						
12 000	4000		2000	1000		600	
	3000		1200		0		

	m	ft
	200	600
	0	0
	2000	6000
	4000	12 000
	m	ft

1:20 000 000

100   0   100   200   300   400   500 miles
100   0   200   400   600   800 km

Projection Bonne   West from Greenwich 0 East from Greenwich

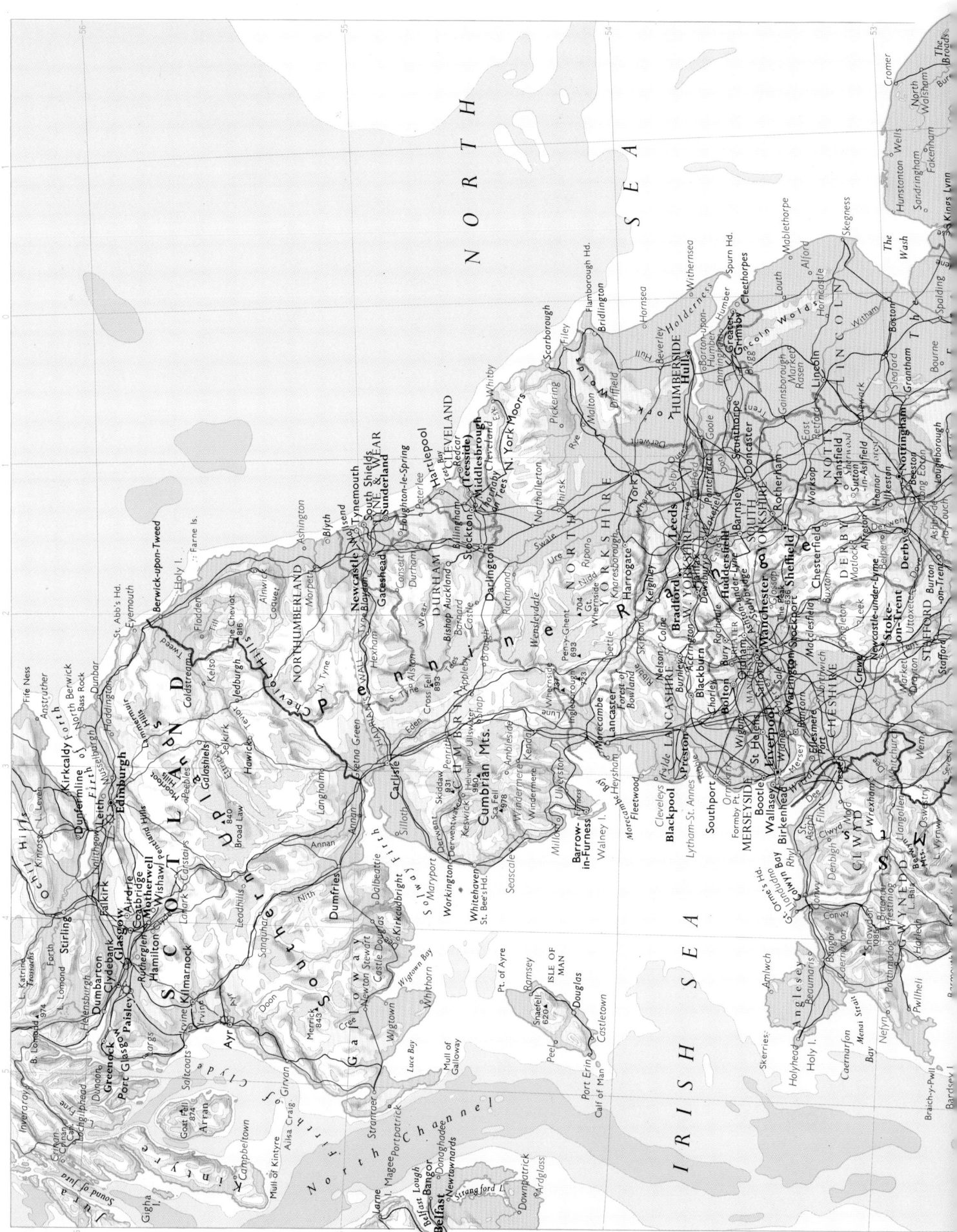
NORTH SEA
IRISH SEA
SCOTLAND
NORTHUMBERLAND
DURHAM
CLEVELAND
CUMBRIA
N. YORKSHIRE
W. YORKSHIRE
S. YORKSHIRE
HUMBERSIDE
LANCASHIRE
MERSEYSIDE
CHESHIRE
DERBY
LINCOLN
CLWYD
GWYNEDD
ISLE OF MAN
Cumbrian Mts.
N. York Moors
Southern Uplands
Pennines
North Channel
Firth of Clyde
Solway Firth
The Wash
Edinburgh
Glasgow
Newcastle
Carlisle
Leeds
Bradford
Manchester
Liverpool
Sheffield
Hull
York
Nottingham
Derby
Lincoln
Belfast
Berwick-upon-Tweed
Sunderland
Middlesbrough
Blackpool
Preston
Douglas

1 : 2 000 000

10   0   10   20   30   40   50 miles
10   0   10 20 30 40 50 60 70 80 km

East from Greenwich. COPYRIGHT. GEORGE PHILIP & SON, LTD.

West from Greenwich

ENGLISH CHANNEL

FRANCE

Rouen
Dieppe
Le Tréport
St-Valery-en-Caux
Fécamp
Étretat
C. d'Antifer
C. de la Hève   Le Havre
Honfleur
Trouville
Arromanches
Caen
Bayeux
Vierville
Isigny
Carentan
Périers
St-Lô
Barfleur
Quineville
Valognes
Cherbourg
C. de la Hague
Barneville
Carteret
Yvetot
Caudebec
Pont l'Évêque
Lisieux
Bernay
Louviers
Elbeuf
Seine

Channel Islands
Alderney
Guernsey
Sark
St. Peter Port
Jersey
St. Helier

SUFFOLK
ESSEX
CAMBRIDGE
BEDFORD
NORTHAMPTON
WARWICK
HERTFORD
BUCKS
OXFORD
BERKS
WILTS
HANTS
SURREY
KENT
EAST SUSSEX
WEST SUSSEX
DORSET
SOMERSET
DEVON
CORNWALL
AVON
GLOUCESTER
WORCESTER
HEREFORD
SHROPSHIRE
GWENT
GLAMORGAN
WEST GLAMORGAN
MID GLAM.
POWYS
DYFED

LONDON
Birmingham
Coventry
Cardiff
Swansea
Bristol
Bath
Gloucester
Cheltenham
Oxford
Reading
Southampton
Portsmouth
Brighton
Hove
Worthing
Eastbourne
Hastings
Bournemouth
Poole
Weymouth
Exeter
Plymouth
Torquay (Torbay)
Penzance
Truro
Camborne
Redruth
Falmouth
Newquay
Padstow
Bude
Barnstaple
Ilfracombe
Minehead
Weston-super-Mare
Newport
Merthyr Tydfil
Aberdare
Rhondda
Pontypool
Monmouth
Hereford
Worcester
Kidderminster
Dudley
Stourbridge
Tipton
West Bromwich
Leamington
Stratford-on-Avon
Banbury
Northampton
Bedford
Milton Keynes
Luton
Cambridge
Colchester
Ipswich
Southend
Basildon
Chelmsford
Harlow
St. Albans
Watford
Hemel Hempstead
High Wycombe
Maidenhead
Windsor
Guildford
Aldershot
Basingstoke
Winchester
Salisbury
Swindon
Chippenham
Trowbridge
Yeovil
Dorchester
Bridport
Lyme Regis
Taunton
Bridgwater
Glastonbury
Wells
Shaftesbury
Blandford
Sherborne
Chard
Honiton
Tiverton
Okehampton
Tavistock
Newton Abbot
Dartmouth
Kingsbridge
Salcombe
St. Austell
St. Ives
Land's End
Lizard

Canterbury
Dover
Folkestone
Deal
Ramsgate
Margate
Herne Bay
Whitstable
Sheerness
Gillingham
Chatham
Rochester
Gravesend
Maidstone
Ashford
Tonbridge
Tunbridge Wells
Royal Tunbridge Wells
Rye
Bexhill
Battle
Lewes
Newhaven
Crawley
Horsham
Chichester
Bognor Regis
Littlehampton
Fareham
Gosport
Ryde
Newport
Cowes
Lymington
Christchurch
Swanage

ISLE OF WIGHT
Ventnor
St. Catherine's Point
The Needles

Beachy Hd.
Dungeness
New Romney
Romney Marsh
North Foreland
South Foreland

The Weald
North Downs
South Downs
Chilterns
Cotswolds
Mendip Hills
Quantock Hills
Exmoor
Dartmoor
Bodmin Moor
Brecon Beacons
Black Mts.
Malvern Hills
Clee Hills
Salisbury Plain
Marlborough Downs
Berkshire Downs
Cleeve Hill

Bristol Channel
Cardigan Bay
Carmarthen Bay
St. Bride's Bay
Milford Haven
St. David's Hd.
Hartland Point
Lundy
Eddystone
Portland Bill
St. Alban's Hd.
Start Pt.

Projection. Conical with two standard parallels.

SCILLY ISLES
On same Scale
Isles of Scilly
St. Mary's
Penzance
St. Ives
Land's End

ft   m
3000 1000
     1200
     600
     400
      200
      150
      0
      50
      100   300
      m   ft

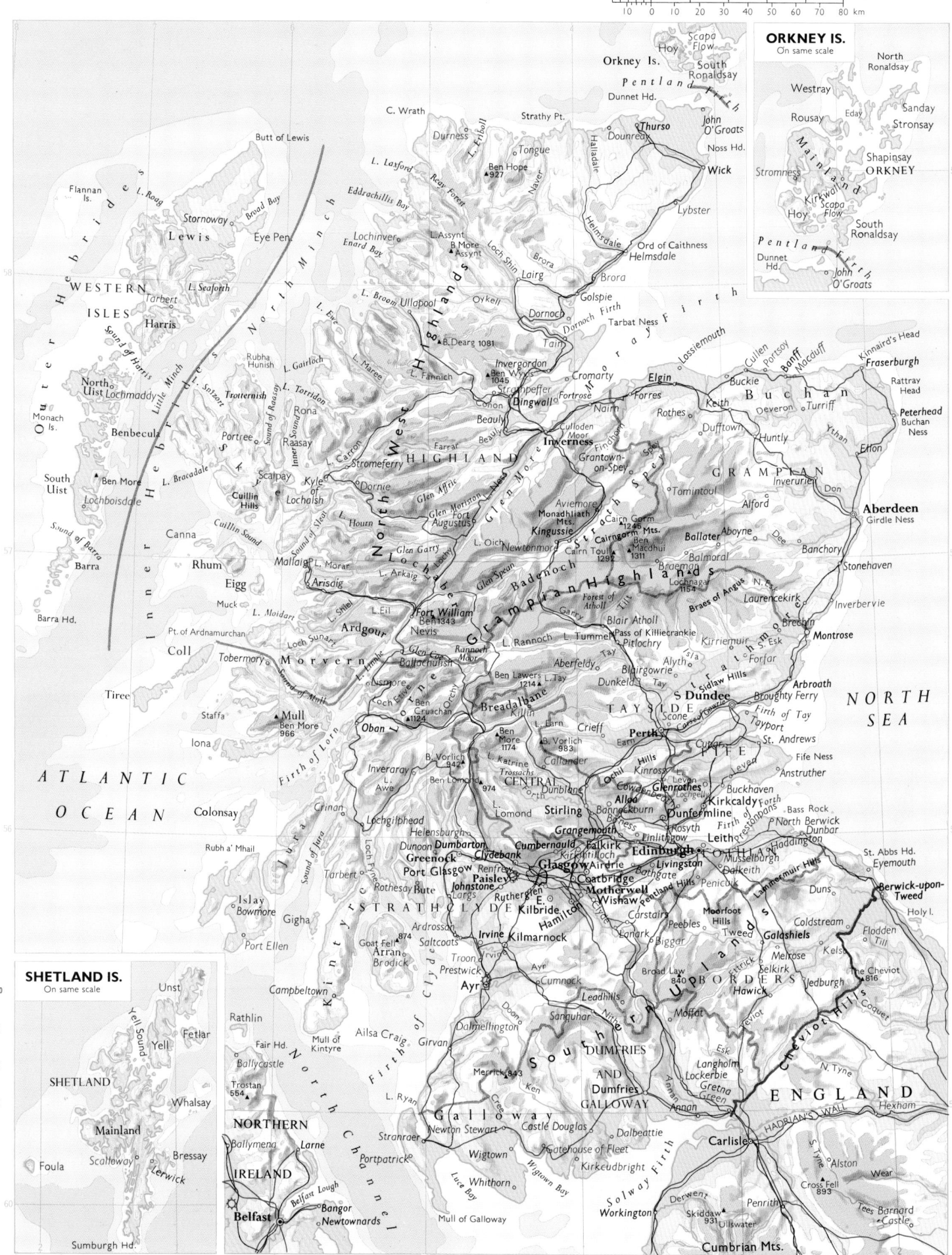

1 : 2 000 000

ORKNEY IS.
On same scale

SHETLAND IS.
On same scale

ATLANTIC OCEAN

NORTH SEA

Projection: Conical with two standard parallels.

West from Greenwich

COPYRIGHT. GEORGE PHILIP & SON. LTD.

1:2 000 000

10 0 10 20 30 40 50 miles
10 0 10 20 30 40 50 60 70 80 km

ATLANTIC OCEAN

IRISH SEA

Kintyre
Campbeltown
Arran
Mull of Kintyre
Ailsa Craig
Rathlin I.
Giant's Causeway
Fair Hd.
Portrush
Stranraer
Portpatrick
I. Magee

Malin Hd.
Lough Swilly
Sheep Haven
Tory I. Horn Hd.
Bloody Foreland
Carndonagh
Inishowen Pen.
Moville
Buncrana
Ballycastle
Ballymoney
Coleraine
Limavady
Ballymena
Larne
554 Trostan
Antrim
Carrickfergus
Belfast L.
Donaghadee
Bangor
Newtownards
Ards Pen.
Belfast
Lisburn
Strangford L.

Gweedore
Errigal 752
Derryveagh Mts.
Letterkenny
Londonderry
Sperrin Mts.
Strabane
Magherafelt
Sawel 683
Bann
Cookstown
Antrim

Aran I.
Gweebarra B.
DONEGAL
Glenties
Bluestack 676
Finn
Lifford
Omagh
ULSTER
NORTHERN IRELAND
Lough Neagh 16
Dungannon
Lurgan (Craigavon)
Portadown
Banbridge
Downpatrick
Dundrum
Newcastle

Rossan Pt.
Rathlin O Birne I.
Killybegs
Donegal
Ballyshannon
Bundoran
L. Erne
Enniskillen
1
Upper Erne
Irvinestown
Blackwater
Armagh
Slieve Donard 852
Mourne Mts.
Warrenpoint
Carlingford L.
Greenore
Dundrum Bay

Donegal Bay
Killala B.
Sligo B.
Sligo
Finn
Clones
Newry 8
Sl. Gullion 577
Castleblayney
Dundalk
Dundalk Bay

Broad Haven
Erris Hd.
Belmullet
Mullet Peninsula
Killala
Ballina
Ox Mts.
SLIGO
Collooney
L. Allen
Arrow
LEITRIM
Leitrim
Carrick-on-Shannon
Boyle
Belturbet
CAVAN
Annalee
Cootehill
Cavan
Carrickmacross
Louth
Ardee
LOUTH

Achill Hd.
Achill
Achill I.
Nephin 806
L. Conn
Castlebar
Clew Bay
Croagh Patrick 765
Westport
CONNACHT
ROSCOMMON
Castlereagh
L. Gowna
Granard
Longford
Oldcastle
An Uaimh (Navan)
Kells
Ceanannas Mor (Kells)
Drogheda
Balbriggan

Inishbofin
Killary Harbour
Mweelrea 819
L. Mask
Ballinrobe
Robe
Roscommon
LONGFORD
L. Ree
Athboy
Trim
MEATH
Boyne
Swords
Lambay I.

Clare I.
Clifden
Twelve Pins
Slyne Hd.
MAYO
L. Corrib
Tuam
GALWAY
Athenry
Ballinasloe
IRELAND
WESTMEATH
Athlone
Mullingar
Maynooth
DUBLIN
Ireland's Eye
Howth Head
Dublin (Baile Atha Cliath)
Dublin Bay

Connemara
Galway
Clare
Galway Bay
Inishmore
Aran Is.
Clare
Loughrea
OFFALY
Tullamore
Clara
Edenderry
Daingean
Droichead Nua
Naas
Celbridge
Liffey
Dun Laoghaire
Bray
Kippure 754
Poulaphouca Res.

Hags Hd.
Ennistymon
Liscannor Bay
Mal Bay
Miltown Malbay
Ennis
CLARE
Gort
Slieve Aughty
Portumna
Shannon
Birr
Sl. Bloom
Mountmellick
Port Laoise
KILDARE
Kildare
Athy
LEINSTER
LAOIS
WICKLOW
Lugnaquillia 923
Wicklow
Wicklow Hd.
Rathdrum
Mizen Hd.

Kilkee
Loop Hd.
Kilrush
Shannonna
Killaloe
Ballina
Nenagh
L. Derg
Roscrea
Templemore
Carlow
Tullow
CARLOW
Muine Bheag
Mt. Leinster 796
Shillelagh
Gorey
Arklow

R. Shannon
Foynes
Rathkeale
LIMERICK
Newcastle
Limerick
Golden Vale
Keeper 694
Ardnacrusha
Thurles
TIPPERARY
Cashel
Kilkenny
KILKENNY
Callan
Enniscorthy
WEXFORD
Cahore Pt.

Kerry Hd.
Brandon Bay
Tralee Bay
Fenit
Listowel
Rath Luirc (Charleville)
Tipperary
Slievenamon
Clonmel
Carrick-on-Suir
New Ross
Wexford
Wexford Harbour
Rosslare
Greenore Pt.
Tuscar Rock
Carnsore Pt.

Brandon Mt. 953
St. Mish
Maine
Tralee
MUNSTER
KERRY
Newmarket
Mitchelstown
Galty Mts. 920
Caher
Knockmealdown Mts. 722
Comeragh Mts.
Waterford
Tramore
Carnsore Pt.
Saltee Is.

Gt. Blasket I.
Dingle
Dingle Bay
Slea Hd.
Killarney
Blackwater
Mallow
Fermoy
Lismore
WATERFORD
Blackwater
Dungarvan
Dungarvan Bay
Hook Hd.
Waterford Harbour

Valentia Harbour
Valentia I.
Skellig Rocks
Macgillycuddy's Reeks
Carrauntuohill 1040
Lakes of Killarney
Boggeragh Mts.
Macroom
Blarney
CORK
Cork
Midleton
Youghal
Youghal Harbour
St. David's Hd.

Ballinskelligs B.
Cahirciveen
Kenmare
Caha Mts.
Glengarriff
Bantry
Lee
Passage West
Cobh
Cork Harbour
Crosshaven

Castletown Bearhaven
Bear I.
Kenmare River
Bantry Bay
Crow Hd.
Dunmanus Bay
Mizen Hd.
Skull
Bandon
Bandon
Kinsale
Clonakilty
Skibbereen
Clonakilty Bay
Old Head of Kinsale
Galley Hd.
Baltimore
Clear I.
C. Clear
Fastnet Rock

St. George's Channel
North Channel

Towns underlined in Northern Ireland give their
names to the Districts in which they stand

The remaining Districts are:—
1 Fermanagh
2 Moyle
3 Newtownabbey
4 North Down
5 Castlereagh
6 Ards
7 Down
8 Newry & Mourne

ft   m
3000 1000
1200 400
600 200
300 100
0   0
100 300
200 600
m   ft

1:4 000 000

20 0 20 40 60 miles
20 0 20 40 60 80 km

ORKNEY
SHETLAND

Kirkwall
59

Lerwick

HIGHLAND
60

The DISTRICTS of Northern Ireland have been numbered and can be identified by reference to this table.

1	Londonderry	14	Craigavon
2	Limavady	15	Armagh
3	Coleraine	16	Newry & Mourne
4	Ballymoney	17	Banbridge
5	Moyle	18	Down
6	Larne	19	Lisburn
7	Ballymena	20	Antrim
8	Magherafelt	21	Newtownabbey
9	Cookstown	22	Carrickfergus
10	Strabane	23	North Down
11	Omagh	24	Ards
12	Fermanagh	25	Castlereagh
13	Dungannon	26	Belfast

WESTERN ISLES

Stornoway

GRAMPIAN
Inverness

HIGHLAND

SCOTLAND

Aberdeen

ATLANTIC OCEAN

TAYSIDE
Dundee

FIFE
Glenrothes

CENTRAL
Stirling

Edinburgh
LOTHIAN

STRATHCLYDE
Glasgow

Newtown
St. Boswells

BORDERS

NORTH SEA

DUMFRIES AND GALLOWAY
Dumfries

NORTHUMBERLAND

Carlisle

Newcastle
TYNE AND WEAR
Durham

DURHAM
CLEVELAND
Middlesbrough

CUMBRIA

Northallerton

ISLE OF MAN
Douglas

NORTH YORKSHIRE

IRISH SEA

LANCASHIRE
Preston

WEST YORKSHIRE
Wakefield

HUMBERSIDE
Hull

GREATER MANCHESTER
MERSEYSIDE
Liverpool
Manchester

Barnsley
SOUTH YORKSHIRE

ENGLAND

Lincoln

Chester
CHESHIRE
DERBYSHIRE
NOTTINGHAMSHIRE
Nottingham
LINCOLNSHIRE

Caernarfon
Mold
CLWYD
Matlock

GWYNEDD

Stafford
STAFFORDSHIRE
WEST MIDLANDS
Birmingham

LEICESTERSHIRE
Leicester

NORFOLK
Norwich

WALES
POWYS
Shrewsbury
SHROPSHIRE

Warwick
WARWICKSHIRE

NORTHAMPTONSHIRE
Northampton

CAMBRIDGESHIRE
Cambridge

SUFFOLK
Ipswich

Llandrindod Wells

HEREFORD AND WORCESTER
Worcester

Bedford
BEDFORDSHIRE

Hertford
HERTFORDSHIRE

ESSEX
Chelmsford

DYFED
Carmarthen

Gloucester
GLOUCESTERSHIRE

Oxford
OXFORDSHIRE

BUCKINGHAMSHIRE
Aylesbury

GREATER LONDON
Kingston

Maidstone
KENT

WEST GLAMORGAN
Swansea
MID GLAMORGAN
SOUTH GLAMORGAN
Cardiff

GWENT
Cwmbran

Bristol
AVON

WILTSHIRE
Trowbridge

BERKSHIRE
Reading

SURREY

EAST SUSSEX
Lewes

SOMERSET
Taunton

HAMPSHIRE
Winchester

WEST SUSSEX
Chichester

DEVON
Exeter

DORSET
Dorchester

Newport
ISLE OF WIGHT

CORNWALL
Truro

Metropolitan Counties :-
On 1st April 1986 the administrative functions of the six metropolitan counties such as planning, education, transportation, libraries and social services were transferred to the city and town boroughs and various non-elected residuary bodies.

NORTHERN IRELAND
DONEGAL
Lifford
Londonderry
Antrim
Tyrone
Fermanagh
Belfast
Down

Sligo
SLIGO
LEITRIM
Monaghan
MONAGHAN
Armagh
Carrick-on-Shannon
Cavan
CAVAN
Dundalk

MAYO
Castlebar

ROSCOMMON
Longford
LONGFORD
LOUTH

An Uaimh (Navan)
Mullingar
WESTMEATH
MEATH

GALWAY
Galway

DUBLIN
Dublin

IRELAND
Tullamore
OFFALY
KILDARE
Naas

LAOIS
Port Laoise

Wicklow
WICKLOW

CLARE
Ennis

Kilkenny
KILKENNY
Carlow
CARLOW

Limerick
TIPPERARY

WEXFORD

LIMERICK
Clonmel
Wexford

Tralee

WATERFORD
Waterford

KERRY

CORK
Cork

NORTH CHANNEL

ST. GEORGE'S CHANNEL

CELTIC SEA

ENGLISH CHANNEL

FRANCE

○ Norwich   Administrative headquarters
MERSEYSIDE Metropolitan counties
Antrim   Former Northern Ireland counties

Projection: Conical with two standard parallels

West from Greenwich 0 East from Greenwich
COPYRIGHT. GEORGE PHILIP & SON. LTD.

ENGLAND

Bideford
South Molton
Bampton
Tiverton
Yeovil
Crewkerne
Sherborne
Romsey
Eastleigh
Midhurst
Haywards Heath
Tenterden
Folk
Bude
Holsworthy
Okehampton
Chard
Blandford
Southampton
Fareham
Chichester
South Downs
Lewes
Battle
Rye
Hythe
Trevose Hd.
Pudstow
Launceston
Princetown
Dartmoor 261
Newton Abbot
Honiton
Dorchester
Lymington
Cowes
I. of Wight
Newport
Ryde
Portsmouth
Bognor Regis
Littlehampton
Worthing
Brighton
Hailsham
Hastings
Bexhill
Eastbourne
Beachy Head
Dungeness
Newquay
Redruth
Camborne
Bodmin
Saltash
Torquay
Paignton
Brixham
Sidmouth
Exmouth
Dawlish
Teignmouth
Weymouth
Lyme Regis
Seaton
Wareham
Bournemouth
Poole
Swanage
The Needles
Sandown
Ventnor
St. Ives
Truro
St. Austell
Fowey
Looe
Dodman Pt.
Kingsbridge
Dartmouth
Start Pt.
Portland Bill
Lyme Bay
Penzance
Helston
Falmouth
Lizard Pt.
Land's End

English Channel

Baie de la

CHANNEL ISLANDS
Casquets
St. Anne
Alderney
Burhou
Guernsey
St. Peter Port
Herm
Sark
Jersey
St. Helier
Roches Douvres
Barnouic
Les Minquiers
Iles Chausey

Cap de la Hague
Auderville
Nez de Jobourg
Octeville
Cherbourg
Pointe de Barfleur
Barfleur
St-Pierre-Église
St-Vaast-la-Hougue
Dielette
Valognes
Montebourg
Iles St-Marcouf
Bricquebec
Ste-Mère-Église
Port-en-Bessin
Barneville-Carteret
St-Sauveur-le-Vicomte
La Haye-du-Puits
Carentan
Périers
Lessay
Coutances
Agon
St-Lô
Torigni
Pointe du Grouin
Bréhal
Granville
Golfe de St-Malo
Cancale
Le Mont-St-Michel
Avranches
Pontaubault
St-Hilaire
Dinard
St-Malo

Baie de la Seine
Arromanches
Courseulles
Villers-sur-Mer
Riva Bella
Quistreham
Caen
Bayeux
Ste-Adresse
Honfleur
Le Havre
Trouville
Deauville
Pont-l'Évêque
Lisieux
Dives-sur-Mer
Cabourg
Pont-Audemer

Dieppe
St-Valery-en-Caux
St-Pierre-en-Port
Fécamp
Étretat
Doudeville
Yvetot
Bolbec
Lillebonne
Rouen
Le Petit-Quevilly
Sotteville-lès-R.
Elbeuf
Louviers
Bernay
Évreux
Dreux

Mer d'Iroise
Ile d'Ouessant
Le Conquet
Camaret
Pte. de St-Mathieu
Brest
Daoulas
Morgat
Crozon
Ile de Sein
Pte. du Raz
Douarnenez
Audierne
Quimper
Pont l'Abbé
Penmarch
Pointe de Penmarch

Brignogan-Plage
Roscoff
Perros-Guirec
St-Pol-de-Léon
Morlaix
Lannion
Tréguier
Paimpol
Lézardrieux
Guingamp
St-Brieuc
Lamballe
Dinan
Combourg
Fougères

Trégastel-Plage
Plestin-les-Grèves
Plouha
Étables-s.-M.
Pléneuf-Val-André
Erquy
Cap Fréhel
Sillon de Talbert
Ile de Bréhat

Monts d'Arrée
Huelgoat
Châteauneuf-du-Faou
Carhaix-Plouguer
Montagne Noire
Gourin
Callac
Quintin
Mur-de-Bretagne
Loudéac
Ploërmel
Rennes
Vitré
Châteaubourg
Laval
Mayenne
Ernée

Scaer
Rosporden
Concarneau
Quimperlé
Pont-Aven
Hennebont
Lorient
Port-Louis
Ile de Groix
Pontivy
Josselin
Malestroit
Vannes
Auray
Redon
Châteaubriant

Guilvinec
Bénodet
Iles de Glénan
Le Pouldu
Groix
Quiberon
Presqu'île de Quiberon
Belle-Ile
Le Palais
Pointe du Croisic
Le Croisic
St-Nazaire
St-Brévin

Baie de Bourgneuf
Noirmoutier
Ile de Noirmoutier
Bourgneuf-en-Retz
Pornic
Nantes
Ancenis
Angers
Saumur
Tours

Port-Joinville
Ile d'Yeu
St-Jean-de-Monts
St-Gilles-Croix-de-Vie
Challans
La Roche-sur-Yon
Cholet
Bressuire
Châtellerault
Poitiers

Les-Sables-d'Olonne
Talmont
Luçon
Fontenay-le-Comte
Niort
Le Blanc

Pertuis Breton
Ile de Ré
La Rochelle
Surgères
Pertuis d'Antioche
Rochefort
Ile d'Oléron
Tonnay-Charente
St-Jean-d'Angély
Saintes
Cognac
Angoulême

Pointe de la Coubre
Royan
Pointe de Grave

ft m
12 000 4000
9000 3000
6000 2000
4500 1500
3000 1000
1200 400
600 200
0
200 600
2000 6000
m ft

DÉPARTEMENTS IN THE PARIS AREA
1 Ville de Paris   3 Val-de-Marne
2 Seine-St-Denis   4 Hauts-de-Seine

Projection: Conical with two standard parallels

West from Greenwich   0   East from Greenwich

1:2 500 000

19

COPYRIGHT GEORGE PHILIP & SON, LTD.

1:2 500 000

10   0   10   20   30   40   50 miles
10   0   10 20 30 40 50 60 70 80 km

SWITZERLAND

FRANCE

ITALY

LIGURIAN SEA

Golfo di Génova

MEDITERRANEAN SEA

CORSICA

Livorno

Elba

MILANO (Milan)

TORINO (Turin)

GENOVA (Genoa)

MARSEILLE

Toulon

Nice

MONACO
Monte-Carlo

Cannes

Grenoble

LYON

St-Étienne

Valence

Avignon

Aix-en-Provence

Bergamo

Brescia

La Spezia

ALPES-DE-HAUTE-PROVENCE

HAUTE-SAVOIE

SAVOIE

VAUCLUSE

DRÔME

ALPES-MARITIMES

VAR

BOUCHES-DU-RHÔNE

Corse du Sud

Haute-Corse

Ajaccio

Bastia

COPYRIGHT GEORGE PHILIP & SON, LTD.

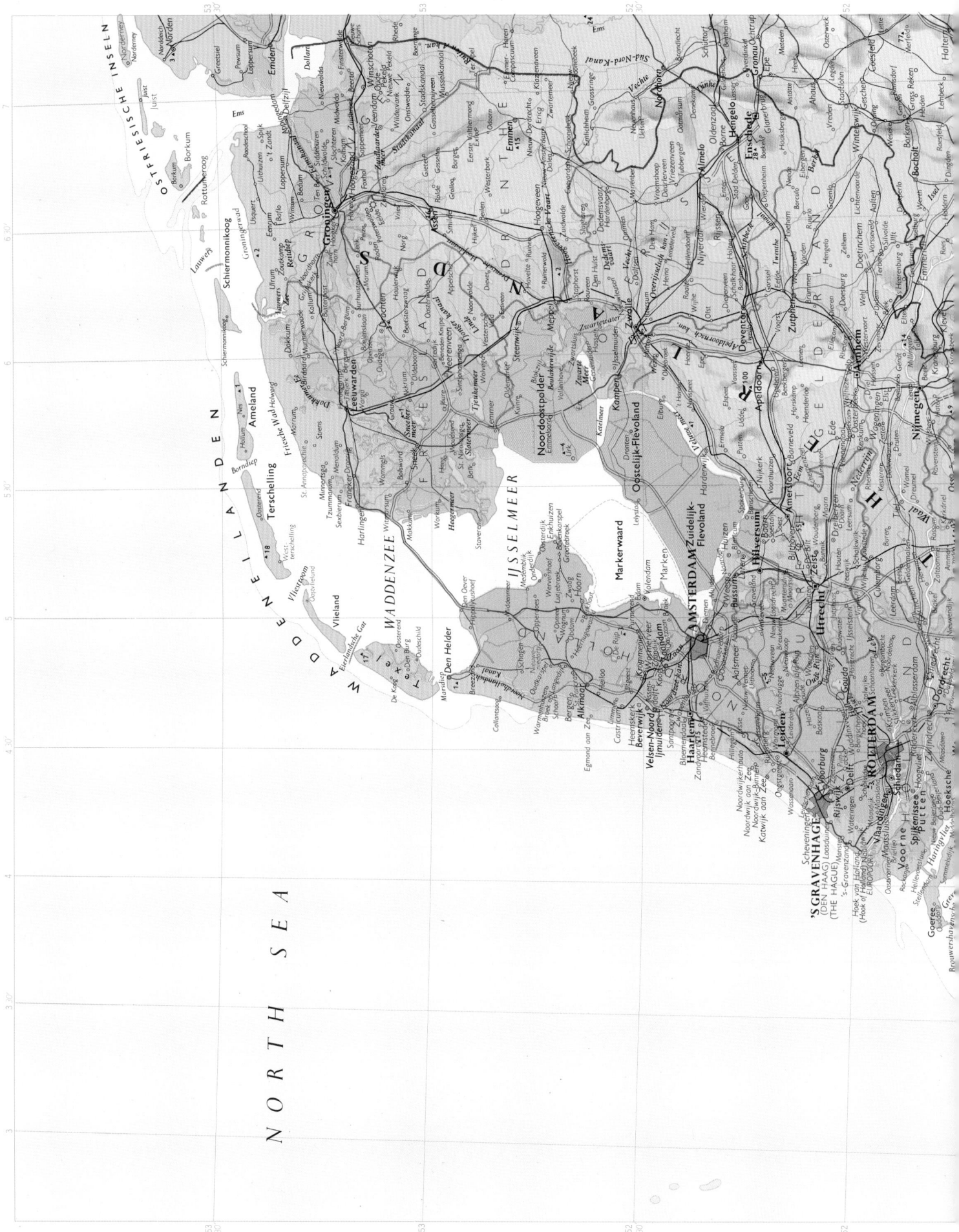
NORTH SEA
WADDENEILANDEN
OSTFRIESISCHE INSELN
WADDENZEE
IJSSELMEER
Markerwaard
Noordoostpolder
Oostelijk-Flevoland
Zuidelijk-Flevoland
AMSTERDAM
ROTTERDAM
'S GRAVENHAGE
(DEN HAAG)
(THE HAGUE)
Utrecht
Haarlem
Leiden
Hilversum
Amersfoort
Apeldoorn
Deventer
Zwolle
Arnhem
Nijmegen
Groningen
Leeuwarden
Assen
Emmen
Hengelo
Enschede
Almelo
Alkmaar
Den Helder
Texel
Vlieland
Terschelling
Ameland
Schiermonnikoog
Borkum
Juist
Emden
Dokkum
Harlingen
Kampen
Hoorn
Zaandam
Gouda
Dordrecht
Schiedam
Vlaardingen
Delft
Voorburg
Rijswijk

1:1 250 000

5 0 5 10 15 20 25 miles

5 0 10 20 30 40 km

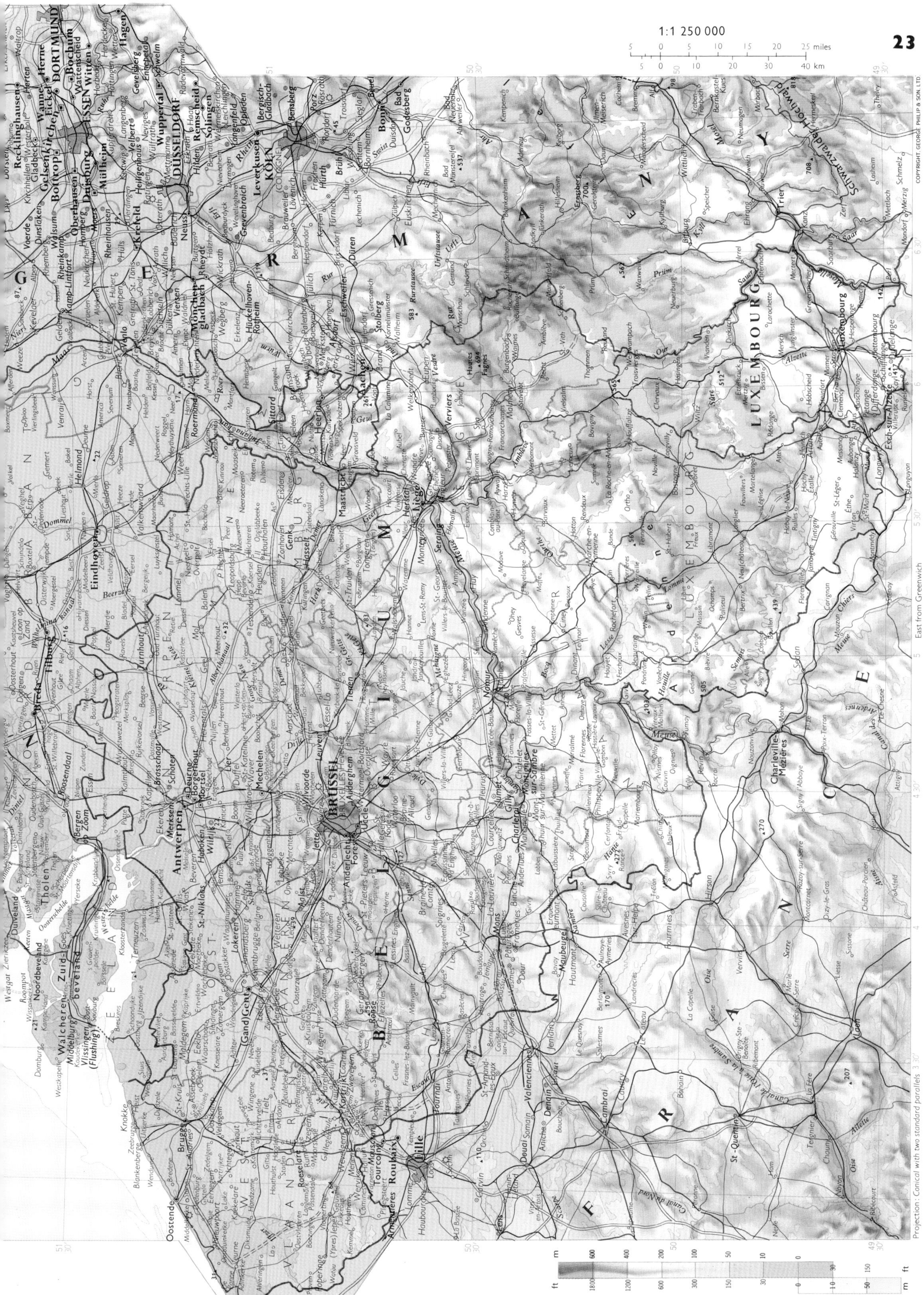

COPYRIGHT GEORGE PHILIP & SON, LTD.

East from Greenwich

Projection: Conical with two standard parallels

G E R M A N Y

B E L G I U M

LUXEMBOURG

F R A N C E

DORTMUND
ESSEN
DÜSSELDORF
KÖLN (COLOGNE)
Bonn
Aachen
Trier
Luxembourg
Liège
BRUSSEL
BRUXELLES
Antwerpen
Gand/Gent
Lille
Roubaix
Tourcoing
Charleroi
Mons
Maubeuge
Valenciennes
Cambrai
St-Quentin
Charleville-Mézières
Sedan
Verviers
Eindhoven
Tilburg
Breda
Bergen op Zoom
Maastricht
Hasselt
Genk
Oostende
Bruges
Leuven

m 600 400 200 100 50 10 0
ft 1800 1200 600 300 150 30 0

ARDENNE

Projection : Conical with two standard parallels

East from Greenwich

1:5 000 000

50   0   50   100 miles

50   0   50   100   150 km

E A
Zatoka
Gdańska
Vejherowo
Sopot
Gdynia
Gdańsk
(Danzig)
Elbląg
Braniewo
Malbork
Starogard
Kwidzyn
Grudziądz
Chełmża
Wąbrzeźno
oszcz
Chełmża
Toruń
Rypin
Lipno
Inowrocław
Włocławek
Gniezno
Płock
(Vistula)
Konin
Koło
Kutno
Łowicz
Warszawa
(Warsaw)
Turek
Łęczyca
Pruszków
Żyrardów
Grójec
Kalisz
Zduńska
Wola
Łódź
Pabianice
Pilica
toszny
Ostrów
Wielkopolski
aw
Wieluń
Warta
Piotrków
Trybunalski
Radom
Kielce
Częstochowa
Opole
Radomsko
Tarnowskie
Góry
Zawiercie
Jędrzejów
Bytom
Sosnowiec
Zabrze
Gliwice
Chorzów
Katowice
Kraków
Raciborz
Wieliczka

Kaliningrad (Königsberg)
Chernyakhovsk
Gusev
Lyna
Zelenogradsk
R.S.F.S.R.
Ketrzyn
Gizycko
309
Suwałki
Pojezierze Mazurskie
Olsztyn
Ostróda
Iława
Mława
Ciechanów
Pułtusk
Łomża
Ostrołęka
Ostrów
Mazowiecka
Brańsk
Białystok
238
Sokółka
Mińsk
Mazowiecki
Siedlce
Otwock
Łuków
Międzyrzec
Podlaski
Biała
Podlaska
Radzyń
Podlaski
Puławy
Kozienice
Włodawa
Lublin
Chełm
Krasnik
Zamość
Sandomierz
Tarnobrzeg
390
San
Dębica
Dąbrowa
Tarnowska
Rzeszów
Tarnów
Przeworsk
Jarosław
Przemyśl
Nowy
Sącz
Jasło
Krosno
Sanok
Dukelský Pr.

LITHUANIAN
S.S.R.
Vilnius
Alitus
Varena
Molodechno
Gorki
Lida
Novogrudok
Grodno
Mosty
Neman
Volkovysk
Slonim
Minsk
Borisov
Berezina
Mogilev
Kriche
B
Y
E
L
O
R
U
S
S
I
A
N
S.S.R.
Bereza
Luninets
Bobruysk
Shchara
Baranovichi
Zhabinka
Brest
Pripyat
Ptich
Kalinkovichi
Gomel
Pripyat
Polsy
Drut
Chernobyl
Desna
316
Dubrovitsa
Sarny
Uzh
Korosten
Goryn
Sluch
Kovel
Styr
Radomyshl
Vladimir
Volynskiy
Lutsk
Rovno
Korets
Novograd-
Volynskiy
Zhitomir
Kiev
Borispol
Sokal
Dubno
Ostrog
Shepetovka
Fastov
Belaya Tserkov
Radekhov
Brody
Kremenets
Berdichev
Kazatin
Lvov
Zolochev
Starokonstantinov
U
K
R
A
I
N
I
A
N
471
Ternopol
Khmelnitskiy
384
Vinnitsa
U. S. S. R.
Buchach
Chortkov
Zhmerinka
Bug
Uman
Gorodok
Kamenka
Bugskaya
Zaleshchiki
Kamenets-Podolskiy
Mogilev-Podolskiy
Pervomaisk
Ivano-Frankovsk
Nadvornaya
1881
Kolomyya
Snyatyn
Khotin
Yedintsy
Soroki
Kotovsk
Chernovtsy
Storozhinets
Beltsy
M
O
L
D
A
V
I
A
N

Ostrava
Frýdek
Místek
Český Těšín
Jablunkovský Pr.
550
1725
a
Západné Beskydy
Vychodné Beskydy
Dnestr
Sambor
Drogobych
Borislav
Stryi
Turka
Gottwaldov
Žilina
Ružomberok
2655
SLOVAK
S.S.R.
Nizké Tatry
Tatry
Vysoké Tatry
Prešov
Košice
Uzhgorod
Mukachevo
931
2061
Storozhinets
Pen.
Yablonitse
S.S.R.
C
a
r
p
a
t
h
Dorohoi
Radauti
Suceava
Botoşani
Iaşi
429
Kishinev
Benderŷ
Tiraspol
S.S.R.
Kremnica
Banská Bystrica
Zvolen
Slovenské Rudohorie
Banská Štiavnica
Lučenec
Nitra
Sajó
Sátoraljaújhely
Beregovo
Khust
Tokaj
Hernád
Sighetu
Marmatiei
Vatra-Dornei
Odessa
N.
Šahy
Žiar
Miskolc
Eger
Nyíregyháza
Satu Mare
Baia Mare
Pietrosul
2305
Bistriţa
2102
Pietrosu
Roman
Vaslui
Bârlad
Belgorod
Dnestrovskiy
Komárno
Esztergom
Vác
Gyöngyös
Hatvan
Mezőkövesd
Hajdúböszörmény
Jászberény
Carei
Someş
Dej
Bistriţa
Piatra
Neamţ
Bacău
Siret
Gyor
Tatabánya
Hegység
Nyírbátor
Debrecen
Karcag
Oradea
Someşul
2533
Cluj-Napoca
Turda
Praid
Tirgu
Mureş
Odorheiu
Secuiesc
Miercurea
Ciuc
Bretcu
Prut
Brăila
467
Budapest
Újpest
Szolnok
Cegléd
Nagykőrös
Mezőtúr
Salonta
Gyula
Criş
Negru
Aiud
Abrud
Mţii Bihor
1848
Tirgu Mureş
Sebeş
H
U
N
G
A
R
Y
Kecskemét
Kiskunfélegyháza
Kőrös
Békéscsaba
Szentes
Hódmezővásárhely
Makó
Criş
Arad
Crişul Alb
Alba-Iulia
Deva
Brad
Medias
Sighişoara
u
l
B4çău
Galaţi
Ismail
Reni
Kagul
Vt. Omul
2535
Vf. Negoiu
2507
Braşov
Rimnicu Sarat
Focşani
Dunărea
(Danube)
Tulcea
Sulina
Szekszárd
Szeged
Subotica
Senta
Kikinda
Zrenjanin
(Petrovgrad)
B
a
n
a
t
Timişoara
Caransebeş
Reşiţa
R
O
M
A
N
I
A
Lugoj
Hunedoara
Simeria
Carpaţii Meridionali
Sibiu
Sfintu Gheorghe
Fâgâraş
P. Turnu Roşu
350
Mehadia
Poarta Orientalis
Peleaga
2509
2618
Paring
Vf. Negoiu
Cimpulung
Tirgovişte
Rimnicu
Vilcea
Braşov
Buzău
S
Buzău
Mangalia
BLACK
SEA
Pécs
Mohács
Osijek
Novi Sad
Petrovaradin
Sombor
Bečej
Vršac
Bela Crkva
Porţile de Fier
Orşova
Turnu-
Severin
Mehedinţi
Tirgu-Jiu
Targu-Jiu
V
l
a
h
i
a
Piteşti
Slatina
Argeş
Bucureşti
(Bucharest)
Ialomiţa
Cernavodă
Constanţa
Călăraşi
Silistra
Dunărea
(Danube)
ovar
Szekszárd
Batászék
Kalocsa
Kiskunhalas
Dunaújváros
Dunaföldvár
Drava
Brod
Odžak
Tuzla
Brčko
Bijeljina
Sremska
Mitrovica
Zemun
Beograd
(Belgrade)
Pančevo
Smederevo
Požarevac
Sava
Morava
Negotin
Bor
Zaječar
Timok
Vidin
Lom
Corabia
Turnu
Măgurele
Giurgiu
Zimnicea
Ruse (Ruschuk)
B
U
L
G
A
R
I
A
Talbukhin
G O S L A V I A
Sarajevo
Titova Užice
1346
Čačak
Kragujevac
Valjevo
Caracal
Vedea
Olteniţa
44
Travnik
ovina

COPYRIGHT. GEORGE PHILIP & SON. LTD.

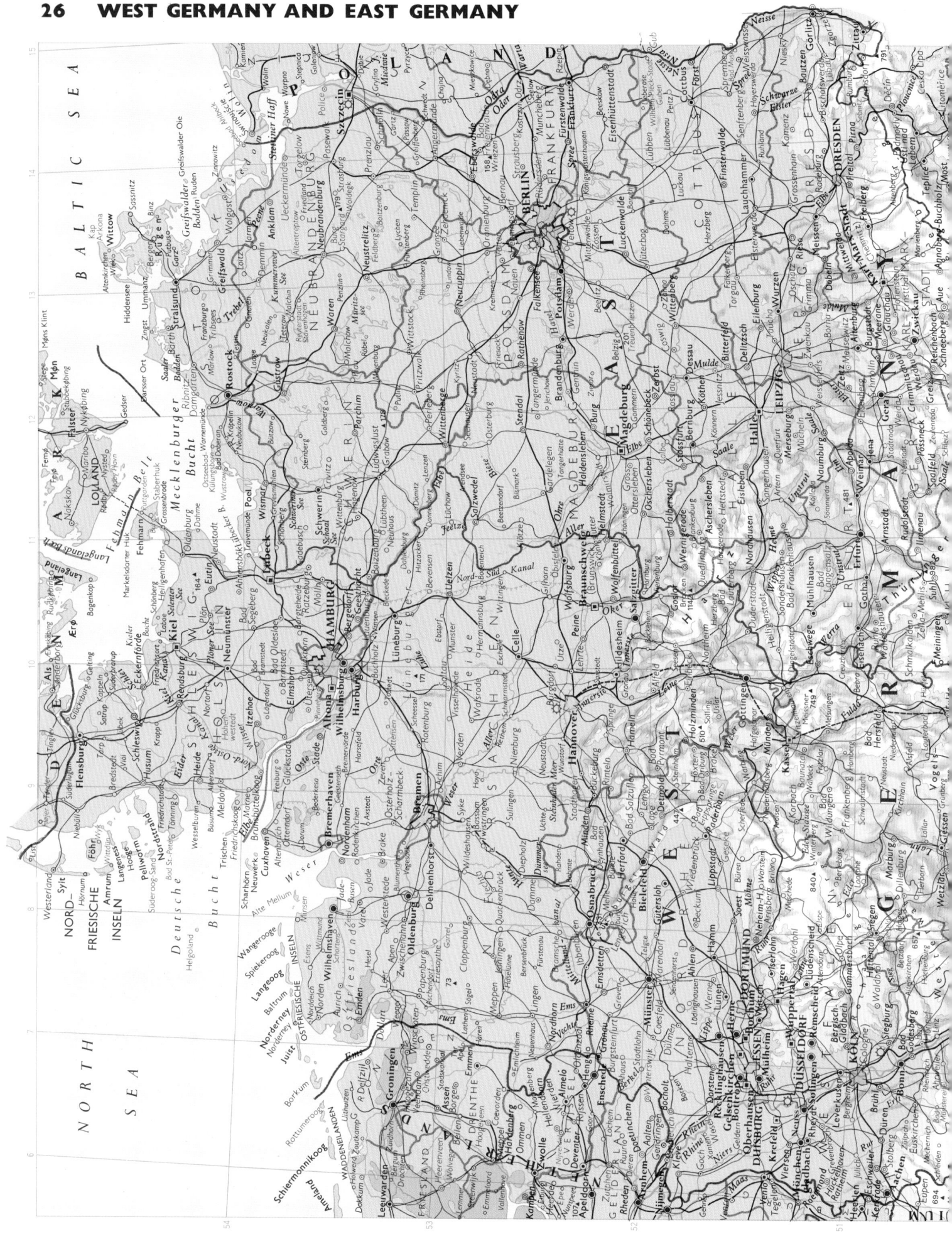
NORTH SEA
BALTIC SEA
Deutsche Bucht
Mecklenburger Bucht
NORDFRIESISCHE INSELN
OSTFRIESISCHE INSELN
DENMARK
POLAND
WEST GERMANY
EAST GERMANY
HAMBURG
BERLIN
DRESDEN
LEIPZIG
DORTMUND
DÜSSELDORF
ESSEN
DUISBURG
KÖLN
Bremen
Hannover
Magdeburg
Rostock
Szczecin

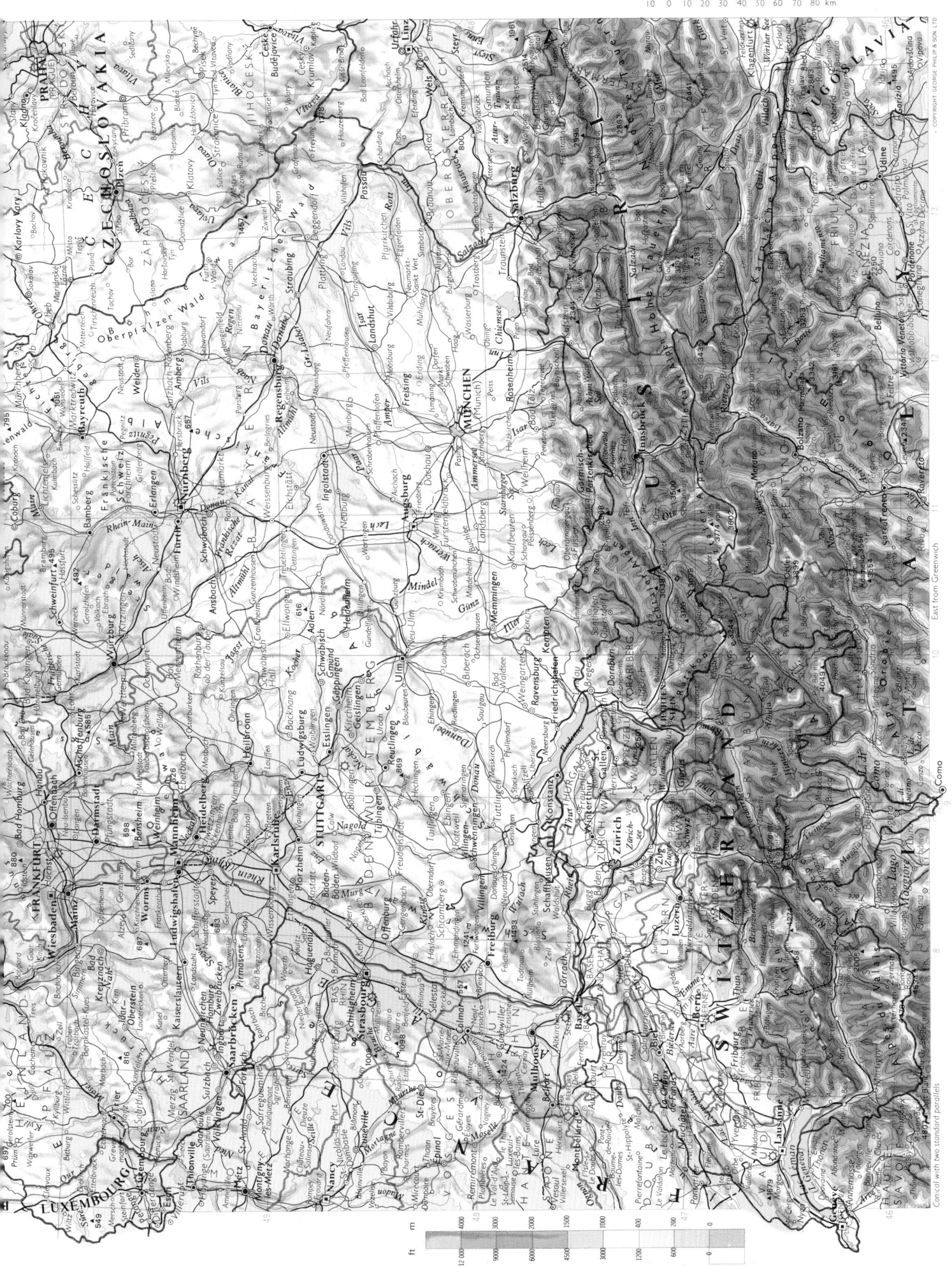

1 : 2 500 000

East from Greenwich

Conical with two standard parallels

Projection: Conical with two standard parallels

1 : 1 000 000

5   0   5   10   15   20   25 miles
5   0   10   20   30   40 km

W.   GERMANY
BAYERN

Bonndorf
im Schwarzwald
Blumb'g
WÜRTTEMBERG
Stockach
Baienfurt
Wolfegg
Leutkirch
Obergünzburg
Schongau
Peiting

SCHAFFHAUSEN
Schaffhausen
Singen
Radolfzell
Überlingen
Meersburg
Markdorf
Ravensburg
Weingarten
Kisslegg
Isny
Altusried
Wildpoldsried
Kempten
St. Mang
Marktoberdorf

Neuhausen
Konstanz
252
Reichenau
Meckenbeuren
Argen
Wangen i.A.
Buchenberg
Durach
Steingaden

THURGAU
Kreuzlingen
396
Steckborn
Stein a. Rhein
Bodensee
(L. Constance)
Friedrichshafen
Langenargen
Tettnang
Lindenberg
i.A.
Weiler-
Simmerberg
Weitnau
Sulzberg
1243
Mittelberg
Rettenberg
1738
Immenstadt
I.A. Blaichach
Nesselwang
Schwangau
Füssen

Rhine
Frauenfeld
Weinfelden
Romanshorn
Amriswil
Lindau
Bregenz
Wolfurt
Egg
Hittisau
Oberstaufen
Sonthofen
Balderschwang
Fischen
I.A.
Oberstdorf
2594
Pfronten
Reutte

Winterthur
Arbon
Rorschach
Rheineck
Lustenau
Dornbirn
Bregenzer Wald
Au
Hochtannb.
2232
Mädelegabel
2645
Hinterhornbach
Imst

ZÜRICH
St. Gallen
Gossau
Teufen
Hohenems
Götzis
Hoher
Freschen
2004
Damüls
Schröcken
Mittelberg
2777

Uster
Wetzikon
Herisau
APPENZELL
Appenzell
Oberriet
Rankweil
VORARLBERG
Rote Wand
2704
AUSTRIA
Parseier Sp.
3036
Landeck

Küsnacht
Wald
Rüti
Rapperswil
Feldkirch
Frastanz
Nenzing
Bludenz
Bürs
Dalaas
Arlberg
Am Arlberg
1793
TIROL
2974

Zug
Einsiedeln
Lachen
Walensee
Churfisten
Buchs
Sevelen
Vaduz
Schesaplana
2817
Montafon
Schruns
3148
Galtür
3099
St. Leonhard
i. Pitztal
3533

SCHWYZ
Näfels
Glarus
Mels
Bad Ragaz
Schiers
St. Antönien
2853
Silvretta-Gruppe
3399
3294
Nauders
3602

Luzern
Schwyz
GLARUS ALPEN
2844
Landquart
Klosters
Prättigau
3312
Unterengadin
Ardez
Weisspitze
3738

Altdorf
2794
3247
Chur
Langwies
Davos
National-
Park
3705

Engelberg
3620
Disentis
Oberland
Flims
Domat/Ems
Arosa
3085
Zernez
National-
Park
3602

GRAUBÜNDEN
Lenzerheide
Wiesen
Serrig
3063
Sta. Maria
Adige

Adula-
Gruppe
Thusis
Tiefencastel
Albula
P. Kesch
3418
Livigno
Ortler
3899

TICINO
Splügenpass
St. Bernardino
2133
Mulegns
P. d'Err
St. Moritz
Julierpass
2284
Silvaplana
P. della Bernina
2323
Bormio
2757

Bellinzona
Chiavenna
Campodolcino
Pzo. Stella
3163
Maloja
Maloggia
Bernina
Poschiavo
Grosio
3006

Locarno
Muralto
Ascona
Giubiasco
Gravedona
Dongo
Sondrio
Tirano
3556

Domodossola
Lugano
Lago di Como
Menaggio
Bellano
Valtellina
Adda
Morbegno
Alpi Orobie
3554

Lago
Maggiore
Luino
Lago
di Lugano
Porlezza
Bellagio
Introbio
3052

Intra
Verbania
Laveno
Mendrisio
Canzo
Lecco
Como
LOMBARDIA
Lago
d'Iseo

Varese
Gallarate
Borgomanero
BERGAMO
Seriate

East from Greenwich

COPYRIGHT. GEORGE. PHILIP & SON. LTD.

Projection: Conical with two standard parallels

1:2 500 000

10   0   10   20   30   40   50 miles
10   0   10   20   30   40   50   60   70   80 km

POLAND

Wrocław (Breslau)

Opole

Częstochowa

KIELCE

Świętokrzyskie Góry

ZAMOŚĆ

KRAKÓW

Kraków

TARNÓW

RZESZÓW

PRZEMYSL

Jarosław

KROSNO

C S R.

SLOVAKIA

ČESKOSLOVENSKÁ

Ostrava

Olomouc

Brno

Tatry

SLOVENSKÁ SOCIALISTICKÁ REPUBLIKA

Žilina

Košice

Uzhgorod

ZAKARPAT

Mukachevo

Bratislava

WIEN (VIENNA)

HUNGARY

Győr

BUDAPEST

Miskolc

Debrecen

SZABOLCS-SZATMAR

Szeged

Timişoara

YUGOSLAVIA

East from Greenwich

COPYRIGHT GEORGE PHILIP & SON LTD.

1: 3 000 000

20 10 0 10 20 30 40 50 60 miles

20 0 20 40 60 80 km

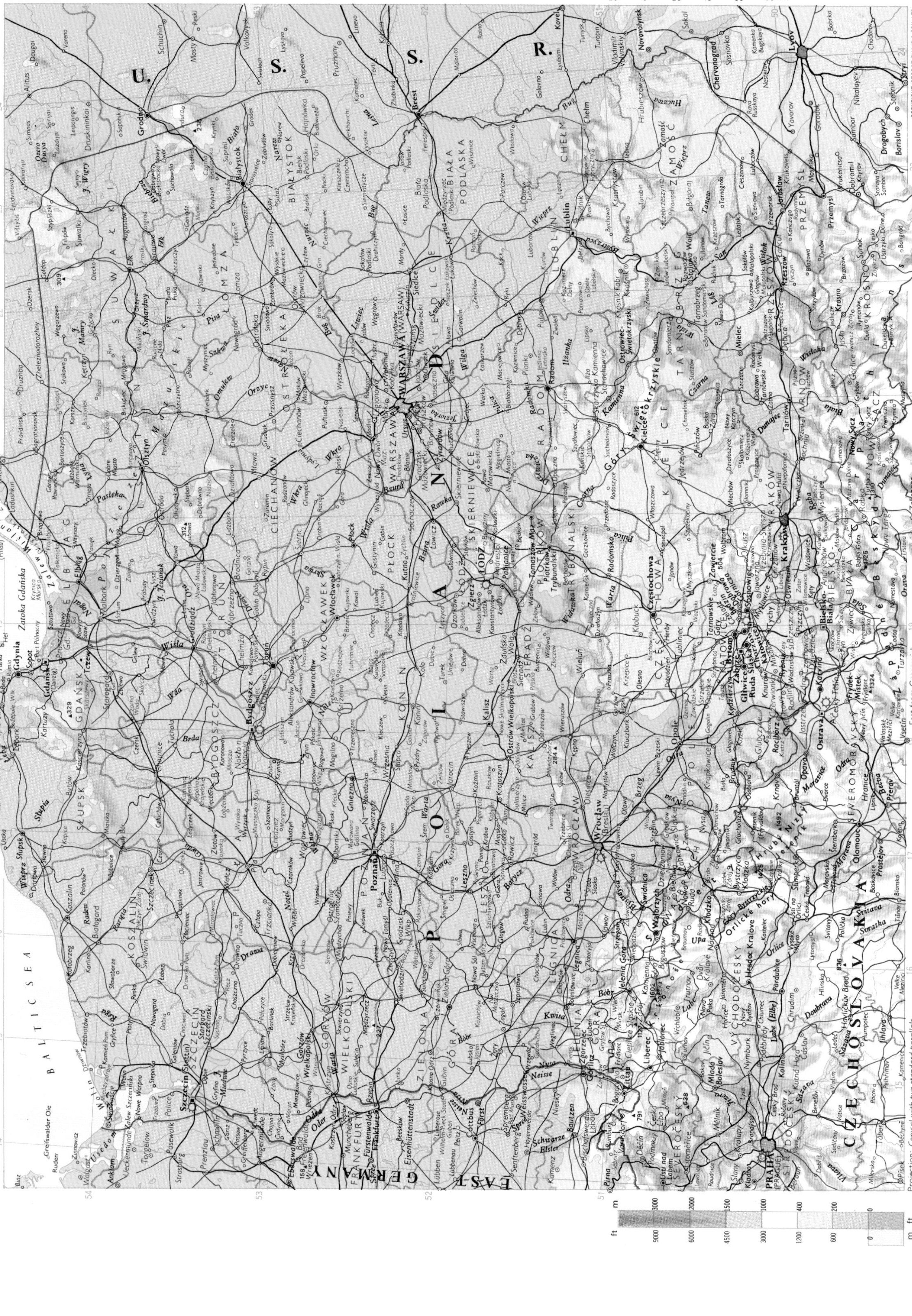
U. S. S. R.
BALTIC SEA
POLAND
EAST GERMANY
CZECHOSLOVAKIA
WARSZAWA (WARSAW)
Kaliningrad (Königsberg)
Gdańsk (Danzig)
Gdynia
Sopot
Szczecin (Stettin)
Poznań
Wrocław (Breslau)
Łódź
Kraków
Lublin
Białystok
Bydgoszcz
Katowice
Częstochowa
Radom
Kielce
Olsztyn
Toruń
Brest
Grodno
Lvov
Praha (Prague)
Ostrava
Zatoka Gdańska
Wisła
Odra
Bug
Warta
Narew
Notéć
Pilica
San
East from Greenwich
Projection: Conical with two standard parallels
COPYRIGHT. GEORGE PHILIP & SON, LTD.
m ft
3000 9000
2000 6000
1500 4500
1000 3000
400 1200
200 600
0 0

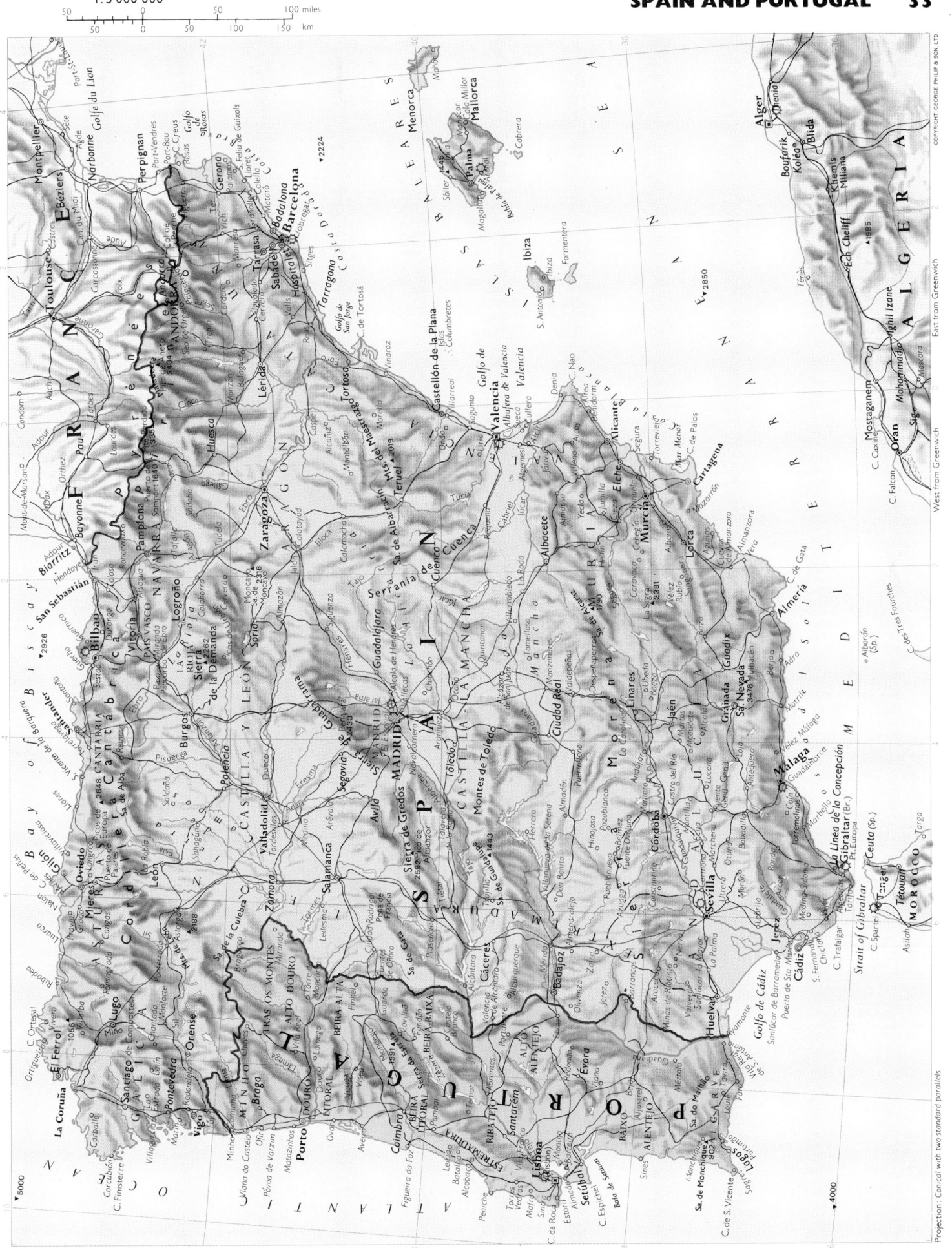

1:5 000 000

50   0   50   100 miles
50   0   50   100   150 km

Projection : Conical with two standard parallels

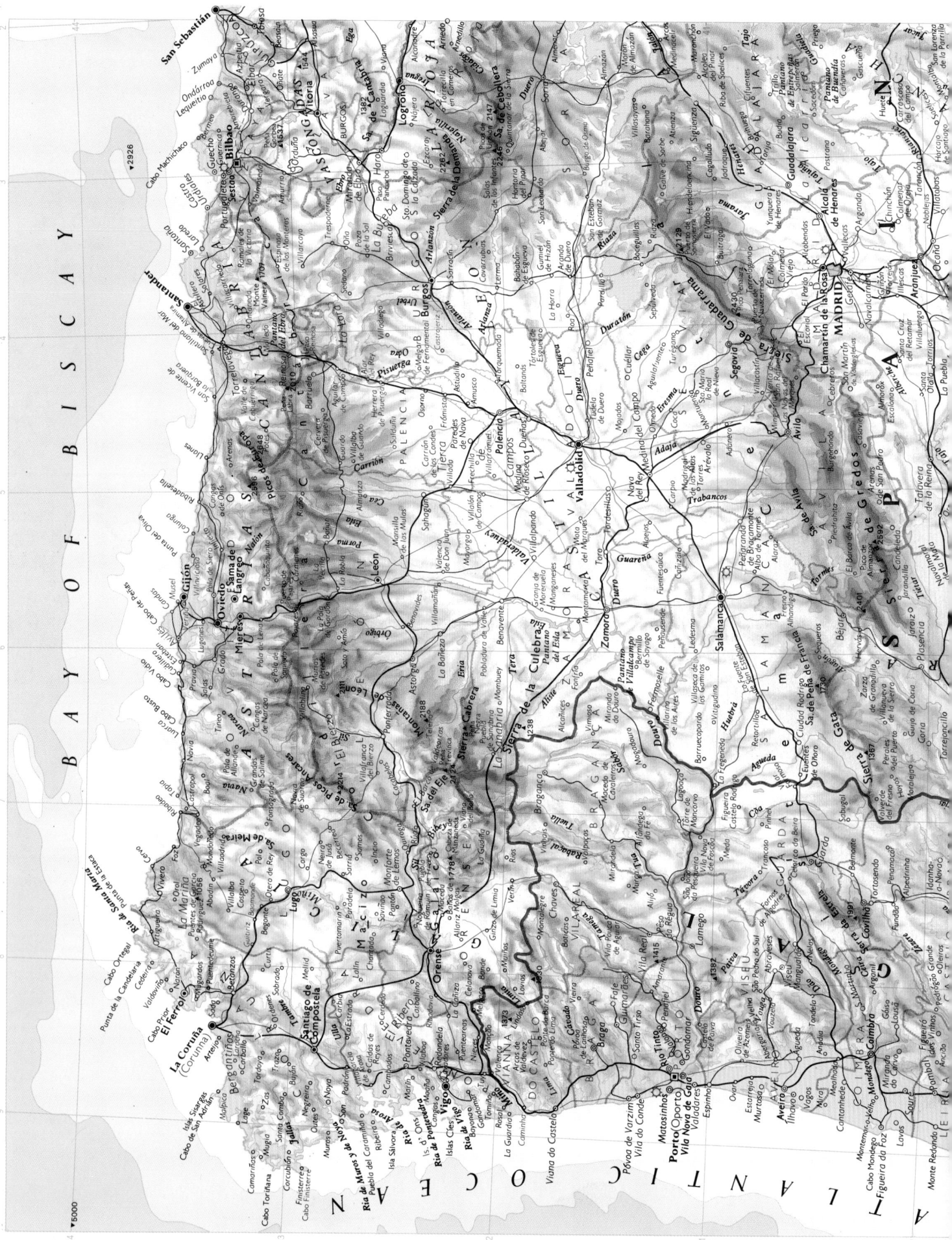

BAY OF BISCAY
ATLANTIC OCEAN
San Sebastián
Bilbao
Santander
Gijón
Oviedo
Mieres
León
Burgos
Vitoria
Logroño
Palencia
Valladolid
Zamora
Salamanca
Segovia
Avila
MADRID
Alcalá de Henares
Guadalajara
Aranjuez
La Coruña (Corunna)
El Ferrol
Lugo
Santiago de Compostela
Orense
Pontevedra
Vigo
Porto (Oporto)
Vila Nova de Gaia
Braga
Aveiro
Coimbra
Figueira da Foz
Viseu
Guarda
Covilhã
Ciudad Rodrigo
Plasencia
Talavera de la Reina
Picos de Europa
Sierra de Gredos
Sierra de Guadarrama
Sierra de Gata
Duero
Douro
Miño
Cabo Ortegal
Cabo Finisterre
Cabo Machichaco

1 : 2 500 000

MEDITERRANEAN

SEA

MOROCCO

West from Greenwich

Projection: Conical with two standard parallels

BAY OF BISCAY
Golfe de Gascogne
FRANCE
SPAIN
BARCELONA
Zaragoza
(Saragossa)
Pamplona
Bilbao
San Sebastián
Toulouse
Perpignan
Lérida
Tarragona
Huesca
Logroño
Burgos
Soria
Guadalajara
MADRID
Castellón de la Plana
Teruel
Gerona
ANDORRA
ROUSSILLON
NAVARRE
BÉARN
CANTABRIA
VASCONGADAS
Golfo de San Jorge
Menorca
(Minorca)
Mallorca
(Majorca)
BALEARES
(BALEARIC ISLANDS)

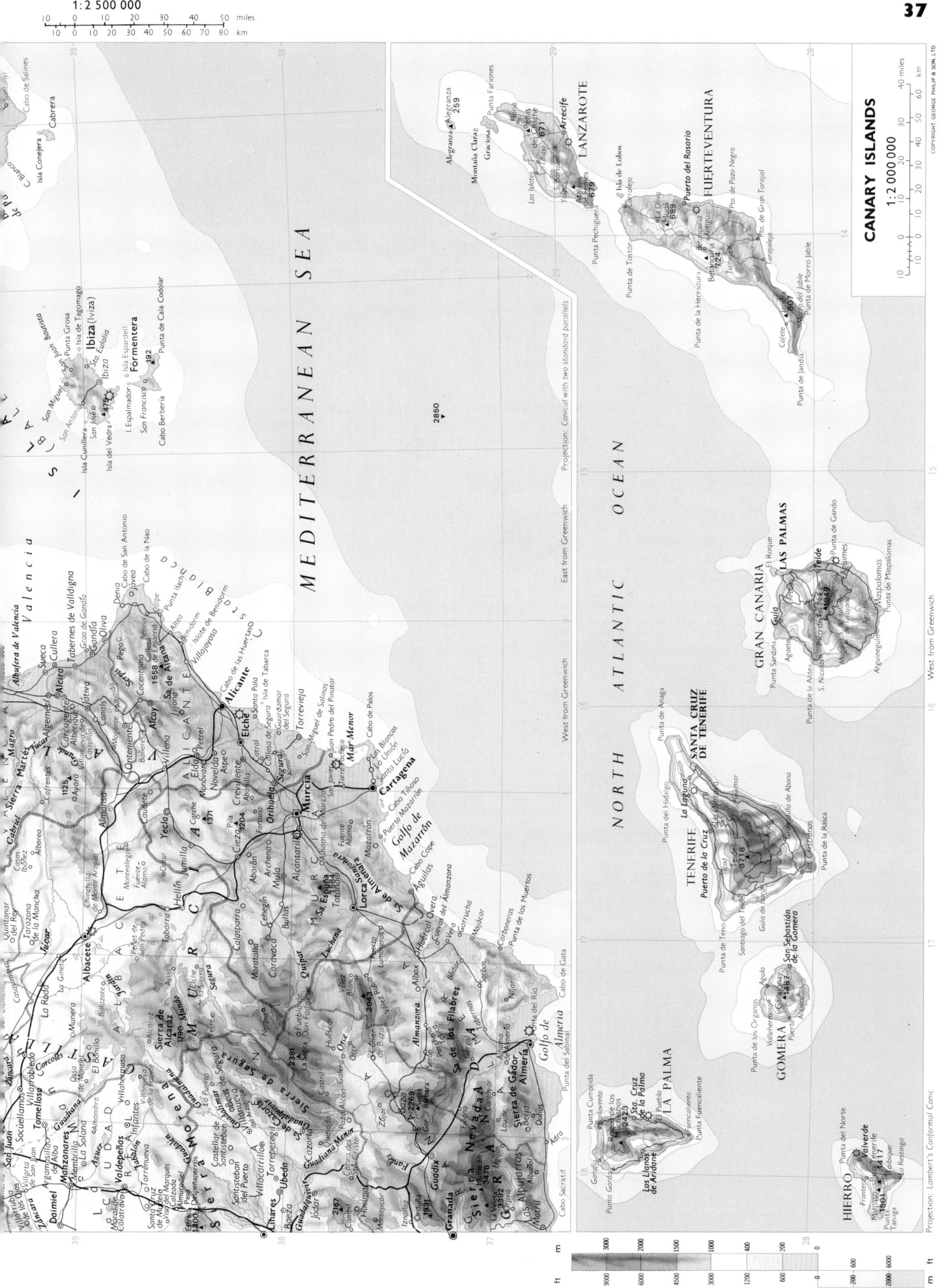

1:2 500 000

10   0   10   20   30   40   50 miles
10   0   10   20   30   40   50   60   70   80 km

MEDITERRANEAN SEA

B A L E A R I C

Isla Conejera   Cabrera
Isla de Salines

Cabo Blanco

San Miguel   San Juan Bautista   Punta Grosa
Isla de Tagomago
Puerto   Santa Eulalia
Ibiza (Iviza)
Ibiza
San Antonio
San José   475
San Francisco   Formentera
I. Espalmador   192
I. Espardell   Punta de Cala Codolar
Isla del Vedra   Cabo Berbería

2850

V a l e n c i a
Albufera de Valencia
Sueca
Alcira   Cullera
Taberns de Valldigna
Denia   Cabo de San Antonio
Gandía   Oliva   Cabo de la Nao
Grao de Gandía   Punta Ifach
Pego   Calpe
Villalonga   Benidorm
1558   Sa. de Aitana   Isiote de Benidorm
Cocentaina   Altea
Ontenniente   Alcoy   Villajoyosa
Alcoy   Santa Pola
Villena   Petrel   Cabo de las Huertas
1125   Eldo   Alicante
Almansa   Monóvar   Elche
Novelda   Guardamar del Segura
Aspe   Crevillente   Torrevieja
Monteagudo   Catral   San Pedro del Pinatar
Yecla   Callosa de Segura   Isla de Tabarca
Jumilla   Orihuela   San Miguel de Salinas
Abanilla   Murcia   Mar Menor
Cieza   1204   Molina de Segura   Cabo de Palos
Abarán   Alcantarilla   La Unión
Mula   Alhama de Murcia   Santa Lucía
Calasparra   Alguazas   Cartagena
Cehegín   Totana   Fuente Alamo   Cabo Tiñoso
Caravaca   Lorca   Mazarrón   Puerto Mazarrón
Bullas   Sa. Espuña   Golfo de Mazarrón
Vélez   Águilas   Cabo Cope
Cabo del Almanzora

NORTH   ATLANTIC   OCEAN

Sierra de Alcaraz
Alcaraz   Riópar
Segura
Puebla de Don Fadrique
Huéscar
Orce   Baza
Albox
Sorbas   Níjar
Cabo de Gata
Vera   Garrucha
Mojácar
Carboneras
Punta de los Muertos

Sierra de los Filabres
Tabernas   Almería
Golfo de Almería
Punta del Sabinal

Sa. de los Filabres
Sa. de Gádor
Almería

Albacete   La Roda
Tomelloso   Socuéllamos
Sierra Morena
Daimiel
Manzanares
Valdepeñas
Guadiana

Sierra Nevada   3478   3392
Guadix   Granada
Sierra de Alpujarras

COPYRIGHT GEORGE PHILIP & SON LTD

CANARY ISLANDS
1:2 000 000

km   10   0   10   20   30   40   50   60
10   0   10   20   30   40 miles

Alegranza   259
Montaña Clara   Graciosa   Punta Fariones
Los Islotes   Peñas del Chache   671
Isla de Lobos   Arrecife   LANZAROTE
Corralejo   Yaiza
La Oliva   689
Punta Pechiguera   619
Puerto del Rosario
FUERTEVENTURA   724
Punta de Tostón
Betancuria   Antigua
Punta de la Herradura
Pto. de Gran Tarajal
Cofete   807
Punta de Jandía   Punta de Morro Jable

GRAN CANARIA
El Roque   LAS PALMAS
Gáldar   Telde   Punta de Gando
Punta Sardina   1949
Agaete   Maspalomas
Punta de la Aldea   Punta de Maspalomas
S. Nicolás   Arguineguín

TENERIFE
Punta de Anaga
SANTA CRUZ
La Laguna   DE TENERIFE
Puerto de la Cruz
Punta del Hidalgo
3718   Güimar
Teide   Golfo de Abona
Punta de Teno   Guía de Isora
Santiago del Teide   Los Cristianos
Punta de la Rasca

GOMERA
Agulo
Hermigua   1487   San Sebastián
Vallehermoso   de la Gomera
Punta de los Órganos   Puerto de Santiago
Punta Falcanei

LA PALMA
Punta Cumplida
Barlovento
2423   Sta. Cruz
Los Sauces   de la Palma
Puerto   Pueblo
Punta Gorda
Los Llanos   Fuencaliente
de Aridane
Punta Fuencaliente

HIERRO
Punta del Norte
1417   Valverde
Frontera
1501   Punta Tamaduste
Punta de Orchilla   Restinga

Projection: Lambert's Conformal Conic

m   3000   2000   1500   1000   400   200   0
ft   9000   6000   4500   3000   1200   600   0

ft   6000   2000   600   0
m   200   0

LONDON
Bristol
Southampton
Plymouth
Brighton
Portsmouth
Land's End
Scilly Is.
Lizard Pt.
English Channel
Channel Is.
Jersey
St-Malo
Cherbourg
Le Havre
Rouen
Caen
Dieppe
Somme
Str. of Dover
Dover
Folkestone
Calais
Boulogne
Dunkerque
Oostende
Vlissingen
Harwich
's-Gravenhage
Hoek van Holland
Amsterdam
Rotterdam
NETH.
Dordrecht
Antwerpen
Mechelen
Gent
BELGIUM
Brussel
Namur
Liège
Aachen
Maas
Ardennes
LUX.
Lille
Arras
Douai
Amiens
St-Quentin
Reims
Verdun
Metz
Nancy
Toul
Épinal
Vosges
Strasbourg
Marne
Châlons
Meuse
I. d'Ouessant
Pte. St-Mathieu
Brest
Pte. de Penmarch
Lorient
Vannes
Belle-Île
St-Nazaire
Rennes
Alençon
Le Mans
Versailles
PARIS
Seine
Orléans
Troyes
Loire
Nantes
Angers
Sarthe
Tours
Cher
Vienne
Poitiers
Bourges
Dijon
Le Creusot
Chalon
Yonne
Belfort
Besançon
La Rochelle
Rochefort
Charente
Gironde
Angoulême
Limoges
Périgueux
Bordeaux
Dordogne
Lot
Garonne
Adour
Toulouse
Tarn
Bay of Biscay
5365
5098
FRANCE
Vichy
Mâcon
Mt. Dore 1886
Auvergne
Clermont-Ferrand
St-Étienne
Lyon
Saône
Rhône
Allier
Cévennes
Isère
Grenoble
Durance
Nîmes
Montpellier
Béziers
Sète
Narbonne
Avignon
Marseille
Toulon
Golfe du Lion
Perpignan
C. Creus
Cannes
MONACO
Nice
Menton
Mt. Blanc 4807
Genève
Lac Léman
Lausanne
Bern
SWITZERLAND
Zürich
Basel
Freiburg
Bodensee
LIECHT.
Jura
W. GERMANY
Hannover
Weser
Osnabrück
Münster
Braunschweig
Dortmund
Essen
Kassel
Düsseldorf
Köln
Bonn
Koblenz
Rhein
Mosel
Wiesbaden
Mainz
Frankfurt
Fulda
Darmstadt
Mannheim
Heidelberg
Karlsruhe
Stuttgart
Schwarzwald
Donau
Ulm
Augsburg
München
Isar
Inn
Würzburg
Nürnberg
Regensburg
Thüringer Wald
E. GERMANY
BERLIN
Potsdam
Spree
Magdeburg
Elbe
Harz
Halle
Leipzig
Mulde
Erfurt
Plauen
Karl-Marx-Stadt (Chemnitz)
Erzgeb.
Dresden
Praha
Plzeň
Böhmerwald
Vltava
Linz
Salzburg
Innsbruck
Brenner 1371
TIROL
Drava
Klagenfurt
Ljubljana
Ortles 3899
Passo del S. Gottardo
Simplonpass
Col du Mt. Cenis 2083
Como
Bergamo
Brescia
Milano
Novara
Torino
Po
Garda
Verona
Vicenza
Trento
Adige
Udine
Gorizia
Isonzo
Trieste
Rijeka
Pádova
Venézia
G. di Venézia
Alessándria
Pavia
Génova
Golfo di Génova
Parma
Réggio
Modena
Ferrara
Bologna
Ravenna
Forlì
Rimini
SAN MARINO
La Spezia
Firenze
Pisa
Livorno
Arno
Siena
Arezzo
Ancona
Perúgia
Ligurian Sea
Elba
Mt. Cinto 2710
Bastia
C. Corse
Ajaccio
Corse (Corsica)
Bouches de Bonifacio
Caprera
Sássari
Olbia
Sardegna (Sardinia)
Mt. del Gennargentu 1834
Cágliari
Civitavécchia
Tevere
ROMA
Mt. Sabini
Gran Sasso 2914
Gaeta
Volturno
Nápoli
Capri
Salerno
Tyrrhenian Sea
3719
Isole Eólie o Lipari (Æolian Is.)
Palermo
Trápani
Ísole Egadi
Marsala
Agrigento
Caltanissetta
Sicilia
3340
Pantelleria (It.)
Gozo
Valletta
MALTA
Lampedusa (It.)
ITALY
ADRIATIC
C. Ortegal
La Coruña
El Ferrol
C. Finisterre
Santiago
Pontevedra
Vigo
Oviedo
Gijón
Picos de Europa
Cordillera Cantábrica
Santander
Bilbao
San Sebastián
Biarritz
Bayonne
Pau
Pamplona
Vitoria
Ebro
Pyrenees
Pico de Aneto 3404
Andorra
Orense
Miño
León
Campos
Braga
Bragança
Porto
Douro
Valladolid
Palencia
Burgos
Duero
Salamanca
Ciudad Rodrigo
Coimbra
Sa. da Estrela
Sa. de Gata
Sa. de Guadarrama
MADRID
Tajo
Tejo
Guadalajara
Zaragoza
Lérida
Barcelona
Tarragona
Tortosa
Torres Vedras
Lisboa
Alcántara
Cáceres
Toledo
Guadiana
Badajoz
Évora
Teruel
Cuenca
Castellón
La Mancha
Ciudad Real
Júcar
Valencia
Albacete
PORTUGAL
SPAIN
Sierra Morena
Córdoba
Linares
Segura
Guadalquivir
Jaén
Huelva
Faro
Tinto
Sevilla
Genil
Granada
Murcia
Lorca
Alicante
C. Nao
Cartagena
Cádiz
Jérez
C. Trafalgar
Str. of Gibraltar
Gibraltar (Br.)
Algeciras
Málaga
Mulhacén
Sa. Nevada 3478
Almería
C. de Gata
Islas Baleares
Ibiza
Formentera
Palma
Mallorca (Majorca)
Cabrera
Menorca (Minorca)
Mahón
MEDITERRANEAN
2887
2850
Tanger
Ceuta (Sp.)
Larache
Tétouan
Alborán (Sp.)
Melilla (Sp.)
Ouezzane
Rabat
Meknès
Fès
Moulouya
Oujda
MOROCCO
Haut Atlas
3737
Mostaganem
Oran
Ghazaouet
Sidi-Bel-Abbès
Tlemcen
Alger
Cheliff
Hauts Plateaux
Chott ech Chergui
Djelfa
Atlas Saharien
Aïn Sefra
Figuig
Bechar
Beni Abbès
ALGERIA
Bejaia
Skikda
Annaba
Constantine
Chott el Hodna
Biskra
Tébessa
O. Djedi
Chott Melrhir
Touggourt
Ghardaïa
Ouargla
Hassi Messaoud
Ft. Lallemand
El Goléa
Bizerte
Tunis
Carthage
C. Bon
G. de Hammamet
Sousse
Kairouan
TUNISIA
Sfax
Iles Kerkenna
Tozeur
Chott Djerid
Gabès
Djerba
Tarābulus
Al Khums
Jabal Nafūsah
Mizdah
LIBYA
ft m
12 000 4000
6000 2000
3000 1000
1200 400
600 200
0 0
200 600
1000 3000
2000 6000
3000 9000
m ft
Projection: Conical with two standard parallels.
West from Greenwich 0 East from Greenwich
10
5
45
40
35
30

1 : 10 000 000

50   0   100   150   200 miles
50   0   100   200   300 km

POLAND
Poznań
Łódź
Radom
Legnica
Wrocław
Chorzów
Kraków
Tarnów
Przemyśl
Ostrava
Banská
Slavkov
Bratislava
Miskolc
Košice
HUNGARY
Kecskemét
Budapest
Debrecen
Oradea
Cluj-Napoca
Szeged
Hódmezővásárhely
Arad
ROMANIA
Timişoara
Subotica
Novi Sad
Zrenjanin
Beograd
Smederevo
Kragujevac
Niš
BULGÁRIA
Sofiya
Plovdiv
Skopje
Bitola
ALBANIA
Tiranë
Durrës
Elbasan
GREECE
Thessaloníki
Thívai
Athínai
Piraiévs
Pátrai
Pelopónnisos
Sparti
Náxos
Kikládhes
Dhodhekánisos
Kríti
Iráklion

Warszawa
Brest
Pinsk
Polesye
Pripyat
Chernigov
Desna
Sumy
Belgorod
Kharkov
Volgograd

Lublin
Lutsko
Rovno
Zhitomir
Kiyev
Poltava
Kremenchug
Shakhty
Novocherkassk

Lvov
Vinnitsa
Kirovograd
Dnepropetrovsk
Donetsk
Rostov
Stavropol

Chernovtsy
MOLDAVIAN
S.S.R.
Kishinev
Odessa
Nikolayev
Kherson
Melitopol
Krasnodar
Maykop

BLACK SEA

Istanbul
Ankara
TURKEY
Konya
Adana
Gaziantep
SYRIA
Halab

CYPRUS
Nicosia
Famagusta
Larnaca
Limassol

Bayrūt
(Beirut)
LEBANON
Dimashq
(Damascus)

Hefa
(Haifa)
Tel Aviv-Yafo
Jerusalem
Amman
JORDAN
ISRAEL

MEDITERRANEAN SEA

EGYPT
El Qâhira
El Iskandarîya
Tanta
Bur Sa'id
El Suweis
Sinai

LIBYA
Banghāzī
Barqa

_ _ _ _ _   Division between Greeks
and Turks in Cyprus;
Turks to the north.

COPYRIGHT. GEORGE PHILIP & SON. LTD.

1 : 5 000 000

50   0   50   100 miles
50   0   50   100   150 km

HUNGARY

Kiskőrös   Szentes   Békéscsaba

Kalocsa   Kiskunhalas   Hódmezővásárhely   Mtii Bihor   Abrud   T r a n s i l v a n i a   Bîrlad

Szekszárd   Makó   Arad   1848   Alba-Iulia   Sighişoara   Bretcu   Tecuci

Baja   Szeged   Deva   Sibiu   Fogăraş   Braşov   Galaţi   Ismail

Pécs   Subotica   Sentao   R O M A N I A   Simeria   Carpaţii Meridionali   2535   Vt. Omul   Braşov   Focşani   Seret (Sereth)   Reni   Ozero Sasyk

Mohács   Sombor   Timişoara   Lugoj   350 Vf. Omul   2507   Rîmnicu Sărat   Brăila   Kiliya

Osijek   Novi Sad   Zrenjanin   B a n a t   Caransebeş   Reşiţa   2518   Tîrgu-Jiu   Cîmpulung   Ploieşti   Buzău   Tulcea

Drava   Petrovaradin   Vršac   2509   Paring   Rîmnicu Vîlcea   Tîrgovişte   Prahova   Mamaia

Brod   Sremska Mitrovica   Pančevo   V a l a h i   Piteşti   Dîmboviţa   Bucureşti   (Bucharest)   Cernavodă   Constanţa

Odžak   YUGOSLAVIA   Zemun   Beograd (Belgrade)   Smederevo   Požarevac   Orşova   Turnu-Severin   Craiova   Slatina   Argeş   Olteniţa   Silistra   Dobrici

Bosna   Bijeljina   Sava   Danube (Dunărea)   Negotin   Vedea   Giurgiu   Turnu Măgurele   Ruse (Ruschuk)   Tutrakan   Tolbukhin   Balchik

Tuzla   Drina   Vidin   Calafăt   Lom   Corabia   Zimnicea   Svishtov   Razgrad   Nos Kaliakra

Sarajevo   Valjevo   Morava   Bor   Oryakhovo   Pleven   Gorna Oryakhovitsa   Türnovo   Kolarovgrad (Shumen)   Varna   BLACK

Višegrad   Užice   Čačak   Kruševac   Niš   Zaječar   Vratsa   S t a r a   P l a n i n a   Türgovishte   SEA

Konjic   Pljevlja   SRBIJA   2168   Pirot   P. Dragoman   Teteven   Vezhen   Shipchenski P.   Sliven   Poljanovgrad   Burgas

Durmitor   Novi Pazar   Kopaonik   Suva Pl.   Gabrovo   Kazanlŭk   Stara Zagora   Aytos

Mostar   Trebinje   2522 Tara   Kosovska Mitrovica   Leskovac   BULGARIA   Sofiya (Sofia)   2198   Musala   Yambol   Elkhovo

Stolac   CRNA GORA   Pec   Priština   Vranje   Pernik   Radomir   Stanke Dimitrov (Marek)   2925   Stara Zagora   Tundzha

Hercegnovi   Titograd Podgorica   Đakovica   Prizren   Kumanovo   Skopje   Kyustendil   Trajanova Vrata   Pazardzhik   Dimitrovgrad   Istranca Dağları   1018   Karadeniz Boğazı

Kotor   Bar   Cetinje   Beli Drim   Tetovo   2496   Titov Veles   Kočani   Stip   Rhodopi Planina   Ploydiv   Haskovo   Kŭrdzhali   Arda   Edirne   Kırklareli   TURKEY   Beykoz

Ulcinj   Skadarsko Jezero   Shkodra   ALBANIA   2259   Korab 2764   Solunska   2540   MAKEDONIJA   Prilep   Vardar   Strumica   Pirin Planina   Smolyan   Zlatograd   Xánthi   Dhidhimótikhon   Komotiní   Tekirdağ   Istanbul   Üsküdar

Bojana   Durrës   Tirana   Jablanica   Ohrid   Bitola (Monastir)   E. Serai   Dráma Philippi   Kavalla   THRÁKI   Ergene   Marmara Denizi   İmralı

Brindisi   Sur.   Elbasan   Ohridsko Jezero   Prespansko Jezero   Florina   Edhessa   M Y i a n n i t s a   Thessaloniki   Polfiyros   Alexandroúpolis   Enez   Saros Körfezi   Gelibolu (Gallipoli)   Çanakkale   Marmara   Bursa

Lecce   Otranto   Sazan   Vlóra   Berat   2480   Korça   Kastoria   Véroia   Kozáni   Áno Platí   1127 Thásos   Samothráki   1600   Gökçeada   2543

Galatina   C. d'Otranto   Gjirokastra   Smólikas   2637   Kalabáka   Pindos   Óros Ólimbos   2917   (Olympus)   Thermaikós Kólpos   Áthos 2033   Ákra Pláka   Ákra Ámbelos   Limnos   Moúdhros   Bozcaada   Troy (Ilium)   Çanakkale Boğazı   Ida 1766   Edremit   Balıkesir   2181

Capo Sta. Maria di Leuca   Kérkira (Corfu)   Ípiros   Ioánnina   Tríkkala   1978   Lárisa   Óssa   Ákra   Áyios Evstrátios   Lésvos   Ayvalık   Edremit Körfezi   Bergama (Pergamum)   2157

Kérkira   THESSALIA   Kardhítsa   Vólos   Pagasitikós Kólpos   Iliodhrómia   Skíros   Voríai Sporádhes   Baba Burun   968   İzmir (Smyrna)   Alaşehir   Sarıgöl

IONIAN   Préveza   Árta   Fársala   1575   TURKEY   Anadolu   Akhisar

SEA   Levkás (Sta. Maura)   Agrínion   Thermopílai   Gióna   2510   Lamía   Dhírfis 1743   Évvoia   Khíos   1297   Çeşme   Çesme   Manisa   Turgutlu

Kefallinía   STEREA   HELLAS   2457   Parnasós   Khalkís   Ákra Kafirévs   Áfro   Kuşadası   Ephesus   Aydın   Büyük Menderes   2308

Itháki   Navpaktos   Thívai   Marathóna   1398   Ákra   İzmir Körfezi   Menemen

Argostólion   Mesolóngion   Patraïkós Kólpos   Korinthiakós Kólpos   Megara   Athínai (Athens)   Pireievs   Ándros   Sámos   Mandalya Körfezi

Zákinthos   Patrai   Aíyion   Killíni   2376 Kórinthos   Salamís   Áyfina   Saronikós Kólpos   Lávrion   Tínos   Ándros   Ikaría   Fournoi   Mugla   2294

Zákinthos   Erímanthos   2224   Mycenae   Mikínai   Áyfina   Kéa   Tínos   Mikonos   Kálimnos   Kerme Körfezi

Pírgos   PELOPÓNNISOS   Olympia   Argos   Návplion   Idhra   Kíthnos   Érmoupolis   Síros   Rínia   Pátmos   Kos

Kiparissiakós Kólpos   Trípolis   Argolikós Kólpos   Kíthnos   Kéa   Sérifos   Páros   Náxos   1001   Amorgós   Kálimnos   Astipálaia   Ródhos

Kiparissía   KIKLÁDHES   Sífnos   Páros   Náxos   D H   O   D   Tílos

Filiatrá   Messíni   Kalamáta   Taïyetos Óros   Síkinos   Míkonos   Thíra   Ródhos 4486

MEDITERRANEAN   5121   Yíthion   Lakonikós Kólpos   Ákra Maléa   Mílos   Thíra   Kárpathos   1215

Pílos   Messiniakós Kólpos   Kíthira   Ákra Tainaron   Kásos

SEA   Andikíthira   Ákra Spátha   Kólpos Khaníon   K R Í T I   Rethímnon   Ákra Stavros   Iráklion   Knossos   Kólpos Merabéllou

East from Greenwich   Lévka Óri   Idhi Óros   Kóra Sfakíon   2456   Dhíkti   2148   Ierápetra   Kólpos Mirabéllou

Ákra Líthinon   2462   COPYRIGHT. GEORGE PHILIP & SON. LTD.

U.S.S.R.   Galaţi   Brăila   Bolgrad   Ozero   Kagul   Prut   Sulina   Gura Portiţei   Nos Kaliakra

LIGURIAN SEA

Golfo di Génova

CORSE

(CORSICA)

HAUTE-CORSE

CORSE-DU-SUD

Arcipelago

Toscano

ft m

12 000 4000

9000 3000

6000 2000

4500 1500

3000 1000

1200 400

600 200

0 0

200 600

2000 6000

m ft

Projection: Conical with two standard parallels

East from Greenwich

1:2 500 000

10   0   10   20   30   40   50 miles

10   0   10   20   30   40   50   60   70   80 km

HUNGARY

Innsbruck

Graz

Klagenfurt

Maribor

Bolzano

FRIULI

VENEZIA GIULIA

Udine

Ljubljana

Zagreb

Trieste

Venézia (Venice)

Pádova (Padua)

Golfo di Venézia

Laguna Veneta

Karlovac

Ferrara

Rijeka (Fiume)

Pula

Ravenna

A D R I A T I C

Velebitski Kanal

Velebit Planina

Zadar

Rímini

SAN MARINO

BOSNA

HERCEGOVINA

Dinara Planina

DALMACIJA

Dugi Otok

Ancona

Split

MARCHE

Brač

Hvar

Vis

Korčula

Pelješac

UMBRIA

Lastovski Kanal

Lastovo

Mljet

S E A

Pescara

ABRUZZI

LAZIO

MOLISE

ROMA (ROME)

Vatican City

COPYRIGHT. GEORGE PHILIP & SON. LTD.

Iles Sanguinaires
Petretq TavJgna
2136 Zonza
Levie

Solenzara

C. d'Ajaccio
C.di Muro
Sartène
Favone

C O R S E

CORSICA

Porto-Vecchio

CORSE-DU-SUD
Iles Cerbicales
I. de Cavallo

G. de Valinco
Propriano

Bonifacio
Bouches de Bonifacio
Maddalena
Santa Teresa Gallura
La Maddalena
Caprera

Punta dello Scorno
Golfo dell' Asinara
Costa Smeralda

Asinara
Pto. Cervo
Arzachena

Coghinas
Ággius
Calangiánus
G. di Olbia

Pórto Tórres
Tempio Pausania
1362
Ólbia

Sorso
M. Limbara
Tavolara

Sennori
Sássari
Óschiri

C. dell'Argentiera
Ittiri
Osilo
L. di Coghinas
Pattada
Posada

Algheri
Villanova
Monteleone
Boriorva 1259
Bitti
Buddusò
Siniscola

C. Comino

Temo
Bosa
Orune
Núoro

Macomer
Dorgali

SARDEGNA
Oliena
Orosei

C. Mannu
Ghilarza
Fonni
Golfo di Orosei

Oristano
Sorgono
SARDEGNA
Monti del
Gennargentu
1834
Baunei
C. di Monte Santu

M. Arci
812
Láconi
Arbatax

Golfo di Oristano
Arborea
Terralba
Múravera
Lanusei

SARDINIA
Ierzu
Villaputzu

Gúspini
Monteale
S. Gavino
Sanluri
Mandas
C. Ferrato
Serpentara

Arbus
1236
M. Linas
Gonnosfanadiga
Villacidro
Seramanna
Sestu
Sinnai 1069
Serdiana

Fluminimaggiore
Siliqua
Dolianova

Iglésias
Cixerri
Gonnesa
Assémini

Portoscuso
Carloforte
Carbónia
1116
Quartu Sant'Elena

San Pietro
Sant'Antioco
Santadi
Cágliari

Sant' Antíoco
Porto Botte
Pula
Golfo di Cágliari
C. Carbonara

G. di Pàlmas
Teulada
C. Spartivento

T Y R R H E N I A N

3719

S E A

3589

Ustica

ROMA
Rome
Tivoli

Vatican City
Palestrina

Fregene
Frascati
Velletri
Angni
Véroli

Lido di Óstia
(Lido di Roma)
Albano
Cori
Ferentino
Frosinone

Prática di Mare
Aprília
Cisterna di Latina
Ceccano

Ánzio
Latina
Priverno

Nettuno
Pontínia
Fondi
1533

Circeo
Sabáudia
Terracina
Fórmia

Monte Circeo
541
Gaeta

Zannone
Golfo di Gaeta

Palmarola
Ponza
Mondrago

Ísole Ponziane
283

Ventotene
Ísch

Scale
ft   m

9000   3000

6000   2000

4500   1500

3000   1000

1200   400

600   200

0   0

200   600

2000   6000

4000   12 000

m   ft

C. San Vito
G. di Castellammare
Favaratta

Levanzo
Trápani
1110
Corino
Móntelepre
PALERMO
Bagheria

Isole Égadi
Érice
Alcamo
S. Giuseppe
Iato
Mortelle

Maréttimo
Favignana
Paceco
Partinico
Camporeale
Marineo

Favignana
Stagnone
Calatafimi
Salemi
Corleone
1613
Lercara
Belsi

Marsala
Castelvetrano
Partanna
Gibellina
Bisacquino Prizzi
SIC

Mazara
del Vallo
Menfi
Sambuca
di Sicilia
Búrgio
Mussomeli
Cast

Campobello di Mazara
Belice
Sciacca
Caltabellotta
Ribera
Platani
Racalmuto
Cal

Sicilian Channel
Cattólica Eráclea
Siculiana
Raffadali
Naro

Porto Empédocle
Agrigento
Favara

Palma di Montechiaro
Campobello

Iles de la
Galite

Bizerte
(Binzert)
C. Blanc Cani

C. Serrat
Plane

Menzel-Bourguiba
Zembra

Mateur
C. Bon

El Kala
Tabarka
Golfe de Tunis

Tébourba
TUNIS
Halq el Oued

ALGERIA
Bou Salem
Béja
Medjerda
Menzel-Temime

Pantelleria
Pantelleria
836 (It.)

T U N I S I A
Nabeul
M E D I T E

Téboursouk
Zaghouan
Hammamet
Soliman
1319

45

1:2 500 000

10   0   10   20   30   40   50 miles
10   0   10   20   30   40   50   60   70   80 km

ADRIATIC

SEA

G. di Manfredónia

Bari

Táranto

Golfo di
Táranto

Lecce

Strait of Otranto

Brindisi

BASILICATA

G. di Salerno

G. di
Policastro

IONIAN

CALABRIA

Cosenza

Crotone

Catanzaro

Golfo di
Sant'Eufémia

Golfo di Squillace

Isole Eólie o Lípari (Æolian Is.)

SEA

Vibo Valéntia

G. di Gióia

Messina
Réggio

Monti Nebrodi

Catánia
Golfo di
Catánia

Siracusa

G. di
Avola
Noto

MEDITERRANEAN SEA

Kérkira
(Corfu)

ALBANIA

Durrës
(Durazzo)

COPYRIGHT GEORGE PHILIP & SON, LTD

HUNGARY
ADRIATIC SEA
ALBANIA
MAKEDONIJA
CRNA GORA (MONTENEGRO)
BOSNA
HERCEGOVINA
SRBIJA
Autonomna Pokrajina Vojvodina
Socijalistička Autonomna Pokrajina Kosovo
Beograd (Belgrade)
Novi Sad
Sarajevo
Zagreb
Skopje
Titograd (Podgorica)
Tirana (Tiranë)
Durrës (Durazzo)
Timişoara
Arad
Szeged
Pécs
Subotica
Osijek
Banja Luka
Tuzla
Zenica
Mostar
Dubrovnik
Niš
Kragujevac
Priština
Prizren
Shkodra (Shkodër)
Elbasani
Ohrid
Bitola
Prilep
Titov Veles
Kumanovo
Leskovac
Kruševac
Čačak
Valjevo
Šabac
Zrenjanin
Pančevo
Vršac
Kikinda
Sombor
Vukovar
Vinkovci
Slavonski Brod
Bihor
Munţii Apuseni
Munţii Zarandului
Caransebeş
Reşiţa
Vidin
Pernik
Kyustendil
Dunav (Danube)
Sava
Drina
Morava
Tisa
Ibar
Vardar
Kopaonik
Durmitor
Prokletije
Skadarsko Jezero
Ohridsko Jezero (L. Ohrid)
Prespansko Jezero (L. Prespa)
Projection: Conical with two standard parallels
East from Greenwich
ft m
9000 3000
6000 2000
4500 1500
3000 1000
1200 400
600 200
0 0
200 600
2000 6000
m ft

1:2 500 000

10 20 30 40 50 miles
10 10 20 30 40 50 60 70 80 km

U.S.S.R.

UKRAINIAN S.S.R.

R O M A N I A

VALAHIA (WALACHIA)

BUCUREŞTI (Bucharest)

Ploieşti · Piteşti · Craiova · Galaţi · Brăila · Constanţa · Tulcea

B U L G A R I A

Sofiya (Sofia) · Plovdiv (Philippopolis) · Stara Zagora · Pleven · Ruse (Ruschuk) · Varna · Burgas · Tolbukhin

Stara Planina

Sredna Gora

T U R K E Y

İSTANBUL · Üsküdar · Edirne (Adrianople) · KIRKLARELI · TEKİRDAĞ

Karadeniz Boğazı (Bosporus)

G R E E C E

Dráma · Xánthi · Komotiní

B L A C K   S E A

Dunărea (Danube)

COPYRIGHT GEORGE PHILIP & SON LTD

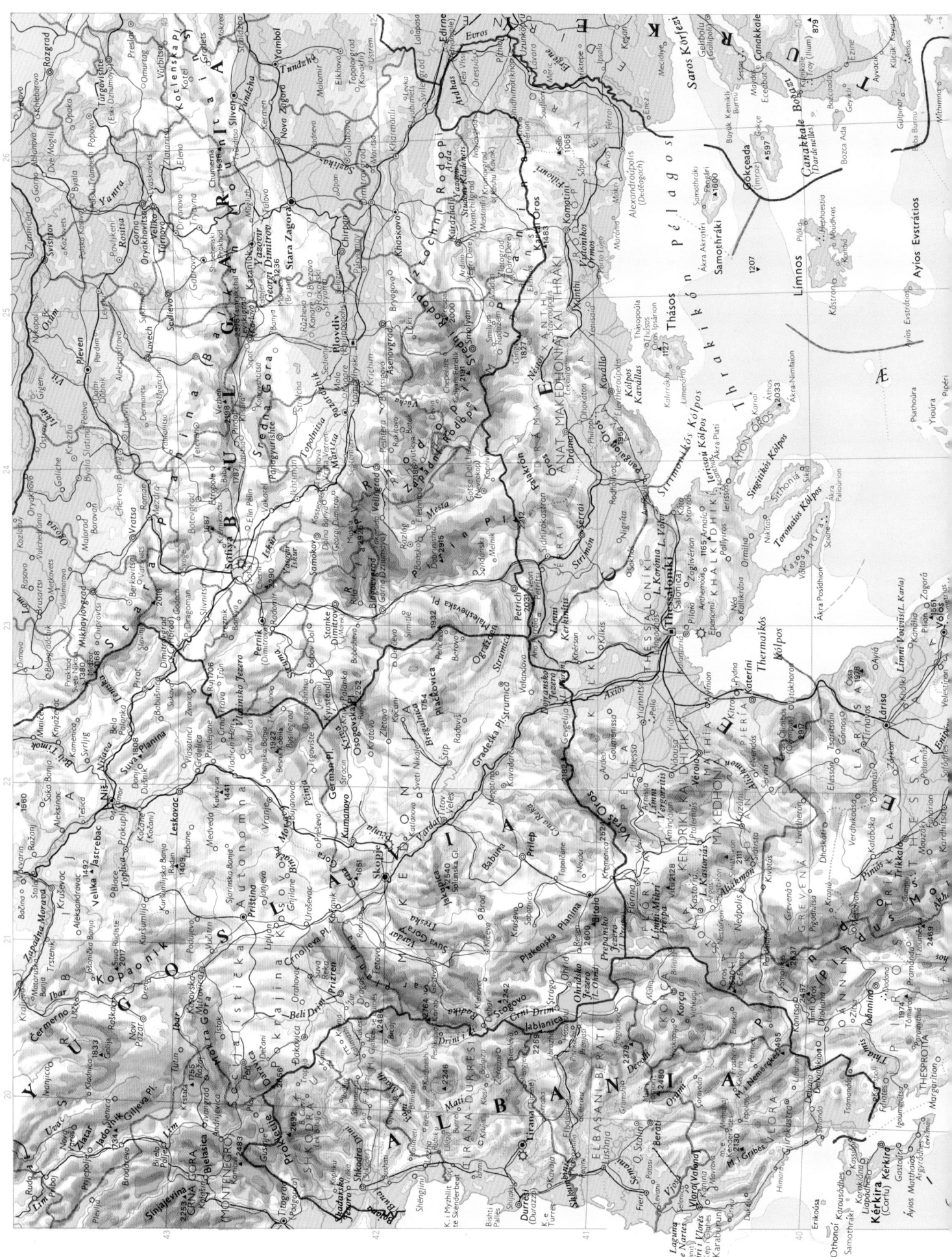
Thessaloníki
Tirana
Skopje
Sofiya
Plovdiv
Thrakikón Pélagos
Límnos
Thásos
Kérkira

1:2 500 000
miles
km
SEA OF CRETE
(Sea of Candia)
KIKLÁDHES
(CYCLADES)
ARKHIPÉLAGOS
DHODHEKÁNISOS
(DODECANESE)
PELOPÓNNISOS KAI DHITIKÍ IPROTIKÍ ELLÁS
ATTIKÍ
ATHÍNAI
(ATHENS)
Piraiévs
(Piræus)
Kallithéa
Kórinthos
(Corinth)
Corinth Canal
Khalkís
(Chalcis)
Pátrai
Kalamáta
Trípolis
Návplion
Pírgos
Agrínion
Lamía
Iráklion
(Candia)
Khaniá
(Canea)
Réthímnon
Ródhos
(Rhodes)
Kárpathos
Kásos
Kos
Sámos
Pátmos
Léros
Kálimnos
Astipálaia
Khíos
(Chios)
Psará
Ikaría
Skíros
Skópelos
Ándros
Tínos
Míkonos
Síros
Kéa
Kíthnos
Sérifos
Sífnos
Mílos
Páros
Náxos
Amorgós
Íos
Thíra
Kíthira
(Cerigo)
Zákinthos
(Zante)
Kefallinía
(Cephalonia)
Itháki
(Ithaca)
Levkás
(Santa Maura)
Korinthiakós Kólpos
Patraïkós Kólpos
Saronikós Kólpos
Argolikós Kólpos
Lakonikós Kólpos
Messiniakós Kólpos
Kiparissiakós Kólpos
Kólpos Kisámou
Kólpos Mesarás
Kólpos Merabéllou
Kerme Körfezi
Mandalya Körfezi
Kuşadasi Körfezi
TURKEY
MUĞLA
Taïyetos Óros
Párnon Óros
Ídhi Óros
Stenón Karpáthos
Stenón Kásos
Continuation Eastwards
on same scale
Projection: Conical with two standard parallels
East from Greenwich
ft
m
COPYRIGHT GEORGE PHILIP & SON LTD

1:2 500 000

EXTENSION WESTWARDS
At the same scale as main map

Projection: Conical with two standard parallels

East from Greenwich

COPYRIGHT GEORGE PHILIP & SON LTD

1:2 500 000

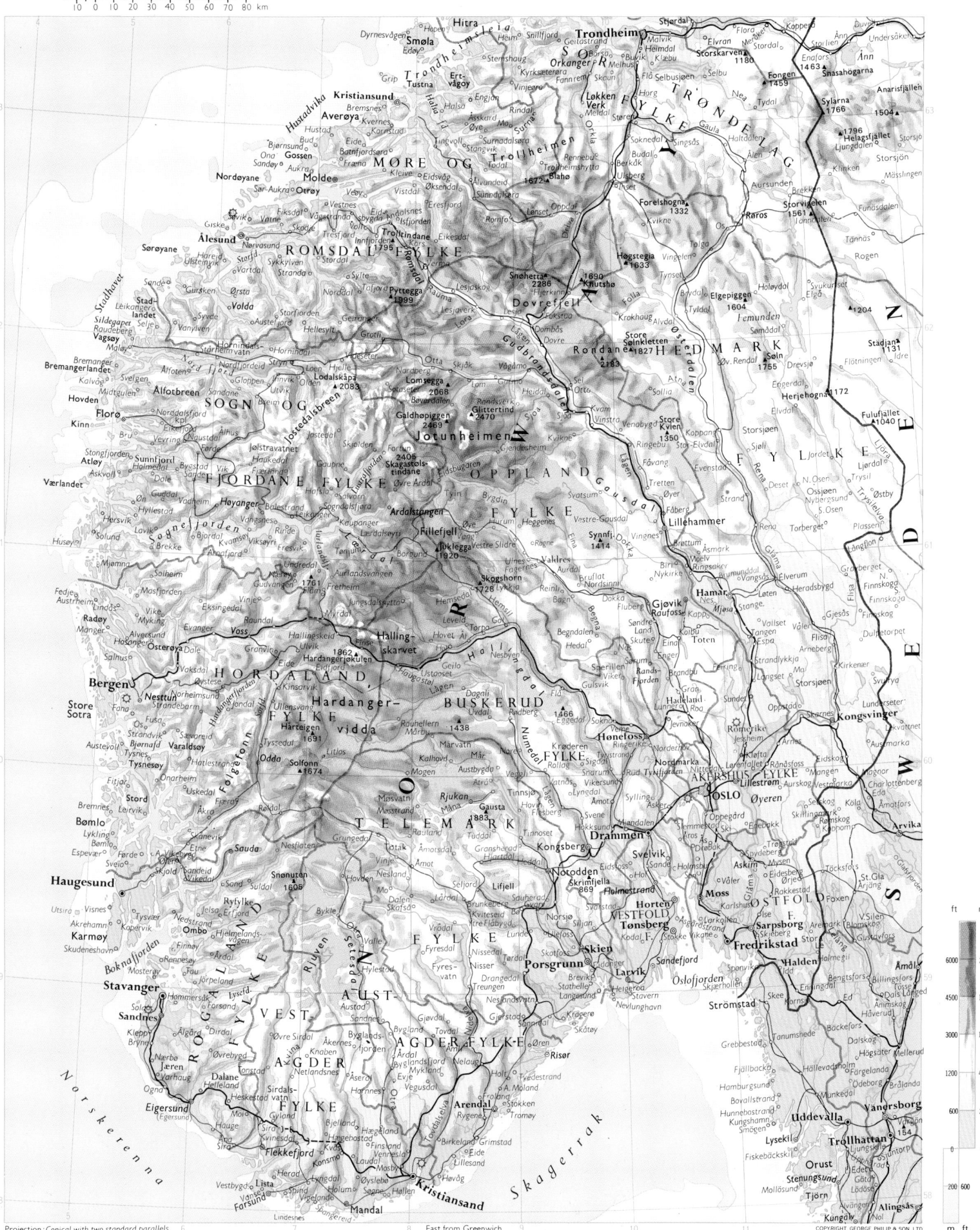

Projection: Conical with two standard parallels

East from Greenwich

COPYRIGHT. GEORGE PHILIP & SON, LTD.

Gulf of Bothnia
NORWAY
SWEDEN
Trondheim
Östersund
Sundsvall
Härnösand
Hudiksvall
Söderhamn
Gävle
Falun
Borlänge
Uppsala
Stockholm
Västerås
Örebro
Karlstad
Oslo
Drammen
Lillehammer
Hamar
Kongsberg
Skien
Porsgrunn
Larvik
Fredrikstad
Sarpsborg
Halden
Moss
JÄMTLANDS LÄN
VÄSTERNORRLANDS LÄN
GÄVLEBORGS LÄN
KOPPARBERGS LÄN
VÄRMLANDS LÄN
VÄSTMANLANDS LÄN
UPPSALA LÄN
STOCKHOLMS LÄN
SÖDERMANLANDS LÄN
ÖREBRO LÄN
HEDMARK
OPPLAND FYLKE
BUSKERUD
TELEMARK
VESTFOLD
ØSTFOLD
AKERSHUS FYLKE
SØR-TRØNDELAG FYLKE
MØRE OG ROMSDAL FYLKE
Jotunheimen
Dovrefjell
Rondane
Gudbrandsdalen
Siljan
Trollheimen

1:2 500 000

10   10   20   30   40   50 miles

10 0 10 20 30 40 50 60 70 80 km

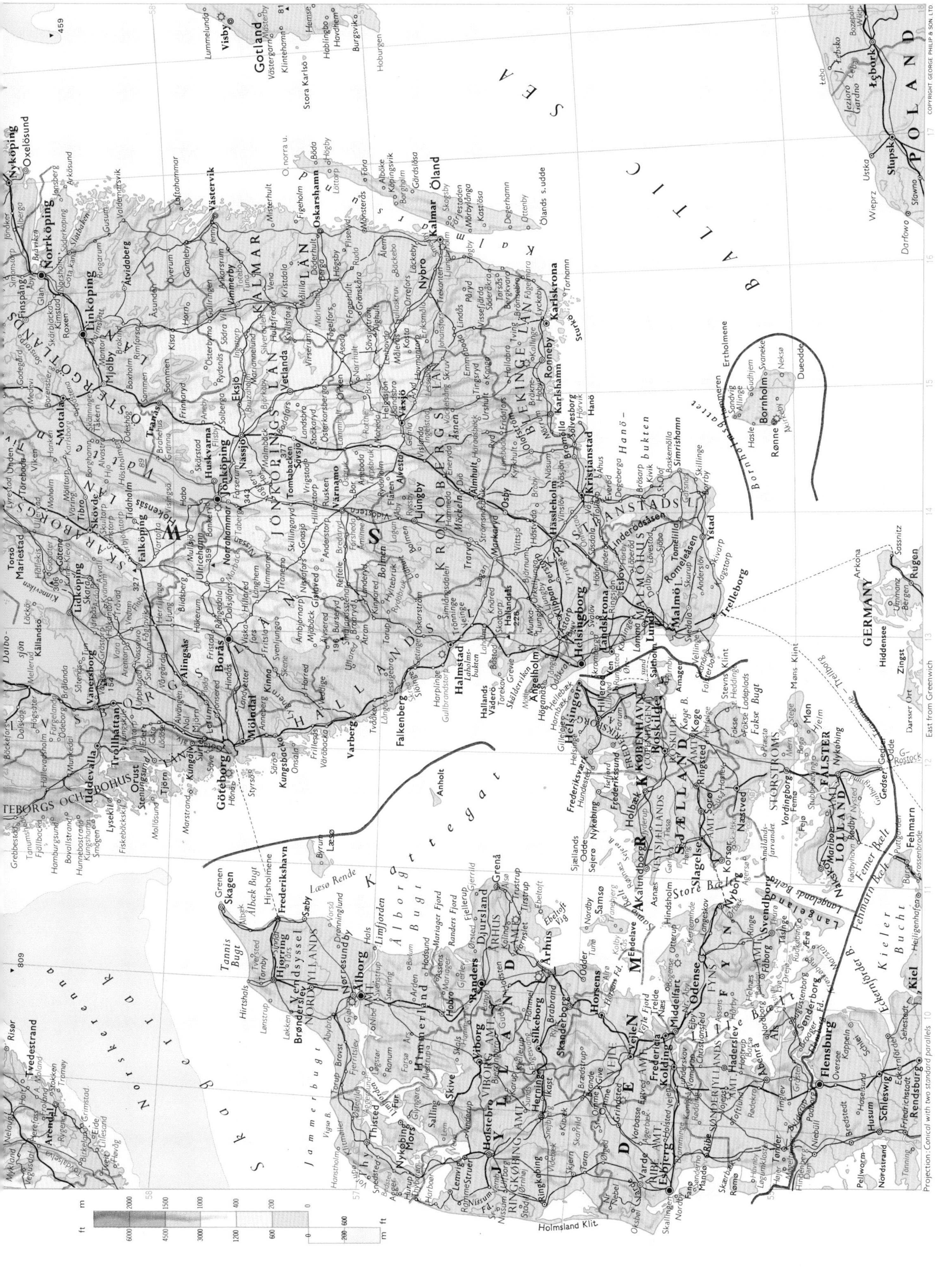

COPYRIGHT GEORGE PHILIP & SON LTD

Projection: Conical with two standard parallels

East from Greenwich

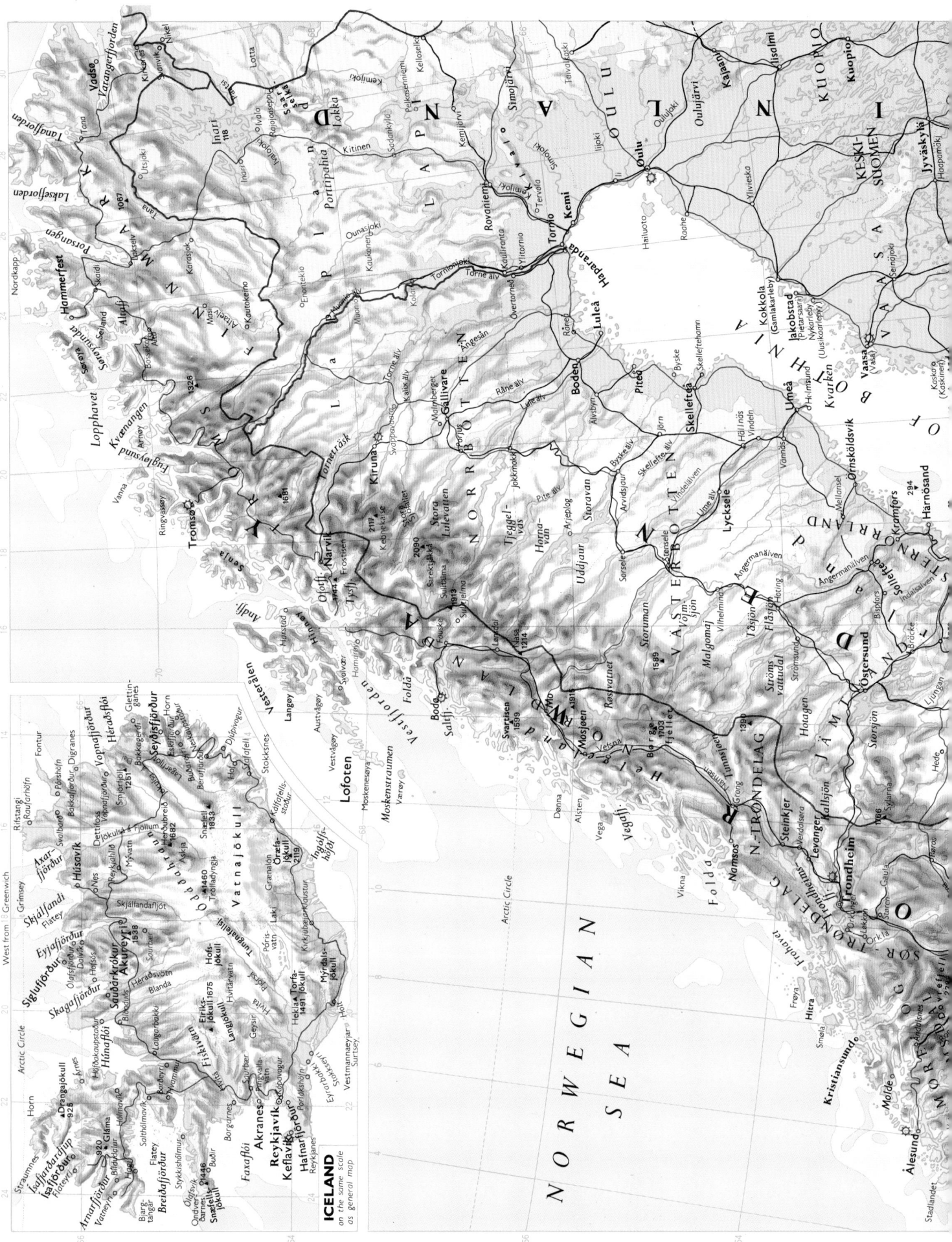
NORWEGIAN SEA
ICELAND
on the same scale
as general map
West from Greenwich
Arctic Circle
Lofoten
Vesterålen
Vestfjorden
Hammerfest
Tromsø
Narvik
Kiruna
Gällivare
Luleå
Boden
Piteå
Skellefteå
Umeå
Örnsköldsvik
Härnösand
Östersund
Trondheim
Kristiansund
Molde
Ålesund
Namsos
Steinkjer
Levanger
Bodø
Mosjøen
Haparanda
Tornio
Kemi
Oulu
Kajaani
Kuopio
Jyväskylä
Vaasa
Kokkola
Jakobstad
Rovaniemi
Inari
Reykjavik
Keflavik
Akranes
Hafnarfjördur
Akureyri
Húsavik
Vatnajökull
Hekla
Faxaflói
Ísafjördur
Vadsø
Tanafjorden
Porsanger
Nordkapp
Loppahavet
Senja
Tornträsk
Stora Lulevatten
Storuman
Hitra
Frøya
Smøla

1 : 5 000 000

```
20        40        60        80     100 miles
40  20  0    40    80    120   160 km
```

COPYRIGHT GEORGE PHILIP & SON LTD

East from Greenwich

Projection : Conical with two standard parallels

Countries / Regions:
FINLAND · HÄME · TURUN JA PORIN · UUDENMAAN · ESTONIAN S.S.R. · R.S.F.S.R. · LATVIAN S.S.R. · LITHUANIAN S.S.R. · POLAND · NORWAY · SWEDEN · DENMARK · EAST GERMANY · WEST GERMANY · NETHERLANDS

Seas / Waters:
GULF OF FINLAND · G. OF BOTHNIA · BALTIC SEA · Rigas Jūras Līcis (Gulf of Riga) · Skagerrak · Kattegat · The Sound · Store Bælt · Lille Bælt · Hardanger Fjorden · Sognefjord

Selected place names:
HELSINKI (Helsingfors) · Tampere · Turku (Åbo) · Rauma · Pori · Lahti · Kotka · Lovisa (Loviisa) · Porvoo · Hämeenlinna · Heinola · Hangö (Hanko) · Mariehamn (Maarianhamina) · Åland (Ahvenanmaa) · Naantali · Uusikaupunki · Tallinn · Haapsalu · Pärnu · Saaremaa (Ösel) · Hiiumaa (Dagö) · Kingisepp · Valga · Viljandi · Rakvere · Paldiski

Riga · Jelgava · Ventspils · Liepaja · Valmiera · Cēsis · Bauska · Šiauliai · Telšiai · Kuldiga

Klaipėda · Kaunas · Vilnius · Kaliningrad · Sovetsk · Chernyakhovsk · Grodno · Białystok · Łomża · Suwałki · Augustów · Grudziądz · Toruń · Bydgoszcz · Gdańsk · Gdynia · Zatoka Gdańska · Elbląg · Malbork · Szczecin (Stettin) · Słupsk · Koszalin · Kołobrzeg · Łódź · Pyrzyce

STOCKHOLM · Uppsala · Gävle · Söderhamn · Hudiksvall · Sundsvall · Falun · Borlänge · Mora · Örebro · Västerås · Eskilstuna · Södertälje · Norrköping · Nyköping · Oxelösund · Linköping · Motala · Jönköping · Växjö · Kalmar · Karlskrona · Karlshamn · Kristianstad · Halmstad · Göteborg · Borås · Trollhättan · Vänersborg · Lidköping · Karlstad · Kristinehamn · Falköping · Skövde · Västervik · Oskarshamn · Visby · Gotland · Öland · Kristinehamn · Filipstad · Arvika · Kongsvinger

OSLO · Bergen · Stavanger · Kristiansand · Drammen · Lillehammer · Hamar · Gjøvik · Skien · Larvik · Tønsberg · Sandefjord · Moss · Halden · Arendal · Grimstad · Lillesand · Mandal · Farsund · Flekkefjord · Egersund (Eigersund) · Haugesund · Kongsberg · Notodden · Kragerø · Risør

KØBENHAVN · Malmö · Helsingør · Helsingborg · Landskrona · Roskilde · Odense · Svendborg · Nykøbing · Korsør · Slagelse · Sjælland · Fyn · Lolland · Falster · Ålborg · Århus · Randers · Horsens · Vejle · Kolding · Esbjerg · Viborg · Herning · Silkeborg · Fredericia · Hjørring · Thisted · Holstebro · Frederikshavn · Skagen · Bornholm · Rønne · Hobro · Frederikshavn

Rostock · Warnemünde · Stralsund · Greifswald · Rügen · Wismar · Schwerin · Lübeck · Kiel · Flensburg · Hamburg · Bremen · Bremerhaven · Wilhelmshaven · Oldenburg · Emden · Groningen · Cuxhaven · Helgoland (Heligoland) · Usedom · Wolin · Nordfriesische Inseln · Ostfriesische Inseln

Elevations: 2469 · 2405 · 1883 · 1933 · 1674 · 809 · 377 · 459 · 285 · 245 · 228 · 309 · 329 · 179 · 173

Kolguyev
P-ov. Kanin
Cheshskaya Guba
Ostrov Morzhovets
M. Kanin Nos
Pechorskaya Guba
Malozemelskaya Tundra
Bolshezemelskaya Tundra
Timanskiy Kryazh
Arctic Circle
Pechora
Naryan-Mar
Ust Tsilma
Ust Usa
Inta
Vorkuta
Salekhard
Labytnangi
Ukhta
Sosnogorsk
Troitsko Pechorsk
Syktyvkar
Kotlas
Velikiy Ustyug
Kirov
Perm
SVERDLOVSK
Nizhniy Tagil
Serov
Krasnoturinsk
Berezniki
Solikamsk
Zlatoust
Miass
Ufa
Magnitogorsk
Beloretsk
Orenburg
Orsk
Novotroitsk
Sterlitamak
Salavat
Votkinsk
Ustinov
Sarapul
Kazan
Yoshkar Ola
Cheboksary
Ulyanovsk
Syzran
KUYBYSHEV
Togliatti
Novokuybyshevsk
Chapayevsk
Saransk
Penza
GORKIY
Dzerzhinsk
Arzamas
Murom
Vladimir
Ivanovo
Kostroma
Kineshma
Yaroslavl
Andropov (Rybinsk)
Vologda
Cherepovets
MOSKVA (Moscow)
Kalinin
Tula
Kaluga
Ryazan
Novomoskovsk
Lipetsk
Tambov
Michurinsk
Orel
Bryansk
Smolensk
Vitebsk
Mogilev
Gomel
Minsk
Bobruysk
Baranovichi
Brest
Grodno
Vilnius
Kaunas
Kaliningrad (Königsberg)
Klaipeda (Memel)
Liepaja
Riga
Tallinn
Tartu
Pskov
Novgorod
LENINGRAD
Kronshtadt
Vyborg
Petrozavodsk
Ladozhskoye Ozero
Onezhskoye Ozero
Beloye More (White Sea)
Arkhangelsk (Archangel)
Severodvinsk (Molotovsk)
Onega
Kandalakshskiy Zaliv
Kolskiy Poluostrov
Murmansk
Monchegorsk
Kirovsk
Apatity
Kandalaksha
P-ov. Rybachiy
Helsinki
Tampere
Turku
Pori
Lahti
Kuopio
Oulu
Kemi
Tornio
Luleå
Piteå
Umeå
Stockholm
Sundsvall
Härnösand
Gällivare
Kiruna
Narvik
Bodø
Åland (Ahvenanmaa)
Hiiumaa (Dagö)
Saaremaa (Ösel)
Gulf of Bothnia
G. of Finland
Inari
L a p p l a n d
F I N L A N D
S W E D E N
N O R W A Y
ESTONIAN S.S.R.
LATVIAN S.S.R.
LITHUANIAN S.S.R.
BYELORUSSIAN S.S.R. (WHITE RUSSIA)
KARELIAN A.S.S.R.
KOMI A.S.S.R.
UDMURT A.S.S.R.
TATAR A.S.S.R.
CHUVASH
MARI A.S.S.R.
MORDOVIAN A.S.S.R.
BASHKIR A.S.S.R.
U r a l s
Severnyye Uvaly
Valdayskaya Vozvyshennost
Polesye (Pripet Marshes)
RUSSIAN SOVIET FEDERATIVE SOCIALIST REPUBLIC
WARSZAWA (Warsaw)
POLAND
Lublin
Białystok

1 : 10 000 000

100   50   0   50   100   150   200 miles
100   0   100   200   300 km

Legend:
1 Kabardino-Balkar A.S.S.R.
2 North Ossetian A.S.S.R. (Azer.)
3 Nakhichevan A.S.S.R.
4 Checheno-Ingush A.S.S.R.
Karagiye Depression

Zaliv Kara Bogaz Gol

C A S P I A N   S E A

B L A C K   S E A

M E D I T E R R A N E A N   S E A

Sea of Azov (Azovskoye More)

KAZAKHSTAN (Kazakhskaya)
KALMYK A.S.S.R.
GEORGIAN S.S.R.
ARMENIAN S.S.R.
AZERBAIJAN
UKRAINE
MOLDAVIAN S.S.R.
ROMANIA
BULGARIA
TURKEY
SYRIA
LEBANON
IRAQ
IRAN (PERSIA)
CYPRUS
DAGESTAN

KIEV KHARKOV ROSTOV VOLGOGRAD (Stalingrad) Astrakhan Guryev
BAKU TEHRAN Baghdad Dimashq (Damascus) Bayrūt (Beirut)
ISTANBUL Ankara Tbilisi Yerevan Grozny Krasnodar
BUCUREŞTI (Bucharest) Odessa Kishinev

Division between Greeks and Turks
in Cyprus: Turks to the North.

Projection: Conical with two standard parallels

East from Greenwich

COPYRIGHT. GEORGE PHILIP & SON, LTD.

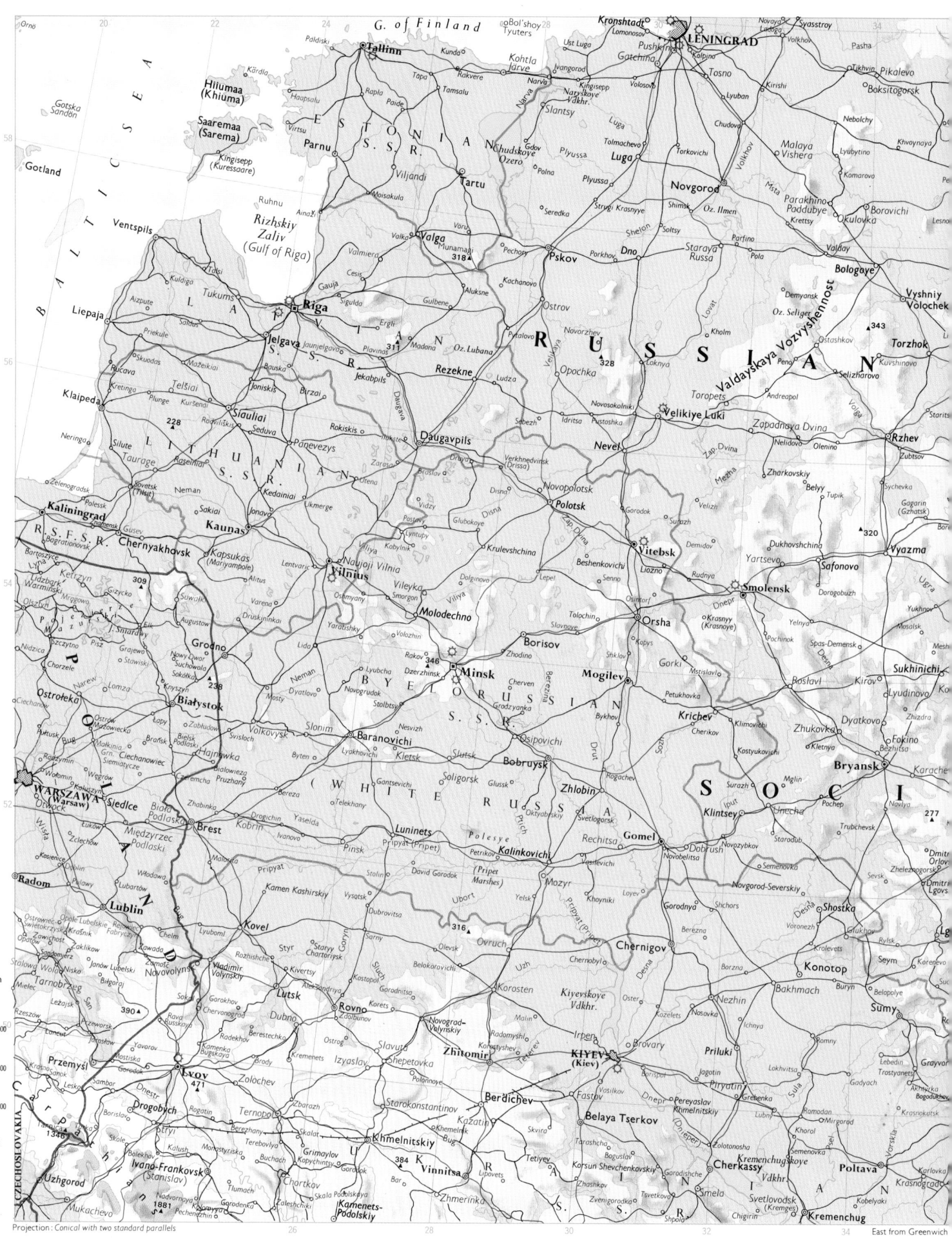
G. of Finland
BALTIC SEA
Gotland
Gotska Sandön
Hiiumaa (Khiuma)
Saaremaa (Sarema)
Kingisepp (Kuressaare)
Ruhnu
Rizhskiy Zaliv (Gulf of Riga)
Kronshtadt
Lomonosov
LENINGRAD
Pushkin
Gatchina
Kolpino
Tosno
Lyuban
Kirishi
Volkhov
Syasstroy
Tikhvin
Pikalevo
Boksitogorsk
Pasha
Tallinn
Paldiski
Kunda
Rakvere
Kohtla Järve
Narva
Ivangorod
Ust Luga
Kingisepp
Narvskoye Vdkhr.
Slantsy
Haapsalu
Rapla
Paide
Tamsalu
Tapa
ESTONIAN S.S.R.
Virtsu
Parnu
Viljandi
Tartu
Chudskoye Ozero
Gdov
Plyussa
Luga
Tolmachevo
Chudovo
Torkovichi
Novgorod
Oz. Ilmen
Shimsk
Malaya Vishera
Nebolchy
Lyubytino
Khvoynaya
Parakhino-Paddubye
Borovichi
Okulovka
Krettsy
Valday
Bologoye
Staraya Russa
Parfino
Pola
Dno
Porkhov
Soltsy
Shelon
Strugi Krasnyye
Seredka
Polna
Pskov
Pechory
Moisakula
Ainazi
Valga
Valka
Voru
Munamagi 318
Valmiera
Cesis
Gauja
Sigulda
Riga
Ventspils
Talsi
Tukums
Kuldiga
Aizpute
Liepaja
Saldus
Priekule
Jelgava
Jaunjelgava
Bauska
Ergli
Plavinas
Madona
Gulbene
Aluksne
Kachanovo
Ostrov
Oz. Lubana
Rezekne
Ludza
Jekabpils
Daugava
LATVIAN S.S.R.
Skuodas
Mazeikiai
Rucava
Kretinga
Telsiai
Plunge
Kursenai
Siauliai
Joniskis
Birzai
Klaipeda
Radviliskis
Seduva
Rokiskis
Panevezys
Neringa
Silute
Taurage
Raseiniai
Zarasai
Daugavpils
LITHUANIAN S.S.R.
Kedainiai
Utena
Ukmerge
Sovetsk (Tilsit)
Zelenogradsk
Kaliningrad
Polessk
Gusev
Neman
Sakiai
Kaunas
Jonava
R.S.F.S.R.
Chernyakhovsk
Bagrationovsk
Kapsukas (Mariyampole)
Lentvaric
Alitus
Vilnius
Naujoji Vilnia
Varena
Druskininkai
Oshmyany
Smorgon
Vileyka
Molodechno
Postavy
Vidzy
Braslav
Drisa
Verkhnedvinsk (Drissa)
Novopolotsk
Polotsk
Glubokoye
Disna
Lyntupy
Kobylnik
Krulevshchina
Dolginovo
Lepel
Beshenkovichi
Vitebsk
Liozno
Gorodok
Surazh
Velizh
Demidov
Nevel
Novosokolniki
Idritsa
Pustoshka
Sebezh
Velikiye Luki
Toropets
Andreapol
Zapadnaya Dvina
Nelidovo
Olenino
Rzhev
Zubtsov
Sychevka
Gagarin (Gzhatsk)
Vyazma
Safonovo
Yartsevo
Dukhovshchina
Smolensk
Rudnya
Krasnyy (Krasnoye)
Dorogobuzh
Yelnya
Pochinok
Spas-Demensk
Kirov
Lyudinovo
Sukhinichi
Roslavl
Zhukovka
Dyatkovo
Fokino
Bryansk
Kletnya
Mglin
Pochep
Unecha
Surazh
Klintsey
Starodub
Trubchevsk
Navlya
Novozybkov
Semenovka
Novgorod-Severskiy
Shostka
Glukhov
Krolevets
Konotop
Bakhmach
Seym
Sumy
Belopolye
Romny
Lebedin
Trostyanets
Akhtyrka
Gadyach
Lokhvitsa
Mirgorod
Khorol
Poltava
Kremenchug
Kremenchugskoye Vdkhr.
Svetlovodsk (Kremges)
Semenovka
Lubny
Grebenka
Piryatin
Priluki
Ichnya
Nezhin
Chernigov
Gorodnya
Shchors
Borzna
Berezna
Desna
Dobrush
Gomel
Novobelitsa
Rechitsa
Svetlogorsk
Zhlobin
Rogachev
Bobruysk
Bykhov
Krichev
Klimovichi
Cherikov
Kostyukovichi
Mogilev
Mstislavl
Gorki
Shklov
Kopys
Orsha
Osintorf
Senno
Tolochin
Slavnoye
Borisov
Zhodino
Cherven
Berezina
Minsk
Dzerzhinsk
Rakov 346
Volozhin
Grodzyanka
Osipovichi
BYELORUSSIAN S.S.R. (WHITE RUSSIA)
Nesvizh
Stolbtsy
Baranovichi
Lyakhovichi
Kletsk
Slutsk
Soligorsk
Glussk
Lyuban
Oktyabrskiy
Ptich
Novogrudok
Lyubcha
Mir
Dyatlovo
Lida
Yuratishki
Neman
Mosty
Grodno
Slonim
Volkovysk
Svisloch
Zelva
Byten
Gantsevichi
Telekhany
Ivatsevichi
Kobrin
Drogichin
Yaselda
Ivanovo
Pinsk
Luninets
Pripyat (Pripet)
Polesye
Petrikov
Kalinkovichi
Pripet Marshes
Mozyr
Yelsk
Khoyniki
Loyev
Vasilevichi
Stolin
David Gorodok
Brest
Zhabinka
Malorita
Pripyat
Kamen Kashirskiy
Vysotsk
Ubort
Dubrovitsa
316
Ovruch
Olevsk
Belokorovichi
Chernobyl
Kiyevskoye Vdkhr.
Korosten
Malin
Radomyshl
Irpen
Brovary
Korostyshev
Teterev
Zhitomir
KIYEV (Kiev)
Borispol
Vasilkov
Fastov
Belaya Tserkov
Pereyaslav Khmelnitskiy
Dnepr
Kanev
Cherkassy
Smela
Zolotonosha
Gorodishche
Korsun Shevchenkovskiy
Boguslav
Tarashcha
Tetiyev
Skvira
Berdichev
Kazatin
Vinnitsa
Lipovets
Zhmerinka
Bar
Khmelnitskiy
Starokonstantinov
Polonnoye
Shepetovka
Slavuta
Izyaslav
Novograd-Volynskiy
Korets
Rovno
Zdolbunov
Ostrog
Kremenets
Dubno
Radekhov
Brody
Zolochev
Lvov 471
Ternopol
Zbarazh
Skalat
Terebovlya
Grimaylov
Kopychintsy
Chortkov
Buchach
Zaleshchiki
Kamenets-Podolskiy
Gorodenka
Kolomyya
Nadvornaya
Ivano-Frankovsk (Stanislav)
Kalush
Dolina
Stryy
Drogobych
Borislav
Sambor
Skole
Tlumach
Mukachevo
Uzhgorod
Goverla 1881
1346
Carpathians
Przemyśl
Jarosław
Łańcut
Rzeszów
Mielec
Tarnobrzeg
Leżajsk
Kovel
Lutsk
Kivertsy
Kostopol
Sarny
Stary Chartoriysk
Goryn
Sluch
Styr
Vladimir Volynskiy
Novovolynsk
Lyuboml
Rava Russkaya
Chervonograd
Sokal
Gorokhov
Berestechko
Zamość
Hrubieszów
Chełm
Krasnik
Lublin
Łuków
Międzyrzec Podlaski
Biała Podlaska
Siedlce
WARSZAWA (Warsaw)
Otwock
Radzymin
Wołomin
Węgrów
Kałuszyn
Radom
Puławy
Dęblin
Włodawa
Lubartów
Wisła
Opatów
Sandomierz
Ostrowiec Swiętokrzyski
Ostrołęka
Ciechanów
Pułtusk
Ostrów Mazowiecka
Łomża
Białystok
Zambrów
Bielsk Podlaski
Hajnówka
Białowieża
Pruzhany
Kamenets
Grajewo
Stawiski
Augustów
Suwałki
Ełk
Gizycko
Pisz
Szczytno
Olsztyn
Kętrzyn
Bartoszyce
Lidzbark Warmiński
Nidzica
Chorzele
Narew
Bug
POLAND
CZECHOSLOVAKIA
RUSSIAN SOVIET
UKRAINIAN S.S.R.
Valdayskaya Vozvyshennost
Oz. Seliger
Demyansk
Ostashkov
Peno
Kholm
Lovat
Novorzhev
Opochka
Velikaya
Loknya
Torzhok
Kuvshinovo
Selizharovo
Volga
Vyshniy Volochek
Bol'shoy Tyuters
Projection: Conical with two standard parallels
East from Greenwich
ft
m
3000
1000
1200
400
600
200
0
0
200
600
m
ft

1:5 000 000

50 0 50 100 miles

50 0 50 100 150 km

S O V I E T   F E D E R A T I V E   S O C I A L I S T   R E P U B L I C

Cherepovets · Vologda · Sokol · Kharovsk · Totma · Nikolsk · Murashi · Vyatka · Peskovka

Kirov · Novovyatsk · Slobodskoy · Kirovo-Chepetsk · Zuyevka · Falenki · Glazov · Omutninsk

Belozersk · Oz. Beloye · Kirillov · Ozero Kubenskoye · Uste · Sheksna · Chebsara · Gryazovets · Suday · Pyshchug · Chernovskoye · Khalturin · Kotelnich · Kumeny · Uni

Ustyuzhna · Vesyegonsk · Rybinskoye Vodokhranilishche · Breytovo · Danilov · Buy · Lyubim · Galich · Neya · Sharya · Leninskoye · Sorvizhi · Sovetsk · Urzhum · Malmyzh · Mozhga

UDMURT A.S.S.R.

Krasnyy Kholm · Androv (Rybinsk) · Tutayev · Kostromskoye Vdkhr. · Antropovo · Manturovo · Unzha · Vetluga · Shakhunya · Yaransk · Nolinsk · Medvedok · Arkul · Kilmez · Liva

Sonkovo · Kashin · Volga · Yaroslavl · Nerekhta · Kostroma · Zavolzhsk · Makaryev · Uren · Yaransk · Tursha · Kilmez

Goritsy · Kalyazin · Rostov · Ivanovo · Kineshma · Vichuga · Gorkovskoye Vdkhr. · Vetluzhskiy · Krasnyye Baki · Yoshkar Ola · MARI A.S.S.R. · Kumar · Vyatskiye Polyany · Arsk

O V I E T   F E D E R A T I V E

Kimry · Dubna · Pereslavl-Zalesskiy · Aleksandrov · Kolchugino · Shuya · Teykovo · Kokhma · Semenov · Voskresenskoye · Cheboksary · Krasnogorskiy · Zelenodolsk · Kazan · TATAR A.S.S.R. · Mamadysh

Klin · Zagorsk · Vladimir · Kovrov · Dzerzhinsk · GORKIY (Gorki) · Kstovo · Lyskovo · Yadrin · Kozmodemyansk · Marinskiy Posad · Volzhsk · Chistopol

Mytishchi · Balashikha · Noginsk · Orekhovo-Zuyevo · Gus-Khrustalnyy · Pavlovo · Bogorodsk · CHUVASH A.S.S.R. · Kanash · Buinsk · Tetyushi · Bilyarsk · Nurlat

MOSKVA (Moscow) · Lyubertsy · Elektrostal · Murom · Vyksa · Kulebaki · Arzamas · Pyana · Sergach · Shumerlya · Kamskoye Ustye · Kuybyshev · Cherdakly

Podolsk · Ramenskoye · Kolomna · Melenki · Kasimov · Temnikov · Pervomaysk · Alatyr · Ulyanovsk · Dimitrovgrad · Sernovodsk

Serpukhov · Stupino · Kashira · Ryazan · Sasovo · Krasnoslobodsk · MORDOVIAN A.S.S.R. · Saransk · Ruzayevka · Inza · Karsun · Sengiley · Sok

Kaluga · Aleksin · Zaraysk · Shilovo · Kobylkino · Kuznetsk · Togliatti · Komsomolskiy · Krasnyy Yar · KUYBYSHEV · Novokuybyshevsk

Tula · Novotulskiy · Novomoskovsk · Skopin · Nizhniy Lomov · Bazarnyy Syzgan · Syzran · Chapayevsk

Shchekino · Uzlovaya · Ryazhsk · Zametchino · Penza · Kamenka · Serdobsk · Volsk · Balakovo · Pugachev

Mtsensk · Yefremov · Michurinsk · Kirsanov · Kotovsk · Rtishchevo · Petrovsk · Khvalynsk · Gornyy

Orel · Yelets · Lipetsk · Gryazi · Tambov · Uvarovo · Turki · Arkadak · Atkarsk · Saratov · Engels · Krasnyy Kut · Orlov Gay

Livny · Usman · Mordovo · Muchkapskiy · Balanda · Balashov · Volgogradskoye Vdkhr. · Novouzensk

Voronezh · Semiluki · Anna · Borisoglebsk · Peski · Samoylovka · Krasnoarmeysk · Kamyshin · Nikolayevsk

Staryy Oskol · Gubkin · Korotoyak · Ostrogozhsk · Novyy Oskol · Georgiu-Dezh · Buzuluk · Novoannenskiy · Kamenskiy · Krasnyy Yar · Pallasovka

Belgorod · Shebekino · Pavlovsk · Kalach · Buturlinovka · Mikhaylovka · Frolovo · Bykovo · Kaztalovka

Kharkov · Kupyansk · Valuyki · Rossosh · Boguchar · Serafimovich · KAZAKH S.S.R.

Rubezhnoye · Starobelsk · Millerovo · Kantemirovka · Veshenskaya · Kletskiy · Dubovka · Urda

Volgograd (Stalingrad) · Krasnoslobodsk · Volzhskiy · Kapustin Yar

COPYRIGHT. GEORGE PHILIP & SON. LTD.

ft   m

12.000 4000

9000   3000

6000   2000

4500   1500

3000   1000

1200   400

600   200

0   0

200   600

2000   6000

m   ft

Projection: Conical with two standard parallels

1:5 000 000

50   0   50   100 miles
50   0   50   100   150 km

East from Greenwich   40   42   44   46   48   COPYRIGHT. GEORGE PHILIP & SON. LTD.

Yelan-Kolenovskiy
Povorino   Peski
 yal   Bobrov   Talovaya   Novokhopersk   Zhirnovsk   Krasnyy Kut
Georgiu-Dezh   Samoylovka
Ostrogozhsk   Buturlinovka   239   Uryupinsk   Yelan   Krasnoarmeysk   Oz. Chalkar   Chalkar
Kamenka   Khrenovoye   Novoannenskiy   Ravnoye   Piterka   Novouzensk   Dzhambeyty
atovskiy   Pavlovsk   Kalach   Buzuluk   Kukvidze   358   Vozyshennost   Aleksandrov Gay   Mergenevsky   Karsha
Rossosh   Boguchar   Novokhopersk   Panfilovo   Krasnyy   Novatka   Kaztalovka   Furmanovo   Antonovka
Kantemirovka   Medvedtsa   Danilovka   Yar   Kamyshin   Nikolayevsk   Bazar-bate
Ust Buzulukskaya   Mikhaylovka   Ilovlya   Bykovo   Dzhanybek   Ari-kovo
Starobelsk   Kazanskaya   Kumylzhenskaya   Frolovo   Elton   K   A   Z   A   K   H   Inderborskiy
Melovoye   Veshenskaya   Serafimovich   Ilovlya   S.   S.   R.
Chertkovo   Kletskiy   Pallasovka
odonetsk   Don   Kletskaya   (Kletskaya)   Dubovka   Urda   Zelënyy   Topoli
sk   Kamenskiy   Sovetskaya   Iloulya (Iloulinskaya)   Pervolzhskaya   Volzhskiy   Kapustin Yar   Shungay   Nizmennost
hanov   Millerovo   Chir   Pichuzinskaya   Volgograd   Krasnoslobodsk   Vladimirovka   Verkhniy Baskunchak   Makhombet
anka   Voroshilovgrad   Dubovskiy   (Stalingrad)   Krasnoarmeysk   Akhtubinsk   (Yamankhalinka)
(Lugansk)   Surovikino   Kalach na Donu   (Petropavlovsk)   Novobogatinskoye
munarsk   Krasnodon   Belaya Kalitva   Krasnadonetskaya   Chernyshkovskiy   Volga
Krasnyy Luch   dlovsk   Morozovsk   Tsimlyanskoye   Guryev
ez   Rovenki   Gukovo   Krasny Sulin   Sinegorskiy   Vdkhr.   -28
nezhnoye   Artemovski   Tsimlyansk   Obilnoye   Koponovka
voshakhtinsk   Shakhty   Ust-Donetskiy   Volgodonsk   Dubovskoye   Yenotayevsk   Aydushkino
Kamenolomni   Konstantinovski   Krasnoye   Krasnyy Yar
Matveyev Kurgan   Tuzlov   Sal   Bolshaya Martynovka   Zimovniki   Zavetnoye   K   A   L   M   Y   K   Astrakhan
nrog   Novocherkassk   Veselovskoye   Manych   KALMYK   Kamyzyak
Azov   Rostov   Bataysk   Vdkhr.   A.S.S.R.   Kirovski
rt Katon   Zernograd   Mechetinskaya   Kuberle   A. S. S. R.   Mumra   C
chek-   Yeya   Kusnchevskaya   Yegorlykskaya   Proletarskaya   Remontnoye   Krasnoye   Liman   A
Stara-   Gigant   Oz. Manych-   Elista   S
minskaya   Salsk   Peschanokopskoye   Gudilo   (Stepnoi)   Beloye Ozero   P   O. Kulaly   Mangyshlakskiy
Pavlovskaya   Yegoryk   Leninskoye   Priyutnoye   R   Kaspiyskiy   I   M. Tyub Karagan   Zaliv
Kanevskaya   Belaya   Divnoye   I   Fort Shevchenko   P-ov.
Glina   Krasnogvardeyskoye   Kalaus   Kuma   A   Mangyshlak
Timashevsk   Tikhoretsk   Novaleksandrovskaya   Ipatovo   Arzgir   Staryy Biryuzyak   S   Kultay
Korenovsk   Kropotkin   Svetlograd   Budennovsk   K   P
Ust-Labinsk   Izobil'nyy   (Petrovskoye)   Blagodarnoye   A   I   O. Chechen
Krasnodar   Armavir   Stavropol   Y   Tyuleniy   Y   Shevchenko
Khadyzhensk   Kurgannsk   Kuban   831   Zelenokumsk   Vladimirovka   S   Bryanskaya   S   O. Chechen
eltegorsk   (Kurgannaya)   Nevinnomyssk   (Vorontsovo-Aleksandrovskoye)   Aleksandriyskaya   K   A   N
se   Apsheronsk   Labinsk   Kursavka   Lapatin   Kizlyar   A   Shevchenko
B   Urup   Cherkessk   Mineralnyye Vody   Y   -28
Sochi   Dakhovskaya   Georgievsk   A   N
o   l   Kislovodsk   Teberda   Yessentuki   Pyatigorsk   Prokhladnyy   Mozdok   CHECHENO-   Terek   S
Adler   s   Karachayevsk   Nalchik   Nartkala   Malgobek   INGUSH   Gudermes   Sulak   800
Gagra   h   Elbrus   Mayskiy   Groznyy   Kizil Yurt   P
ABKHAZ   5633   KABARDINO-   Elkhotovo   Baslan   A.S.S.R.   Khasavyurt   Makhachkala   I
Novyy Afon   C   BALKAR   NORTH   Kumtorkala   A
Gudata   a   A.S.S.R.   OSSETIN   Kaspiysk   N
Sukhumi   u   5203   Ordzhonikidze   Sagopshin   Buynaksk   S
Ochamchire   c   Kazbek   Izberbash   E
a   5047   K   Tebulos   Agvali   Novokayakent   A
Andkia   s   GEORGIA   4492   Akusha   Dagestanskiye Ogni
Kutaisi   u   o   Khunzakh   Kakhib   Derbent
Mikha-Tskhakaya   Tribuli   Sachkhere   Tskhinvali   u   Modzod   D
Poti   s   Zestafoni   (Stalinir)   Dusheti   n   A
Samtredia   Chiatura   Ushkul   t   Kasumkent   G
S.S.R.   Shorapani   Gori   a   Tlyarata   E
Kobuleti   Makharadze   Borzhomi   Kaspi   Mtskheta   i   S   Kuba   S
Batumi   Khulo   Tbilisi   Telavi   n   Jakhy   T
ADZHAR   Akhaltsikhe   Khrami   Rustavi   Signakhi   Alazan   Divichi   A
A.S.S.R.   Akhalkalaki   Marneuli   lori   Citeli   k   Khachmas   N
Hopa   Pazar   Shoumyani   Ckaro   Mirzaani   Shekl   (Nukha)   Baba dag.   Siazan   S
Görele   Akçaabat   Ardahan   Cildir   Akstafa   Sheki   Mingechaurskoye   Bazar Dyuzi   S
Tirebolu   Artvin   Y   Ardanuç   Kura   Tauz   4486   Mashtaga   R
Trabzon   Rize   Şavşat   3192   Alaverdi   Mingechaur   Agdash   Genkchay   3629   Sumgait   Surokhom-   Artem
Sürmene   Kars   Kirovakan   Kirovabad   Yevlakh   Vdkhr.   BAKU
Çamlıhemşin   Ispir   Selim   AZERBAIJAN   Lyaki   zyrya
Çakirgol   Leninakan   Ağri   Aktti   Dashkesan   Mir-Bashi   Barda   Kyurdamir   Kazi Magomed
3063   Oltu   Narman   Sarikamiş   Aragats   Chaterevtshen   Ozero   S.S.R.   Sabirabad   Ali-Bayramly
Gümüşhane   D   Y   4090   Sevan   Terter   Agdzhabedi   Agsu
Bayburt   Çoruh   Kağizman   Digor   Sarikamiş   Echmiadzin   Mattun   Imishly   Surakhani
D   E   g   l   a   r   Yerevan   Aras   Agdam   Zhdanovsk   M. Byandovan
Aras

1:5 000 000

50   0   50   100 miles

50   0   50   100   150 km

KOMI A.S.S.R.

Gora Denezhkin Kamen ▲1493

Obyachevo   Vishera   Gora Denezhkin Kamen
Kazhim   Krasnovishersk   Severouralsk   Massava
Lesnoy   Cherdyn   Pokrovsk-Uralskiy   Soma   Shaim   Konda
Kay   Gayny   Krasnoturinsk   Lozva
Nagorsk   Kosa   Karpinsk   Serov   Pelym   Mezhdurechenskiy
Rudnichnyy   Borovsk   Gora Konzhakovskiy Kamen ▲1569   Pelym
Vyatka   Kirs   Solikamsk   Lobva   Gari
Belaya   Berezniki   Lyalya   Novaya Lyalya
Kholunitsa   Chernaya Kholunitsa   Peskovka   Usolye   Kytlym   Verkhoturye   Sosva   Tavda
Kirov   Slobodskoy   Kama   Kizel   Lobva   Tabory
Novovyatsk   Afanasyevo   Kamskoye Vdkhr.   Gubakha   Malomalsk   Bolotovskoye
Zuyevka   Falenki   Chermoz   Malomalsk   Kochkanar   Turinsk   Tavda
Kumeny   Omutninsk   Dobryanka   Krasnouralsk   Tagil
Glazov   Krasnokamsk   Chusovoy   Kushva
Nolinsk   Balezino   Vereshchagino   Kungur   Nizh. Salda   Turinsk
Medvedok   Kez   Nytva   Lysva   Nizhniy Tagil   Verkhnyaya Salda
Arkul   Igra   Perm   Nevyansk   Alapayevsk   Irbit   Nitsa
Uzhum   UDMURT A.S.S.R.   Verkhniy Tagil   Rezh   Artemovskiy   Tyumen
Shurma   Kilmez   Zura   Kungur   Shalya   Bulanash   Troitskiy   Pyshma
Kilmez   Votkinsk   Osa   Kuzino   Pervouralsk   Asbest   Sukhoy Log   Kamyshlov
Malmyzh   Uva   Yokshur Bodya   Votkinskoye Vdkhr.   Krasnoufimsk   Nizhniye Sergi   Revda   SVERDLOVSK   Beloyarskiy   Talitsa
Mozhga   Ustinov   Chaykovskiy   Achit   Polevskoy   Bogdanovich   KAMENSK URALSKIY
Vyatskiye Polyany   Sarapul   Chernushka   Mikhaylovskiy   Sysert   Dalmatova   Shadrinsk
Kukmor   Agryz   Kambarka   Yanaul   Askino   Ufa   Nyazepetrovsk   Verkhniy Ufaley   Isel
Mamadysh   Yelabuga   Menzelinsk   Burayevo   Duvan   Kasli   Techa   Uksyanskoye   Kargapolye
Kuybyshevskoye Vdkhr.   Buklyan   BASHKIR   Verkhniye Kigi   Kyshtym   Argayash   Brodokalmak   Miass   Mishkino   Kurgan
Chistopol   Brezhnev   Birsk   Krasnyy Klyuch   Kusa   Karabash   Chelyabinsk
Bilyarsk   TATAR   Kushnarenkovo   Ay   Kropachevo   Zlatoust   Miass   Shchuchye   Shumikha
Aktash   A.S.S.R.   Blagoveshchensk   Minyar   Yuryuzan   Satka   Miass   Kopeysk   Kurtamysh   Tobol
Almetyevsk   Tumutuk   Chishmy   Asha   Katav Ivanovsk   Bakal   Chebarkul   Korkino
Leninogorsk   Tuymazy   Ufa   Iglino   Gora Iremel ▲1582   Yemanzhelinsk   Zverinogolovskoye
Bugulma   Belebey   Chernikovsk   Gora Yamantau ▲1638   Uchaly   Yuzhno-Uralsk   Plast   Uvelskiy
Nurlat   Oktyabrskiy   A.S.S.R.   Inzer   Tirlyanskiy   Stepnoye   Uy
Sernovodsk   Davlekanovo   Krasnousolskiy   Beloretsk   Verkhneuralsk   Troitsk   Vvedenka
Isakly   Rayevskiy   Zirgazinskiy   Uy   Komsomolets   Borovskoye
Buguruslan   Abdulino   Petrovskoye   Gora Bol. Shatan ▲1270   Magnitogorsk   Varna   Toguzak   Fedorovka
KUYBYSHEV   Sterlitamak   Ishimbay   Verkhniy Avzyan   Agapovka   Kustanay
Novokuybyshevsk   Koltubanovskiy   Tok   Ivanovka   Salavat   Bakr Uzyak   Aktobe   Rudnyy
Buzuluk   Grachevka   Ponomarevka   Meleuz   Sibay   Kizilskoye   Kartaly   Tobol
Alekseyevka   Samara   Kumertau   Mrakovo   Baymak   Bredy   Denisovka   Ozero Kushmurun
Bolshaya Glushitsa   Sorochinsk   Andreyevka   Bulanovo   Tyulgan   Zhaima   Ozero Kushmurun
Nova-Sergiyevskiy   Sakmara   Sakmara   Buribay   Iriklinskoye Vdkhr.   Dzhetygara   Livanovka   Ozero Sarymoin
Orenburg   Saraktash   Krasnoyarskiy   Tobol   Ozero Aksuat
Uralsk   Ural   Iletsk   Krasnyy Kholm   Kuvandyk   Gay   Iriklinskiy   Shilda   Adamovka
Darinskoye   Ilek   Dubenskiy   Mednogorsk   Orsk   Novoorsk   Ozernyy   Oz. Ayke
Sol Iletsk   Akbulak   Novotroitsk   Kumak   Oz. Zhetykol   Oz. Shalkar Yega Kara
Chili   Grigoryevka   Svetlyy   Dombarovskiy   Suykbulak   Ozera Sarykopa
Chapayevo   Utva   Martuk   Bol. Kumak   Iletsk   Batamshinskiy   Oz. Shalkar Karashatau
Mergenevo   Chalkar   Dzhambeyty   Khromtau   Zharkol
Oz. Chalkar   Aktyubinsk   Alga   Karabutak   Turgay
Karsha   Ural   Novoalekseyevka   Turgay
KAZAKH S.S.R.
Karatobe

Projection: Conical with two standard parallels

East from Greenwich

COPYRIGHT. GEORGE PHILIP & SON. LTD.

Sredniy (Central Ural)

Yuzhnyy (Southern) Ural

ft   m
4500   1500
3000   1000
1200   400
600   200
0   0

1:5 000 000

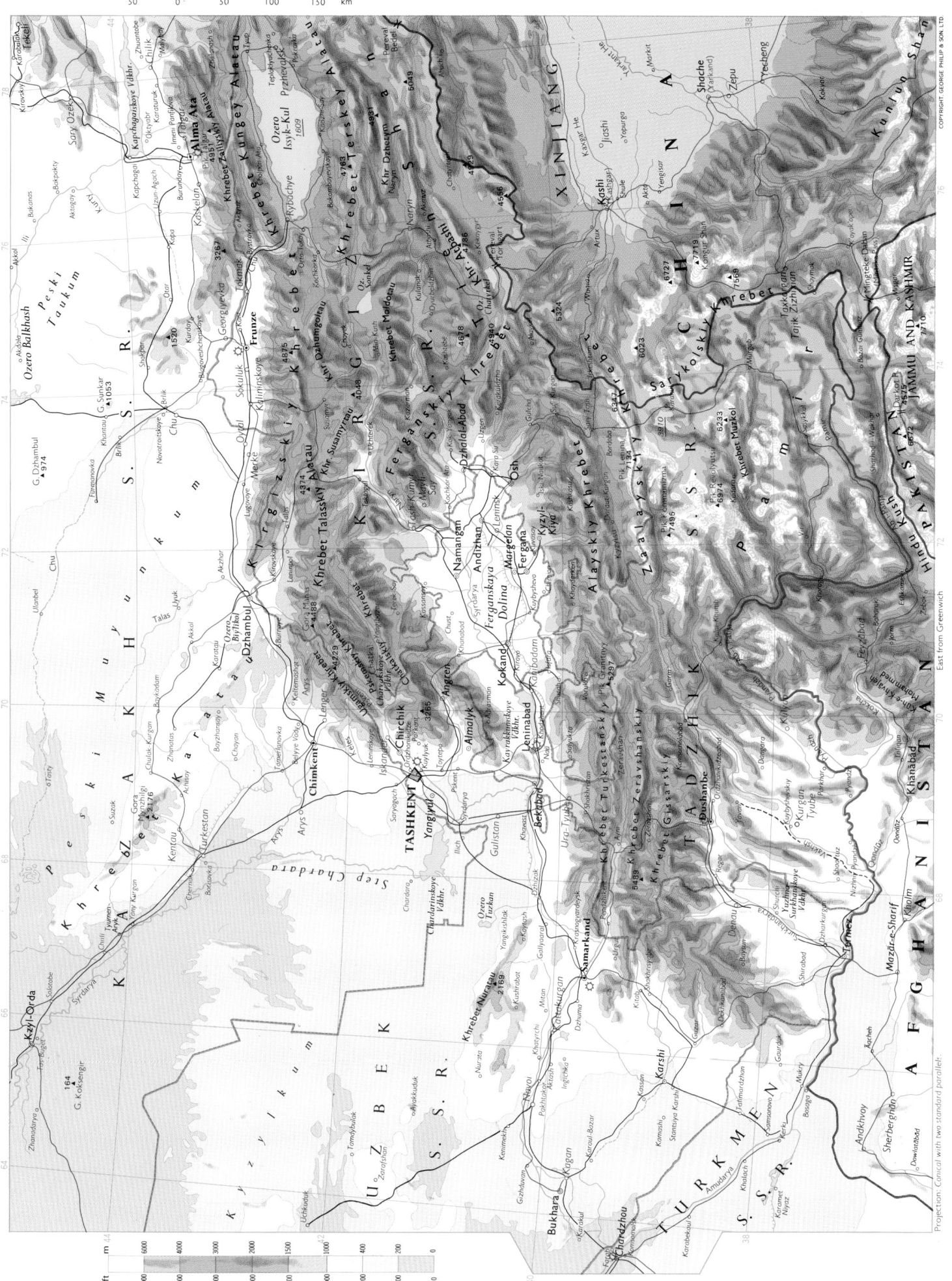

Projection: Conical with two standard parallels

East from Greenwich

R.S.F.S.R.
1. Daghestan A.S.S.R.
2. Kabardino–Balkar A.S.S.R.
3. Mari A.S.S.R.
4. Mordovian A.S.S.R.
5. North Ossetian A.S.S.R.
6. Tatar A.S.S.R.
7. Udmurt A.S.S.R.
8. Chuvash A.S.S.R.
9. Checheno–Ingush A.S.S.R.
AZERBAIJAN
10. Nakhichevan A.S.S.R.
GEORGIA
11. Abkhaz A.S.S.R.
12. Adzhar A.S.S.R.

Projection: Conical Orthomorphic with two standard parallels

East from Greenwich

1:20 000 000
miles
km
Boundaries of U.S.S.R.
Boundaries of S.S.R.
Boundaries of A.S.S.R.
Mys Dezhneva (East C.)
St. Lawrence I. (U.S.A.)
Chukotskoye More
Ostrov Vrangelya
East Siberian Sea
Chukotskiy Khrebet
Anadyrskiy Zaliv
Koryakskiy Khrebet
Bering Sea
Komandorskiye Ostrova
Poluostrov Kamchatka
Petropavlovsk-Kamchatskiy
Sea of Okhotsk
Zaliv Shelikhova
Gizhiginskaya Guba
Penzhinskaya Guba
Magadan
Okhotsk
Khrebet Cherskogo
Verkhoyanskiy Khrebet
Novosibirskiye Ostrova
Ostrova Delong
Lyakhovskiye Ostrova
Proliv Dmitriya Lapteva
Laptev Sea
OCEAN
Severnaya Zemlya
Ostrov Komsomolets
Ostrov Oktyabrskoy Revolyutsii
Ostrov Bolshevik
Proliv Vilkitskogo
Poluostrov Taymyr
Gory Byrranga
Nordvik
Tiksi
Verkhoyansk
Srednekolymsk
Arctic Circle
YAKUT A.S.S.R.
Yakutsk
Vilyuysk
Olekminsk
Stanovoy Khrebet
Dzhugdzhur
Sakhalin
Yuzhno-Sakhalinsk
Nikolayevsk-na-Amure
Komsomolsk
Khabarovsk
Sikhote Alin
Kurilskiye Ostrova
Hokkaido
Sapporo
Hakodate
Honshū
Nii-gata
Kanazawa
To-yama
Sea of JAPAN
Vladivostok
Nakhodka
Ussuriysk
Harbin
Qiqihar
Dongbei
Changchun
Jilin
Siping
Fushun
Shenyang
Anshan
Dandong
Dalian
Yingkou
Beijing
Zhangjiakou
Baotou
NORTH KOREA
P'yongyang
Wŏnsan
Chongjin
Sŏul
Inch'on
SOUTH KOREA
Taejŏn
Pusan
Da Hinggan Ling
Hulun Nur
MONGOLIA
Ulaanbaatar (Ulan Bator)
Hangayn Nuruu
Hentiyn Nuruu
GOBI
Gurvan Sayhan
Ulan Ude
BURYAT A.S.S.R.
Chita
Irkutsk
Angarsk
Bratsk
Krasnoyarsk
Kirensk
Khrebet Yablonovyy
Blagoveshchensk
Birobidzhan
Nizhneudinsk
Cheremkhovo
Vostochnyy Sayan
Hovsgol Nuur
Uvs Nuur
Edrengiyn Nuruu
Hami
SOCIALIST REPUBLIC

1 : 50 000 000

250	0	250	500	750	1000 miles
250	0	500	1000	1500	km

PACIFIC OCEAN

ARCTIC OCEAN

INDIAN OCEAN

South China Sea

Bay of Bengal

Arabian Sea

Plateau of Tibet

Himalaya

Kunlun Shan

Tien Shan

West Siberian Plain

Steppe

Caspian Sea

Black Sea

Mediterranean Sea

Red Sea

Libyan Desert

Projection: Bonne

COPYRIGHT GEORGE PHILIP & SON LTD

m										ft
	6000	4000	2000	1000	400	200	0			
18 000	12 000	6000	3000	1200	600	0	200	2000	6000	18 000

1:50 000 000

250 0 250 500 750 1000 miles
250 0 500 1000 1500 km

PACIFIC OCEAN

ARCTIC OCEAN

INDIAN OCEAN

U. S. S. R.

CHINA

MONGOLIA

INNER MONGOLIA

MANCHURIA

INDIA

PAKISTAN

AFGHANISTAN

IRAN (PERSIA)

IRAQ

SAUDI ARABIA

TURKEY

XIZANG (TIBET)

XINJIANG UYGUR

NEPAL

BHUTAN

BANGLADESH

BURMA

THAILAND (SIAM)

VIETNAM

CAMBODIA

LAOS

MALAYSIA

INDONESIA

PHILIPPINES

SRI LANKA (CEYLON)

AUSTRALIA

EUROPE

AFRICA

Tōkyō · Yokohama · Ōsaka · Kyōto · Kōbe · Kitakyūshū · Nagasaki · Sapporo · Pusan · Sŏul · Beijing · Tianjin · Dalian · Qingdao · Shanghai · Nanjing · Wuhan · Xi'an · Chengdu · Chongqing · Kunming · Changsha · Fuzhou · Guangzhou · Hong Kong · Macau (Port.) · Zhanjiang · Hainan · Taiwan (Formosa)

Khabarovsk · Vladivostok · Nikolayevsk · Petropavlovsk-Kamchatskiy · Yakutsk · Irkutsk · Ulan-Ude · Chita · Ulaanbaatar (Ulan Bator) · Krasnoyarsk · Kemerovo · Tomsk · Novosibirsk · Barnaul · Semipalatinsk · Omsk · Tobolsk · Sverdlovsk · Chelyabinsk · Magnitogorsk · Alma Ata · Tashkent · Samarkand · Bukhara · Khiva · Ashkhabad · Krasnovodsk · Mary

Moskva · Leningrad · Murmansk · Arkhangelsk · Orenburg · Astrakhan · Baku · Tbilisi · Yerevan · Rostov · Odessa · Istanbul · Ankara · Izmir · Bursa · Erzurum · Tabriz · Tehran · Eşfahān · Shīrāz · Būshehr · Mashhad · Herāt · Kābul · Qandahār · Quetta · Zāhedān · Gwadar · Karachi · Peshāwar · Lahore · Delhi · Agra · Kānpur · Allāhābād · Lucknow · Vārānasi · Calcutta · Dhaka · Hyderābād · Bombay · Ahmadābād · Madras · Pondicherry · Bangalore · Colombo

Baghdād · Al Başrah · Kuwait · Bahrain · Qatar · Ar Riyāḍ · Al Madīnah · Makkah (Mecca) · Oman · Masqat · United Arab Emirates · South Yemen · Yemen · Halab · Dimashq · Bayrūt · Jerusalem · Jordan · Syria · Lebanon · Israel · Cyprus · Athínai · Thessaloníki · Beograd · Warszawa · Wien · Berlin · Paris · London · Roma

EGYPT · LIBYA · SUDAN · ETHIOPIA · SOMALI REP · KENYA · TANZANIA · UGANDA · ZAIRE · ZAMBIA · MALAWI · ICELAND · UNITED KINGDOM

El Qāhira · El Iskandariya · El Khartûm · Addis Abeba · Nairobi · Mombasa · Dar es Salaam

Bering Sea · Sea of Okhotsk · Sea of Japan · East China Sea · South China Sea · Yellow Sea · Bay of Bengal · Arabian Sea · Red Sea · G. of Aden · G. of Oman · The Gulf · Caspian Sea · Black Sea · Mediterranean Sea · Baltic Sea · North Sea · Aral Sea · Kara Sea · Laptev Sea · Barents Sea · Celebes Sea · Sulu Sea · Banda Sea · Flores Sea · Java Sea

Tropic of Cancer · Equator · Arctic Circle · East from Greenwich

Projection: Bonne

1:15 000 000

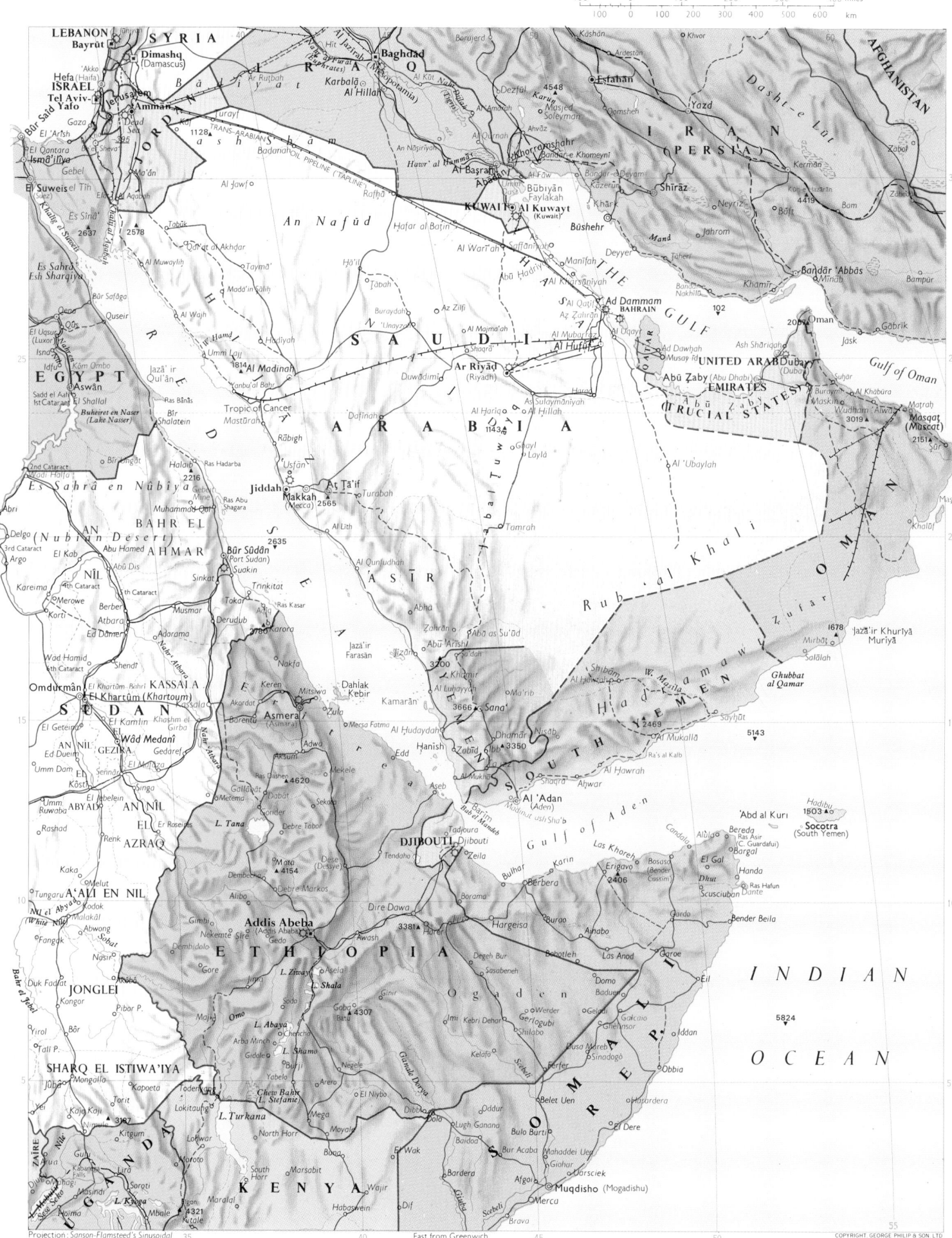

1:1 000 000

10 5 0 10 20 miles

10 0 10 20 30 km

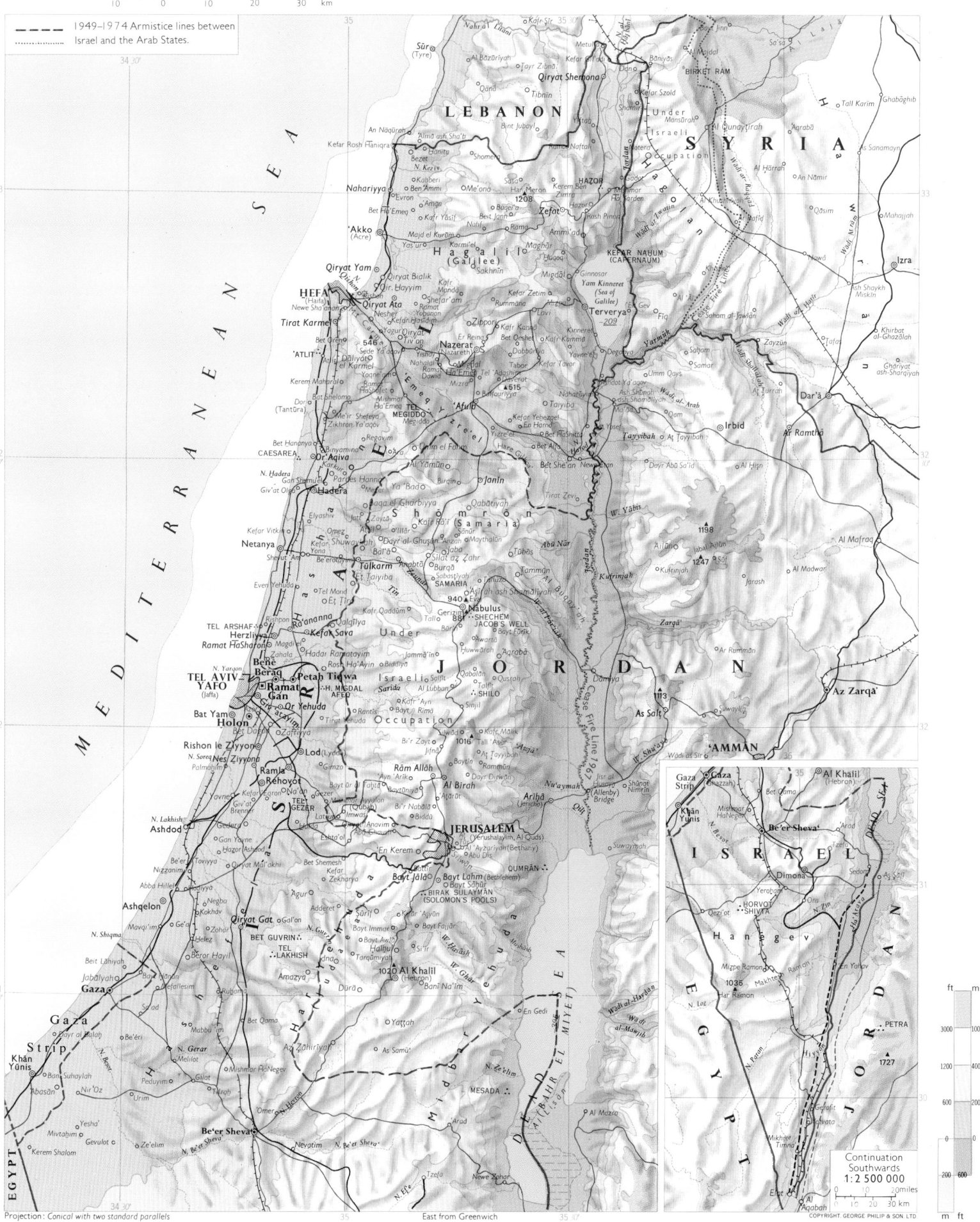

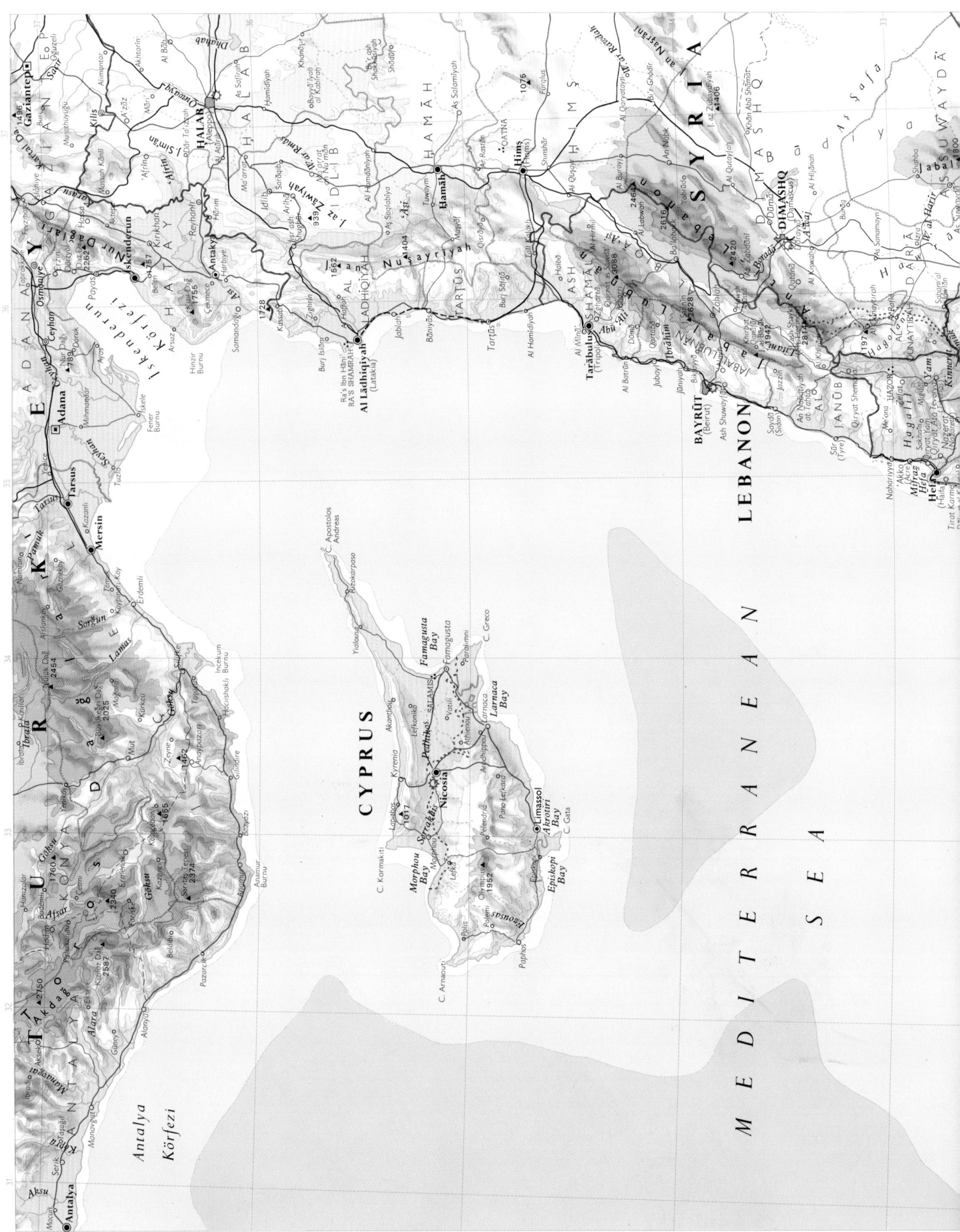
TURKEY
SYRIA
LEBANON
CYPRUS
MEDITERRANEAN SEA
Antalya Körfezi
İskenderun Körfezi
Antalya
Mersin
Tarsus
Adana
Ceyhan
İskenderun
Antakya
Gaziantep
Kilis
HALAB (Aleppo)
Ḥamāh
Ḥimṣ (Homs)
Al Lādhiqīyah (Latakia)
Ṭarṭūs
Bāniyās
Jablah
Ṭarābulus (Tripoli)
BAYRŪT (Beirut)
Ṣaydā (Sidon)
Ṣūr (Tyre)
DIMASHQ (Damascus)
Ḥefa (Haifa)
Nicosia
Famagusta
Famagusta Bay
Larnaca
Larnaca Bay
Limassol
Akrotiri Bay
Episkopi Bay
Morphou Bay
Paphos
Kyrenia
C. Apostolos Andreas
C. Greco
C. Gata
C. Arnaouti
C. Kormakiti
Anamur Burnu
Silifke
Alanya
Manavgat
Serik
Aksu
Kinneret

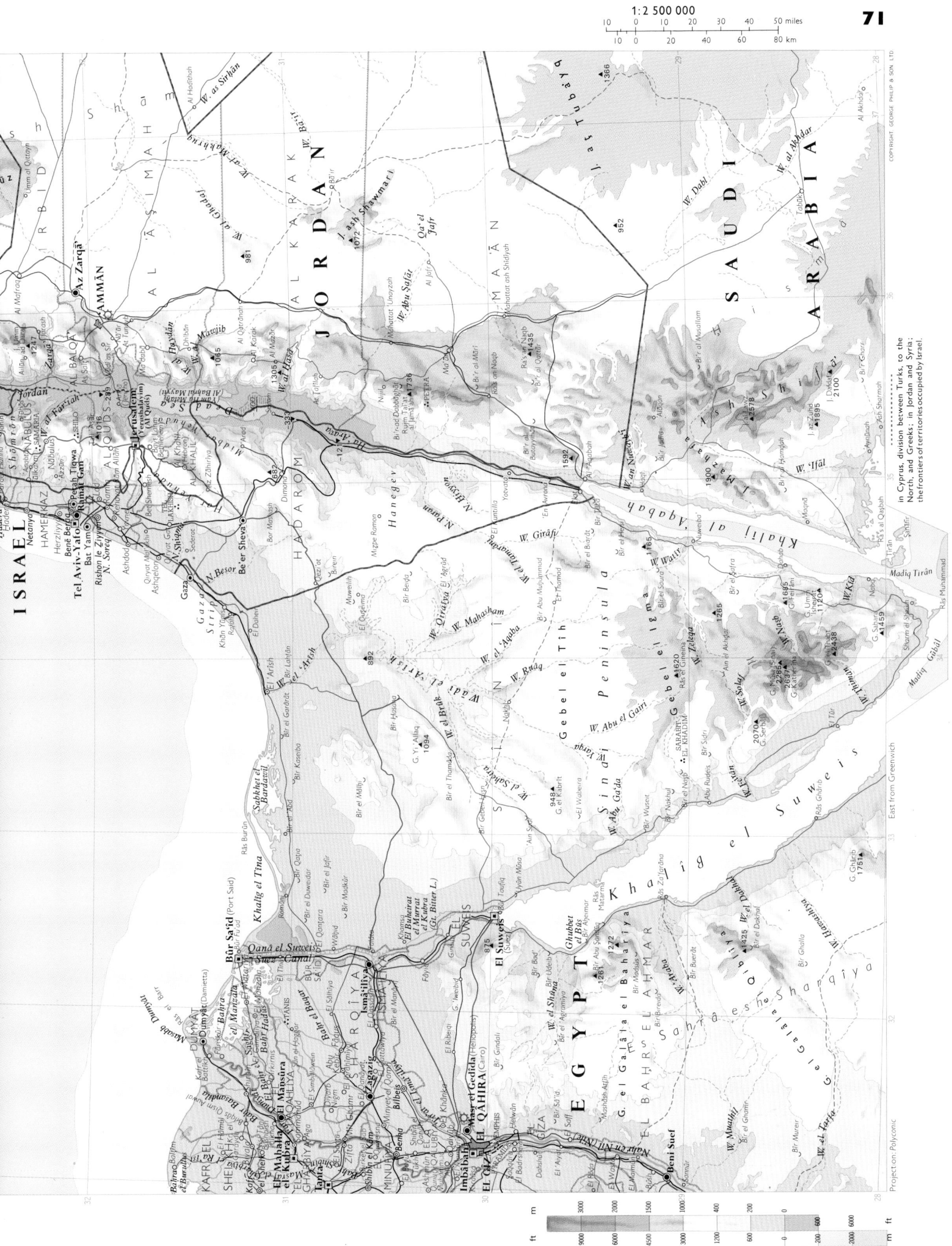

1:2 500 000

| 10 | 0 | 10 | 20 | 30 | 40 | 50 miles |

| 10 | 0 | 20 | 40 | 60 | 80 km |

in Cyprus, division between Turks, to the
North, and Greeks; in Jordan and Syria:
the frontiers of territories occupied by Israel.

East from Greenwich

Projection Polyconic

ISRAEL

JORDAN

EGYPT

SAUDI ARABIA

Sinai Peninsula

m	
3000	
2000	
1500	
1000	
400	
200	
0	

ft	
9000	
6000	
4500	
3000	
1200	
600	
0	

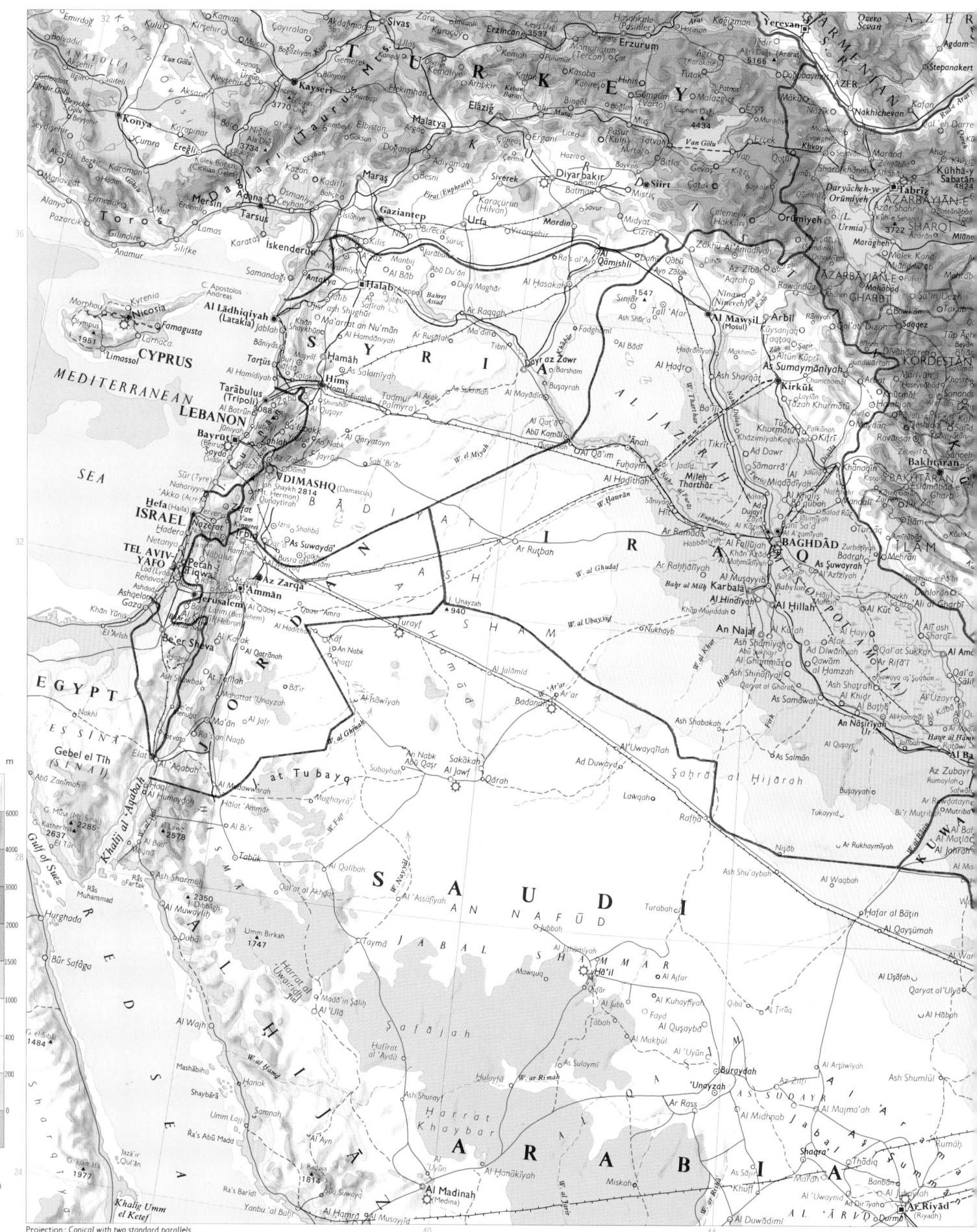

Projection: Conical with two standard parallels

1 : 7 000 000

50   0   50   100   150   200 miles
50 0 50 100 150 200 250 300 km

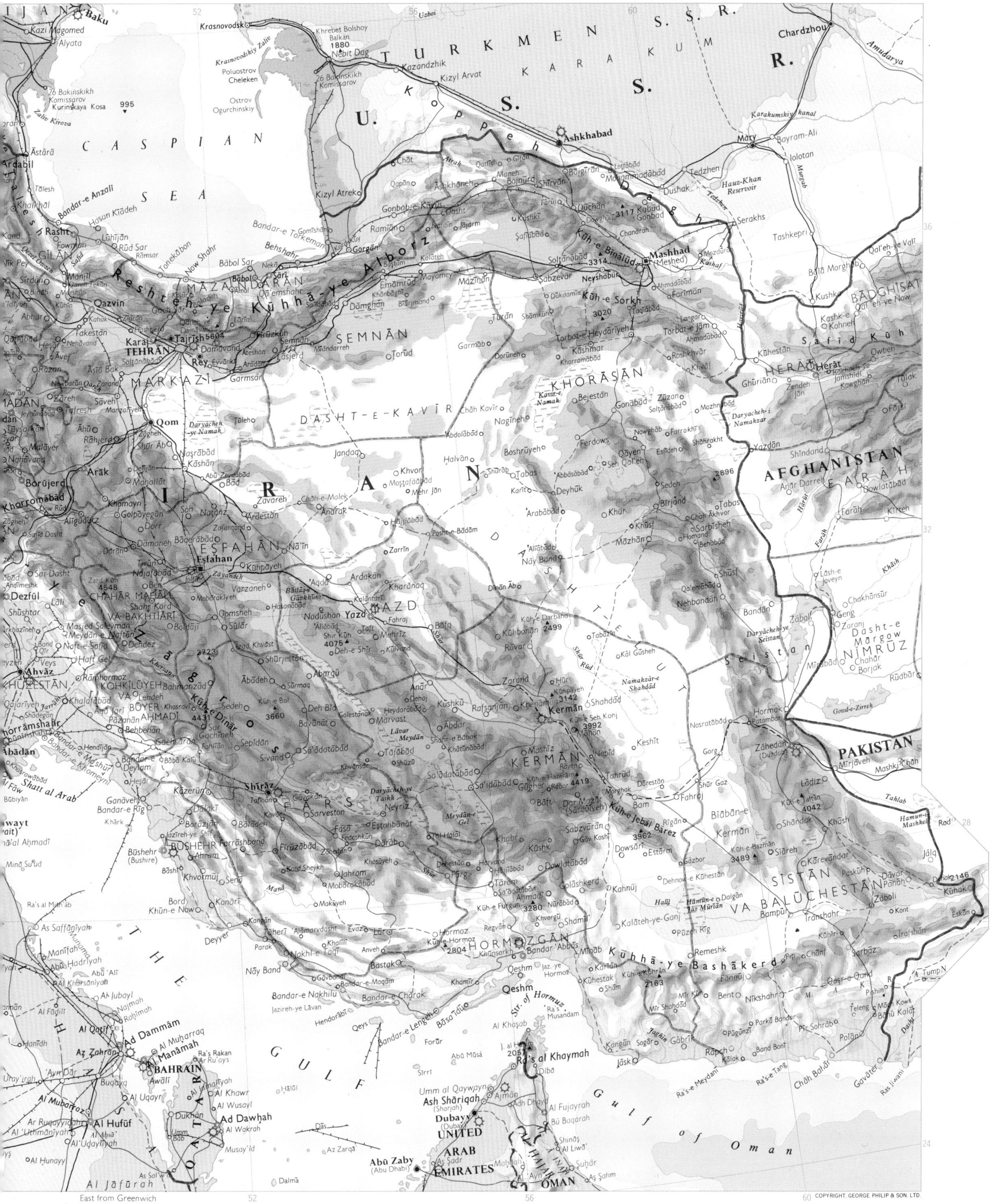

Baku
Krasnovodsk
Kazi Magomed
Alyata
Krasnovodskiy Zaliv
Khrebet Bolshoy Balkan
1880
Nebit Dag
Poluostrov Cheleken
Ostrov Ogurchinskiy
26 Bakinskikh Komissarov
Kurinskaya Kosa
995
Kizyl Arvat
Kazandzhik

TURKMEN S.S.R.
KARA KUM
U.
S.
S.
R.
Chardzhou
Amudarya
Karakumskiy kanal

Ashkhabad
Mary
Bayram-Ali
Iolotan
Tedzhen
Hauz-Khan Reservoir
Dushak
Tashkepri
Serakhs

CASPIAN
SEA

Āstārā
Ardabīl
Tālesh
Khalkhāl
Bandar-e Anzalī
Hasan Kīādeh
Rasht
Fowman
Lāhījān
Rūd Sar
Rāmsar
Now Shahr
Bābol Sar
Neka
Bandar-e Torkeman
Gorgān
Gonbad-e Kāvūs
Bandar-e Torkeman

Qazvīn
Karaj
TEHRĀN
Tajrīsh 5604
Rey
Damāvand
MARKAZĪ
Qom

RESHTEH-YE KŪHHĀ-YE ALBORZ
MĀZANDARĀN
Bābol
Bāmol
Behshahr
Sārī
Dāmghān
Semnān
SEMNĀN
Shāhrūd

KHORĀSĀN
Mashhad (Meshed)
3314
Neyshābūr
Sabzevār
Kāshmar
Torbat-e Heydarīyeh
Torbat-e Jām
Kūh-e Sorkh
3020

AFGHANISTAN
HERĀT
Herāt
BĀDGHĪSĀT
Ghūrīān

DASHT-E KAVĪR
Chāh Kavīr
Naqīneh
Jandaq
Abdolābād
Halvān
Tabas
Ferdows
Boshrūyeh
Bejestān
Gonābād
Soltānābād

IRAN
ESFAHĀN
Esfahan
Nā'īn
Ardestān
Nāṭanz
Ardekān
Kāshān
Zavāreh
Anārak

YAZD
Yazd
Taft
Mehrīz
Bāfq
Kharānaq
Abarqū

Shīrāz
FĀRS
Marvdasht
Neyrīz
Eṣṭahbānāt
Fasā
Dārāb
Jahrom
Fīrūzābād
Kāzerūn

Kermān
KERMĀN
Rafsanjān
Bam
Sīrjān
Shahr-e Bābak
Bāft

AHVĀZ
KHŪZESTĀN
Dezfūl
Shūshtar
Rāmhormoz
Behbehān
Gachsārān

Būshehr (Bushire)
Bandar-e Rīg
Ganāveh
Borāzjān
Bandar-e Deylam

ZĀGROS
Kūh-e Dīnār 4431
3660

Khorramshahr
Ābādān
Shatt al Arab
BĀKHTIĀRĪ
CHAHĀR MAHĀL VA BAKHTIĀRĪ

HORMOZGĀN
Bandar-e 'Abbās
Mīnāb
Qeshm
Bandar-e Lengeh
Jāsk

Gulf of Oman
SĪSTĀN VA BALŪCHESTĀN
PAKISTAN
Zāhedān (Duzdāb)
Mīrjāveh
Khāsh
Īrānshahr
Bampūr

THE
GULF
Ra's al Mish'āb
Manīfah
Al Jubayl
Az Zahrān
Ad Dammām
Al Muḥarraq
Al Manāmah
BAHRAIN
Awālī
Al Qaṭīf
Al Hufūf
Ar Ruqayyiqah
QATAR
Dukhān
Ad Dawḥah
Al Wakrah

Umm al Qaywayn
Ash Shāriqah (Sharjah)
Ajmān
Dubayy (Dubai)
UNITED ARAB EMIRATES
Abū Zaby (Abu Dhabi)
Ra's al Khaymah
Al Fujayrah
OMAN
Ṣuḥār

Gulf of Oman

East from Greenwich
COPYRIGHT. GEORGE PHILIP & SON. LTD.

EGYPT
SUDAN
ETHIOPIA
ERITREA
YEMEN
RED SEA
HIJAZ
ASIR
Al Madinah
(Medina)
Makkah
Jiddah
At Ta'if
Ar-Riyad
(Riyadh)
Sana'
Al'Adan (Aden)
Ta'izz
Al Hudaydah
Abha
Bûr Sûdân
(Port Sudan)
Asmera
(Asmara)
Mitsiwa
(Massawa)
Kassala
Keren
Aksum
Gonder
L. Tana
Aseb
(Assab)
Danakil
Depression
Jaza'ir
Farasan
(Farasan Is.)
Bab el Mandeb
Little Aden
Ramlat as Sab'atayn
Ma'rib
Buraydah
'Unayzah
Harrat Khaybar
Harrat al Kishb
Harrat Nawasif
NAFUD AD DAHY
Yanbu 'al Bahr
Al Wajh
Rabigh
Al Lith
Al Qunfudhah
Jizan
Sabya
Khamis Mushayt
Najran
Sa'dah
Al Mukha
Zabid
Dhamar
Ibb
Yarim
Halaib
Suakin
Tokar
Agordat
Tesseney
Adi Ugri
Mekele
Dahlak Kebir
Mitsiwa Channel
Ras Kasar
Karora
Muhammad Qol
Al Khamasin
As Sulayyil
Tathlith
Al Hariq
Al Hillah
Ad Dir'iyah
Ft
m
12 000
9000
6000
4500
3000
1200
600
0
200
2000
4000
4000
3000
2000
1500
1000
400
200
0
600
6000
12 000
m
ft
Projection: Conical with two standard parallels
40
44

1:7 000 000

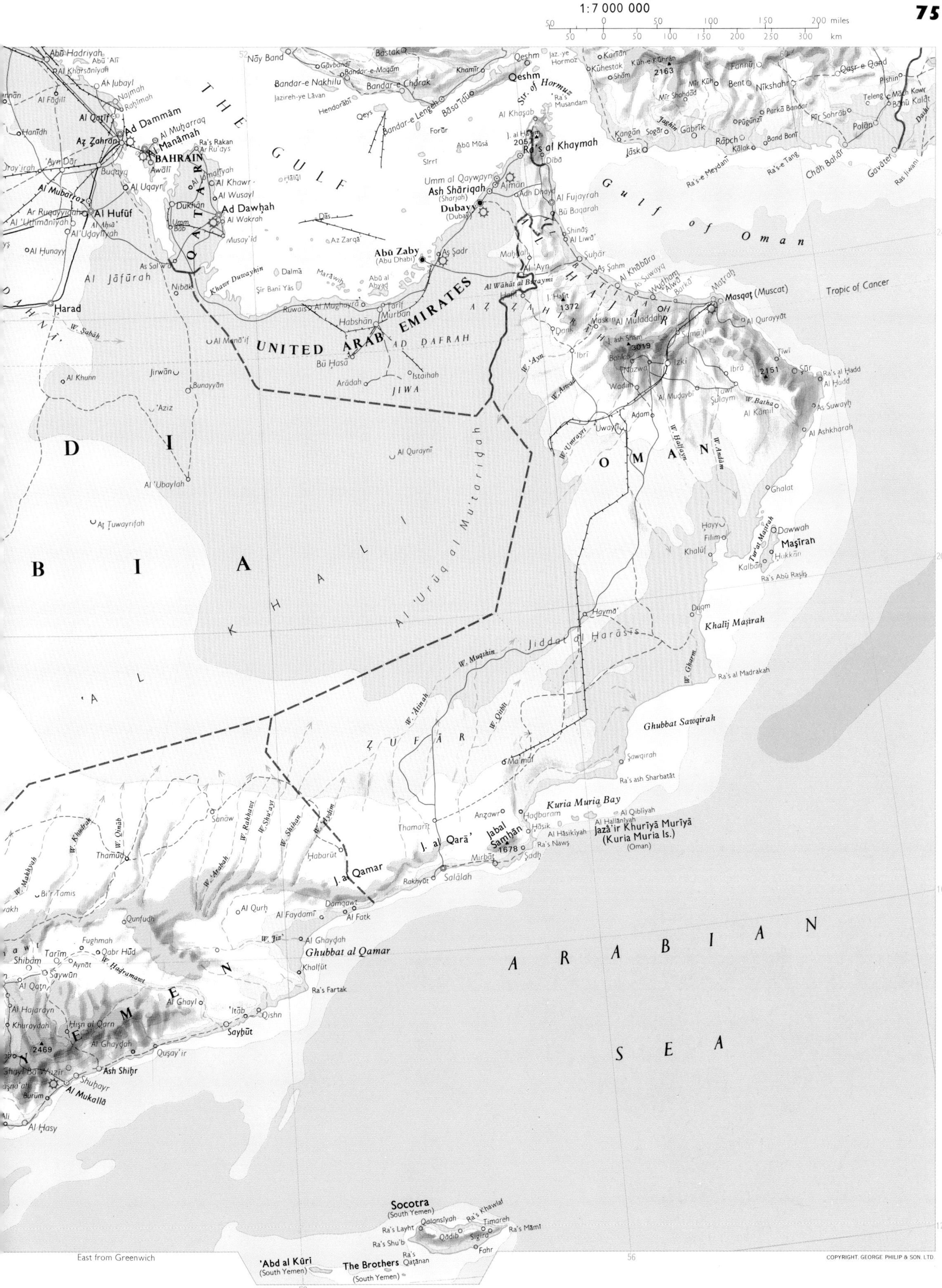

Tropic of Cancer

THE GULF

Str. of Hormuz

Gulf of Oman

UNITED ARAB EMIRATES

OMAN

ARABIA

AL KHALI

YEMEN

ARABIAN SEA

Socotra
(South Yemen)

'Abd al Kūri
(South Yemen)

The Brothers
(South Yemen)

East from Greenwich

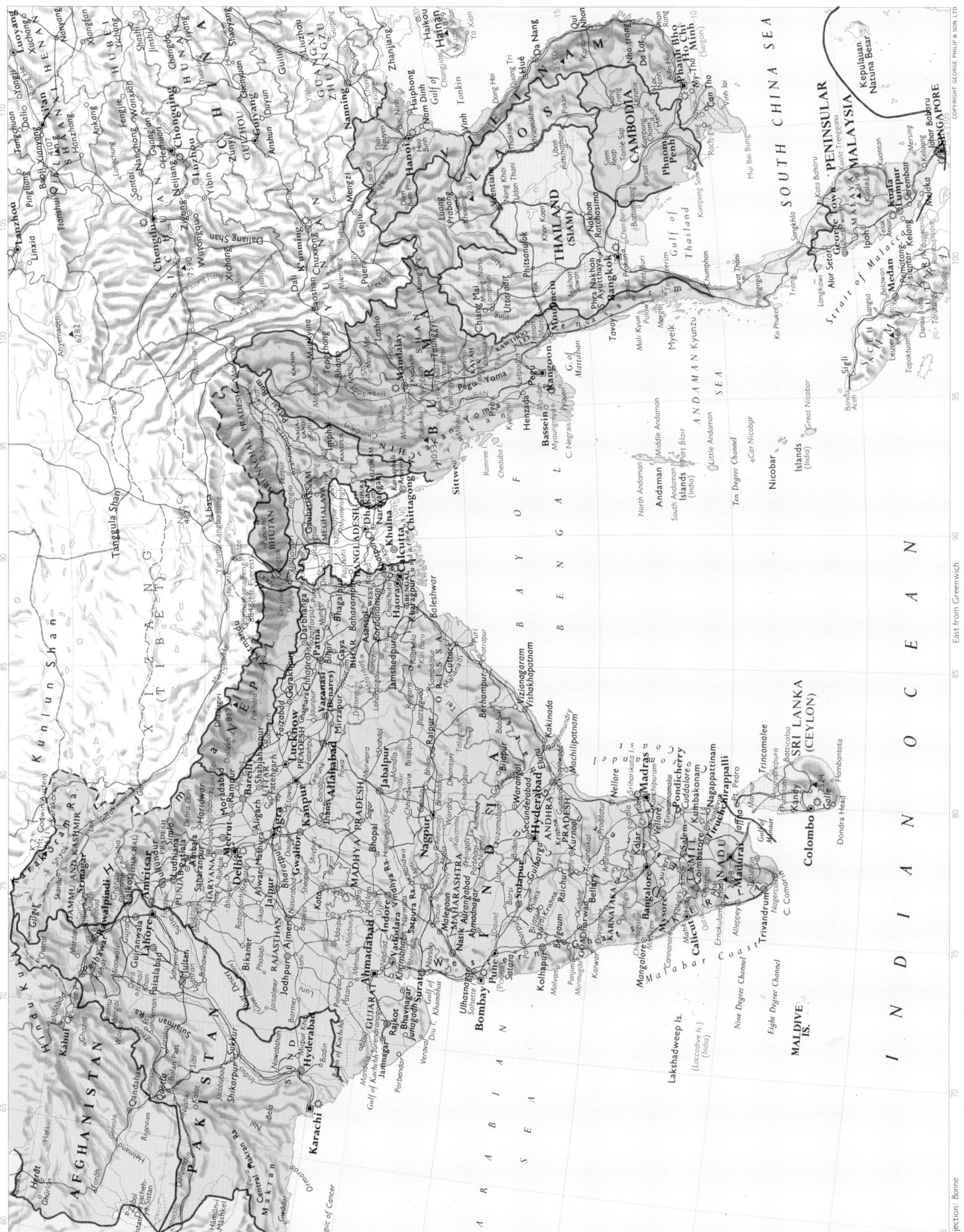

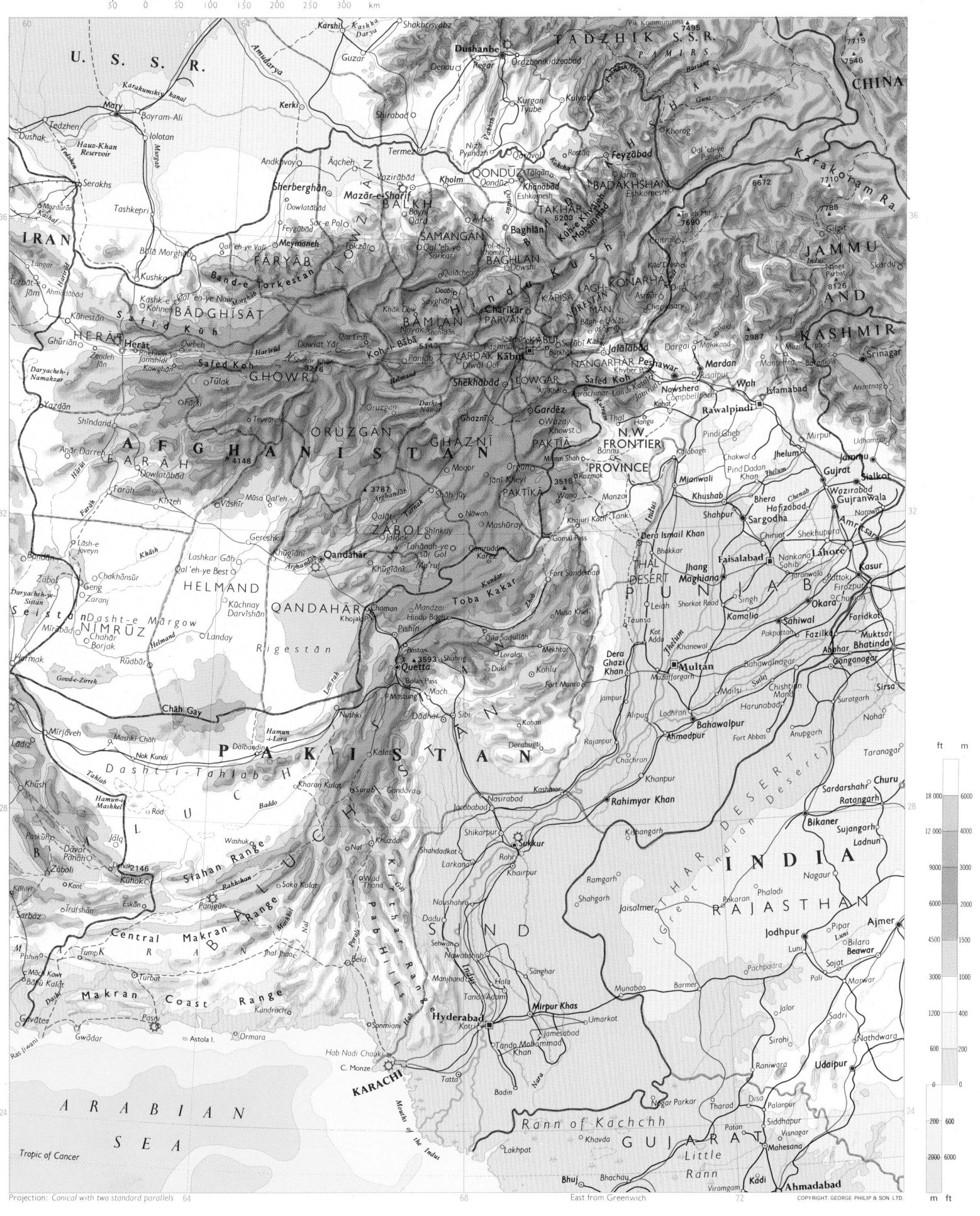

1:7 000 000

Projection: *Conical with two standard parallels*

East from Greenwich

COPYRIGHT. GEORGE PHILIP & SON. LTD.

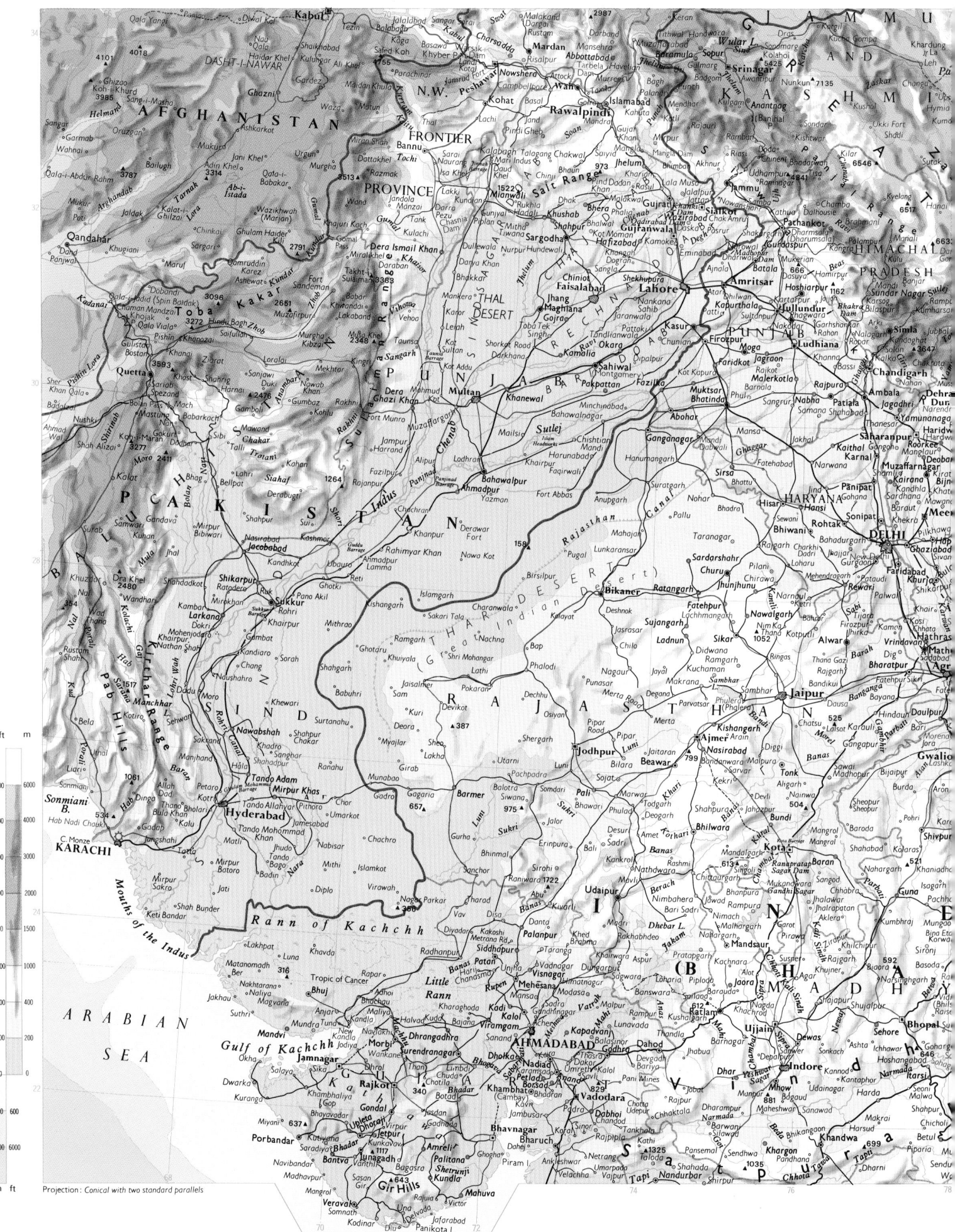
AFGHANISTAN
DASHT-I-NAWAR
Kabul
Ghazni
Qandahar
N.W. FRONTIER PROVINCE
Peshawar
Rawalpindi
Islamabad
Salt Range
Lahore
Amritsar
Ludhiana
Chandigarh
PUNJAB
HIMACHAL PRADESH
JAMMU AND KASHMIR
Srinagar
Jammu
Multan
Faisalabad
THAL DESERT
Quetta
BALUCHISTAN
PAKISTAN
Sulaiman Range
Toba Kakar
Indus
Chenab
Sutlej
Bahawalpur
Sukkur
Larkana
Kirthar Range
Pab Hills
SIND
Hyderabad
KARACHI
Mouths of the Indus
Rann of Kachchh
Little Rann
Gulf of Kachchh
ARABIAN SEA
Tropic of Cancer
THAR DESERT (Great Indian Desert)
RAJASTHAN
Bikaner
Jodhpur
Jaipur
Ajmer
Udaipur
DELHI
HARYANA
Agra
Gwalior
Kota
Ahmadabad
Vadodara
Rajkot
Bhavnagar
Gir Hills
Indore
Ujjain
Bhopal
MADHYA PRADESH
Vindhya Range
Satpura Range
Narmada
Tapi
Projection: Conical with two standard parallels
ft m
18 000 6000
12 000 4000
9000 3000
6000 2000
4500 1500
3000 1000
1200 400
600 200
0 0
200 600
2000 6000
m ft

1:6 000 000

50   50   100   150 miles
50   0   50   100   150   200   250 km

JAMMU AND KASHMIR
On same scale as Main Map

CHINESE REPUBLIC

PUNJAB

Rawalpindi
Islamabad
Srinagar
Anantnag
Wular L.
Baramula
Muzaffarabad
Abbottabad
Jammu
Sialkot
Gujrat
Wazirabad
Amritsar
HIMACHAL PRADESH

Kunlun Shan
Karakoram Range
Gilgit
Nanga Parbat
Skardu
Leh
Zaskar Mountains
Deosai Mountains
SODA PLAINS
Aksai Chin

Ngangiong Kangri
Gangdise Shan
Mapam Yumco

Moradabad
Rampur
Bareilly
Lucknow
KANPUR
Allahabad
Varanasi
Mirzapur
Panna Hills
Kaimur Hills
Jabalpur
Bilaspur
Raigarh
Raurkela
Sambalpur

Katmandu
Lalitpur
Bhaktapur
NEPAL
Mt. Everest 8848
Kanchenjunga
SIKKIM
Gangtok
Darjiling
BHUTAN
Thimphu
XIZANG
Xigaze

Gorakhpur
Darbhanga
Muzaffarpur
Patna
Gaya
Bihar
Munger
Bhagalpur
Hazaribag
Bokaro
Dhanbad
Asansol
Durgapur
Ranchi
Jamshedpur
Kharagpur

ASSAM
Koch Bihar
Rangpur
DHAKA
Rajshahi
BANGLADESH
Khulna
Barisal
CALCUTTA
Haora
Mouths of the Ganga
The Sandheads
Sunderbans

INDIA

East from Greenwich

COPYRIGHT. GEORGE PHILIP & SON. LTD.

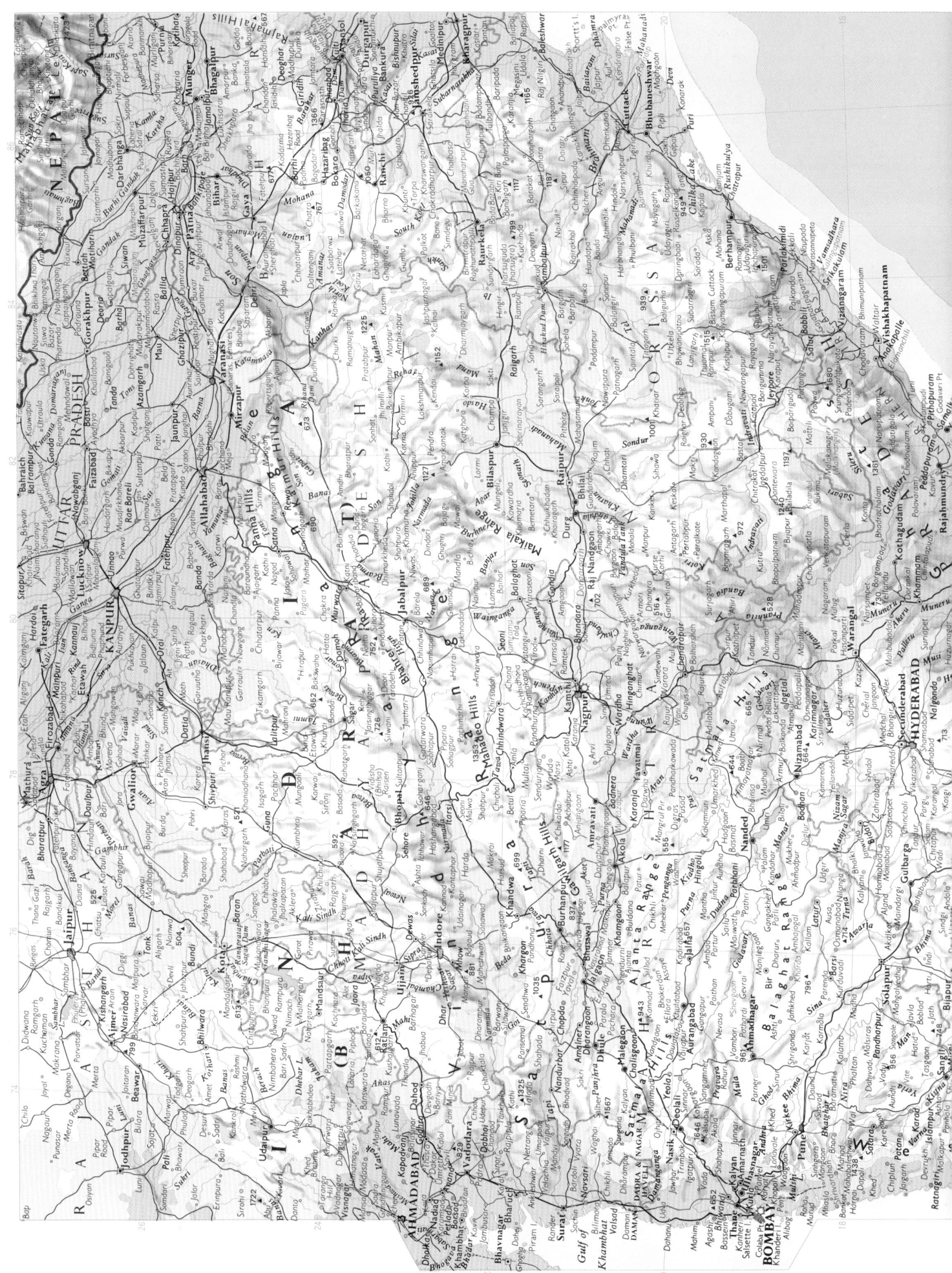
NEPAL
UTTAR PRADESH
MADHYA PRADESH
ORISSA
RAJASTHAN
KANPUR
Lucknow
Allahabad
Varanasi
Patna
Jabalpur
Nagpur
Raipur
Cuttack
Bhubaneshwar
Vishakhapatnam
HYDERABAD
Secunderabad
BOMBAY
Pune
AHMADABAD
Vadodara
Surat
Indore
Bhopal
Jaipur
Agra
Gwalior
Jhansi
Gulf of Khambhat
Satpura Range
Mahadeo Hills
Maikala Range
Ajanta Range
Balaghat Range
Vindhya Range

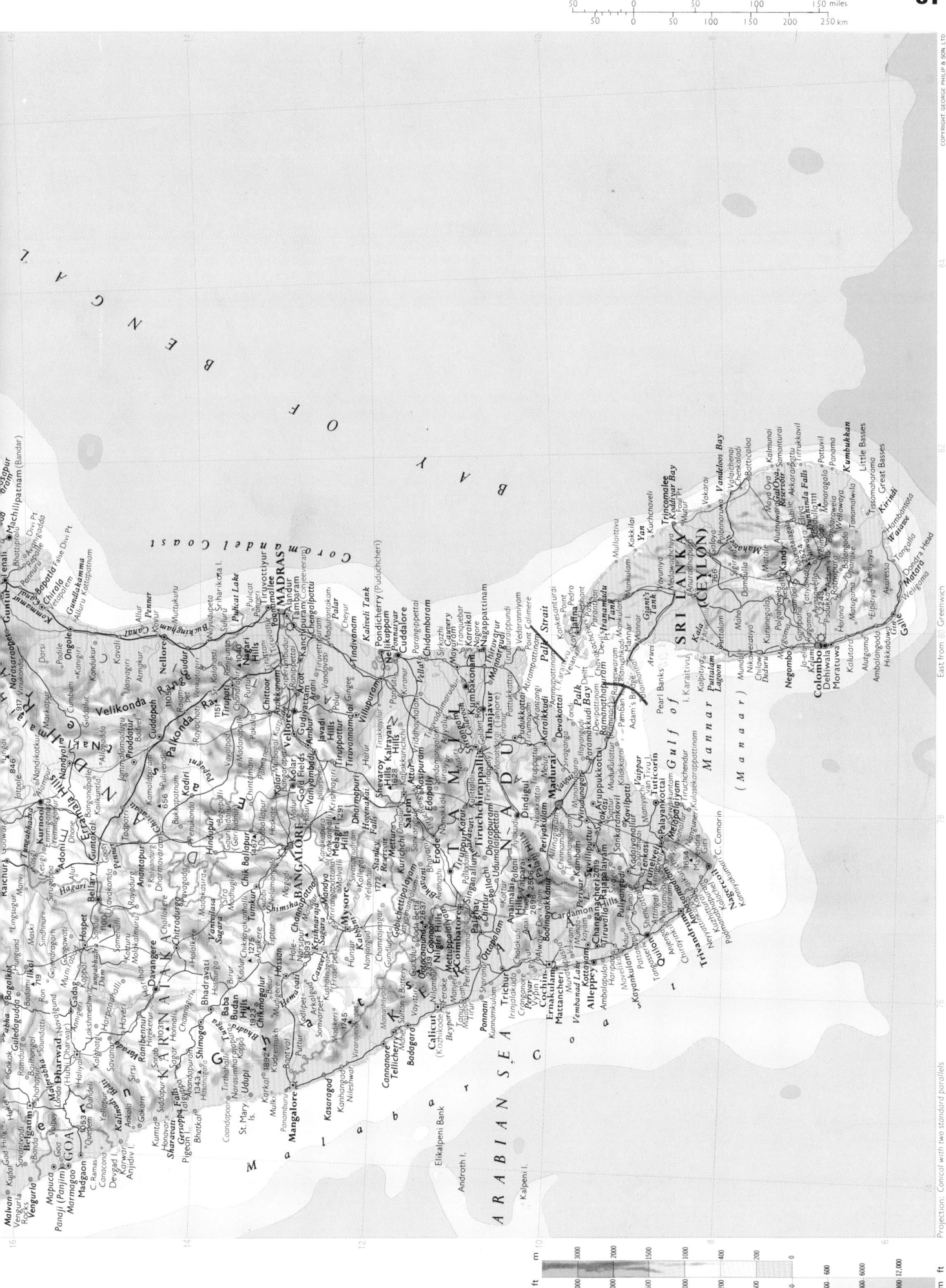

1:6 000 000

East from 80 Greenwich

Projection Conical with two standard parallels

1:6 000 000

Projection: Conical with two standard parallels

East from Greenwich

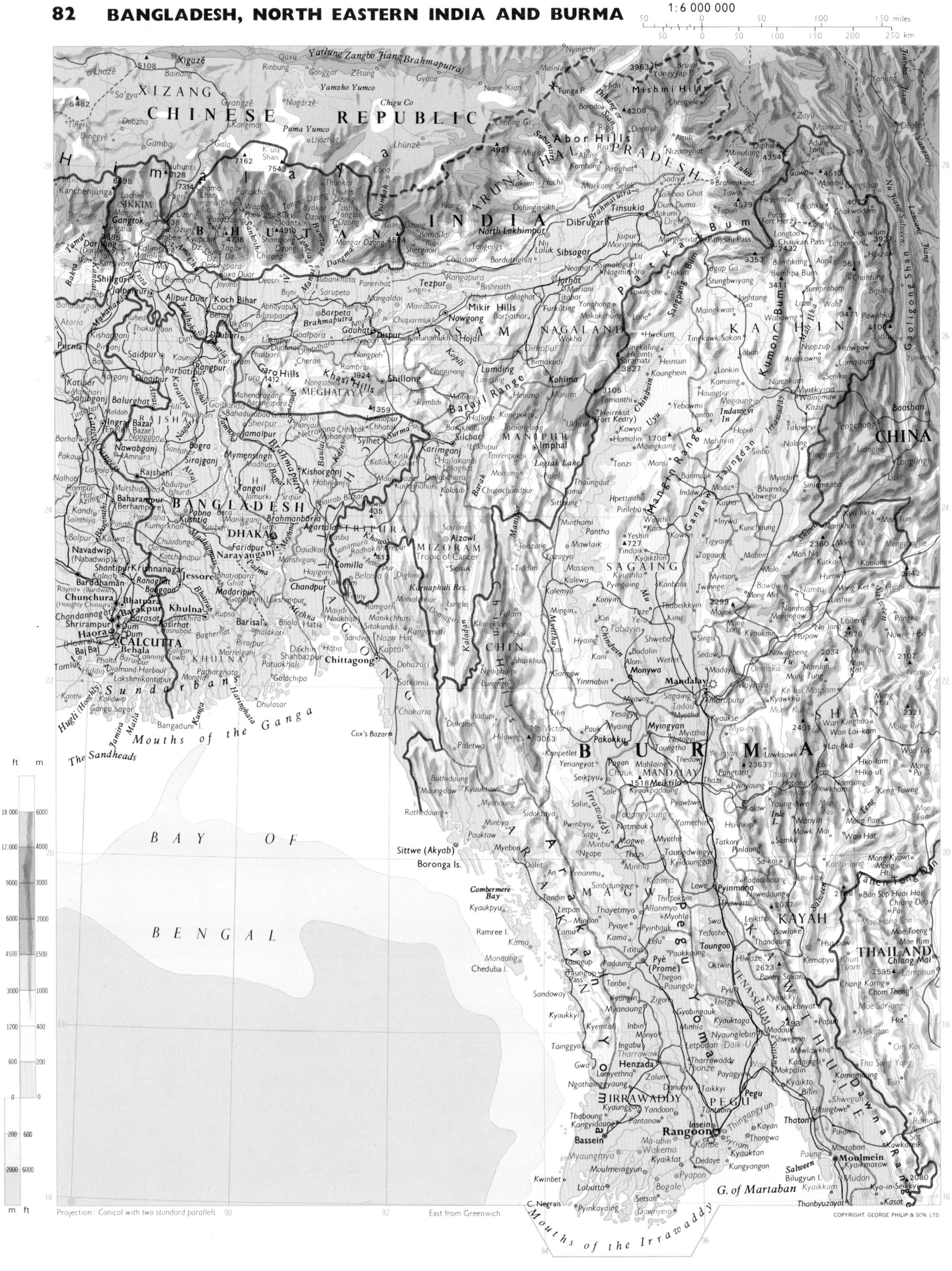

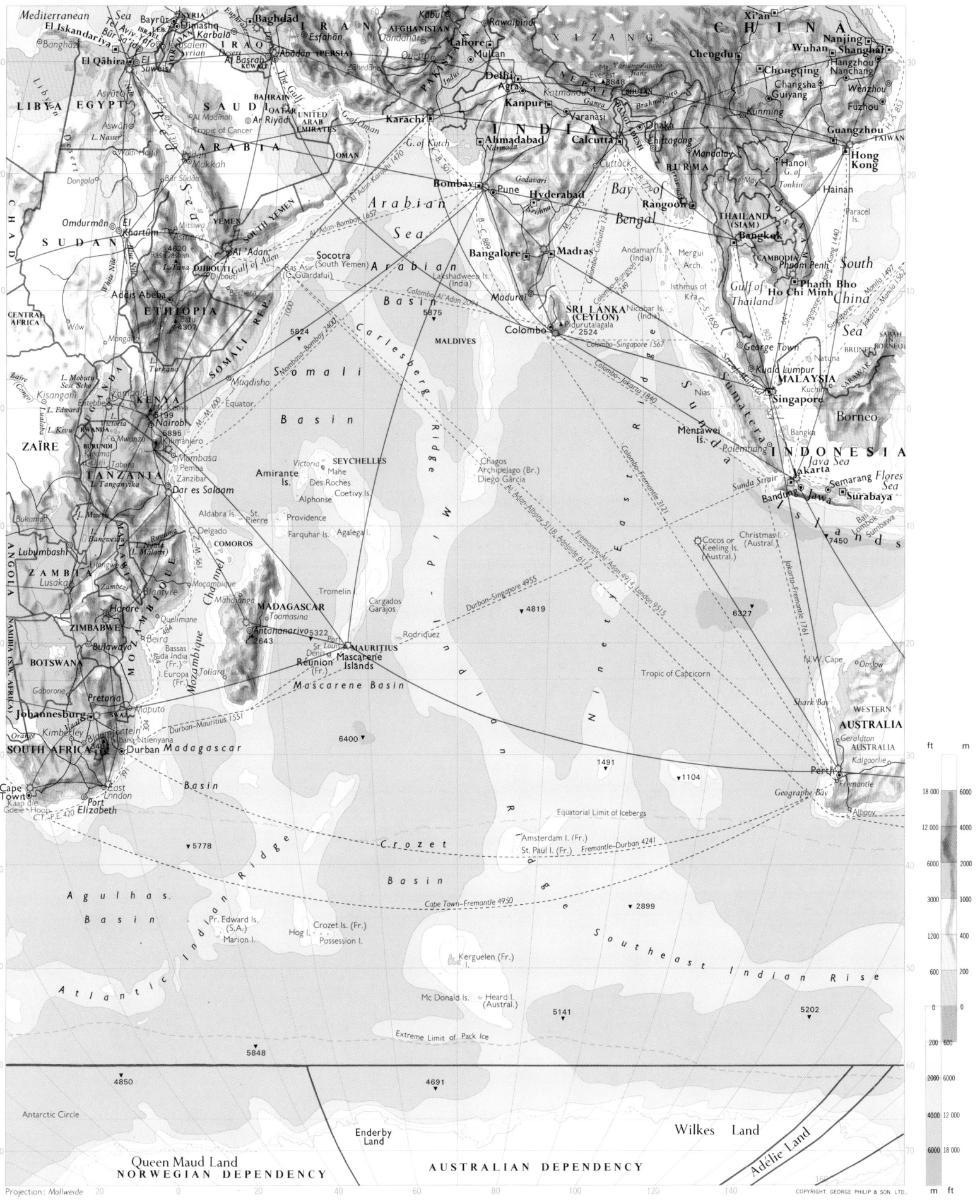

Mediterranean Sea
El Iskandariya
Banghazi
El Qâhira El Suweis
LIBYA EGYPT
Aswân
L. Nasser
Wâdi Halfa
Dongola
CHAD
Omdurmân El Khartûm
SUDAN
CENTRAL AFRICA
Addis Abeba
ETHIOPIA
ZAÏRE
Kisangani
UGANDA
KENYA
Nairobi
TANZANIA
Dar es Salaam
ANGOLA
Lubumbashi
ZAMBIA
Lusaka
ZIMBABWE
Bulawayo
Harare
BOTSWANA
Gaborone
Pretoria
Johannesburg
Kimberley
SOUTH AFRICA
Durban
Cape Town
East London
Port Elizabeth

Bayrût
SYRIA
Dimashq
Baghdad
IRAN
IRAQ
Al Basrah
SAUDI ARABIA
Al Madinah
Ar Riyâd
Makkah
YEMEN
SOUTH YEMEN
Al 'Adan
DJIBOUTI
Berbera
Socotra (South Yemen)
Ras Asir (C. Guardafui)
Mogdisho
SOMALI REP.
Equator

AFGHANISTAN
Kabul
Quetta
PAKISTAN
Multan
Karachi
Delhi
Agra
Kanpur
INDIA
Ahmadabad
Bombay
Pune
Hyderabad
Bangalore
Madras
Madurai
SRI LANKA (CEYLON)
Colombo

CHINA
Xi'an
Chengdu
Chongqing
Wuhan
Nanjing
Shanghai
Guangzhou
Hong Kong
TAIWAN
Hainan
BURMA
Mandalay
Rangoon
THAILAND (SIAM)
Bangkok
CAMBODIA
Phnom Penh
Ho Chi Minh
Hanoi
South China Sea
MALAYSIA
Kuala Lumpur
Singapore
INDONESIA
Sumatera
Jakarta
Bandung
Surabaya
Java
Borneo

Arabian Sea
Arabian Basin
MALDIVES
Carlesberg Ridge
Somali Basin
SEYCHELLES
Amirante Is.
Mahe
Aldabra Is.
COMOROS
MADAGASCAR
Antananarivo
MAURITIUS
Réunion (Fr.)
Mascarene Islands
Mascarene Basin
Chagos Archipelago (Br.)
Diego Garcia
Cocos or Keeling Is. (Austral.)
Christmas I. (Austral.)

Madagascar Basin
Agulhas Basin
Atlantic Indian Ridge
Crozet Basin
Pr. Edward Is. (S.A.)
Marion I.
Crozet Is. (Fr.)
Kerguelen (Fr.) I.
Mc Donald Is.
Heard I. (Austral.)
Amsterdam I. (Fr.)
St. Paul I. (Fr.)
Southeast Indian Rise
Ninety East Ridge
Tropic of Capricorn
WESTERN AUSTRALIA
Perth
Fremantle

Equatorial Limit of Icebergs
Extreme Limit of Pack Ice
Antarctic Circle
Queen Maud Land
NORWEGIAN DEPENDENCY
Enderby Land
AUSTRALIAN DEPENDENCY
Wilkes Land
Adélie Land

Projection: Mollweide

COPYRIGHT GEORGE PHILIP & SON, LTD.

Gulf of Tonkin
Hainan
HANOI
Haiphong
Vientiane
BANGKOK (Krung Thep)
Rangoon
Gulf of Martaban
Moulmein
Mandalay
Da Nang (Tourane)

1:6 000 000

50 0 50 100 150 miles
50 0 50 100 150 200 250 km

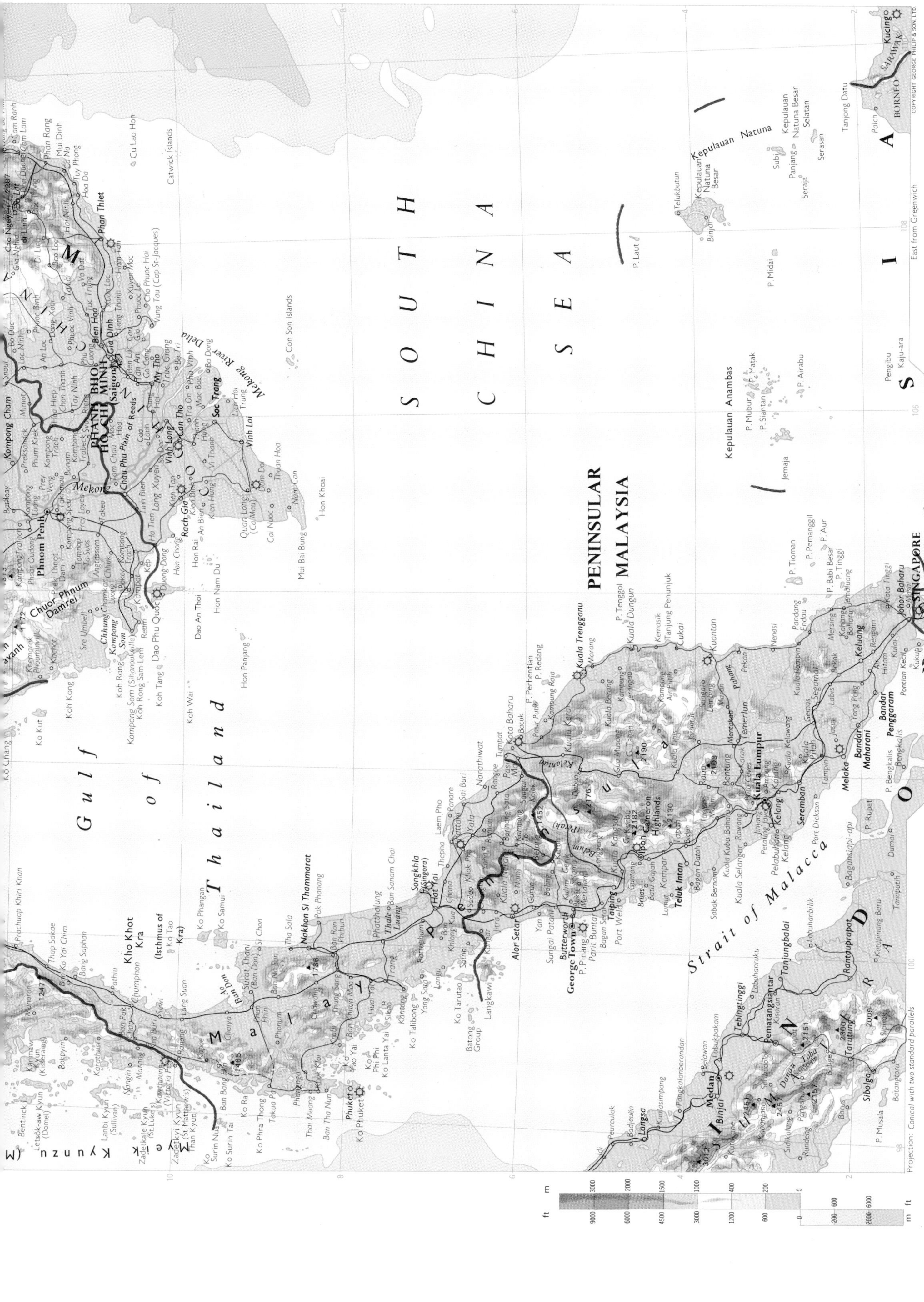

SOUTH CHINA SEA

Gulf of Thailand

Thailand

Malaya

Isthmus of Kra

Kho Khot Kra

PENINSULAR MALAYSIA

Strait of Malacca

BORNEO
SARAWAK
Kuching
Tanjung Datu

Kepulauan Natuna
Kepulauan Natuna Besar
Natuna Selatan
Subi
Panjang
Serasan
Seraja
Telukbutun
Binjai
P. Laut
P. Midai

Kepulauan Anambas
P. Mubur
P. Matak
P. Siantan
P. Airabu
Jemaja

Pengibu
Kaju-ara

SINGAPORE
Johor Baharu
Tanjungpinang
P. Bintan
P. Batam
P. Bulan

Kuala Trengganu
Marang
Kuala Dungun
P. Tenggol
Kemasik
Cukai
Kuantan
Pekan
P. Tioman
P. Pemanggil
P. Aur
P. Babi Besar
P. Tinggi

Kota Baharu
P. Perhentian
Pasir Putih
P. Redang
Bacok
Kampong Raja
Tumpat
Tanah Merah
Kuala Krai
Kuala Lipis
Temerluh
Kuala Kerai
Raub
Bentong
Kuala Lumpur
Klang
Kelang
Petaling Jaya
Batu Caves
Seremban
Port Dickson
Melaka
Muar
Bandar Maharani
Batu Pahat
Bandar Penggaram
Kluang
Kulai
Pontian Kechil
Kukup

George Town
P. Pinang
Butterworth
Bagan Serai
Taiping
Ipoh
Cameron Highlands
Kuala Kangsar
Teluk Intan
Teluk Anson
Sungkai
Tapah
Bidor
Tanjung Malim

Alor Setar
Sungai Petani
Kangar
Langkawi
Yan
Kroh
Kuala Nerang
Padang Besar

Songkhla
Hat Yai
Pattani
Yala
Narathiwat
Sadao
Thepha
Saba Yoi
Ranot

Nakhon Si Thammarat
Phatthalung
Thung Song
Ron Phibun
Trang
Satun
Sai Buri
Sungai Kolok

Surat Thani (Ban Don)
Ko Samui
Ko Phangan
Chaiya
Ko Tao

Chumphon
Lang Suan
Bang Saphan
Prachuap Khiri Khan
Thap Sakae

Phuket
Ko Phuket
Phangnga
Krabi
Ko Lanta Yai
Ko Talibong
Ko Phi Phi
Ko Yao

Takua Pa
Phang Nga
Ko Phra Thong

South China Sea

Con Son Islands
Con Son
Hon Khoai
Hon Nam Du
Mui Bai Bung

HO CHI MINH CITY
Saigon
PHANH BHO
Bien Hoa
Gia Dinh
My Tho
Can Tho
Vinh Long
Soc Trang
Rach Gia
Vinh Loi

Phnom Penh
Kompong Cham
Kompong Som
Chhung Kompong Som
Koh Kong
Ko Kut
Ko Chang

Chuor Phnum Damrei

Phan Rang
Phan Thiet
Cam Ranh
Mui Dinh
Cu Lao Hon
Catwick Islands

Mekong River Delta
Chau Phu Plain of Reeds
Quan Long (Ca Mau)
Dao Phu Quoc
Dao An Thoi

Myeik Kyunzu
Zadetkyi Kyun (St. Matthew's)
Lanbi Kyun (Sullivan's)
Kadan Kyun (King I.)

Projection: Conical with two standard parallels

East from Greenwich

ft m
9000 3000
6000 2000
4500 1500
3000 1000
1200 400
600 200
0
600 200
6000 2000
ft m

East from Greenwich

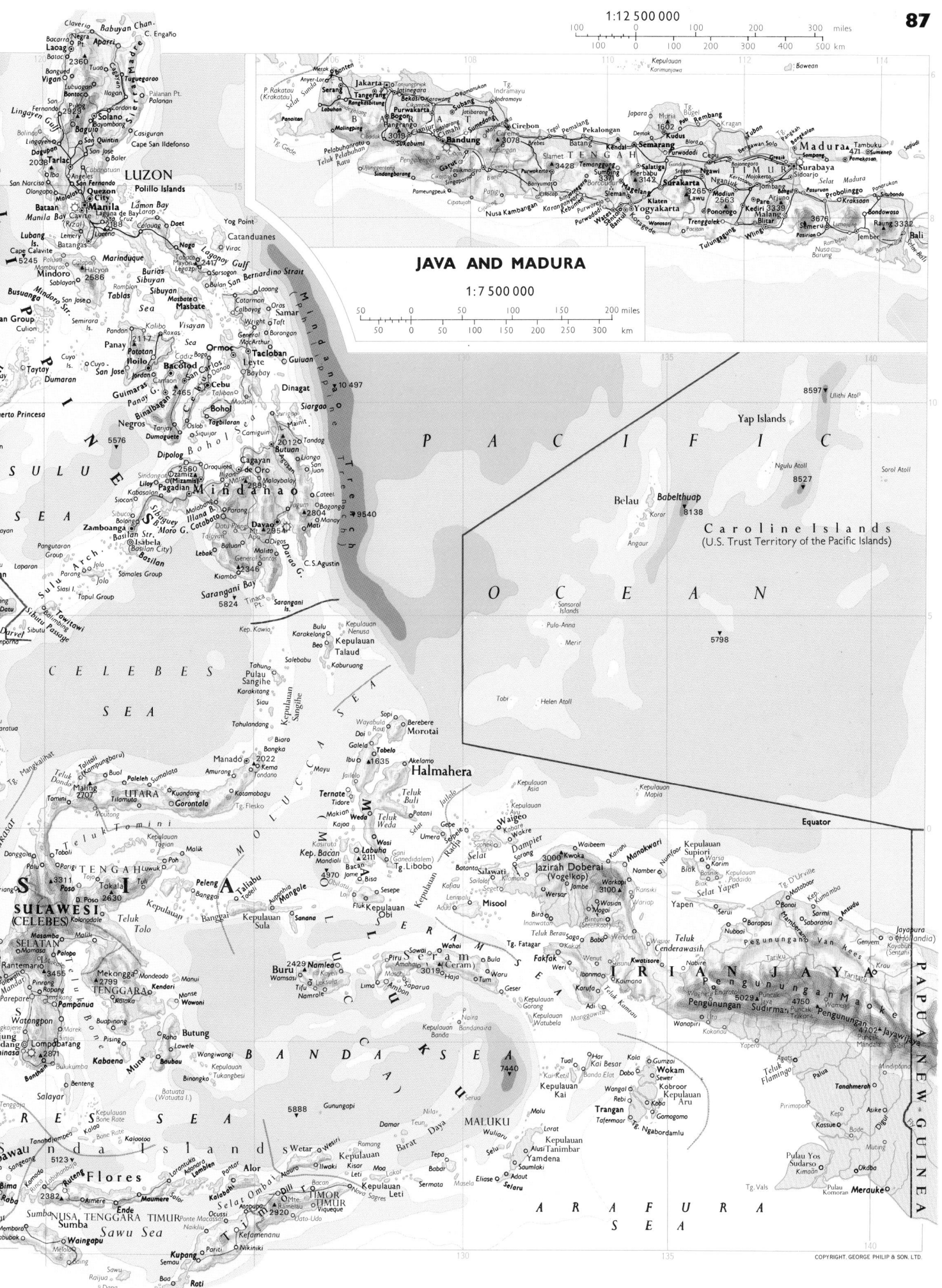

1:12 500 000
100 0 100 200 300 miles
100 0 100 200 300 400 500 km
JAVA AND MADURA
1:7 500 000
50 0 50 100 150 200 miles
50 0 50 100 150 200 250 300 km
Jakarta
Bandung
Semarang
Surakarta
Yogyakarta
Surabaya
Madura
Malang
Cirebon
Bogor
Serang
Kediri
Madiun
Jember
Bali
Nusa Kambangan
LUZON
Polillo Islands
Manila
Quezon City
Baguio
Mindoro
Marinduque
Catanduanes
Samar
Leyte
Panay
Negros
Cebu
Bohol
Mindanao
Zamboanga
Davao
Cagayan de Oro
SULU SEA
CELEBES SEA
MOLUCCA SEA
BANDA SEA
ARAFURA SEA
PACIFIC OCEAN
Yap Islands
Belau
Babelthuap
Caroline Islands
(U.S. Trust Territory of the Pacific Islands)
Equator
Halmahera
Morotai
Ternate
SULAWESI (CELEBES)
Manado
Kepulauan Talaud
Kepulauan Sula
Buru
Seram
Ambon
Misool
Jazirah Doberai (Vogelkop)
Manokwari
Yapen
IRIAN JAYA
Jayapura (Hollandia)
Pegunungan Sudirman
Pegunungan Jayawijaya
Teluk Cenderawasih
Kepulauan Aru
Kepulauan Kai
Kepulauan Tanimbar
Yamdena
MALUKU
Flores
Sumba
Timor
Sawu Sea
Kupang
Roti
Alor
PAPUA NEW GUINEA
Merauke

THAILAND

SOUTH

MA

PENINSULAR
MALAYSIA

Batong
Group
Savu
Pattani
Yala
Langkawi
Kangar
Kuala Nerang
Narathiwat
PERLIS
Alor Setar
KEDAH
Kota Baharu
Pasir Mas
Tanah Merah

Sabang
We
Banda Aceh
(Kutaraja)
Breueh
Seulimeum
Sigli
Meureudu
Bireuen
Lhokseumawe
Idi
Sungai Petani
Kuala Kerai
Kuala Trengganu

Lhokkruet
Geumpang
Peureulak
Langsa
George Town
PINANG
Butterworth
Kulim
Gerik
G. Chamah
2170
Dabung
Marang

Calang
Geureudong
2858
Takengon
Kualasimpang
Bukit Mertajam
Parit Buntar
Taiping
PERAK
748
Besar
KELANTAN
TRENGGANU
Kuala Dungun

Meulaboh
ACEH
Abongabong
2985
Pangkalansusu
Pangkalanbrandan
Port Weld
Kuala Kangsar
Ipoh
2182
G. Korbu
2190
G. Tahan
2108
Cameron Highlands
2130 G. Batu Puteh

Ujung Raja
3381
Leuser
Blangpidie
Bohorok
Belawan
Batu Gajah
Kampar
Tapah
Kuala Lipis

Tapaktuan
Kabanjahe
Binjai
Medan
Lumut
Teluk Anson
Bernam
Raub
Jerantut
Cukai
Kuantan

Kadang
Bakungan
Sidikalang
Tebingtinggi
Kisaran
Tanjong Malim
Kuala Kubu Baharu
Benom
Benting
PAHANG
Temerloh
Pekan

Sibigo
Simeulue
Sinabang
Seabudolak
Samosir
Pematangsiantar
Prapat
Tanjungbalai
SELANGOR
Kuala Selangor
Shah Alam
Kelang
Kajang
Kuala Lumpur
Rompin
Pahang

Lasia
Kepulauan
Banyak
Danau
Toba
Balige
Rantauprapat
Telok Datok
Seremban
NEGERI
Kuala Pilah
SEMBILAN
Gemas
Kuala Rompin
Pandang Endau
P. Tioman

Singkil
Tarutung
SUMATERA
UTARA
Kopinang
Labuhanbilik
Port Dickson
Rembau
Tampin
MELAKA
1276
G. Ledang
Segamat
Mersing

Gunungsitoli
Nias
Sibolga
Siplongot
Bagansiapiapi
Rupat
Dumai
Melaka
Muar
JOHOR
Keluang
Labis

Sirombu
Padangsidempuan
Sibuhuan
Lubuk
Rantaukampar
Padang
Batu Pahat
Kota Tinggi

Teluhdalem
Natal
Kotatengah
Sungaipakning
Rangsang
Teberau
Tebingtinggi
Johor Baharu
Nee Soon
Changi
SINGAPORE

Pini
Rao
Rohan
Siksrindrapura
Siak
Batam
Bintan
Tanjungpinang

Lubuksikaping
Pekanbaru
Bangkinang
Kampar
Minas
Kundur
Kepulauan
Riau
Kepulauan
Badas

Equator
Tanahmasa
Bukittinggi
Payakumbuh
Lipatkain
RIAU
Sebangka
Kepulauan
Lingga

Kepulauan
Batu
Tanahbala
Padangpanjang
Batusangkar
Sawahlunto
Airmolek
Rengat
Tembilahan
Lingga
Dabo
Sinkep

Pariaman
Solok
Muaro
Sijunjung
Teluk
Cerenti
Kualatungkal
Muarasabak
Selat Berhala

Padang
BARAT
Kotabaru
SUMATERA

Siberut
Sabulubek
Pasarkuok
Panjang
Muarabungo
Muaratebo
Batanghari
Jambi (Telanaipura)
Kenaliasam
Muaratembesi
Belinyu

Kepulauan
Mentawai
3805
Kerinci
BUKI
JAMBI
Sungaipenuh
Indrapura
Bangko
Tembesi
Lalang
Jebus
Sungailiat
Muntok
Pangkalpinang

Pulau Pagai
Utara
Mukomuko
2833
Masurai
Sarolangun
Sungsang
Bangka
Koba
Selat Bangka

Pulau Pagai
Selatan
Sipora
Ipuh
Seblat
2383
Muaraupi
Muaradaman
Musi
Sekayu
Palembang
Toboali
Tg. Paku

INDIAN
Argamakmur
Curup
SELATAN
Lubuklinggau
Perabumilih
Kayuagung
Pendopo
Tg. Lumut

Bengkulu
BENGKULU
Lahat
Muaraenim
Ogan
Baturaja
Dempo
3159
Tais
Martapura
Tulangbawang
Menggala

OCEAN
Manna
BUKIT BARISAN
D.
Ranau
Baturmin
LAMPUNG
Kotabumi
N
G

Bintuhan
Enggano
6073
Metro
Sukadana
Kotaagung
Kruk
Tanjungkarang
Telukbetung

Tg. Cina
Krakatau
Anyer
JAKA
Kotajawa
Kalianda

Selat Sunda
Pulau Rakata
Pandeglang
Labuhan
Bonten
Serang
Tangerang

Panaitan
Tg. Gede
Rangkasbitung
Bogor
Sukabumi

Java Trench
6650
Teluk
Pelabuhan
Ratu
Pelabuha
Ujunggenteng
Sindangba

ft	m
9000	3000
6000	2000
4500	1500
3000	1000
1200	400
600	200
0	0
200	600
2000	6000
4000	12 000
6000	18 000
m	ft

Projection: Mercator

East from Green

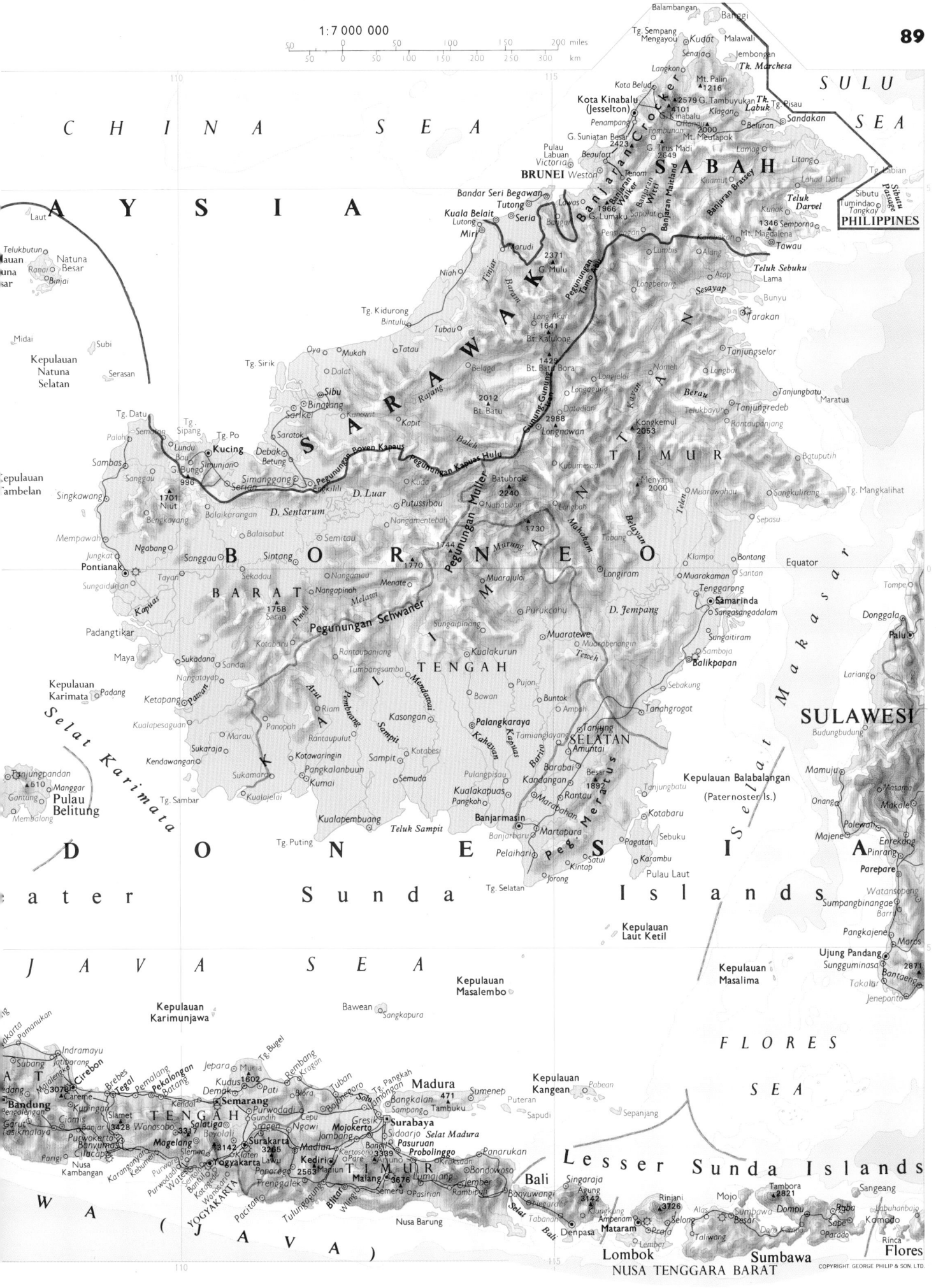

1 : 7 000 000

50   0   50   100   150   200 miles
50 0 50 100 150 200 250 300 km

C H I N A   S E A

SULU
SEA

Balambangan
Tg. Sempang
Mengayou   Kudat   Malawali   Banggi
Langkon   Tk. Marchesa
Mt. Palin
▲1216
Kota Belud   Crocker   G. Tambuyukan   Tk.
Kota Kinabalu   ▲2579   Labuk   Tg. Risau
(Jesselton)   ▲4101   G. Kinabalu   Klagan   Sandakan
Penampang   Mt. Meutapok
2000
Beaufort   Mt. Trus Madi   Banjaran   Litang   Tg. Labian
Pulau   G. Suniatan Besar   2649   Lamag   SABAH
Labuan   2423   Tenom   G. Lumaku   Sapulut   Kunak   Teluk   Sibutu
Victoria   Weston   1966   Tambunan   Lahad Datu   Darvel   Tumindao   Passage
BRUNEI   Lawas   Keningau   Wirti   1346 Semporna   Tangkay
Bandar Seri Begawan   Tutong   Maitand   Mt. Magdalena   PHILIPPINES
Kuala Belait   Seria   Lawas   Banjaran Brassey   Tawau
Lutong   Marudi   Pensiangan   Teluk Sebuku
Miri   Lama
Niah   2371   G. Mulu   Longberang   Sesayap   Bunyu
Tg. Kidurong   Tinjar   Atap   Tarakan
Bintulu   Tubau   Long Akah   Pegunungan   Iran
Oya   Mukah   Tatau   1641   Berau   Tanjungredeb   Maratua
Tg. Sirik   Dalat   Bt. Kalulong   Tanjungbatu
Sibu   Belaga   1429   Longjelai   Kongkemul   Batuputih
Binatang   Kanowit   Bt. Batu Bora   2012   Gunung   2053   Tg. Mangkalihat
Sarikei   Kapit   Bt. Batu   2988   Longnawan   Menyapa
Saratok   Rajang   Baleh   Longnawan   TIMUR   2000
Debak   Boyen Kapuas   Pegunungan Kapuas Hulu   Kubumesaai   Muarawahau   Sangkulirang
Betung   Batubrok   Sepasu
Semangga   Simanggang   Kuda   2240   Tg. Datu   Simunjan   Nahabuan   Telen   Klampo   Bontang   Santan
Lundu   Kucing   Putussibau   Longbob   Samarinda
Paloh   G. Bungo   Serian   1730   Murung   Bilayan   Balikpapan
Sambas   996   Balaikarangan   Nangamentebah   Longiram   Muarakaman   Equator
Singkawang   Niut ▲1701   D. Luar   1744   Tenggarong   Donggala
Bengkayang   D. Sentarum   1770   Pegunungan Muller   Muarajuloi   Palu
Ngabang   Balaisabut   Semitau   Makaham   Sangasangadalam
Mempawah   Sintang   Pontianak   Sekadau   Muarawewe   Tengah   Sungaitiram
BORNEO   Tayan   Nangamau   Menate   Purukcahu   D. Jempang   Samboja
BARAT   1758   Nangapinoh   Melatan   Tanahgrogot   SULAWESI
Padangtikar   Saran   Sungaipinang   Teweh   Sebakung
Kotabaru   Pegunungan Schwaner   Budungbudung
Maya   Sukadana   Rantaubanjang   Kualakurun   Buntok   Ampah   Mamuju
Kepulauan   Nangatayap   Pinoh   Tumbangsamba   Bawan   Pujon   Onang
Karimata   Padang   Arut   Riam   Kasongan   Kepulauan Balabalangan   Makale
Ketapang   Pembuang   Sampit   (Paternoster Is.)   Polewali
Kualapesaguan   Marau   Rantaupulut   Sampit   Tamianglayang   Majene
Kendawangan   Panopah   Mendawai   Palangkaraya   Kotabaru   Enrekang
Tg. Sambar   Sukaraja   Kotawaringin   Sampit   SELATAN   Pinrang
Tanjungpandan   Sukamara   Pangkalanbuun   Semuda   Barabai   Sebuku   Parepare
Manggar   510   Kumai   Pulangpisau   Kandangan   Pagatan
Gantung   Pulau   Kualapembuang   Kualakapuas   1892   Pulau Laut   Watansopeng
Belitung   Kualajelai   Pangkoh   Marabahan   Rantau   Tanjungbatu   Sumpangbinangae
Membalong   Teluk Sampit   Banjarmasin   Martapura   Peg. Meratus   Karambu   Barri
Tg. Puting   Banjarbaru   Kotabaru   Pangkajene
INDONESIA   Pelaihari   Satui   Maros
Greater   Sunda   Islands   Jorong   Kintap   Ujung Pandang
Tg. Selatan   Kepulauan   Sungguminasa   2871   Bantaeng
Kepulauan   Laut Ketil   Takalar   Jeneponto
Laut Ketil
JAVA   SEA   Kepulauan   FLORES   SEA
Masalembo   Masalima
Kepulauan   Bawean
Karimunjawa   Sangkapura

Indramayu   Tg. Bugel   Jepara   Muria   Rembang   Kepulauan
Subang   Jatibarang   Pekalongan   Kudus 1602   Krogan   Kangean   Pabean
Cirebon   Brebes   Tegal   Pemalong   Batang   Demak   Pati   Tuban   Madura   Sumenep
Pamanukan   Careme   Pekalongan   Kendal   Gundih   Cepu   Tg. Pangkah   Bangkalan   Sampang   Tambuku   Puteran
3078   Semarang   Purwodadi   Blora   Ngawi   Bojonegoro   Sapudi   Panaruban   Lesser   Sunda   Islands
Bandung   Ciamis   TENGAH   Salatiga   Gundih   Sragen   Jombang   Gresik   Selat Madura   Sepanjang
3428   Slamet   3339   Boyolali   Solo   Mojokerto   Surabaya   Kepulauan   Sangeang
Tasikmalaya   Purwokerto   Wonosobo   Magelang   3142   3265   Madiun   Kediri   Sidoarjo   Pasuruan   Singaraja   Agung   Rinjani   Tambora   ▲2821
Garut   Purwodadi   3676   Klaten   Yogyakarta   2563   Malang   Probolinggo   Panarukan   Bali   3142   ▲3726   Mojo   Sumbawa   Dompu   Ruba   Labuhanbajo
Nusa   Kambangan   Wates   Surakarta   Ponorogo   TIMUR   Blitar   Semeru   Bondowoso   Clungkung   Alas   Besar   Sape
Parigi   Cilacap   Karanganyar   Trenggalek   Tulungagung   Jember   Pasirian   Negara   Ampenan   Selong   Rinca
YOGYAKARTA   Pacitan   Blitar   Rambipuji   Tabanan   Mataram   Praya   Taliwang   Parado   Flores
WA   (J A V A)   Nusa Barung   Denpasar   Bali   Lombok   Sumbawa   Flores
NUSA TENGGARA BARAT

1 : 4 000 000

20   0   20   40   60 miles
20   0   20   40   60   80 km

Continuation Northwards
on same scale

Batanes Islands
BATANES
Itbayat
Bosco
Batan I.
Sabtang I.
Balintang Is.
Balintang Channel
Babuyan I.
Calayan I.
Calayan
Camiguin I.
Dalupiri I.
Babuyan Islands
Fuga I.
Babuyan Channel

PACIFIC OCEAN

Mindanao Trench

SOUTH CHINA SEA

LUZON

Babuyan I.
Calayan I.
Fuga I.
Calayan
Babuyan Islands
Camiguin I.
Dalupiri I.
Babuyan Channel

CAGAYAN
Namuac
Aparri
Pamplona
Ballesteros
Port San Vicente
Cape Engaño
Escarpada Pt.
San Ana
Labig Pt.
Pasuquin
Bacarra
Laoag
San Nicolas
Sarrat
ILOCOS NORTE
Batac
Dingras
Solsona
Buguey
Abulug
Lal-lo
Gonzaga
Alcala
Tuguegarao
Ilagan
ISABELA
Mt. Cresta
Palanan Pt.
Palanan Bay
Palanan
Cauayan
Roxas
Cabagan
San Mateo
Cordon
Cabarroguis
Cagayan
Cosiguran
Cape San Ildefonso

Vigan
Narvacan
Santa Maria
Candon
ILOCOS SUR
Tagudin
ABRA
Bangued
MOUNTAIN
Baguio
BENGUET
KALINGA
APAYAO
IFUGAO
NUEVA VIZCAYA
Bayombong
Solano
Bambang
QUIRINO
Baler
Dingalan Bay
AURORA
Dingalan

LA UNION
San Fernando
Agoo
PANGASINAN
Lingayen
Dagupan
San Carlos
Urdaneta
Rosales
TARLAC
Tarlac
Camiling
NUEVA ECIJA
Cabanatuan
Gapan
San Jose
Santa Rosa
Talavera
Guimba
Muñoz

ZAMBALES
Iba
San Felipe
San Antonio
Olongapo
Botolan
Cape Bolinao
Cabangan

Masinloc
BATAAN
Balanga
Morong
Dinalupihan
Bagac Bay
Mariveles

PAMPANGA
Angeles
San Fernando
Guagua
Arayat
BULACAN
Malolos
Baliuag
Caloocan
Quezon City
MANILA
Pasay
Pasig
RIZAL
Marikina
Antipolo

CAVITE
Cavite
Bacoor
Trece Martires
Tanza
Maragondon
LAGUNA
Calamba
Santa Cruz
Pagsanjan
San Pablo
BATANGAS
Batangas
Lipa
Tanauan
Balayan
Lemery
Calaca
Nasugbu

QUEZON
Tayabas
Lucena
Lucban
Mauban
Atimonan
Gumaca
Lopez
Calauag

Polillo
Polillo Islands
Polillo Strait
Burias Bay
Lamon Bay

CAMARINES NORTE
Daet
Mercedes
Jose Panganiban
Paracale
CAMARINES SUR
Naga
Iriga
Libmanan
Nabua
Goa
Sipocot
Calabanga
Pasacao
Pili
Ragay
Tigaon
Caramoan
CATANDUANES
Virac
Pandan
Panganiban
Gigmoto
Yog Pt.
Maqueda Channel

Lagonoy Gulf
Tabaco
Legazpi
ALBAY
Mt. Mayon
Ligao
Guinobatan
Polangui
Daraga
Tiwi
Sorsogon
SORSOGON
Bulan
Magallanes
Donsol
Gubat
Bulusan
Matnog
Irosin

MASBATE
Masbate
Mandaon
Aroroy
Cataingan
Placer
Dimasalang
Balud
Milagros

NORTHERN SAMAR
Laoang
Catarman
Bobon
Allen
Gamay
Catubig

Burias I.
Ticao I.
San Miguel

Ragay Gulf

MINDORO
Calapan
MINDORO ORIENTAL
Naujan
Pinamalayan
Pola
Bongabong
Roxas
Bansud
Mansalay
Bulalacao
MINDORO OCCIDENTAL
Mamburao
San Jose
Sablayan
Calintaan
Magsaysay
Abra de Ilog

Lubang
Lubang Islands

Calavite Pass
Verde I.
Verde I. Pass
Maricaban I.
Puerta Galera

Mindoro Strait
Apo West Pass
Apo East Pass
San José

MARINDUQUE
Boac
Santa Cruz
Gasan
Buenavista
Torrijos
Mogpog
Banton I.

ROMBLON
Romblon
Tablas I.
Sibuyan I.
Tablas Strait

SIBUYAN SEA

Sibuyan

Mompog Pass

PACIFIC OCEAN

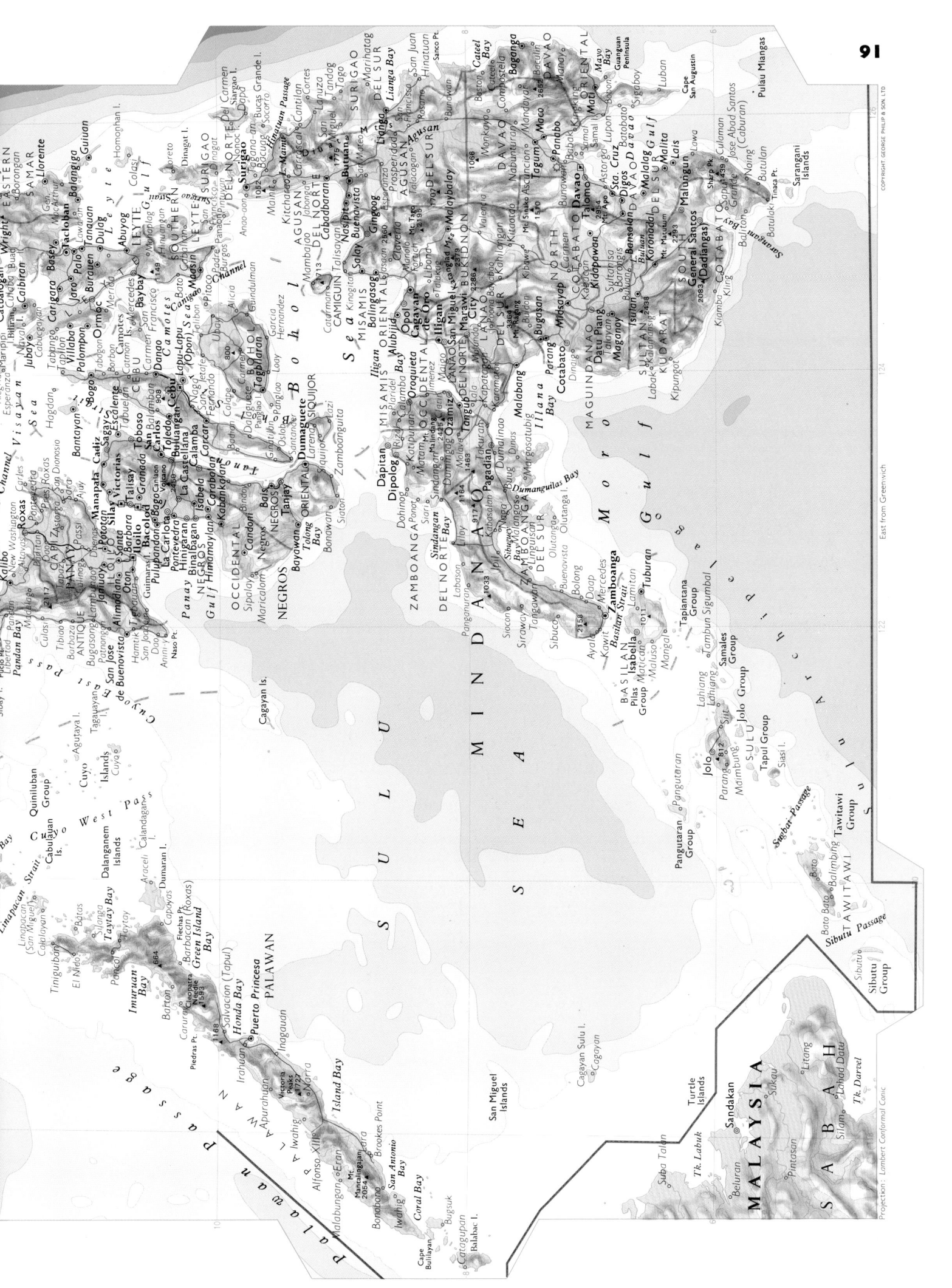

Palawan Passage
PALAWAN
Puerto Princesa
Honda Bay
Imuruan Bay
Green Island Bay
Island Bay
Coral Bay
Balabac I.
Cuyo Islands
Cuyo West Pass
Cuyo East Pass
Cagayan Is.
San Miguel Islands
Cagayan Sulu I.
S U L U   S E A
M I N D A N A O
Moro Gulf
Illana Bay
Sulu Archipelago
Bohol Sea
Visayan Sea
Leyte Gulf
Camotes Sea
Panay Gulf
PANAY
NEGROS
CEBU
BOHOL
LEYTE
SAMAR
SIQUIJOR
CAMIGUIN
BASILAN
SULU
TAWITAWI
Jolo
Zamboanga
Isabella
Dipolog
Dapitan
Pagadian
Ozamiz
Iligan
Cagayan de Oro
Marawi City
Malaybalay
Butuan
Surigao
Cotabato
Davao
General Santos (Dadiangas)
Iloilo
Bacolod
Cebu
Dumaguete
Tagbilaran
Tacloban
Ormoc
Roxas
Kalibo
MALAYSIA
S A B A H
Sandakan
Turtle Islands
Sibutu Group
Sibutu Passage
Projection: Lambert Conformal Conic
East from Greenwich
COPYRIGHT GEORGE PHILIP & SON, LTD

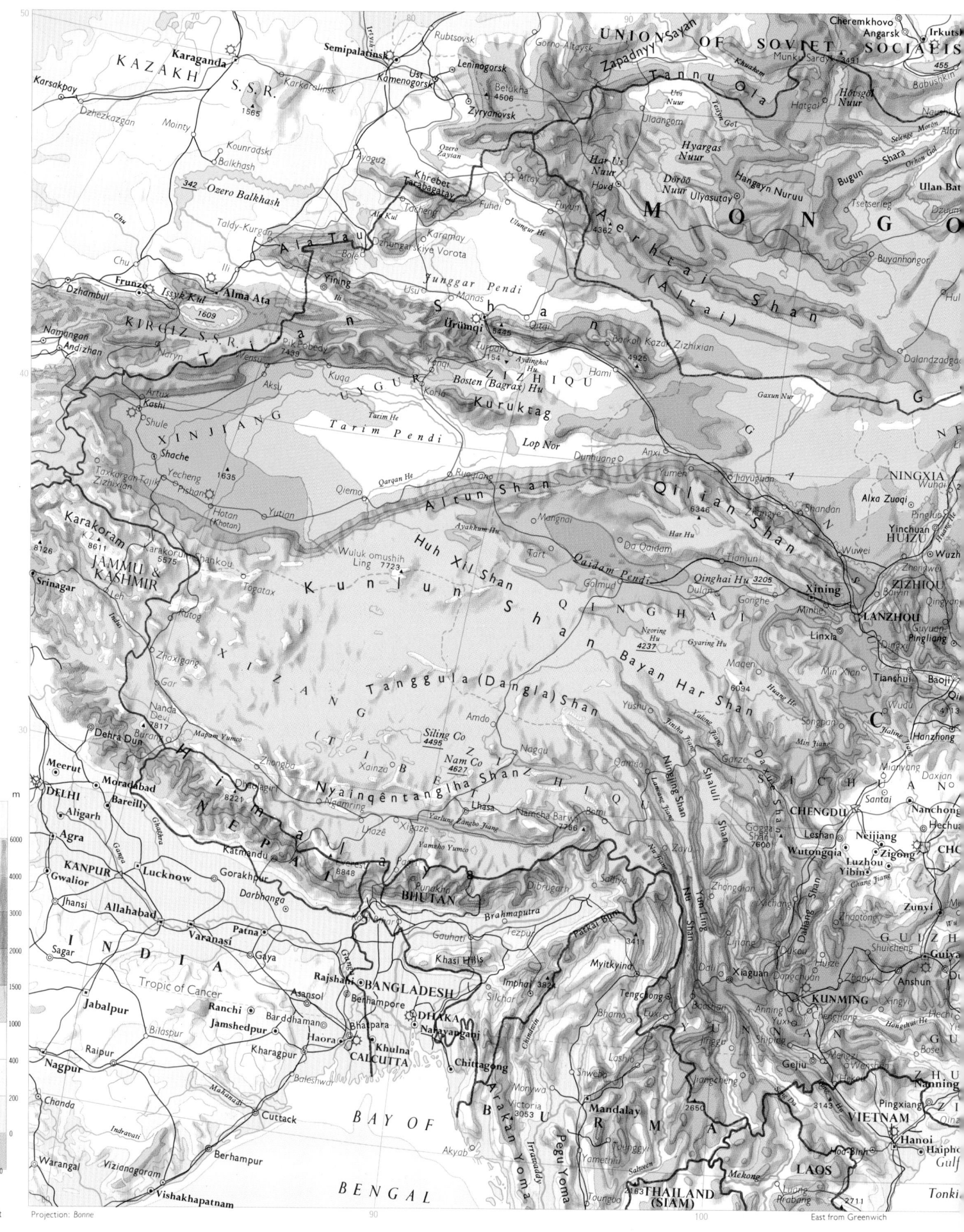

KAZAKH S.S.R.
UNION OF SOVIET SOCIALIST
MONGOLIA
KIRGIZ S.S.R.
XINJIANG UYGUR ZIZHIQU
XIZANG ZIZHIQU (TIBET)
QINGHAI
JAMMU & KASHMIR
NEPAL
BHUTAN
BANGLADESH
INDIA
BURMA
THAILAND (SIAM)
LAOS
VIETNAM
NINGXIA HUIZU
YUNNAN
Tian Shan
Kunlun Shan
Altun Shan
Qilian Shan
Himalaya
Tanggula (Dangla) Shan
Bayan Har Shan
Nyainqêntanglha Shan
Huh Xil Shan
Karakoram
Aerhtai Shan (Altai)
Tarim Pendi
Junggar Pendi
Qaidam Pendi
Lop Nor
Kuruktag
Tropic of Cancer
BAY OF BENGAL
Karaganda
Semipalatinsk
Ust Kamenogorsk
Alma Ata
Frunze
Ürümqi
Kashi
LANZHOU
CHENGDU
KUNMING
DELHI
KANPUR
CALCUTTA
DHAKA
Lhasa
Xining
Everest 8848
Projection: Bonne
East from Greenwich

1:15 000 000

100   0   100   200   300   400 miles
100   0   100   200   300   400   500   600 km

Sakhalin

REPUBLICS   Chita
an Ude
Baykal

Bukachacha
Yablonovy Khrebet
Sretensk
Nerchinsk
Oloyyannaya
Borzya
Manzhouli
Hailar
Hulun
Nur

Dutulun Shan

Choybalsan
Kerülen
Buir
Nur

Saynshand

Dzamin Üüd   Erenhot

ONGGOL

Hohhot
Datong
otou

WALL
Baoding
Yuoping

TAIYUAN
Fenyang
Yangquan

Changzhi
Tongchuan
Luoyang
Xinxiang

XI'AN   ZHENGZHOU
Pingdingshan   Luohe
Sanmenxia

Nanyang
Han Shui
Zhumadian

Xiangfan
Dabie Shan
Zhongxiang

Yichang

Shashi
WUHAN
Huangshi

Changde
Yiyang

Dongting
Hu
Yueyang

HUNAN
Xiangtan
Changsha
Pingxiang

Shaoyang
Hengyang

Nan Ling

Guilin
ou

Wuzhou
Zhaoqing

ZU
QU
Jiangmen
Maoming
Zhanjiang
Haixia

Haikou
Hainan Dao

Shimanovsk
Svobodny
Chegdomyn
Aleksandrovsk
Poronaysk
C. Terpeniya

Oroqen Zizhiqi
Blagoveshchensk
Bureya
Komsomolsk
L. Bolon
Dolinsk
Yuzhno-Sakhalinsk

Aihui
Troitskoye
Birobidzhan
Khabarovsk
Kholmsk
La Perouse Str.

Yilehuli
Shan
Nenjiang
Bei'an
Yichun
Obluchye
Amur
Bikin
Wakkanai

HEILONGJIANG
Butha Qi
Qiqihar
Jiamusi
Shuangyashan
Mishan
Ozero
Khanka
Asahigawa
2290
Hokkaido

Horqin Youyi
Qianqi
(Ulan Hot)
Baicheng
Anda
Suihua
HARBIN
Shuangcheng
Jixi
Ussuriysk
SAPPORO
Otaru
Kushiro

Solon
Arxan
Tao'an
Manchuria
Mudanjiang
Artem
Muroran
C. Erimo

JILIN
CHANGCHUN
Jilin
Dunhua
Vladivostok
Nakhodka
Hakodate

ZIZHIQU DA Hinggan Ling
1949
Linxi
Shuangliao
Liaoyuan
Songhua
Yanji
Hunchun
Tsugaru-kaikyō
Aomori
Hachinohe

Tongliao
Siping
Paektu
2744
Chongjin
Morioka

Fuxin
FUSHUN
SHENYANG
Yonghung
Akita
Sakata
Ishinomaki

Duolun
Chifeng
Chaoyang
Liaoyang
Benxi
NORTH
Sado
Niigata
Kōriyama

SEA OF

JAPAN

Jining
Zhangjiakou
Xuanhua
Chengde
Jinzhou
ANSHAN
Dandong
KOREA
Hungnam
Wajima
Sendai
Utsunomiya

Qinhuangdao
Yingkou
Liaodong
Wan
Yalu Jiang
Wŏnsan
Toyama
Kanazawa
TOKYO

BEIJING (Peking)
BEIJING SHI
Tangshan
Liaodong Bandao
Korea Bay
P'YŎNGYANG
Kaesong
SŎUL
NAGOYA
KYOTO
KOBE
YOKOHAMA
Kawasaki
Yokosuka

HEBEI
TIANJIN
TIANJIN SHI
Cangzhou
DALIAN
Inch'ŏn
SOUTH
Fuji 3776
OSAKA
Shizuoka
Hamamatsu

2894
Shijiazhuang
Bo Hai
Yantai
Weihai
Taejŏn
Sakai
Wakayama

Handan
Dezhou
Ye Xian
Weifang
TAEGU
PUSAN
Okayama
HiroshimaKure

JINAN
Tai'an
Zibo
YELLOW
Masan
1915
Shimonoseki
Kobe
Kōchi
Matsuyama

Jining
QINGDAO
SEA
Kwangju
KITAKYUSHU
FUKUOKA
SHIKOKU

Kaifeng
Zaozhuang
Lianyungang
Cheju Do
1950
Sasebo
Kumamoto

Shangqiu
Xuzhou
Qingjiang
Yancheng
Nagasaki
Kyushu

HENAN
Shangshui
Bengbu
Yangzhou
Taizhou
Changzhou
Kagoshima

Huainan
NANJING
Ma'anshan
Wuxi
Suzhou
SHANGHAI SHI

Hefei
Wuhu
Wuxing
SHANGHAI
Tanega-shima

ANHUI
Tongling
Jiaxing

Anqing
Hangzhou
Hangzhou Wan

Tunxi
Shaoxing
Ningbo

Jiujiang
Jingdezhen
Jinhua
Qu Xian
Linhai

Nanchang
ZHEJIANG

JIANGXI
Shangrao
Wenzhou

EAST CHINA
Amami-ō-Shima

SEA

Ji'an
WUYI Shan
2120
Nanping

RYŪKYŪ-rettō

PACIFIC

Ganzhou
Sanming

Ruijin
FUJIAN
Longyan
Fuzhou
Jilong

Naha
Okinawa

Shaoguan
Zhangzhou
Quanzhou
TAIBEI
Sakashima Gunto

Mei Xian
Xiamen
Taizhong

Tropic of Cancer

GUANGDONG
Chao'an
Jiayi
Yu Shan
3997

GUANGZHOU
Huizhou
Shantou
Tainan
TAIWAN

HONG KONG (Br.)
Macau (Port.)
Gaoxiong
Pingdong

OCEAN

Pratas
Batan Is.

SOUTH CHINA
Babuyan Is.

SEA

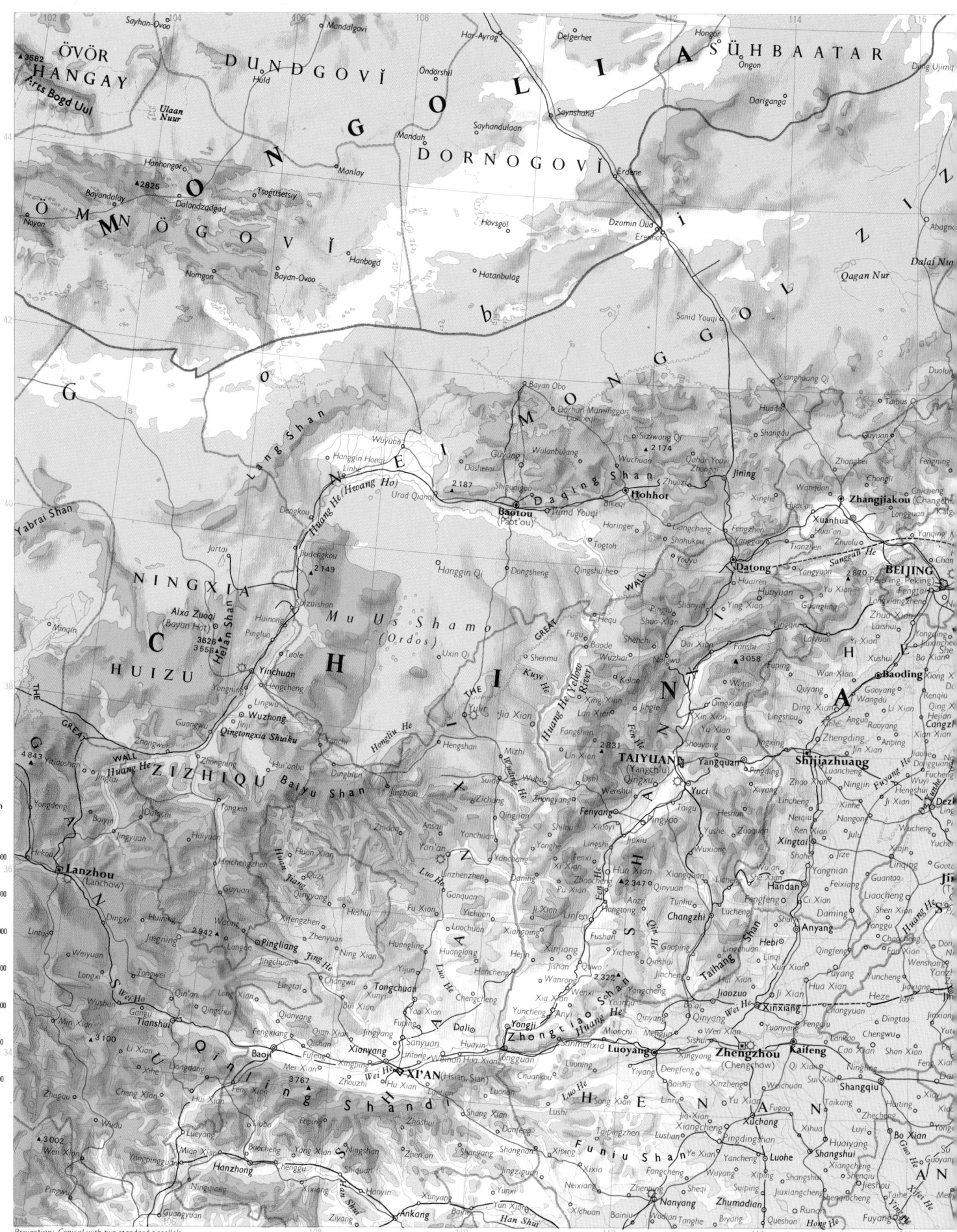

ft   m

12,000 4000

9000   3000

6000   2000

4500   1500

3000   1000

1200   400

600   200

0   0

200   600

2000   6000

m ft

Projection: Conical with two standard parallels

1:6 000 000

50   0   50   100   150 miles

50   0   50   100   150   200   km

HEILONGJIANG

HARBIN
(Haerhpin)

U.S.S.R.

Ozero Khanka

Vladivostok

JILIN

Changchun

Jilin

Zhangguangcai Ling
(Manchuria)

Mudanjiang

Ning'an

Ussuriysk
(Voroshilov)

Shuangliao

Siping

Liaoyuan

Changbai Shan

Yanji

Tumen

NEI

Changchun

Paektu-san

Chongjin

Kyŏngsŏng

Fushun

SHENYANG
(Mukden)

Benxi

Yalu
Jiang

NORTH
KOREA

Kimch'aek

Tanchŏn

Pukch'ŏng

Jinzhou

Anshan

Dandong

Sinŭiju

Kanggye

Changjin-
chosuji

Hamhung

Hŭngnam

Liaodong
Wan.

Liaodong
Bandao

Yalu Jiang

P'yŏngyang

Tongjosŏn
Man

SEA   OF
JAPAN

Tangshan

Lüshun

DALIAN
(Lüda)

Korea
Bay

Anju

Wŏnsan

TIANJIN (Tientsin)
(T'ienching)

Bo Hai
(Gulf of Chihli)

Chinnampo

Kaesŏng

Paengnyong-do

Cease Fire Line

SEOUL
(Seoul)

Inch'ŏn

Chunchŏn

Kangnŭng

Ullung-do

Huang He

Laizhou
Wan

Yantai

Weihai

Wŏnju

SOUTH
KOREA

SHANDONG

Zibo

Weifang

Shandong Bandao

Taejŏn

Andong

Pohang

QINGDAO
(Ch'ingtao)

Chŏnju

Taegu

Kyongju

Ulsan

HUANG   HAI
(Yellow Sea)

Kwangju

Chinju

Masan

Chinhae

PUSAN

Lianyungang
(Hsinhailien)

Mokpo

Cheju
Cheju-do

Tsushima

Korea
Strait

Tsushima-kaikyō

JAPAN
Sasebo

Nagasaki

JIANGSU

ft m
12,000 4000
9000 3000
6000 2000
4500 1500
3000 1000
1200 400
600 200
0 0
200 600
2000 6000
m ft
GANSU
SHAANXI
SICHUAN
GUIZHOU
YUNNAN
GUANGXI
KACHIN
BURMA
SHAN STATE
LAOS
VIETNAM
THAILAND
CHENGDU
(Ch'engtu; Tch'eng-tou)
CHONGQING
(Ch'ungch'ing; Tch'ong-k'ing)
Zigong
(Tzukong)
Guiyang
(Kueiyang)
Kunming
Nanning
Hanoi
Haiphong
Nanchong
Wanxian
Neijiang
Luzhou
Yibin
Zunyi
Anshun
Liuzhou
Luang Prabang
Nam Dinh
Gulf of Tonkin
Leizhou Bandao
Weizhou Dao
Fai Tsi Long Archipelago
Ningjing Shan
Shaluli Shan
Daxue Shan
Qionglai Shan
Daliang Shan
Dalou Shan
Daba Shan
Ailao Shan
Wuliang Shan
Yun Ling
Nu Shan
Gaoligong Shan
Lancang Jiang
Jinsha Jiang
Yalong Jiang
Min Jiang
Mekong
Salween
Hong (Red)
Da (Black)
Sip Song Chau Thai
Gongga Shan
7600
5500
6500
4038
3054
2683
3143
3570
3233
2320
4600
Projection: Conical with two standard parallels
102
104
106
108
20
22
24
26
28
30
32

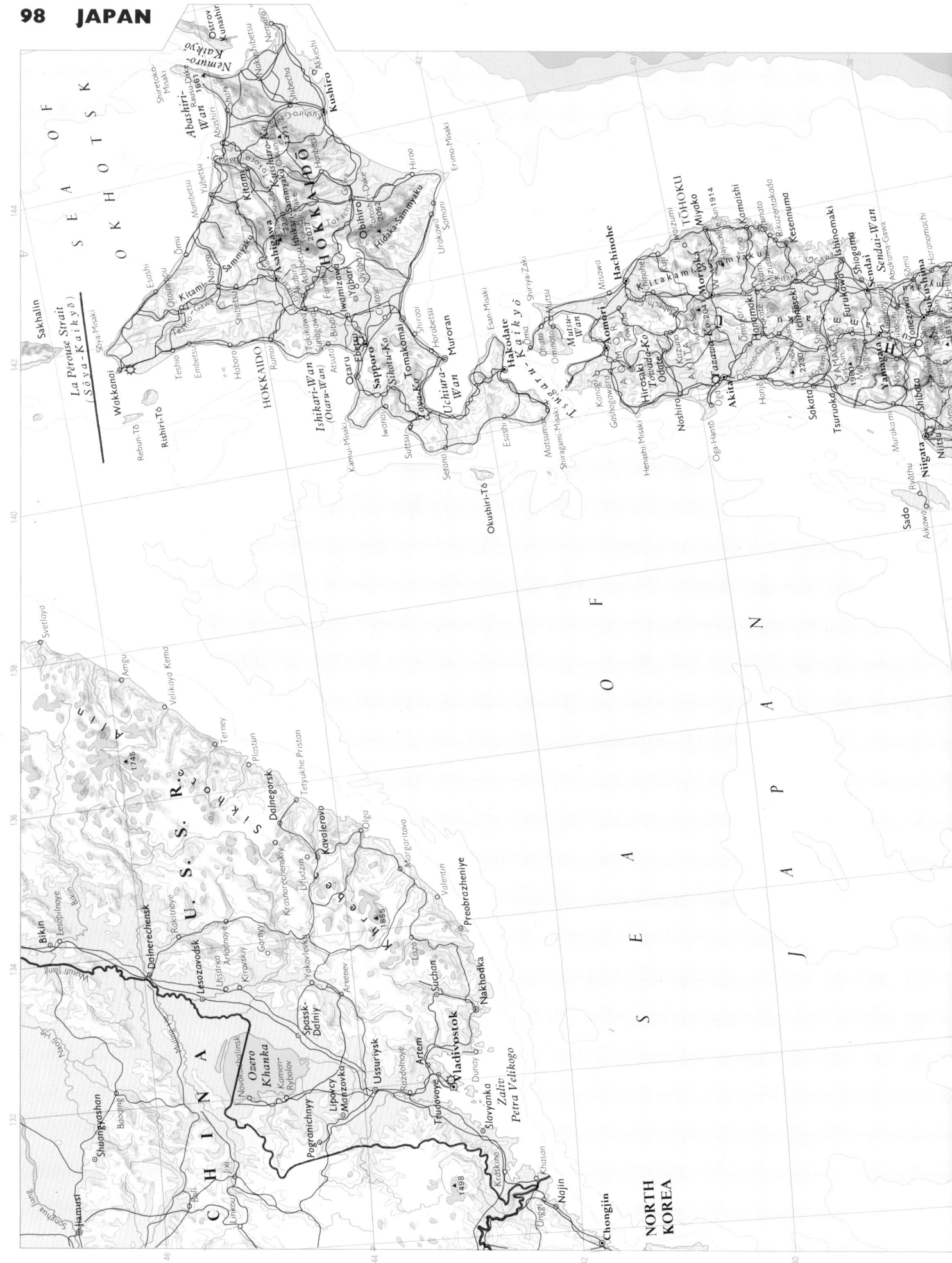
SEA OF OKHOTSK
SEA OF JAPAN
Sakhalin
La Pérouse Strait
(Sōya-Kaikyō)
Sōya-Misaki
Wakkanai
Rebun-Tō
Rishiri-Tō
Abashiri-Wan
Nemuro-Kaikyō
Ostrov Kunashir
Shiretoko-Misaki
Rausu-Dake 1661
Nemuro
Kushiro
Kitami
Asahikawa
HOKKAIDŌ
HOKKAIDO
Rumoi
Sapporo
Otaru
Ishikari-Wan
(Otaru-Wan)
Sikotu-Ko
Tōya-Ko
Tomakomai
Muroran
Uchiura-Wan
Hakodate
Esan-Misaki
Tsugaru-Kaikyō
Obihiro
Hidaka-Sammyaku
Hiroo
Erimo-Misaki
Okushiri-Tō
Mutsu-Wan
Aomori
Hachinohe
Hirosaki
Towada-Ko
Odate
Noshiro
Akita
Tazawa-Ko
TŌHOKU
Morioka
Miyako
Kamaishi
Kesennuma
Ichinoseki
Ishinomaki
Sendai
Sendai-Wan
Shiogama
Sakata
Tsuruoka
Yamagata
Yonezawa
Fukushima
Shibata
Niigata
Sado
U. S. S. R.
CHINA
NORTH KOREA
Vladivostok
Nakhodka
Ussuriysk
Artem
Ozero Khanka
Zaliv Petra Velikogo
Spassk-Dalniy
Lesozavodsk
Dalnerechensk
Bikin
Dalnegorsk
Kavalerovo
Preobrazheniye
Arsenev
Suchan
Pogranichnyy
Lipovcy
Manzovka
Slavyanka
Shuangyashan
Jiamusi
Chongjin
Najin
Svetlaya
Terney
Olga

1:5 000 000

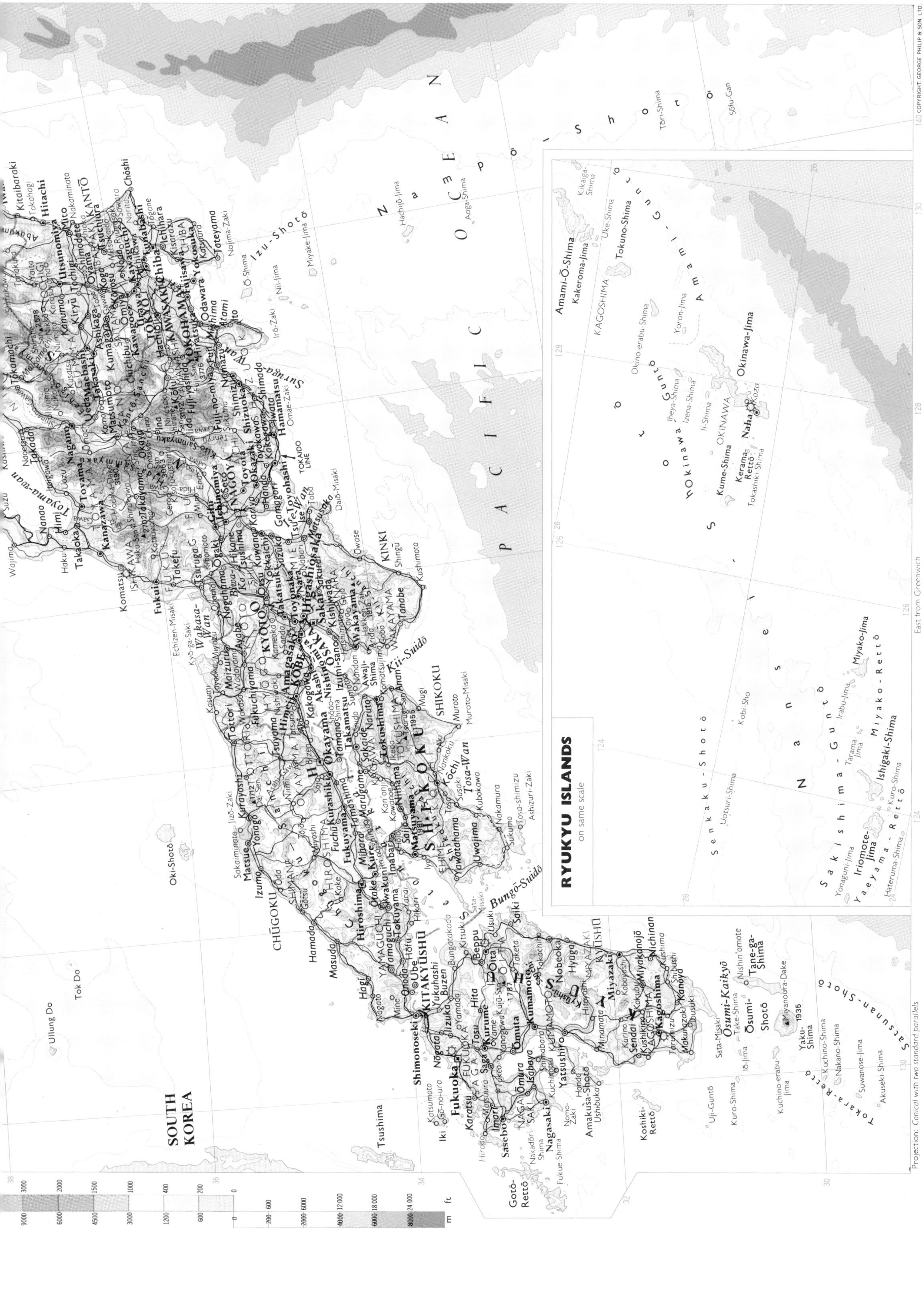

50   0   50   100 miles

50   0   50   100   150   km

RYUKYU ISLANDS
on same scale

SOUTH
KOREA

PACIFIC OCEAN

Izu-Shotō

KANTŌ

TŌKYŌ
YOKOHAMA
KAWASAKI
CHIBA

NAGOYA
KYOTO
ŌSAKA
KOBE

KINKI

CHŪGOKU

SHIKOKU

KYŪSHŪ

Fukuoka
KITAKYŪSHŪ
Shimonoseki
Nagasaki
Sasebo
Kumamoto
KAGOSHIMA
Miyazaki
Ōita
Beppu

Hiroshima
YAMAGUCHI

Matsue
Tottori
Izumo

Kanazawa
Fukui
Toyama
Takaoka

Tsushima

Ullung Do
Tok Do

Gotō-Rettō

Koshiki-Rettō

Tokara-Rettō

Ōsumi-Shotō
Ōsumi-Kaikyō
Yaku-Shima
Tane-ga-Shima

Satsunan-Shotō

Amami-Ō-Shima
Kakeroma-Jima
KAGOSHIMA
Tokuno-Shima
Okino-erabu-Shima

Okinawa-Guntō
OKINAWA
Okinawa-Jima
Naha
Kume-Shima
Kerama-Rettō

Senkaku-Shotō

Sakishima-Guntō
Miyako-Rettō
Miyako-Jima
Ishigaki-Shima
Iriomote-Jima
Yaeyama-Rettō
Yonaguni-Jima

Nansei-Shotō

East from Greenwich

Projection: Conical with two standard parallels

COPYRIGHT GEORGE PHILIP & SON, LTD.

ft
9000
6000
4500
3000
1500
1200
600
0

m
24 000
18 000
12 000
6000
2000
1000
400
200
0
200
600

SEA OF JAPAN

SOUTH KOREA

H O N S

CHŪGOKU-DISTRICT

Oki-Shotō
Dōgo ▲608
Saigō
Daimanji-San

Shimane-Hantō
Jizō-Zaki
Iwami
Kasumi
Toyooka
Matsue
Yonago
Kurayoshi
Tottori
Hidaka
Hirata
Shinji
Sakaiminato
Dai-Sen ▲
Yasugi
Wakasa
Wadayama
Hi-no-Misaki
Taisha
Shinji-Ko
Izumo
Daito
TOTTORI
Katsuyama
Yamazaki
HYŌG
Nishiw
Ōda
Niimi
Tsuyama
Yunotsu
Sanbe-San
Gotsu
Ochiai
Tojo
Shobara
Takahashi
Okayama
Bizen
Aioi
Himeji
Or
Hamada
SHIMANE
Miyoshi
Saidaiji
Kakogawa
Mi-Shima
Kake
Fuchū
Ibara
Sōja
Takasago
Akō
Masuda
Chūgo
Ōta-Gawa
HIROSHIMA
Kannabe
Kurashiki
Shōdo-Shima
Harima-Nada
Aka
Aono-Yama ▲
HIROSHIMA
Itsukaichi
Saijo
Kasaoka
Tamano
Tonoshō
Awaji-Shima
Sumoto
Nagato
YAMAGUCHI
Ōmi-Shima
Hagi
Kanmuri-Yama ▲ 339
Takehara
Mihara
Onomichi
Tomo
In'no-shima
Marugame
Sakaide
Takamatsu
Hibiki-Nada
Tsuno-Shima
Toyoura
Kure
Kaita
Iyo-shima
Kan'onji
Naruto
Narumi-Kaik-yo
Mine
Ogōri
Hōfu
Nan'yō
Ōtake
Ōsaki
Zentsūji
Kotohira
KAGAWA
Hiketa
Tokushin
Shimonoseki
San'yō
Onoda
Iwakuni
Tokuyama
Yanai
Kurahashi-Jima
Aki-Nada
Imabari
Saijo
Niihama
Sannuki-Sammyaku
Anabuki
Komatsujima
KITAKYŪSHŪ
Ube
Kudamatsu
Hikari
Suō-Nada
Naga-Shima
Iwai-Jima
Ōshima
Yashiro-Jima
Hōjō
Hiuchi-Nada
Iyo-mishima
TOKUSHIMA
Anan
Nakama
Nōgata
Yukuhashi
Hime-Jima
Heigun-To
Matsuyama
Matsusaki
Iyo
Mishima-Yama ▲
Shikoku-Sanchi
KŌCHI
Gami
FUKUOKA
Iizuka
Takawa
Buzen
Kunisaki
Iyo-Nada
Nagahama
SHIKOKU
Yobuko
Miyota
Yamada
Nakatsu
Putago-yama ▲ 721
Ozu
Saijo
Kochi
Tosa-yamada
Muro
Karatsu
Umi
Usa
Bungotakada
Sada-Misaki-Hantō
Yawatahama
Sagawa
Tosa
Nankoku
Aki
FUKUO
Tsuki
Amagi
Hiji
Kitsuki
Kusu
Uchiko
Tosa
SAGA
Tsukushi-Sanchi
Tosu
Hira
Yufu-Dake ▲ 584
Beppu-Wan
Uwajima
Hiromi
Kubokawa
Tosa-Wan
Sasebo
Takeo
Taku
Saga
Yame
Kurogi
Kuju
Beppu
Tsurusaki
SHIKOKU
Imari
Kurume
Setaka
ŌITA
Ōita
SHIKOKU-DISTRICT
Kashima
Okawa
Yanagawa
Chikugo
Oguni
Kuju-San ▲ 1787
Usuki
Ōshima
Sobo-Yama
Ekawasaki
Sukumo
Tara
Omura-Wan ▲983
Ōmuta
Yamaga
Aso
Taketa
Tsukumi
Saga
Nakamura
Tara-Dake
Arao
Kikuchi
Tsurumi-Saki
NAGASAKI
Tamana
Ōzu
Chiyomiya ▲
Sobo-Yama ▲1758
Saiki
Kamae
Tosa-shimizu
Isahaya
Kumamoto
Mashiki
Takachiho
Oki-no-Shima
Ashizuri-Zaki
Omura
KUMAMOTO
Uto
Kunimi-Dake ▲
Nagasaki
Unzen-Dake ▲
Shimabara
Oyama
Misumi
Hirokase
Nobeoka
Nomo-Zaki
Obama
Kuchinotsu
Amakusa-
Hondo
Kami-
Jima
Yatsushiro
Itsuki
Shiba
Hyūga
Amakusa-
Shoto-
Jima
Yunome
Kyūshū-Sanchi
Hososhima
Nada
Ushibuka
Yatsushiro-Kai
MIYAZAKI
Naga-Shima
Minamata
Hitoyoshi
KYŪSHŪ
Kami-koshiki-Jima
Akune
Izumi
Ebino
Saito
Takanabe
KYŪSHŪ-DISTRICT
Ōkuchi
Yoshimatsu
Kobayashi
Koshiki-
Rettō
Sendai
Kirishima-Yama ▲1700
Miyazaki
Shimo-koshiki-Jima
Kushikino
Ijuin
Kajiki
Kokubu
Miyakonojō
Nichinan
KAGOSHIMA
On-Take ▲1118
Kagoshima
Shibushi
Aburatsu
Taniyama
KAGOSHIMA
Tarumizu
Kanoya
Kushima
Fukiage
Kaseda
Chiran
Satsuma-Hantō
Kagoshima-Wan
Shibushi-Wan
Noma-Saki
Makurazaki
Ibusuki
Kōyama
Ōsumi-Hantō
Bō-no-Misaki
Kaimon-Dake ▲924
Yamagawa

Projection:
Lambert's Conformal
Conic

Sata-Misaki

1 : 2 500 000

10 0 10 20 30 40 50 miles
10 0 20 40 60 80 km

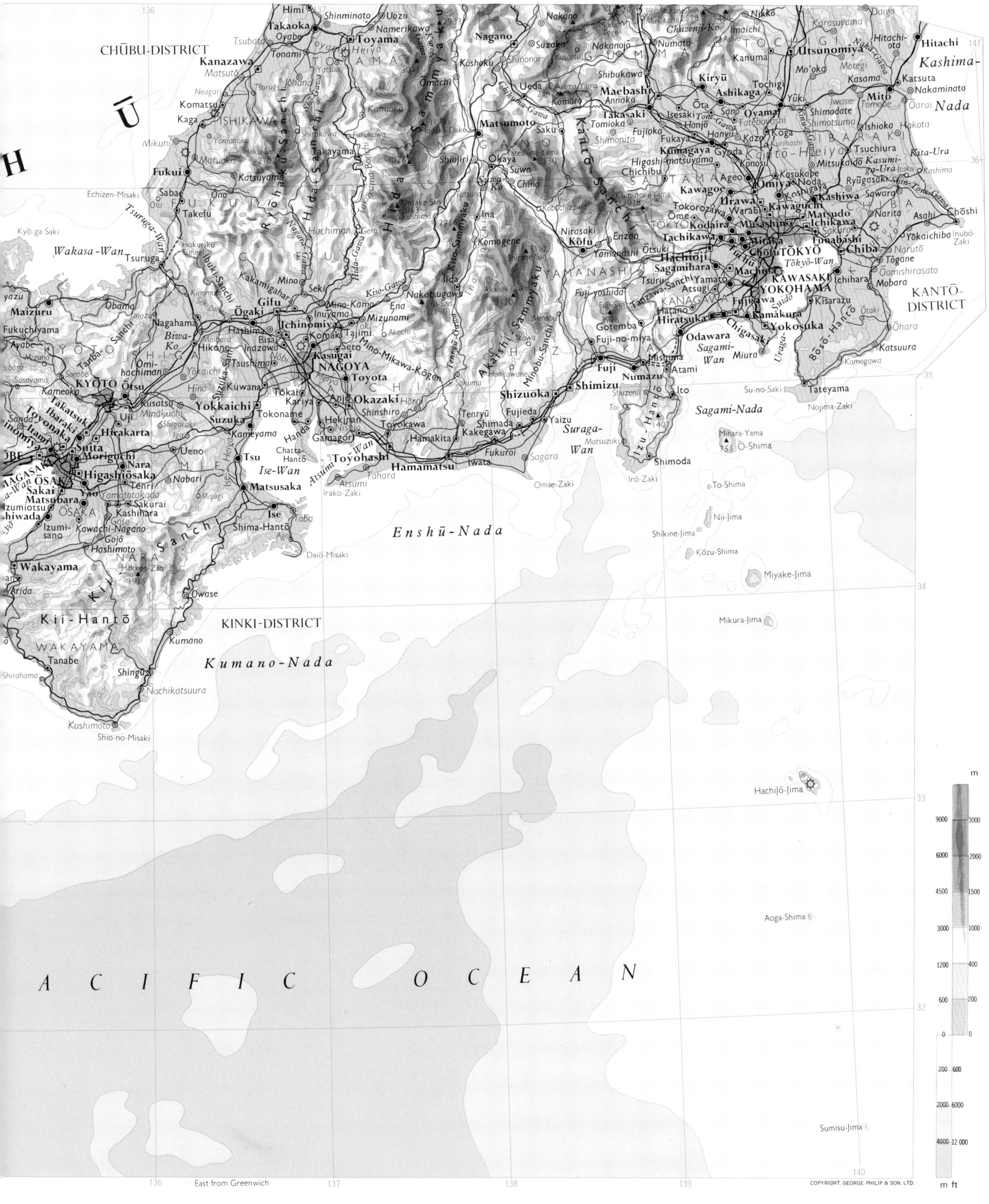

101

CHŪBU-DISTRICT

KANTŌ-DISTRICT

KINKI-DISTRICT

Kashima-Nada

Enshū-Nada

Kumano-Nada

Sagami-Nada

Wakasa-Wan

Biwa-Ko

Ise-Wan

Suruga-Wan

Tōkyō-Wan

Kii-Hantō

Shima-Hantō

Bōsō-Hantō

Izu-Hantō

PACIFIC OCEAN

East from Greenwich

COPYRIGHT. GEORGE PHILIP & SON. LTD.

Kanazawa, Toyama, Takaoka, Himi, Nagano, Matsumoto, Maebashi, Takasaki, Ashikaga, Kiryū, Utsunomiya, Nikko, Hitachi, Mito, Fukui, Gifu, Ōgaki, Ichinomiya, NAGOYA, Toyota, Okazaki, Toyohashi, Hamamatsu, Shizuoka, Shimizu, Fuji, Numazu, Odawara, Hiratsuka, Hachiōji, TOKYO, KAWASAKI, YOKOHAMA, Kamakura, Yokosuka, Chiba, Funabashi, Ichikawa, Matsudo, Urawa, Ōmiya, Kawagoe, Kasukabe, KYŌTO, Ōtsu, Yokkaichi, Suzuka, Tsu, Matsusaka, Ise, Nara, Higashiosaka, OSAKA, Sakai, Wakayama, Kōfu, Chōshi

Himi, Shinminato, Uozu, Namerikawa, Nakano, Nakanojō, Numata, Daigo, Karasuyama, Hitachi-ōta, Nakaminato, Ōarai, Tsuruga, Obama, Maizuru, Fukuchiyama, Kumano, Tanabe, Shingū, Nachikatsuura, Kushimoto, Shio-no-Misaki

Ō-Shima, To-Shima, Nii-Jima, Kōzu-Shima, Miyake-Jima, Mikura-Jima, Hachijō-Jima, Aoga-Shima, Sumisu-Jima

m ft
9000 / 3000
6000 / 2000
4500 / 1500
3000 / 1000
1200 / 400
600 / 200
0
200 / 600
2000 / 6000
4000 / 12 000

1:45 000 000

200   0   200   400   600   800   1000 miles
250   0   500   1000   1500 km

U.S.S.R.
Irkutsk
Ozero Baykal
Chita
Ulan Ude
Da Hinggan Ling
Blagoveshchensk
Khabarovsk
Sakhalin
SEA OF OKHOTSK
Kuril Islands
MONGOLIA
Ulan Bator (Ulaanbaatar)
Qiqihar
Harbin
Changchun
Jilin
Shenyang
Fushun
Anshan
Chongjin
P'yongyang
Vladivostok
Hokkaido
La Pérouse Str.
Sapporo
Hami
Alxa Zuoqi
Hohhot
Baotou
NEI MONGGOL
BEIJING (Peking)
TIANJIN
Dalian
Inch'on
SŎUL (Seoul)
KOREA
S. KOREA
Niigata
Sendai
HONSHU
Qilian Shan 6346
Taiyuan
Shijiazhuang
Qingdao
Pusan
Taegu
Nagoya
TOKYO
Kyoto
Yokohama
Lanzhou
Jinan
YELLOW SEA
Kitakyushu
Osaka
Kobe
Fukuoka
Hiroshima
Shikoku
Xi'an
Zhengzhou
Kaifeng
Xuzhou
Kyushu
Qin Ling
Huang
CHINA
Nanjing
Suzhou
Shanghai
SEA OF JAPAN
Chengdu 7590
Daliang Shan
Chongqing
Wuhan
Hangzhou
Nanchang
EAST CHINA SEA
INDIA
Guiyang
Hengyang
Changsha
Fuzhou
Ryūkyū-retto
Kunming
Wuyi Shan
Bonin Is.
Nu
Myitkyina
Nanning
Guangzhou
Xiamen
Taipei
TAIWAN
Volcano Is.
BURMA
Mandalay
Hanoi
Macau (Port.)
Hong Kong (Br.)
Tainan
Kaohsiung
Chiengmai
LAOS
Da Nang
Hainan
Bashi Channel
Wake I.
Irrawaddy
RANGOON
Vientiane
C. Engano
THAILAND (SIAM)
VIETNAM
2928
Luzon
Northern Marianas
Bassein
Moulmein
BANGKOK
CAMBODIA
Guam (U.S.)
TRUST TERRITORY OF
Bikini Atoll
Mergui
Phnom Penh
MANILA
PHILIPPINES
THE PACIFIC ISLANDS
Marshall Is.
Phanh Bho
Ho Chi Minh
Mindoro
Iloilo
Samar
Cebu
Yap
(U.S.)
Gulf of Thailand
George Town
Kota Baharu
SOUTH CHINA SEA
Palawan
Sulu Sea
Zamboanga
Mindanao
Davao
Belau
Truk
Caroline Islands
Pohnpei
KIRIBATI (Gilbert Is.)
Equator
PENINSULAR MALAYSIA
Kuala Lumpur
Kep. Natuna
Kota Kinabalu 4101
BRUNEI
Bandar Seri Begawan
SABAH
Celebes Sea
Halmahera
Medan
Melaka
MALAYSIA
SARAWAK
Kuching
Selat Dampier
NAURU
Singapore
Pontianak
Borneo Kalimantan
Maluku
Seram
Admiralty Is.
Bismarck Arch.
New Ireland
Sumatra
3800
Palembang
Sulawesi
Buru
Irian Jaya 5029
Bougainville
SOLOMON IS.
Sunda
INDONESIA
Banjarmasin
Selat Makasar
Banda Sea
Kep. Aru
PAPUA
New Guinea
Madang
New Britain
Java Sea
Semarang
Ujung Pandang
Flores Sea
NEW GUINEA
JAKARTA
Bandung
Surabaya
Surakarta
Malang
Bali
Flores
Santa Cruz I.
Java
Sumbawa
Timor
Arafura Sea
Torres Strait
Port Moresby
VANUATU
FIJI
Sumba
Louisiade Arch.
Suva
Cocos (Keeling) Is. (Aust.)
Timor Sea
Darwin
C. Arnhem
Cape York Pen.
Coral Sea
INDIAN
Arnhem Land
Gulf of Carpentaria
Great Barrier Reef
Wyndham
Larrimah
Cairns
Chesterfield Is.
New Caledonia (Fr.)
OCEAN
P. Hedland
Great Sandy Desert
NORTHERN TERRITORY
QUEENSLAND
Townsville
Noumea
Karratha
N.W. Cape
WESTERN
Mt. Isa
Mackay
Tropic of Capricorn
Shark Bay
AUSTRALIA
Macdonnell Ra.
Alice Springs
Rockhampton
Maryborough
Norfolk I. (Aust.)
AUSTRALIA
AUSTRALIA
Oodnadatta
Great Dividing Range
Brisbane
Geraldton
SOUTH AUSTRALIA
L. Eyre
Kalgoorlie-Boulder
Nullarbor Plain
Tarcoola
Flinders Ra.
NEW SOUTH WALES
Lord Howe I. (Aust.)
Perth
Darling Ra.
Bourke
New England Ra.
Fremantle
P. Pirie
Broken Hill
Newcastle
Albany
Great Australian Bight
Adelaide
Murray
Sydney
Wollongong
Tasman Sea
NORTH ISLAND
Encounter Bay
VICTORIA
Ballarat
CANBERRA
Auckland
Geelong
Australian Alps
Melbourne
Hamilton
Bass Strait
Palmerston N.
Wellington
NEW ZEALAND
SOUTHERN OCEAN
TASMANIA
Launceston
Hobart
Nelson
SOUTH ISLAND
Cook Str.
Christchurch
Invercargill
Southern Alps
Oamaru
Dunedin

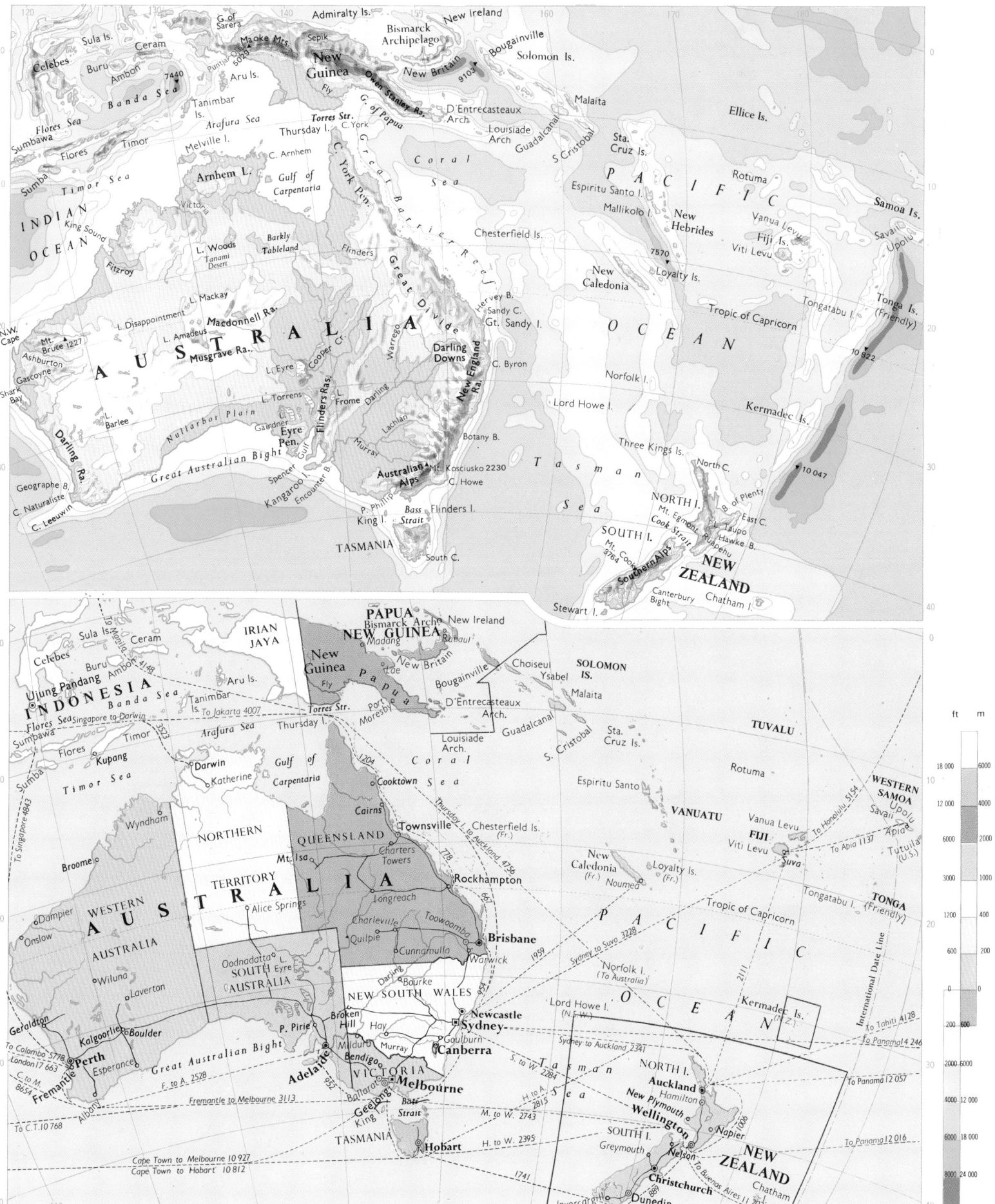

1:40 000 000

200   0   200   400   600   800 miles
200   0   200   400   600   800 1000 1200 km

Projection: Bonne

East from Greenwich   West from Greenwich   COPYRIGHT. GEORGE PHILIP & SON. LTD.

ft	m
18 000	6000
12 000	4000
6000	2000
3000	1000
1200	400
600	200
0	0
200	600
2000	6000
4000	12 000
6000	18 000
8000	24 000
m	ft

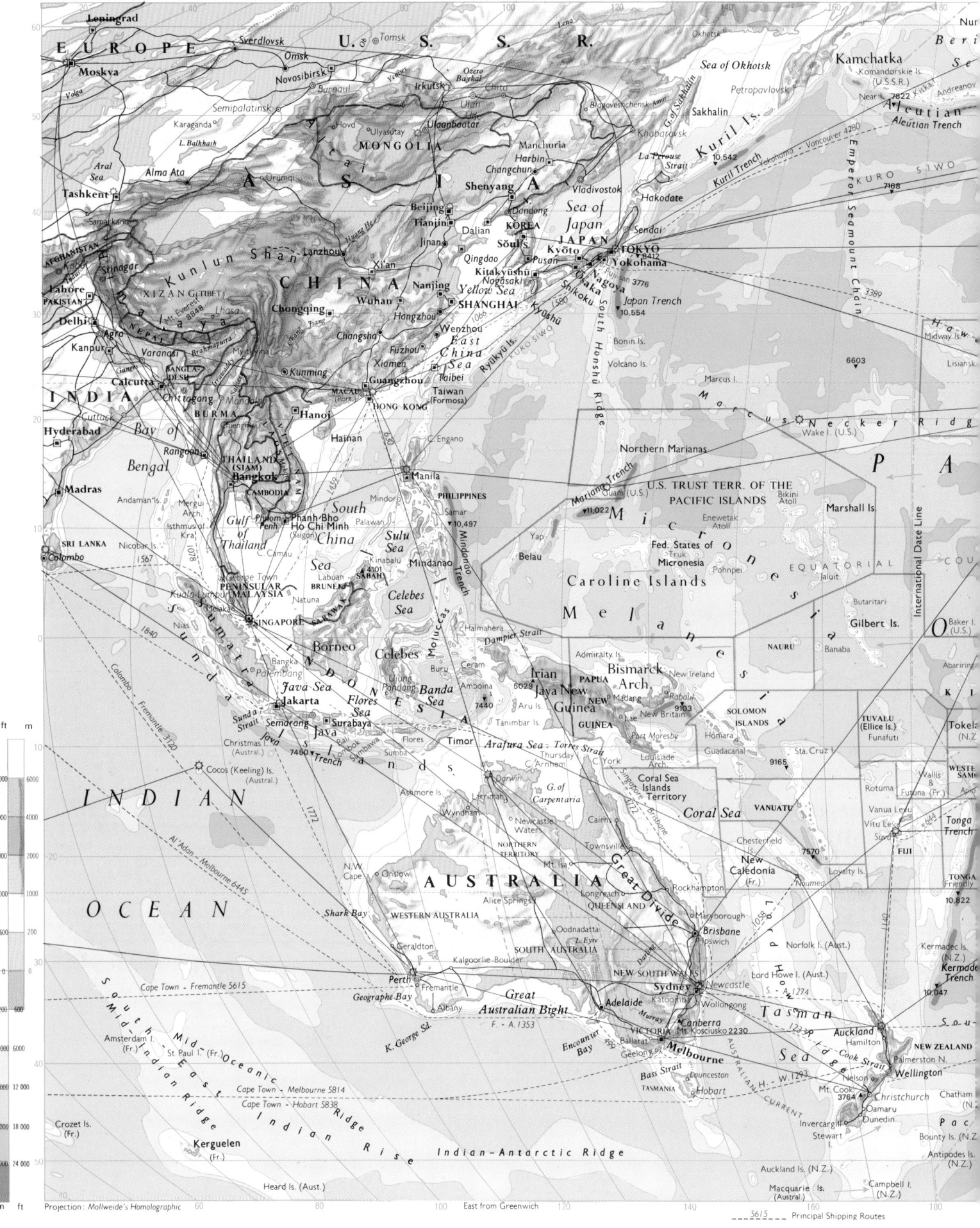

EUROPE
U. S. S. R.
ASIA
Leningrad
Moskva
Sverdlovsk
Omsk
Novosibirsk
Tomsk
Irkutsk
Ozero Baykal
Barnaul
Semipalatinsk
Karaganda
L. Balkhash
Aral Sea
Alma Ata
Tashkent
Urumqi
Ulaanbaatar
MONGOLIA
Hovd
Ulyasutay
Chita
Ulan Ude
Manchuria
Harbin
Changchun
Shenyang
Vladivostok
Blagoveshchensk
Khabarovsk
Sea of Okhotsk
Okhotsk
Sakhalin
Kuril Is.
Kamchatka
Petropavlovsk
Komandorskie Is. (U.S.S.R.)
Aleutian Trench
La Perouse Strait
Kuril Trench
Hakodate
Sea of Japan
JAPAN
TOKYO
Yokohama
Kyōto
Ōsaka
Nagoya
Sendai
Japan Trench
Emperor Seamount Chain
KURO SIWO
Beijing
Tianjin
Dalian
KOREA
Sŏul
Pusan
Jinan
Qingdao
Kitakyūshū
Nagasaki
Yellow Sea
SHANGHAI
Nanjing
Lanzhou
Xi'an
Kunlun Shan
CHINA
XIZANG (TIBET)
Lhasa
Mt. Everest 8848
Himalaya
NEPAL
Chongqing
Wuhan
Hangzhou
Wenzhou
Changsha
Fuzhou
Xiamen
East China Sea
Taibei
Taiwan (Formosa)
Guangzhou
MACAU (Port.)
HONG KONG
Kunming
Hanoi
Hainan
Ryūkyū Is.
Kyūshū
Shikoku
Bonin Is.
Volcano Is.
Marcus I.
South Honshū Ridge
Marcus Necker Ridge
Wake I. (U.S.)
Midway Is.
Lisiansk
AFGHANISTAN
Samarkand
Srinagar
Lahore
PAKISTAN
Delhi
Agra
Kanpur
Varanasi
BANGLADESH
Calcutta
Chittagong
INDIA
Hyderabad
Madras
Cuttack
Bay of Bengal
BURMA
Rangoon
Mandalay
THAILAND (SIAM)
Bangkok
CAMBODIA
VIETNAM
Phnom Penh
Ho Chi Minh (Saigon)
Gulf of Thailand
Andaman Is.
Mergui Arch.
Isthmus of Kra
Nicobar Is.
SRI LANKA
Colombo
South China Sea
Mindoro
Manila
PHILIPPINES
Samar
Palawan
Sulu Sea
Mindanao
Mindanao Trench
C. Engano
George Town
PENINSULAR MALAYSIA
Kuala Lumpur
Melaka
SINGAPORE
SABAH
BRUNEI
SARAWAK
Labuan
Kinabalu 4101
Natuna
Celebes Sea
Borneo
Celebes
INDONESIA
Sumatra
Nias
Bangka
Palembang
Java Sea
Jakarta
Semarang
Surabaya
Java
Bali
Lombok
Sumbawa
Flores Sea
Flores
Sumba
Timor
Banda Sea
Ujung Pandang
Buru
Ceram
Amboina
Moluccas
Halmahera
Dampier Strait
Irian Jaya
PAPUA NEW GUINEA
New Guinea
Aru Is.
Tanimbar Is.
Arafura Sea
Torres Strait
Java Trench
Sunda Strait
Christmas I. (Austral.)
Cocos (Keeling) Is. (Austral.)
Northern Marianas
Mariana Trench
Guam (U.S.)
U.S. TRUST TERR. OF THE PACIFIC ISLANDS
Micronesia
Bikini Atoll
Enewetak Atoll
Marshall Is.
Yap
Belau
Fed. States of Micronesia
Truk
Pohnpei
Jaluit
Caroline Islands
EQUATORIAL
Melanesia
Butaritari
Gilbert Is.
NAURU
Banaba
Baker I. (U.S.)
Admiralty Is.
Bismarck Arch.
New Ireland
Madang
Rabaul
New Britain
Lae
Port Moresby
SOLOMON ISLANDS
Honiara
Guadacanal
Sta. Cruz I.
TUVALU (Ellice Is.)
Funafuti
Tokelau
International Date Line
Coral Sea Islands Territory
Coral Sea
VANUATU
Louisiade Arch.
Thursday I.
C. Arnhem
C. York
G. of Carpentaria
Darwin
Wyndham
Ashmore Is.
Newcastle Waters
NORTHERN TERRITORY
Mt. Isa
Cairns
Townsville
Great Divide
AUSTRALIA
Alice Springs
Longreach
QUEENSLAND
Rockhampton
Maryborough
Brisbane
Ipswich
WESTERN AUSTRALIA
N.W. Cape
Onslow
Shark Bay
Geraldton
Kalgoorlie-Boulder
Oodnadatta
L. Eyre
SOUTH AUSTRALIA
NEW SOUTH WALES
Perth
Fremantle
Albany
Geographe Bay
Great Australian Bight
K. George Sd.
Adelaide
Murray
Darling
Sydney
Newcastle
Wollongong
Katoomba
Canberra
Mt. Kosciusko 2230
VICTORIA
Ballarat
Geelong
Melbourne
Encounter Bay
Bass Strait
TASMANIA
Launceston
Hobart
AUSTRALIAN CURRENT
New Caledonia (Fr.)
Chesterfield Is.
Noumea
Loyalty Is.
Norfolk I. (Aust.)
Lord Howe I. (Aust.)
Lord Howe Ridge
Tasman Sea
Rotuma
Wallis & Futuna (Fr.)
WESTERN SAMOA
Vanua Levu
Viti Levu
Suva
FIJI
Tonga Trench
TONGA
Kermadec Is. (N.Z.)
Kermadec Trench
Auckland
Hamilton
NEW ZEALAND
Palmerston N.
Cook Strait
Wellington
Nelson
Mt. Cook 3764
Christchurch
Oamaru
Dunedin
Invercargill
Stewart I.
Chatham Is. (N.Z.)
Bounty Is. (N.Z.)
Antipodes Is. (N.Z.)
Auckland Is. (N.Z.)
Macquarie Is. (Austral.)
Campbell I. (N.Z.)
INDIAN OCEAN
Amsterdam I. (Fr.)
St. Paul I. (Fr.)
Mid-Indian Ridge
South-East Mid-Oceanic Ridge
Indian Rise
Indian-Antarctic Ridge
Crozet Is. (Fr.)
Kerguelen (Fr.)
Heard Is. (Aust.)
Colombo - Fremantle 3120
Al 'Adan - Melbourne 6445
Cape Town - Fremantle 5615
Cape Town - Melbourne 5814
Cape Town - Hobart 5838
F. - A. 1353
Yokohama - Vancouver 4280
Singapore - Brisbane
S. - A. 1274
H. - W. 1293
ft m
18 000 6000
12 000 4000
6000 2000
3000 1000
600 200
0 0
200 600
2000 6000
4000 12 000
6000 18 000
8000 24 000
m ft
Projection: Mollweide's Homolographic
East from Greenwich
5615 Principal Shipping Routes

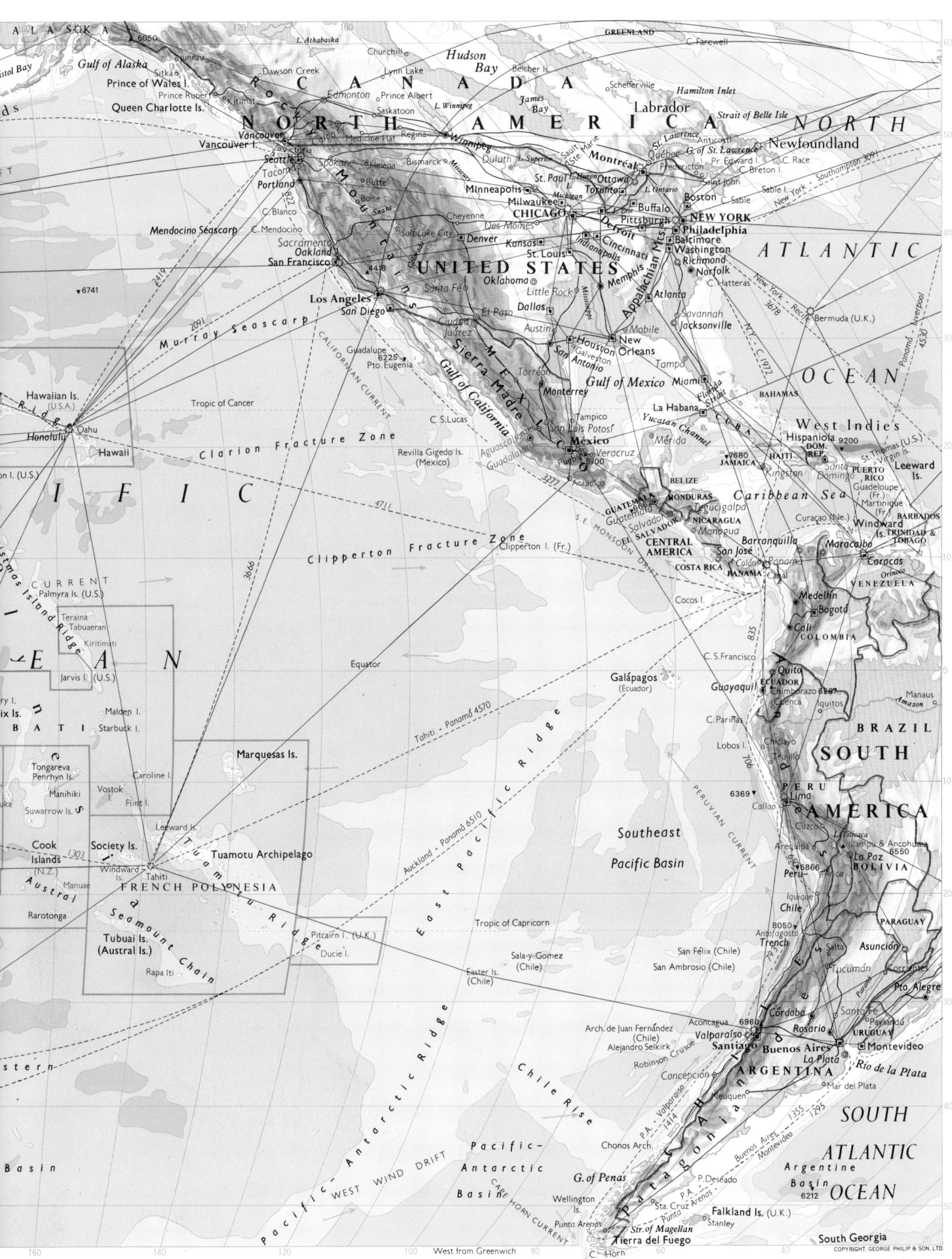

ALASKA
6050
Gulf of Alaska
Sitka
Prince of Wales I.
Juneau
Prince Rupert
Ki imat
Queen Charlotte Is.

GREENLAND
C. Farewell

CANADA
NORTH AMERICA
Dawson Creek
Churchill
Lynn Lake
Hudson Bay
Belcher Is.
James Bay
Labrador
Hamilton Inlet
Strait of Belle Isle
NORTH
Edmonton
Prince Albert
L. Athabaska
Saskatoon
L. Winnipeg
Scheffenville
Newfoundland
Medicine Hat
Regina
Winnipeg
Ste. Marie
Montréal
Québec
Anticosti
G. of St. Lawrence
Pr. Edward I.
Fredericton
C. Breton I.
C. Race
3091
Vancouver
Victoria
Seattle
Spokane
Helena
Bismarck
Duluth
L. Superior
Huron
Toronto
St. Lawrence
Saint John
Sable I.
New York
Southampton
Vancouver I.
Tacoma
Butte
Boise
Snake
Missouri
St. Paul
Minneapolis
Milwaukee
Michigan
Ottawa
L. Ontario
Buffalo
Boston
Pr. Edward
New
ATLANTIC
Portland
C. Blanco
Cheyenne
Des Moines
CHICAGO
Detroit
Pittsburgh
Philadelphia
NEW YORK
Mendocino Seascarp
C. Mendocino
Salt Lake City
Denver
Kansas
St. Louis
Indianapolis
Cincinnati
Washington
Baltimore
Richmond
New York
Sacramento
Oakland
San Francisco
4418
UNITED STATES
Santa Fé
Oklahoma
Memphis
Atlanta
Norfolk
C. Hatteras
6741
Los Angeles
San Diego
Ciudad Juárez
El Paso
Dallas
Little Rock
Mississippi
Savannah
Jacksonville
Bermuda (U.K.)
3678
OCEAN
Murray Seascarp
2091
Guadalupe
6225
Pto. Eugenia
Austin
San Antonio
Houston
Galveston
New Orleans
Mobile
Tampa
Miami
N.Y.-C 1972
Panama-Liverpool
4530
Sierra Madre
Torreón
Monterrey
Gulf of Mexico
BAHAMAS
Tropic of Cancer
C.S.Lucas
Tampico
La Habana
CUBA
West Indies
Hispaniola
9200
Gulf of California
San Luis Potosí
Yucatán Channel
Mérida
Florida Strait
DOM. REP.
HAITI
St. Thomas (U.S.)
Virgin Is.
PUERTO RICO
Leeward
Clarion Fracture Zone
Aguascalientes
MÉXICO
Veracruz
JAMAICA
Santo Domingo
Kingston
Hawaiian Is.
(U.S.A.)
Revilla Gigedo Is.
(Mexico)
Guadalajara
7680
3171
5700
BELIZE
Caribbean Sea
Guadeloupe (Fr.)
Martinique (Fr.)
BARBADOS
Ridge
Honolulu
Oahu
Hawaii
Acapulco
S.E. MONSOON
GUATEMALA
6865
Guatemala
Tegucigalpa
HONDURAS
Managua
NICARAGUA
Curaçao (Ne.)
Windward
IS. TRINIDAD & TOBAGO
I. (U.S.)
4711
SALVADOR
San José
COSTA RICA
CENTRAL AMERICA
PANAMA
Barranquilla
Panamá
Cartagena
Maracaibo
Caracas
IFIC
Clipperton Fracture Zone
Clipperton I. (Fr.)
PANAMA Canal
Colón
10
VENEZUELA
CURRENT
Palmyra Is. (U.S.)
Cocos I.
Medellín
Bogotá
Orinoco
Teraina
Tabuaeran
Kiritimati
Galápagos
(Ecuador)
C.S. Francisco
Cali
COLOMBIA
Jarvis I. (U.S.)
Equator
Quito
ECUADOR
Chimborazo 6267
Manaus
Amazon
E
A
N
Malden I.
Guayaquil
Cuenca
Iquitos
BATI
Starbuck I.
C. Parinas
BRAZIL
ix Is.
SOUTH
Tongareva
Penrhyn Is.
Caroline I.
Tahiti - Panamá 4570
Chiclayo
Trujillo
Manihiki
Vostok I.
Flint I.
PERU
6369
Lima
Callao
AMERICA
Suwarrow Is.
Marquesas Is.
Lobos I.
Cuzco
Leeward Is.
Society Is.
Tuamotu Archipelago
Cook Islands
(N.Z.)
1303
Windward Is.
Tahiti
Auckland - Panamá 6510
L. Titicaca
Illampu & Ancohuma
6550
La Paz
BOLIVIA
Manuae
FRENCH POLYNESIA
East Pacific Ridge
6866
Arica
Peru
Rarotonga
Austral
Seamount Chain
Southeast
Pacific Basin
Iquique
Chile
Tubuai Is.
(Austral Is.)
Pitcairn I. (U.K.)
Rapa Iti
Ducie I.
Tropic of Capricorn
8050
Trench
Antofagasta
Salta
Tucumán
PARAGUAY
Asunción
Corrientes
Sala-y-Gomez
(Chile)
San Félix (Chile)
San Ambrosio (Chile)
Easter Is.
(Chile)
Pto. Alegre
Arch. de Juan Fernández
(Chile)
Alejandro Selkirk
Aconcagua 6960
Valparaíso
Santiago
Córdoba
Rosario
Santa Fé
Payandú
URUGUAY
Montevideo
Robinson Crusoe
Buenos Aires
La Plata
Río de la Plata
Concepción
ARGENTINA
Mar del Plata
Basin
Neuquén
Chile Rise
SOUTH
Pacific - Antarctic Ridge
WEST WIND DRIFT
Pacific - Antarctic Basin
G. of Penas
Chonos Arch.
Buenos Aires - Montevideo
1355
1795
ATLANTIC
Argentine Basin
6212
OCEAN
P. Deseado
Basin
CAPE HORN CURRENT
Wellington Is.
Sta. Cruz Arenas
Punta Arenas
Falkland Is. (U.K.)
Stanley
South Georgia
Str. of Magellan
Tierra del Fuego
C. Horn

1 : 5 000 000

20   0   20   40   60   80 miles
20   0   20   40   80   120 km

1 : 1 000 000

5   0   5   10   15 miles
5   0   5   10   15   20 25 km

NEW CALEDONIA AND LOYALTY ISLANDS
1 : 5 000 000

Î. Baaba
Î. Neba
Yandé
Balabio
Pte. Nendiarene
Poum
Ouégoa
Ouabatche
Recif de la Gazelle
Î. Beautemps-Beaupré
C. Rossel
Île Ouvéa
St. Pierre
Î. Loyauté (Loyalty Is.)
Fayaoué
C. Escarpé
Chépénéhé
Î. Lifu
Wé
C. de Flotte
Î. Tiga
Ra
C. Roussin
Néce
Î. Maré
C. Wabao
C. Boyer

Koumac
Kaala-Gomen
Mt. Panié 1628
Hienghène
Tauha
Poindimié
Ponérihouen
Paagoumène
Voh
Massif de Tchingou
Kone
Me Maoya 1385
Houailou
Pouembout
Poya
3566
Me Maoya 1508
Canala
Bouloupari
Moindou
1441 1610
La Foa
2212
Paita Dombéa
Nouméa
Mont-Dore
Île Ouen
Cap N'doua
Île des Pins 110

Nouvelle-Calédonie
(New Caledonia)

OKINAWA
1 : 1 000 000

Yanaha-shima
Izena-shima
Hedo-misaki
Hedo
Oku
Uka
Oku
Sosu
Ie-shima
421
Tona
Hentona
Ada
Akamaru-saki
Aha
Ogimi
Mjoka
498
Yonaha-dake
Bise-zaki
Kouri-shima
Unten
Smoya
Taiho
Taira
Arakawa
Seseko-jima
Urasaki
Minna-shima
Toguchi
470
Yabu
400
Nakaoshi
Arume-wan
Kayo
Banno-saki
Awa
Nago
Kushi
Kyoda
Ora
Oura-wan
Maeki-saki
Yamada
Kanna
366
Tancha
Kin-misaki
Ikei-shima
Zampa-misaki
Ishikawa
Kin
Takabanare-shima
Nagahama
Higashi Onna
Kin-wan
Takashippu
Kadena
Chibana
Gushikawa
Henza-shima
Nagunna-shima
Kina
Koza
Misato
Tsuken-jima
Futemmi
Henna
Kamiyama-shima
Nakama
Atsuta
Oroku
Shuri
Naha
Yonabaru
Nakagusuku-wan
Kochinda
Azama
Rukan-sho
Chinen
Itoman
Tomori
Hyakuna
Kudaka-shima
Kiyan
Mabuni

EAST CHINA SEA

BELAU
1 : 1 000 000

Kayangel Islands
Kayangel Passage
Northwest Reef
North Entrance
Kossol Reef
Kossol Passage East
Cormoran Entrance Reef
Ngaregur
Ngarmegei Pas
Konrei
Arekalong Peninsula
Galap
Ngardmau Bay
Ngardmau
239
Reklau
Namai Bay
Pkulagalid Pt.
Melekeiok
Ngatpang
BABELTHUAP I.
Komebail Lagoon
Arakabesan
Mukeru
Goikul
224
Koror
Garreru
Madalai
Koror I.
Malakal Harbor
Auluptagel
Uruktapel
Aulong
Apurashokoru
Ngobasangel
Sar Passage
Orukuizu
El Malk I.
Ngemelis Islands
Ngesebus I.
Ngardololok
Ngergoi I.
Kongauru I.
Ngerong
Peleliu I.
Ngarekeukl I.
Saipan
Angaur I.

FIJI
1 : 5 000 000

Great Sea Reef
Udu Pt.
Ringgold Isles
Yasawa
Lambasa
1031
Natewa Bay
Rambi
Yasawa Group
Vanua Levu
Savusavu
Ngamea
Namuka Passage
Taveuni
Nambouwalu
Somosomo Str.
Vanua Mbalavu
Naviti
Waya
Bligh Water
Koro
Lomaloma
Lautoka
Nandi
1322
Tomaniivi
Levuka
Ovalau
Thithia
Mango
Viti Levu
Ngau
Tuvutha
Nandrau
Singatoka
Nausori
Suva
Nayau
Lakemba Passage
Lakemba
Vatulele
Mbengga
Moala
Matuku
Kandavu Passage
Kandavu
Vunisea
Ono
Totoya
Kambara
Ongea Levu

KORO SEA
F I J I
LAU (EAST)

YAP
1 : 1 000 000

Rumung
Omin
Runu
Map
Tageren Canal
Gatjapar
Okau
187
Gagil-Tomil
YAP
Tomil
Kanif
Tomil Harbor
Nif
Tabunifi
Gorror

TAHITI AND MOORÉA
1 : 1 000 000

Baie de Opunohu
Pte. Aroa
Baie de Matavai
Pte. Vénus
Papenoo
Tahiti 1207
Mahina
Tiarei
Papeete
Orohena 2241
Hitida
Moorea
Punaauia
1799
Pte. Nuupere
Paea
Tahiti
Isthme de Taravao
Papara
Mataiea
Tautira
Pte. Tatatua
Port Phaeton
Teahupoo
Mt. Roonu 1332
Presqu'île de Taiarapu

GUAM
1 : 1 000 000

Ritidian Pt.
Pati Pt.
Tumon Bay
Mt. Santa Rosa 252
Tamuning
Dededo
Cabras I.
Agana Bay
Apra Harbor
Agana
Barrigada
Orote Peninsula
Piti
Toto
Agat Bay
Yona
Pago Bay
Agat
Santa Rita
Fena Valley
Talofofo
Facpi Pt.
Mt. Lamlam 406
Inarajan
Talofofo Bay
Cetti Bay
Umatac
Merizo
Cocos I.

TUTUILA
1 : 1 000 000

Pola I.
Vatia
Cape Matatula
Pago Pago
Aua
Fagasa
652
Leloaloa
Nu'uuli
600
Fagatogo
Pago Pago Harbor
Amanave
Tafuna
Leone
Vaitogi
Steps Pt.
Aputapu

MANUA
1 : 1 000 000

Ofu
484
639
Olosega
Ta'u
Olosega
Aunu'u
Lumu
631
Ta'u
Leusoalii

AMERICAN SAMOA

TRUK ISLANDS
1 : 1 000 000

Pis
North Pass
Holap I.
Falas I.
Northeast Islands
Mor I.
Northeast Pass
Yawata
Falo I.
Moen I.
370
Ulalu I.
Eot I.
Shiki
Dublon
Shichiyo
Udot
Param
Islands
Lemotol B.
Tol I.
452
Fefan Islands
Falabeguets I.
Tarik I.
Uman I.
Tsis I.
Ollan I.
Fanan I.
Uijec I.
Otta I.
Mesegon I.
South Pass

PACIFIC OCEAN LOCATOR MAP

Tokyo
JAPAN
Shanghai
CHINA
Okinawa
Taibei
TAIWAN (FORMOSA)
Manila
PHILIPPINES
Los Angeles
UNITED STATES
MEXICO
HAWAII
Tropic of Cancer
U.S. TRUST TERR. OF THE PACIFIC IS
Guam
Yap
Truk
Belau
NAURU
INDONESIA
PAPUA NEW GUINEA
SOLOMON IS.
TUVALU
KIRIBATI
Equator
WESTERN SAMOA
AMER. SAMOA
FRENCH POLYNESIA
Tahiti
VANUATU
FIJI
TONGA
AUSTRALIA
New Caledonia
Tropic of Capricorn
Sydney
International Date Line

ft m
6000 2000
4500 1500
3000 1000
1200 400
600 200
0
200 600
2000 6000
4000 12 000
m ft

1:6 500 000

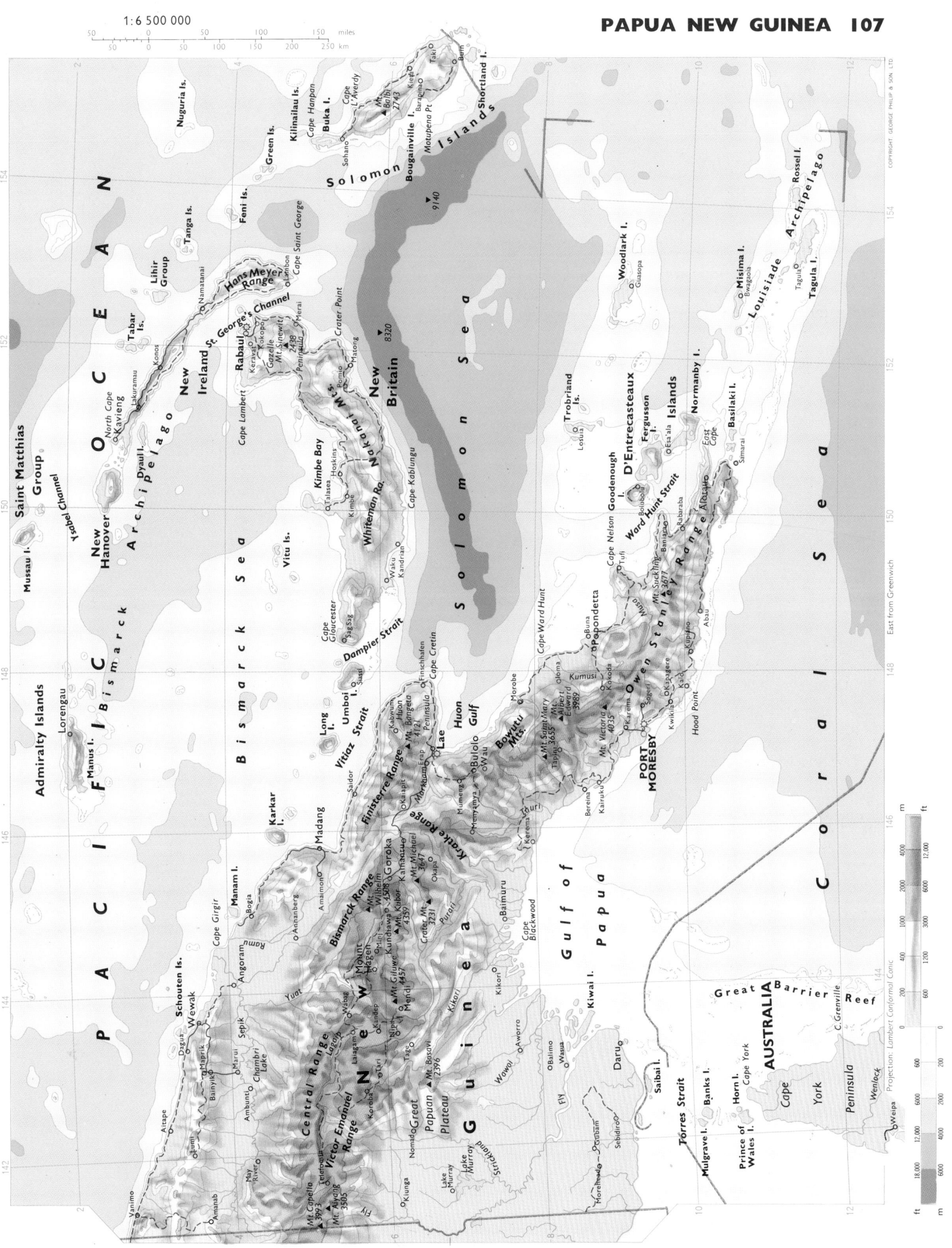

PACIFIC OCEAN
Bismarck Archipelago
Bismarck Sea
Solomon Sea
Coral Sea
Gulf of Papua
Solomon Islands
New Guinea
Admiralty Islands
Manus I.
Lorengau
Mussau I.
Saint Matthias Group
Ysabel Channel
New Hanover
Kavieng
North Cape
Dyaul I.
New Ireland
Lakuramau
Konos
Namatanai
Hans Meyer Range
Tabar Is.
Lihir Group
Tanga Is.
Feni Is.
Green Is.
Nuguria Is.
Kilinailau Is.
Buka I.
Cape Hanpan
Sohano
Cape L'Averdy
Mt. Balbi 2743
Kieta
Buin
Bougainville I.
Motupena Pt
Shortland I.
St. George's Channel
Cape Saint George
Rabaul
Kokopo
Gazelle Peninsula
Mt. Sinewit 2438
Cape Lambert
New Britain
Nakanai Mts.
Whiteman Ra.
Kimbe Bay
Hoskins
Talasea
Kimbe
Cape Kablunga
Kandrian
Cape Gloucester
Dampier Strait
Umboi I.
Long I.
Vitiaz Strait
Vitu Is.
Karkar I.
Madang
Manam I.
Bogia
Cape Girgir
Schouten Is.
Wewak
Angoram
Ramu
Sepik
Yuat
Maprik
Chambri Lake
Ambunti
Aitape
Vanimo
Amanab
Finisterre Range
Huon Peninsula
Mt. Bangeta 4121
Finschhafen
Cape Cretin
Lae
Huon Gulf
Markham
Kratke Range
Bismarck Range
Mt. Wilhelm 4508
Goroka
Kainantu
Mt. Michael 3647
Mount Hagen
Mt. Kubor 4359
Kundiawa
Mt. Giluwe 4457
Mendi
Crater Mt. 3231
Purari
Bulolo
Wau
Bowutu Mts.
Mt. Saint Mary 3655
Mt. Albert Edward 3989
Mt. Victoria 4035
Owen Stanley Range
Kokoda
Kumusi
Popondetta
Buna
Cape Ward Hunt
Morobe
PORT MORESBY
Hood Point
Kerema
Cape Blackwood
Baimuru
Kikori
Kiwai I.
Daru
Balimo
Fly
Wawoi
Mt. Bosavi 2396
Great Papuan Plateau
Strickland
Lake Murray
Kiunga
Nomad
Central Range
Victor Emanuel Range
Telefomin
Mt. Capella 3993
Mt. Aiyang 3505
Lagaip
Torres Strait
Saibai I.
Mulgrave I.
Banks I.
Prince of Wales I.
Horn I.
Cape York
AUSTRALIA
Cape York Peninsula
Weipa
Great Barrier Reef
C. Grenville
Cape Nelson
Tufi
Mt. Suckling 3677
Ward Hunt Strait
Goodenough I.
D'Entrecasteaux Islands
Fergusson I.
Normanby I.
Trobriand Is.
Losuia
East Cape
Alotau
Samarai
Basilaki I.
Woodlark I.
Guasopa
Misima I.
Bwagaoia
Louisiade Archipelago
Tagula I.
Rossel I.
9140
8320
East from Greenwich
Projection: Lambert Conformal Conic
COPYRIGHT GEORGE PHILIP & SON LTD

NORTHERN TERRITORY

Tanami Desert

Great Sandy Desert

TIMOR SEA

INDONESIA

INDIAN OCEAN

Timor

Sumba

Lombok

Melville I.

Bathurst I.

Darwin

King Leopold Ranges

Joseph Bonaparte Gulf

Cambridge Gulf

Bonaparte Archipelago

Port Hedland

Karratha

Hamersley Range

Tropic of Capricorn

MacDonnell Ranges

Lake Mackay

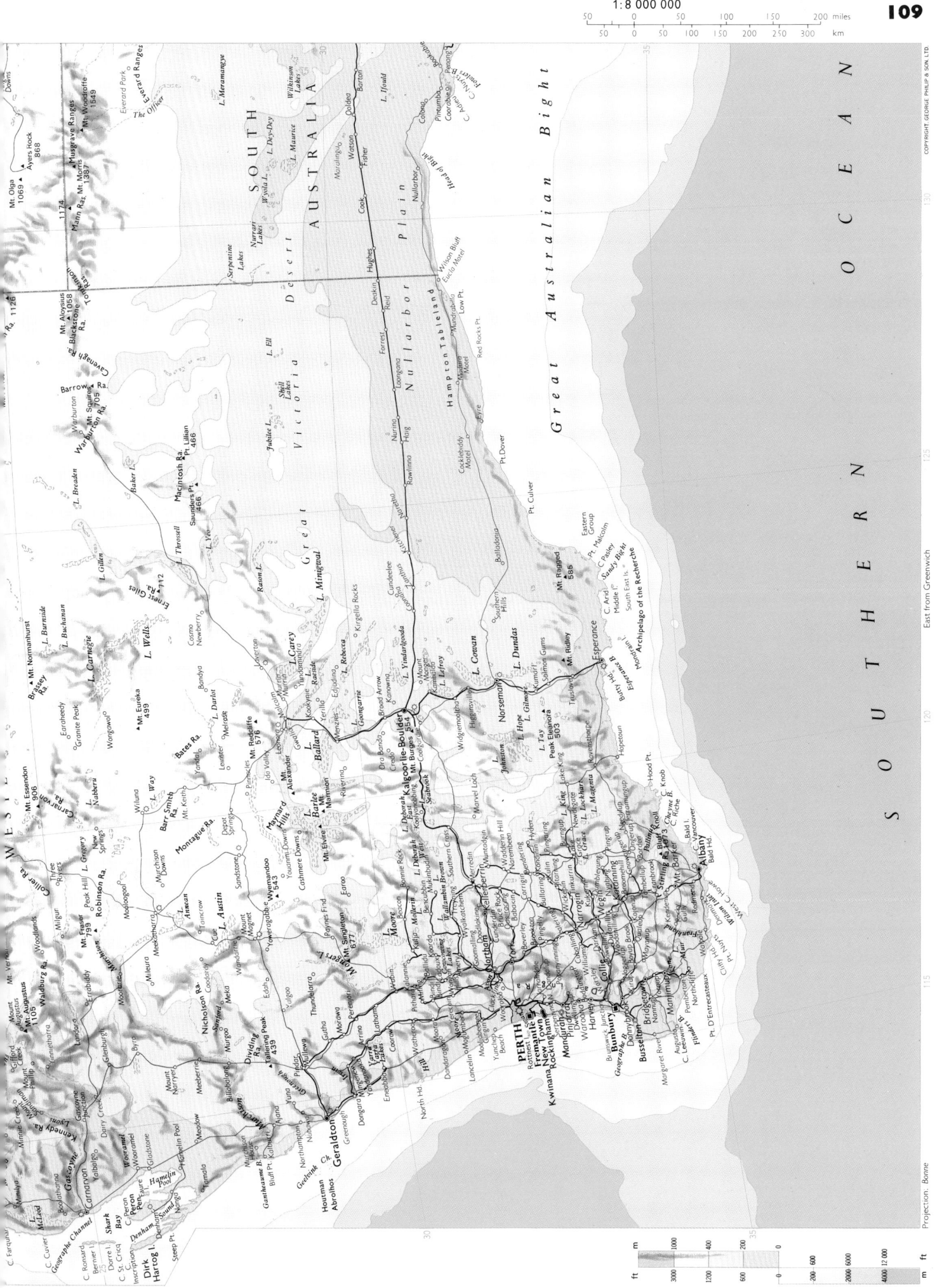

1:8 000 000

50   0   50   100   150   200 miles

50   0   50   100   150   200   250   300   km

S O U T H

A U S T R A L I A

W E S T   A U S T R A L I A

Gibson   Desert

Great   Victoria   Desert

Nullarbor   Plain

Hampton Tableland

Great   Australian   Bight

S O U T H E R N   O C E A N

PERTH
Fremantle
New Town
Rockingham
Kwinana

Geraldton

Bunbury
Busselton

Albany

Esperance

Norseman

Kalgoorlie-Boulder

Carnarvon

Shark Bay

Denham

Dirk Hartog I.

Mt. Olga
1069

Ayers Rock
868

Musgrave Ranges

Mt. Woodroffe
1549

Mann Ra. Mt. Morris
1387

Everard Ranges

East from Greenwich

Projection. Bonne

COPYRIGHT GEORGE PHILIP & SON. LTD.

ft   m
3000   1000
1200   400
600   200
0   0
600   200
2000   600
6000   2000
12 000   4000
m

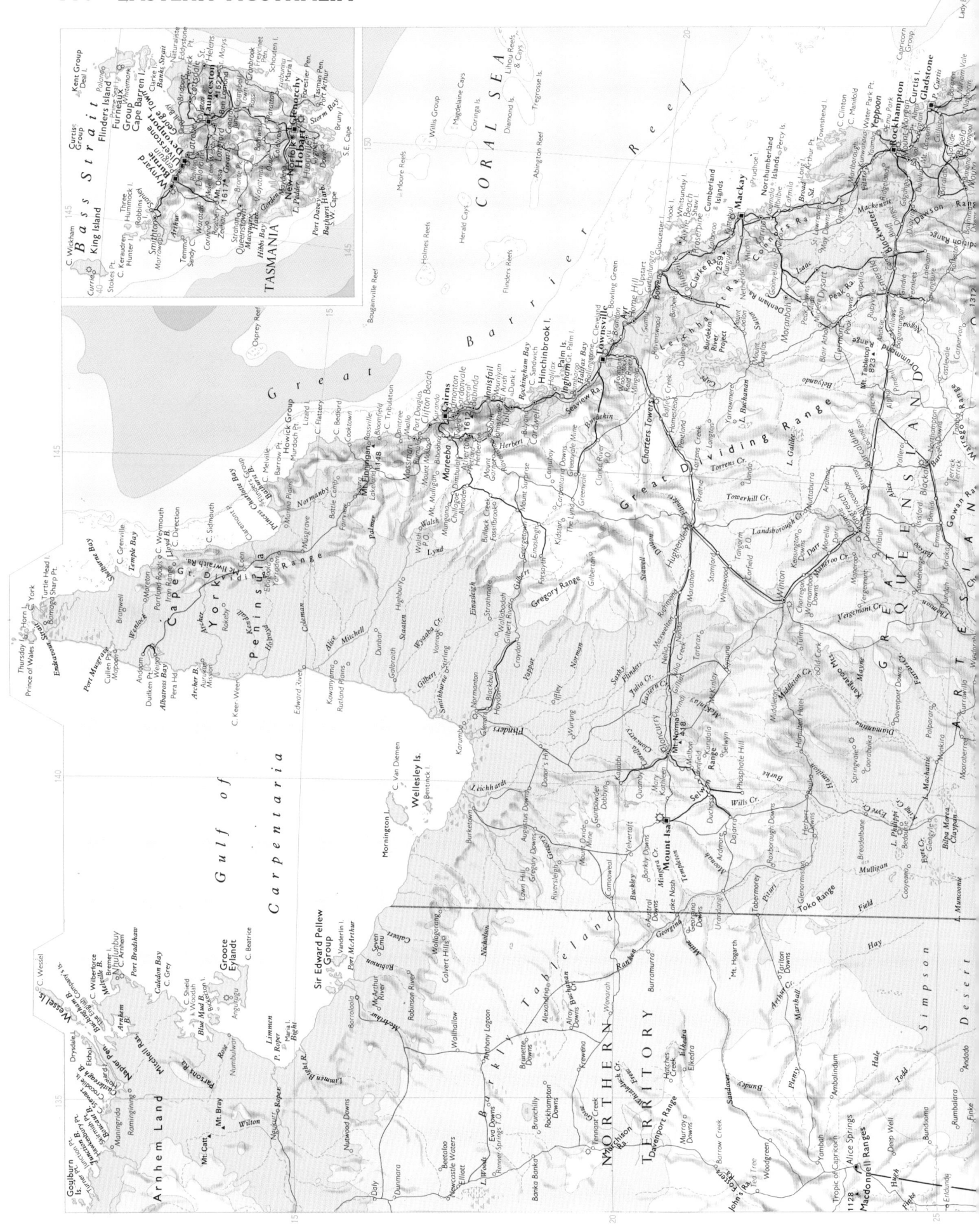

Bass Strait
TASMANIA
King Island
Flinders Island
Furneaux Group
Cape Barren I.
Launceston
Hobart
Devonport
Burnie
Storm Bay
CORAL SEA
Great Barrier Reef
Gulf of Carpentaria
Cape York Peninsula
Arnhem Land
Groote Eylandt
Sir Edward Pellew Group
Wellesley Is.
Mornington I.
NORTHERN TERRITORY
GREAT QUEENSLAND
Great Dividing Range
Barkly Tableland
Simpson Desert
Macdonnell Ranges
Alice Springs
Tropic of Capricorn
Mount Isa
Cloncurry
Townsville
Cairns
Mackay
Rockhampton
Gladstone
Charters Towers
Hughenden
Winton
Longreach
Tennant Creek
Normanton
Cooktown
Bowen
Ingham
Hinchinbrook I.
Whitsunday I.
Cumberland Islands
Northumberland Islands
Curtis I.
Selwyn Range
Gregory Range
Dawson Range
Wessel Is.

III

1:8 000 000

50   0   50   100   150   200 miles
50 0 50 100 150 200 250 300 km

COPYRIGHT. GEORGE PHILIP & SON LTD.

T A S M A N   S E A

Projection: Bonne

East from Greenwich

ft
4500
3000
1200
600
0
200
2000
4000

m
1500
1000
400
200
0
600
6000
12 000

SOUTH AUSTRALIA
NE
VIC
Parakylia
Leigh Creek South
Mt. Deception 685
Benbonyathe 1058
Copley
Mt. Hack 1083
Beltana
Lake Torrens
Flinders Ranges
Lake Frome
Barrier Range
Packsaddle
Caradoc
Peri Lake
L. Younghusband
L. Hanson
Arcoona
L. Hart
Woomera
Nilpena
Parachilna
Broughams Gate
White Cliffs
Koonawarra
Momba
McDougalls Well
Glen Gowrie
Kalkaroo
Frome Downs
Benagerie
Mulga Valley
Sturts Meadows
Grassmere
Menamurtee
Wirraminna
Pimba
Island Lagoon
Pernatty Lagoon
Wilpena
St. Mary Pk. 1165
Wilpena Cr.
Mooleulooloo
Wilangee
Langidoon
Wilcannia
Wongal
Volo
Goonalga
Lake Gairdner
Woocalla
Cotabena
Hawker
Glenorchy
Boolcoomata
Silverton
Stephens Creek
Cawkers Well
Wahratta
Broken Hill
Slamannon
L. Macfarlane
Hesso
Gordon
Mount Victor
Mingary
Cockburn
Olary
Mannahill
Mutooroo
Menindee L.
Leonora Downs
Menindee
Cawndilla L.
Tandou L.
Teryaweyna L.
Mount Manara
Baden Park
Mt. Ive
Mt. Brown 965
Quorn
Carrieton
Eurelia
Port Augusta West
Port Augusta
Siam
Wilmington
Orroroo
Paratoo
Yunta
Nackara
Netley Gap
Kimberley
Boolaboolka L.
Gum Lake
Darnick
Beilpajah
Gypsum
Lake Gilles
Iron Knob
Nectar Brook
969 Mt. Remarkable
Booleroo Centre
Black Rock
Peterborough
Tartna Point
Buckleboo
Iron Baron
Whyalla
Port Pirie
Napperby
Laura
Jamestown
Gladstone
Terowie
Quondong
Oakbank
L. Popilta
Popio L.
Kimba
Braemar
Morgan Vale
Traveller's Lake
Poonacarie
Manfred
Clare
Crystal Brook
Hallett
Mt. Bryan 934
Canopus
Gulnare
Spalding
Belmore
Lethero
Darke Peak
Pondooma
Port Broughton
Brinkworth
Burra
Bulpunga
Burtundy
Arumpo
Magenta
Cowell
Rudall
Snowtown
Clare
Blyth
Gluepot
Spencer Gulf
Bute
Farrell Flat
L. Victoria
Hatfield P.O.
Arno Bay
Wallaroo
Willamulka
Kadina
Hoyleton
Robertstown
Point Pass
Morgan
Wentworth
Bidura
Renmark
Merbein
Mildura
Irymple
Red Cliffs
Moonta
Bowmans
Riverton
Waikerie
Berri
Yamba
Oxley
Ungarra
Port Wakefield
Owen
Balaklava
Kapunda
Eudunda
Holder
Barmera
Meringur
Werrimull
Pitarpunga L.
Murrumbidgee
Maitland
Hamley Bridge
Nuriootpa
Truro
Maggea
Loxton
Nangiloc
Benanee
Tumby Bay
Ardrossan
Mallala
Tanunda
Angaston
Mantung
Taplan
Robinvale
Balranald
Koppio
Port Victoria
Gawler
Sedan
Swan Reach
Veitch
Nowingi
Bannerton
Wanbi
Meribah
Gulf
Salisbury
Elizabeth
Sanderston
Copeville
Kunlara
Alawoona
Hattah
Annuello
Koorioonong
Perekerten
Minlaton
C. Donington
Port Lincoln
Port Adelaide
ADELAIDE
Glenelg
Mount Lofty Ranges
Mannum
Kalyan
Sandalwood
Peebinga
Kulwin
Natya
Moulamein
Corny Pt.
THISTLE I.
Woodside
Murray Bridge
Brighton
St.
Mt. Barker
McLaren Vale
Walpeup
Ouyen
Piangil
Nyah West
Yorke Peninsula
Karoonda
Cowangie
West Pt.
Edithburgh
Marion Bay
Monteith
Tailem Bend
Marama
Pinnaroo
Tutye
Underbool
Pier Millan
Niemur
GAMBIER IS.
Willunga
Strathalbyn
Peake
Lameroo
Patchewollock
Speed
L. Tyrrell
Waitchie
Swan Hill
C. Spencer
Investigator Strait
Vincent
Finniss
Milang
L. Alexandrina
Cooke Plains
Geranium
Yarto
Ultima
Meatian
Normanville
Goolwa
L. Albert
Yumali
Berriwillock
Culgoa
Kerang
Kondrook
Cohuna
Nepean Bay
Backstairs Passage
Victor Harbor
Cape Jervis
Encounter Bay
Meningie
Coonalpyn
Hopetoun
Tyrrell
Western River
Kingscote
Penneshaw
L. Albacutya
Yaapeet
Curyo
Quambatook
Tragowel
C. Borda
KANGAROO I.
Culburra
Tintinara
Rainbow
Birchip
Avoca
D'Estrees Bay
Younghusband Peninsula
The Coorong
Lake Hindmarsh
Mincha
Vivonne
Vivonne Bay
Keith
Yanac
Jeparit
Brim
Wycheproof
C. du Couedic
C. Gantheaume
Salt Creek
Bordertown
Diapur
Nhill
Antwerp
Warracknabeal
Litchfield
Charlton
Mitiamo
Wolseley
Kaniva
Dimboola
Donald
Wedderburn
Korong Vale
Minyip
Cope Cope
Wimmera
Murtoa
Inglewood
Bridgewater
Lacepede Bay
Frances
Goroke
Natimuk
St. Arnaud
Eaglehawk
Morea (Carpolac)
Noradjuha
Horsham
Bolangum
Emu
Kingston S.E.
C. Jaffa
Kybybolite
The Grampians
Glenorchy
Dunolly
Maldon
Reedy Creek
Naracoorte
Toolondo
Deep Lead
Stawell
Maryborough
Avoca
Castlemaine
Glenelg
Balmoral
Mt. William 1167
Ararat
Talbot
Clunes
Kyneton
Glenroy
Waubra
Daylesford
Creswick
Penola
Maroona
Beaufort
BALLARAT
Beachport
George
Rivoli B.
Kalangadoo
Casterton
Coleraine
Englefield
Cavendish
Willaura
Millicent
Nangwarry
Mininera
Scarsdale
Elaine
Hamilton
Dunkeld
Skipton
L. Bonney
Mount Gambier
Dartmoor
Branxholme
Condah
Penshurst
Derrinallum
Mortlake
Leigh
C. Northumberland
Port MacDonnell
Heywood
Macarthur
Cressy
Inverleigh
GEELONG
Discovery Bay
Koroit
Terang
Camperdown
Alvie
Winchelsea
Portland
Portland Bay
Cobden
Colac
C. Bridgewater
C. Nelson
Port Fairy
Warrnambool
Allansford
Timboon
Forrest
Lorne
Aireys Inlet
Port Campbell
Lavers Hill
Apollo Bay
C. Otway
ft m
6000 2000
4500 1500
3000 1000
1200 400
600 200
0 0
200 600
2000 6000
4000 12 000
m ft
138
140
142
144
32
34
36
38
Projection: Alber's Equal area with two standard parallels

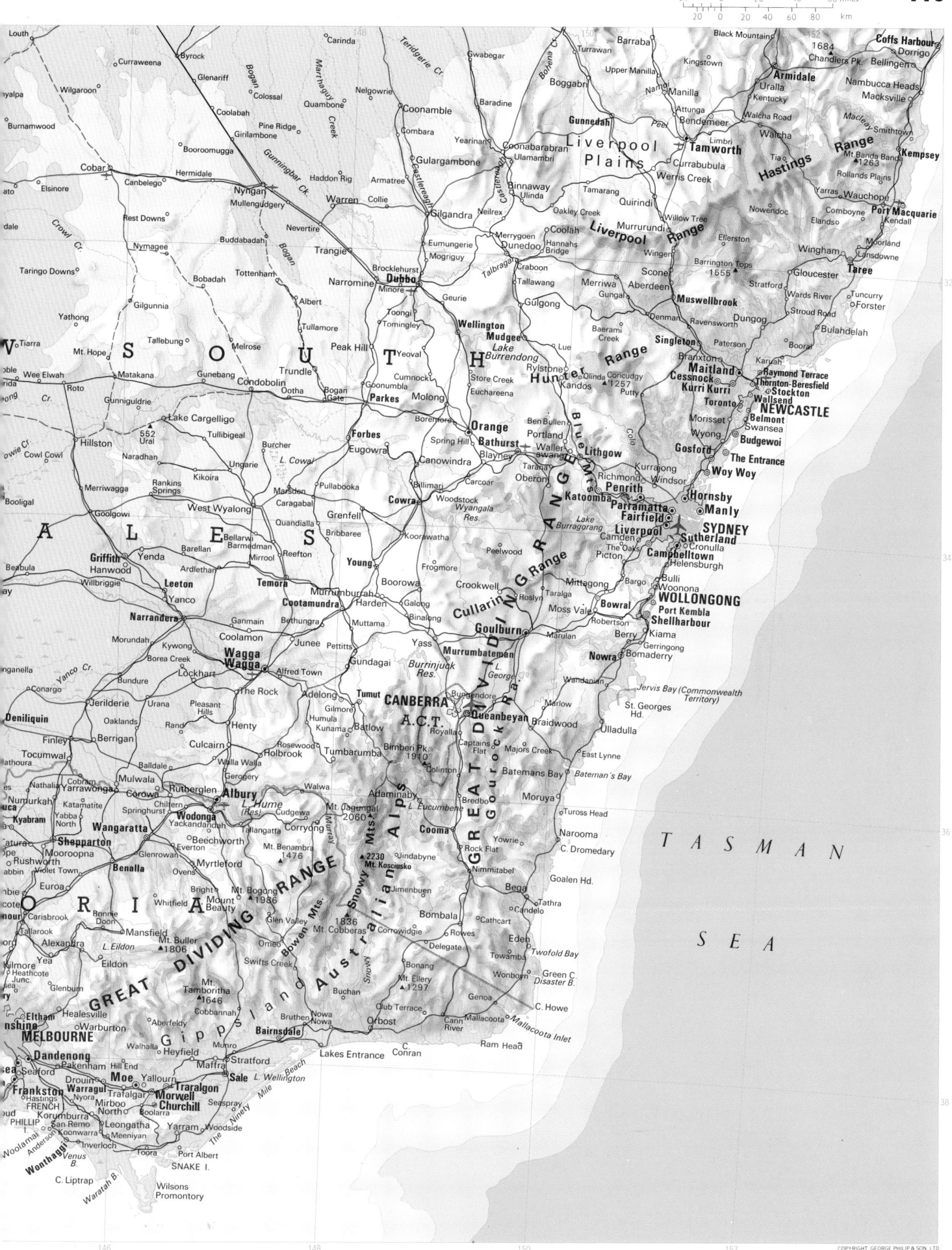

1 : 4 000 000

20   0   20   40   60 miles
20   0   20   40   60   80
km

TASMAN

SEA

1 : 3 500 000

20   0   20   40   60   80 miles
20   0   20   40   60   80   100   120km

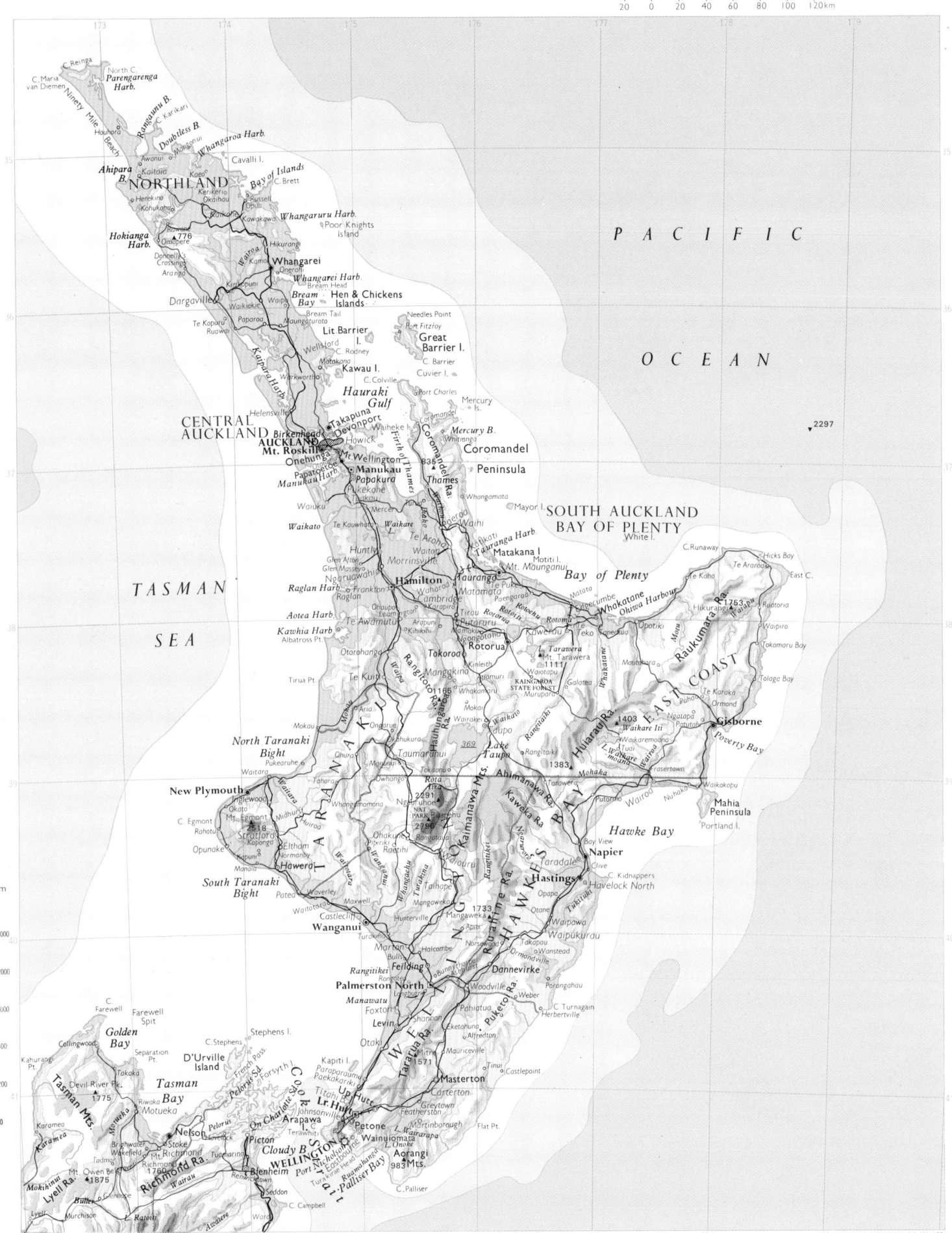

C. Maria
van Diemen
North C.
Parengarenga Harb.
C. Reinga
Ninety Mile Beach
Rangaunu B.
C. Karikari
Doubtless B.
Whangaroa Harb.
Ahipara B.
Hauhora
Awanui
Kaitaia
Kaeo
Cavalli I.
Bay of Islands
NORTHLAND
Herekino
Kerikeri
Okaihau
Russell
Opua
C. Brett
Kohukohu
Kawakawa
Hokianga Harb.
Donnelly
Crossing
Omapere
Rawene
776
Waiotira
Kamo
Hikurangi
Poor Knights Island
Aranga
Kaikohe
Hikurangi
Whangarei
PACIFIC
Dargaville
Waikiekie
Waipu
Whangarei Harb.
Onerahi
Bream Head
Bream Bay
Hen & Chickens Islands
Te Kopuru
Paparoa
Maungaturoto
Bream Tail
Needles Point
Port Fitzroy
OCEAN
Ruawai
Lit. Barrier I.
Great Barrier I.
Wellsford
C. Rodney
Motakana
C. Barrier
Kaiwaka
Cuvier I.
Kaipara Harb.
C. Colville
Port Charles
Kawau I.
Warkworth
2297
Helensville
Hauraki Gulf
Mercury Is.
CENTRAL
AUCKLAND
Takapuna
Birkenhead
Devonport
Waiheke I.
C. Coromandel
Coromandel
Mercury B.
Whitianga
AUCKLAND
Howick
Port Charles
Mt. Roskill
Mt. Wellington
Coromandel
Coromandel Peninsula
Onehunga
836
Papatoetoe
Manukau
Thames
Whangamata
Papakura
Manukau Harb.
Pukekohe
Firth of Thames
Mayor I.
SOUTH AUCKLAND
Waiuku
Mercer
Waikato
Te Kauwhata
Waikare L.
Paeroa
Waihi
White I.
BAY OF PLENTY
Te Aroha
TASMAN
Huntly
Waiton
Tauranga Harb.
C. Runaway
Hicks Bay
Glen Afton
Morrinsville
Matakana I.
Motiti I.
Te Kaha
Ngaruawahia
Mt. Maunganui
Bay of Plenty
Te Araroa
East C.
Hamilton
Tauranga
Raukumara Ra.
Raglan Harb.
Wahotao
Te Puke
Te Matata
Whakatane
1753
Ruatoria
Raglan
Frankton
Cambridge
Matamata
Paengaroa
Edgecumbe
Ohiwa Harbour
Hikurangi
Waipiro
SEA
Aotea Harb.
Te Awamutu
Arapuni
Karapiro
Tirau
Rotorua
Rotoma
Opotiki
EAST
Tokomaru Bay
Otorohanga
Kihikihi
Putaruru
L. Rotorua
Motu
COAST
Tolaga Bay
Kawhia Harb.
Albatross Pt.
Tokoroa
Rotorua
Kawerau
Teko
Waioeka
Tirua Pt.
Te Kuiti
Mangakino
1165
Kinleith
L. Tarawera
1111
Galatea
Ngatapa
1403
Waikare Iti
Putatutu
Ormond
Gisborne
Aria
Whakamaru
KAINGAROA
STATE FOREST
Murupara
Rangitaiki
Poverty Bay
Mokau
Ongarue
Waikato
Waikato
Taupo
1383
Hikurangi
Mahia Peninsula
North Taranaki Bight
Taumarunui
369
Lake Taupo
Ahimanawa Mts.
Portland I.
Waitara
Pukearuhe
Ohura
Rangitaiki
Waikokopu
New Plymouth
TARANAKI
Whangamomona
Raurimu
Rota
2291
NAT.
PARK
Ruapehu
Kaimanawa Mts.
Kaweka Ra.
Mohaka
Nuhaka
Inglewood
Okato
Midhirst
Ohakune
2796
Rangataua
Hawke Bay
C. Egmont
Mt. Egmont
Pipiriki
Bay View
Mt. Egmont
2518
Stratford
Kopuaranga
Raetihi
Rangitikei
Napier
Clive
Opunake
Rahotu
Eltham
Taihape
Taradale
Hastings
Kaponga
Normanby
Havelock North
C. Kidnappers
Opapa
South Taranaki Bight
Hawera
Patea
Maxwell
Mangaweka
Otane
Waipawa
Castlecliff
1733
RUAHINE RA.
Waipukurau
Waverley
Hunterville
Wanganui
Turakina
Waiouru
Dannevirke
Marton
Halcombe
Porangahau
Bulls
Rangitikei
Feilding
Woodville
Weber
Palmerston North
WELLINGTON
Ormondville
C. Turnagain
Manawatu
Longburn
Herbertville
Foxton
Pahiatua
Levin
Shannon
Eketahuna
Otaki
Alfredton
Kapiti I.
Mauriceville
Paraparaumu
Tararua Ra.
Paekakariki
1571
Masterton
Golden Bay
C. Farewell
Farewell Spit
C. Stephens
Stephens I.
Mt. Bruce
Tinui
Carterton
Castlepoint
Collingwood
Kahurangi Pt.
D'Urville Island
French Pass
Forsyth I.
Cook Strait
Greytown
Featherston
Flat Pt.
C. Takaka
Separation Pt.
Queen Charlotte Sd.
Upper Hutt
Titahi
Martinborough
Tasman Mts.
Devil River Pk.
1775
Riwaka
Pelorus Sd.
Lr. Hutt
L. Wairarapa
Tasman Bay
Motueka
Arapawa
Johnsonville
Petone
L. Onoke
Wainuiomata
Nelson
Pelorus
Terawhiti
Picton
Cloudy B.
WELLINGTON
Palliser Bay
Brightwater
Stoke
On Charlotte
Aorangi
983 Mts.
Wakefield
Richmond
Port Nicholson
Tuamarina
Turakirae Head
C. Palliser
Mokihinui
Richmond Ra.
Blenheim
1875
Renwick
Mt. Owen
Wairau
Lyell Ra.
1730
Lyell
Butler
Seddon
Murchison
Rai
Anakoa
Ward
C. Campbell

TASMAN SEA

ft   m
9000 3000
6000 2000
3000 1000
1200 400
600   200
0   0
200   600
2000 6000
m   ft

Projection: Conical with two standard parallels   East from Greenwich   COPYRIGHT GEORGE PHILIP & SON LTD

1:3 500 000

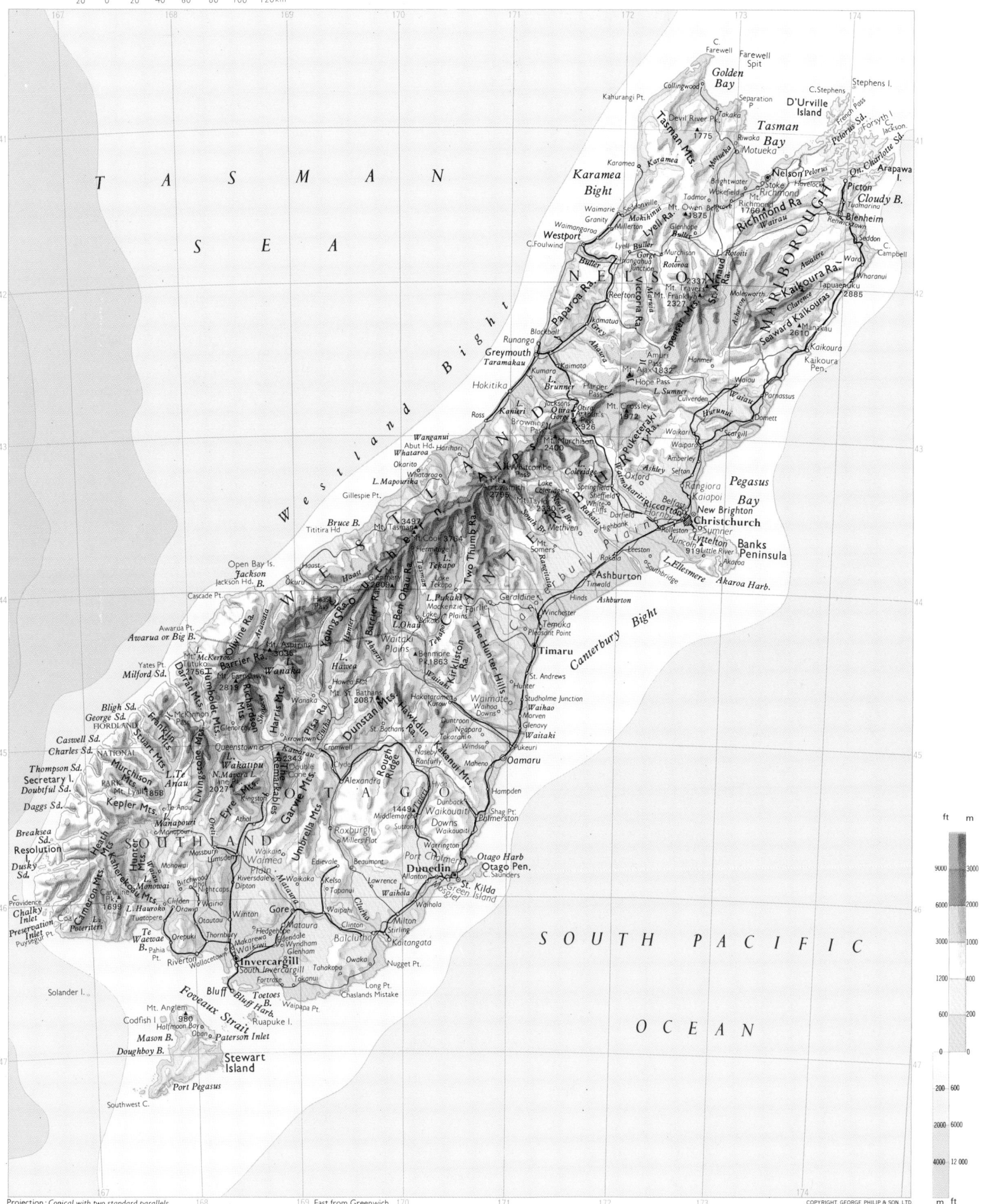

East from Greenwich

COPYRIGHT. GEORGE PHILIP & SON. LTD.

1:40 000 000

200 0 200 400 600 800 1000 miles
200 0 200 400 600 800 1000 1200 1400 1600 km

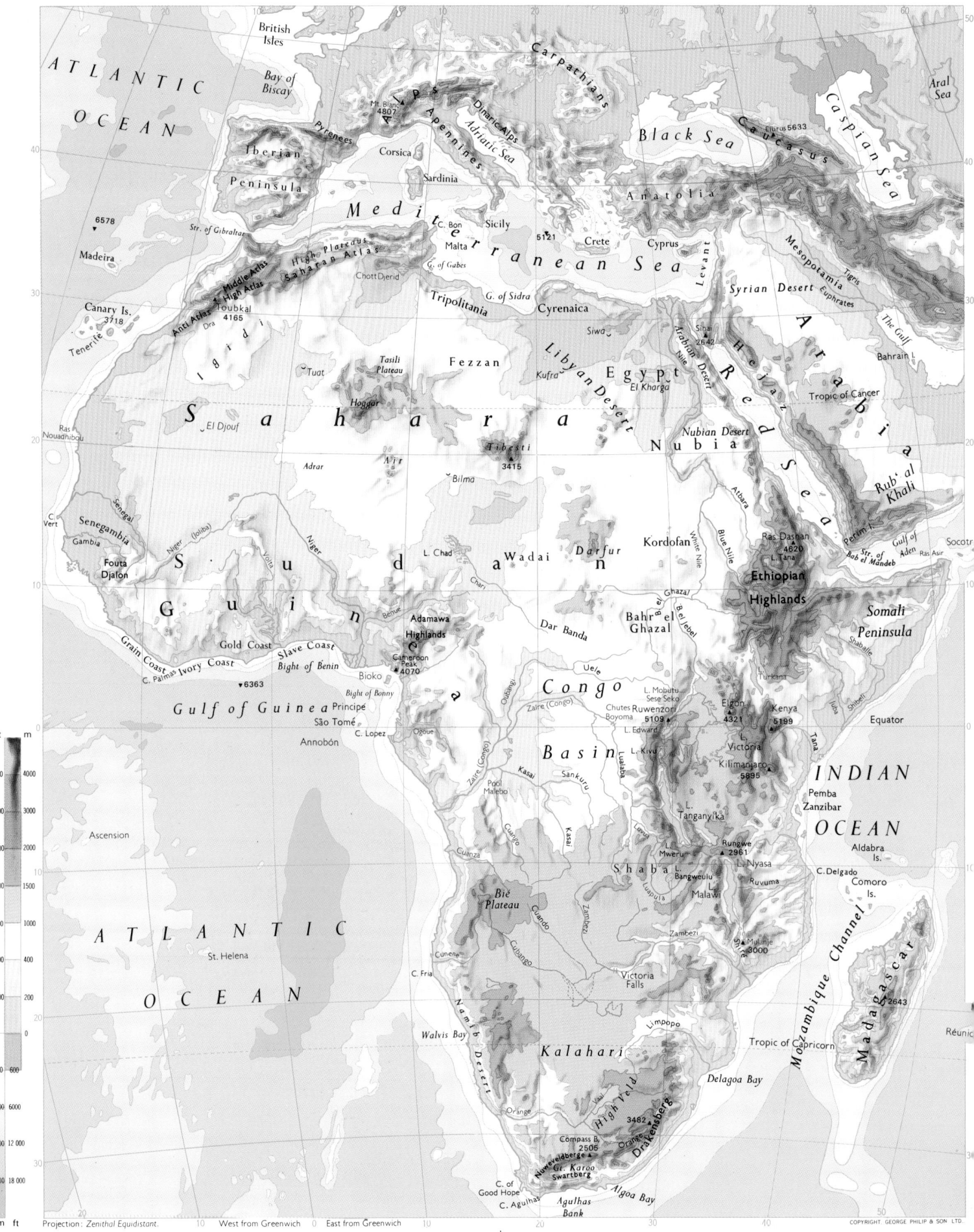

ATLANTIC OCEAN

British Isles

Bay of Biscay

Carpathians

Alps
Mt. Blanc 4807
Pyrenees
Apennines
Dinaric Alps
Adriatic Sea

Black Sea

Caucasus
Elbrus 5633

Caspian Sea

Aral Sea

Iberian Peninsula

Corsica

Sardinia

Anatolia

▼6578

Madeira

Str. of Gibraltar

C. Bon
Sicily
Malta
5121
Crete
Cyprus

Mediterranean Sea

Mesopotamia
Tigris
Euphrates

Syrian Desert

Canary Is.
Tenerife 3718

Middle Atlas
High Atlas
Toubkal
Anti Atlas 4165
Dra

High Plateaus
Saharan Atlas
Chott Djerid
G. of Gabes
Tripolitania
G. of Sidra
Cyrenaica

Libyan Desert

Egypt
Siwa
El Kharga
Kufra

Sinai 2642

Nile

Arabian Desert

Hejaz

Red Sea

Arabia

The Gulf

Bahrain I.

Tropic of Cancer

Ras Nouadhibou

Igidi

Tuat

Tasili Plateau

Fezzan

S a h a r a

El Djouf

Hoggar

Adrar

Aïr

Tibesti
3415

Bilma

Nubian Desert

N u b i a

Rub' al Khali

Perim I.
Str. of Bab el Mandeb
Gulf of Aden
Ras Asir

Socotra

C. Vert
Senegal
Senegambia
Gambia
Fouta Djalon

Niger (Joliba)

S u d

L. Chad
Wadai
Darfur
Kordofan
White Nile
Atbara
Blue Nile

Ras Dashan 4620
L. Tana

Ethiopian Highlands

Somali Peninsula

G u i n e a

Volta
Niger
Benue
Chari

a n
Dar Banda
Bahr el Ghazal
Bahr el Ghazal
Bahr el Jebel

Gold Coast
Grain Coast
Ivory Coast
C. Palmas
Slave Coast
Bight of Benin

Adamawa Highlands
Cameroon Peak 4070
Bioko

Uele
Oubangi
Zaire (Congo)

L. Mobutu Sese Seko
Chutes Ruwenzori
Boyoma 5109
Ruwenzori
L. Edward

Turkana

Elgon 4321
Kenya 5199

▼6363

Bight of Bonny
Gulf of Guinea
Príncipe
São Tomé
C. Lopez
Annobón

Ogoué

Congo

Basin

Zaïre (Congo)
Kasai
Sankuru

Pool Malebo

Kasai

Lualaba
L. Kivu

L. Victoria
Kilimanjaro 5895

INDIAN
OCEAN

Pemba
Zanzibar

Ascension

ATLANTIC

OCEAN

St. Helena

Cuanza

Cuango

Kasai

Shaba

Bié Plateau

Cuando

Zambezi

Lomani
L. Mweru
L. Bangweulu
Lupula
Malawi

Rungwe 2961
L. Nyasa
Ruvuma

L. Tanganyika

C. Delgado
Comoro Is.

Aldabra Is.

Victoria Falls

Cunene
Cubango

Zambezi

Mulanje 3000
Shire

Mozambique Channel

Madagascar
▲2643

C. Fria

Namib Desert

Kalahari

Orange
Vaal
High Veld

Limpopo

Victoria Falls

Walvis Bay

Tropic of Capricorn

Delagoa Bay

Réunion

Orange

Drakensberg 3482

Compass B. 2505
Nuweveldberge
Gr. Karoo
Swartberg

C. of Good Hope
C. Agulhas
Agulhas Bank

Algoa Bay

---

ft m

2 000 4000

9000 3000

6000 2000

4500 1500

3000 1000

1200 400

600 200

0 0

200 600

2000 6000

4000 12 000

6000 18 000

m ft

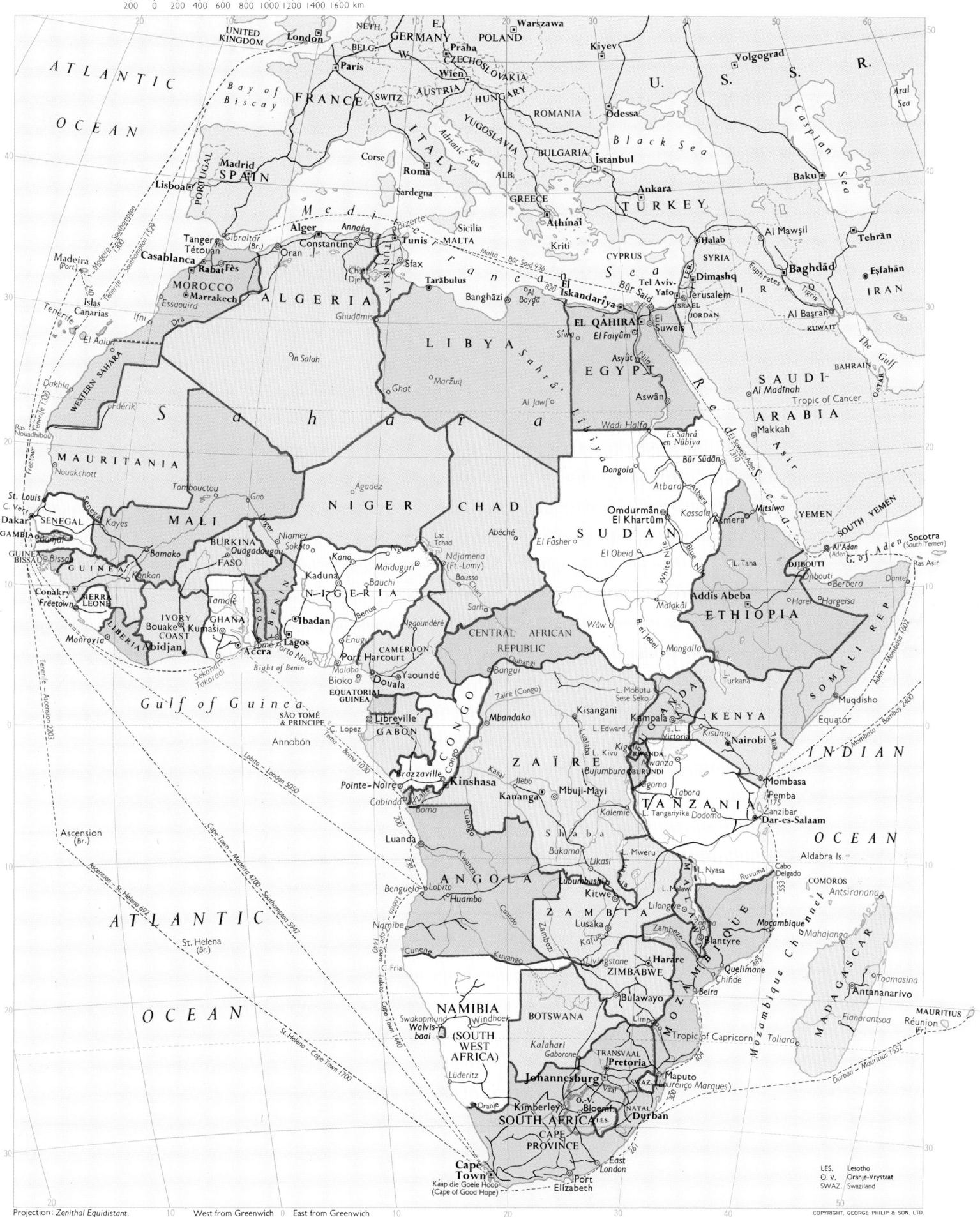

1 : 40 000 000

200 0 200 400 600 800 1000 miles

200 0 200 400 600 800 1000 1200 1400 1600 km

ATLANTIC OCEAN

UNITED KINGDOM London NETH. GERMANY POLAND Warszawa Kiyev Volgograd

Bay of Biscay FRANCE BELG. W. Praha CZECHOSLOVAKIA Kiyev U. S. S. R.

Paris SWITZ. AUSTRIA HUNGARY ROMANIA Odessa Caspian Sea

Madrid SPAIN ITALY Corse Roma Adriatic Sea YUGOSLAVIA BULGARIA Black Sea İstanbul Ankara Baku Aral Sea

Lisboa PORTUGAL Sardegna ALB. GREECE TURKEY Athínaì Kriti

Madeira (Port.) Tanger Tétouan Alger Constantine Annaba Bizerte Tunis MALTA Sicilia CYPRUS SYRIA Halab Al Mawşil Tehrān

Casablanca Rabat Fès Oran TUNISIA Sfax Tarābulus Bûr Said 936 El Iskandarîya Tel Aviv-Yafo Dimashq Baghdād Eşfahān

MOROCCO Marrakech Djel... ALGERIA LIBYA Banghāzī Al Bayda EL QÂHIRA Jerusalem ISRAEL JORDAN El Başrah IRAN

Essaouira Ghudāmis Sahrā El Suwei Siwa El Faiyûm KUWAIT The Gulf

El Aaiun Ifni Dra In Salah Marzūq EGYPT Aswân Tropic of Cancer SAUDI- BAHRAIN

WESTERN SAHARA Ghat Al Jawf Aswân Al Madînah ARABIA QATAR

Dakhla Frdérik S a h a r a Wadi Halfa Es Sahrâ en Nûbiya Bûr Sûdân Makkah Asir

MAURITANIA Nouakchott Dongola Atbara Mitsiwa YEMEN SOUTH YEMEN Socotra (South Yemen)

St. Louis Tombouctou Gaó Agadez El Fâsher SUDAN Kassala Asmera Al 'Adan (Aden) Ras Asir G. of Aden

C. Verde Dakar SENEGAL Kayes MALI NIGER CHAD El Obeid DJIBOUTI Berbera Hargeisa

GAMBIA Bamako BURKINA Niamey Sokoto Abéché Omdurmân El Khartûm Djibouti L. Tana Dante

GUINEA BISSAU Bissau GUINEA Kankan FASO Ouagadougou Kano Maiduguri Lac Tchad Ndjamena (Ft.-Lamy) Bousso Addis Abeba Harer ETHIOPIA

Conakry Freetown SIERRA LEONE Tamale Kaduna Bauchi Sarh Wāw Malakal Mongalla L. Turkana SOMALI REP

LIBERIA Monrovia IVORY COAST Bouake GHANA Kumasi NIGERIA Ibadan Benue Nggoundéré CAMEROON CENTRAL AFRICAN REPUBLIC Bangui Oubangi Muqdisho

Abidjan Accra Porto Novo Lagos Port Harcourt Enugu Yaoundé Douala Bangui Zaïre (Congo) Mombasa Bombay 2400 INDIAN OCEAN

Sekondi-Takoradi Bight of Benin EQUATORIAL GUINEA Malabo Bioko São Tomé & Príncipe Libreville GABON CONGO Mbandaka Kisangani UGANDA Kampala L. Victoria KENYA Nairobi Equator

Gulf of Guinea C. Lopez Annobón Brazzaville Kinshasa ZAÏRE L. Edward L. Kivu Kigali RWANDA Kisumu Mwanza Mombasa

Ascension (Br.) Pointe-Noire Cabinda Boma Ilebo Kananga Mbuji-Mayi Bujumbura BURUNDI Kigoma Tabora TANZANIA Dodoma Pemba 175 Zanzibar Dar-es-Salaam

St. Helena (Br.) Luanda Kasai Shaba Kalemie L. Tanganyika OCEAN

Benguela Lobito ANGOLA Bukama Likasi Mweru L. Nyasa Cabo Delgado 553 COMOROS Antsiranana

Namibe Huambo Lubumbashi Kitwe ZAMBIA L. Malawi Lilongwe Moçambique Mahajanga

NAMIBIA Swakopmund Windhoek BOTSWANA Lusaka Kafue Zambeze Blantyre MALAWI MOZAMBIQUE Toamasina MADAGASCAR MAURITIUS Réunion (Fr.)

Walvis-baai (SOUTH WEST AFRICA) Kalahari Gaborone Harare ZIMBABWE Bulawayo Limpopo Quelimane Chinde Beira Antananarivo Fianarantsoa

Lüderitz Cunene Kuvango TRANSVAAL Pretoria Maputo SWAZ. Lourenço Marques Toliara

ATLANTIC OCEAN Oranje Johannesburg Vaal Tropic of Capricorn

Kimberley Bloemf. NATAL Durban

SOUTH AFRICA CAPE PROVINCE O.V. LES. East London

Cape Town Port Elizabeth Kaap die Goeie Hoop (Cape of Good Hope)

LES. Lesotho
O.V. Oranje-Vrystaat
SWAZ. Swaziland

Projection: Zenithal Equidistant. West from Greenwich East from Greenwich

COPYRIGHT. GEORGE PHILIP & SON. LTD.

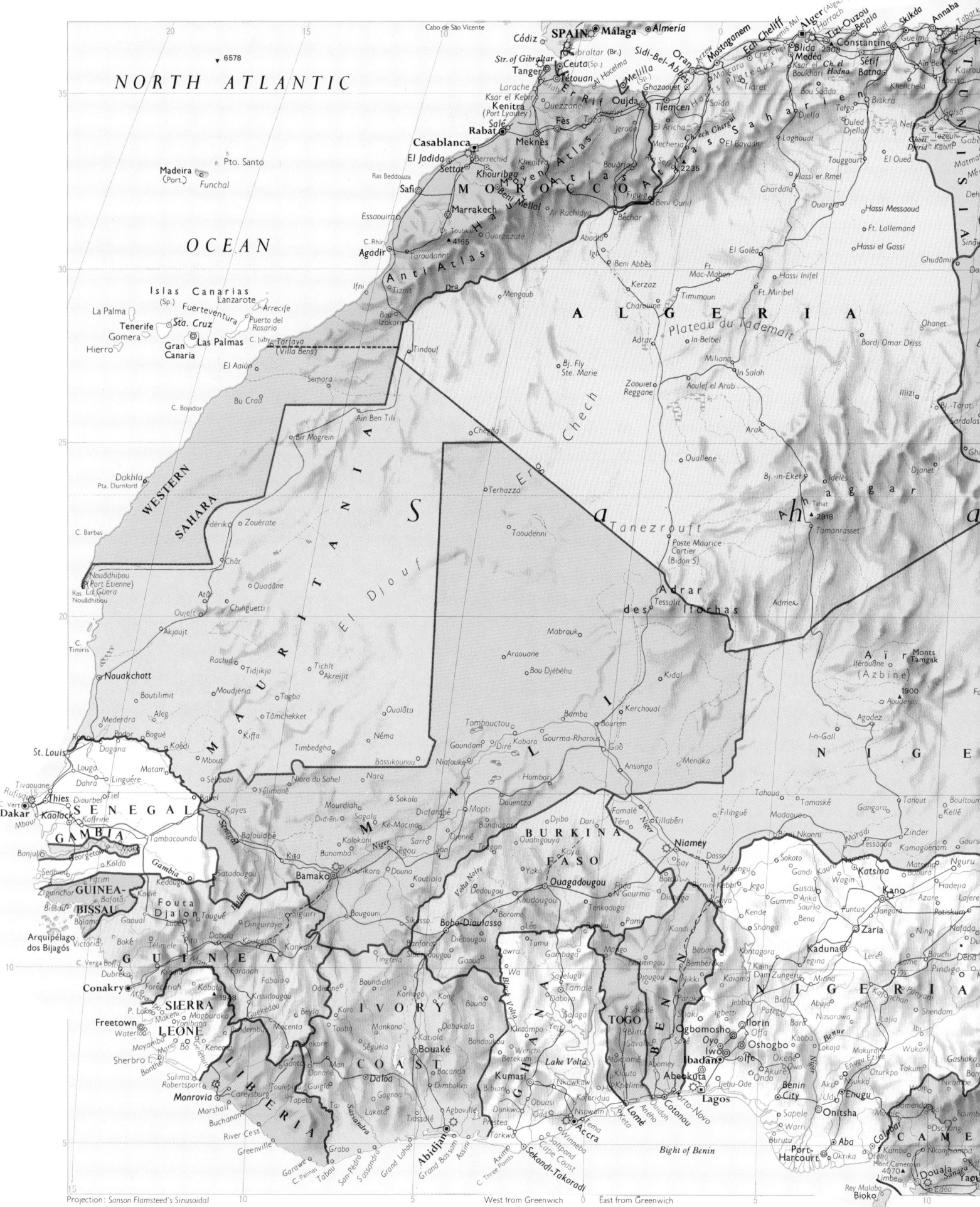

NORTH ATLANTIC

OCEAN

SPAIN

MOROCCO

WESTERN SAHARA

MAURITANIA

ALGERIA

MALI

SENEGAL

GAMBIA

GUINEA-BISSAU

GUINEA

SIERRA LEONE

LIBERIA

IVORY COAST

BURKINA FASO

GHANA

TOGO

BENIN

NIGERIA

NIGER

1:15 000 000

100 0 100 200 300 400 miles
100 0 100 200 300 400 500 600 km

MEDITERRANEAN SEA

TURKEY
Antalya
Antalya Körfezi
Ródhos
Karpathos
İskenderun Körfezi
İskenderun
Al Ladhiqiya
CYPRUS
Nikosia
Limassol
Hama'
Homs
Tarabulus
LEBANON
Bayrūt
Dimashq (Damascus)
'Akko
Haifa
ISRAEL
Tel Aviv-Yafo
Jerusalem (Al Quds)
Gaza
Ammān
JORDAN
Ar Rutbah
IRAQ
Al Mawşil (Mosul)
Nahr Dijlah (Tigris)
Mesopotamia
Nahr al Furāt
Bādiyat ash Shām

Sicily
Ragusa
C. Passero
MALTA
Lampedusa (It.)
Pantelleria (It.)
Menzel-Temime
C. Bon

Tarābulus (Tripoli)
Al Khums
Zlītan
Misrātah
Al Qaşabt
Gharyān
968
Banī Walīd
Mizdah
Zuwārah
Jādū

Banghāzī (Benghazi)
Suluq
Al Bu'ayrāt
878
Al Mar
Tūkrah
Tulmaythah (Cyrene)
Shahhāt
Apollonia
Marsá Susah
Darnah
Khalīj Bunbah
Tubruq (Tobruk)
Bardia
Sīdī Barrāni
Khalīg el Sallūm
Salūm
Marsá Matrūh
El Daba
El Alamein
(Rosetta) Rashīd
El Iskandarīya (Alexandria)
Damanhûr
El Mansûra
El Mahalla el Kubra
Dumyât
Bûr Sa'îd
El Qantara
Ismâ'îlîya
El 'Arîsh

Surt
Khalīj Surt
Ajdābiyah
Marsa Brega
Ra's Al-Unuf
Al 'Uqaylah
Zueitina

Tarābulus
Al Jaghbûb
Siwa
Qâra
EL QÂHIRA (Cairo)
Zagazig
El Gîza
Helwân
El Suweis
El Faiyûm
Beni Suef

LIBYA
Hûn
Marādah
Awjilah
Al 'Iraq
Zillah
Munkhafed el Qattâra (Qattâra Depression)
El Bawîti
Beni Mazâr
El Minya
Mallawi
Manfalût
Asyût
Dairût
Abu Tig
Esh Sharqîya
Es Sahrâ'
El Tîh
Gebel
Sînâ'
An Nafūd
Tabūk
Mādā'in Sālih

SAUDI ARABIA
Taymā'

Sabhā
Brach
Adri
Tasāwah
Marzūq
Tmassah
Wāw al Kabīr
Al Qatrūn
Al Jazirah
Rebiana
Al Jawf
Al Kufrah

Fezzan
Zawīa
Idehan
Marzūq

EGYPT
Sahrâ' Lîbîya
Cyrenaica
1200
Qasr Farâfra
El Wâhât el-Dakhla
El Qasr
Mût
El Wâhât el-Khârga
Bâris
El Khârga
Qena
El Uqsur (Luxor)
Qûs
Isnâ
Idfû
Kôm Ombo
Aswân
Aswân High Dam
Sadd el Aali
Dunqul
El Shallal
Buheiret en Naser (Lake Nasser)

Akhmim
Sohâg
Girga
Tahta
Bûr Safâga
Quseir
El Wejh
Umm Laj
Al Madinah
Yanbu' al Bahr

RED SEA
Râs Bânâs
Bîr Shalatein
Halaib
Ras Hadarba
Rabigh Qasr
At Tâ'if
Jiddah
Makkah (Mecca)
Al Lith

Tropic of Cancer
Toummo
Madama
Aozou
Bardai
3150 Tarso Emissi
Ma'ton es Sarra
Uweinat
1893
Ayn al 'Uwaynat
El Wâhât el Selîma
2nd Cataract
Wadi Halfa
Es Sahrâ en Nûbiya
Bîr Ungât
Bîr Shalatein
Emi Koussi 3415
Gouri

Tibesti
Zouar
Anaye
Bilma
Kosha
Abri
Delgo
(Nubian Desert)
Nukheila
Bir 'Atrun
Laqiya Arba'în
3rd Cataract
Argo
Dongola
El Kab
Abu Hamed
Abû Dis
4th Cataract
BAHR EL AHMAR
Bûr Sûdân (Port Sudan)
2635
Suakin
Sinkat
Muhammad Qol
Ras Abu Shagara
Gebeit Mine
Haiya Junction
Tokar
Trinkitat
Ras Kasar

Borkou
Ounianga-Kébir
Ounianga Sérir
Depression du Mourdi
Faya-Largeau
Fada
Ennedi

SHAMÂL DÂRFÛR
El Khandaq
Kareima
Merowe
Korti
Berber
Atbara
Ed Dâmer
Musmar
Adarama
Derudeb
Karora
El Khandaq
Ed Debba

Djourab
Oum Chalouba
Zigey
Biltine
Tiné
Iriba
Kutum
Hamrata esh Sheykh
Sodiri

CHAD
Rig-Rig
Arada
Harazé
Abéché
Adré
El Junaynah
Kabkabiyah
El Fasher
Umm Keddada
Umm Bel
Bara
SHAMÂL KORDOFAN
Ed Dueim
El Geteina
Rufa'a
Kassala
Khashm el Girba
Gedaref
El Gezira
Wâd Medanî
Mafâza

Eritrea
Kerem
Nakfa
Akordat
Barentu
Asmera
Mitsiwa
Zula

6th Cataract
Shendi
Geili
El Khartûm Bahri (Khartoum)
Omdurmân
El Khartûm
SUDAN

Lac Tchad
Bol
Kukawa
Massakory
Massaguet
Ndjamena (Fort Lamy)
Bokoro
Ati
Oum Hadjer
Am Dam
Mongo
Guéréda
Goz Beida
Biltine
Zalingei
Marrah 3088
Nyâlâ
Wad Banda
En Nahud
Abû Zabad
Er Rahad
El Obeid
Rashad
Dilling
El Laqâwa
Heiban
Kadugli
Talodi
Kaka
Renk
Malakâl
Melut
Kodok
A'ÂLI EN NIL
Tungaru

Dikwa
Kousséri
Massénya
Bousso
Melfi
Am Timan
Haraze
Aouka
Rahad al Bardî
Buram
Abu Matariq
Muglad
JANUB DÂRFÛR
Iddl Ghanam
JANUB KORDOFAN
El Oddiya

Bongor
Guelengdeng
Léré
Pala
Kélo
Lai
Doba
Moundou
Bénoye
Moïssala
Sarh
Kyabé
Kaélé
Koumra
Ndélé
Kafia Kingi
Nyâmlêll
Birao
Songo
BAHR EL GHAZAL
Râga
Aweil
Gogrial
Wâw
Deim Zubeir
Tonj
BUHEIRAT
Rumbêk
Yirol
Bôr
JONGLEI
Kongor
Pibor P.

CENTRAL AFRICAN REPUBLIC
Markounda
Batangafo
Kaga Bandoro
Bria
Bozoum
Bocaranga
Bouca
Bakala
Yalinga
Ippy
Bambari
Grimari
Bakouma
Djema
Rafaï
Obo
Amâdi
GHARB EL ISTIWA'IYA
Maridî
Tombura
Yambio
Tali P.
Nagishot
SHARQ EL ISTIWA'IYA
Jûba
Mongalla
Kapoeta
Torit

Bangui
Mbaiki
Bimbo
Mobaye
Bangassou
Zémio
Yakoma
Bondo
ZAÏRE (CONGO)
Uele
Doruma
Niangara
Dungu
Faradje
Kajo Kaji
KENYA
Lokitaung
L. Turkana

Addis Abeba (Addis Ababa)
ETHIOPIA
Nekemte
Gimbi
Gore
Gambela
L. Tana
Debre Tabor
Mekdela
Mota
Debre Markos
L. Zwai
4200 L. Shamo
L. Abaya
Chew Bahir (L. Stefanie)
Yabelo
Mega

COPYRIGHT. GEORGE PHILIP & SON. LTD.

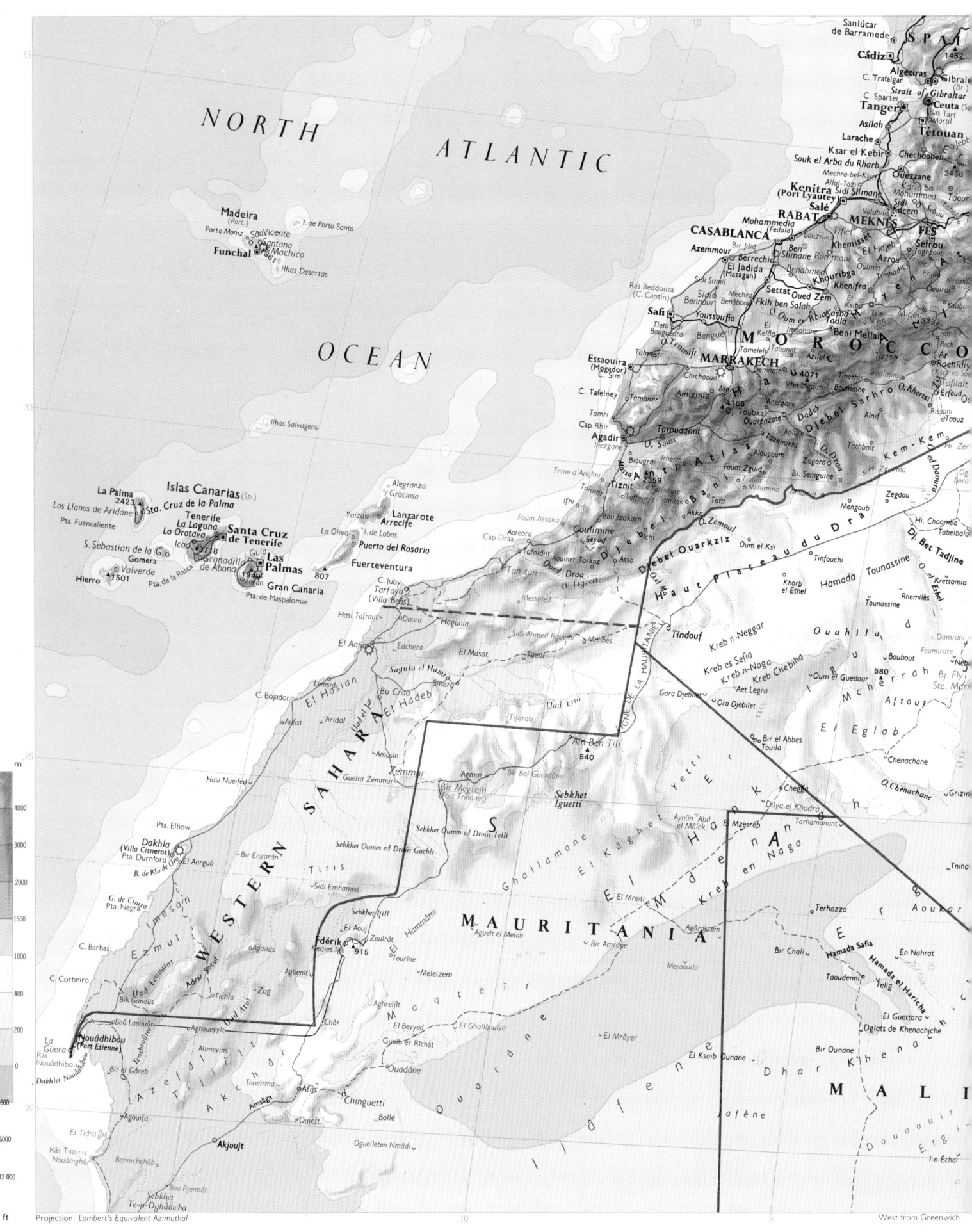

NORTH

ATLANTIC

OCEAN

Madeira (Port.)
Porto Moniz São Vicente I. de Porto Santo
Santana Machico
Funchal 667
Ilhas Desertas

Ilhas Salvagens

Islas Canarias (Sp.)
La Palma 2423 Alegranza
Los Llanos de Aridane Sta. Cruz de la Palma Graciosa
Pta. Fuencaliente Tenerife Lanzarote
La Laguna Arrecife
La Orotava Santa Cruz La Oliva I. de Lobos
S. Sebastian de la G. Icod 3718 de Tenerife Puerto del Rosario
Gomera Guia Las Fuerteventura
Valverde Granadilla Palmas
Hierro 1501 de Abona 807
Pta. de la Rasca 1940 Gran Canaria
Pta. de Maspalomas

WESTERN SAHARA

MAURITANIA

MALI

Projection: Lambert's Equivalent Azimuthal

West from Greenwich

SPAI
Sanlúcar de Barrameda
Cádiz 1452
Algeciras C. Trafalgar Gibral (Br.)
C. Spartel Strait of Gibraltar
Tanger Ceuta (S
C. Tarf
Asilah Tétouan
Larache Chechaouen Martil
Ksar el Kebir
Souk el Arba du Rharb
Mechra-bel-Ksiri
Allal-Tazi Quezzane 2456
Kenitra Sidi Slimane Karia ba Taour
(Port Lyautey) Salé Sidi
RABAT MEKNES FES
Mohammedia Volubilis Sefrou
CASABLANCA (Fedala) El Hajeb
Azemmour Bir Jdid Ben Khemisset El Azrou
Berrechid Slimane Rommani
El Jadida Benahmed Khouribga
(Mazagan) Settat Oued Zem
Sidi Smail Bennour Mechra Fkih ben Salah Kasba-M Midel
Safi Youssoufia Oum er Rbia Beni Mellal 3737
Tleta Sidi Bo, Kasba T
Bouguedra Benguerir Kelâa El Kba Rich
Ras Beddouza Tamelelt Imi
(C. Cantin) MARRAKECH Demnate Rachidiy
Essaouira Chichaoua 4071 Tinerhir Erfoud
(Mogador) Tafilalt
C. Tafelney Amizmiz Asni Irhil Mgoun Boumalne Rissani
Tamanar Taroudannt 4185 Ouarzazate Dades Taouz
Tamri Toubkal Anergane Aloujoum Tazenakht Djebel Sarhro O. Rheris
Cap Rhir Argana Biougra Zagora Hi. Zer
Agadir O. Souss Irhem Foum Zguid O. Draa Kem-Kem
Inezgane Taliouine Tazenakht Zegdou
Tiznit 2359 Mirhamin O. Dao
Ifni Tafraout Imitek Tata Bera
Goulimine Bou Izakarn Akka Hamada Mengoub Hi. Chagmba
Foum Assaka Aoreora Assa Tinfouchi Tabelbal
Cap Draa Tafnidilt Aouinet Torkoz Tounassine Dj. Bet Tadjine
Tan-tan Tafudirt Oued Draa Oum el Ksi Khorb Krettamia
O. Tigzerte Djebel Ouarkziz el Ethel Rhemilès
Messeied Haut Plateau du Dra Tounassine
C. Juby Sidi Ahmed Rouein Malibes Tindouf Kreb r. Neggar Ouahila Damrani
Tarfaya Tueat Kreb es Sefia Foumirate
(Villa Bens) Kreb n-Naga Oum el Guedour 580
Hasi Tafraut Hagunia Kreb Chebiha Bj. Fly
Daora Aet Legra Mcherrah Ste. Mar
El Aaiún Edchera El Masat Gara Djebilet Oum el Guedour Aftout
Lemsidi Saguia el Hamra Oro Djebilet El Eglab
C. Bojador Bu Craa Smara Uad Erni Bir el Abbes El Eglab
El Hasian El Hadeb Touila Chenachane
Aridal Tifarati Ain Ben Tili Chegga
Aufist 540 Chegga O. Chenachane
Hasi Nueifed Amasin Agmar Bir Bel Guerdâne Dâya el Khadra
Zemmur Bir el Abbes Tarhamanant Grizin
Guelta Zemmur Sebkhet Ayoûn 'Abd Mzereeb
Pta. Elbow Iguetti el Mâlek Terhazza
Dakhla Sebkhet Oumm ed Drous Telli Mzereeb Bir el Abbes En Nahrat
(Villa Cisneros) Sebkhet Oumm ed Drous Guebli El Kâghet Kreb en Naga
Pta. Durnford El Aargub Ghallamane Hamada Safia
B. de Río de Oro Bir Enzarán El Mreiti Terjemt Yelig
G. de Cintra Tiris Sidi Emhamed Bir Chali
Pta. Negra El Mraver Taoudenni El Guettara
C. Barbas Sebkhet Ijill Hammâmi Bir Amrâne Mejaâuda Bir Ounane Dglats de Khenachiche
El Aouj Zouirât Agârektoum El Ksaib Ounane
Agailas Fdérik 915 Aguelt el Melah
C. Corbeiro Mediet Ijill Tourine Terhazza
Aguenit Meleizem Taoudenni
Bir Gandús Adrar Tichla Zug Châr Maqtein El Ksaib Ounane
Uad Tenuilar Aghueylit M Dhar
Nouâdhibou Boû Lanouâr El Beyyed El Mrâyer
La Güera (Port Etienne) Aghreijit Ouarâne Khenachich
Rás Bir el Gâreb Gueib er Richât MALI
Nouâdhibou Dakhlet Naou Ahmeyim Ouadâne El Ksaib Dunane Ifâfène
Agouita Toueirma Chinguetti Tâfène
Amsâga Oujeft Bollé
Et Tidra Isi Oguelleten Nmâdi Douaouir Ergâ
Rás Tmiris Akjoujt In-n-Échaï
Nouâmghar Bou Rjeimât Bennichchâb
Sebkhet
Te-n-Dghâmcha

Scale bar (elevation legend):
ft m
12.000 4000
9000 3000
6000 2000
4500 1500
3000 1000
1200 400
600 200
0 0
200 600
2000 6000
4000 12 000
m ft

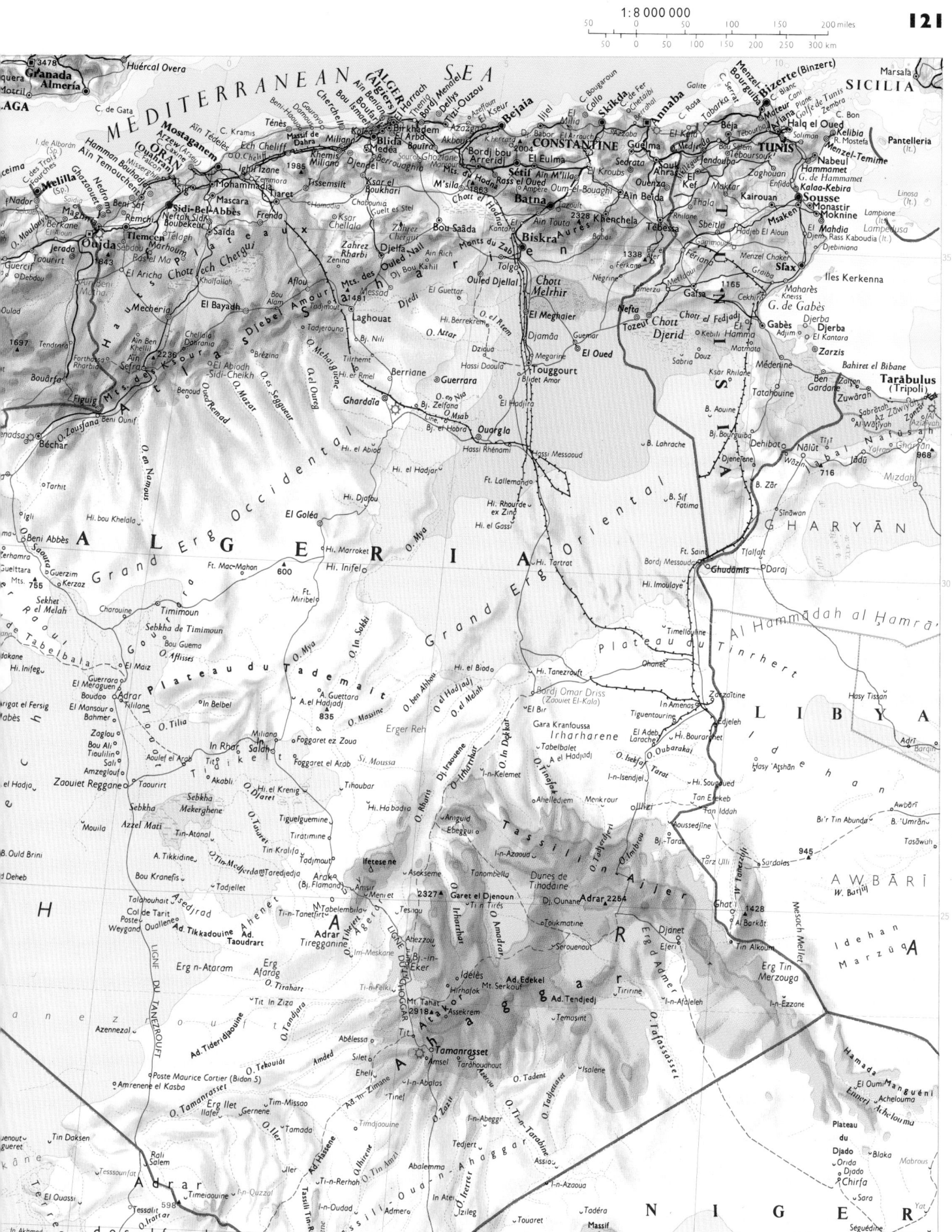

1:8 000 000

50   0   50   100   150   200 miles
50   0   50   100   150   200   250   300 km

MEDITERRANEAN SEA

SICILIA

ALGERIA

LIBYA

NIGER

TUNISIA

GHARYĀN

AWBĀRĪ

COPYRIGHT. GEORGE PHILIP & SON. LTD

East from Greenwich

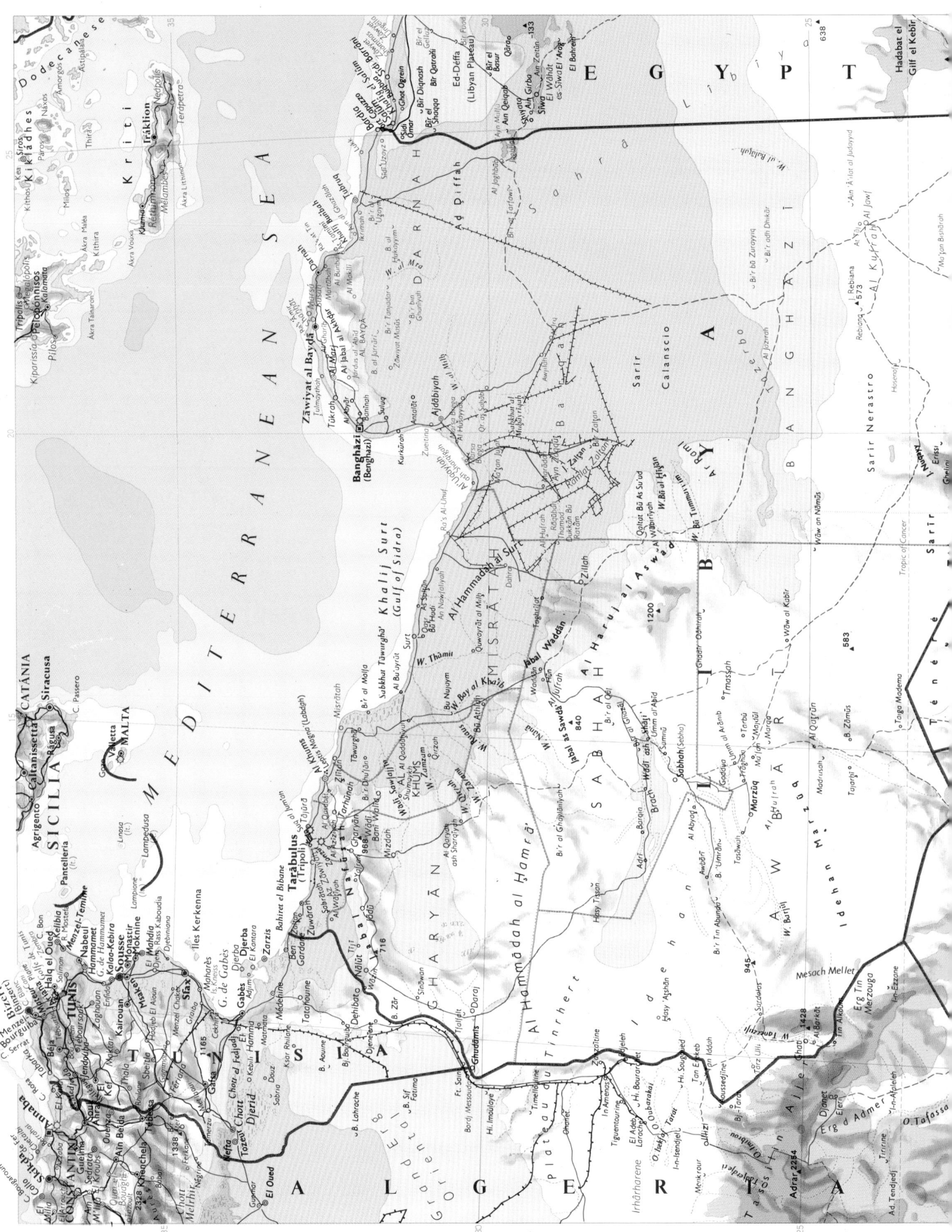
MEDITERRANEAN SEA
EGYPT
LIBYA
ALGERIA
TUNISIA
SICILIA
Agrigento
Caltanissetta
CATÁNIA
Siracusa
Ragusa
C. Passero
Pantelleria
Linosa
Lampedusa
Lampione
Gozo
Valletta
MALTA
Kríti
Iráklion
Khaniá
Réthimnon
Kikládhes
Dodecanese
Pelopónnisos
Kalamata
Tripolis
Megalópolis
Kiparissía
Pílos
Kithira
Skikda
Annaba
CONSTANTINE
Bizerte (Binzert)
Menzel Bourguiba
Béja
Halq el Oued
TUNIS
Kelibia
C. Bon
Nabeul
Hammamet
G. de Hammamet
Menzel-Temime
Kairouan
Sousse
Monastir
Moknine
Mahdia
Msaken
Sfax
Iles Kerkenna
G. de Gabès
Gabès
Djerba
Zarzis
Gafsa
Tozeur
Nefta
Chott Djerid
Chott el Fedjadj
Tébessa
Khenchela
El Oued
Médenine
Tataouine
Ben Gardane
Bahiret el Bibane
Zuwārah
Ţarābulus (Tripoli)
Al Khums
Leptis Magna (Labdah)
Misrātah
Gharyān
Tarhūnah
Jabal Nafūsah
Nālūt
Jādū
Mizdah
GHARYĀN
AL KHUMS
Wādī Sawfajjīn
Sabkhat Tāwurghā'
Khalij Surt (Gulf of Sidra)
Surt
Al Hammādah al Surt
MISRĀTAH
Banghāzī (Benghazi)
Zāwiyat al Bayḍā
Al Marj
Al Jabal al Akhdar
Darnah
Ţubruq
Bardia
Sidi Barrānī
Salūm
Ajdābiyah
DARNAH
Ad Diffah
Ed-Déffa (Libyan Plateau)
Sīwa
El Wâhât es-Sīwa
Ghudāmis
Grand Erg Oriental
Plateau du Tinrhert
Al Hammādah al Hamrā'
SABHAH
Jabal as Sawdā
Jabal Waddān
Al Harūj al Aswad
Zillah
Ramlat Zaltan
Sarir Calanscio
Sabhah (Sebha)
Wādī ash Shāţi'
Idehan
Marzūq
AWBĀRĪ
Idehan Marzūq
Mesach Mellet
Erg Tin Merzouga
Tassili n Ajjer
Adrar 2254
Djanet
Ghāt
BANGHĀZĪ
Tazerbo
Al Kufrah
Sarīr Nerastro
Tropic of Cancer
Ténéré
Hadabat el Gilf el Kebīr

1 : 8 000 000

50 0 50 100 150 200 miles

50 0 50 100 150 200 250 300 km

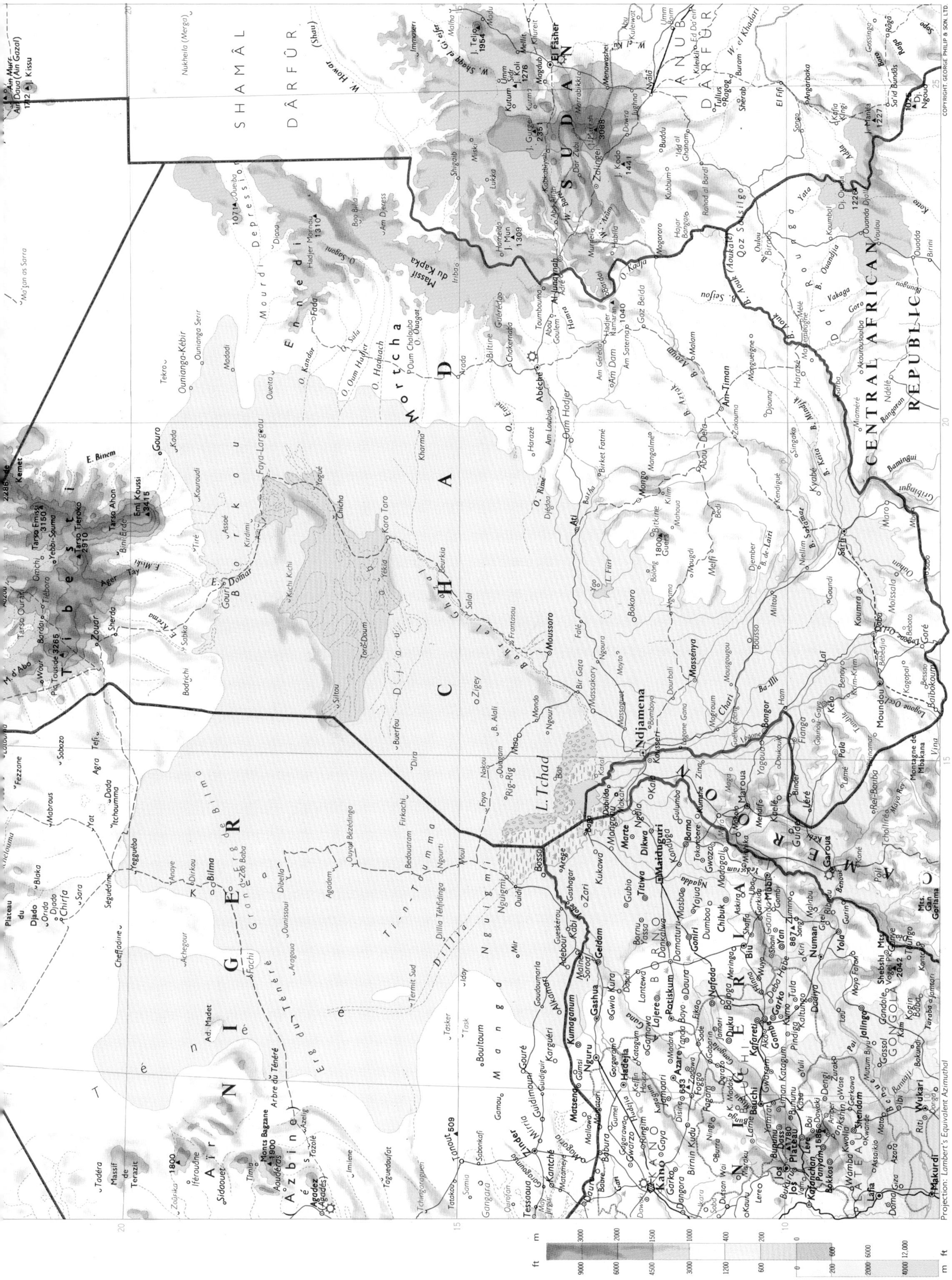

COPYRIGHT GEORGE PHILIP & SON LTD.

Projection: Lambert's Equivalent Azimuthal

SHAMÂL DÂRFÛR

S U D A N

JANÛB DÂRFÛR

CENTRAL AFRICAN REPUBLIC

C H A D

N I G E R

N I G E R I A

C A M E R O O N

T I B E S T I

Ennedi

Mortcha

Borkou

Djourab

Erg du Ténéré

L. Tchad

Ndjamena

Abéché

El Fasher

Nyâlâ

Kano

Maiduguri

Zinder

Agadez

Yola

Garoua

Moundou

BORNO

GONGOLA

Emi Koussi 3415

Kamet 22,867

m ft

3000 9000

2000 6000

1500 4500

1000 3000

400 1200

200 600

0 0

200 6000

2000 12,000

4000

THE NILE DELTA
1:4 000 000
MEDITERRANEAN SEA
EL ISKANDARÎYA (Alexandria)
Bûr Sa'îd (Port Said)
Dumyât (Damietta)
Rashîd (Rosetta)
El Mansûra
Tanta
Zagazig
Ismâ'iliya
El Suweis (Suez)
Heliopolis
EL QÂHIRA (Cairo)
El Gîza
Imbâbah
Helwân
Beni Suef
El Faiyûm
Birket Qârûn
Damanhûr
Benha
Shibîn el Kôm
East from Greenwich
MEDITERRANEAN SEA
EGYPT
Es Sahrâ' el Gharbîya
(Western Desert)
Munkhafad el Qattâra (Qattara Depression)
Marsá Matrûh
Siwa
El Wâhât el-Khârga
Buheiret en Naser (Lake Nasser)
Aswân
El Uqsur (Luxor)
Qena
Asyût
El Minyâ
Khalîg el Suweis
Tel Aviv-Yafo
Jerusalem (Al Quds)
'Ammân
JORDAN
ISRAEL
SAUDI ARABIA
Al Madînah (Medina)
Makkah (Mecca)
Jiddah
Tropic of Cancer
Bûr Sûdân (Port Sudan)
Berber
Second Cataract
Third Cataract
Fourth Cataract
Fifth Cataract
Es Sahrâ en Nûbîya (Nubian Desert)
BAHR EL AHMAR
Hadabat el Gilf el Kebîr
SHAMÂLÎYA
Gebel Abyad

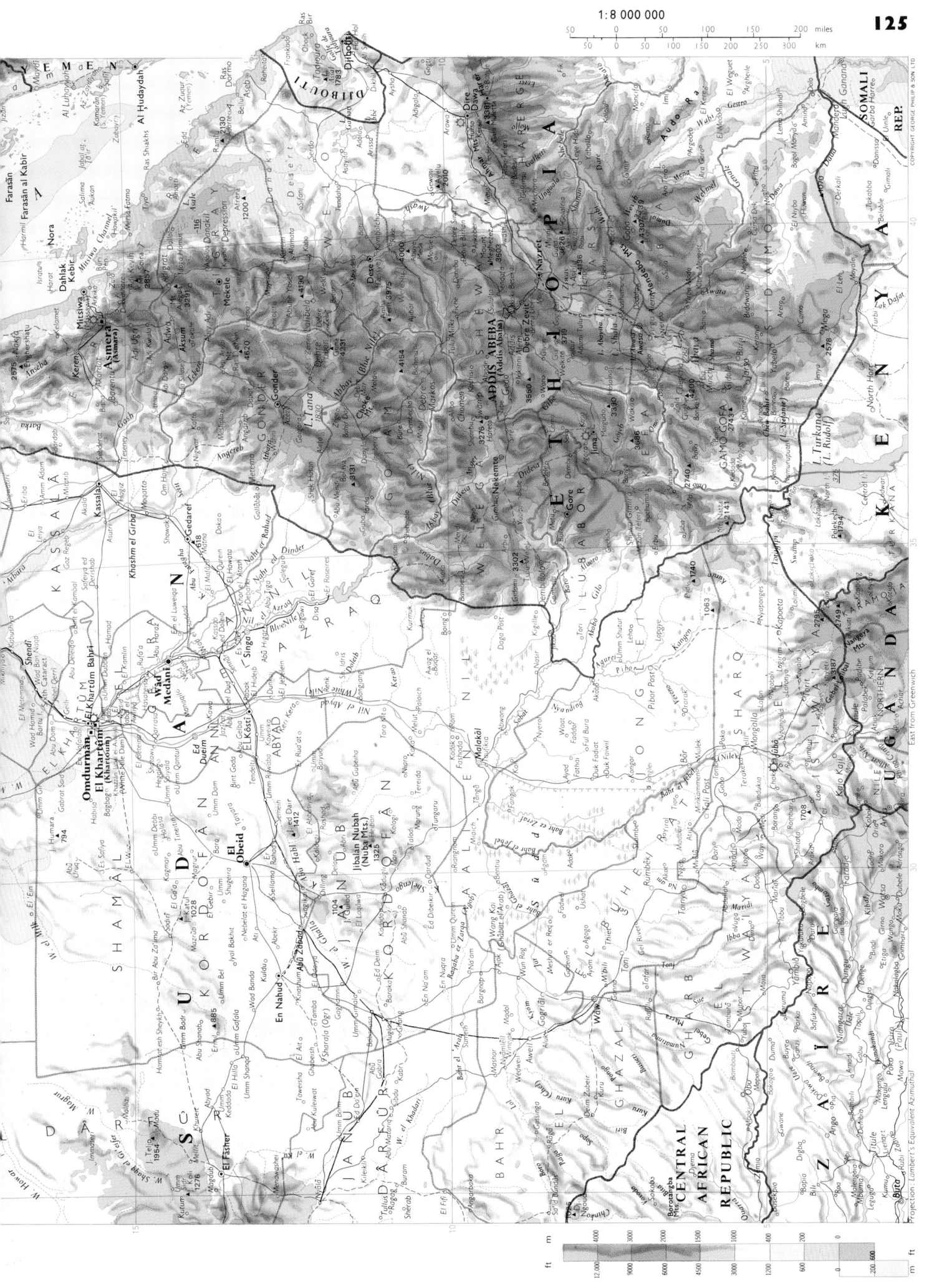
1:8 000 000
50 0 50 100 150 200 miles
50 0 50 100 150 200 250 300 km
YEMEN
DJIBOUTI
E T H I O P I A
S U D A N
K E N Y A
U G A N D A
Z A Ï R E
CENTRAL AFRICAN REPUBLIC
SOMALI REP.
ADDIS ABEBA (Addis Ababa)
Omdurmân
El Khartûm (Khartoum)
El Khartûm Bahri
Asmera (Asmara)
Djibouti
Dire Dawa
Gonder
Dese
Nazret
Jima
Gore
Nekemte
Wad Medani
Kassala
Gedaref
El Obeid
En Nahud
El Fasher
Malakâl
Wâw
Jûbâ
L. Tana
L. Turkana (L. Rudolf)
Projection: Lambert's Equivalent Azimuthal
East from Greenwich
m 4000 3000 2000 1500 1000 400 200 0
ft 12 000 9000 6000 4500 3000 1200 600 0
200 600
COPYRIGHT GEORGE PHILIP & SON. LTD

MAURITANIA

SENEGAL

GAMBIA

GUINEA-BISSAU

GUINEA

SIERRA LEONE

LIBERIA

IVORY COAST

Nouakchott

DAKAR

St. Louis

Bamako

Conakry

Freetown

Monrovia

Abidjan

Projection: Lambert's Equivalent Azimuthal

West from Gre

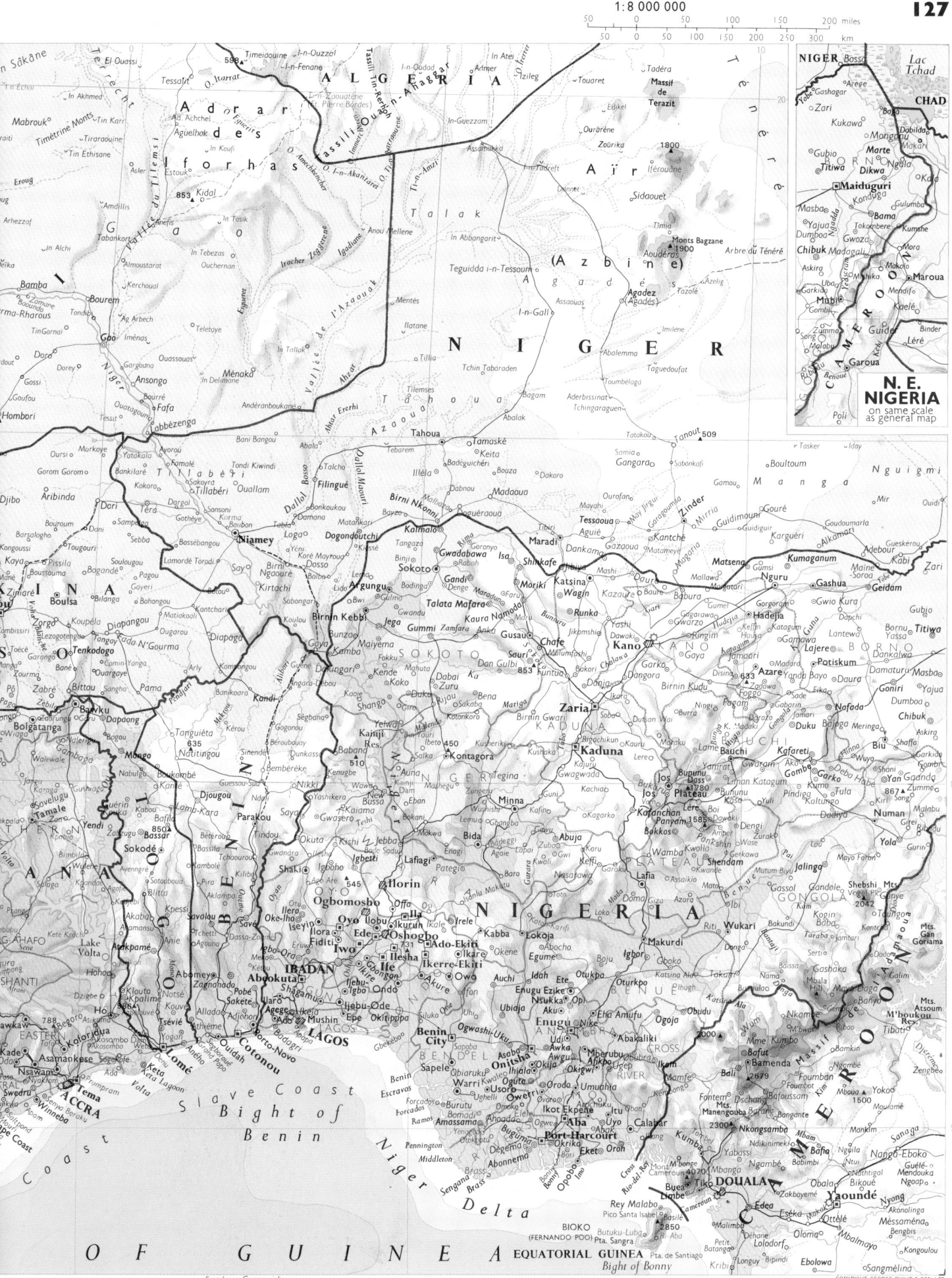

1:8 000 000

N. E. NIGERIA
on same scale
as general map

East from Greenwich

COPYRIGHT GEORGE PHILIP & SON, LTD.

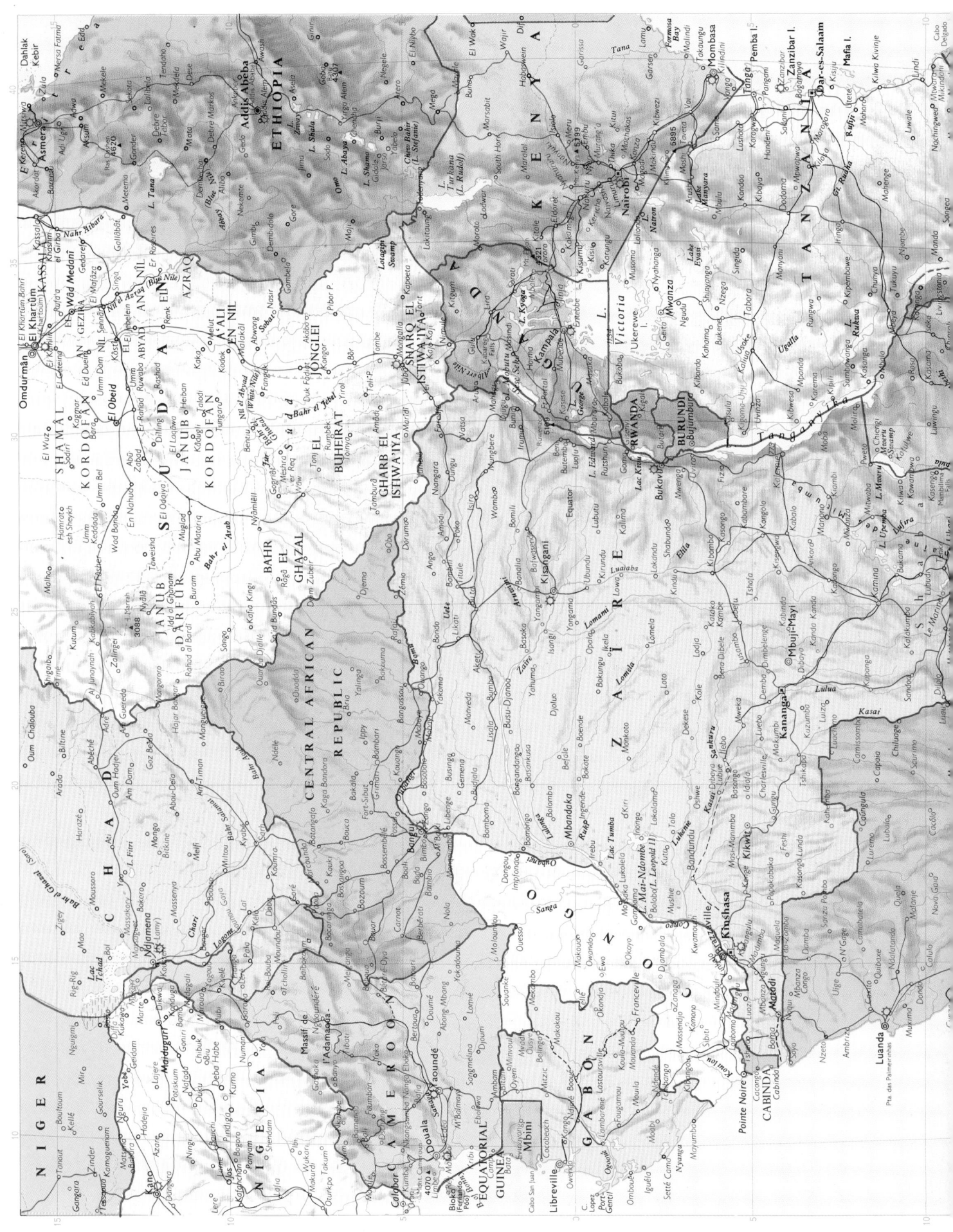
NIGER
CHAD
NIGERIA
CAMEROON
CENTRAL AFRICAN REPUBLIC
SUDAN
ETHIOPIA
KENYA
UGANDA
TANZANIA
RWANDA
BURUNDI
ZAÏRE
CONGO
GABON
EQUATORIAL GUINEA
CABINDA
SHAMÂL KORDOFÂN
JANUB KORDOFÂN
JANUB DARFÛR
BAHR EL GHAZAL
EL BUHEIRAT
JONGLEI
GHARB EL ISTIWA'IYA
SHARQ EL ISTIWA'IYA
A'ALI EN NIL
AN NÎL EL AZRAQ
KASSALA
GEZIRA
Omdurmân
El Khartûm
Wad Medanî
El Obeid
Addis Abeba
Asmera
Nairobi
Mombasa
Dar-es-Salaam
Zanzibar I.
Pemba I.
Mafia I.
Kampala
Kisangani
Kinshasa
Brazzaville
Luanda
Libreville
Douala
Yaoundé
Bangui
Ndjamena
Kano
Maiduguri
Bukavu
Bujumbura
Kananga
Mbuji-Mayi
Mbandaka
Kikwit
Pointe Noire
Matadi
Mwanza
Lac Tchad
L. Victoria
L. Turkana (L. Rudolf)
L. Tana
L. Mobutu Sese Seko
L. Kyoga
L. Edward
L. George
Lac Kivu
Tanganyika
L. Rukwa
L. Mweru
L. Mai-Ndombe (L. Leopold II)
Lac Tumba
Massif de l'Adamaoua
Mbini
Bioko (Fernando Póo)
Dahlak Kebir

1:15 000 000

100   0   100   200   300   400 miles
100   0 100 200 300 400 500 600 km

MADAGASCAR
On same scale as General Map

INDIAN OCEAN

Tropic of Capricorn

Îles Glorieuses
(Reunion)

Nosy Mitsio
Nosy Bé

Antsiranana

5349

Vohimarina
Antalaha

Sambava

Andoany
Ambilobe

Ambanja

Analalava
Antsohihy

Sofia

Maroantsetra

Mandritsara

Nosy Boraha

Toamasina
(Tamatave)

Mahajanga
Port-Bergé

Marovoay

Boriziny

Andriba

Mananara

Maevatanana

Ambatondrazaka

2876

Antananarivo(Tananarive)
Vohibinany

Soalala

Morovoay

Maintirano

Besalampy

Maevatanana
Miandrivazo

Ambatolampy

Morondava

Mahabo

Manja

Belo-Tsiribihina

Belo

Fianarantsoa

2643

Antsirabe

Ambositra

Mananjary

Nosy-Varika

Morombe

Manakara

Beroroha

Farafangana

Ankazoabo

2658

Vangaindrano

Ampanihy

Betioky

Sakaraha

Ihosy

Betroka

Ranomafana

Toliara

Monombo

Onilahy

Ambovombe

Tsihombe

Faradofay

Tanjon'i Vohimena

INDIAN OCEAN

Tropic of Capricorn

East from Greenwich

Projection: Sanson Flamsteed's Sinusoidal

ATLANTIC OCEAN

5283

INDIAN OCEAN

Mozambique

Mozambique Channel

ZIMBABWE

Harare (Salisbury)

Bulawayo

Victoria Falls

Livingstone

ZAMBIA

Kitwe
Ndola
Luanshya
Lusaka
Kabwe

Kariba Lake

L. Nyasa
(Malawi)

Blantyre
Lilongwe

Beira

Maputo
(Lourenço Marques)

SWAZILAND

TRANSVAAL

Pretoria
Johannesburg
Benoni
Springs
Germiston
Vereeniging

Soweto

ORANGE
FREE
STATE

Bloemfontein

Kimberley

LESOTHO

3482

NATAL

Pietermaritzburg
Durban

Port Shepstone

East London

King William's Town
Port Alfred
Port Elizabeth
St. Francis

CAPE PROVINCE

BOTSWANA

Gaborone

Kalahari

NAMIBIA
(SOUTH WEST AFRICA)

Windhoek
2483

Kalahari

Namaland

Namib Desert

Walvis Bay
Swakopmund

Lüderitz

Orange

SOUTH AFRICA

Cape Town
(Kaapstad)

Table Mt.

Kaap die Goeie Hoop
(C. of Good Hope)

C. Agulhas

Tropic of Capricorn

ANGOLA

Benguela

Namibe
Tombua

SOMALI REP.

ETHIOPIA

KENYA

UGANDA

TANZANIA

RWANDA

BURUNDI

CENTRAL AFRICAN REPUBLIC

NAIROBI

MOMBASA

DAR ES SALAAM

Zanzibar

Pemba I.

Kampala

Kisangani

L. Turkana (L. Rudolf)

Lake Victoria

L. Tanganyika

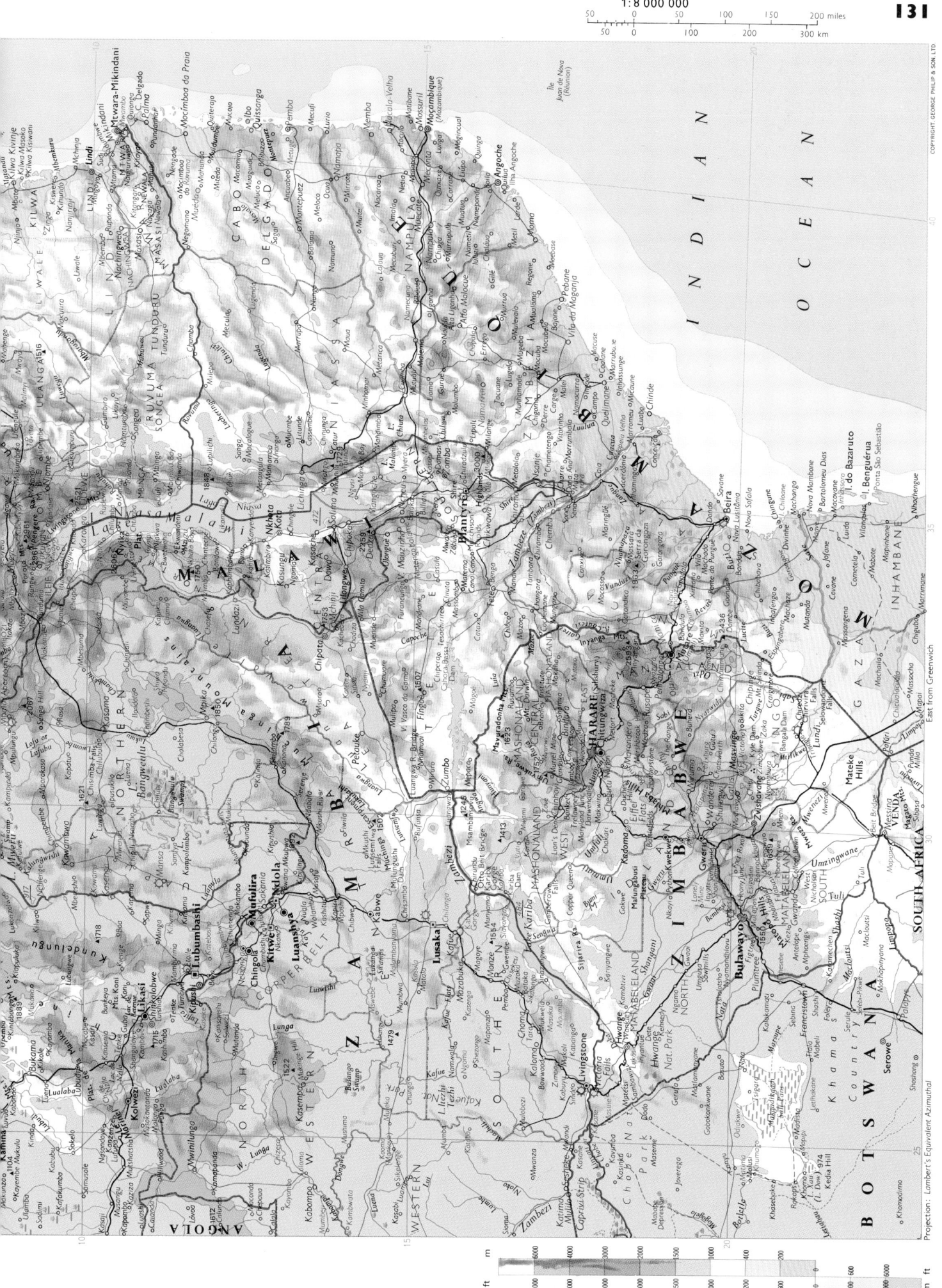

1:8 000 000

Projection: Lambert's Equivalent Azimuthal

East from Greenwich

I N D I A N   O C E A N

MOÇAMBIQUE

MALAWI

ZAMBIA

ZIMBABWE

BOTSWANA

SOUTH AFRICA

ANGOLA

Harare

Bulawayo

Lusaka

Beira

Lindi

Livingstone

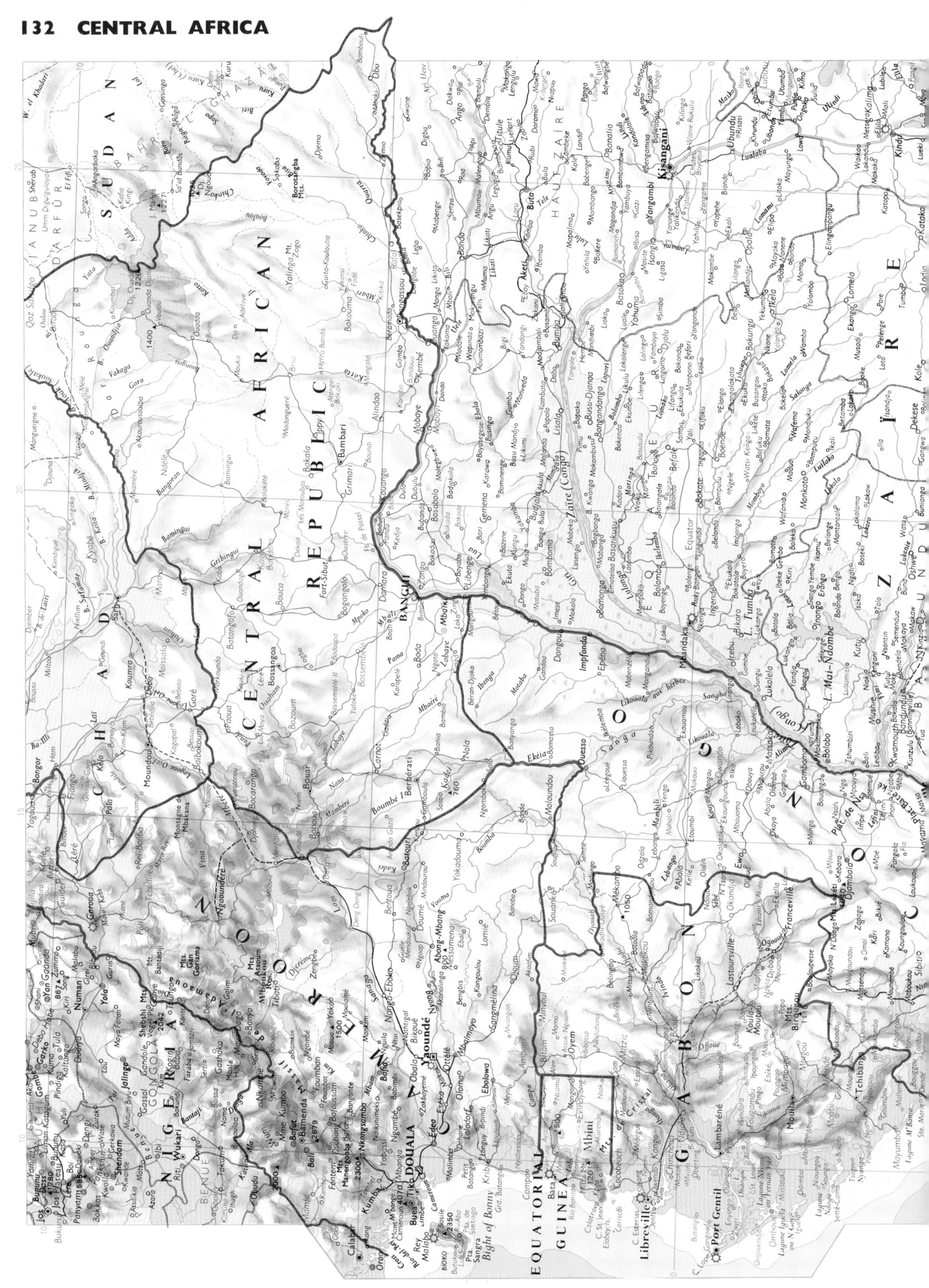

SUDAN
CENTRAL AFRICAN REPUBLIC
CHAD
NIGERIA
CAMEROON
EQUATORIAL GUINEA
GABON
CONGO
ZAÏRE
BANGUI
Yaoundé
DOUALA
Libreville
Port Gentil
Bata
Mbini
BIOKO
Bight of Bonny
Kisangani
Mbandaka
Ouesso
Berbérati
Bambari
Bangassou
Moundou
Sarh
Garoua
Ngaoundere
Franceville
Lambaréné
Zaïre (Congo)
Equator
HAUT ZAÏRE
DARFŪR
L. Mai-Ndombe
L. Tumba

1:8 000 000

50   100   150   200 miles

50   0   50   100   150   200   250   300 km

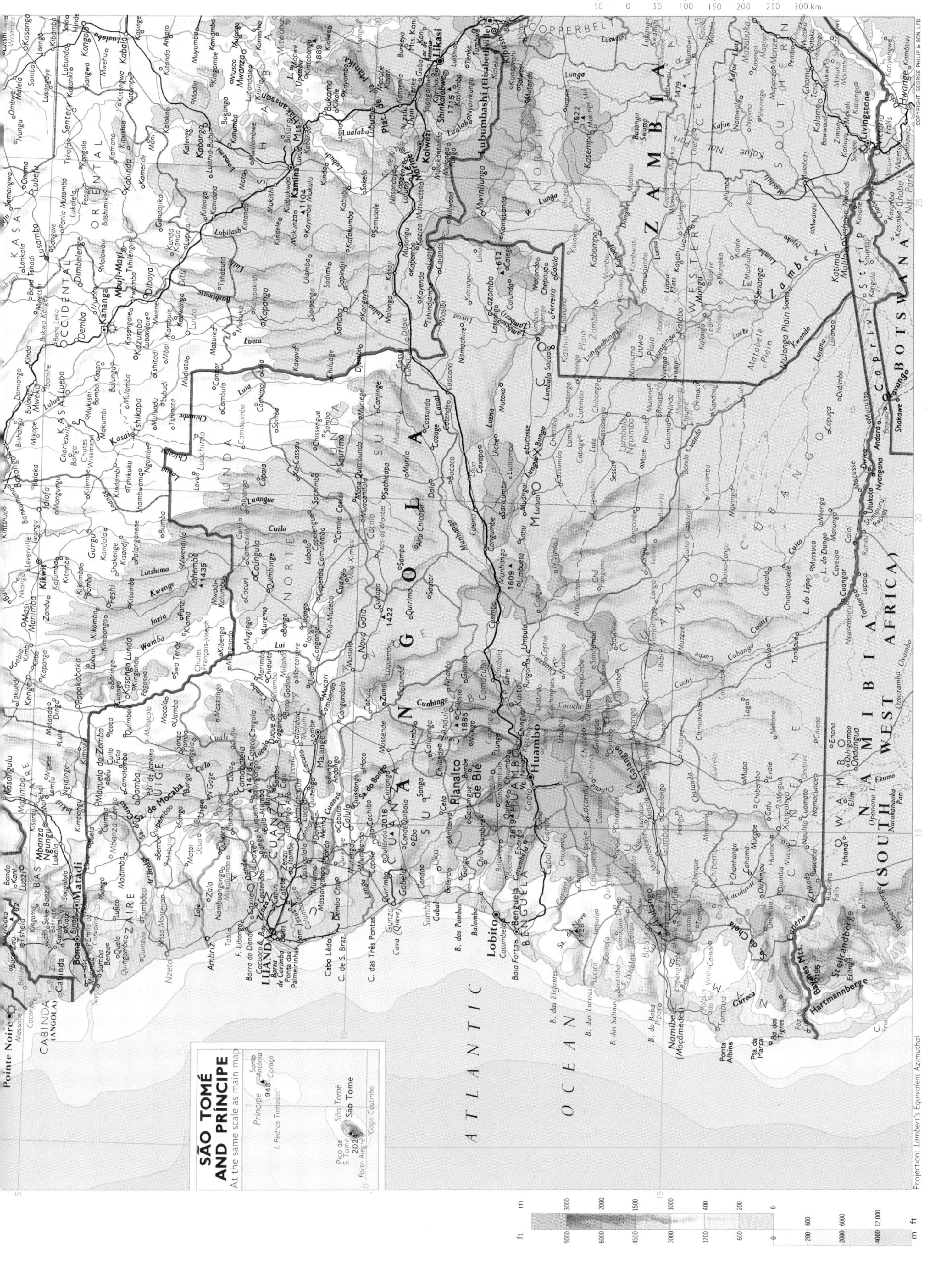

COPPERBELT

ZAMBIA

NORTH WESTERN

CENTRAL

SOUTHERN

WESTERN

ANGOLA

LUNDA NORTE

LUNDA SUL

MOXICO

CUANDO CUBANGO

KASAI OCCIDENTAL

KASAI ORIENTAL

ZAIRE

CABINDA (ANGOLA)

BOTSWANA

NAMIBIA (SOUTH WEST AFRICA)

OVAMBO

CUNENE

HUÍLA

BENGUELA

HUAMBO

BIÉ

CUANZA NORTE

CUANZA SUL

MALANGE

UÍGE

BAS ZAIRE

Pointe Noire

Lubumbashi (Elisabethville)

Likasi

Kolwezi

Kamina

Kananga

Mbuji-Mayi

Livingstone

Lobito

Benguela

Luanda

Matadi

Huambo

Planalto de Bié

Namibe (Moçâmedes)

ATLANTIC OCEAN

Projection: Lambert's Equivalent Azimuthal

COPYRIGHT GEORGE PHILIP & SON, LTD.

SÃO TOMÉ AND PRÍNCIPE
At the same scale as main map

Príncipe
948 Pico de Santo António
I. Pedras Tinhosas
São Tomé
Pico de S. Tomé 2024
S. Tomé
Porto Alegre
Gago Coutinho

m 3000 2000 1500 1000 400 200 0
ft 9000 6000 4500 3000 1200 600 200
m
ft 12,000 6000 4000 2000 600 200 0

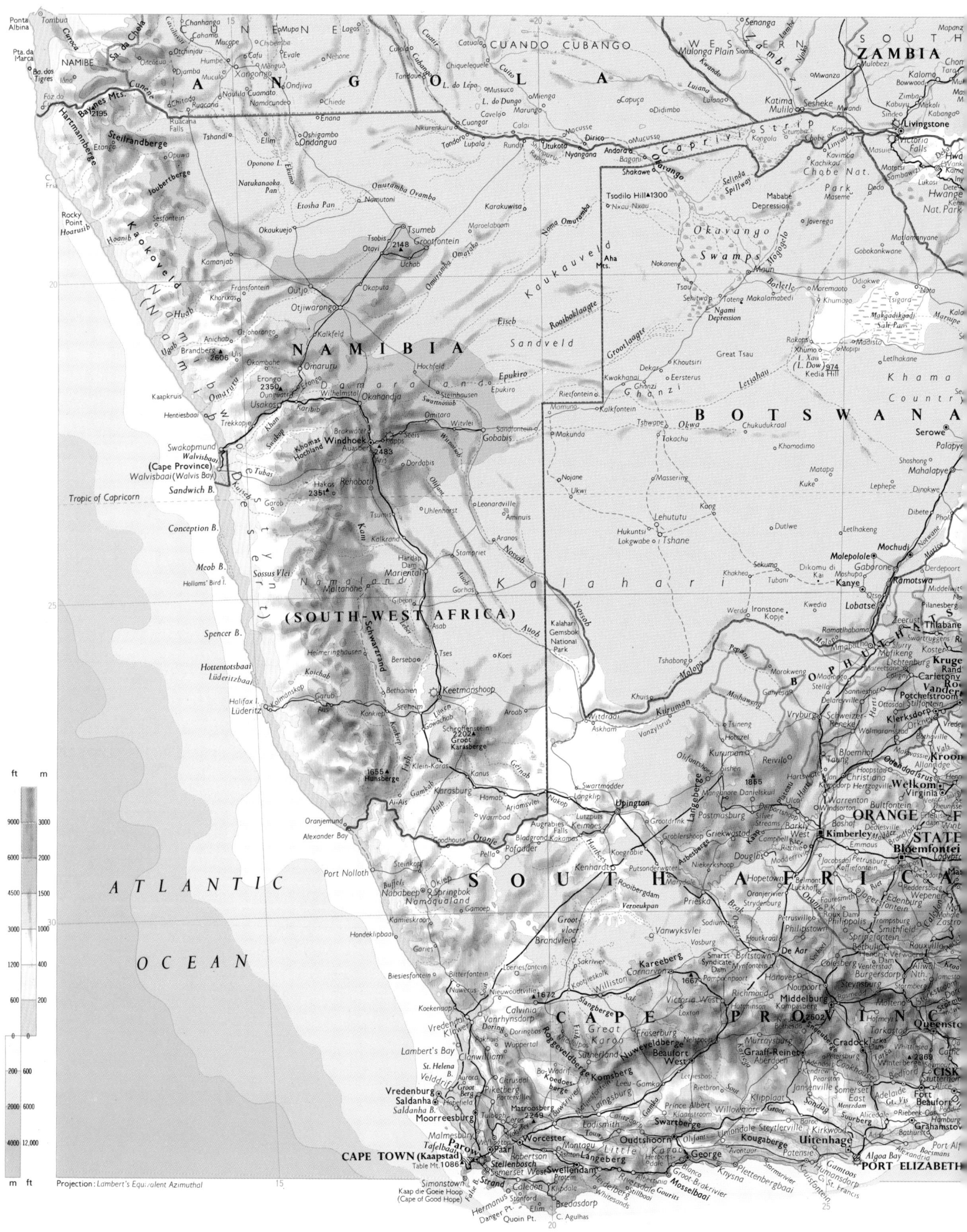
ANGOLA
ZAMBIA
NAMIBIA
(SOUTH-WEST AFRICA)
BOTSWANA
SOUTH AFRICA
CAPE PROVINCE
ORANGE FREE STATE
ATLANTIC
OCEAN
Tropic of Capricorn
CUANDO CUBANGO
Caprivi Strip
Okavango Swamps
Kalahari
Namib Desert
Kaokoveld
Damaraland
Namaland
Great Karoo
Little Karoo
Ngami Depression
Etosha Pan
Kalahari Gemsbok National Park
Windhoek
Swakopmund
Walvisbaai
(Cape Province)
Walvisbaai (Walvis Bay)
Lüderitz
Keetmanshoop
Tsumeb
Grootfontein
Otjiwarongo
Okahandja
Rehoboth
Mariental
Gobabis
Maun
Ghanzi
Kanye
Lobatse
Gaborone
Molepolole
Mochudi
Serowe
Livingstone
Victoria Falls
Upington
Kimberley
Bloemfontein
Welkom
Vryburg
Mafikeng
Klerksdorp
Springbok
Port Nolloth
Alexander Bay
Oranjemund
De Aar
Beaufort West
Graaff-Reinet
Cradock
Middelburg
Oudtshoorn
George
Mosselbaai
Worcester
Paarl
Stellenbosch
CAPE TOWN (Kaapstad)
Table Mt. 1086
Kaap die Goeie Hoop
(Cape of Good Hope)
C. Agulhas
Uitenhage
PORT ELIZABETH
Algoa Bay
Grahamstown
Saldanha
Vredenburg
Moorreesburg
Calvinia
Swellendam
Knysna
Plettenbergbaai
Kareeberg
Nuweveldberge
Komsberg
Langeberg
Swartberge
Projection: Lambert's Equivalent Azimuthal
ft
m
9000
3000
6000
2000
4500
1500
3000
1000
1200
400
600
200
0
200
600
2000
6000
4000
12,000
m
ft

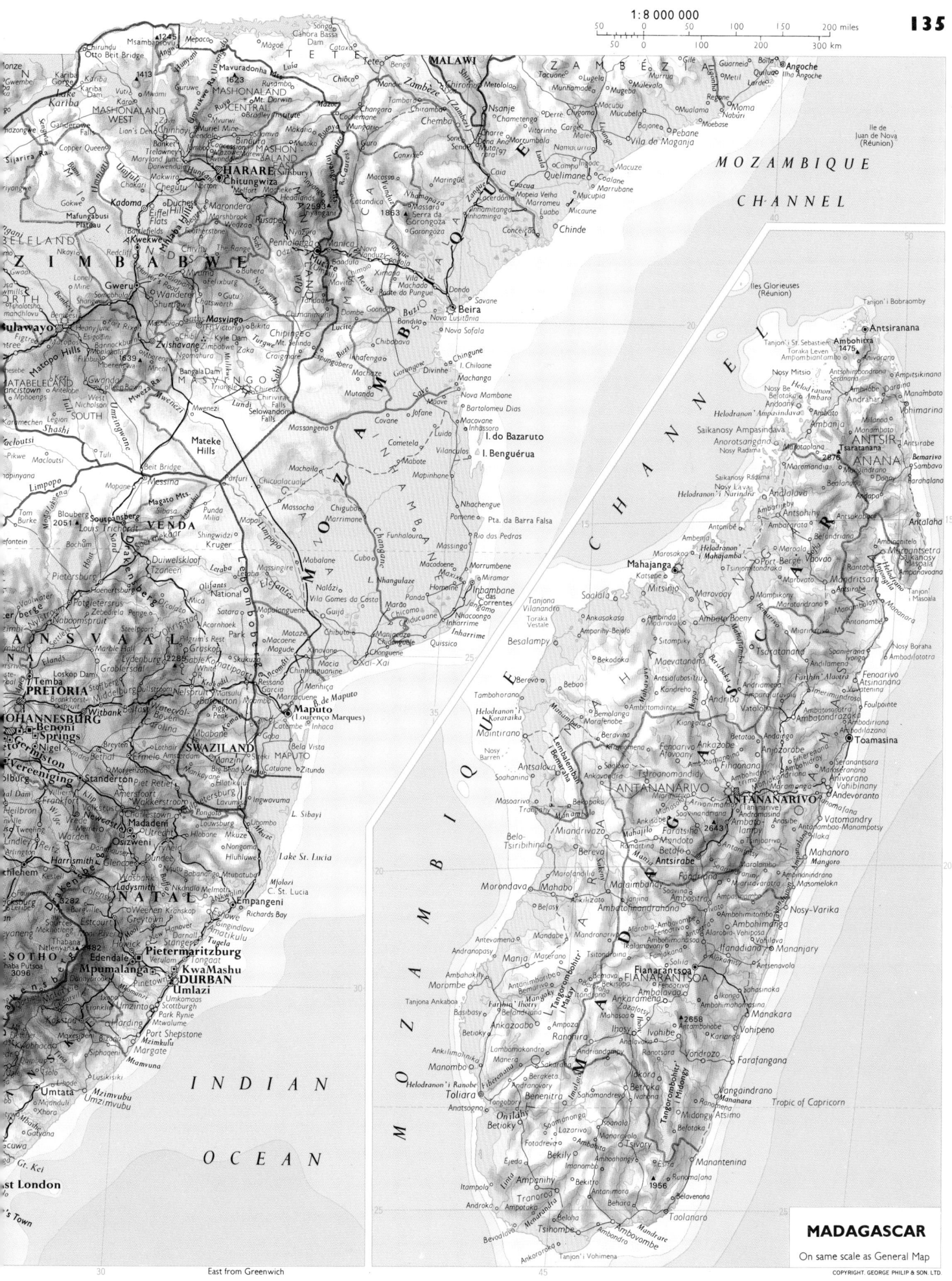

1 : 8 000 000

50   0   50   100   150   200 miles
50   0   100   200   300 km

MOZAMBIQUE

CHANNEL

M O Z A M B I Q U E

I N D I A N

O C E A N

MADAGASCAR

On same scale as General Map

East from Greenwich

COPYRIGHT. GEORGE PHILIP & SON. LTD

1:8 000 000

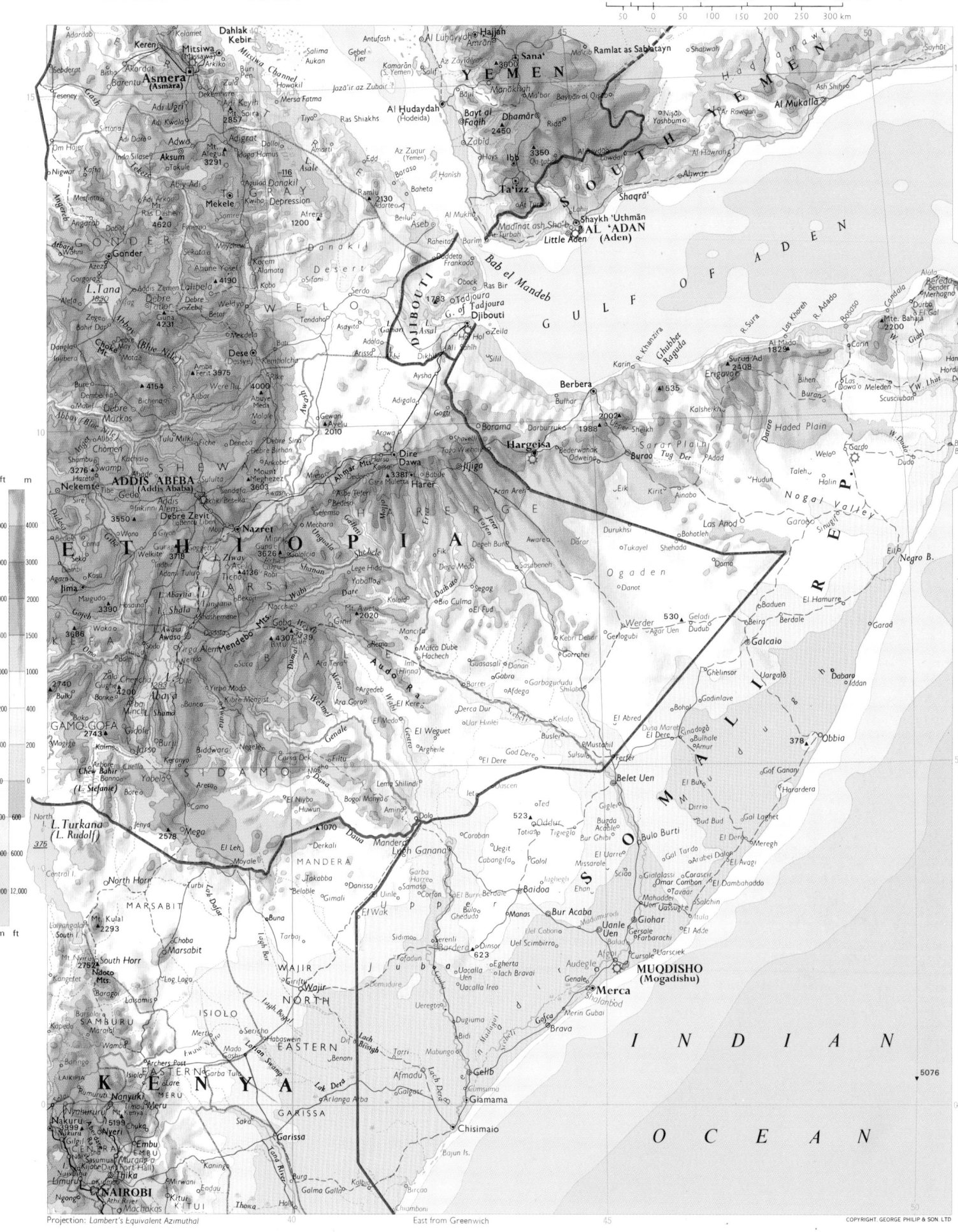

Projection: Lambert's Equivalent Azimuthal

East from Greenwich

1:60 000 000

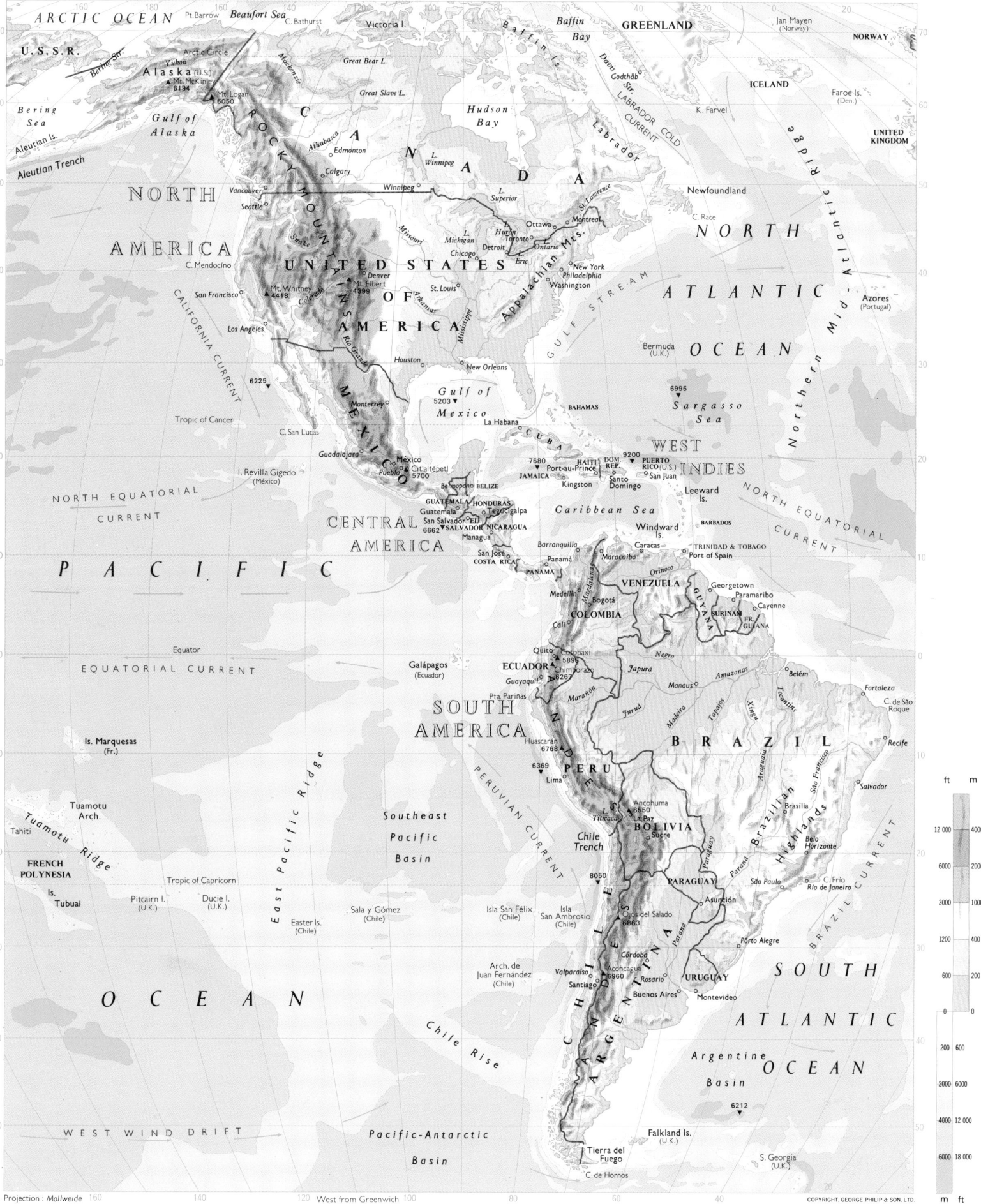

ARCTIC OCEAN   Pt.Barrow   Beaufort Sea   C. Bathurst   Victoria I.   Baffin Is.   Baffin Bay   GREENLAND   Jan Mayen (Norway)   NORWAY

U.S.S.R.   Bering Str.   Arctic Circle   Yukon   Alaska (U.S.)   ▲Mt. McKinley 6194   ▲Mt Logan 6050   Great Bear L.   Great Slave L.   Mackenzie   Hudson Bay   Danish Str.   Godthåb   K. Farvel   ICELAND   Faroe Is. (Den.)   UNITED KINGDOM

Bering Sea   Aleutian Is.   Gulf of Alaska   Athabasca   Edmonton   Calgary   C A N A D A   L. Winnipeg   L. Superior   St. Lawrence   Newfoundland   C. Race   Labrador Current Cold   Labrador

Aleutian Trench   NORTH   Vancouver   Seattle   ROCKY MOUNTAINS   Snake   Winnipeg   L. Michigan   L. Huron   Toronto   Detroit   Ottawa   Montreal   Ontario   St. Lawrence Mts.   NORTH   Northern Mid-Atlantic Ridge

AMERICA   C. Mendocino   UNITED STATES   Missouri   L. Erie   New York   Philadelphia   Washington   Appalachian Mts.   ATLANTIC   Azores (Portugal)

San Francisco   Mt. Whitney ▲4418   Colorado   Denver   Mt. Elbert ▲4399   OF   St. Louis   Arkansas   Mississippi   GULF STREAM   OCEAN

Los Angeles   Rio Grande   AMERICA   Houston   Bermuda (U.K.)   Sargasso Sea

CALIFORNIA CURRENT   6225▼   MEXICO   5203▼   Gulf of Mexico   New Orleans

Tropic of Cancer   C. San Lucas   Monterrey   La Habana   BAHAMAS   6995▼   WEST   INDIES

Guadalajara   México   Citlaltépetl   Puebla 5700   CUBA   7680▼   HAITI   DOM. REP.   9200▼ PUERTO RICO (U.S.)   San Juan   Leeward Is.   NORTH EQUATORIAL

I. Revilla Gigedo (México)   Port-au-Prince   Santo Domingo   CURRENT

NORTH EQUATORIAL   Belmopan BELIZE   JAMAICA   Kingston

CURRENT   GUATEMALA HONDURAS   Caribbean Sea   Windward Is.   BARBADOS

CENTRAL   Guatemala   Tegucigalpa   TRINIDAD & TOBAGO   Port of Spain

San Salvador   EL   6662▼ SALVADOR NICARAGUA   Barranquilla   Caracas

AMERICA   Managua   San José   Panamá   Maracaibo   Orinoco   Georgetown   Paramaribo   Cayenne

P A C I F I C   COSTA RICA   PANAMA   Medellín   VENEZUELA   GUYANA   SURINAM   FR. GUIANA

Bogotá   COLOMBIA   Cali   Negro   Japurá   Amazonas   Belém   Fortaleza

Equator   EQUATORIAL CURRENT   Galápagos (Ecuador)   Quito   Cotopaxi   ECUADOR 5896   Japurá   Manaus   Madeira   C. de São Roque

Guayaquil ▲6267   Marañón   Juruá   BRAZIL   Recife

Pta. Parinas   SOUTH   PERUVIAN CURRENT   Huascarán ▲6768   Tapajós   Xingu   Tocantins   Brazilian   São Francisco   Salvador

AMERICA   6369▼   PERU   Lima   Highlands

Is. Marquesas (Fr.)   Brasília   Belo Horizonte

Tuamotu Arch.   Ancohuma 6550   BOLIVIA   Titicaca La Paz   Sucre

Tahiti   East Pacific Ridge   Southeast Pacific Basin   Chile Trench   Paraguay   São Paulo   C. Frío   Río de Janeiro   BRAZIL CURRENT

FRENCH POLYNESIA   Tuamotu Ridge   8050▼   PARAGUAY   Paraná   Asunción   Porto Alegre

Is. Tubuai   Tropic of Capricorn   Pitcairn I. (U.K.)   Ducie I. (U.K.)   Sala y Gómez (Chile)   Isla San Félix (Chile)   Isla San Ambrosio (Chile)   Ojos del Salado 6863   Paraná

Easter Is. (Chile)   Córdoba   SOUTH

Arch. de Juan Fernández (Chile)   Aconcagua ▲6960   Rosario   URUGUAY   ATLANTIC

Valparaíso   Santiago   ARGENTINA   Buenos Aires   Montevideo

OCEAN   CHILE   ANDES   Argentine Basin   6212▼   OCEAN

Chile Rise   Falkland Is. (U.K.)

WEST WIND DRIFT   Pacific-Antarctic Basin   Tierra del Fuego   S. Georgia (U.K.)

C. de Hornos

Projection: Mollweide   160   140   120   West from Greenwich 100   80   60   40   20   COPYRIGHT. GEORGE PHILIP & SON. LTD.   m ft

ft   m
12 000   4000
6000   2000
3000   1000
1200   400
600   200
0
200   600
2000   6000
4000   12 000
6000   18 000

1:35 000 000

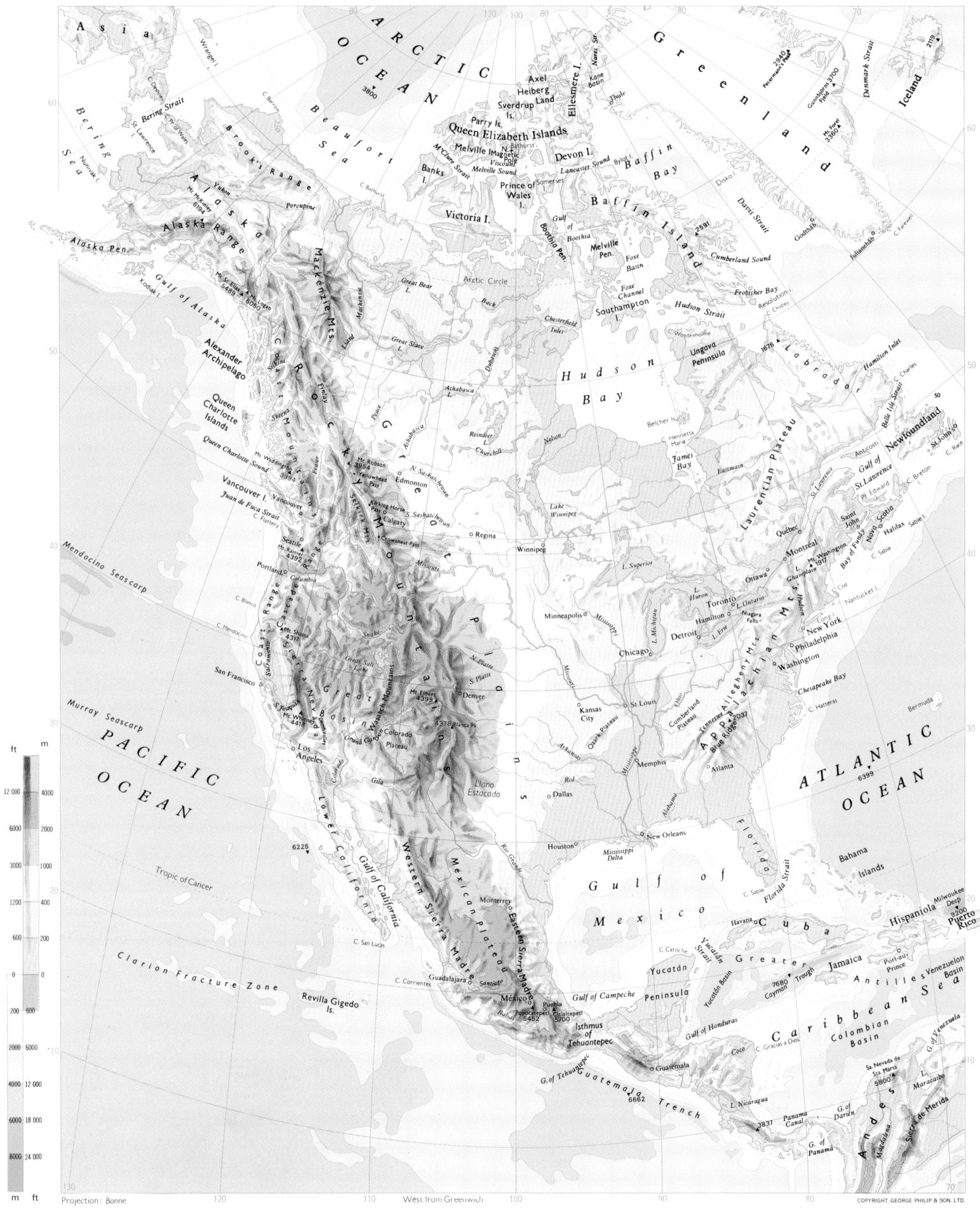

PACIFIC OCEAN

ATLANTIC OCEAN

ARCTIC OCEAN

Projection: Bonne   West from Greenwich   COPYRIGHT GEORGE PHILIP & SON LTD.

1:35 000 000

200   0   200   400   600   800 miles
400   0   400   800   1200 km

ARCTIC OCEAN

U.S.S.R.

Bering Strait

Bering Sea

ALASKA
Yukon

Arctic Circle

Porcupine

Fairbanks

Anchorage

Gulf of Alaska

Beaufort Sea

Queen Elizabeth Is.

Ellesmere I.

GREENLAND (Denmark)

Baffin Bay

Denmark Strait

ICELAND

Reykjavik

Godthåb

C. Farvel

Davis Strait

Baffin I.

BAFFIN

KITIKMEOT

Victoria I.

INUVIK

YUKON TERRITORY

Whitehorse

Juneau

Liard

NORTHWEST TERRITORIES

Great Bear L.

FORT SMITH

Yellowknife

Great Slave L.

Back

Dubawnt

KEEWATIN

Hudson Strait

NEWFOUNDLAND

Hudson Bay

Labrador

SPM

St. John's

BRITISH COLUMBIA

ALBERTA

Peace

Athabasca

Edmonton

N. Saskatchewan

Calgary

S. Saskatchewan

Skeena

Fraser

Finlay

CANADA

Churchill

Nelson

MANITOBA

L. Winnipeg

Eastmain

QUÉBEC

St. Lawrence

Québec

Montréal

Ottawa

PR. EDWARD I.

Charlottetown

NEW BRUNS-WICK

NOVA SCOTIA

Halifax

Fredericton

MAINE

Augusta

VER.

Montpelier

Concord

N.H.

Boston

MASS.

Providence

R.I.

Hartford

C

Albany

NEW YORK

Victoria

Vancouver

Regina

SASKATCHEWAN

Winnipeg

ONTARIO

L. Superior

Toronto

L. Ontario

Buffalo

Huron

L. Michigan

NEW YORK

Trenton

N.J.

Philadelphia

WASHINGTON

Olympia

Seattle

Columbia

Portland

Salem

OREGON

MONTANA

Helena

Missouri

NORTH DAKOTA

Bismarck

MINNESOTA

St. Paul

Minneapolis

WISCONSIN

Madison

MICHIGAN

Lansing

Detroit

Cleveland

Toledo

PENNSYLVANIA

Pittsburgh

Harrisburg

Baltimore

MD.

D.C.

Dover

Annapolis

IDAHO

Boise

Snake

WYOMING

Cheyenne

SOUTH DAKOTA

Pierre

N. Platte

NEBRASKA

Lincoln

I O W A

Des Moines

Chicago

ILLINOIS

Springfield

INDIANA

Indianapolis

Columbus

OHIO

Frankfort

Cincinnati

WEST VIRGINIA

Charleston

Ohio

Richmond

VIRGINIA

Washington

Raleigh

Sacramento

San Francisco

San Jose

Carson City

Salt Lake City

NEVADA

UTAH

UNITED STATES

Denver

COLORADO

Arkansas

KANSAS

Topeka

Kansas City

MISSOURI

St. Louis

Jefferson City

KENTUCKY

Nashville

Tennessee

NORTH CAROLINA

Columbia

Bermuda

ATLANTIC OCEAN

PACIFIC OCEAN

CALIFORNIA

Las Vegas

LOS ANGELES

San Diego

Colorado

Santa Fe

ARIZONA

Phoenix

Tucson

Gila

Albuquerque

NEW MEXICO

El Paso

Oklahoma City

OKLAHOMA

Red River

ARKANSAS

Little Rock

Memphis

TENNESSEE

MISSISSIPPI

Jackson

ALABAMA

Montgomery

GEORGIA

Atlanta

SOUTH CAROLINA

Birmingham

Dallas

TEXAS

Austin

LOUISIANA

Baton Rouge

New Orleans

Mississippi

Jacksonville

FLORIDA

Tallahassee

Tampa

Miami

C. Sable

Str. of Florida

BAHAMAS

Nassau

Houston

Tropic of Cancer

Rio Grande

Monterrey

M E X I C O

Gulf of Mexico

Havana

C U B A

Guadalajara

MEXICO

Caribbean Sea

HAITI

Port-au-Prince

DOMINICAN REP.

Santo Domingo

San Juan

PUERTO RICO

JAMAICA

Kingston

Belmopan

BELIZE

GUATEMALA

Guatemala

San Salvador

EL SALVADOR

HONDURAS

Tegucigalpa

NICARAGUA

L. Nicaragua

Managua

COSTA RICA

San José

PANAMA

Panamá

Maracaibo

Barranquilla

VENEZUELA

COLOMBIA

Medellín

Bogotá

SOUTH AMERICA

State capital ⊙

C   CONNECTICUT
D.   DELAWARE
D.C.   DISTRICT OF COLUMBIA
M.   MARYLAND
MASS.   MASSACHUSETTS

N.H.   NEW HAMPSHIRE
N.J.   NEW JERSEY
R.I.   RHODE ISLAND
VER.   VERMONT
SPM   ST. PIERRE ET MIQUELON

PACIFIC OCEAN
ALASKA
YUKON TERRITORY
BRITISH COLUMBIA
ALBERTA
SASKATCHEWAN
MANITOBA
NORTHWEST TERRITORIES
INUVIK
KITIKMEOT
KEEWATIN
FORT SMITH
UNITED STATES
WASHINGTON
MONTANA
NORTH DAKOTA
SOUTH DAKOTA
MINNESOTA
NEBRASKA
WYOMING
Rocky Mountains
Mackenzie Mountains
Coast Mountains
Cassiar Mountains
Banks Island
Victoria Island
Prince of Wales Island
Amundsen Gulf
Coronation Gulf
Queen Maud Gulf
Great Bear Lake
Great Slave L.
Lake Athabasca
Queen Charlotte Is.
Vancouver
Victoria
Seattle
Tacoma
Spokane
Calgary
Edmonton
Saskatoon
Regina
Winnipeg
Minneapolis
Omaha
Whitehorse
Yellowknife
Fairbanks
Anchorage
Juneau
Projection: Bonne
ALASKA
1:30 000 000
100 0 100 200 300 miles
100 0 200 400 km
BERING SEA
GULF OF ALASKA
PACIFIC OCEAN
Brooks Range
Aleutian Is.
West from Greenwich
ft
m
9000
3000
6000
2000
4500
1500
3000
1000
1200
400
600
200
0
0
200
600
2000
6000
m
ft

1:15 000 000

100 50 0   100   200   300   400 miles
100   0   100   200   300   400   500   600 km

Devon Island
Lancaster Sound
Arctic Bay
Bylot I.
1890
Pond Inlet
Pond Inlet
2136
Svartenhuk
Halvø
Broderor
Peninsula
Milne
Inlet
Scott I.
C. Hewett
Clyde
Baffin Bay
Disko
Disko
B.
Christianshåb
G
Sandre Strømfjord
2850
Angmagssalik
R
Godthåb
E
E
Fury & Hecla Str.
Igloolik
Island
Hall
Lake
2591
Melville
Prince
Charles
Cumberland
Peninsula
C. Dyer
Dyer
C. Dyer
Davis Strait
Holsteinsborg
Sukkertoppen
N
Repulse
Bay
Committee B.
Peninsula
Foxe
Basin
Pond Inlet
Foxe
Penin.
Amadjuak
L.
C. Mercy
Cumberland Sd.
Hoare B.
Godthåb
L
Sandre Strømfjord
Kong Frederik VI Kyst
Frederikshåb
Ivigtut
A
Rae Isthmus
oBay
Foxe
Channel
C. Dorchester
Amadjuak
L.
Foxe
Penin.
Cape Dorset
Lake
Harbour
Frobisher Bay
Resolution I.
Julianehåb
Nanortalik
Kap Farvel
N
Wager B.
Roes Welcome Str.
Southampton
I.
Coral Harbour
Bell
Pen.
Coats
I.
Digges Is.
Mansel
I.
Saglouc
(Sugluk)
Maricourt
(Wakeham)
Koartac (Notre Dame
de Koartac)
Akpatok
I.
C. Chidley
Hudson Strait
T I N
Nottingham
Baker's
Dozen
King
George Is.
Sleeper Is.
Ottawa
Isl.
257
Hudson
Bay
King George Is.
Belcher
Is.
C. Henrietta
Maria
Pte.
Louis-XIV
Portland
Promontory
Inoucdjouac
(Port Harrison)
P e n i n s u l a
Payne
Feuilles
Minto
Mélèzes
Kaniapiskau
Arnaud (Bellin)
(Payne Bay)
Ungava Bay
Payne
1676
Port-Nouveau
George
Whale
U n g a v a
Hebron
Nutak
Nain
Hopedale
N
C. Harrison
Indian Harbour
Rigolet
Mulville
Cartwright
L'Eau Claire
Poste-de-
la-Baleine
(Great Whole River)
Grand Baleine
Kanaaupscow
Ft. George
La Grande
4128
Goynon
Scheffervillle
Petitsikapau
L.
COAST OF LABRADOR
Smallwood
Reservoir
North West
Churchill
Falls
Churchill
Lobstick L.
Ashuanipi
Battle Harb.
Belle Isle
North West
L
Winisk
Severn
Big
Trout L.
D
A
James Bay
Akimiski
I.
Charlton
I.
Attawapiskat
Nouveau Comptoir
(Point Hills)
Lac Bienville
Eastmain
Q U E B E C
Kaniapiskau
L. Albanel
Mistassini
Péribonca
Romaine
Natashquan
Natashquan
R
St-Augustin
Saguenay
Strait of Belle Isle
N E W F O U N D L A N D
Grand
Falls
Buchans
Twillingate
Lewisporte
Gander
Bonavista
Notre Dame B.
814
Grand
Banks
Harbour Grace
Carbonear
St. John's
Placentia
Trinity B.
Placentia B.
Trepassey
C. Race
Port
aux Basques
Cabot Str.
St-Pierre
et MIQUELON
(Fr.)
Moisie
Mingan
I. d'Anticosti
Sept Îles
Port-Cartier
Manitougan
Mingan
Moisie
Baie-Comeau
Betsiamites
Gulf of
St. Lawrence
Îs. de la Madeleine
Cape Breton
Glace Bay
Sydney
Port Hawkesbury
Mulgrave
Sable I.
(Nova Scotia)
6309
O
C
E
A
N
A T L A N T I C
3809
Missinaibi
Nakina
Longlac
Hearst
Cochrane
Rés. de Gouin
Roberval
Lac St-Jean
Chicoutimi
Jonquière
Dolbeau
St-Jean
Saguenay
Rivière-
du-Loup
Rimouski
Matane
Ste. Anne
Pén. de Gaspé
C. de Gaspé
Chaleur Bay
Campbellton
Bathurst
Newcastle
Chatham
Summerside
PR. EDWARD I.
Charlottetown
Northumberland Str.
Pictou
N O V A   S C O T I A
New Glasgow
Antigonish
Truro
Windsor
Dartmouth
Halifax
Bridgewater
Liverpool
Shelburne
C. Sable
Yarmouth
B. of Fundy
Digby
Kentville
Amherst
Springhill
Moncton
NEW
BRUNSWICK
Fredericton
Woodstock
St. Leonard
Edmundston
Saint
John
MAINE
Bangor
Augusta
Portland
NEW
HAMPSHIRE
Concord
Manchester
VERMONT
Montpelier
Boston
C. Cod
Lowell
Worcester
Providence
MASS.
Springfield
Hartford
CONN.
New Haven
Bridgeport
R. I.
Thunder Bay
Michipicoten
Heron Bay
Franz
Oba
Longlac
Mattawa
L. Abitibi
Noranda
Taschereau
Senneterre
Val-d'Or
Kirkland Lake
Timmins
Matagami
Rouyn
La Tuque
Shawinigan
Trois-Rivières
Rés. de
Cabonga
Haileybury
Cobalt
Témiscamingue
Québec
Lévis
Thetford Mines
Drummondville
St. Hyacinthe
Sherbrooke
Woodstock
Sorel
Joliette
Lachine
MONTRÉAL
Hull
Ottawa
Cornwall
Arnprior
Pembroke
North Bay
Sudbury
Copper Cliff
Sault Ste. Marie
Sault Ste. Marie
Parry
Sound
Georgian
Bay
North Chan.
L. Champlain
1917
Glens Falls
Plattsburgh
Watertown
Kingston
Burlington
Belleville
Brockville
Cobourg
Peterboro
Orillia
Owen Sound
Lake
Huron
Cheboygan
Petoskey
Traverse
City
Cadillac
Ludington
Muskegon
Manistee
Manistique
Escanaba
Menominee
Antigo
Wausau
Green
Bay
Appleton
Manitowoc
Sheboygan
Milwaukee
Racine
Kenosha
Evanston
ICAGO
Gary
INDIANA
South Bend
Toledo
DETROIT
Windsor
Erie
Cleveland
Akron
Youngstown
Jamestown
OHIO
PENNSYLVANIA
Reading
Allentown
Trenton
Williamsport
Scranton
Binghamton
Elmira
Corning
NEW JERSEY
Newark
Jersey City
NEW YORK
NEW YORK
Poughkeepsie
Waterbury
Buffalo
Rochester
Syracuse
Utica
Albany
Schenectady
Niagara
Falls
St. Catharines
Hamilton
Brantford
London
Guelph
Kitchener
Stratford
TORONTO
Oshawa
L. Ontario
ARIO
Lake Erie
Copper Harbour
Keweenaw
Pt.
Marquette
Iron Mt.
Menominee
Kalamazoo
Grand
Rapids
Saginaw
Bay City
Flint
Lansing
Battle
Creek
L. Superior
Thunder Bay
Nipigon
Heron Bay
Nakina
Longlac

West from Greenwich

COPYRIGHT. GEORGE PHILIP & SON. LTD.

N. W. TERRITORIES
MANITOBA
ONTARIO
HUDSON BAY
JAMES BAY
Belcher Islands
North Belcher Is.
Baker's Dozen Is.
Nastapoka Is.
Akimiski I.
Charlton I.
POLAR BEAR PROVINCIAL PARK
C. Henrietta Maria
Fort Severn
Fort Albany
Moosonee
Moose Factory
Hannah B.
Rupert B.
Eastmain
Fort Rupert (Rupert House)
Nouveau Comptoir
Fort George
La Grande
Grand Baleine
Lac Bienville
L. Minto
Kapuskasing
Hearst
Cochrane
Timmins
Kirkland Lake
Rouyn
Val-d'Or
Amos
Chibougamau
Mistassini
L. Nipigon
Thunder Bay
Isle Royale
LAKE SUPERIOR
Duluth
Superior
Michipicoten I.
Marquette
Sault Ste. Marie
Elliot Lake
Sudbury
North Bay
Manitoulin I.
Georgian Bay
LAKE HURON
LAKE MICHIGAN
LAKE ONTARIO
LAKE ERIE
Green Bay
Milwaukee
Madison
Rockford
CHICAGO
Gary
South Bend
Kalamazoo
Grand Rapids
Flint
Lansing
Saginaw
Bay City
Port Huron
DETROIT
Windsor
Toledo
CLEVELAND
Erie
London
Kitchener
TORONTO
HAMILTON
St. Catharines
BUFFALO
Niagara Falls
Rochester
Syracuse
Utica
Albany
Binghamton
Kingston
OTTAWA
Pembroke
Trois-Rivières
Shawinigan
Adirondack Mountains
Catskill Mts.
WISCONSIN
MICHIGAN
NEW YORK
ILLINOIS
Q
Lambert's Equivalent Azimuthal
INDIANA
OHIO
PENNSYLVANIA
ft m
4500 1500
3000 1000
1200 400
600 200
0 0
200 600
2000 6000
4000 12 000
m ft

50 0 50 100 150 200 miles
50 0 50 100 150 200 250 300 km

N E W

C O A S T   O F

South Aulatsivik I.
High I.
Paul I.
Erlandson L.
Whale L.
George L.
Fraser
Nain
Voisey's I.

Fort McKenzie
Nachicapau
Kogaluk
Tûnungayualuk I.
Davis Inlet
Nunaksaluk I.

Chakonipau L.
Otelnuk L.
Wheeler
Kaniapiskau
L. Champdoré
Mistastin L.
Big Bay
Hopedale
Kaipokok B.
Makkovik
Adlavik I.
C. Harrison

L. de la Hutte Sauvage
Tudor
610
Whitegull L.
Harp L.
Holton
Indian Harbour
Groswater

Attikamagen L.
Kanairiktok
Nakaupi
Seal L.
Nipishish
Hamilton Inlet
Rigolet
Table B.

Scheffervile
Petitsikapau L.
Michikamau Lake
North-West River
L. Melville
Mealy Mts.
Cartwright
Sandwich B.
Island of Ponds

Woods L.
Lobstick L.
Churchill Falls
Goose
Happy Valley-Goose Bay
Separation Point
Eagle
Paradise
Square Islands

O U N D

Neret L.
Kaniapiskau Lake
L. Bermen
Ossokmanuan
Churchill
Winokapau L.
L A B R A D O R
Alexis
St. Lewis
St. Mary's Harbour
Battle Harbour
Belle I.

Itcheqoun L.
Opiscoteo L.
Opiskotish L.
Shabogamo L.
Lac Joseph
Atikonak L.
Minipi L.
Little Mecatina
St. Paul
St. Lunaire-Griquet
Red Bay
Str. of Belle Isle

Naococane L.
Labrador City
Ashuanipi L.
Burnt L.
Mecatina
Anse au Loup
Forteau
St. Anthony
Hare B.

1128
Moisie
Petit Lac Manicouagan
West Maître
Maître
Romaine
St-Augustin-Saguenay
Bradore Bay
Lourdes-de-Blanc-Sablon
Flower's Cove
Groais I.
Conche
Engle
Bell I.

Plétipi L.
Gagnon
Rés. Manicouagan
1048
L. Manitou
Natashquan
Aguanus
Olomani
St-Augustin
Port Saunders
Great Harbour Deep
White B.
Roddickton
Englee
Horse I.

Manouane L.
Ste-Marguerite
L. Jean
Lac Allard
Musquaro
I. du Petit-Mécatina
Harrington Harbour
Daniel's Harbour
Seal Cove
Baie Verte
La Scie
C. St. John
Notre Dame B.
Twillingate
Fogo I.
C. Freels

Clarke City
Moisie
Sheldrake
Mingan
Havre-St-Pierre
Aguanish
Kegaske
Gethsémani
Etamamu
GROS MORNE NAT. PARK
Springdale
Botwood
Lewisporte
Glenwood
Wesleyville
Bonavista B.

Port-Cartier
Ste-Anne-des-Monts
Pte. Ouest
Port-Menier
Dét. de Jacques-Cartier
Trout River
Deer Lake
Howley
Grand Falls
Windsor
Gander
C. Bonavista
Bonavista
Catalina

Rivière-Pentecôte
Baie-Trinité
Pte. des Monts
Mont-Louis
Grande-Vallée
Î. d'Anticosti
Jupiter
Heath Pt.
Bay of Islands
Corner Brook
814
Buchans
Red Indian L.
Grand L.
Dark Cove
Glovertown
Trinity B.

Godbout
Cap-Chat
Rivière-au-Renard
Pte. Sud
Long Pt.
C. St. George
Deer Lake
Stephenville
Victoria
NEWFOUNDLAND
Blandford
C. Content
Carbonear
Trinity

Baie-Comeau
Matane
1268 Mt. Jacques-Cartier
Gaspé
Grande-Rivière
GULF OF
572
St. George's B.
Grey Res.
Salmon
381
Clarenville
Content
Grace
Pouch Cove

Manicouagan
PARC PROV. DE LA GASPÉSIE
Pén. de Gaspé
Chandler
Percé
ST. LAWRENCE
St. George's
St. David's
South Branch
White Bear Res.
St. Alban's
Terrenceville
Bay de Verde
Bell I.
Torbay
St. John's
Mt. Pearl

Mont-Joli
Sayabec
Mts. Chic-Chocs
Bonaventure
Douglastown
St. Andrew's
Long Range Mts.
Rose Blanche
Belleoram
Marystown
Spaniard's Bay
Conception B.

Rimouski
Amqui
Matapédia
Pespébiac
Miscou I.
Î. Brion
C. Ray
Channel-Port aux Basques
Burgeo
Ramea
Fortune B.
Grand Bank
Placentia
Avalon

Bic
Trois-Pistoles
Causapscal
Dalhousie
Chaleur Bay
Lamèque I.
Shippegan
Cap-aux-Meules
St. Paul I.
C. North
Cabot Strait
Grand Banks
Bank
Burin
Placentia B.
St. Mary's B.
C. Race

Rivière-du-Loup
Cabano
Campbellton
Atholville
Tracadie
Îs. de la Madeleine
(Quebec)
Havre-Aubert
Miquelon
Marystown
St. Lawrence
C. St. Mary's
Trepassey

Edmundston
Kedgwick
Bathurst
Miramichi B.
Pleasant Bay
Langlade
SAINT-PIERRE ET MIQUELON (Fr.)
St. Pierre

St-Léonard 819
Grand Falls
St. Arthur
North Pt.
Tignish
CAPE BRETON NAT. PARK
532
Chéticamp
Ingonish

Clair
St-Quentin
Plaster Rock
NEW
Newcastle
Chatham
Richibucto
Alberton
PRINCE EDWARD
Pleasant Bay
Sydney Mines
New Waterford

St. John
Van Buren
Caribou
BRUNSWICK
Buctouche
Summerside
Kensington
ISLAND
East Pt.
Inverness
N. Sydney
Glace Bay

Ashland
Presque Isle
Boiestown
Notre Dame
Shediac
Borden
Charlottetown
Souris
Murray Hr.
Port Hood
Sydney

Houlton
Chipman
Moncton
Cape Tormentine
Georgetown
Brasd'Or
Cape Breton
Louisbourg

Eagle L.
Stanley
Grand L.
Havelock
Amherst
Pictou
L.
Island

Island Falls
Woodstock
Minto
Sussex
Springhill
New Glasgow
Stellarton
Î. Madame

Chesuncook
1606
Fredericton
Gagetown
Elgin
Parrsboro
Truro
St. Peters
Canso

Moosehead
Millinocket
Oromocto
Sussex
Minas Basin
Sherbrooke
Chedabucto B.

MAINE
Lincoln
NOVA SCOTIA
Upper Musquodoboit
Musquodoboit

Greenville
Mattawamkeag
St. Martins
Windsor
Sheet Hr.

Dover-Foxcroft
Old Town
Blacks Hr.
Saint John
Bridgetown
Middleton
Dartmouth
Musquodoboit Hr.

Brewer
Machias
Eastport
Grand Manan I.
Annapolis Royal
Kentville

Binghamham
Bangor
Ellsworth
Fundy Bay
Mahone Bay
Halifax

Moosehead L.
Waterville
Bar Harbor
Mt. Desert I.
Weymouth
Lunenburg
Bridgewater

Rumford
Berlin
Bethel
Augusta
Belfast
Digby
Rossignol Res.
Liverpool
Port Mouton

Waterville
Camden
Rockland
St. Mary's B.
Freeport
Shelburne

Auburn
Lewiston
Bath
Yarmouth
Wedgeport
Lockeport

Sebago L.
Brunswick
Rockland
Clark's Harbour
C. Sable

Portland
Sanford
Saco
Biddeford
Sable I.
(Nova Scotia)

Rochester
Dover
Portsmouth

Manchester
Nashua
Haverhill
Lawrence
C. Ann

Lowell
Lynn
Gloucester

BOSTON
Brockton

A T L A N T I C

O C E A N

GULF OF
ST. LAWRENCE

Q U E B E C

M A I N E

N E W
B R U N S W I C K

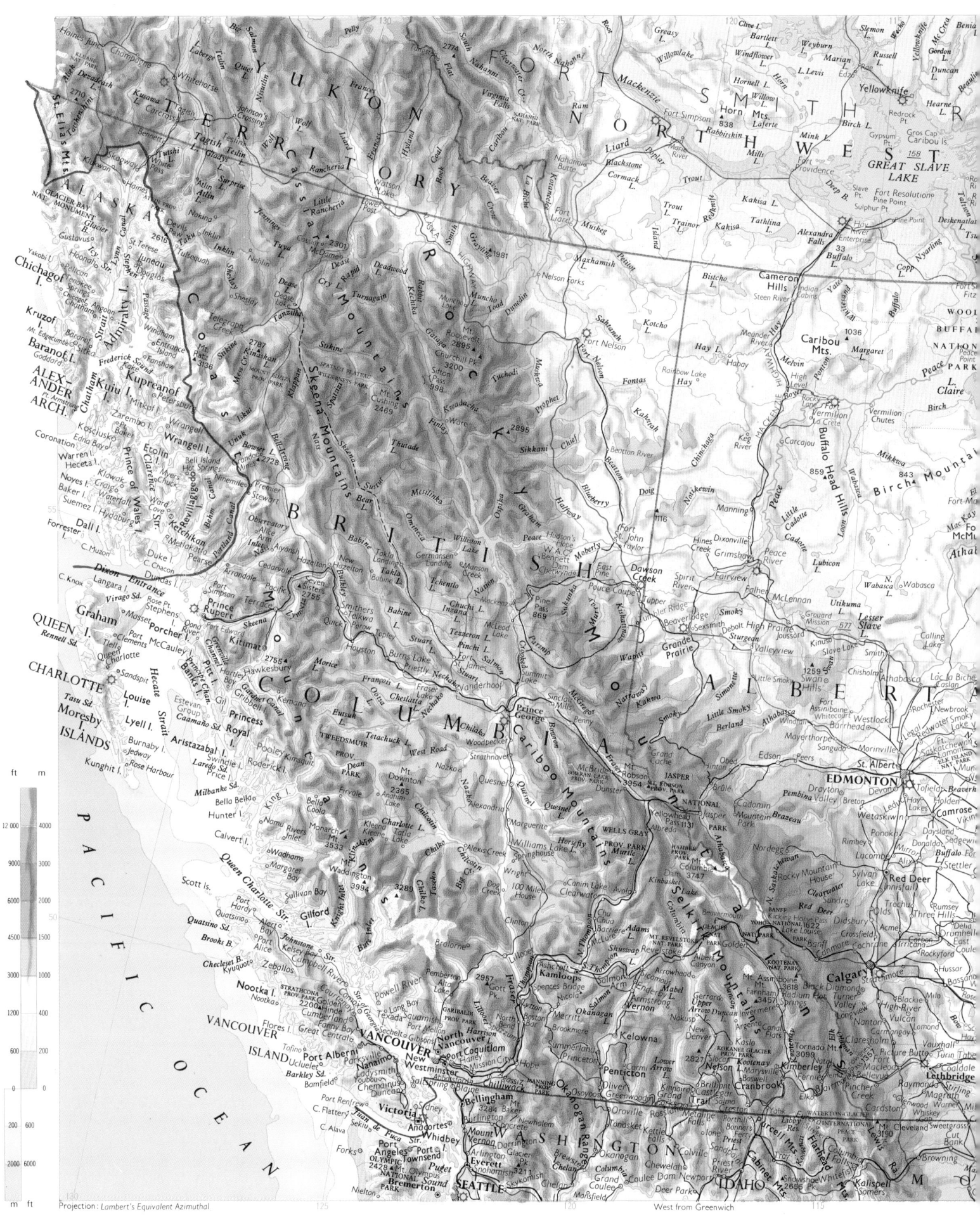
YUKON TERRITORY
NORTHWEST TERRITORIES
FORT SMITH
BRITISH COLUMBIA
ALBERTA
ALASKA
WASHINGTON
IDAHO
PACIFIC OCEAN
GREAT SLAVE LAKE
QUEEN CHARLOTTE ISLANDS
VANCOUVER ISLAND
ALEXANDER ARCH.
Coast Mountains
Cassiar Mountains
Skeena Mountains
Rocky Mountains
Cariboo Mountains
Selkirk Mountains
Omineca Mountains
Birch Mountains
Caribou Mts.
Horn Mts.
Dixon Entrance
Hecate Strait
Queen Charlotte Str.
Juan de Fuca Str.
Whitehorse
Yellowknife
Fort Simpson
Fort Nelson
Dawson Creek
Prince Rupert
Prince George
Kamloops
Kelowna
Penticton
VANCOUVER
North Vancouver
New Westminster
Victoria
Nanaimo
Port Alberni
Kitimat
EDMONTON
Calgary
Red Deer
Lethbridge
Grande Prairie
Peace River
Bellingham
Everett
SEATTLE
Mt. Robson 3954
Mt. Waddington 3994
Juneau
Chichagof I.
Baranof I.
Kupreanof I.
Graham I.
Moresby I.
ft
m
12 000
9000
6000
4500
3000
1200
600
0
200
2000
4000
1500
1000
400
Projection: Lambert's Equivalent Azimuthal
West from Greenwich

1:7 000 000

50 0 50 100 150 200 miles
50 0 50 100 150 200 250 300 km

KEEWATIN

REGION

TERRITORIES

HUDSON BAY

MANITOBA

SASKATCHEWAN

ONTARIO

LAKE WINNIPEG

NORTH DAKOTA

MINNESOTA

MONTANA

WINNIPEG

Regina

Saskatoon

Prince Albert

Brandon

Moose Jaw

Duluth

Churchill

Flin Flon

The Pas

Lake Athabasca

Reindeer L.

Southern Indian L.

Lake Winnipegosis

Lake Manitoba

Cedar Lake

Lake of the Woods

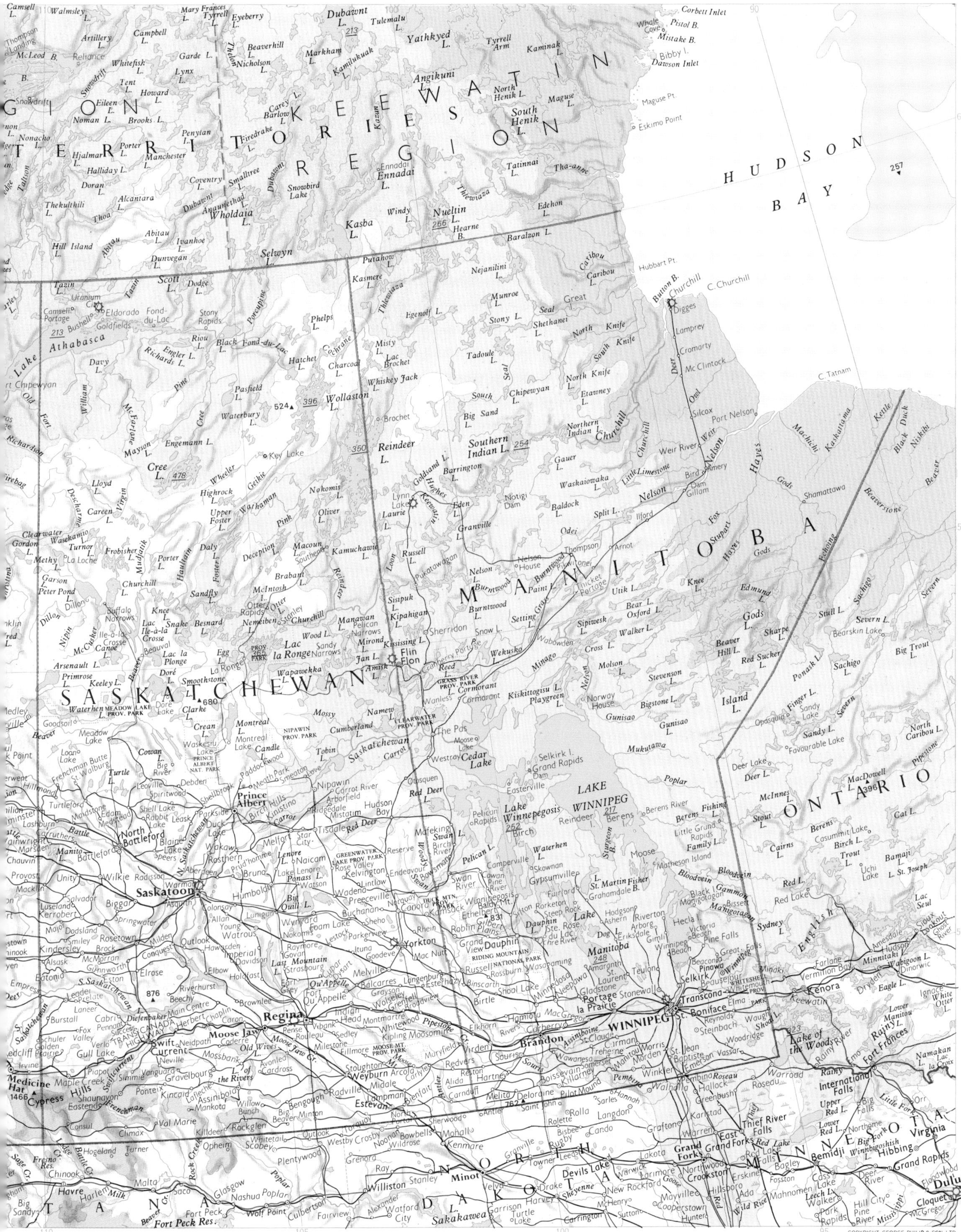

HAWAII
1:10 000 000

Projection : Albers' Equal Area with two standard parallels

West from Greenwich

1:12 000 000

50   100   150   200   250   300 miles
50 0 50 100 150 200 250 300 350 400 450 km

COPYRIGHT. GEORGE PHILIP & SON. LTD.

QUEBEC

VERMONT

NEW HAMPSHIRE

MASS.

MONTREAL

Ottawa

ONTARIO

LAKE ONTARIO

NEW YORK

TORONTO

Hamilton

LAKE ERIE

LAKE HURON

Georgian Bay

Parry Sound

LAKE SUPERIOR

MICHIGAN

DETROIT

WISCONSIN

MILWAUKEE

CHICAGO

ILLINOIS

INDIANA

INDIANAPOLIS

OHIO

COLUMBUS

CINCINNATI

CLEVELAND

PITTSBURGH

PENNSYLVANIA

PHILADELPHIA

NEW JERSEY

NEW YORK CITY

BOSTON

CONN.

R.I.

MARYLAND

BALTIMORE

WASHINGTON, D.C.

DELAWARE

VIRGINIA

Richmond

WEST VIRGINIA

KENTUCKY

Louisville

Chesapeake Bay

1:6 000 000

50   0   50   100 miles

50   0   50   100   150 km

Continuation
Eastwards
On same scale

M A I N E

NEW HAMPSHIRE

CANADA

NORTH CAROLINA

TENNESSEE

SOUTH CAROLINA

G E O R G I A

A L A B A M A

MISSISSIPPI

F L O R I D A

Wilmington

Raleigh

Charlotte

Columbia

ATLANTA

Savannah

JACKSONVILLE

Orlando

Tampa

St. Petersburg

Miami

Montgomery

Birmingham

Knoxville

Nashville

Chattanooga

Mobile

Pensacola

A T L A N T I C   O C E A N

G U L F   O F   M E X I C O

BAHAMAS

Great Abaco I.

Grand Bahama I.

Freeport

Settlement Pt.

West from Greenwich

Projection: Alber's Equal Area with two standard parallels

COPYRIGHT GEORGE PHILIP & SON, LTD

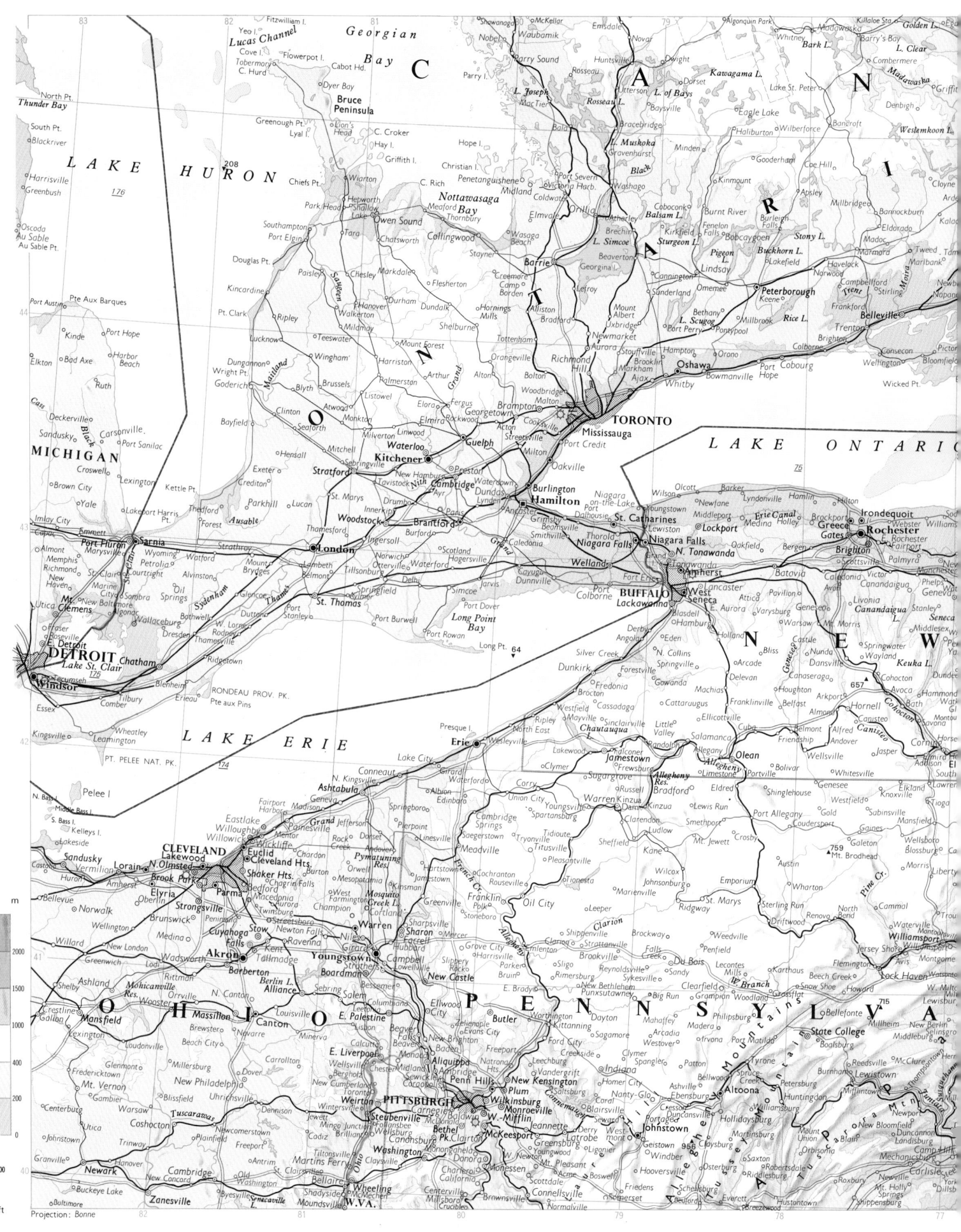

Georgian Bay
LAKE HURON
LAKE ONTARIO
LAKE ERIE
MICHIGAN
ONTARIO
OHIO
PENNSYLVANIA
NEW
Bruce Peninsula
Lucas Channel
Thunder Bay
Lake St. Clair
Long Point Bay
L. Simcoe
L. Muskoka
L. of Bays
L. Scugog
Rice L.
Nottawasaga Bay
TORONTO
Mississauga
Hamilton
Burlington
Oakville
St. Catharines
Niagara Falls
BUFFALO
Lackawanna
Rochester
Irondequoit
Lockport
Erie Canal
Kitchener
Waterloo
Guelph
Cambridge
Brantford
Woodstock
London
Stratford
St. Thomas
Sarnia
Port Huron
DETROIT
Windsor
Chatham
Barrie
Orillia
Peterborough
Oshawa
Belleville
Owen Sound
Collingwood
Erie
Jamestown
Olean
Bradford
CLEVELAND
Lakewood
Euclid
Parma
Lorain
Elyria
Akron
Canton
Youngstown
Warren
Mansfield
Sandusky
Ashtabula
PITTSBURGH
Butler
New Castle
Altoona
Johnstown
State College
Williamsport
Lock Haven
Wheeling
W.VA.
Steubenville
Washington
Zanesville
Newark
Coshocton
Allegheny Mountains
Tuscarora Mtn.
Allegheny Res.
Projection: Bonne
ft
m
6000
4500
3000
1200
600
0
200
2000
1500
1000
400

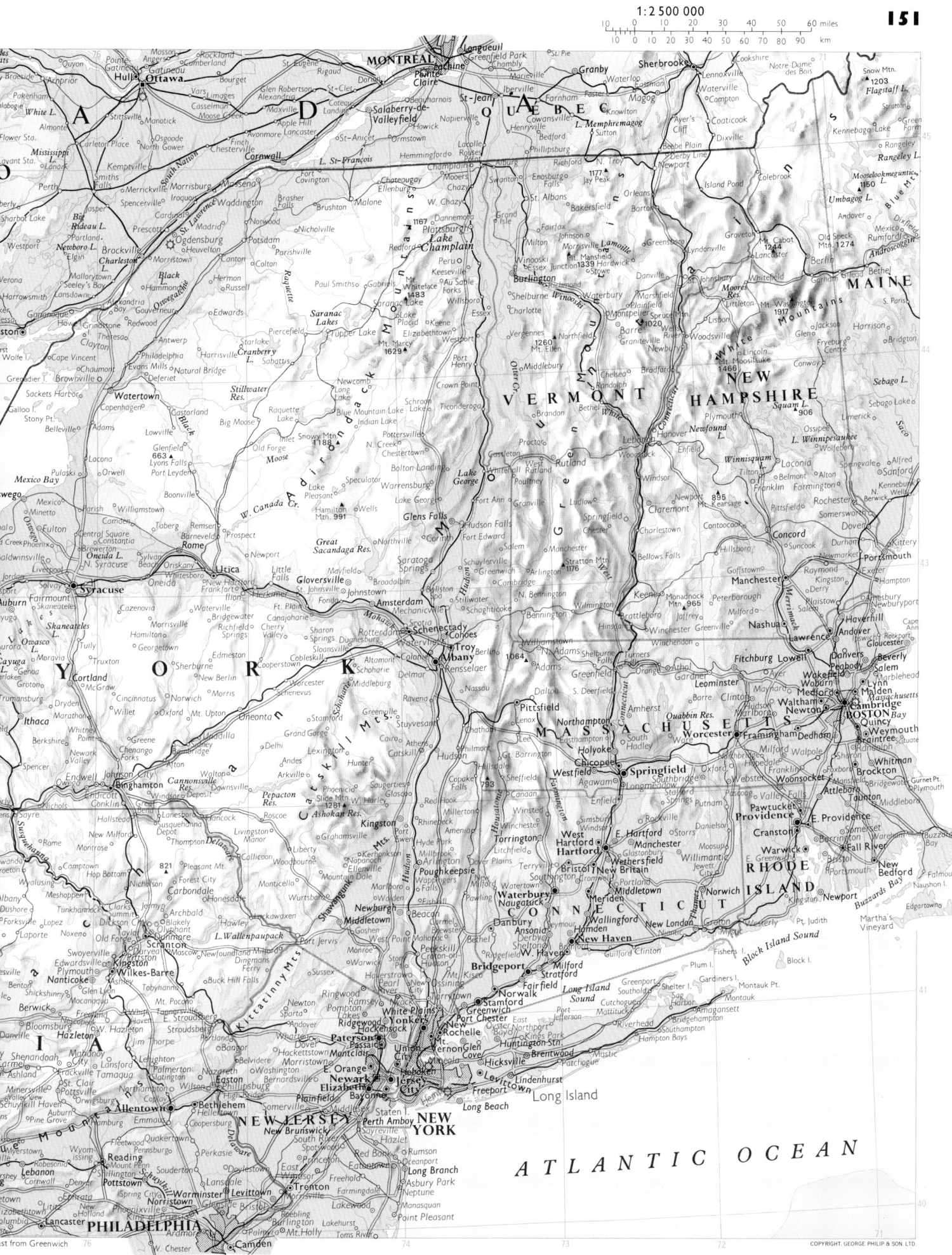

1:2 500 000

10 0 10 20 30 40 50 60 miles
10 0 10 20 30 40 50 60 70 80 90 km

MONTREAL

QUEBEC

CANADA

VERMONT

NEW HAMPSHIRE

MAINE

NEW YORK

MASSACHUSETTS

Syracuse

Albany

Boston

Springfield

Worcester

Providence

RHODE ISLAND

CONNECTICUT

Hartford

New Haven

Bridgeport

Long Island Sound

Long Island

NEW JERSEY

NEW YORK

Newark

Trenton

PHILADELPHIA

Camden

ATLANTIC OCEAN

COPYRIGHT GEORGE PHILIP & SON, LTD

st from Greenwich

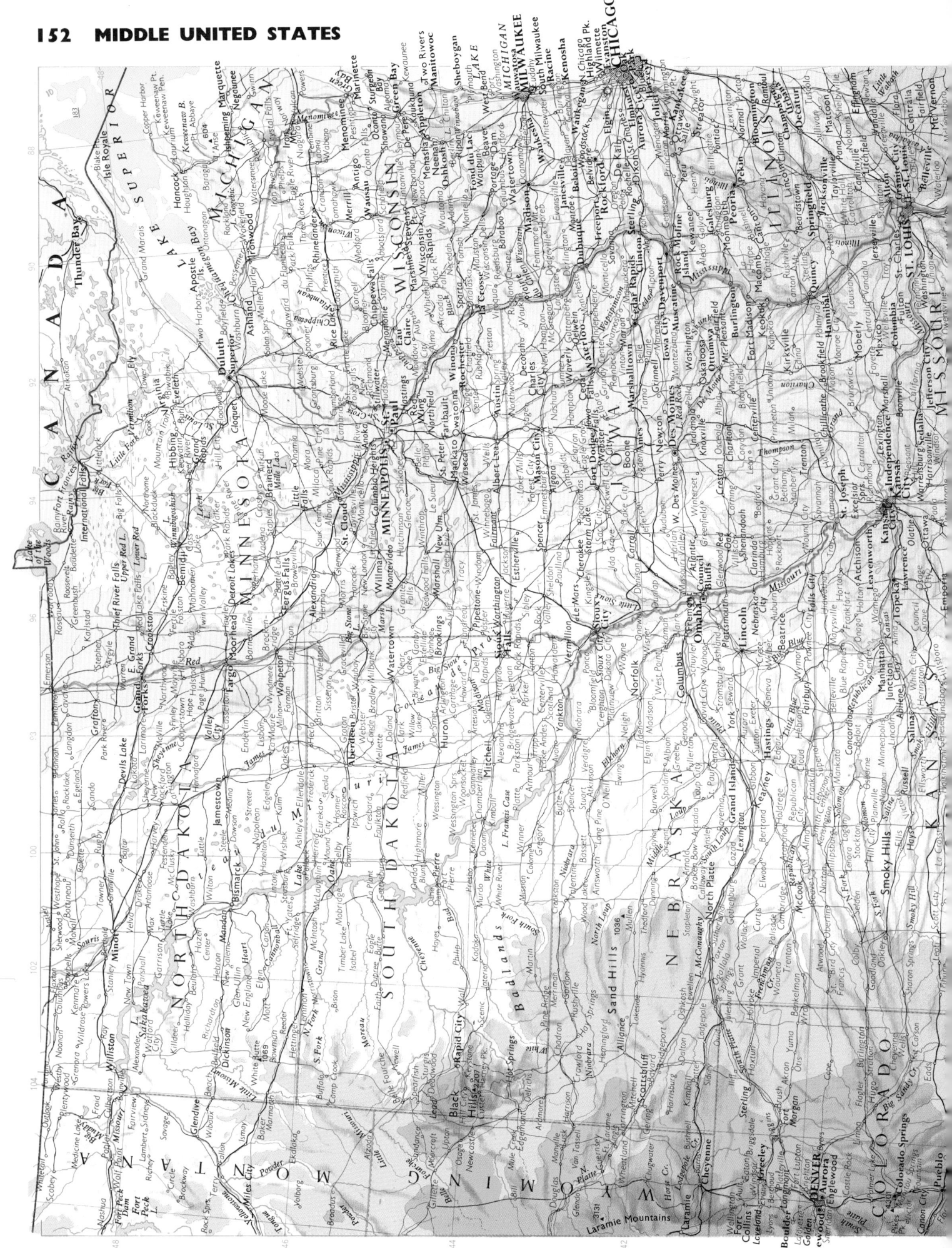

CANADA
LAKE SUPERIOR
LAKE MICHIGAN
MICHIGAN
WISCONSIN
MINNESOTA
NORTH DAKOTA
SOUTH DAKOTA
IOWA
ILLINOIS
NEBRASKA
MISSOURI
KANSAS
COLORADO
WYOMING
MONTANA
CHICAGO
MILWAUKEE
MINNEAPOLIS
St. Paul
DENVER
ST. LOUIS
Kansas City
Des Moines
Omaha
Lincoln
Duluth
Superior
Madison
Green Bay
Rockford
Peoria
Springfield
Sioux City
Sioux Falls
Fargo
Bismarck
Rapid City
Cheyenne
Colorado Springs
Pueblo
Topeka
Thunder Bay
Lake of the Woods
Black Hills
Badlands
Sand Hills
Smoky Hills
Laramie Mountains

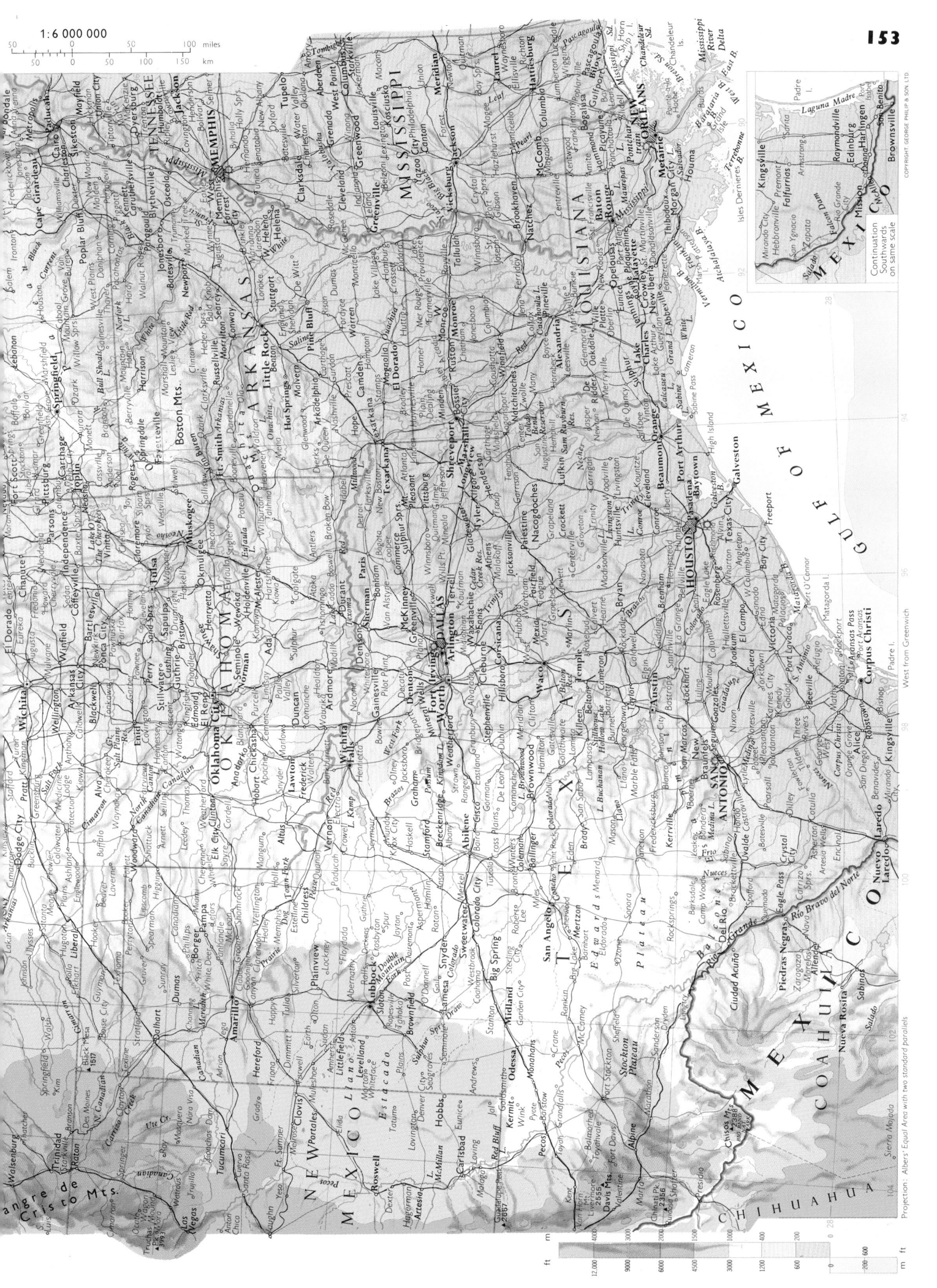
1:6 000 000
miles
km
OKLAHOMA
ARKANSAS
TENNESSEE
MISSISSIPPI
LOUISIANA
TEXAS
NEW MEXICO
MEXICO
COAHUILA
CHIHUAHUA
GULF OF MEXICO
Edwards Plateau
Llano Estacado
Stockton Plateau
Sangre de Cristo Mts.
Boston Mts.
Oklahoma City
Tulsa
Wichita
Amarillo
Lubbock
Dallas
Fort Worth
Arlington
Houston
San Antonio
Austin
Waco
Corpus Christi
Galveston
Beaumont
Port Arthur
Shreveport
Little Rock
Memphis
Jackson
New Orleans
Baton Rouge
Laredo
Nuevo Laredo
Brownsville
Abilene
San Angelo
Midland
Odessa
Continuation Southwards on same scale
Projection: Albers' Equal Area with two standard parallels
West from Greenwich

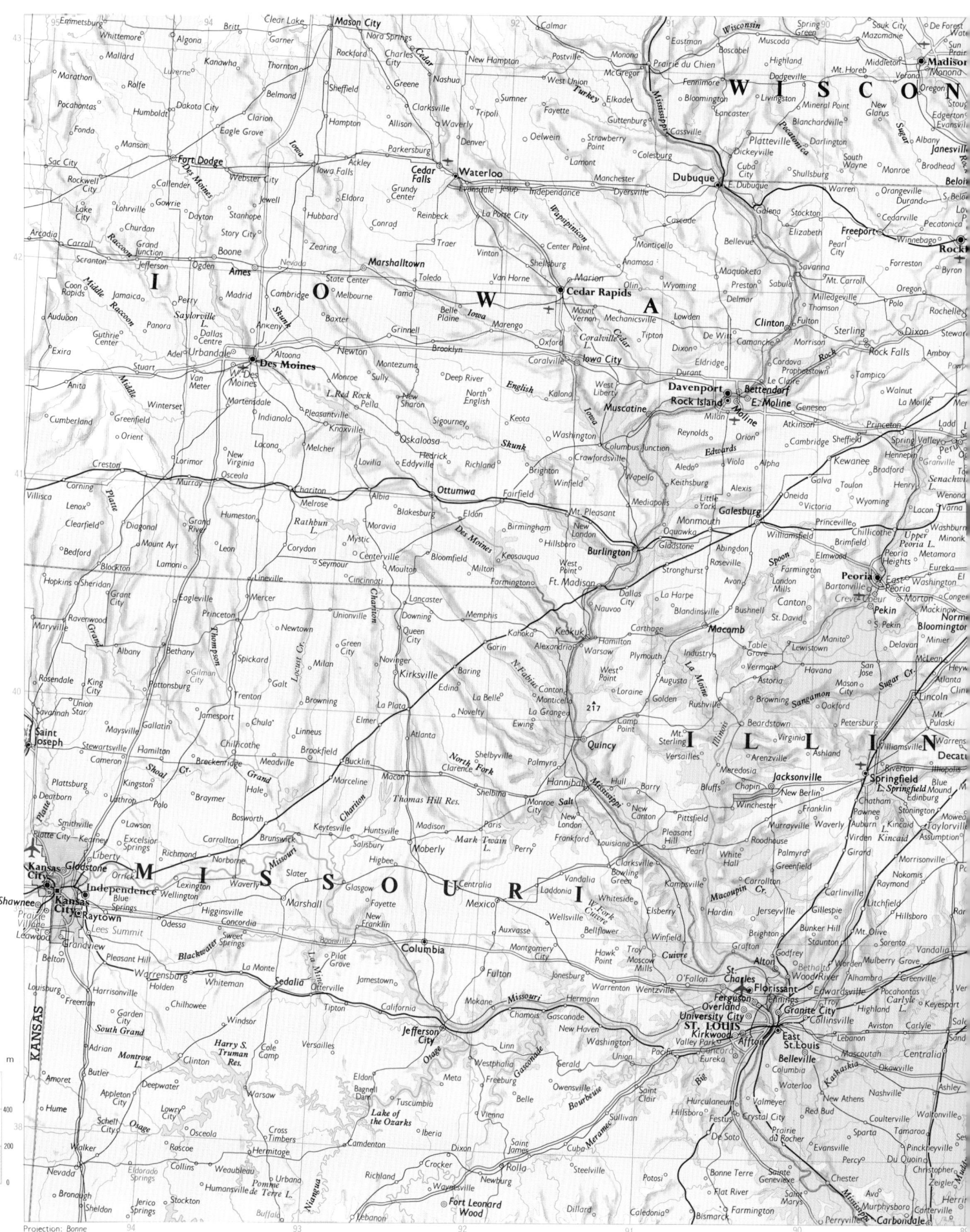
IOWA
MISSOURI
ILLIN
WISCON
KANSAS
Mason City
Clear Lake
Emmetsburg
Algona
Britt
Garner
Nora Springs
Charles City
Rockford
Thornton
Sheffield
Greene
Nashua
New Hampton
Calmar
Postville
Monona
McGregor
Prairie du Chien
Eastman
Wisconsin
Boscobel
Muscoda
Spring Green
Sauk City
Mazomanie
De Forest
Sun Prairie
Madison
Monona
Middleton
Verona
Oregon
Mt. Horeb
Highland
Dodgeville
Fennimore
Bloomington
Livingston
Mineral Point
New Glarus
Lancaster
Blanchardville
Cassville
Platteville
Darlington
Dickeyville
Albany
Janesville
Cuba City
South Wayne
Monroe
Brodhead
Beloit
Shullsburg
Whittemore
Mallard
Kanawha
Marathon
Rolfe
Pocahontas
Humboldt
Dakota City
Belmond
Clarion
Hampton
Clarksville
Allison
Waverly
Sumner
Tripoli
West Union
Fayette
Turkey
Elkader
Guttenburg
Oelwein
Strawberry Point
Colesburg
Lamont
Fonda
Manson
Eagle Grove
Parkersburg
Denver
Fort Dodge
Webster City
Iowa Falls
Ackley
Cedar Falls
Waterloo
Grundy Center
Evansdale
Jesup
Independence
Manchester
Dyersville
Dubuque
E. Dubuque
Sac City
Rockwell City
Callender
Gowrie
Lohrville
Lake City
Dayton
Stanhope
Jewell
Eldora
Hubbard
Conrad
Reinbeck
La Porte City
Wapsipinicon
Cascade
Galena
Stockton
Warren
Orangeville
Durand
Cedarville
Elizabeth
Freeport
Pecatonica
Winnebago
Rockford
Arcadia
Carroll
Churdan
Grand Junction
Story City
Boone
Zearing
Traer
Vinton
Center Point
Monticello
Bellevue
Pearl City
Scranton
Jefferson
Ogden
Ames
Nevada
Marshalltown
State Center
Toledo
Tama
Van Horne
Shellsburg
Marion
Anamosa
Maquoketa
Savanna
Forreston
Byron
Coon Rapids
Jamaica
Perry
Madrid
Cambridge
Melbourne
Belle Plaine
Marengo
Cedar Rapids
Olin
Wyoming
Preston
Sabula
Mt. Carroll
Delmar
Milledgeville
Thomson
Oregon
Polo
Rochelle
Audubon
Panora
Saylorville L.
Ankeny
Baxter
Grinnell
Mount Vernon
Mechanicsville
Lowden
Clinton
Fulton
Sterling
Dixon
Guthrie Center
Dallas Centre
Tipton
De Witt
Camanche
Morrison
Rock Falls
Amboy
Exira
Adel
Urbandale
Des Moines
Altoona
Newton
Brooklyn
Oxford
Coralville
Coralville L.
Iowa City
Dixon
Eldridge
Cordova
Port Byron
Prophetstown
Tampico
Stuart
Van Meter
W. Des Moines
Monroe
Sully
Montezuma
Deep River
English
Kalona
West Liberty
Durant
Le Claire
Davenport
Bettendorf
Rock Island
E. Moline
Moline
Milan
Geneseo
Walnut
La Moille
Anita
Winterset
Martensdale
L. Red Rock
Pella
New Sharon
North English
Muscatine
Cumberland
Greenfield
Orient
Indianola
Pleasantville
Knoxville
Sigourney
Keota
Washington
Reynolds
Orion
Atkinson
Cambridge
Sheffield
Princeton
Spring Valley
Peru
Ladd
Lacona
Melcher
Oskaloosa
Columbus Junction
Edwards
Skunk
Hennepin
New Virginia
Hedrick
Crawfordsville
Aledo
Viola
Alpha
Kewanee
Bradford
Granville
Creston
Lorimor
Osceola
Lovilia
Eddyville
Richland
Brighton
Winfield
Wapello
Keithsburg
Alexis
Galva
Toulon
Henry
Senachwine L.
Corning
Murray
Chariton
Albia
Ottumwa
Fairfield
Mediapolis
Little York
Oneida
Victoria
Wyoming
Wenona
Villisca
Lenox
Platte
Melrose
Blakesburg
Eldon
Mt. Pleasant
Galesburg
Lacon
Varna
Humeston
Rathbun L.
Moravia
Birmingham
New London
Monmouth
Princeville
Chillicothe
Washburn
Minonk
Clearfield
Diagonal
Grand River
Mystic
Hillsboro
Oquawka
Williamsfield
Brimfield
Upper Peoria L.
Metamora
Bedford
Mount Ayr
Leon
Corydon
Centerville
Bloomfield
Keosauqua
Burlington
Gladstone
Abingdon
Elmwood
Peoria Heights
Lamoni
Seymour
Moulton
Milton
West Point
Spoon
Eureka
Blockton
Lineville
Cincinnati
Farmington
Ft. Madison
Stronghurst
Roseville
Farmington
Peoria
East Peoria
Washington
Hopkins
Sheridan
Grant City
Eagleville
Mercer
Lancaster
Dallas City
La Harpe
Avon
London Mills
Bartonville
Creve Coeur
Morton
Congerville
Princeton
Unionville
Chariton
Downing
Memphis
Nauvoo
Blandinsville
Bushnell
Canton
St. David
Pekin
Mackinaw
Normal
Bloomington
Ravenwood
Maryville
Grand
Thompson
Newtown
Green City
Queen City
Kahoka
Keokuk
Hamilton
Carthage
Macomb
S. Pekin
Manito
Minier
Albany
Bethany
Spickard
Milan
Novinger
Kirksville
Gorin
Alexandria
Warsaw
Plymouth
Industry
Table Grove
Lewistown
Delavan
McLean
Gilman City
Baring
West Point
Vermont
Havana
San Jose
Atlanta
Rosendale
King City
Pattonsburg
Galt
Locust Cr.
Edina
La Belle
N. Fabius
Canton
Monticello
Loraine
Augusta
La Moine
Astoria
Mason City
Clinton
Union Star
Trenton
Browning
La Plata
Novelty
La Grange
Golden
Rushville
Browning
Sangamon
Oakford
Sugar Cr.
Lincoln
Savannah
Jamesport
Chula
Linneus
Elmer
Ewing
Camp Point
Beardstown
Petersburg
Mt. Pulaski
Saint Joseph
Maysville
Gallatin
Chillicothe
Brookfield
Atlanta
Shelbyville
Quincy
Mt. Sterling
Virginia
Williamsville
Warrensburg
Decatur
Stewartsville
Hamilton
Cameron
Meadville
Bucklin
North Fork
Palmyra
Versailles
Arenzville
Ashland
Plattsburg
Kingston
Shoal
Breckenridge
Grand
Marceline
Macon
Clarence
Shelbina
Hannibal
Hull
Barry
Meredosia
Jacksonville
Riverton
Springfield
Illiopolis
Dearborn
Lathrop
Braymer
Hale
Thomas Hill Res.
Monroe City
Salt
New Canton
Bluffs
Chapin
New Berlin
L. Springfield
Blue Mound
Edinburg
Polo
Lawson
Bosworth
Chariton
Keytesville
Huntsville
Madison
Paris
Mark Twain L.
New London
Pittsfield
Winchester
Franklin
Chatham
Pawnee
Stonington
Mowequa
Taylorville
Smithville
Platte City
Kearney
Excelsior Springs
Carrollton
Brunswick
Salisbury
Moberly
Perry
Frankford
Louisiana
Pleasant Hill
Murrayville
Waverly
Auburn
Kincaid
Virden
Assumption
Liberty
Richmond
Norborne
Missouri
Higbee
Clarksville
Pearl
White Hall
Roodhouse
Palmyra
Girard
Kansas City
Gladstone
Orrick
Lexington
Waverly
Slater
Vandalia
Bowling Green
Carrollton
Greenfield
Morrisonville
Nokomis
Raymond
Shawnee
Independence
Wellington
Blue Springs
Glasgow
Centralia
Laddonia
Whiteside
Kampsville
Macoupin Cr.
Carlinville
Litchfield
Prairie Village
Leawood
Raytown
Lees Summit
Higginsville
Concordia
Marshall
Fayette
New Franklin
Mexico
Wellsville
W. Fork Cuivre
Elsberry
Hardin
Jerseyville
Gillespie
Hillsboro
Odessa
Grandview
Sweet Springs
Boonville
Columbia
Auxvasse
Bellflower
Winfield
Brighton
Bunker Hill
Staunton
Mt. Olive
Sorento
Belton
Pleasant Hill
Blackwater
La Monte
La Mine
Pilot Grove
Montgomery City
Hawk Point
Troy
Moscow Mills
Cuivre
Grafton
Godfrey
Alton
Bethalto
Worden
Mulberry Grove
Vandalia
Warrensburg
Whiteman
Sedalia
Jamestown
Fulton
Jonesburg
Warrenton
Wentzville
O'Fallon
St. Charles
Florissant
Wood River
Alhambra
Greenville
Louisburg
Harrisonville
Holden
Otterville
Freeman
Chilhowee
Tipton
California
Mokane
Missouri
Hermann
Ferguson
Overland
Jennings
Edwardsville
Troy
Pocahontas
Carlyle L.
Keyesport
Garden City
Windsor
Jefferson City
Chamois
Gasconade
University City
ST. LOUIS
Granite City
Collinsville
Highland
Aviston
Carlyle
South Grand
New Haven
Washington
Kirkwood
Affton
East St. Louis
Lebanon
Adrian
Montrose L.
Clinton
Harry S. Truman Res.
Cole Camp
Versailles
Osage
Linn
Union
Pacific
Valley Park
Concord
Eureka
Belleville
Mascoutah
Centralia
Okawville
Butler
Westphalia
Gasconade
Gerald
Freeburg
Columbia
Kaskaskia
Amoret
Deepwater
Eldon
Meta
Bagnell Dam
Tuscumbia
Owensville
Bourbeuse
Saint Clair
Big
Waterloo
New Athens
Nashville
Ashley
Hume
Appleton City
Warsaw
Lowry City
Lake of the Ozarks
Belle
Vienna
Sullivan
Hurculaneum
Hillsboro
Valmeyer
Red Bud
Coulterville
Waltonville
Schell City
Osage
Osceola
Cross Timbers
Iberia
Meramec
Festus
Crystal City
Prairie du Rocher
Sparta
Tamaroa
Walker
Roscoe
Hermitage
Camdenton
Dixon
Saint James
Cuba
De Soto
Evansville
Pinckneyville
Nevada
Collins
Eldorado Springs
Weaubleau
Urbana
Pomme de Terre L.
Niangua
Crocker
Richland
Rolla
Waynesville
Newburg
Steelville
Potosi
Bonne Terre
Sainte Genevieve
Percy
Du Quoin
Chester
Christopher
Zeigler
Humansville
Fort Leonard Wood
Flat River
Saint Marys
Ava
Murphysboro
Herrin
Carterville
Bronaugh
Sheldon
Jerico Springs
Stockton
Buffalo
Lebanon
Dillard
Caledonia
Bismarck
Farmington
Perryville
Carbondale
Mississippi
Rock
Pecatonica
Sugar
Cedar
Iowa
Des Moines
Raccoon
Middle Raccoon
Middle
Skunk
Illinois
Projection: Bonne
95
94
93
92
91
90
89
43
42
41
40
38
217
ft
m
1200
600
0
400
200
0

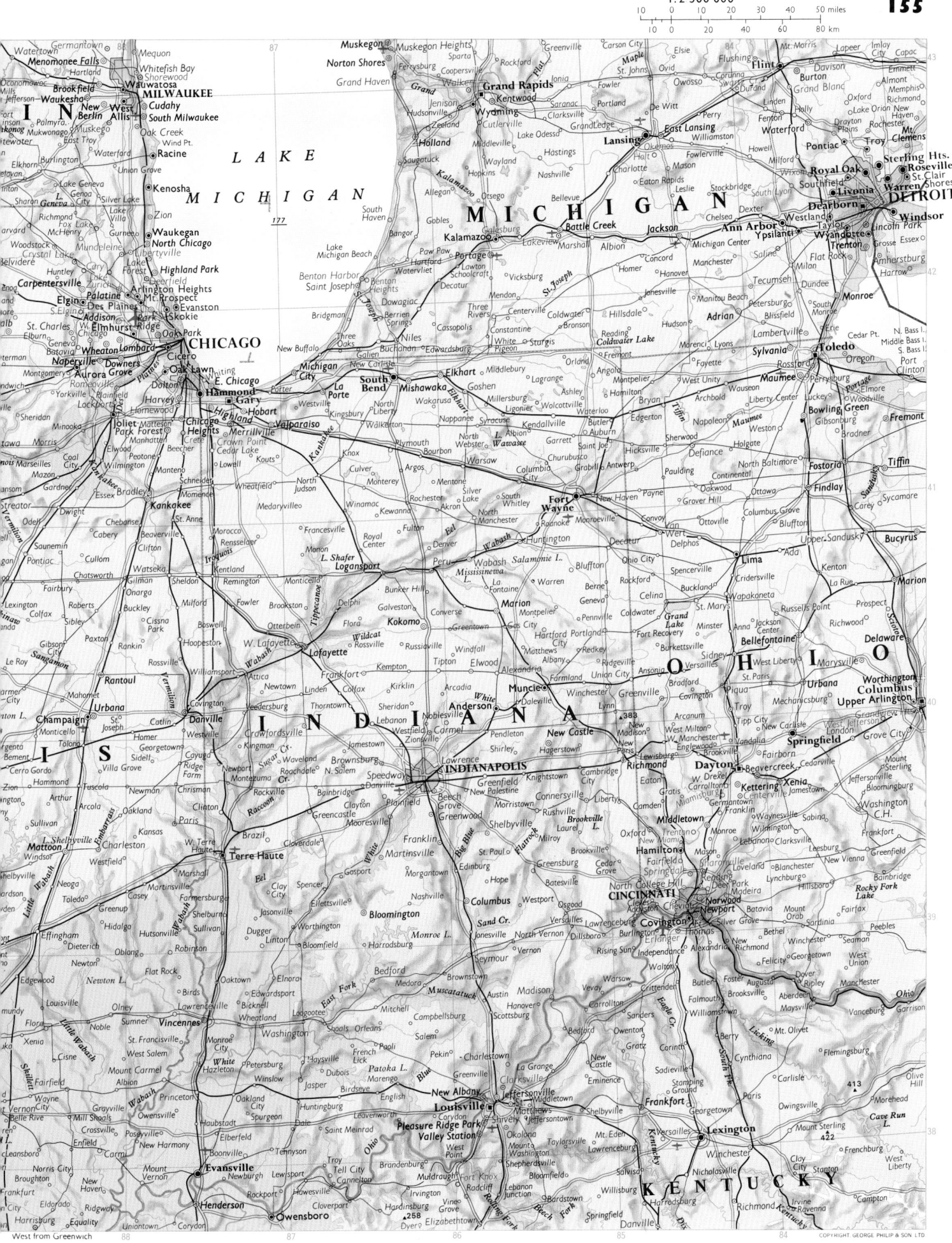

1: 2 500 000

COPYRIGHT GEORGE PHILIP & SON LTD

1:6 000 000

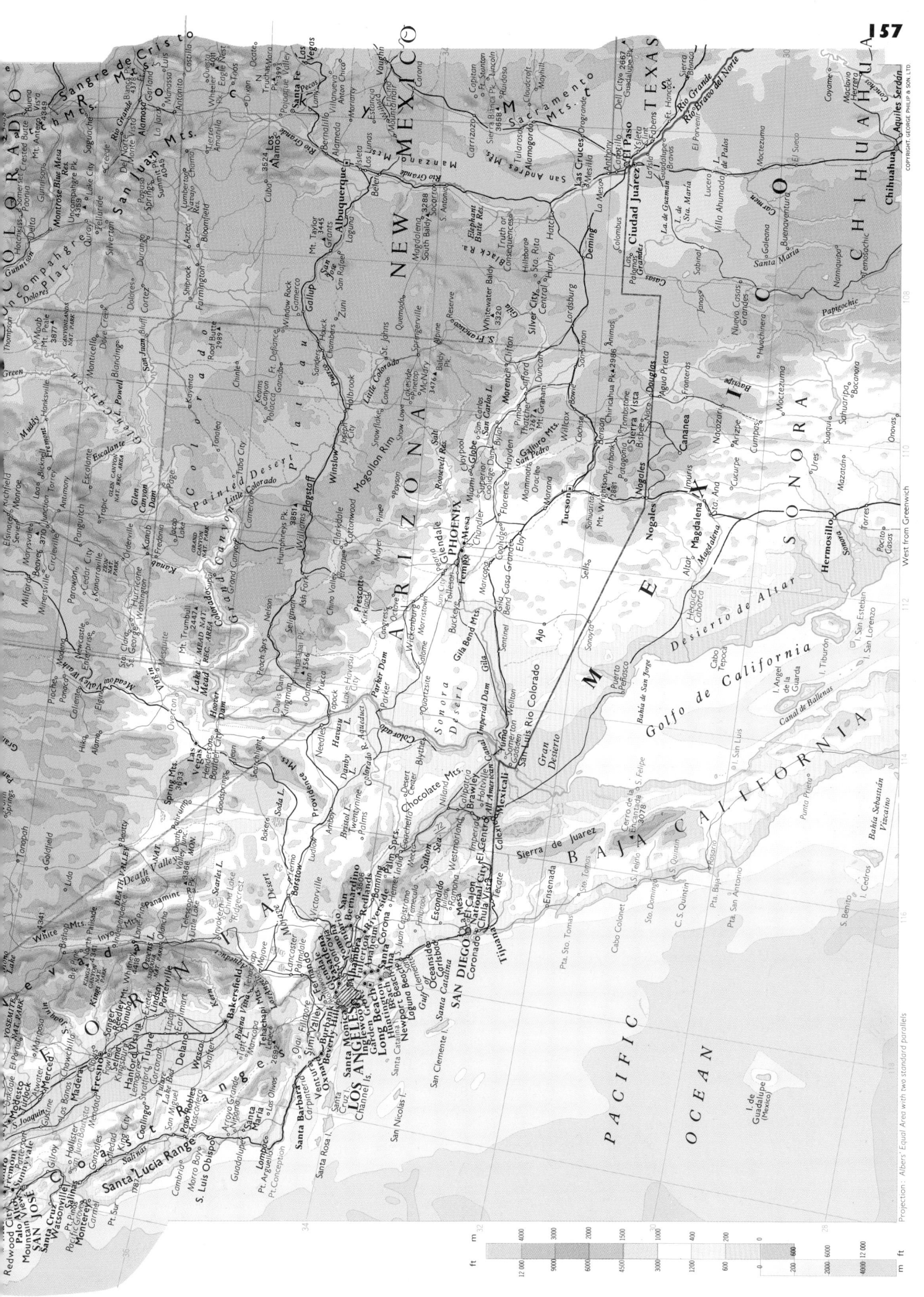

West from Greenwich

Projection: Albers' Equal Area with two standard parallels

SEATTLE-PORTLAND REGION
On same scale
PACIFIC OCEAN
WASHINGTON
OREGON
SEATTLE
Tacoma
Olympia
PORTLAND
Vancouver
Victoria
Vancouver Island
Juan de Fuca Strait
Strait of Georgia
Olympic Mountains
White Mts.
Inyo Mts.
Sierra Nevada
Mono L.
L. Tahoe
Reno
Sacramento
Stockton
Modesto
Merced
Fresno
SAN FRANCISCO
Oakland
Berkeley
SAN JOSE
Monterey
Salinas
Santa Lucia Range
Diablo Range
Coast Ranges
CALIFORNIA

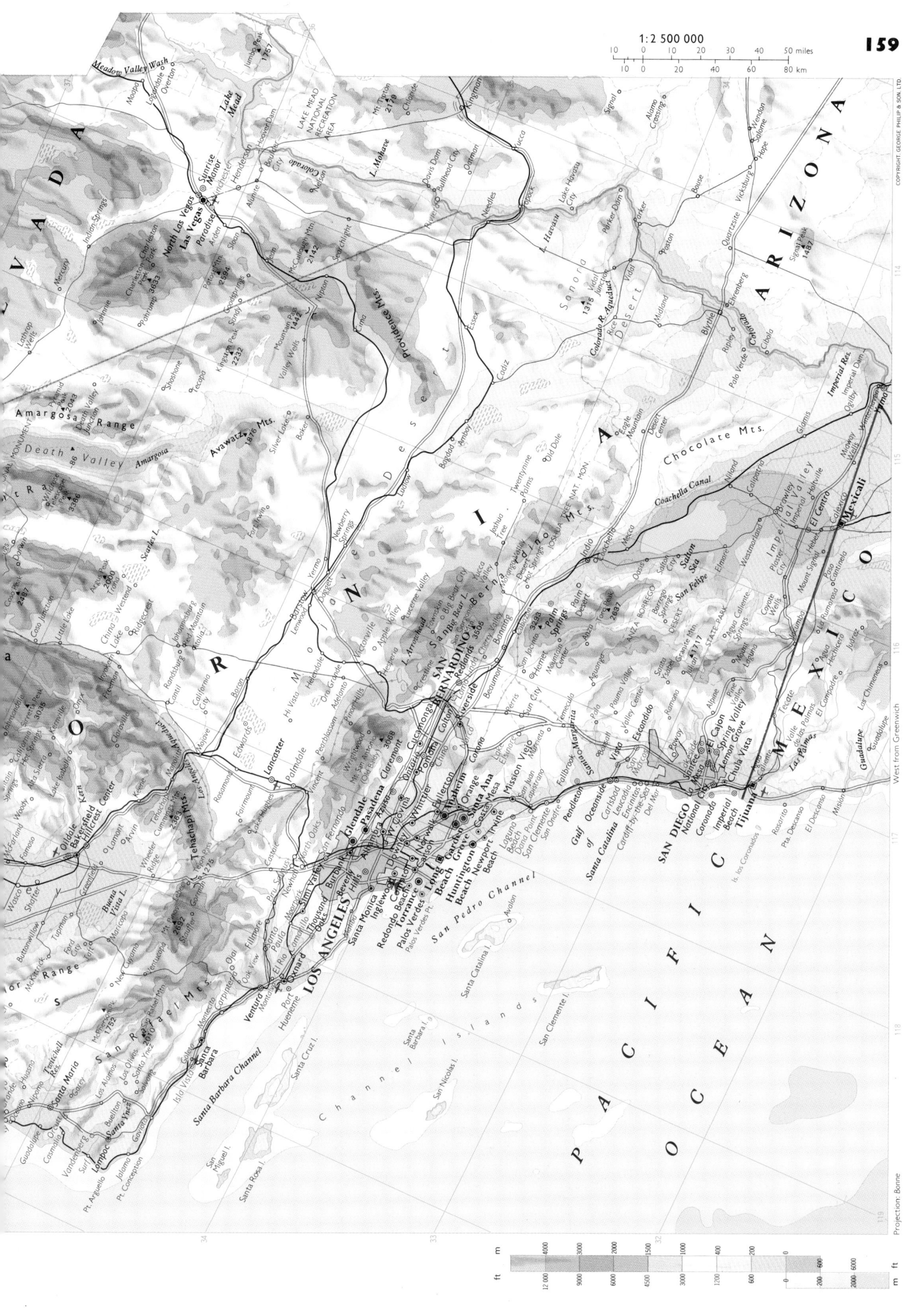

1:2 500 000

10   0   10   20   30   40   50 miles
10   0   20   40   60   80 km

COPYRIGHT GEORGE PHILIP & SON, LTD.

N E V A D A

A R I Z O N A

C A L I F O R N I A

M E X I C O

P A C I F I C   O C E A N

Meadow Valley Wash

Lake Mead

LAKE MEAD NATIONAL RECREATION AREA

Las Vegas
North Las Vegas
Sunrise Manor
Paradise
Henderson

Hoover Dam
Davis Dam
Colorado

L. Mohave

Bullhead City
Oatman
Kingman

Needles
Topock
Lake Havasu City
Parker Dam

Amargosa Range

Death Valley

Avawatz Mts.

Providence Mts.

Sonora Desert

Chocolate Mts.

Imperial Res.
Imperial Dam
Yuma
Mexicali

Coachella Canal

Salton Sea

SAN BERNARDINO
Redlands
Riverside
Colton

Lancaster
Palmdale
Edwards

Santa Monica
LOS ANGELES
Pasadena
Glendale
Long Beach
Torrance
Redondo Beach
Palos Verdes Pt.
Huntington Beach
Newport Beach
Santa Ana
Anaheim
Orange
Fullerton
Pomona

Santa Catalina I.
San Pedro Channel

Santa Barbara
Santa Barbara Channel

Channel Islands

San Miguel I.
Santa Rosa I.
Santa Cruz I.
Santa Barbara I.
San Nicolas I.
San Clemente I.

SAN DIEGO
National City
Chula Vista
Coronado
Imperial Beach
Tijuana

El Cajon
Escondido
Oceanside
Carlsbad

Santa Maria
Lompoc
Pt. Conception

Ventura
Oxnard

Bakersfield

San Rafael Mts.

Tehachapi Mts.

West from Greenwich

Projection: Bonne

m   ft
4000   12 000
3000   9000
2000   6000
1500   4500
1000   3000
600   1200
200   600
0   0
200   600
2000   6000
6000   m ft

ARIZONA
NEW MEXICO
UNITED STATES
TIJUANA
MEXICALI
Ensenada
Yuma
San Luis Río Colorado
TUCSON
Nogales
Douglas
Agua Prieta
CIUDAD JUÁREZ
EL PASO
Las Cruces
Deming
Lordsburg
Roswell
Carlsbad
Hobbs
Lubbock
Big Spring
Sweetwater
Van Horn
BAJA CALIFORNIA NORTE
Sierra de Juárez
Sierra de San Pedro Mártir
Puerto Peñasco
San Felipe
Golfo de California
Caborca
Magdalena
Cananea
Santa Ana
I. Ángel de la Guarda
I. Tiburón
Hermosillo
SONORA
Guaymas
Empalme
Ciudad Obregón
Navojoa
Huatabampo
I. Cedros
Bahía Sebastián Vizcaíno
Desierto de Vizcaíno
Sierra Vizcaíno
Santa Rosalía
Laguna San Ignacio
Pta. Abreojos
BAJA CALIFORNIA SUR
Sierra de la Giganta
Llano de la Magdalena
I. Carmen
I. San José
I. Espíritu Santo
I. Cerralvo
I. Santa Magdalena
B. Magdalena
I. Santa Margarita
La Paz
Todos Santos
San José del Cabo
C. San Lucas
Los Mochis
El Fuerte
Guasave
Guamúchil
Culiacán
Navolato
SINALOA
Mazatlán
Rosario
Escuinapa
Acaponeta
Tecuala
CHIHUAHUA
Nuevo Casas Grandes
Cuauhtémoc
Delicias
Meoqui
Ciudad Camargo
Jiménez
Hidalgo del Parral
Santa Bárbara
Sierra Madre Occidental
Bolsón de Mapimí
COAHUILA
Piedras Negras
Acuña
Nueva Rosita
Sabinas
Monclova
Saltillo
TORREÓN
Gómez Palacio
Lerdo
San Pedro de las Colonias
DURANGO
Victoria de Durango
Santiago Papasquiaro
Fresnillo
Zacatecas
ZACATECAS
Aguascalientes
NAYARIT
Tepic
Santiago Ixcuintla
Compostela
Islas Tres Marías
Puerto Vallarta
B. de Banderas
C. Corrientes
JALISCO
GUADALAJARA
Tlaquepaque
Ocotlán
L. de Chapala
LEÓN
Lagos de Moreno
Irapuato
Ciudad Guzmán
Autlán
Colima
Manzanillo
COLIMA
Tecomán
Uruapan
Zamora
Apatzingán
MICHOACÁN
Zihuatanejo
Is. de Revillagigedo (Mexico)
San Benedicto
Socorro
Roca Partida
PACIFIC OCEAN
REFERENCE TO NUMBERS
1 Federal District
2 Aguascalientes
3 Guanajuato
4 Hidalgo
5 México
6 Morelos
7 Querétaro
8 Tlaxcala
Projection: Bi-polar oblique Conical Orthomorphic
West from Greenwich
110
105

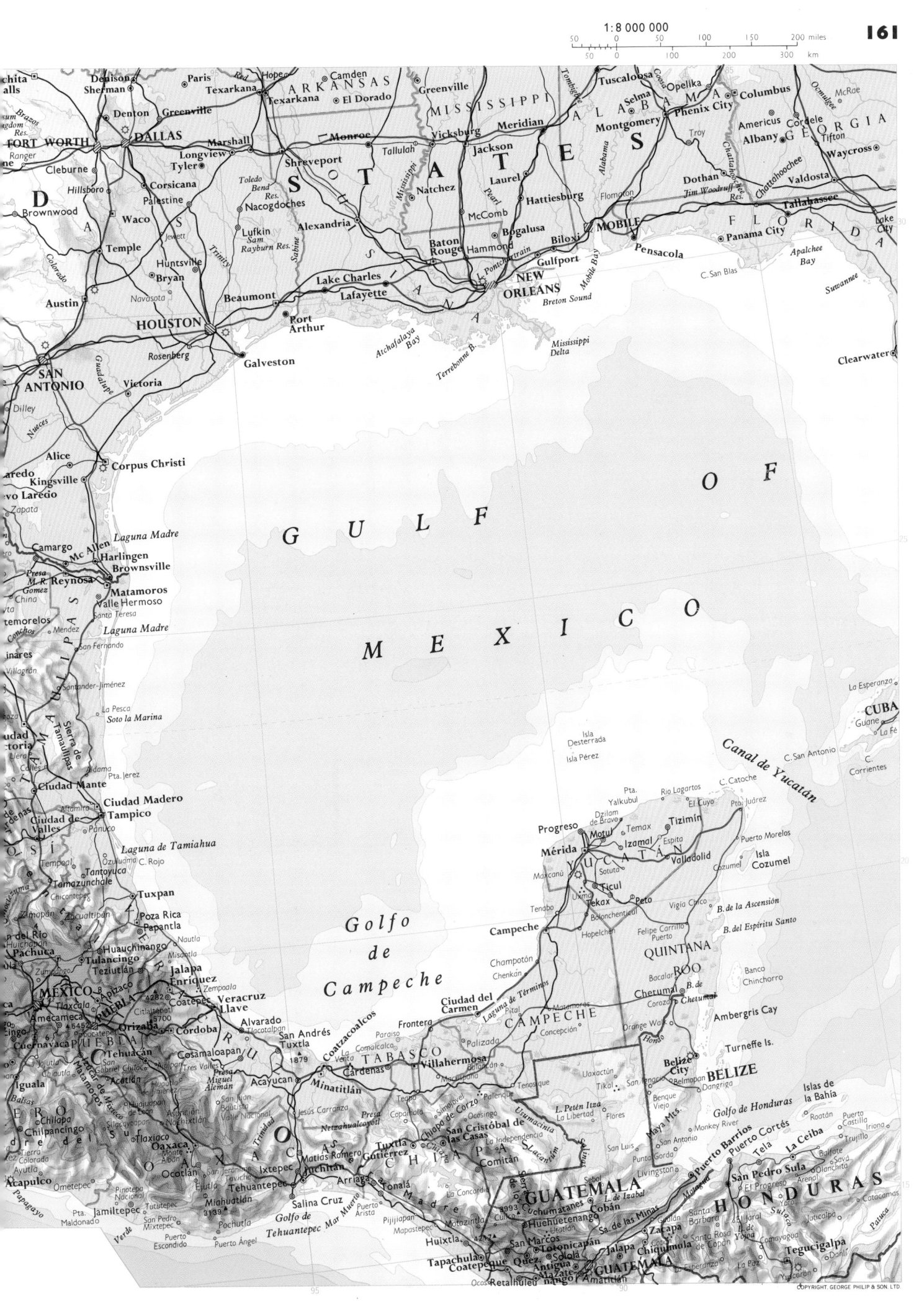

1:8 000 000

50   0   50   100   150   200 miles
50   0   100   200   300   km

chita
alls
Denison
Sherman   Paris   Texarkana   Camden   Greenville   Tuscaloosa   Opelika   Columbus   McRae
sum   Brazos   Denton   Greenville   Texarkana   El Dorado   MISSISSIPPI   Selma   Columbus   Ormulgee
agdom   Res.   ARKANSAS   Greenville   Montgomery   Americus   Cordele
Ranger   FORT WORTH   DALLAS   Marshall   Monroe   Vicksburg   Meridian   Troy   Albany   GEORGIA   Tifton
ne   Cleburne   Longview   Shreveport   S   T   A   T   E   S   Chattahoochee   Waycross
Tyler   Tallulah   Jackson   Montgomery   Dothan   Valdosta
D   Hillsboro   Corsicana   Toledo   Jim Woodruff   Tallahassee   Lake
Brownwood   Palestine   Bend   Natchez   Laurel   Flomaton   Res.   City
Waco   Nacogdoches   Res.   A   L   A   B   A   M   A   FLORIDA
Temple   Lufkin   Alexandria   McComb   MOBILE   Pensacola   Panama City   Apalachee
Huntsville   Sam   Baton   Bogalusa   Bay
Austin   Bryan   Rayburn Res.   Rouge Hammond   Biloxi   Gulfport   C. San Blas   Suwannee
Lake Charles   NEW   Pontchartrain   Breton Sound   Clearwater
HOUSTON   Beaumont   Lafayette   ORLEANS   Mississippi
SAN   Port   Delta
ANTONIO   Arthur   Atchafalaya   Terrebonne B.
Rosenberg   Bay
Dilley   Galveston
Victoria

G   U   L   F   O   F

Alice
Laredo   Kingsville   Corpus Christi
vo Laredo
Zapata   Laguna Madre
Camargo   Mc Allen   Harlingen   M   E   X   I   C   O
Presa   Brownsville
M.R.Reynosa   Matamoros
Gomez   Valle Hermoso
China   Santa Teresa
temorelos   Mendez   Laguna Madre
Conchos   San Fernando
inares   Villagrán   La Esperanza
Santander-Jiménez   CUBA
La Pesca   Guane   La Fé
Soto la Marina   C. San Antonio
dad   Isla   Canal de Yucatán   C.
toria   Sierra de   Desterrada   Corrientes
Aldama   Tamaulipas   Isla Pérez   Rio Lagartos   C. Catoche
llera   Pta. Jerez   Pta.   El Cuyo   Pta. Juárez
Ciudad Mante   Yalkubul   Puerto Morelos
Ciudad Madero   Dzilam   Tizimín
Ciudad de   Tampico   Progreso   de Bravo   Temax   Espita
Valles   Pánuco   Motul   Izamal   Isla
OSI   Laguna de Tamiahua   Mérida   YUCATÁN   Valladolid   Cozumel
Tempoal   C. Rojo   Maxcanú   Sotuta   Cozumel
Tamazunchale   Ozuluama   Ticul   Peto   Vigia Chico   B. de la Ascensión
Tantoyuca   Uxmal   Tekax   Bolonchenticul   B. del Espíritu Santo
Chicontepec   Tuxpan   Tenabo   Hopelchen   QUINTANA
Zacualtipan   Poza Rica   Campeche   Felipe Carrillo   ROO
del Rio   Papantla   Golfo   Champotón   Puerto   Banco
Pachuca   Huauchinango   Nautla   de   Chenkán   Bacalar   Chinchorro
Tulancingo   Misantla   Campeche   QUINTANA   B. de
Teziutlán   Jalapa   Ciudad del   Laguna de Términos   Chetumal   Chetumal
MÉXICO   Enriquez   Carmen   Pital   Matamoros   ROO   Corozal
Tlaxcala   Apizaco   Zempoala   Frontera   Belize
Amecameca   PUEBLA   Coatepec   Veracruz   Ambergris Cay
Citlaltepetl   Llave   CAMPECHE   Orange Walk
Cuernavaca   Orizaba   Alvarado   San Andrés   Paraiso   Concepción   Turneffe Is.
PUEBLA   Córdoba   Tlacotalpan   Tuxtla   Coatzacoalcos   Palizada   Hondo
Iguala   Tehuacán   Cosamaloapan   Comalcalco   Belize   BELIZE
Balsas   1879   TABASCO   La Venta   Palenque   City
ERO   Acatlán   Acayucan   Minatitlán   Cárdenas   Villahermosa   Uaxactún   Dangriga
Chilapa   Tres Valles   Tenosique   Tikal   San   Belmopan
Chilpancingo   Miguel   Teapa   Benque   Islas de
dre del   Tlaxiaco   Alemán   Jesús Carranza   Presa   Chiapa de Corzo   Viejo   la Bahía
Ayutla   San Juan   Capalhá   Ocosingo   L. Petén Itza   Golfo de Honduras
Oaxaca   Bautista   Netzahualcoyotl   Palenque   La Libertad   Roatán   Puerto
Acapulco   Nochixtlán   OAXACA   Ixtepec   Usumacinta   Flores   Castilla
Ometepec   Ejutla   San Jeronimo   Tuxtla   San Cristóbal de   La Independencia   Maya Mts.   Puerto   Trujillo
Pinotepa   Ocotlán   Gutiérrez   las Casas   CHIAPA   San   Puerto Barrios   Puerto Cortés   La Ceiba
Nacional   Miahuatlán   Comitán   Sierra   Antonio   Livingston   El Progreso   Olanchito
Pta. Jamiltepec   Tututepec   3139   Salina Cruz   Mar Muerto   Madre   Punta   San Pedro Sula   HONDURAS
Maldonado   Mixtepec   Golfo de   Arista   La Concordia   Gorda   GUATEMALA   Cobán   Santa   Catacamas
Puerto   Tehuantepec   Pijijiapan   Cuchumatanes   Barbara
Escondido   Pochutla   Motozintla   3993   Sa. de las Minas   Zacapa   Yoro
Verde   Huixtla   San Marcos   Huehuetenango   Chiquimula   Santa Rosa   Comayagua   Patuca
Mapastepec   GUATEMALA   Jalapa   Tegucigalpa
Tapachula   Coatepeque   Quez.   Totonicapán   Sololá   Antigua   GUATEMALA   La Paz
Ocós   Retalhuleu   nango   Amatitlán   Yuscarán
COPYRIGHT GEORGE PHILIP & SON, LTD.

GULF OF MEXICO

West Palm Beach
Fort Myers
Naples
C. Romano
Everglades
Hialeah
MIAMI
C. Sable
Florida City
Florida Bay
Key West
Dry Tortugas
Florida Keys
Straits of Florida

Little Abaco I.
West End
Freeport
Grand Bahama I.
Hope Town
Great Abaco I.
Great Guana Cay
Bimini Is.
Berry Is.
Nassau
New Providence I.
Adelaide
Eleuthera I.
Andros Town
Andros Island
Great Exuma
Northwest Providence Channel
Northeast Providence Channel
GREAT BAHAMA BANK

Isla Desterrada
Isla Pérez
Canal de Yucatán
C. San Antonio

(Havana) LA HABANA
MARIANAO
San Antonio de los Baños
Guanajay
Guanabacoa
Santa Cruz del Norte
Matanzas
Canal Nicolás
Cay Sal Bank
Santarén Channel

Progreso
Pta. Yalkubul
Dzilam de Bravo
Dzibilchaltún
Motul
Temax
Izamal
Tizimín
El Cuyo
C. Catoche
Pto. Juárez
Mérida
Maxcanú
Calkiní
Tekax
Ticul
Chichén Itzá
Valladolid
Puerto Morel s
Río Lagartos
Espita
El Diaz

Campeche
Champotón
Chenkan
San José Carpizo
Vigía Chico
B. de la Ascensión
Isla Cozumel
Cozumel

La Esperanza
Bahía Honda
Guane
La Fé
Pinar del Río
San Luis
Nueva Gerona
Isla de la Juventud
Los Palacios
Corrientes
Archipiélago de los Canarreos

Güines
Batabanó
Jagüey Grande
Playa Larga
Cienfuegos
Cárdenas
Colón
Jovellanos
Sagua la Grande
Santa Clara
Caibarién
Placetas
Morón
Trinidad
Sancti-Spíritus
Júcaro
Ciego de Avila
Cayo Romano
Nuevitas
Puerto
Arch. de los Jardines de la Reina
Tunas de Zaza
Camagüey
Santa Cruz del Sur
Victoria de las Tunas
Golfo de Guacanayabo
Manzanillo
Gibara
HOLG
Bayam
Palm
Sorian
Sierra Maestra
SANTI DE C
C. Cruz
2000
GREATER
CUBA

Ciudad del Carmen
Laguna de Términos
Pital
Palizada
Concepción
Matamoros
Juárez
Pedro Antonio Santos
Bacalar
B. de Chetumal
Banco Chinchorro
Hondo
QUINTANA ROO
CAMPECHE
Chetumal
Corozal
Orange Walk
Ambergris Cay
Turneffe Is.
Belize City
San Ignacio
Belmopan
BELIZE
Middlesex
Dangriga
Benque Viejo

Cayman Islands (Br.)
Georgetown
Grand Cayman
Cayman Brac
Little Cayman

Montego Bay
Lucea
Falmouth
St. Ann's Bay
Port Mari
Annotto
Savanna la Mar
South Negril Pt.
Black River
Cambri
Mandeville
May Pen
JAMAICA
Spanish Town
KINGS
Pedro Cays (Jamaica)

Palenque
Ocosingo
Tenosique
Uaxactún
Tikal
L. Petén Itzá
La Libertad
Flores
Sayaxché
Comitán
La Independencia
Lacantún
Usumacinta
GUATEMALA
Cuchumatanes
Huehuetenango
Cobán
L. de Izabal
Livingston
Puerto Barrios
Puerto Cortés
Tela
Golfo de Honduras
Monkey River
Punta Gorda
San Antonio
Maya Mts.
San Luis
Roatán
Islas de la Bahía
Puerto Castilla
Trujillo
La Ceiba
Iriona
C. Camarón
Pta. Patuca
Brus Laguna
Swan Islands (U.S.A. & Honduras)
Bajo Nuevo (Colombia)

San Marcos
Totonicapán
Quezaltenango
Sololá
Antigua
GUATEMALA
Coatepeque
Retalhuleu
Mazatenango
Jalapa
Chiquimula
Zacapa
Santa Bárbara
El Progreso
San Pedro Sula
HONDURAS
Santa Rosa de Copán
Comayagua
Tegucigalpa
Juticalpa
Catacamas
Pta. Lempira
C. Falso
Mosquitia
C. Gracias á Dios
Puerto Cabo Gracias á Dios
Cayos Miskitos (Nicaragua)
Pta. Gorda
CARI
CARI

Ahuachapán
Santa Ana
Suchitoto
Cojutepeque
Zacatecoluca
SAN SALVADOR
Usulután
EL SALVADOR
San Miguel
La Unión
Golfo de Fonseca
Chinandega
Corinto
León
La Paz Centro
Boaco
MANAGUA
Masaya
Diriamba
Granada
Jinotepe
Rivas
Lago de Managua
Estelí
Cord. Isabella
Matagalpa
Muy Muy
Juigalpa
Santo Domingo
Rama
Bluefields
El Bluff
Pta. Mico
Cord. de Yolaina
NICARAGUA
Puerto Cabezas
Prinzapolca
Río Grande
Siuna
Bonanza
Tunga
San Pedro del Norte
Siquia
Islas del Maíz (Nicaragua, U.S.A.)
I. de Providencia (U.S.A. & Colombia)
I. de San Andrés (Colombia)
Cayos Roncador (U.S.A. & Colombia)
Cayos de Albuquerque (Colombia)

San Juan del Sur
B. de Salinas
C. Sta. Elena
Golfo de Papagayo
C. Velas
Liberia
Santa Cruz
C. Blanco
Pen. de Nicoya
Golfo de Nicoya
Puntarenas
Espartaza
Alajuela
San José
Cartago
Puerto Quepos
Bahía de Coronado
Pen. de Osa
Golfo Dulce
Puerto Armuelles
Pta. Burica
Golfo de Chiriquí
David
Santiago
Chitré
Pen. de Azuero
Pta. Mala
Pta. Mariato
I. de Coiba
I. de Cebaco
I. Jicarón
Lago de Nicaragua
Isla de Ometepe
San Carlos
San Juan
San Juan del Norte
Bahía de San Juan del Norte
COSTA RICA
Cord. de Guanacaste
Cord. Central
Cord. de Talamanca
Limón
Pta. Mona
Siquirres
Guápiles
Bocas del Toro
Almirante
Laguna de Chiriquí
Golfo de los Mosquitos
Serranía de Tabasará
PANAMÁ
Colón
Nombre de Dios
Portobelo
Archipiélago de las Mulatas
Golfo del Darién
Gatun L.
Balboa
La Chorrea
Chimán
San Miguel I. del Rey
Arch. de las Perlas
Golfo de Panamá
Las Tablas
Pocrí
Garachine
La Palma
Sierranía del Darien
Turbo
El Real
Jaque
Golfo de Uraba
CART
CART
Is. de San Berna

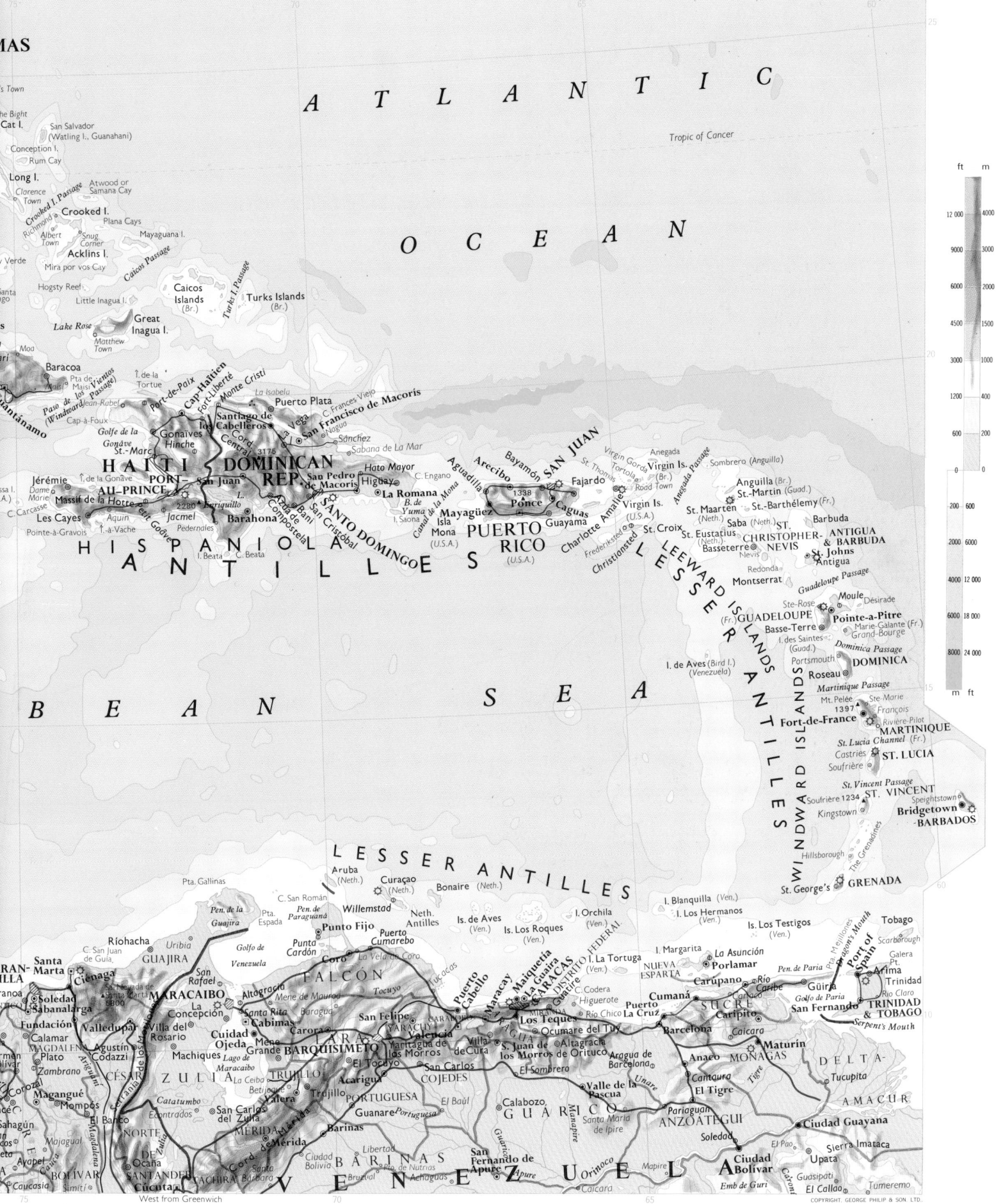

1 : 8 000 000

50   0   50   100   150   200 miles

50   0   100   200   300 km

A T L A N T I C

Tropic of Cancer

O C E A N

MAS

's Town
Cat I.
The Bight
San Salvador
(Watling I., Guanahani)
Conception I.
Rum Cay
Long I.
Clarence Town
Crooked I. Passage
Crooked I.
Richmond
Plana Cays
Albert Town
Snug Corner
Mayaguana I.
Acklins I.
Mira por vos Cay
Hogsty Reef
Little Inagua I.
Caicos Passage
Caicos Islands (Br.)
Turks Islands (Br.)
Turks I. Passage
Great Inagua I.
Lake Rose
Matthew Town
Moa
Baracoa
Pta. de Maisi
Î. de la Tortue
Port-de-Paix
Cap-Haïtien
Fort-Liberté
Monte Cristi
La Isabela
Puerto Plata
C. Francés Viejo
San Francisco de Macorís
Nagua
Santiago de los Cabelleros
Vega
Sánchez
Sabana de La Mar
Paso de los Vientos
(Windward) Passage
Jean-Rabel
Cap-à-Foux
Golfe de la Gonâve
Gonaïves
Hinche
Cord. Central 3175
Hato Mayor
Aguadilla
Arecibo
Bayamón
SAN JUAN
Virgin Gorda
Anegada
Virgin Is.
Sombrero (Anguilla)
Anguilla (Br.)
St. Thomas
Road Town
(Br.)
Anegada Passage
Guantánamo
HAITI
DOMINICAN REP.
San Juan
San Pedro de Macorís
Higüey
C. Engaño
Fajardo
Virgin Is.
St.-Martin (Guad.)
St-Barthélemy (Fr.)
Jérémie
Î. de la Gonâve
PORT-AU-PRINCE
L.
Ponce
Caguas
1338
St. Maarten (Neth.)
Saba (Neth.)
Barbuda
Massif de la Hotte
2280 Enriquillo
La Romana
B. de Yuma
Mayagüez
Guayama
Charlotte Amalie
St. Croix
St. Eustatius
(Neth.)
ST. CHRISTOPHER-NEVIS
ANTIGUA & BARBUDA
Les Cayes
Aquin
Jacmel
San Cristóbal
Baní
Compostela
Isla Mona
Canal de la Mona
& la Saona
Christiansted
Frederiksted
Basseterre
Nevis
St. Johns
Antigua
Pointe-à-Gravois
Î.-à-Vache
Barahona
Pedernales
SANTO DOMINGO
PUERTO RICO
(U.S.A.)
(U.S.A.)
Redonda
Montserrat
HISPANIOLA
Î. Beata
C. Beata
Guadeloupe Passage
A N T I L L E S
Ste-Rose
Moule
Désirade
L E S S E R
Pointe-à-Pitre
GUADELOUPE (Fr.)
Basse-Terre
Marie-Galante (Fr.)
Grand-Bourg
Î. des Saintes (Guad.)
Dominica Passage
B E A N   S E A
I. de Aves (Bird I.)
(Venezuela)
L E E W A R D   I S L A N D S
Portsmouth
Roseau
DOMINICA
A N T I L L E S
Martinique Passage
Mt. Pelée 1397
Ste-Marie
François
Rivière-Pilot
Fort-de-France
MARTINIQUE (Fr.)
St. Lucia Channel (Fr.)
Castries
ST. LUCIA
W I N D W A R D   I S L A N D S
Soufrière
St. Vincent Passage
Soufrière 1234
ST. VINCENT
Speightstown
Kingstown
Bridgetown
BARBADOS
Hillsborough
The Grenadines
L E S S E R   A N T I L L E S
St. George's
GRENADA
Pta. Gallinas
Aruba (Neth.)
Curaçao (Neth.)
Bonaire (Neth.)
I. Blanquilla (Ven.)
Tobago
C. San Román
Willemstad
Neth. Antilles
I. Orchila (Ven.)
I. Los Hermanos (Ven.)
I. Los Testigos (Ven.)
Scarborough
Pen. de la Guajira
Pta. Espada
Pen. de Paraguaná
Punto Fijo
Puerto Cumarebo
Is. de Aves (Ven.)
Is. Los Roques (Ven.)
Port of Spain
Galera Pt.
Ríohacha
Uribia
C. San Juan de Guía
GUAJIRA
Pta. Cardón
Coro
La Vela de Coro
I. Margarita
La Asunción
NUEVA ESPARTA
Porlamar
Pta. Peñas
Pen. de Paria
Arima
Trinidad
Golfo de Venezuela
Cuchuás
Maiquetía
La Guaira
CARACAS
I. La Tortuga (Ven.)
Carúpano
Río Caribe
Güiria
Golfo de Paria
San Fernando
TRINIDAD & TOBAGO
Santa Marta
Ciénaga
Santa Rosa de
San Rafael
Altagracia
Mene de Mauroa
FALCÓN
Tocuyo
Puerto Cabello
Maracay
DISTRITO FEDERAL
C. Codera
Higuerote
Puerto La Cruz
Cumaná
SUCRE
Caripito
Serpent's Mouth
Soledad
Sabanalarga
MARACAIBO
La Concepción
Santa Rita
Cabimas
San Felipe
YARACUY
Los Teques
Ocumare del Tuy
Río Chico
Barcelona
Maturín
MONAGAS
DELTA-
Fundación
Calamar
Ciudad Ojeda
Mene Grande
BARQUISIMETO
Carora
Yaritagua de los Morros
Villa de Cura
San Juan de los Morros
Aragua de Barcelona
Anaco
Caicara
Tucupita
AMACUR
Valledupar
Villa del Rosario
Machiques
Lago de Maracaibo
La Ceiba
LARA
El Tocuyo
San Carlos
El Sombrero
Valle de la Pascua
El Tigre
Cantaura
Magangué
Mompós
El Banco
CÉSAR
ZULIA
Trujillo
Betijoque
Acarigua
COJEDES
Calabozo
ANZOÁTEGUI
Ciudad Guayana
Sierra Imataca
Sahagún
Agustín Codazzi
Plato
Zambrano
Valera
Trujillo
PORTUGUESA
El Baúl
GUÁRICO
Santa María de Ipire
Pariaguán
Soledad
Upata
Guasipati
Coroza
NORTE DE SANTANDER
Ocaña
Cord. de Mérida
MÉRIDA
Guanare
Portuguesa
Orinoco
Ciudad Bolívar
El Pao
El Callao
Tumeremo
BOLÍVAR
Simití
Cúcuta
TÁCHIRA
BARINAS
Barinas
Libertad
Ciudad Bolivia
San Fernando de Apure
Achaguas
Zipire
Mapire
Emb. de Guri
Caroní
Ayapel
Majagual
San Cristóbal
Santa Bárbara
V E N E Z U E L A
Cáceres
Caicara

ft   m
12 000   4000
9000   3000
6000   2000
4500   1500
3000   1000
1200   400
600   200
0
200   600
600   200
2000   6000
4000   12 000
6000   18 000
8000   24 000
m   ft

West from Greenwich

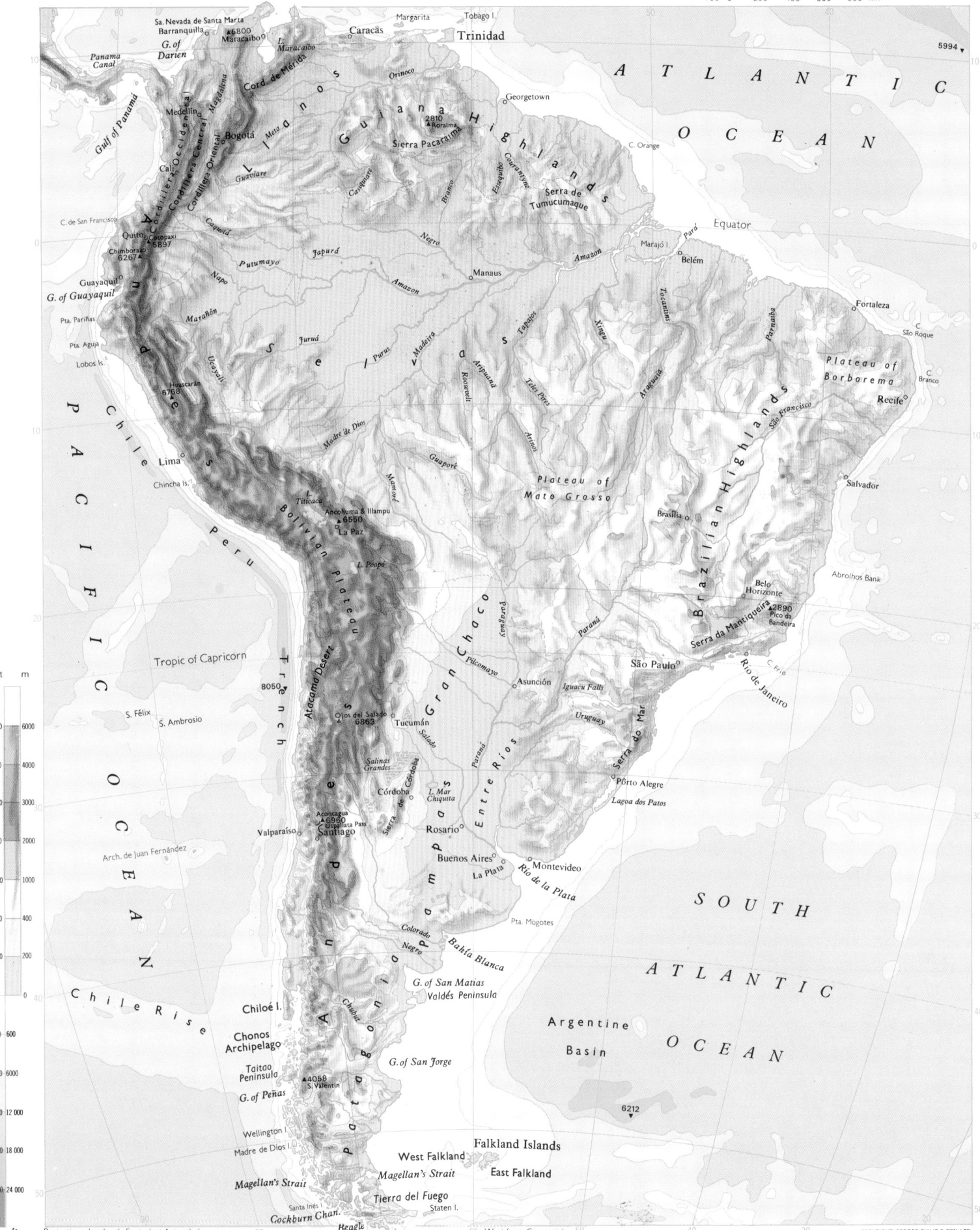

1:30 000 000

100 0 100 200 300 400 500 miles
100 0 200 400 600 800 km

5994 ▼

A T L A N T I C

O C E A N

Equator

Panama
Canal
Sa. Nevada de Santa Marta
Barranquilla
Maracaibo   5800
G. of
Darien
Margarita
Caracas
Tobago I.
Trinidad

Medellín
Cali
Bogotá
Cord. de Mérida
L. Maracaibo
Orinoco

Llanos
Meta
Guaviare
Casiquiare
Branco
Guiana Highlands
Sierra Pacaraima
2810
Roraima
Serra de
Tumucumaque
Georgetown
C. Orange
Courantyne
Essequibo
Berbice

Cordillera Occidental
Cordillera Central Magdalena
Cordillera Oriental

C. de San Francisco
Quito
Cotopaxi
5897
Chimborazo
6267
Guayaquil
G. of Guayaquil
Pta. Pariñas
Pta. Aguja
Lobos Is.

Napo
Caquetá
Putumayo
Japurá
Marañón
Ucayali
Juruá
Purus
Negro
Madre de Dios
Amazon
Manaus
Marajó I.
Pará
Belém

S   e   l   v   a   s
Roosevelt
Tapajós
Xingu
Telles Pires
Araguaia
Tocantins
Parnaíba
Fortaleza
São Roque
Plateau of
Borborema
Recife
C. Branco

Huascarán
6768

Lima
Chincha Is.
Titicaca
Ancohuma & Illampu
6550
La Paz
L. Poopó
Bolivian Plateau
Madeira
Aripuanã
Arinos
Guaporé
Mamoré
Plateau of
Mato Grosso
São Francisco
Brasília
Salvador
Abrolhos Bank
Belo
Horizonte
2890
Pico da
Bandeira
Brazilian Highlands
Serra da Mantiqueira

C H I L E

Chile
Peru
Trench

8050
Atacama Desert
Ojos del Salado
6863
Tucumán
Salado
Salinas
Grandes
Gran Chaco
Pilcomayo
Bermejo
Paraguay
Paraná
São Paulo
Asunción
Iguacu Falls
Uruguay
Serra do Mar
Pôrto Alegre
Lagoa dos Patos
Rio de Janeiro
C. Frio

Tropic of Capricorn

S. Félix
S. Ambrosio
Arch. de Juan Fernández
Aconcagua
6960
Uspallata Pass
Santiago
Valparaíso
Sierra de Córdoba
Córdoba
L. Mar
Chiquita
Rosario
Entre Ríos
Paraná
Buenos Aires
La Plata
Montevideo
Río de la Plata
Pta. Mogotes

P A C I F I C

O C E A N

Chile Rise

P   a   m   p   a   s
Colorado
Negro
Bahía Blanca
G. of San Matias
Valdés Peninsula

S O U T H

A T L A N T I C

O C E A N

Argentine
Basin

Chiloé I.
Chonos
Archipelago
Taitao
Peninsula
G. of Peñas
Wellington I.
Madre de Dios I.
Chubut
4058
S. Valentin
Andes
Patagonia
G. of San Jorge
6212 ▼

Magellan's Strait
Santa Inés I.
Cockburn Chan.
Beagle
Chan.
C. Horn
Staten I.
Tierra del Fuego
Magellan's Strait
West Falkland
East Falkland
Falkland Islands

ft   m

18 000 ... 6000
12 000 ... 4000
9000 ... 3000
6000 ... 2000
3000 ... 1000
1200 ... 400
600 ... 200
0 ... 0
200 ... 600
2000 ... 6000
4000 ... 12000
6000 ... 18000
8000 ... 24000

m   ft

Projection: Lambert's Equivalent Azimuthal

West from Greenwich

COPYRIGHT. GEORGE PHILIP & SON. LTD.

1:30 000 000

100   0   100   200   300   400   500 miles
100   0   200   400   600   800 km

Projection: *Lambert's Equivalent Azimuthal*

West from Greenwich

COPYRIGHT. GEORGE PHILIP & SON. LTD.

A T L A N T I C   O C E A N

Equator

6059

FR. GUIANA

AMAPÁ

Paramaribo
Nieuw Amsterdam
St. Laurent
Cayenne
C. Orange
Kaw
Approuague
St. Georges
Oiapoque
Camopi

Amapá
Serra do Navio
Macapá
Mazagão
Ilha Caviana
Estuario do Rio Amazonas
Ilha de Marajó
C. do Norte
Ilha de Maracá
Ilha Mexiana
C. Maguarinho
Salinópolis
Curuçá
Bragança
Viseu
Vigia
Chaves
Souré
Afuá
Anajás
I. Grande de Gurupá
Breves
Muaná
Guimarães
Alcântara
Cururupu
Turiaçu
Acará
Abaetetuba

Belém (Pará)
Santarém
Óbidos
Monte Alegre
Almeirim
Gurupá
Pôrto de Moz
Cametá
Baião
Tucuruí
Cametá

Amazonas (Amazon)
Aveiro
Brasília Legal
Itaituba
Altamira
Pôrto Nacional

São Luís (Maranhão)
B. de São Marcos
Rosário
Barreirinhas
Tutóia
Parnaíba
Luís Correia
Camocim
Granja
Fortaleza (Ceará)
Sobral
Maranguape
Aracati
Macau
Mossoró
Areia Branca
Ceará Mirim
Natal
C. de São Roque
Cruz
Canguaretama
Mamanguape
Cabedelo
João Pessoa (Paraíba)
Campina Grande
RECIFE (Pernambuco)
Ponta de Santo Antão
Barreiros
Palmares
Garanhuns
Maceió
ALAGOAS
Penedo
SERGIPE
Capela
Aracaju
São Cristóvão
Estância

PARÁ
MARANHÃO
Viana
Itapecuru-Mirim
Brejo
Caxias
Codó
Bacabal
Coroatá
Timbiras
Barra do Corda
Grajaú
Imperatriz
Marabá
Sa. dos Carajás
Tocantinópolis
Pôrto Franco
Carolina
Riachão

Teresina
Piripiri
Piracuruca
Campo Maior
União
Amarante
Floriano
Oeiras
PIAUÍ
Uruçuí
São João do Piauí
Paulistana
Valença do Piauí
Picos
Jaicós
CEARÁ
Crateús
Senador Pompeu
Iguatú
Caucaia
Quixadá
Russas
Limoeiro do Norte
Icó
Cedro
Crato
Juàzeiro do Norte
Cajazeiras
Souza
Patos
PARAÍBA
Caruaru
PERNAMBUCO
Petrolândia
Vitória
Garanhuns
Ouricuri
Petrolina
Remanso
Casa Nova
Juàzeiro
Paulo Afonso
Pal. dos Índios

B R A Z I L
GOIÁS
BAHIA
Barreiras
Ibotirama
Paratinga
Bom Jesus da Lapa
Caetité
Brumado
Xique-Xique
Santo Inácio
Jacobina
Jacuípe
Feira de Santana
Alagoinhas
Santo Amaro
Cachoeira
Castro Alves
Nazaré
Valença
Jequié
Ubaitaba
Salvador (Bahia)
B. de Todos os Santos
Amargosa
Itaberaba
Mundo Novo
Serrinha
Itapicuru
Senhor do Bonfim
Queimadas
Campo Formoso

Pôrto Nacional
Natividade
Peixe
Paranã
Campos Belos
São Domingos
Sta. Maria da Vitória
Correntina
Posse
Niquelândia
DIST. FED. Brasília
Formosa
Corumbá
Goiânia
Anápolis
Luziânia
Vianópolis
Ipameri
Catalão
Araguari
MINAS GERAIS
Uberlândia
Patrocínio
Patos de Minas
Paracatu
Pirapora
Montes Claros
Januária
Monte Azul
Salinas
Teófilo Otoni
Nanuque
Caravelas
Mucuri
Abrolhos
Prado
Pôrto Seguro
Belmonte
Canavieiras
Ilhéus
Itabuna
Vitória da Conquista
Jequitinhonha
Conceição da Barra
São Mateus
Nova Venécia
Gov. Valadares
Diamantina
Belo Horizonte
Uberaba
Araxá
Franca
Ribeirão Prêto
São José do Rio Prêto
Araçatuba
Marília
Bauru
Piracicaba
SÃO PAULO
Campinas
Vitória
Cachoeiro de Itapemirim
ESPÍRITO SANTO
Campos
Macaé
Cabo Frio
Petrópolis
Niterói
RIO DE JANEIRO
Juiz de Fora
Barbacena
Poços de Caldas
Lavras
Ouro Prêto
Nova Lima
Itabira

MATO GROSSO
Planalto do Mato Grosso
Rondonópolis
Baliza
Aruanã
GOIÁS
Jataí
Rio Verde
Morrinhos
Itumbiara
Araguari

MATO GROSSO DO SUL
Campo Grande
Agua Clara
Três Lagoas
Andradina
Pres. Prudente
Pres. Epitácio
Dourados
Ponta Porã

Planalto Brasileiro

Serra do Roncador

Fernando de Noronha (Braz.)
Rocas
Trindade (Braz.)

CARIBBEAN SEA

PACIFIC OCEAN

PANAMA

COLOMBIA

VENEZUELA

ECUADOR

PERU

Projection: Lambert's Equivalent Azimuthal

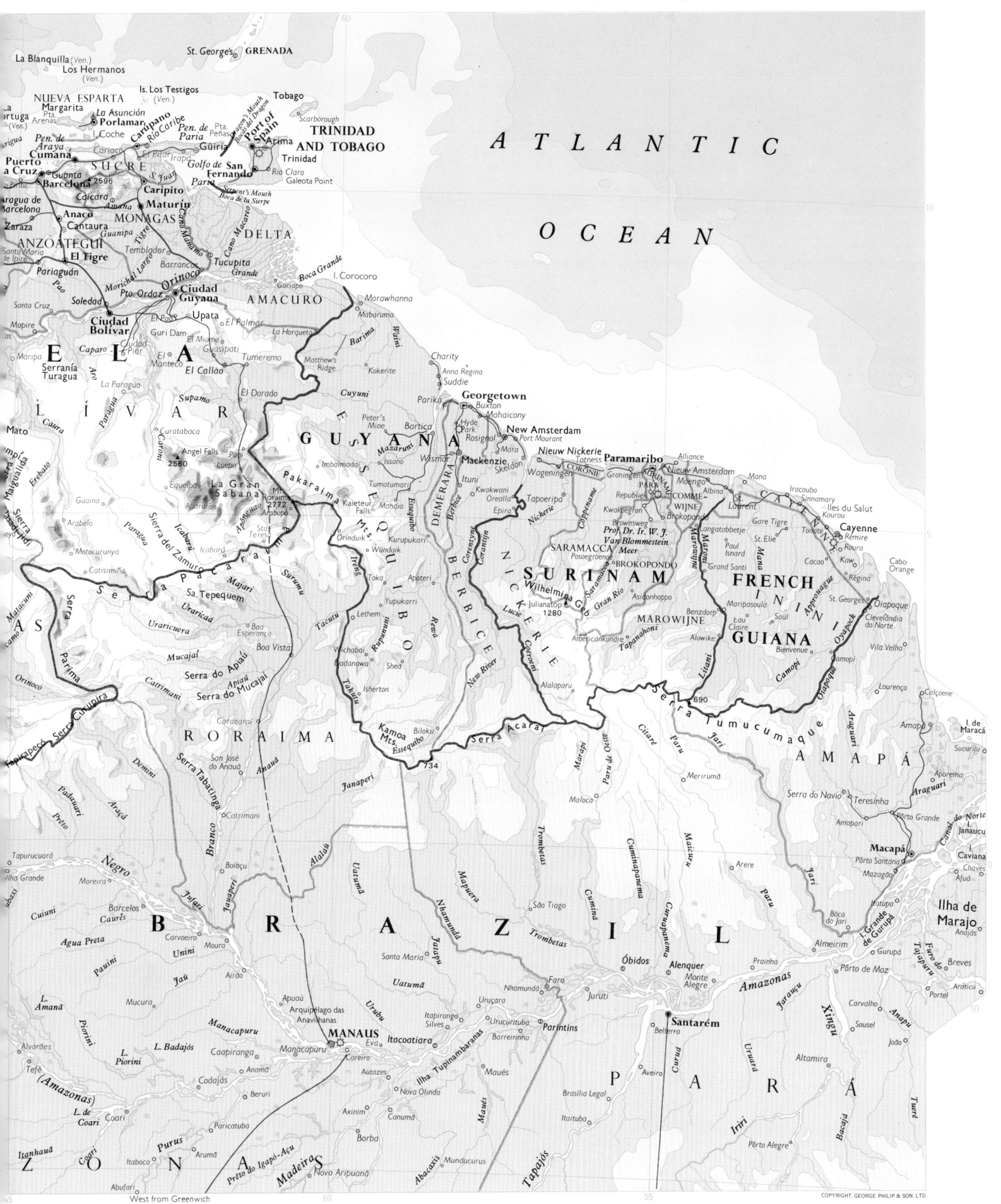

1:8,000,000

50   0   50   100   150   200 miles
50   0   100   200   300 km

ATLANTIC

OCEAN

La Blanquilla (Ven.)
Los Hermanos (Ven.)
St. George's GRENADA
NUEVA ESPARTA
Margarita
La Asunción
Is. Los Testigos (Ven.)
Porlamar
Tobago
Scarborough
Pen. de Araya
La Tortuga (Ven.)
Carúpano
Río Caribe
Pta. Peñas
Carúpano
TRINIDAD AND TOBAGO
Cumaná
SUCRE
Güiria
Port of Spain
Arima
Pen. de Paria
Golfo de Paria
San Fernando
Trinidad
Puerto la Cruz
Guanta
Barcelona
2596
Caicara
Caripito
Maturín
Río Claro
Galeota Point
Anaco
Cantaura
MONAGAS
Serpent's Mouth
Boca de la Sierpe
Zaraza
ANZOÁTEGUI
El Tigre
Temblador
DELTA
Tucupita
Boca Grande
Guijapo
I. Corocoro
Pariaguán
Orinoco
Barrancas
Caño Mariusa
Morawhanna
Pao
Morichal Largo
Mabaruma
Soledad
Pto. Ordaz
Ciudad Guyana
AMACURO
Barima
Santa Cruz
Ciudad Bolívar
El Pao
Upata
El Palmar
Wini
Charity
Caparo
Guri Dam
El Miamo
La Horqueta
Anna Regina
Mapire
El Merey
Guasipati
Matthew's Ridge
Kokerite
Suddie
Maripa
Serranía Turagua
La Paragua
El Dorado
Cuyuni
Parika
Georgetown
Buxton
Mahaicony
E L A
La Paragua
Manteco
El Callao
Peter's Mine
Bartica
Hyde Park
New Amsterdam
Port Mourant
B O L Í V A R
Supamo
Imbaimadai
Issano
Wismar
Rosignol
Mara
Mato
Caura
Curataraca
Angel Falls
Papi
Luepa
GUYANA
Mazaruni
Mackenzie
Wagenigen
Nieuw Nickerie
Totness
Paramaribo
Nieuw Amsterdam
Alliance
Mana
2560
La Gran Sabana
Apanau
Roraima 2772
Kaieteur Falls
Tumatumari
Skeldon
CORONIE
Groningen
SURINAM
Moengo
Albina
Iracoubo
Sinnamary
Sierra del Zamuro
Icabaru
Sta. Teresa
Orinduik
Mts. Kanuku
Kurupukari
Apoteri
Kwakwani
Oreala
Epira
Ituni
Nickerie
Tapoeripa
Republiek
PARA
COMMEWIJNE
Brokopondo
Brownsweg
St. Laurent
Gare Tigre
Îles du Salut
Kourou
Cayenne
Rémire
Icabarú
Wündik
Yupukarí
Prof. Dr. Ir. W. J.
Van Blommestein
Meer
SARAMACCA
Posoegroenoe
BROKOPONDO
Paul Isnard
Grand Santi
St. Élie
Roura
Majari
Sa. Tepequem
Uraricad
Lethem
Toka
Rewa
SURINAM
Wilhelmina Geb.
Julianatop 1280
Gran Rio
Asidonhoppo
FRENCH
ININI
GUIANA
Maripasoula
Cacao
Kaw
Urariccuera
Boa Esperança
Wichabai
Dadanawa
Shea
New River
Lucie
Saramacca
Americankondre
MAROWIJNE
Bénzdorp
Saul
Cabo Orange
Mucajaí
Boa Vista
Isherton
Tapanahoni
Alowike
Bienvenue
Maroni
Camopi
Vila Velha
Serra do Apiaú
Apiaú
Serra do Mucajaí
Kamoa Mts.
Biloku
Essequibo
Serra Acaraí
Alalaparu
Coeroeni
Serra Tumucumaque
690
Oyapock
Lourenço
Calçoene
Catrimani
Caroebari
734
Janaperi
Maloca
Manari
Paru de Oeste
Citaré
Paru
Jari
AMAPÁ
I. de Maracá
Sucuriju
Serra Cucuipira
RORAIMA
San José do Anauá
Anauá
Meirumá
Serra do Navio
Teresinha
Aporema
Araguari
Demini
Serra Tabatinga
Trombetas
Cuminapanema
Amapari
Pôrto Grande
Araguari
Tapurucuará
Araçá
Branco
Boiaçu
Alalaú
Uatumã
Mapuera
Maicuru
Arere
Macapá
Amapá
Itaúba
I. Grande de Gurupá
Canal do Norte
Januaçu
Caviana
Negro
Catrimani
Jatapu
São Tiago
Cuminá
Jari
Bôca do Jari
Afuá
Padauiri
Prêto
Nhamundá
Óbidos
Prainha
Almeirim
Pôrto de Moz
Ilha de Marajó
Cuiuni
Barcelos
Caurés
Carvoeiro
Moura
Santa Maria
Uatumã
Jatapu
Nhamundá
Alenquer
Monte Alegre
Amazonas
Jaraçu
Anajás
Ilha Grande
Agua Preta
Unini
Airão
Uracurituba
Faro
Juruti
Breves
Pauini
Jaú
Apuaú
Urucará
Silves
Barreirinha
Parintins
Santarém
Belterra
Xingu
Sousel
Carvalho
Arataiú
Portel
L. Amanã
Mucura
Manacapuru
Arquipélago das Anavilhanas
Urubu
Itapiranga
Uatumã
Santarém
João
Alvarães
L. Piorini
Caapiranga
Manacapuru
Anamã
MANAUS
Itacoatiara
Maués
Curuá
Aveiro
B R A Z I L
Tefé
L. Badajós
Codajós
Beruri
Careiro
Evá
Ilha Tupinambaranas
Nova Olinda
Brasília Legal
P A R Á
(Amazonas)
Coari
Autazes
Maués
Itaituba
Iriri
Bacajá
L. de Coari
Caapiranga
Paricatuba
Axinim
Canumã
Tapajós
Tauarí
Itanhauá
Z O N A S
Purus
Arumã
Itaboca
Prêto do Igapó-Açu
Borba
Abacaxis
Munducurus
Pôrto Alegre
Abufari
Madeiras
Novo Aripuaná

West from Greenwich

COPYRIGHT GEORGE PHILIP & SON. LTD.

ATLANTIC OCEAN
AMAPÁ
Macapá
I. de Maracá
Cabo do Norte
I. Bailique
I. Caviana
I. Mexiana
Cabo Maguarinho
Ilha de Marajó
Soure
Baía de Marajó
BELÉM (Pará)
Icoraci
Abaetetuba
Vigia
Bragança
Capanema
Castanhal
Xingu
Altamira
Tocantins
Tucuruí
PARÁ
Serra do Gurupi
Sa. do Tiracambu
Marabá
Imperatriz
Tocantinópolis
Araguaia
Serra dos Carajás
Serra dos Gradaús
Serra do Estrondo
SÃO LUÍS
Ribamar
Rosário
Pinheiro
Viana
Pindaré Mirim
Vitorino Friere
Bacabal
Pedreiras
Codó
Caxias
Coroatá
MARANHÃO
Carolina
Balsas
Timon
Teresina
Campo Maior
Piripiri
Parnaíba
Floriano
Oeiras
Picos
PIAUÍ
Camocim
Granja
Sobral
Massapê
Itapipoca
FORTALEZA (Ceará)
Parangaba
Maranguape
Baturité
Quixadá
Russas
Aracati
Crateús
Quixeramobim
Senador Pompeu
Iguatu
Icó
Crato
Juàzeiro do Norte
CEARÁ
Mossoró
Areia Branca
Macau
Açu
RIO GRANDE DO NORTE
NATAL
Ceará-Mirim
Caicó
Currais Novos
Santa Cruz
Nova Cruz
Patos
Cajazeiras
Sousa
Campina Grande
João Pessoa (Paraíba)
Cabedelo
Guarabira
Timbaúba
Goiana
Carpina
Paulista
Olinda
RECIFE (Pernambuco)
Jaboatão
Vitória de S. Antão
Limoeiro
Caruaru
Gravatá
Pesqueira
Arcoverde
Serra Talhada
Salgueiro
Escada
Palmares
Barreiros
Garanhuns
PERNAMBUCO
Petrolina
Juàzeiro
Paulo Afonso
Senhor do Bofim
Xique-Xique
Barra
Francisco
Palmeira dos Índios
Arapiraca
MACEIÓ
ALAGOAS
Penedo
Propriá
Aracaju
São Cristóvão
SERGIPE
Chapada das Mangabeiras
BRAZIL

1:8 000 000

50 0 50 100 150 200 miles
50 0 100 200 300 km

ATLANTIC OCEAN

Tropic of Capricorn

ESPÍRITO SANTO

West from Greenwich

Projection: Lambert's Equivalent Azimuthal

SALVADOR (Bahia)
Feira de Santana
Alagoinhas
Itabuna
Ilhéus
Vitória da Conquista
Montes Claros
Teófilo Otoni
Gov. Valadares
Caratinga
Vitória
Vila Velha
CAMPOS
BELO HORIZONTE
Curvelo
Diamantina
Juiz de Fora
Nova Friburgo
Petrópolis
NITERÓI
RIO DE JANEIRO
Angra dos Reis
BRASÍLIA
DISTRITO FEDERAL
Anápolis
GOIÂNIA
Rio Verde
Jataí
Uberlândia
Uberaba
Araxá
Ribeirão Prêto
Araraquara
SÃO PAULO
SANTO ANDRÉ
SANTOS
São Vicente
CAMPINAS
Sorocaba
Bauru
Marília
Presidente Prudente
Londrina
Maringá
Ponta Grossa
CURITIBA
Guarapuava

GOIÁS
MINAS GERAIS
SÃO PAULO
PARANÁ
Serra Geral de Goiás

 m ft
6000 2000
4500 1500
3000 1000
1200 400
600 200
0 0
200 600
2000 6000
4000 12 000
ft m

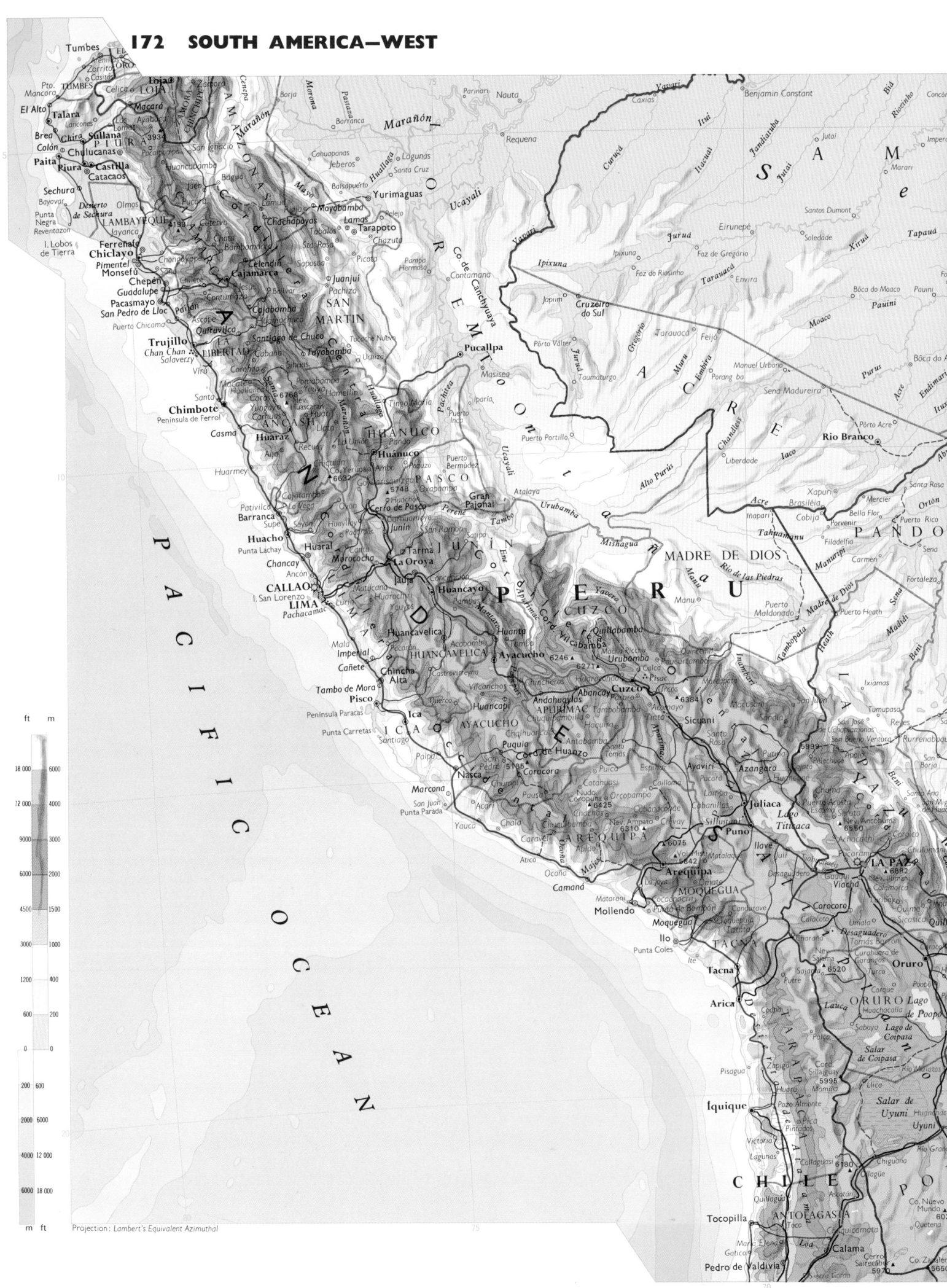

PACIFIC OCEAN

PERU

CHILE

MADRE DE DIOS

CUZCO

AREQUIPA

MOQUEGUA

TACNA

ORURO

Projection: Lambert's Equivalent Azimuthal

1:8 000 000

173

50   0   50   100   150   200miles
50 0   100   200   300 km

L. de Coari Coari
Itanhauá
Coari
Purus
Paricatuba
Aximim
Canumã
Itaituba
Pôrto Alegre
Baagia
Irriri

Z O N A S
á
B R A Z I L
P A R Á

Tapauá
Jaburú
Itatuba
Tapauá
Santa Maria das Marmelos
Manicoré
Capoeira
Madeira
Borba
Munducurus
Tapajós
Tucunaré
Entre Rios
Nazaré
São Félix

Purus
Lábrea
Majuriã
Mucim
Ipixuna
Humaitá
Maici
Marmelos
Prainha
Canudos
Sai-Cinza
Crepori
Serra do Cachimbo
Cachimbo
Xingu
Riosinho

Itui
Irãndô
Calama
Madeira
Jamari
Tabajara
Recreio
Teles Pires
Barracão do Barreto
S. Benedito
Alto Iriri
Liberdade

Pôrto Velho
404
Jaciparaná
Cantianas
Aripuanã
Jurúena
Peixoto de Azeredo
Iriri Novo

Abuná
Bella
Guajará-Mirim
Guayaramerin
Sa. dos Pacaás Novos
Nova Vida
Jaru
Jaru
Rondônia
Presidente Hermes
Serra do Norte
Arinos
Manitsaud-Missu
Campo de Diauarum

R O N D Ô N I A
Serra
Pimenta Bueno
Barão de Melgaço
Alpidiá
663 Vilhena
Serra do Tombador
Serra dos Caiabis
Serra Formosa
Pôrto Cajueiro
Pouso Alegre
Arinos
Arraias
Xingu
Suiá Missu
Serra do Roncador

Princípe da Beira
Versalles
Pedras Negras
Nhambiquara
Juruena
Utiariti
Saluemma
Telés Peres
Verde
Romuro
Pôrto dos Meinacos
Chavantina

Puerto Siles
Lago Rogoaguado
San Joaquin
Magdalena
Guaporé
Camararé
M A T O G R O S S O
Arinos
Planalto
do
Aruanã

San Ramón
Boures
Puerto Villazón
669
Nortelândia
Arenápolis
Diamantino
Cuiabá
Alto Paraguai
Serra Azul
Chavantina

Lago de San Luis
El Carmen
San Joaquin
San Martin
Paraguá
Serrania de Huanchaca
Mato Grosso
Guaporé
Tapirapuã
Barra do Bugres
Rosário Oeste
M a t o G r o s s o
915
Chapada dos Guimarães
Mortes
Aruanã
Araguaia

B O L I V I A
San Javier
San Ignacio
Trinidad
Blanco
1995
Acorizal
Várzea Grande Cuiabá
Nossa Senhora do Livramento
Santo Antônio do Levergé
Coronel Ponce
Barro do Garças
Araguaiana
Aragarças

de Mojos
Loreto
San Miguel
Negro
Añez
Santa Rosa de la Roca
Guaporé
Pôrto Esperidião
Cáceres
Poconé
Barão de Melgaço
Jaciara
Poxoreu
Rio das Garças
Tesouro
Guiratinga
Baliza
Ipora
Ivolândia
Sa. das Divisões

Cochabamba
Chapare
Ichilo
San Javier
Concepción
Santa Ana
Aguapei
San Matías
Itiquira
São Lourenço
Rondonópolis
Ponte Branca
Alto Garças
Caiapônia
Rio Verde
Jataí

Totora
S A N T A C R U Z
Portachuelo
Montero Warnes
El Cerro
San José
Laguna Concepción
San Ignacio
San Miguel
Lagoa Uberaba
Pôrto Jofre
Pantanal do São Lourenço
Correntes
Itiquira
Alto Araguaia
Santa Rita do Araguaia
Mineiros

Santa Cruz
Cotoca
Buena Vista
El Palmar
Llanos de Chiquitos
1425 Roboré
Serra de Santiago
Santo Corazón
La Cal
Lagoa Mandioré
Taquari
M A T O G R O S S O
Coxim
Baús
Serra do Verde
Claro
Itarumã
Açu
Cachoeira Alta

Pampa Grande
Villegrande
Abapó
Bañados de Izozog
Santa Ana
Puerto Suárez
Corumbá
Ladário
Nhecolândia
Pantanal do Rio Negro
Rio Verde de Mato Grosso
D O S U L
Paraíso
Alto Sucuri
Aporé
Cassilândia
Aporé

Padilla
Gutiérrez
Parapeti
Fortin General Pando
Albuquerque
Pôrto Esperança
Negro
Sucuri
Paranaiba
Rubineia

Camiri
Charagua
Fortín Ingavi
Coimbra
Miranda
Corguinho
Rochedo
Ribas do Rio Pardo
Agua Clara
Aparecida do Taboado

CHUQUISACA
Carandaiti
Fortín Coronel Eugenio Garay
Bahía Negra
Sa. da Bodoquena
Aquidauana
Jango
Terenos
Campo Grande
Garcas
Pereira Barreto

Villa Montes
Fortín Madrejón
O L I M P O
Fuerte Olimpo
Bonito
Nioaque
Sidrolândia
Três Lagoas
Mirandópolis
Andradina

Tarija
S A L T A
La Esmeralda
Puerto Guaraní
C h a c o B o r e a l
P A R A G U A Y
B O Q U E R Ó N
Pôrto Murtinho
Jardim
Guia Lopes da Laguna
Maracaju
Anhandui
Xavantina
Panorama
Aguapei

5603
Tartagal
West from Greenwich
COPYRIGHT GEORGE PHILIP & SON LTD.

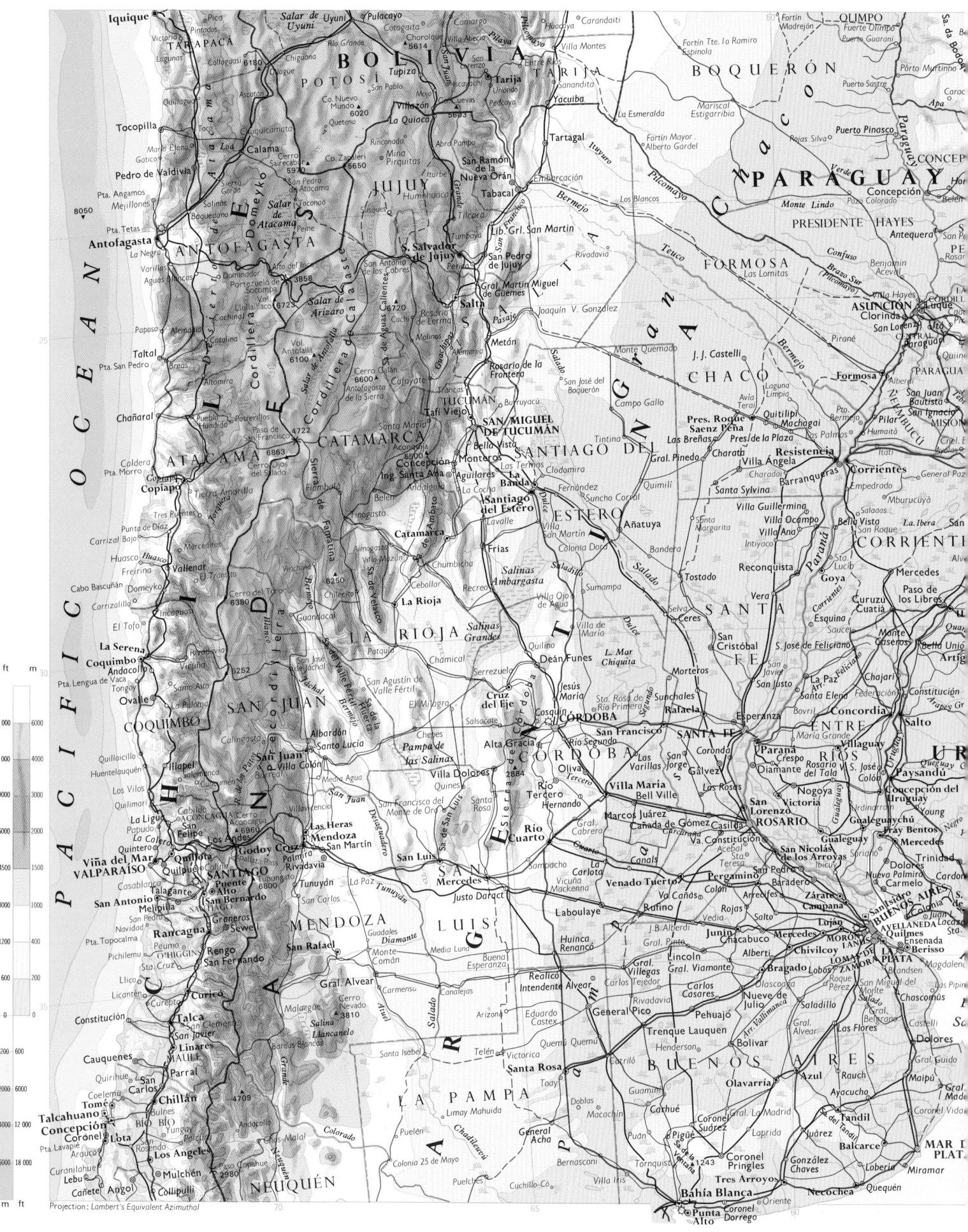
PACIFIC OCEAN
BOLIVIA
PARAGUAY
ARGENTINA
CHILE
ANDES
Gran Chaco
BOQUERÓN
PRESIDENTE HAYES
POTOSÍ
TARIJA
JUJUY
SALTA
ANTOFAGASTA
ATACAMA
CATAMARCA
TUCUMÁN
SANTIAGO DEL ESTERO
CHACO
FORMOSA
CORRIENTES
SANTA FE
ENTRE RÍOS
LA RIOJA
SAN JUAN
CÓRDOBA
COQUIMBO
MENDOZA
SAN LUIS
LA PAMPA
BUENOS AIRES
NEUQUÉN
Iquique
Tocopilla
Antofagasta
Taltal
Chañaral
Copiapó
Vallenar
La Serena
Coquimbo
Ovalle
Viña del Mar
VALPARAÍSO
SANTIAGO
Rancagua
Curicó
Talca
Linares
Chillán
Concepción
Talcahuano
Los Angeles
Tarija
Yacuiba
Tupiza
Salta
S. Salvador de Jujuy
SAN MIGUEL DE TUCUMÁN
Catamarca
Santiago del Estero
La Rioja
San Juan
Mendoza
San Luis
San Rafael
CÓRDOBA
Río Cuarto
Villa María
Santa Rosa
ROSARIO
SANTA FE
Paraná
Resistencia
Corrientes
Formosa
ASUNCIÓN
Concepción
Posadas
Concordia
Paysandú
Salto
BUENOS AIRES
LA PLATA
Bahía Blanca
MAR DEL PLATA
Olavarría
Tandil
Necochea
Aconcagua 6960
Projection: Lambert's Equivalent Azimuthal

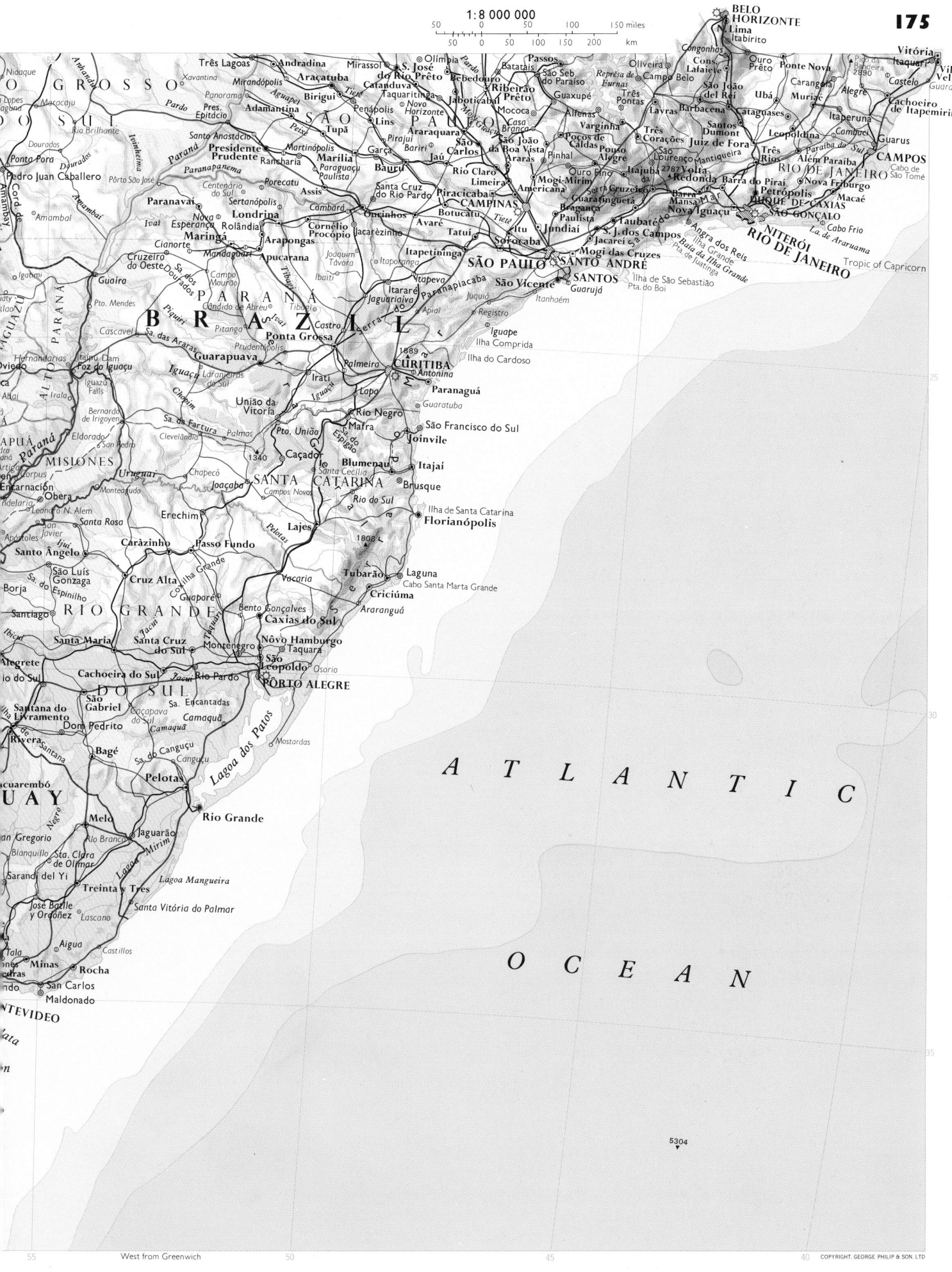

1:8 000 000

50   0   50   100   150 miles
50   0   50 100 200
km

BELO
HORIZONTE
Lima
Itabirito
Congonhas
Cons.
Lafaiete
Ouro
Prêto
Ponte Nova
Vitória
Itaquari
Vila
Velha
Guarapari

MATO GROSSO
DO SUL

Três Lagoas
Andradina
Aracatuba
Mirassol
Olímpia
S. José
do Rio Prêto
Passos
Batatais
São Seb
do Paraiso
Oliveira
Campo Belo
Reprêsa de
Furnas
São João
del Rei
Carangola
Castelo
Cachoeiro
de Itapemirim

Xavantina
Mirandópolis
Birigui
Catanduva
Taquaritinga
Guaxupé
Alegre

Panorama
Adamantina
Penápolis
Jaboticabal
Mococa
Três
Pontas
Lavras
Barbacena
Cataguases
Itaperuna
Cambuci

SÃO
PAULO
Lins
Novo
Horizonte
Casa
Branca
Varginha
Santos
Dumont
Leopoldina

Presidente
Prudente
Martinópolis
Marilia
Garça
Jaú
São
Carlos
Araras
Pinhal
Poços de
Caldas
Pouso
Alegre
Três
Corações
Juiz de Fora
Leopoldina
Muriaé

Santo Anastácio
Rancharia
Paraguaçu
Paulista
Bauru
Araraquara
Limeira
Rio Claro
Mogi-Mirim
Mantiqueira
Três
Rios
Além Paraíba
Guarus

Paranavaí
Assis
Piracicaba
Americana
Ouro Fino
Itajubá
Volta
Redonda
Barra do Pirai
Nova Friburgo
CAMPOS
Cabo de
São Tomé

Nova
Esperança
Porecatu
Londrina
Cambará
Ourinhos
CAMPINAS
Botucatu
Bragança
Guaratinguetá
Barra
Mansa
Nova Iguaçu
DUQUE DE CAXIAS
Macaé

Maringá
Cianorte
Rolândia
Cornélio
Procópio
Jacarezinho
Avaré
Tatuí
Itu
Jundiaí
Paulista
S. J. dos Campos
Angra dos Reis
SÃO GONÇALO
Cabo Frio
La. de Araruama

Apucarana
Mandaguari
Joaquim
Tavora
Itapetininga
Sorocaba
Mogi das Cruzes
Ilha Grande
NITERÓI
RIO DE JANEIRO
Tropic of Capricorn

Cruzeiro
do Oeste
Campo
Mourão
Ibaiti
SÃO PAULO
SANTO ANDRÉ
Petrópolis
Baía da Ilha Grande
Pta. de Juatinga

PARANÁ
BRAZIL
Itararé
Itapeva
Paranapiacaba
São Vicente
SANTOS
Guarujá
Ilha de São Sebastião
Pta. do Boi

Guaíra
Guarapuava
Pitanga
Castro
Jaguariaíva
Apiaí
Juquiá
Itanhaém

Foz do Iguaçu
Iguaçu
Falls
Itaipu Dam
Ponta Grossa
Prudentópolis
Registro
Iguape
Ilha Comprida

União da
Vitória
Irati
Palmeira
Lapa
CURITIBA
Antonina
Ilha do Cardoso

Chapecó
Caçador
Mafra
Rio Negro
Guaratuba
Paranaguá
São Francisco do Sul

Erechim
Joaçaba
Campos
Novos
BLUMENAU
Itajaí
Joinvile

RIO GRANDE
Passo Fundo
Lajes
Brusque
SANTA
CATARINA
Santa Cecília
Rio do Sul
Ilha de Santa Catarina
Florianópolis

Caràzinho
Vacaria
Tubarão
Laguna
Cabo Santa Marta Grande

Cruz Alta
Bento Gonçalves
Criciúma
Araranguá
Caxias do Sul

Santa Maria
Santa Cruz
do Sul
Montenegro
Nôvo Hamburgo
Taquara

Cachoeira do Sul
São
Leopoldo
Osorio
Rio Pardo
PÔRTO ALEGRE

DO SUL
São Gabriel
Caçapava
do Sul
Encantadas
Sa. Encantadas
Camaquã
Lagoa dos Patos
Mostardas

Bagé
Sa. do Canguçu
Canguçu
Pelotas

Rio Grande

A T L A N T I C

O C E A N

5304

1:8 000 000

50   0   50   100   150 miles
50   0   100   200   km

Major labels

LA PAMPA

BUENOS AIRES

ARAUCANIA

NEUQUÉN

RÍO NEGRO

LOS LAGOS

CHUBUT

SANTA CRUZ

MAGALLANES

SOUTH ATLANTIC OCEAN

PACIFIC OCEAN

SOUTHERN OCEAN

FALKLAND ISLANDS
(ISLAS MALVINAS)

West Falkland

East Falkland

Isla de Chiloé

Archipiélago de los Chonos

Península de Taitao

Golfo de Penas

Archipiélago Guayaneco

Isla Grande de Tierra del Fuego

TIERRA DEL FUEGO

Strait of Magellan

Estrecho de Magallanes

Cabo de Hornos (Cape Horn)

Canal Beagle

Cities and towns

Arauco, Cañete, Angol, Colliputli, Mulchén, Victoria, Traiguén, Curacautín, Temuco, Lautaro, Capitán Pastene, I. Mocha, Carahue, Puerto Saavedra, Nueva Imperial, Pitrufquén, Tolten, Valdivia, Corral, Pta. Galera, La Unión, Osorno, Río Bueno, Puerto Varas, Puerto Montt, Maullín, Ancud, Castro, Puerto Quellón, C. Quilán

Colonia 25 de Mayo, Puelches, Bernasconi, Tornquist, Villa Iris, Coronel Pringles, Juárez, Balcarce, González Chaves, Loberia, Daqueén, Coronel Dorrego, Tres Arroyos, Necochea, Bahía Blanca, Punta Alta, B. Blanca, I. Trinidad

Neuquén, Cipolletti, Allen, Gral. Roca, Choele Choel, Lamarque, Río Colorado, Viedma, Carmen de Patagones, San Antonio Oeste, Valcheta, Los Menucos, Maquinchao, Ingeniero Jacobacci, El Cain, Cona Niyeu

San Carlos de Bariloche, El Bolsón, El Maitén, Esquel, Tecka, Las Plumas, Trelew, Rawson, Gaimán, Puerto Madryn, Puerto Pirámides, Pen. Valdés

Golfo San Matías, Golfo San José, Golfo Nuevo, Golfo San Jorge

Comodoro Rivadavia, Caleta Olivia, Colonia Las Heras, Pico Truncado, Puerto Deseado, Sarmiento, Río Mayo, Perito Moreno, Los Antiguos, Las Heras

Gob. Gregores, San Julián, Puerto Coig, Río Gallegos, Puerto Natales, El Turbio, Gallegos, Monte Dinero, Calafate, Lago Argentino, Tres Lagos, Santa Cruz, Esperanza, Puerto Coig

Punta Arenas, Porvenir, Río Grande, Ushuaia, San Sebastián

Coihaique, Puerto Aisén, Balmaceda, Chile Chico, Cochrane

Stanley, Port Darwin, Weddell I., Pebble I., Jason Is., King George B., Queen Charlotte B., Beauchêne I.

Elevations

Mt. Fitzroy 3375, Mte. San Lorenzo 3700, Cerro San Valentín 4058, Monte Tronador 3554, Mte. Darwin 2469, Mt. Adam 700, Mt. Usborne 705

Water bodies and features

L. Nahuel Huapi, L. Llanquihue, L. Ranco, Lago Ranco, L. Fontana, L. La Plata, L. Buenos Aires, L. Pueyrredón, L. Posadas, L. Cardiel, L. Viedma, L. San Martín, L. Musters, L. Colhué Huapi, Lago Argentino

Golfo de Ancud, Golfo de Corcovado, Boca del Guafo, Canal Moraleda, Canal Baker, Canal Messier, Canal Wellington, Canal Concepción

Projection: Lambert's Equivalent Azimuthal

West from Greenwich

COPYRIGHT. GEORGE PHILIP & SON, LTD.

Index

Abbreviations used

A.S.S.R. - *Autonomous Soviet Socialist Republic*
Adr. S. - *Adriatic Sea*
Aeg. S. - *Aegean Sea*
Ala. - *Alabama*
Alta. - *Alberta*
Amer. - *America, American*
Ang. - *Angola*
Arch. - *Archipelago*
Arg. - *Argentina*
Ariz. - *Arizona*
Ark. - *Arkansas*
Atl. Oc. - *Atlantic Ocean*
B. - *Baie, Bahia, Bay, Boca, Bucht, Bugt*
B.C. - *British Columbia*
Br. - *British*
C. - *Cabo, Cap, Cape, Coast, Costa*
C.A.R. - *Central African Republic*
C.H. - *Court House*
C. Prov. - *Cape Province*
Calif. - *California*
Cat. - *Cataract*
Cent. - *Central*
Chan. - *Channel*
Col. - *Colombia*
Colo. - *Colorado*
Conn. - *Connecticut*
Cord. - *Cordillera*
Czech. - *Czechoslovakia*
D.C. - *District of Columbia*
Del. - *Delaware*
Dep. - *Dependency*
Des. - *Desert*
Dist. - *District*
Dj. - *Djebel*
Dom. Rep. - *Dominican Republic*
E. - *East, Eastern*
El Salv. - *El Salvador*
Eq. Guin. - *Equatorial Guinea*
Falk. Is. - *Falkland Is.*
Fd. - *Fjord*
Fed. - *Federal, Federation*
Fla. - *Florida*
Fr. - *France, French*
Fr. Gui. - *French Guiana*
G. - *Golfe, Golfo, Gulf, Guba, Gebel*
Ga. - *Georgia*

Gt. - *Great*
Guat. - *Guatemala*
H.K. - *Hong Kong*
H.P. - *Himachal Pradesh*
Hants. - *Hampshire*
Hd. - *Head*
Hts. - *Heights*
I.(s) - *Ile, Ilha, Insel, Isla Island(s)*
I. of W. - *Isle of Wight*
Ill. - *Illinois*
Ind. Res. - *Indian Reservation*
Ind. - *Indiana*
J. - *Jabal, Jazira*
K. - *Kap. Kapp*
Kans. - *Kansas*
Kep. - *Kepulauan*
Kól. - *Kólpos*
Ky. - *Kentucky*
L. - *Lac, Lacul, Lago, Lagoa, Lake, Limni, Loch, Lough*
La. - *Louisiana*
Lag. - *Laguna*
Ld. - *Land*
Mad. P. - *Madhya Pradesh*
Man. - *Manitoba*
Mass. - *Massachusetts*
Md. - *Maryland*
Mich. - *Michigan*
Minn. - *Minnesota*
Miss. - *Mississippi*
Mo. - *Missouri*
Mozam. - *Mozambique*
Mont. - *Montana*
Mt.(s) - *Mont, Monta, Monti, Muntii, Montaña, Mount, Mountain(s)*
Mys. - *Mysore*
N. - *North, Northern*
N.B. - *New Brunswick*
N.C. - *North Carolina*
N. Dak. - *North Dakota*
N.H. - *New Hampshire*
N.Ire. - *Northern Ireland*
N.J. - *New Jersey*
N. Mex - *New Mexico*
N.S. - *Nova Scotia*
N.S.W. - *New South Wales*
N.W.T. - *North West Territories*
N.Y. - *New York*

N.Z. - *New Zealand*
Nat. For. - *National Forest*
Nat. Park - *National Park*
Nat. Rec. Area - *National Recreation Area*
Nebr. - *Nebraska*
Neth. - *Netherlands*
Nev. - *Nevada*
Newf. - *Newfoundland*
Nic. - *Nicaragua*
Nig. - *Nigeria*
O. - *Oued, Ouadi*
O.F.S. - *Orange Free State*
Okla. - *Oklahoma*
Ont. - *Ontario*
Oreg. - *Oregon*
Os. - *Ostrov*
Oz. - *Ozero*
P. - *Pass, Passo, Pasul, Pulau*
P.E.I. - *Prince Edward Island*
P. Rico - *Puerto Rico*
Pa. - *Pennsylvania*
Pac. Oc. - *Pacific Ocean*
Pak. - *Pakistan*
Papua N.G. - *Papua New Guinea*
Pass. - *Passage*
Pen. - *Peninsula*
Pk. - *Peak*
Plat. - *Plateau*
Port. - *Portugal, Portuguese*
P-ov. - *Poluostrov*
Prov. - *Province, Provincial*
Pt. - *Point*
Pta. - *Ponta, Punta*
Pte. - *Pointe*
Qué. - *Québec*
Queens. - *Queensland*
R. - *Rio, River, Rivière*
R.I. - *Rhode Island*
R.S.F.S.R. - *Russian Soviet Federative Socialist Republic*
Ra.(s) - *Range(s)*
Raj. - *Rajasthan*
Reg. - *Region*
Rep. - *Republic*
Res. - *Reserve, Reservoir, Reservation*
S. - *South, Southern, Sea, Sur*
S.C. - *South Carolina*
S.S.R. - *Soviet Socialist Republic*

S. Africa - *South Africa*
S. Dak. - *South Dakota*
S. Leone - *Sierra Leone*
Sa. - *Serra, Sierra*
Salop. - *Shropshire*
Sask. - *Saskatchewan*
Scot. - *Scotland*
Sd. - *Sound*
Sev. - *Severnaya*
Si. Arabia - *Saudi Arabia*
Sib. - *Siberia*
Sp. - *Spain, Spanish*
Sprgs. - *Springs*
St. - *Saint*
Sta. - *Santa*
Ste. - *Sainte*
Sto. - *Santo*
Str. - *Strait, Stretto*
Switz. - *Switzerland*
Tanz. - *Tanzania*
Tas. - *Tasmania*
Tenn. - *Tennessee*
Terr. - *Territory*
Tex. - *Texas*
Tg. - *Tanjung*
Trin. & Tob. - *Trinidad and Tobago*
U.K. - *United Kingdom*
U.S.A. - *United States of America*
U.S.S.R. - *Union of Soviet Socialist Republics*
Ut. P. - *Uttar Pradesh*
V.S. - *Vozvyshennost*
Va. - *Virginia*
Vdkhr. - *Vodokhranilishche*
Ven. - *Venezuela*
Vf. - *Virful*
Vic. - *Victoria*
Vol. - *Volcano*
Vt. - *Vermont*
Wash. - *Washington*
W. - *West, Western, Wadi*
W. Va. - *West Virginia*
Wis. - *Wisconsin*
Wlkp. - *Wielkopolski*
Worcs. - *Worcestershire*
Wyo. - *Wyoming*
Yorks. - *Yorkshire*
Yug. - *Yugoslavia*

Introduction to Index

The number in bold type which follows each name in the index refers to the number of the map-page where that feature or place will be found. This is usually the largest scale on which the place or feature appears.

Rivers have been indexed to their mouth or to where they join another river. All river names are followed by the symbol →.

The geographical co-ordinates which follow the place name are sometimes only approximate but are close enough for the place name to be located.

A solid square ■ follows the name of a country while an open square □ refers to a first order administrative area.

Alphabetical Order

The alphabetical order of names composed of two or more words is governed primarily by the first word and then by the second. This is an example of the rule:

> East Tawas
> Eastbourne
> Easter Is.
> Eastern Ghats
> Eastmain →.

Physical features composed of a proper name (*Mexico*) and a description (*Gulf of*) are positioned alphabetically by the proper name. The description is positioned after the proper name and is usually abbreviated:

> Mexico, G. of
> Midi, Canal de
> Pacaraima, Sa.

Where a description forms part of a settlement or administrative name however it is always written in full and put in its true alphabetic position:

> Lake Placid
> Mount Vernon
> Sturgeon Bay

Names composed of the definite article (*Le, La, Les, L'*) and a proper name are usually alphabetised by the proper name.

> Havre, Le
> Spezia, La
> Wash, The

Names beginning with M', Mc are all indexed as if they were spelled Mac. All names beginning St. are alphabetised under Saint, but Sankt, Sint, Sant', Santa and San are all spelt in full and are alphabetised accordingly.

If the same place name occurs two or more times in the index and all are in the same country, each is followed by the name of the administrative subdivision in which it is located. The names are placed in the alphabetical order of the subdivisions. For example:

> Bear L., Alta., Canada
> Bear L., B.C., Canada
> Bear L., Man., Canada

If the same place name occurs twice or more in the index and the places are in different countries, they will be followed by the country names and the latter in alphabetical order.

> Ben Lomond, Australia
> Ben Lomond, U.K.

If there is a mixture of these situations, the primary order is fixed by the alphabetical sequence of the countries and the secondary order by that of the country subdivisions.

> Rosario, Arg.
> Rosario, Brazil
> Rosario, Baja Calif. N., Mexico
> Rosario, Baja Calif. S., Mexico
> Rosario, Sinaloa, Mexico
> Rosario, Paraguay

Foreign Place Names

The atlas uses the local spellings for most place names, that is the name by which a place or feature is known within the country in which it occurs. For example:

> Roma
> 's-Gravenhage.

In the index the English form is cross-referenced to the local spelling:

> Rome = Roma
> Hague, The = 's-Gravenhage

Spellings of names are in the form given in the latest official lists and generally agree with the rules of the Permanent Committee on Geographical Names and the U.S. Board on Geographic Names.

Where languages do not use Roman alphabets certain rules are used to transcribe these languages into Roman alphabet. These rules are based largely on pronunciation.

The Pronunciation of Foreign Place Names

English speaking people usually have no difficulty in reading and pronouncing correctly American and English place names. However, foreign place name pronunciations may present many problems. Such problems can be minimised by following some simple rules. However, these rules cannot be applied to all situations, and there will be many exceptions.

1. In general, stress each syllable equally, unless your experience suggests otherwise.
2. Pronounce the letter 'a' as a broad 'a' as in 'arm'
3. Pronounce the letter 'e' as a short 'e' as in 'elm'
4. Pronounce the letter 'i' as a cross between a short 'i' and long 'e', as the two 'i's' in 'California'.
5. Pronounce the letter 'o' as an intermediate 'o' as in 'soft'
6. Pronounce the letter 'u' as an intermediate 'u' as in 'sure'
7. Pronounce consonants hard, except in the Romance-language areas where 'g's are likely to be pronounced softly like 'j' in 'jam'; 'j' itself may be pronounced as 'y'; and 'x's' may be pronounced as 'h'.

Moreover, English has no diacritical marks (accent and pronunciation signs), although some languages do. The following is a brief and general guide to the pronunciation of those most frequently used in the Western European languages.

		Pronunciation as in
French	é	day and shows that the e is to be pronounced e.g. Orléans.
	è	mare
	î	used over any vowel and does not affect pronunciation; shows contraction of the name, usually ommission of 's' following a vowel.
	ç	's' before 'a', 'o' and 'u'
	¨	over 'e', 'i', and 'u' when they are used with another vowel and shows that each is to be pronounced.
German	ä	fat
	ö	fur
	ü	no English equivalent; like French 'tu'
Italian	à, é	over vowels and indicates stress.
Portuguese	ã, õ	vowels pronounced nasally.
	ç	boss
	á	shows stress.
	ô	shows that a vowel has an 'i' or 'u' sound combined with it.
Spanish	ñ	canyon
	ü	pronounced as w and separately from adjoining vowels.
	á	usually indicates that this is a stressed vowel
Swedish	å	law
	ä	fat
	ö	fur

The problem of place name pronunciation is more difficult where the written form of the name is a transliteration (changing of a letter or letters of one alphabet into corresponding characters of another alphabet or language) from a non-Roman alphabet. Early English-speaking travellers and traders to such countries as China, Japan, and Russia prepared written forms of the names that they heard there. Although not based upon a formal system, many of these written forms have become conventional place name spellings.

More advanced study of particular languages has produced complex transliteration rules. These attempt to retain the nuances of the language concerned. One of the more difficult languages from the standpoint of both transliteration and pronunciation, is Chinese. Following are four examples of place names in three commonly used transliteration systems.

Chinese Postal System	Wade-Giles (pronunciation)	Pinyin
Peking	Pei-ching (ba-jing)	Beijing
Shanghai	Shang-hai (shäng-hi)	Shanghai
Canton	Kuang-chou (gwäng-jo)	Guangzhou

The Pinyin system, as developed by the Peking government, is the most recent system. It is the one adopted by the U.S. Board on Geographic Names and is used in this atlas. The Postal system contains the conventional place name spellings and does not require diacritical markings. It is listed by the U.S. Board on Geographic Names as an alternative to the Pinyin system for many place names in China.

The Chinese place-name problem is complicated further by actual changes in place-names over the years. For example, Mukden is now known as Shenyang.

In contrast to Chinese, Japanese romanization commonly employs only one diacritical mark, a line over 'o's and 'u's, which marks these as long vowels. Diacritical marks employed in the romanization of other languages not based on the Roman alphabet (such as Vietnamese and Hindi) are not commonly employed in general reference atlases as yet.

Geographical Co-ordinates

In the index, each place name is followed by its geographical co-ordinates which allow the reader to find the place on the map. These co-ordinates give the latitude and the longitude of a particular place.

The latitude (or parallel) is the distance of a point north or south of the Equator measured as an angle with the centre of the earth. The Equator is latitude 0°, the North Pole is 90°N, and the South Pole 90°S. On a globe, the lines could be drawn as concentric circles parallel to the Equator, decreasing in diameter from the Equator until they become a point at the poles. On the maps, these lines of latitude are usually represented as lines running across the map from East to West in smooth curves. They are numbered on the sides of the map. North of the Equator the numbers increase northwards, to the south they increase southwards. The degree interval between them depends on the scale of the map. On a large scale map (for example 1:2 500 000), the interval is one degree, but on a small scale map, (for example 1:40 000 000) the interval will be ten degrees.

Lines of longitude (or meridians) cut the latitude lines at right angles on the globe and intersect with one another at the poles. Longitude is measured by an angle at the centre of the earth between it and the meridian of origin which runs through Greenwich (0°). It may be a measurement East or West of this line from 0° to 180° in each direction. The longitude line of 180° runs North – South through the Pacific Ocean. On a particular map, the interval between the lines of longitude is always the same as that between the lines of latitude. Normally, the meridians are drawn vertically. They are numbered in the top and bottom margins and a note states East or West from Greenwich.

The unit of measurement for latitude and longitude is the degree, and it is subdivided into 60 minutes. An index entry states the position of a place in degrees and minutes, a space being left between the degrees and minutes. The latitude is followed by N(orth) or S(outh) and the longitude by E(ast) or W(est).

The diagrams below illustrate how the reader has to estimate the required distance from the nearest line of latitude or longitude. In the case of the first diagram, there is one degree, or 60 minutes between the lines and so to find the position of Newport an estimate has to be made. 28 parts of 60 north of the 41 degree latitude line and 19 parts of 60, or 19 minutes west of the 71 degree longitude line. In the case of the second diagram, it is a little more difficult to estimate since there are 10 degrees between the lines. In the example of Anchorage, the reader has to estimate 1 degree 13 minutes north of 60° and 9° 53 minutes west of 140°.

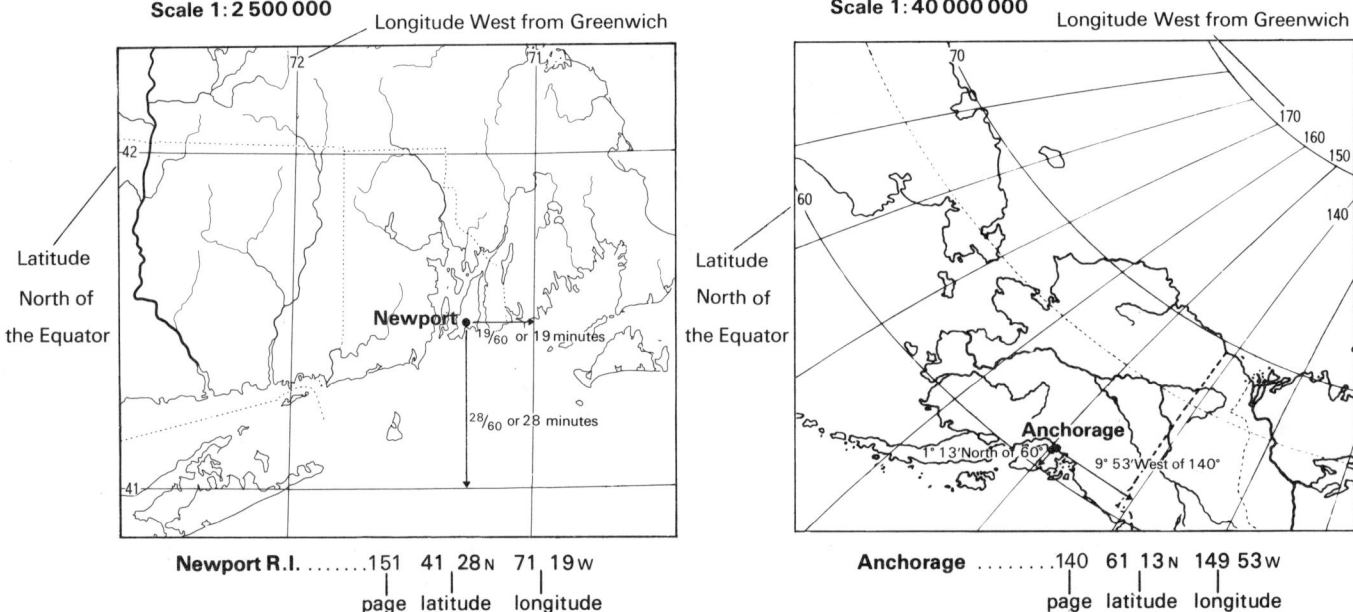

Afándou

A

Aachen **26** 50 47N 6 4 E
Aadorf **29** 47 30N 8 55 E
Aalborg = Ålborg **53** 57 2N 9 54 E
Aalen **27** 48 49N 10 6 E
A'âli en Nîl □ **125** 9 30N 31 30 E
Aalsmeer **22** 52 17N 4 43 E
Aalst, Belgium **23** 50 56N 4 2 E
Aalst, Neth. **23** 51 23N 5 29 E
Aalten **22** 51 56N 6 35 E
Aalter **23** 51 5N 3 28 E
Aarau **28** 47 23N 8 4 E
Aarberg **28** 47 2N 7 16 E
Aardenburg **23** 51 16N 3 28 E
Aare → **28** 47 33N 8 14 E
Aargau □ **28** 47 26N 8 10 E
Aarhus = Århus **53** 56 8N 10 11 E
Aarle **23** 51 30N 5 38 E
Aarschot **23** 50 59N 4 49 E
Aarsele **23** 51 0N 3 26 E
Aartrijke **23** 51 7N 3 6 E
Aarwangen **28** 47 15N 7 46 E
Aba, China **96** 32 59N 101 42 E
Aba, Nigeria **127** 5 10N 7 19 E
Aba, Zaïre **130** 3 58N 30 17 E
Âbâ, Jazîrat **125** 13 30N 32 31 E
Abacaxis → **169** 3 54 S 58 47W
Ābādān **73** 30 22N 48 20 E
Abade **125** 9 22N 38 3 E
Ābādeh **73** 31 8N 52 40 E
Abadin **34** 43 21N 7 29W
Abadla **121** 31 2N 2 45W
Abaeté **171** 19 9 S 45 27W
Abaeté → **171** 18 2 S 45 12W
Abaetetuba **170** 1 40 S 48 50W
Abagnar Qi **94** 43 52N 116 2 E
Abai **175** 25 58 S 55 54W
Abak **127** 4 58N 7 50 E
Abakaliki **127** 6 22N 8 2 E
Abakan **65** 53 40N 91 10 E
Abalemma **127** 16 12N 7 50 E
Abancay **172** 13 35 S 72 55W
Abanilla **37** 38 12N 1 3W
Abano Terme **43** 45 22N 11 46 E
Abapó **173** 18 48 S 63 25W
Abarán **37** 38 12N 1 23W
Abariringa **104** 2 50 S 171 40W
Abarqū **73** 31 10N 53 20 E
'Abasān **69** 31 19N 34 21 E
Abashiri **98** 44 0N 144 15 E
Abashiri-Wan **98** 44 0N 144 30 E
Abau **107** 10 11 S 148 46 E
Abaújszántó **31** 48 16N 21 12 E
Abay **64** 49 38N 72 53 E
Abaya, L. **125** 6 30N 37 50 E
Abaza **64** 52 39N 90 6 E
Abbadia San Salvatore **43** 42 53N 11 40 E
'Abbāsābād **73** 33 34N 58 23 E
Abbay = Nîl el Azraq → **125** 15 38N 32 31 E
Abbaye, Pt. **148** 46 58N 88 4W
Abbé, L. **125** 11 8N 41 47 E
Abbeville, France **19** 50 6N 1 49 E
Abbeville, La., U.S.A. **153** 30 0N 92 7W
Abbeville, S.C., U.S.A. **149** 34 12N 82 21W
Abbiategrasso **42** 45 23N 8 55 E
Abbieglassie **111** 27 15 S 147 28 E
Abbot Ice Shelf **7** 73 0 S 92 0W
Abbotsford, Canada **144** 49 5N 122 20W
Abbotsford, U.S.A. **152** 44 55N 90 20W
Abbottabad **78** 34 10N 73 15 E
Abcoude **22** 52 17N 4 59 E
Abd al Kūrī **75** 12 5N 52 20 E
Ābdar **73** 30 16N 55 19 E
'Abdolābād **73** 34 12N 56 30 E
Abdulino **62** 53 42N 53 40 E
Abéché **123** 13 50N 20 35 E
Abejar **36** 41 48N 2 47W
Abekr **125** 12 45N 28 50 E
Abêlessa **121** 22 58N 4 47 E
Abengourou **126** 6 42N 3 27W
Åbenrå **53** 55 3N 9 25 E
Abensberg **27** 48 49N 11 51 E
Abeokuta **127** 7 3N 3 19 E
Aber **130** 2 12N 32 25 E
Aberaeron **13** 52 15N 4 16W
Aberayron = Aberaeron **13** 52 15N 4 16W
Abercorn = Mbala **131** 8 46 S 31 24 E
Abercorn **111** 25 12 S 151 5 E
Aberdare **13** 51 43N 3 27W
Aberdare Ra. **130** 0 15 S 36 50 E
Aberdeen, Australia **111** 32 9 S 150 56 E
Aberdeen, Canada **145** 52 20N 106 8W
Aberdeen, S. Africa **134** 32 28 S 24 2 E
Aberdeen, U.K. **14** 57 9N 2 6W
Aberdeen, Ala., U.S.A. **149** 33 49N 88 33W
Aberdeen, Idaho, U.S.A. **156** 42 57N 112 50W
Aberdeen, Ohio, U.S.A. **155** 38 39N 83 46W
Aberdeen, S. Dak., U.S.A. **152** 45 30N 98 30W
Aberdeen, Wash., U.S.A. **158** 47 0N 123 50W
Aberdovey **13** 52 33N 4 3W
Aberfeldy, Australia **113** 37 42 S 146 22 E
Aberfeldy, U.K. **14** 56 37N 3 50W
Abergaria-a-Velha **34** 40 41N 8 32W
Abergavenny **13** 51 49N 3 1W
Abernathy **153** 33 49N 101 49W
Abert, L. **156** 42 40N 120 8W
Aberystwyth **13** 52 25N 4 6W
Abha **124** 18 0N 42 34 E
Abhar **73** 36 9N 49 13 E
Abhayapuri **82** 26 24N 90 38 E
Abidiya **124** 18 18N 34 3 E
Abidjan **126** 5 26N 3 58W
Abilene, Kans., U.S.A. **152** 39 0N 97 16W
Abilene, Tex., U.S.A. **153** 32 22N 99 40W
Abingdon, U.K. **13** 51 40N 1 17W
Abingdon, Ill., U.S.A. **154** 40 53N 90 23W
Abingdon, Va., U.S.A. **149** 36 46N 81 56W
Abington Reef **110** 18 0 S 149 35 E
Abitau → **145** 59 53N 109 3W
Abitau L. **145** 60 27N 107 15W
Abitibi L. **142** 48 40N 79 40W
Abiy Adi **125** 13 39N 39 3 E
Abkhaz A.S.S.R. □ **61** 43 0N 41 0 E
Abkit **65** 64 10N 157 10 E
Abminga **111** 26 8 S 134 51 E
Abnûb **124** 27 18N 31 4 E
Abo, Massif d' **123** 21 41N 16 8 E
Abocho **127** 7 35N 6 56 E
Abohar **78** 30 10N 74 10 E
Aboisso **126** 5 30N 3 5W
Abolo **132** 0 8N 14 16 E
Abomey **127** 7 10N 2 5 E
Abondance **21** 46 18N 6 43 E
Abong-Mbang **132** 4 0N 13 8 E
Abongabong **88** 4 15N 96 48 E
Abonnema **127** 4 41N 6 49 E
Abony **31** 47 12N 20 3 E
Aboso **126** 5 23N 1 57W
Abou-Deïa **123** 11 20N 19 20 E
Abou Goulem **123** 13 37N 21 38 E
Aboyne **14** 57 4N 2 48W
Abra □ **90** 17 35N 120 45 E
Abra de Ilog **90** 13 27N 120 44 E
Abra Pampa **174** 22 43 S 65 42W
Abrantes **35** 39 24N 8 7W
Abraveses **34** 40 41N 7 55W
Abreojos, Pta. **160** 26 50N 113 40W
Abreschviller **19** 48 39N 7 6 E
Abrets, Les **21** 45 32N 5 35 E
Abri, Esh Shamâliya, Sudan **124** 20 50N 30 27 E
Abri, Janub Kordofân, Sudan **125** 11 40N 30 21 E
Abrolhos, Banka **171** 18 0 S 38 0W
Abrud **50** 46 19N 23 5 E
Abruzzi □ **43** 42 15N 14 0 E
Absaroka Ra. **156** 44 40N 110 0W
Abū al Khaşīb **72** 30 25N 48 0 E
Abū 'Alī **73** 27 20N 49 27 E
Abū 'Alī → **70** 34 25N 35 50 E
Abu 'Arīsh **74** 16 53N 42 48 E
Abû Ballas **124** 24 26N 27 36 E
Abu Deleiq **125** 15 57N 33 48 E
Abu Dhabi = Abū Z̧āby **75** 24 28N 54 22 E
Abū Dīs, Jordan **69** 31 47N 35 16 E
Abû Dis, Sudan **124** 19 12N 33 38 E
Abû Dom **125** 16 18N 32 25 E
Abū Du'ān **72** 36 25N 38 15 E
Abu el Gairi, W. → **71** 29 35N 33 30 E
Abû Gabra **125** 11 2N 26 50 E
Abu Ga'da, W. → **71** 29 15N 32 53 E
Abû Ghaush **69** 31 48N 35 6 E
Abû Gubeiha **125** 11 30N 31 15 E
Abu Habl, Khawr → **125** 12 37N 31 0 E
Abū Ḩadrīyah **73** 27 20N 48 58 E
Abu Hamed **124** 19 32N 33 13 E
Abu Haraz, An Nîl el Azraq, Sudan **125** 14 35N 33 30 E
Abû Haraz, Esh Shamâliya, Sudan **124** 19 8N 32 18 E
Abû Higar **125** 12 50N 33 59 E
Abū Kamāl **72** 34 30N 41 0 E
Abū Madd, Ra's **72** 24 50N 37 7 E
Abu Matariq **125** 10 59N 26 9 E
Abu Qir **124** 31 18N 30 0 E
Abu Qireiya **124** 24 5N 35 28 E
Abu Qurqâs **124** 28 1N 30 44 E
Abū Raşāş, Ra's **75** 20 10N 58 38 E
Abū Rubayq **74** 23 44N 39 42 E
Abu Rudeis **71** 28 54N 33 11 E
Abu Şafāt, W. → **71** 30 24N 36 7 E
Abû Simbel **124** 22 18N 31 40 E
Abū Şukhayr **72** 31 54N 44 30 E
Abu Tig **124** 27 4N 31 15 E
Abu Tiga **125** 12 47N 34 12 E
Abû Zabad **125** 12 25N 29 10 E
Abū Z̧āby **75** 24 28N 54 22 E
Abū Zeydābād **73** 33 54N 51 45 E
Abufari **173** 5 25 S 62 59W
Abuja **127** 9 16N 7 2 E
Abukuma-Gawa → **98** 38 6N 140 52 E
Abukuma-Sammyaku **98** 37 30N 140 45 E
Abulug **90** 18 27N 121 27 E
Abumombazi **132** 3 42N 22 10 E
Abunã **173** 9 40 S 65 20W
Abunã → **173** 9 41 S 65 20W
Abung **90** 13 46N 121 26 E
Aburatsu **100** 31 34N 131 24 E
Aburo, Mt. **130** 2 4N 30 53 E
Abut Hd. **115** 43 7 S 170 15 E
Abwong **125** 9 2N 32 14 E
Åby **53** 58 40N 16 10 E
Aby, Lagune **126** 5 15N 3 14W
Acacías **168** 3 59N 73 46W
Acajutla **162** 13 36N 89 50W
Açallândia **170** 5 0 S 47 50W
Acámbaro **160** 20 0N 100 40W
Acanthus **48** 40 27N 23 47 E
Acaponeta **160** 22 30N 105 20W
Acapulco **161** 16 51N 99 56W
Acarai, Serra **169** 1 50N 57 50W
Acaraú **170** 2 53 S 40 7W
Acari, Brazil **170** 6 31 S 36 38W
Acarí, Peru **172** 15 25 S 74 36W
Acarigua **168** 9 33N 69 12W
Acatlán **161** 18 10N 98 3W
Acayucan **161** 17 59N 94 58W
Accéglio **42** 44 28N 6 59 E
Accomac **148** 37 43N 75 40W
Accous **20** 43 0N 0 36W
Accra **127** 5 35N 0 6W
Accrington **12** 53 46N 2 22W
Acebal **174** 33 20 S 60 50W
Aceh □ **86** 4 15N 97 30 E
Acerenza **45** 40 50N 15 58 E
Acerra **45** 40 57N 14 22 E
Aceuchal **35** 38 39N 6 30W
Achacachi **172** 16 3 S 68 43W
Achaguas **168** 7 46N 68 14W
Achalpur **78** 21 22N 77 32 E
Achao **176** 42 28 S 73 30W
Achel **23** 51 15N 5 29 E
Acheng **95** 45 30N 126 58 E
Achenkirch **30** 47 32N 11 45 E
Achensee **30** 47 26N 11 45 E
Acher **78** 23 10N 72 32 E
Achern **27** 48 37N 8 5 E
Acheron → **115** 42 16 S 173 4 E
Achill **15** 53 56N 9 55W
Achill Hd. **15** 53 59N 10 15W
Achill I. **15** 53 58N 10 5W
Achill Sound **15** 53 53N 9 55W
Achim **26** 53 1N 9 2 E
Achinsk **65** 56 20N 90 20 E
Achisay **63** 43 35N 68 53 E
Achit **62** 56 48N 57 54 E
Achol **125** 6 35N 31 32 E
Acireale **45** 37 37N 15 9 E
Ackerman **153** 33 20N 89 8W
Ackley **154** 42 33N 93 3W
Acklins I. **163** 22 30N 74 0W
Acme **144** 51 33N 113 30W
Acobamba **172** 12 52 S 74 35W
Acomayo **172** 13 55 S 71 38W
Aconcagua □, Argentina **174** 32 50 S 70 0W
Aconcagua □, Chile **174** 32 15 S 70 30W
Aconcagua, Cerro **174** 32 39 S 70 0W
Aconquija, Mt. **174** 27 0 S 66 0W
Acopiara **170** 6 6 S 39 27W
Açores, Is. dos = Azores **8** 38 44N 29 0W
Acorizal **173** 15 12 S 56 22W
Acquapendente **43** 42 45N 11 50 E
Acquasanta **43** 42 46N 13 24 E
Acquaviva delle Fonti **45** 40 53N 16 50 E
Acqui **42** 44 40N 8 28 E
Acre = 'Akko **69** 32 55N 35 4 E
Acre □ **172** 9 1 S 71 0W
Acre → **172** 8 45 S 67 22W
Acri **45** 39 29N 16 23 E
Acs **31** 47 42N 18 0 E
Actium **48** 38 57N 20 45 E
Acton **150** 43 38N 80 3W
Açu **170** 5 34 S 36 54W
Ad Dahnā **75** 24 30N 48 10 E
Aḑ Ḑāli' **74** 13 42N 44 44 E
Ad Dammām **73** 26 20N 50 5 E
Ad Darb **74** 18 2N 43 7 E
Ad Dawhah **75** 25 15N 51 35 E
Ad Dawr **72** 34 27N 43 47 E
Aḑ Ḑiffah **122** 30 30N 25 30 E
Ad Dilam **74** 23 55N 47 10 E
Ad Dir'īyah **72** 24 44N 46 35 E
Ad Dīwānīyah **72** 32 0N 45 0 E
Ad Dujayl **72** 33 51N 44 14 E
Ad Durūz, J. **71** 32 35N 36 40 E
Ada, Ghana **127** 5 44N 0 40 E
Ada, Minn., U.S.A. **152** 47 20N 96 30W
Ada, Ohio, U.S.A. **155** 40 46N 83 49W
Ada, Okla., U.S.A. **153** 34 50N 96 45W
Ada, Yugoslavia **46** 45 49N 20 9 E
Adad **136** 9 27N 46 49 E
Adaja → **34** 41 32N 4 52W
Ådalslinden **52** 63 27N 16 55 E
Adam **75** 22 15N 57 28 E
Adam, Mt. **176** 51 34 S 60 4W
Adamantina **171** 21 42 S 51 4W
Adamaoua, Massif de l' **127** 7 20N 12 20 E
Adamawa Highlands = Adamaoua, Massif de l' **127** 7 20N 12 20 E
Adamello, Mt. **42** 46 10N 10 34 E
Adami Tulu **125** 7 53N 38 41 E
Adaminaby **113** 36 0 S 148 45 E
Adamovka **62** 51 32N 59 56 E
Adams, Phil. **90** 18 28N 120 54 E
Adams, Mass., U.S.A. **151** 42 38N 73 8W
Adams, N.Y., U.S.A. **151** 43 50N 76 3W
Adams, Wis., U.S.A. **152** 43 59N 89 50W
Adams, Mt. **158** 46 10N 121 28W
Adam's Bridge **81** 9 15N 79 40 E
Adams L. **144** 51 10N 119 40W
Adam's Peak **81** 6 48N 80 30 E
Adamuz **35** 38 2N 4 32W
Adana **57** 37 0N 35 16 E
Adana □ **70** 37 0N 35 30 E
Adanero **34** 40 56N 4 36W
Adapazarı **57** 40 48N 30 25 E
Adarama **125** 17 10N 34 52 E
Adare, C. **7** 71 0 S 171 0 E
Adaut **87** 8 8 S 131 7 E
Adavale **111** 25 52 S 144 32 E
Adda → **42** 45 8N 9 53 E
Addis Ababa = Addis Abeba **125** 9 2N 38 42 E
Addis Abeba **125** 9 2N 38 42 E
Addis Alem **125** 9 0N 38 17 E
Addison, Ill., U.S.A. **155** 41 56N 88 2W
Addison, N.Y., U.S.A. **150** 42 9N 77 15W
Addo **134** 33 32 S 25 45 E
Addu Atoll **67** 0 30 S 73 0 E
Addyston **155** 39 8N 84 43W
Adebour **127** 13 17N 11 50 E
Ādeh **72** 37 42N 45 11 E
Adel, Ga., U.S.A. **149** 31 10N 83 28W
Adel, Iowa, U.S.A. **154** 41 37N 94 1W
Adelaide, Australia **112** 34 52 S 138 30 E
Adelaide, Bahamas **162** 25 0N 77 31W
Adelaide, S. Africa **135** 32 42 S 26 20 E
Adelaide I. **7** 67 15 S 68 30W
Adelaide Pen. **140** 68 15N 97 30W
Adelaide River **108** 13 15 S 131 7 E
Adelanto **159** 34 35N 117 22W
Adelboden **28** 46 29N 7 33 E
Adele, I. **108** 15 32 S 123 9 E
Adélie, Terre **7** 68 0 S 140 0 E
Ademuz **36** 40 5N 1 13W
Aden = Al 'Adan **74** 12 45N 45 0 E
Aden, G. of **68** 12 30N 47 30 E
Adendorp **134** 32 15 S 24 30 E
Adgz **120** 30 47N 6 30W
Adh Dhayd **75** 25 17N 55 53 E
Adhoi **78** 23 26N 70 32 E
Adi **87** 4 15 S 133 30 E
Adi Daro **125** 14 20N 38 14 E
Adi Keyih **125** 14 51N 39 22 E
Adi Kwala **125** 14 38N 38 48 E
Adi Ugri **125** 14 58N 38 48 E
Adieu, C. **109** 32 0 S 132 10 E
Adieu Pt. **108** 15 14 S 124 35 E
Adigala **125** 10 24N 42 15 E
Adige → **43** 45 9N 12 20 E
Adigrat **125** 14 20N 39 26 E
Adilabad **80** 19 33N 78 20 E
Adin **156** 41 10N 121 0W
Adinkerke **23** 51 5N 2 36 E
Adirondack Mts. **151** 44 0N 74 15W
Adjim **121** 33 47N 10 50 E
Adjohon **127** 6 41N 2 32 E
Adjud **50** 46 7N 27 10 E
Adjumani **130** 3 20N 31 50 E
Adlavik Is. **143** 55 2N 57 45W
Adler **61** 43 28N 39 52 E
Adliswil **29** 47 19N 8 32 E
Admer **121** 20 21N 5 27 E
Admer, Erg d' **121** 24 0N 9 5 E
Admiralty G. **108** 14 20 S 125 55 E
Admiralty I. **140** 57 40N 134 35W
Admiralty Inlet **156** 48 0N 122 40W
Admiralty Is. **107** 2 0 S 147 0 E
Ado **127** 6 36N 2 56 E
Ado Ekiti **127** 7 38N 5 12 E
Adok **125** 8 10N 30 20 E
Adola **125** 11 14N 41 44 E
Adonara **87** 8 15 S 123 5 E
Adoni **81** 15 33N 77 18W
Adony **31** 47 6N 18 52 E
Adour → **20** 43 32N 1 32W
Adra, India **79** 23 30N 86 42 E
Adra, Spain **37** 36 43N 3 3W
Adrano **45** 37 40N 14 49 E
Adrar **121** 27 51N 0 11W
Adrasman **63** 40 38N 69 58 E
Adré **123** 13 40N 22 20 E
Adrī **122** 27 32N 13 2 E
Ádria **43** 45 4N 12 3 E
Adrian, Mich., U.S.A. **155** 41 55N 84 0W
Adrian, Mo., U.S.A. **154** 38 24N 94 21W
Adrian, Tex., U.S.A. **153** 35 19N 102 37W
Adriatic Sea **38** 43 0N 16 0 E
Adua **87** 1 45 S 129 50 E
Adula **29** 46 30N 9 3 E
Adung Long **82** 28 7N 97 42 E
Adur **81** 9 8N 76 40 E
Adwa **125** 14 15N 38 52 E
Adzhar A.S.S.R. □ **61** 42 0N 42 0 E
Adzopé **126** 6 7N 3 49W
Ægean Sea **39** 37 0N 25 0 E
Æolian Is. = Eólie, Is. **45** 38 30N 14 50 E
Aerht'ai Shan **92** 46 40N 92 45 E
Ærø **53** 54 52N 10 25 E
Ærøskøbing **53** 54 53N 10 24 E
Aesch **28** 47 28N 7 36 E
Aëtós **49** 37 15N 21 50 E
Afafi, Massif d' **123** 22 11N 15 10 E
'Afak **72** 32 4N 45 15 E
Afanasyevo **62** 58 52N 53 15 E
Afándou **49** 36 18N 28 12 E

Afarag, Erg

Afarag, Erg **121** 23 50N 2 47 E
Afareaitu **106** 17 33 S 149 47W
Afars & Issas, Terr. of
= Djibouti ■ **125** 12 0N 43 0 E
Afdega **136** 6 4N 43 30 E
Affreville = Khemis
Miliana **121** 36 11N 2 14 E
Affton **154** 38 33N 90 20W
Afghanistan ■ **77** 33 0N 65 0 E
Afgoi **136** 2 7N 44 59 E
'Afif **74** 23 53N 42 56 E
Afikpo **127** 5 53N 7 54 E
Aflou **121** 34 7N 2 3 E
Afmadu **136** 0 31N 42 4 E
Afogados da Ingàzeira **170** 7 45 S 37 39W
Afognak I. **140** 58 10N 152 50W
Afragola **45** 40 54N 14 15 E
Afrera **125** 13 16N 41 5 E
Africa **116** 10 0N 20 0 E
'Afrīn **70** 36 32N 36 50 E
'Afrīn → **70** 36 20N 36 35 E
Afşar → **70** 37 2N 32 35 E
Afton **151** 42 14N 75 31W
Aftout **120** 26 50N 3 45W
Afuá **170** 0 15 S 50 20W
Afula **69** 32 37N 35 17 E
Afyonkarahisar **57** 38 45N 30 33 E
Aga **124** 30 55N 31 10 E
Agadès = Agadez **127** 16 58N 7 59 E
Agadez **127** 16 58N 7 59 E
Agadir **120** 30 28N 9 55W
Agaete **37** 28 6N 15 43W
Agailás **120** 22 37N 14 22W
Agana **106** 13 28N 144 45 E
Agapa **65** 71 27N 89 15 E
Agapovka **62** 53 18N 59 8 E
Agar **78** 23 40N 76 2 E
Agaro **125** 7 50N 36 38 E
Agartala **82** 23 50N 91 23 E
Ağaş **50** 46 28N 26 15 E
Agassiz **144** 49 14N 121 46W
Agats **87** 5 33 S 138 0 E
Agattu I. **140** 52 25N 172 30 E
Agbélouvé **127** 6 35N 1 14 E
Agboville **126** 5 55N 4 15W
Agcogan **90** 12 4N 121 57 E
Agdam **61** 40 0N 46 58 E
Agdash **61** 40 44N 47 22 E
Agde **20** 43 19N 3 28 E
Agde, C. d' **20** 43 16N 3 28 E
Agdzhabedi **61** 40 5N 47 27 E
Agen **20** 44 12N 0 38 E
Ageo **101** 35 58N 139 36 E
Ager Tay **123** 20 0N 17 41 E
Agersø **52** 55 13N 11 12 E
Ageyevo **59** 54 10N 36 27 E
Agger **53** 56 47N 8 13 E
Aggius **44** 40 56N 9 4 E
Āgh Kand **73** 37 15N 48 4 E
Aghil Mts. **79** 36 0N 77 0 E
Aghoueyyît **120** 21 10N 15 6W
Aginskoye **65** 51 6N 114 32 E
Agira **45** 37 40N 14 30 E
Agly → **20** 42 46N 3 3 E
Agnibilékrou **126** 7 10N 3 11W
Agnita **50** 45 59N 24 40 E
Agnone **45** 41 49N 14 20 E
Ago **101** 34 20N 136 51 E
Agofie **127** 8 27N 0 15 E
Agogna → **42** 45 4N 8 52 E
Agogo **125** 7 50N 28 45 E
Agon, France **18** 49 2N 1 34W
Agön, Sweden **52** 61 34N 17 23 E
Agoo **90** 16 20N 120 22 E
Ágordo **43** 46 18N 12 2 E
Agout → **20** 43 47N 1 41 E
Agra **78** 27 17N 77 58 E
Agramunt **36** 41 48N 1 6 E
Agreda **36** 41 51N 1 55W
Agri → **45** 40 13N 16 44 E
Ağri Daği **57** 39 50N 44 15 E
Ağri Karakose **57** 39 44N 43 3 E
Agrigento **44** 37 19N 13 33 E
Agrinion **49** 38 37N 21 27 E
Agrópoli **45** 40 23N 14 59 E
Agryz **62** 56 33N 53 2 E
Água Branca **170** 5 50 S 42 40W
Agua Caliente,
Baja Calif. N., Mexico **159** 32 29N 116 59W
Agua Caliente, Sinaloa,
Mexico **160** 26 30N 108 20W
Agua Caliente Springs **159** 32 56N 116 19W
Água Clara **173** 20 25 S 52 45W
Agua Hechicero **159** 32 26N 116 14W
Agua Preta → **169** 1 41 S 63 48W
Agua Prieta **160** 31 20N 109 32W
Aguachica **168** 8 19N 73 38W
Aguada Cecilio **176** 40 51 S 65 51W
Aguadas **168** 5 40N 75 38W
Aguadilla **163** 18 27N 67 10W
Aguadulce **162** 8 15N 80 32W
Aguanga **159** 33 27N 116 51W
Aguanish **143** 50 14N 62 2W
Aguanus → **143** 50 13N 62 5W
Aguapeí **173** 16 12 S 59 43W
Aguapeí → **171** 21 0 S 51 0W
Aguapey → **174** 29 7 S 56 36W
Aguaray Guazú → **174** 24 47 S 57 19W
Aguarico → **168** 0 59 S 75 11W
Aguas → **36** 41 20N 0 30W
Aguas Blancas **174** 24 15 S 69 55W
Aguas Calientes, Sierra
de **174** 25 26 S 66 40W
Águas Formosas **171** 17 5 S 40 57W
Aguascalientes **160** 21 53N 102 12W
Aguascalientes □ **160** 22 0N 102 20W
Agudo **35** 38 59N 4 52W
Águeda **34** 40 34N 8 27W
Agueda → **34** 41 2N 6 56W
Aguié **127** 13 31N 7 46 E
Aguilafuente **34** 41 13N 4 7W
Aguilar **35** 37 31N 4 40W
Aguilar de Campóo **34** 42 47N 4 15W
Aguilares **174** 27 26 S 65 35W
Aguilas **37** 37 23N 1 35W
Agüimes **37** 27 58N 15 27W
Aguja, C. de la **168** 11 18N 74 12W
Agulaa **125** 13 40N 39 40 E
Agulhas, C. **134** 34 52 S 20 0 E
Agulo **37** 28 11N 17 12W
Agung **89** 8 20 S 115 28 E
'Agur, Israel **69** 31 42N 34 55 E
Agur, Uganda **130** 2 28N 32 55 E
Agusan → **91** 9 0N 125 30 E
Agusan del Norte □ **91** 9 20N 125 10 E
Agusan del Sur □ **91** 8 30N 125 30 E
Agustín Codazzi **168** 10 2N 73 14W
Agutaya I. **91** 11 9N 120 58 E
Agvali **61** 42 36N 46 8 E
Aha Mts. **134** 19 45 S 21 0 E
Ahaggar **121** 23 0N 6 30 E
Ahamansu **127** 7 38N 0 35 E
Ahar **72** 38 35N 47 0 E
Ahaura → **115** 42 21 S 171 34 E
Ahaus **26** 52 4N 7 1 E
Ahelledjem **121** 26 37N 6 58 E
Ahipara B. **114** 35 5 S 173 5 E
Ahiri **80** 19 30N 80 0 E
Ahlen **26** 51 45N 7 52 E
Ahmad Wal **78** 29 18N 65 58 E
Ahmadabad, India **78** 23 0N 72 40 E
Aḥmadābād, Khorāsān,
Iran **73** 35 3N 60 50 E
Aḥmadābād, Khorāsān,
Iran **73** 35 49N 59 42 E
Aḥmadī **73** 27 56N 56 42 E
Ahmadnagar **80** 19 7N 74 46 E
Ahmadpur **78** 29 12N 71 10 E
Ahmar Mts. **125** 9 20N 41 15 E
Ahmedabad =
Ahmadabad **78** 23 0N 72 40 E
Ahmednagar =
Ahmadnagar **80** 19 7N 74 46 E
Ahoada **127** 5 8N 6 36 E
Ahome **160** 25 55N 109 11W
Ahr → **26** 50 33N 7 17 E
Ahram **73** 28 52N 51 16 E
Ahrensbök **26** 54 0N 10 34 E
Ahrweiler **26** 50 31N 7 3 E
Āhū **73** 34 33N 50 2 E
Ahuachapán **162** 13 54N 89 52W
Ahuriri → **115** 44 31 S 170 12 E
Åhus **53** 55 56N 14 18 E
Ahvāz **73** 31 20N 48 40 E
Ahvenanmaa = Åland **55** 60 15N 20 0 E
Aḥwar **74** 13 30N 46 40 E
Ahzar **127** 15 30N 3 20 E
Aiari → **168** 1 22N 68 36W
Aichach **27** 48 28N 11 9 E
Aichi □ **101** 35 0N 137 15 E
Aidone **45** 37 26N 14 26 E
Aiello Cálabro **45** 39 6N 16 12 E
Aigle **28** 46 18N 6 58 E
Aigle, L' **18** 48 46N 0 38 E
Aignay-le-Duc **19** 47 40N 4 43 E
Aigoual, Mt. **20** 44 8N 3 35 E
Aigre **20** 45 54N 0 1 E
Aigua **175** 34 13 S 54 46W
Aigueperse **20** 46 3N 3 13 E
Aigues → **21** 44 7N 4 43 E
Aigues-Mortes **21** 43 35N 4 12 E
Aigues-Mortes, G. d' **21** 43 31N 4 3 E
Aiguilles **21** 44 47N 6 51 E
Aiguillon **20** 44 18N 0 21 E
Aiguillon-sur-Mer, L' **20** 46 20N 1 18W
Aigurande **20** 46 27N 1 49 E
Aihui **93** 50 10N 127 30 E
Aija **172** 9 50 S 77 45W
Aikawa **98** 38 2N 138 15 E
Aiken **149** 33 34N 81 50W
Ailao Shan **96** 24 0N 101 20 E
Aillant-sur-Tholon **19** 47 52N 3 20 E
Aillik **143** 55 11N 59 18W
Ailly-sur-Noye **19** 49 45N 2 20 E
Ailsa Craig **14** 55 15N 5 7W
'Ailūn **69** 32 18N 35 47 E
Aim **65** 59 0N 133 55 E
Aimere **87** 8 45 S 121 3 E
Aimogasta **174** 28 33 S 66 50W
Aimorés **171** 19 30 S 41 4W
Ain □ **21** 46 5N 5 20 E
Ain → **21** 45 45N 5 11 E
Aïn Beïda **121** 35 50N 7 29 E
Aïn Ben Khellil **121** 33 15N 0 49W
Aïn Ben Tili **120** 25 59N 9 27W
Aïn Beni Mathar **121** 34 1N 2 0W
Aïn Benian **121** 36 48N 2 55 E
Aïn Dalla **124** 27 20N 27 23 E
'Ain el Akhḍar **71** 28 50N 33 55 E
Ain el Mafki **124** 27 30N 28 15 E
Ain Girba **124** 29 20N 25 14 E
Aïn M'lila **121** 36 2N 6 35 E
Ain Qeiqab **124** 29 42N 24 55 E
Aïn-Sefra **121** 32 47N 0 37W
Ain Sheikh Murzûk **124** 26 47N 27 45 E
'Ain Sudr **71** 29 50N 33 6 E
Ain Sukhna **124** 29 32N 32 20 E
Aïn Tédelès **121** 36 0N 0 21 E
Aïn-Témouchent **121** 35 16N 1 8W
Aïn Touta **121** 35 26N 5 54 E
Ain Zeitûn **124** 29 10N 25 48 E
Aïn Zorah **121** 34 37N 3 32W
Ainabo **136** 9 0N 46 25 E
Ainaži **58** 57 50N 24 24 E
Aínos Óros **49** 38 10N 20 35 E
Ainsworth **152** 42 33N 99 52W
Aioi **100** 34 48N 134 28 E
Aipe **168** 3 13N 75 15W
Aiquile **173** 18 10 S 65 10W
Aïr **127** 18 30N 8 0 E
Air Hitam **85** 1 55N 103 11 E
Airaines **19** 49 58N 1 55 E
Airão **169** 1 56 S 61 22W
Airdrie **14** 55 53N 3 57W
Aire →, France **19** 49 18N 4 49 E
Aire →, U.K. **12** 53 42N 0 55W
Aire, I. del **36** 39 48N 4 16 E
Aire-sur-la-Lys **19** 50 37N 2 22 E
Aire-sur-l'Adour **20** 43 42N 0 15W
Aireys Inlet **112** 38 29 S 144 5 E
Airlie Beach **110** 20 16 S 148 43 E
Airolo **29** 46 32N 8 37 E
Airvault **18** 46 50N 0 8W
Aisch → **27** 49 46N 11 1 E
Aisen □ **176** 46 30 S 73 0W
Aisne □ **19** 49 42N 3 40 E
Aisne → **19** 49 26N 2 50 E
Aitana, Sierra de **37** 38 35N 0 24W
Aitape **107** 3 11 S 142 22 E
Aitkin **152** 46 32N 93 43W
Aitolía Kai Akarnanía □ **49** 38 45N 21 18 E
Aitolikón **49** 38 26N 21 21 E
Aiuaba **170** 6 38 S 40 7W
Aiud **50** 46 19N 23 44 E
Aix-en-Provence **21** 43 32N 5 27 E
Aix-la-Chapelle =
Aachen **26** 50 47N 6 4 E
Aix-les-Bains **21** 45 41N 5 53 E
Aixe-sur-Vienne **20** 45 47N 1 9 E
Aiyang, Mt. **107** 5 10 S 141 20 E
Aiyansh **144** 55 17N 129 2W
Áíyina **49** 37 45N 23 26 E
Aiyínion **48** 40 28N 22 28 E
Aiyion **49** 38 15N 22 5 E
Aizawl **82** 23 40N 92 44 E
Aizenay **18** 46 44N 1 38W
Aizpute **58** 56 43N 21 40 E
Aizuwakamatsu **98** 37 30N 139 56 E
Ajaccio **21** 41 55N 8 40 E
Ajaccio, G. d' **21** 41 52N 8 40 E
Ajaju → **168** 0 59N 72 20W
Ajalpan **161** 18 22N 97 15W
Ajanta Ra. **80** 20 28N 75 50 E
Ajax **150** 43 50N 79 1W
Ajax, Mt. **115** 42 35 S 172 5 E
Ajdâbiyah **122** 30 54N 20 4 E
Ajdovščina **43** 45 54N 13 54 E
Ajibar **125** 10 35N 38 36 E
Ajka **31** 47 4N 17 31 E
'Ajmān **75** 25 25N 55 30 E
Ajmer **78** 26 28N 74 37 E
Ajo **157** 32 18N 112 54W
Ajoie **28** 47 22N 7 0 E
Ajok **125** 9 15N 28 28 E
Ajuy **91** 11 10N 123 1 E
Akaba **127** 8 10N 1 2 E
Akabira **98** 43 33N 142 5 E
Akabli **121** 26 49N 1 31 E
Akaishi-Dake **101** 35 27N 138 9 E
Akaishi-Sammyaku **101** 35 25N 138 10 E
Akaki Beseka **125** 8 55N 38 45 E
Akala **125** 15 39N 36 13 E
Akanthou **70** 35 22N 33 45 E
Akaroa **115** 43 49 S 172 59 E
Akasha **124** 21 10N 30 32 E
Akashi **100** 34 45N 135 0 E
Akbou **121** 36 31N 4 31 E
Akbulak **62** 51 1N 55 37 E
Akchâr **120** 20 20N 14 28W
Akdağ **70** 37 0N 32 0 E
Akdala **63** 45 2N 74 35 E
Akechi **101** 35 18N 137 23 E
Akelamo **87** 1 35N 129 40 E
Åkernes **51** 58 45N 7 30 E
Akershus fylke □ **51** 60 0N 11 10 E
Akeru → **80** 17 25N 80 0 E
Aketi **132** 2 38N 23 47 E
Akhaïa □ **49** 38 5N 21 45 E
Akhalkalaki **61** 41 27N 43 25 E
Akhaltsikhe **61** 41 40N 43 0 E
Akharnaí **49** 38 5N 23 44 E
Akhelóös → **49** 38 36N 21 14 E
Akhendria **49** 34 58N 25 16 E
Akhéron → **48** 39 20N 20 29 E
Akhladhókambos **49** 37 31N 22 35 E
Akhmîm **124** 26 31N 31 47 E
Akhnur **79** 32 52N 74 45 E
Akhtarīn **70** 36 31N 37 20 E
Akhtopol **47** 42 6N 27 56 E
Akhtubinsk **61** 48 13N 46 7 E
Akhty **61** 41 30N 47 45 E
Akhtyrka **58** 50 25N 35 0 E
Aki **100** 33 30N 133 54 E
Aki-Nada **100** 34 5N 132 40 E
Akiéni **132** 1 11 S 13 53 E
Akimiski I. **142** 52 50N 81 30W
Akimovka **60** 46 44N 35 0 E
Åkirkeby **53** 55 4N 14 55 E
Akita **98** 39 45N 140 7 E
Akita □ **98** 39 40N 140 30 E
Akjoujt **126** 19 45N 14 15W
Akka **120** 29 22N 8 9W
Akkeshi **98** 43 2N 144 51 E
'Akko **69** 32 55N 35 4 E
Akkol, Kazakh S.S.R.,
U.S.S.R. **63** 43 36N 70 45 E
Akkol, Kazakh S.S.R.,
U.S.S.R. **64** 45 0N 75 39 E
Akköy **49** 37 30N 27 18 E
Akkrum **22** 53 3N 5 50 E
Aklampa **127** 8 15N 2 10 E
Aklan □ **91** 11 50N 122 30 E
Aklavik **140** 68 12N 135 0W
Akmonte **35** 37 13N 6 38W
Akmuz **63** 41 15N 76 10 E
Aknoul **121** 34 40N 3 55W
Akō, Japan **100** 34 45N 134 24 E
Ako, Nigeria **127** 10 19N 10 48 E
Akobo → **125** 7 48N 33 3 E
Akola **78** 20 42N 77 2 E
Akonolinga **127** 3 50N 12 18 E
Akordat **125** 15 30N 37 40 E
Akosombo Dam **127** 6 20N 0 5 E
Akot, India **78** 21 10N 77 10 E
Akot, Sudan **125** 6 31N 30 9 E
Akpatok I. **141** 60 25N 68 8W
Akranes **54** 64 19N 21 58W
Åkrehamn **51** 59 15N 5 10 E
Akreïjit **126** 18 19N 9 11W
Akrítas Venétiko, Ákra **49** 36 43N 21 54 E
Akron, Colo., U.S.A. **152** 40 13N 103 15W
Akron, Ind., U.S.A. **155** 41 2N 86 1W
Akron, Ohio, U.S.A. **150** 41 7N 81 31W
Akrotíri, Ákra **48** 40 26N 25 27 E
Akrotiri Bay **70** 34 35N 33 10 E
Aksai Chih **79** 35 15N 79 55 E
Aksarka **64** 66 31N 67 50 E
Aksay **62** 51 11N 53 0 E
Aksek **70** 37 2N 31 47 E
Aksenovo Zilovskoye **65** 53 20N 117 40 E
Akstafa **61** 41 7N 45 27 E
Aksu **92** 41 5N 80 10 E
Aksu → **70** 36 54N 30 54 E
Aksuat, Ozero **62** 51 32N 64 34 E
Aksum **125** 14 5N 38 40 E
Aktash, R.S.F.S.R.,
U.S.S.R. **62** 55 2N 52 7 E
Aktash, Uzbek S.S.R.,
U.S.S.R. **63** 39 55N 65 55 E
Aktepe **70** 36 42N 36 27 E
Aktogay,
Kazakh S.S.R.,
U.S.S.R. **62** 46 57N 79 40 E
Aktogay,
Kazakh S.S.R.,
U.S.S.R. **63** 44 25N 76 44 E
Aktyubinsk **57** 50 17N 57 10 E
Aktyuz **63** 42 54N 76 7 E
Aku **127** 6 40N 7 18 E
Akula **132** 2 22N 20 12 E
Akune **100** 32 1N 130 12 E
Akure **127** 7 15N 5 5 E
Akureyri **54** 65 40N 18 6W
Akuseki-Shima **99** 29 27N 129 37 E
Akusha **61** 42 18N 47 30 E
Akyab = Sittwe **82** 20 18N 92 45 E
Akzhar **63** 43 8N 71 37 E
Al Abyār **122** 32 9N 20 29 E
Al 'Adan **74** 12 45N 45 0 E
Al Aḥsā **73** 25 50N 49 0 E
Al Ajfar **72** 27 26N 43 0 E
Al Akhḍar **71** 28 4N 37 9 E
Al Akhḍar, W. → **71** 28 30N 36 36 E
Al Amādīyah **72** 37 5N 43 30 E
Al Amārah **72** 31 55N 47 15 E
Al 'Aqabah **69** 29 31N 35 0 E
Al' Aqīq **74** 20 39N 41 25 E
Al Arak **72** 34 38N 38 35 E
Al 'Aramah **72** 25 30N 46 0 E
Al 'Ariḍah **74** 17 3N 43 5 E
Al Arṭāwīyah **72** 26 31N 45 20 E
Al Ashkhara **75** 21 50N 59 30 E
Al 'Āṣimah □ **71** 31 40N 36 30 E
Al' Assāfīyah **72** 28 17N 38 59 E
Al Atārib **70** 36 9N 36 49 E
Al 'Ayn, Oman **75** 24 15N 55 45 E
Al 'Ayn, Si. Arabia **72** 25 4N 38 6 E
Al 'Ayzarīyah **69** 31 47N 35 15 E
Al A'ẓamīyah **72** 33 22N 44 22 E
Al 'Azīzīyah, Iraq **72** 32 54N 45 4 E
Al 'Azīzīyah, Libya **122** 32 30N 13 1 E
Al Bāb **70** 36 23N 37 29 E
Al Bad' **72** 28 28N 35 1 E
Al Bādī, Iraq **72** 35 56N 41 32 E
Al Badī', Si. Arabia **74** 22 0N 46 35 E
Al Baḥrah **72** 29 40N 47 52 E

Aleksandrovac

Al Balqā' □ 71 32 5N 35 45 E
Al Barkāt 122 24 56N 10 14 E
Al Bārūk, J. 70 33 39N 35 40 E
Al Baṣrah 72 30 30N 47 50 E
Al Baṭḥā 72 31 6N 45 53 E
Al Batrūn 70 34 15N 35 40 E
Al Bayāḍ 74 22 0N 47 0 E
Al Bayḍā' 74 14 5N 45 42 E
Al Bayḍā □ 122 32 0N 21 30 E
Al Bāzūrīyah 69 33 15N 35 16 E
Al Bi'ār 74 22 39N 39 40 E
Al Biqā □ 70 34 0N 36 5 E
Al Bi'r 72 28 51N 36 16 E
Al Bīrah 69 31 55N 35 12 E
Al Birk 74 18 13N 41 33 E
Al Bu'ayrāt 122 31 24N 15 44 E
Al Buqay'ah 69 32 15N 35 30 E
Al Burayj 70 34 15N 36 46 E
Al Fallūjah 72 33 20N 43 55 E
Al Fatk 75 16 31N 52 41 E
Al Fāw 73 30 0N 48 30 E
Al Faydamī 75 16 25N 52 26 E
Al Fujayrah 75 25 7N 56 18 E
Al Ghadaf, W. → 71 31 26N 36 43 E
Al Ghammās 72 31 45N 44 37 E
Al Gharīb 122 32 35N 21 11 E
Al Ghayḍah, S. Yemen 75 16 13N 52 11 E
Al Ghayḍah, S. Yemen 75 14 55N 50 0 E
Al Ghayl 75 15 30N 50 54 E
Al Hābah 72 27 10N 47 0 E
Al Ḥadd 75 22 32N 59 48 E
Al Ḥaddār 74 21 58N 45 57 E
Al Ḥadīthah, Iraq 72 34 0N 41 13 E
Al Ḥadīthah, Si. Arabia 72 31 28N 37 8 E
Al Haffah 70 35 36N 36 1 E
Al Hājānah 70 33 20N 36 33 E
Al Hajarayn 75 15 29N 48 20 E
Al Hallānīyah 75 17 30N 56 1 E
Al Hāmad 72 31 30N 39 30 E
Al Ḥamar 74 22 26N 46 12 E
Al Hamdānīyah 70 35 25N 36 50 E
Al Hamidīyah 70 34 42N 35 57 E
Al Hammādah al Ḥamrā' 122 29 30N 12 0 E
Al Ḥammār 72 30 57N 46 51 E
Al Ḥamrā' 74 24 2N 38 55 E
Al Ḥarīq 74 23 29N 46 27 E
Al Harīr, W. → 69 32 44N 35 59 E
Al Harūj al Aswad 122 27 0N 17 10 E
Al Ḥasā, W. → 71 31 4N 35 29 E
Al Ḥasakah 72 36 35N 40 45 E
Al Hāsikīyah 75 17 28N 55 36 E
Al Ḥasy 75 14 3N 48 40 E
Al Ḥawrah 74 13 50N 47 35 E
Al Ḥawṭah 74 14 23N 47 24 E
Al Ḥawṭah □ 74 23 30N 47 0 E
Al Haydān, W. → 71 31 29N 35 34 E
Al Ḥayy 72 32 5N 46 5 E
Al Ḥijāz 74 26 0N 37 30 E
Al Ḥillah, Iraq 72 32 30N 44 25 E
Al Ḥillah, Si. Arabia 74 23 35N 46 50 E
Al Hirmil 70 34 26N 36 24 E
Al Ḥiṣnn 69 32 29N 35 52 E
Al Hoceïma 121 35 8N 3 58W
Al Ḥudaydah 74 14 50N 43 0 E
Al Ḥufrah, Awbārī, Libya 122 25 32N 14 1 E
Al Ḥufrah, Misrātah, Libya 122 29 5N 18 3 E
Al Hufūf 73 25 25N 49 45 E
Al Ḥulwah 74 23 24N 46 48 E
Al Ḥumayḍah 72 29 14N 34 56 E
Al Ḥunayy 73 25 58N 48 45 E
Al Ḥurayḍah 75 15 36N 48 12 E
Al Husayyāt 122 30 24N 20 37 E
Al Hūwah 74 23 2N 45 48 E
Al Ḥuwaymī 74 13 23N 44 28 E
Al Irq 122 29 5N 21 35 E
Al 'Irqah 74 13 39N 47 22 E
Al Īsāwīyah 72 30 43N 37 59 E
Al Ittihad = Madīnat ash Sha'b 74 12 50N 45 0 E
Al Jabal al Akhḍar 122 32 0N 21 30 E
Al Jafr 71 30 18N 36 14 E
Al Jaghbūb 122 29 42N 24 38 E
Al Jahrah 72 29 25N 47 40 E
Al Jalāmīd 72 31 20N 39 45 E
Al Jamalīyah 75 25 37N 51 5 E
Al Janūb □ 70 33 20N 35 20 E
Al Jawf, Libya 122 24 10N 23 24 E
Al Jawf, Si. Arabia 72 29 55N 39 40 E
Al Jazirah, Asia 72 33 30N 44 0 E
Al Jazirah, Libya 122 26 10N 21 20 E
Al Jithāmīyah 72 27 41N 41 43 E
Al Jubayl 73 27 0N 49 50 E
Al Jubaylah 72 24 55N 46 25 E
Al Jubb 72 27 11N 42 17 E
Al Jumūm 74 21 37N 39 42 E
Al Junaynah 123 13 27N 22 45 E
Al Kabā'ish 72 30 58N 47 0 E
Al Kāmil 75 22 13N 59 12 E
Al Karak 71 31 11N 35 42 E
Al Karak □ 71 31 0N 36 0 E
Al Kāẓim Tyah 72 33 22N 44 12 E
Al Khābūra 75 23 57N 57 5 E
Al Khalīl 69 31 32N 35 6 E
Al Khalīl □ 71 31 35N 35 5 E
Al Khalūf 68 20 30N 58 13 E
Al Khamāsīn 74 20 29N 44 46 E
Al Kharāb 74 16 29N 44 18 E
Al Kharfah 74 22 0N 46 35 E
Al Kharj 74 24 0N 47 0 E
Al Khāṣirah 74 23 30N 43 47 E
Al Khawr 75 25 41N 51 30 E
Al Khiḍr 72 31 12N 45 33 E
Al Khiyām 70 33 20N 35 36 E
Al Khums 122 32 40N 14 17 E
Al Khums □ 122 31 20N 14 10 E
Al Kiswah 70 33 23N 36 14 E
Al Kufrah 122 24 17N 23 15 E
Al Kuhayfīyah 72 27 12N 43 3 E
Al Kūt 72 32 30N 46 0 E
Al Kuwayt 72 29 30N 48 0 E
Al Labwah 70 34 11N 36 20 E
Al Lādhiqīyah 70 35 30N 35 45 E
Al Ladhiqīyah □ 70 35 45N 36 0 E
Al Lawz, J. 71 28 40N 35 20 E
Al Līth 74 20 9N 40 15 E
Al Liwā' 75 24 31N 56 36 E
Al Lubban 69 32 9N 35 14 E
Al Luḥayyah 74 15 45N 42 40 E
Al Madīnah, Iraq 72 30 57N 47 16 E
Al Madīnah, Si. Arabia 72 24 35N 39 52 E
Al-Mafraq 69 32 17N 36 14 E
Al Maghārīm 74 15 1N 47 49 E
Al Maḥmūdīyah 72 33 3N 44 21 E
Al Majma'ah 72 25 57N 45 22 E
Al Makhruq, W. → 71 31 28N 37 0 E
Al Makḥūl 72 26 37N 42 39 E
Al Makīlī 122 32 10N 22 17 E
Al Manā'if 75 23 49N 51 20 E
Al Manāmah 75 26 10N 50 30 E
Al Manṣūrī 74 14 17N 45 16 E
Al Maqwa' 72 29 10N 47 59 E
Al Marj 122 32 25N 20 30 E
Al Maṭlā 72 29 24N 47 40 E
Al Mawjib, W. → 71 31 28N 35 36 E
Al Mawṣil 72 36 15N 43 5 E
Al Mayādin 72 35 1N 40 27 E
Al Mazār 71 31 4N 35 41 E
Al Mazra 69 31 16N 35 31 E
Al Midhnab 72 25 50N 44 18 E
Al Mīfá 74 18 54N 41 57 E
Al Minā' 70 34 24N 35 49 E
Al Miqdādīyah 72 34 0N 45 0 E
Al Mubarraz 73 25 30N 49 40 E
Al Muḍaybī 75 22 34N 58 7 E
Al Mughayrā' 75 24 5N 53 32 E
Al Muḥarraq 75 26 15N 50 40 E
Al Mukallā 75 14 33N 49 2 E
Al Mukha 74 13 18N 43 15 E
Al Muladdah 75 23 45N 57 34 E
Al Musayjīd 72 24 5N 39 5 E
Al Musayyib 72 32 40N 44 25 E
Al Muwayliḥ 72 27 40N 35 30 E
Al Owuho = Otukpa 127 7 9N 7 41 E
Al Qaddāhiyah 122 31 15N 15 9 E
Al Qaḍīmah 74 22 20N 39 13 E
Al Qaḥmah 74 18 0N 41 41 E
Al Qā'im 72 34 21N 41 7 E
Al Qalībah 72 28 24N 37 42 E
Al Qaryah ash Sharqīyah 122 30 28N 13 40 E
Al Qaryatayn 70 34 12N 37 13 E
Al Qaṣabát 122 32 39N 14 1 E
Al Qaṭ'ā 72 34 40N 40 48 E
Al Qaṭīf 73 26 35N 50 0 E
Al Qaṭn 75 15 51N 48 26 E
Al Qatrānah 71 31 14N 36 26 E
Al Qaṭrūn 122 24 56N 15 3 E
Al Qayṣūmah 72 28 20N 46 7 E
Al Qiblīyah 75 17 30N 56 20 E
Al Quds = Jerusalem 69 31 47N 35 10 E
Al Quds □ 71 31 50N 35 20 E
Al Qunaytirah 70 32 55N 35 45 E
Al Qunfudhah 74 19 3N 41 4 E
Al Qurḥ 75 16 44N 51 29 E
Al Qurnah 72 31 1N 47 25 E
Al Quṣayr, Iraq 72 30 39N 45 50 E
Al Quṣayr, Syria 70 34 31N 36 34 E
Al Qutayfah 70 33 44N 36 36 E
Al Quway'īyah 74 24 3N 45 15 E
Al 'Ubaylah 75 21 59N 50 57 E
Al' Uḍaylīyah 73 25 8N 49 18 E
Al 'Ulā 72 26 35N 38 0 E
Al 'Ulayyah 74 19 39N 41 54 E
Al Uqaylah ash Sharqīgah 122 30 12N 19 10 E
Al Uqayr 73 25 40N 50 15 E
Al 'Uwaynid 72 24 50N 46 0 E
Al' 'Uwayqīlah 72 30 30N 42 10 E
Al 'Uyūn, Si. Arabia 72 26 30N 43 50 E
Al 'Uyūn, Si. Arabia 72 24 33N 39 35 E
Al Wajh 72 26 10N 36 30 E
Al Wakrah 75 25 10N 51 40 E
Al Wannān 73 26 55N 48 24 E
Al Waqbah 72 28 48N 45 33 E
Al Wari'āh 72 27 51N 47 25 E
Al Wātīyah 122 32 28N 11 57 E
Al Wusayl 75 25 29N 51 29 E
Al Yāmūn 69 32 29N 35 14 E
Ala 42 45 46N 11 0 E
Alabama □ 149 33 0N 87 0W
Alabama → 149 31 8N 87 57W
Alaçati 49 38 16N 26 23 E
Alaejos 34 41 18N 5 13W
Alagna Valsésia 42 45 51N 7 56 E
Alagoa Grande 170 7 3 S 35 35W
Alagoas □ 170 9 0 S 36 0W
Alagoinhas 171 12 7 S 38 20W
Alagón 36 41 46N 1 12W
Alagón → 35 39 44N 6 53W
Alajero 37 28 3N 17 13W
Alajuela 162 10 2N 84 8W
Alakamisy 135 21 19 S 47 14 E
Alakurtti 56 67 0N 30 30 E
Alalapura 169 2 20N 56 25W
Alalaú → 169 0 30 S 61 9W
Alameda, Spain 35 37 12N 4 39W
Alameda, Calif., U.S.A. 158 37 46N 122 15W
Alameda, N. Mex., U.S.A. 157 35 10N 106 43W
Alaminos 90 16 10N 119 59 E
Alamo 159 36 21N 115 10W
Alamo Crossing 159 34 16N 113 33W
Alamogordo 157 32 59N 106 0W
Alamos 160 27 0N 109 0W
Alamosa 157 37 30N 106 0W
Åland, Finland 55 60 15N 20 0 E
Aland, India 80 17 36N 76 35 E
Alandroal 35 38 41N 7 24W
Alandur 81 13 0N 80 15 E
Alange, Presa de 35 38 45N 6 18W
Alanis 35 38 3N 5 43W
Alanya 57 36 38N 32 0 E
Alaotra, Farihin' 135 17 30 S 48 30 E
Alapayevsk 62 57 52N 61 42 E
'Alāqán 71 29 10N 35 21 E
Alar del Rey 34 42 38N 4 20W
Alara → 70 36 38N 31 39 E
Alaraz 34 40 45N 5 17W
Alaşehir 57 38 23N 28 30 E
Alaska □ 140 65 0N 150 0W
Alaska, G. of 140 58 0N 145 0W
Alaska Highway 144 60 0N 130 0W
Alaska Pen. 140 56 0N 160 0W
Alaska Range 140 62 50N 151 0W
Alássio 42 44 1N 8 10 E
Alatri 44 41 44N 13 21 E
Alatyr 59 54 45N 46 35 E
Alatyr → 59 54 52N 46 36 E
Alausi 168 2 0 S 78 50W
Álava □ 35 42 48N 2 28W
Alava, C. 156 48 10N 124 40W
Alaverdi 61 41 15N 44 37 E
Alawoona 112 34 45 S 140 30 E
'Alayh 70 33 46N 35 33 E
Alaykel 63 40 15N 74 25 E
Alayor 36 39 57N 4 8 E
Alayskiy Khrebet 63 39 45N 72 0 E
Alazan → 61 41 5N 46 40 E
Alba 42 44 41N 8 1 E
Alba □ 50 46 10N 23 30 E
Alba de Tormes 34 40 50N 5 30W
Alba Iulia 50 46 8N 23 39 E
Albac 50 46 28N 23 1 E
Albacete 37 39 0N 1 50W
Albacete □ 37 38 50N 2 0W
Albacutya, L. 112 35 45 S 141 58 E
Ålbæk 53 57 36N 10 25 E
Ålbæk Bugt 53 57 35N 10 40 E
Albaida 37 38 51N 0 31W
Albalate de las Nogueras 36 40 22N 2 18W
Albalate del Arzobispo 36 41 6N 0 31W
Albania ■ 48 41 0N 20 0 E
Albano Laziale 44 41 44N 12 40 E
Albany, Australia 109 35 1 S 117 58 E
Albany, Ga., U.S.A. 149 31 40N 84 10W
Albany, Ind., U.S.A. 155 40 18N 85 13W
Albany, Minn., U.S.A. 152 45 37N 94 38W
Albany, Mo., U.S.A. 154 40 15N 94 20W
Albany, N.Y., U.S.A. 151 42 35N 73 47W
Albany, Oreg., U.S.A. 156 44 41N 123 0W
Albany, Tex., U.S.A. 153 32 45N 99 20W
Albany, Wis., U.S.A. 154 42 43N 89 26W
Albany → 142 52 17N 81 31W
Albardón 174 31 20 S 68 30W
Albarracín 36 40 25N 1 26W
Albarracín, Sierra de 36 40 30N 1 30W
Albatross B. 110 12 45 S 141 30 E
Albatross Pt. 114 38 7 S 174 44 E
Albay □ 90 13 13N 123 33 E
Albegna → 43 42 30N 11 11 E
Albemarle 149 35 27N 80 15W
Albemarle Sd. 149 36 0N 76 30W
Albenga 42 44 3N 8 12 E
Alberche → 34 39 58N 4 46W
Alberdi 174 26 14 S 58 20W
Alberes, Mts. 36 42 28N 2 56 E
Alberique 37 39 7N 0 31W
Albersdorf 26 54 8N 9 19 E
Albert, Australia 113 32 22 S 147 30 E
Albert, France 19 50 0N 2 38 E
Albert, L. = Mobutu Sese Seko, L. 130 1 30N 31 0 E
Albert, L. 112 35 30 S 139 10 E
Albert Canyon 144 51 8N 117 41W
Albert Edward, Mt. 107 8 20 S 147 24 E
Albert Edward Ra. 108 18 17 S 127 57 E
Albert Lea 152 43 32N 93 20W
Albert Nile → 130 3 36N 32 2 E
Albert Town 163 22 37N 74 33 E
Alberta □ 144 54 40N 115 0W
Alberti 174 35 1 S 60 16W
Albertinia 134 34 11 S 21 34 E
Albertirsa 31 47 14N 19 37 E
Albertkanaal → 23 51 14N 4 26 E
Alberton 143 46 50N 64 0W
Albertville = Kalemie 130 5 55 S 29 9 E
Albertville 21 45 40N 6 22 E
Albi 20 43 56N 2 9 E
Albia 154 41 0N 92 50W
Albina 169 5 37N 54 15W
Albina, Ponta 133 15 52 S 11 44 E
Albino 42 45 47N 9 48 E
Albion, Idaho, U.S.A. 156 42 21N 113 37W
Albion, Ill., U.S.A. 155 38 23N 88 4W
Albion, Ind., U.S.A. 155 41 24N 85 25W
Albion, Mich., U.S.A. 155 42 15N 84 45W
Albion, Nebr., U.S.A. 152 41 47N 98 0W
Albion, Pa., U.S.A. 150 41 53N 80 21W
Alblasserdam 22 51 52N 4 40 E
Albocácer 36 40 21N 0 1 E
Alböke 53 56 57N 16 47 E
Alborán 35 35 57N 3 0W
Alborea 37 39 17N 1 24W
Ålborg 53 57 2N 9 54 E
Ålborg Bugt 53 56 50N 10 35 E
Alborz, Reshteh-ye Kūhhā-ye 73 36 0N 52 0 E
Albox 37 37 23N 2 8W
Albreda 144 52 35N 119 10W
Albuera, La 35 38 45N 6 49W
Albufeira 35 37 5N 8 15W
Albula → 29 46 38N 9 30 E
Albuñol 37 36 48N 3 11W
Albuquerque, Brazil 173 19 23 S 57 26W
Albuquerque, U.S.A. 157 35 5N 106 47W
Albuquerque, Cayos de 162 12 10N 81 50W
Alburg 151 44 58N 73 19W
Alburno, Mte. 45 40 32N 15 15 E
Alburquerque 35 39 15N 6 59W
Albury 113 36 3 S 146 56 E
Alby 52 62 30N 15 28 E
Alcácer do Sal 35 38 22N 8 33W
Alcaçovas 35 38 23N 8 9W
Alcala 90 17 54N 121 39 E
Alcalá de Chisvert 36 40 19N 0 13 E
Alcalá de Guadaira 35 37 20N 5 50W
Alcalá de Henares 36 40 28N 3 22W
Alcalá de los Gazules 35 36 29N 5 43W
Alcalá la Real 35 37 27N 3 57W
Alcamo 44 37 59N 12 55 E
Alcanadre 36 42 24N 2 7W
Alcanadre → 36 41 43N 0 12W
Alcanar 36 40 33N 0 28 E
Alcanede 35 39 25N 8 49W
Alcanena 35 39 27N 8 40W
Alcañices 34 41 41N 6 21W
Alcaníz 36 41 2N 0 8W
Alcântara, Brazil 170 2 20 S 44 30W
Alcántara, Spain 35 39 41N 6 57W
Alcantara L. 145 60 57N 108 9W
Alcantarilla 37 37 59N 1 12W
Alcaracejos 35 38 24N 4 58W
Alcaraz 37 38 40N 2 29W
Alcaraz, Sierra de 37 38 40N 2 20W
Alcarria, La 36 40 31N 2 45W
Alcaudete 35 37 35N 4 5W
Alcázar de San Juan 37 39 24N 3 12W
Alcira 37 39 9N 0 30W
Alcoa 149 35 50N 84 0W
Alcobaça 35 39 32N 9 0W
Alcobendas 36 40 32N 3 38W
Alcolea del Pinar 36 41 2N 2 28W
Alcora 36 40 5N 0 14W
Alcoutim 35 37 25N 7 28W
Alcova 156 42 37N 106 52W
Alcoy 37 38 43N 0 30W
Alcubierre, Sierra de 36 41 45N 0 22W
Alcublas 36 39 48N 0 43W
Alcudia 36 39 51N 3 7 E
Alcudia, B. de 36 39 47N 3 15 E
Alcudia, Sierra de la 35 38 34N 4 30W
Aldabra Is. 83 9 22 S 46 28 E
Aldama 161 23 0N 98 4W
Aldan 65 58 40N 125 30 E
Aldan → 65 63 28N 129 35 E
Aldea, Pta. de la 37 28 0N 15 50W
Aldeburgh 13 52 9N 1 35 E
Aldeia Nova 35 37 55N 7 24W
Alder 156 45 27N 112 3W
Alder Pk. 158 35 53N 121 22W
Alderney 18 49 42N 2 12W
Aldershot 13 51 15N 0 43W
Aledo 154 41 10N 90 50W
Alefa 125 11 55N 36 55 E
Aleg 126 17 3N 13 55W
Alegranza 37 29 23N 13 32W
Alegranza, I. 37 29 23N 13 32W
Alegre 171 20 50 S 41 30W
Alegrete 175 29 40 S 56 0W
Alegria 91 11 47N 124 3 E
Aleisk 64 52 40N 83 0 E
Alejandro Selkirk, I. 105 33 50 S 80 15W
Aleksandriya, Ukraine S.S.R., U.S.S.R. 58 50 37N 26 19 E
Aleksandriya, Ukraine S.S.R., U.S.S.R. 60 48 42N 33 3 E
Aleksandriyskaya 61 43 59N 47 0 E
Aleksandrov 59 56 23N 38 44 E
Aleksandrovac, Srbija, Yugoslavia 46 43 28N 21 3 E
Aleksandrovac, Srbija, Yugoslavia 46 44 28N 21 13 E

Angamos, Punta

Amâdi, Sudan .... **125** 5 29N 30 25 E
Amadi, Zaïre .... **130** 3 40N 26 40 E
Amadjuak **141** 64 0N 72 39W
Amadjuak L. **141** 65 0N 71 8W
Amadora **35** 38 45N 9 13W
Amagasaki .... **101** 34 42N 135 20 E
Amager .... **52** 55 37N 12 35 E
Amagi .... **100** 33 25N 130 39 E
Amaimon .... **107** 5 12 S 145 30 E
Amakusa-Nada .... **100** 32 35N 130 5 E
Amakusa-Shotō ...... **100** 32 15N 130 10 E
Åmål .... **52** 59 3N 12 42 E
Amalapuram .... **81** 16 35N 81 55 E
Amalfi, Colombia **168** 6 55N 75 4W
Amalfi, Italy .... **45** 40 39N 14 34 E
Amaliás .... **49** 37 47N 21 22 E
Amalner .... **78** 21 5N 75 5 E
Amambaí .... **175** 23 5 S 55 13W
Amambaí → .... **175** 23 22 S 53 56W
Amambay □ .... **175** 23 0 S 56 0W
Amambay, Cordillera de **175** 23 0 S 55 45W
Amami-Guntō .... **99** 28 16N 129 21 E
Amami-Ō-Shima ...... **99** 28 0N 129 0 E
Amana → **169** 9 45N 62 39W
Amaná, L. .... **169** 2 35 S 64 40W
Amanab .... **107** 3 40 S 141 14 E
Amanda Park **158** 47 28N 123 55W
Amándola .... **43** 42 59N 13 21 E
Amangeldy .... **64** 50 10N 65 10 E
Amantea .... **45** 39 8N 16 3 E
Amapá **170** 2 5N 50 50W
Amapá □ **170** 1 40N 52 0W
Amapari **169** 0 37N 51 39W
Amara .... **125** 10 25N 34 10 E
Amarante, Brazil ...... **170** 6 14 S 42 50W
Amarante, Portugal ... **34** 41 16N 8 5W
Amarante do Maranhão **170** 5 36 S 46 45W
Amaranth **145** 50 36N 98 43W
Amarapura .... **82** 21 54N 96 3 E
Amaravati → .... **81** 11 0N 78 15 E
Amareleja **35** 38 12N 7 13W
Amargosa .... **171** 13 2 S 39 36W
Amargosa → **159** 36 14N 116 51W
Amargosa Ra. **159** 36 25N 116 40W
Amarillo **153** 35 14N 101 46W
Amarnath .... **80** 19 12N 73 22 E
Amaro, Mt. .... **43** 42 5N 14 6 E
Amaro Leite .... **171** 13 58 S 49 9W
Amarpur .... **79** 25 5N 87 0 E
Amassama .... **127** 5 1N 6 2 E
Amataurá .... **168** 3 29 S 68 6W
Amatikulu .... **135** 29 3 S 31 33 E
Amatitlán **162** 14 29N 90 38W
Amatrice .... **43** 42 38N 13 16 E
Amay .... **23** 50 33N 5 19 E
Amazon =
Amazonas → ...... **169** 0 5 S 50 0W
Amazonas □, Brazil ... **172** 4 0 S 62 0W
Amazonas □, Peru .... **172** 5 0 S 78 0W
Amazonas □, Venezuela **168** 3 30N 66 0W
Amazonas → .... **169** 0 5 S 50 0W
Ambad .... **80** 19 38N 75 50 E
Ambahakily .... **135** 21 36 S 43 41 E
Ambala .... **78** 30 23N 76 56 E
Ambalangoda .... **81** 6 15N 80 5 E
Ambalapulai .... **81** 9 25N 76 25 E
Ambalavao .... **135** 21 50 S 46 56 E
Ambalindum .... **110** 23 23 S 135 0 E
Ambam .... **132** 2 20N 11 15 E
Ambanja .... **135** 13 40 S 48 27 E
Ambarchik .... **65** 69 40N 162 20 E
Ambarijeby .... **135** 14 56 S 47 41 E
Ambaro, Helodranon' . **135** 13 23 S 48 38 E
Ambartsevo .... **64** 57 30N 83 52 E
Ambasamudram ...... **81** 8 43N 77 25 E
Ambato .... **168** 1 5 S 78 42W
Ambato, Sierra de .... **174** 28 25 S 66 10W
Ambato Boeny .... **135** 16 28 S 46 43 E
Ambatofinandrahana .. **135** 20 33 S 46 48 E
Ambatolampy .... **135** 19 20 S 47 35 E
Ambatondrazaka ...... **135** 17 55 S 48 28 E
Ambatosoratra .... **135** 17 37 S 48 31 E
Ambenja .... **135** 15 17 S 46 58 E
Amberg .... **27** 49 25N 11 52 E
Ambergris Cay **161** 18 0N 88 0W
Ambérieu-en-Bugey ... **21** 45 57N 5 20 E
Amberley .... **115** 43 9 S 172 44 E
Ambert .... **20** 45 33N 3 44 E
Ambidédi **126** 14 35N 11 47W
Ambikapur .... **79** 23 15N 83 15 E
Ambikol .... **124** 21 20N 30 50 E
Ambilobé .... **135** 13 10 S 49 3 E
Ambinanindrano ...... **135** 20 5 S 48 23 E
Ambjörnarp .... **53** 57 25N 13 17 E
Ambleside **12** 54 26N 2 58W
Amblève .... **23** 50 21N 6 10 E
Amblève → .... **23** 50 25N 5 45 E
Ambo, Ethiopia .... **125** 12 20N 37 30 E
Ambo, Peru .... **172** 10 5 S 76 10W
Ambodifototra .... **135** 16 59 S 49 52 E
Ambodilazana .... **135** 18 6 S 49 10 E
Ambohimahasoa ...... **135** 21 7 S 47 13 E
Ambohimanga .... **135** 20 52 S 47 36 E
Ambohitra .... **135** 12 30 S 49 10 E
Ambon .... **87** 3 35 S 128 20 E
Amboseli L. .... **130** 2 40 S 37 10 E
Ambositra .... **135** 20 31 S 47 25 E
Ambovombé .... **135** 25 11 S 46 5 E
Amboy, Calif., U.S.A. **159** 34 33N 115 51W
Amboy, Ill., U.S.A. ... **154** 41 44N 89 20W
Amboyna I. .... **86** 7 50N 112 50 E
Ambridge **150** 40 36N 80 15W
Ambriz .... **133** 7 48 S 13 8 E
Ambunti .... **107** 4 13 S 142 52 E
Ambur .... **81** 12 48N 78 43 E
Amby .... **111** 26 30 S 148 11 E
Amchitka I. **140** 51 30N 179 0W
Amderma .... **64** 69 45N 61 30 E
Ameca **160** 20 30N 104 0W
Ameca → **160** 20 40N 105 15W
Amecameca **161** 19 7N 98 46W
Ameland .... **22** 53 27N 5 45 E
Amélia .... **43** 42 34N 12 25 E
Amélie-les-Bains-Palalda **20** 42 29N 2 41 E
Amen .... **65** 68 45N 180 0 E
Amendolaro .... **45** 39 58N 16 34 E
America .... **23** 51 27N 5 59 E
American Falls **156** 42 46N 112 56W
American Falls Res. ... **156** 43 0N 112 50W
American Highland .... **7** 73 0 S 75 0 E
American Samoa ■ ... **105** 14 20 S 170 40W
Americana .... **175** 22 45 S 47 20W
Americus **149** 32 0N 84 10W
Amersfoort, Neth. .... **22** 52 9N 5 23 E
Amersfoort, S. Africa . **135** 26 59 S 29 53 E
Amery, Australia ..... **109** 31 9 S 117 5 E
Amery, Canada **145** 56 34N 94 3W
Amery Ice Shelf ...... **7** 69 30 S 72 0 E
Ames **154** 42 0N 93 40W
Amesbury **151** 42 50N 70 52W
Amfíklia .... **49** 38 38N 22 35 E
Amfilokhía .... **49** 38 52N 21 9 E
Amfípolis .... **48** 40 48N 23 52 E
Ámfissa .... **49** 38 32N 22 22 E
Amga .... **65** 60 50N 132 0 E
Amga → .... **65** 62 38N 134 32 E
Amgu .... **65** 45 45N 137 15 E
Amgun → .... **65** 52 56N 139 38 E
Amherst, Canada **143** 45 48N 64 8W
Amherst, Mass., U.S.A. **151** 42 21N 72 30W
Amherst, N.Y., U.S.A. **150** 42 59N 78 48W
Amherst, Ohio, U.S.A. **150** 41 23N 82 15W
Amherst, Tex., U.S.A. **153** 34 0N 102 24W
Amherst I. **151** 44 8N 76 43W
Amherstburg **142** 42 6N 83 6W
Amiata, Mte. .... **43** 42 54N 11 40 E
Amiens .... **19** 49 54N 2 16 E
Amigdhalokefáli ...... **49** 35 23N 23 30 E
Amili .... **82** 28 25N 95 52 E
Amindaion .... **48** 40 42N 21 42 E
Amīrābād .... **72** 33 20N 46 16 E
Amirante Is. .... **83** 6 0 S 53 0 E
Amisk L. **145** 54 35N 102 15W
Amistad, Presa de la .. **160** 29 24N 101 0W
Amite **153** 30 47N 90 31W
Amizmiz **120** 31 12N 8 15W
Åmli .... **51** 58 45N 8 32 E
Amlwch **12** 53 24N 4 21W
Amm Adam .... **125** 16 20N 36 1 E
'Ammān .... **69** 31 57N 35 52 E
Ammanford **13** 51 48N 4 0W
Ammerån .... **52** 63 9N 16 13 E
Ammerån → .... **52** 63 9N 16 13 E
Ammersee .... **27** 48 0N 11 7 E
Ammerzoden .... **22** 51 45N 5 13 E
Ammi'ad .... **69** 32 55N 35 32 E
Amnat Charoen ...... **84** 15 51N 104 38 E
Amo Jiang → ...... **96** 23 0N 101 50 E
Āmol .... **73** 36 23N 52 20 E
Amorebieta **36** 43 13N 2 44W
Amoret **154** 38 15N 94 35W
Amorgós .... **49** 36 50N 25 57 E
Amory **149** 33 59N 88 29W
Amos **142** 48 35N 78 5W
Åmot, Buskerud,
Norway .... **51** 59 54N 9 54 E
Åmot, Telemark,
Norway .... **51** 59 34N 8 0 E
Åmotsdal .... **51** 59 37N 8 26 E
Amour, Djebel .... **121** 33 42N 1 37 E
Amoy = Xiamen ...... **97** 24 25N 118 4 E
Ampang .... **85** 3 8N 101 45 E
Ampanihy .... **135** 24 40 S 44 45 E
Ampasindava,
Helodranon' .... **135** 13 40 S 48 15 E
Ampasindava, Saikanosy **135** 13 42 S 47 55 E
Ampato, Nevado ...... **172** 15 40 S 71 56W
Ampenan .... **89** 8 35 S 116 13 E
Amper .... **127** 9 25N 9 40 E
Amper → .... **27** 48 30N 11 57 E
Ampère .... **121** 35 44N 5 27 E
Ampezzo .... **43** 46 25N 12 48 E
Amposta .... **36** 40 43N 0 34 E
Ampotaka .... **135** 25 3 S 44 41 E
Ampoza .... **135** 22 20 S 44 44 E
Amqa .... **69** 32 59N 35 10 E
Amqui **143** 48 28N 67 27W
'Amrān .... **74** 15 41N 43 55 E
Amravati .... **78** 20 55N 77 45 E
Amreli .... **78** 21 35N 71 17 E
Amrenene el Kasba ... **121** 22 10N 0 30 E
Amriswil .... **29** 47 33N 9 18 E
Amritsar .... **78** 31 35N 74 57 E
Amroha .... **79** 28 53N 78 30 E
Amrum .... **26** 54 37N 8 21 E
Amsel .... **121** 22 47N 5 29 E
Amsterdam, Neth. .... **22** 52 23N 4 54 E
Amsterdam, U.S.A. ... **151** 42 58N 74 10W
Amsterdam, I. .... **83** 38 30 S 77 30 E
Amstetten .... **30** 48 7N 14 51 E
Amudarya → .... **64** 43 40N 59 0 E
Amulung .... **90** 17 50N 121 43 E
Amund Ringnes I. **6** 78 20N 96 25W
Amundsen Gulf **140** 71 0N 124 0W
Amundsen Sea .... **7** 72 0 S 115 0W
Amungen .... **52** 61 10N 15 40 E
Amuntai .... **89** 2 28 S 115 25 E
Amur .... **136** 5 16N 46 30 E
Amur → .... **65** 52 56N 141 10 E
Amurang .... **87** 1 5N 124 40 E
Amuri Pass .... **115** 42 31 S 172 11 E
Amurrio **36** 43 3N 3 0W
Amursk .... **65** 50 14N 136 54 E
Amurzet .... **65** 47 50N 131 5 E
Amusco **34** 42 10N 4 28W
Amutag .... **90** 12 23N 123 16 E
Amvrakikós Kólpos ... **49** 39 0N 20 55 E
Amvrosiyevka .... **61** 47 43N 38 30 E
Amzeglouf .... **121** 26 50N 0 1 E
An **82** 19 48N 94 0W
An Bien .... **85** 9 45N 105 0 E
An Hoa .... **84** 15 40N 108 5 E
An Khe .... **84** 13 57N 108 39 E
An Nabatīyah at Tahta **70** 33 23N 35 27 E
An Nabk, Si. Arabia .. **72** 31 20N 37 20 E
An Nabk, Syria .... **70** 34 2N 36 44 E
An Nabk Abū Qaşr ... **72** 30 21N 38 34 E
An Nafūd .... **72** 28 15N 41 0 E
An Najaf .... **72** 32 3N 44 15 E
An Naqb, Ra's .... **71** 29 48N 35 44 E
An Nāqūrah .... **69** 33 7N 35 8 E
An Nāşirīyah .... **72** 31 0N 46 15 E
An Naşrānī, J. .... **70** 34 3N 37 20 E
An Nawfalīyah .... **122** 30 54N 17 58 E
An Nhon .... **84** 13 55N 109 7 E
An Nîl □ .... **124** 19 30N 33 0 E
An Nîl el Abyad □ .... **125** 14 0N 32 15 E
An Nîl el Azraq □ .... **125** 12 30N 34 30 E
An Nimāş .... **74** 19 7N 42 8 E
An Nu'ayrīyah .... **73** 27 30N 48 30 E
An Nuşayrīyah, J. .... **70** 35 20N 36 13 E
An Nuwayb'ī, W. → . **71** 29 18N 34 57 E
An Thoi, Dao .... **85** 9 58N 104 0 E
An Uaimh **15** 53 39N 6 40W
Åna-Sira .... **51** 58 17N 6 25 E
Anabar → .... **65** 73 8N 113 36 E
'Anabtā .... **69** 32 19N 35 7 E
Anabuki .... **100** 34 2N 134 11 E
Anaco **169** 9 27N 64 28W
Anaconda **156** 46 7N 113 0W
Anacortes **144** 48 30N 122 40W
Anacuao, Mt. .... **90** 16 16N 121 53 E
Anadarko **153** 35 4N 98 15W
Anadia, Brazil .... **170** 9 42 S 36 18W
Anadia, Portugal **34** 40 26N 8 27W
Anadolu .... **57** 38 0N 30 0 E
Anadyr .... **65** 64 35N 177 20 E
Anadyr → .... **65** 64 55N 176 5 E
Anadyrskiy Zaliv ..... **65** 64 0N 180 0 E
Anáfi .... **49** 36 22N 25 48 E
Anafópoulo .... **49** 36 17N 25 50 E
Anaga, Pta. de **37** 28 34N 16 9W
Anagni .... **44** 41 44N 13 8 E
'Ānah .... **72** 34 25N 42 0 E
Anaheim **159** 33 50N 118 0W
Anahim Lake **144** 52 28N 125 18W
Anáhuac **160** 27 14N 100 9W
Anai Mudi, Mt. .... **81** 10 12N 77 4 E
Anaimalai Hills ...... **81** 10 20N 76 40 E
Anajás .... **170** 0 59 S 49 57W
Anajatuba .... **170** 3 16 S 44 37W
Anakapalle .... **80** 17 42N 83 6 E
Anakie .... **110** 23 32 S 147 45 E
Anaklia .... **61** 42 22N 41 35 E
Analalava .... **135** 14 35 S 48 0 E
Anamã .... **169** 3 35 S 61 22W
Anambar → .... **78** 30 15N 68 50 E
Anambas, Kepulauan .. **88** 3 20N 106 30 E
Anamoose **152** 47 55N 100 20W
Anamosa **154** 42 7N 91 30W
Anamur .... **57** 36 8N 32 58 E
Anamur Burnu .... **70** 36 2N 32 47 E
Anan .... **100** 33 54N 134 40 E
Anand .... **78** 22 32N 72 59 E
Anandpur .... **79** 21 16N 86 13 E
Anánes .... **49** 36 33N 24 9 E
Anantapur .... **81** 14 39N 77 42 E
Anantnag .... **79** 33 45N 75 10 E
Ananyev .... **60** 47 44N 29 47 E
Anao-aon .... **91** 9 47N 125 25 E
Anapa .... **60** 44 55N 37 25 E
Anápolis .... **171** 16 15 S 48 50W
Anapu → .... **169** 1 53 S 50 53W
Anār .... **73** 30 55N 55 13 E
Anār Darreh .... **77** 32 46N 61 39 E
Anārak .... **73** 33 25N 53 40 E
Anatolia = Anadolu ... **57** 38 0N 30 0 E
Anatone **156** 46 9N 117 4W
Anatsogno .... **135** 23 33 S 43 46 E
Añatuya .... **174** 28 20 S 62 50W
Anauá → **169** 0 58N 61 21W
Anaunethad L. **145** 60 55N 104 25W
Anavilhanas,
Arquipélago das .... **169** 2 42 S 60 45W
Anaye .... **123** 19 15N 12 50 E
Anaypazarı .... **70** 36 20N 33 24 E
Anbyŏn .... **95** 39 1N 127 35 E
Ancash □ .... **172** 9 30 S 77 45W
Ancenis **18** 47 21N 1 10W
Ancho, Canal .... **176** 50 0 S 74 20W
Anchor Bay **158** 38 48N 123 34W
Anchorage **140** 61 13N 149 53W
Anci .... **94** 39 20N 116 40 E
Ancohuma, Nevada ... **172** 16 0 S 68 50W
Ancón .... **172** 11 50 S 77 10W
Ancona .... **43** 43 37N 13 30 E
Ancud .... **176** 42 0 S 73 50W
Ancud, G. de .... **176** 42 0 S 73 0W
Anda, China .... **93** 46 24N 125 19 E
Anda, Phil. .... **90** 16 17N 119 57 E
Andacollo, Argentina .. **174** 37 10 S 70 42W
Andacollo, Chile ...... **174** 30 5 S 71 10W
Andado .... **110** 25 25 S 135 15 E
Andahuaylas .... **172** 13 40 S 73 25W
Andalgalá .... **174** 27 40 S 66 30W
Åndalsnes .... **51** 62 35N 7 43 E
Andalucía □ **35** 37 35N 5 0W
Andalusia **149** 31 19N 86 30W
Andalusia □ =
Andalucía □ **35** 37 35N 5 0W
Andaman Is. .... **76** 12 30N 92 30 E
Andaman Sea .... **86** 13 0N 96 0 E
Andara .... **134** 18 2 S 21 9 E
Andaraí .... **171** 12 48 S 41 20W
Andeer .... **29** 46 36N 9 26 E
Andelfingen .... **29** 47 36N 8 41 E
Andelot .... **19** 48 15N 5 18 E
Andelys, Les .... **18** 49 15N 1 25 E
Andenne .... **23** 50 30N 5 5 E
Andéranboukane ...... **127** 15 26N 3 2 E
Anderlecht .... **23** 50 50N 4 19 E
Anderlues .... **23** 50 25N 4 16 E
Andermatt .... **29** 46 38N 8 35 E
Andernach .... **26** 50 24N 7 25 E
Andernos-les-Bains **20** 44 44N 1 6W
Anderslöv .... **52** 55 26N 13 19 E
Anderson, Calif.,
U.S.A. **156** 40 30N 122 19W
Anderson, Ind., U.S.A. **155** 40 5N 85 40W
Anderson, Mo., U.S.A. **153** 36 43N 94 29W
Anderson, S.C., U.S.A. **149** 34 32N 82 40W
Anderson → **140** 69 42N 129 0W
Anderson, Mt. .... **135** 25 5 S 30 42 E
Anderstorp .... **53** 57 19N 13 39 E
Andes **172** 5 40N 75 53W
Andes, Cord. de los ... **172** 20 0 S 68 0W
Andfjorden .... **54** 69 10N 16 20 E
Andhra, L. .... **80** 18 54N 73 32 E
Andhra Pradesh □ .... **81** 16 0N 79 0 E
Andikíthira .... **49** 35 52N 23 15 E
Andīmeshk .... **73** 32 27N 48 21 E
Andímilos .... **49** 36 47N 24 12 E
Andíparos .... **49** 37 0N 25 3 E
Andípaxoi .... **49** 39 9N 20 13 E
Andípsara .... **49** 38 30N 25 29 E
Andírrion .... **49** 38 24N 21 46 E
Andizhan .... **63** 41 10N 72 0 E
Andkhvoy .... **77** 36 52N 65 8 E
Andoany .... **135** 13 25 S 48 16 E
Andoas .... **168** 2 55 S 76 25W
Andol .... **80** 17 51N 78 4 E
Andong .... **95** 36 40N 128 43 E
Andongwei .... **95** 35 6N 119 20 E
Andorra ■ .... **36** 42 30N 1 30 E
Andorra La Vella ..... **36** 42 31N 1 32 E
Andover, U.K. **13** 51 13N 1 29W
Andover, Mass., U.S.A. **151** 42 40N 71 8W
Andover, N.Y., U.S.A. **150** 42 11N 77 48W
Andover, Ohio, U.S.A. **150** 41 35N 80 35W
Andradina .... **171** 20 54 S 51 23W
Andrahary, Mt. .... **135** 13 37 S 49 17 E
Andraitx .... **36** 39 39N 2 25 E
Andramasina .... **135** 19 11 S 47 35 E
Andranopasy .... **135** 21 17 S 43 44 E
Andreanof Is. **140** 52 0N 178 0W
Andreapol .... **58** 56 40N 32 17 E
Andrespol .... **32** 51 45N 19 34 E
Andrewilla .... **111** 26 31 S 139 17 E
Andrews, S.C., U.S.A. **149** 33 29N 79 30W
Andrews, Tex., U.S.A. **153** 32 18N 102 33W
Andreyevka .... **62** 52 19N 51 55 E
Ándria .... **45** 41 13N 16 17 E
Andriba .... **135** 17 30 S 46 58 E
Andrijevica .... **46** 42 45N 19 48 E
Andrítsaina .... **49** 37 29N 21 52 E
Androka .... **135** 24 58 S 44 2 E
Andropov .... **59** 58 5N 38 50 E
Ándros .... **49** 37 50N 24 57 E
Andros I. **162** 24 30N 78 0W
Andros Town **162** 24 43N 77 47W
Andrychów .... **32** 49 51N 19 18 E
Andújar **35** 38 3N 4 5W
Andulo .... **133** 11 25 S 16 45 E
Aneby .... **53** 57 48N 14 49 E
Anegada, B. .... **176** 40 20 S 62 20W
Anegada I. **163** 18 45N 64 20W
Anegada Passage **163** 18 15N 63 45W
Aného .... **127** 6 12N 1 34 E
Añelo .... **176** 38 20 S 68 45W
Anergane **120** 31 4N 7 14W
Aneto, Pico de .... **36** 42 37N 0 40 E
Añez .... **173** 15 40 S 63 10W
Anfu .... **97** 27 21N 114 40 E
Ang Thong .... **84** 14 35N 100 31 E
Angadanan .... **90** 16 45N 121 45 E
Angamos, Punta ...... **174** 23 1 S 70 32W

Aragua □ 168 10 0N 67 10W
Aragua de Barcelona 169 9 28N 64 49W
Araguacema 170 8 50S 49 20W
Araguaçu 171 12 49S 49 51W
Araguaia → 171 5 21S 48 41W
Araguaiana 173 15 43S 51 51W
Araguaína 170 7 12S 48 12W
Araguari 171 18 38S 48 11W
Araguari → 170 1 15N 49 55W
Araguatins 170 5 38S 48 7W
Araioses 170 2 53S 41 55W
Arak, Algeria 121 25 20N 3 45 E
Arāk, Iran 73 34 0N 49 40 E
Arakan □ 82 19 0N 94 15 E
Arakan Yoma 82 20 0N 94 40 E
Arákhova 49 38 28N 22 35 E
Arakkonam 81 13 7N 79 43 E
Araks = Aras, Rūd-e → 72 39 10N 47 10 E
Aral Sea = Aralskoye More 64 44 30N 60 0 E
Aralsk 64 46 50N 61 20 E
Aralskoye More 64 44 30N 60 0 E
Aramac 110 22 58S 145 14 E
Arambag 79 22 53N 87 48 E
Aran Areh 136 9 2N 43 54 E
Aran I. 15 55 0N 8 30W
Aran Is. 15 53 5N 9 42W
Aranda de Duero 36 41 39N 3 42W
Arandān 72 35 23N 46 55 E
Arand-elovac 46 44 18N 20 27 E
Aranga 114 35 44S 173 40 E
Arani 81 12 43N 79 19 E
Aranjuez 34 40 1N 3 40W
Aranos 134 24 9S 19 7 E
Aransas Pass 153 27 55N 97 9W
Aranzazu 168 5 16N 75 30W
Arao 100 32 59N 130 25 E
Araouane 126 18 55N 3 30W
Arapahoe 152 40 22N 99 53W
Arapari 170 5 34S 49 15W
Arapey Grande → 174 30 55S 57 49W
Arapiraca 170 9 45S 36 39W
Arapongas 175 23 29S 51 28W
Ar'ar 72 30 59N 41 2 E
Araracuara 168 0 24S 72 17W
Araranguá 175 29 0S 49 30W
Araraquara 171 21 50S 48 0W
Ararás, Serra das 175 25 0S 53 10W
Ararat 112 37 16S 143 0 E
Ararat, Mt. = Ağri Daği 57 39 50N 44 15 E
Arari 170 3 28S 44 47W
Araria 79 26 9N 87 33 E
Araripe, Chapada do 170 7 20S 40 0W
Araripina 170 7 33S 40 34W
Araruama, L. de 171 22 53S 42 12W
Araruna 170 6 52S 35 44W
Aras, Rūd-e → 72 39 10N 47 10 E
Araticu 170 1 58S 49 51W
Arauca 168 7 0N 70 40W
Arauca □ 168 6 40N 71 0W
Arauca → 168 7 24N 66 35W
Arauco 174 37 16S 73 25W
Arauco □ 174 37 40S 73 25W
Araújos 171 19 56S 45 14W
Arauquita 168 7 2N 71 25W
Araure 168 9 34N 69 13W
Arawa 125 9 57N 41 58 E
Arawata → 115 44 0S 168 40 E
Araxá 171 19 35S 46 55W
Araya, Pen. de 169 10 40N 64 0W
Arayat 90 15 10N 120 46 E
Arba Minch 125 6 0N 37 30 E
Arbat 72 35 25N 45 35 E
Arbatax 44 39 57N 9 42 E
Arbaza 65 52 40N 92 30 E
Arbedo 29 46 12N 9 3 E
Arbīl 72 36 15N 44 5 E
Arboga 52 59 24N 15 52 E
Arbois 19 46 55N 5 46 E
Arboletes 168 8 51N 76 26W
Arbon 29 47 31N 9 26 E
Arbore 125 5 3N 36 50 E
Arborea 44 39 46N 8 34 E
Arborfield 145 53 6N 103 39W
Arborg 145 50 54N 97 13W
Arbrå 52 61 28N 16 22 E
Arbresle, L' 21 45 50N 4 36 E
Arbroath 14 56 34N 2 35W
Arbuckle 158 39 3N 122 2W
Arbus 44 39 30N 8 33 E
Arbuzinka 60 47 0N 31 59 E
Arc 19 47 28N 5 34 E
Arc → 21 45 34N 6 12 E
Arcachon 20 44 40N 1 10W
Arcachon, Bassin d' 20 44 42N 1 10W
Arcade, Calif., U.S.A. 158 34 2N 118 15W
Arcade, U.S.A. 150 42 34N 78 25W
Arcadia, Fla., U.S.A. 149 27 20N 81 50W
Arcadia, Ind., U.S.A. 155 40 10N 86 1W
Arcadia, Iowa, U.S.A. 154 42 5N 95 3W
Arcadia, La., U.S.A. 153 32 34N 92 53W
Arcadia, Nebr., U.S.A. 152 41 29N 99 4W
Arcadia, Pa., U.S.A. 150 40 46N 78 54W
Arcadia, Wis., U.S.A. 152 44 13N 91 29W
Arcanum 155 39 59N 84 33W
Arcata 156 40 55N 124 4W
Arcévia 43 43 29N 12 58 E
Archangel = Arkhangelsk 56 64 40N 41 0 E
Archar 46 43 50N 22 54 E
Archbald 151 41 30N 75 31W
Archbold 155 41 31N 84 18W
Archena 37 38 9N 1 16W
Archer → 110 13 28S 141 41 E
Archer B. 110 13 20S 141 30 E
Archers Post 130 0 35N 37 35 E
Archidona 35 37 6N 4 22W
Arci, Monte 44 39 47N 8 44 E
Arcidosso 43 42 51N 11 30 E
Arcila = Asilah 120 35 29N 6 0W
Arcis-sur-Aube 19 48 32N 4 10 E
Arckaringa 111 27 56S 134 45 E
Arckaringa Cr. → 111 28 10S 135 22 E
Arco, Italy 42 45 55N 10 54 E
Arco, U.S.A. 156 43 45N 113 16W
Arcola, Canada 145 49 40N 102 30W
Arcola, U.S.A. 155 39 41N 88 19W
Arcoona 112 31 2S 137 1 E
Arcos 36 41 12N 2 16W
Arcos de los Frontera 35 36 45N 5 49W
Arcos de Valdevez 34 41 55N 8 22W
Arcot 81 12 53N 79 20 E
Arcoverde 170 8 25S 37 4W
Arcs, Les 21 43 27N 6 29 E
Arctic Bay 141 73 1N 85 7W
Arctic Ocean 6 78 0N 160 0W
Arctic Red River 140 67 15N 134 0W
Arda →, Bulgaria 47 41 40N 26 29 E
Arda →, Italy 42 44 53N 9 52 E
Ardabīl 73 38 15N 48 18 E
Ardakān = Sepīdān 73 30 20N 52 5 E
Årdal, Aust-Agder, Norway 51 58 42N 7 48 E
Årdal, Rogaland, Norway 51 59 9N 6 13 E
Ardales 35 36 53N 4 51W
Årdalstangen 51 61 14N 7 43 E
Ardatov 59 54 51N 46 15 E
Ardea 48 40 58N 22 3 E
Ardèche □ 21 44 42N 4 16 E
Ardèche → 21 44 16N 4 39 E
Ardee 15 53 51N 6 32W
Arden, Canada 150 44 43N 76 56W
Arden, Calif., U.S.A. 158 38 36N 121 33W
Arden, U.S.A. 159 36 1N 115 14W
Arden Stby. 53 56 46N 9 52 E
Ardenne 23 50 0N 5 10 E
Ardennes □ 19 49 35N 4 40 E
Ardentes 19 46 45N 1 50 E
Ardestān 73 33 20N 52 25 E
Ardgour 14 56 45N 5 25W
Árdhas → 48 41 36N 26 25 E
Ardila → 35 38 12N 7 28W
Ardino 47 41 34N 25 9 E
Ardlethan 113 34 22S 146 53 E
Ardmore, Australia 110 21 39S 139 11 E
Ardmore, Okla., U.S.A. 153 34 10N 97 5W
Ardmore, Pa., U.S.A. 151 39 58N 75 18W
Ardmore, S. Dak., U.S.A. 152 43 0N 103 40W
Ardnacrusha 15 52 43N 8 38W
Ardnamurchan, Pt. of 14 56 44N 6 14W
Ardooie 23 50 59N 3 13 E
Ardore Marina 45 38 11N 16 10 E
Ardres 19 50 50N 2 0 E
Ardrossan, Australia 112 34 26S 137 53 E
Ardrossan, U.K. 14 55 39N 4 50W
Ards □ 15 54 35N 5 30W
Ards Pen. 15 54 30N 5 25W
Ardud 50 47 37N 22 52 E
Ardunac 61 41 8N 42 5 E
Åre 52 63 22N 13 15 E
Arecibo 163 18 29N 66 42W
Areia Branca 170 5 0S 37 0W
Aremark 51 59 15N 11 42 E
Arena, Pt. 158 38 57N 123 44W
Arenales, Cerro 176 47 5S 73 40W
Arenápolis 173 14 26S 56 49W
Arenas 34 43 17N 4 50W
Arenas de San Pedro 34 40 12N 5 5W
Arendal 51 58 28N 8 46 E
Arendonk 23 51 19N 5 5 E
Arendsee 26 52 52N 11 27 E
Arenillas 168 3 33S 80 10W
Arenys de Mar 36 41 35N 2 33 E
Arenzano 42 44 24N 8 40 E
Arenzville 154 39 53N 90 22W
Areópolis 49 36 40N 22 22 E
Arequipa 172 16 20S 71 30W
Arequipa □ 172 16 0S 72 50W
Arere 169 0 16S 53 52W
Arero 125 4 41N 38 50 E
Arès 20 44 47N 1 8W
Arévalo 34 41 3N 4 43W
Arezzo 43 43 28N 11 50 E
Arga → 36 42 18N 1 47W
Argalastí 48 39 13N 23 13 E
Argamakmur 88 3 35S 102 0 E
Argamasilla de Alba 37 39 8N 3 5W
Arganda 36 40 19N 3 26W
Arganil 34 40 13N 8 3W
Argayash 62 55 29N 60 52 E
Argelès-Gazost 20 43 0N 0 6W
Argelès-sur-Mer 20 42 34N 3 1 E
Argens → 21 43 24N 6 44 E
Argent-sur-Sauldre 19 47 33N 2 25 E
Argenta, Italy 43 44 37N 11 50 E
Argenta, U.S.A. 155 39 59N 88 49W
Argentan 18 48 45N 0 1W
Argentário, Mte. 43 42 23N 11 11 E
Argentat 20 45 6N 1 56 E
Argentera 42 44 23N 6 58 E
Argentera, Monte del 42 44 12N 7 5 E
Argenteuil 19 48 57N 2 14 E
Argentia 143 47 18N 53 58W
Argentiera, C. dell' 44 40 44N 8 8 E
Argentière, Aiguilles d' 28 45 58N 7 2 E
Argentière-la-Bessée, L' 21 44 47N 6 33 E
Argentina ■ 176 35 0S 66 0W
Argentina Is. 7 66 0S 64 0W
Argentino, L. 176 50 10S 73 0W
Argenton-Château 18 46 59N 0 27W
Argenton-sur-Creuse 20 46 36N 1 30 E
Argeş □ 50 45 0N 24 45 E
Argeş → 50 44 12N 26 14 E
Arghandab → 77 31 30N 64 15 E
Argo 124 19 28N 30 30 E
Argolikós Kólpos 49 37 20N 22 52 E
Argolís □ 49 37 38N 22 50 E
Argonne 19 49 10N 5 0 E
Árgos, Greece 49 37 40N 22 43 E
Argos, U.S.A. 155 41 14N 86 15W
Árgos Orestikón 48 40 27N 21 26 E
Argostólion 49 38 12N 20 33 E
Arguedas 36 42 11N 1 36W
Arguello, Pt. 159 34 34N 120 40W
Arguineguín 37 27 46N 15 41W
Argun → 65 53 20N 121 28 E
Argungu 127 12 40N 4 31 E
Argus Pk. 159 35 52N 117 26W
Argyle 152 48 23N 96 49W
Argyle, L. 108 16 20S 128 40 E
Argyrádhes 48 39 27N 19 58 E
Århus 53 56 8N 10 11 E
Århus Amtskommune □ 53 56 15N 10 15 E
Aria 114 38 33S 175 0 E
Ariadnoye 98 45 8N 134 25 E
Ariamsvlei 134 28 9S 19 51 E
Ariana 121 36 52N 10 12 E
Ariano Irpino 45 41 10N 15 4 E
Ariano nel Polèsine 43 44 56N 12 5 E
Ariari → 168 2 35N 72 47W
Aribinda 127 14 17N 0 52W
Arica, Chile 172 18 32S 70 20W
Arica, Colombia 168 2 0S 71 50W
Arico 37 28 9N 16 29W
Arid, C. 109 34 1S 123 10 E
Arida 101 34 5N 135 8 E
Ariège □ 20 42 56N 1 30 E
Ariège → 20 43 30N 1 25 E
Arieş → 50 46 24N 23 20 E
Arīḩā 70 35 49N 36 35 E
Arilje 46 43 44N 20 7 E
Arima 163 10 38N 61 17W
Aringay 90 16 26N 120 21 E
Arinos → 173 10 25S 58 20W
Ario de Rosales 160 19 12N 102 0W
Aripuanã 173 9 25S 60 30W
Aripuanã → 173 5 7S 60 25W
Ariquemes 173 9 55S 63 6W
Arisaig 14 56 55N 5 50W
Arîsh, W. el → 124 31 9N 33 49 E
Arismendi 168 8 29N 68 22W
Arissa 125 11 10N 41 35 E
Aristazabal I. 144 52 40N 129 10W
Arita 100 33 11N 129 54 E
Aritao 90 16 18N 121 2 E
Arivaca 157 31 37N 111 25W
Arivonimamo 135 19 1S 47 11 E
Ariyalur 81 11 8N 79 8 E
Ariza 100 41 19N 2 3W
Arizaro, Salar de 174 24 40S 67 50W
Arizona 174 35 45S 65 25W
Arizona □ 157 34 20N 111 30W
Arizpe 160 30 20N 110 11W
Årjäng 52 59 24N 12 8 E
Arjeplog 54 66 3N 18 2 E
Arjona, Colombia 168 10 14N 75 22W
Arjona, Spain 35 37 56N 4 4W
Arjuno 89 7 49S 112 34 E
Arka 65 60 15N 142 0 E
Arkadak 59 51 58N 43 19 E
Arkadelphia 153 34 5N 93 0W
Arkadhía □ 49 37 30N 22 20 E
Arkaig, L. 14 56 58N 5 10W
Arkalyk 64 50 13N 66 50 E
Arkansas □ 153 35 0N 92 30W
Arkansas → 153 33 48N 91 4W
Arkansas City 153 37 4N 97 3W
Árkathos → 48 39 20N 21 4 E
Arkhángelos 49 36 13N 28 7 E
Arkhangelsk 56 64 40N 41 0 E
Arkhangelskoye 59 51 32N 40 58 E
Arkiko 125 15 33N 39 30 E
Arklow 15 52 48N 6 10W
Árkoi 49 37 24N 26 44 E
Arkona, Kap 26 54 41N 13 26 E
Arkösund 53 58 29N 16 56 E
Arkoúdhi 49 38 33N 20 43 E
Arkticheskiy, Mys 65 81 10N 95 0 E
Arkul 59 57 17N 50 3 E
Arlanc 20 45 25N 3 42 E
Arlanza → 34 42 6N 4 9W
Arlanzón → 34 42 3N 4 17W
Arlberg Pass 27 47 9N 10 12 E
Arlee 156 47 10N 114 4W
Arles 21 43 41N 4 40 E
Arlesheim 28 47 30N 7 37 E
Arlington, S. Africa 135 28 1S 27 53 E
Arlington, Oreg., U.S.A. 156 45 48N 120 6W
Arlington, S. Dak., U.S.A. 152 44 25N 97 4W
Arlington, Va., U.S.A. 148 38 52N 77 5W
Arlington, Wash., U.S.A. 144 48 11N 122 4W
Arlington Heights 155 42 5N 87 59W
Arlon 23 49 42N 5 49 E
Arlöv 52 55 38N 13 5 E
Arly 127 11 35N 1 28 E
Armagh 15 54 22N 6 40W
Armagh □ 15 54 18N 6 37W
Armagnac 20 43 50N 0 10 E
Armançon → 19 47 59N 3 30 E
Armavir 61 45 2N 41 7 E
Armenia 168 4 35N 75 45W
Armenian S.S.R. □ 61 40 0N 44 0 E
Armeniş 50 45 13N 22 17 E
Armentières 19 50 40N 2 50 E
Armidale 111 30 30S 151 40 E
Armour 152 43 20N 98 25W
Armstrong, B.C., Canada 144 50 25N 119 10W
Armstrong, Ont., Canada 142 50 18N 89 4W
Armstrong, U.S.A. 153 26 59N 97 48W
Armstrong Cr. → 108 16 35S 131 40 E
Armur 80 18 48N 78 16 E
Arnaía 48 40 30N 23 40 E
Arnaouti, C. 70 35 6N 32 17 E
Arnarfjörður 54 65 48N 23 40W
Arnaud → 141 60 0N 70 0W
Arnay-le-Duc 19 47 10N 4 27 E
Arnedillo 36 42 13N 2 14W
Arnedo 36 42 12N 2 5W
Arnemuiden 23 51 30N 3 40 E
Årnes, Iceland 54 66 1N 21 31W
Årnes, Norway 51 60 7N 11 28 E
Arnett 153 36 9N 99 44W
Arnhem 22 51 58N 5 55 E
Arnhem, C. 110 12 20S 137 30 E
Arnhem B. 110 12 20S 136 10 E
Arnhem Land 110 13 10S 134 30 E
Árnissa 48 40 47N 21 49 E
Arno → 42 43 41N 10 17 E
Arno Bay 112 33 54S 136 34 E
Arnold, Calif., U.S.A. 158 38 15N 120 20W
Arnold, Nebr., U.S.A. 152 41 29N 100 10W
Arnoldstein 30 46 33N 13 43 E
Arnon → 19 47 13N 2 1 E
Arnot 145 55 56N 96 41W
Arnøy 54 70 9N 20 40 E
Arnprior 142 45 26N 76 21W
Arnsberg 26 51 25N 8 2 E
Arnstadt 26 50 50N 10 56 E
Aro → 169 8 1N 64 11W
Aroab 134 26 41S 19 39 E
Aroánia Óri 49 37 56N 22 12 E
Aroche 35 37 56N 6 57W
Aroeiras 170 7 31S 35 41W
Arolla 28 46 2N 7 29 E
Arolsen 26 51 23N 9 1 E
Aron → 20 46 50N 3 28 E
Arona 42 45 45N 8 32 E
Aroroy 90 12 31N 123 24 E
Arosa 29 46 47N 9 41 E
Arosa, Ria de → 34 42 28N 8 57W
Arpajon 19 48 36N 2 15 E
Arpajon-sur-Cère 20 44 53N 2 28 E
Arpino 44 41 40N 13 35 E
Arque 172 17 48S 66 23W
Arrabury 111 26 45S 141 0 E
Arraias 171 12 56S 46 57W
Arraias →, Mato Grosso, Brazil 173 11 10S 53 35W
Arraias →, Pará, Brazil 170 7 30S 49 20W
Arraiolos 35 38 44N 7 59W
Arran 14 55 34N 5 12W
Arrandale 144 54 57N 130 0W
Arras 19 50 17N 2 46 E
Arrats → 20 44 6N 0 52 E
Arreau 20 42 54N 0 22 E
Arrecife 37 28 57N 13 37W
Arrecifes 174 34 6S 60 9W
Arrée, Mts. d' 18 48 26N 3 55W
Arriaga, Chiapas, Mexico 161 16 15N 93 52W
Arriaga, San Luis Potosí, Mexico 160 21 55N 101 23W
Arrilalah P.O. 110 23 43S 143 54 E
Arrino 109 29 30S 115 40 E
Arrojado → 171 13 24S 44 20W
Arromanches-les-Bains 18 49 20N 0 38W
Arronches 35 39 8N 7 16W
Arros → 20 43 40N 0 2W
Arrou 18 48 6N 1 8 E
Arrow, L. 15 54 3N 8 20W
Arrow Rock Res. 156 43 45N 115 50W
Arrowhead 144 50 40N 117 55W
Arrowhead, L. 159 34 16N 117 10W
Arrowsmith, Mt. 115 43 20S 170 55 E
Arrowtown 115 44 57S 168 50 E
Arroyo de la Luz 35 39 30N 6 38W
Arroyo Grande 159 35 9N 120 32W
Års, Denmark 53 56 48N 9 30 E

Ars, Iran 72 37 9N 47 46 E
Ars-en-Ré 20 46 12N 1 31W
Ars-sur-Moselle 19 49 5N 6 4 E
Arsenault L. 145 55 6N 108 32W
Arsenev 98 44 10N 133 15 E
Arsi □ 125 7 45N 39 0 E
Arsiero 43 45 49N 11 22 E
Arsikere 81 13 15N 76 15 E
Arsk 59 56 10N 49 50 E
Arslanköy 70 37 0N 34 17 E
Arsuz 70 36 24N 35 51 E
Árta, Greece 49 39 8N 21 2 E
Artá, Spain 36 39 41N 3 21 E
Árta □ 48 39 15N 21 5 E
Arteaga 160 18 50N 102 20W
Arteche 90 12 30N 125 35 E
Arteijo 34 43 19N 8 29W
Artem 98 43 22N 132 13 E
Artem, Ostrov 61 40 28N 50 20 E
Artemovsk, R.S.F.S.R., U.S.S.R. 65 54 45N 93 35 E
Artemovsk, Ukraine S.S.R., U.S.S.R. 60 48 35N 38 0 E
Artemovski 61 47 45N 40 16 E
Artemovskiy 62 57 21N 61 54 E
Artenay 19 48 5N 1 50 E
Artern 26 51 22N 11 18 E
Artesa de Segre 36 41 54N 1 3 E
Artesia = Mosomane 134 24 2 S 26 19 E
Artesia 153 32 55N 104 25W
Artesia Wells 153 28 17N 99 18W
Artesian 152 44 2N 97 54W
Arth 29 47 4N 8 31 E
Arthez-de-Béarn 20 43 29N 0 38W
Arthington 126 6 35N 10 45W
Arthur 155 39 43N 88 28W
Arthur → 110 41 2 S 144 40 E
Arthur Cr. → 110 22 30 S 136 25 E
Arthur Pt. 110 22 7 S 150 3 E
Arthur's Pass 115 42 54 S 171 35 E
Arthur's Town 163 24 38N 75 42W
Artigas 174 30 20 S 56 30W
Artik 61 40 38N 43 58 E
Artillery L. 145 63 9N 107 52W
Artois 19 50 20N 2 30 E
Artotína 49 38 42N 22 2 E
Artsiz 60 46 4N 29 26 E
Artvin 61 41 14N 41 44 E
Aru, Kepulauan 87 6 0 S 134 30 E
Aru Meru □ 130 3 20 S 36 50 E
Arua 130 3 1N 30 58 E
Aruanã 171 14 54 S 51 10W
Aruba 163 12 30N 70 0W
Arucas 37 28 7N 15 32W
Arudy 20 43 7N 0 28W
Arumã 169 4 44 S 62 8W
Arumpo 112 33 48 S 142 55 E
Arun → 79 26 55N 87 10 E
Arunachal Pradesh □ 82 28 0N 95 0 E
Aruppukkottai 81 9 31N 78 8 E
Arusha 130 3 20 S 36 40 E
Arusha □ 130 4 0 S 36 30 E
Arusha Chini 130 3 32 S 37 20 E
Arut → 89 2 42 S 111 34 E
Aruvi → 81 8 48N 79 53 E
Aruwimi → 130 1 13N 23 36 E
Arvada 156 44 43N 106 6W
Arvakalu 81 8 20N 79 58 E
Arve → 21 46 11N 6 8 E
Arvi 78 20 59N 78 16 E
Arvida 143 48 25N 71 14W
Arvidsjaur 54 65 35N 19 10 E
Arvika 52 59 40N 12 36 E
Arvin 159 35 12N 118 50W
Arxan 93 47 11N 119 57 E
Arys 63 42 26N 68 48 E
Arys → 63 42 45N 68 15 E
Arzachena 44 41 5N 9 27 E
Arzamas 59 55 27N 43 55 E
Arzew 121 35 50N 0 23W
Arzgir 61 45 18N 44 23 E
Arzignano 43 45 30N 11 20 E
As, Belgium 23 51 1N 5 35 E
Aš, Czech. 30 50 13N 12 12 E
Aş Şadr 75 24 40N 54 41 E
Aş Şafā 70 33 10N 37 0 E
'As Saffānīyah 73 28 5N 48 50 E
Aş Şāfī 69 31 2N 35 28 E
As Safīrah 70 36 5N 37 21 E
Aş Şahm 75 24 10N 56 53 E
As Sājir 72 25 11N 44 36 E
As Salamīyah, Si. Arabia 74 24 12N 47 18 E
As Salamīyah, Syria 70 35 1N 37 2 E
As Salt 69 32 2N 35 43 E
As Sal'w'a 75 24 23N 50 50 E
As Samāwah 72 31 15N 45 15 E
As Samū' 69 31 24N 35 4 E
As Sanamayn 69 33 3N 36 10 E
Aş Saqlabīya 70 35 23N 36 23 E
Aş Sawādah 74 22 24N 44 28 E
As Sayl al Kabīr 74 21 38N 40 25 E
As Sukhnah 72 34 52N 38 52 E
As Sulaymānīyah 74 24 9N 47 18 E
As Sulaymī 72 26 17N 41 21 E
As Sulayyil 74 20 27N 45 34 E
As Sulţan 122 31 4N 17 8 E
As Sumaymānīyah 72 35 35N 45 29 E
As Summān 72 25 0N 47 0 E
As Sūq 74 21 54N 42 3 E
Aş Şurrah 74 13 57N 46 14 E
As Suwaydā' 70 32 40N 36 30 E
As Suwaydā' □ 70 32 45N 36 45 E
As Suwayh 75 22 10N 59 33 E
As Suwayq 75 23 51N 57 26 E
As Şuwayrah 72 32 55N 45 0 E
Asab 134 25 30 S 18 0 E
Asaba 127 6 12N 6 38 E
Asafo 126 6 20N 2 40W
Asahi 101 35 43N 140 39 E
Asahi-Gawa → 100 34 36N 133 58 E
Asahigawa 98 43 46N 142 22 E
Asale, L. 125 14 0N 40 20 E
Asama-Yama 101 36 24N 138 31 E
Asamankese 127 5 50N 0 40W
Asansol 79 23 40N 87 1 E
Åsarna 52 62 39N 14 22 E
Asbe Teferi 125 9 4N 40 49 E
Asbesberge 134 29 0 S 23 0 E
Asbest 62 57 0N 61 30 E
Asbestos 143 45 47N 71 58W
Asbury Park 151 40 15N 74 1W
Ascensión 160 31 6N 107 59W
Ascensión, B. de la 161 19 50N 87 20W
Ascension I. 9 8 0 S 14 15W
Aschach 30 48 22N 14 2 E
Aschaffenburg 27 49 58N 9 8 E
Aschendorf 26 53 2N 7 22 E
Aschersleben 26 51 45N 11 28 E
Asciano 43 43 14N 11 32 E
Áscoli Piceno 43 42 51N 13 34 E
Áscoli Satriano 45 41 11N 15 32 E
Ascona 29 46 9N 8 46 E
Ascope 172 7 46 S 79 8W
Ascotán 174 21 45 S 68 17W
Asuncion 91 7 35N 125 45 E
Aseb 125 13 0N 42 40 E
Åseda 53 57 10N 15 20 E
Asedjrad 121 24 51N 1 29 E
Asela 125 8 0N 39 0 E
Asenovgrad 47 42 1N 24 51 E
Aseral 51 58 37N 7 25 E
Asfeld 19 49 27N 4 5 E
Asfûn el Matâ'na 124 25 26N 32 30 E
Åsgårdstrand 51 59 22N 10 27 E
Ash Fork 157 35 14N 112 32W
Ash Grove 153 37 21N 93 36W
Ash Shamāl □ 70 34 25N 36 0 E
Ash Shāmīyah 72 31 55N 44 35 E
Ash Sha'rā' 74 24 16N 44 11 E
Ash Shāriqah 75 25 23N 55 26 E
Ash Sharmah 71 28 1N 35 16 E
Ash Sharqāt 72 35 27N 43 16 E
Ash Shaţrah 72 31 30N 46 10 E
Ash Shawbak 72 30 32N 35 34 E
Ash Shawmari, J. 71 30 35N 36 35 E
Ash Shaykh, J. 70 33 25N 35 50 E
Ash Shifā' 71 28 30N 35 30 E
Ash Shiḩr 75 14 45N 49 36 E
Ash Shināfīyah 72 31 35N 44 39 E
Ash Shu'aybah 72 27 53N 44 43 E
Ash Shumlūl 72 26 31N 47 20 E
Ash Shūnah ash Shamālīyah 69 32 37N 35 34 E
Ash Shuqayq 74 17 44N 42 1 E
Ash Shūr'a 72 35 58N 43 13 E
Ash Shurayf 72 25 43N 39 14 E
Ash Shuwayfāt 70 33 45N 35 30 E
Asha 62 55 0N 57 16 E
Ashanti □ 127 7 30N 1 30W
Ashau 84 16 6N 107 22 E
Ashburn 149 31 42N 83 40W
Ashburton 115 43 53 S 171 48 E
Ashburton → 108 21 40 S 114 56 E
Ashburton, North Branch → 115 43 54 S 171 44 E
Ashburton, South Branch → 115 43 54 S 171 44 E
Ashburton Downs 108 23 25 S 117 4 E
Ashby-de-la-Zouch 12 52 45N 1 29W
Ashcroft 144 50 40N 121 20W
Ashdod 69 31 49N 34 35 E
Ashdot Yaaqov 69 32 39N 35 35 E
Asheboro 149 35 43N 79 46W
Asherton 153 28 25N 99 43W
Asheville 149 35 39N 82 30W
Asheweig → 142 54 17N 87 12W
Ashford, Australia 111 29 15 S 151 3 E
Ashford, U.K. 13 51 8N 0 53 E
Ashford, U.S.A. 156 46 45N 122 2W
Ashibetsu 98 43 31N 142 11 E
Ashikaga 101 36 28N 139 29 E
Ashio 101 36 38N 139 27 E
Ashizuri-Zaki 100 32 44N 133 0 E
Ashkarkot 78 33 3N 67 58 E
Ashkhabad 64 38 0N 57 50 E
Ashland, Ill., U.S.A. 154 39 53N 90 0W
Ashland, Kans., U.S.A. 153 37 13N 99 43W
Ashland, Ky., U.S.A. 148 38 25N 82 40W
Ashland, Maine, U.S.A. 143 46 34N 68 26W
Ashland, Mont., U.S.A. 156 45 41N 106 12W
Ashland, Nebr., U.S.A. 152 41 5N 96 27W
Ashland, Ohio, U.S.A. 150 40 52N 82 20W
Ashland, Oreg., U.S.A. 156 42 10N 122 38W
Ashland, Pa., U.S.A. 151 40 45N 76 22W
Ashland, Va., U.S.A. 148 37 46N 77 30W
Ashland, Wis., U.S.A. 152 46 40N 90 52W
Ashley, Ill., U.S.A. 154 38 20N 89 11W
Ashley, Ind., U.S.A. 155 41 32N 85 4W
Ashley, N. Dak., U.S.A. 152 46 3N 99 23W
Ashley, Pa., U.S.A. 151 41 12N 75 55W
Ashmont 144 54 7N 111 35W
Ashmore Reef 108 12 14 S 123 5 E
Ashmûn 124 30 18N 30 55 E
Ashq'elon 69 31 42N 34 35 E
Ashtabula 150 41 52N 80 50W
Ashti 80 18 50N 75 15 E
Ashton, S. Africa 134 33 50 S 20 5 E
Ashton, U.S.A. 156 44 6N 111 30W
Ashton-under-Lyne 12 53 30N 2 8W
Ashuanipi, L. 143 52 45N 66 15W
Ashurst 114 40 16 S 175 45 E
'Āşī →, Syria 70 36 0N 36 22 E
Asi →, Turkey 70 36 2N 35 57 E
Asia 66 45 0N 75 0 E
Asia, Kepulauan 87 1 0N 131 13 E
Āsīā Bak 73 35 19N 50 30 E
Asiago 43 45 52N 11 30 E
Asidonhoppo 169 3 50N 55 30W
Asifabad 80 19 20N 79 24 E
Asike 87 6 39 S 140 24 E
Asilah 120 35 29N 6 0W
Asinara 44 41 5N 8 15 E
Asinara, G. dell' 44 41 0N 8 30 E
Asino 64 57 0N 86 0 E
'Asīr □ 74 18 40N 42 30 E
Asir, Ras 136 11 55N 51 10 E
Aska 80 19 2N 84 42 E
Asker 51 59 50N 10 26 E
Askersund 53 58 53N 14 55 E
Askham 134 26 59 S 20 47 E
Askim 51 59 35N 11 10 E
Askino 62 56 5N 56 34 E
Askja 54 65 3N 16 48W
Asl 124 29 33N 32 44 E
Asmār 77 35 10N 71 27 E
Asmara = Asmera 125 15 19N 38 55 E
Asmera 125 15 19N 38 55 E
Asnæs 52 55 40N 11 0 E
Asni 120 31 17N 7 58W
Aso 100 33 0N 131 5 E
Aso-Zan 100 32 53N 131 6 E
Asola 42 45 12N 10 25 E
Asoteriba, Jebel 124 21 51N 36 30 E
Asotin 156 46 20N 117 3W
Aspe 37 38 20N 0 40W
Aspen 157 39 12N 106 56W
Aspermont 153 33 11N 100 15W
Aspiring, Mt. 115 44 23 S 168 46 E
Aspres-sur-Buëch 21 44 32N 5 44 E
Aspromonte 45 38 10N 16 0 E
Aspur 78 23 58N 74 7 E
Asquith 145 52 8N 107 13W
Assa 120 28 35N 9 6W
Assâba 126 16 10N 11 45W
Assam □ 82 26 0N 93 0 E
Assamakka 127 19 21N 5 38 E
Asse 23 50 24N 4 10 E
Assebroek 23 51 11N 3 17 E
Assekrem 121 23 16N 5 49 E
Assémini 44 39 18N 9 0 E
Assen 22 53 0N 6 35 E
Assendelft 22 52 29N 4 45 E
Assenede 23 51 14N 3 46 E
Assens, Fyn, Denmark 53 56 41N 10 3 E
Assens, Fyn, Denmark 53 55 16N 9 55 E
Assesse 23 50 22N 5 2 E
Assini 126 5 9N 3 17W
Assiniboia 145 49 40N 105 59W
Assiniboine → 145 49 53N 97 8W
Assis 175 22 40 S 50 20W
Assisi 43 43 4N 12 36 E
Ássos 49 38 22N 20 33 E
Assumption 154 39 31N 89 3W
Assus 48 39 32N 26 22 E
Assynt, L. 14 58 25N 5 15W
Astaffort 20 44 4N 0 40 E
Astakidha 49 35 53N 26 50 E
Astara 57 38 30N 48 50 E
Asten 23 51 24N 5 45 E
Asti 42 44 54N 8 11 E
Astipálaia 49 36 32N 26 22 E
Astorga, Mindanao, Phil. 91 6 54N 125 27 E
Astorga, Panay, Phil. 91 11 15N 122 48 E
Astorga, Spain 34 42 29N 6 8W
Astoria, Ill., U.S.A. 154 40 14N 90 21W
Astoria, Oreg., U.S.A. 158 46 16N 123 50W
Åstorp 52 56 6N 12 55 E
Astrakhan 61 46 25N 48 5 E
Astrakhan-Bazàr 57 39 14N 48 30 E
Astudillo 34 42 12N 4 22W
Asturias 34 43 15N 6 0W
Asunción 174 25 10 S 57 30W
Asunción, La 169 11 2N 63 53W
Asunción Nochixtlán 161 17 28N 97 14W
Asutri 125 15 25N 35 45 E
Aswa → 130 3 43N 31 55 E
Aswad, Ras al 74 21 20N 39 0 E
Aswân 124 24 4N 32 57 E
Aswân High Dam = Sadd el Aali 124 23 54N 32 54 E
Asyût 124 27 11N 31 4 E
Asyûti, Wadi → 124 27 11N 31 16 E
Aszód 31 47 39N 19 28 E
At Ţafīlah 71 30 45N 35 30 E
At Tā'if 74 21 5N 40 27 E
At Tāj 122 24 13N 23 18 E
At Tamīmī 122 32 20N 23 4 E
Aţ Ţirāq 72 27 19N 44 33 E
Aţ Tubayq 71 29 30N 37 0 E
Aţ Ţur 69 31 47N 35 14 E
At Turbah, S. Yemen 74 12 40N 43 30 E
At Turbah, Yemen 74 13 13N 44 7 E
Aţ Ţurrah 69 32 39N 35 59 E
Aţ Ţuwayrifah 75 21 30N 49 35 E
Atacama □ 174 27 30 S 70 0W
Atacama, Desierto de 174 24 0 S 69 20W
Atacama, Salar de 174 23 30 S 68 20W
Ataco 168 3 35N 75 23W
Atakor 121 23 27N 5 31 E
Atakpamé 127 7 31N 1 13 E
Atalándi 49 38 39N 22 58 E
Atalaya 172 10 45 S 73 50W
Atalaya de Femes 37 28 56N 13 47W
Ataléia 171 18 3 S 41 6W
Atami 101 35 5N 139 4 E
Atankawng 82 25 50N 97 47 E
Atapupu 87 9 0 S 124 51 E
Atâr 120 20 30N 13 5W
Atara 65 63 10N 129 10 E
Ataram, Erg n- 121 23 57N 2 0 E
Atarfe 35 37 13N 3 40W
Atascadero, Calif., U.S.A. 158 35 29N 120 40W
Atascadero, U.S.A. 157 35 32N 120 44W
Atasu 64 48 30N 71 0 E
Atauro 87 8 10 S 125 30 E
Atbara 124 17 42N 33 59 E
'Atbara → 124 17 40N 33 56 E
Atbasar 64 51 48N 68 20 E
Atbashi 63 41 10N 75 48 E
Atbashi, Khrebet 63 40 50N 75 30 E
Atchafalaya B. 153 29 30N 91 20W
Atchison 152 39 40N 95 10W
Atebubu 127 7 47N 1 0W
Ateca 36 41 20N 1 49W
Aterno → 43 42 11N 13 51 E
Atesine, Alpi 42 46 55N 11 30 E
Atessa 43 42 5N 14 27 E
Ath 23 50 38N 3 47 E
Athabasca 144 54 45N 113 20W
Athabasca → 145 58 40N 110 50W
Athabasca, L. 145 59 15N 109 15W
Athboy 15 53 37N 6 55W
Athenry 15 53 18N 8 45W
Athens = Athínai 49 37 58N 23 46 E
Athens, Ala., U.S.A. 149 34 49N 86 58W
Athens, Ga., U.S.A. 149 33 56N 83 24W
Athens, N.Y., U.S.A. 151 42 15N 73 48W
Athens, Ohio, U.S.A. 148 39 25N 82 6W
Athens, Pa., U.S.A. 151 41 57N 76 36W
Athens, Tenn., U.S.A. 149 35 45N 84 38W
Athens, Tex., U.S.A. 153 32 11N 95 48W
Atherley 150 44 37N 79 20W
Atherton 110 17 17 S 145 30 E
Athiéme 127 6 37N 1 40 E
Athienou 70 35 3N 33 32 E
Athínai 49 37 58N 23 46 E
Athlone 15 53 26N 7 57W
Athni 80 16 44N 75 6 E
Athol 115 45 30 S 168 35 E
Atholl, Forest of 14 56 51N 3 50W
Atholville 143 47 59N 66 43W
Áthos 48 40 9N 24 22 E
Athus 23 49 34N 5 50 E
Athy 15 53 0N 7 0W
Ati, Chad 123 13 13N 18 20 E
Ati, Sudan 125 13 5N 29 2 E
Atiak 130 3 12N 32 2 E
Atiamuri 114 38 24 S 176 5 E
Atico 172 16 14 S 73 40W
Atienza 36 41 12N 2 52W
Atikokan 142 48 45N 91 37W
Atikonak L. 143 52 40N 64 32W
Atimonan 90 14 0N 121 55 E
'Ātinah, W. → 75 18 23N 53 28 E
Atirampattinam 81 10 28N 79 20 E
Atka 65 60 50N 151 48 E
Atkarsk 59 51 55N 45 2 E
Atkinson, Ill., U.S.A. 154 41 25N 90 1W
Atkinson, Nebr., U.S.A. 152 42 35N 98 59W
Atlanta, Ga., U.S.A. 149 33 50N 84 24W
Atlanta, Ill., U.S.A. 154 40 16N 89 14W
Atlanta, Mo., U.S.A. 154 39 54N 92 29W
Atlanta, Tex., U.S.A. 153 33 7N 94 8W
Atlantic 152 41 25N 95 0W
Atlantic City 148 39 25N 74 25W
Atlantic Ocean 8 0 0 20 0W
Atlántico □ 168 10 45N 75 0W
Atlas Mts. = Haut Atlas 120 32 30N 5 0W
Atlin 140 59 31N 133 41W
Atlin, L. 144 59 26N 133 45W
'Atlit 69 32 42N 34 56 E
Atløy 51 61 21N 4 58 E
Atmakur 81 14 37N 79 40 E
Atmore 149 31 2N 87 30W
Atna → 51 61 44N 10 49 E
Atō 100 34 25N 131 40 E
Atok 90 16 35N 120 41 E
Atoka 153 34 22N 96 10W
Atókos 49 38 28N 20 49 E
Atolia 159 35 19N 117 37W
Atouguia 35 39 20N 9 20W

Babak

Atoyac → 161 16 30N 97 31W
Atrak → 73 37 50N 57 0 E
Ätran 53 57 7N 12 57 E
Atrato → 168 8 17N 76 58W
Atrauli 78 28 2N 78 20 E
Atri 43 42 35N 14 0 E
Atsbi 125 13 52N 39 50 E
Atsoum, Mts. 127 6 41N 12 57 E
Atsugi 101 35 25N 139 21 E
Atsumi 101 34 35N 137 4 E
Atsumi-Wan 101 34 44N 137 13 E
Atsuta 98 43 24N 141 26 E
Attalla 149 34 2N 86 5W
Attawapiskat 142 52 56N 82 24W
Attawapiskat → 142 52 57N 82 18W
Attawapiskat, L. 142 52 18N 87 54W
Attendorn 26 51 8N 7 54 E
Attersee 30 47 55N 13 32 E
Attert 23 49 45N 5 47 E
Attica 155 40 20N 87 15W
Attichy 19 49 25N 3 3 E
Attigny 19 49 28N 4 35 E
Attikamagen L. 143 55 0N 66 30W
Attikí □ 49 38 10N 23 40 E
'Attīl 69 32 23N 35 4 E
Attleboro 151 41 56N 71 18W
Attock 78 33 52N 72 20 E
Attopeu 84 14 48N 106 50 E
Attunga 113 30 55 S 150 50 E
Attur 81 11 35N 78 30 E
'Atūd 75 14 53N 48 10 E
Atuel → 174 36 17 S 66 50W
Åtvidaberg 53 58 12N 16 0 E
Atwater 158 37 21N 120 37W
Atwood, Canada 150 43 40N 81 1W
Atwood, U.S.A. 152 39 52N 101 3W
Au Sable → 148 44 25N 83 20W
Au Sable Pt. 142 46 40N 86 10W
Aubagne 21 43 17N 5 37 E
Aubange 23 49 34N 5 48 E
Aube □ 19 48 15N 4 10 E
Aube → 19 48 34N 3 43 E
Aubel 23 50 42N 5 51 E
Aubenas 21 44 37N 4 24 E
Aubenton 19 49 50N 4 12 E
Auberry 158 37 7N 119 29W
Aubigny-sur-Nère 19 47 30N 2 24 E
Aubin 20 44 33N 2 15 E
Aubrac, Mts. d' 20 44 40N 3 2 E
Auburn, Ala., U.S.A. 149 32 37N 85 30W
Auburn, Calif., U.S.A. 158 38 53N 121 4W
Auburn, Ill., U.S.A. 154 39 36N 89 45W
Auburn, Ind., U.S.A. 155 41 20N 85 0W
Auburn, N.Y., U.S.A. 151 42 57N 76 39W
Auburn, Nebr., U.S.A. 152 40 25N 95 50W
Auburn, Wash., U.S.A. 158 47 18N 122 13W
Auburn Range 111 25 15 S 150 30 E
Auburndale 149 28 5N 81 45W
Aubusson 20 45 57N 2 11 E
Auch 20 43 39N 0 36 E
Auchel 19 50 30N 2 29 E
Auchi 127 7 6N 6 13 E
Auckland 114 36 52 S 174 46 E
Auckland □ 114 38 35 S 177 0 E
Auckland Is. 104 50 40 S 166 5 E
Aude □ 20 43 8N 2 28 E
Aude → 20 43 13N 3 14 E
Audegle 136 1 59N 44 50 E
Auden 142 50 14N 87 53W
Auderghem 23 50 49N 4 26 E
Auderville 18 49 43N 1 57W
Audierne 18 48 1N 4 34W
Audincourt 19 47 30N 6 50 E
Audo Ra. 125 6 20N 41 50 E
Audubon 154 41 43N 94 56W
Aue 26 50 34N 12 43 E
Auerbach 26 50 30N 12 25 E
Aueti Paraná → 168 1 51 S 65 37W
Aufist 120 25 44N 14 39W
Augathella 111 25 48 S 146 35 E
Augrabies Falls 134 28 35 S 20 20 E
Augsburg 27 48 22N 10 54 E
Augusta, Italy 45 37 14N 15 12 E
Augusta, Ark., U.S.A. 153 35 17N 91 25W
Augusta, Ga., U.S.A. 149 33 29N 81 59W
Augusta, Ill., U.S.A. 154 40 14N 90 57W
Augusta, Kans., U.S.A. 153 37 40N 97 0W
Augusta, Ky., U.S.A. 155 38 47N 84 0W
Augusta, Maine, U.S.A. 143 44 20N 69 46W
Augusta, Mont., U.S.A. 156 47 30N 112 29W
Augusta, Wis., U.S.A. 152 44 41N 91 8W
Augustenborg 53 54 57N 9 53 E
Augustów 32 53 51N 23 0 E
Augustus, Mt. 109 24 20 S 116 50 E
Augustus Downs 110 18 35 S 139 55 E
Augustus I. 108 15 20 S 124 30 E
Aukan 125 15 29N 40 50 E
Aukum 158 38 34N 120 43W
Aulla 42 44 12N 10 0 E
Aulnay 20 46 2N 0 22W
Aulne → 18 48 17N 4 16W
Aulnoye-Aymeries 19 50 12N 3 50 E
Ault, France 18 50 8N 1 26 E
Ault, U.S.A. 152 40 40N 104 42W
Aulus-les-Bains 20 42 49N 1 19 E
Aumale 19 49 46N 1 46 E
Aumont-Aubrac 20 44 43N 3 17 E
Auna 127 10 9N 4 42 E
Aundh 80 17 33N 74 23 E
Aunis 20 46 5N 0 50W
Auponhia 87 1 58 S 125 27 E
Aups 21 43 37N 6 15 E
Aur, P. 85 2 35N 104 10 E
Aura 82 26 59N 97 57 E
Auraiya 79 26 28N 79 33 E
Aurangabad, Bihar, India 79 24 45N 84 18 E
Aurangabad, Maharashtra, India 80 19 50N 75 23 E
Auray 18 47 40N 2 59W
Aurès 121 35 8N 6 30 E
Aurich 26 53 28N 7 30 E
Aurilândia 171 16 44 S 50 28W
Aurillac 20 44 55N 2 26 E
Aurlandsvangen 51 60 55N 7 12 E
Auronza 43 46 33N 12 27 E
Aurora, Canada 150 44 0N 79 28W
Aurora, Isabela, Phil. 90 16 59N 121 38 E
Aurora, Quezon, Phil. 90 13 21N 122 31 E
Aurora, S. Africa 134 32 40 S 18 29 E
Aurora, Colo., U.S.A. 152 39 44N 104 55W
Aurora, Ill., U.S.A. 155 41 42N 88 12W
Aurora, Mo., U.S.A. 153 36 58N 93 42W
Aurora, Nebr., U.S.A. 152 40 55N 98 0W
Aurora, Ohio, U.S.A. 150 41 21N 81 20W
Aurskog 51 59 55N 11 26 E
Aurukun Mission 110 13 20 S 141 45 E
Aus 134 26 35 S 16 12 E
Aust-Agder fylke □ 51 58 55N 7 40 E
Austad 51 58 58N 7 37 E
Austerlitz = Slavkov 31 49 10N 16 52 E
Austevoll 51 60 5N 5 13 E
Austin, Ind., U.S.A. 155 38 45N 85 49W
Austin, Minn., U.S.A. 152 43 37N 92 59W
Austin, Nev., U.S.A. 156 39 30N 117 1W
Austin, Pa., U.S.A. 150 41 40N 78 7W
Austin, Tex., U.S.A. 153 30 20N 97 45W
Austin, L. 109 27 40 S 118 0 E
Austral Downs 110 20 30 S 137 45 E
Austral Is. = Tubuai Is. 105 25 0 S 150 0W
Austral Seamount Chain 105 24 0 S 150 0W
Australia ■ 103 23 0 S 135 0 E
Australian Alps 113 36 30 S 148 30 E
Australian Dependency □ 7 73 0 S 90 0 E
Austria ■ 30 47 0N 14 0 E
Austvågøy 54 68 20N 14 40 E
Autazes 169 3 35 S 59 8W
Autelbas 23 49 39N 5 52 E
Auterive 20 43 21N 1 29 E
Authie → 19 50 22N 1 38 E
Authon-du-Perche 18 48 12N 0 54 E
Autlán 160 19 40N 104 30W
Autun 19 46 58N 4 17 E
Auvelais 23 50 27N 4 38 E
Auvergne, Australia 108 15 39 S 130 1 E
Auvergne, France 20 45 20N 3 15 E
Auvergne, Mts. d' 20 45 20N 2 55 E
Auvézére → 20 45 12N 0 50 E
Auxerre 19 47 48N 3 32 E
Auxi-le-Château 19 50 15N 2 8 E
Auxonne 19 47 10N 5 20 E
Auxvasse 154 39 1N 91 54W
Auzances 20 46 2N 2 30 E
Auzat-sur-Allier 20 45 27N 3 19 E
Ava 154 37 53N 89 30W
Avallon 19 47 30N 3 53 E
Avalon 159 33 21N 118 20W
Avalon Pen. 143 47 30N 53 20W
Avanigadda 81 16 0N 80 56 E
Avaré 175 23 4 S 48 58W
Åvas 48 40 57N 25 56 E
Avawatz Mts. 159 35 30N 116 20W
Aveiro, Brazil 169 3 10 S 55 5W
Aveiro, Portugal 34 40 37N 8 38W
Aveiro □ 34 40 40N 8 35W
Āvej 73 35 40N 49 15 E
Avelgem 23 50 47N 3 27 E
Avellaneda 174 34 50 S 58 10W
Avellino 45 40 54N 14 46 E
Avenal 158 36 0N 120 8W
Avenches 28 46 53N 7 2 E
Averøya 51 63 0N 7 35 E
Aversa 45 40 58N 14 11 E
Avery 156 47 22N 115 56W
Aves, I. de 163 15 45N 63 55W
Aves, Is. de 163 12 0N 67 30W
Avesnes-sur-Helpe 19 50 8N 3 55 E
Avesta 52 60 9N 16 10 E
Aveyron □ 20 44 22N 2 45 E
Aveyron → 20 44 5N 1 16 E
Avezzano 43 42 2N 13 24 E
Avgó 49 35 33N 25 37 E
Aviá Terai 174 26 45 S 60 50W
Aviano 43 46 3N 12 35 E
Avigliana 42 45 7N 7 13 E
Avigliano 45 40 44N 15 41 E
Avignon 21 43 57N 4 50 E
Ávila 34 40 39N 4 43W
Ávila □ 34 40 30N 5 0W
Ávila, Sierra de 34 40 40N 5 0W
Avila Beach 159 35 11N 120 44W
Avilés 34 43 35N 5 57W
Avionárion 49 38 31N 24 8 E
Avisio → 43 46 7N 11 5 E
Aviston 154 38 36N 89 36W
Aviz 35 39 4N 7 53W
Avize 19 48 59N 4 0 E
Avoca, Ireland 15 52 52N 6 13W
Avoca, U.S.A. 150 42 24N 77 25W
Avoca → 112 35 40 S 143 43 E
Avola, Canada 144 51 45N 119 19W
Avola, Italy 45 36 56N 15 7 E
Avon, Ill., U.S.A. 154 40 40N 90 26W
Avon, N.Y., U.S.A. 150 42 55N 77 42W
Avon, S. Dak., U.S.A. 152 43 0N 98 3W
Avon □ 13 51 30N 2 40W
Avon →, Australia 109 31 40 S 116 7 E
Avon →, Avon, U.K. 13 51 30N 2 43W
Avon →, Hants., U.K. 13 50 44N 1 45W
Avon →, Warwick, U.K. 13 52 0N 2 9W
Avondale 131 17 43 S 30 58 E
Avonlea 145 50 0N 105 0W
Avonmore 151 45 10N 74 58W
Avonmouth 13 51 30N 2 42W
Avramov 47 42 45N 26 38 E
Avranches 18 48 40N 1 20W
Avre → 18 48 47N 1 22 E
Avrig 50 45 43N 24 21 E
Avtovac 46 43 9N 18 35 E
Awag el Baqar 125 10 10N 33 10 E
A'waj → 70 33 23N 36 20 E
Awaji 101 34 32N 135 1 E
Awaji-Shima 100 34 30N 134 50 E
'Awālī 75 26 0N 50 30 E
Awantipur 79 33 55N 75 3 E
Awanui 114 35 4 S 173 17 E
Awarja → 80 17 5N 76 15 E
'Awartā 69 32 10N 35 17 E
Awarua Pt. 115 44 15 S 168 5 E
Awasa, L. 125 7 0N 38 30 E
Awash 125 9 1N 40 10 E
Awash → 125 11 45N 41 5 E
Awaso 126 6 15N 2 22W
Awatere → 115 41 37 S 174 10 E
Awbārī 122 26 46N 12 57 E
Awbārī □ 122 26 35N 12 46 E
Awe, L. 14 56 15N 5 15W
Aweil 125 8 42N 27 20 E
Awgu 127 6 4N 7 24 E
Awjilah 122 29 8N 21 7 E
Aworro 107 7 43 S 143 11 E
Ax-les-Thermes 20 42 44N 1 50 E
Axarfjörður 54 66 15N 16 45W
Axel 23 51 16N 3 55 E
Axel Heiberg I. 6 80 0N 90 0W
Axim 126 4 51N 2 15W
Axinim 169 4 2 S 59 22W
Axintele 50 44 37N 26 47 E
Axioma 173 6 45 S 64 31W
Axiós → 48 40 57N 22 35 E
Axmarsbruk 52 61 3N 17 10 E
Axminster 13 50 47N 3 1W
Axstedt 26 53 26N 8 43 E
Axvall 53 58 23N 13 34 E
Aÿ 19 49 3N 4 0 E
Ay → 62 56 8N 57 40 E
Ayaantang 132 1 58N 10 24 E
Ayabaca 172 4 40 S 79 53W
Ayabe 101 35 20N 135 20 E
Ayacucho, Argentina 174 37 5 S 58 20W
Ayacucho, Peru 172 13 0 S 74 0W
Ayaguz 64 48 10N 80 0 E
Ayakkuduk 63 41 12N 65 12 E
Ayakudi 81 10 28N 77 56 E
Ayala 91 6 57N 121 57 E
Ayamonte 35 37 12N 7 24W
Ayan 65 56 30N 138 16 E
Ayancık 60 41 57N 34 18 E
Ayapel 168 8 19N 75 9W
Ayas, Adana, Turkey 70 36 46N 35 46 E
Ayas, Ankara, Turkey 60 40 10N 32 14 E
Ayaviri 172 14 50 S 70 35W
Āybak 77 36 15N 68 5 E
Aydim, W. → 75 18 8N 53 8 E
Aye 23 50 14N 5 18 E
Ayenngré 127 8 40N 1 1 E
Ayer's Cliff 151 45 10N 72 3W
Ayers Rock 109 25 23 S 131 5 E
Ayiá 48 39 43N 22 45 E
Ayía Ánna 49 38 52N 23 24 E
Ayía Marína, Kásos, Greece 49 35 27N 26 53 E
Ayía Marína, Leros, Greece 49 37 11N 26 48 E
Ayía Paraskeví 48 39 14N 26 16 E
Ayía Rouméli 49 35 14N 23 58 E
Ayiássos 49 39 5N 26 23 E
Áyion Óros 48 40 25N 24 6 E
Áyios Andréas 49 37 21N 22 45 E
Áyios Evstrátios, Greece 48 39 30N 25 0 E
Áyios Evstrátios, Greece 48 39 34N 24 58 E
Áyios Ioannis, Ákra 49 35 20N 25 40 E
Áyios Kiríkos 49 37 34N 26 17 E
Áyios Matthaíos 48 39 30N 19 47 E
Áyios Mírono 49 35 15N 25 1 E
Áyios Nikólaos 49 35 11N 25 41 E
Áyios Pétros 49 38 38N 20 33 E
Áyios Yeóryios 49 37 28N 23 57 E
Aykathonisi 49 37 28N 27 0 E
Ayke, Ozero 62 50 57N 61 36 E
Aykin 56 62 15N 49 56 E
Aylesbury 13 51 48N 0 49W
Aylmer 150 42 46N 80 59W
Aylmer L. 140 64 0N 110 8W
'Ayn al Ghazālah 122 32 10N 23 20 E
'Ayn 'Arīk 69 31 54N 35 8 E
'Ayn Zaqqūt 122 29 0N 19 30 E
Ayna 37 38 34N 2 3W
Aynāt 75 16 4N 49 9 E
Ayni 63 39 23N 68 32 E
'Aynūnah 71 28 5N 35 8 E
Ayolas 174 27 10 S 56 59W
Ayom 125 7 49N 28 23 E
Ayon, Ostrov 65 69 50N 169 0 E
Ayora 37 39 3N 1 3W
Ayr, Australia 110 19 35 S 147 25 E
Ayr, U.K. 14 55 28N 4 37W
Ayr → 14 55 29N 4 40W
Ayre, Pt. of 12 54 27N 4 21W
Aysha 125 10 50N 42 23 E
Aytos 47 42 42N 27 16 E
Aytoska Planina 47 42 45N 27 30 E
Ayu, Kepulauan 87 0 35N 131 5 E
Ayutla, Guat. 162 14 40N 92 10W
Ayutla, Mexico 161 16 58N 99 17W
Ayvalık 57 39 20N 26 46 E
Aywaille 23 50 28N 5 40 E
Az Zabdānī 70 33 43N 36 5 E
Aẓ Ẓāhirīyah 71 31 25N 34 58 E
Aẓ Ẓahrān 73 26 10N 50 7 E
Az Zarqā 69 32 5N 36 4 E
Az Zāwiyah 122 32 52N 12 56 E
Az Zāwīyah, J. 70 35 45N 36 35 E
Az Zaydīyah 74 15 20N 43 1 E
Az Zibār 72 36 52N 44 4 E
Az-Zilfī 72 26 12N 44 52 E
Az Zubaydīyah, J. 70 33 45N 37 1 E
Az Zubayr 72 30 20N 47 50 E
Az Zuhd, J. 71 28 20N 35 17 E
Az Zuqur 74 14 0N 42 45 E
Azambuja 35 39 4N 8 51W
Azamgarh 79 26 5N 83 13 E
Azangaro 172 14 55 S 70 13W
Azaouak, Vallée de l' 127 15 50N 3 20 E
Āzār Shahr 72 37 45N 45 59 E
Āzarbāyjān-e Gharbī □ 72 37 0N 44 30 E
Āzarbāyjān-e Sharqī □ 72 37 20N 47 0 E
Azare 127 11 55N 10 10 E
Azay-le-Rideau 18 47 16N 0 30 E
A'zāz 70 36 36N 37 4 E
Azazga 121 36 48N 4 22 E
Azbine = Aïr 127 18 30N 8 0 E
Azefal 120 21 0N 14 45W
Azeffoun 121 36 51N 4 26 E
Azemmour 120 33 20N 9 20W
Azerbaijan S.S.R. □ 61 40 20N 48 0 E
Azezo 125 12 28N 37 15 E
Azilal 120 32 0N 6 30W
Azimganj 79 24 14N 88 16 E
Aznalcóllar 35 37 32N 6 17W
Azogues 168 2 35 S 78 0W
Azor 69 32 2N 34 48 E
Azores 8 38 44N 29 0W
Azov 61 47 3N 39 25 E
Azov Sea = Azovskoye More 60 46 0N 36 30 E
Azovskoye More 60 46 0N 36 30 E
Azovy 64 64 55N 64 35 E
Azpeitia 36 43 12N 2 19W
Azrou 120 33 28N 5 19W
Aztec 157 36 54N 108 0W
Azúa de Compostela 163 18 25N 70 44W
Azuaga 35 38 16N 5 39W
Azuara 36 41 15N 0 53W
Azuay □ 168 2 55 S 79 0W
Azuer → 35 39 8N 3 36W
Azuero, Pen. de 162 7 30N 80 30W
Azul 174 36 42 S 59 43W
Azul, Serra 173 14 50 S 54 50W
Azurduy 173 19 59 S 64 29W
Azusa 159 34 8N 117 52W
Azzaba 121 36 48N 7 6 E
Azzano Décimo 43 45 53N 12 46 E
'Azzūn 71 32 10N 35 2 E

B

Ba Don 84 17 45N 106 26 E
Ba Dong 85 9 40N 106 33 E
Ba Ngoi = Cam Lam 85 11 54N 109 10 E
Ba Ria 85 10 30N 107 10 E
Ba Tri 85 10 2N 106 36 E
Ba Xian 94 39 8N 116 22 E
Baa 87 10 50 S 123 0 E
Baaba, I. 106 20 3 S 164 59 E
Baamonde 34 43 7N 7 44W
Baao 90 13 27N 123 22 E
Baar 29 47 12N 8 32 E
Baarle Nassau 23 51 27N 4 56 E
Baarlo 23 51 20N 6 6 E
Baarn 22 52 12N 5 17 E
Bab el Mandeb 74 12 35N 43 25 E
Baba 47 42 44N 23 59 E
Baba Burnu 48 39 29N 26 2 E
Baba dag 61 41 0N 48 19W
Bābā Kalū 73 30 7N 50 49 E
Babaçulândia 170 7 13 S 47 46W
Babadag 50 44 53N 28 44 E
Babaeski 47 41 26N 27 6 E
Babahoyo 168 1 40 S 79 30W
Babak 91 7 8N 125 41 E

Babakin

Babakin **109** 32 7 S 118 1 E
Babana **127** 10 31N 3 46 E
Babar, Algeria **121** 35 10N 7 6 E
Babar, Indonesia **87** 8 0 S 129 30 E
Babar, Pakistan **78** 31 7N 69 32 E
Babarkach **78** 29 45N 68 0 E
Babayevo **59** 59 24N 35 55 E
Babb **156** 48 56N 113 27W
Babenhausen **27** 49 57N 8 56 E
Babi Besar, P. **85** 2 25N 103 59 E
Babia Gora **32** 49 38N 19 38 E
Babian Jiang → **96** 22 55N 101 47 E
Babile **125** 9 16N 42 11 E
Babinda **110** 17 20 S 145 56 E
Babine **144** 55 22N 126 37W
Babine → **144** 55 45N 127 44W
Babine L. **144** 54 48N 126 0W
Babo **87** 2 30 S 133 30 E
Babócsa **31** 46 2N 17 21 E
Bābol **73** 36 40N 52 50 E
Bābol Sar **73** 36 45N 52 45 E
Baborów **32** 50 7N 18 1 E
Baboua **132** 5 49N 14 58 E
Babuna **46** 41 30N 21 40 E
Babura **127** 12 51N 8 59 E
Babusar Pass **79** 35 12N 73 59 E
Babušnica **46** 43 7N 22 27 E
Babuyan Chan. **90** 18 40N 121 30 E
Babuyan I. **90** 19 32N 121 57 E
Babuyan Is. **90** 19 15N 121 40 E
Babylon **72** 32 40N 44 30 E
Bač **46** 45 29N 19 17 E
Bac Can **84** 22 8N 105 49 E
Bac Giang **84** 21 16N 106 11 E
Bac Ninh **84** 21 13N 106 4 E
Bac Phan **84** 22 0N 105 0 E
Bac Quang **84** 22 30N 104 48 E
Bacabal **170** 4 15 S 44 45W
Bacacay **90** 13 18N 123 47 E
Bacajá → **169** 3 25 S 51 50W
Bacalar **161** 18 50N 87 27W
Bacan **87** 8 27 S 126 27 E
Bacan, Kepulauan **87** 0 35 S 127 30 E
Bacan, Pulau **87** 0 50 S 127 30 E
Bacarra **90** 18 15N 120 37 E
Bacău **50** 46 35N 26 55 E
Bacău □ **50** 46 30N 26 45 E
Baccarat **19** 48 28N 6 42 E
Bacchus Marsh **112** 37 43 S 144 27 E
Bacerac **160** 30 18N 108 50W
Băceşti **50** 46 50N 27 11 E
Bach Long Vi, Dao **84** 20 10N 107 40 E
Bachaquero **168** 9 56N 71 8W
Bacharach **27** 50 3N 7 46 E
Bachelina **64** 57 45N 67 20 E
Bachuma **125** 6 48N 35 53 E
Bačina **46** 43 42N 21 23 E
Back → **140** 65 10N 104 0W
Bačka Palanka **46** 45 17N 19 27 E
Bačka Topola **46** 45 49N 19 39 E
Bäckefors **53** 58 48N 12 9 E
Bački Petrovac **46** 45 29N 19 32 E
Backnang **27** 48 57N 9 26 E
Backstairs Passage **112** 35 40 S 138 5 E
Baco, Mt. **90** 12 49N 121 10 E
Bacolod **91** 10 40N 122 57 E
Bacon **90** 13 3N 124 3 E
Bacoor **90** 14 28N 120 56 E
Bacqueville-en-Caux **18** 49 47N 1 0 E
Bacs-Kiskun □ **31** 46 43N 19 30 E
Bácsalmás **31** 46 8N 19 17 E
Bacuag **91** 9 36N 125 38 E
Bacuk **85** 6 4N 102 25 E
Baculin **91** 7 27N 126 35 E
Bād **73** 33 41N 52 1 E
Bad → **152** 44 22N 100 22W
Bad Aussee **30** 47 43N 13 45 E
Bad Axe **150** 43 48N 82 59W
Bad Bergzabern **27** 49 6N 8 0 E
Bad Bramstedt **26** 53 56N 9 53 E
Bad Doberan **26** 54 6N 11 55 E
Bad Driburg **26** 51 44N 9 0 E
Bad Ems **27** 50 22N 7 44 E
Bad Frankenhausen **26** 51 21N 11 3 E
Bad Freienwalde **26** 52 47N 14 3 E
Bad Godesberg **26** 50 41N 7 4 E
Bad Hersfeld **26** 50 52N 9 42 E
Bad Hofgastein **30** 47 17N 13 6 E
Bad Homburg **27** 50 17N 8 33 E
Bad Honnef **26** 50 39N 7 13 E
Bad Ischl **30** 47 44N 13 38 E
Bad Kissingen **27** 50 11N 10 5 E
Bad Kreuznach **27** 49 47N 7 47 E
Bad Lands **152** 43 40N 102 10W
Bad Langensalza **26** 51 6N 10 40 E
Bad Lauterberg **26** 51 38N 10 29 E
Bad Leonfelden **30** 48 31N 14 18 E
Bad Lippspringe **26** 51 47N 8 46 E
Bad Mergentheim **27** 49 29N 9 47 E
Bad Münstereifel **26** 50 33N 6 46 E
Bad Muskau **26** 51 33N 14 43 E
Bad Nauheim **27** 50 24N 8 45 E
Bad Oeynhausen **26** 52 16N 8 45 E
Bad Oldesloe **26** 53 48N 10 22 E
Bad Orb **27** 50 16N 9 21 E
Bad Pyrmont **26** 51 59N 9 15 E
Bad Ragaz **29** 47 0N 9 30 E
Bad Reichenhall **27** 47 44N 12 53 E
Bad St.-Peter **26** 54 23N 8 32 E
Bad Salzuflen **26** 52 8N 8 44 E
Bad Segeberg **26** 53 58N 10 16 E
Bad Tölz **27** 47 43N 11 34 E
Bad Waldsee **27** 47 56N 9 46 E
Bad Wildungen **26** 51 7N 9 10 E
Bad Wimpfen **27** 49 12N 9 10 E
Bad Windsheim **27** 49 29N 10 25 E
Badagara **81** 11 35N 75 40 E
Badagri **127** 6 25N 2 55 E
Badajós, L. **169** 3 15 S 62 50W
Badajoz **35** 38 50N 6 59W
Badajoz □ **35** 38 40N 6 30W
Badakhshān □ **77** 36 30N 71 0 E
Badalona **36** 41 26N 2 15 E
Badalzai **78** 29 50N 65 35 E
Badampahar **79** 22 10N 86 10 E
Badanah **72** 30 58N 41 30 E
Badarinath **79** 30 45N 79 30 E
Badas **86** 4 33N 114 25 E
Badas, Kepulauan **88** 0 45N 107 5 E
Baddo → **77** 28 0N 64 20 E
Bade **87** 7 10 S 139 35 E
Bademli **70** 37 1N 32 41 E
Baden, Austria **31** 48 1N 16 13 E
Baden, Switz. **29** 47 28N 8 18 E
Baden-Baden **27** 48 45N 8 15 E
Baden Park **112** 32 8 S 144 12 E
Baden-Württemberg □ **27** 48 40N 9 0 E
Badgastein **30** 47 7N 13 9 E
Badger, Canada **143** 49 0N 56 4W
Badger, U.S.A. **158** 36 38N 119 1W
Bādghīsāt □ **77** 35 0N 63 0 E
Badgom **79** 34 1N 74 45 E
Badhoevedorp **22** 52 20N 4 47 E
Badia Polèsine **43** 45 6N 11 30 E
Badian **91** 9 55N 123 24 E
Badin **77** 24 38N 68 54 E
Badnera **78** 20 48N 77 44 E
Badoc **90** 17 56N 120 28 E
Badogo **126** 11 2N 8 13W
Badong **97** 31 1N 110 23 E
Badr Ḥunayn **74** 23 44N 38 46 E
Baduen **136** 7 15N 47 40 E
Badulla **81** 7 1N 81 7 E
Badupi **82** 21 36N 93 27 E
Baena **35** 37 37N 4 20W
Baerami Creek **113** 32 27 S 150 27 E
Baexem **23** 51 13N 5 53 E
Baeza, Ecuador **168** 0 25 S 77 53W
Baeza, Spain **37** 37 57N 3 25W
Bafa Gölü **49** 37 30N 27 29 E
Bafang **127** 5 9N 10 11 E
Bafatá **126** 12 8N 14 40W
Baffin B. **6** 72 0N 64 0W
Baffin I. **141** 68 0N 75 0W
Bafia **127** 4 40N 11 10 E
Bafilo **127** 9 22N 1 22 E
Bafing → **126** 13 49N 10 50W
Bafliyūn **72** 36 37N 36 59 E
Baflo **22** 53 22N 6 31 E
Bafoulabé **126** 13 50N 10 55W
Bafoussam **127** 5 28N 10 25 E
Bāfq **73** 31 40N 55 25 E
Bafra **60** 41 34N 35 54 E
Bafra, C. **60** 41 44N 35 58 E
Bāft **73** 29 15N 56 38 E
Bafut **127** 6 6N 10 2 E
Bafwasende **130** 1 3N 27 5 E
Bagabag **90** 16 30N 121 15 E
Bagac **90** 14 36N 120 23 E
Bagac Bay **90** 14 36N 120 20 E
Bagalkot **81** 16 10N 75 40 E
Bagamoyo **130** 6 28 S 38 55 E
Bagamoyo □ **130** 6 20 S 38 30 E
Bagan Datoh **85** 3 59N 100 47 E
Bagan Serai **85** 5 1N 100 32 E
Baganga **91** 7 34N 126 33 E
Bagani **134** 18 7 S 21 41 E
Bagansiapiapi **88** 2 12N 100 50 E
Bagasra **78** 21 30N 71 0 E
Bagata **132** 3 44 S 17 57 E
Bagawi **125** 12 20N 34 18 E
Bagdad **159** 34 35N 115 53W
Bagdarin **65** 54 26N 113 36 E
Bagé **175** 31 20 S 54 15W
Bagenalstown = Muine Bheag **15** 52 42N 6 57W
Baggs **156** 41 8N 107 46W
Bagh **79** 33 59N 73 45 E
Baghdād **72** 33 20N 44 30 E
Bagherhat **82** 22 40N 89 47 E
Bagheria **44** 38 5N 13 30 E
Baghlān **77** 36 12N 69 0 E
Baghlān □ **77** 36 0N 68 30 E
Bagley **152** 47 30N 95 22W
Bagnacavallo **43** 44 25N 11 58 E
Bagnara Cálabra **45** 38 16N 15 49 E
Bagnell Dam **154** 38 14N 92 36W
Bagnères-de-Bigorre **20** 43 5N 0 9 E
Bagnères-de-Luchon **20** 42 47N 0 38 E
Bagni di Lucca **42** 44 1N 10 37 E
Bagno di Romagna **43** 43 50N 11 59 E
Bagnoles-de-l'Orne **18** 48 32N 0 25W
Bagnoli di Sopra **43** 45 13N 11 55 E
Bagnolo Mella **42** 45 27N 10 14 E
Bagnols-sur-Cèze **21** 44 10N 4 36 E
Bagnorégio **43** 42 38N 12 7 E
Bago **91** 10 32N 122 50 E
Bagolino **42** 45 49N 10 28 E
Bagotville **143** 48 22N 70 54W
Bagrdan **46** 44 5N 21 11 E
Bagua **172** 5 35 S 78 22W
Baguio **90** 16 26N 120 34 E
Bahabón de Esgueva **36** 41 52N 3 43W
Bahadurabad Ghat **82** 25 11N 89 44 E
Bahadurgarh **78** 28 40N 76 57 E
Bahama, Canal Viejo de **162** 22 10N 77 30W
Bahamas ■ **163** 24 0N 75 0W
Baharampur **79** 24 2N 88 27 E
Baharîya, El Wâhât al **124** 28 0N 28 50 E
Bahau **85** 2 48N 102 26 E
Bahawalnagar **77** 30 0N 73 15 E
Bahawalpur **77** 29 24N 71 40 E
Baheri **79** 28 45N 79 34 E
Bahi **130** 5 58 S 35 21 E
Bahi Swamp **130** 6 10 S 35 0 E
Bahía = Salvador **171** 13 0 S 38 30W
Bahía □ **171** 12 0 S 42 0W
Bahía, Is. de la **162** 16 45N 86 15W
Bahía Blanca **174** 38 35 S 62 13W
Bahía de Caráquez **168** 0 40 S 80 27W
Bahía Honda **162** 22 54N 83 10W
Bahía Laura **176** 48 10 S 66 30W
Bahía Negra **173** 20 5 S 58 5W
Bahir Dar **125** 11 37N 37 10 E
Bahlah **75** 22 58N 57 18 E
Bahmanzād **73** 31 15N 51 47 E
Bahmer **121** 27 32N 0 10W
Bahönye **31** 46 25N 17 28 E
Bahr Aouk → **132** 8 40N 19 0 E
Bahr el Ahmar □ **124** 20 0N 35 0 E
Bahr el Ghazâl □ **125** 7 0N 28 0 E
Bahr Salamat → **123** 9 20N 18 0 E
Bahr Yûsef → **124** 28 25N 30 35 E
Bahra el Burullus **124** 31 28N 30 48 E
Bahraich **79** 27 38N 81 37 E
Bahrain ■ **75** 26 0N 50 35 E
Bahret Assad **72** 36 0N 38 15 E
Bahror **78** 27 51N 76 20 E
Bāhū Kalāt **73** 25 43N 61 25 E
Bai **126** 13 35N 3 28W
Bai Bung, Mui **85** 8 38N 104 44 E
Bai Duc **84** 18 3N 105 49 E
Bai Thuong **84** 19 54N 105 23 E
Baia Farta **133** 12 40 S 13 11 E
Baia Mare **50** 47 40N 23 35 E
Baia-Sprie **50** 47 41N 23 43 E
Baião **170** 2 40 S 49 40W
Baïbokoum **123** 7 46N 15 43 E
Baicheng **95** 45 38N 122 42 E
Băicoi **50** 45 3N 25 52 E
Baidoa **136** 3 8N 43 30 E
Baie Comeau **143** 49 12N 68 10W
Baie-St-Paul **143** 47 28N 70 32W
Baie Trinité **143** 49 25N 67 20W
Baie Verte **143** 49 55N 56 12W
Baignes-Ste.-Radegonde **20** 45 23N 0 25W
Baigneux-les-Juifs **19** 47 31N 4 39 E
Baihe, China **94** 32 50N 110 5 E
Baihe, Taiwan **97** 23 24N 120 24 E
Ba'ījī **72** 35 0N 43 30 E
Baikal, L. = Baykal, Oz. **65** 53 0N 108 0 E
Bailadila, Mt. **80** 18 43N 81 15 E
Baile Atha Cliath = Dublin **15** 53 20N 6 18W
Bailei **125** 6 44N 40 18 E
Bailén **35** 38 8N 3 48W
Băileşti **50** 44 1N 23 20 E
Baileux **23** 50 2N 4 23 E
Bailhongal **81** 15 55N 74 53 E
Bailique, Ilha **170** 1 2N 49 58W
Bailleul **19** 50 44N 2 41 E
Bailundo **133** 12 10 S 15 50 E
Baima **96** 33 0N 100 26 E
Baimuru **107** 7 35 S 144 51 E
Bain-de-Bretagne **18** 47 50N 1 40W
Bainbridge, Ga., U.S.A. **149** 30 53N 84 34W
Bainbridge, Ind., U.S.A. **155** 39 46N 86 49W
Bainbridge, N.Y., U.S.A. **151** 42 17N 75 29W
Bainbridge, Ohio, U.S.A. **155** 39 14N 83 16W
Baing **87** 10 14 S 120 34 E
Bainiu **94** 32 50N 112 15 E
Bainville **152** 48 8N 104 10W
Bainyik **107** 3 40 S 143 4 E
Bā'ir **71** 30 45N 36 55 E
Bā'ir, W. → **71** 30 59N 37 24 E
Baird **153** 32 25N 99 25W
Baird Mts. **140** 67 10N 160 15W
Bairin Youqi **95** 43 30N 118 35 E
Bairin Zuoqi **95** 43 58N 119 15 E
Bairnsdale **113** 37 48 S 147 36 E
Bais **91** 9 35N 123 7 E
Baisha **94** 34 20N 112 32 E
Baïsole → **20** 43 26N 0 25 E
Baissa **127** 7 14N 10 38 E
Baitadi **79** 29 35N 80 25 E
Baixa Grande **171** 11 57 S 40 11W
Baiyin **94** 36 45N 104 14 E
Baiyü **96** 31 16N 98 50 E
Baiyu Shan **94** 37 15N 107 30 E
Baiyuda **124** 17 35N 32 7 E
Baj Baj **79** 22 30N 88 5 E
Baja **31** 46 12N 18 59 E
Baja, Pta. **160** 29 50N 116 0W
Baja California **160** 31 10N 115 12W
Bajana **78** 23 7N 71 49 E
Bājgīrān **73** 37 36N 58 24 E
Bājil **74** 15 4N 43 17 E
Bajimba, Mt. **111** 29 17 S 152 6 E
Bajina Bašta **46** 43 58N 19 35 E
Bajmok **46** 45 57N 19 24 E
Bajo Nuevo **162** 15 40N 78 50W
Bajoga **127** 10 57N 11 20 E
Bajool **110** 23 40 S 150 35 E
Bak **31** 46 43N 16 51 E
Bakal **62** 54 56N 58 48 E
Bakala **132** 6 15N 20 20 E
Bakanas **63** 44 50N 76 15 E
Bakar **43** 45 18N 14 32 E
Bakchar **64** 57 1N 82 5 E
Bakel, Neth. **23** 51 30N 5 45 E
Bakel, Senegal **126** 14 56N 12 20W
Baker, Calif., U.S.A. **159** 35 16N 116 8W
Baker, Mont., U.S.A. **152** 46 22N 104 12W
Baker, Oreg., U.S.A. **156** 44 50N 117 55W
Baker, Canal **176** 47 45 S 74 45W
Baker, L., Australia **109** 26 54 S 126 5 E
Baker, L., Canada **140** 64 0N 96 0W
Baker I. **104** 0 10N 176 35W
Baker Lake **140** 64 20N 96 3W
Baker Mt. **156** 48 50N 121 49W
Bakers Creek **110** 21 13 S 149 7 E
Baker's Dozen Is. **142** 56 45N 78 45W
Bakersfield, Calif., U.S.A. **159** 35 25N 119 0W
Bakersfield, Vt., U.S.A. **151** 44 46N 72 48W
Bakhchisaray **60** 44 40N 33 45 E
Bakhmach **58** 51 10N 32 45 E
Bākhtarān **72** 34 23N 47 0 E
Bākhtarān □ **72** 34 0N 46 30 E
Bakırköy **47** 40 59N 28 53 E
Bakkafjörður **54** 66 2N 14 48W
Bakkagerði **54** 65 31N 13 49W
Bakony → **31** 47 35N 17 54 E
Bakony Forest = Bakony Hegyseg **31** 47 10N 17 30 E
Bakony Hegyseg **31** 47 10N 17 30 E
Bakori **127** 11 34N 7 25 E
Bakouma **132** 5 40N 22 56 E
Bakov **30** 50 27N 14 55 E
Bakpakty **63** 44 35N 76 40 E
Bakr Uzyak **62** 52 59N 58 38 E
Baku **61** 40 25N 49 45 E
Bakun **90** 16 48N 120 40 E
Bakutis Coast **7** 74 0 S 120 0W
Bakwa-Kenge **133** 4 51 S 22 4 E
Bala, Canada **150** 45 1N 79 37W
Bal'ā, Jordan **69** 32 20N 35 6 E
Bala, L. = Tegid, L. **12** 52 53N 3 38W
Bālā Morghāb **77** 35 35N 63 20 E
Balabac, Str. **86** 7 53N 117 5 E
Balabac I. **91** 8 0N 117 0 E
Balabagh **78** 34 25N 70 12 E
Balabakk **70** 34 0N 36 10 E
Balabalangan, Kepulauan **89** 2 20 S 117 30 E
Balabio, I. **106** 20 7 S 164 11 E
Bălăciţa **50** 44 23N 23 8 E
Balad **72** 34 1N 44 9 E
Balad Rūz **72** 33 42N 45 5 E
Bālādeh, Fārs, Iran **73** 29 17N 51 56 E
Baladeh, Māzandaran, Iran **73** 36 12N 51 48 E
Balaghat **79** 21 49N 80 12 E
Balaghat Ra. **80** 18 50N 76 30 E
Balaguer **36** 41 50N 0 50 E
Balakété **132** 6 56N 19 54 E
Balakhna **59** 56 25N 43 32 E
Balaklava, Australia **112** 34 7 S 138 22 E
Balaklava, U.S.S.R. **60** 44 30N 33 30 E
Balakleya **60** 49 28N 36 55 E
Balakovo **59** 52 4N 47 55 E
Balamban **91** 10 30N 123 43 E
Balancán **161** 17 48N 91 32W
Balanda **59** 51 30N 44 40 E
Balangiga **91** 11 7N 125 23 E
Balangir **79** 20 43N 83 35 E
Balapur **78** 20 40N 76 45 E
Balashikha **59** 55 49N 37 59 E
Balashov **59** 51 30N 43 10 E
Balasinor **78** 22 57N 73 23 E
Balasore = Baleshwar **79** 21 35N 87 3 E
Balassagyarmat **31** 48 4N 19 15 E
Balât **124** 25 36N 29 19 E
Balaton **31** 46 50N 17 40 E
Balatonfüred **31** 46 58N 17 54 E
Balatonszentgyörgy **31** 46 41N 17 19 E
Balayan **90** 13 57N 120 44 E
Balazote **37** 38 54N 2 9W
Balbalan **90** 17 27N 121 12 E
Balbi, Mt. **107** 5 55 S 154 58 E
Balboa **162** 9 0N 79 30W
Balbriggan **15** 53 35N 6 10W
Balcarce **174** 38 0 S 58 10W
Balcarres **145** 50 50N 103 35W
Balchik **47** 43 28N 28 11 E
Balclutha **115** 46 15 S 169 45 E
Bald Hd. **109** 35 6 S 118 1 E
Bald I. **109** 34 57 S 118 27 E
Bald Knob **153** 35 20N 91 35W
Baldock L. **145** 56 33N 97 57W
Baldwin, Fla., U.S.A. **149** 30 15N 82 10W
Baldwin, Mich., U.S.A. **148** 43 54N 85 53W
Baldwinsville **151** 43 10N 76 19W

Baranovichi

Bale **43** 45 4N 13 46 E
Bale □ **125** 6 20N 41 30 E
Baleares □ **36** 39 30N 3 0 E
Baleares, Is. **36** 39 30N 3 0 E
Balearic Is. = Baleares, Is. **36** 39 30N 3 0 E
Baleia,Punta da **171** 17 40 S 39 7W
Balen **23** 51 10N 5 10 E
Băleni **50** 45 48N 27 51 E
Baler **90** 15 46N 121 34 E
Baler Bay **90** 15 50N 121 35 E
Balerna **29** 45 52N 9 0 E
Baleshwar **79** 21 35N 87 3 E
Balezino **62** 58 2N 53 6 E
Balfate **162** 15 48N 86 25W
Balfe's Creek **110** 20 12 S 145 55 E
Balfour **135** 26 38 S 28 35 E
Balfouriyya **69** 32 38N 35 18 E
Balharshah **80** 19 50N 79 23 E
Bali, Cameroon **127** 5 54N 10 0 E
Bali, Indonesia **89** 8 20 S 115 0 E
Bali □ **86** 8 20 S 115 0 E
Bali, Selat **89** 8 18 S 114 25 E
Balicuatro Is. **90** 12 39N 124 24 E
Baligród **32** 49 20N 22 17 E
Balikesir **57** 39 35N 27 58 E
Balikpapan **89** 1 10 S 116 55 E
Balimbing **91** 5 5N 119 58 E
Balimo **107** 8 6 S 142 57 E
Baling **85** 5 41N 100 55 E
Balintang Channel **90** 19 49N 121 40 E
Balintang Is. **90** 19 58N 122 9 E
Baliton **91** 5 44N 125 14 E
Baliza **173** 16 0 S 52 20W
Baljurshi **74** 19 51N 41 33 E
Balk **22** 52 54N 5 35 E
Balkan Mts. = Stara Planina **47** 43 15N 23 0 E
Balkan Pen. **10** 42 0N 22 0 E
Balkh □ **77** 36 30N 67 0 E
Balkhash **64** 46 50N 74 50 E
Balkhash, Ozero **64** 46 0N 74 50 E
Ballachulish **14** 56 40N 5 10W
Balladonia **109** 32 27 S 123 51 E
Ballara **112** 32 19 S 140 45 E
Ballard, L. **109** 29 20 S 120 10 E
Ballater **14** 57 2N 3 2W
Balldale **113** 35 50 S 146 33 E
Ballenas, Canal de las **160** 29 10N 113 45W
Balleny Is. **7** 66 30 S 163 0 E
Ballesteros **90** 18 25N 121 31 E
Ballia **79** 25 46N 84 12 E
Ballidu **109** 30 35 S 116 45 E
Ballina, Australia **111** 28 50 S 153 31 E
Ballina, Mayo, Ireland **15** 54 7N 9 10W
Ballina, Tipp., Ireland **15** 52 49N 8 27W
Ballinasloe **15** 53 20N 8 12W
Ballinger **153** 31 45N 99 58W
Ballinrobe **15** 53 36N 9 13W
Ballinskelligs B. **15** 51 46N 10 11W
Ballon **18** 48 10N 0 14 E
Ballycastle **15** 55 12N 6 15W
Ballymena **15** 54 53N 6 18W
Ballymena □ **15** 54 53N 6 18W
Ballymoney **15** 55 5N 6 30W
Ballymoney □ **15** 55 5N 6 23W
Ballyshannon **15** 54 30N 8 10W
Balmaceda **176** 46 0 S 71 50W
Balmazújváros **31** 47 37N 21 21 E
Balmhorn **28** 46 26N 7 42 E
Balmoral, Australia **112** 37 15 S 141 48 E
Balmoral, U.K. **14** 57 3N 3 13W
Balmorhea **153** 31 2N 103 41W
Balombo **133** 12 21 S 14 46 E
Balonne —► **111** 28 47 S 147 56 E
Balrampur **79** 27 30N 82 20 E
Balranald **112** 34 38 S 143 33 E
Balş **50** 44 22N 24 5 E
Balsapuerto **172** 5 48 S 76 33W
Balsas **161** 18 0N 99 40W
Balsas —►, Goiás, Brazil **170** 9 58 S 47 52W
Balsas —►, Maranhão, Brazil **170** 7 15 S 44 35W
Balsas —►, Mexico **160** 17 55N 102 10W
Bålsta **52** 59 35N 17 30 E
Balsthal **28** 47 19N 7 41 E
Balston Spa **151** 43 0N 73 52W
Balta, Romania **50** 44 54N 22 38 E
Balta, U.S.A. **152** 48 12N 100 7W
Balta, R.S.F.S.R., U.S.S.R. **61** 42 58N 44 32 E
Balta, Ukraine S.S.R., U.S.S.R. **60** 48 2N 29 45 E
Baltanás **34** 41 56N 4 15W
Baltic Sea **55** 56 0N 20 0 E
Baltîm **124** 31 35N 31 10 E
Baltimore, Ireland **15** 51 29N 9 22W
Baltimore, U.S.A. **148** 39 18N 76 37W
Baltit **79** 36 15N 74 40 E
Baltrum **26** 53 43N 7 25 E
Baluchistan □ **77** 27 30N 65 0 E
Balud **90** 12 2N 123 12 E
Balurghat **79** 25 15N 88 44 E
Balygychan **65** 63 56N 154 12 E
Balzar **168** 2 2 S 79 54W
Bam **73** 29 7N 58 14 E
Bama, China **96** 24 8N 107 12 E
Bama, Nigeria **127** 11 33N 13 41 E
Bamako **126** 12 34N 7 55W
Bamba, Mali **127** 17 5N 1 24W
Bamba, Zaïre **133** 5 45 S 18 23 E
Bambam **90** 15 40N 120 20 E
Bambamarca **172** 6 36 S 78 32W
Bambang **90** 16 23N 121 6 E
Bambari **132** 5 40N 20 35 E
Bambaroo **110** 18 50 S 146 10 E
Bamberg, Germany **27** 49 54N 10 53 E
Bamberg, U.S.A. **149** 33 19N 81 1W
Bambesi **125** 9 45N 34 40 E
Bambey **126** 14 42N 16 28W
Bambili **130** 3 40N 26 0 E
Bambuí **171** 20 1 S 45 58W
Bamenda **127** 5 57N 10 11 E
Bamfield **144** 48 45N 125 10W
Bāmīān □ **77** 35 0N 67 0 E
Bamiancheng **95** 43 15N 124 2 E
Bamingui **132** 7 34N 20 11 E
Bamkin **127** 6 3N 11 27 E
Bampūr **73** 27 15N 60 21 E
Ban Aranyaprathet **84** 13 41N 102 30 E
Ban Ban **84** 19 31N 103 30 E
Ban Bang Hin **85** 9 32N 98 35 E
Ban Chiang Klang **84** 19 25N 100 55 E
Ban Chik **84** 17 15N 102 22 E
Ban Choho **84** 15 2N 102 9 E
Ban Dan Lan Hoi **84** 17 0N 99 35 E
Ban Don = Surat Thani **85** 9 6N 99 20 E
Ban Don **84** 12 53N 107 48 E
Ban Don, Ao **85** 9 20N 99 25 E
Ban Dong **84** 19 30N 100 59 E
Ban Hong **84** 18 18N 98 50 E
Ban Kaeng **84** 17 29N 100 7 E
Ban Keun **84** 18 22N 102 35 E
Ban Khai **84** 12 46N 101 18 E
Ban Kheun **84** 20 13N 101 7 E
Ban Khlong Kua **85** 6 57N 100 8 E
Ban Khuan Mao **85** 7 50N 99 37 E
Ban Khun Yuam **84** 18 49N 97 57 E
Ban Ko Yai Chim **85** 11 17N 99 26 E
Ban Kok **84** 16 40N 103 40 E
Ban Laem **84** 13 13N 99 59 E
Ban Lao Ngam **84** 15 28N 106 10 E
Ban Le Kathe **84** 15 49N 98 53 E
Ban Mae Chedi **84** 19 11N 99 31 E
Ban Mae Laeng **84** 20 1N 99 17 E
Ban Mae Sariang **84** 18 10N 97 56 E
Ban Mi **84** 15 3N 100 32 E
Ban Muong Mo **84** 19 4N 103 58 E
Ban Na Mo **84** 17 7N 105 40 E
Ban Na San **85** 8 53N 99 52 E
Ban Na Tong **84** 20 56N 101 47 E
Ban Nam Bac **84** 20 38N 102 20 E
Ban Nam Ma **84** 22 2N 101 37 E
Ban Ngang **84** 15 59N 106 11 E
Ban Nong Bok **84** 17 5N 104 48 E
Ban Nong Boua **84** 15 40N 106 33 E
Ban Nong Pling **84** 15 40N 100 10 E
Ban Pak Chan **85** 10 32N 98 51 E
Ban Phai **84** 16 4N 102 44 E
Ban Pong **84** 13 50N 99 55 E
Ban Ron Phibun **85** 8 9N 99 51 E
Ban Sanam Chai **85** 7 33N 100 25 E
Ban Sangkha **84** 14 37N 103 52 E
Ban Tak **84** 17 2N 99 4 E
Ban Tako **84** 14 5N 102 40 E
Ban Tha Dua **84** 17 59N 98 39 E
Ban Tha Li **84** 17 37N 101 25 E
Ban Tha Nun **85** 8 12N 98 18 E
Ban Thahine **84** 14 12N 105 33 E
Ban Xien Kok **84** 20 54N 100 39 E
Ban Yen Nhan **84** 20 57N 106 2 E
Baña, Punta de la **36** 40 33N 0 40 E
Banā, W. —► **74** 13 3N 45 24 E
Banaba **104** 0 45 S 169 50 E
Banalia **130** 1 32N 25 5 E
Banam **85** 11 20N 105 17 E
Banamba **126** 13 29N 7 22W
Banana **110** 24 28 S 150 8 E
Bananal, I. do **171** 11 30 S 50 30W
Banaras = Varanasi **79** 25 22N 83 0 E
Banas —►, Gujarat, India **78** 23 45N 71 25 E
Banas —►, Mad. P., India **79** 24 15N 81 30 E
Bânâs, Ras **124** 23 57N 35 50 E
Banbān **72** 25 1N 46 35 E
Banbridge **15** 54 21N 6 17W
Banbridge □ **15** 54 21N 6 16W
Banbury **13** 52 4N 1 21W
Banchory **14** 57 3N 2 30W
Bancroft **142** 45 3N 77 51W
Band **50** 46 30N 24 25 E
Band Boni **73** 25 30N 59 33 E
Band-e Torkestān **77** 35 30N 64 0 E
Band Qīr **73** 31 39N 48 53 E
Banda, Cameroon **132** 3 58N 14 32 E
Banda, India **79** 25 30N 80 26 E
Banda, Kepulauan **87** 4 37 S 129 50 E
Banda, La **174** 27 45 S 64 10W
Banda Aceh **88** 5 35N 95 20 E
Banda Banda, Mt. **111** 31 10 S 152 28 E
Banda Elat **87** 5 40 S 133 5 E
Banda Sea **87** 6 0 S 130 0 E
Bandai-San **98** 37 36N 140 4 E
Bandama —► **126** 6 32N 5 30W
Bandān **73** 31 23N 60 44 E
Bandanaira **87** 4 32 S 129 54 E
Bandanwara **78** 26 9N 74 38 E
Bandar = Machilipatnam **81** 16 12N 81 8 E
Bandār 'Abbās **73** 27 15N 56 15 E
Bandar-e Anzalī **73** 37 30N 49 30 E
Bandar-e Chārak **73** 26 45N 54 20 E
Bandar-e Deylam **73** 30 5N 50 10 E
Bandar-e Khomeyni **73** 30 30N 49 5 E
Bandar-e Lengeh **73** 26 35N 54 58 E
Bandar-e Maqām **73** 26 56N 53 29 E
Bandar-e Ma'shur **73** 30 35N 49 10 E
Bandar-e Nakhīlū **73** 26 58N 53 30 E
Bandar-e Rīg **73** 29 29N 50 38 E
Bandar-e Torkeman **73** 37 0N 54 10 E
Bandar Maharani = Muar **85** 2 3N 102 34 E
Bandar Penggaram = Batu Pahat **85** 1 50N 102 56 E
Bandar Seri Begawan **86** 4 52N 115 0 E
Bandawe **131** 11 58 S 34 5 E
Bande, Belgium **23** 50 10N 5 25 E
Bande, Spain **34** 42 3N 7 58W
Bandeira, Pico da **171** 20 26 S 41 47W
Bandeirante **171** 13 41 S 50 48W
Bandera, Argentina **174** 28 55 S 62 20W
Bandera, U.S.A. **153** 29 45N 99 3W
Banderas, B. de **160** 20 40N 105 30W
Bandia —► **80** 19 2N 80 28 E
Bandiagara **126** 14 12N 3 29W
Bandırma **57** 40 20N 28 0 E
Bandon **15** 51 44N 8 45W
Bandon —► **15** 51 40N 8 41W
Bandoua **132** 4 39N 21 42 E
Bandula **131** 19 0 S 33 7 E
Bandundu **132** 3 15 S 17 22 E
Bandung **89** 6 54 S 107 36 E
Bandya **109** 27 40 S 122 5 E
Băneasa **50** 45 56N 27 55 E
Bāneh **72** 35 59N 45 53 E
Bañeres **37** 38 44N 0 38W
Banes **163** 21 0N 75 42W
Bañeza, La **34** 42 17N 5 54W
Banff, Canada **144** 51 10N 115 34W
Banff, U.K. **14** 57 40N 2 32W
Banff Nat. Park **144** 51 30N 116 15W
Banfora **126** 10 40N 4 40W
Bang Fai —► **84** 16 57N 104 45 E
Bang Hieng —► **84** 16 10N 105 10 E
Bang Krathum **84** 16 34N 100 18 E
Bang Lamung **84** 13 3N 100 56 E
Bang Mun Nak **84** 16 2N 100 23 E
Bang Pa In **84** 14 14N 100 35 E
Bang Rakam **84** 16 45N 100 7 E
Bang Saphan **85** 11 14N 99 28 E
Bangala Dam **131** 21 7 S 31 25 E
Bangalore **81** 12 59N 77 40 E
Bangante **127** 5 8N 10 32 E
Bangaon **79** 23 0N 88 47 E
Bangassou **132** 4 55N 23 7 E
Bangeta, Mt. **107** 6 21 S 147 3 E
Banggai **87** 1 40 S 123 30 E
Banggi, P. **86** 7 17N 117 12 E
Banghāzī **122** 32 11N 20 3 E
Banghāzī □ **122** 32 7N 20 4 E
Bangil **89** 7 36 S 112 50 E
Bangjang **125** 11 23N 32 41 E
Bangka, Pulau, Sulawesi, Indonesia **88** 1 50N 125 5 E
Bangka, Pulau, Sumatera, Indonesia **86** 2 0 S 105 50 E
Bangka, Selat **88** 2 30 S 105 30 E
Bangkalan **89** 7 2 S 112 46 E
Bangkinang **88** 0 18N 101 5 E
Bangko **88** 2 5 S 102 9 E
Bangkok **84** 13 45N 100 35 E
Bangladesh ■ **82** 24 0N 90 0 E
Bangolo **126** 7 1N 7 29W
Bangor, N. Ireland, U.K. **15** 54 40N 5 40W
Bangor, Wales, U.K. **12** 53 13N 4 9W
Bangor, Maine, U.S.A. **143** 44 48N 68 42W
Bangor, Mich., U.S.A. **155** 42 18N 86 7W
Bangor, Pa., U.S.A. **151** 40 51N 75 13W
Bangu **132** 0 3S 19 12 E
Bangued **90** 17 40N 120 37 E
Bangui, C.A.R. **132** 4 23N 18 35 E
Bangui, Phil. **90** 18 32N 120 46 E
Banguru **130** 0 30N 27 10 E
Bangweulu, L. **131** 11 0 S 30 0 E
Bangweulu Swamp **131** 11 20 S 30 15 E
Bani, Dom. Rep. **163** 18 16N 70 22W
Bani, Phil. **90** 16 11N 119 52 E
Bani —► **126** 14 30N 4 12W
Bani, Djebel **120** 29 16N 8 0W
Bani Bangou **127** 15 3N 2 42 E
Banī Na'īm **69** 31 31N 35 10 E
Banī Sa'd **72** 33 34N 44 32 E
Banī Sār **74** 20 6N 41 27 E
Banī Suhaylah **69** 31 21N 34 19 E
Banī Walīd **122** 31 36N 13 53 E
Bania **126** 9 4N 3 6W
Baniara **107** 9 44 S 149 54 E
Banihal Pass **79** 33 30N 75 12 E
Banīnah **122** 32 0N 20 12 E
Bāniyās **70** 35 10N 36 0 E
Banja Luka **46** 44 49N 17 11 E
Banjar **89** 7 24 S 108 30 E
Banjarmasin **89** 3 20 S 114 35 E
Banjarnegara **89** 7 24 S 109 42 E
Banjul **126** 13 28N 16 40W
Banka Banka **110** 18 50 S 134 0 E
Bankeryd **53** 57 53N 14 6 E
Banket **131** 17 27 S 30 19 E
Bankilaré **127** 14 35N 0 44 E
Bankipore **79** 25 35N 85 10 E
Banks I., B.C., Canada **144** 53 20N 130 0W
Banks I., N.W.T., Canada **140** 73 15N 121 30W
Banks I., Papua N. G. **107** 10 10 S 142 15 E
Banks Pen. **115** 43 45 S 173 15 E
Banks Str. **110** 40 40 S 148 10 E
Bankura **79** 23 11N 87 18 E
Bankya **46** 42 43N 23 8 E
Bann —►, Down, U.K. **15** 54 30N 6 31W
Bann —►, Londonderry, U.K. **15** 55 10N 6 34W
Banna **90** 17 59N 120 39 E
Bannalec **18** 47 57N 3 42W
Bannang Sata **85** 6 16N 101 16 E
Bannerton **112** 34 42 S 142 47 E
Banning **159** 33 58N 116 52W
Banningville = Bandundu **132** 3 15 S 17 22 E
Bannockburn, Canada **150** 44 39N 77 33W
Bannockburn, U.K. **14** 56 5N 3 55W
Bannockburn, Zambia **131** 20 17 S 29 48 E
Bannu **77** 33 0N 70 18 E
Bañolas **36** 42 16N 2 44 E
Banon **21** 44 2N 5 38 E
Baños de la Encina **35** 38 10N 3 46W
Baños de Molgas **34** 42 15N 7 40W
Bánovce **31** 48 44N 18 16 E
Bansilan □ **91** 6 40N 121 40 E
Banská Bystrica **31** 48 46N 19 14 E
Banská Štiavnica **31** 48 25N 18 55 E
Bansko **47** 41 52N 23 28 E
Banswara **78** 23 32N 74 24 E
Bantayan **91** 11 10N 123 43 E
Bantayan I. **91** 11 13N 123 44 E
Banten **88** 6 5 S 106 8 E
Banton I. **90** 12 56N 122 4 E
Bantry **15** 51 40N 9 28W
Bantry, B. **15** 51 35N 9 50W
Bantul **89** 7 55 S 110 19 E
Bantva **78** 21 29N 70 12 E
Bantval **81** 12 55N 75 0 E
Banya **47** 42 33N 24 50 E
Banyak, Kepulauan **88** 2 10N 97 10 E
Banyo **127** 6 52N 11 45 E
Banyuls-sur-Mer **20** 42 28N 3 8 E
Banyumas **87** 7 32 S 109 18 E
Banyuwangi **89** 8 13 S 114 21 E
Banzare Coast **7** 68 0 S 125 0 E
Banzyville = Mobayi **132** 4 15N 21 8 E
Bao Ha **84** 22 11N 104 21 E
Bao Lac **84** 22 57N 105 40 E
Bao Loc **85** 11 32N 107 48 E
Bao'an **97** 22 27N 114 10 E
Baocheng **94** 33 12N 106 56 E
Baode **94** 39 1N 111 5 E
Baodi **95** 39 38N 117 20 E
Baoding **94** 38 50N 115 28 E
Baoji **94** 34 20N 107 5 E
Baojing **96** 28 45N 109 41 E
Baokang **97** 31 54N 111 12 E
Baoro **132** 5 40N 15 58 E
Baoshan, Shanghai, China **97** 31 27N 121 26 E
Baoshan, Yunnan, China **96** 25 10N 99 5 E
Baotou **94** 40 32N 110 2 E
Baoying **95** 33 17N 119 20 E
Bap **78** 27 23N 72 18 E
Bapatla **81** 15 55N 80 30 E
Bapaume **19** 50 7N 2 50 E
Bāqa el Gharbīyya **69** 32 25N 35 2 E
Bāqerābād **73** 33 2N 51 58 E
Ba'qūbah **72** 33 45N 44 50 E
Baquedano **174** 23 20 S 69 52W
Bar, U.S.S.R. **60** 49 4N 27 40 E
Bar, Yugoslavia **46** 42 8N 19 8 E
Bar Bigha **79** 25 21N 85 47 E
Bar Harbor **143** 44 15N 68 20W
Bar-le-Duc **19** 48 47N 5 10 E
Bar-sur-Aube **19** 48 14N 4 40 E
Bar-sur-Seine **19** 48 7N 4 20 E
Barabai **89** 2 32 S 115 34 E
Barabinsk **64** 55 20N 78 20 E
Baraboo **152** 43 28N 89 46W
Baracoa **163** 20 20N 74 30W
Baradero **174** 33 52 S 59 29W
Baradine **113** 30 56 S 149 4 E
Baraga **152** 46 49N 88 29W
Barahona, Dom. Rep. **163** 18 13N 71 7W
Barahona, Spain **36** 41 17N 2 39W
Baraka —► **124** 18 13N 37 35 E
Barakot **79** 21 33N 84 59 E
Barakpur **79** 22 44N 88 30 E
Barakula **111** 26 30 S 150 33 E
Baralaba **110** 24 13 S 149 50 E
Baralzon L. **145** 60 0N 98 3W
Baramati **80** 18 11N 74 33 E
Baramba **79** 20 25N 85 23 E
Barameiya **124** 18 32N 36 38 E
Baramula **79** 34 15N 74 20 E
Baran **78** 25 9N 76 40 E
Baranoa **168** 10 48N 74 55W
Baranof I. **140** 57 0N 135 10W
Baranovichi **58** 53 10N 26 0 E

Baranów Sandomierski

Baranów Sandomierski **32** 50 29N 21 30 E
Baranya □ **31** 46 0N 18 15 E
Barão de Cocais **171** 19 56 S 43 28W
Barão de Grajaú **170** 6 45 S 43 1W
Barão de Melgaço, Mato Grosso, Brazil **173** 16 14 S 55 52W
Barão de Melgaço, Rondônia, Brazil **173** 11 50 S 60 45W
Baraolt **50** 46 5N 25 34 E
Barapasi **87** 2 15 S 137 5 E
Barapina **107** 6 21 S 155 25 E
Barasat **79** 22 46N 88 31 E
Barat Daya, Kepulauan **87** 7 30 S 128 0 E
Barataria B. **153** 29 15N 89 45W
Baraut **78** 29 13N 77 7 E
Baraya **168** 3 10N 75 4W
Barbacan **91** 10 20N 119 21 E
Barbacena **171** 21 15 S 43 56W
Barbacoas, Colombia **168** 1 45N 78 0W
Barbacoas, Venezuela **168** 9 29N 66 58W
Barbados ■ **163** 13 0N 59 30W
Barbalha **170** 7 19 S 39 17W
Barban **43** 45 5N 14 4 E
Barbastro **36** 42 2N 0 5 E
Barbate **35** 36 13N 5 56W
Barbaza **91** 11 12N 122 2 E
Barberino di Mugello **43** 44 1N 11 15 E
Barberton, S. Africa **135** 25 42 S 31 2 E
Barberton, U.S.A. **150** 41 0N 81 40W
Barbezieux **20** 45 28N 0 9W
Barbosa **168** 5 57N 73 37W
Barbourville **149** 36 57N 83 52W
Barbuda I. **163** 17 30N 61 40W
Barca, La **160** 20 20N 102 40W
Barcaldine **110** 23 43 S 145 6 E
Barcarès, Le **20** 42 47N 3 2 E
Barcarrota **35** 38 31N 6 51W
Barcellona Pozzo di Gotto **45** 38 8N 15 15 E
Barcelona, Spain **36** 41 21N 2 10 E
Barcelona, Venezuela **169** 10 10N 64 40W
Barcelona □ **36** 41 30N 2 0 E
Barcelonette **21** 44 23N 6 40 E
Barcelos **169** 1 0 S 63 0W
Barcin **32** 52 52N 17 55 E
Barcoo → **110** 25 30 S 142 50 E
Barcs **31** 45 58N 17 28 E
Barczewo **32** 53 50N 20 42 E
Barda **61** 40 25N 47 10 E
Barda del Medio **176** 38 45 S 68 11W
Bardai **123** 21 25N 17 0 E
Bardas Blancas **174** 35 49 S 69 45W
Barddhaman **79** 23 14N 87 39 E
Bardejov **31** 49 18N 21 15 E
Bardera **136** 2 20N 42 27 E
Bardi **42** 44 38N 9 43 E
Bardia **122** 31 45N 25 0 E
Bardo **32** 50 31N 16 42 E
Bardoli **78** 21 12N 73 5 E
Bardolino **42** 45 33N 10 43 E
Bardsey I. **12** 52 46N 4 47W
Bardstown **155** 37 50N 85 29W
Bareilly **79** 28 22N 79 27 E
Barellan **113** 34 16 S 146 24 E
Barentin **18** 49 33N 0 58 E
Barenton **18** 48 38N 0 50W
Barents Sea **6** 73 0N 39 0 E
Barentu **125** 15 2N 37 35 E
Barfleur **18** 49 40N 1 17W
Barfleur, Pte. de **18** 49 42N 1 16W
Barga **42** 44 5N 10 30 E
Bargal **136** 11 25N 51 0 E
Bargara **110** 24 50 S 152 25 E
Barge **42** 44 43N 7 19 E
Barge, La **156** 42 12N 110 4W
Bargnop **125** 9 32N 28 25 E
Bargo **113** 34 18 S 150 35 E
Bargteheide **26** 53 42N 10 13 E
Barguzin **65** 53 37N 109 37 E
Barh **79** 25 29N 85 46 E
Barhaj **79** 26 18N 83 44 E
Barhi **79** 24 15N 85 25 E
Bari, India **78** 26 39N 77 39 E
Bari, Italy **45** 41 6N 16 52 E
Bari Doab **78** 30 20N 73 0 E
Bariadi □ **130** 2 45 S 34 40 E
Barīm **74** 12 39N 43 25 E
Barima → **169** 8 33N 60 25W
Barinas **168** 8 36N 70 15W
Barinas □ **168** 8 10N 69 50W
Baring **154** 40 15N 92 12W
Baring, C. **140** 70 0N 117 30W
Baringa **132** 0 45N 20 52 E
Baringo **130** 0 47N 36 16 E
Baringo □ **130** 0 55N 36 0 E
Baringo, L. **130** 0 47N 36 16 E
Barinitas **168** 8 45N 70 25W
Baripada **79** 21 57N 86 45 E
Bariri **171** 22 4 S 48 44W
Bârîs **124** 24 42N 30 31 E
Barisal **82** 22 45N 90 20 E
Barisan, Bukit **86** 3 30 S 102 15 E
Barito → **86** 4 0 S 114 50 E
Barjac **21** 44 20N 4 22 E
Barjols **21** 43 34N 6 2 E
Barjūj, Wadi → **122** 25 26N 12 12 E
Bark L. **150** 45 27N 77 51W
Barka = Baraka → **124** 18 13N 37 35 E
Barkam **96** 31 51N 102 28 E
Barker **150** 43 20N 78 35W
Barkley Sound **144** 48 50N 125 10W
Barkly Downs **110** 20 30 S 138 30 E
Barkly East **134** 30 58 S 27 33 E
Barkly Tableland **110** 17 50 S 136 40 E
Barkly West **134** 28 5 S 24 31 E
Barkol **92** 43 37N 93 2 E
Barkol, Wadi → **124** 17 40N 32 0 E
Barksdale **153** 29 47N 100 2W
Barlee, L. **109** 29 15 S 119 30 E
Barletta **45** 41 20N 16 17 E
Barlinek **32** 53 0N 15 15 E
Barlovento **37** 28 48N 17 48W
Barlow L. **145** 62 0N 103 0W
Barmedman **113** 34 9 S 147 21 E
Barmer **78** 25 45N 71 20 E
Barmera **112** 34 15 S 140 28 E
Barmouth **12** 52 44N 4 3W
Barmstedt **26** 53 47N 9 46 E
Barnagar **78** 23 7N 75 19 E
Barnard Castle **12** 54 33N 1 55W
Barnato **113** 31 38 S 145 0 E
Barnaul **64** 53 20N 83 40 E
Barnesville **149** 33 6N 84 9W
Barnet **13** 51 37N 0 15W
Barneveld, Neth. **22** 52 7N 5 36 E
Barneveld, U.S.A. **151** 43 16N 75 14W
Barneville-Cartevert **18** 49 23N 1 46W
Barngo **110** 25 3 S 147 20 E
Barnhart **153** 31 10N 101 8W
Barnsley **12** 53 33N 1 29W
Barnstaple **13** 51 5N 4 3W
Barnsville **152** 46 43N 96 28W
Baro **127** 8 35N 6 18 E
Baro → **125** 8 26N 33 13 E
Baroda = Vadodara **78** 22 20N 73 10 E
Baroda **78** 25 29N 76 35 E
Baroe **134** 33 13 S 24 33 E
Baron Ra. **108** 23 30 S 127 45 E
Barpali **79** 21 11N 83 35 E
Barpathar **82** 26 17N 93 53 E
Barpeta **82** 26 20N 91 10 E
Barqin **122** 27 33N 13 34 E
Barques, Pte. aux **148** 44 5N 82 55W
Barquinha **35** 39 28N 8 25W
Barquísimeto **168** 10 4N 69 19W
Barr **19** 48 25N 7 28 E
Barra, Brazil **170** 11 5 S 43 10W
Barra, U.K. **14** 57 0N 7 30W
Barra, Sd. of **14** 57 4N 7 25W
Barra da Estiva **171** 13 38 S 41 19W
Barra de Navidad **160** 19 12N 104 41W
Barra do Corda **170** 5 30 S 45 10W
Barra do Dande **133** 8 28 S 13 22 E
Barra do Mendes **171** 11 43 S 42 4W
Barra do Piraí **171** 22 30 S 43 50W
Barra Falsa, Pta. da **135** 22 58 S 35 37 E
Barra Hd. **14** 56 47N 7 40W
Barra Mansa **175** 22 35 S 44 12W
Barraba **111** 30 21 S 150 35 E
Barracão do Barreto **173** 8 48 S 58 24W
Barrackpur = Barakpur **79** 22 44N 88 30 E
Barrafranca **45** 37 22N 14 10 E
Barranca, Lima, Peru **172** 10 45 S 77 50W
Barranca, Loreto, Peru **168** 4 50 S 76 50W
Barrancabermeja **168** 7 0N 73 50W
Barrancas, Colombia **168** 10 57N 72 50W
Barrancas, Venezuela **169** 8 55N 62 5W
Barrancos **35** 38 10N 6 58W
Barranqueras **174** 27 30 S 59 0W
Barranquilla **168** 11 0N 74 50W
Barras, Brazil **170** 4 15 S 42 18W
Barras, Colombia **168** 1 45 S 73 13W
Barraute **142** 48 26N 77 38W
Barre **151** 44 15N 72 30W
Barre do Bugres **173** 15 0 S 57 11W
Barreal **174** 31 33 S 69 28W
Barrei **136** 6 10N 42 49 E
Barreiras **171** 12 8 S 45 0W
Barreirinha **169** 2 47 S 57 3W
Barreirinhas **170** 2 30 S 42 50W
Barreiro **35** 38 40N 9 6W
Barreiros **170** 8 49 S 35 12W
Barrême **21** 43 57N 6 23 E
Barren, Nosy **135** 18 25 S 43 40 E
Barretos **171** 20 30 S 48 35W
Barrhead **144** 54 10N 114 24W
Barrie **142** 44 24N 79 40W
Barrier, C. **114** 36 25 S 175 32 E
Barrier Ra., Australia **112** 31 0 S 141 30 E
Barrier Ra., N.Z. **115** 44 5 S 169 42 E
Barrière **144** 51 12N 120 7W
Barrington **151** 41 43N 71 20W
Barrington L. **145** 56 55N 100 15W
Barrington Tops **111** 32 6 S 151 28 E
Barringun **111** 29 1 S 145 41 E
Barro do Garças **173** 15 54 S 52 16W
Barrow **140** 71 16N 156 50W
Barrow → **15** 52 10N 6 57W
Barrow Creek **110** 21 30 S 133 55 E
Barrow I. **108** 20 45 S 115 20 E
Barrow-in-Furness **12** 54 8N 3 15W
Barrow Pt. **110** 14 20 S 144 40 E
Barrow Ra. **109** 26 0 S 127 40 E
Barrow Str. **6** 74 20N 95 0W
Barruecopardo **34** 41 4N 6 40W
Barruelo **34** 42 54N 4 17W
Barry, U.K. **13** 51 23N 3 19W
Barry, U.S.A. **154** 39 42N 91 2W
Barry's Bay **142** 45 29N 77 41W
Barsalogho **127** 13 25N 1 3W
Barsat **79** 36 10N 72 45 E
Barsham **72** 35 21N 40 33 E
Barsi **80** 18 10N 75 50 E
Barsø **53** 55 7N 9 33 E
Barstow, Calif., U.S.A. **159** 34 58N 117 2W
Barstow, Tex., U.S.A. **153** 31 28N 103 24W
Barth **26** 54 20N 12 36 E
Barthélemy, Col **84** 19 26N 104 6 E
Bartica **169** 6 25N 58 40W
Bartlesville **153** 36 50N 95 58W
Bartlett, Calif., U.S.A. **158** 36 29N 118 2W
Bartlett, Tex., U.S.A. **153** 30 46N 97 30W
Bartlett, L. **144** 63 5N 118 20W
Bartolomeu Dias **131** 21 10 S 35 8 E
Barton, Australia **109** 30 31 S 132 39 E
Barton, Phil. **91** 10 24N 119 8 E
Barton-upon-Humber **12** 53 41N 0 27W
Bartonville **154** 40 39N 89 39W
Bartoszyce **32** 54 15N 20 55 E
Bartow **149** 27 53N 81 49W
Barú, I. de **168** 10 15N 75 35W
Barú, Volcan **162** 8 55N 82 35W
Barumba **130** 1 3N 23 37 E
Baruth **26** 52 3N 13 31 E
Barvaux **23** 50 21N 5 29 E
Barvenkovo **60** 48 57N 37 0 E
Barwani **78** 22 2N 74 57 E
Barycz → **32** 51 42N 16 15 E
Barysh **59** 53 39N 47 8 E
Barzān **72** 36 55N 44 3 E
Bas-Rhin □ **19** 48 40N 7 30 E
Bašaid **46** 45 38N 20 25 E
Bāsa'idū **73** 26 35N 55 20 E
Basal **78** 33 33N 72 13 E
Basankusa **132** 1 5N 19 50 E
Basawa **78** 34 15N 70 50 E
Bascharage **23** 49 34N 5 55 E
Basco **90** 20 27N 121 58 E
Bascuñán, C. **174** 28 52 S 71 35W
Basècles **23** 50 32N 3 39 E
Basel **28** 47 35N 7 35 E
Basel-Stadt □ **28** 47 35N 7 35 E
Baselland □ **28** 47 26N 7 45 E
Basento → **45** 40 21N 16 50 E
Basey **91** 11 17N 125 4 E
Bāshī **73** 28 41N 51 4 E
Bashkir A.S.S.R. □ **62** 54 0N 57 0 E
Basilaki I. **107** 10 35 S 151 0 E
Basilan **91** 6 35N 122 0 E
Basilan □ **91** 6 33N 122 4 E
Basilan Str. **91** 6 50N 122 0 E
Basildon **13** 51 34N 0 29 E
Basilicata □ **45** 40 30N 16 0 E
Basim = Washim **80** 20 3N 77 0 E
Basin **156** 44 22N 108 2W
Basingstoke **13** 51 15N 1 5W
Basirhat **82** 22 40N 88 54 E
Baška **43** 44 58N 14 45 E
Baskatong, Rés. **142** 46 46N 75 50W
Basle = Basel **28** 47 35N 7 35 E
Basmat **80** 19 15N 77 12 E
Basoda **78** 23 52N 77 54 E
Basodino **29** 46 25N 8 28 E
Basoka **130** 1 16N 23 40 E
Basongo **133** 4 15 S 20 20 E
Basque, Pays **20** 43 15N 1 20W
Basque Provinces = Vascongadas □ **36** 42 50N 2 45W
Basra = Al Başrah **72** 30 30N 47 50 E
Bass Rock **14** 56 5N 2 40W
Bass Str. **110** 39 15 S 146 30 E
Bassano **144** 50 48N 112 20W
Bassano del Grappa **43** 45 45N 11 45 E
Bassar **127** 9 19N 0 57 E
Basse Santa-Su **126** 13 13N 14 15W
Basse-Terre **163** 16 0N 61 40W
Bassecourt **28** 47 20N 7 15 E
Bassée, La **19** 50 31N 2 49 E
Bassein, Burma **82** 16 45N 94 30 E
Bassein, India **80** 19 26N 72 48 E
Basseterre **163** 17 17N 62 43W
Bassett, Nebr., U.S.A. **152** 42 37N 99 30W
Bassett, Va., U.S.A. **149** 36 48N 79 59W
Bassevelde **23** 51 15N 3 41 E
Bassi **78** 30 44N 76 21 E
Bassigny **19** 48 0N 5 30 E
Bassikounou **126** 15 55N 6 1W
Bassilly **23** 50 40N 3 56 E
Bassum **26** 52 50N 8 42 E
Båstad **53** 56 25N 12 51 E
Bastak **73** 27 15N 54 25 E
Baştām **73** 36 29N 55 4 E
Bastar **80** 19 15N 81 40 E
Bastelica **21** 42 1N 9 3 E
Basti **79** 26 52N 82 55 E
Bastia **21** 42 40N 9 30 E
Bastia Umbra **43** 43 4N 12 34 E
Bastide-Puylaurent, La **20** 44 35N 3 55 E
Bastogne **23** 50 1N 5 43 E
Bastrop **153** 30 5N 97 22W
Basyanovskiy **62** 58 19N 60 44 E
Bat Yam **69** 32 2N 34 44 E
Bata, Eq. Guin. **132** 1 57N 9 50 E
Bata, Romania **50** 46 1N 22 4 E
Bataan **90** 14 40N 120 25 E
Batabanó **162** 22 40N 82 20W
Batabanó, G. de **162** 22 30N 82 30W
Batac **90** 18 3N 120 34 E
Batagoy **65** 67 38N 134 38 E
Batak **47** 41 57N 24 12 E
Batalha **35** 39 40N 8 50W
Batam **88** 1 5N 104 3 E
Batama **130** 0 58N 26 33 E
Batamay **65** 63 30N 129 15 E
Batamshinskiy **62** 50 36N 58 16 E
Batan I. **90** 20 30N 121 50 E
Batanes □ **90** 20 40N 121 55 E
Batanes Is. **90** 20 30N 121 50 E
Batang, China **96** 30 1N 99 0 E
Batang, Indonesia **89** 6 55 S 109 45 E
Batangafo **132** 7 25N 18 20 E
Batangas **90** 13 35N 121 10 E
Batangas □ **90** 13 15N 121 5 E
Batanghari **88** 1 36 S 103 37 E
Batanta **87** 0 55 S 130 40 E
Batas **91** 11 10N 119 37 E
Batas I. **91** 11 10N 119 36 E
Batatais **175** 20 54 S 47 37W
Batavia, Ind., U.S.A. **155** 41 55N 88 17W
Batavia, N.Y., U.S.A. **150** 43 0N 78 10W
Batavia, Ohio, U.S.A. **155** 39 5N 84 11W
Bataysk **61** 47 3N 39 45 E
Batchelor **108** 13 4 S 131 1 E
Batéké, Plateau **132** 3 30 S 15 45 E
Bateman's B. **113** 35 40 S 150 12 E
Batemans Bay **113** 35 44 S 150 11 E
Batesburg **149** 33 54N 81 32W
Batesville, Ark., U.S.A. **153** 35 48N 91 40W
Batesville, Ind., U.S.A. **155** 39 18N 85 13W
Batesville, Miss., U.S.A. **153** 34 17N 89 58W
Batesville, Tex., U.S.A. **153** 28 59N 99 38W
Bath, U.K. **13** 51 22N 2 22W
Bath, Maine, U.S.A. **143** 43 50N 69 49W
Bath, N.Y., U.S.A. **150** 42 20N 77 17W
Batheay **85** 11 59N 104 57 E
Bathgate **14** 55 54N 3 38W
Bathmen **22** 52 15N 6 29 E
Bathurst = Banjul **126** 13 28N 16 40W
Bathurst, Australia **113** 33 25 S 149 31 E
Bathurst, Canada **143** 47 37N 65 43W
Bathurst, S. Africa **134** 33 30 S 26 50 E
Bathurst, C. **140** 70 34N 128 0W
Bathurst B. **110** 14 16 S 144 25 E
Bathurst Harb. **110** 43 15 S 146 10 E
Bathurst I., Australia **108** 11 30 S 130 10 E
Bathurst I., Canada **6** 76 0N 100 30W
Bathurst Inlet **140** 66 50N 108 1W
Batie **126** 9 53N 2 53W
Batlow **113** 35 31 S 148 9 E
Batna **121** 35 34N 6 15 E
Bato, Leyte, Phil. **91** 10 13N 124 48 E
Bato, Sulu, Phil. **91** 5 15N 120 3 E
Bato Bato **91** 5 6N 119 49 E
Batoala **132** 0 48N 13 27 E
Batobato **91** 6 50N 126 5 E
Batočina **46** 44 7N 21 5 E
Batoka **131** 16 45 S 27 15 E
Baton Rouge **153** 30 30N 91 5W
Batong, Ko **85** 6 32N 99 12 E
Bátonyterenye **31** 48 3N 19 50 E
Batopilas **160** 27 0N 107 45W
Batouri **132** 4 30N 14 25 E
Battambang **84** 13 7N 103 12 E
Batticaloa **81** 7 43N 81 45 E
Battice **23** 50 39N 5 50 E
Battipáglia **45** 40 38N 15 0 E
Battīr **69** 31 44N 35 8 E
Battle **13** 50 55N 0 30 E
Battle → **145** 52 43N 108 15W
Battle Camp **110** 15 20 S 144 40 E
Battle Creek **155** 42 20N 85 6W
Battle Ground **158** 45 47N 122 32W
Battle Harbour **143** 52 16N 55 35W
Battle Lake **152** 46 20N 95 43W
Battle Mountain **156** 40 45N 117 0W
Battlefields **131** 18 37 S 29 47 E
Battleford **145** 52 45N 108 15W
Battonya **31** 46 16N 21 3 E
Batu **125** 6 55N 39 45 E
Batu, Kepulauan **88** 0 30 S 98 25 E
Batu Caves **85** 3 15N 101 40 E
Batu Gajah **85** 4 28N 101 3 E
Batu Pahat **85** 1 50N 102 56 E
Batuata **87** 6 12 S 122 42 E
Batulaki **91** 5 34N 125 19 E
Batumi **61** 41 30N 41 30 E
Baturaja **88** 4 11 S 104 15 E
Baturité **170** 4 28 S 38 45W
Batusangkar **88** 0 27 S 100 35 E
Bau **86** 1 25N 110 9 E
Bauang **90** 16 31N 120 20 E
Baubau **87** 5 25 S 122 38 E
Bauchi **127** 10 22N 9 48 E
Bauchi □ **127** 10 30N 10 0 E
Baud **18** 47 52N 3 1W
Baudette **152** 48 46N 94 35W
Baudour **23** 50 29N 3 50 E
Bauer, C. **111** 32 44 S 134 4 E
Baugé **18** 47 31N 0 8W
Bauhinia Downs **110** 24 35 S 149 18 E
Baule, La **18** 47 17N 2 24W
Bauma **29** 47 23N 8 53 E
Baume-les-Dames **19** 47 22N 6 22 E
Baunatal **26** 51 13N 9 25 E
Baunei **44** 40 2N 9 41 E
Baures **173** 13 35 S 63 35W

Bellefontaine

Bauru 175 22 10 S 49 0W
Baús 173 18 22 S 52 47W
Bauska 58 56 24N 25 15 E
Bautzen 26 51 11N 14 25 E
Baux-de-Provence, Les 21 43 45N 4 51 E
Bavānāt 73 30 28N 53 27 E
Bavanište 46 44 49N 20 53 E
Bavaria = Bayern □ 27 49 7N 11 30 E
Båven 52 59 0N 16 56 E
Bavi Sadri 78 24 28N 74 30 E
Bavispe → 160 29 30N 109 11W
Bawdwin 82 23 5N 97 20 E
Bawean 89 5 46 S 112 35 E
Bawku 127 11 3N 0 19W
Bawlake 82 19 11N 97 21 E
Bawolung 96 28 50N 101 16 E
Baxley 149 31 43N 82 23W
Baxoi 96 30 1N 96 50 E
Baxter 154 41 49N 93 9W
Baxter Springs 153 37 3N 94 45W
Bay, L. de 87 14 20N 121 11 E
Bay Bulls 143 47 19N 52 50W
Bay City, Mich., U.S.A. 148 43 35N 83 51W
Bay City, Oreg., U.S.A. 156 45 45N 123 58W
Bay City, Tex., U.S.A. 153 28 59N 95 55W
Bay de Verde 143 48 5N 52 54W
Bay Minette 149 30 54N 87 43W
Bay St. Louis 153 30 18N 89 22W
Bay Springs 153 31 58N 89 18W
Bay View 114 39 25 S 176 50 E
Baya 131 11 53 S 27 25 E
Bayambang 90 15 49N 120 27 E
Bayamo 162 20 20N 76 40W
Bayamón 163 18 24N 66 10W
Bayan Har Shan 92 34 0N 98 0 E
Bayan Hot = Alxa Zuoqi 94 38 50N 105 40 E
Bayan Obo 94 41 52N 109 59 E
Bayan-Ovoo 94 42 55N 106 5 E
Bayana 78 26 55N 77 18 E
Bayanaul 64 50 45N 75 45 E
Bayandalay 94 43 30N 103 29 E
Bayard 152 41 48N 103 17W
Bayawan 91 9 46N 122 45 E
Baybay 91 10 40N 124 55 E
Bayerischer Wald 27 49 0N 13 0 E
Bayern □ 27 49 7N 11 30 E
Bayeux 18 49 17N 0 42W
Bayfield, Canada 150 43 34N 81 42W
Bayfield, U.S.A. 152 46 50N 90 48W
Bayḩān al Qiṣāb 74 15 48N 45 44 E
Baykadam 63 43 48N 69 58 E
Baykal, Oz. 65 53 0N 108 0 E
Baykit 65 61 50N 95 50 E
Baykonur 64 47 48N 65 50 E
Baymak 62 52 36N 58 19 E
Baynes Mts. 134 17 15 S 13 0 E
Bayombong 90 16 30N 121 10 E
Bayon 19 48 30N 6 20 E
Bayona 34 42 6N 8 52W
Bayonne, France 20 43 30N 1 28W
Bayonne, U.S.A. 151 40 41N 74 7W
Bayovar 172 5 50 S 81 0W
Bayram-Ali 64 37 37N 62 10 E
Bayreuth 27 49 56N 11 35 E
Bayrischzell 27 47 39N 12 1 E
Bayrūt 70 33 53N 35 31 E
Baysun 63 38 12N 67 12 E
Bayt al Faqīh 74 14 31N 43 19 E
Bayt Awlá 69 31 37N 35 2 E
Bayt Fajjār 69 31 38N 35 9 E
Bayt Fūrīk 69 32 11N 35 20 E
Bayt Ḩānūn 69 31 32N 34 32 E
Bayt Jālā 69 31 43N 35 11 E
Bayt Lahm 69 31 43N 35 12 E
Bayt Rīma 69 32 2N 35 6 E
Bayt Sāḩūr 69 31 42N 35 13 E
Bayt Ummar 69 31 38N 35 7 E
Bayt 'ūr al Taḩtā 69 31 54N 35 5 E
Baytīn 69 31 56N 35 14 E
Baytown 153 29 42N 94 57W
Baytūniyā 69 31 54N 35 10 E
Bayyā'iyah al Kabīrah 70 35 44N 37 6 E
Bayzhansay 63 43 14N 69 54 E
Bayzo 127 13 52N 4 35 E
Baza 37 37 30N 2 47W
Bazar Dyuzi 61 41 12N 47 50 E
Bazarny Karabulak 59 52 15N 46 20 E
Bazarnyy Syzgan 59 53 45N 46 40 E
Bazartobe 61 49 26N 51 45 E
Bazaruto, I. do 135 21 40 S 35 28 E
Bazas 20 44 27N 0 13W
Bazhong 96 31 52N 106 46 E
Bazmān, Kūh-e 73 28 4N 60 1 E
Beabula 113 34 26 S 145 9 E
Beach 152 46 57N 103 58W
Beach City 150 40 38N 81 35W
Beachport 112 37 29 S 140 0 E
Beachy Head 13 50 44N 0 16 E
Beacon, Australia 109 30 26 S 117 52 E
Beacon, U.S.A. 151 41 32N 73 58W
Beaconia 145 50 25N 96 31W
Beagle, Canal 176 55 0 S 68 30W
Beagle Bay 108 16 58 S 122 40 E
Bealanana 135 14 33N 48 44 E
Beamsville 150 43 12N 79 28W
Bear → 158 38 56N 121 36W
Béar, C. 20 42 31N 3 8 E
Bear I. 15 51 38N 9 50W
Bear L., B.C., Canada 144 56 10N 126 52W
Bear L., Man., Canada 145 55 8N 96 0W
Bear L., U.S.A. 156 42 0N 111 20W
Bearcreek 156 45 11N 109 6W
Beardmore 142 49 36N 87 57W
Beardmore Glacier 7 84 30 S 170 0 E
Beardstown 154 40 0N 90 25W
Béarn 20 43 20N 0 30W
Bearpaw Mts. 156 48 15N 109 30W
Bearskin Lake 142 53 58N 91 2W
Beas de Segura 37 38 15N 2 53W
Beasain 36 43 3N 2 11W
Beata, C. 163 17 40N 71 30W
Beata, I. 163 17 34N 71 31W
Beatrice, U.S.A. 152 40 20N 96 40W
Beatrice, Zambia 131 18 15 S 30 55 E
Beatrice, C. 110 14 20 S 136 55 E
Beatton → 144 56 15N 120 45W
Beatton River 144 57 26N 121 20W
Beatty 158 36 58N 116 46W
Beaucaire 21 43 48N 4 39 E
Beauce, Plaine de la 19 48 10N 1 45 E
Beauceville 143 46 13N 70 46W
Beauchêne, I. 176 52 55 S 59 15W
Beaudesert 111 27 59 S 153 0 E
Beaufort, Australia 112 37 25 S 143 25 E
Beaufort, Malaysia 86 5 30N 115 40 E
Beaufort, N.C., U.S.A. 149 34 45N 76 40W
Beaufort, S.C., U.S.A. 149 32 25N 80 40W
Beaufort Sea 6 72 0N 140 0W
Beaufort West 134 32 18 S 22 36 E
Beaugency 19 47 47N 1 38 E
Beauharnois 142 45 20N 73 52W
Beaujeu 21 46 10N 4 35 E
Beaulieu → 144 62 3N 113 11W
Beaulieu-sur-Dordogne 20 44 58N 1 50 E
Beaulieu-sur-Mer 21 43 42N 7 20 E
Beauly 14 57 29N 4 27W
Beauly → 14 57 26N 4 28W
Beaumaris 12 53 16N 4 7W
Beaumetz-lès-Loges 19 50 15N 2 38 E
Beaumont, Belgium 23 50 15N 4 14 E
Beaumont, France 20 44 45N 0 46 E
Beaumont, N.Z. 115 45 50 S 169 33 E
Beaumont, Calif., U.S.A. 159 33 56N 116 58W
Beaumont, Tex., U.S.A. 153 30 5N 94 8W
Beaumont-de-Lomagne 20 43 53N 1 0 E
Beaumont-le-Roger 18 49 4N 0 47 E
Beaumont-sur-Oise 19 49 9N 2 17 E
Beaumont-sur-Sarthe 18 48 13N 0 8 E
Beaune 19 47 2N 4 50 E
Beaune-la-Rolande 19 48 4N 2 25 E
Beaupréau 18 47 12N 0 59W
Beauraing 23 50 7N 4 57 E
Beauséjour 145 50 5N 96 35W
Beausset, Le 21 43 12N 5 48 E
Beautemps-Beaupré, I. 106 20 24 S 166 9 E
Beauvais 19 49 25N 2 8 E
Beauval 145 55 9N 107 37W
Beauvoir-sur-Mer 18 46 55N 2 2W
Beauvoir-sur-Niort 20 46 12N 0 30W
Beaver, Alaska, U.S.A. 140 66 20N 147 30W
Beaver, Okla., U.S.A. 153 36 52N 100 31W
Beaver, Pa., U.S.A. 150 40 40N 80 18W
Beaver, Utah, U.S.A. 157 38 20N 112 45W
Beaver →, B.C., Canada 144 59 52N 124 20W
Beaver →, Ont., Canada 142 55 55N 87 48W
Beaver →, Sask., Canada 145 55 26N 107 45W
Beaver City 152 40 13N 99 50W
Beaver Dam 152 43 28N 88 50W
Beaver Falls 150 40 44N 80 20W
Beaver Hill L. 145 54 5N 94 50W
Beaver I. 148 45 40N 85 31W
Beavercreek 155 39 43N 84 11W
Beaverhill L., Alta., Canada 144 53 27N 112 32W
Beaverhill L., N.W.T., Canada 145 63 2N 104 22W
Beaverlodge 144 55 11N 119 29W
Beavermouth 144 51 32N 117 23W
Beaverstone → 142 54 59N 89 25W
Beaverton, Canada 150 44 26N 79 9W
Beaverton, U.S.A. 158 45 29N 122 48W
Beaverville 155 40 57N 87 39W
Beawar 78 26 3N 74 18 E
Bebedouro 175 21 0 S 48 25W
Beboa 135 17 22 S 44 33 E
Bebra 26 50 59N 9 48 E
Beccles 13 52 27N 1 33 E
Bečej 46 45 36N 20 3 E
Beceni 50 45 23N 26 48 E
Becerreá 34 42 51N 7 10W
Béchar 121 31 38N 2 18W
Bechyně 30 49 17N 14 29 E
Beckley 148 37 50N 81 8W
Beckum 26 51 46N 8 3 E
Bečva → 31 49 31N 17 40 E
Bédar 37 37 11N 1 59W
Bédarieux 20 43 37N 3 10 E
Bédarrides 21 44 2N 4 54 E
Beddouza, Ras 120 32 33N 9 9W
Bedel, Pereval 63 41 26N 78 26 E
Bedele 125 8 31N 36 23 E
Bederkesa 26 53 37N 8 50 E
Bederwanak 136 9 34N 44 23 E
Bedeso 125 9 58N 40 52 E
Bedford, Canada 142 45 7N 72 59W
Bedford, S. Africa 134 32 40 S 26 10 E
Bedford, U.K. 13 52 8N 0 29W
Bedford, Ind., U.S.A. 155 38 50N 86 30W
Bedford, Iowa, U.S.A. 154 40 40N 94 41W
Bedford, Ky., U.S.A. 155 38 36N 85 19W
Bedford, Ohio, U.S.A. 150 41 23N 81 32W
Bedford, Pa., U.S.A. 150 40 1N 78 30W
Bedford, Va., U.S.A. 148 37 25N 79 30W
Bedford □ 13 52 4N 0 28W
Bedford, C. 110 15 14 S 145 21 E
Bedford Downs 108 17 19 S 127 20 E
Bedi 123 11 6N 18 33 E
Będków 32 51 36N 19 44 E
Bednja → 43 46 12N 16 25 E
Bednodemyanovsk 59 53 55N 43 15 E
Bedónia 42 44 28N 9 36 E
Bedourie 110 24 30 S 139 30 E
Bedretto 29 46 31N 8 31 E
Bedum 22 53 18N 6 36 E
Będzin 32 50 19N 19 7 E
Beech Fork → 155 37 55N 85 50W
Beech Grove 155 39 40N 86 2W
Beecher 155 41 21N 87 38W
Beechworth 113 36 22 S 146 43 E
Beechy 145 50 53N 107 24W
Beek, Gelderland, Neth. 22 51 55N 6 11 E
Beek, Limburg, Neth. 23 50 57N 5 48 E
Beek, Noord-Brabant, Neth. 23 51 32N 5 38 E
Beekbergen 22 52 10N 5 58 E
Beelitz 26 52 14N 12 58 E
Beenleigh 111 27 43 S 153 10 E
Be'er Menuḥa 72 30 19N 35 8 E
Be'er Sheva' 69 31 15N 34 48 E
Be'er Sheva' → 69 31 12N 34 40 E
Be'er Toviyya 69 31 44N 34 42 E
Be'eri 69 31 25N 34 30 E
Be'erotayim 69 32 19N 34 59 E
Beersheba = Be'er Sheva' 69 31 15N 34 48 E
Beerta 22 53 11N 7 6 E
Beerze → 22 51 39N 5 20 E
Beesd 22 51 53N 5 11 E
Beeskow 26 52 9N 14 14 E
Beeston 12 52 55N 1 11W
Beetaloo 110 17 15 S 133 50 E
Beetsterzwaag 22 53 4N 6 5 E
Beetzendorf 26 52 42N 11 6 E
Beeville 153 28 27N 97 44W
Befale 132 0 25N 20 45 E
Befandriana 135 21 55 S 44 0 E
Befotaka 135 23 49 S 47 0 E
Bega 113 36 41 S 149 51 E
Bega, Canalul 46 45 37N 20 46 E
Bégard 18 48 38N 3 18W
Bègles 20 44 45N 0 35W
Begna → 51 60 41N 10 0 E
Begonte 34 43 10N 7 40W
Begusarai 79 25 24N 86 9 E
Behābād 73 32 24N 59 47 E
Behara 135 24 55 S 46 20 E
Behbehān 73 30 30N 50 15 E
Behshahr 73 36 45N 53 35 E
Bei Jiang → 97 23 2N 112 58 E
Bei'an 93 48 10N 126 20 E
Beigang 97 23 38N 120 16 E
Beihai 96 21 28N 109 6 E
Beijing 94 39 55N 116 20 E
Beijing □ 94 39 55N 116 20 E
Beilen 22 52 52N 6 27 E
Beiliu 97 22 41N 110 21 E
Beilngries 27 49 1N 11 27 E
Beilpajah 112 32 54 S 143 52 E
Beilul 125 13 2N 42 20 E
Beipiao 95 41 52N 120 32 E
Beira, Mozam. 131 19 50 S 34 52 E
Beira, Somalia 136 6 57N 47 19 E
Beirut = Bayrūt 70 33 53N 35 31 E
Beit Lāhiyah 69 31 32N 34 30 E
Beitaolaizhao 95 44 58N 125 58 E
Beitbridge 131 22 12 S 30 0 E
Beiuş 50 46 40N 22 21 E
Beizhen, Liaoning, China 95 41 38N 121 54 E
Beizhen, Shandong, China 95 37 20N 118 2 E
Beizhengzhen 95 44 31N 123 30 E
Beja, Portugal 35 38 2N 7 53W
Béja, Tunisia 121 36 43N 9 12 E
Beja □ 35 37 55N 7 55W
Bejaia 121 36 42N 5 2 E
Béjar 34 40 23N 5 46W
Bejestān 73 34 30N 58 5 E
Bekaa = Al Biqā □ 70 34 0N 36 5 E
Bekabad 63 40 13N 69 14 E
Bekasi 88 6 14 S 106 59 E
Békés 31 46 47N 21 9 E
Békés □ 31 46 45N 21 0 E
Békéscsaba 31 46 40N 21 5 E
Bekily 135 24 13 S 45 19 E
Bekkevoort 23 50 57N 4 58 E
Bekoji 125 7 40N 39 17 E
Bekok 85 2 20N 103 7 E
Bekwai 127 6 30N 1 34W
Bela, India 79 25 50N 82 0 E
Bela, Pakistan 77 26 12N 66 20 E
Bela Crkva 46 44 55N 21 27 E
Bela Palanka 46 43 13N 22 17 E
Bela Vista, Brazil 174 22 12 S 56 20W
Bela Vista, Mozam. 135 26 10 S 32 44 E
Bélâbre 20 46 34N 1 8 E
Belalcázar 35 38 35N 5 10W
Belanovica 46 44 15N 20 23 E
Belas 133 8 55 S 13 9 E
Belau Is. 106 7 30N 134 30 E
Belavenona 135 24 50 S 47 4 E
Belawan 88 3 33N 98 32 E
Belaya → 62 56 0N 54 32 E
Belaya, Mt. 125 11 25N 36 8 E
Belaya Glina 61 46 5N 40 48 E
Belaya Kalitva 61 48 13N 40 50 E
Belaya Kholunitsa 59 58 41N 50 13 E
Belaya Tserkov 58 49 45N 30 10 E
Belayan → 89 0 14 S 116 36 E
Belceşti 50 47 19N 27 7 E
Bełchatów 32 51 21N 19 22 E
Belcher Is. 142 56 15N 78 45W
Belchite 36 41 18N 0 43W
Belden 158 40 2N 121 17W
Beldibi 70 36 25N 32 26 E
Belebey 62 54 7N 54 7 E
Belém 170 1 20 S 48 30W
Belém de São Francisco 170 8 46 S 38 58W
Belén, Argentina 174 27 40 S 67 5W
Belén, Colombia 168 1 26N 75 56W
Belén, Paraguay 174 23 30 S 57 6W
Belen, Turkey 70 36 31N 36 10 E
Belen, U.S.A. 157 34 40N 106 50W
Belene 47 43 39N 25 10 E
Bélesta 20 42 55N 1 56 E
Belet Uen 136 4 30N 45 5 E
Belev 59 53 50N 36 5 E
Belfair 158 47 27N 122 50W
Belfast, N.Z. 115 43 27 S 172 39 E
Belfast, S. Africa 135 25 42 S 30 2 E
Belfast, U.K. 15 54 35N 5 56W
Belfast, Maine, U.S.A. 143 44 30N 69 0W
Belfast, N.Y., U.S.A. 150 42 21N 78 9W
Belfast □ 15 54 35N 5 56W
Belfast, L. 15 54 40N 5 50W
Belfeld 23 51 18N 6 6 E
Belfield 152 46 54N 103 11W
Belfort 19 47 38N 6 50 E
Belfry 156 45 10N 109 2W
Belgaum 81 15 55N 74 35 E
Belgioioso 42 45 9N 9 21 E
Belgium ■ 23 50 30N 5 0 E
Belgorod 60 50 35N 36 35 E
Belgorod-Dnestrovskiy 60 46 11N 30 23 E
Belgrade = Beograd 46 44 50N 20 37 E
Belgrade 156 45 50N 111 10W
Belgrove 115 41 27 S 172 59 E
Belhaven 149 35 34N 76 35W
Beli Drim → 46 42 6N 20 25 E
Beli Manastir 46 45 45N 18 36 E
Beli Timok → 46 43 53N 22 14 E
Belice → 44 37 35N 12 55 E
Belin-Béliet 20 44 29N 0 47W
Belinga 132 1 10N 13 2 E
Belinskiy 59 53 0N 43 25 E
Belinţ 50 45 48N 21 54 E
Belinyu 88 1 35 S 105 50 E
Belitung 89 3 10 S 107 50 E
Beliu 50 46 30N 22 0 E
Belize ■ 161 17 0N 88 30W
Belize City 161 17 25N 88 0W
Beljanica 46 44 8N 21 43 E
Belkovskiy, Ostrov 65 75 32N 135 44 E
Bell → 142 49 48N 77 38W
Bell Bay 110 41 6 S 146 53 E
Bell I. 143 50 46N 55 35W
Bell-Irving → 144 56 12N 129 5W
Bell Peninsula 141 63 50N 82 0W
Bell Ville 174 32 40 S 62 40W
Bella Bella 144 52 10N 128 10W
Bella Coola 144 52 25N 126 40W
Bella Flor 172 11 9 S 67 49W
Bella Unión 174 30 15 S 57 40W
Bella Vista, Corrientes, Argentina 174 28 33 S 59 0W
Bella Vista, Tucuman, Argentina 174 27 10 S 65 25W
Bellac 20 46 7N 1 3 E
Bellágio 42 45 59N 9 15 E
Bellaire 150 40 1N 80 46W
Bellary 81 15 10N 76 56 E
Bellata 111 29 53 S 149 46 E
Belle 154 38 17N 91 43W
Belle, La, Fla., U.S.A. 149 26 45N 81 22W
Belle, La, Mo., U.S.A. 154 40 7N 91 55W
Belle Fourche 152 44 43N 103 52W
Belle Fourche → 152 44 25N 102 19W
Belle Glade 149 26 43N 80 38W
Belle-Ile 18 47 20N 3 10W
Belle Isle 143 51 57N 55 25W
Belle Isle, Str. of 143 51 30N 56 30W
Belle-Isle-en-Terre 18 48 33N 3 23W
Belle Plaine, Iowa, U.S.A. 154 41 51N 92 18W
Belle Plaine, Minn., U.S.A. 152 44 35N 93 48W
Belle Rive 155 38 14N 88 45W
Belle Yella 126 7 24N 10 0W
Belledonne, Chaîne de 21 45 20N 6 10 E
Belledune 143 47 55N 65 50W
Bellefontaine 155 40 20N 83 45W

Bîr el Heisi

Bessarabka 60 46 21N 28 58 E
Bessèges 21 44 18N 4 8 E
Bessemer, Ala., U.S.A. 149 33 25N 86 57W
Bessemer, Mich., U.S.A. 152 46 27N 90 0W
Bessin 18 49 18N 1 0W
Bessines-sur-Gartempe 20 46 6N 1 22 E
Best 23 51 31N 5 23 E
Bet Alfa 69 32 31N 35 25 E
Bet Dagan 69 32 1N 34 49 E
Bet Guvrin 69 31 37N 34 54 E
Bet Ha'Emeq 69 32 58N 35 8 E
Bet Hashitta 69 32 31N 35 27 E
Bet Qeshet 69 32 41N 35 21 E
Bet She'an 69 32 30N 35 30 E
Bet Shemesh 69 31 44N 35 0 E
Bet Tadjine, Djebel 120 29 0N 3 30W
Bet Yosef 69 32 34N 35 33 E
Betafo 135 19 50 S 46 51 E
Betancuria 37 28 25N 14 3W
Betanzos, Bolivia 173 19 34 S 65 27W
Betanzos, Spain 34 43 15N 8 12W
Bétaré Oya 132 5 40N 14 5 E
Bétera 36 39 35N 0 28W
Bethal 135 26 27 S 29 28 E
Bethanien 134 26 31 S 17 8 E
Bethany = Al 'Ayzarīyah 69 31 47N 35 15 E
Bethany, S. Africa 134 29 34 S 25 59 E
Bethany, Ill., U.S.A. 155 39 39N 88 45W
Bethany, Mo., U.S.A. 154 40 18N 94 0W
Bethel, Alaska, U.S.A. 140 60 50N 161 50W
Bethel, Ohio, U.S.A. 155 38 58N 84 5W
Bethel, Vt., U.S.A. 151 43 50N 72 37W
Bethel Park 150 40 20N 80 2W
Bethlehem = Bayt Lahm 69 31 43N 35 12 E
Bethlehem, S. Africa 135 28 14 S 28 18 E
Bethlehem, U.S.A. 151 40 39N 75 24W
Bethulie 134 30 30 S 25 59 E
Béthune 19 50 30N 2 38 E
Béthune → 18 49 53N 1 9 E
Bethungra 113 34 45 S 147 51 E
Betijoque 168 9 23N 70 44W
Betim 171 19 58 S 44 7W
Betioky 135 23 48 S 44 20 E
Beton-Bazoches 19 48 42N 3 15 E
Betong 85 5 45N 101 5 E
Betoota 110 25 45 S 140 42 E
Betroka 135 23 16 S 46 0 E
Betsiamites 143 48 56N 68 40W
Betsiamites → 143 48 56N 68 38W
Betsiboka → 135 16 3 S 46 36 E
Betsjoeanaland 134 26 30 S 22 30 E
Bettembourg 23 49 31N 6 6 E
Bettendorf 154 41 32N 90 30W
Bettiah 79 26 48N 84 33 E
Bèttola 42 44 42N 9 32 E
Betul 78 21 58N 77 59 E
Betung 86 1 24N 111 31 E
Betzdorf 26 50 47N 7 53 E
Beuca 50 44 14N 24 56 E
Beuil 21 44 6N 6 59 E
Beulah 152 47 18N 101 47W
Beuvron → 18 47 29N 1 15 E
Bevensen 26 53 5N 10 34 E
Beveren 23 51 12N 4 16 E
Beverley, Australia 109 32 9 S 116 56 E
Beverley, U.K. 12 53 52N 0 26W
Beverlo 23 51 7N 5 13 E
Beverly, Mass., U.S.A. 151 42 32N 70 50W
Beverly, Wash., U.S.A. 156 46 55N 119 59W
Beverly Hills 159 34 4N 118 29W
Beverwijk 22 52 28N 4 38 E
Bex 28 46 15N 7 0 E
Beyānlū 72 36 0N 47 51 E
Beyin 126 5 1N 2 41W
Beykoz 47 41 8N 29 7 E
Beyla 126 8 30N 8 38W
Beynat 20 45 8N 1 44 E
Beyneu 57 45 10N 55 3 E
Beypazarı 57 40 10N 31 56 E
Beypore → 81 11 10N 75 47 E
Beyşehir Gölü 57 37 40N 31 45 E
Bezdan 46 45 50N 18 57 E
Bezet 69 33 4N 35 8 E
Bezhetsk 59 57 47N 36 39 E
Bezhitsa 58 53 19N 34 17 E
Béziers 20 43 20N 3 12 E
Bezwada = Vijayawada 81 16 31N 80 39 E
Bhadarwah 79 32 58N 75 46 E
Bhadra → 81 14 0N 75 20 E
Bhadrakh 79 21 10N 86 30 E
Bhadravati 81 13 49N 75 40 E
Bhagalpur 79 25 10N 87 0 E
Bhainsa 80 19 10N 77 58 E
Bhairab → 82 22 51N 89 34 E
Bhairab Bazar 82 24 4N 90 58 E
Bhakkar 77 31 40N 71 5 E
Bhakra Dam 78 31 30N 76 45 E
Bhamo 82 24 15N 97 15 E
Bhamragarh 80 19 30N 80 40 E
Bhandara 79 21 5N 79 42 E
Bhanrer Ra. 78 23 40N 79 45 E
Bharat = India ■ 76 20 0N 78 0 E
Bharatpur 78 27 15N 77 30 E
Bharuch 78 21 47N 73 0 E
Bhatghar L. 80 18 10N 73 48 E
Bhatiapara Ghat 82 23 13N 89 42 E
Bhatinda 78 30 15N 74 57 E
Bhatkal 81 13 58N 74 35 E
Bhatpara 79 22 50N 88 25 E
Bhattiprolu 81 16 7N 80 45 E
Bhaun 78 32 55N 72 40 E
Bhaunagar = Bhavnagar 78 21 45N 72 10 E
Bhavani 81 11 27N 77 43 E
Bhavani → 81 11 0N 78 15 E
Bhavnagar 78 21 45N 72 10 E
Bhawanipatna 80 19 55N 80 10 E
Bhera 78 32 29N 72 57 E
Bhilsa = Vidisha 78 23 28N 77 53 E
Bhilwara 78 25 25N 74 38 E
Bhima → 80 16 25N 77 17 E
Bhimavaram 81 16 30N 81 30 E
Bhimbar 79 32 59N 74 3 E
Bhind 79 26 30N 78 46 E
Bhiwandi 80 19 20N 73 0 E
Bhiwani 78 28 50N 76 9 E
Bhola 82 22 45N 90 35 E
Bhongir 80 17 30N 78 56 E
Bhopal 78 23 20N 77 30 E
Bhor 80 18 12N 73 53 E
Bhubaneshwar 79 20 15N 85 50 E
Bhuj 78 23 15N 69 49 E
Bhumibol Dam 84 17 15N 98 58 E
Bhusaval 78 21 3N 75 46 E
Bhutan ■ 82 27 25N 90 30 E
Biá → 168 3 28 S 67 23W
Biafra, B. of = Bonny, Bight of 127 3 30N 9 20 E
Biak 87 1 10 S 136 6 E
Biała 32 50 24N 17 40 E
Biała →, Białystok, Poland 32 53 11N 23 4 E
Biała →, Tarnów, Poland 32 50 3N 20 55 E
Biała Piska 32 53 37N 22 5 E
Biała Podlaska 32 52 4N 23 6 E
Biała Podlaska □ 32 52 0N 23 0 E
Biała Rawska 32 51 48N 20 29 E
Białobrzegi 32 52 27N 21 3 E
Białogard 32 54 2N 15 58 E
Białowieża 32 52 41N 23 49 E
Biały Bór 32 53 53N 16 51 E
Białystok 32 53 10N 23 10 E
Białystok □ 32 53 9N 23 10 E
Biancavilla 45 37 39N 14 50 E
Bīārjmand 73 36 6N 55 53 E
Biaro 87 2 5N 125 26 E
Biarritz 20 43 29N 1 33W
Biasca 29 46 22N 8 58 E
Biba 124 28 55N 31 0 E
Bibai 98 43 19N 141 52 E
Bibala 133 14 44 S 13 24 E
Bibane, Bahiret el 121 33 16N 11 13 E
Bibassé 132 1 27N 11 37 E
Bibbiena 43 43 43N 11 50 E
Bibby I. 145 61 55N 93 0W
Biberach 27 48 5N 9 49 E
Biberist 28 47 11N 7 34 E
Bibey → 34 42 24N 7 13W
Bibiani 126 6 30N 2 8W
Bibile 81 7 10N 81 25 E
Biboohra 110 16 56 S 145 25 E
Bibungwa 130 2 40 S 28 15 E
Bic 143 48 20N 68 41W
Bicaj 48 42 0N 20 25 E
Bicaz 50 46 53N 26 5 E
Biccari 45 41 23N 15 12 E
Biche, La → 144 59 57N 123 50W
Bichena 125 10 28N 38 10 E
Bickerton I. 110 13 45 S 136 10 E
Bicknell, Ind., U.S.A. 155 38 50N 87 20W
Bicknell, Utah, U.S.A. 157 38 16N 111 35W
Bida, Nigeria 127 9 3N 5 58 E
Bida, Zaïre 132 4 55N 19 56 E
Bidar 80 17 55N 77 35 E
Biddeford 143 43 30N 70 28W
Biddiyā 69 32 7N 35 4 E
Biddū 69 31 50N 35 8 E
Biddwara 125 5 11N 38 34 E
Bideford 13 51 1N 4 13W
Bidon 5 = Poste Maurice Cortier 121 22 14N 1 2 E
Bidor 85 4 6N 101 15 E
Bidura 112 34 10 S 143 21 E
Bié □ 133 12 30 S 17 0 E
Bié, Planalto de 133 12 0 S 16 0 E
Bieber 156 41 4N 121 6W
Biebrza → 32 53 13N 22 25 E
Biecz 32 49 44N 21 15 E
Biel 28 47 8N 7 14 E
Bielawa 32 50 43N 16 37 E
Bielé Karpaty 31 49 5N 18 0 E
Bielefeld 26 52 2N 8 31 E
Bielersee 28 47 6N 7 5 E
Biella 42 45 33N 8 3 E
Bielsk Podlaski 32 52 47N 23 12 E
Bielsko-Biała 32 49 50N 19 2 E
Bielsko-Biała □ 32 49 45N 19 15 E
Bien Hoa 85 10 57N 106 49 E
Bienfait 145 49 10N 102 50W
Bienne = Biel 28 47 8N 7 14 E
Bienvenida 35 38 18N 6 12W
Bienvenue 169 3 0N 52 30W
Bienville, L. 142 55 5N 72 40W
Biescas 36 42 37N 0 20W
Biese → 26 52 53N 11 46 E
Biesiesfontein 134 30 57 S 17 58 E
Bietigheim 27 48 57N 9 8 E
Bievre 23 49 57N 5 1 E
Biferno → 45 41 59N 15 2 E
Bifoum 132 0 20 S 10 23 E
Big →, Canada 143 54 50N 58 55W
Big →, U.S.A. 154 38 27N 90 37W
Big B. 143 55 43N 60 35W
Big Bear City 159 34 16N 116 51W
Big Bear L. 159 34 15N 116 56W
Big Beaver 145 49 10N 105 10W
Big Belt Mts. 156 46 50N 111 30W
Big Bend 135 26 50 S 31 58 E
Big Bend Nat. Park 153 29 15N 103 15W
Big Black → 153 32 0N 91 5W
Big Blue →, Ind., U.S.A. 155 39 12N 85 56W
Big Blue →, Kans., U.S.A. 152 39 11N 96 40W
Big Cr. → 144 51 42N 122 41W
Big Creek 158 37 11N 119 14W
Big Cypress Swamp 149 26 12N 81 10W
Big Falls 152 48 11N 93 48W
Big Fork → 152 48 31N 93 43W
Big Horn Mts. = Bighorn Mts. 156 44 30N 107 30W
Big Lake 153 31 12N 101 25W
Big Moose 151 43 49N 74 58W
Big Muddy →, Ill., U.S.A. 154 38 0N 89 0W
Big Muddy →, Mont., U.S.A. 152 48 8N 104 36W
Big Pine 158 37 12N 118 17W
Big Piney 156 42 32N 110 3W
Big Quill L. 145 51 55N 104 50W
Big Rapids 148 43 42N 85 27W
Big River 145 53 50N 107 0W
Big Run 150 40 57N 78 55W
Big Sable Pt. 148 44 5N 86 30W
Big Sand L. 145 57 45N 99 45W
Big Sandy 156 48 12N 110 9W
Big Sandy Cr. → 152 38 6N 102 29W
Big Sioux → 152 42 30N 96 25W
Big Spring 153 32 10N 101 25W
Big Springs 152 41 4N 102 3W
Big Stone City 152 45 20N 96 30W
Big Stone Gap 149 36 52N 82 45W
Big Stone L. 152 45 30N 96 35W
Big Sur 158 36 15N 121 48W
Big Timber 156 45 53N 110 0W
Big Trout L. 142 53 40N 90 0W
Biganos 20 44 39N 0 59W
Bigfork 156 48 3N 114 2W
Biggar, Canada 145 52 4N 108 0W
Biggar, U.K. 14 55 38N 3 31W
Bigge I. 108 14 35 S 125 10 E
Biggenden 111 25 31 S 152 4 E
Biggs 158 39 24N 121 43W
Bighorn 156 46 11N 107 25W
Bighorn → 156 46 9N 107 28W
Bighorn Mts. 156 44 30N 107 30W
Bignona 126 12 52N 16 14W
Bigorre 20 43 10N 0 5 E
Bigstone L. 145 53 42N 95 44W
Bigwa 130 7 10 S 39 10 E
Bihać 43 44 49N 15 57 E
Bihar 79 25 5N 85 40 E
Bihar □ 79 25 0N 86 0 E
Biharamulo 130 2 25 S 31 25 E
Biharamulo □ 130 2 30 S 31 20 E
Biharkeresztes 31 47 8N 21 44 E
Bihor □ 50 47 0N 22 10 E
Bihor, Munţii 50 46 29N 22 47 E
Bijagós, Arquipélago dos 126 11 15N 16 10W
Bijaipur 78 26 2N 77 20 E
Bijapur, Karnataka, India 80 16 50N 75 55 E
Bijapur, Mad. P., India 80 18 50N 80 50 E
Bījār 72 35 52N 47 35 E
Bijeljina 46 44 46N 19 17 E
Bijelo Polje 46 43 1N 19 45 E
Bijie 96 27 20N 105 16 E
Bijni 82 26 30N 90 40 E
Bijnor 78 29 27N 78 11 E
Bikaner 78 28 2N 73 18 E
Bikapur 79 26 30N 82 7 E
Bikeqi 94 40 43N 111 20 E
Bikfayyā 70 33 55N 35 41 E
Bikin 65 46 50N 134 20 E
Bikin → 98 46 51N 134 2 E
Bikini Atoll 104 12 0N 167 30 E
Bikoro 132 0 48 S 18 15 E
Bikoué 127 3 55N 11 50 E
Bilara 78 26 14N 73 53 E
Bilaspara 82 26 13N 90 14 E
Bilaspur, Mad. P., India 79 22 2N 82 15 E
Bilaspur, Punjab, India 78 31 19N 76 50 E
Bilauk Taungdan 84 13 0N 99 0 E
Bilbao 36 43 16N 2 56W
Bilbeis 124 30 25N 31 34 E
Bilbor 50 47 6N 25 30 E
Bíldudalur 54 65 41N 23 36W
Bileća 46 42 53N 18 27 E
Bilecik 57 40 5N 30 5 E
Biłgoraj 32 50 33N 22 42 E
Bilibino 65 68 3N 166 20 E
Bilibiza 131 12 30 S 40 20 E
Bilin 82 17 14N 97 15 E
Bilir 65 65 40N 131 20 E
Biliran I. 91 11 35N 124 28 E
Bilishti 48 40 37N 21 2 E
Bill 152 43 18N 105 18W
Billabalong 109 27 25 S 115 49 E
Billiluna 108 19 37 S 127 41 E
Billingham 12 54 36N 1 18W
Billings 156 45 43N 108 29W
Billingsfors 52 58 59N 12 15 E
Billiton Is. = Belitung 89 3 10 S 107 50 E
Billom 20 45 43N 3 20 E
Bilma 123 18 50N 13 30 E
Bilo Gora 46 45 53N 17 15 E
Biloela 110 24 24 S 150 31 E
Biloku 169 1 50N 58 25W
Biloxi 153 30 24N 88 53W
Bilpa Morea Claypan 110 25 0 S 140 0 E
Bilthoven 22 52 8N 5 12 E
Biltine 123 14 40N 20 50 E
Bilugyun 82 16 24N 97 32 E
Bilyana 110 18 5 S 145 50 E
Bilyarsk 59 54 58N 50 22 E
Bilzen 23 50 52N 5 31 E
Bima 89 8 22 S 118 49 E
Bimban 124 24 24N 32 54 E
Bimberi Peak 113 35 44 S 148 51 E
Bimbila 127 8 54N 0 5 E
Bimbo 132 4 15N 18 33 E
Bimini Is. 162 25 42N 79 25W
Bin Xian, Heilongjiang, China 95 45 42N 127 32 E
Bin Xian, Shaanxi, China 94 35 2N 108 4 E
Bina-Etawah 78 24 13N 78 14 E
Bināb 73 36 35N 48 41 E
Binalbagan 91 10 12N 122 50 E
Binalong 113 34 40 S 148 39 E
Bīnālūd, Kūh-e 73 36 30N 58 30 E
Binatang 86 2 10N 111 40 E
Binbee 110 20 19 S 147 56 E
Binche 23 50 26N 4 10 E
Binchuan 96 25 42N 100 38 E
Binda, Australia 111 27 52 S 147 21 E
Binda, Zaïre 133 5 52 S 13 14 E
Bindi Bindi 109 30 37 S 116 22 E
Bindle 111 27 40 S 148 45 E
Bindoy 91 9 48N 123 5 E
Bindura 131 17 18 S 31 18 E
Bingara, N.S.W., Australia 111 29 52 S 150 36 E
Bingara, Queens., Australia 111 28 10 S 144 37 E
Bingen 27 49 57N 7 53 E
Bingerville 126 5 18N 3 49W
Bingham 143 45 5N 69 50W
Bingham Canyon 156 40 31N 112 10W
Binghamton 151 42 9N 75 54W
Binh Dinh = An Nhon 84 13 55N 109 7 E
Binh Khe 84 13 57N 108 51 E
Binh Son 84 15 20N 108 40 E
Binhai 95 34 2N 119 49 E
Binjai 88 3 20N 98 30 E
Binnaway 111 31 28 S 149 24 E
Binongko 87 5 55 S 123 55 E
Binscarth 145 50 37N 101 17W
Bint Jubayl 69 33 8N 35 25 E
Bintan 88 1 0N 104 0 E
Bintulu 86 3 10N 113 0 E
Bintuni 87 2 7 S 133 32 E
Binyamina 69 32 32N 34 56 E
Binyang 96 23 12N 108 47 E
Binz 26 54 23N 13 37 E
Binza 133 4 21 S 15 14 E
Binzert = Bizerte 121 37 15N 9 50 E
Bío Bío □ 174 37 35 S 72 0W
Biograd 43 43 56N 15 29 E
Bioko 127 3 30N 8 40 E
Biokovo 46 43 23N 17 0 E
Biougra 120 30 15N 9 14W
Biq'at Bet Netofa 69 32 49N 35 22 E
Bir 80 19 4N 75 46 E
Bir, Ras 125 12 0N 43 20 E
Bîr Abu Hashim 124 23 42N 34 6 E
Bîr Abu M'nqar 124 26 33N 27 33 E
Bîr Abu Muḩammad 71 29 44N 34 14 E
Bi'r ad Dabbāghāt 71 30 26N 35 32 E
Bîr Adal Deib 124 22 35N 36 10 E
Bi'r al Butayyihāt 71 29 47N 35 20 E
Bi'r al Ḩamḑah 71 28 30N 34 55 E
Bi'r al Malfa 122 31 58N 15 18 E
Bi'r al Mārī 71 30 4N 35 33 E
Bi'r al Musallam 71 28 56N 35 38 E
Bi'r al Qattār 71 29 47N 35 32 E
Bir 'Ali 75 14 1N 48 20 E
Bir Aouine 121 32 25N 9 18 E
Bîr 'Asal 124 25 55N 34 20 E
Bi'r ash Shakkūsīyah 70 35 23N 37 26 E
Bir Autrun 124 18 15N 26 40 E
Bîr Beiḑa 71 30 25N 34 29 E
Bi'r Dhu'fān 122 31 59N 14 32 E
Bîr Diqnash 124 31 3N 25 23 E
Bir el Abbes 120 26 7N 6 9W
Bîr el 'Abd 71 31 2N 33 0 E
Bir el Ater 121 34 46N 8 3 E
Bîr el Basur 124 29 51N 25 49 E
Bîr el Biarât 71 29 30N 34 43 E
Bîr el Duweidar 71 30 56N 32 32 E
Bîr el Garârât 71 31 3N 33 34 E
Bîr el Gellaz 124 30 50N 26 40 E
Bîr el Heisi 71 29 22N 34 36 E

Bîr el Jafir

Bîr el Jafir 71 30 50N 32 41 E
Bîr el Mâlḥi 71 30 38N 33 19 E
Bîr el Naṣb 71 29 3N 33 2 E
Bîr el Ṣafra 71 28 45N 34 21 E
Bîr el Saura 71 29 9N 34 30 E
Bîr el Shaqqa 124 30 54N 25 1 E
Bîr el Thamâda 71 30 12N 33 27 E
Bîr Fuad 124 30 35N 26 28 E
Bîr Gara 123 13 11N 15 58 E
Bîr Gebeil Ḥiṣn 71 30 2N 33 18 E
Bi'r Ghadīr 70 34 6N 37 3 E
Bi'r Gharr 71 28 7N 35 32 E
Bîr Haimur 124 22 45N 33 40 E
Bîr Ḥasana 71 30 29N 33 46 E
Bi'r Idimah 74 18 31N 44 12 E
Bi'r Jadīd, Iraq 72 34 1N 42 54 E
Bi'r Jadīd, Si. Arabia 71 29 10N 35 6 E
Bir Jdid 120 33 26N 8 0W
Bîr Kanayis 124 24 59N 33 15 E
Bîr Kaseiba 71 31 0N 33 17 E
Bîr Kerawein 124 27 10N 28 25 E
Bîr Lahfân 71 31 0N 33 51 E
Bir Lahrache 121 32 1N 8 12 E
Bîr Madkûr 71 30 44N 32 33 E
Bîr Maql 124 23 7N 33 40 E
Bîr Misaha 124 22 13N 27 59 E
Bir Mogrein 120 25 10N 11 25W
Bîr Murr 124 23 28N 30 10 E
Bi'r Muṭribah 72 29 54N 47 17 E
Bi'r Nabālā 69 31 52N 35 12 E
Bîr Nakheila 124 24 1N 30 50 E
Bîr Nakhul 71 29 5N 33 16 E
Bîr Qaṭia 71 30 58N 32 45 E
Bîr Qatrani 124 30 55N 26 10 E
Bîr Ranga 124 24 25N 35 15 E
Bîr Sahara 124 22 54N 28 40 E
Bîr Seiyâla 124 26 10N 33 50 E
Bir Semguine 120 30 1N 5 39W
Bîr Shalatein 124 23 5N 35 25 E
Bîr Shebb 124 22 25N 29 40 E
Bîr Shût 124 23 50N 35 15 E
Bîr Sidri 71 28 53N 33 28 E
Bîr Tâba 71 29 29N 34 53 E
Bi'r Tamis 75 16 45N 48 48 E
Bîr Terfawi 124 22 57N 28 55 E
Bîr Umm Qubûr 124 24 35N 34 2 E
Bîr Ungât 124 22 8N 33 48 E
Bîr Wuseit 71 29 14N 33 1 E
Bîr Za'farâna 124 29 10N 32 40 E
Bîr Zāmûs 122 24 16N 15 6 E
Bi'r Zayt 69 31 59N 35 11 E
Bîr Zeidûn 124 25 45N 33 40 E
Bira, Indonesia 87 2 3 S 132 2 E
Bîra, Romania 50 47 2N 27 3 E
Birak Sulaymān 69 31 42N 35 7 E
Biramféro 126 11 40N 9 10W
Birao 132 10 20N 22 47 E
Birawa 130 2 20 S 28 48 E
Bîrca 50 43 59N 23 36 E
Birch Hills 145 52 59N 105 25W
Birch I. 145 52 26N 99 54W
Birch L., N.W.T., Canada 144 62 4N 116 33W
Birch L., Ont., Canada 142 51 23N 92 18W
Birch L., U.S.A. 142 47 48N 91 43W
Birch Mts. 144 57 30N 113 10W
Birch River 145 52 24N 101 6W
Birchip 112 35 56 S 142 55 E
Birchiş 50 45 58N 22 9 E
Birchwood 115 45 55 S 167 53 E
Bird 145 56 30N 94 13W
Bird City 152 39 48N 101 33W
Bird I. = Aves, I. de 163 15 45N 63 55W
Bird I. 134 32 3 S 18 17 E
Birdaard 22 53 18N 5 53 E
Birdlip 13 51 50N 2 7W
Birds 155 38 50N 87 40W
Birdseye 155 38 19N 86 42W
Birdsville 110 25 51 S 139 20 E
Birdum 108 15 39 S 133 13 E
Birein 71 30 50N 34 28 E
Bireuen 88 5 14N 96 39 E
Birifo 126 13 30N 14 0W
Birigui 175 21 18 S 50 16W
Birini 132 7 51N 22 24 E
Birkenfeld 27 49 39N 7 11 E
Birkenhead, N.Z. 114 36 49 S 174 46 E
Birkenhead, U.K. 12 53 24N 3 1W
Birket Qârûn 124 29 30N 30 40 E
Birkfeld 30 47 21N 15 45 E
Birkhadem 121 36 43N 3 3 E
Bîrlad 50 46 15N 27 38 E
Birmingham, U.K. 13 52 30N 1 55W
Birmingham, Ala., U.S.A. 149 33 31N 86 50W
Birmingham, Iowa, U.S.A. 154 40 53N 91 57W
Birmitrapur 79 22 24N 84 46 E
Birni Ngaouré 127 13 5N 2 51 E
Birni Nkonni 127 13 55N 5 15 E
Birnin Gwari 127 11 0N 6 45 E
Birnin Kebbi 127 12 32N 4 12 E
Birnin Kudu 127 11 30N 9 29 E
Birobidzhan 65 48 50N 132 50 E
Birougou, Mts. 132 1 51 S 12 20 E
Birqîn 69 32 27N 35 15 E
Birr 15 53 7N 7 55W
Birrie → 111 29 43 S 146 37 E
Birs → 28 47 24N 7 32 E
Birsilpur 78 28 11N 72 15 E
Birsk 62 55 25N 55 30 E
Birtin 50 46 59N 22 31 E
Birtle 145 50 30N 101 5W
Biryuchiy 60 46 10N 35 0 E
Birzai 58 56 11N 24 45 E
Bîrzava 50 46 7N 21 59 E
Bisa 87 1 15 S 127 28 E
Bisáccia 45 41 0N 15 20 E
Bisacquino 44 37 42N 13 13 E
Bisai 101 35 16N 136 44 E
Bisalpur 79 28 14N 79 48 E
Bisbal, La 36 41 58N 3 2 E
Bisbee 157 31 30N 110 0W
Biscarrosse et de Parentis, Étang de 20 44 21N 1 10W
Biscay, B. of 38 45 0N 2 0W
Biscayne B. 149 25 40N 80 12W
Biscéglie 45 41 14N 16 30 E
Bischofshofen 30 47 26N 13 14 E
Bischofswerda 26 51 8N 14 11 E
Bischofszell 29 47 29N 9 15 E
Bischwiller 19 48 46N 7 50 E
Biscoe Bay 7 77 0 S 152 0W
Biscoe Is. 7 66 0 S 67 0W
Biscostasing 142 47 18N 82 9W
Biscucuy 168 9 22N 69 59W
Biševo 43 42 57N 16 3 E
Bisha 125 15 30N 37 31 E
Bishah, W. → 74 21 24N 43 26 E
Bishan 96 29 33N 106 12 E
Bishnupur 79 23 8N 87 20 E
Bisho 135 32 50 S 27 23 E
Bishop, Calif., U.S.A. 158 37 20N 118 26W
Bishop, Tex., U.S.A. 153 27 35N 97 49W
Bishop Auckland 12 54 40N 1 40W
Bishop's Falls 143 49 2N 55 30W
Bishop's Stortford 13 51 52N 0 11 E
Bisignano 45 39 30N 16 17 E
Bisina, L. 130 1 38N 33 56 E
Biskra 121 34 50N 5 44 E
Biskupiec 32 53 53N 20 58 E
Bislig 87 8 15N 126 27 E
Bismarck, Mo., U.S.A. 154 37 46N 90 38W
Bismarck, N. Dak., U.S.A. 152 46 49N 100 49W
Bismarck Arch. 107 2 30 S 150 0 E
Bismarck Ra. 107 5 35 S 145 0 E
Bismarck Sea 107 4 10 S 146 50 E
Bismark 26 52 39N 11 31 E
Biso 130 1 44N 31 26 E
Bison 152 45 34N 102 28W
Bīsotūn 72 34 23N 47 26 E
Bispgården 52 63 2N 16 40 E
Bissagos = Bijagós, Arquipélago dos 126 11 15N 16 10W
Bissau 126 11 45N 15 45W
Bissett 145 51 2N 95 41W
Bissikrima 126 10 50N 10 58W
Bistcho L. 144 59 45N 118 50W
Bistreţu 50 43 54N 23 23 E
Bistrica = Ilirska-Bistrica 43 45 34N 14 14 E
Bistriţa 50 47 9N 24 35 E
Bistriţa → 50 46 30N 26 57 E
Bistriţa Năsăud □ 50 47 15N 24 30 E
Bistriţei, Munţii 50 47 15N 25 40 E
Biswan 79 27 29N 81 2 E
Bisztynek 32 54 8N 20 53 E
Bitam 132 2 5N 11 25 E
Bitburg 27 49 58N 6 32 E
Bitche 19 49 2N 7 25 E
Bitkine 123 11 59N 18 13 E
Bitlis 57 38 20N 42 3 E
Bitola 46 41 5N 21 10 E
Bitolj = Bitola 46 41 5N 21 10 E
Bitonto 45 41 7N 16 40 E
Bitter Creek 156 41 39N 108 36W
Bitter L. = Buheirat-Murrat-el-Kubra 124 30 15N 32 40 E
Bitterfeld 26 51 36N 12 20 E
Bitterfontein 134 31 1 S 18 32 E
Bitterroot → 156 46 52N 114 6W
Bitterroot Range 156 46 0N 114 20W
Bitterwater 158 36 23N 121 0W
Bitti 44 40 29N 9 20 E
Bittou 127 11 17N 0 18W
Biu 127 10 40N 12 3 E
Bivolari 50 47 31N 27 27 E
Bivolu 50 47 16N 25 58 E
Biwa-Ko 101 35 15N 136 10 E
Biwabik 152 47 33N 92 19W
Bixad 50 47 56N 23 28 E
Biyang 94 32 38N 113 21 E
Biylikol, Ozero 63 43 5N 70 45 E
Biysk 64 52 40N 85 0 E
Bizana 135 30 50 S 29 52 E
Bizen 100 34 43N 134 8 E
Bizerte 121 37 15N 9 50 E
Bjargtangar 54 65 30N 24 30W
Bjelasica 46 42 50N 19 40 E
Bjelašnica 46 43 43N 18 9 E
Bjelovar 46 45 56N 16 49 E
Bjerringbro 53 56 23N 9 39 E
Björbo 52 60 27N 14 44 E
Björneborg 52 59 14N 14 16 E
Bjørnøya 6 74 30N 19 0 E
Bjuv 52 56 5N 12 55 E
Blace 46 43 18N 21 17 E
Blachownia 32 50 49N 18 56 E
Black → = Da → 84 21 15N 105 20 E
Black →, Canada 150 44 42N 79 19W
Black →, Ark., U.S.A. 153 35 38N 91 19W
Black →, N.Y., U.S.A. 151 43 59N 76 4W
Black →, Wis., U.S.A. 152 43 52N 91 22W
Black Diamond 144 50 45N 114 14W
Black Forest = Schwarzwald 27 48 0N 8 0 E
Black Hills 152 44 0N 103 50W
Black I. 145 51 12N 96 30W
Black L., Canada 145 59 12N 105 15W
Black L., U.S.A. 148 45 28N 84 15W
Black Mesa, Mt. 153 36 57N 102 55W
Black Mt. = Mynydd Du 13 51 45N 3 45W
Black Mountain 113 30 18 S 151 39 E
Black Mts. 13 51 52N 3 5W
Black Range 157 33 30N 107 55W
Black River 162 18 0N 77 50W
Black River Falls 152 44 23N 90 52W
Black Rock 112 32 50 S 138 44 E
Black Sea 39 43 30N 35 0 E
Black Volta → 126 8 41N 1 33W
Black Warrior → 149 32 32N 87 51W
Blackall 110 24 25 S 145 45 E
Blackball 115 42 22 S 171 26 E
Blackbull 110 17 55 S 141 45 E
Blackburn 12 53 44N 2 30W
Blackduck 152 47 43N 94 32W
Blackfoot 156 43 13N 112 12W
Blackfoot → 156 46 52N 113 53W
Blackfoot Res. 156 43 0N 111 35W
Blackie 144 50 36N 113 37W
Blackpool 12 53 48N 3 3W
Blackriver 150 44 46N 83 17W
Blacks Harbour 143 45 3N 66 49W
Blacksburg 148 37 17N 80 23W
Blacksod B. 15 54 6N 10 0W
Blackstone 148 37 6N 78 0W
Blackstone → 144 61 5N 122 55W
Blackstone Ra. 109 26 0 S 128 30 E
Blackville 143 46 44N 65 50W
Blackwater 110 23 35 S 148 53 E
Blackwater →, Ireland 15 51 55N 7 50W
Blackwater →, U.K. 15 54 31N 6 35W
Blackwater →, U.S.A. 154 38 59N 92 59W
Blackwater Cr. → 111 25 56 S 144 30 E
Blackwell 153 36 55N 97 20W
Blackwells Corner 159 35 37N 119 47W
Blackwood, C. 107 7 49 S 144 31 E
Bladel 23 51 22N 5 13 E
Blaenau Ffestiniog 12 53 0N 3 57W
Blagaj 46 43 16N 17 55 E
Blagodarnoye 61 45 7N 43 37 E
Blagoevgrad 46 42 2N 23 5 E
Blagoveshchensk, Amur, U.S.S.R. 65 50 20N 127 30 E
Blagoveshchensk, Urals, U.S.S.R. 62 55 1N 55 59 E
Blagoveshchenskoye 63 43 18N 74 12 E
Blain 18 47 29N 1 45W
Blaine 144 48 59N 122 43W
Blaine Lake 145 52 51N 106 52W
Blainville-sur-l'Eau 19 48 33N 6 23 E
Blair 152 41 38N 96 10W
Blair Athol 110 22 42 S 147 31 E
Blair Atholl 14 56 46N 3 50W
Blairgowrie 14 56 36N 3 20W
Blairmore 144 49 40N 114 25W
Blairsden 158 39 47N 120 37W
Blairsville 150 40 27N 79 15W
Blaj 50 46 10N 23 57 E
Blake Pt. 152 48 12N 88 27W
Blakely 149 31 22N 85 0W
Blakesburg 154 40 58N 92 38W
Blâmont 19 48 35N 6 50 E
Blanc, C. 121 37 15N 9 56 E
Blanc, Le 20 46 37N 1 3 E
Blanc, Mont 21 45 48N 6 50 E
Blanca, B. 176 39 10 S 61 30W
Blanca Peak 157 37 35N 105 29W
Blanchard 153 35 8N 97 40W
Blanchardville 154 42 48N 89 52W
Blanche, C. 111 33 1 S 134 9 E
Blanche L., S. Austral., Australia 111 29 15 S 139 40 E
Blanche L., W. Austral., Australia 108 22 25 S 123 17 E
Blanchester 155 39 17N 83 59W
Blanco, S. Africa 134 33 55 S 22 23 E
Blanco, U.S.A. 153 30 7N 98 30W
Blanco → 174 30 20 S 68 42W
Blanco, C., C. Rica 162 9 34N 85 8W
Blanco, C., Spain 37 39 21N 2 51 E
Blanco, C., U.S.A. 156 42 50N 124 40W
Blanda → 54 65 20N 19 40W
Blandford Forum 13 50 52N 2 10W
Blanding 157 37 35N 109 30W
Blandinsville 154 40 33N 90 52W
Blanes 36 41 40N 2 48 E
Blangy-sur-Bresle 19 49 55N 1 37 E
Blanice → 30 49 10N 14 5 E
Blankenberge 23 51 20N 3 9 E
Blankenburg 26 51 46N 10 56 E
Blanquefort 20 44 55N 0 38W
Blanquilla, La 169 11 51N 64 37W
Blanquillo 175 32 53 S 55 37W
Blansko 31 49 22N 16 40 E
Blantyre 131 15 45 S 35 0 E
Blaricum 22 52 16N 5 14 E
Blarney 15 51 57N 8 35W
Błaski 32 51 38N 18 30 E
Blatná 30 49 25N 13 52 E
Blatnitsa 47 43 41N 28 32 E
Blato 43 42 56N 16 48 E
Blatten 28 46 20N 7 50 E
Blaubeuren 27 48 24N 9 47 E
Blaydon 12 54 56N 1 47W
Blaye 20 45 8N 0 40W
Blaye-les-Mines 20 44 1N 2 8 E
Blayney 113 33 32 S 149 14 E
Blaze, Pt. 108 12 56 S 130 11 E
Blazowa 32 49 53N 22 7 E
Bleckede 26 53 18N 10 43 E
Bled 43 46 27N 14 7 E
Blednaya, Gora 64 76 20N 65 0 E
Bléharis 23 50 31N 3 25 E
Bleiburg 30 46 35N 14 49 E
Blejeşti 50 44 19N 25 27 E
Blekinge län □ 53 56 20N 15 20 E
Blenheim, Canada 150 42 20N 82 0W
Blenheim, N.Z. 115 41 38 S 173 57 E
Bléone → 21 44 5N 6 0 E
Blerick 23 51 22N 6 9 E
Bletchley 13 51 59N 0 44W
Bleymard, Le 20 44 30N 3 42 E
Blida 121 36 30N 2 49 E
Blidet Amor 121 32 59N 5 58 E
Blidö 52 59 37N 18 53 E
Blidsberg 53 57 56N 13 30 E
Bligh Sound 115 44 47 S 167 32 E
Bligh Water 106 17 0 S 178 0 E
Blind River 142 46 10N 82 58W
Blinishti 48 41 52N 19 58 E
Blinnenhorn 29 46 26N 8 19 E
Blissfield 155 41 50N 83 52W
Blitar 89 8 5 S 112 11 E
Blitta 127 8 23N 1 6 E
Block I. 151 41 11N 71 35W
Block Island Sd. 151 41 17N 71 35W
Blockton 154 40 37N 94 29W
Blodgett Iceberg Tongue 7 66 8 S 130 35 E
Bloemendaal 22 52 24N 4 39 E
Bloemfontein 134 29 6 S 26 7 E
Bloemhof 134 27 38 S 25 32 E
Blois 18 47 35N 1 20 E
Blokziji 22 52 43N 5 58 E
Blomskog 52 59 16N 12 2 E
Blönduós 54 65 40N 20 12W
Blonie 32 52 12N 20 37 E
Bloodvein → 145 51 47N 96 43W
Bloody Foreland 15 55 10N 8 18W
Bloomer 152 45 8N 91 30W
Bloomfield, Australia 110 15 56 S 145 22 E
Bloomfield, Canada 150 43 59N 77 14W
Bloomfield, Ind., U.S.A. 155 39 1N 86 57W
Bloomfield, Iowa, U.S.A. 154 40 44N 92 26W
Bloomfield, Ky., U.S.A. 155 37 55N 85 19W
Bloomfield, N. Mex., U.S.A. 157 36 46N 107 59W
Bloomfield, Nebr., U.S.A. 152 42 38N 97 40W
Bloomingburg 155 39 36N 83 24W
Bloomington, Ill., U.S.A. 154 40 27N 89 0W
Bloomington, Ind., U.S.A. 155 39 10N 86 30W
Bloomington, Wis., U.S.A. 154 42 53N 90 55W
Bloomsburg 151 41 0N 76 30W
Blora 89 6 57 S 111 25 E
Blossburg 150 41 40N 77 4W
Blouberg 135 23 8 S 28 59 E
Blountstown 149 30 28N 85 5W
Bludenz 30 47 10N 9 50 E
Blue → 155 38 11N 86 18W
Blue Island 148 41 40N 87 40W
Blue Lake 156 40 53N 124 0W
Blue Mesa Res. 157 38 30N 107 15W
Blue Mound 154 39 42N 89 7W
Blue Mts., Australia 113 33 40 S 150 0 E
Blue Mts., Oreg., U.S.A. 156 45 15N 119 0W
Blue Mts., Pa., U.S.A. 151 40 30N 76 30W
Blue Mud B. 110 13 30 S 136 0 E
Blue Nile = An Nîl el Azraq □ 125 12 30N 34 30 E
Blue Nile = Nîl el Azraq → 125 15 38N 32 31 E
Blue Rapids 152 39 41N 96 39W
Blue Ridge Mts. 149 36 30N 80 15W
Blue Springs 154 39 1N 94 17W
Blue Stack Mts. 15 54 46N 8 5W
Blueberry → 144 56 45N 120 49W
Bluefield 148 37 18N 81 14W
Bluefields 162 12 20N 83 50W
Blueskin B. 115 45 44 S 170 38 E
Bluff, Australia 110 23 35 S 149 4 E
Bluff, N.Z. 115 46 37 S 168 20 E
Bluff, U.S.A. 157 37 17N 109 33W
Bluff Harbour 115 46 36 S 168 21 E
Bluff Knoll 109 34 24 S 118 15 E
Bluff Pt. 109 27 50 S 114 5 E
Bluffs 154 39 45N 90 32W
Bluffton, Ind., U.S.A. 155 40 43N 85 9W

Borgarnes

Bluffton, Ohio, U.S.A. **155** 40 54N 83 54W
Bluford **155** 38 20N 88 45W
Blumenau **175** 27 0S 49 0W
Blumenthal **26** 53 5N 8 20 E
Blümisalphorn **28** 46 30N 7 47 E
Blunt **152** 44 32N 100 0W
Bly **156** 42 23N 121 0W
Blyberg **52** 61 9N 14 11 E
Blyth, Australia **112** 33 49S 138 28 E
Blyth, Canada **150** 43 44N 81 26W
Blyth, U.K. **12** 55 8N 1 32W
Blythe **159** 33 40N 114 33W
Bø, Norway **51** 59 25N 9 3 E
Bo, S. Leone **126** 7 55N 11 50W
Bo Duc **85** 11 58N 106 50 E
Bo Hai **95** 39 0N 120 0 E
Bō-no-Misaki **100** 31 15N 130 13 E
Bo Xian **94** 33 50N 115 45 E
Boa Esperança **169** 3 21N 61 23W
Boa Nova **171** 14 22S 40 10W
Boa Viagem **170** 5 7S 39 44W
Boa Vista **169** 2 48N 60 30W
Boac **90** 13 27N 121 50 E
Boaco **162** 12 29N 85 35W
Bo'ai **94** 35 10N 113 3 E
Boal **34** 43 25N 6 49W
Boali **132** 4 48N 18 7 E
Boardman **150** 41 2N 80 40W
Boatman **111** 27 16S 146 55 E
Bobadah **113** 32 19S 146 41 E
Bobai **96** 22 17N 109 59 E
Bobbili **80** 18 35N 83 30 E
Bóbbio **42** 44 47N 9 22 E
Bobcaygeon **142** 44 33N 78 33W
Böblingen **27** 48 41N 9 1 E
Bobo-Dioulasso **126** 11 8N 4 13W
Boboc **50** 45 13N 26 59 E
Bobolice **32** 53 58N 16 37 E
Bobon, Davao, Phil. **91** 6 53N 126 19 E
Bobon, Samar, Phil. **90** 12 32N 124 34 E
Bobonaza → **168** 2 36S 76 38W
Boboshevo **46** 42 9N 23 0 E
Bobov Dol **46** 42 20N 23 0 E
Bóbr → **32** 52 4N 15 4 E
Bobraomby, Tanjon' i **135** 12 40S 49 10 E
Bobrinets **60** 48 4N 32 5 E
Bobrov **59** 51 5N 40 2 E
Bobruysk **58** 53 10N 29 15 E
Bobures **168** 9 15N 71 11W
Boca de Drago **169** 11 0N 61 50W
Boca de Uracoa **168** 9 8N 62 20W
Bôca do Acre **172** 8 50S 67 27W
Bôca do Jari **169** 1 7S 51 58W
Bôca do Moaco **172** 7 41S 68 17W
Boca Grande **169** 8 40N 60 40W
Boca Raton **149** 26 21N 80 5W
Bocaiúva **171** 17 7S 43 49W
Bocanda **126** 7 5N 4 31W
Bocaranga **132** 7 0N 15 35 E
Bocas del Toro **162** 9 15N 82 20W
Boceguillas **36** 41 20N 3 39W
Bochnia **32** 49 58N 20 27 E
Bocholt, Belgium **23** 51 10N 5 35 E
Bocholt, Germany **26** 51 50N 6 35 E
Bochov **30** 50 9N 13 3 E
Bochum **26** 51 28N 7 12 E
Bockenem **26** 52 1N 10 8 E
Boćki **32** 52 39N 23 3 E
Bocognano **21** 42 5N 9 4 E
Boconó **168** 9 15N 70 16W
Boconó → **168** 8 43N 69 34W
Bocoyna **160** 27 52N 107 35W
Bocq → **23** 50 20N 4 55 E
Bocşa **46** 45 21N 21 47 E
Boda, C.A.R. **132** 4 19N 17 26 E
Böda, Sweden **53** 57 15N 17 3 E
Bodafors **53** 57 48N 14 23 E
Bodaybo **65** 57 50N 114 0 E
Boddington **109** 32 50S 116 30 E
Bodega Bay **158** 38 20N 123 3W
Bodegraven **22** 52 5N 4 46 E
Boden **54** 65 50N 21 42 E
Bodensee **29** 47 35N 9 25 E
Bodenteich **26** 52 49N 10 41 E
Bodhan **80** 18 40N 77 44 E
Bodinayakkanur **81** 10 2N 77 10 E
Bodinga **127** 12 58N 5 10 E
Bodio **29** 46 23N 8 55 E
Bodmin **13** 50 28N 4 44W
Bodmin Moor **13** 50 33N 4 36W
Bodø **54** 67 17N 14 24 E
Bodoquena, Serra da **173** 21 0S 56 50W
Bodoupa **132** 5 43N 17 36 E
Bodrog → **31** 48 15N 21 35 E
Bódva → **31** 48 19N 20 45 E
Boechout **23** 51 10N 4 30 E
Boegoebergdam **134** 29 7S 22 9 E
Boekelo **22** 52 12N 6 49 E
Boelenslaan **22** 53 10N 6 10 E
Boembé **132** 2 54S 15 39 E
Boën **21** 45 44N 4 0 E
Boende **132** 0 24S 21 12 E
Boerne **153** 29 48N 98 41W
Boertange **22** 53 1N 7 12 E
Boezinge **23** 50 54N 2 52 E
Boffa **126** 10 16N 14 3W
Bogale **82** 16 17N 95 24 E
Bogalusa **153** 30 50N 89 55W
Bogan → **113** 29 59S 146 17 E
Bogan Gate **113** 33 7S 147 49 E
Bogangolo **132** 5 34N 18 15 E
Bogantungan **110** 23 41S 147 17 E
Bogata **153** 33 26N 95 10W
Bogatić **46** 44 51N 19 30 E
Bogdanovitch **62** 56 47N 62 1 E
Bogense **53** 55 34N 10 5 E
Boggabilla **111** 28 36S 150 24 E
Boggabri **111** 30 45S 150 0 E
Boggeragh Mts. **15** 52 2N 8 55W
Bogia **107** 4 9S 145 0 E
Bognor Regis **13** 50 47N 0 40W
Bogø, Denmark **53** 54 55N 12 2 E
Bogo, Phil. **91** 11 3N 124 0 E
Bogodukhov **58** 50 9N 35 33 E
Bogong, Mt. **113** 36 47S 147 17 E
Bogor **88** 6 36S 106 48 E
Bogoroditsk **59** 53 47N 38 8 E
Bogorodsk **59** 56 4N 43 30 E
Bogorodskoye **65** 52 22N 140 30 E
Bogoso **126** 5 38N 2 3W
Bogotá **168** 4 34N 74 0W
Bogotol **64** 56 15N 89 50 E
Bogra **82** 24 51N 89 22 E
Boguchany **65** 58 40N 97 30 E
Boguchar **61** 49 55N 40 32 E
Bogué **126** 16 45N 14 10W
Boguslav **60** 49 47N 30 53 E
Boguszów **32** 50 45N 16 12 E
Bohain-en-Vermandois **19** 49 59N 3 28 E
Bohemia **30** 50 0N 14 0 E
Bohemia Downs **108** 18 53S 126 14 E
Bohemian Forest = Böhmerwald **27** 49 30N 12 40 E
Bohena Cr. → **111** 30 17S 149 42 E
Bohinjska Bistrica **43** 46 17N 14 1 E
Böhmerwald **27** 49 30N 12 40 E
Bohmte **26** 52 24N 8 20 E
Bohol, Phil. **91** 9 50N 124 10 E
Bohol, Somalia **136** 5 45N 46 9 E
Bohol Sea **87** 9 0N 124 0 E
Bohol Str. **91** 9 45N 123 40 E
Bohotleh **136** 8 20N 46 25 E
Boi **127** 9 35N 9 27 E
Boi, Pta. de **175** 23 55S 45 15W
Boiaçu **169** 0 27S 61 46W
Boiano **45** 41 28N 14 29 E
Boileau, C. **108** 17 40S 122 7 E
Boinitsa **46** 43 58N 22 32 E
Boipeba, I. de **171** 13 39S 38 55W
Bois → **171** 18 35S 50 2W
Bois, Les **28** 47 11N 6 50 E
Boischot **23** 51 3N 4 47 E
Boise **156** 43 43N 116 9W
Boise City **153** 36 45N 102 30W
Boissevain **145** 49 15N 100 5W
Boite → **43** 46 5N 12 5 E
Boitzenburg **26** 53 16N 13 36 E
Boizenburg **26** 53 22N 10 42 E
Bojador C. **120** 26 0N 14 30W
Bojana → **46** 41 52N 19 22 E
Bojanowo **32** 51 43N 16 42 E
Bojnūrd **73** 37 30N 57 20 E
Bojonegoro **89** 7 11S 111 54 E
Boju **127** 7 22N 7 55 E
Boka **46** 45 22N 20 52 E
Boka Kotorska **46** 42 23N 18 32 E
Bokada **132** 4 8N 19 23 E
Bokala **126** 8 31N 4 33W
Bokatola **132** 0 38S 18 46 E
Boké **126** 10 56N 14 17W
Bokhara → **111** 29 55S 146 42 E
Bokkos **127** 9 17N 9 1 E
Boknafjorden **51** 59 14N 5 40 E
Bokombayevskoye **63** 42 10N 76 55 E
Bokoro **123** 12 25N 17 14 E
Bokote **132** 0 12S 21 8 E
Boksitogorsk **58** 59 32N 33 56 E
Bokungu **132** 0 35S 22 50 E
Bol, Chad **123** 13 30N 15 0 E
Bol, Yugoslavia **43** 43 18N 16 38 E
Bolama **126** 11 30N 15 30W
Bolan Pass **77** 29 50N 67 20 E
Bolangum **112** 36 42S 142 54 E
Bolaños → **160** 21 14N 104 8W
Bolbec **18** 49 30N 0 30 E
Boldāji **73** 31 56N 51 3 E
Boldeşti **50** 45 3N 26 2 E
Bole, China **92** 45 11N 81 37 E
Bole, Ethiopia **125** 6 36N 37 20 E
Bolekhov **58** 49 0N 24 0 E
Bolesławiec **32** 51 17N 15 37 E
Bolgatanga **127** 10 44N 0 53W
Bolgrad **60** 45 40N 28 32 E
Boli **125** 6 2N 28 48 E
Bolinao **90** 16 23N 119 54 E
Bolinao C. **90** 16 23N 119 55 E
Boliney **90** 17 24N 120 48 E
Bolívar, Argentina **174** 36 15S 60 53W
Bolívar, Antioquía, Colombia **168** 5 50N 76 1W
Bolívar, Cauca, Colombia **168** 2 0N 77 0W
Bolívar, Peru **172** 7 18S 77 48W
Bolivar, Mo., U.S.A. **153** 37 38N 93 22W
Bolivar, Tenn., U.S.A. **153** 35 14N 89 0W
Bolívar □, Colombia **168** 9 0N 74 40W
Bolívar □, Ecuador **168** 1 15S 79 5W
Bolívar □, Venezuela **169** 6 20N 63 30W
Bolivia ■ **173** 17 6S 64 0W
Bolivian Plateau **164** 20 0S 67 30W
Boljevac **46** 43 51N 21 58 E
Bolkhov **59** 53 25N 36 0 E
Bollène **21** 44 18N 4 45 E
Bollnäs **52** 61 21N 16 24 E
Bollon **111** 28 2S 147 29 E
Bollstabruk **52** 63 1N 17 40 E
Bollullos **35** 37 19N 6 32W
Bolmen **53** 56 55N 13 40 E
Bolobo **132** 2 6S 16 20 E
Bologna **43** 44 30N 11 20 E
Bologne **19** 48 10N 5 8 E
Bologoye **58** 57 55N 34 0 E
Bolomba **132** 0 35N 19 0 E
Bolonchenticul **161** 20 0N 89 49W
Bolong **91** 7 6N 122 14 E
Bolotovskoye **62** 58 31N 62 28 E
Boloven, Cao Nguyen **84** 15 10N 106 30 E
Bolpur **79** 23 40N 87 45 E
Bolsena **43** 42 40N 11 58 E
Bolsena, L. di **43** 42 35N 11 55 E
Bolshaya Glushitsa **59** 52 28N 50 30 E
Bolshaya Khobda → **62** 50 56N 54 34 E
Bolshaya Kinel → **62** 53 14N 50 30 E
Bolshaya Martynovka **61** 47 12N 41 46 E
Bolshaya Shatan, Gora **62** 53 37N 58 3 E
Bolshaya Vradiyevka **60** 47 50N 30 40 E
Bolshereche **64** 56 4N 74 45 E
Bolshevik, Ostrov **65** 78 30N 102 0 E
Bolshezemelskaya Tundra **56** 67 0N 56 0 E
Bolshoi Kavkas **61** 42 50N 44 0 E
Bolshoy Anyuy → **65** 68 30N 160 49 E
Bolshoy Atlym **64** 62 25N 66 50 E
Bolshoy Begichev, Ostrov **65** 74 20N 112 30 E
Bolshoy Lyakhovskiy, Ostrov **65** 73 35N 142 0 E
Bolshoy Tokmak **60** 47 16N 35 42 E
Bol'shoy Tyuters, Ostrov **58** 59 51N 27 13 E
Bolsward **22** 53 3N 5 32 E
Boltaña **36** 42 28N 0 4 E
Boltigen **28** 46 38N 7 24 E
Bolton, Canada **150** 43 54N 79 45W
Bolton, U.K. **12** 53 35N 2 26W
Bolu **57** 40 45N 31 35 E
Bolubolu **107** 9 21S 150 20 E
Boluo **97** 23 3N 114 21 E
Bolvadin **57** 38 45N 31 4 E
Bolzano **43** 46 30N 11 20 E
Bom Comércio **173** 9 45S 65 54W
Bom Conselho **170** 9 10S 36 41W
Bom Despacho **171** 19 43S 45 15W
Bom Jesus **170** 9 4S 44 22W
Bom Jesus da Gurguéia, Serra **170** 9 0S 43 0W
Bom Jesus da Lapa **171** 13 15S 43 25W
Boma **133** 5 50S 13 4 E
Bomaderry **113** 34 52S 150 37 E
Bomandjokou **132** 0 34N 14 23 E
Bomassa **132** 2 12N 16 12 E
Bomba, La **160** 31 53N 115 2W
Bombala **113** 36 56S 149 15 E
Bombarral **35** 39 15N 9 9W
Bombay **80** 18 55N 72 50 E
Bomboma **132** 2 25N 18 55 E
Bombombwa **130** 1 40N 25 40 E
Bomi Hills **126** 7 1N 10 38W
Bomili **130** 1 45N 27 5 E
Bommel **22** 51 43N 4 26 E
Bomokandi → **130** 3 39N 26 8 E
Bomongo **132** 1 27N 18 21 E
Bomu → **132** 4 40N 22 30 E
Bon, C. **121** 37 1N 11 2 E
Bon Sar Pa **84** 12 24N 107 35 E
Bonaduz **29** 46 49N 9 25 E
Bonaire **163** 12 10N 68 15W
Bonang **113** 37 11S 148 41 E
Bonanza **162** 13 54N 84 35W
Bonaparte Archipelago **108** 14 0S 124 30 E
Boñar **34** 42 52N 5 19W
Bonaventure **143** 48 5N 65 32W
Bonavista **143** 48 40N 53 5W
Bonavista, C. **143** 48 42N 53 5W
Bonawan **91** 9 8N 122 55 E
Bondeno **43** 44 53N 11 22 E
Bondo **130** 3 55N 23 53 E
Bondoukou **126** 8 2N 2 47W
Bondowoso **89** 7 55S 113 49 E
Bondyug **62** 60 29N 55 56 E
Bone, Teluk **87** 4 10S 120 50 E
Bone Rate **87** 7 25S 121 5 E
Bone Rate, Kepulauan **87** 6 30S 121 10 E
Bonefro **45** 41 42N 14 55 E
Bo'ness **14** 56 0N 3 38W
Bong Son = Hoai Nhon **84** 14 28N 109 1 E
Bongabon **90** 15 38N 121 8 E
Bongabong **90** 12 45N 121 29 E
Bongandanga **132** 1 24N 21 3 E
Bongo **132** 1 47S 17 41 E
Bongor **123** 10 35N 15 20 E
Bongouanou **126** 6 42N 4 15W
Bonham **153** 33 30N 96 10W
Bonheiden **23** 51 1N 4 32 E
Bonifacio **21** 41 24N 9 10 E
Bonifacio, Bouches de **44** 41 12N 9 15 E
Bonin Is. **104** 27 0N 142 0 E
Bonke **125** 6 5N 37 16 E
Bonn **26** 50 43N 7 6 E
Bonnat **20** 46 20N 1 54 E
Bonne Terre **154** 37 57N 90 33W
Bonners Ferry **156** 48 38N 116 21W
Bonnétable **18** 48 11N 0 25 E
Bonneuil-Matours **18** 46 41N 0 34 E
Bonneval **18** 48 11N 1 24 E
Bonneville **21** 46 4N 6 24 E
Bonney, L. **112** 37 50S 140 20 E
Bonnie Doon **113** 37 2S 145 53 E
Bonnie Downs **110** 22 7S 143 50 E
Bonnie Rock **109** 30 29S 118 22 E
Bonny **127** 4 25N 7 13 E
Bonny → **127** 4 20N 7 10 E
Bonny, Bight of **127** 3 30N 9 20 E
Bonny-sur-Loire **19** 47 33N 2 50 E
Bonnyville **145** 54 20N 110 45W
Bonobono **91** 8 40N 117 36 E
Bonoi **87** 1 45S 137 41 E
Bonorva **44** 40 25N 8 47 E
Bonsall **159** 33 16N 117 14W
Bontang **89** 0 10N 117 30 E
Bonthain **87** 5 34S 119 56 E
Bonthe **126** 7 30N 12 33W
Bontoc **90** 17 7N 120 58 E
Bonyeri **126** 5 1N 2 46W
Bonyhád **31** 46 18N 18 32 E
Bonython Ra. **108** 23 40S 128 45 E
Boogardie **109** 28 2S 117 45 E
Bookabie **109** 31 50S 132 41 E
Booker **153** 36 29N 100 30W
Boolaboolka, L. **112** 32 38S 143 10 E
Boolarra **113** 38 20S 146 20 E
Boolcoomata **112** 31 57S 140 33 E
Booleroo Centre **112** 32 53S 138 21 E
Booligal **113** 33 58S 144 53 E
Boom **23** 51 6N 4 20 E
Boonah **111** 27 58S 152 41 E
Boone, Iowa, U.S.A. **154** 42 5N 93 53W
Boone, N.C., U.S.A. **149** 36 14N 81 43W
Booneville, Ark., U.S.A. **153** 35 10N 93 54W
Booneville, Miss., U.S.A. **149** 34 39N 88 34W
Boonville, Calif., U.S.A. **158** 39 1N 123 22W
Boonville, Ind., U.S.A. **155** 38 3N 87 13W
Boonville, Mo., U.S.A. **154** 38 57N 92 45W
Boonville, N.Y., U.S.A. **151** 43 31N 75 20W
Booral **113** 32 30S 151 56 E
Boorindal **111** 30 22S 146 11 E
Booroomugga **113** 31 17S 146 27 E
Boorowa **113** 34 28S 148 44 E
Boothia, Gulf of **141** 71 0N 90 0W
Boothia Pen. **140** 71 0N 94 0W
Bootle, Cumbria, U.K. **12** 54 17N 3 24W
Bootle, Merseyside, U.K. **12** 53 28N 3 1W
Booué **132** 0 5S 11 55 E
Bophuthatswana □ **134** 25 49S 25 30 E
Boppard **27** 50 13N 7 36 E
Boquerón □ **173** 21 30S 60 0W
Boquete **162** 8 46N 82 27W
Boquilla, Presa de la **160** 27 40N 105 30W
Boquillas del Carmen **160** 29 17N 102 53W
Bor, Czech. **30** 49 41N 12 45 E
Bôr, Sudan **125** 6 10N 31 40 E
Bor, Sweden **53** 57 9N 14 10 E
Bor, Yugoslavia **46** 44 8N 22 7 E
Bor Mashash **71** 31 7N 34 50 E
Boradā → **70** 33 33N 36 34 E
Borah, Pk. **156** 44 19N 113 46W
Borama **136** 9 55N 43 7 E
Borang **125** 4 50N 30 59 E
Borangapara **82** 25 14N 90 14 E
Borås **53** 57 43N 12 56 E
Borāzjān **73** 29 22N 51 10 E
Borba, Brazil **169** 4 12S 59 34W
Borba, Portugal **35** 38 50N 7 26W
Borbon **91** 10 50N 124 2 E
Borborema, Planalto da **170** 7 0S 37 0W
Borçka **61** 41 25N 41 41 E
Borculo **22** 52 7N 6 31 E
Bord Khūn-e Now **73** 28 3N 51 28 E
Borda, C. **112** 35 45S 136 34 E
Bordeaux **20** 44 50N 0 36W
Borden, Australia **109** 34 3S 118 12 E
Borden, Canada **143** 46 18N 63 47W
Borden I. **6** 78 30N 111 30W
Borders □ **14** 55 35N 2 50W
Bordertown **112** 36 19S 140 45 E
Borðeyri **54** 65 12N 21 6W
Bordighera **42** 43 47N 7 40 E
Bordj bou Arreridj **121** 36 4N 4 45 E
Bordj Bourguiba **121** 32 12N 10 2 E
Bordj el Hobra **121** 32 9N 4 51 E
Bordj Fly Ste. Marie **120** 27 19N 2 32W
Bordj-in-Eker **121** 24 9N 5 3 E
Bordj Menaiel **121** 36 46N 3 43 E
Bordj Messouda **121** 30 12N 9 25 E
Bordj Nili **121** 33 28N 3 2 E
Bordj Omar Driss **121** 28 10N 6 40 E
Bordj-Tarat **121** 25 55N 9 3 E
Bordj Zelfana **121** 32 27N 4 15 E
Bordoba **63** 39 31N 73 16 E
Borea Creek **113** 35 5S 146 35 E
Borek Wielkopolski **32** 51 54N 17 11 E
Boremore **113** 33 15S 149 0 E
Borensberg **53** 58 34N 15 17 E
Borgarnes **54** 64 32N 21 55W

Borger

Borger, Neth. .... **22** 52 54N 6 44 E
Borger, U.S.A. **153** 35 40N 101 20W
Borgerhout .... **23** 51 12N 4 28 E
Borghamn .... **53** 58 23N 14 41 E
Borgholm .... **53** 56 52N 16 39 E
Bórgia .... **45** 38 50N 16 30 E
Borgloon .... **23** 50 48N 5 21 E
Borgo San Dalmazzo .. **42** 44 19N 7 29 E
Borgo San Lorenzo .... **43** 43 57N 11 21 E
Borgo Valsugano ...... **43** 46 3N 11 27 E
Borgomanero .... **42** 45 41N 8 28 E
Borgonovo Val Tidone . **42** 45 1N 9 28 E
Borgorose .... **43** 42 12N 13 14 E
Borgosésia .... **42** 45 43N 8 17 E
Borgvattnet .... **52** 63 26N 15 48 E
Borikhane .... **84** 18 33N 103 43 E
Borislav .... **58** 49 18N 23 28 E
Borisoglebsk .... **59** 51 27N 42 5 E
Borisoglebskiy .... **59** 56 28N 43 59 E
Borisov .... **58** 54 17N 28 28 E
Borisovka .... **63** 43 15N 68 10 E
Borispol .... **58** 50 21N 30 59 E
Borja, Peru .... **168** 4 20 S 77 40W
Borja, Spain **36** 41 48N 1 34W
Borjas Blancas .... **36** 41 31N 0 52 E
Borken .... **26** 51 51N 6 52 E
Borkou .... **123** 18 15N 18 50 E
Borkum .... **26** 53 36N 6 42 E
Borlänge .... **52** 60 29N 15 26 E
Borley, C. .... **7** 66 15 S 52 30 E
Bormida ➝ .... **42** 44 23N 8 13 E
Bórmio .... **42** 46 28N 10 22 E
Born .... **23** 51 2N 5 49 E
Borna .... **26** 51 8N 12 31 E
Borndiep .... **22** 53 27N 5 35 E
Borne .... **22** 52 18N 6 46 E
Bornem .... **23** 51 6N 4 14 E
Borneo .... **86** 1 0N 115 0 E
Bornholm .... **53** 55 10N 15 0 E
Bornholmsgattet ...... **53** 55 15N 14 20 E
Borno □ .... **127** 12 30N 12 30 E
Bornos **35** 36 48N 5 42W
Bornu Yassa .... **127** 12 14N 12 25 E
Borobudur .... **89** 7 36 S 110 13 E
Borodino .... **58** 55 31N 35 40 E
Borogontsy .... **65** 62 42N 131 8 E
Boromo **126** 11 45N 2 58W
Boron **159** 35 0N 117 39W
Boronga Is. .... **82** 19 58N 93 6 E
Borongan .... **91** 11 37N 125 26 E
Bororen .... **110** 24 13 S 151 33 E
Borotangba Mts. ...... **125** 6 30N 25 0 E
Borovan .... **47** 43 27N 23 45 E
Borovichi .... **58** 58 25N 33 55 E
Borovsk, Moskva, U.S.S.R. .... **59** 55 12N 36 24 E
Borovsk, Urals, U.S.S.R. .... **62** 59 43N 56 40 E
Borovskoye .... **62** 53 48N 64 12 E
Borrby .... **53** 55 27N 14 10 E
Borrego Springs **159** 33 15N 116 23W
Borriol **36** 40 4N 0 4W
Borroloola .... **110** 16 4 S 136 17 E
Borşa .... **50** 47 41N 24 50 E
Borsod-Abaúj-Zemplén □ .... **31** 48 20N 21 0 E
Borssele .... **23** 51 26N 3 45 E
Bort-les-Orgues .... **20** 45 24N 2 29 E
Borth **13** 52 29N 4 3W
Borujerd .... **73** 33 55N 48 50 E
Borzhomi .... **61** 41 48N 43 28 E
Borzna .... **58** 51 18N 32 26 E
Borzya .... **65** 50 24N 116 31 E
Bosa .... **44** 40 17N 8 32 E
Bosaga .... **63** 37 33N 65 41 E
Bosanska Brod .... **46** 45 10N 18 0 E
Bosanska Dubica ...... **43** 45 10N 16 50 E
Bosanska Gradiška .... **46** 45 10N 17 15 E
Bosanska Kostajnica ... **43** 45 11N 16 33 E
Bosanska Krupa ...... **43** 44 53N 16 10 E
Bosanski Novi .... **43** 45 2N 16 22 E
Bosanski Šamac .... **46** 45 3N 18 29 E
Bosansko Grahovo .... **43** 44 12N 16 26 E
Bosansko Petrovac .... **43** 44 35N 16 21 E
Bosaso .... **136** 11 12N 49 18 E
Bosavi, Mt. .... **107** 6 30 S 142 49 E
Boscastle **13** 50 42N 4 42W
Boscobel **154** 43 8N 90 42W
Boscotrecase .... **45** 40 46N 14 28 E
Bose .... **96** 23 53N 106 35 E
Boshan .... **95** 36 28N 117 49 E
Boshoek .... **134** 25 30 S 27 9 E
Boshof .... **134** 28 31 S 25 13 E
Boshrūyeh .... **73** 33 50N 57 30 E
Bosilegrad .... **46** 42 30N 22 27 E
Boskoop .... **22** 52 4N 4 40 E
Boskovice .... **31** 49 29N 16 40 E
Bosna ➝ .... **46** 45 4N 18 29 E
Bosna i Hercegovina □ **46** 44 0N 18 0 E
Bosnia = Bosna i Hercegovina □ ...... **46** 44 0N 18 0 E
Bosnik .... **87** 1 5 S 136 10 E
Bōsō-Hantō .... **101** 35 20N 140 20 E
Bosobolo .... **132** 4 15N 19 50 E
Bosporus = Karadeniz Boğazı .... **57** 41 10N 29 10 E
Bossangoa .... **132** 6 35N 17 30 E
Bossekop .... **54** 69 57N 23 15 E
Bossembélé .... **132** 5 25N 17 40 E
Bossembélé II .... **132** 5 41N 16 38 E
Bossier City **153** 32 28N 93 48W
Bosso .... **127** 13 43N 13 19 E
Bostānābād .... **72** 37 50N 46 50 E
Bosten Hu .... **92** 41 55N 87 40 E
Boston, Phil. .... **91** 7 52N 126 22 E
Boston, U.K. **12** 52 59N 0 2W
Boston, U.S.A. **151** 42 20N 71 0W
Boston Bar **144** 49 52N 121 30W
Bosusulu .... **132** 0 50N 20 45 E
Bosut ➝ .... **46** 45 20N 19 0 E
Boswell, Canada **144** 49 28N 116 45W
Boswell, Ind., U.S.A. . **155** 40 30N 87 23W
Boswell, Okla., U.S.A. **153** 34 1N 95 50W
Boswell, Pa., U.S.A. .. **150** 40 9N 79 2W
Bosworth **154** 39 28N 93 20W
Botad .... **78** 22 15N 71 40 E
Botene .... **84** 17 35N 101 12 E
Botevgrad .... **47** 42 55N 23 47 E
Bothaville .... **134** 27 23 S 26 34 E
Bothnia, G. of .... **54** 63 0N 20 0 E
Bothwell, Australia .... **110** 42 20 S 147 1 E
Bothwell, Canada **150** 42 38N 81 52W
Boticas **34** 41 41N 7 40W
Botletle ➝ .... **134** 20 10 S 23 15 E
Botolan .... **90** 15 17N 120 1 E
Botoroaga .... **50** 44 8N 25 32 E
Botoşani .... **50** 47 42N 26 41 E
Botoşani □ .... **50** 47 50N 26 50 E
Botro **126** 7 51N 5 19W
Botswana ■ .... **134** 22 0 S 24 0 E
Bottineau **152** 48 49N 100 25W
Bottrop .... **26** 51 34N 6 59 E
Botucatu .... **175** 22 55 S 48 30W
Botwood **143** 49 6N 55 23W
Bou Alam .... **121** 33 50N 1 26 E
Bou Ali **121** 27 11N 0 4W
Bou Djébéha **126** 18 25N 2 45W
Bou Guema .... **121** 28 49N 0 19 E
Bou Ismael .... **121** 36 38N 2 42 E
Bou Izakarn **120** 29 12N 9 46W
Boû Lanouâr **120** 21 12N 16 34W
Bou Saâda .... **121** 35 11N 4 9 E
Bou Salem .... **122** 36 45N 9 2 E
Bouaké **126** 7 40N 5 2W
Bouanga .... **132** 2 7 S 16 8 E
Bouar .... **132** 6 0N 15 40 E
Bouârfa .... **121** 32 32N 1 58 E
Bouca .... **132** 6 45N 18 25 E
Boucau **20** 43 32N 1 29W
Boucaut B. .... **110** 12 0 S 134 25 E
Bouches-du-Rhône □ .. **21** 43 37N 5 2 E
Bouda **121** 27 50N 0 27W
Boudenib **121** 31 59N 3 31W
Boudry .... **28** 46 57N 6 50 E
Boufarik .... **121** 36 34N 2 58 E
Bougainville C. .... **108** 13 57 S 126 4 E
Bougainville I. .... **107** 6 0 S 155 0 E
Bougainville Reef ..... **110** 15 30 S 147 5 E
Bougaroun, C. .... **121** 37 6N 6 30 E
Bougie = Bejaia ...... **121** 36 42N 5 2 E
Bougouni **126** 11 30N 7 20W
Bouillon .... **23** 49 44N 5 3 E
Bouïra .... **121** 36 20N 3 59 E
Boulder, Colo., U.S.A. **152** 40 3N 105 10W
Boulder, Mont., U.S.A. **156** 46 14N 112 4W
Boulder City **159** 35 58N 114 50W
Boulder Creek **158** 37 7N 122 7W
Boulder Dam = Hoover Dam **159** 36 0N 114 45W
Boulembo .... **132** 1 26 S 12 0 E
Bouli **126** 15 17N 12 18W
Boulia .... **110** 22 52 S 139 51 E
Bouligny .... **19** 49 17N 5 45 E
Boulogne ➝ **18** 47 12N 1 47W
Boulogne-sur-Gesse ... **20** 43 18N 0 38 E
Boulogne-sur-Mer ..... **19** 50 42N 1 36 E
Bouloire .... **18** 47 59N 0 45 E
Bouloupari .... **106** 21 52 S 166 4 E
Boulsa **127** 12 39N 0 34W
Boultoum .... **127** 14 45N 10 25 E
Boumalne **120** 31 25N 6 0W
Boun Neua .... **84** 21 38N 101 54 E
Boun Tai .... **84** 21 23N 101 58 E
Bouna **126** 9 10N 3 0W
Boundary Pk. **158** 37 51N 118 21W
Boundiali **126** 9 30N 6 20W
Bountiful **156** 40 57N 111 58W
Bounty I. .... **104** 48 0 S 178 30 E
Bourail .... **106** 21 34 S 165 30 E
Bourbeuse ➝ **154** 38 24N 90 54W
Bourbon **155** 41 18N 86 7W
Bourbon-Lancy .... **20** 46 37N 3 45 E
Bourbon-l'Archambault **20** 46 36N 3 4 E
Bourbonnais .... **20** 46 28N 3 0 E
Bourbonne-les-Bains ... **19** 47 54N 5 45 E
Bourem **127** 17 0N 0 24W
Bourg **20** 45 3N 0 34W
Bourg-Argental .... **21** 45 18N 4 32 E
Bourg-de-Péage .... **21** 45 2N 5 3 E
Bourg-en-Bresse ...... **21** 46 13N 5 12 E
Bourg-St.-Andéol ..... **21** 44 23N 4 39 E
Bourg-St.-Maurice .... **21** 45 35N 6 46 E
Bourg-St.-Pierre ...... **28** 45 57N 7 12 E
Bourganeuf .... **20** 45 57N 1 45 E
Bourges .... **19** 47 9N 2 25 E
Bourget **151** 45 26N 75 9W
Bourget, L. du .... **21** 45 44N 5 52 E
Bourgneuf, B. de **18** 47 3N 2 10W
Bourgneuf-en-Retz **18** 47 2N 1 58W
Bourgneuf-la-Fôret, Le **18** 48 10N 0 59W
Bourgogne .... **19** 47 0N 4 50 E
Bourgoin-Jallieu ...... **21** 45 36N 5 17 E
Bourgueil .... **18** 47 17N 0 10 E
Bourke .... **111** 30 8 S 145 55 E
Bournemouth **13** 50 43N 1 53W
Bourriot-Bergonce **20** 44 7N 0 14W
Bouscat, Le **20** 44 53N 0 37W
Bouse **159** 33 55N 114 0W
Boussac .... **20** 46 22N 2 13 E
Boussens .... **20** 43 12N 0 58 E
Bousso .... **123** 10 34N 16 52 E
Boussu .... **23** 50 26N 3 48 E
Boutilimit **126** 17 45N 14 40W
Bouvet I. = Bouvetøya **7** 54 26 S 3 24 E
Bouvetøya .... **7** 54 26 S 3 24 E
Bouznika **120** 33 46N 7 6W
Bouzonville .... **19** 49 17N 6 32 E
Bova Marina .... **45** 37 59N 15 56 E
Bovalino Marina ...... **45** 38 9N 16 10 E
Bovec .... **43** 46 20N 13 33 E
Bovenkarspel .... **22** 52 41N 5 14 E
Bovigny .... **23** 50 12N 5 55 E
Bovill **156** 46 58N 116 27W
Bovino .... **45** 41 15N 15 20 E
Bow Island **144** 49 50N 111 23W
Bowbells **152** 48 47N 102 19W
Bowdle **152** 45 30N 99 40W
Bowelling .... **109** 33 25 S 116 30 E
Bowen .... **110** 20 0 S 148 16 E
Bowen Mts. .... **113** 37 0 S 148 0 E
Bowie, Ariz., U.S.A. .. **157** 32 15N 109 30W
Bowie, Tex., U.S.A. .. **153** 33 33N 97 50W
Bowkān .... **72** 36 31N 46 12 E
Bowland, Forest of **12** 54 0N 2 30W
Bowling Green, Ky., U.S.A. **148** 37 0N 86 25W
Bowling Green, Mo., U.S.A. **154** 39 21N 91 12W
Bowling Green, Ohio, U.S.A. **155** 41 22N 83 40W
Bowling Green, C. .... **110** 19 19 S 147 25 E
Bowman **152** 46 12N 103 21W
Bowman I. .... **7** 65 0 S 104 0 E
Bowmans .... **112** 34 10 S 138 17 E
Bowmanville **142** 43 55N 78 41W
Bowmore **14** 55 45N 6 18W
Bowral .... **113** 34 26 S 150 27 E
Bowraville .... **111** 30 37 S 152 52 E
Bowron ➝ **144** 54 3N 121 50W
Bowser L. **144** 56 30N 129 30W
Bowsman **145** 52 14N 101 12W
Bowutu Mts. .... **107** 7 45 S 147 10 E
Bowwood .... **131** 17 5 S 26 20 E
Boxholm .... **53** 58 12N 15 3 E
Boxmeer .... **23** 51 38N 5 56 E
Boxtel .... **23** 51 36N 5 20 E
Boyabat .... **60** 41 28N 34 42 E
Boyabo .... **132** 3 43N 18 46 E
Boyaca □ **168** 5 30N 72 30W
Boyce **153** 31 25N 92 39W
Boyer ➝ **144** 58 27N 115 57W
Boyer, C. .... **106** 21 37 S 168 6 E
Boyle **15** 53 58N 8 19W
Boyne ➝ **15** 53 43N 6 15W
Boyne City **148** 45 13N 85 1W
Boyni Qara .... **77** 36 20N 67 0 E
Boynton Beach **149** 26 31N 80 3W
Boyolali .... **89** 7 32 S 110 35 E
Boyoma, Chutes ...... **130** 0 35N 25 23 E
Boyup Brook .... **109** 33 50 S 116 23 E
Bozburun .... **49** 36 43N 28 8 E
Bozcaada .... **48** 39 49N 26 3 E
Bozeman **156** 45 40N 111 0W
Bozen = Bolzano ..... **43** 46 30N 11 20 E
Bozene .... **132** 2 56N 19 12 E
Bożepole Wielkopolski . **32** 54 33N 17 56 E
Boževac .... **46** 44 32N 21 24 E
Bozouls .... **20** 44 28N 2 43 E
Bozoum .... **132** 6 25N 16 35 E
Bozovici .... **50** 44 56N 22 1 E
Bozyazı .... **70** 36 6N 33 0 E
Bra .... **42** 44 41N 7 50 E
Brabant □ .... **23** 50 46N 4 30 E
Brabant L. **145** 55 58N 103 43W
Brabrand .... **53** 56 9N 10 7 E
Brač .... **43** 43 20N 16 40 E
Bracadale, L. **14** 57 20N 6 30W
Bracciano .... **43** 42 6N 12 10 E
Bracciano, L. di .... **43** 42 8N 12 11 E
Bracebridge **142** 45 2N 79 19W
Brach .... **122** 27 31N 14 20 E
Bracieux .... **19** 47 30N 1 30 E
Bräcke .... **52** 62 45N 15 26 E
Brackettville **153** 29 21N 100 20W
Bracki Kanal .... **43** 43 24N 16 40 E
Brad .... **50** 46 10N 22 50 E
Brădano ➝ .... **45** 40 23N 16 51 E
Bradenton **149** 27 25N 82 35W
Bradford, Canada **150** 44 7N 79 34W
Bradford, U.K. **12** 53 47N 1 45W
Bradford, Ill., U.S.A. . **154** 41 11N 89 39W
Bradford, Ohio, U.S.A. **155** 40 8N 84 27W
Bradford, Pa., U.S.A. . **150** 41 58N 78 41W
Bradford, Vt., U.S.A. . **151** 43 59N 72 9W
Brădiceni .... **50** 45 3N 23 4 E
Bradley, Ark., U.S.A. . **153** 33 7N 93 39W
Bradley, Calif., U.S.A. **158** 35 52N 120 48W
Bradley, Ill., U.S.A. .. **155** 41 9N 87 52W
Bradley, S. Dak., U.S.A. **152** 45 10N 97 40W
Bradley Institute ...... **131** 17 7 S 31 25 E
Bradore Bay **143** 51 27N 57 18W
Bradshaw .... **108** 15 21 S 130 16 E
Brady **153** 31 8N 99 25W
Brædstrup .... **53** 55 58N 9 37 E
Braemar .... **112** 33 12 S 139 35 E
Braeside **151** 45 28N 76 24W
Braga **34** 41 35N 8 25W
Braga □ **34** 41 30N 8 30W
Bragado .... **174** 35 2 S 60 27W
Bragança, Brazil ...... **170** 1 0 S 47 2W
Bragança, Portugal **34** 41 48N 6 50W
Bragança □ **34** 41 30N 6 45W
Bragança Paulista ..... **175** 22 55 S 46 32W
Brahmanbaria .... **82** 23 58N 91 15 E
Brahmani ➝ .... **79** 20 39N 86 46 E
Brahmaputra ➝ ...... **79** 24 2N 90 59 E
Braich-y-pwll **12** 52 47N 4 46W
Braidwood .... **113** 35 27 S 149 49 E
Brăila .... **50** 45 19N 27 59 E
Brăila □ .... **50** 45 5N 27 30 E
Braine-l'Alleud ...... **23** 50 42N 4 23 E
Braine-le-Comte ...... **23** 50 37N 4 8 E
Brainerd **152** 46 20N 94 10W
Braintree, U.K. .... **13** 51 53N 0 34 E
Braintree, U.S.A. **151** 42 11N 71 0W
Brak ➝ .... **134** 29 35 S 22 55 E
Brake, Niedersachsen, Germany .... **26** 53 19N 8 30 E
Brake, Nordrhein-Westfalen, Germany .... **26** 51 43N 9 12 E
Brakel .... **22** 51 49N 5 5 E
Bräkne-Hoby .... **53** 56 14N 15 6 E
Brakwater .... **134** 22 28 S 17 3 E
Brålanda .... **53** 58 34N 12 21 E
Bralorne **144** 50 50N 122 50W
Bramberg .... **27** 50 6N 10 40 E
Bramminge .... **53** 55 28N 8 42 E
Brämön .... **52** 62 14N 17 40 E
Brampton **142** 43 45N 79 45W
Bramsche .... **26** 52 25N 7 58 E
Bramwell .... **110** 12 8 S 142 37 E
Branco ➝ .... **169** 1 20 S 61 50W
Branco, C. .... **170** 7 9 S 34 47W
Brande .... **53** 55 57N 9 8 E
Brandenburg, Germany **26** 52 24N 12 33 E
Brandenburg, U.S.A. .. **155** 38 0N 86 10W
Brandfort .... **134** 28 40 S 26 30 E
Brandon, Canada **145** 49 50N 99 57W
Brandon, U.S.A. **151** 43 48N 73 4W
Brandon, Mt. **15** 52 15N 10 15W
Brandon B. **15** 52 17N 10 8W
Brandsen .... **174** 35 10 S 58 15W
Brandval .... **51** 60 19N 12 1 E
Brandvlei .... **134** 30 25 S 20 30 E
Brandýs .... **30** 50 10N 14 40 E
Branford **151** 41 15N 72 48W
Braniewo .... **32** 54 25N 19 50 E
Bransfield Str. .... **7** 63 0 S 59 0W
Brańsk .... **32** 52 45N 22 50 E
Branson, Colo., U.S.A. **153** 37 4N 103 53W
Branson, Mo., U.S.A. . **153** 36 40N 93 18W
Brantford **142** 43 10N 80 15W
Brantôme .... **20** 45 22N 0 39 E
Branxholme .... **112** 37 52 S 141 49 E
Branxton .... **113** 32 38 S 151 21 E
Branzi .... **42** 46 0N 9 46 E
Bras d'Or, L. **143** 45 50N 60 50W
Brasil, Planalto .... **164** 18 0 S 46 30W
Brasiléia .... **172** 11 0 S 68 45W
Brasília .... **171** 15 47 S 47 55 E
Brasília Legal .... **169** 3 49 S 55 36W
Braslav .... **58** 55 38N 27 0 E
Braslovce .... **43** 46 21N 15 3 E
Braşov .... **50** 45 38N 25 35 E
Braşov □ .... **50** 45 45N 25 15 E
Brass .... **127** 4 35N 6 14 E
Brass ➝ .... **127** 4 15N 6 13 E
Brassac-les-Mines ..... **20** 45 24N 3 20 E
Brasschaat .... **23** 51 19N 4 27 E
Brassey, Banjaran ..... **86** 5 0N 117 15 E
Brassey Ra. .... **109** 25 8 S 122 15 E
Brasstown Bald, Mt. ... **149** 34 54N 83 45W
Brassus, Le .... **28** 46 35N 6 13 E
Bratan = Morozov .... **47** 42 30N 25 10 E
Bratislava .... **31** 48 10N 17 7 E
Bratsigovo .... **47** 42 1N 24 22 E
Bratsk .... **65** 56 10N 101 30 E
Brattleboro **151** 42 53N 72 37W
Braţul Chilia ➝ ..... **50** 45 25N 29 20 E
Bratul Sfîntu Gheorghe ➝ ..... **50** 45 0N 29 20 E
Braţul Sulina ➝ ..... **50** 45 10N 29 20 E
Bratunac .... **46** 44 13N 19 21 E
Braunau .... **30** 48 15N 13 3 E
Braunschweig .... **26** 52 17N 10 28 E
Braunton **13** 51 6N 4 9W
Brava .... **136** 1 20N 44 8 E
Bråviken .... **52** 58 38N 16 32 E
Bravo del Norte ➝ ... **160** 25 57N 97 9W
Brawley **159** 32 58N 115 30W
Bray **15** 53 12N 6 6W
Bray, Mt. .... **110** 14 0 S 134 30 E
Bray, Pays de .... **19** 49 46N 1 26 E
Bray-sur-Seine .... **19** 48 25N 3 14 E

Bryansk

Braymer 154 39 35N 93 48W
Brazeau → 144 52 55N 115 14W
Brazil 155 39 32N 87 8W
Brazil ■ 171 12 0S 50 0W
Brazilian Highlands = Brasil, Planalto 164 18 0S 46 30W
Brazo Sur → 174 25 21S 57 42W
Brazos → 153 28 53N 95 23W
Brazzaville 133 4 9S 15 12E
Brčko 46 44 54N 18 46E
Brda → 32 53 8N 18 8E
Brea 172 4 40S 81 7W
Breadalbane, Australia 110 23 50S 139 35E
Breadalbane, U.K. 14 56 30N 4 15W
Breaden, L. 109 25 51S 125 28E
Breaksea Sd. 115 45 35S 166 35E
Bream Bay 114 35 56S 174 28E
Bream Head 114 35 51S 174 36E
Bream Tail 114 36 3S 174 36E
Breas 174 25 29S 70 24W
Brebes 89 6 52S 109 3E
Brechin, Canada 150 44 32N 79 10W
Brechin, U.K. 14 56 44N 2 40W
Brecht 23 51 21N 4 38E
Breckenridge, Colo., U.S.A. 156 39 30N 106 2W
Breckenridge, Minn., U.S.A. 152 46 20N 96 36W
Breckenridge, Mo., U.S.A. 154 39 46N 93 48W
Breckenridge, Tex., U.S.A. 153 32 48N 98 55W
Brecknock, Pen. 176 54 35S 71 30W
Břeclav 31 48 46N 16 53E
Brecon 13 51 57N 3 23W
Brecon Beacons 13 51 53N 3 27W
Breda 23 51 35N 4 45E
Bredaryd 53 57 10N 13 45E
Bredasdorp 134 34 33S 20 2E
Bredbo 113 35 58S 149 10E
Bredene 23 51 14N 2 59E
Bredstedt 26 54 37N 8 59E
Bredy 62 52 26N 60 21E
Bree 23 51 8N 5 35E
Breezand 22 52 53N 4 49E
Bregalnica → 46 41 43N 22 9E
Bregenz 30 47 30N 9 45E
Bregovo 46 44 9N 22 39E
Bréhal 18 48 53N 1 30W
Bréhat, I. de 18 48 51N 3 0W
Breiðafjörður 54 65 15N 23 15W
Breil-sur-Roya 21 43 56N 7 31E
Breisach 27 48 2N 7 37E
Brejinho de Nazaré 170 11 1S 48 34W
Brejo 170 3 41S 42 47W
Brekke 51 61 1N 5 26E
Bremangerlandet 51 61 51N 5 0E
Bremen 26 53 4N 8 47E
Bremen □ 26 53 6N 8 46E
Bremer I. 110 12 5S 136 45E
Bremerhaven 26 53 34N 8 35E
Bremerton 158 47 30N 122 38W
Bremervörde 26 53 28N 9 10E
Bremnes 51 59 47N 5 8E
Bremsnes 51 63 6N 7 40E
Brenes 35 37 32N 5 54W
Brenham 153 30 5N 96 27W
Brenner Pass 30 47 0N 11 30E
Breno 42 45 57N 10 20E
Brent, Canada 142 46 2N 78 29W
Brent, U.K. 13 51 33N 0 18W
Brenta → 43 45 11N 12 18E
Brentwood, U.K. 13 51 37N 0 19E
Brentwood, U.S.A. 151 40 47N 73 15W
Bréscia 42 45 33N 10 13E
Breskens 23 51 23N 3 33E
Breslau = Wrocław 32 51 5N 17 5E
Bresle → 18 50 4N 1 22E
Bresles 19 49 25N 2 13E
Bressanone 43 46 43N 11 40E
Bressay I. 14 60 10N 1 5W
Bresse 19 46 50N 5 10E
Bresse, La 19 48 0N 6 53E
Bressuire 18 46 51N 0 30W
Brest, France 18 48 24N 4 31W
Brest, U.S.S.R. 58 52 10N 23 40E
Bretagne 18 48 0N 3 0W
Bretçu 50 46 7N 26 18E
Breteuil, Eure, France 18 48 50N 0 53E
Breteuil, Oise, France 19 49 38N 2 18E
Breton 144 53 7N 114 28W
Breton, Pertuis 20 46 17N 1 25W
Breton Sd. 153 29 40N 89 12W
Brett, C. 114 35 10S 174 20E
Bretten 27 49 2N 8 43E
Breukelen 22 52 10N 5 0E
Brevard 149 35 19N 82 42W
Breves 170 1 40S 50 29W
Brevik 51 59 4N 9 42E
Brewarrina 111 30 0S 146 51E
Brewer 143 44 43N 68 50W
Brewer, Mt. 158 36 44N 118 28W
Brewster, N.Y., U.S.A. 151 41 23N 73 37W
Brewster, Wash., U.S.A. 156 48 10N 119 51W
Brewster, Kap 6 70 7N 22 0W
Brewton 149 31 9N 87 2W
Breyten 135 26 16S 30 0E
Breytovo 59 58 18N 37 50E
Brezhnev 62 55 42N 52 19E
Brežice 43 45 54N 15 35E
Brézina 121 33 4N 1 14E
Březnice 30 49 32N 13 57E
Breznik 46 42 44N 22 50E
Brezno 31 48 50N 19 40E
Brezovo 47 42 21N 25 5E
Bria 132 6 30N 21 58E
Briançon 21 44 54N 6 39E
Briare 19 47 38N 2 45E
Bribbaree 113 34 10S 147 51E
Bribie I. 111 27 0S 152 58E
Bricquebec 18 49 28N 1 38W
Bridgehampton 151 40 56N 72 19W
Bridgend 13 51 30N 3 35W
Bridgeport, Calif., U.S.A. 158 38 14N 119 15W
Bridgeport, Conn., U.S.A. 151 41 12N 73 12W
Bridgeport, Nebr., U.S.A. 152 41 42N 103 10W
Bridgeport, Tex., U.S.A. 153 33 15N 97 45W
Bridger 156 45 20N 108 58W
Bridgeton 148 39 29N 75 10W
Bridgetown, Australia 109 33 58S 116 7E
Bridgetown, Barbados 163 13 0N 59 30W
Bridgetown, Canada 143 44 55N 65 18W
Bridgewater, Australia 112 36 36S 143 59E
Bridgewater, Canada 143 44 25N 64 31W
Bridgewater, Mass., U.S.A. 151 41 59N 70 56W
Bridgewater, S. Dak., U.S.A. 152 43 34N 97 29W
Bridgewater, C. 112 38 23S 141 23E
Bridgman 155 41 57N 86 33W
Bridgnorth 13 52 33N 2 25W
Bridgton 151 44 5N 70 41W
Bridgwater 13 51 7N 3 0W
Bridlington 12 54 6N 0 11W
Bridport, Australia 110 40 59S 147 23E
Bridport, U.K. 13 50 43N 2 45W
Brie, Plaine de la 19 48 35N 3 10E
Brie-Comte-Robert 19 48 40N 2 35E
Briec 18 48 6N 4 0W
Brielle 22 51 54N 4 10E
Brienne-le-Château 19 48 24N 4 30E
Brienon-sur-Armançon 19 47 59N 3 38E
Brienz 28 46 46N 8 2E
Brienzersee 28 46 44N 7 53E
Briey 19 49 14N 5 57E
Brig 28 46 18N 7 59E
Brigg 12 53 33N 0 30W
Briggsdale 152 40 40N 104 20W
Brigham City 156 41 30N 112 1W
Bright 113 36 42S 146 56E
Brighton, Australia 112 35 5S 138 30E
Brighton, Canada 142 44 2N 77 44W
Brighton, U.K. 13 50 50N 0 9W
Brighton, Colo., U.S.A. 152 39 59N 104 50W
Brighton, Ill., U.S.A. 154 39 2N 90 8W
Brighton, Iowa, U.S.A. 154 41 10N 91 49W
Brightwater 115 41 22S 173 9E
Brignogan-Plage 18 48 40N 4 20W
Brignoles 21 43 25N 6 5E
Brihuega 36 40 45N 2 52W
Brikama 126 13 15N 16 45W
Brilliant, Canada 144 49 19N 117 38W
Brilliant, U.S.A. 150 40 15N 80 39W
Brilon 26 51 23N 8 32E
Brim 112 36 3S 142 27E
Brimfield 154 40 50N 89 53W
Bríndisi 45 40 39N 17 55E
Brinje 43 45 0N 15 9E
Brinkley 153 34 55N 91 15W
Brinkworth 112 33 42S 138 26E
Brinnon 158 47 41N 122 54W
Brion, I. 143 47 46N 61 26W
Brionne 18 49 11N 0 43E
Brionski 43 44 55N 13 45E
Brioude 20 45 18N 3 24E
Briouze 18 48 42N 0 23W
Brisbane 111 27 25S 153 2E
Brisbane → 111 27 24S 153 9E
Brisighella 43 44 14N 11 46E
Bristol, U.K. 13 51 26N 2 35W
Bristol, Conn., U.S.A. 151 41 44N 72 57W
Bristol, Pa., U.S.A. 151 40 6N 74 52W
Bristol, R.I., U.S.A. 151 41 40N 71 15W
Bristol, S. Dak., U.S.A. 152 45 25N 97 43W
Bristol, Tenn., U.S.A. 149 36 36N 82 11W
Bristol B. 140 58 0N 160 0W
Bristol Channel 13 51 18N 4 30W
Bristol I. 7 58 45S 28 0W
Bristol L. 157 34 23N 116 50W
Bristow 153 35 55N 96 28W
British Antarctic Territory □ 7 66 0S 45 0W
British Columbia □ 144 55 0N 125 15W
British Guiana = Guyana ■ 172 5 0N 59 0W
British Honduras = Belize ■ 161 17 0N 88 30W
British Isles 10 55 0N 4 0W
Brits 135 25 37S 27 48E
Britstown 134 30 37S 23 30E
Britt, Canada 142 45 46N 80 34W
Britt, U.S.A. 154 43 6N 93 48W
Brittany = Bretagne 18 48 0N 3 0W
Britton 152 45 50N 97 47W
Brive-la-Gaillarde 20 45 10N 1 32E
Briviesca 36 42 32N 3 19W
Brixton 110 23 32S 144 57E
Brlik, Kazakh S.S.R., U.S.S.R. 63 43 40N 73 49E
Brlik, Kazakh S.S.R., U.S.S.R. 63 44 5N 73 31E
Brno 31 49 10N 16 35E
Bro 52 59 31N 17 38E
Broach = Bharuch 78 21 47N 73 0E
Broad → 149 33 59N 82 39W
Broad Arrow 109 30 23S 121 15E
Broad B. 14 58 14N 6 16W
Broad Haven 15 54 20N 9 55W
Broad Law 14 55 30N 3 22W
Broad Sd. 110 22 0S 149 45E
Broadford 113 37 14S 145 4E
Broadhurst Ra. 108 22 30S 122 30E
Broads, The 12 52 45N 1 30E
Broadus 152 45 28N 105 27W
Broadview 145 50 22N 102 35W
Broager 53 54 53N 9 40E
Broaryd 53 57 7N 13 15E
Brochet 145 57 53N 101 40W
Brochet, L. 145 58 36N 101 35W
Brock 145 51 26N 108 43W
Brocken 26 51 48N 10 40E
Brocklehurst 113 32 9S 148 38E
Brockport 150 43 12N 77 56W
Brockton 151 42 8N 71 2W
Brockville 142 44 35N 75 41W
Brockway, Mont., U.S.A. 152 47 18N 105 46W
Brockway, Pa., U.S.A. 150 41 14N 78 48W
Brocton 150 42 25N 79 26W
Brod 46 41 35N 21 17E
Brodarevo 46 43 14N 19 44E
Brodeur Pen. 141 72 30N 88 10W
Brodhead 154 42 37N 89 22W
Brodick 14 55 34N 5 9W
Brodnica 32 53 15N 19 25E
Brodokalmak 62 55 35N 62 6E
Brody 58 50 5N 25 10E
Broechem 23 51 11N 4 38E
Broek 22 52 26N 5 0E
Broek op Langedijk 22 52 41N 4 49E
Brogan 156 44 14N 117 32W
Broglie 18 49 0N 0 30E
Brok 32 52 43N 21 52E
Broken Bow, Nebr., U.S.A. 152 41 25N 99 35W
Broken Bow, Okla., U.S.A. 153 34 2N 94 43W
Broken Hill = Kabwe 131 14 30S 28 29E
Broken Hill 112 31 58S 141 29E
Brokind 53 58 13N 15 42E
Brokopondo 169 5 3N 54 59W
Brokopondo □ 169 4 30N 55 30W
Bromfield 13 52 25N 2 45W
Bromley 13 51 20N 0 5E
Bromölla 53 56 5N 14 28E
Bronaugh 154 37 41N 94 28W
Brønderslev 53 57 16N 9 57E
Brong-Ahafo □ 126 7 50N 2 0W
Bronkhorstspruit 135 25 46S 28 45E
Bronnitsy 59 55 27N 38 10E
Bronson 155 41 52N 85 12W
Bronte, Italy 45 37 48N 14 49E
Bronte, U.S.A. 153 31 54N 100 18W
Bronte Park 110 42 8S 146 30E
Brook Park 150 41 24N 80 51W
Brookes Point 91 8 47N 117 50E
Brookfield 154 39 50N 93 4W
Brookhaven 153 31 40N 90 25W
Brookings, Oreg., U.S.A. 156 42 4N 124 10W
Brookings, S. Dak., U.S.A. 152 44 20N 96 45W
Brooklin 150 43 55N 78 55W
Brooklyn 154 41 44N 92 27W
Brookmere 144 49 52N 120 53W
Brooks 144 50 35N 111 55W
Brooks B. 144 50 15N 127 55W
Brooks L. 145 61 55N 106 35W
Brooks Ra. 140 68 40N 147 0W
Brookston 155 40 36N 86 52W
Brooksville, Fla., U.S.A. 149 28 32N 82 21W
Brooksville, Ky., U.S.A. 155 38 41N 84 4W
Brookville 155 39 25N 85 0W
Brooloo 111 26 30S 152 43E
Broom, L. 14 57 55N 5 15W
Broome 108 18 0S 122 15E
Broomehill 109 33 51S 117 39E
Broons 18 48 20N 2 16W
Brora 14 58 0N 3 50W
Brora → 14 58 4N 3 52W
Brösarp 53 55 43N 14 6E
Brosna → 15 53 8N 8 0W
Broşteni 50 47 14N 25 43E
Brotas de Macaúbas 171 12 0S 42 38W
Brothers 156 43 56N 120 39W
Brøttum 51 61 2N 10 34E
Brou 18 48 13N 1 11E
Broughams Gate 112 30 51S 140 59E
Broughton 155 37 56N 88 27W
Broughton Island 141 67 33N 63 0W
Broughty Ferry 14 56 29N 2 50W
Broumov 31 50 35N 16 20E
Brouwershaven 22 51 45N 3 55E
Brouwershavensche Gat 22 51 46N 3 50E
Brovary 58 50 34N 30 48E
Brovst 53 57 6N 9 31E
Browerville 152 46 3N 94 50W
Brown, Mt. 112 32 30S 138 0E
Brown, Pt. 111 32 32S 133 50E
Brown Willy 13 50 35N 4 34W
Brownfield 153 33 10N 102 15W
Browning, Ill., U.S.A. 154 40 7N 90 22W
Browning, Mo., U.S.A. 154 40 3N 93 12W
Browning, Mont., U.S.A. 156 48 35N 113 0W
Brownlee 145 50 43N 106 1W
Brownsburg 155 39 50N 86 26W
Brownstown 155 38 53N 86 3W
Brownsville, Oreg., U.S.A. 156 44 29N 123 0W
Brownsville, Tenn., U.S.A. 153 35 35N 89 15W
Brownsville, Tex., U.S.A. 153 25 56N 97 25W
Brownsweg 169 5 5N 55 15W
Brownwood 153 31 45N 99 0W
Brownwood, L. 153 31 51N 98 35W
Browse I. 108 14 7S 123 33E
Broye → 28 46 52N 6 58E
Brozas 35 39 37N 6 47W
Bru 51 61 32N 5 11E
Bruas 85 4 30N 100 47E
Bruay-en-Artois 19 50 29N 2 33E
Bruce, Mt. 108 22 37S 118 8E
Bruce B. 115 43 35S 169 42E
Bruce Pen. 150 45 0N 81 30W
Bruce Rock 109 31 52S 118 8E
Bruche → 19 48 34N 7 43E
Bruchsal 27 49 9N 8 39E
Bruck an der Leitha 31 48 1N 16 47E
Bruck an der Mur 30 47 24N 15 16E
Brückenau 27 50 17N 9 48E
Brue → 13 51 10N 2 59W
Brugelette 23 50 35N 3 52E
Bruges = Brugge 23 51 13N 3 13E
Brugg 28 47 29N 8 11E
Brugge 23 51 13N 3 13E
Brühl 26 50 49N 6 51E
Bruinisse 23 51 40N 4 5E
Brûlé 144 53 15N 117 58W
Brûlon 18 47 58N 0 15W
Brûly 23 49 58N 4 32E
Brumado 171 14 14S 41 40W
Brumado → 171 14 13S 41 40W
Brumath 19 48 43N 7 40E
Brummen 22 52 5N 6 10E
Brumunddal 51 60 53N 10 56E
Brunchilly 110 18 50S 134 30E
Brundidge 149 31 43N 85 45W
Bruneau 156 42 57N 115 55W
Bruneau → 156 42 57N 115 58W
Brunei = Bandar Seri Begawan 86 4 52N 115 0E
Brunei ■ 86 4 50N 115 0E
Brunette Downs 110 18 40S 135 55E
Brunflo 52 63 5N 14 50E
Brunico 43 46 50N 11 55E
Brünig, P. 28 46 46N 8 8E
Brunkeberg 51 59 26N 8 28E
Brunna 52 59 52N 17 25E
Brunnen 29 46 59N 8 37E
Brunner, L. 115 42 37S 171 27E
Brunnsvik 52 60 12N 15 8E
Bruno 145 52 20N 105 30W
Brunsbüttelkoog 26 53 52N 9 13E
Brunssum 23 50 57N 5 59E
Brunswick = Braunschweig 26 52 17N 10 28E
Brunswick, Ga., U.S.A. 149 31 10N 81 30W
Brunswick, Maine, U.S.A. 143 43 53N 69 50W
Brunswick, Md., U.S.A. 148 39 20N 77 38W
Brunswick, Mo., U.S.A. 154 39 26N 93 10W
Brunswick, Ohio, U.S.A. 150 41 15N 81 50W
Brunswick, Pen. de 176 53 30S 71 30W
Brunswick B. 108 15 15S 124 50E
Brunswick Junction 109 33 15S 115 50E
Bruntál 31 50 0N 17 27E
Bruny I. 110 43 20S 147 15E
Brus Laguna 162 15 47N 84 35W
Brusartsi 46 43 40N 23 5E
Brush 152 40 17N 103 33W
Brushton 151 44 50N 74 32W
Brusio 29 46 14N 10 8E
Brusque 175 27 5S 49 0W
Brussel 23 50 51N 4 21E
Brussels = Brussel 23 50 51N 4 21E
Brussels 150 43 44N 81 15W
Brustem 23 50 48N 5 14E
Bruthen 113 37 42S 147 50E
Bruxelles = Brussel 23 50 51N 4 21E
Bruyères 19 48 10N 6 40E
Brwinów 32 52 9N 20 40E
Bryagovo 47 41 58N 25 8E
Bryan, Ohio, U.S.A. 155 41 30N 84 30W
Bryan, Tex., U.S.A. 153 30 40N 96 27W
Bryan, Mt. 112 33 30S 139 0E
Bryanka 61 48 32N 38 45E
Bryansk 58 53 13N 34 25E

Caleta Olivia

Burriana 36 39 50N 0 4W
Burrinjuck Res. 113 35 0 S 148 36 E
Burro, Serranías del 160 29 0N 102 0W
Burrundie 108 13 32 S 131 42 E
Burruyacú 174 26 30 S 64 40W
Burry Port 13 51 41N 4 17W
Bursa 57 40 15N 29 5 E
Burseryd 53 57 12N 13 17 E
Burstall 145 50 39N 109 54W
Burton 155 43 0N 83 40W
Burton L. 142 54 45N 78 20W
Burton-upon-Trent 12 52 48N 1 39W
Burtundy 112 33 45 S 142 15 E
Buru 87 3 30 S 126 30 E
Buruanga 91 11 51N 121 53 E
Burullus, Bahra el 124 31 25N 31 0 E
Burûm 75 14 22N 48 59 E
Burûn, Râs 71 31 14N 33 7 E
Burunday 63 43 20N 76 51 E
Burundi ■ 130 3 15 S 30 0 E
Bururi 130 3 57 S 29 37 E
Burutu 127 5 20N 5 29 E
Burwell 152 41 49N 99 8W
Bury 12 53 36N 2 19W
Bury St. Edmunds 13 52 15N 0 42 E
Buryat A.S.S.R. □ 65 53 0N 110 0 E
Buryn 58 51 13N 33 50 E
Burzenin 32 51 28N 18 47 E
Busalla 42 44 34N 8 58 E
Busango Swamp 131 14 15 S 25 45 E
Buşayrah 72 35 9N 40 26 E
Buşayyah 72 30 0N 46 10 E
Busca 42 44 31N 7 29 E
Bushati 48 41 58N 19 34 E
Būshehr 73 28 55N 50 55 E
Būshehr □ 73 28 20N 51 45 E
Bushell 145 59 31N 108 45W
Bushenyi 130 0 35 S 30 10 E
Bushire = Būshehr 73 28 55N 50 55 E
Bushnell, Ill., U.S.A. 152 40 32N 90 30W
Bushnell, Nebr., U.S.A. 152 41 18N 103 50W
Busia □ 130 0 25N 34 6 E
Busie 126 10 29N 2 22W
Businga 132 3 16N 20 59 E
Buskerud fylke □ 51 60 13N 9 0 E
Busko Zdrój 32 50 28N 20 42 E
Buslei 136 5 28N 44 25 E
Busoga □ 130 0 5N 33 30 E
Busovača 46 44 6N 17 53 E
Busra ash Shām 71 32 30N 36 25 E
Bussang 19 47 50N 6 50 E
Busselton 109 33 42 S 115 15 E
Busseto 42 44 59N 10 2 E
Bussigny 28 46 33N 6 33 E
Bussum 22 52 16N 5 10 E
Bustamante, B. 176 45 5 S 66 18W
Busto, C. 34 43 34N 6 28W
Busto Arsizio 42 45 40N 8 50 E
Busu-Djanoa 132 1 43N 21 23 E
Busuanga 90 12 10N 120 0 E
Büsum 26 54 7N 8 50 E
Buta 130 2 50N 24 53 E
Butare 130 2 31 S 29 52 E
Butaritari 104 3 30N 174 0 E
Bute, Australia 112 33 51 S 138 2 E
Bute, U.K. 14 55 48N 5 2W
Bute Inlet 144 50 40N 124 53W
Butemba 130 1 9N 31 37 E
Butembo 130 0 9N 29 18 E
Butera 45 37 10N 14 10 E
Bütgenbach 23 50 26N 6 12 E
Butha Qi 93 48 0N 122 32 E
Buthidaung 82 20 52N 92 32 E
Butiaba 130 1 50N 31 20 E
Butkhāk 77 34 30N 69 22 E
Butler, Ind., U.S.A. 155 41 26N 84 52W
Butler, Ky., U.S.A. 155 38 47N 84 22W
Butler, Mo., U.S.A. 154 38 17N 94 18W
Butler, Pa., U.S.A. 150 40 52N 79 52W
Butom Odrzánski 32 51 44N 15 48 E
Bütschwil 29 47 23N 9 5 E
Butte, Mont., U.S.A. 156 46 0N 112 31W
Butte, Nebr., U.S.A. 152 42 56N 98 54W
Butte Creek → 158 39 12N 121 56W
Butterworth = Gcuwa 135 32 20 S 28 11 E
Butterworth 85 5 24N 100 23 E
Buttfield, Mt. 109 24 45 S 128 9 E
Button B. 145 58 45N 94 23W
Buttonwillow 159 35 24N 119 28W
Butty Hd. 109 33 54 S 121 39 E
Butuan 91 8 57N 125 33 E
Butuku-Luba 127 3 29N 8 33 E
Butulan 91 5 38N 125 26 E
Butung 87 5 0 S 122 45 E
Buturlinovka 59 50 50N 40 35 E
Butzbach 26 50 24N 8 40 E
Bützow 26 53 51N 11 59 E
Buug 91 7 40N 123 2 E
Buxar 79 25 34N 83 58 E
Buxton, Guyana 169 6 48N 58 2W
Buxton, S. Africa 134 27 38 S 24 42 E
Buxton, U.K. 12 53 16N 1 54W
Buxy 19 46 44N 4 40 E
Buy 59 58 28N 41 28 E
Buyaga 65 59 50N 127 0 E
Buynaksk 61 42 48N 47 7 E
Büyük Çekmece 47 41 2N 28 35 E
Büyük Kemikli Burun 48 40 20N 26 15 E
Büyükeğri Dağ 70 36 45N 33 33 E
Buzançais 18 46 54N 1 25 E
Buzău 50 45 10N 26 50 E
Buzău □ 50 45 20N 26 30 E
Buzău → 50 45 26N 27 44 E
Buzău, Pasul 50 45 35N 26 12 E
Buzen 100 33 35N 131 5 E
Buzet 43 45 24N 13 58 E
Buzi → 131 19 50 S 34 43 E
Buziaş 50 45 38N 21 36 E
Buzuluk 62 52 48N 52 12 E
Buzuluk → 59 50 15N 42 7 E
Buzzards Bay 151 41 45N 70 38W
Bwagaoia 107 10 40 S 152 52 E
Bwana Mkubwe 131 13 8 S 28 38 E
Byala, Ruse, Bulgaria 47 43 28N 25 44 E
Byala, Varna, Bulgaria 47 42 53N 27 55 E
Byala Slatina 47 43 26N 23 55 E
Byandovan, Mys 61 39 45N 49 28 E
Bychawa 32 51 1N 22 36 E
Byczyna 32 51 7N 18 12 E
Bydgoszcz 32 53 10N 18 0 E
Bydgoszcz □ 32 53 16N 17 33 E
Byelorussian S.S.R. □ 58 53 30N 27 0 E
Byers 152 39 46N 104 13W
Byesville 150 39 56N 81 32W
Bygland 51 58 50N 7 48 E
Byglandsfjord 51 58 40N 7 50 E
Byglandsfjorden 51 58 44N 7 50 E
Byhalia 153 34 53N 89 41W
Bykhov 58 53 31N 30 14 E
Bykle 51 59 20N 7 22 E
Bykovo 61 49 50N 45 25 E
Bylas 157 33 11N 110 9W
Bylderup 53 54 57N 9 6 E
Bylot I. 141 73 13N 78 34W
Byrd, C. 7 69 38 S 76 7W
Byrd Land 7 79 30 S 125 0W
Byrd Sub-Glacial Basin 7 82 0 S 120 0W
Byro 109 26 5 S 116 11 E
Byrock 113 30 40 S 146 27 E
Byron 154 42 8N 89 15W
Byron Bay 111 28 43 S 153 37 E
Byrranga, Gory 65 75 0N 100 0 E
Byrum 53 57 16N 11 0 E
Bystrovka 63 42 47N 75 42 E
Bystrzyca →, Lublin, Poland 32 51 21N 22 46 E
Bystrzyca →, Wrocław, Poland 32 51 12N 16 55 E
Bystrzyca Kłodzka 32 50 19N 16 39 E
Byten 58 52 50N 25 27 E
Bytom 32 50 25N 18 54 E
Bytów 32 54 10N 17 30 E
Byumba 130 1 35 S 30 4 E
Bzenec 31 48 58N 17 18 E
Bzura → 32 52 25N 20 15 E

C

Ca → 84 18 45N 105 45 E
Ca Mau = Quan Long 85 9 7N 105 8 E
Ca Mau, Mui = Bai Bung, Mui 85 8 38N 104 44 E
Ca Na 85 11 20N 108 54 E
Caacupé 174 25 23 S 57 5W
Caála 133 12 46 S 15 30 E
Caamano Sd. 144 52 55N 129 25W
Caapiranga 169 3 18 S 61 13W
Caazapá 174 26 8 S 56 19W
Caazapá □ 175 26 10 S 56 0W
Cabadbaran 91 9 10N 125 38 E
Cabagan 90 17 26N 121 46 E
Cabalian 91 10 16N 125 10 E
Caballeria, C. de 36 40 5N 4 5 E
Cabana 172 8 25 S 78 5W
Cabanaconde 172 15 38 S 71 58W
Cabañaquinta 34 43 10N 5 38W
Cabanatuan 90 15 30N 120 58 E
Cabanes 36 40 9N 0 2 E
Cabangon 90 15 10N 120 3 E
Cabanillas 172 15 36 S 70 28W
Cabano 143 47 40N 68 56W
Čabar 43 45 36N 14 39 E
Cabarroquis 90 16 50N 121 30 E
Cabarruyan I. 90 16 18N 119 59 E
Cabazon 159 33 55N 116 47W
Cabcaben 90 14 27N 120 35 E
Cabedelo 170 7 0 S 34 50W
Cabery 155 40 59N 88 12W
Cabeza del Buey 35 38 44N 5 13W
Cabildo 174 32 30 S 71 5W
Cabimas 168 10 23N 71 25W
Cabinda 133 5 33 S 12 11 E
Cabinda □ 133 5 0 S 12 30 E
Cabinet Mts. 156 48 0N 115 30W
Cabiri 133 8 52 S 13 39 E
Cabo Blanco 176 47 15 S 65 47W
Cabo Frio 171 22 51 S 42 3W
Cabo Pantoja 168 1 0 S 75 10W
Cabo Raso 176 44 20 S 65 15W
Cabonga, Réservoir 142 47 20N 76 40W
Cabool 153 37 10N 92 8W
Caboolture 111 27 5 S 152 58 E
Cabora Bassa Dam 131 15 20 S 32 50 E
Caborca 160 30 40N 112 10W
Cabot, Mt. 151 44 30N 71 25W
Cabot Strait 143 47 15N 59 40W
Cabra 35 37 30N 4 28W
Cabra del Santo Cristo 37 37 42N 3 16W
Cábras 44 39 57N 8 30 E
Cabrera, I. 37 39 8N 2 57 E
Cabrera, Sierra 34 42 12N 6 40W
Cabri 145 50 35N 108 25W
Cabriel → 37 39 14N 1 3W
Cabruta 168 7 50N 66 10W
Cabucgayan 91 11 29N 124 34 E
Cabuga 90 17 48N 120 27 E
Cabulauan Is. 91 11 25N 120 8 E
Caburan = Jose Abad Santos 91 5 55N 125 39 E
Cabuyaro 168 4 18N 72 49W
Cacabelos 34 42 36N 6 44W
Čačak 46 43 54N 20 20 E
Cacao 169 4 33N 52 26W
Cáceres, Brazil 173 16 5 S 57 40W
Cáceres, Colombia 168 7 35N 75 20W
Cáceres, Spain 35 39 26N 6 23W
Cáceres □ 35 39 45N 6 0W
Cache Bay 142 46 22N 80 0W
Cache Cr. → 158 38 45N 121 43W
Cachepo 35 37 20N 7 49W
Cachéu 126 12 14N 16 8W
Cachi 174 25 5 S 66 10W
Cachimbo 173 8 57 S 54 54W
Cachimbo, Serra do 173 9 30 S 55 0W
Cachingues 133 13 5 S 16 43 E
Cachoeira 171 12 30 S 39 0W
Cachoeira Alta 171 18 48 S 50 58W
Cachoeira de Itapemirim 175 20 51 S 41 7W
Cachoeira do Sul 175 30 3 S 52 53W
Cachoeiro do Arari 170 1 1 S 48 58W
Cachopo 35 37 20N 7 49W
Cachuela Esperanza 173 10 32 S 65 38W
Cacólo 133 10 9 S 19 21 E
Caconda 133 13 48 S 15 8 E
Cacongo 133 5 11 S 12 5 E
Caçu 171 18 37 S 51 4W
Cacula 133 14 29 S 14 10 E
Caculé 171 14 30 S 42 13W
Cacuso 133 9 25 S 15 45 E
Cadarache 21 43 41N 5 43 E
Čadca 31 49 26N 18 45 E
Caddo 153 34 8N 96 18W
Cadell Cr. → 110 22 35 S 141 51 E
Cadenazzo 29 46 9N 8 57 E
Cader Idris 12 52 43N 3 56W
Cadí, Sierra del 36 42 17N 1 42 E
Cadibarrawirracanna, L. 111 28 52 S 135 27 E
Cadillac, Canada 142 48 14N 78 23W
Cadillac, France 20 44 38N 0 20W
Cadillac, U.S.A. 148 44 16N 85 25W
Cadiz, Phil. 91 10 57N 123 15 E
Cádiz, Spain 35 36 30N 6 20W
Cadiz, U.S.A. 150 40 13N 81 0W
Cádiz □ 35 36 36N 5 45W
Cádiz, G. de 35 36 40N 7 0W
Cadney Park 111 27 55 S 134 3 E
Cadomin 144 53 2N 117 20W
Cadotte → 144 56 43N 117 10W
Cadours 20 43 44N 1 2 E
Cadoux 109 30 46 S 117 7 E
Caen 18 49 10N 0 22W
Caernarfon 12 53 8N 4 17W
Caernarfon B. 12 53 4N 4 40W
Caernarvon = Caernarfon 12 53 8N 4 17W
Caerphilly 13 51 34N 3 13W
Caesarea 69 32 30N 34 53 E
Caeté 171 19 55 S 43 40W
Caetité 171 13 50 S 42 32W
Cafayate 174 26 2 S 66 0W
Cafifi 168 5 13N 71 4W
Cafu 133 16 30 S 15 8 E
Cagayan □ 90 18 0N 121 50 E
Cagayan → 90 18 25N 121 42 E
Cagayan de Oro 91 8 30N 124 40 E
Cagayan Is. 91 9 40N 121 16 E
Cagayan Sulu I. 91 7 1N 118 30 E
Cagli 43 43 32N 12 38 E
Cágliari 44 39 15N 9 6 E
Cágliari, G. di 44 39 8N 9 10 E
Cagnano Varano 45 41 49N 15 47 E
Cagnes-sur-Mer 21 43 40N 7 9 E
Caguán → 168 0 8 S 74 18W
Caguas 163 18 14N 66 4W
Caha Mts. 15 51 45N 9 40W
Cahama 133 16 17 S 14 19 E
Caher 15 52 23N 7 56W
Cahersiveen 15 51 57N 10 13W
Cahore Pt. 15 52 34N 6 11W
Cahors 20 44 27N 1 27 E
Cahuapanas 172 5 15 S 77 0W
Cahuinari → 168 1 21 S 70 44W
Cai Bau, Dao 84 21 10N 107 27 E
Cai Nuoc 85 8 56N 105 1 E
Caia 131 17 51 S 35 24 E
Caiabis, Serra dos 173 11 30 S 56 30W
Caianda 131 11 2 S 23 31 E
Caiapó, Serra do 173 17 0 S 52 0W
Caiapônia 173 16 57 S 51 49W
Caibarién 162 22 30N 79 30W
Caibiran 91 11 34N 124 35 E
Caicara, Bolívar, Venezuela 168 7 38N 66 10W
Caicara, Monagas, Venezuela 169 9 52N 63 38W
Caicó 170 6 20 S 37 0W
Caicos Is. 163 21 40N 71 40W
Caicos Passage 163 22 45N 72 45W
Cailloma 172 15 9 S 71 45W
Caine → 173 18 23 S 65 21W
Caird Coast 7 75 0 S 25 0W
Cairn Gorm 14 57 7N 3 40W
Cairn Toul 14 57 3N 3 44W
Cairngorm Mts. 14 57 6N 3 42W
Cairns 110 16 57 S 145 45 E
Cairo = El Qâhira 124 30 1N 31 14 E
Cairo, Ga., U.S.A. 149 30 52N 84 12W
Cairo, Ill., U.S.A. 153 37 0N 89 10W
Cairo Montenotte 42 44 23N 8 16 E
Caithness, Ord of 14 58 9N 3 37W
Caiundo 133 15 50 S 17 28 E
Caiza 173 20 2 S 65 40W
Cajabamba 172 7 38 S 78 4W
Cajamarca 172 7 5 S 78 28W
Cajamarca □ 172 6 15 S 78 50W
Cajapió 170 2 58 S 44 48W
Cajarc 20 44 29N 1 50 E
Cajatambo 172 10 30 S 77 2W
Cajàzeiras 170 6 52 S 38 30W
Čajetina 46 43 47N 19 42 E
Cajidiocan 90 12 22N 122 41 E
Čajniče 46 43 34N 19 5 E
Çakirgol 61 40 33N 39 40 E
Čakovec 43 46 23N 16 26 E
Cal, La → 173 17 27 S 58 15W
Cala 35 37 59N 6 21W
Cala → 35 37 38N 6 5W
Cala Cadolar, Punta de 37 38 38N 1 35 E
Calabanga 90 13 42N 123 17 E
Calabar 127 4 57N 8 20 E
Calabozo 168 9 0N 67 28W
Calábria □ 45 39 24N 16 30 E
Calaburras, Pta. de 35 36 30N 4 38W
Calaceite 36 41 1N 0 11 E
Calacota 172 17 16 S 68 38W
Calafat 50 43 58N 22 59 E
Calafate 176 50 19 S 72 15W
Calahorra 36 42 18N 1 59W
Calais, France 19 50 57N 1 56 E
Calais, U.S.A. 143 45 11N 67 20W
Calais, Pas de 19 51 0N 1 20 E
Calalaste, Cord. de 174 25 0 S 67 0W
Calalayan 91 11 30N 119 38 E
Calama, Brazil 173 8 0 S 62 50W
Calama, Chile 174 22 30 S 68 55W
Calamar, Bolívar, Colombia 168 10 15N 74 55W
Calamar, Vaupés, Colombia 168 1 58N 72 32W
Calamarca 172 16 55 S 68 9W
Calamba, Cavite, Phil. 91 8 35N 123 39 E
Calamba, Misamis, Phil. 91 10 11N 123 17 E
Calamba, Negros, Phil. 90 14 13N 121 10 E
Calamian Group 90 11 50N 119 55 E
Calamocha 36 40 50N 1 17W
Calañas 35 37 40N 6 53W
Calanda 36 40 56N 0 15W
Calandagan I. 91 10 39N 120 15 E
Calandula 133 9 6 S 15 57 E
Calang 88 4 37N 95 37 E
Calangiánus 44 40 56N 9 12 E
Calanscio, Sarīr 122 27 0N 21 30 E
Calapan 90 13 25N 121 7 E
Calape 91 9 54N 123 52 E
Călăraşi 50 44 12N 27 20 E
Călăraşi □ 50 44 10N 27 0 E
Calasparra 37 38 14N 1 41W
Calatafimi 44 37 56N 12 50 E
Calatagan 90 13 50N 120 38 E
Calatayud 36 41 20N 1 40W
Calato = Kálathos 49 36 9N 28 8 E
Calauag 90 13 55N 122 15 E
Calavà, C. 45 38 11N 14 55 E
Calavite, Cape 90 13 26N 120 20 E
Calavite Pass 90 13 36N 120 25 E
Calayan 90 19 16N 121 28 E
Calayan I. 90 19 20N 121 27 E
Calbayog 90 12 4N 124 38 E
Calbe 26 51 57N 11 47 E
Calca 172 13 22 S 72 0W
Calcasieu L. 153 30 0N 93 17W
Calci 42 43 44N 10 31 E
Calcutta 79 22 36N 88 24 E
Caldaro 43 46 23N 11 15 E
Caldas □ 168 5 15N 75 30W
Caldas da Rainha 35 39 24N 9 8W
Caldas de Reyes 34 42 36N 8 39W
Caldas Novas 171 17 45 S 48 38W
Calder → 12 53 44N 1 21W
Caldera 174 27 5 S 70 55W
Caldwell, Idaho, U.S.A. 156 43 45N 116 42W
Caldwell, Kans., U.S.A. 153 37 5N 97 37W
Caldwell, Tex., U.S.A. 153 30 30N 96 42W
Caledon 134 34 14 S 19 26 E
Caledon → 134 30 31 S 26 5 E
Caledon B. 110 12 45 S 137 0 E
Caledonia, Canada 150 43 7N 79 58W
Caledonia, Mo., U.S.A. 154 37 45N 90 46W
Caledonia, N.Y., U.S.A. 150 42 57N 77 54W
Calella 36 41 37N 2 40 E
Calemba 134 16 0 S 15 44 E
Calenzana 21 42 31N 8 51 E
Calera, La 174 32 50 S 71 10W
Caleta Olivia 176 46 25 S 67 25W

Calexico

Calexico 159 32 40N 115 33W
Calf of Man 12 54 4N 4 48W
Calgary 144 51 0N 114 10W
Calhoun 149 34 30N 84 55W
Cali 168 3 25N 76 35W
Calicut 81 11 15N 75 43 E
Caliente 157 37 36N 114 34W
California, Mo., U.S.A. 154 38 37N 92 30W
California, Pa., U.S.A. 150 40 5N 79 55W
California □ 157 37 25N 120 0W
California, Baja 160 32 10N 115 12W
California, Baja, T.N. □ 160 30 0N 115 0W
California, Baja, T.S. □ 160 25 50N 111 50W
California, G. de 160 27 0N 111 0W
California, Lr. = California, Baja 160 32 10N 115 12W
California City 159 35 7N 117 57W
California Hot Springs 159 35 51N 118 41W
Călimăneşti 50 45 14N 24 20 E
Călimani, Munţii 50 47 12N 25 0 E
Călineşti 50 45 21N 24 18 E
Calingasta 174 31 15 S 69 30W
Calinog 91 11 7N 122 32 E
Calintaan 90 12 35N 120 57 E
Calipatria 159 33 8N 115 30W
Calistoga 158 38 36N 122 32W
Calitri 45 40 54N 15 25 E
Calitzdorp 134 33 33 S 21 42 E
Callabonna, L. 111 29 40 S 140 5 E
Callac 18 48 25N 3 27W
Callan 15 52 33N 7 25W
Callander 14 56 15N 4 14W
Callang 90 17 2N 121 38 E
Callantsoog 22 52 50N 4 42 E
Callao 172 12 0 S 77 0W
Callaway 152 41 20N 99 56W
Callender 154 42 22N 94 17W
Calles 161 23 2N 98 42W
Callide 110 24 18 S 150 28 E
Calling Lake 144 55 15N 113 12W
Calliope 110 24 0 S 151 16 E
Callosa de Ensarriá 37 38 40N 0 8W
Callosa de Segura 37 38 7N 0 53W
Calmar 154 43 11N 91 52W
Calne 12 51 26N 2 0W
Calola 133 16 25 S 17 48 E
Calolbon 90 13 36N 124 6 E
Caloocan 90 14 39N 120 58 E
Calore → 45 41 11N 14 28 E
Caloundra 111 26 45 S 153 10 E
Calpe 37 38 39N 0 3 E
Calpella 158 39 14N 123 12W
Calpine 158 39 40N 120 27W
Calstock 142 49 47N 84 9W
Caltabellotta 44 37 36N 13 11 E
Caltagirone 45 37 13N 14 30 E
Caltanissetta 45 37 30N 14 3 E
Calucinga 133 11 18 S 16 12 E
Calulo 133 10 1 S 14 56 E
Calumet 148 47 14N 88 27W
Calunda 133 12 7 S 23 36 E
Caluquembe 133 13 47 S 14 44 E
Caluso 42 45 18N 7 52 E
Caluya I. 91 11 55N 121 34 E
Calvados □ 18 49 5N 0 15W
Calvert 153 30 59N 96 40W
Calvert → 110 16 17 S 137 44 E
Calvert Hills 110 17 15 S 137 20 E
Calvert I. 144 51 30N 128 0W
Calvert Ra. 108 24 0 S 122 30 E
Calvi 21 42 34N 8 45 E
Calvillo 160 21 51N 102 43W
Calvinia 134 31 28 S 19 45 E
Calw 27 48 43N 8 44 E
Calwa 158 36 42N 119 46W
Calzada Almuradiel 37 38 32N 3 28W
Calzada de Calatrava 35 38 42N 3 46W
Cam → 13 52 21N 0 16 E
Cam Lam 85 11 54N 109 10 E
Cam Pha 84 21 7N 107 18 E
Cam Ranh 85 11 54N 109 12 E
Cam Xuyen 84 18 15N 106 0 E
Camabatela 133 8 20 S 15 26 E
Camacá 171 15 24 S 39 30W
Camaçari 171 12 41 S 38 18W
Camacho 160 24 25N 102 18W
Camacupa 133 11 58 S 17 22 E
Camagüán 168 8 6N 67 36W
Camagüey 162 21 20N 78 0W
Camaiore 42 43 57N 10 18 E
Camamu 171 13 57 S 39 7W
Camaná 172 16 30 S 72 50W
Camanche 154 41 47N 90 15W
Camanche Res. 158 38 16N 120 51W
Camanongue 133 11 24 S 20 17 E
Camaquã → 175 31 17 S 51 47W
Camararé → 173 12 15 S 58 55W
Camarat, C. 21 43 12N 6 41 E
Camaret 18 48 16N 4 37W
Camargo 173 20 38 S 65 15 E
Camargue 21 43 34N 4 34 E
Camarillo 159 34 13N 119 2W
Camariñas 34 43 8N 9 12W
Camarines Norte □ 90 14 10N 122 45 E
Camarines Sur □ 90 13 40N 123 20 E
Camarón, C. 162 16 0N 85 0W
Camarones 176 44 50 S 65 40W
Camarones, B. 176 44 45 S 65 35W
Camas 158 45 35N 122 24W
Camas Valley 156 43 0N 123 46W
Camaxilo 133 8 21 S 18 56 E
Cambados 34 42 31N 8 49W
Cambamba 133 8 53 S 14 44 E
Cambará 175 23 2 S 50 5W
Cambay = Khambhat 78 22 23N 72 33 E
Cambil 37 37 40N 3 33W
Cambo-les-Bains 20 43 22N 1 23W
Cambodia ■ 84 12 15N 105 0 E
Camborne 13 50 13N 5 18W
Cambrai 19 50 11N 3 14 E
Cambria 158 35 39N 121 6W
Cambrian Mts. 13 52 25N 3 52W
Cambridge, Canada 142 43 23N 80 15W
Cambridge, Jamaica 162 18 18N 77 54W
Cambridge, N.Z. 114 37 54 S 175 29 E
Cambridge, U.K. 13 52 13N 0 8 E
Cambridge, Idaho, U.S.A. 156 44 36N 116 40W
Cambridge, Ill., U.S.A. 154 41 18N 90 12W
Cambridge, Iowa, U.S.A. 154 41 54N 93 32W
Cambridge, Mass., U.S.A. 151 42 20N 71 8W
Cambridge, Md., U.S.A. 148 38 33N 76 2W
Cambridge, Minn., U.S.A. 152 45 34N 93 15W
Cambridge, N.Y., U.S.A. 151 43 2N 73 22W
Cambridge, Nebr., U.S.A. 152 40 20N 100 12W
Cambridge, Ohio, U.S.A. 150 40 1N 81 35W
Cambridge Bay 140 69 10N 105 0W
Cambridge City 155 39 49N 85 10W
Cambridge Gulf 108 14 55 S 128 15 E
Cambridge Springs 150 41 47N 80 4W
Cambridgeshire □ 13 52 12N 0 7 E
Cambrils 36 41 8N 1 3 E
Cambuci 171 21 35 S 41 55W
Camden, Australia 113 34 1 S 150 43 E
Camden, Ala., U.S.A. 149 31 59N 87 15W
Camden, Ark., U.S.A. 153 33 40N 92 50W
Camden, Maine, U.S.A. 143 44 14N 69 6W
Camden, N.J., U.S.A. 151 39 57N 75 7W
Camden, Ohio, U.S.A. 155 39 38N 84 39W
Camden, S.C., U.S.A. 149 34 17N 80 34W
Camden Sound 108 15 27 S 124 25 E
Camdenton 154 38 1N 92 45W
Camembert 18 48 53N 0 10 E
Cámeri 42 45 30N 8 40 E
Camerino 43 43 10N 13 4 E
Cameron, Ariz., U.S.A. 157 35 55N 111 31W
Cameron, La., U.S.A. 153 29 50N 93 18W
Cameron, Mo., U.S.A. 154 39 42N 94 14W
Cameron, Tex., U.S.A. 153 30 53N 97 0W
Cameron Falls 142 49 8N 88 19W
Cameron Highlands 85 4 27N 101 22 E
Cameron Hills 144 59 48N 118 0W
Cameron Mts. 115 46 1 S 167 0 E
Cameroon ■ 132 6 0N 12 30 E
Camerota 45 40 2N 15 21 E
Cameroun → 127 4 0N 9 35 E
Cameroun, Mt. 127 4 13N 9 10 E
Cametá 170 2 12 S 49 30W
Camiguin □ 91 9 11N 124 42 E
Camiguin I. 90 18 56N 121 55 E
Camiling 90 15 42N 120 24 E
Caminha 34 41 50N 8 50W
Camino 158 38 47N 120 40W
Camira Creek 111 29 15 S 152 58 E
Camiranga 170 1 48 S 46 17W
Camiri 173 20 3 S 63 31W
Camissombo 133 8 7 S 20 38 E
Cammal 150 41 24N 77 28W
Camoa Mts. 169 1 30N 58 50W
Camocim 170 2 55 S 40 50W
Camogli 42 44 21N 9 9 E
Camooweal 110 19 56 S 138 7 E
Camopi 169 3 12N 52 17W
Camopi → 169 3 10N 52 20W
Camotes Is. 91 10 40N 124 24 E
Camotes Sea 91 10 30N 124 15 E
Camp Crook 152 45 36N 103 59W
Camp Nelson 159 36 8N 118 39W
Camp Point 154 40 3N 91 4W
Camp Wood 153 29 41N 100 0W
Campagna 45 40 40N 15 5 E
Campana 174 34 10 S 58 55W
Campana, I. 176 48 20 S 75 20W
Campanario 35 38 52N 5 36W
Campania □ 45 40 50N 14 45 E
Campbell, S. Africa 134 28 48 S 23 44 E
Campbell, Calif., U.S.A. 158 37 17N 121 57W
Campbell, Ohio, U.S.A. 150 41 5N 80 36W
Campbell, C. 115 41 47 S 174 18 E
Campbell I. 104 52 30 S 169 0 E
Campbell L. 145 63 14N 106 55W
Campbell River 144 50 5N 125 20W
Campbell Town 110 41 52 S 147 30 E
Campbellford 150 44 18N 77 48W
Campbellpur 78 33 46N 72 26 E
Campbellsburg 155 38 39N 86 16W
Campbellsville 148 37 23N 85 21W
Campbellton 143 47 57N 66 43W
Campbelltown 113 34 4 S 150 49 E
Campbeltown 14 55 25N 5 36W
Campeche 161 19 50N 90 32W
Campeche □ 161 19 50N 90 32W
Campeche, B. de 161 19 30N 93 0W
Camperdown 112 38 14 S 143 9 E
Camperville 145 51 59N 100 9W
Campi Salentina 45 40 22N 18 2 E
Campidano 44 39 30N 8 40 E
Campíglia Maríttima 42 43 4N 10 37 E
Campillo de Altobuey 36 39 36N 1 49W
Campillo de Llerena 35 38 30N 5 50W
Campillos 35 37 4N 4 51W
Campiña, La 35 37 45N 4 45W
Campina Grande 170 7 20 S 35 47W
Campina Verde 171 19 31 S 49 28W
Campinas 175 22 50 S 47 0W
Campine 23 51 8N 5 20 E
Campli 43 42 44N 13 40 E
Campo, Cameroon 132 2 22N 9 50 E
Campo, Spain 36 42 25N 0 24 E
Campo Belo 171 20 52 S 45 16W
Campo de Criptana 37 39 24N 3 7W
Campo de Diauarum 173 11 12 S 53 14W
Campo de Gibraltar 35 36 15N 5 25W
Campo Flórido 171 19 47 S 48 35W
Campo Formoso 170 10 30 S 40 20W
Campo Grande 173 20 25 S 54 40W
Campo Maíor, Brazil 170 4 50 S 42 12W
Campo Maior, Portugal 35 38 59N 7 7W
Campo Mourão 175 24 3 S 52 22W
Campo Tencia 29 46 26N 8 43 E
Campo Túres 43 46 53N 11 55 E
Campoalegre 168 2 41N 75 20W
Campobasso 45 41 34N 14 40 E
Campobello di Licata 44 37 16N 13 55 E
Campobello di Mazara 44 37 38N 12 45 E
Campofelice 44 37 54N 13 53 E
Camporeale 44 37 53N 13 3 E
Campos 171 21 50 S 41 20W
Campos Altos 171 19 47 S 46 10W
Campos Belos 171 13 10 S 47 3W
Campos del Puerto 37 39 26N 3 1 E
Campos Novos 175 27 21 S 51 50W
Campos Sales 170 7 4 S 40 23W
Camprodón 36 42 19N 2 23 E
Campton 155 37 44N 83 33W
Camptonville 158 39 27N 121 3W
Campuya → 168 1 40 S 73 30W
Camrose 144 53 0N 112 50W
Camsell Portage 145 59 37N 109 15W
Can Gio 85 10 25N 106 58 E
Can Tho 85 10 2N 105 46 E
Canaan 151 42 1N 73 20W
Canada ■ 140 60 0N 100 0W
Cañada de Gómez 174 32 40 S 61 30W
Canadian 153 35 56N 100 25W
Canadian → 153 35 27N 95 3W
Çanakkale 48 40 8N 26 30 E
Çanakkale Boğazı 48 40 3N 26 12 E
Canal Flats 144 50 10N 115 48W
Canala 106 21 32 S 165 57 E
Canalejas 174 35 15 S 66 34W
Canals, Argentina 174 33 35 S 62 53W
Canals, Spain 37 38 58N 0 35W
Canandaigua 150 42 55N 77 18W
Cananea 160 31 0N 110 20W
Cañar 168 2 33 S 78 56W
Cañar □ 168 2 30 S 79 0W
Canarias, Is. 120 28 30N 16 0W
Canarreos, Arch. de los 162 21 35N 81 40W
Canary Is. = Canarias, Is. 120 28 30N 16 0W
Canastra, Serra da 171 20 0 S 46 20W
Canatlán 160 24 31N 104 47W
Canaveral, C. 149 28 28N 80 31W
Cañaveras 36 40 27N 2 24W
Canavieiras 171 15 39 S 39 0W
Canbelego 113 31 32 S 146 18 E
Canberra 113 35 15 S 149 8 E
Canby, Calif., U.S.A. 156 41 26N 120 58W
Canby, Minn., U.S.A. 152 44 44N 96 15W
Canby, Oreg., U.S.A. 158 45 16N 122 42W
Cancale 18 48 40N 1 50W
Canche → 19 50 31N 1 39 E
Canchyuaya, Cordillera de 172 7 30 S 74 0W
Candala 136 11 30N 49 58 E
Candarave 172 17 15 S 70 13W
Candas 34 43 35N 5 45W
Candé 18 47 34N 1 0W
Candeias → 173 8 39 S 63 31W
Candela 45 41 8N 15 31 E
Candelaria, Argentina 175 27 29 S 55 44W
Candelaria, Phil. 90 13 56N 121 25 E
Candelaria, Pta. de la 34 43 45N 8 0W
Candeleda 34 40 10N 5 14W
Candelo 113 36 47 S 149 43 E
Candia = Iráklion 49 35 20N 25 12 E
Candia, Sea of = Crete, Sea of 49 36 0N 25 0 E
Cândido de Abreu 171 24 35 S 51 20W
Cândido Mendes 170 1 27 S 45 43W
Candle L. 145 53 50N 105 18W
Candlemas I. 7 57 3 S 26 40W
Cando 152 48 30N 99 14W
Candon 90 17 12N 120 27 E
Candoni 91 9 48N 122 30 E
Canea = Khaniá 49 35 30N 24 4 E
Canela 170 10 15 S 48 25W
Canelli 42 44 44N 8 18 E
Canelones 175 34 32 S 56 17W
Canet-Plage 20 42 41N 3 2 E
Cañete, Chile 174 37 50 S 73 30W
Cañete, Peru 172 13 8 S 76 30W
Cañete, Spain 36 40 3N 1 54W
Cañete de las Torres 35 37 53N 4 19W
Canfranc 36 42 42N 0 31W
Cangamba 133 13 40 S 19 54 E
Cangandala 133 9 45 S 16 33 E
Cangas 34 42 16N 8 47W
Cangas de Narcea 34 43 10N 6 32W
Cangas de Onís 34 43 21N 5 8W
Cangoa 133 13 8 S 18 30 E
Cangombo 133 14 24 S 19 59 E
Cangongo 133 9 24 S 17 30 E
Canguaretama 170 6 20 S 35 5W
Canguçu 175 31 22 S 52 43W
Cangxi 96 31 47N 105 59 E
Cangyuan 96 23 12N 99 14 E
Cangzhou 94 38 19N 116 52 E
Canhoca 133 9 15 S 14 41 E
Cani, I. 121 36 21N 10 5 E
Canicattì 44 37 21N 13 50 E
Canicattini 45 37 1N 15 3 E
Canigao Channel 91 10 15N 124 42 E
Canim Lake 144 51 47N 120 54W
Canindé 170 4 22 S 39 19W
Canindé → 170 6 15 S 42 52W
Canipaan 86 8 33N 117 15 E
Canisteo 150 42 17N 77 37W
Canisteo → 150 42 5N 77 8W
Cañitas 160 23 36N 102 43W
Cañiza, La 34 42 13N 8 16W
Cañizal 34 41 12N 5 22W
Canjáyar 37 37 1N 2 44W
Canjinge 133 10 12 S 21 17 E
Çankırı 57 40 40N 33 37 E
Cankuzo 130 3 10 S 30 31 E
Canmore 144 51 7N 115 18W
Cann River 113 37 35 S 149 7 E
Canna 14 57 3N 6 33W
Cannanore 81 11 53N 75 27 E
Cannelton 155 37 55N 86 45W
Cannes 21 43 32N 7 0 E
Canning Town = Port Canning 79 22 23N 88 40 E
Cannington 150 44 20N 79 2W
Cannock 12 52 42N 2 2W
Cannon Ball → 152 46 20N 100 38W
Cannondale, Mt. 110 25 13 S 148 57 E
Caño Colorado 168 2 18N 68 22W
Canoe L. 145 55 10N 108 15W
Canon City 152 38 27N 105 14W
Canopus 112 33 29 S 140 42 E
Canora 145 51 40N 102 30W
Canosa di Púglia 45 41 13N 16 4 E
Canourgue, Le 20 44 26N 3 13 E
Canowindra 113 33 35 S 148 38 E
Canso 143 45 20N 61 0W
Canta 172 11 29 S 76 37W
Cantabria □ 34 43 10N 4 0W
Cantabria, Sierra de 36 42 40N 2 30W
Cantabrian Mts. = Cantábrica, Cordillera 34 43 0N 5 10W
Cantábrica, Cordillera 34 43 0N 5 10W
Cantal □ 20 45 5N 2 45 E
Cantal, Plomb du 20 45 3N 2 45 E
Cantanhede 34 40 20N 8 36W
Cantaura 169 9 19N 64 21W
Cantavieja 36 40 31N 0 25W
Čantavir 46 45 55N 19 46 E
Canterbury, Australia 110 25 23 S 141 53 E
Canterbury, U.K. 13 51 17N 1 5 E
Canterbury □ 115 43 45 S 171 19 E
Canterbury Bight 115 44 16 S 171 55 E
Canterbury Plains 115 43 55 S 171 22 E
Cantil 159 35 18N 117 58W
Cantilan 91 9 20N 125 58 E
Cantillana 35 37 36N 5 50W
Canto do Buriti 170 8 7 S 42 58W
Canton = Guangzhou 97 23 5N 113 10 E
Canton, Ga., U.S.A. 149 34 13N 84 29W
Canton, Ill., U.S.A. 154 40 32N 90 0W
Canton, Miss., U.S.A. 153 32 40N 90 1W
Canton, Mo., U.S.A. 154 40 10N 91 33W
Canton, N.Y., U.S.A. 151 44 32N 75 3W
Canton, Ohio, U.S.A. 150 40 47N 81 22W
Canton, Okla., U.S.A. 153 36 5N 98 36W
Canton, S. Dak., U.S.A. 152 43 20N 96 35W
Canton L. 153 36 12N 98 40W
Cantù 42 45 44N 9 8 E
Canudos 173 7 13 S 58 5W
Canumã, Amazonas, Brazil 169 4 2 S 59 4W
Canumã, Amazonas, Brazil 173 6 8 S 60 10W
Canumã → 173 3 55 S 59 10W
Canutama 173 6 30 S 64 20W
Canutillo 157 31 58N 106 36W
Canyon, Tex., U.S.A. 153 35 0N 101 57W
Canyon, Wyo., U.S.A. 156 44 43N 110 36W
Canyonlands Nat. Park 157 38 25N 109 30W
Canyonville 156 42 55N 123 14W
Canzo 42 45 54N 9 18 E
Cao Bang 84 22 40N 106 15 E
Cao He → 95 40 10N 124 32 E
Cao Lanh 85 10 27N 105 38 E
Cao Xian 94 34 50N 115 35 E
Caoayan 90 17 37N 120 23 E
Cáorle 43 45 36N 12 51 E
Cap-aux-Meules 143 47 23N 61 52W

Casiquiare

Cap-Chat 143 49 6N 66 40W
Cap-de-la-Madeleine 142 46 22N 72 31W
Cap-Haïtien 163 19 40N 72 20W
Cap St.-Jacques = Vung Tau 85 10 21N 107 4 E
Capa 84 22 21N 103 50 E
Capa Stilo 45 38 25N 16 35 E
Capáccio 45 40 26N 15 4 E
Capaia 133 8 27 S 20 13 E
Capalonga 90 14 20N 122 30 E
Capanaparo → 168 7 1N 67 7W
Capanema 170 1 12 S 47 11W
Caparo →, Barinas, Venezuela 168 7 46N 70 23W
Caparo →, Bolívar, Venezuela 169 7 30N 64 0W
Capatárida 168 11 11N 70 37W
Capayas 91 10 28N 119 39 E
Capbreton 20 43 39N 1 26W
Capdenac 20 44 34N 2 5 E
Cape → 110 20 49 S 146 51 E
Cape Barren I. 110 40 25 S 148 15 E
Cape Breton Highlands Nat. Park 143 46 50N 60 40W
Cape Breton I. 143 46 0N 60 30W
Cape Charles 148 37 15N 75 59W
Cape Coast 127 5 5N 1 15W
Cape Dorset 141 64 14N 76 32W
Cape Dyer 141 66 30N 61 22W
Cape Fear → 149 34 30N 78 25W
Cape Girardeau 153 37 20N 89 30W
Cape Jervis 112 35 40 S 138 5 E
Cape May 148 39 1N 74 53W
Cape Palmas 126 4 25N 7 49W
Cape Preston 108 20 51 S 116 12 E
Cape Province □ 134 32 0 S 23 0 E
Cape Tormentine 143 46 8N 63 47W
Cape Town 134 33 55 S 18 22 E
Cape Verde Is. ■ 8 17 10N 25 20W
Cape Vincent 151 44 9N 76 21W
Cape York Peninsula 110 12 0 S 142 30 E
Capela 170 10 30 S 37 0W
Capela de Campo 170 4 40 S 41 55W
Capele 133 13 39 S 14 53 E
Capelinha 171 17 42 S 42 31W
Capella 110 23 2 S 148 1 E
Capella, Mt. 107 5 4 S 141 8 E
Capelle, La 19 49 59N 3 50 E
Capenda Camulemba 133 9 24 S 18 27 E
Capendu 20 43 11N 2 31 E
Capernaum = Kefar Nahum 69 32 54N 35 34 E
Capestang 20 43 20N 3 2 E
Capim 170 1 41 S 47 47W
Capim → 170 1 40 S 47 47W
Capinópolis 171 18 41 S 49 35W
Capinota 172 17 43 S 66 14W
Capitan 157 33 33N 105 41W
Capitán Aracena, I. 176 54 10 S 71 20W
Capitan Arturo Prat 7 63 0 S 60 15W
Capitán Pastene 176 38 13 S 73 1W
Capitola 158 36 59N 121 57W
Capivara, Serra da 171 14 35 S 45 0W
Capiz □ 91 11 35N 122 30 E
Capizzi 45 37 50N 14 26 E
Čapljina 46 43 10N 17 43 E
Capoche → 131 15 35 S 33 0 E
Capoeira 173 5 37 S 59 33W
Capolo 133 10 22 S 14 7 E
Capraia 42 43 2N 9 50 E
Caprarola 43 42 21N 12 11 E
Capreol 142 46 43N 80 56W
Caprera 44 41 12N 9 28 E
Capri 45 40 34N 14 15 E
Capricorn Group 110 23 30 S 151 55 E
Capricorn Ra. 108 23 20 S 116 50 E
Caprino Veronese 42 45 37N 10 47 E
Caprivi Strip 134 18 0 S 23 0 E
Captainganj 79 26 55N 83 45 E
Captain's Flat 113 35 35 S 149 27 E
Captieux 20 44 18N 0 16W
Capu-Lapu 91 10 20N 123 55 E
Cápua 45 41 7N 14 15 E
Capul I. 90 12 26N 124 10 E
Caquetá □ 168 1 0N 74 0W
Caquetá → 168 1 15 S 69 15W
Carabalan 91 10 6N 122 57 E
Carabao I. 90 12 4N 121 56 E
Carabobo 168 10 2N 68 5W
Carabobo □ 168 10 10N 68 5W
Caracal 50 44 8N 24 22 E
Caracaraí 169 1 50N 61 8W
Caracas 168 10 30N 66 55W
Caracol 170 9 15 S 43 22W
Caracollo 172 17 39 S 67 10W
Caradoc 112 30 35 S 143 5 E
Caragabal 113 33 49 S 147 45 E
Caráglio 42 44 25N 7 25 E
Carahue 176 38 43 S 73 12W
Caraí 171 17 12 S 41 42W
Carajás, Serra dos 170 6 0 S 51 30W
Caramoan 90 13 46N 123 52 E
Caranapatuba 173 6 38 S 62 34W
Carandaiti 173 20 45 S 63 4W
Carangola 171 20 44 S 42 5W
Carani 109 30 57 S 116 28 E
Caransebeş 50 45 28N 22 18 E
Carantec 18 48 40N 3 55W
Caraparaná → 168 1 45 S 73 13W
Carapelle → 45 41 3N 15 55 E
Caras 172 9 3 S 77 47W
Caraş Severin □ 46 45 10N 22 10 E
Caraşova 46 45 11N 21 51 E
Caratasca, L. 162 15 20N 83 40W
Caratinga 171 19 50 S 42 10W
Caraúbas 170 5 43 S 37 33W
Caravaca 37 38 8N 1 52W
Caravággio 42 45 30N 9 39 E
Caravelas 171 17 45 S 39 15W
Caraveli 172 15 45 S 73 25W
Caràzinho 175 28 16 S 52 46W
Carballino 34 42 26N 8 5W
Carballo 34 43 13N 8 41W
Carberry 145 49 50N 99 25W
Carbia 34 42 48N 8 14W
Carbó 160 29 42N 110 58W
Carbon 144 51 30N 113 9W
Carbonara, C. 44 39 8N 9 30 E
Carbondale, Colo., U.S.A. 156 39 30N 107 10W
Carbondale, Ill., U.S.A. 154 37 45N 89 10W
Carbondale, Pa., U.S.A. 151 41 37N 75 30W
Carbonear 143 47 42N 53 13W
Carboneras 37 37 0N 1 53W
Carboneras de Guadazaón 36 39 54N 1 50W
Carbonia 44 39 10N 8 30 E
Carcabuey 35 37 27N 4 17W
Carcagente 37 39 8N 0 28W
Carcajou 144 57 47N 117 6W
Carcar 91 10 6N 123 38 E
Carcasse, C. 163 18 30N 74 28W
Carcassonne 20 43 13N 2 20 E
Carche 37 38 26N 1 9W
Carchi □ 168 0 45N 78 0W
Carcoar 113 33 36 S 149 8 E
Carcross 140 60 13N 134 45W
Cardabia 108 23 2 S 113 48 E
Cardamon Hills 81 9 30N 77 15 E
Cárdenas, Cuba 162 23 0N 81 30W
Cárdenas, San Luis Potosí, Mexico 161 22 0N 99 41W
Cárdenas, Tabasco, Mexico 161 17 59N 93 21W
Cardenete 36 39 46N 1 41W
Cardiel, L. 176 48 55 S 71 10W
Cardiff 13 51 28N 3 11W
Cardiff-by-the-Sea 159 33 1N 117 17W
Cardigan 13 52 6N 4 41W
Cardigan B. 13 52 30N 4 30W
Cardinal 151 44 47N 75 23W
Cardón, Punta 168 11 37N 70 14W
Cardona, Spain 36 41 56N 1 40 E
Cardona, Uruguay 174 33 53 S 57 18W
Cardoner → 36 41 41N 1 51 E
Cardross 145 49 50N 105 40W
Cardston 144 49 15N 113 20W
Cardwell 110 18 14 S 146 2 E
Careen L. 145 57 0N 108 11W
Carei 50 47 40N 22 29 E
Careiro 169 3 12 S 59 45W
Careme 89 6 55 S 108 27 E
Carentan 18 49 19N 1 15W
Carey, Idaho, U.S.A. 156 43 19N 113 58W
Carey, Ohio, U.S.A. 155 40 58N 83 22W
Carey, L. 109 29 0 S 122 15 E
Carey L. 145 62 12N 102 55W
Careysburg 126 6 34N 10 30W
Cargados Garajos 83 17 0 S 59 0 E
Cargèse 21 42 7N 8 35 E
Carhaix-Plouguer 18 48 18N 3 36W
Carhuamayo 172 10 51 S 76 4W
Carhuas 172 9 15 S 77 39W
Carhué 174 37 10 S 62 50W
Cariango 133 10 37 S 15 20 E
Caribbean Sea 163 15 0N 75 0W
Cariboo Mts. 144 53 0N 121 0W
Caribou 143 46 55N 68 0W
Caribou →, Man., Canada 145 59 20N 94 44W
Caribou →, N.W.T., Canada 144 61 27N 125 45W
Caribou I. 142 47 22N 85 49W
Caribou Is. 144 61 55N 113 15W
Caribou L., Man., Canada 145 59 21N 96 10W
Caribou L., Ont., Canada 142 50 25N 89 5W
Caribou Mts. 144 59 12N 115 40W
Carichic 160 27 56N 107 3W
Carigara 91 11 18N 124 41 E
Carignan 19 49 38N 5 10 E
Carignano 42 44 55N 7 40 E
Carillo 160 26 50N 103 55W
Carin 136 10 59N 49 13 E
Carinda 113 30 28 S 147 41 E
Cariñena 36 41 20N 1 13W
Carinhanha 171 14 15 S 44 46W
Carinhanha → 171 14 20 S 43 47W
Carini 44 38 9N 13 10 E
Carinola 44 41 11N 13 58 E
Carinthia □ = Kärnten □ 30 46 52N 13 30 E
Caripito 169 10 8N 63 6W
Caritianas 173 9 20 S 63 6W
Carlbrod = Dimitrovgrad 46 43 0N 22 48 E
Carlentini 45 37 15N 15 2 E
Carles 91 11 34N 123 8 E
Carleton Place 142 45 8N 76 9W
Carletonville 134 26 23 S 27 22 E
Carlin 156 40 44N 116 5W
Carlingford, L. 15 54 0N 6 5W
Carlinville 154 39 20N 89 55W
Carlisle, U.K. 12 54 54N 2 55W
Carlisle, Ky., U.S.A. 155 38 18N 84 1W
Carlisle, Pa., U.S.A. 150 40 12N 77 10W
Carlit, Pic 20 42 35N 1 55 E
Carloforte 44 39 10N 8 18 E
Carlos Casares 174 35 32 S 61 20W
Carlos Chagas 171 17 43 S 40 45W
Carlos Tejedor 174 35 25 S 62 25W
Carlota, La, Argentina 174 33 30 S 63 20W
Carlota, La, Phil. 91 10 25N 122 55 E
Carlow 15 52 50N 6 58W
Carlow □ 15 52 43N 6 50W
Carlsbad, Calif., U.S.A. 159 33 11N 117 25W
Carlsbad, N. Mex., U.S.A. 153 32 20N 104 14W
Carlyle, Canada 145 49 40N 102 20W
Carlyle, U.S.A. 152 38 38N 89 23W
Carlyle Resr. 154 38 37N 89 21W
Carmacks 140 62 5N 136 16W
Carmagnola 42 44 50N 7 42 E
Carman 145 49 30N 98 0W
Carmangay 144 50 10N 113 10W
Carmanville 143 49 23N 54 19W
Carmarthen 13 51 52N 4 20W
Carmarthen B. 13 51 40N 4 30W
Carmaux 20 44 3N 2 10 E
Carmel, Ind., U.S.A. 155 39 59N 86 8W
Carmel, N.Y., U.S.A. 151 41 25N 73 38W
Carmel-by-the-Sea 158 36 38N 121 55W
Carmel Mt. 69 32 45N 35 3 E
Carmel Valley 158 36 29N 121 43W
Carmelo 174 34 0 S 58 20W
Carmen, Bolivia 172 11 40 S 67 51W
Carmen, Colombia 168 9 43N 75 8W
Carmen, Paraguay 175 27 13 S 56 12W
Carmen, Bohol, Phil. 91 9 50N 124 12 E
Carmen, Cebu, Phil. 91 10 35N 124 1 E
Carmen, Mindanao, Phil. 91 7 13N 124 45 E
Carmen → 160 30 42N 106 29W
Carmen, I. 160 26 0N 111 20W
Carmen de Patagones 176 40 50 S 63 0W
Cármenes 34 42 58N 5 34W
Carmensa 174 35 15 S 67 40W
Carmi 155 38 6N 88 10W
Carmichael 158 38 38N 121 19W
Carmila 110 21 55 S 149 24 E
Carmona 35 37 28N 5 42W
Carnarvon, Queens., Australia 110 24 48 S 147 45 E
Carnarvon, W. Austral., Australia 109 24 51 S 113 42 E
Carnarvon, S. Africa 134 30 56 S 22 8 E
Carnarvon Ra., Queens., Australia 110 25 15 S 148 30 E
Carnarvon Ra., W. Austral., Australia 109 25 20 S 120 45 E
Carnation 158 47 39N 121 55W
Carnaxide 35 38 43N 9 14W
Carndonagh 15 55 15N 7 16W
Carnduff 145 49 10N 101 50W
Carnegie 150 40 24N 80 4W
Carnegie, L. 109 26 5 S 122 30 E
Carnic Alps = Karnische Alpen 30 46 36N 13 0 E
Carnot 132 4 59N 15 56 E
Carnot B. 108 17 20 S 122 15 E
Carnsore Pt. 15 52 10N 6 20W
Caro 148 43 29N 83 27W
Carol City 149 25 5N 80 16W
Carolina, Brazil 170 7 10 S 47 30W
Carolina, S. Africa 135 26 5 S 30 6 E
Carolina, La 35 38 17N 3 38W
Caroline I. 105 9 15 S 150 3W
Caroline Is. 104 8 0N 150 0 E
Caroline Pk. 115 45 57 S 167 15 E
Caron 145 50 30N 105 50W
Caroni → 169 8 21N 62 43W
Caroona 111 31 24 S 150 26 E
Carora 168 10 11N 70 5W
Carovigno 45 40 42N 17 40 E
Carpathians, Mts. 50 49 30N 21 0 E
Carpaţii Meridionali 50 45 30N 25 0 E
Carpenédolo 42 45 22N 10 25 E
Carpentaria, G. of 110 14 0 S 139 0 E
Carpentaria Downs 110 18 44 S 144 20 E
Carpentersville 155 42 6N 88 17W
Carpentras 21 44 3N 5 2 E
Carpi 42 44 47N 10 52 E
Carpina 170 7 51 S 35 15W
Carpino 45 41 50N 15 51 E
Carpinteria 159 34 25N 119 31W
Carpio 34 41 13N 5 7W
Carpolac = Morea 112 36 45 S 141 18 E
Carr Boyd Ra. 108 16 15 S 128 35 E
Carrabelle 149 29 52N 84 40W
Carranglan 90 15 58N 121 4 E
Carranya 108 19 14 S 127 46 E
Carrara 42 44 5N 10 7 E
Carrascal 91 9 22N 125 56 E
Carrascosa del Campo 36 40 2N 2 45W
Carrauntoohill, Mt. 15 52 0N 9 49W
Carretas, Punta 172 14 12 S 76 17W
Carrick-on-Shannon 15 53 57N 8 7W
Carrick-on-Suir 15 52 22N 7 30W
Carrickfergus 15 54 43N 5 50W
Carrickfergus □ 15 54 43N 5 49W
Carrickmacross 15 54 0N 6 43W
Carrieton 112 32 25 S 138 31 E
Carrington 152 47 30N 99 7W
Carrión → 34 41 53N 4 32W
Carrión de los Condes 34 42 20N 4 37W
Carrizal Bajo 174 28 5 S 71 20W
Carrizalillo 174 29 5 S 71 30W
Carrizo Cr. → 153 36 30N 103 40W
Carrizo Springs 153 28 28N 99 50W
Carrizozo 157 33 40N 105 57W
Carroll 154 42 2N 94 55W
Carrollton, Ga., U.S.A. 149 33 36N 85 5W
Carrollton, Ill., U.S.A. 152 39 20N 90 25W
Carrollton, Ky., U.S.A. 155 38 40N 85 10W
Carrollton, Mo., U.S.A. 154 39 19N 93 24W
Carrollton, Ohio, U.S.A. 150 40 31N 81 9W
Carron → 14 57 30N 5 30W
Carron, L. 14 57 22N 5 35W
Carrot → 145 53 50N 101 17W
Carrot River 145 53 17N 103 35W
Carrouges 18 48 34N 0 10W
Carruthers 145 52 52N 109 16W
Carse of Gowrie 14 56 30N 3 10W
Carsoli 43 42 7N 13 3 E
Carson, Calif., U.S.A. 159 33 48N 118 17W
Carson, U.S.A. 152 46 27N 101 29W
Carson → 158 39 45N 118 40W
Carson City, Mich., U.S.A. 155 43 11N 84 51W
Carson City, Nev., U.S.A. 158 39 12N 119 46W
Carson Sink 156 39 50N 118 40W
Carstairs 14 55 42N 3 41W
Cartagena, Colombia 168 10 25N 75 33W
Cartagena, Spain 37 37 38N 0 59W
Cartago, Colombia 168 4 45N 75 55W
Cartago, C. Rica 162 9 50N 85 52W
Cartaxo 35 39 10N 8 47W
Cartaya 35 37 16N 7 9W
Carteret 18 49 23N 1 47W
Cartersville 149 34 11N 84 48W
Carterton 114 41 2 S 175 31 E
Carterville 154 37 46N 89 5W
Carthage, Ark., U.S.A. 153 34 4N 92 32W
Carthage, Ill., U.S.A. 154 40 25N 91 10W
Carthage, Mo., U.S.A. 153 37 10N 94 20W
Carthage, S. Dak., U.S.A. 152 44 14N 97 38W
Carthage, Tex., U.S.A. 153 32 8N 94 20W
Cartier I. 108 12 31 S 123 29 E
Cartwright 143 53 41N 56 58W
Caruaru 170 8 15 S 35 55W
Carubig 90 12 24N 125 3 E
Carúpano 169 10 39N 63 15W
Caruray 91 10 20N 119 0 E
Carutapera 170 1 13 S 46 1W
Caruthersville 153 36 10N 89 40W
Carvalho 169 2 16 S 51 29W
Carvin 19 50 30N 2 57 E
Carvoeiro 169 1 30 S 61 59W
Carvoeiro, C. 35 39 21N 9 24W
Casa Branca, Brazil 171 21 46 S 47 4W
Casa Branca, Portugal 35 38 29N 8 12W
Casa Grande 157 32 53N 111 51W
Casa Nova 170 9 25 S 41 5W
Casablanca, Chile 174 33 20 S 71 25W
Casablanca, Morocco 120 33 36N 7 36W
Casacalenda 45 41 45N 14 50 E
Casal di Principe 45 41 0N 14 8 E
Casalbordino 43 42 10N 14 34 E
Casale Monferrato 42 45 8N 8 28 E
Casalmaggiore 42 44 59N 10 25 E
Casalpusterlengo 42 45 10N 9 40 E
Casamance → 126 12 33N 16 46W
Casamássima 45 40 58N 16 55 E
Casanare → 168 6 2N 69 51W
Casarano 45 40 0N 18 10 E
Casares 35 36 27N 5 16W
Casas Grandes 160 30 22N 108 0W
Casas Ibañez 37 39 17N 1 30W
Casasimarro 37 39 22N 2 3W
Casatejada 34 39 54N 5 40W
Casavieja 34 40 17N 4 46W
Cascade, Idaho, U.S.A. 156 44 30N 116 2W
Cascade, Iowa, U.S.A. 154 42 18N 91 0W
Cascade, Mont., U.S.A. 156 47 16N 111 46W
Cascade Locks 158 45 44N 121 54W
Cascade Pt. 115 44 1 S 168 20 E
Cascade Ra. 158 47 0N 121 30W
Cascais 35 38 41N 9 25W
Cáscina 42 43 40N 10 32 E
Caselle Torinese 42 45 12N 7 39 E
Caserta 45 41 5N 14 20 E
Cashel 15 52 31N 7 53W
Cashmere 156 47 31N 120 30W
Cashmere Downs 109 28 57 S 119 35 E
Casibare → 168 3 48N 72 18W
Casiguran 90 16 22N 122 7 E
Casiguran Sound 90 16 6N 121 58 E
Casilda 174 33 10 S 61 10W
Casimcea 50 44 45N 28 23 E
Casino 111 28 52 S 153 3 E
Casiquiare → 168 2 1N 67 7W

Châtillon-Coligny

Ceres, Italy 42 45 19N 7 22 E
Ceres, S. Africa 134 33 21 S 19 18 E
Ceres, U.S.A. 158 37 35N 120 57W
Céret 20 42 30N 2 42 E
Cereté 168 8 53N 75 48W
Cerfontaine 23 50 11N 4 26 E
Cerignola 45 41 17N 15 53 E
Cerigo = Kíthira 49 36 9N 23 0 E
Cérilly 20 46 37N 2 50 E
Cerisiers 19 48 8N 3 30 E
Cerizay 18 46 50N 0 40W
Cerknica 43 45 48N 14 21 E
Cermerno 46 43 35N 20 25 E
Cerna 50 45 4N 28 17 E
Cerna → 50 44 45N 24 0 E
Cernavodă 50 44 22N 28 3 E
Cernay 19 47 44N 7 10 E
Cernik 46 45 17N 17 22 E
Cerralvo 160 24 20N 109 45 E
Cerreto Sannita 45 41 17N 14 34 E
Cerritos 160 22 27N 100 20W
Cerro Gordo 155 39 53N 88 44W
Cerro Sombrero 176 52 45 S 69 15W
Certaldo 42 43 32N 11 2 E
Cervaro → 45 41 30N 15 52 E
Cervera 36 41 40N 1 16 E
Cervera de Pisuerga 34 42 51N 4 30W
Cervera del Río Alhama 36 42 2N 1 58W
Cérvia 43 44 15N 12 20 E
Cervignano del Friuli 43 45 49N 13 20 E
Cervinara 45 41 2N 14 36 E
Cervione 21 42 20N 9 29 E
Cervo 34 43 40N 7 24W
César □ 168 9 0N 73 30W
Cesaro 45 37 50N 14 38 E
Cesena 43 44 9N 12 14 E
Cesenático 43 44 12N 12 22 E
Cēsis 58 57 17N 25 28 E
Česká Lípa 30 50 45N 14 30 E
Česka Socialistická Republika □ 30 49 30N 14 40 E
Česká Třebová 31 49 54N 16 27 E
České Budějovice 30 48 55N 14 25 E
České Velenice 30 48 45N 15 1 E
Ceskomoravská Vrchovina 30 49 30N 15 40 E
Český Brod 30 50 4N 14 52 E
Český Krumlov 30 48 43N 14 21 E
Český Těšin 31 49 45N 18 39 E
Çeşme 49 38 20N 26 23 E
Cessnock 113 32 50 S 151 21 E
Cestos → 126 5 40N 9 10W
Cetate 50 44 7N 23 2 E
Cétin Grad 43 45 9N 15 45 E
Cetina → 43 43 26N 16 42 E
Cetinje 46 42 23N 18 59 E
Çetmı 70 36 52N 32 38 E
Cetraro 45 39 30N 15 56 E
Ceuta 120 35 52N 5 18W
Ceva 42 44 23N 8 3 E
Cévennes 20 44 10N 3 50 E
Ceyhan 70 37 4N 35 47 E
Ceyhan → 57 36 38N 35 40 E
Ceylon = Sri Lanka ■ 81 7 30N 80 50 E
Cèze → 21 44 6N 4 43 E
Cha-am 84 12 48N 99 58 E
Chá Pungana 133 13 44 S 18 39 E
Chaam 23 51 30N 4 52 E
Chabeuil 21 44 54N 5 3 E
Chablais 21 46 20N 6 36 E
Chablis 19 47 47N 3 48 E
Chabounia 121 35 30N 2 38 E
Chacabuco 174 34 40 S 60 27W
Chachapoyas 172 6 15 S 77 50W
Chachasp 172 15 30 S 72 15W
Chachoengsao 84 13 42N 101 5 E
Chachro 78 25 5N 70 15 E
Chaco □ 174 26 30 S 61 0W
Chad ■ 123 15 0N 17 15 E
Chad, L. = Tchad, L. 123 13 30N 14 30 E
Chadan 65 51 17N 91 35 E
Chadarinskoye Vdkhr. 63 41 0N 68 20 E
Chadileuvú → 174 37 46 S 66 0W
Chadiza 131 14 45 S 32 27 E
Chadron 152 42 50N 103 0W
Chadyr-Lunga 60 46 3N 28 51 E
Chae Hom 84 18 43N 99 35 E
Chaem → 84 18 11N 98 38 E
Chaeryŏng 95 38 24N 125 36 E
Chagda 65 58 45N 130 38 E
Chagny 19 46 57N 4 45 E
Chagoda 58 59 10N 35 15 E
Chagos Arch. 66 6 0 S 72 0 E
Chāh Ākhvor 73 32 41N 59 40 E
Chāh Bahār 73 25 20N 60 40 E
Chāh-e-Malek 73 28 35N 59 7 E
Chāh Gay Hills 77 29 30N 64 0 E
Chāh Kavīr 73 31 45N 54 52 E
Chahār Borjak 77 30 17N 62 3 E
Chahtung 82 26 41N 98 10 E
Chaillé-les-Marais 20 46 25N 1 2W
Chainat 84 15 11N 100 8 E
Chaise-Dieu, La 20 45 18N 3 42 E
Chaitén 176 42 55 S 72 43W
Chaiya 85 9 23N 99 14 E
Chaize-le-Vicomte, La 18 46 40N 1 18W
Chaj Doab 78 32 15N 73 0 E
Chajari 174 30 42 S 58 0W
Chakaria 82 21 45N 92 5 E
Chake Chake 130 5 15 S 39 45 E
Chakhānsūr 77 31 10N 62 0 E
Chakonipau, L. 143 56 18N 68 30W
Chakradharpur 79 22 45N 85 40 E
Chakwadam 82 27 29N 98 31 E
Chakwal 77 32 56N 72 53 E
Chala 172 15 48 S 74 20W
Chalais 20 45 16N 0 3 E
Chalakudi 81 10 18N 76 20 E
Chalchihuites 160 23 29N 103 53W
Chalcis = Khalkís 49 38 27N 23 42 E
Chaleur B. 143 47 55N 65 30W
Chalfant 158 37 32N 118 21W
Chalhuanca 172 14 15 S 73 15W
Chalindrey 19 47 43N 5 26 E
Chaling 97 26 58N 113 30 E
Chalisgaon 80 20 30N 75 10 E
Chalkar 61 50 40N 51 53 E
Chalkar, Ozero 61 50 50N 51 50 E
Chalky Inlet 115 46 3 S 166 31 E
Challans 18 46 50N 1 52W
Challapata 172 18 53 S 66 50W
Challis 156 44 32N 114 25W
Chalna 79 22 36N 89 35 E
Chalon-sur-Saône 19 46 48N 4 50 E
Chalonnes-sur-Loire 18 47 20N 0 45W
Châlons-sur-Marne 19 48 58N 4 20 E
Châlus 20 45 39N 0 58 E
Chalyaphum 84 15 48N 102 2 E
Cham, Germany 27 49 12N 12 40 E
Cham, Switz. 29 47 11N 8 28 E
Cham, Cu Lao 84 15 57N 108 30 E
Chama 157 36 54N 106 35W
Chaman 77 30 58N 66 25 E
Chamartín de la Rosa 36 40 28N 3 40W
Chamba, India 78 32 35N 76 10 E
Chamba, Tanzania 131 11 37 S 37 0 E
Chambal → 79 26 29N 79 15 E
Chamberlain 152 43 50N 99 21W
Chamberlain → 108 15 30 S 127 54 E
Chambers 157 35 13N 109 30W
Chambersburg 148 39 53N 77 41W
Chambéry 21 45 34N 5 55 E
Chambly 151 45 27N 73 17W
Chambon-Feugerolles, Le 21 45 24N 4 19 E
Chambord 143 48 25N 72 6W
Chambri L. 107 4 15 S 143 10 E
Chamchamal 72 35 32N 44 50 E
Chamela 160 19 32N 105 5W
Chamical 174 30 22 S 66 27W
Chamkar Luong 85 11 0N 103 45 E
Chamois 154 38 41N 91 46W
Chamonix-Mont-Blanc 21 45 55N 6 51 E
Champa 79 22 2N 82 43 E
Champagne, Canada 144 60 49N 136 30W
Champagne, France 19 48 40N 4 20 E
Champagne, Plaine de 19 49 0N 4 30 E
Champagnole 19 46 45N 5 55 E
Champaign 155 40 8N 88 14W
Champassak 84 14 53N 105 52 E
Champaubert 19 48 50N 3 45 E
Champdeniers 20 46 29N 0 25W
Champeix 20 45 37N 3 8 E
Champlain, Canada 148 46 27N 72 24W
Champlain, U.S.A. 151 44 59N 73 27W
Champlain, L. 151 44 30N 73 20W
Champotón 161 19 20N 90 50W
Chamrajnagar 81 11 52N 76 52 E
Chamusca 35 39 21N 8 29W
Chan Chan 172 8 7 S 79 0W
Chana 85 6 55N 100 44 E
Chañaral 174 26 23 S 70 40W
Chanārān 73 36 39N 59 6 E
Chanasma 78 23 44N 72 5 E
Chancay 172 11 32 S 77 25W
Chancy 28 46 8N 6 0 E
Chandalar 140 67 30N 148 35W
Chandannagar 79 22 52N 88 24 E
Chandausi 79 28 27N 78 49 E
Chandeleur Is. 153 29 48N 88 51W
Chandeleur Sd. 153 29 58N 88 40W
Chandigarh 78 30 43N 76 47 E
Chandler, Australia 111 27 0 S 133 19 E
Chandler, Canada 143 48 18N 64 46W
Chandler, Ariz., U.S.A. 157 33 20N 111 56W
Chandler, Okla., U.S.A. 153 35 43N 96 53W
Chandlers Peak 113 30 15 S 151 48 E
Chandless → 172 9 8 S 69 51W
Chandpur, Bangla. 82 23 8N 90 45 E
Chandpur, India 78 29 8N 78 19 E
Chandrapur 80 19 57N 79 25 E
Chānf 73 26 38N 60 29 E
Chang 78 26 59N 68 30 E
Chang, Ko 85 12 0N 102 23 E
Chang Jiang → 97 31 48N 121 10 E
Changa 79 33 53N 77 35 E
Changanacheri 81 9 25N 76 31 E
Changane → 135 24 30 S 33 30 E
Changbai 95 41 25N 128 5 E
Changbai Shan 95 42 20N 129 0 E
Changchiak'ou = Zhangjiakou 94 40 48N 114 55 E
Ch'angchou = Changzhou 97 31 47N 119 58 E
Changchun 95 43 57N 125 17 E
Changchunling 95 45 18N 125 27 E
Changde 97 29 4N 111 35 E
Changdo-ri 95 38 30N 127 40 E
Changfeng 97 32 28N 117 10 E
Changhai = Shanghai 97 31 15N 121 26 E
Changhua 97 30 12N 119 12 E
Changhŭng 95 34 41N 126 52 E
Changhŭngni 95 40 24N 128 19 E
Changjiang 84 19 20N 108 55 E
Changjin 95 40 23N 127 15 E
Changjin-chŏsuji 95 40 30N 127 15 E
Changle 97 25 59N 119 27 E
Changli 95 39 40N 119 13 E
Changling 95 44 20N 123 58 E
Changlun 85 6 25N 100 26 E
Changning, Hunan, China 97 26 28N 112 22 E
Changning, Yunnan, China 96 24 45N 99 30 E
Changping 94 40 14N 116 12 E
Changsha 97 28 12N 113 0 E
Changshan 97 28 55N 118 27 E
Changshou 96 29 51N 107 8 E
Changshu 97 31 38N 120 43 E
Changshun 96 26 3N 106 25 E
Changtai 97 24 35N 117 42 E
Changting 97 25 50N 116 22 E
Changwu 94 35 10N 107 45 E
Changxing 97 31 0N 119 55 E
Changyang 97 30 30N 111 10 E
Changyi 95 36 40N 119 30 E
Changyŏn 95 38 15N 125 6 E
Changyuan 94 35 15N 114 42 E
Changzhi 94 36 10N 113 6 E
Changzhou 97 31 47N 119 58 E
Chanhanga 133 16 0 S 14 8 E
Chanlar 61 40 25N 46 10 E
Channapatna 81 12 40N 77 15 E
Channel Is., U.K. 18 49 30N 2 40W
Channel Is., U.S.A. 159 33 55N 119 26W
Channel-Port aux Basques 143 47 30N 59 9W
Channing, Mich., U.S.A. 148 46 9N 88 1W
Channing, Tex., U.S.A. 153 35 45N 102 20W
Chantada 34 42 36N 7 46W
Chanthaburi 84 12 38N 102 12 E
Chantilly 19 49 12N 2 29 E
Chantonnay 18 46 40N 1 3W
Chantrey Inlet 140 67 48N 96 20W
Chanute 153 37 45N 95 25W
Chanza → 35 37 32N 7 30W
Chao Hu 97 31 30N 117 30 E
Chao Phraya → 84 13 32N 100 36 E
Chao Phraya Lowlands 84 15 30N 100 0 E
Chao Xian 97 31 38N 117 50 E
Chao'an 97 23 42N 116 32 E
Chaocheng 94 36 4N 115 37 E
Chaoyang, Guangdong, China 97 23 17N 116 30 E
Chaoyang, Liaoning, China 95 41 35N 120 22 E
Chapada dos Guimarães 173 15 26 S 55 45W
Chapala 131 15 50 S 37 35 E
Chapala, L. de 160 20 10N 103 20W
Chaparé → 173 15 58 S 64 42W
Chaparmukh 82 26 12N 92 31 E
Chaparral 168 3 43N 75 28W
Chapayevo 61 50 25N 51 10 E
Chapayevsk 59 53 0N 49 40 E
Chapecó 175 27 14 S 52 41W
Chapel Hill 149 35 53N 79 3W
Chapelle d'Angillon, La 19 47 21N 2 25 E
Chapelle-Glain, La 18 47 38N 1 11W
Chapeyevo 62 50 12N 51 10 E
Chapin 154 39 46N 90 24W
Chapleau 142 47 50N 83 24W
Chaplin 145 50 28N 106 40W
Chaplino 60 48 8N 36 15 E
Chaplygin 59 53 15N 40 0 E
Châr 120 21 32N 12 45 E
Chara 65 56 54N 118 20 E
Charadai 174 27 35 S 60 0W
Charagua 173 19 45 S 63 10W
Charalá 168 6 17N 73 10W
Charambirá, Punta 168 4 16N 77 32W
Charaña 172 17 30 S 69 25W
Charapita 168 0 37 S 74 21W
Charata 174 27 13 S 61 14W
Charcas 160 23 10N 101 20W
Charcoal L. 145 58 49N 102 22W
Chard 13 50 52N 2 59W
Chardara 63 41 16N 67 59 E
Chardara, Step 63 42 20N 68 0 E
Chardarinskoye Vdkhr. 63 41 10N 68 15 E
Chardon 150 41 34N 81 17W
Charduar 82 26 51N 92 46 E
Chardzhou 63 39 6N 63 34 E
Charente □ 20 45 50N 0 16 E
Charente → 20 45 57N 1 5W
Charente-Maritime □ 20 45 45N 0 45W
Charentsavan 61 40 35N 44 41 E
Chari → 123 12 58N 14 31 E
Chārīkār 77 35 0N 69 10 E
Charité-sur-Loire, La 19 47 10N 3 1 E
Chariton 154 41 1N 93 19W
Chariton → 154 39 19N 92 58W
Charity 169 7 24N 58 36W
Charkhari 79 25 24N 79 45 E
Charkhi Dadri 78 28 37N 76 17 E
Charleroi, Belgium 23 50 24N 4 27 E
Charleroi, U.S.A. 150 40 8N 79 54W
Charles, C. 148 37 10N 75 59W
Charles City 154 43 2N 92 41W
Charles L. 145 59 50N 110 33W
Charles Town 148 39 20N 77 50W
Charleston, Ill., U.S.A. 148 39 30N 88 10W
Charleston, Ill., U.S.A. 155 39 30N 88 10W
Charleston, Miss., U.S.A. 153 34 2N 90 3W
Charleston, Mo., U.S.A. 153 36 52N 89 20W
Charleston, S.C., U.S.A. 149 32 47N 79 56W
Charleston, W. Va., U.S.A. 148 38 24N 81 36W
Charleston Park 159 36 17N 115 37W
Charleston Pk. 159 36 16N 115 42W
Charlestown, S. Africa 135 27 26 S 29 53 E
Charlestown, U.S.A. 155 38 29N 85 40W
Charlesville 133 5 27 S 20 59 E
Charleville = Rath Luirc 15 52 21N 8 40W
Charleville 111 26 24 S 146 15 E
Charleville-Mézières 19 49 44N 4 40 E
Charlevoix 148 45 19N 85 14W
Charlieu 21 46 10N 4 10 E
Charlotte, Mich., U.S.A. 155 42 36N 84 48W
Charlotte, N.C., U.S.A. 149 35 16N 80 46W
Charlotte Amalie 163 18 22N 64 56W
Charlotte Harbor 149 26 58N 82 4W
Charlottenberg 52 59 54N 12 17 E
Charlottesville 148 38 1N 78 30W
Charlottetown 143 46 14N 63 8W
Charlton, Australia 112 36 16 S 143 24 E
Charlton, U.S.A. 152 40 59N 93 20W
Charlton I. 142 52 0N 79 20W
Charmes 19 48 22N 6 17 E
Charny 143 46 43N 71 15W
Charolles 21 46 27N 4 16 E
Chârost 19 46 58N 2 7 E
Charouine 121 29 0N 0 15W
Charre 131 17 13 S 35 10 E
Charroux 20 46 9N 0 25 E
Charsadda 78 34 7N 71 45 E
Charters Towers 110 20 5 S 146 13 E
Chartre-sur-le-Loir, La 18 47 44N 0 34 E
Chartres 18 48 29N 1 30 E
Charvakskoye Vdkhr. 63 41 35N 70 0 E
Chascomús 174 35 30 S 58 0W
Chasefu 131 11 55 S 33 8 E
Chaslands Mistake 115 46 38 S 169 22 E
Chasovnya-Uchurskaya 65 57 15N 132 50 E
Chasseneuil-sur-Bonnieure 20 45 52N 0 29 E
Chāt 73 37 59N 55 16 E
Châtaigneraie, La 20 46 39N 0 44W
Chatal Balkan = Udvoy Balkan 47 42 50N 26 50 E
Château-Arnoux 21 44 6N 6 0 E
Château-Chinon 19 47 4N 3 56 E
Château d'Oex 28 46 28N 7 8 E
Château-d'Oléron, Le 20 45 54N 1 12W
Château-du-Loir 18 47 40N 0 25 E
Château-Gontier 18 47 50N 0 48W
Château-la-Vallière 18 47 30N 0 20 E
Château-Landon 19 48 8N 2 40 E
Château-Porcien 19 49 31N 4 13 E
Château-Renault 18 47 36N 0 56 E
Château-Salins 19 48 50N 6 30 E
Château-Thierry 19 49 3N 3 20 E
Châteaubourg 18 48 7N 1 25W
Châteaubriant 18 47 43N 1 23W
Châteaudun 18 48 3N 1 20 E
Châteaugiron 18 48 3N 1 30W
Châteaulin 18 48 11N 4 8W
Châteaumeillant 20 46 35N 2 12 E
Châteauneuf-du-Faou 18 48 11N 3 50W
Châteauneuf-en-Thymerais 18 48 35N 1 13 E
Châteauneuf-sur-Charente 20 45 36N 0 3W
Châteauneuf-sur-Cher 19 46 52N 2 18 E
Châteauneuf-sur-Loire 19 47 52N 2 13 E
Châteaurenard, Bouches-du-Rhône, France 21 43 53N 4 51 E
Châteaurenard, Loiret, France 19 47 56N 2 55 E
Châteauroux 19 46 50N 1 40 E
Châtel-St.-Denis 28 46 32N 6 54 E
Châtelaillon-Plage 20 46 5N 1 5W
Châtelard, Le 28 46 4N 6 57 E
Châtelaudren 18 48 33N 2 59W
Chatelet 23 50 24N 4 32 E
Châtelet, Le 20 46 38N 2 16 E
Châtelet-en-Brie, Le 19 48 31N 2 48 E
Châtelguyon 20 45 55N 3 4 E
Châtellerault 18 46 50N 0 30 E
Châtelus-Malvaleix 20 46 18N 2 1 E
Chatfield 152 43 15N 91 58W
Chatham, N.B., Canada 143 47 2N 65 28W
Chatham, Ont., Canada 142 42 24N 82 11W
Chatham, U.K. 13 51 22N 0 32 E
Chatham, Ill., U.S.A. 154 39 40N 89 42W
Chatham, La., U.S.A. 153 32 22N 92 26W
Chatham, N.Y., U.S.A. 151 42 21N 73 32W
Chatham, I. 176 50 40 S 74 25W
Chatham Is. 104 44 0 S 176 40W
Chatham Str. 144 57 0N 134 40W
Chatillon 42 45 45N 7 40 E
Châtillon-Coligny 19 47 50N 2 51 E

Châtillon-en-Bazois

Châtillon-en-Bazois 19 47 3N 3 39 E
Châtillon-en-Diois 21 44 41N 5 29 E
Châtillon-sur-Indre 18 46 59N 1 10 E
Châtillon-sur-Loire 19 47 35N 2 44 E
Châtillon-sur-Marne 19 49 6N 3 44 E
Châtillon-sur-Seine 19 47 50N 4 33 E
Chatkal → 63 41 38N 70 1 E
Chatkalskiy Khrebet 63 41 30N 70 45 E
Chatmohar 79 24 15N 89 15 E
Chatra 79 24 12N 84 56 E
Chatrapur 79 19 22N 85 2 E
Châtre, La 20 46 35N 2 0 E
Chats, L. des 151 45 30N 76 20W
Chatsworth, Canada 150 44 27N 80 54W
Chatsworth, U.S.A. 155 40 45N 88 18W
Chatsworth, Zambia 131 19 38 S 31 13 E
Chatta-Hantō 101 34 45N 136 55 E
Chattahoochee → 149 30 43N 84 51W
Chattanooga 149 35 2N 85 17W
Chaturat 84 15 40N 101 51 E
Chatyrkel, Ozero 63 40 40N 75 18 E
Chatyrtash 63 40 55N 76 25 E
Chau Doc 85 10 42N 105 7 E
Chaudanne, Barr. de 21 43 51N 6 32 E
Chaudes-Aigues 20 44 51N 3 1 E
Chauffailles 21 46 13N 4 20 E
Chauk 82 20 53N 94 49 E
Chaukan Pass 82 27 8N 97 10 E
Chaulnes 19 49 48N 2 47 E
Chaumont, France 19 48 7N 5 8 E
Chaumont, U.S.A. 151 44 4N 76 9W
Chaumont-en-Vexin 19 49 16N 1 53 E
Chaumont-sur-Loire 18 47 29N 1 11 E
Chaunay 20 46 13N 0 9 E
Chauny 19 49 37N 3 12 E
Chausey, Is. 18 48 52N 1 49W
Chaussin 19 46 59N 5 22 E
Chautauqua L. 150 42 7N 79 30W
Chauvigny 18 46 34N 0 39 E
Chauvin 145 52 45N 110 10W
Chaux-de-Fonds, La 28 47 7N 6 50 E
Chavantina 173 14 40 S 52 21W
Chaves, Brazil 170 0 15 S 49 55W
Chaves, Portugal 34 41 45N 7 32W
Chavuma 133 13 4 S 22 40 E
Chawang 85 8 25N 99 30 E
Chayan 63 43 5N 69 25 E
Chayek 63 41 55N 74 30 E
Chaykovskiy 62 56 47N 54 9 E
Chazelles-sur-Lyon 21 45 39N 4 22 E
Chazuta 172 6 30 S 76 0W
Chazy 151 44 52N 73 28W
Cheb 30 50 9N 12 28 E
Chebanse 155 41 0N 87 54W
Chebarkul 62 55 0N 60 25 E
Cheboksary 62 56 8N 47 12 E
Cheboygan 148 45 38N 84 29W
Chebsara 59 59 10N 38 59 E
Chech, Erg 120 25 0N 2 15W
Chechaouen 120 35 9N 5 15W
Chechen, Os. 61 43 59N 47 40 E
Checheno-Ingush A.S.S.R. □ 61 43 30N 45 29 E
Chechon 95 37 8N 128 12 E
Chęciny 32 50 46N 20 28 E
Checleset B. 144 50 5N 127 35W
Checotah 153 35 31N 95 30W
Chedabucto B. 143 45 25N 61 8W
Cheduba I. 82 18 45N 93 40 E
Cheepie 111 26 33 S 145 1 E
Chef-Boutonne 20 46 7N 0 4W
Chegdomyn 65 51 7N 133 1 E
Chegga 120 25 27N 5 40W
Chegutu 131 18 10 S 30 14 E
Chehalis 158 46 44N 122 59W
Cheiron, Mt. 21 43 49N 6 58 E
Cheju Do 95 33 29N 126 34 E
Chekalin 59 54 10N 36 10 E
Chekiang = Zhejiang □ 97 29 0N 120 0 E
Chel = Kuru, Bahr el → 125 8 10N 26 50 E
Chela, Sa. da 133 16 20 S 13 20 E
Chelan 156 47 49N 120 0W
Chelan, L. 156 48 5N 120 30W
Cheleken 57 39 26N 53 7 E
Chelforó 176 39 0 S 66 33W
Chéliff, O. → 121 36 0N 0 8 E
Chelkar 64 47 48N 59 39 E
Chelkar Tengiz, Solonchak 64 48 0N 62 30 E
Chellala Dahrania 121 33 2N 0 1 E
Chelles 19 48 52N 2 33 E
Chełm 32 51 8N 23 30 E
Chełm □ 32 51 15N 23 30 E
Chełmek 32 50 6N 19 16 E
Chełmno 32 53 20N 18 30 E
Chelmsford 13 51 44N 0 29 E
Chelmsford Dam 135 27 55 S 29 59 E
Chełmża 32 53 10N 18 39 E
Chelsea, Australia 113 38 5 S 145 8 E
Chelsea, Mich., U.S.A. 155 42 19N 84 1W
Chelsea, Okla., U.S.A. 153 36 35N 95 35W
Chelsea, Vt., U.S.A. 151 43 59N 72 27W
Cheltenham 13 51 55N 2 5W
Chelva 36 39 45N 1 0W
Chelyabinsk 62 55 10N 61 24 E
Chelyuskin, C. 66 77 30N 103 0 E
Chemainus 144 48 55N 123 42W
Chembar = Belinskiy 59 53 0N 43 25 E
Chemillé 18 47 14N 0 45W
Chemnitz = Karl-Marx-Stadt 26 50 50N 12 55 E
Chemult 156 43 14N 121 47W
Chen, Gora 65 65 16N 141 50 E
Chen Xian 97 25 47N 113 1 E
Chenab → 77 30 23N 71 2 E
Chenachane, O. → 120 25 20N 3 20W
Chenango Forks 151 42 15N 75 51W
Chencha 125 6 15N 37 32 E
Chenchiang = Zhenjiang 97 32 11N 119 26 E
Chênée 23 50 37N 5 37 E
Cheney 156 47 29N 117 34W
Cheng Xian 94 33 43N 105 42 E
Chengalpattu 81 12 42N 79 58 E
Chengbu 97 26 18N 110 16 E
Chengcheng 94 35 8N 109 56 E
Chengchou = Zhengzhou 94 34 45N 113 34 E
Chengde 95 40 59N 117 58 E
Chengdong Hu 97 32 15N 116 20 E
Chengdu 96 30 38N 104 2 E
Chengele 82 28 47N 96 16 E
Chenggong 96 24 52N 102 56 E
Chenggu 94 33 10N 107 21 E
Chengjiang 96 24 39N 103 0 E
Chengkou 96 31 54N 108 31 E
Ch'engtu = Chengdu 96 30 38N 104 2 E
Chengwu 94 34 58N 115 50 E
Chengxi Hu 97 32 15N 116 10 E
Chengyang 95 36 18N 120 21 E
Chenjiagang 95 34 23N 119 47 E
Chenkán 161 19 8N 90 58W
Chenoa 155 40 45N 88 42W
Chenxi 97 28 2N 110 12 E
Cheo Reo 84 13 25N 108 28 E
Cheom Ksan 84 14 13N 104 56 E
Chepelare 47 41 44N 24 40 E
Chepén 172 7 15 S 79 23W
Chépénéhé 106 20 47 S 167 9 E
Chepes 174 31 20 S 66 35W
Chepo 162 9 10N 79 6W
Cheptsa → 59 58 36N 50 4 E
Cheptulil, Mt. 130 1 25N 35 35 E
Chequamegon B. 152 46 40N 90 30W
Cher □ 19 47 10N 2 30 E
Cher → 18 47 21N 0 29 E
Cheran 82 25 45N 90 44 E
Cherasco 42 44 39N 7 50 E
Cheratte 23 50 40N 5 41 E
Cheraw 149 34 42N 79 54W
Cherbourg 18 49 39N 1 40W
Cherchell 121 36 35N 2 12 E
Cherdakly 59 54 25N 48 50 E
Cherdyn 62 60 24N 56 29 E
Cheremkhovo 65 53 8N 103 1 E
Cherepanovo 64 54 15N 83 30 E
Cherepovets 59 59 5N 37 55 E
Chergui, Chott ech 121 34 21N 0 25 E
Cherikov 58 53 32N 31 20 E
Cherkassy 60 49 27N 32 4 E
Cherkessk 61 44 15N 42 5 E
Cherlak 64 54 15N 74 55 E
Chermoz 62 58 46N 56 10 E
Chernak 63 43 24N 68 2 E
Chernaya Kholunitsa 59 58 51N 51 52 E
Cherni 47 42 35N 23 18 E
Chernigov 58 51 28N 31 20 E
Chernikovsk 62 54 48N 56 8 E
Chernobyl 58 51 13N 30 15 E
Chernogorsk 65 53 49N 91 18 E
Chernomorskoye 60 45 31N 32 40 E
Chernovskoye 59 58 48N 47 20 E
Chernovtsy 60 48 15N 25 52 E
Chernoye 65 70 30N 89 10 E
Chernushka 62 56 29N 56 3 E
Chernyakhovsk 58 54 36N 21 48 E
Chernyshkovskiy 61 48 30N 42 13 E
Chernyshovskiy 65 63 0N 112 30 E
Cherokee, Iowa, U.S.A. 152 42 40N 95 30W
Cherokee, Okla., U.S.A. 153 36 45N 98 25W
Cherokees, L. O'The 153 36 50N 95 12W
Cherquenco 176 38 35 S 72 0W
Cherry Creek 156 39 50N 114 58W
Cherry Valley 159 33 59N 116 57W
Cherryvale 153 37 20N 95 33W
Cherskiy 65 68 45N 161 18 E
Cherskogo Khrebet 65 65 0N 143 0 E
Chertkovo 61 49 25N 40 19 E
Cherven 58 53 45N 28 28 E
Cherven-Bryag 47 43 17N 24 7 E
Chervonograd 58 50 25N 24 10 E
Cherwell → 13 51 46N 1 18W
Chesapeake 148 36 43N 76 15W
Chesapeake Bay 148 38 0N 76 12W
Cheshire □ 12 53 14N 2 30W
Cheshskaya Guba 56 67 20N 47 0 E
Cheslatta L. 144 53 49N 125 20W
Chesley 150 44 17N 81 5W
Chesne, Le 19 49 30N 4 45 E
Cheste 37 39 30N 0 41W
Chester, U.K. 12 53 12N 2 53W
Chester, Calif., U.S.A. 156 40 22N 121 14W
Chester, Ill., U.S.A. 154 37 58N 89 50W
Chester, Mont., U.S.A. 156 48 31N 111 0W
Chester, Pa., U.S.A. 148 39 54N 75 20W
Chester, S.C., U.S.A. 149 34 44N 81 13W
Chesterfield 12 53 14N 1 26W
Chesterfield, Îles 104 19 52 S 158 15 E
Chesterfield Inlet 140 63 30N 90 45W
Chesterton Range 111 25 30 S 147 27 E
Chesterville 151 45 6N 75 14W
Chesuncook L. 143 46 0N 69 10W
Chetaibi 121 37 1N 7 20 E
Chéticamp 143 46 37N 60 59W
Chetumal 161 18 30N 88 20W
Chetumal, B. de 161 18 40N 88 10W
Chetwynd 144 55 45N 121 36W
Chevanceaux 20 45 18N 0 14W
Cheviot 155 39 10N 84 37W
Cheviot, The 12 55 29N 2 8W
Cheviot Hills 12 55 20N 2 30W
Cheviot Ra. 110 25 20 S 143 45 E
Chew Bahir 125 4 40N 36 50 E
Chewelah 156 48 17N 117 43W
Cheyenne, Okla., U.S.A. 153 35 35N 99 40W
Cheyenne, Wyo., U.S.A. 152 41 9N 104 49W
Cheyenne → 152 44 40N 101 15W
Cheyenne Wells 152 38 51N 102 10W
Cheylard, Le 21 44 55N 4 25 E
Cheyne B. 109 34 35 S 118 50 E
Chhabra 78 24 40N 76 54 E
Chhapra 79 25 48N 84 44 E
Chhata 78 27 42N 77 30 E
Chhatak 82 25 5N 91 37 E
Chhatarpur 79 24 55N 79 35 E
Chhep 84 13 45N 105 24 E
Chhindwara 79 22 2N 78 59 E
Chhlong 85 12 15N 105 58 E
Chhuk 85 10 46N 104 28 E
Chi → 84 15 11N 104 43 E
Chiamis 87 7 20 S 108 21 E
Chiamussu = Jiamusi 93 46 40N 130 26 E
Chiang Dao 84 19 22N 98 58 E
Chiang Kham 84 19 32N 100 18 E
Chiang Khan 84 17 52N 101 36 E
Chiang Khong 84 20 17N 100 24 E
Chiang Mai 84 18 47N 98 59 E
Chiang Saen 84 20 16N 100 5 E
Chiange 133 15 35 S 13 40 E
Chiapa → 161 16 42N 93 0W
Chiapa de Corzo 161 16 42N 93 0W
Chiapas □ 161 17 0N 92 45W
Chiaramonte Gulfi 45 37 1N 14 41 E
Chiaravalle 43 43 38N 13 17 E
Chiaravalle Centrale 45 38 41N 16 25 E
Chiari 42 45 31N 9 55 E
Chiasso 29 45 50N 9 0 E
Chiatura 61 42 15N 43 17 E
Chiautla 161 18 18N 98 34W
Chiávari 42 44 20N 9 20 E
Chiavenna 42 46 18N 9 23 E
Chiba 101 35 30N 140 7 E
Chiba □ 101 35 30N 140 20 E
Chibabava 135 20 17 S 33 35 E
Chibatu 87 7 6 S 107 59 E
Chibemba, Cunene, Angola 133 15 48 S 14 8 E
Chibemba, Huila, Angola 133 16 20 S 15 20 E
Chibia 133 15 10 S 13 42 E
Chibougamau 142 49 56N 74 24W
Chibougamau L. 142 49 50N 74 20W
Chibuk 127 10 52N 12 50 E
Chic-Chocs, Mts. 143 48 55N 66 0W
Chicacole = Srikakulam 80 18 14N 83 58 E
Chicago 155 41 53N 87 40W
Chicago Heights 155 41 29N 87 37W
Chichagof I. 144 58 0N 136 0W
Chichaoua 120 31 32N 8 44W
Chicheng 94 40 55N 115 55 E
Chichester 13 50 50N 0 47W
Chichibu 101 36 5N 139 10 E
Ch'ich'ihaerh = Qiqihar 93 47 26N 124 0 E
Chickasha 153 35 0N 98 0W
Chiclana de la Frontera 35 36 26N 6 9W
Chiclayo 172 6 42 S 79 50W
Chico 158 39 45N 121 54W
Chico →, Chubut, Argentina 176 44 0 S 67 0W
Chico →, Santa Cruz, Argentina 176 50 0 S 68 30W
Chicomo 135 24 31 S 34 6 E
Chicontepec 161 20 58N 98 10W
Chicopee 151 42 6N 72 37W
Chicoutimi 143 48 28N 71 5W
Chicualacuala 135 22 6 S 31 42 E
Chidambaram 81 11 20N 79 45 E
Chidenguele 135 24 55 S 34 11 E
Chidley, C. 141 60 23N 64 26W
Chiede 133 17 15 S 16 22 E
Chiefs Pt. 150 44 41N 81 18W
Chiem Hoa 84 22 12N 105 17 E
Chiemsee 27 47 53N 12 27 E
Chiengi 131 8 45 S 29 10 E
Chiengmai = Chiang Mai 84 18 47N 98 59 E
Chiengo 133 13 20 S 21 55 E
Chienti → 43 43 18N 13 45 E
Chieri 42 45 0N 7 50 E
Chiers → 19 49 39N 5 0 E
Chiese → 42 45 8N 10 25 E
Chieti 43 42 22N 14 10 E
Chièvres 23 50 35N 3 48 E
Chifeng 95 42 18N 118 58 E
Chigasaki 101 35 19N 139 24 E
Chigirin 60 49 4N 32 38 E
Chignecto B. 143 45 30N 64 40W
Chigorodó 168 7 41N 76 42W
Chiguana 174 21 0 S 67 58W
Chiha-ri 95 38 40N 126 30 E
Chihli, G. of = Bo Hai 95 39 0N 120 0 E
Chihuahua 160 28 40N 106 3W
Chihuahua □ 160 28 40N 106 3W
Chiili 63 44 20N 66 15 E
Chik Bollapur 81 13 25N 77 45 E
Chikhli 78 20 20N 76 18 E
Chikmagalur 81 13 15N 75 45 E
Chikodi 81 16 26N 74 38 E
Chikugo 100 33 14N 130 28 E
Chikuma-Gawa → 101 36 59N 138 35 E
Chikwawa 131 16 2 S 34 50 E
Chilac 161 18 20N 97 24W
Chilako → 144 53 53N 122 57W
Chilam Chavki 79 35 5N 75 5 E
Chilanga 131 15 33 S 28 16 E
Chilapa 161 17 40N 99 11W
Chilas 79 35 25N 74 5 E
Chilcotin → 144 51 44N 122 23W
Childers 111 25 15 S 152 17 E
Childress 153 34 30N 100 15W
Chile ■ 176 35 0 S 72 0W
Chile Chico 176 46 33 S 71 44W
Chile Rise 105 38 0 S 92 0W
Chilecito 174 29 10 S 67 30W
Chilete 172 7 10 S 78 50W
Chilhowee 154 38 36N 93 51W
Chilik, Kazakh S.S.R., U.S.S.R. 62 51 7N 53 55 E
Chilik, Kirgiz S.S.R., U.S.S.R. 63 43 33N 78 17 E
Chililabombwe 131 12 18 S 27 43 E
Chilin = Jilin 95 43 44N 126 30 E
Chilka L. 79 19 40N 85 25 E
Chilko → 144 52 0N 123 40W
Chilko, L. 144 51 20N 124 10W
Chillagoe 110 17 7 S 144 33 E
Chillán 174 36 40 S 72 10W
Chillicothe, Ill., U.S.A. 154 40 55N 89 32W
Chillicothe, Mo., U.S.A. 154 39 45N 93 30W
Chillicothe, Ohio, U.S.A. 148 39 20N 82 58W
Chilliwack 144 49 10N 121 54W
Chilo 78 27 25N 73 32 E
Chiloane, I. 135 20 40 S 34 55 E
Chiloé □ 176 43 0 S 73 0W
Chiloé, I. de 176 42 30 S 73 50W
Chilonda 133 11 19 S 16 12 E
Chilpancingo 161 17 30N 99 30W
Chiltern 113 36 10 S 146 36 E
Chiltern Hills 13 51 44N 0 42W
Chilton 148 44 1N 88 12W
Chiluage 133 9 30 S 21 50 E
Chilubula 131 10 14 S 30 51 E
Chilumba 131 10 28 S 34 12 E
Chilwa, L. 131 15 15 S 35 40 E
Chimaltitán 160 21 46N 103 50W
Chimán 162 8 45N 78 40W
Chimay 23 50 3N 4 20 E
Chimbay 64 42 57N 59 47 E
Chimborazo 168 1 29 S 78 55W
Chimborazo □ 168 1 0 S 78 40W
Chimbote 172 9 0 S 78 35W
Chimion 63 40 15N 71 32 E
Chimishliya 50 46 34N 28 44 E
Chimkent 63 42 18N 69 36 E
Chimoio 131 19 4 S 33 30 E
Chimpembe 131 9 31 S 29 33 E
Chin □ 82 22 0N 93 0 E
Chin Hills 82 22 30N 93 30 E
Chin Ling Shan = Qinling Shandi 94 33 50N 108 10 E
China 161 25 40N 99 20W
China ■ 93 30 0N 110 0 E
China Lake 159 35 44N 117 37W
Chinacota 168 7 37N 72 36W
Chinan = Jinan 94 36 38N 117 1 E
Chinandega 162 12 35N 87 12W
Chinati Pk. 153 30 0N 104 25W
Chincha Alta 172 13 25 S 76 7W
Chinchilla 111 26 45 S 150 38 E
Chinchilla de Monte Aragón 37 38 53N 1 40W
Chinchón 36 40 9N 3 26W
Chinchorro, Banco 161 18 35N 87 20W
Chinchou = Jinzhou 95 41 5N 121 3 E
Chinchoua 132 0 1N 9 48 E
Chincoteague 148 37 58N 75 21W
Chinde 131 18 35 S 36 30 E
Chindo 95 34 28N 126 15 E
Chindwin → 82 21 26N 95 15 E
Chineni 79 33 2N 75 15 E
Chinga 131 15 13 S 38 35 E
Chingola 131 12 31 S 27 53 E
Chingole 131 13 4 S 34 17 E
Chingoroi 133 13 37 S 14 1 E
Ch'ingtao = Qingdao 95 36 5N 120 20 E
Chinguar 133 12 25 S 16 45 E
Chinguetti 120 20 25N 12 24W
Chingune 135 20 33 S 35 0 E
Chinhae 95 35 9N 128 47 E
Chinhanguanine 135 25 21 S 32 30 E
Chinhoyi 131 17 20 S 30 8 E
Chiniot 77 31 45N 73 0 E

Claremore

Claremore **153** 36 40N 95 37W
Claremorris **15** 53 45N 9 0W
Clarence **154** 39 45N 92 16W
Clarence →, Australia **111** 29 25 S 153 22 E
Clarence →, N.Z. . . . . **115** 42 10 S 173 56 E
Clarence, I. . . . . **176** 54 0 S 72 0W
Clarence I. . . . . **7** 61 10 S 54 0W
Clarence Str., Australia **108** 12 0 S 131 0 E
Clarence Str., U.S.A. . . **144** 55 40N 132 10W
Clarence Town **163** 23 6N 74 59W
Clarendon, Ark.,
U.S.A. **153** 34 41N 91 20W
Clarendon, Tex., U.S.A. **153** 34 58N 100 54W
Clarenville **143** 48 10N 54 1W
Claresholm **144** 50 0N 113 33W
Clarie Coast . . . . **7** 68 0 S 135 0 E
Clarin . . . . **91** 8 12N 123 52 E
Clarinda **152** 40 45N 95 0W
Clarion, Iowa, U.S.A. . **154** 42 41N 93 46W
Clarion, Pa., U.S.A. . . **150** 41 12N 79 22W
Clarion → **150** 41 9N 79 41W
Clarion Fracture Zone . **105** 20 0N 120 0W
Clark **152** 44 55N 97 45W
Clark, Pt. **150** 44 4N 81 45W
Clark Fork **156** 48 9N 116 9W
Clark Fork → **156** 48 9N 116 15W
Clark Hill Res. **149** 33 45N 82 20W
Clarkdale **157** 34 53N 112 3W
Clarke City **143** 50 12N 66 38W
Clarke I. . . . . **110** 40 32 S 148 10 E
Clarke L. **145** 54 24N 106 54W
Clarke Ra. . . . . **110** 20 45 S 148 20 E
Clark's Fork → **156** 45 39N 108 43W
Clark's Harbour **143** 43 25N 65 38W
Clarks Summit **151** 41 31N 75 44W
Clarksburg **148** 39 18N 80 21W
Clarksdale **153** 34 12N 90 33W
Clarkston **156** 46 28N 117 2W
Clarksville, Ark.,
U.S.A. **153** 35 29N 93 27W
Clarksville, Iowa,
U.S.A. **154** 42 47N 92 40W
Clarksville, Mich.,
U.S.A. **155** 42 50N 85 15W
Clarksville, Ohio,
U.S.A. **155** 39 24N 83 59W
Clarksville, Tenn.,
U.S.A. **149** 36 32N 87 20W
Clarksville, Tex., U.S.A. **153** 33 37N 94 59W
Claro → . . . . **171** 19 8 S 50 40W
Clatskanie **158** 46 9N 123 12W
Claude **153** 35 8N 101 22W
Claveria, Cagayan, Phil. **90** 12 54N 123 15 E
Claveria, Masbate, Phil. **91** 8 38N 124 55 E
Claveria, Mindanao,
Phil. . . . . **90** 18 37N 121 4 E
Clay **158** 38 17N 121 10W
Clay Center **152** 39 27N 97 9W
Clay City, Ind., U.S.A. **155** 39 17N 87 7W
Clay City, Ky., U.S.A. **155** 37 52N 83 55W
Clayette, La . . . . **21** 46 17N 4 19 E
Claypool **157** 33 27N 110 55W
Claysville **150** 40 5N 80 25W
Clayton, Idaho, U.S.A. **156** 44 12N 114 31W
Clayton, Ind., U.S.A. . **155** 39 41N 86 31W
Clayton, N. Mex.,
U.S.A. **153** 36 30N 103 10W
Cle Elum **156** 47 15N 120 57W
Clear, C. **15** 51 26N 9 30W
Clear I. **15** 51 26N 9 30W
Clear L. **158** 39 5N 122 47W
Clear Lake, Iowa,
U.S.A. **154** 43 8N 93 23W
Clear Lake, S. Dak.,
U.S.A. **152** 44 48N 96 41W
Clear Lake, Wash.,
U.S.A. **156** 48 27N 122 15W
Clear Lake Res. **156** 41 55N 121 10W
Clearfield, Iowa, U.S.A. **154** 40 48N 94 29W
Clearfield, Pa., U.S.A. **148** 41 0N 78 27W
Clearfield, Utah, U.S.A. **156** 41 10N 112 0W
Clearlake Highlands . . . **158** 38 57N 122 38W
Clearmont **156** 44 43N 106 29W
Clearwater, Canada . . . **144** 51 38N 120 2W
Clearwater, U.S.A. **149** 27 58N 82 45W
Clearwater →, Alta.,
Canada **144** 52 22N 114 57W
Clearwater →, Alta.,
Canada **145** 56 44N 111 23W
Clearwater Cr. → **144** 61 36N 125 30W
Clearwater Mts. **156** 46 20N 115 30W
Clearwater Prov. Park . **145** 54 0N 101 0W
Cleburne **153** 32 18N 97 25W
Cleethorpes **12** 53 33N 0 2W
Cleeve Cloud **13** 51 56N 2 0W
Clelles . . . . **21** 44 50N 5 38 E
Clemency . . . . **23** 49 35N 5 53 E
Cleopatra Needle . . . . . **91** 10 7N 118 58 E
Clerke Reef . . . . **108** 17 22 S 119 20 E
Clerks Rocks . . . . **7** 56 0 S 34 30W
Clermont, Australia . . . **110** 22 49 S 147 39 E
Clermont, France . . . . . **19** 49 23N 2 24 E
Clermont-en-Argonne . **19** 49 5N 5 4 E
Clermont-Ferrand . . . . . **20** 45 46N 3 4 E
Clermont-l'Hérault . . . . **20** 43 38N 3 26 E
Clerval . . . . **19** 47 25N 6 30 E
Clervaux . . . . **23** 50 4N 6 2 E
Cléry-St.-André . . . . . . **19** 47 50N 1 46 E
Cles . . . . **42** 46 21N 11 4 E
Cleveland, Australia . . . **111** 27 30 S 153 15 E
Cleveland, Miss.,
U.S.A. **153** 33 43N 90 43W
Cleveland, Ohio, U.S.A. **150** 41 28N 81 43W
Cleveland, Okla.,
U.S.A. **153** 36 21N 96 33W
Cleveland, Tenn.,
U.S.A. **149** 35 9N 84 52W
Cleveland, Tex., U.S.A. **153** 30 18N 95 0W
Cleveland □ . . . . **12** 54 35N 1 8 E
Cleveland, C. . . . . **110** 19 11 S 147 1 E
Cleveland Heights **150** 41 32N 81 30W
Clevelândia . . . . **175** 26 24 S 52 23W
Clevelândia do Norte . . **169** 3 49N 51 52W
Cleves **155** 39 10N 84 45W
Clew B. **15** 53 54N 9 50W
Clewiston **149** 26 44N 80 50W
Clifden, Ireland **15** 53 30N 10 2W
Clifden, N.Z. . . . . **115** 46 1 S 167 42 E
Cliffdell **158** 46 56N 121 5W
Clifton, Australia . . . . . **111** 27 59 S 151 53 E
Clifton, Ariz., U.S.A. . **157** 33 8N 109 23W
Clifton, Ill., U.S.A. . . . **155** 40 56N 87 56W
Clifton, Tex., U.S.A. . . **153** 31 46N 97 35W
Clifton Beach . . . . **110** 16 46 S 145 39 E
Clifton Forge **148** 37 49N 79 51W
Clifton Hills . . . . **111** 27 1 S 138 54 E
Climax **145** 49 10N 108 20W
Clinch → **149** 36 0N 84 29W
Clingmans Dome **149** 35 35N 83 30W
Clint **157** 31 37N 106 11W
Clinton, B.C., Canada . **144** 51 6N 121 35W
Clinton, Ont., Canada . **142** 43 37N 81 32W
Clinton, N.Z. . . . . **115** 46 12 S 169 23 E
Clinton, Ark., U.S.A. . . **153** 35 37N 92 30W
Clinton, Ill., U.S.A. . . . **152** 40 8N 89 0W
Clinton, Ind., U.S.A. . . **155** 39 40N 87 22W
Clinton, Iowa, U.S.A. . **154** 41 50N 90 12W
Clinton, Mass., U.S.A. **151** 42 26N 71 40W
Clinton, Mo., U.S.A. . . **154** 38 20N 93 46W
Clinton, N.C., U.S.A. . **149** 35 5N 78 15W
Clinton, Okla., U.S.A. **153** 35 30N 99 0W
Clinton, S.C., U.S.A. . **149** 34 30N 81 54W
Clinton, Tenn., U.S.A. **149** 36 6N 84 10W
Clinton, Wash., U.S.A. **158** 47 59N 122 22W
Clinton, Wis., U.S.A. . **155** 42 34N 88 52W
Clinton C. . . . . **110** 22 30 S 150 45 E
Clinton Colden L. **140** 63 58N 107 27W
Clintonville **152** 44 35N 88 46W
Clipperton, I. **105** 10 18N 109 13W
Clipperton Fracture
Zone **105** 19 0N 122 0W
Clisson **18** 47 5N 1 16W
Clive . . . . **114** 39 36 S 176 58 E
Clive L. **144** 63 13N 118 54W
Cliza . . . . **173** 17 36 S 65 56W
Cloates, Pt. . . . . **108** 22 43 S 113 40 E
Clocolan . . . . **135** 28 55 S 27 34 E
Clodomira . . . . **174** 27 35 S 64 14W
Clonakilty **15** 51 37N 8 53W
Clonakilty B. **15** 51 33N 8 50W
Cloncurry . . . . **110** 20 40 S 140 28 E
Cloncurry → . . . . **110** 18 37 S 140 40 E
Clones **15** 54 10N 7 13W
Clonmel **15** 52 22N 7 42W
Cloppenburg . . . . **26** 52 50N 8 3 E
Cloquet **152** 46 40N 92 30W
Clorinda . . . . **174** 25 16 S 57 45W
Cloud Peak **156** 44 23N 107 10W
Cloudcroft **157** 33 0N 105 48W
Cloudy B. . . . . **115** 41 25 S 174 10 E
Cloverdale, Calif.,
U.S.A. **158** 38 49N 123 0W
Cloverdale, Ind., U.S.A. **155** 39 31N 86 47W
Cloverport **155** 37 50N 86 38W
Clovis, Calif., U.S.A. . . **158** 36 47N 119 45W
Clovis, N. Mex., U.S.A. **153** 34 20N 103 10W
Cloyes-sur-le-Loir . . . . **18** 48 0N 1 14 E
Club Terrace . . . . **113** 37 35 S 148 58 E
Cluj □ . . . . **50** 46 45N 23 30 E
Cluj-Napoca . . . . **50** 46 47N 23 38 E
Clunes . . . . **112** 37 20 S 143 45 E
Cluny . . . . **21** 46 26N 4 38 E
Cluses . . . . **21** 46 5N 6 35 E
Clusone . . . . **42** 45 54N 9 58 E
Clutha → . . . . **115** 46 20 S 169 49 E
Clwyd □ **12** 53 5N 3 20W
Clwyd → **12** 53 20N 3 30W
Clyde, N.Z. . . . . **115** 45 12 S 169 20 E
Clyde, U.S.A. **150** 43 8N 76 52W
Clyde → **14** 55 56N 4 29W
Clyde, Firth of **14** 55 20N 5 0W
Clyde River **141** 70 30N 68 30W
Clydebank **14** 55 54N 4 25W
Clymer **150** 42 3N 79 39W
Côa → **34** 41 5N 7 6W
Coachella **159** 33 44N 116 13W
Coachella Canal **159** 32 43N 114 57W
Coahoma **153** 32 17N 101 20W
Coahuayana → **160** 18 41N 103 45W
Coahuayutla **160** 18 19N 101 42W
Coahuila □ **160** 27 0N 103 0W
Coal → **144** 59 39N 126 57W
Coal City **155** 41 17N 88 17W
Coal I. . . . . **115** 46 8 S 166 40 E
Coalane . . . . **131** 17 48 S 37 2 E
Coalcomán **160** 18 40N 103 10W
Coaldale **144** 49 45N 112 35W
Coalgate **153** 34 35N 96 13W
Coalinga **158** 36 10N 120 21W
Coalville, U.K. **12** 52 43N 1 21W
Coalville, U.S.A. **156** 40 58N 111 24W
Coaraci . . . . **171** 14 38 S 39 32W
Coari . . . . **169** 4 8 S 63 7W
Coari → . . . . **169** 4 30 S 63 33W
Coari, L. de . . . . **169** 4 15 S 63 22W
Coast □ . . . . **130** 2 40 S 39 45 E
Coast Mts. **144** 40 0N 123 0W
Coast Ranges **158** 41 0N 123 0W
Coastal Plains Basin . . . **109** 30 10 S 115 30 E
Coatbridge **14** 55 52N 4 2W
Coatepec **161** 19 27N 96 58W
Coatepeque **162** 14 46N 91 55W
Coatesville **148** 39 59N 75 55W
Coaticook **143** 45 10N 71 46W
Coats I. **141** 62 30N 83 0W
Coats Land . . . . **7** 77 0 S 25 0W
Coatzacoalcos **161** 18 7N 94 25W
Cobadin . . . . **50** 44 5N 28 13 E
Cobalt **142** 47 25N 79 42W
Cobán **162** 15 30N 90 21W
Cobar . . . . **113** 31 27 S 145 48 E
Cobberas, Mt. . . . . **113** 36 53 S 148 12 E
Cobden . . . . **112** 38 20 S 143 3 E
Cóbh **15** 51 50N 8 18W
Cobham . . . . **111** 30 18 S 142 7 E
Cobija . . . . **172** 11 0 S 68 50W
Cobleskill **151** 42 40N 74 30W
Coboconk **150** 44 39N 78 48W
Cobourg **142** 43 58N 78 10W
Cobourg Pen. . . . . **108** 11 20 S 132 15 E
Cobram . . . . **113** 35 54 S 145 40 E
Cobre **156** 41 6N 114 25W
Cóbué . . . . **131** 12 0 S 34 58 E
Coburg . . . . **27** 50 15N 10 58 E
Coca **34** 41 13N 4 32W
Coca → . . . . **168** 0 29 S 76 58W
Cocachacra . . . . **172** 17 5 S 71 45W
Cocal . . . . **170** 3 28 S 41 34W
Cocanada = Kakinada . **80** 16 57N 82 11 E
Cocentaina **37** 38 45N 0 27W
Cocha, La . . . . **174** 27 50 S 65 40W
Cochabamba . . . . **173** 17 26 S 66 10W
Coche, I. **169** 10 47N 63 56W
Cochem . . . . **27** 50 8N 7 7 E
Cochemane . . . . **131** 17 0 S 32 54 E
Cochin . . . . **81** 9 59N 76 22 E
Cochin China = Nam-
Phan . . . . **85** 10 30N 106 0 E
Cochise **157** 32 6N 109 58W
Cochran **149** 32 25N 83 23W
Cochrane, Alta., Canada **144** 51 11N 114 30W
Cochrane, Ont., Canada **142** 49 0N 81 0W
Cochrane → **145** 59 0N 103 40W
Cochrane, L. . . . . **176** 47 10 S 72 0W
Cockburn . . . . **112** 32 5 S 141 0 E
Cockburn, Canal . . . . . . **176** 54 30 S 72 0W
Cockburn I. **142** 45 55N 83 22W
Cockburn Ra. . . . . **108** 15 46 S 128 0 E
Cocklebiddy Motel . . . . **109** 32 0 S 126 3 E
Coco → **162** 15 0N 83 8W
Coco, Pta. **168** 2 58N 77 43W
Cocoa **149** 28 22N 80 40W
Cocobeach . . . . **132** 0 59N 9 34 E
Cocora . . . . **50** 44 45N 27 3 E
Côcos . . . . **171** 14 10 S 44 33W
Côcos → . . . . **171** 12 44 S 44 48W
Cocos I., Guam . . . . . . **106** 13 14N 144 39 E
Cocos I., Pac. Oc. **105** 5 25N 87 55W
Cocos Is. . . . . **83** 12 10 S 96 55 E
Cod, C. **147** 42 8N 70 10W
Codajás . . . . **169** 3 55 S 62 0W
Codera, C. **168** 10 35N 66 4W
Coderre **145** 50 11N 106 31W
Codigoro . . . . **43** 44 50N 12 5 E
Codó . . . . **170** 4 30 S 43 55W
Codogno . . . . **42** 45 10N 9 42 E
Codpa . . . . **172** 18 50 S 69 44W
Codróipo . . . . **43** 45 57N 13 0 E
Codru, Munții . . . . **50** 46 30N 22 15 E
Cody **156** 44 35N 109 0W
Coe Hill **142** 44 52N 77 50W
Coelemu . . . . **174** 36 30 S 72 48W
Coelho Neto . . . . **170** 4 15 S 43 0W
Coen . . . . **110** 13 52 S 143 12 E
Coeroeni → **169** 3 21N 57 31W
Coesfeld . . . . **26** 51 56N 7 10 E
Coetivy Is. . . . . **83** 7 8 S 56 16 E
Cœur d'Alene **156** 47 45N 116 51W
Cœur d'Alene L. **156** 47 32N 116 48W
Coevorden . . . . **22** 52 40N 6 44 E
Cofete **37** 28 6N 14 23W
Coffeyville **153** 37 0N 95 40W
Coffs Harbour . . . . **111** 30 16 S 153 5 E
Cofrentes **37** 39 13N 1 5W
Cogealac . . . . **50** 44 36N 28 36 E
Coghinas → . . . . **44** 40 55N 8 48 E
Coghinas, L. di . . . . **44** 40 46N 9 3 E
Cognac **20** 45 41N 0 20W
Cogne . . . . **42** 45 37N 7 21 E
Cogolludo **36** 40 59N 3 10W
Cohagen **156** 47 2N 106 36W
Cohoes **151** 42 47N 73 42W
Cohuna . . . . **112** 35 45 S 144 15 E
Coiba, I. **162** 7 30N 81 40W
Coig → . . . . **176** 51 0 S 69 10W
Coihaique . . . . **176** 45 30 S 71 45W
Coimbatore . . . . **81** 11 2N 76 59 E
Coimbra, Brazil . . . . . . **172** 19 55 S 57 48W
Coimbra, Portugal **34** 40 15N 8 27W
Coimbra □ **34** 40 12N 8 25W
Coín **35** 36 40N 4 48W
Coipasa, L. de . . . . **172** 19 12 S 68 7W
Coipasa, Salar de . . . . . **172** 19 26 S 68 9W
Cojata . . . . **172** 15 2 S 69 25W
Cojedes □ **168** 9 20N 68 20W
Cojedes → **168** 8 34N 68 5W
Cojimies **172** 0 20N 80 0W
Cojocna . . . . **50** 46 45N 23 50 E
Cojutepequé **162** 13 41N 88 54W
Čoka . . . . **46** 45 57N 20 12 E
Cokeville **156** 42 4N 111 0W
Colaba Pt. . . . . **80** 18 54N 72 47 E
Colac . . . . **112** 38 21 S 143 35 E
Colachel = Kolachel . . . **81** 8 10N 77 15 E
Colares **35** 38 48N 9 30W
Colasi . . . . **91** 10 43N 125 44 E
Colatina . . . . **171** 19 32 S 40 37W
Colbeck, C. . . . . **7** 77 6 S 157 48W
Colbinabbin . . . . **113** 36 38 S 144 48 E
Colborne **150** 44 0N 77 53W
Colby **152** 39 27N 101 2W
Colchagua □ . . . . **174** 34 30 S 71 0W
Colchester . . . . **13** 51 54N 0 55 E
Coldstream **14** 55 39N 2 14W
Coldwater, Canada **150** 44 42N 79 40W
Coldwater, Kans.,
U.S.A. **153** 37 18N 99 24W
Coldwater, Mich.,
U.S.A. **155** 41 57N 85 0W
Coldwater, Ohio,
U.S.A. **155** 40 29N 84 38W
Coldwater, L. **155** 41 48N 84 59W
Cole Camp **154** 38 28N 93 12W
Colebrook, Australia . . **110** 42 31 S 147 21 E
Colebrook, U.S.A. **151** 44 54N 71 29W
Coleman, Canada **144** 49 40N 114 30W
Coleman, U.S.A. **153** 31 52N 99 30W
Coleman → . . . . **110** 15 6 S 141 38 E
Colenso . . . . **135** 28 44 S 29 50 E
Coleraine, Australia . . . **112** 37 36 S 141 40 E
Coleraine, U.K. **15** 55 8N 6 40W
Coleraine □ . . . . **15** 55 8N 6 40 E
Coleridge, L. . . . . **115** 43 17 S 171 30 E
Coleroon → . . . . **81** 11 25N 79 50 E
Colesberg . . . . **134** 30 45 S 25 5 E
Colesburg **154** 42 38N 91 12W
Coleville **158** 38 34N 119 30W
Colfax, Calif., U.S.A. . **158** 39 6N 120 57W
Colfax, Ill., U.S.A. . . . **155** 40 34N 88 37W
Colfax, Ind., U.S.A. . . **155** 40 12N 86 40W
Colfax, La., U.S.A. . . . **153** 31 35N 92 39W
Colfax, Wash., U.S.A. . **156** 46 57N 117 28W
Colhué Huapi, L. . . . . . **176** 45 30 S 69 0W
Cólico . . . . **42** 46 8N 9 22 E
Coligny, France . . . . **21** 46 23N 5 21 E
Coligny, S. Africa . . . . **135** 26 17 S 26 15 E
Colima **160** 19 10N 103 40W
Colima □ **160** 19 10N 103 40W
Colima, Nevado de **160** 19 35N 103 45W
Colina . . . . **174** 33 13 S 70 45W
Colina do Norte **126** 12 28N 15 0W
Colinas, Goiás, Brazil . **171** 14 15 S 48 2W
Colinas, Maranhão,
Brazil . . . . **170** 6 0 S 44 10W
Colinton . . . . **113** 35 50 S 149 10 E
Coll **14** 56 40N 6 35W
Collaguasi . . . . **174** 21 5 S 68 45W
Collarada, Peña **36** 42 43N 0 29W
Collarenebri . . . . **111** 29 33 S 148 34 E
Collbran **157** 39 16N 107 58W
Colle di Val d'Elsa . . . . **43** 43 25N 11 7 E
Colle Salvetti . . . . **42** 43 34N 10 27 E
Colle Sannita . . . . **45** 41 22N 14 48 E
Collécchio . . . . **42** 44 45N 10 10 E
Colleen Bawn . . . . **131** 21 0 S 29 12 E
College Park **149** 33 42N 84 27W
Collette **143** 46 40N 65 30W
Collie, N.S.W.,
Australia . . . . **113** 31 41 S 148 18 E
Collie, W. Austral.,
Australia . . . . **109** 33 22 S 116 8 E
Collier B. . . . . **108** 16 10 S 124 15 E
Collier Ra. . . . . **109** 24 45 S 119 10 E
Colline Metallifere . . . . **42** 43 10N 11 0 E
Collingwood, Canada . . **150** 44 29N 80 13W
Collingwood, N.Z. . . . . **115** 40 41 S 172 40 E
Collins, Canada **142** 50 17N 89 27W
Collins, U.S.A. **154** 37 54N 93 37W
Collinsville, Australia . . **110** 20 30 S 147 56 E
Collinsville, U.S.A. . . . **154** 38 40N 89 59W
Collipulli . . . . **174** 37 55 S 72 30W
Collo . . . . **121** 36 58N 6 37 E
Collonges . . . . **21** 46 9N 5 52 E
Collooney **15** 54 11N 8 28W
Colmar . . . . **19** 48 5N 7 20 E
Colmars . . . . **21** 44 11N 6 39 E
Colmenar **35** 36 54N 4 20W
Colmenar de Oreja **36** 40 6N 3 25W
Colmenar Viejo **34** 40 39N 3 47W
Colne **12** 53 51N 2 11W
Colo → . . . . **113** 33 25 S 150 52 E
Cologna Véneta . . . . **43** 45 19N 11 21 E
Cologne = Köln . . . . . . **26** 50 56N 6 58 E
Coloma **158** 38 49N 120 53W
Colomb-Béchar =
Béchar **121** 31 38N 2 18W

Corinto

Corinto, Brazil 171 18 20 S 44 30W
Corinto, Nic. 162 12 30N 87 10W
Corj □ 50 45 5N 23 25 E
Cork 15 51 54N 8 30W
Cork □ 15 51 50N 8 50W
Cork Harbour 15 51 46N 8 16W
Corlay 18 48 20N 3 5W
Corleone 44 37 48N 13 16 E
Corleto Perticara 45 40 23N 16 2 E
Çorlu 47 41 11N 27 49 E
Cormack L. 144 60 56N 121 37W
Cormóns 43 45 58N 13 29 E
Cormorant 145 54 14N 100 35W
Cormorant L. 145 54 15N 100 50W
Corn Is. = Maiz, Is. del 162 12 15N 83 4W
Cornélio Procópio 175 23 7 S 50 40W
Cornell, Ill., U.S.A. 155 40 58N 88 43W
Cornell, Wis., U.S.A. 152 45 10N 91 8W
Corner Brook 143 48 57N 57 58W
Corníglio 42 44 29N 10 5 E
Corning, Ark., U.S.A. 153 36 27N 90 34W
Corning, Calif., U.S.A. 156 39 56N 122 9W
Corning, Iowa, U.S.A. 154 40 57N 94 40W
Corning, N.Y., U.S.A. 150 42 10N 77 3W
Corno, Monte 43 42 28N 13 34 E
Cornwall 142 45 2N 74 44W
Cornwall □ 13 50 26N 4 40W
Cornwallis I. 6 75 8N 95 0W
Corny Pt. 112 34 55 S 137 0 E
Coro 168 11 25N 69 41W
Coroaci 171 18 35 S 42 17W
Coroatá 170 4 8 S 44 0W
Coroban 136 3 58N 42 44 E
Corocoro 172 17 15 S 68 28W
Corocoro, I. 169 8 30N 60 10W
Coroico 172 16 0 S 67 50W
Coromandel, Brazil 171 18 28 S 47 13W
Coromandel, N.Z. 114 36 45 S 175 31 E
Coromandel Coast 81 12 30N 81 0 E
Coromandel Pen. 114 37 0 S 175 45 E
Coromandel Ra. 114 37 0 S 175 40 E
Coron 90 12 0N 120 12 E
Coron Bay 91 11 54N 120 8 E
Coron I. 91 11 55N 120 14 E
Corona, Australia 111 31 16 S 141 24 E
Corona, Calif., U.S.A. 159 33 49N 117 36W
Corona, N. Mex., U.S.A. 157 34 15N 105 32W
Coronada 159 32 45N 117 9W
Coronado, B. de 162 9 0N 83 40W
Coronados, G. de los 176 41 40 S 74 0W
Coronados, Is. los 159 32 25N 117 15W
Coronation 144 52 5N 111 27W
Coronation Gulf 140 68 25N 110 0W
Coronation I., Antarct. 7 60 45 S 46 0W
Coronation I., U.S.A. 144 55 52N 134 20W
Coronation Is. 108 14 57 S 124 55 E
Coronda 174 31 58 S 60 56W
Coronel 174 37 0 S 73 10W
Coronel Bogado 174 27 11 S 56 18W
Coronel Dorrego 174 38 40 S 61 10W
Coronel Fabriciano 171 19 31 S 42 38W
Coronel Murta 171 16 37 S 42 11W
Coronel Oviedo 174 25 24 S 56 30W
Coronel Ponce 173 15 34 S 55 1W
Coronel Pringles 174 38 0 S 61 30W
Coronel Suárez 174 37 30 S 61 52W
Coronel Vidal 174 37 28 S 57 45W
Corongo 172 8 30 S 77 53W
Coronie □ 169 5 55N 56 20W
Coropuna, Nevado 172 15 30 S 72 41W
Çorovoda 48 40 31N 20 14 E
Corowa 113 35 58 S 146 21 E
Corozal, Belize 161 18 23N 88 23W
Corozal, Colombia 168 9 19N 75 18W
Corps 21 44 50N 5 56 E
Corpus 175 27 10 S 55 30W
Corpus Christi 153 27 50N 97 28W
Corpus Christi, L. 153 28 5N 97 54W
Corque 172 18 20 S 67 41W
Corral 176 39 52 S 73 26W
Corral de Almaguer 36 39 45N 3 10W
Corralejo 37 28 43N 13 53W
Corréggio 42 44 46N 10 47 E
Corrente 170 10 27 S 45 10W
Corrente → 171 13 8 S 43 28W
Correntes → 173 17 38 S 55 8W
Correntes, C. das 135 24 6 S 35 34 E
Correntina 171 13 20 S 44 39W
Corrèze □ 20 45 20N 1 45 E
Corrèze → 20 45 10N 1 28 E
Corrib, L. 15 53 5N 9 10W
Corrientes 174 27 30 S 58 45W
Corrientes □ 174 28 0 S 57 0W
Corrientes →, Argentina 174 30 42 S 59 38W
Corrientes →, Peru 172 3 43 S 74 35W
Corrientes, C., Colombia 168 5 30N 77 34W
Corrientes, C., Cuba 162 21 43N 84 30W
Corrientes, C., Mexico 160 20 25N 105 42W
Corrigan 153 31 0N 94 48W
Corrigin 109 32 20 S 117 53 E
Corrowidgie 113 36 56 S 148 50 E
Corry 150 41 55N 79 39W
Corryong 113 36 12 S 147 53 E
Corse 21 42 0N 9 0 E
Corse, C. 21 43 1N 9 25 E
Corse-du-Sud □ 21 41 45N 9 0 E
Corsica = Corse 21 42 0N 9 0 E
Corsicana 153 32 5N 96 30W
Corte 21 42 19N 9 11 E
Corte do Pinto 35 37 42N 7 29W
Cortegana 35 37 52N 6 49W
Cortes 91 9 17N 126 11 E
Cortez 157 37 24N 108 35W
Cortina d'Ampezzo 43 46 32N 12 9 E
Cortland 151 42 35N 76 11W
Cortona 43 43 16N 12 0 E
Coruche 35 38 57N 8 30W
Çorum 57 40 30N 34 57 E
Corumbá 173 19 0 S 57 30W
Corumbá → 171 18 19 S 48 55W
Corumbá de Goiás 171 16 0 S 48 50W
Corumbaíba 171 18 9 S 48 34W
Coruña, La 34 43 20N 8 25W
Coruña, La □ 34 43 10N 8 30W
Corund 50 46 30N 25 13 E
Corunna = Coruña, La 34 43 20N 8 25W
Corunna 155 42 59N 84 7W
Corvallis 156 44 36N 123 15W
Corvette, L. de la 142 53 25N 74 3W
Corydon, Ind., U.S.A. 155 38 13N 86 7W
Corydon, Iowa, U.S.A. 154 40 42N 93 22W
Corydon, Ky., U.S.A. 155 37 44N 87 43W
Cosalá 160 24 28N 106 40W
Cosamaloapan 161 18 23N 95 50W
Cosenza 45 39 17N 16 14 E
Coşereni 50 44 38N 26 35 E
Coshocton 150 40 17N 81 51W
Cosmo Newberry 109 28 0 S 122 54 E
Cosne-sur-Loire 19 47 24N 2 54 E
Coso Junction 159 36 3N 117 57W
Coso Pk. 159 36 13N 117 44W
Cospeito 34 43 12N 7 34W
Cosquín 174 31 15 S 64 30W
Cossato 42 45 34N 8 10 E
Cossé-le-Vivien 18 47 57N 0 54W
Cosson → 18 47 30N 1 15 E
Costa Blanca 37 38 25N 0 10W
Costa Brava 36 41 30N 3 0 E
Costa del Sol 35 36 30N 4 30W
Costa Dorada 36 40 45N 1 15 E
Costa Mesa 159 33 39N 117 55W
Costa Rica ■ 162 10 0N 84 0W
Costa Smeralda 44 41 5N 9 35 E
Costigliole d'Asti 42 44 48N 8 11 E
Costilla 157 37 0N 105 30W
Coştiui 50 47 53N 24 2 E
Cosumnes → 158 38 14N 121 25W
Coswig 26 51 52N 12 31 E
Cotabato 91 7 14N 124 15 E
Cotabena 112 31 42 S 138 11 E
Cotacajes → 172 16 0 S 67 1W
Cotagaita 174 20 45 S 65 40W
Cotahuasi 172 15 12 S 72 50W
Côte, La 28 46 25N 6 15 E
Côte d'Azur 21 43 25N 7 10 E
Côte d'Or 19 47 10N 4 50 E
Côte-d'Or □ 19 47 30N 4 50 E
Côte-St.-André, La 21 45 24N 5 15 E
Coteau des Prairies 152 44 30N 97 0W
Coteau du Missouri 152 47 0N 101 0W
Coteau Landing 151 45 15N 74 13W
Cotegipe 171 12 2 S 44 15W
Cotentin 18 49 15N 1 30W
Côtes de Meuse 19 49 15N 5 22 E
Côtes-du-Nord □ 18 48 25N 2 40W
Cotiella 36 42 31N 0 19 E
Cotina → 46 43 36N 18 50 E
Cotoca 173 17 49 S 63 3W
Cotonou 127 6 20N 2 25 E
Cotopaxi □ 168 0 5 S 78 55W
Cotopaxi, Vol. 168 0 40 S 78 30W
Cotronei 45 39 9N 16 45 E
Cotswold Hills 13 51 42N 2 10W
Cottage Grove 156 43 48N 123 2W
Cottbus 26 51 44N 14 20 E
Cottbus □ 26 51 43N 13 30 E
Cottonwood 157 34 48N 112 1W
Cotulla 153 28 26N 99 14W
Coubre, Pte. de la 20 45 42N 1 15W
Couches 19 46 53N 4 30 E
Couço 35 38 59N 8 17W
Coudersport 150 41 45N 78 1W
Couedic, C. du 112 36 5 S 136 40 E
Couëron 18 47 13N 1 44W
Couesnon → 18 48 38N 1 32W
Couhé 20 46 17N 0 11 E
Coulanges-sur-Yonne 19 47 31N 3 33 E
Coulee City 156 47 36N 119 18W
Coulman I. 7 73 35 S 170 0 E
Coulommiers 19 48 50N 3 3 E
Coulonge → 142 45 52N 76 46W
Coulonges-sur-l'Autize 20 46 29N 0 36W
Coulterville, Calif., U.S.A. 158 37 42N 120 12W
Coulterville, Ill., U.S.A. 154 38 11N 89 36W
Council, Alaska, U.S.A. 140 64 55N 163 45W
Council, Idaho, U.S.A. 156 44 44N 116 26W
Council Bluffs 152 41 20N 95 50W
Council Grove 152 38 41N 96 30W
Coupeville 158 48 13N 122 41W
Courantyne → 172 5 55N 57 5W
Courcelles 23 50 28N 4 22 E
Courçon 20 46 15N 0 50W
Couronne, C. 21 43 19N 5 3 E
Cours-la-Ville 21 46 7N 4 19 E
Coursan 20 43 14N 3 4 E
Courseulles-sur-Mer 18 49 20N 0 29W
Court-St.-Etienne 23 50 38N 4 34 E
Courtenay 144 49 45N 125 0W
Courtine-le-Trucq, La 20 45 41N 2 15 E
Courtland 158 38 20N 121 34W
Courtrai = Kortrijk 23 50 50N 3 17 E
Courtright 150 42 49N 82 28W
Courville-sur-Eure 18 48 28N 1 15 E
Coushatta 153 32 0N 93 21W
Coutances 18 49 3N 1 28W
Couterne 18 48 30N 0 25W
Coutras 20 45 3N 0 8W
Coutts 144 49 0N 111 57W
Couvet 28 46 57N 6 38 E
Couvin 23 50 3N 4 29 E
Covarrubias 36 42 4N 3 31W
Covasna 50 45 50N 26 10 E
Covasna □ 50 45 50N 26 0 E
Coveñas 168 9 24N 75 44W
Coventry 13 52 25N 1 31W
Coventry L. 145 61 15N 106 15W
Covilhã 34 40 17N 7 31W
Covington, Ga., U.S.A. 149 33 36N 83 50W
Covington, Ind., U.S.A. 155 40 9N 87 24W
Covington, Ky., U.S.A. 155 39 5N 84 30W
Covington, Ohio, U.S.A. 155 40 8N 84 20W
Covington, Okla., U.S.A. 153 36 21N 97 36W
Covington, Tenn., U.S.A. 153 35 34N 89 39W
Cowal, L. 113 33 40 S 147 25 E
Cowan 145 52 5N 100 45W
Cowan, L. 109 31 45 S 121 45 E
Cowan L. 145 54 0N 107 15W
Cowangie 112 35 12 S 141 26 E
Cowansville 151 45 14N 72 46W
Cowarie 111 27 45 S 138 15 E
Cowcowing Lakes 109 30 55 S 117 20 E
Cowden 155 39 15N 88 52W
Cowdenbeath 14 56 7N 3 20W
Cowell 112 33 39 S 136 56 E
Cowes 13 50 45N 1 18W
Cowl Cowl 113 33 36 S 145 18 E
Cowlitz → 158 46 5N 122 53W
Cowra 113 33 49 S 148 42 E
Coxilha Grande 175 28 18 S 51 30W
Coxim 173 18 30 S 54 55W
Coxim → 173 18 34 S 54 46W
Cox's Bazar 82 21 26N 91 59 E
Cox's Cove 143 49 7N 58 5W
Coyame 160 29 28N 105 6W
Coyote Wells 159 32 44N 115 58W
Coyuca de Benítez 161 17 1N 100 8W
Coyuca de Catalan 160 18 18N 100 41W
Cozad 152 40 55N 99 57W
Cozumel 161 20 31N 86 55W
Cozumel, I. de 161 20 30N 86 40W
Craboon 111 32 3 S 149 30 E
Cracow = Kraków 32 50 4N 19 57 E
Cracow 111 25 17 S 150 17 E
Cradock 134 32 8 S 25 36 E
Craig, Alaska, U.S.A. 144 55 30N 133 5W
Craig, Colo., U.S.A. 156 40 32N 107 33W
Craigmore 131 20 28 S 32 50 E
Crailsheim 27 49 7N 10 5 E
Craiova 50 44 21N 23 48 E
Cramsie 110 23 20 S 144 15 E
Cranberry Portage 145 54 35N 101 23W
Cranbrook, Tas., Australia 110 42 0 S 148 5 E
Cranbrook, W. Austral., Australia 109 34 18 S 117 33 E
Cranbrook, Canada 144 49 30N 115 46W
Crandon 152 45 32N 88 52W
Crane, Oreg., U.S.A. 156 43 21N 118 39W
Crane, Tex., U.S.A. 153 31 26N 102 27W
Cranston 151 41 47N 71 27W
Craon 18 47 50N 0 58W
Craonne 19 49 27N 3 46 E
Craponne-sur-Arzon 20 45 19N 3 51 E
Crasna 50 46 32N 27 51 E
Crasna → 50 47 44N 22 35 E
Crasnei, Munţii 50 47 0N 23 20 E
Crater, L. 156 42 55N 122 3W
Crater Mt. 107 6 37 S 145 7 E
Crater Pt. 107 5 25 S 152 9 E
Crateús 170 5 10 S 40 39W
Crati → 45 39 41N 16 30 E
Crato, Brazil 170 7 10 S 39 25W
Crato, Portugal 35 39 16N 7 39W
Crau, La 21 43 32N 4 40 E
Cravo Norte 168 6 18N 70 12W
Cravo Norte → 168 6 18N 70 12W
Crawford 152 42 40N 103 25W
Crawfordsville 155 40 2N 86 51W
Crawley 13 51 7N 0 10W
Crazy Mts. 156 46 14N 110 30W
Crean L. 145 54 5N 106 9W
Crécy-en-Brie 19 48 50N 2 53 E
Crécy-en-Ponthieu 19 50 15N 1 53 E
Crediton 150 43 17N 81 33W
Credo 109 30 28 S 120 45 E
Cree →, Canada 145 58 57N 105 47W
Cree →, U.K. 14 54 51N 4 24W
Cree L. 145 57 30N 106 30W
Creede 157 37 56N 106 59W
Creel 160 27 45N 107 38W
Creighton 152 42 30N 97 52W
Creil 19 49 15N 2 29 E
Crema 42 45 21N 9 40 E
Cremona 42 45 8N 10 2 E
Crepaja 46 45 1N 20 38 E
Crepori → 173 5 42 S 57 8W
Crépy 19 49 35N 3 32 E
Crépy-en-Valois 19 49 14N 2 54 E
Cres 43 44 58N 14 25 E
Cresbard 152 45 13N 98 57W
Crescent, Okla., U.S.A. 153 35 58N 97 36W
Crescent, Oreg., U.S.A. 156 43 30N 121 37W
Crescent City 156 41 45N 124 12W
Crescentino 42 45 11N 8 7 E
Crespino 43 44 59N 11 51 E
Crespo 174 32 2 S 60 19W
Cressy 112 38 2 S 143 40 E
Crest 21 44 44N 5 2 E
Cresta, Mt. 90 17 17N 122 6 E
Crested Butte 157 38 57N 107 0W
Crestline, Calif., U.S.A. 159 34 14N 117 18W
Crestline, Ohio, U.S.A. 150 40 46N 82 45W
Creston, Canada 144 49 10N 116 31W
Creston, Calif., U.S.A. 158 35 32N 120 33W
Creston, Iowa, U.S.A. 154 41 0N 94 20W
Creston, Wash., U.S.A. 156 47 47N 118 36W
Crestview, Calif., U.S.A. 158 37 46N 118 58W
Crestview, Fla., U.S.A. 149 30 45N 86 35W
Creswick 112 37 25 S 143 58 E
Crete = Kríti 49 35 15N 25 0 E
Crete 152 40 38N 96 58W
Crete, La 144 58 11N 116 24W
Crete, Sea of 49 36 0N 25 0 E
Cretin, C. 107 6 40 S 147 53 E
Creus, C. 36 42 20N 3 19 E
Creuse □ 20 46 10N 2 0 E
Creuse → 20 47 0N 0 34 E
Creusot, Le 19 46 48N 4 24 E
Creuzburg 26 51 3N 10 15 E
Crevalcore 43 44 41N 11 10 E
Crèvecœur-le-Grand 19 49 37N 2 5 E
Crevillente 37 38 12N 0 48W
Crewe 12 53 6N 2 28W
Criciúma 175 28 40 S 49 23W
Cridersville 155 40 39N 84 9W
Crieff 14 56 22N 3 50W
Crikvenica 43 45 11N 14 40 E
Crimea = Krymskiy Poluostrov 60 45 0N 34 0 E
Crimmitschau 26 50 48N 12 23 E
Crinan 14 56 6N 5 34W
Cristal, Mts. de 132 0 30N 10 30 E
Cristalândia 170 10 36 S 49 11W
Cristeşti 50 47 15N 26 33 E
Cristino Castro 170 8 49 S 44 13W
Crişu Alb → 46 46 42N 21 17 E
Crişu Negru → 50 46 42N 21 16 E
Crişul Repede → 50 46 55N 20 59 E
Crittenden 155 38 47N 84 36W
Crivitz 26 53 35N 11 39 E
Crixás 171 14 27 S 49 58W
Crna Gora 46 42 10N 21 30 E
Crna Gora □ 46 42 40N 19 20 E
Crna Reka → 46 41 33N 21 59 E
Crna Trava 46 42 49N 22 19 E
Crni Drim → 46 41 17N 20 40 E
Crni Timok → 46 43 53N 22 15 E
Crnoljeva Planina 46 42 20N 21 0 E
Črnomelj 43 45 33N 15 10 E
Croaghpatrick 15 53 46N 9 40W
Croatia = Hrvatska □ 43 45 20N 18 0 E
Crocker 154 37 57N 92 16W
Crocker, Banjaran 86 5 40N 116 30 E
Crocker I. 109 11 12 S 132 32 E
Crockett 153 31 20N 95 30W
Crocodile = Krokodil → 135 25 14 S 32 18 E
Crocodile Is. 110 12 3 S 134 58 E
Crocq 20 45 52N 2 21 E
Croisette, C. 21 43 14N 5 22 E
Croisic, Le 18 47 18N 2 30W
Croisic, Pte. du 18 47 19N 2 31W
Croix, La, L. 142 48 20N 92 15W
Croker, C. 108 10 58 S 132 35 E
Cromarty, Canada 145 58 3N 94 9W
Cromarty, U.K. 14 57 40N 4 2W
Cromer 12 52 56N 1 18 E
Cromwell 115 45 3 S 169 14 E
Cronat 19 46 43N 3 40 E
Cronulla 113 34 3 S 151 8 E
Crooked →, Canada 144 54 50N 122 54W
Crooked →, U.S.A. 156 44 30N 121 16W
Crooked I. 163 22 50N 74 10W
Crooked Island Passage 163 23 0N 74 30W
Crookston, Minn., U.S.A. 152 47 50N 96 40W
Crookston, Nebr., U.S.A. 152 42 56N 100 45W
Crooksville 148 39 45N 82 8W
Crookwell 113 34 28 S 149 24 E
Crosby, Minn., U.S.A. 152 46 28N 93 57W
Crosby, N. Dak., U.S.A. 145 48 55N 103 18W
Crosby, Pa., U.S.A. 150 41 45N 78 23W
Crosbyton 153 33 37N 101 12W
Cross → 127 4 42N 8 21 E
Cross City 149 29 35N 83 5W
Cross Fell 12 54 44N 2 29W
Cross L. 145 54 45N 97 30W
Cross Plains 153 32 8N 99 7W
Cross River □ 127 6 0N 8 0 E
Cross Sound 140 58 20N 136 30W

Dalachi

Cross Timbers 154 38 1N 93 14W
Crosse, La, Kans., U.S.A. 152 38 33N 99 20W
Crosse, La, Wis., U.S.A. 152 43 48N 91 13W
Crossett 153 33 10N 91 57W
Crossfield 144 51 25N 114 0W
Crosshaven 15 51 48N 8 19W
Crossley, Mt. 115 42 50 S 172 5 E
Crossville 155 38 10N 88 4W
Croton-on-Hudson 151 41 12N 73 55W
Crotone 45 39 5N 17 6 E
Crow —► 144 59 41N 124 20W
Crow Agency 156 45 40N 107 30W
Crow Hd. 15 51 34N 10 9W
Crowell 153 33 59N 99 45W
Crowl Creek 113 32 0 S 145 30 E
Crowley 153 30 15N 92 20W
Crowley, L. 158 37 33N 118 42W
Crown Point 155 41 24N 87 23W
Crows Landing 158 37 23N 121 6W
Crows Nest 111 27 16 S 152 4 E
Crowsnest Pass 144 49 40N 114 40W
Croydon, Australia 110 18 13 S 142 14 E
Croydon, U.K. 13 51 18N 0 5W
Crozet Is. 83 46 27 S 52 0 E
Crozon 18 48 15N 4 30W
Cruz, C. 162 19 50N 77 50W
Cruz, La, C. Rica 162 11 4N 85 39W
Cruz, La, Mexico 160 23 55N 106 54W
Cruz Alta 175 28 45 S 53 40W
Cruz das Almas 171 12 0 S 39 6W
Cruz de Malta 170 8 15 S 40 20W
Cruz del Eje 174 30 45 S 64 50W
Cruzeiro 171 22 33 S 45 0W
Cruzeiro do Oeste 175 23 46 S 53 4W
Cruzeiro do Sul 172 7 35 S 72 35W
Cry L. 144 58 45N 129 0W
Crystal Bay 158 39 15N 119 58W
Crystal Brook 112 33 21 S 138 12 E
Crystal City, Mo., U.S.A. 154 38 15N 90 23W
Crystal City, Tex., U.S.A. 153 28 40N 99 50W
Crystal Falls 148 46 9N 88 11W
Crystal Lake 155 42 14N 88 19W
Crystal River 149 28 54N 82 35W
Crystal Springs 153 31 59N 90 25W
Csongrád 31 46 43N 20 12 E
Csongrád □ 31 46 32N 20 15 E
Csorna 31 47 38N 17 18 E
Csurgo 31 46 16N 17 9 E
Cu Lao Hon 85 10 54N 108 18 E
Cua Rao 84 19 16N 104 27 E
Cuácua —► 131 17 54 S 37 0 E
Cuamato 133 17 2 S 15 7 E
Cuamba 131 14 45 S 36 22 E
Cuando —► 133 17 30 S 23 15 E
Cuando Cubango □ 133 16 25 S 20 0 E
Cuangar 133 17 36 S 18 39 E
Cuango 133 6 15 S 16 42 E
Cuanza —► 116 9 2 S 13 30 E
Cuanza Norte □ 133 8 50 S 14 30 E
Cuanza Sul □ 133 10 50 S 14 50 E
Cuarto —► 174 33 25 S 63 2W
Cuatrociénegas 160 26 59N 102 5W
Cuauhtémoc 160 28 25N 106 52W
Cuba, Portugal 35 38 10N 7 54W
Cuba, Mo., U.S.A. 154 38 4N 91 24W
Cuba, N. Mex., U.S.A. 157 36 0N 107 0W
Cuba, N.Y., U.S.A. 150 42 12N 78 18W
Cuba ■ 162 22 0N 79 0W
Cuba City 154 42 36N 90 26W
Cubal 133 12 26 S 14 3 E
Cuballing 109 32 50 S 117 10 E
Cubango —► 133 18 50 S 22 25 E
Cubanja 133 14 49 S 21 20 E
Cubia 133 15 58 S 21 42 E
Cucamonga 159 34 10N 117 30W
Cuchi 133 14 37 S 16 58 E
Cuchillo-Có 176 38 20 S 64 37W
Cuchivero —► 168 7 40N 65 57W
Cuchumatanes, Sierra de los 162 15 35N 91 25W
Cucuí 168 1 12N 66 50W
Cucurpe 160 30 20N 110 43W
Cucurrupí 168 4 23N 76 56W
Cúcuta 168 7 54N 72 31W
Cudahy 155 42 54N 87 50W
Cudalbi 50 45 46N 27 41 E
Cuddalore 81 11 46N 79 45 E
Cuddapah 81 14 30N 78 47 E
Cuddapan, L. 110 25 45 S 141 26 E
Cudgewa 113 36 10 S 147 42 E
Cudillero 34 43 33N 6 9W
Cue 109 27 25 S 117 54 E
Cuéllar 34 41 23N 4 21W
Cuemba 133 11 50 S 17 42 E
Cuenca, Ecuador 168 2 50 S 79 9W
Cuenca, Spain 36 40 5N 2 10W
Cuenca □ 36 40 0N 2 0W
Cuenca, Serranía de 36 39 55N 1 50W
Cuerdo del Pozo, Pantano de la 36 41 51N 2 44W
Cuernavaca 161 18 50N 99 20W
Cuero 153 29 5N 97 17W
Cuers 21 43 14N 6 5 E
Cuervo 153 35 5N 104 25W
Cuesmes 23 50 26N 3 56 E
Cuevas, Cerro 173 22 0 S 65 12W
Cuevas del Almanzora 37 37 18N 1 58W
Cuevo 172 20 15 S 63 30W
Cugir 50 45 48N 23 25 E
Cuiabá 173 15 30 S 56 0W
Cuiabá —► 173 17 5 S 56 36W
Cuilco 162 15 24N 91 58W
Cuillin Hills 14 57 14N 6 15W
Cuillin Sd. 14 57 4N 6 20W
Cuima 133 13 25 S 15 45 E
Cuiseaux 21 46 30N 5 22 E
Cuité 170 6 29 S 36 9W
Cuito —► 133 18 1 S 20 48 E
Cuito Cuanavale 133 15 10 S 19 10 E
Cuitzeo, L. de 160 19 55N 101 5W
Cuiuni —► 169 0 45 S 63 7W
Cuivre —► 154 38 55N 90 44W
Cuivre, West Fork —► 154 39 2N 90 58W
Cujmir 50 44 13N 22 57 E
Cukai 85 4 13N 103 25 E
Culaba 91 11 40N 124 32 E
Culan 20 46 34N 2 20 E
Culasi 91 11 26N 122 3 E
Culauan 91 5 58N 125 40 E
Culbertson 152 48 9N 104 30W
Culburra 112 35 50 S 139 58 E
Culebra, Sierra de la 34 41 55N 6 20W
Culemborg 22 51 58N 5 14 E
Culgoa 112 35 44 S 143 6 E
Culgoa —► 111 29 56 S 146 20 E
Culiacán 160 24 50N 107 23W
Culiacán —► 160 24 30N 107 42W
Culion 91 11 54N 120 1 E
Culiseu —► 173 12 14 S 53 17W
Cúllar de Baza 37 37 35N 2 34W
Cullarin Range 113 34 30 S 149 30 E
Cullen, Australia 108 13 58 S 131 54 E
Cullen, U.K. 14 57 45N 2 50W
Cullen Pt. 110 11 57 S 141 54 E
Cullera 37 39 9N 0 17W
Cullman 149 34 13N 86 50W
Culloden Moor 14 57 29N 4 7W
Cullom 155 40 53N 88 16W
Culoz 21 45 47N 5 46 E
Culpataro 112 33 40 S 144 22 E
Culpeper 148 38 29N 77 59W
Culuene —► 173 12 56 S 52 51W
Culver 155 41 13N 86 25W
Culver, Pt. 109 32 54 S 124 43 E
Culverden 115 42 47 S 172 49 E
Cuma 133 12 52 S 15 5 E
Cumali 49 36 42N 27 28 E
Cumaná 169 10 30N 64 5W
Cumare 168 0 49N 72 32W
Cumari 171 18 16 S 48 11W
Cumberland, Canada 144 49 40N 125 0W
Cumberland, Iowa, U.S.A. 154 41 16N 94 52W
Cumberland, Md., U.S.A. 148 39 40N 78 43W
Cumberland, Wis., U.S.A. 152 45 32N 92 3W
Cumberland —► 149 36 15N 87 0W
Cumberland I. 149 30 52N 81 30W
Cumberland Is. 110 20 35 S 149 10 E
Cumberland L. 145 54 3N 102 18W
Cumberland Pen. 141 67 0N 64 0W
Cumberland Plateau 149 36 0N 84 30W
Cumberland Sd. 141 65 30N 66 0W
Cumborah 111 29 40 S 147 45 E
Cumbres Mayores 35 38 4N 6 39W
Cumbria □ 12 54 35N 2 55W
Cumbrian Mts. 12 54 30N 3 0W
Cumbum 81 15 40N 79 10 E
Cuminá —► 169 1 30 S 56 0W
Cuminapanema —► 169 1 9 S 54 54W
Cummings Mt. 159 35 2N 118 34W
Cumnock, Australia 113 32 59 S 148 46 E
Cumnock, U.K. 14 55 27N 4 18W
Cumpas 160 30 0N 109 48W
Cumplida, Pta. 37 28 50N 17 48W
Cuncumén 174 31 53 S 70 38W
Cundeelee 109 30 43 S 123 26 E
Cunderdin 109 31 37 S 117 12 E
Cundinamarca □ 168 5 0N 74 0W
Cunene □ 133 16 30 S 15 0 E
Cunene —► 133 17 20 S 11 50 E
Cúneo 42 44 23N 7 31 E
Cunhinga 133 12 11 S 16 47 E
Cunillera, I. 37 38 59N 1 13 E
Cunjamba 133 15 27 S 20 10 E
Cunlhat 20 45 38N 3 32 E
Cunnamulla 111 28 2 S 145 38 E
Cuorgnè 42 45 23N 7 39 E
Cupar, Canada 145 50 57N 104 10W
Cupar, U.K. 14 56 20N 3 0W
Cupica, G. de 168 6 25N 77 30W
Ćuprija 46 43 57N 21 26 E
Curaçá 170 8 59 S 39 54W
Curaçao 163 12 10N 69 0W
Curacautín 176 38 26 S 71 53W
Curahuara de Carangas 172 17 52 S 68 26W
Curanilahue 174 37 29 S 73 28W
Curaray —► 168 2 20 S 74 5W
Curatabaca 169 6 19N 62 51W
Cure —► 19 47 40N 3 41 E
Curepto 174 35 8 S 72 1W
Curiapo 172 8 33N 61 5W
Curicó 174 34 55 S 71 20W
Curicó □ 174 34 50 S 71 15W
Curicuriari —► 168 0 14 S 66 48W
Curimatá 170 10 2 S 44 17W
Curiplaya 168 0 16N 74 52W
Curitiba 175 25 20 S 49 10W
Currabubula 111 31 16 S 150 44 E
Currais Novos 170 6 13 S 36 30W
Curralinho 170 1 45 S 49 46W
Currant 156 38 51N 115 32W
Curranyalpa 113 30 53 S 144 39 E
Curraweena 113 30 47 S 145 54 E
Currawilla 110 25 10 S 141 20 E
Current —► 153 37 15N 91 10W
Currie, Australia 110 39 56 S 143 53 E
Currie, U.S.A. 156 40 16N 114 45W
Currie, Mt. 135 30 29 S 29 21 E
Currituck Sd. 149 36 20N 75 50W
Cursole 136 2 14N 45 25 E
Curtea de Argeş 50 45 12N 24 42 E
Curtis, Spain 34 43 7N 8 4W
Curtis, U.S.A. 152 40 41N 100 32W
Curtis Group 110 39 30 S 146 37 E
Curtis I. 110 23 35 S 151 10 E
Curuá —►, Pará, Brazil 169 2 24 S 54 5W
Curuá —►, Pará, Brazil 173 5 23 S 54 22W
Curuá, I. 170 0 48N 50 10W
Curuaés —► 173 7 30 S 54 45W
Curuápanema —► 169 2 25 S 55 2W
Curuçá 170 0 43 S 47 50W
Curuguaty 175 24 31 S 55 42W
Çürüksu Çayi —► 57 37 27N 27 11 E
Curup 88 4 26 S 102 13 E
Curupira, Serra 169 1 25N 64 30W
Cururu —► 173 7 12 S 58 3W
Cururupu 170 1 50 S 44 50W
Curuzú Cuatiá 174 29 50 S 58 5W
Curvelo 171 18 45 S 44 27W
Curyo 112 35 50 S 142 47 E
Cushing 153 35 59N 96 46W
Cushing, Mt. 144 57 35N 126 57W
Cusihuiriáchic 160 28 10N 106 50W
Cusna, Monte 42 44 13N 10 25 E
Cusset 20 46 8N 3 28 E
Custer 152 43 45N 103 38W
Cut Bank 156 48 40N 112 15W
Cutervo 172 6 25 S 78 55W
Cuthbert 149 31 47N 84 47W
Cutler 158 36 31N 119 17W
Cutral-Có 176 38 58 S 69 15W
Cutro 45 39 1N 16 58 E
Cuttaburra —► 111 29 43 S 144 22 E
Cuttack 79 20 25N 85 57 E
Cuvelai 133 15 44 S 15 50 E
Cuvier, C. 109 23 14 S 113 22 E
Cuvier I. 114 36 27 S 175 50 E
Cuxhaven 26 53 51N 8 41 E
Cuyabeno 168 0 16 S 75 53W
Cuyahoga Falls 150 41 8N 81 30W
Cuyapo 90 15 46N 120 40 E
Cuyo 91 10 50N 121 5 E
Cuyo East Pass 91 11 0N 121 28 E
Cuyo I. 91 10 51N 121 2 E
Cuyo West Pass 91 11 0N 120 30 E
Cuyuni —► 169 6 23N 58 41W
Cuzco, Bolivia 172 20 0 S 66 50W
Cuzco, Peru 172 13 32 S 72 0W
Cuzco □ 172 13 31 S 71 59W
Čvrsnica 46 43 36N 17 35 E
Cwmbran 13 51 39N 3 0W
Cyangugu 130 2 29 S 28 54 E
Cybinka 32 52 12N 14 46 E
Cyclades = Kikládhes 49 37 20N 24 30 E
Cygnet 110 43 8 S 147 1 E
Cynthiana 155 38 23N 84 10W
Cypress Hills 145 49 40N 109 30W
Cyprus ■ 70 35 0N 33 0 E
Cyrene = Shaḩḩāt 122 32 48N 21 54 E
Czaplinek 32 53 34N 16 14 E
Czar 145 52 27N 110 50W
Czarna —►, Piotrkow Trybunalski, Poland 32 51 18N 19 55 E
Czarna —►, Tarnobrzeg, Poland 32 50 3N 21 21 E
Czarna Woda 32 53 51N 18 6 E
Czarne 32 53 42N 16 58 E
Czarnków 32 52 55N 16 38 E
Czechoslovakia ■ 31 49 0N 17 0 E
Czechowice-Dziedzice 32 49 54N 18 59 E
Czeladz 32 50 16N 19 2 E
Czempiń 32 52 9N 16 33 E
Czeremcha 32 52 31N 23 21 E
Czersk 32 53 46N 17 58 E
Czerwieńsk 32 52 1N 15 13 E
Czerwionka 32 50 7N 18 37 E
Częstochowa 32 50 49N 19 7 E
Częstochowa □ 32 50 45N 19 0 E
Człopa 32 53 6N 16 6 E
Człuchów 32 53 41N 17 22 E
Czyzew 32 52 48N 22 19 E

D

Da —► 84 21 15N 105 20 E
Da Hinggan Ling 93 48 0N 121 0 E
Da Lat 85 11 56N 108 25 E
Da Nang 84 16 4N 108 13 E
Da Qaidam 92 37 50N 95 15 E
Da Yunhe —► 95 34 25N 120 5 E
Da'an 95 45 30N 124 7 E
Daap 91 7 4N 122 12 E
Daarlerveen 22 52 26N 6 34 E
Dab'a, Râs el 124 31 3N 28 31 E
Daba Shan 96 32 0N 109 0 E
Dabai 127 11 25N 5 15 E
Dabajuro 168 11 2N 70 40W
Dabakala 126 8 15N 4 20W
Dabaro 136 6 21N 48 43 E
Dabbūriya 69 32 42N 35 22 E
Dabeiba 168 7 1N 76 16W
Dabhoi 78 22 10N 73 20 E
Dąbie, Konin, Poland 32 52 5N 18 50 E
Dąbie, Szczecin, Poland 32 53 27N 14 45 E
Dabie Shan 97 31 20N 115 20 E
Dabl, W. —► 71 29 5N 36 16 E
Dabo 88 0 30 S 104 33 E
Dabola 126 10 50N 11 5W
Dabou 126 5 20N 4 23W
Daboya 127 9 30N 1 20W
Dabrowa Górnicza 32 50 15N 19 10 E
Dabrowa Tarnówska 32 50 10N 20 59 E
Dąbrówno 32 53 27N 20 2 E
Dabu 97 24 22N 116 41 E
Dabung 85 5 23N 102 1 E
Dabus —► 125 10 48N 35 10 E
Dacato —► 125 7 25N 42 40 E
Dacca = Dhaka 82 23 43N 90 26 E
Dacca □ = Dhaka 82 24 25N 90 25 E
Dachau 27 48 16N 11 27 E
Dadanawa 169 2 50N 59 30W
Daday 60 41 28N 33 27 E
Dade City 149 28 20N 82 12W
Dades, Oued —► 120 30 58N 6 44W
Dadiya 127 9 35N 11 24 E
Dadra and Nagar Haveli □ 78 20 5N 73 0 E
Dadri = Charkhi Dadri 78 28 37N 76 17 E
Dadu 77 26 45N 67 45 E
Dadu He —► 96 29 31N 103 46 E
Dăeni 50 44 51N 28 10 E
Daet 90 14 2N 122 55 E
Dafang 96 27 9N 105 39 E
Dafdaf, J. 71 28 16N 35 35 E
Dagana 126 16 30N 15 35W
Dagash 124 19 19N 33 25 E
Dagestanskiye Ogni 61 42 6N 48 12 E
Dagg Sd. 115 45 23 S 166 45 E
Daggett 159 34 52N 116 52W
Daghestan A.S.S.R. □ 61 42 30N 47 0 E
Daghfeli 124 19 18N 32 40 E
Dagö = Hiiumaa 58 58 50N 22 45 E
Dagu 95 38 59N 117 40 E
Dagua 107 3 27 S 143 20 E
Daguan 96 27 43N 103 56 E
Dagupan 90 16 3N 120 20 E
Dahab 71 28 31N 34 31 E
Dahlak Kebir 125 15 50N 40 10 E
Dahlenburg 26 53 11N 10 43 E
Dahlgren 155 38 12N 88 41W
Dahlonega 149 34 35N 83 59W
Dahme, E. Germany 26 51 51N 13 25 E
Dahme, W. Germany 26 54 13N 11 5 E
Dahod 78 22 50N 74 15 E
Dahomey = Benin ■ 127 10 0N 2 0 E
Dahong Shan 97 31 25N 113 0 E
Dahra 126 15 22N 15 30W
Dahra, Massif de 121 36 7N 1 21 E
Daḩy, Nafūd ad 74 22 0N 45 25 E
Dai Hao 84 18 1N 106 25 E
Dai-Sen 100 35 22N 133 32 E
Dai Shan 97 30 25N 122 10 E
Dai Xian 94 39 4N 112 58 E
Daicheng 94 38 42N 116 38 E
Daigo 101 36 46N 140 21 E
Daimanji-San 100 36 14N 133 20 E
Daimiel 37 39 5N 3 35W
Daingean 15 53 18N 7 15W
Dainkog 96 32 30N 97 58 E
Daintree 110 16 20 S 145 20 E
Daiō-Misaki 101 34 15N 136 45 E
Dairût 124 27 34N 30 43 E
Daisetsu-Zan 98 43 30N 142 57 E
Daitari 79 21 10N 85 46 E
Daito 100 35 19N 132 58 E
Dajarra 110 21 42 S 139 30 E
Dajia 97 24 22N 120 37 E
Dajin Chuan —► 96 31 16N 101 59 E
Dak Dam 84 12 20N 107 21 E
Dak Nhe 84 15 28N 107 48 E
Dak Pek 84 15 4N 107 44 E
Dak Song 85 12 19N 107 35 E
Dak Sui 84 14 55N 107 43 E
Dakar 126 14 34N 17 29W
Dakhla 120 23 50N 15 53W
Dakhla, El Wâhât el- 124 25 30N 28 50 E
Dakhovskaya 61 44 13N 40 13 E
Dakingari 127 11 37N 4 1 E
Dakor 78 22 45N 73 11 E
Dakoro 127 14 31N 6 46 E
Dakota City, Iowa, U.S.A. 154 42 43N 94 12W
Dakota City, Nebr., U.S.A. 152 42 27N 96 28W
Đakovica 46 42 22N 20 26 E
Đakovo 46 45 19N 18 24 E
Dala 133 11 3 S 20 17 E
Dalaba 126 10 42N 12 15W
Dalachi 94 36 48N 105 0 E

Dalaguete

Dalaguete 91 9 46N 123 32 E
Dalai Nur 94 43 20N 116 45 E
Dālakī 73 29 26N 51 17 E
Dalandzadgad 94 43 27N 104 30 E
Dalanganem Is. 91 10 40N 120 17 E
Dālbandīn 77 29 0N 64 23 E
Dalbeattie 14 54 55N 3 50W
Dalbosjön 53 58 40N 12 45 E
Dalby, Australia 111 27 10 S 151 17 E
Dalby, Sweden 52 55 40N 13 22 E
Dale, Norway 51 61 22N 5 23 E
Dale, U.S.A. 155 38 10N 86 59W
Dalen, Neth. 22 52 42N 6 46 E
Dalen, Norway 51 59 26N 8 0 E
Dalet 82 19 59N 93 51 E
Daletme 82 21 36N 92 46 E
Daleville 155 40 7N 85 33W
Dalfsen 22 52 31N 6 16 E
Dalga 124 27 39N 30 41 E
Dalgān 73 27 31N 59 19 E
Dalgaranger, Mt. 109 27 50 S 117 5 E
Dalhart 153 36 10N 102 30W
Dalhousie, Canada 143 48 5N 66 26W
Dalhousie, India 78 32 38N 76 0 E
Dali, Shaanxi, China 94 34 48N 109 58 E
Dali, Yunnan, China 96 25 40N 100 10 E
Dalian 95 38 50N 121 40 E
Daliang Shan 96 28 0N 102 45 E
Dalias 37 36 49N 2 52W
Daling He → 95 40 55N 121 40 E
Dāliyat el Karmel 69 32 43N 35 2 E
Dalj 46 45 29N 18 59 E
Dalkeith 14 55 54N 3 5W
Dall I. 144 54 59N 133 25W
Dallarnil 111 25 19 S 152 2 E
Dallas, Oreg., U.S.A. 156 45 0N 123 15W
Dallas, Tex., U.S.A. 153 32 50N 96 50W
Dallas Center 154 41 41N 93 58W
Dallas City 154 40 38N 91 10W
Dallol 125 14 14N 40 17 E
Dalmacija □ 46 43 20N 17 0 E
Dalmatia = Dalmacija □ 46 43 20N 17 0 E
Dalmatovo 62 56 16N 62 56 E
Dalmellington 14 55 20N 4 25W
Dalnegorsk 65 44 32N 135 33 E
Dalneretchensk 65 45 50N 133 40 E
Daloa 126 7 0N 6 30W
Dalou Shan 96 28 15N 107 0 E
Dalsjöfors 53 57 46N 13 5 E
Dalskog 53 58 44N 12 18 E
Daltenganj 79 24 0N 84 4 E
Dalton, Canada 142 48 11N 84 1W
Dalton, Ga., U.S.A. 149 34 47N 84 58W
Dalton, Mass., U.S.A. 151 42 28N 73 11W
Dalton, Nebr., U.S.A. 152 41 27N 103 0W
Dalton Iceberg Tongue 7 66 15 S 121 30 E
Dalupiri I., Cagayan, Phil. 90 19 5N 121 12 E
Dalupiri I., N. Samar, Phil. 90 12 25N 124 16 E
Dalvík 54 65 58N 18 32W
Daly → 108 13 35 S 130 19 E
Daly City 158 37 42N 122 28W
Daly L. 145 56 32N 105 39W
Daly Waters 110 16 15 S 133 24 E
Dam Doi 85 8 50N 105 12 E
Dam Ha 84 21 21N 107 36 E
Daman 78 20 25N 72 57 E
Daman □ 78 20 25N 72 58 E
Dāmaneh 73 33 1N 50 29 E
Damanhûr 124 31 0N 30 30 E
Damanzhuang 94 38 5N 116 35 E
Damar 87 7 7 S 128 40 E
Damara 132 4 58N 18 42 E
Damaraland 134 21 0 S 17 0 E
Damascus = Dimashq 70 33 30N 36 18 E
Damaturu 127 11 45N 11 55 E
Damāvand 73 35 47N 52 0 E
Damāvand, Qolleh-ye 73 35 56N 52 10 E
Damba 133 6 44 S 15 20 E
Dame Marie 163 18 36N 74 26W
Dāmghān 73 36 10N 54 17 E
Dămienesti 50 46 44N 27 1 E
Damietta = Dumyât 124 31 24N 31 48 E
Daming 94 36 15N 115 6 E
Damīr Qābū 72 36 58N 41 51 E
Dāmīya 69 32 6N 35 34 E
Dammarie 18 48 20N 1 30 E
Dammartin-en-Goële 19 49 3N 2 41 E
Dammastock 29 46 38N 8 24 E
Damme 26 52 32N 8 12 E
Damodar → 79 23 17N 87 35 E
Damoh 79 23 50N 79 28 E
Damous 121 36 31N 1 42 E
Dampier 108 20 41 S 116 42 E
Dampier, Selat 87 0 40 S 131 0 E
Dampier Arch. 108 20 38 S 116 32 E
Dampier Str. 107 5 50 S 148 0 E
Damqawt 75 16 34N 52 50 E
Damrei, Chuor Phnum 85 11 30N 103 0 E
Damville 18 48 51N 1 5 E
Damvillers 19 49 20N 5 21 E
Dan-Gulbi 127 11 40N 6 15 E
Dana 87 11 0 S 122 52 E
Dana, L. 142 50 53N 77 20W
Dana, Mt. 158 37 54N 119 12W
Danakil Depression 125 12 45N 41 0 E
Danao, Cebu, Phil. 91 10 31N 124 1 E
Danao, Sorsogon, Phil. 90 12 44N 123 51 E
Danbury 151 41 23N 73 29W
Danby L. 157 34 17N 115 0W
Dand 78 31 28N 65 32 E
Dandaragan 109 30 40 S 115 40 E
Dandeldhura 79 29 20N 80 35 E
Dandenong 113 38 0 S 145 15 E
Dandong 95 40 10N 124 20 E
Danfeng 94 33 45N 110 25 E
Danforth 143 45 39N 67 57W
Dangan Liedao 97 22 2N 114 8 E
Dangara 63 38 6N 69 22 E
Danger Is. = Pukapuka 105 10 53 S 165 49W
Danger Pt. 134 34 40 S 19 17 E
Dangla 125 11 18N 36 56 E
Dangora 127 11 30N 8 7 E
Dangrek, Phnom 84 14 15N 105 0 E
Dangriga 161 17 0N 88 13W
Dangshan 94 34 27N 116 22 E
Dangtu 97 31 32N 118 25 E
Dangyang 97 30 52N 111 44 E
Daniel 156 42 56N 110 2W
Daniel's Harbour 143 50 13N 57 35W
Danielskuil 134 28 11 S 23 33 E
Danielson 151 41 50N 71 52W
Danilov 59 58 16N 40 13 E
Danilovgrad 46 42 38N 19 9 E
Danilovka 59 50 25N 44 12 E
Daning 94 36 28N 110 45 E
Danissa 130 3 15N 40 58 E
Danja 127 11 21N 7 30 E
Danje-ia-Menha 133 9 32 S 14 39 E
Ḍank 75 23 33N 56 16 E
Dankalwa 127 11 52N 12 12 E
Dankama 127 13 20N 7 44 E
Dankov 59 53 20N 39 5 E
Danleng 96 30 1N 103 31 E
Danlí 162 14 4N 86 35W
Dannemora, Sweden 52 60 12N 17 51 E
Dannemora, U.S.A. 151 44 41N 73 44W
Dannenberg 26 53 7N 11 4 E
Dannevirke 114 40 12 S 176 8 E
Dannhauser 135 28 0 S 30 3 E
Danot 136 7 33N 45 17 E
Danshui 97 25 12N 121 25 E
Dansville 150 42 32N 77 41W
Dantan 79 21 57N 87 20 E
Dante 68 10 25N 51 16 E
Danube → 50 45 20N 29 40 E
Danubyu 82 17 15N 95 35 E
Danukandi 82 23 32N 90 43 E
Danvers 151 42 34N 70 55W
Danville, Ill., U.S.A. 155 40 10N 87 40W
Danville, Ind., U.S.A. 155 39 46N 86 32W
Danville, Ky., U.S.A. 155 37 40N 84 45W
Danville, Va., U.S.A. 149 36 40N 79 20W
Danyang 97 32 0N 119 31 E
Danzhai 96 26 11N 107 48 E
Danzig = Gdańsk 32 54 22N 18 40 E
Dao, Antiqe, Phil. 91 10 30N 121 57 E
Dao, Capiz, Phil. 91 11 24N 122 41 E
Dão → 34 40 20N 8 11W
Dao Xian 97 25 36N 111 31 E
Daocheng 96 29 0N 100 10 E
Daora 120 27 5N 12 59W
Daoud = Aïn Beïda 121 35 50N 7 29 E
Daoulas 18 48 22N 4 17W
Dapa 91 9 46N 126 3 E
Dapitan 91 8 39N 123 25 E
Dapong 127 10 55N 0 16 E
Daqing Shan 94 40 40N 111 0 E
Daqu Shan 97 30 25N 122 20 E
Dar es Salaam 130 6 50 S 39 12 E
Dar Mazār 73 29 14N 57 20 E
Dār Ta'izzah 70 36 20N 36 52 E
Dar'ā 69 32 36N 36 7 E
Dar'ā □ 70 32 55N 36 10 E
Dārāb 73 28 50N 54 30 E
Darabani 50 48 10N 26 39 E
Daraj 122 30 10N 10 28 E
Dārān 73 32 59N 50 24 E
Daraut Kurgan 63 39 33N 72 11 E
Daravica 46 42 32N 20 8 E
Daraw 124 24 22N 32 51 E
Dārayyā 70 33 28N 36 15 E
Darazo 127 11 1N 10 24 E
Darband 78 34 20N 72 50 E
Darband, Kūh-e 73 31 34N 57 8 E
Darbhanga 79 26 15N 85 55 E
Darburruk 136 9 44N 44 31 E
Darby 156 46 2N 114 7W
Darda 46 45 40N 18 41 E
Dardanelle, Ark., U.S.A. 153 35 12N 93 9W
Dardanelle, Calif., U.S.A. 158 38 15N 119 50W
Dardanelles = Çanakkale Boğazı 48 40 3N 26 12 E
Dārestān 73 29 9N 58 42 E
Darfield 115 43 29 S 172 7 E
Darfo 42 45 52N 10 11 E
Dargai 77 34 25N 71 55 E
Dargan Ata 64 40 29N 62 10 E
Dargaville 114 35 57 S 173 52 E
Darhan Muminggan Lianheqi 94 41 40N 110 28 E
Dari 125 5 48N 30 26 E
Darién, G. del 168 9 0N 77 0W
Darién, Serranía del 168 8 30N 77 30W
Dariganga 94 45 21N 113 45 E
Darinskoye 62 51 20N 51 44 E
Darjeeling = Darjiling 79 27 3N 88 18 E
Darjiling 79 27 3N 88 18 E
Dark Cove 143 48 47N 54 13W
Darkan 109 33 20 S 116 43 E
Darke Peak 112 33 27 S 136 12 E
Darkhazīneh 73 31 54N 48 39 E
Darkot Pass 79 36 45N 73 26 E
Darling → 112 34 4 S 141 54 E
Darling Downs 111 27 30 S 150 30 E
Darling Ra. 109 32 30 S 116 0 E
Darlington, U.K. 12 54 33N 1 33W
Darlington, S.C., U.S.A. 149 34 18N 79 50W
Darlington, Wis., U.S.A. 154 42 43N 90 7W
Darlot, L. 109 27 48 S 121 35 E
Darłowo 32 54 25N 16 25 E
Dărmăneşti 50 46 21N 26 33 E
Darmstadt 27 49 51N 8 40 E
Darnah 122 32 40N 22 35 E
Darnah □ 122 31 0N 23 40 E
Darnall 135 29 23 S 31 18 E
Darnétal 18 49 25N 1 10 E
Darney 19 48 5N 6 2 E
Darnick 112 32 48 S 143 38 E
Darnley, C. 7 68 0 S 69 0 E
Darnley B. 140 69 30N 123 30W
Daroca 36 41 9N 1 25W
Darr 110 23 13 S 144 7 E
Darr → 110 23 39 S 143 50 E
Darran Mts. 115 44 37 S 167 59 E
Darrington 156 48 14N 121 37W
Darror → 68 10 30N 50 0 E
Darsana 82 23 35N 88 48 E
Darsi 81 15 46N 79 44 E
Darsser Ort 26 54 29N 12 31 E
Dart → 13 50 24N 3 36W
Dart, C. 7 73 6 S 126 20W
Dartmoor, Australia 112 37 56 S 141 19 E
Dartmoor, U.K. 13 50 36N 4 0W
Dartmouth, Australia 110 23 31 S 144 44 E
Dartmouth, Canada 143 44 40N 63 30W
Dartmouth, U.K. 13 50 21N 3 35W
Dartmouth, L. 111 26 4 S 145 18 E
Dartuch, C. 36 39 55N 3 49 E
Daru 107 9 3 S 143 13 E
Daruvar 46 45 35N 17 14 E
Darvaza 64 40 11N 58 24 E
Darvel, Teluk 87 4 50N 118 20 E
Darwha 78 20 15N 77 45 E
Darwin, Australia 108 12 25 S 130 51 E
Darwin, U.S.A. 159 36 15N 117 35W
Darwin, Mt. 176 0 10 S 69 55W
Darwin River 108 12 50 S 130 58 E
Daryapur 78 20 55N 77 20 E
Dās 75 25 20N 53 30 E
Dashetai 94 41 0N 109 5 E
Dashkesan 61 40 40N 46 0 E
Dasht 73 37 17N 56 7 E
Dasht → 77 25 10N 61 40 E
Dasht-i-Nawar 78 33 52N 68 0 E
Daska 78 32 20N 74 20 E
Dassa-Zoume 127 7 46N 2 14 E
Dasseneiland 134 33 25 S 18 3 E
Datça 49 36 46N 27 40 E
Datia 79 25 39N 78 27 E
Datian 97 25 40N 117 50 E
Datong, Anhui, China 97 30 48N 117 44 E
Datong, Shanxi, China 94 40 6N 113 18 E
Dattapur = Dhamangaon 78 20 45N 78 15 E
Datu, Tanjung 89 2 5N 109 39 E
Datu Piang 91 7 2N 124 30 E
Daugava → 58 57 4N 24 3 E
Daugavpils 58 55 53N 26 32 E
Daulatabad 80 19 57N 75 15 E
Daule 168 1 56 S 79 56W
Daule → 168 2 10 S 79 52W
Daulpur 78 26 45N 77 59 E
Daun 27 50 10N 6 53 E
Daund 80 18 26N 74 40 E
Dauphin 145 51 9N 100 5W
Dauphin I. 149 30 16N 88 10W
Dauphin L. 145 51 20N 99 45W
Dauphiné 21 45 15N 5 25 E
Daura, Borno, Nigeria 127 11 31N 11 24 E
Daura, Kaduna, Nigeria 127 13 2N 8 21 E
Dausa 78 26 52N 76 20 E
Davangere 81 14 25N 75 55 E
Davao 91 7 0N 125 40 E
Davao □ 91 7 0N 125 55 E
Davao, G. of 91 6 30N 125 48 E
Davao del Sur □ 91 6 30N 125 25 E
Davao Oriental □ 91 7 10N 126 30 E
Dāvar Panāh 73 27 25N 62 15 E
Davenport, Calif., U.S.A. 158 37 1N 122 12W
Davenport, Iowa, U.S.A. 154 41 30N 90 40W
Davenport, Wash., U.S.A. 156 47 40N 118 5W
Davenport Downs 110 24 8 S 141 7 E
Davenport Ra. 110 20 28 S 134 0 E
David 162 8 30N 82 30W
David City 152 41 18N 97 10W
David Gorodok 58 52 4N 27 8 E
Davidson 145 51 16N 105 59W
Davis, Antarct. 7 68 34 S 17 55 E
Davis, U.S.A. 158 38 33N 121 44W
Davis Dam 159 35 11N 114 35W
Davis Inlet 143 55 50N 60 59W
Davis Mts. 153 30 42N 104 15W
Davis Sea 7 66 0 S 92 0 E
Davis Str. 141 65 0N 58 0W
Davlekanovo 62 54 13N 55 3 E
Davos 29 46 48N 9 49 E
Davy L. 145 58 53N 108 18W
Dawa → 125 4 11N 42 6 E
Dawaki, Bauchi, Nigeria 127 9 25N 9 33 E
Dawaki, Kano, Nigeria 127 12 5N 8 23 E
Dawes Ra. 110 24 40 S 150 40 E
Dawna Range 82 16 30N 98 30 E
Dawnyein 82 15 54N 95 36 E
Dawqah 74 19 36N 40 54 E
Dawson, Canada 140 64 10N 139 30W
Dawson, Ga., U.S.A. 149 31 45N 84 28W
Dawson, N. Dak., U.S.A. 152 46 56N 99 45W
Dawson, I. 176 53 50 S 70 50W
Dawson Creek 144 55 45N 120 15W
Dawson Inlet 145 61 50N 93 25W
Dawson Range 110 24 30 S 149 48 E
Dawu 96 30 55N 101 10 E
Dawwah 75 20 33N 58 48 E
Dax 20 43 44N 1 3W
Daxi 97 24 52N 121 20 E
Daxian 96 31 15N 107 23 E
Daxin 96 22 50N 107 11 E
Daxindian 95 37 30N 120 50 E
Daxinggou 95 43 25N 129 40 E
Daxue Shan, Sichuan, China 96 30 30N 101 30 E
Daxue Shan, Yunnan, China 96 23 42N 99 48 E
Dayao 96 25 43N 101 20 E
Daye 97 30 6N 114 58 E
Dayi 96 30 41N 103 29 E
Daylesford 112 37 21 S 144 9 E
Dayong 97 29 11N 110 30 E
Dayr Abū Sa'īd 69 32 30N 35 42 E
Dayr al-Ghuşūn 69 32 21N 35 4 E
Dayr az Zawr 72 35 20N 40 5 E
Dayr Dirwān 69 31 55N 35 15 E
Daysland 144 52 50N 112 20W
Dayton, Iowa, U.S.A. 154 42 14N 94 6W
Dayton, Ky., U.S.A. 155 39 47N 84 28W
Dayton, Nev., U.S.A. 158 39 15N 119 34W
Dayton, Ohio, U.S.A. 148 39 45N 84 10W
Dayton, Pa., U.S.A. 150 40 54N 79 18W
Dayton, Tenn., U.S.A. 149 35 30N 85 1W
Dayton, Wash., U.S.A. 156 46 20N 118 10W
Daytona Beach 149 29 14N 81 0W
Dayu 97 25 24N 114 22 E
Dayville 156 44 33N 119 37W
Daz Dağ 70 36 49N 36 20 E
Dazhu 96 30 41N 107 15 E
Dazu 96 29 40N 105 42 E
De Aar 134 30 39 S 24 0 E
De Bilt 22 52 6N 5 11 E
De Forest 154 43 15N 89 20W
De Funiak Springs 149 30 42N 86 10W
De Grey 108 20 12 S 119 12 E
De Grey → 108 20 12 S 119 13 E
De Kalb 155 41 55N 88 45W
De Koog 22 53 6N 4 46 E
De Land 149 29 1N 81 19W
De Leon 153 32 9N 98 35W
De Panne 23 51 6N 2 34 E
De Pere 148 44 28N 88 1W
De Queen 153 34 3N 94 24W
De Quincy 153 30 30N 93 27W
De Ridder 153 30 48N 93 15W
De Rijp 22 52 33N 4 51 E
De Smet 152 44 25N 97 35W
De Soto 154 38 7N 90 33W
De Tour 148 45 59N 83 56W
De Witt, Ark., U.S.A. 153 34 19N 91 20W
De Witt, Iowa, U.S.A. 154 41 49N 90 33W
De Witt, Mich., U.S.A. 155 42 50N 84 33W
Dead Sea 69 31 30N 35 30 E
Deadwood 152 44 23N 103 44W
Deadwood L. 144 59 10N 128 30W
Deakin 109 30 46 S 128 58 E
Deal 13 51 13N 1 25 E
Deal I. 110 39 30 S 147 20 E
Dealesville 134 28 41 S 25 44 E
De'an 97 29 21N 115 46 E
Dean, Forest of 13 51 50N 2 35W
Deán Funes 174 30 20 S 64 20W
Dearborn, Mich., U.S.A. 142 42 18N 83 15W
Dearborn, Mo., U.S.A. 154 39 32N 94 46W
Dease → 144 59 56N 128 32W
Dease L. 144 58 40N 130 5W
Dease Lake 144 58 25N 130 6W
Death Valley 159 36 19N 116 52W
Death Valley Junc. 159 36 21N 116 30W
Death Valley Nat. Monument 159 36 30N 117 0W
Deauville 18 49 23N 0 2 E
Deba Habe 127 10 14N 11 20 E
Debaltsevo 60 48 22N 38 26 E
Debao 96 23 21N 106 46 E
Debar 46 41 31N 20 30 E
Debden 145 53 30N 106 50W
Debdou 121 33 59N 3 0W
Debessy 62 57 39N 53 49 E

Diamantina

Dębica 32 50 2N 21 25 E
Dęblin 32 51 34N 21 50 E
Debno 32 52 44N 14 41 E
Débo, L. 126 15 14N 4 15W
Debolt 144 55 12N 118 1W
Deborah East, L. 109 30 45 S 119 0 E
Deborah West, L. 109 30 45 S 118 50 E
Debre 46 44 38N 19 53 E
Debre Birhan 125 9 41N 39 31 E
Debre Markos 125 10 20N 37 40 E
Debre May 125 11 20N 37 25 E
Debre Sina 125 9 51N 39 50 E
Debre Tabor 125 11 50N 38 26 E
Debre Zebit 125 11 48N 38 30 E
Debrecen 31 47 33N 21 42 E
Dečani 46 42 30N 20 10 E
Decatur, Ala., U.S.A. 149 34 35N 87 0W
Decatur, Ga., U.S.A. 149 33 47N 84 17W
Decatur, Ill., U.S.A. 154 39 50N 89 0W
Decatur, Ind., U.S.A. 155 40 50N 84 56W
Decatur, Mich., U.S.A. 155 42 7N 85 58W
Decatur, Tex., U.S.A. 153 33 15N 97 35W
Decazeville 20 44 34N 2 15 E
Deccan 80 18 0N 79 0 E
Deception, Mt. 112 30 42 S 138 16 E
Deception I. 7 63 0 S 60 15W
Deception L. 145 56 33N 104 13W
Dechang 96 27 25N 102 11 E
Děčín 30 50 47N 14 12 E
Decize 19 46 50N 3 28 E
Deckerville 150 43 33N 82 46W
Decollatura 45 39 2N 16 21 E
Decorah 152 43 20N 91 50W
Deda 50 46 56N 24 50 E
Dedaye 82 16 24N 95 53 E
Dedéagach = Alexandroúpolis 48 40 50N 25 54 E
Dedemsvaart 22 52 36N 6 28 E
Dedham 151 42 14N 71 10W
Dedilovo 59 53 59N 37 50 E
Dédougou 126 12 30N 3 25W
Deduru Oya 81 7 32N 79 50 E
Dedza 131 14 20 S 34 20 E
Dee ~▸, Scotland, U.K. 14 57 4N 2 7W
Dee ~▸, Wales, U.K. 12 53 15N 3 7W
Deep B. 144 61 15N 116 35W
Deep Lead 112 37 0 S 142 43 E
Deep River 154 41 35N 92 22W
Deep Well 110 24 20 S 134 0 E
Deepwater, Australia 111 29 25 S 151 51 E
Deepwater, U.S.A. 154 38 18N 93 46W
Deer ~▸ 145 58 23N 94 13W
Deer Lake, Nfld., Canada 143 49 11N 57 27W
Deer Lake, Ont., Canada 145 52 36N 94 20W
Deer Lodge 156 46 25N 112 40W
Deer Park, Ohio, U.S.A. 155 39 13N 84 23W
Deer Park, Wash., U.S.A. 156 47 55N 117 21W
Deer River 152 47 21N 93 44W
Deeral 110 17 14 S 145 55 E
Deerdepoort 134 24 37 S 26 27 E
Deerlijk 23 50 51N 3 22 E
Deferiet 151 44 2N 75 41W
Defiance 155 41 20N 84 20W
Deganya 69 32 43N 35 34 E
Dêgê 96 31 44N 98 39 E
Degebe ~▸ 35 38 13N 7 29W
Degeh Bur 136 8 11N 43 31 E
Degema 127 4 50N 6 48 E
Degersheim 29 47 23N 9 12 E
Deggendorf 27 48 49N 12 59 E
Deh Bīd 73 30 39N 53 11 E
Deh-e Shīr 73 31 29N 53 45 E
Dehaj 73 30 42N 54 53 E
Dehak 77 27 11N 62 37 E
Dehdez 73 31 43N 50 17 E
Dehestān 73 28 30N 55 35 E
Dehgolān 72 35 17N 47 25 E
Dehibat 121 32 0N 10 47 E
Dehiwala 81 6 50N 79 51 E
Dehlorān 72 32 41N 47 16 E
Dehnow-e Kūhestān 73 27 58N 58 32 E
Dehra Dun 78 30 20N 78 4 E
Dehri 79 24 50N 84 15 E
Dehua 97 25 26N 118 14 E
Dehui 95 44 30N 125 40 E
Deinze 23 50 59N 3 32 E
Dej 50 47 10N 23 52 E
Deje 52 59 35N 13 29 E
Dejiang 96 28 18N 108 7 E
Dekemhare 125 15 6N 39 0 E
Dekese 132 3 24 S 21 24 E
Dekhkanabad 63 38 21N 66 30 E
Dekoa 132 6 19N 19 4 E
Del Carmen 91 9 50N 126 0 E
Del Mar 159 32 58N 117 16W
Del Norte 157 37 40N 106 27W
Del Rio 153 29 23N 100 50W
Delai 124 17 21N 36 6 E
Delano 159 35 48N 119 13W
Delareyville 134 26 41 S 25 26 E
Delavan, Ill., U.S.A. 154 40 22N 89 33W
Delavan, Wis., U.S.A. 155 42 40N 88 39W
Delaware 155 40 20N 83 0W
Delaware □ 148 39 0N 75 40W
Delaware ~▸ 148 39 20N 75 25W
Delčevo 46 41 58N 22 46 E
Delegate 113 37 4 S 148 56 E
Delémont 28 47 22N 7 20 E
Delft 22 52 1N 4 22 E
Delft I. 81 9 30N 79 40 E
Delfzijl 22 53 20N 6 55 E
Delgado, C. 131 10 45 S 40 40 E
Delgerhet 94 45 50N 110 30 E
Delgo 124 20 6N 30 40 E
Delhi, Canada 150 42 51N 80 30W
Delhi, India 78 28 38N 77 17 E
Delhi, U.S.A. 151 42 17N 74 56W
Deli Jovan 46 44 13N 22 9 E
Delia 144 51 38N 112 23W
Delice ~▸ 57 39 45N 34 15 E
Delicias 160 28 10N 105 30W
Delījān 73 33 59N 50 40 E
Delitzsch 26 51 32N 12 22 E
Dell City 157 31 58N 105 19W
Dell Rapids 152 43 53N 96 44W
Delle 19 47 30N 7 2 E
Dellys 121 36 57N 3 57 E
Delmar, Iowa, U.S.A. 154 42 0N 90 37W
Delmar, N.Y., U.S.A. 151 42 37N 73 47W
Delmenhorst 26 53 3N 8 37 E
Delmiro Gouveia 170 9 24 S 38 6W
Delnice 43 45 23N 14 50 E
Delong, Ostrova 65 76 40N 149 20 E
Deloraine, Australia 110 41 30 S 146 40 E
Deloraine, Canada 145 49 15N 100 29W
Delphi, Greece 49 38 28N 22 30 E
Delphi, U.S.A. 155 40 37N 86 40W
Delphos 155 40 51N 84 17W
Delportshoop 134 28 22 S 24 20 E
Delray Beach 149 26 27N 80 4W
Delsbo 52 61 48N 16 32 E
Delta, Colo., U.S.A. 157 38 44N 108 5W
Delta, Utah, U.S.A. 156 39 21N 112 29W
Delta Amacuro □ 169 8 30N 61 30W
Delungra 111 29 39 S 150 51 E
Delvina 48 39 59N 20 4 E
Delvinákion 48 39 57N 20 32 E
Demak 89 6 53 S 110 38 E
Demanda, Sierra de la 36 42 15N 3 0W
Demba 133 5 28 S 22 15 E
Demba Chio 133 9 41 S 13 41 E
Dembecha 125 10 32N 37 30 E
Dembi 125 8 5N 36 25 E
Dembia 130 3 33N 25 48 E
Dembidolo 125 8 34N 34 50 E
Demer ~▸ 23 50 57N 4 42 E
Demerara □ 169 6 0N 58 30W
Demetrias 48 39 22N 23 1 E
Demidov 58 55 16N 31 30 E
Deming, N. Mex., U.S.A. 157 32 10N 107 50W
Deming, Wash., U.S.A. 158 48 49N 122 13W
Demini ~▸ 169 0 46 S 62 56W
Demmin 26 53 54N 13 2 E
Demnate 120 31 44N 6 59W
Demonte 42 44 18N 7 18 E
Demopolis 149 32 30N 87 48W
Dempo, Mt. 88 4 2 S 103 15 E
Demyansk 58 57 40N 32 27 E
Den Burg 22 53 3N 4 47 E
Den Chai 84 17 59N 100 4 E
Den Dungen 23 51 41N 5 22 E
Den Haag = 's-Gravenhage 22 52 7N 4 17 E
Den Ham 22 52 28N 6 30 E
Den Helder 22 52 57N 4 45 E
Den Hulst 22 52 36N 6 16 E
Den Oever 22 52 56N 5 2 E
Denain 19 50 20N 3 22 E
Denair 158 37 32N 120 48W
Denau 63 38 16N 67 54 E
Denbigh 12 53 12N 3 26W
Dendang 89 3 7 S 107 56 E
Dender ~▸ 23 51 2N 4 6 E
Denderhoutem 23 50 53N 4 2 E
Denderleeuw 23 50 54N 4 5 E
Dendermonde 23 51 2N 4 5 E
Deneba 125 9 47N 39 10 E
Denekamp 22 52 22N 7 1 E
Denezhkin Kamen, Gora 62 60 25N 59 32 E
Deng Deng 132 5 12N 13 31 E
Deng Xian 97 32 34N 112 4 E
Dengchuan 96 25 59N 100 3 E
Denge 127 12 52N 5 21 E
Dengfeng 94 34 25N 113 2 E
Dengi 127 9 25N 9 55 E
Dengkou 94 40 18N 106 55 E
Denham 109 25 56 S 113 31 E
Denham Ra. 110 21 55 S 147 46 E
Denham Sd. 109 25 45 S 113 15 E
Denia 37 38 49N 0 8 E
Denial B. 111 32 14 S 133 32 E
Deniliquin 113 35 30 S 144 58 E
Denison, Iowa, U.S.A. 152 42 0N 95 18W
Denison, Tex., U.S.A. 153 33 50N 96 40W
Denison Plains 108 18 35 S 128 0 E
Denisovka 62 52 28N 61 46 E
Denizli 57 37 42N 29 2 E
Denman 113 32 24 S 150 42 E
Denman Glacier 7 66 45 S 99 25 E
Denmark 109 34 59 S 117 25 E
Denmark ■ 53 55 30N 9 0 E
Denmark Str. 6 66 0N 30 0W
Dennison 150 40 21N 81 21W
Denpasar 86 8 45 S 115 14 E
Denton, Mont., U.S.A. 156 47 25N 109 56W
Denton, Tex., U.S.A. 153 33 12N 97 10W
D'Entrecasteaux Is. 107 9 0 S 151 0 E
D'Entrecasteaux Pt. 109 34 50 S 115 57 E
Dents du Midi 28 46 10N 6 56 E
Denu 127 6 4N 1 8 E
Denver, Colo., U.S.A. 152 39 45N 105 0W
Denver, Ind., U.S.A. 155 40 52N 86 5W
Denver, Iowa, U.S.A. 154 42 40N 92 20W
Denver City 153 32 58N 102 48W
Deoband 78 29 42N 77 43 E
Deobhog 80 19 53N 82 44 E
Deogarh 79 21 32N 84 45 E
Deoghar 79 24 30N 86 42 E
Deolali 80 19 58N 73 50 E
Deoli = Devli 78 25 50N 75 20 E
Deoria 79 26 31N 83 48 E
Deosai Mts. 79 35 40N 75 0 E
Deping 95 37 25N 116 58 E
Deposit 151 42 5N 75 23W
Depot Springs 109 27 55 S 120 3 E
Deputatskiy 65 69 18N 139 54 E
Dêqên 96 28 34N 98 51 E
Deqing 97 23 8N 111 42 E
Dera Ghazi Khan 77 30 5N 70 43 E
Dera Ismail Khan 77 31 50N 70 50 E
Derbent 54 42 5N 48 15 E
Derby, Australia 108 17 18 S 123 38 E
Derby, U.K. 12 52 55N 1 28W
Derby, Conn., U.S.A. 151 41 20N 73 5W
Derby, N.Y., U.S.A. 150 42 40N 78 59W
Derby □ 12 52 55N 1 28W
Derecske 31 47 20N 21 33 E
Derg ~▸ 15 54 42N 7 26W
Derg, L. 15 53 0N 8 20W
Dergachi 59 50 9N 36 11 E
Dermantsi 47 43 8N 24 17 E
Dernieres Isles 153 29 0N 90 45W
Dêrong 96 28 44N 99 9 E
Derrinallum 112 37 57 S 143 15 E
Derry = Londonderry 15 55 0N 7 20W
Derryveagh Mts. 15 55 0N 8 40W
Derudub 124 17 31N 36 7 E
Derval 18 47 40N 1 41W
Dervéni 49 38 8N 22 25 E
Derventa 46 44 59N 17 55 E
Derwent 145 53 41N 110 58W
Derwent ~▸, Derby, U.K. 12 52 53N 1 17W
Derwent ~▸, N. Yorks., U.K. 12 53 45N 0 57W
Derwent Water, L. 12 54 35N 3 9W
Des Moines, Iowa, U.S.A. 154 41 35N 93 37W
Des Moines, N. Mex., U.S.A. 153 36 50N 103 51W
Des Moines ~▸ 152 40 23N 91 25W
Des Plaines 155 42 3N 87 52W
Des Plaines ~▸ 155 41 23N 88 15W
Desaguadero ~▸, Argentina 174 34 30 S 66 46W
Desaguadero ~▸, Bolivia 172 18 24 S 67 5W
Desaguadero ~▸, Peru 172 16 35 S 69 5W
Descanso, Pta. 159 32 21N 117 3W
Descartes 20 46 59N 0 42 E
Deschaillons 143 46 32N 72 7W
Descharme ~▸ 145 56 51N 109 13W
Deschutes ~▸ 156 45 30N 121 0W
Dese 125 11 5N 39 40 E
Deseado, C. 176 52 45 S 74 42W
Desenzano del Gardo 42 45 28N 10 32 E
Desert Center 159 33 45N 115 27W
Desert Hot Springs 159 33 58N 116 30W
Désirade, I. 163 16 18N 61 3W
Deskenatlata L. 144 60 55N 112 3W
Desna ~▸ 58 50 33N 30 32 E
Desnătui ~▸ 50 44 15N 23 27 E
Desolación, I. 176 53 0 S 74 0W
Despeñaperros, Paso 37 38 24N 3 30W
Despotovac 46 44 6N 21 30 E
Dessau 26 51 49N 12 15 E
Dessel 23 51 15N 5 7 E
Dessye = Dese 125 11 5N 39 40 E
D'Estrees B. 112 35 55 S 137 45 E
Desuri 78 25 18N 73 35 E
Desvres 19 50 40N 1 48 E
Det Udom 84 14 54N 105 5 E
Deta 46 45 24N 21 13 E
Dete 131 18 38 S 26 50 E
Detinja ~▸ 46 43 51N 19 45 E
Detmold 26 51 55N 8 50 E
Detour Pt. 148 45 37N 86 35W
Detroit, Mich., U.S.A. 150 42 23N 83 5W
Detroit, Tex., U.S.A. 153 33 40N 95 10W
Detroit Lakes 152 46 50N 95 50W
Deurne, Belgium 23 51 12N 4 24 E
Deurne, Neth. 23 51 27N 5 49 E
Deutsche Bucht 26 54 0N 8 0 E
Deutschlandsberg 30 46 49N 15 14 E
Deux-Sèvres □ 18 46 35N 0 20W
Deva 50 45 53N 22 55 E
Devakottai 81 9 55N 78 45 E
Devaprayag 79 30 13N 78 35 E
Dévaványa 31 47 2N 20 59 E
Deveci Daği 60 40 10N 36 0 E
Devecser 31 47 6N 17 26 E
Deventer 22 52 15N 6 10 E
Deveron ~▸ 14 57 40N 2 31W
Devesel 50 44 28N 22 41 E
Devgad, I. 81 14 48N 74 5 E
Devgadh Bariya 78 22 40N 73 55 E
Devil River Pk. 115 40 56 S 172 37 E
Devils Den 158 35 46N 119 58W
Devils Lake 152 48 5N 98 50W
Devils Paw 144 58 47N 134 0W
Devil's Pt. 81 9 26N 80 6 E
Devin 47 41 44N 24 24 E
Devizes 13 51 21N 2 0W
Devli 78 25 50N 75 20 E
Devnya 47 43 13N 27 33 E
Devolii ~▸ 48 40 57N 20 15 E
Devon 144 53 24N 113 44W
Devon I. 6 75 10N 85 0W
Devonport, Australia 110 41 10 S 146 22 E
Devonport, N.Z. 114 36 49 S 174 49 E
Devonport, U.K. 13 50 23N 4 11W
Devonshire □ 13 50 50N 3 40W
Dewas 78 22 59N 76 3 E
Dewetsdorp 134 29 33 S 26 39 E
Dewsbury 12 53 42N 1 38W
Dexing 97 28 46N 117 30 E
Dexter, Mich., U.S.A. 155 42 20N 83 53W
Dexter, Mo., U.S.A. 153 36 50N 90 0W
Dexter, N. Mex., U.S.A. 153 33 15N 104 25W
Dey-Dey, L. 109 29 12 S 131 4 E
Deyang 96 31 3N 104 27 E
Deyhūk 73 33 15N 57 30 E
Deyyer 73 27 55N 51 55 E
Dezadeash L. 144 60 28N 136 58W
Dezfūl 73 32 20N 48 30 E
Dezhneva, Mys 65 66 5N 169 40W
Dezhou 94 37 26N 116 18 E
Dháfni 49 37 48N 22 1 E
Dhahab ~▸ 70 36 5N 37 30 E
Dhahaban 74 21 58N 39 3 E
Dhahiriya = Aẓ Ẓāhiriyah 71 31 25N 34 58 E
Dhahran = Aẓ Ẓahrān 73 26 10N 50 7 E
Dhaka 82 23 43N 90 26 E
Dhaka □ 82 24 25N 90 25 E
Dhamangaon 78 20 45N 78 15 E
Dhamar 74 14 30N 44 20 E
Dhamási 48 39 43N 22 11 E
Dhampur 79 29 19N 78 33 E
Dhamtari 79 20 42N 81 35 E
Dhanbad 79 23 50N 86 30 E
Dhankuta 79 26 55N 87 40 E
Dhanora 79 20 20N 80 22 E
Dhar 78 22 35N 75 26 E
Dharampur, Gujarat, India 80 20 32N 73 17 E
Dharampur, Mad. P., India 78 22 13N 75 18 E
Dharamsala = Dharmsala 78 32 16N 76 23 E
Dharapuram 81 10 45N 77 34 E
Dharmapuri 81 12 10N 78 10 E
Dharmavaram 81 14 29N 77 44 E
Dharmsala 78 32 16N 76 23 E
Dharwad 81 15 22N 75 15 E
Dhaulagiri 79 28 39N 83 28 E
Dhebar, L. 78 24 10N 74 0 E
Dhenkanal 79 20 45N 85 35 E
Dhenoúsa 49 37 8N 25 48 E
Dheskáti 48 39 55N 21 49 E
Dhespotikó 49 36 57N 24 58 E
Dhestina 49 38 25N 22 31 E
Dhībān 71 31 30N 35 46 E
Dhidhimótikhon 48 41 22N 26 29 E
Dhíkti 49 35 8N 25 22 E
Dhilianáta 49 38 15N 20 34 E
Dhílos 49 37 23N 25 15 E
Dhimitsána 49 37 36N 22 3 E
Dhírfis 49 38 40N 23 54 E
Dhodhekánisos 49 36 35N 27 0 E
Dhokós 49 37 20N 23 20 E
Dholiana 48 39 54N 20 32 E
Dholka 78 22 44N 72 29 E
Dhomokós 49 39 10N 22 18 E
Dhoraji 78 21 45N 70 37 E
Dhoxáton 48 41 9N 24 16 E
Dhragonísi 49 37 27N 25 29 E
Dhrangadhra 78 22 59N 71 31 E
Dhriopís 49 37 25N 24 35 E
Dhrol 78 22 33N 70 25 E
Dhubāb 74 12 56N 43 25 E
Dhuburi 82 26 2N 89 59 E
Dhulasar 82 21 52N 90 14 E
Dhule 78 20 58N 74 50 E
Dhupdhara 82 26 10N 91 4 E
Di Linh 85 11 35N 108 4 E
Di Linh, Cao Nguyen 85 11 30N 108 0 E
Día 49 35 26N 25 13 E
Diablerets, Les 28 46 22N 7 10 E
Diablo, Mt. 158 37 53N 121 56W
Diablo Range 158 37 0N 121 5W
Diafarabé 126 14 9N 4 57W
Diagonal 154 40 49N 94 20W
Diala 126 14 10N 10 0W
Dialakoro 126 12 18N 7 54W
Diallassagou 126 13 47N 3 41W
Diamante 174 32 5 S 60 40W
Diamante ~▸ 174 34 30 S 66 46W
Diamantina 171 18 17 S 43 40W
Diamantina ~▸ 111 26 45 S 139 10 E

Diamantino

Diamantino 173 14 30 S 56 30W
Diamond Harbour 79 22 11N 88 14 E
Diamond Is. 110 17 25 S 151 5 E
Diamond Mts. 156 40 0N 115 58W
Diamond Springs 158 38 42N 120 49W
Diamondville 156 41 51N 110 30W
Dianbai 97 21 33N 111 0 E
Diancheng 97 21 30N 111 4 E
Diano Marina 42 43 55N 8 3 E
Dianópolis 171 11 38 S 46 50W
Dianra 126 8 45N 6 14W
Diapaga 127 12 5N 1 46 E
Diapangou 127 12 5N 0 10 E
Diapur 112 36 19 S 141 29 E
Diariguila 126 10 35N 10 2W
Dībā 75 25 45N 56 16 E
Dibaya 133 6 30 S 22 57 E
Dibaya-Lubue 133 4 12 S 19 54 E
Dibbi 125 4 10N 41 52 E
Dibble Glacier Tongue 7 66 8 S 134 32 E
Dibete 134 23 45 S 26 32 E
Dibrugarh 82 27 29N 94 55 E
Dickeyville 154 42 38N 90 36W
Dickinson 152 46 50N 102 48W
Dickson, U.S.A. 149 36 5N 87 22W
Dickson, U.S.S.R. 64 73 40N 80 5 E
Dickson City 151 41 29N 75 40W
Dicomano 43 43 53N 11 30 E
Didam 22 51 57N 6 8 E
Didesa, W. → 125 10 2N 35 32 E
Didiéni 126 13 53N 8 6W
Didsbury 144 51 35N 114 10W
Didwana 78 27 23N 17 36 E
Die 21 44 47N 5 22 E
Diébougou 126 11 0N 3 15W
Diefenbaker L. 145 51 0N 106 55W
Diego Garcia 83 7 50 S 72 50 E
Diekirch 23 49 52N 6 10 E
Diélette 18 49 33N 1 52W
Diéma 126 14 32N 9 12W
Diémbéring 126 12 29N 16 47W
Diemen 22 52 21N 4 58 E
Dien Ban 84 15 53N 108 16 E
Dien Bien 84 21 20N 103 0 E
Dien Khanh 85 12 15N 109 6 E
Diepenbeek 23 50 54N 5 25 E
Diepenheim 22 52 12N 6 33 E
Diepenveen 22 52 18N 6 9 E
Diepholz 26 52 37N 8 22 E
Diepoldsau 29 47 23N 9 40 E
Dieppe 18 49 54N 1 4 E
Dieren 22 52 3N 6 6 E
Dierks 153 34 9N 94 0W
Diessen 23 51 29N 5 10 E
Diessenhofen 29 47 42N 8 46 E
Diest 23 50 58N 5 4 E
Dieterich 155 39 4N 88 23W
Dietikon 29 47 24N 8 24 E
Dieulefit 21 44 32N 5 4 E
Dieuze 19 48 49N 6 43 E
Diever 22 52 51N 6 19 E
Differdange 23 49 31N 5 54 E
Diffun 90 16 36N 121 33 E
Dig 78 27 28N 77 20 E
Digba 130 4 25N 25 48 E
Digboi 82 27 23N 95 38 E
Digby 143 44 38N 65 50W
Digges 145 58 40N 94 0W
Digges Is. 141 62 40N 77 50W
Dighinala 82 23 15N 92 5 E
Dighton 152 38 30N 100 26W
Diglur 80 18 34N 77 33 E
Digne 21 44 5N 6 12 E
Digoin 20 46 29N 3 58 E
Digos 91 6 45N 125 20 E
Digranes 54 66 4N 14 44 E
Digras 80 20 6N 77 45 E
Digul → 87 7 7 S 138 42 E
Dīhōk 72 36 55N 38 57 E
Dijlah, Nahr → 72 31 0N 47 25 E
Dijle → 23 50 58N 4 41 E
Dijon 19 47 20N 5 0 E
Dikala 125 4 45N 31 28 E
Dikkil 125 11 8N 42 20 E
Dikomu di Kai 134 24 58 S 24 36 E
Diksmuide 23 51 2N 2 52 E
Dikson = Dickson 64 73 40N 80 5 E
Dikwa 127 12 4N 13 30 E
Dila 125 6 21N 38 22 E
Dilbeek 23 50 51N 4 17 E
Dili 87 8 39 S 125 34 E
Dilizhan 61 40 46N 44 57 E
Dilj 46 45 29N 18 1 E
Dillard 154 37 44N 91 13W
Dillenburg 26 50 44N 8 17 E
Dilley 153 28 40N 99 12W
Dilling 125 12 3N 29 35 E
Dillingen 27 48 32N 10 29 E
Dillon, Canada 145 55 56N 108 35W
Dillon, Mont., U.S.A. 156 45 9N 112 36W
Dillon, S.C., U.S.A. 149 34 26N 79 20W
Dillon → 145 55 56N 108 56W
Dillsboro 155 39 1N 85 4W
Dilolo 133 10 28 S 22 18 E
Dilsen 23 51 2N 5 44 E
Dilston 110 41 22 S 147 10 E
Dimapur 82 25 54N 93 45 E
Dimas 160 23 43N 106 47W
Dimasalang 90 12 12N 123 51 E
Dimashq 70 33 30N 36 18 E
Dimashq □ 70 33 30N 36 30 E
Dimbaza 135 32 50 S 27 14 E
Dimbelenge 133 5 33 S 23 7 E
Dimbokro 126 6 45N 4 46W
Dimboola 112 36 28 S 142 7 E
Dîmbovița □ 50 45 0N 25 30 E
Dîmbovița → 50 44 5N 26 35 E
Dîmbovnic → 50 44 28N 25 18 E
Dimbulah 110 17 8 S 145 4 E
Dimitrovgrad, Bulgaria 47 42 5N 25 35 E
Dimitrovgrad, U.S.S.R. 59 54 14N 49 39 E
Dimitrovgrad, Yugoslavia 46 43 0N 22 48 E
Dimitrovo = Pernik 46 42 35N 23 2 E
Dimmitt 153 34 36N 102 16W
Dimo 125 5 19N 29 10 E
Dimona 69 31 2N 35 1 E
Dimovo 46 43 43N 22 50 E
Dinagat 91 10 10N 125 40 E
Dinaig 91 7 11N 124 10 E
Dinajpur 82 25 33N 88 43 E
Dinalupihan 90 14 52N 120 28 E
Dinan 18 48 28N 2 2W
Dīnān Āb 73 32 4N 56 49 E
Dinant 23 50 16N 4 55 E
Dinapur 79 25 38N 85 5 E
Dinara Planina 43 44 0N 16 30 E
Dinard 18 48 38N 2 6W
Dinaric Alps = Dinara Planina 43 44 0N 16 30 E
Dinas 91 7 38N 123 20 E
Dinder, Nahr ed → 125 14 6N 33 40 E
Dindi → 81 16 24N 78 15 E
Dindigul 81 10 25N 78 0 E
Ding Xian 94 38 30N 114 59 E
Dingalan 90 15 18N 121 25 E
Dingalan Bay 90 15 18N 121 25 E
Dingbian 94 37 35N 107 32 E
Dingelstädt 26 51 19N 10 19 E
Dinghai 97 30 1N 122 6 E
Dingle 15 52 9N 10 17W
Dingle B. 15 52 3N 10 20W
Dingmans Ferry 151 41 13N 74 55W
Dingnan 97 24 45N 115 0 E
Dingo 110 23 38 S 149 19 E
Dingolfing 27 48 38N 12 30 E
Dingras 90 18 6N 120 42 E
Dingtao 94 35 5N 115 35 E
Dinguiraye 126 11 18N 10 49W
Dingwall 14 57 36N 4 26W
Dingxi 94 35 30N 104 33 E
Dingxiang 94 38 30N 112 58 E
Dingyuan 97 32 32N 117 41 E
Dinh, Mui 85 11 22N 109 1 E
Dinh Lap 84 21 33N 107 6 E
Dinhata 82 26 8N 89 27 E
Dinkel → 22 52 30N 6 58 E
Dinokwe 134 23 29 S 26 37 E
Dinosaur National Monument 156 40 30N 108 58W
Dinslaken 23 51 34N 6 41 E
Dinsor 136 2 24N 42 59 E
Dintel → 23 51 39N 4 22 E
Dinteloord 23 51 38N 4 22 E
Dinuba 158 36 31N 119 22W
Dinxperlo 22 51 52N 6 30 E
Dio 53 56 37N 14 15 E
Diósgyör 31 48 7N 20 43 E
Diosig 50 47 18N 22 2 E
Diourbel 126 14 39N 16 12W
Dipaculao 90 15 51N 121 32 E
Diphu Pass 82 28 9N 97 20 E
Diplo 78 24 35N 69 35 E
Dipolog 91 8 36N 123 20 E
Dipșa 50 46 58N 24 27 E
Dipton 115 45 54 S 168 22 E
Dir 77 35 8N 71 59 E
Diré 126 16 20N 3 25W
Dire Dawa 125 9 35N 41 45 E
Diriamba 162 11 51N 86 19W
Dirico 133 17 50 S 20 42 E
Dirk Hartog I. 109 25 50 S 113 5 E
Dirkou 123 19 1N 12 53 E
Dirranbandi 111 28 33 S 148 17 E
Dirs 74 18 32N 42 5 E
Disa, India 78 24 18N 72 10 E
Disa, Sudan 125 12 5N 34 15 E
Disappointment, C. 156 46 20N 124 0W
Disappointment L. 108 23 20 S 122 40 E
Disaster B. 113 37 15 S 150 0 E
Discovery B. 112 38 10 S 140 40 E
Disentis 29 46 42N 8 50 E
Dishna 124 26 9N 32 32 E
Disina 127 11 35N 9 50 E
Disko 6 69 45N 53 30W
Disko Bugt 6 69 10N 52 0W
Disna 58 55 32N 28 11 E
Disna → 58 55 34N 28 12 E
Dison 23 50 37N 5 51 E
Disteghil Sar 79 36 20N 75 12 E
Distrito Federal □, Brazil 171 15 45 S 47 45W
Distrito Federal □, Venezuela 168 10 30N 66 55W
Disûq 124 31 8N 30 35 E
Ditu 133 5 23 S 21 27 E
Diu 78 20 45N 70 58 E
Diuata Mts. 91 9 0N 125 50 E
Dīvāndarreh 72 35 55N 47 2 E
Dives → 18 49 18N 0 7W
Dives-sur-Mer 18 49 18N 0 8W
Divi Pt. 81 15 59N 81 9 E
Divichi 61 41 15N 48 57 E
Divide 156 45 48N 112 47W
Dividing Ra. 109 27 45 S 116 0 E
Divinópolis 171 20 10 S 44 54W
Divisões, Serra dos 171 17 0 S 51 0W
Divnoye 61 45 55N 43 21 E
Divo 126 5 48N 5 15W
Dīwāl Kol 77 34 23N 67 52 E
Dix → 155 37 49N 84 44W
Dixie Mt. 158 39 55N 120 16W
Dixon, Calif., U.S.A. 158 38 27N 121 49W
Dixon, Ill., U.S.A. 154 41 50N 89 30W
Dixon, Iowa, U.S.A. 154 41 45N 90 47W
Dixon, Mo., U.S.A. 154 37 59N 92 6W
Dixon, Mont., U.S.A. 156 47 19N 114 25W
Dixon, N. Mex., U.S.A. 157 36 15N 105 57W
Dixon Entrance 144 54 30N 132 0W
Dixonville 144 56 32N 117 40W
Diyarbakir 57 37 55N 40 18 E
Djado 123 21 4N 12 14 E
Djado, Plateau du 123 21 29N 12 21 E
Djakarta = Jakarta 88 6 9 S 106 49 E
Djamâa 121 33 32N 5 59 E
Djamba 133 16 45 S 13 58 E
Djambala 132 2 32 S 14 30 E
Djanet 121 24 35N 9 32 E
Djaul I. 107 2 58 S 150 57 E
Djawa = Jawa 88 7 0 S 110 0 E
Djebiniana 121 35 1N 11 0 E
Djédaa 123 13 31N 18 34 E
Djelfa 121 34 40N 3 15 E
Djema 130 6 3N 25 15 E
Djember 123 10 25N 17 50 E
Djendel 121 36 15N 2 25 E
Djeneïene 121 31 45N 10 9 E
Djenné 126 14 0N 4 30W
Djenoun, Garet el 121 25 4N 5 31 E
Djerba 121 33 52N 10 51 E
Djerba, I. de 70 33 50N 10 48 E
Djerid, Chott 121 33 42N 8 30 E
Djiba 132 1 20 S 13 9 E
Djibo 127 14 9N 1 35W
Djibouti 136 11 30N 43 5 E
Djibouti ■ 125 12 0N 43 0 E
Djolu 132 0 35N 22 5 E
Djougou 127 9 40N 1 45 E
Djoum 132 2 41N 12 35 E
Djourab 123 16 40N 18 50 E
Djugu 130 1 55N 30 35 E
Djúpivogur 54 64 39N 14 17W
Djursholm 52 59 25N 18 6 E
Djursland 53 56 27N 10 45 E
Dmitriev-Lgovskiy 58 52 10N 35 0 E
Dmitriya Lapteva, Proliv 65 73 0N 140 0 E
Dmitrov 59 56 25N 37 32 E
Dmitrovsk-Orlovskiy 58 52 29N 35 10 E
Dnepr → 60 46 30N 32 18 E
Dneprodzerzhinsk 60 48 32N 34 37 E
Dneprodzerzhinskoye Vdkhr. 60 49 0N 34 0 E
Dnepropetrovsk 60 48 30N 35 0 E
Dneprorudnoye 60 47 21N 34 58 E
Dnestr → 60 46 18N 30 17 E
Dnestrovski = Belgorod 60 50 35N 36 35 E
Dnieper = Dnepr → 60 46 30N 32 18 E
Dniester = Dnestr → 60 46 18N 30 17 E
Dno 58 57 50N 29 58 E
Doabi 77 36 1N 69 32 E
Doan Hung 84 21 30N 105 10 E
Doba 123 8 40N 16 50 E
Dobbiaco 43 46 44N 12 13 E
Dobbyn 110 19 44 S 140 2 E
Dobczyce 32 49 52N 20 25 E
Döbeln 26 51 7N 13 10 E
Doberai, Jazirah 87 1 25 S 133 0 E
Dobiegniew 32 52 59N 15 45 E
Doblas 174 37 5 S 64 0W
Dobo 87 5 45 S 134 15 E
Doboj 46 44 46N 18 6 E
Dobra, Konin, Poland 32 51 55N 18 37 E
Dobra, Szczecin, Poland 32 53 34N 15 20 E
Dobra, Dîmbovita, Romania 50 44 52N 25 40 E
Dobra, Hunedoara, Romania 50 45 54N 22 36 E
Dobre Miasto 32 53 58N 20 26 E
Dobrinishta 47 41 49N 23 34 E
Dobříš 30 49 46N 14 10 E
Dobrodzień 32 50 45N 18 25 E
Dobropole 60 48 25N 37 2 E
Dobruja 50 44 30N 28 15 E
Dobrush 59 52 28N 30 19 E
Dobryanka 62 58 27N 56 25 E
Dobrzyń nad Wisłą 32 52 39N 19 22 E
Dobtong 125 6 25N 31 40 E
Doc, Mui 84 17 58N 106 30 E
Doce → 171 19 37 S 39 49W
Doda 79 33 10N 75 34 E
Dodecanese = Dhodhekánisos 49 36 35N 27 0 E
Dodewaard 22 51 55N 5 39 E
Dodge Center 152 44 1N 92 50W
Dodge City 153 37 42N 100 0W
Dodge L. 145 59 50N 105 36W
Dodgeville 154 42 55N 90 8W
Dodo 125 5 10N 29 57 E
Dodola 125 6 59N 39 11 E
Dodoma 130 6 8 S 35 45 E
Dodoma □ 130 6 0 S 36 0 E
Dodona 48 39 40N 20 46 E
Dodsland 145 51 50N 108 45W
Dodson 156 48 23N 108 16W
Doesburg 22 52 1N 6 9 E
Doetinchem 22 51 59N 6 18 E
Doftana 50 45 11N 25 45 E
Dog Creek 144 51 35N 122 14W
Dog L., Man., Canada 145 51 2N 98 31W
Dog L., Ont., Canada 142 48 48N 89 30W
Doğanbey 49 37 40N 27 10 E
Dogger Bank 10 54 50N 2 0 E
Dogliani 42 44 35N 7 55 E
Dōgo 100 36 15N 133 16 E
Dōgo-San 100 35 2N 133 13 E
Dogondoutchi 127 13 38N 4 2 E
Dogran 78 31 48N 73 35 E
Doguéraoua 127 14 0N 5 31 E
Dohinog 91 8 32N 123 12 E
Doi 87 2 14N 127 49 E
Doi Luang 84 18 30N 101 0 E
Doi Saket 84 18 52N 99 9 E
Doig → 144 56 25N 120 40W
Dois Irmãos, Sa. 170 9 0 S 42 30W
Dojransko Jezero 46 41 13N 22 44 E
Dokka 51 60 49N 10 7 E
Dokka → 51 61 7N 10 0 E
Dokkum 22 53 20N 5 59 E
Dokkumer Ee → 22 53 18N 5 52 E
Dokri 78 27 25N 68 7 E
Dol-de-Bretagne 18 48 34N 1 47W
Doland 152 44 55N 98 5W
Dolbeau 143 48 53N 72 18W
Dole 19 47 7N 5 31 E
Doleib, Wadi → 125 12 10N 33 15 E
Dolgellau 12 52 44N 3 53W
Dolgelley = Dolgellau 12 52 44N 3 53W
Dolginovo 58 54 39N 27 29 E
Dolianova 44 39 23N 9 11 E
Dolinskaya 60 48 6N 32 46 E
Dolj □ 50 44 10N 23 30 E
Dollart 22 53 20N 7 10 E
Dolna Banya 47 42 18N 23 44 E
Dolni Dŭbnik 47 43 24N 24 26 E
Dolo, Ethiopia 125 4 11N 42 3 E
Dolo, Italy 43 45 25N 12 4 E
Dolomites = Dolomiti 43 46 30N 11 40 E
Dolomiti 43 46 30N 11 40 E
Dolores, Argentina 174 36 20 S 57 40W
Dolores, Phil. 90 12 2N 125 29 E
Dolores, Uruguay 174 33 34 S 58 15W
Dolores, U.S.A. 157 37 30N 108 30W
Dolores → 157 38 49N 108 17W
Đolovo 46 44 55N 20 52 E
Dolphin, C. 176 51 10 S 59 0W
Dolphin and Union Str. 140 69 5N 114 45W
Dolsk 32 51 59N 17 3 E
Dolton 155 41 38N 87 36W
Dom 28 46 6N 7 50 E
Dom Joaquim 171 18 57 S 43 16W
Dom Pedrito 175 31 0 S 54 40W
Dom Pedro 170 4 59 S 44 27W
Doma 127 8 25N 8 18 E
Domasi 131 15 15 S 35 22 E
Domat Ems 29 46 50N 9 27 E
Domazlice 30 49 28N 13 0 E
Dombarovskiy 62 50 46N 59 32 E
Dombasle-sur-Meurthe 19 48 38N 6 21 E
Dombes 21 46 0N 5 0 E
Dombóvár 31 46 21N 18 9 E
Dombrád 31 48 13N 21 54 E
Domburg 23 51 34N 3 30 E
Domérat 20 46 21N 2 32 E
Domett 115 42 53 S 173 12 E
Domeyko 174 29 0 S 71 0W
Domeyko, Cordillera 174 24 30 S 69 0W
Domfront 18 48 37N 0 40W
Dominador 174 24 21 S 69 20W
Dominica ■ 163 15 20N 61 20W
Dominica Passage 163 15 10N 61 20W
Dominican Rep. ■ 163 19 0N 70 30W
Domiongo 133 4 37 S 21 15 E
Dömitz 26 53 9N 11 13 E
Domme 20 44 48N 1 12 E
Dommel → 23 51 30N 5 20 E
Domo 136 7 50N 47 10 E
Domodóssola 42 46 6N 8 19 E
Dompaire 19 48 14N 6 14 E
Dompierre-sur-Besbre 20 46 31N 3 41 E
Dompim 126 5 10N 2 5W
Domrémy-la-Pucelle 19 48 26N 5 40 E
Domsjö 52 63 16N 18 41 E
Domville, Mt. 111 28 1 S 151 15 E
Domvraína 49 38 15N 22 59 E
Domžale 43 46 9N 14 35 E
Don →, India 81 16 20N 76 15 E
Don →, England, U.K. 12 53 41N 0 51W
Don →, Scotland, U.K. 14 57 14N 2 5W
Don →, U.S.S.R. 61 47 4N 39 18 E
Don, C. 108 11 18 S 131 46 E
Don Benito 35 38 53N 5 51W
Don Duong 85 11 51N 108 35 E
Don Martín, Presa de 160 27 30N 100 50W
Dona Ana 131 17 25 S 35 5 E
Donaghadee 15 54 38N 5 32W

Dumanguilas Bay

Donald 112 36 23 S 143 0 E
Donalda 144 52 35N 112 34W
Donaldsonville 153 30 2N 91 0W
Donalsonville 149 31 3N 84 52W
Donau → 25 48 10N 17 0 E
Donaueschingen 27 47 57N 8 30 E
Donauwörth 27 48 42N 10 47 E
Donawitz 30 47 22N 15 4 E
Doncaster 12 53 31N 1 9W
Dondo, Angola 133 9 45 S 14 25 E
Dondo, Mozam. 131 19 33 S 34 46 E
Dondo, Zaïre 132 4 11N 21 39 E
Dondo, Teluk 87 0 29N 120 30 E
Dondra Head 81 5 55N 80 40 E
Donegal 15 54 39N 8 8W
Donegal □ 15 54 53N 8 0W
Donegal B. 15 54 30N 8 35W
Donets → 61 47 33N 40 55 E
Donetsk 60 48 0N 37 45 E
Dong Ba Thin 85 12 8N 109 13 E
Dong Dang 84 21 54N 106 42 E
Dong Giam 84 19 25N 105 31 E
Dong Ha 84 16 55N 107 8 E
Dong Hene 84 16 40N 105 18 E
Dong Hoi 84 17 29N 106 36 E
Dong Jiang → 97 23 6N 114 0 E
Dong Khe 84 22 26N 106 27 E
Dong Ujimqin Qi 94 45 32N 116 55 E
Dong Van 84 23 16N 105 22 E
Dong Xoai 85 11 32N 106 55 E
Donga 127 7 45N 10 2 E
Dong'an 97 26 23N 111 12 E
Dongara 109 29 14 S 114 57 E
Dongargarh 79 21 10N 80 40 E
Dongbei 95 42 0N 125 0 E
Dongchuan 96 26 8N 103 1 E
Dongen 23 51 38N 4 56 E
Donges 18 47 18N 2 4W
Dongfang 84 18 50N 108 33 E
Dongfeng 95 42 40N 125 34 E
Donggala 87 0 30 S 119 40 E
Donggan 96 23 22N 105 9 E
Donggou 95 39 52N 124 10 E
Dongguan 97 22 58N 113 44 E
Dongguang 94 37 50N 116 30 E
Donghai Dao 97 21 0N 110 15 E
Dongjingcheng 95 44 0N 129 10 E
Donglan 96 24 30N 107 21 E
Dongliu 97 30 13N 116 55 E
Dongmen 96 22 20N 107 48 E
Dongning 95 44 2N 131 5 E
Dongnyi 96 28 3N 100 15 E
Dongo 133 14 36 S 15 48 E
Dongola 124 19 9N 30 22 E
Dongou 132 2 0N 18 5 E
Dongping 94 35 55N 116 20 E
Dongshan 97 23 43N 117 30 E
Dongsheng 94 39 50N 110 0 E
Dongshi 97 24 18N 120 49 E
Dongtai 95 32 51N 120 21 E
Dongting Hu 97 29 18N 112 45 E
Dongxiang 97 28 11N 116 34 E
Dongxing 96 21 34N 108 0 E
Dongyang 97 29 13N 120 15 E
Dongzhi 97 30 9N 117 0 E
Donington, C. 112 34 45 S 136 0 E
Doniphan 153 36 40N 90 50W
Donja Stubica 43 45 59N 16 0 E
Donji Dušnik 46 43 12N 22 5 E
Donji Miholjac 46 45 45N 18 10 E
Donji Milanovac 46 44 28N 22 6 E
Donji Vakuf 46 44 8N 17 24 E
Donjon, Le 20 46 22N 3 48 E
Donna 153 26 12N 98 2W
Donnaconna 143 46 41N 71 41W
Donnelly's Crossing 114 35 42 S 173 38 E
Donnybrook, Australia 109 33 34 S 115 48 E
Donnybrook, S. Africa 135 29 59 S 29 48 E
Donora 150 40 11N 79 50W
Donor's Hill 110 18 42 S 140 33 E
Donque 133 15 28 S 14 6 E
Donskoy 59 53 55N 38 15 E
Donsol 90 12 54N 123 36 E
Donya Lendava 43 46 35N 16 25 E
Donzère 21 44 28N 4 43 E
Donzère-Mondragon, Barr. de 21 44 13N 4 42 E
Donzy 19 47 20N 3 6 E
Doon → 14 55 26N 4 41W
Doorn 22 52 2N 5 20 E
Dor 69 32 37N 34 55 E
Dora, L. 108 22 0 S 123 0 E
Dora Báltea → 42 45 11N 8 5 E
Dora Riparia → 42 45 5N 7 44 E
Dorada, La 168 5 30N 74 40W
Doran L. 145 61 13N 108 6W
Dorat, Le 20 46 14N 1 5 E
Dorchester 13 50 42N 2 28W
Dorchester, C. 141 65 27N 77 27W
Dordogne □ 20 45 5N 0 40 E
Dordogne → 20 45 2N 0 36W
Dordrecht, Neth. 22 51 48N 4 39 E
Dordrecht, S. Africa 134 31 20 S 27 3 E
Dore → 20 45 50N 3 35 E
Dore, Mts. 20 45 32N 2 50 E
Doré L. 145 54 46N 107 17W
Doré Lake 145 54 38N 107 36W
Dores do Indaiá 171 19 27 S 45 36W
Dorfen 27 48 16N 12 10 E
Dorgali 44 40 18N 9 35 E
Dori 127 14 3N 0 2W
Doring → 134 31 54 S 18 39 E
Doringbos 134 31 59 S 19 16 E
Dorion 142 45 23N 74 3W
Dormaa-Ahenkro 126 7 15N 2 52W
Dormo, Ras 125 13 14N 42 35 E
Dornach 28 47 29N 7 37 E
Dornberg 43 55 45N 13 50 E
Dornbirn 30 47 25N 9 45 E
Dornes 19 46 48N 3 18 E
Dornoch 14 57 52N 4 0W
Dornoch Firth 14 57 52N 4 0W
Dornogovĭ □ 94 44 0N 110 0 E
Doro 127 16 9N 0 51W
Dorog 31 47 42N 18 45 E
Dorogobuzh 58 54 50N 33 18 E
Dorohoi 50 47 56N 26 30 E
Döröö Nuur 92 48 0N 93 0 E
Dorr 73 33 17N 50 38 E
Dorre I. 109 25 13 S 113 12 E
Dorrigo 111 30 20 S 152 44 E
Dorris 156 41 59N 121 58W
Dorset, Canada 150 45 14N 78 54W
Dorset, U.S.A. 150 41 4N 80 40W
Dorset □ 13 50 48N 2 25W
Dorsten 26 51 40N 6 55 E
Dortmund 26 51 32N 7 28 E
Doruk 70 36 53N 35 45 E
Dorum 26 53 40N 8 33 E
Doruma 130 4 42N 27 33 E
Dorūneh 73 35 10N 57 18 E
Dos Bahías, C. 176 44 58 S 65 32W
Dos Hermanas 35 37 16N 5 55W
Dos Palos 158 36 59N 120 37W
Dosso 127 13 0N 3 13 E
Dothan 149 31 10N 85 25W
Dottignies 23 50 44N 3 19 E
Doty 158 46 38N 123 17W
Douai 19 50 21N 3 4 E
Douala 127 4 0N 9 45 E
Douarnenez 18 48 6N 4 21W
Douăzeci Şi Trei August 50 43 55N 28 40 E
Double Island Pt. 111 25 56 S 153 11 E
Doubrava → 30 49 40N 15 30 E
Doubs □ 19 47 10N 6 20 E
Doubs → 19 46 53N 5 1 E
Doubtful Sd. 115 45 20 S 166 49 E
Doubtless B. 114 34 55 S 173 26 E
Doudeville 18 49 43N 0 47 E
Doué-la-Fontaine 18 47 11N 0 16W
Douentza 126 14 58N 2 48W
Douglas, S. Africa 134 29 4 S 23 46 E
Douglas, U.K. 12 54 9N 4 29W
Douglas, Alaska, U.S.A. 144 58 23N 134 24W
Douglas, Ariz., U.S.A. 157 31 21N 109 30W
Douglas, Ga., U.S.A. 149 31 32N 82 52W
Douglas, Wyo., U.S.A. 152 42 45N 105 20W
Douglastown 143 48 46N 64 24W
Douglasville 149 33 46N 84 43W
Douirat 121 33 2N 4 11W
Doukáton, Ákra 49 38 34N 20 30 E
Doulevant-le-Château 19 48 23N 4 55 E
Doullens 19 50 10N 2 20 E
Doumé 132 4 15N 13 25 E
Douna 126 13 13N 6 0W
Dounan 97 23 41N 120 26 E
Dounguila 132 2 53 S 11 58 E
Dounreay 14 58 34N 3 44W
Dour 23 50 24N 3 46 E
Dourada, Serra 171 13 10 S 48 45W
Dourados 175 22 9 S 54 50W
Dourados → 175 21 58 S 54 18W
Dourdan 19 48 30N 2 1 E
Douro → 34 41 8N 8 40W
Douvaine 21 46 19N 6 16 E
Douz 122 33 25N 9 0 E
Douze → 20 43 54N 0 30W
Dove → 12 52 51N 1 36W
Dove Creek 157 37 46N 108 59W
Dover, Australia 110 43 18 S 147 2 E
Dover, U.K. 13 51 7N 1 19 E
Dover, Del., U.S.A. 148 39 10N 75 31W
Dover, Ky., U.S.A. 155 38 43N 83 52W
Dover, N.H., U.S.A. 151 43 12N 70 51W
Dover, N.J., U.S.A. 151 40 53N 74 34W
Dover, Ohio, U.S.A. 150 40 32N 81 30W
Dover, Pt. 109 32 32 S 125 32 E
Dover, Str. of 18 51 0N 1 30 E
Dover-Foxcroft 143 45 14N 69 14W
Dover Plains 151 41 43N 73 35W
Dovey → 13 52 32N 4 0W
Dovre 51 61 58N 9 15 E
Dovrefjell 51 62 15N 9 33 E
Dow Rūd 73 33 28N 49 4 E
Dowa 131 13 38 S 33 58 E
Dowagiac 155 41 58N 86 8W
Dowgha'i 73 36 54N 58 32 E
Dowlat Yār 77 34 30N 65 45 E
Dowlatābād, Farāh, Afghan. 77 32 47N 62 40 E
Dowlatābād, Fāryāb, Afghan. 77 36 26N 64 55 E
Dowlatābād, Iran 73 28 20N 56 40W
Down □ 15 54 20N 6 0W
Downers Grove 155 41 49N 88 1W
Downey, Calif., U.S.A. 159 42 26N 112 7W
Downey, U.S.A. 156 42 29N 112 3W
Downham Market 13 52 36N 0 22 E
Downieville 158 39 34N 120 50W
Downing 154 40 29N 92 22W
Downpatrick 15 54 20N 5 43W
Downpatrick Hd. 15 54 20N 9 21W
Dowsārī 73 28 25N 57 59 E
Dowshī 77 35 35N 68 43 E
Doyle 158 40 2N 120 6W
Doylestown 151 40 21N 75 10W
Draa, C. 120 28 47N 11 0W
Draa, Oued → 120 28 40N 11 10W
Drac → 21 45 12N 5 42 E
Drachten 22 53 7N 6 5 E
Drăgăneşti 50 44 9N 24 32 E
Drăgăneşti-Viaşca 50 44 5N 25 33 E
Dragaš 46 42 5N 20 35 E
Drăgăsani 50 44 39N 24 17 E
Dragina 46 44 30N 19 25 E
Dragocvet 46 44 0N 21 15 E
Dragoman, Prokhod 46 43 0N 22 53 E
Dragonera, I. 36 39 35N 2 19 E
Dragovishtitsa 46 42 22N 22 39 E
Draguignan 21 43 32N 6 27 E
Drain 156 43 45N 123 17W
Drake, Australia 111 28 55 S 152 25 E
Drake, U.S.A. 152 47 56N 100 21W
Drake Passage 7 58 0 S 68 0W
Drakensberg 135 31 0 S 28 0 E
Dráma 48 41 9N 24 10 E
Dráma □ 48 41 20N 24 0 E
Drammen 51 59 42N 10 12 E
Drangajökull 54 66 9N 22 15W
Drangedal 51 59 6N 9 3 E
Dranov, Ostrov 50 44 55N 29 30 E
Dras 79 34 25N 75 48 E
Drau = Drava → 30 45 33N 18 55 E
Drava → 30 45 33N 18 55 E
Draveil 19 48 41N 2 25 E
Dravograd 43 46 36N 15 5 E
Drawa → 32 52 52N 15 59 E
Drawno 32 53 13N 15 46 E
Drawsko Pomorskie 32 53 35N 15 50 E
Drayton Plains 155 42 42N 83 23W
Drayton Valley 144 53 12N 114 58W
Dreibergen 22 52 3N 5 17 E
Dren 46 43 8N 20 44 E
Drenthe □ 22 52 52N 6 40 E
Drentsche Hoofdvaart 22 52 39N 6 4 E
Dresden, Canada 150 42 35N 82 11W
Dresden, Germany 26 51 2N 13 45 E
Dresden □ 26 51 12N 14 0 E
Dreux 18 48 44N 1 23 E
Drexel 155 39 45N 84 18W
Drezdenko 32 52 50N 15 49 E
Driel 22 51 57N 5 49 E
Driffield 12 54 0N 0 25W
Driftwood 150 41 22N 78 9W
Driggs 156 43 50N 111 8W
Drin i zi → 48 41 37N 20 28 E
Drina → 46 44 53N 19 21 E
Drincea → 50 44 20N 22 55 E
Drînceni 50 46 49N 28 10 E
Drini → 48 42 20N 20 0 E
Drinjača → 46 44 15N 19 8 E
Driva → 51 62 33N 9 38 E
Drivstua 51 62 26N 9 47 E
Drniš 43 43 51N 16 10 E
Drøbak 51 59 39N 10 39 E
Drobin 32 52 42N 19 58 E
Drogheda 15 53 45N 6 20W
Drogichin 58 52 15N 25 8 E
Drogobych 58 49 20N 23 30 E
Drohiczyn 32 52 24N 22 39 E
Droichead Nua 15 53 11N 6 50W
Droitwich 13 52 16N 2 10W
Drôme □ 21 44 38N 5 15 E
Drôme → 21 44 46N 4 46 E
Dromedary, C. 113 36 17 S 150 10 E
Dronero 42 44 29N 7 22 E
Dronfield 110 21 12 S 140 3 E
Dronne → 20 45 2N 0 9W
Dronning Maud Land 7 72 30 S 12 0 E
Dronninglund 53 57 10N 10 19 E
Dronrijp 22 53 11N 5 39 E
Dropt → 20 44 35N 0 6W
Drosendorf 30 48 52N 15 37 E
Drouin 113 38 10 S 145 53 E
Drouzhba 47 43 15N 28 0 E
Drumbo 150 43 16N 80 35W
Drumheller 144 51 25N 112 40W
Drummond 156 46 40N 113 4W
Drummond I. 142 46 0N 83 40W
Drummond Pt. 111 34 9 S 135 16 E
Drummond Ra. 110 23 45 S 147 10 E
Drummondville 142 45 55N 72 25W
Drumright 153 35 59N 96 38W
Drunen 23 51 41N 5 8 E
Druskininkai 58 54 3N 23 58 E
Drut → 58 53 3N 30 42 E
Druten 22 51 53N 5 36 E
Druya 58 55 45N 27 28 E
Druzhina 65 68 14N 145 18 E
Drvar 43 44 21N 16 23 E
Drvenik 43 43 27N 16 3 E
Drwęca → 32 53 0N 18 42 E
Dry Tortugas 162 24 38N 82 55W
Dryanovo 47 42 59N 25 28 E
Dryden, Canada 145 49 47N 92 50W
Dryden, U.S.A. 153 30 3N 102 3W
Drygalski I. 7 66 0 S 92 0 E
Drysdale → 108 13 59 S 126 51 E
Drysdale I. 110 11 41 S 136 0 E
Drzewiczka → 32 51 36N 20 36 E
Dschang 127 5 32N 10 3 E
Du Bois 150 41 8N 78 46W
Du Quoin 154 38 0N 89 10W
Duanesburg 151 42 45N 74 11W
Duaringa 110 23 42 S 149 42 E
Ḑubā 72 27 10N 35 40 E
Dubai = Dubayy 75 25 18N 55 20 E
Dubawnt → 145 64 33N 100 6W
Dubawnt, L. 145 63 4N 101 42W
Dubayy 75 25 18N 55 20 E
Dubbeldam 22 51 47N 4 43 E
Dubbo 113 32 11 S 148 35 E
Dubele 130 2 56N 29 35 E
Dübendorf 29 47 24N 8 37 E
Dubenskiy 62 51 27N 56 38 E
Dubica 43 45 11N 16 48 E
Dublin, Ireland 15 53 20N 6 18W
Dublin, Ga., U.S.A. 149 32 30N 82 34W
Dublin, Tex., U.S.A. 153 32 0N 98 20W
Dublin □ 15 53 24N 6 20W
Dublin B. 15 53 18N 6 5W
Dublon I. 106 7 23N 151 53 E
Dubna, R.S.F.S.R., U.S.S.R. 59 54 8N 36 59 E
Dubna, R.S.F.S.R., U.S.S.R. 59 56 44N 37 10 E
Dubno 58 50 25N 25 45 E
Dubois, Idaho, U.S.A. 156 44 7N 112 9W
Dubois, Ind., U.S.A. 155 38 26N 86 48W
Dubossary 60 47 15N 29 10 E
Dubossary Vdkhr. 60 47 30N 29 0 E
Dubovka 61 49 5N 44 50 E
Dubovskoye 61 47 28N 42 46 E
Dubrajpur 79 23 48N 87 25 E
Dubréka 126 9 46N 13 31W
Dubrovitsa 58 51 31N 26 35 E
Dubrovnik 46 42 39N 18 6 E
Dubrovskoye 65 58 55N 111 10 E
Dubulu 132 4 18N 20 16 E
Dubuque 154 42 30N 90 41W
Duchang 97 29 18N 116 12 E
Duchesne 156 40 14N 110 22W
Duchess 110 21 20 S 139 50 E
Ducie I. 105 24 40 S 124 48W
Duck Cr. → 108 22 37 S 116 53 E
Duck Lake 145 52 50N 106 16W
Duck Mt. Prov. Parks 145 51 45N 101 0W
Duckwall, Mt. 158 37 58N 120 7W
Düdelange 23 49 29N 6 5 E
Duderstadt 26 51 30N 10 15 E
Dudhnai 82 25 59N 90 47 E
Düdingen 28 46 52N 7 12 E
Dudinka 65 69 30N 86 13 E
Dudley 13 52 30N 2 5W
Dudna → 80 19 17N 76 54 E
Dudo 136 9 20N 50 12 E
Dudub 136 6 55N 46 43 E
Duenas, Phil. 91 11 4N 122 37 E
Dueñas, Spain 34 41 52N 4 33W
Dueodde 53 54 59N 15 4 E
Dueré 171 11 20 S 49 17W
Duero → 34 41 8N 8 40W
Dūfah, W. → 74 18 45N 41 49 E
Duffel 23 51 6N 4 30 E
Dufftown 14 57 26N 3 9W
Dufourspitz 28 45 56N 7 52 E
Dugger 155 39 4N 87 16W
Dugi 43 44 0N 15 0 E
Dugiuma 136 1 15N 42 34 E
Dugo Selo 43 45 51N 16 18 E
Duifken Pt. 110 12 33 S 141 38 E
Duisburg 26 51 27N 6 42 E
Duitama 168 5 50N 73 2W
Duiveland 23 51 38N 4 0 E
Duiwelskloof 135 23 42 S 30 10 E
Dukati 48 40 16N 19 32 E
Dūkdamīn 73 35 59N 57 43 E
Duke I. 144 54 50N 131 20W
Dukelskýprůsmyk 31 49 25N 21 42 E
Dukhān 75 25 25N 50 50 E
Dukhovshchina 58 55 15N 32 27 E
Duki 77 30 14N 68 25 E
Dukla 32 49 30N 21 35 E
Duku, Bauchi, Nigeria 127 10 43N 10 43 E
Duku, Sokoto, Nigeria 127 11 11N 4 55 E
Dulag 91 10 57N 125 2 E
Dulce → 174 30 32 S 62 33W
Dulce, G. 162 8 40N 83 20W
Dulf 72 35 7N 45 51 E
Dŭlgopol 47 43 3N 27 22 E
Dulit, Banjaran 86 3 15N 114 30 E
Duliu 94 39 2N 116 55 E
Dullewala 78 31 50N 71 25 E
Dülmen 26 51 49N 7 18 E
Dulovo 47 43 48N 27 9 E
Dulq Maghār 72 36 22N 38 39 E
Dululu 110 23 48 S 150 15 E
Duluth 152 46 48N 92 10W
Dum Dum 79 22 39N 88 33 E
Dum Hadjer 123 13 18N 19 41 E
Dūmā, Lebanon 70 34 12N 35 50 E
Dūmā, Syria 70 33 34N 36 24 E
Dumaguete 91 9 17N 123 15 E
Dumai 88 1 35N 101 28 E
Dumalinao 91 7 49N 123 23 E
Dumanguilas Bay 91 7 34N 123 4 E

Dumaran

Dumaran 91 10 33N 119 50 E
Dumas, Ark., U.S.A. 153 33 52N 91 30W
Dumas, Tex., U.S.A. 153 35 50N 101 58W
Dumbarton 14 55 58N 4 35W
Dumbea 106 22 10 S 166 27 E
Dumbleyung 109 33 17 S 117 42 E
Dumbo 133 14 6 S 17 24 E
Dumbrăveni 50 46 14N 24 34 E
Dumfries 14 55 4N 3 37W
Dumfries & Galloway □ 14 55 0N 4 0W
Dumingag 91 8 20N 123 20 E
Dumka 79 24 12N 87 15 E
Dümmersee 26 52 30N 8 21 E
Dumoine → 142 46 13N 77 51W
Dumoine L. 142 46 55N 77 55W
Dumraon 79 25 33N 84 8 E
Dumyât 124 31 24N 31 48 E
Dumyât, Masabb 124 31 28N 31 51 E
Dun Laoghaire 15 53 17N 6 9W
Dun-le-Palestel 20 46 18N 1 39 E
Dun-sur-Auron 19 46 53N 2 33 E
Duna → 31 45 51N 18 48 E
Dunaföldvár 31 46 50N 18 57 E
Dunaj → 31 48 5N 17 10 E
Dunajec → 32 50 15N 20 44 E
Dunajska Streda 31 48 0N 17 37 E
Dunapatai 31 46 39N 19 4 E
Dunărea → 50 45 20N 29 40 E
Dunaszekcső 31 46 6N 18 45 E
Dunaújváros 31 47 0N 18 57 E
Dunav → 46 44 47N 21 20 E
Dunavtsi 46 43 57N 22 53 E
Dunay 98 42 52N 132 22 E
Dunback 115 45 23 S 170 36 E
Dunbar, Australia 110 16 0 S 142 22 E
Dunbar, U.K. 14 56 0N 2 32W
Dunblane 14 56 10N 3 58W
Duncan, Canada 144 48 45N 123 40W
Duncan, Ariz., U.S.A. 157 32 46N 109 6W
Duncan, Okla., U.S.A. 153 34 25N 98 0W
Duncan, L. 142 53 29N 77 58W
Duncan L. 144 62 51N 113 58W
Duncan Town 162 22 15N 75 45W
Duncannon 150 40 23N 77 2W
Dundalk, Canada 150 44 10N 80 24W
Dundalk, Ireland 15 54 1N 6 25W
Dundalk Bay 15 53 55N 6 15W
Dundas 142 43 17N 79 59W
Dundas, L. 109 32 35 S 121 50 E
Dundas I. 144 54 30N 130 50W
Dundas Str. 108 11 15 S 131 35 E
Dundee, S. Africa 135 28 11 S 30 15 E
Dundee, U.K. 14 56 29N 3 0W
Dundee, U.S.A. 155 41 57N 83 40W
Dundgovĭ □ 94 45 10N 106 0 E
Dundoo 111 27 40 S 144 37 E
Dundrum 15 54 17N 5 50W
Dundrum B. 15 54 12N 5 40W
Dundwara 79 27 48N 79 9 E
Dunedin, N.Z. 115 45 50 S 170 33 E
Dunedin, U.S.A. 149 28 1N 82 45W
Dunedin → 144 59 30N 124 5W
Dunfermline 14 56 5N 3 28W
Dungannon, Canada 150 43 51N 81 36W
Dungannon, U.K. 15 54 30N 6 47W
Dungannon □ 15 54 30N 6 55W
Dungarpur 78 23 52N 73 45 E
Dungarvan 15 52 6N 7 40W
Dungarvan Bay 15 52 5N 7 35W
Dungeness 13 50 54N 0 59 E
Dungo, L. do 133 17 15 S 19 0 E
Dungog 113 32 22 S 151 46 E
Dungu 130 3 40N 28 32 E
Dungunâb 124 21 10N 37 9 E
Dungunâb, Khalij 124 21 5N 37 12 E
Dunhinda Falls 81 7 5N 81 6 E
Dunhua 95 43 20N 128 14 E
Dunhuang 92 40 8N 94 36 E
Dunières 21 45 13N 4 20 E
Dunk I. 110 17 59 S 146 29 E
Dunkeld, Australia 112 37 40 S 142 22 E
Dunkeld, U.K. 14 56 34N 3 36W
Dunkerque 19 51 2N 2 20 E
Dunkery Beacon 13 51 15N 3 37W
Dunkirk = Dunkerque 19 51 2N 2 20 E
Dunkirk 150 42 30N 79 18W
Dunkuj 125 12 50N 32 49 E
Dunkwa, Central, Ghana 126 6 0N 1 47W
Dunkwa, Central, Ghana 127 5 30N 1 0W
Dunlap 152 41 50N 95 36W
Dúnleary = Dun Laoghaire 15 53 17N 6 9W
Dunmanus B. 15 51 31N 9 50W
Dunmara 110 16 42 S 133 25 E
Dunmore 151 41 27N 75 38W
Dunmore Hd. 15 52 10N 10 35W
Dunmore Town 162 25 30N 76 39W
Dunn 149 35 18N 78 36W
Dunnellon 149 29 4N 82 28W
Dunnet Hd. 14 58 38N 3 22W
Dunning 152 41 52N 100 4W
Dunnville 150 42 54N 79 36W
Dunolly 112 36 51 S 143 44 E
Dunoon 14 55 57N 4 56W
Dunqul 124 23 26N 31 37 E
Duns 14 55 47N 2 20W
Dunseith 152 48 49N 100 2W
Dunsmuir 156 41 10N 122 18W
Dunstable 13 51 53N 0 31W
Dunstan Mts. 115 44 53 S 169 35 E
Dunster 144 53 8N 119 50W
Duntroon 115 44 51 S 170 40 E
Dunvegan L. 145 60 8N 107 10W
Duolun 94 42 12N 116 28 E
Duong Dong 85 10 13N 103 58 E
Dupax 90 16 17N 121 5 E
Dupree 152 45 4N 101 35W
Dupuyer 156 48 11N 112 31W
Duqm 75 19 39N 57 42 E
Duque de Caxias 171 22 45 S 43 19W
Duque de York, I. 176 50 37 S 75 25W
Dūrā 69 31 31N 35 1 E
Durack → 108 15 33 S 127 52 E
Durack Range 108 16 50 S 127 40 E
Durance → 21 43 55N 4 45 E
Durand, Ill., U.S.A. 154 42 26N 89 20W
Durand, Mich., U.S.A. 155 42 54N 83 58W
Durango, Spain 36 43 13N 2 40W
Durango, U.S.A. 157 37 16N 107 50W
Durango □ 160 25 0N 105 0W
Duranillin 109 33 30 S 116 45 E
Durant, Iowa, U.S.A. 154 41 36N 90 54W
Durant, Okla., U.S.A. 153 34 0N 96 25W
Duratón → 34 41 37N 4 7W
Durazno 174 33 25 S 56 31W
Durazzo = Durrësi 48 41 19N 19 28 E
Durban, France 20 42 59N 2 49 E
Durban, S. Africa 135 29 49 S 31 1 E
Durbo 136 11 37N 50 20 E
Dúrcal 35 37 0N 3 34W
Đurd-evac 46 46 2N 17 3 E
Düren 26 50 48N 6 30 E
Durg 79 21 15N 81 22 E
Durgapur 79 23 30N 87 20 E
Durham, Canada 150 44 10N 80 49W
Durham, U.K. 12 54 47N 1 34W
Durham, Calif., U.S.A. 158 39 39N 121 48W
Durham, N.C., U.S.A. 149 36 0N 78 55W
Durham □ 12 54 42N 1 45W
Durham Downs 111 26 6 S 141 47 E
Durmä 74 24 37N 46 8 E
Durmitor 38 43 10N 19 0 E
Durness 14 58 34N 4 45W
Durrësi 48 41 19N 19 28 E
Durrie 110 25 40 S 140 15 E
Durtal 18 47 40N 0 18W
Duru 130 4 14N 28 50 E
D'Urville, Tanjung 87 1 28 S 137 54 E
D'Urville I. 115 40 50 S 173 55 E
Duryea 151 41 20N 75 45W
Dusa Mareb 136 5 30N 46 15 E
Dûsh 124 24 35N 30 41 E
Dushak 64 37 13N 60 1 E
Dushan 96 25 48N 107 30 E
Dushanbe 63 38 33N 68 48 E
Dusheti 61 42 10N 44 42 E
Dusky Sd. 115 45 47 S 166 30 E
Dussejour, C. 108 14 45 S 128 13 E
Düsseldorf 26 51 15N 6 46 E
Dussen 22 51 44N 4 59 E
Duszniki-Zdrój 32 50 24N 16 24 E
Dutch Harbor 140 53 54N 166 35W
Dutlwe 134 23 58 S 23 46 E
Dutsan Wai 127 10 50N 8 10 E
Dutton 150 42 39N 81 30W
Dutton → 110 20 44 S 143 10 E
Duvan 62 55 42N 57 54 E
Duved 52 63 24N 12 55 E
Duvno 46 43 42N 17 13 E
Duyun 96 26 18N 107 29 E
Duzdab = Zāhedān 73 29 30N 60 50 E
Dve Mogili 47 43 35N 25 55 E
Dvina, Sev. → 56 64 32N 40 30 E
Dvinsk = Daugavpils 58 55 53N 26 32 E
Dvinskaya Guba 56 65 0N 39 0 E
Dvor 43 45 4N 16 22 E
Dvorce 31 49 50N 17 34 E
Dvur Králové 30 50 27N 15 50 E
Dwarka 78 22 18N 69 8 E
Dwellingup 109 32 43 S 116 4 E
Dwight, Canada 150 45 20N 79 1W
Dwight, U.S.A. 155 41 5N 88 25W
Dyakovskoya 59 60 5N 41 12 E
Dyatkovo 58 53 40N 34 27 E
Dyatlovo 58 53 28N 25 28 E
Dyer 155 37 24N 86 13W
Dyer, C. 141 66 40N 61 0W
Dyer Plateau 7 70 45 S 65 30W
Dyerbeldzhin 63 41 13N 74 54 E
Dyersburg 153 36 2N 89 20W
Dyersville 154 42 29N 91 8W
Dyfed □ 13 52 0N 4 30W
Dyje → 31 48 37N 16 56 E
Dyle → 23 50 58N 4 41 E
Dynevor Downs 111 28 10 S 144 20 E
Dynów 32 49 50N 22 11 E
Dysart 145 50 57N 104 2W
Dyurtyuli 62 55 9N 54 4 E
Dzamin Üüd 94 43 50N 111 58 E
Dzerzhinsk, Byelorussian S.S.R., U.S.S.R. 58 53 40N 27 1 E
Dzerzhinsk, R.S.F.S.R., U.S.S.R. 59 56 14N 43 30 E
Dzhalal-Abad 63 40 56N 73 0 E
Dzhalinda 65 53 26N 124 0 E
Dzhambeyty 61 50 16N 52 35 E
Dzhambul 63 42 54N 71 22 E
Dzhambul, Gora 63 44 54N 73 0 E
Dzhankoi 60 45 40N 34 20 E
Dzhanybek 61 49 25N 46 50 E
Dzhardzhan 65 68 10N 124 10 E
Dzharkurgan 63 37 31N 67 25 E
Dzhelinde 65 70 0N 114 20 E
Dzhetygara 62 52 11N 61 12 E
Dzhetym, Khrebet 63 41 30N 77 0 E
Dzhezkazgan 64 47 44N 67 40 E
Dzhikimde 65 59 1N 121 47 E
Dzhizak 63 40 6N 67 50 E
Dzhugdzur, Khrebet 65 57 30N 138 0 E
Dzhuma 63 39 42N 66 40 E
Dzhumgoltau, Khrebet 63 42 15N 74 30 E
Dzhungarskiye Vorota 64 45 0N 82 0 E
Dzhvari 61 42 42N 42 4 E
Działdowo 32 53 15N 20 15 E
Działoszyce 32 50 22N 20 20 E
Działoszyn 32 51 6N 18 50 E
Dzierzgoń 32 53 58N 19 20 E
Dzierzoniów 32 50 45N 16 39 E
Dzilam de Bravo 161 21 24N 88 53W
Dzioua 121 33 14N 5 14 E
Dziwnów 32 54 2N 14 45 E
Dzungarian Gates = Dzhungarskiye Vorota 64 45 0N 82 0 E
Dzuumod 92 47 45N 106 58 E

E

Eabamet, L. 142 51 30N 87 46W
Eads 152 38 30N 102 46W
Eagle, Alaska, U.S.A. 140 64 44N 141 7W
Eagle, Colo., U.S.A. 156 39 39N 106 55W
Eagle → 143 53 36N 57 26W
Eagle Butt 152 45 1N 101 12W
Eagle Cr. → 155 38 36N 85 4W
Eagle Grove 154 42 37N 93 53W
Eagle L., Calif., U.S.A. 156 40 35N 120 50W
Eagle L., Maine, U.S.A. 143 46 23N 69 22W
Eagle Lake 153 29 35N 96 21W
Eagle Mountain 159 33 52N 115 26W
Eagle Nest 157 36 33N 105 13W
Eagle Pass 153 28 45N 100 35W
Eagle Pk. 158 38 10N 119 25W
Eagle Pt. 108 16 11 S 124 23 E
Eagle River 152 45 55N 89 17W
Eagleville 154 40 28N 93 59W
Ealing 13 51 30N 0 19W
Earaheedy 109 25 34 S 121 29 E
Earl Grey 145 50 57N 104 43W
Earle 153 35 18N 90 26W
Earlimart 159 35 53N 119 16W
Earlville 155 41 35N 88 55W
Earn → 14 56 20N 3 19W
Earn, L. 14 56 23N 4 14W
Earnslaw, Mt. 115 44 32 S 168 27 E
Earoo 109 29 34 S 118 22 E
Earth 153 34 18N 102 30W
Easley 149 34 52N 82 35W
East Angus 143 45 30N 71 40W
East Aurora 150 42 46N 78 38W
East B. 153 29 2N 89 16W
East Beskids = Vychodné Beskydy 31 49 30N 22 0 E
East Brady 150 40 59N 79 36W
East C., N.Z. 114 37 42 S 178 35 E
East C., Papua N. G. 107 10 13 S 150 53 E
East Chicago 155 41 40N 87 30W
East China Sea 93 30 5N 126 0 E
East Coast Bays 114 36 40 S 174 40 E
East Coulee 144 51 23N 112 27W
East Dubuque 154 42 29N 90 39W
East Falkland 176 51 30 S 58 30W
East Germany ■ 26 52 0N 12 0 E
East Grand Forks 152 47 55N 97 5W
East Greenwich 151 41 39N 71 27W
East Hartford 151 41 45N 72 39W
East Helena 156 46 37N 111 58W
East Indies 66 0 0 120 0 E
East Jordan 148 45 10N 85 7W
East Kilbride 14 55 46N 4 10W
East Lansing 155 42 44N 84 29W
East Liverpool 150 40 39N 80 35W
East London 135 33 0 S 27 55 E
East Lynne 113 35 35 S 150 16 E
East Main = Eastmain 142 52 10N 78 30W
East Moline 154 41 31N 90 25W
East Orange 151 40 46N 74 13W
East Pacific Ridge 105 15 0 S 110 0W
East Pakistan = Bangladesh ■ 82 24 0N 90 0 E
East Palestine 150 40 50N 80 32W
East Peoria 154 40 40N 89 34W
East Pine 144 55 48N 120 12W
East Pt. 143 46 27N 61 58W
East Point 149 33 40N 84 28W
East Providence 151 41 48N 71 22W
East Retford 12 53 19N 0 55W
East St. Louis 154 38 37N 90 4W
East Schelde → = Oosterschelde 23 51 33N 4 0 E
East Siberian Sea 65 73 0N 160 0 E
East Stroudsburg 151 41 1N 75 11W
East Sussex □ 13 51 0N 0 20 E
East Tawas 148 44 17N 83 31W
East Toorale 111 30 27 S 145 28 E
East Troy 155 42 47N 88 24W
East Walker → 158 38 52N 119 10W
Eastbourne, N.Z. 114 41 19 S 174 55 E
Eastbourne, U.K. 13 50 46N 0 18 E
Eastend 145 49 32N 108 50W
Easter Islands 105 27 0 S 109 0W
Eastern □, Kenya 130 0 0 38 30 E
Eastern □, Uganda 130 1 50N 33 45 E
Eastern Cr. → 110 20 40 S 141 35 E
Eastern Ghats 81 14 0N 78 50 E
Eastern Group = Lau 106 17 0 S 178 30W
Eastern Group 109 33 30 S 124 30 E
Eastern Province □ 126 8 15N 11 0W
Eastern Samar □ 91 11 40N 125 40 E
Easterville 145 53 8N 99 49W
Easthampton 151 42 15N 72 41W
Eastland 153 32 26N 98 45W
Eastleigh 13 50 58N 1 21W
Eastmain 142 52 10N 78 30W
Eastmain → 142 52 27N 78 26W
Eastman, Canada 151 45 18N 72 19W
Eastman, Ga., U.S.A. 149 32 13N 83 20W
Eastman, Wis., U.S.A. 154 43 10N 91 1W
Easton, Md., U.S.A. 148 38 47N 76 7W
Easton, Pa., U.S.A. 151 40 41N 75 15W
Easton, Wash., U.S.A. 158 47 14N 121 8W
Eastport 143 44 57N 67 0W
Eastsound 158 48 42N 122 55W
Eaton, Colo., U.S.A. 152 40 35N 104 42W
Eaton, Ohio, U.S.A. 155 39 45N 84 38W
Eaton Rapids 155 42 31N 84 39W
Eatonia 145 51 13N 109 25W
Eatonton 149 33 22N 83 24W
Eatontown 151 40 18N 74 7W
Eatonville 158 46 52N 122 16W
Eau Claire, Fr. Gui. 169 3 30N 53 40W
Eau Claire, U.S.A. 152 44 46N 91 30W
Eauze 20 43 53N 0 7 E
Ebagoola 110 14 15 S 143 12 E
Eban 127 9 40N 4 50 E
Ebangalakata 132 0 29 S 21 29 E
Ebbw Vale 13 51 47N 3 12W
Ebebiyín 132 2 9N 11 20 E
Ebeggui 121 26 2N 6 0 E
Ebel 132 0 7N 11 5 E
Ebensburg 150 40 29N 78 43W
Ebensee 30 47 48N 13 46 E
Eberbach 27 49 27N 8 59 E
Eberswalde 26 52 49N 13 50 E
Ebetsu 98 43 7N 141 34 E
Ebian 96 29 11N 103 13 E
Ebikon 29 47 5N 8 21 E
Ebingen 27 48 13N 9 1 E
Ebino 100 32 2N 130 48 E
Ebnat-Kappel 29 47 16N 9 7 E
Eboli 45 40 39N 15 2 E
Ebolowa 127 2 55N 11 10 E
Ebrach 27 49 50N 10 30 E
Ébrié, Lagune 126 5 12N 4 26W
Ebro → 36 40 43N 0 54 E
Ebro, Pantano del 34 43 0N 3 58W
Ebstorf 26 53 2N 10 23 E
Ecaussines-d' Enghien 23 50 35N 4 11 E
Eceabat 48 40 11N 26 21 E
Ech Cheliff 121 36 10N 1 20 E
Echallens 28 46 38N 6 38 E
Échelles, Les 21 45 26N 5 46 E
Echeng 97 30 23N 114 50 E
Echigo-Sammyaku 99 36 50N 139 50 E
Echizen-Misaki 101 35 59N 135 57 E
Echmiadzin 61 40 12N 44 19 E
Echo Bay, N.W.T., Canada 140 66 5N 117 55W
Echo Bay, Ont., Canada 142 46 29N 84 4W
Echoing → 145 55 51N 92 5W
Echt 23 51 7N 5 52 E
Echternach 23 49 49N 6 25 E
Echuca 113 36 10 S 144 20 E
Ecija 35 37 30N 5 10W
Eckernförde 26 54 26N 9 50 E
Eclipse Is. 108 13 54 S 126 19 E
Écommoy 18 47 50N 0 17 E
Ecoporanga 171 18 23 S 40 50W
Écos 19 49 9N 1 35 E
Écouché 18 48 42N 0 10W
Ecuador ■ 168 2 0 S 78 0W
Écueillé 18 47 5N 1 21 E
Ed 53 58 55N 11 55 E
Ed Dabbura 124 17 40N 34 15 E
Ed Dâmer 124 17 27N 34 0 E
Ed Debba 124 18 0N 30 51 E
Ed-Déffa 124 30 40N 26 30 E
Ed Deim 125 10 10N 28 20 E
Ed Dueim 125 14 0N 32 10 E
Edah 109 28 16 S 117 10 E
Edam, Canada 145 53 11N 108 46W
Edam, Neth. 22 52 31N 5 3 E
Edapally 81 11 19N 78 3 E
Eday 14 59 11N 2 47W
Edd 125 14 0N 41 38 E
Eddrachillis B. 14 58 16N 5 10W
Eddystone 13 50 11N 4 16W
Eddystone Pt. 110 40 59 S 148 20 E
Eddyville 154 41 9N 92 38W
Ede, Neth. 22 52 4N 5 40 E
Ede, Nigeria 127 7 45N 4 29 E

Elburn

Édea 127 3 51N 10 9 E
Edegem 23 51 10N 4 27 E
Edehon L. 145 60 25N 97 15W
Edekel, Adrar 121 23 56N 6 47 E
Eden, Australia 113 37 3 S 149 55 E
Eden, N.C., U.S.A. 149 36 29N 79 53W
Eden, N.Y., U.S.A. 150 42 39N 78 55W
Eden, Tex., U.S.A. 153 31 16N 99 50W
Eden, Wyo., U.S.A. 156 42 2N 109 27W
Eden → 12 54 57N 3 2W
Eden L. 145 56 38N 100 15W
Edenburg 134 29 43 S 25 58 E
Edendale, N.Z. 115 46 19 S 168 48 E
Edendale, S. Africa 135 29 39 S 30 18 E
Edenderry 15 53 21N 7 3W
Edenton 149 36 5N 76 36W
Edenville 135 27 37 S 27 34 E
Eder → 26 51 15N 9 25 E
Ederstausee 26 51 11N 9 0 E
Edgar 152 40 25N 98 0W
Edgartown 151 41 22N 70 28W
Edge Hill 13 52 7N 1 28W
Edgecumbe 114 37 59 S 176 47 E
Edgefield 149 33 50N 81 59W
Edgeley 152 46 27N 98 41W
Edgemont 152 43 15N 103 53W
Edgeøya 6 77 45N 22 30 E
Edgerton, Ohio, U.S.A. 155 41 27N 84 45W
Edgerton, Wis., U.S.A. 154 42 50N 89 4W
Edgewood 155 38 55N 88 40W
Edhessa 48 40 48N 22 5 E
Edievale 115 45 49 S 169 22 E
Edina, Liberia 126 6 0N 10 10W
Edina, U.S.A. 154 40 6N 92 10W
Edinburg, Ill., U.S.A. 154 39 39N 89 23W
Edinburg, Ind., U.S.A. 155 39 21N 85 58W
Edinburg, Tex., U.S.A. 153 26 22N 98 10W
Edinburgh 14 55 57N 3 12W
Edirne 47 41 40N 26 34 E
Edison 158 48 33N 122 27W
Edithburgh 112 35 5 S 137 43 E
Edjeleh 121 28 38N 9 50 E
Edjudina 109 29 48 S 122 23 E
Edmeston 151 42 42N 75 15W
Edmond 153 35 37N 97 30W
Edmonds 158 47 47N 122 22W
Edmonton, Australia 110 17 2 S 145 46 E
Edmonton, Canada 144 53 30N 113 30W
Edmund L. 145 54 45N 93 17W
Edmundston 143 47 23N 68 20W
Edna 153 29 0N 96 40W
Edna Bay 144 55 55N 133 40W
Edolo 42 46 10N 10 21 E
Edsbyn 52 61 23N 15 49 E
Edsel Ford Ra. 7 77 0 S 143 0W
Edsele 52 63 25N 16 32 E
Edson 144 53 35N 116 28W
Eduardo Castex 174 35 50 S 64 18W
Edward → 112 35 0 S 143 30 E
Edward, L. 130 0 25 S 29 40 E
Edward I. 142 48 22N 88 37W
Edward VII Land 7 80 0 S 150 0W
Edwards 159 34 55N 117 51W
Edwards → 154 41 10N 90 59W
Edwards Plateau 153 30 30N 101 5W
Edwardsburg 155 41 48N 86 6W
Edwardsport 155 38 49N 87 15W
Edwardsville, Ill., U.S.A. 154 38 49N 89 57W
Edwardsville, Pa., U.S.A. 151 41 15N 75 56W
Edzo 144 62 49N 116 4W
Eefde 22 52 10N 6 13 E
Eekloo 23 51 11N 3 33 E
Eel →, Ind., U.S.A. 155 39 7N 86 58W
Eel →, Ind., U.S.A. 155 40 45N 86 22W
Eelde 22 53 8N 6 34 E
Eem → 22 52 16N 5 20 E
Eems → 22 53 26N 6 57 E
Eems Kanaal 22 53 18N 6 46 E
Eenrum 22 53 22N 6 28 E
Eernegem 23 51 8N 3 2 E
Eerste Valthermond 22 52 53N 6 58 E
Ef'e, Nahal 69 31 9N 35 13 E
Eferding 30 48 18N 14 1 E
Eferi 121 24 30N 9 28 E
Effingham 155 39 8N 88 30W
Effretikon 29 47 25N 8 42 E
Eforie Sud 50 44 1N 28 37 E
Ega → 36 42 19N 1 55W
Égadi, Ísole 44 37 55N 12 16 E
Eganville 142 45 32N 77 5W
Egeland 152 48 42N 99 6W
Egenolf L. 145 59 3N 100 0W
Eger = Cheb 30 50 9N 12 28 E
Eger 31 47 53N 20 27 E
Eger → 31 47 38N 20 50 E
Egersund 51 58 26N 6 1 E
Egg L. 145 55 5N 105 30W
Eggenburg 30 48 38N 15 50 E
Eggenfelden 27 48 24N 12 46 E
Eggiwil 28 46 52N 7 47 E
Egherta 136 2 4N 43 11 E
Éghezée 23 50 35N 4 55 E
Eginbah 108 20 53 S 119 47 E
Egito 133 12 4 S 13 58 E
Égletons 20 45 24N 2 3 E
Eglisau 29 47 35N 8 31 E
Egmond-aan-Zee 22 52 37N 4 38 E
Egmont, C. 114 39 16 S 173 45 E
Egmont, Mt. 114 39 17 S 174 5 E
Eğridir 57 37 52N 30 51 E
Eğridir Gölü 57 37 53N 30 50 E
Egtved 53 55 38N 9 18 E
Éguas → 171 13 26 S 44 14W
Egume 127 7 30N 7 14 E
Éguzon 20 46 27N 1 33 E
Egvekinot 65 66 19N 179 50W
Egyek 31 47 39N 20 52 E
Egypt ■ 124 28 0N 31 0 E
Eha Amufu 127 6 30N 7 46 E
Ehime □ 100 33 30N 132 40 E
Ehingen 27 48 16N 9 43 E
Ehrenberg 159 33 36N 114 31W
Ehrwald 30 47 24N 10 56 E
Eibar 36 43 11N 2 28W
Eibergen 22 52 6N 6 39 E
Eichstatt 27 48 53N 11 12 E
Eida 51 60 32N 6 43 E
Eider → 26 54 19N 8 58 E
Eidsvold 111 25 25 S 151 12 E
Eifel 27 50 10N 6 45 E
Eiffel Flats 131 18 20 S 30 0 E
Eigg 14 56 54N 6 10W
Eighty Mile Beach 108 19 30 S 120 40 E
Eil 136 8 0N 49 50 E
Eil, L. 14 56 50N 5 15W
Eil Malk 106 7 10N 134 23 E
Eildon 113 37 14 S 145 55 E
Eileen L. 145 62 16N 107 37W
Eilenburg 26 51 28N 12 38 E
Ein el Luweiqa 125 14 5N 33 50 E
Einasleigh 110 18 32 S 144 5 E
Einasleigh → 110 17 30 S 142 17 E
Einbeck 26 51 48N 9 50 E
Eindhoven 23 51 26N 5 30 E
Einsiedeln 29 47 7N 8 46 E
Eire ■ 15 53 0N 8 0W
Eiríksjökull 54 64 46N 20 24W
Eirlandsche Gat 22 53 12N 4 54 E
Eirunepé 172 6 35 S 69 53W
Eisden 23 50 59N 5 42 E
Eisenach 26 50 58N 10 18 E
Eisenberg 26 50 59N 11 50 E
Eisenerz 30 47 32N 14 54 E
Eisenhüttenstadt 26 52 9N 14 41 E
Eisenkappel 30 46 29N 14 36 E
Eisenstadt 31 47 51N 16 31 E
Eiserfeld 26 50 50N 7 59 E
Eisfeld 26 50 25N 10 54 E
Eisleben 26 51 31N 11 31 E
Ejby 53 55 25N 9 56 E
Eje, Sierra del 34 42 24N 6 54W
Ejea de los Caballeros 36 42 7N 1 9W
Ejutla 161 16 34N 96 44W
Ekalaka 152 45 55N 104 30W
Ekalla 132 1 27 S 14 0 E
Ekanga 132 2 23 S 23 14 E
Ekawasaki 100 33 13N 132 46 E
Ekeren 23 51 17N 4 25 E
Eket 127 4 38N 7 56 E
Eketahuna 114 40 38 S 175 43 E
Ekhínos 48 41 16N 25 1 E
Ekibastuz 64 51 50N 75 10 E
Ekimchan 65 53 0N 133 0W
Ekoli 130 0 23 S 24 13 E
Eksel 23 51 9N 5 24 E
Eksere 70 36 48N 32 0 E
Eksjö 53 57 40N 14 58W
Ekwan → 142 53 12N 82 15W
Ekwan Pt. 142 53 16N 82 7W
El Aaiún 120 27 9N 13 12W
El Aargub 120 23 37N 15 52W
El Aat 69 32 50N 35 45 E
El Abiodh-Sidi-Cheikh 121 32 53N 0 31 E
El Adde 136 2 35N 46 9 E
El 'Agrûd 71 30 14N 34 24 E
El Aïoun 121 34 33N 2 30W
El 'Aiyat 124 29 36N 31 15 E
El Alamein 124 30 48N 28 58 E
El Alto 172 4 15 S 81 14W
El 'Aqaba, W. → 71 30 7N 33 54 E
El 'Arag 124 28 40N 26 20 E
El Arahal 35 37 15N 5 33W
El Aricha 121 34 13N 1 10W
El Arīhā 69 31 52N 35 27 E
El Arish, Australia 110 17 35 S 146 1 E
El 'Arîsh, Egypt 71 31 8N 33 50 E
El 'Arîsh, W. → 71 31 8N 33 47 E
El Arrouch 121 36 37N 6 53 E
El Asnam = Ech Cheliff 121 36 10N 1 20 E
El Astillero 34 43 24N 3 49W
El Badâri 124 27 4N 31 25 E
El Bahrein 124 28 30N 26 25 E
El Ballâs 124 26 2N 32 43 E
El Balyana 124 26 10N 32 3 E
El Banco 168 9 0N 73 58W
El Baqeir 124 18 40N 33 40 E
El Barco de Ávila 34 40 21N 5 31W
El Barco de Valdeorras 34 42 23N 7 0W
El Bauga 124 18 18N 33 52 E
El Baúl 168 8 57N 68 17W
El Bawiti 124 28 25N 28 45 E
El Bayadh 121 33 40N 1 1 E
El Bierzo 34 42 45N 6 30W
El Bluff 162 11 59N 83 40W
El Bolsón 176 41 55 S 71 30W
El Bonillo 37 38 57N 2 35W
El Brûk, W. → 71 30 15N 33 50 E
El Buheirat □ 125 7 0N 30 0 E
El Bur 136 4 40N 46 37 E
El Caín 176 41 38 S 68 19W
El Cajon 159 32 49N 117 0W
El Callao 169 7 18N 61 50W
El Camp 36 41 5N 1 10 E
El Campo 153 29 10N 96 20W
El Carmen, Bolivia 173 13 40 S 63 55W
El Carmen, Venezuela 168 1 16N 66 52W
El Castillo 35 37 41N 6 19W
El Centro 159 32 50N 115 40W
El Cerro, Bolivia 173 17 30 S 61 40W
El Cerro, Spain 35 37 45N 6 57W
El Cocuy 168 6 25N 72 27W
El Compadre 159 32 20N 116 14W
El Corcovado 176 43 25 S 71 35W
El Coronil 35 37 5N 5 38W
El Cuy 176 39 55 S 68 25W
El Cuyo 161 21 30N 87 40W
El Dab'a 124 31 0N 28 27 E
El Daheir 71 31 13N 34 10 E
El Dambahaddo 136 3 17N 46 40 E
El Deir 124 25 25N 32 20 E
El Dere, Ethiopia 136 5 6N 43 5 E
El Dere, Somalia 136 3 50N 47 8 E
El Dere, Somalia 136 5 22N 46 11 E
El Descanso 159 32 12N 116 58W
El Desemboque 160 30 30N 112 57W
El Dilingat 124 30 50N 30 31 E
El Diviso 168 1 22N 78 14W
El Djem 121 35 18N 10 42 E
El Dorado, Ark., U.S.A. 153 33 10N 92 40W
El Dorado, Kans., U.S.A. 153 37 55N 96 56W
El Dorado, Venezuela 169 6 55N 61 37W
El Eglab 120 26 20N 4 30W
El Escorial 34 40 35N 4 7W
El Eulma 121 36 9N 5 42 E
El Faiyûm 124 29 19N 30 50 E
El Fâsher 125 13 33N 25 26 E
El Fashn 124 28 50N 30 54 E
El Ferrol 34 43 29N 8 15W
El Fifi 125 10 4N 25 0 E
El Fud 136 7 15N 42 52 E
El Fuerte 160 26 30N 108 40W
El Gal 136 10 58N 50 20 E
El Gebir 125 13 40N 29 40 E
El Gedida 124 25 40N 28 30 E
El Geteina 125 14 50N 32 27 E
El Gezira □ 125 15 0N 33 0 E
El Gineina, Râs 71 29 4N 33 54 E
El Gîza 124 30 0N 31 10 E
El Goléa 121 30 30N 2 50 E
El Guettar 121 34 5N 4 38 E
El Hadeb 120 25 51N 13 0W
El Hadjira 121 32 36N 5 30 E
El Hagiz 125 15 15N 35 50 E
El Hajeb 120 33 43N 5 13W
El Hammam 124 30 52N 29 25 E
El Hammâmi 120 23 3N 11 30W
El Hamurre 97 7 13N 48 54 E
El Hank 120 24 30N 7 0W
El Harrach 121 36 45N 3 5 E
El Hasian 120 26 20N 14 0W
El Hawata 125 13 25N 34 42 E
El Heiz 124 27 50N 28 40 E
El 'Idisât 124 25 30N 32 35 E
El Igma, G. 71 29 10N 34 0 E
El Iskandarîya 124 31 0N 30 0 E
El Jadida 120 33 11N 8 17W
El Jebelein 125 12 40N 32 55 E
El Kab 124 19 27N 32 46 E
El Kabrît, G. 71 29 42N 33 16 E
El Kala 121 36 50N 8 30 E
El Kalâa 120 32 4N 7 27W
El Kamlin 125 15 3N 33 11 E
El Kantara, Algeria 121 35 14N 5 45 E
El Kantara, Tunisia 121 33 45N 10 58 E
El Karaba 124 18 32N 33 41 E
El Kef 121 36 12N 8 47 E
El Khandaq 124 18 30N 30 30 E
El Khârga 124 25 30N 30 33 E
El Khartûm 125 15 31N 32 35 E
El Khartûm □ 125 16 0N 33 0 E
El Khartûm Bahrî 125 15 40N 32 31 E
El-Khroubs 121 36 10N 6 55 E
El Kseur 121 36 46N 4 49 E
El Ksiba 120 32 45N 6 1W
El Kuntilla 71 30 1N 34 45 E
El Laqâwa 125 11 25N 29 1 E
El Laqeita 124 25 50N 33 15 E
El Leiya 125 16 15N 35 28 E
El Mafâza 125 13 38N 34 30 E
El Mahalla el Kubra 124 31 0N 31 0 E
El Mahârîq 124 25 35N 30 35 E
El Mahmûdîya 124 31 10N 30 32 E
El Maitén 176 42 3 S 71 10W
El Maiz 121 28 19N 0 9W
El-Maks el-Bahari 124 24 30N 30 40 E
El Manshâh 124 26 26N 31 50 E
El Mansour 121 27 47N 0 14W
El Mansûra 124 31 0N 31 19 E
El Mantico 169 7 38N 62 45W
El Manzala 124 31 10N 31 50 E
El Marâgha 124 26 35N 31 10 E
El Masid 125 15 15N 33 0 E
El Matariya 124 31 15N 32 0 E
El Meghaier 121 33 55N 5 58 E
El Meraguen 121 28 0N 0 7W
El Metemma 125 16 50N 33 10 E
El Miamo 169 7 39N 61 46W
El Milagro 174 30 59 S 65 59W
El Milia 121 36 51N 6 13 E
El Minyâ 124 28 7N 30 33 E
El Molar 36 40 42N 3 45W
El Mreyye 126 18 0N 6 0W
El Nido 91 11 10N 119 25 E
El Obeid 125 13 8N 30 10 E
El Odaiya 125 12 8N 28 12 E
El Oro 161 19 48N 100 8W
El Oro □ 168 3 30 S 79 50W
El Oued 121 33 20N 6 58 E
El Palmar, Bolivia 173 17 50 S 63 9W
El Palmar, Venezuela 169 7 58N 61 53W
El Palmito, Presa 160 25 40N 105 30W
El Panadés 36 41 10N 1 30 E
El Pardo 34 40 31N 3 47W
El Paso, Ill., U.S.A. 154 40 44N 89 1W
El Paso, Tex., U.S.A. 157 31 50N 106 30W
El Paso Robles 158 35 38N 120 41W
El Pedernoso 37 39 29N 2 45W
El Pedroso 35 37 51N 5 45W
El Pobo de Dueñas 36 40 46N 1 39W
El Portal 158 37 44N 119 49W
El Porvenir 160 31 15N 105 51W
El Prat de Llobregat 36 41 18N 2 3 E
El Progreso 162 15 26N 87 51W
El Provencío 37 39 23N 2 35W
El Pueblito 160 29 3N 105 4W
El Pueblo 37 28 36N 17 47W
El Qâhira 124 30 1N 31 14 E
El Qantara 71 30 51N 32 20 E
El Qasr 124 25 44N 28 42 E
El Quseima 71 30 40N 34 15 E
El Qusîya 124 27 29N 30 44 E
El Râshda 124 25 36N 28 57 E
El Reno 153 35 30N 98 0W
El Ribero 34 42 30N 8 30W
El Rîdisiya 124 24 56N 32 51 E
El Rio 159 34 14N 119 10W
El Ronquillo 35 37 44N 6 10W
El Roque, Pta. 37 28 10N 15 25W
El Rosarito 160 28 38N 114 4W
El Rubio 35 37 22N 5 0W
El Saff 124 29 34N 31 16 E
El Saheira, W. → 71 30 5N 33 25 E
El Salto 160 23 47N 105 22W
El Salvador ■ 162 13 50N 89 0W
El Sancejo 35 37 4N 5 6W
El Sauce 162 13 0N 86 40W
El Shallal 124 24 0N 32 53 E
El Simbillawein 124 30 48N 31 13 E
El Sombrero 168 9 23N 67 3W
El Suweis 124 29 58N 32 31 E
El Tamarâni, W. → 71 30 7N 34 43 E
El Thabt, G. 71 28 17N 34 1 E
El Thamad 71 29 40N 34 28 E
El Tigre 169 8 44N 64 15W
El Tîh, G. 71 29 40N 33 50 E
El Tîna, Khalîg 71 31 10N 32 40 E
El Tocuyo 168 9 47N 69 48W
El Tofo 174 29 22 S 71 18W
El Tránsito 174 28 52 S 70 17W
El Tûr 71 28 14N 33 36 E
El Turbio 176 51 45 S 72 5W
El Uinle 136 3 4N 41 42 E
El Uqsur 124 25 41N 32 38 E
El Vado 36 41 2N 3 18W
El Vallés 36 41 35N 2 20 E
El Venado 160 22 56N 101 10W
El Vigía 168 8 38N 71 39W
El Wabeira 71 29 34N 33 6 E
El Wak, Kenya 130 2 49N 40 56 E
El Wak, Somalia 136 2 44N 41 1 E
El Waqf 124 25 45N 32 15 E
El Wâsta 124 29 19N 31 12 E
El Weguet 125 5 28N 42 17 E
El Wuz 125 15 0N 30 7 E
Elafónisos 49 36 29N 22 56 E
Elaine 112 37 44 S 144 2 E
Elamanchili 80 17 33N 82 50 E
Elands 113 31 37 S 152 20 E
Elandsvlei 134 32 19 S 19 31 E
Élassa 49 35 18N 26 21 E
Elassón 48 39 53N 22 12 E
Elat 69 29 30N 34 56 E
Eláthia 49 38 37N 22 46 E
Elâzığ 57 38 37N 39 14 E
Elba, Italy 42 42 48N 10 15 E
Elba, U.S.A. 149 31 27N 86 4W
Elbasani 48 41 9N 20 9 E
Elbasani-Berati □ 48 40 58N 20 0 E
Elbe 158 46 45N 122 10W
Elbe → 26 53 50N 9 0 E
Elberfeld 155 38 10N 87 27W
Elbert, Mt. 157 39 5N 106 27W
Elberta 148 44 35N 86 14W
Elberton 149 34 7N 82 51W
Elbeuf 18 49 17N 1 2 E
Elbing = Elbląg 32 54 10N 19 25 E
Elbląg 32 54 10N 19 25 E
Elbląg □ 32 54 15N 19 30 E
Elbow 145 51 7N 106 35W
Elbrus 61 43 21N 42 30 E
Elburg 22 52 26N 5 50 E
Elburn 155 41 54N 88 28W

Elburz Mts.

Elburz Mts. = Alborz, Reshteh-ye Kūhhā-ye **73** 36 0N 52 0 E
Elche **37** 38 15N 0 42W
Elche de la Sierra **37** 38 27N 2 3W
Elcho I. **110** 11 55 S 135 45 E
Elda **37** 38 29N 0 47W
Eldon, Mo., U.S.A. **154** 38 20N 92 38W
Eldon, Wash., U.S.A. **158** 47 32N 123 4W
Eldora **154** 42 20N 93 5W
Eldorado, Argentina **175** 26 28 S 54 43W
Eldorado, Canada **145** 59 35N 108 30W
Eldorado, Mexico **160** 24 20N 107 22W
Eldorado, Ill., U.S.A. **155** 37 50N 88 25W
Eldorado, Tex., U.S.A. **153** 30 52N 100 35W
Eldorado Springs **154** 37 54N 93 59W
Eldoret **130** 0 30N 35 17 E
Eldred **150** 41 57N 78 24W
Eldridge **154** 41 39N 90 35W
Electra **153** 34 0N 99 0W
Elefantes → **135** 24 10 S 32 40 E
Elefantes, G. **176** 46 28 S 73 49W
Elektrogorsk **59** 55 56N 38 50 E
Elektrostal **59** 55 41N 38 32 E
Elele **127** 5 5N 6 50 E
Elena **47** 42 55N 25 53 E
Elephant Butte Res. **157** 33 45N 107 30W
Elephant I. **7** 61 0 S 55 0W
Elephant Pass **81** 9 35N 80 25 E
Elesbão Veloso **170** 6 13 S 42 8W
Eleshnitsa **47** 41 52N 23 36 E
Eleuthera **162** 25 0N 76 20W
Elevsís **49** 38 4N 23 26 E
Elevtheroúpolis **48** 40 52N 24 20 E
Elgepiggen **51** 62 10N 11 21 E
Elgeyo-Marakwet □ **130** 0 45N 35 30 E
Elgg **29** 47 29N 8 52 E
Elgin, N.B., Canada **143** 45 48N 65 10W
Elgin, Ont., Canada **151** 44 36N 76 13W
Elgin, U.K. **14** 57 39N 3 20W
Elgin, Ill., U.S.A. **155** 42 0N 88 20W
Elgin, N. Dak., U.S.A. **152** 46 24N 101 46W
Elgin, Nebr., U.S.A. **152** 41 58N 98 3W
Elgin, Nev., U.S.A. **157** 37 21N 114 20W
Elgin, Oreg., U.S.A. **156** 45 37N 118 0W
Elgin, Tex., U.S.A. **153** 30 21N 97 22W
Elgon, Mt. **130** 1 10N 34 30 E
Eliase **87** 8 21 S 130 48 E
Elida **153** 33 56N 103 41W
Elikón, Mt. **49** 38 18N 22 45 E
Elim **134** 34 35 S 19 45 E
Elin Pelin **47** 42 40N 23 36 E
Elisabethville = Lubumbashi **131** 11 40 S 27 28 E
Eliseu Martins **170** 8 13 S 43 42W
Elista **61** 46 16N 44 14 E
Elizabeth, Australia **112** 34 42 S 138 41 E
Elizabeth, Ill., U.S.A. **154** 42 19N 90 13W
Elizabeth, N.J., U.S.A. **151** 40 37N 74 12W
Elizabeth City **149** 36 18N 76 16W
Elizabethton **149** 36 20N 82 13W
Elizabethtown, Ky., U.S.A. **148** 37 40N 85 54W
Elizabethtown, N.Y., U.S.A. **151** 44 13N 73 36W
Elizabethtown, Pa., U.S.A. **151** 40 8N 76 36W
Elizondo **36** 43 12N 1 30W
Elk **32** 53 50N 22 21 E
Elk → **32** 53 41N 22 28 E
Elk City **153** 35 25N 99 25W
Elk Creek **158** 39 36N 122 32W
Elk Grove **158** 38 25N 121 22W
Elk Island Nat. Park **144** 53 35N 112 59W
Elk Lake **142** 47 40N 80 25W
Elk Point **145** 53 54N 110 55W
Elk River, Idaho, U.S.A. **156** 46 50N 116 8W
Elk River, Minn., U.S.A. **152** 45 17N 93 34W
Elkader **154** 42 51N 91 24W
Elkedra **110** 21 9 S 135 33 E
Elkedra → **110** 21 8 S 136 22 E
Elkhart, Ind., U.S.A. **155** 41 42N 85 55W
Elkhart, Kans., U.S.A. **153** 37 3N 101 54W
Elkhart → **155** 41 41N 85 58W
Elkhorn, Canada **145** 49 59N 101 14W
Elkhorn, U.S.A. **155** 42 40N 88 33W
Elkhorn → **152** 41 7N 98 15W
Elkhotovo **61** 43 19N 44 15 E
Elkhovo **47** 42 10N 26 40 E
Elkin **149** 36 17N 80 50W
Elkins **148** 38 53N 79 53W
Elko, Canada **144** 49 20N 115 10W
Elko, U.S.A. **156** 40 50N 115 50W
Ell, L. **109** 29 13 S 127 46 E
Ellecom **22** 52 2N 6 6 E
Ellef Ringnes I. **6** 78 30N 102 2W
Ellendale, Australia **108** 17 56 S 124 48 E
Ellendale, U.S.A. **152** 46 3N 98 30W
Ellensburg **156** 47 0N 120 30W
Ellenville **151** 41 42N 74 23W
Ellerston **113** 31 49 S 151 20 E
Ellery, Mt. **113** 37 28 S 148 47 E
Ellesmere I. **6** 79 30N 80 0W
Ellesworth Land **7** 76 0 S 89 0W
Ellettsville **155** 39 14N 86 38W
Ellezelles **23** 50 44N 3 42 E
Ellice Is. = Tuvalu ■ **104** 8 0 S 178 0 E
Ellinwood **152** 38 27N 98 37W
Elliot, Australia **110** 17 33 S 133 32 E
Elliot, S. Africa **135** 31 22 S 27 48 E
Elliot Lake **142** 46 25N 82 35W
Elliotdale = Xhora **135** 31 55 S 28 38 E
Ellis **152** 39 0N 99 39W
Ellisville **153** 31 38N 89 12W
Ellon **14** 57 21N 2 5W
Ellore = Eluru **80** 16 48N 81 8 E
Ells → **144** 57 18N 111 40W
Ellsworth **152** 38 47N 98 15W
Ellsworth Land **7** 76 0 S 89 0W
Ellsworth Mts. **7** 78 30 S 85 0W
Ellwangen **27** 48 57N 10 9 E
Ellwood City **150** 40 52N 80 19W
Elm **29** 46 54N 9 10 E
Elma, Canada **145** 49 52N 95 55W
Elma, U.S.A. **158** 47 0N 123 30W
Elmalı **57** 36 44N 29 56 E
Elmer **154** 39 57N 92 39W
Elmhurst **155** 41 52N 87 58W
Elmina **127** 5 5N 1 21W
Elmira, Canada **150** 43 36N 80 33W
Elmira, U.S.A. **150** 42 8N 76 49W
Elmore, Australia **112** 36 30 S 144 37 E
Elmore, Calif., U.S.A. **159** 33 7N 115 49W
Elmore, Minn., U.S.A. **155** 41 29N 83 18W
Elmshorn **26** 53 44N 9 40 E
Elmvale **150** 44 35N 79 52W
Elmwood **154** 40 47N 90 0W
Elne **20** 42 36N 2 58 E
Elnora **155** 38 53N 87 5W
Elora **150** 43 41N 80 26W
Elorza **168** 7 3N 69 31W
Elos **49** 36 46N 22 43 E
Eloy **157** 32 46N 111 33W
Éloyes **19** 48 6N 6 36 E
Elrose **145** 51 12N 108 0W
Elsas **142** 48 32N 82 55W
Elsie **158** 45 52N 123 35W
Elsinore = Helsingør **52** 56 2N 12 35 E
Elsinore, Australia **113** 31 35 S 145 11 E
Elsinore, U.S.A. **157** 38 40N 112 2W
Elspe **26** 51 10N 8 1 E
Elspeet **22** 52 17N 5 48 E
Elst **22** 51 55N 5 51 E
Elster → **26** 51 25N 11 57 E
Elsterwerda **26** 51 27N 13 32 E
Elten **22** 51 52N 6 9 E
Eltham, Australia **113** 37 43 S 145 12 E
Eltham, N.Z. **114** 39 26 S 174 19 E
Elton **61** 49 5N 46 52 E
Eluanbi **97** 21 51N 120 50 E
Eluru **80** 16 48N 81 8 E
Elvas **35** 38 50N 7 10W
Elven **18** 47 44N 2 36W
Elverum **51** 60 53N 11 34 E
Elvire → **108** 17 51 S 128 11 E
Elvo → **42** 45 23N 8 21 E
Elvran **51** 63 24N 11 3 E
Elwood, Ill., U.S.A. **155** 41 24N 88 7W
Elwood, Ind., U.S.A. **155** 40 20N 85 50W
Elwood, Nebr., U.S.A. **152** 40 38N 99 51W
Ely, U.K. **13** 52 24N 0 16 E
Ely, Minn., U.S.A. **152** 47 54N 91 52W
Ely, Nev., U.S.A. **156** 39 10N 114 50W
Elyashiv **69** 32 23N 34 55 E
Elyria **150** 41 22N 82 8W
Elyrus **49** 35 15N 23 45 E
Elz → **27** 48 21N 7 45 E
Emådalen **52** 61 20N 14 44 E
Emāmrūd **73** 36 30N 55 0 E
Emba **64** 48 50N 58 8 E
Emba → **57** 46 38N 53 14 E
Embarcación **174** 23 10 S 64 0W
Embarras Portage **145** 58 27N 111 28W
Embarrass → **155** 38 39N 87 37W
Embetsu **98** 44 44N 141 47 E
Embira → **172** 7 19 S 70 15W
Embóna **49** 36 13N 27 51 E
Embrach **29** 47 30N 8 36 E
Embrun **21** 44 34N 6 30 E
Embu **130** 0 32 S 37 38 E
Embu □ **130** 0 30 S 37 35 E
Emden **26** 53 22N 7 12 E
'Emeq Yizre'el **69** 32 35N 35 12 E
Emerald **110** 23 32 S 148 10 E
Emerson **145** 49 0N 97 10W
Emery **157** 38 59N 111 17W
Emi Koussi **123** 20 0N 18 55 E
Emilia-Romagna □ **42** 44 33N 10 40 E
Emilius, Mte. **42** 45 41N 7 23 E
Eminabad **78** 32 2N 74 8 E
Emine, Nos **47** 42 40N 27 56 E
Eminence **155** 38 22N 85 11W
Emlenton **150** 41 11N 79 41W
Emlichheim **26** 52 37N 6 51 E
Emmaboda **53** 56 37N 15 32 E
Emme → **28** 47 0N 7 42 E
Emmeloord **22** 52 44N 5 46 E
Emmen **22** 52 48N 6 57 E
Emmendingen **27** 48 7N 7 51 E
Emmental **28** 47 0N 7 35 E
Emmer-Compascuum **22** 52 49N 7 2 E
Emmerich **26** 51 50N 6 12 E
Emmet **110** 24 45 S 144 30 E
Emmetsburg **154** 43 3N 94 40W
Emmett **156** 43 51N 116 33W
Emöd **31** 47 57N 20 47 E
Emona **47** 42 43N 27 53 E
Empalme **160** 28 1N 110 49W
Empangeni **135** 28 50 S 31 52 E
Empedrado **174** 28 0 S 58 46W
Emperor Seamount Chain **104** 40 0N 170 0 E
Empoli **42** 43 43N 10 57 E
Emporia, Kans., U.S.A. **152** 38 25N 96 10W
Emporia, Va., U.S.A. **149** 36 41N 77 32W
Emporium **150** 41 30N 78 17W
Empress **145** 50 57N 110 0W
Emptinne **23** 50 19N 5 8 E
Ems → **26** 53 22N 7 15 E
Emsdale **150** 45 32N 79 19W
Emsdetten **26** 52 11N 7 31 E
Emu, Australia **112** 36 44 S 143 26 E
Emu, China **95** 43 40N 128 6 E
Emu Park **110** 23 13 S 150 50 E
'En 'Avrona **71** 29 43N 35 0 E
En Gedi **69** 31 28N 35 25 E
En Gev **69** 32 47N 35 38 E
En Harod **69** 32 33N 35 22 E
'En Kerem **69** 31 47N 35 6 E
En Nahud **125** 12 45N 28 25 E
Ena **101** 35 25N 137 25 E
Ena-San **101** 35 26N 137 36 E
Enafors **52** 63 17N 12 20 E
Enambú **168** 1 1N 70 17W
Enana **134** 17 30 S 16 23 E
Enånger **52** 61 30N 17 9 E
Enaratoli **87** 3 55 S 136 21 E
Enard B. **14** 58 5N 5 20W
Encantadas, Serra **175** 30 40 S 53 0W
Encanto, C. **87** 15 45N 121 38 E
Encarnación **175** 27 15 S 55 50W
Encarnación de Diaz **160** 21 30N 102 13W
Enchi **126** 5 53N 2 48W
Encinal **153** 28 3N 99 25W
Encinitas **159** 33 3N 117 17W
Encino **157** 34 38N 105 40W
Encontrados **168** 9 3N 72 14W
Encounter B. **112** 35 45 S 138 45 E
Encruzilhada **171** 15 31 S 40 54W
Ende **87** 8 45 S 121 40 E
Endeavour **145** 52 10N 102 39W
Endeavour Str. **110** 10 45 S 142 0 E
Endelave **53** 55 46N 10 18 E
Enderbury I. **104** 3 8 S 171 5W
Enderby **144** 50 35N 119 10W
Enderby I. **108** 20 35 S 116 30 E
Enderby Land **7** 66 0 S 53 0 E
Enderlin **152** 46 37N 97 41W
Endicott, N.Y., U.S.A. **151** 42 6N 76 2W
Endicott, Wash., U.S.A. **156** 47 0N 117 45W
Endimari → **172** 8 46 S 66 7W
Endröd **31** 46 55N 20 47 E
Endyalgout I. **108** 11 40 S 132 35 E
Ene → **172** 11 10 S 74 18W
Enewatak **104** 11 30N 162 15 E
Enez **48** 40 45N 26 5 E
Enfida **121** 36 6N 10 28 E
Enfield, U.K. **13** 51 39N 0 4W
Enfield, U.S.A. **155** 38 6N 88 20W
Engadin **29** 46 45N 10 10 E
Engaño, C., Dom. Rep. **163** 18 30N 68 20W
Engaño, C., Phil. **90** 18 35N 122 23 E
Engcobo **135** 31 37 S 28 0 E
Engelberg **29** 46 48N 8 26 E
Engels **59** 51 28N 46 6 E
Engemann L. **145** 58 0N 106 55W
Enger **51** 60 35N 10 20 E
Enggano **88** 5 20 S 102 40 E
Enghien **23** 50 37N 4 2 E
Engil **120** 33 12N 4 32W
Engkilili **86** 1 3N 111 42 E
England **153** 34 30N 91 58W
England □ **16** 53 0N 2 0W
Englee **143** 50 45N 56 5W
Englefield **112** 37 21 S 141 48 E
Englehart **142** 47 49N 79 52W
Engler L. **145** 59 8N 106 52W
Englewood, Colo., U.S.A. **152** 39 40N 105 0W
Englewood, Kans., U.S.A. **153** 37 7N 99 59W
Englewood, Ohio, U.S.A. **155** 39 53N 84 18W
English **155** 38 20N 86 28W
English →, Canada **145** 50 35N 93 30W
English →, U.S.A. **154** 41 29N 91 32W
English Bazar = Ingraj Bazar **79** 24 58N 88 10 E
English Channel **13** 50 0N 2 0W
English River **142** 49 14N 91 0W
Enid **153** 36 26N 97 52W
Enipévs → **48** 39 22N 22 17 E
Enkhuizen **22** 52 42N 5 17 E
Enköping **52** 59 37N 17 4 E
Enle **96** 24 0N 101 9 E
Enna **45** 37 34N 14 15 E
Ennadai **145** 61 8N 100 53W
Ennadai L. **145** 61 0N 101 0W
Ennedi **123** 17 15N 22 0 E
Enngonia **111** 29 21 S 145 50 E
Ennis, Ireland **15** 52 51N 8 59W
Ennis, Mont., U.S.A. **156** 45 20N 111 42W
Ennis, Tex., U.S.A. **153** 32 15N 96 40W
Enniscorthy **15** 52 30N 6 35W
Enniskillen **15** 54 20N 7 40W
Ennistimon **15** 52 56N 9 18W
Enns **30** 48 12N 14 28 E
Enns → **30** 48 14N 14 32 E
Enping **97** 22 16N 112 21 E
Enrile **90** 17 34N 121 42 E
Enriquillo, L. **163** 18 20N 72 5W
Ens **22** 52 38N 5 50 E
Enschede **22** 52 13N 6 53 E
Ensenada, Argentina **174** 34 55 S 57 55W
Ensenada, Mexico **160** 31 50N 116 50W
Ensenada, La **176** 41 12 S 72 33W
Enshi **96** 30 18N 109 29 E
Enshū-Nada **101** 34 27N 137 38 E
Ensisheim **19** 47 50N 7 20 E
Entebbe **130** 0 4N 32 28 E
Enter **22** 52 17N 6 35 E
Enterprise, Canada **144** 60 47N 115 45W
Enterprise, Oreg., U.S.A. **156** 45 30N 117 18W
Enterprise, Utah, U.S.A. **157** 37 37N 113 36W
Entlebuch **28** 46 59N 8 4 E
Entre Ríos, Bolivia **174** 21 30 S 64 25W
Entre Rios, Bahia, Brazil **171** 11 56 S 38 5W
Entre Rios, Pará, Brazil **173** 5 24 S 54 21W
Entre Ríos □ **174** 30 30 S 58 30W
Entrecasteaux, Pt. d' **114** 34 50 S 115 56 E
Entrepeñas, Pantano de **36** 40 34N 2 42W
Enugu **127** 6 20N 7 30 E
Enugu Ezike **127** 7 0N 7 29 E
Enumclaw **158** 47 12N 122 0W
Envermeu **18** 49 53N 1 15 E
Envigado **168** 6 10N 75 35W
Envira **172** 7 18 S 70 13W
Enz → **27** 49 1N 9 6 E
Enza → **42** 44 54N 10 31 E
Enzan **101** 35 42N 138 44 E
Eólie, Is. **45** 38 30N 14 50 E
Epanomí **48** 40 25N 22 59 E
Epe, Neth. **22** 52 21N 5 59 E
Epe, Nigeria **127** 6 36N 3 59 E
Epéna **132** 1 22N 17 29 E
Épernay **19** 49 3N 3 56 E
Épernon **19** 48 35N 1 40 E
Ephesus **49** 37 50N 27 33 E
Ephraim **156** 39 21N 111 37W
Ephrata **156** 47 20N 119 32W
Epidaurus Limera **49** 36 46N 23 0 E
Epila **36** 41 36N 1 17W
Épinac-les-Mines **19** 46 59N 4 31 E
Épinal **19** 48 10N 6 27 E
Epira **169** 5 5N 57 20W
Episcopia Bihorului **50** 47 12N 21 55 E
Episkopi **70** 34 40N 32 54 E
Episkopi Bay **70** 34 35N 32 50 E
Epitálion **49** 37 37N 21 30 E
Epping **13** 51 42N 0 8 E
Epukiro **134** 21 40 S 19 9 E
Equality **155** 37 44N 88 20W
Equatorial Guinea ■ **132** 2 0N 8 0 E
Equeipa **169** 5 22N 62 43W
Er Rahad **125** 12 45N 30 32 E
Er Rif **121** 35 1N 4 1W
Er Roseires **125** 11 55N 34 30 E
Er Yébigué **123** 22 30N 17 30 E
Eran **91** 9 4N 117 42 E
Erandol **78** 20 56N 75 20 E
Erap **107** 6 37 S 146 51 E
Erāwadī Myit → = Irrawaddy → **82** 15 50N 95 6 E
Erba, Italy **42** 45 49N 9 12 E
Erba, Sudan **124** 19 5N 36 51 E
Ercha **65** 69 45N 147 20 E
Erciyaş Dağı **57** 38 30N 35 30 E
Erdao Jiang → **95** 43 0N 127 0 E
Erdemli **70** 36 36N 34 19 E
Erdene **94** 44 13N 111 10 E
Erding **27** 48 18N 11 55 E
Erdre → **18** 47 13N 1 32W
Erebato → **169** 5 54N 64 16W
Erebus, Mt. **7** 77 35 S 167 0 E
Erechim **175** 27 35 S 52 15W
Ereğli, Turkey **57** 41 15N 31 30 E
Ereğli, Turkey **57** 37 31N 34 4 E
Erei, Monti **45** 37 20N 14 20 E
Erembodegem **23** 50 56N 4 4 E
Erenhot **94** 43 48N 111 59 E
Eresma → **34** 41 26N 40 45W
Eressós **49** 39 11N 25 57 E
Erfenisdam **134** 28 30 S 26 50 E
Erfjord **51** 59 20N 6 14 E
Erfoud **121** 31 30N 4 15W
Erft → **26** 51 11N 6 44 E
Erfurt **26** 50 58N 11 2 E
Erfurt □ **26** 51 10N 10 30 E
Ergene → **47** 41 1N 26 22 E
Ergeni Vozvyshennost **61** 47 0N 44 0 E
Ergli **58** 56 54N 25 38 E
Eria → **34** 42 3N 5 44W
Eriba **125** 16 40N 36 10 E
Eriboll, L. **14** 58 28N 4 41W
Erica **22** 52 43N 6 56 E
Érice **44** 38 4N 12 34 E
Erie, Mich., U.S.A. **155** 41 47N 83 31W
Erie, Pa., U.S.A. **150** 42 10N 80 7W
Erie, L. **150** 42 15N 81 0W
Erie Canal **150** 43 15N 78 0W
Erieau **150** 42 16N 81 57W
Erigavo **136** 10 35N 47 20 E

Fagnières

Erikoúsa **48** 39 55N 19 14 E
Eriksdale **145** 50 52N 98 7W
Erikslund **52** 62 31N 15 54 E
Erímanthos **49** 37 57N 21 50 E
Erimo-misaki **98** 41 50N 143 15 E
Eriswil **28** 47 5N 7 46 E
Erithraí **49** 38 13N 23 20 E
Eritrea □ **125** 14 0N 38 30 E
Erjas → **35** 39 40N 7 1W
Erlangen **27** 49 35N 11 0 E
Erldunda **110** 25 14 S 133 12 E
Erlin **97** 23 55N 120 21 E
Ermelo, Neth. **22** 52 18N 5 35 E
Ermelo, S. Africa **135** 26 31 S 29 59 E
Ermenak **70** 36 38N 33 0 E
Ermióni **49** 37 23N 23 15 E
Ermoúpolis = Síros **49** 37 28N 24 57 E
Ernakulam = Cochin **81** 9 59N 76 22 E
Erne → **15** 54 30N 8 16W
Erne, Lough **15** 54 26N 7 46W
Ernée **18** 48 18N 0 56W
Ernest Giles Ra. **109** 27 0 S 123 45 E
Ernstberg **27** 50 14N 6 46 E
Erode **81** 11 24N 77 45 E
Eromanga **111** 26 40 S 143 11 E
Erongo **134** 21 39 S 15 58 E
Erp **23** 51 36N 5 37 E
Erquelinnes **23** 50 19N 4 8 E
Erquy **18** 48 38N 2 29W
Erquy, C. d' **18** 48 39N 2 29W
Err, Piz d' **29** 46 34N 9 43 E
Errabiddy **109** 25 25 S 117 5 E
Erramala Hills **81** 15 30N 78 15 E
Errer → **125** 7 32N 42 35 E
Errigal, Mt. **15** 55 2N 8 8W
Erris Hd. **15** 54 19N 10 0W
Erseka **48** 40 22N 20 40 E
Erskine **152** 47 37N 96 0W
Erstein **19** 48 25N 7 38 E
Erstfeld **29** 46 50N 8 38 E
Ertil **59** 51 55N 40 50 E
Ertvågøy **51** 63 13N 8 26 E
Ertvelde **23** 51 11N 3 45 E
Eruwa **127** 7 33N 3 26 E
Ervy-le-Châtel **19** 48 2N 3 55 E
Erwin **149** 36 10N 82 28W
Eryuan **96** 26 7N 99 57 E
Erzgebirge **26** 50 25N 13 0 E
Erzin, Turkey **70** 36 57N 36 11 E
Erzin, U.S.S.R. **65** 50 15N 95 10 E
Erzincan **57** 39 46N 39 30 E
Erzurum **57** 39 57N 41 15 E
Es Sahrâ' Esh Sharqîya **124** 27 30N 32 30 E
Es Sînâ' **124** 29 0N 34 0 E
Es Sûkî **125** 13 20N 33 58 E
Esa'ala **107** 9 45 S 150 49 E
Esambo **130** 3 48 S 23 30 E
Esan-Misaki **98** 41 40N 141 10 E
Esashi, Hokkaidō, Japan **98** 44 56N 142 35 E
Esashi, Hokkaidō, Japan **98** 41 52N 140 7 E
Esbjerg **53** 55 29N 8 29 E
Escada **170** 8 22 S 35 8W
Escalante **157** 37 47N 111 37W
Escalante → **157** 37 17N 110 53W
Escalente **91** 10 50N 123 33 E
Escalón **160** 26 46N 104 20W
Escalona **34** 40 9N 4 29W
Escambia → **149** 30 32N 87 15W
Escanaba **148** 45 44N 87 5W
Escarparda Pt. **90** 18 31N 122 13 E
Escarpé, C. **106** 20 41 S 167 13 E
Escaut → **23** 51 2N 3 45 E
Esch-sur-Alzette **23** 49 32N 6 0 E
Eschallens **28** 46 39N 6 38 E
Eschede **26** 52 44N 10 13 E
Escholzmatt **28** 46 55N 7 56 E
Eschwege **26** 51 10N 10 3 E
Eschweiler **26** 50 49N 6 14 E
Escoma **172** 15 40 S 69 8W
Escondida, La **160** 24 6N 99 55W
Escondido **159** 33 9N 117 4W
Escuinapa **160** 22 50N 105 50W
Escuintla **162** 14 20N 90 48W
Eséka **127** 3 41N 10 44 E
Esens **26** 53 40N 7 35 E
Esera → **36** 42 6N 0 15 E
Eşfahān **73** 33 0N 51 30 E
Esfīdeh **73** 33 39N 59 46 E
Esgueva → **34** 41 40N 4 43W
Esh Sham = Dimashq **70** 33 30N 36 18 E
Esh Shamâlîya □ **124** 19 0N 29 0 E
Eshan **96** 24 11N 102 24 E
Eshkamesh **77** 36 23N 69 19 E
Eshowe **135** 28 50 S 31 30 E
Eshta'ol **69** 31 47N 35 0 E
Esiama **126** 4 56N 2 25W
Esino → **43** 43 39N 13 22 E
Esk →, Dumf. & Gall., U.K. **14** 54 58N 3 4W
Esk →, N. Yorks., U.K. **12** 54 27N 0 36W
Eskān **77** 26 48N 63 9 E
Eskifjörður **54** 65 3N 13 55W
Eskilstuna **52** 59 22N 16 32 E
Eskimo Pt. **145** 61 10N 94 15W
Eskişehir **57** 39 50N 30 35 E
Esla → **34** 41 29N 6 3W
Esla, Pantano del **34** 41 29N 6 3W
Eslāmābād-e Gharb **72** 34 10N 46 30 E
Eslöv **52** 55 50N 13 20 E
Esmeralda, I. **176** 48 55 S 75 25W
Esmeralda, La **174** 22 16 S 62 33W
Esmeraldas **168** 1 0N 79 40W
Esmeraldas □ **168** 0 40N 79 30W
Esmeraldas → **168** 0 58N 79 38W
Esneux **23** 50 32N 5 33 E
Espada, Pta. **168** 12 5N 71 7W
Espalion **20** 44 32N 2 47 E
Espalmador, I. **37** 38 47N 1 26 E
Espanola **142** 46 15N 81 46W
Espardell, I. del **37** 38 48N 1 29 E
Esparraguera **36** 41 33N 1 52 E
Esparta **162** 9 59N 84 40W
Espejo **35** 37 40N 4 34W
Esperança **170** 7 1 S 35 51W
Esperance **109** 33 45 S 121 55 E
Esperance B. **109** 33 48 S 121 55 E
Esperantinópolis **170** 4 53 S 44 53W
Esperanza, Antarct. **7** 65 0 S 55 0W
Esperanza, Santa Cruz, Argentina **176** 51 1 S 70 49W
Esperanza, Santa Fe, Argentina **174** 31 29 S 61 3W
Esperanza, Masbate, Phil. **91** 11 45N 124 3 E
Esperanza, Mindanao, Phil. **91** 8 43N 125 36 E
Esperanza, La, Argentina **176** 40 26 S 68 32W
Esperanza, La, Cuba **162** 22 46N 83 44W
Esperanza, La, Hond. **162** 14 15N 88 10W
Espéraza **20** 42 56N 2 14 E
Espevær **51** 59 35N 5 7 E
Espichel, C. **35** 38 22N 9 16W
Espiel **35** 38 11N 5 1W
Espigão, Serra do **175** 26 35 S 50 30W
Espinal **168** 4 9N 74 53W
Espinar **172** 14 51 S 71 24W
Espinazo, Sierra del = Espinhaço, Serra do **171** 17 30 S 43 30W
Espinhaço, Serra do **171** 17 30 S 43 30W
Espinho **34** 41 1N 8 38W
Espinilho, Serra do **175** 28 30 S 55 0W
Espino **168** 8 34N 66 1W
Espinosa de los Monteros **34** 43 5N 3 34W
Espírito Santo □ **171** 20 0 S 40 45W
Espíritu Santo, B. del **161** 19 15N 87 0W
Espíritu Santo, I. **160** 24 30N 110 23W
Espita **161** 21 1N 88 19W
Esplanada **171** 11 47 S 37 57W
Espluga de Francolí **36** 41 24N 1 7 E
Espuña, Sierra **37** 37 51N 1 35W
Espungabera **135** 20 29 S 32 45 E
Esquel **176** 42 55 S 71 20W
Esquina **174** 30 0 S 59 30W
Essaouira **120** 31 32N 9 42W
Essarts, Les **18** 46 47N 1 12W
Essebie **130** 2 58N 30 40 E
Essen, Belgium **23** 51 28N 4 28 E
Essen, W. Germany **26** 51 28N 6 59 E
Essequibo □ **169** 7 0N 59 0W
Essequibo → **169** 6 50N 58 30W
Essex, Canada **150** 42 10N 82 49W
Essex, Calif., U.S.A. **159** 34 44N 115 15W
Essex, Ill., U.S.A. **155** 41 11N 88 11W
Essex, N.Y., U.S.A. **151** 44 17N 73 21W
Essex □ **13** 51 48N 0 30 E
Esslingen **27** 48 43N 9 19 E
Essonne □ **19** 48 30N 2 20 E
Essvik **52** 62 18N 17 24 E
Estaca, Pta. del **34** 43 46N 7 42W
Estadilla **36** 42 4N 0 16 E
Estados, I. de Los **176** 54 40 S 64 30W
Estagel **20** 42 47N 2 40 E
Eşṭahbānāt **73** 29 8N 54 4 E
Estância, Brazil **170** 11 16 S 37 26W
Estancia, U.S.A. **157** 34 50N 106 1W
Estārm **73** 28 21N 58 21 E
Estarreja **34** 40 45N 8 35W
Estats, Pic d' **36** 42 40N 1 24 E
Estavayer-le-Lac **28** 46 51N 6 51 E
Estcourt **135** 29 0 S 29 53 E
Este **43** 45 12N 11 40 E
Esteban **34** 43 33N 6 5W
Estelí **162** 13 9N 86 22W
Estella **36** 42 40N 2 0W
Estelline, S. Dak., U.S.A. **152** 44 39N 96 52W
Estelline, Tex., U.S.A. **153** 34 35N 100 27W
Estena → **35** 39 23N 4 44W
Estepa **35** 37 17N 4 52W
Estepona **35** 36 24N 5 7W
Esterhazy **145** 50 37N 102 5W
Esternay **19** 48 44N 3 33 E
Esterri de Aneu **36** 42 38N 1 5 E
Estevan **145** 49 10N 102 59W
Estevan Group **144** 53 3N 129 38W
Estherville **152** 43 25N 94 50W
Estissac **19** 48 16N 3 48 E
Eston **145** 51 8N 108 40W
Estonian S.S.R. □ **58** 58 30N 25 30 E
Estoril **35** 38 42N 9 23W
Estouk **127** 18 14N 1 2 E
Estrada, La **34** 42 43N 8 27W
Estrêla, Serra da **34** 40 10N 7 45W
Estrella **37** 38 25N 3 35W
Estremoz **35** 38 51N 7 39W
Estrondo, Serra do **170** 7 20 S 48 0W
Esztergom **31** 47 47N 18 44 E
Et Tîdra **126** 19 45N 16 20W
Eṭ Ṭîra **69** 32 14N 34 56 E
Étables-sur-Mer **18** 48 38N 2 51W
Etadunna **111** 28 43 S 138 38 E
Etah **79** 27 35N 78 40 E
Étain **19** 49 13N 5 38 E
Etalle **23** 49 40N 5 36 E
Etamamu **143** 50 18N 59 59W
Étampes **19** 48 26N 2 10 E
Étang-sur-Arroux **21** 46 51N 4 11 E
Etanga **134** 17 55 S 13 0 E
Étaples **19** 50 30N 1 39 E
Etawah **79** 26 48N 79 6 E
Etawah → **149** 34 20N 84 15W
Etawney L. **145** 57 50N 96 50W
Eteh **127** 7 2N 7 28 E
Éthe **23** 49 35N 5 35 E
Ethel **158** 46 32N 122 46W
Ethel, Oued el → **120** 28 31N 3 37W
Ethel Creek **108** 23 5 S 120 11 E
Ethelbert **145** 51 32N 100 25W
Ethiopia ■ **136** 8 0N 40 0 E
Ethiopian Highlands **116** 10 0N 37 0 E
Etive, L. **14** 56 30N 5 12W
Etna **45** 37 45N 15 0 E
Etne **51** 59 40N 5 56 E
Etoile **131** 11 33 S 27 30 E
Etolin I. **144** 56 5N 132 20W
Etosha Pan **134** 18 40 S 16 30 E
Etoumbi **132** 0 1 S 14 57 E
Etowah **149** 35 20N 84 30W
Étrépagny **19** 49 18N 1 36 E
Étretat **18** 49 42N 0 12 E
Étroits, Les **143** 47 24N 68 54W
Etropole **47** 42 50N 24 0 E
Ettelbruck **23** 49 51N 6 5 E
Etten **23** 51 34N 4 38 E
Ettlingen **27** 48 58N 8 25 E
Ettrick Water **14** 55 31N 2 55W
Etuku **130** 3 42 S 25 45 E
Etzatlán **160** 20 48N 104 5W
Eu **18** 50 3N 1 26 E
Euboea = Évvoia **49** 38 30N 24 0 E
Euchareena **113** 32 57 S 149 6 E
Euclid **150** 41 32N 81 31W
Euclides da Cunha **170** 10 31 S 39 1W
Eucumbene, L. **113** 36 2 S 148 40 E
Eudora **153** 33 5N 91 17W
Eudunda **112** 34 12 S 139 7 E
Eufaula, Ala., U.S.A. **149** 31 55N 85 11W
Eufaula, Okla., U.S.A. **153** 35 20N 95 33W
Eufaula, L. **153** 35 15N 95 28W
Eugene **156** 44 0N 123 8W
Eugowra **113** 33 22 S 148 24 E
Eulo **111** 28 10 S 145 3 E
Eumungerie **113** 31 56 S 148 36 E
Eunice, La., U.S.A. **153** 30 35N 92 28W
Eunice, N. Mex., U.S.A. **153** 32 30N 103 10W
Eupen **23** 50 37N 6 3 E
Euphrates = Furāt, Nahr al → **72** 31 0N 47 25 E
Eure □ **18** 49 10N 1 0 E
Eure → **18** 49 18N 1 12 E
Eure-et-Loir □ **18** 48 22N 1 30 E
Eureka, Canada **6** 80 0N 85 56W
Eureka, Calif., U.S.A. **156** 40 50N 124 0W
Eureka, Ill., U.S.A. **154** 40 43N 89 16W
Eureka, Kans., U.S.A. **153** 37 50N 96 20W
Eureka, Mo., U.S.A. **154** 38 30N 90 38W
Eureka, Mont., U.S.A. **156** 48 53N 115 6W
Eureka, Nev., U.S.A. **156** 39 32N 116 2W
Eureka, S. Dak., U.S.A. **152** 45 49N 99 38W
Eureka, Utah, U.S.A. **156** 40 0N 112 9W
Eureka, Mt. **109** 26 35 S 121 35 E
Eurelia **112** 32 33 S 138 35 E
Euroa **113** 36 44 S 145 35 E
Europa, Picos de **34** 43 10N 4 49W
Europa, Pta. de **35** 36 3N 5 21W
Europa Pt. = Europa, Pta. de **35** 36 3N 5 21W
Europe **10** 50 0N 20 0 E
Europoort **22** 51 57N 4 10 E
Euskirchen **26** 50 40N 6 45 E
Eustis **149** 28 54N 81 36W
Eutin **26** 54 7N 10 38 E
Eutsuk L. **144** 53 20N 126 45W
Eva **169** 3 9 S 59 56W
Eva Downs **110** 18 1 S 134 52 E
Eval **69** 32 15N 35 15 E
Evale **133** 16 33 S 15 44 E
Evanger **51** 60 39N 6 7 E
Evans **152** 40 25N 104 43W
Evans Head **111** 29 7 S 153 27 E
Evans L. **142** 50 50N 77 0W
Evans Mills **151** 44 6N 75 48W
Evansdale **154** 42 30N 92 17W
Evanston, Ill., U.S.A. **155** 42 0N 87 40W
Evanston, Wyo., U.S.A. **156** 41 10N 111 0W
Evansville, Ill., U.S.A. **154** 38 5N 89 56W
Evansville, Ind., U.S.A. **155** 38 0N 87 35W
Evansville, Wis., U.S.A. **154** 42 47N 89 18W
Évaux-les-Bains **20** 46 12N 2 29 E
Evaz **73** 27 46N 53 59 E
Eveleth **152** 47 29N 92 46W
Even Yahuda **69** 32 16N 34 53 E
Evensk **65** 62 12N 159 30 E
Evenstad **51** 61 25N 11 7 E
Everard, L. **111** 31 30 S 135 0 E
Everard Ras. **109** 27 5 S 132 28 E
Everdale **113** 31 52 S 144 46 E
Evere **23** 50 52N 4 25 E
Everest, Mt. **79** 28 5N 86 58 E
Everett, Pa., U.S.A. **150** 40 2N 78 24W
Everett, Wash., U.S.A. **158** 48 0N 122 10W
Evergem **23** 51 7N 3 43 E
Everglades **149** 26 0N 80 30W
Everglades City **149** 25 52N 81 23W
Everglades Nat. Park. **149** 25 27N 80 53W
Evergreen **149** 31 28N 86 55W
Everson **156** 48 57N 122 22W
Everton **113** 36 25 S 146 33 E
Evesham **13** 52 6N 1 57W
Évian-les-Bains **21** 46 24N 6 35 E
Evinayong **132** 1 26N 10 35 E
Évinos → **49** 38 27N 21 40 E
Évisa **21** 42 15N 8 48 E
Evje **51** 58 36N 7 51 E
Évora **35** 38 33N 7 57W
Évora □ **35** 38 33N 7 50W
Evowghlī **72** 38 43N 45 13 E
Évreux **18** 49 0N 1 8 E
Evritanía □ **49** 39 5N 21 30 E
Évron **18** 48 10N 0 24W
Évros □ **48** 41 10N 26 0 E
Evrótas → **49** 36 50N 22 40 E
Évvoia **49** 38 30N 24 0 E
Évvoia □ **49** 38 40N 23 40 E
Ewe, L. **14** 57 49N 5 38W
Ewing, Mo., U.S.A. **154** 40 0N 91 43W
Ewing, Nebr., U.S.A. **152** 42 18N 98 22W
Ewo **132** 0 48 S 14 45 E
Exaltación **173** 13 10 S 65 20W
Excelsior Springs **154** 39 20N 94 10W
Excideuil **20** 45 20N 1 4 E
Exe → **13** 50 38N 3 27W
Exeter, Canada **150** 43 21N 81 29W
Exeter, U.K. **13** 50 43N 3 31W
Exeter, Calif., U.S.A. **158** 36 17N 119 9W
Exeter, N.H., U.S.A. **151** 43 0N 70 58W
Exeter, Nebr., U.S.A. **152** 40 43N 97 30W
Exira **154** 41 35N 94 52W
Exloo **22** 52 53N 6 52 E
Exmes **18** 48 45N 0 10 E
Exmoor **13** 51 10N 3 59W
Exmouth, Australia **108** 21 54 S 114 10 E
Exmouth, U.K. **13** 50 37N 3 26W
Exmouth G. **108** 22 15 S 114 15 E
Expedition Range **110** 24 30 S 149 12 E
Extremadura □ **35** 39 30N 6 5W
Exuma Sound **162** 24 30N 76 20W
Eyasi, L. **130** 3 30 S 35 0 E
Eyeberry L. **145** 63 8N 104 43W
Eyemouth **14** 55 53N 2 5W
Eygurande **20** 45 40N 2 26 E
Eyjafjörður **54** 66 15N 18 30W
Eymet **20** 44 40N 0 25 E
Eymoutiers **20** 45 40N 1 45 E
Eyrarbakki **54** 63 52N 21 9W
Eyre **109** 32 15 S 126 18 E
Eyre (North), L. **111** 28 30 S 137 20 E
Eyre (South), L. **111** 29 18 S 137 25 E
Eyre Cr. → **111** 26 40 S 139 0 E
Eyre Mts. **115** 45 25 S 168 25 E
Eyvānkī **73** 35 24N 51 56 E
Eyzies-de-Tayac-Sireuil, Les **20** 44 56N 1 1 E
Ez Zeidab **124** 17 25N 33 55 E
Ezcaray **36** 42 19N 3 0W
Ezine **48** 39 48N 26 12 E
Ezmul **120** 22 15N 15 40W
Ezousas → **70** 34 44N 32 27 E

F

Fabens **157** 31 30N 106 8W
Fåborg **53** 55 6N 10 15 E
Fabriano **43** 43 20N 12 52 E
Făcăeni **50** 44 32N 27 53 E
Facatativá **168** 4 49N 74 22W
Fachi **123** 18 6N 11 34 E
Facture **20** 44 39N 0 58W
Fada **123** 17 13N 21 34 E
Fada-n-Gourma **127** 12 10N 0 30 E
Fadd **31** 46 28N 18 49 E
Faddeyevskiy, Ostrov **65** 76 0N 150 0 E
Fadghāmī **72** 35 53N 40 52 E
Fadlab **124** 17 42N 34 2 E
Faenza **43** 44 17N 11 53 E
Fafa **127** 15 22N 0 48 E
Fafe **34** 41 27N 8 11W
Fagam **127** 11 1N 10 1 E
Făgăras **50** 45 48N 24 58 E
Făgăras, Munţii **50** 45 40N 24 40 E
Fagatogo **106** 14 17 S 170 41W
Fågelsjö **52** 61 50N 14 35 E
Fagerhult **53** 57 8N 15 40 E
Fagersta **52** 60 1N 15 46 E
Făget **50** 45 52N 22 10 E
Făget, Munţii **50** 47 40N 23 10 E
Fagnano, L. **176** 54 30 S 68 0W
Fagnano Castello **45** 39 31N 16 4 E
Fagnières **19** 48 58N 4 20 E

Fahlīān

Fahlīān 73 30 11N 51 28 E
Fahr 75 12 26N 54 8 E
Fahraj, Kermān, Iran 73 29 0N 59 0 E
Fahraj, Yazd, Iran 73 31 46N 54 36 E
Faido 29 46 29N 8 48 E
Fair Hd. 15 55 14N 6 10W
Fair Oaks 158 38 39N 121 16W
Fairbank 157 31 44N 110 12W
Fairbanks 140 64 50N 147 50W
Fairborn 155 39 52N 84 2W
Fairbury, Ill., U.S.A. 155 40 45N 88 31W
Fairbury, Nebr., U.S.A. 152 40 5N 97 5W
Faire 90 17 53N 121 34 E
Fairfax, Ohio, U.S.A. 155 39 5N 83 37W
Fairfax, Okla., U.S.A. 153 36 37N 96 45W
Fairfield, Australia 113 33 53 S 150 57 E
Fairfield, Ala., U.S.A. 149 33 30N 87 0W
Fairfield, Calif., U.S.A. 158 38 14N 122 1W
Fairfield, Conn., U.S.A. 151 41 8N 73 16W
Fairfield, Idaho, U.S.A. 156 43 21N 114 46W
Fairfield, Ill., U.S.A. 155 38 20N 88 20W
Fairfield, Iowa, U.S.A. 154 41 0N 91 58W
Fairfield, Mont., U.S.A. 156 47 40N 112 0W
Fairfield, Ohio, U.S.A. 155 39 21N 84 34W
Fairfield, Tex., U.S.A. 153 31 40N 96 0W
Fairford 145 51 37N 98 38W
Fairhope 149 30 35N 87 50W
Fairlie 115 44 5 S 170 49 E
Fairmead 158 37 5N 120 10W
Fairmont, Minn., U.S.A. 152 43 37N 94 30W
Fairmont, W. Va., U.S.A. 148 39 29N 80 10W
Fairmount 159 34 45N 118 26W
Fairplay 157 39 9N 105 40W
Fairport, N.Y., U.S.A. 150 43 8N 77 29W
Fairport, Ohio, U.S.A. 150 41 45N 81 17W
Fairview, Australia 110 15 31 S 144 17 E
Fairview, Canada 144 56 5N 118 25W
Fairview, N. Dak., U.S.A. 152 47 49N 104 7W
Fairview, Okla., U.S.A. 153 36 19N 98 30W
Fairview, Utah, U.S.A. 156 39 50N 111 0W
Fairweather, Mt. 140 58 55N 137 45W
Faisalabad 77 31 30N 73 5 E
Faith 152 45 2N 102 4W
Faizabad 79 26 45N 82 10 E
Faizpur 78 21 14N 75 49 E
Fajardo 163 18 20N 65 39W
Fakam 74 16 38N 43 49 E
Fakfak 87 3 0 S 132 15 E
Fakiya 47 42 10N 27 6 E
Fakobli 126 7 23N 7 23W
Fakse 52 55 15N 12 8 E
Fakse B. 52 55 11N 12 15 E
Fakse Ladeplads 52 55 11N 12 9 E
Faku 95 42 32N 123 21 E
Falaise 18 48 54N 0 12W
Falaise, Mui 84 19 6N 105 45 E
Falakrón Óros 48 41 15N 23 58 E
Falam 82 23 0N 93 45 E
Falces 36 42 24N 1 48W
Fălciu 50 46 17N 28 7 E
Falcón □ 168 11 0N 69 50W
Falcon, C. 121 35 50N 0 50W
Falcon Dam 153 26 50N 99 20W
Falconara Marittima 43 43 37N 13 23 E
Falconer 150 42 7N 79 13W
Faléa 126 12 16N 11 17W
Falenki 59 58 22N 51 35 E
Faleshty 60 47 32N 27 44 E
Falfurrias 153 27 14N 98 8W
Falher 144 55 44N 117 15W
Falkenberg, Germany 26 51 34N 13 13 E
Falkenberg, Sweden 53 56 54N 12 30 E
Falkensee 26 52 35N 13 6 E
Falkenstein 26 50 27N 12 24 E
Falkirk 14 56 0N 3 47W
Falkland, East, I. 176 51 40 S 58 30W
Falkland, West, I. 176 51 40 S 60 0W
Falkland Is. 176 51 30 S 59 0W
Falkland Is. Dependency □ 7 57 0 S 40 0W
Falkland Sd. 176 52 0 S 60 0W
Falkonéra 49 36 50N 23 52 E
Falköping 53 58 12N 13 33 E
Fall River 151 41 45N 71 5W
Fall River Mills 156 41 1N 121 30W
Fallbrook, U.S.A. 157 33 25N 117 12W
Fallbrook, U.S.A. 159 33 23N 117 15W
Fallon, Mont., U.S.A. 152 46 52N 105 8W
Fallon, Nev., U.S.A. 156 39 31N 118 51W
Falls City, Nebr., U.S.A. 152 40 0N 95 40W
Falls City, Oreg., U.S.A. 156 44 54N 123 29W
Falls Creek 150 41 8N 78 49W
Falmouth, Jamaica 162 18 30N 77 40W
Falmouth, U.K. 13 50 9N 5 5W
Falmouth, U.S.A. 155 38 40N 84 20W
False B. 134 34 15 S 18 40 E
False Divi Pt. 81 15 43N 80 50 E
Falset 36 41 7N 0 50 E
Falso, C. 162 15 12N 83 21W
Falster 53 54 45N 11 55 E
Falsterbo 52 55 23N 12 50 E
Fălticeni 50 47 21N 26 20 E
Falun 52 60 37N 15 37 E
Famagusta 70 35 8N 33 55 E
Famagusta Bay 70 35 15N 34 0 E
Famatina, Sierra de 174 27 30 S 68 0W
Family L. 145 51 54N 95 27W
Famoso 159 35 37N 119 12W
Fan Xian 94 35 55N 115 38 E
Fana, Mali 126 13 0N 6 56W
Fana, Norway 51 60 16N 5 20 E
Fanárion 48 39 24N 21 47 E
Fandriana 135 20 14 S 47 21 E
Fang 84 19 55N 99 13 E
Fang Xian 97 32 3N 110 40 E
Fangchang 97 31 5N 118 4 E
Fangcheng, Guangxi Zhuangzu, China 96 21 42N 108 21 E
Fangcheng, Henan, China 94 33 18N 112 59 E
Fangliao 97 22 22N 120 38 E
Fangshan 94 38 3N 111 25 E
Fangzi 95 36 33N 119 10 E
Fani i Madh → 48 41 56N 20 16 E
Fanjiatun 95 43 40N 125 0 E
Fannich, L. 14 57 40N 5 0W
Fannūj 73 26 35N 59 38 E
Fanny Bay 144 49 37N 124 48W
Fanø, Denmark 53 55 25N 8 25 E
Fano, Italy 43 43 50N 13 0 E
Fanshaw 144 57 11N 133 30W
Fanshi 94 39 12N 113 20 E
Fao = Al Fāw 73 30 0N 48 30 E
Faqirwali 78 29 27N 73 0 E
Fara in Sabina 43 42 13N 12 44 E
Farab 63 39 9N 63 36 E
Faradje 130 3 50N 29 45 E
Faradofay 135 25 2 S 47 0 E
Farafangana 135 22 49 S 47 50 E
Farâfra, El Wâhât el- 124 27 15N 28 20 E
Farāh 77 32 20N 62 7 E
Farāh □ 77 32 25N 62 10 E
Farahalana 135 14 26 S 50 10 E
Faraid, Gebel 124 23 33N 35 19 E
Faramana 126 11 56N 4 45W
Faranah 126 10 3N 10 45W
Farasān, Jazā'ir 74 16 45N 41 55 E
Faratsiho 135 19 24 S 46 57 E
Farbarachi 136 2 30N 45 30 E
Fardes → 37 37 35N 3 0W
Fareham 13 50 52N 1 11W
Farewell, C. 115 40 29 S 172 43 E
Farewell C. = Farvel, Kap 6 59 48N 43 55W
Farewell Spit 115 40 35 S 173 0 E
Fargo 152 46 52N 96 40W
Fari'a → 69 32 12N 35 27 E
Faribault 152 44 15N 93 19W
Faridkot 78 30 44N 74 45 E
Faridpur 82 23 15N 89 55 E
Färila 52 61 48N 15 50 E
Farim 126 12 27N 15 9W
Farīmān 73 35 40N 59 49 E
Farina 111 30 3 S 138 15 E
Faringe 52 59 55N 18 7 E
Farinha → 170 6 51 S 47 30W
Fariones, Pta. 37 29 13N 13 28W
Fariske 70 36 37N 32 32 E
Fāriskūr 124 31 20N 31 43 E
Farmakonisi 49 37 17N 27 8 E
Farmer City 155 40 15N 88 39W
Farmersburg 155 39 15N 87 23W
Farmerville 153 32 48N 92 23W
Farmington, Calif., U.S.A. 158 37 56N 121 0W
Farmington, Ill., U.S.A. 154 40 42N 90 0W
Farmington, Iowa, U.S.A. 154 40 38N 91 44W
Farmington, Mo., U.S.A. 154 37 47N 90 25W
Farmington, N.H., U.S.A. 151 43 25N 71 7W
Farmington, N. Mex., U.S.A. 157 36 45N 108 28W
Farmington, Utah, U.S.A. 156 41 0N 111 12W
Farmington → 151 41 51N 72 38W
Farmland 155 40 15N 85 5W
Farmville 148 37 19N 78 22W
Farnborough 13 51 17N 0 46W
Farne Is. 12 55 38N 1 37W
Farnham 151 45 17N 72 59W
Faro, Brazil 169 2 10 S 56 39W
Faro, Portugal 35 37 2N 7 55W
Faro □ 35 37 12N 8 10W
Faroe Is. = Føroyar 8 62 0N 7 0W
Farquhar, C. 109 23 50 S 113 36 E
Farquhar Is. 83 11 0 S 52 0 E
Farrar → 14 57 30N 4 30W
Farrars Cr. → 110 25 35 S 140 43 E
Farrāshband 73 28 57N 52 5 E
Farrell 150 41 13N 80 29W
Farrell Flat 112 33 48 S 138 48 E
Farrokhī 73 33 50N 59 31 E
Farrukhabad-cum-Fatehgarh 79 27 30N 79 32 E
Fārs □ 73 29 30N 55 0 E
Fársala 48 39 17N 22 23 E
Fārsī 77 33 47N 63 15 E
Farsø 53 56 46N 9 19 E
Farsund 51 58 5N 6 55 E
Fartak, Ra's, S. Yemen 75 15 38N 52 15 E
Fartak, Râs, Si. Arabia 72 28 5N 34 34 E
Fartura, Serra da 175 26 21 S 52 52W
Faru 127 12 48N 6 12 E
Fārūj 73 37 14N 58 14 E
Farum 52 55 49N 12 21 E
Farvel, Kap 6 59 48N 43 55W
Farwell 153 34 25N 103 0W
Fāryāb □ 77 36 0N 65 0 E
Fasā 73 29 0N 53 39 E
Fasano 45 40 50N 17 20 E
Fashoda 125 9 50N 32 2 E
Fastnet Rock 15 51 22N 9 37W
Fastov 58 50 7N 29 57 E
Fatagar, Tanjung 87 2 46 S 131 57 E
Fatehgarh 79 27 25N 79 35 E
Fatehpur, Raj., India 78 28 0N 74 40 E
Fatehpur, Ut. P., India 79 25 56N 81 13 E
Fatesh 59 52 8N 35 57 E
Fatick 126 14 19N 16 27W
Fatima, Canada 143 47 24N 61 53W
Fátima, Portugal 35 39 37N 8 39W
Fatoya 126 11 37N 9 10W
Faucille, Col de la 21 46 22N 6 2 E
Faulkton 152 45 4N 99 8W
Faulquemont 19 49 3N 6 36 E
Fauquembergues 19 50 36N 2 5 E
Faure I. 109 25 52 S 113 50 E
Făurei 50 45 6N 27 19 E
Fauresmith 134 29 44 S 25 17 E
Fauvillers 23 49 51N 5 40 E
Fåvang 51 61 27N 10 11 E
Favara 44 37 19N 13 39 E
Favignana 44 37 56N 12 18 E
Favignana, I. 44 37 56N 12 18 E
Favourable Lake 142 52 50N 93 39W
Fawn → 142 55 20N 87 35W
Fawnskin 159 34 16N 116 56W
Faxaflói 54 64 29N 23 0W
Faya-Largeau 123 17 58N 19 6 E
Fayaoué 106 20 38 S 166 33 E
Fayd 72 27 1N 42 52 E
Fayence 21 43 38N 6 42 E
Fayette, Ala., U.S.A. 149 33 40N 87 50W
Fayette, Iowa, U.S.A. 154 42 51N 91 48W
Fayette, Mo., U.S.A. 154 39 10N 92 40W
Fayette, Ohio, U.S.A. 155 41 40N 84 20W
Fayetteville, Ark., U.S.A. 153 36 0N 94 5W
Fayetteville, N.C., U.S.A. 149 35 0N 78 58W
Fayetteville, Tenn., U.S.A. 149 35 8N 86 30W
Fayón 36 41 15N 0 20 E
Fazenda Libongo 133 8 24 S 13 24 E
Fazenda Nova 171 16 11 S 50 48W
Fazilka 78 30 27N 74 2 E
Fazilpur 78 29 18N 70 29 E
Fdérik 120 22 40N 12 45W
Fé, La 162 22 2N 84 15W
Feale → 15 52 26N 9 40W
Fear, C. 149 33 51N 78 0W
Feather → 156 38 47N 121 36W
Feather Falls 158 39 36N 121 16W
Featherston 114 41 6 S 175 20 E
Featherstone 131 18 42 S 30 55 E
Fécamp 18 49 45N 0 22 E
Fedala = Mohammedia 120 33 44N 7 21W
Federación 174 31 0 S 57 55W
Fedeshkūh 73 28 49N 53 50 E
Fedjadj, Chott el 121 33 52N 9 14 E
Fedje 51 60 47N 4 43 E
Fedorovka 62 53 38N 62 42 E
Fefan I. 106 7 21N 151 51 E
Fehérgyarmat 31 48 0N 22 30 E
Fehmarn 26 54 26N 11 10 E
Fei Xian 95 35 18N 117 59 E
Feijó 172 8 9 S 70 21W
Feilding 114 40 13 S 175 35 E
Feira de Santana 171 12 15 S 38 57W
Feirân, W. → 71 28 39N 33 12 E
Feirâni, G. 71 28 31N 34 19 E
Feixiang 94 36 30N 114 45 E
Fejér □ 31 47 9N 18 30 E
Fejø 52 54 55N 11 30 E
Fekete → 31 45 47N 18 15 E
Felanitx 37 39 28N 3 9 E
Feldbach 30 46 57N 15 52 E
Feldberg, E. Germany 26 53 20N 13 26 E
Feldberg, W. Germany 27 47 51N 7 58 E
Feldkirch 30 47 15N 9 37 E
Feldkirchen 30 46 44N 14 6 E
Felicity 155 38 51N 84 6W
Felipe Carrillo Puerto 161 19 38N 88 3W
Felixlândia 171 18 47 S 44 55W
Felixstowe 13 51 58N 1 22 E
Felletin 20 45 53N 2 11 E
Felton 158 37 3N 122 4W
Feltre 43 46 1N 11 55 E
Femø 52 54 58N 11 53 E
Femunden 51 62 10N 11 53 E
Fen He → 94 35 36N 110 42 E
Fenelon Falls 150 44 32N 78 45W
Fener Burnu 70 36 32N 35 21 E
Feneroa 125 13 5N 39 3 E
Feng Xian, Jiangsu, China 94 34 43N 116 35 E
Feng Xian, Shaanxi, China 94 33 54N 106 40 E
Fengári 48 40 25N 25 32 E
Fengcheng, Jiangxi, China 97 28 12N 115 48 E
Fengcheng, Liaoning, China 95 40 28N 124 5 E
Fengdu 96 29 55N 107 41 E
Fengfeng 94 36 28N 114 8 E
Fenggang 96 27 57N 107 47 E
Fenghua 97 29 40N 121 25 E
Fenghuang 96 27 57N 109 29 E
Fenghuangzui 96 33 30N 109 23 E
Fengjie 96 31 5N 109 36 E
Fengkai 97 23 24N 111 30 E
Fengle 97 31 29N 112 29 E
Fengning 94 41 10N 116 33 E
Fengqing 96 24 38N 99 55 E
Fengqiu 94 35 2N 114 25 E
Fengrun 95 39 48N 118 8 E
Fengshan, Guangxi Zhuangzu, China 96 24 39N 109 15 E
Fengshan, Guangxi Zhuangzu, China 96 24 31N 107 3 E
Fengtai, Anhui, China 97 32 50N 116 40 E
Fengtai, Beijing, China 94 39 50N 116 18 E
Fengxian 97 30 55N 121 26 E
Fengxiang 94 34 29N 107 25 E
Fengxin 97 28 41N 115 18 E
Fengyang 95 32 51N 117 29 E
Fengyi 96 25 37N 100 20 E
Fengzhen 94 40 25N 113 2 E
Feni Is. 107 4 0 S 153 40 E
Fenit 15 52 17N 9 51W
Fennimore 154 42 58N 90 41W
Fenny 82 22 55N 91 32 E
Feno, C. de 21 41 58N 8 33 E
Fenoarivo Afovoany 135 18 26 S 46 34 E
Fenoarivo Atsinanana 135 17 22 S 49 25 E
Fens, The 12 52 45N 0 2 E
Fenton 142 42 47N 83 44W
Fenxi 94 36 40N 111 31 E
Fenyang 94 37 18N 111 48 E
Fenyi 97 27 45N 114 47 E
Feodosiya 60 45 2N 35 28 E
Fer, C. de 121 37 3N 7 10 E
Ferdows 73 33 58N 58 2 E
Fère, La 19 49 39N 3 21 E
Fère-Champenoise 19 48 45N 4 0 E
Fère-en-Tardenois 19 49 10N 3 30 E
Ferentino 44 41 42N 13 14 E
Ferfer 136 5 4N 45 9 E
Fergana 63 40 23N 71 19 E
Ferganskaya Dolina 63 40 50N 71 30 E
Ferganskiy Khrebet 63 41 0N 73 50 E
Fergus 142 43 43N 80 24W
Fergus Falls 152 46 18N 96 7W
Ferguson 154 38 45N 90 18W
Fergusson I. 107 9 30 S 150 45 E
Fériana 121 34 59N 8 33 E
Feričanci 46 45 32N 18 0 E
Ferkane 121 34 37N 7 26 E
Ferkéssédougou 126 9 35N 5 6W
Ferlach 30 46 32N 14 18 E
Ferland 142 50 19N 88 27W
Ferlo, Vallée du 126 15 15N 14 15W
Fermanagh □ 15 54 21N 7 40W
Fermo 43 43 10N 13 42 E
Fermoselle 34 41 19N 6 27W
Fermoy 15 52 4N 8 18W
Fernán Nuñéz 35 37 40N 4 44W
Fernández 174 27 55 S 63 50W
Fernandina Beach 149 30 40N 81 30W
Fernando de Noronha 170 4 0 S 33 10W
Fernando Póo = Bioko 127 3 30N 8 40 E
Fernandópolis 171 20 16 S 50 14W
Ferndale, Calif., U.S.A. 156 40 37N 124 12W
Ferndale, Wash., U.S.A. 158 48 51N 122 41W
Fernie 144 49 30N 115 5W
Fernlees 110 23 51 S 148 7 E
Fernley 156 39 36N 119 14W
Feroke 81 11 9N 75 46 E
Ferozepore = Firozpur 78 30 55N 74 40 E
Férrai 48 40 53N 26 10 E
Ferrandina 45 40 30N 16 28 E
Ferrara 43 44 50N 11 36 E
Ferrato, C. 44 39 18N 9 39 E
Ferreira do Alentejo 35 38 4N 8 6W
Ferreñafe 172 6 42 S 79 50W
Ferret, C. 20 44 38N 1 15W
Ferrette 19 47 30N 7 20 E
Ferriday 153 31 35N 91 33W
Ferrières 19 48 5N 2 48 E
Ferriete 42 44 40N 9 30 E
Ferrol, Pen. de 172 9 10 S 78 35W
Ferron 157 39 3N 111 3W
Ferros 171 19 14 S 43 2W
Ferryland 143 47 2N 52 53W
Ferrysburg 155 43 5N 86 13W
Ferté-Bernard, La 18 48 10N 0 40 E
Ferté-Macé, La 18 48 35N 0 22W
Ferté-St.-Aubin, La 19 47 42N 1 57 E
Ferté-sous-Jouarre, La 19 48 56N 3 8 E
Ferté-Vidame, La 18 48 37N 0 53 E
Fertile 152 47 31N 96 18W
Fertília 44 40 37N 8 13 E
Fertőszentmiklós 31 47 35N 16 53 E
Fès 120 34 0N 5 0W
Feschaux 23 50 9N 4 54 E
Feshi 133 6 8 S 18 10 E

Fort Kent

Fessenden 152 47 42N 99 38W
Festus 154 38 13N 90 24W
Feteşti 50 44 22N 27 51 E
Fetlar 14 60 36N 0 52W
Feuerthalen 29 47 37N 8 38 E
Feuilles → 141 58 47N 70 4W
Feurs 21 45 45N 4 13 E
Fevzipaşa 70 37 6N 36 37 E
Feyẕābād, Badākhshān, Afghan. 77 37 7N 70 33 E
Feyẕābād, Fāryāb, Afghan. 77 36 17N 64 52 E
Fezzan 116 27 0N 15 0 E
Ffestiniog 12 52 58N 3 56W
Fiambalá 174 27 45 S 67 37W
Fianarantsoa 135 21 26 S 47 5 E
Fianarantsoa □ 135 19 30 S 47 0 E
Fianga 123 9 55N 15 9 E
Fibiş 50 45 57N 21 26 E
Fichtelgebirge 27 50 10N 12 0 E
Ficksburg 135 28 51 S 27 53 E
Fidenza 42 44 51N 10 3 E
Fiditi 127 7 45N 3 53 E
Field 142 46 31N 80 1W
Field → 110 23 48 S 138 0 E
Field I. 108 12 5 S 132 23 E
Fieri 48 40 43N 19 33 E
Fiesch 28 46 25N 8 12 E
Fife □ 14 56 13N 3 2W
Fife Ness 14 56 17N 2 35W
Fifth Cataract 124 18 22N 33 50 E
Figeac 20 44 37N 2 2 E
Figline Valdarno 43 43 37N 11 28 E
Figtree 131 20 22 S 28 20 E
Figueira Castelo Rodrigo 34 40 57N 6 58W
Figueira da Foz 34 40 7N 8 54W
Figueiró dos Vinhos 34 39 55N 8 16W
Figueras 36 42 18N 2 58 E
Figuig 121 32 5N 1 11W
Fihaonana 135 18 36 S 47 12 E
Fiherenana 135 18 29 S 48 24 E
Fiherenana → 135 23 19 S 43 37 E
Fiji ■ 106 17 20 S 179 0 E
Fika 127 11 15N 11 13 E
Filabres, Sierra de los 37 37 13N 2 20W
Filadelfia, Bolivia 172 11 20 S 68 46W
Filadélfia, Brazil 170 7 21 S 47 30W
Filadélfia, Italy 45 38 47N 16 17 E
Fil'akovo 31 48 17N 19 50 E
Filer 156 42 30N 114 35W
Filey 12 54 13N 0 18W
Filiaşi 50 44 32N 23 31 E
Filiátes 48 39 38N 20 16 E
Filiatrá 49 37 9N 21 35 E
Filicudi 45 38 35N 14 33 E
Filim 75 20 37N 58 12 E
Filiourí → 48 41 15N 25 40 E
Filipów 32 54 11N 22 37 E
Filipstad 52 59 43N 14 9 E
Filisur 29 46 41N 9 40 E
Fillmore, Canada 145 49 50N 103 25W
Fillmore, Calif., U.S.A. 159 34 23N 118 58W
Fillmore, Utah, U.S.A. 157 38 58N 112 20W
Filottrano 43 43 28N 13 20 E
Filyos 60 41 34N 32 4 E
Finale Lígure 42 44 10N 8 21 E
Finale nell' Emília 43 44 50N 11 18 E
Fiñana 37 37 10N 2 50W
Finch 151 45 11N 75 7W
Findhorn → 14 57 38N 3 38W
Findlay 155 41 0N 83 41W
Finger L. 145 53 33N 93 30W
Fíngõe 131 14 55 S 31 50 E
Finistère □ 18 48 20N 4 0W
Finisterre 34 42 54N 9 16W
Finisterre, C. 34 42 50N 9 19W
Finisterre Ra. 107 6 0 S 146 30 E
Finke 110 25 34 S 134 35 E
Finke → 111 27 0 S 136 10 E
Finland ■ 56 63 0N 27 0 E
Finland, G. of 55 60 0N 26 0 E
Finlay → 144 57 0N 125 10W
Finley, Australia 113 35 38 S 145 35 E
Finley, U.S.A. 152 47 35N 97 50W
Finn → 15 54 50N 7 55W
Finnigan, Mt. 110 15 49 S 145 17 E
Finniss 112 35 24 S 138 48 E
Finniss, C. 111 33 8 S 134 51 E
Finnmark fylke □ 54 69 30N 25 0 E
Finschhafen 107 6 33 S 147 50 E
Finse 51 60 36N 7 30 E
Finsteraarhorn 28 46 31N 8 10 E
Finsterwalde 26 51 37N 13 42 E
Finsterwolde 22 53 12N 7 6 E
Fiora → 43 42 20N 11 35 E
Fiordland National Park 115 45 0 S 167 50 E
Fiorenzuola d'Arda 42 44 56N 9 54 E
Fīq 69 32 46N 35 41 E
Fire River 142 48 47N 83 21W
Firebag → 145 57 45N 111 21W
Firebaugh 158 36 52N 120 27W
Firedrake L. 145 61 25N 104 30W
Firenze 43 43 47N 11 15 E
Firk → 72 30 59N 44 34 E
Firmi 20 44 33N 2 19 E
Firminy 21 45 23N 4 18 E
Firozabad 79 27 10N 78 25 E
Firozpur 78 30 55N 74 40 E
Fīrūzābād 73 28 52N 52 35 E
Fīrūzkūh 73 35 50N 52 50 E
Firvale 144 52 27N 126 13W
Fish →, Namibia 134 28 7 S 17 10 E
Fish →, S. Africa 134 31 30 S 20 16 E
Fisher 109 30 30 S 131 0 E
Fisher B. 145 51 35N 97 13W
Fishguard 13 51 59N 4 59W
Fishing L. 145 52 10N 95 24W
Fismes 19 49 20N 3 40 E
Fitchburg 151 42 35N 71 47W
Fitero 36 42 4N 1 52W
Fitjar 51 59 55N 5 17 E
Fitri, L. 123 12 50N 17 28 E
Fitz Roy 176 47 0 S 67 0W
Fitzgerald, Canada 144 59 51N 111 36W
Fitzgerald, U.S.A. 149 31 45N 83 16W
Fitzmaurice → 108 14 45 S 130 5 E
Fitzroy →, Queens., Australia 110 23 32 S 150 52 E
Fitzroy →, W. Austral., Australia 108 17 31 S 123 35 E
Fitzroy Crossing 108 18 9 S 125 38 E
Fitzwilliam I. 150 45 30N 81 45W
Fiume = Rijeka 43 45 20N 14 21 E
Fiumefreddo Brúzio 45 39 14N 16 4 E
Five Points 158 36 26N 120 6W
Fivizzano 42 44 12N 10 11 E
Fizi 130 4 17 S 28 55 E
Fjæra 51 59 52N 6 22 E
Fjellerup 53 56 29N 10 34 E
Fjerritslev 53 57 5N 9 15 E
Fkih ben Salah 120 32 32N 6 45W
Flå, Buskerud, Norway 51 60 25N 9 28 E
Flå, Sør-Trøndelag, Norway 51 63 13N 10 18 E
Flagler 152 39 20N 103 4W
Flagstaff 157 35 10N 111 40W
Flaherty I. 142 56 15N 79 15W
Flambeau → 152 45 18N 91 15W
Flamborough Hd. 12 54 8N 0 4W
Flaming Gorge Dam 156 40 50N 109 46W
Flaming Gorge Res. 156 41 15N 109 30W
Flamingo, Teluk 87 5 30 S 138 0 E
Flanagan 155 40 53N 88 52W
Flanders = West-Vlaanderen □ 23 51 0N 3 0 E
Flandre Occidentale □ = West-Vlaanderen □ 23 51 0N 3 0 E
Flandre Orientale □ = Oost-Vlaanderen □ 23 51 5N 3 50 E
Flandreau 152 44 5N 96 38W
Flanigan 158 40 10N 119 53W
Flåsjön 54 64 5N 15 40 E
Flat →, Canada 144 61 33N 125 18W
Flat →, U.S.A. 155 42 56N 85 20W
Flat River 153 37 50N 90 30W
Flat Rock, Ill., U.S.A. 155 38 54N 87 40W
Flat Rock, Mich., U.S.A. 155 42 4N 83 15W
Flatey, Barðastrandarsýsla, Iceland 54 66 10N 17 52W
Flatey, Suður-þingeyjarsýsla, Iceland 54 65 22N 22 56W
Flathead L. 156 47 50N 114 0W
Flatrock → 155 38 46N 86 10W
Flattery, C., Australia 110 14 58 S 145 21 E
Flattery, C., U.S.A. 158 48 21N 124 43W
Flavy-le-Martel 19 49 43N 3 12 E
Flawil 29 47 26N 9 11 E
Flaxton 152 48 52N 102 24W
Flechas Pt. 91 10 22N 119 34 E
Flèche, La 18 47 42N 0 4W
Fleetwood 12 53 55N 3 1W
Flekkefjord 51 58 18N 6 39 E
Flémalle 23 50 36N 5 28 E
Flemingsburg 155 38 25N 83 45W
Flemington 150 41 7N 77 28W
Flensborg Fjord 53 54 50N 9 40 E
Flensburg 26 54 46N 9 28 E
Flers 18 48 47N 0 33W
Flesherton 150 44 16N 80 33W
Flesko, Tanjung 87 0 29N 124 30 E
Fletton 13 52 34N 0 13W
Fleurance 20 43 52N 0 40 E
Fleurier 28 46 54N 6 35 E
Fleurus 23 50 29N 4 32 E
Flims 29 46 50N 9 17 E
Flin Flon 145 54 46N 101 53W
Flinders → 110 17 36 S 140 36 E
Flinders B. 109 34 19 S 115 19 E
Flinders Group 110 14 11 S 144 15 E
Flinders I. 110 40 0 S 148 0 E
Flinders Ranges 112 31 30 S 138 30 E
Flinders Reefs 110 17 37 S 148 31 E
Flint, U.K. 12 53 15N 3 7W
Flint, U.S.A. 142 43 5N 83 40W
Flint → 149 30 52N 84 38W
Flint, I. 105 11 26 S 151 48W
Flinton 111 27 55 S 149 32 E
Fliseryd 53 57 6N 16 15 E
Flix 36 41 14N 0 32 E
Flixecourt 19 50 0N 2 5 E
Flobecq 23 50 44N 3 45 E
Flodden 12 55 37N 2 8W
Floodwood 152 46 55N 92 55W
Flora, Norway 51 63 27N 11 22 E
Flora, Ill., U.S.A. 148 38 40N 88 30W
Flora, Ind., U.S.A. 155 40 33N 86 31W
Florac 20 44 20N 3 37 E
Florala 149 31 0N 86 20W
Florânia 170 6 8 S 36 49W
Floreffe 23 50 26N 4 46 E
Florence = Firenze 43 43 47N 11 15 E
Florence, Ala., U.S.A. 149 34 50N 87 40W
Florence, Ariz., U.S.A. 157 33 0N 111 25W
Florence, Colo., U.S.A. 152 38 26N 105 0W
Florence, Oreg., U.S.A. 156 44 0N 124 3W
Florence, S.C., U.S.A. 149 34 12N 79 44W
Florence, L. 111 28 53 S 138 9 E
Florennes 23 50 15N 4 35 E
Florensac 20 43 23N 3 28 E
Florenville 23 49 40N 5 19 E
Flores, Brazil 170 7 51 S 37 59W
Flores, Guat. 162 16 59N 89 50W
Flores, Indonesia 87 8 35 S 121 0 E
Flores I. 144 49 20N 126 10W
Flores Sea 86 6 30 S 124 0 E
Floresta 170 8 40 S 37 26W
Floresville 153 29 10N 98 10W
Floriano 170 6 50 S 43 0W
Florianópolis 175 27 30 S 48 30W
Florida, Cuba 162 21 32N 78 14W
Florida, Uruguay 175 34 7 S 56 10W
Florida □ 149 28 30N 82 0W
Florida, Straits of 162 25 0N 80 0W
Florida B. 162 25 0N 81 20W
Florida Keys 162 25 0N 80 40W
Florídia 45 37 6N 15 9 E
Floridsdorf 31 48 14N 16 22 E
Flórina 48 40 48N 21 26 E
Flórina □ 48 40 45N 21 20 E
Florissant 154 38 48N 90 20W
Florø 51 61 35N 5 1 E
Flower Sta. 151 45 10N 76 41W
Flower's Cove 143 51 14N 56 46W
Floydada 153 33 58N 101 18W
Fluk 87 1 42 S 127 44 E
Flumen → 36 41 43N 0 9W
Flumendosa → 44 39 26N 9 38 E
Fluminimaggiore 44 39 25N 8 30 E
Flushing = Vlissingen 23 51 26N 3 34 E
Flushing 155 43 4N 83 51W
Fluviá → 36 42 12N 3 7 E
Fly → 107 8 25 S 143 0 E
Flying Fish, C. 7 72 6 S 102 29W
Foam Lake 145 51 40N 103 32W
Foča 46 43 31N 18 47 E
Focşani 50 45 41N 27 15 E
Fogang 97 23 52N 113 30 E
Foggaret el Arab 121 27 13N 2 49 E
Foggaret ez Zoua 121 27 20N 2 53 E
Fóggia 45 41 28N 15 31 E
Foggo 127 11 21N 9 57 E
Foglia → 43 43 55N 12 54 E
Fogo 143 49 43N 54 17W
Fogo I. 143 49 40N 54 5W
Fohnsdorf 30 47 12N 14 40 E
Föhr 26 54 40N 8 30 E
Foia 35 37 19N 8 37W
Foix 20 42 58N 1 38 E
Fojnica 46 43 59N 17 51 E
Fokino 58 53 30N 34 22 E
Fokís □ 49 38 30N 22 15 E
Fokstua 51 62 7N 9 17 E
Folda, Nord-Trøndelag, Norway 54 64 41N 10 50 E
Folda, Nordland, Norway 54 67 38N 14 50 E
Földeák 31 46 19N 20 30 E
Folégandros 49 36 40N 24 55 E
Foleyet 142 48 15N 82 25W
Folgefonn 51 60 3N 6 23 E
Foligno 43 42 58N 12 40 E
Folkestone 13 51 5N 1 11 E
Folkston 149 30 55N 82 0W
Follett 153 36 30N 100 12W
Follette, La 149 36 23N 84 9W
Follónica 42 42 55N 10 45 E
Follónica, G. di 42 42 50N 10 40 E
Folsom Res. 158 38 42N 121 9W
Fond-du-Lac, Canada 145 59 19N 107 12W
Fond du Lac, U.S.A. 152 43 46N 88 26W
Fond-du-Lac → 145 59 17N 106 0W
Fonda, Iowa, U.S.A. 154 42 35N 94 51W
Fonda, N.Y., U.S.A. 151 42 57N 74 23W
Fondi 44 41 21N 13 25 E
Fonfría 34 41 37N 6 9W
Fongen 51 63 11N 11 38 E
Fonni 44 40 5N 9 16 E
Fonsagrada 34 43 8N 7 4W
Fonseca, G. de 162 13 10N 87 40W
Fontaine, La 155 40 40N 85 43W
Fontaine-Française 19 47 32N 5 21 E
Fontainebleau 19 48 24N 2 40 E
Fontana, L. 176 44 55 S 71 30W
Fontas → 144 58 14N 121 48W
Fonte Boa 168 2 33 S 66 0W
Fontem 127 5 32N 9 52 E
Fontenay-le-Comte 20 46 28N 0 48W
Fontur 54 66 23N 14 32W
Fonyód 31 46 44N 17 33 E
Foochow = Fuzhou 97 26 5N 119 16 E
Foping 94 33 41N 108 0 E
Foppiano 42 46 21N 8 24 E
Föra 53 57 1N 16 51 E
Forbach 19 49 10N 6 52 E
Forbes 113 33 22 S 148 0 E
Forbesganj 79 26 17N 87 18 E
Forcados 127 5 26N 5 26 E
Forcados → 127 5 25N 5 19 E
Forcall → 36 40 51N 0 16W
Forcalquier 21 43 58N 5 47 E
Forchheim 27 49 42N 11 4 E
Forclaz, Col de la 28 46 3N 7 1 E
Ford City, Calif., U.S.A. 159 35 10N 119 27W
Ford City, Pa., U.S.A. 150 40 47N 79 31W
Førde 51 61 27N 5 53 E
Ford's Bridge 111 29 41 S 145 29 E
Fordyce 153 33 50N 92 20W
Forécariah 126 9 28N 13 10W
Forel, Mt. 6 66 52N 36 55W
Foremost 144 49 26N 111 34W
Forenza 45 40 50N 15 50 E
Forest, Belgium 23 50 49N 4 20 E
Forest, Canada 150 43 6N 82 0W
Forest, U.S.A. 153 32 21N 89 27W
Forest City, Iowa, U.S.A. 152 43 12N 93 39W
Forest City, N.C., U.S.A. 149 35 23N 81 50W
Forest City, Pa., U.S.A. 151 41 39N 75 29W
Forest Grove 158 45 31N 123 4W
Forestburg 144 52 35N 112 1W
Foresthill 158 39 1N 120 49W
Forestier Pen. 110 43 0 S 148 0 E
Forestville, Canada 143 48 48N 69 2W
Forestville, Calif., U.S.A. 158 38 28N 122 54W
Forestville, Wis., U.S.A. 148 44 41N 87 29W
Forez, Mts. du 20 45 40N 3 50 E
Forfar 14 56 40N 2 53W
Forges-les-Eaux 19 49 37N 1 30 E
Forks 158 47 56N 124 23W
Forlì 43 44 14N 12 2 E
Forman 152 46 9N 97 43W
Formazza 42 46 23N 8 26 E
Formby Pt. 12 53 33N 3 7W
Formentera 37 38 43N 1 27 E
Formentor, C. de 36 39 58N 3 13 E
Fórmia 44 41 15N 13 34 E
Formiga 171 20 27 S 45 25W
Formigine 42 44 37N 10 51 E
Formiguères 20 42 37N 2 5 E
Formosa = Taiwan ■ 97 23 30N 121 0 E
Formosa, Argentina 174 26 15 S 58 10W
Formosa, Brazil 171 15 32 S 47 20W
Formosa □ 174 25 0 S 60 0W
Formosa, Serra 173 12 0 S 55 0W
Formosa Bay 130 2 40 S 40 20 E
Formoso → 171 10 34 S 49 56W
Fornells 36 40 3N 4 7 E
Fornos de Algodres 34 40 38N 7 32W
Fornovo di Taro 42 44 42N 10 7 E
Føroyar 8 62 0N 7 0W
Forres 14 57 37N 3 38W
Forrest, Vic., Australia 112 38 33 S 143 47 E
Forrest, W. Austral., Australia 109 30 51 S 128 6 E
Forrest, Mt. 109 24 48 S 127 45 E
Forrest City 153 35 0N 90 50W
Forreston 154 42 8N 89 35W
Forrières 23 50 8N 5 17 E
Fors 52 60 14N 16 20 E
Forsa 52 61 44N 16 55 E
Forsand 51 58 54N 6 5 E
Forsayth 110 18 33 S 143 34 E
Forserum 53 57 42N 14 30 E
Forshaga 52 59 33N 13 29 E
Forskacka 52 60 39N 16 54 E
Forsmo 52 63 16N 17 11 E
Forst 26 51 43N 14 37 E
Forster 111 32 12 S 152 31 E
Forsyth, Ga., U.S.A. 149 33 4N 83 55W
Forsyth, Mont., U.S.A. 156 46 14N 106 37W
Forsyth I. 115 40 58 S 174 5 E
Fort Albany 142 52 15N 81 35W
Fort Apache 157 33 50N 110 0W
Fort Assiniboine 144 54 20N 114 45W
Fort Atkinson 155 42 56N 88 50W
Fort Augustus 14 57 9N 4 40W
Fort Beaufort 134 32 46 S 26 40 E
Fort Benton 156 47 50N 110 40W
Fort Bragg 156 39 28N 123 50W
Fort Bridger 156 41 22N 110 20W
Fort Chipewyan 145 58 42N 111 8W
Fort Collins 152 40 30N 105 4W
Fort-Coulonge 142 45 50N 76 45W
Fort Davis 153 30 38N 103 53W
Fort-de-France 163 14 36N 61 2W
Fort de Possel = Possel 132 5 5N 19 10 E
Fort Defiance 157 35 47N 109 4W
Fort Dodge 152 42 29N 94 10W
Fort Edward 151 43 16N 73 35W
Fort Frances 145 48 36N 93 24W
Fort Franklin 140 65 10N 123 30W
Fort Garland 157 37 28N 105 30W
Fort George 142 53 50N 79 0W
Fort Good-Hope 140 66 14N 128 40W
Fort Hancock 157 31 19N 105 56W
Fort Hertz = Putao 82 27 28N 97 30 E
Fort Hope 142 51 30N 88 0W
Fort Irwin 159 35 16N 116 34W
Fort Jameson = Chipata 131 13 38 S 32 28 E
Fort Kent 143 47 12N 68 30W

Gardanne

Fuding 97 27 20N 120 12 E
Fuencaliente, Canary Is. 37 28 28N 17 50W
Fuencaliente, Spain 35 38 25N 4 18W
Fuencaliente, Pta. 37 28 27N 17 51W
Fuengirola 35 36 32N 4 41W
Fuente Alamo, Albacete, Spain 37 38 44N 1 24W
Fuente Álamo, Murcia, Spain 37 37 42N 1 6W
Fuente de Cantos 35 38 15N 6 18W
Fuente de San Esteban, La 34 40 49N 6 15W
Fuente del Maestre 35 38 31N 6 28W
Fuente el Fresno 35 39 14N 3 46W
Fuente Ovejuna 35 38 15N 5 25W
Fuentes de Andalucía 35 37 28N 5 20W
Fuentes de Ebro 36 41 31N 0 38W
Fuentes de León 35 38 5N 6 32W
Fuentes de Oñoro 34 40 33N 6 52W
Fuentesaúco 34 41 15N 5 30W
Fuerte → 160 25 50N 109 25W
Fuerte Olimpo 174 21 0 S 57 51W
Fuerteventura 37 28 30N 14 0W
Fufeng 94 34 22N 108 0 E
Fuga I. 90 18 52N 121 20 E
Fughmah 75 16 9N 49 26 E
Fugløysund 54 70 15N 20 20 E
Fugong 96 27 5N 98 47 E
Fugou 94 34 3N 114 25 E
Fugu 94 39 2N 111 3 E
Fuhai 92 47 2N 87 25 E
Fuḩaymī 72 34 16N 42 10 E
Fuji 101 35 9N 138 39 E
Fuji-no-miya 101 35 10N 138 40 E
Fuji-San 101 35 22N 138 44 E
Fuji-yoshida 101 35 30N 138 46 E
Fujian □ 97 26 0N 118 0 E
Fujieda 101 34 52N 138 16 E
Fujioka 101 36 15N 139 5 E
Fujisawa 101 35 22N 139 29 E
Fukaya 101 36 12N 139 12 E
Fukien = Fujian □ 97 26 0N 118 0 E
Fukuchiyama 101 35 19N 135 9 E
Fukue-Shima 99 32 40N 128 45 E
Fukui 101 36 0N 136 10 E
Fukui □ 101 36 0N 136 12 E
Fukuma 100 33 46N 130 28 E
Fukuoka 100 33 39N 130 21 E
Fukuoka □ 100 33 30N 131 0 E
Fukuroi 101 34 45N 137 55 E
Fukushima 98 37 44N 140 28 E
Fukushima □ 98 37 30N 140 15 E
Fukuyama 100 34 35N 133 20 E
Fulda 26 50 32N 9 41 E
Fulda → 26 51 27N 9 40 E
Fuling 96 29 40N 107 20 E
Fullerton, Calif., U.S.A. 159 33 52N 117 58W
Fullerton, Nebr., U.S.A. 152 41 25N 98 0W
Fulongquan 95 44 20N 124 42 E
Fulton, Ill., U.S.A. 154 41 52N 90 11W
Fulton, Ind., U.S.A. 155 40 57N 86 16W
Fulton, Mo., U.S.A. 154 38 50N 91 55W
Fulton, N.Y., U.S.A. 151 43 20N 76 22W
Fulton, Tenn., U.S.A. 149 36 31N 88 53W
Fuluälven 52 61 18N 13 4 E
Fulufjället 52 61 32N 12 41 E
Fumay 19 50 0N 4 40 E
Fumel 20 44 30N 0 58 E
Fumin 96 25 10N 102 20 E
Funabashi 101 35 45N 140 0 E
Funafuti 104 8 30 S 179 0 E
Fundación 168 10 31N 74 11W
Fundão, Brazil 171 19 55 S 40 24W
Fundão, Portugal 34 40 8N 7 30W
Fundy, B. of 143 45 0N 66 0W
Funing, Hebei, China 95 39 53N 119 12 E
Funing, Jiangsu, China 95 33 45N 119 50 E
Funing, Yunnan, China 96 23 35N 105 45 E
Funiu Shan 94 33 30N 112 20 E
Funsi 126 10 21N 1 54W
Funtua 127 11 30N 7 18 E
Fuping, Hebei, China 94 38 48N 114 12 E
Fuping, Shaanxi, China 94 34 42N 109 10 E
Fuqing 97 25 41N 119 21 E
Fuquan 96 26 40N 107 27 E
Fur 53 56 50N 9 0 E
Furano 98 43 21N 142 23 E
Furāt, Nahr al → 72 31 0N 47 25 E
Fūrg 73 28 18N 55 13 E
Furkapass 29 46 34N 8 35 E
Furmanov 59 57 10N 41 9 E
Furmanovka 63 44 17N 72 57 E
Furmanovo 61 49 42N 49 25 E
Furnas, Reprêsa de 171 20 50 S 45 0W
Furneaux Group 110 40 10 S 147 50 E
Furness 12 54 12N 3 10W
Furqlus 70 34 36N 37 8 E
Fürstenau 26 52 32N 7 40 E
Fürstenberg 26 53 11N 13 9 E
Fürstenfeld 30 47 3N 16 3 E
Fürstenfeldbruck 27 48 10N 11 15 E
Fürstenwalde 26 52 20N 14 3 E
Fürth 27 49 29N 11 0 E
Furth im Wald 27 49 19N 12 51 E
Furtwangen 27 48 3N 8 14 E
Furudal 52 61 10N 15 11 E
Furukawa 101 38 34N 140 58 E
Furusund 52 59 40N 18 55 E
Fury and Hecla Str. 141 69 56N 84 0W
Fusa 51 60 12N 5 37 E
Fusagasuga 168 4 21N 74 22W
Fuscaldo 45 39 25N 16 1 E
Fushan, Shandong, China 95 37 30N 121 15 E
Fushan, Shanxi, China 94 35 58N 111 51 E
Fushë Arrëzi 48 42 4N 20 2 E
Fushun, Liaoning, China 95 41 50N 123 56 E
Fushun, Sichuan, China 96 29 13N 104 52 E
Fusio 29 46 27N 8 40 E
Fusong 95 42 20N 127 15 E
Füssen 27 47 35N 10 43 E
Fusui 96 22 40N 107 56 E
Futago-Yama 100 33 35N 131 36 E
Futrono 176 40 8 S 72 24W
Futuna 104 14 25 S 178 20 E
Fuwa 124 31 12N 30 33 E
Fuxin 95 42 5N 121 48 E
Fuyang, Anhui, China 94 33 0N 115 48 E
Fuyang, Zhejiang, China 97 30 5N 119 57 E
Fuyang He → 94 38 12N 117 0 E
Fuying Dao 97 26 34N 120 9 E
Fuyu 95 45 12N 124 43 E
Fuyuan 96 25 40N 104 16 E
Füzesgyarmat 31 47 6N 21 14 E
Fuzhou 97 26 5N 119 16 E
Fylde 12 53 50N 2 58W
Fyn 53 55 20N 10 30 E
Fyne, L. 14 56 0N 5 20W
Fyns Amtskommune □ 53 55 15N 10 30 E
Fyresvatn 51 59 6N 8 10 E

G

Gaanda 127 10 10N 12 27 E
Gabarin 127 11 8N 10 27 E
Gabas → 20 43 46N 0 42W
Gabela 133 11 0 S 14 24 E
Gabès 121 33 53N 10 2 E
Gabès, G. de 121 34 0N 10 30 E
Gabgaba, W. → 124 22 10N 33 5 E
Gabin 32 52 23N 19 41 E
Gabon ■ 132 0 10 S 10 0 E
Gaborone 134 24 45 S 25 57 E
Gabriels 151 44 26N 74 12W
Gābrīk 73 25 44N 58 28 E
Gabro 136 6 18N 43 16 E
Gabrovo 47 42 52N 25 19 E
Gacé 18 48 49N 0 20 E
Gāch Sār 73 36 7N 51 19 E
Gachsārān 73 30 15N 50 45 E
Gacko 46 43 10N 18 33 E
Gadag 81 15 30N 75 45 E
Gadamai 125 17 11N 36 10 E
Gadap 78 25 5N 67 28 E
Gadarwara 79 22 50N 78 50 E
Gadebusch 26 53 41N 11 6 E
Gadein 125 8 10N 28 45 E
Gadhada 78 22 0N 71 35 E
Gadmen 29 46 45N 8 16 E
Gádor, Sierra de 37 36 57N 2 45W
Gadsden, Ala., U.S.A. 149 34 1N 86 0W
Gadsden, Ariz., U.S.A. 157 32 35N 114 47W
Gadwal 81 16 10N 77 50 E
Gadyach 58 50 21N 34 0 E
Gadzi 132 4 47N 16 42 E
Găeşti 50 44 48N 25 19 E
Gaeta 44 41 12N 13 35 E
Gaeta, G. di 44 41 0N 13 25 E
Gaffney 149 35 3N 81 40W
Gafsa 121 34 24N 8 43 E
Gagarin 58 55 38N 35 0 E
Gagetown 143 45 46N 66 10W
Gagil-Tomil, I. 106 9 31N 138 12 E
Gagino 59 55 15N 45 1 E
Gagliano del Capo 45 39 50N 18 23 E
Gagnef 52 60 36N 15 5 E
Gagnoa 126 6 56N 5 16W
Gagnon 143 51 50N 68 5W
Gagnon, L. 145 62 3N 110 27W
Gagra 61 43 20N 40 10 E
Gahini 130 1 50 S 30 30 E
Gahmar 79 25 27N 83 49 E
Gai Xian 95 40 22N 122 20 E
Gaibanda 82 25 20N 89 36 E
Gaïdhouronísi 49 34 53N 25 41 E
Gail 153 32 48N 101 25W
Gail → 30 46 36N 13 53 E
Gaillac 20 43 54N 1 54 E
Gaillon 18 49 10N 1 20 E
Gaima 107 8 20 S 142 59 E
Gaimán 176 43 10 S 65 25W
Gaines 150 41 46N 77 35W
Gainesville, Fla., U.S.A. 149 29 38N 82 20W
Gainesville, Ga., U.S.A. 149 34 17N 83 47W
Gainesville, Mo., U.S.A. 153 36 35N 92 26W
Gainesville, Tex., U.S.A. 153 33 40N 97 10W
Gainsborough 12 53 23N 0 46W
Gairdner L. 112 31 30 S 136 0 E
Gairloch, L. 14 57 43N 5 45W
Gais 29 47 22N 9 27 E
Gaj 46 45 28N 17 3 E
Gakuch 79 36 7N 73 45 E
Gal Laghet 136 4 9N 47 10 E
Gal Oya Res. 81 7 5N 81 30 E
Gal Tardo 136 3 34N 45 58 E
Galachipa 82 22 8N 90 26 E
Galán, Cerro 174 25 55 S 66 52W
Galana → 130 3 9 S 40 8 E
Galangue 133 13 42 S 16 9 E
Galangue, Serra 133 14 18 S 15 52 E
Galanta 31 48 11N 17 45 E
Galápagos 105 0 0 89 0W
Galashiels 14 55 37N 2 50W
Galatás 49 37 30N 23 26 E
Galatea 114 38 24 S 176 45 E
Galaţi 50 45 27N 28 2 E
Galaţi □ 50 45 45N 27 30 E
Galatina 45 40 10N 18 10 E
Galátone 45 40 8N 18 3 E
Galax 149 36 42N 80 57W
Galaxídhion 49 38 22N 22 23 E
Galbraith 110 16 25 S 141 30 E
Galcaio 68 6 30N 47 30 E
Galdhøpiggen 51 61 38N 8 18 E
Galeana 160 24 50N 100 4W
Galela 87 1 50N 127 49 E
Galena 154 42 25N 90 26W
Galera 37 37 45N 2 33W
Galera, Pta. 176 39 59 S 73 43W
Galera Point 163 10 8N 61 0W
Galesburg, Ill., U.S.A. 154 40 57N 90 23W
Galesburg, Mich., U.S.A. 155 42 17N 85 26W
Galeton 150 41 43N 77 40W
Galgasc 136 0 11N 41 38 E
Galheirâo → 171 12 23 S 45 5W
Galheiros 171 13 18 S 46 25W
Gali 61 42 37N 41 46 E
Galicea Mare 50 44 4N 23 19 E
Galich 59 58 23N 42 12 E
Galiche 47 43 34N 23 50 E
Galicia □ 34 42 43N 7 45W
Galien 155 41 48N 86 30W
Galilee = Hagalil 69 32 53N 35 18 E
Galilee, L. 110 22 20 S 145 50 E
Galilee, Sea of = Yam Kinneret 69 32 45N 35 35 E
Galion 150 40 43N 82 48W
Galite, Is. de la 121 37 30N 8 59 E
Galiuro Mts. 157 32 40N 110 30W
Gallabat 125 12 58N 36 11 E
Gallardon 19 48 32N 1 42 E
Gallarte 42 45 40N 8 48 E
Gallatin, Mo., U.S.A. 154 39 55N 93 58W
Gallatin, Tenn., U.S.A. 149 36 24N 86 27W
Galle 81 6 5N 80 10 E
Gállego → 36 41 39N 0 51W
Gallegos → 176 51 35 S 69 0W
Galley Hd. 15 51 32N 8 56W
Galliate 42 45 27N 8 44 E
Gallinas, Pta. 168 12 28N 71 40W
Gallipoli = Gelibolu 48 40 28N 26 43 E
Gallípoli 45 40 8N 18 0 E
Gallipolis 148 38 50N 82 10W
Gällivare 54 67 9N 20 40 E
Gallo, C. 44 38 13N 13 19 E
Gallocanta, L. de 36 40 58N 1 30W
Galloway 14 55 0N 4 25W
Galloway, Mull of 14 54 38N 4 50W
Gallup 157 35 30N 108 45W
Gallur 36 41 52N 1 19W
Gallyaaral 63 40 2N 67 35 E
Gal'on 69 31 38N 34 51 E
Galong 113 34 37 S 148 34 E
Galt, Calif., U.S.A. 158 38 15N 121 18W
Galt, Mo., U.S.A. 154 40 8N 93 23W
Galtström 52 62 10N 17 30 E
Galtür 30 46 58N 10 11 E
Galty Mts. 15 52 22N 8 10W
Galtymore 15 52 22N 8 12W
Galva 154 41 10N 90 0W
Galvarino 176 38 24 S 72 47W
Galve de Sorbe 36 41 13N 3 10W
Galveston, Ind., U.S.A. 155 40 35N 86 11W
Galveston, Tex., U.S.A. 153 29 15N 94 48W
Galveston B. 153 29 30N 94 50W
Gálvez, Argentina 174 32 0 S 61 14W
Gálvez, Spain 35 39 42N 4 16W
Galway 15 53 16N 9 4W
Galway □ 15 53 16N 9 3W
Galway B. 15 53 10N 9 20W
Gam → 84 21 55N 105 12 E
Gamagori 101 34 50N 137 14 E
Gamari, L. 125 11 32N 41 40 E
Gamawa 127 12 10N 10 31 E
Gamay 90 12 23N 125 18 E
Gamay Bay 90 12 21N 125 21 E
Gamba 133 11 42 S 17 14 E
Gambaga 127 10 30N 0 28W
Gambat 78 27 17N 68 26 E
Gambela 125 8 14N 34 38 E
Gambia ■ 126 13 25N 16 0W
Gambia → 126 13 28N 16 34W
Gambier, C. 108 11 56 S 130 57 E
Gambier Is. 112 35 3 S 136 30 E
Gambo 132 4 39N 22 16 E
Gamboli 78 29 53N 68 24 E
Gamboma 132 1 55 S 15 52 E
Gamboula 132 4 8N 15 9 E
Gamerco 157 35 33N 108 56W
Gamlakarleby = Kokkola 54 63 50N 23 8 E
Gammon → 145 51 24N 95 44W
Gammouda 121 35 3N 9 39 E
Gamoda-Saki 100 33 50N 134 45 E
Gamu-Gofa □ 125 5 40N 36 40 E
Gan 20 43 12N 0 27W
Gan Gan 176 42 30 S 68 10W
Gan Goriama, Mts. 127 7 44N 12 45 E
Gan Jiang → 97 29 15N 116 0 E
Gan Shemu'el 69 32 28N 34 56 E
Gan Yavne 69 31 48N 34 42 E
Ganado, Ariz., U.S.A. 157 35 46N 109 41W
Ganado, Tex., U.S.A. 153 29 4N 96 31W
Gananoque 142 44 20N 76 10W
Ganaveh 73 29 35N 50 35 E
Gand = Gent 23 51 2N 3 42 E
Ganda 133 13 3 S 14 35 E
Gandak → 79 25 39N 85 13 E
Gandara 90 12 1N 124 49 E
Gandava 77 28 32N 67 32 E
Gander 143 48 58N 54 35W
Gander L. 143 48 58N 54 35W
Ganderowe Falls 131 17 20 S 29 10 E
Gandesa 36 41 3N 0 26 E
Gandhi Sagar 78 24 40N 75 40 E
Gandi 127 12 55N 5 49 E
Gandía 37 38 58N 0 9W
Gandino 42 45 50N 9 52 E
Gando, Pta. 37 27 55N 15 22W
Gandole 127 8 28N 11 35 E
Gandu 171 13 45 S 39 30W
Ganedidalem = Gani 87 0 48 S 128 14 E
Ganetti 124 18 0N 31 10 E
Ganga → 79 23 20N 90 30 E
Ganga, Mouths of the 79 21 30N 90 0 E
Ganganagar 78 29 56N 73 56 E
Gangapur 78 26 32N 76 49 E
Gangara 127 14 35N 8 29 E
Gangaw 82 22 5N 94 5 E
Gangawati 81 15 30N 76 36 E
Gangdisê Shan 79 31 20N 81 0 E
Ganges = Ganga → 79 23 20N 90 30 E
Ganges 20 43 56N 3 42 E
Gangoh 78 29 46N 77 18 E
Gangtok 82 27 20N 88 37 E
Gangu 94 34 40N 105 15 E
Gangyao 95 44 12N 126 37 E
Gani 87 0 48 S 128 14 E
Ganj 79 27 45N 78 57 E
Gannat 20 46 7N 3 11 E
Gannett Pk. 156 43 15N 109 38W
Gannvalley 152 44 3N 98 57W
Ganquan 94 36 20N 109 20 E
Gänserdorf 31 48 20N 16 43 E
Ganshui 96 28 40N 106 40 E
Gansu □ 94 36 0N 104 0 E
Ganta 126 7 15N 8 59W
Gantheaume, C. 112 36 4 S 137 32 E
Gantheaume B. 109 27 40 S 114 10 E
Gantsevichi 58 52 49N 26 30 E
Ganyem 87 2 46 S 140 12 E
Ganyu 95 34 50N 119 8 E
Ganyushkino 61 46 35N 49 20 E
Ganzhou 97 25 51N 114 56 E
Gao □ 127 18 0N 1 0 E
Gao Xian 96 28 21N 104 32 E
Gao'an 97 28 26N 115 17 E
Gaohe 97 22 46N 112 57 E
Gaohebu 97 30 43N 116 49 E
Gaokeng 97 27 40N 113 58 E
Gaolan Dao 97 21 55N 113 10 E
Gaoligong Shan 96 24 45N 98 45 E
Gaomi 95 36 20N 119 42 E
Gaoping 94 35 45N 112 55 E
Gaotang 94 36 50N 116 15 E
Gaoua 126 10 20N 3 8W
Gaoual 126 11 45N 13 25W
Gaoxiong 97 22 38N 120 18 E
Gaoyang 94 38 40N 115 45 E
Gaoyou 97 32 47N 119 26 E
Gaoyou Hu 95 32 45N 119 20 E
Gaoyuan 95 37 8N 117 58 E
Gaozhou 97 21 58N 110 50 E
Gap 21 44 33N 6 5 E
Gapan 90 15 19N 120 57 E
Gar 92 32 10N 79 58 E
Garachiné 162 8 0N 78 12W
Garad 136 6 57N 49 24 E
Garafia 37 28 48N 17 57W
Garajonay 37 28 7N 17 14W
Garanhuns 170 8 50 S 36 30W
Garawe 126 4 35N 8 0W
Garba Harre 136 3 19N 42 13 E
Garba Tula 130 0 30N 38 32 E
Garbagududu 136 6 12N 43 50 E
Garber 153 36 30N 97 36W
Garberville 156 40 11N 123 50W
Garça 171 22 14 S 49 37W
Garças →, Mato Grosso, Brazil 173 15 54 S 52 16W
Garças →, Pernambuco, Brazil 170 8 43 S 39 41W
Garchitorena 90 13 52N 123 40 E
Garcia Hernandez 91 9 37N 124 18 E
Garcias 173 20 34 S 52 13W
Gard 136 9 30N 49 6 E
Gard □ 21 44 2N 4 10 E
Gard → 21 43 51N 4 37 E
Garda, L. di 42 45 40N 10 40 E
Gardanne 21 43 27N 5 27 E

Hamer Koke

Gumlu **110** 19 53 S 147 41 E
Gumma □ **101** 36 30N 138 20 E
Gummersbach **26** 51 2N 7 32 E
Gummi **127** 12 4N 5 9 E
Gümüşhaciköy **60** 40 50N 35 18 E
Gumzai **87** 5 28 S 134 42 E
Guna **78** 24 40N 77 19 E
Guna Mt. **125** 11 50N 37 40 E
Gundagai **113** 35 3 S 148 6 E
Gundelfingen **27** 48 33N 10 22 E
Gundih **89** 7 10 S 110 56 E
Gundlakamma → **81** 15 30N 80 15 E
Gunebang **113** 33 1 S 146 38 E
Güney **70** 36 40N 31 52 E
Gungal **113** 32 17 S 150 32 E
Gungu **133** 5 43 S 19 20 E
Gunisao → **145** 53 56N 97 53W
Gunisao L. **145** 53 33N 96 15W
Gunnedah **111** 30 59 S 150 15 E
Gunniguldrie **113** 33 12 S 146 8 E
Gunningbar Cr. → **113** 31 14 S 147 6 E
Gunnison, Colo., U.S.A. **157** 38 32N 106 56W
Gunnison, Utah, U.S.A. **156** 39 11N 111 48W
Gunnison → **157** 39 3N 108 30W
Guntakal **81** 15 11N 77 27 E
Guntersville **149** 34 18N 86 16W
Guntong **85** 4 36N 101 3 E
Guntur **81** 16 23N 80 30 E
Gunungapi **87** 6 45 S 126 30 E
Gunungsitoli **88** 1 15N 97 30 E
Gunupur **80** 19 5N 83 50 E
Günz → **27** 48 27N 10 16 E
Gunza **133** 10 50 S 13 50 E
Günzburg **27** 48 27N 10 16 E
Gunzenhausen **27** 49 6N 10 45 E
Guo He → **95** 32 59N 117 10 E
Guoyang **94** 33 32N 116 12 E
Gupis **79** 36 15N 73 20 E
Gura Humorului **50** 47 35N 25 53 E
Gura-Teghii **50** 45 30N 26 25 E
Gurag **125** 8 20N 38 20 E
Gurdaspur **78** 32 5N 75 31 E
Gurdon **153** 33 55N 93 10W
Gurdzhaani **61** 41 43N 45 52 E
Gurgaon **78** 28 27N 77 1 E
Gurghiu, Munţii **50** 46 41N 25 15 E
Gurguéia → **170** 6 50 S 43 24W
Gurha **78** 25 12N 71 39 E
Guri Dam **169** 7 50N 62 52W
Gurk → **30** 46 35N 14 31 E
Gurkha **79** 28 5N 84 40 E
Gurley **111** 29 45 S 149 48 E
Gurnee **155** 42 22N 87 55W
Gurué **131** 15 25 S 36 58 E
Gurun **85** 5 49N 100 27 E
Gurupá **170** 1 25 S 51 35W
Gurupá, I. Grande de **169** 1 25 S 51 45W
Gurupi **171** 11 43 S 49 4W
Gurupi → **170** 1 13 S 46 6W
Gurupi, Serra do **170** 5 0 S 47 30W
Guryev **61** 47 5N 52 0 E
Gus-Khrustalnyy **59** 55 42N 40 44 E
Gusau **127** 12 12N 6 40 E
Gusev **58** 54 35N 22 10 E
Gushan **95** 39 50N 123 35 E
Gushi **97** 32 11N 115 41 E
Gushiago **127** 9 55N 0 15W
Gushikawa **106** 26 22N 127 52 E
Gusinje **46** 42 35N 19 50 E
Gúspini **44** 39 32N 8 38 E
Gusselby **52** 59 38N 15 14 E
Güssing **31** 47 3N 16 20 E
Gustanj **43** 46 36N 14 49 E
Gustine **158** 37 14N 121 0W
Güstrow **26** 53 47N 12 12 E
Gusum **53** 58 16N 16 30 E
Guta = Kalárovo **31** 47 54N 18 0 E
Gütersloh **26** 51 54N 8 25 E
Gutha **109** 28 58 S 115 55 E
Guthalongra **110** 19 52 S 147 50 E
Guthrie **153** 35 55N 97 30W
Guthrie Center **154** 41 41N 94 30W
Gutian **97** 26 32N 118 43 E
Gutiérrez **173** 19 25 S 63 34W
Guttannen **29** 46 38N 8 18 E
Guttenberg **154** 42 46N 91 10W
Guyana ■ **172** 5 0N 59 0W
Guyang **94** 41 0N 110 5 E
Guyenne **20** 44 30N 0 40 E
Guymon **153** 36 45N 101 30W
Guyra **111** 30 15 S 151 40 E
Guyuan, Hebei, China **94** 41 37N 115 40 E
Guyuan, Ningxia Huizu, China **94** 36 0N 106 20 E
Guzar **63** 38 36N 66 15 E
Guzhang **96** 28 42N 109 58 E
Guzhen **95** 33 22N 117 18 E
Guzmán, L. de **160** 31 25N 107 25W
Gwa **82** 17 36N 94 34 E
Gwaai **131** 19 15 S 27 45 E
Gwabegar **111** 30 31 S 149 0 E
Gwadabawa **127** 13 28N 5 15 E
Gwādar **77** 25 10N 62 18 E
Gwagwada **127** 10 15N 7 15 E
Gwalia **109** 28 54 S 121 20 E
Gwalior **78** 26 12N 78 10 E
Gwanda **131** 20 55 S 29 0 E
Gwandu **127** 12 30N 4 41 E
Gwane **130** 4 45N 25 48 E
Gwaram **127** 10 15N 10 25 E
Gwarzo **127** 12 20N 8 55 E
Gwda → **32** 53 3N 16 44 E
Gweebarra B. **15** 54 52N 8 21W
Gweedore **15** 55 4N 8 15W
Gwent □ **13** 51 45N 2 55W
Gweru **131** 19 28 S 29 45 E
Gwi **127** 9 0N 7 10 E
Gwinn **148** 46 15N 87 29W
Gwio Kura **127** 12 40N 11 2 E
Gwol **126** 10 58N 1 59W
Gwoza **127** 11 5N 13 40 E
Gwydir → **111** 29 27 S 149 48 E
Gwynedd □ **12** 53 0N 4 0W
Gyaring Hu **92** 34 50N 97 40 E
Gydanskiy P-ov. **64** 70 0N 78 0 E
Gyland **51** 58 24N 6 45 E
Gympie **111** 26 11 S 152 38 E
Gyobingauk **82** 18 13N 95 39 E
Gyoda **101** 36 10N 139 30 E
Gyoma **31** 46 56N 20 50 E
Gyöngyös **31** 47 48N 19 56 E
Györ **31** 47 41N 17 40 E
Györ-Sopron □ **31** 47 40N 17 20 E
Gypsum Palace **112** 32 37 S 144 9 E
Gypsum Pt. **144** 61 53N 114 35W
Gypsumville **145** 51 45N 98 40W
Gyttorp **52** 59 31N 14 58 E
Gyula **31** 46 38N 21 17 E
Gzhatsk = Gagarin **58** 55 38N 35 0 E

H

Ha 'Arava → **69** 30 50N 35 20 E
Ha Coi **84** 21 26N 107 46 E
Ha Dong **84** 20 58N 105 46 E
Ha Giang **84** 22 50N 104 59 E
Ha Tien **85** 10 23N 104 29 E
Ha Tinh **84** 18 20N 105 54 E
Ha Trung **84** 20 0N 105 50 E
Haacht **23** 50 59N 4 37 E
Haag **27** 48 11N 12 12 E
Haaksbergen **22** 52 9N 6 45 E
Haaltert **23** 50 55N 4 1 E
Haamstede **23** 51 42N 3 45 E
Haapamäki **54** 62 18N 24 28 E
Haapsalu **58** 58 56N 23 30 E
Haarlem **22** 52 23N 4 39 E
Haast **115** 43 51 S 169 1 E
Haast → **115** 43 50 S 169 2 E
Haast P. **115** 44 6 S 169 21 E
Haastrecht **22** 52 0N 4 47 E
Hab Nadi Chauki **78** 25 0N 66 50 E
Habana, La **162** 23 8N 82 22W
Ḩabarūt **75** 17 18N 52 44 E
Habaswein **130** 1 2N 39 30 E
Ḩabawnah, W. → **74** 17 57N 44 58 E
Habay **144** 58 50N 118 44W
Habay-la-Neuve **23** 49 44N 5 38 E
Ḩabbān **74** 14 21N 47 5 E
Habbānīyah **72** 33 17N 43 29 E
Habiganj **82** 24 24N 91 30 E
Hablingbo **53** 57 12N 18 16 E
Habo **53** 57 55N 14 6 E
Haboro **98** 44 22N 141 42 E
Haccourt **23** 50 44N 5 40 E
Hachenburg **26** 50 40N 7 49 E
Hachijō-Jima **101** 33 5N 139 45 E
Hachinohe **98** 40 30N 141 29 E
Hachiōji **101** 35 40N 139 20 E
Hachōn **95** 41 29N 129 2 E
Hachy **23** 49 42N 5 41 E
Hacıushaklı **70** 36 12N 33 39 E
Hackensack **151** 40 53N 74 3W
Hadali **78** 32 16N 72 11 E
Hadarba, Ras **124** 22 4N 36 51 E
Hadarom □ **71** 31 0N 35 0 E
Ḩaḑbaram **75** 17 27N 55 15 E
Hadd, Ras al **75** 22 35N 59 50 E
Ḩaddā **74** 21 27N 39 34 E
Haddington **14** 55 57N 2 48W
Haddon Rig **113** 31 27 S 147 52 E
Haded Plain **136** 9 46N 48 2 E
Hadejia **127** 12 30N 10 5 E
Hadejia → **127** 12 50N 10 51 E
Haden **111** 27 13 S 151 54 E
Ḩadera **69** 32 27N 34 55 E
Ḩadera, N. → **69** 32 28N 34 52 E
Haderslev **53** 55 15N 9 30 E
Hadházteglas **31** 47 40N 21 40 E
Hadhramaut = Haḑramawt **75** 15 30N 49 30 E
Hadım **70** 36 58N 32 26 E
Hadjeb El Aïoun **121** 35 21N 9 32 E
Hadong **95** 35 5N 127 44 E
Haḑramawt **75** 15 30N 49 30 E
Ḩaḑramawt, W. → **75** 16 0N 48 53 E
Ḩadrānīyah **72** 35 38N 43 14 E
Hadrians Wall **12** 55 0N 2 30W
Hadsten **53** 56 19N 10 3 E
Hadsund **53** 56 44N 10 8 E
Haeju **95** 38 3N 125 45 E
Haenam **95** 34 34N 126 35 E
Haerhpin = Harbin **95** 45 48N 126 40 E
Hafar al Bāţin **72** 28 25N 46 0 E
Ḩafīrat al 'Aydā **72** 26 26N 39 12 E
Ḩafit **75** 23 59N 55 49 E
Hafizabad **78** 32 5N 73 40 E
Haflong **82** 25 10N 93 5 E
Hafnarfjörður **54** 64 4N 21 57W
Hafun, Ras **68** 10 29N 51 30 E
Hagalil **69** 32 53N 35 18 E
Hagari → **81** 15 40N 77 0 E
Hagdan **91** 11 20N 123 54 E
Hagen **26** 51 21N 7 29 E
Hagenow **26** 53 25N 11 10 E
Hagerman **153** 33 5N 104 22W
Hagerstown, Ind., U.S.A. **155** 39 55N 85 10W
Hagerstown, Md., U.S.A. **148** 39 39N 77 46W
Hagetmau **20** 43 39N 0 37W
Hagfors **52** 60 3N 13 45 E
Häggenås **52** 63 24N 14 55 E
Hagi, Iceland **54** 65 28N 23 25W
Hagi, Japan **100** 34 30N 131 22 E
Hagolan **69** 33 0N 35 45 E
Hagonoy **90** 14 50N 120 44 E
Hags Hd. **15** 52 57N 9 30W
Hague, C. de la **18** 49 44N 1 56W
Hague, The = 's-Gravenhage **22** 52 7N 4 17 E
Haguenau **19** 48 49N 7 47 E
Hai □ **130** 3 10 S 37 10 E
Hai Duong **84** 20 56N 106 19 E
Hai'an, Guangdong, China **97** 20 18N 110 11 E
Hai'an, Jiangsu, China **97** 32 37N 120 27 E
Haicheng, Fujian, China **97** 24 23N 117 48 E
Haicheng, Liaoning, China **95** 40 50N 122 45 E
Haidar Khel **78** 33 58N 68 38 E
Haifa = Ḩefa **69** 32 46N 35 0 E
Haifeng **97** 22 58N 115 10 E
Haig **109** 30 55 S 126 10 E
Haiger **26** 50 44N 8 12 E
Haikang **97** 20 52N 110 8 E
Haikou **84** 20 1N 110 16 E
Ḩā'il **72** 27 28N 41 45 E
Hailakandi **82** 24 42N 92 34 E
Hailar **93** 49 10N 119 38 E
Hailey **156** 43 30N 114 15W
Haileybury **142** 47 30N 79 38W
Hailin **95** 44 37N 129 30 E
Hailing Dao **97** 21 35N 111 47 E
Hailong **95** 42 32N 125 40 E
Haimen, Guangdong, China **97** 23 15N 116 38 E
Haimen, Jiangsu, China **97** 31 52N 121 10 E
Haimen, Zhejiang, China **97** 28 40N 121 24 E
Hainan Dao **84** 19 0N 109 30 E
Hainaut □ **23** 50 30N 4 0 E
Hainburg **31** 48 9N 16 56 E
Haines **156** 44 51N 117 59W
Haines City **149** 28 6N 81 35W
Haines Junction **144** 60 45N 137 30W
Hainfeld **30** 48 3N 15 48 E
Haining **97** 30 28N 120 40 E
Haiphong **84** 20 47N 106 41 E
Haiti ■ **163** 19 0N 72 30W
Haiya Junction **124** 18 20N 36 21 E
Haiyan **97** 30 28N 120 58 E
Haiyang **95** 36 47N 121 9 E
Haiyuan, Guangxi Zhuangzu, China **96** 22 8N 107 35 E
Haiyuan, Ningxia Huizu, China **94** 36 35N 105 52 E
Haizhou **95** 34 37N 119 7 E
Haizhou Wan **95** 34 50N 119 20 E
Haja **87** 3 19 S 129 37 E
Hajar Bangar **123** 10 40N 22 45 E
Hajdú-Bihar □ **31** 47 30N 21 30 E
Hajdúböszörmény **31** 47 40N 21 30 E
Hajdúdurog **31** 47 48N 21 30 E
Hajdúnánás **31** 47 50N 21 26 E
Hajdúsámson **31** 47 37N 21 42 E
Hajdúszobaszló **31** 47 27N 21 22 E
Hajiganj **82** 23 15N 90 50 E
Hajipur **79** 25 45N 85 13 E
Ḩajjah **74** 15 42N 43 36 E
Ḩājjī Muḩsin **72** 32 35N 45 29 E
Ḩājjīābād, Eşfahan, Iran **73** 33 41N 54 50 E
Ḩājjīābād, Hormozgān, Iran **73** 28 19N 55 55 E
Hajówka **32** 52 47N 23 35 E
Ḩajrah **74** 20 14N 41 3 E
Haka **82** 22 39N 93 37 E
Hakansson, Mts. **131** 8 40 S 25 45 E
Håkantorp **53** 58 18N 12 55 E
Hakataramea **115** 44 43 S 170 30 E
Ḩakkan **75** 20 22N 58 47 E
Hakken-Zan **101** 34 10N 135 54 E
Hakodate **98** 41 45N 140 44 E
Hakota **101** 36 5N 140 30 E
Haku-San **101** 36 9N 136 46 E
Hakui **99** 36 53N 136 47 E
Hakun **82** 26 46N 95 42 E
Hala **77** 25 43N 68 20 E
Ḩalab **70** 36 10N 37 15 E
Ḩalab □ **70** 36 10N 37 10 E
Ḩalaban **74** 23 29N 44 23 E
Ḩalabjah **72** 35 10N 45 58 E
Halaib **124** 22 12N 36 30 E
Halanzy **23** 49 33N 5 44 E
Hālat 'Ammār **72** 29 10N 36 4 E
Halbā **70** 34 34N 36 6 E
Halberstadt **26** 51 53N 11 2 E
Halcombe **114** 40 8 S 175 30 E
Halcon, Mt. **90** 13 0N 121 30 E
Halden **51** 59 9N 11 23 E
Haldensleben **26** 52 17N 11 30 E
Haldwani **79** 29 31N 79 30 E
Hale **154** 39 36N 93 20W
Hale → **110** 24 56 S 135 53 E
Haleakala Crater **146** 20 43N 156 12W
Halen **23** 50 57N 5 6 E
Haleyville **149** 34 15N 87 40W
Half Assini **126** 5 1N 2 50W
Halfmoon Bay **115** 46 50 S 168 5 E
Halfway → **144** 56 12N 121 32W
Ḩalḩul **69** 31 35N 35 7 E
Haliburton **142** 45 3N 78 30W
Halicarnassus **49** 37 3N 27 30 E
Halifax, Australia **110** 18 32 S 146 22 E
Halifax, Canada **143** 44 38N 63 35W
Halifax, U.K. **12** 53 43N 1 51W
Halifax B. **110** 18 50 S 147 0 E
Halifax I. **134** 26 38 S 15 4 E
Halīl → **73** 27 40N 58 30 E
Halin **136** 9 6N 48 37 E
Hall **30** 47 17N 11 30 E
Hall Beach **141** 68 46N 81 12W
Hall Pt. **108** 15 40 S 124 23 E
Hallabro **53** 56 22N 15 5 E
Hallands län □ **53** 56 50N 12 50 E
Hallands Väderö **53** 56 27N 12 34 E
Hallandsås **53** 56 22N 13 0 E
Halle, Belgium **23** 50 44N 4 13 E
Halle, Halle, Germany **26** 51 29N 12 0 E
Halle, Nordrhein-Westfalen, Germany **26** 52 4N 8 20 E
Halle □ **26** 51 28N 11 58 E
Hällefors **52** 59 47N 14 31 E
Hallein **30** 47 40N 13 5 E
Hällekis **53** 58 38N 13 27 E
Hallett **112** 33 25 S 138 55 E
Hallettsville **153** 29 28N 96 57W
Hällevadsholm **53** 58 35N 11 33 E
Halley Bay **7** 75 31 S 26 36W
Hallia → **80** 16 55N 79 20 E
Halliday **152** 47 20N 102 25W
Halliday L. **145** 61 21N 108 56W
Hallim **95** 33 24N 126 15 E
Hallingskeid **51** 60 40N 7 17 E
Hällnäs **54** 64 19N 19 36 E
Hallock **145** 48 47N 97 0W
Halls Creek **108** 18 16 S 127 38 E
Hallsberg **52** 59 5N 15 7 E
Hallstahammar **52** 59 38N 16 15 E
Hallstatt **30** 47 33N 13 38 E
Hallstavik **52** 60 5N 18 37 E
Hallstead **151** 41 56N 75 45W
Halmahera **87** 0 40N 128 0 E
Halmeu **50** 47 57N 23 2 E
Halmstad **53** 56 41N 12 52 E
Halq el Oued **121** 36 53N 10 18 E
Hals **53** 56 59N 10 18 E
Halsa **51** 63 3N 8 14 E
Halsafjorden **51** 63 5N 8 10 E
Hälsingborg = Helsingborg **52** 56 3N 12 42 E
Halstad **152** 47 21N 96 50W
Haltdalen **51** 62 56N 11 8 E
Haltern **26** 51 44N 7 10 E
Halul **75** 25 40N 52 40 E
Ḩalvān **73** 33 57N 56 15 E
Ham **19** 49 45N 3 4 E
Ham Tan **85** 10 40N 107 45 E
Ham Yen **84** 22 4N 105 3 E
Hamab **134** 28 7 S 19 16 E
Hamad **125** 15 20N 33 32 E
Hamada **100** 34 56N 132 4 E
Hamadān **73** 34 52N 48 32 E
Hamadān □ **73** 35 0N 49 0 E
Hamadia **121** 35 28N 1 57 E
Ḩamāh **70** 35 5N 36 40 E
Ḩamāh □ **70** 35 10N 37 0 E
Hamakita **101** 34 45N 137 47 E
Hamamatsu **101** 34 45N 137 45 E
Hamar **51** 60 48N 11 7 E
Hamarøy **54** 68 5N 15 38 E
Hamâta, Gebel **124** 24 17N 35 0 E
Hamber Prov. Park **144** 52 20N 118 0W
Hamburg, Germany **26** 53 32N 9 59 E
Hamburg, Ark., U.S.A. **153** 33 15N 91 47W
Hamburg, Iowa, U.S.A. **152** 40 37N 95 38W
Hamburg, N.Y., U.S.A. **150** 42 44N 78 50W
Hamburg, Pa., U.S.A. **151** 40 33N 76 0W
Hamburg □ **26** 53 30N 10 0 E
Ḩamḑ, W. al → **72** 24 55N 36 20 E
Ḩamḑah **74** 19 2N 43 36 E
Ḩamdānah **74** 19 59N 40 34 E
Hamden **151** 41 21N 72 56W
Hämeen lääni □ **55** 61 24N 24 10 E
Hämeenlinna **54** 61 0N 24 28 E
Hamélé **126** 10 56N 2 45W
Hamelin Pool **109** 26 22 S 114 20 E
Hamelin Pool Bay **109** 26 10 S 114 5 E
Hameln **26** 52 7N 9 24 E
Hamer Koke **125** 5 15N 36 45 E

Hevron

Haverhill 151 42 50N 71 2W
Haveri 81 14 53N 75 24 E
Havering 13 51 33N 0 20 E
Haverstraw 151 41 12N 73 58W
Håverud 53 58 50N 12 28 E
Havîrna 50 48 4N 26 43 E
Havlíčkův Brod 30 49 36N 15 33 E
Havneby 53 55 5N 8 34 E
Havre 156 48 34N 109 40W
Havre, Le 18 49 30N 0 5 E
Havre-Aubert 143 47 12N 61 56W
Havre-St.-Pierre 143 50 18N 63 33W
Haw → 149 35 36N 79 3W
Hawaii □ 146 20 30N 157 0W
Hawaii I. 146 20 0N 155 0W
Hawaiian Is. 146 20 30N 156 0W
Hawaiian Ridge 105 24 0N 165 0W
Hawarden, Canada 145 51 25N 106 36W
Hawarden, U.S.A. 152 43 2N 96 28W
Hawea Flat 115 44 40 S 169 19 E
Hawea Lake 115 44 28 S 169 19 E
Hawera 114 39 35 S 174 19 E
Hawesville 155 37 54N 86 45W
Hawick 14 55 25N 2 48W
Hawk Junction 142 48 5N 84 38W
Hawk Point 154 38 58N 91 8W
Hawkdun Ra. 115 44 53 S 170 5 E
Hawke B. 114 39 25 S 177 20 E
Hawker 112 31 59 S 138 22 E
Hawke's Bay □ 114 39 45 S 176 35 E
Hawkesbury 142 45 37N 74 37W
Hawkesbury I. 144 53 37N 129 3W
Hawkesbury Pt. 110 11 55 S 134 5 E
Hawkinsville 149 32 17N 83 30W
Hawkwood 111 25 45 S 150 50 E
Hawley 152 46 58N 96 20W
Hawrān 69 32 45N 36 15 E
Hawsh Mūssá 70 33 45N 35 55 E
Hawthorne 156 38 31N 118 37W
Hawzen 125 13 58N 39 28 E
Haxtun 152 40 40N 102 39W
Hay 113 34 30 S 144 51 E
Hay →, Australia 110 24 50 S 138 0 E
Hay →, Canada 144 60 50N 116 26W
Hay, C. 108 14 5 S 129 29 E
Hay L. 144 58 50N 118 50W
Hay Lakes 144 53 12N 113 2W
Hay-on-Wye 13 52 4N 3 9W
Hay River 144 60 51N 115 44W
Hay Springs 152 42 40N 102 38W
Hayachine-San 98 39 34N 141 29 E
Hayange 19 49 20N 6 2 E
Hayato 100 31 40N 130 43 E
Hayden, Ariz., U.S.A. 157 33 2N 110 48W
Hayden, Colo., U.S.A. 156 40 30N 107 22W
Haydon 110 18 0 S 141 30 E
Haye-du-Puits, La 18 49 17N 1 33W
Hayes 152 44 22N 101 1W
Hayes → 145 57 3N 92 12W
Hayjān 74 16 40N 44 5 E
Haymā' 75 19 56N 56 19 E
Haynan 75 15 50N 48 18 E
Haynesville 153 33 0N 93 7W
Ḥayrān 74 16 8N 43 5 E
Hays, Canada 144 50 6N 111 48W
Hays, U.S.A. 152 38 55N 99 25W
Ḥays, Yemen 74 13 56N 43 29 E
Haysville 155 38 28N 86 55W
Hayward, Calif., U.S.A. 158 37 40N 122 5W
Hayward, Wis., U.S.A. 152 46 2N 91 30W
Hayward's Heath 13 51 0N 0 5W
Ḥayy 75 20 46N 58 18 E
Hazafon □ 70 32 40N 35 20 E
Hazarām, Kūh-e 73 29 30N 57 18 E
Hazard 148 37 18N 83 10W
Hazaribag 79 23 58N 85 26 E
Hazaribag Road 79 24 12N 85 57 E
Hazebrouck 19 50 42N 2 31 E
Hazelton, Canada 144 55 20N 127 42W
Hazelton, U.S.A. 152 46 30N 100 15W
Hazen, N. Dak., U.S.A. 152 47 18N 101 38W
Hazen, Nev., U.S.A. 156 39 37N 119 2W
Hazerswoude 22 52 5N 4 36 E
Hazlehurst, Ga., U.S.A. 149 31 50N 82 35W
Hazlehurst, Miss., U.S.A. 153 31 52N 90 24W
Hazleton, Ind., U.S.A. 155 38 29N 87 34W
Hazleton, Pa., U.S.A. 151 40 58N 76 0W
Hazlett, L. 108 21 30 S 128 48 E
Hazor 69 33 2N 35 32 E
He Xian, Anhui, China 97 31 45N 118 20 E
He Xian, Guangxi Zhuangzu, China 97 24 27N 111 30 E
Head of Bight 109 31 30 S 131 25 E
Headlands 131 18 15 S 32 2 E
Healdsburg 158 38 33N 122 51W
Healdton 153 34 16N 97 31W
Healesville 113 37 35 S 145 30 E
Heanor 12 53 1N 1 20W
Heard I. 83 53 0 S 74 0 E
Hearne 153 30 54N 96 35W
Hearne B. 145 60 10N 99 10W
Hearne L. 144 62 20N 113 10W
Hearst 142 49 40N 83 41W
Heart → 152 46 40N 100 51W
Heart's Content 143 47 54N 53 27W
Heath → 172 12 31 S 68 38W
Heath Mts. 115 45 39 S 167 9 E
Heath Pt. 143 49 8N 61 40W
Heath Steele 143 47 17N 66 5W
Heathcote 113 36 56 S 144 45 E
Heavener 153 34 54N 94 36W
Hebbronville 153 27 20N 98 40W
Hebei □ 94 39 0N 116 0 E
Hebel 111 28 58 S 147 47 E
Heber 159 32 44N 115 32W
Heber Springs 153 35 29N 91 59W
Hebert 145 50 30N 107 10W
Hebgen, L. 156 44 50N 111 15W
Hebi 94 35 57N 114 7 E
Hebrides 14 57 30N 7 0W
Hebrides, Inner Is. 14 57 20N 6 40W
Hebrides, Outer Is. 14 57 30N 7 40W
Hebron = Al Khalīl 69 31 32N 35 6 E
Hebron, Canada 141 58 5N 62 30W
Hebron, N. Dak., U.S.A. 152 46 56N 102 2W
Hebron, Nebr., U.S.A. 152 40 15N 97 33W
Heby 52 59 56N 16 53 E
Hecate Str. 144 53 10N 130 30W
Hechi 96 24 40N 108 2 E
Hechingen 27 48 20N 8 58 E
Hechtel 23 51 8N 5 22 E
Hechuan 96 30 2N 106 12 E
Hecla 152 45 56N 98 8W
Hecla I. 145 51 10N 96 43W
Heddal 51 59 36N 9 9 E
Hédé, France 18 48 18N 1 49W
Hede, Sweden 52 62 23N 13 30 E
Hedemora 52 60 18N 15 58 E
Hedgehope 115 46 12 S 168 34 E
Hedley 153 34 53N 100 39W
Hedmark fylke □ 51 61 17N 11 40 E
Hedo 106 26 52N 128 15 E
Hedrick 154 41 11N 92 19W
Hedrum 51 59 7N 10 5 E
Heeg 22 52 58N 5 37 E
Heegermeer 22 52 56N 5 32 E
Heemskerk 22 52 31N 4 40 E
Heemstede 22 52 22N 4 37 E
Heer 23 50 50N 5 43 E
Heerde 22 52 24N 6 2 E
's Heerenburg 22 51 53N 6 16 E
Heerenveen 22 52 57N 5 55 E
Heerhugowaard 22 52 40N 4 51 E
Heerlen 23 50 55N 6 0 E
Heers 23 50 45N 5 18 E
Heesch 22 51 44N 5 32 E
Heestert 23 50 47N 3 25 E
Heeze 23 51 23N 5 35 E
Ḥefa 69 32 46N 35 0 E
Ḥefa □ 70 32 40N 35 0 E
Hefei 97 31 52N 117 18 E
Hegang 93 47 20N 130 19 E
Hegyalja 31 48 25N 21 25 E
Heichengzhen 94 36 24N 106 3 E
Heide 26 54 10N 9 7 E
Heidelberg, Germany 27 49 23N 8 41 E
Heidelberg, C. Prov., S. Africa 134 34 6 S 20 59 E
Heidelberg, Trans., S. Africa 135 26 30 S 28 23 E
Heidenheim 27 48 40N 10 10 E
Heigun-To 100 33 47N 132 14 E
Heijing 96 25 22N 101 44 E
Heilbron 135 27 16 S 27 59 E
Heilbronn 27 49 8N 9 13 E
Heiligenblut 30 47 2N 12 51 E
Heiligenhafen 26 54 21N 10 58 E
Heiligenstadt 26 51 22N 10 9 E
Heilongjiang □ 95 48 0N 126 0 E
Heilunkiang = Heilongjiang □ 95 48 0N 126 0 E
Heim 51 63 26N 9 5 E
Heino 22 52 26N 6 14 E
Heinola 55 61 13N 26 2 E
Heinsch 23 49 42N 5 44 E
Heinsun 82 25 52N 95 35 E
Heirnkut 82 25 14N 94 44 E
Heishan 95 41 40N 122 5 E
Heishui, Liaoning, China 95 42 8N 119 30 E
Heishui, Sichuan, China 96 32 4N 103 2 E
Heist 23 51 20N 3 15 E
Heist-op-den-Berg 23 51 5N 4 44 E
Hejaz = Al Ḥijāz 74 26 0N 37 30 E
Hejian 94 38 25N 116 5 E
Hejiang 96 28 43N 105 46 E
Hejin 94 35 35N 110 42 E
Hekelegem 23 50 55N 4 7 E
Hekinan 101 34 52N 137 0 E
Hekla 54 63 56N 19 35W
Hekou, Gansu, China 94 36 10N 103 28 E
Hekou, Guangdong, China 97 23 13N 112 45 E
Hel 32 54 37N 18 47 E
Helagsfjället 52 62 54N 12 25 E
Helan Shan 94 39 0N 105 55 E
Helchteren 23 51 4N 5 22 E
Helden 23 51 19N 6 0 E
Helechosa 35 39 22N 4 53W
Helena, Ark., U.S.A. 153 34 30N 90 35W
Helena, Mont., U.S.A. 156 46 40N 112 0W
Helendale 159 34 44N 117 19W
Helensburgh, Australia 113 34 11 S 151 1 E
Helensburgh, U.K. 14 56 0N 4 44W
Helensville 114 36 41 S 174 29 E
Helez 69 31 36N 34 39 E
Helgasjön 53 57 0N 14 50 E
Helgeroa 51 59 0N 9 45 E
Helgoland 26 54 10N 7 51 E
Heligoland = Helgoland 26 54 10N 7 51 E
Heliopolis 124 30 6N 31 17 E
Hellebæk 52 56 4N 12 32 E
Helleland 51 58 33N 6 7 E
Hellendoorn 22 52 24N 6 27 E
Hellevoetsluis 22 51 50N 4 8 E
Hellín 37 38 31N 1 40W
Helmand □ 77 31 20N 64 0 E
Helmand → 77 31 12N 61 34 E
Helme → 26 51 40N 11 20 E
Helmond 23 51 29N 5 41 E
Helmsdale 14 58 7N 3 40W
Helmstedt 26 52 16N 11 0 E
Helnæs 53 55 9N 10 0 E
Helong 95 42 40N 129 0 E
Helper 156 39 44N 110 56W
Helsingborg 52 56 3N 12 42 E
Helsinge 52 56 2N 12 12 E
Helsingfors 55 60 15N 25 3 E
Helsingør 52 56 2N 12 35 E
Helsinki 55 60 15N 25 3 E
Helska, Mierzeja 32 54 45N 18 40 E
Helston 13 50 7N 5 17W
Helvellyn 12 54 31N 3 1W
Helvoirt 23 51 38N 5 14 E
Helwân 124 29 50N 31 20 E
Hemavati → 81 12 30N 76 20 E
Hemet 159 33 45N 116 59W
Hemingford 152 42 21N 103 4W
Hemphill 153 31 21N 93 49W
Hempstead 153 30 5N 96 5W
Hemse 53 57 15N 18 22 E
Hemsö 52 62 43N 18 5 E
Hen & Chickens Is. 114 35 58 S 174 45 E
Henan □ 94 34 0N 114 0 E
Henares → 36 40 24N 3 30W
Henashi-Misaki 98 40 37N 139 51 E
Hendaye 20 43 23N 1 47W
Henderson, Argentina 174 36 18 S 61 43W
Henderson, Ky., U.S.A. 155 37 50N 87 38W
Henderson, N.C., U.S.A. 149 36 20N 78 25W
Henderson, Nev., U.S.A. 159 36 2N 115 0W
Henderson, Pa., U.S.A. 149 35 25N 88 40W
Henderson, Tex., U.S.A. 153 32 5N 94 49W
Hendersonville 149 35 21N 82 28W
Hendījān 73 30 14N 49 43 E
Hendon 111 28 5 S 151 50 E
Hendorf 50 46 4N 24 55 E
Heng Xian 96 22 40N 109 17 E
Hengcheng 94 38 18N 106 28 E
Hengdaohezi 95 44 52N 129 0 E
Hengelo, Gelderland, Neth. 22 52 3N 6 19 E
Hengelo, Overijssel, Neth. 22 52 16N 6 48 E
Hengfeng 97 28 12N 115 48 E
Hengshan, Hunan, China 97 27 16N 112 45 E
Hengshan, Shaanxi, China 94 37 58N 109 5 E
Hengshui 94 37 41N 115 40 E
Hengyang, Hunan, China 97 26 52N 112 33 E
Hengyang, Hunan, China 97 26 59N 112 22 E
Hénin-Beaumont 19 50 25N 2 58 E
Henlopen, C. 148 38 48N 75 5W
Hennan 52 62 3N 15 46 E
Hennebont 18 47 49N 3 19W
Hennenman 134 27 59 S 27 1 E
Hennepin 154 41 15N 89 21W
Hennessey 153 36 8N 97 53W
Hennigsdorf 26 52 38N 13 13 E
Henrichemont 19 47 20N 2 30 E
Henrietta 153 33 50N 98 15W
Henrietta, Ostrov 65 77 6N 156 30 E
Henrietta Maria C. 142 55 9N 82 20W
Henry 154 41 5N 89 20W
Henryetta 153 35 30N 96 0W
Hensall 150 43 26N 81 30W
Hentiyn Nuruu 93 48 30N 108 30 E
Henzada 82 17 38N 95 26 E
Hephaestia 48 39 55N 25 14 E
Heping 97 24 29N 115 0 E
Heppner 156 45 21N 119 34W
Hepu 96 21 40N 109 12 E
Hepworth 150 44 37N 81 9W
Heqing 96 26 37N 100 11 E
Hequ 94 39 20N 111 15 E
Herad 51 58 8N 6 47 E
Héraðsflói 54 65 42N 14 12W
Héraðsvötn → 54 65 45N 19 25W
Herald Cays 110 16 58 S 149 9 E
Herāt 77 34 20N 62 7 E
Herāt □ 77 35 0N 62 0 E
Hérault □ 20 43 34N 3 15 E
Hérault → 20 43 17N 3 26 E
Herbault 18 47 36N 1 8 E
Herbert → 110 18 31 S 146 17 E
Herbert Downs 110 23 7 S 139 9 E
Herberton 110 17 20 S 145 25 E
Herbiers, Les 18 46 52N 1 1W
Herbignac 18 47 27N 2 18W
Herborn 26 50 40N 8 19 E
Herby 32 50 45N 18 50 E
Hercegnovi 46 42 30N 18 33 E
Hercegovina = Bosna i Hercegovina □ 46 44 0N 18 0 E
Herculaneum 154 38 16N 90 23W
Herðubreið 54 65 11N 16 21W
Hereford, U.K. 13 52 4N 2 42W
Hereford, U.S.A. 153 34 50N 102 28W
Hereford and Worcester □ 13 52 10N 2 30W
Herefoss 51 58 32N 8 23 E
Herekino 114 35 18 S 173 11 E
Herent 23 50 54N 4 40 E
Herentals 23 51 12N 4 51 E
Herenthout 23 51 8N 4 45 E
Herfølge 52 55 26N 12 9 E
Herford 26 52 7N 8 40 E
Héricourt 19 47 32N 6 45 E
Herington 152 38 43N 97 0W
Herisau 29 47 22N 9 17 E
Hérisson 20 46 32N 2 42 E
Herk → 23 50 56N 5 12 E
Herkenbosch 23 51 9N 6 4 E
Herkimer 151 43 0N 74 59W
Herlong 158 40 8N 120 8W
Herm 18 49 30N 2 28W
Hermagor-Pressegger See 30 46 38N 13 23 E
Herman 152 45 51N 96 8W
Hermann 152 38 40N 91 25W
Hermannsburg 26 52 49N 10 6 E
Hermannsburg Mission 108 23 57 S 132 45 E
Hermanus 134 34 27 S 19 12 E
Herment 20 45 45N 2 24 E
Hermidale 113 31 30 S 146 42 E
Hermiston 156 45 50N 119 16W
Hermitage, N.Z. 115 43 44 S 170 5 E
Hermitage, U.S.A. 154 37 56N 93 19W
Hermite, I. 176 55 50 S 68 0W
Hermon, Mt. = Ash Shaykh, J. 70 33 25N 35 50 E
Hermosillo 160 29 10N 111 0W
Hernád → 31 47 56N 21 8 E
Hernandarias 175 25 20 S 54 40W
Hernandez 158 36 24N 120 46W
Hernando, Argentina 174 32 28 S 63 40W
Hernando, U.S.A. 153 34 50N 89 59W
Herne, Belgium 23 50 44N 4 2 E
Herne, Germany 26 51 33N 7 12 E
Herne Bay 13 51 22N 1 8 E
Herning 53 56 8N 8 58 E
Heroica = Caborca 160 30 40N 112 10W
Heroica Nogales = Nogales 160 31 20N 110 56W
Heron Bay 142 48 40N 86 25W
Herradura, Pta. de la 37 28 26N 14 8W
Herreid 152 45 53N 100 5W
Herrera 35 37 26N 4 55W
Herrera de Alcántar 35 39 39N 7 25W
Herrera de Pisuerga 34 42 35N 4 20W
Herrera del Duque 35 39 10N 5 3W
Herrick 110 41 5 S 147 55 E
Herrin 154 37 50N 89 0W
Herrljunga 53 58 5N 13 1 E
Hersbruck 27 49 30N 11 25 E
Herseaux 23 50 43N 3 15 E
Herselt 23 51 3N 4 53 E
Herstal 23 50 40N 5 38 E
Hersvik 51 61 10N 4 53 E
Hertford 13 51 47N 0 4W
Hertford □ 13 51 51N 0 5W
's-Hertogenbosch 23 51 42N 5 17 E
Hertzogville 134 28 9 S 25 30 E
Hervás 34 40 16N 5 52W
Herve 23 50 38N 5 48 E
Hervey Bay 110 25 3 S 153 5 E
Herwijnen 22 51 50N 5 7 E
Herzberg, Cottbus, Germany 26 51 40N 13 13 E
Herzberg, Niedersachsen, Germany 26 51 38N 10 20 E
Herzele 23 50 53N 3 53 E
Herzliyya 69 32 10N 34 50 E
Herzogenbuchsee 28 47 11N 7 42 E
Herzogenburg 30 48 17N 15 41 E
Ḥeşār, Fārs, Iran 73 29 52N 50 16 E
Ḥeşār, Markazī, Iran 73 35 49N 49 24 E
Hesdin 19 50 21N 2 0 E
Hesel 26 53 18N 7 36 E
Heshui 94 36 0N 108 0 E
Heshun 94 37 22N 113 32 E
Heskestad 51 58 28N 6 22 E
Hesperange 23 49 35N 6 10 E
Hesperia 159 34 25N 117 18W
Hesse = Hessen □ 26 50 40N 9 20 E
Hessen □ 26 50 40N 9 20 E
Hetch Hetchy Aqueduct 158 37 36N 121 25W
Hettinger 152 46 0N 102 38W
Hettstedt 26 51 39N 11 30 E
Heugem 23 50 49N 5 42 E
Heule 23 50 51N 3 15 E
Heusden, Belgium 23 51 2N 5 17 E
Heusden, Neth. 22 51 44N 5 8 E
Hève, C. de la 18 49 30N 0 5 E
Heverlee 23 50 52N 4 42 E
Heves □ 31 47 50N 20 0 E
Hevron → 69 31 12N 34 42 E

Huinan

Huinan 95 42 40N 126 2 E
Huinca Renancó 174 34 51 S 64 22W
Huining 94 35 38N 105 0 E
Huinong 94 39 5N 106 35 E
Huiroa 114 39 15 S 174 30 E
Huise 23 50 54N 3 36 E
Huishui 96 26 7N 106 38 E
Huisne → 18 47 59N 0 11 E
Huissen 22 51 57N 5 57 E
Huiting 94 34 5N 116 5 E
Huitong 96 26 51N 109 45 E
Huixtla 161 15 9N 92 28W
Huize 96 26 24N 103 15 E
Huizen 22 52 18N 5 14 E
Huizhou 97 23 0N 114 23 E
Hukou 97 29 45N 116 21 E
Hukuntsi 134 23 58 S 21 45 E
Hula 125 6 33N 38 30 E
Ḥulayfā' 72 25 58N 40 45 E
Huld 94 45 5N 105 30 E
Ḥulda 69 31 50N 34 51 E
Hulin He → 95 45 0N 122 10 E
Hull, Canada 142 45 25N 75 44W
Hull, U.K. 12 53 45N 0 20W
Hull, U.S.A. 154 39 43N 91 13W
Hull → 12 53 43N 0 25W
Hulst 23 51 17N 4 2 E
Hultsfred 53 57 30N 15 52 E
Hulun Nur 93 49 0N 117 30 E
Humahuaca 174 23 10 S 65 25W
Humaitá, Brazil 173 7 35 S 63 1W
Humaitá, Paraguay 174 27 2 S 58 31W
Humansdorp 134 34 2 S 24 46 E
Humansville 154 37 48N 93 35W
Humbe 133 16 40 S 14 55 E
Humber → 12 53 40N 0 10W
Humberside □ 12 53 50N 0 30W
Humbert River 108 16 30 S 130 45 E
Humble 153 29 59N 93 18W
Humboldt, Canada 145 52 15N 105 9W
Humboldt, Iowa, U.S.A. 154 42 42N 94 15W
Humboldt, Tenn., U.S.A. 153 35 50N 88 55W
Humboldt → 156 40 2N 118 31W
Humboldt Gletscher 6 79 30N 62 0W
Humboldt Mts. 115 44 30 S 168 15 E
Humbolt, Massif du 106 21 53 S 166 25 E
Hume, Calif., U.S.A. 158 36 48N 118 54W
Hume, Kans., U.S.A. 154 38 5N 94 35W
Hume, L. 113 36 0 S 147 0 E
Humenné 31 48 55N 21 50 E
Humeston 154 40 51N 93 30W
Humpata 133 15 2 S 13 24 E
Humphreys, Mt. 158 37 17N 118 40W
Humphreys Pk. 157 35 24N 111 38W
Humpolec 30 49 31N 15 20 E
Humptulips 158 47 14N 123 57W
Humula 113 35 30 S 147 46 E
Hūn 122 29 2N 16 0 E
Hun Jiang → 95 40 50N 125 38 E
Húnaflói 54 65 50N 20 50W
Hunan □ 97 27 30N 112 0 E
Hunchun 95 42 52N 130 28 E
Hundested 52 55 58N 11 52 E
Hundred Mile House 144 51 38N 121 18W
Hunedoara 50 45 40N 22 50 E
Hunedoara □ 50 45 50N 22 54 E
Hünfeld 26 50 40N 9 47 E
Hung Yen 84 20 39N 106 4 E
Hungary ■ 31 47 20N 19 20 E
Hungary, Plain of 10 47 0N 20 0 E
Hungerford 111 28 58 S 144 24 E
Hŭngnam 95 39 49N 127 45 E
Huni Valley 126 5 33N 1 56W
Hunsberge 134 27 45 S 17 12 E
Hunsrück 27 49 30N 7 0 E
Hunstanton 12 52 57N 0 30 E
Hunsur 81 12 16N 76 16 E
Hunte → 26 52 30N 8 19 E
Hunter, N.Z. 115 44 36 S 171 2 E
Hunter, N. Dak., U.S.A. 152 47 12N 97 17W
Hunter, N.Y., U.S.A. 151 42 13N 74 13W
Hunter → 115 44 21 S 169 27 E
Hunter Hills, The 115 44 26 S 170 46 E
Hunter I., Australia 110 40 30 S 144 45 E
Hunter I., Canada 144 51 55N 128 0W
Hunter Mts. 115 45 43 S 167 25 E
Hunter Ra. 113 32 45 S 150 15 E
Hunters Road 131 19 9 S 29 49 E
Hunterville 114 39 56 S 175 35 E
Huntingburg 155 38 20N 86 58W
Huntingdon, Canada 142 45 6N 74 10W
Huntingdon, U.K. 13 52 20N 0 11W
Huntingdon, U.S.A. 150 40 28N 78 1W
Huntington, Ind., U.S.A. 155 40 52N 85 30W
Huntington, N.Y., U.S.A. 151 40 52N 73 25W
Huntington, Oreg., U.S.A. 156 44 22N 117 21W
Huntington, Utah, U.S.A. 156 39 24N 111 1W
Huntington, W. Va., U.S.A. 148 38 20N 82 30W
Huntington Beach 159 33 40N 118 0W
Huntington Park 157 33 58N 118 15W
Huntley 155 42 10N 88 26W
Huntly, N.Z. 114 37 34 S 175 11 E
Huntly, U.K. 14 57 27N 2 48W
Huntsville, Canada 142 45 20N 79 14W
Huntsville, Ala., U.S.A. 149 34 45N 86 35W
Huntsville, Mo., U.S.A. 154 39 26N 92 33W
Huntsville, Tex., U.S.A. 153 30 45N 95 35W
Hunyani → 131 15 57 S 30 39 E
Hunyuan 94 39 42N 113 42 E
Hunza → 79 35 54N 74 20 E
Huo Xian 94 36 36N 111 42 E
Huon, G. 107 7 0 S 147 30 E
Huon Pen. 107 6 20 S 147 30 E
Huong Hoa 84 16 37N 106 45 E
Huong Khe 84 18 13N 105 41 E
Huonville 110 43 0 S 147 5 E
Huoqiu 97 32 20N 116 12 E
Huoshan, Anhui, China 97 32 28N 118 30 E
Huoshan, Anhui, China 97 31 25N 116 20 E
Huoshao Dao 97 22 40N 121 30 E
Hupeh □ = Hubei 97 31 0N 112 0 E
Ḥūr 73 30 50N 57 7 E
Hurbanovo 31 47 51N 18 11 E
Hure Qi 95 42 45N 121 45 E
Hurezani 50 44 49N 23 40 E
Hurghada 124 27 15N 33 50 E
Hurley, N. Mex., U.S.A. 157 32 45N 108 7W
Hurley, Wis., U.S.A. 152 46 26N 90 10W
Huron, Calif., U.S.A. 158 36 12N 120 6W
Huron, Ohio, U.S.A. 150 41 22N 82 34W
Huron, S. Dak., U.S.A. 152 44 22N 98 12W
Huron, L. 150 45 0N 83 0W
Hurricane 157 37 10N 113 12W
Hurso 125 9 35N 41 33 E
Hurum, Buskerud, Norway 51 59 36N 10 23 E
Hurum, Oppland, Norway 51 61 9N 8 46 E
Hurunui → 115 42 54 S 173 18 E
Hurup 53 56 46N 8 25 E
Húsavík 54 66 3N 17 21W
Huşi 50 46 41N 28 7 E
Huskvarna 53 57 47N 14 15 E
Husøy 51 61 3N 4 44 E
Hussar 144 51 3N 112 41W
Hustopéce 31 48 57N 16 43 E
Husum, Germany 26 54 27N 9 3 E
Husum, Sweden 52 63 21N 19 12 E
Hutchinson, Kans., U.S.A. 153 38 3N 97 59W
Hutchinson, Minn., U.S.A. 152 44 50N 94 22W
Ḥūth 74 16 14N 43 58 E
Hutsonville 155 39 6N 87 40W
Huttenberg 30 46 56N 14 33 E
Hüttental 26 50 52N 8 1 E
Huttig 153 33 5N 92 10W
Hutton, Mt. 111 25 51 S 148 20 E
Huttwil 28 47 7N 7 50 E
Huwun 125 4 23N 40 6 E
Ḥuwwārah 69 32 9N 35 15 E
Huy 23 50 31N 5 15 E
Hvaler 51 59 4N 11 1 E
Hvammur 54 65 13N 21 49W
Hvar 43 43 11N 16 28 E
Hvarski Kanal 43 43 15N 16 35 E
Hvítá 54 64 40N 21 5W
Hvítá → 54 64 0N 20 58W
Hvítárvatn 54 64 37N 19 50W
Hvitsten 51 59 35N 10 42 E
Hwachon-chosuji 95 38 5N 127 50 E
Hwang Ho = Huang He → 95 37 55N 118 50 E
Hwange 131 18 18 S 26 30 E
Hwange Nat. Park 134 19 0 S 26 30 E
Hwekum 82 26 7N 95 22 E
Hyannis 152 42 0N 101 45W
Hyargas Nuur 92 49 0N 93 0 E
Hybo 52 61 49N 16 15 E
Hyde 115 45 18 S 170 16 E
Hyde Park 169 6 30N 58 16W
Hyden 109 32 24 S 118 53 E
Hyderabad, India 80 17 22N 78 29 E
Hyderabad, Pakistan 77 25 23N 68 24 E
Hyères 21 43 8N 6 9 E
Hyères, Is. d' 21 43 0N 6 20 E
Hyesan 95 41 20N 128 10 E
Hyland → 144 59 52N 128 12W
Hylestad 51 59 6N 7 29 E
Hyltebruk 53 56 59N 13 15 E
Hymia 79 33 40N 78 2 E
Hyndman Pk. 156 43 50N 114 10W
Hyōgo □ 100 35 15N 135 0 E
Hyrum 156 41 35N 111 56W
Hysham 156 46 21N 107 11W
Hythe 13 51 4N 1 5 E
Hyūga 100 32 25N 131 35 E
Hyvinge = Hyvinkää 55 60 38N 24 50 E
Hyvinkää 55 60 38N 24 50 E

I

I-n-Échaï 120 20 10N 2 5W
I-n-Gall 127 16 51N 7 1 E
Iabès, Erg 121 27 30N 2 2W
Iaco → 172 9 3 S 68 34W
Iacobeni 50 47 25N 25 20 E
Iaçu 171 12 45 S 40 13W
Iakora 135 23 6 S 46 40 E
Ialomiţa □ 50 44 30N 27 30 E
Ialomiţa → 50 44 42N 27 51 E
Ianca 50 45 6N 27 29 E
Iara 50 46 31N 23 35 E
Iaşi 50 47 10N 27 40 E
Iaşi □ 50 47 20N 27 0 E
Iauaretê 168 0 36N 69 12W
Iba 90 15 22N 120 0 E
Ibadan 127 7 22N 3 58 E
Ibagué 168 4 20N 75 20W
Ibaiti 171 23 50 S 50 10W
Ibajay 91 11 49N 122 10 E
Iballja 48 42 12N 20 0 E
Ibăneşti 50 46 45N 24 50 E
Ibar → 46 43 43N 20 45 E
Ibara 100 34 36N 133 28 E
Ibaraki 101 34 49N 135 34 E
Ibaraki □ 101 36 10N 140 10 E
Ibarra 168 0 21N 78 7W
Ibba 125 4 49N 29 2 E
Ibba, Bahr el → 125 5 30N 28 55 E
Ibbenbüren 26 52 16N 7 41 E
Ibembo 130 2 35N 23 35 E
Ibera, L. 174 28 30 S 57 9W
Iberia 154 38 5N 92 18W
Iberian Peninsula 10 40 0N 5 0W
Iberville 142 45 19N 73 17W
Iberville, Lac D' 142 55 55N 73 15W
Ibi 127 8 15N 9 44 E
Ibiá 171 19 30 S 46 30W
Ibicaraí 171 14 51 S 39 36W
Ibicuí 171 14 51 S 39 59W
Ibicuy 174 33 55 S 59 10W
Ibioapaba, Sa. da 170 4 0 S 41 30W
Ibipetuba 170 11 0 S 44 32W
Ibitiara 171 12 39 S 42 13W
Ibiza 37 38 54N 1 26 E
Íblei, Monti 45 37 15N 14 45 E
Ibn Hāni', Ra's 70 35 35N 35 43 E
Ibo 131 12 22 S 40 40 E
Ibonma 87 3 29 S 133 31 E
Ibotirama 171 12 13 S 43 12W
İbradi 70 37 4N 31 35 E
Ibrāhīm → 70 34 4N 35 38 E
İbrala 70 37 9N 33 30 E
'Ibrī 75 23 14N 56 30 E
İbriktepe 48 41 2N 26 33 E
Ibshawâi 124 29 21N 30 40 E
Ibu 87 1 35N 127 33 E
Ibuki-Sanchi 101 35 25N 136 18 E
Iburg 26 52 10N 8 3 E
Ibusuki 100 31 12N 130 40 E
Icá 172 14 0 S 75 48W
Ica □ 172 14 20 S 75 30W
Iça → 172 2 55 S 67 58W
Icabarú 169 4 20N 61 45W
Icabarú → 169 4 45N 62 15W
Içana 168 0 21N 67 19W
Içana → 168 0 26N 67 19W
Icatu 170 2 46 S 44 4W
İçel □ 70 36 45N 34 0 E
Iceland ■ 54 65 0N 19 0W
Icha 65 55 30N 156 0 E
Ich'ang = Yichang 97 30 40N 111 20 E
Ichchapuram 80 19 10N 84 40 E
Ichihara 101 35 28N 140 5 E
Ichikawa 101 35 44N 139 55 E
Ichilo → 173 15 57 S 64 50W
Ichinohe 98 40 13N 141 17 E
Ichinomiya, Gifu, Japan 101 35 18N 136 48 E
Ichinomiya, Kumamoto, Japan 100 32 58N 131 5 E
Ichinoseki 98 38 55N 141 8 E
Ichnya 58 50 52N 32 24 E
Ichŏn 95 37 17N 127 27 E
Icht 120 29 6N 8 54W
Ichtegem 23 51 5N 3 1 E
Icó 170 6 24 S 38 51W
Icod 37 28 22N 16 43W
Icoraci 170 1 18 S 48 28W
Icy Str. 144 58 20N 135 30W
Ida Grove 152 42 20N 95 25W
Ida Valley 109 28 42 S 120 29 E
Idabel 153 33 53N 94 50W
Idaga Hamus 125 14 13N 39 48 E
Idah 127 7 5N 6 40 E
Idaho □ 156 44 10N 114 0W
Idaho City 156 43 50N 115 52W
Idaho Falls 156 43 30N 112 1W
Idaho Springs 156 39 49N 105 30W
Idanha-a-Nova 34 39 50N 7 15W
Idar-Oberstein 27 49 43N 7 19 E
Idd el Ghanam 123 11 30N 24 19 E
Iddan 136 6 10N 48 55 E
Idehan 122 27 10N 11 30 E
Idehan Marzūq 122 24 50N 13 51 E
Idelès 121 23 50N 5 53 E
Idfû 124 25 0N 32 49 E
Ídhi Óros 49 35 15N 24 45 E
Ídhra 49 37 20N 23 28 E
Idi 88 5 2N 97 37 E
Idiofa 133 4 55 S 19 42 E
Idkerberget 52 60 22N 15 15 E
Idku, Bahra el 124 31 18N 30 18 E
Idlib 70 35 55N 36 36 E
Idlib □ 70 35 45N 36 45 E
Idna 69 31 34N 34 58 E
Idria 158 36 25N 120 41W
Idrija 43 46 0N 14 5 E
Idritsa 58 56 25N 28 30 E
Idstein 27 50 13N 8 17 E
Idutywa 135 32 8 S 28 18 E
Ieper 23 50 51N 2 53 E
Ierápetra 49 35 0N 25 44 E
Ierissós 48 40 22N 23 52 E
Ierissóu Kólpos 48 40 27N 23 57 E
Ierzu 44 39 48N 9 32 E
Ieshima-Shotō 100 34 40N 134 32 E
Iesi 43 43 32N 13 12 E
Ifach, Punta 37 38 38N 0 5 E
'Ifāl, W. al → 72 28 7N 35 3 E
Ifanadiana 135 21 19 S 47 39 E
Ife 127 7 30N 4 31 E
Iférouâne 127 19 5N 8 24 E
Iffley 110 18 53 S 141 12 E
Ifni 120 29 29N 10 12W
Ifon 127 6 58N 5 40 E
Iforas, Adrar des 127 19 40N 1 40 E
Ifrane 120 33 33N 5 7W
Ifugao □ 90 16 40N 121 10 E
Iga 101 34 45N 136 10 E
Iganga 130 0 37N 33 28 E
Igara Paraná → 168 2 9 S 71 47W
Igarapava 171 20 3 S 47 47W
Igarapé Açu 170 1 4 S 47 33W
Igarapé-Mirim 170 1 59 S 48 58W
Igarka 65 67 30N 86 33 E
Igatimi 175 24 5 S 55 40W
Igatpuri 80 19 40N 73 35 E
Igbetti 127 8 44N 4 8 E
Igbo-Ora 127 7 29N 3 15 E
Igboho 127 8 53N 3 50 E
Iggesund 52 61 39N 17 10 E
Ighil Izane 121 35 44N 0 31 E
Iglésias 44 39 19N 8 27 E
Igli 121 30 25N 2 19W
Iglino 62 54 50N 56 26 E
Igloolik 141 69 20N 81 49W
Igma, Gebel el 124 28 55N 34 0 E
Ignace 142 49 30N 91 40W
Igoshevo 59 59 25N 42 35 E
Igoumenítsa 48 39 32N 20 18 E
Igra 62 57 33N 53 7 E
Iguaçu → 175 25 36 S 54 36W
Iguaçu, Cat. del 175 25 41 S 54 26W
Iguaçu Falls = Iguaçu, Cat. del 175 25 41 S 54 26W
Iguala 161 18 20N 99 40W
Igualada 36 41 37N 1 37 E
Iguape 171 24 43 S 47 33W
Iguassu = Iguaçu → 175 25 36 S 54 36W
Iguatu 170 6 20 S 39 18W
Iguéla 132 2 0 S 9 16 E
Iguig 90 17 45N 121 44 E
Igunga □ 130 4 20 S 33 45 E
Iheya-Shima 99 27 4N 127 58 E
Ihiala 127 5 51N 6 55 E
Ihosy 135 22 24 S 46 8 E
Ihotry, L. 135 21 56 S 43 41 E
Ii-Shima 99 26 43N 127 47 E
Iida 101 35 35N 137 50 E
Iisalmi 54 63 32N 27 10 E
Iiyama 99 36 51N 138 22 E
Iizuka 100 33 38N 130 42 E
Ijâfene 120 20 40N 8 0W
Ijebu-Igbo 127 6 56N 4 1 E
Ijebu-Ode 127 6 47N 3 58 E
IJmuiden 22 52 28N 4 35 E
IJssel → 22 52 35N 5 50 E
IJsselmeer 22 52 45N 5 20 E
IJsselmuiden 22 52 34N 5 57 E
IJsselstein 22 52 1N 5 2 E
Ijuí → 175 27 58 S 55 20W
Ijūin 100 31 37N 130 24 E
IJzendijke 23 51 19N 3 37 E
IJzer → 23 51 9N 2 44 E
Ik → 62 55 55N 52 36 E
Ikale 127 7 40N 5 37 E
Ikare 127 7 32N 5 40 E
Ikaría 49 37 35N 26 10 E
Ikast 53 56 8N 9 10 E
Ikawa 101 35 13N 138 15 E
Ikeda 100 34 1N 133 48 E
Ikeja 127 6 36N 3 23 E
Ikela 132 1 6 S 23 6 E
Ikenge 132 0 8 S 18 8 E
Ikerre-Ekiti 127 7 25N 5 19 E
Ikhtiman 47 42 27N 23 48 E
Iki 100 33 45N 129 42 E
Iki-Kaikyō 100 33 40N 129 45 E
Ikimba L. 130 1 30 S 31 20 E
Ikire 127 7 23N 4 15 E
Ikitsuki-Shima 100 33 23N 129 26 E
Ikom 127 6 0N 8 42 E
Ikopa → 135 16 45 S 46 40 E
Ikot Ekpene 127 5 12N 7 40 E
'Ikrimah 122 32 2N 23 41 E
Ikungu 130 1 33 S 33 42 E
Ikuno 100 35 10N 134 48 E
Ikurun 127 7 54N 4 40 E
Ila 127 8 0N 4 39 E
Ilagan 90 17 7N 121 53 E
Īlām, Iran 72 33 0N 46 0 E
Ilam, Nepal 79 26 58N 87 58 E
Ilanskiy 65 56 14N 96 3 E
Ilanz 29 46 46N 9 12 E
Ilaro 127 6 53N 3 3 E

Iriri Novo

Ilawa 32 53 36N 19 34 E
Ilayangudi 81 9 34N 78 37 E
Ilbilbie 110 21 45 S 149 20 E
Île-à-la Crosse 145 55 27N 107 53W
Île-à-la-Crosse, Lac 145 55 40N 107 45W
Île-Bouchard, L' 18 47 7N 0 26 E
Île-de-France 19 49 0N 2 20 E
Ile-Rousse, L' 21 42 38N 8 57 E
Ilebo 133 4 17 S 20 55 E
Ileje □ 131 9 30 S 33 25 E
Ilek 62 51 32N 53 21 E
Ilek → 62 51 30N 53 22 E
Ilero 127 8 0N 3 20 E
Ilesha, Kwara, Nigeria 127 8 57N 3 28 E
Ilesha, Oyo, Nigeria 127 7 37N 4 40 E
Ilford 145 56 4N 95 35W
Ilfov □ 50 44 20N 26 0 E
Ilfracombe, Australia 110 23 30 S 144 30 E
Ilfracombe, U.K. 13 51 13N 4 8W
Ilha Grande 169 0 27 S 65 2W
Ilha Grande, B. da 171 23 9 S 44 30W
Ílhavo 34 40 33N 8 43W
Ilhéus 171 14 49 S 39 2W
Ili → 63 45 53N 77 10 E
Ilia 50 45 57N 22 40 E
Ilia □ 49 37 45N 21 35 E
Ilich 63 40 50N 68 27 E
Iliff 152 40 50N 103 3W
Iligan 91 8 12N 124 13 E
Iligan Bay 91 8 25N 124 5 E
Ilíki, L. 49 38 24N 23 15 E
Ilin I. 90 12 14N 121 5 E
Iliodhrómia 48 39 12N 23 50 E
Ilion 151 43 0N 75 3W
Ilirska-Bistrica 43 45 34N 14 14 E
Ilkal 81 15 57N 76 8 E
Ilkeston 12 52 59N 1 19W
Illampu = Ancohuma, Nevada 172 16 0 S 68 50W
Illana B. 91 7 35N 123 45 E
Illapel 174 32 0 S 71 10W
'Illär 69 32 23N 35 7 E
Ille-et-Vilaine □ 18 48 10N 1 30W
Ille-sur-Têt 20 42 40N 2 38 E
Iller → 27 48 23N 9 58 E
Illescas 34 40 8N 3 51W
Illiers-Combray 18 48 18N 1 15 E
Illimani 172 16 30 S 67 50W
Illinois □ 147 40 15N 89 30W
Illinois → 147 38 55N 90 28W
Illiopolis 154 39 51N 89 15W
Illium = Troy 48 39 57N 26 12 E
Illizi 121 26 31N 8 32 E
Illora 35 37 17N 3 53W
Ilm → 26 51 7N 11 45 E
Ilmen, Oz. 58 58 15N 31 10 E
Ilmenau 26 50 41N 10 55 E
Ilo 172 17 40 S 71 20W
Ilobu 127 7 45N 4 25 E
Ilocos Norte □ 90 18 10N 120 45 E
Ilocos Sur □ 90 17 20N 120 35 E
Iloilo 91 10 45N 122 33 E
Iloilo □ 91 11 0N 122 40 E
Ilok 46 45 15N 19 20 E
Ilora 127 7 45N 3 50 E
Ilorin 127 8 30N 4 35 E
Iloulya 61 49 15N 44 2 E
Ilovatka 59 50 30N 45 50 E
Ilovlya → 61 49 14N 43 54 E
Ilowa 32 51 30N 15 10 E
Ilubabor □ 125 7 25N 35 0 E
Ilukste 58 55 55N 26 20 E
Ilva Mică 50 47 17N 24 40 E
Ilwaco 158 46 19N 124 3W
Ilwaki 87 7 55 S 126 30 E
Ilyichevsk 60 46 10N 30 35 E
Ilza 32 51 10N 21 15 E
Ilzanka → 32 51 14N 21 48 E
Imabari 100 34 4N 133 0 E
Imaichi 101 36 43N 139 46 E
Imaloto → 135 23 27 S 45 13 E
Imandra, Oz. 56 67 30N 33 0 E
Imari 100 33 15N 129 52 E
Imasa 124 18 0N 36 12 E
Imathía □ 48 40 30N 22 15 E
Imbâbah 124 30 5N 31 12 E
Imbabura □ 168 0 30N 78 45W
Imbaimadai 169 5 44N 60 17W
Imbler 156 45 31N 118 0W
Imdahane 120 32 8N 7 0W
imeni 26 Bakinskikh Komissarov, Azerbaijan, U.S.S.R. 57 39 19N 49 12 E
imeni 26 Bakinskikh Komissarov, Turkmen S.S.R., U.S.S.R. 57 39 22N 54 10 E
Imeni Panfilova 63 43 23N 77 7 E
Imeni Poliny Osipenko 65 52 30N 136 29 E
Imeri, Serra 168 0 50N 65 25W
Imerimandroso 135 17 26 S 48 35 E
Imesan 120 22 54N 15 30W
Imi 125 6 28N 42 10 E
Imishly 61 39 49N 48 4 E
Imitek 120 29 43N 8 10W
Imlay 156 40 45N 118 9W
Imlay City 150 43 0N 83 2W
Immenstadt 27 47 34N 10 13 E
Immingham 12 53 37N 0 12W
Immokalee 149 26 25N 81 26W
Imo □ 127 5 15N 7 20 E
Imola 43 44 20N 11 42 E
Imotski 46 43 27N 17 12 E
Imperatriz, Amazonas, Brazil 172 5 18 S 67 11W
Imperatriz, Maranhão, Brazil 170 5 30 S 47 29W
Impéria 42 43 52N 8 0 E
Imperial, Canada 145 51 21N 105 28W
Imperial, Peru 172 13 4 S 76 21W
Imperial, Calif., U.S.A. 159 32 52N 115 34W
Imperial, Nebr., U.S.A. 152 40 38N 101 39W
Imperial Beach 159 32 35N 117 8W
Imperial Dam 159 32 50N 114 30W
Imperial Res. 159 32 53N 114 28W
Imperial Valley 159 32 55N 115 30W
Imperieuse Reef 108 17 36 S 118 50 E
Impfondo 132 1 40N 18 0 E
Imphal 82 24 48N 93 56 E
Imphy 20 46 55N 3 16 E
İmroz = Gökçeada 48 40 10N 25 50 E
Imst 30 47 15N 10 44 E
Imuruan B. 91 10 40N 119 10 E
In Belbel 121 27 55N 1 12 E
In Delimane 127 15 52N 1 31 E
In Rhar 121 27 10N 1 59 E
In Salah 121 27 10N 2 32 E
In Tallak 127 16 19N 3 15 E
Ina 101 35 50N 138 0 E
Ina-Bonchi 101 35 45N 137 58 E
Inagauan 91 9 33N 118 39 E
Inajá 170 8 54 S 37 49W
Inangahua Junc. 115 41 52 S 171 59 E
Inanwatan 87 2 10 S 132 14 E
Iñapari 172 11 0 S 69 40W
Inari 54 68 54N 27 5 E
Inawashiro-Ko 98 37 29N 140 6 E
Inazawa 101 35 15N 136 47 E
Inca 36 39 43N 2 54 E
Incaguasi 174 29 12 S 71 5W
İnce-Burnu 60 42 7N 34 56 E
İncekum Burnu 70 36 13N 33 57 E
Inchon 95 37 27N 126 40 E
Incio 34 42 39N 7 21W
Incomáti → 135 25 46 S 32 43 E
Incudine, L' 21 41 50N 9 12 E
Inda Silase 125 14 10N 38 15 E
Indalsälven → 52 62 36N 17 30 E
Indaw 82 24 15N 96 5 E
Indbir 125 8 7N 37 52 E
Independence, Calif., U.S.A. 158 36 51N 118 14W
Independence, Iowa, U.S.A. 154 42 27N 91 52W
Independence, Kans., U.S.A. 153 37 10N 95 43W
Independence, Ky., U.S.A. 155 38 57N 84 33W
Independence, Mo., U.S.A. 154 39 3N 94 25W
Independence, Oreg., U.S.A. 156 44 53N 123 12W
Independence Fjord 6 82 10N 29 0W
Independence Mts. 156 41 30N 116 2W
Independência 170 5 23 S 40 19W
Independencia, La 161 16 31N 91 47W
Independenţa 50 45 25N 27 42 E
Inderborskiy 61 48 30N 51 42 E
Index 158 47 50N 121 33W
India ■ 76 20 0N 78 0 E
Indian → 149 27 59N 80 34W
Indian-Antarctic Ridge 104 49 0 S 120 0 E
Indian Cabins 144 59 52N 117 40W
Indian Harbour 143 54 27N 57 13W
Indian Head 145 50 30N 103 41W
Indian Ocean 83 5 0 S 75 0 E
Indian Springs 159 36 35N 115 40W
Indiana 150 40 38N 79 9W
Indiana □ 155 40 0N 86 0W
Indianapolis 155 39 42N 86 10W
Indianola, Iowa, U.S.A. 154 41 20N 93 32W
Indianola, Miss., U.S.A. 153 33 27N 90 40W
Indiapora 171 19 57 S 50 17W
Indiga 56 67 50N 48 50 E
Indigirka → 65 70 48N 148 54 E
Ind-ija 46 45 6N 20 7 E
Indio 159 33 46N 116 15W
Indonesia ■ 86 5 0 S 115 0 E
Indore 78 22 42N 75 53 E
Indramayu 89 6 20 S 108 19 E
Indravati → 80 19 20N 80 20 E
Indre □ 19 46 50N 1 39 E
Indre → 18 47 16N 0 11 E
Indre-et-Loire □ 18 47 20N 0 40 E
Indungo 133 14 48 S 16 17 E
Indus → 77 24 20N 67 47 E
Indus, Mouth of the 77 24 0N 68 0 E
Industry 154 40 20N 90 36W
İnebolu 57 41 55N 33 40 E
Inés, Mt. 176 48 30 S 69 40W
Ineu 50 46 26N 21 51 E
Inezgane 120 30 25N 9 29W
Infanta 90 14 45N 121 39 E
Infante, Kaap 134 34 27 S 20 51 E
Infantes 37 38 43N 3 1W
Infiernillo, Presa del 160 18 9N 102 0W
Infiesto 34 43 21N 5 21W
Inganda 132 0 5 S 20 57 E
Ingapirca 168 2 38 S 78 56W
Ingelmunster 23 50 56N 3 16 E
Ingende 132 0 12 S 18 57 E
Ingeniero Jacobacci 176 41 20 S 69 36W
Ingenio 37 27 55N 15 26W
Ingenio Santa Ana 174 27 25 S 65 40W
Ingersoll 150 43 4N 80 55W
Ingham 110 18 43 S 146 10 E
Ingichka 63 39 47N 65 58 E
Ingleborough 12 54 11N 2 23W
Inglewood, Queens., Australia 111 28 25 S 151 2 E
Inglewood, Vic., Australia 112 36 29 S 143 53 E
Inglewood, N.Z. 114 39 9 S 174 14 E
Inglewood, U.S.A. 159 33 58N 118 21W
Ingólfshöfði 54 63 48N 16 39W
Ingolstadt 27 48 45N 11 26 E
Ingomar 156 46 35N 107 21W
Ingonish 143 46 42N 60 18W
Ingore 126 12 24N 15 48W
Ingraj Bazar 79 24 58N 88 10 E
Ingrid Christensen Coast 7 69 30 S 76 0 E
Ingul → 60 46 50N 32 15 E
Ingulec 60 47 42N 33 14 E
Ingulets → 60 46 41N 32 48 E
Inguri → 61 42 38N 41 35 E
Ingwavuma 135 27 9 S 31 59 E
Inhaca, I. 135 26 1 S 32 57 E
Inhafenga 135 20 36 S 33 53 E
Inhambane 135 23 54 S 35 30 E
Inhambane □ 135 22 30 S 34 20 E
Inhambupe 171 11 47 S 38 21W
Inhaminga 131 18 26 S 35 0 E
Inharrime 135 24 30 S 35 0 E
Inharrime → 135 24 30 S 35 0 E
Inhuma 170 6 40 S 41 42W
Inhumas 171 16 22 S 49 30W
Iniesta 37 39 27N 1 45W
Ining = Yining 92 43 58N 81 10 E
Inini □ 169 4 0N 53 0W
Inírida → 168 3 55N 67 52W
Inishbofin 15 53 35N 10 12W
Inishmore 15 53 8N 9 45W
Inishowen 15 55 14N 7 15W
Injune 111 25 53 S 148 32 E
Inklin 144 58 56N 133 5W
Inklin → 144 58 50N 133 10W
Inkom 156 42 51N 112 15W
Inle L. 82 20 30N 96 58 E
Inn → 27 48 35N 13 28 E
Innamincka 111 27 44 S 140 46 E
Inner Hebrides 14 57 0N 6 30W
Inner Mongolia = Nei Monggol Zizhiqu □ 94 42 0N 112 0 E
Inner Sound 14 57 30N 5 55W
Innerkip 150 43 13N 80 42W
Innerkirchen 28 46 43N 8 14 E
Innerste → 26 52 45N 9 40 E
Innetalling I. 142 56 0N 79 0W
Innisfail, Australia 110 17 33 S 146 5 E
Innisfail, Canada 144 52 0N 113 57W
In'no-shima 100 34 19N 133 10 E
Innsbruck 30 47 16N 11 23 E
Inny → 15 53 30N 7 50W
Ino 100 33 33N 133 26 E
Inocência 171 19 47 S 51 48W
Inongo 132 1 55 S 18 30 E
Inoni 132 3 4 S 15 39 E
Inoucdjouac 141 58 25N 78 15W
Inowrocław 32 52 50N 18 12 E
Inpundong 95 41 25N 126 34 E
Inquisivi 172 16 50 S 67 10W
Ins 28 47 1N 7 7 E
Inscription, C. 109 25 29 S 112 59 E
Insein 82 16 50N 96 5 E
Însurăţei 50 44 50N 27 40 E
Inta 56 66 5N 60 8 E
Intendente Alvear 174 35 12 S 63 32W
Interior 152 43 46N 101 59W
Interlaken 28 46 41N 7 50 E
International Falls 152 48 36N 93 25W
Intiyaco 174 28 43 S 60 5W
Intragna 29 46 11N 8 42 E
Intutu 168 3 32 S 74 48W
Inubō-Zaki 101 35 42N 140 52 E
Inútil, B. 176 53 30 S 70 15W
Inuvik 140 68 16N 133 40W
Inuyama 101 35 23N 136 56 E
Inveraray 14 56 13N 5 5W
Inverbervie 14 56 50N 2 17W
Invercargill 115 46 24 S 168 24 E
Inverell 111 29 45 S 151 8 E
Invergordon 14 57 41N 4 10W
Inverleigh 112 38 6 S 144 3 E
Invermere 144 50 30N 116 2W
Inverness, Canada 143 46 15N 61 19W
Inverness, U.K. 14 57 29N 4 12W
Inverness, U.S.A. 149 28 50N 82 20W
Inverurie 14 57 15N 2 21W
Inverway 108 17 50 S 129 38 E
Investigator Group 111 34 45 S 134 20 E
Investigator Str. 112 35 30 S 137 0 E
Inya 64 50 28N 86 37 E
Inyanga 131 18 12 S 32 40 E
Inyangani 131 18 5 S 32 50 E
Inyantue 131 18 30 S 26 40 E
Inyo Mts. 157 37 0N 118 0W
Inyokern 159 35 38N 117 48W
Inywa 82 23 56N 96 17 E
Inza 59 53 55N 46 25 E
Inzer 62 54 14N 57 34 E
Inzhavino 59 52 22N 42 30 E
Iō-Jima 99 30 48N 130 18 E
Ioánnina 48 39 42N 20 47 E
Ioánnina □ 48 39 39N 20 57 E
Iola 153 38 0N 95 20W
Ioma 107 8 19 S 147 52 E
Ion Corvin 50 44 7N 27 50 E
Iona 14 56 20N 6 25W
Ione, Calif., U.S.A. 158 38 20N 120 56W
Ione, Wash., U.S.A. 156 48 44N 117 29W
Ionia 155 42 59N 85 7W
Ionian Is. = Iónioi Nísoi 49 38 40N 20 0 E
Ionian Sea 39 37 30N 17 30 E
Iónioi Nísoi 49 38 40N 20 0 E
Iori → 61 41 3N 46 17 E
Íos 49 36 41N 25 20 E
Iowa □ 152 42 18N 93 30W
Iowa → 154 41 10N 91 1W
Iowa City 154 41 40N 91 35W
Iowa Falls 154 42 30N 93 15W
Ipala 130 4 30 S 32 52 E
Ipameri 171 17 44 S 48 9W
Iparía 172 9 17 S 74 29W
Ipáti 49 38 52N 22 14 E
Ipatovo 61 45 45N 42 50 E
Ipel → 31 48 10N 19 35 E
Ipiales 168 0 50N 77 37W
Ipiaú 171 14 8 S 39 44W
Ipil 91 7 47N 122 35 E
Ipin = Yibin 96 28 45N 104 32 E
Ipirá 171 12 10 S 39 44W
Ipiranga 168 3 13 S 65 57W
Ípiros □ 48 39 30N 20 30 E
Ipixuna 172 7 0 S 71 40W
Ipixuna →, Amazonas, Brazil 172 7 11 S 71 51W
Ipixuna →, Amazonas, Brazil 173 5 45 S 63 2W
Ipoh 85 4 35N 101 5 E
Iporá 171 11 23 S 50 40W
Ippy 132 6 5N 21 7 E
Ipsala 48 40 55N 26 23 E
Ipsárion Óros 48 40 40N 24 40 E
Ipswich, Australia 111 27 35 S 152 40 E
Ipswich, U.K. 13 52 4N 1 9 E
Ipswich, Mass., U.S.A. 151 42 40N 70 50W
Ipswich, S. Dak., U.S.A. 152 45 28N 99 1W
Ipu 170 4 23 S 40 44W
Ipueiras 170 4 33 S 40 43W
Ipupiara 171 11 49 S 42 37W
Iput → 58 52 26N 31 2 E
Iquique 172 20 19 S 70 5W
Iquitos 168 3 45 S 73 10W
Irabu-Jima 99 24 50N 125 10 E
Iracoubo 169 5 30N 53 10W
Īrafshān 73 26 42N 61 56 E
Irahuan 91 9 48N 118 41 E
Iráklia 49 36 50N 25 28 E
Iráklion 49 35 20N 25 12 E
Iráklion □ 49 35 10N 25 10 E
Irako-Zaki 101 34 35N 137 1 E
Irala 175 25 55 S 54 35W
Iramba □ 130 4 30 S 34 30 E
Iran ■ 73 33 0N 53 0 E
Iran, Gunung-Gunung 86 2 20N 114 50 E
Iranamadu Tank 81 9 23N 80 29 E
Īrānshahr 73 27 15N 60 40 E
Irapa 169 10 34N 62 35W
Irapuato 160 20 40N 101 30W
Iraq ■ 72 33 0N 44 0 E
Irarrar, O. → 121 20 0N 1 30 E
Irati 175 25 25 S 50 38W
Irbid 69 32 35N 35 48 E
Irbid □ 71 32 15N 36 35 E
Irbit 62 57 41N 63 3 E
Irebu 132 0 40 S 17 46 E
Irecê 170 11 18 S 41 52W
Iregua → 36 42 27N 2 24 E
Ireland ■ 15 53 0N 8 0W
Ireland's Eye 15 53 25N 6 4W
Irele 127 7 40N 5 40 E
Iremel, Gora 62 54 33N 58 50 E
Ireng → 169 3 33N 59 51W
Iret 65 60 3N 154 20 E
Irgiz, Bolshaya → 59 52 10N 49 10 E
Irhârharene 121 27 37N 7 30 E
Irharrhar, O. → 121 28 3N 6 15 E
Irherm 120 30 7N 8 18W
Irhil Mgoun 120 31 30N 6 28W
Irhyangdong 95 41 15N 129 30 E
Iri 95 35 59N 127 0 E
Irian Jaya □ 87 4 0 S 137 0 E
Iriba 123 15 7N 22 15 E
Irid, Mt. 90 14 47N 121 19 E
Irié 126 8 15N 9 10W
Iriga 90 13 25N 123 25 E
Iriklinskiy 62 51 39N 58 38 E
Iriklinskoye Vdkhr. 62 52 0N 59 0 E
Iringa 130 7 48 S 35 43 E
Iringa □ 130 7 48 S 35 43 E
Irinjalakuda 81 10 21N 76 14 E
Iriomote-Jima 99 24 19N 123 48 E
Iriona 162 15 57N 85 11W
Iriri → 169 3 52 S 52 37W
Iriri Novo → 173 8 46 S 53 22W

Irish Republic

Irish Republic ■ 15 53 0N 8 0W
Irish Sea 12 54 0N 5 0W
Irkeshtam ...... 63 39 41N 73 55 E
Irkineyeva ...... 65 58 30N 96 49 E
Irkutsk ...... 65 52 18N 104 20 E
Irma 145 52 55N 111 14W
Irō-Zaki ...... 101 34 36N 138 51 E
Iroise, Mer d' 18 48 15N 4 45W
Iron Baron ...... 112 32 58 S 137 11 E
Iron Gate = Portile de Fier ...... 50 44 42N 22 30 E
Iron Knob ...... 112 32 46 S 137 8 E
Iron Mountain 148 45 49N 88 4W
Iron River 152 46 6N 88 40W
Ironbridge 13 52 38N 2 29W
Irondequoit 150 43 13N 77 35W
Ironstone Kopje ...... 134 25 17 S 24 5 E
Ironton, Mo., U.S.A. 153 37 40N 90 40W
Ironton, Ohio, U.S.A. 148 38 35N 82 40W
Ironwood 152 46 30N 90 10W
Iroquois → 155 41 5N 87 49W
Iroquois Falls 142 48 46N 80 41W
Irosin ...... 90 12 42N 124 2 E
Irpen ...... 58 50 30N 30 15 E
Irrara Cr. → ...... 111 29 35 S 145 31 E
Irrawaddy □ ...... 82 17 0N 95 0 E
Irrawaddy → ...... 82 15 50N 95 6 E
Irsina ...... 45 40 45N 16 15 E
Irtysh → ...... 64 61 4N 68 52 E
Irumu ...... 130 1 32N 29 53 E
Irún 36 43 20N 1 52W
Irurzun 36 42 55N 1 50W
Irvine, Canada 145 49 57N 110 16W
Irvine, U.K. 14 55 37N 4 40W
Irvine, Calif., U.S.A. 159 33 41N 117 46W
Irvine, U.S.A. 155 37 42N 83 58W
Irvinestown 15 54 28N 7 38W
Irvington 155 37 53N 86 17W
Irvona 150 40 46N 78 35W
Irwin → ...... 109 29 15 S 114 54 E
Irwin, Pt. ...... 109 35 5 S 116 55 E
Irymple ...... 112 34 14 S 142 8 E
Is-sur-Tille ...... 19 47 30N 5 8 E
Isa ...... 127 13 14N 6 24 E
Isaac → ...... 110 22 55 S 149 20 E
Isabel 152 45 27N 101 22W
Isabela ...... 91 10 12N 122 59 E
Isabela □ ...... 90 17 0N 122 0 E
Isabela, I. 160 21 51N 105 55W
Isabela, La 163 19 58N 71 2W
Isabella ...... 91 6 40N 122 10 E
Isabella, Cord. 162 13 30N 85 25W
Isabella Ra. ...... 108 21 0 S 121 4 E
Ísafjarðardjúp 54 66 10N 23 0W
Ísafjörður 54 66 5N 23 9W
Isagarh ...... 78 24 48N 77 51 E
Isahaya ...... 100 32 52N 130 2 E
Isaka ...... 130 3 56 S 32 59 E
Isakly ...... 62 54 8N 51 32 E
Isana → 168 0 26N 67 19W
Isangi ...... 132 0 52N 24 10 E
Isar → ...... 27 48 49N 12 58 E
Isarco → ...... 43 46 57N 11 18 E
Íṣari ...... 49 37 22N 22 0 E
Isbergues ...... 19 50 36N 2 28 E
Isbiceni ...... 50 43 45N 24 40 E
Iscayachi ...... 173 21 31 S 65 3W
Íschia ...... 44 40 45N 13 51 E
Iscuandé 168 2 28N 77 59W
Isdell → ...... 108 16 27 S 124 51 E
Ise ...... 101 34 25N 136 45 E
Ise-Heiya ...... 101 34 40N 136 30 E
Ise-Wan ...... 101 34 43N 136 43 E
Isefjord ...... 52 55 53N 11 50 E
Iseltwald ...... 28 46 43N 7 58 E
Isenthal ...... 29 46 55N 8 34 E
Iseo ...... 42 45 40N 10 3 E
Iseo, L. d' ...... 42 45 45N 10 3 E
Iseramagazi ...... 130 4 37 S 32 10 E
Isère □ ...... 21 45 15N 5 40 E
Isère → ...... 21 44 59N 4 51 E
Iserlohn ...... 26 51 22N 7 40 E
Isérnia ...... 45 41 35N 14 12 E
Isesaki ...... 101 36 19N 139 12 E
Iset → ...... 62 56 36N 66 24 E
Iseyin ...... 127 8 0N 3 36 E
Isfara ...... 63 40 7N 70 38 E
Isherton 169 2 20N 59 25W
Ishigaki-Shima ...... 99 24 20N 124 10 E
Ishikari-Gawa → ...... 98 43 15N 141 23 E
Ishikari-Sammyaku ...... 98 43 30N 143 0 E
Ishikari-Wan ...... 98 43 25N 141 1 E
Ishikawa ...... 106 26 25N 127 48 E
Ishikawa □ ...... 101 36 30N 136 30 E
Ishim ...... 64 56 10N 69 30 E
Ishim → ...... 64 57 45N 71 10 E
Ishimbay ...... 62 53 28N 56 2 E
Ishinomaki ...... 98 38 32N 141 20 E
Ishioka ...... 101 36 11N 140 16 E
Ishizuchi-Yama ...... 100 33 45N 133 6 E
Ishkashim ...... 63 36 44N 71 37 E
Ishkuman ...... 79 36 30N 73 50 E
Ishmi ...... 48 41 33N 19 34 E
Ishpeming 148 46 30N 87 40W
Ishurdi ...... 82 24 9N 89 3 E
Isigny-sur-Mer 18 49 19N 1 6W
Isil Kul ...... 64 54 55N 71 16 E
Isiolo ...... 130 0 24N 37 33 E
Isiolo □ ...... 130 2 30N 37 30 E
Isipingo Beach ...... 135 30 0 S 30 57 E
Isiro ...... 130 2 53N 27 40 E
Isisford ...... 110 24 15 S 144 21 E
Iskander ...... 63 41 36N 69 41 E
İskele ...... 70 36 34N 35 23 E
İskenderun ...... 57 36 32N 36 10 E
İskenderun Körfezi ...... 57 36 40N 35 50 E
Iski-Naukat ...... 63 40 16N 72 36 E
İskilip ...... 60 40 50N 34 20 E
Iskŭr → ...... 47 43 45N 24 25 E
Iskŭr, Yazovir ...... 47 42 23N 23 30 E
Iskut → 144 56 45N 131 49W
Isla → 14 56 32N 3 20W
Isla Cristina 35 37 13N 7 17W
Isla Vista 159 34 27N 119 52W
İslâhiye ...... 70 37 0N 36 35 E
Islamabad ...... 77 33 40N 73 10 E
Islamkot ...... 78 24 42N 70 13 E
Islampur ...... 80 17 2N 74 20 E
Island → 144 60 25N 121 12W
Island Bay ...... 91 9 6N 118 10 E
Island Falls, Canada 142 49 35N 81 20W
Island Falls, U.S.A. 143 46 0N 68 16W
Island L. 145 53 47N 94 25W
Island Lagoon ...... 112 31 30 S 136 40 E
Island Pt. ...... 109 30 20 S 115 1 E
Island Pond 151 44 50N 71 50W
Islands, B. of, Canada 143 49 11N 58 15W
Islands, B. of, N.Z. ...... 114 35 15 S 174 6 E
Islay 14 55 46N 6 10W
Isle → 20 44 55N 0 15W
Isle-Adam, L' ...... 19 49 6N 2 14 E
Isle aux Morts 143 47 35N 59 0W
Isle-Jourdain, L', Gers, France ...... 20 43 36N 1 5 E
Isle-Jourdain, L', Vienne, France ...... 20 46 13N 0 31 E
Isle of Wight □ 13 50 40N 1 20W
Isle Royale 152 48 0N 88 50W
Isle-sur-le-Doubs, L' ...... 19 47 26N 6 34 E
Isleta 157 34 58N 106 46W
Isleton 158 38 10N 121 37W
Ismail ...... 60 45 22N 28 46 E
Ismâ'ilîya ...... 124 30 37N 32 18 E
Ismaning ...... 27 48 14N 11 41 E
Ismay 152 46 33N 104 44W
Isna ...... 124 25 17N 32 30 E
Isogstalo ...... 79 34 15N 78 46 E
Isola del Gran Sasso d'Italia ...... 43 42 30N 13 40 E
Ísola del Liri ...... 44 41 39N 13 32 E
Ísola della Scala ...... 42 45 16N 11 0 E
Ísola di Capo Rizzuto ...... 45 38 56N 17 5 E
Isparta ...... 57 37 47N 30 30 E
Isperikh ...... 47 43 43N 26 50 E
Íspica ...... 45 36 47N 14 53 E
İspir ...... 61 40 40N 40 50 E
Israel ■ ...... 69 32 0N 34 50 E
Issano 169 5 49N 59 26W
Isseka ...... 109 28 30 S 114 35 E
Issia 126 6 33N 6 33W
Issoire ...... 20 45 32N 3 15 E
Issoudun ...... 19 46 57N 2 0 E
Issyk-Kul, Ozero ...... 63 42 25N 77 15 E
Ist ...... 43 44 17N 14 47 E
Istaihah ...... 75 23 19N 54 4 E
İstanbul ...... 57 41 0N 29 0 E
Istiaía ...... 49 38 57N 23 9 E
Istmina 168 5 10N 76 39W
Istok ...... 46 42 45N 20 24 E
Istokpoga, L. 149 27 22N 81 14W
Istra, U.S.S.R. ...... 59 55 55N 36 50 E
Istra, Yugoslavia ...... 43 45 10N 14 0 E
Istranca Dağları ...... 47 41 48N 27 30 E
Istres ...... 21 43 31N 4 59 E
Istria = Istra ...... 43 45 10N 14 0 E
Isulan ...... 91 6 30N 124 29 E
Itá ...... 174 25 29 S 57 21W
'Itāb ...... 75 15 20N 51 29 E
Itabaiana, Paraíba, Brazil ...... 170 7 18 S 35 19W
Itabaiana, Sergipe, Brazil ...... 170 10 41 S 37 37W
Itabaianinha ...... 170 11 16 S 37 47W
Itaberaba ...... 171 12 32 S 40 18W
Itaberaí ...... 171 16 2 S 49 48W
Itabira ...... 171 19 37 S 43 13W
Itabirito ...... 171 20 15 S 43 48W
Itaboca ...... 169 4 50 S 62 40W
Itabuna ...... 171 14 48 S 39 16W
Itacajá ...... 170 8 19 S 47 46W
Itacaunas → ...... 170 5 21 S 49 8W
Itacoatiara ...... 169 3 8 S 58 25W
Itacuaí → ...... 172 4 20 S 70 12W
Itaguaçu ...... 171 19 48 S 40 51W
Itaguari → ...... 171 14 11 S 44 40W
Itaguatins ...... 170 5 47 S 47 29W
Itaim → ...... 170 7 2 S 42 2W
Itainópolis ...... 170 7 24 S 41 31W
Itaipu Dam ...... 175 25 30 S 54 30W
Itaituba ...... 169 4 10 S 55 50W
Itajaí ...... 175 27 50 S 48 39W
Itajubá ...... 171 22 24 S 45 30W
Itajuípe ...... 171 14 41 S 39 22W
Itaka ...... 131 8 50 S 32 49 E
Itako ...... 101 35 56N 140 33 E
Italy ■ ...... 40 42 0N 13 0 E
Itamataré ...... 170 2 16 S 46 24W
Itambacuri ...... 171 18 1 S 41 42W
Itambé ...... 171 15 15 S 40 37W
Itampolo ...... 135 24 41 S 43 57 E
Itanhauã → ...... 169 4 45 S 63 48W
Itanhém ...... 171 17 9 S 40 20W
Itano ...... 100 34 7N 134 28 E
Itapaci ...... 171 14 57 S 49 34W
Itapagé ...... 170 3 41 S 39 34W
Itaparica, I. de ...... 171 12 54 S 38 42W
Itapebi ...... 171 15 56 S 39 32W
Itapecuru-Mirim ...... 170 3 24 S 44 20W
Itaperuna ...... 171 21 10 S 41 54W
Itapetinga ...... 171 15 15 S 40 15W
Itapetininga ...... 175 23 36 S 48 7W
Itapeva ...... 175 23 59 S 48 59W
Itapicuru →, Bahia, Brazil ...... 170 11 47 S 37 32W
Itapicuru →, Maranhão, Brazil ...... 170 2 52 S 44 12W
Itapinima ...... 173 5 25 S 60 44W
Itapipoca ...... 170 3 30 S 39 35W
Itapiranga ...... 169 2 45 S 58 1W
Itapiúna ...... 170 4 33 S 38 57W
Itaporanga ...... 170 7 18 S 38 0W
Itapuá □ ...... 175 26 40 S 55 40W
Itapuranga ...... 171 15 40 S 49 59W
Itaquari ...... 171 20 20 S 40 25W
Itaquatiara ...... 172 2 58 S 58 30W
Itaquí ...... 174 29 8 S 56 30W
Itararé ...... 175 24 6 S 49 23W
Itarsi ...... 78 22 36N 77 51 E
Itarumã ...... 171 18 42 S 51 25W
Itatí ...... 174 27 16 S 58 15W
Itatira ...... 170 4 30 S 39 37W
Itatuba ...... 173 5 46 S 63 20W
Itatupa ...... 169 0 37 S 51 12W
Itaueira ...... 170 7 36 S 43 2W
Itaueira → ...... 170 6 41 S 42 55W
Itaúna ...... 171 20 4 S 44 34W
Itbayat ...... 90 20 47N 121 51 E
Itbayat I. ...... 90 20 46N 121 50 E
Itchen → 13 50 57N 1 20W
Ite ...... 172 17 55 S 70 57W
Itéa ...... 49 38 25N 22 25 E
Ithaca = Itháki ...... 49 38 25N 20 40 E
Ithaca 151 42 25N 76 30W
Itháki ...... 49 38 25N 20 40 E
Itinga ...... 171 16 36 S 41 47W
Itiquira ...... 173 17 12 S 54 7W
Itiquira → ...... 173 17 18 S 56 44W
Itiruçu ...... 171 13 31 S 40 9W
Itiúba ...... 170 10 43 S 39 51W
Ito ...... 101 34 58N 139 5 E
Itoigawa ...... 99 37 2N 137 51 E
Itoman ...... 106 26 7N 127 40 E
Iton → ...... 18 49 9N 1 12 E
Itonamas → ...... 172 12 28 S 64 24W
Itsa ...... 124 29 15N 30 47 E
Itsukaichi ...... 100 34 22N 132 22 E
Itsuki ...... 100 32 24N 130 50 E
İttiri ...... 44 40 38N 8 32 E
Itu, Brazil ...... 175 23 17 S 47 15W
Itu, Nigeria ...... 127 5 10N 7 58 E
Ituaçu ...... 171 13 50 S 41 18W
Ituango 168 7 4N 75 45W
Ituiutaba ...... 171 19 0 S 49 25W
Itumbiara ...... 171 18 20 S 49 10W
Ituna 145 51 10N 103 24W
Itunge Port ...... 131 9 40 S 33 55 E
Ituni 169 5 28N 58 15W
Itupiranga ...... 170 5 9 S 49 20W
Iturama ...... 171 19 44 S 50 11W
Iturbe ...... 174 23 0 S 65 25W
Ituri → ...... 130 1 40N 27 1 E
Iturup, Ostrov ...... 65 45 0N 148 0 E
Ituverava ...... 171 20 20 S 47 47W
Ituxi → ...... 173 7 18 S 64 51W
Ituyuro → ...... 174 22 40 S 63 50W
Itzehoe ...... 26 53 56N 9 31 E
Iuka 155 38 37N 88 47W
Ivaí → ...... 175 23 18 S 53 42W
Ivalo ...... 54 68 38N 27 35 E
Ivalojoki → ...... 54 68 40N 27 40 E
Ivangorod ...... 58 59 37N 28 40 E
Ivangrad ...... 46 42 51N 19 52 E
Ivanhoe, N.S.W., Australia ...... 112 32 56 S 144 20 E
Ivanhoe, N. Terr., Australia ...... 108 15 41 S 128 41 E
Ivanhoe, U.S.A. 158 36 25N 119 13W
Ivanhoe L. 145 60 25N 106 30W
Ivanić Grad ...... 43 45 41N 16 25 E
Ivanjica ...... 46 43 35N 20 12 E
Ivanjšcice ...... 43 46 12N 16 13 E
Ivankoyskoye Vdkhr. ...... 59 56 37N 36 32 E
Ivano-Frankovsk ...... 58 48 40N 24 40 E
Ivanovka ...... 62 52 34N 53 23 E
Ivanovo, Byelorussian S.S.R., U.S.S.R. ...... 58 52 7N 25 29 E
Ivanovo, R.S.F.S.R., U.S.S.R. ...... 59 57 5N 41 0 E
Ivato ...... 135 20 37 S 47 10 E
Ivaylovgrad ...... 47 41 32N 26 8 E
Ivdel ...... 56 60 42N 60 24 E
Ivindo → ...... 132 0 9 S 12 9 E
Ivinheima → ...... 175 23 14 S 53 42W
Iviza = Ibiza ...... 37 38 54N 1 26 E
Ivohibe ...... 135 22 31 S 46 57 E
Ivolândia ...... 171 16 34 S 50 51W
Ivory Coast ■ 126 7 30N 5 0W
Ivösjön ...... 53 56 8N 14 25 E
Ivrea ...... 42 45 30N 7 52 E
Ivugivik 141 62 24N 77 55W
Iwahig, Palawan, Phil. ...... 86 8 36N 117 32 E
Iwahig, Palawan, Phil. ...... 91 9 19N 118 5 E
Iwai-Jima ...... 100 33 47N 131 58 E
Iwaizumi ...... 98 39 50N 141 45 E
Iwaki ...... 99 37 3N 140 55 E
Iwakuni ...... 100 34 15N 132 8 E
Iwami ...... 100 35 32N 134 15 E
Iwamizawa ...... 98 43 12N 141 46 E
Iwanai ...... 98 42 58N 140 30 E
Iwase ...... 101 36 21N 140 6 E
Iwata ...... 101 34 42N 137 51 E
Iwate □ ...... 98 39 30N 141 30 E
Iwate-San ...... 98 39 51N 141 0 E
Iwo ...... 127 7 39N 4 9 E
Iwonicz-Zdrój ...... 32 49 37N 21 47 E
Iwungu ...... 133 5 16 S 19 17 E
Ixiamas ...... 172 13 50 S 68 5W
Ixopo ...... 135 30 11 S 30 5 E
Ixtepec 161 16 32N 95 10W
Ixtlán del Río 160 21 5N 104 21W
'Iyādh ...... 74 14 59N 46 51 E
Iyo ...... 100 33 45N 132 45 E
Iyo-mishima ...... 100 33 58N 133 30 E
Iyo-Nada ...... 100 33 40N 132 20 E
Izabel, L. de 162 15 30N 89 10W
Izamal 161 20 56N 89 1W
Izberbash ...... 61 42 35N 47 52 E
Izbica ...... 32 50 53N 23 10 E
Izbica Kujawska ...... 32 52 25N 18 30 E
Izegem ...... 23 50 55N 3 12 E
Izena-Shima ...... 106 26 56N 127 56 E
Izgrev ...... 47 43 36N 26 58 E
Izh → ...... 62 55 58N 52 38 E
Izhevsk = Ustinov ...... 62 56 51N 53 14 E
Izkī ...... 75 22 56N 27 46 E
İzmir ...... 57 38 25N 27 8 E
İzmit ...... 57 40 45N 29 50 E
Iznajar 35 37 15N 4 19W
Iznalloz 37 37 24N 3 30W
Izobil'nyy ...... 61 45 25N 41 44 E
Izola ...... 43 45 32N 13 39 E
Izozog, Bañados de ...... 173 18 48 S 62 10W
Izra ...... 69 32 51N 36 15 E
Iztochni Rodopi ...... 47 41 45N 25 30 E
Izu-Hantō ...... 101 34 45N 139 0 E
Izu-Shotō ...... 99 34 30N 140 0 E
Izuhara ...... 100 34 12N 129 17 E
Izumi ...... 100 32 5N 130 22 E
Izumi-sano ...... 101 34 23N 135 18 E
Izumiotsu ...... 101 34 30N 135 24 E
Izumo ...... 100 35 20N 132 46 E
Izyaslav ...... 58 50 5N 26 50 E
Izyum ...... 60 49 12N 37 19 E

J

J.F. Rodrigues ...... 170 2 55 S 50 20W
Jaba, Ethiopia ...... 125 6 20N 35 7 E
Jaba', Jordan ...... 69 32 20N 35 13 E
Jabal el Awliya ...... 125 15 10N 32 31 E
Jabal Lubnān ...... 70 33 45N 35 40 E
Jabalón → 35 38 53N 4 5W
Jabalpur ...... 79 23 9N 79 58 E
Jabālyah ...... 69 31 32N 34 27 E
Jabbūl ...... 72 36 4N 37 30 E
Jablah ...... 70 35 20N 36 0 E
Jablanac ...... 43 44 42N 14 56 E
Jablonec ...... 30 50 43N 15 10 E
Jablonica ...... 31 48 37N 17 26 E
Jabłonowo ...... 32 53 23N 19 10 E
Jaboatão ...... 170 8 7 S 35 1W
Jabonga ...... 91 9 20N 125 32 E
Jaboticabal ...... 175 21 15 S 48 17W
Jabukovac ...... 46 44 22N 22 21 E
Jaburu ...... 173 5 30 S 64 0W
Jaca 36 42 35N 0 33W
Jacaré → ...... 170 10 3 S 42 13W
Jacareí ...... 175 23 20 S 46 0W
Jacarèzinho ...... 175 23 5 S 50 0W
Jáchymov ...... 30 50 22N 12 55 E
Jaciara ...... 173 15 59 S 54 57W
Jacinto ...... 171 16 10 S 40 17W
Jaciparaná ...... 173 9 15 S 64 23W
Jackman 143 45 35N 70 17W
Jacksboro 153 33 14N 98 15W
Jackson, Australia ...... 111 26 39 S 149 39 E
Jackson, Ala., U.S.A. 149 31 32N 87 53W
Jackson, Calif., U.S.A. 158 38 19N 120 47W
Jackson, Ky., U.S.A. 148 37 35N 83 22W
Jackson, Mich., U.S.A. 155 42 18N 84 25W
Jackson, Minn., U.S.A. 152 43 35N 95 0W
Jackson, Miss., U.S.A. 153 32 20N 90 10W
Jackson, Mo., U.S.A. 153 37 25N 89 42W
Jackson, Ohio, U.S.A. 148 39 0N 82 40W
Jackson, Tenn., U.S.A. 149 35 40N 88 50W
Jackson, Wyo., U.S.A. 156 43 30N 110 49W
Jackson, C. ...... 115 40 59 S 174 20 E
Jackson, L. 156 43 55N 110 40W
Jackson Bay ...... 115 43 58 S 168 42 E
Jackson Center 155 40 27N 84 4W
Jacksons ...... 115 42 46 S 171 32 E
Jacksonville, Ala., U.S.A. 149 33 49N 85 45W
Jacksonville, Calif., U.S.A. 158 37 52N 120 24W

Jacksonville, Fla., U.S.A. 149 30 15N 81 38W
Jacksonville, Ill., U.S.A. 154 39 42N 90 15W
Jacksonville, N.C., U.S.A. 149 34 50N 77 29W
Jacksonville, Oreg., U.S.A. 156 42 19N 122 56W
Jacksonville, Tex., U.S.A. 153 31 58N 95 19W
Jacksonville Beach 149 30 19N 81 26W
Jacmel 163 18 14N 72 32W
Jacob Lake 157 36 45N 112 12W
Jacobabad 77 28 20N 68 29 E
Jacobina 170 11 11 S 40 30W
Jacob's Well 69 32 13N 35 13 E
Jacques-Cartier, Mt. 143 48 57N 66 0W
Jacqueville 126 5 12N 4 25W
Jacuí → 175 30 2 S 51 15W
Jacumba 159 32 37N 116 11W
Jacundá → 170 1 57 S 50 26W
Jade 26 53 22N 8 14 E
Jadebusen 26 53 30N 8 15 E
Jadoigne 23 50 43N 4 52 E
Jadotville = Likasi 131 10 55 S 26 48 E
Jadovnik 46 43 20N 19 45 E
Jadów 32 52 28N 21 38 E
Jadraque 36 40 55N 2 55W
Jādū 122 32 0N 12 0 E
Jaén, Peru 172 5 25 S 78 40W
Jaén, Spain 35 37 44N 3 43W
Jaén □ 35 37 50N 3 30W
Jærens rev 51 58 45N 5 45 E
Jafène 120 20 35N 5 30W
Jaffa = Tel Aviv-Yafo 69 32 4N 34 48 E
Jaffa, C. 112 36 58 S 139 40 E
Jaffna 81 9 45N 80 2 E
Jagadhri 78 30 10N 77 20 E
Jagadishpur 79 25 30N 84 21 E
Jagdalpur 80 19 3N 82 0 E
Jagersfontein 134 29 44 S 25 27 E
Jagst → 27 49 14N 9 11 E
Jagtial 80 18 50N 79 0 E
Jaguaquara 171 13 32 S 39 58W
Jaguariaíva 175 24 10 S 49 50W
Jaguaribe 170 5 53 S 38 37W
Jaguaribe → 170 4 25 S 37 45W
Jaguaruana 170 4 50 S 37 47W
Jagüey Grande 162 22 35N 81 7W
Jagungal, Mt. 113 36 8 S 148 22 E
Jahangirabad 78 28 19N 78 4 E
Jahrom 73 28 30N 53 31 E
Jaicós 170 7 21 S 41 8W
Jailolo 87 1 5N 127 30 E
Jailolo, Selat 87 0 5N 129 5 E
Jaintiapur 82 25 8N 92 7 E
Jaipur 78 27 0N 75 50 E
Jājarm 73 36 58N 56 27 E
Jajce 46 44 19N 17 17 E
Jajpur 79 20 53N 86 22 E
Jakarta 88 6 9 S 106 49 E
Jakobstad 54 63 40N 22 43 E
Jakupica 46 41 45N 21 22 E
Jal 153 32 8N 103 8W
Jalalabad, Afghan. 77 34 30N 70 29 E
Jalalabad, India 79 27 41N 79 42 E
Jalalpur Jattan 78 32 38N 74 11 E
Jalama 159 34 29N 120 29W
Jalapa 162 14 39N 89 59W
Jalapa Enríquez 161 19 32N 96 55W
Jalaun 79 26 8N 79 25 E
Jaldak 77 31 58N 66 43 E
Jales 171 20 10 S 50 33W
Jaleswar 79 26 38N 85 48 E
Jalgaon, Maharashtra, India 78 21 2N 76 31 E
Jalgaon, Maharashtra, India 78 21 0N 75 42 E
Jalhay 23 50 33N 5 58 E
Jalībah 72 30 35N 46 32 E
Jalingo 127 8 55N 11 25 E
Jalisco □ 160 20 0N 104 0W
Jalkot 79 35 14N 73 24 E
Jallas → 34 42 54N 9 8W
Jallumba 112 36 55 S 141 57 E
Jalna 80 19 48N 75 38 E
Jalón → 36 41 47N 1 4W
Jalpa 160 21 38N 102 58W
Jalpaiguri 82 26 32N 88 46 E
Jalq 77 27 35N 62 46 E
Jaluit I. 104 6 0N 169 30 E
Jalūlā 72 34 16N 45 10 E
Jamaari 127 11 44N 9 53 E
Jamaica 154 41 51N 94 18W
Jamaica ■ 162 18 10N 77 30W
Jamalpur, Bangla. 82 24 52N 89 56 E
Jamalpur, India 79 25 18N 86 28 E
Jamalpurganj 79 23 2N 88 1 E
Jamanxim → 173 4 43 S 56 18W
Jamari 173 8 45 S 63 27W
Jamari → 173 8 27 S 63 30W
Jambe 87 1 15 S 132 10 E
Jambes 23 50 27N 4 52 E
Jambi 88 1 38 S 103 30 E
Jambi □ 88 1 30 S 102 30 E
Jambusar 78 22 3N 72 51 E
James → 152 42 52N 97 18W
James B. 142 51 30N 80 0W
James Ranges 108 24 10 S 132 30 E
James Ross I. 7 63 58 S 57 50W
Jamesport 154 39 58N 93 48W
Jamestown, Australia 112 33 10 S 138 32 E
Jamestown, S. Africa 134 31 6 S 26 45 E
Jamestown, Ind., U.S.A. 155 39 56N 86 38W
Jamestown, Ky., U.S.A. 148 37 0N 85 5W
Jamestown, Mo., U.S.A. 154 38 48N 92 30W
Jamestown, N. Dak., U.S.A. 152 46 54N 98 42W
Jamestown, N.Y., U.S.A. 150 42 5N 79 18W
Jamestown, Ohio, U.S.A. 155 39 39N 83 44W
Jamestown, Pa., U.S.A. 150 41 32N 80 27W
Jamestown, Tenn., U.S.A. 149 36 25N 85 0W
Jamīlābād 73 34 24N 48 28 E
Jamiltepec 161 16 17N 97 49W
Jamkhandi 80 16 30N 75 15 E
Jammā'īn 69 32 8N 35 12 E
Jammalamadugu 81 14 51N 78 25 E
Jammerbugt 53 57 15N 9 20 E
Jammu 78 32 43N 74 54 E
Jammu & Kashmir □ 79 34 25N 77 0 E
Jamnagar 78 22 30N 70 6 E
Jamner 78 20 45N 75 52 E
Jamoigne 23 49 41N 5 24 E
Jampur 77 29 39N 70 40 E
Jamrud 77 33 59N 71 24 E
Jamshedpur 79 22 44N 86 12 E
Jamtara 79 23 59N 86 49 E
Jämtlands län □ 52 62 40N 13 50 E
Jamuna → 82 23 51N 89 45 E
Jamurki 82 24 9N 90 2 E
Jan Kempdorp 134 27 55 S 24 51 E
Jan L. 145 54 56N 102 55W
Jan Mayen Is. 6 71 0N 9 0W
Janaúba 171 15 48 S 43 19W
Janaucu, I. 170 0 30N 50 10W
Jand 78 33 30N 72 6 E
Janda, L. de la 35 36 15N 5 45W
Jandaia 171 17 6 S 50 7W
Jandaq 73 34 3N 54 22 E
Jandia 37 28 6N 14 21W
Jandia, Pta. de 37 28 3N 14 31W
Jandiatuba → 168 3 28 S 68 42W
Jandola 78 32 20N 70 9 E
Jandowae 111 26 45 S 151 7 E
Jandrain-Jandrenouilles 23 50 40N 4 58 E
Jándula → 35 38 3N 4 6W
Jane Pk. 115 45 15 S 168 20 E
Janesville 154 42 39N 89 1W
Janga 127 10 5N 1 0W
Jango 173 20 27 S 55 29W
Jangoon 80 17 44N 79 5 E
Janhtang Ga 82 26 32N 96 38 E
Jānī Kheyl 77 32 46N 68 24 E
Janikowo 32 52 45N 18 7 E
Janīn 69 32 28N 35 18 E
Janinà = Ioánnina □ 48 39 39N 20 57 E
Janiuay 91 10 58N 122 30 E
Janja 46 44 40N 19 17 E
Janjevo 46 42 35N 21 19 E
Janjina 46 42 58N 17 25 E
Janos 160 30 45N 108 10W
Jánoshalma 31 46 18N 19 21 E
Jánosháza 31 47 8N 17 12 E
Jánossomorja 31 47 47N 17 11 E
Janów 32 50 44N 19 27 E
Janów Lubelski 32 50 48N 22 23 E
Janów Podlaski 32 52 11N 23 11 E
Janowiec Wielkopolski 32 52 45N 17 30 E
Januária 171 15 25 S 44 25W
Janub Dârfûr □ 125 11 0N 25 0 E
Janub Kordofân □ 125 12 0N 30 0 E
Janville 19 48 10N 1 50 E
Janzé 18 47 55N 1 28W
Jaora 78 23 40N 75 10 E
Japan ■ 99 36 0N 136 0 E
Japan, Sea of 98 40 0N 135 0 E
Japan Trench 104 32 0N 142 0 E
Japen = Yapen 87 1 50 S 136 0 E
Japurá → 168 3 8 S 64 46W
Jaque 168 7 27N 78 8W
Jara, La 157 37 16N 106 0W
Jarābulus 72 36 49N 38 1 E
Jaraguá 171 15 45 S 49 20W
Jaraguari 173 20 9 S 54 35W
Jaraicejo 35 39 40N 5 49W
Jaraiz 34 40 4N 5 45W
Jarama → 36 40 2N 3 39W
Jaramillo 176 47 10 S 67 7W
Jarandilla 34 40 8N 5 39W
Jaranwala 77 31 15N 73 26 E
Jarash 69 32 17N 35 54 E
Jarauçu → 169 1 48 S 52 22W
Jardas al 'Abīd 122 32 18N 20 59 E
Jardim 174 21 28 S 56 2W
Jardín → 37 38 50N 2 10W
Jardines de la Reina, Is. 162 20 50N 78 50W
Jargalang 95 43 5N 122 55 E
Jargalant = Hovd 92 48 2N 91 37 E
Jargeau 19 47 50N 2 1 E
Jari → 169 1 9 S 51 54W
Jarīr, W. al → 72 25 38N 42 30 E
Jarmen 26 53 56N 13 20 E
Jarnac 20 45 40N 0 11W
Jarny 19 49 9N 5 53 E
Jaro 91 11 11N 124 47 E
Jarocin 32 51 59N 17 29 E
Jaroměř 30 50 22N 15 52 E
Jarosław 32 50 2N 22 42 E
Järpås 53 58 23N 12 57 E
Järpen 52 63 21N 13 26 E
Jarrahdale 109 32 24 S 116 5 E
Jarres, Plaine des 84 19 27N 103 10 E
Jarso 125 5 15N 37 30 E
Jartai 94 39 45N 105 48 E
Jaru 173 10 26 S 62 27W
Jaru → 173 10 5 S 61 59W
Jarud Qi 95 44 28N 120 50 E
Jarvis 150 42 53N 80 6W
Jarvis I. 105 0 15 S 159 55W
Jarvornik 31 50 23N 17 2 E
Jarwa 79 27 38N 82 30 E
Jaša Tomić 46 45 26N 20 50 E
Jasaan 91 8 39N 124 45 E
Jasien 32 51 46N 15 0 E
Jāsimīyah 72 33 45N 44 41 E
Jasin 85 2 20N 102 26 E
Jāsk 73 25 38N 57 45 E
Jasło 32 49 45N 21 30 E
Jason, Is. 176 51 0 S 61 0W
Jasonville 155 39 10N 87 13W
Jasper, Alta., Canada 144 52 55N 118 5W
Jasper, Ont., Canada 151 44 52N 75 57W
Jasper, Ala., U.S.A. 149 33 48N 87 16W
Jasper, Fla., U.S.A. 149 30 31N 82 58W
Jasper, Ind., U.S.A. 155 38 24N 86 56W
Jasper, Minn., U.S.A. 152 43 52N 96 22W
Jasper, Tex., U.S.A. 153 30 59N 93 58W
Jasper Nat. Park 144 52 50N 118 8W
Jassy = Iaşi 50 47 10N 27 40 E
Jastrebarsko 43 45 41N 15 39 E
Jastrowie 32 53 26N 16 49 E
Jastrzębie Zdrój 32 49 57N 18 35 E
Jászapáti 31 47 32N 20 10 E
Jászárokszállás 31 47 39N 20 1 E
Jászberény 31 47 30N 19 55 E
Jászkiser 31 47 27N 20 20 E
Jászladány 31 47 23N 20 10 E
Jataí 171 17 58 S 51 48W
Jatapu → 169 2 13 S 58 17W
Jati 78 24 20N 68 19 E
Jatibarang 89 6 28 S 108 18 E
Jatinegara 88 6 13 S 106 52 E
Játiva 37 39 0N 0 32W
Jatobal 170 4 35 S 49 33W
Jatt 69 32 24N 35 2 E
Jáu, Angola 133 15 12 S 13 31 E
Jaú, Brazil 175 22 10 S 48 30W
Jaú → 169 1 54 S 61 26W
Jauaperí → 169 1 26 S 61 35W
Jauche 23 50 41N 4 57 E
Jauja 172 11 45 S 75 15W
Jaunjelgava 58 56 35N 25 0 E
Jaunpur 79 25 46N 82 44 E
Jauru → 173 16 22 S 57 46W
Java = Jawa 88 7 0 S 110 0 E
Java Sea 89 4 35 S 107 15 E
Java Trench 88 10 0 S 110 0W
Javadi Hills 81 12 40N 78 40 E
Jávea 37 38 48N 0 10 E
Javhlant = Ulyasutay 92 47 56N 97 28 E
Javier, I. 176 47 5 S 74 25W
Javla 80 17 18N 75 9 E
Javron 18 48 25N 0 25W
Jawa 88 7 0 S 110 0 E
Jawf, W. al → 74 15 50N 45 30 E
Jawor 32 51 4N 16 11 E
Jaworzno 32 50 13N 19 11 E
Jay 153 36 25N 94 46W
Jaya, Puncak 87 3 57 S 137 17 E
Jayanca 172 6 24 S 79 50W
Jayanti 82 26 45N 89 40 E
Jayapura 87 2 28 S 140 38 E
Jayawijaya, Pegunungan 87 5 0 S 139 0 E
Jayrūd 72 33 49N 36 44 E
Jayton 153 33 17N 100 35W
Jazīreh-ye Shīf 73 29 4N 50 54 E
Jazminal 160 24 56N 101 25W
Jazzīn 70 33 31N 35 35 E
Jean 159 35 47N 115 20W
Jean Marie River 140 61 32N 120 38W
Jean Rabel 163 19 50N 73 5W
Jeanerette 153 29 52N 91 38W
Jeanette, Ostrov 65 76 43N 158 0 E
Jeannette 150 40 20N 79 36W
Jebba, Morocco 120 35 11N 4 43W
Jebba, Nigeria 127 9 9N 4 48 E
Jebel, Bahr el → 125 9 30N 30 25 E
Jebel Qerri 125 16 16N 32 50 E
Jeberos 172 5 15 S 76 10W
Jedburgh 14 55 28N 2 33W
Jedda = Jiddah 74 21 29N 39 10 E
Jedlicze 32 49 43N 21 40 E
Jedlnia-Letnisko 32 51 25N 21 19 E
Jędrzejów 32 50 35N 20 15 E
Jedwabne 32 53 17N 22 18 E
Jedway 144 52 17N 131 14W
Jeetze → 26 53 9N 11 6 E
Jefferson, Iowa, U.S.A. 154 42 3N 94 25W
Jefferson, Ohio, U.S.A. 150 41 40N 80 46W
Jefferson, Tex., U.S.A. 153 32 45N 94 23W
Jefferson, Wis., U.S.A. 155 43 0N 88 49W
Jefferson, Mt., Nev., U.S.A. 156 38 51N 117 0W
Jefferson, Mt., Oreg., U.S.A. 156 44 45N 121 50W
Jefferson City, Mo., U.S.A. 154 38 34N 92 10W
Jefferson City, Tenn., U.S.A. 149 36 8N 83 30W
Jeffersontown 155 38 17N 85 44W
Jeffersonville, Ind., U.S.A. 155 38 20N 85 42W
Jeffersonville, Ohio, U.S.A. 155 39 38N 83 34W
Jega 127 12 15N 4 23 E
Jekabpils 58 56 29N 25 57 E
Jelenia Góra 32 50 50N 15 45 E
Jelenia Góra □ 32 51 0N 15 30 E
Jelgava 58 56 41N 23 49 E
Jelica 46 43 50N 20 17 E
Jelli 125 5 25N 31 45 E
Jellicoe 142 49 40N 87 30W
Jelšava 31 48 37N 20 15 E
Jemaja 88 3 5N 105 45 E
Jemaluang 85 2 16N 103 52 E
Jemappes 23 50 27N 3 54 E
Jember 89 8 11 S 113 41 E
Jembongan 86 6 45N 117 20 E
Jemeppe 23 50 37N 5 30 E
Jemnice 30 49 1N 15 34 E
Jena, Germany 26 50 56N 11 33 E
Jena, U.S.A. 153 31 41N 92 7W
Jenbach 30 47 24N 11 47 E
Jendouba 121 36 29N 8 47 E
Jenkins 148 37 13N 82 41W
Jenner 158 38 27N 123 7W
Jennings, La., U.S.A. 153 30 10N 92 45W
Jennings, Mo., U.S.A. 154 38 43N 90 16W
Jennings → 144 59 38N 132 5W
Jenny 53 57 47N 16 35 E
Jepara 89 7 40 S 109 14 E
Jeparit 112 36 8 S 142 1 E
Jequié 171 13 51 S 40 5W
Jequitaí → 171 17 4 S 44 50W
Jequitinhonha 171 16 30 S 41 0W
Jequitinhonha → 171 15 51 S 38 53W
Jerada 121 34 17N 2 10W
Jerantut 85 3 56N 102 22 E
Jérémie 163 18 40N 74 10W
Jeremoabo 170 10 4 S 38 21W
Jerez, Punta 161 22 58N 97 40W
Jerez de García Salinas 160 22 39N 103 0W
Jerez de la Frontera 35 36 41N 6 7W
Jerez de los Caballeros 35 38 20N 6 45W
Jericho = Arīḥā 70 35 49N 36 35 E
Jericho = El Arīhā 69 31 52N 35 27 E
Jericho 110 23 38 S 146 6 E
Jerichow 26 52 30N 12 2 E
Jerico Springs 154 37 37N 94 1W
Jerilderie 113 35 20 S 145 41 E
Jermyn 151 41 31N 75 31W
Jerome 157 34 50N 112 0W
Jersey, I. 18 49 13N 2 7W
Jersey City 151 40 41N 74 8W
Jersey Shore 150 41 17N 77 18W
Jerseyville 154 39 5N 90 20W
Jerusalem 69 31 47N 35 10 E
Jervis B. 113 35 8 S 150 46 E
Jesenice 43 46 28N 14 3 E
Jeseník 31 50 0N 17 8 E
Jesenké 31 48 20N 20 10 E
Jesselton = Kota Kinabalu 89 6 0N 116 4 E
Jessnitz 26 51 42N 12 19 E
Jessore 82 23 10N 89 10 E
Jesup, U.S.A. 149 31 36N 81 54W
Jesup, U.S.A. 154 42 29N 92 4W
Jesús 172 7 15 S 78 25W
Jesús Carranza 161 17 28N 95 1W
Jesús María 174 30 59 S 64 5W
Jetafe 91 10 9N 124 9 E
Jetmore 153 38 10N 99 57W
Jetpur 78 21 45N 70 10 E
Jette 23 50 53N 4 20 E
Jevnaker 51 60 15N 10 26 E
Jewell 154 42 20N 93 39W
Jewett, Ohio, U.S.A. 150 40 22N 81 2W
Jewett, Tex., U.S.A. 153 31 20N 96 8W
Jewett City 151 41 36N 71 58W
Jeyḥūnābād 73 34 58N 48 59 E
Jeypore 80 18 50N 82 38 E
Jeziorak, Jezioro 32 53 40N 19 35 E
Jeziorany 32 53 58N 20 46 E
Jeziorka → 32 51 59N 20 57 E
Jhajjar 78 28 37N 76 42 E
Jhal Jhao 77 26 20N 65 35 E
Jhalakati 82 22 39N 90 12 E
Jhalawar 78 24 40N 76 10 E
Jhang Maghiana 77 31 15N 72 22 E
Jhansi 79 25 30N 78 36 E
Jharia 79 23 45N 86 26 E
Jharsuguda 79 21 56N 84 5 E
Jhelum 77 33 0N 73 45 E
Jhelum → 78 31 20N 72 10 E
Jhunjhunu 78 28 10N 75 30 E
Ji Xian, Hebei, China 94 37 35N 115 30 E
Ji Xian, Henan, China 94 35 22N 114 5 E
Ji Xian, Shanxi, China 94 36 7N 110 40 E
Jia Xian, Henan, China 94 33 59N 113 12 E
Jia Xian, Shaanxi, China 94 38 12N 110 28 E
Jiading 97 31 22N 121 15 E
Jiahe 97 25 38N 112 19 E
Jiali 97 23 12N 120 10 E
Jialing Jiang → 96 29 30N 106 20 E
Jiamusi 93 46 40N 130 26 E
Ji'an, Jiangxi, China 97 27 6N 114 59 E
Ji'an, Jilin, China 95 41 5N 126 10 E

Jianchang

Jianchang 95 40 55N 120 35 E
Jianchangying 95 40 10N 118 50 E
Jianchuan 96 26 38N 99 55 E
Jiande 97 29 23N 119 15 E
Jiangbei 96 29 40N 106 34 E
Jiangcheng 96 22 36N 101 52 E
Jiangdi 96 26 57N 103 37 E
Jiange 96 32 4N 105 32 E
Jiangjin 96 29 14N 106 14 E
Jiangkou 96 27 40N 108 49 E
Jiangle 97 26 42N 117 23 E
Jiangling 97 30 25N 112 12 E
Jiangmen 97 22 32N 113 0 E
Jiangshan 97 28 40N 118 37 E
Jiangsu □ 95 33 0N 120 0 E
Jiangxi □ 97 27 30N 116 0 E
Jiangyin 97 31 54N 120 17 E
Jiangyong 97 25 20N 111 22 E
Jiangyou 96 31 44N 104 43 E
Jianhe 96 26 37N 108 31 E
Jianli 97 29 46N 112 56 E
Jianning 97 26 50N 116 50 E
Jian'ou 97 27 3N 118 17 E
Jianshi 96 30 37N 109 38 E
Jianshui 96 23 36N 102 43 E
Jianyang, Fujian, China 97 27 20N 118 5 E
Jianyang, Sichuan, China 96 30 24N 104 33 E
Jiao Xian 95 36 18N 120 1 E
Jiaohe, Hebei, China 94 38 2N 116 20 E
Jiaohe, Jilin, China 95 43 40N 127 22 E
Jiaoling 97 24 41N 116 12 E
Jiaozhou Wan 95 36 5N 120 10 E
Jiaozuo 94 35 16N 113 12 E
Jiashan 97 32 46N 117 59 E
Jiawang 95 34 28N 117 26 E
Jiaxiang 94 35 25N 116 20 E
Jiaxing 97 30 49N 120 45 E
Jiayi 97 23 30N 120 24 E
Jiayu 97 29 55N 113 55 E
Jibão, Serra do 171 14 48 S 45 0W
Jibiya 127 13 5N 7 12 E
Jibou 50 47 15N 23 17 E
Jibuti = Djibouti ■ 125 12 0N 43 0 E
Jicarón, I. 162 7 10N 81 50W
Jičín 30 50 25N 15 28 E
Jiddah 74 21 29N 39 10 E
Jieshou 94 33 18N 115 22 E
Jiexiu 94 37 2N 111 55 E
Jieyang 97 23 35N 116 21 E
Jifnā 69 31 58N 35 13 E
Jihlava 30 49 28N 15 35 E
Jihlava → 30 48 55N 16 36 E
Jihočeský □ 30 49 8N 14 35 E
Jihomoravský □ 31 49 5N 16 30 E
Jijel 121 36 52N 5 50 E
Jijiga 136 9 20N 42 50 E
Jijona 37 38 34N 0 30W
Jikamshi 127 12 12N 7 45 E
Jilin 95 43 44N 126 30 E
Jilin □ 95 44 0N 124 0 E
Jiloca → 36 41 21N 1 39W
Jilong 97 25 8N 121 42 E
Jílové 30 49 52N 14 29 E
Jima 125 7 40N 36 47 E
Jimbolia 50 45 47N 20 43 E
Jimena de la Frontera 35 36 27N 5 24W
Jimenbuen 113 36 42 S 148 53 E
Jiménez, Mexico 160 27 10N 104 54W
Jimenez, Phil. 91 8 20N 123 50 E
Jimo 95 36 23N 120 30 E
Jin Jiang → 97 28 24N 115 48 E
Jin Xian, Hebei, China 94 38 2N 115 2 E
Jin Xian, Liaoning, China 95 38 55N 121 42 E
Jinan 94 36 38N 117 1 E
Jincheng 94 35 29N 112 50 E
Jinchuan 96 31 30N 102 3 E
Jind 78 29 19N 76 22 E
Jindabyne 113 36 25 S 148 35 E
Jindrichuv Hradeç 30 49 10N 15 2 E
Jing He → 94 34 27N 109 4 E
Jing Shan 97 31 20N 111 35 E
Jing Xian, Anhui, China 97 30 38N 118 25 E
Jing Xian, Hunan, China 96 26 33N 109 40 E
Jing'an 97 28 50N 115 17 E
Jingbian 94 37 20N 108 30 E
Jingchuan 94 35 20N 107 20 E
Jingde 97 30 15N 118 27 E
Jingdezhen 97 29 20N 117 11 E
Jingdong 96 24 23N 100 47 E
Jinggu 96 23 35N 100 41 E
Jinghai 94 38 55N 116 55 E
Jinghong 96 22 0N 100 45 E
Jingjiang 97 32 2N 120 16 E
Jingle 94 38 20N 111 55 E
Jingmen 97 31 0N 112 10 E
Jingning 94 35 30N 105 43 E
Jingpo Hu 95 43 55N 128 55 E
Jingshan 97 31 1N 113 7 E
Jingtai 94 37 10N 104 6 E
Jingxi 96 23 8N 106 27 E
Jingxing 94 38 2N 114 8 E
Jingyang 94 34 30N 108 50 E
Jingyu 95 42 25N 126 45 E
Jingyuan 94 36 30N 104 40 E
Jingziguan 94 33 15N 111 0 E
Jinhua 97 29 8N 119 38 E
Jining, Nei Mongol Zizhiqu, China 94 41 5N 113 0 E
Jining, Shandong, China 94 35 22N 116 34 E
Jinja 130 0 25N 33 12 E
Jinjang 85 3 13N 101 39 E
Jinji 94 37 58N 106 8 E
Jinjiang, Fujian, China 97 24 43N 118 33 E
Jinjiang, Yunnan, China 96 26 14N 100 34 E
Jinjie 96 23 15N 107 18 E
Jinjini 126 7 26N 3 42W
Jinkou 97 30 20N 114 8 E
Jinmen Dao 97 24 25N 118 25 E
Jinning 96 24 38N 102 38 E
Jinotega 162 13 6N 85 59W
Jinotepe 162 11 50N 86 10W
Jinping, Guizhou, China 96 26 41N 109 10 E
Jinping, Yunnan, China 96 22 45N 103 18 E
Jinsha 96 27 29N 106 12 E
Jinsha Jiang → 96 28 50N 104 36 E
Jinshan 97 30 54N 121 10 E
Jinshi 97 29 40N 111 50 E
Jintan 97 31 42N 119 36 E
Jintotolo Channel 91 11 48N 123 5 E
Jinxi, Jiangxi, China 97 27 56N 116 45 E
Jinxi, Liaoning, China 95 40 52N 120 50 E
Jinxian 97 28 26N 116 17 E
Jinxiang 94 35 5N 116 22 E
Jinyun 97 28 35N 120 5 E
Jinzhai 97 31 40N 115 53 E
Jinzhou 95 41 5N 121 3 E
Jiparaná → 173 8 3 S 62 52W
Jipijapa 168 1 0 S 80 40W
Jiquilpan 160 19 57N 102 42W
Jirwān 75 23 27N 50 53 E
Jishan 94 35 34N 110 58 E
Jishou 96 28 21N 109 43 E
Jishui 97 27 12N 115 8 E
Jisr al Ḥusayn 69 31 53N 35 33 E
Jisr ash Shughūr 70 35 49N 36 18 E
Jitarning 109 32 48 S 117 57 E
Jitra 85 6 16N 100 25 E
Jiu → 50 43 47N 23 48 E
Jiudengkou 94 39 56N 106 40 E
Jiujiang, Guangdong, China 97 22 50N 113 0 E
Jiujiang, Jiangxi, China 97 29 42N 115 58 E
Jiuling Shan 97 28 40N 114 40 E
Jiulong 96 28 57N 101 31 E
Jiutai 95 44 10N 125 50 E
Jiuxiangcheng 94 33 12N 114 50 E
Jiuxincheng 94 39 17N 115 59 E
Jiuyuhang 97 30 18N 119 56 E
Jixi, Anhui, China 97 30 5N 118 34 E
Jixi, Heilongjiang, China 95 45 20N 130 50 E
Jiyang 95 37 0N 117 12 E
Jiz', W. → 75 16 12N 52 14 E
Jīzān 74 17 0N 42 20 E
Jize 94 36 54N 114 56 E
Jizera → 30 50 10N 14 43 E
Jizō-Zaki 100 35 34N 133 20 E
Joaçaba 175 27 5 S 51 31W
Joaíma 171 16 39 S 41 2W
João 170 2 46 S 50 59W
João Amaro 171 12 46 S 40 22W
João Câmara 170 5 32 S 35 48W
João Pessoa 170 7 10 S 34 52W
João Pinheiro 171 17 45 S 46 10W
Joaquim Távora 171 23 30 S 49 58W
Joaquín V. González 174 25 10 S 64 0W
Jobourg, Nez de 18 49 41N 1 57W
Jódar 37 37 50N 3 21W
Jodhpur 78 26 23N 73 8 E
Joensuu 56 62 37N 29 49 E
Jœuf 19 49 12N 6 0 E
Jofane 135 21 15 S 34 18 E
Joggins 143 45 42N 64 27W
Jogjakarta = Yogyakarta 89 7 49 S 110 22 E
Jōhana 101 36 30N 136 57 E
Johannesburg, S. Africa 135 26 10 S 28 2 E
Johannesburg, U.S.A. 159 35 26N 117 38W
Johansfors 53 56 42N 15 32 E
Jōhen 100 32 58N 132 32 E
John Day 156 44 25N 118 57W
John Day → 156 45 44N 120 39W
John H. Kerr Res. 149 36 20N 78 30W
John o' Groats 14 58 39N 3 3W
Johnnie 159 36 25N 116 5W
Johnson 153 37 35N 101 48W
Johnson City, Ill., U.S.A. 154 37 49N 88 56W
Johnson City, N.Y., U.S.A. 151 42 7N 75 57W
Johnson City, Tenn., U.S.A. 149 36 18N 82 21W
Johnson City, Tex., U.S.A. 153 30 15N 98 24W
Johnsonburg 150 41 30N 78 40W
Johnsondale 159 35 58N 118 32W
Johnson's Crossing 144 60 29N 133 18W
Johnsonville 114 41 13 S 174 48 E
Johnston, L. 109 32 25 S 120 30 E
Johnston Falls = Mambilima Falls 131 10 31 S 28 45 E
Johnston I. 105 17 10N 169 8W
Johnstone Str. 144 50 28N 126 0W
Johnstown, N.Y., U.S.A. 151 43 1N 74 20W
Johnstown, Pa., U.S.A. 150 40 19N 78 53W
Johor Baharu 85 1 28N 103 46 E
Joigny 19 47 58N 3 20 E
Joinvile 175 26 15 S 48 55 E
Joinville 19 48 27N 5 10 E
Joinville I. 7 65 0 S 55 30W
Jojutla 161 18 37N 99 11W
Jokkmokk 54 66 35N 19 50 E
Jökulsá á Dal → 54 65 40N 14 16W
Jökulsá Fjöllum → 54 66 10N 16 30W
Jolfā, Āzarbājān-e Sharqī, Iran 72 38 57N 45 38 E
Jolfā, Eşfahan, Iran 73 32 58N 51 37 E
Joliet 155 41 30N 88 0W
Joliette 142 46 3N 73 24W
Jolo 91 6 0N 121 0 E
Jolo Group 91 6 0N 121 9 E
Jolon 158 35 58N 121 9W
Jomalig 90 14 42N 122 22 E
Jombang 87 7 33 S 112 14 E
Jomda 96 31 28N 98 12 E
Jome 87 1 16 S 127 30 E
Jomfruland 53 58 52N 9 36 E
Jönåker 53 58 44N 16 40 E
Jonava 53 55 8N 24 12 E
Jones 90 16 33N 121 42 E
Jones Sound 6 76 0N 85 0W
Jonesboro, Ark., U.S.A. 153 35 50N 90 45W
Jonesboro, Ill., U.S.A. 153 37 26N 89 18W
Jonesboro, La., U.S.A. 153 32 15N 92 41W
Jonesburg 154 38 51N 91 18W
Jonesport 143 44 32N 67 38W
Jonesville, Ind., U.S.A. 155 39 5N 85 54W
Jonesville, Mich., U.S.A. 155 41 59N 84 40W
Jonglei 125 6 25N 30 50 E
Jonglei □ 125 7 30N 32 30 E
Joniskis 58 56 13N 23 35 E
Jönköping 53 57 45N 14 10 E
Jönköpings län □ 53 57 30N 14 30 E
Jonquière 143 48 27N 71 14W
Jonsberg 53 58 30N 16 48 E
Jonsered 53 57 45N 12 10 E
Jonzac 20 45 27N 0 28W
Joplin 153 37 0N 94 31W
Jordan 156 47 25N 106 58W
Jordan ■ 71 31 0N 36 0 E
Jordan → 69 31 48N 35 32 E
Jordan Valley 156 43 0N 117 2W
Jordânia 171 15 55 S 40 11W
Jordanów 32 49 41N 19 49 E
Jorge, C. 176 51 40 S 75 35W
Jorhat 82 26 45N 94 12 E
Jorm 77 36 50N 70 52 E
Jörn 54 65 4N 20 1 E
Jorong 89 3 58 S 114 56 E
Jørpeland 51 59 3N 6 1 E
Jorquera → 174 28 3 S 69 58W
Jos 127 9 53N 8 51 E
Jošanička Banja 46 43 24N 20 47 E
Jose Abad Santos 91 5 55N 125 39 E
José Batlle y Ordóñez 175 33 20 S 55 10W
José de San Martín 176 44 4 S 70 26W
Jose Panganiban 90 14 17N 122 41 E
Joseni 50 46 42N 25 29 E
Joseph 156 45 27N 117 13W
Joseph, L., Nfld., Canada 143 52 45N 65 18W
Joseph, L., Ont., Canada 150 45 10N 79 44W
Joseph Bonaparte G. 108 14 35 S 128 50 E
Joseph City 157 35 0N 110 16W
Joshua Tree 159 34 8N 116 19W
Joshua Tree Nat. Mon. 159 33 56N 116 5W
Josselin 18 47 57N 2 33W
Jostedal 51 61 35N 7 15 E
Jotunheimen 51 61 35N 8 25 E
Jourdanton 153 28 54N 98 32W
Joure 22 52 58N 5 48 E
Joussard 144 55 22N 115 50W
Jovellanos 162 22 40N 81 10W
Jovellar 90 13 4N 123 36 E
Jowai 82 25 26N 92 12 E
Jowzjān □ 77 36 10N 66 0 E
Joya, La 172 16 43 S 71 52W
Joyeuse 21 44 29N 4 16 E
Józefów 32 52 10N 21 11 E
Ju Xian 95 36 35N 118 20 E
Juan Aldama 160 24 20N 103 23W
Juan Bautista Alberdi 174 34 26 S 61 48W
Juan de Fuca Str. 158 48 15N 124 0W
Juan de Nova 135 17 3 S 43 45 E
Juan Fernández, Arch. de 164 33 50 S 80 0W
Juan José Castelli 174 25 27 S 60 57W
Juan L. Lacaze 174 34 26 S 57 25W
Juanjuí 172 7 10 S 76 45W
Juárez, Argentina 174 37 40 S 59 43W
Juárez, Mexico 159 32 20N 115 57W
Juárez, Sierra de 160 32 0N 116 0W
Juatinga, Ponta de 171 23 17 S 44 30W
Juàzeiro 170 9 30 S 40 30W
Juàzeiro do Norte 170 7 10 S 39 18W
Jubay 91 11 33N 124 18 E
Jubayl 70 34 5N 35 39 E
Jubbah 72 28 2N 40 56 E
Jubbulpore = Jabalpur 79 23 9N 79 58 E
Jübek 26 54 31N 9 24 E
Jubga 61 44 19N 38 48 E
Jubilee L. 109 29 0 S 126 50 E
Júcar → 37 39 5N 0 10W
Júcaro 162 21 37N 78 51W
Juchitán 161 16 27N 95 5W
Judaea = Har Yehuda 69 31 35N 34 57 E
Judenburg 30 47 12N 14 38 E
Judith → 156 47 44N 109 38W
Judith Gap 156 46 40N 109 46W
Judith Pt. 151 41 20N 71 30W
Jufari → 169 1 13 S 62 0W
Jugoslavia = Yugoslavia ■ 41 44 0N 20 0 E
Juigalpa 162 12 6N 85 26W
Juillac 20 45 20N 1 19 E
Juist 26 53 40N 7 0 E
Juiz de Fora 171 21 43 S 43 19W
Jujuy □ 174 23 20 S 65 40W
Julesburg 152 41 0N 102 20W
Juli 172 16 10 S 69 25W
Julia Cr. → 110 20 0 S 141 11 E
Julia Creek 110 20 39 S 141 44 E
Juliaca 172 15 25 S 70 10W
Julian 159 33 4N 116 38W
Julian Alps = Julijske Alpe 43 46 15N 14 1 E
Julianakanaal 23 51 6N 5 52 E
Julianatop 169 3 40N 56 30W
Julianehåb 6 60 43N 46 0W
Jülich 26 50 55N 6 20 E
Julierpass 29 46 28N 9 32 E
Julijske Alpe 43 46 15N 14 1 E
Julimes 160 28 25N 105 27W
Jullundur 78 31 20N 75 40 E
Julu 94 37 15N 115 2 E
Jumbo 131 17 30 S 30 58 E
Jumbo Pk. 159 36 12N 114 11W
Jumentos Cays 163 23 0N 75 40 E
Jumet 23 50 27N 4 25 E
Jumilla 37 38 28N 1 19W
Jumla 79 29 15N 82 13 E
Jumna = Yamuna → 79 25 30N 81 53 E
Junagadh 78 21 30N 70 30 E
Junaynah 74 22 33N 46 18 E
Junction, Tex., U.S.A. 153 30 29N 99 48W
Junction, Utah, U.S.A. 157 38 10N 112 15W
Junction B. 110 11 52 S 133 55 E
Junction City, Kans., U.S.A. 152 39 4N 96 55W
Junction City, Oreg., U.S.A. 156 44 14N 123 12W
Junction Pt. 110 11 45 S 133 50 E
Jundah 110 24 46 S 143 2 E
Jundiaí 175 24 30 S 47 0W
Juneau 140 58 20N 134 20W
Junee 113 34 53 S 147 35 E
Jungfrau 28 46 32N 7 58 E
Junglinster 23 49 43N 6 15 E
Jungshahi 78 24 52N 67 44 E
Juniata → 150 40 30N 77 40W
Junín, Argentina 174 34 33 S 60 57W
Junín, Peru 172 11 12 S 76 0W
Junín □ 172 11 30 S 75 0W
Junín de los Andes 176 39 45 S 71 0W
Jūniyah 70 33 59N 35 38 E
Junnar 80 19 12N 73 58 E
Junquera, La 36 42 25N 2 53 E
Junta, La 153 38 0N 103 30W
Juntura 156 43 44N 118 4W
Juparanã, L. 171 19 16 S 40 8W
Jupiter → 143 49 29N 63 37W
Juquiá 171 24 19 S 47 38W
Jur, Nahr el → 125 8 45N 29 15 E
Jura, Europe 19 46 35N 6 5 E
Jura, U.K. 14 56 0N 5 50W
Jura □ 19 46 47N 5 45 E
Jura, Mts. 21 46 40N 6 5 E
Jura, Sd. of 14 55 57N 5 45W
Jura Suisse 28 47 10N 7 0 E
Jurado 168 7 7N 77 46W
Jurilovca 50 44 46N 28 52 E
Jūrong 97 31 57N 119 9 E
Juruá → 168 2 37 S 65 44W
Juruena 173 13 0 S 58 10W
Juruena → 173 7 20 S 58 3W
Juruti 169 2 9 S 56 4W
Jussey 19 47 50N 5 55 E
Justo Daract 174 33 52 S 65 12W
Jutaí 172 5 11 S 68 54W
Jutaí → 168 2 43 S 66 57W
Jüterbog 26 52 0N 13 6 E
Juticalpa 162 14 40N 86 12W
Jutland = Jylland 53 56 25N 9 30 E
Jutphaas 22 52 2N 5 6 E
Juventud, I. de la 162 21 40N 82 40W
Juvigny-sous-Andaine 18 48 32N 0 30W
Juvisy-sur-Orge 19 48 42N 2 22 E
Jūy Zar 72 33 50N 46 18 E
Juye 94 35 22N 116 5 E
Juzennecourt 19 48 10N 4 58 E
Jylland 53 56 25N 9 30 E
Jyväskylä 54 62 14N 25 50 E

K

K2, Mt. 79 35 58N 76 32 E
Kaala-Gomén 106 20 40 S 164 25 E
Kaap die Goeie Hoop 134 34 24 S 18 30 E
Kaap Plateau 134 28 30 S 24 0 E
Kaapkruis 134 21 55 S 13 57 E
Kaapstad = Cape Town 134 33 55 S 18 22 E
Kaatsheuvel 23 51 39N 5 2 E
Kabacan 91 7 8N 124 49 E

Kampuchea

Kabaena **87** 5 15 S 122 0 E
Kabala **126** 9 38N 11 37W
Kabale **130** 1 15 S 30 0 E
Kabalo **130** 6 0 S 27 0 E
Kabambare **130** 4 41 S 27 39 E
Kabango **131** 8 35 S 28 30 E
Kabanjahe **88** 3 6N 98 30 E
Kabankalan **91** 9 59N 122 49 E
Kabara **126** 16 40N 2 50W
Kabardinka **60** 44 40N 37 57 E
Kabardino-Balkar-
A.S.S.R. □ **61** 43 30N 43 30 E
Kabare **87** 0 4 S 130 58 E
Kabarega Falls **130** 2 15N 31 30 E
Kabasalan **91** 7 47N 122 44 E
Kabba **127** 7 50N 6 3 E
Kabe **100** 34 31N 132 31 E
Kabi **123** 13 30N 12 35 E
Kabin Buri **84** 13 57N 101 43 E
Kabinakagami L. **142** 48 54N 84 25W
Kabīr, Zab al → **72** 36 0N 43 0 E
Kabkabīyah **123** 13 50N 24 0 E
Kablungu, C. **107** 6 20 S 150 1 E
Kabna **124** 19 6N 32 40 E
Kabo **132** 7 35N 18 38 E
Kabompo **131** 13 36 S 24 14 E
Kabondo **131** 8 58 S 25 40 E
Kabongo **130** 7 22 S 25 33 E
Kabou **127** 9 28N 0 55 E
Kaboudia, Rass **121** 35 13N 11 10 E
Kabra **110** 23 25 S 150 25 E
Kabūd Gonbad **73** 37 5N 59 45 E
Kabugao **90** 18 2N 121 11 E
Kābul **77** 34 28N 69 11 E
Kābul □ **77** 34 30N 69 0 E
Kabul → **77** 33 55N 72 14 E
Kabunga **130** 1 38 S 28 3 E
Kaburuang **87** 3 50N 126 30 E
Kabushiya **125** 16 54N 33 41 E
Kabwe **131** 14 30 S 28 29 E
Kabwum **107** 6 11 S 147 15 E
Kačanik **46** 42 13N 21 12 E
Kachanovo **58** 57 25N 27 38 E
Kachchh, Gulf of **78** 22 50N 69 15 E
Kachchh, Rann of **78** 24 0N 70 0 E
Kachebera **131** 13 50 S 32 50 E
Kachin □ **82** 26 0N 97 30 E
Kachira, L. **130** 0 40 S 31 7 E
Kachiry **64** 53 10N 75 50 E
Kachisi **125** 9 40N 37 50 E
Kachkanar **62** 58 42N 59 33 E
Kachot **85** 11 30N 103 3 E
Kackar **61** 40 45N 41 10 E
Kadaingti **82** 17 37N 97 32 E
Kadaiyanallur **81** 9 3N 77 22 E
Kadan Kyun **86** 12 30N 98 20 E
Kadanai → **78** 31 22N 65 45 E
Kadarkút **31** 46 13N 17 39 E
Kade **127** 6 7N 0 56W
Kadi **78** 23 18N 72 23 E
Kadina **112** 34 0 S 137 43 E
Kadiri **81** 14 12N 78 13 E
Kadiyevka = Stakhanov **61** 48 35N 38 40 E
Kadoka **152** 43 50N 101 31W
Kadom **59** 54 37N 42 30 E
Kadoma **131** 18 20 S 29 52 E
Kâdugli **125** 11 0N 29 45 E
Kaduna **127** 10 30N 7 21 E
Kaduna □ **127** 11 0N 7 30 E
Kadzhi-Say **63** 42 8N 77 10 E
Kaédi **126** 16 9N 13 28W
Kaelé **127** 10 7N 14 27 E
Kaeng Khoï **84** 14 35N 101 0 E
Kaeo **114** 35 6 S 173 49 E
Kaesŏng **95** 37 58N 126 35 E
Kāf **72** 31 25N 37 29 E
Kafakumba **133** 9 38 S 23 46 E
Kafan **57** 39 18N 46 15 E
Kafanchan **127** 9 40N 8 20 E
Kafareti **127** 10 25N 11 12 E
Kaffrine **126** 14 8N 15 36W
Kafia Kingi **132** 9 20N 24 25 E
Kafinda **131** 12 32 S 30 20 E
Kafirévs, Ákra **49** 38 9N 24 38 E
Kafr 'Ayn **69** 32 3N 35 7 E
Kafr el Dauwâr **124** 31 8N 30 8 E
Kafr el Sheikh **124** 31 15N 30 50 E
Kafr Kammā **69** 32 44N 35 26 E
Kafr Kannā **69** 32 45N 35 20 E
Kafr Mālik **69** 32 0N 35 18 E
Kafr Mandā **69** 32 49N 35 15 E
Kafr Quaddūm **69** 32 14N 35 7 E
Kafr Rā'ī **69** 32 23N 35 9 E
Kafr Şīr **69** 33 19N 35 23 E
Kafr Yāsīf **69** 32 58N 35 10 E
Kafue **131** 15 46 S 28 9 E
Kafue Flats **131** 15 40 S 27 25 E
Kafulwe **131** 9 0 S 29 1 E
Kaga, Afghan. **78** 34 14N 70 10 E
Kaga, Japan **101** 36 16N 136 15 E
Kaga Bandoro **132** 7 0N 19 10 E
Kagan **63** 39 43N 64 33 E
Kagawa □ **100** 34 15N 134 0 E
Kagera □ **130** 2 0 S 31 30 E
Kagera → **130** 0 57 S 31 47 E
Kagoshima **100** 31 35N 130 33 E
Kagoshima □ **100** 31 30N 130 30 E
Kagoshima-Wan **100** 31 25N 130 40 E
Kagul **60** 45 50N 28 15 E
Kahak **73** 36 6N 49 46 E
Kahama **130** 4 8 S 32 30 E
Kahama □ **130** 3 50 S 32 0 E
Kahang **85** 2 12N 103 32 E
Kahayan → **89** 3 40 S 114 0 E
Kahe **130** 3 30 S 37 25 E
Kahemba **133** 7 18 S 18 55 E
Kaherekoau Mts. **115** 45 45 S 167 15 E
Kahil, Djebel bou **121** 34 26N 4 0 E
Kahilangan **91** 7 48N 124 48 E
Kahniah → **144** 58 15N 120 55W
Kahnūj **73** 27 55N 57 40 E
Kahoka **154** 40 25N 91 42W
Kahoolawe **146** 20 33N 156 35W
Kahurangi, Pt. **115** 40 50 S 172 10 E
Kahuta **78** 33 35N 73 24 E
Kai, Kepulauan **87** 5 55 S 132 45W
Kai Besar **87** 5 35 S 133 0 E
Kai-Ketil **87** 5 45 S 132 40 E
Kai Xian **96** 31 11N 108 21 E
Kaiama **127** 9 36N 4 1 E
Kaiapit **107** 6 18 S 146 18 E
Kaiapoi **115** 42 24 S 172 40 E
Kaibara **101** 35 8N 135 5 E
Kaieteur Falls **169** 5 1N 59 10W
Kaifeng **94** 34 48N 114 21 E
Kaihua **97** 29 12N 118 20 E
Kaiingveld **134** 30 0 S 22 0 E
Kaikohe **114** 35 25 S 173 49 E
Kaikoura **115** 42 25 S 173 43 E
Kaikoura Pen. **115** 42 25 S 173 43 E
Kaikoura Ra. **115** 41 59 S 173 41 E
Kailahun **126** 8 18N 10 39W
Kailashahar **82** 24 19N 92 0 E
Kaili **96** 26 33N 107 59 E
Kailu **95** 43 38N 121 18 E
Kailua **146** 19 39N 156 0W
Kaimana **87** 3 39 S 133 45 E
Kaimanawa Mts. **114** 39 15 S 175 56 E
Kaimata **115** 42 34 S 171 28 E
Kaimganj **79** 27 33N 79 24 E
Kaimon-Dake **100** 31 11N 130 32 E
Kaimur Hill **79** 24 30N 82 0 E
Kainan **100** 34 9N 135 12 E
Kainantu **107** 6 18 S 145 52 E
Kaingaroa Forest **114** 38 24 S 176 30 E
Kainji Res. **127** 10 1N 4 40 E
Kaipara Harbour **114** 36 25 S 174 14 E
Kaiping **97** 22 23N 112 42 E
Kaipokok B. **143** 54 54N 59 47W
Kairana **78** 29 24N 77 15 E
Kaironi **87** 0 47 S 133 40 E
Kairouan **121** 35 45N 10 5 E
Kairuku **107** 8 51 S 146 35 E
Kaiserslautern **27** 49 30N 7 43 E
Kaitaia **114** 35 8 S 173 17 E
Kaitangata **115** 46 17 S 169 51 E
Kaithal **78** 29 48N 76 26 E
Kaitu → **78** 33 10N 70 30 E
Kaiwi Channel **146** 21 13N 157 30W
Kaiyang **96** 27 4N 106 59 E
Kaiyuan, Liaoning,
China **95** 42 28N 124 1 E
Kaiyuan, Yunnan, China **96** 23 40N 103 12 E
Kajaani **54** 64 17N 27 46 E
Kajabbi **110** 20 0 S 140 1 E
Kajana = Kajaani **54** 64 17N 27 46 E
Kajang **85** 2 59N 101 48 E
Kajiado **130** 1 53 S 36 48 E
Kajiado □ **130** 2 0 S 36 30 E
Kajiki **100** 31 44N 130 40 E
Kajo Kaji **125** 3 58N 31 40 E
Kaka **125** 10 38N 32 10 E
Kakabeka Falls **142** 48 24N 89 37W
Kakamas **134** 28 45 S 20 33 E
Kakamega **130** 0 20N 34 46 E
Kakamega □ **130** 0 20N 34 46 E
Kakamigahara **101** 35 28N 136 48 E
Kakanj **46** 44 9N 18 7 E
Kakanui Mts. **115** 45 10 S 170 30 E
Kake **100** 34 36N 132 19 E
Kakegawa **101** 34 45N 138 1 E
Kakeroma-Jima **99** 28 8N 129 14 E
Kakhib **61** 42 28N 46 34 E
Kakhovka **60** 46 40N 33 15 E
Kakhovskoye Vdkhr. **60** 47 5N 34 16 E
Kakinada **80** 16 57N 82 11 E
Kakisa → **144** 61 3N 118 10W
Kakisa L. **144** 60 56N 117 43W
Kakogawa **100** 34 46N 134 51 E
Kakwa → **144** 54 37N 118 28W
Kāl Gūsheh **73** 30 59N 58 12 E
Kal Safīd **72** 34 52N 47 23 E
Kala **127** 12 2N 14 40 E
Kala Oya → **81** 8 20N 79 45 E
Kala Shank'ou **79** 35 42N 78 20 E
Kalaa-Kebira **121** 35 59N 10 32 E
Kalabagh **77** 33 0N 71 28 E
Kalabahi **87** 8 13 S 124 31 E
Kalabáka **48** 39 42N 21 39 E
Kalabo **133** 14 58 S 22 40 E
Kalach **59** 50 22N 41 0 E
Kalach na Donu **61** 48 43N 43 32 E
Kaladar **150** 44 37N 77 5W
Kalagua Is. **90** 14 30N 122 55 E
Kalahari **134** 24 0 S 21 30 E
Kalahari Gemsbok Nat.
Park **134** 25 30 S 20 30 E
Kalai-Khumb **63** 38 28N 70 46 E
Kālak **73** 25 29N 59 22 E
Kalakamati **135** 20 40 S 27 25 E
Kalakan **65** 55 15N 116 45 E
Kalakh **72** 34 55N 36 10 E
K'alak'unlun Shank'ou **79** 35 33N 77 46 E
Kalam **79** 35 34N 72 30 E
Kalama, U.S.A. **158** 46 0N 122 55W
Kalama, Zaïre **130** 2 52 S 28 35 E
Kalamansig **91** 6 33N 124 3 E
Kalamariá **48** 40 33N 22 55 E
Kalamata **49** 37 3N 22 10 E
Kalamazoo **155** 42 20N 85 35W
Kalamazoo → **155** 42 40N 86 12W
Kalamb **80** 18 3N 74 48 E
Kalambo Falls **131** 8 37 S 31 35 E
Kálamos, Attiki, Greece **49** 38 17N 23 52 E
Kálamos, Pelopónnisos,
Greece **49** 38 37N 20 55 E
Kalamoti **49** 38 15N 26 4 E
Kalangadoo **112** 37 34 S 140 41 E
Kalannie **109** 30 22 S 117 5 E
Kalāntarī **73** 32 10N 54 8 E
Kalao **87** 7 21 S 121 0 E
Kalaotoa **87** 7 20 S 121 50 E
Kälarne **52** 62 59N 16 8 E
Kalárovo **31** 47 54N 18 0 E
Kalasin **84** 16 26N 103 30 E
Kalat **77** 29 8N 66 31 E
Kalāteh **73** 36 33N 55 41 E
Kalāteh-ye-Ganj **73** 27 31N 57 55 E
Kálathos **49** 36 9N 28 8 E
Kalaus → **61** 45 40N 44 7 E
Kalávrita **49** 38 3N 22 8 E
Kalaw **82** 20 38N 96 34 E
Kalbān **75** 20 18N 58 38 E
Kalbarri **109** 27 40 S 114 10 E
Kalecik **60** 40 4N 33 26 E
Kalehe **130** 2 6 S 28 50 E
Kalema **130** 1 12 S 31 55 E
Kalemie **130** 5 55 S 29 9 E
Kalemyo **82** 23 11N 94 4 E
Kalety **32** 50 35N 18 52 E
Kalewa **82** 23 10N 94 15 E
Kálfafellsstaður **54** 64 11N 15 53W
Kalgan = Zhangjiakou **94** 40 48N 114 55 E
Kalgoorlie-Boulder **109** 30 40 S 121 22 E
Kaliakra, Nos **47** 43 21N 28 30 E
Kalianda **88** 5 50 S 105 45 E
Kalibo **91** 11 43N 122 22 E
Kaliganj Town **79** 22 25N 89 8 E
Kalima **130** 2 33 S 26 32 E
Kalimantan **89** 0 0 114 0 E
Kalimantan Barat □ **89** 0 0 110 30 E
Kalimantan Selatan □ **89** 2 30 S 115 30 E
Kalimantan Tengah □ **89** 2 0 S 113 30 E
Kalimantan Timur □ **89** 1 30N 116 30 E
Kálimnos **49** 37 0N 27 0 E
Kalimpong **79** 27 4N 88 35 E
Kalinadi → **81** 14 50N 74 7 E
Kalinga □ **90** 17 30N 121 20 E
Kalinin **59** 56 55N 35 55 E
Kaliningrad **58** 54 42N 20 32 E
Kalininskoye **63** 42 50N 73 49 E
Kalinkovichi **58** 52 12N 29 20 E
Kalinovik **46** 43 31N 18 29 E
Kalipetrovo **47** 44 5N 27 14 E
Kaliro **130** 0 56N 33 30 E
Kalirrákhi **48** 40 40N 24 35 E
Kalispell **156** 48 10N 114 22W
Kalisz **32** 51 45N 18 8 E
Kalisz □ **32** 51 30N 18 0 E
Kalisz Pomorski **32** 53 17N 15 55 E
Kaliua **130** 5 5 S 31 48 E
Kaliveli Tank **81** 12 5N 79 50 E
Kalix → **54** 65 50N 23 11 E
Kalka **78** 30 46N 76 57 E
Kalkaroo **112** 31 12 S 143 54 E
Kalkaska **148** 44 44N 85 11W
Kalkfeld **134** 20 57 S 16 14 E
Kalkfontein **134** 22 4 S 20 57 E
Kalkrand **134** 24 1 S 17 35 E
Kallakkurichchi **81** 11 44N 79 1 E
Kållandsö **53** 58 40N 13 5 E
Kallia **69** 31 46N 35 30 E
Kallidaikurichi **81** 8 38N 77 31 E
Kallinge **53** 56 15N 15 18 E
Kallithéa **49** 37 55N 23 41 E
Kallmeti **48** 41 51N 19 41 E
Kalloní, Kólpos **49** 39 10N 26 10 E
Kalmalo **127** 13 40N 5 20 E
Kalmar **53** 56 40N 16 20 E
Kalmar län □ **53** 57 25N 16 0 E
Kalmar sund **53** 56 40N 16 25 E
Kalmthout **23** 51 23N 4 29 E
Kalmyk A.S.S.R. □ **61** 46 5N 46 1 E
Kalmykovo **61** 49 0N 51 47 E
Kalna **79** 23 13N 88 25 E
Kalo **107** 10 1 S 147 48 E
Kalocsa **31** 46 32N 19 0 E
Kalofer **47** 42 37N 24 59 E
Kaloko **130** 6 47 S 25 48 E
Kalol, Gujarat, India **78** 22 37N 73 31 E
Kalol, Gujarat, India **78** 23 15N 72 33 E
Kalolímnos **49** 37 4N 27 8 E
Kalomo **131** 17 0 S 26 30 E
Kalona **154** 41 29N 91 43W
Kalonerón **49** 37 20N 21 38 E
Kalpi **79** 26 8N 79 47 E
Kalrayan Hills **81** 11 45N 78 40 E
Kalsubai **80** 19 35N 73 45 E
Kaltbrunn **29** 47 13N 9 2 E
Kaltungo **127** 9 48N 11 19 E
Kalu **78** 25 5N 67 39 E
Kaluga **59** 54 35N 36 10 E
Kalulushi **131** 12 50 S 28 3 E
Kalundborg **52** 55 41N 11 5 E
Kalush **58** 49 3N 24 23 E
Kałuszyn **32** 52 13N 21 52 E
Kalutara **81** 6 35N 80 0 E
Kalwaria **32** 49 53N 19 41 E
Kalya **62** 60 15N 59 59 E
Kalyan, Australia **112** 34 55 S 139 49 E
Kalyan, India **78** 20 30N 74 3 E
Kalyazin **59** 57 15N 37 55 E
Kama, Burma **82** 19 1N 95 4 E
Kama, Zaïre **130** 3 30 S 27 5 E
Kama → **62** 55 45N 52 0 E
Kamachumu **130** 1 37 S 31 37 E
Kamae **100** 32 48N 131 56 E
Kamaing **82** 25 26N 96 35 E
Kamaishi **98** 39 16N 141 53 E
Kamakura **101** 35 19N 139 33 E
Kamalia **78** 30 44N 72 42 E
Kamamaung **82** 17 21N 97 40 E
Kamandorskiye Ostrava **65** 55 0N 167 0 E
Kamapanda **131** 12 5 S 24 0 E
Kamaran **74** 15 21N 42 35 E
Kamashi **63** 38 51N 65 23 E
Kamativi **131** 18 15 S 27 27 E
Kamba **127** 11 50N 3 45 E
Kambalda **109** 31 10 S 121 37 E
Kambam **81** 9 45N 77 16 E
Kambar **78** 27 37N 68 1 E
Kambarka **62** 56 15N 54 11 E
Kambia **126** 9 3N 12 53W
Kambolé **131** 8 47 S 30 48 E
Kambove **131** 10 51 S 26 33 E
Kambuie **133** 6 59 S 22 19 E
Kamchatka, P-ov. **65** 57 0N 160 0 E
Kamen **64** 53 50N 81 30 E
Kamen Kashirskiy **58** 51 39N 24 56 E
Kamen-Rybolov **98** 44 46N 132 2 E
Kamenets-Podolskiy **60** 48 45N 26 10 E
Kamenica, Srbija,
Yugoslavia **46** 43 27N 22 27 E
Kamenica, Srbija,
Yugoslavia **46** 44 25N 19 40 E
Kamenice **30** 49 18N 15 2 E
Kamenjak, Rt. **43** 44 47N 13 55 E
Kamenka, R.S.F.S.R.,
U.S.S.R. **56** 65 58N 44 0 E
Kamenka, R.S.F.S.R.,
U.S.S.R. **59** 53 10N 44 5 E
Kamenka, R.S.F.S.R.,
U.S.S.R. **59** 50 47N 39 20 E
Kamenka,
Ukraine S.S.R.,
U.S.S.R. **60** 49 3N 32 6 E
Kamenka Bugskaya **58** 50 8N 24 16 E
Kamenka Dneprovskaya **60** 47 29N 34 14 E
Kameno **47** 42 34N 27 18 E
Kamenolomini **61** 47 40N 40 14 E
Kamensk-Shakhtinskiy **61** 48 23N 40 20 E
Kamensk Uralskiy **62** 56 25N 62 2 E
Kamenskiy, R.S.F.S.R.,
U.S.S.R. **59** 50 48N 45 25 E
Kamenskiy, R.S.F.S.R.,
U.S.S.R. **61** 49 20N 41 15 E
Kamenskoye **65** 62 45N 165 30 E
Kamenyak **47** 43 24N 26 57 E
Kamenz **26** 51 17N 14 7 E
Kameoka **101** 35 0N 135 35 E
Kameyama **101** 34 51N 136 27 E
Kami **48** 42 17N 20 18 E
Kami-Jima **100** 32 27N 130 20 E
Kami-koshiki-Jima **100** 31 50N 129 52 E
Kamiah **156** 46 12N 116 2W
Kamień Krajeński **32** 53 32N 17 32 E
Kamień Pomorski **32** 53 57N 14 43 E
Kamienna → **32** 51 6N 21 47 E
Kamienna Góra **32** 50 47N 16 2 E
Kamiensk **32** 51 12N 19 29 E
Kamieskroon **134** 30 9 S 17 56 E
Kamiita **100** 34 6N 134 22 E
Kamilukuak, L. **145** 62 22N 101 40W
Kamina **131** 8 45 S 25 0 E
Kaminak L. **145** 62 10N 95 0W
Kaminoyama **98** 38 9N 140 17 E
Kamioka **101** 36 25N 137 15 E
Kamituga **130** 3 2 S 28 10 E
Kamloops **144** 50 40N 120 20W
Kamnik **43** 46 14N 14 37 E
Kamo, Japan **98** 37 39N 139 3 E
Kamo, N.Z. **114** 35 42 S 174 20 E
Kamo, U.S.S.R. **61** 40 21N 45 7 E
Kamogawa **101** 35 5N 140 5 E
Kamoke **78** 32 4N 74 4 E
Kamp → **30** 48 23N 15 42 E
Kampala **130** 0 20N 32 30 E
Kampar **85** 4 18N 101 9 E
Kampar → **88** 0 30N 103 8 E
Kampen **22** 52 33N 5 53 E
Kamperland **23** 51 34N 3 43 E
Kamphaeng Phet **84** 16 28N 99 30 E
Kampolombo, L. **131** 11 37 S 29 42 E
Kampong To **85** 6 3N 101 13 E
Kampot **85** 10 36N 104 10 E
Kampsville **154** 39 18N 90 37W
Kamptee **78** 21 9N 79 19 E
Kampti **126** 10 7N 3 25W
Kampuchea =
Cambodia ■ **84** 12 15N 105 0 E

Kampung

Kampung → **87** 5 44 S 138 24 E
Kampung Air Putih **85** 4 15N 103 10 E
Kampung Jerangau **85** 4 50N 103 10 E
Kampung Raja **85** 5 45N 102 35 E
Kampungbaru = Tolitoli **87** 1 5N 120 50 E
Kamrau, Teluk **87** 3 30 S 133 36 E
Kamsack **145** 51 34N 101 54W
Kamskoye Ustye **59** 55 10N 49 20 E
Kamskoye Vdkhr. **56** 58 0N 56 0 E
Kamuchawie L. **145** 56 18N 101 59W
Kamui-Misaki **98** 43 20N 140 21 E
Kāmyārān **72** 34 47N 46 56 E
Kamyshin **59** 50 10N 45 24 E
Kamyshlov **62** 56 50N 62 43 E
Kamyzyak **61** 46 4N 48 10 E
Kan **82** 22 25N 94 5 E
Kanaaupscow **142** 54 2N 76 30W
Kanab **157** 37 3N 112 29W
Kanab Creek **157** 37 0N 112 40W
Kanagawa □ **101** 35 20N 139 20 E
Kanagi **98** 40 54N 140 27 E
Kanairiktok → **143** 55 2N 60 18W
Kanakapura **81** 12 33N 77 28 E
Kanália **48** 39 30N 22 53 E
Kananga **133** 5 55 S 22 18 E
Kanarraville **157** 37 34N 113 12W
Kanash **59** 55 30N 47 32 E
Kanaskat **158** 47 19N 121 54W
Kanastraíon, Ákra **48** 39 57N 23 45 E
Kanawha → **148** 38 50N 82 8W
Kanazawa **101** 36 30N 136 38 E
Kanbalu **82** 23 12N 95 31 E
Kanchanaburi **84** 14 2N 99 31 E
Kanchenjunga **79** 27 50N 88 10 E
Kanchipuram **81** 12 52N 79 45 E
Kańczuga **31** 49 59N 22 25 E
Kanda Kanda **133** 6 52 S 23 48 E
Kandahar = Qandahār **77** 31 32N 65 30 E
Kandalaksha **56** 67 9N 32 30 E
Kandalakshkiy Zaliv **56** 66 0N 35 0 E
Kandangan **89** 2 50 S 115 20 E
Kandanos **49** 35 19N 23 44 E
Kandavu **106** 19 0 S 178 15 E
Kandavu Passage **106** 18 45 S 178 0 E
Kandep **107** 5 54 S 143 32 E
Kander → **28** 46 33N 7 38 E
Kandersteg **28** 46 30N 7 40 E
Kandhíla **49** 37 46N 22 22 E
Kandhkot **78** 28 16N 69 8 E
Kandhla **78** 29 18N 77 19 E
Kandi, Benin **127** 11 7N 2 55 E
Kandi, India **79** 23 58N 88 5 E
Kandla **78** 23 0N 70 10 E
Kandos **113** 32 45 S 149 58 E
Kandrian **107** 6 14 S 149 37 E
Kandy **81** 7 18N 80 43 E
Kane **150** 41 39N 78 53W
Kane Basin **6** 79 1N 73 0W
Kanevskaya **61** 46 3N 39 3 E
Kanfanar **43** 45 7N 13 50 E
Kangaba **126** 11 56N 8 25W
Kangān, Fārs, Iran **73** 27 50N 52 3 E
Kangān, Hormozgān, Iran **73** 25 48N 57 28 E
Kangar **85** 6 27N 100 12 E
Kangaroo I. **112** 35 45 S 137 0 E
Kangaroo Mts. **110** 23 25 S 142 0 E
Kangavar **73** 34 40N 48 0 E
Kangding **96** 30 2N 101 57 E
Kāngdong **95** 39 9N 126 5 E
Kangean, Kepulauan **89** 6 55 S 115 23 E
Kangerdlugsuak **6** 68 10N 32 20W
Kanggye **95** 41 0N 126 35 E
Kanggyŏng **95** 36 10N 127 0 E
Kanghwa **95** 37 45N 126 30 E
Kangnŭng **95** 37 45N 128 54 E
Kango **132** 0 11N 10 5 E
Kangoya **133** 9 55 S 22 48 E
Kangping **95** 42 43N 123 18 E
Kangpokpi **82** 25 8N 93 58 E
Kangyidaung **82** 16 56N 94 54 E
Kanhangad **81** 12 21N 74 58 E
Kanheri **80** 19 13N 72 50 E
Kani **126** 8 29N 6 36W
Kaniama **130** 7 30 S 24 12 E
Kaniapiskau → **143** 56 40N 69 30W
Kaniapiskau L. **143** 54 10N 69 55W
Kanibadam **63** 40 17N 70 25 E
Kanin, P-ov. **56** 68 0N 45 0 E
Kanin Nos, Mys **56** 68 45N 43 20 E
Kanina **48** 40 23N 19 30 E
Kaniva **112** 36 22 S 141 18 E
Kanjiža **46** 46 3N 20 4 E
Kanjut Sar **79** 36 7N 75 25 E
Kankakee **155** 41 6N 87 50W
Kankakee → **155** 41 23N 88 16W
Kankan **126** 10 23N 9 15W
Kanker **80** 20 10N 81 40 E
Kankunskiy **65** 57 37N 126 8 E
Kanmuri-Yama **100** 34 30N 132 4 E
Kannabe **100** 34 32N 133 23 E
Kannapolis **149** 35 32N 80 37W
Kannauj **79** 27 3N 79 56 E
Kano **127** 12 2N 8 30 E
Kano □ **127** 11 45N 9 0 E
Kan'onji **100** 34 7N 133 39 E
Kanoroba **126** 9 7N 6 8W
Kanowha **154** 42 57N 93 47W
Kanowit **86** 2 14N 112 20 E
Kanowna **109** 30 32 S 121 31 E
Kanoya **100** 31 25N 130 50 E
Kanpetlet **82** 21 10N 93 59 E
Kanpur **79** 26 28N 80 20 E
Kansas **155** 39 33N 87 56W
Kansas □ **152** 38 40N 98 0W
Kansas → **152** 39 7N 94 36W
Kansas City, Kans., U.S.A. **154** 39 0N 94 40W
Kansas City, Mo., U.S.A. **154** 39 3N 94 30W
Kansenia **131** 10 20 S 26 0 E
Kansk **65** 56 20N 95 37 E
Kansŏng **95** 38 24N 128 30 E
Kansu = Gansu □ **94** 36 0N 104 0 E
Kant **63** 42 53N 74 51 E
Kantang **85** 7 25N 99 31 E
Kantché **127** 13 31N 8 30 E
Kanté **127** 9 57N 1 3 E
Kantemirovka **61** 49 43N 39 55 E
Kantharalak **84** 14 39N 104 39 E
Kantō □ **101** 36 15N 139 30 E
Kantō-Heiya **101** 36 0N 139 30 E
Kantō-Sanchi **101** 35 59N 138 50 E
Kantu-long **82** 19 57N 97 36 E
Kanturk **15** 52 10N 8 55W
Kanuma **101** 36 34N 139 42 E
Kanus **134** 27 50 S 18 39 E
Kanye **134** 25 0 S 25 28 E
Kanzenze **131** 10 30 S 25 12 E
Kanzi, Ras **130** 7 1 S 39 33 E
Kaohsiung = Gaoxiong **97** 22 38N 120 18 E
Kaokoveld **134** 19 15 S 14 30 E
Kaolack **126** 14 5N 16 8W
Kaoshan **95** 44 38N 124 50 E
Kaouar **123** 19 5N 12 52 E
Kapadvanj **78** 23 5N 73 0 E
Kapagere **107** 9 46 S 147 42 E
Kapanga **133** 8 30 S 22 40 E
Kapatagan **91** 7 52N 123 44 E
Kapchagai **63** 43 51N 77 14 E
Kapchagaiskoye Vdkhr. **63** 43 45N 77 50 E
Kapellen **23** 51 19N 4 25 E
Kapéllo, Ákra **49** 36 9N 23 3 E
Kapema **131** 10 45 S 28 22 E
Kapfenberg **30** 47 26N 15 18 E
Kapia **133** 4 17 S 19 46 E
Kapiri Mposhi **131** 13 59 S 28 43 E
Kāpīsā □ **77** 35 0N 69 20 E
Kapiskau → **142** 52 47N 81 55W
Kapit **86** 2 0N 112 55 E
Kapiti I. **114** 40 50 S 174 56 E
Kapka, Massif du **123** 15 7N 21 45 E
Kaplice **30** 48 42N 14 30 E
Kapoe **85** 9 34N 98 32 E
Kapoeta **125** 4 50N 33 35 E
Kápolnásnyék **31** 47 16N 18 41 E
Kaponga **114** 39 29 S 174 9 E
Kapos → **31** 46 44N 18 30 E
Kaposvár **31** 46 25N 17 47 E
Kapowsin **158** 46 59N 122 13W
Kappeln **26** 54 37N 9 56 E
Kapps **134** 22 32 S 17 18 E
Kaprije **43** 43 42N 15 43 E
Kaprijke **23** 51 13N 3 38 E
Kapsan **95** 41 4N 128 19 E
Kapsukas **58** 54 33N 23 19 E
Kapuas **89** 3 10 S 114 5 E
Kapuas → **89** 0 25 S 109 20 E
Kapuas Hulu, Pegunungan **86** 1 30N 113 30 E
Kapulo **131** 8 18 S 29 15 E
Kapunda **112** 34 20 S 138 56 E
Kapurthala **78** 31 23N 75 25 E
Kapuskasing **142** 49 25N 82 30W
Kapuskasing → **142** 49 49N 82 0W
Kapustin Yar **61** 48 37N 45 40 E
Kaputar, Mt. **111** 30 15 S 150 10 E
Kaputir **130** 2 5N 35 28 E
Kapuvár **31** 47 36N 17 1 E
Kara, Turkey **49** 36 58N 27 30 E
Kara, U.S.S.R. **64** 69 10N 65 0 E
Kara Bogaz Gol, Zaliv **57** 41 0N 53 30 E
Kara Burun **49** 38 41N 26 28 E
Kara Kalpak A.S.S.R. □ **64** 43 0N 60 0 E
Kara Kum = Karakum, Peski **64** 39 30N 60 0 E
Kara-Saki **100** 34 41N 129 30 E
Kara Sea **64** 75 0N 70 0 E
Kara Su **63** 40 44N 72 53 E
Karabash **62** 55 29N 60 14 E
Karabekaul **63** 38 30N 64 8 E
Karabük **60** 41 12N 32 37 E
Karabulak **63** 44 54N 78 30 E
Karaburuni **48** 40 25N 19 20 E
Karabutak **62** 49 59N 60 14 E
Karachala **61** 39 45N 48 53 E
Karachayevsk **61** 43 50N 42 0 E
Karachev **58** 53 10N 35 5 E
Karachi **77** 24 53N 67 0 E
Karád, Hungary **31** 46 41N 17 51 E
Karad, India **80** 17 15N 74 10 E
Karadeniz Boğazı **57** 41 10N 29 10 E
Karaga **127** 9 58N 0 28W
Karaganda **64** 49 50N 73 10 E
Karagayly **64** 49 26N 76 0 E
Karaginskiy, Ostrov **65** 58 45N 164 0 E
Karagiye Depression **57** 43 27N 51 45 E
Karagwe □ **130** 2 0 S 31 0 E
Karaikal **81** 10 59N 79 50 E
Karaikkudi **81** 10 0N 78 45 E
Karaitivu, I. **81** 9 45N 79 52 E
Karaj **73** 35 48N 51 0 E
Karak **85** 3 25N 102 2 E
Karakas **64** 48 20N 83 30 E
Karakitang **87** 3 14N 125 28 E
Karakoram Pass **79** 35 33N 77 50 E
Karakoram Ra. **79** 35 30N 77 0 E
Karakul, Tadzhik S.S.R., U.S.S.R. **63** 39 2N 73 33 E
Karakul, Uzbek S.S.R., U.S.S.R. **63** 39 22N 63 50 E
Karakuldzha **63** 40 39N 73 26 E
Karakulino **60** 56 1N 53 43 E
Karakum, Peski **64** 39 30N 60 0 E
Karal **123** 12 50N 14 46 E
Karalon **65** 57 5N 115 50 E
Karaman **57** 37 14N 33 13 E
Karamay **92** 45 30N 84 58 E
Karambu **89** 3 53 S 116 6 E
Karamea **115** 41 14 S 172 6 E
Karamea → **115** 41 13 S 172 26 E
Karamea Bight **115** 41 22 S 171 40 E
Karamet Niyaz **63** 37 45N 64 34 E
Karamoja □ **130** 3 0N 34 15 E
Karamsad **78** 22 35N 72 50 E
Karand **72** 34 16N 46 15 E
Karanganyar **89** 7 38 S 109 37 E
Karanja **78** 20 29N 77 31 E
Karapiro **114** 37 53 S 175 32 E
Karasburg **134** 28 0 S 18 44 E
Karasino **64** 66 50N 86 50 E
Karasu → **70** 36 37N 36 27 E
Karasuk **64** 53 44N 78 2 E
Karasuyama **101** 36 39N 140 9 E
Karatau **63** 43 10N 70 28 E
Karatau, Khrebet **63** 43 30N 69 30 E
Karativu **81** 8 22N 79 47 E
Karatobe **62** 49 44N 53 30 E
Karatoya → **82** 24 7N 89 36 E
Karaturuk **63** 43 35N 78 0 E
Karaul-Bazar **63** 39 30N 64 48 E
Karauli **78** 26 30N 77 4 E
Karávi **49** 36 49N 23 37 E
Karawa **132** 3 18N 20 17 E
Karawang **89** 6 30 S 107 15 E
Karawanken **30** 46 30N 14 40 E
Karazhal **64** 48 2N 70 49 E
Karbalā **72** 32 36N 44 3 E
Kårböle **52** 61 59N 15 22 E
Karcag **31** 47 19N 20 57 E
Karcha → **79** 34 45N 76 10 E
Karda **65** 55 0N 103 16 E
Kardhámila **49** 38 35N 26 5 E
Kardhítsa **48** 39 23N 21 54 E
Kardhítsa □ **48** 39 15N 21 50 E
Kärdla **58** 58 50N 22 40 E
Kareeberge **134** 30 59 S 21 50 E
Kareima **124** 18 30N 31 49 E
Karelian A.S.S.R. □ **56** 65 30N 32 30 E
Karema **107** 9 12 S 147 18 E
Kärevändar **73** 27 53N 60 44 E
Kargapolye **62** 55 57N 64 24 E
Kargasok **64** 59 3N 80 53 E
Kargat **64** 55 10N 80 15 E
Kargı **60** 41 11N 34 30 E
Kargil **79** 34 32N 76 12 E
Kargopol **56** 61 30N 38 58 E
Kargowa **32** 52 5N 15 51 E
Karguéri **127** 13 27N 10 30 E
Karia ba Mohammed **120** 34 22N 5 12W
Kariaí **48** 40 14N 24 19 E
Karīān **73** 26 57N 57 14 E
Kariba **131** 16 28 S 28 50 E
Kariba Dam **131** 16 30 S 28 35 E
Kariba Gorge **131** 16 30 S 28 50 E
Kariba L. **131** 16 40 S 28 25 E
Karibib **134** 22 0 S 15 56 E
Karimata, Kepulauan **89** 1 25 S 109 0 E
Karimata, Selat **89** 2 0 S 108 40 E
Karimnagar **80** 18 26N 79 10 E
Karimunjawa, Kepulauan **89** 5 50 S 110 30 E
Karin **136** 10 50N 45 52 E
Káristos **49** 38 1N 24 29 E
Karīt **73** 33 29N 56 55 E
Kariya **101** 34 58N 137 1 E
Karkal **81** 13 15N 74 56 E
Karkar I. **107** 4 40 S 146 0 E
Karkaralinsk **64** 49 26N 75 30 E
Karkinitskiy Zaliv **60** 45 56N 33 0 E
Karkur **69** 32 29N 34 57 E
Karkur Tohl **124** 22 5N 25 5 E
Karl Libknekht **58** 51 40N 35 35 E
Karl-Marx-Stadt **26** 50 50N 12 55 E
Karl-Marx-Stadt □ **26** 50 45N 13 0 E
Karla, L. = Voiviis Límni **48** 39 30N 22 45 E
Karlino **32** 54 3N 15 53 E
Karlobag **43** 44 32N 15 5 E
Karlovac **43** 45 31N 15 36 E
Karlovka **60** 49 29N 35 8 E
Karlovy Vary **30** 50 13N 12 51 E
Karlsborg **53** 58 33N 14 33 E
Karlshamn **53** 56 10N 14 51 E
Karlskoga **52** 59 22N 14 33 E
Karlskrona **53** 56 10N 15 35 E
Karlsruhe **27** 49 3N 8 23 E
Karlstad, Sweden **52** 59 23N 13 30 E
Karlstad, U.S.A. **152** 48 38N 96 30W
Karlstadt **27** 49 57N 9 46 E
Karmøy **51** 59 15N 5 15 E
Karnal **78** 29 42N 77 2 E
Karnali → **79** 29 0N 83 20 E
Karnaphuli Res. **82** 22 40N 92 20 E
Karnataka □ **81** 13 15N 77 0 E
Karnes City **153** 28 53N 97 53W
Karnische Alpen **30** 46 36N 13 0 E
Kärnten □ **30** 46 52N 13 30 E
Karo **126** 12 16N 3 18W
Karoi **131** 16 48 S 29 45 E
Karomatan **91** 7 55N 123 44 E
Karonga **131** 9 57 S 33 55 E
Karoonda **112** 35 1 S 139 59 E
Karora **124** 17 44N 38 15 E
Káros **49** 36 54N 25 40 E
Karousádhes **48** 39 47N 19 45 E
Kárpathos **49** 35 37N 27 10 E
Karpáthos, Stenón **49** 36 0N 27 30 E
Karpinsk **62** 59 45N 60 1 E
Karpogory **56** 63 59N 44 27 E
Karrebæk **52** 55 12N 11 39 E
Kars **60** 40 40N 43 5 E
Karsakpay **64** 47 55N 66 40 E
Karsha **61** 49 45N 51 35 E
Karshi **63** 38 53N 65 48 E
Karsiyang **79** 26 56N 88 18 E
Karst **43** 45 35N 14 0 E
Karsun **59** 54 14N 46 57 E
Kartal Dağları **70** 37 4N 36 55 E
Kartál Óros **48** 41 15N 25 13 E
Kartaly **62** 53 3N 60 40 E
Kartapur **78** 31 27N 75 32 E
Karthaus **150** 41 8N 78 9W
Kartuzy **32** 54 22N 18 10 E
Karuah **113** 32 37 S 151 56 E
Karufa **87** 3 50 S 133 20 E
Karumba **110** 17 31 S 140 50 E
Karumo **130** 2 25 S 32 50 E
Karumwa **130** 3 12 S 32 38 E
Karungu **130** 0 50 S 34 10 E
Karup **53** 56 19N 9 10 E
Karur **81** 10 59N 78 2 E
Karviná **31** 49 53N 18 25 E
Karwi **79** 25 12N 80 57 E
Kasache **131** 13 25 S 34 20 E
Kasai **100** 34 55N 134 52 E
Kasai → **133** 3 30 S 16 10 E
Kasai Occidental □ **133** 6 0 S 22 0 E
Kasai Oriental □ **130** 5 0 S 24 30 E
Kasaji **131** 10 25 S 23 27 E
Kasama, Japan **101** 36 23N 140 16 E
Kasama, Zambia **131** 10 16 S 31 9 E
Kasan-dong **95** 41 18N 126 55 E
Kasane **134** 17 34 S 24 50 E
Kasanga **131** 8 30 S 31 10 E
Kasangulu **133** 4 33 S 15 15 E
Kasaoka **100** 34 30N 133 30 E
Kasaragod **81** 12 30N 74 58 E
Kasat **82** 15 56N 98 13 E
Kasba **82** 23 45N 91 2 E
Kasba L. **145** 60 20N 102 10W
Kasba Tadla **120** 32 36N 6 17W
Kaseda **100** 31 25N 130 19 E
Kâseh Garān **72** 34 5N 46 2 E
Kasempa **131** 13 30 S 25 44 E
Kasenga **131** 10 20 S 28 45 E
Kasese **130** 0 13N 30 3 E
Kasewa **131** 14 28 S 28 53 E
Kasganj **79** 27 48N 78 42 E
Kashabowie **142** 48 40N 90 26W
Kāshān **73** 34 5N 51 30 E
Kashi **92** 39 30N 76 2 E
Kashihara **101** 34 27N 135 46 E
Kashima, Ibaraki, Japan **101** 35 58N 140 38 E
Kashima, Saga, Japan **100** 33 7N 130 6 E
Kashima-Nada **101** 36 0N 140 45 E
Kashimbo **131** 11 12 S 26 19 E
Kashin **59** 57 20N 37 36 E
Kashipur, Orissa, India **80** 19 16N 83 3 E
Kashipur, Ut. P., India **79** 29 15N 79 0 E
Kashira **59** 54 45N 38 10 E
Kashiwa **101** 35 52N 139 59 E
Kashiwazaki **99** 37 22N 138 33 E
Kashk-e Kohneh **77** 34 55N 62 30 E
Kashkasu **63** 39 54N 72 44 E
Kāshmar **73** 35 16N 58 26 E
Kashmir **79** 34 0N 76 0 E
Kashmor **77** 28 28N 69 32 E
Kashpirovka **59** 53 0N 48 30 E
Kashun Noerh = Gaxun Nur **92** 42 22N 100 30 E
Kasimov **59** 54 55N 41 20 E
Kasinge **130** 6 15 S 26 58 E
Kasiruta **87** 0 25 S 127 12 E
Kaskaskia → **154** 37 58N 89 57W
Kaskattama → **145** 57 3N 90 4W
Kaskelan **63** 43 20N 76 35 E
Kaskinen **54** 62 22N 21 15 E
Kaskö **54** 62 22N 21 15 E
Kasli **62** 55 53N 60 46 E
Kaslo **144** 49 55N 116 55W
Kasmere L. **145** 59 34N 101 10W
Kasongan **89** 2 0 S 113 23 E
Kasongo **130** 4 30 S 26 33 E
Kasongo Lunda **133** 6 35 S 16 49 E
Kásos **49** 35 20N 26 55 E
Kasos, Stenón **49** 35 30N 26 30 E
Kaspi **61** 41 54N 44 17 E
Kaspichan **47** 43 18N 27 11 E

Kesennuma

Kaspiysk 61 42 52N 47 40 E
Kaspiyskiy 61 45 22N 47 23 E
Kassab 70 35 55N 35 59 E
Kassab ed Doleib 125 13 30N 33 35 E
Kassaba 124 22 40N 29 55 E
Kassala 125 15 30N 36 0 E
Kassalâ □ 125 15 20N 36 26 E
Kassan 63 39 2N 65 35 E
Kassándra 48 40 0N 23 30 E
Kassansay 63 41 15N 71 31 E
Kassel 26 51 19N 9 32 E
Kassinger 124 18 46N 31 51 E
Kassue 87 6 58 S 139 21 E
Kastamonu 57 41 25N 33 43 E
Kastav 43 45 22N 14 20 E
Kastélli 49 35 29N 23 38 E
Kastéllion 49 35 12N 25 20 E
Kastellorizon = Megiste 39 36 8N 29 34 E
Kastellou, Ákra 49 35 30N 27 15 E
Kasterlee 23 51 15N 4 59 E
Kastlösa 53 56 26N 16 25 E
Kastóri 49 37 10N 22 17 E
Kastoría 48 40 30N 21 19 E
Kastoría □ 48 40 30N 21 15 E
Kastorías, L. 48 40 30N 21 20 E
Kastornoye 59 51 55N 38 2 E
Kastós 49 38 35N 20 55 E
Kástron 48 39 50N 25 2 E
Kastrosikiá 49 39 6N 20 36 E
Kasugai 101 35 12N 136 59 E
Kasukabe 101 35 58N 139 49 E
Kasulu 130 4 37 S 30 5 E
Kasulu □ 130 4 37 S 30 5 E
Kasumi 100 35 38N 134 38 E
Kasumiga-Ura 101 36 0N 140 25 E
Kasumkent 61 41 47N 48 15 E
Kasungu 131 13 0 S 33 29 E
Kasur 77 31 5N 74 25 E
Kata 65 58 46N 102 40 E
Kataba 131 16 5 S 25 10 E
Katako Kombe 130 3 25 S 24 20 E
Katákolon 49 37 38N 21 19 E
Katale 130 4 52 S 31 7 E
Katamatite 113 36 6 S 145 41 E
Katanda, Kivu, Zaïre 130 0 55 S 29 21 E
Katanda, Shaba, Zaïre 130 7 52 S 24 13 E
Katangi 79 21 56N 79 50 E
Katanglad Mts. 91 8 6N 124 54 E
Katangli 65 51 42N 143 14 E
Katapakishi 133 8 15 S 22 49 E
Katastári 49 37 50N 20 45 E
Katav Ivanovsk 62 54 45N 58 12 E
Katavi Swamp 130 6 50 S 31 10 E
Katchiungo 133 12 35 S 16 13 E
Kateríni 48 40 18N 22 37 E
Katherîna 128 28 31N 33 57 E
Katherîna, Gebel 124 28 30N 33 57 E
Katherine 108 14 27 S 132 20 E
Kathiawar 78 22 20N 71 0 E
Kathua 79 32 23N 75 30 E
Kati 126 12 41N 8 4W
Katihar 79 25 34N 87 36 E
Katima Mulilo 134 17 28 S 24 13 E
Katimbira 131 12 40 S 34 0 E
Katingan = Mendawai → 89 3 30 S 113 0 E
Katiola 126 8 10N 5 10W
Katipunan 91 8 31N 123 17 E
Katkopberg 134 30 0 S 20 0 E
Katlanovo 46 41 52N 21 40 E
Katmandu 79 27 45N 85 20 E
Kato Akhaïa 49 38 8N 21 33 E
Káto Stavros 48 40 39N 23 43 E
Katol 78 21 17N 78 38 E
Katompe 130 6 2 S 26 23 E
Katonga → 130 0 34N 31 50 E
Katoomba 113 33 41 S 150 19 E
Katowice 32 50 17N 19 5 E
Katowice □ 32 50 10N 19 0 E
Katrine, L. 14 56 15N 4 30W
Katrineholm 52 59 9N 16 12 E
Katsepe 135 15 45 S 46 15 E
Katsina 127 13 0N 7 32 E
Katsina Ala → 127 7 10N 9 20 E
Katsumoto 100 33 51N 129 42 E
Katsuta 101 36 25N 140 31 E
Katsuura 101 35 10N 140 20 E
Katsuyama 101 36 3N 136 30 E
Kattakurgan 63 39 55N 66 15 E
Kattegatt 53 57 0N 11 20 E
Katumba 130 7 40 S 25 17 E
Katungu 130 2 55 S 40 3 E
Katwa 79 23 30N 88 5 E
Katwijk-aan-Zee 22 52 12N 4 24 E
Katy 32 51 2N 16 45 E
Kauai 146 22 0N 159 30W
Kauai Chan. 146 21 45N 158 50W
Kaub 27 50 5N 7 46 E
Kaufbeuren 27 47 50N 10 37 E
Kaufman 153 32 35N 96 20W
Kaukauna 148 44 20N 88 13W
Kaukauveld 134 20 0 S 20 15 E
Kauliranta 54 66 27N 23 41 E
Kaunas 58 54 54N 23 54 E
Kaunghein 82 25 41N 95 26 E
Kaura Namoda 127 12 37N 6 33 E
Kautokeino 54 69 0N 23 4 E
Kavacha 65 60 16N 169 51 E
Kavadarci 46 41 26N 22 3 E
Kavaja 48 41 11N 19 33 E
Kavalerovo 98 44 15N 135 4 E
Kavali 81 14 55N 80 1 E
Kavála 48 40 57N 24 28 E
Kavála □ 48 41 5N 24 30 E
Kavála Kólpos 48 40 50N 24 25 E
Kavār 73 29 11N 52 44 E
Kavarna 47 43 26N 28 22 E
Kavieng 107 2 36 S 150 51 E
Kavkaz, Bolshoi 61 42 50N 44 0 E
Kavoúsi 49 35 7N 25 51 E
Kaw 169 4 30N 52 15W
Kawa 125 13 42N 32 34 E
Kawachi-Nagano 101 34 28N 135 31 E
Kawagama L. 150 45 18N 78 45W
Kawagoe 101 35 55N 139 29 E
Kawaguchi 101 35 52N 139 45 E
Kawaihae 146 20 3N 155 50W
Kawakawa 114 35 23 S 174 6 E
Kawambwa 131 9 48 S 29 3 E
Kawanoe 100 34 1N 133 34 E
Kawarau 115 45 3 S 168 45 E
Kawardha 79 22 0N 81 17 E
Kawasaki 101 35 35N 139 42 E
Kawau I. 114 36 25 S 174 52 E
Kawene 142 48 45N 91 15W
Kawerau 114 38 7 S 176 42 E
Kawhia Harbour 114 38 5 S 174 51 E
Kawio, Kepulauan 87 4 30N 125 30 E
Kawit 91 6 57N 121 58 E
Kawkabān 74 15 30N 43 54 E
Kawkareik 82 16 33N 98 14 E
Kawlin 82 23 47N 95 41 E
Kawthoolei □ = Kawthule □ 82 18 0N 97 30 E
Kawthule □ 82 18 0N 97 30 E
Kawya 82 24 50N 94 58 E
Kay 62 59 57N 52 59 E
Kaya 127 13 4N 1 10W
Kayah □ 82 19 15N 97 15 E
Kayan 82 16 54N 96 34 E
Kayan → 89 2 55N 117 35 E
Kayankulam 81 9 10N 76 33 E
Kayapa 90 16 22N 120 53 E
Kaycee 156 43 45N 106 46W
Kayeli 87 3 20 S 127 10 E
Kayenta 157 36 46N 110 15W
Kayes, Congo 133 4 25 S 11 41 E
Kayes, Mali 126 14 25N 11 30W
Kayima 126 8 54N 11 15W
Kayl 23 49 29N 6 2 E
Kayoa 87 0 1N 127 28 E
Kayomba 131 13 11 S 24 2 E
Kayoro 127 11 0N 1 28W
Kayrakkumskoye Vdkhr. 63 40 20N 70 0 E
Kayrunnera 111 30 40 S 142 30 E
Kaysatskoye 61 49 47N 46 49 E
Kayseri 57 38 45N 35 30 E
Kaysville 156 41 2N 111 58W
Kayuagung 88 3 24 S 104 50 E
Kazachinskoye 65 56 16N 107 36 E
Kazachye 65 70 52N 135 58 E
Kazakh S.S.R. □ 60 50 0N 70 0 E
Kazan 59 55 48N 49 3 E
Kazanci 70 36 29N 32 51 E
Kazanlı 70 36 49N 34 43 E
Kazanlúk 47 42 38N 25 20 E
Kazanskaya 61 49 50N 41 10 E
Kazarman 63 41 24N 73 59 E
Kazatin 60 49 45N 28 50 E
Kazbek 61 42 42N 44 30 E
Kāzerūn 73 29 38N 51 40 E
Kazhim 62 60 21N 51 33 E
Kazi Magomed 61 40 3N 49 0 E
Kazimierz Dolny 32 51 19N 21 57 E
Kazimierza Wielka 32 50 15N 20 30 E
Kazincbarcika 31 48 17N 20 36 E
Kazo 101 36 7N 139 36 E
Kaztalovka 61 49 47N 48 43 E
Kazu 82 25 27N 97 46 E
Kazumba 133 6 25 S 22 5 E
Kazuno 98 40 10N 140 45 E
Kazym → 64 63 54N 65 50 E
Kcynia 32 53 0N 17 30 E
Ke-hsi Mansam 82 21 56N 97 50 E
Ké-Macina 126 13 58N 5 22W
Kéa 49 37 35N 24 22 E
Keams Canyon 157 35 53N 110 9W
Kearney, Mo., U.S.A. 154 39 22N 94 22W
Kearney, Nebr., U.S.A. 152 40 45N 99 3W
Keban 57 38 50N 38 50 E
Kébi 126 9 18N 6 37W
Kebili 121 33 47N 9 0 E
Kebnekaise 54 67 53N 18 33 E
Kebri Dehar 136 6 45N 44 17 E
Kebumen 89 7 42 S 109 40 E
Kecel 31 46 31N 19 16 E
Kechika → 144 59 41N 127 12W
Kecskemét 31 46 57N 19 42 E
Kedada 125 5 25N 35 58 E
Kedainiai 58 55 15N 24 2 E
Kedgwick 143 47 40N 67 20W
Kedia Hill 134 21 28 S 24 37 E
Kediri 89 7 51 S 112 1 E
Kédougou 126 12 35N 12 10W
Kedzierzyn 32 50 20N 18 12 E
Keeler 158 36 29N 117 52W
Keeley L. 145 54 54N 108 8W
Keeling Is. = Cocos Is. 83 12 10 S 96 55 E
Keene, Calif., U.S.A. 159 35 13N 118 33W
Keene, N.H., U.S.A. 151 42 57N 72 17W
Keeper Hill 15 52 46N 8 17W
Keer-Weer, C. 110 14 0 S 141 32 E
Keerbergen 23 51 1N 4 38 E
Keeseville 151 44 29N 73 30W
Keeten Mastgat 23 51 36N 4 0 E
Keetmanshoop 134 26 35 S 18 8 E
Keewatin 152 47 23N 93 0W
Keewatin □ 145 63 20N 95 0W
Keewatin → 145 56 29N 100 46W
Kefa □ 125 6 55N 36 30 E
Kefallinía 49 38 20N 20 30 E
Kefamenanu 87 9 28 S 124 29 E
Kefar 'Eqron 69 31 52N 34 49 E
Kefar Ḥasīdim 69 32 47N 35 5 E
Kefar Naḥum 69 32 54N 35 34 E
Kefar Sava 69 32 11N 34 54 E
Kefar Szold 69 33 11N 35 39 E
Kefar Vitkin 69 32 22N 34 53 E
Kefar Yehezqel 69 32 34N 35 22 E
Kefar Yona 69 32 20N 34 54 E
Kefar Zekharya 69 31 43N 34 57 E
Kefar Zetim 69 32 48N 35 27 E
Keffi 127 8 55N 7 43 E
Keflavík 54 64 2N 22 35W
Keg River 144 57 54N 117 55W
Kegalla 81 7 15N 80 21 E
Kegaska 143 50 9N 61 18W
Kehl 27 48 34N 7 50 E
Keighley 12 53 52N 1 54W
Keimoes 134 28 41 S 20 59 E
Keita 127 14 46N 5 56 E
Keith, Australia 112 36 6 S 140 20 E
Keith, U.K. 14 57 33N 2 58W
Keith Arm 140 64 20N 122 15W
Keithsburg 154 41 6N 90 56W
Kekaygyr 63 40 42N 75 32 E
Kekri 78 26 0N 75 10 E
Kël 65 69 30N 124 10 E
Kelamet 125 16 0N 38 30 E
Kelan 94 38 43N 111 31 E
Kelang 85 3 2N 101 26 E
Kelani Ganga → 81 6 58N 79 50 E
Kelantan → 85 6 13N 102 14 E
Këlcyra 48 40 22N 20 12 E
Keles → 63 41 1N 68 37 E
Kelheim 27 48 58N 11 57 E
Kelibia 121 36 50N 11 3 E
Kellé 132 0 8 S 14 38 E
Keller 156 48 2N 118 44W
Kellerberrin 109 31 36 S 117 38 E
Kellett C. 6 72 0N 126 0W
Kelleys I. 150 41 35N 82 42W
Kellogg 156 47 30N 116 5W
Kelloselkä 54 66 56N 28 53 E
Kells = Ceanannus Mor 15 53 42N 6 53W
Kélo 123 9 10N 15 45 E
Kelowna 144 49 50N 119 25W
Kelsey Bay 144 50 25N 126 0W
Kelseyville 158 38 59N 122 50W
Kelso, N.Z. 115 45 54 S 169 15 E
Kelso, U.K. 14 55 36N 2 27W
Kelso, U.S.A. 158 46 10N 122 57W
Keltemashat 63 42 25N 70 8 E
Keluang 85 2 3N 103 18 E
Kelvington 145 52 10N 103 30W
Kem 56 65 0N 34 38 E
Kem → 56 64 57N 34 41 E
Kem-Kem 120 30 40N 4 30W
Kema 87 1 22N 125 8 E
Kemano 144 53 35N 128 0W
Kemapyu 82 18 49N 97 19 E
Kemasik 85 4 25N 103 27 E
Kembé 132 4 36N 21 54 E
Kembolcha 125 11 2N 39 42 E
Kemerovo 64 55 20N 86 5 E
Kemi älv = Kemijoki → 54 65 47N 24 32 E
Kemijärvi 54 66 43N 27 22 E
Kemijoki → 54 65 47N 24 32 E
Kemmel 23 50 47N 2 50 E
Kemmerer 156 41 52N 110 30W
Kemmuna = Comino 40 36 0N 14 20 E
Kemp L. 153 33 45N 99 15W
Kemp Land 7 69 0 S 55 0 E
Kempsey 111 31 1 S 152 50 E
Kempt, L. 142 47 25N 74 22W
Kempten 27 47 42N 10 18 E
Kempton 155 40 16N 86 14W
Kemptville 142 45 0N 75 38W
Kenadsa 121 31 48N 2 26W
Kendal, Indonesia 89 6 56 S 110 14 E
Kendal, U.K. 12 54 19N 2 44W
Kendall 111 31 35 S 152 44 E
Kendall → 110 14 4 S 141 35 E
Kendallville 155 41 25N 85 15W
Kendari 87 3 50 S 122 30 E
Kendawangan 89 2 32 S 110 17 E
Kende 127 11 30N 4 12 E
Kendenup 109 34 30 S 117 38 E
Kendervicës, Mal e. 48 40 15N 19 52 E
Kendrapara 79 20 35N 86 30 E
Kendrew 134 32 32 S 24 30 E
Kendrick 156 46 43N 116 41W
Kene Thao 84 17 44N 101 10 E
Kenedy 153 28 49N 97 51W
Kenema 126 7 50N 11 14W
Keng Kok 84 16 26N 105 12 E
Keng Tawng 82 20 45N 98 18 E
Kengani 132 2 59 S 17 36 E
Kenge 133 4 50 S 17 4 E
Kengeja 130 5 26 S 39 45 E
Kenhardt 134 29 19 S 21 12 E
Kenimekh 63 40 16N 65 7 E
Kenitra 120 34 15N 6 40W
Kenli 95 37 30N 118 20 E
Kenmare, Ireland 15 51 52N 9 35W
Kenmare, U.S.A. 152 48 40N 102 4W
Kenmare → 15 51 40N 10 0W
Kennebec 152 43 56N 99 54W
Kennedy 131 18 52 S 27 10 E
Kennedy Ra. 109 24 45 S 115 10 E
Kennet → 13 51 24N 0 58W
Kenneth Ra. 109 23 50 S 117 8 E
Kennett 153 36 7N 90 0W
Kennewick 156 46 11N 119 2W
Kénogami 143 48 25N 71 15W
Kenogami → 142 51 6N 84 28W
Kenora 145 49 47N 94 29W
Kenosha 155 42 33N 87 48W
Kensington, Canada 143 46 28N 63 34W
Kensington, U.S.A. 152 39 48N 99 2W
Kensington Downs 110 22 31 S 144 19 E
Kent, Ohio, U.S.A. 150 41 8N 81 20W
Kent, Oreg., U.S.A. 156 45 11N 120 45W
Kent, Tex., U.S.A. 153 31 5N 104 12W
Kent, Wash., U.S.A. 158 47 23N 122 14W
Kent □ 13 51 12N 0 40 E
Kent Group 110 39 30 S 147 20 E
Kent Pen. 140 68 30N 107 0W
Kentau 63 43 32N 68 36 E
Kentland 155 40 45N 87 25W
Kenton 155 40 40N 83 35W
Kentucky 113 30 45 S 151 28 E
Kentucky □ 148 37 20N 85 0W
Kentucky → 155 38 41N 85 11W
Kentucky L. 149 36 25N 88 0W
Kentville 143 45 6N 64 29W
Kentwood, Mich., U.S.A. 155 30 56N 90 31W
Kentwood, U.S.A. 153 31 0N 90 30W
Kenya ■ 130 1 0N 38 0 E
Kenya, Mt. 130 0 10 S 37 18 E
Kenzou 132 4 10N 15 2 E
Keo Neua, Deo 84 18 23N 105 10 E
Keokuk 154 40 25N 91 24W
Keosauqua 154 40 44N 91 58W
Keota 154 41 22N 91 57W
Kep, Cambodia 85 10 29N 104 19 E
Kep, Vietnam 84 21 24N 106 16 E
Kepi 87 6 32 S 139 19 E
Kepice 32 54 16N 16 51 E
Kepler Mts. 115 45 25 S 167 20 E
Kępno 32 51 18N 17 58 E
Kerala □ 81 11 0N 76 15 E
Kerama-Rettō 99 26 5N 127 15 E
Keran 79 34 35N 73 59 E
Kerang 112 35 40 S 143 55 E
Keratéa 49 37 48N 23 58 E
Keraudren, C. 108 19 58 S 119 45 E
Keravat 107 4 17 S 152 2 E
Kerch 60 45 20N 36 20 E
Kerchenskiy Proliv 60 45 10N 36 30 E
Kerchoual 127 17 12N 0 20 E
Kerem Maharal 69 32 39N 34 59 E
Kerema 107 7 58 S 145 50 E
Keren 125 15 45N 38 28 E
Kerewan 126 13 29N 16 10W
Kerguelen 83 49 15 S 69 10 E
Keri 49 37 40N 20 49 E
Keri Kera 125 12 21N 32 42 E
Kericho 130 0 22 S 35 15 E
Kericho □ 130 0 30 S 35 15 E
Kerikeri 114 35 12 S 173 59 E
Kerinci 88 1 40 S 101 15 E
Kerkdriel 22 51 47N 5 20 E
Kerkenna, Is. 121 34 48N 11 11 E
Kerki 63 37 50N 65 12 E
Kerkinítis, Límni 48 41 12N 23 10 E
Kérkira 48 39 38N 19 50 E
Kerkrade 23 50 53N 6 4 E
Kerma 124 19 33N 30 32 E
Kermadec Is. 104 30 0 S 178 15W
Kermadec Trench 104 30 30 S 176 0W
Kermān, Iran 73 30 15N 57 1 E
Kerman, U.S.A. 158 36 43N 120 4W
Kermān □ 73 30 0N 57 0 E
Kermānshāh = Bākhtarān 72 34 23N 47 0 E
Kerme Körfezi 49 36 55N 27 50 E
Kermen 47 42 30N 26 16 E
Kermit 153 31 56N 103 3W
Kern → 159 35 16N 119 18W
Kerns 29 46 54N 8 17 E
Kernville 159 35 45N 118 26W
Keroh 85 5 43N 101 1 E
Kerrobert 145 51 56N 109 8W
Kerrville 153 30 1N 99 8W
Kerry □ 15 52 7N 9 35W
Kerry Hd. 15 52 26N 9 56W
Kersa 125 9 28N 41 48 E
Kerteminde 53 55 28N 10 39 E
Kertosono 89 7 38 S 112 9 E
Kerulen → 93 48 48N 117 0 E
Kerzaz 121 29 29N 1 37W
Kerzers 28 46 59N 7 12 E
Kesagami → 142 51 40N 79 45W
Kesagami L. 142 50 23N 80 15W
Keşan 48 40 49N 26 38 E
Kesch, Piz 29 46 38N 9 53 E
Kesennuma 98 38 54N 141 35 E

Kočane

Kineshma **59** 57 30N 42 5 E
Kinesi **130** 1 25 S 33 50 E
King, L. **109** 33 10 S 119 35 E
King, Mt. **110** 25 10 S 147 30 E
King City, Calif., U.S.A. **158** 36 11N 121 8W
King City, Mo., U.S.A. **154** 40 3N 94 31W
King Cr. → **110** 24 35 S 139 30 E
King Edward → **108** 14 14 S 126 35 E
King Frederick VI Land = Kong Frederik VI.s Kyst **6** 63 0N 43 0W
King George B. **176** 51 30 S 60 30W
King George I. **7** 60 0 S 60 0W
King George Is. **141** 57 20N 80 30W
King I. = Kadan Kyun **86** 12 30N 98 20 E
King I., Australia **110** 39 50 S 144 0 E
King I., Canada **144** 52 10N 127 40W
King Leopold Ranges **108** 17 30 S 125 45 E
King Sd. **108** 16 50 S 123 20 E
King William I. **140** 69 10N 97 25W
King William's Town **134** 32 51 S 27 22 E
Kingaroy **111** 26 32 S 151 51 E
Kingfisher **153** 35 50N 97 55W
Kingirbān **72** 34 40N 44 54 E
Kingisepp, Estonia, U.S.S.R. **58** 58 15N 22 30 E
Kingisepp, R.S.F.S.R., U.S.S.R. **58** 59 25N 28 40 E
Kingking **91** 7 9N 125 54 E
Kingman, Ariz., U.S.A. **159** 35 12N 114 2W
Kingman, Ind., U.S.A. **155** 39 58N 87 18W
Kingman, Kans., U.S.A. **153** 37 41N 98 9W
Kings → **158** 36 10N 119 50W
Kings Canyon National Park **158** 37 0N 118 35W
King's Lynn **12** 52 45N 0 25 E
Kings Mountain **149** 35 13N 81 20W
King's Peak **156** 40 46N 110 27W
Kingsbridge **13** 50 17N 3 46W
Kingsburg **158** 36 35N 119 36W
Kingsbury **155** 41 31N 86 42W
Kingscote **112** 35 40 S 137 38 E
Kingscourt **15** 53 55N 6 48W
Kingsley **152** 42 37N 95 58W
Kingsport **149** 36 33N 82 36W
Kingston, Canada **142** 44 14N 76 30W
Kingston, Jamaica **162** 18 0N 76 50W
Kingston, N.Z. **115** 45 20 S 168 43 E
Kingston, Mo., U.S.A. **154** 39 38N 94 2W
Kingston, N.Y., U.S.A. **151** 41 55N 74 0W
Kingston, Pa., U.S.A. **151** 41 19N 75 58W
Kingston, R.I., U.S.A. **151** 41 29N 71 30W
Kingston Pk. **159** 35 45N 115 54W
Kingston South East **112** 36 51 S 139 55 E
Kingston-upon-Thames **13** 51 23N 0 20W
Kingstown, Australia **113** 30 29 S 151 6 E
Kingstown, St. Vinc. **163** 13 10N 61 10W
Kingstree **149** 33 40N 79 48W
Kingsville, Canada **142** 42 2N 82 45W
Kingsville, U.S.A. **153** 27 30N 97 53W
Kingussie **14** 57 5N 4 2W
Kinistino **145** 52 57N 105 2W
Kinkala **133** 4 18 S 14 49 E
Kinki □ **101** 33 30N 136 0 E
Kinleith **114** 38 20 S 175 56 E
Kinmount **150** 44 48N 78 45W
Kinmundy **155** 38 46N 88 51W
Kinn **51** 61 34N 4 45 E
Kinna **53** 57 32N 12 42 E
Kinnaird **144** 49 17N 117 39W
Kinnairds Hd. **14** 57 40N 2 0W
Kinnared **53** 57 2N 13 7 E
Kinneret **69** 32 44N 35 34 E
Kino **160** 28 45N 111 59W
Kinogitan **91** 9 0N 124 48 E
Kinoje → **142** 52 8N 81 25W
Kinomoto **101** 35 30N 136 13 E
Kinoni **130** 0 41 S 30 28 E
Kinrooi **23** 51 9N 5 45 E
Kinross **14** 56 13N 3 25W
Kinsale **15** 51 42N 8 31W
Kinsale, Old Hd. of **15** 51 37N 8 32W
Kinsarvik **51** 60 22N 6 43 E
Kinshasa **133** 4 20 S 15 15 E
Kinsley **153** 37 57N 99 30W
Kinston **149** 35 18N 77 35W
Kintampo **127** 8 5N 1 41W
Kintap **89** 3 51 S 115 13 E
Kintore Ra. **108** 23 15 S 128 47 E
Kintyre **14** 55 30N 5 35W
Kintyre, Mull of **14** 55 17N 5 55W
Kinu **82** 22 46N 95 37 E
Kinu-Gawa → **101** 35 36N 139 57 E
Kinushseo → **142** 55 15N 83 45W
Kinuso **144** 55 20N 115 25W
Kinyangiri **130** 4 25 S 34 37 E
Kinzig → **27** 48 37N 7 49 E
Kinzua **150** 41 52N 78 58W
Kinzua Dam **150** 41 53N 79 0W
Kióni **49** 38 27N 20 41 E
Kiosk **142** 46 6N 78 53W
Kiowa, Kans., U.S.A. **153** 37 3N 98 30W
Kiowa, Okla., U.S.A. **153** 34 45N 95 50W
Kipahigan L. **145** 55 20N 101 55W
Kipanga **130** 6 15 S 35 20 E
Kiparissía **49** 37 15N 21 40 E
Kiparissiakós Kólpos **49** 37 25N 21 25 E
Kipembawe **130** 7 38 S 33 27 E
Kipengere Ra. **131** 9 12 S 34 15 E
Kipili **130** 7 28 S 30 32 E
Kipini **130** 2 30 S 40 32 E
Kipling **145** 50 6N 102 38W
Kippure **15** 53 11N 6 23W
Kipungot **91** 6 24N 124 4 E
Kipushi **131** 11 48 S 27 12 E
Kirandul **80** 18 33N 81 10 E
Kiratpur **78** 29 32N 78 12 E
Kirchberg **28** 47 5N 7 35 E
Kirchhain **26** 50 49N 8 54 E
Kirchheim **27** 48 38N 9 20 E
Kirchheim-Bolanden **27** 49 40N 8 0 E
Kirchschlag **31** 47 30N 16 19 E
Kirensk **65** 57 50N 107 55 E
Kirgella Rocks **109** 30 5 S 122 50 E
Kirgiz S.S.R. □ **63** 42 0N 75 0 E
Kirgiziya Steppe **57** 50 0N 55 0 E
Kiri **132** 1 29 S 19 0 E
Kiri Buru **79** 22 0N 85 0 E
Kiribati ■ **104** 1 0N 176 0 E
Kırıkhan **70** 36 31N 36 21 E
Kırıkkale **57** 39 51N 33 32 E
Kirikopuni **114** 35 50 S 174 1 E
Kirillov **59** 59 51N 38 14 E
Kirin = Jilin **95** 43 44N 126 30 E
Kirin □ = Jilin **95** 44 0N 124 0 E
Kirindi → **81** 6 15N 81 20 E
Kirishi **58** 59 28N 31 59 E
Kirishima-Yama **100** 31 58N 130 55 E
Kiritimati **105** 1 58N 157 27W
Kirkcaldy **14** 56 7N 3 10W
Kirkcudbright **14** 54 50N 4 3W
Kirkee **80** 18 34N 73 56 E
Kirkenær **51** 60 27N 12 3 E
Kirkenes **54** 69 40N 30 5 E
Kirkintilloch **14** 55 57N 4 10W
Kirkjubæjarklaustur **54** 63 47N 18 4W
Kirkland, Ariz., U.S.A. **157** 34 29N 112 46W
Kirkland, Ill., U.S.A. **155** 42 5N 88 51W
Kirkland Lake **142** 48 9N 80 2W
Kırklareli **47** 41 44N 27 15 E
Kirklin **155** 40 12N 86 22W
Kirkliston Ra. **115** 44 25 S 170 34 E
Kirksville **154** 40 8N 92 35W
Kirkūk **72** 35 30N 44 21 E
Kirkwall **14** 58 59N 2 59W
Kirkwood, S. Africa **134** 33 22 S 25 15 E
Kirkwood, U.S.A. **154** 38 35N 90 24W
Kirlampudi **80** 17 12N 82 12 E
Kirn **27** 49 46N 7 29 E
Kirov, R.S.F.S.R., U.S.S.R. **58** 54 3N 34 20 E
Kirov, R.S.F.S.R., U.S.S.R. **59** 58 35N 49 40 E
Kirovabad **61** 40 45N 46 20 E
Kirovakan **61** 40 48N 44 30 E
Kirovo **63** 40 26N 70 36 E
Kirovo-Chepetsk **59** 58 28N 50 0 E
Kirovograd **60** 48 35N 32 20 E
Kirovsk, R.S.F.S.R., U.S.S.R. **56** 67 48N 33 50 E
Kirovsk, Turkmen S.S.R., U.S.S.R. **64** 37 42N 60 23 E
Kirovsk, Ukraine S.S.R., U.S.S.R. **61** 48 35N 38 30 E
Kirovski **61** 45 51N 48 11 E
Kirovskiy, Kamchatka, U.S.S.R. **65** 54 27N 155 42 E
Kirovskiy, Kazakh S.S.R., U.S.S.R. **63** 44 52N 78 12 E
Kirovskiy, R.S.F.S.R., U.S.S.R. **98** 45 7N 133 30 E
Kirovskoye **63** 42 39N 71 35 E
Kirriemuir **14** 56 41N 3 0W
Kirs **62** 59 21N 52 14 E
Kirsanov **59** 52 35N 42 40 E
Kırşehir **57** 39 14N 34 5 E
Kirstonia **134** 25 30 S 23 45 E
Kirtachi **127** 12 52N 2 30 E
Kīrteh **77** 32 15N 63 0 E
Kirthar Range **77** 27 0N 67 0 E
Kiruna **54** 67 52N 20 15 E
Kirundu **130** 0 50 S 25 35 E
Kirup **109** 33 40 S 115 50 E
Kirya **59** 55 5N 46 45 E
Kiryū **101** 36 24N 139 20 E
Kisa **53** 58 0N 15 39 E
Kisaga **130** 4 30 S 34 23 E
Kisalaya **162** 14 40N 84 3W
Kisambo **133** 6 25 S 18 14 E
Kisámou, Kólpos **49** 35 30N 23 38 E
Kisanga **130** 2 30N 26 35 E
Kisangani **130** 0 35N 25 15 E
Kisantu **133** 5 7 S 15 5 E
Kisar **87** 8 5 S 127 10 E
Kisaran **88** 3 0N 99 37 E
Kisarawe **130** 6 53 S 39 0 E
Kisarawe □ **130** 7 3 S 39 0 E
Kisarazu **101** 35 23N 139 55 E
Kisbér **31** 47 30N 18 0 E
Kiselevsk **64** 54 5N 86 39 E
Kishanganga → **79** 34 18N 73 28 E
Kishanganj **79** 26 3N 88 14 E
Kishangarh **78** 27 50N 70 30 E
Kishi **127** 9 1N 3 52 E
Kishinev **60** 47 0N 28 50 E
Kishiwada **101** 34 28N 135 22 E
Kishon **69** 32 49N 35 2 E
Kishorganj **82** 24 26N 90 40 E
Kishtwar **79** 33 20N 75 48 E
Kishwaukee → **154** 42 12N 89 8W
Kisii **130** 0 40 S 34 45 E
Kisii □ **130** 0 40 S 34 45 E
Kisiju **130** 7 23 S 39 19 E
Kısır, Dağ **61** 41 0N 43 5 E
Kisizi **130** 1 0 S 29 58 E
Kiska I. **140** 52 0N 177 30 E
Kiskatinaw → **144** 56 8N 120 10W
Kiskittogisu L. **145** 54 13N 98 20W
Kiskomárom = Zalakomár **31** 46 33N 17 10 E
Kiskörös **31** 46 37N 19 20 E
Kiskundorozsma **31** 46 16N 20 5 E
Kiskunfélegyháza **31** 46 42N 19 53 E
Kiskunhalas **31** 46 28N 19 37 E
Kiskunmajsa **31** 46 30N 19 48 E
Kislovodsk **61** 43 50N 42 45 E
Kismayu = Chisimaio **136** 0 22 S 42 32 E
Kiso-Gawa → **101** 35 20N 136 45 E
Kiso-Sammyaku **101** 35 45N 137 45 E
Kisofukushima **101** 35 52N 137 43 E
Kisoro **130** 1 17 S 29 48 E
Kispest **31** 47 27N 19 9 E
Kissidougou **126** 9 5N 10 0W
Kissimmee **149** 28 18N 81 22W
Kissimmee → **149** 27 20N 80 55W
Kississing L. **145** 55 10N 101 20W
Kistanje **43** 43 58N 15 55 E
Kisújszállás **31** 47 12N 20 50 E
Kisuki **100** 35 17N 132 54 E
Kisumu **130** 0 3 S 34 45 E
Kisvárda **31** 48 14N 22 4 E
Kiswani **130** 4 5 S 37 57 E
Kiswere **131** 9 27 S 39 30 E
Kit Carson **152** 38 48N 102 45W
Kita **126** 13 5N 9 25W
Kita-Ura **101** 36 0N 140 34 E
Kitab **63** 39 7N 66 52 E
Kitaibaraki **99** 36 50N 140 45 E
Kitakami **98** 39 20N 141 10 E
Kitakami-Gawa → **98** 38 25N 141 19 E
Kitakami-Sammyaku **98** 39 30N 141 30 E
Kitakata **98** 37 39N 139 52 E
Kitakyūshū **100** 33 50N 130 50 E
Kitale **130** 1 0N 35 0 E
Kitami **98** 43 48N 143 54 E
Kitami-Sammyaku **98** 44 22N 142 43 E
Kitangiri, L. **130** 4 5 S 34 20 E
Kitano-Kaikyō **100** 34 17N 134 58 E
Kitaotao **91** 7 40N 125 1 E
Kitaya **131** 10 38 S 40 8 E
Kitcharao **91** 9 27N 125 36 E
Kitchener, Australia **109** 30 55 S 124 8 E
Kitchener, Canada **142** 43 27N 80 29W
Kitega = Gitega **130** 3 26 S 29 56 E
Kitengo **130** 7 26 S 24 8 E
Kiteto □ **130** 5 0 S 37 0 E
Kitgum **130** 3 17N 32 52 E
Kíthira **49** 36 9N 23 0 E
Kíthnos **49** 37 26N 24 27 E
Kitikmeot □ **140** 70 0N 110 0W
Kitimat **144** 54 3N 128 38W
Kitiyab **125** 17 13N 33 35 E
Kítros **48** 40 22N 22 34 E
Kitsuki **100** 33 25N 131 37 E
Kittakittaooloo, L. **111** 28 3 S 138 14 E
Kittanning **150** 40 49N 79 30W
Kittatinny Mts. **151** 41 0N 75 0W
Kittery **151** 43 7N 70 42W
Kitui **130** 1 17 S 38 0 E
Kitui □ **130** 1 30 S 38 25 E
Kitwe **131** 12 54 S 28 13 E
Kitzbühel **30** 47 27N 12 24 E
Kitzingen **27** 49 44N 10 9 E
Kivarli **78** 24 33N 72 46 E
Kivotós **48** 40 13N 21 26 E
Kivu □ **130** 3 10 S 27 0 E
Kivu, L. **130** 1 48 S 29 0 E
Kiwai I. **107** 8 35 S 143 30 E
Kiyev **58** 50 30N 30 28 E
Kiyevskoye Vdkhr. **58** 51 0N 30 0 E
Kizel **62** 59 3N 57 40 E
Kiziguru **130** 1 46 S 30 23 E
Kizil Dağ **70** 36 19N 35 57 E
Kızıl Irmak → **60** 39 15N 36 0 E
Kizil Jilga **79** 35 26N 78 50 E
Kizil Yurt **61** 43 13N 46 54 E
Kızılcahamam **60** 40 30N 32 30 E
Kızıllar **70** 37 8N 33 36 E
Kızılöz Dağ **70** 36 44N 32 21 E
Kizilskoye **62** 52 44N 58 54 E
Kizimkazi **130** 6 28 S 39 30 E
Kizlyar **61** 43 51N 46 40 E
Kizyl-Arvat **64** 38 58N 56 15 E
Kjellerup **53** 56 17N 9 25 E
Kladanj **46** 44 14N 18 42 E
Kladnica **46** 43 23N 20 2 E
Kladno **30** 50 10N 14 7 E
Kladovo **46** 44 36N 22 33 E
Klaeng **84** 12 47N 101 39 E
Klagenfurt **30** 46 38N 14 20 E
Klagshamn **53** 55 32N 12 53 E
Klagstorp **52** 55 22N 13 23 E
Klaipeda **58** 55 43N 21 10 E
Klamath → **156** 41 40N 124 4W
Klamath Falls **156** 42 20N 121 50W
Klamath Mts. **156** 41 20N 123 0W
Klangklang **82** 22 41N 93 26 E
Klanjec **43** 46 3N 15 45 E
Klappan → **144** 58 0N 129 43W
Klaten **89** 7 43 S 110 36 E
Klatovy **30** 49 23N 13 18 E
Klawak **144** 55 35N 133 0W
Klawer **134** 31 44 S 18 36 E
Klazienaveen **22** 52 44N 7 0 E
Kłecko **32** 52 38N 17 25 E
Kleczew **32** 52 22N 18 9 E
Kleena Kleene **144** 52 0N 124 59W
Klein **156** 46 26N 108 31W
Klein-Karas **134** 27 33 S 18 7 E
Kleine Gette → **23** 50 51N 5 6 E
Kleine Nete → **23** 51 12N 4 46 E
Klekovača **43** 44 25N 16 32 E
Klenovec, Czech. **31** 48 36N 19 54 E
Klenovec, Yugoslavia **46** 41 32N 20 49 E
Klerksdorp **134** 26 53 S 26 38 E
Kleszczele **32** 52 35N 23 19 E
Kletnya **58** 53 23N 33 12 E
Kletsk **58** 53 5N 26 45 E
Kletskiy **61** 49 20N 43 0 E
Kleve **26** 51 46N 6 10 E
Klickitat **156** 45 50N 121 10W
Klickitat → **158** 45 42N 121 17W
Klimovichi **58** 53 36N 32 0 E
Klin **59** 56 20N 36 48 E
Klinaklini → **144** 51 21N 125 40W
Kling **91** 5 58N 124 42 E
Klintsey **58** 52 50N 32 10 E
Klipdale **134** 34 19 S 19 57 E
Klipplaat **134** 33 1 S 24 22 E
Klisura **47** 42 40N 24 28 E
Klitmøller **53** 57 3N 8 30 E
Kljajićevo **46** 45 45N 19 17 E
Ključ **43** 44 32N 16 48 E
Kłobuck **32** 50 55N 18 55 E
Kłodawa **32** 52 15N 18 55 E
Kłodzko **32** 50 28N 16 38 E
Kloetinge **23** 51 30N 3 56 E
Klondike **140** 64 0N 139 26W
Kloosterzande **23** 51 22N 4 1 E
Klosi **48** 41 28N 20 10 E
Klosterneuburg **31** 48 18N 16 19 E
Klosters **29** 46 52N 9 52 E
Kloten **29** 47 27N 8 35 E
Klötze **26** 52 38N 11 9 E
Klouto **127** 6 57N 0 44 E
Kluane L. **140** 61 15N 138 40W
Kluczbork **32** 50 58N 18 12 E
Klundert **23** 51 40N 4 32 E
Klyuchevskaya, Guba **65** 55 50N 160 30 E
Knaresborough **12** 54 1N 1 29W
Knee L., Man., Canada **145** 55 3N 94 45W
Knee L., Sask., Canada **145** 55 51N 107 0W
Kneïss, Is. **121** 34 22N 10 18 E
Knesselare **23** 51 9N 3 26 E
Knezha **47** 43 30N 24 5 E
Knić **46** 43 53N 20 45 E
Knight Inlet **144** 50 45N 125 40W
Knighton **13** 52 21N 3 2W
Knights Ferry **158** 37 50N 120 40W
Knight's Landing **158** 38 50N 121 43W
Knightstown **155** 39 49N 85 32W
Knin **43** 44 1N 16 17 E
Knittelfeld **30** 47 13N 14 51 E
Knjaževac **46** 43 35N 22 18 E
Knob, C. **109** 34 32 S 119 16 E
Knockmealdown Mts. **15** 52 16N 8 0W
Knokke **23** 51 20N 3 17 E
Knossos **49** 35 16N 25 10 E
Knox **155** 41 18N 86 36W
Knox, C. **144** 54 11N 133 5W
Knox City **153** 33 26N 99 49W
Knox Coast **7** 66 30 S 108 0 E
Knoxville, Iowa, U.S.A. **154** 41 20N 92 55W
Knoxville, Tenn., U.S.A. **149** 35 58N 83 57W
Knurów **32** 50 13N 18 38 E
Knutshø **51** 62 18N 9 41 E
Knysna **134** 34 2 S 23 2 E
Knyszyn **32** 53 20N 22 56 E
Ko Kha **84** 18 11N 99 24 E
Kō-Saki **100** 34 5N 129 13 E
Ko Tao **85** 10 6N 99 48 E
Koartac **141** 60 55N 69 40W
Koba, Aru, Indonesia **87** 6 37 S 134 37 E
Koba, Bangka, Indonesia **88** 2 26 S 106 14 E
Kobarid **43** 46 15N 13 30 E
Kobayashi **100** 31 56N 130 59 E
Kobdo = Hovd **92** 48 2N 91 37 E
Kōbe **101** 34 45N 135 10 E
Kobelyaki **60** 49 11N 34 9 E
København **52** 55 41N 12 34 E
Kōbi-Sho **99** 25 56N 123 41 E
Koblenz, Germany **27** 50 21N 7 36 E
Koblenz, Switz. **28** 47 37N 8 14 E
Kobo, Ethiopia **125** 12 2N 39 56 E
Kobo, Zaïre **133** 4 54 S 17 9 E
Kobrin **58** 52 15N 24 22 E
Kobroor, Kepulauan **87** 6 10 S 134 30 E
Kobuchizawa **101** 35 52N 138 19 E
Kobuleti **61** 41 55N 41 45 E
Kobylin **32** 51 43N 17 12 E
Kobyłka **32** 52 21N 21 10 E
Kobylkino **59** 54 8N 43 56 E
Kobylnik **58** 54 58N 26 39 E
Kočane **46** 43 12N 21 52 E

Kočani

Kočani **46** 41 55N 22 25 E
Koçarlı **49** 37 45N 27 43 E
Koceljevo **46** 44 28N 19 50 E
Kočevje **43** 45 39N 14 50 E
Koch Bihar **82** 26 22N 89 29 E
Kochang **95** 35 41N 127 55 E
Kochas **79** 25 15N 83 56 E
Kocher → **27** 49 14N 9 12 E
Kocheya **65** 52 32N 120 42 E
Kōchi **100** 33 30N 133 35 E
Kōchi □ **100** 33 40N 133 30 E
Kōchi-Heiya **100** 33 28N 133 30 E
Kochiu = Gejiu **96** 23 20N 103 10 E
Kochkor-Ata **63** 41 1N 72 29 E
Kochkorka **63** 42 13N 75 46 E
Kock **32** 51 38N 22 27 E
Kodaira **101** 35 44N 139 29 E
Koddiyar Bay **81** 8 33N 81 15 E
Kodiak **140** 57 30N 152 45W
Kodiak I. **140** 57 30N 152 45W
Kodinar **78** 20 46N 70 46 E
Kodori → **61** 42 47N 41 10 E
Koekelare **23** 51 5N 2 59 E
Koersel **23** 51 3N 5 17 E
Koes **134** 26 0 S 19 15 E
Koffiefontein **134** 29 30 S 25 0 E
Kofiau **87** 1 11 S 129 50 E
Köflach **30** 47 4N 15 5 E
Koforidua **127** 6 3N 0 17W
Kōfu **101** 35 40N 138 30 E
Koga **101** 36 11N 139 43 E
Kogaluk → **143** 56 12N 61 44W
Kogan **111** 27 2 S 150 40 E
Kogin Baba **127** 7 55N 11 35 E
Koh-i-Bābā **77** 34 30N 67 0 E
Koh-i-Khurd **78** 33 30N 65 59 E
Kohat **77** 33 40N 71 29 E
Kohima **82** 25 35N 94 10 E
Kohkīlūyeh va Būyer Ahmadi □ **73** 31 30N 50 30 E
Kohler Ra. **7** 77 0 S 110 0W
Kohtla Järve **58** 59 20N 27 20 E
Kohukohu **114** 35 22 S 173 38 E
Koin-dong **95** 40 28N 126 18 E
Kojetín **31** 49 21N 17 20 E
Kojima **100** 34 30N 133 50 E
Kōjo, Japan **100** 34 33N 133 55 E
Kojŏ, N. Korea **95** 38 58N 127 58 E
Kojonup **109** 33 48 S 117 10 E
Kojūr **73** 36 23N 51 43 E
Kok Yangak **63** 41 2N 73 12 E
Koka **124** 20 5N 30 35 E
Kokand **63** 40 30N 70 57 E
Kokanee Glacier Prov. Park **144** 49 47N 117 10W
Kokas **87** 2 42 S 132 26 E
Kokava **31** 48 35N 19 50 E
Kokchetav **64** 53 20N 69 25 E
Kokemäenjoki → **55** 61 32N 21 44 E
Kokerite **169** 7 12N 59 35W
Kokhma **59** 56 55N 41 18 E
Kokiri **115** 42 29 S 171 25 E
Kokkola **54** 63 50N 23 8 E
Koko **127** 11 28N 4 29 E
Kokoda **107** 8 54 S 147 47 E
Kokolopozo **126** 5 8N 6 5W
Kokomo **155** 40 30N 86 6W
Kokonau **87** 4 43 S 136 26 E
Kokopo **107** 4 22 S 152 19 E
Kokoro **127** 14 12N 0 55 E
Koksan **95** 38 46N 126 40 E
Koksengir, Gora **63** 44 21N 65 6 E
Koksoak → **141** 58 30N 68 10W
Kokstad **135** 30 32 S 29 29 E
Kokubu **100** 31 44N 130 46 E
Kokuora **65** 71 35N 144 50 E
Kola, Indonesia **87** 5 35 S 134 30 E
Kola, U.S.S.R. **56** 68 45N 33 8 E
Kola Pen. = Kolskiy Poluostrov **56** 67 30N 38 0 E
Kolachel **81** 8 10N 77 15 E
Kolahoi **79** 34 12N 75 22 E
Kolahun **126** 8 15N 10 4W
Kolaka **87** 4 3 S 121 46 E
Kolar **81** 13 12N 78 15 E
Kolar Gold Fields **81** 12 58N 78 16 E
Kolarovgrad **47** 43 18N 26 55 E
Kolašin **46** 42 50N 19 31 E
Kolby Kås **53** 55 48N 10 32 E
Kolchugino **59** 56 17N 39 22 E
Kolda **126** 12 55N 14 57W
Kolding **53** 55 30N 9 29 E
Kole **132** 3 16 S 22 42 E
Koléa **121** 36 38N 2 46 E
Kolepom = Yos Sudarso, Pulau **87** 8 0 S 138 30 E
Kolguyev, Ostrov **56** 69 20N 48 30 E
Kolham **22** 53 11N 6 44 E
Kolhapur **80** 16 43N 74 15 E
Kolia **126** 9 46N 6 28W
Kolín **30** 50 2N 15 9 E
Kolind **53** 56 21N 10 34 E
Kölleda **26** 51 11N 11 14 E
Kollegal **81** 12 9N 77 9 E
Kolleru L. **80** 16 40N 81 10 E
Kollum **22** 53 17N 6 10 E
Kolmanskop **134** 26 45 S 15 14 E
Köln **26** 50 56N 6 58 E
Kolno **32** 53 25N 21 56 E
Koło **32** 52 14N 18 40 E
Kołobrzeg **32** 54 10N 15 35 E
Kologriv **59** 58 48N 44 25 E
Kolokani **126** 13 35N 7 45W
Kolomna **59** 55 8N 38 45 E
Kolomyya **60** 48 31N 25 2 E
Kolondiéba **126** 11 5N 6 54W
Kolonodale **87** 2 3 S 121 25 E
Kolosib **82** 24 15N 92 45 E
Kolpashevo **64** 58 20N 83 5 E
Kolpino **58** 59 44N 30 39 E
Kolpny **59** 52 12N 37 10 E
Kolskiy Poluostrov **56** 67 30N 38 0 E
Kolskiy Zaliv **56** 69 23N 34 0 E
Koltubanovskiy **62** 52 57N 52 2 E
Kolubara → **46** 44 35N 20 15 E
Kolumna **32** 51 36N 19 14 E
Koluszki **32** 51 45N 19 46 E
Kolwezi **131** 10 40 S 25 25 E
Kolyberovo **59** 55 15N 38 40 E
Kolyma → **65** 69 30N 161 0 E
Kolymskoye, Okhotsko **65** 63 0N 157 0 E
Kôm Ombo **124** 24 25N 32 52 E
Komagene **101** 35 44N 137 58 E
Komaki **101** 35 17N 136 55 E
Komárno **31** 47 49N 18 5 E
Komárom **31** 47 43N 18 7 E
Komárom □ **31** 47 35N 18 20 E
Komarovo **58** 58 38N 33 40 E
Komatipoort **135** 25 25 S 31 55 E
Komatsu **101** 36 25N 136 30 E
Komatsujima **100** 34 0N 134 35 E
Kombissiri **127** 12 4N 1 20W
Kombo **132** 0 20 S 12 22 E
Kombori **126** 13 26N 3 56W
Kombóti **49** 39 6N 21 5 E
Komebail Lagoon **106** 7 25N 134 25 E
Komen **43** 45 49N 13 45 E
Komenda **127** 5 4N 1 28W
Komi A.S.S.R. □ **62** 64 0N 55 0 E
Komiža **43** 43 3N 16 11 E
Komló **31** 46 15N 18 16 E
Kommamur Canal **81** 16 0N 80 25 E
Kommunarsk **61** 48 30N 38 45 E
Kommunizma, Pik **63** 39 0N 72 2 E
Komnes **51** 59 30N 9 55 E
Komodo **87** 8 37 S 119 20 E
Komoé **126** 5 12N 3 44W
Komono **132** 3 10 S 13 20 E
Komoran, Pulau **87** 8 18 S 138 45 E
Komoro **101** 36 19N 138 26 E
Komotini **48** 41 9N 25 26 E
Komovi **46** 42 41N 19 39 E
Kompasberg **134** 31 45 S 24 32 E
Kompong Bang **85** 12 24N 104 40 E
Kompong Cham **85** 12 0N 105 30 E
Kompong Chhnang **85** 12 20N 104 35 E
Kompong Chikreng **84** 13 5N 104 18 E
Kompong Kleang **84** 13 6N 104 8 E
Kompong Luong **85** 11 49N 104 48 E
Kompong Pranak **84** 13 35N 104 55 E
Kompong Som **85** 10 38N 103 30 E
Kompong Som, Chhung **85** 10 50N 103 32 E
Kompong Speu **85** 11 26N 104 32 E
Kompong Sralao **84** 14 5N 105 46 E
Kompong Thom **84** 12 35N 104 51 E
Kompong Trabeck, Cambodia **84** 13 6N 105 14 E
Kompong Trabeck, Cambodia **85** 11 9N 105 28 E
Kompong Trach **85** 11 25N 105 48 E
Kompong Tralach **85** 11 54N 104 47 E
Komrat **60** 46 18N 28 40 E
Komsberg **134** 32 40 S 20 45 E
Komsomolabad **63** 38 50N 69 55 E
Komsomolets **62** 53 45N 62 2 E
Komsomolets, Ostrov **65** 80 30N 95 0 E
Komsomolsk, R.S.F.S.R., U.S.S.R. **59** 57 2N 40 20 E
Komsomolsk, R.S.F.S.R., U.S.S.R. **65** 50 30N 137 0 E
Komsomolsk, Turkmen S.S.R., U.S.S.R. **63** 39 2N 63 36 E
Komsomolskiy **59** 53 30N 49 30 E
Konakovo **59** 56 52N 36 45 E
Konarhá □ **77** 35 30N 71 3 E
Konārī **73** 28 13N 51 36 E
Konawa **153** 34 59N 96 46W
Konch **79** 26 0N 79 10 E
Kondagaon **80** 19 35N 81 35 E
Kondakovo **65** 69 36N 152 0 E
Konde **130** 4 57 S 39 45 E
Kondiá **48** 39 49N 25 10 E
Kondinin **109** 32 34 S 118 8 E
Kondo **133** 5 35 S 13 0 E
Kondoa **130** 4 55 S 35 50 E
Kondoa □ **130** 5 0 S 36 0 E
Kondopaga **56** 62 12N 34 17 E
Kondratyevo **65** 57 22N 98 15 E
Konduga **127** 11 35N 13 26 E
Kondukur **81** 15 12N 79 57 E
Koné **106** 21 4 S 164 52 E
Konevo **56** 62 8N 39 20 E
Kong **126** 8 54N 4 36W
Kong → **84** 13 32N 105 58 E
Kong, Koh **85** 11 20N 103 0 E
Kong Christian IX.s Land **6** 68 0N 36 0W
Kong Christian X.s Land **6** 74 0N 29 0W
Kong Franz Joseph Fd. **6** 73 20N 24 30W
Kong Frederik IX.s Land **6** 67 0N 52 0W
Kong Frederik VI.s Kyst **6** 63 0N 43 0W
Kong Frederik VIII.s Land **6** 78 30N 26 0W
Kong Oscar Fjord **6** 72 20N 24 0W
Konga **53** 56 30N 15 6 E
Kongbo **132** 4 44N 21 23 E
Kongeå **53** 55 24N 9 39 E
Kongju **95** 36 30N 127 0 E
Kongkemul **89** 1 52N 112 11 E
Konglu **82** 27 13N 97 57 E
Kongolo, Kasai Or., Zaïre **130** 5 26 S 24 49 E
Kongolo, Shaba, Zaïre **130** 5 22 S 27 0 E
Kongor **125** 7 1N 31 27 E
Kongoussi **127** 13 19N 1 32W
Kongsberg **51** 59 39N 9 39 E
Kongsvinger **51** 60 12N 12 2 E
Kongwa **130** 6 11 S 36 26 E
Koni **131** 10 40 S 27 11 E
Koni, Mts. **131** 10 36 S 27 10 E
Koniecpol **32** 50 46N 19 40 E
Königsberg = Kaliningrad **58** 54 42N 20 32 E
Königshofen **27** 50 18N 10 29 E
Königslutter **26** 52 14N 10 50 E
Königswusterhausen **26** 52 19N 13 38 E
Konin **32** 52 12N 18 15 E
Konin □ **32** 52 15N 18 30 E
Konispoli **48** 39 42N 20 10 E
Kónitsa **48** 40 5N 20 48 E
Köniz **28** 46 56N 7 25 E
Konjic **46** 43 42N 17 58 E
Konjice **43** 46 20N 15 28 E
Konkiep **134** 26 49 S 17 15 E
Konkouré → **126** 9 50N 13 42W
Könnern **26** 51 40N 11 45 E
Konnur **81** 16 14N 74 49 E
Kono **126** 8 30N 11 5W
Konolfingen **28** 46 54N 7 38 E
Konongo **127** 6 40N 1 15W
Konos **107** 3 10 S 151 44 E
Konosha **56** 61 0N 40 5 E
Kōnosu **101** 36 3N 139 31 E
Konotop **58** 51 12N 33 7 E
Końskie **32** 51 15N 20 23 E
Konsmo **51** 58 16N 7 23 E
Konstantinovka **60** 48 32N 37 39 E
Konstantinovski **61** 47 33N 41 10 E
Konstantynów Łódźki **32** 51 45N 19 20 E
Konstanz **27** 47 39N 9 10 E
Kont **73** 26 55N 61 50 E
Kontagora **127** 10 23N 5 27 E
Kontich **23** 51 8N 4 26 E
Kontum **84** 14 24N 108 0 E
Kontum, Plateau du **84** 14 30N 108 0 E
Konya **57** 37 52N 32 35 E
Konyin **82** 22 58N 94 42 E
Konz **27** 49 41N 6 36 E
Konza **130** 1 45 S 37 7 E
Konzhakovskiy Kamen, Gora **62** 59 38N 59 8 E
Kookynie **109** 29 17 S 121 22 E
Kooline **108** 22 57 S 116 20 E
Kooloonong **112** 34 48 S 143 10 E
Koolyanobbing **109** 30 48 S 119 36 E
Koondrook **112** 35 33 S 144 8 E
Koorawatha **113** 34 2 S 148 33 E
Koorda **109** 30 48 S 117 35 E
Kooskia **156** 46 9N 115 59W
Kootenai → **156** 49 15N 117 39W
Kootenay L. **144** 49 45N 116 50W
Kootenay Nat. Park **144** 51 0N 116 0W
Kootjieskolk **134** 31 15 S 20 21 E
Kopa **63** 43 31N 75 50 E
Kopanovka **61** 47 28N 46 50 E
Kopaonik Planina **46** 43 10N 21 50 E
Kopargaon **80** 19 51N 74 28 E
Kópavogur **54** 64 6N 21 55W
Koper **43** 45 31N 13 44 E
Kopervik **51** 59 17N 5 17 E
Kopeysk **62** 55 7N 61 37 E
Kopi **111** 33 24 S 135 40 E
Köping **52** 59 31N 16 3 E
Kopiste **43** 42 48N 16 42 E
Kopliku **48** 42 15N 19 25 E
Köpmanholmen **52** 63 10N 18 35 E
Koppal **81** 15 23N 76 5 E
Koppang **51** 61 34N 11 3 E
Kopparbergs län □ **52** 61 20N 14 15 E
Kopperå **51** 63 24N 11 50 E
Koppies **135** 27 20 S 27 30 E
Koppio **112** 34 26 S 135 51 E
Koppom **52** 59 43N 12 10 E
Koprivlen **47** 41 36N 23 53 E
Koprivnica **43** 46 12N 16 45 E
Koprivshtitsa **47** 42 40N 24 19 E
Köprü → **70** 36 48N 31 11 E
Kopychintsy **58** 49 7N 25 58 E
Kopys **58** 54 20N 30 17 E
Korab **46** 41 44N 20 40 E
Korakiána **48** 39 42N 19 45 E
Koraput **80** 18 50N 82 40 E
Korba **79** 22 20N 82 45 E
Korbach **26** 51 17N 8 50 E
Korbu, G. **85** 4 41N 101 18 E
Korça **48** 40 37N 20 50 E
Korça □ **48** 40 40N 20 50 E
Korce = Korça **48** 40 37N 20 50 E
Korčula **43** 42 57N 17 8 E
Korčulanski Kanal **43** 43 3N 16 40 E
Kord Kūy **73** 36 48N 54 7 E
Kord Sheykh **73** 28 31N 52 53 E
Kordestān □ **72** 36 0N 47 0 E
Korea, North ■ **95** 40 0N 127 0 E
Korea, South ■ **95** 36 0N 128 0 E
Korea Bay **95** 39 0N 124 0 E
Korea Strait **95** 34 0N 129 30 E
Koregaon **80** 17 40N 74 10 E
Korenevo **58** 51 27N 34 55 E
Korenovsk **61** 45 30N 39 22 E
Korets **58** 50 40N 27 5 E
Korgus **124** 19 16N 33 29 E
Korhogo **126** 9 29N 5 28W
Koribundu **126** 7 41N 11 46W
Korim **87** 0 58 S 136 10 E
Korinthía □ **49** 37 50N 22 35 E
Korinthiakós Kólpos **49** 38 16N 22 30 E
Kórinthos **49** 37 56N 22 55 E
Korioumé **126** 16 35N 3 0W
Kōriyama **98** 37 24N 140 23 E
Korkino **62** 54 54N 61 23 E
Korla **92** 41 45N 86 4 E
Kormakiti, C. **70** 35 23N 32 56 E
Körmend **31** 47 5N 16 35 E
Kornat **43** 43 50N 15 20 E
Korneshty **60** 47 21N 28 1 E
Korneuburg **31** 48 20N 16 20 E
Kornsjø **51** 58 57N 11 39 E
Kornstad **51** 62 59N 7 27 E
Koro, Fiji **106** 17 19 S 179 23 E
Koro, Ivory C. **126** 8 32N 7 30W
Koro, Mali **126** 14 1N 2 58W
Koro Sea **106** 17 30 S 179 45W
Koro Toro **123** 16 5N 18 30 E
Koroba **107** 5 44 S 142 47 E
Korocha **59** 50 55N 37 30 E
Korogwe **130** 5 5 S 38 25 E
Korogwe □ **130** 5 0 S 38 20 E
Koroit **112** 38 18 S 142 24 E
Koronadal **91** 6 12N 125 1 E
Korong Vale **112** 36 22 S 143 45 E
Koróni **49** 36 48N 21 57 E
Korónia, Limni **48** 40 47N 23 37 E
Koronís **49** 37 12N 25 35 E
Koronowo **32** 53 19N 17 55 E
Koror **87** 7 20N 134 28 E
Körös → **31** 46 43N 20 12 E
Köröstarcsa **31** 46 53N 21 3 E
Korosten **58** 50 57N 28 25 E
Korotoyak **59** 51 1N 39 2 E
Korraraika, Helodranon' i **135** 17 45 S 43 57 E
Korsakov **65** 46 36N 142 42 E
Korshunovo **65** 58 37N 110 10 E
Korsun Shevchenkovskiy **60** 49 26N 31 16 E
Korsze **32** 54 11N 21 9 E
Kortemark **23** 51 2N 3 3 E
Kortessem **23** 50 52N 5 23 E
Korti **124** 18 6N 31 33 E
Kortrijk **23** 50 50N 3 17 E
Korumburra **113** 38 26 S 145 50 E
Korwai **78** 24 7N 78 5 E
Koryakskiy Khrebet **65** 61 0N 171 0 E
Koryŏng **95** 35 44N 128 15 E
Kos **49** 36 50N 27 15 E
Kosa, Ethiopia **125** 7 50N 36 50 E
Kosa, U.S.S.R. **62** 59 56N 55 0 E
Kosa → **62** 60 11N 55 10 E
Kosaya Gora **59** 54 10N 37 30 E
Koschagyl **57** 46 40N 54 0 E
Kościan **32** 52 5N 16 40 E
Kościerzyna **32** 54 8N 17 59 E
Kosciusko **153** 33 3N 89 34W
Kosciusko, Mt. **113** 36 27 S 148 16 E
Kosciusko I. **144** 56 0N 133 40W
Köseçobanlı **70** 36 30N 33 9 E
Kösély → **31** 47 25N 21 5 E
Kosgi **80** 16 58N 77 43 E
Kosha **124** 20 50N 30 30 E
Koshigaya **101** 35 54N 139 48 E
K'oshih = Kashi **92** 39 30N 76 2 E
Koshiki-Rettō **100** 31 45N 129 49 E
Koshkonong, L. **155** 42 53N 88 58W
Kōshoku **101** 36 38N 138 6 E
Koshtëbë **63** 41 5N 74 15 E
Kosi **78** 27 48N 77 29 E
Kosi-meer **135** 27 0 S 32 50 E
Košice **31** 48 42N 21 15 E
Kosjerić **46** 44 0N 19 55 E
Koslan **56** 63 28N 48 52 E
Kosŏng **95** 38 40N 128 22 E
Kosovo, Soc. Aut. Pokrajina □ **46** 42 30N 21 0 E
Kosovska-Mitrovica **46** 42 54N 20 52 E
Kostajnica **43** 45 17N 16 30 E
Kostamuksa **56** 62 34N 32 44 E
Kostanjevica **43** 45 51N 15 27 E
Kostelec **31** 50 14N 16 35 E
Kostenets **47** 42 15N 23 52 E
Koster **134** 25 52 S 26 54 E
Kôstî **125** 13 8N 32 43 E
Kostolac **46** 44 37N 21 15 E
Kostopol **58** 50 51N 26 22 E
Kostroma **59** 57 50N 40 58 E
Kostromskoye Vdkhr. **59** 57 52N 40 49 E
Kostrzyn, Gorzow Wlkp., Poland **32** 52 35N 14 39 E

Kukësi

Kostrzyn, Poznań, Poland **32** 52 24N 17 14 E
Kostyukovichi **58** 53 20N 32 4 E
Koszalin **32** 54 11N 16 8 E
Koszalin □ **32** 53 40N 16 10 E
Kőszeg **31** 47 23N 16 33 E
Kot Addu **77** 30 30N 71 0 E
Kot Moman **78** 32 13N 73 0 E
Kota **78** 25 14N 75 49 E
Kota Baharu **85** 6 7N 102 14 E
Kota Belud **86** 6 21N 116 26 E
Kota Kinabalu **89** 6 0N 116 4 E
Kota Tinggi **85** 1 44N 103 53 E
Kotaagung **88** 5 38 S 104 29 E
Kotabaru **89** 3 20 S 116 20 E
Kotabumi **88** 4 49 S 104 54 E
Kotagede **89** 7 54 S 110 26 E
Kotamobagu **87** 0 57N 124 31 E
Kotaneelee → **144** 60 11N 123 42W
Kotawaringin **89** 2 28 S 111 27 E
Kotchandpur **82** 23 24N 89 1 E
Kotcho L. **144** 59 7N 121 12W
Kotel **47** 42 52N 26 26 E
Kotelnich **59** 58 20N 48 10 E
Kotelnikovo **61** 47 38N 43 8 E
Kotelnyy, Ostrov **65** 75 10N 139 0 E
Kothagudam **80** 17 30N 80 40 E
Kothapet **80** 19 21N 79 28 E
Köthen **26** 51 44N 11 59 E
Kothi **79** 24 45N 80 40 E
Kotiro **78** 26 17N 67 13 E
Kotka **55** 60 28N 26 58 E
Kotlas **56** 61 15N 47 0 E
Kotlenska Planina **47** 42 56N 26 30 E
Kotli **78** 33 30N 73 55 E
Kotmul **79** 35 32N 75 10 E
Kotohira **100** 34 11N 133 49 E
Kotonkoro **127** 11 3N 5 58 E
Kotor **46** 42 25N 18 47 E
Kotor Varoš **46** 44 38N 17 22 E
Kotoriba **43** 46 23N 16 48 E
Kotovo **59** 50 22N 44 45 E
Kotovsk **60** 47 45N 29 35 E
Kotputli **78** 27 43N 76 12 E
Kotri **77** 25 22N 68 22 E
Kotri → **80** 19 15N 80 35 E
Kótronas **49** 36 38N 22 29 E
Kötschach-Mauthen **30** 46 41N 13 1 E
Kottayam **81** 9 35N 76 33 E
Kottur **81** 10 34N 76 56 E
Kotuy → **65** 71 54N 102 6 E
Kotzebue **140** 66 50N 162 40W
Kouango **132** 5 0N 20 10 E
Koudekerke **23** 51 29N 3 33 E
Koudougou **126** 12 10N 2 20W
Koufonísi **49** 34 56N 26 8 E
Koufonísia **49** 36 57N 25 35 E
Kougaberge **134** 33 48 S 23 50 E
Kouibli **126** 7 15N 7 14W
Kouilou → **133** 4 10 S 12 5 E
Kouki **132** 7 22N 17 3 E
Koula Moutou **132** 1 15 S 12 25 E
Koulen **84** 13 50N 104 40 E
Koulikoro **126** 12 40N 7 50W
Koumac **106** 20 33 S 164 17 E
Koumala **110** 21 38 S 149 15 E
Koumankou **126** 11 58N 6 6W
Koumbia, Burkina Faso **126** 11 10N 3 50W
Koumbia, Guinea **126** 11 48N 13 29W
Koumboum **126** 10 25N 13 0W
Koumpenntoum **126** 13 59N 14 34W
Koumra **123** 8 50N 17 35 E
Koundara **126** 12 29N 13 18W
Koundé **132** 6 7N 14 38 E
Kounradskiy **64** 46 59N 75 0 E
Kountze **153** 30 20N 94 22W
Koupéla **127** 12 11N 0 21W
Kourizo, Passe de **122** 22 28N 15 27 E
Kourou **169** 5 9N 52 39W
Kouroussa **126** 10 45N 9 45W
Koussané **126** 14 53N 11 14W
Kousseri **123** 12 0N 14 55 E
Koutiala **126** 12 25N 5 23W
Kouto **126** 9 53N 6 25W
Kouts **155** 41 18N 87 2W
Kouvé **127** 6 25N 1 25 E
Kovačica **46** 45 5N 20 38 E
Kovdor **56** 67 34N 30 24 E
Kovel **58** 51 10N 24 20 E
Kovilpatti **81** 9 10N 77 50 E
Kovin **46** 44 44N 20 59 E
Kovrov **59** 56 25N 41 25 E
Kovur, Andhra Pradesh, India **80** 17 3N 81 39 E
Kovur, Andhra Pradesh, India **81** 14 30N 80 1 E
Kowal **32** 52 32N 19 7 E
Kowalewo Pomorskie **32** 53 10N 18 52 E
Kowghān **77** 34 12N 63 2 E
Kowkash **142** 50 20N 87 12W
Kowloon **97** 22 20N 114 15 E
Kowŏn **95** 39 26N 127 14 E
Koyabuti **87** 2 36 S 140 37 E
Kōyama **100** 31 20N 130 56 E
Köypınarı Köy **70** 36 42N 34 16 E
Koytash **63** 40 11N 67 19 E
Koyuk **140** 64 55N 161 20W
Koyukuk → **140** 64 56N 157 30W
Koyulhisar **60** 40 20N 37 52 E
Koza **106** 26 19N 127 46 E
Kozáni **48** 40 19N 21 47 E
Kozáni □ **48** 40 18N 21 45 E
Kozara **43** 45 0N 17 0 E
Kozarac **43** 44 58N 16 48 E
Kozelsk **58** 54 2N 35 48 E
Kozhikode = Calicut **81** 11 15N 75 43 E
Kozhva **56** 65 10N 57 0 E
Koziegłowy **32** 50 37N 19 8 E
Kozienice **32** 51 35N 21 34 E
Kozje **43** 46 5N 15 35 E
Kozle **32** 50 20N 18 8 E
Kozloduy **47** 43 45N 23 42 E
Kozlovets **47** 43 30N 25 20 E
Koźmin **32** 51 48N 17 27 E
Kozmodemyansk **59** 56 20N 46 36 E
Kōzu-Shima **101** 34 13N 139 10 E
Kozuchów **32** 51 45N 15 31 E
Kpabia **127** 9 10N 0 20W
Kpalimé **127** 6 57N 0 44 E
Kpandae **127** 8 30N 0 2W
Kpessi **127** 8 4N 1 16 E
Kra, Isthmus of = Kra, Kho Khot **85** 10 15N 99 30 E
Kra, Kho Khot **85** 10 15N 99 30 E
Kra Buri **85** 10 22N 98 46 E
Krabbendijke **23** 51 26N 4 7 E
Krabi **85** 8 4N 98 55 E
Kragan **89** 6 43 S 111 38 E
Kragerø **51** 58 52N 9 25 E
Kragujevac **46** 44 2N 20 56 E
Krajenka **32** 53 18N 16 59 E
Krakatau = Rakata, Pulau **88** 6 10 S 105 20 E
Krakor **84** 12 32N 104 12 E
Kraków **32** 50 4N 19 57 E
Kraków □ **31** 50 0N 20 0 E
Kraksaan **89** 7 43 S 113 23 E
Kråkstad **51** 59 39N 10 55 E
Kralanh **84** 13 35N 103 25 E
Králiky **31** 50 6N 16 45 E
Kraljevo **46** 43 44N 20 41 E
Kralovice **30** 49 59N 13 29 E
Královský Chlmec **31** 48 27N 22 0 E
Kralupy **30** 50 13N 14 20 E
Kramatorsk **60** 48 50N 37 30 E
Kramfors **52** 62 55N 17 48 E
Kramis, C. **121** 36 26N 0 45 E
Krångede **52** 63 9N 16 10 E
Kraniá **48** 39 53N 21 18 E
Kranídhion **49** 37 20N 23 10 E
Kranj **43** 46 16N 14 22 E
Kranjska Gora **43** 46 29N 13 48 E
Krankskop **135** 28 0 S 30 47 E
Krapina **43** 46 10N 15 52 E
Krapina → **43** 45 50N 15 50 E
Krapivna **59** 53 58N 37 10 E
Krapkowice **32** 50 29N 17 56 E
Krasavino **56** 60 58N 46 29 E
Krashyy Klyuch **62** 55 23N 56 39 E
Kraskino **65** 42 44N 130 48 E
Kraslice **30** 50 19N 12 31 E
Krasnaya Gorbatka **59** 55 52N 41 45 E
Krasnaya Polyana **61** 43 40N 40 13 E
Kraśnik **32** 50 55N 22 5 E
Kraśnik Fabryczny **32** 50 58N 22 11 E
Krasnoarmeisk **60** 48 18N 37 11 E
Krasnoarmeysk, R.S.F.S.R., U.S.S.R. **59** 51 0N 45 42 E
Krasnoarmeysk, R.S.F.S.R., U.S.S.R. **61** 48 30N 44 25 E
Krasnodar **61** 45 5N 39 0 E
Krasnodon **61** 48 17N 39 44 E
Krasnodonetskaya **61** 48 5N 40 50 E
Krasnogorskiy **59** 56 10N 48 28 E
Krasnograd **60** 49 27N 35 27 E
Krasnogvardeysk **63** 39 46N 67 16 E
Krasnogvardeyskoye **61** 45 52N 41 33 E
Krasnogvardyesk **60** 45 32N 34 16 E
Krasnokamsk **62** 58 4N 55 48 E
Krasnokutsk **58** 50 10N 34 50 E
Krasnoperekopsk **60** 46 0N 33 54 E
Krasnorechenskiy **98** 44 41N 135 14 E
Krasnoselkupsk **64** 65 20N 82 10 E
Krasnoslobodsk, R.S.F.S.R., U.S.S.R. **59** 54 25N 43 45 E
Krasnoslobodsk, R.S.F.S.R., U.S.S.R. **61** 48 42N 44 33 E
Krasnoturinsk **56** 59 46N 60 12 E
Krasnoufimsk **62** 56 57N 57 46 E
Krasnouralsk **62** 58 21N 60 3 E
Krasnousolskiy **62** 53 54N 56 27 E
Krasnovishersk **62** 60 23N 57 3 E
Krasnovodsk **57** 40 0N 52 52 E
Krasnoyarsk **65** 56 8N 93 0 E
Krasnoyarskiy **62** 51 58N 59 55 E
Krasnoye = Krasnyy **58** 54 25N 31 30 E
Krasnoye, Kalmyk A.S.S.R., U.S.S.R. **61** 46 16N 45 0 E
Krasnoye, R.S.F.S.R., U.S.S.R. **59** 59 15N 47 40 E
Krasnozavodsk **59** 56 27N 38 25 E
Krasny Liman **60** 48 58N 37 50 E
Krasny Sulin **61** 47 52N 40 8 E
Krasnystaw **32** 50 57N 23 5 E
Krasnyy **58** 54 25N 31 30 E
Krasnyy Kholm, R.S.F.S.R., U.S.S.R. **59** 58 10N 37 10 E
Krasnyy Kholm, R.S.F.S.R., U.S.S.R. **62** 51 35N 54 9 E
Krasnyy Kut **59** 50 50N 47 0 E
Krasnyy Luch **61** 48 13N 39 0 E
Krasnyy Profintern **59** 57 45N 40 27 E
Krasnyy Yar, Kalmyk A.S.S.R., U.S.S.R. **61** 46 43N 48 23 E
Krasnyy Yar, R.S.F.S.R., U.S.S.R. **59** 53 30N 50 22 E
Krasnyy Yar, R.S.F.S.R., U.S.S.R. **59** 50 42N 44 45 E
Krasnyye Baki **59** 57 8N 45 10 E
Krasnyyoskolskoye Vdkhr. **60** 49 30N 37 30 E
Kraszna → **31** 48 0N 22 20 E
Kratie **84** 12 32N 106 10 E
Kratke Ra. **107** 6 45 S 146 0 E
Kratovo **46** 42 6N 22 10 E
Krau **87** 3 19 S 140 5 E
Kravanh, Chuor Phnum **85** 12 0N 103 32 E
Krawang **87** 6 19N 107 18 E
Krefeld **26** 51 20N 6 32 E
Krémaston, Límni **49** 38 52N 21 30 E
Kremenchug **60** 49 5N 33 25 E
Kremenchugskoye Vdkhr. **60** 49 20N 32 30 E
Kremenets **60** 50 8N 25 43 E
Kremenica **46** 40 55N 21 25 E
Kremennaya **60** 49 1N 38 10 E
Kremges = Svetlovodsk **58** 49 2N 33 13 E
Kremikovtsi **47** 42 46N 23 28 E
Kremmen **26** 52 45N 13 1 E
Kremmling **156** 40 10N 106 30W
Kremnica **31** 48 45N 18 50 E
Krems **30** 48 25N 15 36 E
Kremsmünster **30** 48 3N 14 8 E
Kretinga **58** 55 53N 21 15 E
Krettamia **120** 28 47N 3 27W
Krettsy **58** 58 15N 32 30 E
Kreuzberg **27** 50 22N 9 58 E
Kreuzlingen **29** 47 38N 9 10 E
Kribi **127** 2 57N 9 56 E
Krichem **47** 42 8N 24 28 E
Krichev **58** 53 45N 31 50 E
Krim **43** 45 53N 14 30 E
Krimpen **22** 51 55N 4 34 E
Krionéri **49** 38 20N 21 35 E
Krishna → **80** 15 57N 80 59 E
Krishnagiri **81** 12 32N 78 16 E
Krishnanagar **79** 23 24N 88 33 E
Krishnaraja Sagara **81** 12 20N 76 30 E
Kristiansand **51** 58 9N 8 1 E
Kristianstad **53** 56 2N 14 9 E
Kristiansund **51** 63 7N 7 45 E
Kristiinankaupunki **54** 62 16N 21 21 E
Kristinehamn **52** 59 18N 14 13 E
Kristinestad **54** 62 16N 21 21 E
Kríti **49** 35 15N 25 0 E
Kritsá **49** 35 10N 25 41 E
Kriva → **46** 42 5N 21 47 E
Kriva Palanka **46** 42 11N 22 19 E
Krivaja → **46** 44 27N 18 9 E
Krivelj **46** 44 8N 22 5 E
Krivoy Rog **60** 47 51N 33 20 E
Križevci **43** 46 3N 16 32 E
Krk **43** 45 8N 14 40 E
Krka → **43** 45 50N 15 30 E
Krkonoše **30** 50 50N 15 35 E
Krnov **31** 50 5N 17 40 E
Krobia **32** 51 47N 16 59 E
Kročehlavy **30** 50 8N 14 9 E
Krøderen **51** 60 9N 9 49 E
Krokawo **32** 54 47N 18 9 E
Krokeaí **49** 36 53N 22 32 E
Krokodil → **135** 25 14 S 32 18 E
Krokom **52** 63 20N 14 30 E
Krolevets **58** 51 35N 33 20 E
Kroměříz **31** 49 18N 17 21 E
Krommenie **22** 52 30N 4 46 E
Krompachy **31** 48 54N 20 52 E
Kromy **58** 52 40N 35 48 E
Kronach **27** 50 14N 11 19 E
Kronobergs län □ **53** 56 45N 14 30 E
Kronprins Olav Kyst **7** 69 0 S 42 0 E
Kronprinsesse Märtha Kyst **7** 73 30 S 10 0 E
Kronshtadt **58** 60 5N 29 45 E
Kroonstad **134** 27 43 S 27 19 E
Kröpelin **26** 54 4N 11 48 E
Kropotkin, R.S.F.S.R., U.S.S.R. **61** 45 28N 40 28 E
Kropotkin, R.S.F.S.R., U.S.S.R. **65** 59 0N 115 30 E
Kropp **26** 54 24N 9 32 E
Krościenko **32** 49 29N 20 25 E
Krośniewice **32** 52 15N 19 11 E
Krosno **32** 49 42N 21 46 E
Krosno □ **32** 49 35N 22 0 E
Krosno Odrzańskie **32** 52 3N 15 7 E
Krotoszyn **32** 51 42N 17 23 E
Krotovka **62** 53 18N 51 10 E
Krraba **48** 41 13N 20 0 E
Krško **43** 45 57N 15 30 E
Krstača **46** 42 57N 20 8 E
Kruger Nat. Park **135** 23 30 S 31 40 E
Krugersdorp **135** 26 5 S 27 46 E
Kruiningen **23** 51 27N 4 2 E
Kruisfontein **134** 33 59 S 24 43 E
Kruishoutem **23** 50 54N 3 32 E
Kruisland **23** 51 34N 4 25 E
Kruja **48** 41 32N 19 46 E
Krulevshchina **58** 55 5N 27 45 E
Kruma **48** 42 14N 20 28 E
Krumbach **27** 48 15N 10 22 E
Krumovgrad **47** 41 29N 25 38 E
Krung Thep = Bangkok **84** 13 45N 100 35 E
Krupanj **46** 44 25N 19 22 E
Krupina **31** 48 22N 19 5 E
Krupinica → **31** 48 15N 18 52 E
Kruševac **46** 43 35N 21 28 E
Kruševo **46** 41 23N 21 19 E
Kruszwica **32** 52 40N 18 20 E
Kruzof I. **144** 57 10N 135 40W
Krylbo **52** 60 7N 16 15 E
Krymsk Abinsk **60** 44 50N 38 0 E
Krymskiy Poluostrov **60** 45 0N 34 0 E
Krynica **32** 49 25N 20 57 E
Krynica Morska **32** 54 23N 19 28 E
Krynki **32** 53 17N 23 43 E
Krzepice **32** 50 58N 18 50 E
Krzeszów **32** 50 24N 22 21 E
Krzeszowice **32** 50 8N 19 37 E
Krzna → **32** 51 59N 22 47 E
Krzywiń **32** 51 58N 16 50 E
Krzyz **32** 52 52N 16 0 E
Ksabi **121** 32 51N 4 13W
Ksar Chellala **121** 35 13N 2 19 E
Ksar el Boukhari **121** 35 51N 2 52 E
Ksar el Kebir **120** 35 0N 6 0W
Ksar es Souk = Ar Rachidiya **121** 31 58N 4 20W
Ksar Rhilane **121** 33 0N 9 39 E
Ksour, Mts. des **121** 32 45N 0 30W
Kstovo **59** 56 12N 44 13 E
Kuala **88** 2 55N 105 47 E
Kuala Berang **85** 5 5N 103 1 E
Kuala Dungun **85** 4 45N 103 25 E
Kuala Kangsar **85** 4 46N 100 56 E
Kuala Kelawang **85** 2 56N 102 5 E
Kuala Kerai **85** 5 30N 102 12 E
Kuala Kubu Baharu **85** 3 34N 101 39 E
Kuala Lipis **85** 4 10N 102 3 E
Kuala Lumpur **85** 3 9N 101 41 E
Kuala Nerang **85** 6 16N 100 37 E
Kuala Pilah **85** 2 45N 102 15 E
Kuala Rompin **85** 2 49N 103 29 E
Kuala Selangor **85** 3 20N 101 15 E
Kuala Trengganu **85** 5 20N 103 8 E
Kualajelai **89** 2 58 S 110 46 E
Kualakapuas **89** 2 55 S 114 20 E
Kualakurun **89** 1 10 S 113 50 E
Kualapembuang **89** 3 14 S 112 38 E
Kualasimpang **88** 4 17N 98 3 E
Kuancheng **95** 40 37N 118 30 E
Kuandang **87** 0 56N 123 1 E
Kuandian **95** 40 45N 124 45 E
Kuangchou = Guangzhou **97** 23 5N 113 10 E
Kuantan **85** 3 49N 103 20 E
Kuba **61** 41 21N 48 32 E
Kuban → **61** 45 20N 37 30 E
Kubenskoye, Oz. **59** 59 40N 39 25 E
Kuberle **61** 47 0N 42 20 E
Kubokawa **100** 33 12N 133 8 E
Kubor, Mt. **107** 6 10 S 144 44 E
Kubrat **47** 43 49N 26 31 E
Kučevo **46** 44 30N 21 40 E
Kucha Gompa **79** 34 25N 76 56 E
Kuchaman **78** 27 13N 74 47 E
Kuchenspitze **30** 47 7N 10 12 E
Kuchino-eruba-Jima **99** 30 28N 130 12 E
Kuchino-Shima **99** 29 57N 129 55 E
Kuchinotsu **100** 32 36N 130 11 E
Kucing **89** 1 33N 110 25 E
Kuçove = Qytet Stalin **48** 40 47N 19 57 E
Kücük Kuyu **48** 39 35N 26 27 E
Kud → **78** 26 5N 66 20 E
Kudalier → **80** 18 35N 79 48 E
Kudamatsu **100** 34 0N 131 52 E
Kudara **63** 38 25N 72 39 E
Kudat **86** 6 55N 116 55 E
Kudayd **74** 19 21N 41 48 E
Kudremukh, Mt. **81** 13 15N 75 20 E
Kudus **89** 6 48 S 110 51 E
Kudymkar **62** 59 1N 54 39 E
Kueiyang = Guiyang **96** 26 32N 106 40 E
Kufrinjah **69** 32 20N 35 41 E
Kufstein **30** 47 35N 12 11 E
Kugong I. **142** 56 18N 79 50W
Kūh-e Dīnār **73** 30 40N 51 0 E
Kūh-e-Hazārām **73** 29 35N 57 20 E
Kūhak **77** 27 12N 63 10 E
Kūhbonān **73** 31 23N 56 19 E
Kūhestak **73** 26 47N 57 2 E
Kūhestān **77** 34 39N 61 12 E
Kūhīn **73** 35 13N 48 25 E
Kūhīrī **73** 26 55N 61 2 E
Kuhnsdorf **30** 46 37N 14 38 E
Kūhpāyeh, Eşfahan, Iran **73** 32 44N 52 20 E
Kūhpāyeh, Kermān, Iran **73** 30 35N 57 15 E
Kui Buri **85** 12 3N 99 52 E
Kuinre **22** 52 47N 5 51 E
Kuito **133** 12 22 S 16 55 E
Kujang **95** 39 57N 126 1 E
Kuji **98** 40 11N 141 46 E
Kujū-San **100** 33 5N 131 15 E
Kujukuri-Heiya **101** 35 45N 140 30 E
Kukavica **46** 42 48N 21 57 E
Kukawa **127** 12 58N 13 27 E
Kukerin **109** 33 13 S 118 0 E
Kukësi **48** 42 5N 20 20 E

L

Lansing

Lachlan → **112** 34 22 S 143 55 E
Lachute **142** 45 39N 74 21W
Lackawanna **150** 42 49N 78 50W
Lacolle **151** 45 5N 73 22W
Lacombe **144** 52 30N 113 44W
Lacon **154** 41 2N 89 24W
Lacona, Iowa, U.S.A. **154** 41 11N 93 23W
Lacona, N.Y., U.S.A. **151** 43 37N 76 5W
Láconi **44** 39 54N 9 4 E
Laconia **151** 43 32N 71 30W
Lacq **20** 43 25N 0 35W
Lacrosse **156** 46 51N 117 58W
Lacub **90** 17 40N 120 53 E
Ladakh Ra. **79** 34 0N 78 0 E
Ladário **173** 19 1 S 57 35W
Ladd **154** 41 23N 89 13W
Laddonia **154** 39 15N 91 39W
Lądekzdrój **32** 50 21N 16 53 E
Ládhon → **49** 37 40N 21 50 E
Ladik **60** 40 57N 35 58 E
Ladismith **134** 33 28 S 21 15 E
Lādīz **73** 28 55N 61 15 E
Ladnun **78** 27 38N 74 25 E
Ladoga, L. = Ladozhskoye Ozero **56** 61 15N 30 30 E
Ladon **19** 48 0N 2 30 E
Ladozhskoye Ozero **56** 61 15N 30 30 E
Ladrillero, G. **176** 49 20 S 75 35W
Lady Grey **134** 30 43 S 27 13 E
Ladybrand **134** 29 9 S 27 29 E
Ladysmith, Canada **144** 49 0N 123 49W
Ladysmith, S. Africa **135** 28 32 S 29 46 E
Ladysmith, U.S.A. **152** 45 27N 91 4W
Lae **107** 6 40 S 147 2 E
Laem Ngop **85** 12 10N 102 26 E
Laem Pho **85** 6 55N 101 19 E
Læsø **53** 57 15N 10 53 E
Læsø Rende **53** 57 20N 10 45 E
Lafayette, Colo., U.S.A. **152** 40 0N 105 2W
Lafayette, Ga., U.S.A. **149** 34 44N 85 15W
Lafayette, Ind., U.S.A. **148** 40 22N 86 52W
Lafayette, Ind., U.S.A. **153** 30 25N 86 54W
Lafayette, La., U.S.A. **153** 30 18N 92 0W
Lafayette, Tenn., U.S.A. **149** 36 35N 86 0W
Laferte → **144** 61 53N 117 44W
Lafia **127** 8 30N 8 34 E
Lafiagi **127** 8 52N 5 20 E
Lafleche **145** 49 45N 106 40W
Lafon **125** 5 5N 32 29 E
Laforsen **52** 61 56N 15 3 E
Lagaip → **107** 5 4 S 142 52 E
Lagan →, Sweden **53** 56 56N 13 58 E
Lagan →, U.K. **15** 54 35N 5 55W
Lagangilang **90** 17 37N 120 44 E
Lagarfljót → **54** 65 40N 14 18W
Lagarto **170** 10 54 S 37 41W
Lagawe **90** 16 49N 121 6 E
Lage, Germany **26** 52 0N 8 47 E
Lage, Spain **34** 43 13N 9 0W
Lage-Mierde **23** 51 25N 5 9 E
Lågen →, Oppland, Norway **51** 61 8N 10 25 E
Lågen →, Vestfold, Norway **51** 59 3N 10 5 E
Lägerdorf **26** 53 53N 9 35 E
Laghmān □ **77** 34 20N 70 0 E
Laghouat **121** 33 50N 2 59 E
Lagnieu **21** 45 55N 5 20 E
Lagny **19** 48 52N 2 44 E
Lago **45** 39 9N 16 8 E
Lago Posadas **176** 47 30 S 71 40W
Lago Ranco **176** 40 19 S 72 30W
Lagôa **35** 37 8N 8 27W
Lagoaça **34** 41 11N 6 44W
Lagodekhi **61** 41 50N 46 22 E
Lagónegro **45** 40 8N 15 45 E
Lagonoy Gulf **90** 13 50N 123 50 E
Lagos, Nigeria **127** 6 25N 3 27 E
Lagos, Portugal **35** 37 5N 8 41W
Lagos de Moreno **160** 21 21N 101 55W
Lagrange, Australia **108** 18 45 S 121 43 E
Lagrange, U.S.A. **155** 41 39N 85 25W
Lagrange B. **108** 18 38 S 121 42 E
Laguardia **36** 42 33N 2 35W
Laguépie **20** 44 8N 1 57 E
Laguna, Brazil **175** 28 30 S 48 50W
Laguna, U.S.A. **157** 35 3N 107 28W
Laguna □ **90** 14 10N 121 20 E
Laguna, La **37** 28 28N 16 18W
Laguna Beach **159** 33 31N 117 52W
Laguna de la Janda **35** 36 15N 5 45W
Laguna Limpia **174** 26 32 S 59 45W
Laguna Madre **161** 27 0N 97 20W
Lagunas, Chile **174** 21 0 S 69 45W
Lagunas, Peru **172** 5 10 S 75 35W
Lagunillas **173** 19 38 S 63 43W
Lahad Datu **87** 5 0N 118 20 E
Lahan Sai **84** 14 25N 102 52 E
Lahanam **84** 16 16N 105 16 E
Laharpur **79** 27 43N 80 56 E
Lahat **88** 3 45 S 103 30 E
Lahe **82** 26 20N 95 26 E
Lahewa **88** 1 22N 97 12 E
Lahiang Lahiang **91** 6 1N 121 23 E
Laḥij **74** 13 4N 44 53 E
Lāhījān **73** 37 10N 50 6 E
Lahn → **27** 50 17N 7 38 E
Laholm **53** 56 30N 13 2 E
Laholmsbukten **53** 56 30N 12 45 E
Lahontan Res. **156** 39 28N 118 58W
Lahore **77** 31 32N 74 22 E
Lahpongsel **82** 27 7N 98 25 E
Lahr **27** 48 20N 7 52 E
Lahti **55** 60 58N 25 40 E
Lahtis = Lahti **55** 60 58N 25 40 E
Laï **123** 9 25N 16 18 E
Lai Chau **84** 22 5N 103 3 E
Lai-hka **82** 21 16N 97 40 E
Laiagam **107** 5 33 S 143 30 E
Lai'an **97** 32 28N 118 30 E
Laibin **96** 23 42N 109 14 E
Laidley **111** 27 39 S 152 20 E
Laifeng **97** 29 27N 109 20 E
Laignes **19** 47 50N 4 20 E
Laikipia □ **130** 0 30N 36 30 E
Laingsburg **134** 33 9 S 20 52 E
Lairg **14** 58 1N 4 24W
Lais **91** 6 20N 125 39 E
Laishui **94** 39 23N 115 45 E
Laiwu **95** 36 15N 117 40 E
Laixi **95** 36 50N 120 31 E
Laiyang **95** 36 59N 120 45 E
Laiyuan **94** 39 20N 114 40 E
Laizhou Wan **95** 37 30N 119 30 E
Laja → **160** 20 55N 100 46W
Lajere **127** 12 10N 11 25 E
Lajes, Rio Grande do N., Brazil **170** 5 41 S 36 14W
Lajes, Sta. Catarina, Brazil **175** 27 48 S 50 20W
Lajinha **171** 20 9 S 41 37W
Lajkovac **46** 44 27N 20 14 E
Lajosmizse **31** 47 3N 19 32 E
Lak Sao **84** 18 11N 104 59 E
Lakaband **78** 31 2N 69 15 E
Lakar **87** 8 15 S 128 17 E
Lake Alpine **158** 38 29N 120 0W
Lake Andes **152** 43 10N 98 32W
Lake Anse **148** 46 42N 88 25W
Lake Arthur **153** 30 8N 92 40W
Lake Cargelligo **113** 33 15 S 146 22 E
Lake Charles **153** 30 15N 93 10W
Lake City, Colo., U.S.A. **157** 38 3N 107 27W
Lake City, Fla., U.S.A. **149** 30 10N 82 40W
Lake City, Iowa, U.S.A. **154** 42 12N 94 42W
Lake City, Mich., U.S.A. **148** 44 20N 85 10W
Lake City, Minn., U.S.A. **152** 44 28N 92 21W
Lake City, Pa., U.S.A. **150** 42 2N 80 20W
Lake City, S.C., U.S.A. **149** 33 51N 79 44W
Lake Coleridge **115** 43 17 S 171 30 E
Lake Forest **155** 42 15N 87 50W
Lake Geneva **155** 42 36N 88 26W
Lake George **151** 43 25N 73 43W
Lake Grace **109** 33 7 S 118 28 E
Lake Harbour **141** 62 50N 69 50W
Lake Havasu City **159** 34 25N 114 29W
Lake Hughes **159** 34 41N 118 26W
Lake Isabella **159** 35 38N 118 28W
Lake King **109** 33 5 S 119 45 E
Lake Lenore **145** 52 24N 104 59W
Lake Louise **144** 51 30N 116 10W
Lake Mead Nat. Rec. Area **159** 36 0N 114 30W
Lake Michigan Beach **155** 42 13N 86 25W
Lake Mills, Iowa, U.S.A. **152** 43 23N 93 33W
Lake Mills, Wis., U.S.A. **155** 43 5N 88 55W
Lake Murray **107** 6 48 S 141 29 E
Lake Nash **110** 20 57 S 138 0 E
Lake Odessa **155** 42 47N 85 8W
Lake Orion **155** 42 47N 83 14W
Lake Providence **153** 32 49N 91 12W
Lake River **142** 54 30N 82 31W
Lake Superior Prov. Park **142** 47 45N 84 45W
Lake Tekapo **115** 44 0 S 170 30 E
Lake Varley **109** 32 48 S 119 30 E
Lake Villa **155** 42 25N 88 5W
Lake Village **153** 33 20N 91 19W
Lake Wales **149** 27 55N 81 32W
Lake Worth **149** 26 36N 80 3W
Lakefield **142** 44 25N 78 16W
Lakeland **149** 28 0N 82 0W
Lakeport **158** 39 1N 122 56W
Lakes Entrance **113** 37 50 S 148 0 E
Lakeside, Ariz., U.S.A. **157** 34 12N 109 59W
Lakeside, Calif., U.S.A. **159** 32 52N 116 55W
Lakeside, Nebr., U.S.A. **152** 42 5N 102 24W
Lakeview **156** 42 15N 120 22W
Lakewood, Colo., U.S.A. **152** 39 44N 105 3W
Lakewood, N.J., U.S.A. **151** 40 5N 74 13W
Lakewood, Ohio, U.S.A. **150** 41 28N 81 50W
Lakewood Center **158** 47 11N 122 32W
Lakhaniá **49** 35 58N 27 54 E
Lákhi **49** 35 24N 23 57 E
Lakhipur, Assam, India **82** 24 48N 93 0 E
Lakhipur, Assam, India **82** 26 2N 90 18 E
Lakhonpheng **84** 15 54N 105 34 E
Lakhpat **78** 23 48N 68 47 E
Laki **54** 64 4N 18 14W
Lakin **153** 37 58N 101 18W
Lakitusaki → **142** 54 21N 82 25W
Lakonía □ **49** 36 55N 22 30 E
Lakonikós Kólpos **49** 36 40N 22 40 E
Lakota, Ivory C. **126** 5 50N 5 30W
Lakota, U.S.A. **152** 48 0N 98 22W
Laksefjorden **54** 70 45N 26 50 E
Lakselv **54** 70 2N 24 56 E
Lakshadweep Is. **76** 10 0N 72 30 E
Laksham **82** 23 14N 91 8 E
Lakshmeshwar **81** 15 9N 75 28 E
Lakshmikantapur **79** 22 5N 88 20 E
Lakshmipur **82** 22 58N 90 50 E
Lakuramau **107** 2 54 S 151 15 E
Lal-lo **90** 18 12N 121 40 E
Lala **91** 7 59N 123 46 E
Lala Musa **78** 32 40N 73 57 E
Lalago **130** 3 28 S 33 58 E
Lalapanzi **131** 19 20 S 30 15 E
Lalganj **79** 25 52N 85 13 E
Lalibela **125** 12 2N 39 2 E
Lalin, China **95** 45 12N 127 0 E
Lalín, Spain **34** 42 40N 8 5W
Lalin He → **95** 45 32N 125 40 E
Lalinde **20** 44 50N 0 44 E
Lalitpur **79** 24 42N 78 28 E
Lam **84** 21 21N 106 31 E
Lam Pao Res. **84** 16 50N 103 15 E
Lama Kara **127** 9 30N 1 15 E
Lamaipum **82** 25 40N 97 57 E
Lamar, Colo., U.S.A. **152** 38 9N 102 35W
Lamar, Mo., U.S.A. **153** 37 30N 94 20W
Lamarque **176** 39 24 S 65 40W
Lamas **172** 6 28 S 76 31W
Lamas → **70** 36 33N 34 15 E
Lamastre **21** 44 59N 4 35 E
Lambach **30** 48 6N 13 51 E
Lamballe **18** 48 29N 2 31W
Lambaréné **132** 0 41 S 10 12 E
Lambasa **106** 16 30 S 179 10 E
Lambay I. **15** 53 30N 6 0W
Lambayeque □ **172** 6 45 S 80 0W
Lambert **152** 47 44N 104 39W
Lambert, C. **107** 4 11 S 151 31 E
Lambert Glacier **7** 71 0 S 70 0 E
Lamberts Bay **134** 32 5 S 18 17 E
Lambesc **21** 43 39N 5 16 E
Lámbia **49** 37 52N 21 53 E
Lambon **107** 4 45 S 152 48 E
Lambro → **42** 45 8N 9 32 E
Lambunao **91** 11 3N 122 29 E
Lame **127** 10 30N 9 20 E
Lame Deer **156** 45 45N 106 40W
Lamego **34** 41 5N 7 52W
Lamèque **143** 47 45N 64 38W
Lameroo **112** 35 19 S 140 33 E
Lamesa **153** 32 45N 101 57W
Lamía **49** 38 55N 22 26 E
Lamitan **91** 6 39N 122 8 E
Lammermuir Hills **14** 55 50N 2 40W
Lamon Bay **90** 14 30N 122 20 E
Lamongan **89** 7 7 S 112 25 E
Lamoni **154** 40 37N 93 56W
Lamont, Canada **144** 53 46N 112 50W
Lamont, Calif., U.S.A. **159** 35 15N 118 55W
Lamont, Iowa, U.S.A. **154** 42 35N 91 40W
Lampa **172** 15 22 S 70 22W
Lampang **84** 18 16N 99 32 E
Lampasas **153** 31 5N 98 10W
Lampaul **18** 48 28N 5 7W
Lampazos de Naranjo **160** 27 2N 100 32W
Lampedusa **38** 35 36N 12 40 E
Lampeter **13** 52 6N 4 6W
Lampione **122** 35 33N 12 20 E
Lampman **145** 49 25N 102 50W
Lamprechtshausen **30** 48 0N 12 58 E
Lamprey **145** 58 33N 94 8W
Lampung □ **88** 5 30 S 104 30 E
Lamu, Burma **82** 19 14N 94 10 E
Lamu, Kenya **130** 2 16 S 40 55 E
Lamu □ **130** 2 0 S 40 45 E
Lamud **172** 6 10 S 77 57W
Lamut **90** 16 39N 121 14 E
Lamy **157** 35 30N 105 58W
Lan Xian **94** 38 15N 111 35 E
Lan Yu **97** 22 5N 121 35 E
Lanai I. **146** 20 50N 156 55W
Lanak La **79** 34 27N 79 32 E
Lanaken **23** 50 53N 5 39 E
Lanak'o Shank'ou = Lanak La **79** 34 27N 79 32 E
Lanao, L. **91** 7 52N 124 15 E
Lanao del Norte □ **91** 8 0N 124 10 E
Lanao del Sur □ **91** 7 40N 124 15 E
Lanark, Canada **151** 45 1N 76 22W
Lanark, U.K. **14** 55 40N 3 48W
Lancang **96** 22 36N 99 58 E
Lancang Jiang → **96** 21 40N 101 10 E
Lancashire □ **12** 53 40N 2 30W
Lancaster, Canada **151** 45 10N 74 30W
Lancaster, U.K. **12** 54 3N 2 48W
Lancaster, Calif., U.S.A. **159** 34 47N 118 8W
Lancaster, Ky., U.S.A. **148** 37 40N 84 40W
Lancaster, Mo., U.S.A. **154** 40 31N 92 32W
Lancaster, N.H., U.S.A. **151** 44 27N 71 33W
Lancaster, N.Y., U.S.A. **150** 42 53N 78 43W
Lancaster, Pa., U.S.A. **151** 40 4N 76 19W
Lancaster, S.C., U.S.A. **149** 34 45N 80 47W
Lancaster, Wis., U.S.A. **154** 42 48N 90 43W
Lancaster Sd. **141** 74 13N 84 0W
Lancer **145** 50 48N 108 53W
Lanchow = Lanzhou **94** 36 1N 103 52 E
Lanciano **43** 42 15N 14 22 E
Lanco **176** 39 24 S 72 46W
Lancones **172** 4 30 S 80 30W
Lancun **95** 36 25N 120 10 E
Łancut **32** 50 10N 22 13 E
Lancy **28** 46 12N 6 8 E
Landau, Bayern, Germany **27** 48 41N 12 41 E
Landau, Rhld-Pfz., Germany **27** 49 12N 8 7 E
Landay **77** 30 31N 63 47 E
Landeck **30** 47 9N 10 34 E
Landen **23** 50 45N 5 3 E
Lander **156** 42 50N 108 49W
Lander → **108** 22 0 S 132 0 E
Landerneau **18** 48 28N 4 17W
Landeryd **53** 57 7N 13 15 E
Landes **20** 44 0N 1 0W
Landes □ **20** 43 57N 0 48W
Landete **36** 39 56N 1 25W
Landi Kotal **77** 34 7N 71 6 E
Landivisiau **18** 48 31N 4 6W
Landor **109** 25 10 S 116 54 E
Landquart **29** 46 58N 9 32 E
Landquart → **29** 46 50N 9 47 E
Landrecies **19** 50 7N 3 40 E
Land's End **13** 50 4N 5 43W
Landsberg **27** 48 3N 10 52 E
Landsborough Cr. → **110** 22 28 S 144 35 E
Landsbro **53** 57 24N 14 56 E
Landshut **27** 48 31N 12 10 E
Landskrona **52** 55 53N 12 50 E
Landstuhl **27** 49 25N 7 34 E
Landvetter **53** 57 41N 12 17 E
Laneffe **23** 50 17N 4 30 E
Lanesboro **151** 41 57N 75 34W
Lanett **149** 33 0N 85 15W
Lang Bay **144** 49 45N 124 21W
Lang Qua **84** 22 16N 104 27 E
Lang Shan **94** 41 0N 106 30 E
Lang Son **84** 21 52N 106 42 E
Lang Suan **85** 9 57N 99 4 E
La'nga Co **79** 30 45N 81 15 E
Långadhás **48** 40 46N 23 2 E
Langádhia **49** 37 43N 22 1 E
Långan → **52** 63 19N 14 44 E
Langar **73** 35 23N 60 25 E
Langara I. **144** 54 14N 133 1W
Langatabbetje **169** 4 59N 54 28W
Langdai **96** 26 6N 105 21 E
Langdon **152** 48 47N 98 24W
Langdorp **23** 50 59N 4 52 E
Langeac **20** 45 7N 3 29 E
Langeais **18** 47 20N 0 24 E
Langeb Baraka → **124** 17 28N 36 50 E
Langeberg **134** 33 55 S 21 0 E
Langeberge **134** 28 15 S 22 33 E
Langeland **53** 54 56N 10 48 E
Langemark **23** 50 55N 2 55 E
Langen **27** 49 59N 8 40 E
Langenburg **145** 50 51N 101 43W
Langeness **26** 54 34N 8 35 E
Langenlois **30** 48 29N 15 40 E
Langenthal **28** 47 13N 7 47 E
Langeoog **26** 53 44N 7 33 E
Langeskov **53** 55 22N 10 35 E
Langesund **51** 59 0N 9 45 E
Länghem **53** 57 36N 13 14 E
Langhirano **42** 44 39N 10 16 E
Langholm **14** 55 9N 2 59W
Langidoon **112** 31 36 S 142 2 E
Langjökull **54** 64 39N 20 12W
Langkawi, P. **85** 6 25N 99 45 E
Langklip **134** 28 12 S 20 20 E
Langkon **86** 6 30N 116 40 E
Langlade **143** 46 50N 56 20W
Langlois **156** 42 54N 124 26W
Langnau **28** 46 56N 7 47 E
Langogne **20** 44 43N 3 50 E
Langon **20** 44 33N 0 16W
Langøya **54** 68 45N 14 50 E
Langres **19** 47 52N 5 20 E
Langres, Plateau de **19** 47 45N 5 3 E
Langsa **88** 4 30N 97 57 E
Långsele **52** 63 12N 17 4 E
Långshyttan **52** 60 27N 16 2 E
Langtao **82** 27 15N 97 34 E
Langting **82** 25 31N 93 7 E
Langtry **153** 29 50N 101 33W
Langu **85** 6 53N 99 47 E
Languedoc **20** 43 58N 4 0 E
Langwies **29** 46 50N 9 44 E
Langxi **97** 31 10N 119 12 E
Langxiangzhen **94** 39 43N 116 8 E
Langzhong **96** 31 38N 105 58 E
Lanigan **145** 51 51N 105 2W
Lankao **94** 34 48N 114 50 E
Lannemezan **20** 43 8N 0 23 E
Lannilis **18** 48 35N 4 32W
Lannion **18** 48 46N 3 29W
Lanouaille **20** 45 24N 1 9 E
Lanping **96** 26 28N 99 15 E
Lansdale **151** 40 14N 75 18W
Lansdowne, Australia **111** 31 48 S 152 30 E
Lansdowne, Canada **151** 44 24N 76 1W
Lansdowne House **142** 52 14N 87 53W
Lansford **151** 40 48N 75 55W
Lanshan **97** 25 24N 112 10 E
Lansing **155** 42 47N 84 40W

Lillestrøm

Lempdes 20 45 22N 3 17 E
Lemsid 120 26 33N 13 51W
Lemvig 53 56 33N 8 20 E
Lemyethna 82 17 36N 95 9 E
Lena → 65 72 52N 126 40 E
Lenartovce 31 48 18N 20 19 E
Lencloître 18 46 50N 0 20 E
Lençóis 171 12 35 S 41 24W
Lendeh 73 30 58N 50 25 E
Lendelede 23 50 53N 3 16 E
Lendinara 43 45 4N 11 37 E
Lenger 63 42 12N 69 54 E
Lengerich 26 52 12N 7 50 E
Lenggong 85 5 6N 100 58 E
Lenggries 27 47 41N 11 34 E
Lengua de Vaca, Pta. 174 30 14 S 71 38W
Lengyeltóti 31 46 40N 17 40 E
Lenhovda 53 57 0N 15 16 E
Lenin 61 48 20N 40 56 E
Lenina, Pik 63 39 20N 72 55 E
Leninabad 63 40 17N 69 37 E
Leninakan 61 40 47N 43 50 E
Leningrad 58 59 55N 30 20 E
Leningradskaya 7 69 50 S 160 0 E
Lenino 60 45 17N 35 46 E
Leninogorsk, Kazakh S.S.R., U.S.S.R. 64 50 20N 83 30 E
Leninogorsk, R.S.F.S.R., U.S.S.R. 62 54 36N 52 30 E
Leninpol 63 42 29N 71 55 E
Leninsk, R.S.F.S.R., U.S.S.R. 61 48 40N 45 15 E
Leninsk, R.S.F.S.R., U.S.S.R. 61 46 10N 43 46 E
Leninsk, Uzbek S.S.R., U.S.S.R. 63 40 38N 72 15 E
Leninsk-Kuznetskiy 64 54 44N 86 10 E
Leninskaya Sloboda 59 56 7N 44 29 E
Leninskoye, R.S.F.S.R., U.S.S.R. 59 58 23N 47 3 E
Leninskoye, R.S.F.S.R., U.S.S.R. 65 47 56N 132 38 E
Leninskoye, Uzbek S.S.R., U.S.S.R. 63 41 45N 69 23 E
Lenk 28 46 27N 7 28 E
Lenkoran 57 39 45N 48 50 E
Lenmalu 87 1 45 S 130 15 E
Lenne → 26 51 25N 7 30 E
Lennox, I. 176 55 18 S 66 50W
Lennoxville 151 45 22N 71 51W
Leno 42 45 24N 10 14 E
Lenoir 149 35 55N 81 36W
Lenoir City 149 35 40N 84 20W
Lenora 152 39 39N 100 1W
Lenore L. 145 52 30N 104 59W
Lenox, Iowa, U.S.A. 154 40 53N 94 34W
Lenox, Mass., U.S.A. 151 42 20N 73 18W
Lens, Belgium 23 50 33N 3 54 E
Lens, France 19 50 26N 2 50 E
Lens St. Remy 23 50 39N 5 7 E
Lensk 65 60 48N 114 55 E
Lenskoye 60 45 3N 34 1 E
Lent 22 51 52N 5 52 E
Lenti 31 46 37N 16 33 E
Lentini 45 37 18N 15 0 E
Lentvaric 58 54 39N 25 3 E
Lenwood 159 34 53N 117 7W
Lenzburg 28 47 23N 8 11 E
Lenzen 26 53 6N 11 26 E
Lenzerheide 29 46 44N 9 34 E
Léo 126 11 3N 2 2W
Leoben 30 47 22N 15 5 E
Leola 152 45 47N 98 58W
Leominster, U.K. 13 52 15N 2 43W
Leominster, U.S.A. 151 42 32N 71 45W
Léon, France 20 43 53N 1 18W
León, Mexico 160 21 7N 101 30W
León, Nic. 162 12 20N 86 51W
León, Spain 34 42 38N 5 34W
Leon, U.S.A. 154 40 40N 93 40W
León □ 34 42 40N 5 55W
León, Montañas de 34 42 30N 6 18W
Leonardtown 148 38 19N 76 39W
Leone, Mte. 28 46 15N 8 5 E
Leonforte 45 37 39N 14 22 E
Leongatha 113 38 30 S 145 58 E
Leonídhion 49 37 9N 22 52 E
Leonora 109 28 49 S 121 19 E
Leonora Downs 112 32 29 S 142 5 E
Léopold II, Lac = Mai-Ndombe, L. 132 2 0 S 18 20 E
Leopoldina 171 21 28 S 42 40W
Leopoldo Bulhões 171 16 37 S 48 46W
Leopoldsburg 23 51 7N 5 13 E
Léopoldville = Kinshasa 133 4 20 S 15 15 E
Leoti 152 38 31N 101 19W
Leoville 145 53 39N 107 33W
Lépa, L. do 133 17 0 S 19 0 E
Lepe 35 37 15N 7 12W
Lepel 58 54 50N 28 40 E
Lepikha 65 64 45N 125 55 E
Leping 97 28 47N 117 7 E
Lepontine, Alpi 29 46 22N 8 27 E
Lepsény 31 47 0N 18 15 E
Leptis Magna 122 32 40N 14 12 E
Lequeitio 36 43 20N 2 32W
Lercara Friddi 44 37 42N 13 36 E
Lerdo 160 25 32N 103 32W
Léré, C.A.R. 132 6 46N 17 25 E
Léré, Chad 123 9 39N 14 13 E
Lere, Nigeria 127 9 43N 9 18 E
Leribe 135 28 51 S 28 3 E
Lérici 42 44 4N 9 58 E
Lérida 36 41 37N 0 39 E
Lérida □ 36 42 6N 1 0 E
Lérins, Is. de 21 43 31N 7 3 E
Lerma 34 42 0N 3 47W
Léros 49 37 10N 26 50 E
Lérouville 19 48 44N 5 30 E
Lerwick 14 60 10N 1 10W
Les 50 46 58N 21 50 E
Lesbos, I. = Lésvos 49 39 10N 26 20 E
Leshan 96 29 33N 103 41 E
Leshukonskoye 56 64 54N 45 46 E
Lésina, L. di 43 41 53N 15 25 E
Lesja 51 62 7N 8 51 E
Lesjaverk 51 62 12N 8 34 E
Lesko 32 49 30N 22 23 E
Leskov I. 7 56 0 S 28 0W
Leskovac 46 43 0N 21 58 E
Leskoviku 48 40 10N 20 34 E
Leslie, Ark., U.S.A. 153 35 50N 92 35W
Leslie, Mich., U.S.A. 155 42 27N 84 26W
Lesna 32 51 0N 15 15 E
Lesneven 18 48 35N 4 20W
Lešnica 46 44 39N 19 20 E
Lesnoy 62 59 47N 52 9 E
Lesnoye 58 58 15N 35 18 E
Lesopilnoye 98 46 44N 134 20 E
Lesotho ■ 135 29 40 S 28 0 E
Lesozavodsk 65 45 30N 133 29 E
Lesparre-Médoc 20 45 18N 0 57W
Lessay 18 49 14N 1 30W
Lesse → 23 50 15N 4 54 E
Lesser Antilles 163 15 0N 61 0W
Lesser Slave L. 144 55 30N 115 25W
Lesser Sunda Is. 87 7 0 S 120 0 E
Lessines 23 50 42N 3 50 E
Lester 158 47 12N 121 29W
Lestock 145 51 19N 103 59W
Lesuer I. 108 13 50 S 127 17 E
Lésvos 49 39 10N 26 20 E
Leszno 32 51 50N 16 30 E
Leszno □ 32 51 45N 16 30 E
Letchworth 13 51 58N 0 13W
Letea, Ostrov 50 45 18N 29 20 E
Lethbridge 144 49 45N 112 45W
Lethem 169 3 20N 59 50W
Lethero 112 33 33 S 142 30 E
Leti, Kepulauan 87 8 10 S 128 0 E
Letiahau → 134 21 16 S 24 0 E
Leticia 168 4 9 S 70 0W
Leting 95 39 23N 118 55 E
Letjiesbos 134 32 34 S 22 16 E
Letlhakeng 134 24 0 S 24 59 E
Letpadan 82 17 45N 95 45 E
Letpan 82 19 28N 94 10 E
Letterkenny 15 54 57N 7 42W
Leu 50 44 10N 24 0 E
Léua 133 11 34 S 20 32 E
Leucadia 159 33 4N 117 18W
Leucate 20 42 56N 3 3 E
Leucate, Étang de 20 42 50N 3 0 E
Leuk 28 46 19N 7 37 E
Leukerbad 28 46 24N 7 36 E
Leupegem 23 50 50N 3 36 E
Leuser, G. 88 3 46N 97 12 E
Leutkirch 27 47 49N 10 1 E
Leuven 23 50 52N 4 42 E
Leuze, Hainaut, Belgium 23 50 36N 3 37 E
Leuze, Namur, Belgium 23 50 33N 4 54 E
Lev Tolstoy 59 53 13N 39 29 E
Levádhia 49 38 27N 22 54 E
Levan 156 39 37N 111 52W
Levanger 51 63 45N 11 19 E
Levani 48 40 40N 19 28 E
Levant, I. du 21 43 3N 6 28 E
Lévanto 42 44 10N 9 37 E
Levanzo 44 38 0N 12 19 E
Levelland 153 33 38N 102 23W
Leven 14 56 12N 3 0W
Leven, L. 14 56 12N 3 22W
Leven, Toraka 135 12 30 S 47 45 E
Levens 21 43 50N 7 12 E
Leveque C. 108 16 20 S 123 0 E
Leverano 45 40 16N 18 0 E
Leverkusen 26 51 2N 6 59 E
Leverville 133 4 50 S 18 44 E
Levet 19 46 56N 2 22 E
Levice 31 48 13N 18 35 E
Levico 43 46 0N 11 18 E
Levie 21 41 40N 9 7 E
Levier 19 46 58N 6 8 E
Levin 114 40 37 S 175 18 E
Lévis 143 46 48N 71 9W
Levis, L. 144 62 37N 117 58W
Levítha 49 37 0N 26 28 E
Levittown, N.Y., U.S.A. 151 40 41N 73 31W
Levittown, Pa., U.S.A. 151 40 10N 74 51W
Levka, Bulgaria 47 41 52N 26 15 E
Lévka, Greece 49 35 18N 24 3 E
Levkás 49 38 40N 20 43 E
Levkímmi 48 39 25N 20 3 E
Levkôsia = Nicosia 70 35 10N 33 25 E
Levoča 31 49 2N 20 35 E
Levroux 19 46 59N 1 38 E
Levski 47 43 21N 25 10 E
Levskigrad 47 42 38N 24 47 E
Levuka 106 17 34 S 179 0 E
Lewe 82 19 38N 96 7 E
Lewellen 152 41 22N 102 5W
Lewes, U.K. 13 50 53N 0 2 E
Lewes, U.S.A. 148 38 45N 75 8W
Lewin Brzeski 32 50 45N 17 37 E
Lewis 14 58 10N 6 40W
Lewis → 158 45 51N 122 48W
Lewis, Butt of 14 58 30N 6 12W
Lewis Ra., Australia 108 20 3 S 128 50 E
Lewis Ra., U.S.A. 156 48 0N 113 15W
Lewisburg, Ohio, U.S.A. 155 39 51N 84 33W
Lewisburg, Pa., U.S.A. 150 40 57N 76 57W
Lewisburg, Tenn., U.S.A. 149 35 29N 86 46W
Lewisport 155 37 56N 86 54W
Lewisporte 143 49 15N 55 3W
Lewiston 156 46 25N 117 0W
Lewistown, Ill., U.S.A. 154 40 24N 90 9W
Lewistown, Mont., U.S.A. 156 47 0N 109 25W
Lewistown, Pa., U.S.A. 150 40 37N 77 33W
Lexington, Ill., U.S.A. 155 40 37N 88 47W
Lexington, Ky., U.S.A. 155 38 6N 84 30W
Lexington, Miss., U.S.A. 153 33 8N 90 2W
Lexington, Mo., U.S.A. 154 39 7N 93 55W
Lexington, N.C., U.S.A. 149 35 50N 80 13W
Lexington, Nebr., U.S.A. 152 40 48N 99 45W
Lexington, Ohio, U.S.A. 150 40 39N 82 35W
Lexington, Oreg., U.S.A. 156 45 29N 119 46W
Lexington, Tenn., U.S.A. 149 35 38N 88 25W
Lexington Park 148 38 16N 76 27W
Leye 96 24 48N 106 29 E
Leyre → 20 44 39N 1 1W
Leysin 28 46 21N 7 0 E
Leyte 91 11 0N 125 0 E
Leyte Gulf 91 10 50N 125 25 E
Lezajsk 32 50 16N 22 25 E
Lezay 20 46 15N 0 1 E
Lezha 48 41 47N 19 42 E
Lezhi 96 30 19N 104 58 E
Lézignan-Corbières 20 43 13N 2 43 E
Lezoux 20 45 49N 3 21 E
Lgov 58 51 42N 35 16 E
Lhasa 92 29 25N 90 58 E
Lhazê 92 29 5N 87 38 E
Lhokkruet 88 4 55N 95 24 E
Lhokseumawe 88 5 10N 97 10 E
Lhuntsi Dzong 82 27 39N 91 10 E
Li 84 17 48N 98 57 E
Li Shui → 97 29 24N 112 1 E
Li Xian, Gansu, China 94 34 10N 105 5 E
Li Xian, Hebei, China 94 38 30N 115 35 E
Li Xian, Hunan, China 97 29 36N 111 42 E
Li Xian, Sichuan, China 96 31 23N 103 13 E
Lia-Moya 132 6 54N 16 17 E
Liádhoi 49 36 50N 26 11 E
Lian 90 14 3N 120 39 E
Lian Xian 97 24 51N 112 22 E
Liancheng 97 25 42N 116 40 E
Lianga 91 8 38N 126 6 E
Lianga Bay 91 8 37N 126 12 E
Liangcheng, Nei Mongol Zizhiqu, China 94 40 28N 112 25 E
Liangcheng, Shandong, China 95 35 32N 119 37 E
Liangdang 94 33 56N 106 18 E
Lianghekou 96 29 11N 108 44 E
Liangping 96 30 38N 107 47 E
Lianhua 97 27 3N 113 54 E
Lianjiang, Fujian, China 97 26 12N 119 27 E
Lianjiang, Guangdong, China 97 21 40N 110 20 E
Lianping 97 24 26N 114 30 E
Lianshan 97 24 38N 112 8 E
Lianshanguan 95 40 53N 123 43 E
Lianshui 95 33 42N 119 20 E
Lianyuan 97 27 40N 111 38 E
Lianyungang 95 34 40N 119 11 E
Liao He → 95 41 0N 121 50 E
Liaocheng 94 36 28N 115 58 E
Liaodong Bandao 95 40 0N 122 30 E
Liaodong Wan 95 40 20N 121 10 E
Liaoning □ 95 42 0N 122 0 E
Liaoyang 95 41 15N 122 58 E
Liaoyuan 95 42 58N 125 2 E
Liaozhong 95 41 23N 122 50 E
Liapádhes 48 39 42N 19 40 E
Liard → 144 61 51N 121 18W
Liari 78 25 37N 66 30 E
Líbano 168 4 55N 75 4W
Libau = Liepaja 58 56 30N 21 0 E
Libby 156 48 20N 115 33W
Libenge 132 3 40N 18 55 E
Liberal, Kans., U.S.A. 153 37 4N 101 0W
Liberal, Mo., U.S.A. 153 37 35N 94 30W
Liberdade 172 10 5 S 70 20W
Liberdade → 173 9 40 S 52 17W
Liberec 30 50 47N 15 7 E
Liberia 162 10 40N 85 30W
Liberia ■ 126 6 30N 9 30W
Libertad, Panay, Phil. 91 11 46N 121 55 E
Libertad, Tablas, Phil. 90 12 27N 122 0 E
Libertad, Venezuela 168 8 20N 69 37W
Libertad, La, Guat. 162 16 47N 90 7W
Libertad, La, Mexico 160 29 55N 112 41W
Libertad, La □ 172 8 0 S 78 30W
Liberty, Ind., U.S.A. 155 39 38N 84 56W
Liberty, Mo., U.S.A. 154 39 15N 94 24W
Liberty, Tex., U.S.A. 153 30 5N 94 50W
Liberty Center 155 41 27N 84 1W
Libertyville 155 42 18N 87 57W
Libiaz 31 50 7N 19 21 E
Libibi 133 14 42 S 17 44 E
Libin 23 49 59N 5 15 E
Libmanan 90 13 42N 123 4 E
Libo 96 25 22N 107 53 E
Libobo, Tanjung 87 0 54 S 128 28 E
Libode 135 31 33 S 29 2 E
Libohava 48 40 3N 20 10 E
Libona 91 8 20N 124 44 E
Libonda 133 14 28 S 23 12 E
Libourne 20 44 55N 0 14W
Libramont 23 49 55N 5 23 E
Librazhdi 48 41 12N 20 22 E
Libreville 132 0 25N 9 26 E
Libya ■ 122 27 0N 17 0 E
Libyan Desert 116 25 0N 25 0 E
Libyan Plateau = Ed-Déffa 124 30 40N 26 30 E
Licantén 174 35 55 S 72 0W
Licata 44 37 6N 13 55 E
Licheng 94 36 28N 113 20 E
Lichfield 12 52 40N 1 50W
Lichinga 131 13 13 S 35 11 E
Lichtaart 23 51 13N 4 55 E
Lichtenburg 134 26 8 S 26 8 E
Lichtenfels 27 50 7N 11 4 E
Lichtenvoorde 22 51 59N 6 34 E
Lichtervelde 23 51 2N 3 9 E
Lichuan, Hubei, China 96 30 18N 108 57 E
Lichuan, Jiangxi, China 97 27 18N 116 55 E
Licking, South Fork → 155 38 40N 84 19W
Licosa, Punta 45 40 15N 14 53 E
Lida, U.S.A. 157 37 30N 117 30W
Lida, U.S.S.R. 58 53 53N 25 15 E
Lidhult 53 56 50N 13 27 E
Lidingö 52 59 22N 18 8 E
Lidköping 53 58 31N 13 14 E
Lidlidda 90 17 15N 120 31 E
Lido, Italy 43 45 25N 12 23 E
Lido, Niger 127 12 54N 3 44 E
Lido di Roma = Óstia, Lido di 44 41 43N 12 17 E
Lidzbark 32 53 15N 19 49 E
Lidzbark Warminski 32 54 7N 20 34 E
Liebenwalde 26 52 51N 13 23 E
Lieberose 26 51 59N 14 18 E
Liebling 50 45 36N 21 20 E
Liechtenstein ■ 29 47 8N 9 35 E
Liederkerke 23 50 52N 4 5 E
Liège 23 50 38N 5 35 E
Liège □ 23 50 32N 5 35 E
Liegnitz = Legnica 32 51 12N 16 10 E
Liempde 23 51 35N 5 23 E
Lienart 130 3 3N 25 31 E
Lienyünchiangshih = Lianyungang 95 34 40N 119 11 E
Lienz 30 46 50N 12 46 E
Liepaja 58 56 30N 21 0 E
Lier 23 51 7N 4 34 E
Lierneux 23 50 17N 5 47 E
Lieshout 23 51 31N 5 36 E
Lieşta 50 45 38N 27 34 E
Liestal 28 47 29N 7 44 E
Liévin 19 50 24N 2 47 E
Lièvre → 142 45 31N 75 26W
Liezen 30 47 34N 14 15 E
Liffey → 15 53 21N 6 20W
Lifford 15 54 50N 7 30W
Liffré 18 48 12N 1 30W
Lifjell 51 59 27N 8 45 E
Lifudzin 98 44 21N 134 58 E
Ligao 90 13 14N 123 32 E
Lightning Ridge 111 29 22 S 148 0 E
Lignano 43 45 42N 13 8 E
Ligny-en-Barrois 19 48 36N 5 20 E
Ligny-le-Châtel 19 47 54N 3 45 E
Ligoúrion 49 37 37N 23 2 E
Ligua, La 174 32 30 S 71 16W
Ligueil 18 47 2N 0 49 E
Liguria □ 42 44 30N 9 0 E
Ligurian Sea 42 43 20N 9 0 E
Lihir Group 107 3 0 S 152 35 E
Lihou Reefs and Cays 110 17 25 S 151 40 E
Lihue 146 21 59N 159 24W
Lijiang 96 26 55N 100 20 E
Likasi 131 10 55 S 26 48 E
Likati 132 3 20N 24 0 E
Likhoslavl 58 57 12N 35 30 E
Likhovski 61 48 10N 40 10 E
Likokou 132 0 12 S 12 48 E
Likoma I. 131 12 3 S 34 45 E
Likumburu 131 9 43 S 35 8 E
Liling 97 27 42N 113 29 E
Lille, Belgium 23 51 15N 4 50 E
Lille, France 19 50 38N 3 3 E
Lille Bælt 53 55 20N 9 45 E
Lillebonne 18 49 30N 0 32 E
Lillehammer 51 61 8N 10 30 E
Lillers 19 50 35N 2 28 E
Lillesand 51 58 15N 8 23 E
Lilleshall 13 52 45N 2 22W
Lillestrøm 51 59 58N 11 5 E

Lovington

Lovington, N. Mex., U.S.A. **153** 33 0N 103 20W
Lovios **34** 41 55N 8 4W
Lovisa **55** 60 28N 26 12 E
Lovosice **30** 50 30N 14 2 E
Lovran **43** 45 18N 14 15 E
Lovrin **50** 45 58N 20 48 E
Lövstabukten **52** 60 35N 17 45 E
Low Pt. **109** 32 25 S 127 25 E
Lowa **130** 1 25 S 25 47 E
Lowa —► **130** 1 24 S 25 51 E
Lowden **154** 41 52N 90 56W
Lowell, Ind., U.S.A. **155** 41 18N 87 25W
Lowell, Mass., U.S.A. **151** 42 38N 71 19W
Lower Arrow L. **144** 49 40N 118 5W
Lower Austria = Niederösterreich □ **30** 48 25N 15 40 E
Lower California = Baja California **160** 31 10N 115 12W
Lower Hutt **114** 41 10 S 174 55 E
Lower L. **156** 41 17N 120 3W
Lower Lake **158** 38 56N 122 36W
Lower Post **144** 59 58N 128 30W
Lower Red L. **152** 48 0N 94 50W
Lower Saxony = Niedersachsen □ **26** 52 45N 9 0 E
Lowestoft **13** 52 29N 1 44 E
Łowicz **32** 52 6N 19 55 E
Lowry City **154** 38 8N 93 44W
Lowville **151** 43 48N 75 30W
Loxton, Australia **112** 34 28 S 140 31 E
Loxton, S. Africa **134** 31 30 S 22 22 E
Loyalton **158** 39 41N 120 14W
Loyalty Is. = Loyauté, Is. **106** 21 0 S 167 30 E
Loyang = Luoyang **94** 34 40N 112 26 E
Loyauté, Is. **106** 21 0 S 167 30 E
Loyev **58** 51 56N 30 46 E
Loyoro **130** 3 22N 34 14 E
Lož **43** 45 43N 14 14 E
Lozère □ **20** 44 35N 3 30 E
Loznica **46** 44 32N 19 14 E
Lozovaya **60** 49 0N 36 20 E
Lozva —► **62** 59 36N 62 20 E
Luachimo **133** 7 23 S 20 48 E
Luacono **133** 11 15 S 21 37 E
Lualaba —► **130** 0 26N 25 20 E
Luampa **131** 15 4 S 24 20 E
Lu'an **97** 31 45N 116 29 E
Luan Chau **84** 21 38N 103 24 E
Luan He —► **95** 39 20N 119 5 E
Luan Xian **95** 39 40N 118 40 E
Luancheng, Guangxi Zhuangzu, China **96** 22 48N 108 55 E
Luancheng, Hebei, China **94** 37 53N 114 40 E
Luanda **133** 8 50 S 13 15 E
Luanda □ **133** 9 0 S 13 10 E
Luang Prabang **84** 19 52N 102 10 E
Luang Thale **85** 7 30N 100 15 E
Luangwa **131** 15 35 S 30 16 E
Luangwa —► **131** 14 25 S 30 25 E
Luangwa Valley **131** 13 30 S 31 30 E
Luanne **95** 40 55N 117 40 E
Luanping **95** 40 53N 117 23 E
Luanshya **131** 13 3 S 28 28 E
Luapula □ **131** 11 0 S 29 0 E
Luapula —► **131** 9 26 S 28 33 E
Luarca **34** 43 32N 6 32W
Luashi **131** 10 50 S 23 36 E
Luau **133** 10 40 S 22 10 E
Luba **90** 17 19N 120 42 E
Lubaczów **32** 50 10N 23 8 E
Lubalo **133** 9 10 S 19 15 E
Luban, Phil. **91** 6 26N 126 13 E
Lubań, Poland **32** 51 5N 15 15 E
Lubana, Ozero **58** 56 45N 27 0 E
Lubang **90** 13 52N 120 7 E
Lubang Is. **90** 13 50N 120 12 E
Lubango **133** 14 55 S 13 30 E
Lubao **90** 14 56N 120 36 E
Lubartów **32** 51 28N 22 42 E
Lubawa **32** 53 30N 19 48 E
Lubbeek **23** 50 54N 4 50 E
Lübben **26** 51 56N 13 54 E
Lübbenau **26** 51 49N 13 59 E
Lubbock **153** 33 40N 101 53W
Lübeck **26** 53 52N 10 41 E
Lübecker Bucht **26** 54 3N 11 0 E
Lubefu **130** 4 47 S 24 27 E
Lubefu —► **130** 4 10 S 23 0 E
Lubero = Luofu **130** 0 10 S 29 15 E
Lubicon L. **144** 56 23N 115 56W
Lubień Kujawski **32** 52 23N 19 9 E
Lubin **32** 51 24N 16 11 E
Lublin **32** 51 12N 22 38 E
Lublin □ **32** 51 5N 22 30 E
Lubliniec **32** 50 43N 18 45 E
Lubnān, J. **70** 33 50N 35 45 E
Lubny **58** 50 3N 32 58 E
Lubon **32** 52 21N 16 51 E
Lubongola **130** 2 35 S 27 50 E
Lubotin **31** 49 17N 20 53 E
Lubraniec **32** 52 33N 18 50 E
Lubsko **32** 51 45N 14 57 E
Lübtheen **26** 53 18N 11 4 E
Lubuagan **90** 17 21N 121 10 E
Lubudi —► **131** 9 0 S 25 35 E
Lubuk Antu **86** 1 3N 111 50 E
Lubuklinggau **88** 3 15 S 102 55 E
Lubuksikaping **88** 0 10N 100 15 E
Lubumbashi **131** 11 40 S 27 28 E
Lubunda **130** 5 12 S 26 41 E
Lubungu **131** 14 35 S 26 24 E
Lubutu **130** 0 45 S 26 30 E
Luc, Le **21** 43 23N 6 21 E
Luc An Chau **84** 22 6N 104 43 E
Luc-en-Diois **21** 44 36N 5 28 E
Lucala **133** 9 7 S 15 58 E
Lucan **150** 43 11N 81 24W
Lucban **90** 14 6N 121 33 E
Lucca **42** 43 50N 10 30 E
Luce Bay **14** 54 45N 4 48W
Lucea **162** 18 25N 78 10W
Lucedale **149** 30 55N 88 34W
Lucena, Phil. **90** 13 56N 121 37 E
Lucena, Spain **35** 37 27N 4 31W
Lucena del Cid **36** 40 9N 0 17W
Lučenec **31** 48 18N 19 42 E
Lucens **28** 46 43N 6 51 E
Lucera **45** 41 30N 15 20 E
Lucerne = Luzern **29** 47 3N 8 18 E
Lucerne **158** 39 6N 122 48W
Lucerne Valley **159** 34 27N 116 57W
Lucero **160** 30 49N 106 30W
Luchena —► **37** 37 44N 1 50W
Lucheng **94** 36 20N 113 11 E
Lucheringo —► **131** 11 43 S 36 17 E
Lüchow **26** 52 58N 11 8 E
Luchuan **97** 22 21N 110 12 E
Lucie —► **169** 13 51 S 12 35 E
Lucira **133** 14 0 S 12 35 E
Luckau **26** 51 50N 13 43 E
Luckenwalde **26** 52 5N 13 11 E
Luckey **155** 41 27N 83 29W
Lucknow **79** 26 50N 81 0 E
Luçon **20** 46 28N 1 10W
Lucusse **133** 12 32 S 20 48 E
Lüda = Dalian **95** 38 50N 121 40 E
Luda Kamchiya —► **47** 43 3N 27 29 E
Ludbreg **43** 46 15N 16 38 E
Lüdenscheid **26** 51 13N 7 37 E
Lüderitz **134** 26 41 S 15 8 E
Ludewe □ **131** 10 0 S 34 50 E
Ludhiana **78** 30 57N 75 56 E
Ludian **96** 27 10N 103 33 E
Luding Qiao **96** 29 53N 102 12 E
Lüdinghausen **26** 51 46N 7 28 E
Ludington **148** 43 58N 86 27W
Ludlow, U.K. **13** 52 23N 2 42W
Ludlow, Calif., U.S.A. **159** 34 43N 116 10W
Ludlow, Vt., U.S.A. **151** 43 25N 72 40W
Ludus **50** 46 29N 24 5 E
Ludvika **52** 60 8N 15 14 E
Ludwigsburg **27** 48 53N 9 11 E
Ludwigshafen **27** 49 27N 8 27 E
Ludwigslust **26** 53 19N 11 28 E
Ludza **58** 56 32N 27 43 E
Lue **113** 32 38 S 149 50 E
Luebo **133** 5 21 S 21 23 E
Lueki **130** 3 20 S 25 48 E
Luena, Angola **133** 12 13 S 19 51 E
Luena, Zaïre **131** 9 28 S 25 43 E
Luena, Zambia **131** 10 40 S 30 25 E
Luepa **169** 5 43N 61 31W
Lüeyang **94** 33 22N 106 10 E
Lufeng, Guangdong, China **97** 22 57N 115 38 E
Lufeng, Yunnan, China **96** 25 0N 102 5 E
Lufico **133** 6 24 S 13 23 E
Lufira —► **131** 9 30 S 27 0 E
Lufkin **153** 31 25N 94 40W
Lufupa **131** 10 37 S 24 56 E
Luga **58** 58 40N 29 55 E
Luga —► **58** 59 40N 28 18 E
Lugang **97** 24 4N 120 23 E
Lugano **29** 46 0N 8 57 E
Lugano, L. di **29** 46 0N 9 0 E
Lugansk = Voroshilovgrad **61** 48 38N 39 15 E
Lugard's Falls **130** 3 6 S 38 41 E
Lugela **131** 16 25 S 36 43 E
Lugenda —► **131** 11 25 S 38 33 E
Lugh Ganana **136** 3 48N 42 34 E
Lugnaquilla **15** 52 58N 6 28W
Lugnvik **52** 62 56N 17 55 E
Lugo, Italy **43** 44 25N 11 53 E
Lugo, Spain **34** 43 2N 7 35W
Lugo □ **34** 43 0N 7 30W
Lugoj **46** 45 42N 21 57 E
Lugones **34** 43 26N 5 50W
Lugovoye **63** 42 55N 72 43 E
Luhe **97** 32 19N 118 50 E
Luhe —► **26** 53 18N 10 11 E
Luhuo **96** 31 21N 100 48 E
Luiana **133** 17 25 S 22 59 E
Luino **42** 46 0N 8 42 E
Luís Correia **170** 3 0 S 41 35W
Luís Gonçalves **170** 5 37 S 50 25W
Luitpold Coast **7** 78 30 S 32 0W
Luiza **133** 7 40 S 22 30 E
Luizi **130** 6 0 S 27 25 E
Luján **174** 34 45 S 59 5W
Lujiang **97** 31 20N 117 15 E
Lukala **133** 5 31 S 14 32 E
Lukanga Swamp **131** 14 30 S 27 40 E
Lukenie —► **132** 3 0 S 18 50 E
Lukhisaral **79** 25 11N 86 5 E
Lŭki **47** 41 50N 24 43 E
Lukk **122** 32 1N 24 46 E
Lukolela, Equateur, Zaïre **132** 1 10 S 17 12 E
Lukolela, Kasai Or., Zaïre **130** 5 23 S 24 32 E
Lukosi **131** 18 30 S 26 30 E
Lukovit **47** 43 13N 24 11 E
Łuków **32** 51 55N 22 23 E
Lukoyanov **59** 55 2N 44 29 E
Lule älv —► **54** 65 35N 22 10 E
Luleå **54** 65 35N 22 10 E
Lüleburgaz **47** 41 23N 27 22 E
Luliang **96** 25 0N 103 40 E
Luling **153** 29 45N 97 40W
Lulong **95** 39 53N 118 51 E
Lulonga —► **132** 1 0N 18 10 E
Lulua —► **133** 4 30 S 20 30 E
Luluabourg = Kananga **133** 5 55 S 22 18 E
Luma **106** 14 15 S 169 32W
Lumai **133** 13 13 S 21 25 E
Lumajang **89** 8 8 S 113 13 E
Lumbala Kaquengue **133** 12 39 S 22 34 E
Lumbala N'guimbo **133** 14 18 S 21 18 E
Lumberton, Miss., U.S.A. **153** 31 4N 89 28W
Lumberton, N.C., U.S.A. **149** 34 37N 78 59W
Lumberton, N. Mex., U.S.A. **157** 36 58N 106 57W
Lumbres **19** 50 40N 2 5 E
Lumbwa **130** 0 12 S 35 28 E
Lumding **82** 25 46N 93 10 E
Lumi **107** 3 30 S 142 2 E
Lummen **23** 50 59N 5 12 E
Lumsden **115** 45 44 S 168 27 E
Lumut **85** 4 13N 100 37 E
Lumut, Tg. **88** 3 50 S 105 58 E
Luna, Luzon, Phil. **90** 18 18N 121 21 E
Luna, Luzon, Phil. **90** 16 51N 120 23 E
Lunan **96** 24 40N 103 18 E
Lunavada **78** 23 8N 73 37 E
Lunca **50** 47 22N 25 1 E
Lund, Sweden **52** 55 44N 13 12 E
Lund, U.S.A. **156** 38 53N 115 0W
Lunda Norte □ **133** 8 0 S 20 0 E
Lunda Sul □ **133** 10 0 S 20 0 E
Lundazi **131** 12 20 S 33 7 E
Lunde **51** 59 17N 9 5 E
Lunderskov **53** 55 29N 9 19 E
Lundi —► **131** 21 43 S 32 34 E
Lundu **86** 1 40N 109 50 E
Lundy **13** 51 10N 4 41W
Lune —► **12** 54 0N 2 51W
Lüneburg **26** 53 15N 10 23 E
Lüneburg Heath = Lüneburger Heide **26** 53 0N 10 0 E
Lüneburger Heide **26** 53 0N 10 0 E
Lunel **21** 43 39N 4 9 E
Lünen **26** 51 36N 7 31 E
Lunenburg **143** 44 22N 64 18W
Lunéville **19** 48 36N 6 30 E
Lunga —► **131** 14 34 S 26 25 E
Lungern **28** 46 48N 8 10 E
Lungi Airport **126** 8 40N 13 17W
Lunglei **82** 22 55N 92 45 E
Lungngo **82** 21 57N 93 36 E
Luni **78** 26 0N 73 6 E
Luni —► **78** 24 41N 71 14 E
Luninets **58** 52 15N 26 50 E
Luning **156** 38 30N 118 10W
Lunino **59** 53 35N 45 6 E
Lunner **51** 60 19N 10 35 E
Lunsemfwa —► **131** 14 54 S 30 12 E
Lunsemfwa Falls **131** 14 30 S 29 6 E
Lunteren **22** 52 5N 5 38 E
Luo He —► **94** 34 35N 110 20 E
Luocheng **96** 24 48N 108 53 E
Luochuan **94** 35 45N 109 26 E
Luoci **96** 25 19N 102 18 E
Luodian **96** 25 24N 106 43 E
Luoding **97** 22 45N 111 40 E
Luodong **97** 24 41N 121 46 E
Luofu **130** 0 10 S 29 15 E
Luohe **94** 33 32N 114 2 E
Luojiang **96** 31 18N 104 33 E
Luonan **94** 34 5N 110 10 E
Luoning **94** 34 35N 111 40 E
Luoshan **97** 32 13N 114 30 E
Luotian **97** 30 46N 115 22 E
Luoyang **94** 34 40N 112 26 E
Luoyuan **97** 26 28N 119 30 E
Luozi **133** 4 54 S 14 0 E
Luozigou **95** 43 42N 130 18 E
Lupeni **50** 45 21N 23 13 E
Lupilichi **131** 11 47 S 35 13 E
Lupire **133** 14 36 S 19 29 E
Łupków **31** 49 15N 22 4 E
Lupoing **96** 24 53N 104 21 E
Lupon **91** 6 54N 126 0 E
Luquan **96** 25 35N 102 25 E
Luque, Paraguay **174** 25 19 S 57 25W
Luque, Spain **35** 37 35N 4 16W
Luray **148** 38 39N 78 26W
Lure **19** 47 40N 6 30 E
Luremo **133** 8 30 S 17 50 E
Lurgan **15** 54 28N 6 20W
Luribay **172** 17 6 S 67 39W
Lurin **172** 12 17 S 76 52W
Lusaka **131** 15 28 S 28 16 E
Lusambo **130** 4 58 S 23 28 E
Lusangaye **130** 4 54 S 26 0 E
Luseland **145** 52 5N 109 24W
Lushan, Henan, China **94** 33 45N 112 55 E
Lushan, Sichuan, China **96** 30 12N 102 52 E
Lushih **94** 34 3N 111 3 E
Lushnja **48** 40 55N 19 41 E
Lushoto **130** 4 47 S 38 20 E
Lushoto □ **130** 4 45 S 38 20 E
Lushui **96** 25 58N 98 44 E
Lüshun **95** 38 45N 121 15 E
Lusignan **20** 46 26N 0 8 E
Lusigny-sur-Barse **19** 48 16N 4 15 E
Lusk **152** 42 47N 104 27W
Lussac-les-Châteaux **20** 46 24N 0 43 E
Lussanvira **171** 20 42 S 51 7W
Luta = Dalian **95** 38 50N 121 40 E
Lutembo **133** 13 26 S 21 16 E
Luton **13** 51 53N 0 24W
Lutong **86** 4 28N 114 0 E
Lutry **28** 46 31N 6 42 E
Lutsk **58** 50 50N 25 15 E
Lutuai **133** 12 41 S 20 7 E
Lützow Holmbukta **7** 69 10 S 37 30 E
Lutzputs **134** 28 3 S 20 40 E
Luverne **152** 43 35N 96 12W
Luvo **133** 5 51 S 14 5 E
Luvua **131** 8 48 S 25 17 E
Luvua —► **130** 6 50 S 27 30 E
Luwegu —► **131** 8 31 S 37 23 E
Luwuk **87** 0 56 S 122 47 E
Luxembourg **23** 49 37N 6 9 E
Luxembourg □ **23** 49 58N 5 30 E
Luxembourg ■ **23** 50 0N 6 0 E
Luxeuil-les-Bains **19** 47 49N 6 24 E
Luxi, Hunan, China **97** 28 20N 110 7 E
Luxi, Yunnan, China **96** 24 40N 103 55 E
Luxi, Yunnan, China **96** 24 27N 98 36 E
Luxor = El Uqsur **124** 25 41N 32 38 E
Luy —► **20** 43 39N 1 9W
Luy-de-Béarn —► **20** 43 39N 0 48W
Luy-de-France —► **20** 43 39N 0 48W
Luyi **94** 33 50N 115 35 E
Luyksgestel **23** 51 17N 5 20 E
Luz-St.-Sauveur **20** 42 53N 0 0 E
Luza **59** 60 39N 47 10 E
Luzern **29** 47 3N 8 18 E
Luzern □ **28** 47 2N 7 55 E
Luzhai **96** 24 29N 109 42 E
Luzhou **96** 28 52N 105 20 E
Luziânia **171** 16 20 S 48 0W
Luzilândia **170** 3 28 S 42 22W
Luzon **90** 16 0N 121 0 E
Luzon Strait **90** 21 0N 122 0 E
Luzy **19** 46 47N 3 58 E
Luzzi **45** 39 28N 16 17 E
Lvov **58** 49 50N 24 0 E
Lwówek **32** 52 28N 16 10 E
Lwówek Śląski **32** 51 7N 15 38 E
Lyakhovichi **58** 53 2N 26 32 E
Lyakhovskiye, Ostrova **65** 73 40N 141 0 E
Lyaki **61** 40 34N 47 22 E
Lyall Mt. **115** 45 16 S 167 32 E
Lyallpur = Faisalabad **77** 31 30N 73 5 E
Lyalya —► **62** 59 9N 61 29 E
Lyaskovets **47** 43 6N 25 44 E
Lychen **26** 53 13N 13 20 E
Lyckeby **53** 56 12N 15 37 E
Lycksele **54** 64 38N 18 40 E
Lycosura **49** 37 20N 22 3 E
Lydda = Lod **69** 31 57N 34 54 E
Lydenburg **135** 25 10 S 30 29 E
Lyell **115** 41 48 S 172 4 E
Lyell I. **144** 52 40N 131 35W
Lyell Range **115** 41 38 S 172 20 E
Lygnern **53** 57 30N 12 15 E
Lykling **51** 59 42N 5 12 E
Lyman **156** 41 24N 110 15W
Lyme Regis **13** 50 44N 2 57W
Lymington **13** 50 46N 1 32W
Łyńa —► **32** 54 37N 21 14 E
Lynchburg, Ohio, U.S.A. **155** 39 15N 83 48W
Lynchburg, Va., U.S.A. **148** 37 23N 79 10W
Lynd —► **110** 16 28 S 143 18 E
Lynd Ra. **111** 25 30 S 149 20 E
Lynden, Canada **150** 43 14N 80 9W
Lynden, U.S.A. **158** 48 56N 122 32W
Lyndhurst **111** 30 15 S 138 18 E
Lyndon —► **109** 23 29 S 114 6 E
Lyndonville, N.Y., U.S.A. **150** 43 19N 78 25W
Lyndonville, Vt., U.S.A. **151** 44 32N 72 1W
Lyngdal, Aust-Agder, Norway **51** 58 8N 7 7 E
Lyngdal, Buskerud, Norway **51** 59 54N 9 32 E
Lynher Reef **108** 15 27 S 121 55 E
Lynn, Ind., U.S.A. **155** 40 3N 84 56W
Lynn, Mass., U.S.A. **151** 42 28N 70 57W
Lynn Canal **144** 58 50N 135 20W
Lynn Lake **145** 56 51N 101 3W
Lynnwood **158** 47 49N 122 19W
Lynton **13** 51 14N 3 50W
Lyntupy **58** 55 4N 26 23 E
Lynx L. **145** 62 25N 106 15W
Lyø **53** 55 3N 10 9 E
Lyon **21** 45 46N 4 50 E
Lyonnais **21** 45 45N 4 15 E
Lyons = Lyon **21** 45 46N 4 50 E
Lyons, Colo., U.S.A. **152** 40 17N 105 15W

Magnetic Pole

Lyons, Ga., U.S.A. 149 32 10N 82 15W
Lyons, Kans., U.S.A. 152 38 24N 98 13W
Lyons, N.Y., U.S.A. 150 43 3N 77 0W
Lyrestad 53 58 48N 14 4 E
Lys → 19 50 39N 2 24 E
Lysá 30 50 11N 14 51 E
Lysekil 53 58 17N 11 26 E
Lyskovo 59 56 0N 45 3 E
Lyss 28 47 4N 7 19 E
Lysva 62 58 7N 57 49 E
Lysvik 52 60 1N 13 9 E
Lytle 153 29 14N 98 46W
Lyttelton 115 43 35 S 172 44 E
Lytton 144 50 13N 121 31W
Lyuban 58 59 16N 31 18 E
Lyubcha 58 53 46N 26 1 E
Lyubertsy 59 55 39N 37 50 E
Lyubim 59 58 20N 40 39 E
Lyubimets 47 41 50N 26 5 E
Lyuboml 58 51 11N 24 4 E
Lyubotin 60 50 0N 36 0 E
Lyubytino 58 58 50N 33 16 E
Lyudinovo 58 53 52N 34 28 E

M

Ma → 84 19 47N 105 56 E
Mā'ad 69 32 37N 35 36 E
Ma'adaba 71 30 43N 35 47 E
Maamba 134 17 17 S 26 28 E
Ma'ān 71 30 12N 35 44 E
Ma'ān □ 71 30 0N 36 0 E
Ma'anshan 97 31 44N 118 29 E
Maarheeze 23 51 19N 5 36 E
Maarn 22 52 3N 5 22 E
Ma'arrat 70 36 2N 36 49 E
Ma'arrat an Nu'mān 70 35 43N 36 43 E
Maarssen 22 52 9N 5 2 E
Maartensdijk 22 52 9N 5 10 E
Maas → 22 51 45N 4 32 E
Maasbracht 23 51 9N 5 54 E
Maasbree 23 51 22N 6 3 E
Maasdam 22 51 48N 4 34 E
Maasdijk 22 51 58N 4 13 E
Maaseik 23 51 6N 5 45 E
Maasland 22 51 57N 4 16 E
Maasniel 23 51 12N 6 1 E
Maassluis 22 51 56N 4 16 E
Maastricht 23 50 50N 5 40 E
Maave 135 21 4 S 34 47 E
Ma'bar 74 14 48N 44 17 E
Mabaruma 169 8 10N 59 50W
Mabein 82 23 29N 96 37 E
Mabel L. 144 50 35N 118 43W
Mabenge 130 4 15N 24 12 E
Mabian 96 28 47N 103 37 E
Mablethorpe 12 53 21N 0 14 E
Maboma 130 2 30N 28 10 E
Maboukou 132 3 39 S 12 31 E
Mabrouk 127 19 29N 1 15W
Mabton 156 46 15N 120 12W
Mabungo 136 0 49N 42 35 E
Mac Bac 85 9 46N 106 7 E
Macachín 174 37 10 S 63 43W
Macaé 171 22 20 S 41 43W
Macaíba 170 5 51 S 35 21W
Macajuba 171 12 9 S 40 22W
Macalelon 90 13 45N 122 8 E
McAlester 153 34 57N 95 46W
McAllen 153 26 12N 98 15W
Macamic 142 48 45N 79 0W
Macão 35 39 35N 7 59W
Macapá 170 0 5N 51 4W
Macará 168 4 23 S 79 57W
Macarani 171 15 33 S 40 24W
Macarena, Serranía de la 168 2 45N 73 55W
Macarthur 112 38 5 S 142 0 E
McArthur → 110 15 54 S 136 40 E
McArthur River 110 16 27 S 136 7 E
Macas 168 2 19 S 78 7W
Macate 172 8 48 S 78 7W
Macau 170 5 0 S 36 40W
Macaúbas 171 13 2 S 42 42W
Macaya → 168 0 59N 72 20W
McBride 144 53 20N 120 19W
McCall 156 44 55N 116 6W
McCamey 153 31 8N 102 15W
McCammon 156 42 41N 112 11W
McCauley I. 144 53 40N 130 15W
McCleary 158 47 3N 123 16W
Macclesfield 12 53 16N 2 9W
McClintock 145 57 50N 94 10W
McClintock Ra. 108 18 44 S 127 38 E
McCloud 156 41 14N 122 5W
McClure 150 40 42N 77 20W
McClure, L. 158 37 35N 120 16W
McClure Str. 6 75 0N 119 0W
McClusky 152 47 30N 100 31W
McComb 153 31 13N 90 30W
McConaughy, L. 152 41 20N 101 40W
McCook 152 40 15N 100 35W
McCullough Mt. 159 35 35N 115 13W
McCusker → 145 55 32N 108 39W
McDame 144 59 44N 128 59W
McDermitt 156 42 0N 117 45W
McDonald Is. 83 53 0 S 73 0 E
Macdonald L. 108 23 30 S 129 0 E
Macdonnell Ranges 108 23 40 S 133 0 E
McDouall Peak 111 29 51 S 134 55 E
Macdougall L. 140 66 0N 98 27W
McDougalls Well 112 31 8 S 141 15 E
MacDowell L. 142 52 15N 92 45W
Macduff 14 57 40N 2 30W
Maceda 34 42 16N 7 39W
Macedonia = Makedhonía □ 48 40 39N 22 0 E
Macedonia = Makedonija □ 46 41 53N 21 40 E
Maceió 170 9 40 S 35 41W
Maceira 35 39 41N 8 55W
Macenta 126 8 35N 9 32W
Macerata 43 43 19N 13 28 E
McFarland 159 35 41N 119 14W
McFarlane → 145 59 12N 107 58W
Macfarlane, L. 112 32 0 S 136 40 E
McGehee 153 33 40N 91 25W
McGill 156 39 27N 114 50W
Macgillycuddy's Reeks 15 52 2N 9 45W
MacGregor 145 49 57N 98 48W
McGregor 154 43 0N 91 15W
McGregor → 144 55 10N 122 0W
McGregor Ra. 111 27 0 S 142 45 E
Māch Kowr 73 25 48N 61 28 E
Machacalis 171 17 5 S 40 45W
Machado = Jiparaná → 173 8 3 S 62 52W
Machagai 174 26 56 S 60 2W
Machakos 130 1 30 S 37 15 E
Machakos □ 130 1 30 S 37 15 E
Machala 168 3 20 S 79 57W
Machanga 135 20 59 S 35 0 E
Machattie, L. 110 24 50 S 139 48 E
Machava 135 25 54 S 32 28 E
Machece 131 19 15 S 35 32 E
Machecoul 18 47 0N 1 49W
Machelen 23 50 55N 4 26 E
Macheng 97 31 12N 115 2 E
McHenry 155 42 21N 88 16W
Machevna 65 61 20N 172 20 E
Machezo 35 39 21N 4 20W
Machias 143 44 40N 67 28W
Machichaco, C. 36 43 28N 2 47W
Machichi → 145 57 3N 92 6W
Machida 101 35 28N 139 23 E
Machilipatnam 81 16 12N 81 8 E
Machine, La 19 46 54N 3 27 E
Machiques 168 10 4N 72 34W
Machupicchu 172 13 8 S 72 30W
Machynlleth 13 52 36N 3 51W
Maciejowice 32 51 36N 21 26 E
McIlwraith Ra. 110 13 50 S 143 20 E
Măcin 50 45 16N 28 8 E
Macina 126 14 50N 5 0W
McIntosh 152 45 57N 101 20W
McIntosh L. 145 55 45N 105 0W
Macintyre → 111 28 37 S 150 47 E
Macizo Galaico 34 42 30N 7 30W
Mackay, Australia 110 21 8 S 149 11 E
Mackay, U.S.A. 156 43 58N 113 37W
MacKay → 144 57 10N 111 38W
Mackay, L. 108 22 30 S 129 0 E
McKay Ra. 108 23 0 S 122 30 E
McKeesport 150 40 21N 79 50W
McKenna 158 46 56N 122 33W
Mackenzie, Canada 144 55 20N 123 5W
Mackenzie, Guyana 169 6 0N 58 17W
McKenzie 149 36 10N 88 31W
Mackenzie →, Australia 110 23 38 S 149 46 E
Mackenzie →, Canada 140 69 10N 134 20W
McKenzie → 156 44 2N 123 6W
Mackenzie City = Linden 172 6 0N 58 10W
Mackenzie Highway 144 58 0N 117 15W
Mackenzie Mts. 140 64 0N 130 0W
Mackenzie Plains 115 44 10 S 170 25W
McKerrow L. 115 44 25 S 168 5 E
Mackinaw 154 40 32N 89 21W
Mackinaw → 154 40 33N 89 44W
Mackinaw City 148 45 47N 84 44W
McKinlay 110 21 16 S 141 18 E
McKinlay → 110 20 50 S 141 28 E
McKinley, Mt. 140 63 2N 151 0W
McKinley Sea 6 84 0N 10 0W
McKinney 153 33 10N 96 40W
Mackinnon Road 130 3 40 S 39 1 E
Mackintosh Ra. 109 27 39 S 125 32 E
Macksville 111 30 40 S 152 56 E
McLaren Vale 112 35 13 S 138 31 E
McLaughlin 152 45 50N 100 50W
Maclean 111 29 26 S 153 16 E
McLean, Ill., U.S.A. 154 40 19N 89 10W
McLean, Tex., U.S.A. 153 35 15N 100 35W
McLeansboro 155 38 5N 88 30W
Maclear 135 31 2 S 28 23 E
Macleay → 111 30 56 S 153 0 E
McLennan 144 55 42N 116 50W
MacLeod, B. 145 62 53N 110 0W
McLeod L. 109 24 9 S 113 47 E
MacLeod Lake 144 54 58N 123 0W
M'Clintock Chan. 140 72 0N 102 0W
McLoughlin, Mt. 156 42 10N 122 19W
McLure 144 51 2N 120 13W
McMechen 150 39 57N 80 44W
McMillan L. 153 32 40N 104 20W
McMinnville, Oreg., U.S.A. 156 45 16N 123 11W
McMinnville, Tenn., U.S.A. 149 35 43N 85 45W
McMorran 145 51 19N 108 42W
McMurdo Sd. 7 77 0 S 170 0 E
McMurray = Fort McMurray 144 56 44N 111 7W
McMurray 158 48 19N 122 19W
McNary 157 34 4N 109 53W
MacNutt 145 51 5N 101 36W
Maco 91 7 20N 125 50 E
Macocolo 133 6 47 S 16 8 E
Macodoene 135 23 32 S 35 5 E
Macomb 154 40 25N 90 40W
Macomer 44 40 16N 8 48 E
Mâcon, France 21 46 19N 4 50 E
Macon, Ga., U.S.A. 149 32 50N 83 37W
Macon, Ill., U.S.A. 154 39 43N 89 0W
Macon, Miss., U.S.A. 149 33 7N 88 31W
Macon, Mo., U.S.A. 154 39 40N 92 26W
Macondo 133 12 37 S 23 46 E
Macossa 131 17 55 S 33 56 E
Macoun L. 145 56 32N 103 40W
Macoupin Cr. → 154 39 11N 90 38W
Macovane 135 21 30 S 35 0 E
McPherson 152 38 25N 97 40W
McPherson Pk. 159 34 53N 119 53W
Macpherson Ra. 111 28 15 S 153 15 E
Macquarie Harbour 110 42 15 S 145 23 E
Macquarie Is. 104 54 36 S 158 55 E
MacRobertson Land 7 71 0 S 64 0 E
Macroom 15 51 54N 8 57W
Macroy 108 20 53 S 118 2 E
MacTier 150 45 9N 79 46W
Macubela 131 16 53 S 37 49 E
Macugnaga 42 45 57N 7 58 E
Macuiza 131 18 7 S 34 29 E
Macujer 168 0 24N 73 10W
Macun 70 36 56N 30 51 E
Macusani 172 14 4 S 70 29W
Macuse 131 17 45 S 37 10 E
Macuspana 161 17 46N 92 36W
Macusse 133 17 48 S 20 23 E
McVille 152 47 46N 98 11W
Madadeni 135 27 43 S 30 3 E
Madadi 123 18 28N 20 45 E
Madagali 127 10 56N 13 33 E
Madagascar ■ 135 20 0 S 47 0 E
Madā'in Sālih 72 26 46N 37 57 E
Madalag 91 11 32N 122 18 E
Madama 123 22 0N 13 40 E
Madame I. 143 45 30N 60 58W
Madan 47 41 30N 24 57 E
Madanapalle 81 13 33N 78 28 E
Madang 107 5 12 S 145 49 E
Madaoua 127 14 5N 6 27 E
Madara 127 11 45N 10 35 E
Madaripur 82 23 19N 90 15 E
Madauk 82 17 56N 96 52 E
Madawaska 150 45 30N 78 0W
Madawaska → 150 45 27N 76 21W
Madaya 82 22 12N 96 10 E
Madbar 125 6 17N 30 45 E
Maddalena, La 44 41 13N 9 25 E
Maddaloni 45 41 4N 14 23 E
Made 23 51 41N 4 49 E
Madeira, Atl. Oc. 120 32 50N 17 0W
Madeira, U.S.A. 155 39 11N 84 22W
Madeira → 169 3 22 S 58 45W
Madeleine, Is. de la 143 47 30N 61 40W
Madera 158 36 58N 120 1W
Madgaon 81 15 12N 73 58 E
Madha 80 18 0N 75 30 E
Madhubani 79 26 21N 86 7 E
Madhumati → 82 22 53N 89 52 E
Madhya Pradesh □ 78 21 50N 81 0 E
Madian 97 33 0N 116 6 E
Madidi → 172 12 32 S 66 52W
Madikeri 81 12 30N 75 45 E
Madill 153 34 5N 96 49W
Madimba, Angola 133 6 36 S 14 23 E
Madimba, Zaïre 133 5 0 S 15 0 E
Ma'din 72 35 45N 39 36 E
Madīnat ash Sha'b 74 12 50N 45 0 E
Madingou 132 4 10 S 13 33 E
Madīq Gûbâl 71 27 47N 33 55 E
Madīq Tirân 71 27 55N 34 30 E
Madirovalo 135 16 26 S 46 32 E
Madison, Calif., U.S.A. 158 38 41N 121 59W
Madison, Fla., U.S.A. 149 30 29N 83 39W
Madison, Ind., U.S.A. 155 38 42N 85 20W
Madison, Mo., U.S.A. 154 39 28N 92 13W
Madison, Nebr., U.S.A. 152 41 53N 97 25W
Madison, Ohio, U.S.A. 150 41 45N 81 4W
Madison, S. Dak., U.S.A. 152 44 0N 97 8W
Madison, Wis., U.S.A. 154 43 5N 89 25W
Madison → 156 45 56N 111 30W
Madisonville, Ky., U.S.A. 148 37 20N 87 30W
Madisonville, Tex., U.S.A. 153 30 57N 95 55W
Madista 134 21 15 S 25 6 E
Madiun 89 7 38 S 111 32 E
Madley 13 52 3N 2 51W
Madol 125 9 3N 27 45 E
Madon → 19 48 36N 6 6 E
Madona 58 56 53N 26 5 E
Madonie, Le 44 37 50N 13 50 E
Madrakah, Ra's al 75 19 0N 57 50 E
Madras = Tamil Nadu □ 81 11 0N 77 0 E
Madras, India 81 13 8N 80 19 E
Madras, U.S.A. 156 44 40N 121 10W
Madre, L., Mexico 161 25 0N 97 30W
Madre, L., U.S.A. 153 26 0N 97 40W
Madre, Sierra, Mexico 161 16 0N 93 0W
Madre, Sierra, Phil. 90 17 0N 122 0 E
Madre de Dios □ 172 12 0 S 70 15W
Madre de Dios → 172 10 59 S 66 8W
Madre de Dios, I. 176 50 20 S 75 10W
Madre del Sur, Sierra 161 17 30N 100 0W
Madre Occidental, Sierra 160 27 0N 107 0W
Madre Oriental, Sierra 160 25 0N 100 0W
Madri 78 24 16N 73 32 E
Madrid, Spain 34 40 25N 3 45W
Madrid, U.S.A. 154 41 53N 93 49W
Madrid □ 34 40 30N 3 45W
Madridejos 35 39 28N 3 33W
Madrigal de las Altas Torres 34 41 5N 5 0W
Madrona, Sierra 35 38 27N 4 16W
Madroñera 35 39 26N 5 42W
Madu 125 14 37N 26 4 E
Madura, Selat 89 7 30 S 113 20 E
Madura Motel 109 31 55 S 127 0 E
Madurai 81 9 55N 78 10 E
Madurantakam 81 12 30N 79 50 E
Madzhalis 61 42 9N 47 47 E
Mae Chan 84 20 9N 99 52 E
Mae Hong Son 84 19 16N 98 1 E
Mae Khlong → 84 13 24N 100 0 E
Mae Phrik 84 17 27N 99 7 E
Mae Ramat 84 16 58N 98 31 E
Mae Rim 84 18 54N 98 57 E
Mae Sot 84 16 43N 98 34 E
Mae Suai 84 19 39N 99 33 E
Mae Tha 84 18 28N 99 8 E
Maebaru 100 33 33N 130 12 E
Maebashi 101 36 24N 139 4 E
Maella 36 41 8N 0 7 E
Măeruş 50 45 53N 25 31 E
Maesteg 13 51 36N 3 40W
Maestra, Sierra 162 20 15N 77 0W
Maestrazgo, Mts. del 36 40 30N 0 25W
Maestre de Campo I. 90 12 56N 121 42 E
Maevatanana 135 16 56 S 46 49 E
Ma'fan 122 25 56N 14 29 E
Mafeking 145 52 40N 101 10W
Maféré 126 5 30N 3 2W
Mafeteng 134 29 51 S 27 15 E
Maffe 23 50 21N 5 19 E
Maffra 113 37 53 S 146 58 E
Mafia I. 130 7 45 S 39 50 E
Mafikeng 134 25 50 S 25 38 E
Mafra, Brazil 175 26 10 S 50 0W
Mafra, Portugal 35 38 55N 9 20W
Mafungabusi Plateau 131 18 30 S 29 8 E
Magadan 65 59 38N 150 50 E
Magadi 130 1 54 S 36 19 E
Magadi, L. 130 1 54 S 36 19 E
Magaliesburg 135 26 0 S 27 32 E
Magallanes 90 12 50N 123 50 E
Magallanes □ 176 52 0 S 72 0W
Magallanes, Estrecho de 176 52 30 S 75 0W
Magangué 168 9 14N 74 45W
Maganoy 91 6 51N 124 31 E
Mağara 70 36 43N 33 52 E
Magaria 127 13 4N 9 5 E
Magburaka 126 8 47N 12 0W
Magdalena, Argentina 174 35 5 S 57 30W
Magdalena, Bolivia 173 13 13 S 63 57W
Magdalena, Malaysia 86 4 25N 117 55 E
Magdalena, Mexico 160 30 50N 112 0W
Magdalena, U.S.A. 157 34 10N 107 20W
Magdalena □ 168 10 0N 74 0W
Magdalena →, Colombia 168 11 6N 74 51W
Magdalena →, Mexico 160 30 40N 112 25W
Magdalena, B. 160 24 30N 112 10W
Magdalena, I. 176 44 40 S 73 0W
Magdalena, Llano de la 160 25 0N 111 30W
Magdeburg 26 52 8N 11 36 E
Magdeburg □ 26 52 20N 11 30 E
Magdelaine Cays 110 16 33 S 150 18 E
Magdi'el 69 32 10N 34 54 E
Magdub 125 13 42N 25 5 E
Magee 153 31 53N 89 45W
Magee, I. 15 54 48N 5 44W
Magelang 89 7 29 S 110 13 E
Magellan's Str. = Magallanes, Estrecho de 176 52 30 S 75 0W
Magenta, Australia 112 33 51 S 143 34 E
Magenta, Italy 42 45 28N 8 53 E
Magenta, L. 109 33 30 S 119 2 E
Maggea 112 34 28 S 140 2 E
Maggia 29 46 15N 8 42 E
Maggia → 29 46 18N 8 36 E
Maggiorasca, Mte. 42 44 33N 9 29 E
Maggiore, L. 42 46 0N 8 35 E
Maghama 126 15 32N 12 57W
Maghār 69 32 54N 35 24 E
Magherafelt 15 54 44N 6 37W
Maghnia 121 34 50N 1 43W
Magione 43 43 10N 12 12 E
Maglaj 46 44 33N 18 7 E
Magliano in Toscana 43 42 36N 11 18 E
Máglie 45 40 8N 18 17 E
Magnac-Laval 20 46 13N 1 11 E
Magnetic Pole (North) 6 77 5N 102 6W
Magnetic Pole (South) 7 65 2 S 139 4 E

Maratua

Man → **80** 17 31N 75 32 E
Man, I. of **12** 54 15N 4 30W
Man Na **82** 23 27N 97 19 E
Man Tun **82** 23 52N 98 38 E
Mana **169** 5 45N 53 55W
Mana →, Fr. Gui. **169** 5 45N 53 55W
Måna →, Norway **51** 59 55N 8 50 E
Manaar, Gulf of = Mannar, G. of **81** 8 30N 79 0 E
Manabí □ **168** 0 40S 80 5W
Manacacías → **168** 4 23N 72 4W
Manacapuru **169** 3 16S 60 37W
Manacapuru → **169** 3 18S 60 37W
Manacor **36** 39 34N 3 13 E
Manado **87** 1 29N 124 51 E
Manage **23** 50 31N 4 15 E
Managua **162** 12 6N 86 20W
Managua, L. **162** 12 20N 86 30W
Manaia **114** 39 33S 174 8 E
Manakara **135** 22 8S 48 1 E
Manakau Mt. **115** 42 15S 173 42 E
Manākhah **74** 15 5N 43 44 E
Manam I. **107** 4 5S 145 0 E
Manambao → **135** 17 35S 44 0 E
Manambato **135** 13 43S 49 7 E
Manambolo → **135** 19 18S 44 22 E
Manambolosy **135** 16 2S 49 40 E
Mananara **135** 16 10S 49 46 E
Mananara → **135** 23 21S 47 42 E
Mananjary **135** 21 13S 48 20 E
Manantenina **135** 24 17S 47 19 E
Manaos = Manaus **169** 3 0S 60 0W
Manapala **91** 10 58N 123 5 E
Manapire → **168** 7 42N 66 7W
Manapouri **115** 45 34S 167 39 E
Manapouri, L. **115** 45 32S 167 32 E
Manar → **80** 18 50N 77 20 E
Manār, Jabal **74** 14 2N 44 17 E
Manas, China **92** 44 17N 85 56 E
Manas, Somalia **136** 2 57N 43 28 E
Manas, Gora **63** 42 22N 71 2 E
Manaslu, Mt. **79** 28 33N 84 33 E
Manasquan **151** 40 7N 74 3W
Manassa **157** 37 12N 105 58W
Manaung **82** 18 45N 93 40 E
Manaus **169** 3 0S 60 0W
Manavgat **70** 36 47N 31 26 E
Manavgat → **70** 36 43N 31 27 E
Manawan L. **145** 55 24N 103 14W
Manawatu → **114** 40 28S 175 12 E
Manay **91** 7 17N 126 33 E
Manbij **72** 36 31N 37 57 E
Mancelona **148** 44 54N 85 5W
Mancha, La **37** 39 10N 2 54W
Mancha Real **35** 37 48N 3 39W
Manche □ **18** 49 10N 1 20W
Manchegorsk **56** 67 40N 32 40 E
Manchester, U.K. **12** 53 30N 2 15W
Manchester, Calif., U.S.A. **158** 38 58N 123 41W
Manchester, Conn., U.S.A. **151** 41 47N 72 30W
Manchester, Ga., U.S.A. **149** 32 53N 84 32W
Manchester, Iowa, U.S.A. **154** 42 28N 91 27W
Manchester, Ky., U.S.A. **148** 37 9N 83 45W
Manchester, Mich., U.S.A. **155** 42 9N 84 2W
Manchester, N.H., U.S.A. **151** 42 58N 71 29W
Manchester, N.Y., U.S.A. **150** 42 56N 77 16W
Manchester, Vt., U.S.A. **151** 43 10N 73 5W
Manchester L. **145** 61 28N 107 29W
Manchuria = Dongbei **95** 42 0N 125 0 E
Manciano **43** 42 35N 11 30 E
Mancifa **125** 6 53N 41 50 E
Mancora, Pta. **172** 4 9S 81 1W
Mand → **73** 28 20N 52 30 E
Manda, Chunya, Tanzania **130** 6 51S 32 29 E
Manda, Ludewe, Tanzania **131** 10 30S 34 40 E
Mandabé **135** 21 0S 44 55 E
Mandaguari **175** 23 32S 51 42W
Mandah **94** 44 27N 108 2 E
Mandal **51** 58 2N 7 25 E
Mandalay **82** 22 0N 96 4 E
Mandale = Mandalay **82** 22 0N 96 4 E
Mandalgovi **94** 45 45N 106 10 E
Mandalī **72** 33 43N 45 28 E
Mandalya Körfezi **49** 37 15N 27 20 E
Mandan **152** 46 50N 101 0W
Mandaon **90** 12 13N 123 17 E
Mandapeta **80** 16 47N 81 56 E
Mandar, Teluk **87** 3 35S 119 15 E
Mandas **44** 39 40N 9 8 E
Mandasor = Mandsaur **78** 24 3N 75 8 E
Mandayar **91** 7 34N 126 14 E
Mandelieu-la-Napoule **21** 43 34N 6 57 E
Mandera **130** 3 55N 41 53 E
Mandera □ **130** 3 30N 41 0 E
Manderfeld **23** 50 20N 6 20 E
Mandi **78** 31 39N 76 58 E
Mandimba **131** 14 20S 35 40 E
Mandioli **87** 0 40S 127 20 E
Mandioré, L. **173** 18 8S 57 33W
Mandji I. = Lopez I. **132** 0 50S 8 47 E
Mandla **79** 22 39N 80 30 E
Mandø **53** 55 18N 8 33 E
Mandoto **135** 19 34S 46 17 E
Mandoúdhion **49** 38 48N 23 29 E
Mandra **78** 33 23N 73 12 E
Mandráki **49** 36 36N 27 11 E
Mandrare → **135** 25 10S 46 30 E
Mandritsara **135** 15 50S 48 49 E
Mandsaur **78** 24 3N 75 8 E
Mandurah **109** 32 36S 115 48 E
Mandúria **45** 40 25N 17 38 E
Mandvi **78** 22 51N 69 22 E
Mandya **81** 12 30N 77 0 E
Mandzai **78** 30 55N 67 6 E
Mané **127** 12 59N 1 21W
Maneh **73** 37 39N 57 7 E
Manengouba, Mts. **127** 5 0N 9 50 E
Maner → **80** 18 30N 79 40 E
Maneroo **110** 23 22S 143 53 E
Maneroo Cr. → **110** 23 21S 143 53 E
Manfalût **124** 27 20N 30 52 E
Manfred **112** 33 19S 143 45 E
Manfredónia **45** 41 40N 15 55 E
Manfredónia, G. di **45** 41 30N 16 10 E
Manga, Brazil **171** 14 46S 43 56W
Manga, Burkina Faso **127** 11 40N 1 4W
Manga, Niger **127** 15 0N 14 0 E
Mangabeiras, Chapada das **170** 10 0S 46 30W
Mangal **91** 6 25N 121 58 E
Mangalagiri **81** 16 26N 80 36 E
Mangaldai **82** 26 26N 92 2 E
Mangalia **50** 43 50N 28 35 E
Mangalore, Australia **113** 36 56S 145 10 E
Mangalore, India **81** 12 55N 74 47 E
Manganeses **34** 41 45N 5 43W
Mangaon **80** 18 15N 73 20 E
Mange **132** 0 54N 20 30 E
Manger **51** 60 38N 5 3 E
Manggar **89** 2 50S 108 10 E
Manggawitu **87** 4 8S 133 32 E
Mangin Range **82** 24 15N 95 45 E
Mangkalihat, Tanjung **89** 1 2N 118 59 E
Mangla Dam **79** 33 9N 73 44 E
Manglares, C. **168** 1 36N 79 2W
Manglaur **78** 29 44N 77 49 E
Mangnai **92** 37 52N 91 43 E
Mango **127** 10 20N 0 30 E
Mangoche **131** 14 25S 35 16 E
Mangoky → **135** 21 29S 43 41 E
Mangole **87** 1 50S 125 55 E
Mangombe **130** 1 20S 26 48 E
Mangonui **114** 35 1S 173 32 E
Mangualde **34** 40 38N 7 48W
Mangueigne **123** 10 30N 21 15 E
Mangueira, L. da **175** 33 0S 52 50W
Manguéni, Hamada **122** 22 35N 12 40 E
Mangum **153** 34 50N 99 30W
Mangyshlak Poluostrov **61** 44 30N 52 30 E
Mangyshlakskiy Zaliv **61** 44 40N 50 50 E
Manhattan **152** 39 10N 96 40W
Manhatten **155** 41 26N 87 59W
Manhiça **135** 25 23S 32 49 E
Manhuaçu **171** 20 15S 42 2W
Manhumirim **171** 20 22S 41 57W
Maní **168** 4 49N 72 17W
Mania → **135** 19 42S 45 22 E
Maniago **43** 46 11N 12 40 E
Manica **135** 18 58S 32 59 E
Manica e Sofala □ **135** 19 10S 33 45 E
Manicaland □ **131** 19 0S 32 30 E
Manicoré **173** 5 48S 61 16W
Manicoré → **173** 5 51S 61 19W
Manicouagan → **143** 49 30N 68 30W
Manīfah **73** 27 44N 49 0 E
Manifold **110** 22 41S 150 40 E
Manifold, C. **110** 22 41S 150 50 E
Maniganggo **96** 31 56N 99 10 E
Manigotagan **145** 51 6N 96 18W
Manihiki **105** 10 24S 161 1W
Manika, Plateau de la **131** 10 0S 25 5 E
Manikganj **82** 23 52N 90 0 E
Manila, Phil. **90** 14 40N 121 3 E
Manila, U.S.A. **156** 41 0N 109 44W
Manila Bay **90** 14 0N 120 0 E
Manilla **111** 30 45S 150 43 E
Manimpé **126** 14 11N 5 28W
Manipur □ **82** 25 0N 94 0 E
Manipur → **82** 23 45N 94 20 E
Manisa **57** 38 38N 27 30 E
Manistee **148** 44 15N 86 20W
Manistee → **148** 44 15N 86 21W
Manistique **148** 45 59N 86 18W
Manito **154** 40 25N 89 47W
Manito L. **145** 52 43N 109 43W
Manitoba □ **145** 55 30N 97 0W
Manitoba, L. **145** 51 0N 98 45W
Manitou **145** 49 15N 98 32W
Manitou Beach **155** 41 58N 84 19W
Manitou I. **142** 47 22N 87 30W
Manitou Is. **148** 45 8N 86 0W
Manitou L. **143** 50 55N 65 17W
Manitou Springs **152** 38 52N 104 55W
Manitoulin I. **142** 45 40N 82 30W
Manitowaning **142** 45 46N 81 49W
Manitowoc **148** 44 8N 87 40W
Manitsauá-Missu → **173** 10 58S 53 20W
Manizales **168** 5 5N 75 32W
Manja **135** 21 26S 44 20 E
Manjacaze **135** 24 45S 34 0 E
Manjakandriana **135** 18 55S 47 47 E
Manjeri **81** 11 7N 76 11 E
Manjhand **77** 25 50N 68 10 E
Manjil **73** 36 46N 49 30 E
Manjimup **109** 34 15S 116 6 E
Manjra → **80** 18 49N 77 52 E
Mankato, Kans., U.S.A. **152** 39 49N 98 11W
Mankato, Minn., U.S.A. **152** 44 8N 93 59W
Mankayan **90** 16 52N 120 47 E
Mankayane **135** 26 40S 31 4 E
Mankono **126** 8 1N 6 10W
Mankota **145** 49 25N 107 5W
Manlay **94** 44 9N 107 0 E
Manlleu **36** 42 2N 2 17 E
Manly **113** 33 48S 151 17 E
Manmad **80** 20 18N 74 28 E
Mann Ranges, Mts. **109** 26 6S 130 5 E
Manna **88** 4 25S 102 55 E
Mannahill **112** 32 25S 140 0 E
Mannar **81** 9 1N 79 54 E
Mannar, G. of **81** 8 30N 79 0 E
Mannar I. **81** 9 5N 79 45 E
Mannargudi **81** 10 45N 79 51 E
Mannduque □ **90** 13 18N 122 0 E
Männedorf **29** 47 15N 8 43 E
Mannheim **27** 49 28N 8 29 E
Manning, Canada **144** 56 53N 117 39W
Manning, Oreg., U.S.A. **158** 45 45N 123 13W
Manning, S.C., U.S.A. **149** 33 40N 80 9W
Manning Prov. Park **144** 49 5N 120 45W
Mannington **148** 39 35N 80 25W
Mannu → **44** 39 15N 9 32 E
Mannu, C. **44** 40 2N 8 24 E
Mannum **112** 34 50S 139 20 E
Mano **126** 8 3N 12 2W
Manoa **173** 9 40S 65 27W
Manokwari **87** 0 54S 134 0 E
Manolás **49** 38 4N 21 21 E
Manolo Fortich **91** 8 28N 124 50 E
Manombo **135** 22 57S 43 28 E
Manono **130** 7 15S 27 25 E
Manosque **21** 43 49N 5 47 E
Manouane, L. **143** 50 45N 70 45W
Manpojin **95** 41 6N 126 24 E
Manresa **36** 41 48N 1 50 E
Mans, Le **18** 48 0N 0 10 E
Mansa, Gujarat, India **78** 23 27N 72 45 E
Mansa, Punjab, India **78** 30 0N 75 27 E
Mansa, Zambia **131** 11 13S 28 55 E
Mansalay **90** 12 31N 121 26 E
Mansehra **78** 34 20N 73 15 E
Mansel I. **141** 62 0N 80 0W
Mansfield, Australia **113** 37 4S 146 6 E
Mansfield, U.K. **12** 53 8N 1 12W
Mansfield, La., U.S.A. **153** 32 2N 93 40W
Mansfield, Mass., U.S.A. **151** 42 2N 71 12W
Mansfield, Ohio, U.S.A. **150** 40 45N 82 30W
Mansfield, Pa., U.S.A. **150** 41 48N 77 4W
Mansfield, Wash., U.S.A. **156** 47 51N 119 44W
Mansi **82** 24 48N 95 52 E
Mansidão **170** 10 43S 44 2W
Mansilla de las Mulas **34** 42 30N 5 25W
Mansle **20** 45 52N 0 12 E
Manso → **171** 13 50S 47 0W
Mansoa **126** 12 0N 15 20W
Manson **154** 42 32N 94 32W
Manson Creek **144** 55 37N 124 32W
Mansoura **121** 36 1N 4 31 E
Manta **168** 1 0S 80 40W
Manta, B. de **168** 0 54S 80 44W
Mantalingajan, Mt. **91** 8 55N 117 45 E
Mantare **130** 2 42S 33 13 E
Manteca **158** 37 50N 121 12W
Mantecal **168** 7 34N 69 17W
Mantena **171** 18 47S 40 59W
Manteno **155** 41 15N 87 50W
Manteo **149** 35 55N 75 41W
Mantes-la-Jolie **19** 49 0N 1 41 E
Manthani **80** 18 40N 79 35 E
Manthelan **18** 47 9N 0 47 E
Manti **156** 39 23N 111 32W
Mantiqueira, Serra da **175** 22 0S 44 0W
Manton **148** 44 23N 85 25W
Mantorp **53** 58 21N 15 20 E
Mántova **42** 45 20N 10 42 E
Mänttä **54** 62 0N 24 40 E
Mantua = Mántova **42** 45 20N 10 42 E
Mantung **112** 34 35S 140 3 E
Manturovo **59** 58 30N 44 30 E
Manu **172** 12 10S 70 51W
Manu → **172** 12 16S 70 55W
Manua Is. **106** 14 13S 169 35W
Manuae **105** 19 30S 159 0W
Manuel Alves → **171** 11 19S 48 28W
Manuel Alves Grande → **170** 7 27S 47 35W
Manuel Urbano **172** 8 53S 69 18W
Manui **87** 3 35S 123 5 E
Manukau **114** 37 1S 174 55 E
Manukau Harbour **114** 37 3S 174 45 E
Manunui **114** 38 54S 175 21 E
Manuripi → **172** 11 6S 67 36W
Manus I. **107** 2 0S 147 0 E
Manvi **81** 15 57N 76 59 E
Manville **152** 42 48N 104 36W
Manwath **80** 19 19N 76 32 E
Many **153** 31 36N 93 28W
Manyara, L. **130** 3 40S 35 50 E
Manych → **61** 47 15N 40 0 E
Manych-Gudilo, Oz. **61** 46 24N 42 38 E
Manyonga → **130** 4 10S 34 15 E
Manyoni **130** 5 45S 34 55 E
Manyoni □ **130** 6 30S 34 30 E
Manzai **77** 32 12N 70 15 E
Manzala, Bahra el **124** 31 10N 31 56 E
Manzanares **37** 39 0N 3 22W
Manzaneda, Cabeza de **34** 42 12N 7 15W
Manzanillo, Cuba **162** 20 20N 77 31W
Manzanillo, Mexico **160** 19 0N 104 20W
Manzanillo, Pta. **162** 9 30N 79 40W
Manzano Mts. **157** 34 30N 106 45W
Manzarīyeh **73** 34 53N 50 50 E
Manzhouli **93** 49 35N 117 25 E
Manzini **135** 26 30S 31 25 E
Mao **123** 14 4N 15 19 E
Maoke, Pegunungan **87** 3 40S 137 30 E
Maolin **95** 43 58N 123 30 E
Maoming **97** 21 50N 110 54 E
Maowen **96** 31 41N 103 49 E
Maoxing **95** 45 28N 124 40 E
Mapam Yumco **79** 30 45N 81 28 E
Mapastepec **161** 15 26N 92 54W
Mapia, Kepulauan **87** 0 50N 134 20 E
Mapimí **160** 25 50N 103 50W
Mapimí, Bolsón de **160** 27 30N 104 15W
Maping **97** 31 34N 113 32 E
Mapinga **130** 6 40S 39 12 E
Mapinhane **135** 22 20S 35 0 E
Mapire **169** 7 45N 64 42W
Maple → **155** 42 58N 84 56W
Maple Creek **145** 49 55N 109 29W
Maple Valley **158** 47 25N 122 3W
Mapleton **156** 44 4N 123 58W
Maprik **107** 3 44S 143 3 E
Mapuca **81** 15 36N 73 46 E
Mapuera → **169** 1 5S 57 2W
Maputing Baybay **90** 12 45N 123 20 E
Maputo **135** 25 58S 32 32 E
Maputo, B. de **135** 25 50S 32 45 E
Maqiaohe **95** 44 40N 130 30 E
Maqnā **71** 28 25N 34 50 E
Maqran, W. → **74** 20 55N 47 12 E
Maqteïr **120** 21 50N 11 40W
Maqueda Channel **90** 13 42N 124 1 E
Maquela do Zombo **133** 6 0S 15 15 E
Maquinchao **176** 41 15S 68 50W
Maquoketa **154** 42 4N 90 40W
Mår → **51** 59 59N 8 46 E
Mar, Serra do **175** 25 30S 49 0W
Mar Chiquita, L. **174** 30 40S 62 50W
Mar del Plata **174** 38 0S 57 30W
Mar Menor, L. **37** 37 40N 0 45W
Mara, Guyana **169** 6 0N 57 36W
Mara, India **82** 28 11N 94 14 E
Mara, Tanzania **130** 1 30S 34 32 E
Mara □ **130** 1 45S 34 20 E
Maraã **168** 1 52S 65 25W
Marabá **170** 5 20S 49 5W
Maracá, I. de **170** 2 10N 50 30W
Maracaibo **168** 10 40N 71 37W
Maracaibo, L. de **168** 9 40N 71 30W
Maracaju **175** 21 38S 55 9W
Maracajú, Serra de **173** 23 57S 55 1W
Maracanã **170** 0 46S 47 27W
Maracás **171** 13 26S 40 18W
Maracay **168** 10 15N 67 28W
Marādah **122** 29 15N 19 15 E
Maradi **127** 13 29N 7 20 E
Maradun **127** 12 35N 6 18 E
Marāgheh **72** 37 30N 46 12 E
Maragogipe **171** 12 46S 38 55W
Maragondon **90** 14 16N 120 44 E
Marāh **72** 25 0N 45 35 E
Marajó, B. de **170** 1 0S 48 30W
Marajó, I. de **170** 1 0S 49 30W
Marākand **72** 38 51N 45 16 E
Maralal **130** 1 0N 36 38 E
Maralinga **109** 30 13S 131 32 E
Marama **112** 35 10S 140 10 E
Marampa **126** 8 45N 12 28W
Maramureș □ **50** 47 45N 24 0 E
Maran **85** 3 35N 102 45 E
Marana **157** 32 30N 111 9W
Maranboy **108** 14 40S 132 39 E
Maranchón **36** 41 6N 2 15W
Marand **72** 38 30N 45 45 E
Marang **85** 5 12N 103 13 E
Maranguape **170** 3 55S 38 50W
Maranhão = São Luís **170** 2 39S 44 15W
Maranhão □ **170** 5 0S 46 0W
Marano, L. di **43** 45 42N 13 13 E
Maranoa → **111** 27 50S 148 37 E
Marañón → **172** 4 30S 73 35W
Marão **135** 24 18S 34 2 E
Marapi → **169** 0 37N 55 58W
Marari **172** 5 43S 67 47W
Maraş **57** 37 37N 36 53 E
Mărășești **50** 45 52N 27 14 E
Maratea **45** 39 59N 15 43 E
Marateca **35** 38 34N 8 40W
Marathókambos **49** 37 43N 26 42 E
Marathon, Australia **110** 20 51S 143 32 E
Marathon, Canada **142** 48 44N 86 23W
Marathón, Greece **49** 38 11N 23 58 E
Marathon, Iowa, U.S.A. **154** 42 52N 94 59W
Marathon, N.Y., U.S.A. **151** 42 25N 76 3W
Marathon, Tex., U.S.A. **153** 30 15N 103 15W
Maratua **89** 2 10N 118 35 E

Médégué

Maski 81 15 56N 76 46 E
Maslen Nos 47 42 18N 27 48 E
Maslinica 43 43 24N 16 13 E
Maşna'ah 75 14 27N 48 17 E
Masnou 36 41 28N 2 20 E
Masoala, Tanjon' i 135 15 59 S 50 13 E
Masoarivo 135 19 3 S 44 19 E
Masohi 87 3 20 S 128 55 E
Masomeloka 135 20 17 S 48 37 E
Mason, Mich., U.S.A. 155 42 35N 84 27W
Mason, Nev., U.S.A. 158 38 56N 119 8W
Mason, Ohio, U.S.A. 155 39 22N 84 19W
Mason, Tex., U.S.A. 153 30 45N 99 15W
Mason B. 115 46 55 S 167 45 E
Mason City, Ill., U.S.A. 154 40 12N 89 42W
Mason City, Iowa, U.S.A. 154 43 9N 93 12W
Maspalomas 37 27 46N 15 35W
Maspalomas, Pta. 37 27 43N 15 36W
Masqat 75 23 37N 58 36 E
Massa, Congo 132 3 45 S 15 29 E
Massa, Italy 42 44 2N 10 7 E
Massa, O. → 120 30 2N 9 40W
Massa Maríttima 42 43 3N 10 52 E
Massachusetts □ 151 42 25N 72 0W
Massachusetts B. 151 42 30N 70 0W
Massada 69 33 41N 35 36 E
Massafra 45 40 35N 17 8 E
Massaguet 123 12 28N 15 26 E
Massah Kānlī 70 36 42N 36 39 E
Massakory 123 13 0N 15 49 E
Massangena 135 21 34 S 33 0 E
Massapê 170 3 31 S 40 19W
Massarosa 42 43 53N 10 17 E
Massat 20 42 53N 1 21 E
Massava 62 60 40N 62 6 E
Massawa = Mitsiwa 125 15 35N 39 25 E
Massena 151 44 52N 74 55W
Massénya 123 11 21N 16 9 E
Masset 144 54 2N 132 10W
Massiac 20 45 15N 3 11 E
Massif Central 20 45 30N 3 0 E
Massillon 150 40 47N 81 30W
Massinga 135 23 15 S 35 22 E
Masson 151 45 32N 75 25W
Masson I. 7 66 10 S 93 20 E
Mastābah 74 20 49N 39 26 E
Mastanli = Momchilgrad 47 41 33N 25 23 E
Masterton 114 40 56 S 175 39 E
Mástikho, Ákra 49 38 10N 26 2 E
Mastuj 79 36 20N 72 36 E
Mastung 77 29 50N 66 56 E
Mastūrah 74 23 7N 38 52 E
Masuda 100 34 40N 131 51 E
Masuika 133 7 37 S 22 32 E
Masvingo 131 20 8 S 30 49 E
Masvingo □ 131 21 0 S 31 30 E
Maswa □ 130 3 30 S 34 0 E
Maşyāf 70 35 4N 36 20 E
Mata de São João 171 12 31 S 38 17W
Matabeleland North □ 131 19 0 S 28 0 E
Matabeleland South □ 131 21 0 S 29 0 E
Mataboor 87 1 41 S 138 3 E
Matachel → 35 38 50N 6 17W
Matachewan 142 47 56N 80 39W
Matacuni → 169 3 2N 65 16W
Matadi 133 5 52 S 13 31 E
Matagalpa 162 13 0N 85 58W
Matagami 142 49 45N 77 34W
Matagami, L. 142 49 50N 77 40W
Matagorda 153 28 43N 96 0W
Matagorda B. 153 28 30N 96 15W
Matagorda I. 153 28 10N 96 40W
Mataguinao 90 12 5N 124 55 E
Matak, P. 85 3 18N 106 16 E
Matakana 113 32 59 S 145 54 E
Matala 133 14 46 S 15 4 E
Matalaque 172 16 26 S 70 49W
Matale 81 7 30N 80 37 E
Matam, Phil. 91 8 25N 123 19 E
Matam, Senegal 126 15 34N 13 17W
Matamata 114 37 48 S 175 47 E
Matameye 127 13 26N 8 28 E
Matamoros, Campeche, Mexico 161 18 50N 90 50W
Matamoros, Coahuila, Mexico 160 25 33N 103 15W
Matamoros, Puebla, Mexico 161 18 2N 98 17W
Matamoros, Tamaulipas, Mexico 161 25 50N 97 30W
Ma'ṭan as Sarra 123 21 45N 22 0 E
Matandu → 131 8 45 S 34 19 E
Matane 143 48 50N 67 33W
Matang 96 23 30N 104 7 E
Matankari 127 13 46N 4 1 E
Matanuska 140 61 39N 149 19W
Matanzas 162 23 0N 81 40W
Matapan, C. = Taínaron, Ákra 49 36 22N 22 27 E
Matapédia 143 48 0N 66 59W
Matara 81 5 58N 80 30 E
Mataram 89 8 41 S 116 10 E
Matarani 172 77 0 S 72 10W
Mataranka 108 14 55 S 133 4 E
Matarma, Râs 71 30 27N 32 44 E
Mataró 36 41 32N 2 29 E
Matarraña → 36 41 14N 0 22 E
Mataruška Banja 46 43 40N 20 45 E
Matata 114 37 54 S 176 48 E
Matatiele 135 30 20 S 28 49 E
Mataura 115 46 11 S 168 51 E
Mataura → 115 46 34 S 168 44 E
Mategua 173 13 1 S 62 48W
Matehuala 160 23 40N 100 40W
Mateira 171 18 54 S 50 30W
Mateke Hills 131 21 48 S 31 0 E
Matélica 43 43 15N 13 0 E
Matera 45 40 40N 16 37 E
Mátészalka 31 47 58N 22 20 E
Matetsi 131 18 12 S 26 0 E
Mateur 122 37 0N 9 40 E
Matfors 52 62 21N 17 2 E
Matha 20 45 52N 0 20W
Matheson Island 145 51 45N 96 56W
Mathis 153 28 4N 97 48W
Mathoura 113 35 50 S 144 55 E
Mathura 78 27 30N 77 40 E
Mati 91 6 55N 126 15 E
Mati → 48 41 40N 20 0 E
Matías Romero 161 16 53N 95 2W
Matibane 131 14 49 S 40 45 E
Matican 91 6 39N 121 53 E
Matima 134 20 15 S 24 26 E
Matlock 12 53 8N 1 32W
Matmata 121 33 37N 9 59 E
Matna 125 13 49N 35 10 E
Matnog 90 12 35N 124 5 E
Mato → 169 7 9N 65 7W
Mato, Serrania de 168 6 25N 65 25W
Mato Grosso □ 173 14 0 S 55 0W
Mato Grosso, Planalto do 173 15 0 S 59 57W
Matochkin Shar 64 73 10N 56 40 E
Matong 107 5 36 S 151 50 E
Matopo Hills 131 20 36 S 28 20 E
Matopos 131 20 20 S 28 29 E
Matosinhos 34 41 11N 8 42W
Matour 21 46 19N 4 29 E
Matrah 75 23 37N 58 30 E
Matsena 127 13 5N 10 5 E
Matsesta 61 43 34N 39 51 E
Matsubara 101 34 33N 135 34 E
Matsudo 101 35 47N 139 54 E
Matsue 100 35 25N 133 10 E
Matsumae 98 41 26N 140 7 E
Matsumoto 101 36 15N 138 0 E
Matsusaka 101 34 34N 136 32 E
Matsutō 101 36 31N 136 34 E
Matsuura 100 33 20N 129 49 E
Matsuyama 100 33 45N 132 45 E
Matsuzaki 101 34 43N 138 50 E
Mattagami → 142 50 43N 81 29W
Mattancheri 81 9 50N 76 15 E
Mattawa 142 46 20N 78 45W
Mattawamkeag 143 45 30N 68 21W
Matterhorn 28 45 58N 7 39 E
Mattersburg 31 47 44N 16 24 E
Matteson 155 41 30N 87 42W
Matthew Town 163 20 57N 73 40W
Matthews 155 40 23N 85 31W
Matthew's Ridge 169 7 37N 60 10W
Mattice 142 49 40N 83 20W
Mattituck 151 40 58N 72 32W
Mattmar 52 63 18N 13 45 E
Matuba 135 24 28 S 32 49 E
Matucana 172 11 55 S 76 25W
Matuku 106 19 10 S 179 44 E
Matun 78 33 22N 69 58 E
Maturín 169 9 45N 63 11W
Matutum, Mt. 91 6 22N 125 5 E
Matveyev Kurgan 61 47 35N 38 47 E
Mau 79 25 56N 83 33 E
Mau Escarpment 130 0 40 S 36 0 E
Mau Ranipur 79 25 16N 79 8 E
Mauban 90 14 12N 121 44 E
Maubeuge 19 50 17N 3 57 E
Maubourguet 20 43 29N 0 1 E
Maud, Pt. 108 23 6 S 113 45 E
Maude 112 34 29 S 144 18 E
Maudheim 7 71 5 S 11 0W
Maués 169 3 20 S 57 45W
Maui 146 20 45N 156 20 E
Maule □ 174 36 5 S 72 30W
Mauléon-Licharre 20 43 14N 0 54W
Maullín 176 41 38 S 73 37W
Maulvibazar 82 24 29N 91 42 E
Maumee 155 41 35N 83 40W
Maumee → 155 41 42N 83 28W
Maumere 87 8 38 S 122 13 E
Maun 134 20 0 S 23 26 E
Mauna Kea 146 19 50N 155 28W
Mauna Loa 146 21 8N 157 10W
Maungaturoto 114 36 6 S 174 23 E
Maungdow 82 20 50N 92 21 E
Maupin 156 45 12N 121 9W
Maure-de-Bretagne 18 47 53N 1 58W
Maurepas L. 153 30 18N 90 35W
Maures 21 43 15N 6 15 E
Mauriac 20 45 13N 2 19 E
Maurice L. 109 29 30 S 131 0 E
Mauriceville 114 40 45 S 175 42 E
Mauritania ■ 120 20 50N 10 0W
Mauritius ■ 83 20 0 S 57 0 E
Mauron 18 48 9N 2 18W
Maurs 20 44 43N 2 12 E
Mauston 152 43 48N 90 5W
Mauterndorf 30 47 9N 13 40 E
Mauvezin 20 43 44N 0 53 E
Mauzé-sur-le-Mignon 20 46 12N 0 41W
Mavaca → 169 2 31N 65 11W
Mavelikara 81 9 14N 76 32 E
Mavinga 133 15 50 S 20 21 E
Mavli 78 24 45N 73 55 E
Mavqi'im 69 31 38N 34 32 E
Mavrova 48 40 26N 19 32 E
Mavuradonha Mts. 131 16 30 S 31 30 E
Mawa 130 2 45N 26 40 E
Mawana 78 29 6N 77 58 E
Mawand 78 29 33N 68 38 E
Mawk Mai 82 20 14N 97 37 E
Mawlaik 82 23 40N 94 26 E
Mawlawkho 82 17 50N 97 38 E
Mawquq 72 27 25N 41 8 E
Mawshij 74 13 43N 43 17 E
Mawson Base 7 67 30 S 62 53 E
Mawson Coast 7 68 30 S 63 0 E
Max 152 47 50N 101 20W
Maxcanú 161 20 40N 92 0W
Maxesibeni 135 30 49 S 29 23 E
Maxhamish L. 144 59 50N 123 17W
Maxixe 135 23 54 S 35 17 E
Maxville 151 45 17N 74 51W
Maxwell, N.Z. 114 39 51 S 174 49 E
Maxwell, U.S.A. 158 39 17N 122 11W
Maxwelton 110 20 43 S 142 41 E
May Downs 110 22 38 S 148 55 E
May Pen 162 17 58N 77 15W
May River 107 4 19 S 141 58 E
Maya, Indonesia 89 1 10 S 109 35 E
Maya, Spain 36 43 12N 1 29W
Maya → 65 54 31N 134 41 E
Maya Mts. 161 16 30N 89 0W
Mayaguana 163 22 30N 72 44W
Mayagüez 163 18 12N 67 9W
Mayahi 127 13 58N 7 40 E
Mayals 36 41 22N 0 30 E
Mayama 132 3 51 S 14 54 E
Mayāmey 73 36 24N 55 42 E
Mayang 96 27 53N 109 49 E
Mayarí 163 20 40N 75 41W
Mayavaram = Mayuram 81 11 3N 79 42 E
Maybell 156 40 30N 108 4W
Maychew 125 12 50N 39 31 E
Maydān 72 34 55N 45 37 E
Maydena 110 42 45 S 146 30 E
Maydī 74 16 19N 42 48 E
Maydos 48 40 13N 26 20 E
Mayen 27 50 18N 7 10 E
Mayenne 18 48 20N 0 38W
Mayenne □ 18 48 10N 0 40W
Mayenne → 18 47 30N 0 32W
Mayer 157 34 28N 112 17W
Mayerthorpe 144 53 57N 115 8W
Mayfield 149 36 45N 88 40W
Mayhill 157 32 58N 105 30W
Maykop 61 44 35N 40 25 E
Mayli-Say 63 41 17N 72 24 E
Maymyo 84 22 2N 96 28 E
Maynard 158 47 59N 122 55W
Maynard Hills 109 28 28 S 119 49 E
Mayne → 110 23 40 S 141 55 E
Maynooth 15 53 22N 6 38W
Mayo 140 63 38N 135 57W
Mayo □ 15 53 47N 9 7W
Mayo →, Argentina 176 45 45 S 69 45W
Mayo →, Peru 172 6 38 S 76 15W
Mayo Bay 91 6 56N 126 22 E
Mayo L. 140 63 45N 135 0W
Mayoko 132 2 18 S 12 49 E
Mayon Volcano 90 13 15N 123 41 E
Mayor I. 114 37 16 S 176 17 E
Mayorga 34 42 10N 5 16W
Mayoyao 90 16 59N 121 14 E
Mayraira Pt. 90 18 39N 120 51 E
Mayskiy 61 43 47N 44 2 E
Mayson L. 145 57 55N 107 10W
Maysville, Ky., U.S.A. 155 38 39N 83 46W
Maysville, Mo., U.S.A. 154 39 53N 94 21W
Maythalūn 69 32 21N 35 16 E
Mayu 87 1 30N 126 30 E
Mayumba 132 3 25 S 10 39 E
Mayuram 81 11 3N 79 42 E
Mayville, N. Dak., U.S.A. 152 47 30N 97 23W
Mayville, N.Y., U.S.A. 150 42 14N 79 31W
Mayya 65 61 44N 130 18 E
Mazabuka 131 15 52 S 27 44 E
Mazagán = El Jadida 120 33 11N 8 17W
Mazagão 169 0 7 S 51 16W
Mazamet 20 43 30N 2 20 E
Mazán 168 3 30 S 73 0W
Māzandarān □ 73 36 30N 52 0 E
Mazapil 160 24 38N 101 34W
Mazar, O. → 121 31 50N 1 36 E
Mazar-e Sharīf 77 36 41N 67 0 E
Mazara del Vallo 44 37 40N 12 34 E
Mazarredo 176 47 10 S 66 50W
Mazarrón 37 37 38N 1 19W
Mazarrón, G. de 37 37 27N 1 19W
Mazaruni → 169 6 25N 58 35W
Mazatán 160 29 0N 110 8W
Mazatenango 162 14 35N 91 30W
Mazatlán 160 23 10N 106 30W
Mažeikiai 58 56 20N 22 20 E
Mazhafa, J. 71 28 52N 35 5 E
Māzhān 73 32 30N 59 0 E
Mazīnān 73 36 19N 56 56 E
Mazoe 131 16 42 S 33 7 E
Mazoe → 131 16 20 S 33 30 E
Mazomanie 154 43 11N 89 48W
Mazon 155 41 14N 88 25W
Mazowe 131 17 28 S 30 58 E
Mazrûb 125 14 0N 29 20 E
Mazu Dao 97 26 10N 119 55 E
Mazurian Lakes = Mazurski, Pojezierze 32 53 50N 21 0 E
Mazurski, Pojezierze 32 53 50N 21 0 E
Mazzarino 45 37 19N 14 12 E
Mba 106 17 33 S 177 41 E
Mbaba 126 14 59N 16 44W
Mbabane 135 26 18 S 31 6 E
Mbagne 126 16 6N 14 47W
M'bahiakro 126 7 33N 4 19W
Mbaïki 132 3 53N 18 1 E
Mbakana, Mt. de 131 7 57N 15 6 E
Mbala 131 8 46 S 31 24 E
Mbale 130 1 8N 34 12 E
Mbalmayo 127 3 33N 11 33 E
Mbamba Bay 131 11 13 S 34 49 E
Mbandaka 132 0 1N 18 18 E
Mbanga 127 4 30N 9 33 E
Mbanza Congo 133 6 18 S 14 16 E
Mbanza Ngungu 133 5 12 S 14 53 E
Mbarara 130 0 35 S 30 40 E
Mbashe → 135 32 15 S 28 54 E
Mbatto 126 6 28N 4 22W
Mbengga 106 18 23 S 178 8 E
Mbenkuru → 131 9 25 S 39 50 E
Mberengwa 131 20 29 S 29 57 E
Mberengwa N. 131 20 37 S 29 55 E
Mberubu 127 6 10N 7 38 E
Mbesuma 131 10 0 S 32 2 E
Mbeya 131 8 54 S 33 29 E
Mbeya □ 130 8 15 S 33 30 E
Mbigou 132 1 53 S 11 56 E
Mbinga 131 10 50 S 35 0 E
Mbinga □ 131 10 50 S 35 0 E
Mbini □ 132 1 30N 10 0 E
Mboki 125 5 19N 25 58 E
Mboli 132 4 8N 23 9 E
Mboro 126 15 9N 16 54W
Mboune 126 14 42N 13 34W
Mbouomo 132 0 52 S 15 4 E
Mbour 126 14 22N 16 54W
Mbout 126 16 1N 12 38W
Mbozi □ 131 9 0 S 32 50 E
Mbrés 132 6 40N 19 48 E
Mbuji-Mayi 130 6 9 S 23 40 E
Mbulu 130 3 45 S 35 30 E
Mbulu □ 130 3 52 S 35 33 E
Mburucuyá 174 28 1 S 58 14W
Mcherrah 120 27 0N 4 30W
Mchinja 131 9 44 S 39 45 E
Mchinji 131 13 47 S 32 58 E
Mdennah 120 24 37N 6 0W
Mdina 40 35 51N 14 25 E
Mead, L. 159 36 1N 114 44W
Meade 153 37 18N 100 25W
Meadow 109 26 35 S 114 40 E
Meadow Lake 145 54 10N 108 26W
Meadow Lake Prov. Park 145 54 27N 109 0W
Meadow Valley Wash → 159 36 39N 114 35W
Meadville, Mo., U.S.A. 154 39 47N 93 18W
Meadville, Pa., U.S.A. 150 41 39N 80 9W
Meaford 142 44 36N 80 35W
Mealhada 34 40 22N 8 27W
Mealy Mts. 143 53 10N 58 0W
Meander River 144 59 2N 117 42W
Meares, C. 156 45 37N 124 0W
Mearim → 170 3 4 S 44 35W
Meath □ 15 53 32N 6 40W
Meath Park 145 53 27N 105 22W
Meatian 112 35 34 S 143 21 E
Meaulne 20 46 36N 2 36 E
Meaux 19 48 58N 2 50 E
Mebechi-Gawa → 98 40 31N 141 31 E
Mecanhelas 131 15 12 S 35 54 E
Mecaya → 168 0 29N 75 11W
Mecca = Makkah 74 21 30N 39 54 E
Mecca 159 33 37N 116 3W
Mechanicsburg 150 40 12N 77 0W
Mechanicsville 154 41 54N 91 16W
Mechanicville 151 42 54N 73 41W
Mechara 125 8 36N 40 20 E
Mechelen, Antwerpen, Belgium 23 51 2N 4 29 E
Mechelen, Limburg, Belgium 23 50 58N 5 41 E
Mecheria 121 33 35N 0 18W
Mechernich 26 50 35N 6 39 E
Mechetinskaya 61 46 45N 40 32 E
Mechra Benâbbou 120 32 39N 7 48W
Mecidiye 48 40 38N 26 32 E
Mecitözü 60 40 32N 35 17 E
Mecklenburger Bucht 26 54 20N 11 40 E
Meconta 131 14 59 S 39 50 E
Meda, Australia 108 17 22 S 123 59 E
Meda, Portugal 34 40 57N 7 18W
Medak 80 18 1N 78 15 E
Medan 88 3 40N 98 38 E
Médanos 176 38 50 S 62 42W
Medanosa, Pta. 176 48 8 S 66 0W
Medaryville 155 41 4N 86 55W
Medawachchiya 81 8 30N 80 30 E
Medéa 121 36 12N 2 50 E
Mededa 46 43 44N 19 15 E
Médégué 132 0 37N 10 8 E

Minden

Mésou Volímais 49 37 53N 20 35 E
Mesquite 157 36 47N 114 6W
Mess Cr. → 144 57 55N 131 14W
Messac 18 47 49N 1 50W
Messad 121 34 8N 3 30 E
Messalo → 131 12 25 S 39 15 E
Méssaména 127 3 48N 12 49 E
Messancy 23 49 36N 5 49 E
Messeue 49 37 12N 21 58 E
Messier, Canal 176 48 20 S 74 33W
Messina, Italy 45 38 10N 15 32 E
Messina, S. Africa 135 22 20 S 30 0 E
Messina, Str. di 45 38 5N 15 35 E
Messíni 49 37 4N 22 1 E
Messínia □ 49 37 10N 22 0 E
Messiniakós, Kólpos 49 36 45N 22 5 E
Messkirch 27 47 59N 9 7 E
Mesta → 47 41 30N 24 0 E
Mestà, Ákra 49 38 16N 25 53 E
Mestanza 35 38 35N 4 4W
Město Teplá 30 49 59N 12 52 E
Mestre 43 45 30N 12 13 E
Mestre, Espigão 171 12 30 S 46 10W
Městys Zelezná Ruda 30 49 8N 13 15 E
Meta 154 38 19N 92 10W
Meta □ 168 3 30N 73 0W
Meta → 168 6 12N 67 28W
Metairie 153 29 59N 90 9W
Metalici, Munţii 50 46 15N 22 50 E
Metaline Falls 156 48 52N 117 22W
Metamora 154 40 47N 89 22W
Metán 174 25 30 S 65 0W
Metangula 131 12 40 S 34 50 E
Metauro → 43 43 50N 13 3 E
Metema 125 12 56N 36 13 E
Metengobalame 131 14 49 S 34 30 E
Méthana 49 37 35N 23 23 E
Methóni 49 36 49N 21 42 E
Methven 115 43 38 S 171 40 E
Methy L. 145 56 28N 109 30W
Metil 131 16 24 S 39 0 E
Metkovets 47 43 37N 23 10 E
Metković 46 43 6N 17 39 E
Metlakatla 144 55 10N 131 33W
Metlaoui 121 34 24N 8 24 E
Metlika 43 45 40N 15 20 E
Metro 88 5 5 S 105 20 E
Metropolis 153 37 10N 88 47W
Métsovon 48 39 48N 21 12 E
Mettet 23 50 19N 4 41 E
Mettuppalaiyam 81 11 18N 76 59 E
Mettur 81 11 48N 77 47 E
Metulla 69 33 17N 35 34 E
Metz 19 49 8N 6 10 E
Meulaboh 88 4 11N 96 3 E
Meulan 19 49 0N 1 55 E
Meung-sur-Loire 19 47 50N 1 40 E
Meureudu 88 5 19N 96 10 E
Meurthe → 19 48 47N 6 9 E
Meurthe-et-Moselle □ 19 48 52N 6 0 E
Meuse □ 19 49 8N 5 25 E
Meuse → 23 50 45N 5 41 E
Meuselwitz 26 51 3N 12 18 E
Mexborough 12 53 29N 1 18W
Mexia 153 31 38N 96 32W
Mexiana, I. 170 0 0 49 30W
Mexicali 160 32 40N 115 30W
México, Mexico 161 19 20N 99 10W
Mexico, Maine, U.S.A. 151 44 35N 70 30W
Mexico, Mo., U.S.A. 154 39 10N 91 55W
México □ 160 19 20N 99 10W
Mexico ■ 160 25 0N 105 0W
Mexico, G. of 161 25 0N 90 0W
Meyenburg 26 53 19N 12 15 E
Meymac 20 45 32N 2 10 E
Meymaneh 77 35 53N 64 38 E
Meyrargues 21 43 38N 5 32 E
Meyrueis 20 44 12N 3 27 E
Meyssac 20 45 3N 1 40 E
Mezdra 47 43 12N 23 42 E
Mèze 20 43 27N 3 36 E
Mezen 56 65 50N 44 20 E
Mezen → 56 66 11N 43 59 E
Mézenc, Mt. 21 44 54N 4 11 E
Mezeş, Munţii 50 47 5N 23 5 E
Mezha → 58 55 50N 31 45 E
Mezhdurechenskiy 62 59 36N 65 56 E
Mézidon 18 49 5N 0 1W
Mézilhac 21 44 49N 4 21 E
Mézin 20 44 4N 0 16 E
Mezöberény 31 46 49N 21 3 E
Mezöfalva 31 46 55N 18 49 E
Mezöhegyes 31 46 19N 20 49 E
Mezökövácsháza 31 46 25N 20 57 E
Mezökövesd 31 47 49N 20 35 E
Mézos 20 44 5N 1 10W
Mezötúr 31 47 0N 20 41 E
Mezquital 160 23 29N 104 23W
Mezzolombardo 42 46 13N 11 5 E
Mgeta 131 8 22 S 36 6 E
Mglin 58 53 2N 32 50 E
Mhlaba Hills 131 18 30 S 30 30 E
Mhow 78 22 33N 75 50 E
Mi-Shima 100 34 46N 131 9 E
Miahuatlán 161 16 21N 96 36W
Miajadas 35 39 9N 5 54W
Miallo 110 16 28 S 145 22 E
Miami, Ariz., U.S.A. 157 33 25N 110 54W
Miami, Fla., U.S.A. 149 25 45N 80 15W
Miami, Tex., U.S.A. 153 35 44N 100 38W
Miami → 148 39 20N 84 40W
Miami Beach 149 25 49N 80 6W
Miamisburg 155 39 40N 84 11W
Mian Xian 94 33 10N 106 32 E
Mianchi 94 34 48N 111 48 E
Mīāndow āb 72 37 0N 46 5 E
Miandrivazo 135 19 31 S 45 29 E
Mīāneh 72 37 30N 47 40 E
Mianning 96 28 32N 102 9 E
Mianwali 77 32 38N 71 28 E
Mianyang, Hubei, China 97 30 25N 113 25 E
Mianyang, Sichuan, China 96 31 22N 104 47 E
Mianzhu 96 31 22N 104 7 E
Miaoli 97 24 37N 120 49 E
Miarinarivo 135 18 57 S 46 55 E
Miass 62 54 59N 60 6 E
Miass → 62 56 6N 64 30 E
Miasteczko Kraj 32 53 7N 17 1 E
Miastko 32 54 0N 16 58 E
Micăsasa 50 46 7N 24 7 E
Michael, Mt. 107 6 27 S 145 22 E
Michalovce 31 48 47N 21 58 E
Michelstadt 27 49 40N 9 0 E
Michigan □ 147 44 40N 85 40W
Michigan, L. 148 44 0N 87 0W
Michigan Center 155 42 14N 84 20W
Michigan City 155 41 42N 86 56W
Michikamau L. 143 54 20N 63 10W
Michipicoten 142 47 55N 84 55W
Michipicoten I. 142 47 40N 85 40W
Michoacan □ 160 19 0N 102 0W
Michurin 47 42 9N 27 51 E
Michurinsk 59 52 58N 40 27 E
Miclere 110 22 34 S 147 32 E
Mico, Pta. 162 12 0N 83 30W
Micronesia 104 11 0N 160 0 E
Mid Glamorgan □ 13 51 40N 3 25W
Mid-Indian Ridge 104 40 0 S 75 0 E
Mid-Oceanic Ridge 104 42 0 S 90 0 E
Midai, P. 85 3 0N 107 47 E
Midale 145 49 25N 103 20W
Middagsfjället 52 63 27N 12 19 E
Middelbeers 23 51 28N 5 15 E
Middelburg, Neth. 23 51 30N 3 36 E
Middelburg, C. Prov., S. Africa 134 31 30 S 25 0 E
Middelburg, Trans., S. Africa 135 25 49 S 29 28 E
Middelfart 53 55 30N 9 43 E
Middelharnis 22 51 46N 4 10 E
Middelkerke 23 51 11N 2 49 E
Middelrode 23 51 41N 5 26 E
Middelwit 134 24 51 S 27 3 E
Middle → 154 41 26N 93 30W
Middle Alkali L. 156 41 30N 120 3W
Middle Andaman I. 76 12 30N 92 30 E
Middle Fork Feather → 158 39 35N 121 25W
Middle Loup → 152 41 17N 98 23W
Middle Raccoon → 154 41 35N 93 35W
Middleboro 151 41 56N 70 52W
Middleburg, N.Y., U.S.A. 151 42 36N 74 19W
Middleburg, Pa., U.S.A. 150 40 46N 77 5W
Middlebury, Ind., U.S.A. 155 41 41N 85 42W
Middlebury, Vt., U.S.A. 151 44 0N 73 9W
Middlemarch 115 45 30 S 170 9 E
Middleport 148 39 0N 82 5W
Middlesboro 149 36 36N 83 43W
Middlesbrough 12 54 35N 1 14W
Middlesex, Belize 162 17 2N 88 31W
Middlesex, U.S.A. 151 40 36N 74 30W
Middleton, Australia 110 22 22 S 141 32 E
Middleton, Canada 143 44 57N 65 4W
Middleton, U.S.A. 154 43 6N 89 30W
Middletown, Calif., U.S.A. 158 38 45N 122 37W
Middletown, Conn., U.S.A. 151 41 37N 72 40W
Middletown, N.Y., U.S.A. 151 41 28N 74 28W
Middletown, Ohio, U.S.A. 155 39 29N 84 25W
Middletown, Pa., U.S.A. 151 40 12N 76 44W
Middleville 155 42 43N 85 28W
Midelt 120 32 46N 4 44W
Midhirst 114 39 17 S 174 18 E
Midi, Canal du → 20 43 45N 1 21 E
Midi d'Ossau 36 42 50N 0 25W
Midi d'Ossau, Pic du 20 42 50N 0 26W
Midland, Australia 111 31 54 S 115 59 E
Midland, Canada 142 44 45N 79 50W
Midland, Calif., U.S.A. 159 33 52N 114 48W
Midland, Mich., U.S.A. 148 43 37N 84 17W
Midland, Pa., U.S.A. 150 40 39N 80 27W
Midland, Tex., U.S.A. 153 32 0N 102 3W
Midlands □ 131 19 40 S 29 0 E
Midleton 15 51 52N 8 12W
Midlothian 153 32 30N 97 0W
Midongy, Tangorombohitr' i 135 23 30 S 47 0 E
Midongy Atsimo 135 23 35 S 47 1 E
Midou → 20 43 54N 0 30W
Midouze → 20 43 48N 0 51W
Midsayap 91 7 12N 124 32 E
Midu 96 25 18N 100 30 E
Midway Is. 104 28 13N 177 22W
Midway Wells 159 32 41N 115 7W
Midwest 156 43 27N 106 19W
Midwolda 22 53 12N 6 52 E
Midzur 46 43 24N 22 40 E
Mie □ 101 34 30N 136 10 E
Miechów 32 50 21N 20 5 E
Miedwie, Jezioro 32 53 17N 14 54 E
Międzybód 32 51 25N 17 34 E
Międzychód 32 52 35N 15 53 E
Międzylesie 32 50 8N 16 40 E
Międzyrzec Podlaski 32 51 58N 22 45 E
Międzyrzecz 32 52 26N 15 35 E
Międzyzdroje 32 53 56N 14 26 E
Miejska 32 51 39N 16 58 E
Miélan 20 43 27N 0 19 E
Mielec 32 50 15N 21 25 E
Mienga 133 17 12 S 19 48 E
Miercurea Ciuc 50 46 21N 25 48 E
Mieres 34 43 18N 5 48W
Mierlo 23 51 27N 5 37 E
Mieroszów 32 50 40N 16 11 E
Mieso 125 9 15N 40 43 E
Mieszkowice 32 52 47N 14 30 E
Mifflintown 150 40 34N 77 24W
Mifraz Ḥefa 70 32 52N 35 0 E
Migdāl 69 32 51N 35 30 E
Migdal Afeq 69 32 5N 34 58 E
Migennes 19 47 58N 3 31 E
Migliarino 43 44 45N 11 56 E
Miguel Alemán, Presa 161 18 15N 96 40W
Miguel Alves 170 4 11 S 42 55W
Miguel Calmon 170 11 26 S 40 36W
Mihara 100 34 24N 133 5 E
Mihara-Yama 101 34 43N 139 23 E
Mihmandar 70 36 51N 35 20 E
Mijares → 36 39 55N 0 1W
Mijas 35 36 36N 4 40W
Mikese 130 6 48 S 37 55 E
Mikha-Tskhakaya 61 42 15N 42 7 E
Mikhailovka 60 47 36N 35 16 E
Mikhaylov 59 54 14N 39 0 E
Mikhaylovgrad 47 43 27N 23 16 E
Mikhaylovka, Azerbaijan, U.S.S.R. 61 41 31N 48 52 E
Mikhaylovka, R.S.F.S.R., U.S.S.R. 59 50 3N 43 5 E
Mikhaylovski 62 56 27N 59 7 E
Mikhnevo 59 55 4N 37 59 E
Miki, Hyōgo, Japan 100 34 48N 134 59 E
Miki, Kagawa, Japan 100 34 12N 134 7 E
Mikínai 49 37 43N 22 46 E
Mikkeli 55 61 43N 27 15 E
Mikkelin lääni □ 54 61 56N 28 0 E
Mikkwa → 144 58 25N 114 46W
Mikniya 125 17 0N 33 45 E
Mikołajki 32 53 49N 21 37 E
Mikołów 31 50 10N 18 50 E
Míkonos 49 37 30N 25 25 E
Mikrí Préspa, Límni 48 40 47N 21 3 E
Mikrón Dhérion 48 41 19N 26 6 E
Mikstat 32 51 32N 17 59 E
Mikulov 31 48 48N 16 39 E
Mikumi 130 7 26 S 37 0 E
Mikun 56 62 20N 50 0 E
Mikuni 101 36 13N 136 9 E
Mikuni-Tōge 101 36 50N 138 50 E
Mikura-Jima 101 33 52N 139 36 E
Milaca 152 45 45N 93 40W
Milagro 168 2 11 S 79 36W
Milagros 90 12 13N 123 30 E
Milan = Milano 42 45 28N 9 10 E
Milan, Ill., U.S.A. 154 41 27N 90 34W
Milan, Mich., U.S.A. 155 42 5N 83 40W
Milan, Mo., U.S.A. 154 40 10N 93 5W
Milan, Tenn., U.S.A. 149 35 55N 88 45W
Milang, S. Austral., Australia 111 32 2 S 139 10 E
Milang, S. Austral., Australia 112 35 24 S 138 58 E
Milange 131 16 3 S 35 45 E
Milano 42 45 28N 9 10 E
Milâs 57 37 20N 27 50 E
Milazzo 45 38 13N 15 13 E
Milbank 152 45 17N 96 38W
Milden 145 51 29N 107 32W
Mildmay 150 44 3N 81 7W
Mildura 112 34 13 S 142 9 E
Mile 96 24 28N 103 20 E
Miléai 48 39 20N 23 9 E
Mileh Tharthār 72 34 0N 43 15 E
Miles, Australia 111 26 40 S 150 9 E
Miles, U.S.A. 153 31 39N 100 11W
Miles City 152 46 24N 105 50W
Milestone 145 49 59N 104 31W
Mileto 45 38 37N 16 3 E
Miletto, Mte. 45 41 26N 14 23 E
Miletus 49 37 20N 27 33 E
Mileura 109 26 22 S 117 20 E
Milevsko 30 49 27N 14 21 E
Milford, Conn., U.S.A. 151 41 13N 73 4W
Milford, Del., U.S.A. 148 38 52N 75 27W
Milford, Ill., U.S.A. 155 40 40N 87 43W
Milford, Mass., U.S.A. 151 42 8N 71 30W
Milford, Mich., U.S.A. 155 42 35N 83 36W
Milford, Pa., U.S.A. 151 41 20N 74 47W
Milford, Utah, U.S.A. 157 38 20N 113 0W
Milford, U.S.A. 158 40 10N 120 22W
Milford Haven 13 51 43N 5 2W
Milford Sd. 115 44 41 S 167 47 E
Milgun 109 25 6 S 118 18 E
Milḥ, Baḥr al 72 32 40N 43 35 E
Miliana, Aïn Salah, Algeria 121 27 20N 2 32 E
Miliana, Médéa, Algeria 121 36 20N 2 15 E
Milicz 32 51 31N 17 19 E
Miling 109 30 30 S 116 17 E
Militello in Val di Catánia 45 37 16N 14 46 E
Milk → 156 48 5N 106 15W
Milk, Wadi el → 124 17 55N 30 20 E
Milk River 144 49 10N 112 5W
Mill 23 51 41N 5 48 E
Mill City 156 44 45N 122 28W
Mill I. 7 66 0 S 101 30 E
Mill Shoals 155 38 15N 88 21W
Mill Valley 158 37 54N 122 32W
Millau 20 44 8N 3 4 E
Millbridge 150 44 41N 77 36W
Millbrook 150 44 10N 78 29W
Mille 149 33 7N 83 15W
Mille Lacs, L. 152 46 10N 93 30W
Mille Lacs, L. des 142 48 45N 90 35W
Milledgeville 154 41 58N 89 46W
Millen 149 32 50N 81 57W
Miller 152 44 35N 98 59W
Millerovo 61 48 57N 40 28 E
Miller's Flat 115 45 39 S 169 23 E
Millersburg, Ind., U.S.A. 155 41 32N 85 42W
Millersburg, Ohio, U.S.A. 150 40 32N 81 52W
Millersburg, Pa., U.S.A. 150 40 32N 76 58W
Millerton, N.Z. 115 41 39 S 171 54 E
Millerton, U.S.A. 151 41 57N 73 32W
Millerton L. 158 37 0N 119 42W
Millevaches, Plateau de 20 45 45N 2 0 E
Millicent 112 37 34 S 140 21 E
Millingen 22 51 52N 6 2 E
Millinocket 143 45 45N 68 45W
Millmerran 111 27 53 S 151 16 E
Mills L. 144 61 30N 118 20W
Millsboro 150 40 0N 80 0W
Milltown Malbay 15 52 51N 9 25W
Millville 148 39 22N 75 0W
Millwood Res. 153 33 45N 94 0W
Milly-la-Forêt 19 48 24N 2 28 E
Milna 43 43 20N 16 28 E
Milne → 110 21 10 S 137 33 E
Milne Inlet 141 72 30N 80 0W
Milnor 152 46 19N 97 29W
Milo 144 50 34N 112 53W
Mílos 49 36 44N 24 25 E
Miloševo 46 45 42N 20 20 E
Miłosław 32 52 12N 17 32 E
Milparinka 111 29 46 S 141 57 E
Milroy 155 39 30N 85 28W
Miltenberg 27 49 41N 9 13 E
Milton, Canada 150 43 31N 79 53W
Milton, N.Z. 115 46 7 S 169 59 E
Milton, U.K. 14 57 18N 4 32W
Milton, Calif., U.S.A. 158 38 3N 120 51W
Milton, Fla., U.S.A. 149 30 38N 87 0W
Milton, Iowa, U.S.A. 154 40 41N 92 10W
Milton, Pa., U.S.A. 150 41 0N 76 53W
Milton, Wis., U.S.A. 155 42 47N 88 56W
Milton-Freewater 156 45 57N 118 24W
Milton Keynes 13 52 3N 0 42W
Miltou 123 10 14N 17 26 E
Milverton 150 43 34N 80 55W
Milwaukee 155 43 9N 87 58W
Milwaukie 158 45 27N 122 39W
Mim 126 6 57N 2 33W
Mimizan 20 44 12N 1 13W
Mimon 30 50 38N 14 43 E
Mimongo 132 1 11 S 11 36 E
Mimoso 171 15 10 S 48 5W
Min Jiang →, Fujian, China 97 26 0N 119 35 E
Min Jiang →, Sichuan, China 96 28 45N 104 40 E
Min-Kush 63 41 4N 74 28 E
Min Xian 94 34 25N 104 0 E
Mina 157 38 21N 118 9W
Mina Pirquitas 174 22 40 S 66 30W
Mīnā Su'ud 72 28 45N 48 28 E
Mīnā'al Aḥmadī 73 29 5N 48 10 E
Mīnāb 73 27 10N 57 1 E
Minago → 145 54 33N 98 59W
Minakami 101 36 49N 138 59 E
Minaki 145 49 59N 94 40W
Minakuchi 101 34 58N 136 10 E
Minamata 100 32 10N 130 30 E
Minas 175 34 20 S 55 10W
Minas, Sierra de las 162 15 9N 89 31W
Minas Basin 143 45 20N 64 12W
Minas de Rio Tinto 35 37 42N 6 35W
Minas de San Quintín 35 38 49N 4 23W
Minas Gerais □ 171 18 50 S 46 0W
Minas Novas 171 17 15 S 42 36W
Minatitlán 161 17 58N 94 35W
Minbu 82 20 10N 94 52 E
Minbya 82 20 22N 93 16 E
Mincio → 42 45 4N 10 59 E
Mindanao 91 8 0N 125 0 E
Mindanao Sea = Bohol Sea 87 9 0N 124 0 E
Mindanao Trench 87 8 0N 128 0 E
Mindel → 27 48 31N 10 23 E
Mindelheim 27 48 4N 10 30 E
Minden, Canada 150 44 55N 78 43W
Minden, Germany 26 52 18N 8 45 E

Minden

Minden, La., U.S.A. 153 32 40N 93 20W
Minden, Nev., U.S.A. 158 38 57N 119 48W
Mindiptana 87 5 55S 140 22 E
Mindon 82 19 21N 94 44 E
Mindoro 90 13 0N 121 0 E
Mindoro Occidental □ 90 13 0N 120 55 E
Mindoro Oriental □ 90 13 0N 121 5 E
Mindoro Strait 90 12 30N 120 30 E
Mindouli 133 4 12S 14 28 E
Mine 100 34 12N 131 7 E
Minehead 13 51 12N 3 29W
Mineiros 173 17 34S 52 34W
Mineola 153 32 40N 95 30W
Mineral King 158 36 27N 118 36W
Mineral Point 154 42 52N 90 11W
Mineral Wells 153 32 50N 98 5W
Mineralnyye Vody 61 44 2N 43 8 E
Minersville, Pa., U.S.A. 151 40 11N 76 17W
Minersville, Utah, U.S.A. 157 38 14N 112 58W
Minerva 150 40 43N 81 8W
Minervino Murge 45 41 6N 16 4 E
Minetto 151 43 24N 76 28W
Mingan 143 50 20N 64 0W
Mingary 112 32 8S 140 45 E
Mingechaur 61 40 45N 47 0 E
Mingechaurskoye Vdkhr. 61 40 56N 47 20 E
Mingela 110 19 52S 146 38 E
Mingenew 109 29 12S 115 21 E
Mingera Cr. → 110 20 38S 137 45 E
Minggang 97 32 24N 114 3 E
Mingin 82 22 50N 94 30 E
Minglanilla 36 39 34N 1 38W
Minglun 96 25 10N 108 21 E
Mingorria 34 40 45N 4 40W
Mingxi 97 26 18N 117 12 E
Mingyuegue 95 43 2N 128 50 E
Minhou 97 26 0N 119 15 E
Minićevo 46 43 42N 22 18 E
Minidoka 156 42 47N 113 34W
Minier 154 40 26N 89 19W
Minigwal L. 109 29 31S 123 14 E
Minilya 109 23 55S 114 0 E
Minilya → 109 23 45S 114 0 E
Mininera 112 37 37S 142 58 E
Minipi, L. 143 52 25N 60 45W
Minj 107 5 54S 144 37 E
Mink L. 144 61 54N 117 40W
Minlaton 112 34 45S 137 35 E
Minna 127 9 37N 6 30 E
Minneapolis, Kans., U.S.A. 152 39 11N 97 40W
Minneapolis, Minn., U.S.A. 152 44 58N 93 20W
Minnedosa 145 50 14N 99 50W
Minnesota □ 152 46 40N 94 0W
Minnesund 51 60 23N 11 14 E
Minnie Creek 109 24 3S 115 42 E
Minnitaki L. 142 49 57N 92 10W
Mino 101 35 32N 136 55 E
Miño → 34 41 52N 8 40W
Mino-Kamo 101 35 23N 137 2 E
Mino-Mikawa-Kōgen 101 35 10N 137 23 E
Minoa 49 35 6N 25 45 E
Minobu 101 35 22N 138 26 E
Minobu-Sanchi 101 35 14N 138 20 E
Minonk 154 40 54N 89 2W
Minooka 155 41 27N 88 16W
Minorca = Menorca 36 40 0N 4 0 E
Minore 113 32 14S 148 27 E
Minot 152 48 10N 101 15W
Minqin 94 38 38N 103 20 E
Minqing 97 26 15N 118 50 E
Minquiers, Les 18 48 58N 2 8W
Minsen 26 53 43N 7 58 E
Minsk 58 53 52N 27 30 E
Mińsk Mazowiecki 32 52 10N 21 33 E
Minster 155 40 24N 84 23W
Mintaka Pass 79 37 0N 74 58 E
Minthami 82 23 55N 94 16 E
Minto 140 64 55N 149 20W
Minton 145 49 10N 104 35W
Mintoum 132 0 27N 12 16 E
Minturn 156 39 35N 106 25W
Minturno 44 41 15N 13 43 E
Minûf 124 30 26N 30 52 E
Minusinsk 65 53 50N 91 20 E
Minutang 82 28 15N 96 30 E
Minvoul 132 2 9N 12 8 E
Minwakh 75 16 48N 48 6 E
Minya el Qamh 124 30 31N 31 21 E
Minyar 62 55 4N 57 33 E
Minyip 112 36 29S 142 36 E
Mionica 46 44 14N 20 6 E
Mir 127 14 5N 11 59 E
Mir-Bashir 61 40 20N 46 58 E
Mīr Kūh 73 26 22N 58 55 E
Mīr Shahdād 73 26 15N 58 29 E
Mira, Italy 43 45 26N 12 9 E
Mira, Portugal 34 40 26N 8 44W
Mira →, Colombia 168 1 36N 79 1W
Mira →, Portugal 35 37 43N 8 47W
Mira por vos Cay 163 22 9N 74 30W
Mīrābād 77 30 25N 61 50 E
Mirabella Eclano 45 41 3N 14 59 E
Miracema do Norte 170 9 33S 48 24W
Mirador 170 6 22S 44 22W
Miraflores 168 1 25N 72 13W
Miraj 80 16 50N 74 45 E
Miram 110 21 15S 148 55 E
Miram Shah 77 33 0N 70 2 E
Miramar, Argentina 174 38 15S 57 50W
Miramar, Mozam. 135 23 50S 35 35 E
Miramas 21 43 33N 4 59 E
Mirambeau 20 45 23N 0 35W
Miramichi B. 143 47 15N 65 0W
Miramont-de-Guyenne 20 44 37N 0 21 E
Miranda 173 20 10S 56 15W
Miranda □ 168 10 15N 66 25W
Miranda → 173 19 25S 57 20W
Miranda de Ebro 36 42 41N 2 57W
Miranda do Corvo 34 40 6N 8 20W
Miranda do Douro 34 41 30N 6 16W
Mirande 20 43 31N 0 25 E
Mirandela 34 41 32N 7 10W
Mirando City 153 27 28N 98 59W
Mirandola 42 44 53N 11 2 E
Mirandópolis 175 21 9S 51 6W
Mirango 131 13 32S 34 58 E
Mirano 43 45 29N 12 6 E
Mirassol 175 20 46S 49 28W
Mirbāṭ 75 17 0N 54 45 E
Mirboo North 113 38 24S 146 10 E
Mirear 124 23 15N 35 41 E
Mirebeau, Côte-d'Or, France 19 47 25N 5 20 E
Mirebeau, Vienne, France 18 46 49N 0 10 E
Mirecourt 19 48 20N 6 10 E
Mirgorod 58 49 58N 33 37 E
Miri 86 4 23N 113 59 E
Miriam Vale 110 24 20S 151 33 E
Mirim, L. 175 32 45S 52 50W
Mirimire 168 11 10N 68 43W
Miriti 173 6 15S 59 0W
Mirnyy, Antarct. 7 66 33S 93 1 E
Mirnyy, U.S.S.R. 65 62 33N 113 53 E
Miroč 46 44 32N 22 16 E
Mirond L. 145 55 6N 102 47W
Mirosławiec 32 53 20N 16 5 E
Mirpur 79 33 32N 73 56 E
Mirpur Bibiwari 78 28 33N 67 44 E
Mirpur Khas 77 25 30N 69 0 E
Mirpur Sakro 78 24 33N 67 41 E
Mirria 127 13 43N 9 7 E
Mirror 144 52 30N 113 7W
Mîrşani 50 44 1N 23 59 E
Mirsk 32 50 58N 15 23 E
Miryang 95 35 31N 128 44 E
Mirzaani 61 41 24N 46 5 E
Mirzapur 79 25 10N 82 34 E
Mirzapur-cum-Vindhyachal = Mirzapur 79 25 10N 82 34 E
Misamis Occidental □ 91 8 20N 123 42 E
Misamis Oriental □ 91 8 45N 125 0 E
Misantla 161 19 56N 96 50W
Misawa 98 40 41N 141 24 E
Miscou I. 143 47 57N 64 31W
Mish'āb, Ra'as al 72 28 15N 48 43 E
Mishagua → 172 11 12S 72 58W
Mishan 93 45 37N 131 48 E
Mishawaka 155 41 40N 86 8W
Mishbih, Gebel 124 22 38N 34 44 E
Mishima 101 35 10N 138 52 E
Mishkino 62 55 20N 63 55 E
Mishmar Ayyalon 69 31 52N 34 57 E
Mishmar Ha' Emeq 69 32 37N 35 7 E
Mishmar Ha Negev 69 31 22N 34 48 E
Mishmar Ha Yarden 69 33 0N 35 36 E
Mishmi Hills 82 29 0N 96 0 E
Misilmeri 44 38 2N 13 25 E
Misima I. 107 10 40S 152 45 E
Misión 159 32 6N 116 53W
Misión, La 160 32 5N 116 50W
Misión Fagnano 176 54 32S 67 17W
Misiones □, Argentina 175 27 0S 55 0W
Misiones □, Paraguay 174 27 0S 56 0W
Miskah 72 24 49N 42 56 E
Miskitos, Cayos 162 14 26N 82 50W
Miskolc 31 48 7N 20 50 E
Misoke 130 0 42S 28 2 E
Misool 87 1 52S 130 10 E
Misrātah 122 32 24N 15 3 E
Misrātah □ 122 29 0N 16 0 E
Missanabie 142 48 20N 84 6W
Missão Velha 170 7 15S 39 10W
Missinaibi → 142 50 43N 81 29W
Missinaibi L. 142 48 23N 83 40W
Mission, S. Dak., U.S.A. 152 43 21N 100 36W
Mission, Tex., U.S.A. 153 26 15N 98 20W
Mission City 144 49 10N 122 15W
Mission Viejo 159 33 41N 117 46W
Missisa L. 142 52 20N 85 7W
Mississagi → 142 46 15N 83 9W
Mississinewa Res. 155 40 46N 86 3W
Mississippi → 153 29 0N 89 15W
Mississippi, Delta of the 153 29 15N 90 30W
Mississippi L. 151 45 5N 76 10W
Mississippi Sd. 153 30 25N 89 0W
Missoula 156 46 52N 114 0W
Missour 120 33 3N 4 0W
Missouri □ 152 38 25N 92 30W
Missouri → 152 38 50N 90 8W
Missouri Valley 152 41 33N 95 53W
Mist 158 45 59N 123 15W
Mistake B. 145 62 8N 93 0W
Mistassini → 143 48 42N 72 20W
Mistassini L. 142 51 0N 73 30W
Mistastin L. 143 55 57N 63 20W
Mistatim 145 52 52N 103 22W
Mistelbach 31 48 34N 16 34 E
Misterbianco 45 37 32N 15 0 E
Mistretta 45 37 56N 14 20 E
Misty L. 145 58 53N 101 40W
Misugi 101 34 31N 136 16 E
Misumi 100 32 37N 130 27 E
Mît Ghamr 124 30 42N 31 12 E
Mitaka 101 35 40N 139 33 E
Mitan 63 40 0N 66 35 E
Mitatib 125 15 59N 36 12 E
Mitchell, Australia 111 26 29S 147 58 E
Mitchell, Canada 150 43 28N 81 12W
Mitchell, Ind., U.S.A. 155 38 42N 86 25W
Mitchell, Nebr., U.S.A. 152 41 58N 103 45W
Mitchell, Oreg., U.S.A. 156 44 31N 120 8W
Mitchell, S. Dak., U.S.A. 152 43 40N 98 0W
Mitchell → 110 15 12S 141 35 E
Mitchell, Mt. 149 35 40N 82 20W
Mitchelstown 15 52 16N 8 18W
Mitha Tiwana 78 32 13N 72 6 E
Míthimna 48 39 20N 26 12 E
Mitiamo 112 36 12S 144 15 E
Mitilíni 49 39 6N 26 35 E
Mitilinoí 49 37 42N 26 56 E
Mito 101 36 20N 140 30 E
Mitsinjo 135 16 1S 45 52 E
Mitsiwa 125 15 35N 39 25 E
Mitsiwa Channel 125 15 30N 40 0 E
Mitsukaidō 101 36 1N 139 59 E
Mittagong 113 34 28S 150 29 E
Mittelland 28 46 50N 7 23 E
Mittelland Kanal 26 52 23N 7 45 E
Mittenwalde 26 52 16N 13 33 E
Mitterteich 27 49 57N 12 15 E
Mittweida 26 50 59N 13 0 E
Mitú 168 1 8N 70 3W
Mituas 168 3 52N 68 49W
Mitumba 130 7 8S 31 2 E
Mitumba, Chaîne des 130 7 0S 27 30 E
Mitwaba 131 8 2S 27 17 E
Mityana 130 0 23N 32 2 E
Mitzic 132 0 45N 11 40 E
Miura 101 35 12N 139 40 E
Mixteco → 161 18 11N 98 30W
Miyagi □ 98 38 15N 140 45 E
Miyâh, W. el →, Egypt 124 25 0N 33 23 E
Miyah, W. el →, Syria 72 34 44N 39 57 E
Miyake-Jima 101 34 0N 139 30 E
Miyako 98 39 40N 141 59 E
Miyako-Jima 99 24 45N 125 20 E
Miyako-Rettō 99 24 24N 125 0 E
Miyakonojō 100 31 40N 131 5 E
Miyanojō 100 31 54N 130 27 E
Miyanoura-Dake 99 30 20N 130 31 E
Miyata 100 33 49N 130 42 E
Miyazaki 100 31 56N 131 30 E
Miyazaki □ 100 32 30N 131 30 E
Miyazu 101 35 35N 135 10 E
Miyet, Bahr el = Dead Sea 69 31 30N 35 30 E
Miyi 96 26 47N 102 9 E
Miyoshi 100 34 48N 132 51 E
Miyun 94 40 28N 116 50 E
Miyun Shuiku 95 40 30N 117 0 E
Mizamis = Ozamis 91 8 15N 123 50 E
Mizdah 122 31 30N 13 0 E
Mizen Hd., Cork, Ireland 15 51 27N 9 50W
Mizen Hd., Wicklow, Ireland 15 52 52N 6 4W
Mizhi 94 37 47N 110 12 E
Mizil 50 44 59N 26 29 E
Mizoram □ 82 23 30N 92 40 E
Mizpe Ramon 69 30 34N 34 49 E
Mizuho, Antarct. 7 70 30S 41 0 E
Mizuho, Japan 101 35 6N 135 17 E
Mizunami 101 35 22N 137 15 E
Mizusawa 98 39 8N 141 8 E
Mjöbäck 53 57 28N 12 53 E
Mjölby 53 58 20N 15 10 E
Mjømna 51 60 55N 4 55 E
Mjörn 53 57 55N 12 25 E
Mjøsa 51 60 48N 11 0 E
Mkata 130 5 45S 38 20 E
Mkokotoni 130 5 55S 39 15 E
Mkomazi 130 4 40S 38 7 E
Mkomazi → 135 30 12S 30 50 E
Mkulwe 131 8 37S 32 20 E
Mkumbi, Ras 130 7 38S 39 55 E
Mkushi 131 14 25S 29 15 E
Mkushi River 131 13 32S 29 45 E
Mkuze 135 27 10S 32 0 E
Mkuze → 135 27 45S 32 30 E
Mladá Boleslav 30 50 27N 14 53 E
Mladenovac 46 44 28N 20 44 E
Mlala Hills 130 6 50S 31 40 E
Mlange 131 16 2S 35 33 E
Mlava → 46 44 45N 21 13 E
Mława 32 53 9N 20 25 E
Mlinište 43 44 15N 16 50 E
Mljet 46 42 43N 17 30 E
Mljetski Kanal 46 42 48N 17 35 E
Mlynąry 32 54 12N 19 46 E
Mmabatho 134 25 49S 25 30 E
Mme 127 6 18N 10 14 E
Mo 51 59 28N 7 50 E
Mo i Rana 54 66 15N 14 7 E
Moa 87 8 0S 128 0 E
Moa → 126 6 59N 11 36 E
Moab 157 38 40N 109 35W
Moabi 132 2 24S 10 59 E
Moaco → 172 7 41S 68 18W
Moala 106 18 36S 179 53 E
Moalie Park 111 29 42S 143 3 E
Moaña 34 42 18N 8 43W
Moba 130 7 0S 29 48 E
Mobara 101 35 25N 140 18 E
Mobārakābād 73 28 24N 53 20 E
Mobārakīyeh 73 35 5N 51 47 E
Mobaye 132 4 25N 21 5 E
Mobayi 132 4 15N 21 8 E
Moberly 154 39 25N 92 25W
Moberly → 144 56 12N 120 55W
Mobile 149 30 41N 88 3W
Mobile B. 149 30 30N 88 0W
Mobridge 152 45 31N 100 28W
Mobutu Sese Seko, L. 130 1 30N 31 0 E
Moc Chau 84 20 50N 104 38 E
Moc Hoa 85 10 46N 105 56 E
Mocaba, Sa. de 133 7 12S 15 0 E
Mocabe Kasari 131 9 58S 26 12 E
Mocajuba 170 2 35S 49 30W
Moçambique 131 15 3S 40 42 E
Moçâmedes = Namibe 133 15 7S 12 11 E
Mocapra → 168 7 56N 66 46W
Mocha, I. 176 38 22S 73 56W
Mochudi 134 24 27S 26 7 E
Mocimboa da Praia 131 11 25S 40 20 E
Mociu 50 46 46N 24 3 E
Möckeln 53 56 40N 14 15 E
Moclips 158 47 14N 124 10W
Mocoa 168 1 7N 76 35W
Mococa 175 21 28S 47 0W
Mocorito 160 25 30N 107 53W
Moctezuma 160 29 50N 109 0W
Moctezuma → 161 21 59N 98 34W
Mocuba 131 16 54S 36 57 E
Mocúzari, Presa 160 27 10N 109 10W
Moda 82 24 22N 96 29 E
Modalen 51 60 49N 5 48 E
Modane 21 45 12N 6 40 E
Modasa 78 23 30N 73 21 E
Modave 23 50 27N 5 18 E
Modder → 134 29 2S 24 37 E
Modderrivier 134 29 2S 24 38 E
Módena, Italy 42 44 39N 10 55 E
Modena, U.S.A. 157 37 55N 113 56W
Modesto 158 37 43N 121 0W
Módica 45 36 52N 14 45 E
Modigliana 43 44 9N 11 48 E
Modjamboli 132 2 28N 22 6 E
Modlin 32 52 24N 20 41 E
Mödling 31 48 5N 16 17 E
Modo 125 5 31N 30 33 E
Modra 31 48 19N 17 20 E
Modriča 46 44 57N 18 17 E
Moe 113 38 12S 146 19 E
Moebase 131 17 3S 38 41 E
Moëlan-sur-Mer 18 47 49N 3 38W
Moengo 169 5 45N 54 20W
Moergestel 23 51 33N 5 11 E
Moësa → 29 46 12N 9 10 E
Moffat 14 55 20N 3 27W
Moga 78 30 48N 75 8 E
Mogadishu = Muqdisho 136 2 2N 45 25 E
Mogador = Essaouira 120 31 32N 9 42W
Mogadouro 34 41 22N 6 47W
Mogalakwena → 135 22 38S 28 40 E
Mogami → 98 38 45N 140 0 E
Mogán 37 27 53N 15 43W
Mogaung 82 25 20N 97 0 E
Møgeltønder 53 54 57N 8 48 E
Mogente 37 38 52N 0 45W
Mogho 125 4 54N 40 16 E
Mogi das Cruzes 175 23 31S 46 11W
Mogi-Guaçu → 175 20 53S 48 10W
Mogi-Mirim 175 22 29S 47 0W
Mogielnica 32 51 42N 20 41 E
Mogilev 58 53 55N 30 18 E
Mogilev-Podolskiy 60 48 20N 27 40 E
Mogilno 32 52 39N 17 55 E
Mogincual 131 15 35S 40 25 E
Mogliano Véneto 43 45 33N 12 15 E
Mogocha 65 53 40N 119 50 E
Mogoi 87 1 55S 133 10 E
Mogok 82 23 0N 96 40 E
Mogriguy 113 32 3S 148 40 E
Moguer 35 37 15N 6 52W
Mogumber 109 31 2S 116 3 E
Mohács 31 45 58N 18 41 E
Mohaka → 114 39 7S 177 12 E
Mohales Hoek 134 30 7S 27 26 E
Mohall 152 48 46N 101 30W
Moḥammadābād 73 37 52N 59 5 E
Mohammadia 121 35 33N 0 3 E
Mohammedia 120 33 44N 7 21W
Mohave, L. 159 35 25N 114 36W
Mohawk → 151 42 47N 73 42W
Moheda 53 57 1N 14 35 E
Möhne → 26 51 29N 7 57 E
Mohnyin 82 24 47N 96 22 E
Moholm 53 58 37N 14 5 E
Mohoro 130 8 6S 39 8 E
Moia 125 5 3N 28 2 E
Moidart, L. 14 56 47N 5 40W
Moille, La 154 41 32N 89 17W
Moinabad 80 17 44N 77 16 E

Montpelier

Moindou **106** 21 42 S 165 41 E
Moine, La → **154** 39 58N 90 32W
Moineşti **50** 46 28N 26 31 E
Mointy **64** 47 10N 73 18 E
Moirans **21** 45 20N 5 33 E
Moirans-en-Montagne **21** 46 26N 5 43 E
Moíres **49** 35 4N 24 56 E
Moisakula **58** 58 3N 25 12 E
Moisie **143** 50 12N 66 1W
Moisie → **143** 50 14N 66 5W
Moissac **20** 44 7N 1 5 E
Moïssala **123** 8 21N 17 46 E
Moita **35** 38 38N 8 58W
Mojácar **37** 37 6N 1 55W
Mojados **34** 41 26N 4 40W
Mojave **159** 35 8N 118 8W
Mojave Desert **159** 35 0N 116 30W
Mojiang **96** 23 37N 101 35 E
Mojo, Bolivia **174** 21 48 S 65 33W
Mojo, Ethiopia **125** 8 35N 39 5 E
Mojokerto **89** 7 28 S 112 26 E
Mojos, Llanos de **173** 15 0 S 65 0W
Moju → **170** 1 40 S 48 25W
Mokai **114** 38 32 S 175 56 E
Mokambo **131** 12 25 S 28 20 E
Mokameh **79** 25 24N 85 55 E
Mokane **154** 38 41N 91 53W
Mokau → **114** 38 35 S 174 35 E
Mokelumne → **158** 38 23N 121 25W
Mokelumne Hill **158** 38 18N 120 43W
Mokhós **49** 35 16N 25 27 E
Mokhotlong **135** 29 22 S 29 2 E
Mokihinui → **115** 41 33 S 171 58 E
Moknine **121** 35 35N 10 58 E
Mokpalin **82** 17 26N 96 53 E
Mokra Gora **46** 42 50N 20 30 E
Mokronog **43** 45 57N 15 9 E
Moksha → **59** 54 45N 41 53 E
Mokshan **59** 53 25N 44 35 E
Mol **23** 51 11N 5 5 E
Mola, C. de la **36** 39 40N 4 20 E
Mola di Bari **45** 41 3N 17 5 E
Moláoi **49** 36 49N 22 56 E
Molat **43** 44 15N 14 50 E
Molave **91** 8 5N 123 30 E
Molchanovo **64** 57 40N 83 50 E
Mold **12** 53 10N 3 10W
Moldava nad Bodvou **31** 48 38N 21 0 E
Moldavia = Moldova **50** 46 30N 27 0 E
Moldavian S.S.R. □ **60** 47 0N 28 0 E
Molde **51** 62 45N 7 9 E
Moldotau, Khrebet **63** 41 35N 75 0 E
Moldova **50** 46 30N 27 0 E
Moldova Nouă **46** 44 45N 21 41 E
Moldoveanu **50** 45 36N 24 45 E
Molepolole **134** 24 28 S 25 28 E
Moléson **28** 46 33N 7 1 E
Molesworth **115** 42 5 S 173 16 E
Molfetta **45** 41 12N 16 35 E
Molina de Aragón **36** 40 46N 1 52W
Moline **154** 41 30N 90 30W
Molinella **43** 44 38N 11 40 E
Molinos **174** 25 28 S 66 15W
Moliro **130** 8 12 S 30 30 E
Molise □ **43** 41 45N 14 30 E
Moliterno **45** 40 14N 15 50 E
Mollahat **79** 22 56N 89 48 E
Mölle **52** 56 17N 12 31 E
Molledo **34** 43 8N 4 6W
Mollendo **172** 17 0 S 72 0W
Mollerin, L. **109** 30 30 S 117 35 E
Mollerusa **36** 41 37N 0 54 E
Mollina **35** 37 8N 4 38W
Mölln **26** 53 37N 10 41 E
Mölltorp **53** 58 30N 14 26 E
Mölndal **53** 57 40N 12 3 E
Molo **82** 23 22N 96 53 E
Molochansk **60** 47 15N 35 35 E
Molochnaya → **60** 47 0N 35 30 E
Molodechno **58** 54 20N 26 50 E
Molokai **146** 21 8N 157 0W
Moloma → **59** 58 20N 48 15 E
Molong **113** 33 5 S 148 54 E
Molopo → **134** 27 30 S 20 13 E
Mólos **49** 38 47N 22 37 E
Molotov = Perm **62** 58 0N 57 10 E
Moloundou **132** 2 8N 15 15 E
Molsheim **19** 48 33N 7 29 E
Molson L. **145** 54 22N 96 40W
Molteno **134** 31 22 S 26 22 E
Molu **87** 6 45 S 131 40 E
Molucca Sea **89** 4 0 S 124 0 E
Moluccas = Maluku **87** 1 0 S 127 0 E
Molundo **91** 7 57N 124 23 E
Moma, Mozam. **131** 16 47 S 39 4 E
Moma, Zaïre **130** 1 35 S 23 52 E
Momba **112** 30 58 S 143 30 E
Mombaça **170** 5 43 S 39 45W
Mombasa **130** 4 2 S 39 43 E
Mombetsu **98** 44 21N 143 22 E
Mombil **82** 27 46N 98 6 E
Mombuey **34** 42 3N 6 20W
Momchilgrad **47** 41 33N 25 23 E
Momence **155** 41 10N 87 40W
Momi **130** 1 42 S 27 0 E
Momignies **23** 50 2N 4 10 E
Mompog Pass **90** 13 34N 122 13 E
Mompós **168** 9 14N 74 26W
Møn **53** 54 57N 12 15 E
Mona, Canal de la **163** 18 30N 67 45W
Mona, I. **163** 18 5N 67 54W
Mona, Pta. **162** 9 37N 82 36W
Mona, Punta **35** 36 43N 3 45W
Mona Quimbundo **133** 9 55 S 19 58 E
Monach Is. **14** 57 32N 7 40W
Monaco ■ **21** 43 46N 7 23 E
Monadhliath Mts. **14** 57 10N 4 4W
Monagas □ **169** 9 20N 63 0W
Monaghan **15** 54 15N 6 58W
Monaghan □ **15** 54 10N 7 0W
Monahans **153** 31 35N 102 50W
Monapo **131** 14 56 S 40 19 E
Monarch Mt. **144** 51 55N 125 57W
Monastier-sur-Gazeille, Le **20** 44 57N 3 59 E
Monastir = Bitola **46** 41 5N 21 10 E
Monastir **121** 35 50N 10 49 E
Monastyriska **58** 49 8N 25 14 E
Moncada, Phil. **90** 15 44N 120 34 E
Moncada, Spain **36** 39 30N 0 24W
Moncalieri **42** 45 0N 7 40 E
Moncalvo **42** 45 3N 8 15 E
Moncão **34** 42 4N 8 27W
Moncarapacho **35** 37 5N 7 46W
Moncayo, Sierra del **36** 41 48N 1 50W
Mönchengladbach **26** 51 12N 6 23 E
Monchique **35** 37 19N 8 38W
Monclova **160** 26 50N 101 30W
Moncontour **18** 48 22N 2 38W
Moncoutant **20** 46 43N 0 35W
Moncton **143** 46 7N 64 51W
Mondego → **34** 40 9N 8 52W
Mondego, C. **34** 40 11N 8 54W
Mondeodo **87** 3 34 S 122 9 E
Mondo **123** 13 47N 15 32 E
Mondolfo **43** 43 45N 13 8 E
Mondoñedo **34** 43 25N 7 23W
Mondoví, Italy **42** 44 23N 7 49 E
Mondovi, U.S.A. **152** 44 37N 91 40W
Mondragon, France **21** 44 13N 4 44 E
Mondragon, Phil. **90** 12 31N 124 45 E
Mondragone **44** 41 8N 13 52 E
Mondrain I. **109** 34 9 S 122 14 E
Monduli □ **130** 3 0 S 36 0 E
Monemvasía **49** 36 41N 23 3 E
Monessen **150** 40 9N 79 50W
Monesterio **35** 38 6N 6 15W
Monestier-de-Clermont **21** 44 55N 5 38 E
Monêtier-les-Bains, Le **21** 44 58N 6 30 E
Monett **153** 36 55N 93 56W
Monfalcone **43** 45 49N 13 32 E
Monflanquin **20** 44 32N 0 47 E
Monforte **35** 39 6N 7 25W
Monforte de Lemos **34** 42 31N 7 33W
Mong Hta **82** 19 50N 98 35 E
Mong Ket **82** 23 8N 98 22 E
Mong Kung **82** 21 35N 97 35 E
Mong Kyawt **82** 19 56N 98 45 E
Mong Nai **82** 20 32N 97 46 E
Mong Ping **82** 21 22N 99 2 E
Mong Pu **82** 20 55N 98 44 E
Mong Ton **82** 20 17N 98 45 E
Mong Tung **82** 22 2N 97 41 E
Mong Yai **82** 22 21N 98 3 E
Monga **132** 4 12N 22 49 E
Mongalla **125** 5 8N 31 42 E
Mongers, L. **109** 29 25 S 117 5 E
Monghyr = Munger **79** 25 23N 86 30 E
Mongla **82** 22 8N 89 35 E
Mongngaw **82** 22 47N 96 59 E
Mongo, Chad **123** 12 14N 18 43 E
Mongó, Eq. Guin. **132** 1 52N 10 10 E
Mongolia ■ **92** 47 0N 103 0 E
Mongomo **132** 1 38N 11 19 E
Mongonu **127** 12 40N 13 32 E
Mongororo **123** 12 3N 22 26 E
Mongu **133** 15 16 S 23 12 E
Môngua **133** 16 43 S 15 20 E
Monistrol-d'Allier **20** 44 58N 3 38 E
Monistrol-sur-Loire **21** 45 17N 4 11 E
Monkayo **91** 7 50N 126 0 E
Monkey Bay **131** 14 7 S 35 1 E
Monkey River **161** 16 22N 88 29W
Mońki **32** 53 23N 22 48 E
Monkira **110** 24 46 S 140 30 E
Monkoto **132** 1 38 S 20 35 E
Monmouth, U.K. **13** 51 48N 2 43W
Monmouth, U.S.A. **154** 40 50N 90 40W
Mono, L. **158** 38 0N 119 9W
Monolith **159** 35 7N 118 22W
Monon **155** 40 52N 86 53W
Monona, Iowa, U.S.A. **154** 43 3N 91 24W
Monona, Wis., U.S.A. **154** 43 4N 89 20W
Monongahela **150** 40 12N 79 56W
Monópoli **45** 40 57N 17 18 E
Monor **31** 47 21N 19 27 E
Monóvar **37** 38 28N 0 53W
Monowai **115** 45 53 S 167 31 E
Monowai, L. **115** 45 53 S 167 25 E
Monqoumba **132** 3 33N 18 40 E
Monreal del Campo **36** 40 47N 1 20W
Monreale **44** 38 6N 13 16 E
Monroe, Ga., U.S.A. **149** 33 47N 83 43W
Monroe, Iowa, U.S.A. **154** 41 31N 93 6W
Monroe, La., U.S.A. **153** 32 32N 92 4W
Monroe, Mich., U.S.A. **155** 41 55N 83 26W
Monroe, N.C., U.S.A. **149** 35 2N 80 37W
Monroe, N.Y., U.S.A. **151** 41 19N 74 11W
Monroe, Ohio, U.S.A. **155** 39 27N 84 22W
Monroe, Utah, U.S.A. **157** 38 45N 112 5W
Monroe, Wash., U.S.A. **158** 47 51N 121 58W
Monroe, Wis., U.S.A. **154** 42 38N 89 40W
Monroe, Res. **155** 39 1N 86 31W
Monroe City **154** 39 40N 91 40W
Monroeville, Ala., U.S.A. **149** 31 33N 87 15W
Monroeville, Ind., U.S.A. **155** 40 59N 84 52W
Monroeville, Pa., U.S.A. **150** 40 26N 79 45W
Monrovia, Liberia **126** 6 18N 10 47W
Monrovia, U.S.A. **157** 34 7N 118 1W
Mons **23** 50 27N 3 58 E
Monsaraz **35** 38 28N 7 22W
Monse **87** 4 0 S 123 10 E
Monsefú **172** 6 52 S 79 52W
Monségur **20** 44 38N 0 4 E
Monsélice **43** 45 16N 11 46 E
Monster **22** 52 1N 4 10 E
Mont-de-Marsan **20** 43 54N 0 31W
Mont Dore **106** 22 16 S 166 34 E
Mont-Dore, Le **20** 45 35N 2 49 E
Mont-Joli **143** 48 37N 68 10W
Mont-Laurier **142** 46 35N 75 30W
Mont-St.-Michel, Le **18** 48 40N 1 30W
Mont-sous-Vaudrey **19** 46 58N 5 36 E
Mont-sur-Marchienne **23** 50 23N 4 24 E
Mont Tremblant Prov. Park **142** 46 30N 74 30W
Montabaur **26** 50 26N 7 49 E
Montagnac **20** 43 29N 3 28 E
Montagnana **43** 45 13N 11 29 E
Montagu **134** 33 45 S 20 8 E
Montagu I. **7** 58 25 S 26 20W
Montague, Canada **143** 46 10N 62 39W
Montague, U.S.A. **156** 41 47N 122 30W
Montague, I. **160** 31 40N 114 56W
Montague I. **140** 60 0N 147 0W
Montague Ra. **109** 27 15 S 119 30 E
Montague Sd. **108** 14 28 S 125 20 E
Montaigu **18** 46 59N 1 18W
Montalbán **36** 40 50N 0 45W
Montalbano di Elicona **45** 38 1N 15 0 E
Montalbano Iónico **45** 40 17N 16 33 E
Montalbo **36** 39 53N 2 42W
Montalcino **43** 43 4N 11 30 E
Montalegre **34** 41 49N 7 47W
Montalto di Castro **43** 42 20N 11 36 E
Montalto Uffugo **45** 39 25N 16 9 E
Montalvo **159** 34 15N 119 12W
Montamarta **34** 41 39N 5 49W
Montaña, Peru **172** 6 0 S 73 0W
Montana, Switz. **28** 46 19N 7 29 E
Montana □ **146** 47 0N 110 0W
Montaña Clara, I. **37** 29 17N 13 33W
Montánchez **35** 39 15N 6 8W
Montañita **168** 1 22N 75 28W
Montargis **19** 47 59N 2 43 E
Montauban **20** 44 0N 1 21 E
Montauk **151** 41 3N 71 57W
Montauk Pt. **151** 41 4N 71 52W
Montbard **19** 47 38N 4 20 E
Montbéliard **19** 47 31N 6 48 E
Montblanch **36** 41 23N 1 4 E
Montbrison **21** 45 36N 4 3 E
Montcalm, Pic de **20** 42 40N 1 25 E
Montceau-les-Mines **19** 46 40N 4 23 E
Montchanin **21** 46 47N 4 30 E
Montclair **151** 40 53N 74 13W
Montcornet **19** 49 40N 4 1 E
Montcuq **20** 44 21N 1 13 E
Montdidier **19** 49 38N 2 35 E
Monte, La **154** 38 47N 93 27W
Monte Albán **161** 17 2N 96 45W
Monte Alegre **169** 2 0 S 54 0W
Monte Alegre de Goiás **171** 13 14 S 47 10W
Monte Alegre de Minas **171** 18 52 S 48 52W
Monte Azul **171** 15 9 S 42 53W
Monte Bello Is. **108** 20 30 S 115 45 E
Monte-Carlo **21** 43 46N 7 23 E
Monte Carmelo **171** 18 43 S 47 29W
Monte Caseros **174** 30 10 S 57 50W
Monte Comán **174** 34 40 S 67 53W
Monte Cristi **163** 19 52N 71 39W
Monte Dinero **176** 52 18 S 68 33W
Monte Lindo → **174** 23 56 S 57 12W
Monte Quemado **174** 25 53 S 62 41W
Monte Redondo **34** 39 53N 8 50W
Monte Rio **158** 38 28N 123 0W
Monte San Giovanni **44** 41 39N 13 33 E
Monte San Savino **43** 43 20N 11 42 E
Monte Sant' Ángelo **45** 41 42N 15 59 E
Monte Santu, C. di **44** 40 5N 9 42 E
Monte Vista **157** 37 40N 106 8W
Monteagudo, Argentina **175** 27 14 S 54 8W
Monteagudo, Bolivia **173** 19 49 S 63 59W
Montealegre **37** 38 48N 1 17W
Montebello **142** 45 40N 74 55W
Montebelluna **43** 45 47N 12 3 E
Montebourg **18** 49 30N 1 20W
Montecastrilli **43** 42 40N 12 30 E
Montecatini Terme **43** 43 55N 10 48 E
Montecito **159** 34 26N 119 40W
Montecristi **168** 1 0 S 80 40W
Montecristo **42** 42 20N 10 20 E
Montefalco **43** 42 53N 12 38 E
Montefiascone **43** 42 31N 12 2 E
Montefrío **35** 37 20N 4 0W
Montegnée **23** 50 38N 5 31 E
Montego Bay **162** 18 30N 78 0W
Montegranaro **43** 43 13N 13 38 E
Monteiro **170** 7 48 S 37 2W
Monteith **112** 35 11 S 139 23 E
Montejicar **37** 37 33N 3 30W
Montejinnie **108** 16 40 S 131 38 E
Montelíbano **168** 8 5N 75 29W
Montélimar **21** 44 33N 4 45 E
Montella **45** 40 50N 15 0 E
Montellano **35** 36 59N 5 36W
Montello **152** 43 49N 89 21W
Montelupo Fiorentino **42** 43 44N 11 2 E
Montemor-o-Novo **35** 38 40N 8 12W
Montemor-o-Velho **34** 40 11N 8 40W
Montemorelos **161** 25 11N 99 42W
Montendre **20** 45 16N 0 26W
Montenegro = Crna Gora □ **46** 42 40N 19 20 E
Montenegro **175** 29 39 S 51 29W
Montenero di Bisaccia **43** 42 0N 14 47 E
Montepuez **131** 13 8 S 38 59 E
Montepuez → **131** 12 32 S 40 27 E
Montepulciano **43** 43 5N 11 46 E
Montereale **43** 42 31N 13 13 E
Montereau-Fault-Yonne **19** 48 22N 2 57 E
Monterey, Calif., U.S.A. **158** 36 35N 121 57W
Monterey, Ind., U.S.A. **155** 41 11N 86 30W
Monterey B. **158** 36 50N 121 55W
Montería **168** 8 46N 75 53W
Montero **173** 17 20 S 63 15W
Monteros **174** 27 11 S 65 30W
Monterotondo **43** 42 3N 12 36 E
Monterrey **160** 25 40N 100 30W
Montes Altos **170** 5 50 S 47 4W
Montes Claros **171** 16 30 S 43 50W
Montesano **158** 46 58N 123 39W
Montesárchio **45** 41 5N 14 37 E
Montescaglioso **45** 40 34N 16 40 E
Montesilvano **43** 42 30N 14 8 E
Montevarchi **43** 43 30N 11 32 E
Montevideo, Uruguay **175** 34 50 S 56 11W
Montevideo, U.S.A. **152** 44 55N 95 40W
Montezuma, Ind., U.S.A. **155** 39 47N 87 22W
Montezuma, Iowa, U.S.A. **154** 41 32N 92 35W
Montfaucon **19** 49 16N 5 8 E
Montfaucon-en-Velay **21** 45 11N 4 20 E
Montfort, France **18** 48 9N 1 58W
Montfort, Neth. **23** 51 7N 5 58 E
Montfort-l'Amaury **19** 48 47N 1 49 E
Montgenèvre **21** 44 56N 6 43 E
Montgomery = Sahiwal **77** 30 45N 73 8 E
Montgomery, U.K. **13** 52 34N 3 9W
Montgomery, Ala., U.S.A. **149** 32 20N 86 20W
Montgomery, Ill., U.S.A. **155** 41 44N 88 21W
Montgomery, W. Va., U.S.A. **148** 38 9N 81 21W
Montgomery City **154** 38 59N 91 30W
Montguyon **20** 45 12N 0 12W
Monthey **28** 46 15N 6 56 E
Monticelli d'Ongina **42** 45 3N 9 56 E
Monticello, Ark., U.S.A. **153** 33 40N 91 48W
Monticello, Fla., U.S.A. **149** 30 35N 83 50W
Monticello, Ill., U.S.A. **155** 40 1N 88 34W
Monticello, Ind., U.S.A. **155** 40 40N 86 45W
Monticello, Iowa, U.S.A. **154** 42 18N 91 12W
Monticello, Ky., U.S.A. **149** 36 52N 84 50W
Monticello, Minn., U.S.A. **152** 45 17N 93 52W
Monticello, Miss., U.S.A. **153** 31 35N 90 8W
Monticello, Mo., U.S.A. **154** 40 7N 91 43W
Monticello, N.Y., U.S.A. **151** 41 37N 74 42W
Monticello, Utah, U.S.A. **157** 37 55N 109 27W
Montichiari **42** 45 28N 10 29 E
Montier-en-Der **19** 48 30N 4 45 E
Montignac **20** 45 4N 1 10 E
Montignies-sur-Sambre **23** 50 24N 4 29 E
Montigny **19** 49 7N 6 10 E
Montigny-sur-Aube **19** 47 57N 4 45 E
Montijo **35** 38 52N 6 39W
Montijo, Presa de **35** 38 55N 6 26W
Montilla **35** 37 36N 4 40W
Montlhéry **19** 48 39N 2 15 E
Montluçon **20** 46 22N 2 36 E
Montmagny **143** 46 58N 70 34W
Montmarault **20** 46 19N 2 57 E
Montmartre **145** 50 14N 103 27W
Montmédy **19** 49 30N 5 20 E
Montmélian **21** 45 30N 6 4 E
Montmirail **19** 48 51N 3 30 E
Montmoreau-St.-Cybard **20** 45 23N 0 8 E
Montmorency **143** 46 53N 71 11W
Montmorillon **20** 46 26N 0 50 E
Montmort **19** 48 55N 3 49 E
Monto **110** 24 52 S 151 6 E
Montoir-sur-le-Loir **18** 47 45N 0 52 E
Montório al Vomano **43** 42 35N 13 38 E
Montoro **35** 38 1N 4 27W
Montour Falls **150** 42 20N 76 51W
Montpelier, Idaho, U.S.A. **156** 42 15N 111 20W

Muqaddam, Wadi

Mount Forest 142 43 59N 80 43W
Mount Gambier 112 37 50 S 140 46 E
Mount Garnet 110 17 37 S 145 6 E
Mount Hagen 107 5 52 S 144 16 E
Mount Hope, N.S.W., Australia 113 32 51 S 145 51 E
Mount Hope, S. Austral., Australia 111 34 7 S 135 23 E
Mount Hope, U.S.A. 148 37 52N 81 9W
Mount Horeb 154 43 0N 89 42W
Mount Howitt 111 26 31 S 142 16 E
Mount Isa 110 20 42 S 139 26 E
Mount Ive 112 32 25 S 136 5 E
Mount Keith 109 27 15 S 120 30 E
Mount Laguna 159 32 52N 116 25W
Mount Larcom 110 23 48 S 150 59 E
Mount Lofty Ra. 112 34 35 S 139 5 E
Mount McKinley Nat. Park 140 64 0N 150 0W
Mount Magnet 109 28 2 S 117 47 E
Mount Manara 112 32 29 S 143 58 E
Mount Margaret 111 26 54 S 143 21 E
Mount Maunganui 114 37 40 S 176 14 E
Mount Molloy 110 16 42 S 145 20 E
Mount Monger 109 31 0 S 122 0 E
Mount Morgan 110 23 40 S 150 25 E
Mount Morris 150 42 43N 77 50W
Mount Mulligan 110 16 45 S 144 47 E
Mount Narryer 109 26 30 S 115 55 E
Mount Olive 154 39 4N 89 44W
Mount Olivet 155 38 32N 84 2W
Mount Orab 155 39 5N 83 56W
Mount Oxide Mine 110 19 30 S 139 29 E
Mount Pearl 143 47 31N 52 47W
Mount Perry 111 25 13 S 151 42 E
Mount Phillips 109 24 25 S 116 15 E
Mount Pleasant, Iowa, U.S.A. 154 40 58N 91 35W
Mount Pleasant, Mich., U.S.A. 148 43 35N 84 47W
Mount Pleasant, Pa., U.S.A. 150 40 9N 79 31W
Mount Pleasant, S.C., U.S.A. 149 32 45N 79 48W
Mount Pleasant, Tenn., U.S.A. 149 35 31N 87 11W
Mount Pleasant, Tex., U.S.A. 153 33 5N 95 0W
Mount Pleasant, Utah, U.S.A. 156 39 40N 111 29W
Mount Pocono 151 41 8N 75 21W
Mount Pulaski 154 40 1N 89 17W
Mount Rainier Nat. Park. 158 46 50N 121 43W
Mount Revelstoke Nat. Park 144 51 5N 118 30W
Mount Robson Prov. Park 144 53 0N 119 0W
Mount Roskill 114 36 55 S 174 45 E
Mount Sandiman 109 24 25 S 115 30 E
Mount Shasta 156 41 20N 122 18W
Mount Signal 159 32 39N 115 37W
Mount Somers 115 43 45 S 171 27 E
Mount Sterling, Ill., U.S.A. 154 39 59N 90 40W
Mount Sterling, Ky., U.S.A. 155 38 3N 83 57W
Mount Sterling, Ohio, U.S.A. 155 39 43N 83 16W
Mount Surprise 110 18 10 S 144 17 E
Mount Union 150 40 22N 77 51W
Mount Vernon, Australia 109 24 9 S 118 2 E
Mount Vernon, Ill., U.S.A. 155 38 19N 88 55W
Mount Vernon, Ind., U.S.A. 155 38 17N 88 57W
Mount Vernon, Iowa, U.S.A. 154 41 55N 91 23W
Mount Vernon, N.Y., U.S.A. 151 40 57N 73 49W
Mount Vernon, Ohio, U.S.A. 150 40 20N 82 30W
Mount Vernon, Wash., U.S.A. 144 48 25N 122 20W
Mount Victor 112 32 11 S 139 44 E
Mount Washington 155 38 3N 85 33W
Mount Wellington 114 36 55 S 174 52 E
Mount Zion 155 39 46N 88 53W
Mountain □ 90 17 20N 121 10 E
Mountain Center 159 33 42N 116 44W
Mountain City, Nev., U.S.A. 156 41 54N 116 0W
Mountain City, Tenn., U.S.A. 149 36 30N 81 50W
Mountain Grove 153 37 5N 92 20W
Mountain Home, Ark., U.S.A. 153 36 20N 92 25W
Mountain Home, Idaho, U.S.A. 156 43 11N 115 45W
Mountain Iron 152 47 30N 92 37W
Mountain Park 144 52 50N 117 15W
Mountain Pass 159 35 29N 115 35W
Mountain View, Ark., U.S.A. 153 35 52N 92 10W
Mountain View, Calif., U.S.A. 157 37 26N 122 5W
Mountain View, Calif., U.S.A. 158 37 23N 122 6W
Mountainair 157 34 35N 106 15W
Mountmellick 15 53 7N 7 20W
Moura, Australia 110 24 35 S 149 58 E
Moura, Brazil 169 1 32 S 61 38W
Moura, Portugal 35 38 7N 7 30W
Mourão 35 38 22N 7 22W
Mourdi, Dépression du 123 18 10N 23 0 E
Mourdiah 126 14 35N 7 25W
Moure, La 152 46 27N 98 17W
Mourenx-Ville-Nouvelle 20 43 22N 0 38W
Mouri 127 5 6N 1 14W
Mourilyan 110 17 35 S 146 3 E
Mourmelon-le-Grand 19 49 8N 4 22 E
Mourne → 15 54 45N 7 39W
Mourne Mts. 15 54 10N 6 0W
Mouscron 23 50 45N 3 12 E
Moussoro 123 13 41N 16 35 E
Mouthe 19 46 44N 6 12 E
Moutier 28 47 16N 7 21 E
Moûtiers 21 45 29N 6 32 E
Moutong 87 0 28N 121 13 E
Mouy 19 49 18N 2 20 E
Mouzáki 48 39 25N 21 37 E
Movas 160 28 10N 109 25W
Moville 15 55 11N 7 3W
Moweaqua 154 39 37N 89 1W
Moxhe 23 50 38N 5 5 E
Moxico □ 133 12 0 S 20 30 E
Moxotó → 170 9 19 S 38 14W
Moy → 15 54 5N 8 50W
Moyale, Ethiopia 125 3 34N 39 4 E
Moyale, Kenya 130 3 30N 39 0 E
Moyamba 126 8 4N 12 30W
Moyen Atlas 121 33 0N 5 0W
Moyle □ 15 55 10N 6 15W
Moyo 86 8 10 S 117 40 E
Moyobamba 172 6 0 S 77 0W
Moyyero → 65 68 44N 103 42 E
Mozambique = Moçambique 131 15 3 S 40 42 E
Mozambique ■ 131 19 0 S 35 0 E
Mozambique Chan. 135 17 30 S 42 30 E
Mozdok 61 43 45N 44 48 E
Mozdūrān 73 36 9N 60 35 E
Mozhaysk 59 55 30N 36 2 E
Mozhga 59 56 26N 52 15 E
Mozhnābād 73 34 7N 60 6 E
Mozirje 43 46 22N 14 58 E
Mozyr 58 52 0N 29 15 E
Mpanda 130 6 23 S 31 1 E
Mpanda □ 130 6 23 S 31 40 E
Mpésoba 126 12 31N 5 39W
Mpika 131 11 51 S 31 25 E
Mpulungu 131 8 51 S 31 5 E
Mpumalanga 135 29 50 S 30 33 E
Mpwapwa 130 6 23 S 36 30 E
Mpwapwa □ 130 6 30 S 36 20 E
Mrągowo 32 53 52N 21 18 E
Mrakovo 62 52 43N 56 38 E
Mramor 46 43 20N 21 45 E
Mrimina 120 29 50N 7 9W
Mrkonjić Grad 46 44 26N 17 4 E
Mrkopalj 43 45 21N 14 52 E
Mrocza 32 53 16N 17 35 E
Msab, Oued en → 121 32 25N 5 20 E
Msaken 121 35 49N 10 33 E
Msambansovu 131 15 50 S 30 3 E
M'sila 121 35 46N 4 30 E
Msoro 131 13 35 S 31 50 E
Msta → 58 58 25N 31 20 E
Mstislavl 58 54 0N 31 50 E
Mszana Dolna 32 49 41N 20 5 E
Mszczonów 32 51 58N 20 33 E
Mtama 131 10 17 S 39 21 E
Mtilikwe → 131 21 9 S 31 30 E
Mtsensk 59 53 25N 36 30 E
Mtskheta 61 41 52N 44 45 E
Mtubatuba 135 28 30 S 32 8 E
Mtwara-Mikindani 131 10 20 S 40 20 E
Mu → 82 21 56N 95 38 E
Mu Gia, Deo 84 17 40N 105 47 E
Mu Us Shamo 94 39 0N 109 0 E
Muacandalo 133 10 2 S 19 40 E
Muaná 170 1 25 S 49 15W
Muanda 133 6 0 S 12 20 E
Muang Chiang Rai 84 19 52N 99 50 E
Muang Lamphun 84 18 40N 99 2 E
Muang Pak Beng 84 19 54N 101 8 E
Muar 85 2 3N 102 34 E
Muarabungo 88 1 28 S 102 52 E
Muaraenim 88 3 40 S 103 50 E
Muarajuloi 89 0 12 S 114 3 E
Muarakaman 89 0 2 S 116 45 E
Muaratebo 88 1 30 S 102 26 E
Muaratembesi 88 1 42 S 103 8 E
Muaratewe 89 0 58 S 114 52 E
Mubarakpur 79 26 6N 83 18 E
Mubende 130 0 33N 31 22 E
Mubi 127 10 18N 13 16 E
Mubur, P. 85 3 20N 106 12 E
Mucajaí → 169 2 25N 60 52W
Mucajaí, Serra do 169 2 23N 61 10W
Mucari 133 9 30 S 16 54 E
Muchachos, Roque de los 37 28 44N 17 52W
Mücheln 26 51 18N 11 49 E
Muchinga Mts. 131 11 30 S 31 30 E
Muchkapskiy 59 51 52N 42 28 E
Muck 14 56 50N 6 15W
Muckadilla 111 26 35 S 148 23 E
Muco → 168 4 15N 70 21W
Mucoma 133 15 18 S 13 39 E
Muconda 133 10 31 S 21 15 E
Mucuim → 173 6 33 S 64 18W
Mucura 169 2 31 S 62 43W
Mucuri 171 18 0 S 39 36W
Mucurici 171 18 6 S 40 31W
Mucusso 133 18 1 S 21 25 E
Muda 37 28 34N 13 57W
Mudan Jiang → 95 46 20N 129 30 E
Mudanjiang 95 44 38N 129 30 E
Mudanya 60 40 25N 28 50 E
Muddy → 157 38 0N 110 22W
Mudgee 113 32 32 S 149 31 E
Mudjatik → 145 56 1N 107 36W
Mudon 82 16 15N 97 44 E
Mudugh □ 136 7 0N 47 30 E
Muecate 131 14 55 S 39 40 E
Muêda 131 11 36 S 39 28 E
Muela, La 36 41 36N 1 7W
Mueller Ra. 108 18 18 S 126 46 E
Muende 131 14 28 S 33 0 E
Muerto, Mar 161 16 10N 94 10W
Muertos, Punta de los 37 36 57N 1 54W
Mufindi □ 131 8 30 S 35 20 E
Mufu Shan 97 29 20N 114 30 E
Mufulira 131 12 32 S 28 15 E
Mufumbiro Range 130 1 25 S 29 30 E
Mugardos 34 43 27N 8 15W
Muge 35 39 3N 8 40W
Muge → 35 39 8N 8 44W
Múggia 43 45 36N 13 47 E
Mughayrā' 72 29 17N 37 41 E
Mugi 100 33 40N 134 25 E
Mugia 34 43 3N 9 10W
Mugila, Mts. 130 7 0 S 28 50 E
Muğla 57 37 15N 28 22 E
Mŭglizh 47 42 37N 25 32 E
Mugu 79 29 45N 82 30 E
Muhammad, Râs 71 27 44N 34 16 E
Muhammad Qol 124 20 53N 37 9 E
Muhammadabad 79 26 4N 83 25 E
Muharraqa = Sa'ad 69 31 28N 34 33 E
Muḩayriqah 74 23 59N 45 4 E
Muhesi → 130 7 0 S 35 20 E
Muheza □ 130 5 0 S 39 0 E
Mühldorf 27 48 14N 12 33 E
Mühlhausen 26 51 12N 10 29 E
Mühlig Hofmann fjella 7 72 30 S 5 0 E
Muhutwe 130 1 35 S 31 45 E
Muiden 22 52 20N 5 4 E
Muikamachi 99 37 15N 138 50 E
Muine Bheag 15 52 42N 6 57W
Muiños 34 41 58N 7 59W
Muir, L. 109 34 30 S 116 40 E
Mukachevo 58 48 27N 22 45 E
Mukah 86 2 55N 112 5 E
Mukawwa, Geziret 124 23 55N 35 53 E
Mukdahan 84 16 32N 104 43 E
Mukden = Shenyang 95 41 48N 123 27 E
Mukhtolovo 59 55 29N 43 15 E
Mukhtuya = Lensk 65 60 48N 114 55 E
Mukinbudin 109 30 55 S 118 5 E
Mukishi 131 8 30 S 24 44 E
Mukomuko 88 2 30 S 101 10 E
Mukomwenze 130 6 49 S 27 15 E
Mukry 63 37 54N 65 12 E
Muktsar 78 30 30N 74 30 E
Mukur 78 32 50N 67 42 E
Mukutawa → 145 53 10N 97 24W
Mukwela 131 17 0 S 26 40 E
Mukwonago 155 42 52N 88 20W
Mula 37 38 3N 1 33W
Mula → 80 18 34N 74 21 E
Mulanay 90 13 31N 122 24 E
Mulange 130 3 40 S 27 10 E
Mulberry Grove 154 38 55N 89 16W
Mulchén 174 37 45 S 72 20W
Mulde → 26 51 50N 12 15 E
Muldraugh 155 37 56N 85 59W
Mule Creek 152 43 19N 104 8W
Muleba 130 1 50 S 31 37 E
Muleba □ 130 2 0 S 31 30 E
Mulegns 29 46 32N 9 38 E
Muleshoe 153 34 17N 102 42W
Mulga Valley 112 31 8 S 141 3 E
Mulgathing 111 30 15 S 134 8 E
Mulgrave 143 45 38N 61 31W
Mulgrave I. 107 10 5 S 142 10 E
Mulhacén 37 37 4N 3 20W
Mülheim 26 51 26N 6 53 E
Mulhouse 19 47 40N 7 20 E
Muli 96 27 52N 101 8 E
Muling 95 44 35N 130 10 E
Mull 14 56 27N 6 0W
Mullaittvu 81 9 15N 80 49 E
Mullen 152 42 5N 101 0W
Mullengudgery 113 31 43 S 147 23 E
Mullens 148 37 34N 81 22W
Muller, Pegunungan 89 0 30N 113 30 E
Mullet Pen. 15 54 10N 10 2W
Mullewa 109 28 29 S 115 30 E
Müllheim 27 47 48N 7 37 E
Mulligan → 111 26 40 S 139 0 E
Mullin 153 31 33N 98 38W
Mullingar 15 53 31N 7 20W
Mullins 149 34 12N 79 15W
Mullsjö 53 57 56N 13 55 E
Mullumbimby 111 28 30 S 153 30 E
Mulobezi 131 16 45 S 25 7 E
Mulshi L. 80 18 30N 73 48 E
Multai 78 21 50N 78 21 E
Multan 77 30 15N 71 36 E
Multrå 52 63 10N 17 24 E
Mulumbe, Mts. 131 8 40 S 27 30 E
Mulungushi Dam 131 14 48 S 28 48 E
Mulvane 153 37 30N 97 15W
Mulwad 124 18 45N 30 39 E
Mulwala 113 35 59 S 146 0 E
Mumbondo 133 10 9 S 14 15 E
Mumbwa 131 15 0 S 27 0 E
Mumeng 107 7 1 S 146 37 E
Mumra 61 45 45N 47 41 E
Mun → 84 15 19N 105 30 E
Muna 87 5 0 S 122 30 E
Munamagi 58 57 43N 27 4 E
Munawwar 79 32 47N 74 27 E
Münchberg 27 50 11N 11 48 E
Müncheberg 26 52 30N 14 9 E
München 27 48 8N 11 33 E
Munchen-Gladbach = Mönchengladbach 26 51 12N 6 23 E
Muncho Lake 144 59 0N 125 50W
Munchŏn 95 39 14N 127 19 E
Münchwilen 29 47 28N 8 59 E
Muncie 155 40 10N 85 20W
Mundakayam 81 9 30N 76 50 E
Mundala 87 4 30 S 141 0 E
Mundare 144 53 35N 112 20W
Munday 153 33 26N 99 39W
Münden 26 51 25N 9 42 E
Mundiwindi 108 23 47 S 120 9 E
Mundo → 37 38 30N 2 15W
Mundo Novo 171 11 50 S 40 29W
Mundra 78 22 54N 69 48 E
Mundrabilla 109 31 52 S 127 51 E
Munducurus 169 4 47 S 58 16W
Munenga 133 10 2 S 14 41 E
Munera 37 39 2N 2 29W
Muneru → 81 16 45N 80 3 E
Mungallala 111 26 28 S 147 34 E
Mungallala Cr. → 111 28 53 S 147 5 E
Mungana 110 17 8 S 144 27 E
Mungaoli 78 24 24N 78 7 E
Mungari 131 17 12 S 33 30 E
Mungbere 130 2 36N 28 28 E
Munger 79 25 23N 86 30 E
Mungindi 111 28 58 S 149 1 E
Munhango 133 12 10 S 18 38 E
Munich = München 27 48 8N 11 33 E
Munising 148 46 25N 86 39W
Munka-Ljungby 53 56 16N 12 58 E
Munkedal 53 58 28N 11 40 E
Munkfors 52 59 50N 13 30 E
Munku-Sardyk 65 51 45N 100 20 E
Münnerstadt 27 50 15N 10 11 E
Munoz 90 15 43N 120 54 E
Muñoz Gamero, Pen. 176 52 30 S 73 5 E
Munro 113 37 56 S 147 11 E
Munroe L. 145 59 13N 98 35W
Munsan 95 37 51N 126 48 E
Munshiganj 82 23 33N 90 32 E
Münsingen 28 46 52N 7 32 E
Munster, France 19 48 2N 7 8 E
Munster, Niedersachsen, Germany 26 52 59N 10 5 E
Münster, Nordrhein-Westfalen, Germany 26 51 58N 7 37 E
Münster, Switz. 29 46 30N 8 17 E
Munster □ 15 52 20N 8 40W
Muntadgin 109 31 45 S 118 33 E
Muntele Mare 50 46 30N 23 12 E
Muntok 88 2 5 S 105 10 E
Munyak 64 43 30N 59 15 E
Munyama 131 16 5 S 28 31 E
Muong Beng 84 20 23N 101 46 E
Muong Boum 84 22 24N 102 49 E
Muong Et 84 20 49N 104 1 E
Muong Hai 84 21 3N 101 49 E
Muong Hiem 84 20 5N 103 22 E
Muong Houn 84 20 8N 101 23 E
Muong Hung 84 20 56N 103 53 E
Muong Kau 84 15 6N 105 47 E
Muong Khao 84 19 38N 103 32 E
Muong Khoua 84 21 5N 102 31 E
Muong Liep 84 18 29N 101 40 E
Muong May 84 14 49N 106 56 E
Muong Ngeun 84 20 36N 101 3 E
Muong Ngoi 84 20 43N 102 41 E
Muong Nhie 84 22 12N 102 28 E
Muong Nong 84 16 22N 106 30 E
Muong Ou Tay 84 22 7N 101 48 E
Muong Oua 84 18 18N 101 20 E
Muong Peun 84 20 13N 103 52 E
Muong Phalane 84 16 39N 105 34 E
Muong Phieng 84 19 6N 101 32 E
Muong Phine 84 16 32N 106 2 E
Muong Sai 84 20 42N 101 59 E
Muong Saiapoun 84 18 24N 101 31 E
Muong Sen 84 19 24N 104 8 E
Muong Sing 84 21 11N 101 9 E
Muong Son 84 20 27N 103 19 E
Muong Soui 84 19 33N 102 52 E
Muong Va 84 21 53N 102 19 E
Muong Xia 84 20 19N 104 50 E
Muonio 54 67 57N 23 40 E
Muotathal 29 46 58N 8 46 E
Mupa 133 16 5 S 15 50 E
Muping 95 37 22N 121 36 E
Muqaddam, Wadi → 124 18 4N 31 30 E

Muqdisho

Muqdisho **136** 2 2N 45 25 E
Muqshin, W. → **75** 19 44N 55 14 E
Muquequete **133** 14 50 S 14 16 E
Mur → **30** 46 35N 16 3 E
Mur-de-Bretagne **18** 48 12N 3 0W
Mura → **43** 46 18N 16 53 E
Murakami **98** 38 14N 139 29 E
Murallón, Cuerro **176** 49 48 S 73 30W
Muralto **29** 46 11N 8 49 E
Muranda **130** 1 52 S 29 20 E
Murang'a **130** 0 45 S 37 9 E
Murashi **59** 59 30N 49 0 E
Murat **20** 45 7N 2 53 E
Murathüyüğü **70** 36 52N 36 55 E
Murau **30** 47 6N 14 10 E
Muravera **44** 39 25N 9 35 E
Murayama **98** 38 30N 140 25 E
Murban **75** 23 50N 53 45 E
Murça **34** 41 24N 7 28W
Murchison **115** 41 49 S 172 21 E
Murchison → **109** 27 45 S 114 0 E
Murchison, Mt. **7** 73 0 S 168 0 E
Murchison Falls = Kabarega Falls **130** 2 15N 31 30 E
Murchison House **109** 27 39 S 114 14 E
Murchison Mts. **115** 45 13 S 167 23 E
Murchison Ra. **110** 20 0 S 134 10 E
Murchison Rapids **131** 15 55 S 34 35 E
Murcia **37** 38 20N 1 10W
Murcia □ **37** 37 50N 1 30W
Murdo **152** 43 56N 100 43W
Murdoch Pt. **110** 14 37 S 144 55 E
Mure, La **21** 44 55N 5 48 E
Mureş □ **50** 46 45N 24 40 E
Mureş → **50** 46 15N 20 13 E
Mureşul = Mureş → **50** 46 15N 20 13 E
Muret **20** 43 30N 1 20 E
Murfatlar **50** 44 10N 28 26 E
Murfreesboro **149** 35 50N 86 21W
Murg **29** 47 6N 9 13 E
Murg → **27** 48 55N 8 10 E
Murgab **63** 38 10N 74 2 E
Murgeni **50** 46 12N 28 1 E
Murgenthal **28** 47 16N 7 50 E
Murgon **111** 26 15 S 151 54 E
Murgoo **109** 27 24 S 116 28 E
Muri **29** 47 17N 8 21 E
Muria **89** 6 36 S 110 53 E
Muriaé **171** 21 8 S 42 23W
Murias de Paredes **34** 42 52N 6 11W
Murici **170** 9 19 S 35 56W
Muriége **133** 9 58 S 21 11 E
Muriel Mine **131** 17 14 S 30 40 E
Murila **133** 10 44 S 20 20 E
Müritz See **26** 53 25N 12 40 E
Murka **130** 3 27 S 38 0 E
Murmansk **56** 68 57N 33 10 E
Murmerwoude **22** 53 18N 6 0 E
Murnau **27** 47 40N 11 11 E
Muro, France **21** 42 34N 8 54 E
Muro, Spain **36** 39 44N 3 3 E
Muro, C. de **21** 41 44N 8 37 E
Muro Lucano **45** 40 45N 15 30 E
Murom **59** 55 35N 42 3 E
Muroran **98** 42 25N 141 0 E
Muros **34** 42 45N 9 5W
Muros y de Noya, Ría de → **34** 42 45N 9 0W
Muroto **100** 33 18N 134 9 E
Muroto-Misaki **100** 33 15N 134 10 E
Murowana Goślina **32** 52 35N 17 0 E
Murphy **156** 43 11N 116 33W
Murphys **158** 38 8N 120 28W
Murphysboro **154** 37 50N 89 20W
Murrat **124** 18 51N 29 33 E
Murray, Iowa, U.S.A. **154** 41 3N 93 57W
Murray, Ky., U.S.A. **149** 36 40N 88 20W
Murray, Utah, U.S.A. **156** 40 41N 111 58W
Murray →, Australia **112** 35 20 S 139 22 E
Murray →, Canada **144** 56 11N 120 45W
Murray, L., Papua N. G. **107** 7 0 S 141 35 E
Murray, L., U.S.A. **149** 34 8N 81 30W
Murray Bridge **112** 35 6 S 139 14 E
Murray Downs **110** 21 4 S 134 40 E
Murray Harbour **143** 46 0N 62 28W
Murray Seascarp **105** 30 0N 135 0W
Murraysburg **134** 31 58 S 23 47 E
Murrayville **154** 39 35N 90 15W
Murree **78** 33 56N 73 28 E
Murrieta **159** 33 33N 117 13W
Murrin Murrin **109** 28 58 S 121 33 E
Murrumbidgee → **112** 34 43 S 143 12 E
Murrumburrah **113** 34 32 S 148 22 E
Murrurundi **111** 31 42 S 150 51 E
Mursala **88** 1 41N 98 28 E
Murshid **124** 21 40N 31 10 E
Murshidabad **79** 24 11N 88 19 E
Murska Sobota **43** 46 39N 16 12 E
Murtazapur **78** 20 40N 77 25 E
Murten **28** 46 56N 7 4 E
Murtensee **28** 46 56N 7 7 E
Murtle L. **144** 52 8N 119 38W
Murtoa **112** 36 35 S 142 28 E
Murtosa **34** 40 44N 8 40W
Muru → **172** 8 9 S 70 45W
Murungu **130** 4 12 S 31 10 E
Murupara **114** 38 28 S 176 42 E
Murwara **79** 23 46N 80 28 E
Murwillumbah **111** 28 18 S 153 27 E
Mürz → **30** 47 30N 15 25 E
Mürzzuschlag **30** 47 36N 15 41 E
Muş **57** 38 45N 41 30 E
Musa **132** 2 40N 19 18 E
Musa → **107** 9 3 S 148 55 E
Mûsa, G. **71** 28 33N 33 59 E
Musa Khel **77** 30 59N 69 52 E
Mūsá Qal'eh **77** 32 20N 64 50 E
Musala **47** 42 13N 23 37 E
Musan **95** 42 12N 129 12 E
Musangu **131** 10 28 S 23 55 E
Musasa **130** 3 25 S 31 30 E
Musashino **101** 35 42N 139 34 E
Musay'īd **75** 25 0N 51 33 E
Musaymīr **74** 13 27N 44 37 E
Muscat = Masqat **75** 23 37N 58 36 E
Muscat & Oman = Oman ■ **75** 23 0N 58 0 E
Muscatine **154** 41 25N 91 5W
Muscoda **154** 43 11N 90 27W
Musel **34** 43 34N 5 42W
Musgrave Ras. **109** 26 0 S 132 0 E
Mushie **132** 2 56 S 16 55 E
Mushin **127** 6 32N 3 21 E
Musi →, India **80** 16 41N 79 40 E
Musi →, Indonesia **88** 2 20 S 104 56 E
Muskeg → **144** 60 20N 123 20W
Muskegon **155** 43 15N 86 17W
Muskegon → **148** 43 25N 86 0W
Muskegon Hts. **155** 43 12N 86 17W
Muskogee **153** 35 50N 95 25W
Muskwa → **144** 58 47N 122 48W
Muslīmiyah **72** 36 19N 37 12 E
Musmar **124** 18 13N 35 40 E
Musofu **131** 13 30 S 29 0 E
Musoma **130** 1 30 S 33 48 E
Musoma □ **130** 1 50 S 34 30 E
Musquaro, L. **143** 50 38N 61 5W
Musquodoboit Harbour **143** 44 50N 63 9W
Mussau I. **107** 1 30 S 149 40 E
Musselburgh **14** 55 57N 3 3W
Musselkanaal **22** 52 57N 7 0 E
Musselshell → **156** 47 21N 107 58W
Mussende **133** 10 32 S 16 5 E
Mussidan **20** 45 2N 0 22 E
Mussolo **133** 9 59 S 17 19 E
Mussomeli **44** 37 35N 13 43 E
Musson **23** 49 33N 5 42 E
Mussoorie **78** 30 27N 78 6 E
Mussuco **133** 17 2 S 19 3 E
Mustahil **136** 5 16N 44 45 E
Mustang **79** 29 10N 83 55 E
Musters, L. **176** 45 20 S 69 25W
Musudan **95** 40 50N 129 43 E
Muswellbrook **113** 32 16 S 150 56 E
Muszyna **31** 49 22N 20 55 E
Mût, Egypt **124** 25 28N 28 58 E
Mut, Turkey **70** 36 40N 33 28 E
Mutanda, Mozam. **135** 21 0 S 33 34 E
Mutanda, Zambia **131** 12 24 S 26 13 E
Mutaray **65** 60 56N 101 0 E
Mutare **131** 18 58 S 32 38 E
Mu'tariḑah, Al 'Urūq al **75** 21 15N 54 0 E
Muting **87** 7 23 S 140 20 E
Mutooroo **112** 32 26 S 140 55 E
Mutoto **133** 5 42 S 22 42 E
Mutshatsha **131** 10 35 S 24 20 E
Mutsu **98** 41 5N 140 55 E
Mutsu-Wan **98** 41 5N 140 55 E
Muttaburra **110** 22 38 S 144 29 E
Muttama **113** 34 46 S 148 8 E
Mutuáli **131** 14 55 S 37 0 E
Mutunópolis **171** 13 40 S 49 15W
Muvatupusha **81** 9 53N 76 35 E
Muweilih **71** 30 42N 34 19 E
Muxima **133** 9 33 S 13 58 E
Muy, Le **21** 43 28N 6 34 E
Muy Muy **162** 12 39N 85 36W
Muya **65** 56 27N 115 50 E
Muyinga **130** 3 14 S 30 33 E
Muyunkum, Peski **63** 44 12N 71 0 E
Muzaffarabad **79** 34 25N 73 30 E
Muzaffargarh **77** 30 5N 71 14 E
Muzaffarnagar **78** 29 26N 77 40 E
Muzaffarpur **79** 26 7N 85 23 E
Muzeze **133** 15 3 S 17 43 E
Muzhi **64** 65 25N 64 40 E
Muzillac **18** 47 35N 2 30W
Muzkol, Khrebet **63** 38 22N 73 20 E
Muzon C. **144** 54 40N 132 40W
Mvadhi-Ousyé **132** 1 13N 13 12 E
Mvam **132** 0 13 S 9 39 E
Mvôlô **125** 6 2N 29 53 E
Mvuma **131** 19 16 S 30 30 E
Mvurwi **131** 17 0 S 30 57 E
Mwadui **130** 3 26 S 33 32 E
Mwambo **131** 10 30 S 40 22 E
Mwandi **131** 17 30 S 24 51 E
Mwanza, Tanzania **130** 2 30 S 32 58 E
Mwanza, Zaïre **130** 7 55 S 26 43 E
Mwanza, Zambia **131** 16 58 S 24 28 E
Mwanza □ **130** 2 0 S 33 0 E
Mwaya **131** 9 32 S 33 55 E
Mweelrea **15** 53 37N 9 48W
Mweka **133** 4 50 S 21 34 E
Mwendjila **133** 7 12 S 18 51 E
Mwene **133** 6 35 S 22 27 E
Mwenezi **131** 21 15 S 30 48 E
Mwenezi → **131** 22 40 S 31 50 E
Mwenga **130** 3 1 S 28 28 E
Mweru, L. **131** 9 0 S 28 40 E
Mweza Range **131** 21 0 S 30 0 E
Mwilambwe **130** 8 7 S 25 0 E
Mwimbi **131** 8 38 S 31 39 E
Mwinilunga **131** 11 43 S 24 25 E
My Tho **85** 10 29N 106 23 E
Mya, O. → **121** 30 46N 4 54 E
Myajlar **78** 26 15N 70 20 E
Myanaung **82** 18 18N 95 22 E
Myaungmya **82** 16 30N 94 40 E
Mycenae = Mikínai **49** 37 43N 22 46 E
Myeik Kyunzu **84** 11 30N 97 30 E
Myerstown **151** 40 22N 76 18W
Myingyan **82** 21 30N 95 20 E
Myitkyina **82** 25 24N 97 26 E
Myittha → **82** 23 12N 94 17 E
Myjava **31** 48 41N 17 37 E
Mymensingh **82** 24 45N 90 24 E
Myndus **49** 37 3N 27 14 E
Mynydd Du **13** 51 45N 3 45W
Mynzhilgi, Gora **63** 43 48N 68 51 E
Myrdal **51** 60 43N 7 10 E
Mýrdalsjökull **54** 63 40N 19 6W
Myrtle Beach **149** 33 43N 78 50W
Myrtle Creek **156** 43 0N 123 9W
Myrtle Point **156** 43 0N 124 4W
Myrtleford **113** 36 34 S 146 44 E
Mysen **51** 59 33N 11 20 E
Myslenice **32** 49 51N 19 57 E
Myślibórz **32** 52 55N 14 50 E
Mysłowice **32** 50 15N 19 12 E
Mysore **81** 12 17N 76 41 E
Mysore □ = Karnataka □ **81** 13 15N 77 0 E
Mystic, Conn., U.S.A. **151** 41 21N 71 58W
Mystic, Iowa, U.S.A. **154** 40 47N 92 57W
Mystishchi **59** 55 50N 37 50 E
Myszków **32** 50 45N 19 22 E
Myszyniec **32** 53 23N 21 21 E
Mythen **29** 47 2N 8 42 E
Myton **156** 40 10N 110 2W
Mývatn **54** 65 36N 17 0W
Mze → **30** 49 46N 13 24 E
Mzimba **131** 11 55 S 33 39 E
Mzimkulu → **135** 30 44 S 30 28 E
Mzimvubu → **135** 31 38 S 29 33 E
Mzuzu **131** 11 30 S 33 55 E

N

N' Dioum **126** 16 31N 14 39W
Na-lang **82** 22 42N 97 33 E
Na Noi **84** 18 19N 100 43 E
Na Phao **84** 17 35N 105 44 E
Na Sam **84** 22 3N 106 37 E
Na San **84** 21 12N 104 2 E
Naab → **27** 49 1N 12 2 E
Naaldwijk **22** 51 59N 4 13 E
Na'am **125** 9 42N 28 27 E
Na'an **69** 31 53N 34 52 E
Naantali **55** 60 29N 22 2 E
Naarden **22** 52 18N 5 9 E
Naas **15** 53 12N 6 40W
Nababiep **134** 29 36 S 17 46 E
Nabadwip = Navadwip **79** 23 34N 88 20 E
Nabari **101** 34 37N 136 5 E
Nabawa **109** 28 30 S 114 48 E
Nabberu, L. **109** 25 50 S 120 30 E
Nabburg **27** 49 27N 12 11 E
Nabeul **121** 36 30N 10 44 E
Nabha **78** 30 26N 76 14 E
Nabīd **73** 29 40N 57 38 E
Nabire **87** 3 15 S 135 26 E
Nabisar **78** 25 8N 69 40 E
Nabisipi → **143** 50 14N 62 13W
Nabiswera **130** 1 27N 32 15 E
Nablus = Nābulus **69** 32 14N 35 15 E
Naboomspruit **135** 24 32 S 28 40 E
Nabq **71** 28 6N 34 25 E
Nabua **90** 13 24N 123 22 E
Nābulus **69** 32 14N 35 15 E
Nābulus □ **71** 32 20N 35 20 E
Nabunturan **91** 7 35N 125 58 E
Nacala-Velha **131** 14 32 S 40 34 E
Nacaome **162** 13 31N 87 30W
Nacaroa **131** 14 22 S 39 56 E
Naches **156** 46 48N 120 42W
Naches → **158** 46 38N 120 31W
Nachikatsuura **101** 33 33N 135 58 E
Nachingwea **131** 10 23 S 38 49 E
Nachingwea □ **131** 10 30 S 38 30 E
Nachna **78** 27 34N 71 41 E
Náchod **31** 50 25N 16 8 E
Nacimiento Res. **158** 35 46N 121 0W
Nacka **52** 59 17N 18 12 E
Nackara **112** 32 48 S 139 12 E
Naco, Mexico **160** 31 20N 109 56W
Naco, U.S.A. **157** 31 24N 109 58W
Nacogdoches **153** 31 33N 94 39W
Nácori Chico **160** 29 39N 109 1W
Nacozari **160** 30 24N 109 39W
Nadi **124** 18 40N 33 41 E
Nadiad **78** 22 41N 72 56 E
Nădlac **50** 46 10N 20 50 E
Nador **121** 35 14N 2 58W
Nadūshan **73** 32 2N 53 35 E
Nadvoitsy **56** 63 52N 34 14 E
Nadvornaya **60** 48 37N 24 30 E
Nadym **64** 65 35N 72 42 E
Nadym → **64** 66 12N 72 0 E
Nærbø **51** 58 40N 5 39 E
Næstved **52** 55 13N 11 44 E
Nafada **127** 11 8N 11 20 E
Näfels **29** 47 6N 9 4 E
Naftshahr **72** 34 0N 45 30 E
Nafūsah, Jabal **122** 32 12N 12 30 E
Nag Hammâdi **124** 26 2N 32 18 E
Naga, Cebu, Phil. **91** 10 13N 123 45 E
Naga, Luzon, Phil. **90** 13 38N 123 15 E
Naga, Zamboanga del S., Phil. **91** 7 46N 122 45 E
Naga, Kreb en **120** 24 12N 6 0W
Naga-Shima, Kagoshima, Japan **100** 32 10N 130 9 E
Naga-Shima, Yamaguchi, Japan **100** 33 49N 132 5 E
Nagagami → **142** 49 40N 84 40W
Nagahama, Ehime, Japan **100** 33 36N 132 29 E
Nagahama, Shiga, Japan **101** 35 23N 136 16 E
Nagai **98** 38 6N 140 2 E
Nagaland □ **82** 26 0N 94 30 E
Nagambie **113** 36 47 S 145 10 E
Nagano **101** 36 40N 138 10 E
Nagano □ **101** 36 15N 138 0 E
Nagaoka **99** 37 27N 138 51 E
Nagappattinam **81** 10 46N 79 51 E
Nagar Parkar **78** 24 28N 70 46 E
Nagara → **101** 35 40N 136 43 E
Nagari Hills **81** 13 3N 79 45 E
Nagarjuna Sagar **81** 16 35N 79 17 E
Nagasaki **100** 32 47N 129 50 E
Nagasaki □ **100** 32 50N 129 40 E
Nagato **100** 34 19N 131 5 E
Nagaur **78** 27 15N 73 45 E
Nagbhir **80** 20 34N 79 55 E
Nagercoil **81** 8 12N 77 26 E
Nagina **79** 29 30N 78 30 E
Nagīneh **73** 34 20N 57 15 E
Nagir **79** 36 12N 74 42 E
Nago **106** 26 36N 128 0 E
Nagold **27** 34 14N 57 2 E
Nagold → **27** 48 52N 8 42 E
Nagoorin **110** 24 17 S 151 15 E
Nagornyy **65** 55 58N 124 57 E
Nagorsk **59** 59 18N 50 48 E
Nagoya **101** 35 10N 136 50 E
Nagpur **78** 21 8N 79 10 E
Nagua **163** 19 23N 69 50W
Nagyatád **31** 46 14N 17 22 E
Nagyecsed **31** 47 53N 22 24 E
Nagykanizsa **31** 46 28N 17 0 E
Nagykörös **31** 47 5N 19 48 E
Nagyléta **31** 47 23N 21 55 E
Naha **106** 26 13N 127 42 E
Nahalal **69** 32 41N 35 12 E
Nahanni Butte **144** 61 2N 123 31W
Nahanni Nat. Park **144** 61 15N 125 0W
Nahariyya **69** 33 1N 35 5 E
Nahāvand **73** 34 10N 48 22 E
Nahe → **27** 49 58N 7 57 E
Nahf **69** 32 56N 35 18 E
Nahîya, Wadi → **124** 28 55N 31 0 E
Nahlin **144** 58 55N 131 38W
Nahuel Huapi, L. **176** 41 0 S 71 32W
Naicá **160** 27 53N 105 31W
Naicam **145** 52 30N 104 30W
Nā'ifah **68** 19 59N 50 46 E
Naila **27** 50 19N 11 43 E
Nain, Canada **143** 56 34N 61 40W
Nā'īn, Iran **73** 32 54N 53 0 E
Naini Tal **79** 29 30N 79 30 E
Naintré **18** 46 46N 0 29 E
Naipu **50** 44 12N 25 47 E
Naira **87** 4 28 S 130 0 E
Nairn **14** 57 35N 3 54W
Nairobi **130** 1 17 S 36 48 E
Naivasha **130** 0 40 S 36 30 E
Naivasha, L. **130** 0 48 S 36 20 E
Najac **20** 44 14N 1 58 E
Najafābād **73** 32 40N 51 15 E
Nájera **36** 42 26N 2 48W
Najerilla → **36** 42 32N 2 48W
Najibabad **78** 29 40N 78 20 E
Najin **95** 42 12N 130 15 E
Najmah **73** 26 42N 50 6 E
Naju **95** 35 3N 126 43 E
Naka → **101** 36 20N 140 36 E
Nakadōri-Shima **99** 32 57N 129 4 E
Nakalagba **130** 2 50N 27 58 E
Nakama **100** 33 56N 130 43 E
Nakaminato **101** 36 21N 140 36 E
Nakamura **100** 33 0N 133 0 E
Nakanai Mts. **107** 5 40 S 151 0 E
Nakano **101** 36 45N 138 22 E
Nakano-Shima **99** 29 51N 129 52 E
Nakanojō **101** 36 35N 138 51 E
Nakashibetsu **98** 43 33N 144 59 E
Nakatsu **100** 33 34N 131 15 E
Nakatsugawa **101** 35 29N 137 30 E
Nakfa **125** 16 40N 38 32 E
Nakhichevan A.S.S.R. □ **57** 39 14N 45 30 E
Nakhl **71** 29 55N 33 43 E
Nakhl-e Taqī **73** 27 28N 52 36 E
Nakhodka **65** 42 53N 132 54 E

Nchanga

Nakhon Nayok **84** 14 12N 101 13 E
Nakhon Pathom **84** 13 49N 100 3 E
Nakhon Phanom **84** 17 23N 104 43 E
Nakhon Ratchasima **84** 14 59N 102 12 E
Nakhon Sawan **84** 15 35N 100 10 E
Nakhon Si Thammarat **85** 8 29N 100 0 E
Nakhon Thai **84** 17 5N 100 44 E
Nakina, B.C., Canada **144** 59 12N 132 52W
Nakina, Ont., Canada **142** 50 10N 86 40W
Nakło nad Notecią **32** 53 9N 17 38 E
Nakodar **78** 31 8N 75 31 E
Nakskov **53** 54 50N 11 8 E
Näkten **52** 62 48N 14 38 E
Naktong → **95** 35 7N 128 57 E
Nakuru **130** 0 15 S 36 4 E
Nakuru □ **130** 0 15 S 35 5 E
Nakuru, L. **130** 0 23 S 36 5 E
Nakusp **144** 50 20N 117 45W
Nal → **77** 25 20N 65 30 E
Nalchik **61** 43 30N 43 33 E
Nälden **52** 63 21N 14 14 E
Näldsjön **52** 63 25N 14 15 E
Nalerigu **127** 10 35N 0 25W
Nalgonda **80** 17 6N 79 15 E
Nalhati **79** 24 17N 87 52 E
Nalinnes **23** 50 19N 4 27 E
Nallamalai Hills **81** 15 30N 78 50 E
Nalón → **34** 43 32N 6 4W
Nālūt **122** 31 54N 11 0 E
Nam Can **85** 8 46N 104 59 E
Nam Co **92** 30 30N 90 45 E
Nam Dinh **84** 20 25N 106 5 E
Nam Du, Hon **85** 9 41N 104 21 E
Nam Ngum Dam **84** 18 35N 102 34 E
Nam-Phan **85** 10 30N 106 0 E
Nam Phong **84** 16 42N 102 52 E
Nam Tha **84** 20 58N 101 30 E
Nam Tok **84** 14 21N 99 4 E
Namachire **133** 11 26 S 22 43 E
Namacunde **133** 17 18 S 15 50 E
Namacurra **135** 17 30 S 36 50 E
Namak, Daryācheh-ye **73** 34 30N 52 0 E
Namak, Kavir-e **73** 34 30N 57 30 E
Namakkal **81** 11 13N 78 13 E
Namaland **134** 24 30 S 17 0 E
Namangan **63** 41 0N 71 40 E
Namapa **131** 13 43 S 39 50 E
Namaqualand **134** 30 0 S 17 25 E
Namasagali **130** 1 2N 33 0 E
Namatanai **107** 3 40 S 152 29 E
Namber **87** 1 2 S 134 49 E
Nambour **111** 26 32 S 152 58 E
Nambucca Heads **111** 30 37 S 153 0 E
Namcha Barwa **92** 29 40N 95 10 E
Namche Bazar **79** 27 51N 86 47 E
Namchonjŏm **95** 38 15N 126 26 E
Namêche **23** 50 28N 5 0 E
Namecunda **131** 14 54 S 37 37 E
Nameh **89** 2 34N 116 21 E
Nameponda **131** 15 50 S 39 50 E
Namerikawa **101** 36 46N 137 20 E
Náměšt' nad Oslavou **31** 49 12N 16 10 E
Námestovo **31** 49 24N 19 25 E
Nametil **131** 15 40 S 39 21 E
Namew L. **145** 54 14N 101 56W
Namhsan **82** 22 48N 97 2 E
Nami **85** 22 58N 97 10 E
Namib Desert = Namibwoestyn **134** 22 30 S 15 0 E
Namibe **133** 15 7 S 12 11 E
Namibe □ **133** 16 35 S 12 30 E
Namibia ■ **134** 22 0 S 18 9 E
Namibwoestyn **134** 22 30 S 15 0 E
Namkhan **82** 23 50N 97 41 E
Namlea **87** 3 18 S 127 5 E
Namoi → **111** 30 12 S 149 30 E
Namous, O. en → **121** 31 0N 0 15W
Nampa **156** 43 34N 116 34W
Nampō-Shotō **99** 30 0N 140 0 E
Nampula **131** 15 6 S 39 15 E
Namrole **87** 3 46 S 126 46 E
Namrun **70** 37 8N 34 35 E
Namse Shankou **79** 30 0N 82 25 E
Namsen → **54** 64 27N 11 42 E
Namtay **65** 62 43N 129 37 E
Namtu **82** 23 5N 97 28 E
Namtumbo **131** 10 30 S 36 4 E
Namu **144** 51 52N 127 50W
Namuac **90** 18 37N 121 10 E
Namur **23** 50 27N 4 52 E
Namur □ **23** 50 17N 5 0 E
Namutoni **134** 18 49 S 16 55 E
Namwala **131** 15 44 S 26 30 E
Namwŏn **95** 35 23N 127 23 E
Namysłów **32** 51 6N 17 42 E
Nan **84** 18 48N 100 46 E
Nan → **84** 15 42N 100 9 E
Nan Xian **97** 29 20N 112 22 E
Nana **50** 44 17N 26 34 E
Nanaimo **144** 49 10N 124 0W
Nanam **95** 41 44N 129 40 E
Nanan **97** 24 59N 118 21 E
Nanango **111** 26 40 S 152 0 E
Nan'ao, China **97** 23 28N 117 5 E
Nanao, Japan **99** 37 0N 137 0 E
Nanbu **96** 31 18N 106 3 E
Nanchang **97** 28 42N 115 55 E
Nancheng **97** 27 33N 116 35 E
Nanchong **96** 30 43N 106 2 E
Nanchuan **96** 29 9N 107 6 E
Nancy **19** 48 42N 6 12 E
Nanda Devi **79** 30 23N 79 59 E
Nandan, China **96** 24 58N 107 29 E
Nandan, Japan **100** 34 10N 134 42 E
Nanded **80** 19 10N 77 20 E
Nandewar Ra. **111** 30 15 S 150 35 E
Nandi □ **130** 0 15N 35 0 E
Nandikotkur **81** 15 52N 78 18 E
Nandura **78** 20 52N 76 25 E
Nandurbar **78** 21 20N 74 15 E
Nandyal **81** 15 30N 78 30 E
Nanfeng, Guangdong, China **97** 23 45N 111 47 E
Nanfeng, Jiangxi, China **97** 27 12N 116 28 E
Nanga **109** 26 7 S 113 45 E
Nanga-Eboko **127** 4 41N 12 22 E
Nanga Parbat **79** 35 10N 74 35 E
Nangade **131** 11 5 S 39 36 E
Nangapinoh **89** 0 20 S 111 44 E
Nangarhár □ **77** 34 20N 70 0 E
Nangatayap **89** 1 32 S 110 34 E
Nangeya Mts. **130** 3 30N 33 30 E
Nangis **19** 48 33N 3 0 E
Nangong **94** 37 23N 115 22 E
Nangwarry **112** 37 33 S 140 48 E
Nanhua **96** 25 13N 101 21 E
Nanhuang **95** 36 58N 121 48 E
Nanhui **97** 31 5N 121 44 E
Nanjangud **81** 12 6N 76 43 E
Nanjeko **131** 15 31 S 23 30 E
Nanji Shan **97** 27 27N 121 4 E
Nanjian **96** 25 2N 100 25 E
Nanjiang **96** 32 28N 106 51 E
Nanjing **97** 24 25N 117 20 E
Nanjirinji **131** 9 41 S 39 5 E
Nankana Sahib **78** 31 27N 73 38 E
Nankang **97** 25 40N 114 45 E
Nankoku **100** 33 39N 133 44 E
Nanling **97** 30 55N 118 20 E
Nanning **96** 22 48N 108 20 E
Nannup **109** 33 59 S 115 48 E
Nanpan Jiang → **96** 25 10N 106 0 E
Nanpara **79** 27 52N 81 33 E
Nanpi **94** 38 2N 116 45 E
Nanping, Fujian, China **97** 26 38N 118 10 E
Nanping, Henan, China **97** 29 55N 112 3 E
Nanri Dao **97** 25 15N 119 25 E
Nanripe **131** 13 52 S 38 52 E
Nansei-Shotō **99** 26 0N 128 0 E
Nansen Sd. **6** 81 0N 91 0W
Nansio **130** 2 3 S 33 4 E
Nant **20** 44 1N 3 18 E
Nantes **18** 47 12N 1 33W
Nanteuil-le-Haudouin **19** 49 9N 2 48 E
Nantiat **20** 46 1N 1 11 E
Nanticoke **151** 41 12N 76 1W
Nanton **144** 50 21N 113 46W
Nantong **97** 32 1N 120 52 E
Nantua **21** 46 10N 5 35 E
Nanuku Passage **106** 16 45 S 179 15W
Nanuque **171** 17 50 S 40 21W
Nanutarra **108** 22 32 S 115 30 E
Nanxiong **97** 25 6N 114 15 E
Nanyang **94** 33 11N 112 30 E
Nanyi Hu **97** 31 5N 119 0 E
Nan'yō **100** 34 3N 131 49 E
Nanyuan **94** 39 44N 116 22 E
Nanyuki **130** 0 2N 37 4 E
Nanzhang **97** 31 45N 111 50 E
Náo, C. de la **37** 38 44N 0 14 E
Naococane L. **143** 52 50N 70 45W
Naoetsu **99** 37 12N 138 10 E
Naogaon **82** 24 52N 88 52 E
Náousa **48** 40 42N 22 9 E
Naozhou Dao **97** 20 55N 110 20 E
Napa **158** 38 18N 122 17W
Napa → **158** 38 10N 122 19W
Napanee **142** 44 15N 77 0W
Napanoch **151** 41 44N 74 22W
Nape **84** 18 18N 105 6 E
Nape Pass = Keo Neua, Deo **84** 18 23N 105 10 E
Naperville **155** 41 46N 88 9W
Napf **28** 47 1N 7 56 E
Napier **114** 39 30 S 176 56 E
Napier Broome B. **108** 14 2 S 126 37 E
Napier Downs **108** 17 11 S 124 36 E
Napier Pen. **110** 12 4 S 135 43 E
Naples = Nápoli **45** 40 50N 14 17 E
Naples **149** 26 10N 81 45W
Napo **96** 23 22N 105 50 E
Napo □ **168** 0 30 S 77 0W
Napo → **168** 3 20 S 72 40W
Napoleon, N. Dak., U.S.A. **152** 46 32N 99 49W
Napoleon, Ohio, U.S.A. **155** 41 24N 84 7W
Nápoli **45** 40 50N 14 17 E
Nápoli, G. di **45** 40 40N 14 10 E
Napopo **130** 4 15N 28 0 E
Nappa Merrie **111** 27 36 S 141 7 E
Nappanee **155** 41 27N 86 0W
Naqâda **124** 25 53N 32 42 E
Naqqāsh **73** 35 40N 49 6 E
Nara, Japan **101** 34 40N 135 49 E
Nara, Mali **126** 15 10N 7 20W
Nara □ **101** 34 30N 136 0 E
Nara, Canal **78** 24 30N 69 20 E
Nara Visa **153** 35 39N 103 10W
Naracoorte **112** 36 58 S 140 45 E
Naradhan **113** 33 34 S 146 17 E
Narasapur **81** 16 26N 81 40 E
Narasaropet **81** 16 14N 80 4 E
Narathiwat **85** 6 30N 101 48 E
Narayanganj **82** 23 40N 90 33 E
Narayanpet **80** 16 45N 77 30 E
Narbonne **20** 43 11N 3 0 E
Narcea → **34** 43 33N 6 44W
Nardīn **73** 37 3N 55 59 E
Nardò **45** 40 10N 18 0 E
Narembeen **109** 32 7 S 118 24 E
Naretha **109** 31 0 S 124 45 E
Narew **32** 52 55N 23 31 E
Narew → **32** 52 26N 20 41 E
Nari → **78** 29 40N 68 0 E
Narindra, Helodranon' i **135** 14 55 S 47 30 E
Narino □ **168** 1 30N 78 0W
Narita **101** 35 47N 140 19 E
Narmada → **78** 21 38N 72 36 E
Narnaul **78** 28 5N 76 11 E
Narni **43** 42 30N 12 30 E
Naro, Ghana **126** 10 22N 2 27W
Naro, Italy **44** 37 18N 13 48 E
Naro Fominsk **59** 55 23N 36 43 E
Narodnaya **56** 65 5N 60 0 E
Narok **130** 1 55 S 33 52 E
Narok □ **130** 1 20 S 36 30 E
Narón **34** 43 32N 8 9W
Narooma **113** 36 14 S 150 4 E
Narowal **77** 32 6N 74 52 E
Narrabri **111** 30 19 S 149 46 E
Narran → **111** 28 37 S 148 12 E
Narrandera **113** 34 42 S 146 31 E
Narraway → **144** 55 44N 119 55W
Narrogin **109** 32 58 S 117 14 E
Narromine **113** 32 12 S 148 12 E
Narsampet **80** 17 57N 79 58 E
Narsimhapur **79** 22 54N 79 14 E
Nartkala **61** 43 33N 43 51 E
Naruto, Kantō, Japan **100** 34 11N 134 37 E
Narutō, Shikoku, Japan **101** 35 36N 140 25 E
Naruto-Kaikyō **100** 34 14N 134 39 E
Narva **58** 59 23N 28 12 E
Narva → **58** 59 27N 28 2 E
Narvacan **90** 17 25N 120 28 E
Narvik **54** 68 28N 17 26 E
Narvskoye Vdkhr. **58** 59 18N 28 14 E
Narwana **78** 29 39N 76 6 E
Naryan-Mar **56** 68 0N 53 0 E
Naryilco **111** 28 37 S 141 53 E
Narym **64** 59 0N 81 30 E
Narymskoye **64** 49 10N 84 15 E
Naryn **63** 41 26N 75 58 E
Naryn → **63** 40 52N 71 36 E
Nasa **54** 66 29N 15 23 E
Nasarawa **127** 8 32N 7 41 E
Năsăud **50** 47 19N 24 29 E
Naşb, W. → **71** 28 29N 34 31 E
Naseby **115** 45 1 S 170 10 E
Naselle **158** 46 22N 123 49W
Naser, Buheirat en **124** 23 0N 32 30 E
Nashua, Iowa, U.S.A. **154** 42 55N 92 34W
Nashua, Mont., U.S.A. **156** 48 10N 106 25W
Nashua, N.H., U.S.A. **151** 42 50N 71 25W
Nashville, Ark., U.S.A. **153** 33 56N 93 50W
Nashville, Ga., U.S.A. **149** 31 3N 83 15W
Nashville, Ill., U.S.A. **154** 38 21N 89 23W
Nashville, Ind., U.S.A. **155** 39 12N 86 14W
Nashville, Mich., U.S.A. **155** 42 36N 85 5W
Nashville, Tenn., U.S.A. **149** 36 12N 86 46W
Našice **46** 45 32N 18 4 E
Nasielsk **32** 52 35N 20 50 E
Nasik **80** 19 58N 73 50 E
Nasipit **91** 8 57N 125 19 E
Nasirabad **78** 26 15N 74 45 E
Naskaupi → **143** 53 47N 60 51W
Naso **45** 38 8N 14 46 E
Naso Pt. **91** 10 25N 121 57 E
Naşriān-e Pā'īn **72** 32 52N 46 52 E
Nass → **144** 55 0N 129 40W
Nassau, Bahamas **162** 25 0N 77 20W
Nassau, U.S.A. **151** 42 30N 73 34W
Nassau, B. **176** 55 20 S 68 0W
Nasser, L. = Naser, Buheirat en **124** 23 0N 32 30 E
Nasser City = Kôm Ombo **124** 24 25N 32 52 E
Nassian **126** 8 28N 3 28W
Nässjö **53** 57 39N 14 42 E
Nasugbu **90** 14 5N 120 38 E
Näsum **53** 56 10N 14 29 E
Näsviken **52** 61 46N 16 52 E
Nata **134** 20 12 S 26 12 E
Natagaima **168** 3 37N 75 6W
Natal, Brazil **170** 5 47 S 35 13W
Natal, Canada **144** 49 43N 114 51W
Natal, Indonesia **88** 0 35N 99 7 E
Natal □ **135** 28 30 S 30 30 E
Natalinci **46** 44 15N 20 49 E
Naţanz **73** 33 30N 51 55 E
Natashquan **143** 50 14N 61 46W
Natashquan → **143** 50 7N 61 50W
Natchez **153** 31 35N 91 25W
Natchitoches **153** 31 47N 93 4W
Naters **28** 46 19N 8 0 E
Nathalia **113** 36 1 S 145 13 E
Nathdwara **78** 24 55N 73 50 E
Natimuk **112** 36 42 S 142 0 E
Nation → **144** 55 30N 123 32W
National City **159** 32 39N 117 7W
Natitingou **127** 10 20N 1 26 E
Natividad, I. **160** 27 50N 115 10W
Natogyi **82** 21 25N 95 39 E
Natoma **152** 39 14N 99 0W
Natonin **90** 17 6N 121 18 E
Natron, L. **130** 2 20 S 36 0 E
Natrona Heights **150** 40 39N 79 43W
Natrûn, W. el → **124** 30 25N 30 13 E
Natuna Besar, Kepulauan **85** 4 0N 108 15 E
Natuna Selatan, Kepulauan **85** 2 45N 109 0 E
Natural Bridge **151** 44 5N 75 30W
Naturaliste C. **110** 40 50 S 148 15 E
Natya **112** 34 57 S 143 13 E
Nau **63** 40 9N 69 22 E
Nau Qala **78** 34 5N 68 5 E
Naubinway **142** 46 7N 85 27W
Naucelle **20** 44 13N 2 20 E
Nauders **30** 46 54N 10 30 E
Nauen **26** 52 36N 12 52 E
Naugatuck **151** 41 28N 73 4W
Naujan **90** 13 20N 121 18 E
Naujoji Vilnia **58** 54 48N 25 27 E
Naumburg **26** 51 10N 11 48 E
Nā'ūr at Tunayb **71** 31 48N 35 57 E
Nauru ■ **104** 1 0 S 166 0 E
Naurzum **62** 51 32N 64 34 E
Naushahra = Nowshera **77** 34 0N 72 0 E
Nausori **106** 18 2 S 178 32 E
Nauta **168** 4 31 S 73 35W
Nautla **161** 20 20N 96 50W
Nauvoo **154** 40 33N 91 23W
Nava **160** 28 25N 100 46W
Nava del Rey **34** 41 22N 5 6W
Navacerrada, Puerto de **34** 40 47N 4 0W
Navadwip **79** 23 34N 88 20 E
Navahermosa **35** 39 41N 4 28W
Navajo Res. **157** 36 55N 107 30W
Naval **91** 11 34N 124 23 E
Navalcarnero **34** 40 17N 4 5W
Navalmoral de la Mata **34** 39 52N 5 33W
Navalvillar de Pela **35** 39 9N 5 24W
Navan = An Uaimh **15** 53 39N 6 40W
Navarino, I. **176** 55 0 S 67 40W
Navarra □ **36** 42 40N 1 40W
Navarre **150** 40 43N 81 31W
Navarrenx **20** 43 20N 0 45W
Navarro **158** 39 10N 123 32W
Navas del Marqués, Las **34** 40 36N 4 20W
Navasota **153** 30 20N 96 5W
Navassa **163** 18 30N 75 0W
Nave **42** 45 35N 10 17 E
Naver → **14** 58 34N 4 15W
Navia **34** 43 35N 6 42W
Navia → **34** 43 15N 6 50W
Navia de Suarna **34** 42 58N 6 59W
Navidad **174** 33 57 S 71 50W
Naviti **106** 17 7 S 177 15 E
Navlya **58** 52 53N 34 30 E
Navoi **63** 40 9N 65 22 E
Navojoa **160** 27 0N 109 30W
Navolato **160** 24 47N 107 42W
Navolok **56** 62 33N 39 57 E
Návpaktos **49** 38 23N 21 50 E
Návplion **49** 37 33N 22 50 E
Navrongo **127** 10 51N 1 3W
Navsari **78** 20 57N 72 59 E
Nawa Kot **78** 28 21N 71 24 E
Nawabganj, Bangla. **82** 24 35N 88 14 E
Nawabganj, Ut. P., India **79** 26 56N 81 14 E
Nawabganj, Ut. P., India **79** 28 32N 79 40 E
Nawabshah **77** 26 15N 68 25 E
Nawada **79** 24 50N 85 33 E
Nāwah **77** 32 19N 67 53 E
Nawakot **79** 27 55N 85 10 E
Nawalgarh **78** 27 50N 75 15 E
Nawanshahr **79** 32 33N 74 48 E
Nawapara **79** 20 46N 82 33 E
Nawāsīf, Harrat **74** 21 20N 42 10 E
Nawi **124** 18 32N 30 50 E
Nawng Hpa **82** 22 30N 98 30 E
Nawş, Ra's **75** 17 15N 55 16 E
Náxos **49** 37 8N 25 25 E
Nay **20** 43 10N 0 18W
Nāy Band **73** 27 20N 52 40 E
Naya → **168** 3 13N 77 22W
Nayakhan **65** 61 56N 159 0 E
Nayarit □ **160** 22 0N 105 0W
Nayé **126** 14 28N 12 12W
Nayong **96** 26 50N 105 20 E
Nayoro **98** 44 21N 142 28 E
Nayyāl, W. → **72** 28 35N 39 4 E
Nazaré, Bahia, Brazil **171** 13 2 S 39 0W
Nazaré, Goiás, Brazil **170** 6 23 S 47 40W
Nazaré, Pará, Brazil **173** 6 25 S 52 29W
Nazaré, Portugal **35** 39 36N 9 4W
Nazareth = Nazerat **69** 32 42N 35 17 E
Nazas **160** 25 10N 104 6W
Nazas → **160** 25 35N 103 25W
Naze, The **13** 51 53N 1 19 E
Nazerat **69** 32 42N 35 17 E
Nāzīk **72** 39 1N 45 4 E
Nazir Hat **82** 22 35N 91 49 E
Nazko **144** 53 1N 123 37W
Nazko → **144** 53 7N 123 34W
Nazret **125** 8 32N 39 22 E
Nazwá **75** 22 56N 57 32 E
Nchanga **131** 12 30 S 27 49 E

Ncheu

Ncheu 131 14 50 S 34 47 E
Ndala 130 4 45 S 33 15 E
Ndalatando 133 9 12 S 14 48 E
Ndali 127 9 50N 2 46 E
Ndareda 130 4 12 S 35 30 E
Ndélé 95 8 25N 20 36 E
Ndendé 132 2 22 S 11 23 E
Ndjamena 123 12 10N 14 59 E
Ndjolé 132 0 10 S 10 45 E
Ndola 131 13 0 S 28 34 E
Ndoto Mts. 130 2 0N 37 0 E
Ndoua, C. 106 22 24 S 166 56 E
Nduguti 130 4 18 S 34 41 E
Nea → 51 63 15N 11 0 E
Néa Epídhavros 49 37 40N 23 7 E
Néa Flippiás 48 39 12N 20 53 E
Néa Kallikrátia 48 40 21N 23 1 E
Néa Víssi 48 41 34N 26 33 E
Neagari 101 36 26N 136 25 E
Neagh, Lough 15 54 35N 6 25W
Neah Bay 158 48 25N 124 40W
Neale L. 108 24 15 S 130 0 E
Neamţ □ 50 47 0N 26 20 E
Neápolis, Kozan, Greece 48 40 20N 21 24 E
Neápolis, Lakonia, Greece 49 36 27N 23 8 E
Near Is. 140 53 0N 172 0 E
Neath 13 51 39N 3 49W
Neba, I. 106 20 9 S 163 56 E
Nebbou 127 11 9N 1 51W
Nebine Cr. → 111 29 27 S 146 56 E
Nebit Dag 57 39 30N 54 22 E
Nebo 110 59 12N 32 25 E
Nebolchy 58 59 8N 33 18 E
Nebraska □ 152 41 30N 100 0W
Nebraska City 152 40 40N 95 52W
Nébrodi, Monti 44 37 55N 14 50 E
Necedah 152 44 2N 90 7W
Nechako → 144 53 30N 122 44W
Neches → 153 29 55N 93 52W
Neckar → 27 49 31N 8 26 E
Necochea 174 38 30 S 58 50W
Nectar Brook 112 32 43 S 137 57 E
Nedelišće 43 46 23N 16 22 E
Neder Rijn → 22 51 57N 6 2 E
Nederbrakel 23 50 48N 3 46 E
Nederweert 23 51 17N 5 45 E
Nédha → 49 37 25N 21 45 E
Nedroma 121 35 1N 1 45W
Nedstrand 51 59 21N 5 49 E
Neede 22 52 8N 6 37 E
Needles 159 34 50N 114 35W
Needles, Pt. 114 36 3 S 175 25 E
Needles, The 13 50 39N 1 35W
Ñeembucú □ 174 27 0 S 58 0W
Neemuch = Nimach 78 24 30N 74 56 E
Neenah 148 44 10N 88 30W
Neepawa 145 50 15N 99 30W
Neer 23 51 16N 5 59 E
Neerpelt 23 51 13N 5 26 E
Neft-chala = imeni 26 Bakinskikh Komissarov 57 39 19N 49 12 E
Nefta 121 33 53N 7 50 E
Neftah Sidi Boubekeur 121 35 1N 0 4 E
Neftegorsk 61 44 25N 39 45 E
Neftenbach 29 47 32N 8 41 E
Neftyannyye Kamni 57 40 20N 50 55 E
Negapatam = Nagappattinam 81 10 46N 79 51 E
Negaunee 148 46 30N 87 36W
Negba 69 31 40N 34 41 E
Negele 125 5 20N 39 36 E
Negev Desert = Hanegev 69 30 50N 35 0 E
Negoiul, Vf. 50 45 38N 24 35 E
Negombo 81 7 12N 79 50 E
Negotin 46 44 16N 22 37 E
Negotino 46 41 29N 22 9 E
Negra, La 174 23 46 S 70 18W
Negra, Peña 34 42 11N 6 30W
Negra, Pta., Maurit. 120 22 54N 16 18W
Negra, Pta., Peru 172 6 6 S 81 10W
Negra Pt. 90 18 40N 120 50 E
Negrais C. 82 16 0N 94 12 E
Negreira 34 42 54N 8 45W
Negreşti 50 46 50N 27 30 E
Négrine 121 34 30N 7 30 E
Negro →, Argentina 176 41 2 S 62 47W
Negro →, Bolivia 173 14 11 S 63 7W
Negro →, Brazil 169 3 0 S 60 0W
Negro →, Uruguay 175 33 24 S 58 22W
Negros 91 9 30N 122 40 E
Negru Vodă 50 43 47N 28 21 E
Nehalem → 158 45 40N 123 56W
Nehāvand 73 35 56N 49 31 E
Nehbandān 73 31 35N 60 5 E
Neheim-Hüsten 26 51 27N 7 58 E
Nehoiaşu 50 45 24N 26 20 E
Nei Monggol Zizhiqu □ 94 42 0N 112 0 E
Neidpath 145 50 12N 107 20W
Neihart 156 47 0N 110 44W
Neijiang 96 29 35N 104 55 E
Neilrex 113 31 44 S 149 20 E
Neilton 156 17 24N 123 52W
Neiqiu 94 37 15N 114 30 E
Neira de Jusá 34 42 53N 7 14W
Neisse → 26 52 4N 14 46 E
Neiva 168 2 56N 75 18W
Neixiang 94 33 10N 111 52 E
Nejanilini L. 145 59 33N 97 48W
Nejo 125 9 30N 35 28 E
Nekā 73 36 39N 53 19 E
Nekemte 125 9 4N 36 30 E
Nêkheb 124 25 10N 32 48 E
Neksø 53 55 4N 15 8 E
Nelas 34 40 32N 7 52W
Nelaug 51 58 39N 8 40 E
Nelia 110 20 39 S 142 12 E
Nelidovo 58 56 13N 32 49 E
Neligh 152 42 11N 98 2W
Nelkan 65 57 40N 136 4 E
Nellikuppam 81 11 46N 79 43 E
Nellore 81 14 27N 79 59 E
Nelma 65 47 39N 139 0 E
Nelson, Canada 144 49 30N 117 20W
Nelson, N.Z. 115 41 18 S 173 16 E
Nelson, U.K. 12 53 50N 2 14W
Nelson, U.S.A. 157 35 35N 113 16W
Nelson □ 115 42 11 S 172 15 E
Nelson → 145 54 33N 98 2W
Nelson, C., Australia 112 38 26 S 141 32 E
Nelson, C., Papua N. G. 107 9 0 S 149 20 E
Nelson, Estrecho 176 51 30 S 75 0W
Nelson Forks 144 59 30N 124 0W
Nelson House 145 55 47N 98 51W
Nelson L. 145 55 48N 100 7W
Nelspoort 134 32 7 S 23 0 E
Nelspruit 135 25 29 S 30 59 E
Néma 126 16 40N 7 15W
Neman → 58 55 25N 21 10 E
Neméa 49 37 49N 22 40 E
Nemeiben L. 145 55 20N 105 20W
Nemira 50 46 17N 26 19 E
Nemours 19 48 16N 2 40 E
Nemunas = Neman → 58 55 25N 21 10 E
Nemuro 98 43 20N 145 35 E
Nemuro-Kaikyō 98 43 30N 145 30 E
Nemuy 65 55 40N 136 9 E
Nen Jiang → 95 45 28N 124 30 E
Nenagh 15 52 52N 8 11W
Nenana 140 64 30N 149 20W
Nenasi 85 3 9N 103 23 E
Nendiarene, Pte. 106 20 14 S 164 19 E
Nene → 12 52 38N 0 13 E
Nenjiang 93 49 10N 125 10 E
Neno 131 15 25 S 34 40 E
Nenusa, Kepulauan 87 4 45N 127 1 E
Neodesha 153 37 30N 95 37W
Neoga 155 39 19N 88 27W
Néon Petrítsi 48 41 16N 23 15 E
Neópolis 170 10 18 S 36 35W
Neosho 153 36 56N 94 28W
Neosho → 153 35 59N 95 10W
Nepal ■ 79 28 0N 84 30 E
Nepalganj 79 28 5N 81 40 E
Nephi 156 39 43N 111 52W
Nephin 15 54 1N 9 21W
Nepomuk 30 49 29N 13 35 E
Neptune City 151 40 13N 74 4W
Néra → 46 44 48N 21 25 E
Nérac 20 44 8N 0 21 E
Nerastro, Sarīr 122 24 20N 20 37 E
Nerchinsk 65 52 0N 116 39 E
Nerchinskiy Zavod 65 51 20N 119 40 E
Nereju 50 45 43N 26 43 E
Nerekhta 59 57 26N 40 38 E
Néret L. 143 54 45N 70 44W
Neretva → 46 43 1N 17 27 E
Neretvanski Kanal 46 43 7N 17 10 E
Neringa 58 55 30N 21 5 E
Nerja 35 36 43N 3 55W
Nerl → 59 56 11N 40 34 E
Nerokoúrou 49 35 29N 24 3 E
Nerpio 37 38 11N 2 16W
Nerva 35 37 42N 6 30W
Nes, Iceland 54 65 53N 17 24W
Nes, Neth. 22 53 26N 5 47 E
Nes Ziyyona 69 31 56N 34 48W
Nesbyen 51 60 34N 9 35 E
Nesebûr 47 42 41N 27 46 E
Nesflaten 51 59 38N 6 48 E
Neskaupstaður 54 65 9N 13 42W
Nesland 51 59 31N 7 59 E
Neslandsvatn 51 58 57N 9 10 E
Nesle 19 49 45N 2 53 E
Nesodden 51 59 48N 10 40 E
Nesque → 21 43 59N 4 59 E
Ness, Loch 14 57 15N 4 30W
Nesslau 29 47 14N 9 13 E
Nestórion 48 40 24N 21 5 E
Néstos → 48 41 20N 24 35 E
Nesttun 51 60 19N 5 21 E
Nesvizh 58 53 14N 26 38 E
Netanya 69 32 20N 34 51 E
Nète → 23 51 7N 4 14 E
Nether Stowey 13 51 0N 3 10W
Netherbury 13 50 46N 2 45W
Netherdale 110 21 10 S 148 33 E
Netherlands ■ 22 52 0N 5 30 E
Netherlands Antilles ■ 163 12 15N 69 0W
Netherlands Guiana = Surinam ■ 169 4 0N 56 0W
Netley Gap 112 32 43 S 139 59 E
Neto → 45 39 13N 17 8 E
Netrakona 82 24 53N 90 47 E
Nettancourt 19 48 51N 4 57 E
Nettilling L. 141 66 30N 71 0W
Nettuno 44 41 29N 12 40 E
Netzahualcoyotl, Presa 161 17 10N 93 30W
Neu-Isenburg 27 50 3N 8 42 E
Neu-Ulm 27 48 23N 10 2 E
Neubrandenburg 26 53 33N 13 17 E
Neubrandenburg □ 26 53 30N 13 20 E
Neubukow 26 54 1N 11 40 E
Neuburg 27 48 43N 11 11 E
Neuchâtel 28 47 0N 6 55 E
Neuchâtel □ 28 47 0N 6 55 E
Neuchâtel, Lac de 28 46 53N 6 50 E
Neudau 30 47 11N 16 6 E
Neuenegg 28 46 54N 7 18 E
Neuenhaus 26 52 30N 6 55 E
Neuf-Brisach 19 48 1N 7 30 E
Neufahrn 27 48 44N 12 11 E
Neufchâteau, Belgium 23 49 50N 5 25 E
Neufchâteau, France 19 48 21N 5 40 E
Neufchâtel-en-Bray 18 49 44N 1 26 E
Neufchâtel-sur-Aisne 19 49 26N 4 1 E
Neuhaus 26 53 16N 10 54 E
Neuhausen 29 47 41N 8 37 E
Neuillé-Pont-Pierre 18 47 33N 0 33 E
Neuilly-St.-Front 19 49 10N 3 15 E
Neukalen 26 53 49N 12 48 E
Neumarkt 27 49 16N 11 28 E
Neumarkt-Sankt Veit 27 48 22N 12 30 E
Neumünster 26 54 4N 9 58 E
Neung-sur-Beuvron 19 47 30N 1 50 E
Neunkirchen, Austria 30 47 43N 16 4 E
Neunkirchen, Germany 27 49 23N 7 12 E
Neuquén 176 38 55 S 68 0 E
Neuquén □ 174 38 0 S 69 50W
Neuquén → 176 38 59 S 68 0W
Neuruppin 26 52 56N 12 48 E
Neuse → 149 35 5N 76 30W
Neusiedl 31 47 57N 16 50 E
Neusiedler See 31 47 50N 16 47 E
Neuss 26 51 12N 6 39 E
Neussargues-Moissac 20 45 9N 3 0 E
Neustadt, Baden-W., Germany 27 47 54N 8 13 E
Neustadt, Bayern, Germany 27 49 42N 12 10 E
Neustadt, Bayern, Germany 27 48 48N 11 47 E
Neustadt, Bayern, Germany 27 49 34N 10 37 E
Neustadt, Bayern, Germany 27 50 23N 11 0 E
Neustadt, Gera, Germany 26 50 45N 11 43 E
Neustadt, Hessen, Germany 26 50 51N 9 9 E
Neustadt, Niedersachsen, Germany 26 52 30N 9 30 E
Neustadt, Potsdam, Germany 26 52 50N 12 27 E
Neustadt, Rhld-Pfz., Germany 27 49 21N 8 10 E
Neustadt, Schleswig-Holstein, Germany 26 54 6N 10 49 E
Neustrelitz 26 53 22N 13 4 E
Neuveville, La 28 47 4N 7 6 E
Neuvic 20 45 23N 2 16 E
Neuville 23 50 11N 4 32 E
Neuville-aux-Bois 19 48 4N 2 3 E
Neuville-de-Poitou 20 46 41N 0 15 E
Neuville-sur-Saône 21 45 52N 4 51 E
Neuvy-le-Roi 18 47 36N 0 36 E
Neuvy-St.-Sépulchre 20 46 35N 1 48 E
Neuvy-sur-Barangeon 19 47 20N 2 15 E
Neuwerk 26 53 55N 8 30 E
Neuwied 26 50 26N 7 29 E
Neva → 56 59 50N 30 30 E
Nevada, Iowa, U.S.A. 154 42 1N 93 27W
Nevada, Mo., U.S.A. 154 37 51N 94 22W
Nevada □ 156 39 20N 117 0W
Nevada, Sierra, Spain 37 37 3N 3 15W
Nevada, Sierra, U.S.A. 156 39 0N 120 30W
Nevada City 158 39 20N 121 0W
Nevada de Sta. Marta, Sa. 172 10 55N 73 50W
Nevado, Cerro 174 35 30 S 68 32W
Nevanka 65 56 31N 98 55 E
Nevasa 80 19 34N 75 0 E
Nevel 58 56 0N 29 55 E
Nevele 23 51 3N 3 33 E
Nevers 19 47 0N 3 9 E
Nevertire 113 31 50 S 147 44 E
Nevesinje 46 43 14N 18 6 E
Neville 145 49 58N 107 39W
Nevinnomyssk 61 44 40N 42 0 E
Nevis 163 17 0N 62 30W
Nevlunghavn 51 55 58N 9 52 E
Nevrokop = Gotse Delchev 47 41 43N 23 46 E
Nevyansk 62 57 30N 60 13 E
New → 169 3 20N 57 37W
New Albany, Ind., U.S.A. 155 38 20N 85 50W
New Albany, Miss., U.S.A. 153 34 30N 89 0W
New Albany, Pa., U.S.A. 151 41 35N 76 28W
New Amsterdam 169 6 15N 57 36W
New Angledool 111 29 5 S 147 55 E
New Athens 154 38 19N 89 53W
New Bedford 151 41 40N 70 52W
New Berlin, Ill., U.S.A. 154 39 44N 89 55W
New Berlin, Wis., U.S.A. 155 42 59N 88 6W
New Bern 149 35 8N 77 3W
New Bethlehem 150 41 0N 79 22W
New Bloomfield 150 40 24N 77 12W
New Boston 153 33 27N 94 21W
New Braunfels 153 29 43N 98 9W
New Brighton, N.Z. 115 43 29 S 172 43 E
New Brighton, U.S.A. 150 40 42N 80 19W
New Britain, Papua N. G. 107 5 50 S 150 20 E
New Britain, U.S.A. 151 41 41N 72 47W
New Brunswick 151 40 30N 74 28W
New Brunswick □ 143 46 50N 66 30W
New Buffalo 155 41 47N 86 45W
New Bussa 127 9 53N 4 31 E
New Caledonia 106 21 0 S 165 0 E
New Canton 154 39 37N 91 8W
New Carlisle, Ind., U.S.A. 155 41 45N 86 32W
New Carlisle, Ohio, U.S.A. 155 39 56N 84 2W
New Castile = Castilla La Nueva 35 39 45N 3 20W
New Castle, Ind., U.S.A. 155 39 55N 85 23W
New Castle, Ky., U.S.A. 155 38 26N 85 10W
New Castle, Pa., U.S.A. 150 41 0N 80 20W
New City 151 41 8N 74 0W
New Cumberland 150 40 30N 80 36W
New Cuyama 159 34 57N 119 38W
New Delhi 78 28 37N 77 13 E
New Denver 144 50 0N 117 25W
New Don Pedro Res. 158 37 43N 120 24W
New England 152 46 36N 102 47W
New England Ra. 111 30 20 S 151 45 E
New Forest 13 50 53N 1 40W
New Franklin 154 39 1N 92 44W
New Glarus 154 42 49N 89 38W
New Glasgow 143 45 35N 62 36W
New Guinea 104 4 0 S 136 0 E
New Hamburg 150 43 23N 80 42W
New Hampshire □ 151 43 40N 71 40W
New Hampton 154 43 2N 92 20W
New Hanover, Papua N. G. 107 2 30 S 150 10 E
New Hanover, S. Africa 135 29 22 S 30 31 E
New Harmony 155 38 7N 87 56W
New Haven, Conn., U.S.A. 151 41 20N 72 54W
New Haven, Ill., U.S.A. 155 37 55N 88 8W
New Haven, Ind., U.S.A. 155 41 4N 85 1W
New Haven, Mich., U.S.A. 150 42 44N 82 46W
New Haven, Mo., U.S.A. 154 38 37N 91 13W
New Hazelton 144 55 20N 127 30W
New Hebrides = Vanuatu ■ 104 15 0 S 168 0 E
New Iberia 153 30 2N 91 54W
New Ireland 107 3 20 S 151 50 E
New Jersey □ 151 40 30N 74 10W
New Kensington 150 40 36N 79 43W
New Lexington 148 39 40N 82 15W
New Liskeard 142 47 31N 79 41W
New London, Conn., U.S.A. 151 41 23N 72 8W
New London, Iowa, U.S.A. 154 40 55N 91 24W
New London, Minn., U.S.A. 152 45 17N 94 55W
New London, Mo., U.S.A. 154 39 35N 91 24W
New London, Ohio, U.S.A. 150 41 4N 82 25W
New London, Wis., U.S.A. 152 44 23N 88 43W
New Madison 155 39 58N 84 43W
New Madrid 153 36 40N 89 30W
New Meadows 156 45 0N 116 32W
New Melones L. 158 37 57N 120 31W
New Mexico □ 146 34 30N 106 0W
New Miami 155 39 26N 84 32W
New Milford, Conn., U.S.A. 151 41 35N 73 25W
New Milford, Pa., U.S.A. 151 41 50N 75 45W
New Norcia 109 30 57 S 116 13 E
New Norfolk 110 42 46 S 147 2 E
New Orleans 153 30 0N 90 5W
New Palestine 155 39 45N 85 52W
New Paris 155 39 55N 84 48W
New Pekin 155 38 31N 86 2W
New Philadelphia 150 40 29N 81 25W
New Plymouth, N.Z. 114 39 4 S 174 5 E
New Plymouth, U.S.A. 156 43 58N 116 49W
New Providence 162 25 25N 78 35W
New Radnor 13 52 15N 3 10W
New Richmond, Ohio, U.S.A. 155 38 57N 84 17W
New Richmond, Wis., U.S.A. 152 45 6N 92 34W
New Roads 153 30 43N 91 30W
New Rochelle 151 40 55N 73 46W
New Rockford 152 47 44N 99 7W
New Ross 15 52 24N 6 58W
New Salem 152 46 51N 101 25W
New Sharon 154 41 28N 92 39W

Nizhniy Lomov

New Siberian Is. = Novosibirskiye Ostrava **65** 75 0N 142 0 E
New Smyrna Beach **149** 29 0N 80 50W
New South Wales □ **111** 33 0 S 146 0 E
New Springs **109** 25 49 S 120 1 E
New Town **152** 48 0N 102 30W
New Ulm **152** 44 15N 94 30W
New Vienna **155** 39 19N 83 42W
New Virginia **154** 41 11N 93 44W
New Washington **91** 11 39N 122 26 E
New Waterford **143** 46 13N 60 4W
New Westminster **144** 49 13N 122 55W
New York □ **151** 42 40N 76 0W
New York City **151** 40 45N 74 0W
New Zealand ■ **114** 40 0 S 176 0 E
Newala **131** 10 58 S 39 18 E
Newala □ **131** 10 46 S 39 20 E
Newark, Del., U.S.A. **148** 39 42N 75 45W
Newark, N.J., U.S.A. **151** 40 41N 74 12W
Newark, N.Y., U.S.A. **150** 43 2N 77 10W
Newark, Ohio, U.S.A. **150** 40 5N 82 24W
Newark-on-Trent **12** 53 6N 0 48W
Newaygo **148** 43 25N 85 48W
Newberg, Mo., U.S.A. **154** 37 55N 91 54W
Newberg, Oreg., U.S.A. **156** 45 22N 123 0W
Newberry, Mich., U.S.A. **148** 46 20N 85 32W
Newberry, S.C., U.S.A. **149** 34 17N 81 37W
Newberry Springs **159** 34 50N 116 41W
Newbrook **144** 54 24N 112 57W
Newburgh, Ind., U.S.A. **155** 37 57N 87 24W
Newburgh, N.Y., U.S.A. **151** 41 30N 74 1W
Newbury, U.K. **13** 51 24N 1 19W
Newbury, U.S.A. **151** 44 7N 72 6W
Newburyport **151** 42 48N 70 50W
Newcastle, Australia **113** 33 0 S 151 46 E
Newcastle, Canada **143** 47 1N 65 38W
Newcastle, S. Africa **135** 27 45 S 29 58 E
Newcastle, U.K. **15** 54 13N 5 54W
Newcastle, Calif., U.S.A. **158** 38 50N 121 8W
Newcastle, Wyo., U.S.A. **152** 43 50N 104 12W
Newcastle Emlyn **13** 52 2N 4 29W
Newcastle Ra. **108** 15 45 S 130 15 E
Newcastle-under-Lyme **12** 53 2N 2 15W
Newcastle-upon-Tyne **12** 54 59N 1 37W
Newcastle Waters **110** 17 30 S 133 28 E
Newdegate **109** 33 6 S 119 0 E
Newe Etan **69** 32 30N 35 32 E
Newe Sha'anan **69** 32 47N 34 59 E
Newe Zohar **69** 31 9N 35 21 E
Newell **152** 44 48N 103 25W
Newenham, C. **140** 58 40N 162 15W
Newfoundland □ **141** 53 0N 58 0W
Newhalem **144** 48 41N 121 16W
Newhall **159** 34 23N 118 32W
Newham **13** 51 31N 0 2 E
Newhaven **13** 50 47N 0 4 E
Newkirk **153** 36 52N 97 3W
Newman, Australia **108** 23 18 S 119 45 E
Newman, Calif., U.S.A. **158** 37 19N 121 1W
Newman, Ill., U.S.A. **155** 39 48N 87 59W
Newmarket, Canada **150** 44 3N 79 28W
Newmarket, Ireland **15** 52 13N 9 0W
Newmarket, U.K. **13** 52 15N 0 23 E
Newmarket, U.S.A. **151** 43 4N 70 57W
Newnan **149** 33 22N 84 48W
Newport, Gwent, U.K. **13** 51 35N 3 0W
Newport, I. of W., U.K. **13** 50 42N 1 18W
Newport, Salop, U.K. **13** 52 47N 2 22W
Newport, Ark., U.S.A. **153** 35 38N 91 15W
Newport, Ind., U.S.A. **155** 39 53N 87 26W
Newport, Ky., U.S.A. **155** 39 5N 84 23W
Newport, N.H., U.S.A. **151** 43 23N 72 8W
Newport, Oreg., U.S.A. **156** 44 41N 124 2W
Newport, Pa., U.S.A. **150** 40 28N 77 8W
Newport, R.I., U.S.A. **151** 41 28N 71 19W
Newport, Tenn., U.S.A. **149** 35 59N 83 12W
Newport, Vt., U.S.A. **151** 44 57N 72 17W
Newport, Wash., U.S.A. **156** 48 11N 117 2W
Newport Beach **159** 33 40N 117 58W
Newport News **148** 37 2N 76 30W
Newquay **13** 50 24N 5 6W
Newry **15** 54 10N 6 20W
Newry & Mourne □ **15** 54 10N 6 15W
Newton, Ill., U.S.A. **155** 38 59N 88 10W
Newton, Iowa, U.S.A. **154** 41 40N 93 3W
Newton, Mass., U.S.A. **148** 42 21N 71 10W
Newton, Mass., U.S.A. **151** 42 21N 71 12W
Newton, Miss., U.S.A. **153** 32 19N 89 10W
Newton, N.C., U.S.A. **149** 35 42N 81 10W
Newton, N.J., U.S.A. **151** 41 3N 74 46W
Newton, Tex., U.S.A. **153** 30 54N 93 42W
Newton Abbot **13** 50 32N 3 37W
Newton Boyd **111** 29 45 S 152 16 E
Newton Stewart **14** 54 57N 4 30W
Newtonmore **14** 57 4N 4 7W
Newtown, U.K. **13** 52 31N 3 19W
Newtown, U.S.A. **154** 40 22N 93 20W
Newtownabbey **15** 54 40N 5 55W
Newtownabbey □ **15** 54 45N 6 0W
Newtownards **15** 54 37N 5 40W
Newville **150** 40 10N 77 24W
Nexon **20** 45 41N 1 11 E
Neya **59** 58 21N 43 49 E
Neyrīz **73** 29 15N 54 19 E
Neyshābūr **73** 36 10N 58 50 E
Neyyattinkara **81** 8 26N 77 5 E
Nezhin **58** 51 5N 31 55 E
Nezperce **156** 46 13N 116 15W
Ngabang **89** 0 23N 109 55 E
Ngabordamlu, Tanjung **87** 6 56 S 134 11 E
N'Gage **133** 7 46 S 15 15 E
Ngaiphaipi **82** 22 14N 93 15 E
Ngambé **127** 5 48N 11 29 E
Ngami Depression **134** 20 30 S 22 46 E
Ngamo **131** 19 3 S 27 32 E
Nganglong Kangri **79** 33 0N 81 0 E
Nganjuk **89** 7 32 S 111 55 E
Ngao **84** 18 46N 99 59 E
Ngaoundéré **132** 7 15N 13 35 E
Ngapara **115** 44 57 S 170 46 E
Ngara **130** 2 29 S 30 40 E
Ngara □ **130** 2 29 S 30 40 E
Ngaruawahia **114** 37 42 S 175 11 E
Ngatapa **114** 38 32 S 177 45 E
Ngathainggyaung **82** 17 24N 95 5 E
Ngauruhoe, Mt. **114** 39 13 S 175 45 E
Ngawi **89** 7 24 S 111 26 E
Nggamea **106** 16 46 S 179 46W
Nghia Lo **84** 21 33N 104 28 E
Ngidinga **133** 5 37 S 15 17 E
Ngo **132** 2 29 S 15 45 E
N'Gola **133** 14 10 S 14 30 E
Ngoma **131** 13 8 S 33 45 E
Ngomahura **131** 20 26 S 30 43 E
Ngomba **131** 8 20 S 32 53 E
Ngop **125** 6 17N 30 9 E
Ngoring Hu **92** 34 55N 97 5 E
Ngorkou **126** 15 40N 3 41W
Ngorongoro **130** 3 11 S 35 32 E
Ngouri **123** 13 38N 15 22 E
Ngourti **123** 15 19N 13 12 E
Ngozi **130** 2 54 S 29 50 E
Ngudu **130** 2 58 S 33 25 E
Nguigmi **123** 14 20N 13 20 E
Ngukurr **110** 14 44 S 134 44 E
Ngunga **130** 3 37 S 33 37 E
Nguru **127** 12 56N 10 29 E
Nguru Mts. **130** 6 0 S 37 30 E
Nguyen Binh **84** 22 39N 105 56 E
Nha Trang **85** 12 16N 109 10 E
Nhacoongo **135** 24 18 S 35 14 E
Nhambiquara **173** 12 50 S 59 49W
Nhamundá **169** 2 14 S 56 43W
Nhamundá → **169** 2 12 S 56 41W
Nhangutazi, L. **135** 24 0 S 34 30 E
Nhecolândia **173** 19 17 S 56 58W
Nhill **112** 36 18 S 141 40 E
Nho Quan **84** 20 18N 105 45 E
Nhulunbuy **110** 12 10 S 137 20 E
Nhundo **133** 14 25 S 21 23 E
Nia-nia **130** 1 30N 27 40 E
Niafounké **126** 16 0N 4 5W
Niagara **148** 45 45N 88 0W
Niagara Falls, Canada **142** 43 7N 79 5W
Niagara Falls, U.S.A. **150** 43 5N 79 0W
Niagara-on-the-Lake **150** 43 15N 79 4W
Niah **86** 3 58N 113 46 E
Niamey **127** 13 27N 2 6 E
Nianforando **126** 9 37N 10 36W
Nianfors **52** 61 36N 16 46 E
Niangara **130** 3 42N 27 50 E
Niangua → **154** 38 0N 92 48W
Nias **88** 1 0N 97 30 E
Niassa □ **131** 13 30 S 36 0 E
Nibāk **75** 24 25N 50 50 E
Nibbiano **42** 44 54N 9 20 E
Nibe **53** 56 59N 9 38 E
Nicaragua ■ **162** 11 40N 85 30W
Nicaragua, L. de **162** 12 0N 85 30W
Nicastro **45** 39 0N 16 18 E
Nice **21** 43 42N 7 14 E
Niceville **149** 30 30N 86 30W
Nichinan **100** 31 38N 131 23 E
Nicholás, Canal **162** 23 30N 80 5W
Nicholasville **155** 37 54N 84 31W
Nichols **151** 42 1N 76 22W
Nicholson, Australia **108** 18 2 S 128 54 E
Nicholson, U.S.A. **151** 41 37N 75 47W
Nicholson → **110** 17 31 S 139 36 E
Nicholson Ra. **109** 27 15 S 116 45 E
Nickerie □ **169** 4 0N 57 0W
Nickerie → **169** 5 58N 57 0W
Nicobar Is. **76** 9 0N 93 0 E
Nicoclí **168** 8 26N 76 48W
Nicola **144** 50 12N 120 40W
Nicolet **142** 46 17N 72 35W
Nicolls Town **162** 25 8N 78 0W
Nicopolis **49** 39 2N 20 37 E
Nicosia, Cyprus **70** 35 10N 33 25 E
Nicosia, Italy **45** 37 45N 14 22 E
Nicótera **45** 38 33N 15 57 E
Nicoya **162** 10 9N 85 27W
Nicoya, G. de **162** 10 0N 85 0W
Nicoya, Pen. de **162** 9 45N 85 40W
Nidau **28** 47 7N 7 15 E
Nidd → **12** 54 1N 1 32W
Nidda **26** 50 24N 9 2 E
Nidda → **27** 50 6N 8 34 E
Nidwalden □ **29** 46 50N 8 25 E
Nidzica **32** 53 25N 20 28 E
Niebüll **26** 54 47N 8 49 E
Nied → **19** 49 23N 6 40 E
Niederaula **26** 50 48N 9 37 E
Niederbipp **28** 47 16N 7 42 E
Niederbronn-les-Bains **19** 48 57N 7 39 E
Niedere Tauern **30** 47 20N 14 0 E
Niedermarsberg **26** 51 28N 8 52 E
Niederösterreich □ **30** 48 25N 15 40 E
Niedersachsen □ **26** 52 45N 9 0 E
Niefang **132** 1 50N 10 14 E
Niekerkshoop **134** 29 19 S 22 51 E
Niel **23** 51 7N 4 20 E
Niellé **126** 10 5N 5 38W
Niem **132** 6 12N 15 14 E
Niemba **130** 5 58 S 28 24 E
Niemcza **32** 50 42N 16 47 E
Niemodlin **32** 50 38N 17 38 E
Niemur **112** 35 17 S 144 9 E
Nienburg **26** 52 38N 9 15 E
Niepołomice **32** 50 3N 20 13 E
Niers → **26** 51 45N 5 58 E
Niesen **28** 46 38N 7 39 E
Niesky **26** 51 18N 14 48 E
Nieszawa **32** 52 52N 18 50 E
Nieu Bethesda **134** 31 51 S 24 34 E
Nieuw-Amsterdam, Neth. **22** 52 43N 6 52 E
Nieuw Amsterdam, Surinam **169** 5 53N 55 5W
Nieuw Beijerland **22** 51 49N 4 20 E
Nieuw-Dordrecht **22** 52 45N 6 59 E
Nieuw Loosdrecht **22** 52 12N 5 8 E
Nieuw Nickerie **169** 6 0N 56 59W
Nieuw-Schoonebeek **22** 52 39N 7 0 E
Nieuw-Vennep **22** 52 16N 4 38 E
Nieuw-Vossemeer **23** 51 34N 4 12 E
Nieuwe-Niedorp **22** 52 44N 4 54 E
Nieuwe-Pekela **22** 53 5N 6 58 E
Nieuwe-Schans **22** 53 11N 7 12 E
Nieuwendijk **22** 51 46N 4 55 E
Nieuwerkerken **23** 50 52N 5 12 E
Nieuwkoop **22** 52 9N 4 48 E
Nieuwleusen **22** 52 34N 6 17 E
Nieuwnamen **23** 51 18N 4 9 E
Nieuwolda **22** 53 15N 6 58 E
Nieuwoudtville **134** 31 23 S 19 7 E
Nieuwpoort **23** 51 8N 2 45 E
Nieuwveen **22** 52 12N 4 46 E
Nieves **34** 42 7N 8 26W
Nieves, Pico de las **37** 27 57N 15 35W
Nièvre □ **19** 47 10N 3 40 E
Nigata **100** 34 13N 132 39 E
Niğde **57** 38 0N 34 40 E
Nigel **135** 26 27 S 28 25 E
Niger □ **127** 10 0N 5 0 E
Niger ■ **127** 17 30N 10 0 E
Niger → **127** 5 33N 6 33 E
Nigeria ■ **127** 8 30N 8 0 E
Nightcaps **115** 45 57 S 168 2 E
Nigríta **48** 40 56N 23 29 E
Nihtaur **79** 29 20N 78 23 E
Nii-Jima **101** 34 20N 139 15 E
Niigata **98** 37 58N 139 0 E
Niigata □ **99** 37 15N 138 45 E
Niihama **100** 33 55N 133 16 E
Niihau **146** 21 55N 160 10W
Niimi **100** 34 59N 133 28 E
Niitsu **98** 37 48N 139 7 E
Níjar **37** 36 53N 2 15W
Nijil **71** 30 32N 35 33 E
Nijkerk **22** 52 13N 5 30 E
Nijlen **23** 51 10N 4 40 E
Nijmegen **22** 51 50N 5 52 E
Nijverdal **22** 52 22N 6 28 E
Nīk Pey **73** 36 50N 48 10 E
Nike **127** 6 26N 7 29 E
Nikel **54** 69 24N 30 12 E
Nikiniki **87** 9 49 S 124 30 E
Nikítas **48** 40 13N 23 34 E
Nikki **127** 9 58N 3 12 E
Nikkō **101** 36 45N 139 35 E
Nikolayev **60** 46 58N 32 0 E
Nikolayevsk **59** 50 0N 45 35 E
Nikolayevsk-na-Amur **65** 53 8N 140 44 E
Nikolsk **59** 59 30N 45 28 E
Nikolskoye **65** 55 12N 166 0 E
Nikopol, Bulgaria **47** 43 43N 24 54 E
Nikopol, U.S.S.R. **60** 47 35N 34 25 E
Niksar **60** 40 31N 37 2 E
Nīkshahr **73** 26 15N 60 10 E
Nikšić **46** 42 50N 18 57 E
Nîl, Nahr en → **124** 30 10N 31 6 E
Nîl el Abyad → **125** 15 38N 32 31 E
Nîl el Azraq → **125** 15 38N 32 31 E
Niland **159** 33 16N 115 30W
Nile = Nîl, Nahr en → **124** 30 10N 31 6 E
Nile □ **130** 2 0N 31 30 E
Nile Delta **124** 31 40N 31 0 E
Niles **150** 41 8N 80 40W
Nilgiri Hills **81** 11 30N 76 30 E
Nilo Peçanha **171** 13 37 S 39 6W
Nilpena **112** 30 58 S 138 20 E
Nimach **78** 24 30N 74 56 E
Nimbahera **78** 24 37N 74 45 E
Nîmes **21** 43 50N 4 23 E
Nimfaíon, Ákra- **48** 40 5N 24 20 E
Nimmitabel **113** 36 29 S 149 15 E
Nimneryskiy **65** 57 50N 125 10 E
Nimule **125** 3 32N 32 3 E
Nin **43** 44 16N 15 12 E
Nīnawá **72** 36 25N 43 10 E
Ninda **133** 14 47 S 21 24 E
Nindigully **111** 28 21 S 148 50 E
Ninemile **144** 56 0N 130 7W
Ninety Mile Beach, The **113** 38 15 S 147 24 E
Nineveh = Nīnawá **72** 36 25N 43 10 E
Ning Xian **94** 35 30N 107 58 E
Ningaloo **108** 22 41 S 113 41 E
Ning'an **95** 44 22N 129 20 E
Ningbo **97** 29 51N 121 28 E
Ningcheng **95** 41 32N 119 53 E
Ningde **97** 26 38N 119 23 E
Ningdu **97** 26 25N 115 59 E
Ninggang **97** 26 42N 113 55 E
Ningguo **97** 30 35N 119 0 E
Ninghai **97** 29 15N 121 27 E
Ninghua **97** 26 14N 116 45 E
Ningjin **94** 37 35N 114 57 E
Ningjing Shan **96** 30 0N 98 20 E
Ninglang **96** 27 20N 100 55 E
Ningling **94** 34 25N 115 22 E
Ningming **96** 22 8N 107 4 E
Ningnan **96** 27 5N 102 36 E
Ningpo = Ningbo **97** 29 51N 121 28 E
Ningqiang **94** 32 47N 106 15 E
Ningshan **94** 33 21N 108 21 E
Ningsia Hui A.R. = Ningxia Huizu Zizhiqu □ **94** 38 0N 106 0 E
Ningwu **94** 39 0N 112 18 E
Ningxia Huizu Zizhiqu □ **94** 38 0N 106 0 E
Ningxiang **97** 28 15N 112 30 E
Ningyang **94** 35 47N 116 45 E
Ningyuan **97** 25 37N 111 57 E
Ninh Binh **84** 20 15N 105 55 E
Ninh Giang **84** 20 44N 106 24 E
Ninh Hoa **84** 12 30N 109 7 E
Ninh Ma **84** 12 48N 109 21 E
Ninove **23** 50 51N 4 2 E
Nioaque **175** 21 5 S 55 50W
Niobrara **152** 42 48N 97 59W
Niobrara → **152** 42 45N 98 0W
Nioki **132** 2 47 S 17 40 E
Niono **126** 14 15N 6 0W
Nioro du Rip **126** 13 40N 15 50W
Nioro du Sahel **126** 15 15N 9 30W
Niort **20** 46 19N 0 29W
Nipa **107** 6 9 S 143 29 E
Nipani **81** 16 20N 74 25 E
Nipawin **145** 53 20N 104 0W
Nipawin Prov. Park **145** 54 0N 104 37W
Nipigon **142** 49 0N 88 17W
Nipigon, L. **142** 49 50N 88 30W
Nipin → **145** 55 46N 108 35W
Nipishish L. **143** 54 12N 60 45W
Nipissing L. **142** 46 20N 80 0W
Nipomo **159** 35 4N 120 29W
Nipton **159** 35 28N 115 16W
Niquelândia **171** 14 33 S 48 23W
Nīr **72** 38 2N 47 59 E
Nira → **80** 17 58N 75 8 E
Nirasaki **101** 35 42N 138 27 E
Nirmal **80** 19 3N 78 20 E
Nirmali **79** 26 20N 86 35 E
Niš **46** 43 19N 21 58 E
Nisa **35** 39 30N 7 41W
Nişāb **72** 14 25N 46 29 E
Nišava → **46** 43 20N 21 46 E
Niscemi **45** 37 8N 14 21 E
Nishi-Sonogi-Hantō **100** 32 55N 129 45 E
Nishinomiya **101** 34 45N 135 20 E
Nishin'omote **99** 30 43N 130 59 E
Nishio **101** 34 52N 137 3 E
Nishiwaki **100** 34 59N 134 58 E
Nísíros **49** 36 35N 27 12 E
Niskibi → **142** 56 29N 88 9W
Nisko **32** 50 35N 22 7 E
Nispen **23** 51 29N 4 28 E
Nisporeny **50** 47 4N 28 10 E
Nisqually → **158** 47 6N 122 42W
Nissafors **53** 57 25N 13 37 E
Nissan → **53** 56 40N 12 51 E
Nissedal **51** 59 10N 8 30 E
Nisser **51** 59 7N 8 28 E
Nissum Fjord **53** 56 20N 8 11 E
Nistelrode **23** 51 42N 5 34 E
Nisutlin → **144** 60 14N 132 34W
Nitchequon **143** 53 10N 70 58W
Niterói **171** 22 52 S 43 0W
Nith → **14** 55 20N 3 5W
Nitra **31** 48 19N 18 4 E
Nitra → **31** 47 46N 18 10 E
Nitsa → **62** 57 29N 64 33 E
Nittedal **51** 60 1N 10 57 E
Nittendau **27** 49 12N 12 16 E
Niue I. **105** 19 2 S 169 54W
Niulan Jiang → **96** 27 30N 103 5 E
Niut **89** 0 55N 110 6 E
Niutou Shan **97** 29 5N 121 59 E
Niuzhuang **95** 40 58N 122 28 E
Nivelles **23** 50 35N 4 20 E
Nivernais **19** 47 0N 3 20 E
Nixon **153** 29 17N 97 45W
Nizam Sagar **80** 18 10N 77 58 E
Nizamabad **80** 18 45N 78 7 E
Nizamghat **82** 28 20N 95 45 E
Nizhiye Sergi **62** 56 40N 59 18 E
Nizhne Kolymsk **65** 68 34N 160 55 E
Nizhneangarsk **65** 55 47N 109 30 E
Nizhnegorskiy **60** 45 27N 34 38 E
Nizhneudinsk **65** 54 54N 99 3 E
Nizhnevartovsk **64** 60 56N 76 38 E
Nizhneyansk **65** 71 26N 136 4 E
Nizhniy Lomov **59** 53 34N 43 38 E

Nizhniy Novgorod

Nizhniy Novgorod =
Gorkiy **59** 56 20N 44 0 E
Nizhniy Pyandzh **63** 37 12N 68 35 E
Nizhniy Tagil **62** 57 55N 59 57 E
Nizhny Salda **62** 58 8N 60 42 E
Nizhnyaya Tunguska → **65** 64 20N 93 0 E
Nizké Tatry **31** 48 55N 20 0 E
Nizza Monferrato **42** 44 46N 8 22 E
Njakwa **131** 11 1 S 33 56 E
Njanji **131** 14 25 S 31 46 E
Njinjo **131** 8 48 S 38 54 E
Njombe **131** 9 20 S 34 50 E
Njombe □ **131** 9 20 S 34 49 E
Njombe → **130** 6 56 S 35 6 E
Nkambe **127** 6 35N 10 40 E
Nkana **131** 12 50 S 28 8 E
Nkawkaw **127** 6 36N 0 49W
Nkayi **131** 19 41 S 29 20 E
Nkhota Kota **131** 12 56 S 34 15 E
Nkolabona **132** 1 14N 11 43 E
Nkone **132** 1 2 S 22 20 E
Nkongsamba **127** 4 55N 9 55 E
Nkunga **133** 4 41 S 18 34 E
Nkurenkuru **134** 17 42 S 18 32 E
Nkwanta **126** 6 10N 2 10W
Nmaushahr **79** 33 11N 74 15 E
Noakhali = Maijdi **82** 22 48N 91 10 E
Noatak **140** 67 32N 162 59W
Nobel **150** 45 25N 80 6W
Nobeoka **100** 32 36N 131 41 E
Nôbi-Heiya **101** 35 15N 136 45 E
Noble **155** 38 42N 88 14W
Noblejas **36** 39 58N 3 26W
Noblesville **155** 40 1N 85 59W
Noce → **42** 46 9N 11 4 E
Nocera Inferiore **45** 40 45N 14 37 E
Nocera Terinese **45** 39 2N 16 9 E
Nocera Umbra **43** 43 8N 12 47 E
Noci **45** 40 47N 17 7 E
Nockatunga **111** 27 42 S 142 42 E
Nocona **153** 33 48N 97 45W
Nocrich **50** 45 55N 24 26 E
Noda **101** 35 56N 139 52 E
Noel **153** 36 36N 94 29W
Nogal Valley **136** 8 35N 48 35 E
Nogales, Mexico **160** 31 20N 110 56W
Nogales, U.S.A. **157** 31 33N 110 56W
Nogat → **32** 54 17N 19 17 E
Nôgata **100** 33 48N 130 44 E
Nogent-en-Bassigny **19** 48 1N 5 20 E
Nogent-le-Rotrou **18** 48 20N 0 50 E
Nogent-sur-Seine **19** 48 30N 3 30 E
Noggerup **109** 33 32 S 116 5 E
Noginsk, Moskva,
U.S.S.R. **59** 55 50N 38 25 E
Noginsk, Sib., U.S.S.R. **65** 64 30N 90 50 E
Nogoa → **110** 23 40 S 147 55 E
Nogoyá **174** 32 24 S 59 48W
Nógrád □ **31** 48 0N 19 30 E
Nogueira de Ramuin **34** 42 21N 7 43W
Noguera Pallaresa → **36** 42 15N 1 0 E
Noguera
Ribagorzana → **36** 41 40N 0 43 E
Nohar **78** 29 11N 74 49 E
Noing **91** 5 40N 125 28 E
Noire, Mt. **18** 48 11N 3 40W
Noirétable **20** 45 48N 3 46 E
Noirmoutier, I. de **18** 46 58N 2 10W
Noirmoutier-en-l'Ile **18** 47 0N 2 14W
Nojane **134** 23 15 S 20 14 E
Nojima-Zaki **101** 34 54N 139 53 E
Nok Kundi **77** 28 50N 62 45 E
Nokaneng **134** 19 40 S 22 17 E
Nokhtuysk **65** 60 0N 117 45 E
Nokomis, Canada **145** 51 35N 105 0W
Nokomis, U.S.A. **154** 39 18N 89 18W
Nokomis L. **145** 57 0N 103 0W
Nokou **123** 14 35N 14 47 E
Nol **53** 57 56N 12 5 E
Nola, C.A.R. **132** 3 35N 16 4 E
Nola, Italy **45** 40 54N 14 29 E
Nolay **19** 46 58N 4 35 E
Noli, C. di **42** 44 12N 8 26 E
Nolinsk **59** 57 28N 49 57 E
Noma Omuramba → **134** 18 52 S 20 53 E
Noma-Saki **100** 31 25N 130 7 E
Nomad **107** 6 19 S 142 13 E
Noman L. **145** 62 15N 108 55W
Nombre de Dios **162** 9 34N 79 28W
Nome **140** 64 30N 165 24W
Nomo-Zaki **100** 32 35N 129 44 E
Nonacho L. **145** 61 42N 109 40W
Nonancourt **18** 48 47N 1 11 E
Nonant-le-Pin **18** 48 42N 0 12 E
Nonda **110** 20 40 S 142 28 E
Nong Chang **84** 15 23N 99 51 E
Nong Het **84** 19 29N 103 59 E
Nong Khai **84** 17 50N 102 46 E
Nong'an **95** 44 25N 125 5 E
Nongoma **135** 27 58 S 31 35 E
Nonoava **160** 27 28N 106 44W
Nonoc I. **91** 9 51N 125 37 E
Nonthaburi **84** 13 51N 100 34 E
Nontron **20** 45 31N 0 40 E
Nonza **21** 42 47N 9 21 E
Noonamah **108** 12 40 S 131 4 E
Noonan **152** 48 51N 102 59W
Noondoo **111** 28 35 S 148 30 E
Noonkanbah **108** 18 30 S 124 50 E
Noord-Bergum **22** 53 14N 6 1 E
Noord Brabant □ **23** 51 40N 5 0 E
Noord Holland □ **22** 52 30N 4 45 E
Noordbeveland **23** 51 35N 3 50 E
Noordeloos **22** 51 55N 4 56 E
Noordhollandsch Kanaal **22** 52 55N 4 48 E
Noordhorn **22** 53 16N 6 24 E
Noordoostpolder **22** 52 45N 5 45 E
Noordwijk aan Zee **22** 52 14N 4 26 E
Noordwijk-Binnen **22** 52 14N 4 27 E
Noordwijkerhout **22** 52 16N 4 30 E
Noordzee Kanaal **22** 52 28N 4 35 E
Noorwolde **22** 52 54N 6 8 E
Nootka **144** 49 38N 126 38W
Nootka I. **144** 49 32N 126 42W
Nóqui **133** 5 55 S 13 30 E
Nora, Ethiopia **125** 16 6N 40 4 E
Nora, Sweden **52** 59 32N 15 2 E
Nora Springs **154** 43 9N 93 0W
Noranda **142** 48 20N 79 0W
Norberg **52** 60 4N 15 56 E
Norborne **154** 39 18N 93 40W
Nórcia **43** 42 50N 13 5 E
Norco **159** 33 56N 117 33W
Nord □ **19** 50 15N 3 30 E
Nord-Ostsee Kanal **26** 54 15N 9 40 E
Nord-Süd Kanal **26** 53 0N 10 32 E
Nord-Trøndelag fylke □ **54** 64 20N 12 0 E
Nordagutu **51** 59 25N 9 20 E
Nordaustlandet **6** 79 14N 23 0 E
Nordborg **53** 55 5N 9 50 E
Nordby, Århus,
Denmark **53** 55 58N 10 32 E
Nordby, Ribe, Denmark **53** 55 27N 8 24 E
Norddal **51** 62 15N 7 14 E
Norddalsfjord **51** 61 39N 5 23 E
Norddeich **26** 53 37N 7 10 E
Nordegg **144** 52 29N 116 5W
Norden **26** 53 35N 7 12 E
Nordenham **26** 53 29N 8 28 E
Norderhov **51** 60 7N 10 17 E
Norderney **26** 53 42N 7 15 E
Nordfjord **51** 61 55N 5 30 E
Nordfriesische Inseln **26** 54 40N 8 20 E
Nordhausen **26** 51 29N 10 47 E
Nordhorn **26** 52 27N 7 4 E
Nordjyllands
Amtskommune □ **53** 57 0N 10 0 E
Nordkapp, Norway **54** 71 10N 25 44 E
Nordkapp, Svalbard **6** 80 31N 20 0 E
Nordkinn **10** 71 8N 27 40 E
Nordland fylke □ **54** 65 40N 13 0 E
Nördlingen **27** 48 50N 10 30 E
Nordrhein-Westfalen □ **26** 51 45N 7 30 E
Nordstrand **26** 54 27N 8 50 E
Nordvik **65** 74 2N 111 32 E
Nore **51** 60 10N 9 0 E
Nore → **15** 52 40N 7 20W
Norefjell **51** 60 16N 9 29 E
Norembega **142** 48 59N 80 43W
Noresund **51** 60 11N 9 37 E
Norfolk, Nebr., U.S.A. **152** 42 3N 97 25W
Norfolk, Va., U.S.A. **148** 36 40N 76 15W
Norfolk □ **12** 52 39N 1 0 E
Norfolk Broads **12** 52 30N 1 15 E
Norfolk I. **104** 28 58 S 168 3 E
Norfork Res. **153** 36 13N 92 15W
Norg **22** 53 4N 6 28 E
Norilsk **65** 69 20N 88 6 E
Norley **111** 27 45 S 143 48 E
Norma, Mt. **110** 20 55 S 140 42 E
Normal **154** 40 30N 89 0W
Norman **153** 35 12N 97 30W
Norman → **110** 17 28 S 140 49 E
Norman Wells **140** 65 17N 126 51W
Normanby **114** 39 32 S 174 18 E
Normanby → **110** 14 23 S 144 10 E
Normanby I. **107** 10 55 S 151 5 E
Normandie **18** 48 45N 0 10 E
Normandie, Collines de **18** 48 55N 0 45W
Normandin **142** 48 49N 72 31W
Normandy = Normandie **18** 48 45N 0 10 E
Normanhurst, Mt. **109** 25 4 S 122 30 E
Normanton **110** 17 40 S 141 10 E
Normanville **112** 35 27 S 138 18 E
Norquay **145** 51 53N 102 5W
Norquinco **176** 41 51 S 70 55W
Norrahammar **53** 57 43N 14 7 E
Nørre Åby **53** 55 27N 9 52 E
Nørre Nebel **53** 55 47N 8 17 E
Nørresundby **53** 57 5N 9 52 E
Norris **156** 45 40N 111 40W
Norris City **155** 37 59N 88 20W
Norristown **151** 40 9N 75 21W
Norrköping **53** 58 37N 16 11 E
Norrtälje **52** 59 46N 18 42 E
Norseman **109** 32 8 S 121 43 E
Norsholm **53** 58 31N 15 59 E
Norsk **65** 52 30N 130 0 E
Norte, Pta. **176** 42 5 S 63 46W
Norte, Pta. del **37** 27 51N 17 57W
Norte de Santander □ **168** 8 0N 73 0W
Nortelândia **173** 14 25 S 56 48W
North Adams **151** 42 42N 73 6W
North Andaman I. **76** 13 15N 92 40 E
North Atlantic Ocean **8** 30 0N 50 0W
North Baltimore **155** 41 11N 83 41W
North Battleford **145** 52 50N 108 17W
North Bay **142** 46 20N 79 30W
North Belcher Is. **142** 56 50N 79 50W
North Bend, Canada **144** 49 50N 121 27W
North Bend, Oreg.,
U.S.A. **156** 43 28N 124 14W
North Bend, Pa.,
U.S.A. **150** 41 20N 77 42W
North Bend, Wash.,
U.S.A. **158** 47 30N 121 47W
North Berwick, U.K. **14** 56 4N 2 44W
North Berwick, U.S.A. **151** 43 18N 70 43W
North Buganda □ **130** 1 0N 32 0 E
North Canadian → **153** 35 17N 95 31W
North C., Canada **143** 47 2N 60 20W
North C., N.Z. **114** 34 23 S 173 4 E
North C., Papua N. G. **107** 2 32 S 150 50 E
North Caribou L. **142** 52 50N 90 40W
North Carolina □ **149** 35 30N 80 0W
North Channel, Br. Is. **14** 55 0N 5 30W
North Channel, Canada **142** 46 0N 83 0W
North Chicago **155** 42 19N 87 50W
North College Hill **155** 39 13N 84 33W
North Cotabato □ **91** 7 10N 125 0 E
North Dakota □ **152** 47 30N 100 0W
North Dandalup **109** 32 30 S 115 57 E
North Down □ **15** 54 40N 5 45W
North Downs **13** 51 17N 0 30 E
North East **150** 42 17N 79 50W
North East Frontier
Agency = Arunachal
Pradesh □ **82** 28 0N 95 0 E
North East Providence
Chan. **162** 26 0N 76 0W
North Eastern □ **130** 1 30N 40 0 E
North English **154** 41 31N 92 5W
North Esk → **14** 56 44N 2 25W
North European Plain **10** 55 0N 20 0 E
North Fabius → **154** 39 54N 91 28W
North Foreland **13** 51 22N 1 28 E
North Fork **158** 37 14N 119 21W
North Fork,
American → **158** 38 45N 121 8W
North Fork, Feather → **158** 39 17N 121 38W
North Fork, Salt → **154** 39 26N 91 53W
North Frisian Is. =
Nordfriesische Inseln **26** 54 40N 8 20 E
North Henik L. **145** 61 45N 97 40W
North Highlands **158** 38 40N 121 25W
North Horr **130** 3 20N 37 8 E
North I., Kenya **130** 4 5N 36 5 E
North I., N.Z. **115** 38 0 S 175 0 E
North Judson **155** 41 13N 86 46W
North Kingsville **150** 41 53N 80 42W
North Knife → **145** 58 53N 94 45W
North Koel → **79** 24 45N 83 50 E
North Korea ■ **95** 40 0N 127 0 E
North Lakhimpur **82** 27 14N 94 7 E
North Las Vegas **159** 36 15N 115 6W
North Liberty **155** 41 32N 86 26W
North Loup → **152** 41 17N 98 23W
North Manchester **155** 41 0N 85 46W
North Minch **14** 58 5N 5 55W
North Nahanni → **144** 62 15N 123 20W
North Olmsted **150** 41 25N 81 56W
North Ossetian
A.S.S.R. □ **61** 43 30N 44 30 E
North Palisade **158** 37 6N 118 32W
North Platte **152** 41 10N 100 50W
North Platte → **152** 41 15N 100 45W
North Pt. **143** 47 5N 64 0W
North Pole **6** 90 0N 0 0 E
North Portal **145** 49 0N 102 33W
North Powder **156** 45 2N 117 59W
North Ronaldsay **14** 59 20N 2 30W
North Saskatchewan → **145** 53 15N 105 5W
North Sea **10** 56 0N 4 0 E
North Sporades = Voríai
Sporádhes **49** 39 15N 23 30 E
North Sydney **143** 46 12N 60 15W
North Thompson → **144** 50 40N 120 20W
North Tonawanda **150** 43 5N 78 50W
North Troy **151** 44 59N 72 24W
North Truchas Pk. **157** 36 0N 105 30W
North Twin I. **142** 53 20N 80 0W
North Tyne → **12** 54 59N 2 7W
North Uist **14** 57 40N 7 15W
North Vancouver **144** 49 25N 123 3W
North Vernon **155** 39 0N 85 35W
North Wabasca L. **144** 56 0N 113 55W
North Walsham **12** 52 49N 1 22 E
North Webster **155** 41 25N 85 48W
North West C. **108** 21 45 S 114 9 E
North West Christmas I.
Ridge **105** 6 30N 165 0W
North West Frontier □ **77** 34 0N 71 0 E
North West Highlands **14** 57 35N 5 2W
North West Providence
Channel **162** 26 0N 78 0W
North West River **143** 53 30N 60 10W
North West
Territories □ **140** 67 0N 110 0W
North Western □ **131** 13 30 S 25 30 E
North York Moors **12** 54 25N 0 50W
North Yorkshire □ **12** 54 15N 1 25W
Northallerton **12** 54 20N 1 26W
Northam **134** 24 56 S 27 18 E
Northampton, Australia **109** 28 27 S 114 33 E
Northampton, U.K. **13** 52 14N 0 54W
Northampton, Mass.,
U.S.A. **151** 42 22N 72 31W
Northampton, Pa.,
U.S.A. **151** 40 38N 75 24W
Northampton □ **13** 52 16N 0 55W
Northampton Downs **110** 24 35 S 145 48 E
Northbridge **151** 42 12N 71 40W
Northcliffe **109** 34 39 S 116 7 E
Northeim **26** 51 42N 10 0 E
Northern □, Malawi **131** 11 0 S 34 0 E
Northern □, Uganda **130** 3 5N 32 30 E
Northern □, Zambia **131** 10 30 S 31 0 E
Northern Circars **80** 17 30N 82 30 E
Northern Indian L. **145** 57 20N 97 20W
Northern Ireland □ **15** 54 45N 7 0W
Northern Light, L. **142** 48 15N 90 39W
Northern Marianas **104** 17 0N 145 0 E
Northern Province □ **126** 9 15N 11 30W
Northern Samar □ **90** 12 30N 124 40 E
Northern Territory □ **108** 16 0 S 133 0 E
Northfield **152** 44 30N 93 10W
Northland □ **114** 35 30 S 173 30 E
Northome **152** 47 53N 94 15W
Northport, Ala., U.S.A. **149** 33 15N 87 35W
Northport, Mich.,
U.S.A. **148** 45 8N 85 39W
Northport, Wash.,
U.S.A. **156** 48 55N 117 48W
Northumberland □ **12** 55 12N 2 0W
Northumberland, C. **112** 38 5 S 140 40 E
Northumberland Is. **110** 21 30 S 149 50 E
Northumberland Str. **143** 46 20N 64 0W
Northwich **12** 53 16N 2 30W
Northwood, Iowa,
U.S.A. **152** 43 27N 93 0W
Northwood, N. Dak.,
U.S.A. **152** 47 44N 97 30W
Norton, U.S.A. **152** 39 50N 99 53W
Norton, Zambia **131** 17 52 S 30 40 E
Norton Sd. **140** 64 0N 164 0W
Norton Shores **155** 43 8N 86 15W
Nortorf **26** 54 14N 9 47 E
Norwalk, Calif., U.S.A. **159** 33 54N 118 5W
Norwalk, Conn., U.S.A. **151** 41 9N 73 25W
Norwalk, Ohio, U.S.A. **150** 41 13N 82 38W
Norway **148** 45 46N 87 57W
Norway ■ **54** 63 0N 11 0 E
Norway House **145** 53 59N 97 50W
Norwegian
Dependency □ **7** 66 0 S 15 0 E
Norwegian Sea **6** 66 0N 1 0 E
Norwich, Canada **150** 42 59N 80 36W
Norwich, U.K. **12** 52 38N 1 17 E
Norwich, Conn., U.S.A. **151** 41 33N 72 5W
Norwich, N.Y., U.S.A. **151** 42 32N 75 30W
Norwood, Canada **150** 44 23N 77 59W
Norwood, U.S.A. **155** 39 10N 84 27W
Noshiro **98** 40 12N 140 0 E
Nosok **64** 70 10N 82 20 E
Nosovka **58** 50 50N 31 37 E
Noss Hd. **14** 58 29N 3 4W
Nossa Senhora da Glória **170** 10 14 S 37 25W
Nossa Senhora das
Dores **170** 10 29 S 37 13W
Nossa Senhora do
Livramento **173** 15 48 S 56 22W
Nossebro **53** 58 12N 12 43 E
Nossob → **134** 26 55 S 20 45 E
Nosy Boraha **135** 16 50 S 49 55 E
Nosy Varika **135** 20 35 S 48 32 E
Noteć → **32** 52 44N 15 26 E
Notigi Dam **145** 56 40N 99 10W
Notikewin → **144** 57 2N 117 38W
Notios Evvoïkos Kólpos **49** 38 20N 24 0 E
Noto **45** 36 52N 15 4 E
Noto, G. di **45** 36 50N 15 10 E
Notodden **51** 59 35N 9 17 E
Notre-Dame **143** 46 18N 64 46W
Notre Dame B. **143** 49 45N 55 30W
Notre Dame de Koartac
= Koartac **141** 60 55N 69 40W
Notre Dame d'Ivugivic
= Ivugivik **141** 62 24N 77 55W
Notsé **127** 7 0N 1 17 E
Nottaway → **142** 51 22N 78 55W
Nøtterøy **51** 59 14N 10 24 E
Nottingham **12** 52 57N 1 10W
Nottingham □ **12** 53 10N 1 0W
Nottoway → **148** 36 33N 76 55W
Notwane → **134** 23 35 S 26 58 E
Nouâdhibou **120** 20 54N 17 0W
Nouâdhibou, Ras **120** 20 50N 17 0W
Nouakchott **126** 18 9N 15 58W
Nouméa **106** 22 17 S 166 30 E
Noupoort **134** 31 10 S 24 57 E
Nouveau Comptoir **142** 53 0N 78 49W
Nouvelle Calédonie =
New Caledonia **106** 21 0 S 165 0 E
Nouzonville **19** 49 48N 4 44 E
Nová Baňa **31** 48 28N 18 39 E
Nová Bystřice **30** 49 2N 15 8 E
Nova Cruz **170** 6 28 S 35 25W
Nova Era **171** 19 45 S 43 3W
Nova Esperança **175** 23 8 S 52 24W
Nova Friburgo **171** 22 16 S 42 30W
Nova Gaia **133** 10 10 S 17 35 E
Nova Gradiška **46** 45 17N 17 28 E
Nova Granada **171** 20 30 S 49 20W
Nova Iguaçu **171** 22 45 S 43 28W
Nova Iorque **170** 7 0 S 44 5W
Nova Lamego **126** 12 19N 14 11W
Nova Lima **175** 19 59 S 43 51W
Nova Lisboa = Huambo **133** 12 42 S 15 54 E
Nova Lusitânia **131** 19 50 S 34 34 E
Nova Mambone **135** 21 0 S 35 3 E

Obyachevo

Nova Mesto **43** 45 47N 15 12 E
Nova Paka **30** 50 29N 15 30 E
Nova Ponte **171** 19 8 S 47 41W
Nova Scotia □ **143** 45 10N 63 0W
Nova Sofala **135** 20 7 S 34 42 E
Nova Varoš **46** 43 29N 19 48 E
Nova Venécia **171** 18 45 S 40 24W
Nova Vida **173** 10 11 S 62 47W
Nova Zagora **47** 42 32N 25 59 E
Novaci, Romania **50** 45 10N 23 42 E
Novaci, Yugoslavia **46** 41 5N 21 29 E
Noval Iorque **170** 6 48 S 44 0W
Novaleksandrovskaya **61** 45 29N 41 17 E
Novannenskiy **59** 50 32N 42 39 E
Novara **42** 45 27N 8 36 E
Novata **158** 38 6N 122 35W
Novaya Kakhovka **60** 46 42N 33 27 E
Novaya Ladoga **56** 60 7N 32 16 E
Novaya Lyalya **62** 59 10N 60 35 E
Novaya Sibir, Ostrov **65** 75 10N 150 0 E
Novaya Zemlya **64** 75 0N 56 0 E
Nové Město **31** 48 45N 17 50 E
Nové Zámky **31** 48 0N 18 8 E
Novelda **37** 38 24N 0 45W
Novellara **42** 44 50N 10 43 E
Novelty **154** 40 1N 92 12W
Noventa Vicentina **43** 45 18N 11 30 E
Novgorod **58** 58 30N 31 25 E
Novgorod-Severskiy **58** 52 2N 33 10 E
Novi Bečej **46** 45 36N 20 10 E
Novi Grad **43** 45 19N 13 33 E
Novi Kneževa **46** 46 4N 20 8 E
Novi Krichim **47** 42 8N 24 31 E
Novi Lígure **42** 44 45N 8 47 E
Novi Pazar, Bulgaria **47** 43 25N 27 15 E
Novi Pazar, Yugoslavia **46** 43 12N 20 28 E
Novi Sad **46** 45 18N 19 52 E
Novi Vinodolski **43** 45 10N 14 48 E
Novigrad **43** 44 10N 15 32 E
Noville **23** 50 4N 5 46 E
Novinger **154** 40 14N 92 43W
Novo Acôrdo **170** 10 10 S 46 48W
Novo Aripuanã **169** 5 8 S 60 22W
Nôvo Cruzeiro **171** 17 29 S 41 53W
Nôvo Hamburgo **175** 29 37 S 51 7W
Novo Horizonte **171** 21 25 S 49 10W
Novo-Sergiyevskiy **62** 52 5N 53 38 E
Novo-Zavidovskiy **59** 56 32N 36 29 E
Novoakrainka **60** 48 25N 31 30 E
Novoalekseyevka **62** 50 8N 55 39 E
Novoaltaysk **64** 53 30N 84 0 E
Novoazovsk **60** 47 15N 38 4 E
Novobelitsa **58** 52 27N 31 2 E
Novobogatinskoye **61** 47 20N 51 11 E
Novocherkassk **61** 47 27N 40 5 E
Novodevichye **59** 53 37N 48 50 E
Novograd-Volynskiy **58** 50 34N 27 35 E
Novogrudok **58** 53 40N 25 50 E
Novokachalinsk **98** 45 5N 132 0 E
Novokayakent **61** 42 30N 47 52 E
Novokazalinsk **64** 45 48N 62 6 E
Novokhopersk **59** 51 5N 41 39 E
Novokuybyshevsk **59** 53 7N 49 58 E
Novokuznetsk **64** 53 45N 87 10 E
Novomirgorod **60** 48 45N 31 33 E
Novomoskovsk, R.S.F.S.R., U.S.S.R. **59** 54 5N 38 15 E
Novomoskovsk, Ukraine S.S.R., U.S.S.R. **60** 48 33N 35 17 E
Novoorsk **62** 51 21N 59 2 E
Novopolotsk **58** 55 32N 28 37 E
Novorossiysk **60** 44 43N 37 46 E
Novorybnoye **65** 72 50N 105 50 E
Novorzhev **58** 57 3N 29 25 E
Novoselitsa **60** 48 14N 26 15 E
Novoshakhtinsk **61** 47 46N 39 58 E
Novosibirsk **64** 55 0N 83 5 E
Novosibirskiye Ostrava **65** 75 0N 142 0 E
Novosil **59** 52 59N 37 2 E
Novosokolniki **58** 56 33N 30 5 E
Novotroitsk **62** 51 10N 58 15 E
Novotroitskoye **63** 43 42N 73 46 E
Novotulskiy **59** 54 10N 37 43 E
Novouzensk **59** 50 32N 48 17 E
Novovolynsk **58** 50 45N 24 4 E
Novovyatsk **59** 58 24N 49 45 E
Novozybkov **58** 52 30N 32 0 E
Novska **46** 45 19N 17 0 E
Novvy Port **64** 67 40N 72 30 E
Novy Bug **60** 47 34N 32 29 E
Nový Bydzov **30** 50 14N 15 29 E
Nowy Dwór Mazowiecki **32** 52 26N 20 44 E
Nový Jičín **31** 49 30N 18 0 E
Novyy Afon **61** 43 7N 40 50 E
Novyy Oskol **59** 50 44N 37 55 E
Now Shahr **73** 36 40N 51 30 E
Nowa Deba **32** 50 26N 21 41 E
Nowa Huta **31** 50 5N 20 30 E
Nowa Nowa **113** 37 44 S 148 3 E
Nowa Ruda **32** 50 35N 16 30 E
Nowa Skalmierzyce **32** 51 43N 18 0 E
Nowa Sól **32** 51 48N 15 44 E
Nowbarān **73** 35 8N 49 42 E
Nowe **32** 53 41N 18 44 E
Nowe Miasteczko **32** 51 42N 15 42 E
Nowe Miasto **32** 51 38N 20 34 E
Nowe Miasto Lubawskie **32** 53 27N 19 33 E
Nowe Warpno **32** 53 42N 14 18 E
Nowendoc **113** 31 32 S 151 44 E
Nowghāb **73** 33 53N 59 4 E
Nowgong **82** 26 20N 92 50 E
Nowingi **112** 34 33 S 142 15 E
Nowogard **32** 53 41N 15 10 E
Nowogród **32** 53 14N 21 53 E
Nowra **113** 34 53 S 150 35 E
Nowshera **77** 34 0N 72 0 E
Nowy Dwór, Białystok, Poland **32** 53 40N 23 30 E
Nowy Dwór, Gdańsk, Poland **32** 54 13N 19 7 E
Nowy Korczyn **32** 50 19N 20 48 E
Nowy Sącz **32** 49 40N 20 41 E
Nowy Sącz □ **32** 49 30N 20 30 E
Nowy Staw **32** 54 13N 19 2 E
Nowy Tomyśl **32** 52 19N 16 10 E
Noxen **151** 41 25N 76 4W
Noxon **156** 48 0N 115 43W
Noya **34** 42 48N 8 53W
Noyant **18** 47 30N 0 6 E
Noyers **19** 47 40N 4 0 E
Noyes I. **144** 55 30N 133 40W
Noyon, France **19** 49 34N 3 0 E
Noyon, Mongolia **94** 43 2N 102 4 E
Nozay **18** 47 34N 1 38W
Nsa, O. en → **121** 32 28N 5 24 E
Nsa, Plateau de **132** 2 26 S 15 20 E
Nsah **132** 2 22 S 15 19 E
Nsanje **131** 16 55 S 35 12 E
Nsawam **127** 5 50N 0 24W
Nsomba **131** 10 45 S 29 51 E
Nsopzup **82** 25 51N 97 30 E
Nsukka **127** 6 51N 7 29 E
Ntoum **132** 0 22N 9 47 E
Nu Jiang → **96** 29 58N 97 25 E
Nu Shan **96** 26 0N 99 20 E
Nuba Mts. = Nubah, Jibalan **125** 12 0N 31 0 E
Nubah, Jibalan **125** 12 0N 31 0 E
Nûbîya, Es Sahrâ En **124** 21 30N 33 30 E
Ñuble □ **174** 37 0 S 72 0W
Nuboai **87** 2 10 S 136 30 E
Nubra → **79** 34 35N 77 35 E
Nueces → **153** 27 50N 97 30W
Nueima → **69** 31 54N 35 25 E
Nueltin L. **145** 60 30N 99 30W
Nuenen **23** 51 29N 5 33 E
Nueva, I. **176** 55 13 S 66 30W
Nueva Antioquia **168** 6 5N 69 26W
Nueva Ecija □ **90** 15 35N 121 0 E
Nueva Esparta □ **169** 11 0N 64 0W
Nueva Gerona **162** 21 53N 82 49W
Nueva Imperial **176** 38 45 S 72 58W
Nueva Palmira **174** 33 52 S 58 20W
Nueva Rosita **160** 28 0N 101 11W
Nueva San Salvador **162** 13 40N 89 18W
Nueva Vizcaya □ **90** 16 20N 121 20 E
Nuéve de Julio **174** 35 30 S 61 0W
Nuevitas **162** 21 30N 77 20W
Nuevo, G. **176** 43 0 S 64 30W
Nuevo Guerrero **161** 26 34N 99 15W
Nuevo Laredo **161** 27 30N 99 30W
Nuevo León □ **160** 25 0N 100 0W
Nuevo Mundo, Cerro **172** 21 55 S 66 53W
Nuevo Rocafuerte **168** 0 55 S 75 27W
Nugget Pt. **115** 46 27 S 169 50 E
Nugrus, Gebel **124** 24 47N 34 35 E
Nuhaka **114** 39 3 S 177 45 E
Nuits-St.-Georges **19** 47 10N 4 56 E
Nukey Bluff, Mt. **111** 32 26 S 135 29 E
Nukheila **124** 19 1N 26 21 E
Nukus **64** 42 20N 59 7 E
Nuland **22** 51 44N 5 26 E
Nulato **140** 64 40N 158 10W
Nules **36** 39 51N 0 9W
Nullagine → **108** 21 20 S 120 20 E
Nullarbor **109** 31 28 S 130 55 E
Nullarbor Plain **109** 31 10 S 129 0 E
Numalla, L. **111** 28 43 S 144 20 E
Numan **127** 9 29N 12 3 E
Numansdorp **22** 51 43N 4 26 E
Numata **101** 36 45N 139 4 E
Numatinna → **125** 7 38N 27 20 E
Numazu **101** 35 7N 138 51 E
Numbulwar **110** 14 15 S 135 45 E
Numfoor **87** 1 0 S 134 50 E
Numurkah **113** 36 5 S 145 26 E
Nunaksaluk I. **143** 55 49N 60 20W
Nuneaton **13** 52 32N 1 29W
Nungo **131** 13 23 S 37 43 E
Nungwe **132** 2 48 S 32 2 E
Nunivak **140** 60 0N 166 0W
Nunkun **79** 33 57N 76 2 E
Nunspeet **22** 52 21N 5 45 E
Nuoro **44** 40 20N 9 20 E
Nuqayy, Jabal **123** 23 11N 19 30 E
Nuqūb **74** 14 59N 45 48 E
Nuquí **168** 5 42N 77 17W
Nur Dağı **70** 36 54N 35 39 E
Nur Dağları **70** 36 50N 36 23 E
Nūrābād **73** 27 47N 57 12 E
Nurata **63** 40 33N 65 41 E
Nuratau, Khrebet **63** 40 40N 66 30 E
Nure → **42** 45 3N 9 49 E
Nuremburg = Nürnberg **27** 49 26N 11 5 E
Nūrestān **77** 35 30N 70 45 E
Nuri **160** 28 2N 109 22W
Nurina **109** 30 56 S 126 33 E
Nuriootpa **112** 34 27 S 139 0 E
Nurlat **59** 54 29N 50 45 E
Nürnberg **27** 49 26N 11 5 E
Nurran, L. = Terewah, L. **111** 29 52 S 147 35 E
Nurrari Lakes **109** 29 1 S 130 5 E
Nurri **44** 39 43N 9 13 E
Nurzec → **32** 52 37N 22 25 E
Nusa Barung **89** 8 10 S 113 30 E
Nusa Kambangan **89** 7 40 S 108 10 E
Nusa Tenggara Barat □ **89** 8 50 S 117 30 E
Nusa Tenggara Timur □ **87** 9 30 S 122 0 E
Nusaybin **57** 37 3N 41 10 E
Nushki **77** 29 35N 66 0 E
Nutak **141** 57 28N 61 59W
Nuth **23** 50 55N 5 53 E
Nutwood Downs **110** 15 49 S 134 10 E
Nuwakot **79** 28 10N 83 55 E
Nuwara Eliya **81** 6 58N 80 48 E
Nuweiba' **71** 28 59N 34 39 E
Nuweveldberge **134** 32 10 S 21 45 E
Nuyts, C. **109** 32 2 S 132 21 E
Nuyts Arch. **111** 32 35 S 133 20 E
Nuzvid **80** 16 47N 80 53 E
Nxau-Nxau **134** 18 57 S 21 4 E
Nyaake **126** 4 52N 7 37W
Nyack **151** 41 5N 73 57W
Nyadal **52** 62 48N 17 59 E
Nyah West **112** 35 16 S 143 21 E
Nyahanga **130** 2 20 S 33 37 E
Nyahua **130** 5 25 S 33 23 E
Nyahururu **130** 0 2N 36 27 E
Nyainqentanglha Shan **92** 30 0N 90 0 E
Nyakanazi **130** 3 2 S 31 10 E
Nyakrom **127** 5 40N 0 50W
Nyâlâ **125** 12 2N 24 58 E
Nyamandhlovu **131** 19 55 S 28 16 E
Nyambiti **130** 2 48 S 33 27 E
Nyamwaga **130** 1 27 S 34 33 E
Nyandekwa **130** 3 57 S 32 32 E
Nyanding → **125** 8 40N 32 41 E
Nyandoma **56** 61 40N 40 12 E
Nyanga → **132** 2 58 S 10 15 E
Nyangana **134** 18 0 S 20 40 E
Nyanguge **130** 2 30 S 33 12 E
Nyankpala **127** 9 21N 0 58W
Nyanza, Burundi **130** 4 21 S 29 36 E
Nyanza, Rwanda **130** 2 20 S 29 42 E
Nyanza □ **130** 0 10 S 34 15 E
Nyarling → **144** 60 41N 113 23W
Nyasa, L. = Malawi, L. **131** 12 30 S 34 30 E
Nyaunglebin **82** 17 52N 96 42 E
Nyazepetrovsk **62** 56 3N 59 36 E
Nyazura **131** 18 40 S 32 16 E
Nyazwidzi → **131** 20 0 S 31 17 E
Nyborg **53** 55 18N 10 47 E
Nybro **53** 56 44N 15 55 E
Nyda **64** 66 40N 72 58 E
Nyeri **130** 0 23 S 36 56 E
Nyerol **125** 8 41N 32 1 E
Nyhem **52** 62 54N 15 37 E
Nyiel **125** 6 9N 31 13 E
Nyinahin **126** 6 43N 2 3W
Nyírbátor **31** 47 49N 22 9 E
Nyíregyháza **31** 47 58N 21 47 E
Nykarleby **54** 63 22N 22 31 E
Nykøbing, Sjælland, Denmark **52** 55 55N 11 40 E
Nykøbing, Storstrøm, Denmark **53** 54 56N 11 52 E
Nykøbing, Viborg, Denmark **53** 56 48N 8 51 E
Nyköping **53** 58 45N 17 0 E
Nykroppa **52** 59 37N 14 18 E
Nykvarn **52** 59 11N 17 25 E
Nyland **52** 63 1N 17 45 E
Nylstroom **135** 24 42 S 28 22 E
Nymagee **113** 32 7 S 146 20 E
Nymburk **30** 50 10N 15 1 E
Nynäshamn **52** 58 54N 17 57 E
Nyon **28** 46 23N 6 14 E
Nyong → **127** 3 17N 9 54 E
Nyons **21** 44 22N 5 10 E
Nyora **113** 38 20 S 145 41 E
Nyord **52** 55 4N 12 13 E
Nyou **127** 12 42N 2 1W
Nysa **32** 50 30N 17 22 E
Nysa → **32** 52 4N 14 46 E
Nyssa **156** 43 56N 117 2W
Nysted **53** 54 40N 11 44 E
Nytva **62** 57 56N 55 20 E
Nyûgawa **100** 33 56N 133 5 E
Nyunzu **130** 5 57 S 27 58 E
Nyurba **65** 63 17N 118 28 E
Nzega **130** 4 10 S 33 12 E
Nzega □ **130** 4 10 S 33 10 E
N'Zérékoré **126** 7 49N 8 48W
Nzeto **133** 7 10 S 12 52 E
Nzilo, Chutes de **131** 10 18 S 25 27 E
Nzubuka **130** 4 45 S 32 50 E

O

Ō-Shima, Fukuoka, Japan **100** 33 54N 130 25 E
Ō-Shima, Nagasaki, Japan **100** 34 29N 129 33 E
Ō-Shima, Shizuoka, Japan **101** 34 44N 139 24 E
Oacoma **152** 43 50N 99 26W
Oahe Dam **152** 44 28N 100 25W
Oahe L. **152** 45 30N 100 25W
Oahu **146** 21 30N 158 0W
Oak Creek, Colo., U.S.A. **156** 40 15N 106 59W
Oak Creek, Wis., U.S.A. **155** 42 52N 87 55W
Oak Harb. **158** 48 20N 122 38W
Oak Hill **148** 38 0N 81 7W
Oak Lawn **155** 41 43N 87 44W
Oak Park, Ill., U.S.A. **155** 41 53N 87 47W
Oak Park, U.S.A. **148** 41 55N 87 45W
Oak Ridge **149** 36 1N 84 12W
Oak View **159** 34 24N 119 18W
Oakan-Dake **98** 43 27N 144 10 E
Oakbank **112** 33 4 S 140 33 E
Oakdale, Calif., U.S.A. **158** 37 45N 120 55W
Oakdale, La., U.S.A. **153** 30 50N 92 38W
Oakengates **12** 52 42N 2 29W
Oakes **152** 46 14N 98 4W
Oakesdale **156** 47 11N 117 15W
Oakey **111** 27 25 S 151 43 E
Oakford **154** 40 6N 89 58W
Oakham **12** 52 40N 0 43W
Oakhurst **158** 37 19N 119 40W
Oakland, Calif., U.S.A. **158** 37 50N 122 18W
Oakland, Ill., U.S.A. **155** 39 39N 88 2W
Oakland, Oreg., U.S.A. **156** 43 23N 123 18W
Oakland City **155** 38 20N 87 20W
Oaklands **113** 35 34 S 146 10 E
Oakley, Idaho, U.S.A. **156** 42 14N 113 55W
Oakley, Kans., U.S.A. **152** 39 8N 100 51W
Oakley Creek **113** 31 37 S 149 46 E
Oakover → **108** 21 0 S 120 40 E
Oakridge **156** 43 47N 122 31W
Oaktown **155** 38 52N 87 27W
Oakville **158** 46 50N 123 14W
Oakwood **155** 41 6N 84 23W
Oamaru **115** 45 5 S 170 59 E
Ōamishirasato **101** 35 31N 140 18 E
Oarai **101** 36 21N 140 34 E
Oasis, Calif., U.S.A. **159** 33 28N 116 6W
Oasis, Nev., U.S.A. **158** 37 29N 117 55W
Oates Coast **7** 69 0 S 160 0 E
Oatman **159** 35 1N 114 19W
Oaxaca **161** 17 2N 96 40W
Oaxaca □ **161** 17 0N 97 0W
Ob → **64** 66 45N 69 30 E
Oba **142** 49 4N 84 7W
Obala **127** 4 9N 11 32 E
Obama, Fukui, Japan **101** 35 30N 135 45 E
Obama, Nagasaki, Japan **100** 32 43N 130 13 E
Oban **14** 56 25N 5 30W
Obbia **136** 5 25N 48 30 E
Obdam **22** 52 41N 4 55 E
Obed **144** 53 30N 117 10W
Ober-Aagau **28** 47 10N 7 45 E
Obera **175** 27 21 S 55 2W
Oberalppass **29** 46 39N 8 35 E
Oberalpstock **29** 46 45N 8 47 E
Oberammergau **27** 47 35N 11 3 E
Oberdrauburg **30** 46 44N 12 58 E
Oberengadin **29** 46 35N 9 55 E
Oberentfelden **28** 47 21N 8 2 E
Oberhausen **26** 51 28N 6 50 E
Oberkirch **27** 48 31N 8 5 E
Oberland **28** 46 30N 7 30 E
Oberlin, Kans., U.S.A. **152** 39 52N 100 31W
Oberlin, La., U.S.A. **153** 30 42N 92 42W
Oberlin, Ohio, U.S.A. **150** 41 15N 82 10W
Obernai **19** 48 28N 7 30 E
Oberndorf **27** 48 17N 8 35 E
Oberon **113** 33 45 S 149 52 E
Oberösterreich □ **30** 48 10N 14 0 E
Oberpfälzer Wald **27** 49 30N 12 25 E
Obersiggenthal **29** 47 29N 8 18 E
Oberstdorf **27** 47 25N 10 16 E
Oberting **132** 0 22 S 9 46 E
Oberwil **28** 47 32N 7 33 E
Obi, Kepulauan **87** 1 23 S 127 45 E
Obiaruku **127** 5 51N 6 9 E
Óbidos, Brazil **169** 1 50 S 55 30W
Óbidos, Portugal **35** 39 19N 9 10W
Obihiro **98** 42 56N 143 12 E
Obilatu **87** 1 25 S 127 20 E
Obilnoye **61** 47 32N 44 30 E
Obing **27** 48 0N 12 25 E
Obisfelde **26** 52 27N 10 57 E
Objat **20** 45 16N 1 24 E
Oblong **155** 39 0N 87 55W
Obluchye **65** 49 1N 131 4 E
Obninsk **59** 55 8N 36 37 E
Obo, C.A.R. **130** 5 20N 26 32 E
Obo, Ethiopia **125** 3 46N 38 52 E
Oboa, Mt. **130** 1 45N 34 45 E
Obock **125** 12 0N 43 20 E
Oborniki **32** 52 39N 16 50 E
Oborniki Śląskie **32** 51 17N 16 53 E
Obouya **132** 0 56 S 15 43 E
Oboyan **59** 51 13N 36 37 E
Obrenovac **46** 44 40N 20 11 E
Obrovac **43** 44 11N 15 41 E
Observatory Inlet **144** 55 10N 129 54W
Obshchi Syrt **10** 52 0N 53 0 E
Obskaya Guba **64** 69 0N 73 0 E
Obuasi **127** 6 17N 1 40W
Obubra **127** 6 8N 8 20 E
Obwalden □ **28** 46 55N 8 15 E
Obyachevo **62** 60 20N 49 37 E

Obzor

Obzor 47 42 50N 27 52 E
Ocala 149 29 11N 82 5W
Ocamo → 169 2 48N 65 14W
Ocampo 160 28 9N 108 24W
Ocaña, Colombia 168 8 15N 73 20W
Ocaña, Spain 36 39 55N 3 30W
Ocanomowoc 152 43 7N 88 30W
Ocate 153 36 12N 104 59W
Occidental, Cordillera, Colombia 168 5 0N 76 0W
Occidental, Cordillera, Peru 172 14 0S 74 0W
Ocean, I. = Banaba 104 0 45 S 169 50 E
Ocean City, N.J., U.S.A. 148 39 18N 74 34W
Ocean City, Wash., U.S.A. 158 47 4N 124 10W
Ocean Park 158 46 30N 124 2W
Oceano 159 35 6N 120 37W
Oceanport 151 40 20N 74 3W
Oceanside 159 33 13N 117 26W
Ochagavia 36 42 55N 1 5W
Ochamchire 61 42 46N 41 32 E
Ochamps 23 49 56N 5 16 E
Ocher 62 57 53N 54 42 E
Ochiai 100 35 1N 133 45 E
Ochil Hills 14 56 14N 3 40W
Ochre River 145 51 4N 99 47W
Ochsenfurt 27 49 38N 10 3 E
Ochsenhausen 27 48 4N 9 57 E
Ocilla 149 31 35N 83 12W
Ockelbo 52 60 54N 16 45 E
Ocmulgee → 149 31 58N 82 32W
Ocna Mureş 50 46 23N 23 55 E
Ocna Sibiului 50 45 52N 24 2 E
Ocnele Mari 50 45 8N 24 18 E
Ocoña 172 16 26 S 73 8W
Ocoña → 172 16 28 S 73 8W
Oconee → 149 31 58N 82 32W
Oconomowoc 155 43 6N 88 30W
Oconto 148 44 52N 87 53W
Oconto Falls 148 44 52N 88 10W
Ocosingo 161 17 10N 92 15W
Ocotal 162 13 41N 86 31W
Ocotlán 160 20 21N 102 42W
Ocquier 23 50 24N 5 24 E
Ocreza → 35 39 32N 7 50W
Ócsa 31 47 17N 19 15 E
Octave 157 34 10N 112 43W
Octeville 18 49 38N 1 40W
Ocumare del Tuy 168 10 7N 66 46W
Ocuri 173 18 45 S 65 50W
Oda, Ghana 127 5 50N 0 51W
Oda, Ehime, Japan 100 33 36N 132 53 E
Ōda, Shimane, Japan 100 35 11N 132 30 E
Oda, Jebel 124 20 21N 36 39 E
Ódáðahraun 54 65 5N 17 0W
Ödåkra 52 56 7N 12 45 E
Odate 98 40 16N 140 34 E
Odawara 101 35 20N 139 6 E
Odda 51 60 3N 6 35 E
Odder 53 55 58N 10 10 E
Oddur 136 4 11N 43 52 E
Ödeborg 53 58 32N 11 58 E
Odei → 145 56 6N 96 54W
Odell 155 41 0N 88 31W
Odemira 35 37 35N 8 40W
Odendaalsrus 134 27 48 S 26 45 E
Odense 53 55 22N 10 23 E
Odenwald 27 49 40N 9 0 E
Oder → 26 53 33N 14 38 E
Oderzo 43 45 47N 12 29 E
Odessa, Canada 151 44 17N 76 43W
Odessa, Mo., U.S.A. 154 39 0N 93 57W
Odessa, Tex., U.S.A. 153 31 51N 102 23W
Odessa, Wash., U.S.A. 156 47 19N 118 35W
Odessa, U.S.S.R. 60 46 30N 30 45 E
Odiakwe 134 20 12 S 25 17 E
Odiel → 35 37 10N 6 55W
Odienné 126 9 30N 7 34W
Odiongan 90 12 24N 121 59 E
Odobeşti 50 45 43N 27 4 E
Odolanów 32 51 34N 17 40 E
O'Donnell, Phil. 90 15 21N 120 27 E
O'Donnell, U.S.A. 153 33 0N 101 48W
Odoorn 22 52 51N 6 51 E
Odorheiu Secuiesc 50 46 21N 25 21 E
Odoyevo 59 53 56N 36 42 E
Odra →, Poland 32 53 33N 14 38 E
Odra →, Spain 34 42 14N 4 17W
Odweina 136 9 25N 45 4 E
Odžaci 46 45 30N 19 17 E
Odžak 46 45 3N 18 18 E
Odzi 135 19 0S 32 20 E
Oedelem 23 51 10N 3 21 E
Oegstgeest 22 52 11N 4 29 E
Oeiras, Brazil 170 7 0S 42 8W
Oeiras, Portugal 35 38 41N 9 18W
Oelrichs 152 43 11N 103 14W
Oelsnitz 26 50 24N 12 11 E
Oelwein 152 42 41N 91 55W
Oenpelli 108 12 20 S 133 4 E
O'Fallon 154 38 50N 90 43W
Ofanto → 45 41 22N 16 13 E
Offa 127 8 13N 4 42 E
Offaly □ 15 53 15N 7 30W
Offenbach 27 50 6N 8 46 E
Offenburg 27 48 29N 7 56 E
Offerdal 52 63 28N 14 0 E
Offida 43 42 56N 13 40 E
Offranville 18 49 52N 1 1 E
Ofidhousa 49 36 33N 26 8 E
Ofotfjorden 54 68 27N 16 40 E
Ofu 106 14 11 S 169 41W
Ōfunato 98 39 4N 141 43 E
Oga 98 39 55N 139 50 E
Oga-Hantō 98 39 58N 139 47 E
Ogaden 136 7 30N 45 30 E
Ogahalla 142 50 6N 85 51W
Ōgaki 101 35 21N 136 37 E
Ogallala 152 41 12N 101 40W
Ogan → 88 3 1S 104 44 E
Ogbomosho 127 8 1N 4 11 E
Ogden, Iowa, U.S.A. 154 42 3N 94 0W
Ogden, Utah, U.S.A. 156 41 13N 112 1W
Ogdensburg 151 44 40N 75 27W
Ogeechee → 149 31 51N 81 6W
Ogilby 159 32 49N 114 50W
Oglesby 154 41 21N 89 3W
Oglio → 42 45 2N 10 39 E
Ogmore 110 22 37 S 149 35 E
Ogna 51 58 31N 5 48 E
Ognon → 19 47 16N 5 28 E
Ogoja 127 6 38N 8 39 E
Ogoki → 142 51 38N 85 57W
Ogoki L. 142 50 50N 87 10W
Ogoki Res. 142 50 45N 88 15W
Ogooué → 132 1 0S 9 0 E
Ōgori 100 34 6N 131 24 E
Ogosta → 47 43 48N 23 55 E
Ogowe = Ogooué → 132 1 0S 9 0 E
Ogr = Sharafa 125 11 59N 27 7 E
Ogražden 46 41 30N 22 50 E
Ogrein 124 17 55N 34 50 E
Ogulin 43 45 16N 15 16 E
Ogun □ 127 7 0N 3 0 E
Oguni 100 33 11N 131 8 E
Oguta 127 5 44N 6 44 E
Oğuzeli 70 36 58N 37 27 E
Ogwashi-Uku 127 6 15N 6 30 E
Ogwe 127 5 0N 7 14 E
Ohai 115 44 55 S 168 0 E
Ohakune 114 39 24 S 175 24 E
Ohanet 121 28 44N 8 46 E
Ōhara 101 35 15N 140 23 E
Ohata 98 41 24N 141 10 E
Ohau, L. 115 44 15 S 169 53 E
Ohaupo 114 37 56 S 175 20 E
Ohey 23 50 26N 5 8 E
Ohio □ 148 40 20N 14 10 E
Ohio → 148 38 0N 86 0W
Ohio City 155 40 46N 84 37W
Ohiwa Harbour 114 37 59 S 177 10 E
Ohre →, Czech. 30 50 30N 14 10 E
Ohre →, Germany 26 52 18N 11 47 E
Ohrid 46 41 8N 20 52 E
Ohridsko, Jezero 46 41 8N 20 52 E
Ohrigstad 135 24 39 S 30 36 E
Öhringen 27 49 11N 9 31 E
Oiapoque → 169 4 8N 51 40W
Oikou 95 38 35N 117 42 E
Oil City 150 41 26N 79 40W
Oildale 159 35 25N 119 1W
Oinousa 49 38 33N 26 14 E
Oirschot 23 51 30N 5 18 E
Oise □ 19 49 28N 2 30 E
Oise → 19 49 0N 2 4 E
Oisterwijk 23 51 35N 5 12 E
Ōita 100 33 14N 131 36 E
Ōita □ 100 33 15N 131 30 E
Oiticica 170 5 3S 41 5W
Ojai 159 34 28N 119 16W
Ojinaga 160 29 34N 104 25W
Ojiya 99 37 18N 138 48 E
Ojos del Salado, Cerro 174 27 0S 68 40W
Oka → 59 56 20N 43 59 E
Okaba 87 8 6S 139 42 E
Okahandja 134 22 0S 16 59 E
Okahukura 104 38 48 S 175 14 E
Okaihau 114 35 19 S 173 47 E
Okanagan L. 144 50 0N 119 30W
Okandja 132 0 35 S 13 45 E
Okanogan 156 48 6N 119 43W
Okanogan → 156 48 6N 119 43W
Okány 31 46 52N 21 21 E
Okapa 107 6 38 S 145 39 E
Okaputa 134 20 5S 17 0 E
Okara 77 30 50N 73 31 E
Okarito 115 43 15 S 170 9 E
Okato 114 39 12 S 173 53 E
Okaukuejo 134 19 10 S 16 0 E
Okavango Swamps 134 18 45 S 22 45 E
Okawa 100 33 9N 130 21 E
Okawville 154 38 26N 89 33W
Okaya 101 36 0N 138 10 E
Okayama 100 34 40N 133 54 E
Okayama □ 100 35 0N 133 50 E
Okazaki 101 34 57N 137 10 E
Oke-Iho 127 8 1N 3 18 E
Okeechobee 149 27 16N 80 46W
Okeechobee, L. 149 27 0N 80 50W
Okefenokee Swamp 149 30 50N 82 15W
Okehampton 17 50 44N 4 1W
Okene 127 7 32N 6 11 E
Oker → 26 52 30N 10 22 E
Okha 65 53 40N 143 0 E
Ókhi Óros 49 38 5N 24 25 E
Okhotsk 65 59 20N 143 10 E
Okhotsk, Sea of 65 55 0N 145 0 E
Okhotskiy Perevoz 65 61 52N 135 35 E
Okhotsko Kolymskoye 65 63 0N 157 0 E
Oki-no-Shima 100 32 44N 132 33 E
Oki-Shotō 100 36 5N 133 15 E
Okiep 134 29 39 S 17 53 E
Okigwi 127 5 52N 7 20 E
Okija 127 5 54N 6 55 E
Okinawa □ 106 26 40N 128 0 E
Okinawa-Guntō 99 26 40N 128 0 E
Okinawa-Jima 99 26 32N 128 0 E
Okino-erabu-Shima 99 27 21N 128 33 E
Okitipupa 127 6 31N 4 50 E
Oklahoma □ 153 35 20N 97 30W
Oklahoma City 153 35 25N 97 30W
Okmulgee 153 35 38N 96 0W
Oknitsa 60 48 25N 27 30 E
Okolo 130 2 37N 31 8 E
Okolona, Ky., U.S.A. 155 38 8N 85 41W
Okolona, Miss., U.S.A. 153 34 0N 88 45W
Okonek 32 53 32N 16 51 E
Okrika 127 4 40N 7 10 E
Oktabrsk 57 49 28N 57 25 E
Oktyabr 63 43 41N 77 12 E
Oktyabrsk 59 53 11N 48 40 E
Oktyabrskiy, Byelorussian S.S.R., U.S.S.R. 58 52 38N 28 53 E
Oktyabrskiy, R.S.F.S.R., U.S.S.R. 62 54 28N 53 28 E
Oktyabrskoy Revolyutsii, Os. 65 79 30N 97 0 E
Oktyabrskoye = Zhovtnevoye 60 46 54N 32 3 E
Oktyabrskoye 64 62 28N 66 3 E
Oku 106 26 35N 127 50 E
Ōkuchi 100 32 4N 130 37 E
Okulovka 58 58 25N 33 19 E
Okuru 115 43 55 S 168 55 E
Okushiri-Tō 98 42 15N 139 30 E
Okuta 127 9 14N 3 12 E
Okwa → 134 22 30 S 23 0 E
Ola 153 35 2N 93 10W
Ólafsfjörður 54 66 4N 18 39W
Ólafsvík 54 64 53N 23 43W
Olancha 159 36 15N 118 1W
Olancha Pk. 159 36 15N 118 7W
Olanchito 162 15 30N 86 30W
Öland 53 56 45N 16 38 E
Olargues 20 43 34N 2 53 E
Olary 112 32 18 S 140 19 E
Olascoaga 174 35 15 S 60 39W
Olathe 152 38 50N 94 50W
Olavarría 174 36 55 S 60 20W
Oława 32 50 57N 17 20 E
Ólbia 44 40 55N 9 30 E
Ólbia, G. di 44 40 55N 9 35 E
Old Bahama Chan. = Bahama, Canal Viejo de 162 22 10N 77 30W
Old Baldy Pk. = San Antonio, Mt. 159 34 17N 117 38W
Old Castile = Castilla La Vieja 34 41 55N 4 0W
Old Castle 15 53 46N 7 10W
Old Cork 110 22 57 S 141 52 E
Old Crow 140 67 30N 140 5 E
Old Dale 159 34 8N 115 47W
Old Dongola 124 18 11N 30 44 E
Old Forge, N.Y., U.S.A. 151 43 43N 74 58W
Old Forge, Pa., U.S.A. 151 41 20N 75 46W
Old Fort → 145 58 36N 110 24W
Old Shinyanga 130 3 33 S 33 27 E
Old Speck, Mt. 151 44 35N 70 57W
Old Town 143 45 0N 68 41W
Old Wives L. 145 50 5N 106 0W
Oldbury 13 51 38N 2 30W
Oldeani 130 3 22 S 35 35 E
Oldenburg, Niedersachsen, Germany 26 53 10N 8 10 E
Oldenburg, Schleswig-Holstein, Germany 26 54 16N 10 53 E
Oldenzaal 22 52 19N 6 53 E
Oldham 12 53 33N 2 8W
Oldman → 144 49 57N 111 42W
Olds 144 51 50N 114 10W
Olean 150 42 8N 78 25W
Olecko 32 54 2N 22 31 E
Oléggio 42 45 36N 8 38 E
Oleiros 34 39 56N 7 56W
Olekma → 65 60 22N 120 42 E
Olekminsk 65 60 25N 120 30 E
Olema 158 38 3N 122 47W
Olen 23 51 9N 4 52 E
Olenegorsk 56 68 9N 33 18 E
Olenek 65 68 28N 112 18 E
Olenek → 65 73 0N 120 10 E
Olenino 58 56 15N 33 30 E
Oléron, I. d' 20 45 55N 1 15W
Oleśnica 32 51 13N 17 22 E
Olesno 32 50 51N 18 26 E
Olevsk 58 51 12N 27 39 E
Olga 65 43 50N 135 14 E
Olga, L. 142 49 47N 77 15W
Olga, Mt. 109 25 20 S 130 50 E
Olgastretet 6 78 35N 25 0 E
Ølgod 53 55 49N 8 36 E
Olhão 35 37 3N 7 48W
Olib 43 44 23N 14 44 E
Oliena 44 40 18N 9 22 E
Oliete 36 41 1N 0 41W
Olifants → 135 23 57 S 31 58 E
Olifantshoek 134 27 57 S 22 42 E
Ólimbos 49 35 44N 27 11 E
Ólimbos, Óros 48 40 6N 22 23 E
Olímpia 175 20 44 S 48 54W
Olimpo □ 174 20 30 S 58 45W
Olin 154 42 0N 91 9W
Olinda 170 8 1S 34 51W
Olindiná 170 11 22 S 38 21W
Olite 36 42 29N 1 40W
Oliva, Argentina 174 32 0S 63 38W
Oliva, Spain 37 38 58N 0 9W
Oliva, La 37 28 36N 13 57W
Oliva, Punta del 34 43 37N 5 28W
Oliva de la Frontera 35 38 17N 6 54W
Olivares 36 39 46N 2 20W
Olive Hill 155 38 18N 83 13W
Olivehurst 158 39 6N 121 34W
Oliveira 171 20 39 S 44 50W
Oliveira de Azemeis 34 40 49N 8 29W
Oliveira dos Brejinhos 171 12 19 S 42 54W
Olivenza 35 38 41N 7 9W
Oliver 144 49 13N 119 37W
Oliver L. 145 56 56N 103 22W
Olivine Ra. 115 44 15 S 168 30 E
Olivone 29 46 32N 8 57 E
Olkhovka 61 49 48N 44 32 E
Olkusz 32 50 18N 19 33 E
Ollagüe 174 21 15 S 68 10W
Olloy 23 50 5N 4 36 E
Olmedo 34 41 20N 4 43W
Olmos 172 5 59 S 79 46W
Olney, Ill., U.S.A. 155 38 40N 88 0W
Olney, Tex., U.S.A. 153 33 25N 98 45W
Olofström 53 56 17N 14 32 E
Oloma 127 3 29N 11 19 E
Olomane → 143 50 14N 60 37W
Olombo 132 1 18 S 15 53 E
Olomouc 31 49 38N 17 12 E
Olonets 56 61 10N 33 0 E
Olongapo 90 14 50N 120 18 E
Oloron, Gave d' → 20 43 33N 1 5W
Oloron-Ste.-Marie 20 43 11N 0 38W
Olosega, I. 106 14 11 S 169 38W
Olot 36 42 11N 2 30 E
Olovo 46 44 8N 18 35 E
Olovyannaya 65 50 58N 115 35 E
Oloy → 65 66 29N 159 29 E
Olpe 26 51 2N 7 50 E
Olshanka 60 48 16N 30 58 E
Olshany 60 50 3N 35 53 E
Olst 22 52 20N 6 7 E
Olsztyn 32 53 48N 20 29 E
Olsztyn □ 32 54 0N 21 0 E
Olsztynek 32 53 34N 20 19 E
Olt □ 50 44 20N 24 30 E
Olt → 50 43 43N 24 51 E
Olten 28 47 21N 7 53 E
Olteniţa 50 44 7N 26 42 E
Olton 153 34 16N 102 7W
Olutanga 91 7 26N 122 54 E
Olutanga I. 91 7 22N 122 52 E
Olvega 36 41 47N 2 0W
Olvera 35 36 55N 5 18W
Olympia, Greece 49 37 39N 21 39 E
Olympia, U.S.A. 158 47 0N 122 58W
Olympic Mts. 158 47 50N 123 45W
Olympic Nat. Park 158 47 48N 123 30W
Olympus, Mt. = Ólimbos, Óros 48 40 6N 22 23 E
Olympus, Mt. 158 47 52N 123 40W
Olyphant 151 41 27N 75 36W
Om → 64 54 59N 73 22 E
Om Hajer 125 14 20N 36 41 E
Om Koi 84 17 48N 98 22 E
Ōma 98 41 45N 141 5 E
Ōmachi 101 36 30N 137 50 E
Omae-Zaki 101 34 36N 138 14 E
Ōmagari 98 39 27N 140 29 E
Omagh 15 54 36N 7 20W
Omagh □ 15 54 35N 7 15W
Omaha 152 41 15N 96 0W
Omak 156 48 24N 119 31W
Oman ■ 75 23 0N 58 0 E
Oman, G. of 73 24 30N 58 30 E
Omar Combon 136 3 10N 45 47 E
Omaruru 134 21 26 S 16 0 E
Omaruru → 134 22 7S 14 15 E
Omate 172 16 45 S 71 0W
Ombai, Selat 87 8 30 S 124 50 E
Ombo 51 59 18N 6 0 E
Omboué 132 1 35 S 9 15 E
Ombrone → 42 42 39N 11 0 E
Omchi 123 21 22N 17 53 E
Omdurmân 125 15 40N 32 28 E
Ōme 101 35 47N 139 15 E
Omegna 42 45 52N 8 23 E
Omeonga 130 3 40 S 24 22 E
Ometepe, I. de 162 11 32N 85 35W
Ometepec 161 16 39N 98 23W
Omez 69 32 22N 35 0 E
Ōmi-Shima, Ehime, Japan 100 34 15N 133 0 E
Ōmi-Shima, Yamaguchi, Japan 100 34 25N 131 9 E
Omihachiman 101 35 7N 136 3 E
Ominato 98 41 17N 141 10 E
Omineca → 144 56 3N 124 16W

Orzinuovi

Omiš .... 43 43 28N 16 40 E
Omišalj .... 43 45 13N 14 32 E
Omitara .... 134 22 16 S 18 2 E
Ōmiya .... 101 35 54N 139 38 E
Omme Å → .... 53 55 56N 8 32 E
Ommen .... 22 52 31N 6 26 E
Ömnögovĭ □ .... 94 43 15N 104 0 E
Omo → .... 125 6 25N 36 10 E
Omolon → .... 65 68 42N 158 36 E
Omono-Gawa → ..... 98 39 46N 140 3 E
Omsk .... 64 55 0N 73 12 E
Omsukchan .... 65 62 32N 155 48 E
Ōmu .... 98 44 34N 142 58 E
Omul, Vf. .... 50 45 27N 25 29 E
Omulew → .... 32 53 5N 21 33 E
Ōmura .... 100 32 56N 130 0 E
Omura-Wan .... 100 32 57N 129 52 E
Omurtag .... 47 43 8N 26 26 E
Ōmuta .... 100 33 0N 130 26 E
Omutninsk .... 59 58 45N 52 4 E
On .... 23 50 11N 5 18 E
On-Take .... 100 31 35N 130 39 E
Oña 36 42 43N 3 25W
Onaga 152 39 32N 96 12W
Onalaska 152 43 53N 91 14W
Onamia 152 46 4N 93 38W
Onancock 148 37 42N 75 49W
Onang .... 87 3 2 S 118 49 E
Onaping L. 142 47 3N 81 30W
Onarga 155 40 43N 88 1W
Onarhā .... 77 35 30N 71 0 E
Onarheim .... 51 59 57N 5 35 E
Oñate 36 43 3N 2 25W
Onavas 160 28 28N 109 30W
Onawa 152 42 2N 96 2W
Onaway 148 45 21N 84 11W
Oncesti .... 50 43 56N 25 52 E
Oncócua .... 133 16 30 S 13 25 E
Onda 36 39 55N 0 17W
Ondaejin .... 95 41 34N 129 40 E
Ondangua .... 134 17 57 S 16 4 E
Ondárroa 36 43 19N 2 25W
Ondas → .... 171 12 8 S 45 0W
Ondava → .... 31 48 27N 21 48 E
Onderdijk .... 22 52 45N 5 8 E
Ondjiva .... 133 16 48 S 15 50 E
Ondo, Japan .... 100 34 11N 132 32 E
Ondo, Nigeria .... 127 7 4N 4 47 E
Ondo □ .... 127 7 0N 5 0 E
Öndörshil .... 94 45 13N 108 5 E
Öndverðarnes 54 64 52N 24 0W
Onega .... 56 64 0N 38 10 E
Onega → .... 56 63 58N 37 55 E
Onega, G. of = Onezhskaya Guba ... 56 64 30N 37 0 E
Onega, L. = Onezhskoye Ozero .. 56 62 0N 35 30 E
Onehunga .... 114 36 55 S 174 48 E
Oneida, Ill., U.S.A. ... 154 41 4N 90 13W
Oneida, N.Y., U.S.A. . 151 43 5N 75 40W
Oneida L. 151 43 12N 76 0W
O'Neill 152 42 30N 98 38W
Onekotan, Ostrov ..... 65 49 25N 154 45 E
Onema .... 130 4 35 S 24 30 E
Oneonta, Ala., U.S.A. 149 33 58N 86 29W
Oneonta, N.Y., U.S.A. 151 42 26N 75 5W
Onerahi .... 114 35 45 S 174 22 E
Onezhskaya Guba ..... 56 64 30N 37 0 E
Onezhskoye Ozero .... 56 62 0N 35 30 E
Ongarue .... 114 38 42 S 175 19 E
Ongea Levu .... 106 19 8 S 178 24W
Ongerup .... 109 33 58 S 118 28 E
Ongjin .... 95 37 56N 125 21 E
Ongkharak .... 84 14 8N 101 1 E
Ongniud Qi .... 95 43 0N 118 38 E
Ongoka .... 130 1 20 S 26 0 E
Ongole .... 81 15 33N 80 2 E
Ongon .... 94 45 41N 113 5 E
Onguren .... 65 53 38N 107 36 E
Onhaye .... 23 50 15N 4 50 E
Oni .... 61 42 33N 43 26 E
Onida 152 44 42N 100 5W
Onilahy → .... 135 23 34 S 43 45 E
Onitsha .... 127 6 6N 6 42 E
Onmaka .... 82 22 17N 96 41 E
Ono, Fiji .... 106 18 55 S 178 29 E
Ono, Fukui, Japan .... 101 35 59N 136 29 E
Ono, Hyōgo, Japan ... 100 34 51N 134 56 E
Onoda .... 100 34 2N 131 25 E
Onomichi .... 100 34 25N 133 12 E
Onpyŏng-ni .... 95 33 25N 126 55 E
Ons, Is. d' 34 42 23N 8 55W
Onsala .... 53 57 26N 12 0 E
Onslow .... 108 21 40 S 115 12 E
Onslow B. 149 34 20N 77 20W
Onstwedde .... 22 53 2N 7 4 E
Ontake-San .... 101 35 53N 137 29 E
Ontaneda 34 43 12N 3 57W
Ontario, Calif., U.S.A. 159 34 2N 117 40W
Ontario, Oreg., U.S.A. 156 44 1N 117 1W
Ontario □ 142 52 0N 88 10W
Ontario, L. 142 43 40N 78 0W
Onteniente 37 38 50N 0 35W
Ontonagon 152 46 52N 89 19W
Ontur 37 38 38N 1 29W
Onyx 159 35 41N 118 14W
Oodnadatta .... 111 27 33 S 135 30 E
Ooldea .... 109 30 27 S 131 50 E
Ooltgensplaat .... 23 51 41N 4 21 E
Oombulgurri .... 108 15 15 S 127 45 E
Oona River 144 53 57N 130 16W
Oordegem .... 23 50 58N 3 54 E
Oorindi .... 110 20 40 S 141 1 E
Oost-Vlaanderen □ .... 23 51 5N 3 50 E
Oost-Vlieland .... 22 53 18N 5 4 E
Oostakker .... 23 51 6N 3 46 E
Oostburg .... 23 51 19N 3 30 E
Oostduinkerke .... 23 51 7N 2 41 E
Oostelijk-Flevoland .... 22 52 31N 5 38 E
Oostende .... 23 51 15N 2 54 E
Oosterbeek .... 22 51 59N 5 51 E
Oosterdijk .... 22 52 44N 5 14 E
Oosterend, Friesland, Neth. .... 22 53 24N 5 23 E
Oosterend, Noord-Holland, Neth. 22 53 5N 4 52 E
Oosterhout, Noord-Brabant, Neth. 23 51 53N 5 50 E
Oosterhout, Noord-Brabant, Neth. 23 51 39N 4 47 E
Oosterschelde .... 23 51 33N 4 0 E
Oosterwolde .... 22 53 0N 6 17 E
Oosterzele .... 23 50 57N 3 48 E
Oostkamp .... 23 51 9N 3 14 E
Oostmalle .... 23 51 18N 4 44 E
Oostrozebekke .... 23 50 55N 3 21 E
Oostvleteven .... 23 50 56N 2 45 E
Oostvoorne .... 22 51 55N 4 5 E
Oostzaan .... 22 52 26N 4 52 E
Ootacamund .... 81 11 30N 76 44 E
Ootha .... 113 33 6 S 147 29 E
Ootmarsum .... 22 52 24N 6 54 E
Ootsa L. 144 53 50N 126 2W
Opaka .... 47 43 28N 26 10 E
Opala, U.S.S.R. ...... 65 51 58N 156 30 E
Opala, Zaïre .... 130 0 40 S 24 20 E
Opalenica .... 32 52 18N 16 24 E
Opan .... 47 42 13N 25 41 E
Opanake .... 81 6 35N 80 40 E
Opapa .... 114 39 47 S 176 42 E
Opasatika 142 49 30N 82 50W
Opasquia 145 53 16N 93 34W
Opatija .... 43 45 21N 14 17 E
Opatów .... 32 50 50N 21 27 E
Opava .... 31 49 57N 17 58 E
Opeinde .... 22 53 8N 6 4 E
Opelousas 153 30 35N 92 7W
Opémisca, L. 142 49 56N 74 52W
Open Bay Is. .... 115 43 51 S 168 51 E
Opglabbeek .... 23 51 3N 5 35 E
Opheim 156 48 52N 106 30W
Ophir 140 63 10N 156 40W
Ophthalmia Ra. .... 108 23 15 S 119 30 E
Opi .... 127 6 36N 7 28 E
Opinaca → 142 52 15N 78 2W
Opinaca L. 142 52 39N 76 20W
Opiskotish, L. 143 53 10N 67 50W
Oploo .... 23 51 37N 5 52 E
Opmeer .... 22 52 42N 4 57 E
Opobo .... 127 4 35N 7 34 E
Opochka .... 58 56 42N 28 45 E
Opoczno .... 32 51 22N 20 18 E
Opol .... 91 8 31N 124 34 E
Opole .... 32 50 42N 17 58 E
Opole □ .... 32 50 40N 17 56 E
Opon = Capu-Lapu ... 91 10 20N 123 55 E
Oporto = Porto 34 41 8N 8 40W
Opotiki .... 114 38 1 S 177 19 E
Opp 149 31 19N 86 13W
Oppegård .... 51 59 48N 10 48 E
Oppenheim .... 27 49 50N 8 22 E
Opperdoes .... 22 52 45N 5 4 E
Óppido Mamertina .... 45 38 16N 15 59 E
Oppland fylke □ ...... 51 61 15N 9 40 E
Oppstad .... 51 60 17N 11 40 E
Oprtalj .... 43 45 23N 13 50 E
Opua .... 114 35 19 S 174 9 E
Opunake .... 114 39 26 S 173 52 E
Opuzen .... 46 43 1N 17 34 E
Oquawka 154 40 56N 90 57W
Or, Le Mont d' .... 19 46 45N 6 18 E
Or Yehuda .... 69 32 2N 34 50 E
Ora, Israel .... 69 30 55N 35 1 E
Ora, Italy .... 43 46 20N 11 19 E
Ora Banda .... 109 30 20 S 121 0 E
Oracle 157 32 36N 110 46W
Oradea .... 50 47 2N 21 58 E
Öræfajökull 54 64 2N 16 39W
Orahovac .... 46 42 24N 20 40 E
Orahovica .... 46 45 35N 17 52 E
Orai .... 79 25 58N 79 30 E
Oraison .... 21 43 55N 5 55 E
Oran, Algeria 121 35 45N 0 39W
Oran, Argentina ...... 174 23 10 S 64 20W
Orange, Australia ..... 113 33 15 S 149 7 E
Orange, France .... 21 44 8N 4 47 E
Orange, Calif., U.S.A. . 159 33 47N 117 51W
Orange, Mass., U.S.A. 151 42 35N 72 15W
Orange, Tex., U.S.A. . 153 30 10N 93 50W
Orange, Va., U.S.A. .. 148 38 17N 78 5W
Orange → = Oranje → .... 134 28 41 S 16 28 E
Orange, C. 169 4 20N 51 30W
Orange Cove 158 36 38N 119 19W
Orange Free State □ .. 134 28 30 S 27 0 E
Orange Grove 153 27 57N 97 57W
Orange Walk 161 18 6N 88 33W
Orangeburg 149 33 35N 80 53W
Orangeville, Canada ... 142 43 55N 80 5W
Orangeville, U.S.A. ... 154 42 28N 89 39W
Orani .... 90 14 49N 120 32 E
Oranienburg .... 26 52 45N 13 15 E
Oranje → .... 134 28 41 S 16 28 E
Oranje Vrystaat □ = Orange Free State □ 134 28 30 S 27 0 E
Oranjemund .... 134 28 38 S 16 29 E
Oranjerivier .... 134 29 40 S 24 12 E
Or'Aquiva .... 69 32 30N 34 54 E
Oras .... 90 12 9N 125 28 E
Orašje .... 46 45 1N 18 42 E
Orăştie .... 50 45 50N 23 10 E
Oraşul Stalin = Braşov 50 45 38N 25 35 E
Orava → .... 31 49 24N 19 20 E
Oravita .... 46 45 2N 21 43 E
Orawia .... 115 46 1 S 167 50 E
Oraya, La .... 172 11 32 S 75 54W
Orb → .... 20 43 15N 3 18 E
Orba → .... 42 44 53N 8 37 E
Ørbæk .... 53 55 17N 10 39 E
Orbe .... 28 46 43N 6 32 E
Orbec .... 18 49 1N 0 23 E
Orbetello .... 43 42 26N 11 11 E
Órbigo → 34 42 5N 5 42W
Orbost .... 113 37 40 S 148 29 E
Örbyhus .... 52 60 15N 17 43 E
Orcadas .... 7 60 44 S 44 37W
Orce 37 37 44N 2 28W
Orce → 37 37 44N 2 28W
Orchies .... 19 50 28N 3 14 E
Orchila, I. 168 11 48N 66 10W
Orco → .... 42 45 10N 7 52 E
Orcopampa .... 172 15 20 S 72 23W
Orcutt 159 34 52N 120 27W
Ord → .... 108 15 33 S 138 15 E
Ord, Mt. .... 108 17 20 S 125 34 E
Ordenes 34 43 5N 8 29W
Orderville 157 37 18N 112 43W
Ordos = Mu Us Shamo 94 39 0N 109 0 E
Orduña, Álava, Spain . 36 42 58N 2 58 E
Orduña, Granada, Spain 37 37 20N 3 30W
Ordway 152 38 15N 103 42W
Ordzhonikidze, N. Ossetian A.S.S.R., U.S.S.R. .... 61 43 0N 44 35 E
Ordzhonikidze, Ukraine S.S.R., U.S.S.R. .... 60 47 39N 34 3 E
Ordzhonikidze, Uzbek S.S.R., U.S.S.R. .... 63 41 21N 69 22 E
Ordzhonikidzeabad .... 63 38 34N 69 1 E
Ore, Sweden .... 52 61 8N 15 10 E
Ore, Zaïre .... 130 3 17N 29 30 E
Ore Mts. = Erzgebirge 26 50 25N 13 0 E
Orealla 169 5 15N 57 23W
Orebić .... 46 43 0N 17 11 E
Örebro .... 52 59 20N 15 18 E
Örebro län □ .... 52 59 27N 15 0 E
Oregon, Ill., U.S.A. ... 154 42 1N 89 20W
Oregon, Ohio, U.S.A. . 155 41 38N 83 25W
Oregon, Wis., U.S.A. . 154 42 56N 89 23W
Oregon □ 156 44 0N 121 0W
Oregon City 158 45 21N 122 35W
Öregrund .... 52 60 21N 18 30 E
Öregrundsgrepen ...... 52 60 25N 18 15 E
Orekhov .... 60 47 30N 35 48 E
Orekhovo-Zuyevo ..... 59 55 50N 38 55 E
Orel .... 59 52 57N 36 3 E
Orel → .... 60 48 30N 34 54 E
Orellana, Canal de 35 39 2N 6 0W
Orellana, Pantano de .. 35 39 5N 5 10W
Orellana la Vieja 35 39 1N 5 32W
Orem 156 40 20N 111 45W
Oren .... 49 37 3N 27 57 E
Orenburg .... 62 51 45N 55 6 E
Orense 34 42 19N 7 55W
Orense □ 34 42 15N 7 51W
Orepuki .... 115 46 19 S 167 46 E
Orestiás .... 48 41 30N 26 33 E
Øresund .... 52 55 45N 12 45 E
Oreti → .... 115 46 28 S 168 14 E
Orford Ness .... 13 52 6N 1 31 E
Orgañà .... 36 42 13N 1 20 E
Organos, Pta. de los ... 37 28 12N 17 17W
Orgaz 35 39 39N 3 53W
Orgeyev .... 60 47 24N 28 50 E
Orgon .... 21 43 47N 5 3 E
Orgūn .... 77 32 55N 69 12 E
Orhon Gol → .... 92 49 30N 106 0 E
Ória .... 45 40 30N 17 38 E
Orient, Australia ..... 111 28 7 S 142 50 E
Orient, U.S.A. 154 41 12N 94 25W
Oriental, Cordillera, Bolivia .... 173 17 0 S 66 0W
Oriental, Cordillera, Colombia 168 6 0N 73 0W
Oriente .... 174 38 44 S 60 37W
Origny-Ste.-Benoîte ... 19 49 50N 3 30 E
Orihuela 37 38 7N 0 55W
Orihuela del Tremedal . 36 40 33N 1 39W
Oriku .... 48 40 20N 19 30 E
Orinduik 169 4 40N 60 3W
Orinoco → 169 9 15N 61 30W
Orion 154 41 21N 90 23W
Orissa □ .... 79 20 0N 84 0 E
Oristano .... 44 39 54N 8 35 E
Oristano, G. di .... 44 39 50N 8 22 E
Orituco → 168 8 45N 67 27W
Orizaba 161 18 50N 97 10W
Orizare .... 47 42 44N 27 39 E
Orizona .... 171 17 3 S 48 18W
Ørje .... 51 59 29N 11 39 E
Orjen .... 46 42 35N 18 34 E
Orjiva 37 36 53N 3 24W
Orkanger .... 51 63 18N 9 52 E
Örkelljunga .... 53 56 17N 13 17 E
Örkény .... 31 47 9N 19 26 E
Orkla → .... 51 63 18N 9 51 E
Orkney .... 134 26 58 S 26 40 E
Orkney □ 14 59 0N 3 0W
Orkney Is. 14 59 0N 3 0W
Orla .... 32 52 42N 23 20 E
Orland, Calif., U.S.A. . 158 39 46N 122 12W
Orland, Ind., U.S.A. .. 155 41 47N 85 12W
Orlando 149 28 30N 81 25W
Orlando, C. d' .... 45 38 10N 14 43 E
Orléanais .... 19 48 0N 2 0 E
Orléans, France .... 19 47 54N 1 52 E
Orleans, U.S.A. 151 44 49N 72 10W
Orléans, I. d' 143 46 54N 70 58W
Orlice → .... 30 50 5N 16 10 E
Orlické Hory .... 31 50 15N 16 30 E
Orlik .... 65 52 30N 99 55 E
Orlov .... 31 49 17N 20 51 E
Orlov Gay .... 59 50 56N 48 19 E
Orlovat .... 46 45 14N 20 33 E
Ormara .... 77 25 16N 64 33 E
Ormea .... 42 44 9N 7 54 E
Ormília .... 48 40 16N 23 39 E
Ormoc .... 91 11 0N 124 37 E
Ormond .... 114 38 33 S 177 56 E
Ormond Beach 149 29 13N 81 5W
Ormondville .... 114 40 5 S 176 19 E
Ormož .... 43 46 25N 16 10 E
Ormstown 151 45 8N 74 0W
Ornans .... 19 47 7N 6 10 E
Orne □ .... 18 48 40N 0 5 E
Orne → 18 49 18N 0 15W
Orneta .... 32 54 8N 20 9 E
Ørnhøj .... 53 56 13N 8 34 E
Ornö .... 52 59 4N 18 24 E
Örnsköldsvik .... 52 63 17N 18 40 E
Oro .... 95 40 1N 127 27 E
Oro → 160 25 35N 105 2W
Oro Grande 159 34 36N 117 20W
Orobie, Alpi .... 42 46 7N 10 0 E
Orocué 168 4 48N 71 20W
Orodo .... 127 5 34N 7 4 E
Orogrande 157 32 20N 106 4W
Orol 34 43 34N 7 39W
Oromocto 143 45 54N 66 29W
Oron, Nigeria .... 127 4 48N 8 14 E
Oron, Switz. .... 28 46 34N 6 50 E
Orono 150 43 59N 78 37W
Oropesa 34 39 57N 5 10W
Oroqen Zizhiqi .... 93 50 34N 123 43 E
Oroquieta .... 91 8 32N 123 44 E
Orós .... 170 6 15 S 38 55W
Orosei, G. di .... 44 40 15N 9 40 E
Orosháza .... 31 46 32N 20 42 E
Orotava, La 37 28 22N 16 31W
Orote Pen. .... 106 13 26N 144 38 E
Orotukan .... 65 62 16N 151 42 E
Oroville, Calif., U.S.A. 158 39 31N 121 30W
Oroville, Wash., U.S.A. 156 48 58N 119 30W
Oroville, Res. 158 39 33N 121 29W
Orrefors .... 53 56 50N 15 45 E
Orrick 154 39 13N 94 7W
Orroroo .... 112 32 43 S 138 38 E
Orrville 150 40 50N 81 46W
Orsa .... 52 61 7N 14 37 E
Orsara di Púglia ...... 45 41 17N 15 16 E
Orsasjön .... 52 61 7N 14 37 E
Orsha .... 58 54 30N 30 25 E
Orsières .... 28 46 2N 7 9 E
Orsk .... 62 51 12N 58 34 E
Ørslev .... 52 55 3N 11 56 E
Orsogna .... 43 42 13N 14 17 E
Orşova .... 50 44 41N 22 25 E
Ørsted .... 53 56 30N 10 20 E
Orta, L. d' .... 42 45 48N 8 21 E
Orta Nova .... 45 41 20N 15 40 E
Orte .... 43 42 28N 12 23 E
Ortegal, C. 34 43 43N 7 52W
Orteguaza → 168 0 43N 75 16W
Orthez 20 43 29N 0 48W
Ortho .... 23 50 8N 5 37 E
Ortigueira 34 43 40N 7 50W
Orting 158 47 6N 122 12W
Ortles .... 42 46 31N 10 33 E
Orto, Tokay .... 63 42 20N 76 1 E
Ortón → .... 172 10 50 S 67 0W
Ortona .... 43 42 21N 14 24 E
Orūmīyeh .... 72 37 40N 45 0 E
Orūmīyeh, Daryācheh-ye 72 37 50N 45 30 E
Orune .... 44 40 25N 9 20 E
Oruro .... 172 18 0 S 67 9W
Oruro □ .... 172 18 40 S 67 30W
Orust .... 53 58 10N 11 40 E
Oruzgān □ .... 77 33 30N 66 0 E
Orvault 18 47 17N 1 38W
Orvieto .... 43 42 43N 12 8 E
Orwell 150 41 32N 80 52W
Orwell → .... 13 52 2N 1 12 E
Oryakhovo .... 47 43 40N 23 57 E
Orzinuovi .... 42 45 24N 9 55 E

Orzyc

Orzyc → **32** 52 46N 21 14 E
Orzysz **32** 53 50N 21 58 E
Os **51** 60 9N 5 30 E
Osa **62** 57 17N 55 26 E
Osa → **32** 53 33N 18 46 E
Osa, Pen. de **162** 8 0N 84 0W
Osage, Iowa, U.S.A. **152** 43 15N 92 50W
Osage, Wyo., U.S.A. **152** 43 59N 104 25W
Osage → **154** 38 35N 91 57W
Osage City **152** 38 43N 95 51W
Ōsaka **101** 34 40N 135 30 E
Ōsaka □ **101** 34 30N 135 30 E
Ōsaka-Wan **101** 34 30N 135 18 E
Osan **95** 37 11N 127 4 E
Osawatomie **152** 38 30N 94 55W
Osborne **152** 39 30N 98 45W
Osby **53** 56 23N 13 59 E
Osceola, Ark., U.S.A. **153** 35 40N 90 0W
Osceola, Iowa, U.S.A. **154** 41 0N 93 20W
Osceola, Mo., U.S.A. **154** 38 3N 93 42W
Oschatz **26** 51 17N 13 8 E
Oschersleben **26** 52 2N 11 13 E
Óschiri **44** 40 43N 9 7 E
Oscoda **150** 44 26N 83 20W
Osečina **46** 44 23N 19 34 E
Ösel = Saaremaa **58** 58 30N 22 30 E
Osëry **59** 54 52N 38 28 E
Osgood **155** 39 8N 85 18W
Osh **63** 40 37N 72 49 E
Oshawa **142** 43 50N 78 50W
Oshima **100** 33 55N 132 14 E
Oshkosh, Nebr., U.S.A. **152** 41 27N 102 20W
Oshkosh, Wis., U.S.A. **152** 44 3N 88 35W
Oshmyany **58** 54 26N 25 52 E
Oshnovīyeh **72** 37 2N 45 6 E
Oshogbo **127** 7 48N 4 37 E
Oshtorīnān **73** 34 1N 48 38 E
Oshwe **132** 3 25 S 19 28 E
Osica de Jos **50** 44 14N 24 20 E
Osieczna **32** 51 55N 16 40 E
Osijek **46** 45 34N 18 41 E
Ósilo **44** 40 45N 8 41 E
Osimo **43** 43 28N 13 30 E
Osintorf **58** 54 40N 30 39 E
Osipenko = Berdyansk **60** 46 45N 36 50 E
Osipovichi **58** 53 19N 28 33 E
Osizweni **135** 27 49 S 30 7 E
Oskaloosa **154** 41 18N 92 40W
Oskarshamn **53** 57 15N 16 27 E
Oskélanéo **142** 48 5N 75 15W
Oskol → **59** 49 6N 37 25 E
Oslo **51** 59 55N 10 45 E
Oslob **91** 9 31N 123 26 E
Oslofjorden **51** 59 20N 10 35 E
Osmanabad **80** 18 5N 76 10 E
Osmancık **60** 40 45N 34 47 E
Osmaniye **57** 37 5N 36 10 E
Ösmo **52** 58 58N 17 55 E
Osnabrück **26** 52 16N 8 2 E
Ośno Lubuskie **32** 52 28N 14 51 E
Osobláha **31** 50 17N 17 44 E
Osogovska Planina **46** 42 10N 22 30 E
Osor **42** 44 42N 14 24 E
Osorio **175** 29 53 S 50 17W
Osorno, Chile **176** 40 25 S 73 0W
Osorno, Spain **34** 42 24N 4 22W
Osorno □ **176** 40 34 S 73 9W
Osorno, Vol. **176** 41 0 S 72 30W
Osoyoos **144** 49 0N 119 30W
Ospika → **144** 56 20N 124 0W
Osprey Reef **110** 13 52 S 146 36 E
Oss **22** 51 46N 5 32 E
Ossa, Mt. **110** 41 52 S 146 3 E
Óssa, Oros **48** 39 47N 22 42 E
Ossa de Montiel **37** 38 58N 2 45W
Ossabaw I. **149** 31 45N 81 8W
Osse → **20** 44 7N 0 17 E
Ossendrecht **23** 51 24N 4 20 E
Ossining **151** 41 9N 73 50W
Ossipee **151** 43 41N 71 9W
Ossokmanuan L. **143** 53 25N 65 0W
Ossora **65** 59 20N 163 13 E
Ostashkov **58** 57 4N 33 2 E
Oste → **26** 53 30N 9 12 E
Ostend = Oostende **23** 51 15N 2 54 E
Oster **58** 50 57N 30 53 E
Osterburg **26** 52 47N 11 44 E
Osterburken **27** 49 26N 9 25 E
Österbybruk **52** 60 13N 17 55 E
Österbymo **53** 57 49N 15 15 E
Östergötlands län □ **53** 58 35N 15 45 E
Osterholz-Scharmbeck **26** 53 14N 8 48 E
Østerild **53** 57 2N 8 51 E
Österkorsberga **53** 57 18N 15 6 E
Ostermundigen **28** 46 58N 7 30 E
Osterøya **51** 60 32N 5 30 E
Östersund **52** 63 10N 14 38 E
Østfold fylke □ **51** 59 25N 11 25 E
Ostfriesische Inseln **26** 53 45N 7 15 E
Ostfriesland **26** 53 20N 7 30 E
Óstia, Lido di **44** 41 43N 12 17 E
Ostiglía **43** 45 4N 11 9 E
Ostra **43** 43 40N 13 5 E
Ostrava **31** 49 51N 18 18 E
Ostróda **32** 53 42N 19 58 E
Ostrog **58** 50 20N 26 30 E
Ostrogozhsk **59** 50 55N 39 7 E
Ostrogróg Szamotuły **32** 52 37N 16 33 E
Ostrołęka **32** 53 4N 21 32 E
Ostrołeka □ **32** 53 0N 21 30 E
Ostrov, Bulgaria **47** 43 40N 24 9 E
Ostrov, Romania **50** 44 6N 27 24 E
Ostrov, U.S.S.R. **58** 57 25N 28 20 E
Ostrów Lubelski **32** 51 29N 22 51 E
Ostrów Mazowiecka **32** 52 50N 21 51 E
Ostrów Wielkopolski **32** 51 36N 17 44 E
Ostrowiec-Świętokrzyski **32** 50 55N 21 22 E
Ostrozac **46** 43 43N 17 49 E
Ostrzeszów **32** 51 25N 17 52 E
Ostseebad-Külungsborn **26** 54 10N 11 40 E
Ostuni **45** 40 44N 17 34 E
Osum → **47** 43 40N 24 50 E
Osumi → **48** 40 40N 20 10 E
Ōsumi-Hantō **100** 31 20N 130 55 E
Ōsumi-Kaikyō **99** 30 55N 131 0 E
Ōsumi-Shotō **99** 30 30N 130 0 E
Osuna **35** 37 14N 5 8W
Oswego **151** 43 29N 76 30W
Oswestry **12** 52 52N 3 3W
Oświecim **32** 50 2N 19 11 E
Ōta **101** 36 18N 139 22 E
Ota-Gawa → **100** 34 21N 132 18 E
Otago □ **115** 44 44 S 169 10 E
Otago Harb. **115** 45 47 S 170 42 E
Otago Pen. **115** 45 48 S 170 39 E
Otahuhu **114** 36 56 S 174 51 E
Ōtake **100** 34 12N 132 13 E
Ōtaki, Japan **101** 35 17N 140 15 E
Otaki, N.Z. **114** 40 45 S 175 10 E
Otane **114** 39 54 S 176 39 E
Otar **63** 43 32N 75 12 E
Otaru **98** 43 10N 141 0 E
Otaru-Wan = Ishikari-Wan **98** 43 25N 141 1 E
Otautau **115** 46 9 S 168 1 E
Otava → **30** 49 26N 14 12 E
Otavalo **168** 0 13N 78 20W
Otavi **134** 19 40 S 17 24 E
Otchinjau **133** 16 30 S 13 56 E
Otelec **50** 45 36N 20 50 E
Otero de Rey **34** 43 6N 7 36W
Othello **156** 46 53N 119 8W
Othonoí **48** 39 52N 19 22 E
Óthris, Óros **49** 39 4N 22 42 E
Otira **115** 42 49 S 171 35 E
Otira Gorge **115** 42 53 S 171 33 E
Otis **152** 40 12N 102 58W
Otjiwarongo **134** 20 30 S 16 33 E
Otmuchów **32** 50 28N 17 10 E
Otočac **43** 44 53N 15 12 E
Otoineppu **98** 44 44N 142 16 E
Oton **91** 10 42N 122 29 E
Otorohanga **114** 38 12 S 175 14 E
Otoskwin → **142** 52 13N 88 6W
Otosquen **145** 53 17N 102 1W
Ōtoyo **100** 33 43N 133 45 E
Otra → **51** 58 8N 8 1 E
Otranto **45** 40 9N 18 28 E
Otranto, C. d' **45** 40 7N 18 30 E
Otranto, Str. of **45** 40 15N 18 40 E
Otse **134** 25 2 S 25 45 E
Otsego **155** 42 27N 85 42W
Ōtsu **101** 35 0N 135 50 E
Ōtsuki **101** 35 36N 138 57 E
Otta **51** 61 46N 9 32 E
Otta → **51** 61 46N 9 31 E
Ottapalam **81** 10 46N 76 23 E
Ottawa, Canada **142** 45 27N 75 42W
Ottawa, Ill., U.S.A. **155** 41 20N 88 55W
Ottawa, Kans., U.S.A. **152** 38 40N 95 6W
Ottawa, Ohio, U.S.A. **155** 41 1N 84 3W
Ottawa → = Outaouais → **142** 45 27N 74 8W
Ottawa Is. **141** 59 35N 80 10W
Ottélé **127** 3 38N 11 19 E
Ottenby **53** 56 15N 16 24 E
Ottensheim **30** 48 21N 14 12 E
Otter L. **145** 55 35N 104 39W
Otter Rapids, Ont., Canada **142** 50 11N 81 39W
Otter Rapids, Sask., Canada **145** 55 38N 104 44W
Otterbein **155** 40 29N 87 6W
Otterberg **27** 49 30N 7 46 E
Otterndorf **26** 53 47N 8 52 E
Otterup **53** 55 30N 10 22 E
Otterville, Canada **150** 42 55N 80 36W
Otterville, U.S.A. **154** 38 42N 93 0W
Ottignies **23** 50 40N 4 33 E
Otto Beit Bridge **131** 15 59 S 28 56 E
Ottosdal **134** 26 46 S 25 59 E
Ottoshoop **134** 25 45 S 25 58 E
Ottoville **155** 40 57N 84 22W
Ottsjö **52** 63 13N 13 2 E
Ottumwa **154** 41 0N 92 25W
Otu **127** 8 14N 3 22 E
Otukpa **127** 7 9N 7 41 E
Oturkpo **127** 7 16N 8 8 E
Otway, B. **176** 53 30 S 74 0W
Otway, C. **112** 38 52 S 143 30 E
Otwock **32** 52 5N 21 20 E
Ötz **30** 47 13N 10 53 E
Ötz → **30** 47 14N 10 50 E
Ötztaler Alpen **30** 46 45N 11 0 E
Ou → **84** 20 4N 102 13 E
Ou Neua **84** 22 18N 101 48 E
Ou-Sammyaku **98** 39 20N 140 35 E
Ouachita → **153** 31 38N 91 49W
Ouachita, L. **153** 34 40N 93 25W
Ouachita Mts. **153** 34 50N 94 30W
Ouaco **106** 20 50 S 164 29 E
Ouadâne **120** 20 50N 11 40W
Ouadda **132** 8 15N 22 20 E
Ouagadougou **127** 12 25N 1 30W
Ouagam **123** 14 22N 14 42 E
Ouahigouya **126** 13 31N 2 25W
Ouahila **120** 27 50N 5 0W
Ouahran = Oran **121** 35 45N 0 39W
Oualâta **126** 17 20N 6 55W
Ouallene **121** 24 41N 1 11 E
Ouanda Djallé **132** 8 55N 22 53 E
Ouandago **132** 7 13N 18 50 E
Ouango **132** 4 19N 22 30 E
Ouarâne **120** 21 0N 10 30W
Ouargla **121** 31 59N 5 16 E
Ouarkziz, Djebel **120** 28 50N 8 0W
Ouarzazate **120** 30 55N 6 50W
Ouatagouna **127** 15 11N 0 43 E
Ouatere **132** 5 30N 19 8 E
Oubangi → **132** 0 30 S 17 50 E
Oubarakai, O. → **121** 27 20N 9 0 E
Oubatche **106** 20 26 S 164 39 E
Ouche → **19** 47 6N 5 16 E
Oud-Beijerland **22** 51 50N 4 25 E
Oud-Gastel **23** 51 35N 4 28 E
Oud Turnhout **23** 51 19N 5 0 E
Ouddorp **22** 51 50N 3 57 E
Oude-Pekela **22** 53 6N 7 0 E
Oude Rijn → **22** 52 12N 4 24 E
Oudega **22** 53 8N 6 0 E
Oudenaarde **23** 50 50N 3 37 E
Oudenbosch **23** 51 35N 4 32 E
Oudenburg **23** 51 11N 3 1 E
Ouderkerk, Utrecht, Neth. **22** 52 18N 4 55 E
Ouderkerk, Zuid-Holland, Neth. **22** 51 56N 4 38 E
Oudeschild **22** 53 2N 4 50 E
Oudewater **22** 52 2N 4 52 E
Oudkarspel **22** 52 43N 4 49 E
Oudon **18** 47 22N 1 19W
Oudtshoorn **134** 33 35 S 22 14 E
Oued Zem **120** 32 52N 6 34W
Ouégoa **106** 20 20 S 164 26 E
Ouellé **126** 7 26N 4 1W
Ouen, I. **106** 22 26 S 166 49 E
Ouenza **121** 35 57N 8 4 E
Ouessa **126** 11 4N 2 47W
Ouessant, I. d' **18** 48 28N 5 6W
Ouesso **132** 1 37N 16 5 E
Ouest, Pte. **143** 49 52N 64 40W
Ouezzane **120** 34 51N 5 35W
Ouffet **23** 50 26N 5 28 E
Ouidah **127** 6 25N 2 0 E
Ouistreham **18** 49 17N 0 18W
Oujda **121** 34 41N 1 55W
Oujeft **120** 20 2N 13 0W
Ould Yenjé **126** 15 38N 12 16W
Ouled Djellal **121** 34 28N 5 2 E
Ouled Naïl, Mts. des **121** 34 30N 3 30 E
Oulmès **120** 33 17N 6 0W
Oulu **54** 65 1N 25 29 E
Oulujärvi **54** 64 25N 27 15 E
Oulujoki → **54** 65 1N 25 30 E
Oulun lääni □ **54** 64 36N 27 20 E
Oulx **42** 45 2N 6 49 E
Oum Chalouba **123** 15 48N 20 46 E
Oum-el-Bouaghi **121** 35 55N 7 6 E
Oum el Ksi **120** 29 4N 6 59W
Oum-er-Rbia, O. → **120** 33 19N 8 21W
Oumè **126** 6 21N 5 27W
Ounane, Dj. **121** 25 4N 7 19 E
Ounasjoki → **54** 66 31N 25 30 E
Ounguati **134** 22 0 S 15 46 E
Ounianga-Kébir **123** 19 4N 20 29 E
Ounianga Sérir **123** 18 54N 20 51 E
Our → **23** 49 55N 6 5 E
Ouray **157** 38 3N 107 40W
Ourcq → **19** 49 1N 3 1 E
Oureg, Oued el → **121** 32 34N 2 10 E
Ourém **170** 1 33 S 47 6W
Ouricuri **170** 7 53 S 40 5W
Ourinhos **175** 23 0 S 49 54W
Ourique **35** 37 38N 8 16W
Ouro Fino **175** 22 16 S 46 25W
Ouro Prêto **175** 20 20 S 43 30W
Ouro Sogui **126** 15 36N 13 19W
Oursi **127** 14 41N 0 27W
Ourthe → **23** 50 29N 5 35 E
Ouse **110** 42 38 S 146 42 E
Ouse →, E. Sussex, U.K. **13** 50 43N 0 3 E
Ouse →, N. Yorks., U.K. **12** 54 3N 0 7 E
Oust **20** 42 52N 1 13 E
Oust → **18** 47 35N 2 6W
Outaouais → **142** 45 27N 74 8W
Outardes → **143** 49 24N 69 30W
Outat Oulad el Haj **121** 33 22N 3 42W
Outer Hebrides **14** 57 30N 7 40W
Outer I. **143** 51 10N 58 35W
Outes **34** 42 52N 8 55W
Outjo **134** 20 5 S 16 7 E
Outlook, Canada **145** 51 30N 107 0W
Outlook, U.S.A. **152** 48 53N 104 46W
Outreau **19** 50 40N 1 36 E
Ouvèze → **21** 43 59N 4 51 E
Ouyen **112** 35 1 S 142 22 E
Ouzouer-le-Marché **19** 47 54N 1 32 E
Ovada **42** 44 39N 8 40 E
Ovalau **106** 17 40 S 178 48 E
Ovalle **174** 30 33 S 71 18W
Ovar **34** 40 51N 8 40W
Ovejas **168** 9 32N 75 14W
Ovens **113** 36 35 S 146 46 E
Overdinkel **22** 52 14N 7 2 E
Overflakkee **22** 51 44N 4 10 E
Overijse **23** 50 47N 4 32 E
Overijssel □ **22** 52 25N 6 35 E
Overijsselsch Kanaal → **22** 52 31N 6 6 E
Overland **154** 38 41N 90 23W
Overpelt **23** 51 12N 5 20 E
Overton **159** 36 32N 114 31W
Overum **53** 58 0N 16 20 E
Ovid, Colo., U.S.A. **152** 41 0N 102 17W
Ovid, Mich., U.S.A. **155** 43 1N 84 22W
Ovidiopol **60** 46 15N 30 30 E
Oviedo **34** 43 25N 5 50W
Oviedo □ **34** 43 20N 6 0W
Oviken **52** 63 0N 14 23 E
Oviksfjällen **52** 63 0N 13 49 E
Övör Hangay □ **94** 45 0N 102 30 E
Ovoro **127** 5 26N 7 16 E
Övre Sirdal **51** 58 48N 6 43 E
Ovruch **58** 51 25N 28 45 E
Owaka **115** 46 27 S 169 40 E
Owando **132** 0 29 S 15 55 E
Owase **101** 34 7N 136 12 E
Owatonna **152** 44 3N 93 10W
Owbeh **77** 34 28N 63 10 E
Owego **151** 42 6N 76 17W
Owen **112** 34 15 S 138 32 E
Owen Falls **130** 0 30N 33 5 E
Owen Mt. **115** 41 35 S 172 33 E
Owen Sound **142** 44 35N 80 55W
Owen Stanley Range **107** 8 30 S 147 0 E
Owendo **132** 0 17N 9 30 E
Owens → **158** 36 32N 117 59W
Owens L. **159** 36 20N 118 0W
Owensboro **155** 37 40N 87 5W
Owensville, Ind., U.S.A. **155** 38 16N 87 41W
Owensville, Mo., U.S.A. **154** 38 20N 91 30W
Owenton **155** 38 32N 84 50W
Owerri **127** 5 29N 7 0 E
Owhango **114** 39 0 S 175 23 E
Owingsville **155** 38 9N 83 46W
Owl → **145** 57 51N 92 44W
Owo **127** 7 10N 5 39 E
Owosso **142** 43 0N 84 10W
Owyhee **156** 42 0N 116 3W
Owyhee → **156** 43 46N 117 2W
Owyhee, L. **156** 43 40N 117 16W
Ox Mts. **15** 54 6N 9 0W
Oxapampa **172** 10 33 S 75 26W
Oxberg **52** 61 7N 14 11 E
Oxelösund **53** 58 43N 17 15 E
Oxford, N.Z. **115** 43 18 S 172 11 E
Oxford, U.K. **13** 51 45N 1 15W
Oxford, Iowa, U.S.A. **154** 41 43N 91 47W
Oxford, Mich., U.S.A. **155** 42 49N 83 16W
Oxford, Miss., U.S.A. **153** 34 22N 89 30W
Oxford, N.C., U.S.A. **149** 36 19N 78 36W
Oxford, Ohio, U.S.A. **155** 39 30N 84 40W
Oxford □ **13** 51 45N 1 15W
Oxford L. **145** 54 51N 95 37W
Oxía **49** 38 16N 21 5 E
Oxílithos **49** 38 35N 24 7 E
Oxley **112** 34 11 S 144 6 E
Oxnard **159** 34 10N 119 14W
Oxus → = Pyandzh → **77** 43 40N 59 1 E
Oya **86** 2 55N 111 55 E
Oyabe **101** 36 47N 136 56 E
Oyama **101** 36 18N 139 48 E
Oyana **100** 32 32N 130 30 E
Oyapock → **169** 4 8N 51 40W
Oyem **132** 1 34N 11 31 E
Oyen **145** 51 22N 110 28W
Öyeren **51** 59 50N 11 15 E
Oykel → **14** 57 55N 4 26W
Oymyakon **65** 63 25N 142 44 E
Oyo **127** 7 46N 3 56 E
Oyo □ **127** 8 0N 3 30 E
Oyón **172** 10 37 S 76 47W
Oyonnax **21** 46 16N 5 40 E
Oyster Bay **151** 40 52N 73 32W
Øystese **51** 60 22N 6 9 E
Oytal **63** 42 54N 73 17 E
Ōyūbari **98** 43 1N 142 5 E
Ozamis **91** 8 15N 123 50 E
Ozark, Ala., U.S.A. **149** 31 29N 85 39W
Ozark, Ark., U.S.A. **153** 35 30N 93 50W
Ozark, Mo., U.S.A. **153** 37 0N 93 15W
Ozark Plateau **153** 37 20N 91 40W
Ozarks, L. of the **154** 38 10N 92 40W
Ózd **31** 48 14N 20 15 E
Ozërnyy **62** 51 8N 60 50 E
Ozette, L. **158** 48 6N 124 38W
Ozieri **44** 40 35N 9 0 E
Ozimek **32** 50 41N 18 11 E
Ozona **153** 30 43N 101 11W
Ozorków **32** 51 57N 19 16 E
Ozren **46** 43 55N 18 29 E
Ozu, Ehime, Japan **100** 33 30N 132 33 E
Ozu, Kumamoto, Japan **100** 32 52N 130 52 E
Ozuluama **161** 21 40N 97 50W
Ozun **50** 45 47N 25 50 E

P

P.K. le Roux Dam **134** 30 4 S 24 40 E
Pa **126** 11 33N 3 19W
Pa-an **82** 16 51N 97 40 E
Pa Mong Dam **84** 18 0N 102 22 E
Paagoumène **106** 20 29 S 164 11 E
Paal **23** 51 2N 5 10 E
Paar → **27** 48 13N 10 59 E
Paarl **134** 33 45 S 18 56 E
Paauilo **146** 20 3N 155 22W
Pab Hills **77** 26 30N 66 45 E
Pabianice **32** 51 40N 19 20 E
Pabna **82** 24 1N 89 18 E
Pabo **130** 3 1N 32 10 E
Pacaás Novos, Serra dos **173** 10 45 S 64 15W
Pacaipampa **172** 5 35 S 79 39W
Pacaja → **170** 1 56 S 50 50W
Pacajus **170** 4 10 S 38 31W
Pacaraima, Sierra **169** 4 0N 62 30W
Pacarán **172** 12 50 S 76 3W
Pacaraos **172** 11 12 S 76 42W
Pacasmayo **172** 7 20 S 79 35W
Pacaudière, La **20** 46 11N 3 52 E
Paceco **44** 37 59N 12 32 E
Pachacamac **172** 12 14 S 77 53W
Pachhar **78** 24 40N 77 42 E
Pachino **45** 36 43N 15 4 E
Pachitea → **172** 8 46 S 74 33W
Pachiza **172** 7 16 S 76 46W
Pacho **168** 5 8N 74 10W
Pachora **78** 20 38N 75 29 E
Pachuca **161** 20 10N 98 40W
Pacific, Canada **144** 54 48N 128 28W
Pacific, U.S.A. **154** 38 29N 90 45W
Pacific-Antarctic Basin **105** 46 0 S 95 0W
Pacific-Antarctic Ridge **105** 43 0 S 115 0W
Pacific Grove **158** 36 38N 121 58W
Pacific Ocean **104** 10 0N 140 0W
Pacifica **158** 37 36N 122 30W
Pacitan **89** 8 12 S 111 7 E
Packsaddle **112** 30 36 S 141 58 E
Packwood **158** 46 36N 121 40W
Pacov **30** 49 27N 15 0 E
Pacsa **31** 46 44N 17 2 E
Pacuí → **171** 16 46 S 45 1W
Paczków **32** 50 28N 17 0 E
Padaido, Kepulauan **87** 1 5 S 138 0 E
Padang **88** 1 0 S 100 20 E
Padangpanjang **88** 0 40 S 100 20 E
Padangsidempuan **88** 1 30N 99 15 E
Padangtikar **89** 0 44 S 109 15 E
Padatchuang **82** 19 46N 94 48 E
Padauari → **169** 0 15 S 64 5W
Padborg **53** 54 49N 9 21 E
Padcaya **173** 21 52 S 64 48W
Paddockwood **145** 53 30N 105 30W
Paderborn **26** 51 42N 8 44 E
Padeşul **50** 45 40N 22 22 E
Padilla **173** 19 19 S 64 20W
Padina **50** 44 50N 27 8 E
Padloping Island **141** 67 0N 62 50W
Padma → **82** 23 22N 90 32 E
Padmanabhapuram **81** 8 16N 77 17 E
Pádova **43** 45 24N 11 52 E
Padra **78** 22 15N 73 7 E
Padrauna **79** 26 54N 83 59 E
Padre Burgos **91** 10 1N 125 0 E
Padre I. **153** 27 0N 97 20W
Padro, Mte. **21** 42 28N 8 59 E
Padrón **34** 42 41N 8 39W
Padstow **12** 50 33N 4 57W
Padua = Pádova **43** 45 24N 11 52 E
Paducah, Ky., U.S.A. **148** 37 0N 88 40W
Paducah, Tex., U.S.A. **153** 34 3N 100 16W
Padul **35** 37 1N 3 38W
Padula **45** 40 20N 15 40 E
Padwa **80** 18 27N 82 47 E
Paekakariki **114** 40 59 S 174 58 E
Paengaroa **114** 37 49 S 176 29 E
Paengnyong-do **95** 37 57N 124 40 E
Paeroa **114** 37 23 S 175 41 E
Paesana **42** 44 40N 7 18 E
Paete **90** 14 23N 121 29 E
Pag **43** 44 30N 14 50 E
Paga **127** 11 1N 1 8W
Pagadian **91** 7 55N 123 30 E
Pagai Selatan **88** 3 0 S 100 15W
Pagai Utara **88** 2 35 S 100 0 E
Pagalu = Annobón **117** 1 25 S 5 36 E
Pagastikós Kólpos **48** 39 15N 23 0 E
Pagatan **89** 3 33 S 115 59 E
Page, Ariz., U.S.A. **157** 36 57N 111 27W
Page, N. Dak., U.S.A. **152** 47 11N 97 37W
Paglieta **43** 42 10N 14 30 E
Pagny-sur-Moselle **19** 48 59N 6 0 E
Pago Pago **106** 14 16 S 170 43W
Pagosa Springs **157** 37 16N 107 4W
Pagwa River **142** 50 2N 85 14W
Pahala **146** 19 12N 155 25W
Pahang → **85** 3 30N 103 9 E
Pahiatua **114** 40 27 S 175 50 E
Pahokee **149** 26 50N 80 40W
Pahrump **159** 36 15N 116 0W
Pahute Mesa **158** 37 25N 116 50W
Pai **84** 19 19N 98 27 E
Paia **146** 20 54N 156 22W
Paicines **158** 36 44N 121 17W
Paide **58** 58 57N 25 31 E
Paignton **13** 50 26N 3 33W
Paiján **172** 7 42 S 79 20W
Päijänne, L. **55** 61 30N 25 30 E
Paimbœuf **18** 47 17N 2 0W
Paimpol **18** 48 48N 3 4W
Painan **88** 1 21 S 100 34 E
Painesville **150** 41 42N 81 18W
Paint Hills = Nouveau Comptoir **142** 53 0N 78 49W
Paint L. **145** 55 28N 97 57W
Paint Rock **153** 31 30N 99 56W
Painted Desert **157** 36 0N 111 30W
Paintsville **148** 37 50N 82 50W
Pais Vasco □ **36** 43 0N 2 30W
Paisley, Canada **150** 44 18N 81 16W
Paisley, U.K. **14** 55 51N 4 27W
Paisley, U.S.A. **156** 42 43N 120 40W
Païta, N. Cal. **106** 22 8 S 166 22 E
Paita, Peru **172** 5 11 S 81 9W
Paiva → **34** 41 4N 8 16W
Paizhou **97** 30 12N 113 55 E
Pajares **34** 43 1N 5 46W
Pajares, Puerto de **34** 43 0N 5 46W
Pajeczno **32** 51 10N 19 0 E
Pak Lay **84** 18 15N 101 27 E
Pak Phanang **85** 8 21N 100 12 E
Pak Sane **84** 18 22N 103 39 E
Pak Song **84** 15 11N 106 14 E
Pak Suong **84** 19 58N 102 15 E
Pakala **81** 13 29N 79 8 E
Pakaraima Mts. **169** 6 0N 60 0W
Pakenham **113** 38 6 S 145 30 E
Pakhtakor **63** 40 2N 65 46 E
Pakistan ■ **77** 30 0N 70 0 E
Pakistan, East = Bangladesh ■ **82** 24 0N 90 0 E
Pakkading **84** 18 19N 103 59 E
Pakokku **82** 21 20N 95 0 E
Pakosc **32** 52 48N 18 6 E
Pakpattan **77** 30 25N 73 27 E
Pakrac **46** 45 27N 17 12 E
Paks **31** 46 38N 18 55 E
Pakse **84** 15 5N 105 52 E
Paktīā □ **77** 33 0N 69 15 E
Paktīkā □ **77** 32 30N 69 0 E
Pakwach **130** 2 28N 31 27 E
Pala, Chad **123** 9 25N 15 5 E
Pala, U.S.A. **159** 33 22N 117 5W
Pala, Zaïre **130** 6 45 S 29 30 E
Palabek **130** 3 22N 32 33 E
Palacios **153** 28 44N 96 12W
Palafrugell **36** 41 55N 3 10 E
Palagiano **45** 40 35N 17 0 E
Palagonía **45** 37 20N 14 43 E
Palagruža **43** 42 24N 16 15 E
Palaiokastron **49** 35 12N 26 18 E
Palaiokhóra **49** 35 16N 23 39 E
Pálairos **49** 38 45N 20 51 E
Palais, Le **18** 47 20N 3 10W
Palakol **81** 16 31N 81 46 E
Palam **80** 19 0N 77 0 E
Palamás **48** 39 26N 22 4 E
Palamós **36** 41 50N 3 10 E
Palampur **78** 32 10N 76 30 E
Palana, Australia **110** 39 45 S 147 55 E
Palana, U.S.S.R. **65** 59 10N 159 59 E
Palanan **90** 17 8N 122 29 E
Palanan Bay **90** 17 9N 122 27 E
Palanan Pt. **90** 17 17N 122 30 E
Palandri **79** 33 42N 73 40 E
Palangkaraya **89** 2 16 S 113 56 E
Palani **81** 10 30N 77 30 E
Palani Hills **81** 10 14N 77 33 E
Palanpur **78** 24 10N 72 25 E
Palapye **134** 22 30 S 27 7 E
Palar → **81** 12 27N 80 13 E
Palas **79** 35 4N 73 14 E
Palatine **155** 42 7N 88 3W
Palatka, U.S.A. **149** 29 40N 81 40W
Palatka, U.S.S.R. **65** 60 6N 150 54 E
Palawan **91** 9 30N 118 30 E
Palawan □ **91** 10 0N 119 0 E
Palawan Passage **91** 10 0N 118 0 E
Palayankottai **81** 8 45N 77 45 E
Palazzo, Pte. **21** 42 28N 8 30 E
Palazzo San Gervásio **45** 40 53N 15 58 E
Palazzolo Acreide **45** 37 4N 14 54 E
Palca **172** 19 7 S 69 9W
Paldiski **58** 59 23N 24 9 E
Pale **46** 43 50N 18 38 E
Palel **82** 24 27N 94 2 E
Paleleh **87** 1 10N 121 50 E
Palembang **88** 3 0 S 104 50 E
Palena → **176** 43 50 S 73 50W
Palena, L. **176** 43 55 S 71 40W
Palencia **34** 42 1N 4 34W
Palencia □ **34** 42 31N 4 33W
Palermo, Colombia **168** 2 54N 75 26W
Palermo, Italy **44** 38 8N 13 20 E
Palermo, U.S.A. **156** 39 30N 121 37W
Palestine, Asia **69** 32 0N 35 0 E
Palestine, U.S.A. **153** 31 42N 95 35W
Palestrina **44** 41 50N 12 52 E
Paletwa **82** 21 10N 92 50 E
Palghat **81** 10 46N 76 42 E
Palgrave, Mt. **108** 23 22 S 115 58 E
Pali **78** 25 50N 73 20 E
Palinit **90** 12 15N 124 20 E
Palinuro, C. **45** 40 1N 15 14 E
Palisade **152** 40 21N 101 10W
Paliseul **23** 49 54N 5 8 E
Palitana **78** 21 32N 71 49 E
Palizada **161** 18 18N 92 8W
Palizzi **45** 37 58N 15 59 E
Palk Bay **81** 9 30N 79 15 E
Palk Strait **81** 10 0N 79 45 E
Palkānah **72** 35 49N 44 26 E
Palkonda **80** 18 36N 83 48 E
Palkonda Ra. **81** 13 50N 79 20 E
Palla Road = Dinokwe **134** 23 29 S 26 37 E
Pallanza = Verbánia **42** 45 56N 8 43 E
Pallasovka **59** 50 4N 47 0 E
Palleru → **80** 16 45N 80 2 E
Pallinup **109** 34 0 S 117 55 E
Pallisa **130** 1 12N 33 43 E
Palliser, C. **114** 41 37 S 175 14 E
Palliser Bay **114** 41 26 S 175 5 E
Pallu **78** 28 59N 74 14 E
Palm Beach **149** 26 46N 80 0W
Palm Desert **159** 33 43N 116 22W
Palm Is. **110** 18 40 S 146 35 E
Palm Springs **159** 33 51N 116 35W
Palma **131** 10 46 S 40 29 E
Palma → **171** 12 33 S 47 52W
Palma, B. de **37** 39 30N 2 39 E
Palma, La, Canary Is. **37** 28 40N 17 50W
Palma, La, Panama **162** 8 15N 78 0W
Palma, La, Spain **35** 37 21N 6 38W
Palma de Mallorca **36** 39 35N 2 39 E
Palma del Río **35** 37 43N 5 17W
Palma di Montechiaro **44** 37 12N 13 46 E
Palma Soriano **162** 20 15N 76 0W
Palmahim **69** 31 56N 34 44 E
Palmanova **43** 45 54N 13 18 E
Palmares **170** 8 41 S 35 28W
Palmarito **168** 7 37N 70 10W
Palmarola **44** 40 57N 12 50 E
Palmas **175** 26 29 S 52 0W
Palmas, C. **126** 4 27N 7 46W
Pálmas, G. di **44** 39 0N 8 30 E
Palmas de Monte Alto **171** 14 16 S 43 10W
Palmdale **159** 34 36N 118 7W
Palmeira **171** 25 25 S 50 0W
Palmeira dos Índios **170** 9 25 S 36 37W
Palmeirais **170** 6 0 S 43 0W
Palmeiras → **171** 12 22 S 47 8W
Palmeirinhas, Pta. das **133** 9 2 S 12 57 E
Palmela **35** 38 32N 8 57W
Palmelo **171** 17 20 S 48 27W
Palmer **140** 61 35N 149 10W
Palmer → **110** 15 34 S 142 26 E
Palmer Arch. **7** 64 15 S 65 0W
Palmer Lake **152** 39 10N 104 52W
Palmer Land **7** 73 0 S 60 0W
Palmerston **150** 43 50N 80 51W
Palmerston North **115** 40 21 S 175 39 E
Palmerton **151** 40 47N 75 36W
Palmetto **149** 27 33N 82 33W
Palmi **45** 38 21N 15 51 E
Palmira, Argentina **174** 32 59 S 68 34W
Palmira, Colombia **168** 3 32N 76 16W
Palmyra = Tudmur **72** 34 36N 38 15 E
Palmyra, Ill., U.S.A. **154** 39 26N 90 0W
Palmyra, Mo., U.S.A. **154** 39 45N 91 30W
Palmyra, N.Y., U.S.A. **150** 43 5N 77 18W
Palmyra, Wis., U.S.A. **155** 42 52N 88 36W
Palmyra Is. **105** 5 52N 162 5W
Palo **91** 11 10N 124 59 E
Palo Alto **158** 37 25N 122 8W
Palo del Colle **45** 41 4N 16 43 E
Palo Verde **159** 33 26N 114 45W
Paloma, La **174** 30 35 S 71 0W
Palombara Sabina **43** 42 4N 12 45 E
Palompon **91** 11 3N 124 23 E
Palopo **87** 3 0 S 120 16 E
Palos, C. de **37** 37 38N 0 40W
Palos Verdes **159** 33 48N 118 23W
Palos Verdes, Pt. **159** 33 43N 118 26W
Palouse **156** 46 59N 117 5W
Palpa **172** 14 30 S 75 15W
Palparara **110** 24 47 S 141 28 E
Pålsboda **53** 59 3N 15 22 E
Palu, Indonesia **87** 1 0 S 119 52 E
Palu, Turkey **57** 38 45N 40 0 E
Paluan **90** 13 26N 120 29 E
Palwal **78** 28 8N 77 19 E
Pama **127** 11 19N 0 44 E
Pamanukan **89** 6 16 S 107 49 E
Pamban I. **81** 9 15N 79 20 E
Pambuhan **90** 13 59N 123 5 E
Pamekasan **89** 7 10 S 113 28 E
Pamiers **20** 43 7N 1 39 E
Pamir → **63** 37 1N 72 41 E
Pamirs **63** 37 40N 73 0 E
Pamlico → **149** 35 25N 76 30W
Pamlico Sd. **149** 35 20N 76 0W
Pampa **153** 35 35N 100 58W
Pampa, La □ **174** 36 50 S 66 0W
Pampa de Agma **176** 43 45 S 69 40W
Pampa de las Salinas **174** 32 1 S 66 58W
Pampa Grande **173** 18 5 S 64 6W
Pampa Hermosa **172** 7 7 S 75 4W
Pampanga □ **90** 15 4N 120 40 E
Pampanua **87** 4 16 S 120 8 E
Pamparato **42** 44 16N 7 54 E
Pampas, Argentina **174** 35 0 S 63 0W
Pampas, Peru **172** 12 20 S 74 50W
Pampas → **172** 13 24 S 73 12W
Pamplona, Colombia **168** 7 23N 72 39W
Pamplona, Phil. **90** 18 31N 121 20 E
Pamplona, Spain **36** 42 48N 1 38W
Pampoenpoort **134** 31 3 S 22 40 E
Pamuk → **70** 37 2N 34 49 E
Pan Xian **96** 25 46N 104 38 E
Pana **154** 39 25N 89 10W
Panabo **91** 7 19N 125 42 E
Panaca **157** 37 51N 114 23W
Panagyurishte **47** 42 30N 24 15 E
Panaitan **88** 6 36 S 105 12 E
Panaji **81** 15 25N 73 50 E
Panamá **162** 9 0N 79 25W
Panama ■ **162** 8 48N 79 55W
Panamá, G. de **162** 8 4N 79 20W
Panama Canal **162** 9 10N 79 37W
Panama City **149** 30 10N 85 41W
Panamint Range **159** 36 20N 117 20W
Panamint Ra. **157** 36 30N 117 20W
Panamint Springs **159** 36 20N 117 28W
Panão **172** 9 55 S 75 55W
Panaon I. **91** 10 3N 125 13 E
Panare **85** 6 51N 101 30 E
Panarea **45** 38 38N 15 3 E
Panaro → **42** 44 55N 11 25 E
Panarukan **89** 7 42 S 113 56 E
Panay **91** 11 10N 122 30 E
Panay, G. **91** 11 0N 122 30 E
Pancake Ra. **157** 38 30N 116 0W
Pančevo **46** 44 52N 20 41 E
Panciu **50** 45 54N 27 8 E
Pancol **91** 10 52N 119 25 E
Pancorbo, Paso **36** 42 32N 3 5W
Pandan, Antiq., Phil. **91** 11 45N 122 10 E
Pandan, Catanduanes, Phil. **90** 14 3N 124 10 E
Pandan Bay **91** 11 43N 122 0 E
Pandegelang **88** 6 25 S 106 0 E
Pandharpur **80** 17 41N 75 20 E
Pandhurna **78** 21 36N 78 35 E
Pandilla **36** 41 32N 3 43W
Pando **175** 34 44 S 56 0W
Pando □ **172** 11 20 S 67 40W
Pando, L. = Hope, L. **111** 28 24 S 139 18 E
Pandu **132** 5 1N 19 16 E
Panevezys **58** 55 42N 24 25 E
Panfilov **64** 44 10N 80 0 E
Panfilovo **59** 50 25N 42 46 E
Panga **130** 1 52N 26 18 E
Pangaíon Óros **48** 40 50N 24 0 E
Pangala **132** 4 1 S 13 52 E
Pangalanes, Canal des **135** 22 48 S 47 50 E
Pangani **130** 5 25 S 38 58 E
Pangani □ **130** 5 25 S 39 0 E
Pangani → **130** 5 26 S 38 58 E
Panganiban **90** 13 55N 124 18 E
Panganuran **91** 8 2N 122 22 E
Pangasinan □ **90** 15 55N 120 20 E
Pangfou = Bengbu **95** 32 58N 117 20 E
Pangil **130** 3 10 S 26 35 E
Pangkah, Tanjung **89** 6 51 S 112 33 E
Pangkai **82** 22 40N 98 40 E
Pangkajene **87** 4 46 S 119 34 E
Pangkalanbrandan **88** 4 1N 98 20 E
Pangkalanbuun **89** 2 41 S 111 37 E
Pangkalansusu **88** 4 2N 98 13 E
Pangkalpinang **88** 2 0 S 106 0 E
Pangkoh **89** 3 5 S 114 8 E
Panglao **91** 9 35N 123 45 E
Panglao I. **91** 9 35N 123 48 E
Pangnirtung **141** 66 8N 65 54W
Pangong Tso **79** 34 0N 78 20 E
Pangrango **88** 6 46 S 107 1 E
Pangsau Pass **82** 27 15N 96 10 E
Pangtara **82** 20 57N 96 40 E
Panguipulli **176** 39 38 S 72 20W
Panguitch **157** 37 52N 112 30W
Pangutaran **91** 6 18N 120 35 E
Pangutaran Group **91** 6 18N 120 34 E
Panhandle **153** 35 23N 101 23W
Pani Mines **78** 22 29N 73 50 E
Pania-Mutombo **130** 5 11 S 23 51 E
Panié, Mt. **106** 20 36 S 164 46 E
Panipat **78** 29 25N 77 2 E
Panitan **91** 11 28N 122 46 E
Panjal Range **78** 32 30N 76 50 E
Panjgur **77** 27 0N 64 5 E
Panjim = Panaji **81** 15 25N 73 50 E
Panjwai **78** 31 26N 65 27 E
Pankshin **127** 9 16N 9 25 E
Panmunjŏm **95** 37 59N 126 38 E
Panna **79** 24 40N 80 15 E
Panna Hills **79** 24 40N 81 15 E
Pano Lefkara **70** 34 53N 33 20 E
Panora **154** 41 41N 94 22W
Panorama **175** 21 21 S 51 51W
Panruti **81** 11 46N 79 35 E
Panshan **95** 41 3N 122 2 E
Panshi **95** 42 58N 126 5 E
Pantao **90** 13 12N 123 20 E
Pantar **87** 8 28 S 124 10 E
Pantelleria **44** 36 52N 12 0 E
Pantha **82** 23 55N 94 35 E
Pantin Sakan **82** 18 38N 97 33 E
Pantón **34** 42 31N 7 37W
Pánuco **161** 22 0N 98 15W
Panukulan **90** 14 56N 121 49 E
Panyam **127** 9 27N 9 8 E
Panyu **97** 22 51N 113 20 E
Pao →, Anzoátegui, Venezuela **169** 8 6N 64 17W

Pao →, Apure, Venezuela **168** 8 33N 68 1W
Páola, Italy **45** 39 21N 16 2 E
Paola, U.S.A. **152** 38 36N 94 50W
Paoli **155** 38 33N 86 28W
Paonia **157** 38 56N 107 37W
Paoting = Baoding **94** 38 50N 115 28 E
Paot'ou = Baotou **94** 40 32N 110 2 E
Paoua **132** 7 9N 16 20 E
Pápa **31** 47 22N 17 30 E
Papagayo → **161** 16 36N 99 43W
Papagayo, G. de **162** 10 30N 85 50W
Papagni → **81** 15 35N 77 45 E
Papakura **114** 37 4 S 174 59 E
Papantla **161** 20 30N 97 30W
Papar **86** 5 45N 116 0 E
Papara **106** 17 45 S 149 21W
Paparoa **115** 36 6 S 174 16 E
Paparoa Range **115** 42 5 S 171 35 E
Pápas, Ákra **49** 38 13N 21 20 E
Papatoetoe **114** 36 59 S 174 51 E
Papeete **106** 17 32 S 149 34W
Papenburg **26** 53 7N 7 25 E
Papenoo **106** 17 30 S 149 25W
Paphos **70** 34 46N 32 25 E
Papien Chiang = Da → **84** 21 15N 105 20 E
Papigochic → **160** 29 9N 109 40W
Paposo **174** 25 0 S 70 30W
Papua, Gulf of **107** 9 0 S 144 50 E
Papua New Guinea ■ **107** 8 0 S 145 0 E
Papuča **43** 44 22N 15 30 E
Papudo **174** 32 29 S 71 27W
Papuk **46** 45 30N 17 30 E
Papun **82** 18 0N 97 30 E
Pará = Belém **170** 1 20 S 48 30W
Pará □, Brazil **173** 3 20 S 52 0W
Pará □, Surinam **169** 40 0 S 53 0W
Parábita **45** 40 3N 18 8 E
Paraburdoo **108** 23 14 S 117 32 E
Paracale **90** 14 17N 122 48 E
Paracas, Pen. **172** 13 53 S 76 20W
Paracatu **171** 17 10 S 46 50W
Paracatu → **171** 16 30 S 45 4W
Parachilna **112** 31 10 S 138 21 E
Parachinar **77** 33 55N 70 5 E
Paraćin **46** 43 54N 21 27 E
Paracuru **170** 3 24 S 39 4W
Parada, Punta **172** 15 22 S 75 11W
Paradas **35** 37 18N 5 29W
Paradela **34** 42 44N 7 37W
Paradip **79** 20 15N 86 35 E
Paradise, Calif., U.S.A. **158** 39 46N 121 37W
Paradise, Mont., U.S.A. **156** 47 27N 114 17W
Paradise, Nev., U.S.A. **159** 36 4N 115 7W
Paradise → **143** 53 27N 57 19W
Paradise Valley **156** 41 30N 117 28W
Parado **89** 8 42 S 118 30 E
Paradyz **32** 51 19N 20 2 E
Paragould **153** 36 5N 90 30W
Paraguá →, Bolivia **173** 13 34 S 61 53W
Paragua →, Venezuela **169** 6 55N 62 55W
Paragua, La **169** 6 50N 63 20W
Paraguaçu → **171** 12 45 S 38 54W
Paraguaçu Paulista **175** 22 22 S 50 35W
Paraguaipoa **168** 11 21N 71 57W
Paraguaná, Pen. de **168** 12 0N 70 0W
Paraguarí **174** 25 36 S 57 0W
Paraguarí □ **174** 26 0 S 57 10W
Paraguay ■ **174** 23 0 S 57 0W
Paraguay → **174** 27 18 S 58 38W
Paraíba = João Pessoa **170** 7 10 S 34 52W
Paraíba □ **170** 7 0 S 36 0W
Paraíba do Sul → **171** 21 37 S 41 3W
Parainen **55** 60 18N 22 18 E
Paraiso **161** 18 24N 93 14W
Parak **73** 27 38N 52 25 E
Parakhino Paddubye **58** 58 26N 33 10 E
Parakou **127** 9 25N 2 40 E
Parakylia **112** 30 24 S 136 25 E
Paralimni **70** 35 2N 33 58 E
Parálion-Astrous **49** 37 25N 22 45 E
Paramakkudi **81** 9 31N 78 39 E
Paramaribo **169** 5 50N 55 10W
Parambu **170** 6 13 S 40 43W
Paramillo, Nudo del **168** 7 4N 75 55W
Paramirim **171** 13 26 S 42 15W
Paramirim → **171** 11 34 S 43 18W
Paramithiá **48** 39 30N 20 35 E
Paramushir, Ostrov **65** 50 24N 156 0 E
Paran → **69** 30 20N 35 10 E
Paraná, Argentina **174** 31 45 S 60 30W
Paranã, Brazil **171** 12 30 S 47 48W
Paraná □ **175** 24 30 S 51 0W
Paraná → **174** 33 43 S 59 15W
Paranaguá **175** 25 30 S 48 30W
Paranaíba → **171** 20 6 S 51 4W
Paranapanema → **175** 22 40 S 53 9W
Paranapiacaba, Serra do **175** 24 31 S 48 35W
Paranavaí **175** 23 4 S 52 56W
Parang, Jolo, Phil. **91** 5 55N 120 54 E
Parang, Mindanao, Phil. **91** 7 23N 124 16 E
Parangaba **170** 3 45 S 38 33W
Parangipettai **81** 11 30N 79 38 E
Paraparauma **114** 40 57 S 175 3 E
Parapóla **49** 36 55N 23 27 E
Paraspóri, Ákra **49** 35 55N 27 15 E
Paratinga **171** 12 40 S 43 10W
Paratoo **112** 32 42 S 139 40 E
Parattah **110** 42 22 S 147 23 E
Paraúna **171** 16 55 S 50 26W
Paray-le-Monial **21** 46 27N 4 7 E
Parbati → **78** 25 50N 76 30 E
Parbatipur **82** 25 39N 88 55 E
Parbhani **78** 19 8N 76 52 E
Parchim **26** 53 25N 11 50 E
Parczew **32** 51 40N 22 52 E
Pardes Hanna **69** 32 28N 34 57 E
Pardilla **34** 41 33N 3 43W
Pardo →, Bahia, Brazil **171** 15 40 S 39 0W
Pardo →, Mato Grosso, Brazil **175** 21 46 S 52 9W
Pardo →, Minas Gerais, Brazil **171** 15 48 S 44 48W
Pardo →, São Paulo, Brazil **171** 20 10 S 48 38W
Pardubice **30** 50 3N 15 45 E
Pare **89** 7 43 S 112 12 E
Pare □ **130** 4 10 S 38 0 E
Pare Mts. **130** 4 0 S 37 45 E
Parecis, Serra dos **173** 13 0 S 60 0W
Paredes de Nava **34** 42 9N 4 42W
Pareh **72** 38 52N 45 42 E
Parelhas **170** 6 41 S 36 39W
Paren **65** 62 30N 163 15 E
Parengarenga Harbour **114** 34 31 S 173 0 E
Parent **142** 47 55N 74 35W
Parent, Lac **142** 48 31N 77 1W
Parentis-en-Born **20** 44 21N 1 4W
Parepare **87** 4 0 S 119 40 E
Parfino **58** 57 59N 31 34 E
Parfuri **135** 22 28 S 31 17 E
Parguba **56** 62 20N 34 27 E
Paria, G. de **168** 10 20N 62 0W
Paria, Pen. de **169** 10 50N 62 30W
Pariaguán **169** 8 51N 64 34W
Pariaman **88** 0 47 S 100 11 E
Paricatuba **169** 4 26 S 61 53W
Paricutín, Cerro **160** 19 28N 102 15W
Parigi, Java, Indonesia **89** 7 42 S 108 29 E
Parigi, Sulawesi, Indonesia **87** 0 50 S 120 5 E
Parika **169** 6 50N 58 20W
Parima, Serra **169** 2 30N 64 0W
Parinari **172** 4 35 S 74 25W
Parincea **50** 46 27N 27 9 E
Paring **50** 45 20N 23 37 E
Parintins **169** 2 40 S 56 50W
Paris, Canada **142** 43 12N 80 25W
Paris, France **19** 48 50N 2 20 E
Paris, Idaho, U.S.A. **156** 42 13N 111 30W
Paris, Ill., U.S.A. **155** 39 36N 87 42W
Paris, Ky., U.S.A. **155** 38 12N 84 12W
Paris, Mo., U.S.A. **154** 39 29N 92 0W
Paris, Tenn., U.S.A. **149** 36 20N 88 20W
Paris, Tex., U.S.A. **153** 33 40N 95 30W
Paris, Ville de □ **19** 48 50N 2 20 E
Parish **151** 43 24N 76 9W
Pariti **87** 10 15 S 123 45 E
Park **158** 48 45N 122 18W
Park City **156** 40 42N 111 35W
Park Falls **152** 45 58N 90 27W
Park Forest **155** 41 29N 87 40W
Park Range **156** 40 0N 106 30W
Park Rapids **152** 46 56N 95 0W
Park Ridge **155** 42 2N 87 51W
Park River **152** 48 25N 97 43W
Park Rynie **135** 30 25 S 30 45 E
Parkā Bandar **73** 25 55N 59 35 E
Parkent **63** 41 18N 69 40 E
Parker, Ariz., U.S.A. **159** 34 8N 114 16W
Parker, S. Dak., U.S.A. **152** 43 25N 97 7W
Parker Dam **159** 34 13N 114 5W
Parkersburg, Iowa, U.S.A. **154** 42 35N 92 47W
Parkersburg, W. Va., U.S.A. **148** 39 18N 81 31W
Parkerview **145** 51 21N 103 18W
Parkes **113** 33 9 S 148 11 E
Parkfield **158** 35 54N 120 26W
Parkhar **63** 37 30N 69 34 E
Parkland **158** 47 9N 122 26W
Parkside **145** 53 10N 106 33W
Parkston **152** 43 25N 98 0W
Parksville **144** 49 20N 124 21W
Parlakimidi **80** 18 45N 84 5 E
Parli **78** 18 50N 76 35 E
Parma, Italy **42** 44 50N 10 20 E
Parma, Idaho, U.S.A. **156** 43 49N 116 59W
Parma, Ohio, U.S.A. **150** 41 25N 81 42W
Parma → **42** 44 56N 10 26 E
Parnaguá **170** 10 10 S 44 38W
Parnaíba, Piauí, Brazil **170** 2 54 S 41 47W
Parnaíba, São Paulo, Brazil **173** 19 34 S 51 14W
Parnaíba → **170** 3 0 S 41 50W
Parnamirim **170** 8 5 S 39 34W
Parnarama **170** 5 31 S 43 6W
Parnassós **49** 38 35N 22 30 E
Parnassus **115** 42 42 S 173 23 E
Párnis **49** 38 14N 23 45 E
Párnon Óros **49** 37 15N 22 45 E
Pärnu **58** 58 28N 24 33 E
Parola **78** 20 47N 75 7 E
Paroo → **111** 31 28 S 143 32 E
Páros **49** 37 5N 25 12 E
Parowan **157** 37 54N 112 56W
Parpaillon **21** 44 30N 6 40 E
Parral **174** 36 10 S 71 52W
Parramatta **113** 33 48 S 151 1 E
Parras **160** 25 30N 102 20W
Parrett → **13** 51 7N 2 58W
Parris I. **149** 32 20N 80 30W
Parrsboro **143** 45 30N 64 25W
Parry Is. **6** 77 0N 110 0W
Parry Sound **142** 45 20N 80 0W
Parsberg **27** 49 10N 11 43 E
Parseta → **32** 54 11N 15 34 E
Parshall **152** 47 56N 102 11W
Parsnip → **144** 55 10N 123 2W
Parsons **153** 37 20N 95 17W
Parsons Ra. **110** 13 30 S 135 15 E
Partabpur **80** 20 0N 80 42 E
Partanna **44** 37 43N 12 51 E
Parthenay **18** 46 38N 0 16W
Partinico **44** 38 3N 13 6 E
Partur **80** 19 40N 76 14 E
Paru →, Brazil **169** 1 33 S 52 38W
Parú →, Venezuela **168** 4 20N 66 27W
Paru de Oeste → **169** 1 30N 56 0W
Parubcan **90** 13 43N 123 45 E
Parucito → **168** 5 18N 65 59W
Parur **81** 10 13N 76 14 E
Paruro **172** 13 45 S 71 50W
Parvān □ **77** 35 0N 69 0 E
Parvatipuram **80** 18 50N 83 25 E
Parys **134** 26 52 S 27 29 E
Pas-de-Calais □ **19** 50 30N 2 10 E
Pasadena, Calif., U.S.A. **159** 34 5N 118 9W
Pasadena, Tex., U.S.A. **153** 29 45N 95 14W
Pasaje **168** 3 23 S 79 50W
Pasaje → **174** 25 39 S 63 56W
Pasay **90** 14 33N 121 0 E
Pascagoula **153** 30 21N 88 30W
Pascagoula → **153** 30 21N 88 35W
Paşcani **50** 47 14N 26 45 E
Pasco **156** 46 10N 119 0W
Pasco □ **172** 10 40 S 75 0W
Pasco, Cerro de **172** 10 45 S 76 10W
Pasewalk **26** 53 30N 14 0 E
Pasfield L. **145** 58 24N 105 20W
Pasha → **58** 60 29N 32 55 E
Pashiwari **79** 34 40N 75 10 E
Pashiya **62** 58 33N 58 26 E
Pashmakli = Smolyan **47** 41 36N 24 38 E
Pasighat **82** 28 4N 95 21 E
Pasing **27** 48 9N 11 27 E
Pasirian **89** 8 13 S 113 8 E
Paskūh **73** 27 34N 61 39 E
Pasłeka → **32** 54 26N 19 46 E
Pasley, C. **109** 33 52 S 123 35 E
Pašman **43** 43 58N 15 20 E
Pasmore → **112** 31 5 S 139 49 E
Pasni **77** 25 15N 63 27 E
Paso Cantinela **159** 32 33N 115 47W
Paso de Indios **176** 43 55 S 69 0W
Paso de los Libres **174** 29 44 S 57 10W
Paso de los Toros **174** 32 45 S 56 30W
Paso Flores **176** 40 35 S 70 38W
Paso Robles **157** 35 40N 120 45W
Pasorapa **173** 18 16 S 64 37W
Paspébiac **143** 48 3N 65 17W
Pasrur **78** 32 16N 74 43 E
Passage West **15** 51 52N 8 20W
Passaic **151** 40 50N 74 8W
Passau **27** 48 34N 13 27 E
Passendale **23** 50 54N 3 2 E
Passero, C. **45** 36 42N 15 8 E
Passi **91** 11 6N 122 38 E
Passo Fundo **175** 28 10 S 52 20W
Passos **171** 20 45 S 46 37W
Passow **26** 53 13N 14 10 E
Passwang **28** 47 22N 7 41 E
Passy **21** 45 55N 6 41 E
Pastaza □ **168** 2 0 S 77 0W
Pastaza → **168** 4 50 S 76 52W
Pastęk **32** 54 3N 19 41 E
Pasto **168** 1 13N 77 17W
Pastos Bons **170** 6 36 S 44 5W
Pastrana **36** 40 27N 2 53W
Pasuquin **90** 18 20N 120 37 E
Pasuruan **89** 7 40 S 112 44 E
Pasym **32** 53 48N 20 49 E
Pásztó **31** 47 52N 19 43 E
Patagonia, Argentina **176** 45 0 S 69 0W
Patagonia, U.S.A. **157** 31 35N 110 45W
Patambar **73** 29 45N 60 17 E
Patan, Gujarat, India **80** 17 22N 73 57 E
Patan, Maharashtra, India **78** 23 54N 72 14 E
Patani **87** 0 20N 128 50 E
Pataudi **78** 28 18N 76 48 E
Patay **19** 48 2N 1 40 E
Patchewollock **112** 35 22 S 142 12 E
Patchogue **151** 40 46N 73 1W
Patea **114** 39 45 S 174 30 E
Pategi **127** 8 50N 5 45 E
Patensie **134** 33 46 S 24 49 E
Paternò **45** 37 34N 14 53 E
Pateros **156** 48 4N 119 58W
Paterson, Australia **113** 32 37 S 151 39 E
Paterson, U.S.A. **151** 40 55N 74 10W
Paterson Inlet **115** 46 56 S 168 12 E
Paterson Ra. **108** 21 45 S 122 10 E
Paterswolde **22** 53 9N 6 34 E
Pathankot **78** 32 18N 75 45 E
Patharghata **82** 22 2N 89 58 E
Pathfinder Res. **156** 42 30N 107 0W
Pathiu **85** 10 42N 99 19 E
Pathum Thani **84** 14 1N 100 32 E
Pati **89** 6 45 S 111 1 E
Patía **168** 2 4N 77 4W
Patía → **168** 2 13N 78 40W
Patiala **78** 30 23N 76 26 E
Patine Kouka **126** 12 45N 13 45W
Pativilca **172** 10 42 S 77 48W
Patkai Bum **82** 27 0N 95 30 E
Pátmos **49** 37 21N 26 36 E
Patna **79** 25 35N 85 12 E
Patnongon **91** 10 55N 122 0 E
Patonga **130** 2 45N 33 15 E
Patos **170** 6 55 S 37 16W
Patos, L. dos **175** 31 20 S 51 0 E
Patos de Minas **171** 18 35 S 46 32W
Patosi **48** 40 42N 19 38 E
Patquía **174** 25 30N 102 11W
Pátrai **49** 38 14N 21 47 E
Pátraikós, Kólpos **49** 38 17N 21 30 E
Patricio Lynch, I. **176** 48 35 S 75 30W
Patrocínio **171** 18 57 S 47 0W
Patta **130** 2 10 S 41 0 E
Pattada **44** 40 35N 9 7 E
Pattanapuram **81** 9 6N 76 50 E
Pattani **85** 6 48N 101 15 E
Patten **143** 45 59N 68 28W
Patterson, Calif., U.S.A. **158** 37 30N 121 9W
Patterson, La., U.S.A. **153** 29 44N 91 20W
Patterson, Mt. **158** 38 29N 119 20W
Patti, India **78** 31 17N 74 54 E
Patti, Italy **45** 38 8N 14 57 E
Pattoki **78** 31 5N 73 52 E
Patton **150** 40 38N 78 40W
Pattonsburg **154** 40 3N 94 8W
Pattukkattai **81** 10 25N 79 20 E
Patu **170** 6 6 S 37 38W
Patuakhali **82** 22 20N 90 25 E
Patuca → **162** 15 50N 84 18W
Patuca, Punta **162** 15 49N 84 14W
Pâturages **23** 50 25N 3 52 E
Pátzcuaro **160** 19 30N 101 40W
Pau **20** 43 19N 0 25W
Pau, Gave de → **20** 43 33N 1 12W
Pau d' Arco **170** 7 30 S 49 22W
Pau dos Ferros **170** 6 7 S 38 10W
Paucartambo **172** 13 19 S 71 35W
Pauillac **20** 45 11N 0 46W
Pauini **172** 7 40 S 66 58W
Pauini → **169** 1 42 S 62 50W
Pauk **82** 21 27N 94 30 E
Paul I. **143** 56 30N 61 20W
Paul Isnard **169** 4 47N 54 1W
Paulding **155** 41 8N 84 35W
Paulhan **20** 43 33N 3 28 E
Paulis = Isiro **130** 2 53N 27 40 E
Paulista **170** 7 57 S 34 53W
Paulistana **170** 8 9 S 41 9W
Paullina **152** 42 55N 95 40W
Paulo Afonso **170** 9 21 S 38 15W
Paulo de Faria **171** 20 2 S 49 24W
Paulpietersburg **135** 27 23 S 30 50 E
Pauls Valley **153** 34 40N 97 17W
Pauma Valley **159** 33 16N 116 58W
Paungde **82** 18 29N 95 30 E
Pauni **79** 20 48N 79 40 E
Pausa **172** 15 16 S 73 22W
Pauto → **168** 5 9N 70 55W
Pāveh **72** 35 3N 46 22 E
Pavelets **59** 53 49N 39 14 E
Pavia **42** 45 10N 9 10 E
Pavlikeni **47** 43 14N 25 20 E
Pavlodar **64** 52 33N 77 0 E
Pavlograd **60** 48 30N 35 52 E
Pavlovo, Gorkiy, U.S.S.R. **59** 55 58N 43 5 E
Pavlovo, Yakut A.S.S.R., U.S.S.R. **65** 63 5N 115 25 E
Pavlovsk **59** 50 26N 40 5 E
Pavlovskaya **61** 46 17N 39 47 E
Pavlovskiy-Posad **59** 55 47N 38 42 E
Pavullo nel Frignano **42** 44 20N 10 50 E
Paw Paw **155** 42 13N 85 53W
Pawahku **82** 26 11N 98 40 E
Pawan → **89** 1 55 S 110 0 E
Pawhuska **153** 36 40N 96 25W
Pawling **151** 41 35N 73 37W
Pawnee, Ill., U.S.A. **154** 39 35N 89 35W
Pawnee, Okla., U.S.A. **153** 36 24N 96 50W
Pawnee City **152** 40 8N 96 10W
Pawpaw **154** 41 41N 88 59W
Pawtucket **151** 41 51N 71 22W
Paximádhia **49** 35 0N 24 35 E
Paxoí **48** 39 14N 20 12 E
Paxton, Ill., U.S.A. **155** 40 25N 88 7W
Paxton, Nebr., U.S.A. **152** 41 12N 101 27W
Payakumbuh **88** 0 20 S 100 35 E
Payas **70** 36 46N 36 11 E
Payerne **28** 46 49N 6 56 E
Payette **156** 44 0N 117 0W
Paymogo **35** 37 44N 7 21W
Payne **155** 41 5N 84 44W
Payne Bay = Bellin **141** 60 0N 70 0W
Payne L. **141** 59 30N 74 30W
Paynes Find **109** 29 15 S 117 42 E
Paynesville, Liberia **126** 6 20N 10 45W
Paynesville, U.S.A. **152** 45 21N 94 44W
Paysandú **174** 32 19 S 58 8W
Payson, Ariz., U.S.A. **157** 34 17N 111 15W
Payson, Utah, U.S.A. **156** 40 8N 111 41W
Paz → **162** 13 44N 90 10W
Paz, B. de la **160** 24 15N 110 25W

Petersburg

Paz, La, Entre Ríos, Argentina 174 30 50 S 59 45W
Paz, La, San Luis, Argentina 174 33 30 S 67 20W
Paz, La, Bolivia 172 16 20 S 68 10W
Paz, La, Hond. 162 14 20N 87 47W
Paz, La, Mexico 160 24 10N 110 20W
Paz, La, Phil. 90 15 26N 120 45 E
Paz, La □ 172 15 30 S 68 0W
Paz Centro, La 162 12 20N 86 41W
Păzanān 73 30 35N 49 59 E
Pazarcık 70 36 16N 32 20 E
Pazardzhik 47 42 12N 24 20 E
Pazin 43 45 14N 13 56 E
Pazña 172 18 36 S 66 55W
Pčinja → 46 41 50N 21 45 E
Pe Ell 158 46 30N 123 18W
Peabody 151 42 31N 70 56W
Peace → 144 59 0N 111 25W
Peace Point 144 59 7N 112 27W
Peace River 144 56 15N 117 18W
Peach Springs 157 35 36N 113 30W
Peak, The 12 53 24N 1 53W
Peak Downs 110 22 14 S 148 0 E
Peak Downs Mine 110 22 17 S 148 11 E
Peak Hill, N.S.W., Australia 113 32 47 S 148 11 E
Peak Hill, W. Austral., Australia 109 25 35 S 118 43 E
Peak Range 110 22 50 S 148 20 E
Peake 112 35 25 S 140 0 E
Peake Cr. → 111 28 2 S 136 7 E
Peale Mt. 157 38 25N 109 12W
Pearblossom 159 34 30N 117 55W
Pearl 154 39 28N 90 38W
Pearl → 153 30 23N 89 45W
Pearl Banks 81 8 45N 79 45 E
Pearl City, Hawaii, U.S.A. 146 21 24N 158 0W
Pearl City, Ill., U.S.A. 154 42 16N 89 50W
Pearsall 153 28 55N 99 8W
Pearse I. 144 54 52N 130 14W
Peary Land 6 82 40N 33 0W
Pease → 153 34 12N 99 7W
Pebane 131 17 10 S 38 8 E
Pebas 168 3 10 S 71 46W
Pebble, I. 176 51 20 S 59 40W
Pebble Beach 158 36 34N 121 57W
Peč 46 42 40N 20 17 E
Peçanha 171 18 33 S 42 34W
Pecatonica 154 42 19N 89 22W
Pecatonica → 154 42 26N 89 17W
Péccioli 42 43 32N 10 43 E
Pechea 50 45 36N 27 49 E
Pechenezhin 60 48 30N 24 48 E
Pechenga 56 69 30N 31 25 E
Pechiguera, Pta. 37 28 51N 13 53W
Pechnezhskoye Vdkhr. 59 50 0N 37 10 E
Pechora → 56 68 13N 54 15 E
Pechorskaya Guba 56 68 40N 54 0 E
Pechory 58 57 48N 27 40 E
Pecica 50 46 10N 21 3 E
Pečka 46 44 18N 19 33 E
Pécora, C. 44 39 28N 8 23 E
Pecos 153 31 25N 103 35W
Pecos → 153 29 42N 102 30W
Pécs 31 46 5N 18 15 E
Peddapalli 80 18 40N 79 24 E
Peddapuram 80 17 6N 8 13 E
Pedder, L. 110 42 55 S 146 10 E
Peddie 135 33 14 S 27 7 E
Pédernales 163 18 2N 71 44W
Pedhikos → 70 35 10N 33 54 E
Pedirka 111 26 40 S 135 14 E
Pedra Azul 171 16 2 S 41 17W
Pedra Grande, Recifes de 171 17 45 S 38 58W
Pedras Negras 173 12 51 S 62 54W
Pedreiras 170 4 32 S 44 40W
Pedrera, La 168 1 18 S 69 43W
Pedro Afonso 170 9 0 S 48 10W
Pedro Cays 162 17 5N 77 48W
Pedro Chico 168 1 4N 70 25W
Pedro de Valdivia 174 22 55 S 69 38W
Pedro Juan Caballero 175 22 30 S 55 40W
Pedro Muñoz 37 39 25N 2 56W
Pedrógão Grande 34 39 55N 8 9W
Peduyim 69 31 20N 34 37 E
Peebinga 112 34 52 S 140 57 E
Peebles, U.K. 14 55 40N 3 12W
Peebles, U.S.A. 155 38 57N 83 23W
Peekskill 151 41 18N 73 57W
Peel 12 54 14N 4 40W
Peel →, Australia 111 30 50 S 150 29 E
Peel →, Canada 140 67 0N 135 0W
Peelwood 113 34 7 S 149 27 E
Peene → 26 54 9N 13 46 E
Peera Peera Poolanna L. 111 26 30 S 138 0 E
Peers 144 53 40N 116 0W
Pegasus Bay 115 43 20 S 173 10 E
Peggau 30 47 12N 15 21 E
Pegnitz 27 49 45N 11 33 E
Pegnitz → 27 49 29N 10 59 E
Pego 37 38 51N 0 8W
Pegu 82 17 20N 96 29 E
Pegu Yoma 82 19 0N 96 0 E
Pehčevo 46 41 41N 22 55 E
Pehuajó 174 35 45 S 62 0W
Pei Xian 94 34 44N 116 55 E
Peine, Chile 174 23 45 S 68 8W
Peine, Germany 26 52 19N 10 12 E
Peip'ing = Beijing 94 39 55N 116 20 E
Peiss 27 47 58N 11 47 E
Peissenberg 27 47 48N 11 4 E
Peitz 26 51 50N 14 23 E
Peixe 171 12 0 S 48 40W
Peixe → 171 21 31 S 51 58W
Peixoto de Azeredo → 173 10 6 S 55 31W
Peize 22 53 9N 6 30 E
Pek → 46 44 45N 21 29 E
Pekalongan 89 6 53 S 109 40 E
Pekan 85 3 30N 103 25 E
Pekanbaru 88 0 30N 101 15 E
Pekin 154 40 35N 89 40W
Peking = Beijing 94 39 55N 116 20 E
Pelabuhan Kelang 85 3 0N 101 23 E
Pelabuhan Ratu, Teluk 88 7 5 S 106 30 E
Pelabuhanratu 88 7 0 S 106 32 E
Pélagos 48 39 17N 24 4 E
Pelaihari 89 3 55 S 114 45 E
Pelat, Mt. 21 44 16N 6 42 E
Pelczyce 32 53 3N 15 16 E
Peleaga 50 45 22N 22 55 E
Pelechuco 172 14 48 S 69 4W
Pelée, Mt. 163 14 48N 61 0W
Pelee, Pt. 142 41 54N 82 31W
Pelee I. 142 41 47N 82 40W
Pelejo 172 6 10 S 75 49W
Pelekech 130 3 52N 35 8 E
Pelendria 70 34 55N 33 0 E
Peleng 87 1 20 S 123 30 E
Pelham 149 31 5N 84 6W
Pelhřimov 30 49 24N 15 12 E
Pelican L. 145 52 28N 100 20W
Pelican Narrows 145 55 10N 102 56W
Pelican Rapids 145 52 45N 100 42W
Peljesac 46 42 55N 17 25 E
Pella, Greece 48 40 46N 22 23 E
Pella, S. Africa 134 29 1 S 19 6 E
Pella, U.S.A. 154 41 30N 93 0W
Pélla □ 48 40 52N 22 0 E
Péllaro 45 38 1N 15 40 E
Pellworm 26 54 30N 8 40 E
Pelly → 140 62 47N 137 19W
Pelly Bay 141 68 38N 89 50W
Pelly L. 140 66 0N 102 0W
Peloponnese = Pelopónnisos □ 49 37 10N 22 0 E
Pelopónnisos □ 49 37 10N 22 0 E
Peloritani, Monti 45 38 2N 15 25 E
Peloro, C. 45 38 15N 15 40 E
Pelorus Sound 115 40 59 S 173 59 E
Pelotas 175 31 42 S 52 23W
Pelòvo 47 43 26N 24 17 E
Pelvoux, Massif de 21 44 52N 6 20 E
Pelym → 62 59 39N 63 26 E
Pemalang 89 6 53 S 109 23 E
Pematangsiantar 88 2 57N 99 5 E
Pemba, Mozam. 131 12 58 S 40 30 E
Pemba, Zambia 131 16 30 S 27 28 E
Pemba Channel 130 5 0 S 39 37 E
Pemba I. 130 5 0 S 39 45 E
Pemberton, Australia 109 34 30 S 116 0 E
Pemberton, Canada 144 50 25N 122 50W
Pembina 145 48 58N 97 15W
Pembina → 145 49 0N 98 12W
Pembine 148 45 38N 87 59W
Pembino 152 48 58N 97 15W
Pembroke, Canada 142 45 50N 77 7W
Pembroke, U.K. 13 51 41N 4 57W
Pembroke, U.S.A. 149 32 5N 81 32W
Pembuang → 89 3 24 S 112 33 E
Pen-y-Ghent 12 54 10N 2 15W
Peña, Sierra de la 36 42 32N 0 45W
Peña de Francia, Sierra de 34 40 32N 6 10W
Penafiel, Portugal 34 41 12N 8 17W
Peñafiel, Spain 34 41 35N 4 7W
Peñaflor 35 37 43N 5 21W
Peñalara, Pico 34 40 51N 3 57W
Penalva 170 3 18 S 45 10W
Penamacôr 34 40 10N 7 10W
Penang = Pinang 85 5 25N 100 15 E
Penápolis 175 21 30 S 50 0W
Peñaranda de Bracamonte 34 40 53N 5 13W
Peñarroya-Pueblonuevo 35 38 19N 5 16W
Peñas, C. de 34 43 42N 5 52W
Penas, G. de 176 47 0 S 75 0W
Peñas, Pta. 169 11 17N 62 0W
Peñas de San Pedro 37 38 44N 2 0W
Peñas del Chache 37 29 6N 13 33W
Peñausende 34 41 17N 5 52W
Pench'i = Benxi 95 41 20N 123 48 E
Pend Oreille → 156 49 4N 117 37W
Pend Oreille, L. 156 48 0N 116 30W
Pendálofon 48 40 14N 21 12 E
Pendelikón 49 38 10N 23 53 E
Pendembu 126 9 7N 12 14W
Pendências 170 5 15 S 36 43W
Pender B. 108 16 45 S 122 42 E
Pendleton, Calif., U.S.A. 159 33 16N 117 23W
Pendleton, Ind., U.S.A. 155 40 0N 85 45W
Pendleton, Oreg., U.S.A. 156 45 35N 118 50W
Pendzhikent 63 39 29N 67 37 E
Penedo 170 10 15 S 36 36W
Penetanguishene 142 44 50N 79 55W
Peng Xian 96 31 4N 103 32 E
Pengalengan 89 7 9 S 107 30 E
Penge, Kasai Or., Zaïre 130 5 30 S 24 33 E
Penge, Kivu, Zaïre 130 4 27 S 28 25 E
Penglai 95 37 48N 120 42 E
Pengshui 96 29 17N 108 12 E
Penguin 110 41 8 S 146 6 E
Pengxi 96 30 44N 105 45 E
Pengze 97 29 52N 116 32 E
Penhalonga 131 18 52 S 32 40 E
Peniche 35 39 19N 9 22W
Penicuik 14 55 50N 3 14W
Penida 89 8 45 S 115 30 E
Peninsular Malaysia □ 85 4 0N 102 0 E
Peñíscola 36 40 22N 0 24 E
Penitente, Serra dos 170 8 45 S 46 20W
Penmarch 18 47 49N 4 21W
Penmarch, Pte. de 18 47 48N 4 22W
Penn Hills 150 40 28N 79 52W
Penn Yan 150 42 39N 77 7W
Pennabilli 43 43 50N 12 17 E
Pennant 145 50 32N 108 14W
Penne 43 42 28N 13 56 E
Penner → 81 14 35N 80 10 E
Penneshaw 112 35 44 S 137 56 E
Pennine, Alpi 42 46 4N 7 30 E
Pennines 12 54 50N 2 20W
Pennington 158 39 15N 121 47W
Pennino, Mte. 43 43 6N 12 54 E
Pennsylvania □ 148 40 50N 78 0W
Pennville 155 40 30N 85 9W
Penny 144 53 51N 121 20W
Peno 58 57 2N 32 49 E
Penola 112 37 25 S 140 21 E
Penonomé 162 8 31N 80 21W
Penrhyn Is. 105 9 0 S 158 30W
Penrith, Australia 113 33 43 S 150 38 E
Penrith, U.K. 12 54 40N 2 45W
Pensacola 149 30 30N 87 10W
Pensacola Mts. 7 84 0 S 40 0W
Pense 145 50 25N 104 59W
Penshurst 112 37 49 S 142 20 E
Pentecoste 170 3 48 S 39 17W
Penticton 144 49 30N 119 38W
Pentland 110 20 32 S 145 25 E
Pentland Firth 14 58 43N 3 10W
Pentland Hills 14 55 48N 3 25W
Penukonda 81 14 5N 77 38 E
Penylan L. 145 61 50N 106 20W
Penza 59 53 15N 45 5 E
Penzance 13 50 7N 5 32W
Penzberg 27 47 46N 11 23 E
Penzhino 65 63 30N 167 55 E
Penzhinskaya Guba 65 61 30N 163 0 E
Penzlin 26 53 32N 13 6 E
Peoria, Ariz., U.S.A. 157 33 40N 112 15W
Peoria, Ill., U.S.A. 154 40 40N 89 40W
Peoria Heights 154 40 45N 89 35W
Peotone 155 41 20N 87 48W
Pepingen 23 50 46N 4 10 E
Pepinster 23 50 34N 5 47 E
Peqini 48 41 4N 19 44 E
Pera Hd. 110 12 55 S 141 37 E
Perabumilih 88 3 27 S 104 15 E
Perakhóra 49 38 2N 22 56 E
Perales de Alfambra 36 40 38N 1 0W
Perales del Puerto 34 40 10N 6 40W
Peralta 36 42 21N 1 49W
Pérama 49 35 20N 24 40 E
Perast 46 42 31N 18 47 E
Percé 143 48 31N 64 13W
Perche 18 48 31N 1 1 E
Perche, Collines du 18 48 30N 0 40 E
Percival Lakes 108 21 25 S 125 0 E
Percy, France 18 48 55N 1 11W
Percy, U.S.A. 154 38 5N 89 41W
Percy Is. 110 21 39 S 150 16 E
Perdido → 176 42 55 S 67 0W
Perdido, Mte. 20 42 40N 0 5 E
Perdu, Mt. 20 42 40N 0 5 E
Pereira 168 4 49N 75 43W
Pereira Barreto 171 20 38 S 51 7W
Perekerten 112 34 55 S 143 40 E
Perekop 60 46 10N 33 42 E
Perené → 172 11 9 S 74 14W
Perenjori 109 29 26 S 116 16 E
Pereslavi-Zalesskiy 59 56 45N 38 50 E
Pereyaslav Khmelnitskiy 58 50 3N 31 28 E
Pérez, I. 161 22 24N 89 42W
Perg 30 48 15N 14 38 E
Pergamino 174 33 52 S 60 30W
Pérgine Valsugano 43 46 4N 11 15 E
Pérgola 43 43 35N 12 50 E
Perham 152 46 36N 95 36W
Perhentian, Kepulauan 85 5 54N 102 42 E
Peri, L. 112 30 45 S 143 35 E
Periam 50 46 2N 20 59 E
Péribonca → 143 48 45N 72 5W
Péribonca, L. 143 50 1N 71 10W
Perico 174 24 20 S 65 5W
Pericos 160 25 3N 107 42W
Périers 18 49 11N 1 25W
Périgord 20 45 0N 0 40 E
Périgueux 20 45 10N 0 42 E
Perijá, Sierra de 168 9 30N 73 3W
Peristéra 49 39 15N 23 58 E
Perito Moreno 176 46 36 S 70 56W
Peritoró 170 4 20 S 44 18W
Perivol = Dragovishtitsa 46 42 22N 22 39 E
Periyakulam 81 10 5N 77 30 E
Periyar → 81 10 15N 76 10 E
Periyar, L. 81 9 25N 77 10 E
Perković 43 43 41N 16 10 E
Perlas, Arch. de las 162 8 41N 79 7W
Perlas, Punta de 162 12 30N 83 30W
Perleberg 26 53 5N 11 50 E
Perlevka 59 51 48N 38 57 E
Perlez 46 45 11N 20 22 E
Perm 62 58 0N 57 10 E
Përmeti 48 40 15N 20 21 E
Pernambuco = Recife 170 8 0 S 35 0W
Pernambuco □ 170 8 0 S 37 0W
Pernatty Lagoon 112 31 30 S 137 12 E
Pernik 46 42 35N 23 2 E
Peron, C. 109 25 30 S 113 30 E
Peron Is. 108 13 9 S 130 4 E
Peron Pen. 109 26 0 S 113 10 E
Péronne 19 49 55N 2 57 E
Péronnes 23 50 27N 4 9 E
Perosa Argentina 42 44 57N 7 11 E
Perouse Str., La 98 45 40N 142 0 E
Perow 144 54 35N 126 10W
Perpendicular Pt. 111 31 37 S 152 52 E
Perpignan 20 42 42N 2 53 E
Perris 159 33 47N 117 14W
Perros-Guirec 18 48 49N 3 28W
Perry, Fla., U.S.A. 149 30 9N 83 40W
Perry, Ga., U.S.A. 149 32 25N 83 41W
Perry, Iowa, U.S.A. 154 41 48N 94 5W
Perry, Maine, U.S.A. 149 44 59N 67 20W
Perry, Mich., U.S.A. 155 42 50N 84 13W
Perry, Mo., U.S.A. 154 39 26N 91 40W
Perry, Okla., U.S.A. 153 36 20N 97 20W
Perrysburg 155 41 34N 83 38W
Perryton 153 36 28N 100 48W
Perryville 154 37 42N 89 50W
Persberg 52 59 47N 14 15 E
Perseverancia 173 14 44 S 62 48W
Persia = Iran ■ 73 33 0N 53 0 E
Persian Gulf = Gulf, The 73 27 0N 50 0 E
Perstorp 52 56 10N 13 25 E
Perth, Australia 109 31 57 S 115 52 E
Perth, Canada 142 44 55N 76 15W
Perth, U.K. 14 56 24N 3 27W
Perth Amboy 151 40 31N 74 16W
Perthus, Le 20 42 30N 2 53 E
Pertuis 21 43 42N 5 30 E
Peru, Ill., U.S.A. 154 41 18N 89 12W
Peru, Ind., U.S.A. 155 40 42N 86 0W
Peru ■ 168 8 0 S 75 0W
Peru-Chile Trench 105 20 0 S 72 0W
Perúgia 43 43 6N 12 24 E
Perušić 43 44 40N 15 22 E
Péruwelz 23 50 31N 3 36 E
Pervomaysk, R.S.F.S.R., U.S.S.R. 59 54 56N 43 58 E
Pervomaysk, Ukraine S.S.R., U.S.S.R. 60 48 10N 30 46 E
Pervouralsk 62 56 55N 60 0 E
Perwez 23 50 38N 4 48 E
Pésaro 43 43 55N 12 53 E
Pesca, La 161 23 46N 97 47W
Pescara 43 42 28N 14 13 E
Pescara → 43 42 28N 14 13 E
Peschanokopskoye 61 46 14N 41 4 E
Péscia 42 43 54N 10 40 E
Pescina 43 42 0N 13 39 E
Peseux 28 46 59N 6 53 E
Peshawar 77 34 2N 71 37 E
Peshkopia 48 41 41N 20 25 E
Peshovka 62 59 4N 52 22 E
Peshtera 47 42 2N 24 18 E
Peshtigo 148 45 4N 87 46W
Peski 59 51 14N 42 29 E
Peskovka 59 59 23N 52 20 E
Pêso da Régua 34 41 10N 7 47W
Pesqueira 170 8 20 S 36 42W
Pessac 20 44 48N 0 37W
Pessoux 23 50 17N 5 11 E
Pest □ 31 47 29N 19 5 E
Pestovo 58 58 33N 35 42 E
Pestravka 59 52 28N 49 57 E
Péta 49 39 10N 21 2 E
Petah Tiqwa 69 32 6N 34 53 E
Petalídhion 49 36 57N 21 55 E
Petaling Jaya 85 3 4N 101 42 E
Petaluma 158 38 13N 122 39W
Petange 23 49 33N 5 55 E
Petatlán 160 17 31N 101 16W
Petauke 131 14 14 S 31 20 E
Petawawa 142 45 54N 77 17W
Petegem 23 50 59N 3 32 E
Petén Itzá, L. 162 16 58N 89 50W
Peter 1st, I. 7 69 0 S 91 0W
Peter Pond L. 145 55 55N 108 44W
Peterbell 142 48 36N 83 21W
Peterborough, Australia 112 32 58 S 138 51 E
Peterborough, Canada 150 44 20N 78 20W
Peterborough, U.K. 13 52 35N 0 14W
Peterborough, U.S.A. 151 42 55N 71 59W
Peterhead 14 57 30N 1 49W
Peter's Mine 169 6 14N 59 20W
Petersburg, Alaska, U.S.A. 140 56 50N 133 0W
Petersburg, Ill., U.S.A. 154 40 1N 89 51W
Petersburg, Ind., U.S.A. 155 38 30N 87 15W
Petersburg, Va., U.S.A. 148 37 17N 77 26W
Petersburg, W. Va., U.S.A. 148 38 59N 79 10W

Petford

Petford **110** 17 20 S 144 58 E
Petília Policastro **45** 39 7N 16 48 E
Petit Bois I. **149** 30 16N 88 25W
Petit-Cap **143** 49 3N 64 30W
Petit Goâve **163** 18 27N 72 51W
Petit Lac Manicouagan **143** 51 25N 67 40W
Petit Saint Bernard, Col du **42** 45 40N 6 52 E
Petitcodiac **143** 45 57N 65 11W
Petite Baleine → **142** 56 0N 76 45W
Petite Saguenay **143** 48 15N 70 4W
Petitsikapau, L. **143** 54 37N 66 25W
Petlad **78** 22 30N 72 45 E
Peto **161** 20 10N 88 53W
Petone **114** 41 13 S 174 53 E
Petoskey **148** 45 22N 84 57W
Petra, Jordan **69** 30 20N 35 22 E
Petra, Spain **36** 39 37N 3 6 E
Petra, Ostrova **6** 76 15N 118 30 E
Petra Velikogo, Zaliv **98** 42 40N 132 0 E
Petralia **45** 37 49N 14 4 E
Petrel **37** 38 30N 0 46W
Petreto-Bicchisano **21** 41 47N 8 58 E
Petrich **47** 41 24N 23 13 E
Petrijanec **43** 46 23N 16 17 E
Petrikov **58** 52 11N 28 29 E
Petrila **50** 45 29N 23 29 E
Petrinja **43** 45 28N 16 18 E
Petrolândia **170** 9 5 S 38 20W
Petrolia **142** 42 54N 82 9W
Petrolina **170** 9 24 S 40 30W
Petromagoúla **49** 38 31N 23 0 E
Petropavlovsk **64** 54 53N 69 13 E
Petropavlovsk-Kamchatskiy **65** 53 3N 158 43 E
Petropavlovskiy = Akhtubinsk **61** 48 13N 46 7 E
Petrópolis **171** 22 33 S 43 9W
Petroşeni **50** 45 28N 23 20 E
Petroskey **148** 45 22N 84 57W
Petrova Gora **43** 45 15N 15 45 E
Petrovac, Crna Gora, Yugoslavia **46** 42 13N 18 57 E
Petrovac, Srbija, Yugoslavia **46** 44 22N 21 26 E
Petrovaradin **46** 45 16N 19 55 E
Petrovsk **59** 52 22N 45 19 E
Petrovsk-Zabaykalskiy **65** 51 20N 108 55 E
Petrovskoye = Svetlograd **61** 45 25N 42 58 E
Petrovskoye **62** 53 37N 56 23 E
Petrozavodsk **56** 61 41N 34 20 E
Petrus Steyn **135** 27 38 S 28 8 E
Petrusburg **134** 29 4 S 25 26 E
Pettitts **113** 34 56 S 148 10 E
Petukhovka **58** 53 42N 30 54 E
Peumo **174** 34 21 S 71 12W
Peureulak **88** 4 48N 97 45 E
Peusangan → **88** 5 16N 96 51 E
Pevek **65** 69 41N 171 19 E
Peveragno **42** 44 20N 7 37 E
Peyrehorade **20** 43 34N 1 7W
Peyruis **21** 44 1N 5 56 E
Pézenas **20** 43 28N 3 24 E
Pezinok **31** 48 17N 17 17 E
Pfaffenhofen **27** 48 31N 11 31 E
Pfäffikon **29** 47 13N 8 46 E
Pfarrkirchen **27** 48 25N 12 57 E
Pfeffenhausen **27** 48 40N 11 58 E
Pforzheim **27** 48 53N 8 43 E
Pfullendorf **27** 47 55N 9 15 E
Pfungstadt **27** 49 47N 8 36 E
Phala **134** 23 45 S 26 50 E
Phalera = Phulera **78** 26 52N 75 16 E
Phalodi **78** 27 12N 72 24 E
Phalsbourg **19** 48 46N 7 15 E
Phan **84** 19 28N 99 43 E
Phan Rang **85** 11 34N 109 0 E
Phan Ri = Hoa Da **85** 11 16N 108 40 E
Phan Thiet **85** 11 1N 108 9 E
Phanae **49** 38 8N 25 57 E
Phanat Nikhom **84** 13 27N 101 11 E
Phangan, Ko **85** 9 45N 100 0 E
Phangnga **85** 8 28N 98 30 E
Phanh Bho Ho Chi Minh **85** 10 58N 106 40 E
Phanom Sarakham **84** 13 45N 101 21 E
Pharenda **79** 27 5N 83 17 E
Phatthalung **85** 7 39N 100 6 E
Phayao **84** 19 11N 99 55 E
Phelps, N.Y., U.S.A. **150** 42 57N 77 5W
Phelps, Wis., U.S.A. **152** 46 2N 89 2W
Phelps L. **145** 59 15N 103 15W
Phenix City **149** 32 30N 85 0W
Phet Buri **84** 13 1N 99 55 E
Phetchabun **84** 16 25N 101 8 E
Phetchabun, Thiu Khao **84** 16 0N 101 20 E
Phi Phi, Ko **85** 7 45N 98 46 E
Phiafay **84** 14 48N 106 0 E
Phibun Mangsahan **84** 15 14N 105 14 E
Phichai **84** 17 22N 100 10 E
Phichit **84** 16 26N 100 22 E
Philadelphia, Miss., U.S.A. **153** 32 47N 89 5W
Philadelphia, N.Y., U.S.A. **151** 44 9N 75 40W
Philadelphia, Pa., U.S.A. **151** 40 0N 75 10W
Philip **152** 44 4N 101 42W
Philippeville **23** 50 12N 4 33 E
Philippi **48** 41 1N 24 16 E
Philippi L. **110** 24 20 S 138 55 E
Philippines ■ **90** 12 0N 123 0 E
Philippolis **134** 30 15 S 25 16 E
Philippopolis = Plovdiv **47** 42 8N 24 44 E
Philipsburg, Mont., U.S.A. **156** 46 20N 113 21W
Philipsburg, Pa., U.S.A. **150** 40 53N 78 10W
Philipstown **134** 30 28 S 24 30 E
Phillip, I. **113** 38 30 S 145 12 E
Phillips, Tex., U.S.A. **153** 35 48N 101 17W
Phillips, Wis., U.S.A. **152** 45 41N 90 22W
Phillipsburg, Kans., U.S.A. **152** 39 48N 99 20W
Phillipsburg, Pa., U.S.A. **151** 40 43N 75 12W
Phillott **111** 27 53 S 145 50 E
Philmont **151** 42 14N 73 37W
Philomath **156** 44 28N 123 21W
Phimai **84** 15 13N 102 30 E
Phitsanulok **84** 16 50N 100 12 E
Phnom Dangrek **84** 14 20N 104 0 E
Phnom Penh **85** 11 33N 104 55 E
Phoenix, Ariz., U.S.A. **157** 33 30N 112 10W
Phoenix, N.Y., U.S.A. **151** 43 13N 76 18W
Phoenix Is. **104** 3 30 S 172 0W
Phoenixville **151** 40 12N 75 29W
Phon **84** 15 49N 102 36 E
Phon Tiou **84** 17 53N 104 37 E
Phong → **84** 16 23N 102 56 E
Phong Saly **84** 21 42N 102 9 E
Phong Tho **84** 22 32N 103 21 E
Phonhong **84** 18 30N 102 25 E
Phonum **85** 8 49N 98 48 E
Photharam **84** 13 41N 99 51 E
Phra Chedi Sam Ong **84** 15 16N 98 23 E
Phra Nakhon Si Ayutthaya **84** 14 25N 100 30 E
Phra Thong, Ko **85** 9 5N 98 17 E
Phrae **84** 18 7N 100 9 E
Phrom Phiram **84** 17 2N 100 12 E
Phu Dien **84** 18 58N 105 31 E
Phu Loi **84** 20 14N 103 14 E
Phu Ly **84** 20 35N 105 50 E
Phu Tho **84** 21 24N 105 13 E
Phuc Yen **84** 21 16N 105 45 E
Phuket **85** 7 52N 98 22 E
Phuket, Ko **85** 8 0N 98 22 E
Phulbari **82** 25 55N 90 2 E
Phulera **78** 26 52N 75 16 E
Phun Phin **85** 9 7N 99 12 E
Piacá **170** 7 42 S 47 18W
Piacenza **42** 45 2N 9 42 E
Piaçubaçu **170** 10 24 S 36 25W
Piádena **42** 45 8N 10 22 E
Pialba **111** 25 20 S 152 45 E
Pian Cr. → **111** 30 2 S 148 12 E
Piana **21** 42 15N 8 34 E
Pianella **43** 42 24N 14 5 E
Piangil **112** 35 5 S 143 20 E
Pianoro **43** 44 20N 11 20 E
Pianosa, Puglia, Italy **43** 42 12N 15 44 E
Pianosa, Toscana, Italy **42** 42 36N 10 4 E
Piapot **145** 49 59N 109 8W
Piare → **43** 45 32N 12 44 E
Pias **35** 38 1N 7 29W
Piaseczno **32** 52 5N 21 2 E
Piaski **32** 51 8N 22 52 E
Piastów **32** 52 12N 20 48 E
Piatã **171** 13 9 S 41 48W
Piatra **50** 43 51N 25 9 E
Piatra Neamţ **50** 46 56N 26 21 E
Piatra Olt **50** 44 22N 24 16 E
Piauí □ **170** 7 0 S 43 0W
Piaui → **170** 6 38 S 42 42W
Piave → **43** 45 32N 12 44 E
Piazza Ármerina **45** 37 21N 14 20 E
Pibor → **125** 7 35N 33 0 E
Pibor Post **125** 6 47N 33 3 E
Pica **172** 20 35 S 69 25W
Picardie **19** 49 50N 3 0 E
Picardie, Plaine de **19** 50 0N 2 0 E
Picardy = Picardie **19** 49 50N 3 0 E
Picayune **153** 30 31N 89 40W
Picerno **45** 40 40N 15 37 E
Pichilemu **174** 34 22 S 72 0W
Pichincha, □ **168** 0 10 S 78 40W
Pickerel L. **142** 48 40N 91 25W
Pickle Lake **142** 51 30N 90 12W
Pico Truncado **176** 46 40 S 68 0W
Picos **170** 7 5 S 41 28W
Picos Ancares, Sierra de **34** 42 51N 6 52W
Picota **172** 6 54 S 76 24W
Picquigny **19** 49 56N 2 10 E
Picton, Australia **113** 34 12 S 150 34 E
Picton, Canada **142** 44 1N 77 9W
Picton, N.Z. **115** 41 18 S 174 3 E
Picton, I. **176** 55 2 S 66 57W
Pictou **143** 45 41N 62 42W
Picture Butte **144** 49 55N 112 45W
Picuí **170** 6 31 S 36 21W
Picún Leufú **176** 39 30 S 69 5W
Pidurutalagala **81** 7 10N 80 50 E
Piedad, La **160** 20 20N 102 1W
Piedecuesta **168** 6 59N 73 3W
Piedicavallo **42** 45 41N 7 57 E
Piedmont = Piemonte □ **42** 45 0N 7 30 E
Piedmont **149** 33 55N 85 39W
Piedmont Plateau **149** 34 0N 81 30W
Piedmonte d'Alife **45** 41 22N 14 22 E
Piedra → **36** 41 18N 1 47W
Piedra del Anguila **176** 40 2 S 70 4W
Piedra Lais **168** 3 10N 65 50W
Piedrabuena **35** 39 0N 4 10W
Piedrahita **34** 40 28N 5 23W
Piedras, R. de las → **172** 12 30 S 69 15W
Piedras Negras **160** 28 35N 100 35W
Piedras Pt. **91** 10 11N 118 48 E
Piemonte □ **42** 45 0N 7 30 E
Piensk **32** 51 16N 15 2 E
Pier Millan **112** 35 14 S 142 40 E
Pierce **156** 46 29N 115 53W
Piercefield **151** 44 13N 74 35W
Piería □ **48** 40 13N 22 25 E
Pierre **152** 44 23N 100 20W
Pierre Benite, Barrage **21** 45 42N 4 49 E
Pierre-de-Bresse **21** 46 54N 5 13 E
Pierrefeu-du-Var **21** 43 13N 6 9 E
Pierrefonds **19** 49 20N 3 0 E
Pierrefontaine-les-Varans **19** 47 14N 6 32 E
Pierrefort **20** 44 55N 2 50 E
Pierrelatte **21** 44 23N 4 43 E
Pieštany **31** 48 38N 17 55 E
Piesting → **31** 48 6N 16 40 E
Pieszyce **32** 50 43N 16 33 E
Piet Retief **135** 27 1 S 30 50 E
Pietarsaari = Jakobstad **54** 63 40N 22 43 E
Pietermaritzburg **135** 29 35 S 30 25 E
Pietersburg **135** 23 54 S 29 25 E
Pietraperzia **45** 37 26N 14 8 E
Pietrasanta **42** 43 57N 10 12 E
Pietrosu **50** 47 12N 25 8 E
Pietrosul **50** 47 35N 24 43 E
Pieve di Cadore **43** 46 25N 12 22 E
Pieve di Teco **42** 44 3N 7 54 E
Pievepélago **42** 44 12N 10 35 E
Pigádhia **49** 35 30N 27 12 E
Pigadhítsa **48** 39 59N 21 23 E
Pigeon **148** 43 50N 83 17W
Pigeon I. **81** 14 2N 74 20 E
Piggott **153** 36 20N 90 10W
Pigna **42** 43 57N 7 40 E
Pigüe **174** 37 36 S 62 25W
Pihani **79** 27 36N 80 15 E
Pijnacker **22** 52 1N 4 26 E
Pikalevo **58** 59 37N 34 0 E
Pikes Peak **152** 38 50N 105 10W
Piketberg **134** 32 55 S 18 40 E
Pikeville **148** 37 30N 82 30W
Pikou **95** 39 18N 122 22 E
Pikwitonei **145** 55 35N 97 9W
Piła, Poland **32** 53 10N 16 48 E
Pila, Spain **37** 38 16N 1 11W
Piła □ **32** 53 0N 17 0 E
Pilaía **48** 40 32N 22 59 E
Pilani **78** 28 22N 75 33 E
Pilão Arcado **170** 10 9 S 42 26W
Pilar, Brazil **170** 9 36 S 35 56W
Pilar, Paraguay **174** 26 50 S 58 20W
Pilas Group **91** 6 45N 121 35 E
Pilawa **32** 51 57N 21 32 E
Pilaya → **173** 20 55 S 64 4W
Pilbara **108** 21 15 S 118 16 E
Pilcomayo → **174** 25 21 S 57 42W
Píli, Greece **49** 36 50N 27 15 E
Pili, Phil. **90** 13 33N 123 19 E
Pilibhit **79** 28 40N 79 50 E
Pilica → **32** 51 52N 21 17 E
Pilion **48** 39 27N 23 7 E
Pilis **31** 47 17N 19 35 E
Pilisvörösvár **31** 47 38N 18 56 E
Pilkhawa **78** 28 43N 77 42 E
Pillaro **168** 1 10 S 78 32W
Pílos **49** 36 55N 21 42 E
Pilot Grove **154** 38 53N 92 55W
Pilot Mound **145** 49 15N 98 54W
Pilot Point **153** 33 26N 97 0W
Pilot Rock **156** 45 30N 118 50W
Pilsen = Plzeň **30** 49 45N 13 22 E
Pilštanj **43** 46 8N 15 39 E
Pilzno **32** 50 0N 21 16 E
Pima **157** 32 54N 109 50W
Pimba **112** 31 18 S 136 46 E
Pimenta Bueno **173** 11 35 S 61 10W
Pimentel **172** 6 45 S 79 55W
Pina **36** 41 29N 0 33W
Pinamalayan **90** 13 2N 121 29 E
Pinang **85** 5 25N 100 15 E
Pinar del Río **162** 22 26N 83 40W
Pincehely **31** 46 41N 18 27 E
Pinchang **96** 31 36N 107 3 E
Pincher Creek **144** 49 30N 113 57W
Pinchi L. **144** 54 38N 124 30W
Pinckneyville **154** 38 5N 89 20W
Pîncota **46** 46 20N 21 45 E
Pińczów **32** 50 32N 20 32 E
Pind Dadan Khan **78** 32 36N 73 7 E
Pindar **109** 28 30 S 115 47 E
Pindaré → **170** 3 17 S 44 47W
Pindaré Mirim **170** 3 37 S 45 21W
Pindi Gheb **78** 33 14N 72 21 E
Pindiga **127** 9 58N 10 53 E
Pindobal **170** 3 16 S 48 25W
Pindos Óros **48** 40 0N 21 0 E
Pindus Mts. = Pindos Óros **48** 40 0N 21 0 E
Pine **157** 34 27N 111 30W
Pine → **145** 58 50N 105 38W
Pine, C. **143** 46 37N 53 32W
Pine, La **156** 43 40N 121 30W
Pine Bluff **153** 34 10N 92 0W
Pine City **152** 45 46N 93 0W
Pine Falls **145** 50 34N 96 11W
Pine Flat Res. **158** 36 50N 119 20W
Pine Pass **144** 55 25N 122 42W
Pine Point **144** 60 50N 114 28W
Pine Ridge, Australia **113** 31 10 S 147 30 E
Pine Ridge, U.S.A. **152** 43 0N 102 35W
Pine River, Canada **145** 51 45N 100 30W
Pine River, U.S.A. **152** 46 43N 94 24W
Pine Valley **159** 32 50N 116 32W
Pinecrest **158** 38 12N 120 1W
Pinedale **158** 36 50N 119 48W
Pinega → **56** 64 8N 46 54 E
Pinehill **110** 23 38 S 146 57 E
Pinerolo **42** 44 47N 7 21 E
Pineto **43** 42 36N 14 4 E
Pinetop **157** 34 10N 109 57W
Pinetown **135** 29 48 S 30 54 E
Pinetree **156** 43 42N 105 52W
Pineville, Ky., U.S.A. **149** 36 42N 83 42W
Pineville, La., U.S.A. **153** 31 22N 92 30W
Piney **19** 48 22N 4 21 E
Ping → **84** 15 42N 100 9 E
Pingaring **109** 32 40 S 118 32 E
Pingba **96** 26 23N 106 12 E
Pingchuan **96** 27 35N 101 55 E
Pingding **94** 37 47N 113 38 E
Pingdingshan **94** 33 43N 113 27 E
Pingdong **97** 22 39N 120 30 E
Pingdu **95** 36 42N 119 59 E
Pingelly **109** 32 32 S 117 5 E
Pingguo **96** 23 19N 107 36 E
Pinghe **97** 24 17N 117 21 E
Pinghu **97** 30 40N 121 2 E
Pingjiang **97** 28 45N 113 36 E
Pingle **97** 24 40N 110 40 E
Pingli **96** 32 27N 109 22 E
Pingliang **94** 35 35N 106 31 E
Pinglu **94** 39 31N 112 30 E
Pingluo **94** 38 52N 106 30 E
Pingnan, Fujian, China **97** 26 55N 119 0 E
Pingnan, Guangxi Zhuangzu, China **97** 23 33N 110 22 E
Pingquan **95** 41 1N 118 37 E
Pingrup **109** 33 32 S 118 29 E
Pingtan **97** 25 31N 119 47 E
Pingtang **96** 25 49N 107 17 E
Pingwu **94** 32 25N 104 30 E
Pingxiang, Guangxi Zhuangzu, China **96** 22 6N 106 46 E
Pingxiang, Jiangxi, China **97** 27 43N 113 48 E
Pingyao **94** 37 12N 112 10 E
Pingyi **95** 35 30N 117 35 E
Pingyin **94** 36 20N 116 25 E
Pingyuan, Guangdong, China **97** 24 37N 115 57 E
Pingyuan, Shandong, China **94** 37 10N 116 22 E
Pingyuanjie **96** 23 45N 103 48 E
Pinhal **175** 22 10 S 46 46W
Pinheiro **170** 2 31 S 45 5W
Pinhel **34** 40 50N 7 1W
Pinhuá → **173** 6 21 S 65 0W
Pini **88** 0 10N 98 40 E
Piniós →, Ilía, Greece **49** 37 48N 21 20 E
Piniós →, Trikkala, Greece **48** 39 55N 22 10 E
Pinjarra **109** 32 37 S 115 52 E
Pink → **145** 56 50N 103 50W
Pinkafeld **31** 47 22N 16 9 E
Pinlebu **82** 24 5N 95 22 E
Pinnacles, Australia **109** 28 12 S 120 26 E
Pinnacles, U.S.A. **158** 36 33N 121 19W
Pinnaroo **112** 35 17 S 140 53 E
Pinneberg **26** 53 39N 9 48 E
Pino Hachado, Paso **176** 38 39 S 70 54W
Pinon Hills **159** 34 26N 117 39W
Pinos **160** 22 20N 101 40W
Pinos, Mt **159** 34 49N 119 8W
Pinos Pt. **157** 36 38N 121 57W
Pinos Puente **35** 37 15N 3 45W
Pinotepa Nacional **161** 16 19N 98 3W
Pinrang **87** 3 46 S 119 41 E
Pins, I. des **106** 22 37 S 167 30 E
Pinsk **58** 52 10N 26 1 E
Pintados **172** 20 35 S 69 40W
Pintumba **109** 31 30 S 132 12 E
Pintuyan **91** 9 57N 125 15 E
Pinukpuk **90** 17 35N 121 22 E
Pinyang **97** 27 42N 120 31 E
Pinyug **56** 60 5N 48 0 E
Pinzolo **42** 46 9N 10 45 E
Pio V. Corpuz **91** 11 55N 124 2 E
Pio XII **170** 3 53 S 45 17W
Pioche **157** 38 0N 114 35W
Pioduran **90** 13 2N 123 25 E
Piombino **42** 42 54N 10 30 E
Piombino, Canale di **42** 42 50N 10 25 E
Pioner, Os. **65** 79 50N 92 0 E
Pionki **32** 51 29N 21 28 E
Piorini → **169** 3 23 S 63 30W
Piorini, L. **169** 3 15 S 62 35W
Piotrków Trybunalski **32** 51 23N 19 43 E
Piotrków Trybunalski □ **32** 51 30N 19 45 E
Piove di Sacco **43** 45 18N 12 1 E
Pīp **73** 26 45N 60 10 E
Pipar **78** 26 25N 73 31 E
Piparia **78** 22 45N 78 23 E

Ponca City

Pipéri 48 39 20N 24 19 E
Pipestone 152 44 0N 96 20W
Pipestone → 142 52 53N 89 23W
Pipestone Cr. → 145 49 38N 100 15W
Pipiriki 114 39 28 S 175 5 E
Pipmuacan, Rés. 143 49 45N 70 30W
Pippingarra 108 20 27 S 118 42 E
Pipriac 18 47 49N 1 58W
Piqua 155 40 10N 84 10W
Piquet Carneiro 170 5 48 S 39 25W
Piquiri → 175 24 3 S 54 14W
Pīr Sohrāb 73 25 44N 60 54 E
Piracanjuba 171 17 18 S 49 1W
Piracicaba 175 22 45 S 47 40W
Piracuruca 170 3 50 S 41 50W
Piræus = Piraiévs 49 37 57N 23 42 E
Piraiévs 49 37 57N 23 42 E
Piraiévs □ 49 37 0N 23 30 E
Piráino 45 38 10N 14 52 E
Pirajuí 175 21 59 S 49 29W
Piran 43 45 31N 13 33 E
Pirané 174 25 42 S 59 6W
Piranhas 170 9 27 S 37 46W
Pirano = Piran 43 45 31N 13 33 E
Pirapemas 170 3 43 S 44 14W
Pirapora 171 17 20 S 44 56W
Piray → 173 16 32 S 63 45W
Pirdop 47 42 40N 24 10 E
Pires do Rio 171 17 18 S 48 17W
Pirganj 82 25 51N 88 24 E
Pírgos, Ilía, Greece 49 37 40N 21 27 E
Pírgos, Messinia, Greece 49 36 50N 22 16 E
Pirgovo 47 43 44N 25 43 E
Piriac-sur-Mer 18 47 22N 2 33W
Piribebuy 174 25 26 S 57 2W
Pirin Planina 47 41 40N 23 30 E
Pirineos 36 42 40N 1 0 E
Piripiri 170 4 15 S 41 46W
Piritu 168 9 23N 69 12W
Pirlerkondu 70 36 54N 32 29 E
Pirmasens 27 49 12N 7 30 E
Pirna 26 50 57N 13 57 E
Pirojpur 82 22 35N 90 1 E
Pirot 46 43 9N 22 39 E
Piru, Indonesia 87 3 4 S 128 12 E
Piru, U.S.A. 159 34 25N 118 48W
Piryatin 58 50 15N 32 25 E
Piryí 49 38 13N 25 59 E
Pisa 42 43 43N 10 23 E
Pisa → 32 53 14N 21 52 E
Pisa Ra. 115 44 52 S 169 12 E
Pisac 172 13 25 S 71 50W
Pisagua 172 19 40 S 70 15W
Pisarovina 43 45 35N 15 50 E
Pisciotta 45 40 7N 15 12 E
Pisco 172 13 50 S 76 12W
Piscu 50 45 30N 27 43 E
Písek 30 49 19N 14 10 E
Pishan 92 37 30N 78 33 E
Pishin Lora → 78 29 9N 64 55 E
Pising 87 5 8 S 121 53 E
Pismo Beach 159 35 9N 120 38W
Pissos 20 44 19N 0 49W
Pisticci 45 40 24N 16 33 E
Pistóia 42 43 57N 10 53 E
Pistol B. 145 62 25N 92 37W
Pisuerga → 34 41 33N 4 52W
Pisz 32 53 38N 21 49 E
Pitalito 168 1 51N 76 2W
Pitanga 171 24 46 S 51 44W
Pitangui 171 19 40 S 44 54 E
Pitarpunga, L. 112 34 24 S 143 30 E
Pitcairn I. 105 25 5 S 130 5W
Pite älv → 54 65 20N 21 25 E
Piteå 54 65 20N 21 25 E
Piterka 59 50 41N 47 29 E
Piteşti 50 44 52N 24 54 E
Pithapuram 80 17 10N 82 15 E
Pithara 109 30 20 S 116 35 E
Píthion 48 41 24N 26 40 E
Pithiviers 19 48 10N 2 13 E
Pitigliano 43 42 38N 11 40 E
Pitlochry 14 56 43N 3 43W
Pitoco 91 10 8N 124 33 E
Pitrufquén 176 38 59 S 72 39W
Pitt I. 144 53 30N 129 50W
Pittem 23 51 1N 3 13 E
Pittsburg, Kans., U.S.A. 153 37 21N 94 43W
Pittsburg, Tex., U.S.A. 153 32 59N 94 58W
Pittsburgh 150 40 25N 79 55W
Pittsfield, Ill., U.S.A. 154 39 35N 90 46W
Pittsfield, Mass., U.S.A. 151 42 28N 73 17W
Pittsfield, N.H., U.S.A. 151 43 17N 71 18W
Pittston 151 41 19N 75 50W
Pittsworth 111 27 41 S 151 37 E
Pituri → 110 22 35 S 138 30 E
Piuí 171 20 28 S 45 58W
Pium 170 10 27 S 49 11W
Piura 172 5 15 S 80 38W
Piura □ 172 5 10 S 80 0W
Piva → 46 43 20N 18 50 E
Pivijay 168 10 28N 74 37W
Piwniczna 32 49 27N 20 42 E
Pixley 158 35 58N 119 18W
Piyai 48 39 17N 21 25 E
Pizarro 168 4 58N 77 22W
Pizol 29 46 57N 9 23 E
Pizzo 45 38 44N 16 10 E
Placentia 143 47 20N 54 0W
Placentia B. 143 47 0N 54 40W
Placer 91 11 52N 123 55 E
Placerville 158 38 47N 120 51W
Placetas 162 22 15N 79 44W
Plačkovica 46 41 45N 22 30 E
Plaffeien 28 46 45N 7 17 E
Plain Dealing 153 32 56N 93 41W
Plainfield, Ill., U.S.A. 155 41 37N 88 12W
Plainfield, N.J., U.S.A. 151 40 37N 74 28W
Plains, Kans., U.S.A. 153 37 20N 100 35W
Plains, Mont., U.S.A. 156 47 27N 114 57W
Plains, Tex., U.S.A. 153 33 11N 102 50W
Plainview, Nebr., U.S.A. 152 42 25N 97 48W
Plainview, Tex., U.S.A. 153 34 10N 101 40W
Plainville 152 39 18N 99 19W
Plainwell 148 42 28N 85 40W
Plaisance 20 43 36N 0 3 E
Pláka 48 40 0N 25 24 E
Plakenska Planina 46 41 14N 21 2 E
Plakhino 64 67 45N 86 5 E
Planá 30 49 50N 12 44 E
Plana Cays 163 22 38N 73 30W
Planada 158 37 18N 120 19W
Plancoët 18 48 32N 2 13W
Plandište 46 45 16N 21 10 E
Planeta Rica 168 8 25N 75 36W
Planina, Slovenija, Yugoslavia 43 46 10N 15 20 E
Planina, Slovenija, Yugoslavia 43 45 47N 14 19 E
Plankinton 152 43 45N 98 27W
Plano 153 33 0N 96 45W
Plant, La 152 45 11N 100 40W
Plant City 149 28 0N 82 8W
Plaquemine 153 30 20N 91 15W
Plaridel 91 8 37N 123 43 E
Plasencia 34 40 3N 6 8W
Plaški 43 45 4N 15 22 E
Plassen 52 61 9N 12 30 E
Plast 62 54 22N 60 50 E
Plaster City 159 32 47N 115 51W
Plaster Rock 143 46 53N 67 22W
Plastun 98 44 45N 136 19 E
Plata, La, Argentina 174 35 0 S 57 55W
Plata, La, Colombia 168 2 23N 75 53W
Plata, La, U.S.A. 154 40 2N 92 29W
Plata, La, L. 176 44 55 S 71 50W
Plata, Río de la 174 34 45 S 57 30W
Platani → 44 37 23N 13 16 E
Plateau □ 127 8 0N 8 30 E
Plateau du Coteau du Missouri 152 47 9N 101 5W
Platí, Ákra 48 40 27N 24 0 E
Plato 168 9 47N 74 47W
Platte 152 43 28N 98 50W
Platte → 154 39 16N 94 50W
Platte, Piz 29 46 30N 9 35 E
Platte City 154 39 22N 94 47W
Platteville, Colo., U.S.A. 152 40 18N 104 47W
Platteville, Wis., U.S.A. 154 42 44N 90 29W
Plattling 27 48 46N 12 53 E
Plattsburg, Miss., U.S.A. 154 39 34N 94 27W
Plattsburg, N.Y., U.S.A. 151 44 41N 73 30W
Plattsmouth 152 41 0N 95 50W
Plau 26 53 27N 12 16 E
Plauen 26 50 29N 12 9 E
Plav 46 42 38N 19 57 E
Plavinas 58 56 35N 25 46 E
Plavnica 46 42 20N 19 13 E
Plavsk 59 53 40N 37 18 E
Playgreen L. 145 54 0N 98 15W
Pleasant Bay 143 46 51N 60 48W
Pleasant Hill, Calif., U.S.A. 158 37 57N 122 4W
Pleasant Hill, Ill., U.S.A. 154 39 27N 90 52W
Pleasant Hill, Mo., U.S.A. 154 38 48N 94 14W
Pleasant Hills 113 35 28 S 146 50 E
Pleasant Pt. 115 44 16 S 171 9 E
Pleasanton 153 29 0N 98 30W
Pleasantville, Iowa, U.S.A. 154 41 23N 93 18W
Pleasantville, N.J., U.S.A. 148 39 25N 74 30W
Pleasure Ridge Park 155 38 9N 85 50W
Pléaux 20 45 8N 2 13 E
Pleiku 84 13 57N 108 0 E
Plélan-le-Grand 18 48 0N 2 7W
Plémet-la-Pierre 18 48 11N 2 36W
Pléneuf-Val-André 18 48 35N 2 32W
Pleniţa 50 44 14N 23 10 E
Plenty → 110 23 25 S 136 31 E
Plenty, Bay of 114 37 45 S 177 0 E
Plentywood 152 48 45N 104 35W
Plesetsk 56 62 40N 40 10 E
Plessisville 143 46 14N 71 47W
Plestin-les-Grèves 18 48 40N 3 39W
Pleszew 32 51 53N 17 47 E
Pleternica 46 45 17N 17 48 E
Pletipi L. 143 51 44N 70 6W
Pleven 47 43 26N 24 37 E
Plevlja 46 43 21N 19 21 E
Ploče 46 43 4N 17 26 E
Płock 32 52 32N 19 40 E
Płock □ 32 52 30N 19 45 E
Plöcken Passo 43 46 37N 12 57 E
Ploegsteert 23 50 44N 2 53 E
Ploemeur 18 47 44N 3 26W
Ploërmel 18 47 55N 2 26W
Ploieşti 50 44 57N 26 5 E
Plomárion 49 38 58N 26 24 E
Plombières-les-Bains 19 47 58N 6 27 E
Plomin 43 45 8N 14 10 E
Plön 26 54 8N 10 22 E
Plöner See 26 54 10N 10 22 E
Plonge, Lac la 145 55 8N 107 20W
Płońsk 32 52 37N 20 21 E
Płoty 32 53 48N 15 18 E
Plouaret 18 48 37N 3 28W
Plouay 18 47 55N 3 21W
Ploučnice → 30 50 46N 14 13 E
Ploudalmézeau 18 48 34N 4 41W
Plougasnou 18 48 42N 3 49W
Plouha 18 48 41N 2 57W
Plouhinec 18 48 0N 4 29W
Plovdiv 47 42 8N 24 44 E
Plum 150 40 29N 79 47W
Plum I. 151 41 10N 72 12W
Plumas 158 39 45N 119 4W
Plummer 156 47 21N 116 59W
Plumtree 131 20 27 S 27 55 E
Plunge 58 55 53N 21 59 E
Pluvigner 18 47 46N 3 1W
Plymouth, U.K. 13 50 23N 4 9W
Plymouth, Calif., U.S.A. 158 38 29N 120 51W
Plymouth, Ill., U.S.A. 154 40 15N 90 58W
Plymouth, Ind., U.S.A. 155 41 20N 86 19W
Plymouth, Mass., U.S.A. 151 41 58N 70 40W
Plymouth, N.C., U.S.A. 149 35 54N 76 46W
Plymouth, N.H., U.S.A. 151 43 44N 71 41W
Plymouth, Pa., U.S.A. 151 41 17N 76 0W
Plymouth, Wis., U.S.A. 148 43 42N 87 58W
Plymouth Sd. 13 50 20N 4 10W
Plynlimon = Pumlumon Fawr 13 52 29N 3 47W
Plyussa 58 58 40N 29 20 E
Plyussa → 58 58 40N 29 0 E
Plzeň 30 49 45N 13 22 E
Pniewy 32 52 31N 16 16 E
Pô 127 11 14N 1 5W
Po → 42 44 57N 12 4 E
Po, Foci del 43 44 55N 12 30 E
Po Hai = Bo Hai 95 39 0N 120 0 E
Pobé 127 7 0N 2 56 E
Pobeda 65 65 12N 146 12 E
Pobedino 65 49 51N 142 49 E
Pobedy Pik 64 40 45N 79 58 E
Pobiedziska 32 52 29N 17 11 E
Pobla de Lillet, La 36 42 16N 1 59 E
Pobla de Segur 36 42 15N 0 58 E
Pobladura de Valle 34 42 6N 5 44W
Pocahontas, Ark., U.S.A. 153 36 18N 91 0W
Pocahontas, Ill., U.S.A. 154 38 50N 89 33W
Pocahontas, Iowa, U.S.A. 154 42 41N 94 42W
Pocatello 156 42 50N 112 25W
Počátky 30 49 15N 15 14 E
Pochep 58 52 58N 33 29 E
Pochinki 59 54 41N 44 59 E
Pochinok 58 54 28N 32 29 E
Pöchlarn 30 48 12N 15 12 E
Pochutla 161 15 50N 96 31W
Poci 169 5 57N 61 29W
Pocinhos 170 7 4 S 36 3W
Pocito Casas 160 28 32N 111 6W
Poções 171 14 31 S 40 21W
Pocomoke City 148 38 4N 75 32W
Poconé 173 16 15 S 56 37W
Poços de Caldas 175 21 50 S 46 33W
Poddebice 32 51 54N 18 58 E
Poděbrady 30 50 9N 15 8 E
Podensac 20 44 40N 0 22W
Podgorač 46 45 27N 18 13 E
Podgorica = Titograd 46 42 30N 19 19 E
Podkamennaya Tunguska → 65 61 50N 90 13 E
Podlapac 43 44 37N 15 47 E
Podmokly 30 50 48N 14 10 E
Podoleni 50 46 46N 26 39 E
Podolínec 31 49 16N 20 31 E
Podolsk 59 55 25N 37 30 E
Podor 126 16 40N 15 2W
Podporozhy 56 60 55N 34 2 E
Podravska Slatina 46 45 42N 17 45 E
Podu Turcului 50 46 11N 27 25 E
Podujevo 46 42 54N 21 10 E
Poel 26 54 0N 11 25 E
Pofadder 134 29 10 S 19 22 E
Pogamasing 142 46 55N 81 50W
Poggiardo 45 40 3N 18 21 E
Poggibonsi 43 43 27N 11 8 E
Pogoanele 50 44 55N 27 0 E
Pogorzela 32 51 50N 17 12 E
Pogoso 133 6 46 S 17 12 E
Pogradeci 48 40 57N 20 37 E
Pogranitšnyi 98 44 25N 131 24 E
Poh 87 0 46 S 122 51 E
Pohang 95 36 1N 129 23 E
Pohorelá 31 48 50N 20 2 E
Pohořelice 31 48 59N 16 31 E
Pohorje 43 46 30N 15 20 E
Poiana Mare 50 43 57N 23 5 E
Poiana Ruscăi, Munţii 50 45 45N 22 25 E
Poindimié 106 20 56 S 165 20 E
Poinsett, C. 7 65 42 S 113 18 E
Point Edward 142 43 0N 82 30W
Point Pass 112 34 5 S 139 5 E
Point Pedro 81 9 50N 80 15 E
Point Pleasant, N.J., U.S.A. 151 40 5N 74 4W
Point Pleasant, W. Va., U.S.A. 148 38 50N 82 7W
Pointe-à-la Hache 153 29 35N 89 55W
Pointe-à-Pitre 163 16 10N 61 30W
Pointe Noire 133 4 48 S 11 53 E
Poirino 42 44 55N 7 50 E
Poisonbush Ra. 108 22 30 S 121 30 E
Poissy 19 48 55N 2 2 E
Poitiers 18 46 35N 0 20 E
Poitou 20 46 40N 0 10W
Poitou, Seuil du 20 46 30N 0 1W
Poix de Picardie 19 49 47N 2 0 E
Poix-Terron 19 49 38N 4 38 E
Pojoaque Valley 157 35 55N 106 0W
Pokataroo 111 29 30 S 148 36 E
Poko, Sudan 125 5 41N 31 55 E
Poko, Zaïre 130 3 7N 26 52 E
Pokrov 59 55 55N 39 7 E
Pokrovka 63 42 20N 78 0 E
Pokrovsk 65 61 29N 126 12 E
Pokrovsk-Uralskiy 62 60 10N 59 49 E
Pol 34 43 9N 7 20W
Pola = Pula 43 44 54N 13 57 E
Pola de Allande 34 43 16N 6 37W
Pola de Gordón, La 34 42 51N 5 41W
Pola de Lena 34 43 10N 5 49W
Pola de Siero 34 43 24N 5 39W
Pola de Somiedo 34 43 5N 6 15W
Polacca 157 35 55N 110 25W
Polan 73 25 30N 61 10 E
Poland ■ 32 52 0N 20 0 E
Polanów 32 54 7N 16 41 E
Polar Sub-Glacial Basin 7 85 0 S 110 0 E
Polcura 174 37 17 S 71 43W
Polcyn Zdrój 32 53 47N 16 5 E
Polden Hills 13 51 7N 2 50W
Polemi 70 34 54N 32 30 E
Polessk 58 54 50N 21 8 E
Polesye 58 52 0N 28 10 E
Polevskoy 62 56 26N 60 11 E
Polewali 87 3 21 S 119 23 E
Polgar 31 47 54N 21 6 E
Pŏlgyo-ri 95 34 51N 127 21 E
Poli 132 8 34N 13 15 E
Políaigos 49 36 45N 24 38 E
Policastro, G. di 45 39 55N 15 35 E
Police 32 53 33N 14 33 E
Polička 31 49 43N 16 15 E
Polignano a Mare 45 41 0N 17 12 E
Poligny 19 46 50N 5 42 E
Políkhnitas 49 39 4N 26 10 E
Polillo 90 14 43N 121 56 E
Polillo Is. 90 14 56N 122 0 E
Polillo Strait 90 14 44N 121 51 E
Polis 70 35 2N 32 26 E
Polístena 45 38 25N 16 4 E
Políyiros 48 40 23N 23 25 E
Polk 150 41 22N 79 57W
Polkowice 32 51 29N 16 3 E
Polla 45 40 31N 15 27 E
Pollachi 81 10 35N 77 0 E
Pollensa 36 39 54N 3 1 E
Pollensa, B. de 36 39 53N 3 8 E
Póllica 45 40 13N 15 3 E
Pollino, Mte. 45 39 54N 16 13 E
Pollock 152 45 58N 100 18W
Polna 58 58 31N 28 0 E
Polnovat 64 63 50N 65 54 E
Polo, Ill., U.S.A. 154 41 59N 89 38W
Polo, Mo., U.S.A. 154 39 33N 94 3W
Pologi 60 47 29N 36 15 E
Polonnoye 58 50 6N 27 30 E
Polotsk 58 55 30N 28 50 E
Polski Trŭmbesh 47 43 20N 25 38 E
Polsko Kosovo 47 43 23N 25 38 E
Polson 156 47 45N 114 12W
Poltava 60 49 35N 34 35 E
Polunochnoye 56 60 52N 60 25 E
Polur 81 12 32N 79 11 E
Polyanovgrad 47 42 39N 26 59 E
Polyarny 56 69 8N 33 20 E
Polynesia 105 10 0 S 162 0W
Pomarance 42 43 18N 10 51 E
Pomarico 45 40 31N 16 33 E
Pomaro 160 18 20N 103 18W
Pombal, Brazil 170 6 45 S 37 50W
Pombal, Portugal 34 39 55N 8 40W
Pómbia 49 35 0N 24 51 E
Pomeroy, Ohio, U.S.A. 148 39 0N 82 0W
Pomeroy, Wash., U.S.A. 156 46 30N 117 33W
Pomio 107 5 32 S 151 33 E
Pomme de Terre, Res. 154 37 54N 93 19W
Pomona 159 34 2N 117 49W
Pomorie 47 42 32N 27 41 E
Pomoshnaya 60 48 13N 31 36 E
Pompano Beach 149 26 12N 80 6W
Pompei 45 40 45N 14 30 E
Pompey 19 48 46N 6 6 E
Pompeys Pillar 156 46 0N 108 0W
Ponape 104 6 55N 158 10 E
Ponask, L. 142 54 0N 92 41W
Ponass L. 145 52 16N 103 58W
Ponca 152 42 38N 96 41W
Ponca City 153 36 40N 97 5W

Pucka, Zatoka

Portuguese Timor ■ =
  Timor **87** 9 0 S 125 0 E
Portumna **15** 53 5N 8 12W
Portville **150** 42 3N 78 21W
Porvenir, Bolivia **172** 11 10 S 68 50W
Porvenir, Chile **176** 53 10 S 70 16W
Porvoo **55** 60 24N 25 40 E
Porzuna **35** 39 9N 4 9W
Posada → **44** 40 40N 9 45 E
Posadas, Argentina **175** 27 30 S 55 50W
Posadas, Spain **35** 37 47N 5 11W
Poschiavo **29** 46 19N 10 4 E
Posets **36** 42 39N 0 25 E
Poseyville **155** 38 10N 87 47W
Poshan = Boshan **95** 36 28N 117 49 E
Posht-e-Badam **73** 33 2N 55 23 E
Posídhion, Ákra **48** 39 57N 23 30 E
Posidium **49** 35 30N 27 10 E
Poso **87** 1 20 S 120 55 E
Posoegroenoe **169** 4 23N 55 43W
Posong **95** 34 46N 127 5 E
Posse **171** 14 4 S 46 18W
Possel **132** 5 5N 19 10 E
Possession I. **7** 72 4 S 172 0 E
Pössneck **26** 50 42N 11 34 E
Post **153** 33 13N 101 21W
Post Falls **156** 47 46N 116 59W
Postavy **58** 55 4N 26 50 E
Poste Maurice Cortier . **121** 22 14N 1 2 E
Postmasburg **134** 28 18 S 23 5 E
Postojna **43** 45 46N 14 12 E
Poston **159** 34 0N 114 24W
Postville **154** 43 5N 91 34W
Potamós, Andikíthira,
  Greece **49** 36 18N 22 58 E
Potamós, Kíthira,
  Greece **49** 36 15N 22 58 E
Potchefstroom **134** 26 41 S 27 7 E
Potcoava **50** 44 30N 24 39 E
Poté **171** 17 49 S 41 49W
Poteau **153** 35 5N 94 37W
Poteet **153** 29 4N 98 35W
Potelu, Lacul **50** 43 44N 24 20 E
Potenza **45** 40 40N 15 50 E
Potenza → **43** 43 27N 13 38 E
Potenza Picena **43** 43 22N 13 37 E
Poteriteri, L. **115** 46 5 S 167 10 E
Potes **34** 43 15N 4 42W
Potgietersrus **135** 24 10 S 28 55 E
Poti **61** 42 10N 41 38 E
Potiraguá **171** 15 36 S 39 53W
Potiskum **127** 11 39N 11 2 E
Potlogi **50** 44 34N 25 34 E
Potomac → **148** 38 0N 76 23W
Potosí, Bolivia **173** 19 38 S 65 50W
Potosi, U.S.A. **154** 37 56N 90 47W
Potosí □ **172** 20 31 S 67 0W
Potosi Mt. **159** 35 57N 115 29W
Pototan **91** 10 54N 122 38 E
Potrerillos **174** 26 30 S 69 30W
Potsdam, Germany **26** 52 23N 13 4 E
Potsdam, U.S.A. **151** 44 40N 74 59W
Potsdam □ **26** 52 40N 12 50 E
Pottenstein **27** 49 46N 11 25 E
Potter **152** 41 15N 103 20W
Pottery Hill = Abû
  Ballas **124** 24 26N 27 36 E
Pottstown **151** 40 17N 75 40W
Pottsville **151** 40 39N 76 12W
Pouancé **18** 47 44N 1 10W
Pouce Coupé **144** 55 40N 120 10W
Pouembout **106** 21 8 S 164 53 E
Poughkeepsie **151** 41 40N 73 57W
Pouilly-sur-Loire **19** 47 17N 2 57 E
Poulaphouca Res. **15** 53 8N 6 30W
Pouldu, Le **18** 47 41N 3 36W
Poulsbo **158** 47 45N 122 39W
Poum **106** 20 14 S 164 2 E
Poumadji **132** 5 56N 22 10 E
Pounga-Nganda **132** 2 58 S 10 51 E
Pourri, Mt. **21** 45 32N 6 52 E
Pouso Alegre,
  Mato Grosso, Brazil . **173** 11 46 S 57 16W
Pouso Alegre,
  Minas Gerais, Brazil . **175** 22 14 S 45 57W
Pouzauges **18** 46 47N 0 50W
Povenets **56** 62 50N 34 50 E
Poverty Bay **114** 38 43 S 178 2 E
Povlen **46** 44 9N 19 44 E
Póvoa de Lanhosa **34** 41 33N 8 15W
Póvoa de Varzim **34** 41 25N 8 46W
Povorino **59** 51 12N 42 5 E
Powassan **142** 46 5N 79 25W
Poway **159** 32 58N 117 2W
Powder → **152** 46 47N 105 12W
Powder River **156** 43 5N 107 0W
Powell **156** 44 45N 108 45W
Powell, L. **157** 37 25N 110 45W
Powell River **144** 49 50N 124 35W
Powers, Mich., U.S.A. **148** 45 40N 87 32W
Powers, Oreg., U.S.A. **156** 42 53N 124 2W
Powers Lake **152** 48 37N 102 38W
Powys □ **13** 52 20N 3 20W
Poxoreu **173** 15 50 S 54 23W
Poyang Hu **97** 29 5N 116 20 E
Poyarkovo **65** 49 36N 128 41 E
Poysdorf **31** 48 40N 16 37 E
Poza de la Sal **36** 42 35N 3 31W
Poza Rica **161** 20 33N 97 27W
Požarevac **46** 44 35N 21 18 E
Požega **46** 43 53N 20 2 E
Pozhva **62** 59 5N 56 5 E
Pozi **97** 23 30N 120 13 E
Poznań **32** 52 25N 16 55 E
Poznań □ **32** 52 50N 17 0 E
Pozo **159** 35 20N 120 24W
Pozo Alcón **37** 37 42N 2 56W
Pozo Almonte **172** 20 10 S 69 50W
Pozo Colorado **174** 23 30 S 58 45W
Pozo del Dátil **160** 30 0N 112 15W
Pozoblanco **35** 38 23N 4 51W
Pozorrubio **90** 16 7N 120 33 E
Pozuzo **172** 10 5 S 75 35W
Pozzallo **45** 36 44N 14 52 E
Pozzuoli **45** 40 46N 14 6 E
Pra → **127** 5 1N 1 37W
Prabuty **32** 53 47N 19 15 E
Prača **46** 43 47N 18 43 E
Prachatice **30** 49 1N 14 0 E
Prachin Buri **84** 14 0N 101 25 E
Prachuap Khiri Khan .. **85** 11 49N 99 48 E
Pradelles **20** 44 46N 3 52 E
Pradera **168** 3 25N 76 15W
Prades **20** 42 38N 2 23 E
Prado **171** 17 20 S 39 13W
Prado del Rey **35** 36 48N 5 33W
Præstø **52** 55 8N 12 2 E
Pragersko **43** 46 27N 15 42 E
Prague = Praha **30** 50 5N 14 22 E
Praha **30** 50 5N 14 22 E
Prahecq **20** 46 19N 0 26W
Prahita → **80** 19 0N 79 55 E
Prahova □ **50** 45 10N 26 0 E
Prahova → **50** 44 50N 25 50 E
Prahovo **46** 44 18N 22 39 E
Praid **50** 46 32N 25 10 E
Prainha, Amazonas,
  Brazil **173** 7 10 S 60 30W
Prainha, Pará, Brazil .. **169** 1 45 S 53 30W
Prairie **110** 20 50 S 144 35 E
Prairie → **153** 34 30N 99 23W
Prairie City **156** 44 27N 118 44W
Prairie du Chien **154** 43 1N 91 9W
Prairie du Rocher **154** 38 5N 90 6W
Pramánda **48** 39 32N 21 8 E
Pran Buri **84** 12 23N 99 55 E
Prang **127** 8 1N 0 56W
Prapat **86** 2 41N 98 58 E
Praszka **32** 51 5N 18 31 E
Prata **171** 19 25 S 48 54W
Pratapgarh **78** 24 2N 74 40 E
Prática di Mare **44** 41 40N 12 26 E
Prätigau **29** 46 56N 9 44 E
Prato **42** 43 53N 11 5 E
Prátola Peligna **43** 42 7N 13 51 E
Pratovécchio **43** 43 44N 11 43 E
Prats-de-Mollo-la-Preste **20** 42 25N 2 27 E
Pratt **153** 37 40N 98 45W
Pratteln **28** 47 31N 7 41 E
Prattville **149** 32 30N 86 28W
Pravara → **80** 19 35N 74 45 E
Pravdinsk **59** 56 29N 43 28 E
Pravia **34** 43 30N 6 12W
Praya **89** 8 39 S 116 17 E
Pré-en-Pail **18** 48 28N 0 12W
Pré St. Didier **42** 45 45N 7 0 E
Precordillera **174** 30 0 S 69 1W
Predáppio **43** 44 7N 11 58 E
Predazzo **43** 46 19N 11 37 E
Predejane **46** 42 51N 22 9 E
Preeceville **145** 51 57N 102 40W
Préfailles **18** 47 9N 2 11W
Pregonero **168** 8 1N 71 46W
Pregrada **43** 46 11N 15 45 E
Preko **43** 44 7N 15 14 E
Prelate **145** 50 51N 109 24W
Prelog **43** 46 18N 16 32 E
Premier **144** 56 4N 129 56W
Premont **153** 27 19N 98 8W
Premuda **43** 44 20N 14 36 E
Prenj **46** 43 33N 17 53 E
Prenjasi **48** 41 6N 20 32 E
Prentice **152** 45 31N 90 19W
Prenzlau **26** 53 19N 13 51 E
Preobrazheniye **98** 42 54N 133 54 E
Prepansko Jezero **46** 40 55N 21 0 E
Přerov **31** 49 28N 17 27 E
Presanella **42** 46 13N 10 40 E
Prescott, Canada **142** 44 45N 75 30W
Prescott, Ariz., U.S.A. **157** 34 35N 112 30W
Prescott, Ark., U.S.A. . **153** 33 49N 93 22W
Preservation Inlet **115** 46 8 S 166 35 E
Preševo **46** 42 19N 21 39 E
Presho **152** 43 56N 100 4W
Presicce **45** 39 53N 18 13 E
Presidencia de la Plaza . **174** 27 0 S 29 50W
Presidencia Roque Saenz
  Peña **174** 26 45 S 60 30W
Presidente Epitácio **171** 21 56 S 52 6W
Presidente Hayes □ **174** 24 0 S 59 0W
Presidente Hermes **173** 11 17 S 61 55W
Presidente Prudente **175** 22 5 S 51 25W
Presidente Roxas **91** 11 26N 122 56 E
Presidio, Mexico **160** 29 29N 104 23W
Presidio, U.S.A. **153** 29 30N 104 20W
Preslav **47** 43 10N 26 52 E
Preslavska Planina **47** 43 10N 26 45 E
Prešov **31** 49 0N 21 15 E
Prespa **47** 41 44N 24 55 E
Prespa, L. = Prepansko
  Jezero **46** 40 55N 21 0 E
Presque Isle **143** 46 40N 68 0W
Presseger See **30** 46 37N 13 26 E
Prestbury **13** 51 54N 2 2W
Prestea **126** 5 22N 2 7W
Presteigne **13** 52 17N 3 0W
Přeštice **30** 49 34N 13 20 E
Presto **173** 18 55 S 64 56W
Preston, Canada **150** 43 23N 80 21W
Preston, U.K. **12** 53 46N 2 42W
Preston, Idaho, U.S.A. **156** 42 10N 111 55W
Preston, Iowa, U.S.A. . **154** 42 6N 90 24W
Preston, Minn., U.S.A. **152** 43 39N 92 3W
Preston, Nev., U.S.A. . **156** 38 59N 115 2W
Preston, C. **108** 20 51 S 116 12 E
Prestonpans **14** 55 58N 3 0W
Prestwick **14** 55 30N 4 38W
Prêto →, Amazonas,
  Brazil **169** 0 8 S 64 6W
Prêto →, Bahia, Brazil **170** 11 21 S 43 52W
Prêto do Igapó-Açu → **169** 4 26 S 59 48W
Pretoria **135** 25 44 S 28 12 E
Preuilly-sur-Claise **18** 46 51N 0 56 E
Préveza **49** 38 57N 20 47 E
Préveza □ **48** 39 20N 20 40 E
Priazovskoye **60** 46 44N 35 40 E
Pribilof Is. **6** 56 0N 170 0W
Priboj **46** 43 35N 19 32 E
Příbram **30** 49 41N 14 2 E
Price **156** 39 40N 110 48W
Price I. **144** 52 23N 128 41W
Prichalnaya **61** 48 57N 44 33 E
Prichard **149** 30 47N 88 5W
Priego **36** 40 26N 2 21W
Priego de Córdoba **35** 37 27N 4 12W
Priekule **58** 57 27N 21 45 E
Prien **27** 47 52N 12 20 E
Prieska **134** 29 40 S 22 42 E
Priest L. **156** 48 30N 116 55W
Priest River **156** 48 11N 116 55W
Priest Valley **158** 36 10N 120 39W
Priestly **144** 54 8N 125 20W
Prieto Diaz **90** 13 2N 124 12 E
Prievidza **31** 48 46N 18 36 E
Prijedor **43** 44 58N 16 41 E
Prijepolje **46** 43 27N 19 40 E
Prikaspiyskaya
  Nizmennost **61** 47 0N 48 0 E
Prilep **46** 41 21N 21 37 E
Priluki **58** 50 30N 32 24 E
Prime Seal I. **110** 40 3 S 147 43 E
Primeira Cruz **170** 2 30 S 43 26W
Primorsko **47** 42 15N 27 44 E
Primorsko-Akhtarsk **60** 46 2N 38 10 E
Primorskoye **60** 47 10N 37 38 E
Primrose L. **145** 54 55N 109 45W
Prince Albert, Canada . **145** 53 15N 105 50W
Prince Albert, S. Africa **134** 33 12 S 22 2 E
Prince Albert Mts. **7** 76 0 S 161 30 E
Prince Albert Nat. Park **145** 54 0N 106 25W
Prince Albert Pen. **140** 72 30N 116 0W
Prince Albert Sd. **140** 70 25N 115 0W
Prince Alfred C. **6** 74 20N 124 40W
Prince Charles I. **141** 67 47N 76 12W
Prince Charles Mts. **7** 72 0 S 67 0 E
Prince Edward I. □ **143** 46 20N 63 20W
Prince Edward Is. **83** 46 35 S 38 0 E
Prince George **144** 53 55N 122 50W
Prince of Wales I.,
  Canada **140** 73 0N 99 0W
Prince of Wales I.,
  U.S.A. **140** 55 30N 133 0W
Prince of Wales Is. **110** 10 40 S 142 10 E
Prince Patrick I. **6** 77 0N 120 0W
Prince Regent Inlet **6** 73 0N 90 0W
Prince Rupert **144** 54 20N 130 20W
Princenhage **23** 51 9N 4 45 E
Princesa Isabel **170** 7 44 S 38 0W
Princess Charlotte B. **110** 14 25 S 144 0 E
Princess May Ranges **108** 15 30 S 125 30 E
Princess Royal I. **144** 53 0N 128 40W
Princeton, Canada **144** 49 27N 120 30W
Princeton, Calif., U.S.A. **158** 39 24N 122 1W
Princeton, Ill., U.S.A. . **154** 41 25N 89 25W
Princeton, Ind., U.S.A. **155** 38 20N 87 35W
Princeton, Ky., U.S.A. **148** 37 6N 87 55W
Princeton, Mo., U.S.A. **154** 40 23N 93 35W
Princeton, N.J., U.S.A. **151** 40 18N 74 40W
Princeton, W. Va.,
  U.S.A. **148** 37 21N 81 8W
Princeville **154** 40 56N 89 46W
Principe, I. de **116** 1 37N 7 27 E
Principe Chan. **144** 53 28N 130 0W
Principe da Beira **173** 12 20 S 64 30W
Prineville **156** 44 17N 120 50W
Prins Harald Kyst **7** 70 0 S 35 1 E
Prinsesse Astrid Kyst .. **7** 70 45 S 12 30 E
Prinsesse Ragnhild Kyst **7** 70 15 S 27 30 E
Prinzapolca **162** 13 20N 83 35W
Prior, C. **34** 43 34N 8 17W
Priozersk **56** 61 2N 30 7 E
Pripet = Pripyat → .. **58** 51 20N 30 9 E
Pripet Marshes =
  Polesye **58** 52 0N 28 10 E
Pripyat → **58** 51 20N 30 9 E
Pripyat Marshes =
  Polesye **58** 52 0N 28 10 E
Prislop, Pasul **50** 47 37N 25 15 E
Pristen **59** 51 15N 36 44 E
Priština **46** 42 40N 21 13 E
Pritzwalk **26** 53 10N 12 11 E
Privas **21** 44 45N 4 37 E
Priverno **44** 41 29N 13 10 E
Privolzhsk **59** 57 23N 41 16 E
Privolzhskaya
  Vozvyshennost **59** 51 0N 46 0 E
Privolzhskiy **59** 51 25N 46 3 E
Privolzhye **59** 52 52N 48 33 E
Priyutnoye **61** 46 12N 43 40 E
Prizren **46** 42 13N 20 45 E
Prizzi **44** 37 44N 13 24 E
Prnjavor **46** 44 52N 17 43 E
Probolinggo **89** 7 46 S 113 13 E
Prochowice **32** 51 17N 16 20 E
Procida **44** 40 46N 14 0 E
Proddatur **81** 14 45N 78 30 E
Proença-a-Nova **35** 39 45N 7 54W
Prof. Van Blommestein
  Meer **169** 4 45N 55 5W
Profondeville **23** 50 23N 4 52 E
Progreso **161** 21 20N 89 40W
Prokhladnyy **61** 43 50N 44 2 E
Prokletije **48** 42 30N 19 45 E
Prokopyevsk **64** 54 0N 86 45 E
Prokuplje **46** 43 16N 21 36 E
Proletarskaya **61** 46 42N 41 50 E
Prome = Pyè **82** 18 49N 95 13 E
Prophet → **144** 58 48N 122 40W
Prophetstown **154** 41 40N 89 56W
Propriá **170** 10 13 S 36 51W
Propriano **21** 41 41N 8 52 E
Proserpine **110** 20 21 S 148 36 E
Prosna **32** 51 1N 18 30 E
Prosperidad **91** 8 34N 125 52 E
Prosser **156** 46 11N 119 52W
Prostějov **31** 49 30N 17 9 E
Prostki **32** 53 42N 22 25 E
Proston **111** 26 8 S 151 32 E
Proszowice **32** 50 13N 20 16 E
Protection **153** 37 16N 99 30W
Próti **49** 37 5N 21 32 E
Provadiya **47** 43 12N 27 30 E
Proven **23** 50 54N 2 40 E
Provence **21** 43 40N 5 46 E
Providence, Ky., U.S.A. **148** 37 25N 87 46W
Providence, R.I.,
  U.S.A. **151** 41 50N 71 28W
Providence Bay **142** 45 41N 82 15W
Providence C. **115** 45 59 S 166 29 E
Providence Mts. **157** 35 0N 115 30W
Providencia **168** 0 28 S 76 28W
Providencia, I. de **162** 13 25N 81 26W
Provideniya **65** 64 23N 173 18W
Provins **19** 48 33N 3 15 E
Provo **156** 40 16N 111 37W
Provost **145** 52 25N 110 20W
Prozor **46** 43 50N 17 34 E
Prudentópolis **171** 25 12 S 50 57W
Prud'homme **145** 52 20N 105 54W
Prudnik **32** 50 20N 17 38 E
Prüm **27** 50 14N 6 22 E
Pruszcz Gd. **32** 54 17N 18 40 E
Pruszków **32** 52 9N 20 49 E
Prut → **50** 45 28N 28 10 E
Pruzhany **58** 52 33N 24 28 E
Prvič **43** 44 55N 14 47 E
Prydz B. **7** 69 0 S 74 0 E
Pryor **153** 36 17N 95 20W
Przasnysz **32** 53 2N 20 45 E
Przedbórz **32** 51 6N 19 53 E
Przedecz **32** 52 20N 18 53 E
Przemysl **32** 49 50N 22 45 E
Przeworsk **32** 50 6N 22 32 E
Przewóz **32** 51 28N 14 57 E
Przhevalsk **63** 42 30N 78 20 E
Przysuchla **32** 51 22N 20 38 E
Psakhná **49** 38 34N 23 35 E
Psará **49** 38 37N 25 38 E
Psathoúra **48** 39 30N 24 12 E
Psel → **60** 49 5N 33 20 E
Pserimos **49** 36 56N 27 12 E
Pskem → **63** 41 38N 70 1 E
Pskemskiy Khrebet **63** 42 0N 70 45 E
Pskent **63** 40 54N 69 20 E
Pskov **58** 57 50N 28 25 E
Psunj **46** 45 25N 17 19 E
Pszczyna **32** 49 59N 18 58 E
Pteleón **49** 39 3N 22 57 E
Ptich → **58** 52 9N 28 52 E
Ptolemaís **48** 40 30N 21 43 E
Ptuj **43** 46 28N 15 50 E
Ptujska Gora **43** 46 23N 15 47 E
Pu Xian **94** 36 24N 111 6 E
Pua **84** 19 11N 100 55 E
Puán, Argentina **174** 37 30 S 62 45W
Pu'an, China **96** 25 46N 104 57 E
Puan, S. Korea **95** 35 44N 126 44 E
Pubei **96** 22 16N 109 31 E
Pucacuro → **168** 3 20 S 74 58W
Pucallpa **172** 8 25 S 74 30W
Pucará, Bolivia **173** 18 43 S 64 11W
Pucará, Peru **172** 15 5 S 70 24W
Pucarani **172** 16 23 S 68 30W
Pucheng **97** 27 59N 118 31 E
Pucheni **50** 45 12N 25 17 E
Pucio Pt. **91** 11 46N 121 51 E
Pučišće **43** 43 22N 16 43 E
Puck **32** 54 45N 18 23 E
Pucka, Zatoka **32** 54 30N 18 40 E

Ramanetaka, B. de

Qinglong **96** 25 49N 105 12 E
Qingping **96** 26 39N 107 47 E
Qingpu **97** 31 10N 121 6 E
Qingshui **94** 34 48N 106 8 E
Qingshuihe **94** 39 55N 111 35 E
Qingtian **97** 28 12N 120 15 E
Qingtongxia Shuiku **94** 37 50N 105 58 E
Qingxi **96** 27 8N 108 43 E
Qingxu **94** 37 34N 112 22 E
Qingyang, Anhui, China **97** 30 38N 117 50 E
Qingyang, Gansu, China **94** 36 2N 107 55 E
Qingyi Jiang → **96** 29 32N 103 44 E
Qingyuan, Guangdong, China **97** 23 40N 112 59 E
Qingyuan, Liaoning, China **95** 42 10N 124 55 E
Qingyuan, Zhejiang, China **97** 27 36N 119 3 E
Qingyun **95** 37 45N 117 20 E
Qingzhen **96** 26 31N 106 25 E
Qinhuangdao **95** 39 56N 119 30 E
Qinling Shandi **94** 33 50N 108 10 E
Qinshui **94** 35 40N 112 8 E
Qinyang **94** 35 7N 112 57 E
Qinyuan **94** 36 29N 112 20 E
Qinzhou **96** 21 58N 108 38 E
Qionghai **84** 19 15N 110 26 E
Qionglai **96** 30 25N 103 31 E
Qionglai Shan **96** 31 0N 102 30 E
Qiongshan **84** 19 51N 110 26 E
Qiongzhou Haixia **84** 20 10N 110 15 E
Qiqihar **93** 47 26N 124 0 E
Qiraîya, W. → **71** 30 27N 34 0 E
Qiryat 'Anavim **69** 31 49N 35 7 E
Qiryat Ata **69** 32 47N 35 6 E
Qiryat Bialik **69** 32 50N 35 5 E
Qiryat Gat **69** 31 32N 34 46 E
Qiryat Ḥayyim **69** 32 49N 35 4 E
Qiryat Mal'akhi **69** 31 44N 34 44 E
Qiryat Shemona **69** 33 13N 35 35 E
Qiryat Yam **69** 32 51N 35 4 E
Qishan, China **94** 34 25N 107 38 E
Qishan, Taiwan **97** 22 52N 120 25 E
Qishn **75** 15 26N 51 40 E
Qishon → **69** 32 49N 35 2 E
Qisrâyâ **70** 34 55N 36 26 E
Qitai **92** 44 2N 89 35 E
Qitbît, W. → **75** 19 15N 54 23 E
Qiubei **96** 24 2N 104 12 E
Qixia **95** 37 17N 120 52 E
Qiyang **97** 26 35N 111 50 E
Qojûr **72** 36 12N 47 55 E
Qom **73** 34 40N 51 0 E
Qomsheh **73** 32 0N 51 55 E
Qondûz **77** 36 50N 68 50 E
Qondûz □ **77** 36 50N 68 50 E
Qu Jiang → **96** 30 1N 106 24 E
Qu Xian, Sichuan, China **96** 30 48N 106 58 E
Qu Xian, Zhejiang, China **97** 28 57N 118 54 E
Quackenbrück **26** 52 40N 7 59 E
Quairading **109** 32 0 S 117 21 E
Quakertown **151** 40 27N 75 20W
Qualeup **109** 33 48 S 116 48 E
Quambatook **112** 35 49 S 143 34 E
Quambone **113** 30 57 S 147 53 E
Quan Long **85** 9 7N 105 8 E
Quanah **153** 34 20N 99 45W
Quandialla **113** 34 1 S 147 47 E
Quang Ngai **84** 15 13N 108 58 E
Quang Yen **84** 20 56N 106 52 E
Quannan **97** 24 45N 114 33 E
Quantock Hills **13** 51 8N 3 10W
Quanzhou, Fujian, China **97** 24 55N 118 34 E
Quanzhou, Guangxi Zhuangzu, China **97** 25 57N 111 5 E
Quaraí **174** 30 15 S 56 20W
Quarré-les-Tombes **19** 47 21N 4 0 E
Quartu Sant' Elena **44** 39 15N 9 10 E
Quartzsite **159** 33 44N 114 16W
Quatsino **144** 50 30N 127 40W
Quatsino Sd. **144** 50 25N 127 58W
Qubab = Mishmar Ayyalon **69** 31 52N 34 57 E
Qûchân **73** 37 10N 58 27 E
Queanbeyan **113** 35 17 S 149 14 E
Québec **143** 46 52N 71 13W
Québec □ **143** 50 0N 70 0W
Quedlinburg **26** 51 47N 11 9 E
Queen Alexandra Ra. **7** 85 0 S 170 0 E
Queen Charlotte **144** 53 15N 132 2W
Queen Charlotte Bay **176** 51 50 S 60 40W
Queen Charlotte Is. **144** 53 20N 132 10W
Queen Charlotte Sd. **115** 41 10 S 174 15 E
Queen Charlotte Str. **144** 51 0N 128 0W
Queen City **154** 40 25N 92 34W
Queen Elizabeth Is. **138** 76 0N 95 0W
Queen Elizabeth Nat. Park **130** 0 0 30 0 E
Queen Mary Land **7** 70 0 S 95 0 E
Queen Maud G. **140** 68 15N 102 30W
Queen Maud Mts. **7** 86 0 S 160 0W
Queens Chan. **108** 15 0 S 129 30 E
Queensland □ **110** 22 0 S 142 0 E
Queenstown, Australia **110** 42 4 S 145 35 E
Queenstown, N.Z. **115** 45 1 S 168 40 E
Queenstown, S. Africa **134** 31 52 S 26 52 E
Queets **158** 47 32N 124 20W
Queguay Grande → **174** 32 9 S 58 9W
Queimadas **170** 11 0 S 39 38W
Quela **133** 9 10 S 16 56 E
Quelimane **131** 17 53 S 36 58 E
Quelpart = Cheju Do **95** 33 29N 126 34 E
Quemado, N. Mex., U.S.A. **157** 34 17N 108 28W
Quemado, Tex., U.S.A. **153** 28 58N 100 35W
Quemú-Quemú **174** 36 3 S 63 36W
Quequén **174** 38 30 S 58 30W
Querco **172** 13 50 S 74 52W
Querétaro **160** 20 40N 100 23W
Querétaro □ **160** 20 30N 100 0W
Querfurt **26** 51 22N 11 33 E
Quesada **37** 37 51N 3 4W
Queshan **94** 32 55N 114 2 E
Quesnel **144** 53 0N 122 30W
Quesnel → **144** 52 58N 122 29W
Quesnel L. **144** 52 30N 121 20W
Quesnoy, Le **19** 50 15N 3 38 E
Questa **157** 36 45N 105 35W
Questembert **18** 47 40N 2 28W
Quetena **172** 22 10 S 67 25W
Quetico Prov. Park **142** 48 30N 91 45W
Quetrequile **176** 41 33 S 69 22W
Quetta **77** 30 15N 66 55 E
Quevedo **168** 1 2 S 79 29W
Quezaltenango **162** 14 50N 91 30W
Quezon □ **90** 14 40N 121 30 E
Quezon City **90** 14 38N 121 0 E
Qufār **72** 27 26N 41 37 E
Qui Nhon **84** 13 40N 109 13 E
Quiaca, La **174** 22 5 S 65 35W
Quibala **133** 10 46 S 14 59 E
Quibaxe **133** 8 24 S 14 27 E
Quibdo **168** 5 42N 76 40W
Quiberon **18** 47 29N 3 9W
Quíbor **168** 9 56N 69 37W
Quick **144** 54 36N 126 54W
Quickborn **26** 53 42N 9 52 E
Quiet L. **144** 61 5N 133 5W
Quiévrain **23** 50 24N 3 41 E
Quiindy **174** 25 58 S 57 14W
Quila **160** 24 23N 107 13W
Quilán, C. **176** 43 15 S 74 30W
Quilcene **158** 47 49N 122 53W
Quilengues **133** 14 12 S 14 12 E
Quilimarí **174** 32 5 S 71 30W
Quilino **174** 30 14 S 64 29W
Quillabamba **172** 12 50 S 72 50W
Quillacollo **172** 17 26 S 66 17W
Quillagua **174** 21 40 S 69 40W
Quillaicillo **174** 31 17 S 71 40W
Quillan **20** 42 53N 2 10 E
Quillebeuf-sur-Seine **18** 49 28N 0 30 E
Quillota **174** 32 54 S 71 16W
Quilmes **174** 34 43 S 58 15W
Quilon **81** 8 50N 76 38 E
Quilpie **111** 26 35 S 144 11 E
Quilpué **174** 33 5 S 71 33W
Quilua **131** 16 17 S 39 54 E
Quimbele **133** 6 17 S 16 41 E
Quimbonge **133** 8 36 S 18 30 E
Quime **172** 17 2 S 67 15W
Quimilí **174** 27 40 S 62 30W
Quimper **18** 48 0N 4 9W
Quimperlé **18** 47 53N 3 33W
Quinault → **158** 47 23N 124 18W
Quincemil **172** 13 15 S 70 40W
Quincy, Calif., U.S.A. **158** 39 56N 120 56W
Quincy, Fla., U.S.A. **149** 30 34N 84 34W
Quincy, Ill., U.S.A. **152** 39 55N 91 20W
Quincy, Mass., U.S.A. **151** 42 14N 71 0W
Quincy, Wash., U.S.A. **156** 47 22N 119 56W
Quines **174** 32 13 S 65 48W
Quinga **131** 15 49 S 40 15 E
Quingey **19** 47 7N 5 52 E
Quiniluban Group **91** 11 27N 120 48 E
Quintana de la Serena **35** 38 45N 5 40W
Quintana Roo □ **161** 19 0N 88 0W
Quintanar de la Orden **36** 39 36N 3 5W
Quintanar de la Sierra **36** 41 57N 2 55W
Quintanar del Rey **37** 39 21N 1 56W
Quintero **174** 32 45 S 71 30W
Quintin **18** 48 26N 2 56W
Quinto **36** 41 25N 0 32W
Quinyambie **111** 30 15 S 141 0 E
Quípar → **37** 38 15N 1 40W
Quipungo **133** 14 37 S 14 40 E
Quirihue **174** 36 15 S 72 35W
Quirimbo **133** 10 36 S 14 12 E
Quirindi **111** 31 28 S 150 40 E
Quirino □ **90** 16 15N 121 40 E
Quiriquire **168** 9 59N 63 13W
Quiroga **34** 42 28N 7 18W
Quiruvilca **172** 8 1 S 78 19W
Quissac **21** 43 55N 4 0 E
Quissanga **131** 12 24 S 40 28 E
Quitapa **133** 10 20 S 18 19 E
Quitilipi **174** 26 50 S 60 13W
Quitman, Ga., U.S.A. **149** 30 49N 83 35W
Quitman, Miss., U.S.A. **149** 32 2N 88 42W
Quitman, Tex., U.S.A. **153** 32 48N 95 25W
Quito **168** 0 15 S 78 35W
Quixadá **170** 4 55 S 39 0W
Quixaxe **131** 15 17 S 40 4 E
Quixeramobim **170** 5 12 S 39 17W
Quixinge **133** 9 52 S 14 23 E
Quizenga **133** 9 21 S 15 28 E
Qujing **96** 25 32N 103 41 E
Qul'ân, Jazâ'ir **124** 24 22N 35 31 E
Qumbu **135** 31 10 S 28 48 E
Qumrān **69** 31 43N 35 27 E
Quneitra **69** 33 7N 35 48 E
Qunfudh **75** 16 39N 49 33 E
Quoin I. **108** 14 54 S 129 32 E
Quoin Pt. **134** 34 46 S 19 37 E
Quondong **112** 33 6 S 140 18 E
Quorn **112** 32 25 S 138 0 E
Qurein **125** 13 30N 34 50 E
Qurnat as Sawdā' **70** 34 18N 36 6 E
Qûs **124** 25 55N 32 50 E
Qusaybah **72** 34 24N 40 59 E
Quṣay'ir **75** 14 55N 50 20 E
Quseir **124** 26 7N 34 16 E
Qūshchī **72** 37 59N 45 3 E
Qusrah **69** 32 5N 35 20 E
Quthing **135** 30 25 S 27 36 E
Qūṭīābād **73** 35 47N 48 30 E
Quwayq → **70** 36 20N 37 10 E
Quwo **94** 35 38N 111 25 E
Quyang **94** 38 35N 114 40 E
Quynh Nhai **84** 21 49N 103 33 E
Quzi **94** 36 20N 107 20 E
Qytet Stalin **48** 40 47N 19 57 E

R

Ra, Ko **85** 9 13N 98 16 E
Råå **52** 56 0N 12 45 E
Raab **30** 48 21N 13 39 E
Raahe **54** 64 40N 24 28 E
Raalte **22** 52 23N 6 16 E
Raamsdonksveer **23** 51 43N 4 52 E
Ra'ananna **69** 32 12N 34 52 E
Raasay **14** 57 25N 6 4W
Raasay, Sd. of **14** 57 30N 6 8W
Rab **43** 44 45N 14 45 E
Raba **87** 8 36 S 118 55 E
Rába →, Hungary **32** 47 38N 17 38 E
Raba →, Poland **31** 50 8N 20 30 E
Rabaçal → **34** 41 30N 7 12W
Rabah **127** 13 5N 5 30 E
Rabai **130** 3 50 S 39 31 E
Rabaraba **107** 9 58 S 149 49 E
Rabastens **20** 43 50N 1 43 E
Rabastens-de-Bigorre **20** 43 23N 0 9 E
Rabat, Malta **40** 35 53N 14 25 E
Rabat, Morocco **120** 34 2N 6 48W
Rabaul **107** 4 24 S 152 18 E
Rabbit → **144** 59 41N 127 12W
Rabbit Lake **145** 53 8N 107 46W
Rabbitskin → **144** 61 47N 120 42W
Râbigh **74** 22 50N 39 5 E
Rabka **32** 49 37N 19 59 E
Râbor **73** 29 17N 56 55 E
Rača **46** 44 14N 21 0 E
Răcale **45** 39 57N 18 6 E
Racalmuto **44** 37 25N 13 41 E
Răcăşdia **46** 44 59N 21 36 E
Racconigi **42** 44 47N 7 41 E
Raccoon → **154** 41 35N 93 37W
Raccoon Cr. → **155** 39 47N 87 23W
Race, C. **143** 46 40N 53 5W
Rach Gia **85** 10 5N 105 5 E
Raciąż **32** 52 46N 20 10 E
Racibórz **32** 50 7N 18 18 E
Racine **155** 42 41N 87 51W
Rackerby **158** 39 26N 121 22W
Radama, Nosy **135** 14 0 S 47 47 E
Radama, Saikanosy **135** 14 16 S 47 53 E
Radan **46** 42 59N 21 29 E
Rădăuţi **50** 47 50N 25 59 E
Radbuza → **30** 49 35N 13 5 E
Radcliff **155** 37 51N 85 57W
Råde **51** 59 21N 10 53 E
Radeburg **26** 51 6N 13 55 E
Radeče **43** 46 5N 15 14 E
Radekhov **58** 50 25N 24 32 E
Radew → **32** 54 2N 15 52 E
Radford **148** 37 8N 80 32W
Radhanpur **78** 23 50N 71 38 E
Radiska → **46** 41 38N 20 37 E
Radisson **145** 52 30N 107 20W
Radium Hot Springs **144** 50 35N 116 2W
Radków **32** 50 30N 16 24 E
Radlin **32** 50 3N 18 29 E
Radna **46** 46 7N 21 41 E
Radnevo **47** 42 17N 25 58 E
Radnice **30** 49 51N 13 35 E
Radnor Forest **13** 52 17N 3 10W
Radolfzell **27** 47 44N 8 58 E
Radom **32** 51 23N 21 12 E
Radom □ **32** 51 30N 21 0 E
Radomir **46** 42 37N 23 4 E
Radomka → **32** 51 31N 21 11 E
Radomsko **32** 51 5N 19 28 E
Radomyshl **58** 50 30N 29 12 E
Radomysl Wielki **32** 50 14N 21 15 E
Radoszyce **32** 51 4N 20 15 E
Radoviš **46** 41 38N 22 28 E
Radovljica **43** 46 22N 14 12 E
Radstadt **30** 47 24N 13 28 E
Radstock **13** 51 17N 2 25W
Radstock, C. **111** 33 12 S 134 20 E
Răducăneni **50** 46 58N 27 54 E
Raduša **46** 42 7N 21 15 E
Radviliškis **58** 55 49N 23 33 E
Radville **145** 49 30N 104 15W
Radymno **32** 49 59N 22 52 E
Radzanów **32** 52 56N 20 8 E
Radziejów **32** 52 40N 18 30 E
Radzymin **32** 52 25N 21 11 E
Radzyń Chełmiński **32** 53 23N 18 55 E
Radzyń Podlaski **32** 51 47N 22 37 E
Rae **144** 62 50N 116 3W
Rae Bareli **79** 26 18N 81 20 E
Rae Isthmus **141** 66 40N 87 30W
Raeren **23** 50 41N 6 7 E
Raeside, L. **109** 29 20 S 122 0 E
Raetihi **114** 39 25 S 175 17 E
Rafaela **174** 31 10 S 61 30W
Rafah **71** 31 18N 34 14 E
Rafai **130** 4 59N 23 58 E
Raffadali **44** 37 23N 13 29 E
Rafḩā **72** 29 35N 43 35 E
Rafsanjān **73** 30 30N 56 5 E
Raft Pt. **108** 16 4 S 124 26 E
Ragag **125** 10 59N 24 40 E
Ragang, Mt. **91** 7 43N 124 32 E
Ragay **90** 13 49N 122 47 E
Ragay G. **90** 13 30N 122 45 E
Ragged Mt. **109** 33 27 S 123 25 E
Raglan, Australia **110** 23 42 S 150 49 E
Raglan, N.Z. **114** 37 55 S 174 55 E
Ragunda **52** 63 6N 16 23 E
Ragusa **45** 36 56N 14 42 E
Raha **87** 4 55 S 123 0 E
Rahad, Nahr ed → **125** 14 28N 33 31 E
Rahad al Bardī **123** 11 20N 23 40 E
Rahaeng = Tak **84** 16 52N 99 8 E
Rahden **26** 52 26N 8 36 E
Raheita **125** 12 46N 43 4 E
Raḩīmah **73** 26 42N 50 4 E
Rahimyar Khan **77** 28 30N 70 25 E
Rāhjerd **73** 34 22N 50 22 E
Rahotu **114** 39 20 S 173 49 E
Raichur **81** 16 10N 77 20 E
Raiganj **79** 25 37N 88 10 E
Raigarh **79** 21 56N 83 25 E
Raighar **80** 19 51N 82 6 E
Raijua **87** 10 37 S 121 36 E
Railton **110** 41 25 S 146 28 E
Rainbow **112** 35 55 S 142 0 E
Rainbow Lake **144** 58 30N 119 23W
Rainier **158** 46 4N 122 58W
Rainier, Mt. **158** 46 50N 121 50W
Rainy L. **145** 48 42N 93 10W
Rainy River **145** 48 43N 94 29W
Raipur **79** 21 17N 81 45 E
Raj Nandgaon **79** 21 5N 81 5 E
Raja, Ujung **88** 3 40N 96 25 E
Raja Ampat, Kepulauan **87** 0 30 S 130 0 E
Rajahmundry **80** 17 1N 81 48 E
Rajajooseppi **54** 68 28N 28 29 E
Rajang → **86** 2 30N 112 0 E
Rajapalaiyam **81** 9 25N 77 35 E
Rajasthan □ **78** 26 45N 73 30 E
Rajasthan Canal **78** 28 0N 72 0 E
Rajauri **79** 33 25N 74 21 E
Rajbari **82** 23 47N 89 41 E
Rajgarh, Mad. P., India **78** 24 2N 76 45 E
Rajgarh, Raj., India **78** 28 40N 75 25 E
Rajgród **32** 53 42N 22 42 E
Rajhenburg **43** 46 1N 15 29 E
Rajkot **78** 22 15N 70 56 E
Rajmahal Hills **79** 24 30N 87 30 E
Rajpipla **78** 21 50N 73 30 E
Rajpura **78** 30 25N 76 32 E
Rajshahi **82** 24 22N 88 39 E
Rajshahi □ **79** 25 0N 89 0 E
Rakaia **115** 43 45 S 172 1 E
Rakaia → **115** 43 36 S 172 15 E
Rakan, Ra's **75** 26 10N 51 20 E
Rakaposhi **79** 36 10N 74 25 E
Rakata, Pulau **88** 6 10 S 105 20 E
Rakhawt, W. → **75** 18 16N 51 50 E
Rakhneh-ye Jamshīdī **77** 34 22N 62 19 E
Rakhni **78** 30 4N 69 56 E
Rakhyūt **75** 16 44N 53 20 E
Rakitnoye **98** 45 36N 134 17 E
Rakitovo **47** 41 59N 24 5 E
Rakkestad **51** 59 25N 11 21 E
Rakoniewice **32** 52 10N 16 16 E
Rakops **134** 21 1 S 24 28 E
Rákospalota **31** 47 30N 19 5 E
Rakov **58** 53 58N 26 59 E
Rakovica **43** 44 59N 15 38 E
Rakovník **30** 50 6N 13 42 E
Rakovski **47** 42 21N 24 57 E
Rakvere **58** 59 30N 26 25 E
Raleigh **149** 35 47N 78 39W
Raleigh B. **149** 34 50N 76 15W
Ralja **46** 44 33N 20 34 E
Ralls **153** 33 40N 101 20W
Ram → **144** 62 1N 123 41W
Rām Allāh **69** 31 55N 35 10 E
Ram Hd. **113** 37 47 S 149 30 E
Rama, Israel **69** 32 56N 35 21 E
Rama, Nic. **162** 12 9N 84 15W
Ramacca **45** 37 24N 14 40 E
Ramachandrapuram **80** 16 50N 82 4 E
Ramales de la Victoria **36** 43 15N 3 28W
Ramalho, Serra do **171** 13 45 S 44 0W
Raman **85** 6 29N 101 18 E
Ramanathapuram **81** 9 25N 78 55 E
Ramanetaka, B. de **135** 14 13 S 47 52 E

Ramas C.

Ramas C. 81 15 5N 73 55 E
Ramat Gan 69 32 4N 34 48 E
Ramat HaSharon 69 32 7N 34 50 E
Ramatlhabama 134 25 37 S 25 33 E
Ramban 79 33 14N 75 12 E
Rambervillers 19 48 20N 6 38 E
Rambi 106 16 30 S 179 59W
Rambipuji 89 8 12 S 113 37 E
Rambla, La 35 37 37N 4 45W
Rambouillet 19 48 39N 1 50 E
Ramdurg 81 15 58N 75 22 E
Ramea 143 47 31N 57 23W
Ramechhap 79 27 25N 86 10 E
Ramelau 87 8 55 S 126 22 E
Ramenskoye 59 55 32N 38 15 E
Ramgarh, Bihar, India 79 23 40N 85 35 E
Ramgarh, Raj., India 78 27 16N 75 14 E
Ramgarh, Raj., India 78 27 30N 70 36 E
Rāmhormoz 73 31 15N 49 35 E
Ramīān 73 37 3N 55 16 E
Ramla 69 31 55N 34 52 E
Ramlat Zalṭan 122 28 30N 19 30 E
Ramlu 125 13 32N 41 40 E
Ramme 53 56 30N 8 11 E
Rammūn 69 31 55N 35 17 E
Ramnad = Ramanathapuram 81 9 25N 78 55 E
Ramnagar 79 32 47N 75 18 E
Ramnäs 52 59 46N 16 12 E
Ramon 59 51 55N 39 21 E
Ramon, Har 69 30 30N 34 38 E
Ramona 159 33 1N 116 56W
Ramore 142 48 30N 80 25W
Ramotswa 134 24 50 S 25 52 E
Rampart 140 65 0N 150 15W
Rampur, H.P., India 78 31 26N 77 43 E
Rampur, Mad. P., India 78 23 25N 73 53 E
Rampur, Orissa, India 79 21 48N 83 58 E
Rampur, Ut. P., India 79 28 50N 79 5 E
Rampur Hat 79 24 10N 87 50 E
Rampura 78 24 30N 75 27 E
Rāmsar 73 36 53N 50 41 E
Ramsel 23 51 2N 4 50 E
Ramsey, Canada 142 47 25N 82 20W
Ramsey, U.K. 12 54 20N 4 21W
Ramsey, U.S.A. 154 39 8N 89 7W
Ramsgate 13 51 20N 1 25 E
Ramshai 82 26 44N 88 51 E
Ramsjö 52 62 11N 15 37 E
Ramtek 79 21 20N 79 15 E
Ramu → 107 4 0 S 144 41 E
Ramvik 52 62 49N 17 51 E
Ranaghat 79 23 15N 88 35 E
Ranahu 78 25 55N 69 45 E
Ranau 86 6 2N 116 40 E
Rancagua 174 34 10 S 70 50W
Rance 23 50 9N 4 16 E
Rance → 18 48 34N 1 59W
Rance, Barrage de la 18 48 30N 2 3W
Rancharia 171 22 15 S 50 55W
Rancheria → 144 60 13N 129 7W
Ranchester 156 44 57N 107 12W
Ranchi 79 23 19N 85 27 E
Ranco, L. 176 40 15 S 72 25W
Rancu 50 44 32N 24 15 E
Rand 113 35 33 S 146 32 E
Randan 20 46 2N 3 21 E
Randazzo 45 37 53N 14 56 E
Randers 53 56 29N 10 1 E
Randers Fjord 53 56 37N 10 20 E
Randfontein 135 26 8 S 27 45 E
Randle 158 46 32N 121 57W
Randolph, Mass., U.S.A. 151 42 10N 71 3W
Randolph, N.Y., U.S.A. 150 42 10N 78 59W
Randolph, Utah, U.S.A. 156 41 43N 111 10W
Randolph, Vt., U.S.A. 151 43 55N 72 39W
Randsfjord 51 60 15N 10 25 E
Råne älv → 54 65 50N 22 20 E
Ranfurly 115 45 7 S 170 6 E
Rangae 85 6 19N 101 44 E
Rangamati 82 22 38N 92 12 E
Rangataua 114 39 26 S 175 28 E
Rangaunu B. 114 34 51 S 173 15 E
Rångedala 53 57 47N 13 9 E
Rangeley 151 44 58N 70 33W
Rangely 156 40 3N 108 53W
Ranger 153 32 30N 98 42W
Rangia 82 26 28N 91 38 E
Rangiora 115 43 19 S 172 36 E
Rangitaiki → 114 37 54 S 176 49 E
Rangitata → 115 43 45 S 171 15 E
Rangitikei → 114 40 17 S 175 15 E
Rangitoto Range 114 38 25 S 175 35 E
Rangkasbitung 88 6 21 S 106 15 E
Rangoon 82 16 45N 96 20 E
Rangpur 82 25 42N 89 22 E
Rangsang 88 1 20N 103 30 E
Rangsit 84 13 59N 100 37 E
Ranibennur 81 14 35N 75 30 E
Raniganj 79 23 40N 87 5 E
Ranippettai 81 12 56N 79 23 E
Rāniyah 72 36 15N 44 53 E
Ranken → 110 20 31 S 137 36 E
Rankin, Ill., U.S.A. 155 40 28N 87 54W
Rankin, Tex., U.S.A. 153 31 16N 101 56W
Rankin Inlet 140 62 30N 93 0W
Rankins Springs 113 33 49 S 146 14 E
Rannoch, L. 14 56 41N 4 20W
Rannoch Moor 14 56 38N 4 48W
Ranobe, Helodranon' i 135 23 3 S 43 33 E
Ranohira 135 22 29 S 45 24 E
Ranomafana, Toamasina, Madag. 135 18 57 S 48 50 E
Ranomafana, Toliara, Madag. 135 24 34 S 47 0 E
Ranong 85 9 56N 98 40 E
Rānsa 73 33 39N 48 18 E
Ransiki 87 1 30 S 134 10 E
Ransom 155 41 9N 88 39W
Rantau 89 2 56 S 115 9 E
Rantauprapat 88 2 15N 99 50 E
Rantekombola 87 3 15 S 119 57 E
Rantīs 69 32 4N 35 3 E
Rantoul 155 40 18N 88 10W
Ranum 53 56 54N 9 14 E
Ranyah, W. → 74 21 18N 43 20 E
Raon l'Étape 19 48 24N 6 50 E
Raoui, Erg er 121 29 0N 2 0W
Raoyang 94 38 15N 115 45 E
Rapa Iti 105 27 35 S 144 20W
Rapallo 42 44 21N 9 12 E
Rāpch 73 25 40N 59 15 E
Rapid → 144 59 15N 129 5W
Rapid City 152 44 0N 103 0W
Rapid River 148 45 55N 87 0W
Rapides des Joachims 142 46 13N 77 43W
Rapla 58 59 1N 24 52 E
Rapperswil 29 47 14N 8 45 E
Rapu Rapu I. 90 13 12N 124 9 E
Rarotonga 105 21 30 S 160 0W
Ra's al' Ayn 72 36 51N 40 4 E
Ra's al Khaymah 75 25 50N 56 5 E
Ra's al Qaşbah 71 28 2N 34 38 E
Ra's al-Unuf 122 30 25N 18 15 E
Ra's an Naqb 71 30 0N 35 29 E
Ras Bânâs 124 23 57N 35 59 E
Ras Dashen 125 13 8N 38 26 E
Ras el Ma 121 34 26N 0 50W
Ras Mallap 124 29 18N 32 50 E
Ra's Shamrah 70 35 35N 35 45 E
Râs Timirist 126 19 21N 16 30W
Rasa, Punta 176 40 50 S 62 15W
Rasca, Pta. de la 37 27 59N 16 41W
Raseiniai 58 55 25N 23 5 E
Rashad 125 11 55N 31 0 E
Rashîd 124 31 21N 30 22 E
Rashîd, Masabb 124 31 22N 30 17 E
Rasht 73 37 20N 49 40 E
Rasi Salai 84 15 20N 104 9 E
Rasipuram 81 11 30N 78 15 E
Raška 46 43 19N 20 39 E
Rason, L. 109 28 45 S 124 25 E
Raşova 50 44 15N 27 55 E
Rasovo 47 43 42N 23 17 E
Rasra 79 25 50N 83 50 E
Rass el Oued 121 35 57N 5 2 E
Rasskazovo 59 52 35N 41 50 E
Rastatt 27 48 50N 8 12 E
Rastu 50 43 53N 23 16 E
Raszków 32 51 43N 17 40 E
Rat Buri 84 13 30N 99 54 E
Rat Is. 140 51 50N 178 15 E
Rat River 144 61 7N 112 36W
Ratangarh 78 28 5N 74 35 E
Raţāwī 72 30 38N 47 13 E
Rath 79 25 36N 79 37 E
Rath Luirc 15 52 21N 8 40W
Rathbun Res. 154 40 49N 92 53W
Rathdrum 15 52 57N 6 13W
Rathedaung 82 20 29N 92 45 E
Rathenow 26 52 38N 12 23 E
Rathkeale 15 52 32N 8 57W
Rathlin I. 15 55 18N 6 14W
Rathlin O'Birne I. 15 54 40N 8 50W
Ratibor = Racibórz 32 50 7N 18 18 E
Rätikon 30 47 0N 9 55 E
Ratlam 78 23 20N 75 0 E
Ratnagiri 80 16 57N 73 18 E
Ratnapura 81 6 40N 80 20 E
Raton 153 37 0N 104 30W
Rattaphum 85 7 8N 100 16 E
Ratten 30 47 28N 15 44 E
Rattray Hd. 14 57 38N 1 50W
Rättvik 52 60 52N 15 7 E
Ratz, Mt. 144 57 23N 132 12W
Ratzeburg 26 53 41N 10 46 E
Raub 85 3 47N 101 52 E
Rauch 174 36 45 S 59 5W
Raufarhöfn 54 66 27N 15 57W
Raufoss 51 60 44N 10 37 E
Raukumara Ra. 114 38 5 S 177 55 E
Raul Soares 171 20 5 S 42 22W
Rauland 51 59 43N 8 0 E
Rauma 55 61 10N 21 30 E
Rauma → 51 62 34N 7 43 E
Raundal 51 60 40N 6 37 E
Raurkela 79 22 14N 84 50 E
Rausu-Dake 98 44 4N 145 7 E
Rava Russkaya 58 50 15N 23 42 E
Ravānsar 72 34 43N 46 40 E
Ravanusa 44 37 16N 13 58 E
Rāvar 73 31 20N 56 51 E
Ravels 23 51 22N 5 0 E
Ravena 151 42 28N 73 49W
Ravenna, Italy 43 44 28N 12 15 E
Ravenna, Ky., U.S.A. 155 37 42N 83 55W
Ravenna, Nebr., U.S.A. 152 41 3N 98 58W
Ravenna, Ohio, U.S.A. 150 41 11N 81 15W
Ravensburg 27 47 48N 9 38 E
Ravenshoe 110 17 37 S 145 29 E
Ravenstein 22 51 47N 5 39 E
Ravensthorpe 109 33 35 S 120 2 E
Ravenswood, Australia 110 20 6 S 146 54 E
Ravenswood, U.S.A. 148 38 58N 81 47W
Ravensworth 113 32 26 S 151 4 E
Ravenwood 154 40 23N 94 41W
Ravi → 78 30 35N 71 49 E
Ravna Gora 43 45 24N 14 50 E
Ravna Reka 46 43 59N 21 35 E
Rawa Mazowiecka 32 51 46N 20 12 E
Rawalpindi 77 33 38N 73 8 E
Rawāndūz 72 36 40N 44 30 E
Rawang 85 3 20N 101 35 E
Rawdon 142 46 3N 73 40W
Rawene 114 35 25 S 173 32 E
Rawicz 32 51 36N 16 52 E
Rawka → 32 52 9N 20 8 E
Rawlinna 109 30 58 S 125 28 E
Rawlins 156 41 50N 107 20W
Rawlinson Range 109 24 40 S 128 30 E
Rawson 176 43 15 S 65 0W
Ray 152 48 21N 103 6W
Ray, C. 143 47 33N 59 15W
Rayachoti 81 14 4N 78 50 E
Rayadurg 81 14 40N 76 50 E
Rayagada 80 19 15N 83 20 E
Raychikhinsk 65 49 46N 129 25 E
Rāyen 73 29 34N 57 26 E
Rayevskiy 62 54 4N 54 56 E
Raymond, Canada 144 49 30N 112 35W
Raymond, Calif., U.S.A. 158 37 13N 119 54W
Raymond, Ill., U.S.A. 154 39 19N 89 34W
Raymond, Wash., U.S.A. 158 46 45N 123 48W
Raymond Terrace 113 32 45 S 151 44 E
Raymondville 153 26 30N 97 50W
Raymore 145 51 25N 104 31W
Rayne 153 30 16N 92 16W
Rayón 160 29 43N 110 35W
Rayong 84 12 40N 101 20 E
Raytown 154 39 1N 94 28W
Rayville 153 32 30N 91 45W
Raz, Pte. du 18 48 2N 4 47W
Razan 73 35 23N 49 2 E
Ražana 46 44 6N 19 55 E
Ražanj 46 43 40N 21 31 E
Razdelna 47 43 13N 27 41 E
Razdel'naya 60 46 50N 30 2 E
Razdolnoye, R.S.F.S.R., U.S.S.R. 98 43 30N 131 52 E
Razdolnoye, Ukraine S.S.R., U.S.S.R. 60 45 46N 33 29 E
Razeh 73 32 47N 48 9 E
Razelm, Lacul 50 44 50N 29 0 E
Razgrad 47 43 33N 26 34 E
Razlog 47 41 53N 23 28 E
Razmak 77 32 45N 69 50 E
Razole 81 16 36N 81 48 E
Ré, I. de 20 46 12N 1 30W
Reading, U.K. 13 51 27N 0 57W
Reading, Mich., U.S.A. 155 41 50N 84 45W
Reading, Ohio, U.S.A. 155 39 13N 84 26W
Reading, Pa., U.S.A. 151 40 20N 75 53W
Real, Cordillera 172 17 0 S 67 10W
Realicó 174 35 0 S 64 15W
Réalmont 20 43 48N 2 10 E
Reata 160 26 8N 101 5W
Rebais 19 48 50N 3 10 E
Rebecca L. 109 30 0 S 122 15 E
Rebi 87 6 23 S 134 7 E
Rebiana 122 24 12N 22 10 E
Rebun-Tō 98 45 23N 141 2 E
Recanati 43 43 24N 13 32 E
Recaş 50 45 46N 21 30 E
Recherche, Arch. of the 109 34 15 S 122 50 E
Rechitsa 58 52 13N 30 15 E
Recht 23 50 20N 6 3 E
Recife 170 8 0 S 35 0W
Recklinghausen 26 51 36N 7 10 E
Reconquista 174 29 10 S 59 45W
Recreio 173 8 0 S 58 25W
Recreo 174 29 25 S 65 10W
Recuay 172 9 43 S 77 28W
Recz 32 53 16N 15 31 E
Red → = Hong → 84 20 17N 106 34 E
Red →, Canada 145 50 24N 96 48W
Red →, Minn., U.S.A. 152 48 10N 97 0W
Red →, Tex., U.S.A. 153 31 0N 91 40W
Red Bank 151 40 21N 74 4W
Red Bay 143 51 44N 56 25W
Red Bluff 156 40 11N 122 11W
Red Bluff L. 153 31 59N 103 58W
Red Bud 154 38 13N 90 0W
Red Cliffs 112 34 19 S 142 11 E
Red Cloud 152 40 8N 98 33W
Red Deer 144 52 20N 113 50W
Red Deer →, Alta., Canada 145 50 58N 110 0W
Red Deer →, Man., Canada 145 52 53N 101 1W
Red Deer L. 145 52 55N 101 20W
Red Indian L. 143 48 35N 57 0W
Red Lake 145 51 3N 93 49W
Red Lake Falls 152 47 54N 96 15W
Red Lodge 156 45 10N 109 10W
Red Mountain 159 35 22N 117 38W
Red Oak 152 41 0N 95 10W
Red Rock 142 48 55N 88 15W
Red Rock, L. 154 41 30N 93 15W
Red Rock's Pt. 109 32 13 S 127 32 E
Red Sea 68 25 0N 36 0 E
Red Slate Mt. 158 37 31N 118 52W
Red Sucker L. 145 54 9N 93 40W
Red Tower Pass = Turnu Rosu Pasul 50 45 33N 24 17 E
Red Wing 152 44 32N 92 35W
Reda 32 54 40N 18 19 E
Rédange 23 49 46N 5 52 E
Redbridge 13 51 35N 0 7 E
Redcar 12 54 37N 1 4W
Redcliff 145 50 10N 110 50W
Redcliffe 111 27 12 S 153 0 E
Redcliffe, Mt. 109 28 30 S 121 30 E
Reddersburg 134 29 41 S 26 10 E
Redding 156 40 30N 122 25W
Redditch 13 52 18N 1 57W
Redenção 170 4 13 S 38 43W
Redfield 152 45 0N 98 30W
Redkey 155 40 21N 85 9W
Redknife → 144 61 14N 119 22W
Redlands 159 34 0N 117 11W
Redmond, Australia 109 34 55 S 117 40 E
Redmond, Oreg., U.S.A. 156 44 19N 121 11W
Redmond, Wash., U.S.A. 158 47 40N 122 7W
Redon 18 47 40N 2 6W
Redonda 163 16 58N 62 19W
Redondela 34 42 15N 8 38W
Redondo 35 38 39N 7 37W
Redondo Beach 158 33 50N 118 23W
Redrock Pt. 144 62 11N 115 2W
Redruth 13 50 14N 5 14W
Redvers 145 49 35N 101 40W
Redwater 144 53 55N 113 6W
Redwood 151 44 18N 75 48W
Redwood City 158 37 30N 122 15W
Redwood Falls 152 44 30N 95 2W
Ree, L. 15 53 35N 8 0W
Reed, L. 145 54 38N 100 30W
Reed City 148 43 52N 85 30W
Reeder 152 46 7N 102 52W
Reedley 158 36 36N 119 27W
Reedsburg 152 43 34N 90 5W
Reedsport 156 43 45N 124 4W
Reedy Creek 112 36 58 S 140 2 E
Reefton, Australia 113 34 15 S 147 27 E
Reefton, N.Z. 115 42 6 S 171 51 E
Reftele 53 57 11N 13 35 E
Refugio 153 28 18N 97 17W
Rega → 32 54 10N 15 18 E
Regalbuto 45 37 40N 14 38 E
Regar 63 38 30N 68 14 E
Regavim 69 32 32N 35 2 E
Regen 27 48 58N 13 9 E
Regen → 27 49 2N 12 6 E
Regeneração 170 6 15 S 42 41W
Regensburg 27 49 1N 12 7 E
Regensdorf 29 47 26N 8 28 E
Réggio di Calábria 45 38 7N 15 38 E
Réggio nell' Emilia 42 44 42N 10 38 E
Regina, Canada 145 50 27N 104 35W
Régina, Fr. Gui. 169 4 19N 52 8W
Registro 175 24 29 S 47 49W
Reguengos de Monsaraz 35 38 25N 7 32W
Rehar → 79 23 55N 82 40 E
Rehoboth 134 23 15 S 17 4 E
Rehovot 69 31 54N 34 48 E
Rei-Bouba 132 8 40N 14 15 E
Reichenbach, Germany 26 50 36N 12 19 E
Reichenbach, Switz. 28 46 38N 7 42 E
Reid 109 30 49 S 128 26 E
Reid River 110 19 40 S 146 48 E
Reiden 28 47 14N 7 59 E
Reidsville 149 36 21N 79 40W
Reigate 13 51 14N 0 11W
Reillo 36 39 54N 1 53W
Reims 19 49 15N 4 1 E
Reina 69 32 43N 35 18 E
Reina Adelaida, Arch. 176 52 20 S 74 0W
Reinach, Aargau, Switz. 28 47 14N 8 11 E
Reinach, Basel, Switz. 28 47 29N 7 35 E
Reinbeck 154 42 18N 92 40W
Reindeer → 145 55 36N 103 11W
Reindeer I. 145 52 30N 98 0W
Reindeer L. 145 57 15N 102 15W
Reine, La 142 48 50N 79 30W
Reinga, C. 114 34 25 S 172 43 E
Reinosa 34 43 2N 4 15W
Reinosa, Paso 34 42 56N 4 10W
Reitdiep 22 53 20N 6 20 E
Reitz 135 27 48 S 28 29 E
Reivilo 134 27 36 S 24 8 E
Rejmyre 53 58 50N 15 55 E
Rejowiec Fabryczny 32 51 5N 23 17 E
Reka → 43 45 40N 14 0 E
Rekinniki 65 60 51N 163 40 E
Rekovac 46 43 51N 21 3 E
Reliance 145 63 0N 109 20W
Remad, Oued → 121 33 28N 1 20W
Rémalard 18 48 26N 0 47 E
Remanso 170 9 41 S 42 4W
Remarkable, Mt. 112 32 48 S 138 10 E
Rembang 89 6 42 S 111 21 E
Remchi 121 35 2N 1 26W
Remedios, Colombia 168 7 2N 74 41W
Remedios, Panama 162 8 15N 81 50W

Ripley

Remeshk 73 26 55N 58 50 E
Remetea 50 46 45N 25 29 E
Remich 23 49 32N 6 22 E
Remington 155 40 45N 87 8W
Rémire 169 4 53N 52 17W
Remiremont 19 48 0N 6 36 E
Remo 125 6 48N 41 20 E
Remontnoye 61 46 34N 43 37 E
Remoulins 21 43 55N 4 35 E
Remscheid 26 51 11N 7 12 E
Ren Xian 94 37 8N 114 40 E
Rena 51 61 8N 11 20 E
Rena → 51 61 8N 11 23 E
Renascença 168 3 50 S 66 21W
Rend L. 154 38 2N 88 58W
Rende 45 39 19N 16 11 E
Rendeux 23 50 14N 5 30 E
Rendína 49 39 4N 21 58 E
Rendsburg 26 54 18N 9 41 E
Rene 65 66 2N 179 25W
Renfrew, Canada 142 45 30N 76 40W
Renfrew, U.K. 14 55 52N 4 24W
Rengat 88 0 30 S 102 45 E
Rengo 174 34 24 S 70 50W
Renhua 97 25 5N 113 40 E
Renhuai 96 27 48N 106 24 E
Reni 60 45 28N 28 15 E
Renigunta 81 13 38N 79 30 E
Renk 125 11 50N 32 50 E
Renkum 22 51 58N 5 43 E
Renmark 112 34 11 S 140 43 E
Rennell Sd. 144 53 23N 132 35W
Renner Springs T.O. 110 18 20 S 133 47 E
Rennes 18 48 7N 1 41W
Rennes, Bassin de 18 48 0N 1 30W
Rennesøy 51 59 6N 5 43 E
Reno 158 39 30N 119 50W
Reno → 43 44 37N 12 17 E
Renovo 150 41 20N 77 47W
Renqiu 94 38 43N 116 5 E
Rensselaer, Ind., U.S.A. 155 40 57N 87 10W
Rensselaer, N.Y., U.S.A. 151 42 38N 73 41W
Rentería 36 43 19N 1 54W
Renton 158 47 30N 122 9W
Renwick 115 41 30 S 173 51 E
Réo 126 12 28N 2 35W
Réole, La 20 44 35N 0 1W
Reotipur 79 25 33N 83 45 E
Repalle 81 16 2N 80 45 E
Répcelak 31 47 24N 17 1 E
Republic, Mich., U.S.A. 148 46 25N 87 59W
Republic, Wash., U.S.A. 156 48 38N 118 42W
Republican → 152 39 3N 96 48W
Republican City 152 40 9N 99 20W
Republiek 169 5 30N 55 13W
Repulse B. 7 64 30 S 99 30 E
Repulse Bay 141 66 30N 86 30W
Requena, Peru 172 5 5 S 73 52W
Requena, Spain 37 39 30N 1 4W
Resele 52 63 20N 17 5 E
Resen 46 41 5N 21 0 E
Reserve, Canada 145 52 28N 102 39W
Reserve, U.S.A. 157 33 50N 108 54W
Resht = Rasht 73 37 20N 49 40 E
Resistencia 174 27 30 S 59 0W
Reşiţa 46 45 18N 21 53 E
Resko 32 53 47N 15 25 E
Resolution I., Canada 141 61 30N 65 0W
Resolution I., N.Z. 115 45 40 S 166 40 E
Resplandes 170 6 17 S 45 13W
Resplendor 171 19 20 S 41 15W
Ressano Garcia 135 25 25 S 32 0 E
Rest Downs 113 31 48 S 146 21 E
Restinga, La 37 27 38N 17 59W
Reston 145 49 33N 101 6W
Reszel 32 54 4N 21 10 E
Retalhuleu 162 14 33N 91 46W
Reteag 50 47 10N 24 0 E
Retenue, L. de 131 11 0 S 27 0 E
Rethel 19 49 30N 4 20 E
Rethem 26 52 47N 9 25 E
Réthímnon 49 35 18N 24 30 E
Réthímnon □ 49 35 23N 24 28 E
Retiche, Alpi 29 46 30N 10 0 E
Retie 23 51 16N 5 5 E
Retiers 18 47 55N 1 23W
Retortillo 34 40 48N 6 21W
Rétság 31 47 58N 19 10 E
Reuland 23 50 12N 6 8 E
Réunion 83 21 0 S 56 0 E
Reus 36 41 10N 1 5 E
Reusel 23 51 21N 5 9 E
Reuss → 29 47 16N 8 24 E
Reuterstadt Stavenhagen 26 53 41N 12 54 E
Reutlingen 27 48 28N 9 13 E
Reutte 30 47 29N 10 42 E
Reuver 23 51 17N 6 5 E
Reval = Tallinn 58 59 22N 24 48 E
Revda 62 56 48N 59 57 E
Revel 20 43 28N 2 0 E
Revelganj 79 25 50N 84 40 E
Revelstoke 144 51 0N 118 10W
Reventazón 172 6 10 S 80 58W
Revigny-sur-Ornain 19 48 49N 4 59 E
Revilla Gigedo, Is. 105 18 40N 112 0W
Revillagigedo I. 144 55 50N 131 20W
Revin 19 49 55N 4 39 E
Revolyutsii, Pix 63 38 31N 72 21 E
Revuè → 131 19 50 S 34 0 E
Rewa 79 24 33N 81 25 E
Rewa → 169 3 19N 58 42W
Rewari 78 28 15N 76 40 E
Rexburg 156 43 55N 111 50W
Rey 73 35 35N 51 25 E
Rey, Rio del → 127 4 30N 8 48 E
Rey Malabo 127 3 45N 8 50 E
Reyes 172 14 19 S 67 23W
Reyes, Pt. 158 37 59N 123 2W
Reyhanlı 70 36 16N 36 35 E
Reykjahlið 54 65 40N 16 55W
Reykjanes 54 63 48N 22 40W
Reykjavík 54 64 10N 21 57 E
Reynolds, Canada 145 49 40N 95 55W
Reynolds, U.S.A. 154 41 20N 90 40W
Reynolds Ra. 108 22 30 S 133 0 E
Reynoldsville 150 41 5N 78 58W
Reynosa 161 26 5N 98 18W
Rezekne 58 56 30N 27 17 E
Rezh 62 57 23N 61 24 E
Rezovo 47 42 0N 28 0 E
Rezvān 73 27 34N 56 6 E
Rgotina 46 44 1N 22 17 E
Rhamnus 49 38 12N 24 3 E
Rharis, O. → 121 26 0N 5 4 E
Rhayader 13 52 19N 3 30W
Rheden 22 52 0N 6 3 E
Rhein 145 51 25N 102 15W
Rhein → 26 51 52N 6 2 E
Rhein-Main-Donau-Kanal → 27 49 1N 11 27 E
Rheinbach 26 50 38N 6 54 E
Rheine 26 52 17N 7 25 E
Rheineck 29 47 28N 9 31 E
Rheinfelden 28 47 32N 7 47 E
Rheinland-Pfalz □ 27 50 0N 7 0 E
Rheinsberg 26 53 6N 12 52 E
Rheinwaldhorn 29 46 30N 9 3 E
Rhenen 22 51 58N 5 33 E
Rheriss, Oued → 121 30 50N 4 34W
Rheydt 26 51 10N 6 24 E
Rhin = Rhein → 26 51 52N 6 2 E
Rhinau 19 48 19N 7 43 E
Rhine = Rhein → 26 51 52N 6 2 E
Rhineland-Palatinate □ = Rheinland-Pfalz □ 27 50 0N 7 0 E
Rhinelander 152 45 38N 89 29W
Rhino Camp 130 3 0N 31 22 E
Rhir, Cap 120 30 38N 9 54W
Rhisnes 23 50 31N 4 48 E
Rho 42 45 31N 9 2 E
Rhode Island □ 151 41 38N 71 37W
Rhodes = Ródhos 49 36 15N 28 10 E
Rhodes' Tomb 131 20 30 S 28 30 E
Rhodesia = Zimbabwe ■ 131 19 0 S 30 0 E
Rhodope Mts. = Rhodopi Planina 47 41 40N 24 20 E
Rhodopi Planina 47 41 40N 24 20 E
Rhondda 13 51 39N 3 30W
Rhône □ 21 45 54N 4 35 E
Rhône → 21 43 28N 4 42 E
Rhum 14 57 0N 6 20W
Rhyl 12 53 19N 3 29W
Rhymney 13 51 32N 3 7W
Ri-Aba 127 3 28N 8 40 E
Riachão 170 7 20 S 46 37W
Riacho de Santana 171 13 37 S 42 57W
Rialma 171 15 18 S 49 34W
Riang 82 27 31N 92 56 E
Riaño 34 42 59N 5 0W
Rians 21 43 37N 5 44 E
Riansares → 36 39 32N 3 18W
Riasi 79 33 10N 74 50 E
Riau □ 86 0 0 102 35 E
Riau, Kepulauan 88 0 30N 104 20 E
Riaza 36 41 18N 3 30W
Riaza → 36 41 42N 3 55W
Riba de Saelices 36 40 55N 2 17W
Ribadavia 34 42 17N 8 8W
Ribadeo 34 43 35N 7 5W
Ribadesella 34 43 30N 5 7W
Ribamar 170 2 33 S 44 3W
Ribas 36 42 19N 2 15 E
Ribas do Rio Pardo 173 20 27 S 53 46W
Ribāţ 74 14 18N 44 15 E
Ribble → 12 54 13N 2 20W
Ribe 53 55 19N 8 44 E
Ribeauvillé 19 48 10N 7 20 E
Ribécourt 19 49 30N 2 55 E
Ribeira 34 42 36N 8 58W
Ribeira do Pombal 170 10 50 S 38 32W
Ribeirão Prêto 175 21 10 S 47 50W
Ribeiro Gonçalves 170 7 32 S 45 14W
Ribemont 19 49 47N 3 27 E
Ribera 44 37 30N 13 13 E
Ribérac 20 45 15N 0 20 E
Riberalta 173 11 0 S 66 0W
Ribnica 43 45 45N 14 45 E
Ribnitz-Damgarten 26 54 14N 12 24 E
Říčany 30 50 0N 14 40 E
Riccarton 115 43 32 S 172 37 E
Riccia 45 41 30N 14 50 E
Riccione 43 44 0N 12 39 E
Rice 159 34 5N 114 51W
Rice L. 150 44 12N 78 10W
Rice Lake 152 45 30N 91 42W
Riceys, Les 19 47 59N 4 22 E
Rich 120 32 16N 4 30W
Rich Hill 153 38 5N 94 22W
Richards Bay 135 28 48 S 32 6 E
Richards L. 145 59 10N 107 10W
Richardson → 145 58 25N 111 14W
Richardson Mts. 115 44 49 S 168 34 E
Richardson Springs 158 39 51N 121 46W
Richardton 152 46 56N 102 22W
Riche, C. 109 34 36 S 118 47 E
Richelieu 18 47 0N 0 20 E
Richey 152 47 42N 105 5W
Richfield, Idaho, U.S.A. 156 43 2N 114 5W
Richfield, Utah, U.S.A. 157 38 50N 112 0W
Richford 151 45 0N 72 40W
Richibucto 143 46 42N 64 54W
Richland, Ga., U.S.A. 149 32 7N 84 40W
Richland, Iowa, U.S.A. 154 41 13N 92 0W
Richland, Mo., U.S.A. 154 37 51N 92 26W
Richland, Oreg., U.S.A. 156 44 49N 117 9W
Richland, Wash., U.S.A. 156 46 15N 119 15W
Richland Center 152 43 21N 90 22W
Richlands 148 37 7N 81 49W
Richmond, N.S.W., Australia 113 33 35 S 150 42 E
Richmond, Queens., Australia 110 20 43 S 143 8 E
Richmond, N.Z. 115 41 20 S 173 12 E
Richmond, S. Africa 135 29 51 S 30 18 E
Richmond, N. Yorks., U.K. 12 54 24N 1 43W
Richmond, Surrey, U.K. 13 51 28N 0 18W
Richmond, Calif., U.S.A. 158 37 58N 122 21W
Richmond, Ind., U.S.A. 155 39 50N 84 50W
Richmond, Ky., U.S.A. 155 37 40N 84 20W
Richmond, Mich., U.S.A. 150 42 47N 82 45W
Richmond, Mo., U.S.A. 152 39 15N 93 58W
Richmond, Tex., U.S.A. 153 29 32N 95 42W
Richmond, Utah, U.S.A. 156 41 55N 111 48W
Richmond, Va., U.S.A. 148 37 33N 77 27W
Richmond, Mt. 115 41 32 S 173 22 E
Richmond Ra., Australia 111 29 0 S 152 45 E
Richmond Ra., N.Z. 115 41 32 S 173 22 E
Richterswil 29 47 13N 8 43 E
Richton 149 31 23N 88 58W
Richwood, Ohio, U.S.A. 155 40 26N 83 18W
Richwood, W. Va., U.S.A. 148 38 17N 80 32W
Ricla 36 41 31N 1 24W
Ricupe 133 14 37 S 21 25 E
Ridā' 74 14 25N 44 50 E
Riddarhyttan 52 59 49N 15 33 E
Ridderkerk 22 51 52N 4 35 E
Riddes 28 46 11N 7 14 E
Ridge Farm 155 39 54N 87 39W
Ridgecrest 159 35 37N 117 40W
Ridgedale 145 53 0N 104 10W
Ridgefield 158 45 49N 122 45W
Ridgeland 149 32 30N 80 58W
Ridgelands 110 23 16 S 150 17 E
Ridgetown 142 42 26N 81 52W
Ridgeville 155 40 18N 85 2W
Ridgewood 151 40 59N 74 7W
Ridgway, Ill., U.S.A. 155 37 48N 88 16W
Ridgway, Pa., U.S.A. 150 41 25N 78 43W
Riding Mt. Nat. Park 145 50 50N 100 0W
Ridley Mt. 109 33 12 S 122 7 E
Ried 30 48 14N 13 30 E
Riedlingen 27 48 9N 9 28 E
Riel 23 51 31N 5 1 E
Rienza → 43 46 49N 11 47 E
Riesa 26 51 19N 13 19 E
Riesco, I. 176 52 55 S 72 40W
Riesi 45 37 16N 14 4 E
Riet → 134 29 0 S 23 54 E
Rieti 43 42 23N 12 50 E
Rieupeyroux 20 44 19N 2 12 E
Riez 21 43 49N 6 6 E
Riffe, L. 158 46 30N 122 20W
Rifle 156 39 40N 107 50W
Rifstangi 54 66 32N 16 12W
Rift Valley □ 130 0 20N 36 0 E
Rig Rig 123 14 13N 14 25 E
Riga 58 56 53N 24 8 E
Riga, G. of = Rigas Jūras Līcis 58 57 40N 23 45 E
Rīgān 73 28 37N 58 58 E
Rīgas Jūras Līcis 58 57 40N 23 45 E
Rigaud 151 45 29N 74 18W
Rigby 156 43 41N 111 58W
Rīgestān □ 77 30 15N 65 0 E
Riggins 156 45 29N 116 26W
Rignac 20 44 25N 2 16 E
Rigolet 143 54 10N 58 23W
Riihimäki 55 60 45N 24 48 E
Riiser-Larsen-halvøya 7 68 0 S 35 0 E
Rijau 127 11 8N 5 17 E
Rijeka 43 45 20N 14 21 E
Rijeka Crnojevica 46 42 24N 19 1 E
Rijen 23 51 35N 4 55 E
Rijkevorsel 23 51 21N 4 46 E
Rijn → 22 52 12N 4 21 E
Rijnsberg 22 52 11N 4 27 E
Rijsbergen 23 51 31N 4 41 E
Rijssen 22 52 19N 6 30 E
Rijswijk 22 52 4N 4 22 E
Rikā', W. ar → 74 22 25N 44 50 E
Rike 125 10 50N 39 53 E
Rikuzentakada 98 39 0N 141 40 E
Rila 47 42 7N 23 7 E
Rila Planina 46 42 10N 23 0 E
Riley 156 43 35N 119 33W
Rima → 127 13 4N 5 10 E
Rimah, Wadi ar → 72 26 5N 41 30 E
Rimavská Sobota 31 48 22N 20 2 E
Rimbey 144 52 35N 114 15W
Rimbo 52 59 44N 18 21 E
Rimforsa 53 58 6N 15 43 E
Rimi 127 12 58N 7 43 E
Rímini 43 44 3N 12 33 E
Rîmna → 50 45 36N 27 3 E
Rîmnicu Sărat 50 45 26N 27 3 E
Rîmnicu Vîlcea 50 45 9N 24 21 E
Rimouski 143 48 27N 68 30W
Rimrock 158 46 38N 121 10W
Rinca 87 8 45 S 119 35 E
Rincón de Romos 160 22 14N 102 18W
Rinconada 174 22 26 S 66 10W
Rineanna 15 52 42N 85 7W
Ringarum 53 58 21N 16 26 E
Ringe 53 55 13N 10 28 E
Ringgold Is. 106 16 15 S 179 25W
Ringim 127 12 13N 9 10 E
Ringkøbing 53 56 5N 8 15 E
Ringling 156 46 16N 110 56W
Ringsaker 51 60 54N 10 45 E
Ringsjön 53 55 55N 13 30 E
Ringsted 52 55 25N 11 46 E
Ringvassøy 54 69 56N 19 15 E
Rinía 49 37 23N 25 13 E
Rinjani 89 8 24 S 116 28 E
Rinteln 26 52 11N 9 3 E
Río, Punta del 37 36 49N 2 24W
Rio Branco, Brazil 172 9 58 S 67 49W
Río Branco, Uruguay 175 32 40 S 53 40W
Rio Brilhante 175 21 48 S 54 33W
Río Bueno 176 40 19 S 72 58W
Río Chico 168 10 19N 65 59W
Rio Claro, Brazil 175 22 19 S 47 35W
Rio Claro, Trin. & Tob. 163 10 20N 61 25W
Río Colorado 176 39 0 S 64 0W
Río Cuarto 174 33 10 S 64 25W
Rio das Pedras 135 23 8 S 35 28 E
Rio de Contas 171 13 36 S 41 48W
Rio de Janeiro 175 23 0 S 43 12W
Rio de Janeiro □ 175 22 50 S 43 0W
Rio do Prado 171 16 35 S 40 34W
Rio do Sul 175 27 13 S 49 37W
Río Gallegos 176 51 35 S 69 15W
Río Grande, Argentina 176 53 50 S 67 45W
Río Grande, Bolivia 172 20 51 S 67 17W
Rio Grande, Brazil 175 32 0 S 52 20W
Río Grande, Mexico 160 23 50N 103 2W
Río Grande, Nic. 162 12 54N 83 33W
Rio Grande → 153 25 57N 97 9W
Rio Grande City 153 26 23N 98 49W
Río Grande del Norte → 146 26 0N 97 0W
Rio Grande do Norte □ 170 5 40 S 36 0W
Rio Grande do Sul □ 175 30 0 S 53 0W
Río Hato 162 8 22N 80 10W
Rio Lagartos 161 21 36N 88 10W
Rio Largo 170 9 28 S 35 50W
Rio Maior 35 39 19N 8 57W
Rio Marina 42 42 48N 10 25 E
Río Mayo 176 45 40 S 70 15W
Río Mulatos 172 19 40 S 66 50W
Río Muni = Mbini □ 132 1 30N 10 0 E
Rio Negro, Brazil 175 26 0 S 50 0W
Río Negro, Chile 176 40 47 S 73 14W
Rio Negro, Pantanal do 173 19 0 S 56 0W
Rio Pardo 175 30 0 S 52 30W
Río Pico 176 44 0 S 70 22W
Río Real 171 11 28 S 37 56W
Río Segundo 174 31 40 S 63 59W
Río Tercero 174 32 15 S 64 8W
Rio Tinto, Brazil 170 6 48 S 35 5W
Rio Tinto, Portugal 34 41 11N 8 34W
Rio Verde, Brazil 171 17 50 S 51 0W
Río Verde, Mexico 161 21 56N 99 59W
Rio Verde de Mato Grosso 173 18 56 S 54 52W
Rio Vista 158 38 11N 121 44W
Ríobamba 168 1 50 S 78 45W
Ríohacha 168 11 33N 72 55W
Rioja 172 6 11 S 77 5W
Rioja, La 174 29 20 S 67 0W
Rioja, La □, Argentina 174 29 30 S 67 0W
Rioja, La □, Spain 36 42 20N 2 20W
Riom 20 45 54N 3 7 E
Riom-ès-Montagnes 20 45 17N 2 39 E
Rion-des-Landes 20 43 55N 0 56W
Rionegro 168 6 9N 75 22W
Rionero in Vúlture 45 40 55N 15 40 E
Rioni → 61 42 5N 41 50 E
Rios 34 41 58N 7 16W
Riosucio, Caldas, Colombia 168 5 30N 75 40W
Ríosucio, Choco, Colombia 168 7 27N 77 7W
Riou L. 145 59 7N 106 25W
Rioz 19 47 26N 6 5 E
Riozinho → 168 2 55 S 67 7W
Riparia, Dora → 42 45 7N 7 24 E
Ripatransone 43 43 0N 13 45 E
Ripley, Canada 150 44 4N 81 35W
Ripley, Calif., U.S.A. 159 33 32N 114 39W
Ripley, N.Y., U.S.A. 150 42 16N 79 44W

Rzhev

Rosas .... 36 42 19N 3 10 E
Roscoe, Miss., U.S.A. . 154 37 58N 93 48W
Roscoe, S. Dak., U.S.A. 152 45 27N 99 20W
Roscoff 18 48 44N 4 0W
Roscommon, Ireland .. 15 53 38N 8 11W
Roscommon, U.S.A. .. 148 44 27N 84 35W
Roscommon □ 15 53 40N 8 15W
Roscrea 15 52 58N 7 50W
Rose → .... 110 14 16 S 135 45 E
Rose Blanche 143 47 38N 58 45W
Rose Harbour 144 52 15N 131 10W
Rose Pt. 144 54 11N 131 39W
Rose Valley 145 52 19N 103 49W
Roseau, Domin. 163 15 20N 61 24W
Roseau, U.S.A. 152 48 51N 95 46W
Rosebery .... 110 41 46 S 145 33 E
Rosebud, Australia .... 113 38 21 S 144 54 E
Rosebud, U.S.A. 153 31 5N 97 0W
Roseburg 156 43 10N 123 20W
Rosedale, Australia ... 110 24 38 S 151 53 E
Rosedale, U.S.A. 153 33 51N 91 0W
Rosée .... 23 50 14N 4 41 E
Roseland 158 38 25N 122 43W
Rosemary 144 50 46N 112 5W
Rosenberg 153 29 30N 95 48W
Rosendaël .... 19 51 3N 2 24 E
Rosendale 154 40 4N 94 51W
Rosenheim .... 27 47 51N 12 9 E
Roseto degli Abruzzi .. 43 42 40N 14 2 E
Rosetown 145 51 35N 107 59W
Rosetta = Rashîd ..... 124 31 21N 30 22 E
Roseville, Calif., U.S.A. 158 38 46N 121 17W
Roseville, Ill., U.S.A. . 154 40 44N 90 40W
Roseville, Mich., U.S.A. 155 42 30N 82 56W
Rosewood, N.S.W., Australia .... 113 35 38 S 147 52 E
Rosewood, N. Terr., Australia .... 108 16 28 S 128 58 E
Rosewood, Queens., Australia .... 111 27 38 S 152 36 E
Rosh Haniqra, Kefar .. 69 33 5N 35 5 E
Rosh Pinna .... 69 32 58N 35 32 E
Roshkhvār .... 73 34 58N 59 37 E
Rosières-en-Santerre ... 19 49 49N 2 42 E
Rosignano Marittimo .. 42 43 23N 10 28 E
Rosignol 169 6 15N 57 30W
Roşiori de Vede ...... 50 44 9N 25 0 E
Rositsa .... 47 43 57N 27 57 E
Rositsa → .... 47 43 10N 25 30 E
Roskilde .... 52 55 38N 12 3 E
Roskilde Amtskommune □ ... 52 55 35N 12 5 E
Roskilde Fjord .... 52 55 50N 12 2 E
Roslavl .... 58 53 57N 32 55 E
Roslyn .... 113 34 29 S 149 37 E
Rosmaninhal 35 39 44N 7 5W
Rosmead .... 134 31 29 S 25 8 E
Røsnæs .... 52 55 44N 10 55 E
Rosolini .... 45 36 49N 14 58 E
Rosporden 18 47 57N 3 50W
Ross, Australia .... 110 42 2 S 147 30 E
Ross, N.Z. .... 115 42 53 S 170 49 E
Ross Dependency □ ... 7 70 0 S 170 5W
Ross I. .... 7 77 30 S 168 0 E
Ross Ice Shelf .... 7 80 0 S 180 0 E
Ross L. 156 48 50N 121 5W
Ross on Wye 13 51 55N 2 34W
Ross Sea .... 7 74 0 S 178 0 E
Rossa .... 29 46 23N 9 8 E
Rossan Pt. 15 54 42N 8 47W
Rossano Cálabro ...... 45 39 36N 16 39 E
Rossburn 145 50 40N 100 49W
Rosseau 150 45 16N 79 39W
Rossel, C. .... 106 20 23 S 166 36 E
Rossford 155 41 36N 83 34W
Rossignol, L. 142 52 43N 73 40W
Rossignol Res. 143 44 12N 65 10W
Rossland 144 49 6N 117 50W
Rosslare 15 52 17N 6 23W
Rosslau .... 26 51 52N 12 15 E
Rosso 126 16 40N 15 45W
Rossosh .... 61 50 15N 39 28 E
Rossport 142 48 50N 87 30W
Rossum .... 22 51 48N 5 20 E
Røssvatnet .... 54 65 45N 14 5 E
Rossville, Australia .... 110 15 48 S 145 15 E
Rossville, U.S.A. 155 40 25N 86 35W
Rostāq .... 77 37 7N 69 49 E
Rosthern 145 52 40N 106 20W
Rostock .... 26 54 4N 12 9 E
Rostock □ .... 26 54 10N 12 30 E
Rostov, Don, U.S.S.R. 61 47 15N 39 45 E
Rostov, Moskva, U.S.S.R. .... 59 57 14N 39 25 E
Rostrenen 18 48 14N 3 21W
Roswell 153 33 26N 104 32W
Rosyth 14 56 2N 3 26W
Rota 35 36 37N 6 20W
Rotälven → .... 52 61 15N 14 3 E
Rotan 153 32 52N 100 30W
Rotem .... 23 51 3N 5 45 E
Rotenburg .... 26 53 6N 9 24 E
Roth .... 27 49 15N 11 6 E
Rothaargebirge .... 24 51 0N 8 20 E
Rothenburg .... 29 47 6N 8 16 E
Rothenburg ob der Tauber .... 27 49 21N 10 11 E
Rother → .... 13 50 59N 0 40 E
Rotherham 12 53 26N 1 21W
Rothes 14 57 31N 3 12W
Rothesay, Canada 143 45 23N 66 0W
Rothesay, U.K. 14 55 50N 5 3W
Rothrist .... 28 47 18N 7 54 E
Roti .... 87 10 50 S 123 0 E
Roto .... 113 33 0 S 145 30 E
Roto Aira L. .... 114 39 3 S 175 45 E
Rotoehu L. .... 114 38 1 S 176 32 E
Rotoiti L. .... 115 41 51 S 172 49 E
Rotoma L. .... 114 38 2 S 176 35 E
Rotondella .... 45 40 10N 16 30 E
Rotoroa, L. .... 115 41 55 S 172 39 E
Rotorua .... 114 38 9 S 176 16 E
Rotorua, L. .... 114 38 5 S 176 18 E
Rotselaar .... 23 50 57N 4 42 E
Rott → .... 27 48 26N 13 26 E
Rotten → .... 28 46 18N 7 36 E
Rottenburg .... 27 48 28N 8 56 E
Rottenmann .... 30 47 31N 14 22 E
Rotterdam .... 22 51 55N 4 30 E
Rottnest I. .... 109 32 0 S 115 27 E
Rottumeroog .... 22 53 33N 6 34 E
Rottweil .... 27 48 9N 8 38 E
Rotuma .... 104 12 25 S 177 5 E
Roubaix .... 19 50 40N 3 10 E
Roudnice .... 30 50 25N 14 15 E
Rouen .... 18 49 27N 1 4 E
Rough Ridge .... 115 45 10 S 169 55 E
Rouillac 20 45 47N 0 4W
Rouleau 145 50 10N 104 56W
Round Mt. .... 111 30 26 S 152 16 E
Round Mountain 156 38 46N 117 3W
Roundup 156 46 25N 108 35W
Roura 169 4 44N 52 20W
Rousay 14 59 10N 3 2W
Rouses Point 151 44 58N 73 22W
Roussillon, Isère, France 21 45 24N 4 49 E
Roussillon, Pyrénées-Or., France 20 42 30N 2 35 E
Roussin, C. .... 106 21 20 S 167 59 E
Rouveen .... 22 52 37N 6 11 E
Rouxville .... 134 30 25 S 26 50 E
Rouyn 142 48 20N 79 0W
Rovaniemi .... 54 66 29N 25 41 E
Rovato .... 42 45 34N 10 0 E
Rovenki .... 61 48 5N 39 21 E
Rovereto .... 42 45 53N 11 3 E
Rovigo .... 43 45 4N 11 48 E
Rovinari .... 50 44 56N 23 10 E
Rovinj .... 43 45 5N 13 40 E
Rovira 168 4 15N 75 20W
Rovno .... 58 50 40N 26 10 E
Rovnoye .... 59 50 52N 46 3 E
Rovuma → .... 131 10 29 S 40 28 E
Row'ān .... 73 35 8N 48 51 E
Rowena .... 111 29 48 S 148 55 E
Rowes .... 113 37 0 S 149 6 E
Rowley Shoals .... 108 17 30 S 119 0 E
Roxa 126 11 15N 15 45W
Roxas = Barbacan .... 91 10 20N 119 21 E
Roxas, Capiz, Phil. .... 91 11 36N 122 49 E
Roxas, Isabela, Phil. .. 90 17 8N 121 36 E
Roxas, Mindoro, Phil. . 90 12 35N 121 31 E
Roxboro 149 36 24N 78 59W
Roxborough Downs ... 110 22 30 S 138 45 E
Roxburgh .... 115 45 33 S 169 19 E
Roxen .... 53 58 30N 15 40 E
Roy, Mont., U.S.A. ... 156 47 17N 109 0W
Roy, N. Mex., U.S.A. . 153 35 57N 104 8W
Roy, Le, Ill., U.S.A. .. 155 40 21N 88 46W
Roy, Le, Kans., U.S.A. 153 38 8N 95 35W
Roy Hill .... 108 22 37 S 119 58 E
Roya, Peña 36 40 25N 0 40W
Royal Center 155 40 52N 86 30W
Royalla .... 113 35 30 S 149 9 E
Royan 20 45 37N 1 2W
Roye .... 19 49 42N 2 48 E
Røyken .... 51 59 45N 10 23 E
Rožaj .... 46 42 50N 20 15 E
Rózan .... 32 52 52N 21 25 E
Rozay-en-Brie .... 19 48 41N 2 58 E
Rozhishche .... 58 50 54N 25 15 E
Rǒžnava .... 31 48 37N 20 35 E
Rozogi .... 32 53 48N 21 9 E
Rozoy-sur-Serre ...... 19 49 40N 4 8 E
Rozwadów .... 32 50 37N 22 2 E
Rrësheni .... 48 41 47N 19 49 E
Rrogozhino .... 48 41 2N 19 50 E
Rtanj .... 46 43 45N 21 50 E
Rtishchevo .... 59 55 16N 43 50 E
Rúa 34 42 24N 7 6W
Ruacaná .... 133 17 20 S 14 12 E
Ruahine Ra. .... 114 39 55 S 176 2 E
Ruamahanga → ..... 114 41 24 S 175 8 E
Ruapehu .... 114 39 17 S 175 35 E
Ruapuke I. .... 115 46 46 S 168 31 E
Ruâq, W. → .... 71 30 0N 33 49 E
Ruatoria .... 114 37 55 S 178 20 E
Ruaus, Wadi → ..... 122 30 26N 15 24 E
Ruawai .... 114 36 8 S 173 59 E
Rub' al Khali .... 75 18 0N 48 0 E
Rubeho Mts. .... 130 6 50 S 36 25 E
Rubezhnoye .... 60 49 6N 38 25 E
Rubh a' Mhail 14 55 55N 6 10W
Rubha Hunish 14 57 42N 6 20W
Rubiataba .... 171 15 8 S 49 48W
Rubicon → 158 38 53N 121 4W
Rubicone → .... 43 44 8N 12 28 E
Rubinéia .... 171 20 13 S 51 2W
Rubino 126 6 4N 4 18W
Rubio 168 7 43N 72 22W
Rubtsovsk .... 64 51 30N 81 10 E
Ruby 140 64 40N 155 35W
Ruby L. 156 40 10N 115 28W
Ruby Mts. 156 40 30N 115 30W
Rucava .... 58 56 9N 21 12 E
Rucheng .... 97 25 33N 113 38 E
Ruciane-Nida .... 32 53 40N 21 32 E
Rud .... 51 60 1N 10 1 E
Rūd Sar .... 73 37 8N 50 18 E
Ruda .... 53 57 6N 16 7 E
Ruda Śląska .... 32 50 16N 18 50 E
Rudall .... 112 33 43 S 136 17 E
Rūdbār .... 77 30 9N 62 36 E
Ruden .... 26 54 13N 13 47 E
Rüdersdorf .... 26 52 28N 13 48 E
Rudewa .... 131 10 7 S 34 40 E
Rudkøbing .... 53 54 56N 10 41 E
Rudna .... 32 51 30N 16 17 E
Rudnichnyy .... 62 59 38N 52 26 E
Rudnik, Bulgaria ...... 47 42 36N 27 30 E
Rudnik, Poland .... 32 50 26N 22 15 E
Rudnik, Yugoslavia ... 46 44 7N 20 35 E
Rudnogorsk .... 65 57 15N 103 42 E
Rudnya .... 58 54 55N 31 7 E
Rudnyy .... 62 52 57N 63 7 E
Rudo .... 46 43 41N 19 23 E
Rudolf, Ostrov .... 64 81 45N 58 30 E
Rudolstadt .... 26 50 44N 11 20 E
Rudong .... 97 32 20N 121 12 E
Rudozem .... 47 41 29N 24 51 E
Rudyard 148 46 14N 84 35W
Rue .... 19 50 15N 1 40 E
Rue, La 155 40 35N 83 23W
Ruelle .... 20 45 41N 0 14 E
Rufa'a .... 125 14 44N 33 22 E
Ruffec .... 20 46 2N 0 12 E
Rufiji □ .... 130 8 0 S 38 30 E
Rufiji → .... 130 7 50 S 39 15 E
Rufino .... 174 34 20 S 62 50W
Rufisque 126 14 40N 17 15W
Rufunsa .... 131 15 4 S 29 34 E
Rugao .... 97 32 23N 120 31 E
Rugby, U.K. 13 52 23N 1 16W
Rugby, U.S.A. 152 48 21N 100 0W
Rügen .... 26 54 22N 13 25 E
Rugles .... 18 48 50N 0 40 E
Ruḫama .... 69 31 31N 34 43 E
Ruhea .... 82 26 10N 88 25 E
Ruhengeri .... 130 1 30 S 29 36 E
Ruhla .... 26 50 53N 10 21 E
Ruhland .... 26 51 27N 13 52 E
Ruhr → .... 26 51 25N 6 44 E
Ruhuhu → .... 131 10 31 S 34 34 E
Rui Barbosa .... 171 12 18 S 40 27W
Rui'an .... 97 27 47N 120 40 E
Ruichang .... 97 29 40N 115 39 E
Ruidosa 153 29 59N 104 39W
Ruidoso 157 33 19N 105 39W
Ruili .... 96 24 1N 97 43 E
Ruinen .... 22 52 46N 6 21 E
Ruinerwold .... 22 52 44N 6 15 E
Ruiten A Kanaal → .. 22 52 54N 7 8 E
Ruj .... 46 42 52N 22 42 E
Rujen .... 46 42 9N 22 30 E
Rujm Tal'at al Jamā'ah 71 30 24N 35 30 E
Ruk .... 78 27 50N 68 42 E
Rukwa □ .... 130 7 0 S 31 30 E
Rukwa L. .... 130 8 0 S 32 20 E
Rulhieres, C. .... 108 13 56 S 127 22 E
Rulles .... 23 49 43N 5 32 E
Rum Cay 162 23 40N 74 58W
Rum Jungle .... 108 13 0 S 130 59 E
Ruma .... 46 45 0N 19 50 E
Rumādah .... 74 13 34N 43 52 E
Rumāḥ .... 72 25 29N 47 10 E
Rumania = Romania ■ 50 46 0N 25 0 E
Rumaylah .... 72 30 47N 47 37 E
Rumaylah, 'Urūq ar ... 74 21 0N 47 30 E
Rumbalara .... 110 25 20 S 134 29 E
Rumbêk .... 125 6 54N 29 37 E
Rumbeke .... 23 50 56N 3 10 E
Rumburk .... 30 50 57N 14 32 E
Rumelange .... 23 49 27N 6 2 E
Rumford 151 44 30N 70 30W
Rumia .... 32 54 37N 18 25 E
Rumilly .... 21 45 53N 5 56 E
Rumoi 98 43 56N 141 39W
Rumonge .... 130 3 59 S 29 26 E
Rumorosa, La 159 32 33N 116 4W
Rumsey 144 51 51N 112 48W
Rumula .... 110 16 35 S 145 20 E
Rumuruti .... 130 0 17N 36 32 E
Runan .... 94 33 0N 114 30 E
Runanga .... 115 42 25 S 171 15 E
Runcorn 12 53 20N 2 44W
Rungwa .... 130 6 55 S 33 32 E
Rungwa → .... 130 7 36 S 31 50 E
Rungwe .... 131 9 11 S 33 32 E
Rungwe □ .... 131 9 25 S 33 32 E
Runka .... 127 12 28N 7 20 E
Runn .... 52 60 30N 15 40 E
Ruoqiang .... 92 38 55N 88 10 E
Rupa .... 82 27 15N 92 21 E
Rupar .... 78 31 2N 76 38 E
Rupat .... 88 1 45N 101 40 E
Rupea .... 50 46 2N 25 13 E
Rupert → 142 51 29N 78 45W
Rupert House = Fort Rupert 142 51 30N 78 40W
Rupsa .... 82 21 44N 89 30 E
Rupununi → 169 4 3N 58 35W
Rur → .... 26 51 20N 6 0 E
Rurrenabaque .... 172 14 30 S 67 32W
Rus → 37 39 30N 2 30W
Rusambo .... 131 16 30 S 32 4 E
Rusape .... 131 18 35 S 32 8 E
Ruschuk = Ruse ...... 47 43 48N 25 59 E
Ruse .... 47 43 48N 25 59 E
Ruşeţu .... 50 44 57N 27 14 E
Rushan .... 95 36 56N 121 30 E
Rushden 13 52 17N 0 37W
Rushford 152 43 48N 91 46W
Rushville, Ill., U.S.A. . 154 40 6N 90 35W
Rushville, Ind., U.S.A. 155 39 38N 85 22W
Rushville, Nebr., U.S.A. 152 42 43N 102 28W
Rushworth .... 113 36 32 S 145 1 E
Rusken .... 53 57 15N 14 20 E
Russas .... 170 4 55 S 37 50W
Russell, Canada 145 50 50N 101 20W
Russell, N.Z. .... 114 35 16 S 174 10 E
Russell, U.S.A. 152 38 56N 98 55W
Russell L., Man., Canada 145 56 15N 101 30W
Russell L., N.W.T., Canada 144 63 5N 115 44W
Russellkonda .... 79 19 57N 84 42 E
Russellville, Ala., U.S.A. 149 34 30N 87 44W
Russellville, Ark., U.S.A. 153 35 15N 93 8W
Russellville, Ky., U.S.A. 149 36 50N 86 50W
Russi .... 43 44 21N 12 1 E
Russian → 158 38 27N 123 8W
Russian S.F.S.R. □ ... 65 62 0N 105 0 E
Russiaville 155 40 25N 86 16W
Russkaya Polyana ..... 64 53 47N 73 53 E
Russkoye Ustie .... 6 71 0N 149 0 E
Rust .... 31 47 49N 16 42 E
Rustam .... 78 34 25N 72 13 E
Rustam Shahr .... 78 26 58N 66 6 E
Rustavi .... 61 41 30N 45 0 E
Rustenburg .... 134 25 41 S 27 14 E
Ruston 153 32 30N 92 58W
Ruswil .... 28 47 5N 8 8 E
Rutana .... 130 3 55 S 30 0 E
Rute 35 37 19N 4 23W
Ruteng .... 87 8 35 S 120 30 E
Ruth, Mich., U.S.A. .. 150 43 42N 82 45W
Ruth, Nev., U.S.A. ... 156 39 15N 115 1W
Rutherford 158 38 26N 122 24W
Rutherglen, Australia .. 113 36 5 S 146 29 E
Rutherglen, U.K. 14 55 50N 4 11W
Rüti .... 29 47 16N 8 51 E
Rutigliano .... 45 41 1N 17 0 E
Rutland Plains .... 110 15 38 S 141 43 E
Rutledge → 145 61 4N 112 0W
Rutledge L. 145 61 33N 110 47W
Rutshuru .... 130 1 13 S 29 25 E
Ruurlo .... 22 52 5N 6 24 E
Ruvo di Púglia .... 45 41 7N 16 27 E
Ruvu .... 130 6 49 S 38 43 E
Ruvu → .... 130 6 23 S 38 52 E
Ruvuma □ .... 131 10 20 S 36 0 E
Ruwais .... 75 24 5N 52 50 E
Ruwenzori .... 130 0 30N 29 55 E
Ruyigi .... 130 3 29 S 30 15 E
Ruyuan .... 97 24 46N 113 16 E
Ruzayevka .... 59 54 4N 45 0 E
Rǔzhevo Konare ...... 47 42 23N 24 46 E
Ružomberok .... 31 49 3N 19 17 E
Rwanda ■ .... 130 2 0 S 30 0 E
Ry .... 53 56 5N 9 45 E
Ryakhovo .... 47 44 0N 26 18 E
Ryan, L. 14 55 0N 5 2W
Ryazan .... 59 54 40N 39 40 E
Ryazhsk .... 59 53 45N 40 3 E
Rybache .... 64 46 40N 81 20 E
Rybachiy Poluostrov ... 56 69 43N 32 0 E
Rybachye .... 63 42 26N 76 12 E
Rybinsk = Andropov .. 59 58 5N 38 50 E
Rybinskoye Vdkhr. .... 59 58 30N 38 25 E
Rybnik .... 32 50 6N 18 32 E
Rybnitsa .... 60 47 45N 29 0 E
Rybnoye .... 59 54 45N 39 30 E
Rychwał .... 32 52 4N 18 10 E
Ryd .... 53 56 27N 14 42 E
Ryde 13 50 44N 1 9W
Ryderwood 158 46 23N 123 3W
Rydöbruk .... 53 56 58N 13 7 E
Rydsnäs .... 53 57 47N 15 9 E
Rydułtowy .... 32 50 4N 18 23 E
Rydzyna .... 32 51 47N 16 39 E
Rye .... 13 50 57N 0 46 E
Rye → 12 54 12N 0 53W
Rye Patch Res. 156 40 38N 118 20W
Ryegate 156 46 21N 109 15W
Ryki .... 32 51 38N 21 56 E
Rylsk .... 58 51 36N 34 43 E
Rylstone .... 113 32 46 S 149 58 E
Rymanów .... 32 49 35N 21 51 E
Ryn .... 32 53 57N 21 34 E
Ryōhaku-Sanchi .... 101 36 9N 136 49 E
Ryōthu .... 98 38 5N 138 26 E
Rypin .... 32 53 3N 19 25 E
Ryūgasaki .... 101 35 54N 140 11 E
Ryūkyū Is. = Nansei-Shotō .... 99 26 0N 128 0 E
Rzepin .... 32 52 20N 14 49 E
Rzeszów .... 32 50 5N 21 58 E
Rzeszów □ .... 32 50 0N 22 0 E
Rzhev .... 58 56 20N 34 20 E

S

Samal

Samal .... 91 7 5N 125 42 E
Samal I. .... 91 7 3N 125 44 E
Samales Group .... 91 6 0N 122 0 E
Samalkot .... 80 17 3N 82 13 E
Samâlût .... 124 28 20N 30 42 E
Samana .... 78 30 10N 76 13 E
Samana Cay 163 23 3N 73 45W
Samandağı .... 70 36 5N 35 59 E
Samanga .... 131 8 20 S 39 13 E
Samangán □ .... 77 36 15N 68 3 E
Samangwa .... 130 4 23 S 24 10 E
Samani .... 98 42 7N 142 56 E
Samar .... 90 12 0N 125 0 E
Samar □ .... 91 11 50N 125 0 E
Samar Sea .... 90 12 0N 124 30 E
Samara → .... 62 53 10N 50 4 E
Samarai .... 107 10 39 S 150 41 E
Samaria = Shōmrōn ... 69 32 15N 35 13 E
Samarinda .... 89 0 30 S 117 9 E
Samarkand .... 63 39 40N 66 55 E
Sāmarrā .... 72 34 12N 43 52 E
Samastipur .... 79 25 50N 85 50 E
Samatan .... 20 43 29N 0 55 E
Samaúma .... 173 7 50 S 60 2W
Samba, Kashmir ...... 79 32 32N 75 10 E
Samba, Zaïre .... 130 4 38 S 26 22 E
Samba Caju .... 133 8 46 S 15 24 E
Sambaíba .... 170 7 8 S 45 21W
Sambalpur .... 79 21 28N 84 4 E
Sambar, Tanjung ...... 89 2 59 S 110 19 E
Sambas .... 89 1 20N 109 20 E
Sambava .... 135 14 16 S 50 10 E
Sambawizi .... 131 18 24 S 26 13 E
Sambhal .... 79 28 35N 78 37 E
Sambhar .... 78 26 52N 75 6 E
Sambiase .... 45 38 58N 16 16 E
Sambonifacio .... 42 45 24N 11 16 E
Sambor, Cambodia .... 84 12 46N 106 0 E
Sambor, U.S.S.R. ...... 58 49 30N 23 10 E
Sambre → .... 23 50 27N 4 52 E
Sambuca di Sicilia ..... 44 37 39N 13 6 E
Samburu □ .... 130 1 10N 37 0 E
Samchŏk .... 95 37 30N 129 10 E
Samchonpo .... 95 35 0N 128 6 E
Same .... 130 4 2 S 37 38 E
Samedan .... 29 46 32N 9 52 E
Samer .... 19 50 38N 1 44 E
Samfya .... 131 11 22 S 29 31 E
Samḥān, Jabal .... 75 17 12N 54 55 E
Sámi .... 49 38 15N 20 39 E
Samnah .... 72 25 10N 37 15 E
Samnaun .... 29 46 57N 10 22 E
Samnū .... 122 27 15N 14 55 E
Samo Alto .... 174 30 22 S 71 0W
Samobor .... 43 45 47N 15 44 E
Samoëns .... 21 46 5N 6 45 E
Samokov .... 47 42 18N 23 35 E
Samoorombón, B. ...... 174 36 5 S 57 20W
Samorogouan 126 11 21N 4 57W
Sámos, Greece .... 49 37 45N 26 50 E
Samos, Spain 34 42 44N 7 20W
Samoš, Yugoslavia .... 46 45 13N 20 49 E
Samosir .... 88 2 55N 98 50 E
Samothráki, Évros, Greece .... 48 40 28N 25 28 E
Samothráki, Ípiros, Greece .... 48 39 48N 19 31 E
Samoylovka .... 59 51 12N 43 43 E
Sampa 126 8 0N 2 36W
Sampacho .... 174 33 20 S 64 50W
Sampang .... 89 7 11 S 113 13 E
Samper de Calanda 36 41 11N 0 28W
Sampit .... 89 2 34 S 113 0 E
Sampit → .... 89 2 44 S 112 54 E
Sampit, Teluk .... 89 3 5 S 113 3 E
Samrée .... 23 50 13N 5 39 E
Samrong, Cambodia ... 84 14 15N 103 30 E
Samrong, Thailand .... 84 15 10N 100 40 E
Samsø .... 53 55 50N 10 35 E
Samsø Bælt .... 53 55 45N 10 45 E
Samsonovo .... 63 37 53N 65 15 E
Samsun .... 57 41 15N 36 22 E
Samsun Dağı .... 49 37 45N 27 10 E
Samtredia .... 61 42 7N 42 24 E
Samui, Ko .... 85 9 30N 100 0 E
Samur → .... 61 41 53N 48 32 E
Samusole .... 131 10 2 S 24 0 E
Samut Prakan .... 84 13 32N 100 40 E
Samut Sakhon .... 84 13 31N 100 13 E
Samut Songkhram → . 84 13 24N 100 1 E
Samwari .... 78 28 30N 66 46 E
San 126 13 15N 4 57W
San →, Cambodia ..... 84 13 32N 105 57 E
San →, Poland ...... 32 50 45N 21 51 E
San Adrián, C. de 34 43 21N 8 50W
San Agustín 168 1 53N 76 16W
San Agustín de Valle Fértil .... 174 30 35 S 67 30W
San Ambrosio .... 164 26 28 S 79 53W
San Andreas 158 38 0N 120 39W
San Andres .... 90 13 19N 122 41 E
San Andrés, I. de 162 12 42N 81 46W
San Andres Mts. 157 33 0N 106 45W
San Andrés Tuxtla 161 18 30N 95 20W
San Angelo 153 31 30N 100 30W
San Anselmo 158 37 59N 122 34W
San Antonio, Belize ... 161 16 15N 89 2W
San Antonio, Chile .... 174 33 40 S 71 40W
San Antonio, Phil. .... 90 14 57N 120 5 E
San Antonio, N. Mex., U.S.A. 157 33 58N 106 57W
San Antonio, Tex., U.S.A. 153 29 30N 98 30W
San Antonio, Venezuela 168 3 30N 66 44W
San Antonio → 153 28 30N 96 50W
San Antonio, C., Argentina .... 174 36 15 S 56 40W
San Antonio, C., Cuba 162 21 50N 84 57W
San Antonio, C. de .... 37 38 48N 0 12 E
San Antonio, Mt. 159 34 17N 117 38W
San Antonio Abad .... 37 38 59N 1 19 E
San Antonio Bay ...... 91 8 38N 117 35 E
San Antonio de los Baños 162 22 54N 82 31W
San Antonio de los Cobres .... 174 24 10 S 66 17W
San Antonio Oeste .... 176 40 40 S 65 0W
San Arcángelo .... 44 40 14N 16 14 E
San Ardo 158 36 1N 120 54W
San Augustín 37 27 47N 15 32W
San Augustin, C. ...... 91 6 20N 126 13 E
San Augustine 153 31 30N 94 7W
San Bartolomé 37 28 59N 13 37W
San Bartolomé de Tirajana 37 27 54N 15 34W
San Bartolomeo in Galdo .... 45 41 23N 15 2 E
San Benedetto .... 42 45 2N 10 57 E
San Benedetto del Tronto .... 43 42 57N 13 52 E
San Benedicto, I. 160 19 18N 110 49W
San Benito 153 26 5N 97 39W
San Benito → 158 36 53N 121 50W
San Benito Mt. 158 36 22N 120 37W
San Bernardino 159 34 7N 117 18W
San Bernardino, Paso del .... 29 46 28N 9 11 E
San Bernardino Mts. .. 159 34 10N 116 45W
San Bernardino Str. ... 90 13 0N 125 0 E
San Bernardo .... 174 33 40 S 70 50W
San Bernardo, I. de ... 168 9 45N 75 50W
San Blas 160 26 4N 108 46W
San Blas, Arch. de 162 9 50N 78 31W
San Blas, C. 149 29 40N 85 12W
San Borja .... 172 14 50 S 66 52W
San Buenaventura, Bolivia .... 172 14 28 S 67 35W
San Buenaventura, Mexico 160 27 5N 101 32W
San Carlos = Butuku-Luba .... 127 3 29N 8 33 E
San Carlos, Argentina . 174 33 50 S 69 0W
San Carlos, Bolivia .... 173 17 24 S 63 45W
San Carlos, Chile ..... 174 36 10 S 72 0W
San Carlos, Mexico 160 29 0N 100 54W
San Carlos, Nic. 162 11 12N 84 50W
San Carlos, Negros, Phil. .... 91 10 29N 123 25 E
San Carlos, Pangasinan, Phil. .... 90 15 55N 120 20 E
San Carlos, Uruguay .. 175 34 46 S 54 58W
San Carlos, U.S.A. 157 33 24N 110 27W
San Carlos, Amazonas, Venezuela 168 1 55N 67 4W
San Carlos, Cojedes, Venezuela 168 9 40N 68 36W
San Carlos de Bariloche 176 41 10 S 71 25W
San Carlos de la Rápita 36 40 37N 0 35 E
San Carlos del Zulia ... 168 9 1N 71 55W
San Carlos L. 157 33 15N 110 25W
San Cataldo .... 44 37 30N 13 58 E
San Celoni .... 36 41 42N 2 30 E
San Clemente, Chile ... 174 35 30 S 71 29W
San Clemente, Spain .. 37 39 24N 2 25W
San Clemente, U.S.A. . 159 33 29N 117 36W
San Clemente I. 159 32 53N 118 30W
San Constanzo .... 43 43 46N 13 5 E
San Cristóbal, Argentina 174 30 20 S 61 10W
San Cristóbal, Colombia 168 2 18 S 73 2W
San Cristóbal, Dom. Rep. 163 18 25N 70 6W
San Cristóbal, Venezuela 168 7 46N 72 14W
San Cristóbal de las Casas 161 16 50N 92 33W
San Damiano d'Asti ... 42 44 51N 8 4 E
San Daniele del Friuli . 43 46 10N 13 0 E
San Demétrio Corone . 45 39 34N 16 22 E
San Diego, Calif., U.S.A. 159 32 43N 117 10W
San Diego, Tex., U.S.A. 153 27 47N 98 15W
San Diego, C. .... 176 54 40 S 65 10W
San Diego de la Unión . 160 21 28N 100 52W
San Dionisio .... 91 11 16N 123 6 E
San Donà di Piave .... 43 45 38N 12 34 E
San Elpídio a Mare .... 43 43 16N 13 41 E
San Emilio .... 90 17 14N 120 37 E
San Estanislao .... 174 24 39 S 56 26W
San Esteban de Gormaz 36 41 34N 3 13W
San Fabian .... 90 16 5N 120 25 E
San Felice sul Panaro .. 42 44 51N 11 9 E
San Felipe, Chile ..... 174 32 43 S 70 42W
San Felipe, Colombia .. 168 1 55N 67 6W
San Felipe, Mexico 160 31 0N 114 52W
San Felipe, Phil. ...... 90 15 4N 120 4 E
San Felipe, Venezuela . 168 10 20N 68 44W
San Felipe → 159 33 12N 115 49W
San Feliu de Guíxols .. 36 41 45N 3 1 E
San Feliu de Llobregat . 36 41 23N 2 2 E
San Félix .... 105 26 23 S 80 0W
San Fernando, Chile ... 174 34 30 S 71 0W
San Fernando, Mexico . 160 30 0N 115 10W
San Fernando, Cebu, Phil. .... 91 10 10N 123 42 E
San Fernando, La Union, Phil. ..... 90 16 40N 120 23 E
San Fernando, Pampanga, Phil. .... 90 15 5N 120 37 E
San Fernando, Tablas, Phil. .... 90 12 18N 122 36 E
San Fernando, Spain .. 35 36 28N 6 17W
San Fernando, Trin. & Tob. 163 10 20N 61 30W
San Fernando, U.S.A. . 159 34 15N 118 29W
San Fernando → 160 24 55N 98 10W
San Fernando de Apure 168 7 54N 67 15W
San Fernando de Atabapo 168 4 3N 67 42W
San Fernando di Púglia 45 41 18N 16 5 E
San Francisco, Argentina 174 31 30 S 62 5W
San Francisco, Bolivia . 173 15 16 S 65 31W
San Francisco, Cebu, Phil. .... 91 10 39N 124 23 E
San Francisco, Leyte, Phil. .... 91 10 4N 125 9 E
San Francisco, Mindanao, Phil. ..... 91 8 30N 125 56 E
San Francisco, U.S.A. . 158 37 47N 122 30W
San Francisco → 157 32 59N 109 22W
San Francisco, Paso de . 174 27 0 S 68 0W
San Francisco de Macorís 163 19 19N 70 15W
San Francisco del Monte de Oro .... 174 32 36 S 66 8W
San Francisco del Oro . 160 26 52N 105 50W
San Francisco Javier ... 37 38 42N 1 26 E
San Francisco Solano, Pta. 168 6 18N 77 29W
San Fratello .... 45 38 1N 14 33 E
San Gabriel 168 0 36N 77 49W
San Gavino Monreale .. 44 39 33N 8 47 E
San Gil 168 6 33N 73 8W
San Gimignano .... 42 43 28N 11 3 E
San Giórgio di Nogaro . 43 45 50N 13 13 E
San Giórgio Iónico .... 45 40 27N 17 23 E
San Giovanni Bianco .. 42 45 52N 9 40 E
San Giovanni in Fiore . 45 39 16N 16 42 E
San Giovanni in Persiceto .... 43 44 39N 11 12 E
San Giovanni Rotondo . 45 41 41N 15 42 E
San Giovanni Valdarno 43 43 32N 11 30 E
San Giuliano Terme ... 42 43 45N 10 26 E
San Gorgonio Mt. 159 34 7N 116 51W
San Gottardo, Paso del 29 46 33N 8 33 E
San Gregorio, Uruguay 175 32 37 S 55 40W
San Gregorio, U.S.A. . 158 37 20N 122 23W
San Guiseppe Iato ..... 44 37 57N 13 11 E
San Ignacio, Belize 161 17 10N 89 0W
San Ignacio, Bolivia ... 173 16 20 S 60 55W
San Ignacio, Mexico ... 160 27 27N 113 0W
San Ignacio, Paraguay . 174 26 52 S 57 3W
San Ignacio, L. 160 26 50N 113 11W
San Ildefonso .... 90 15 5N 120 56 E
San Ildefonso, C. ..... 90 16 0N 122 1 E
San Isidro .... 174 34 29 S 58 31W
San Jacinto, Colombia . 168 9 50N 75 8W
San Jacinto, Phil. ..... 90 12 34N 123 44 E
San Jacinto, U.S.A. ... 159 33 47N 116 57W
San Javier, Misiones, Argentina .... 175 27 55 S 55 5W
San Javier, Santa Fe, Argentina .... 174 30 40 S 59 55W
San Javier, Beni, Bolivia 173 14 34 S 64 42W
San Javier, Santa Cruz, Bolivia .... 173 16 18 S 62 30W
San Javier, Chile ...... 174 35 40 S 71 45W
San Javier, Spain 37 37 49N 0 50W
San Jerónimo, Sa. de .. 168 8 0N 75 50W
San Jeronimo Taviche . 161 16 38N 96 32W
San Joaquín, Bolivia ... 173 13 4 S 64 49W
San Joaquin, Phil. ..... 91 10 35N 122 8 E
San Joaquin, U.S.A. ... 158 36 36N 120 11W
San Joaquín, Venezuela 168 10 16N 67 47W
San Joaquín →, Bolivia 173 13 8 S 63 41W
San Joaquin →, U.S.A. 158 38 4N 121 51W
San Joaquin Valley 158 37 0N 120 30W
San Jorge .... 174 31 54 S 61 50W
San Jorge, B. de 160 31 20N 113 20W
San Jorge, G. .... 176 46 0 S 66 0W
San Jorge, G. de 36 40 50N 0 55W
San José, Bolivia ...... 173 17 53 S 60 50W
San José, C. Rica 162 10 0N 84 2W
San José, Guat. 162 14 0N 90 50W
San José, Mexico 160 25 0N 110 50W
San Jose, Luzon, Phil. . 90 15 45N 120 55 E
San Jose, Mindoro, Phil. 90 12 27N 121 4 E
San José, Spain .... 37 38 55N 1 18 E
San Jose, Calif., U.S.A. 158 37 20N 121 53W
San Jose, Ill., U.S.A. .. 154 40 18N 89 36W
San Jose → 157 34 58N 106 7W
San José de Feliciano .. 174 30 26 S 58 46W
San José de Jáchal .... 174 30 15 S 68 46W
San José de Mayo .... 174 34 27 S 56 40W
San José de Ocune 168 4 15N 70 20W
San José de Uchapiamonas ...... 172 14 13 S 68 5W
San José del Cabo 160 23 0N 109 40W
San José del Guaviare . 168 2 35N 72 38W
San José do Anauá 169 0 58N 61 22W
San Juan, Argentina ... 174 31 30 S 68 30W
San Juan, Colombia ... 168 8 46N 76 32W
San Juan, Mexico 160 21 20N 102 50W
San Juan, Ica, Peru .... 172 15 22 S 75 7W
San Juan, Puno, Peru .. 172 14 2 S 69 19W
San Juan, Luzon, Phil. . 90 16 40N 120 20 E
San Juan, Mindanao, Phil. .... 91 8 25N 126 20 E
San Juan, Puerto Rico . 163 18 28N 66 8W
San Juan □, Argentina 174 31 9 S 69 0W
San Juan □, Dom. Rep. 163 18 45N 71 25W
San Juan →, Argentina 174 32 20 S 67 25W
San Juan →, Bolivia .. 173 21 2 S 65 19W
San Juan →, Colombia 168 4 3N 77 27W
San Juan →, Nic. 162 10 56N 83 42W
San Juan →, Calif., U.S.A. 158 36 14N 121 9W
San Juan →, Utah, U.S.A. 157 37 20N 110 20W
San Juan →, Venezuela 169 10 14N 62 38W
San Juan, C. .... 132 1 5N 9 20 E
San Juan Bautista, Paraguay .... 174 26 37 S 57 6W
San Juan Bautista, Spain 37 39 5N 1 31 E
San Juan Bautista, U.S.A. 158 36 51N 121 32W
San Juan Bautista Valle Nacional 161 17 47N 96 19W
San Juan Capistrano ... 159 33 29N 117 40W
San Juan de Guadalupe 160 24 38N 102 44W
San Juan de los Morros 168 9 55N 67 21W
San Juan del César 168 10 46N 73 1W
San Juan del Norte 162 10 58N 83 40W
San Juan del Norte, B. de 162 11 0N 83 40W
San Juan del Puerto ... 35 37 20N 6 50W
San Juan del Río 161 20 25N 100 0W
San Juan del Sur 162 11 20N 85 51W
San Juan I. 158 48 32N 123 5W
San Juan Mts. 157 38 30N 108 30W
San Julián, Argentina .. 176 49 15 S 67 45W
San Julian, Phil. ...... 91 11 45N 125 27 E
San Just, Sierra de 36 40 45N 0 49W
San Justo .... 174 30 47 S 60 30W
San Kamphaeng .... 84 18 45N 99 8 E
San Lázaro, C. 160 24 50N 112 18W
San Lázaro, Sa. 160 23 25N 110 0W
San Leandro 158 37 40N 122 6W
San Leonardo 36 41 51N 3 5W
San Lorenzo, Argentina 174 32 45 S 60 45W
San Lorenzo, Beni, Bolivia .... 173 15 22 S 65 48W
San Lorenzo, Tarija, Bolivia .... 173 21 26 S 64 47W
San Lorenzo, Ecuador . 168 1 15N 78 50W
San Lorenzo, Paraguay 174 25 20 S 57 32W
San Lorenzo, Venezuela 168 9 47N 71 4W
San Lorenzo → 160 24 15N 107 24W
San Lorenzo, I., Mexico 160 28 35N 112 50W
San Lorenzo, I., Peru .. 172 12 7 S 77 15W
San Lorenzo, Mt. ..... 176 47 40 S 72 20W
San Lorenzo de la Parrilla 36 39 51N 2 22W
San Lorenzo de Morunys 36 42 8N 1 35 E
San Lucas, Bolivia .... 173 20 5 S 65 7W
San Lucas, Baja Calif. S., Mexico 160 22 53N 109 54W
San Lucas, Baja Calif. S., Mexico 160 27 10N 112 14W
San Lucas, U.S.A. 158 36 8N 121 1W
San Lucas, C. 160 22 50N 110 0W
San Lúcido .... 45 39 18N 16 3 E
San Luis, Argentina ... 174 33 20 S 66 20W
San Luis, Cuba 162 22 17N 83 46W
San Luis, Guat. 162 16 14N 89 27W
San Luis, U.S.A. 157 37 3N 105 26W
San Luis □ .... 174 34 0 S 66 0W
San Luis, I. 160 29 58N 114 26W
San Luis, L. de .... 173 13 45 S 64 0W
San Luis, Sierra de .... 174 32 30 S 66 10W
San Luis de la Paz 160 21 19N 100 32W
San Luis Obispo, Calif., U.S.A. 159 35 17N 120 40W
San Luis Obispo, U.S.A. 157 35 21N 120 38W
San Luis Potosí 160 22 9N 100 59W
San Luis Potosí □ 160 22 10N 101 0W
San Luis Res. 158 37 4N 121 5W
San Luis Río Colorado . 160 32 29N 114 58W
San Manuel .... 90 16 4N 120 40 E
San Marco Argentano . 45 39 34N 16 8 E
San Marco dei Cavoti .. 45 41 20N 14 50 E
San Marco in Lámis ... 45 41 43N 15 38 E
San Marcos, Colombia . 168 8 39N 75 8W
San Marcos, Guat. 162 14 59N 91 52W
San Marcos, Mexico ... 160 27 13N 112 6W
San Marcos, U.S.A. ... 153 29 53N 98 0W
San Marino ■ .... 43 43 56N 12 25 E
San Martin, Antarct. .. 7 68 11 S 67 0W
San Martín, Argentina . 174 33 5 S 68 28W
San Martín, Colombia . 168 3 42N 73 42W
San Martin → .... 173 13 8 S 63 43W
San Martín, L. .... 176 48 50 S 72 50W
San Martín de los Andes 176 40 10 S 71 20W
San Martín de Valdeiglesias 34 40 21N 4 24W
San Martino de Calvi .. 42 45 57N 9 41 E
San Mateo, Agusan del N., Phil. . 91 8 48N 125 33 E
San Mateo, Isabela, Phil. .... 90 16 54N 121 33 E
San Mateo, Spain ..... 36 40 28N 0 10 E

Santa Maria da Vitória

Santa Maria da Vitória . 171 13 24 S 44 12W
Santa María de Ipire ... 169 8 49N 65 19W
Santa Maria di Leuca, C. ... 45 39 48N 18 20 E
Santa Maria do Suaçuí . 171 18 12 S 42 25W
Santa Maria dos Marmelos ... 173 6 7 S 61 51W
Santa María la Real de Nieva ... 34 41 4N 4 24W
Santa Marta, Colombia 168 11 15N 74 13W
Santa Marta, Spain 35 38 37N 6 39W
Santa Marta, Ría de ... 34 43 44N 7 45W
Santa Marta, Sierra Nevada de ... 168 10 55N 73 50W
Santa Marta Grande, C. 175 28 43 S 48 50W
Santa Maura = Levkás 49 38 40N 20 43 E
Santa Monica ... 159 34 0N 118 30W
Santa Olalla, Huelva, Spain ... 35 37 54N 6 14W
Santa Olalla, Toledo, Spain ... 34 40 2N 4 25W
Sant' Onofrio ... 45 38 42N 16 10 E
Santa Pola ... 37 38 13N 0 35W
Santa Quitéria ... 170 4 20 S 40 10W
Santa Rita, U.S.A. 157 32 50N 108 0W
Santa Rita, Guarico, Venezuela ... 168 8 8N 66 16W
Santa Rita, Zulia, Venezuela ... 168 10 32N 71 32W
Santa Rita do Araquaia 173 17 20 S 53 12W
Santa Rosa, La Pampa, Argentina ... 174 36 40 S 64 17W
Santa Rosa, San Luis, Argentina ... 174 32 21 S 65 10W
Santa Rosa, Bolivia ... 172 10 36 S 67 20W
Santa Rosa, Brazil ... 175 27 52 S 54 29W
Santa Rosa, Colombia . 168 3 32N 69 48W
Santa Rosa, Ecuador .. 168 3 27 S 79 58W
Santa Rosa, Peru ... 172 14 30 S 70 50W
Santa Rosa, Phil. ... 90 15 25N 120 57 E
Santa Rosa, Calif., U.S.A. ... 158 38 26N 122 43W
Santa Rosa, N. Mex., U.S.A. ... 153 34 58N 104 40W
Santa Rosa, Venezuela 168 1 29N 66 55W
Santa Rosa de Cabal .. 168 4 52N 75 38W
Santa Rosa de Copán .. 162 14 47N 88 46W
Santa Rosa de Osos ... 168 6 39N 75 28W
Santa Rosa de Río Primero ... 174 31 8 S 63 20W
Santa Rosa de Viterbo . 168 5 53N 72 59W
Santa Rosa del Palmar . 173 16 54 S 62 24W
Santa Rosa I., Calif., U.S.A. ... 159 34 0N 120 6W
Santa Rosa I., Fla., U.S.A. ... 149 30 23N 87 0W
Santa Rosa Ra. ... 156 41 45N 117 30W
Santa Rosalía ... 160 27 20N 112 20W
Santa Sofia ... 43 43 57N 11 55 E
Santa Sylvina ... 174 27 50 S 61 10W
Santa Tecla = Nueva San Salvador ... 162 13 40N 89 18W
Santa Teresa, Argentina 174 33 25 S 60 47W
Santa Teresa, Brazil ... 171 19 55 S 40 36W
Santa Teresa, Mexico .. 161 25 17N 97 51W
Santa Teresa, Venezuela 169 4 43N 61 4W
Santa Teresa di Riva .. 45 37 58N 15 21 E
Santa Teresa Gallura .. 44 41 14N 9 12 E
Santa Vitória ... 171 18 50 S 50 8W
Santa Vitória do Palmar 175 33 32 S 53 25W
Santa Ynez ... 159 34 37N 120 5W
Santa Ynez → ... 159 34 37N 120 41W
Santa Ysabel ... 159 33 7N 116 40W
Santadi ... 44 39 5N 8 42 E
Santahar ... 82 24 48N 88 59 E
Santai ... 96 31 5N 104 58 E
Santaluz ... 170 11 15 S 39 22W
Santana ... 171 13 2 S 44 5W
Santana, Coxilha de ... 175 30 50 S 55 35W
Santana do Ipanema ... 170 9 22 S 37 14W
Santana do Livramento 175 30 55 S 55 30W
Santanayi ... 37 39 20N 3 5 E
Santander, Colombia .. 168 3 1N 76 28W
Santander, Phil. ... 91 9 25N 123 20 E
Santander, Spain ... 34 43 27N 3 51W
Santander □ ... 34 43 25N 4 0W
Santander Jiménez ... 161 24 11N 98 29W
Santaquin ... 156 40 0N 111 51W
Santarém, Brazil ... 169 2 25 S 54 42W
Santarém, Portugal ... 35 39 12N 8 42W
Santarém □ ... 35 39 10N 8 40W
Santaren Channel ... 162 24 0N 79 30W
Santee ... 159 32 50N 116 58W
Santéramo in Colle ... 45 40 48N 16 45 E
Santerno → ... 43 44 10N 11 38 E
Santhia ... 42 45 20N 8 10 E
Santiago, Bolivia ... 173 18 19 S 59 34W
Santiago, Brazil ... 175 29 11 S 54 52W
Santiago, Chile ... 174 33 24 S 70 40W
Santiago, Panama ... 162 8 0N 81 0W
Santiago, Peru ... 172 14 11 S 75 43W
Santiago, Ilocos S., Phil. 90 17 18N 120 27 E
Santiago, Isabela, Phil. 90 16 41N 121 33 E
Santiago □ ... 174 33 30 S 70 50W
Santiago → ... 168 4 27 S 77 38W
Santiago, C. ... 176 50 46 S 75 27W
Santiago, Punta de ... 127 3 12N 8 40 E
Santiago, Serranía de .. 173 18 25 S 59 25W
Santiago de Chuco ... 172 8 9 S 78 11W
Santiago de Compostela 34 42 52N 8 37W
Santiago de Cuba ... 162 20 0N 75 49W
Santiago de los Cabelleros ... 163 19 30N 70 40W
Santiago del Estero ... 174 27 50 S 64 15W
Santiago del Estero □ . 174 27 40 S 63 15W
Santiago del Teide ... 37 28 17N 16 48W
Santiago do Cacém ... 35 38 1N 8 42W
Santiago Ixcuintla ... 160 21 50N 105 11W
Santiago Papasquiaro .. 160 25 0N 105 20W
Santiaguillo, L. de ... 160 24 50N 104 50W
Santillana del Mar ... 34 43 24N 4 6W
Säntis ... 29 47 15N 9 22 E
Santisteban del Puerto . 37 38 17N 3 15W
Santo → ... 172 8 56 S 78 37W
Santo Amaro ... 171 12 30 S 38 43W
Santo Anastácio ... 175 21 58 S 51 39W
Santo André ... 175 23 39 S 46 29W
Santo Ângelo ... 175 28 15 S 54 15W
Santo Antonio ... 173 15 50 S 56 0W
Santo Antônio de Jesus 171 12 58 S 39 16W
Santo Antônio do Içá .. 168 3 5 S 67 57W
Santo Antônio do Leverger ... 173 15 52 S 56 5W
Santo Corazón ... 173 18 0 S 58 45W
Santo Domingo, Dom. Rep. ... 163 18 30N 69 59W
Santo Domingo, Baja Calif. N., Mexico 160 30 43N 116 2W
Santo Domingo, Baja Calif. S., Mexico 160 25 32N 112 2W
Santo Domingo, Nic. .. 162 12 14N 84 59W
Santo Domingo de la Calzada ... 36 42 26N 2 57W
Santo Domingo de los Colorados ... 168 0 15 S 79 9W
Santo Nino I. ... 91 11 55N 124 27 E
Santo Stéfano di Camastro ... 45 38 1N 14 22 E
Santo Stino di Livenza . 43 45 45N 12 40 E
Santo Tirso ... 34 41 21N 8 28W
Santo Tomás, Mexico .. 160 31 33N 116 24W
Santo Tomás, Peru ... 172 14 26 S 72 8W
Santo Tomé ... 175 28 40 S 56 5W
Santo Tomé de Guayana = Ciudad Guayana .. 169 8 0N 62 30W
Santol ... 90 16 47N 120 27 E
Santoña ... 34 43 29N 3 27W
Santos ... 175 24 0 S 46 20W
Santos, Sierra de los ... 35 38 7N 5 12W
Santos Dumont ... 175 22 55 S 43 10W
Santpoort ... 22 52 26N 4 39 E
Sānūr ... 69 32 22N 35 15 E
Sanvignes-les-Mines ... 19 46 40N 4 18 E
San'yō ... 100 34 2N 131 5 E
Sanyuan ... 94 34 35N 108 58 E
Sanyuki-Sammyaku ... 100 34 5N 133 0 E
Sanza Pombo ... 133 7 18 S 15 56 E
São Anastácio ... 175 22 0 S 51 40W
São Bartolomeu de Messines ... 35 37 15N 8 17W
São Benedito ... 170 4 3 S 40 53W
São Bento ... 170 2 42 S 44 50W
São Bento do Norte ... 170 5 4 S 36 2W
São Borja ... 175 28 39 S 56 0W
São Bras d'Alportel ... 35 37 8N 7 37W
São Caitano ... 170 8 21 S 36 6W
São Carlos ... 175 22 0 S 47 50W
São Cristóvão ... 170 11 1 S 37 15W
São Domingos ... 171 13 25 S 46 19W
São Domingos do Maranhão ... 170 5 42 S 44 22W
São Félix ... 171 11 36 S 50 39W
São Francisco ... 171 16 0 S 44 50W
São Francisco → ... 170 10 30 S 36 24W
São Francisco do Maranhão ... 170 6 15 S 42 52W
São Francisco do Sul .. 175 26 15 S 48 36W
São Gabriel ... 175 30 20 S 54 20W
São Gabriel da Palha .. 171 18 47 S 40 39W
São Gonçalo ... 171 22 48 S 43 5W
São Gotardo ... 171 19 19 S 46 3W
Sao Hill ... 131 8 20 S 35 12 E
São João da Boa Vista . 175 22 0 S 46 52W
São João da Pesqueira . 34 41 8N 7 24W
São João da Ponte ... 171 15 56 S 44 1W
São João del Rei ... 171 21 8 S 44 15W
São João do Araguaia . 170 5 23 S 48 46W
São João do Paraíso .. 171 15 19 S 42 1W
São João do Piauí ... 170 8 21 S 42 15W
São João dos Patos ... 170 6 30 S 43 42W
São Joaquim da Barra . 171 20 35 S 47 53W
São José, B. de ... 170 2 38 S 44 4W
São José da Laje ... 170 9 1 S 36 3W
São José de Mipibu ... 170 6 5 S 35 15W
São José do Peixe ... 170 7 24 S 42 34W
São José do Rio Prêto . 175 20 50 S 49 20W
São José dos Campos .. 175 23 7 S 45 52W
São Leopoldo ... 175 29 50 S 51 10W
São Lourenço ... 171 22 7 S 45 3W
São Lourenço → ... 173 17 53 S 57 27W
São Lourenço, Pantanal do ... 173 17 30 S 56 20W
São Luís ... 170 2 39 S 44 15W
São Luís do Curu ... 170 3 40 S 39 14W
São Luís Gonzaga ... 175 28 25 S 55 0W
São Marcos → ... 171 18 15 S 47 37W
São Marcos, B. de ... 170 2 0 S 44 0W
São Martinho ... 34 40 18N 8 8W
São Mateus ... 171 18 44 S 39 50W
São Mateus → ... 171 18 35 S 39 44W
São Miguel do Araguaia 171 13 19 S 50 13W
São Miguel dos Campos 170 9 47 S 36 5W
São Nicolau → ... 170 5 45 S 42 2W
São Paulo ... 175 23 32 S 46 37W
São Paulo □ ... 175 22 0 S 49 0W
Sao Paulo, I. ... 8 0 50N 31 40W
São Paulo de Olivença . 168 3 27 S 68 48W
São Pedro do Sul ... 34 40 46N 8 4W
São Rafael ... 170 5 47 S 36 55W
São Raimundo das Mangabeiras ... 170 7 1 S 45 29W
São Raimundo Nonato . 170 9 1 S 42 42W
São Romão ... 171 16 22 S 45 4W
São Roque, C. de ... 170 5 30 S 35 16W
São Sebastião, I. de ... 175 23 50 S 45 18W
São Sebastião do Paraíso 175 20 54 S 46 59W
São Simão ... 171 18 56 S 50 30W
São Teotónio ... 35 37 30N 8 42W
São Tomé, Atl. Oc. ... 116 0 10N 6 39 E
São Tomé, Brazil ... 170 5 58 S 36 4W
São Tomé, C. de ... 171 22 0 S 40 59W
São Tomé & Principe ■ 117 0 12N 6 39 E
São Vicente ... 175 23 57 S 46 23W
São Vicente, C. de ... 35 37 0N 9 0W
Saona, I. ... 163 18 10N 68 40W
Saône → ... 21 45 44N 4 50 E
Saône-et-Loire □ ... 19 46 30N 4 50 E
Saonek ... 87 0 22 S 130 55 E
Saoura, O. → ... 121 29 0N 0 55W
Sápai ... 48 41 2N 25 43 E
Sapão → ... 170 11 1 S 45 32W
Saparua ... 87 3 33 S 128 40 E
Sapé ... 170 7 6 S 35 13W
Sapele ... 127 5 50N 5 40 E
Sapelo I. ... 149 31 28N 81 15W
Sapiéntza ... 49 36 45N 21 43 E
Sapone ... 127 12 3N 1 35W
Saposoa ... 172 6 55 S 76 45W
Sapozhok ... 59 53 59N 40 41 E
Sappemeer ... 22 53 10N 6 48 E
Sappho ... 158 48 4N 124 16W
Sapporo ... 98 43 0N 141 21 E
Sapri ... 45 40 5N 15 37 E
Sapu Grande ... 91 5 55N 125 16 E
Sapudi ... 89 7 6 S 114 20 E
Sapulpa ... 153 36 0N 96 0W
Saqqez ... 72 36 15N 46 20 E
Sar Dasht ... 73 32 32N 48 52 E
Sar-e Pol ... 77 36 10N 66 0 E
Sar Gachīneh ... 73 30 31N 51 31 E
Sar Planina ... 46 42 10N 21 0 E
Sara, Burkina Faso ... 126 11 40N 3 53W
Sara, Phil. ... 91 11 16N 123 1 E
Sara Buri ... 84 14 30N 100 55 E
Sarāb, Iran ... 72 38 0N 47 30 E
Sarab, S. Yemen ... 75 14 51N 48 31 E
Sarabadi ... 72 33 1N 44 48 E
Sarabit el Khadim ... 71 29 2N 33 25 E
Saragossa = Zaragoza . 36 41 39N 0 53W
Saraguro ... 168 3 35 S 79 16W
Saraipali ... 79 21 20N 82 59 E
Sarajevo ... 46 43 52N 18 26 E
Saraktash ... 62 51 47N 56 22 E
Saralu ... 50 44 43N 28 10 E
Saramacca □ ... 169 5 0N 56 0W
Saramacca → ... 169 5 50N 55 55W
Saramati ... 82 25 44N 95 2 E
Saran, G. ... 89 0 30 S 111 25 E
Saranac ... 155 42 56N 85 13W
Saranac Lake ... 151 44 20N 74 10W
Saranda, Albania ... 48 39 52N 19 55 E
Saranda, Tanzania ... 130 5 45 S 34 59 E
Sarandí del Yi ... 175 33 18 S 55 38W
Sarandí Grande ... 174 33 44 S 56 20W
Sarangani B. ... 91 6 0N 125 13 E
Sarangani Is. ... 91 5 25N 125 25 E
Sarangarh ... 79 21 30N 83 5 E
Saransk ... 59 54 10N 45 10 E
Sarapul ... 62 56 28N 53 48 E
Sarāqib ... 70 35 52N 36 47 E
Sarar Plain ... 136 9 25N 46 17 E
Sarasota ... 149 27 20N 82 30W
Saratoga, Calif., U.S.A. 158 37 16N 122 2W
Saratoga, Wyo., U.S.A. 156 41 30N 106 48W
Saratoga Springs ... 151 43 5N 73 47W
Saratov ... 59 51 30N 46 2 E
Saravane ... 84 15 43N 106 25 E
Sarawak □ ... 86 2 0N 113 0 E
Saraya ... 126 12 50N 11 45W
Sarbāz ... 73 26 38N 61 19 E
Sarbīsheh ... 73 32 30N 59 40 E
Sârbogârd ... 31 46 50N 18 40 E
Sarca → ... 42 45 52N 10 52 E
Sardalas ... 122 25 50N 10 34 E
Sardarshahr ... 78 28 30N 74 29 E
Sardegna ... 44 39 57N 9 0 E
Sardhana ... 78 29 9N 77 39 E
Sardina, Pta. ... 37 28 9N 15 44W
Sardinata ... 168 8 5N 72 48W
Sardinia = Sardegna ... 44 39 57N 9 0 E
Sardinia ... 155 39 0N 83 49W
Sārdūīyeh = Dar Mazār 73 29 14N 57 20 E
Šarengrad ... 46 45 14N 19 16 E
Saréyamou ... 126 16 7N 3 10W
Sargasso Sea ... 8 27 0N 72 0W
Sargent ... 152 41 42N 99 24W
Sargodha ... 77 32 10N 72 40 E
Sarh ... 123 9 5N 18 23 E
Sarhro, Djebel ... 120 31 6N 5 0W
Sārī ... 73 36 30N 53 4 E
Sária ... 49 35 54N 27 17 E
Saricumbe ... 133 12 12 S 19 46 E
Sarida → ... 69 32 4N 34 45 E
Sarikei ... 86 2 8N 111 30 E
Sarina ... 110 21 22 S 149 13 E
Sariñena ... 36 41 47N 0 10W
Sarīr Tibasti ... 122 22 50N 18 30 E
Sarita ... 153 27 14N 97 49W
Saritaş Tepesi ... 70 36 20N 32 38 E
Sariwŏn ... 95 38 31N 125 46 E
Sariyer ... 47 41 10N 29 3 E
Sark ... 18 49 25N 2 20W
Sarkad ... 31 46 47N 21 23 E
Sarlat-la-Canéda ... 20 44 54N 1 13 E
Sarles ... 152 48 58N 99 0W
Sărmaşu ... 50 46 45N 24 13 E
Sarmi ... 87 1 49 S 138 44 E
Sarmiento ... 176 45 35 S 69 5W
Särna ... 52 61 41N 13 8 E
Sarnano ... 43 43 2N 13 17 E
Sarnen ... 28 46 53N 8 13 E
Sarnia ... 142 42 58N 82 23W
Sarno ... 45 40 48N 14 35 E
Sarnowa ... 32 51 39N 16 53 E
Sarny ... 58 51 17N 26 40 E
Särö ... 53 57 31N 11 57 E
Sarolangun ... 88 2 19 S 102 42 E
Saronikós Kólpos ... 49 37 45N 23 45 E
Saronno ... 42 45 38N 9 2 E
Saros Körfezi ... 48 40 30N 26 15 E
Sárospatak ... 31 48 18N 21 33 E
Sarosul Românesc ... 46 45 34N 21 43 E
Sarova ... 59 54 55N 43 19 E
Sarpsborg ... 51 59 16N 11 12 E
Sarracín ... 36 42 15N 3 45W
Sarralbe ... 19 49 0N 7 1 E
Sarrat ... 90 18 9N 120 39 E
Sarraz, La ... 28 46 38N 6 30 E
Sarre = Saar → ... 19 49 41N 6 32 E
Sarre, La ... 142 48 45N 79 15W
Sarre-Union ... 19 48 57N 7 4 E
Sarrebourg ... 19 48 43N 7 3 E
Sarreguemines ... 19 49 5N 7 4 E
Sarriá ... 34 42 49N 7 29W
Sarrión ... 36 40 9N 0 49W
Sarro ... 126 13 40N 5 15W
Sarstedt ... 26 52 13N 9 50 E
Sartène ... 21 41 38N 8 58 E
Sarthe □ ... 18 47 58N 0 10 E
Sarthe → ... 18 47 33N 0 31W
Sartilly ... 18 48 45N 1 28W
Sartynya ... 64 63 22N 63 11 E
Sárvár ... 31 47 15N 16 56 E
Sarvestān ... 73 29 20N 53 10 E
Särvfjället ... 52 62 42N 13 30 E
Sárviz → ... 31 46 24N 18 41 E
Sary Ozek ... 63 44 22N 77 59 E
Sary-Tash ... 63 39 44N 73 15 E
Saryagach ... 63 41 27N 69 9 E
Sarych, Mys. ... 60 44 25N 33 45 E
Sarykolskiy Khrebet ... 63 38 30N 74 30 E
Sarykopa, Ozero ... 62 50 22N 64 6 E
Sarymoin, Ozero ... 62 51 36N 64 30 E
Saryshagan ... 64 46 12N 73 38 E
Sarzana ... 42 44 5N 9 59 E
Sarzeau ... 18 47 31N 2 48W
Sas van Gent ... 23 51 14N 3 48 E
Sasa ... 69 33 2N 35 23 E
Sasabeneh ... 136 7 59N 44 43 E
Sasaram ... 79 24 57N 84 5 E
Sasayama ... 101 35 4N 135 13 E
Sasca Montană ... 46 44 50N 21 45 E
Sasebo ... 100 33 10N 129 43 E
Saser Mt. ... 79 34 50N 77 50 E
Saskatchewan □ ... 145 54 40N 106 0W
Saskatchewan → ... 145 53 37N 100 40W
Saskatoon ... 145 52 10N 106 38W
Saskylakh ... 65 71 55N 114 1 E
Sasnovka ... 59 56 20N 51 4 E
Sasolburg ... 135 26 46 S 27 49 E
Sasovo ... 59 54 25N 41 55 E
Sassandra ... 126 5 0N 6 8W
Sassandra → ... 126 4 58N 6 5W
Sássari ... 44 40 44N 8 33 E
Sassenheim ... 22 52 14N 4 31 E
Sassnitz ... 26 54 29N 13 39 E
Sasso Marconi ... 43 44 22N 11 12 E
Sassocorvaro ... 43 43 47N 12 30 E
Sassoferrato ... 43 43 26N 12 51 E
Sassuolo ... 42 44 31N 10 47 E
Sástago ... 36 41 19N 0 21W
Sastown ... 126 4 45N 8 27W
Sasumua Dam ... 130 0 45 S 36 40 E
Sasyk, Ozero ... 50 45 45N 30 0 E
Sasykkul ... 63 37 41N 73 11 E
Sata-Misaki ... 100 30 59N 130 40 E
Satadougou ... 126 12 25N 11 25W
Satanta ... 153 37 30N 101 0W
Satara ... 80 17 44N 73 58 E
Satilla → ... 149 30 59N 81 28W
Satipo ... 172 11 15 S 74 25W
Satka ... 62 55 3N 59 1 E
Satkania ... 82 22 4N 92 3 E
Satkhira ... 82 22 43N 89 8 E
Satmala Hills ... 80 20 15N 74 40 E
Satna ... 79 24 35N 80 50 E
Šator ... 43 44 11N 16 37 E
Sátoraljaújhely ... 31 48 25N 21 41 E
Satpura Ra. ... 78 21 25N 76 10 E
Satrup ... 26 54 39N 9 38 E

Seilles

Satsuma-Hantō 100 31 25N 130 25 E
Satsuna-Shotō 99 30 0N 130 0 E
Sattahip 84 12 41N 100 54 E
Sattenapalle 81 16 25N 80 6 E
Satu Mare 50 47 46N 22 55 E
Satu Mare □ 50 47 45N 23 0 E
Satui 89 3 50 S 115 27 E
Satun 85 6 43N 100 2 E
Saturnina → 173 12 15 S 58 10W
Sauce 174 30 5 S 58 46W
Sauceda 160 25 55N 101 18W
Saucillo 160 28 1N 105 17W
Sauda 51 59 40N 6 20 E
Saúde 170 10 56 S 40 24W
Sauðarkrókur 54 65 45N 19 40W
Saudi Arabia ■ 74 26 0N 44 0 E
Saugatuck 155 42 40N 86 12W
Saugeen → 150 44 30N 81 22W
Saugerties 151 42 4N 73 58W
Saugues 20 44 58N 3 32 E
Sauherad 51 59 25N 9 15 E
Saujon 20 45 41N 0 55W
Sauk Centre 152 45 42N 94 56W
Sauk City 154 43 17N 89 43W
Sauk Rapids 152 45 35N 94 10W
Saül 169 3 37N 53 12W
Saulgau 27 48 4N 9 32 E
Saulieu 19 47 17N 4 14 E
Sault 21 44 6N 5 24 E
Sault Ste. Marie, Canada 142 46 30N 84 20W
Sault Ste. Marie, U.S.A. 148 46 27N 84 22W
Saumlaki 87 7 55 S 131 20 E
Saumur 18 47 15N 0 5W
Saunders C. 115 45 53 S 170 45 E
Saunders I. 7 57 48 S 26 28W
Saunders Point, Mt. 109 27 52 S 125 38 E
Saunemin 155 40 54N 88 24W
Saurbær, Borgarfjarðarsýsla, Iceland 54 64 24N 21 35W
Saurbær, Eyjafjarðarsýsla, Iceland 54 65 27N 18 13W
Sauri 127 11 42N 6 44 E
Saurimo 133 9 40 S 20 12 E
Sausalito 158 37 51N 122 29W
Sautatá 168 7 50N 77 4W
Sauveterre-de-Béarn 20 43 24N 0 57W
Sauzé-Vaussais 20 46 8N 0 8 E
Savá, Hond. 162 15 32N 86 15W
Sava, Yugoslavia 43 40 28N 17 32 E
Sava → 46 44 50N 20 26 E
Savage 152 47 27N 104 20W
Savage I. = Niue I. 105 19 2 S 169 54W
Savalou 127 7 57N 1 58 E
Savane 131 19 37 S 35 8 E
Savanna 154 42 5N 90 10W
Savanna la Mar 162 18 10N 78 10W
Savannah, Ga., U.S.A. 149 32 4N 81 4W
Savannah, Mo., U.S.A. 154 39 55N 94 46W
Savannah, Tenn., U.S.A. 149 35 12N 88 18W
Savannah → 149 32 2N 80 53W
Savannakhet 84 16 30N 104 49 E
Savant L. 142 50 16N 90 44W
Savant Lake 142 50 14N 90 40W
Savantvadi 81 15 55N 73 54 E
Savanur 81 14 59N 75 21 E
Savda 78 21 9N 75 56 E
Savé 127 8 2N 2 29 E
Save →, France 20 43 47N 1 17 E
Save →, Mozam. 135 21 16 S 34 0 E
Sāveh 73 35 2N 50 20 E
Savelugu 127 9 38N 0 54W
Savenay 18 47 20N 1 55W
Saverdun 20 43 14N 1 34 E
Saverne 19 48 43N 7 20 E
Savièse 28 46 17N 7 22 E
Savigliano 42 44 39N 7 40 E
Savigny-sur-Braye 18 47 53N 0 49 E
Saviñao 34 42 35N 7 38W
Savio → 43 44 19N 12 20 E
Šavnik 46 42 59N 19 10 E
Savognin 29 46 36N 9 37 E
Savoie □ 21 45 26N 6 25 E
Savona 42 44 19N 8 29 E
Savonlinna 56 61 52N 28 53 E
Sävsjö 53 57 20N 14 40 E
Sävsjøström 53 57 1N 15 25 E
Savusavu 106 16 34 S 179 15 E
Savusavu B. 106 16 45 S 179 15 E
Sawahlunto 88 0 40 S 100 52 E
Sawai 87 3 0 S 129 5 E
Sawai Madhopur 78 26 0N 76 25 E
Sawang Daen Din 84 17 28N 103 28 E
Sawankhalok 84 17 19N 99 50 E
Sawara 101 35 55N 140 30 E
Sawatch Mts. 157 38 30N 106 30W
Sawdā, Jabal as 122 28 51N 15 12 E
Sawel, Mt. 15 54 48N 7 5W
Sawfajjin, W. → 122 31 46N 14 30 E
Sawi 85 10 14N 99 5 E
Sawmills 131 19 30 S 28 2 E
Şawqirah 75 18 7N 56 32 E
Sawqirah, Ghubbat 75 18 35N 57 0 E
Sawu 87 10 35 S 121 50 E
Sawu Sea 87 9 30 S 121 50 E
Saxby → 110 18 25 S 140 53 E
Saxon 28 46 9N 7 11 E
Saxony, Lower = Niedersachsen □ 26 52 45N 9 0 E
Saxton 150 40 12N 78 18W
Say 127 13 8N 2 22 E
Saya 127 9 30N 3 18 E
Sayabec 143 48 35N 67 41W
Sayaboury 84 19 15N 101 45 E
Sayán 172 11 8 S 77 12W
Sayan, Vostochnyy 65 54 0N 96 0 E
Sayan, Zapadnyy 65 52 30N 94 0 E
Sayasan 61 42 56N 46 15 E
Saydā 70 33 35N 35 25 E
Sayghān 77 35 10N 67 55 E
Sayhan-Ovoo 94 45 27N 103 54 E
Sayhandulaan 94 44 40N 109 1 E
Sayḥut 75 15 12N 51 10 E
Saylorville Res. 154 41 43N 93 41W
Saynshand 94 44 55N 110 11 E
Sayō 100 34 59N 134 22 E
Sayre, Okla., U.S.A. 153 35 20N 99 40W
Sayre, Pa., U.S.A. 151 42 0N 76 30W
Sayula 160 19 50N 103 40W
Saywūn 75 15 56N 48 47 E
Sazan 48 40 30N 19 20 E
Sázava → 30 49 53N 14 24 E
Sazin 79 35 35N 73 30 E
Sazlika → 47 41 59N 25 50 E
Sbeïtla 121 35 12N 9 7 E
Scaër 18 48 2N 3 42W
Scafell Pikes 12 54 26N 3 14W
Scalea 45 39 49N 15 47 E
Scalpay 14 57 51N 6 40W
Scandia 144 50 20N 112 0W
Scandiano 42 44 36N 10 40 E
Scandinavia 10 64 0N 12 0 E
Scansano 43 42 40N 11 20 E
Scapa Flow 14 58 52N 3 6W
Scappoose 158 45 45N 122 53W
Scarborough, Trin. & Tob. 163 11 11N 60 42W
Scarborough, U.K. 12 54 17N 0 24W
Scargill 115 42 56 S 172 58 E
Scarsdale 112 37 41 S 143 39 E
Šćedro 43 43 6N 16 43 E
Scenic 152 43 49N 102 32W
Schaal See 26 53 40N 10 57 E
Schaan 29 47 10N 9 31 E
Schaesberg 23 50 54N 6 0 E
Schaffen 23 51 0N 5 5 E
Schaffhausen 29 47 42N 8 39 E
Schaffhausen □ 29 47 42N 8 36 E
Schagen 22 52 49N 4 48 E
Schaijk 22 51 44N 5 38 E
Schalkhaar 22 52 17N 6 12 E
Schalkwijk 22 52 0N 5 11 E
Schangnau 28 46 50N 7 47 E
Schänis 29 47 10N 9 3 E
Schärding 30 48 27N 13 27 E
Scharhörn 26 53 58N 8 24 E
Scharnitz 30 47 23N 11 15 E
Scheessel 26 53 10N 9 33 E
Schefferville 143 54 48N 66 50W
Scheibbs 30 48 1N 15 9 E
Schelde → 23 51 15N 4 16 E
Schell City 154 38 1N 94 7W
Schell Creek Ra. 156 39 15N 114 30W
Schenectady 151 42 50N 73 58W
Scherfede 26 51 32N 9 2 E
Scherpenheuvel 23 50 58N 4 58 E
Scherpenisse 23 51 33N 4 6 E
Scherpenzeel 22 52 5N 5 30 E
Schesaplana 29 47 5N 9 43 E
Schesslitz 27 49 59N 11 2 E
Scheveningen 22 52 6N 4 16 E
Schiedam 22 51 55N 4 25 E
Schiermonnikoog 22 53 30N 6 15 E
Schiers 29 46 58N 9 41 E
Schifferstadt 27 49 22N 8 23 E
Schifflange 23 49 30N 6 1 E
Schijndel 23 51 37N 5 27 E
Schiltigheim 19 48 35N 7 45 E
Schio 43 45 42N 11 21 E
Schipbeek 22 52 14N 6 10 E
Schipluiden 22 51 59N 4 19 E
Schirmeck 19 48 29N 7 12 E
Schladming 30 47 23N 13 41 E
Schlei → 26 54 45N 9 52 E
Schleiden 26 50 32N 6 26 E
Schleiz 26 50 35N 11 49 E
Schleswig 26 54 32N 9 34 E
Schleswig-Holstein □ 26 54 10N 9 40 E
Schlieren 29 47 26N 8 27 E
Schlüchtern 27 50 20N 9 32 E
Schmalkalden 26 50 43N 10 28 E
Schmölin 26 50 54N 12 22 E
Schmölln 26 53 15N 14 6 E
Schneeberg, Austria 30 47 47N 15 48 E
Schneeberg, Germany 26 50 35N 12 39 E
Schneider 155 41 13N 87 28W
Schoenberg 23 50 17N 6 16 E
Schofield 152 44 54N 89 39W
Scholls 158 45 24N 122 56W
Schönberg, Rostock, Germany 26 53 50N 10 55 E
Schönberg, Schleswig-Holstein, Germany 26 54 23N 10 20 E
Schönebeck 26 52 2N 11 42 E
Schönenwerd 28 47 23N 8 0 E
Schongau 27 47 49N 10 54 E
Schöningen 26 52 8N 10 57 E
Schoolcraft 155 42 7N 85 38W
Schoondijke 23 51 21N 3 33 E
Schoonebeek 22 52 39N 6 52 E
Schoonhoven 22 51 57N 4 51 E
Schoorl 22 52 42N 4 42 E
Schortens 26 53 37N 7 51 E
Schoten 23 51 16N 4 30 E
Schouten I. 110 42 20 S 148 20 E
Schouwen 23 51 43N 3 45 E
Schramberg 27 48 12N 8 24 E
Schrankogl 30 47 3N 11 7 E
Schreckhorn 28 46 36N 8 7 E
Schreiber 142 48 45N 87 20W
Schrobenhausen 27 48 33N 11 16 E
Schruns 30 47 5N 9 56 E
Schuler 145 50 20N 110 6W
Schuls 29 46 48N 10 18 E
Schumacher 142 48 30N 81 16W
Schüpfen 28 47 2N 7 24 E
Schüpfheim 28 46 57N 8 2 E
Schurz 156 38 57N 118 48W
Schuyler 152 41 30N 97 3W
Schuylkill Haven 151 40 37N 76 11W
Schwabach 27 49 19N 11 3 E
Schwäbisch Gmünd 27 48 49N 9 48 E
Schwäbisch Hall 27 49 7N 9 45 E
Schwäbische Alb 27 48 30N 9 30 E
Schwabmünchen 27 48 11N 10 45 E
Schwanden 29 46 58N 9 5 E
Schwandorf 27 49 20N 12 7 E
Schwaner, Pegunungan 89 1 0 S 112 30 E
Schwarmstedt 26 52 41N 9 37 E
Schwarzach → 30 46 56N 12 35 E
Schwärze 26 52 50N 13 49 E
Schwarzenberg 26 50 31N 12 49 E
Schwarzenburg 28 46 49N 7 20 E
Schwarzwald 27 48 0N 8 0 E
Schwaz 30 47 20N 11 44 E
Schwedt 26 53 4N 14 18 E
Schweinfurt 27 50 3N 10 12 E
Schweizer Mittelland 28 47 0N 7 15 E
Schweizer-Reneke 134 27 11 S 25 18 E
Schwerin 26 53 37N 11 22 E
Schwerin □ 26 53 35N 11 20 E
Schweriner See 26 53 45N 11 26 E
Schwetzingen 27 49 22N 8 35 E
Schwyz 29 47 2N 8 39 E
Schwyz □ 29 47 2N 8 39 E
Sciacca 44 37 30N 13 3 E
Sciao 136 3 26N 45 21 E
Scicli 45 36 48N 14 41 E
Scie, La 143 49 57N 55 36W
Scilla 45 38 18N 15 44 E
Scilly, Isles of 13 49 55N 6 15W
Ścinawa 32 51 25N 16 26 E
Scione 48 39 57N 23 36 E
Scioto → 148 38 44N 83 0W
Scobey 152 48 47N 105 30W
Scone, Australia 111 32 5 S 150 52 E
Scone, U.K. 14 56 25N 3 26W
Scordia 45 37 19N 14 50 E
Scoresbysund 6 70 20N 23 0W
Scorno, Punta dello 44 41 7N 8 23 E
Scotia, Calif., U.S.A. 156 40 36N 124 4W
Scotia, N.Y., U.S.A. 151 42 50N 73 58W
Scotia Sea 7 56 5 S 56 0W
Scotland 152 43 10N 97 45W
Scotland □ 14 57 0N 4 0W
Scotland Neck 149 36 6N 77 32W
Scott 7 77 0 S 165 0 E
Scott, C. 108 13 30 S 129 49 E
Scott City 152 38 30N 100 52W
Scott Glacier 7 66 15 S 100 5 E
Scott I. 7 67 0 S 179 0 E
Scott Inlet 141 71 0N 71 0W
Scott Is. 144 50 48N 128 40W
Scott L. 145 59 55N 106 18W
Scott Reef 108 14 0 S 121 50 E
Scottburgh 135 30 15 S 30 47 E
Scottdale 150 40 8N 79 35W
Scottsbluff 152 41 55N 103 35W
Scottsboro 149 34 40N 86 0W
Scottsburg 155 38 40N 85 46W
Scottsdale 110 41 9 S 147 31 E
Scottsville, Ky., U.S.A. 149 36 48N 86 10W
Scottsville, N.Y., U.S.A. 150 43 2N 77 47W
Scottville 148 43 57N 86 18W
Scranton, Iowa, U.S.A. 154 42 1N 94 33W
Scranton, Pa., U.S.A. 151 41 22N 75 41W
Scugog, L. 150 44 10N 78 55W
Scunthorpe 12 53 35N 0 38W
Scuol 29 46 48N 10 17 E
Scusciuban 136 10 18N 50 12 E
Scutari = Üsküdar 57 41 0N 29 5 E
Seabra 171 12 25 S 41 46W
Seabrook, L. 109 30 55 S 119 40 E
Seaford, Australia 113 38 10 S 145 11 E
Seaford, U.S.A. 148 38 37N 75 36W
Seaforth 142 43 35N 81 25W
Seagraves 153 32 56N 102 30W
Seal → 145 59 4N 94 48W
Seal Cove 143 49 57N 56 22W
Seal L. 143 54 20N 61 30W
Sealy 153 29 46N 96 9W
Seaman 155 38 57N 83 34W
Searchlight 159 35 31N 114 55W
Searcy 153 35 15N 91 45W
Searles L. 159 35 47N 117 17W
Seaside, Calif., U.S.A. 158 36 37N 121 50W
Seaside, Oreg., U.S.A. 158 45 59N 123 55W
Seaspray 113 38 25 S 147 15 E
Seattle 158 47 41N 122 15W
Seaview Ra. 110 18 40 S 145 45 E
Seaward Kaikouras, Mts. 115 42 10 S 173 44 E
Sebangka 88 0 7N 104 36 E
Sebastián Vizcaíno, B. 160 28 0N 114 30W
Sebastopol = Sevastopol 60 44 35N 33 30 E
Sebastopol 158 38 24N 122 49W
Sebderat 125 15 26N 36 42 E
Sebdou 121 34 38N 1 19W
Sebeş 50 45 58N 23 34 E
Sebeşului, Munţii 50 45 36N 23 40 E
Sebewaing 148 43 45N 83 27W
Sebezh 58 56 14N 28 22 E
Sébi 126 15 50N 4 12W
Şebinkarahisar 60 40 22N 38 28 E
Sebiş 50 46 23N 22 13 E
Sebkhet Te-n-Dghâmcha 126 18 30N 15 55W
Sebkra Azzel Mati 121 26 10N 0 43 E
Sebkra Mekerghene 121 26 21N 1 30 E
Seblat 88 3 14 S 101 38 E
Sebnitz 26 50 58N 14 17 E
Sebou, Oued → 120 34 16N 6 40W
Sebring, Fla., U.S.A. 149 27 30N 81 26W
Sebring, Ohio, U.S.A. 150 40 55N 81 2W
Sebringville 150 43 24N 81 4W
Sebta = Ceuta 120 35 52N 5 18W
Sebuku 89 3 30 S 116 25 E
Sebuku, Teluk 86 4 0N 118 10 E
Sečanj 46 45 25N 20 47 E
Secchia → 42 44 4N 11 0 E
Sechelt 144 49 25N 123 42W
Sechura 172 5 39 S 80 50W
Sechura, Desierto de 172 6 0 S 80 30W
Seclin 19 50 33N 3 2 E
Secondigny 18 46 37N 0 26W
Sečovce 31 48 42N 21 40 E
Secretary I. 115 45 15 S 166 56 E
Secunderabad 80 17 28N 78 30 E
Sécure → 173 15 10 S 64 52W
Sedalia 154 38 40N 93 18W
Sedan, Australia 112 34 34 S 139 19 E
Sedan, France 19 49 43N 4 57 E
Sedan, U.S.A. 153 37 10N 96 11W
Sedano 36 42 43N 3 49W
Seddon 115 41 40 S 174 7 E
Seddonville 115 41 33 S 172 1 E
Sede Ya'aqov 69 32 43N 35 7 E
Sedeh, Fārs, Iran 73 30 45N 52 11 E
Sedeh, Khorāsān, Iran 73 33 20N 59 14 E
Sederot 71 31 32N 34 37 E
Sedgewick 144 52 48N 111 41W
Sedhiou 126 12 44N 15 30W
Sedičany 30 49 40N 14 25 E
Sedico 43 46 8N 12 6 E
Sedienie 47 42 16N 24 33 E
Sedley 145 50 10N 104 0W
Sedom 69 31 5N 35 20 E
Sedova, Pik 64 73 29N 54 58 E
Sedrata 121 36 7N 7 31 E
Sedro Woolley 158 48 30N 122 15W
Seduva 58 55 45N 23 45 E
Sedziszów Malapolski 32 50 5N 21 45 E
Seebad Ahlbeck 26 53 56N 14 10 E
Seefeld 30 47 19N 11 13 E
Seehausen 26 52 52N 11 43 E
Seeheim 134 26 50 S 17 45 E
Seekoei → 134 30 18 S 25 1 E
Seelaw 26 52 32N 14 22 E
Sées 18 48 38N 0 10 E
Seesen 26 51 53N 10 10 E
Sefadu 126 8 35N 10 58W
Séfeto 126 14 8N 9 49W
Sefrou 120 33 52N 4 52W
Sefton 115 43 15 S 172 41 E
Sefuri-San 100 33 28N 130 18 E
Sefwi Bekwai 126 6 10N 2 25W
Seg-ozero 58 63 0N 33 10 E
Segag 136 7 39N 42 50 E
Segamat 85 2 30N 102 50 E
Segarcea 50 44 6N 23 43 E
Segbwema 126 8 0N 11 0W
Seget 87 1 24 S 130 58 E
Segezha 56 63 44N 34 19 E
Seggueur, O. → 121 32 4N 2 4 E
Segonzac 20 45 36N 0 14W
Segorbe 36 39 50N 0 30W
Ségou 126 13 30N 6 16W
Segovia = Coco → 162 15 0N 83 8W
Segovia, Colombia 168 7 7N 74 42W
Segovia, Spain 34 40 57N 4 10W
Segovia □ 34 40 55N 4 10W
Segré 18 47 40N 0 52W
Segre → 36 41 40N 0 43 E
Séguéla 126 7 55N 6 40W
Seguin 153 29 34N 97 58W
Segundo → 174 30 53 S 62 44W
Segura → 37 38 6N 0 54W
Segura, Sierra de 37 38 5N 2 45W
Seh Qal'eh 73 33 40N 58 24 E
Sehitwa 134 20 30 S 22 30 E
Sehore 78 23 10N 77 5 E
Sehwan 77 26 28N 67 53 E
Şeica Mare 50 46 1N 24 7 E
Seikpyu 82 20 54N 94 48 E
Seiling 153 36 10N 98 56W
Seille → 21 46 31N 4 57 E
Seilles 23 50 30N 5 6 E

Szendrö

Szendrö 31 48 24N 20 41 E
Szentendre 31 47 39N 19 4 E
Szentes 31 46 39N 20 21 E
Szentgotthárd 31 46 58N 16 19 E
Szentlörinc 31 46 3N 18 1 E
Szerencs 31 48 10N 21 12 E
Szigetvár 31 46 3N 17 46 E
Szikszó 31 48 12N 20 56 E
Szkwa → 32 53 11N 21 43 E
Szlichtyngowa 32 51 42N 16 15 E
Szob 31 47 48N 18 53 E
Szolnok 31 47 10N 20 15 E
Szolnok □ 31 47 15N 20 30 E
Szombathely 31 47 14N 16 38 E
Szprotawa 32 51 33N 15 35 E
Sztum 32 53 55N 19 1 E
Sztutowo 32 54 20N 19 15 E
Szubin 32 53 1N 17 45 E
Szydłowiec 32 51 15N 20 51 E
Szypliszki 32 54 17N 23 2 E

T

't Harde 22 52 24N 5 54 E
't Zandt 22 53 22N 6 46 E
Ta Khli Khok 84 15 18N 100 20 E
Ta Lai 85 11 24N 107 23 E
Tabacal 174 23 15 S 64 15W
Tabaco 90 13 22N 123 44 E
Tabagné 126 7 59N 3 4W
Ṭābah 72 26 55N 42 38 E
Tabajara 173 8 56 S 62 8W
Tabalos 172 6 26 S 76 37W
Tabango 91 11 19N 124 22 E
Tabar Is. 107 2 50 S 152 0 E
Tabarca, I. de 37 38 17N 0 30W
Tabarka 121 36 56N 8 46 E
Ṭabas, Khorāsān, Iran 73 32 48N 60 12 E
Ṭabas, Khorāsān, Iran 73 33 35N 56 55 E
Tabasará, Serranía de 162 8 35N 81 40W
Tabasco □ 161 17 45N 93 30W
Tabatinga, Serra da 170 10 30 S 44 0W
Tabayin 82 22 42N 95 20 E
Tabāzīn 73 31 12N 57 54 E
Tabelbala, Kahal de 121 28 47N 2 0W
Taber 144 49 47N 112 8W
Tabernas 37 37 4N 2 26W
Tabernes de Valldigna 37 39 5N 0 13W
Tabi 133 8 10 S 13 18 E
Tabira 170 7 35 S 37 33W
Tablas 90 12 25N 122 2 E
Tablas Strait 90 12 40N 121 48 E
Table B. = Tafelbaai 134 33 35 S 18 25 E
Table B. 143 53 40N 56 25W
Table Grove 154 40 20N 90 27W
Table Mt. 134 34 0 S 18 22 E
Table Top, Mt. 110 23 24 S 147 11 E
Tableland 108 17 16 S 126 51 E
Tabogon 91 10 57N 124 2 E
Tábor, Czech. 30 49 25N 14 39 E
Tabor, Israel 69 32 42N 35 24 E
Tabora 130 5 2 S 32 50 E
Tabora □ 130 5 0 S 33 0 E
Tabory 62 58 31N 64 33 E
Tabou 126 4 30N 7 20W
Tabrīz 72 38 7N 46 20 E
Tabuelan 91 10 49N 123 52 E
Tabuenca 36 41 42N 1 33W
Tabuk, Phil. 90 17 24N 121 25 E
Tabūk, Si. Arabia 71 28 23N 36 36 E
Tacámbaro de Codallos 160 19 14N 101 28W
Tacheng 92 46 40N 82 58 E
Tachibana-Wan 100 32 45N 130 7 E
Tachikawa 101 35 42N 139 25 E
Tach'ing Shan = Daqing Shan 94 40 40N 111 0 E
Tachira 168 8 7N 72 15 E
Táchira □ 168 8 7N 72 15W
Tachov 30 49 47N 12 39 E
Tácina → 45 38 57N 16 55 E
Tacloban 91 11 15N 124 58 E
Tacna 172 18 0 S 70 20W
Tacna □ 172 17 40 S 70 20W
Tacoma 158 47 15N 122 30W
Tacuarembó 175 31 45 S 56 0W
Tacutu → 169 3 1N 60 29W
Tademaït, Plateau du 121 28 30N 2 30 E
Tadent, O. → 121 22 25N 6 40 E
Tadjerdjeri, O. → 121 26 0N 8 0W
Tadjerouna 121 33 31N 2 3 E
Tadjettaret, O. → 121 21 20N 7 22 E
Tadjmout, Oasis, Algeria 121 33 52N 2 30 E
Tadjmout, Saoura, Algeria 121 25 37N 3 48 E
Tadjoura 125 11 50N 42 55 E
Tadjoura, Golfe de 125 11 50N 43 0 E
Tadmor 115 41 27 S 172 45 E
Tadotsu 100 34 16N 133 45 E
Tadoule, L. 145 58 36N 98 20W
Tadoussac 143 48 11N 69 42W
Tadzhik S.S.R. □ 63 35 30N 70 0 E
Taechŏn-ni 95 36 21N 126 36 E
Taegu 95 35 50N 128 37 E
Taegwan 95 40 13N 125 12 E
Taejŏn 95 36 20N 127 28 E
Tafalla 36 42 30N 1 41W
Tafar 125 6 52N 28 15 E
Ṭafas 69 32 44N 36 5 E
Tafassasset, O. → 121 22 0N 9 57 E
Tafelbaai 134 33 35 S 18 25 E
Tafelney, C. 120 31 3N 9 51W
Tafermaar 87 6 47 S 134 10 E
Taffermit 120 29 37N 9 15W
Tafí Viejo 174 26 43 S 65 17W
Tafīhān 73 29 25N 52 39 E
Tafiré 126 9 4N 5 4W
Tafnidilt 120 28 47N 10 58W
Tafraoute 120 29 50N 8 58W
Taft, Iran 73 31 45N 54 14 E
Taft, Phil. 91 11 57N 125 30 E
Taft, Calif., U.S.A. 159 35 9N 119 28W
Taft, Tex., U.S.A. 153 27 58N 97 23W
Taga Dzong 82 27 5N 89 55 E
Tagana-an 91 9 42N 125 35 E
Taganrog 61 47 12N 38 50 E
Taganrogskiy Zaliv 60 47 0N 38 30 E
Tagânt 126 18 20N 11 0W
Tagap Ga 82 26 56N 96 13 E
Tagapula I. 90 12 4N 124 12 E
Tagatay 90 14 6N 120 56 E
Tagauayan I. 91 10 58N 121 13 E
Tagbilaran 91 9 39N 123 51 E
Tage 107 6 19 S 143 20 E
Tággia 42 43 52N 7 50 E
Taghrīfat 122 29 5N 17 26 E
Taghzout 120 33 30N 4 49W
Tagish 144 60 19N 134 16W
Tagish L. 140 60 10N 134 20W
Tagkawayan 90 13 58N 122 32 E
Tagliacozzo 43 42 4N 13 13 E
Tagliamento → 43 45 38N 13 5 E
Táglio di Po 43 45 0N 12 12 E
Tagna 168 2 24 S 70 37W
Tago 91 9 2N 126 13 E
Tago, Mt. 91 8 23N 125 5 E
Tagomago, I. de 37 39 2N 1 39 E
Tagua, La 168 0 3N 74 40W
Taguatinga 171 12 16 S 42 26W
Tagudin 90 16 56N 120 27 E
Tagula 107 11 22 S 153 15 E
Tagula I. 107 11 30 S 153 30 E
Tagum 91 7 33N 125 53 E
Tagus = Tajo → 33 38 40N 9 24W
Tahakopa 115 46 30 S 169 23 E
Tahala 121 34 0N 4 28W
Tahan, Gunong 85 4 34N 102 17 E
Tahānah-ye sūr Gol 77 31 43N 67 53 E
Tahara 101 34 40N 137 16 E
Tahat 121 23 18N 5 33 E
Tāherī 73 27 43N 52 20 E
Tahiti 106 17 37 S 149 27W
Tahoe, L. 158 39 0N 120 9W
Tahoe City 158 39 12N 120 9W
Taholah 158 47 21N 124 17W
Tahora 114 39 2 S 174 49 E
Tahoua 127 14 57N 5 16 E
Tahta 124 26 44N 31 32 E
Tahuamanu → 172 11 6 S 67 36W
Tahulandang 87 2 27N 125 23 E
Tahuna 87 3 38N 125 30 E
Taï 126 5 55N 7 30W
Tai Shan 95 36 25N 117 20 E
Tai Xian 97 32 30N 120 7 E
Tai'an 95 36 12N 117 8 E
Taibei 97 25 4N 121 29 E
Taibique 37 27 42N 17 58W
Taibus Qi 94 41 54N 115 22 E
T'aichung = Taizhong 97 24 12N 120 35 E
Taidong 97 22 43N 121 9 E
Taieri → 115 46 3 S 170 12 E
Taiga Madema 122 23 46N 15 25 E
Taigu 94 37 28N 112 30 E
Taihang Shan 94 36 0N 113 30 E
Taihape 114 39 41 S 175 48 E
Taihe, Anhui, China 94 33 20N 115 42 E
Taihe, Jiangxi, China 97 26 47N 114 52 E
Taihu 97 30 22N 116 20 E
Taijiang 96 26 39N 108 21 E
Taikang 94 34 5N 114 50 E
Taikkyi 82 17 20N 96 0 E
Tailem Bend 112 35 12 S 139 29 E
Tailfingen 27 48 15N 9 1 E
Taimyr = Taymyr, Poluostrov 65 75 0N 100 0 E
Taimyr, Oz. 65 74 20N 102 0 E
Tain 14 57 49N 4 4W
Tainan 97 23 17N 120 18 E
Taínaron, Ákra 49 36 22N 22 27 E
Tainggyo 82 17 49N 94 29 E
Taining 97 26 54N 117 9 E
Taintignies 23 50 33N 3 22 E
Taiobeiras 171 15 49 S 42 14W
T'aipei = Taibei 97 25 4N 121 29 E
Taiping, China 97 30 15N 118 6 E
Taiping, Malaysia 85 4 51N 100 44 E
Taipingzhen 94 33 35N 111 42 E
Taipu 170 5 37 S 35 36W
Taisha 100 35 24N 132 40 E
Taishan 97 22 14N 112 41 E
Taishun 97 27 30N 119 42 E
Taita □ 130 4 0 S 38 30 E
Taita Hills 130 3 25 S 38 15 E
Taitao, C. 176 45 53 S 75 5W
Taitao, Pen. de 176 46 30 S 75 0W
Taiwan ■ 97 23 30N 121 0 E
Taiwan Shan 97 23 40N 121 20 E
Taixing 97 32 11N 120 0 E
Taïyetos Óros 49 37 0N 22 23 E
Taiyib → 69 31 55N 35 17 E
Taiyiba 69 32 36N 35 27 E
Taiyuan 94 37 52N 112 33 E
Taizhong 97 24 12N 120 35 E
Taizhou 97 32 28N 119 55 E
Taizhou Liedao 97 28 30N 121 55 E
Ta'izz 74 13 35N 44 2 E
Tājābād 73 30 2N 54 24 E
Tajapuru, Furo do 170 1 50 S 50 25W
Tajarḥī 122 24 21N 14 28 E
Tajima 99 37 12N 139 46 E
Tajimi 101 35 19N 137 8 E
Tajo → 33 38 40N 9 24W
Tajrīsh 73 35 48N 51 25 E
Tājūrā 122 32 51N 13 21 E
Tak 84 16 52N 99 8 E
Takāb 72 36 24N 47 7 E
Takachiho 100 32 42N 131 18 E
Takada 99 37 7N 138 15 E
Takahagi 99 36 43N 140 45 E
Takahashi 100 34 51N 133 39 E
Takaka 115 40 51 S 172 50 E
Takamatsu 100 34 20N 134 5 E
Takanabe 100 32 8N 131 30 E
Takaoka 101 36 47N 137 0 E
Takapau 114 40 2 S 176 21 E
Takapuna 114 36 47 S 174 47 E
Takasago 100 34 45N 134 48 E
Takasaki 101 36 20N 139 0 E
Takase 100 34 7N 133 48 E
Takatsuki 101 34 51N 135 37 E
Takaungu 130 3 38 S 39 52 E
Takawa 100 33 38N 130 51 E
Takayama 101 36 18N 137 11 E
Takayama-Bonchi 101 36 0N 137 18 E
Take-Shima 99 30 49N 130 26 E
Takefu 101 35 50N 136 10 E
Takehara 100 34 21N 132 55 E
Takengon 88 4 45N 96 50 E
Takeo, Cambodia 85 10 59N 104 47 E
Takeo, Japan 100 33 12N 130 1 E
Tåkern 53 58 22N 14 45 E
Tākestān 73 36 0N 49 40 E
Taketa 100 32 58N 131 24 E
Takh 79 33 6N 77 32 E
Takhār □ 77 36 40N 70 0 E
Takhman 85 11 29N 104 57 E
Taki 107 6 29 S 155 52 E
Takikawa 98 43 33N 141 54 E
Takla L. 144 55 15N 125 45W
Takla Landing 144 55 30N 125 50W
Takla Makan 66 39 0N 83 0 E
Taku 100 33 18N 130 3 E
Taku → 144 58 30N 133 50W
Takua Pa 85 7 18N 9 59 E
Takum 127 7 18N 9 36 E
Takuma 100 34 13N 133 40 E
Takundi 133 4 45 S 16 34 E
Takuran 91 7 51N 123 34 E
Takutu → 169 3 1N 60 29W
Tal Halāl 73 28 54N 55 1 E
Tala 175 34 21 S 55 46W
Talacogan 91 8 32N 125 39 E
Talagante 174 33 40 S 70 50W
Talaïnt 120 29 41N 9 40W
Talak 127 18 0N 5 0 E
Talakag 91 8 16N 124 37 E
Talamanca, Cordillera de 162 9 20N 83 20W
Talara 172 4 38 S 81 18 E
Talas 63 42 30N 72 13 E
Talas → 63 44 0N 70 20 E
Talasea 107 5 20 S 150 2 E
Talasskiy, Khrebet 63 42 15N 72 0 E
Talâta 71 30 36N 30 20 E
Talata Mafara 127 12 38N 6 4 E
Talaud, Kepulauan 87 4 30N 127 10 E
Talavera de la Reina 34 39 55N 4 46W
Talawana 108 22 51 S 121 9 E
Talawgyi 82 25 4N 97 19 E
Talayan 91 6 52N 124 24 E
Talbert, Sillon de 18 48 53N 3 5W
Talbot, C. 108 13 48 S 126 43 E
Talbragar → 113 32 12 S 148 37 E
Talca 174 35 28 S 71 40W
Talca □ 174 35 20 S 71 46W
Talcahuano 174 36 40 S 73 10W
Talcher 79 21 0N 85 18 E
Talcho 127 14 44N 3 28 E
Taldy Kurgan 64 45 10N 78 45 E
Talesh 73 37 58N 48 58 E
Ṭalesh, Kūhhā-ye 73 39 0N 48 30 E
Talfīt 69 32 5N 35 17 E
Talgar 63 43 19N 77 15 E
Talgar, Pic 63 43 5N 77 20 E
Talguharai 124 18 19N 35 56 E
Tali Post 125 5 55N 30 44 E
Taliabu 87 1 45 S 125 0 E
Talibon 91 10 9N 124 20 E
Talibong, Ko 85 7 15N 99 23 E
Talihina 153 34 45N 95 1W
Talikota 81 16 29N 76 17 E
Talimardzhan 63 38 23N 65 37 E
Talisay 91 10 44N 122 58 E
Talisayan 91 9 0N 124 55 E
Talitsa 62 57 0N 63 43 E
Taliwang 86 8 50 S 116 55 E
Talkeetna 140 62 20N 150 9W
Tall 69 33 0N 35 6 E
Tall 'Asūr 69 31 59N 35 17 E
Tall Kalakh 70 34 41N 36 15 E
Talla 124 28 5N 30 43 E
Talladega 149 33 28N 86 2W
Tallahassee 149 30 25N 84 15W
Tallangatta 113 36 15 S 147 19 E
Tallarook 113 37 5 S 145 6 E
Tallawang 113 32 12 S 149 28 E
Tällberg 52 60 51N 15 2 E
Tallering Pk. 109 28 6 S 115 37 E
Tallinn 58 59 22N 24 48 E
Tallulah 153 32 25N 91 12W
Ṭallūzā 69 32 17N 35 18 E
Tălmaciu 50 45 38N 24 19 E
Talmest 120 31 48N 9 21W
Talmont 20 46 27N 1 37W
Talnoye 60 48 50N 30 44 E
Taloda 78 21 34N 74 11 E
Talodi 125 10 35N 30 22 E
Talomo 91 7 3N 125 32 E
Talovaya 59 51 6N 40 45 E
Talpa de Allende 160 20 23N 104 51W
Tālqān 77 36 44N 69 33 E
Talsi 58 57 10N 22 30 E
Talsinnt 121 32 33N 3 27W
Taltal 174 25 23 S 70 33W
Taltson → 144 61 24N 112 46W
Talwood 111 28 29 S 149 29 E
Talyawalka Cr. → 112 32 28 S 142 22 E
Tam Chau 85 10 48N 105 12 E
Tam Ky 84 15 34N 108 29 E
Tam Quan 84 14 35N 109 3 E
Tama 154 41 56N 92 37W
Tamala 109 26 42 S 113 47 E
Tamalameque 168 8 52N 73 49W
Tamale 127 9 22N 0 50W
Taman 60 45 14N 36 41 E
Tamana 100 32 58N 130 32 E
Tamanar 120 31 1N 9 46W
Tamano 100 34 29N 133 59 E
Tamanrasset 121 22 50N 5 30 E
Tamanrasset, O. → 121 22 0N 2 0 E
Tamanthi 82 25 19N 95 17 E
Tamaqua 151 40 46N 75 58W
Tamar → 13 50 33N 4 15W
Támara 168 5 50N 72 10W
Tamarang 111 31 27 S 150 5 E
Tamarite de Litera 36 41 52N 0 25 E
Tamaroa 154 38 8N 89 14W
Tamashima 100 34 32N 133 40 E
Tamási 31 46 40N 18 18 E
Tamaské 127 14 49N 5 43 E
Tamaulipas □ 161 24 0N 99 0W
Tamaulipas, Sierra de 161 23 30N 98 20W
Tamazula 160 24 55N 106 58W
Tamazunchale 161 21 16N 98 47W
Tamba-Dabatou 126 11 50N 10 40W
Tambacounda 126 13 45N 13 40W
Tambelan, Kepulauan 88 1 0N 107 30 E
Tambellup 109 34 4 S 117 37 E
Tambo, Australia 110 24 54 S 146 14 E
Tambo, Peru 172 12 57 S 74 1W
Tambo → 172 10 42 S 73 47W
Tambo de Mora 172 13 30 S 76 8W
Tambobamba 172 13 54 S 72 8W
Tambohorano 135 17 30 S 43 58 E
Tambopata → 172 13 21 S 69 36W
Tambora 86 8 12 S 118 5 E
Tamboritha, Mt. 113 37 31 S 146 40 E
Tambov 59 52 45N 41 28 E
Tambre → 34 42 49N 8 53W
Tambuku 89 7 8 S 113 40 E
Tambun Sigumbal 91 6 5N 121 47 E
Tamburâ 125 5 40N 27 25 E
Tâmchekket 126 17 25N 10 40W
Tamdybulak 63 41 46N 64 36 E
Tame 168 6 28N 71 44W
Tamega → 34 41 5N 8 21W
Tamelelt 120 31 50N 7 32W
Tamenglong 82 25 0N 93 35 E
Tamerlanovka 63 42 36N 69 17 E
Tamerza 121 34 23N 7 58 E
Tamiahua, L. de 161 21 30N 97 30W
Tamil Nadu □ 81 11 0N 77 0 E
Tamines 23 50 26N 4 36 E
Tamluk 79 22 18N 87 58 E
Tammerfors = Tampere 55 61 30N 23 50 E
Tammisaari 55 60 0N 23 26 E
Ṭammūn 69 32 18N 35 23 E
Tämnaren 52 60 10N 17 25 E
Tamo Abu, Pegunungan 86 3 10N 115 0 E
Tampa 149 27 57N 82 38W
Tampa B. 149 27 40N 82 40W
Tampere 55 61 30N 23 50 E
Tampico, Mexico 161 22 20N 97 50W
Tampico, U.S.A. 154 41 38N 89 47W
Tampin 85 2 28N 102 13 E
Tamrah 74 20 24N 45 25 E
Tamri 120 30 49N 9 50W
Tamrida = Qādib 75 12 37N 53 57 E
Tamsalu 58 59 11N 26 8 E
Tamsweg 30 47 7N 13 49 E
Tamuja → 35 39 38N 6 29W
Tamworth, Australia 111 31 7 S 150 58 E
Tamworth, U.K. 13 52 38N 1 41W
Tamyang 95 35 19N 126 59 E
Tan An 85 10 32N 106 25 E
Tan-tan 120 28 29N 11 1W
Tana 54 70 26N 28 14 E

Taz → **64** 67 32N 78 40 E
Taza **121** 34 16N 4 6W
Tāzah Khurmātū **72** 35 18N 44 20 E
Tazawa-Ko **98** 39 43N 140 40 E
Taze **82** 22 57N 95 24 E
Tazenakht **120** 30 35N 7 12W
Tazerbo **122** 25 45N 21 0 E
Tazin L. **145** 59 44N 108 42W
Tazoult **121** 35 29N 6 11 E
Tazovskiy **64** 67 30N 78 44 E
Tbilisi **61** 41 43N 44 50 E
Tchad = Chad ■ **123** 15 0N 17 15 E
Tchad, L. **123** 13 30N 14 30 E
Tchaourou **127** 8 58N 2 40 E
Tch'eng-tou = Chengdu **96** 30 38N 104 2 E
Tchentlo L. **144** 55 15N 125 0W
Tchibanga **132** 2 45 S 11 0 E
Tchien **126** 5 59N 8 15W
Tchikala-Tcholohanga **133** 12 38 S 16 3 E
Tchin Tabaraden **127** 15 58N 5 56 E
Tchingou, Massif de **106** 20 54 S 165 0 E
Tchollíré **132** 8 24N 14 10 E
Tch'ong-k'ing = Chongqing **96** 29 35N 106 25 E
Tczew **32** 54 8N 18 50 E
Te Anau, L. **115** 45 15 S 167 45 E
Te Araroa **114** 37 39 S 178 25 E
Te Aroha **114** 37 32 S 175 44 E
Te Awamutu **114** 38 1 S 175 20 E
Te Kaha **114** 37 44 S 177 52 E
Te Karaka **114** 38 26 S 177 53 E
Te Kauwhata **114** 37 25 S 175 9 E
Te Kopuru **114** 36 2 S 173 56 E
Te Kuiti **114** 38 20 S 175 11 E
Te Puke **114** 37 46 S 176 22 E
Te Waewae B. **115** 46 13 S 167 33 E
Tea → **168** 0 30 S 65 9W
Tea Tree **110** 22 5 S 133 22 E
Teaca **50** 46 55N 24 30 E
Teague **153** 31 40N 96 20W
Teano **45** 41 15N 14 1 E
Teapa **161** 18 35N 92 56W
Teba **35** 36 59N 4 55W
Tebakang **86** 1 6N 110 30 E
Teberda **61** 43 30N 41 46 E
Tébessa **121** 35 22N 8 8 E
Tebicuary → **174** 26 36 S 58 16W
Tebingtinggi **88** 3 20N 99 9 E
Tebintingii **88** 1 0N 102 45 E
Tébourba **121** 36 49N 9 51 E
Téboursouk **121** 36 29N 9 10 E
Tebulos **61** 42 36N 45 17 E
Tecate **160** 32 34N 116 38W
Tech → **20** 42 36N 3 3 E
Techa → **62** 56 13N 62 58 E
Techiman **126** 7 35N 1 58W
Techirghiol **50** 44 4N 28 32 E
Tecka **176** 7 35N 1 43W
Tecomán **160** 18 55N 103 53W
Tecopa **159** 35 51N 116 14W
Tecoripa **160** 28 37N 109 57W
Tecuala **160** 22 23N 105 27W
Tecuci **50** 45 51N 27 27 E
Tecumseh **155** 42 1N 83 59W
Ted **136** 4 24N 43 55 E
Tedzhen **64** 37 23N 60 31 E
Tees → **12** 54 36N 1 25W
Teesside **12** 54 37N 1 13W
Teeswater **150** 43 59N 81 17W
Tefé **169** 3 25 S 64 50W
Tefé → **169** 3 35 S 64 47W
Tegal **89** 6 52 S 109 8 E
Tegelen **23** 51 20N 6 9 E
Tegernsee **27** 47 43N 11 46 E
Teggiano **45** 40 24N 15 32 E
Teghra **79** 25 30N 85 34 E
Tegid, L. **12** 52 53N 3 38W
Tegina **127** 10 5N 6 11 E
Tegucigalpa **162** 14 5N 87 14W
Tehachapi **159** 35 11N 118 29W
Tehachapi Mts. **159** 35 0N 118 40W
Tehamiyam **124** 18 20N 36 32 E
Tehilla **124** 17 42N 36 6 E
Téhini **126** 9 39N 3 40W
Tehrān **73** 35 44N 51 30 E
Tehuacán **161** 18 30N 97 30W
Tehuantepec **161** 16 21N 95 13W
Tehuantepec, G. de **161** 15 50N 95 0W
Tehuantepec, Istmo de **161** 17 0N 94 30W
Teide **37** 28 15N 16 38W
Teifi → **13** 52 4N 4 14W
Teign → **13** 50 41N 3 42W
Teignmouth **13** 50 33N 3 30W
Teil, Le **21** 44 33N 4 40 E
Teilleul, Le **18** 48 32N 0 53W
Teiuş **50** 46 12N 23 40 E
Teixeira **170** 7 13 S 37 15W
Teixeira Pinto **126** 12 3N 16 0W
Tejo → **35** 38 40N 9 24W
Tejon Pass **159** 34 49N 118 53W
Tekamah **152** 41 48N 96 22W
Tekapo, L. **115** 43 53 S 170 33 E
Tekax **161** 20 11N 89 18W
Tekeli **63** 44 50N 79 0 E
Tekeze → **125** 14 20N 35 50 E
Tekija **46** 44 42N 22 26 E
Tekirdağ **57** 40 58N 27 30 E
Tekkali **80** 18 37N 84 15 E
Tekoa **156** 47 19N 117 4W
Tekouiât, O. → **121** 22 25N 2 35 E
Tel Adashim **69** 32 30N 35 17 E
Tel Aviv-Yafo **69** 32 4N 34 48 E
Tel Lakhish **69** 31 34N 34 51 E
Tel Megiddo **69** 32 35N 35 11 E
Tel Mond **69** 32 15N 34 56 E
Tela **162** 15 40N 87 28W
Télagh **121** 34 51N 0 32W
Telanaipura = Jambi **88** 1 38 S 103 30 E
Telavi **61** 42 0N 45 30 E
Telciu **50** 47 25N 24 24 E
Telde **37** 27 59N 15 25W
Telefomin **107** 5 10 S 141 31 E
Telegraph Cr. → **144** 58 0N 131 10W
Telekhany **58** 52 30N 25 46 E
Telemark fylke □ **51** 59 25N 8 30 E
Telén **174** 36 15 S 65 31W
Telen → **89** 0 10 S 117 20 E
Teleng **73** 25 47N 61 3 E
Teleño **34** 42 23N 6 22W
Teleorman □ **50** 44 0N 25 0 E
Teleorman → **50** 44 15N 25 20 E
Teles Pires → **173** 7 21 S 58 3W
Telescope Peak **159** 36 6N 117 7W
Teletaye **127** 16 31N 1 30 E
Telford **12** 52 42N 2 31W
Telfs **30** 47 19N 11 4 E
Telgte **26** 51 59N 7 46 E
Télimélé **126** 10 54N 13 2W
Telkwa **144** 54 41N 127 5W
Tell City **155** 38 0N 86 44W
Tellicherry **81** 11 45N 75 30 E
Tellin **23** 50 5N 5 13 E
Telluride **157** 37 58N 107 48W
Teloloapán **161** 18 21N 99 51W
Telpos Iz **56** 63 35N 57 30 E
Telsen **176** 42 30 S 66 50W
Telšiai **58** 55 59N 22 14 E
Teltow **26** 52 24N 13 15 E
Teluk Anson **85** 4 3N 101 0 E
Teluk Betung = Tanjungkarang Telukbetung **88** 5 20 S 105 10 E
Teluk Intan = Teluk Anson **85** 4 3N 101 0 E
Telukbutun **85** 4 13N 108 12 E
Telukdalem **88** 0 33N 97 50 E
Tema **127** 5 41N 0 0 E
Temanggung **89** 7 18 S 110 10 E
Temapache **161** 21 4N 97 38W
Temax **161** 21 10N 88 50W
Temba **135** 25 20 S 28 17 E
Tembe **130** 0 16 S 28 14 E
Tembesi **88** 1 43 S 103 6 E
Tembilahan **88** 0 19 S 103 9 E
Temblador **169** 8 59N 62 44W
Tembleque **36** 39 41N 3 30W
Temblor Ra. **159** 35 30N 120 0W
Teme → **13** 52 23N 2 15W
Temecula **159** 33 26N 117 6W
Temerloh **85** 3 27N 102 25 E
Temir **64** 49 21N 57 3 E
Temirtau, Kazakh S.S.R., U.S.S.R. **64** 50 5N 72 56 E
Temirtau, R.S.F.S.R., U.S.S.R. **64** 53 10N 87 30 E
Témiscaming **142** 46 44N 79 5W
Temma **110** 41 12 S 144 48 E
Temnikov **59** 54 40N 43 11 E
Temo → **44** 40 20N 8 30 E
Temora **113** 34 30 S 147 30 E
Temosachic **160** 28 58N 107 50W
Tempe **157** 33 26N 111 59W
Tempe Downs **108** 24 22 S 132 24 E
Tempio Pausania **44** 40 53N 9 6 E
Tempiute **158** 37 39N 115 38W
Temple **153** 31 5N 97 22W
Temple B. **110** 12 15 S 143 3 E
Templemore **15** 52 48N 7 50W
Templeton **158** 35 33N 120 42W
Templeton → **110** 21 0 S 138 40 E
Templeuve **23** 50 39N 3 17 E
Templin **26** 53 8N 13 31 E
Tempoal **161** 21 31N 98 23W
Temryuk **60** 45 15N 37 24 E
Temse **23** 51 7N 4 13 E
Temska → **46** 43 17N 22 33 E
Temuco **176** 38 45 S 72 40W
Temuka **115** 44 14 S 171 17 E
Ten Boer **22** 53 16N 6 42 E
Tena **168** 0 59 S 77 49W
Tenabo **161** 20 2N 90 12W
Tenaha **153** 31 57N 94 25W
Tenali **81** 16 15N 80 35 E
Tenancingo **161** 19 0N 99 33W
Tenango **161** 19 7N 99 33W
Tenasserim **85** 12 6N 99 3 E
Tenasserim □ **84** 14 0N 98 30 E
Tenay **21** 45 55N 5 31 E
Tenby **13** 51 40N 4 42W
Tenda, Col di **21** 44 7N 7 36 E
Tendaho **125** 11 48N 40 54 E
Tende **21** 44 5N 7 35 E
Tendelti **125** 13 1N 31 55 E
Tendjedi, Adrar **121** 23 41N 7 32 E
Tendrara **121** 33 3N 1 58W
Tendre, Mt. **28** 46 35N 6 18 E
Teneida **124** 25 30N 29 19 E
Tenente Marques → **173** 11 10 S 59 56W
Ténéré **127** 19 0N 10 30 E
Ténéré, Erg du **123** 17 35N 10 55 E
Tenerife **37** 28 15N 16 35W
Tenerife, Pico **37** 27 43N 18 1W
Ténès **121** 36 31N 1 14 E
Teng Xian, Guangxi Zhuangzu, China **97** 23 21N 110 56 E
Teng Xian, Shandong, China **95** 35 5N 117 10 E
Tengah □ **87** 2 0 S 122 0 E
Tengah Kepulauan **89** 7 5 S 118 15 E
Tengchong **96** 25 0N 98 28 E
Tengchowfu = Penglai **95** 37 48N 120 42 E
Tenggara □ **87** 3 0 S 122 0 E
Tenggarong **89** 0 24 S 116 58 E
Tenggol, P. **85** 4 48N 103 41 E
Tengiz, Ozero **64** 50 30N 69 0 E
Tenigerbad **29** 46 42N 8 57 E
Tenino **158** 46 51N 122 51W
Tenkasi **81** 8 55N 77 20 E
Tenke, Shaba, Zaïre **131** 11 22 S 26 40 E
Tenke, Shaba, Zaïre **131** 10 32 S 26 7 E
Tenkodogo **127** 11 54N 0 19W
Tenna → **43** 43 12N 13 47 E
Tennant Creek **110** 19 30 S 134 15 E
Tennessee □ **147** 36 0N 86 30W
Tennessee → **148** 37 4N 88 34W
Tenneville **23** 50 6N 5 32 E
Tennille **149** 32 58N 82 50W
Tennsift, Oued → **120** 32 3N 9 28W
Tennyson **155** 38 5N 87 7W
Teno, Pta. de **37** 28 21N 16 55W
Tenom **86** 5 4N 115 57 E
Tenosique **161** 17 30N 91 24W
Tenri **101** 34 39N 135 49 E
Tenryū **101** 34 52N 137 49 E
Tenryū-Gawa → **101** 35 39N 137 48 E
Tent L. **145** 62 25N 107 54W
Tenterfield **111** 29 0 S 152 0 E
Teófilo Otoni **171** 17 50 S 41 30W
Teotihuacán **161** 19 44N 98 50W
Tepa **87** 7 52 S 129 31 E
Tepalcatepec → **160** 18 35N 101 59W
Tepehuanes **160** 25 21N 105 44W
Tepelena **48** 40 17N 20 2 E
Tepequem, Serra **169** 3 45N 61 45W
Tepetongo **160** 22 28N 103 9W
Tepic **160** 21 30N 104 54W
Teplice **30** 50 40N 13 48 E
Teploklyuchenka **63** 42 30N 78 30 E
Tepoca, C. **160** 30 20N 112 25W
Tequila **160** 20 54N 103 47W
Ter → **36** 42 0N 3 12 E
Ter Apel **22** 52 53N 7 5 E
Téra **127** 14 0N 0 45 E
Tera → **34** 41 54N 5 44W
Teraina, I. **105** 4 43N 160 25W
Téramo **43** 42 40N 13 40 E
Terang **112** 38 15 S 142 55 E
Terawhiti, C. **114** 41 16 S 174 38 E
Terazit, Massif de **123** 20 2N 8 30 E
Terborg **22** 51 56N 6 22 E
Tercero → **174** 32 58 S 61 47W
Terdal **80** 16 33N 75 3 E
Terebovlya **58** 49 18N 25 44 E
Teregova **50** 45 10N 22 16 E
Terek → **61** 44 0N 47 30 E
Terek-Say **63** 41 30N 71 11 E
Terenos **173** 20 26 S 54 50W
Tereshka → **59** 51 48N 46 26 E
Teresina **170** 5 9 S 42 45W
Teresinha **169** 0 58N 52 2W
Terespol **32** 52 5N 23 37 E
Terewah, L. **111** 29 52 S 147 35 E
Terges → **35** 37 49N 7 41W
Tergnier **19** 49 40N 3 17 E
Terhazza **120** 23 38N 5 22W
Terheijden **23** 51 38N 4 45 E
Teridgerie Cr. → **111** 30 25 S 148 50 E
Terifa **74** 14 24N 43 48 E
Terlizzi **45** 41 8N 16 32 E
Terme **60** 41 11N 37 0 E
Termez **63** 37 15N 67 15 E
Términi Imerese **44** 37 58N 13 42 E
Términos, L. de **161** 18 35N 91 30W
Térmoli **43** 42 0N 15 0 E
Ternate **87** 0 45N 127 25 E
Terneuzen **23** 51 20N 3 50 E
Terney **65** 45 3N 136 37 E
Terni **43** 42 34N 12 38 E
Ternitz **30** 47 43N 16 2 E
Ternopol **58** 49 30N 25 40 E
Terra Bella **159** 35 58N 119 3W
Terra Nova B. **7** 74 50 S 164 40 E
Terrace **144** 54 30N 128 35W
Terrace Bay **142** 48 47N 87 5W
Terracina **44** 41 17N 13 12 E
Terralba **44** 39 42N 8 38 E
Terranova = Ólbia **44** 40 55N 9 30 E
Terranuova Bracciolini **43** 43 31N 11 35 E
Terrasini Favarotta **44** 38 10N 13 4 E
Terrasson-la-Villedieu **20** 45 8N 1 18 E
Terre Haute **155** 39 28N 87 24W
Terrebonne B. **153** 29 15N 90 28W
Terrecht **121** 20 10N 0 10W
Terrell **153** 32 44N 96 19W
Terrenceville **143** 47 40N 54 44W
Terrick Terrick **110** 24 44 S 145 5 E
Territoire de Belfort □ **19** 47 40N 6 55 E
Terry **152** 46 47N 105 20W
Terschelling **22** 53 25N 5 20 E
Terskey Alatau, Khrebet **63** 41 50N 77 0 E
Terter → **61** 40 35N 47 22 E
Teruel **36** 40 22N 1 8W
Teruel □ **36** 40 48N 1 0W
Tervel **47** 43 45N 27 28 E
Tervola **54** 66 6N 24 49 E
Teryaweyna L. **112** 32 18 S 143 22 E
Tešanj **46** 44 38N 17 59 E
Teseney **125** 15 5N 36 42 E
Tesha → **59** 55 38N 42 9 E
Teshio **98** 44 53N 141 44 E
Teshio-Gawa → **98** 44 53N 141 45 E
Tešica **46** 43 27N 21 45 E
Tesiyn Gol → **92** 50 40N 93 20 E
Teslić **46** 44 37N 17 54 E
Teslin **140** 60 10N 132 43W
Teslin → **144** 61 34N 134 35W
Teslin L. **144** 60 15N 132 57W
Tesouro **173** 16 4 S 53 34W
Tessalit **127** 20 12N 1 0 E
Tessaoua **127** 13 47N 7 56 E
Tessenderlo **23** 51 4N 5 5 E
Tessin **26** 54 2N 12 28 E
Tessit **127** 15 13N 0 18 E
Test → **13** 51 7N 1 30W
Testa del Gargano **45** 41 50N 16 10 E
Teste, La **20** 44 37N 1 8W
Tét **31** 47 30N 17 33 E
Têt → **20** 42 44N 3 2 E
Tetachuck L. **144** 53 18N 125 55W
Tetas, Pta. **174** 23 31 S 70 38W
Tete **131** 16 13 S 33 33 E
Tete □ **131** 15 15 S 32 40 E
Teterev → **58** 51 1N 30 5 E
Teteringen **23** 51 37N 4 49 E
Teterow **26** 53 45N 12 34 E
Teteven **47** 42 58N 24 17 E
Tethul → **144** 60 35N 112 12W
Tetiyev **60** 49 22N 29 38 E
Teton → **156** 47 58N 111 0W
Tétouan **120** 35 35N 5 21W
Tetovo **46** 42 1N 21 2 E
Tetuán = Tétouan **120** 35 35N 5 21W
Tetyukhe Pristan **98** 44 22N 135 48 E
Tetyushi **59** 54 55N 48 49 E
Teuco → **174** 25 35 S 60 11W
Teufen **29** 47 24N 9 23 E
Teulada **44** 38 59N 8 47 E
Teulon **145** 50 23N 97 16W
Teun **87** 6 59 S 129 8 E
Teutoburger Wald **24** 52 5N 8 20 E
Tevere → **43** 41 44N 12 14 E
Teverya **69** 32 47N 35 32 E
Teviot → **14** 55 21N 2 51W
Tewantin **111** 26 27 S 153 3 E
Tewkesbury **13** 51 59N 2 8W
Texada I. **144** 49 40N 124 25W
Texarkana, Ark., U.S.A. **153** 33 25N 94 0W
Texarkana, Tex., U.S.A. **153** 33 25N 94 3W
Texas **111** 28 49 S 151 9 E
Texas □ **153** 31 40N 98 30W
Texas City **153** 29 20N 94 55W
Texel **22** 53 5N 4 50 E
Texhoma **153** 36 32N 101 47W
Texline **153** 36 26N 103 0W
Texoma L. **153** 34 0N 96 38W
Teykovo **59** 56 55N 40 30 E
Teyvareh **77** 33 30N 64 24 E
Teza → **59** 56 32N 41 53 E
Tezin **78** 34 24N 69 30 E
Teziutlán **161** 19 50N 97 22W
Tezpur **82** 26 40N 92 45 E
Tezzeron L. **144** 54 43N 124 30W
Tha-anne → **145** 60 31N 94 37W
Tha Deua, Laos **84** 17 57N 102 53 E
Tha Deua, Laos **84** 19 26N 101 50 E
Tha Pla **84** 17 48N 100 32 E
Tha Rua **84** 14 34N 100 44 E
Tha Sala **85** 8 40N 99 56 E
Tha Song Yang **84** 17 34N 97 55 E
Thaba Nchu **134** 29 17 S 26 52 E
Thaba Putsoa **135** 29 45 S 28 0 E
Thabana Ntlenyana **135** 29 30 S 29 16 E
Thabazimbi **135** 24 40 S 27 21 E
Thabeikkyin **82** 22 53N 95 59 E
Thai Binh **84** 20 35N 106 1 E
Thai Hoa **84** 19 20N 105 20 E
Thai Muang **85** 8 24N 98 16 E
Thai Nguyen **84** 21 35N 105 55 E
Thailand ■ **84** 16 0N 102 0 E
Thailand, G. of **85** 11 30N 101 0 E
Thakhek **84** 17 25N 104 45 E
Thakurgaon **82** 26 2N 88 34 E
Thal **77** 33 28N 70 33 E
Thal Desert **78** 31 10N 71 30 E
Thala **121** 35 35N 8 40 E
Thalabarivat **84** 13 33N 105 57 E
Thalkirch **29** 46 39N 9 17 E
Thallon **111** 28 39 S 148 49 E
Thalwil **29** 47 17N 8 35 E
Thamarīt **75** 17 39N 54 2 E
Thame → **13** 51 35N 1 8W
Thames **114** 37 7 S 175 34 E
Thames →, Canada **142** 42 20N 82 25W
Thames →, U.K. **13** 51 30N 0 35 E
Thames →, U.S.A. **151** 41 18N 72 9W
Thames, Firth of **114** 37 0 S 175 25 E
Thamesford **150** 43 4N 81 0W

Tinglayan

Thamesville **150** 42 33N 81 59W
Thâmit, W. → **122** 30 51N 16 14 E
Thamūd **75** 17 18N 49 55 E
Than Uyen **84** 22 0N 103 54 E
Thanbyuzayat **82** 15 58N 97 44 E
Thane **80** 19 12N 72 59 E
Thanesar **78** 30 1N 76 52 E
Thanet, I. of **13** 51 21N 1 20 E
Thangoo **108** 18 10 S 122 22 E
Thangool **110** 24 38 S 150 42 E
Thanh Hoa **84** 19 48N 105 46 E
Thanh Hung **85** 9 55N 105 43 E
Thanh Pho Ho Chi Minh = Phanh Bho Ho Chi Minh **85** 10 58N 106 40 E
Thanh Thuy **84** 22 55N 104 51 E
Thanjavur **81** 10 48N 79 12 E
Thann **19** 47 48N 7 5 E
Thaon-les-Vosges **19** 48 15N 6 24 E
Thap Sakae **85** 11 30N 99 37 E
Thap Than **84** 15 27N 99 54 E
Thar Desert **78** 28 0N 72 0 E
Tharad **78** 24 30N 71 44 E
Thargomindah **111** 27 58 S 143 46 E
Tharrawaddy **82** 17 38N 95 48 E
Tharrawaw **82** 17 41N 95 28 E
Tharthar, W. → **72** 33 59N 43 12 E
Thasopoúla **48** 40 49N 24 45 E
Thásos **48** 40 40N 24 40 E
That Khe **84** 22 16N 106 28 E
Thatcher, Ariz., U.S.A. **157** 32 54N 109 46W
Thatcher, Colo., U.S.A. **153** 37 38N 104 6W
Thaton **82** 16 55N 97 22 E
Thau, Bassin de **20** 43 23N 3 36 E
Thaungdut **82** 24 30N 94 40 E
Thayer **153** 36 34N 91 34W
Thayetmyo **82** 19 20N 95 10 E
Thayngen **29** 47 49N 8 43 E
The Alberga → **111** 27 6 S 135 33 E
The Bight **163** 24 19N 75 24W
The Brothers **75** 12 8N 53 10 E
The Dalles **156** 45 40N 121 11W
The English Company's Is. **110** 11 50 S 136 32 E
The Entrance **113** 33 21 S 151 30 E
The Frome → **111** 29 8 S 137 54 E
The Grenadines, Is. **163** 12 40N 61 20W
The Hague = 's-Gravenhage **22** 52 7N 4 17 E
The Hamilton → **111** 26 40 S 135 19 E
The Lynd **110** 19 12 S 144 20 E
The Macumba → **111** 27 52 S 137 12 E
The Neales → **111** 28 8 S 136 47 E
The Oaks **113** 34 3 S 150 34 E
The Officer → **109** 27 46 S 132 30 E
The Pas **145** 53 45N 101 15W
The Range **131** 19 2 S 31 2 E
The Salt Lake **111** 30 6 S 142 8 E
The Stevenson → **111** 27 6 S 135 33 E
The Warburton → **111** 28 4 S 137 28 E
Thebes = Thívai **49** 38 19N 23 19 E
Thebes **124** 25 40N 32 35 E
Thedford, Canada **150** 43 9N 81 51W
Thedford, U.S.A. **152** 41 59N 100 31W
Theebine **111** 25 57 S 152 34 E
Theil, Le **18** 48 16N 0 42 E
Thekulthili L. **145** 61 3N 110 0W
Thelon → **145** 62 35N 104 3W
Thénezay **18** 46 44N 0 2W
Thenia **121** 36 44N 3 33 E
Thenon **20** 45 9N 1 4 E
Theodore **110** 24 55 S 150 3 E
Thepha **85** 6 52N 100 58 E
Thérain → **19** 49 15N 2 27 E
Theresa **151** 44 13N 75 50W
Thermaïkos Kólpos **48** 40 15N 22 45 E
Thermopolis **156** 43 35N 108 10W
Thermopylae P. **49** 38 48N 22 35 E
Thesprotía □ **48** 39 27N 20 22 E
Thessalía □ **48** 39 30N 22 0 E
Thessalon **142** 46 20N 83 30W
Thessaloníki **48** 40 38N 22 58 E
Thessaloníki □ **48** 40 45N 23 0 E
Thessaloniki, Gulf of = Thermaïkos Kólpos **48** 40 15N 22 45 E
Thessaly = Thessalía □ **48** 39 30N 22 0 E
Thetford **13** 52 25N 0 44 E
Thetford Mines **143** 46 8N 71 18W
Theun → **84** 18 19N 104 0 E
Theunissen **134** 28 26 S 26 43 E
Theux **23** 50 32N 5 49 E
Thevenard **111** 32 9 S 133 38 E
Thiámis → **48** 39 15N 20 6 E
Thiberville **18** 49 8N 0 27 E
Thibodaux **153** 29 48N 90 49W
Thicket Portage **145** 55 19N 97 42W
Thief River Falls **152** 48 15N 96 48W
Thiel Mts. **7** 85 15 S 91 0W
Thiene **43** 45 42N 11 29 E
Thiérache **19** 49 51N 3 45 E
Thiers **20** 45 52N 3 33 E
Thies **126** 14 50N 16 51W
Thiet **125** 7 37N 28 49 E
Thika **130** 1 1 S 37 5 E
Thille-Boubacar **126** 16 31N 15 5W
Thillot, Le **19** 47 53N 6 46 E
Thimân, W. → **71** 28 4N 33 45 E
Thimphu **82** 27 31N 89 45 E
þingvallavatn **54** 64 11N 21 9W
Thio **106** 21 37 S 166 14 E
Thionville **19** 49 20N 6 10 E
Thíra **49** 36 23N 25 27 E
Thirasía **49** 36 26N 25 21 E
Thirsk **12** 54 15N 1 20W
Thiruvarur **81** 10 46N 79 38 E
Thistle I. **112** 35 0 S 136 8 E
Thitgy **82** 18 15N 96 13 E
Thithia **106** 17 45 S 179 18W
Thitpokpin **82** 19 24N 95 58 E
Thívai **49** 38 19N 23 19 E
Thiviers **20** 45 25N 0 54 E
Thizy **21** 46 2N 4 18 E
þjórsá → **54** 63 47N 20 48W
Thlewiaza →, Man., Canada **145** 59 43N 100 5W
Thlewiaza →, N.W.T., Canada **145** 60 29N 94 40W
Thmar Puok **84** 13 57N 103 4 E
Tho Vinh **84** 19 16N 105 42 E
Thoa → **145** 60 31N 109 47W
Thoen **84** 17 43N 99 12 E
Thoeng **84** 19 41N 100 12 E
Thoissey **21** 46 12N 4 48 E
Tholdi **79** 35 5N 76 6 E
Tholen **23** 51 32N 4 13 E
Thomas, Okla., U.S.A. **153** 35 48N 98 48W
Thomas, W. Va., U.S.A. **148** 39 10N 79 30W
Thomas, L. **111** 26 4 S 137 58 E
Thomas Hill Res. **154** 39 34N 92 39W
Thomaston **149** 32 54N 84 20W
Thomasville, Ala., U.S.A. **149** 31 55N 87 42W
Thomasville, Ga., U.S.A. **149** 30 50N 84 0W
Thomasville, N.C., U.S.A. **149** 35 55N 80 4W
Thommen **23** 50 14N 6 5 E
Thompson, Canada **145** 55 45N 97 52W
Thompson, U.S.A. **157** 39 0N 109 50W
Thompson →, Canada **144** 50 15N 121 24W
Thompson →, U.S.A. **152** 39 46N 93 37W
Thompson Falls **156** 47 37N 115 20W
Thompson Landing **145** 62 56N 110 40W
Thompson Pk. **156** 41 0N 123 3W
Thomson **154** 41 58N 90 6W
Thomson → **110** 25 11 S 142 53 E
Thomson's Falls = Nyahururu **130** 0 2N 36 27 E
Thon Buri **85** 13 43N 100 29 E
Thônes **21** 45 54N 6 18 E
Thongwa **82** 16 45N 96 33 E
Thonon-les-Bains **21** 46 22N 6 29 E
Thonze **82** 17 38N 95 47 E
Thorez **61** 48 4N 38 34 E
þórisvatn **54** 64 20N 18 55W
þorlákshöfn **54** 63 51N 21 22W
Thornaby on Tees **12** 54 36N 1 19W
Thornbury, Canada **150** 44 34N 80 26W
Thornbury, N.Z. **115** 46 17 S 168 9 E
Thornton **154** 42 57N 93 23W
Thornton-Beresfield **113** 32 50 S 151 40 E
Thorntown **155** 40 8N 86 36W
Thorold **150** 43 7N 79 12W
þórshöfn **54** 66 12N 15 20W
Thouarcé **18** 47 17N 0 30W
Thouars **18** 46 58N 0 15W
Thouin, C. **108** 20 20 S 118 10 E
Thousand Oaks **159** 34 10N 118 50W
Thrace = Thráki □ **48** 41 9N 25 30 E
Thráki □ **48** 41 9N 25 30 E
Thrakikón Pélagos **48** 40 30N 25 0 E
Three Forks **156** 45 55N 111 32W
Three Hills **144** 51 43N 113 15W
Three Hummock I. **110** 40 25 S 144 55 E
Three Lakes **152** 45 48N 89 10W
Three Oaks **155** 41 48N 86 36W
Three Points, C. **126** 4 42N 2 6W
Three Rivers, Australia **109** 25 10 S 119 5 E
Three Rivers, Calif., U.S.A. **158** 36 26N 118 54W
Three Rivers, Mich., U.S.A. **155** 41 57N 85 38W
Three Rivers, Tex., U.S.A. **153** 28 30N 98 10W
Three Sisters, Mt. **156** 44 10N 121 46W
Throssell, L. **109** 27 33 S 124 10 E
Throssell Ra. **108** 22 3 S 121 43 E
Thrun Pass **30** 47 20N 12 25 E
Thuan Hoa **85** 8 58N 105 30 E
Thubun Lakes **145** 61 30N 112 0W
Thueyts **21** 44 41N 4 9 E
Thuillies **23** 50 18N 4 20 E
Thuin **23** 50 20N 4 17 E
Thuir **20** 42 38N 2 45 E
Thule, Antarct. **7** 59 27 S 27 19W
Thule, Greenland **6** 77 40N 69 0W
Thun **28** 46 45N 7 38 E
Thundelarra **109** 28 53 S 117 7 E
Thunder B. **150** 45 0N 83 20W
Thunder Bay **142** 48 20N 89 15W
Thunersee **28** 46 43N 7 39 E
Thung Song **85** 8 10N 99 40 E
Thunkar **82** 27 55N 91 0 E
Thuong Tra **84** 16 2N 107 42 E
Thur → **29** 47 32N 9 10 E
Thurgau □ **29** 47 34N 9 10 E
Thüringer Wald **26** 50 35N 11 0 E
Thurles **15** 52 40N 7 53W
Thurloo Downs **111** 29 15 S 143 30 E
Thurn P. **27** 47 20N 12 25 E
Thursday I. **110** 10 30 S 142 3 E
Thurso, Canada **142** 45 36N 75 15W
Thurso, U.K. **14** 58 34N 3 31W
Thurston I. **7** 72 0 S 100 0W
Thury-Harcourt **18** 48 59N 0 30W
Thusis **29** 46 42N 9 26 E
Thutade L. **144** 57 0N 126 55W
Thuy, Le **84** 17 14N 106 49 E
Thyborøn **53** 56 42N 8 12 E
Thylungra **111** 26 4 S 143 28 E
Thyolo **131** 16 7 S 35 5 E
Thysville = Mbanza Ngungu **133** 5 12 S 14 53 E
Ti-n-Barraouene, O. → **127** 18 40N 4 5 E
Ti-n-Medjerdam, O. → **121** 25 45N 1 30 E
Ti-n-Tarabine, O. → **121** 21 0N 7 25 E
Ti-n-Toumma **123** 16 4N 12 40 E
Ti-n-Zaouatène **121** 20 0N 2 55 E
Tia **111** 31 10 S 150 34 E
Tiahuanacu **172** 16 33 S 68 42W
Tian Shan **92** 43 0N 84 0 E
Tianchang **97** 32 40N 119 0 E
Tiandong **96** 23 36N 107 8 E
Tian'e **96** 25 1N 107 9 E
Tianguá **170** 3 44 S 40 59W
Tianhe **96** 24 48N 108 40 E
Tianjin **95** 39 8N 117 10 E
Tiankoura **126** 10 47N 3 17W
Tianlin **96** 24 21N 106 12 E
Tianmen **97** 30 39N 113 9 E
Tianquan **96** 30 7N 102 43 E
Tianshui **94** 34 32N 105 40 E
Tiantai **97** 29 10N 121 2 E
Tianyang **96** 23 42N 106 53 E
Tianzhen **94** 40 24N 114 5 E
Tianzhu **96** 26 54N 109 11 E
Tianzhuangtai **95** 40 43N 122 5 E
Tiaret **121** 35 20N 1 21 E
Tiarra **113** 32 46 S 145 1 E
Tiassalé **126** 5 58N 4 57W
Tibagi **175** 24 30 S 50 24W
Tibagi → **175** 22 47 S 51 1W
Tibati **127** 6 22N 12 30 E
Tiber = Tevere → **43** 41 44N 12 14 E
Tiber Res. **156** 48 20N 111 15W
Tiberias = Teverya **69** 32 47N 35 32 E
Tiberias, L. = Yam Kinneret **69** 32 45N 35 35 E
Tibesti **123** 21 0N 17 30 E
Tibiao **91** 11 17N 122 2 E
Tibiri **127** 13 34N 7 4 E
Ţibleş **50** 47 32N 24 15 E
Tibnī **72** 35 36N 39 50 E
Tibnīn **69** 33 12N 35 24 E
Tibooburra **111** 29 26 S 142 1 E
Tibro **53** 58 28N 14 10 E
Tibugá, G. de **168** 5 45N 77 20W
Tiburón **160** 29 0N 112 30W
Ticao I. **90** 12 31N 123 42 E
Tîchît **126** 18 21N 9 29W
Tichla **120** 21 36N 14 58W
Ticho **125** 7 50N 39 32 E
Ticino □ **29** 46 20N 8 45 E
Ticino → **42** 45 9N 9 14 E
Ticonderoga **151** 43 50N 73 28W
Ticul **161** 20 20N 89 31W
Tidaholm **53** 58 12N 13 55 E
Tiddim **82** 23 28N 93 45 E
Tideridjaouine, Adrar **121** 23 0N 2 15 E
Tidikelt **121** 26 58N 1 30 E
Tidjikja **126** 18 29N 11 35W
Tidore **87** 0 40N 127 25 E
Tiébissou **126** 7 9N 5 10W
Tiéboro **123** 21 20N 17 7 E
Tiefencastel **29** 46 40N 9 33 E
Tiel, Neth. **22** 51 53N 5 26 E
Tiel, Senegal **126** 14 55N 15 5W
Tieling **95** 42 20N 123 55 E
Tielt **23** 51 0N 3 20 E
Tien Shan **63** 42 0N 80 0 E
Tien-tsin = Tianjin **95** 39 8N 117 10 E
Tien Yen **84** 21 20N 107 24 E
T'ienching = Tianjin **95** 39 8N 117 10 E
Tienen **23** 50 48N 4 57 E
Tiénigbé **126** 8 11N 5 43W
Tientsin = Tianjin **95** 39 8N 117 10 E
Tierp **52** 60 20N 17 30 E
Tierra Amarilla, Chile **174** 27 28 S 70 18W
Tierra Amarilla, U.S.A. **157** 36 42N 106 33W
Tierra Colorada **161** 17 10N 99 35W
Tierra de Barros **35** 38 40N 6 30W
Tierra de Campos **34** 42 10N 4 50W
Tierra del Fuego □ **176** 54 0 S 67 45W
Tierra del Fuego, I. Gr. de **176** 54 0 S 69 0W
Tierralta **168** 8 11N 76 4W
Tiétar → **34** 39 50N 6 1W
Tieté → **175** 20 40 S 51 35W
Tieyon **111** 26 12 S 133 52 E
Tifarit **120** 26 9N 10 33W
Tiffin **155** 41 8N 83 10W
Tiffin → **155** 41 20N 84 24W
Tiflèt **120** 33 54N 6 20W
Tiflis = Tbilisi **61** 41 43N 44 50 E
Tifrah **69** 31 19N 34 42 E
Tifton **149** 31 28N 83 32W
Tifu **87** 3 39 S 126 24 E
Tiga, I. **106** 21 7 S 167 49 E
Tigaon **90** 13 38N 123 30 E
Tigbauan **91** 10 41N 122 27 E
Tigil **65** 57 49N 158 40 E
Tignish **143** 46 58N 64 2W
Tigray □ **125** 13 35N 39 15 E
Tigre →, Peru **172** 4 30 S 74 10W
Tigre →, Venezuela **169** 9 20N 62 30W
Tigris = Dijlah, Nahr → **72** 31 0N 47 25 E
Tiguentourine **121** 27 52N 9 8 E
Tigveni **50** 45 10N 24 31 E
Tigyaing **82** 23 45N 96 10 E
Tigzerte, O. → **120** 28 10N 9 37W
Tîh, Gebel el **124** 29 32N 33 26 E
Tihodaine, Dunes de **121** 25 15N 7 15 E
Tijesno **43** 43 48N 15 39 E
Tiji **122** 32 0N 11 18 E
Tijuana **160** 32 30N 117 10W
Tikal **162** 17 13N 89 24W
Tikamgarh **79** 24 44N 78 50 E
Tikhoretsk **61** 45 56N 40 5 E
Tikhvin **58** 59 35N 33 30 E
Tikkadouine, Adrar **121** 24 28N 1 30 E
Tiko **127** 4 4N 9 20 E
Tikrīt **72** 34 35N 43 37 E
Tiksi **65** 71 40N 128 45 E
Tilamuta **87** 0 32N 122 23 E
Tilburg **23** 51 31N 5 6 E
Tilbury, Canada **142** 42 17N 82 23W
Tilbury, U.K. **13** 51 27N 0 24 E
Tilcara **174** 23 36 S 65 23W
Tilden, Nebr., U.S.A. **152** 42 3N 97 45W
Tilden, Tex., U.S.A. **153** 28 28N 98 33W
Tilemses **127** 15 37N 4 44 E
Tilemsi, Vallée du **127** 17 42N 0 15 E
Tilhar **79** 28 0N 79 45 E
Tilia, O. → **121** 27 32N 0 55 E
Tilichiki **65** 60 27N 166 5 E
Tiligul → **60** 47 4N 30 57 E
Tililane **121** 27 49N 0 6W
Tilin **82** 21 41N 94 6 E
Tílissos **49** 35 2N 25 0 E
Till → **12** 55 35N 2 3W
Tillabéri **127** 14 28N 1 28 E
Tillamook **156** 45 29N 123 55W
Tillberga **52** 59 52N 16 39 E
Tillia **127** 16 8N 4 47 E
Tillsonburg **142** 42 53N 80 44W
Tílos **49** 36 27N 27 27 E
Tilrhemt **121** 33 9N 3 22 E
Tilsit = Sovetsk **58** 55 6N 21 50 E
Tilt → **14** 56 50N 3 50W
Tilton **151** 43 25N 71 36W
Timagami L. **142** 47 0N 80 10W
Timanskiy Kryazh **56** 65 58N 50 5 E
Timareh **75** 12 37N 54 17 E
Timaru **115** 44 23 S 171 14 E
Timashevo **62** 53 22N 51 9 E
Timashevsk **61** 45 35N 39 0 E
Timau, Italy **43** 46 35N 13 0 E
Timau, Kenya **130** 0 4N 37 15 E
Timbákion **49** 35 4N 24 45 E
Timbaúba **170** 7 31 S 35 19W
Timbedgha **126** 16 17N 8 16W
Timber Lake **152** 45 29N 101 6W
Timber Mt. **158** 37 6N 116 28W
Timbío **168** 2 20N 76 40W
Timbiqui **168** 2 46N 77 42W
Timboon **112** 38 30 S 142 58 E
Timbuktu = Tombouctou **126** 16 50N 3 0W
Timellouline **121** 29 22N 8 55 E
Timétrine Montagnes **127** 19 25N 1 0W
Timfi Óros **48** 39 59N 20 45 E
Timfristós, Óros **49** 38 57N 21 50 E
Timhadit **120** 33 15N 5 4W
Tîmia **127** 18 4N 8 40 E
Timimoun **121** 29 14N 0 16 E
Timiş □ **50** 45 40N 21 30 E
Timiş → **50** 45 30N 21 0 E
Timişoara **50** 45 43N 21 15 E
Timmins **142** 48 28N 81 25W
Timok → **46** 44 10N 22 40 E
Timon **170** 5 8 S 42 52W
Timor **87** 9 0 S 125 0 E
Timor □ **87** 9 0 S 125 0 E
Timor Sea **108** 10 0 S 127 0 E
Tin Alkoum **121** 24 42N 10 17 E
Tin Gornai **127** 16 38N 0 38W
Tin Gornaï → **127** 20 30N 4 35 E
Tin Mt. **158** 36 54N 117 28W
Tîna, Khalîg el **124** 31 20N 32 42 E
Tinabog **90** 12 1N 120 25 E
Tinaca Pt. **91** 5 30N 125 25 E
Tinaco **168** 9 42N 68 26W
Tinafak, O. → **121** 27 10N 7 0 E
Tinajo **37** 29 4N 13 42W
Tinaquillo **168** 9 55N 68 18W
Tinca **50** 46 46N 21 58 E
Tinchebray **18** 48 47N 0 45W
Tindivanam **81** 12 15N 79 41 E
Tindouf **120** 27 42N 8 10W
Tinée → **21** 43 55N 7 11 E
Tineg **90** 17 48N 120 56 E
Tineo **34** 43 21N 6 27W
Tinerhir **120** 31 29N 5 31W
Tinfouchi **120** 28 52N 5 49W
Ting Jiang → **97** 24 45N 116 35 E
Tinggi, Pulau **85** 2 18N 104 7 E
Tingkawk Sakan **82** 26 4N 96 44 E
Tinglayan **90** 17 15N 121 9 E

Tinglev

Tinglev **53** 54 57N 9 13 E
Tingo Maria **172** 9 10 S 75 54W
Tingsryd **53** 56 31N 15 0 E
Tinh Bien **85** 10 36N 104 57 E
Tinharé, I. de **171** 13 30 S 38 58W
Tiniguiban **91** 11 22N 119 30 E
Tinkurrin **109** 32 59 S 117 46 E
Tinnevelly = Tirunelveli **81** 8 45N 77 45 E
Tinnoset **51** 59 55N 9 3 E
Tinnsjø **51** 59 55N 8 54 E
Tinogasta **174** 28 5 S 67 32W
Tínos **49** 37 33N 25 8 E
Tiñoso, C. **37** 37 32N 1 6W
Tinsukia **82** 27 29N 95 20 E
Tinta **172** 14 3 S 71 20W
Tintigny **23** 49 41N 5 31 E
Tintina **174** 27 2 S 62 45W
Tintinara **112** 35 48 S 140 2 E
Tinto → **35** 37 12N 6 55W
Tinui **114** 40 52 S 176 5 E
Tinwald **115** 43 55 S 171 43 E
Tioga **150** 41 54N 77 9W
Tioman, Pulau **85** 2 50N 104 10 E
Tione di Trento **42** 46 3N 10 44 E
Tionesta **150** 41 29N 79 28W
Tior **125** 6 26N 31 11 E
Tioulilin **121** 27 1N 0 2W
Tipp City **155** 39 58N 84 11W
Tippecanoe → **155** 40 31N 86 47W
Tipperary **15** 52 28N 8 10W
Tipperary □ **15** 52 37N 7 55W
Tipton, U.K. **13** 52 32N 2 4W
Tipton, Calif., U.S.A. **158** 36 3N 119 19W
Tipton, Ind., U.S.A. **155** 40 17N 86 0W
Tipton, Iowa, U.S.A. **154** 41 45N 91 12W
Tipton, Mo., U.S.A. **154** 38 41N 92 48W
Tipton, Mt. **159** 35 32N 114 16W
Tiptonville **153** 36 22N 89 30W
Tiptur **81** 13 15N 76 26 E
Tiquié → **168** 0 5N 68 25W
Tiracambu, Serra do **170** 3 15 S 46 30W
Tirān, Iran **73** 32 45N 51 8 E
Tirân, Si. Arabia **71** 27 57N 34 32 E
Tirana **48** 41 18N 19 49 E
Tirana-Durrësi □ **48** 41 35N 20 0 E
Tiranë = Tirana **48** 41 18N 19 49 E
Tirano **42** 46 13N 10 11 E
Tiraspol **60** 46 55N 29 35 E
Tirat Karmel **69** 32 46N 34 58 E
Tirat Yehuda **69** 32 1N 34 56 E
Tirat Zevi **69** 32 26N 35 31 E
Tiratimine **121** 25 56N 3 37 E
Tirdout **127** 16 7N 1 5W
Tirebolu **57** 40 58N 38 45 E
Tiree **14** 56 31N 6 55W
Tîrgovişte **50** 44 55N 25 27 E
Tîrgu Frumos **50** 47 12N 27 2 E
Tîrgu-Jiu **50** 45 5N 23 19 E
Tîrgu Mureş **50** 46 31N 24 38 E
Tîrgu Neamţ **50** 47 12N 26 25 E
Tîrgu Ocna **50** 46 16N 26 39 E
Tîrgu Secuiesc **50** 46 0N 26 10 E
Tirich Mir **77** 36 15N 71 55 E
Tiriola **45** 38 57N 16 32 E
Tiririca, Serra da **171** 17 6 S 47 6W
Tiris **120** 23 10N 13 20W
Tirlyanskiy **62** 54 14N 58 35 E
Tirna → **80** 18 4N 76 57 E
Tîrnava Mare → **50** 46 15N 24 30 E
Tîrnava Mică → **50** 46 17N 24 30 E
Tîrnăveni **50** 46 19N 24 13 E
Tírnavos **48** 39 45N 22 18 E
Tîrnova **50** 45 23N 22 1 E
Tirodi **79** 21 40N 79 44 E
Tirol □ **30** 47 3N 10 43 E
Tiros **171** 19 0 S 45 58W
Tirschenreuth **27** 49 51N 12 20 E
Tirso → **44** 39 52N 8 33 E
Tirso, L. del **44** 40 8N 8 56 E
Tirua, Pt. **114** 38 25 S 174 40 E
Tiruchchendur **81** 8 30N 78 11 E
Tiruchchirappalli **81** 10 45N 78 45 E
Tiruchengodu **81** 11 23N 77 56 E
Tirumangalam **81** 9 49N 77 58 E
Tirunelveli **81** 8 45N 77 45 E
Tirupati **81** 13 39N 79 25 E
Tiruppattur **81** 12 30N 78 30 E
Tiruppur **81** 11 5N 77 22 E
Tirutturaippundi **81** 10 32N 79 41 E
Tiruvadaimarudur **81** 11 2N 79 27 E
Tiruvallar **81** 13 9N 79 57 E
Tiruvannamalai **81** 12 15N 79 5 E
Tiruvettipuram **81** 12 39N 79 33 E
Tiruvottiyur **81** 13 10N 80 22 E
Tisa → **46** 45 15N 20 17 E
Tisdale **145** 52 50N 104 0W
Tishomingo **153** 34 14N 96 38W
Tisjön **52** 60 56N 13 0 E
Tisnaren **53** 58 58N 15 56 E
Tišnov **31** 49 21N 16 25 E
Tisovec **31** 48 41N 19 56 E
Tissemsilt **121** 35 35N 1 50 E
Tissint **120** 29 57N 7 16W
Tissø **52** 55 35N 11 18 E
Tista → **82** 25 23N 89 43 E
Tisza → **31** 46 8N 20 2 E
Tiszaföldvár **31** 47 0N 20 14 E
Tiszafüred **31** 47 38N 20 50 E
Tiszalök **31** 48 0N 21 10 E
Tiszavasvári **31** 47 58N 21 18 E
Tit, Ahaggar, Algeria **121** 23 0N 5 10 E
Tit, Tademait, Algeria **121** 27 0N 1 29 E
Tit-Ary **65** 71 55N 127 2 E
Titaguas **36** 39 53N 1 6W
Titahi Bay **114** 41 6 S 174 50 E
Titel **46** 45 10N 20 18 E
Tithwal **79** 34 21N 73 50 E
Titicaca, L. **172** 15 30 S 69 30W
Titiwa **127** 12 14N 12 53 E
Titlagarh **80** 20 15N 83 11 E
Titlis **29** 46 46N 8 27 E
Titograd **46** 42 30N 19 19 E
Titov Veles **46** 41 46N 21 47 E
Titova Korenica **43** 44 45N 15 41 E
Titovo Užice **46** 43 55N 19 50 E
Titule **130** 3 15N 25 31 E
Titumate **168** 8 19N 77 5W
Titusville, Fla., U.S.A. **149** 28 37N 80 49W
Titusville, Pa., U.S.A. **150** 41 35N 79 39W
Tivaouane **126** 14 56N 16 45W
Tivat **46** 42 28N 18 43 E
Tiveden **53** 58 50N 14 30 E
Tiverton **13** 50 54N 3 30W
Tívoli **43** 41 58N 12 45 E
Tiwī **74** 22 45N 59 12 E
Tiyo **125** 14 41N 40 15 E
Tizga **120** 32 1N 5 9W
Ti'zi N'Isli **120** 32 28N 5 47W
Tizi-Ouzou **121** 36 42N 4 3 E
Tizimín **161** 21 0N 88 1W
Tiznados → **168** 8 16N 67 47W
Tiznit **120** 29 48N 9 45W
Tjeggelvas **54** 66 37N 17 45 E
Tjeukemeer **22** 52 53N 5 48 E
Tjirebon = Cirebon **89** 6 45 S 108 32 E
Tjøme **51** 59 8N 10 26 E
Tjonger Kanaal **22** 52 52N 5 52 E
Tjörn **53** 58 0N 11 35 E
Tkibuli **61** 42 26N 43 0 E
Tkvarcheli **61** 42 47N 41 42 E
Tlacotalpan **161** 18 37N 95 40W
Tlahualilo **160** 26 20N 103 30W
Tlaquepaque **160** 20 39N 103 19W
Tlaxcala **161** 19 20N 98 14W
Tlaxcala □ **161** 19 30N 98 20W
Tlaxiaco **161** 17 18N 97 40W
Tlell **144** 53 34N 131 56W
Tlemcen **121** 34 52N 1 21W
Tleta Sidi Bouguedra **120** 32 16N 9 59W
Tlumach **60** 48 51N 25 0 E
Tłuszcz **32** 52 25N 21 25 E
Tlyarata **61** 42 9N 46 26 E
Tmassah **122** 26 19N 15 51 E
Tnine d'Anglou **120** 29 50N 9 50W
To Bong **84** 12 45N 109 16 E
To-Shima **101** 34 31N 139 17 E
Toad → **144** 59 25N 124 57W
Toamasina **135** 18 10 S 49 25 E
Toamasina □ **135** 18 0 S 49 0 E
Toay **174** 36 43 S 64 38W
Toba **101** 34 30N 136 51 E
Toba Kakar **77** 31 30N 69 0 E
Toba Tek Singh **78** 30 55N 72 25 E
Tobago **163** 11 10N 60 30W
Tobarra **37** 38 37N 1 44W
Tobelo **87** 1 45N 127 56 E
Tobermorey **110** 22 12 S 138 0 E
Tobermory, Canada **142** 45 12N 81 40W
Tobermory, U.K. **14** 56 37N 6 4W
Tobin **158** 39 55N 121 19W
Tobin, L. **108** 21 45 S 125 49 E
Tobin L. **145** 53 35N 103 30W
Toboali **88** 3 0 S 106 25 E
Tobol **62** 52 40N 62 39 E
Tobol → **64** 58 10N 68 12 E
Toboli **87** 0 38 S 120 5 E
Tobolsk **64** 58 15N 68 10 E
Toboso **91** 10 43N 123 31 E
Tobruk = Tubruq **122** 32 7N 23 55 E
Tobyhanna **151** 41 10N 75 25W
Tocache Nuevo **172** 8 9 S 76 26W
Tocantínia **170** 9 33 S 48 22W
Tocantinópolis **170** 6 20 S 47 25W
Tocantins → **170** 1 45 S 49 10W
Toccoa **149** 34 32N 83 17W
Toce → **42** 45 56N 8 29 E
Tochigi **101** 36 25N 139 45 E
Tochigi □ **101** 36 45N 139 45 E
Tocina **35** 37 37N 5 44W
Tocopilla **174** 22 5 S 70 10W
Tocumwal **113** 35 51 S 145 31 E
Tocuyo → **168** 11 3N 68 23W
Tocuyo de la Costa **168** 11 2N 68 23W
Todd → **110** 24 52 S 135 48 E
Todeli **87** 1 38 S 124 34 E
Todenyang **130** 4 35N 35 56 E
Todi, Italy **43** 42 47N 12 24 E
Tödi, Switz. **29** 46 48N 8 55 E
Todos los Santos, B. de **171** 12 48 S 38 38W
Todos Santos **160** 23 27N 110 13W
Todtnau **27** 47 50N 7 56 E
Toecé **127** 11 50N 1 16W
Toetoes B. **115** 46 42 S 168 41 E
Tofield **144** 53 25N 112 40W
Tofino **144** 49 11N 125 55W
Töfsingdalens nationalpark **52** 62 15N 12 44 E
Toftlund **53** 55 11N 9 2 E
Tōgane **101** 35 33N 140 22 E
Togba **126** 17 26N 10 12W
Togbo **132** 6 0N 17 27 E
Toggenburg **29** 47 16N 9 9 E
Togian, Kepulauan **87** 0 20 S 121 50 E
Togliatti **59** 53 32N 49 24 E
Togo ■ **127** 8 30N 1 35 E
Togtoh **94** 40 15N 111 10 E
Toguzak → **62** 54 3N 62 44 E
Tōhoku □ **98** 39 50N 141 45 E
Toi **101** 34 54N 138 47 E
Toinya **125** 6 17N 29 46 E
Tojo, Indonesia **87** 1 20 S 121 15 E
Tōjō, Japan **100** 34 53N 133 16 E
Tok → **62** 52 46N 52 22 E
Toka **169** 3 58N 59 17W
Tokaanu **114** 38 58 S 175 46 E
Tokachi-Dake **98** 43 17N 142 5 E
Tokachi-Gawa → **98** 42 44N 143 42 E
Tokai **101** 35 2N 136 55 E
Tokaj **31** 48 8N 21 27 E
Tokala **87** 1 30 S 121 40 E
Tōkamachi **99** 37 8N 138 43 E
Tokanui **115** 46 34 S 168 56 E
Tokar **124** 18 27N 37 56 E
Tokara-Rettō **99** 29 37N 129 43 E
Tokarahi **115** 44 56 S 170 39 E
Tokashiki-Shima **99** 26 11N 127 21 E
Tŏkchŏn **95** 39 45N 126 18 E
Tokeland **158** 46 42N 123 59W
Tokelau Is. **104** 9 0 S 171 45W
Toki **101** 35 18N 137 8 E
Tokmak **63** 42 49N 75 15 E
Toko Ra. **110** 23 5 S 138 20 E
Tokomaru Bay **114** 38 8 S 178 22 E
Tokoname **101** 34 53N 136 51 E
Tokoro-Gawa → **98** 44 7N 144 5 E
Tokoroa **114** 38 13 S 175 50 E
Tokorozawa **101** 35 47N 139 28 E
Toktogul **63** 41 50N 72 50 E
Tokuji **100** 34 11N 131 42 E
Tokuno-Shima **99** 27 56N 128 55 E
Tokushima **100** 34 4N 134 34 E
Tokushima □ **100** 34 15N 134 0 E
Tokuyama **100** 34 3N 131 50 E
Tōkyō **101** 35 45N 139 45 E
Tōkyō □ **101** 35 40N 139 30 E
Tōkyō-Wan **101** 35 25N 139 47 E
Tokzār **77** 35 52N 66 26 E
Tol I. **106** 7 20N 151 35 E
Tolbukhin **47** 43 37N 27 49 E
Toledo, Phil. **91** 10 23N 123 38 E
Toledo, Spain **34** 39 50N 4 2W
Toledo, Ill., U.S.A. **155** 39 16N 88 15W
Toledo, Iowa, U.S.A. **154** 42 0N 92 35W
Toledo, Ohio, U.S.A. **155** 41 37N 83 33W
Toledo, Oreg., U.S.A. **156** 44 40N 123 59W
Toledo, Wash., U.S.A. **156** 46 29N 122 51W
Toledo, Montes de **35** 39 33N 4 20W
Tolentino **43** 43 12N 13 17 E
Tolga, Algeria **121** 34 40N 5 22 E
Tolga, Norway **51** 62 26N 11 1 E
Toliara **135** 23 21 S 43 40 E
Toliara □ **135** 21 0 S 45 0 E
Tolima □ **168** 3 45N 75 15W
Tolima, Vol. **168** 4 40N 75 19W
Tolitoli **87** 1 5N 120 50 E
Tolkamer **22** 51 52N 6 6 E
Tolkmicko **32** 54 19N 19 31 E
Tollarp **53** 55 55N 13 58 E
Tolleson **157** 33 29N 112 10W
Tollhouse **158** 37 1N 119 24W
Tolmachevo **58** 58 56N 29 51 E
Tolmezzo **43** 46 23N 13 0 E
Tolmin **43** 46 11N 13 45 E
Tolna **31** 46 25N 18 48 E
Tolna □ **31** 46 30N 18 30 E
Tolo **132** 2 55 S 18 34 E
Tolo, Teluk **87** 2 20 S 122 10 E
Tolochin **58** 54 25N 29 42 E
Tolong Bay **91** 9 20N 122 49 E
Tolono **155** 39 59N 88 16W
Tolosa **36** 43 8N 2 5W
Tolox **35** 36 41N 4 54W
Toltén **176** 39 13 S 74 14W
Toluca **161** 19 20N 99 40W
Tom Burke **135** 23 5 S 28 0 E
Tom Price **108** 22 40 S 117 48 E
Tomah **152** 43 59N 90 30W
Tomahawk **152** 45 28N 89 40W
Tomakomai **98** 42 38N 141 36 E
Tomales **158** 38 15N 122 53W
Tomales B. **158** 38 15N 123 58W
Tomar **35** 39 36N 8 25W
Tómaros Óros **48** 39 29N 20 48 E
Tomás Barrón **172** 17 35 S 67 31W
Tomaszów Mazowiecki **32** 51 30N 19 57 E
Tomatlán **160** 19 56N 105 15W
Tombador, Serra do **173** 12 0 S 58 0W
Tombé **125** 5 53N 31 40 E
Tombigbee → **149** 31 4N 87 58W
Tombôco **133** 6 48 S 13 18 E
Tombouctou **126** 16 50N 3 0W
Tombstone **157** 31 40N 110 4W
Tombua **133** 15 55 S 11 55 E
Tomé **174** 36 36 S 72 57W
Tomé-Açu **170** 2 25 S 48 9W
Tomelilla **53** 55 33N 13 58 E
Tomelloso **37** 39 10N 3 2W
Tomil Harbor **106** 9 30N 138 10 E
Tomingley **113** 32 6 S 148 16 E
Tomini **87** 0 30N 120 30 E
Tomini, Teluk **87** 0 10 S 122 0 E
Tominian **126** 13 17N 4 35W
Tomiño **34** 41 59N 8 46W
Tomioka **101** 37 20N 141 0 E
Tomkinson Ranges **109** 26 11 S 129 5 E
Tommot **65** 59 4N 126 20 E
Tomnavoulin **14** 57 19N 3 18W
Tomnop Ta Suos **85** 11 20N 104 15 E
Tomo, Colombia **168** 2 38N 67 32W
Tomo, Japan **100** 34 23N 133 23 E
Tomo → **168** 5 20N 67 48W
Tomobe **101** 36 20N 140 20 E
Toms Place **158** 37 34N 118 41W
Toms River **151** 39 59N 74 12W
Tomsk **64** 56 30N 85 5 E
Tomtabacken **53** 57 30N 14 30 E
Tömük **70** 36 42N 34 23 E
Tonalá **161** 16 8N 93 41W
Tonale, Passo del **42** 46 15N 10 34 E
Tonalea **157** 36 17N 110 58W
Tonami **101** 36 40N 136 58 E
Tonantins **168** 2 45 S 67 45W
Tonasket **156** 48 45N 119 30W
Tonate **169** 5 0N 52 28W
Tonawanda **150** 43 0N 78 54W
Tonbridge **13** 51 12N 0 18 E
Tondano **87** 1 35N 124 54 E
Tondela **34** 40 31N 8 5W
Tønder **53** 54 58N 8 50 E
Tondi **81** 9 45N 79 4 E
Tondi Kiwindi **127** 14 28N 2 2 E
Tondibi **127** 16 39N 0 14W
Tonekābon **73** 36 45N 51 12 E
Tong Xian **94** 39 55N 116 35 E
Tonga ■ **104** 19 50 S 174 30W
Tonga Trench **104** 18 0 S 175 0W
Tongaat **135** 29 33 S 31 9 E
Tongala **113** 36 14 S 144 56 E
Tong'an **97** 24 37N 118 8 E
Tongareva **105** 9 0 S 158 0W
Tongbai **97** 32 20N 113 23 E
Tongcheng, Anhui, China **97** 31 4N 116 56 E
Tongcheng, Hubei, China **97** 29 15N 113 50 E
Tongchŏn-ni **95** 39 50N 127 25 E
Tongchuan **94** 35 6N 109 3 E
Tongdao **96** 26 10N 109 42 E
Tongeren **23** 50 47N 5 28 E
Tonggu **97** 28 31N 114 20 E
Tongguan **94** 34 40N 110 25 E
Tonghai **96** 24 10N 102 53 E
Tonghua **95** 41 42N 125 58 E
Tongjiang **96** 31 58N 107 11 E
Tongjosŏn Man **95** 39 30N 128 0 E
Tongking, G. of = Tonkin, G. of **84** 20 0N 108 0 E
Tongliang **96** 29 50N 106 3 E
Tongliao **95** 43 38N 122 18 E
Tongling **97** 30 55N 117 48 E
Tonglu **97** 29 45N 119 37 E
Tongnae **95** 35 12N 129 5 E
Tongnan **96** 30 9N 105 50 E
Tongobory **135** 23 32 S 44 20 E
Tongoy **174** 30 16 S 71 31W
Tongren **96** 27 43N 109 11 E
Tongres = Tongeren **23** 50 47N 5 28 E
Tongsa Dzong **82** 27 31N 90 31 E
Tongue **14** 58 29N 4 25W
Tongue → **152** 46 24N 105 52W
Tongwei **94** 35 0N 105 5 E
Tongxin **94** 36 59N 105 58 E
Tongyang **95** 39 9N 126 53 E
Tongyu **95** 44 45N 123 4 E
Tongzi **96** 28 9N 106 49 E
Tonica **154** 41 13N 89 4W
Tonj **125** 7 20N 28 44 E
Tonk **78** 26 6N 75 54 E
Tonkawa **153** 36 44N 97 22W
Tonkin = Bac Phan **84** 22 0N 105 0 E
Tonkin, G. of **84** 20 0N 108 0 E
Tonlé Sap **84** 13 0N 104 0 E
Tonnay-Charente **20** 45 56N 0 55W
Tonneins **20** 44 23N 0 19 E
Tonnerre **19** 47 51N 3 59 E
Tönning **26** 54 18N 8 57 E
Tono **98** 39 19N 141 32 E
Tonopah **157** 38 4N 117 12W
Tonoshō **100** 34 29N 134 11 E
Tonosí **162** 7 20N 80 20W
Tønsberg **51** 59 19N 10 25 E
Tonstad **51** 58 40N 6 45 E
Tonzang **82** 23 36N 93 42 E
Tonzi **82** 24 39N 94 57 E
Tooele **156** 40 30N 112 20W
Toolondo **112** 36 58 S 141 58 E
Toompine **111** 27 15 S 144 19 E
Toongi **113** 32 28 S 148 30 E
Toonpan **110** 19 28 S 146 48 E
Toora **113** 38 39 S 146 23 E
Toora-Khem **65** 52 28N 96 17 E
Toowoomba **111** 27 32 S 151 56 E
Top-ozero **56** 65 35N 32 0 E
Topalu **50** 44 31N 28 3 E
Topaz **158** 38 41N 119 30W
Topeka **152** 39 3N 95 40W
Topki **64** 55 20N 85 35 E
Topl'a → **31** 48 45N 21 45 E
Topley **144** 54 49N 126 18W
Toplica → **46** 43 15N 21 49 E

Tripoli

Tripoli 154 42 49N 92 16W
Trípolis 49 37 31N 22 25 E
Tripp 152 43 16N 97 58W
Tripura □ 82 24 0N 92 0 E
Trischen 26 54 3N 8 32 E
Tristan da Cunha 9 37 6 S 12 20W
Trivandrum 81 8 41N 77 0 E
Trivento 45 41 48N 14 31 E
Trnava 31 48 23N 17 35 E
Trobriand Is. 107 8 30 S 151 0 E
Trochu 144 51 50N 113 13W
Trodely I. 142 52 15N 79 26W
Troezen 49 37 25N 23 15 E
Trogir 43 43 32N 16 15 E
Troglav 43 43 56N 16 36 E
Trøgstad 51 59 37N 11 16 E
Tróia 45 41 22N 15 19 E
Troilus, L. 142 50 50N 74 35W
Troina 45 37 47N 14 34 E
Trois Fourches, Cap des 121 35 26N 2 58W
Trois-Pistoles 143 48 5N 69 10W
Trois-Riviéres 142 46 25N 72 34W
Troisvierges 23 50 8N 6 0 E
Troitsk 62 54 10N 61 35 E
Troitskiy 62 55 29N 37 18 E
Troitsko Pechorsk 56 62 40N 56 10 E
Trölladyngja 54 64 54N 17 16W
Trollhättan 53 58 17N 12 20 E
Trollheimen 51 62 46N 9 1 E
Trombetas → 169 1 55 S 55 35W
Tromelin I. 83 15 52 S 54 25 E
Troms fylke □ 54 68 56N 19 0 E
Tromsø 54 69 40N 18 56 E
Trona 159 35 46N 117 23W
Tronador 176 41 10 S 71 50W
Trondheim 51 63 36N 10 25 E
Trondheimsfjorden 51 63 35N 10 30 E
Trönninge 53 56 37N 12 51 E
Trönö 52 61 22N 16 54 E
Tronto → 43 42 54N 13 55 E
Troon 14 55 33N 4 40W
Tropea 45 38 40N 15 53 E
Tropic 157 37 36N 112 4W
Tropoja 48 42 23N 20 10 E
Trossachs, The 14 56 14N 4 24W
Trostan 15 55 4N 6 10W
Trostberg 27 48 2N 12 33 E
Trostyanets 58 50 33N 34 59 E
Trotternish 14 57 32N 6 15W
Troup 153 32 10N 95 3W
Trout → 144 61 19N 119 51W
Trout L., N.W.T., Canada 144 60 40N 121 14W
Trout L., Ont., Canada 145 51 20N 93 15W
Trout Lake, Mich., U.S.A. 142 46 10N 85 2W
Trout Lake, Wash., U.S.A. 158 46 0N 121 32W
Trout River 143 49 29N 58 8W
Trouville-sur-Mer 18 49 21N 0 5 E
Trowbridge 13 51 18N 2 12W
Troy, Turkey 48 39 57N 26 12 E
Troy, Ala., U.S.A. 149 31 50N 85 58W
Troy, Idaho, U.S.A. 156 46 44N 116 46W
Troy, Ill., U.S.A. 154 38 44N 89 54W
Troy, Ind., U.S.A. 155 38 0N 86 48W
Troy, Kans., U.S.A. 152 39 47N 95 2W
Troy, Mich., U.S.A. 155 42 37N 83 9W
Troy, Mo., U.S.A. 154 38 56N 90 59W
Troy, Mont., U.S.A. 156 48 30N 115 58W
Troy, N.Y., U.S.A. 151 42 45N 73 39W
Troy, Ohio, U.S.A. 155 40 0N 84 10W
Troyan 47 42 57N 24 43 E
Troyes 19 48 19N 4 3 E
Trpanj 46 43 1N 17 15 E
Trstena 31 49 21N 19 37 E
Trstenik 46 43 36N 21 0 E
Trubchevsk 58 52 33N 33 47 E
Trucial States = United Arab Emirates ■ 75 23 50N 54 0 E
Truckee 158 39 20N 120 11W
Trujillo, Colombia 168 4 10N 76 19W
Trujillo, Hond. 162 16 0N 86 0W
Trujillo, Peru 172 8 6 S 79 0W
Trujillo, Spain 35 39 28N 5 55W
Trujillo, U.S.A. 153 35 34N 104 44W
Trujillo, Venezuela 168 9 22N 70 38W
Trujillo □ 168 9 25N 70 30W
Truk 104 7 25N 151 46 E
Trumann 153 35 42N 90 32W
Trumbull, Mt. 157 36 25N 113 8W
Trŭn, Bulgaria 46 42 51N 22 38 E
Trun, France 18 48 50N 0 2 E
Trun, Switz. 29 46 45N 8 59 E
Trundle 113 32 53 S 147 35 E
Trung-Phan 84 16 0N 108 0 E
Truro, Australia 112 34 24 S 139 9 E
Truro, Canada 143 45 21N 63 14W
Truro, U.K. 13 50 17N 5 2W
Truslove 109 33 20 S 121 45 E
Trustrup 53 56 20N 10 46 E
Truth or Consequences 157 33 9N 107 16W
Trutnov 30 50 37N 15 54 E
Truyère → 20 44 38N 2 34 E
Tryavna 47 42 54N 25 25 E
Tryon 149 35 15N 82 16W
Tryonville 150 41 42N 79 48W
Trzcianka 32 53 3N 16 25 E
Trzciel 32 52 23N 15 50 E
Trzcińsko Zdrój 32 52 58N 14 35 E
Trzebiatów 32 54 3N 15 18 E
Trzebiez 32 53 38N 14 31 E
Trzebinia-Siersza 32 50 11N 19 18 E
Trzebnica 32 51 20N 17 1 E
Trzemeszno 32 52 33N 17 48 E
Tržič 43 46 22N 14 18 E
Tsageri 61 42 39N 42 46 E
Tsamandás 48 39 46N 20 21 E
Tsaratanana 135 16 47 S 47 39 E
Tsaratanana, Mt. de 135 14 0 S 49 0 E
Tsarevo = Michurin 47 42 9N 27 51 E
Tsarichanka 60 48 55N 34 30 E
Tsaritsáni 48 39 53N 22 14 E
Tsau 134 20 8 S 22 22 E
Tsebrikovo 60 47 9N 30 10 E
Tselinograd 64 51 10N 71 30 E
Tsetserleg 92 47 36N 101 32 E
Tshabong 134 26 2 S 22 29 E
Tshane 134 24 5 S 21 54 E
Tshela 133 4 57 S 13 4 E
Tshesebe 135 21 51 S 27 32 E
Tshibeke 130 2 40 S 28 35 E
Tshibinda 130 2 23 S 28 43 E
Tshikapa 133 6 28 S 20 48 E
Tshilenge 130 6 17 S 23 48 E
Tshinsenda 131 12 20 S 28 0 E
Tshofa 130 5 13 S 25 16 E
Tshwane 134 22 24 S 22 1 E
Tsigara 134 20 22 S 25 54 E
Tsihombe 135 25 18 S 45 29 E
Tsimlyansk 61 47 40N 42 6 E
Tsimlyanskoye Vdkhr. 61 48 0N 43 0 E
Tsinan = Jinan 94 36 38N 117 1 E
Tsineng 134 27 5 S 23 5 E
Tsínga 48 41 23N 24 44 E
Tsinghai = Qinghai □ 92 36 0N 98 0 E
Tsingtao = Qingdao 95 36 5N 120 20 E
Tsinjomitondraka 135 15 40 S 47 8 E
Tsiroanomandidy 135 18 46 S 46 2 E
Tsivilsk 59 55 50N 47 25 E
Tsivory 135 24 4 S 46 5 E
Tskhinvali 61 42 14N 44 1 E
Tsna → 59 54 55N 41 58 E
Tso Moriri, L. 79 32 50N 78 20 E
Tsodilo Hill 134 18 49 S 21 43 E
Tsogttsetsiy 94 43 43N 105 35 E
Tsolo 135 31 18 S 28 37 E
Tsomo 135 32 0 S 27 42 E
Tsu 101 34 45N 136 25 E
Tsu L. 144 60 40N 111 52W
Tsuchiura 101 36 5N 140 15 E
Tsugaru-Kaikyō 98 41 35N 141 0 E
Tsukumi 100 33 4N 131 52 E
Tsukushi-Sanchi 100 33 25N 130 30 E
Tsumeb 134 19 9 S 17 44 E
Tsumis 134 23 39 S 17 29 E
Tsuna 100 34 28N 134 56 E
Tsuno-Shima 100 34 21N 130 52 E
Tsuru 101 35 31N 138 57 E
Tsuruga 101 35 45N 136 2 E
Tsuruga-Wan 101 35 50N 136 3 E
Tsurugi 101 36 29N 136 37 E
Tsurugi-San 100 33 51N 134 6 E
Tsurumi-Saki 100 32 56N 132 5 E
Tsuruoka 98 38 44N 139 50 E
Tsurusaki 100 33 14N 131 41 E
Tsushima, Gifu, Japan 101 35 10N 136 43 E
Tsushima, Nagasaki, Japan 100 34 20N 129 20 E
Tsvetkovo 60 49 8N 31 33 E
Tu → 82 21 50N 96 15 E
Tua → 34 41 13N 7 26W
Tuai 114 38 47 S 177 10 E
Tuakau 114 37 16 S 174 59 E
Tual 87 5 38 S 132 44 E
Tuam 15 53 30N 8 50W
Tuamarina 115 41 25 S 173 59 E
Tuamotu Arch. 105 17 0 S 144 0W
Tuamotu Ridge 105 20 0 S 138 0W
Tuanfeng 97 30 38N 114 52 E
Tuanxi 96 27 28N 107 8 E
Tuao 90 17 55N 122 22 E
Tuapse 61 44 5N 39 10 E
Tuatapere 115 46 8 S 167 41 E
Tuba City 157 36 8N 111 18W
Tuban 89 6 54 S 112 3 E
Tubarão 175 28 30 S 49 0W
Tūbās 69 32 20N 35 22 E
Tubau 86 3 10N 113 40 E
Tubbergen 22 52 24N 6 48 E
Tübingen 27 48 31N 9 4 E
Tubize 23 50 42N 4 13 E
Tubruq 122 32 7N 23 55 E
Tubuaeran I. 105 3 51N 159 22W
Tubuai Is. 105 25 0 S 150 0W
Tuburan 91 6 39N 122 16 E
Tuc Trung 85 11 1N 107 12 E
Tucacas 168 10 48N 68 19W
Tucano 170 10 58 S 38 48W
Tuchang 97 24 59N 121 30 E
Tuchodi → 144 58 17N 123 42W
Tuchola 32 53 33N 17 52 E
Tuchów 32 49 54N 21 1 E
Tucson 157 32 14N 110 59W
Tucumán □ 174 26 48 S 66 2W
Tucumcari 153 35 12N 103 45W
Tucunaré 173 5 18 S 55 51W
Tucupido 168 9 17N 65 47W
Tucupita 169 9 2N 62 3W
Tucuruí 170 3 42 S 49 44W
Tuczno 32 53 13N 16 10 E
Tudela 36 42 4N 1 39W
Tudela de Duero 34 41 37N 4 39W
Tudmur 72 34 36N 38 15 E
Tudor, L. 143 55 50N 65 25W
Tudora 50 47 31N 26 45 E
Tuella → 34 41 30N 7 12W
Tuen 111 28 33 S 145 37 E
Tueré → 170 2 48 S 50 59W
Tufi 107 9 8 S 149 19 E
Tugela → 135 29 14 S 31 30 E
Tuguegarao 90 17 35N 121 42 E
Tugur 65 53 44N 136 45 E
Tuineje 37 28 19N 14 3W
Tukangbesi, Kepulauan 87 6 0 S 124 0 E
Tukarak I. 142 56 15N 78 45W
Tukayyid 72 29 47N 45 36 E
Tûkh 124 30 21N 31 12 E
Tukobo 126 5 1N 2 47W
Tūkrah 122 32 30N 20 37 E
Tuktoyaktuk 140 69 27N 133 2W
Tukums 58 57 2N 23 10 E
Tukuyu 131 9 17 S 33 35 E
Tula, Hidalgo, Mexico 161 20 0N 99 20W
Tula, Tamaulipas, Mexico 161 23 0N 99 40W
Tula, Nigeria 127 9 51N 11 27 E
Tula, U.S.S.R. 59 54 13N 37 38 E
Tulak 77 33 55N 63 40 E
Tulancingo 161 20 5N 99 22W
Tulangbawang → 88 4 24 S 105 52 E
Tulare 158 36 15N 119 26W
Tulare Lake Bed 158 36 0N 119 48W
Tularosa 157 33 4N 106 1W
Tulbagh 134 33 16 S 19 6 E
Tulcán 168 0 48N 77 43W
Tulcea 50 45 13N 28 46 E
Tulcea □ 50 45 0N 29 0 E
Tulchin 60 48 41N 28 49 E
Tūleh 73 34 35N 52 33 E
Tulemalu L. 145 62 58N 99 25W
Tulgheş 50 46 58N 25 45 E
Tuli, Indonesia 87 1 24 S 122 26 E
Tuli, Zambia 131 21 58 S 29 13 E
Tulia 153 34 35N 101 44W
Ţulkarm 69 32 19N 35 2 E
Tullahoma 149 35 23N 86 12W
Tullamore, Australia 113 32 39 S 147 36 E
Tullamore, Ireland 15 53 17N 7 30W
Tulle 20 45 16N 1 46 E
Tullibigeal 113 33 25 S 146 44 E
Tullins 21 45 18N 5 29 E
Tulln 30 48 20N 16 4 E
Tullow 15 52 48N 6 45W
Tullus 125 11 7N 24 31 E
Tully 110 17 56 S 145 55 E
Ţulmaythah 122 32 40N 20 55 E
Tulmur 110 22 40 S 142 20 E
Tulnici 50 45 51N 26 38 E
Tulovo 47 42 33N 25 32 E
Tulsa 153 36 10N 96 0W
Tulsequah 144 58 39N 133 35W
Tulu Milki 125 9 55N 38 20 E
Tulu Welel 125 8 56N 34 47 E
Tulua 168 4 6N 76 11W
Tulun 65 54 32N 100 35 E
Tulungagung 89 8 5 S 111 54 E
Tum 87 3 36 S 130 21 E
Tuma 59 55 10N 40 30 E
Tuma → 162 13 6N 84 35W
Tumaco 168 1 50N 78 45W
Tumaco, Ensenada 168 1 55N 78 45W
Tumatumari 169 5 20N 58 55W
Tumauini 90 17 17N 121 49 E
Tumba 52 59 12N 17 48 E
Tumba, L. 132 0 50 S 18 0 E
Tumbarumba 113 35 44 S 148 0 E
Tumbaya 174 23 50 S 65 26W
Túmbes 172 3 37 S 80 27W
Tumbes □ 172 3 50 S 80 30W
Tumbwe 131 11 25 S 27 15 E
Tumby Bay 112 34 21 S 136 8 E
Tumd Youqi 94 40 30N 110 30 E
Tumen 95 43 0N 129 50 E
Tumen Jiang → 95 42 20N 130 35 E
Tumeremo 169 7 18N 61 30W
Tumiritinga 171 18 58 S 41 38W
Tumkur 81 13 18N 77 6 E
Tummel, L. 14 56 43N 3 55W
Tump 77 26 7N 62 16 E
Tumpat 85 6 11N 102 10 E
Tumsar 79 21 26N 79 45 E
Tumu 126 10 56N 1 56W
Tumucumaque, Serra 169 2 0N 55 0W
Tumupasa 172 14 9 S 67 55W
Tumut 113 35 16 S 148 13 E
Tumutuk 62 55 1N 53 19 E
Tumwater 156 47 0N 122 58W
Tunas de Zaza 162 21 39N 79 34W
Tunbridge Wells 13 51 7N 0 16 E
Tuncurry 111 32 17 S 152 29 E
Tunduru 131 11 8 S 37 25 E
Tunduru □ 131 11 5 S 37 22 E
Tundzha → 47 41 40N 26 35 E
Tune 51 59 16N 11 2 E
Tunga → 81 15 0N 75 50 E
Tunga Pass 82 29 0N 94 14 E
Tungabhadra → 81 15 57N 78 15 E
Tungabhadra Dam 81 15 0N 75 50 E
Tungaru 125 10 9N 30 52 E
Tungi 82 23 53N 90 24 E
Tungla 162 13 24N 84 21W
Tungnafellsjökull 54 64 45N 17 55W
Tungsten 144 61 57N 128 16W
Tungurahua □ 168 1 15 S 78 35W
Tunguska, Nizhnyaya → 65 65 48N 88 4 E
Tunguska, Podkamennaya → 65 61 36N 90 18 E
Tuni 80 17 22N 82 36 E
Tunia 168 2 41N 76 31W
Tunica 153 34 43N 90 23W
Tunis 121 36 50N 10 11 E
Tunis, Golfe de 121 37 0N 10 30 E
Tunisia ■ 122 33 30N 9 10 E
Tunja 168 5 33N 73 25W
Tunkhannock 151 41 32N 75 46W
Tunliu 94 36 13N 112 52 E
Tunnsjøen 54 64 45N 13 25 E
Tunungayualok I. 143 56 0N 61 0W
Tunuyán 174 33 35 S 69 0W
Tunuyán → 174 33 33 S 67 30W
Tunxi 97 29 42N 118 25 E
Tuo Jiang → 96 28 50N 105 35 E
Tuolumne 158 37 59N 120 16W
Tuolumne → 158 37 36N 121 13W
Tuoy-Khaya 65 62 32N 111 25 E
Tūp Āghāj 72 36 3N 47 50 E
Tupã 175 21 57 S 50 28W
Tupaciguara 171 18 35 S 48 42W
Tupelo 149 34 15N 88 42W
Tupik, R.S.F.S.R., U.S.S.R. 58 55 42N 33 22 E
Tupik, R.S.F.S.R., U.S.S.R. 65 54 26N 119 57 E
Tupinambaranas 169 3 0 S 58 0W
Tupirama 170 8 58 S 48 12W
Tupiratins 170 8 23 S 48 8W
Tupiza 174 21 30 S 65 40W
Tupižnica 46 43 43N 22 10 E
Tupman 159 35 18N 119 21W
Tupper 144 55 32N 120 1W
Tupper Lake 151 44 18N 74 30W
Tupungato, Cerro 174 33 15 S 69 50W
Tuquan 95 45 18N 121 38 E
Tuque, La 142 47 30N 72 50W
Túquerres 168 1 5N 77 37W
Tura, India 82 25 30N 90 16 E
Tura, U.S.S.R. 65 64 20N 100 17 E
Tura → 62 57 12N 66 56 E
Turabah 72 28 20N 43 15 E
Turagua, Serranía 169 7 20N 64 35W
Turaiyur 81 11 9N 78 38 E
Turakina 114 40 3 S 175 16 E
Turakirae Hd. 114 41 26 S 174 56 E
Tūrān, Iran 73 35 39N 56 42 E
Turan, U.S.S.R. 65 51 55N 95 0 E
Turayf 72 31 41N 38 39 E
Turbacz 31 49 30N 20 8 E
Turbe 46 44 15N 17 35 E
Turbenthal 29 47 27N 8 51 E
Turda 50 46 34N 23 47 E
Turégano 34 41 9N 4 1W
Turek 32 52 3N 18 30 E
Turen 168 9 17N 69 6W
Turfan = Turpan 92 43 58N 89 10 E
Turgay 62 49 38N 63 30 E
Turgay → 62 48 1N 62 45 E
Tŭrgovishte 47 43 17N 26 38 E
Turgutlu 57 38 30N 27 48 E
Turhal 60 40 24N 36 5 E
Turia → 37 39 27N 0 19W
Turiaçu 170 1 40 S 45 19W
Turiaçu → 170 1 36 S 45 19W
Turiec → 31 49 7N 18 55 E
Turin = Torino 42 45 4N 7 40 E
Turin 144 49 58N 112 31W
Turinsk 62 58 3N 63 42 E
Turka 58 49 10N 23 2 E
Turkana □ 130 3 0N 35 30 E
Turkana, L. 130 3 30N 36 5 E
Turkestan 63 43 17N 68 16 E
Turkestanskiy, Khrebet 63 39 35N 69 0 E
Tŭrkeve 31 47 6N 20 44 E
Turkey ■ 57 39 0N 36 0 E
Turkey → 154 42 43N 91 2W
Turkey Creek 108 17 2 S 128 12 E
Turki 59 52 0N 43 15 E
Turkmen S.S.R. □ 64 39 0N 59 0 E
Turks Is. 163 21 20N 71 20W
Turks Island Passage 163 21 30N 71 30W
Turku 55 60 30N 22 19 E
Turkwe → 130 3 6N 36 6 E
Turlock 158 37 30N 120 55W
Turnagain → 144 59 12N 127 35W
Turnagain, C. 114 40 28 S 176 38 E
Turneffe Is. 161 17 20N 87 50W
Turner, Australia 108 17 52 S 128 16 E
Turner, U.S.A. 156 48 52N 108 25W
Turner Pt. 110 11 47 S 133 32 E
Turner Valley 144 50 40N 114 17W
Turners Falls 151 42 36N 72 34W
Turnhout 23 51 19N 4 57 E
Türnitz 30 47 55N 15 29 E
Turnor L. 145 56 35N 108 35W
Turnov 30 50 34N 15 10 E
Tŭrnovo 47 43 5N 25 41 E
Turnu Măgurele 50 43 46N 24 56 E
Turnu Rosu Pasul 50 45 33N 24 17 E
Turnu-Severin 50 44 39N 22 41 E

Union Springs

Turobin 32 50 50N 22 44 E
Turon 153 37 48N 98 27W
Tuross Head 113 36 3 S 150 8 E
Turpan 92 43 58N 89 10 E
Turrës, Kalaja e 48 41 10N 19 28 E
Turriff 14 57 32N 2 28W
Tursāq 72 33 27N 45 47 E
Tursha 59 56 55N 47 36 E
Tursi 45 40 15N 16 27 E
Turtle Hd. I. 110 10 56 S 142 37 E
Turtle Is. 91 6 7N 118 14 E
Turtle L. 145 53 36N 108 38W
Turtle Lake, N. Dak., U.S.A. 152 47 30N 100 55W
Turtle Lake, Wis., U.S.A. 152 45 22N 92 10W
Turtleford 145 53 23N 108 57W
Turua 114 37 14 S 175 35 E
Turukhansk 65 65 21N 88 5 E
Turun ja Porin lääni □ 55 60 27N 22 15 E
Turzovka 31 49 25N 18 35 E
Tuscaloosa 149 33 13N 87 31W
Tuscània 43 42 25N 11 53 E
Tuscany = Toscana 42 43 30N 11 5 E
Tuscola, Ill., U.S.A. 155 39 48N 88 15W
Tuscola, Tex., U.S.A. 153 32 15N 99 48W
Tuscumbia, Ala., U.S.A. 149 34 42N 87 42W
Tuscumbia, Mo., U.S.A. 154 38 14N 92 28W
Tuskar Rock 15 52 12N 6 10W
Tuskegee 149 32 24N 85 39W
Tustna 51 63 10N 8 5 E
Tuszyn 32 51 36N 19 33 E
Tutayev 59 57 53N 39 32 E
Tuticorin 81 8 50N 78 12 E
Tutin 46 43 0N 20 20 E
Tutóia 170 2 45 S 42 20W
Tutong 86 4 47N 114 40 E
Tutova → 50 46 20N 27 30 E
Tutrakan 47 44 2N 26 40 E
Tutshi L. 144 59 56N 134 30W
Tuttle 152 47 9N 100 0W
Tuttlingen 27 47 59N 8 50 E
Tutuala 87 8 25 S 127 15 E
Tutuila 106 14 19 S 170 50W
Tutuko Mt. 115 44 35 S 168 1 E
Tututepec 161 16 9N 97 38W
Tutye 112 35 12 S 141 29 E
Tuva A.S.S.R. □ 65 51 30N 95 0 E
Tuvalu ■ 104 8 0 S 178 0 E
Tuvutha 106 17 40 S 178 48W
Tūwal 74 22 17N 39 6 E
Tuwaym 70 35 10N 36 32 E
Tuxpan 161 20 58N 97 23W
Tuxtla Gutiérrez 161 16 50N 93 10W
Tuy 34 42 3N 8 39W
Tuy An 84 13 17N 109 16 E
Tuy Duc 85 12 15N 107 27 E
Tuy Hoa 84 13 5N 109 10 E
Tuy Phong 85 11 14N 108 43 E
Tuya L. 144 59 7N 130 35W
Tuyen Hoa 84 17 50N 106 10 E
Tuyen Quang 84 21 50N 105 10 E
Tuymazy 62 54 36N 53 42 E
Tūysarkān 73 34 33N 48 27 E
Tuz Gölü 57 38 45N 33 30 E
Ţūz Khurmātū 72 34 56N 44 38 E
Tuzkan, Ozero 63 40 35N 67 28 E
Tuzla, Turkey 70 36 42N 35 6 E
Tuzla, Yugoslavia 46 44 34N 18 41 E
Tuzlov → 61 47 28N 39 45 E
Tvååker 53 57 4N 12 25 E
Tvedestrand 51 58 38N 8 58 E
Tvŭrditsa 47 42 42N 25 53 E
Twain 158 40 1N 121 3W
Twain Harte 158 38 2N 120 14W
Twardogóra 32 51 23N 17 28 E
Tweed 150 44 29N 77 19W
Tweed → 14 55 42N 2 10W
Tweed Heads 111 28 10 S 153 31 E
Tweedsmuir Prov. Park 144 53 0N 126 20W
Twello 22 52 14N 6 6 E
Twentynine Palms 159 34 10N 116 4W
Twillingate 143 49 42N 54 45W
Twin Bridges 156 45 33N 112 23W
Twin Falls 156 42 30N 114 30W
Twin Valley 152 47 18N 96 15W
Twinnge 82 23 10N 96 2 E
Twisp 156 48 21N 120 5W
Twistringen 26 52 48N 8 38 E
Two Harbors 152 47 1N 91 40W
Two Hills 144 53 43N 111 52W
Two Rivers 148 44 10N 87 31W
Two Thumbs Ra. 115 43 45 S 170 44 E
Twofold B. 113 37 8 S 149 59 E
Tychy 32 50 9N 18 59 E
Tyczyn 32 49 58N 22 2 E
Tydal 51 63 4N 11 34 E
Tykocin 32 53 13N 22 46 E
Tyldal 51 62 8N 10 48 E
Tyler, Minn., U.S.A. 152 44 18N 96 8W
Tyler, Tex., U.S.A. 153 32 18N 95 18W
Týn nad Vltavou 30 49 13N 14 26 E
Tynda 65 55 10N 124 43 E
Tyne → 12 54 58N 1 28W
Tyne & Wear □ 12 54 55N 1 35W
Tynemouth 12 55 1N 1 27W
Tynset 51 62 17N 10 47 E
Tyre = Sûr 69 33 19N 35 16 E
Tyrifjorden 51 60 2N 10 8 E
Tyringe 52 56 9N 13 35 E
Tyristrand 51 60 5N 10 5 E
Tyrnyauz 61 43 21N 42 45 E
Tyrol = Tirol □ 30 47 3N 10 43 E
Tyrone 150 40 39N 78 10W
Tyrrell → 112 35 26 S 142 51 E
Tyrrell, L. 112 35 20 S 142 50 E
Tyrrell Arm 145 62 27N 97 30W
Tyrrell L. 145 63 7N 105 27W
Tyrrhenian Sea 38 40 0N 12 30 E
Tysfjorden 54 68 7N 16 25 E
Tysnes 51 60 1N 5 30 E
Tysnesøy 51 60 0N 5 35 E
Tyssedal 51 60 7N 6 35 E
Tystberga 53 58 51N 17 15 E
Tyub Karagan, M. 61 44 40N 50 19 E
Tyuleniy 61 44 28N 47 30 E
Tyulgan 62 52 22N 56 12 E
Tyumen 62 57 11N 65 29 E
Tyumen-Aryk 63 44 2N 67 1 E
Tyup 63 42 45N 78 20 E
Tywi → 13 51 48N 4 20W
Tywyn 13 52 36N 4 5W
Tzaneen 135 23 47 S 30 9 E
Tzermíadhes Neápolis 50 35 11N 25 29 E
Tzoumérka, Óros 48 39 30N 21 26 E
Tzukong = Zigong 96 29 15N 104 48 E
Tzummarum 22 53 14N 5 32 E

U

U Taphao 84 12 35N 101 0 E
Uacalla Iero 136 1 48N 42 38 E
Uachadi, Sierra 169 4 54N 65 18W
Uainambi 168 1 43N 69 51W
Uanda 110 21 37 S 144 55 E
Uanle Uen 136 2 37N 44 54 E
Uarsciek 136 2 28N 45 55 E
Uascen 136 4 11N 43 13 E
Uasin □ 130 0 30N 35 20 E
Uato-Udo 87 9 7 S 125 36 E
Uatumã → 169 2 26 S 57 37W
Uauá 170 9 50 S 39 28W
Uaupés 168 0 8 S 67 5W
Uaupés → 168 0 2N 67 16W
Uaxactún 162 17 25N 89 29W
Ub 46 44 28N 20 6 E
Ubá 175 21 8 S 43 0W
Ubaitaba 171 14 18 S 39 20W
Ubangi = Oubangi → 132 0 30 S 17 50 E
Ubaté 168 5 19N 73 49W
Ubauro 78 28 15N 69 45 E
Ubay 91 10 3N 124 28 E
'Ubaydīyah 74 13 7N 43 20 E
Ubaye → 21 44 28N 6 18 E
Ube 100 33 56N 131 15 E
Ubeda 37 38 3N 3 23W
Uberaba 171 19 50 S 47 55W
Uberaba, L. 173 17 30 S 57 50W
Uberlândia 171 19 0 S 48 20W
Überlingen 27 47 46N 9 10 E
Ubiaja 127 6 41N 6 22 E
Ubolratna Phong, L. 84 16 45N 102 30 E
Ubombo 135 27 31 S 32 4 E
Ubon Ratchathani 84 15 15N 104 50 E
Ubondo 130 0 55 S 25 42 E
Ubort → 58 52 6N 28 30 E
Ubrique 35 36 41N 5 27W
Ubundu 130 0 22 S 25 30 E
Ucayali → 172 4 30 S 73 30W
Uccle 23 50 48N 4 22 E
Uchaly 62 54 19N 59 27 E
Uchi Lake 145 51 5N 92 35W
Uchiko 100 33 33N 132 39 E
Uchiura-Wan 98 42 25N 140 40 E
Uchiza 172 8 25 S 76 20W
Uchte 26 52 29N 8 52 E
Uchterek 63 41 45N 73 12 E
Uchur → 65 58 48N 130 35 E
Ucluelet 144 48 57N 125 32W
Ucuriş 50 46 41N 21 58 E
Uda → 65 54 42N 135 14 E
Udaipur 78 24 36N 73 44 E
Udaipur Garhi 79 27 0N 86 35 E
Udbina 43 44 31N 15 47 E
Uddeholm 52 60 1N 13 38 E
Uddel 22 52 15N 5 48 E
Uddevalla 53 58 21N 11 55 E
Uddjaur 54 65 25N 21 15 E
Uden 23 51 40N 5 37 E
Udgir 80 18 25N 77 5 E
Udhampur 79 33 0N 75 5 E
Udi 127 6 17N 7 21 E
Údine 43 46 5N 13 10 E
Udmurt A.S.S.R. □ 62 57 30N 52 30 E
Udon Thani 84 17 29N 102 46 E
Udumalaippettai 81 10 35N 77 15 E
Udupi 81 13 25N 74 42 E
Udvoy Balkan 47 42 50N 26 50 E
Udzungwa Range 131 9 30 S 35 10 E
Ueckermünde 26 53 45N 14 1 E
Ueda 101 36 24N 138 16 E
Uedineniya, Os. 6 78 0N 85 0 E
Uel Scimbirro 136 2 23N 44 14 E
Uele → 132 3 45N 24 45 E
Uelen 65 66 10N 170 0W
Uelzen 26 53 0N 10 33 E
Ueno 101 34 45N 136 8 E
Uetendorf 28 46 47N 7 34 E
Ufa 62 54 45N 55 55 E
Ufa → 62 54 40N 56 0 E
Uffenheim 27 49 32N 10 15 E
Ugab → 134 20 55 S 13 30 E
Ugalla → 130 5 8 S 30 42 E
Ugamskiy, Khrebet 63 42 20N 70 30 E
Uganda ■ 130 2 0N 32 0 E
Ugchelen 22 52 11N 5 56 E
Ugento 45 39 55N 18 10 E
Ugep 127 5 53N 8 2 E
Ugie 135 31 10 S 28 13 E
Ugíjar 37 36 58N 3 7W
Ugine 21 45 45N 6 25 E
Uglegorsk 65 49 5N 142 2 E
Uglich 59 57 33N 38 20 E
Ugljane 43 43 35N 16 46 E
Ugolyak 65 64 33N 120 30 E
Ugra → 58 54 30N 36 7 E
Ugûn Mûsa 71 29 53N 32 40 E
Ugŭrchin 47 43 6N 24 26 E
Uh → 31 48 7N 21 25 E
Uherske Hradiště 31 49 4N 17 30 E
Uhersky Brod 31 49 1N 17 40 E
Úhlava → 30 49 45N 13 24 E
Uhrichsville 150 40 23N 81 22W
Uíge 133 7 30 S 14 40 E
Uige □ 133 7 0 S 16 0 E
Uijŏngbu 95 37 48N 127 0 E
Ŭiju 95 40 15N 124 35 E
Uinta Mts. 156 40 45N 110 30W
Uitenhage 134 33 40 S 25 28 E
Uitgeest 22 52 32N 4 43 E
Uithoorn 22 52 14N 4 50 E
Uithuizen 22 53 24N 6 41 E
Uitkerke 23 51 18N 3 9 E
Újfehértó 31 47 49N 21 41 E
Ujh → 79 32 40N 75 30 E
Ujhani 79 28 0N 79 6 E
Uji 101 34 53N 135 48 E
Uji-guntō 99 31 15N 129 25 E
Ujjain 78 23 9N 75 43 E
Újpest 31 47 32N 19 6 E
Újszász 31 47 19N 20 7 E
Ujung Pandang 87 5 10 S 119 20 E
Uka 65 57 50N 162 0 E
Ukara I. 130 1 50 S 33 0 E
Uke-Shima 99 28 2N 129 14 E
Ukerewe □ 130 2 0 S 32 30 E
Ukerewe I. 130 2 0 S 33 0 E
Ukholovo 59 53 47N 40 30 E
Ukhrul 82 25 10N 94 25 E
Ukhta 56 63 55N 54 0 E
Ukiah 158 39 10N 123 9W
Ukki Fort 79 33 28N 76 54 E
Ukmerge 58 55 15N 24 45 E
Ukrainian S.S.R. □ 60 49 0N 32 0 E
Uksyanskoye 62 55 57N 63 1 E
Uku 133 11 24 S 14 22 E
Ukwi 134 23 29 S 20 30 E
Ulaanbaatar 92 47 55N 106 53 E
Ulaangom 92 50 0N 92 10 E
Ulamambri 113 31 19 S 149 23 E
Ulamba 131 9 3 S 23 38 E
Ulan Bator = Ulaanbaatar 92 47 55N 106 53 E
Ulan Ude 65 51 45N 107 40 E
Ulanbel 63 44 50N 71 7 E
Ulanga □ 131 8 40 S 36 50 E
Ulanów 32 50 30N 22 16 E
Ulaya, Morogoro, Tanzania 130 7 3 S 36 55 E
Ulaya, Tabora, Tanzania 130 4 25 S 33 30 E
Ulcinj 46 41 58N 19 10 E
Ulco 134 28 21 S 24 15 E
Ulefoss 51 59 17N 9 16 E
Ulëza 48 41 46N 19 57 E
Ulfborg 53 56 16N 8 20 E
Ulft 22 51 53N 6 23 E
Ulhasnagar 80 19 15N 73 10 E
Ulinda 113 31 35 S 149 30 E
Uljma 46 45 2N 21 10 E
Ulla → 34 42 39N 8 44W
Ulladulla 113 35 21 S 150 29 E
Ullånger 52 62 58N 18 10 E
Ullapool 14 57 54N 5 10W
Ullared 53 57 8N 12 42 E
Ulldecona 36 40 36N 0 20 E
Ullswater 12 54 35N 2 52W
Ullung-do 95 37 30N 130 30 E
Ulm 27 48 23N 10 0 E
Ulmarra 111 29 37 S 153 4 E
Ulmeni 50 45 4N 26 40 E
Ulonguè 131 14 37 S 34 19 E
Ulricehamn 53 57 46N 13 26 E
Ulrum 22 53 22N 6 20 E
Ulsan 95 35 20N 129 15 E
Ulsberg 51 62 45N 9 59 E
Ulsteinvik 51 62 21N 5 53 E
Ulster □ 15 54 35N 6 30W
Ulstrem 47 42 1N 26 27 E
Ultima 112 35 30 S 143 18 E
Ulubaria 79 22 31N 88 4 E
Uluguru Mts. 130 7 15 S 37 40 E
Ulungur → 92 47 1N 87 24 E
Ulutau 64 48 39N 67 1 E
Ulvenhout 23 51 33N 4 48 E
Ulverston 12 54 13N 3 7W
Ulverstone 110 41 11 S 146 11 E
Ulvik 51 60 35N 6 54 E
Ulya 65 59 10N 142 0 E
Ulyanovsk 59 54 20N 48 25 E
Ulyasutay 92 47 56N 97 28 E
Ulysses 153 37 39N 101 25W
Umag 43 45 26N 13 31 E
Umala 172 17 25 S 68 5W
Uman 60 48 40N 30 12 E
Umarkhed 80 19 37N 77 46 E
Umatac 106 13 18N 144 39 E
Umatilla 156 45 58N 119 17W
Umba 56 66 50N 34 20 E
Umbertide 43 43 18N 12 20 E
Umboi I. 107 5 40 S 148 0 E
Umbrella Mts. 115 45 35 S 169 5 E
Umbria □ 43 42 53N 12 30 E
Ume älv → 54 63 45N 20 20 E
Umeå 54 63 45N 20 20 E
Umera 87 0 12 S 129 37 E
Umfuli → 131 17 30 S 29 23 E
Umgusa 131 19 29 S 27 52 E
Umi 100 33 34N 130 30 E
Umka 46 44 40N 20 19 E
Umkomaas 135 30 13 S 30 48 E
Umm ad Daraj, J. 71 32 18N 35 48 E
Umm al Arānib 122 26 10N 14 43 E
Umm al Qaywayn 75 25 30N 55 35 E
Umm al Qittayn 71 32 18N 36 40 E
Umm Arda 125 15 17N 32 31 E
Umm Bāb 75 25 12N 50 48 E
Umm Bel 125 13 35N 28 0 E
Umm Dubban 125 15 23N 32 52 E
Umm el Fahm 69 32 31N 35 9 E
Umm 'Isheirât, G. 71 28 21N 34 18 E
Umm Koweika 125 13 10N 32 16 E
Umm Lajj 72 25 0N 37 23 E
Umm Merwa 124 18 4N 32 30 E
Umm Qays 69 32 40N 35 41 E
Umm Ruwaba 125 12 50N 31 20 E
Umm Sidr 125 14 29N 25 10 E
Umm Thalwīwah 74 21 9N 40 48 E
Ummanz 26 54 29N 13 9 E
Umnak 140 53 20N 168 20W
Umniati → 131 16 49 S 28 45 E
Umpqua → 156 43 42N 124 3W
Umpulo 133 12 38 S 17 42 E
Umred 78 20 51N 79 18 E
Umreth 78 22 41N 73 4 E
Umshandige Dam 131 20 10 S 30 40 E
Umtata 135 31 36 S 28 49 E
Umuahia 127 5 33N 7 29 E
Umvukwe Ra. 131 16 45 S 30 45 E
Umzimvubu = Port St. Johns 135 31 38 S 29 33 E
Umzingwane → 131 22 12 S 29 56 E
Umzinto 135 30 15 S 30 45 E
Una 78 20 46N 71 8 E
Una → 43 45 16N 16 55 E
Unac → 43 44 30N 16 9 E
Unadilla 151 42 20N 75 17W
Unalaska 140 53 40N 166 40W
Uncastillo 36 42 21N 1 8W
Uncía 172 18 25 S 66 40W
Uncompahgre Pk. 157 38 5N 107 32W
Unden 53 58 45N 14 25 E
Underberg 135 29 50 S 29 22 E
Underbool 112 35 10 S 141 51 E
Undersaker 52 63 19N 13 21 E
Undersvik 52 61 36N 16 20 E
Undredal 51 60 57N 7 6 E
Unecha 58 52 50N 32 37 E
Uneiuxi → 168 0 37 S 65 34W
Ungarie 113 33 38 S 146 56 E
Ungarra 112 34 12 S 136 2 E
Ungava B. 141 59 30N 67 30W
Ungava Pen. 141 60 0N 74 0W
Ungeny 60 47 11N 27 51 E
Unggi 95 42 16N 130 28 E
Ungwatiri 125 16 52N 36 10 E
Uni 59 56 44N 51 47 E
União da Vitória 175 26 13 S 51 5W
União dos Palmares 170 9 10 S 36 2W
Uniejów 32 51 59N 18 46 E
Unije 43 44 40N 14 15 E
Unimak 140 55 0N 164 0W
Unimak Pass. 140 53 30N 165 15W
Unini → 169 1 41 S 61 31W
Union, Miss., U.S.A. 153 32 34N 89 14W
Union, Mo., U.S.A. 154 38 25N 91 0W
Union, S.C., U.S.A. 149 34 43N 81 39W
Unión, La, Chile 176 40 10 S 73 0W
Unión, La, Colombia 168 1 35N 77 5W
Unión, La, El Salv. 162 13 20N 87 50W
Unión, La, Mexico 160 17 58N 101 49W
Unión, La, Peru 172 9 43 S 76 45W
Unión, La, Spain 37 37 38N 0 53W
Union, La □ 90 16 30N 120 25 E
Union, Mt. 157 34 34N 112 21W
Union City, Calif., U.S.A. 158 37 36N 122 1W
Union City, N.J., U.S.A. 151 40 47N 74 5W
Union City, Pa., U.S.A. 150 41 53N 79 50W
Union City, Tenn., U.S.A. 153 36 25N 89 0W
Union Gap 156 46 38N 120 29W
Union Grove 155 42 41N 88 3W
Union of Soviet Socialist Republics ■ 65 60 0N 100 0 E
Union Springs 149 32 9N 85 44W

Union Star

Union Star **154** 39 59N 94 36W
Uniondale **134** 33 39 S 23 7 E
Uniontown, Ky., U.S.A. **155** 37 47N 87 56W
Uniontown, Pa., U.S.A. **148** 39 54N 79 45W
Unionville **154** 40 29N 93 1W
Unirea **50** 44 15N 27 35 E
United Arab Emirates ■ **75** 23 50N 54 0 E
United Kingdom ■ **16** 55 0N 3 0W
United States of America ■ **147** 37 0N 96 0W
United States Trust Terr. of the Pacific Is. □ **104** 10 0N 160 0 E
Unity **145** 52 30N 109 5W
Universales, Mtes. **36** 40 18N 1 33W
University City **154** 38 40N 90 20W
Unjha **78** 23 46N 72 24 E
Unnao **79** 26 35N 80 30 E
Uno, Ilha **126** 11 15N 16 13W
Unst **14** 60 50N 0 55W
Unstrut → **26** 51 10N 11 48 E
Unter-engadin **29** 46 48N 10 20 E
Unterägeri **29** 47 8N 8 36 E
Unterkulm **28** 47 18N 8 7 E
Unterseen **28** 46 41N 7 50 E
Unterwaldner Alpen **29** 46 55N 8 15 E
Unuk → **144** 56 5N 131 3W
Ünye **60** 41 5N 37 15 E
Unzen-Dake **100** 32 45N 130 17 E
Unzha **59** 58 0N 44 0 E
Unzha → **59** 57 30N 43 40 E
Uors **29** 46 42N 9 12 E
Uozu **101** 36 48N 137 24 E
Upa → **31** 50 35N 16 15 E
Upata **169** 8 1N 62 24W
Upemba, L. **131** 8 30 S 26 20 E
Upernavik **6** 72 49N 56 20W
Upington **134** 28 25 S 21 15 E
Upleta **78** 21 46N 70 16 E
Upper Alkali Lake **156** 41 47N 120 8W
Upper Arlington **155** 40 0N 83 4W
Upper Arrow L. **144** 50 30N 117 50W
Upper Austria = Oberösterreich □ **30** 48 10N 14 0 E
Upper Foster L. **145** 56 47N 105 20W
Upper Hutt **114** 41 8 S 175 5 E
Upper Juba □ **136** 3 0N 43 0 E
Upper Klamath L. **156** 42 16N 121 55W
Upper L. Erne **15** 54 14N 7 22W
Upper Lake **158** 39 10N 122 55W
Upper Manilla **113** 30 38 S 150 40 E
Upper Musquodoboit **143** 45 10N 62 58W
Upper Red L. **152** 48 0N 95 0W
Upper Sandusky **155** 40 50N 83 17W
Upper Sheikh **136** 9 56N 45 13 E
Upper Taimyr → **65** 74 15N 99 48 E
Upper Volta = Burkina Faso ■ **126** 12 0N 1 0W
Upphärad **53** 58 9N 12 19 E
Uppsala **52** 59 53N 17 38 E
Uppsala län □ **52** 60 0N 17 30 E
Upshi **79** 33 48N 77 52 E
Upstart, C. **110** 19 41 S 147 45 E
Upton **152** 44 8N 104 35W
Ur **72** 30 55N 46 25 E
Ura-Tyube **63** 39 55N 69 1 E
Urabá, G. de **168** 8 25N 76 53W
Uracara **172** 2 20 S 57 50W
Urach **27** 48 29N 9 25 E
Urad Qianqi **94** 40 40N 108 30 E
Uraga-Suidō **101** 35 13N 139 45 E
Urakawa **98** 42 9N 142 47 E
Ural → **57** 47 0N 51 48 E
Ural, Mt. **113** 33 21 S 146 12 E
Ural Mts. = Uralskie Gory **56** 60 0N 59 0 E
Uralla **111** 30 37 S 151 29 E
Uralsk **62** 51 20N 51 20 E
Uralskie Gory **56** 60 0N 59 0 E
Urambo **130** 5 4 S 32 0 E
Urambo □ **130** 5 0 S 32 0 E
Urana **113** 35 15 S 146 21 E
Urandangi **110** 21 32 S 138 14 E
Uranium City **145** 59 34N 108 37W
Uraricaá → **169** 3 20N 61 56W
Uraricuera → **169** 3 2N 60 30W
Uravakonda **81** 14 57N 77 12 E
Urawa **101** 35 50N 139 40 E
Uray **64** 60 5N 65 15 E
'Uray'irah **73** 25 57N 48 53 E
Urbana, Ill., U.S.A. **155** 40 7N 88 12W
Urbana, Mo., U.S.A. **154** 37 51N 93 10W
Urbana, Ohio, U.S.A. **155** 40 9N 83 44W
Urbana, La **168** 7 8N 66 56W
Urbandale **154** 41 38N 93 43W
Urbánia **43** 43 40N 12 31 E
Urbano Santos **170** 3 12 S 43 23W
Urbel → **36** 42 21N 3 40W
Urbino **43** 43 43N 12 38 E
Urbión, Picos de **36** 42 1N 2 52W
Urcos **172** 13 40 S 71 38W
Urda, Spain **35** 39 25N 3 43W
Urda, U.S.S.R. **61** 48 52N 47 23 E
Urdaneta **90** 15 59N 120 34 E
Urdinarrain **174** 32 37 S 58 52W
Urdos **20** 42 51N 0 35W
Urdzhar **64** 47 5N 81 38 E
Ure → **12** 54 20N 1 25W
Uren **59** 57 35N 45 55 E
Urengoy **64** 65 58N 28 25 E
Ures **160** 29 30N 110 30W
Ureshino **100** 33 6N 129 59 E
Urfa **57** 37 12N 38 50 E
Urfahr **30** 48 19N 14 17 E
Urgench **64** 41 40N 60 41 E
Urgut **63** 39 23N 67 15 E
Uri **79** 34 8N 74 2 E
Uri □ **29** 46 43N 8 35 E
Uribante → **168** 7 25N 71 50W
Uribe **168** 3 13N 74 24W
Uribia **168** 11 43N 72 16W
Urim **69** 31 18N 34 32 E
Uriondo **174** 21 41 S 64 41W
Urique **160** 27 13N 107 55W
Urique → **160** 26 29N 107 58W
Urirotstock **29** 46 52N 8 32 E
Urk **22** 52 39N 5 36 E
Urlati **50** 44 59N 26 15 E
Urmia = Orūmīyeh **72** 37 40N 45 0 E
Urmia, L. = Orūmīyeh, Daryācheh-ye **72** 37 50N 45 30 E
Urner Alpen **29** 46 45N 8 45 E
Uroševac **46** 42 23N 21 10 E
Urrao **168** 6 20N 76 11W
Urshult **53** 56 31N 14 50 E
Ursus **32** 52 12N 20 53 E
Uruaçu **171** 14 30 S 49 10W
Uruana **171** 15 30 S 49 41W
Uruapan **160** 19 30N 102 0W
Uruará → **169** 2 6 S 53 38W
Urubamba **172** 13 20 S 72 10W
Urubamba → **172** 10 43 S 73 48W
Urubaxi → **169** 0 31 S 64 50W
Urubu → **169** 2 55 S 58 25W
Uruçara **169** 2 32 S 57 45W
Uruçuí **170** 7 20 S 44 28W
Uruçuí, Serra do **170** 9 0 S 44 45W
Uruçuí Prêto → **170** 7 20 S 44 38W
Urucuia → **171** 16 8 S 45 5W
Urucurituba **169** 2 41 S 57 40W
Uruguai → **175** 26 0 S 53 30W
Uruguaiana **174** 29 50 S 57 0W
Uruguay ■ **174** 32 30 S 56 30W
Uruguay → **174** 34 12 S 58 18W
Urukthapel I. **106** 7 17N 134 25 E
Urumchi = Ürümqi **92** 43 45N 87 45 E
Ürümqi **92** 43 45N 87 45 E
Urup → **61** 46 0N 41 10 E
Urup, Os. **65** 46 0N 151 0 E
Urutaí **171** 17 28 S 48 12W
Uryung-Khaya **65** 72 48N 113 23 E
Uryupinsk **59** 50 45N 41 58 E
Urzhum **59** 57 10N 49 56 E
Urziceni **50** 44 40N 26 42 E
Usa **100** 33 31N 131 21 E
Usa → **56** 65 57N 56 55 E
Uşak **57** 38 43N 29 28 E
Usakos **134** 21 54 S 15 31 E
Usborne, Mt. **176** 51 42 S 58 50W
Ušče **46** 43 30N 20 39 E
Usedom **26** 53 50N 13 55 E
'Usfān **74** 21 58N 39 27 E
Ush-Tobe **64** 45 16N 78 0 E
Ushakova, O. **6** 82 0N 80 0 E
Ushant = Ouessant, I. d' **18** 48 28N 5 6W
Ushashi **130** 1 59 S 33 57 E
Ushat **125** 7 59N 29 28 E
Ushibuka **100** 32 11N 130 1 E
Ushuaia **176** 54 50 S 68 23W
Ushumun **65** 52 47N 126 32 E
Usk → **13** 51 37N 2 56W
Uskedal **51** 59 56N 5 53 E
Üsküdar **57** 41 0N 29 5 E
Uslar **26** 51 39N 9 39 E
Usman **59** 52 5N 39 48 E
Usoke **130** 5 8 S 32 24 E
Usolye **62** 59 28N 56 31 E
Usolye Sibirskoye **65** 52 48N 103 40 E
Usoro **127** 5 33N 6 11 E
Uspallata, P. de **174** 32 37 S 69 22W
Uspenskiy **64** 48 41N 72 43 E
Usquert **22** 53 24N 6 36 E
Ussel **20** 45 32N 2 18 E
Ussuri → **98** 48 27N 135 0 E
Ussuriysk **65** 43 48N 131 59 E
Ussurka **98** 45 12N 133 31 E
Ust-Aldan = Batamay **65** 63 30N 129 15 E
Ust Amginskoye = Khandyga **65** 62 42N 135 35 E
Ust-Bolsheretsk **65** 52 50N 156 15 E
Ust Buzulukskaya **59** 50 8N 42 11 E
Ust chaun **65** 68 47N 170 30 E
Ust-Donetskiy **61** 47 35N 40 55 E
Ust'-Ilga **65** 55 5N 104 55 E
Ust Ilimpeya = Yukti **65** 63 26N 105 42 E
Ust-Ilimsk **65** 58 3N 102 39 E
Ust Ishim **64** 57 45N 71 10 E
Ust-Kamchatsk **65** 56 10N 162 28 E
Ust-Kamenogorsk **64** 50 0N 82 36 E
Ust-Karenga **65** 54 25N 116 30 E
Ust Khayryuzova **65** 57 15N 156 45 E
Ust-Kut **65** 56 50N 105 42 E
Ust Kuyga **65** 70 1N 135 43 E
Ust-Labinsk **61** 45 15N 39 41 E
Ust Luga **58** 59 35N 28 20 E
Ust Maya **65** 60 30N 134 28 E
Ust-Mil **65** 59 40N 133 11 E
Ust-Nera **65** 64 35N 143 15 E
Ust-Nyukzha **65** 56 34N 121 37 E
Ust Olenek **65** 73 0N 119 48 E
Ust-Omchug **65** 61 9N 149 38 E
Ust Port **64** 69 40N 84 26 E
Ust Tsilma **56** 65 25N 52 0 E
Ust-Tungir **65** 55 25N 120 36 E
Ust Urt = Ustyurt, Plato **64** 44 0N 55 0 E
Ust Usa **56** 66 0N 56 30 E
Ust-Uyskoye **62** 54 16N 63 54 E
Ust Vorkuta **64** 67 24N 64 0 E
Ustaoset **51** 60 30N 8 2 E
Ustaritz **20** 43 24N 1 27W
Uste **59** 59 35N 39 40 E
Uster **29** 47 22N 8 43 E
Ústí nad Labem **30** 50 41N 14 3 E
Ústí nad Orlicí **31** 49 58N 16 24 E
Ustica **44** 38 42N 13 10 E
Ustinov **62** 56 51N 53 14 E
Ustka **32** 54 35N 16 55 E
Ustroń **31** 49 43N 18 48 E
Ustrzyki Dolne **32** 49 27N 22 40 E
Ustye **65** 57 46N 94 37 E
Ustyurt, Plato **64** 44 0N 55 0 E
Ustyuzhna **59** 58 50N 36 32 E
Usu **92** 44 27N 84 40 E
Usuki **100** 33 8N 131 49 E
Usulután **162** 13 25N 88 28W
Usumacinta → **161** 17 0N 91 0W
Usumbura = Bujumbura **130** 3 16 S 29 18 E
Usure **130** 4 40 S 34 22 E
Usva **62** 58 41N 57 37 E
Uta **87** 4 33 S 136 0 E
Utah □ **156** 39 30N 111 30W
Utah, L. **156** 40 10N 111 58W
Ute Cr. → **153** 35 21N 103 45W
Utena **58** 55 27N 25 40 E
Ütersen **26** 53 40N 9 40 E
Utete **130** 8 0 S 38 45 E
Uthai Thani **84** 15 22N 100 3 E
Uthal **78** 25 44N 66 40 E
Utiariti **173** 13 0 S 58 10W
Utica, N.Y., U.S.A. **151** 43 5N 75 18W
Utica, Ohio, U.S.A. **150** 40 13N 82 26W
Utiel **36** 39 37N 1 11W
Utik L. **145** 55 15N 96 0W
Utikuma L. **144** 55 50N 115 30W
Utinga **171** 12 6 S 41 5W
Uto **100** 32 41N 130 40 E
Utrecht, Neth. **22** 52 5N 5 8 E
Utrecht, S. Africa **135** 27 38 S 30 20 E
Utrecht □ **22** 52 6N 5 7 E
Utrera **35** 37 12N 5 48W
Utsjoki **54** 69 51N 26 59 E
Utsunomiya **101** 36 30N 139 50 E
Uttar Pradesh □ **79** 27 0N 80 0 E
Uttaradit **84** 17 36N 100 5 E
Uttoxeter **12** 52 53N 1 50W
Utva → **62** 51 28N 52 40 E
Ütze **26** 52 28N 10 11 E
Uusikaupunki **55** 60 47N 21 25 E
Uva **59** 56 59N 52 13 E
Uvá → **168** 3 41N 70 3W
Uvac → **46** 43 35N 19 40 E
Uvalde **153** 29 15N 99 48W
Uvarovo **59** 51 59N 42 14 E
Uvat **64** 59 5N 68 50 E
Uvelskiy **62** 54 26N 61 22 E
Uvinza **130** 5 5 S 30 24 E
Uvira **130** 3 22 S 29 3 E
Uvs Nuur **92** 50 20N 92 30 E
Uwa **100** 33 22N 132 31 E
Uwajima **100** 33 10N 132 35 E
'Uwayfī **75** 22 15N 56 59 E
Uweinat, Jebel **124** 21 54N 24 58 E
Uxbridge **150** 44 6N 79 7W
Uxin Qi **94** 38 50N 109 5 E
Uxmal **161** 20 22N 89 46W
Uyandi **65** 69 19N 141 0 E
Uyo **127** 5 1N 7 53 E
Uyu → **82** 24 51N 94 57 E
Uyuk **63** 43 36N 71 16 E
Uyuni **172** 20 28 S 66 47W
Uzbek S.S.R. □ **63** 41 30N 65 0 E
Uzen **57** 43 27N 53 10 E
Uzen, Bol. → **59** 50 0N 49 30 E
Uzen, Mal. → **59** 50 0N 48 30 E
Uzerche **20** 45 25N 1 34 E
Uzès **21** 44 1N 4 26 E
Uzgen **63** 40 46N 73 18 E
Uzh → **58** 51 15N 30 12 E
Uzhgorod **58** 48 36N 22 18 E
Uzlovaya **59** 54 0N 38 5 E
Uzun-Agach **63** 43 35N 76 20 E
Uzunköprü **47** 41 16N 26 43 E
Uzwil **29** 47 26N 9 9 E

V

Vaal → **134** 29 4 S 23 38 E
Vaal Dam **135** 27 0 S 28 14 E
Vaals **23** 50 46N 6 1 E
Vaalwater **135** 24 15 S 28 8 E
Vaasa **54** 63 6N 21 38 E
Vaasan lääni □ **54** 63 2N 22 50 E
Vaassen **22** 52 17N 5 58 E
Vabre **20** 43 42N 2 24 E
Vác **31** 47 49N 19 10 E
Vacaria **175** 28 31 S 50 52W
Vacaville **158** 38 21N 122 0W
Vaccarès, Étang de **21** 43 32N 4 34 E
Vach → **64** 60 45N 76 45 E
Vache, I.-à- **163** 18 2N 73 35W
Väddö **52** 59 55N 18 50 E
Vadnagar **78** 23 47N 72 40 E
Vado Lígure **42** 44 16N 8 26 E
Vadodara **78** 22 20N 73 10 E
Vadsø **54** 70 3N 29 50 E
Vadstena **53** 58 28N 14 54 E
Vaduz **29** 47 8N 9 31 E
Værøy **54** 67 40N 12 40 E
Vagnhärad **52** 58 57N 17 33 E
Vagos **34** 40 33N 8 42W
Váh → **31** 47 55N 18 0 E
Vahsel B. **7** 75 0 S 35 0W
Vaigach **64** 70 10N 59 0 E
Vaigai → **81** 9 15N 79 10 E
Vaiges **18** 48 2N 0 30W
Vaihingen **27** 48 55N 8 58 E
Vaijapur **80** 19 58N 74 45 E
Vaikam **81** 9 45N 76 25 E
Vailly-sur-Aisne **19** 49 24N 3 31 E
Vaippar → **81** 9 0N 78 25 E
Vaison-la-Romaine **21** 44 14N 5 4 E
Vaitogi **106** 14 21 S 170 44W
Vajpur **78** 21 24N 73 17 E
Vakarel **47** 42 35N 23 40 E
Vakhsh → **63** 37 6N 68 18 E
Vaksdal **51** 60 29N 5 45 E
Vál **31** 47 22N 18 40 E
Val-d'Ajol, Le **19** 47 55N 6 30 E
Val-de-Marne □ **19** 48 45N 2 28 E
Val-d'Oise □ **19** 49 5N 2 10 E
Val d'Or **142** 48 7N 77 47W
Val Marie **145** 49 15N 107 45W
Valadares **34** 41 5N 8 38W
Valahia **50** 44 35N 25 0 E
Valais □ **28** 46 12N 7 45 E
Valais, Alpes du **28** 46 5N 7 35 E
Valandovo **46** 41 19N 22 34 E
Valašské Meziříčí **31** 49 29N 17 59 E
Valáxa **49** 38 50N 24 29 E
Vălcani **46** 46 0N 20 26 E
Valcheta **176** 40 40 S 66 8W
Valdagno **43** 45 38N 11 18 E
Valday **58** 57 58N 33 9 E
Valdayskaya Vozvyshennost **58** 57 0N 33 30 E
Valdeazogues → **35** 38 45N 4 55W
Valdemarsvik **53** 58 14N 16 40 E
Valdepeñas, Ciudad Real, Spain **35** 38 43N 3 25W
Valdepeñas, Jaén, Spain **35** 37 33N 3 47W
Valderaduey → **34** 41 31N 5 42W
Valderrobres **36** 40 53N 0 9 E
Valdés, Pen. **176** 42 30 S 63 45W
Valdez, Ecuador **168** 1 15N 79 0W
Valdez, U.S.A. **140** 61 14N 146 17W
Valdivia, Chile **176** 39 50 S 73 14W
Valdivia, Colombia **168** 7 11N 75 27W
Valdivia □ **176** 40 0 S 73 0W
Valdobbiádene **43** 45 53N 12 0 E
Valdosta **149** 30 50N 83 20W
Valdoviño **34** 43 36N 8 8W
Valdres **51** 60 55N 9 28 E
Vale, U.S.A. **156** 44 0N 117 15W
Vale, U.S.S.R. **61** 41 30N 42 58 E
Valea lui Mihai **50** 47 32N 22 11 E
Valença, Brazil **171** 13 20 S 39 5W
Valença, Portugal **34** 42 1N 8 34W
Valença do Piauí **170** 6 20 S 41 45W
Valençay **19** 47 9N 1 34 E
Valence, Drôme, France **21** 44 57N 4 54 E
Valence, Tarn-et-Garonne, France **20** 44 6N 0 53 E
Valencia, Phil. **91** 7 57N 125 3 E
Valencia, Spain **37** 39 27N 0 23W
Valencia, Venezuela **168** 10 11N 68 0W
Valencia □ **37** 39 20N 0 40W
Valencia, Albufera de **37** 39 20N 0 27W
Valencia, G. de **37** 39 30N 0 20 E
Valencia de Alcántara **35** 39 25N 7 14W
Valencia de Don Juan **34** 42 17N 5 31W
Valencia del Ventoso **35** 38 15N 6 29W
Valenciennes **19** 50 20N 3 34 E
Văleni **50** 44 15N 24 45 E
Valensole **21** 43 50N 5 59 E
Valentia Harbour **15** 51 56N 10 17W
Valentia I. **15** 51 54N 10 22W
Valentim, Sa. do **170** 6 0 S 43 30W
Valentin **98** 43 8N 134 17 E
Valentine, Nebr., U.S.A. **152** 42 50N 100 35W
Valentine, Tex., U.S.A. **153** 30 36N 104 28W
Valenza **42** 45 2N 8 39 E
Våler **51** 60 41N 11 50 E
Valera **168** 9 19N 70 37W
Valga **58** 57 44N 26 0 E
Valguarnera Caropepe **45** 37 30N 14 22 E
Valier **156** 48 25N 112 9W
Valinco, G. de **21** 41 40N 8 52 E
Valjevo **46** 44 18N 19 53 E
Valkenburg **23** 50 52N 5 50 E
Valkenswaard **23** 51 21N 5 29 E
Vall de Uxó **36** 39 49N 0 15W
Valla **52** 59 2N 16 20 E
Valladolid, Mexico **161** 20 40N 88 11W
Valladolid, Spain **34** 41 38N 4 43W

Vereshchagino

Valladolid □ **34** 41 38N 4 43W
Vallata **45** 41 3N 15 16 E
Valldemosa **36** 39 43N 2 37 E
Valle **51** 59 13N 7 33 E
Valle d'Aosta □ **42** 45 45N 7 22 E
Valle de Arán **36** 42 50N 0 55 E
Valle de Cabuérniga **34** 43 14N 4 18W
Valle de la Pascua **168** 9 13N 66 0W
Valle de las Palmas **159** 32 20N 116 43W
Valle de Santiago **160** 20 25N 101 15W
Valle de Suchil **160** 23 38N 103 55W
Valle de Zaragoza **160** 27 28N 105 49W
Valle del Cauca □ **168** 3 45N 76 30W
Valle Fértil, Sierra del **174** 30 20 S 68 0W
Valle Hermoso **161** 25 35N 97 40W
Vallecas **34** 40 23N 3 41W
Valledupar **168** 10 29N 73 15W
Vallehermoso **37** 28 10N 17 15W
Vallejo **158** 38 12N 122 15W
Vallenar **174** 28 30 S 70 50W
Valleraugue **20** 44 6N 3 39 E
Vallet **18** 47 10N 1 15W
Valletta **38** 35 54N 14 30 E
Valley Center **159** 33 13N 117 2W
Valley City **152** 46 57N 98 0W
Valley Falls **156** 42 33N 120 16W
Valley Park **154** 38 33N 90 29W
Valley Springs **158** 38 11N 120 50W
Valley Station **155** 38 10N 85 50W
Valley Wells **159** 35 27N 115 46W
Valleyview **144** 55 5N 117 17W
Valli di Comácchio **43** 44 40N 12 15 E
Vallimanca, Arroyo **174** 35 40 S 59 10W
Vallo della Lucánia **45** 40 14N 15 16 E
Vallon-Pont-d'Arc **21** 44 24N 4 24 E
Vallorbe **28** 46 42N 6 20 E
Valls **36** 41 18N 1 15 E
Vallsta **52** 61 31N 16 22 E
Valmaseda **36** 43 11N 3 12W
Valmeyer **154** 38 18N 90 19W
Valmiera **58** 57 37N 25 29 E
Valmont **18** 49 45N 0 30 E
Valmontone **44** 41 48N 12 55 E
Valmy **19** 49 5N 4 45 E
Valnera, Mte. **36** 43 9N 3 40W
Valognes **18** 49 30N 1 28W
Valona = Vlóra **48** 40 32N 19 28 E
Valongo **34** 41 8N 8 30W
Valpaços **34** 41 36N 7 17W
Valparaíso, Chile **174** 33 2 S 71 40W
Valparaíso, Mexico **160** 22 50N 103 32W
Valparaiso, U.S.A. **155** 41 27N 87 2W
Valparaíso □ **174** 33 2 S 71 40W
Valpovo **46** 45 39N 18 25 E
Valréas **21** 44 24N 5 0 E
Vals **29** 46 39N 9 11 E
Vals → **134** 27 23 S 26 30 E
Vals, Tanjung **87** 8 26 S 137 25 E
Vals-les-Bains **21** 44 42N 4 24 E
Valsad **78** 20 40N 72 58 E
Valskog **52** 59 27N 15 57 E
Válta **48** 40 3N 23 25 E
Valtellina **42** 46 9N 9 55 E
Valuyki **59** 50 10N 38 5 E
Valverde **37** 27 48N 17 55W
Valverde del Camino **35** 37 35N 6 47W
Valverde del Fresno **34** 40 15N 6 51W
Vama **50** 47 34N 25 42 E
Vámos **49** 35 24N 24 13 E
Vamsadhara → **80** 18 21N 84 8 E
Van **57** 38 30N 43 20 E
Van, L. = Van Gölü **57** 38 30N 43 0 E
Van Alstyne **153** 33 25N 96 36W
Van Bruyssel **143** 47 56N 72 9W
Van Buren, Canada **143** 47 10N 67 55W
Van Buren, Ark., U.S.A. **153** 35 28N 94 18W
Van Buren, Maine, U.S.A. **149** 47 10N 68 1W
Van Buren, Mo., U.S.A. **153** 37 0N 91 0W
Van Canh **84** 13 37N 109 0 E
Van Diemen, C., N. Terr., Australia **108** 11 9 S 130 24 E
Van Diemen, C., Queens., Australia **110** 16 30 S 139 46 E
Van Diemen G. **108** 11 45 S 132 0 E
Van Gölü **57** 38 30N 43 0 E
Van Horn **153** 31 3N 104 55W
Van Horne **154** 42 1N 92 4W
Van Ninh **84** 12 42N 109 14 E
Van Reenen P. **135** 28 22 S 29 27 E
Van Rees, Pegunungan **87** 2 35 S 138 15 E
Van Tassell **152** 42 40N 104 3W
Van Tivu **81** 8 51N 78 15 E
Van Wert **155** 40 52N 84 31W
Van Yen **84** 21 4N 104 42 E
Vanavara **65** 60 22N 102 16 E
Vanceburg **155** 38 36N 83 19W
Vancouver, Canada **144** 49 15N 123 10W
Vancouver, U.S.A. **158** 45 44N 122 41W
Vancouver, C. **109** 35 2 S 118 11 E
Vancouver I. **144** 49 50N 126 0W
Vandalia, Ill., U.S.A. **154** 38 57N 89 4W
Vandalia, Mo., U.S.A. **154** 39 18N 91 30W
Vandalia, Ohio, U.S.A. **155** 39 54N 84 12W
Vandavasi **81** 12 30N 79 30 E
Vandeloos Bay **81** 8 0N 81 45 E
Vandenburg **159** 34 35N 120 33W
Vanderbijlpark **135** 26 42 S 27 54 E
Vandergrift **150** 40 36N 79 33W
Vanderhoof **144** 54 0N 124 0W
Vanderlin I. **110** 15 44 S 137 2 E
Vandyke **110** 24 10 S 147 51 E
Vänern **53** 58 47N 13 30 E
Vänersborg **53** 58 26N 12 19 E
Vang Vieng **84** 18 58N 102 32 E
Vanga **130** 4 35 S 39 12 E
Vangaindrano **135** 23 21 S 47 36 E
Vanguard **145** 49 55N 107 20W
Vanier **142** 45 27N 75 40W
Vanimo **107** 2 42 S 141 21 E
Vanivilasa Sagara **81** 13 45N 76 30 E
Vaniyambadi **81** 12 46N 78 44 E
Vankarem **65** 67 51N 175 50 E
Vankleek Hill **142** 45 32N 74 40W
Vanna **54** 70 6N 19 50 E
Vännäs **54** 63 58N 19 48 E
Vannes **18** 47 40N 2 47W
Vanoise, Massif de la **21** 45 25N 6 40 E
Vanrhynsdorp **134** 31 36 S 18 44 E
Vanrook **110** 16 57 S 141 57 E
Vans, Les **21** 44 25N 4 7 E
Vansbro **52** 60 32N 14 15 E
Vanse **51** 58 6N 6 41 E
Vansittart B. **108** 14 3 S 126 17 E
Vanthli **78** 21 28N 70 25 E
Vanua Levu **106** 16 33 S 179 15 E
Vanuatu ■ **104** 15 0 S 168 0 E
Vanwyksvlei **134** 30 18 S 21 49 E
Vanylven **51** 62 5N 5 33 E
Vanzylsrus **134** 26 52 S 22 4 E
Vapnyarka **60** 48 32N 28 45 E
Var □ **21** 43 27N 6 18 E
Var → **21** 43 39N 7 12 E
Vara **53** 58 16N 12 55 E
Varada → **81** 15 0N 75 40 E
Varades **18** 47 25N 1 1W
Varaita → **42** 44 49N 7 36 E
Varaldsøy **51** 60 6N 5 59 E
Varallo **42** 45 50N 8 13 E
Varanasi **79** 25 22N 83 0 E
Varangerfjorden **54** 70 3N 29 25 E
Varaždin **43** 46 20N 16 20 E
Varazze **42** 44 21N 8 36 E
Varberg **53** 57 6N 12 20 E
Vardar → **46** 40 35N 22 50 E
Varde **53** 55 38N 8 29 E
Varde Å **53** 55 35N 8 19 E
Varel **26** 53 23N 8 9 E
Varella, Mui **84** 12 54N 109 26 E
Varena **58** 54 12N 24 30 E
Varennes-sur-Allier **20** 46 19N 3 24 E
Vareš **46** 44 12N 18 23 E
Varese **42** 45 49N 8 50 E
Varese Lígure **42** 44 22N 9 33 E
Vårgårda **53** 58 2N 12 49 E
Vargem Bonita **171** 20 20 S 46 22W
Vargem Grande **170** 3 33 S 43 56W
Varginha **175** 21 33 S 45 25W
Vargön **53** 58 22N 12 20 E
Varhaug **51** 58 37N 5 41 E
Variadero **153** 35 43N 104 17W
Varillas **174** 24 0 S 70 10W
Väring **53** 58 30N 14 0 E
Värmeln **52** 59 35N 12 54 E
Värmlands län □ **52** 60 0N 13 20 E
Varna, Bulgaria **47** 43 13N 27 56 E
Varna, U.S.A. **154** 41 2N 89 14W
Varna, U.S.S.R. **62** 53 24N 60 58 E
Varna → **80** 16 48N 74 32 E
Värnamo **53** 57 10N 14 3 E
Varnsdorf **30** 50 55N 14 35 E
Värö **53** 57 16N 12 11 E
Vars **151** 45 21N 75 21W
Varsseveld **22** 51 56N 6 29 E
Varteig **51** 59 23N 11 12 E
Varvarin **46** 43 43N 21 20 E
Varzaneh **73** 32 25N 52 40 E
Várzea Alegre **170** 6 47 S 39 17W
Várzea da Palma **171** 17 36 S 44 44W
Várzea Grande **173** 15 39 S 56 8W
Varzi **42** 44 50N 9 12 E
Varzo **42** 46 12N 8 15 E
Varzy **19** 47 22N 3 20 E
Vas □ **31** 47 10N 16 55 E
Vasa **54** 63 6N 21 38 E
Vasa Barris → **170** 11 10 S 37 10W
Vásárosnamény **31** 48 9N 22 19 E
Vascão → **35** 37 31N 7 31W
Vaşcău **50** 46 28N 22 30 E
Vascongadas □ **36** 42 50N 2 45W
Väse **52** 59 23N 13 52 E
Vāshīr **77** 32 16N 63 51 E
Vasht = Khāsh **73** 28 15N 61 15 E
Vasilevichi **58** 52 15N 29 50 E
Vasilikón **49** 38 25N 23 40 E
Vasilkov **58** 50 7N 30 15 E
Vaslui **50** 46 38N 27 42 E
Vaslui □ **50** 46 30N 27 45 E
Väsman **52** 60 9N 15 5 E
Vassar, Canada **145** 49 10N 95 55W
Vassar, U.S.A. **148** 43 23N 83 33W
Västeräs **52** 59 37N 16 38 E
Västerbottens län □ **54** 64 58N 18 0 E
Västernorrlands län □ **52** 63 30N 17 30 E
Västervik **53** 57 43N 16 43 E
Västmanlands län □ **52** 59 45N 16 20 E
Vasto **43** 42 8N 14 40 E
Vasvár **31** 47 3N 16 47 E
Vatan **19** 47 4N 1 50 E
Vathí, Itháki, Greece **49** 38 18N 20 40 E
Vathí, Sámos, Greece **49** 37 46N 27 1 E
Váthia **49** 36 29N 22 29 E
Vatican City ■ **43** 41 54N 12 27 E
Vaticano, C. **44** 38 40N 15 48 E
Vatili **70** 35 6N 33 40 E
Vatin **46** 45 12N 21 20 E
Vatnajökull **54** 64 30N 16 48W
Vatnås **51** 59 58N 9 37 E
Vatne **51** 62 33N 6 38 E
Vatneyri **54** 65 35N 24 0W
Vatoloha, Mt. **135** 17 52 S 47 48 E
Vatomandry **135** 19 20 S 48 59 E
Vatra-Dornei **50** 47 22N 25 22 E
Vättern **53** 58 25N 14 30 E
Vättis **29** 46 55N 9 27 E
Vatulele **106** 18 33 S 177 37 E
Vaucluse □ **21** 43 50N 5 20 E
Vaucouleurs **19** 48 37N 5 40 E
Vaud □ **28** 46 35N 6 30 E
Vaughn, Mont., U.S.A. **156** 47 37N 111 36W
Vaughn, N. Mex., U.S.A. **157** 34 37N 105 12W
Vaulruz **28** 46 38N 7 0 E
Vaupe □ **168** 1 0N 71 0W
Vaupés → = Uaupés → **168** 0 2N 67 16W
Vauvert **21** 43 42N 4 17 E
Vauxhall **144** 50 5N 112 9W
Vavoua **126** 7 23N 6 29W
Vaxholm **52** 59 25N 18 20 E
Växjö **53** 56 52N 14 50 E
Vaygach, Ostrov **64** 70 0N 60 0 E
Vazovgrad **47** 42 39N 24 45 E
Veadeiros **171** 14 7 S 47 31W
Vechta **26** 52 47N 8 18 E
Vechte → **26** 52 34N 6 6 E
Vecilla, La **34** 42 51N 5 27W
Vecsés **31** 47 26N 19 19 E
Vedaranniyam **81** 10 25N 79 50 E
Veddige **53** 57 17N 12 20 E
Vedea → **50** 43 53N 25 59 E
Vedia **174** 34 30 S 61 31W
Vedra, I. del **37** 38 52N 1 12 E
Vedrin **23** 50 30N 4 52 E
Veendam **22** 53 5N 6 52 E
Veenendaal **22** 52 2N 5 34 E
Veerle **23** 51 4N 4 59 E
Vefsna → **54** 65 48N 13 10 E
Vega, Norway **54** 65 40N 11 55 E
Vega, U.S.A. **153** 35 18N 102 26W
Vega, La, Dom. Rep. **163** 19 20N 70 30W
Vega, La, Peru **172** 10 41 S 77 44W
Vegadeo **34** 43 27N 7 4W
Vegafjorden **54** 65 37N 12 0 E
Vegesack **26** 53 10N 8 38 E
Veggli **51** 60 3N 9 9 E
Veghel **23** 51 37N 5 32 E
Vegorritis, Límni **48** 40 45N 21 45 E
Vegreville **144** 53 30N 112 5W
Vegusdal **51** 58 32N 8 10 E
Veii **43** 42 0N 12 24 E
Veitch **112** 34 39 S 140 31 E
Vejen **53** 55 30N 9 9 E
Vejer de la Frontera **35** 36 15N 5 59W
Vejle **53** 55 43N 9 30 E
Vejle Fjord **53** 55 40N 9 50 E
Vela, La **168** 11 27N 69 34W
Vela Luka **43** 42 59N 16 44 E
Velanai I. **81** 9 45N 79 45 E
Velas, C. **162** 10 21N 85 52W
Velasco, Sierra de **174** 29 20 S 67 10W
Velay, Mts. du **20** 45 0N 3 40 E
Velddrif **134** 32 42 S 18 11 E
Veldegem **23** 51 7N 3 10 E
Velden **23** 51 25N 6 10 E
Veldhoven **23** 51 24N 5 25 E
Velebit Planina **43** 44 50N 15 20 E
Velebitski Kanal **43** 44 45N 14 55 E
Veleka → **47** 42 4N 27 58 E
Velenje **43** 46 23N 15 8 E
Velestínon **48** 39 23N 22 43 E
Veleta, La **35** 37 1N 3 22W
Vélez, Colombia **168** 6 1N 73 41W
Velež, Yugoslavia **46** 43 19N 18 2 E
Vélez Blanco **37** 37 41N 2 5W
Vélez Málaga **35** 36 48N 4 5W
Vélez Rubio **37** 37 41N 2 5W
Velhas → **171** 17 13 S 44 49W
Velika **46** 45 27N 17 40 E
Velika Gorica **43** 45 44N 16 5 E
Velika Gradište **46** 44 46N 21 29 E
Velika Kapela **43** 45 10N 15 5 E
Velika Kladuša **43** 45 11N 15 48 E
Velika Morava → **46** 44 43N 21 3 E
Velika Plana **46** 44 20N 21 1 E
Velikaya → **58** 57 48N 28 20 E
Velikaya Kema **98** 45 30N 137 12 E
Velikaya Lepetikha **60** 47 2N 33 58 E
Veliké Kapušany **31** 48 34N 22 5 E
Velike Lašče **43** 45 49N 14 45 E
Veliki Backa Kanal **46** 45 45N 19 15 E
Veliki Jastrebac **46** 43 25N 21 30 E
Veliki Popović **46** 44 8N 21 18 E
Veliki Ustyug **56** 60 47N 46 20 E
Velikiye Luki **58** 56 25N 30 32 E
Velikonda Range **81** 14 45N 79 10 E
Velikoye, Oz. **59** 55 15N 40 10 E
Velingrad **47** 42 4N 23 58 E
Velino, Mte. **43** 42 10N 13 20 E
Velizh **58** 55 36N 31 11 E
Velké Karlovice **31** 49 20N 18 17 E
Velke Meziřici **30** 49 21N 16 1 E
Vel'ký Žitný ostrov **31** 48 5N 17 20 E
Vellar → **81** 11 30N 79 36 E
Velletri **44** 41 43N 12 43 E
Vellinge **52** 55 29N 13 0 E
Vellore **81** 12 57N 79 10 E
Velp **22** 52 0N 5 59 E
Velsen-Noord **22** 52 27N 4 40 E
Velsk **56** 61 10N 42 5 E
Velten **26** 52 40N 13 11 E
Veluwe Meer **22** 52 24N 5 44 E
Velva **152** 48 6N 100 56W
Velvendós **48** 40 15N 22 6 E
Vembanad L. **81** 9 36N 76 15 E
Veme **51** 60 14N 10 7 E
Ven **52** 55 55N 12 45 E
Vena **53** 57 31N 16 0 E
Venaco **21** 42 14N 9 11 E
Venado Tuerto **174** 33 50 S 62 0W
Venafro **45** 41 28N 14 3 E
Venarey-les-Laumes **19** 47 32N 4 26 E
Venaria **42** 45 6N 7 39 E
Venčane **46** 44 24N 20 28 E
Vence **21** 43 43N 7 6 E
Venda □ **135** 22 40 S 30 35 E
Vendas Novas **35** 38 39N 8 27W
Vendée □ **18** 46 50N 1 35W
Vendée → **18** 46 20N 1 10W
Vendéen, Bocage **20** 46 40N 1 20W
Vendeuvre-sur-Barse **19** 48 14N 4 28 E
Vendôme **18** 47 47N 1 3 E
Vendrell **36** 41 10N 1 30 E
Vendsyssel **53** 57 22N 10 0 E
Véneta, L. **43** 45 23N 12 25 E
Véneto □ **43** 45 40N 12 0 E
Venev **59** 54 22N 38 17 E
Venézia **43** 45 27N 12 20 E
Venézia, G. di **43** 45 20N 13 0 E
Venezuela ■ **168** 8 0N 66 0W
Venezuela, G. de **168** 11 30N 71 0W
Vengurla **81** 15 53N 73 45 E
Vengurla Rocks **81** 15 55N 73 22 E
Venice = Venézia **43** 45 27N 12 20 E
Venkatagiri **81** 14 0N 79 35 E
Venkatapuram **80** 18 20N 80 30 E
Venlo **23** 51 22N 6 11 E
Vennesla **51** 58 15N 8 0 E
Venraij **23** 51 31N 6 0 E
Venta, La **161** 18 8N 94 3W
Venta de Cardeña **35** 38 16N 4 20W
Venta de San Rafael **34** 40 42N 4 12W
Ventana, Punta de la **160** 24 4N 109 48W
Ventana, Sa. de la **174** 38 0 S 62 30W
Ventersburg **134** 28 7 S 27 9 E
Venterstad **134** 30 47 S 25 48 E
Ventimíglia **42** 43 50N 7 39 E
Ventnor **13** 50 35N 1 12W
Ventotene **44** 40 48N 13 25 E
Ventoux, Mt. **21** 44 10N 5 17 E
Ventspils **58** 57 25N 21 32 E
Ventuarí → **168** 3 58N 67 2W
Ventucopa **159** 34 50N 119 29W
Ventura **159** 34 16N 119 18W
Ventura, La **160** 24 38N 100 54W
Venturosa, La **168** 6 8N 68 48W
Venus B. **113** 38 40 S 145 42 E
Vera, Argentina **174** 29 30 S 60 20W
Vera, Spain **37** 37 15N 1 51W
Veracruz **161** 19 10N 96 10W
Veracruz □ **161** 19 0N 96 15W
Veraval **78** 20 53N 70 27 E
Verbánia **42** 45 56N 8 43 E
Verbicaro **45** 39 46N 15 54 E
Verbier **28** 46 6N 7 13 E
Vercelli **42** 45 19N 8 25 E
Verchovchevo **60** 48 32N 34 10 E
Verde →, Argentina **176** 41 56 S 65 5W
Verde →, Goiás, Brazil **171** 19 11 S 50 44W
Verde →, Goiás, Brazil **171** 18 1 S 50 14W
Verde →, Mato Grosso, Brazil **173** 11 54 S 55 48W
Verde →, Mato Grosso, Brazil **173** 21 25 S 56 20W
Verde →, Chihuahua, Mexico **160** 26 29N 107 58W
Verde →, Oaxaca, Mexico **161** 15 59N 97 50W
Verde →, Veracruz, Mexico **160** 21 10N 102 50W
Verde →, Paraguay **174** 23 9 S 57 37W
Verde, Cay **162** 23 0N 75 5W
Verde Grande → **171** 16 13 S 43 49W
Verde I. **90** 13 33N 121 5 E
Verde I. Pass **90** 13 34N 120 51 E
Verde Pequeno → **171** 14 48 S 43 31W
Verden **26** 52 58N 9 18 E
Verdhikoúsa **48** 39 47N 21 59 E
Verdi **158** 39 31N 119 59W
Verdigre **152** 42 38N 98 0W
Verdon → **21** 43 43N 5 46 E
Verdon-sur-Mer, Le **20** 45 33N 1 4W
Verdun **19** 49 9N 5 24 E
Verdun-sur-le-Doubs **19** 46 54N 5 2 E
Vereeniging **135** 26 38 S 27 57 E
Vérendrye, Parc Prov. de la **142** 47 20N 76 40W
Vereshchagino **62** 58 5N 54 40 E

Verga, C.

Verga, C. 126 10 30N 14 10W
Vergato 42 44 18N 11 8 E
Vergemont 110 23 33 S 143 1 E
Vergemont Cr. → 110 24 16 S 143 16 E
Vergennes 151 44 9N 73 15W
Vergt 20 45 2N 0 43 E
Verín 34 41 57N 7 27W
Veriña 34 43 32N 5 43W
Verkhnedvinsk 58 55 45N 27 58 E
Verkhneuralsk 62 53 53N 59 13 E
Verkhnevilyuysk 65 63 27N 120 18 E
Verkhneye Kalinino 65 59 54N 108 8 E
Verkhniy-Avzyan 62 53 32N 57 33 E
Verkhniy Baskunchak 61 48 14N 46 44 E
Verkhniy Tagil 62 57 22N 59 56 E
Verkhniy Ufaley 62 56 4N 60 14 E
Verkhniye Kigi 62 55 25N 58 37 E
Verkhnyaya Salda 62 58 2N 60 33 E
Verkhoturye 62 58 52N 60 48 E
Verkhovye 59 52 55N 37 15 E
Verkhoyansk 65 67 35N 133 25 E
Verkhoyansk Ra. = Verkhoyanskiy Khrebet 65 66 0N 129 0 E
Verkhoyanskiy Khrebet 65 66 0N 129 0 E
Verlo 145 50 19N 108 35W
Verma 51 62 21N 8 3 E
Vermenton 19 47 40N 3 42 E
Vermilion 145 53 20N 110 50W
Vermilion →, Alta., Canada 145 53 22N 110 51W
Vermilion →, Qué., Canada 142 47 38N 72 56W
Vermilion →, Ill., U.S.A. 154 41 19N 89 5W
Vermilion →, Ind., U.S.A. 155 39 57N 87 27W
Vermilion, B. 153 29 45N 91 55W
Vermilion Bay 145 49 51N 93 34W
Vermilion Chutes 144 58 22N 114 51W
Vermilion L. 152 47 53N 92 25W
Vermillion 152 42 50N 96 56W
Vermont 154 40 18N 90 26W
Vermont □ 151 43 40N 72 50W
Vernal 156 40 28N 109 35W
Vernalis 158 37 36N 121 17W
Vernayaz 28 46 8N 7 3 E
Verner 142 46 25N 80 8W
Verneuil-sur-Avre 18 48 45N 0 55 E
Verneukpan 134 30 0 S 21 0 E
Vernier 28 46 13N 6 5 E
Vernon, Canada 144 50 20N 119 15W
Vernon, France 18 49 5N 1 30 E
Vernon, Ill., U.S.A. 154 38 48N 89 5W
Vernon, Ind., U.S.A. 155 38 59N 85 36W
Vernon, Tex., U.S.A. 153 34 10N 99 20W
Vernonia 158 45 52N 123 11W
Vero Beach 149 27 39N 80 23W
Véroia 48 40 34N 22 12 E
Verolanuova 42 45 20N 10 5 E
Véroli 44 41 43N 13 24 E
Verona, Italy 42 45 27N 11 0 E
Verona, U.S.A. 154 42 59N 89 32W
Veropol 65 65 15N 168 40 E
Verrières, Les 28 46 55N 6 28 E
Versailles, France 19 48 48N 2 8 E
Versailles, Ill., U.S.A. 154 39 53N 90 39W
Versailles, Ind., U.S.A. 155 39 4N 85 15W
Versailles, Ky., U.S.A. 155 38 3N 84 44W
Versailles, Mo., U.S.A. 154 38 26N 92 51W
Versailles, Ohio, U.S.A. 155 40 13N 84 29W
Versalles 173 12 44 S 63 18W
Versoix 28 46 17N 6 10 E
Vert, C. 126 14 45N 17 30W
Vertou 18 47 10N 1 28W
Vertus 19 48 54N 4 0 E
Verulam 135 29 38 S 31 2 E
Verviers 23 50 37N 5 52 E
Vervins 19 49 50N 3 53 E
Verzej 43 46 34N 16 13 E
Vescavoto 21 42 30N 9 27 E
Vesdre → 23 50 36N 6 0 E
Veselí nad Lužnicí 30 49 12N 14 43 E
Veseliye 47 42 18N 27 38 E
Veselovskoye Vdkhr. 61 47 0N 41 0 E
Veshenskaya 61 49 35N 41 44 E
Vesle → 19 49 23N 3 28 E
Veslyana → 62 60 20N 54 0 E
Vesoul 19 47 40N 6 11 E
Vessigebro 53 56 58N 12 40 E
Vest-Agder fylke □ 51 58 30N 7 15 E
Vesta 162 9 43N 83 3W
Vestby 51 59 37N 10 45 E
Vesterålen 54 68 45N 15 0 E
Vestersche Veld 22 52 52N 6 9 E
Vestfjorden 54 67 55N 14 0 E
Vestfold fylke □ 51 59 15N 10 0 E
Vestmannaeyjar 54 63 27N 20 15W
Vestmarka 51 59 56N 11 59 E
Vestnes 51 62 39N 7 5 E
Vestone 42 45 43N 10 25 E
Vestsjællands Amtskommune □ 52 55 30N 11 20 E
Vestspitsbergen 6 78 40N 17 0 E
Vestvågøy 54 68 18N 13 50 E
Vesuvio 45 40 50N 14 22 E
Vesuvius, Mt. = Vesuvio 45 40 50N 14 22 E
Vesyegonsk 59 58 40N 37 16 E
Veszprém 31 47 8N 17 57 E
Veszprém □ 31 47 5N 17 55 E
Vésztö 31 46 55N 21 16 E
Vetapalem 81 15 47N 80 18 E
Vetlanda 53 57 24N 15 3 E
Vetluga 59 57 53N 45 45 E
Vetluzhskiy 59 57 17N 45 12 E
Vetovo 47 43 42N 26 16 E
Vetralia 43 42 20N 12 2 E
Vetren 47 42 15N 24 3 E
Vettore, Monte 43 42 49N 13 16 E
Veurne 23 51 5N 2 40 E
Vevay 155 38 45N 85 4W
Vevey 28 46 28N 6 51 E
Vévi 48 40 47N 21 38 E
Veynes 21 44 32N 5 49 E
Veys 73 31 30N 49 0 E
Vézelise 19 48 30N 6 5 E
Vézère → 20 44 53N 0 53 E
Vezhen 47 42 50N 24 20 E
Vi Thanh 85 9 42N 105 26 E
Viacha 172 16 39 S 68 18W
Viadana 42 44 55N 10 30 E
Viana, Brazil 170 3 13 S 45 0W
Viana, Spain 36 42 31N 2 22W
Viana del Bollo 34 42 11N 7 6W
Viana do Alentejo 35 38 17N 7 59W
Viana do Castelo 34 41 42N 8 50W
Vianden 23 49 56N 6 12 E
Vianen 22 51 59N 5 5 E
Vianna do Castelo □ 34 41 50N 8 30W
Vianópolis 171 16 40 S 48 35W
Viar → 35 37 36N 5 50W
Viaréggio 42 43 52N 10 13 E
Viaur → 20 44 8N 1 58 E
Vibank 145 50 20N 103 56W
Vibo Valéntia 45 38 40N 16 5 E
Viborg 53 56 27N 9 23 E
Vibraye 18 48 3N 0 44 E
Vic-en-Bigorre 20 43 24N 0 3 E
Vic-Fézensac 20 43 47N 0 19 E
Vic-sur-Cère 20 44 59N 2 38 E
Vicenza 43 45 32N 11 31 E
Vich 36 41 58N 2 19 E
Vichada □ 168 5 0N 69 30W
Vichada → 168 4 55N 67 50W
Vichuga 59 57 12N 41 55 E
Vichy 20 46 9N 3 26 E
Vicksburg, Ariz., U.S.A. 159 33 45N 113 45W
Vicksburg, Mich., U.S.A. 155 42 10N 85 30W
Vicksburg, Miss., U.S.A. 153 32 22N 90 56W
Vico, L. di 43 42 20N 12 10 E
Vico del Gargaro 45 41 54N 15 57 E
Viçosa 170 9 28 S 36 14W
Viçosa do Ceará 170 3 34 S 41 5W
Vicosoprano 29 46 22N 9 38 E
Victor, India 78 21 0N 71 30 E
Victor, Colo., U.S.A. 152 38 43N 105 7W
Victor, N.Y., U.S.A. 150 42 58N 77 24W
Victor Emanuel Ra. 107 5 20 S 142 15 E
Victoria, Argentina 174 32 40 S 60 10W
Victoria, Canada 144 48 30N 123 25W
Victoria, Chile 176 38 13 S 72 20W
Victoria, Guinea 126 10 50N 14 32W
Victoria, Ind. Oc. 83 5 0 S 55 40 E
Victoria, Malaysia 86 5 20N 115 14 E
Victoria, Mindoro, Phil. 90 13 12N 121 12 E
Victoria, Tarlac, Phil. 90 15 35N 120 41 E
Victoria, Ill., U.S.A. 154 41 2N 90 6W
Victoria, Kans., U.S.A. 152 38 52N 99 8W
Victoria, Tex., U.S.A. 153 28 50N 97 0W
Victoria □ 112 37 0 S 144 0 E
Victoria → 108 15 10 S 129 40 E
Victoria, Grand L. 142 47 31N 77 30W
Victoria, L., Australia 112 33 57 S 141 15 E
Victoria, L., E. Afr. 130 1 0 S 33 0 E
Victoria, La 168 10 14N 67 20W
Victoria, Mt., Burma 82 21 15N 93 55 E
Victoria, Mt., Papua N. G. 107 8 55 S 147 32 E
Victoria Beach 145 50 40N 96 35W
Victoria de Durango 160 24 3N 104 39W
Victoria de las Tunas 162 20 58N 76 59W
Victoria Falls 131 17 58 S 25 52 E
Victoria Harbour 142 44 45N 79 45W
Victoria I. 140 71 0N 111 0W
Victoria Ld. 7 75 0 S 160 0 E
Victoria Nile → 130 2 14N 31 26 E
Victoria Peaks 91 9 22N 118 20 E
Victoria Ra. 115 42 12 S 172 7 E
Victoria Res. 143 48 20N 57 27W
Victoria River Downs 108 16 25 S 131 0 E
Victoria West 134 31 25 S 23 4 E
Victorias 91 10 54N 123 5 E
Victoriaville 143 46 4N 71 56W
Victorica 174 36 20 S 65 30W
Victorville 159 34 32N 117 18W
Vicuña 174 30 0 S 70 50W
Vicuña Mackenna 174 33 53 S 64 25W
Vidal 159 34 7N 114 31W
Vidal Junction 159 34 11N 114 34W
Vidalia 149 32 13N 82 25W
Vidauban 21 43 25N 6 27 E
Vidigueira 35 38 12N 7 48W
Vidin 46 43 59N 22 50 E
Vidio, C. 34 43 35N 6 14W
Vidisha 78 23 28N 77 53 E
Vidöstern 53 57 5N 14 0 E
Vidra 50 45 56N 26 55 E
Viduša 46 42 55N 18 21 E
Vidzy 58 55 23N 26 37 E
Viechtach 27 49 5N 12 53 E
Viedma 176 40 50 S 63 0W
Viedma, L. 176 49 30 S 72 30W
Vieira 34 41 38N 8 8W
Viella 36 42 43N 0 44 E
Vielsalm 23 50 17N 5 54 E
Vienenburg 26 51 57N 10 35 E
Vieng Pou Kha 84 20 41N 101 4 E
Vienna = Wien 31 48 12N 16 22 E
Vienna, Ill., U.S.A. 153 37 29N 88 54W
Vienna, Mo., U.S.A. 154 38 11N 91 57W
Vienne 21 45 31N 4 53 E
Vienne □ 20 46 30N 0 42 E
Vienne → 18 47 13N 0 5 E
Vientiane 84 17 58N 102 36 E
Vientos, Paso de los 163 20 0N 74 0W
Vierlingsbeek 23 51 36N 6 1 E
Viersen 26 51 15N 6 23 E
Vierwaldstättersee 29 47 0N 8 30 E
Vierzon 19 47 13N 2 5 E
Vieste 44 41 52N 16 14 E
Vietnam ■ 84 19 0N 106 0 E
Vieux-Boucau-les-Bains 20 43 48N 1 23W
Vif 21 45 5N 5 41 E
Vigan 90 17 35N 120 28 E
Vigan, Le 20 43 59N 3 36 E
Vigévano 42 45 18N 8 50 E
Vigia 170 0 50 S 48 5W
Vigía Chico 161 19 46N 87 35W
Vignemale, Pic du 20 42 47N 0 10W
Vigneulles-lès-Hattonchâtel 19 48 59N 5 43 E
Vignola 42 44 29N 11 0 E
Vigo 34 42 12N 8 41W
Vigo, Ría de 34 42 15N 8 45W
Vihiers 18 47 10N 0 30W
Vijayadurg 80 16 30N 73 25 E
Vijayawada 81 16 31N 80 39 E
Vijfhuizen 22 52 22N 4 41 E
Vikedal 51 59 30N 5 55 E
Viken 53 58 39N 14 20 E
Vikersund 51 59 58N 10 2 E
Viking 144 53 7N 111 50W
Vikramasingapuram 81 8 40N 76 47 E
Viksjö 52 62 45N 17 26 E
Vikulovo 64 56 50N 70 40 E
Vila da Maganja 131 17 18 S 37 30 E
Vila de João Belo = Xai-Xai 135 25 6 S 33 31 E
Vila de Manica 131 18 58 S 32 59 E
Vila de Rei 35 39 41N 8 9W
Vila do Bispo 35 37 5N 8 53W
Vila do Chibuto 135 24 40 S 33 33 E
Vila do Conde 34 41 21N 8 45W
Vila Franca de Xira 35 38 57N 8 59W
Vila Gamito 131 14 12 S 33 0 E
Vila Gomes da Costa 135 24 20 S 33 37 E
Vila Machado 131 19 15 S 34 14 E
Vila Mouzinho 131 14 48 S 34 25 E
Vila Nova de Foscôa 34 41 5N 7 9W
Vila Nova de Ourém 35 39 40N 8 35W
Vila Novo de Gaia 34 41 4N 8 40W
Vila Pouca de Aguiar 34 41 30N 7 38W
Vila Real 34 41 17N 7 48W
Vila Real de Santo António 35 37 10N 7 28W
Vila Vasco da Gama 131 14 54 S 32 14 E
Vila Velha, Amapá, Brazil 169 3 13N 51 13W
Vila Velha, Espirito Santo, Brazil 171 20 20 S 40 17W
Vila Viçosa 35 38 45N 7 27W
Vilaboa 34 42 21N 8 39W
Vilaine → 18 47 30N 2 27W
Vilanandro, Tanjona 135 16 11 S 44 27 E
Vilanculos 135 22 1 S 35 17 E
Vilar Formosa 34 40 38N 6 45W
Vilareal □ 34 41 36N 7 35W
Vilaseca-Salou 36 41 7N 1 9 E
Vilcabamba, Cordillera 172 13 0 S 73 0W
Vilcanchos 172 13 40 S 74 25W
Vilcea □ 50 45 0N 24 10 E
Vileyka 58 54 30N 26 53 E
Vilhelmina 54 64 35N 16 39 E
Vilhena 173 12 40 S 60 5W
Viliga 65 61 36N 156 56 E
Viliya → 58 55 54N 23 53 E
Viljandi 58 58 28N 25 30 E
Vilkovo 60 45 28N 29 32 E
Villa Abecia 174 21 0 S 68 18W
Villa Ahumada 160 30 38N 106 30W
Villa Ana 174 28 28 S 59 40W
Villa Ángela 174 27 34 S 60 45W
Villa Bella 173 10 25 S 65 22W
Villa Bens = Tarfaya 120 27 55N 12 55W
Villa Cañás 174 34 0 S 61 35W
Villa Cisneros = Dakhla 120 23 50N 15 53W
Villa Colón 174 31 38 S 68 20W
Villa Constitución 174 33 15 S 60 20W
Villa de Cura 168 10 2N 67 29W
Villa de María 174 29 55 S 63 43W
Villa del Rosario 168 10 19N 72 19W
Villa Dolores 174 31 58 S 65 15W
Villa Frontera 160 26 56N 101 27W
Villa Grove 155 39 52N 88 10W
Villa Guillermina 174 28 15 S 59 29W
Villa Hayes 174 25 0 S 57 20W
Villa Iris 174 38 12 S 63 12W
Villa Juárez 160 27 37N 100 44W
Villa María 174 32 20 S 63 10W
Villa Mazán 174 28 40 S 66 30W
Villa Minozzo 42 44 21N 10 30 E
Villa Montes 174 21 10 S 63 30W
Villa Ocampo, Argentina 174 28 30 S 59 20W
Villa Ocampo, Mexico 160 26 29N 105 30W
Villa Ojo de Agua 174 29 30 S 63 44W
Villa San Giovanni 45 38 13N 15 38 E
Villa San José 174 32 12 S 58 15W
Villa San Martín 174 28 15 S 64 9W
Villa Santina 43 46 25N 12 55 E
Villa Unión 160 23 12N 106 14W
Villaba 91 11 13N 124 24 E
Villablino 34 42 57N 6 19W
Villacañas 36 39 38N 3 20W
Villacarlos 36 39 53N 4 17 E
Villacarriedo 36 43 14N 3 48W
Villacarrillo 37 38 7N 3 3W
Villacastín 34 40 46N 4 25W
Villach 30 46 37N 13 51 E
Villaciado 44 39 27N 8 45 E
Villada 34 42 15N 4 59W
Villadiego 34 42 31N 4 1W
Villadóssola 42 46 4N 8 16 E
Villafeliche 36 41 10N 1 30W
Villafranca 36 42 17N 1 46W
Villafranca de los Barros 35 38 35N 6 18W
Villafranca de los Caballeros 37 39 26N 3 21W
Villafranca del Bierzo 34 42 38N 6 50W
Villafranca del Cid 36 40 26N 0 16W
Villafranca del Panadés 36 41 21N 1 40 E
Villafranca di Verona 42 45 20N 10 51 E
Villagarcía de Arosa 34 42 34N 8 46W
Villagrán 161 24 29N 99 29W
Villaguay 174 32 0 S 59 0W
Villaharta 35 38 9N 4 54W
Villahermosa, Mexico 161 18 0N 92 50W
Villahermosa, Spain 37 38 46N 2 52W
Villaines-la-Juhel 18 48 21N 0 20W
Villajoyosa 37 38 30N 0 12W
Villalba 34 43 26N 7 40W
Villalba de Guardo 34 42 42N 4 49W
Villalcampo, Pantano de 34 41 31N 6 0W
Villalón de Campos 34 42 5N 5 4W
Villalpando 34 41 51N 5 25W
Villaluenga 34 40 2N 3 54W
Villamanán 34 42 19N 5 35W
Villamartín 35 36 52N 5 38W
Villamayor 36 39 50N 2 59W
Villamblard 20 45 2N 0 32 E
Villanova Monteleone 44 40 30N 8 28 E
Villanueva, Colombia 168 10 37N 72 59W
Villanueva, U.S.A. 157 35 16N 105 23W
Villanueva de Castellón 37 39 5N 0 31W
Villanueva de Córdoba 35 38 20N 4 38W
Villanueva de la Fuente 37 38 42N 2 42W
Villanueva de la Serena 35 38 59N 5 50W
Villanueva de la Sierra 34 40 12N 6 24W
Villanueva de los Castillejos 35 37 30N 7 15W
Villanueva del Arzobispo 37 38 10N 3 0W
Villanueva del Duque 35 38 20N 5 0W
Villanueva del Fresno 35 38 23N 7 10W
Villanueva y Geltrú 36 41 13N 1 40 E
Villaodrid 34 43 20N 7 11W
Villaputzu 44 39 28N 9 33 E
Villar del Arzobispo 36 39 44N 0 50W
Villar del Rey 35 39 7N 6 50W
Villarcayo 36 42 56N 3 34W
Villard-Bonnot 21 45 14N 5 53 E
Villard-de-Lans 21 45 3N 5 33 E
Villarino de los Aires 34 41 18N 6 23W
Villarosa 45 37 36N 14 9 E
Villarramiel 34 42 2N 4 55W
Villarreal 36 39 55N 0 3W
Villarrica, Chile 176 39 15 S 72 15W
Villarrica, Paraguay 174 25 40 S 56 30W
Villarrobledo 37 39 18N 2 36W
Villarroya de la Sierra 36 41 27N 1 46W
Villarrubia de los Ojos 37 39 14N 3 36W
Villars-les-Dombes 21 46 0N 5 3 E
Villarta de San Juan 37 39 15N 3 25W
Villasayas 36 41 24N 2 39W
Villaseca de los Gamitos 34 41 2N 6 7W
Villastar 36 40 17N 1 9W
Villatobas 36 39 54N 3 20W
Villavicencio, Argentina 174 32 28 S 69 0W
Villavicencio, Colombia 168 4 9N 73 37W
Villaviciosa 34 43 32N 5 27W
Villazón 174 22 0 S 65 35W
Ville-Marie 142 47 20N 79 30W
Ville Platte 153 30 45N 92 17W
Villedieu-les-Poëlles 18 48 50N 1 13W
Villefort 20 44 28N 3 56 E
Villefranche-de-Lauragais 20 43 25N 1 44 E
Villefranche-de-Rouergue 20 44 21N 2 2 E
Villefranche-du-Périgord 20 44 38N 1 5 E
Villefranche-sur-Cher 19 47 18N 1 46 E
Villefranche-sur-Saône 21 45 59N 4 43 E
Villegrande 173 18 30 S 64 10W
Villel 36 40 14N 1 12W
Villemaur-sur-Vanne 19 48 15N 3 44 E
Villemur-sur-Tarn 20 43 51N 1 31 E

Vyazemskiy

Vyazemskiy **65** 47 32N 134 45 E
Vyazma **58** 55 10N 34 15 E
Vyborg **56** 60 43N 28 47 E
Vychegda → **56** 61 18N 46 36 E
Vychodné Beskydy **31** 49 30N 22 0 E
Východočeský □ **30** 50 20N 15 45 E
Východoslovenský □ **31** 48 50N 21 0 E
Vyg-ozero **56** 63 30N 34 0 E
Vyksa **59** 55 19N 42 11 E
Vypin **81** 10 10N 76 15 E
Vyrnwy, L. **12** 52 48N 3 30W
Vyshniy Volochek **58** 57 30N 34 30 E
Vyshzha = imeni 26 Bakinskikh Komissarov **57** 39 22N 54 10 E
Vyškov **31** 49 17N 17 0 E
Vysoké Mýto **31** 49 58N 10 10 E
Vysokovsk **59** 56 22N 36 30 E
Vysotsk **58** 51 43N 26 32 E
Vyšší Brod **30** 48 37N 14 19 E
Vytegra **56** 61 0N 36 27 E

W

W.A.C. Bennett Dam **144** 56 2N 122 6W
Wa **126** 10 7N 2 25W
Waal → **22** 51 59N 4 30 E
Waalwijk **23** 51 42N 5 4 E
Waarschoot **23** 51 10N 3 36 E
Waasmunster **23** 51 6N 4 5 E
Wabag **107** 5 32 S 143 40 E
Wabakimi L. **142** 50 38N 89 45W
Wabana **143** 47 40N 53 0W
Wabao, C. **106** 21 35 S 167 53 E
Wabasca **144** 55 57N 113 56W
Wabash **155** 40 48N 85 46W
Wabash → **148** 37 46N 88 2W
Wabawng **82** 26 20N 97 25 E
Wabeno **148** 45 25N 88 40W
Wabi → **125** 7 45N 40 50 E
Wabigoon L. **145** 49 44N 92 44W
Wabowden **145** 54 55N 98 38W
Wąbrzeźno **32** 53 16N 18 57 E
Wabu Hu **97** 32 20N 116 50 E
Wabuk Pt. **142** 55 20N 85 5W
Wabush **143** 52 55N 66 52W
Wabuska **156** 39 9N 119 13W
Wachtebeke **23** 51 11N 3 52 E
Wächtersbach **27** 50 16N 9 18 E
Waco **153** 31 33N 97 5W
Waconichi, L. **142** 50 8N 74 0W
Wad Ban Naqa **125** 16 32N 33 9 E
Wad Banda **125** 13 10N 27 56 E
Wad el Haddad **125** 13 50N 33 30 E
Wad en Nau **125** 14 10N 33 34 E
Wad Hamid **125** 16 30N 32 45 E
Wâd Medanî **125** 14 28N 33 30 E
Wad Thana **77** 27 22N 66 23 E
Wadayama **100** 35 19N 134 52 E
Waddān **122** 29 9N 16 10 E
Waddān, Jabal **122** 29 0N 16 15 E
Waddeneilanden **22** 53 25N 5 10 E
Waddenzee **22** 53 6N 5 10 E
Wadderin Hill **109** 32 0 S 118 25 E
Waddington **151** 44 51N 75 12W
Waddington, Mt. **144** 51 23N 125 15W
Waddinxveen **22** 52 2N 4 40 E
Waddy Pt. **111** 24 58 S 153 21 E
Wadena, Canada **145** 51 57N 103 47W
Wadena, U.S.A. **152** 46 25N 95 8W
Wädenswil **29** 47 14N 8 40 E
Wadesboro **149** 35 2N 80 2W
Wadhams **144** 51 30N 127 30W
Wādī as Sīr **71** 31 56N 35 49 E
Wādī ash Shāţi' **122** 27 30N 15 0 E
Wādī Banī Walīd **122** 31 49N 14 0 E
Wadi Gemâl **124** 24 35N 35 10 E
Wadi Halfa **124** 21 53N 31 19 E
Wadian **97** 32 42N 112 29 E
Wadim **75** 22 40N 57 21 E
Wadlew **32** 51 31N 19 23 E
Wadowice **32** 49 52N 19 30 E
Wadsworth **156** 39 38N 119 22W
Waegwan **95** 35 59N 128 23 E
Wafrah **72** 28 33N 47 56 E
Wagenberg **23** 51 40N 4 46 E
Wageningen, Neth. **22** 51 58N 5 40 E
Wageningen, Surinam **169** 5 50N 56 50W
Wager B. **141** 65 26N 88 40W
Wager Bay **141** 65 56N 90 49W
Wagga Wagga **113** 35 7 S 147 24 E
Waghete **87** 4 10 S 135 50 E
Wagin **109** 33 17 S 117 25 E
Wagon Mound **153** 36 1N 104 44W
Wagoner **153** 36 0N 95 20W
Wagrowiec **32** 52 48N 17 11 E
Wah **77** 33 45N 72 40 E
Wahai **87** 2 48 S 129 35 E
Wahiawa **146** 21 30N 158 2W
Wâḥid **71** 30 48N 32 21 E
Wahnai **78** 32 40N 65 50 E
Wahoo **152** 41 15N 96 35W
Wahpeton **152** 46 20N 96 35W
Wahratta **112** 31 58 S 141 50 E
Wai **80** 17 56N 73 57 E
Wai, Koh **85** 9 55N 102 55 E
Waiai → **115** 46 12 S 167 38 E
Waiau **115** 42 39 S 173 5 E
Waiau → **115** 42 47 S 173 22 E
Waiawe Ganga → **81** 6 15N 81 0 E
Waibeem **87** 0 30 S 132 59 E
Waiblingen **27** 48 49N 9 20 E
Waidhofen, Niederösterreich, Austria **30** 48 49N 15 17 E
Waidhofen, Niederösterreich, Austria **30** 47 57N 14 46 E
Waigeo **87** 0 20 S 130 40 E
Waihao → **115** 44 52 S 171 11 E
Waihao Downs **115** 44 48 S 170 55 E
Waiheke Islands **114** 36 48 S 175 6 E
Waihi **114** 37 23 S 175 52 E
Waihola **115** 46 1 S 170 8 E
Waihola L. **115** 45 59 S 170 8 E
Waihou → **115** 37 15 S 175 40 E
Waika **130** 2 22 S 25 42 E
Waikabubak **87** 9 45 S 119 25 E
Waikaia **115** 45 44 S 168 51 E
Waikaka **115** 45 55 S 169 1 E
Waikare, L. **114** 37 26 S 175 13 E
Waikaremoana **114** 38 42 S 177 12 E
Waikaremoana L. **114** 38 49 S 177 9 E
Waikari **115** 42 58 S 172 41 E
Waikato → **114** 37 23 S 174 43 E
Waikerie **112** 34 9 S 140 0 E
Waikiekie **114** 35 57 S 174 16 E
Waikokopu **114** 39 3 S 177 52 E
Waikouaiti **115** 45 36 S 170 41 E
Waimangaroa **115** 41 43 S 171 46 E
Waimarie **115** 41 35 S 171 58 E
Waimate **115** 44 45 S 171 3 E
Waimea Plain **115** 45 55 S 168 35 E
Waimes **23** 50 25N 6 7 E
Wainganga → **79** 18 50N 79 55 E
Waingapu **87** 9 35 S 120 11 E
Waingmaw **82** 25 21N 97 26 E
Waini → **169** 8 20N 59 50W
Wainuiomata **114** 41 17 S 174 56 E
Wainwright, Canada **145** 52 50N 110 50W
Wainwright, U.S.A. **140** 70 39N 160 1W
Waiotapu **114** 38 21 S 176 25 E
Waiouru **114** 39 28 S 175 41 E
Waipahi **115** 46 6 S 169 15 E
Waipapa Pt. **115** 46 40 S 168 51 E
Waipara **115** 43 3 S 172 46 E
Waipawa **114** 39 56 S 176 38 E
Waipiro **114** 38 2 S 178 22 E
Waipu **114** 35 59 S 174 29 E
Waipukurau **114** 40 1 S 176 33 E
Wairakei **114** 38 37 S 176 6 E
Wairarapa, L. **114** 41 14 S 175 15 E
Wairau → **115** 41 32 S 174 7 E
Wairio **115** 45 59 S 168 3 E
Wairoa **114** 39 3 S 177 25 E
Wairoa → **114** 36 5 S 173 59 E
Waitaha **115** 43 0 S 170 45 E
Waitaki → **115** 44 56 S 171 7 E
Waitaki Plains **115** 44 22 S 170 0 E
Waitara **114** 38 59 S 174 15 E
Waitchie **112** 35 22 S 143 8 E
Waitoa **114** 37 37 S 175 35 E
Waitotara **114** 39 49 S 174 44 E
Waitsburg **156** 46 15N 118 0W
Waiuku **114** 37 15 S 174 45 E
Waiyevo **106** 16 48 S 179 59W
Wajima **99** 37 30N 137 0 E
Wajir **130** 1 42N 40 5 E
Wajir □ **130** 1 42N 40 20 E
Waka **132** 1 1N 20 13 E
Wakarusa **155** 41 32N 86 1W
Wakasa **100** 35 20N 134 24 E
Wakasa-Wan **101** 35 40N 135 30 E
Wakatipu, L. **115** 45 5 S 168 33 E
Wakaw **145** 52 39N 105 44W
Wakayama **101** 34 15N 135 15 E
Wakayama-ken □ **101** 33 50N 135 30 E
Wake **100** 34 48N 134 8 E
Wake Forest **149** 35 58N 78 30W
Wake I. **104** 19 18N 166 36 E
Wakefield, N.Z. **115** 41 24 S 173 5 E
Wakefield, U.K. **12** 53 41N 1 31W
Wakefield, Mass., U.S.A. **151** 42 30N 71 3W
Wakefield, Mich., U.S.A. **152** 46 28N 89 53W
Wakema **82** 16 30N 95 11 E
Wakkanai **98** 45 28N 141 35 E
Wakkerstroom **135** 27 24 S 30 10 E
Wakool **112** 35 28 S 144 23 E
Wakool → **112** 35 5 S 143 33 E
Wakre **87** 0 19 S 131 5 E
Waku **107** 6 5 S 149 9 E
Wakuach L. **143** 55 34N 67 32W
Walamba **131** 13 30 S 28 42 E
Wałbrzych **32** 50 45N 16 18 E
Walbury Hill **13** 51 22N 1 28W
Walcha **111** 30 55 S 151 31 E
Walcha Road **113** 30 55 S 151 24 E
Walcheren **23** 51 30N 3 35 E
Walcott **156** 41 50N 106 55W
Wałcz **32** 53 17N 16 27 E
Wald **29** 47 17N 8 56 E
Waldbröl **26** 50 52N 7 36 E
Waldburg Ra. **109** 24 40 S 117 35 E
Waldeck **26** 51 12N 9 4 E
Walden, Colo., U.S.A. **156** 40 47N 106 20W
Walden, N.Y., U.S.A. **151** 41 32N 74 13W
Waldenburg **28** 47 23N 7 45 E
Waldport **156** 44 30N 124 2W
Waldron **153** 34 52N 94 4W
Waldshut **27** 47 37N 8 12 E
Walembele **126** 10 30N 1 58W
Walensee **29** 47 7N 9 13 E
Walenstadt **29** 47 8N 9 19 E
Wales □ **13** 52 30N 3 30W
Walewale **127** 10 21N 0 50W
Walgett **111** 30 0 S 148 5 E
Walgreen Coast **7** 75 15 S 105 0W
Walhalla, Australia **113** 37 56 S 146 29 E
Walhalla, U.S.A. **145** 48 55N 97 55W
Walkaway **109** 28 59 S 114 48 E
Walker, Minn., U.S.A. **152** 47 4N 94 35W
Walker, Mo., U.S.A. **154** 37 54N 94 14W
Walker L., Man., Canada **145** 54 42N 95 57W
Walker L., Qué., Canada **143** 50 20N 67 11W
Walker L., U.S.A. **156** 38 56N 118 46W
Walkerston **110** 21 11 S 149 8 E
Walkerton, Canada **150** 44 10N 81 10W
Walkerton, U.S.A. **155** 41 28N 86 29W
Wall **152** 44 0N 102 14W
Walla Walla, Australia **113** 35 45 S 146 54 E
Walla Walla, U.S.A. **156** 46 3N 118 25W
Wallabadah **110** 17 57 S 142 15 E
Wallace, Idaho, U.S.A. **156** 47 30N 116 0W
Wallace, N.C., U.S.A. **149** 34 44N 77 59W
Wallace, Nebr., U.S.A. **152** 40 51N 101 12W
Wallaceburg **142** 42 34N 82 23W
Wallacetown **115** 46 21 S 168 19 E
Wallachia = Valahia **50** 44 35N 25 0 E
Wallal **111** 26 32 S 146 7 E
Wallal Downs **108** 19 47 S 120 40 E
Wallambin, L. **109** 30 57 S 117 35 E
Wallaroo **112** 33 56 S 137 39 E
Wallasey **12** 53 26N 3 2W
Walldürn **27** 49 34N 9 23 E
Wallerawang **113** 33 25 S 150 4 E
Wallhallow **110** 17 50 S 135 50 E
Wallingford, U.K. **12** 51 40N 1 15W
Wallingford, U.S.A. **151** 41 27N 72 50W
Wallis & Futuna **104** 13 18 S 176 10W
Wallisellen **29** 47 25N 8 36 E
Wallowa **156** 45 40N 117 35W
Wallowa, Mts. **156** 45 20N 117 30W
Wallsend, Australia **113** 32 55 S 151 40 E
Wallsend, U.K. **12** 54 59N 1 30W
Wallula **156** 46 3N 118 59W
Wallumbilla **111** 26 33 S 149 9 E
Walmsley, L. **145** 63 25N 108 36W
Walney, Isle of **12** 54 5N 3 15W
Walnut **154** 41 33N 89 36W
Walnut Creek **158** 37 54N 122 4W
Walnut Ridge **153** 36 7N 90 58W
Walpeup **112** 35 7 S 142 2 E
Walsall **13** 52 36N 1 59W
Walsenburg **153** 37 42N 104 45W
Walsh **153** 37 28N 102 15W
Walsh → **110** 16 31 S 143 42 E
Walsh P.O. **110** 16 40 S 144 0 E
Walshoutem **23** 50 43N 5 4 E
Walsrode **26** 52 51N 9 37 E
Waltair **80** 17 44N 83 23 E
Walterboro **149** 32 53N 80 40W
Walters **153** 34 25N 98 20W
Waltershausen **26** 50 53N 10 33 E
Waltham **151** 42 22N 71 12W
Waltham Sta. **142** 45 57N 76 57W
Waltman **156** 43 8N 107 15W
Walton, Ky., U.S.A. **155** 38 52N 84 37W
Walton, N.Y., U.S.A. **151** 42 12N 75 9W
Waltonville **154** 38 13N 89 2W
Walu **82** 26 28N 98 2 E
Walvisbaai **134** 23 0 S 14 28 E
Walwa **113** 35 59 S 147 44 E
Wamba, Kenya **130** 0 58N 37 19 E
Wamba, Zaïre **130** 2 10N 27 57 E
Wamego **152** 39 14N 96 22W
Wamena **87** 4 4 S 138 57 E
Wamsasi **87** 3 27 S 126 7 E
Wan Hat **82** 20 14N 97 53 E
Wan Kinghao **82** 21 34N 98 17 E
Wan Lai-kam **82** 21 21N 98 22 E
Wan Tup **82** 21 13N 98 42 E
Wan Xian **94** 38 47N 115 7 E
Wana **77** 32 20N 69 32 E
Wanaaring **111** 29 38 S 144 9 E
Wanaka L. **115** 44 33 S 169 7 E
Wan'an **97** 26 26N 114 49 E
Wanapiri **87** 4 30 S 135 59 E
Wanapitei L. **142** 46 45N 80 40W
Wanbi **112** 34 46 S 140 17 E
Wandaik **169** 4 27N 59 35W
Wandanian **113** 35 6 S 150 30 E
Wanderer **131** 19 36 S 30 1 E
Wandoan **111** 26 5 S 149 55 E
Wandre **23** 50 40N 5 39 E
Wanfercée-Baulet **23** 50 28N 4 35 E
Wanfu **95** 40 8N 122 38 E
Wang → **84** 17 8N 99 2 E
Wang Kai **125** 9 3N 29 23 E
Wang Noi **84** 14 13N 100 44 E
Wang Saphung **84** 17 18N 101 46 E
Wang Thong **84** 16 50N 100 26 E
Wanga **130** 2 58N 29 12 E
Wangal **87** 6 8 S 134 9 E
Wanganella **113** 35 6 S 144 49 E
Wanganui **114** 39 56 S 175 3 E
Wanganui →, N.I., N.Z. **114** 39 55 S 175 4 E
Wanganui →, S.I., N.Z. **115** 43 3 S 170 26 E
Wangaratta **113** 36 21 S 146 19 E
Wangcang **96** 32 18N 106 20 E
Wangdu **94** 38 40N 115 7 E
Wangdu Phodrang **82** 27 28N 89 54 E
Wangerooge **26** 53 47N 7 52 E
Wangi **130** 1 58 S 40 58 E
Wangiwangi **87** 5 22 S 123 37 E
Wangjiang **97** 30 10N 116 42 E
Wangmo **96** 25 11N 106 5 E
Wangqing **95** 43 12N 129 42 E
Wankaner **78** 22 35N 71 0 E
Wanless **145** 54 11N 101 21W
Wannian **97** 28 42N 117 4 E
Wanon Niwat **84** 17 38N 103 46 E
Wanquan **94** 40 50N 114 40 E
Wanrong **94** 35 25N 110 50 E
Wanshan **96** 27 30N 109 12 E
Wanshengchang **96** 28 57N 106 53 E
Wanssum **23** 51 32N 6 5 E
Wanstead **114** 40 8 S 176 30 E
Wanxian **96** 30 42N 108 20 E
Wanyin **82** 20 23N 97 15 E
Wanyuan **96** 32 4N 108 3 E
Wanzai **97** 28 7N 114 30 E
Wanze **23** 50 32N 5 13 E
Wapakoneta **155** 40 35N 84 10W
Wapato **156** 46 30N 120 25W
Wapawekka L. **145** 54 55N 104 40W
Wapello **154** 41 11N 91 11W
Wapikopa L. **142** 52 56N 87 53W
Wappingers Falls **151** 41 35N 73 56W
Wapsipinicon → **154** 41 44N 90 19W
Warabi **101** 35 49N 139 41 E
Warangal **80** 17 58N 79 35 E
Waratah **110** 41 30 S 145 30 E
Warburg **26** 51 29N 9 10 E
Warburton, Vic., Australia **113** 37 47 S 145 42 E
Warburton, W. Austral., Australia **109** 26 8 S 126 35 E
Warburton Ra. **109** 25 55 S 126 28 E
Ward **115** 41 49 S 174 11 E
Ward → **111** 26 28 S 146 6 E
Ward Cove **144** 55 25N 132 43W
Ward Hunt, C. **107** 8 2 S 148 10 E
Ward Hunt Str. **107** 9 30 S 150 0 E
Ward Mt. **158** 37 12N 118 54W
Warden **135** 27 50 S 29 0 E
Wardha **78** 20 45N 78 39 E
Wardlow **144** 50 56N 111 31W
Wards River **113** 32 11 S 151 56 E
Ware, Canada **144** 57 26N 125 41W
Ware, U.S.A. **151** 42 16N 72 15W
Waregem **23** 50 53N 3 27 E
Wareham **151** 41 45N 70 44W
Waremme **23** 50 43N 5 15 E
Waren **26** 53 30N 12 41 E
Warendorf **26** 51 57N 8 0 E
Warialda **111** 29 29 S 150 33 E
Wariap **87** 1 30 S 134 5 E
Warin Chamrap **84** 15 12N 104 53 E
Warka **32** 51 47N 21 12 E
Warkopi **87** 1 12 S 134 9 E
Warkworth **114** 36 24 S 174 41 E
Warley **13** 52 30N 2 0W
Warm Springs **157** 38 16N 116 32W
Warman **145** 52 19N 106 30W
Warmbad, Namibia **134** 28 25 S 18 42 E
Warmbad, S. Africa **135** 24 51 S 28 19 E
Warmenhuizen **22** 52 43N 4 44 E
Warmeriville **19** 49 20N 4 13 E
Warmond **22** 52 12N 4 30 E
Warnambool Downs **110** 22 48 S 142 52 E
Warnemünde **26** 54 9N 12 5 E
Warner **144** 49 17N 112 12W
Warner Mts. **156** 41 30N 120 20W
Warner Robins **149** 32 41N 83 36W
Warnes **173** 17 30 S 63 10W
Warneton **23** 50 45N 2 57 E
Warnow → **26** 54 6N 12 9 E
Warnsveld **22** 52 8N 6 14 E
Waroona **109** 32 50 S 115 58 E
Warora **80** 20 14N 79 1 E
Warracknabeal **112** 36 9 S 142 26 E
Warragul **113** 38 10 S 145 58 E
Warrawagine **108** 20 51 S 120 42 E
Warrego → **111** 30 24 S 145 21 E
Warrego Ra. **110** 24 58 S 146 0 E
Warren, Australia **113** 31 42 S 147 51 E
Warren, Ark., U.S.A. **153** 33 35N 92 3W
Warren, Ill., U.S.A. **154** 42 30N 89 59W
Warren, Mich., U.S.A. **155** 42 31N 83 2W
Warren, Minn., U.S.A. **152** 48 12N 96 46W
Warren, Ohio, U.S.A. **150** 41 18N 80 52W
Warren, Pa., U.S.A. **150** 41 52N 79 10W
Warrenpoint **15** 54 7N 6 15W
Warrensburg, Ill., U.S.A. **154** 39 56N 89 4W
Warrensburg, Mo., U.S.A. **152** 38 45N 93 45W
Warrenton, S. Africa **134** 28 9 S 24 47 E
Warrenton, Mo., U.S.A. **154** 38 49N 91 9W
Warrenton, Oreg., U.S.A. **158** 46 11N 123 59W

Wesel

Wesel **26** 51 39N 6 34 E
Weser → **26** 53 33N 8 30 E
Wesiri **87** 7 30 S 126 30 E
Wesley Vale **157** 35 3N 106 2W
Wesleyville, Canada **143** 49 8N 53 36W
Wesleyville, U.S.A. **150** 42 9N 80 1W
Wessel, C. **110** 10 59 S 136 46 E
Wessel Is. **110** 11 10 S 136 45 E
Wesselburen **26** 54 11N 8 53 E
Wessem **23** 51 11N 5 49 E
Wessington **152** 44 30N 98 40W
Wessington Springs **152** 44 10N 98 35W
West **153** 31 50N 97 5W
West Allis **155** 43 1N 87 0W
West B. **153** 29 5N 89 27W
West Baines → **108** 15 38 S 129 59 E
West Bend **148** 43 25N 88 10W
West Bengal □ **79** 23 0N 88 0 E
West Branch **148** 44 16N 84 13W
West Bromwich **13** 52 32N 2 1W
West Cape Howe **109** 35 8 S 117 36 E
West Carrollton **155** 39 40N 84 17W
West Chazy **151** 44 49N 73 28W
West Chester **148** 39 58N 75 36W
West Chicago **155** 41 53N 88 12W
West Columbia **153** 29 10N 95 38W
West Covina **159** 34 4N 117 54W
West Des Moines **154** 41 30N 93 45W
West End **162** 26 41N 78 58W
West Falkland **176** 51 40 S 60 0W
West Frankfurt **154** 37 56N 89 0W
West Germany ■ **26** 52 0N 9 0 E
West Glamorgan □ **13** 51 40N 3 55W
West Hartford **151** 41 45N 72 45W
West Haven **151** 41 18N 72 57W
West Helena **153** 34 30N 90 40W
West Ice Shelf **7** 67 0 S 85 0 E
West Indies **163** 15 0N 70 0W
West Lafayette **155** 40 27N 86 55W
West Liberty, Iowa, U.S.A. **154** 41 34N 91 16W
West Liberty, Ky., U.S.A. **155** 37 55N 83 16W
West Liberty, Ohio, U.S.A. **155** 40 15N 83 45W
West Lorne **150** 42 36N 81 36W
West Lunga → **131** 13 6 S 24 39 E
West Manchester **155** 39 55N 84 38W
West Memphis **153** 35 5N 90 11W
West Midlands □ **13** 52 30N 1 55W
West Mifflin **150** 40 22N 79 52W
West Milton **155** 39 58N 84 20W
West Monroe **153** 32 32N 92 7W
West Moors **12** 50 49N 1 50W
West Newton **150** 40 14N 79 46W
West Nicholson **131** 21 2 S 29 20 E
West Palm Beach **149** 26 44N 80 3W
West Plains **153** 36 45N 91 50W
West Pt. **112** 35 1 S 135 56 E
West Point, Ga., U.S.A. **149** 32 54N 85 10W
West Point, Ill., U.S.A. **154** 40 15N 91 11W
West Point, Iowa, U.S.A. **154** 40 43N 91 27W
West Point, Ky., U.S.A. **155** 37 59N 85 57W
West Point, Miss., U.S.A. **149** 33 36N 88 38W
West Point, Nebr., U.S.A. **152** 41 50N 96 43W
West Point, Va., U.S.A. **148** 37 35N 76 47W
West Pokot □ **130** 1 30N 35 15 E
West Road → **144** 53 18N 122 53W
West Rutland **151** 43 38N 73 0W
West Salem **155** 38 31N 88 1W
West Schelde → = Westerschelde → **23** 51 25N 3 25 E
West Seneca **150** 42 51N 78 48W
West Siberian Plain **66** 62 0N 75 0 E
West Sussex □ **13** 50 55N 0 30W
West Terre Haute **155** 39 27N 87 27W
West-Terschelling **22** 53 22N 5 13 E
West Union, Iowa, U.S.A. **154** 42 57N 91 49W
West Union, Ohio, U.S.A. **155** 38 48N 83 33W
West Unity **155** 41 35N 84 26W
West Virginia □ **148** 39 0N 81 0W
West-Vlaanderen □ **23** 51 0N 3 0 E
West Walker → **158** 38 54N 119 9W
West Wyalong **113** 33 56 S 147 10 E
West Yellowstone **156** 44 47N 111 4W
West Yorkshire □ **12** 53 45N 1 40W
Westall Pt. **111** 32 55 S 134 4 E
Westbrook, Maine, U.S.A. **149** 43 40N 70 22W
Westbrook, Tex., U.S.A. **153** 32 25N 101 0W
Westbury **110** 41 30 S 146 51 E
Westby **152** 48 52N 104 3W
Westend **159** 35 42N 117 24W
Westerbork **22** 52 51N 6 37 E
Westerland **26** 54 51N 8 20 E
Western □, Kenya **130** 0 30N 34 30 E
Western □, Uganda **130** 1 45N 31 30 E
Western □, Zambia **131** 15 15 S 24 30 E
Western Australia □ **109** 25 0 S 118 0 E
Western Ghats **81** 14 0N 75 0 E
Western Isles □ **14** 57 30N 7 10W
Western River **112** 35 42 S 136 56 E
Western Sahara ■ **120** 25 0N 13 0W
Western Samoa ■ **104** 14 0 S 172 0W
Westernport **148** 39 30N 79 5W
Westerschelde → **23** 51 25N 3 25 E
Westerstede **26** 53 15N 7 55 E
Westervoort **22** 51 58N 5 59 E
Westerwald **26** 50 39N 8 0 E
Westfield, Ill., U.S.A. **155** 39 27N 88 0W
Westfield, Ind., U.S.A. **155** 40 2N 86 8W
Westfield, Mass., U.S.A. **151** 42 9N 72 49W
Westfield, N.Y., U.S.A. **150** 42 20N 79 38W
Westfield, Pa., U.S.A. **150** 41 54N 77 32W
Westgat **23** 51 39N 3 44 E
Westhope **152** 48 55N 101 0W
Westkapelle, Belgium **23** 51 19N 3 19 E
Westkapelle, Neth. **23** 51 31N 3 28 E
Westland **155** 42 15N 83 20W
Westland □ **115** 43 33 S 169 59 E
Westland Bight **115** 42 55 S 170 5 E
Westlock **144** 54 9N 113 55W
Westmalle **23** 51 18N 4 42 E
Westmeath □ **15** 53 30N 7 30W
Westminster **148** 39 34N 77 1W
Westmorland **157** 33 2N 115 42W
Weston, Malaysia **86** 5 10N 115 35 E
Weston, Ohio, U.S.A. **155** 41 21N 83 47W
Weston, Oreg., U.S.A. **156** 45 50N 118 30W
Weston, W. Va., U.S.A. **148** 39 3N 80 29W
Weston I. **142** 52 33N 79 36W
Weston-super-Mare **13** 51 20N 2 59W
Westphalia **154** 38 26N 92 0W
Westport, Canada **151** 44 40N 76 25W
Westport, Ireland **15** 53 44N 9 31W
Westport, N.Z. **115** 41 46 S 171 37 E
Westport, Ind., U.S.A. **155** 39 11N 85 34W
Westport, Oreg., U.S.A. **158** 46 10N 123 23W
Westport, Wash., U.S.A. **156** 46 48N 124 4W
Westray, Canada **145** 53 36N 101 24W
Westray, U.K. **14** 59 18N 3 0W
Westree **142** 47 26N 81 34W
Westville, Calif., U.S.A. **158** 39 8N 120 42W
Westville, Ill., U.S.A. **155** 40 3N 87 36W
Westville, Ind., U.S.A. **155** 41 35N 86 55W
Westville, Okla., U.S.A. **153** 36 0N 94 33W
Westwood **156** 40 26N 121 0W
Wetar **87** 7 30 S 126 30 E
Wetaskiwin **144** 52 55N 113 24W
Wethersfield **151** 41 43N 72 40W
Wetlet **82** 22 20N 95 53 E
Wetteren **23** 51 0N 3 52 E
Wettingen **29** 47 28N 8 20 E
Wetzikon **29** 47 19N 8 48 E
Wetzlar **26** 50 33N 8 30 E
Wevelgem **23** 50 49N 3 12 E
Wewak **107** 3 38 S 143 41 E
Wewaka **153** 35 10N 96 35W
Wexford **15** 52 20N 6 28W
Wexford □ **15** 52 20N 6 25W
Wexford Harbour **15** 52 20N 6 25W
Weyburn **145** 49 40N 103 50W
Weyburn L. **144** 63 0N 117 59W
Weyer **30** 47 51N 14 40 E
Weyib → **125** 7 15N 40 15 E
Weymouth, Canada **143** 44 30N 66 1W
Weymouth, U.K. **13** 50 36N 2 28W
Weymouth, U.S.A. **151** 42 13N 70 53W
Weymouth, C. **110** 12 37 S 143 27 E
Wezemaal **23** 50 57N 4 45 E
Wezep **22** 52 28N 6 0 E
Whakamaru **114** 38 23 S 175 50 E
Whakatane **114** 37 57 S 177 1 E
Whale → **143** 58 15N 67 40W
Whale Cove **140** 62 11N 92 36W
Whales, B. of **7** 78 0 S 165 0W
Whalsay **14** 60 22N 1 0W
Whangamata **114** 37 12 S 175 53 E
Whangamomona **114** 39 8 S 174 44 E
Whangarei **114** 35 43 S 174 21 E
Whangarei Harbour **114** 35 45 S 174 28 E
Whangaroa Harb. **114** 35 4 S 173 46 E
Wharanui **115** 41 55 S 174 6 E
Wharfe → **12** 53 55N 1 30W
Wharfedale **12** 54 7N 2 4W
Wharton, N.J., U.S.A. **151** 40 53N 74 36W
Wharton, Pa., U.S.A. **150** 41 31N 78 1W
Wharton, Tex., U.S.A. **153** 29 20N 96 6W
Whataroa **115** 43 18 S 170 24 E
Whataroa → **115** 43 7 S 170 16 E
Wheatfield **155** 41 13N 87 4W
Wheatland, Calif., U.S.A. **158** 39 1N 121 25W
Wheatland, Ind., U.S.A. **155** 38 40N 87 19W
Wheatland, Wyo., U.S.A. **152** 42 4N 104 58W
Wheatley **150** 42 6N 82 27W
Wheaton, Ill., U.S.A. **155** 41 52N 88 6W
Wheaton, Minn., U.S.A. **152** 45 50N 96 29W
Wheelbarrow Pk. **158** 37 26N 116 5W
Wheeler, Oreg., U.S.A. **156** 45 50N 123 57W
Wheeler, Tex., U.S.A. **153** 35 29N 100 15W
Wheeler → **145** 57 25N 105 30W
Wheeler Pk., N. Mex., U.S.A. **157** 36 34N 105 25W
Wheeler Pk., Nev., U.S.A. **157** 38 57N 114 15W
Wheeler Ridge **159** 35 0N 118 57W
Wheeling **150** 40 2N 80 41W
Whernside **12** 54 14N 2 24W
Whidbey I. **144** 48 15N 122 40W
Whiskey Gap **144** 49 0N 113 3W
Whiskey Jack L. **145** 58 23N 101 55W
Whistleduck Cr. → **110** 20 15 S 135 18 E
Whitby, Canada **150** 43 52N 78 56W
Whitby, U.K. **12** 54 29N 0 37W
White →, Ark., U.S.A. **153** 33 53N 91 3W
White →, Colo., U.S.A. **156** 40 8N 109 41W
White →, Ind., U.S.A. **155** 38 25N 87 45W
White →, S. Dak., U.S.A. **152** 43 45N 99 30W
White →, Wash., U.S.A. **158** 47 12N 122 15W
White, East Fork → **155** 38 33N 87 14W
White B. **143** 50 0N 56 35W
White Bear Res. **143** 48 10N 57 5W
White Bird **156** 45 46N 116 21W
White Butte **152** 46 23N 103 19W
White City **152** 38 50N 96 45W
White Cliffs **112** 30 50 S 143 10 E
White Deer **153** 35 30N 101 8W
White Hall **154** 39 25N 90 27W
White Haven **151** 41 3N 75 47W
White I. **114** 37 30 S 177 13 E
White L., Canada **151** 45 18N 76 31W
White L., U.S.A. **153** 29 45N 92 30W
White Mts., Calif., U.S.A. **158** 37 30N 118 15W
White Mts., N.H., U.S.A. **151** 44 15N 71 15W
White Nile = Nîl el Abyad → **125** 15 38N 32 31 E
White Nile Dam = Khazzân Jabal el Awliyâ **125** 15 24N 32 20 E
White Otter L. **142** 49 5N 91 55W
White Pass, Canada **140** 59 40N 135 3W
White Pass, U.S.A. **158** 46 38N 121 24W
White Pigeon **155** 41 48N 85 39W
White Plains **151** 41 2N 73 44W
White River, Canada **142** 48 35N 85 20W
White River, S. Africa **135** 25 20 S 31 0 E
White River, U.S.A. **152** 43 34N 100 45W
White Russia = Byelorussian S.S.R. □ **58** 53 30N 27 0 E
White Sea = Beloye More **56** 66 30N 38 0 E
White Sulphur Springs, Mont., U.S.A. **156** 46 35N 110 54W
White Sulphur Springs, W. Va., U.S.A. **148** 37 50N 80 16W
White Swan **158** 46 23N 120 44W
White Volta → **127** 9 10N 1 15W
Whitecliffs **115** 43 26 S 171 55 E
Whitecourt **144** 54 10N 115 45W
Whiteface **153** 33 35N 102 40W
Whitefield **151** 44 23N 71 37W
Whitefish **156** 48 25N 114 22W
Whitefish Bay **155** 43 23N 87 54W
Whitefish L. **145** 62 41N 106 48W
Whitefish Pt. **148** 46 45N 85 0W
Whitegull, L. **143** 55 27N 64 17W
Whitehall, Mich., U.S.A. **148** 43 21N 86 20W
Whitehall, Mont., U.S.A. **156** 45 52N 112 4W
Whitehall, N.Y., U.S.A. **151** 43 32N 73 28W
Whitehall, Wis., U.S.A. **152** 44 20N 91 19W
Whitehaven **12** 54 33N 3 35W
Whitehorse **140** 60 43N 135 3W
Whitehorse, Vale of **13** 51 37N 1 30W
Whiteman **154** 38 45N 93 40W
Whiteman Ra. **107** 5 55 S 150 0 E
Whitemark **110** 40 7 S 148 3 E
Whitemouth **145** 49 57N 95 58W
Whiteplains **126** 6 28N 10 40W
Whitesboro, N.Y., U.S.A. **151** 43 8N 75 20W
Whitesboro, Tex., U.S.A. **153** 33 40N 96 58W
Whiteshell Prov. Park **145** 50 0N 95 40W
Whiteside **154** 39 12N 91 2W
Whiteside, Canal **176** 53 55 S 70 15W
Whitetail **152** 48 54N 105 15W
Whiteville **149** 34 20N 78 40W
Whitewater **155** 42 50N 88 45W
Whitewater Baldy, Mt. **157** 33 20N 108 44W
Whitewater L. **142** 50 50N 89 10W
Whitewood, Australia **110** 21 28 S 143 30 E
Whitewood, Canada **145** 50 20N 102 20W
Whitfield **113** 36 42 S 146 24 E
Whithorn **14** 54 44N 4 25W
Whitianga **114** 36 47 S 175 41 E
Whiting **155** 41 41N 87 29W
Whitman **151** 42 4N 70 55W
Whitmire **149** 34 33N 81 40W
Whitney **150** 45 31N 78 14W
Whitney, Mt. **158** 36 35N 118 14W
Whitney Point **151** 42 19N 75 59W
Whitstable **13** 51 21N 1 2 E
Whitsunday I. **110** 20 15 S 149 4 E
Whittemore **154** 43 4N 94 26W
Whittier, Calif., U.S.A. **159** 33 58N 118 3W
Whittier, U.S.A. **140** 60 46N 148 48W
Whittlesea **113** 37 27 S 145 9 E
Whitwell **149** 35 15N 85 30W
Wholdaia L. **145** 60 43N 104 20W
Whyalla **112** 33 2 S 137 30 E
Whyjonta **111** 29 41 S 142 28 E
Wiarton **150** 44 40N 81 10W
Wiawso **126** 6 10N 2 25W
Wiazów **32** 50 50N 17 10 E
Wibaux **152** 47 0N 104 13W
Wichabai **169** 2 57N 59 35W
Wichian Buri **84** 15 39N 101 7 E
Wichita **153** 37 40N 97 20W
Wichita Falls **153** 33 57N 98 30W
Wick **14** 58 26N 3 5W
Wickenburg **157** 33 58N 112 45W
Wickepin **109** 32 50 S 117 30 E
Wickham, C. **110** 39 35 S 143 57 E
Wickliffe **150** 41 36N 81 29W
Wicklow **15** 53 0N 6 2W
Wicklow □ **15** 52 59N 6 25W
Wicklow Hd. **15** 52 59N 6 3W
Wicklow Mts. **15** 53 0N 6 30W
Widawa **32** 51 27N 18 51 E
Widawka **32** 51 7N 19 36 E
Widgiemooltha **109** 31 30 S 121 34 E
Widnes **12** 53 22N 2 44W
Więcbork **32** 53 21N 17 30 E
Wiedenbrück **26** 51 52N 8 15 E
Wiek **26** 54 37N 13 17 E
Wielbark **32** 53 24N 20 55 E
Wieleń **32** 52 53N 16 9 E
Wieliczka **32** 50 0N 20 5 E
Wieluń **32** 51 15N 18 34 E
Wien **31** 48 12N 16 22 E
Wiener Neustadt **31** 47 49N 16 16 E
Wieprz →, Koszalin, Poland **32** 54 26N 16 35 E
Wieprz →, Lublin, Poland **32** 51 34N 21 49 E
Wierden **22** 52 22N 6 35 E
Wiers **23** 50 30N 3 32 E
Wieruszów **32** 51 19N 18 9 E
Wiesbaden **27** 50 7N 8 17 E
Wiesental **27** 49 15N 8 30 E
Wigan **12** 53 33N 2 38W
Wiggins, Colo., U.S.A. **152** 40 16N 104 3W
Wiggins, Miss., U.S.A. **153** 30 53N 89 9W
Wight, I. of **13** 50 40N 1 20W
Wigry, Jezioro **32** 54 2N 23 8 E
Wigtown **14** 54 52N 4 27W
Wigtown B. **14** 54 46N 4 15W
Wijchen **22** 51 48N 5 44 E
Wijhe **22** 52 23N 6 8 E
Wijk bij Duurstede **22** 51 59N 5 21 E
Wil **29** 47 28N 9 3 E
Wilamowice **31** 49 55N 19 9 E
Wilangee **112** 31 28 S 141 20 E
Wilber **152** 40 34N 96 59W
Wilberforce **150** 45 2N 78 13W
Wilberforce, C. **110** 11 54 S 136 35 E
Wilburton **153** 34 55N 95 15W
Wilcannia **112** 31 30 S 143 26 E
Wilcox **150** 41 34N 78 43W
Wildbad **27** 48 44N 8 32 E
Wildcat Creek → **155** 40 28N 86 48W
Wildervank **22** 53 5N 6 52 E
Wildeshausen **26** 52 54N 8 25 E
Wildhorn **28** 46 22N 7 21 E
Wildon **30** 46 52N 15 31 E
Wildrose, Calif., U.S.A. **159** 36 14N 117 11W
Wildrose, N. Dak., U.S.A. **152** 48 36N 103 11W
Wildspitze **30** 46 53N 10 53 E
Wildstrubel **28** 46 24N 7 32 E
Wildwood **148** 38 59N 74 46W
Wilga → **32** 51 52N 21 18 E
Wilgaroon **113** 30 52 S 145 42 E
Wilge → **135** 27 3 S 28 20 E
Wilhelm II Coast **7** 68 0 S 90 0 E
Wilhelm Mt. **107** 5 50 S 145 1 E
Wilhelm-Pieck-Stadt Guben **26** 51 59N 14 48 E
Wilhelmina, Geb. **169** 3 50N 56 30W
Wilhelmina Kanaal **23** 51 36N 5 6 E
Wilhelmsburg, Austria **30** 48 6N 15 36 E
Wilhelmsburg, Germany **26** 53 28N 10 1 E
Wilhelmshaven **26** 53 30N 8 9 E
Wilhelmstal **134** 21 58 S 16 21 E
Wilkes Barre **151** 41 15N 75 52W
Wilkes Land **7** 69 0 S 120 0 E
Wilkes Sub-Glacial Basin **7** 75 0 S 130 0 E
Wilkesboro **149** 36 10N 81 9W
Wilkie **145** 52 27N 108 42W
Wilkinsburg **150** 40 26N 79 50W
Wilkinson Lakes **109** 29 40 S 132 39 E
Willamina **156** 45 9N 123 32W
Willamulka **112** 33 55 S 137 52 E
Willandra Billabong Creek → **112** 33 22 S 145 52 E
Willapa, B. **156** 46 44N 124 0W
Willapa Hills **158** 46 35N 123 25W
Willard, N. Mex., U.S.A. **157** 34 35N 106 1W
Willard, Utah, U.S.A. **156** 41 28N 112 1W
Willaura **112** 37 31 S 142 45 E
Willbriggie **113** 34 28 S 146 2 E
Willcox **157** 32 13N 109 53W
Willebroek **23** 51 4N 4 22 E
Willemstad **163** 12 5N 69 0W
Willeroo **108** 15 14 S 131 37 E
William → **145** 59 8N 109 19W
William, Mt. **112** 37 17 S 142 35 E
William Creek **111** 28 58 S 136 22 E
Williambury **109** 23 45 S 115 12 E
Williams, Australia **109** 33 2 S 116 52 E
Williams, Ariz., U.S.A. **157** 35 16N 112 11W

Wrightson, Mt.

Williams, Calif., U.S.A. **158** 39 9N 122 9W
Williams Lake **144** 52 10N 122 10W
Williamsburg, Ky., U.S.A. **149** 36 45N 84 10W
Williamsburg, Pa., U.S.A. **150** 40 27N 78 14W
Williamsburg, Va., U.S.A. **148** 37 17N 76 44W
Williamsfield **154** 40 55N 90 1W
Williamson, N.Y., U.S.A. **150** 43 14N 77 15W
Williamson, W. Va., U.S.A. **148** 37 46N 82 17W
Williamsport, Ind., U.S.A. **155** 40 17N 87 17W
Williamsport, Pa., U.S.A. **150** 41 18N 77 1W
Williamston, Mich., U.S.A. **155** 42 41N 84 17W
Williamston, S.C., U.S.A. **149** 35 50N 77 5W
Williamstown, Australia **113** 37 51 S 144 52 E
Williamstown, Ky., U.S.A. **155** 38 38N 84 34W
Williamstown, Mass., U.S.A. **151** 42 41N 73 12W
Williamstown, N.Y., U.S.A. **151** 43 25N 75 54W
Williamsville, Ill., U.S.A. **154** 39 57N 89 33W
Williamsville, Mo., U.S.A. **153** 37 0N 90 33W
Willimantic **151** 41 45N 72 12W
Willis Group **110** 16 18 S 150 0 E
Willisau **28** 47 7N 8 0 E
Willisburg **155** 37 49N 85 8W
Williston, S. Africa **134** 31 20 S 20 53 E
Williston, Fla., U.S.A. **149** 29 25N 82 28W
Williston, N. Dak., U.S.A. **152** 48 10N 103 35W
Williston L. **144** 56 0N 124 0W
Willits **156** 39 28N 123 17W
Willmar **152** 45 5N 95 0W
Willoughby **150** 41 38N 81 26W
Willow Bunch **145** 49 20N 105 35W
Willow L. **144** 62 10N 119 8W
Willow Lake **152** 44 40N 97 40W
Willow Springs **153** 37 0N 92 0W
Willow Tree **113** 31 40 S 150 45 E
Willow Wall, The **95** 42 10N 122 0 E
Willowlake → **144** 62 42N 123 8W
Willowmore **134** 33 15 S 23 30 E
Willows, Australia **110** 23 39 S 147 25 E
Willows, U.S.A. **158** 39 30N 122 10W
Willowvale = Gatyana **135** 32 16 S 28 31 E
Wills, L. **108** 21 25 S 128 51 E
Wills Cr. → **110** 22 43 S 140 2 E
Wills Point **153** 32 42N 95 57W
Willunga **112** 35 15 S 138 30 E
Wilmette **148** 42 6N 87 44W
Wilmington, Australia **112** 32 39 S 138 7 E
Wilmington, Del., U.S.A. **148** 39 45N 75 32W
Wilmington, Ill., U.S.A. **155** 41 19N 88 10W
Wilmington, N.C., U.S.A. **149** 34 14N 77 54W
Wilmington, Ohio, U.S.A. **155** 39 27N 83 50W
Wilpena Cr. → **112** 31 25 S 139 29 E
Wilrijk **23** 51 9N 4 22 E
Wilsall **156** 45 59N 110 40W
Wilson **149** 35 44N 77 54W
Wilson →, Queens., Australia **111** 27 38 S 141 24 E
Wilson →, W. Austral., Australia **108** 16 48 S 128 16 E
Wilson Bluff **109** 31 41 S 129 0 E
Wilsons Promontory **113** 38 55 S 146 25 E
Wilster **26** 53 55N 9 23 E
Wilton, U.K. **13** 51 5N 1 52W
Wilton, U.S.A. **152** 47 12N 100 47W
Wilton → **110** 14 45 S 134 33 E
Wiltshire □ **13** 51 20N 2 0W
Wiltz **23** 49 57N 5 55 E
Wiluna **109** 26 36 S 120 14 E
Wimereux **19** 50 45N 1 37 E
Wimmera → **112** 36 8 S 141 56 E
Winam G. **130** 0 20 S 34 15 E
Winamac **155** 41 3N 86 36W
Winburg **134** 28 30 S 27 2 E
Winchelsea **112** 38 10 S 144 1 E
Winchendon **151** 42 40N 72 3W
Winchester, N.Z. **115** 44 11 S 171 17 E
Winchester, U.K. **13** 51 4N 1 19W
Winchester, Conn., U.S.A. **151** 41 53N 73 9W
Winchester, Idaho, U.S.A. **156** 46 11N 116 32W
Winchester, Ill., U.S.A. **154** 39 38N 90 27W
Winchester, Ind., U.S.A. **155** 40 10N 84 56W
Winchester, Ky., U.S.A. **155** 38 0N 84 8W
Winchester, N.H., U.S.A. **151** 42 47N 72 22W
Winchester, Nev., U.S.A. **159** 36 6N 115 10W
Winchester, Ohio, U.S.A. **155** 38 57N 83 40W
Winchester, Tenn., U.S.A. **149** 35 11N 86 8W
Winchester, Va., U.S.A. **148** 39 14N 78 8W
Wind → **156** 43 8N 108 12W
Wind Pt. **155** 42 47N 87 46W
Wind River Range **156** 43 0N 109 30W
Windber **150** 40 14N 78 50W
Windermere, L. **12** 54 20N 2 57W
Windfall, Canada **144** 54 12N 116 13W
Windfall, U.S.A. **155** 40 22N 85 57W
Windflower L. **144** 62 52N 118 30W
Windhoek **134** 22 35 S 17 4 E
Windischgarsten **30** 47 42N 14 21 E
Windom **152** 43 48N 95 3W
Windorah **110** 25 24 S 142 36 E
Window Rock **157** 35 47N 109 4W
Windrush → **13** 51 48N 1 35W
Windsor, Australia **113** 33 37 S 150 50 E
Windsor, N.S., Canada **143** 44 59N 64 5W
Windsor, Nfld., Canada **143** 48 57N 55 40W
Windsor, Ont., Canada **142** 42 18N 83 0W
Windsor, N.Z. **115** 44 59 S 170 49 E
Windsor, U.K. **13** 51 28N 0 36W
Windsor, Colo., U.S.A. **152** 40 33N 104 45W
Windsor, Conn., U.S.A. **151** 41 50N 72 40W
Windsor, Ill., U.S.A. **155** 39 26N 88 36W
Windsor, Mo., U.S.A. **154** 38 32N 93 31W
Windsor, N.Y., U.S.A. **151** 42 5N 75 37W
Windsor, Vt., U.S.A. **151** 43 30N 72 25W
Windsorton **134** 28 16 S 24 44 E
Windward Is., Atl. Oc. **163** 13 0N 63 0W
Windward Is., Pac. Oc. **105** 18 0 S 149 0W
Windward Passage = Vientos, Paso de los **163** 20 0N 74 0W
Windy L. **145** 60 20N 100 2W
Winefred L. **145** 55 30N 110 30W
Winejok **125** 9 1N 27 30 E
Winfield, Ill., U.S.A. **154** 41 5N 91 30W
Winfield, Kans., U.S.A. **153** 37 15N 97 0W
Winfield, Mo., U.S.A. **154** 39 0N 90 44W
Wingate Mts. **108** 14 25 S 130 40 E
Wingen **111** 31 54 S 150 54 E
Wingene **23** 51 3N 3 17 E
Wingham, Australia **111** 31 48 S 152 22 E
Wingham, Canada **142** 43 55N 81 20W
Winifred **156** 47 30N 109 28W
Winisk **142** 55 20N 85 15W
Winisk → **142** 55 17N 85 5W
Winisk L. **142** 52 55N 87 22W
Wink **153** 31 49N 103 9W
Winkler **145** 49 10N 97 56W
Winklern **30** 46 52N 12 52 E
Winlock **158** 46 29N 122 56W
Winneba **127** 5 25N 0 36W
Winnebago, Ill., U.S.A. **154** 42 15N 89 18W
Winnebago, Minn., U.S.A. **152** 43 43N 94 8W
Winnebago L. **148** 44 0N 88 20W
Winnecke Cr. → **108** 18 35 S 131 34 E
Winnemucca **156** 41 0N 117 45W
Winnemucca, L. **156** 40 25N 119 21W
Winner **152** 43 23N 99 52W
Winnett **156** 47 2N 108 21W
Winnfield **153** 31 57N 92 38W
Winnibigoshish L. **152** 47 25N 94 12W
Winning **108** 23 9 S 114 30 E
Winnipeg **145** 49 54N 97 9W
Winnipeg → **145** 50 38N 96 19W
Winnipeg, L. **145** 52 0N 97 0W
Winnipeg Beach **145** 50 30N 96 58W
Winnipegosis **145** 51 39N 99 55W
Winnipegosis L. **145** 52 30N 100 0W
Winnipesaukee, L. **151** 43 38N 71 21W
Winnsboro, La., U.S.A. **153** 32 10N 91 41W
Winnsboro, S.C., U.S.A. **149** 34 23N 81 5W
Winnsboro, Tex., U.S.A. **153** 32 56N 95 15W
Winokapau, L. **143** 53 15N 62 50W
Winona, Miss., U.S.A. **153** 33 30N 89 42W
Winona, Wis., U.S.A. **152** 44 2N 91 39W
Winooski **151** 44 31N 73 11W
Winschoten **22** 53 9N 7 3 E
Winsen **26** 53 21N 10 11 E
Winslow, Ariz., U.S.A. **157** 35 2N 110 41W
Winslow, Ind., U.S.A. **155** 38 23N 87 13W
Winslow, Wash., U.S.A. **158** 47 37N 122 31W
Winsted **151** 41 55N 73 5W
Winston-Salem **149** 36 7N 80 15W
Winsum **22** 53 20N 6 32 E
Winter Garden **149** 28 33N 81 35W
Winter Haven **149** 28 0N 81 42W
Winter Park **149** 28 34N 81 19W
Winterberg **26** 51 12N 8 30 E
Winterhaven **159** 32 47N 114 39W
Winters, Calif., U.S.A. **158** 38 32N 121 58W
Winters, Tex., U.S.A. **153** 31 58N 99 58W
Winterset **154** 41 18N 94 0W
Wintersville **150** 40 22N 80 38W
Winterswijk **22** 51 58N 6 43 E
Winterthur **29** 47 30N 8 44 E
Winthrop, Minn., U.S.A. **152** 44 31N 94 25W
Winthrop, Wash., U.S.A. **156** 48 27N 120 6W
Winton, Australia **110** 22 24 S 143 3 E
Winton, N.Z. **115** 46 8 S 168 20 E
Winton, U.S.A. **149** 36 25N 76 58W
Wintzenheim **19** 48 4N 7 17 E
Wipper → **26** 51 17N 11 10 E
Wirral **12** 53 25N 3 0W
Wirraminna **112** 31 12 S 136 13 E
Wirrulla **111** 32 24 S 134 31 E
Wisbech **12** 52 39N 0 10 E
Wisconsin □ **152** 44 30N 90 0W
Wisconsin → **152** 43 0N 91 15W
Wisconsin Dells **152** 43 38N 89 45W
Wisconsin Rapids **152** 44 25N 89 50W
Wisdom **156** 45 37N 113 27W
Wishaw **14** 55 46N 3 55W
Wishek **152** 46 20N 99 35W
Wisła **31** 49 38N 18 53 E
Wisła → **32** 54 22N 18 55 E
Wisłok → **31** 50 13N 22 32 E
Wisłoka → **31** 50 27N 21 23 E
Wismar, Germany **26** 53 53N 11 23 E
Wismar, Guyana **169** 5 59N 58 18W
Wisner **152** 42 0N 96 46W
Wissant **19** 50 52N 1 40 E
Wissembourg **19** 49 2N 7 57 E
Wissenkerke **23** 51 35N 3 45 E
Wistoka → **32** 49 50N 21 28 E
Wisznice **32** 51 48N 23 13 E
Witbank **135** 25 51 S 29 14 E
Witdraai **134** 26 58 S 20 48 E
Witham → **12** 53 3N 0 8W
Withernsea **12** 53 43N 0 2 E
Witkowo **32** 52 26N 17 45 E
Witmarsum **22** 53 6N 5 28 E
Witney **13** 51 47N 1 29W
Witnossob → **134** 26 55 S 20 37 E
Wittdün **26** 54 38N 8 23 E
Witten **26** 51 26N 7 19 E
Wittenberg **26** 51 51N 12 39 E
Wittenberge **26** 53 0N 11 44 E
Wittenburg **26** 53 30N 11 4 E
Wittenoom **108** 22 15 S 118 20 E
Wittingen **26** 52 43N 10 43 E
Wittlich **27** 50 0N 6 54 E
Wittmund **26** 53 39N 7 45 E
Wittow **26** 54 37N 13 21 E
Wittstock **26** 53 10N 12 30 E
Witzenhausen **26** 51 20N 9 50 E
Wkra → **32** 52 27N 20 44 E
Władysławowo **32** 54 48N 18 25 E
Wlen **32** 51 0N 15 39 E
Wlingi **89** 8 5 S 112 25 E
Włocławek **32** 52 40N 19 3 E
Włocławek □ **32** 52 50N 19 10 E
Włodawa **32** 51 33N 23 31 E
Włoszczowa **32** 50 50N 19 55 E
Woburn **151** 42 31N 71 7W
Wodian **94** 32 50N 112 35 E
Wodonga **113** 36 5 S 146 50 E
Wodzisław Śląski **32** 50 1N 18 26 E
Woerden **22** 52 5N 4 54 E
Woerth **19** 48 57N 7 45 E
Woëvre **19** 49 15N 5 45 E
Wognum **22** 52 40N 5 1 E
Wohlen **29** 47 21N 8 17 E
Woinbogoin **96** 32 51N 98 39 E
Wokam **87** 5 45 S 134 28 E
Wokha **82** 26 6N 94 16 E
Wolbrom **32** 50 24N 19 45 E
Wolcottville **155** 41 32N 85 22W
Wołczyn **32** 51 1N 18 3 E
Woldegk **26** 53 27N 13 35 E
Wolf → **144** 60 17N 132 33W
Wolf Creek **156** 47 1N 112 2W
Wolf L. **144** 60 24N 131 40W
Wolf Point **152** 48 6N 105 40W
Wolfe I. **142** 44 7N 76 20W
Wolfenbüttel **26** 52 10N 10 33 E
Wolfheze **22** 52 0N 5 48 E
Wolfsberg **30** 46 50N 14 52 E
Wolfsburg **26** 52 27N 10 49 E
Wolgast **26** 54 3N 13 46 E
Wolhusen **28** 47 4N 8 4 E
Wolin **32** 53 50N 14 37 E
Wollaston, Is. **176** 55 40 S 67 30W
Wollaston L. **145** 58 7N 103 10W
Wollaston Pen. **140** 69 30N 115 0W
Wollogorang **110** 17 13 S 137 57 E
Wollongong **113** 34 25 S 150 54 E
Wolmaransstad **134** 27 12 S 25 59 E
Wolmirstedt **26** 52 15N 11 35 E
Wołomin **32** 52 19N 21 15 E
Wołów **32** 51 20N 16 38 E
Wolseley, Australia **112** 36 23 S 140 54 E
Wolseley, Canada **145** 50 25N 103 15W
Wolseley, S. Africa **134** 33 26 S 19 7 E
Wolstenholme Fjord **6** 76 0N 70 0W
Wolsztyn **32** 52 8N 16 5 E
Wolvega **22** 52 52N 6 0 E
Wolverhampton **13** 52 35N 2 6W
Wommels **22** 53 6N 5 36 E
Wonarah **110** 19 55 S 136 20 E
Wonboyn **113** 37 15 S 149 55 E
Wonck **23** 50 46N 5 38 E
Wondai **111** 26 20 S 151 49 E
Wondelgem **23** 51 5N 3 44 E
Wonder Gorge **131** 14 40 S 29 0 E
Wongalarroo L. **112** 31 32 S 144 0 E
Wongan Hills **109** 30 51 S 116 37 E
Wongawol **109** 26 5 S 121 55 E
Wŏnju **95** 37 22N 127 58 E
Wonosari **89** 7 58 S 110 36 E
Wonosobo **89** 7 22 S 109 54 E
Wŏnsan **95** 39 11N 127 27 E
Wonthaggi **113** 38 37 S 145 37 E
Woocalla **112** 31 42 S 137 12 E
Wood Buffalo Nat. Park **144** 59 0N 113 41W
Wood Is. **108** 16 24 S 123 19 E
Wood L. **145** 55 17N 103 17W
Wood Lake **152** 42 38N 100 14W
Wood River **154** 38 52N 90 5W
Woodah I. **110** 13 27 S 136 10 E
Woodanilling **109** 33 31 S 117 24 E
Woodbridge **150** 43 47N 79 36W
Woodburn **111** 29 6 S 153 23 E
Woodenbong **111** 28 24 S 152 39 E
Woodend **112** 37 20 S 144 33 E
Woodfords **158** 38 47N 119 50W
Woodgreen **110** 22 26 S 134 12 E
Woodlake **158** 36 25N 119 6W
Woodland **158** 38 40N 121 50W
Woodlands **109** 24 46 S 118 8 E
Woodlark I. **107** 9 10 S 152 50 E
Woodpecker **144** 53 30N 122 40W
Woodridge **145** 49 20N 96 9W
Woodroffe, Mt. **109** 26 20 S 131 45 E
Woodruff, Ariz., U.S.A. **157** 34 51N 110 1W
Woodruff, Utah, U.S.A. **156** 41 30N 111 4W
Woods, L., Australia **110** 17 50 S 133 30 E
Woods, L., Canada **143** 54 30N 65 13W
Woods, L. of the **145** 49 15N 94 45W
Woodside, S. Austral., Australia **112** 34 58 S 138 52 E
Woodside, Vic., Australia **113** 38 31 S 146 52 E
Woodstock, N.S.W., Australia **113** 33 45 S 148 53 E
Woodstock, Queens., Australia **110** 19 35 S 146 50 E
Woodstock, W. Austral., Australia **108** 21 41 S 118 57 E
Woodstock, N.B., Canada **143** 46 11N 67 37W
Woodstock, Ont., Canada **142** 43 10N 80 45W
Woodstock, U.K. **13** 51 51N 1 20W
Woodstock, Ill., U.S.A. **155** 42 17N 88 30W
Woodstock, Vt., U.S.A. **151** 43 37N 72 31W
Woodsville **151** 44 10N 72 0W
Woodville, N.Z. **114** 40 20 S 175 53 E
Woodville, Ohio, U.S.A. **155** 41 27N 83 22W
Woodville, Tex., U.S.A. **153** 30 45N 94 25W
Woodward **153** 36 24N 99 28W
Woody **159** 35 42N 118 50W
Woolamai, C. **113** 38 30 S 145 23 E
Woolgoolga **111** 30 6 S 153 11 E
Woombye **111** 26 40 S 152 55 E
Woomera **112** 31 30 S 137 10 E
Woonona **113** 34 21 S 150 54 E
Woonsocket, R.I., U.S.A. **151** 42 0N 71 30W
Woonsocket, S. Dak., U.S.A. **152** 44 5N 98 15W
Wooramel **109** 25 45 S 114 17 E
Wooramel → **109** 25 47 S 114 10 E
Wooroloo **109** 31 48 S 116 18 E
Wooster **150** 40 48N 81 55W
Worb **28** 46 56N 7 33 E
Worcester, S. Africa **134** 33 39 S 19 27 E
Worcester, U.K. **13** 52 12N 2 12W
Worcester, Mass., U.S.A. **151** 42 14N 71 49W
Worcester, N.Y., U.S.A. **151** 42 35N 74 45W
Worden **154** 38 56N 89 50W
Wörgl **30** 47 29N 12 3 E
Workington **12** 54 39N 3 34W
Worksop **12** 53 19N 1 9W
Workum **22** 52 59N 5 26 E
Worland **156** 44 0N 107 59W
Wormerveer **22** 52 30N 4 46 E
Wormhoudt **19** 50 52N 2 28 E
Worms **27** 49 37N 8 21 E
Wörth **27** 49 1N 12 24 E
Wortham **153** 31 48N 96 27W
Wörther See **30** 46 37N 14 10 E
Worthing **13** 50 49N 0 21W
Worthington, Ind., U.S.A. **155** 39 7N 86 59W
Worthington, Minn., U.S.A. **152** 43 35N 95 36W
Worthington, Ohio, U.S.A. **155** 40 5N 83 1W
Wosi **87** 0 15 S 128 0 E
Wou-han = Wuhan **97** 30 31N 114 18 E
Woubrugge **22** 52 10N 4 39 E
Woudenberg **22** 52 5N 5 25 E
Woudsend **22** 52 56N 5 38 E
Wour **123** 21 14N 16 0 E
Wouw **23** 51 31N 4 23 E
Wowoni **87** 4 5 S 123 5 E
Woy Woy **113** 33 30 S 151 19 E
Wozniki **32** 50 35N 19 4 E
Wrangel I. **66** 71 0N 180 0 E
Wrangell **140** 56 30N 132 25W
Wrangell, I. **144** 56 20N 132 10W
Wrangell Mts. **140** 61 40N 143 30W
Wrath, C. **14** 58 38N 5 0W
Wray **152** 40 8N 102 18W
Wrekin, The **12** 52 41N 2 35W
Wrens **149** 33 13N 82 23W
Wrexham **12** 53 5N 3 0W
Wriezen **26** 52 43N 14 9 E
Wright, Canada **144** 51 52N 121 40W
Wright, Phil. **91** 11 42N 125 2 E
Wrightson, Mt. **157** 31 43N 110 56W

Z